AUSTRALIA
LBC Information Services
Brisbane • Sydney • Melbourne • Perth

CANADA
Carswell
Ottawa • Toronto • Calgary • Montreal • Vancouver

Agents:
Steimatzky's Agency Ltd., Tel Aviv
N.M. Tripathi (Private) Ltd., Bombay
Eastern Law House (Private) Ltd., Calcutta
M.P.P. House, Bangalore
Universal Book Traders, Delhi
Aditya Books, Delhi
MacMillan Shupan KK, Tokyo
Pakistan Law House, Karachi, Lahore

Current Law

YEAR BOOK
1996

VOLUME TWO

Sweet & Maxwell

W Green

Current Law

YEAR BOOK 1996

Being a Comprehensive Statement of the Law of 1996

SWEET & MAXWELL EDITORIAL TEAM

Shirley Archer
Melanie Bhagat
Ala Kuzmicki
Carol Locke
Rachael Lockley
Sophie Lowe
Christine Miskin
Ceri Pickering
Janice Sayer
Suzanne Warren

W. GREEN EDITORIAL TEAM

Janie Brash
Charlotte Hall
Peter Nicholson

Editors

English and Commonwealth Law

NICHOLAS BAATZ, M.A., B.C.L., *Barrister*
CATHERINE BARNARD, B.A., LL.M.
IAN FERRIER, M.A., *Barrister*
SHAUN FERRIS, B.A., *Barrister*
ALASTAIR HUDSON, LL.B., LL.M., *Barrister*
CHARLES JOSEPH, B.A., *Barrister, FCI Arb*
SIOBHAN McGRATH, B.A. *Barrister*
PETER MANTLE, *Barrister*
VANESSA MIDDLETON LL.B., *Solicitor, Davenport Lyons*
ALEXANDRA MILLBROOK, B.A., *Barrister*
JULIE O'MALLEY, LL.B., *Barrister*
CHARLES SCOTT, LL.B., *Solicitor*
JOHN TATE, LL.B. *Barrister*
WILLIAM UPTON, M.A., LL.M., *Barrister*
WILLIAM VANDYKE, B.A. *Barrister*

English and Commonwealth Law (cont.)

GORDON WIGNALL, M.A., *Barrister*

European Communities:

ALISON GREEN, LL.M., *Barrister*
CONOR QUIGLEY, LL.B., *Barrister*

Northern Ireland

RALPH ERSKINE, LL.B., *Barrister*

Scotland

MALCOLM THOMSON, Q.C. LL.B.
PENNY DICKMAN M.A., LL.B.

Damages Awards

PETER MANTLE, *Barrister*
DAVID KEMP, Q.B., B.A., *Barrister*

Sweet & Maxwell
W Green

The Mode of Citation
of the Current Law Year Book is
[1996] 2 C.L.Y. 1282
The 1996 Year Book is published in two volumes.

Published in 1997 by
Sweet & Maxwell Limited of
100 Avenue Road, Swiss Cottage, London NW3 3PF
Typeset by Legal Information Resources Limited,
Mytholmroyd, Hebden Bridge
Printed by The Bath Press, Bath, Avon.

A CIP catalogue record for this book is available from the British Library

ISBN: This volume only: 0-421-605006
With volume 2 and Case Citator: 0-421-605103

No natural forests were destroyed to make this product; farmed timber was used and then replanted.

PREFACE

This volume completes 49 years of Current Law publishing. It supersedes the issues of *Current Law Monthly Digest* for 1996 and covers the law from January 1 to December 31 of that year.

Citators

The *Case Citator* and the *Legislation Citators* are contained in separate volumes, issued with this volume.

The new *Current Law Citators* cover cases, statutes and statutory instruments, for the year 1996. There are permanent bound volumes covering cases during the periods 1947-76, 1977-88 and 1989-1995 and statutes during 1947-71, 1972-88 and 1989-1995. Separate volumes were published in the *Scottish Current Law* series covering the years 1948-76 and 1977-88 (cases) and 1948-71 and 1972-88 (statutes).

The present volume contains a table of cases digested and reported in 1996, the usual tables covering 1996 statutory instruments, athough the table showing their effect on the orders of earlier years has been superseded by the *Statutory Instruments Citator*, and is therefore no longer included in the Year Book, and tables of Northern Ireland Statutory Rules and Orders.

Books and Articles

Details of the books and articles published in 1996 are included in this volume. The full title, reference and the name of the author are given in each case and arranged under *Current Law* headings. Scottish books and articles are included in the Scottish section under their appropriate subject heading. A separate list of books arranged by author is included in the back of volume two.

Index

The subject-matter index in this volume adapts the new, improved format introduced at the beginning of 1991 in the monthly digest. The 30-year Index from 1947-76 may be found in the 1976 *Current Law Year Book*. The Scottish Index for the years 1972-86 may be found in the Scottish 1986 *Year Book*. Scottish material prior to 1972 can be found in the *Scottish Current Law Year Book Master Volumes*, published in 1956, 1961, 1966 and 1971.

Statutes

75 Acts received the Royal Assent during the year. A complete list of Statutes appears under the subject heading Legislation.

Cases

The number of cases digested exceeds 4,000. This figure does not include the short reports showing what damages have been awarded in English cases of injury or death. These decisions have been collected and edited by Mr. David Kemp. The *Quantum* of Damages Table at the front of this volume provides a guide to the personal injury decisions reported in 1996.

The Year Book again includes a selection of cases of persuasive force from the courts of the Commonwealth and from the English county courts.

Jurisdictions

The text of the *Current Law Year Book* is divided into three sections, covering respectively U.K., England and Wales and E.U. (which includes material applicable to Great Britain or the U.K. as a whole); Northern Ireland; and Scotland. Coverage of European Union cases takes the form of digests of European Court of Justice and Court of First Instance decisions. Coverage of English and European journals dealing with the law of the European Communities and the national law of European states is now contained in *European Current Law*, which began publication of monthly digests in January 1992 and which publishes its own year Book.

Northern Ireland

All Northern Irish Acts and Orders and the cases reported from the courts of Northern Ireland have been digested, together with a selection of the cases reported from the courts of the Republic of Ireland.

Scotland

The Scottish text is prepared by Penny Dickman using material supplied by the W. Green editorial team in Edinburgh. Case digests are prepared by our case editor in Scotland, Malcolm Thomson, Q.C. Users should note that the *Current Law Year Book* does not repeat the references to cases noted in *Green's Weekly Digest* which appear in the Scottish section of *Current Law Monthly Digest*. *Green's Weekly Digest* is purely a precis of recent judgments of the Scottish courts; cases of legal significance will be digested in *Current Law* through their appearance in one of the series of law reports proper.

Cases "ex relatione"

We welcome short reports of cases submitted by members of both branches of the legal profession. They are noted as *"Ex rel. A.B., Barrister"* or *"Ex rel. C.D., Solicitors"*, as the case may be. These reports, we believe, are of considerable value to the profession, since the contributor can properly be regarded as having first-hand knowledge of the facts. Unfortunately, occasional instances have been brought to our notice in which reports of this kind have been misleading or even incorrect. We are grateful to those who bring such matters to our attention and we seek to correct the report in a later issue or in the *Current Law Year Book*. We must stress, however, that we are entirely dependent on the contributor for the accuracy of his or her report. it is impracticable for us independently to check the facts stated to us.

The General Editor thanks those who have pointed out errors and those who have sent in notes of interesting cases.

June 1997

CONTENTS

VOLUME 1

VOLUME 2

INSOLVENCY

3438. Administration–department store–shop within shop concessions–takings of some licensees paid into separate account–whether other licensees could trace into general account–whether separate account a trust

[Insolvency Act 1986 s.14, s.238, s.239.]

The litigation concerned an application for directions under Insolvency Act 1986 s.14(3) by the joint administrators of a department store. Various licensees had "shop within a shop" concessions some of whose takings had been paid into a separate bank account. The issues for the court were (1) whether a licensee whose takings were not paid into a separate account could trace funds into the company's general bank account; (2) whether paying takings into segregated accounts created a trust in favour of licensees and (3) whether such a trust was a preference or transaction at an undervalue or infringed the pari passu rule of distribution.

Held, giving directions, that (1) the licensees could make a claim to trace funds back into the company's general bank account; (2) opening an account did not create a trust in itself but an inference could be drawn that the company intended the monies to be trust monies and (3) the trust did not infringe the pari passu rule or the Insolvency Act 1986 s.238 or s.239 on preferences or transactions at an undervalue.

LEWIS'S OF LEICESTER LTD, *Re* [1995] 1 B.C.L.C. 428, Robert Walker, J., Ch D.

3439. Administration orders–distribution of assets to creditors

[Insolvency Act 1986 Sch.1.]

The administrators of two companies sought the court's approval of distributions of the assets of the companies. In the case of the first company the administrators were able to pay all the creditors in full. In the case of the second company the proposal was to pay off all those who would be preferential creditors in any liquidation and make payments to the remaining unsecured creditors on a pari passu basis. There was a possibility of a further substantial realisation for the second company which would be lost if it was wound up.

Held, sanctioning the payments, that the powers in the Insolvency Act 1986 Sch.1 para.13 were wide enough to permit such a distribution where, unless such a distribution were made, there would be significant prejudice to the creditors who had approved the application and where there was no significant risk of other creditors emerging thereafter.

WBSL REALISATIONS 1992 LTD, *Re*; SUB NOM. WARD GROUP PLC, *Re* [1995] 2 B.C.L.C. 576, Knox, J., Ch D.

3440. Administration orders–whether administrator could pay pre-administration debts

Held, that an administrator had the power to pay off the pre-administration debts in full so as to ensure the survival of the company as a going concern.

JOHN SLACK LTD, *Re* [1995] B.C.C. 1116, Scott, J., Ch D.

3441. Applications–ex parte applications under the Insolvency Act 1986

[Insolvency Act 1986 s.236.]

The company was financed by a loan from H. The loan was secured by a lease in favour of H over the company's premises. The premises were leased back to the company by H, the rent being the interest and then capital repayments on the loan. The company became unable to meet the rental payments and weekly meetings were held between directors of the company and officers from H. All receipts of the company were paid into an account in H's name with transfers out made to the company. The company went into liquidation and the liquidators sent questionnaires to H's officers to determine their involvement in the running of the company. One questionnaire was answered but the officers declined to answer a supplementary questionnaire aimed at discovering whether the company had been trading while insolvent and whether the officers had been acting as shadow directors of the company so that a report could be made that they should be disqualified from acting as directors. The liquidators obtained an ex parte order under the Insolvency Act 1986 s.236 that the questionnaires be answered and the officers appealed.

Held, allowing the appeal, that the examination of the officers was directed at showing that they had acted as shadow directors of the company but no prima facie case had been made out against them and they had merely been acting in the interests of H. The supplementary questionnaire was oppressive and the order should be set aside.

PFTZM LTD, *Re*; SUB NOM. JOURDAIN v. PAUL [1995] 2 B.C.L.C. 354, Paul Baker, J., Ch D.

3442. Assignment–debt on bankruptcy–assignment a sham, champertous or fraudulent

QVD applied for leave to appeal against an order dismissing their application for summary judgment. QVD were in administrative receivership. Their sole asset was an insurance claim for £13 million following the destruction by fire of their property. The claim was assigned to G in return for the cancellation of their indebtedness to G of £30,000. QVD had argued that G's gain was out of proportion to the debt and she had been given the assignment to the exclusion of the other creditors. QVD argued that the trial judge had erred in finding there to be a triable issue as to whether the assignment was a sham or was champertous, or was intended to exclude the other creditors. QVD also applied for leave to amend the notice of appeal. QVD argued that G was only assigned the interest in the action and as the action was now dismissed, the totality of G's interest no longer existed.

Held, allowing the applications for leave to appeal and to amend the notice of appeal, that (1) it was arguable that the assignment was a sham and champertous and intended to exclude fraudulently the other creditors and (2) the fact that QVD enjoyed the whole of the interest of the policy did not mean that the whole of the interest was assigned to G. Although G had been given belated notice of the amendment, she could not oppose the amendment as it merely reproduced the language of the assignment.

QUO VADIS DEVELOPMENTS LTD v. GATTY, Trans. Ref: LTA 95/5135/B, February 2, 1995, Leggatt, L.J., CA.

3443. Bankruptcy–bankrupt failing to provide business accounts–public examination reinstated and immediately adjourned to permit private examination to continue–irregular procedure justified on facts

[Insolvency Act 1986 s.333; Insolvency Rules 1986.]

In bankruptcy proceedings the district judge restored the public examination of the bankrupt and then immediately adjourned it again and also suspended the discharge of the bankruptcy until the conclusion of the private examination. The public examination had been adjourned initially because of the bankrupt's failure to provide the accounts of his business. A private examination was carried out and when the trustee obtained the accounts he thought that there were grounds for an income payment. Accordingly, the trustee applied to reinstate the public examination so that the discharge of the bankrupt could be suspended. The bankrupt appealed arguing that the district judge had no jurisdiction to restore the examination with the sole intention of suspending the discharge of the bankruptcy and that he had been wrong to do so because there had been no default sufficient to justify a suspension.

Held, dismissing the appeal, that the bankrupt had failed to comply with his obligations under the Insolvency Act 1986 s.333 and the Insolvency Rules 1986 and therefore the court had sufficient material upon which to justify exercising its discretion to suspend the automatic discharge. It was an odd use of procedure to do so by reinstating the public examination only to adjourn it, but, on the facts of the case, it had been proper to do so.

DEBTOR (NO.26 OF 1991), *Re*; SUB NOM. HOLMES v. OFFICIAL RECEIVER [1996] B.C.C. 246, Judge Maddocks, Ch D.

3444. Bankruptcy–claims of breach of duty against solicitors'–limitation defences available–lease to commence proceedings nunc pro tune granted

[Insolvency Act 1986 s.130, s.285.]

Bankruptcy orders had been made against S and B, solicitors. The plaintiffs were former clients of S and B who had brought a number of claims of breach of duty against S and B in ignorance of the solicitors' bankruptcy. Leave to commence proceedings had been granted under the Insolvency Act 1986 s.285(3). By the time the bankruptcies were known to the plaintiffs, limitation defences were available to S and B. The plaintiffs sought leave to commence the existing proceedings retrospectively or nunc pro tunc.

Held, allowing the applications, granting leave to commence proceedings nunc pro tunc, that the existing proceedings were not a nullity, *Wilson v. Banner Scaffolding Ltd* [1982] C.L.Y. 1853 and *National Employers Mutual General Insurance Association Ltd, Re* [1995] 1 B.C.L.C. 232, [1996] C.L.Y 3460 not followed. Further, a literal construction of s.285(3) and s.130(2) of the 1986 Act led to absurdities therefore the sections were capable of purposive construction. As the words were capable of more than one meaning they were to be given a meaning which would effect the purpose of the statute. A literal interpretation of the sections would frustrate the statutory intention.

BRISTOL & WEST BUILDING SOCIETY v. SAUNDERS AND BEARMAN; SUB NOM. SAUNDERS (A BANKRUPT), *Re*; BEARMAN (A BANKRUPT), RE [1996] 3 W.L.R. 473, Lindsay, J., Ch D.

3445. Bankruptcy–creditor's solicitor authorised to assist trustee in bankruptcy–minimal risk of conflict of interest

Judgment was obtained against S by a creditor, C, in a contested action in which S was found guilty of fraud and dishonesty. S was later adjudicated bankrupt due to his inability to satisfy the judgment. Certain matters remained in connection with the main action. The district judge authorised the trustee in bankruptcy to retain C's solicitor to advise and assist in the administration of S's estate, subject to an exception requiring another firm to be retained in relation to certain unfinished business. S applied for the authorisation to be set aside, contending that the use of C's solicitor created a conflict of interest. The application was dismissed and S appealed.

Held, dismissing S's appeal, that (1) it was not unreasonable for the trustee to retain C's solicitor, particularly where there were anticipated difficulties in identifying and tracing S's assets. C's solicitor was already aware of these difficulties and this could be advantageous to all creditors, not just C. If C was the largest creditor and no difficulties were expected in quantifying the provable debt, the risk of a conflict of interest was only a distant possibility. If a conflict of interest were to be identified, but there was no real risk of confidential information being misused, a balancing exercise might be appropriate to determine whether the conflict was something the court would permit and (2) the retainer of separate solicitors to deal with the unfinished business was a sensible one and averted any risk of conflict of interest. The district judge had not erred in the exercise of his discretion.

SCHUPPAN (A BANKRUPT), *Re*; SUB NOM. BANKRUPT (NO.400 OF 1995), *Re* [1996] 2 All E.R. 664, Robert Walker, J., Ch D.

3446. Bankruptcy–creditors rescission of bankruptcy order–support by majority of creditors–relevant change in circumstances

[Insolvency Act s.375.]

C was made bankrupt on March 21 by A. At the time of his bankruptcy, C had five creditors, the largest of which was his local authority landlord, B, in respect of rent arrears for his council flat. The debt owed to B represented 30 per cent of the total debts owed by C. After consideration of the facts, C decided there were no grounds for seeking an annulment of the bankruptcy order, neither were there grounds for seeking a voluntary arrangement, because of B's opposition. Accordingly, C made an application, pursuant to the Insolvency Act s.375, to rescind the bankruptcy order. The basis of the application was that since the making of the order there had been "a change in circumstances", the change being that A and all of C's other creditors, except B, agreed to support the application in return for payment of 65 per cent of their debt following rescission. The Official Receiver raised no objections to the proposed application.

Held, that the application should succeed notwithstanding the objections of B, as the interest of the creditors who represented 70 per cent of the total debts outweighed B's considerations, particularly where B had been promised payment of its debt in full, and its objections were for ulterior reasons.

COBB v. OFFICIAL RECEIVER, August 21, 1996, Registrar Pymm, Bankruptcy Registry. [*Ex rel.* Bolt Burden, Solicitors].

3447. Bankruptcy–criminal injuries compensation–application prior to bankruptcy–trustee claiming payment on basis of future or contingent interest–compensation not "property" within Insolvency Act s.436–statutory interpretation

[Insolvency Act 1986 s.436.]

C, who was adjudicated bankrupt, received £182,150 compensation from the Criminal Injuries Compensation Board (after deduction of an interim payment). The court, following an examination under the Insolvency Act 1986 ordered payment of the sum with interest to the trustee, on the ground that it fell within the definition of "property" in s.436 (a) of the 1986 Act and therefore formed part of her estate at the time of the bankruptcy order. C obtained rescission of the order on the basis that the award made after her bankruptcy could not form part of her estate. The trustee appealed contending that at the time of the bankruptcy order C had a future or contingent interest in "property" within the meaning of the 1986 Act.

Held, dismissing the appeal, that the word "property" in the 1986 Act was not intended to describe anything other than an existing item and could not refer to something which might possibly come into existence on the occurrence of some uncertain future event this situation was distinct from one involving a future or contingent interest in property involving an underlying existing property susceptible to a proprietary interest; the mere prospect of an award from the board was therefore not, at the time of the bankruptcy order, "property" within the meaning of the 1986 Act.

CAMPBELL (A BANKRUPT), *Re*; SUB NOM. BANKRUPT (NO.145 OF 1995), *Re* [1997] Ch. 14, Knox, J., Ch D.

3448. Bankruptcy–debtor's home used as security–whether bankruptcy proceedings or Law of Property Act s.30 afforded best method for bank to realign security

[Insolvency Act 1986 s.269; Law of Property Act 1925 s.30.]

Z and his wife, executed security over their home in favour of BCCI. After BCCI's compulsory winding up, it began proceedings to enforce the security. Z's wife alleged that the security was unenforceable against her on the grounds of undue influence. The size of the security was sufficient to discharge the debt owed to BCCI. BCCI presented a bankruptcy petition against Z containing a statement under the Insolvency Act 1986 s.269 that it would give up its security in the event that a bankruptcy order were made. Z and his wife contended that the bankruptcy order should not be allowed to be used to circumvent their other claims under other heads against BCCI. Z's wife appealed against the award of the bankruptcy order.

Held, dismissing the appeal, that BCCI could enforce its security over the property by virtue of the Law of Property Act 1925 s.30 without recourse to bankruptcy proceedings. On such an application, the claims of BCCI would prevail over those of Z and his wife. Z would therefore be in no worse position if the bankruptcy petition were made. Section 269 of the 1986 Act was available to BCCI even if the debtor had no other creditors and there was no improper use by BCCI of the bankruptcy procedure.

ZANDFARID v. BANK OF CREDIT AND COMMERCE INTERNATIONAL SA (IN LIQUIDATION); SUB NOM. ZANDFARID, *Re* [1996] 1 W.L.R. 1420, Parker, J., Ch D.

3449. Bankruptcy–judgment debts–cheques banked in part satisfaction–no value received

[Insolvency Act 1986 s.284.]

In October 1994, cheques amounting to £10,000 were sent to D by B, in full and final settlement of an action commenced against him. On March 9, 1995, a bankruptcy petition was presented against B. On March 10, 1995, D obtained a judgment in the action, and on March 15 banked the cheques in part satisfaction of the judgment. The trustees in bankruptcy sought an order that the payments were void by virtue of the Insolvency Act 1986 s.284, and should be returned. D submitted that the payment fell within s.284(4), since it was for value. A question arose as to whether payment of the sums in part satisfaction of judgment debts was for value.

Held, that value has to be looked at in the practical sense, and should not be given the same meaning as the word "consideration". There were two stages to assessing the question. Firstly, was a payment made that reduced the assets for creditors, and secondly, was there value, were the creditors any worse off as a result of the payment? If the answer to both questions was yes, the recipient must seek ratification of the payment, since no value has been received.

TRUSTEE IN BANKRUPTCY OF DR BULLEN v. BEETHAM, April 22, 1996, District Judge Wolfson, CC (Liverpool). [*Ex rel.* James Dawson, Barrister].

3450. Bankruptcy–partnerships–bankruptcy order not annulled where agreement to pay VAT by bankrupt's partner did not amount to compounding of bankrupt's own debts

[Insolvency Act 1986 s.282.]

The bankrupt's former wife applied under the Insolvency Act 1986 s.282 for the annulment of a bankruptcy order made against her ex-husband, on the grounds that it had been wrongly made. The bankrupt's business partner had reached agreement with Customs and Excise Commissioners to pay £13,326, by a succession of post-dated cheques, in satisfaction of the partnership's VAT debts. However, the bankrupt had given notice of opposition, stating that he could pay his own genuine debts, although these were estimated by the deputy official receiver to be £216,056 against assets of £26,250.

Held, dismissing the application, that the facts showed the bankrupt to be insolvent. Whereas an outright payment of the joint partnership debt would have discharged the bankrupt's liabilities, the payment arrangement made by his business partner did not relate to the bankrupt's own liabilities or amount to anything more than an agreement to compound for the debt.

ARTMAN v. ARTMAN; SUB NOM. BANKRUPT (NO.622 OF 1995), *Re* [1996] B.P.I.R. 511, Robert Walker, J., Ch D.

3451. Bankruptcy–review of decision to set aside statutory demand dismissed–time for appealing expired–discretion to adjourn petition–whether issue estoppel

[Insolvency Rules 1986 r.6.25.]

A debtor's application to set aside a statutory demand failed when a district judge ruled that there were no substantial grounds upon which the debt could be disputed. The debtor's application for a review of the decision was dismissed because he should have appealed. By the date the application failed the time for appealing had expired. A district judge then refused to make a bankruptcy order and adjourned the hearing of the petition. The creditor appealed.

Held, dismissing the appeal, that the debtor had reasonably not anticipated a full hearing on the date set and there was a real prospect of the debtor adducing further relevant evidence. A bankruptcy court had a duty to ensure that its discretion to make a bankruptcy order was not exercised so as to cause injustice. There was no issue estoppel from the earlier bankruptcy proceedings.

EBERHARDT & CO LTD v. MAIR [1995] 1 W.L.R. 1180, Evans-Lombe, J., Ch D.

3452. Bankruptcy–time at which doctrine of relation back operated to sever joint tenancy

Mr and Mrs D were joint tenants of two properties. Mr D committed an act of bankruptcy in September 1982 and in December 1982 a bankruptcy petition was presented against him. In February 1983 Mrs D died leaving her properties to her children. A receiving order was made in May 1983 and D was adjudicated bankrupt in November 1983. D's trustees argued that D's property was not alienated until the adjudication and therefore the right of survivorship applied with regard to Mrs D's share and the whole estate now vested in the trustees in bankruptcy. Mrs D's personal representatives claimed that the doctrine of relation back applied and alienation applied at D's bankruptcy and therefore the joint tenancy had been severed prior to Mrs D's death and her share passed to her children.

Held, allowing the appeal of Mrs D's representatives, that the act of bankruptcy did sever the joint tenancy. The doctrine of relation back did apply and therefore the joint tenancy had been severed prior to Mrs D's death and one half of the properties formed part of Mrs D's estate.

DENNIS (A BANKRUPT), *Re*; SUB NOM. DENNIS v. GOODMAN [1995] 3 W.L.R. 367, Sir Thomas Bingham, M.R., CA.

3453. Bankruptcy–trustee in bankruptcy–entitlement to investment profits

When the partners of FCJ committed an act of bankruptcy, J, the wife of one of the partners, invested money taken from a bank account in the name of her husband and another partner. She appealed against an order that the profits derived from its investment in commodities dealing were the property of the trustee in bankruptcy. J accepted that the Official Receiver was entitled to the money paid into the original account with the commodity brokers, but argued that he was not entitled to profits from J's investments.

Held, dismissing the appeal, that J had no legal title to the money and was merely in possession of it. Title had passed to the Official Receiver who had a right to trace the profits made by using the money and to bring an action in common law for money received, *Lipkin Gorman v. Karpnale Ltd* [1991] 2 A.C. 548, [1991] C.L.Y. 502 and *Clarke v. Shee and Johnson* (1774) 1 Cowp. 197 followed.

TRUSTEE OF THE PROPERTY OF FC JONES & SONS v. JONES [1996] 3 W.L.R. 703, Millett, L.J., CA.

3454. Choses in action–whether trustee in bankruptcy obliged to dispose of an asset where offer derisory

[Insolvency Act 1986 s.303.]

K applied for leave to appeal against the dismissal of his application, under the Insolvency Act 1986 s.303, that the Official Receiver, OR, should assign a chose in action to him. K had a right in action against his solicitors before his bankruptcy when the right became vested in OR. The judge found that the sum of £1,000 offered by K in return for the right was derisory for such a major claim.

Held, dismissing the application, that a trustee in bankruptcy was not obliged to accept the only offer made for an asset if that offer was derisory. K would be unlikely to have the funds to pursue the action and the creditors had not indicated that they would fund it.

KHAN v. OFFICIAL RECEIVER [1997] B.P.I.R. 109, Nourse, L.J., CA.

3455. Comfort letters–interpretation of paragraph–whether warranty as to present intentions or promise of future conduct

A gave two letters of comfort to the bank, NAB. The letters provided that if AML, a subsidiary of A, was unable to meet its commitments to the bank then A would take steps to ensure that the subsidiary company's present and future obligations to the bank were met. The letters included a statement that the paragraph concerned was "an expression of present intention by way of comfort only". A then entered into an arrangement which rejected the bank's claims as a creditor. The bank sought to reverse the decision.

Held, dismissing the application, that the letters were construed as not giving rise to an enforceable obligation. The qualification in the final paragraph indicated that the common intention of the parties was that the letters should be no more than a warranty as to present intentions by way of comfort only and not a promise as to future conduct.

ATLANTIC COMPUTERS PLC (IN ADMINISTRATION), *Re*; SUB NOM. NATIONAL AUSTRALIA BANK LTD v. SODEN [1995] B.C.C. 696, Chadwick, J., Ch D.

3456. Companies–conduct of directors–reporting requirements

INSOLVENT COMPANIES (REPORTS ON CONDUCT OF DIRECTORS) RULES 1996, SI 1996 1909; made under the Insolvency Act 1986 s.411; and the Company Directors Disqualification Act 1986 s.21. In force: September 30, 1996; £3.70.

These Rules revoke and replace the Insolvent Companies (Reports on Conduct of Directors) No.2 Rules 1986 (SI 1986 2134). They make provision for the manner in which a voluntary liquidator, administrative receiver or administrator of a company is to make a report to the Secretary of State in relation to persons who have been directors or shadow directors of insolvent companies and whose conduct appears to be unfit to be concerned with company management. They also make provision for returns to be made to the Secretary of State when a report has not already been made in respect of such persons.

3457. Company registration–dissolution of company void and restoration to register completed despite knowledge of liquidator of asset–cause of action assigned elsewhere

[Companies Act 1985 s.651.]

Before the company was dissolved the liquidator assigned to W any cause of action the company had against A with respect to the supply of defective goods. An application was made to restore the company to the register which was opposed by A which argued that the liquidator had no power to make the assignment which was defective.

Held, granting the application, that the application fell within the general purpose of the Companies Act 1985 s.651. The company would therefore be restored. Whether that restoration would serve any purpose was a matter for another tribunal at a later date.

OAKLEAGUE LTD, *Re* [1995] 2 B.C.L.C. 624, Walker, J., Ch D.

3458. Company voluntary arrangements–creditor knew of meeting though not by formal notice–voluntary arrangement binding on creditor who had opportunity to vote

[Insolvency Act 1986 s.5; Insolvency Rules 1986 r.12.]

The company, BG, incurred a costs liability to M. Thereafter a company voluntary arrangement was approved at a meeting of BG's creditors. M had been aware of the meeting from other sources but denied receipt of the formal notice of the meeting which BG asserted had been sent out. M did not seek to vote at the meeting but later sought to present a winding up petition. The applicant applied to restrain M from proceedings any further for BG's winding upon the grounds that M was bound by the company voluntary arrangement.

Held, allowing the application, that M had received the requisite notice of the meeting from the press and by word of mouth although he did not receive the document by post. However, the document was properly posted to his address according to the Insolvency Rules 1986 r.12. Therefore, no injustice would be caused by regarding him as having had notice in accordance with the rules. As M had notice of the meeting and would have been entitled to vote in accordance with the rules had he intended, under the Insolvency Act 1986 s.5(2) he was bound by the company voluntary arrangement, *Cranley Mansions Ltd, Re* [1995] 1 B.C.L.C. 290, [1995] 1 C.L. 212 and *Doorbar v. Alltime Securities* [1995] 1 B.C.L.C. 316, [1995] 1 C.L.Y. 2842 considered.

BEVERLEY GROUP PLC v. McCLUE [1996] B.P.I.R. 25, Knox, J., Ch D.

3459. Compensation orders–VAT offences–power of magistrates to commit for non-payment in face of individual voluntary arrangement

[Insolvency Act 1986 s.252.]

P applied for judicial review of an order that he should be held in custody until he had paid compensation of £20,467 owed to HM Customs and Excise following his conviction of 10 VAT offences. P paid the money on the same day as the order was made and was released from custody. P argued that the order should be quashed and the money repaid as the Customs and Excise Commissioners were bound by an earlier interim order and voluntary arrangement approved by P's creditors. In such circumstances the Insolvency Act 1986 s.252(2) prevented an execution or legal process against P's property without leave of the court. P argued that the proceedings by the magistrates amounted to such and, as no leave was obtained, the proceedings were unlawful.

Held, dismissing the application, that the proceedings referred to in the 1986 Act s.252(2) related to the provisions of the voluntary arrangement. In this case the person to whom the compensation was owed was not in the same position as an ordinary creditor.

R. v. BARNET MAGISTRATES' COURT, *ex p.* PHILIPPOU [1997] B.P.I.R. 134, Saville, L.J., QBD.

3460. Compulsory winding up–action commenced without knowledge of petition–proceedings null and void

[Insolvency Act 1986 s.130.]

On October 3, 1990 a compulsory winding up order was made in respect of the company. On May 21, 1992 F commenced an action against the company not knowing of the existence of the winding up order. That matter did not come to F's notice until July 1994 whereupon an application was made to the court for retrospective leave to commence and continue the action against the company. The application was dismissed by the Registrar on the ground that obtaining leave was a pre-requisite to commencing the proceedings against the company and that therefore the proceedings were a nullity and could not be validated by some retrospective leave of the court. F appealed.

Held, dismissing F's appeal, that the Insolvency Act 1986 s.130 provided an absolute bar to the commencement of proceedings without the leave of the court where the company was the subject of a compulsory winding up order.

The proceedings were a nullity and could not be validated by a subsequent application for leave. F could not rely on lack of knowledge of the winding up order as it was a matter of public record appearing on the register maintained by the Registrar of Companies, *Wilson v. Banner Scaffolding Ltd* [1982] C.L.Y. 1853 followed.

NATIONAL EMPLOYERS MUTUAL GENERAL INSURANCE ASSOCIATION LTD (IN LIQUIDATION), *Re* [1995] 1 B.C.L.C. 232, Rattee, J., Ch D.

3461. Corporate insolvency–appointment of investigators to inquire into company's affairs–agreement not to become involved in management of company–whether agreement precluded appointment as receivers

SC, a company in financial difficulties, who at the instigation of TSB had agreed to the appointment in 1993 of a firm of accountants, SW, to investigate their affairs, appealed against a refusal to renew an injunction granted ex parte to restrain SW from also acting as their receivers.

Held, allowing the appeal, that SW's letter of appointment contained a clear provision that they would not take any responsibility, either at that time or in the future, for the management of SC's affairs. The provision was a precaution against investigators deciding that a company should go into receivership in the hope that they would then be appointed receivers. That undertaking had not lost any of its force in the three years since it was made and SC was entitled to renewal of the injunction, *Doherty v. Allman* (1878) 3 App. Cas. 709 followed.

SHEPPARD & COOPER LTD v. TSB BANK PLC [1996] B.C.C. 653, Sir John Balcombe, CA.

3462. Corporate insolvency–company name–directors not disqualified–application to trade under prohibited name should not consider suitability of directors

[Insolvency Act 1986 s.216; Company Directors Disqualification Act 1986; Insolvency Rules 1986 r.4.]

P1 and P2 had been directors of HCH Ltd, which went into liquidation in June 1995 because it was unable to pay its debts. When the company ceased to trade in September 1994 they took advice from a licensed insolvency practitioner and decided to incorporate a new company, HCH(H) Ltd, with a paid up share capital of £2, which then purchased the assets of the old company on the basis of an independent valuation. Some of the liabilities of the old company were also assumed by the new one. The report of the Official Receiver into the failure of the old company concluded that it was due to lack of capital, inexperienced management and unwise expansion rather than to any misconduct on the part of P1 or P2. On July 3, 1995 P1 and P2, applied under the Insolvency Act 1986 s.216(3), for leave to be directors of the new company which had a prohibited name within s.216(2) of the 1986 Act. That application was refused on the basis that the proposed trading, through an undercapitalised company with inexperienced management, exposed the creditors of that company to an unacceptable risk.

Held, allowing the appeal and granting the application for leave, that it was not appropriate, when considering an application for leave under the Insolvency Act 1986 s.216(3), to take into account factors, such as the risk that the new company will fail by reason of lack of experience of its directors and undercapitalisation. That would be relevant when considering an application for leave under the Company Directors Disqualification Act 1986 s.17. The disqualification imposed by the Insolvency Act 1986 s.216 was not imposed for any of the reasons to be found in the Company Directors Disqualification Act 1986 s.2 to s.6. It was imposed simply because the applicant wished to continue trading through a limited company with a prohibited name. Provided the requirements of the exceptions contained in the Insolvency Rules 1986, relating to measures to be taken to protect the position of the creditors of the old company, were satisfied, and there were no grounds for disqualification under the Company Directors Disqualification Act 1986, then leave must be granted.

PENROSE v. OFFICIAL RECEIVER; SUB NOM. PENROSE v. SECRETARY OF STATE FOR TRADE AND INDUSTRY [1996] 2 All E.R. 96, Chadwick, J., Ch D.

3463. Corporate insolvency–loan secured by charges over third party deposit–letters of charge unclear on whether principal debtor repaid in full–when bank insolvent whether deposits set off against debts–whether total debt recoverable

[Insolvency Rules 1986 r.4.90.]

Over several years BCCI lent money to many customers under arrangements whereby a third party, usually the controlling shareholder of a particular customer, would purport to provide collateral security for BCCI by depositing money with BCCI and providing a charge over that deposit. The terms of the letters of charge did not provide any express guarantee on the part of the depositor or any personal covenant to repay the indebtedness of the customer in question. In 1993 BCCI went into liquidation with many of the loans outstanding. Two test cases were brought in which the liquidators sought directions as to whether they should attempt to recover the whole of the outstanding loans and leave the depositor to prove the amount of the deposit in the liquidation, or whether they should set off the amount of the outstanding loan against the deposit under the terms of the Insolvency Rules 1986 r.4.90 and claim from the customers only so much of the outstanding loan as exceeded the amount of the deposit. At first instance the judge held that the liquidators were not required to set off the amount of the deposit against the outstanding loan.

Held, dismissing the appeal, that the operation of the rules as to set off in the Insolvency Rules 1986 r.4.90 was mandatory, automatic and immediate on the bankruptcy or liquidation taking place, *National Westminster Bank Ltd v. Halesowen Presswork and Assemblies Ltd* [1972] 1 All E.R. 641 followed. However, there could be no set off if there was no mutuality of dealings between the two parties, and the benefit of set off could not be made available to third parties. Even if all the parties had agreed that BCCI should set off the amounts in question, it could not have done so after the bankruptcy, since in the absence of the necessary mutuality, the set off would have contravened the statutory scheme of distribution in insolvency. The judge was correct to dismiss the customers' claims that they should be discharged from their principal debt since the bank could not repay the deposits at face value, for two reasons: first the rule stated in *Ellis & Co's Trustee v. Dixon-Johnson* [1925] A.C. 489, that a secured creditor could not have judgment for a debt where he had lost or improperly made away with the security, did not apply where, as in the instant case, the security had not been lost or stolen but had simply diminished in value as a result of the creditor's insolvency; secondly, the loss of securities discharged the debtor who provided them, but that could not assist a principal debtor when the security was provided by a surety.

Observed that, the effect of a charge-back was that it did not create and vest in the chargee a proprietary interest in the debt which he owed to the chargor, and accordingly it was not a charge properly so called within the meaning of the Companies Act 1985 s.395, *Charge Card Services Ltd, Re* [1986] 3 All E.R. 289, [1988] C.L.Y. 416 affirmed.

BANK OF CREDIT AND COMMERCE INTERNATIONAL SA (NO.8), *Re*; SUB NOM. MORRIS v. AGRICHEMICALS LTD [1996] Ch. 245, Rose, L.J., CA.

3464. Costs–personal liability of liquidators

The liquidator of M appealed against an order that he personally pay part of the costs of an action after an application for security for costs had succeeded on appeal.

Held, allowing the appeal, that there was a jurisdiction to order a non-party to pay costs personally, but it would only be exercised in exceptional cases where impropriety had been shown. Public interest required that extra caution be shown in the case of liquidators, *Symphony Group Plc v. Hodgson* [1994] Q.B. 179, [1993] C.L.Y. 3153 followed.

METALLOY SUPPLIES LTD (IN LIQUIDATION) v. MA (UK) LTD [1997] 1 All E.R. 418, Waller, L.J., CA.

3465. Costs–trustee in bankruptcy must be brought in once bankruptcy order made–whether able to proceed against him for costs

[Insolvency Rules 1986 r.7.39; Insolvency Act 1986 s.284.]

Proceedings were originally brought against the Official Receiver under the Insolvency Act 1986 s.284 and the trustee in bankruptcy was later brought into the proceedings after a bankruptcy order had been made. The successful party, M, the bankrupt's wife, sought a direction under Insolvency Rules 1986 r.739 that the trustee in bankruptcy should pay the costs of the proceedings personally.

Held, dismissing the application, that there was no good reason for making a costs order against the trustee in bankruptcy. The trustee became joined as a defendant not because M applied to have him joined but because he inevitably became a party by operation of law, however, this was not sufficient reason to award costs against the trustee. Costs would be awarded against a third party creditor, the building society, which had directly caused M to initiate the proceedings when seeking to protect its position by means of which the court disapproved.

MORDANT (A BANKRUPT), *Re* (1994); SUB NOM. MORDANT v. HALLS [1995] 2 B.C.L.C. 647, Sir Donald Nicholls V.C., Ch D.

3466. County Court–directors' disqualification–whether court had jurisdiction

[Company Directors Disqualification Act 1986 s.6.]

F and WP were companies in voluntary liquidation. DF went into compulsory liquidation. In each case proceedings were commenced in the county court seeking the disqualification of persons who had been directors of the companies. In F's case the proceedings were commenced after the liquidator's final return to the Registrar of Companies but before the expiry of the three month period provided for before the company was dissolved. In the other two cases, the proceedings were commenced before the liquidator's final return was made and in the case of DF resulted in a disqualification order made after the final dissolution of the company. An issue arose as to the extent of the jurisdiction of the county court to entertain and continue disqualification proceedings where the winding up of a company was completed. It was contended by the respondents that once the winding up of the companies was concluded the county court's jurisdiction ceased so that the court had no power to make the disqualification order made in DF and in the other cases the proceedings had to be transferred to the High Court.

Held, that the Company Directors Disqualification Act 1986 s.6 gave "the court" power to make a disqualification order. By virtue of s.6(3) "the court", in the case of a company being wound up, was the court having jurisdiction to wind up the company. In any other case "the court" was the High Court. In the instant cases, the county court had jurisdiction to wind up each of the companies and at the commencement of the disqualification proceedings each of them were still being wound up. Parliament could not have intended that disqualification proceedings properly commenced in the county court should cease simply because the winding up of the company was complete. The words "for the purposes of the commencement of the proceedings" should be regarded as implicit in s.6(3) of the Act. The county court was entitled to entertain the proceedings and continue them to their conclusion. The winding up of a company ceased on the date upon which it was formally dissolved by the Registrar of Companies three months after the submission of the liquidator's final return. Until that time the company remained in existence. Accordingly the proceedings in relation to F were properly commenced and continued in the county court.

WORKING PROJECT LTD, *Re*; FOSTERDOWN LTD, *Re*; DAVIES FLOORING (SOUTHERN) LTD, RE [1995] 1 B.C.L.C. 226, Carnwath, J., Ch D.

3467. Courts–insolvency proceedings–reciprocity

CO-OPERATION OF INSOLVENCY COURTS (DESIGNATION OF RELEVANT COUNTRIES) ORDER 1996, SI 1996 253; made under the Insolvency Act 1986 s.426. In force: March 1, 1996; £0.65.

The courts of countries designated by this Order will have the right under the Insolvency Act 1986 s.426 to request assistance in matters of insolvency law from courts having jurisdiction in relation to insolvency law in any part of the United Kingdom. The designated countries are Malaysia and the Republic of South Africa.

3468. Creditors–applications to continue proceedings when company wound up–writs in rem–order for sale

[Insolvency Act 1986 s.130.]

A creditor, TO, arrested the ship, Bolivia. D issued a writ in rem and thereafter further creditors also issued writs in rem. D then presented a petition to wind up the company L. TO obtained judgment in default and an order for the appraisement and sale of the ship subject to the leave of the Companies Court which was granted. L was ordered to be wound up but by the date of the winding up order only one of the writs in rem had been served. The applicants applied for leave to continue their actions in the Admiralty Court so as to receive a share of the proceedings of the sale of the ship.

Held, granting the applications, that by arresting the ship prior to the presentation of D's petition, TO had security and could not object to the enforcement of that security by an order for sale. The effect of an order for sale by the Admiralty Court was to convert the company's interest in the ship into a right to receive the balance of the proceeds of the sale after satisfaction of the prior claimants. On that basis leave was not required under the Insolvency Act 1986 s.130(2) as the applicants were not proceeding against the company or its property. If leave were needed it would be equitable to grant it because the order for sale showed that the Admiralty Court contemplated that the proceeds of sale would be distributed in the ordinary way. The writs were validly issued. A refusal of leave would prevent the applicants enforcing security enabling the other claimants to "scoop the pool" and a better price would be obtained by selling it through the Admiralty Marshal than by a liquidator.

LINEAS NAVIERAS BOLIVIANAS SAM, *Re* [1995] 1 B.C.L.C. 440, Arden, J., Ch D.

3469. Creditors–proxy form faxed to chairman of creditors' meeting–whether form signed as required

The Inland Revenue sent a form of proxy directing the chairman of a creditors' meeting to vote against the debtor's proposals. On the morning of the meeting the Revenue faxed the form to the chairman who decided not to act on the form as it was not the original document. The Revenue sought reversal of that decision and revocation of the approval of the debtor's arrangement. The district judge dismissed the application holding that the faxed proxy was not "signed" as required. The Revenue appealed.

Held, allowing the appeal, that a proxy form was signed if it bore some distinctive or personal mark placed there by the creditor. A form that had been faxed to the chairman of a creditors' meeting was a valid proxy form.

INLAND REVENUE COMMISSIONERS v. CONBEER; SUB NOM. DEBTOR (NO.2021 OF 1995), *Re*; DEBTOR (NO. 2022 OF 1995), RE [1996] 2 All E.R. 345, Laddie, J., Ch D.

3470. Creditors–voluntary liquidation under way–majority of creditors group members–conflicting claims of petitioning and opposing creditors–whether protection afforded by independent scrutiny overrode potential delay

The company was a member of a large group of companies based in Europe which went into creditors' voluntary liquidation and appointed a liquidator. One of the creditors suspected that assets had been extracted from the company and that payments had been made to group members including STBS as favoured creditors before the voluntary liquidation. He applied for a compulsory winding up of the company and sought the removal of the liquidator. Other creditors opposed.

Held, granting the application for compulsory winding up, that, in deciding whether to grant such an order when the company was already in voluntary liquidation, the court had to take account of the quantity and quality of claims made by the petitioning and opposing creditors. Fairness and commercial morality might make it desirable for a large, non group member creditor, who suspected sharp practice, to be afforded the protection given by the independent scrutiny that followed a compulsory order even if the voluntary liquidation was well under way and where the order sought might cause delay. On the facts a compulsory order was justified.

GORDON & BREACH SCIENCE PUBLISHERS LTD, *Re* [1995] 2 B.C.L.C. 189, Walker, J., Ch D.

3471. Debts–statutory demand for £1.6 million debt–failure to state security held for debt–whether demand could be set aside due to non-compliance with Insolvency Rules 1986

[Insolvency Rules 1986 r.6.1; Insolvency Rules 1986 r.6.5.]

Pursuant to a judgment, the debtor, K, owed in excess of £1.6 million to his creditor BS for failing to repurchase shares from BS. BS served a statutory demand. The demand failed to state that BS held security for the debt, in breach of the Insolvency Rules 1986 r.6.1 (5). The security was an unpaid vendor's lien over the shares or the value of that security under r.6.5(4). K applied to set aside the demand on the ground of failure to comply with r.6.1 (5).

Held, dismissing the application, that r.6.5(4) granted the court a permissive power to set aside the statutory demand. The legislature must therefore have intended there to be situations where a statutory demand was able to stand even though it did not refer to security held by the creditor. Those circumstances were where the debtor had suffered no prejudice by the omission. There was no evidence of prejudice on these facts.

KHAN v. BREEZEVALE SARL; SUB NOM. DEBTOR (NO.106 OF 1992), *Re* [1996] B.P.I.R. 190, Evans-Lombe, J., Ch D.

3472. Disclosure–corporate insolvency–transcripts of evidence to DTI inspectors–witnesses' right to oppose disclosure

[Companies Act 1985 s.432; Insolvency Act 1986 s.236, s.434.]

Two inspectors were appointed by the DTI under the Companies Act 1985 s.432 in respect of the administration of Atlantic Computers Plc, A, which had been acquired by British and Commonwealth Holdings Plc, BC. The inspectors found that A's principal product was flawed and that its accounting principles had led to an overvaluation of the company. BC sought to bring actions against numerous parties and sought disclosure of evidence given to the inspectors on the basis that it was necessary for the efficient conduct of BC's litigation. The two issues were whether s.236 of the 1986 Act bound the Crown and, if so, whether the court could exercise its discretion to order disclosure of the transcripts without giving the relevant witnesses an opportunity to be heard.

Held, allowing the application, that s.236 was binding on the Crown in respect of remedies against the company and individuals under the terms of s.434 of the 1986 Act. When exercising its discretion under s.236, the court would not order disclosure of the transcripts by the DTI without giving the witnesses the opportunity to raise objections. There was a qualified duty of confidence attaching to information obtained as a result of compulsory powers. In the circumstances, the court would order disclosure of the transcripts. However, no disclosure of the transcript of the evidence of any director of BC would be ordered before the determination of any objections of such witnesses, *British and Commonwealth Holdings Plc (Nos.1 and 2), Re* [1993] A.C. 426, [1993] C.L.Y. 2317 and *Arrows Ltd (No.4), Re* [1995] 2 A.C. 75, [1994] C.L.Y. 678 considered.

SODEN v. BURNS; SUB NOM. R. v. SECRETARY OF STATE FOR TRADE AND INDUSTRY, *ex p.* SODEN [1996] 1 W.L.R. 1512, Robert Walker, J., Ch D.

3473. Disqualification orders–directors–proceedings issued without full evidence–extension of time granted–whether good reason shown to grant leave

The company went into liquidation and the receiver's report was sent to the Secretary of State after 13 months. A decision was made in principle to commence disqualification proceedings but the matter was delayed pending attempts to secure evidence from the Serious Fraud Office. Disqualification proceedings were commenced at the end of the two year period allowed but only with outline evidence and without any supporting documentation. The Secretary of State then sought an extension of time to file evidence. The registrar granted the application and the directors appealed.

Held, dismissing the appeal, that the case against the directors was serious and it was in the public interest for it to be pursued. A delay that had not affected the defendant's ability to defend themselves should not prevent that. The disqualification proceedings were always going to take less priority than the criminal proceedings brought by the SFO and so the delay in waiting for that information had not added to the delay in the case.

BLACKSPUR GROUP PLC, *Re* [1995] B.C.C. 835, Carnwath, J., Ch D.

3474. Disqualification orders–directors–whether directors unfit

[Prevention of Fraud (Investments) Act 1958.]

The two directors ran a company operating commodities and financial futures syndicates which went into creditors' voluntary liquidation. The Secretary of State relied on six grounds for bringing disqualification proceedings: misapplication of clients' funds; failure to maintain proper client trust accounts; permitting trading whilst insolvent; permitting excessive remuneration to directors; convictions of the company under the Prevention of Fraud (Investments) Act 1958 and failures to file accounts and returns on time.

Held, disqualifying the directors for six and two years respectively, that one had taken no steps to see that his functions in the company were properly carried out while the other had taken some, inadequate steps. It could not be said that there had been a lack of moral probity in allowing the company to continue to trade, there being a real prospect of an injection of fresh capital at the time. No blame attached to the directors in relation to the conviction.

SECRETARY OF STATE FOR TRADE AND INDUSTRY v. VAN HENGEL; SUB NOM. CSTC LTD, *Re* [1995] 1 B.C.L.C. 545, Robert Reid Q.C., Ch D.

3475. Floating charges–fixed charges–priorities–crystallisation of floating charge on business cessation–assets sold post cessation subject to fixed charge

The company charged all its property to C by way of floating charge in 1988 to secure a principal sum of £100,000 from O. In 1991 the company created a fixed and floating charge over its property in favour of N. In 1994 joint administrative receivers were appointed under the 1991 charge. The company's business was sold to RMP which then created a debenture in favour of B which included fixed and floating charges over RMP's assets. The proceeds of the sale of the business went to pay N, preferential creditors and receivership costs. The book debts collected by RMP amounted to £117,000. The receiver appointed under the 1988 charge applied to determine whether RMP had acquired the business subject to the 1988 charge and whether that charge took priority over the terms of the debenture to B. The receiver argued that the book debts which were the subject of the 1988 charge had been used to pay trade creditors who could not have expected to have been paid before a secured creditor had the company been wound up or placed in receivership. RMP argued that the book debts would not have been recoverable in a receivership unless the business was sold as a going concern and that there had been no alternative to the sale. The fact that O had received nothing reflected the worthlessness of O's security.

Held, that B was liable to account to C for monies received to the credit of RMP's account insofar as they represented the proceeds of the book debts owed to RMP in respect of the business, that the 1988 charge impliedly provided for the crystallisation on demand following cessation of business. That term could be excluded only by a clear and unequivocal express term. In the absence of such term the charge crystallised on sale and so, prima facie, the assets were sold and transferred to RMP subject to a fixed charge in favour of C. That made B liable to account to C for the proceeds of the book debts as B was fixed with constructive knowledge of such matters as would have been discovered had reasonable enquiries been made by B. The assets derived from those assets transferred to RMP were held on trust for C as were assets acquired since the sale, where it could not be shown they were acquired outside, *Bank of Credit and Commerce International SA v. BRS Kumar Brothers Ltd* [1994] 1 B.C.L.C. 211, [1995] 1 C.L.Y. 2826 followed.

REAL MEAT CO LTD (IN RECEIVERSHIP), *Re* [1996] B.C.C. 254, Chadwick, J., Ch D.

3476. Guarantees–covenants–guarantor covenanting to perform lessee's obligations on default–covenant could not be set aside where Insolvency Rules r.6.5 did not apply

[Insolvency Rules 1986 r.6.5.]

A assigned his tenancy to C in return for a covenant that C would pay the rent and indemnify A against all proceedings in respect of non-payment of rent. C assigned the residue of the lease to S who covenanted directly with the landlord to comply with A's obligation under the lease. D guaranteed S's obligations by covenanting to perform them in the event of S's default. C and S then became insolvent and the lease was disclaimed. A paid certain arrears and then served a statutory demand on D which D unsuccessfully sought to set aside before the district judge. D appealed on the basis that it was arguable that the original tenant was not entitled to indemnity from the guarantor of a later assignee.

Held, dismissing the appeal, that a statutory demand should be set aside only under the Insolvency Rules 1986 r.6.5(4)(b) where the amount unpaid had to be resolved at trial or, possibly, where there was a complex issue of law with implications beyond the particular case. This was not the position here. D's obligation to pay arose from the court's approach to S who was ultimately liable for the debt, and not due to any contract with A.

CALE v. ASSUIDOMAN KPS (HARROW) LTD [1996] B.P.I.R. 245, Evans-Lombe, J., Ch D.

3477. ICE conditions of contract–contractor's plant left on site–equitable charge over plant not requiring registration–not reclaimable by administrator

[Companies Act 1985 s.395.]

The company was employed by the respondent under a contract to undertake various engineering works in a land reclamation project. To carry out the work, the company placed a coal washing plant on the site. The company suffered financial problems and abandoned the site and the plant. The company's administrator sought to reclaim the plant or obtain payment from the respondent for its use. The respondent refused on the basis that the contract, following the ICE conditions of Contract and Forms of Tender, Agreement and Bond for use with

Works of Civil Engineering Construction, fifth edition, provided that all plant owned by the contractor shall, when on site, be deemed to be the property of the employer and that if the contractor went into liquidation the employer, after giving notice, could enter the site and use or sell the plant. The administrator argued that the contract created only an equitable security interest in the plant, not absolute ownership, and that the interest thus created was a floating charge which was void against the administrator for want of registration under the Companies Act 1985 s.395.

Held, dismissing the administrator's application, that the contract, properly construed, did not transfer legal ownership of the plant to the respondent but the equitable charge created by the contract was not a floating charge because the chargor did not have unfettered freedom to carry on his business in the usual way because the plant could not be removed from the site at the will of the contractor. The contract created a specific equitable charge on relevant plant which did not have to be registered.

COSSLETT (CONTRACTORS) LTD, *Re*; SUB NOM. CLARK v. MID GLAMORGAN CC [1996] 3 W.L.R. 299, Jonathan Parker, J., Ch D.

3478. Indemnities–receivers–order for extension of time to lodge security after expiry of time for lodging–authority to act as receiver determined on expiry of time–whether appointment could be revived by later order–correct form for such orders and validating interim acts of receiver

[Rules of the Supreme Court Ord.3 r.5.]

K appealed against an order granting a receiver, R, an extension of time to lodge security required by the court order appointing R receiver and manager. The application was made after the period of time for lodging the security had expired and the judge held that, although a receiver ceased to have the authority to be a receiver on expiry of the time limit, the order extending the time retrospectively had the effect of reviving the appointment so that R continued to be a receiver and therefore his actions as a receiver in the interim period were validated. R relied upon the Rules of the Supreme Court Ord.3 r.5 para.1 and para.2 which gave the court the discretion to extend the time for complying with orders.

Held, allowing the appeal in part, that (1) if a receiver did not comply with the requirements of an order in relation to security then his appointment was determined. That fact was made clear in a resolution of the Chancery judges of February 22, 1916; (2) the judge was entitled to extend the time for lodging the security under Ord.3 r.5, but that had no effect upon R's status as a receiver in the interim period. The judge could not revive R's previous appointment, which he purported to do, but an order could be made to reappoint R and the court had the inherent jurisdiction to validate and confirm the acts of R which he had performed without authority. Such a jurisdiction was also available in respect of the validation of acts done in excess of the authorised powers of a receiver. Such a form of order was referred to in a practice note of 1943, [1943] W.N. 71, and in an article in the Law Journal (November 27, 1959), and (3) the correct form of order had the same effect as the order made by the judge so nothing had been achieved by the appeal. However, the order was amended to reflect the correct Chancery practice.

SMITH v. KEELY, Trans. Ref: CHANI 95/0042/B, June 14, 1996, Millett, L.J., CA.

3479. Individual voluntary arrangements–defendant not given requisite 14 day's notice of IVA–notice given to defendant's solicitor of no effect in absence of authority to accept it

[Insolvency Rules 1986 r.5.13.]

The landlords were owed substantial sums in respect of rent by the debtor and sued the defendant original lessees when the debtor failed to pay. The defendants relied on an indemnity proferred to them by the debtor. The debtor contended that the defendants were bound by the terms of an individual voluntary arrangement entered into by the debtor with his creditors. The defendants contended inter alia that they were not bound by the IVA because they had not been given 14 days notice of it in accordance with the Insolvency Rules 1986 r.5.13(2).

Held, in favour of the defendant, granting a declaration, that the requirement in r 5.13(2) of the 1986 Rules was clear and should not be clouded by notions like "substantial compliance". Here the creditor had not received 14 day's notice of the IVA and therefore could not be bound by it. Notice given to the creditors' solicitors would not be sufficient unless they had been given authority to accept such notice.

MYTRE INVESTMENTS LTD v. REYNOLDS (NO.2) [1996] B.P.I.R. 464, Blackburne, J., Ch D.

3480. Inland Revenue–statutory demand–whether grounds for setting aside

The Inland Revenue served a statutory demand on N, based in part on a judgment. A Deputy Registrar dismissed N's application to set it aside and authorised the presentation of a bankruptcy petition. N was also pursuing an appeal against a master's decision refusing to set aside the judgment and requested a stay of presentation of the bankruptcy petition, which was refused. On the hearing of his appeal against the refusal of the deputy registrar to set aside the statutory demand, N also sought the admission of further evidence.

Held, dismissing the appeal and refusing to admit further evidence, that the petition should proceed after the hearing of the appeal against the judgment. The judgment was valid as it stood and the statutory demand had its basis in several matters not affected by the judgment itself.

DEBTOR (NO.383-SD-92), *Re*; SUB NOM. NEELY v. INLAND REVENUE COMMISSIONERS 66 T.C. 131, Harman, J., Ch D.

3481. Insolvency practitioners–orders applied for by insolvency practitioners to vacate office must satisfy various criteria–appointing replacements by creditors agreement at a meeting or by court–illness and changing firms required different remedies

[Insolvency Act 1986.]

B and H were insolvency practitioners who acted as trustees in bankruptcy, supervisors of individual voluntary arrangements and liquidators of companies. B retired and H moved to another firm. B wished to be removed from his various offices while H sought to have his offices transferred to another individual. Both applied to the court for appropriate orders.

Held, that the Insolvency Act 1986 provided various forms of protection to creditors. In particular the creditors were entitled to be given an account of the office holder's administration of the winding up or bankruptcy, they were entitled to accept or reject any proposed resignation by an office holder and they were entitled to appoint a new liquidator. The appointment in such cases was a personal one. If an office holder sought to vacate his office he should ordinarily call a meeting of the creditors. The applications would not be granted unless the court could ensure that the creditors would have the same protection as they would have had if there had been a meeting and if the benefit to the creditors in considering the matter at a meeting was outweighed by the inconvenience and expense of holding a meeting. So far as B was concerned he was in ill health and unable to act. Even if his resignation was refused by the creditors the court would be bound to grant such an application. The order sought by B would be granted in respect of the liquidations and bankruptcies. H sought to be replaced only because he was changing firms. In that situation the creditors ought to be consulted.

SANKEY FURNITURE LTD, *ex p.* HARDING, *Re*; CALORIFIQUE LTD, *ex p.* BETTS, *Re* [1995] 2 B.C.L.C. 594, Chadwick, J., Ch D.

3482. Interim orders–creditors meeting failed to reach a voluntary agreement–whether court had jurisdiction to order a second meeting

[Insolvency Act 1986 s.253, s.257; Insolvency Rules 1986 r.5.19.]

The county court made an interim order under the Insolvency Act 1986 s.253 and considered the nominee's report after which it extended the period of the interim order. At the creditors' meeting the debtor's proposal failed to attract the required 75 per cent support. The nominee decided to adjourn the meeting for 14 days but that meeting was cancelled and the nominee lodged a report with the court. The court considered the report and extended the interim order for a further 28 days with a direction for a further creditors' meeting. At that meeting the debtor's modified proposals were passed. One creditor, K, appealed on the grounds that there was no jurisdiction to order a fresh meeting.

Held, allowing the appeal, that a creditors' meeting summoned under s.257 of the 1986 Act could only be adjourned according to the provisions of the Insolvency Rules r.5.19. The second creditors' meeting could not be said to have been an adjourned meeting from the first occasion. The court had no jurisdiction to call a second meeting or to call for a second report from the nominee. The 1986 Act contemplated a single report and that the outcome of the process would be decisive. The second meeting was invalid and the proposal approved was not a valid voluntary arrangement.

SYMES (A DEBTOR), *Re*; SUB NOM. KENT CARPETS LTD v. SYMES [1995] 2 B.C.L.C. 651, James Munby Q.C., Ch D.

3483. Interlocutory injunctions–bankruptcy–suspected failure to make full disclosure of assets–prohibited from leaving jurisdiction

[Insolvency Act 1986 s.333, s.366; Companies Act 1985.]

CM, MM's trustee in bankruptcy, commenced proceedings to commit MM for contempt and obtained an interlocutory injunction restraining MM from leaving the jurisdiction. MM sought to set aside the injunction on the basis that there was no jurisdiction to make the order and that it was made without disclosure of all the relevant facts. The judge found that there was jurisdiction to grant the order and exercised his discretion to order its continuance. MM appealed. CM was not satisfied that MM had made full disclosure under the Insolvency Act 1986 s.333. It was submitted that the statutory duty to cooperate, give information and produce documents, did not give rise to a cause of action and that an interlocutory injunction must be incidental to, and dependent upon, the enforcement of a substantial right giving rise to a cause of action.

Held, dismissing the appeal, that there was ample jurisdiction to grant the injunction. A trustee had the right to enforce the statutory duty owed by a bankrupt. It was not possible to distinguish between the statutory duty under s.333 and an order made under s.366 for the purposes of injunctive relief. It would be extraordinary, moreover, were a trustee to be able to obtain an order for arrest but not the less severe remedy of preventing the bankrupt from leaving the jurisdiction. There was no section corresponding to s.333 of the 1986 Act in the Companies Act 1985, *Oriental Credit Ltd, Re* [1988] Ch. 204, [1988] C.L.Y. 2870 distinguished. The instant litigation was not like cases involving the private rights of litigants, *Siskina (Owners of Cargo Lately Laden on Board) v. Distos Compania Naviera SA* [1979] A.C. 210, [1977] C.L.Y. 2344 and *Mercedes Benz AG v. Leiduck* [1995] 3 W.L.R. 718 distinguished. The position of the trustee, under s.333, fulfilled the requirements for the issue of injunctive relief because the statutory duty founded a sufficient interest.

MORRIS v. MURJANI [1996] 1 W.L.R. 848, Peter Gibson, L.J., CA.

3484. Leases–liquidators disclaiming onerous property–qualifying loss and interest due to landlord–applicable rates–termination of leasehold rights and obligations by disclaimer

[Judgments Act 1838; Insolvency Act 1986 s.178, s.189; Insolvency Rules 1986 r.11.13.]

L, the landlord, granted a 25 year lease of office premises to PA, the rent being set for the first five years with upward only reviews five yearly thereafter. The property market was such that by 1994/5 the rent was substantially in excess of the current rental value. PA entered into a members voluntary winding up and its joint liquidators gave notice under the Insolvency Act 1986 s.178 of disclaimer of the lease as onerous property. L applied for an order quantifying loss or damage for the purposes of the Insolvency Act 1986 s.178(6), and to determine whether the interest on sums outstanding was payable at the lease rate.

Held, giving judgment for L, that (1) the Insolvency Rules 1986 r.11.13 applied only to debts payable in the future and so not here, where the act of disclaimer had created an immediate debt due to L; (2) the proper way to calculate L's loss was to calculate, as at the date of disclaimer, the value of the rent, insurance rent, rates etc. payable by PA to which L would have been entitled during the term, to apply a "market risk rate" to reflect the current worth of payments due in the future, then give credit for what was left to L for the residue of the lease, then, if PA was in breach of repairing covenants, add the cost of any repairs necessary for securing a re-letting on terms equivalent to the original lease and (3) interest under the Insolvency Act 1986 s.189(4)(a) was payable at the rate specified in the Judgments Act 1838, not under the lease, as the disclaimer brought an end to all rights and obligations contained in the lease, *Llynvi Coal and Iron Co, ex p. Hide, Re* (1871) L.R. 7 Ch. App. 28 considered.

PARK AIR SERVICES PLC, *Re*; SUB NOM. CHRISTOPHER MORAN HOLDINGS LTD v. BAIRSTOW AND RUDDOCK [1996] 1 W.L.R. 649, Ferris, J., Ch D.

3485. Legacies–after-acquired property–trustee in bankruptcy–delay in serving notice

[Insolvency Act 1986 s.307, s.333, s.379.]

M, who was made bankrupt in November 1993, became entitled to a substantial legacy after his father's death in May 1995. The Insolvency Service were informed by the executor's solicitors of the legacy on February 1, 1996. Under the Insolvency Act 1986 s.307, there were 42 days thereafter for the trustee in bankruptcy, T, to serve notice on M claiming the legacy as after-acquired property, ie. by March 13. Meanwhile T became aware that M had moved to the USA without informing T of his new address. T wrote to M's last address on March 7, although M did not receive the letter. However, proper notice under s.307 was not sent to the old address until April 10, 28 days out of time, and this was returned unopened. M returned to the UK at the end of May. T applied under s.309 and s.379 for leave to serve out of time.

Held, that although T was not blameless in having missed the time limit, M's opposition to the application had be to viewed in the light of his own failure under s.333 to keep T informed of his address, and to notify T personally of the legacy within 21 days of knowing the relevant facts. M had displayed a laissez faire attitude and would only be inconvenienced rather than prejudiced if leave were granted, whereas the unsecured creditors would be severely prejudiced if leave were refused. In all the circumstances, 28 days delay, though significant, was not substantial, and the court would exercise its discretion in T's favour.

MATTHEW (A BANKRUPT), *Re*, September 10, 1996, District Judge Geddes, CC (Burnley). [*Ex rel.* John G Baldwin, Barrister].

3486. Liquidation–conflict of laws–director of insolvent Bermudian company facing bankruptcy proceedings in England–English courts under no duty to assist liquidators

[Insolvency Act 1986 s.426; Companies Act 1981 (Bermuda).]

The liquidators of F, a Bermudian insurance company compulsorily wound up pursuant to the Companies Act 1981 of Bermuda, applied to the English courts for orders against H, a former director of F, under the Insolvency Act 1986 s.426(4). The liquidators had obtained a judgment against H for $20 million and a Mareva injunction against disposal of assets, having also commenced bankruptcy proceedings against H in England.

Held, dismissing the application, that s.426(4) of the 1986 Act gave an English court a mandatory obligation to assist the courts of any "relevant country or territory", which included Bermuda, although the type of assistance was not specified, and the obligation should be complied with unless a good reason existed for not doing so, *Dallhold Estates, Re* [1992] B.C.L.C. 621, [1993] C.L.Y. 2323 and *Bank of Credit and Commerce International SA (No.9), Re* [1994] 3 All. E.R. 764, [1995] 1 C.L.Y. 2870 considered. A dichotomy arose between the duties of the liquidator and those of a trustee in bankruptcy under English law, however, which created an inconsistency between the orders the liquidators sought and F's status as the main creditor. The liquidator had to remit the net proceeds less expenses but the trustee had a duty to get in the assets and the fact of the bankruptcy itself served to prevent any recovery of a judgment debt. An element of oppression also arose, in that if the s.426 orders were granted, H could be exposed to an obligation to provide the same information both to the Bermudian liquidators and for the purposes of English bankruptcy proceedings.

FOCUS INSURANCE CO LTD, *Re* [1996] B.C.C. 659, Sir Richard Scott V.C., Ch D.

3487. Liquidation–deposit payments not held on trust for customers–payment giving rise to creditor and debtor relationship

The company traded in the promotion of holidays as gifts in connection with competitions run by others. The prize winner would be required to provide a refundable £150 deposit to the company to cover unpaid bar and telephone bills. The company operated two accounts, a current account and a business call account. The latter was used as a current account and the deposits were paid into the business call account but were repaid from the current account. The company went into liquidation and the question arose whether the money left in the business call account was held on trust for those who had paid deposits to the company.

Held, directing that the moneys were not held on trust, that there had been no intention in the contract with the customers that the money should be held on trust and no reason to imply such a term. The money was to form part of the general assets of the company. The payment of the deposit created a relationship of debtor and creditor only and the company was free to use the money as it pleased subject to its obligation to repay.

HOLIDAY PROMOTIONS (EUROPE) LTD, *Re* [1996] 2 B.C.L.C. 618, Timothy Lloyd Q.C., Ch D.

3488. Liquidation–property development company–financial difficulties–leases granted to directors–whether directors could rebut presumption that the transfer was a preference to a connected person

The company had been developing a property comprising a restaurant and six flats. The property was used to secure a loan and the respondent directors acted as guarantors of the company's overdraft. Four months before the company went into liquidation the company granted leases of the flats to the directors in discharge of sums owed by the company to the directors. Two of the flats were charged to the bank to secure the company's overdraft. The liquidator sought to reverse the company's disposition of the flats.

Held, granting the liquidator's application and ordering the return of the flats, that the directors had failed to displace the presumption that the transfers constituted a preference to a connected person. The transfers by way of the leases had put the directors in a better position than they would have been in an insolvent liquidation. That was the case even for the two flats charged to the bank for that transaction operated so as to limit the directors' liabilities as guarantors of the overdraft.

WEISGARD v. PILKINGTON [1995] B.C.C. 1108, Maddocks, J., Ch D.

3489. Liquidators–assignment of action for wrongful trading champertous

[Insolvency Act 1986 s.214, s.436, Sch.4.]

A and others, sometime directors or alleged shadow directors of a company Oasis Merchandising Ltd, O, successfully appealed against an order that their liquidator, W, had authority to enter into an agreement with London Wall Litigation Claims Ltd, L, to finance wrongful trading proceedings brought in terms of the Insolvency Act 1986 s.214. L appealed on the grounds that, although the agreement was champertous, by virtue of the 1986 Act Sch.4 para.6 under which the liquidator had power to sell any of the company's property, the liquidator had statutory authority to sell the fruits of the s.214 action. Alternatively, the agreement was an act necessary for winding up O's affairs and distributing its assets and was an act the liquidator therefore had the requisite power to do in terms of the 1986 Act Sch.4 para.13. The respondents contended that the s.214 action was not company property.

Held, dismissing the appeal, that (1) in answering the primary question of construing the statutory power of sale it was necessary to decide what constituted company property. In terms of the 1986 Act s.436, company property did not include a s.214 action. A distinction had to be drawn between assets which were the property of the company at the time of commencement of the liquidation and assets which only arose after the liquidation and were recoverable only by the liquidator pursuant to statutory powers, *Re Movitor Pty Ltd v. Sims* (1995) 19 A.C.S.R. 440 distinguished and (2) the agreement the liquidator entered into was an attempt to restrict his conduct of the action. Public policy demanded that it be regarded as champertous and Sch.4 did not authorise the agreement as being necessary for the winding up of the company's affairs.

WARD v. AITKEN; SUB NOM. OASIS MERCHANDISING SERVICES LTD, *Re*, *The Times*, October 14, 1996, Peter Gibson, L.J., CA.

3490. Liquidators–assignment of rights in liquidated company at undervalue–right of unsecured creditors to seek directions from court–test for whether assignment should be set aside

[Insolvency Act 1986 s.167, s.168.]

V, the assignee of a right of action belonging to E, a company in liquidation, whose shares he held, appealed against a decision which upheld the setting aside of the assignment and which removed from office the liquidator who made the assignment. E's rights had been assigned at an undervalue despite the objections of unsecured creditors who argued that the realisation of E's assets could be better achieved had they been given the opportunity to make a better offer. V contended that unsecured creditors did not have the right to seek a direction of the court, under the Insolvency Act 1986 s.167(3), to impugn the assignment by the liquidator as unsecured creditors were not "persons aggrieved" within the 1986 Act s.168(5).

Held, allowing the appeal in part, that it was unnecessary to define a class of "persons aggrieved" by an action or decision of a liquidator but, in the instant case, unsecured creditors clearly fell within that category as their interests were prejudiced by the disposal of assets to V. The correct test had been applied by the judge below in reaching the conclusion that, in assigning E's right of action without making inquiry as to whether a better offer was available, the liquidator had acted in a way that no reasonable person would have done. However, it was not appropriate to remove the liquidator from office as there were insufficient grounds to show that creditors had lost confidence in his abilities and that such loss of confidence was reasonable, *Keypack Homecare Ltd, Re* [1987] B.C.L.C. 409, [1987] C.L.Y. 373 considered.

EDENNOTE LTD, *Re*; SUB NOM. TOTTENHAM HOTSPUR PLC v. RYMAN [1996] 2 B.C.L.C. 389, Nourse, L.J., CA.

3491. Liquidators–assignment to creditor–rights to and choses in action concerning dispositions of company–whether liquidator had such a power

[Insolvency Act 1986 s.127, Sch.4.]

The company contracted to build a conference centre in Kuwait and arranged financing through the National Bank of Kuwait. A condition of that financing required the bank to assign rights of all moneys due to the company from the project. The work was completed but final settlement delayed pending resolution of some defects. The company gave the bank irrevocable instructions for the allocation of the remaining sums due. The company was then wound up and a question arose as to the bank's right to retain the money subsequently paid to them on final completion of the project. M, a creditor, brought an application for relief, the liquidator being without funds to pursue an application. The liquidator then assigned to M all rights to and choses in action. The question of the liquidator's power to assign rights to have the dispositions of the company's property declared void was taken as a preliminary issue.

Held, that the liquidator could not assign such rights to a creditor. Although the assets of a company were assignable by sale, under the Insolvency Act 1986 Sch.4, the rights that were conferred on a liquidator in relation to the conduct of litigation were not assignable as they were incidental to the office of liquidator under s.127.

AYALA HOLDINGS LTD (NO.2), *Re* [1996] 1 B.C.L.C. 467, Knox, J., Ch D.

3492. Liquidators–liabilities–payment made to parent company in advance of company's creditors–extent of liability to repay on admitted creditor's proofs

[Insolvency Act 1986 s.212; Insolvency Rules 1986 r.4.85.]

A, a wholly owned subsidiary of Minstar, M, went into a members' voluntary liquidation. Ellis, E, the appointed liquidator, paid £920,000 to M before he had paid all A's creditors and in particular the landlords, L, of the premises demised to A. Eventually E disclaimed the lease, admitted L's proof of debt in the sum of £572,444 and paid £200,000 on account of that sum. E could not pay any more than that because he no longer had funds available and M refused to return any part of the £920,000. At L's instigation E was removed as liquidator and Cohen, C, was appointed in his place. C admitted L's proof of debt in the sum of £759,511 and then sought an order against E, under the Insolvency Act 1986 s.212, to secure repayment of the sum paid to M. E admitted that he was in breach of his duty as liquidator in paying M before the creditors but contended that he was liable to repay only such sum as L could establish to be the true debt and loss sustained. C contended that E was liable to repay the sum comprised in the admitted proof of debt, ie. £759,511, less the £200,000 already paid.

Held, declaring the extent of E's liability, that E was not a contributory and therefore not entitled to appeal under the Insolvency Rules 1986 r.4.85 against C's acceptance of L's proof of debt in the sum of £759,511. In fixing the extent of E's liability to repay, for the purposes of s.212(3) of the 1986 Act, the court was bound to have regard to the fact that if E had not paid £920,000 to M, C would have paid L the amount of the admitted proof of debt without further inquiry. In the absence of fraud or bad faith on the part of the creditors or the new liquidator, the court could not go behind decisions reached in the ordinary course of the liquidation in accordance with the provisions of the Act and the

Rules. Accordingly E was bound by C's acceptance of L's proof of debt and was not entitled to dispute the valuation.

AMF INTERNATIONAL LTD (NO.2), *Re*; SUB NOM. COHEN v. ELLIS [1996] 1 W.L.R. 77, Ferris, J., Ch D.

3493. Liquidators–powers to appoint new liquidator on withdrawal of authorisation by Secretary of State–whether power applicable to creditors' voluntary liquidation and individual voluntary arrangements

[Insolvency Act 1986 s.108, s.373; Insolvency Rules 1986 r.5.]

Held, when an insolvency practitioner ceased to act after his authority was withdrawn by the Secretary of State he vacated his office as liquidator and ceased to be qualified to act as a supervisor of voluntary arrangements. The court could appoint a new liquidator, under the Insolvency Act 1986 s.108(1), in existing winding up proceedings on an application by the Secretary of State but the court had no jurisdiction, on such an application, to appoint a new supervisor in relation to existing individual voluntary arrangements. Jurisdiction over such matters lay with the county court allocated under the Insolvency Rules 1986 r.5.5A(1), whose jurisdiction was confirmed under s.373(3) of the 1986 Act.

BRIDGEND GOLDSMITHS LTD, *Re* [1995] 2 B.C.L.C. 208, Blackburne, J., Ch D.

3494. Liquidators–remuneration and costs application–compulsory winding up

[Insolvency Rules 1986 r.4.127; Insolvency Rules 1986 r.4.130 Insolvency Regulations 1986.]

The applicant was appointed as voluntary liquidator for a period of eight weeks, after which a compulsory order was made on the petition of a creditor. No liquidation committee met and so the applicant's remuneration fell to be determined by the scale laid down in the Insolvency Regulations 1986. The applicant applied for his remuneration and costs to be treated and allowed as an expense of the compulsory winding up. The compulsory liquidator objected to the claim.

Held, allowing the claim and referring the assessment to the registrar, that if a voluntary liquidator could show that the remuneration to which he was entitled under the Insolvency Rules 1986 r.4.127 was insufficient and that the case was a proper one for an increase the court had a discretion under the Insolvency Rules 1986 r.4.130 to enhance the remuneration of the voluntary liquidator. The applicant was entitled to an allowance for his work even if it had to be duplicated by the compulsory liquidator. The applicant would be entitled to his costs and disbursements and the question of the level of his remuneration would be referred to the registrar.

TONY ROWSE NMC LTD, *Re* [1996] 2 B.C.L.C. 225, ME Mann Q.C., Ch D.

3495. Liquidators–remuneration forming winding up expenses–method of determining remuneration–whether amount reasonable–whether company insolvent at point that it went into liquidation given level of winding up expenses

[Company Directors Disqualification Act 1986 s.6; Insolvency Act 1986; Insolvency Rules 1986 r.4; Insolvency Regulations 1986 Reg.19.]

The respondents were directors of G. The company went into compulsory liquidation with debts of £528,461 and assets of £636,643. The liquidator had considerable difficulty in recovering debts due to the company and his fees were fixed at £102,354 in accordance with the provisions of the Insolvency Rules 1986 r.4.127(2)(a). Payments made by the liquidator, other than by way of distributions to creditors, totalled £184,410. The Official Receiver applied to disqualify the respondents under the Company Directors Disqualification Act 1986 s.6. An issue arose as to whether the company had been insolvent as defined by s.6(2)(a) on the date it went into liquidation. The issue was what liquidator's fees were to be included within the phrase "expenses of winding up" and the method to be used to fix such fees. The judge held that "reasonable" fees would be included within the expenses of the winding up and that these should be determined by applying the scale laid down for the Official Receiver, which gave a fee of either £53,241 or £61,000. An inquiry was directed as to whether the company had been insolvent at the time that it had gone into liquidation.

Held, finding the company had been insolvent, that the expression "expenses of the winding up" included the liquidator's fees payable under the 1986 Regulations and Rules as applicable. There was no reason why such expenses should be determined differently for Company Directors Disqualification Act 1986 or Insolvency Act 1986 purposes. The fee charged by the liquidator, although high, was properly allowed under the rules and even if this was incorrect, the Official Receiver's scale, as found in the Insolvency Regulations 1986 Reg.19, would have been reasonable. In either event, the winding up expenses were in excess of G's surplus, therefore it followed that the company had been insolvent when it went into liquidation.

GOWER ENTERPRISES LTD, *Re* [1995] 2 B.C.L.C. 107, Blackburne, J., Ch D.

3496. Liquidators' liabilities–distributions made to parent company–subsequently disclaiming lease–liability for costs of lessor's claim

[Insolvency Act 1986 s.178.]

AMF went into members' voluntary liquidation and a liquidator, E, was appointed. E made distributions to AMF's parent company and took an indemnity from them. The applicant was the assignee of the reversion on AMF's business premises which E viewed as a liability and disclaimed. The applicant claimed under the Insolvency Act 1986 s.178(6). The liquidator was removed at a creditors' meeting under the Insolvency Act 1986 s.95. A new liquidator was appointed and the applicant sought to claim the costs of the application from E personally.

Held, allowing the claim, that E should be personally liable for the costs incurred. He had erred in making payments to the parent company without providing for any liabilities under the lease and could be held liable for any deficiencies to the new liquidator if the company failed to honour the indemnity. Accordingly, the liquidator had brought the claim upon himself.

AMF INTERNATIONAL LTD, *Re*; SUB NOM. AMF INTERNATIONAL LTD v. ELLIS; CHONTOW v. ELLES [1995] 2 B.C.L.C. 529, Ferris, J., Ch D.

3497. Loan agreements–winding up provision–whether contributor's liability varied–list of contributors

[Insolvency Rules 1986 r.4.]

An arrangement was entered into whereby the applicants subscribed £245,000 for shares in the company of which only £100,000 were paid up. C, a company owned by the applicants, loaned £145,000 to the company. The loan agreement provided that on winding up the money owed by the company to C was to be treated as having been paid and the applicants treated as having paid an amount equivalent to the sum outstanding on their share subscription. The company was wound up and the applicants sought an order, under the Insolvency Rules 1986 r.4, to alter the list of contributors so that they were shown as having paid in full for the shares.

Held, dismissing the application, that the agreement did not discharge the applicants' liability and they should remain on the list of contributors. The effect of the agreement was to subordinate C as a lender to the level held by the applicants had they paid the remainder of the sums owed on the share subscription. The agreement did not provide that each debt should cancel out the other.

PINECORD LTD (IN LIQUIDATION), *Re*; SUB NOM. BENNETT v. ROLPH [1995] 2 B.C.L.C. 57, Lightman, J., Ch D.

3498. Misrepresentation–winding up–parent company seeking damages for misrepresentation in purchase of subsidiary–subordination

[Insolvency Act 1986 s.74.]

S and another, administrators of the insolvent Atlantic Computers, AC, appealed against a decision in an action brought by BC, AC's parent company, for damages arising from negligent misrepresentation. BC argued that they had been induced, by misleading and false representations, to purchase shares in AC which were, in fact, worthless. S sought determination as to whether BC's claim was made in its character as a member of the company, which would subordinate its claim to the claims of unsecured creditors pursuant to the Insolvency Act 1986 s.74(2)(f), which provided that sums due to company members by way of dividends or profits were not deemed to be a debt of the company.

Held, dismissing the appeal, that the principle of s.74(2)(f) was that members' rights were subordinated to those of creditors, but a claim by a member was not prevented provided that it was analogous to dividends or profits. However, BC's claim was not a claim for sums owed in its character as a member of AC, as the damages sought could not be construed as being due by way of dividends or profits. Section 74 also applied to a claim for unliquidated damages, *Webb Distributors (Aust) Pty Ltd v. State of Victoria* (1993) 11 A.C.S.R. 731 and *Addlestone Linoleum Co, Re* (1887) 37 Ch. 191 considered.

SODEN v. BRITISH AND COMMONWEALTH HOLDINGS PLC (IN ADMINISTRATION) [1996] 3 All E.R. 951, Peter Gibson, L.J., CA.

3499. Non-domestic business rates–rates due after date of voluntary liquidation formed part of liquidation expenses

[Insolvency Act 1986 s.112.]

The company elected to pay its business rates in instalments. On October 29, 1990 the company went into voluntary liquidation and the liquidator continued to trade from the company's premises until June 1991. There was a dispute as to how the rates from October 30, 1990 were to be dealt with, whether they were an expense of the liquidation or whether the respondent had to prove in the liquidation. The liquidator applied, under the Insolvency Act 1986 s.112, for a determination of the matter.

Held, that any claim which accrued before the winding up and fell due before the date of the commencement of the winding up had to be proved in the liquidation. Rates which fell due after October 29, 1990 in respect of the property where the liquidator retained possession should be paid as expenses of the liquidation.

NOLTON BUSINESS CENTRES LTD, *Re*; SUB NOM. ELIADES v. CITY OF LONDON COMMON COUNCIL [1996] 1 B.C.L.C. 400, Judge Weeks Q.C., Ch D.

3500. Partnerships

INSOLVENT PARTNERSHIPS (AMENDMENT) ORDER 1996, SI 1996 1308; made under the Insolvency Act 1986 s.420; and the Company Directors Disqualification Act 1986 s.21. In force: June 14, 1996; £0.65.

This Order amends the Insolvent Partnerships Order 1994 (SI 1994 2421) which provides for the winding up of insolvent partnerships. The amendment to Art.7 of the Order, which provides for the winding up of an insolvent partnership, as an unregistered company, on the petition of a creditor, a responsible insolvency practitioner or the Secretary of State, where no concurrent petition is presented against a member, extends the list of petitioners to include any person other than a member. This will include the Bank of England and the Securities and Investments Board, entitled under the Banking Act 1987 and the Financial Services Act 1986 respectively, to present a petition for the winding up of an insolvent partnership.

3501. Practice Directions–appeals–single judge of High Court

[Insolvency Rules 1986 r.7.48; Rules of the Supreme Court Ord.59.]

A Practice Direction was released for the procedure and hearing of appeals from the decision of a circuit or district judge of the county court or a registrar in bankruptcy to a single High Court judge under Insolvency Rules 1986 r.7.48(2). Provision is made for the allocation of such appeals, for the application of Rules of the Supreme Court Ord.59 to such appeals and for the procedural steps for bringing such an appeal.

PRACTICE DIRECTION (INSOLVENCY APPEALS: INDIVIDUALS) [1995] 1 W.L.R. 1323, Sir Donald Nicholls, V.C., Ch D.

3502. Practice Directions–compulsory winding up–advertisement of petition–penalities

[Insolvency Rules 1986 r.4.11.]

The attention of practitioners is drawn to Insolvency Rules 1986 r.4.11 (2) (b) (SI 1986 1925). The rule is mandatory, and designed to ensure that the class remedy of winding up by the court is duly made available to all creditors, and is not used as a means of putting pressure on the company to pay the petitioner's debt. Failure to comply with the rule, without good reason accepted by the court, may lead to the summary dismissal of the petition on the return date, r.4.11 (5). If the court, in its discretion, grants an adjournment, this will be on condition that the petition is advertised in due time for the adjourned hearing. No further adjournment for the purpose of advertisement will normally be granted.

PRACTICE DIRECTION (COMPANY: ADVERTISEMENT OF COMPULSORY WINDING-UP PETITION) [1996] 1 W.L.R. 1255, Chief Bankruptcy Registrar, Ch D.

3503. Receivership–indemnifier's liabilities for receiver's costs and fees–statutory interpretation–jurisdiction of companies court to make orders under the Insolvency Act 1986

[Insolvency Act 1986 s.35.]

M, an indemnifier, appealed against a refusal to rescind an order requiring payment of £109,770 to L, the joint receiver of TS. Prior to L's appointment M had agreed to indemnify L, inter alia, for costs, fees and liabilities incurred in the administration, in reliance on which L had sought £110,000 from M in respect of an unexpected insurance claim shortfall. L had also obtained an order from the companies court, under the Insolvency Act 1986 s.35, as to M's liability towards him as the indemnifier.

Held, dismissing the appeal, that s.35 of the Act was widely drafted and permitted the court to make declarations as to an indemnifier's liabilities for receivership costs. As a result, the order made was not beyond the power of the court, as M had contended.

THERM-A-STOR LTD (IN ADMINISTRATIVE RECEIVERSHIP), *Re*; SUB NOM. MORRIS v. LEWIS [1996] 1 W.L.R. 1338, Laddie, J., Ch D.

3504. Sale of land–mortgagees duty to mortgagor to obtain best price–duty of administrative receiver

Bank Leumi (UK) Ltd, BL, the second defendant, appealed against the dismissal of their summons to strike out E's statement of claim. E brought an action against BL and B, the administrative receiver appointed by BL in respect of properties charged to BL as security for a loan to E. E had claimed that BL and B had breached their duty to E to try to get the best price for the properties which E claimed were sold at undervalue at auction. It was claimed that B had operated under the directions of BL. The judge found that E's allegations were not made out but decided that it was not a case where E's statement of claim should be struck out.

Held, dismissing the appeal, that various aspects of the conduct of the auction showed a triable issue as to whether BL had breached their duty by directing the sale. Evidence that solicitors advising E on the sale were also advising BL on the sale and the solicitor's attendance note stating that he rang

BL before the auction began supported that conclusion. Additionally, E's claim that BL had threatened to ruin him both personally and financially was not disputed by BL's employee in his affidavit. Accordingly, there was an issue as to whether or not the threat was made.

EBERT v. BOWIE; SUB NOM. EBERT v. BANK LEUMI (UK) LTD, Trans. Ref: 94/1247/C; 94/1248/C, November 14, 1995, Morritt, L.J., CA.

3505. Set off–guarantor of overdraft seeking to set off debt against sums in other bank accounts–whether had sufficient mutuality or reciprocity

[Insolvency Rules 1986 r.4.90.]

BCCI sought to recover money from AS pursuant to a guarantee given by him in respect of an overdrawn balance owed to BCCI by a company. AS contended that he should be allowed to set off certain sums held in other BCCI accounts on the grounds of his beneficial entitlement to those sums. AS had been granted leave to defend an action to recover the money commenced by BCCI's liquidators, but this had been overturned on appeal. AS appealed.

Held, dismissing the appeal, that, under the Insolvency Rules 1986 r.4.90 and following the rule in *Willis, Percival & Co, ex p. Morier, Re* (1879) 12 Ch. D. 491, not all debts eligible for proof under r.4.90 were eligible for set off in the absence of the mutuality or reciprocity of such debts. Owing to the uncertain nature of the bank accounts in question, some inquiry would be required to settle ownership of the sums involved. In the absence of a clear entitlement by AS to the sums, there was insufficient mutuality or reciprocity to permit set off against the amount sought under the guarantee contract.

BANK OF CREDIT AND COMMERCE INTERNATIONAL SA (IN LIQUIDATION) v. AL-SAUD [1997] B.C.C. 63, Neill, L.J., CA.

3506. Set off–winding up proceedings–whether court had power to disapply set off rules to allow application of foreign insolvency law

[Insolvency Act 1986 s.125; Insolvency Rules 1986 r.4.90 (SI 1986 1925).]

The English liquidators of BCCI applied for directions as to whether the Insolvency Rules 1986 r.4.90 could be disapplied before transferring assets to the principal foreign liquidator in Luxembourg to be distributed pari passu between the creditors in the course of winding up proceedings. BCCI was incorporated in Luxembourg, where different rules of set off applied, with the effect that a creditor would receive only a dividend of the sum due after paying his debts in full, whereas in England a creditor could, in accordance with r.4.90, set off his debt to the company and have his own debt satisfied in full.

Held, that a court had no power, under either the Insolvency Act 1986 s.125 or the 1986 Rules, to disapply the statutory winding up scheme notwithstanding that the applicant was the "ancillary" liquidator rather than the "principal". The English courts maintained a duty to apply English insolvency law and thus the ancillary liquidator should retain sufficient funds to protect the position of net creditors and debtors proved in the English liquidation and entitled to set off, prior to the transfer of assets to the Luxembourg liquidators.

BANK OF CREDIT AND COMMERCE INTERNATIONAL SA (IN LIQUIDATION) (NO.10), *Re* [1996] 4 All E.R. 796, Sir Richard Scott, V.C., Ch D.

3507. Statutory demands–credit agreement regulated by the Consumer Credit Act 1974–no judgment obtained in the county court–whether creditor entitled to issue a statutory demand

[Consumer Credit Act 1974; Insolvency Act 1986.]

M, the debtor under an agreement regulated by the Consumer Credit Act 1974, appealed against the refusal to set aside a decision that, G the creditor, was entitled to use a statutory demand under the Insolvency Act 1986 without having first obtained judgment in the County Court.

Held, dismissing the appeal, that the 1986 Act did not require a creditor to obtain a judgment in the County Court before he could serve a statutory demand. A creditor was entitled to present a bankruptcy petition provided that it was in relation to a debt that was over £750 and was for a liquidated sum and the debtor was either unable to pay or had no reasonable prospect of paying. The word "debt" did not exclude debts protected by the 1974 Act.

MILLS v. GROVE SECURITIES LTD [1996] C.C.L.R. 74, Peter Gibson, L.J., CA.

3508. Surveyors–alleged negligent valuation of property–surveyors going into liquidation–insurance policy void–action for disclosure relating to policy

[Third Parties (Rights Against Insurers) Act 1930 s.1, s.2.]

W commenced proceedings against S, who were surveyors, for damages for breach of contract and professional negligence in connection with the valuation of a property against which W had advanced monies. S defended the claim on the ground that it had not been negligent and was not responsible for the loss claimed by W. S had a policy of professional indemnity insurance with I. After the commencement of the action S went into creditors' voluntary liquidation. Thereafter both the liquidator of S and I wrote to W indicating that insurance cover was not available to meet W's claim as I had avoided the policy for material non-disclosure. W wished to ascertain whether there was any merit in I's position before expending further monies in pursuing S for what might prove to be a worthless judgment. W sought disclosure from the liquidator and I of the policy and all documents relating to the avoidance of the same by I. Both parties refused to provide the information requested whereupon W issued proceedings seeking a declaration that they were bound to do so pursuant to the provisions of the Third Parties (Rights Against Insurers) Act 1930 s.1 and s.2.

Held, dismissing W's claim, that it was impossible to tell whether S had incurred any liability to W until after the determination of that issue in the action by W against S. Accordingly it was impossible to tell whether the triggering event of "any such liability is incurred by the insured" within s.1 (1) of the Act had occurred so as to give rise to an obligation to provide information under s.2 of the Act, *Post Office v. Norwich Union Fire Insurance Society Ltd* [1967] 2 Q.B. 363, [1967] C.L.Y. 2038; *Nigel Upchurch Associates v. Aldridge Estates Investment Co Ltd* [1993] 1 Lloyd's Rep. 535, [1993] C.L.Y. 3213 considered.

WOOLWICH BUILDING SOCIETY v. TAYLOR [1995] 1 B.C.L.C. 132, Lindsay, J., Ch D.

3509. Transactions at an undervalue–accountant's alleged professional negligence avoided by indemnity policy–transfers of property to wife–true intention behind transfers–discretion of court to grant relief

[Insolvency Act 1986 s.423.]

An application was made under the Insolvency Act 1986 s.423 by individuals who were pursuing civil claims against F. F had been accountant to the applicants who had allegedly caused them loss by professional negligence. Criminal charges had been brought against F in the wake of an Inland Revenue investigation. It was likely that F's professional indemnity insurance policy would be avoided and that he would therefore have to meet the award out of his own assets. In expectation of this, F had transferred all his assets (including the matrimonial home) into the name of his wife, the second respondent. These transfers included the acquisition of a flat by the wife, with money given to her by F, which was then put in their joint names. There were letters exchanged between husband and wife that these gifts were in fact in recognition for all the help she had given him in building up his accountancy practice. The applicants claimed that the true purpose of the transfers was to put assets out of the reach of creditors.

Held, that (1) there was no doubt that these transactions complained of were transactions at an undervalue which could only be construed as gifts. The acquisition of the flat was similarly a transaction at an undervalue; (2) the second respondent's belief that the transfers to her were in consideration for her assistance in building up F's accountancy practice was irrelevant. The crucial question was F's intention. On the evidence, the intention was to put assets out of the reach of the applicants, and (3) the court had wide discretion to grant relief under s.423 and s.425 of the 1986 Act. The cash, £5,000, still held by the second respondent was to be transferred into a joint bank account held between both parties' solicitors. No order would be made with respect to the matrimonial home or the flat until the civil claims had reached their conclusion. However, further dealings with the matrimonial home and the flat would be restrained until the completion of the civil proceedings.

MOON v. FRANKLIN [1996] B.P.I.R. 196, Mervyn Davies, J., Ch D.

3510. Transactions at an undervalue–assignment of agricultural tenancy and sale of assets to sons–whether purpose to frustrate bank–whether documents between defendants and solicitors discoverable

[Insolvency Act 1986 s.423.]

E owned land, which E and M farmed together with other land they occupied as tenants. In 1992 the bank granted a 20 year loan to purchase further land, secured on the freehold land. Further funds were secured by converting the loan to a 12 month facility and charging the agricultural assets. In March 1994 the Inland Revenue distrained goods on the farm. A week later, E and M, without informing the bank, assigned the tenancy and agreed to sell agricultural assets to E's sons. The bank applied for declarations, under the Insolvency Act 1986 s.423, that the transactions were void and unenforceable and for discovery of all communications between E and M and their legal advisers relating to the transactions. The judge ordered discovery. E and M appealed.

Held, dismissing the appeal, that (1) before an order could be made under s.423 the court had to be satisfied that a transaction had been entered into at an undervalue and for a prohibited purpose. Here there was a strong prima facie case that the purpose of the transactions was to frustrate the bank's interest and (2) it must have been obvious to E and M that once the bank learnt of the transactions it would commence proceedings. The dominant purpose of the legal advice was not to explain the legal effect of what had been done, or for use in contemplated proceedings, but to stop the bank interfering with what they regarded as their family assets. That purpose was sufficiently iniquitous for public policy to require that legal professional privilege should not apply and that the communications in relation to the setting up of the transactions should be discoverable.

BARCLAYS BANK PLC v. EUSTICE [1995] 1 W.L.R. 1238, Schiemann, L.J., CA.

3511. Transactions at an undervalue–test for determining–purpose of transferor to be investigated–whether prima facie case

[Insolvency Act 1986 s.423.]

L remortgaged his home after proceedings had been issued against him by RSL for the debts of his business. The home had been remortgaged after L had transferred it to his wife and stepson. RSL applied to have the remortgage set aside on the ground that the transaction was an attempt to defraud creditors under the Insolvency Act 1986 s.423. The transaction was held to be fraudulent because it was at a substantial undervalue and only occurred three days before RSL obtained summary judgment. However, there was evidence that the purpose was to raise money rather than defraud. L appealed.

Held, allowing the appeal, that the test under s.423 was not only an objective one and the purpose of the transferor had to be investigated. RSL had failed to show that, prima facie, the objective of the remortgage had been to put the assets beyond the reach of the creditors.

ROYSCOTT SpA LEASING LTD v. LOVETT [1995] B.C.C. 502, Beldam, L.J., CA.

3512. Travel agents–holding money on trust for customers–provider in liquidation–commission payments due to agents–whether deductible before payment–nature of trust money

ILG provided package holidays through travel agents. Under agreements between ILG and the travel agents it was provided that the agents held money received from the customers as trustee until the contract was confirmed, whereupon the travel agents held the money on an express trust for ILG. The travel agents were entitled to a 10 per cent commission. ILG's liquidator brought proceedings against travel agents who held money claiming that it was held on trust and was to be paid over without deduction for commission or set off.

Held, that the agreements created a charge in equity over the monies to secure payment of the agents' indebtedness to ILG. The travel agents were entitled to deduct from the monies the sums owed to them by ILG. If that were not the case then the money owed to the travel agents could be set off against the travel agents' indebtedness to ILG. The agreement had created a bare trust and could not destroy the mutuality of dealings between the parties. The use of the expression "express trust" was not enough to oust the mutuality of dealings.

ILG TRAVEL LTD (IN ADMINISTRATION), *Re* [1995] 2 B.C.L.C. 128, Jonathan Parker, J., Ch D.

3513. Trusts–matrimonial home settled on wife and children–commercial venture failed–trust merely a sham to put property beyond reach of creditors

[Insolvency Act 1986 s.423.]

W settled the matrimonial home on trust for his wife and daughters in June 1987. W at no time informed the bank, his business partners or the solicitors of the declaration of trust. His wife stated that she left all financial matters to her husband and that she would probably not have signed the documentation if she had known what she was signing. W set up a company four years later as a commercial venture which then went into liquidation. W sought to rely on the declaration of trust against the claim of the creditor bank in bankruptcy.

Held, that the burden of proof that this was a sham transaction or that the declaration of trust was voidable, under the Insolvency Act 1986 s.423, fell on MB. The court must be satisfied as to the true nature or object of the transaction in question. On the facts, W had no intention of endowing his children or his wife with an interest in the property. It was created so as to protect his family from long term financial risk should he set up his own company. As such, the declaration of trust was not what it purported to be but a pretence or sham. Even if the transaction was entered into without fraudulent motive or on the basis of mistaken advice, it was still void and therefore an unenforceable transaction. The declaration therefore fell within s.423 of the Act and was voidable, being for the purpose of putting property beyond the reach of creditors.

MIDLAND BANK PLC v. WYATT [1995] 1 F.L.R. 697, DEM Young Q.C., Ch D.

3514. Voluntary arrangements–application to set aside approval abandoned–scope of review under the Insolvency Act 1986

[Insolvency Act 1986 s.375.]

On May 30, 1990, an individual voluntary arrangement with respect to the affairs of Mr and Mrs F was approved by a meeting of creditors. S, a creditor, applied in person to set aside the approval, to remove the supervisor and to convene a new meeting on November 5, 1990. On March 7, 1991, the district judge dismissed the application. With the benefit of solicitor's and counsel's advice, S appealed but on July 2, 1991, by consent, the appeal was withdrawn. S applied under the Insolvency Act 1986 s.375(1) to review the district judge's order. The district judge declined. S appealed.

Held, that the ability to review, under s.375(1) of the 1986 Act, was a valuable one which should not be unduly limited. There was judicial discretion with reference to wastage of costs and the public policy requirement of finality of decision. However, the review procedure was not a gateway for allowing late appeals. It was for the appellant to establish a compelling and preferably fresh case for permission to proceed after the time for appeal had passed, explaining the reasons for delay. On the merits, special circumstances leading to some manifest injustice had to be shown. On the facts, no special circumstances existed given that there was nothing which could not have been argued on the abandoned appeal.

DEBTORS (NOS.VA7 AND VA8 OF 1990), *ex p.* STEVENS, *Re* [1996] B.P.I.R. 101, Lindsay, J., Ch D.

3515. Voluntary arrangements–assignee of lease–liability of original lessee for rent–effect of voluntary arrangement

[Insolvency Act 1986 s.5.]

H, the assignee of a lease, entered into a voluntary arrangement with its creditors pursuant to the Insolvency Act 1986 s.5(2). The claims of H's preferential creditors were so large that the landlords, RA, could not recover any rent or service charges owing from H. The creditors' meeting approved the voluntary arrangement, under which it was proposed that each of H's lessors would accept a surrender of their respective leases, and take steps to mitigate their losses. RA did not attend this meeting and instead pursued M, the original lessee, for all outstanding sums due under the lease. M conceded that it was liable under the lease until the voluntary arrangement was entered into, but argued that at that point RA had accepted a surrender of the lease and M's liability was extinguished by that surrender.

Held, giving judgment for RA, that although RA was deemed to be a party to the voluntary arrangement and bound by it by virtue of s.5(2) of the 1986 Act, the effect of the arrangement was limited to the parties to it and could provide no assistance to an outsider such as M unless and until an act was done in reliance on the arrangement. It would be unfair if a solvent debtor escaped liability as a sidewind of the voluntary arrangement system, *Hill v. East and West India Dock Co* (1884) 9 App Cas 448 and *Levy Ex p. Walton, Re* (1881) 17 Ch. D. 746 considered. The fact that RA was bound by the terms of the voluntary arrangement did not mean that it had voluntarily accepted a different performance of M's obligations other than payment of rent due, *Deanplan Ltd v. Mahmoud* [1992] 3 All E.R. 945, [1992] C.L.Y. 497 considered.

RA SECURITIES LTD v. MERCANTILE CREDIT CO LTD [1995] 3 All E.R. 581, Jacob, J., Ch D.

3516. Voluntary arrangements–debtor failed to make payments and provide information–different trustee appointed–correct distribution of money held by former supervisor

[Insolvency Act 1986 s.264.]

D entered into an individual voluntary arrangement, IVA, on November 12, 1992. He failed to make payments and provide information as required under the IVA, therefore, his supervisor petitioned for bankruptcy under the Insolvency Act 1986 s.264(1)(c). A different insolvency practitioner was appointed to be trustee. The former supervisor sought directions as to how he was to deal with £20,000 which remained in his hands. The question was whether it should be distributed according to the IVA or handed over to the trustee in bankruptcy. The registrar held that the bankruptcy did not terminate the IVA. The trustee in bankruptcy appealed.

Held, that where the supervisor of the IVA petitioned for D's bankruptcy under s.264(1)(c), the making of the order must terminate the IVA, *Bradley-Hole, Re* [1995] B.C.C. 418, [1995] 1 C.L.Y. 428 and *McKeen, Re* [1995] B.C.C. 412, [1996] C.L.Y. 3517 distinguished. The funds held by the supervisor, subject to the supervisor's expenses, must be handed over to the trustee in bankruptcy for distribution among all the creditors of the bankrupt.

HUSSEIN (ESSENGIN), *Re* [1996] B.P.I.R. 160, Blackburne, J., Ch D.

3517. Voluntary arrangements–effect of bankruptcy order–whether arrangement terminated–whether creditors bound by arrangement

[Insolvency Act 1986 s.282, s.382.]

M along with a partner carried on a business as a recruitment agency. Due to the insolvency of other debtors the partnership itself became insolvent. M drew up an approved voluntary arrangement to settle the debts. After the arrangement was set up rent fell due for the business premises and the landlord served a statutory demand and obtained a bankruptcy order. M applied to have the order annulled, under the Insolvency Act 1986 s.282(1) (b), on the ground that the debts due to the landlord had been paid under the voluntary arrangement. The judge found that the debts due to the creditors bound by the voluntary arrangement were bankruptcy debts under s.382(1) and had not been paid in full. M appealed on the ground, inter alia, that the bankruptcy order did not terminate the voluntary arrangement.

Held, allowing the application, that (1) the voluntary arrangement had not been terminated by the bankruptcy order. The assets in the arrangement vested in the trustee in bankruptcy who took the property subject to the rights of the creditors in the voluntary arrangement; (2) the debts under the voluntary arrangement were not bankruptcy debts within s.382(1) and H was not subject to any liabilities regarding them and (3) the voluntary arrangement had been agreed by the creditors and by doing so they had precluded themselves from making any claims in respect of bankruptcy as long as the arrangement continued.

McKEEN (A DEBTOR), *Re* [1995] B.C.C. 412, Morritt, L.J., Ch D.

3518. Voluntary arrangements–partial settlement of arrears–no provision for forfeiture–disclaimer or variation of lease–whether landlord could recover against original lessees

The landlords, M entered into a lease of business premises with the original lessees, R and G, in 1981. R and G then sublet the premises to B, who subsequently fell into financial difficulties. In 1994 B entered into an individual voluntary arrangement which bound those of his creditors who had notice of it, including M. The arrangement provided only a partial settlement of the arrears owing to MI by B under the lease, and M issued a writ for summary judgment for the remainder against R and G. The writ was struck out at first instance, M appealed.

Held, allowing the appeal, that the entry into an individual voluntary arrangement which makes no provision for the forfeiture or the disclaimer or the variation of the lease and which makes no express provision in relation to the original lessees, leaves open the right of the landlord to recover against the original lessees, *RA Securities Ltd v. Mercantile Credit Co Ltd* [1995] 3 All E.R. 581, [1995] 1 C.L.Y. 2844, *Deanplan Ltd v. Mahmoud* [1992] 3 All E.R. 945, [1992] C.L.Y. 497, *Burford Midland Properties Ltd v. Marley Extrusion Ltd* [1994] B.C.C. 604, [1995] 1 C.L.Y. 2843 and *Naeem (A Bankrupt) (No.18 of 1988), Re* [1990] 1 W.L.R. 48, [1990] C.L.Y. 280 considered.

MYTRE INVESTMENTS LTD v. REYNOLDS [1995] 3 All E.R. 588, Michael Burton Q.C., QBD.

3519. Voluntary arrangements–rent liabilites–whether landlord bound by arrangement–whether landlord had forfeited lease

The creditors of AGB had approved a voluntary arrangement without making provision for arrears of rent or prospective rent payments under the terms of a lease with R. R sought a declaration that it was not bound by the arrangement and that the lease on the premises subsisted. R argued that it was entitled to future payments of rent and argued that the arrangement should be revoked. The administrators argued that the lease had been forfeited by the grant of a new lease by R. R replied that the new lease had been executed without the administrators' consent and so took effect subject to the original lease in favour of AGB.

Held, dismissing the application, that the grant of a new lease by R operated to forfeit the original lease. The administrators could have relied upon the failure to obtain their consent as a ground for claiming that the original lease had not been forfeited but R, having exercised its right of re-entry could not claim that the original lease was still in existence.

AGB RESEARCH PLC, *Re*; SUB NOM. REDLEAF INVESTMENTS LTD v. TALBOT [1995] B.C.C. 1091, Vinelott, J., Ch D.

3520. Voluntary arrangements–rent liabilities–right of landlord–underlease exercisable on bankruptcy–whether landlord unfairly prejudiced by arrangement

[Insolvency Act 1986 s.262, s.286.]

At a debtor's voluntary arrangement meeting the landlord argued that the value of its debt should be assessed by reference to future rent obligations but the chairman of the meeting valued the debt only at one year's rent. The voluntary arrangement was approved and the landlord sought to revoke the decision. The district judge held that there had been unfair prejudice because the landlord could not rely on a clause requiring the debtor's wife to take a new lease in the event of bankruptcy if there was no bankruptcy. The landlord's application was granted. The debtor appealed.

Held, allowing the appeal, that the landlord's right of re-entry under the lease was unaffected by the voluntary arrangement by virtue of the Insolvency Act 1986 s.286. The unfairness mentioned in s.262 was unfairness arising from the terms of the arrangement. The landlord's rights under the lease lay against a person other than the debtor and arose on determination of the lease and were therefore a substitute for the indebtedness not a constituent part of it. The landlord's rights were therefore not within the ambit of interests of a creditor. If there had been any consideration of the question of unfairness it was necessary to balance the loss by the landlord of the rights against the debtor's wife against the disadvantage to the whole body of creditors in being prevented from having the benefit of the voluntary arrangement which included future payments of rent. Any prejudice to the landlord would not be unfair as it held security against the debtor in the right to re-enter.

DOORBAR v. ALLTIME SECURITIES LTD (NO.2); SUB NOM. DEBTOR (NO.162 OF 1993) (NO.2), *Re* [1995] B.C.C. 728, Knox, J., Ch D.

3521. Voluntary arrangements–rent liabilities–voting rights–whether landlord bound where unascertained claim–estimated value of debt

[Insolvency Rules 1986 r.5.17.]

AS, the creditor and landlord company of commercial premises leased to D, who had fallen into arrears with the rent and made the subject of a bankruptcy petition, appealed against a finding that it was bound by D's proposals for a voluntary arrangement which included liability for future rent. At a creditors' meeting, the majority of creditors voted in favour of the arrangement, with the effect that AS would not be able to proceed with the bankruptcy petition against D or require the lease to be taken for the remainder of its term. AS argued that it was not bound by the arrangement as to future liability as the chairman had not agreed with the company to put an estimated minimum value on the debt for the purposes of entitling them to vote, pursuant to r.5.17(3) of the Insolvency Rules 1986, which provided that a creditor shall not vote in respect of an unascertained debt except where the chairman agreed to put a minimum value on the debt.

Held, dismissing the appeal, that r.5.17(3) was to be construed as placing a general prohibition on voting by a creditor with an unascertained claim unless the chairman had agreed to an exception. The agreement did not have to be with another creditor but needed only to be an expression of willingness by the chairman to place an estimated value on the debt, *Cranley Mansions, Re* [1994] 1 W.L.R. 1610, [1994] C.L.Y. 2600 not followed. As the chairman had indicated that he would allow AS to vote in relation to future rent liabilities restricted to a period of one year, the requirement in r.5.17(3) was satisfied and AS was bound by the arrangement.

DOORBAR v. ALLTIME SECURITIES LTD (NOS.1 AND 2) [1996] 1 W.L.R. 456, Peter Gibson, L.J., CA.

3522. Voluntary arrangements–subsequent bankruptcy order–consequence of order on money held by supervisor

[Insolvency Act 1986 s.264.]

Held, that the making of a bankruptcy order on the petition of the supervisor of a voluntary arrangement under the Insolvency Act 1986 s.264(1)(c) terminated the voluntary arrangement. Money in the hands of the supervisor became part of the debtor's estate payable to the trustee in bankruptcy subject to any claim by the person who provided it for the purposes of the arrangement if not the debtor.

DAVIS v. MARTIN-SKLAN [1995] B.C.C. 1122, Blackburne, J., Ch D.

3523. Voluntary liquidation–compulsory winding up–director favoured by voluntary liquidation–petition necessary to protect creditors

O, a company controlled by W, commenced proceedings against M, a company controlled by F, seeking to recover the sum of £175,000 from M on the ground that it was a loan. The action was commenced because W and F had, after working together for some years, fallen out with each other. The proceedings were contested by M. Three months later, in October 1993, M entered into a three year fixed term service contract with F pursuant to which M agreed to pay F £80,000 per annum. M's directors were F and his wife. M did not have any great assets and its trading activities were small. In the following December F came to the conclusion, on advice, that M was insolvent. A meeting of creditors was called in January 1994 and H was appointed as the liquidator of the company. F was the principal creditor in the sum of £240,000, due under the service agreement. In the meantime, O pressed on with its claim and in February 1994 obtained judgment in default of M answering interrogatories. O then petitioned for a compulsory winding up order based on the unpaid judgment debt.

Held, making the usual compulsory winding up order, that in the ordinary course of events the court would not make a compulsory order where a company was already in a creditors' voluntary liquidation but might do so where justice might not properly be seen to be done in the voluntary liquidation. In the present case, the liquidator had been appointed at the behest of F, who himself became the principal creditor through the execution of a service agreement which did not appear justifiable on ordinary commercial criteria. F's conduct was the subject of a considerable number of complaints by W which the court could not deal with on a winding up petition. F's claim against the company was of limited value in any event as he was only entitled to damages rather than all the sums which would have been payable under the service contract. It was an exceptional case in which the liquidation ought to be undertaken by a liquidator appointed by the court in the exercise of its power to make a compulsory winding up order, *Lowerstoft Traffic Services Ltd, Re* [1986] B.C.L.C. 81; *Falcon RJ Developments Ltd, Re* [1987] B.C.L.C. 437, [1987] C.L.Y. 383 considered.

MAGNUS CONSULTANTS LTD, *Re* [1995] 1 B.C.L.C. 203, Roger Cooke, J., Ch D.

3524. Wasted costs orders–petition to wind up company–proceedings found an abuse of process–solicitor wrongly swearing affidavit with no evidence

[Insolvency Act 1986; Supreme Court Act 1981 s.51.]

The petitioner, P, was carrying out sub-contracting work at a site having been engaged by the company, C. P left the site without completing the work, and sought payment from C of £196,000 for work performed without accounting for interim payments already made. C agreed to pay £143,000 but contended that it had already paid £147,412 by way of interim payments. P later sought payment of £48,000 in respect of direct loss and expense. P then presented a petition, under the Insolvency Act 1986, for C to be wound up, claiming that it was indebted to the petitioner in the sum of £44,010.91. The petitioner's solicitor had sworn an affidavit that the company appeared to be unable to pay its debts on perusal of accounts shown to him and on the strength of his client's instructions.

However, he also advised P that this was a high risk strategy and that the petition was likely to be struck out. The petition was struck out as an abuse of process and the judge directed a further hearing to consider C's application for an order with respect to wasted costs under the Supreme Court Act 1981 s.51 (6).

Held, granting the application, that (1) the court would be slow to infer from mere non-payment of a debt, which had never been demanded, that a company was unable to pay its debts as they fell due; (2) the solicitor acted improperly and unreasonably in swearing an affidavit in support of a winding up petition where there were no grounds upon which a competent solicitor could reach that view on the material available to him. The solicitor acted unreasonably knowing that the petition was bound to fail if fought out on its merits and would pay the whole of the wasted costs, *Ridehalgh v. Horsefield* [1994] Ch. 205, [1994] C.L.Y. 3623 applied.

COMPANY (NO.006798 OF 1995), *Re* [1996] 1 W.L.R. 491, Chadwick, J., Ch D.

3525. Winding up–assets vested in Crown–disclaimed–nature of guarantee given by applicants

[Insolvency Act 1986 s.181.]

The applicant directors had acted as guarantors of the company to obtain an overdraft from the bank. The company was wound up as insolvent and the bank took proceedings to enforce its guarantee. The company's assets vested in the Crown as bona vacantia and the Crown disclaimed them. The applicants sought a vesting order under the Insolvency Act 1986 s.181 claiming that they were under a liability in respect of the disclaimed property. The application was dismissed by the registrar and the applicants appealed.

Held, dismissing the appeal, that the liability arose because of the guarantees given by the applicants and it was not a liability in respect of the assets in question.

SPIRIT MOTORSPORT LTD (IN LIQUIDATION), *Re* [1996] 1 B.C.L.C. 684, Laddie, J., Ch D.

3526. Winding up–contribution agreement compromising claims between company and majority shareholders–asset pooling agreement–liquidators seeking authorisation to execute

This was an application to permit the execution of a contribution agreement between BCCI companies and the majority shareholders and an agreement pooling the assets of BCCI companies made in June 1992. Both agreements were conditional on the approval of the Luxembourg court which agreed to the pooling agreement but overturned the contribution agreement. The liquidators sought authority to execute a revised contribution agreement.

Held, allowing the application, that the liquidators could execute the two agreements as it was the only means by which any of the creditors could hope to have some of their money returned. This was demonstrated by the approval of the majority of the creditors to the agreements.

BANK OF CREDIT AND COMMERCE INTERNATIONAL SA (NO.4), *Re* [1995] B.C.C. 453, Sir Richard Scott V.C., Ch D.

3527. Winding up–creditors not at first hearing entitled to have order rescinded where probable voluntary arrangement negotiable

[Insolvency Rules 1986 r.4.16; Insolvency Rules 1986 r.7.47.]

The Inland Revenue presented winding up petitions against eight companies for non-payment of tax. A request for a second adjournment of the proceedings to investigate the possibility of a voluntary arrangement was rejected and, in the absence of any other creditors, winding up orders were made by the registrar. The companies sought to have the orders rescinded.

Held, granting the application, that the court had a discretion, under the Insolvency Rules 1986 r.4.16(5), to allow creditors who had not attended the initial proceedings to be heard at the application to rescind the orders since it was important for the court to know the views of the companies' creditors. If there was a real prospect that proposals in a voluntary arrangement would command the necessary creditor approval then the court would rescind the winding up order under r.7.47(1) of the 1986 Rules.

DOLLAR LAND (FELTHAM) LTD, *Re* [1995] 2 B.C.L.C. 370, Blackburne, J., Ch D.

3528. Winding up–delay–applicant seeking costs against directors on ground that petition improperly presented to prevent investigation–refusal to pierce corporate veil

The applicant brought a winding up petition against the company. On the day before the petition was to be heard the directors of the company presented and served a petition for an administration order. Both petitions were adjourned. On the day before the adjourned hearing the directors withdrew their petition and the winding up order was made unopposed. The applicant applied for his costs to be paid personally by the directors on the grounds that they had improperly presented the petition to prevent an investigation into their running of the company.

Held, dismissing the application, that the court would only go behind the corporate veil and order directors to pay the costs of another party where it could summarily be established that the directors had caused costs to be incurred for an improper purpose. That could not be shown in the present case and so no order would be made.

TAJIK AIR LTD, *Re* [1996] 1 B.C.L.C. 317, Martin Mann Q.C., Ch D.

3529. Winding up–injunction to prevent petition from being presented–whether statutory demand was disputed–no bias where counsel acted as recorder on same circuit as judge

G appealed against injunctions made in favour of Y preventing him from presenting petitions to wind up Y without leave of the court. Y enforced a legal charge when a receiving order was made against G. Y were entitled to repayment on demand and, when G failed to pay £23,967 owed, they obtained a possession order for G's land and exercised their power of sale to recoup the money from the proceeds. G unsuccessfully attempted to have the possession order set aside on a number of occasions. He then presented Y with a statutory demand for rent for the property, less his debt, which amounted to £103,532. The judge held the demand to be disputed and therefore granted the injunctions. G argued that there was a breach of natural justice as the judge was based on the North Eastern circuit and counsel for Y was a recorder based on the same circuit. G also argued that the judge was wrong to hold that his case against Y could be disputed.

Held, dismissing the appeal, that (1) representing a client as counsel was distinct from performing duties as a recorder. There was, therefore, no connection between the judge and the counsel which would invoke the *Code of Conduct of the Bar of England and Wales* r.501 and (2) the terms of Y's legal charge fully entitled them to act in the way they did and therefore the debt was a disputed one. It was damaging for a company to have a winding up petition presented against it and the judge was correct to conclude that such a petition would be misconceived.

YORKSHIRE BANK PLC v. GARDNER, Trans. Ref: CHANF 95/0820/B, March 15, 1996, Hirst, L.J., CA.

3530. Winding up–liquidator of companies within group–whether one application for directions could cover all the companies

[Insolvency Act 1986 s.112.]

Held, that a liquidator of more than one company in the same group of companies who wished to issue a number of applications under the Insolvency Act 1986 s.112 did not have to issue a large number of separate applications but was entitled to issue one application in the matter of all the relevant companies if the subject matter of each application was the same.

WILLIAM PICKLES PLC (IN LIQUIDATION), *Re* [1996] 1 B.C.L.C. 681, Rattee, J., Ch D.

3531. Winding up–order sought where company devoid of assets–order granted to enable investigation of company affairs

[Insolvency Act 1986 s.125.]

The liquidator of company P sought the winding up of the respondent company, R, of which P was a creditor in the sum of £6.24 million under the Insolvency Act 1986 s.125. Both companies were members of the same group of companies that had granted securities over its properties in favour of various banks. One of the banks appointed administrative receivers in respect of companies in the group including P and R. The liquidator wished to investigate the circumstances in which the securities had been granted to the banks and sought to challenge them on the grounds that at the time they were granted the companies had been insolvent. The liquidator sought access to documents to investigate the matter. R's administrative receivers and the bank opposed the application on the basis that (1) the winding up was a device to avoid claims for legal professional privilege in the documents, (2) P was not a creditor of R because the debt arose after the debenture was granted to the bank and was therefore subject to a floating charge under the terms of the debenture giving P no standing to present a petition and (3) the winding up would lead to no financial advantage, as R had no assets and so the court should not grant the order.

Held, granting the order, that a debenture holder whose security was under attack could not rely on that security to defeat a petition brought by an unsecured creditor to enable the company through its liquidator to attack that security. The courts could and often did make a winding up order where the company had no assets, as permitted under the Insolvency Act 1986 s.125, if the purpose of the order was to enable an investigation to take place into the company's affairs. Lack of assets could not of itself be a ground for refusing to make such an order.

BELL GROUP FINANCE (PTY) LTD (IN LIQUIDATION) v. BELL GROUP (UK) HOLDINGS LTD [1996] 1 B.C.L.C. 304, Chadwick, J., Ch D.

3532. Winding up–petition–advertised before hearing–whether that amounted to an abuse of process of the court

T and L, cohabitees, formed a company which entered into a factoring agreement with BCS. T and L's relationship broke up and L telephoned various creditors telling them that she was going to have the company wound up. She also telephoned the Inland Revenue and BCS who then suspended the factoring agreement and froze the company's funds. L refused T's offers to buy her shares in the company. When L did present a petition to wind up the company the company applied to have it struck out because L had conducted a campaign of advertising in advance of the petition which was an abuse of the process of the court. The company further contended that an alternative remedy was available and that L was acting vexatiously.

Held, striking out the petition, that in telephoning people as she had done, L had deprived the court of the opportunity to determine whether the petition should be advertised or not. Given the harm that she had done to the company and the abuse of the process of the court the petition would be struck out.

DOREEN BOARDS LTD, *Re* [1996] 1 B.C.L.C. 501, Laddie, J., Ch D.

3533. Winding up–petition–advertising prior to presentation

[Insolvency Rules 1986.]

Held, that although the Insolvency Rules 1986 made no express provision prohibiting a contributory from advertising its petition to wind up a company before the petition had been presented, it was inherent that there should be no advertisement before the return date.

COMPANY (No.62 OF 1995), *Re*, *The Times*, February 15, 1996, Laddie, J., Ch D.

3534. Winding up–petition alleged company insolvent–expectation of management in quasi partnership–whether entitled to striking out

The company sought to strike out a contributory's winding up petition as disclosing no cause of action. Allegations in the petitions that the company was insolvent were inconsistent with the need to aver that the petitioners had a tangible interest in the winding up and the petition merely alleged that the company was a quasi partnership which had broken down and did not describe how the quasi partnership arose.

Held, striking out the petition, that the petitioners had shown sufficient locus standi. They were unable to state whether there was some tangible interest available to them on a winding up but that was due to lack of information. There was no need for a petition to go further and show or aver that there was a likelihood of an entitlement to a tangible interest where it was alleged that the company was in default in providing information. However, it was not sufficient for the petitioner simply to aver that there was a legitimate expectation of taking part in the management. That was not enough to specify the grounds of the petition. It was necessary to state how the expectation arose and what agreement or understanding existed. In the absence of such detail the petition failed to disclose a cause of action.

COMPANY (No.007936 OF 1994), *Re* [1995] B.C.C. 705, Roger Kaye Q.C., Ch D.

3535. Winding up–register of petitions–application to make multiple searches for purpose of creating duplicate register–Appeal Court's jurisdiction to hear renewed application

[Insolvency Rules 1986 r.7.28; Rules of the Supreme Court Ord.59 r.14; Supreme Court Act 1981 s.18.]

A had made an ex parte application, under the Insolvency Rules 1986 r.7.28, to inspect and make multiple searches of the records of insolvency proceedings held at Liverpool District Registry in order to make the information available to its customers and subscribers for credit control purposes. Parker, J. had refused the application, as not being an inspection for a proper purpose under r.7.28(2) because it involved abstracting all the information on the register, thereby creating a duplicate register which would not be subject to control by the courts. A made a renewed application, under the Rules of the Supreme Court Ord.59 r.14(3), contending that, whilst r.7.28(3) of the 1986 Rules stated that the judge's decision was final, the court was not prevented by the Supreme Court Act 1981 s.18(1)(c) from considering the application because (1) r.7.28 was contained in subordinate legislation, rather than an Act, and (2) s.18(1)(c) referred to appeals where the decision of the lower court was final, whereas this was an application.

Held, dismissing the application, that s.18(1)(c) of the 1981 Act applied equally to subordinate legislation as to the primary legislation authorising it, in this case the Insolvency Act 1986. An application under RSC Ord.59 r.14(3) was one that was incidental to a substantive appeal and therefore there was no jurisdiction to entertain it where the substantive appeal could not be heard because of s.18(1)(c).

Observed, that r.7.28 did not envisage the type of search proposed by A which was now possible because of computerisation of the records and advances in information technology, a fact which should be considered by the Insolvency Rules Committee.

AUSTINTEL LTD, *Re*, Trans. Ref: FC3 96/6288/B, October 31, 1996, Morritt, L.J., CA.

3536. Winding up–unfair prejudice petition–remedies–cour[t] ...

[Companies Act 1985 s.459, s.461.]

Held, that under the Companies Act 1985 s.461 the court had a ... to the relief that it granted if it found that an unfair prejudice petition und[er] ... of the Act was well founded. If no relief to constitute a specific remedy co[uld] be devised the court could refuse to grant any relief whatsoever and where no course other than a winding up order was advantageous then only a winding up order would be made without any other relief being ordered.

FULL CUP INTERNATIONAL TRADING LTD, *Re* [1995] B.C.C. 682, Ferris, J., Ch D.

3537. Articles

A piece of the action: champerty and maintenance in insolvency *(Jeremy Goldring* and *Katherine Theobald)*: I.L. & P. 1996, 12(2), 48-51. (Circumstances in which office holder can assign cause of action).

Administration orders: extraterritorial scope and restrictions on the enforcement of claims abroad *(Richard Obank)*: B.J.I.B. & F.L. 1996, 11 (2), 60-64. (Problems facing English administrators appointed to manage companies which have a foreign involvement).

Administration orders: M. Advice 1996, 42, 16-17. (Guidance for money advisers on applying for administration orders or composition orders, court hearings and reviews of orders).

Bankruptcy and insolvency *(Ian Stevens)*: L.S.G. 1996, 93(35), 30. (Effect of bankruptcy, individual voluntary arrangements and partnership voluntary arrangements on practising certificates of solicitors).

Bankruptcy petitions and statutory demands: what the cases say: Insolv. L. & P. 1996, 1 (2), 10-13. (Grounds on which petitions and demands may be liable to challenge under 1986 Act for failure to comply with required formalities).

Casting the net wide: the liability of company officers in French insolvency procedures *(Anker Sorensen)*: I.C.C.L.R. 1996, 7(1), 17-21. (Amendments to concept of mismanagement and negligence by directors and shadow directors, liability and criminal penalties imposed by 1994 Act).

Cross-border insolvency UK style *(Harry Rajak)*: I.B.L. 1996, 24(5), 246-248. (Helpful approach of courts in UK to foreign companies and creditors in insolvency proceedings).

DPR Futures Limited *(Cary Kochberg* and *Martin Fishman)*: I.L. & P. 1996, 12(4), 131-135. (Account of liquidation of investment company following its collapse in 1988, problems of many small but complicated claims and negotiations leading to global compromise).

EC Convention on insolvency proceedings: C. & F.L. 1996, 8(7), 44-47. (Provisions of Convention particularly as it affects English set off rules).

Equitable proprietary rights in insolvency: the ebbing tide? *(Janet Ulph)*: J.B.L. 1996, Sep, 482-506. (Careful balancing by courts in insolvency cases reluctant to extend equitable proprietary rights at expense of ordinary creditors and policy issue about banks' regulatory role).

Greater clarity in insolvency–set off: C. & F.L. 1996, 8(9), 57-60. (Application to contingent liabilities, mutuality and charge backs).

Insolvency and directors' and officers' insurance *(Allan Blake)*: I.L. & P. 1996, 12(4), 127-128. (Growth of liability insurance and its scope in relation to insolvency practitioners).

Insolvency law reform for economies in transition: a comparative law perspective *(Manfred Balz* and *Henry N. Schiffman)*: B.J.I.B. & F.L. 1996, 11 (1), 19-26. (Elements of current western insolvency legislation recommended as appropriate for countries making the transition into market economies where companies suffering structural and financial burdens from past regimes must be reorganised).

Insolvency of financial institutions *(Christopher Grierson)*: I.B.L. 1996, 24(5), 212-216. (Major institutional insolvencies in which insolvency professionals have found innovative solutions include BCCI pooling agreements, Barings acquisition and KWELM insurers' scheme of arrangement).

[illegible] of travel agents–consequences in criminal and civil law *(Paul [illegible])*: T.L.J. 1996, 3, 100-102. (Whether offence committed when travel [illegible]nts use customers' money to pay off debts rather than paying it to carrier and whether carrier can recover from third party).

Insolvent companies and TUPE *(David Pollard)*: I.L.J. 1996, 25(3), 191-210. (Issues to be considered by insolvency practitioners when dealing with transfers of undertakings and employees of insolvent company).

Is administration necessary? *(Steven A. Frieze)*: Insolv. Int. 1996, 9(6), 44-45. (Whether administration order is necessary where its only purpose is to give company protection from creditors while it proposes CVA).

Litigation against bankrupt companies *(Jonathan Middleton)*: L.S.G. 1996, 93(36), 33. (Necessity to obtain leave to litigate and whether such leave can be given retrospectively).

Pursuing insolvent companies *(Robert Barron)*: P. & P. 1996, 1(Feb), 9-11. (Procedural steps to be taken in order to obtain judgment against insurers of insolvent company).

Receivers' liabilities *(Edward Bannister)*: E.G. 1996, 9604, 122-123. (When receiver is liable for rates payable in respect of receivership property).

Safeguarding assets in international litigation: the insolvency option *(Philip St. Smart)*: L.Q.R. 1996, 112(Jul), 397-401. (Use of winding up proceedings to prevent removal of local assets from jurisdiction where Mareva injunction is unavailable because defendant has no connection with UK).

Security considerations for the administrative receiver and debenture holder: Insolv. L. & P. 1996, 1(1), 13-17. (Relative priorities of floating charges and other security).

Set off and cash collateral: three important cases of 1995 *(Dermot Turing)*: J.I.B.L. 1996, 11(4), 170-176. (Circumstances in which debtors may be denied set off on creditors' insolvency).

The administrator, morality and the court *(Ian Dawson)*: J.B.L. 1996, Sep, 437-462. (Need to clarify application of ethics to insolvency administrators in role as officers of court by subsuming relevant case law within law of restitution such that law and not morality would determine responsibilities).

The case for a European Convention in insolvency *(Paul J. Omar)*: I.C.C.L.R. 1996, 7(5), 163-169. (History and principal provisions of draft Convention including jurisdiction and law applicable, recognition of insolvency proceedings, secondary proceedings and creditors' information and proof of claims).

The challenges ahead: address to the Insolvency Lawyers' Association *(Justice Lightman)*: J.B.L. 1996, Mar, 113-126. (Comments on high costs in insolvency matters, law relating to administrative receivers, need for cooperation between insolvency profession and court, conditional fee agreements, length of trials and qualification of directors).

The corporate way of death *(Sally Wheeler)*: Law & Crit. 1996, 7(2), 217-244. (Rituals surrounding liquidation procedure and legal treatment of corporate insolvency).

The decisions on wrongful trading to date: Insolv. L. & P. 1996, 1(3), 14-15. (Directors' liability to contribute to insolvent company's assets, whether expectations of financial recovery were reasonable and implications of managing director's death).

The European Convention on Insolvency Proceedings and the administrative receiver: a missed opportunity? *(Frederique Dahan)*: Co. Law. 1996, 17(6), 181-186. (Provisions of 1995 Convention and its failure to deal with status of administrative receiver in international insolvencies).

The European Union Convention on Insolvency Proceedings: a critique of the Convention's corporate rescue paradigm *(Gordon W. Johnson)*: I.I.R. 1996, 5(1), 80-107. (Effectiveness of Convention scheme for rehabilitation of companies in context of cross border insolvency).

The French experience of corporate voluntary arrangements *(Paul J. Omar and Anker Sorensen)*: I.C.C.L.R. 1996, 7(3), 97-103. (Procedures of amicable resolution and ad hoc mandate allow for rescue of French companies in trouble).

The London approach *(Colin Bird)*: I.L. & P. 199… whereby recovery is achieved without formal rec… procedures but consensus agreed with creditors and banks).

The residual status of directors in receivership *(Louis G. Doyle)*: Co. …ss 17(5), 131-138. (Powers and duties of directors of company in … receivership).

The winding up procedure: cautionary tales *(David Milman)*: P.I.C. 1996, 8(Sep), 1-2. (Issues relating to advertisement of winding up petitions where creditors are
using procedure in order to collect debts and defence of substantial dispute on bona fide grounds).

Transactional avoidance on corporate insolvency *(David Milman)*: P.I.C. 1996, 3(Mar), 1-2. (Recent cases on transactions at an undervalue, particularly s.423 actions).

US considerations respecting financial institution insolvency *(Robert J. Rosenberg* and *Marla S. Becker)*: J.F.R. & C. 1996, 4(1), 47-66. (FIRREA provisions introduced to improve investor protection following savings and loan scandals, impact on role and powers of FDIC and treatment of foreign financial institutions' liquidations).

Voluntary arrangements and notice of creditors' meetings *(Michael Woollard* and *Steven Fennell)*: I.L. & P. 1996, 12(3), 94-97. (Court's strict interpretation of rules concerning notices of creditors' meetings when ruling that creditor was not bound by voluntary arrangement where notice was sent out one day late).

3538. Books

Andrews, Mark; Barnett, Nigel–Insolvency Litigation Strategies. Paperback: £65.00. ISBN 0-7520-0233-3. FT Law & Tax.

Bailey, Edward; Groves, Hugo; Smith, Cormac–Bailey, Groves and Smith: Corporate Insolvency - Law and Practice. Hardback: £125.00. ISBN 0-406-08142-5. Butterworth Law.

Bhandari, Jagdeep S.; Adler, Barry E.; Weiss, Lawrence A.–Corporate Bankruptcy. Hardback: £55.00. ISBN 0-521-45107-8. Paperback: £19.95. ISBN 0-521-45717-3. Cambridge University Press.

Cooper, Neil; Jarvis, Rebecca–Cross-border Insolvency: a Guide to Recognition and Enforcement in International Practice. Commercial law. Paperback: £39.95. ISBN 0-471-96310-0. Chancery Wiley Law Publications.

Loose, Peter; Griffiths, Michael–Loose on Liquidators. Hardback: £55.00. ISBN 0-85308-234-0. Jordan.

McBride, J. Michael–Purchase and Sale of Assets in Bankruptcy. Hardback: £102.95. ISBN 0-471-13321-3. John Wiley and Sons.

McCormack, Gerald–Proprietary Claims in Insolvency. Hardback: £65.00. ISBN 0-421-56480-6. Sweet & Maxwell.

Palmer's Corporate Insolvency. Unbound/looseleaf: £195.00. ISBN 0-421-56500-4. Sweet & Maxwell.

Rajak, Harry; Davis, Richard–Insolvency - a Business by Business Guide. Paperback: £45.00. ISBN 0-406-02231-3. Butterworth Law.

INSURANCE

3539. Agents–political risks insurance–extent of agent's powers to bind pool–agent having independent capacity from pool members–absence of contract between insured and pool

Y was a company which became interested in a timber concession in Liberia granted by the Liberian government. The first defendant, LRF, was a French company acting as an insurer and reinsurer in the international market writing insurance for political risks. The fourth to nineteenth defendants were members

..ciation, PARIS, which acted as a vehicle for a pooled operation for ..iting political insurance risks on behalf of its members. LRF and other ..X insurers placed restrictions on the authority PARIS possessed to ..derwrite certain risks. UIC acted as agent for LRF and the pool. Insurance was effected over Y's risk in Liberia. There was an insurrection in Liberia which led to Y leaving its interest in the convention. The preliminary issue arose as to UIC's authority to bind PARIS and as to PARIS's authority to bind the pool.

Held, that it could not be accepted that, in the light of the restriction on PARIS's authority by the GAREX insurers, PARIS had unlimited authority to bind the pool. On the facts PARIS did not at any time purport to give UIC authority to write the political risks in issue. The relevant committee of PARIS did not give any such authority to UIC. UIC put LRF forward as insurer but PARIS was not made aware that the pool had been preferred as co-insurer of the risk. There was nothing to support a suggestion that Y had acted to its detriment on the belief that it had insurance from the pool. UIC was acting as an independent agent and was understood by Y to be acting in that capacity. There was no binding contract between Y and the pool in any event. Y's silence in response to the offer of insurance could not be accepted as acceptance of any such offer.

YONA INTERNATIONAL LTD v. LA REUNION FRANCAISE SOCIETE ANONYME D'ASSURANCES ET DE REASSURANCES [1996] 2 Lloyd's Rep. 84, Moore-Bick, J., QBD (Comm Ct).

3540. Consequential loss insurance–material damage proviso–claimant did not have insurable interest amounting to personal property interest

NU, the insurer of a consequential loss insurance policy, appealed against a decision on a claim brought by G, the owners of a property under redevelopment which suffered a fire, arising from the resultant loss of rental income from the property. The fire destroyed architects' drawings which were not insured and caused substantial delay in the development. The issue was whether a proviso contained in G's policy, that at the time of the damage the claimant must have "an insurance covering the interest of the insured in the property at the premises against such damage", could be construed as giving G an insurable interest in the architects' drawings, even though they were not the owners.

Held, dismissing the appeal, that the word "interest" contained in the proviso should be construed in context, depending on the assured's relation to the damaged property. An insured could recover if he had rights in existence at the time of the loss which were affected by the damage, eg. profits from a forward sale, but the architects' drawings were not property in which G had a personal interest at the time of the fire. They were the property of the architects and G were under no obligation to insure themselves against their loss, *Lucena v. Craufurd* (1806) 2 B. & P. 269 and *Sharp v. Sphere Drake Insurance Plc (The Moonacre)* [1992] 2 Lloyd's Rep. 501, [1993] C.L.Y. 3614 considered.

GLENGATE-KG PROPERTIES LTD v. NORWICH UNION FIRE INSURANCE SOCIETY LTD [1996] 2 All E.R. 487, Neill, L.J., CA.

3541. Costs–indemnity basis–no liability on insurer to pay costs given defence provided under insurer's rules

[Supreme Court Act 1981 s.51.]

T obtained judgment against B and T was awarded costs on an indemnity basis. B's, P & I club (its mutual insurer), would normally have paid the costs incurred by a member which it had agreed to support unless, under r.9 of its rules, "such costs and expenses become payable by the personal neglect or default of the member". The club had supported the defence for a period, but withdrew support at a later stage. B maintained its defence in a lengthy trial, in which its allegations of fraud were disproved. T applied for an order under the Supreme Court Act 1981 s.51 (1), and on the basis of *Aiden Shipping Co Ltd v. Interbulk Ltd (The Vimeira) (No.2)*

[1986] 1 A.C. 965, [1986] C.L.Y. 2606, that B's P a
costs of the action.

Held, dismissing the application, that the defence containe rules was sufficient to protect the club from liability to pay T's costs. he could find no grounds to make an order for costs against the club which w be exceptional in the circumstances.

THARROS SHIPPING CO LTD AND DEN NORSKE BANK PLC v. BIAS SHIPPING LTD (NO.3) [1995] 1 Lloyd's Rep. 541, Rix, J., QBD (Comm Ct).

3542. Death–drinking heavily to relieve pain of back injury–asphyxia due to vomit inhalation–following alcohol consumption–meaning of "bodily injury"–statutory interpretation

D's wife sustained a back injury at work and began drinking heavily to relieve the pain, six months later she died in her sleep after consuming a large quantity of alcohol. An inquest recorded a verdict of death by misadventure and cause of death as acute alcoholism and misadventure. D's wife was insured under a personal accident policy which provided for payment in respect of inter alia 'bodily injury resulting in death... caused directly or indirectly by the accident..." "Bodily injury" was defined as being caused by accidental means. D's claim was rejected by I. D brought proceedings against I to recover the amount under the policy. The court found that the cause of death was asphyxia resulting from the inhalation of vomit and dismissed the claim on the grounds that death in these circumstances did not amount to bodily injury. D appealed to the Court of Appeal, arguing that his wife had sustained a bodily injury and had done so as a result of an accident since no distinction was to be drawn between an accidental result and accidental means and even if such a distinction were drawn, the effective cause of death was the inhalation of vomit and not the deliberate consuming of alcohol.

Held, dismissing the appeal, that in order to make a successful claim D had to establish that his wife had sustained a bodily injury by accidental means which resulted in death. Bodily injury was not restricted to injury to the exterior of the body and could include the introduction of foreign matter into the body causing harmful physiological changes to the body. Thus asphyxia resulting from the inhalation of vomit was a bodily injury. However, whether an injury was caused by accident depended on whether it was the natural result of a fortuitous and unexpected cause or the fortuitous or unexpected result of a natural cause. It was not accidental if it was the natural and direct consequence of a deliberate act or calculated risk taken by the assured. On the facts, D's wife had been a nurse and must have been well aware of the risks of consuming excess alcohol. Thus her injury had not been caused by accidental means.

DHAK v. INSURANCE CO OF NORTH AMERICA (UK) LTD [1996] 1 W.L.R. 936, Neill, L.J., CA.

3543. Disclosure–whether knowledge that agents intended to withhold commission was imputed to principal–material non-disclosure

[Marine Insurance Act 1906 s.18.]

K and other insurance companies, the plaintiffs, were members of a pool whose reinsurance was arranged by underwriting agents Weavers. K claimed indemnity under the treaty but N raised the defence that K had failed to disclose a material fact which was deemed to be within their knowledge under the Marine Insurance Act 1906 s.18, ie. that Weavers' directors intended not to pay K the agreed commission. K applied to strike out the allegations of non-disclosure.

Held, allowing the application, that under s.18 the reinsured could not be deemed to have knowledge of the agent's intention not to pay commission because in the ordinary course of business it could not be inferred that agents would inform their principals of their intended breach of duty. The criteria for imputing deemed knowledge under s.18 were whether the information concerned was of a kind which the agent had a duty to obtain for the principal

...w of the particular information, whether it could be inferred that the ...ould have discharged the duty by informing the principal.

...GSCROFT v. NISSAN FIRE AND MARINE INSURANCE CO LTD, *Lloyd's List*, ...ay 16, 1996 (I.D.), Colman, J., QBD (Comm Ct).

...44. Duty of care–insurance brokers–exclusion clauses–insurance broker had duty to bring exclusion clause to insured's attention

T, a developer, and M&M, his insurance broker, sued C, insurance brokers who had placed an insurance policy for T's Bahamas leisure development with the following market. M&M instructed C to obtain cover and approved the terms obtained, which included an exclusion clause applicable to any part of the works for which a completion certificate had been issued before the damage occurred. In 1992 Hurricane Andrew damaged the completed marina and a guest house on which work was still in progress. The following market relied on the exclusion clause to deny the claim for damage to the marina. M&M sued on the ground that C had breached their duty of care by allowing the exclusion clause to appear in the policy, but C argued that M&M were guilty of contributory negligence for failing to inspect the policy carefully or object to the clause.

Held, apportioning liability one third to M&M and two thirds to C, that C were in breach of their duty of care by failing to make clear to the following market that full cover for the project should include any phases which might be completed before the others. As prudent brokers, C should have drawn the instructing broker's attention specifically to the exclusion clause which represented a potential problem. To rely on M&M to inspect the policy carefully was insufficient. However, M&M had also failed in their duty to inspect the terms properly before approving the policy. Both breaches contributed to causing the loss.

TUDOR JONES v. CROWLEY COLOSSO [1996] 2 Lloyd's Rep. 619, Langley, J., QBD (Comm Ct).

3545. Duty of care–negligent maintenance of vehicle–policy condition that the insured take reasonable care–concept of recklessness not applicable

A was constructing an air force runway when there was a collision between a tractor unit driven by A's employee and a landing aircraft. A was held liable in negligence and sought indemnity from its insurers, C. C alleged A was in breach of the condition of the policy that A "take all reasonable precautions to... maintain [the tractor unit] in an efficient and roadworthy condition", the tractor having faults in the clutch and handbrake. The Master ordered trial of a preliminary issue as to whether, to succeed in its defence, C had to prove material acts or omissions of A (as opposed to A's employees) which were reckless and not merely negligent, ie. that A recognised a danger existed and did not care whether or not that danger was averted.

Held, deciding the preliminary issues, that (1) the words of the condition were plain and meant the insurers were not covering nor intending to cover A for liability arising out of negligent maintenance of the vehicle and (2) it was not enough to establish a causal act of negligence on the part of an employee. C had to show negligence, not recklessness, on the part of the relevant officer or officers of A in failing to ensure that the unit was maintained in an efficient and roadworthy condition, *Woolfall & Rimmer Ltd v. Moyle* [1942] 1 K.B. 66 and *Sofi v. Prudential Assurance Co* [1993] 2 Lloyd's Rep. 559, [1994] C.L.Y. 2702 considered.

AMEY PROPERTIES LTD v. CORNHILL INSURANCE PLC [1996] L.R.L.R. 259, Tucker, J., QBD (Comm Ct).

...46. Exclusion clauses–insurance policies–construction of indemnity exclusion–damage sustained due to design defect

CU appealed against a refusal to allow reliance on an indemnity exclusion clause, limiting their liability for repair costs, due to defects arising in the course of a quay construction project. CP was a subcontractor building continuous walls and bored piling forming part of a series of quays. The work was done by reclaiming an area from the sea by depositing pumped sand to form a large area of berm, then building walls and dredging out sand from the area inside the walls. During the work it was discovered that sand retained by the wall was escaping through the walls into the newly constructed dock. CP had to carry out extensive work to remedy this problem and make good the damage. The escape was caused by defects in design, materials and workmanship. CP claimed on their insurance policy. That policy contained an indemnity "in respect of physical loss of or damage to the property insured however caused". It also contained an exception relating to the cost of rectifying defects in design, materials or workmanship unless the property insured suffered actual loss, destruction or damage as a result of such defects. The insurers paid for the removal of sand which had escaped into the dock and grouting and filling of the voids created behind the walls when the sand fill had escaped on the grounds that this constituted damage to the dock and damage to the berm behind the walls. CU however refused to pay for the gaps and voids in the walls themselves, contending that these were defects not damage and as such were not covered by the policy.

Held, dismissing the appeal, that the obligation to indemnify had to be construed in the light of the exception. When so construed the first possible meaning of the indemnity was to be preferred, namely that the costs of rectifying defects which caused the physical damage were included in the obligation to indemnify and that the defects in the walls came within the cover.

CEMENTATION PILING AND FOUNDATION LTD v. COMMERCIAL UNION INSURANCE CO PLC; SUB NOM. CEMENTATION PILING AND FOUNDATION LTD v. AEGON INSURANCE LTD [1995] 1 Lloyd's Rep. 97, Sir Ralph Gibson, CA.

3547. Extra statutory concessions–transfer–annuities

The Inland Revenue issued a press release entitled *Transfers of long-term insurance business: transitional relief for losses incurred in general annuity business: new extra-statutory concession*, published on October 17, 1996. A new extra statutory concession on transfers of long term insurance permits the carrying forward of unrelieved losses incurred by the transferring company in general annuity business prior to 1992.

3548. Fire insurance–mortgages–covenant to insure in name of bank–policy in mortgagor's name–whether mortgagee entitled to proceeds of policy

[Property Law Act 1952 Sch.4 (New Zealand).]

A bank granted a second mortgage on a property subject to a covenant that the mortgagors would insure it against fire in the name of the bank. One of the mortgagors effected a policy in his own name. The bank notified the insurers of its interest and obtained from the insurers a certificate that it was a party interested in the insurance. After a fire, the first mortgagees exercised their right of sale; the bank claimed the outstanding sum secured by the second mortgage from the insurers, who paid the mortgagor. The bank successfully claimed entitlement to the proceeds of the policy at first instance and the New Zealand Court of Appeal upheld that decision. The insurer appealed.

Held, dismissing the appeal, that the insurance covenant gave the bank mortgagee an interest by way of charge in the proceeds of the insurance policy and operated, with the Property Law Act 1952 Sch.4 (New Zealand), to give the bank an assignment of the mortgagor's interest; further the bank had given sufficient notice of its equitable interest and so was entitled to the proceeds of the policy, *Dearle v. Hall* (1828) 3 Russ. 1; *Durham Bros v. Robertson* [1898] 1 Q.B. 765 applied.

COLONIAL MUTUAL GENERAL INSURANCE CO LTD v. ANZ BANKING GROUP (NEW ZEALAND) LTD [1995] 1 W.L.R. 1140, Lord Hoffmann, PC.

3549. Fire insurance–proposal form question as to security alarm–affirmative answer not constituting implied warranty as to use

B, an underwriter, appealed against a refusal to dismiss H's claim under a Lloyd's fire policy. H completed a proposal form which contained a question as to whether he had a security alarm fitted in the premises, to which H answered in the affirmative. B submitted that this implied a continuing warranty that the alarm would be set when H left the premises and H's failure to do so breached the policy.

Held, dismissing the appeal, that no principle existed in insurance law which implied continuing promises from answers given on proposal forms. To impose a continuing warranty, breach of which would lead to the automatic cancellation of cover, was a draconian measure and if underwriters required such protection then it should be stipulated in clear terms on the proposal forms.

HUSSAIN v. BROWN [1996] 1 Lloyd's Rep. 627, Saville, L.J., CA.

3550. Forfeiture–husband convicted of wife's manslaughter–joint endowment life policy–wife's policy could be varied under the Forfeiture Act 1982 to create a trust for son

[Married Women's Property Act 1882 s.11; Forfeiture Act 1982 s.1, s.2.]

H and W married in 1985 and had a son in 1988. In 1991 they took out a joint life insurance endowment policy under which the sum assured was payable either on the death of the first of them or on May 31, 2016, whichever event was the first to occur. In 1993 H killed W and was convicted of manslaughter on grounds of diminished responsibility and was detained in a mental hospital. Although H was disentitled from deriving any benefit under the endowment policy by reason of the rule contained in the Forfeiture Act 1982 s.1(1) he sought an order for the modification of that rule under s.2(1) of the Act to have the proceeds of the policy put in trust for his son.

Held, granting the application and making the order sought, that (1) the true view of the joint life insurance endowment policy was that it created in effect two separate policies, one by H on his life for the exclusive benefit of W, the other by W on her life for the exclusive benefit of H. The notional separate policy on W's life created a trust for H under the Married Women's Property Act 1882 s.11, *Griffiths v. Fleming* [1909] 1 K.B. 805 applied. H's interest under that trust fell within the Forfeiture Act 1882 s.2(4)(b) and (2) it was appropriate to grant H's application for modification of the forfeiture rule set out in s.1(1) of the Act since his responsibility for the crime was substantially impaired by abnormality of mind, the order sought would not benefit H but rather his son, and there was no one else interested in the policy.

S (DECEASED) (FORFEITURE RULE), *Re* [1996] 1 W.L.R. 235, Rattee, J., Ch D.

3551. Home income plans–value of bonds dropped–whether insurance company owed investor a duty of care

S, an investor, raised money by mortgaging his property and then invested it in bonds with a view to securing an income which would support mortgage repayments and provide additional income. ARH was the broker and SMA was the insurance company managing the investments. The bonds dropped in value and S claimed against both ARH and SMA, alleging that SMA owed him a duty to manage the investments properly, to ensure he was given proper advice by the brokers and not to permit their products to be used as part of a home income policy without first ensuring that the scheme was safe. SMA applied to have the claim against them struck out.

Held, striking out the claim against SMA, that (1) a duty could only be placed on SMA by statute or by clear assumption of a duty by them. There was no such statute and SMA did not owe a duty merely by virtue of that status; (2) there was no real prospect of S showing the necessary degree of proximity and assumption of responsibility and it would not be just or reasonable to place such a novel duty of care on SMA and (3) there was no reason to displace the common law position that agents and brokers acted as agents of the insured even if the broker's commission might be deducted from the premium.

SEARLE v. AR HALES & CO LTD; HAND v. AR HALES & CO LTD [1996] L.R.L.R. 68, Adrian Whitfield Q.C., QBD.

3552. Insurance brokers–compulsory winding up–application by Secretary of State–business not in public interest

[Insurance Companies Act 1982 s.2.]

The company acted in the position of a broker placing business with a Lebanese and a Lithuanian insurance company. In both instances the business was wholly reinsured with two Belgian reinsurers. The company, which had binding authorities from the insurers to write business as their agents, dealt with the collection of premiums and issuing policy documentation and also dealt with the receipt and settlement of claims. The company did not do business with the general public but provided commercial insurance to other brokers and insurance companies. The Secretary of State for Trade and Industry presented a petition to wind up the company in the public interest on the ground that it was carrying on unauthorised insurance business in breach of the Insurance Companies Act 1982 s.2(1).

Held, dismissing the petition, that the company was not carrying on insurance business within the meaning of s.2(1) of the Act. Carrying on insurance business referred to the risk bearing activity embarked on by an insurer rather than the activities undertaken by the company. The insurance business was being carried on by the Lebanese and Lithuanian companies. As neither was authorised to do so, the company was guilty of aiding and abetting their unlawful conduct in carrying on that business. In the ordinary course of events that of itself should suffice to lead the court to make an order winding up the company in the public interest of preserving the system of statutory regulation of the conduct of insurance business. In the present case it was not appropriate to make such an order as there was no suggestion that the business was conducted in anything other than a proper manner by experienced persons dealing with reputable reinsurers who were capable of meeting any claims that might be made. In addition, since the directors of the company became aware of the difficulty all renewal business had been placed with authorised insurers, *Walter L Jacob & Co Ltd, Re* [1989] B.C.L.C. 345, [1994] C.L.Y. 403; *R. v. Jefferson* [1994] 1 All E.R. 270, [1994] C.L.Y. 952 applied.

COMPANY (NO.007923 OF 1994) (NO.2), *Re*; COMPANY (NO.007924 OF 1994) (NO.2), *Re* [1995] 1 B.C.L.C. 594, Knox, J., Ch D.

3553. Insurance brokers–investments

INSURANCE BROKERS REGISTRATION COUNCIL (CONDUCT OF INVESTMENT BUSINESS) RULES APPROVAL ORDER 1996, SI 1996 1151; made under the Insurance Brokers (Registration) Act 1977 s.27, s.28. In force: May 17, 1996; £0.65.

This Order, which revokes the Insurance Brokers Registration Council (Conduct of Investment Business) Rules Approval Order 1988 (SI 1988 950), approves the new Conduct of Investment Business Rules drawn up by the Insurance Brokers Registration Council for the purposes of the Insurance Brokers (Registration) Act 1977. Provision is made for the authorisation by virtue of a certificate granted under these Rules of registered insurance brokers to carry on certain investment business, for the issue, withdrawal and enforcement of such certificates and for the conduct of investment business, client relations and record keeping by certified persons. Copies of the Rules can be obtained from the Insurance Brokers Registration Council, 15, St Helen's Place, London EC3A 6DS.

3554. Insurance claims–third party liability–householders indemnified by insurance company after house damaged by heave–insurer gained right of subrogation on discharge of claim

B appealed against a decision which held that their insurers, R, could not succeed by subrogation in an action for damages against A, B's house builder. The house suffered damage through heave and R indemnified B by buying the house from them for its full market value prior to the damage. R then sold it at a much lower price. At the preliminary issues hearing the third party, the engineer who had designed the foundations, argued that B had suffered no loss having been indemnified by R. They also claimed that R could not be subrogated since the claim against them no longer existed.

Held, allowing the appeal, that (1) R would not have paid the full value of the house unless they were legally obliged to indemnify B for the diminution in obliged value; (2) the third party's argument that this money was paid under the contract of sale was not accepted, as neither justice nor principle demanded it and (3) third party reliance on *Edwards v. Motor Union Insurance* [1922] 2 K.B. 249, seeking to limit the doctrine of subrogation to actual payment of the sum due under the policy was not a correct interpretation of the case. If insurers discharge a claim, they become subrogated, B were only in a position to obtain the full value of the house because they had paid the premiums on their policy and there was no reason why the third party should benefit from that.

BROWN AND BROWN v. ALBANY CONSTRUCTION CO [1995] N.P.C. 100, Stuart Smith, L.J., CA.

3555. Insurance claims–water pollution–sewage undertaker not entitled to recover cost of remedial works intended to mitigate further loss

Y, a sewerage undertaker and wholly owned subsidiary of YW, appealed against a decision on a preliminary issue relating to the enforcement of public liability insurance policies, arising from the deposit of a large quantity of sewage sludge into a river which subsequently affected a nearby ICI chemical works. Y carried out remedial works at a cost of over £4 million and settled a claim with ICI in the sum of £300,000. They argued that the cost of the flood alleviation work could be recovered under public liability policies issued to YW, as the work constituted measures taken to mitigate further loss which the insurers might have to meet, and that under the implied terms of the insurance policies, they were entitled to indemnity in respect of that expenditure.

Held, dismissing the appeal, that there was no implied term in the insurance policies which would allow Y to recover the cost of remedial works which might mitigate a loss which the insurers might have to meet in the future, as a reasonable and proportional cost of damage which had not yet occurred could not be quantified.

YORKSHIRE WATER SERVICES LTD v. SUN ALLIANCE & LONDON INSURANCE PLC [1997] Env. L.R. D4, Stuart-Smith, L.J., CA.

3556. Insurance companies

INSURANCE COMPANIES (AMENDMENT) REGULATIONS 1996, SI 1996 942; made under the Insurance Companies Act 1982 s.78, s.90, s.96, s.97. In force: April 30, 1996; £2.80.

These Regulations, which amend the Insurance Companies Regulations 1994 (SI 1994 1516), concern the treatment of assets and liabilities of UK insurance companies authorised for the purpose of the Companies Act 1982, the determination of a minimum margin of solvency and the methods by which benefits payable to policyholders under linked long term contracts of insurance may be determined. Regulations 2 to Reg.10 are concerned with the treatment of cumulative preference share capital, Reg.11 amends the definition and scope of the provision for adverse changes under Reg.61 of the 1994 Regulations, Reg.12 makes an amendment for the purposes of determining the margin of solvency required, Reg.13 is concerned with reference values which may be used for the determination of policyholder bene... and Reg.14 makes changes to the rules for the calcula... certain assets can be take into account.

ANCE

...ts

3557. Insurance companies

INSURANCE COMPANIES (AMENDMENT NO.2) REGULATIONS 1996, SI 1996 944; made under the European Communities Act 1972 s.2. In force: April 30, 1996; £1.55.

These Regulations implement the Agreement on the European Economic Area (Cm.2073) as regards the application of Council Directive 92/49 ([1992] OJ L228/1) and Council Directive 92/96 ([1992] OJ L360/1) to Liechtenstein. One of the principal purposes of these Directives was to introduce for direct insurance business the principle of home state control whereby each member state is required to assume sole responsibility for the authorisation and supervision of the business carried on throughout the EC by undertakings having their head office in that State. These Regulations also make minor amendments to the Insurance Companies (Accounts and Statements) Regulations 1983 (SI 1983 1811), the Insurance Companies Regulations 1994 (SI 1994 1516) (both of which partly implemented the Directives) and the Insurance Companies Act 1982.

3558. Insurance companies–accounts and statements

INSURANCE COMPANIES (ACCOUNTS AND STATEMENTS) REGULATIONS 1996, SI 1996 943; made under the Insurance Companies Act 1982 s.17, s.18, s.21, s.96, s.97. In force: Reg.34: April 30, 1996; Remainder: December 23, 1996; £13.30.

These Regulations, which consolidate, with amendments, the Insurance Companies (Accounts and Statements) Regulations 1983 (SI 1983 1811), as amended, prescribe the form and content of annual returns for submission by those insurance companies to which the Insurance Companies Act 1982 Part II applies. The principal changes relate to a general re-organisation and updating of forms, the replacement of form based reporting of other than long term business re-insurance protections by a new free form reporting, a new form for reporting assets used as the basis for discounting liabilities, a reduction in the volume of reporting in certain areas, the transfer of several forms to Sch.4 of the regulations with the result that those forms need no longer be subject to audit and the omission of the prescribed form of the quinquennial statement of long term business.

3559. Insurance companies–claims reserves–taxation–reliefs

The Inland Revenue issued a press release entitled *Equalisation reserves for non-life insurance companies*, published on November 28, 1996. Following consultation with the insurance industry, the Finance Act 1996 has introduced provisions for relief on taxation on transfers into equalisation reserves held by insurers under new supervisory rules. These require insurers writing certain types of business deemed to be volatile to transfer a portion of the premiums into an equalisation reserve each year until a mandatory limit is achieved. These will be deductible in assessing taxable profits. The types of business for which this will be required are credit insurance, those insurers using different accounting methods for DTI returns and tax returns, mutuals, UK insurers operating wholly overseas, and overseas insurers trading in the UK through a branch. The new Regulations came into force on December 23, 1996.

companies–deregulation

EGULATION (INSURANCE COMPANIES ACT 1982) ORDER 1996, SI 1996 2; made under the Deregulation and Contracting Out Act 1994 s.1. In force: ecember 23, 1996; £1.10.

This Order repeals the Insurance Companies Act 1982 s.18(3) which requires insurance companies to which Part II of the 1982 Act applies which carry on long term business to prepare a statement of that business once in every period of five years. It repeals s.42(1)(c) which enables the Secretary of State to require a company to prepare a statement of its long term business, and s.22(2) which requires an insurance company to which Part II of the 1982 Act applies to deposit with the Secretary of State details of certain persons connected with that company. In addition it amends s.22(1), the requirement to deposit five copies of certain printed documents with the Secretary of State so that an insurance company has a choice whether to deposit five printed copies or one printed copy together with one copy in a form approved by the Secretary of State, and s.42 and s.82 so that an insurance company has a choice as to the form in which it submits the required copies.

3561. Insurance companies–fees

INSURANCE (FEES) REGULATIONS 1996, SI 1996 546; made under the Insurance Companies Act 1982 s.94A, s.96, s.97. In force: April 1, 1996; £1.95.

These Regulations revoke the Insurance (Fees) Regulations 1995 (SI 1995 688) and set out the fees to be paid to the Secretary of State by insurance companies when they deposit their accounts and other documents as a requirement of the Insurance Companies Act 1992 and by the Council of Lloyd's. Levels of fees are fixed according to the amount of gross premiums receivable in respect of an insurance company's global business or UK business.

3562. Insurance companies–gilts–accounting for tax on interest

INSURANCE COMPANIES (GILT-EDGED SECURITIES) (PERIODIC ACCOUNTING FOR TAX ON INTEREST) (AMENDMENT) REGULATIONS 1996, SI 1996 1180; made under the Income and Corporation Taxes Act 1988 s.51B; and the Finance Act 1996 Sch.6 para.4. In force: May 21, 1996; £1.10.

In consequence of provisions in the Finance Act 1996, these Regulations amend the Insurance Companies (Gilt-edged Securities) (Periodic Accounting for Tax on Interest) Regulations 1995 (SI 1995 3223). Regulation 6 of the principal Regulations is amended to take account of an amendment to the Income and Corporation Taxes Act 1988 s.51B, by the Finance Act 1996 Sch.6 para.4, which provides for interest to be charged to tax at the lower rate instead of at the basic rate in relation to all payments of interest on relevant gilt-edged securities made without deduction of tax on or after April 6, 1996. Additional specific provision is made for the case of a provisional repayment period which begins before, but includes April 6, 1996. Regulation 8(3) of the principal Regulations is amended to take account of amendments to ICTA 1988 Sch.19AB by the Finance Act 1996 Sch.34.

3563. Insurance companies–pensions–taxation of investment income–repayments

INSURANCE COMPANIES (PENSIONS BUSINESS) (TRANSITIONAL PROVISIONS) (AMENDMENT) REGULATIONS 1996, SI 1996 1; made under the Income and Corporation Taxes Act 1988 Sch.19AB. In force: January 24, 1996; £1.10.

These Regulations amend the Insurance Companies (Pensions Business) (Transitional Provisions) Regulations 1992 (SI 1992 2326), under the Income and Corporation Taxes Act 1988 Sch.19AB, which entitles insurance companies to provisional tax repayments on pension business investment income. As a result of provisions made in the Insurance Companies (Gilt edged Securities) (Periodic Accounting for Tax on Interest) Regulations 1995 (SI 1995 3223), the 1992 Regulations are extended to notional repayments of tax on pension business investment income from interest on gilt e... provisional repayments. A minor drafting amendment is a... 1988 Part XII Ch.I refers to pension business rather than pensio...

3564. **Insurance companies–reserves**

INSURANCE COMPANIES (RESERVES) REGULATIONS 1996, SI 1996 946; made under the Insurance Companies Act 1982 s.17, s.34A, s.90, s.96, s.97. In force: December 23, 1996; £3.20.

These Regulations, which amend the Companies Act 1985 Sch.9A para.50, the Companies (Northern Ireland) Order 1986 (SI 1986 1032) (NI 6) and the Insurance Companies Regulations 1994 (SI 1994 1516), are made primarily under the Insurance Companies Act 1982 s.34A and require insurance companies carrying on general business of a prescribed description to maintain an equalisation reserve to provide against above average fluctuations in claims. Part II applies in respect of prescribed business other than credit insurance business, Part III applies in relation to credit insurance business, Sch.1 sets out the methods of calculating the equalisation reserve and Sch.2 sets out the method of calculating the equalisation reserve for credit insurance business.

3565. **Insurance companies–taxation–equalisation reserves**

INSURANCE COMPANIES (RESERVES) (TAX) REGULATIONS 1996, SI 1996 2991; made under the Income and Corporation Taxes Act 1988 s.444BA, s.444BB, s.444BC, s.444BD. In force: December 23, 1996; £2.80.

These Regulations make provision for the taxation of two different types of equalisation reserve which are required to be maintained by insurance companies.

3566. **Insurance companies–unauthorised insurance business–illegal contracts–effect of Financial Services Act 1986–remoteness of damage**

[Insurance Companies Act 1974; Insurance Companies Act 1981; Insurance Companies Act 1982 s.132; Financial Services Act 1986.]

P were Lloyd's underwriters who between 1981 and 1983 placed stop loss policies with D, a substantial Finnish reinsurance company, through a broker, B. D was not authorised to carry on insurance business in the UK under the Insurance Companies Act 1974 or the Insurance Companies Act 1981. As a result of *Phoenix General Insurance Co of Greece SA v. Halvanon Insurance Co Ltd* [1988] 1 Q.B. 216, [1987] C.L.Y. 2050, it was held that contracts of insurance made by such an insurer were illegal and unenforceable. The Financial Services Act 1986 s.132 was enacted to reverse the judgment and came into effect on January 12, 1987. The question arose as to whether s.132 applied retrospectively and, if so, whether it applied to contracts which contravened the 1974 and 1981 Acts as well as the Insurance Companies Act 1982.

Held, that (1) the policies were effected and carried out in the UK within the meaning of the relevant Insurance Companies Acts and that the policies were void for illegality and unenforceable, *Phoenix General Insurance Co of Greece SA v. Halvanon Insurance Co Ltd* [1988] 1 Q.B. 216, [1987] C.L.Y. 2050 applied; (2) there was nothing unfair in restoring the parties in 1987 to the contractual position they had both assumed and acted upon and Parliament clearly intended to reverse the mischief created by the *Phoenix* decision, *DR Insurance Co v. Seguros America Banamex* [1993] 1 Lloyd's Rep. 120, [1993] C.L.Y. 2415 not followed; *Boucraa, The* [1994] 1 Lloyd's Rep. 251, [1994] C.L.Y. 221 applied; (3) accordingly, s.132 was intended to be retrospective in effect; (4) the retrospectivity extended to the 1974 and 1981 Acts and the Insurance Companies Act 1982; (5) alternatively, if the 1986 Act did not apply retrospectively, B had a duty to use reasonable care to ensure that the stop loss policies did not infringe the Insurance Companies Acts and no reasonably well informed and competent broker would have failed to realise that the scheme contravened the Insurance Companies Acts and B was liable to P for damage flowing from the breach of duty in contract and tort and (6) in 1981 to 1983 B have contemplated that there was a real danger that D would plead ...breach of the Insurance Companies Acts against a policyholder and the ...laimed against B was too remote to be recoverable, *Parsons (Livestock) ... v. Uttley Ingham & Co Ltd* [1978] 1 Q.B. 791, [1978] C.L.Y. 789 and *The Heron II* [1969] 1 A.C. 350, [1967] C.L.Y. 3623 applied.

BATES v. ROBERT BARROW LTD; ANSELL v. ROBERT BARROW LTD [1995] 1 Lloyd's Rep. 680, Gatehouse, J., QBD (Comm Ct).

3567. **Insurance companies–unauthorised insurance business–negotiation of contract came within statutory provisions–statutory interpretation**

[Insurance Companies Act 1982 s.2.]

W appealed against conviction of carrying on an insurance business without authorisation, for which he was sentenced to 100 hours' community service and disqualified from being a director for five years. The issue was whether the Insurance Companies Act 1982 s.2 could be contravened before a contract had actually been formed.

Held, dismissing the appeal, that the word "effecting" in the statutory definitions included the negotiation of a contract which could be said to have begun when the invitation to treat had been made. The soliciting of insurance business was also covered by the words "carrying on [an] insurance business" in s.2 of the Act, *United General Commercial Insurance Corp Ltd, Re* [1927] 2 Ch. 51 considered.

R. v. WILSON (RUPERT) [1996] 1 All E.R. 119, Evans, L.J., CA (Crim Div).

3568. **Insurance companies–unauthorised insurance business–reinsurance contracts–effect of non-authorisation–alleged fraud and material non-disclosure–relevant test for knowledge of material fact where fraud alleged**

[Insurance Companies Act 1974; Insurance Companies Act 1982 s.2; Financial Services Act 1986 s.132; Marine Insurance Act 1906 s.18.]

Between 1974 and 1976 W, an underwriting agency, arranged reinsurance contracts between a number of UK insurance companies and GJ, a Belgian reinsurance firm. GJ was not authorised under either the Insurance Companies Act 1974 or the Insurance Companies Act 1982 to carry on insurance business in Great Britain. In 1983 GJ arranged with W for certain loss reserves held in respect of those reinsurance contracts to be paid over to GJ, in return for which GJ arranged for the opening of letters of credit for W. In order to draw down on the letters of credit W was required to submit debit notes stating that GJ were liable for the sums in question under the reinsurance contracts. GJ then brought proceedings against W, seeking an interim injunction to prevent them from drawing down on the letters of credit on the basis that the reinsurance contracts were illegal because GJ was not authorised to carry on insurance business in Great Britain, and the contracts were avoided for material non-disclosure, namely that three senior employees of W were retaining for themselves commission that should have been credited to the insured companies, and the reinsured companies were aware or should have been aware of this fraud. Both arguments were rejected at first instance. GJ appealed.

Held, dismissing the appeal, that (1) although the reinsurance contracts were illegal, void and unenforceable on the dates when they were made, the effect of the Financial Services Act 1986 s.132(1) and s.132(6) was that a contract of insurance made in contravention of s.2 of the 1982 Act was unenforceable on the part of the insurers only, or in this case, the reinsurers. The contract was still enforceable on the part of the insured. Although s.132(1) of the 1986 Act may in its direct effect apply only to contracts made after the 1982 Act, s.132(6) of the 1986 Act encompassed the carrying out as well as the making of contracts in contravention of the 1982 Act. Section 132 of the 1986 Act applied to contracts entered into both before and after the passing of the 1982 Act, *Bates v. Robert Barrow Ltd* [1995] 1 Lloyd's Rep. 680, [1996] C.L.Y. 3566 followed, *DR Insurance Co v. Seguros America Banamex* [1993] 1 Lloyd's Rep. 120, [1993] C.L.Y. 2415 disapproved. It followed that W and the insured companies were entitled to draw down on the letters of credit and (2) there was no failure to

disclose any material fact that ought to have b[illegible]
Insurance Act 1906 s.18, *PCW Syndicates v. PCW* [illegible]
774, [1995] 2 C.L.Y. 4535 followed. The proposition that, unde[illegible] reinsured companies in this case ought in the ordinary course of business to have known that they were being defrauded offended common sense. The test under s.18 was whether there were natural persons whose knowledge of the alleged material circumstances was to be attributed to the reinsured companies. Where the natural persons in question were the alleged fraudsters, the essence of the principle as stated in *Hampshire Land Co, Re* [1896] 2 Ch. 743 was that the court would not infer that a company had knowledge of a fact known to an agent or director of a company where, because of the agent's or director's fraud or other breach of duty to the company, it would offend common sense to draw such inference.

GROUP JOSI *Re* v. WALBROOK INSURANCE CO LTD; DEUTSCHE RUCKVERSICHERUNG AG v. WALBROOK INSURANCE CO LTD [1996] 1 All E.R. 791, Staughton, L.J., CA.

3569. Insurance Companies (Reserves) Act 1995–Commencement Order

INSURANCE COMPANIES (RESERVES) ACT 1995 COMMENCEMENT ORDER 1996, SI 1996 945 (C.17); made under the Insurance Companies (Reserves) Act 1995 s.4. In force: bringing into force various provisions of the Act on April 30, 1996; £0.65.

This Order brings into force the Insurance Companies (Reserves) Act 1995 s.1 and s.3 on April 30, 1996.

3570. Insurance contracts–aviation–war risk–maximum amount payable in respect of ground risks–ground limit qualified by contract term–contract did not include spare parts as separate entities to planes

Fifteen planes owned by K were positioned on Kuwait Airport when it was captured by the Iraqi army in the Gulf War. K made a claim with their war risk insurers as to the planes themselves and spare parts. The insurers sought to pay only the maximum recoverable under the ground limit in the insurance contract. The issue arose whether this ground limit was qualified by the words "any one occurrence, any one location" and whether the contract covered the spare parts as well as the planes themselves.

Held, dismissing the appeal, that there was unity of time and place when the aircraft were lost. The capture of K's planes constituted one occurrence and therefore the maximum recovery here was the amount of the ground limit. On its proper construction the contract covered spares as well as planes. However, there was no separate cover for spares under the terms of the contract.

KUWAIT AIRWAYS CORP v. KUWAIT INSURANCE CO SAK [1996] 1 Lloyd's Rep. 664, Rix, J., QBD (Comm Ct).

3571. Insurance contracts–guarantee protection scheme–replacement services–whether company was carrying on insurance business–failure to comply with DTI cessation request

[Insolvency Act 1986 s.124A; Insurance Companies Act 1982 s.2.]

S's principal business was the operation of a guarantee protection scheme whereby it undertook to guarantee the supply contracts of subscribers. In practice, it procured the supply of replacement services rather than paying money to the subscriber. The Department of Trade and Industry took the view that S was operating an insurance business in breach of the Insurance Companies Act 1982 s.2(1), and requested that it either cease carrying on that business, that the business be transferred to a company authorised under s.2(1) or that S seek authorisation for the business. S not only continued the business but

...nded it. The Secretary of State petitioned under the Insolvency Act 1986 s.124A for the winding up of the company.

Held, allowing the petition, that S undertook for a consideration to provide the customer with compensation in kind for loss suffered in an uncertain event. Such a contract was in essence a contract of insurance, *Seaton v. Heath* [1899] 1 Q.B. 782 considered. It was immaterial that S provided services in kind rather than money, *Department of Trade and Industry v. St Christopher Motorists' Association Ltd* [1974] 1 W.L.R. 99, [1974] C.L.Y. 1900 and *Prudential Insurance Co v. Inland Revenue Commissioners* [1904] 2 K.B. 658 considered. Since S was not authorised under the terms of s.2(1) of the 1982 Act, it was just and equitable that it be wound up under s.124A of the 1986 Act.

SENTINEL SECURITIES PLC, *Re* [1996] 1 W.L.R. 316, Rattee, J., Ch D.

3572. **Insurance contracts–interpretation–employee dishonesty insurance–joint and several nature of cover provided to group companies–extent of duty of disclosure where contracts continued over several years**

On an appeal and cross-appeal, brought by the insurers on the one side and the claimant companies on the other, a series of preliminary issues arose as to the construction of employee dishonesty insurance contracts. Insurance cover was provided under the contracts by NH and others, including C, whose evidence of insurance consisted of a series of slips, one provided for each year of cover. The issues were whether C's cover formed part of the layered insurance provided by NH and the other insurers, the cover applied to individual group companies and the extent of the duty of disclosure given the continuing nature of the contracts.

Held, dismissing the appeal and the cross-appeal, that (1) as the terms of C's policy contradicted the information given in the slips, acceptance of the risk could not be inferred from silence on the part of the claimants and that C's policy did not form part of the contracts for the years in question; (2) the cover provided under the contracts extended to all the group companies identified in the wording, and the use of "and/or" in the description of the insured was interpreted as including all or any one company in the group, given the joint interest of the parties to the joint insurance, *General Accident Fire and Life Assurance Corp v. Midland Bank Ltd* [1940] 2 K.B. 388 considered. Differing definitions employed by the insurers in later years still carried this interpretation, based on the intentions of the parties. Losses suffered or assets transferred due to an employee's theft or fraud by one group company and received by another were covered by the policies, given the joint and several nature of the cover provided and (3) where the insurance continued over several years the continuing nature of the duty of disclosure was subject to the fact that, unless an event occurred prior to the contract coming into force or before renewal, disclosure could only create a sense of foreboding as to potential future losses. No extension of the duty arose on account of an insurer's cancellation rights, as to do so would serve to enlarge the scope for oppression on the part of the insurer, *Commercial Union Insurance Co v. Niger Co Ltd* [1922] 12 Ll. L. Rep. 75 applied, *Black King Shipping Corp v. Massie (The Litsion Pride)* [1985] 1 Lloyd's Rep. 437, [1985] C.L.Y. 3208 not followed.

NEW HAMPSHIRE INSURANCE CO v. MGN LTD; MAXWELL COMMUNICATION CORP PLC (IN ADMINISTRATION) v. NEW HAMPSHIRE INSURANCE CO, Trans. Ref: QBCMF 96/0765/B, September 6, 1996, Staughton, L.J., CA.

3573. **Insurance policies–"compensation" included exemplary damages awarded for acts of public servants–public policy considerations**

M appealed against a decision that L was entitled to be indemnified, under an insurance policy, for exemplary damages awarded against them as a result of criminal acts by public servants, in this case local authority employees and police officers. M argued that "compensation" did not include awards for exemplary damages, as such damages did not compensate the plaintiff but punished the defendant. M also argued that it was contrary to public policy to award compensation for exemplary damages.

Held, dismissing the appeal, that (1) the meaning of "compensation" was not clear cut. On its proper construction it included exemplary damages, as the torts included for compensation were of a type which attracted such damages. Additionally, where there was ambiguity over the construction of a document it should be resolved against the maker; (2) although it was wrong for someone to be able to insure against liability which arose from the commission of a criminal act, there was nothing to suggest that vicarious liability could not be covered by insurance, and (3) it was not appropriate to prohibit indemnity against exemplary damages. The defendant was still punished, as it would be harder for him to obtain future insurance, and the plaintiff would receive payment. The courts should not create new public policy rules when exemplary damages were being considered in a Law Commission consultation paper.

LANCASHIRE CC v. MUNICIPAL MUTUAL INSURANCE LTD [1996] 3 W.L.R. 493, Simon Brown, L.J., CA.

3574. Insurance policies–disclosure–insured failed to disclose circumstances likely to increase risk under policy–policy clause stated common law position–whether insurer could repudiate policy

E appealed against a finding that they were liable under the terms of an insurance policy to indemnify K for damage to her shop. E had repudiated liability on the grounds that K had failed to tell them of a change of circumstances, namely an increased risk of damage to the property, as required by a clause of the policy. K had failed to inform E that the tenants had threatened to damage the shop and that K, for a time, believed a window, not covered by the policy, had been broken by the tenants. E subsequently contended that, under the clause, damage arising from the changed circumstances was excluded. The judge found that the clause was effective during the time that K believed that the tenant had broken the window and made threats.

Held, dismissing the appeal, that the clause merely stated the common law position regarding a change in circumstances. Cover was ineffective only if changes had occurred which could not be said to be covered on the interpretation of the existing policy, and for an insured peril to be excluded by the cover there had to be an extreme change of circumstances. The risk of the occurrence was dealt with by the insurers when calculating the premium. Their miscalculation in assessing the risk could not lead to the claim being excluded.

KAUSAR v. EAGLE STAR INSURANCE CO LTD; SUB NOM. EAGLE STAR INSURANCE CO LTD v. KAUSAR [1996] 5 Re L.R. 191, Saville, L.J., CA.

3575. Insurance policies–public liability–explosion arising from landfill waste disposal

HC, a waste disposal company, deposited waste between 1979 and 1982 in a landfill site. Landfill gas formed as normal but, because of the land's geological structure, some of the gas did not seep away in the manner expected but accumulated underneath M's house. In 1986, after HC had ceased operations and sold the site, the gas caused an explosion which destroyed the house. HC were found liable to M but succeeded in third party proceedings against their insurers Commercial Union, CU, claiming indemnity under their liability policy. CU appealed on the grounds of an endorsement in the policy which excluded liability for damage arising from "the disposal of waste materials in the way the insured intended to dispose of them unless such claim arises from an accident in the method of disposal". CU argued the escape of the landfill gas was accidental but was not "in the method of disposal".

Held, allowing the appeal, that the endorsement must be interpreted as excluding liability when an accident resulted from an underground accumulation of gas from a landfill site. The waste disposal procedure had been carried out exactly in the way intended and the method of disposal must be considered to have been completed at that point. A subsequent gas escape which occurred because the site chosen was unsafe could not be part of the method of disposal within the meaning of the insurance cover.

MIDDLETON v. WIGGIN [1996] L.R.L.R. 129, Hutchison, L.J., CA.

3576. Insurers–joinder with insured as defendant to personal injury claim–joinder not prejudicial to plaintiff's claim

[Third Parties (Rights Against Insurers) Act 1930; Rules of the Supreme Court Ord.15; Warsaw Convention on International Carriage by Air 1929 Art.29.]

W brought a claim against PT, owners of a helicopter which crashed in 1991, in respect of injuries received in the crash which had killed the pilot, contending his injuries were caused by the pilot's negligence. H, a representative underwriter, applied to be joined in the action on the ground that if PT did not enter a defence, W could gain judgment by default and then commence an action against the insurers under the Third Parties (Rights Against Insurers) Act 1930. H contended, inter alia, that PT's liability was in issue, as a question arose as to whether W had actually been flying the helicopter at the time of the crash, and also that W's right of action had been extinguished two years after the accident under the Warsaw Convention on International Carriage by Air 1929 Art.29 as amended. Leave was granted for H to be joined in the action and W appealed.

Held, dismissing the appeal, that (1) the issue between W and PT fell within the Rules of the Supreme Court Ord.15 r.6(2)(b)(ii), in that the right of action could exist between H and each of the other parties; (2) joinder of H with PT had the same effect as if H was to exercise his right under the subrogation clause. This would allow H to take proceedings in PT's name, giving him sole conduct of the defence and (3) granting joinder would not be prejudicial to W's claim.

WOOD v. PERFECTION TRAVEL LTD [1996] L.R.L.R. 233, Hirst, L.J., CA.

3577. Letters of credit–reinsurers–bank accounts–bank exercising discretion was entitled to discharge liability from principal's account

Agreements between insurance companies and W, an underwriting agency, enabled W to accept business, settle claims and arrange reinsurance collectively on their behalf. L wrote insurance through W's underwriting pool. C, a bank, operated a letter of credit, LOC, scheme enabling reinsurers to substitute LOCs for cash advances required by US state regulators for security. C required W to maintain accounts with C as collateral for LOCs issued by C for W. The LOCs and, initially, the accounts, were not broken down between the various companies who wrote through the W pool. In 1986 L established a segregated account agreeing with C to maintain a share of the aggregate notified by W, with C enabled to retain such margin in the accounts as it considered appropriate if W failed to notify an amount. If no other solution was effected within a period considered by C to be reasonable, C was entitled to debit L's accounts for payment drawn under any LOC, allocating the drawings between W and L as the bank considered appropriate in its sole discretion. In 1989 W transferred its underwriting business to S, a company, by agreement as opposed to a formal assignment of the agency agreement. W went into liquidation. With a growing deficit in the pool, C asserted its right to allocate drawings and debited L's accounts with interest in an apportionment relying on information provided by S. L claimed that no right had arisen or that C's exercise of its discretion was unreasonable.

Held, giving judgment against L, that (1) C was not bound by any notification from S, S not being W's successor; (2) C's decision could be attacked only if it was arbitrary, capricious or unreasonable, which it was not. C was entitled to maintain a conservative attitude to the security pending a resolution between the principals, and to avoid the release of collateral to one principal in such a way as imposed higher liability on another and (3) C had acted reasonably in apportioning in reliance on information supplied by S. If L had a complaint about the apportionment the complaint was not valid against C.

LUDGATE INSURANCE CO LTD v. CITIBANK NA [1996] L.R.L.R. 247, Waller, J., QBD (Comm Ct).

3578. Life insurance–failure to transpose Directive 90/619–European Union

[Treaty of Rome 1957; Council Directive 90/619; Council Directive 79/267.]

The Commission sought a declaration that, by failing to communicate the measures necessary to comply with Council Directive 90/619 relating to direct life insurance, laying down provisions to facilitate the effective exercise of freedom to provide services and amending Council Directive 79/267, Spain had failed to fulfil its obligations under the Treaty of Rome 1957.

Held, that Spain, by failing to implement Directive 90/619, had failed to fulfil its obligations under the 1957 Treaty.

COMMISSION OF THE EUROPEAN COMMUNITIES v. SPAIN (C242/94), October 12, 1995, Judge not specified, ECJ (Sixth Chamber).

3579. Life insurance–policy containing right to determine on death and under other circumstances–whether policy amounted to life assurance policy

[Life Assurance Act 1774 s.1.]

A appealed against a judgment which determined, on a preliminary issue, that an insurance contract providing for the amount insured to be payable to the insured on demand, not just following his death, where those amounts were the same, did not conform with the requirements of the Life Assurance Act 1774 s.1 and therefore did not constitute a life assurance policy. A argued that (1) it did not matter that the same benefit was payable in the case of death as in other circumstances because, inter alia, the right to surrender depended on the continuance of life; (2) on death, the amount was immediately payable on notification whereas a six month postponement was allowed for under other conditions; (3) a discontinuance charge was not payable if the death occurred within the first five years; (4) when considered as a whole, the policy with the insurance element of the charge was an insurance policy and (5) on death, there was no option whether to continue and the benefits were crystallised.

Held, allowing the appeal, that the policy was a life policy within s.1 of the 1774 Act. A life assurance policy was characterised by the fact that benefits depended on life or death. The instant case was an obvious example but other cases sufficiently relating to the uncertainties of life and death included survival to a certain date, *Joseph v. Law Integrity Insurance Co Ltd* [1912] 2 Ch. 597 considered, and an option to determine the policy by the personal representatives of the policy holder, *National Standard Life Assurance Corp, Re* [1918] 1 Ch. 427 considered. There was no reason why a policy which contained a right to benefit on death and benefit on surrender should be precluded from being a life policy. It made no difference that the calculation of benefits was made in the same way, especially as fluctuations in the market would mean that it would be unlikely that the surrender value would be the same.

FUJI FINANCE INC v. AETNA LIFE INSURANCE CO LTD [1996] 3 W.L.R. 871, Morritt, L.J., CA.

3580. Lloyd's–agents and auditors–standard of care required

[Law Reform (Contributory Negligence) Act 1945 s.1.]

P, were Lloyd's names who were members of a syndicate. The first defendants, D1, were underwriting agents who acted either as agents or sub-agents in writing reinsurance business on their behalf. The second defendants, D2, were auditors to the syndicate. The syndicate suffered heavy losses during the 1980s on long tail risks, and sued D1 for writing such business on their behalf, and D2 for drawing up the accounts by way of reinsurance to close, RITC. In *Henderson v. Merrett Syndicates Ltd* [1994] 3 All E.R. 506, [1994] C.L.Y. 3362, the court held that D1 owed a duty of care in tort, without deciding liability. In the present proceedings P claimed that both D1 and D2 had breached the relevant standard of care, which was denied. D2 further claimed that, if they were liable, the measure of that liability was to be reduced by the contributory negligence of P in leaving the writing of risks to D1, in accordance with the Law Reform (Contributory Negligence) Act 1945 s.1.

Held, giving judgment in favour of P that (1) the standard of care required of D1 was that of reasonably competent Lloyd's managing agents specialising in the writing of long tail risks. The standard of care required of D2 was that of reasonably competent Lloyd's panel auditors, *Bolam v. Friern Hospital Management Committee* [1957] 1 W.L.R. 582, [1957] C.L.Y. 2431, *Saif Ali v. Sydney Mitchell & Co* [1980] A.C. 198, [1978] C.L.Y. 2323 and *Eckersley v. Binnie* [1988] 18 Con. L.R. 1 considered; (2) the standards should be determined at the time of the alleged acts or omissions and not with the benefit of hindsight; (3) a professional person should command the corpus of knowledge which forms part of the professional equipment of the ordinary member of his profession. He should be alert to the hazards and risks in any professional task that he undertakes to the extent that other ordinarily competent members of the profession would be alert and (4) having regard to the relevant agency and sub-agency agreements, the audit engagement, the regulatory regime and particularly the role of the managing agents on one hand and the role of the auditors on the other in relation to a RITC, P could not be said to have suffered damage "partly as a result of their own fault" within the meaning of the Law Reform (Contributory Negligence) Act 1945 s.1 (1). Alternatively it would not be just and equitable that damages should be reduced having regard to P's share in responsibility for the damage.

HENDERSON v. MERRETT SYNDICATES LTD (NO.2) [1996] 1 P.N.L.R. 32, Cresswell, J., QBD (Comm Ct).

3581. Lloyd's–indemnities–errors and omissions–underwriters for agents–liability to negligent underwriters and to Lloyds Names–priorities if losses cannot be paid in full

Errors and omissions underwriters of Lloyd's members' and managing agents sought determination of matters arising out of judgments obtained by some Names, so as to avoid risking a double payment in respect of the same loss, namely: (1) whether the same claim could be pressed against original and reinstated level of cover where "claim" meant either liability within the scope of a notice of claim under the policy or liability arising from one originating cause; (2) whether, when a claim was pressed against a reinstated level of cover but recovery was affected by the per cause limit and there remained available cover in respect of other causes, the claim could be pressed against the next layer of cover notwithstanding that the lower layer was not exhausted and, if the gap defeated the claim, (i) whether the gap could be filled by subsequent claims and (ii) whether the next layer would respond to the first claim in priority to the others and (3) whether, where there were a number of quantified losses insured with insufficient cover, the assured or the underwriters could determine the sequence of claims to be enforced, or whether pro-rating should be applied.

Held, deciding the preliminary issues as follows, that (1) whichever meaning of "claim" was adopted, there was nothing in the automatic reinstatement clause in the policy to suggest a claim could not be pressed both against the original and reinstated cover. To interpret the policy so as to limit claims would be inconsistent with the provision that reinstatement was to apply "from the date of notice of claim". A claim could therefore be pressed against both covers subject to the policy limits; (2) the first part of (2) was answered in the negative and parts 2(i) and 2(ii) in the affirmative and (3) it was the assured, rather than the underwriter, who should determine whether and in what order to exercise his remedies unless the contract specifically provided otherwise, which in the instant case it did not, *Edmunds v. Lloyds Italico and L'Ancora Compagnia di Assicurazione e Ressicurazione SpA* [1986] 1 W.L.R. 492, [1986] C.L.Y. 2656 considered. Where the rules of a Names' action group did not govern the sequence in which claims could be enforced, there might be nothing to govern their priority except the principle "equality is equity". Where quantified losses were established in a group judgment against at least two agents, each agent would recover rateably against the policy cover and if one agent was insolvent his rights would be transferred to the Names, who would recover rateably with the solvent agent, *Cox v. Bankside Agency Ltd* [1995] 2 Lloyd's Rep. 437, [1995] 2 C.L.Y. 4122 considered. How pro-rating should be carried out could not be specified in advance for each possible case, except that the primary consideration should be to achieve a fair distribution between the different assured or Names claiming through them, taking into account the policy cover and wording.

COX v. DEENY [1996] L.R.L.R. 288, Judge Diamond Q.C., QBD (Comm Ct).

3582. Lloyd's–litigation

A statement was given on progress and management of the Lloyd's litigation since a similar statement was issued on April 12, 1995. The statement includes developments in LMX cases, long tail cases, personal stop loss cases, portfolio selection cases and central fund litigation.

LLOYD'S LITIGATION: REPORT ON PROGRESS AND MANAGEMENT, *The Times*, April 5, 1996, Cresswell, J., QBD (Comm Ct).

3583. Lloyd's–litigation–losses–names not prevented from bringing action due to failure to discharge claims fully–Lloyd's Agency Agreements Byelaws 1985–funds

Claims arose between Lloyd's Names and their agents. The Names claimed loss and damage from their agents in connection with losses made in insurance business. The agents claimed that the Names were precluded from bringing actions in relation to claims which they had not fully discharged by reason of cl.9 of byelaw 1 of the Lloyd's Agency Agreements Byelaws 1985. The agents contended that the Names had not kept them in funds as required by that byelaw.

Held, dismissing the appeal, that the purpose of the byelaw was to protect the policyholders so that the policyholders would be paid promptly and not required to wait for the Name to put the agent in funds. The byelaw prevented the Name from using matters between him and the agent as a reason for failing to pay. The claims which the Names were pursuing against the agents for negligence were not precluded by the byelaws.

ARBUTHNOTT v. FAGAN (1993); DEENY v. GOODA WALKER LTD [1996] L.R.L.R. 135, Sir Thomas Bingham, M.R., CA.

3584. Lloyd's–litigation–negligence–underwriting–defendants exposed Names to excessive risk–names to accept that underwriting was risk business–assessment of loss

The plaintiffs were Names at Lloyd's; the defendants were managing agents. The Names lost a considerable amount of money on some syndicates. They brought an action in negligence against the defendants on the basis that the defendants had failed to observe certain fundamental principles of underwriting such that the plaintiffs were exposed to excessive risk. Furthermore, where a Name was exposed to excess risk, that could only be permissible where the Name was made aware of such risk. The defendants contended that the Names exposed themselves knowingly to unlimited liability, underwriting was a risk business, the losses suffered in the late 1980's were unprecedented, the underwriters were not required to reinsure risks and there was no requirement of Lloyd's that probable maximum loss calculations be performed.

Held, allowing the application, that (1) while the investor agreed to expose himself to unlimited liability, he did not expect that that would be the risk to which the underwriter would deliberately expose him. On the contrary, the Name would expect the underwriter to exercise reasonable skill and care to avoid such liability. If a Name was to be exposed to such risk, he should be informed of the fact. The competent excess of loss underwriter would consider horizontal as well as vertical loss; he would consider probable maximum loss as a factor considering the number of covers exposed to each risk and not simply look to aggregates. It was a fundamental principle of all insurance business that the underwriter should ensure that the premium was commensurate with the risk. In the context of the spiral market in the late 1980's an irrational rating structure had been created. The exposure faced by the Names was not negligent per se but it was unplanned and unjustified by any proper analysis of the risk and (2) it was for the plaintiffs to demonstrate that their losses were caused by the defendants' incompetent underwriting. The recoverable loss would be that attributable to the inadequacy of the vertical extent of the cover. This loss would be reduced by the amount of a notional premium in respect of this notional cover. Stop loss insurance had no relevance to the measure of the plaintiffs' damages nor to causation.

DEENY v. GOODA WALKER LTD [1996] L.R.L.R. 183, Phillips, J., QBD (Comm Ct).

3585. Lloyd's–litigation–negligence–whether Names could claim discovery of documents which were transcripts of evidence given to loss review committee–documents not of a class protected by statutory confidentiality

[Rules of the Supreme Court Ord.24 r.13.]

The plaintiff members of Lloyd's were suing the defendant agents on the basis that they negligently allowed the Names to remain in the Feltrim syndicates. The Names sought discovery of documents which were transcripts of evidence given to a loss review committee appointed under the Lloyd's byelaws. The defendants contended that the documents should not be disclosed on the basis of statutory confidentiality under the Information and Confidentiality Byelaw 21 of 1993, that the documents were not relevant and that discovery of the documents was not necessary for the fair disposal of the matter in issue.

Held, dismissing the appeal, that a document would not be exempt from discovery solely on the basis that it was confidential although confidentiality was a relevant consideration for a determination under the Rules of the Supreme Court Ord.24 r.13. However, for a document to be exempt one of the existing heads of privilege or immunity must apply or there must be legislation having the same result. It was doubtful whether the byelaw was concerned with confidentiality in discovery in a civil action. While there would be a restriction on those on the committee disclosing the documents, the members' agents could disclose them. There was a prima facie case of relevance here.

ARBUTHNOTT v. FAGAN (1994) [1996] L.R.L.R. 143, Sir Stephen Brown, CA.

3586. Lloyd's–litigation–orders made after majority acceptance of settlement offer

Held, that the date fixed for the hearing of further actions in the Lloyd's litigation was vacated after 94 per cent of the plaintiff Names accepted the settlement offer. Time was extended for compliance with directions previously made and any plaintiff wishing to pursue a claim was to submit details for service and apply to the court for further directions within 21 days. No application for costs would be made against those plaintiffs who had given notice of withdrawal during that period.

AARONS v. ARTHUR ANDERSEN; ARBUTHNOT v. WMD UNDERWRITING AGENCIES LTD; HARRY ALLEN v. WMD UNDERWRITING AGENCIES LTD, *The Times*, October 8, 1996, Cresswell, J., QBD (Comm Ct).

3587. Lloyd's–litigation–solicitors' advice to plaintiffs on pursuing individual claims against Lloyd's

Held, in a statement issued by the Commercial Court, and aimed primarily at the following parties in Lloyd's litigation cases: Wellington, Macmillan, Janson Green 1, King, Pulbrook 90, Poland and Secretan, that plaintiffs in the outstanding Lloyd's litigation cases who had not accepted the market settlement should be advised by their solicitors on their position, particularly in relation to costs, should they opt to continue the litigation individually. Where no plaintiffs wished to pursue their claims, a consent order should be drafted to vacate the dates fixed. Where it was not clear whether claims would be pursued, the parties should apply to the court for directions as soon as possible, unless they agreed an order couched in terms similar to those in *Aarons v. Arthur Andersen* [1996] C.L.Y. 3586: (1) vacating the trial date; (2) extending the time for meeting any outstanding directions; (3) providing that application be made to the court for further direction within a specified time where claims were to be pursued; (4) providing that where no such application was made, the action was to be stayed or dismissed, and (5) directing that the order's effect should be communicated by the plaintiffs' solicitor to all plaintiffs who had not settled as soon as possible.

LLOYD'S LITIGATION: OUTSTANDING CASES (NO.2), *The Times*, November 8, 1996, Cresswell, J., QBD (Comm Ct).

3588. Lloyd's–negligence–causation–failure to report poor underwriting not cause of losses incurred six years later–broker's duty to prospective Names–auditor's duty

D, Lloyd's Names, alleged in an earlier action that in 1983 and 1984 that W, an underwriter, used Time and Distance policies to misrepresent his poor underwriting in order to induce them to join, continue or increase their participation in certain syndicates, and consequentially they obtained judgment against him. In a further action against G, a broker, it was alleged that G's participation in the "fraud" of W was an effective cause of D's losses in 1989 and 1990 arising out of W's poor underwriting and that G owed a duty to report to Lloyd's or another suitable person W's propensity for negligent underwriting. It was alleged that G owed a duty not just to Names on the syndicate which then employed him, but to those who would in the next year be Names of that syndicate. In a further action against L, an auditor, it was alleged that L was negligent in failing to discover or report W's earlier misconduct and that L's negligence was the effective cause of D's losses over the 1989 and 1990 underwriting. G and L applied to strike out parts of the points of claim on the basis that they disclosed no reasonable cause of action.

Held, granting the application in part, that (1) in the earlier action against W there had been a finding of negligence, not of fraud, and so G did not participate in any fraud; (2) G owed no duty to report the alleged propensity; (3) in any event, at most the 1983 and 1984 actions merely set the stage for the later losses and on any common sense view were not an effective cause of them, *Galoo Ltd v. Bright Grahame Murray* [1994] 1 W.L.R. 1360, [1995] 2 C.L.Y. 3691 applied; (4) similarly, any defaults of the auditors in respect of the 1983 and 1984 actions could not be said to be effective causes of the later losses and so such claims against L should be struck out; and (5) there was no arguable claim on a contract between G and the reinsurers, it not being permissible to infer one *Pryke v. Gibbs Hartley Cooper Ltd* [1991] 1 Lloyd's Rep. 602, [1992] C.L.Y. 2594 applied and (6) G owed no duty to future Names of a syndicate for whom he acted.

DEENY v. WALKER; DEENY v. LITTLEJOHN & CO [1996] L.R.L.R. 276, Gatehouse, J., QBD (Comm Ct).

3589. Lloyd's–negligence–lawfully avoided reinsurance–no interim payments for calls following avoidance

Following an arbitration award that found that a reinsurance contract had been lawfully avoided due to material non-disclosure by the tenth defendants' managing agents, Pulbrook Underwriting Management Ltd, PUM, Lloyd's Names of syndicate 334 sought to appeal. The syndicate disputed the findings in a series of preliminary issues, that although PUM and SW, as members' agents, owed duties based in either contract or tort to virtually all the names, all except 11 claims were statute barred. It was also found that if the material facts had been disclosed, run-off reinsurance would have been available, albeit at a higher premium than that provided under the avoided contract. A appealed, contending that an interim award made under the prima facie rule in *Deeny v. Gooda Walker Ltd (No.3)* [1995] 1 W.L.R. 1206, [1995] 1 C.L.Y. 1613 should be based on the calls made on the Names on the basis of declared losses for the year ended December 31, 1993, being: (1) calls that would not have occurred but for PUM's negligence and (2) calls that had arisen due to the absence of reinsurance. SW and PUM submitted, however, that the Names were not out of pocket until claims were paid and any interim payment made on the basis of calls already made would represent a double recovery based on the interest earned on that sum and that recovery on any basis other than a paid claims basis was a windfall.

Held, dismissing the appeal, that although the judge below may have been mistaken in finding that A's claim did not fall wholly within the exception to the prima facie rule as expressed in *Deeny*, an interim award based on the calls already made could not be founded on the basis of that exception. An interim award is made in respect of damages for which the plaintiff has a likelihood of recovery, and although the Names had to pay money in response to the calls, that did not mean that the sums would automatically represent damages as the money paid remained the Names' property. Where a claim had been incurred, but not notified to the Names, an interim payment could not be made, given the speculative nature of a claim which was incapable of precise assessment and where payment would amount to a windfall. Additionally, an interim award could not be made in respect of notified claims, as these amounted to "long tail" claims where it would not be just for sums to be paid by way of damages for losses that had not yet been suffered, *Deeny v. Gooda Walker Ltd (No.4)* [1996] L.R.L.R. 168, [1996] C.L.Y. 5579 considered.

AIKEN v. STEWART WRIGHTSON MEMBERS AGENCY LTD [1996] 2 Lloyd's Rep. 577, Neill, L.J., CA.

3590. Lloyd's–obligation to pay into Central Fund–fund operations as decision of an association of undertakings–arrangements not competitive restriction between Member States

[Treaty of Rome 1957 Art.85.]

C, a Name at Lloyd's, was obliged by his agreement with Lloyd's to provide sums of money to the Central Fund. Lloyd's sued him under the terms of that agreement. C contended that the arrangements for the Central Fund and their by laws were contrary to the Treaty of Rome 1957 Art.85(2).

Held, giving judgment for Lloyd's and dismissing C's counterclaim that the conduct of insurance business fell within Art.85 of the EC Treaty. Lloyd's was an association of undertakings within Art.85 and its decisions as to the withdrawal of funds from the Central Fund were "decisions of an association of undertakings" within Art.85. The relevant markets were the worldwide marine, aviation and reinsurance markets. The Central Fund arrangements had not had a direct or indirect influence, whether actual or potential, on the pattern of trade between Member States. The Central Fund arrangements did not have as their purpose the restriction or distortion of competition between Member States. C's losses were not caused by any of the matters of which he complained.

SOCIETY OF LLOYD'S v. CLEMENTSON (NO.3) [1996] 5 Re L.R. 215, Cresswell, J., QBD (Comm Ct).

3591. Lloyd's–premium trust deeds–trust funds to discharge debts–litigation recoveries for negligent underwriting–validity of amendment to PTD

[Insurance Companies Act 1982 s.83.]

Two cases were brought before the court, *Napier and Ettrick (Lord) v. RF Kershaw Ltd* [1993] A.C. 713, [1993] C.L.Y. 2422 and *Society of Lloyd's v. Woodard* [1996] C.L.Y. 3592 that the premiums trust deed, PTD, signed by all "Names" did not include damages for negligence recovered from their agent underwriters, and (2) that a new clause 2(d) in the PTD was invalid, because there was not sufficient power in cl.22, under which it was purportedly introduced.

Held, allowing the appeal in *Napier* and granting the appropriate extension of time and dismissing the appeal in part by a majority in *Woodard,* Hobhouse, L.J. dissenting, that (1) cl.2(1)(a) of the PTD provided that all money becoming payable to Names in connection with the underwriting business could be applied to the central trust fund. Money recovered in litigation in respect of negligent underwriting was effectively a replacement for any items such as lost reinsurance, salvage monies, excesses or premiums and as such clearly fell within cl.2(a)(i) of the PTD, *Deeny v. Gooda Walker Ltd* [1996] 1 W.L.R. 426, [1995] 1 C.L.Y. 2761 distinguished as not concerned with cl.2(a)(i); (2) it was clear from the recital that the PTD was intended to comply with the Insurance Companies Act 1982 s.83(2) and therefore should include all the receipts of the underwriting business, including those received under cl.2(a)(i) as defined above. However, in *Woodard* other categories were advanced including recovery against member's agents in respect of omissions to advise or put in place stop loss insurance or negligence in selection of syndicates and the amended cl.2(d) sought to introduce all litigation recoveries. But the amendment was too wide, because it attempted to include litigation recoveries that were personal to the Name and not part of his underwriting business. This could not have reasonably been within the contemplation of the parties when the contract was made, *Lloyds v. Morris* [1993] 2 Re L. R. 217 and *Hole v. Garnsey* [1930] A.C. 472 followed, and (3) the extension of time for allowing the appeal in *Napier* and the delay in giving reasons was due to the fact that Lloyd's did not appreciate in 1992 the seriousness and necessity of recovering litigation monies to the solvency of Lloyd's.

NAPIER AND ETTRICK (LORD) v. RF KERSHAW LTD; SOCIETY OF LLOYD'S v. WOODARD, *The Times,* November 7, 1996, Nourse, L.J., CA.

3592. Lloyd's–premium trust deeds–trust funds to discharge debts–Lloyd's power to amend trust deeds to include litigation recoveries

Lloyd's applied by originating summons to determine whether they were entitled to amend Names' trust deeds so as to include in the trust funds moneys, to the extent that the Names were indebted to Lloyd's, which might be recovered by Names in litigation in respect of underwriting business. Some of the Names had recovered damages but failed to use them to discharge their debts. The Council of Lloyd's asserted that sums recovered in litigation were moneys becoming payable to the Name in connection with underwriting, within the meaning of cl.2(a)(i) of the premium trust deeds, and purported to exercise powers under cl.22 to vary or amend all or any of the provisions of the deeds.

Held, denying the declaration sought, that cl.2(a)(i) could not be construed as including recoveries from litigation and therefore the amendments were invalid because the Council had exceeded its powers, *Lloyd's v. Morris* [1993] 2 Re. L.R. 217 and *Napier and Ettrick (Lord) v. RF Kershaw Ltd* [1993] A.C. 713, [1993] C.L.Y. 2422 followed. The dicta in *Morris* were not obiter but were binding. Since the trust deeds were identical, a judicial construction of one deed must apply in law to all the others and although cl.22 conferred apparently unlimited powers of amendment, nevertheless they had to be exercised consistently with the commercial purpose of the deed, which was to ensure that business receipts from underwriting were available to meet the losses and expenses of the Names' underwriting. To include litigation damages would make the trust funds serve an additional purpose. Lloyd's had contractual powers to require Names to supplement their funds to discharge their debts, but to do so they would have to reach agreement or take court action. The power to amend was not a means which was available for this purpose.

SOCIETY OF LLOYD'S v. WOODARD, *The Times,* May 24, 1996, Sir Richard Scott V.C., Ch D.

3593. Lloyd's–regulatory requirements

INSURANCE (LLOYD'S) REGULATIONS 1996, SI 1996 3011; made under the European Communities Act 1972 s.2; and the Insurance Companies Act 1982 s.83, s.86, s.96, s.97. In force: December 24, 1996; £1.95.

These Regulations amend the Insurance Companies Act 1982 and the Insurance (Lloyd's) Regulations 1983 (SI 1983 224), as amended by the Insurance Companies Regulations 1994 (SI 1994 1516) to clarify certain aspects of the regulatory arrangements for members and former members of the Society of Lloyd's and to update the prescribed form of returns on behalf of members of Lloyd's and by the Council of Lloyd's to the Secretary of State.

3594. Lloyd's–reinsurance contracts–claim for underwriting losses–whether delay in presenting claim for recovery constituted breach of contract–leave to amend conditional upon making of interim payment to plaintiffs

J, a member of Lloyd's Syndicate 164, appealed against a decision granting M and other reinsurers unconditional leave to defend a claim under two reinsurance contracts for payment of six collection notes totalling more than $19 million relating to underwriting losses incurred in 1992 and 1993, and refusing an application for interim payment. M sought to rely on two defences, namely that Syndicate 164 had failed to give credit for a quota share agreement under which another syndicate provided 25 per cent reinsurance cover and, further, that Syndicate 164 had acted in breach of contract by failing to recover reinsurance amounts from the reinsurers so as to reduce the ultimate net loss claimed.

Held, allowing the appeal in part, that although there had been delay in presenting the claim to support the defence of breach of contract, there was no evidence to show that a greater amount would have been submitted had the plaintiffs acted more promptly to recover reinsurances. As the computation of Syndicate 164's claim was unverified and inaccurate, further evidence was required to ascertain whether delay resulted in insurance losses. Leave to defend was made subject to the condition that interim payments be made to the plaintiffs.

JUDD v. MERRETT, *Lloyd's List*, June 13, 1996 (I.D.), Leggatt, L.J., CA.

3595. Lloyd's–reinsurance contracts–duty of care–prudent underwriter of catastrophe risks–assessment of probable maximum loss–duty to provide sufficient reinsurance

W were Lloyd's Names of Syndicate 475 who proceeded for negligence against B, their active underwriter RJB; the managing agents who employed him and their predecessor, C. W alleged B had exposed them to improper and unjustified levels of catastrophe risks, by failing to consider and monitor their probable maximum loss, PML, and acquire sufficient vertical reinsurance so that the syndicate was not exposed to a net loss greater than that which was reasonably to be expected. RJB and C were sued in contract and tort for breach of their duties to manage the underwriting business with reasonable skill and care. W made a discrete claim against C, who had undertaken to Lloyd's to provide such administrative support as RJB or Lloyd's considered necessary.

Held, giving judgment for W against B and RJB that, a prudent underwriter should have assessed the PML and ensured that there was sufficient level of cover to match it, less only the risk of loss to which it was appropriate to expose his Names. This syndicate was presented as being balanced internally and by other accounts. There was no suggestion that any unprotected, let alone exceptional, exposure was being run. B should have ensured that the syndicate was not exposed to an unprotected risk on the PML of greater than 50 per cent of the stamp capacity and ensured that such risk arose at the top of some protection programme which should have been acquired. On the discrete claim, C owed no duty to W, as W had neither relied on nor known of the undertaking. In any event there was no evidence to suggest either RJB or Lloyd's considered support necessary.

WYNNIATT-HUSEY v. RJ BROMLEY (UNDERWRITING AGENCIES) PLC [1996] L.R.L.R. 310, Langley, J., QBD (Comm Ct).

3596. Lloyd's–reinsurance contracts–duty of care–whether underwriters failed to act with reasonable care and skill–calculation of loss–vertical reinsurance

The plaintiffs were Lloyd's Names or their agents, who participated in the Lloyd's insurance market through the defendants, who were a Lloyd's members' agency. The plaintiffs claimed that the defendants had failed to act with reasonable care and skill in the conduct and management of the underwriting for two relevant years of account, 1988 and 1989. Mr Bullen, the main managing agent, operated on behalf of the syndicate in the LMX market. Risk in that market was placed in such a way that reinsurance was effected by people who already had exposure to that risk producing a spiral effect.

Held, allowing the application, that (1) every sensible underwriter who specialised in LMX business was aware of the depressed state of the market after the Piper Alpha disaster and should also have recognised the danger of the spiral effect. Therefore, Mr Bullen bore a duty to calculate his probable maximum loss and to make a consequent judgement on the amount of vertical reinsurance required and the amount of exposure he proposed to run net for the account of his Names. The reinsurance purchased by Mr Bullen was not based on such a calculation but rather on a feel for what the market would do. Mr Bullen elected to run a real exposure to a foreseeable catastrophe. The plaintiffs therefore succeeded under this head and (2) the plaintiffs were entitled to be placed in the position they would have occupied if a competent underwriter had competently calculated the probable maximum loss and PNE, and consequently obtained the requisite amount of vertical reinsurance. The loss which the plaintiffs would have suffered on that basis would be subtracted from the loss actually suffered, to arrive at the recoverable loss.

BERRIMAN v. ROSE THOMSON YOUNG (UNDERWRITING) LTD [1996] L.R.L.R. 426, Morison, J., QBD (Comm Ct).

3597. Lloyd's–reinsurance contracts–excess of loss–extent of syndicate's risk acceptance under MIPI lineslip–binding nature of cover period defined in lineslip

D sued F, reinsurers, in respect of three layers of whole account excess of loss reinsurance, each layer expressed to cover losses during a defined period "in respect of risks written prior to October 22, 1982". D claimed that F's syndicate had subscribed to a MIPI lineslip through P, D's syndicate's underwriter prior to October 22, 1982. P had stamped for two syndicates but only signed in one place putting five per cent without dividing it. Thereafter, and after P was suspended from underwriting, insurances were declared under or pursuant to the MIPI lineslip in respect of losses occurring during periods wholly after October 1982. On the trial of preliminary issues F argued that only one syndicate was on risk, the declarations were "risks written" as the lineslip was merely authority to enter into contracts of insurance, that authority was cancellable and that because the endorsement was put forward by D the doctrine of contra proferentum should apply.

Held, giving judgment for D on the preliminary issues, that the failure to divide the five per cent between the two syndicates meant only that they were equally on risk, the words "risk written" were not ambiguous and so the doctrine of contra proferentum was not applicable. The MIPI risk was written on the date when the subscription to the lineslip was made, not the later declarations. Anyone subscribing to the slip at Lloyd's would understand that he was giving irrevocable authority to be bound, not retaining a right to withdraw authority at any stage.

DENBY v. FULLER [1996] 5 Re. L.R. 175, Waller, J., QBD (Comm Ct).

3598. Lloyd's–reinsurance contracts–excess of loss–lineslip–risk written at date of subscription rather than subsequent date of declaration

M were reinsurers of Lloyd's syndicates 700 and 701 covering losses "in respect of risks written prior to October 22, 1982". D sued on behalf of the members of those syndicates who claimed that, through the underwriter, they had subscribed to the MIPI lineslip prior to October 22, 1982, although all declarations were made after that date and 701 later took on 1.48 per cent out of the five per cent written. On a trial of preliminary issues, M argued the declarations were the "risks written" and therefore not covered. Further, 701 reduced a two per cent line on the first excess all classes to 1.4 per cent in May 1983, there being a change of policy number, and M argued that this created a new contract, there being no liability on them thereafter.

Held, deciding the preliminary issues, that (1) the MIPI risk was written when the subscription to the lineslip was made, the syndicate giving at that point irrevocable authority to bind it during the specified period; (2) it must have been intended that 701 would be a party to the lineslip, its stamp having been placed on the lineslip. The fact that the percentage was not divided meant only that the five per cent taken would be evenly split between the syndicates. The later taking of 1.48 per cent was merely a reduction in 701's percentage and (3) the reduction from two per cent to 1.4 per cent was properly seen as a simple reduction in 701's participation in an existing contract, rather than a new one, notwithstanding the new policy number.

DENBY v. MJ MARCHANT [1996] L.R.L.R. 301, Waller, J., QBD (Comm Ct).

3599. Lloyd's–reinsurance contracts–interpretation of contract terms–scope of originating causes and events

Under what was known as "the LMX spiral", syndicates of Lloyd's Names wrote substantial excess of loss business, the effect of which was that the same loss could in certain events circulate through a chain or chain of reinsurances, ultimately exhausting successive layers of cover and leaving the reinsured without any protection. Numerous members of syndicates who suffered heavy losses as a result of the LMX spiral sued their managing agents in negligence, claiming that they had either failed to recognise the effects of the spiral or take proper precautions against its adverse effects. In the course of the various litigations a question arose as to the manner in which losses could be aggregated for the purpose of reinsurance policies. The relevant policy referred to losses arising "out of one event". An originating summons was issued asking whether the loss settlement provisions were governed by the decision in *Cox v. Bankside Members Agency Ltd* [1995] 2 Lloyd's Rep. 437, [1995] 2 C.L.Y. 4122 where the policy covered claims arising from "one originating cause", Phillips J held that since there were three underwriters, each of whom had been negligent, there were three "originating causes" and the claims could not therefore be aggregated. At first instance and before the Court of Appeal that question was answered in the affirmative. The reinsurer appealed.

Held, allowing the appeal, that the expressions "originating cause" and "one event" are not all the same, for two reasons; (1) an event is something which happens at a particular time, in a particular place, in a particular way. A cause can be a continuing state of affairs or it can be an absence of something happening and (2) the word "originating" was consciously chosen to open up the widest possible search for a unifying factor in the history of the losses which it is sought to aggregate. "Originating cause" has a far wider connotation than "one event".

AXA REINSURANCE (UK) PLC v. FIELD [1996] 1 W.L.R. 1026, Lord Mustill, HL.

3600. Lloyd's–reinsurance contracts–interpretation of Lloyd's syndicate–result of termination of contract on risks insured for more than one year–whether reinsurers should pay costs of defending and investigating claims–correct rate of interest to award

BS, the reinsurers, appealed against decisions relating to a reinsurance contract dated April 10, 1957. In 1984 BS stopped paying some of the claims and in 1988 it ceased to pay any of the claims. B sued on behalf of members of syndicate 947 at Lloyd's and cross-appealed on one issue. Evidence of the contract was by means of an obscure cover note and, although it was intended, no formal agreement was drawn up. The issues arising on appeal were; (1) the meaning of the words "United States and Canadian Business" in the cover note; (2) the consequence of termination of the contract in the case of those risks insured for more than one year; (3) whether BS were obliged to pay a share of the costs of investigating and defending claims and (4) whether the rate of interest for these proceedings should have been awarded at two per cent above the Citibank dollar base rate or whether it should have been the normal Commercial Court rate of one per cent over base rate.

Held, dismissing the appeal and the cross-appeal, that (1) the judge was correct to interpret "United States and Canadian Business" with reference to the business of the syndicate rather than the business of those insured. It therefore meant business from a North American broker or a broker specialising in such business which had a US or Canadian corporation as the primary insured and was business which the syndicate reasonably considered to be part of its North American business; (2) the membership of syndicates changed from year to year owing to deaths and resignations. The syndicate was entitled to change its proportions from time to time with no reference to BS. The benefit and burden of the contract could be passed to the syndicate as newly constituted each year. The underwriters of the first year of a risk could be reinsured by the underwriters of the second year of the risk and so on; (3) the costs of investigating and defending claims was not recoverable from BS. There was not an implied term which extended the indemnity to costs incurred. Such a term would be implied only in special circumstances, eg. where the reinsurers had requested that the claim be defended, *British Dominions General Insurance Co Ltd v. Duder* [1915] 2 K.B. 394 not followed, *Scottish Metropolitan Assurance v. Groom* (1924) 20 Ll. L. Rep. 44 followed and (4) the presumption of awarding interest at one per cent over base rate could be rebutted if unfairness to either party could be demonstrated. The judge was correct to decide that the syndicate should be awarded interest for having been kept out of its money and that it did not matter that the syndicate had not borrowed at that rate throughout the period. It was a correct exercise of discretion for the judge to award interest on the basis of evidence of the rate at which a person with the syndicate's general attributes could have borrowed money over that period.

BAKER v. BLACK SEA & BALTIC GENERAL INSURANCE CO LTD; SUB NOM. BLACK SEA & BALTIC GENERAL INSURANCE CO LTD v. BAKER [1996] L.R.L.R. 353, Staughton, L.J., CA.

3601. Lloyd's–reinsurance contracts–ultimate net loss clause–interpretation of "sum actually paid"–no requirement of prior disbursement imposed–legal interpretation

F and other members of Lloyd's syndicates appealed against the dismissal of their appeal from a decision that they were liable under the ultimate net loss clause of a reinsurance contract for "sums actually paid" by C, the reinsurers, who were in liquidation. F argued that the clause created a condition that syndicates incurred liability only when C had made actual disbursements under the original policies, and they could not be liable when the reinsurers would never be in a position to make any payments.

Held, dismissing the appeal, that the words "sums actually paid" had to be construed by considering the contract as a whole. The policy identified four layers of insurance and the fixing of the ultimate net loss clause was provisional, to be determined when the limits of each layer were exceeded. Provided that an insured event occurring within the period of the contract produced a loss sufficient to bring particular layers of insurance into operation when ultimately calculated, an indemnity would fall to be paid. Therefore, the policy required only that the claim was established to be ascertainable and immediately payable, and did not impose a precondition of prior disbursement, *Eddystone Marine Insurance Co, ex p. Western Insurance Co, Re* [1892] Ch. 423 considered.

CHARTER REINSURANCE CO LTD (IN LIQUIDATION) v. FAGAN [1996] 2 W.L.R. 726, Lord Mustill, HL.

3602. Lloyd's–underwriting agent failing to warn Lloyd's Name of risks–extent of duty to warn–measure of damages

B was a Lloyd's Name who had suffered substantial losses as a direct result of becoming involved in excess of loss syndicates chosen by himself. B claimed that K, who was the members' agent acting for him, had acted negligently and in breach of contract in failing to warn him of the dangers of such syndicates. At no time did K warn him of the risks involved in excess loss syndicates despite his requests in 1988 and 1989 for a review of his premium allocations and advice on the balance of his portfolio. B was generally aware of the high risk nature of excess loss syndicates by 1990 but continued to invest, although at a reduced level of exposure. The judge held that a Lloyd's Name was entitled to expect a warning of the inherent dangers. However even if such a warning had been received, B probably would have allocated about 30 per cent of his premium income limit to excess of loss syndicates and the damages should therefore be reduced pro rata. K appealed and B cross-appealed on the question of allocation.

Held, dismissing the appeal and allowing the cross-appeal, that (1) a members' agent owed a duty to a Lloyd's Name, when recommending a percentage of his premium income limit to high risk excess of loss syndicates, to provide proper information and advice about the character and extra risk of the business underwritten by such syndicates; (2) where a members' agent was in breach of its duty to provide appropriate information and advice to a Lloyd's Name, the question of causation was to be approached by identifying first what specific advice the Name ought to have received and then what the name could prove on the balance of probabilities, would have been the consequence of his receipt of such information and advice; (3) although the scale of the loss was unprecedented that fact did not preclude B from recovering damages in respect of it since the loss was of a type or kind that was foreseeable and therefore not too remote. The balance of probabilities was that B would have allocated the market average of 22 per cent of his premium to excess of loss syndicates if he had been properly advised, dictum of Bingham, M.R. in *Banque Bruxelles Lambert SA v. Eagle Star Insurance Co Ltd* [1995] 2 All.E.R. 769, [1994] C.L.Y. 3379 applied and (4) on the issue of set-off, it was clear that B had a separate cause of action in respect of each of the three loss making years and that each cause gave rise to a contractual right. The judge was not therefore entitled to set-off underwriting profits for 1986 and 1987 against those losses incurred in subsequent years, *Bartlett v. Barclays Bank Trust Co Ltd* [1980] 1 All E.R. 139, [1980] C.L.Y. 2404 considered.

BROWN v. KMR SERVICES LTD; SWORD DANIELS v. PITEL [1995] 4 All E.R. 598, Hobhouse, L.J., CA.

3603. Lloyd's–underwriting losses due to negligence–assessment of damages for future losses postponed

[Rules of the Supreme Court Ord.33 r.3, Ord.33 r.4.]

Lloyd's Names, including C, obtained a judgment against managing and underwriting agents for damages to be assessed for losses representing known and future claims. Lloyd's had discharged part of the liabilities of Names, including C, and then commenced proceedings against them to recover the sums paid out, in which it had been ruled that C had an arguable defence. The agents applied under the Rules of the Supreme Court Ord.33 r.3 and r.4 for the asses... losses to be postponed pending judgment in the proceedings again...

Held, granting the application, that the court had jurisdiction to postpone... assessment of the future losses and that, although the desirability of bringing... end to litigation normally made it appropriate to make a single award of damages including an assessment of future loss, the possible dissipation of the damages before the claims were made meant that the damages for future claims should be assessed when the claims were made, *Trans Trust SPRL v. Danubian Trading Co Ltd* [1952] 2 Q.B. 297, [1952] C.L.Y. 895 applied; *Murphy v. Stone-Wallwork (Charlton) Ltd* [1969] 1 W.L.R. 1023, [1969] C.L.Y. 901, *Parry v. Cleaver* [1970] A.C. 1, [1969] C.L.Y. 906 distinguished.

DEENY v. GOODA WALKER LTD (NO.3) [1995] 1 W.L.R. 1206, Phillips, J., QBD (Comm Ct).

3604. Lloyd's Names–losses–settlements

The Association of Lloyd's Members issued a press release entitled *The Lloyd's settlement offer–ALM Committee recommendation*, published on July 2, 1996. The Association has recommended acceptance of the offer to Names, since the offer is adjudged to be better than the offer put to loss making Names in 1994. It notes that the funding requires a greater input from agents, but the Association is confident that this will be forthcoming. The ALM's recommendations take into account that the settlement offers a better compensation package than could reasonably be anticipated from legal proceedings; that the distribution of the offer follows previous recommendations of the Names Committee; that confidence in the plans to reinsure old year liabilities is growing; that Names' losses have been effectively capped; that there are facilities in place to assist hard hit Names; and that there is no better way forward in prospect. The individual action groups have still to decide on the package, but the ALM believes that most of them will accept the settlement offer. The ALM also agrees that the chairmen and committee members of such action groups should be adequately recompensed for their efforts on behalf of their Names.

3605. Marine insurance–cargo insurance under floating policy–contaminated cargo–claim settled and insurance assigned–whether assignees entitled to claim

[Marine Insurance Act 1906 s.50.]

CV insured a cargo of naptha under a floating policy on Institute Cargo Clauses (All Risks) terms. It was a term of the bearer policy that it included "all particular...clauses of the floating policy". Clause 5.3.4 allowed CV to deduct indemnities received from any responsible person or third party to the benefit of the assured and cl.5.4 of the floating policy allowed CV to be subrogated to any indemnity received by the assured by way of compromise settlements. The cargo was found to be contaminated on arrival in the UK as a result of negligence of the shipper in respect of its shorelines prior to shipment. The indorsee claimed against the shipper and the latter settled the claim, on condition that the rights under the insurance policy be assigned to it. The shipper then claimed on the policy as assignee and as co-assured. CV argued that the payment by the shipper to the indorsee was an indemnity and sought a declaration that CV was entitled under the Marine Insurance Act 1906 s.50(2) to make a deduction in respect of it.

Held, granting CV's declaration, that (1) the purpose of the payment was not a gift, *Burnand v. Rodocanachi* (1882) 7 App. Cas. 333 distinguished, but was the consideration for a compromise of disputed claims; (2) it was not necessary for an insurer to be entitled to have a sum brought into account in diminution of the loss, that the sum was the product of a right existing in the assured at the time of the loss, at least where payment has been made pursuant to a subsequent agreement specifically directed at compensating the assured for the very losses insured against, *Castellain v. Preston* (1883) 11 Q.B.D. 380 considered; (3) the words "all particular...clauses of the floating policy" were intended to incorporate all of the special clauses of the floating policy, including

...nd the latter was plainly apt to cover the indemnity received by the ...ee; (4) the shipper was a responsible person or third party for the purpose ...the clause and (5) the policy was not effected on behalf of the shipper, nor was it intended to benefit thereunder, as the policy named as assured an intermediate c.i.f. seller (and its subsidiaries).

COLONIA VERSICHERUNG AG v. AMOCO OIL CO (THE WIND STAR) [1995] 1 Lloyd's Rep. 570, Potter, J., QBD (Comm Ct).

3606. Marine insurance–loss of EEC subsidy due to rejection of cargo–subject of insurance–whether subsidy recoverable under policy–need for cargo to be rejected because of insured peril

In 1989, P insured a cargo of frozen meat under D's marine policy. The meat was rejected by Egyptian buyers and had to be resold to Russian buyers. P claimed for a loss of EEC subsidies which would have been available for exports to Egypt. Section 2 of the policy covered non-payment of "EEC subsidy", in the event that non-payment was "due to a peril covered by the standard form of marine policy" and there were references to the Institute Cargo Clauses. There was also an optional "EEC restitution payments clause". The question was whether P had to prove the cargo was rejected because it was affected by a peril insured against and whether the subject matter of the policy was the goods or the subsidy.

Held, that (1) the nature of the EEC subsidy was analogous to an anticipated profit on resale; (2) it was a matter of construction in each case whether that which was insured was the goods on which profits will accrue or the anticipated profits themselves; (3) in no case under the "EEC restitution payments clause" was the subject matter of the insurance the EEC payment; (4) under s.2, it was the intention of the parties that it was the impact on the meat itself of the perils insured under those clauses which was to be the fortuity which formed the basis of indemnity; (5) the reference to the "standard form of marine policy" and to the Institute Cargo Clauses showed that the cargo must be the subject matter because the perils in question, as identified by the SG policy and the forms were specifically appropriate to meat products and inappropriate if the subject matter were the EEC restitution and (6) accordingly, P had to show that the proximate cause of the rejection of the meat was that it had been affected by an insured peril.

AGRA TRADING LTD v. McAUSLIN (THE FRIO CHILE) [1995] 1 Lloyd's Rep. 182, Colman, J., QBD (Comm Ct).

3607. Marine insurance–loss of hire insurance–subject matter of the policy–insurable interest–whether vessel would have been employed in absence of insured damage–whether action should be struck out for failure to make full discovery

[Marine Insurance Act 1906 s.3, s.6, s.26; Rules of the Supreme Court Ord.24 r.16.]

CS effected a loss of hire insurance with GR, on the ILU marine policy which incorporated GR's general conditions. The policy covered six reefer vessels for differing six month periods for "loss of earnings and/or expenses and/or hire". In May, the crew discovered generator damage caused by an insured peril. Between June and October, the generator was repaired while the vessel was at a layup berth. The summer period was generally an off season in the reefer trade with many vessels being laid up, although CS argued that it hoped to use the vessel if the market improved. CS claimed for 60 days' loss of hire on the basis that it was irrelevant whether the vessel would have been employed on the market. GS denied liability under the policy, disputed CS's insurable interest and applied for the action to be struck out for failure to make full discovery.

Held that (1) the policy could not be construed on the basis that GR must have accepted that layup was covered unless specifically excluded; (2) the subject matter of the policy under the Marine Insurance Act 1906 s.26(1) was the income which the vessel could have made in trading; (3) the "marine adventure" under s.3(1)(b) of the 1906 Act contemplated by the policy was one in which the earning capacity was endangered by perils insured against; (4) the subject matter of the policy was loss of trading income caused by the damage and the policy contemplated a vessel with an earning capacity which was intended to be, and would have been, employed in trade; (5) under s.6 of the 1906 Act, CS's insurable interest, even assessed on a day to day continuing basis, would have constituted a novel and extended interest, involving a substantial element of speculation, and it was unlikely that the parties had agreed on such an interest and (6) it was not necessary to consider GR's application to dismiss the action under the Rules of the Supreme Court Ord.24 r.16 for failure to make proper discovery, since the application was made at the close of the trial when GR had already established its factual case and was not thereby prejudiced.

CEPHEUS SHIPPING CORP v. GUARDIAN ROYAL EXCHANGE ASSURANCE PLC (THE CAPRICORN) [1995] 1 Lloyd's Rep. 622, Mance, J., QBD.

3608. Marine insurance–privity of assured–vessel unseaworthy–duty of utmost good faith ends once insurer rejects claim–claim corporate responsibility–responsibility of company for its officers

[Marine Insurance Act 1906 s.17, s.19, s.39.]

M insured its ship with U for marine perils. The vessel caught fire and became a constructive total loss. U alleged that the vessel had been "sent to sea in an unseaworthy state...with the privity of the assured", within the Marine Insurance Act 1906 s.39(5), and that M was in breach of the duty of utmost good faith in respect of witness statements prepared for the trial. M was a one ship company, beneficially owned by the K family. F was a director of a ship management company employed by M to run the vessel. M had experienced fires on other of its ships.

Held, that (1) the ship was unseaworthy in that it had a defective fire pump and the master was incompetent, being ignorant of the proper working of the CO2 system; (2) the defects in the pump were not causative, but proper use of the CO2 system would have extinguished the fire, had the engine room been effectively sealed; (3) in deciding which person was the assured, it was necessary to ask who had full discretion or autonomy in relation to the acts or omissions in question; (4) although the K family could be regarded as the assured, F had sufficient autonomy to be one of the headmen of M; (5) the superintendent, technical manager, general manager and port captain were not headmen who could be considered as the assured; (6) the knowledge required by s.39 was both positive knowledge and turning a blind eye and "privity" did not carry any connotations of fault, *Eurysthenes, The* [1977] Q.B. 49, [1976] C.L.Y. 2571 applied; (7) F should have highlighted the deficiencies in safety and fire fighting equipment which had become apparent from the earlier fires and instructed superintendents to carry out inspections on the equipment and crew; (8) the inadequate response to the fires demonstrated blind-eye knowledge in that M did not want to know about unseaworthiness in relevant aspects; (9) but for the unseaworthiness resulting in the improper use of the CO2 system, the damage would have been $1.7 million and the claim of $3.2 million for a constructive total loss failed; (10) M's alternative claim for partial loss under s.19(3) of the 1906 Act did not entitle it to a diminution in market value, e.g. the repair costs plus 30 per cent and the value of the claim was $1.7 million; (11) salvage costs were not recoverable as they were incurred as a result of the fire caused by unseaworthiness and (12) although s.17 of the 1906 Act imposed no time limit on the duty of utmost good faith, once insurers had rejected a claim, the duty in relation to that claim had come to an end.

MANIFEST SHIPPING & CO LTD v. UNI-POLARIS INSURANCE CO LTD (THE STAR SEA) [1995] 1 Lloyd's Rep. 651, Tuckey, J., QBD (Comm Ct).

3609. Marine insurance–vessel ran aground and caught fire–allegation that vessel deliberately set on fire with owner's connivance–burden of proof

[Marine Insurance Act 1906 s.30, s.55.]

NJ's vessel was insured with PA for perils of the sea, fire and barratry. The vessel ran aground and caught fire and NJ claimed for an actual or constructive total loss. NJ claimed that loss by fire included loss by deliberate fire, or that if the fire must be accidental, the vessel was lost by the barratrous acts of master and crew. PA alleged that the vessel was deliberately run aground and set on fire by, or with the connivance of, those beneficially interested in NJ. The judge held that the grounding was not deliberate but due to negligent navigation by the master and that PA had not satisfied the burden of showing that the vessel was deliberately set on fire, or that NJ were privy to such an action and, in any event, NJ had disproved privity. PA appealed.

Held, allowing the appeal, that (1) the vessel was deliberately run aground; (2) the vessel was deliberately set on fire and (3) there was clear evidence of a motive for scuttling, no evidence that the crew had any reason to act on their own account to the prejudice of NJ and the overwhelming inference was that NJ authorised the scuttling.

NATIONAL JUSTICE COMPANIA NAVIERA SA v. PRUDENTIAL ASSURANCE CO LTD (THE IKARIAN REEFER) [1995] 1 Lloyd's Rep. 455, Stuart-Smith, L.J., CA.

3610. Marine policies–disclosure–failure of insured to disclose all material information–underwriter not liable under policy written on basis of undisclosed information

MR brought an action against P, the underwriters of a marine insurance policy. MR had instructed its brokers to obtain demurrage liability cover for its vessels. Cover was obtained with P but MR volunteered no information, nor did P request any, relating to the incidence of demurrage liability or their previous loss experience. A substantial claim arose and P denied liability on the ground that MR had not disclosed the relevant information concerning loss experience. MR submitted that the failure to disclose was irrelevant as the insurers would have proceeded in any event and were not induced to write the policy by the non-disclosure.

Held, dismissing the action, that the non-disclosure was relevant to the contract of insurance as P had shown they had been induced into writing the contract on the basis of it. Although it had been shown that the underwriter was both imprudent and negligent, if he had been aware of the loss experience the terms of the contract would have been written differently.

MARC RICH & CO AG v. PORTMAN [1996] 1 Lloyd's Rep. 430, Potter, J., QBD (Comm Ct).

3611. Mortgage indemnity insurance–agents–duty of disclosure to insurers

Held, that where a bank appointed an underwriter as agent in obtaining mortgage indemnity insurance for loans secured by mortgages, the agent alone carried the duty of disclosure where the policies defined the duty of disclosure as falling on the insured. The agent was obliged to discharge the duty with reasonable care and was solely liable if he defaulted. The bank was not the insured for the purpose of disclosure and owed no duty to the insurers.

SUMITOMO BANK LTD v. BANQUE BRUXELLES LAMBERT SA [1996] E.G.C.S. 150, Langley, J., QBD (Comm Ct).

3612. Mortgage indemnity insurance–subrogated right of insurance company to claim in name of mortgagee

Held, that where indemnity insurance was paid to a mortgagee by an insurance company, the indemnity was for the benefit of the mortgagee and the mortgagor could not credit any sums paid towards the discharge of the mortgage debt but remained liable for the full sum owed. The insurance company had a right by subrogation to claim the money from the mortgagor in the name of the mortgagee.

WOOLWICH BUILDING SOCIETY v. BROWN, *The Independent*, January 22, 1996 (C.S.), Waller, J., QBD (Comm Ct).

3613. Motor insurance–legislation governing requirements of insurance policy–liability in respect of personal injuries–driver liability excluded

[Road Traffic Act 1988 s.145; Motor Vehicles (Compulsory Insurance) Regulations 1992; Third Council Directive 90/232 relating to insurance against civil liability in respect of the use of motor vehicles.]

NIGC applied for judicial review of the Secretary of State's refusal to amend the Road Traffic Act 1988 s.145(4A), inserted into the 1988 Act by virtue of the Motor Vehicles (Compulsory Insurance) Regulations 1992, made in order to implement Council Directive 90/232. NIGC pointed to the absence of the word "passenger" in the 1992 Regulations and contended that the words in s.145 of the 1988 Act, which were concerned with insurance cover in respect of liability for personal injuries and referred to persons carried in or upon motor vehicles, were capable of covering a driver.

Held, dismissing the application, that although s.145(4A) could possibly have been drafted so as to conform to the Directive in a clearer manner, there was no reason why it should not have been drafted to conform with prior legislation. On examining the precise words used in the legislation, it was clearly the intention to exclude liability to a driver.

R. v. SECRETARY OF STATE FOR TRANSPORT, *ex p.* NATIONAL INSURANCE GUARANTEE CORP PLC [1996] C.O.D. 425, Popplewell, J., QBD.

3614. Motor insurance–Spain–insurer's joint liability–exclusion clauses–drunk driver–European Union

[Council Directive 72/166 relating to insurance against civil liability in respect of the use of motor vehicles Art.3.]

RB had caused a road accident in Spain due to intoxication. RB's insurer was absolved from liability to cover damage caused by an intoxicated driver. The public prosecutor sought an order that the defendant's insurer was jointly liable with RB. The Seville Provincial Court stayed the proceedings and referred a question for a preliminary ruling to the European Court of Justice whether the Council Directive 72/166 relating to insurance against civil liability in respect of the use of motor vehicles Art.3(1) allowed compulsory insurance contracts to absolve the insurer from liability in cases where the insured was intoxicated.

Held, that the aim of Directive 72/166 was (1) to ensure free movement of vehicles normally based on Community territory and their occupants and (2) to guarantee that victims of accidents caused by those vehicles received comparable treatment irrespective of where in the Community the accident had occurred. Article 3(1) therefore had to be interpreted as meaning that compulsory motor insurance must enable third party victims of accidents to be compensated for damage to property and personal injuries. Any other interpretation would enable Member States to impose different interpretations on the Directive leading to different means of compensating damages. Therefore, a contract of insurance could not provide that the insurer was not liable to pay in connection with an insured who caused an accident while intoxicated. However, the contract might lawfully provide for the insurer to have a right of recovery against the insured.

CRIMINAL PROCEEDINGS AGAINST BERNALDEZ (C129/94) [1996] All E.R. (EC) 741, DAO Edward (President), ECJ.

3615. Motor Insurers Bureau–uninsured vehicle–pillion passenger injured–whether passenger a "user" of vehicle for purposes of MIB liability

[Road Traffic Act 1988 s.143; Road Traffic Act 1988 Part VI.]

The Motor Insurers' Bureau, MIB, appealed against a decision that the plaintiff, who had suffered injuries while travelling as a pillion passenger on an uninsured motorcycle driven by the first defendant, was not a "user" of the vehicle within the meaning of the Motor Insurers' Bureau (Compensation of Victims of Uninsured Drivers) Agreement 1972 cl.6 (1) (c) (ii).

Held, dismissing the appeal, that the Road Traffic Act 1988 s.143 created an absolute offence where the user of a vehicle failed to provide adequate insurance, and that the term "user" had the same meaning in cl.6 of the Agreement as in Part VI of the 1988 Act. The definition of "user" was subject to necessary restrictions, however, as otherwise many passengers could potentially, but unwittingly, commit s.143 offences. An injured passenger's claim against the MIB would not fail on the basis that the passenger had knowledge that the vehicle was not insured unless he also had additional liability as owner or user to insure the vehicle. A plan or agreement to undertake a journey in an uninsured vehicle could not amount to "user" status in the absence of a sufficient degree of control or management of the vehicle, *Brown v. Roberts* [1965] 1 Q.B., [1963] C.L.Y. 3071 applied, *Stinton v. Stinton* [1995] R.T.R. 167, [1995] 2 C.L.Y. 3726 distinguished.

HATTON v. HALL, *The Times*, May 15, 1996, Henry, L.J., CA.

3616. Professional indemnity insurance–legal professional privilege–communications between assured

B, a solicitor, was insured under a professional indemnity policy with GR. There was an exclusion under the policy in respect of dishonesty or fraud and cl.8 (c) of the policy provided that GR could require solicitors' reports to be submitted directly to it. A claim was made against B, which he referred to GR. GR consented to its brokers appointing RPC as solicitors. After negotiations, GR repudiated liability under the policy and RPC ceased to act on B's behalf. In arbitration proceedings under the policy GR pleaded dishonesty by B. GR asked for discovery of RPC's file for the period when they were acting for B, including communications between B and RPC and instructions to counsel. The judge ruled that the documents were privileged and GR appealed. It was accepted that the documents were privileged against anyone other than GR.

Held, that (1) the effect of cl.8 was that any communication which RPC received from B or third parties concerning the subject matter of the claim were to be disclosable to GR; (2) in particular, GR was entitled to reports as to everything which RPC had learned about the claim and was not limited to matters relevant to the claim against B as opposed to the liability of GR and (3) GR was entitled to demand reports on whatever transpired in the course of RPC's retainer, even when the demands were made after the termination of the retainer.

BROWN v. GUARDIAN ROYAL EXCHANGE ASSURANCE PLC [1994] 2 Lloyd's Rep. 325, Hoffman, L.J., CA.

3617. Reinsurance–arbitration–summary judgment–aviation quota share treaties–marine excess of loss treaties–portfolio transfer clause–dispute whether claims made–late request for disclosure

T, the reinsured, and O, the reinsurer, entered into various aviation quota share treaties and marine excess of loss treaties of reinsurance. O contended that on the figures there was a dispute which should be referred to arbitration and sought summary judgment. O sought a stay of the action.

Held, refusing summary judgment, that it did appear that there was a genuine dispute as to whether or not aviation claims had been paid. No request for inspection of the records concerning marine claims had been made before reaching the door of the court. A stay would be granted in respect of the

aviation treaties but not in respect of ‹
would be judgment for the sums claimeo
TRINITY INSURANCE CO LTD v. OVERS... L.R.L.R. 156, Longmore, J., QBD (Comm Ct).

...RANCE

3618. Reinsurance–excess of loss–whether each member of the syndicate had separate arbitration agreements–action to be stayed under the Arbitration Act 1975 s.1 (2)

[Arbitration Act 1975 s.1.]

H, an insurance syndicate member, sued on excess of loss reinsurance policies and sought summary judgment. AA, the reinsurers, sought a stay on the basis of an arbitration clause, arguing that because some of the members of the syndicate were not UK nationals, the court was bound to grant a stay under the Arbitration Act 1975 s.1 (2) as it had an arguable defence.

Held, granting the stay, that (1) each member of the syndicate had a separate contract with AA; (2) there were not, however, separate arbitration agreements as neither party could have intended that each member of the syndicate could insist on a different arbitrator; (3) there was, therefore, one arbitration agreement and, as H conceded that some of the members were foreign nationals, s.1 of the 1975 Act applied; (4) there was a "difference" between the parties where AA had an arguable case, although it was permissible for H to give detailed analysis of the evidence to show that it could readily be demonstrated that AA had no arguable defence and (5) on the facts, there was an arguable defence and so the action must be stayed.

HUME v. AA MUTUAL INTERNATIONAL INSURANCE CO LTD [1996] L.R.L.R. 19, Clarke, J., QBD (Comm Ct).

3619. Reinsurance–implied negative covenant as to confidentiality–arbitration award in favour reassured–whether reassured could disclose award to following reinsurers

LS reinsured a risk with I, a leading reinsurance underwriter, and obtained an arbitration award in their favour. LS wanted to disclose the award to the following reinsurers in order to persuade them to accept liability. I applied for an injunction restraining LS. The question was whether it was open to a reassured, as of right, to disclose to reinsurers who constitute the following market, an arbitration award and reasons made in an arbitration award between the reassured and the leading reinsurance underwriter.

Held, granting the injunction, that (1) there was nothing in the reinsurance contracts by which the following market agreed to be bound by the leading underwriter's settlement; (2) there was an implied duty of confidence between I and LS in respect of the award, *Hassneh Insurance Co of Israel v. Stuart J Mew* [1993] 2 Lloyd's Rep. 243, [1994] C.L.Y. 3662 applied; (3) the mere fact that the arbitration award would be persuasive on the following market did not bring the award within any exception to the *Hassneh* case and it was only necessary to disclose the award if the right in question could not be enforced or protected unless the award and its reasons were disclosed to a stranger; (4) there was no justification for the implication of a wider qualification in the sphere of the reinsurance market as the award and its reasons were not necessary elements in the establishment of LS's claim; (5) where there was an implied negative covenant as to confidentiality, it was not necessary to prove specific loss and damage in order to obtain an injunction, unless enforcement would impose severe hardship on LS and (6) there was no unconscionability on the facts sufficient to deprive I of an injunction.

INSURANCE CO v. LLOYD'S SYNDICATE [1995] 1 Lloyd's Rep. 272, Colman, J., QBD (Comm Ct).

...e–interpretation of follow settlements clause–extent of ...urance cover–issues requiring trial between parties precluded ... summary judgment

[Rules of the Supreme Court Ord.14.]

H, a Lloyd's syndicate, wrote excess of loss reinsurance contracts covering reinsurance risks on war risks policies in respect of Kuwaiti aircraft lost or damaged in August 1990. M, reinsured H with a follow settlements clause expressed to apply only to settlements "within the terms and conditions" of the original policies and of the reinsurance with M. H sought summary judgment for the appropriate proportions of the full insured value and declarations that M was in any event bound to follow H's settlements. The judge gave M unconditional leave to defend. The Court of Appeal allowed H's appeal and M appealed to the House of Lords.

Held, allowing the appeal, that on a true construction of the clause and having regard to the distinction between settlements within the terms of the original policies and settlements within the terms of the reinsurance, M was entitled to defend H's claims on the basis that any loss settlements made by H were not within the cover provided by M. Further, there were issues to be tried as to whether H had made any settlements, so that summary judgment should be refused.

HILL v. MERCANTILE AND GENERAL REINSURANCE CO PLC; BERRY v. MERCANTILE AND GENERAL REINSURANCE CO PLC [1996] 1 W.L.R. 1239, Lord Mustill, HL.

3621. Reinsurance–liability to indemnify losses occurring under underlying policy–relevant event giving rise to obligation to indemnify must occur within relevant period covered by reinsurance contract under which liability was claimed

M sought to recover the reinsured part of a sum paid to its insured, the Port of Sunderland Authority, S, as a result of losses suffered by a third party between 1987 and 1989, for which M was liable to provide an indemnity under an underlying insurance policy. The reinsurers contended that they were only liable to pay on losses referable to a relevant policy year, and that as liability under the underlying policy had only been established in 1992, M's claim lay beyond the reinsurance policies sued on, or, in the alternative, if S's liability was related to events occurring between 1987 and 1989, these were individual events in respect of which the deduction, under either the underlying or reinsurance policies, should be applied.

Held, allowing the claim in part, that (1) under the underlying policy, the payments were compensation for which S was legally liable, and for which recovery was available if losses could be shown to have occurred during a relevant policy period. On the facts, S had been ordered to pay compensation in respect of a series of acts of vandalism but the compensation was not divisible by reference to each particular act; (2) the indemnity entitlement was related to the compensation for which S was liable, being an amount to which the £500 deduction applied and (3) a settlement or payment not attributable to a particular policy year did not bind the reinsurers as M had not agreed with S which year the claim related to, and the reinsurance policies all related to different years. However, M was entitled to claim against the reinsurers in respect of the policy year 1987 to 1988 for loss or damage relating to that particular insurance year.

MUNICIPAL MUTUAL INSURANCE LTD v. SEA INSURANCE CO LTD [1996] L.R.L.R. 265, Waller, J., QBD (Comm Ct).

Ord.11 r.1 (1) (d) as it was not an application to annul the relevant contract. They further submitted that New York law was the proper law of the contract.

Held, that (1) to establish that the court had jurisdiction to grant leave to serve out of the jurisdiction, D had to establish that it had a good arguable case. The evidence, taken as a whole, indicated there was a good arguable case that that any contractual rights assigned to D succeeded under the agreement of bulk assurance. The word "contract" within the meaning of Ord.11 r.1 (1) (d) should be construed broadly enough to include agreements entered into between the parties with intent to create legal relations. The court could, therefore, grant leave to serve out of the jurisdiction if it thought it appropriate to do so and (2) the Insurance Acts applied whatever the proper law of the contract was. There were more pointers to indicate that English law was the proper law rather than New York law. The essential question was whether D needed to assert before the Court the wrongful act of his predecessor in title on these facts. If he did, the principle ex turpi causa non oritur actio applied to the same extent as if it were seeking to rely on its own wrongful act. However, the parties had disclosed that there were serious issues to be tried.

DR INSURANCE CO v. CENTRAL NATIONAL INSURANCE CO [1996] 1 Lloyd's Rep. 74, Martin Moor-Bick Q.C., QBD.

3627. Summary judgments–standard agency agreements–Lloyd's Name liable for cash calls made by managing agents–obligation to pay debts

[Treaty of Rome 1957 Art.85.]

H, a Lloyd's Name, appealed against a summary judgment in the sum of £6,000 given in favour of M, his managing agent, in relation to cash calls made on H in respect of the 1990 and 1991 underwriting years of account. H had argued that a "pay now, sue later" clause in the standard managing agents' agreement was invalid in that it breached the Treaty of Rome 1957 Art.85.

Held, dismissing the appeal, that the clause contained in the standard agency agreement was not unlawful as H was obliged to pay his debts and make funds available to M so that valid claims could be met. Such an obligation was vital in order for Lloyd's to function and was not anti competitive as managing agents were in competition with each other but not with other agents outside Lloyd's.

MARCHANT & ELIOT UNDERWRITING LTD v. HIGGINS; SUB NOM. HIGGINS v. MARCHANT & ELIOT UNDERWRITING LTD [1996] 2 Lloyd's Rep. 31, Leggatt, L.J., CA.

3628. Theft–insurance policies–theft by persons on premises–securities handed over to employee on false representation by company–whether company a person on premises

[Law of Property Act 1925 s.61.]

B and other insurers appealed against a Court of Appeal decision that a bank, DG, was entitled to recover under a Lloyd's insurance policy which provided cover for financial losses through theft "committed by persons present on the premises". DG had agreed to the withdrawal of securities worth £9 million by a merchant bank upon receipt of a signed undertaking by its chairman, S, that alternative securities would be delivered. The undertaking was handed over by a junior employee on the bank's premises but the alternative securities were never received. B argued that the bank's policy was not effective because S himself was guilty of the theft, the only person present on the premises being the junior employee whose involvement had been entirely innocent, and it was incorrect to take the view that the employee was "the company" for the purposes of liability.

Held, allowing the appeal, that the insurance policy only related to crimes committed by natural persons and did not extend to the artificial concept of a company committing theft on the premises through its representative. Although the Law of Property Act 1925 s.61 provided that in all contracts "person" included a corporation, it was not reasonable to assume that B had contemplated theft by a company in the bank, but only that the policy clause was intended solely for theft by an actual live person. If S could not be held to have been present, then neither could the company.

DEUTSCHE GENOSSENSCHAFTSBANK v. BURNHOPE [1995] 1 W.L.R. 1580, Lord Keith of Kinkel, HL.

3629. Articles

Carrying on insurance business: UK activities: Ins. L.M. 1996, 8(10), 1-4. (Whether unauthorised offshore insurance companies were carrying on business in UK for purposes of s.2 and whether section applied to UK underwriting agents and brokers acting on behalf of offshore insurers).

Claims-made policies: European occurrences *(Robert G. Lee)*: Env. Liability 1996, 4(1), 25-28. (Use of claims-made policies for environmental liabilities where claims may only be made during period of insurance or within specified period thereafter and opposition in various countries to such policies).

Communications with insurers about claims: are they discoverable in the United Kingdom? *(Michael Brown)*: Int. I.L.R. 1996, 4(7), 221-223. (Precautions to minimise danger of confidential communications about claims being vulnerable to discovery).

Corporate finance: end of the phoney war *(John Young)*: I.H.L. 1996, 44(Oct), 31-33. (Pressure on life insurance mutuals to demutualise, how demutualisation works and whether s.49 of 1982 Act entirely suitable for purpose).

Defences to an insurer's subrogated action *(Charles Mitchell)*: L.M.C.L.Q. 1996, 3(Aug), 343-367. (Defences available for third parties and insured by establishing that insurer is not entitled to pursue subrogated action or that third parties are not liable to insured).

Demutualisation in the UK life industry *(Katherine Coates* and *Rosemary Sutherland)*: Int. I.L.R. 1996, 4(4), 114-120. (State of UK life industry, pressure for demutualisation and demutualisation procedure under s.49 including valuation, due diligence process, documentation, terms of scheme and advertising and notification requirements).

Directors' liabilities for derivatives transactions *(David Southern)*: E.F.S.L. 1996, 3(6), 179-180. (Whether there is need to purchase directors liability insurance to cover possible personal liability to company, shareholders, bond holders or third parties).

Fraudulent claims: Claims and Underwriting Exchange *(Mark Allen)*: Int. I.L.R. 1996, 4(2), G31-34. (Creation of Claims and Underwriting Exchange database of insurance claims to combat bogus claims).

Health insurance–the OFT reports: Cons. L. Today 1996, 19(10), 3-5. (Recommendations on need to make private medical insurance plans clearer and draw up standard benchmark products to facilitate comparison of premiums).

Insurance coverage for continuing losses *(Todd A. Picker)*: Int. I.L.R. 1996, 4(10), 307-311. (Theories in US law as to when damage can be said to have occurred for the purposes of making insurance claim for long term harm that is not immediately discovered, with particular reference to personal injury and property damage cases).

Insurance policies and material facts *(Michael Griffiths)*: N.L.J. 1996, 146(6752), 1037-1038. (What constitutes a material fact requiring insured to make disclosure to insurer to form basis of insurance contract in light of CTI and St Paul cases).

Insuring pollution in the UK *(Antonia Layard)*: Env. Liability 1996, 4(1), 17-24. (Types of insurance cover for pollution, use of exclusion clauses, extent of insured's liability, compulsory insurance option, underwriting risks and implications for role of insurers).

IPR and insurance *(Ernest Kay)*: C.I.P.A.J. 1996, 25(9), 623-631. (Rise in value of intellectual property rights, survey of insurance policies covering infringement of rights and their effectiveness).

Making insurers pay for joyriders *(Peter Anderson)*: J.P.I.L. 1996, Apr, 29-40. (Difficulties in obtaining compensation from insurance company or Motor Insurers Bureau for personal injuries caused by drivers of stolen vehicles).

Marine insurance–Inchmaree clause–Institute additional perils clauses *(Charles Macdonald)*: Int. M.L. 1996, 3(1), 7-9. (Whether fatigue cracks in legs of accommodation platform caused by insured peril and whether repair costs insured).

Mortgage indemnity insurance: are the terms unfair? *(Damian Falkowski)*: S.J. 1996, 140(42), 1080-1081. (Validity of lenders' requirement that borrower take out mortgage indemnity guarantee to protect mortgagee in event of borrower defaulting on repayments).

Pros and cons of panel games *(Daniel Bush)*: Legal Bus. 1996, 64(May), 73. (Importance of panel system in allocating large volumes of insurance work and impact on law firms).

Reducing the burden of premiums *(Peter Atkinson)*: E.G. 1996, 9636, 140-141. (Increased property insurance costs for terrorism, extent to which tenants can challenge landlord on insurance premiums and other methods of reducing costs).

The EC conflict of laws regime for insurance contracts *(Ademuni Odeke)*: P.N. 1996, 12(1), 7-14. (Complex choice of law in field of insurance contracts according to whether contract is governed by common law, EC Insurance Directives or Rome Convention).

The future of legal expenses insurance *(Vivien Prais)*: Litigator 1996, Jul, 212-26. (Low take up of legal expenses insurance in UK compared with Europe and future prospects in light of Woolf recommendation for fixed costs).

The issues involved in employers liability cover *(Chris Williams)*: Ins. L. & C. 1996, 9, 20-23. (Importance of reviewing level of indemnity in light of increase in costs of claims).

The lessons learned by underwriters *(Phil Bell)*: P.L.I. 1996, 18(6), 83-85. (Underwriters have not learnt from recent escalating employers liability insurance claims, and need to work on basis of projected claims and risk management).

The new DTI returns *(Andrew Chamberlain)*: Actuary 1996, 7(1), 23-24. (Information required on returns for insurance companies' long term business, effective from December 23, 1996).

The production account of insurance enterprises in the EU *(August Gotzfried* and *John Walton)*: E.F.S.L. 1996, 3(5), 144-146. (Methods used by Eurostat to derive macro economic production account of insurance enterprises from their business accounts).

The underwriter's filing cabinet? Lloyd's brokers as document custodians *(Rory Philips)*: Int. I.L.R. 1996, 4(4), 121-125. (Implied term that brokers have duty to collect claims and scope of duty with particular regard to retention and preservation of documents).

Third Life and Non-Life Insurance Directives: has a single European market been achieved? *(Laura Butler)*: Int. I.L.R. 1996, 4(6), 180-188. (Extent to which Directives have eliminated restrictions on cross border trade with details of legislation implementing them in Member States).

Third Party (Rights Against Insurers) Act 1930, together with section 651 of the Companies Act 1985 (as amended) *(Richard J. Bragg)*: Insolv. L. 1996, 17(Jun), 2-7. (Insurance and company law issues raised in situations where claim is made against entity which becomes insolvent either subsequent or prior to action being commenced).

Title insurance *(Phillip H. Kenny)*: Conv. 1996, Mar/Apr, 79-81. (Whether UK home purchasers would benefit from title insurance as used in US).

Trustees' personal liability and the role of liability insurance *(Colin Baxter)*: Conv. 1996, Jan/Feb, 12-23. (Need for, and evaluation of, trustees' personal liability insurance policies for charity trustees).

3630. Books

Bannister, Jim–How to Manage Risk. A DYP textbook. Hardback. ISBN 1-85978-060-1. DYP Insurance Publications.
Bennett, Howard–The Law of Marine Insurance. Hardback: £30.00. ISBN 0-19-826244-2. Paperback: £60.00. ISBN 0-19-825844-5. Clarendon Press.
Clarke, Malcolm A.–The Law of Insurance Contracts: Supplement. Spiral bound: £42.00. ISBN 1-85978-054-7. LLP Limited.
Craighead, David–Financial Analysis of a Reinsurance Office. Spiral bound. ISBN 1-85978-067-9. LLP Limited.
Enright, Ian–Professional Indemnity Insurance Law. Insurance practitioners library. Hardback: £135.00. ISBN 0-421-38240-6. Sweet & Maxwell.
Ivamy, E.R. Hardy–Fire and Motor Insurance. Hardback: £98.50. ISBN 0-406-04838-X. Butterworth Law.
Macleod, J.S.; Levitt, A.R.–MacLeod and Levitt: Taxation of Insurance Business. Unbound/looseleaf: £120.00. ISBN 0-406-04606-9. Butterworth Law.
Park, Semin–The Duty of Disclosure in Insurance Contract Law. Hardback: £42.50. ISBN 1-85521-923-9. Dartmouth.

INTELLECTUAL PROPERTY

3631. Comparative advertising–use of trade mark–reference to rival's trade mark in advertising literature–dishonesty–onus of proof

[Trade Marks Act 1994 s.10.]

BB applied for an interlocutory injunction restraining RBS from referring to the registered trade mark "Barclaycard" in literature promoting their own Visa credit card. BB claimed that in its promotional literature RBS referred to services provided by competitors, in particular " Barclaycard Visa", and as a result would gain an unfair market advantage. RBS argued that even though BB only had to show an arguable case, *American Cyanamid Co v. Ethicon Ltd* [1975] A.C. 396, [1995] 1 C.L.Y. 2640 considered, they did not have such a case, and in the alternative that if such a case did exist, it was too weak to justify relief being granted.

Held, refusing the application, that although the Trade Marks Act 1994 s.10(6) had been badly drafted, its objective was to allow comparative advertising where use of the competitor's mark was judged to be honest by the members of a reasonable audience. Honesty was to be measured by what the general public would normally expect from an advertisement for the goods or services in question. The advertising literature communicated only RBS's belief that its card offered customers a better deal than others on the market. The court agreed with RBS that BB had slender prospects of winning and therefore interlocutory relief should not be granted.

BARCLAYS BANK PLC v. RBS ADVANTA [1996] R.P.C. 307, Laddie, J., Ch D.

3632. Designs–commissioned drawings–joint authorship–ownership–substantial reproduction–inducing breach of implied term–additional damages allowed for flagrant infringement

[Copyright, Designs and Patents Act 1988 s.97.]

RD, C's design director, produced a series of house designs with drawings of elevations and floor plans for each (the 1985 drawings). In 1987, C decided to standardise designs throughout the regional companies and instructed a firm of technical draughtsmen (CH) to produce design drawings based on RD's detailed instructions (the 1987 drawings). C claimed that RD and CH were joint authors of the 1987 drawings. R, another director joined AM, a competitor. He instructed CH to produce drawings for a new range of house designs for AM. C's 1987 drawings were produced at a meeting between R and CH and examined in detail before CH produced the drawings for AM. C claimed that AM's new designs infringed copyright in both the 1985 and 1987 drawings and sought additional damages for flagrancy. C also contended that there was an implied term of exclusivity in the contract with CH that they would not use the 1987 designs for a third party and that AM had induced a breach of contract by CH. AM denied that the 1985 and 1987 drawings were original because they were based on pre-existing drawings and further claimed that C had to identify the particular drawings which they claimed were infringed.

Held, finding that AM had infringed copyright and induced a breach of contract, that (1) C did not have to identify the precise drawings allegedly infringed. If many slightly different versions of a copyright work had been produced, it would frequently be almost impossible to identify precisely which was copied. Even if a drawing could be identified, that drawing was probably largely copied from preceding drawings and not the first in the sequence. Copying of a substantial part of the design depicted in one drawing would therefore infringe the copyright in the first of the series, *King Features Syndicate Inc v. O&M Kleeman Ltd* [1940] Ch. 523 considered; (2) RD employed significant skill and effort in producing one of the 1985 drawings based on an earlier house design so that the 1985 drawing had copyright of its own. AM's designs substantially reproduced the 1985 drawings; (3) the 1987 drawings were also protected by copyright which AM's designs infringed; (4) RD told CH exactly what features to incorporate into each drawing and CH prepared them in accordance with his instructions; (5) copyright in a drawing protected not only the skill of making marks on paper, but also the skill and effort involved in creating, selecting or gathering together the detailed concepts, data or emotions which the words or lines had fixed in a tangible form. Where two or more people collaborated to create a work and each contributed a significant part of the skill and labour, they were joint authors. Here, RD was a joint author of the 1987 drawings; (6) if C had not owned the copyright, the court would have found an implied term that the 1987 drawings were exclusively for C and that AM had procured a breach of that implied exclusivity and (7) additional damages were not restricted to cases where the infringer knew or had reason to believe that copyright had been infringed. Under the Copyright, Designs and Patents Act 1988 s.97(2) the court could increase the damages to register disapproval of the infringer's actions.

CALA HOMES (SOUTH) LTD v. ALFRED McALPINE HOMES EAST LTD [1995] F.S.R. 818, Laddie, J., Ch D.

3633. Designs–confidentiality–defendant's design offered for sale–offer non-confidential–offer pre-dating plaintiff's registration

C sued L for infringement of copyright, unregistered design right and registered design right in its steering wheel lock device. L claimed independent design, and also that its design was disclosed other than in confidence prior to the registration by C of its design, therefore rendering C's registration invalid for want of novelty. The judge decided to try as preliminary issues whether L's design was offered for sale to a third party buyer on a date prior to the registration of C's design, and whether C's design was shown to the buyer other than in confidence.

Held, giving judgment for L, that (1) the design was offered for sale to the buyer on the date prior to C's registration; (2) there was no significant evidence that L's design was copied from C's design; (3) on the question of confidence, the court had to choose between a subjective approach, by asking whether the parties themselves thought a duty of confidence had been imposed, or an objective approach, by asking what a reasonable man would have thought; (4) in relation to the equitable obligation of confidence, the preferred approach was the subjective view; (5) the parties to the disclosure meeting did not consider that an obligation of confidence had been imposed; (6) on an objective approach, a reasonable man would not think that a duty of confidence was imposed each time a prototype was offered for sale, but would know that the prototype would be the subject of independent protection through intellectual property rights and (7) accordingly, on either approach, no obligation of confidence was imposed, and C's action was therefore dismissed, although C's registered design remained on the register leaving open the question of its validity.

CARFLOW PRODUCTS (UK) LTD v. LINWOOD SECURITIES (BIRMINGHAM) LTD [1996] F.S.R. 424, Jacob, J., Pat Ct.

3634. Designs–whether undertaking not to breach copyright was wide enough to cover product which was of similar design

S appealed against a decision that he had breached an undertaking which had been recorded in a consent order to settle a copyright action. S was held to have breached H's copyright with regard to the production of goods made from reconstituted stone and undertook not to "manufacture, advertise, sell, offer or expose for sale or distribute any article... of the same design". The design at issue was for an urn, which it was accepted S was entitled to produce in conformity with a general style. H, however, claimed that S had gone further and included many of H's features so that the two urns were of the same design.

Held, allowing the appeal, that the judge had adopted the wrong test in asking whether the ordinary man would differentiate between the two urns. This was not the relevant question as the instant case was not a passing off action or for infringement of a registered design. The undertaking related to a product "of the same design" not one of "substantially the same design" nor "of similar design", and therefore it could not be said that S had breached the undertaking by producing a similar urn.

HADDONSTONE LTD v. SHARP [1996] F.S.R. 767, Stuart-Smith, L.J., CA.

3635. Passing off–inverse passing off–school's study notes

P1 was a well known school providing courses in social development and self improvement. P2, who owned the exclusive rights to franchise P1's name, licensed P1's name to D in 1983. The franchise was terminated in 1988 and D set up her own school for social development and self improvement. P1 started proceedings, alleging copyright infringement of P1's manual and syllabus and passing off. P1 also alleged inverse passing off based on two grounds. First, that D had passed off P1's study notes as her own. Secondly, that she had passed off the achievements of P1 as her own through misrepresentation in her resume. The judicial commissioner dismissed the copyright infringement claim but upheld P1's claim of inverse passing off and granted a permanent injunction. D appealed.

Held, dismissing the appeal, that (1) although D's resume gave the impression that her school was more experienced than it actually was, it was in very general terms. There was no specific mention of particular courses or training programmes and no particular achievements could be identified as P1's. D did not appropriate to herself any credit which rightly belonged to P1. The resume did not amount to passing off, *John Henderson & Sons v. Alexander Munro Co* [1905] 7 F. 636 distinguished; (2) the essential elements of passing off applied to inverse passing off as well. Therefore, to succeed in an action for inverse passing off a plaintiff must prove that there was goodwill attached to their goods or services; that the defendants misrepresented themselves as the commercial source of the goods or services in question; and that the plaintiff's goodwill was damaged as a consequence and (3) the elements of passing off had been made out. P1's name was well known in the context of self-improvement and social development courses and D did not seriously contend that P1 lacked goodwill and reputation in Singapore. By leaving P1's study notes on shelves that were easily accessible to the students, D was holding out to her students and customers that the notes were the product of her own efforts, which was clearly a misrepresentation. D's passing off was likely to cause damage to P and should be restrained by an injunction preventing D from passing off P1's notes as her own. *Bristol Conservatories Ltd v. Conservatories Custom Built Ltd* [1989] R.P.C. 455, [1990] C.L.Y. 4320, *Attorney General v.*

Manchester Corp [1893] 2 Ch. 87 and *Hooper v. Rogers* [1975] Ch. 43, [1976] C.L.Y. 2966 followed.

JOHN ROBERT POWERS SCHOOL INC v. TESSENSOHN [1995] F.S.R. 947, LP Thean, J.A., CA.

3636. Passing off–lenses described as "to suit" plaintiff's product–whether misrepresentation that use of spares would comply with COSHH regulations–whether gave rise to cause of action–interlocutory injunction refused

[Control of Substances Hazardous to Health Regulations 1994.]

HC sold safety helmets for use in sandblasting which were approved by the Health and Safety Executive as complying with the Control of Substances Hazardous to Health Regulations 1994. It was unlawful to use equipment which did not comply with the Regulations. A sold lenses described as "to suit" HC's helmets. A's lenses did not have HSE approval. Other third parties had sold replacement lenses for HC's helmets with their knowledge, but had not described them as "to suit" HC's helmets. HC applied for an interlocutory injunction to restrain A from passing off the lenses as complying with the Regulations. A claimed that "to suit" merely meant that the lenses would fit HC's helmets.

Held, refusing an interlocutory injunction, that (1) the case was on the outer limits of passing off. If there was a misrepresentation, then HC had met the necessary standards for an application for an interlocutory injunction; (2) it was arguable that selling lenses without warning to a customer who was required to comply with the Regulations amounted to a misrepresentation that A's lenses could be lawfully used; (3) in respect of damage, HC could only suggest an accident might occur with one of A's lenses which would harm HC's goodwill. This was very speculative, particularly in the light of the evidence that A's lenses would shortly be given HSE approval and (4) the balance of justice fell just on the side of A. HC had not taken any action against other third parties who sold spare lenses for their helmets and they could not show that A would be unable to pay damages for any loss of sales, whereas an interlocutory injunction would be a hardship on A when other third parties could continue trading. HC's suggestion that they should supply A with lenses pending trial was unworkable.

HODGE CLEMCO LTD v. AIRBLAST LTD [1995] F.S.R. 806, Jacob, J., Ch D.

3637. Passing off–software–likelihood of confusion–foreign plaintiffs–whether goodwill in UK

P was an American company that developed and made project specific software templates. It had an established goodwill in the US in relation to its product BizPlan Builder, a software template designed to enable businesses to produce a business plan. D was engaged in the business of republishing for use in the UK software prepared abroad. In 1994 discussions took place between P and D regarding D undertaking an anglicisation of BizPlan Builder but these discussions came to nothing. Subsequently, D launched its own product, called BusinessPlan Builder, designed to enable businesses in the UK to produce a business plan. P had made it clear in the earlier negotiations that it claimed ownership of the names BizPlan Builder and BusinessPlan Builder. P sought interlocutory relief to restrain the use of the name BusinessPlan Builder. D resisted the grant of an injunction on the grounds that there was no sufficient goodwill in the UK in BizPlan Builder to support an action for passing off and that the name BizPlan Builder was descriptive and on the evidence there was no likelihood of confusion. Since the launch of BizPlan Builder in 1988 P had sold 127 units to purchasers in the UK, many through some connection with the US. P had no place of business in the UK nor did it have any employees there selling BizPlan Builder.

Held, granting an injunction, that (1) in order to succeed in a passing off action a foreign plaintiff had to show that he had customers in the UK. The number of customers which P was shown to have within the jurisdiction was sufficient to establish an arguable case that P had goodwill in the UK; (2) the names BizPlan Building and BusinessPlan Builder were not entirely descriptive and there was an arguable case that confusion was likely; (3) damages would not be an adequate remedy. P's loss would not be limited just to loss of royalties and D would suffer unquantifiable loss if they were ultimately successful after being forced to change names and (4) D had taken a calculated risk in using the name BusinessPlan Builder and the balance of convenience favoured P, *Erven Warnink v. J Townend & Sons (Hull) Ltd* [1979] A.C. 731, [1979] C.L.Y. 2690; *Star Industrial Co Ltd v. Yap Kwee Kor* [1976] F.S.R. 256, [1977] C.L.Y. 3040 and other authorities considered; *Games Workshop Ltd v. Transworld Publishers Ltd* [1993] F.S.R. 705, [1994] C.L.Y. 4489 referred to.

JIAN TOOLS FOR SALES INC v. RODERICK MANHATTAN GROUP LTD [1995] F.S.R. 924, Knox, J., Ch D.

3638. Passing off–use of MAFF number denoting Government approval–whether unauthorised use of number gave rise to cause of action on behalf of authorised traders

[Rules of the Supreme Court Ord.14, Ord.18 r.19.]

S marketed a fungicide containing a product known as CTL, for which they had obtained approval from the Minister of Agriculture, Fisheries and Foods, MAFF, entitling them to use a MAFF number in respect of the fungicide. P marketed CTL using a different formula and sold it using a MAFF number which they had no authority from MAFF to use. Both S and P's products were grey and were to be used on peas. S alleged P had passed off their product (1) as S's product; (2) as being identical to or of the same quality as S's product; (3) as a product of a trader entitled to use a MAFF number; and (4) as a product that was a parallel import of a product having a MAFF number. S applied for summary judgment in respect of (3), alleging damage to the goodwill of the class of traders entitled to use MAFF numbers, of which S was a member. P applied to strike out all four allegations under the Rules of the Supreme Court Ord.18 r.19.

Held, refusing S's summary judgment application and P's motion to strike out, that the fact that both containers were marked as suitable for use on peas could not amount to a misrepresentation that P's product was S's product, but it was just arguable that by using the grey colour, P were passing off their product as S's product; (2) was really a sub-category of allegation (1) and the same conclusion must therefore be reached; (3), whilst S may have had a good cause of action in passing off, the case was not sufficiently clear as to be fit for judgment under RSC Ord.14, and difficult points of law arose which were not fit to be decided under either Ord.14 or Ord.18 r.19. There was a real argument as to whether or not passing off should be extended to give traders who were licensed under legislation a cause of action against those who wrongly stated they had such a licence, *Erven Warnink BV v. J Townend & Sons (Hull) Ltd* [1980] R.P.C. 31, [1979] C.L.Y. 2690; *Anheuser-Busch Inc v. Budejovicky Budvar NP* [1984] F.S.R. 413, [1984] C.L.Y. 3528 considered and (4) there was no practical difference between allegations (3) and (4) and therefore would be treated in a similar way.

SDS BIOTECH UK LTD v. POWER AGRICHEMICALS LTD [1995] F.S.R. 797, Aldous, J., Ch D.

3639. Performing Right Society–monopolies

The Department of Trade and Industry issued a press release entitled *MMC report on performing rights* (Press notice P/96/77), published on February 1, 1996. A report from the Monopolies and Mergers Commission states that the Performing Rights Society is operating a monopolistic system in administering performing rights and film synchronization rights which is against the public interest. As a result of the report, Consumer Affairs Minister John Taylor is to ask the Director General of Fair Trading to obtain undertakings from the Society and that its articles of association be amended to make it clear that members can elect to self administer certain categories of rights, as specified in decisions of the European Commission. Copies of the MMC's report *Performing Rights: A Report on the Supply in the UK of the Services of Administering Performing Rights and Film Synchronization Rights*, Cm 3147 are available from HMSO, price £27.

3640. Plant breeders rights

PLANT BREEDERS' RIGHTS (APPLICATIONS IN DESIGNATED COUNTRIES) ORDER 1996, SI 1996 1811; made under the Plant Varieties and Seeds Act 1964 Sch.2 Part I. In force: August 1, 1996; £1.10.

The Plant Varieties and Seeds Act 1964 Sch.2 Part I para.2 enables an application for a grant of plant breeders' rights, made in a country to which that paragraph applies, to be treated as if made in the United Kingdom and the Isle of Man for the purpose of establishing priority between applicants for rights in a variety. This Order revokes and consolidates the Plant Breeders' Rights (Applications in Designated Countries) Order 1982 (SI 1982 1094) and the Plant Breeders' Rights (Applications in Designated Countries) (Variation) Order 1985 (SI 1985 1098) and adds Argentina, Australia, Austria, Canada, Chile, the Czech Republic, Finland, Norway, Poland, Portugal, Slovakia, Ukraine and Uruguay to the list of countries designated for the purposes of that paragraph.

3641. Trade names–passing off–charity enjoying reputation and goodwill–injunction restraining other from using similar name–whether reputation exclusive

The BDA was established as an unincorporated charity in 1934 under the name of the "Diabetic Association", later incorporating and changing its name to "British Diabetic Association". The second and third defendants established a new charity for diabetes after disagreement with the BDA. The BDA brought an action against the defendants for passing off and seeking, inter alia, to prevent them from using the name "Diabetic Society" or "British Diabetic Society". The action was bought on the basis that the BDA enjoyed exclusive reputation and goodwill in those names or, alternatively, that the name was deceptively similar to the BDA's.

Held, granting the application, that (1) passing off incorporated the deception of the public by one fund-raising charity in a way that would damage another charity's goodwill. That goodwill would be the charity's "attractive force" in obtaining financial support; (2) on the balance of probabilities, the BDA did not enjoy reputation and goodwill other than in the name "British Diabetic Association" or "Diabetic Association". While mistakes in the BDA's name were made from time to time they did not amount to anything more than a sporadic or erroneous usage and (3) on the facts of this case there was insufficient differentiation between "association" and "society" as they were of similar derivation and meaning and not wholly dissimilar in form. Therefore, the defendant's usage of the name "British Diabetic Society" would amount to deception calculated to damage the BDA's reputation and goodwill.

BRITISH DIABETIC ASSOCIATION v. DIABETIC SOCIETY LTD [1995] 4 All E.R. 812, Robert Walker, J., Ch D.

3642. Articles

A positive future for arbitration of IP disputes *(David Plant)*: I.C. Lit. 1996, Sep, 15-18. (Advantages of using arbitration as means of resolving intellectual property disputes).

Anton Piller orders, intellectual property rights and a diminished burden of proof: Part 1 *(Joanna K. Jowitt)*: Lit. 1996, 15(3), 93-99. (Legal requirements for obtaining prohibitive interlocutory injunctions and Anton Piller orders and evolution of latter).

Anton Piller orders, intellectual property rights and a diminished burden of proof: Part 2 *(Joanna K. Jowitt)*: Lit. 1996, 15(4), 141-150. (Whether infringer's consent to entry, search and seizure and privilege against self incrimination are unfairly prejudiced by ex parte Anton Piller orders and proposals for reform).

Arbitrability of intellectual property disputes *(Marc Blessing)*: Arbitration Int. 1996, 12(2), 191-221. (Problems facing national courts and tribunals, remedies available and recent cases).

Assignment/reservation of UK intellectual property rights *(Chris Ryan)*: I.B.L. 1996, 24(7), 326-330. (Analysis of Government policy towards retention of intellectual property rights when awarding defence and IT contracts and its use of model agreements).

Commission Regulation 240/96 on the application of Art.85(3) of the Treaty to certain categories of technology transfer agreements: IIC 1996, 27(5), 675-691. (Text of technology licensing block exemption which replaces block exemptions for patent and know how licensing).

Comparison of copyright and patent protection *(Martin D. White)*: C.I.P.A.J. 1996, 25(1), 64-66. (Disparity between term of copyright for author and term of patent for inventor).

Copyright: protected against risk *(Ernest Kay)*: C.W. 1996, 59, 25-29. (Development of new insurance cover for legal expenses incurred in intellectual property actions).

Design right, but where to dispute it? *(Andrew J. Margiotta-Mills* and *Nicolas Bragge)*: Litigator 1996, Sep, 297-302. (Nature of design rights and under-used jurisdiction of Comptroller-General of Patent Office).

Dilution and passing off: cause for concern *(Hazel Carty)*: L.Q.R. 1996, 112(Oct), 632-666. (Conflicting dicta in CA on concept of dilution of trade mark and effect on law of passing off).

If not a rocket docket, what? *(Robin Jacob)*: C.I.P.A.J. 1996, 25(3), 149-162. (Address by Mr Justice Jacob at the 702nd OGM of the Chartered Institute of Patent Agents on various aspects of civil procedure relating to intellectual property, including Lord Woolf's proposals).

Intellectual property antitrust *(Daniel F. Kolb)*: I.C. Lit. 1996, Jan, Supp USL 8-13. (Application of US competition rules to intellectual property with antitrust analysis of intellectual property acquisition and licensing arrangements and enforcement of rights).

Intellectual property in artificial neural networks in particular under the European Patent Convention *(Timothy Watkin* and *Albrecht Rau)*: IIC 1996, 27(4), 447-469. (Introduction to neural networks and extent to which neural inventions can be protected by EC copyright and patent law).

Intellectual property insurance *(Ernest Kay)*: Ins. L. & C. 1996, 9, 24, 26, 28. (Importance of insured understanding proposal form and policy for ensuring adequate intellectual property cover).

Intellectual property resources on the global Internet *(Arthur Purcell)*: P.W. 1996, 83, 18-26. (Legal and government resources of interest to intellectual property practitioners including appendix of valuable links to intellectual property resources and reference sites).

Intellectual property rights and information technology: the impact of the Uruguay Round on developing countries *(Rohini Acharya)*: I. & C.T.L. 1996, 5(2), 149-166. (Economics of technological change and relationship between intellectual property rights and country's level of development).

Intellectual property rights and treatment of media *(Stephan Le Goueff* and *Patrizio Menchetti)*: C.L.S.R. 1996, 12(5), 287-289. (IP issues raised by provision of multimedia services by means of digital telecommunications networks).

Know-how and trade secrets (with special reference to franchising) *(Aldo Frignani)*: J.I.F.D.L. 1996, 10(2), 59-67. (EU legal framework, definitions of know how and its transfer and protection in international franchising agreements).

Lawyers beware: complying with EU law can be against the best interests of intellectual property owners *(Mark Abell)*: T.W. 1996, 90, 31-35. (Whether following provisions of block exemptions to Art.85 EC in drafting agreements involving intellectual property can unnecessarily limit protection, with reference to post termination restrictive covenants in franchising).

OECD transfer pricing guidelines: intangible property and intra group services *(Jonathan S. Schwarz)*: W.T.R. 1996, 21 (June), 102-106. (OECD draft guidelines Part 2 on application of arm's length principle to sale or licence transfers of intellectual property, price determination methods and test for determining rendering of intra group services).

Public procurement and intellectual property rights *(Stephen Kahn)*: I.B.L. 1996, 24(7), 320-321. (Problems peculiar to procurement of intellectual property rights in research and development).

Security interests in intellectual property: international law and practice *(Lanning G. Bryer)*: C.W. 1996, 63, 32-37. (Creation and enforcement of security interests in various representative jurisdictions).

Security interests in intellectual property: international law and practice *(Lanning G. Bryer)*: T.W. 1996, 88, 26-31. (Use of intellectual property rights as security for loans in various countries).

The anti-trust threat to rights owners: M.I.P. 1996, 58, 38-45. (Comparison of effect of competition policy on intellectual property rights in 11 key jurisdictions).

The compulsory licensing of intellectual property rights and computers: recent developments in UK, EC and international law *(David L. Perrott)*: I. & C.T.L. 1996, 5(2), 111-132. (Development of compulsory licence of right under UK law and position under Art.86 EC and TRIPs).

The diminishing domain *(Jeremy Phillips)*: E.I.P.R. 1996, 18(8), 429-430. (Whether public domain is under threat from intellectual property law and what can be done to keep it alive).

The new technology transfer block exemption–a whiter shade of grey? *(Justine Antill* and *Michael Burdon)*: P.W. 1996, 80, 14-21. (Theory behind Regulation, general format of block exemption, summary of exempted and non exempted clauses, market share limits, territorial provisions and application of s.44 of 1977 Act).

The technology transfer regulation *(Michael Burnside)*: C.I.P.A.J. 1996, 25(3), 162-164. (Provisions and effect of Technology Transfer Regulation which comes into effect from April 1, 1996).

The TRIPs Agreement and information technologies: implications for developing countries *(Carlos M. Correa)*: I. & C.T.L. 1996, 5(2), 133-147. (Effect of provisions relating to computer software, databases and layout design of integrated circuits).

"Utilisation of patent protection in Europe": EPO script 3–a comment: P.W. 1996, 82, 20-25. (Findings of EPO study into causes for lack of innovation and inadequate patent activity in Europe and comments by Institute of Professional Representatives before the European Patent Office (EPI).

3643. Books

Adams, John N.–Character Merchandising. Hardback: £105.00. ISBN 0-406-07767-3. Butterworth Law.

Bainbridge, David–Intellectual Property. Paperback: £27.99. ISBN 0-273-62279-X. Pitman Publishing.

Bainbridge, David; Pearce, Graham; Platten, Nick–Bainbridge, Pearce and Platten: European Data Protection Directive. Paperback: £90.00. ISBN 0-406-01447-7. Butterworth Law.

Beier, F.-K; Schricker, G.; Fikentscher, W.–German Industrial Property, Copyright and Antitrust Laws. Unbound/looseleaf: £52.00. ISBN 3-527-28730-2. VCH.

Bezold, G.–Protection of Biotechnological Matter Under European and German Law. Paperback: £54.00. ISBN 3-527-28781-7. VCH.

Blakeney, Michael–Trade Related Aspects of Intellectual Property Rights. Intellectual property in practice. Hardback: £55.00. ISBN 0-421-53630-6. Sweet & Maxwell.

Boyle, James–Shamans, Software and Spleens. Hardback: £21.95. ISBN 0-674-80522-4. Harvard University Press.

Budden, Michael Craig–Protecting Trade Secrets Under the Uniform Trade Secrets Act. Hardback: £43.95. ISBN 1-56720-016-8. Quorum Books.

Carter, Mary E.–Electronic Highway Robbery. Paperback: £18.95. ISBN 0-201-88393-7. Peachpit Press.

Clark, Robert; Smyth, Shane–Clark and Smyth: Intellectual Property Law. Hardback: £55.00. ISBN 1-85475-138-7. Butterworth Law (Ireland).

Cornish, W.R.–Cases and Materials on Intellectual Property. Paperback: £35.00. ISBN 0-421-53530-X. Sweet & Maxwell.

Cornish, W.R.–Intellectual Property. Paperback: £30.00. ISBN 0-421-53520-2. Sweet & Maxwell.

Drahos, Peter–A Philosophy of Intellectual Property. Applied Legal Philosophy Series. Hardback: £39.50. ISBN 1-85521-240-4. Dartmouth.

Endeshaw, Assafa–Intellectual Property for Non-industrial Countries. Law, Social Change and Development. Hardback: £45.00. ISBN 1-85521-754-6. Dartmouth.

Farringdon, Jill M.; Morton, Andrew Q.; Farringdon, Michael; Baker, M. David–Analyzing for Authorship. Hardback: £35.00. ISBN 0-7083-1324-8. University of Wales Press.

Firth, Alison–The Prehistory and Development of Intellectual Property Systems. Perspectives on intellectual property, Vol 1. Paperback: £18.50. ISBN 0-421-58030-5. Sweet & Maxwell.

Franzosi, Mario; Hirsch, Marc Roger; Hoyng, Willem A.; Levin, Marianne; Ohlgart, Dietrich C.; Phillips, Jeremy; Posner, Bernhard; Scordamaglia, Vincenzo–European Design Protection. Hardback: £112.50. ISBN 90-411-0112-8. Kluwer Law International.

Fysh, M; Wilson-Thomas, R.–Intellectual Property Citator: 1982-1995. Hardback: £135.00. ISBN 0-421-52820-6. Sweet & Maxwell.

Hearle, Liz–World Guide to Intellectual Property Organisations. Key resources series. Paperback. ISBN 0-7123-0819-9. British Library (Science Reference and Information Service).

Holyoak, Jon; Torremans, Paul–Intellectual Property Law. Butterworths student statutes series. Paperback: £8.95. ISBN 0-406-99376-9. Butterworth Law.

Jeremiah, Joanna R.–Merchandising Intellectual Property Rights. Intellectual property law. Hardback: £65.00. ISBN 0-471-96579-0. John Wiley and Sons.

Jones, Hugh–Essential Law for Publishers. Hardback: £35.00. ISBN 1-85713-000-6. Routledge.

Luckman, Michael–Intellectual Property in Commercial Transactions. Commercial series. Hardback: £65.00. ISBN 0-7520-0131-0. FT Law & Tax.

Mostert, Frederick–Mostert: Famous and Well-known Marks. Hardback: £100.00. ISBN 0-406-99734-9. Butterworth Law.

Parr, Russell L.; Sullivan, Patrick H.–Technology Licensing Strategies. Hardback: £50.00. ISBN 0-471-13081-8. John Wiley and Sons.

Phillips, J.–The Inventor's Guide. Information in focus. Paperback: £25.00. ISBN 0-7123-0793-1. British Library (Science Reference and Information Service).

Schlicher, John W.–Licensing Intellectual Property Rights. Intellectual property library. Hardback: £100.00. ISBN 0-471-15312-5. John Wiley and Sons.

Tatham, David; Richards, William; Gielen, Charles–ECTA Guide to EU Trade Mark Legislation. Hardback: £85.00. ISBN 0-421-52880-X. Sweet & Maxwell.

Turner, Mark; Williams, Alan–Multimedia Contracts Rights and Licensing. Special Report. Hardback: £125.00. ISBN 0-7520-0177-9. FT Law & Tax.

Webster, Andrew–Innovation and the Intellectual Property System. Nijhoff law specials. Paperback: £65.00. ISBN 90-411-0907-2. Kluwer Law International.

INTERNATIONAL LAW

3644. Chemical weapons

CHEMICAL WEAPONS (NOTIFICATION) REGULATIONS 1996, SI 1996 2503; made under the Chemical Weapons Act 1996 s.23. In force: November 1, 1996; £1.55.

These Regulations describe certain persons who have to identify themselves to the Secretary of State as being persons on whom it is likely the Secretary of State will want to serve a notice under the Chemical Weapons Act 1996 s.22.

3645. Chemical weapons

CHEMICAL WEAPONS (NOTIFICATION) (AMENDMENT) REGULATIONS 1996, SI 1996 2669; made under the Chemical Weapons Act 1996 s.23. In force: October 31, 1996; £0.65.

The Chemical Weapons (Notification) Regulations 1996 (SI 1996 2503) described certain persons who have to identify themselves to the Secretary of State as being persons on whom it is likely the Secretary of State will want to serve a notice under the Chemical Weapons Act 1996 s.22. These Regulations provide that they come into force on November 1, 1996.

3646. Chemical weapons–licences

CHEMICALS WEAPONS (LICENCE APPEAL PROVISIONS) ORDER 1996, SI 1996 3030; made under the Chemical Weapons Act 1996 s.20. In force: January 1, 1997; £1.10.

This Order adopts the model rules concerning the conduct of appeals set out in the Deregulation (Model Appeal Provisions) Order 1996 (SI 1996 1678) for the purposes of the Chemical Weapons Act 1996 s.20(4) subject to modifications.

3647. Chemical Weapons Act 1996–Commencement Order

CHEMICAL WEAPONS ACT 1996 (COMMENCEMENT) ORDER 1996, SI 1996 2054 (C.47); made under the Chemical Weapons Act 1996 s.39. In force: bringing into force various provisions of the Act on September 16, 1996; £0.65.

This Order brings into force the provisions of the Chemical Weapons Act 1996 on September 16, 1996 with the exception of s.39, which came into force on Royal Assent.

3648. Chemical Weapons Act 1996 (c.6)

Act to promote the control of chemical weapons and of certain toxic chemicals and their precursors, ratifying the UN Convention on the Prohibition of the Development, Production, Stockpiling and Use of Chemical Weapons and on their Destruction, signed at Paris on January 13, 1993.

This Act received Royal Assent on April 3, 1996.

3649. Consuls–fees

CONSULAR FEES ORDER 1996, SI 1996 1915; made under the Consular Fees Act 1980 s.1. In force: August 14, 1996; £1.95.

This Order revokes and replaces the Consular Fees Order 1995 (SI 1995 1617). Following a review of the costs involved in providing for various services some consular fees are being increased and some decreased, with the eventual aim of full cost recovery.

3650. Explosives–labelling

MARKING OF PLASTIC EXPLOSIVES FOR DETECTION REGULATIONS 1996, SI 1996 890; made under the Health and Safety at Work etc. Act 1974 s.15, s.82, Sch.3 para.1, Sch.3 para.2. In force: in accordance with Reg.1; £1.55.

These Regulations implement in part the Convention on the Marking of Plastic Explosives for the Purpose of Detection, done at Montreal on March 1, 1991. They make provision for ensuring that plastic explosives are marked in such a way that they are detectable. Regulation 2 provides that a marked explosive is one which contains a detection agent. Regulation 2 and Sch.1 further provide for the definition of explosive and the type and concentration of detection agent which must be contained in an explosive in order for that explosive to be marked. Regulation 3 prohibits the manufacture of any explosive, the finished product of which is unmarked. Regulation 4 prohibits the possession and transfer of possession of an unmarked explosive save where the explosive is in the process of being manufactured. There is transitional provision for persons who possess or transfer unmarked explosives manufactured before the Regulations came into force for a period of three years after that date. Regulation 5 prohibits the importation of unmarked explosives.

3651. Extradition–agreements

EUROPEAN CONVENTION ON EXTRADITION ORDER 1990 (AMENDMENT) ORDER 1996, SI 1996 2596; made under the Extradition Act 1989 s.4. In force: on a date to be notified in the London, Edinburgh and Belfast Gazettes; £1.95.

This Order amends the European Convention on Extradition Order 1990 (SI 1990 1507), as regards its operation between the United Kingdom and Germany, Netherlands, Luxembourg and Spain, so that its terms are qualified by the terms of the Agreement between Member States of the European Communities on the Simplification and Modernisation of Methods of Transmitting Extradition Requests.

3652. Extradition–dependent territories

EUROPEAN CONVENTION ON EXTRADITION (DEPENDENT TERRITORIES) ORDER 1996, SI 1996 2875; made under the Extradition Act 1870 s.21; and the Extradition Act 1989 s.4, s.30, s.37. In force: in accordance with Art.1 (1); £1.10.

This Order extends the European Convention on Extradition Order 1990 (SI 1990 1507), in relation to the States Parties to the Convention listed in Sch.1 Part I to the Order, to the territories listed in Part II.

3653. Extradition–evidence from accomplices under plea bargains in the US–whether evidence should have been excluded

[Police and Criminal Evidence Act 1984 s.78.]

The evidence in support of an application by the United States Government for the extradition of F was largely from eight alleged accomplices who had entered into plea bargains with the United States prosecuting authorities. F sought to exclude their evidence under the Police and Criminal Evidence Act 1984 s.78 on the grounds of unfairness. The magistrate accepted the applicability of the section but refused to exclude the evidence in the exercise of his discretion, and committed F to await the directions of the Secretary of State. F applied for habeas corpus.

Held, dismissing the application, that extradition proceedings were not criminal proceedings. Section 78 applied only to criminal proceedings. Therefore the evidence could not have been excluded under the section, *R. v. Governor of Pentonville Prison, ex p. Lee* [1993] 1 W.L.R. 1294, [1993] C.L.Y. 1870 considered; *R. v. King's Lynn Justices, ex p. Holland* [1993] 1 W.L.R. 324, [1993] C.L.Y. 717a distinguished.

R. v. GOVERNOR OF BELMARSH PRISON, *ex p.* FRANCIS [1995] 1 W.L.R. 1121, McCowan, L.J., QBD.

3654. Extradition–political offences–dominant motive the determinant factor in ascertaining whether offence political

[Extradition Act 1989 s.6.]

D, a Kurd suspected of organising a series of attacks against Turkish property in Germany, applied for a writ of habeas corpus to quash a committal order made pending the signing of an extradition order requested by Germany.

Held, dismissing the application, that regard must be given to the motives behind the offences committed and where several motives existed the dominant factor was the determinant one. D's attacks were aimed at the Turkish government, their motive being to force a change of policy, and as the German government was not the main target, the acts could not be political offences under the Extradition Act 1989 s.6(1)(a), which required the actions to be directed against the requesting state, ie. Germany. There was no reason to suspect the German authorities of bad faith or that D would not receive a fair trial and therefore the application must be dismissed.

R. v. GOVERNOR OF BELMARSH PRISON, *ex p.* DUNLAYICI, *The Times*, August 2, 1996, Henry, L.J., QBD.

3655. Extradition–warrants–policy not to give reasons for issue of warrant whether policy wrong

[Extradition Act 1989 s.16.]

C and another applied for a writ of habeas corpus under the Extradition Act 1989 s.16(1), following the signing by the Secretary of State of warrants for their return to Canada to face criminal charges, on the grounds that the warrants had not been returned within the statutory time limits. They also renewed their applications for judicial review of his decision not to give reasons for agreeing the extradition warrants until after leave to apply had been granted.

Held, dismissing the application, that proceedings for judicial review were instituted when notice of an application for leave was filed with the Crown Office. However, the Secretary of State's policy not to give reasons until after the grant of leave was arguably wrong as it gave an offender no opportunity to know the grounds for the decision before making a challenge.

CHETTA, *Re*; SUB NOM. R. v. SECRETARY OF STATE FOR THE HOME DEPARTMENT, *ex p.* CHETTA [1996] C.O.D. 463, Henry, L.J., QBD.

3656. International Court of Justice–advisory opinion–nuclear weapons–legality of threat or use of nuclear weapons

[United Nations Charter 1945 Art.2, Art.51.]

The General Assembly of the United Nations requested an advisory opinion from the International Court of Justice on the legality of the threat or use of nuclear weapons.

Held, that the United Nations Charter, together with international law relating to the conduct of hostilities and any treaties specifically concerned with nuclear weapons, were the laws most closely applicable. Any use of force or the threat to use force which breached Art.2 para.4 of the Charter and could not be justified under Art.51 was unlawful. Whilst there was no specific prohibition on the use of nuclear weapons in international law, most of the principles of international and humanitarian law in armed conflict having been established before their invention, there was no reason why those principles should not apply to the threat or use of nuclear weapons. Any provisions in treaties specifically relating to nuclear weapons had to be observed, and there was also a duty to both advance and conclude negotiations on nuclear disarmament.

LEGALITY OF THE THREAT OR USE OF NUCLEAR WEAPONS (UNITED NATIONS), *The Times*, July 18, 1996, Judge Bedjaoui (President), ICJ.

3657. International Court of Justice–advisory opinions–ICJ had no jurisdiction to deal with question posed by the World Health Organisation on legality of use of nuclear weapons

Held, that the International Court of Justice, ICJ, had jurisdiction to give an advisory opinion only when the question posed was within the functions of the body requesting the opinion. In the case of a request by the World Health Organisation, WHO, for an advisory opinion on the legality of the use of nuclear weapons in armed conflict, the ICJ was unable to give an opinion because WHO, although having authority to ask for advisory opinions, was not concerned with the legality of the use of nuclear weapons, only with the effects of such weapons on health.

LEGALITY OF THE USE BY A STATE OF NUCLEAR WEAPONS IN ARMED CONFLICT (WHO), *The Times*, July 18, 1996, Judge Bedjaoui (President), ICJ.

3658. Limitations–Abu Dhabi company's claim to recover a bribe paid by English companies to the president to secure a construction contract–application of limitation periods under law of Abu Dhabi to claims in tort, contract and quasi contract

[Civil Code of the United Arab Emirates 1986 Art.298 (United Arab Emirates); Abu Dhabi Civil Violations Act 1966.]

AMF appealed against a decision that their claim in respect of a payment of $1.848 million, held to be a bribe, was defeated by limitation, *Arab Monetary Fund v. Hashim (No.9)* [1993] 1 Lloyd's Rep. 543, [1994] C.L.Y. 3555. H, president and director general of AMF for a period of five years, had been paid the bribe by two other defendants, English companies, in return for the award of a tender for the construction of the AMF headquarters in Abu Dhabi. AMF argued that their claim was not defeated by limitation because they had not acquired the requisite knowledge on the date determined by the judge. They argued that the judge had applied the wrong test of knowledge required by the Civil Code of the United Arab Emirates 1986 Art.298(1) which was the date on which "the victim became aware of the occurrence of the harm". AMF contended that they were entitled to recover damages in tort against the companies and H, to recover the amount of the bribe from H due to unjust enrichment and to recover damages from H due to breach of contract.

Held, allowing the appeal in relation to the claim in contract only, that (1) the claims in tort and quasi contract were governed by the law of Abu Dhabi; (2) the judge was entitled to find that AMF had knowledge of the bribe and the identity of the recipient at the earliest on April 15, 1986 and the latest April 17, 1986 by which date the Civil Code 1986 was in force. The three year limitation period provided by the Civil Code 1986 Art.298(1) applied and the limitation period expired on April 16 or April 17 1989. The writ was not issued until April 21, 1989 and consequently the claims in tort and unjust enrichment were statute barred. Awareness of the bribe needed to be actual knowledge, being constituted by sufficient knowledge to justify a belief that the act had occurred; the allegation did not need to be proved. The receipt by AMF of a schedule of payments made into H's bank account, which included the sum of $1.848 million from the English company, coupled with an awareness of strong rumours of the bribe and knowledge that H had transferred other sums from AMF into his accounts provided sufficient actual knowledge. The judge below was correct to decide that, on receipt of the schedule, AMF knew about the bribe and that they did not merely suspect that it had occurred and (3) the judge below was wrong to apply the same three year limitation period to a claim for breach of contract. A contractual claim was made subject to the Islamic *Shari'a* which allowed a limitation period of 15 years. None of the expert evidence suggested that the Abu Dhabi Civil Violations Act 1966 nor the Civil Code 1986 applied to claims in contract.

ARAB MONETARY FUND v. HASHIM (NO.11) [1996] 1 Lloyd's Rep. 589, Nourse, L.J., CA.

3659. Locus standi–Arab Organisation for Industrialisation–breach of treaty

AOI was established by treaty between four Arab states in 1975, with significant assets to produce an Arab arms industry. The treaty made AOI independent to the laws of participating states. As a result of the 1978 Egyptian-Israeli peace treaty, Arab states agreed sanctions against Egypt, at a time when contracts had been made with WH. Three Gulf states party to AOI purported to terminate the activities of AOI. Egypt denied the effectiveness of such termination in respect of AOI as incorporated in Egypt and by a 1979 decree law changed the constitution of AOI and declared that Egyptians would conduct the affairs of the organisation (AOI 1979). WH claimed that its contracts were ended and claimed compensation from AOI, although AOI 1979 insisted that they continue. WH obtained an ICC arbitration award in its favour against AOI. WH, as judgment creditor, obtained garnishee orders nisi against banks in respect of accounts held with them by D. The Cairo based AOI 1979 claimed to intervene, on the basis that it was the same organisation as AOI, in order to challenge the ICC award. AOI 1979 claimed that the constitution and representation of AOI were governed by Egyptian law and continued by the 1979 decree. WH disputed the locus standi of AOI 1979.

Held, that (1) the English courts could not determine whether there had been a breach of the treaty as this would be contrary to the principle of non-justiciability of disputes between sovereign states, *Buttes Gas & Oil Co v. Hammer (No.3)* [1982] A.C. 888, [1980] C.L.Y. 2184 applied; (2) English law will only recognise a foreign entity as having legal personality if such a body has been accorded legal personality under a law of a foreign state recognised by the UK and, in the case of an international organisation, the English courts will treat it as having the legal capacity of a corporation when some or all of its member states have accorded to it such legal capacity, *Arab Monetary Fund v. Hashim (No.3)* [1991] 2 A.C. 114, [1991] C.L.Y. 2200 applied; (3) it was irrelevant to consider domicile or nationality once it was accepted that a friendly foreign state had accorded such personality and the English courts would recognise the legal personality of such an international organisation, *Arab Monetary Fund v. Hashim (No.3)* [1991] 2 A.C. 114, [1991] C.L.Y. 2200 distinguished; (4) accordingly, the court was entitled to consider the governing law of AOI; (5) although the English courts will generally apply the law of the place of incorporation as the governing law, where a friendly foreign state has clothed an international organisation with legal personality and has thereby created a foreign corporation, that body is no ordinary domestic entity but an international body created by treaty and questions as to the meaning, effect and operation of its constitution, at least so far as they arise between the parties to the treaty, can only be determined by reference to the treaty and the principles of public international law and not by any body of domestic law, *International Tin Council, Re* [1989] 1 Ch. 309, [1989] C.L.Y. 274 considered; (6) it followed that, in the absence of any countervailing common law principle, it would be contrary to principle to hold that the proper law of the constitution of an international organisation was the law of its seat state and the proper law governing the existence, constitution and authority of its officers to represent AOI was public international law and (7) obiter, if Egyptian law were applied, the effect of the 1979 law was to continue the existence of AOI and not to create a new organisation.

WESTLAND HELICOPTERS LTD v. ARAB ORGANISATION FOR INDUSTRIALISATION [1995] Q.B. 282, Colman, J., QBD.

3660. Private International Law (Miscellaneous Provisions) Act 1995–Commencement Order

PRIVATE INTERNATIONAL LAW (MISCELLANEOUS PROVISIONS) ACT 1995 (COMMENCEMENT) ORDER 1996, SI 1996 995 (C.16); made under the Private International Law (Miscellaneous Provisions) Act 1995 s.16. In force: bringing into force various provisions of the Act on May 1, 1996; £0.65.

This Order appoints May 1, 1996 as the day on which the Private International Law (Miscellaneous Provisions) Act 1995 Part III shall come into force for the whole of the United Kingdom. Part III establishes new choice of law rules in relation to proceedings brought in England and Wales, Scotland or Northern Ireland in respect of a tort or delict.

3661. Private International Law (Miscellaneous Provisions) Act 1995–Commencement No.2 Order

PRIVATE INTERNATIONAL LAW (MISCELLANEOUS PROVISIONS) ACT 1995 (COMMENCEMENT NO.2) ORDER 1996, SI 1996 2515 (C.69); made under the Private International Law (Miscellaneous Provisions) Act 1995 s.16. In force: bringing into force various provisions of the Act on November 1, 1996; £0.65.

This Order appoints November 1, 1996 as the day on which the Private International Law (Miscellaneous Provisions) Act 1995 s.1, s.2 and s.4 shall come into force. The provisions establish for the High Court and county courts new rules relating to interest on judgment debts. The effect of the Order is to bring into force all those provisions of the Act which are not already in force, excepting s.3 which relates to interest on arbitral awards.

3662. Space law–Gibraltar

OUTER SPACE ACT 1986 (GIBRALTAR) ORDER 1996, SI 1996 1916; made under the Outer Space Act 1986 s.15. In force: August 23, 1996; £1.10.

This Order extends the Outer Space Act 1986 to Gibraltar.

3663. State immunity–Kuwait–allegations of kidnap and torture–entitlement to state immunity

[State Immunity Act 1978 s.1.]

A appealed against a decision entitling Kuwait to state immunity. During the Iraqi occupation, A, a member of the Kuwaiti Air Force, stayed in Kuwait with the resistance and came into possession of video material embarrassing to a member of the Kuwaiti Royal Family. After the liberation, A was allegedly kidnapped and subjected to torture by state security guards. For the purposes of the hearing and to determine jurisdiction, it was accepted that Kuwait was vicariously liable for the guards' actions. The State Immunity Act 1978 s.1 provided express immunity to Kuwait, but A contended that immunity could only be granted provided the state was acting within the law and that torture amounted to a fundamental breach of human rights under international law for which he should be compensated.

Held, dismissing the appeal, that (1) although the 1978 Act modified the absolute common law bar against suing a sovereign state, it was a comprehensive code by which Kuwait was entitled to immunity, *Alcom v. Republic of Columbia* [1984] 1 A.C. 580 [1984] C.L.Y. 349 considered, and (2) as the draftsman of s.1 must have been aware of the international agreements on torture, it must not have been intended that s.1 of the Act should be subject to any overriding provisions. Persuasive authorities from the United States also militated against finding that torture was an exception, *Argentine Republic v. Amerada Hess Shipping Corp* (1989) 48 U.S. 428 and *Siderman de Blake v. Argentine Republic* (1992) 965 F. (2d) 699 considered. It was highly unlikely that Kuwait would submit to the court's jurisdiction and if absent from proceedings there was no possibility of testing the claim or making a determination on the facts.

AL-ADSANI v. KUWAIT, *The Times*, March 29, 1996, Stuart-Smith, L.J., CA.

3664. Territorial waters

TERRITORIAL SEA (AMENDMENT) ORDER 1996, SI 1996 1628; made under the Territorial Sea Act 1987 s.1. In force: August 1, 1996; £0.65.

The Order amends the Schedule to the Territorial Waters Order in Council 1964 by redefining specified points between Cape Wrath and the Mull of Kintyre which are joined by geodesics to form baselines from which the breadth of the territorial sea adjacent thereto is measured. The amendments make minor changes to two points which have been shown to be necessary by the publication of a new larger scale chart of part of the area.

3665. United Nations–international tribunals

UNITED NATIONS (INTERNATIONAL TRIBUNAL) (FORMER YUGOSLAVIA) ORDER 1996, SI 1996 716; made under the United Nations Act 1946 s.1. In force: May 1, 1996; £4.70.

This Order makes provision as respects the United Kingdom to implement a resolution of the Security Council of the United Nations relating to the former Yugoslavia. The Order has effect for the purpose of enabling the United Kingdom to cooperate with the International Tribunal for the Prosecution of Persons Responsible for Serious Violations of International Humanitarian Law Committed in the Territory of the Former Yugoslavia since 1991 established by Resolution 827 (1993) of the Security Council of the United Nations (International Tribunal) in the investigation and prosecution of persons accused of committing International Tribunal crimes and the punishment of persons convicted of such crimes.

3666. United Nations–international tribunals

UNITED NATIONS (INTERNATIONAL TRIBUNAL) (RWANDA) ORDER 1996, SI 1996 1296; made under the United Nations Act 1946 s.1. In force: May 17, 1996; £4.70.

This Order makes provision as respects the United Kingdom to implement a resolution of the Security Council of the United Nations relating to Rwanda. The Order has effect for the purpose of enabling the United Kingdom to cooperate with the International Criminal Tribunal for the Prosecution of Persons Responsible for Genocide and Other Serious Violations of International Humanitarian Law Committed in the Territory of Rwanda and Rwandan citizens responsible for genocide and other such violations committed in the territory of neighbouring states, between January 1, 1994 and December 31, 1994, established by Resolution 955 (1994) of the Security Council of the United National International Tribunal) in the investigation and prosecution of persons accused of committing International Tribunal crimes and the punishment of persons convicted of such crimes.

3667. Articles

Drug trafficking under control: CJ Europe 1996, 6(2), 11-12. (Role of UN International Drug Control Program in coordinating action against international drug trafficking).

EIA and the precautionary principle *(John Salter)*: O.G.L.T.R. 1996, 14(3), 131-135. (Whether France breached international environmental law by failing to assess consequences of nuclear testing at Moruroa Atoll with particular regard to Euratom and other treaties and customary international law).

Ideology, historiography and international legal theory *(Oscar L. Alcantara)*: I.J.S.L. 1996, 9(25), 39-79. (Philosophical structures underpinning development of theory of international law).

International aspects of antitrust enforcement *(Roscoe B. Starek)*: W. Comp. 1996, 19(3), 29-42. (Effect of 1994 Act on international cooperation and problems of enforcing competition law worldwide).

International organisations and non-justiciability *(Alan Berg)*: I.F.L. Rev. 1996, 15(1), 32-34. (English courts' reluctance to decide issues arising from constitution of organisations established by treaties).

Interpretation and application of tax treaties by tax courts *(C. Van Raad)*: Euro. Tax. 1996, 36(1), 3-7. (Van Brunschot lecture on treaty interpretation rules, case law and use of foreign decisions by US, German and Dutch national courts and potential for setting up CD ROM database and or advisory body on international interpretation).

New international law: silence, defence or deliverance? *(Outi Korhonen)*: E.J.I.L. 1996, 7(1), 1-28. (Evolution of meaning and significance of international law through interpretation, how it should be studied and whether there is justification for study and practice of normative international law).

Observations on international nuclear law ten years after Chernobyl *(Philippe Sands)*: R.E.C.I.E.L. 1996, 5(3), 199-204. (International law has failed to develop comprehensive approach to nuclear substances).

"Sex tourism" *(Ronald Cottrell)*: J.P. 1996, 160(12), 201-202. (Whether UK government will take action to enable prosecution of those who perpetrate child abuse abroad).

Subalternity and international law: the problems of global community and the incommensurability of difference *(Dianne Otto)*: S. & L.S. 1996, 5(3), 337-364. (Whether possible for non-state individuals and groupings to participate as subjects of international law).

The 1995 Wilberforce Lecture: the future of international judicial institutions *(Gilbert Guillaume)*: Arbitration 1996, 62(2), 116-122. (Current role of International Court of Justice and other international judicial institutions and how unity of international law can be maintained).

The access of individuals to international trade dispute settlement *(Bernd-Roland Killmann)*: J. Int. Arb. 1996, 13(3), 143-169. (How and why standing of individuals neglected in international trade law, analysis of different methods employed in US and EU, how dispute settlement regime affects private enterprises and whether they benefit from Marrakesh Agreements).

The evolution of public international law since 1914: permanence and transformations *(Jacques-Michel Grossen)*: Hold. L.R. 1991-2, 15(1), 36-54. (Comparison of old and new literature on international law illustrates changes in subject matter and enforcement theory).

The International Criminal Tribunal for Yugoslavia: the decision of the Appeals Chamber on the interlocutory appeal on jurisdiction in the Tadic case *(Peter Rowe)*: I.C.L.Q. 1996, 45(3), 691-701. (Whether Security Council had power to establish Tribunal and whether Tribunal had jurisdiction over crimes committed during internal armed conflict).

The law and practice of water management offshore *(Keith Hayes)*: O.G.L.T.R. 1996, 14(3), 105-111. (Treaties and domestic law affecting discharges at oil into sea from offshore installations).

The potential direct effect of GATT 1994 in European Community law *(Philip Lee* and *Brian Kennedy)*: J.W.T. 1996, 30(1), 67-89. (Whether enforcement mechanisms of GATT have direct effect in national courts).

The relationship between general and particular customary international law *(Olufemi Elias)*: R.A.D.I.C. 1996, 8(1), 67-88.

The right to property *(Jeremy McBride)*: E.L.R. 1996, Supp HRS, 40-50. (Protection provided under ECHR Protocol 1 Art.1 against state's power to expropriate and control property and to levy taxes and general right to peaceful enjoyment of property).

3668. Books

Academie de Droit International de la Haye–Recueil des Cours/Collected Courses: Vol 253. 1995. Recueil Des Cours. Hardback: £96.00. ISBN 90-411-0279-5. Martinus Nijhoff Publishers.

Adlam, J.C.–Iran-US Claims Tribunal Reports. Iran-US Claims Tribunal Reports. Paperback: £95.00. ISBN 0-521-46338-6. Cambridge University Press.

Amerasinghe, C.F.–Principles of the Institutional Law of International Organizations. Cambridge Studies in International and Comparative Law, 1. Hardback: £60.00. ISBN 0-521-56254-6. Cambridge University Press.

Amirahmadi, Hooshang–Small Islands, Big Politics. Hardback: £29.50. ISBN 0-333-68019-7. Macmillan Press.

Anaya, S. James–Indigenous Peoples in International Law. Hardback: £32.50. ISBN 0-19-508620-1. Oxford University Press Inc, USA.

Beck, Robert J.; Arend, Anthony Clark; Lugt, Robert D. Vander–International Rules. Paperback: £15.99. ISBN 0-19-508540-X. Hardback: £27.50. ISBN 0-19-508539-6. Oxford University Press Inc, USA.

Bethlehem, Daniel; Weller, Marc–The "Yugoslav" Crisis in International Law: Part III. Human Rights and War Crimes. Cambridge International Documents Series. Hardback: £75.00. ISBN 0-521-47509-0. Cambridge University Press.

Bourantonis, Dimitris; Evriviades, Marios–A United Nations for the Twenty-first Century. Nijhoff law specials. Hardback: £103.00. ISBN 90-411-0312-0. Kluwer Law International.

Brahm, Laurence; Daoran, Li–The Business Guide to China. Paperback: £11.99. ISBN 981-00-7079-9. Butterworth-Heinemann.

Brownlie, Ian; Crawford, James–The British Year Book of International Law: Vol 66. 1995. Hardback: £95.00. ISBN 0-19-825882-8. Clarendon Press.

Bulterman, M.K.–Compliance with Judgments of International Courts. Hardback: £61.00. ISBN 90-411-0157-8. Martinus Nijhoff Publishers.

Chatterjee, C.–Public International Law. Cracknell's statutes. Paperback: £7.95. ISBN 1-85836-023-4. Old Bailey Press.

Chatterjee, C.; Davies, D.R.–Public International Law. Cracknell's law students' companions. Paperback: £9.95. ISBN 1-85836-038-2. Old Bailey Press.

Chayes, Abram; Chayes, Antonia Handler–The New Sovereignity. Hardback: £31.50. ISBN 0-674-61782-7. Harvard University Press.

Colliver, Douglas; Proctor, Charles–Norton Rose: Cross Border Security. Hardback: £125.00. ISBN 0-406-05463-0. Butterworth Law.

Conforti, Benedetto–The Law and Practice of the United Nations. Hardback: £65.00. ISBN 90-411-0233-7. Kluwer Law International.

Cotran, Eugene–The Arab-Israeli Accords. Centre of Islamic & Middle Eastern law series (Cimel). Hardback: £79.00. ISBN 90-411-0902-1. Kluwer Law International.

De Nooy, Gert–The Role of European Naval Forces After the Cold War. Nijhoff law specials. Paperback: £43.00. ISBN 90-411-0227-2. Kluwer Law International.

Denters, Erik M.G.–Law and Policy of IMF Conditionality. Hardback: £65.00. ISBN 90-411-0211-6. Kluwer Law International.

Dixon, Martin–Textbook on International Law. Hardback: £16.95. ISBN 1-85431-444-0. Blackstone Press.

Dnes, A.W.–Economics of Law. Paperback: £17.99. ISBN 0-412-62800-7. Chapman and Hall.

Dobinson, Ian; Roebuck, Derek–Introduction to Law in the Hong Kong SAR. Paperback: £30.00. ISBN 0-421-56880-1. Sweet & Maxwell.

Elagab, Omar Y, DPhil–Public International Law. Questions and answers. Paperback: £8.95. ISBN 1-874241-37-6. Cavendish Publishing Ltd.

Evans, M.–International Law Documents. £13.95. ISBN 1-85431-565-X. Blackstone Press.

Evans, Malcom D.–Aspects of Statehood and Institutionalism in Contemporary Europe. EC/International Law Forum II. Hardback: £45.00. ISBN 1-85521-928-X. Dartmouth.

Gardner, Anthony Laurence–A New Era in US-EU Relations. Hardback: £30.00. ISBN 1-85972-530-9. Avebury.

Gessner, Volkmar–Foreign Courts: Civil Litigation in Foreign Legal Cultures. Onati International Series in Law and Society. Hardback: £40.00. ISBN 1-85521-808-9. Paperback: £16.50. ISBN 1-85521-812-7. Dartmouth.

Gold, Joseph–Interpretation: the IMF and International Law. Hardback: £124.00. ISBN 90-411-0887-4. Kluwer Law International.

Gomaa, Mohammed M.–Suspension or Termination of Treaties on Grounds of Breach. Hardback: £65.00. ISBN 90-411-0226-4. Martinus Nijhoff Publishers.

Goodwin-Gill, Guy S.–The Refugee in International Law. Hardback: £18.99. ISBN 0-19-826020-2. Paperback: £45.00. ISBN 0-19-826019-9. Oxford University Press.

Greenfield, Jeanette–The Return of Cultural Treasures. Hardback: £55.00. ISBN 0-521-47170-2. Paperback: £19.95. ISBN 0-521-47746-8. Cambridge University Press.

Greig, D.W.; Balkin, Rosemary–Grieg: International Law. Paperback: £25.95. ISBN 0-406-59185-7. Butterworth Law.

Gunther, Teubner–Global Law Without a State. Studies in Modern Law and Policy. Hardback: £45.00. ISBN 1-85521-879-8. Dartmouth.

Higgins, Rosalyn; Flory, Maurice–Terrorism and International Law. Hardback: £65.00. ISBN 0-415-11606-6. Routledge.

Hillier, Tim–Sourcebook on Public International Law. Sourcebook series. Paperback: £20.95. ISBN 1-85941-050-2. Cavendish Publishing Ltd.

International Labour Conventions and Recommendations: 1919-1995. Hardback: £67.50. ISBN 92-2-109192-9. International Labour Office.

Jackson, Sherman A.–Islamic Law and the State. Studies in Islamic law and society, 1. Hardback. ISBN 90-04-10458-5. E.J. Brill.

Jennings, Robert; Watts, Arthur–International Law: Vol 1. Peace. International law, Vol 1. Paperback: £75.00. ISBN 0-582-30245-5. Addison-Wesley Longman Higher Education.

Joubert, Chantal–Schengen Investigated. Hardback: £119.00. ISBN 90-411-0266-3. Kluwer Law International.

Kadish, Alon–The Corn Laws. Fine binding: £375.00. ISBN 1-85196-410-X. Pickering & Chatto.

Khan, L. Ali–The Extinction of Nation-states. Developments in International Law, 21. Hardback: £74.50. ISBN 90-411-0198-5. Kluwer Law International.

Kime's International Law Directory: 1997. Hardback: £77.00. ISBN 0-7520-0238-4. FT Law & Tax.

Korman, Sharon–The Right of Conquest. Hardback: £40.00. ISBN 0-19-828007-6. Clarendon Press.

Lauterpacht, E.J., QC; Greenwood, C.J.–International Law Reports: Vol 101. Hardback: £85.00. ISBN 0-521-49648-9. Cambridge University Press.

Lauterpacht, E.J.; Greenwood, C.J.–International Law Reports: Vol 102. Hardback: £85.00. ISBN 0-521-55199-4. Cambridge University Press.

Lauterpacht, E.J.; Greenwood, C.J.–International Law Reports. Hardback: £95.00. ISBN 0-521-56229-5. Cambridge University Press.

Leibowitz, Arnold H.–Embattled Island. Hardback: £43.95. ISBN 0-275-95390-4. Praeger Publishers.

Leitner, Peter M.–Reforming the Law of the Sea Treaty. Paperback: £33.50. ISBN 0-7618-0394-7. Hardback: £49.50. ISBN 0-7618-0393-9. University Press of America.

Lowe, Vaughan; Fitzmaurice, Malgosia–Fifty Years of the International Court of Justice. Cambridge Studies in International and Comparative Law. Hardback: £75.00. ISBN 0-521-55093-9. Cambridge University Press.

Lowenfeld, Andreas F.–International Litigation and the Quest for Reasonableness. Hardback: £40.00. ISBN 0-19-826059-8. Clarendon Press.

MacCormack, Geoffrey–The Spirit of Traditional Chinese Law. The Spirit of the Laws. Hardback:

£35.50. ISBN 0-8203-1722-5. University of Georgia Press.

MacLean, Robert M.–Public International Law: Textbook 1996-1997. Bachelor of Laws (LLB). Paperback: £18.95. ISBN 0-7510-0699-8. HLT Publications.

MacLean, Robert M.–Public International Law: Casebook 1996-1997. Bachelor of Laws (LLB). Paperback: £18.95. ISBN 0-7510-0665-3. HLT Publications.

Majid, Amir A.–Legal Status of International Institutions. Hardback: £45.00. ISBN 1-85521-761-9. Dartmouth.

Mastel, Greg–American Trade Laws After the Uraguay Round. Paperback: £19.50. ISBN 1-56324-896-4. Hardback: £47.50. ISBN 1-56324-895-6. M.E. Sharpe.

McCoubrey, Hilaire; White, Nigel D.–The Blue Helmets: Legal Regulation of United Nations Military Operations. Hardback: £40.00. ISBN 1-85521-626-4. Dartmouth.

Meessen, Karl M.–Extraterritorial Jurisdiction in Theory and Practice. Hardback: £89.00. ISBN 90-411-0899-8. Kluwer Law International.

Muneer Goolam Fareed–Legal Reform in the Muslim World. Paperback: £31.95. ISBN 1-57292-002-5. Hardback: £47.95. ISBN 1-57292-003-3. Austin and Winfield.

Pritchard, Robert–Economic Development, Foreign Investment and the Law. Hardback: £65.00. ISBN 90-411-0891-2. Kluwer Law International.

Public International Law - LLB: Suggested Solutions (1991- 1995). Bachelor of Laws (LLB). Paperback: £6.95. ISBN 0-7510-0733-1. HLT Publications.

Public International Law: Suggested Solutions - Single Paper (June 1995). Paperback: £3.00. ISBN 0-7510-0632-7. HLT Publications.

Reich, Peter Lester–Mexico's Hidden Revolution. Hardback: £23.50. ISBN 0-268-01418-3. University of Notre Dame Press.

Rogers, Major General A.P.V.–The Law of the Battlefield. Melland Schill studies in international law. Hardback: £35.00. ISBN 0-7190-4784-6. Paperback: £16.99. ISBN 0-7190-4785-4. Manchester University Press.

Rogowski, Ralf–German Law. Paperback: £21.95. ISBN 0-406-02291-7. Butterworth Law.

Rossmanith, H.P.–Structural Failure: Technical, Legal and Insurance Aspects. Hardback: £50.00. ISBN 0-419-20710-4. E & FN Spon (An imprint of Chapman & Hall).

Rothwell, Donald R.–The Polar Regions and the Development of International Law. Cambridge Studies in International and Comparative Law. Hardback: £60.00. ISBN 0-521-56182-5. Cambridge University Press.

Sato, Tetsuo–Evolving Constitutions of International Organizations. International Law in Japanese perspective. Hardback: £79.00. ISBN 90-411-0202-7. Kluwer Law International.

Sellers, M.N.S.–The New World Order. Baltimore studies in nationalism and internationalism. Hardback: £39.95. ISBN 1-85973-059-0. Paperback: £14.95. ISBN 1-85973-064-7. Berg Publishers.

Stamp, Mark–International Insider Dealing. Hardback: £125.00. ISBN 0-7520-0179-5. FT Law & Tax.

Steele, Keith–Anti-dumping Under the WTO. Hardback: £85.00. ISBN 90-411-0915-3. Kluwer Law International.

T.M.C. Asser Instituut–Netherlands Yearbook of International Law: Vol 26. 1995. Netherlands yearbook of international law. Hardback: £88.00. ISBN 90-411-0196-9. Martinus Nijhoff Publishers.

Toman, Jiri–Protection of Cultural Property in the Event of Armed Conflict. Hardback: £40.00. ISBN 1-85521-793-7. Paperback: £28.00. ISBN 1-85521-800-3. Dartmouth.

Wheatley, S.–SWOT International Law. £8.95. ISBN 1-85431-501-3. Blackstone Press.

White, Nigel–The Law of International Organisations. Studies in International Law. Hardback: £40.00. ISBN 0-7190-4339-5. Paperback: £14.99. ISBN 0-7190-4340-9. Manchester University Press.

Zweigert, K.–International Encyclopedia of Comparative Law: Instalment 30. International encyclopedia of comparative law. Paperback: £198.00. ISBN 90-411-0174-8. Martinus Nijhoff Publishers.

INTERNATIONAL TRADE

3669. Commercial policy–Common Customs Tariff–repeal of a Council Regulation–European Union

[Commission Regulation 482/74; Council Regulation 950/68; Council Regulation 2658/87 Art.15.]

The CEC had adopted Commission Regulation 482/74 pursuant to Council Regulation 950/68 on the common customs tariff. The Council repealed that Regulation in 1987 and replaced it with Council Regulation 2658/87 Art.15, which implicitly replaced existing legislation, although it empowered the CEC to amend any such legislation to bring it up to date. The CEC did not amend Regulation 482/74. It was therefore contended that this Regulation was implicitly repealed.

Held, that since Commission Regulation 482/74 was not amended by the CEC in accordance with Council Regulation 2658/87 Art.15(1) it could not be applied to declarations concerning importations after January 1, 1988 inasmuch as failure to amend the former Regulation prevented individuals from determining its precise scope.

GEBROEDERS VAN ES DOUANE AGENTEN BV v. INSPECTEUR DER INVOERRECHTEN EN ACCIJNZEN (C143/93), February 13, 1996, Judge not specified, ECJ.

3670. Customs and Excise–statistics of trade

STATISTICS OF TRADE (CUSTOMS AND EXCISE) (AMENDMENT) REGULATIONS 1996, SI 1996 2968; made under the European Communities Act 1972 s.2. In force: January 1, 1997; £0.65.

The collection of statistics relating to the trading of goods between Member States is governed by Council Regulation 3330/91 ([1991] OJ L316/1). Article 28 makes provision for the application of statistical thresholds. Thresholds are to be set annually in accordance with Commission Regulation 2256/92 ([1992] OJ L219/40). Traders whose annual value of trade with other Member States exceeds the assimilation thresholds set for trade in goods dispatched, or for goods received, will be required to provide additional statistical information in the form of supplementary declarations. These Regulations amend the Statistics of Trade (Customs and Excise) Regulations 1992 (SI 1992 2790) Reg.3(1) by substituting, as an assimilation threshold, the amount of £195,000 for the previous level of £160,000. The Statistics of Trade (Customs and Excise) (Amendment) Regulations 1995 (SI 1995 2946) are revoked.

3671. Customs duty–processed goods–exemption from duty–Canary Islands–European Union

[Council Regulation 3033/80 laying down trade arrangements applicable to certain goods resulting from the processing of agricultural products; Act of Accession of Spain and Portugal Protocol 2 Art.1.]

Council Regulation 3033/80 provided that, on importation into the Community, processed agricultural goods were to be subject to a charge consisting of an ad valorem duty and a variable component. The variable components was intended to reflect, for the quantities of basic products considered to have been used in the manufacture of those goods, the difference between the price of those basic products in the EC and the price if imported from third countries, when the total cost of those quantities of basic products was higher in the EC. The Act of Accession of Spain and Portugal Protocol 2 Art.1 (3) provided that EC customs legislation applied to trade between the EC and the Canary Islands except that under Art.2 of the Protocol products originating in the Canary Islands were exempted from customs duty when released for free circulation in Spain. A dispute arose relating to the application of the Protocol.

Held, that the variable component of the charge concerning processed agricultural goods fell within the arrangements laid down in Art.1 of the Protocol and was not covered by the exemption laid down in Art.2.

TIRMA SA v. ADMINISTRACION GENERAL DEL ESTADO (C300/94), February 29, 1996, Judge not specified, ECJ.

3672. Dumping–anti-dumping duty–injury to Community industry–European Union

[Council Regulation 2849/92; Council Regulation 1739/85; Council Regulation 2423/88 Art.7.]

Two Japanese producers of ball bearings sought annulment of Council Regulation 2849/92 modifying the definitive anti-dumping duty imposed on imports of ball bearings originating in Japan, as provided for in Council Regulation 1739/85. Regulation 2849/92 was based on Council Regulation 2423/88 on protection against dumped or subsidised imports from countries not members of the EEC.

Held, that the reasons given by Council Regulation 2849/92 for finding a threat of material injury, within the meaning of Council Regulation 2423/88

Art.4(1), to the Community ball bearing industry contained errors of fact or law or were misleading because they were incomplete. It was possible that in the absence of those errors, the Council would not have found a threat of injury justifying adoption of the contested Regulation. There was also a breach of Council Regulation 2423/88 Art.7(9)(a) owing to its failure to conclude the review proceedings within a reasonable period.

NTN CORP v. EUROPEAN COUNCIL (T163/94), *Financial Times*, May 23, 1995, Judge not specified, ECJ.

3673. Dumping–imports from non-market economy countries–validity of single duty in respect of all imports from state–European Union

[Council Regulation 2423/88 on protection against dumped or subsidised imports from countries not members of the European Economic Community; Council Regulation 3664/93 imposing a definitive anti-dumping duty on importers into the Community of photo albums in bookbound form originating in China.]

CPC sought the annulment of Council Regulation 3664/93, contending, inter alia, that Council Regulation 2423/88 required EU institutions to grant individual treatment and not to impose a single blanket duty in respect of undertakings from non-market economy countries, especially where the undertaking had complied with an anti-dumping investigation.

Held, dismissing the application, that Regulation 2423/88 did not prohibit the imposition of single anti-dumping duties for state trading countries. Article 13(2) of the Regulation, which provided for a specific supplier to be named "if practicable", had been correctly interpreted. Where the need arose for a single duty in order to prevent the circumvention of anti-dumping duties, individual treatment was not practicable. The imposition of a single duty was particularly relevant where, following an appraisal of the situation, the Community institutions were not satisfied that the exporter was acting independently of the state.

CLIMAX PAPER CONVERTERS LTD v. COUNCIL OF THE EUROPEAN UNION (T155/94) [1996] All E.R. (EC) 781, Judge not specified, CFI.

3674. Export controls

EXPORT OF GOODS (CONTROL) (AMENDMENT) ORDER 1996, SI 1996 1341; made under the Import, Export and Customs Powers (Defence) Act 1939 s.1. In force: June 10, 1996; £0.65.

This Order removes references to the Bosnian-Serb areas of Bosnia-Herzegovina from the exclusions in the Export of Goods (Control) Order 1994 (SI 1994 1191) from the provisions in that Order on goods in transit. The Order also adds Serbia and Montenegro as destinations to which the vehicles specified in Group 3 of Part I of Sch.1 to the 1994 Order, may not be exported without a licence from the Secretary of State. The prohibition was formerly contained in the Serbia and Montenegro (United Nations Sanctions) Order 1992 Art.4, the effect of which has been suspended by United Nations Security Council Resolution 1022 (1995).

3675. Export controls

EXPORT OF GOODS (CONTROL) (AMENDMENT NO.2) ORDER 1996, SI 1996 2663; made under the Import, Export and Customs Powers (Defence) Act 1939 s.1. In force: November 1, 1996; £3.20.

This Order further amends the Export of Goods (Control) Order 1994 (SI 1994 1191) by replacing Sch.1 Part III. The new Part III consists exclusively of what used to be Group 1 of Part III, except for the introduction of a new General Technology Note and the alteration of the entry numbers for some goods.

3676. Export controls–dual-use goods

DUAL-USE AND RELATED GOODS (EXPORT CONTROL) REGULATIONS 1996, SI 1996 2721; made under the European Communities Act 1972 s.2. In force: November 15, 1996; £3.20.

These Regulations revoke and replace the Dual-Use and Related Goods (Export Control) Regulations 1995 (SI 1995 271) as amended. They give effect to certain provisions of Council Regulation 3381/94 on the control of exports of dual-use goods, and make certain additional provisions relating to the export of dual-use goods.

3677. Export controls–dual-use goods

DUAL-USE AND RELATED GOODS (EXPORT CONTROL) (AMENDMENT) REGULATIONS 1996, SI 1996 1124; made under the European Communities Act 1972 s.2. In force: May 13, 1996; £3.20.

The Dual-Use and Related Goods (Export Control) Regulations 1995 (SI 1995 271) (the principal Regulations) contain provisions arising from Council Regulation 3381/94) ([1994] OJ L367/1) on the control of exports of dual-use goods, which in turn makes provision in respect of the goods listed in Annexes I and IV to Council Decision 94/942/CFSP ([1994] OJ L367/8) on the joint action concerning the control and exports of dual-use foods. Schedule 1 and Sch.2 to the principal Regulations reproduce Annexes I and IV. Annexes I and IV have been amended by Council Decision 96/173/CFSP ([1996] OJ L52/1). These Regulations make equivalent amendments to Sch.1 and Sch.2 of the principal Regulations.

3678. Export controls–dual-use goods

DUAL-USE AND RELATED GOODS (EXPORT CONTROL) (AMENDMENT NO.2) REGULATIONS 1996, SI 1996 1736; made under the European Communities Act 1972 s.2. In force: August 1, 1996; £1.10.

These Regulations make equivalent amendments to Sch.1 and Sch.2 to the Dual-Use and Related Goods (Export Control) Regulations 1995 (SI 1995 271) which contain provisions arising from Council Regulation 3381/94 ([1994] OJ L367/1) on the control of exports of dual-use goods, which in turn makes provision in respect of the goods listed in Council Decision 94/942/CFSP ([1994] OJ L367/8) on the joint action concerning the control of exports of dual-use goods. The 1995 Regulations reproduce Annex I and Annex IV which have been amended by Council Decision 96/423/CFSP ([1996] OJ L176/1). These Regulations make equivalent amendments to Sch.1 and Sch.2 to the 1995 Regulations and amend Sch.3.

3679. Exports–dual use of goods–common commercial policy–regulation 2603/69–European Union

[Council Regulation 2603/69 Art.11; Treaty of Rome 1957 Art.113.]

FWI had received an order to supply a vacuum induction smelting and cast oven as well as induction spools for that oven to Libya, where it had installed a repair shop with a foundry. FWI applied to the German authorities for an export licence, but the licence was refused on the ground that supplying those goods would seriously jeopardise the interests to be protected under a domestic law on foreign trade. FWI sued Germany for damages.

Held, that Art.113 and Council Regulation 2603/69 Art.11, establishing common rules for exports, did not preclude national provisions applicable to trade with non-member countries under which the export of a product capable of being used for military purposes was subject to the issue of a licence on the ground that this was necessary in order to avoid the risk of a serious disturbance to its foreign relations which might affect the public security of a Member State within the meaning of Art.11.

FRITZ WERNER INDUSTRIE AUSRUSTUNGEN GmbH v. GERMANY, October 17, 1995, Judge not specified, ECJ.

3680. GATT–Fourth Lome Convention–direct effect–taxation on bananas–prohibition on comparative increase–European Union

[Fourth ACP-EEC Convention (Lome IV).]

In 1964 Italy introduced a special tax on imported bananas which was increased over the years several times. The tax was abolished in 1990. In proceedings before the Italian courts for recovery of the tax on the ground that it was contrary to various provisions of EC and international law, the question arose of the direct effect of GATT in the national court, as well as the effect of other provisions of EC law.

Held, that the provisions of GATT were not capable of direct effect, in particular because of the flexibility of those provisions. However, the Fourth ACP-EEC Convention did contain provisions which might be capable of direct effect so that national provisions which were contrary to them might be challenged in the national courts. In particular, the Convention precluded increases in internal taxation after 1976 on bananas originating in the ACP states where their effect was to put those banana exports in a situation less favourable than before as regards access to their traditional markets and the advantages they enjoyed on those markets.

AMMINISTRAZIONE DELLE FINANZE DELLO STATO v. CHIQUITA ITALIA SpA (C469/93), December 12, 1995, Judge not specified, ECJ.

3681. Hong Kong Economic and Trade Office Act 1996 (c.63)

The Act provides for an Economic and Trade Office to be established in the UK from July 1, 1997 by the government of the Hong Kong Special Administrative Region, and confers certain privileges and immunities on this Office.

This Act received Royal Assent on December 18, 1996.

3682. Sanctions–United States–protection of trading interests

EXTRATERRITORIAL US LEGISLATION (SANCTIONS AGAINST CUBA, IRAN AND LIBYA) (PROTECTION OF TRADING INTERESTS) ORDER 1996, SI 1996 3171; made under the European Communities Act 1972 s.2. In force: January 28, 1997; £1.10.

This Order makes it an offence to breach Council Regulation 2271/96 ([1996] OJ L309/1) Art.2 or Art.5 protecting against the effects of the extraterritorial application of legislation adopted by a third country, and disapplies the Protection of Trading Interests Act 1980 s.1 (1) (3), s.2 and s.6 to the extent that the Council Regulation applies.

3683. State aid–aid to Central and Eastern Europe–PHARE Programme–restricted invitation to tender–action for annulment of Commission Decision–EEA Agreement–action for damages–European Union

[Agreement on a European Economic Area 1992.]

G applied for annulment of the Commission's Decision of March 10, 1994 rejecting its tender for the supply of electronic tachometers in Romania on the ground that G's equipment did not originate in a Member State of the Community or in a beneficiary country of the PHARE Programme. The equipment originated in Sweden and G had assumed that the criteria concerning the origin of the goods changed following the entry into force on January 1, 1994 of the Agreement on a European Economic Area 1992. G therefore claimed damages for breach of the EEA Agreement.

Held, dismissing the application, that there was no Commission Decision capable of forming the subject matter of an action for annulment, because the power to award a contract lay with the beneficiary country under the PHARE Programme, notwithstanding a refusal on the part of the European Commission to grant Community aid. The legal framework for the contract awarding procedure had been established in June 1993 and was not affected by the entry into force of the EEA Agreement. Moreover, the EEA Agreement could not apply to contracts governed by legal relations to which a State that was not a signatory to the EEA Agreement was party.

GEOTRONICS SA v. COMMISSION OF THE EUROPEAN COMMUNITIES, October 26, 1995, Judge not specified, CFI (Fourth Chamber).

3684. United Nations–arms embargoes

UNITED NATIONS ARMS EMBARGOES (FORMER YUGOSLAVIA) (AMENDMENT) ORDER 1996, SI 1996 1629; made under the United Nations Act 1946 s.1. In force: July 30, 1996; £1.10.

This Order amends the United Nations Arms Embargoes (Liberia, Somalia and the Former Yugoslavia) Order 1993 (SI 1993 1787) by revoking restrictions on the delivery and supply of arms and related material to the territories of the former Yugoslavia. The Order implements the decision of the Security Council of the United Nations to terminate the arms embargo in respect of the territories of the former Yugoslavia. In addition, the opportunity has been taken to bring the definition of prohibited goods into line with recent legislation and to take account of the termination of the United Nations Operation in Somalia II.

3685. United Nations–arms embargoes

UNITED NATIONS ARMS EMBARGOES (SOMALIA, LIBERIA AND RWANDA) (CHANNEL ISLANDS) ORDER 1996, SI 1996 3154; made under the United Nations Act 1946 s.1. In force: December 21, 1996; £3.20.

This Order gives effect in the Channel Islands to the imposition of restrictions pursuant to decisions of the Security Council of the United Nations in Resolution No.733 of January 23, 1992 which provided for the States to "implement a general and complete embargo on all deliveries of weapons and military equipment" in relation to Somalia, Resolution No.788 of November 19, 1992 which made similar provision in relation to Liberia, and Resolution No.918 of May 17, 1994 which made similar provision in relation to Rwanda.

3686. United Nations–arms embargoes

UNITED NATIONS ARMS EMBARGOES (SOMALIA, LIBERIA AND RWANDA) (ISLE OF MAN) ORDER 1996, SI 1996 3153; made under the United Nations Act 1946 s.1. In force: December 21, 1996; £2.80.

This Order gives effect in the Isle of Man to the imposition of restrictions pursuant to decisions of the Security Council of the United Nations in Resolution No.733 of January 23, 1992 which provided for States to "implement a general and complete embargo on all deliveries of weapons and military equipment" in relation to Somalia, Resolution No.788 of November 19, 1992 which made similar provision in relation to Liberia, and Resolution No.918 of May 17, 1994 which made similar provision in relation to Rwanda.

3687. Articles

Case law on UNCITRAL texts *(Spiros V. Bazinas)*: I.B.L. 1996, 24(7), 333-335. (Reasons for publishing and publication of case law on United Nations Commission on International Trade Law conventions and model law).

Clinton clamps Iran and Libya traders *(Joseph P. Griffin)*: I.H.L. 1996, 44(Oct), 80-81. (Sanctions against those who trade with or invest in Libya and Iran beyond certain financial limits).

Competition rules in commercial aviation and WTO competition rules: a comparative analysis *(Ruwantissa I.R. Abeyratne)*: W. Comp. 1996, 19(3), 137-186. (Failure of 1994 Convention to provide multilateral guidelines relating to commercial carriers' air traffic rights, developments leading to 1992 World Wide Air Transport Conference and provisions in GATS relevant to air transport services).

Complaining to the WTO *(Guy Baring)*: Eur. Counsel 1996, 1 (3), 17. (Adoption of Trade Barrier Regulation which allows individual firms to apply to CEC to uphold international trade rules).

Connected lender liability–a domestic remedy only? *(Jonathan Gidney)*: N.L.J. 1996, 146(6745), 762-763. (Whether customers have cause of action against credit card company for breach of contract by foreign supplier).

Doing deals cross-border *(Richard Godden* and *Alec Burnside)*: Eur. Counsel 1996, 1 (1), 20-26. (Obstacles to mergers and acquisitions across national boundaries because of divergent legal systems, accounting practices, regulation, taxation and culture).

Draft UNCITRAL Convention on independent guarantees *(Lars Gorton)*: L.M.C.L.Q. 1996, 1 (Feb), 42-49. (Evaluation of structure and rules).

Dumping, anti dumping and antitrust *(Bernard M. Hoekman* and *Petros C. Mavroidis)*: J.W.T. 1996, 30(1), 27-52. (Arguments in favour of negotiated multilateral agreement on competition policy).

Eco-labelling, environment treaties are UK priorities for trade summit: ENDS 1996, 252, 29-30. (Proposals for more multilateral environmental agreements to prevent international trade rules from undermining environmental protection measures will be put forward at WTO summit December 1996).

GATT and the World Trade Organization–what they mean for franchising *(Michael G. Brennan* and *Wayne H. Elowe)*: J.I.F.D.L. 1996, 10(1), 2-14. (Creation of WTO, Multilateral Agreements and dispute settlement will improve environment for franchising among member countries as well as improving world trade generally and increasing competition for franchises).

General Agreement on Trade in Services: Int. T.L.R. 1996, 2(4), Supp i-xvi. (Text including annexes).

International competition rules for governments and for private business: the case for linking future WTO negotiations on investment, competition and environmental rules to reforms of anti dumping laws *(Ernst-Ulrich Petersmann)*: J.W.T. 1996, 30(3), 5-35. (Need to reduce inconsistencies between trade and competition rules).

Labour rights and international trade: IDS Emp. E. 1996, 419, 19-20. (International and EU provisions within trade law designed to exert pressure on developing countries to adhere to core labour standards).

Litigation process under the GATT dispute settlement system: lessons for the World Trade Organization? *(Christopher Thomas)*: J.W.T. 1996, 30(2), 53-81. (Development of dispute settlement procedures under GATT and how these relate to WTO's dispute resolution processes).

Market access: a European Community instrument to break down barriers to trade *(Alistair Stewart)*: Int. T.L.R. 1996, 2(4), 121-123. (Use of Trade Barriers Regulation allowing Community companies to request that EU take action to enforce rights of access to markets of trading partners which implement practices hindering or preventing such access).

Microeconometric analysis for determination of injury: recent beef trade disputes adjudicated by the Canadian International Trade Tribunal *(Hsin C. Huang)*: J.W.T. 1996, 30(2), 133-160. (Use of economic tests for demonstrating causal link between dumped beef imports and injury suffered by industry within framework of GATT codes).

Mutual recognition agreements *(John Clarke)*: Int. T.L.R. 1996, 2(2), 31-36. (Emergence of technical barriers to trade in EU, concept of mutual recognition agreements regarding product testing and standards, benefits derived by contracting states and conditions imposed).

Private participation in the enforcement of WTO law: the new EC Trade Barriers Regulation *(Marco C.E.J. Bronckers)*: C.M.L. Rev. 1996, 33(2), 299-318. (Provisions of Regulation 3286/94, which introduces rights for private parties to complain about illegal trade practices of third countries, compared with New Commercial Policy Instrument from 1984-1994 and scope for judicial review).

Procedural rights in EC anti dumping proceedings *(Ulrich M. Gassner)*: W. Comp. 1996, 19(4), 19-44. (Structure of new anti dumping procedure and rights accorded by it, including access to information, duty to give reasons, disclosure, confidentiality and locus standi).

Reform of the European Community's generalized system of preferences: a missed opportunity *(Steve Peers)*: J.W.T. 1995, 29(6), 79-96. (Effect on international trade of new scheme for industrial products since its inception in January 1995).

Rehabilitating anti dumping and other trade remedies through cost-benefit analyses *(Marco C.E.J. Bronckers)*: J.W.T. 1996, 30(2), 5-37. (GATT and OECD proposals on comprehensive cost benefit analysis, comparison with current WTO and EU framework and argument that comprehensive analysis should be mandatory for governments considering trade remedies).

Social clauses in international trade: the debate in the European Union *(Paul Waer)*: J.W.T. 1996, 30(4), 25-42. (Current EU practice and whether lack of social standards in international trade give competitive edge when exporting).

The death of exclusive competence? *(Nicholas Emiliou)*: E.L.R. 1996, 21(4), 294-311. (Extent of Community competence in field of commercial policy with particular reference to competence to conclude WTO Agreement).

The impact of the General Agreement on Trade in Services on the OECD Multilateral Agreement on Investment *(Ansgar M. Wimmer)*: W. Comp. 1996, 19(4), 109-120. (Implications for investor protection and domestic regulation).

The origins of bills of exchange in international trade revisited *(Samuel O. Maduegbuna)*: R.A.D.I.C. 1995, 7(4), 886-894. (History and development of payment system).

The strengthening of the multilateral system: Article 23 of the WTO Dispute Settlement Understanding: dismantling unilateral retaliation under section 301 of the 1974 Trade Act? *(Christian Schede)*: W. Comp. 1996, 20(1), 109-138. (Conflict between US protectionist trade policy and its obligations under WTO dispute resolution procedures).

The Transatlantic Business Dialogue: driving to make EU and US businesses more competitive *(Craig Burchell)*: Int. T.L.R. 1996, 2(4), 124-132. (Origins of TABD and recommendations in Sevile declaration of 1995 for removal of obstacles to transatlantic trade with particular reference to standards, certification and regulatory requirements).

Trade-related aspects of international taxation: a new WTO code of conduct? *(Asif H. Qureshi)*: J.W.T. 1996, 30(2), 161-194. (Requirement for new WTO Code to address problems of violation of tax regimes).

Transatlantic business dialogue: working to keep US and EU businesses competitive *(Craig Burchell)*: Co. Law. 1996, 17(7), 214-216. (Work of Transatlantic Business Dialogue (TABD) which aims to focus attention on need to reduce costly transatlantic trade barrriers to increase competitiveness).

World trade disputes settlement and the exhaustion of local remedies rule *(Rutsel Silvestre J. Martha)*: J.W.T. 1996, 30(4), 107-130. (Applicability

of international law as embodied in GATT and EU treaties in providing for international trade dispute resolution applicable to international organisations).

3688. Books

Brack, Duncan–International Trade and the Montreal Protocol. Hardback: £35.00. Earthscan.

Ciambella, Franca–Investment in South East Asia. Hardback: £35.00. ISBN 981-00-6798-4. Butterworth-Heinemann.

Comair-Obeid, Nayla–The Law of Business Contracts in the Arab Middle East. Arab and Islamic laws. Hardback: £77.00. ISBN 90-411-0216-7. Kluwer Law International.

Dromgoole, Sarah–International Trade Law. Paperback: £24.95. ISBN 0-273-61112-7. Pitman Publishing.

Gabriel, M.; Gilles, P.–International Trade and Business Law Annual: Vol II. Paperback: £19.95. ISBN 1-85941-291-2. Cavendish Publishing Ltd.

Hindley, Brian; Messerlin, Patrick–Antidumping Industrial Policy. Paperback: £7.95. ISBN 0-8447-7046-9. American Enterprise Institute.

Konstadinidis, Stratos V.–The Legal Regulation of the European Community's External Relations After the Completion of the Internal Market. EC/ International Law Forum I. Hardback: £45.00. ISBN 1-85521-695-7. Dartmouth.

Law of International Trade: Suggested Solutions (1991-1995). Bar examinations. Paperback: £9.95. ISBN 0-7510-0743-9. HLT Publications.

Law of International Trade: Suggested Solutions - Single Paper (Trinity 1995). Bar Examinations. Paperback: £3.95. ISBN 0-7510-0643-2. HLT Publications.

McCahery, Joseph; Bratton, William W.; Picciotto, Sol; Scott, C.–International Regulatory Competition and Coordination. Hardback: £55.00. ISBN 0-19-826035-0. Clarendon Press.

Miller, Grady–The Legal and Economic Basis of International Trade. Hardback: £51.95. ISBN 0-89930-918-6. Quorum Books.

Qureshi, Asif H.–The World Trade Organisation. Melland Studies in International Law. Hardback: £50.00. ISBN 0-7190-3191-5. Manchester University Press.

Sellman, Pamela–Law of International Trade. Cracknell's law students' companions. Paperback: £9.95. ISBN 1-85836-044-7. Old Bailey Press.

Sellman, Pamela–Law of International Trade: Textbook 1996-1997. Bachelor of Laws (LLB). Paperback: £18.95. ISBN 0-7510-0694-7. HLT Publications.

Sellman, Pamela–Law of International Trade: Casebook 1996-1997. Bachelor of Laws (LLB). Paperback: £14.95. ISBN 0-7510-0660-2. Paperback: £15.95. ISBN 0-7510-0681-5. HLT Publications.

JURISPRUDENCE

3689. Articles

A "terrible beauty", the Irish Supreme Court, and dying *(Dermot Feenan)*: E.J.H.L. 1996, 3(1), 29-48. (Constitutional and human rights arguments used by Irish court in its decision to allow withdrawal of artificial nutrition and hydration of woman who had been brain damaged 23 years ago).

An autobiographical apercu of legal philosophy *(Norberto Bobbio)*: Ratio Juris 1996, 9(2), 121-124. (Italian author's increasing interest in jurisprudence and changes in approach of natural law and legal positivist theorists over past 60 years).

Berkshire goes ethical with 6 million: Occ. Pen. 1996, 112, 6-9. (Background to Investment by Berkshire County Council pension fund in ethically screened pooled fund and leading cases on ethical investment).

Brothers in arms: sport, the law and the construction of gender identity *(David McArdle)*: Int. J. Soc. L. 1996, 24(2), 145-162. (Theory that organised sport remains fundamental to creation and maintenance of patriarchal society characterised by laws which differentiate between sexes and subordinate women).

Can a competitive company be ethical? *(Peter G. Cowap)*: E.F.S.L. 1996, 3(10), 268-271. (Importance of ethical considerations for senior managers in financial services sector).

Discourse theory and human rights *(Robert Alexy)*: Ratio Juris 1996, 9(3), 209-235. (Justification of discourse rules and use as foundation of human rights and attempt to define Kantian position which shares principles of universality and autonomy).

Discrimination as injustice *(John Gardner)*: O.J.L.S. 1996, 16(3), 353-367. (Application of concepts of corrective and distributive justice to indirect discrimination).

Dworkin on paternalism and well-being *(T.M. Wilkinson)*: O.J.L.S. 1996, 16(3), 433-444. (Critique of paternalistic theory that forcing people to act against their ultimate wishes can do them good).

Ethics: a moral dilemma *(Brian F. Kingshott)*: Pol. J. 1996, 69(2), 163-166. (Whether police personnel and training professionals should be making greater effort to promote ethical behaviour in their organizations).

Football and the civilizing process: penal discourse and the ethic of collective responsibility in sports law *(Biko Agozino)*: Int. J. Soc. L. 1996, 24(2), 163-188. (Nature of punishment, guilt and innocence in sport, society and law and ways in which power to punish in sports reflects social inequalities of criminal justice administration).

John Chipman Gray–precursor of American realism *(L.B. Curzon)*: S.L.R. 1996, 17(Spr), 51-53. (Profile of American jurist, founder of American Realism school of thought and critic of natural law theories).

Jorgensen's dilemma and how to face it *(Robert Walter)*: Ratio Juris 1996, 9(2), 168-171. (Theory on problems of drawing conclusions from imperatives).

Legal analysis as institutional imagination *(Roberto Mangabeira Unger)*: M.L.R. 1996, 59(1), 1-23. (Arrested development of legal thought by failure to move from concern with enjoyment of rights to develop changes in institutional arrangements and rationalisation of legal analysis).

Legal realism for legal realists *(Neil Duxbury)*: Ratio Juris 1996, 9(2), 198-203. (Review article of American Legal Realism and Empirical Social Science, 1995 by John Henry Schlegel).

On the implications of Kelsen's doctrine of hierarchical structure *(Stanley L. Paulson)*: Liverpool L.R. 1996, 18(1), 49-62. (Failure of Kelsen's search for ideal linguistic form of legal norm).

The limits of justice: finding fault in the criminal law *(Alan W. Norrie)*: M.L.R. 1996, 59(4), 540-556. (Theory of criminal justice and problems with concepts of retribution and deterrence, leading to critical realist approach balancing criminal responsibility with social considerations).

The philosopher-judge: some friendly criticisms of Richard Posner's jurisprudence *(Matthew H. Kramer)*: M.L.R. 1996, 59(3), 465-478. (Review article of Overcoming Law, 1995 by Richard A Posner).

Victimology and rights theories *(Robert E. Mackay)*: I.R.V. 1996, 4(3), 183-194. (Protection of rights in countering victimisation and need to protect vulnerable in rights conflict situations in light of De Las Casas' and Finnis' rights theories, natural law perspective and moral imperatives behind legal protection).

3690. Books

Applying Psychology to the Legal World. £5.99. ISBN 0-340-64759-0. Hodder & Stoughton Educational.

Austin, John–The Province of Jurisprudence Determined. Classical Jurisprudence. Hardback: £40.00. ISBN 1-85521-649-3. Dartmouth.

Bagnall, Gary–Law As Art. Applied legal philosophy. Hardback: £39.50. ISBN 1-85521-758-9. Dartmouth.

Bauman, Richard W.–Critical Legal Studies. Hardback: £40.95. ISBN 0-8133-8980-1. Westview Press.

Bentham, Jeremy; Burns, J.H.; Hart, H.L.A.–The Collected Works of Jeremy Bentham: an Introduction to the Principles of Morals and Legislation. Paperback: £17.99. ISBN 0-19-820516-3. Clarendon Press.

Bentley, Lionel; Flynn, Leo–Law and the Senses. Law and social theory. Hardback: £45.00. ISBN 0-7453-1069-9. Paperback: £14.99. ISBN 0-7453-1068-0. Pluto Press.

Bix, Brian–Jurisprudence: Theory and Context. Modern legal studies. Paperback: £18.95. ISBN 0-421-52660-2. Sweet & Maxwell.

Boorstin, Daniel J.–The Mysterious Science of the Law. Paperback: £11.95. ISBN 0-226-06498-0. University of Chicago Press.

Brooks, Peter; Gewirtz, Paul–Law's Stories. Hardback: £20.00. ISBN 0-300-06675-9. Yale University Press.

Burgess-Jackson, Keith–Rape: a Philosophical Investigation. Appied Legal Philosophy. Hardback: £42.50. ISBN 1-85521-485-7. Dartmouth.

Campbell, Tom D.–The Legal Theory of Ethical Positivism. Applied Legal Philosophy Series. Hardback: £39.50. ISBN 1-85521-171-8. Dartmouth.

Davies, Margaret–Delimiting the Law. Law and social theory. Hardback: £40.00. ISBN 0-7453-1100-8. Paperback: £12.99. ISBN 0-7453-0769-8. Pluto Press.

Edwards, S.–Sex and Gender in the Legal Process. £15.00. ISBN 1-85431-507-2. Blackstone Press.

Faulhaber, Gregory M.–Politics, Law and the Church. Distinguished Research Series/Catholic Scholars Press. Paperback: £39.95. ISBN 1-57309-102-2. Hardback: £55.95. ISBN 1-57309-103-0. International Scholars Publications.

Fentiman, Richard G.–Conflict of Laws. International Library of Essays in Law and Legal Theory. Hardback: £100.00. ISBN 1-85521-191-2. Dartmouth.

Fletcher, George P.–The Basic Concepts of Legal Thought. Hardback: £25.00. ISBN 0-19-508335-0. Paperback: £10.99. ISBN 0-19-508336-9. Oxford University Press Inc, USA.

French, D–How to Cite Legal Authorities. Paperback: £14.95. ISBN 1-85431-315-0. Blackstone Press.

Gaffney, Paul–Ronald Dworkin on Law As Integrity. Hardback: £49.95. ISBN 0-7734-2268-4. Edwin Mellen Press.

George, Robert P.–Natural Law, Liberalism, and Morality. Hardback: £40.00. ISBN 0-19-825984-0. Clarendon Press.

George, Robert P.–The Autonomy of Law. Hardback: £40.00. ISBN 0-19-825786-4. Clarendon Press.

Gorringe, Timothy–God's Just Vengeance. Cambridge Studies in Ideology and Religion, 9. Hardback: £35.00. ISBN 0-521-55301-6. Paperback: £12.95. ISBN 0-521-55762-3. Cambridge University Press.

Gray, John Chipman–The Nature and Sources of the Law. Classical Jurisprudence. Hardback: £40.00. ISBN 1-85521-651-5. Dartmouth.

Guest, Stephen–Positivism Today. Issues in Law and Society. Hardback: £37.50. ISBN 1-85521-689-2. Dartmouth.

Habermas, Jurgen–Between Facts and Norms. Hardback: £45.00. ISBN 0-7456-1229-6. Polity Press.

Haley, John Owen–Authority Without Power. Paperback: £10.99. ISBN 0-19-509257-0. Oxford University Press Inc, USA.

Hay, David–Words and Phrases Legally Defined: 1996. Supplement. Paperback: £29.50. ISBN 0-406-99731-4. Butterworth Law.

Hobson, Charles F.–The Great Chief Justice. American Political Thought. Hardback: £27.95. ISBN 0-7006-0788-9. University Press of Kansas.

Hockett, Jeffrey D.–New Deal Justice. Studies in American Constitutionalism. Hardback: £55.50. ISBN 0-8476-8210-2. Paperback: £21.50. ISBN 0-8476-8211-0. Rowman & Littlefield.

Hogan, Patrick Colm–On Interpretation. Hardback: £35.50. ISBN 0-8203-1724-1. University of Georgia Press.

Holland, James–Learning Legal Rules. Paperback: £13.00. ISBN 1-85431-535-8. Blackstone Press.

Inness, Julie–Privacy, Intimacy, and Isolation. Paperback: £8.99. ISBN 0-19-510460-9. Oxford University Press Inc, USA.

Jackson, Bernard S.–Making Sense in Jurisprudence. Legal semiotics monographs, Vol V. Hardback: £39.50. ISBN 0-9513793-8-0. Paperback: £16.95. ISBN 0-9513793-9-9. Deborah Charles Publications.

Jurisprudence and Legal Theory - LLB: Suggested Solutions (1991-1995). Bachelor of Laws (LLB). Paperback: £6.95. ISBN 0-7510-0726-9. HLT Publications.

Jurisprudence and Legal Theory: Suggested Solutions - Single Paper (June 1995). Paperback: £3.00. ISBN 0-7510-0625-4. HLT Publications.

Jurisprudence and Legal Theory: Textbook 1996-1997. Bachelor of Laws (LLB). Paperback: £16.95. ISBN 0-7510-0691-2. HLT Publications.

Kalman, Laura–The Strange Career of Legal Liberalism. Hardback: £25.00. ISBN 0-300-06369-5. Yale University Press.

Kapur, Ratna–Feminist Terrains in Legal Domains. Hardback. ISBN 81-85107-83-1. Kali for Women.

Kelsen, Hans–Introduction to the Problems of Legal Theory. Paperback: £16.99. ISBN 0-19-826565-4. Clarendon Press.

Keynes, Edward–Liberty, Property, and Privacy. Hardback: £31.95. ISBN 0-271-01509-8. Paperback: £13.50. ISBN 0-271-01510-1. Penn State Press.

Klabbers, Jan–The Concept of Treaty in International Law. Developments in international law. Hardback: £74.25. ISBN 90-411-0244-2. Kluwer Law International.
McCoubrey, Hilaire–Textbook on Jurisprudence. Paperback: £15.95. ISBN 1-85431-582-X. Blackstone Press.
McCoubrey, Hilaire–The Obligation to Obey in Legal Theory. Hardback: £39.50. ISBN 1-85521-825-9. Dartmouth.
McLean, Sheila A. M.–Contemporary Issues in Law, Medicine and Ethics. Medico-legal series. Hardback: £42.50. ISBN 1-85521-586-1. Dartmouth.
Mohammad Hashim Kamali–Principles of Islamic Jurisprudence. Hardback: £45.00. ISBN 0-946621-23-3. Paperback: £18.95. ISBN 0-946621-24-1. The Islamic Texts Society.
Morison, John; Bell, Christine–Tall Stories? Reading Law and Literature. Applied Legal Philosophy. Hardback: £39.50. ISBN 1-85521-741-4. Dartmouth.
Muhammad Mustafa Azami–On Schacht's "Origins of Muhammadan Jurisprudence". Paperback: £14.95. ISBN 0-946621-46-2. The Islamic Texts Society.
Nelken, David–Law As Communication. Issues in Law and Society. Hardback: £35.00. ISBN 1-85521-719-8. Paperback: £15.00. ISBN 1-85521-722-8. Dartmouth.
Patterson, Dennis–Companion to Philosophy of Law and Legal Theory. Blackwell companions to philosophy. Hardback: £65.00. ISBN 1-55786-535-3. Blackwell Publishers.
Patterson, Dennis–Law and Truth. Hardback: £30.00. ISBN 0-19-508323-7. Oxford University Press Inc, USA.
Petersen, Hanne–Home Knitted Law. Socio-legal studies. Hardback: £40.00. ISBN 1-85521-837-2. Dartmouth.
Pongo, Kodzp Tita–Expectation As Fulfillment. Hardback: £29.50. ISBN 0-7618-0227-4. University Press of America.
Popple, James–A Pragmatic Legal Expert System. Applied Legal Philosophy. Hardback: £45.00. ISBN 1-85521-739-2. Dartmouth.
Schultz, David A.; Smith, Christopher E.–The Jurisprudential Vision of Justice Antonin Scalia.
Studies in American Constitutionalism. Hardback: £50.50. ISBN 0-8476-8131-9. Paperback: £19.50. ISBN 0-8476-8132-7. Rowman & Littlefield.
Sells, Benjamin–The Soul of the Law. Paperback: £9.99. ISBN 1-85230-796-X. Element Books Ltd.
Smith, Roger–Achieving Civil Justice. Paperback: £9.95. ISBN 0-905099-75-3. The Legal Action Group.
Stavropoulos, Nicos–Objectivity in Law. Hardback: £35.00. ISBN 0-19-825899-2. Clarendon Press.
Sunstein, Cass R.–Legal Reasoning and Political Conflict. Hardback: £18.99. ISBN 0-19-510082-4. Oxford University Press Inc, USA.
Thornton, Margaret–Public and Private. Paperback: £15.99. ISBN 0-19-553662-2. OUP Australia.
Unger, Roberto Mangabeira–What Should Legal Analysis Become? Hardback: £34.95. ISBN 1-85984-969-5. Paperback: £11.95. ISBN 1-85984-100-7. Verso.
Uniacke, Suzanne–Permissible Killing. Cambridge Studies in Philosophy and Law. Paperback: £12.95. ISBN 0-521-56458-1. Cambridge University Press.
Wai Chee Dimock–Residues of Justice. Hardback: £40.00. ISBN 0-520-20243-0. University of California Press.
Weisberg, D. Kelly–Applications of Feminist Legal Theory to Women's Lives: Vol 2. Women in the Political Economy Series. Hardback: £63.95. ISBN 1-56639-423-6. Paperback: £27.95. ISBN 1-56639-424-4. Temple University Press.
White, G. Edward–Justice Oliver Wendell Holmes. Paperback: £12.99. ISBN 0-19-510128-6. Oxford University Press Inc, USA.
Wiethoff, William E.–A Peculiar Humanism. Studies in the Legal History of the South. Hardback: £29.50. ISBN 0-8203-1797-7. University of Georgia Press.
Young, Peter–Punishment, Money and Legal Order. Edinburgh law and society series. Hardback: £35.00. ISBN 0-7486-0534-7. Edinburgh University Press.

LANDLORD AND TENANT

3691. Adverse possession–claim based on tenancy agreement not capable of creating legal estate–ineffective as parol lease

[Limitation Act 1980 s.15 Sch.1 para.5; Law of Property Act 1925 s.54.]

In 1975 agents acting for T's predecessor in title wrote to L confirming that they were prepared to grant a quarterly tenancy of shop premises. L endorsed a copy of the letter, the tenancy agreement, to the effect that he agreed to the terms and returned it to the landlord. In 1977, L ceased to pay rent. He remained in possession notwithstanding T's notice to quit and in 1995 L commenced proceedings against T seeking a declaration that he was beneficially entitled to the premises and for rectification of the proprietorship register on the basis of adverse possession. T's application to strike out the claim succeeded as first instance and L appealed, claiming that as he had paid no rent since 1977, the right of action was statute-barred by virtue of the 12 year limitation period under the Limitation Act 1980 s.15(1). T, however, contended that the tenancy document was a lease in writing within Sch.1 para.5 of the 1980 Act so that the limitation period began to run from 1984, when L's tenancy was brought to an end by the expiry of the notice to quit.

Held, allowing the appeal, that a written document was not a lease in writing, it was merely evidence of the existence of a lease. The document had to create a leasehold estate in land in law. The agreement was not executed as a deed, and so could only take effect as a lease creating a legal estate in land if it operated as a lease taking effect in possession for a term not exceeding three years in accordance with the Law of Property Act 1925 s.54. The tenancy document did not confer on L an immediate right to take possession as it amounted to a reversionary lease not made by deed and incapable of taking effect as a parol lease which did not create a legal estate in the land. In the absence of any other arguable grounds upon which L's claim could be struck out, L was entitled to have his claim determined at trial.

LONG v. TOWER HAMLETS LBC [1996] 3 W.L.R. 317, James Munby Q.C., Ch D.

3692. Adverse possession–squatting–lessee's right to recover possession

[Renewable Leases Ordinance (Hong Kong).]

L owned from July 1, 1973 a lease of Crown lands in the New Territories of Hong Kong, under the Renewable Leases Ordinance. Proceedings were issued against K who claimed that he had been living on the land, rent free, since 1959. K, therefore, had been living on the land for more than 20 years before the proceedings were commenced but not for 20 years before the original lease expired in 1973. K and others appealed against the decision of the Court of Appeal that L was entitled to possession.

Held, allowing the appeal, that where squatters were in adverse possession of a property, the lessee of the property was barred from asserting his rights to renew the lease during the prescribed period of dispossession. He was only entitled to oust the trespasser and recover possession once a new lease had been granted by the landlord or he exercised an option to renew the lease, by which he acquired a new legal estate under which the squatters' rights were extinguished. The Renewable Leases Ordinance operated as a deemed renewal of the lease pursuant to a right of renewal. However, where an option to renew was exercised, a right to recover the land arose not from the date when the lease was granted but on the date of dispossession, *Taylor v. Twinberrow* [1930] 2 K.B. 16 followed.

CHUNG PING KWAN v. LAM ISLAND DEVELOPMENT CO LTD [1996] 3 W.L.R. 448, Lord Nicholls of Birkenhead, PC.

3693. Adverse possession–tenant paying no rent–whether had correct intention to possess land

[Limitation Act 1980 Sch.1 para.8.]

In 1969 L was granted an oral tenancy of land by W's predecessor in title. In 1970 the landlord consented to the quarterly rent being paid half yearly but L paid no rent from 1974 onwards. L brought a claim for title to the land by adverse possession which was rejected on the ground that L believed until 1981 that he was in the position of tenant to the landlord. L appealed against the decision.

Held, allowing the appeal, that L's possession of the land after he ceased to pay rent was adverse for the purposes of the Limitation Act 1980 Sch.1 para.8(1). To establish adverse possession the tenant needs to show that he had the correct animus possidendi or intention to possess the land, not an intention to become the owner of the land. L had the necessary intention despite the fact that he believed he still had a tenancy and therefore the landlord's title to the land had been extinguished, *Moses v. Lovegrove* [1952] 2 Q.B. 533, [1952] C.L.Y. 1975, *Hayward v. Chaloner* [1968] 1 Q.B. 107, [1967] C.L.Y. 2316 considered.

LODGE v. WAKEFIELD MDC [1995] 38 E.G. 136, Balcombe, L.J., CA.

3694. Agricultural holdings–planning permission–conversion of old farm buildings for sale and provision of new buildings for tenant–permission only granted for old buildings–whether landlord estopped from giving notice to quit

[Agricultural Holdings Act 1986.]

J was an agricultural tenant of a dairy farm. G, the landlord, proposed to J that planning permission be obtained to convert some old buildings (which would be sold) and erect some new farm buildings of which he would have the use. The unopposed planning application was successful only in part and the parties fell into dispute. G then gave notice to quit which he was entitled to do under the Agricultural Holdings Act 1986 on the grounds of the planning application actually granted. J objected that G was estopped from relying on the planning permission to convert the old buildings unless replacement buildings had been provided to the tenant first without cost. The judge found for G and on J's appeal G argued that the necessary shared assumption of the parties must be created by the person to be estopped and secondly that the tenant had to prove his reliance on the assumption was in fact to his detriment, not merely that it might have been so.

Held, allowing the appeal, that (1) J had altered his legal position on the shared assumption that he would remain in possession of the old buildings until he was provided with new buildings. It was not the law that the shared assumptions in such estoppels should be created by the person to be estopped, *Amalgamated Investment & Property Co v. Texas Commerce International Bank* [1982] 1 Q.B. 84, [1981] C.L.Y. 1273 and *Taylor Fashions v. Liverpool Victoria Friendly Society* [1981] 1 Q.B. 133, [1979] C.L.Y. 1619 considered and (2) on the facts of the case, J had lost his opportunity to object. G's second point also failed since detriment to J had been clearly demonstrated on the facts.

JOHN v. GEORGE AND WALTON (1996) 71 P. & C.R. 375, Simon Brown, L.J., CA.

3695. Assignment–leases–validity of unregistered transfer

[Land Registration Act 1925 s.22.]

In 1989 S granted a 25 year lease to B1, a partly owned subsidiary of B2. The lease was registered at the Land Registry and entitled the lessee to give notice expiring at the end of the seventh year. In 1993 B1 became wholly owned by B2 and S granted a licence to assign the lease, B2 bearing the lease obligations. The conveyancing documents were executed and B2 paid the rent, but the assignment was not registered at the Land Registry. Under the Land Registration Act 1925 s.22(1) B1 was deemed to remain proprietor until the transfer was registered. S refused to accept B1's purported notice of termination of the lease, and B1 sought a declaration that the notice was valid.

Held, refusing the declaration, that the assignment took place on the date it was completed because the assignor then gave up the property and had no control over the submission to the Land Registry; thereafter, B1 could not terminate the lease.

BROWN & ROOT TECHNOLOGY LTD v. SUN ALLIANCE AND LONDON ASSURANCE CO LTD [1995] 3 W.L.R. 558, Paul Baker Q.C., Ch D.

3696. Assured shorthold tenancies–death of tenant–succession to tenancy–acquisition of assured shorthold tenancy not periodic assured tenancy–possession proceedings commenced before expiry of notice invalid

[Housing Act 1988 s.20, s.21.]

J appealed against a decision that her tenancy was not a periodic assured tenancy acquired by succession. L had acquired the property and let it to C while awaiting planning permission for development. The tenancy was an assured shorthold tenancy under the Housing Act 1988 s.20. J had moved in with C. Following C's death L claimed possession of the property against J who was the statutory successor to C's tenancy. The judge dismissed L's claim as invalid as there was no date on the notice. The judge also refused a declaration that J had a periodic assured tenancy. L cross-appealed for possession.

Held, dismissing the appeal and the cross-appeal, that (1) by virtue of s.20(4) of the 1988 Act. C was the tenant of an assured shorthold tenancy vested in J on C's death and (2) under s.21 (4) (a) of the 1988 Act, a notice for possession had to state the date that possession was required. That had to be the last day of a period of the tenancy. The date could also not be more than two months before the time when the notice was served. Proceedings had been commenced before the notice had expired.

LOWER STREET PROPERTIES LTD v. JONES (1996) 28 H.L.R. 877, Kennedy, L.J., CA.

3697. Assured tenancies–students

ASSURED AND PROTECTED TENANCIES (LETTINGS TO STUDENTS) (AMENDMENT) REGULATIONS 1996, SI 1996 458; made under the Housing Act 1988 Sch.1 para.8. In force: March 22, 1996; £0.65.

These Regulations amend the Assured and Protected Tenancies (Lettings to Students) Regulations 1988 (SI 1988 2236) Sch.2 to specify the House of St. Gregory and St. Macrina Oxford Ltd for the purposes of the Housing Act 1988 Sch.1 para.8. The effect of specification is that a tenancy granted by the body to a student at an educational institution specified in the 1988 Regulations is not an assured tenancy for the purposes of the 1988 Act.

3698. Assured tenancies–students

ASSURED AND PROTECTED TENANCIES (LETTINGS TO STUDENTS) (AMENDMENT) (NO.2) REGULATIONS 1996, SI 1996 2198; made under the Housing Act 1988 Sch.1 para.8. In force: September 20, 1996; £0.65.

These Regulations amend the Assured and Protected Tenancies (Lettings to Students) Regulations 1988 (SI 1988 2236) to specify Derbyshire Student Residences Limited for the purposes of the Housing Act 1988 Sch.1 para.8. The effect of specification is that a tenancy granted by the body to a student at an educational institution specified in the 1988 Regulations is not an assured tenancy for the purposes of the 1988 Act.

3699. Bailment–goods at landlord's premises–failure by landlord to secure property as agreed–burglary–duty of care

B was granted a tenancy by BHA in an area known to have a strong racist element. Within a day of moving into the premises, B and her family were subjected to racial harassment and abuse from neighbours. B therefore arranged to be rehoused through the local authority, and BHA agreed to release her from the tenancy. Not all her belongings could be removed at once. BHA agreed that B could leave some of her belongings at the premises and that the front door would be secured by a metal grill being fixed across its front. On this basis, B agreed to surrender the keys to the premises. However, when she attended the premises to hand over the keys to BHA's contractor, she saw that there was no metal grill and that the doors and windows of the premises had merely been boarded up with wood. BHA's contractor, however, promised to fix a grill over the door and B duly surrendered the keys. Later that day, before any grill had been attached to the front door, burglars effected entry by forcing open the front door, and stole B's belongings. B brought an action in negligence against BHA, contending that BHA owed her a duty of care in tort to take reasonable care of her belongings, further or alternatively, that BHA owed her a duty to take reasonable care of her belongings as bailee of the same from the surrender of the premises and the keys, and that BHA owed her a duty in contract to fix the premises with a metal grill.

Held, that the claim in contract failed, because there was no consideration for the promise to secure the door with a metal grill. However, there was a clear bailment when BHA took up possession of the premises with B's belongings inside. By not fixing a metal grill, BHA was in breach of its duty to take reasonable care of the goods as bailee, and was liable in damages for the loss of B's goods. Quaere: whether, apart from the bailment, BHA owed B a duty of care in tort, *Blount v. War Office* [1953] 1 W.L.R. 736, [1953] C.L.Y. 239 applied, *Smith v. Littlewoods Organisation* [1987] A.C. 241,[1987] C.L.Y. 2597 and *Reed v. Doncaster MBC* [1995] 2 C.L.Y. 3668 distinguished.

BENOIT v. BROOMLEIGH HOUSING ASSOCIATION, December 5, 1995, Recorder Jacob, CC (Bromley). [*Ex rel.* Stephen Shay, Barrister].

3700. Business tenancies–break clauses–defect in notice

[Landlord and Tenant Act 1730; Distress for Rent Act 1737.]

DB, the tenant, applied for a declaration that all three of its leases had determined on June 24, 1995. The leases were executed by DB and all three leases contained a break clause, allowing DB to terminate the lease by giving not less than nine months' notice. In 1990 DB became a wholly owned subsidiary of the second plaintiff, P2, and ceased to trade. There was no assignment of the leases from DB to P2 although DB remained in occupation. The 1990 rent review was greater than the market rent value and two notices were addressed to PM by DB to effect operation of the break clause on June 24, 1995. By the time DB became aware of the defect in the assignment it could not be corrected in time to meet the deadline and rent was paid although not at the penalty rate.

Held, granting the declaration, but dismissing the counterclaim, that (1) though DB was the actual tenant and the break notices were issued by P2 they were still valid, *Jones v. Phipps* (1868) L.R. 3 Q.B. 567 and *Peel Developments (South) Ltd v. Siemens Plc* [1992] 2 E.G.L.R. 85, [1993] C.L.Y. 2455 applied; (2) DB was a mere shell, it had ceased to trade and those assets which it retained were held on a bare trust, thus P2 was a general agent of DB; (3) lack of wilfulness on DB's part initiated liability on DB's part under the Landlord and Tenant Act 1730 where the tenant was liable to double value for "wilfully" withholding rent beyond the end of the term and (4) acceptance of the single rent amounted to a waiver of P's double rent demand under the Distress for Rent Act 1737.

DUN & BRADSTREET SOFTWARE SERVICES (ENGLAND) LTD v. PROVIDENT MUTUAL LIFE ASSURANCE ASSOCIATION [1996] E.G.C.S. 62, Knox, J., Ch D.

3701. Business tenancies–break clauses–wrong termination date in notice

In 1990 M was granted a 20 year term for an industrial building, and clause 8 of the lease stated that M could determine the lease after the expiration of five years by giving W not less than 12 months' notice. On January 21, 1994 M wrote to W stating that they were enclosing a notice determining the lease on March 23, 1995.

However the notice they enclosed determined the lease on March 23, 1994 and referred to clause 8. M applied for a declaration that the lease would determine on June 23, 1995.

Held, allowing the application, that the letter and the notice would be effective. W on reading the documents would be aware that the only possible date of determination was June 23, 1995 and they would not have been misled by the wrong dates. There was no requirement placed on M to specify a date and consequently the notice was valid, *Carradine Properties Ltd v. Aslam* [1976] 1 W.L.R. 442 applied.

MICROGRAFIX v. WOKING 8 LTD [1995] 37 E.G. 179, Jacob, J., Ch D.

3702. Business tenancies–covenants–bus station–a clause in the lease did not require tenant to keep the public lavatories open to the public–no implied obligation to provide lavatory facilities

R, the tenant of a bus station, appealed against a decision that it was in breach of one of the covenants of the lease having closed the public lavatories within the premises following repeated incidents of vandalism. An injunction was granted requiring R to reopen the lavatories. The lease, granted by C, contained a covenant, cl.2(e), requiring the premises, including the lavatories, to be "conducted in a decent respectable and orderly manner". The judge construed the word "conducted" to mean "kept open". He further held that, if he was wrong on that count, there was an implied term to the same effect. Under the test in *Shirlaw v. Southern Foundries (1962) Ltd* [1939] 2 K.B. 206, the judge found that the officious bystander would have decided that there should have been such a clause when the lease was executed.

Held, allowing the appeal, that (1) if the word "conducted" meant "kept open", it would also mean that the offices of the bus station should be kept open to the public. A further covenant required R not to use the premises for any other reason except that of a bus station without the consent of C, that covenant did not impose a positive obligation on R to continue operating as a bus station. Clause 2(e) contained obligations on the part of R in relation to the physical premises and not the conduct of business. R was obliged to conduct any activities in the manner stated, but was not obliged to conduct the activities themselves and (2) it was not certain that an officious bystander would have unhesitatingly answered yes to the question of whether R should be obliged to keep open the lavatories. An implied term requiring the lavatories to be kept open would not have been necessary for the sake of business efficacy as R would obviously not be opposed to the term if that was the case. The lease worked without the term and C only had an interest as a local authority in the provision of lavatories; it was of no concern to it as a landlord. Lavatory facilities were for the benefit of the tenant and the landlord would not have required a positive obligation in the lease.

CHORLEY BC v. RIBBLE MOTOR SERVICES (1996) 72 P. & C.R. D32, Millett, L.J., CA.

3703. Business tenancies–covenants–forfeiture–landlord's claim was struck out despite being detrimental to landlord's interests

G applied to have a judgment, allowing E's claim for possession and mesne profits, set aside. E granted G a lease of commercial premises for a period of 30 years at a rent of £861,500 p.a. The lease contained covenants; (1) not to assign or part with possession of the premises and (2) not to underlet the whole of the premises. Both landlord and tenant also had options to serve notice after November 16, 1995 doubling the rents applicable at that date and requiring the landlords to pay the tenants £7.75 million in respect thereof. G subsequently activated that provision and assigned the right of payment to Barclays Bank which obtained a fixed charge over the lease. G became insolvent and was unable to pay the rent. E in return alleged breach of covenant.

Held, allowing the appeal, that (1) the receivers appointed by G had authority to defend the action and apply to have the judgment set aside; (2) the charge allowed repayment of the chargee's debts; (3) if the lease was held not to have been forfeited, the liquidators' exclusion clause would allow E to claim the amount of the difference in the double rent accrued in excess of £10 million and would also require them to pay the bank £7.75 million as a windfall. Such considerations though, were immaterial to the court's decision to set aside judgment; (4) the injustice to landlords, liquidators and third parties might provide grounds to prevent the bank receiving payment in separate proceedings and (5) the evidence failed to show a breach of covenant and E's action would therefore be struck out.

GROSVENOR (MAYFAIR) ESTATE v. EDWARD ERDMAN PROPERTY INVESTMENT LTD [1996] E.G.C.S. 83, Lightman, J., Ch D.

3704. Business tenancies–final assignee insolvent–disclaimer of lease–guarantor of intermediary assignee–effect of disclaimer on liability of guarantor and original tenant–interpretation of disclaimer provisions

[Bankruptcy Act 1883; Insolvency Act 1986 s.178.]

The liquidator of an intermediary assignee, CIT, of a business tenancy and their guarantor who were the second and third defendants in an action for rent arrears due under the lease, appealed against a judgment, in favour of the landlord, H, that a disclaimer for rent by the final assignee's liquidator did not discharge the original tenant and the guarantor from liability for the unpaid arrears. The defendants sought clarification of which of two conflicting precedents was to be preferred: *Hill v. East and West India Dock Co* (1884) 9 App. Cas. 448, which ruled that the original tenant remained liable for rent notwithstanding the disclaimer, or *Stacey v. Hill* [1901] 1 K.B. 660 which held that the guarantor was not liable following the disclaimer of the lease.

Held, dismissing the appeal, that there was no distinction between the liability of the original tenant and that of the guarantor. Although it was a general proposition that the release of a debtor discharged his guarantor, the Insolvency Act 1986 s.178(4)(b) provided that a disclaimer did not affect the rights or liabilities of a third person so that the general rule did not apply, a rationale in accordance with the Bankruptcy Act 1883. To relieve a guarantor from liability would defeat the fundamental purpose of a guarantee, that the risk of insolvency should not fall on the creditor. Furthermore, to follow *Stacey* would give rise to the unacceptable anomaly that the guarantor would not be held liable had he guaranteed the obligations of the final assignee who was the principal debtor, but would remain liable in respect of CIT's insolvency, *Hill v. East and West India Dock Co* affirmed and *Stacey v. Hill* overruled.

HINDCASTLE LTD v. BARBARA ATTENBOROUGH ASSOCIATES LTD [1996] 2 W.L.R. 262, Lord Nicholls of Birkenhead, HL.

3705. Business tenancies–fixed term tenancy–period of notice–whether tenancy continued after expiry of contractual term

[Landlord and Tenant Act 1954 s.24, s.27.]

The plaintiffs, E and B, granted a lease and underlease respectively of business premises to PA for a five year period expiring on February 14, 1993. In December 1992, PA ceased to occupy the premises for business purposes and served notices on E and B, pursuant to the Landlord and Tenant Act 1954 s.27 and s.24 to the effect that it did not wish to continue its tenancy. PA had paid the rent up until February 14, 1993 but E and B claimed they were entitled to rent up until June 24, 1993, which was the expiry date of the period of notice given by PA. PA appealed against a decision that the tenancy did not expire until the end of the notice period.

Held, allowing the appeal, that, where a company had ceased occupation before the expiry of the fixed term, the tenancy ended on the date given in the contract for expiry of the lease, and s.24 of the Act did not have the effect of continuing the tenancy beyond that date by requiring notice to be given under s.27. Section 24 could not be construed as including business tenancies that had, in the past, fallen within the ambit of the section but had now expired through common law effluxion of time, *Long Acre Securities Ltd v. Electro*

Acoustic Industries Ltd [1990] 1 E.G.L.R. 91, [1990] C.L.Y. 2778 not followed, *Morrison Holdings Ltd v. Manders Ltd* [1976] 1 W.L.R. 533, [1976] C.L.Y. 1534 followed.

ESSELTE AB v. PEARL ASSURANCE PLC (1997) 73 P. & C.R. D18, Morritt, L.J., CA.

3706. Business tenancies–insolvency of assignee–voluntary arrangement–effect on lessor as creditor–landlord entitled to arrears of rent

[Insolvency Act 1986.]

M, a landlord, sought summary judgment against G for arrears of rent. G had assigned the residue of a 25 year lease to E, a company which in 1995 became insolvent, owing a substantial amount in rent arrears. The directors of E presented a petition for an administration order under the Insolvency Act 1986 and subsequently a scheme of arrangement was approved at a creditors' meeting. The question at issue was the effect of this voluntary arrangement on the rights of M.

Held, giving judgment for M, that for the purposes of s.4(3) of the Act, M, as lessor, was a secured creditor in respect of its right of re-entry, and its right to forfeit the lease if rent was unpaid remained effective despite the voluntary arrangement, *Doorbar v. Alltime Securities Ltd (No.2)* [1995] B.C.C. 728, [1996] C.L.Y. 3521 considered. Since M had not surrendered its rights against E, G's liability towards M remained unaffected, and M was entitled to summary judgment for the unpaid rent.

MARCH ESTATES PLC v. GUNMARK LTD [1996] 2 B.C.L.C. 1, Lightman, J., Ch D.

3707. Business tenancies–invalid notice to determine–notice specified date before expiry but after option to determine–whether notice effective

[Landlord and Tenant Act 1954 s.26.]

On September 29, 1988 S assigned to G a lease dated July 10, 1985 for a term of 20 years from June 24, 1985, terminable by G on the expiration of the tenth year with at least six months' notice. On October 4, 1994 G gave notice to determine on July 9, 1995 and sought a new tenancy under the Landlord and Tenant Act 1954 s.26. G then applied for a declaration that he was entitled to a new tenancy because the contractual term of the lease had been validly determined by notice, or alternatively pursuant to s.26(5) of the 1954 Act, as no valid notice was given prior to the request for a new tenancy.

Held, refusing the declaration, that the contractual notice was not valid as it named the anniversary date of the lease as opposed to the start of the term. G could not rely on the proviso in s.26 of the 1954 Act as it contemplated only a date on which a tenancy would come to an end by effluxion of time or, in the case of a lease for a fixed term granted from year to year, the date on which the lease could be determined by a notice to quit from the lessee. G's notice specified a date earlier than that on which the tenancy would come to an end apart from the 1954 Act.

GARSTON v. SCOTTISH WIDOWS FUND AND LIFE ASSURANCE SOCIETY [1996] 1 W.L.R. 834, Rattee, J., Ch D.

3708. Business tenancies–landlord undertaking construction work–trespass–measure of damages–breach of covenant for quiet enjoyment

[Landlord and Tenant Act 1954 s.24.]

L appealed against a ruling relating to a dispute between themselves as tenants carrying out a retail business and the defendant landlord HB. During the period of the tenancy, HB had undertaken construction work on the whole of the building, which included adding two further floors on top of the single storey extension at the front of the house, part of which was leased by L. Four issues were appealed: (1) did the construction by HB constitute trespass and, if so, what damages were appropriate. Whilst trespass was accepted nominal damages of £20 were disputed. L submitted that the judge below had erroneously concluded that substantial damage had not been established and had failed to adopt the correct approach to assessing damages; (2) with regard to HB being in breach of the covenant for quiet enjoyment, it was not necessary to determine this as no damage had been proved; (3) where HB had derogated from the grant expressed in the lease by carrying out the building work, the judge had held that L had not established their case and made no order for damages and (4) there was a dispute over what was an appropriate interim rent payable by L under the Landlord and Tenant Act 1954 s.24.

Held, allowing the appeal so as to provide for an award of damages for trespass of £8,100 and an interim annual rent of £6,251, that (1) on the issue of trespass, damages were to be assessed upon the *Whitwham* principle of compensation for invasion of the plaintiffs' right, *Whitwham v. Westminster Brymbo Coal and Coke Co* [1896] 2 Ch. 538 followed. There was no further head of damage established in respect of loss of profits or diminution of the value of the lease. L should be allowed to put forward a claim for damage on the *Whitwham* principle, it was appropriate to consider the bargain that would have been struck by a willing lessee and a willing lessor, *Swordheath Properties Ltd v. Tabet* [1979] 1 W.L.R. 285, [1979] C.L.Y. 1626; (2) there was breach of the covenant for quiet enjoyment, but no loss as pleaded proved; (3) there was no derogation from grant following from the building of an upper storey and (4) the market rent was appropriately chosen in terms of the 1954 Act s.24.

LAWSON v. HARTLEY-BROWN (1996) 71 P. & C.R. 242, Aldous, L.J., CA.

3709. Business tenancies–notice to quit–tenant vacating before termination of contractual term–tenant required to serve s.27(2) notice

[Landlord and Tenant Act 1954 s.27.]

G occupied premises for a term of years under an underlease and informed P that it would vacate the premises at the expiry of the underlease on June 21, 1994. G actually quit the premises on May 21, 1994. P agreed that G's letter had determined the tenancy on September 29, 1994. P claimed that, under the Landlord and Tenant Act 1954 s.27(2), G was obliged to serve notice to quit.

Held, giving judgment for P, that G was not bound by P's longer notice period but G could not negate its obligation to pay rent merely by vacating the premises. The tenant was therefore obliged to serve notice under s.27(2) of the 1954 Act and the date on which the tenancy determined was accordingly September 29, 1994, *Esselte AB v. Pearl Assurance Plc* [1995] 2 E.G.L.R. 61, [1996] C.L.Y. 3716 and *Long Acre Securities Ltd v. Electro Acoustic Industries Ltd* [1990] 1 E.G.L.R. 91, [1990] C.L.Y. 2778 applied.

PROVIDENT MUTUAL LIFE ASSURANCE ASSOCIATION v. GREATER LONDON EMPLOYERS' ASSOCIATION LTD [1996] 1 E.G.L.R. 106, Lightman, J., Ch D.

3710. Business tenancies–rates–surrender of lease–liability for non-domestic rates–whether handing over the keys amounted to surrender of the lease

B appealed by way of case stated against a decision that he had not effectively surrendered a lease of commercial premises and was therefore liable to pay £5,451 in non-domestic rates. B had handed back the keys of the premises to the landlord and contended that such an action constituted the surrender of the lease. The landlord denied that the lease had been surrendered.

Held, allowing the appeal, that (1) for a lease to be surrendered by operation of law, a party had to do an act which was inconsistent with the continuation of the lease to which the other party assented. In addition, there had to be an acceptance of the termination and an intention by the landlord to take possession and (2) the handing over of keys by itself could amount to a surrender of the lease in certain circumstances. However, in this case, the magistrates failed to give adequate consideration to the evidence which pointed to the surrender. There was, inter alia, a letter sent by recorded delivery from B which spelt out the terms of the surrender and showed that B would not be responsible for any future liabilities or rent. The decision was quashed and remitted back to a differently constituted bench.

BARAKAT v. EALING LBC [1996] 36 R.V.R. 138, Brooke, J., QBD.

3711. Business tenancies–rates–whether tenant liable for rates after vacated property as result of forfeiture proceedings

[Local Government Finance Act 1988 s.45.]

K appealed against the decision that M was not liable for failure to pay non-domestic rates for business premises under the Local Government Finance Act 1988 s.45. After a dispute, M's landlord issued proceedings against M for damages and forfeiture. M only defended the damages proceedings and then vacated the premises and gave written notice to the landlord of his intention to relinquish the tenancy. K proceeded against M for payment of non-domestic rates for the period following vacation of the premises, claiming that, until a court order had been obtained confirming the end of the landlord tenant relationship, M was still entitled to possession and was therefore liable for the rates.

Held, dismissing the appeal, that M's acceptance of the forfeiture by vacating the premises terminated his liability toward the property. From such time the landlord became responsible for any liabilities arising from the property, including the payment of non-domestic rates.

KINGSTON UPON THAMES RBC v. MARLOW [1996] 1 E.G.L.R. 101, Simon Brown, L.J., QBD.

3712. Business tenancies–restrictive covenants–right of freehold pre-emption–quantification of damages for loss resulting from breach

H appealed against a decision refining specific performance of a leasehold covenant. The covenant granted H pre-emption rights over freehold premises in which H occupied the top floor as tenant under a 999 year lease with a peppercorn rent at an initial price of £119,000. H claimed that S, the freehold owner, who operated a commercial garage business from the ground floor of the premises, was in breach of the covenant for leasing the ground floor to another party for a 16 year term, without notifying H of his pre emption rights. G, the owner of an adjoining property, had offered H £300,000 for a 100 year lease of the ground floor, on the exercise of his pre-emption.

Held, allowing the appeal, that (1) the court had to determine whether the loss sustained by H was recoverable, bearing in mind the circumstances and giving a meaning to the parties' bargain consistent with their intentions; (2) a pre-emption right had been agreed by the parties based on an open market value which was to fixed in default by an arbitrator applying RICS guidelines. That did not mean that the purchase of the property by buyers with a special interest in it was not in the reasonable contemplation of the parties; (3) the increase in the value of the property was due to competitive market forces; in particular the demand for commercial property near the West End. Fluctuations in value owing to market forces must have been within the reasonable contemplation of the parties when H's lease was granted and (4) the judge was wrong to refuse H's claim and damages were assessed in the sum of £102,500.

HOMSY v. MURPHY; SUB NOM. HOMSEY v. SEARLE [1996] E.G.C.S. 43, Beldam, L.J., CA.

3713. Business tenancies–restrictive covenants–without prejudice statement in letter did not negate appellants' right to amend pleadings

[Law of Property Act 1925 s.146.]

M applied for leave to amend their defence in proceedings where P claimed injunctive relief and damages against M for breach of a covenant in a lease by using a site as a car park. P granted the lease of the site to M in order to build a hotel. The development was delayed and in the meantime the vacant site was used as a car park. P served a notice under the Law of Property Act 1925 s.146 and, just before its expiry, M issued an originating summons for relief from forfeiture. M wrote to P requesting P's consent for the temporary use of the land as a car park, on the basis that the request was made "without prejudice" to the application under the s.146 notice. The phrase was included in the body of the letter rather than being at its head. M's application to amend their defence, allowing them to plead unreasonable withholding of consent was refused, owing to the use of the "without prejudice" phrase in the letter to P.

Held, allowing the appeal, that (1) the phrase "without prejudice" could have more than one meaning. When used in the compromise process it usually appeared in the heading of a letter, not within the text; (2) since the phrase was used within the body of the text its other meanings had to be considered and it could be used without any compromise regarding previous rights or claims and (3) from the context in which "without prejudice" was used in the letter and other subsequent correspondence the phrase was clearly given with the latter meaning. It did not indicate the commencement of litigation but merely indicated an intention to seek compromise without giving up the right to seek redress through the courts.

PETERBOROUGH CITY COUNCIL v. MANCHESTER DEVELOPMENTS LTD [1996] E.G.C.S. 50, Waite, L.J., CA.

3714. Business tenancies–service charges–building of leisure units did not entitle landlords to demand higher service charges

C claimed arrears of service charges plus interest owed to them by M. C owned a shopping centre, part of which it leased to M for use as an indoor leisure complex. M covenanted to pay a proportionate part of the service charge. Under the preamble to the sixth schedule of the lease C was obliged to make sure that leisure tenants paid a reasonable proportion of the maintained area service costs and to pass on to them any exceptional costs of maintaining services and facilities. M disputed the charge and claimed that the lease did not reflect the true intention of the parties.

Held, giving judgment for C, that (1) the lease did not place retail tenants under an obligation to pay a greater service charge than would have been the case if the leisure units had never been built; (2) for the purposes of rectification there was no prior agreement which the lease had failed to incorporate, the terms of the leases being specifically referred to in the sixth schedule; (3) the commercial object of the lease was to give effect to C's obligations, as already undertaken in the project's earlier phases, not to separate retail and other uses and (4) the landlord's claim for indemnity costs was disallowed with costs being awarded on the standard basis, *Church Commissioners for England v. Ibrahim* [1996] E.G.C.S. 25, [1997] 4 C.L. 401 distinguished.

CHURCH COMMISSIONERS FOR ENGLAND v. METROLAND LTD [1996] E.G.C.S. 44, Judge Baker Q.C., Ch D.

3715. Business tenancies–supermarkets–keep open covenant–specific performance

CIS, the landlord of a retail premises used as a supermarket comprising the main unit in a shopping centre, appealed against an order for damages and a refusal to grant specific performance requiring the tenant, AS, to keep the supermarket open for the remainder of the 35 year lease which began in 1979. AS had made a loss and decided to sell, whereupon the supermarket had been stripped out. CIS argued that a "keep open" covenant in the lease should be enforced as prolonged closure of the premises would have a harmful effect on the rest of the shopping centre.

Held, allowing the appeal, that although an award of damages was usually the appropriate remedy for breach of a "keep open" covenant, in the circumstances specific performance should be ordered as the terms of the covenant were clearly defined and AS was a substantial company who had undertaken to keep the premises open for a stipulated period, *Braddon Towers Ltd v. International Stores Ltd* [1987] 1 E.G.L.R. 209 considered. Furthermore CIS had made provision that the lease could be assigned to another tenant. Its loss would not be fully compensated by an award of damages and the losses of other business tenants in the centre were irrecoverable. Millett, L.J., dissenting, argued that an order for specific performance for an indefinite period was oppressive where a company would be compelled to continue an unviable business and might be exposed to losses disproportionate to the nature of the breach.

COOPERATIVE INSURANCE SOCIETY LTD v. ARGYLL STORES (HOLDINGS) LTD [1996] Ch. 286, Leggatt, L.J., CA.

3716. Business tenancies–termination–continuation after contractual expiry due to operation of Landlord and Tenant Act 1954–statutory interpretation

[Landlord and Tenant Act 1954 s.24, s.27.]

The second plaintiffs sub-underlet part of an office block to the defendants. The first plaintiffs sub-let the whole of the office block on the same day to the defendant, subject to the sub-lease. The parties were in dispute as to the termination of the underlease and the sub-underlease further to the Landlord and Tenant Act 1954. The defendants contended that the lease terminated contractually on February 14, 1993. The defendants vacated the premises by February 15, 1993 and contended that by that time s.24 of the 1954 Act could not prolong the tenancy. No notice which satisfied s.27 of the 1954 Act had been served by that date.

Held, that where the issue is whether the Act has affected the respective positions of the parties, it will usually be enough to enquire whether the tenancy has been caught by the Act at some point during its duration. While s.24(1) operates in one sense so as to extend the life of the tenancy only after the contractual term date, it has already operated before that date to the extent that it has provided a substitute for the common law method of terminating the tenancy, the common law method of termination, effluxion of time, having been replaced by the apparatus of notices. On the facts, the tenancy continued pursuant to the provisions of the Act, notwithstanding cessor of business occupation, *Long Acre Securities v. Electro Acoustic Industries* [1990] E.G.L.R. 91, [1990] C.L.Y. 2778 followed.

ESSELTE AB v. PEARL ASSURANCE PLC (1996) 72 P. & C.R. 21, Judge Colyer Q.C., Ch D.

3717. Business tenancies–termination–notice served on January 12 although anniversary of lease was on 13th–whether notice valid

M, the tenants, and E, the landlord, entered into two leases. A term stated that M could determine the lease on January 13, 1995, provided that not less than six months' notice in writing was given. By two letters dated June 24, 1994, M gave notice to E to determine the lease on January 12, 1995. The High Court held that these notices, though expressed to determine the lease on January 12, were effective to determine them on January 13, 1995. E appealed. M argued that, although the notices referred to January 12 it was clear that their effect was to determine the leases on January 13, being the only date on which they could have been determined. Alternatively, the notices did not take effect until that moment of time which was both the last moment of January 12, and the first moment of January 13, so that they did determine the lease on January 13.

Held, allowing the appeal, that the notices were invalid. *Hankey v. Clavering* [1942] 2 K.B. 326 and *Carradine Properties Ltd v. Aslam* [1976] 1 W.L.R. 442, [1976] C.L.Y. 1551 applied. If a notice clearly and specifically purported to determine a demise for a fixed term on a date not authorised by the lease, the date could not be corrected simply because it was clear what the correct date ought to be, that the wrong date was inserted and that the recipient might guess or even be certain that that was what had happened. An exception could only be made where the date specified was an impossibility, either because it had passed or because on some other ground it was inconceivable that it was the date intended. The notices in the present case, having clearly and specifically purported to determine the lease on a date which had not passed and could conceivably have been the date intended, did not fall within the exception. The two moments of time, although only one day apart, had always been treated as separate.

MANNAI INVESTMENT CO LTD v. EAGLE STAR LIFE ASSURANCE CO LTD [1995] 1 W.L.R. 1508, Nourse, L.J., CA.

3718. Business tenancies–warrant for possession issued in respect of rent assets–failure to enforce possession order–whether letter concerning new lease gave rise to binding agreement for new lease–whether possession order could be enforced

[Law of Property (Miscellaneous Provisions) Act 1989 s.2.]

E appealed against an order setting aside a warrant for possession of property consisting of a shop and residential accommodation let to E and two others. E had failed to enforce a possession order issued in view of £34,000 rent arrears. However, E wrote to the third named defendant, P, and expressed the letter as being without prejudice and subject to contract. The letter referred to the need to complete a new lease by a specified date, gave the main terms of it, and asked P to return an acceptance slip. A year later, E applied for leave to issue a warrant for possession. P had this set aside on the basis that E had made an offer to the defendants to commence a new agreement, under new terms, that the defendants had accepted the offer, and that a new lease comprising both premises had come into force. Two bankers' orders were drafted, one related to the paying off of the arrears and the second the proposed rent under the new lease.

Held, allowing the appeal, that (1) E did not negotiate the banker's drafts which in fact were insufficient to cover either the arrears or new rent and (2) the letter concerning the new lease was very obviously on a "without prejudice" and "subject to contract" basis, thereby making it part of prior negotiations to a draft lease being drawn up. Thus, there was no new formal letting arrangement between the parties.

ENFIELD LBC v. ARAJAH [1995] E.G.C.S. 164, Sir Thomas Bingham, M.R., CA.

3719. Closing orders–local authority decision to make closure order–whether unreasonable due to loss of rental income–decision based on economic and socio environmental assessments

[Housing Act 1985.]

Following years of complaints by C to S about the state of disrepair of their rented accommodation, S determined that for the purposes of the Housing Act 1985 Part.VI and Part.IX an order for closure was "the most satisfactory course of action". S had carried out an economic assessment which showed closure to be more economically favourable than repair, and a socio environmental assessment the result of which was neutral as between closure and repair. C's application for judicial review on the basis that S had acted unreasonably in failing to take into account, inter alia, the possible rent that might be earned by the property during the statutory thirty year period, was dismissed at first instance.

Held, dismissing the appeal, that the judge was right to conclude that this was not a case which entitled the court to interfere with S's decision by way of judicial review. In respect of both the economic and socio environmental assessments, no evidence revealed errors in either the calculations or the proper weight given to the occupiers' wishes. The matters referred to by C in support of their argument, such as the possibility of the property becoming vacant within the thirty year period, were such as could affect both sides of the equation.

R. v. SOUTHWARK LBC, *ex p.* CORDWELL (1995) 27 H.L.R. 594, Balcombe, L.J., CA.

3720. Damages–breach of landlord's repair covenant–whether mortgagee suffered loss

R, the landlord, appealed against an order that he pay to C, the second mortgagees of the lease, the sum of £30,000 in damages for breach of a landlord's repairing covenant in a long lease of a flat. The first mortgage was for £17,000 and the second for £2,000. The tenants defaulted on their repayments and C went into possession with the first mortgagee's agreement. The property suffered from subsidence and the first mortgagee was paid £23,000 under an insurance policy for loss caused by subsidence. C and the tenants had no such insurance cover. R argued that his failure to repair the subsidence caused C no loss because if the work had been done and the flat sold, C would have received nothing from the proceeds.

Held, allowing the appeal, that if R had effected the repairs and the lease was sold it would have raised £34,500. Once the first mortgagee had redeemed its mortgage, C would have been entitled to the amount due under the second mortgage which amounted to £4,520. That figure had to be set against two thirds of the cost of the repairs which C were liable to pay to R under the lease. That would have left C with nothing. C could have argued that the tenants would have been entitled to the sums recovered under the first mortgagee's insurance policy for the cost of the repairs; however, no argument was made on that point and no policy was adduced in evidence. The order for damages was quashed and replaced with an order for £2.

CASTLE PHILLIPS FINANCE CO LTD v. RAJA, Trans. Ref: QBENI 95/0200/E, March 19, 1996, Sir Ralph Gibson, CA.

3721. Damages–nuisance–cockroach infestation–distress and anxiety–premises declared prejudicial to health

[Environmental Protection Act 1990 s.79.]

P had a secure tenancy from January 1982 to December 1991 in a Southwark council flat. From 1986, the flat was seriously infested with ants and cockroaches. Despite numerous complaints to S, treatment was slow in coming, and ineffectual. By 1990 the infestation was extremely serious, cockroaches were in the fridge, freezer and oven. The furniture had cockroaches nesting in it. Cockroaches crawled out of the TV and the telephones. The bedding had to be checked every day. P kept little food in the flat, and stopped heating it. She and her young daughter increasingly ate out and stayed with relatives. Finally, in July 1991, P, receiving medical treatment for depression related to her housing situation, moved out. In November, an Environmental Health Officer inspected the premises and declared it to be prejudicial to health, and constituting a nuisance under the Environmental Protection Act 1990 s.79(1)(a). P was offered alternative accommodation in December 1991, but was advised not to take her possessions with her as they could infest the new property, so she abandoned all her possessions and was therefore unable to furnish the new flat.

Held, that she was entitled to general damages of £17,490, and special damages of £11,160, *Clark v. Wandsworth LBC* L.A.G. June 1994 and 1995 applied.

McGUIGAN v. SOUTHWARK LBC; CLARK v. WANDSWORTH LBC, September 15, 1995, Recorder Rose, CC. [*Ex rel.* Tracy Bloom, Barrister].

3722. Damages–quiet enjoyment–breach by landlord–measure of damages

M, who shared a property with a group of others, owed C, their landlord, arrears of rent of about £400. C sent M a fax at her work demanding that she leave the property within the following four days. This was followed by something purporting to be a "notice before action", demanding £4,807, which represented the amount owed in respect of the entire property for the remaining term of the tenancy. C, who claimed to run a large property company, knew that he was not entitled to immediate possession, and that such a sum could not have been payable. M, whose duties at work included security, felt embarrassed by the letters, particularly the suggestion that she was substantially in debt.

Held, the district judge found that the letters had been sent for the purpose of embarrassing M, and that this constituted a breach of the covenant of quiet enjoyment. He awarded M £750, to be offset against £220 rent arrears, and £92 for dilapidation owed to C. M was also awarded £5 for a trifling trespass by C.

MOLYNEUX-CHILD v. COE, September 13, 1996, District Judge Stephen Gold, CC (Guildford). [*Ex rel.* Richard Colbey, Barrister].

3723. Damages–residential tenancies–deterioration of bedsit–uninhabitable

P rented a bedsit for £30 per week. Rainwater came through the kitchen roof, a leaking sink and broken gutter caused a damp patch in the bed/sitting room. Owing to the damp, there was mould on the kitchen carpet and wallpaper had peeled off the bed/sitting room wall. After the entry of judgment in default, the court found that the bedsit had deteriorated over a period of six years so that at the end of that period it bordered on the uninhabitable. General damages were assessed at an average annual rate of £1,500 over six years. Had it not been statute-barred, the judge would have awarded annual general damages of £300 for the pre *Limitation Act* period. With special damages, the total award was £10,000.

PIERRE v. GASPER, March 7, 1996, H.H.J. Goldstein, CC (Bow). [*Ex rel.* Jon Holbrook, Barrister].

3724. Damages–residential tenancies–negligence–landlord failing to deal with leak on premises

On the night of December 30, 1995, a 64 year old woman suffering from osteoporosis and cancer awoke to discover water coming through her ceiling. She reported this immediately to LBC who failed to enter the property above, owned by A, for a further five days. After seven days the water ceased to come through the ceiling into M's bedroom. Liability was conceded by LBC. M was impecunious and could not afford to replace her orthopaedic bed that had been irretrievably damaged by the water. She slept on the sofa or the floor for three months and then a friend lent her a bed which she slept on for the remaining seven months until the trial. That bed was not orthopaedic and was therefore not as comfortable as M's previous bed. The district judge awarded general damages of £700 of which £140 was for the first week, £260 for the next three months and £300 for the seven months to trial. In making an award of this size the judge took into account M's ill health, and her history of depression that had been aggravated by this incident and its sequelae. Special damages of £326 were also awarded.

MACKIE v. AFFIYRE AND LAMBETH LBC, October 19, 1996, District Judge Jacey, CC (Lambeth). [*Ex rel.* David McIlroy, Barrister].

3725. Damages–residential tenancies–premises in disrepair–landlord's failure to act

R let a flat to L on January 10, 1993 at a rent of £200 per month (paid in large part by the local authority). The flat had a large and small bedroom, a shower room, a kitchen and a living room. L had a 20 month old son. The flat had severe damp penetration and condensation which caused mould growth on walls, bedding and clothing. R was put on notice of the defects by a solicitor's letter of March 19, 1993. Further correspondence followed and on July 16, 1993 a surveyor's report detailing the defects was served on R. On July 26, 1993 the local council serviced a notice on R requiring her to carry out re-plastering to damp areas in the living room, large bedroom and shower room. In September 1993 the works to the living room were completed in accordance with the council's notice but R chose to use antifungal paint in the large bedroom and bathroom and did not renew the plaster. The works to the living room took three weeks instead of three days. The damp problem was rectified in the living room, but remained in the large bedroom and shower room. L's son suffered an exacerbation of his asthma and frequent colds as a result of the damp conditions. On most weekends L stayed at her mother's premises and she went out most days. L left the premises in August 1994 and and proceedings were commenced later in 1994.

Held, that the letter of March 19, 1993 constituted notice of the defects and a reasonable time for completion was by mid-May 1993. The premises were in disrepair as a result of the damp penetration which significantly contributed to the condensation problems at the flat because it made the walls cold (and therefore susceptible to condensation) and because it increased the moisture content in the atmosphere within the flat. The value of the tenancy was diminished by 30 per cent of the rental value, ie. £60 per month which from mid-May to August amounted to £900. The judge awarded £1,500 damages for distress, inconvenience and ill-health over that 15 month period, assessed at £100 per month. An order was also made for the return of part of the bond and special damages were awarded. Although the total award was less than £3,000, the judge accepted that the case was of sufficient complexity, involving expert evidence and taking two full days, to warrant an order for costs in L's favour on Scale 2.

LLOYD v. REES, September 12, 1996, H.H.J. Morton, CC (Pontypridd). [*Ex rel.* Robert O'Leary, Barrister].

3726. Damages–residential tenancies–property in poor condition

The tenants and their two young children occupied an old terraced house from May 1991 to May 1994. The landlord accepted at the outset of the tenancy that the property was in poor condition and agreed to pay for the costs of labour and materials for any work carried out by the tenants. The cellars were extremely damp, the front door was draughty, there was damaged plasterwork throughout the house, the kitchen floor was damp, most of the windows were rotten and dilapidated, there was penetrating damp into two of the bedrooms, the toilet leaked, the gas fire in the rear bedroom was not working, and there was penetrating damp into both attic rooms. In August 1993, the landlord sent round a workman who commenced installing Velux windows in the attic and stripped the slates off half the roof. The workman then left, leaving the Velux windows unfinished and half the roof unslated. During the following winter, rain and snow penetrated into the attic and the rest of the house.

Held, that the following damages be awarded: diminution in value at 50 per cent from May 1991 to August 1993 and at 75 per cent from August 1993 to May 1994. The total award for diminution of value was £7,260; inconvenience, discomfort and distress; £1,000 for each plaintiff up to August 1993, and £759 for each plaintiff for the remainder of the tenancy (one of the children was a plaintiff). The total per plaintiff for inconvenience, discomfort and distress was £3,000; special damages for damage to property, £400; personal injury damage for exacerbation of the second plaintiff's asthma, £150, and for exacerbation of the third plaintiff's asthma, £500. The total damages, excluding interest, were £15,092.

SHIELDS v. HUSSAIN, March 19, 1996, District Judge Heath, CC (Leeds). [*Ex rel.* Sarah Greenan, Barrister].

3727. Distress–walking possession agreement executed–possession of hire van–whether in reputed ownership of tenants

[Law of Distress Amendment Act 1908 s.4.]

B were the owners of factory premises which they leased to tenants. On February 26, 1992 B distrained for rent and executed a walking possession agreement on goods on the premises. On May 5, 1992 B took close possession of a Mercedes van hired by the tenants but which was owned by S. S served a notice on B under the Law of Distress Amendment Act 1908 s.1 but B proceeded to sell the van for £6100. S appealed against the decision that the van was in the reputed ownership of the tenants.

Held, allowing the appeal, that the van was not in the ownership of the tenants but merely on hire to them. B were required to show that the tenants owned the van and it was not sufficient to just prove probability. Therefore B could not rely on the protection afforded by the Law of Distress Amendment Act 1908 s.4, *Fox, Re* [1948] Ch. 407, [1947-51] C.L.C. 704 applied.

SALFORD VAN HIRE (CONTRACTS) LTD v. BOCHOLT DEVELOPMENTS LTD [1996] R.T.R. 103, Hirst, L.J., CA.

3728. Eviction–damages for unlawful eviction–value of landlord's interest

[Housing Act 1988 s.27, s.28; Housing Act 1985 s.609.]

B, a landlord, appealed against an award of damages to M, a tenant, under the Housing Act 1988 s.27 and s.28 in respect of her unlawful eviction from part of a freehold property owned by B. The property had originally been owned by the local authority and B's predecessor in title acquired the freehold on the basis of a restrictive covenant forbidding use of the premises other than as a private dwelling house in single occupation. Despite the existence of this covenant, there were already two other people occupying part of the premises when M was granted a secure shorthold tenancy. When B evicted M by excluding her from the property and removing her possessions, the county court recorder awarded damages of £15,000 based on an estimate by M's valuer, in accordance with s.28, of the difference between the landlord's interest in the property immediately before M's eviction and the value of that interest once M had ceased to occupy the premises. B's valuer had proposed a smaller figure, but both valuers had, in carrying out their assessment, assumed vacant possession and ignored the existence of the other occupants. B contended, relying on *Jones & Lee v. Miah & Miah* (1992) 24 H.L.R. 578, [1992] C.L.Y. 2675, that the comparison undertaken by the valuers should have been on a factual rather than a notional basis, and should have taken account of the interests of those occupants. M argued that the Housing Act 1985 s.609 gave the local authority the right to enforce the restrictive covenant against those remaining in occupation and that their interests should be regarded as frustrated.

Held, allowing the appeal, that whilst under s.609 of the 1985 Act the local authority had a right to enforce the covenants against the successors in title of the convenantor, they had no such right against the occupants. There was nothing in the 1988 Act to prevent a conclusion that a landlord might not have increased his interest in the property as a result of the eviction. Clearly, had the valuers taken into account the existence of the other occupants, they would have concluded that the value of B's interest had not increased. The award of £15,000 would be set aside.

MELVILLE v. BRUTON [1996] E.G.C.S. 57, Hutchison, L.J., CA.

3729. Eviction–hotel accommodation–whether a tenancy existed for protection under the Housing Act 1988–whether a licence existed for protection under the Protection from Eviction Act 1977

[Housing Act 1988; Protection from Eviction Act 1977.]

B appealed against a decision rejecting his application for an injunction preventing his eviction from a hotel. B argued that he was a tenant and protected from eviction by the Housing Act 1988 and the Protection from Eviction Act 1977.

Held, dismissing the appeal, that (1) to claim protection under the 1988 Act it was necessary to demonstrate the existence of a tenancy. Due to the lack of exclusive possession shown by B, who had taken advantage of some of the facilities of the hotel, a tenancy did not exist and (2) B could claim protection under the 1977 Act by showing that he was a licensee. However, on consideration of all the circumstances of the case, the judge held that B was merely a hotel guest booking accommodation at a daily rate.

BRILLOUET v. LANDLESS (1996) 28 H.L.R. 836, Russell, L.J., CA.

3730. Eviction–removal of beds and fridge–refusal to allow collection of clothes and personal possessions

P were joint assured tenants of a three bedroomed flat owned by D. Six months after P moved in, the council had paid no housing benefit to P, and P had not paid their rent to D (£135 per week). D moved into the flat with his wife and two children in a peaceful eviction. The day after this, D's wife refused to allow P to pick up some clothes and personal possessions. D then failed to respond to a request for readmission from P's solicitors. After obtaining an interlocutory injunction, P were readmitted 15 days later. During this time, P had been sleeping on the floors and sofas of friends, had been denied access to all their possessions, and on getting back into the flat, realised that D had thrown out the beds and fridge which he had previously provided.

Held, that each plaintiff should receive general damages of £2,250 (assessed as £150 per night), and aggravated damages of £1,000 (owing to D's failure to readmit P as requested, and owing to the removal of the beds and fridge). From this total award of £6,500 was set off an agreed sum of £3,392 in unpaid rent, leaving a net balance of £3,108 to be shared by P.

ALTUN AND ULKER v. PATEL, November 20, 1995, Tibber, J., CC. [*Ex rel.* Jon Holbrook, Barrister].

3731. Flats–flat sharing facilities–written agreement–services provided–defendant moved to another room–services wound down–whether tenancy or licence

R appealed against a decision which found that he was a licensee of a room in a flat owned by H and that H was entitled to possession. R had originally entered into an agreement to occupy another room in the flat which did not constitute a tenancy. The rent included laundry and cleaning services. The move to the new room was not recorded by further documentation. H had a key and the services provided were wound down gradually.

Held, dismissing the appeal, that (1) before the judge could decide whether possession could be resisted it was necessary to determine whether the occupation amounted to a licence or a tenancy; (2) the judge had looked at the differences between the contracts for the two rooms; (3) the relationship was that of licensee and licensor due to the provision of services and access to the room; (4) R was still entitled to services and (5) the right to access was not a sham and the same contractual rules applied when R changed rooms.

HUWYLER v. RUDDY (1996) 28 H.L.R. 550, Peter Gibson, L.J., CA.

3732. Flats–grant of new lease–storeroom on different floor an "appurtenance" and within new lease–statutory interpretation

[Leasehold Reform Act 1967; Leasehold Reform, Housing and Urban Development Act 1993 s.62.]

C, the landlord, appealed against a decision that a storeroom was an "appurtenance" of a flat within the Leasehold Reform, Housing and Urban Development Act 1993 s.62(2) which meant that it formed part of a new lease granted to M under the provisions of the 1993 Act. M had entered into a separate agreement for use of the storeroom on the same date on which the lease was entered. C argued that, to be an appurtenance, the storeroom had to be within the curtilage of the flat and had to be capable of passing under an assignment of the flat without express reference.

Held, dismissing the appeal, that (1) the storeroom was not part of the flat, as the flat was on the second floor and the storeroom was on the sixth floor and could just as well be used by tenants of other flats; (2) the storeroom was not an outhouse as an outhouse had to be outside the building and within its grounds and (3) the storeroom was an "appurtenance" and did not need to be able to pass under an assignment without express mention, but had to belong to or be enjoyed with the flat. The 1993 Act applied to flats, whereas the definition relied upon by C in *Methuen-Campbell v. Walters* [1979] Q.B. 525,

[1979] C.L.Y. 1607 related to the Leasehold Reform Act 1967 which concerned houses, *Methuen-Campbell* distinguished. It was adequate that the storeroom was within the premises of which the flat was part or was within the curtilage of the block of flats. That definition was borne out by the fact that Parliament would not have intended a storeroom to be excluded if the tenants of a block of flats had exercised their collective rights.

CADOGAN v. McGIRK; SUB NOM. VISCOUNT CHELSEA & CADOGAN ESTATES v. McGIRK [1996] 4 All E.R. 643, Millett, L.J., CA.

3733. Housing management–multiple occupation–collection of housing benefit cheques did not amount to receipt of rent–payments included meter monies–statutory interpretation of "other payments"

[Housing Act 1985 s.398; Housing (Management of Houses in Multiple Occupation) Regulations 1990.]

J appealed by way of case stated against conviction of offences under the Housing (Management of Houses in Multiple Occupation) Regulations 1990 for which he was fined £200. J was found to be the "person managing" the property within the Housing Act 1985 s.398(6) as amended. J had collected money from gas and electricity meters, arrears of rent, and top-up payments where the tenant was in receipt of housing benefit. J argued that no inference could be drawn that he was the person managing the property as he had not collected arrears or top-up payments since 1990. Furthermore, the collection of housing benefit cheques made payable to the landlord and their payment into the landlord's bank account did not constitute the receipt of rents or other payments within the terms of s.398(6) of the 1985 Act. He also argued that the meter monies did not come within the definition of "other payments" in s.398(6)(b). The words should be narrowly interpreted as meaning the same type of payment as rent.

Held, dismissing the appeal, that (1) payments had not been received by J since 1990, and no inference could be drawn that he was still in receipt of them; (2) there was insufficient evidence that J was the "person managing" in terms of s.398(6)b) of the 1985; (3) the collection of housing benefit cheques, as in the facts of the present case, did not amount to receipt of rent or other payments and (4) "other payments" in terms of s.398(6)(b) were monies, other than rent, received by the landlord in the ordinary course of the lease or licence. In this case the meter monies were included in such payments.

JACQUES v. LIVERPOOL CITY COUNCIL (1996) 72 P. & C.R. D19, McKinnon, J., QBD.

3734. Injunctions–harassment by landlord–wrongfully entering property–measure of damages

[Leasehold Reform, Housing and Urban Development Act 1993 s.76.]

The plaintiffs were long leaseholders of three holiday chalets in a marina development of approximately 100 chalets owned and managed by IM. The plaintiffs, and many other members of the Resident's Association, were in dispute with the landlord concerning service charges and the association had arranged a management audit under the Leasehold Reform, Housing and Urban Development Act 1993 s.76. Despite the fact that other tenants had applied for an injunction against harassment, in respect of which undertakings had been given by the landlord only six months earlier, that proceedings had been issued by the association against the landlord for repayment of excessive charges, and that the landlord had issued proceedings against the plaintiffs for non-payment of the service charges for the present year, the landlord arranged for workmen wrongfully to enter the sub-floor of each chalet and saw one foot lengths out of each sewage pipe, rendering the plaintiff's premises uninhabitable. A notice was then sent to each plaintiff explaining what had been done. Use by the plaintiffs, or lettings to third parties, was prevented for about a week, and the plaintiffs were put to inconvenience in organising repairs and re-arranging visits.

Held, that although the damage caused was not substantial, aggravated damages of £500 would be awarded to each plaintiff. Had the landlord not warned the plaintiffs of what it had done, but merely left them to find out for themselves later, then the incident would have been viewed as more serious.

KING JACKSON & DODD v. ISLEHAM MARINA LTD, October 8, 1996, District Judge Kirby, CC (Cambridge). [*Ex rel.* Graham Sinclair, Barrister].

3735. Insolvency–assignment–repairs–whether flat owner should be permitted to take up right of action under assignment

[Rules of the Supreme Court Ord.15 r.7.]

S appealed against the decision of the court below in refusing to make an order under the Rules of the Supreme Court Ord.15 r.7(2) which would allow S to carry on proceedings after the freehold company which was partly owned by S assigned its right of action against C following its liquidation. CM had employed C to carry out major repair and refurbishment works on the communal parts of the leasehold flat which it managed. S was employed as an architectural consultant and it was proposed that S would pay 46 per cent of the cost of incorporating her flat into the common parts of the project and that C was to supervise repairs to be carried out by the builders. C further reached an agreement with a firm of architects employed by D in relation to their supervisory duties as architects. Certificates for work done were issued by C, however, S's flat was in a badly damaged state when the certification of completion was issued. The company claimed damages of £46,000 against S, but S counterclaimed against them and included C as a third party.

Held, allowing the appeal, that (1) the court had to balance any potential damage to the administration of justice against damage caused to the parties where there was further delay; (2) the official referee failed to consider the damage to S if she was prevented from continuing her claim and (3) the damage caused to S was the overriding consideration.

SAIGOL v. CRANLEY MANSIONS LTD [1996] E.G.C.S. 81, Henry, L.J., CA.

3736. Joint tenancies–trustees–notice to acquire freehold–both tenants to be joined in notice or one to authorise service by other

[Leasehold Reform Act 1967 s.8, s.6.]

W, one of two joint tenants of a house, served a notice on C, the landlord, of a claim under the Leasehold Reform Act 1967 s.8(1) to acquire the freehold. C contested the validity of the notices contending that W and his wife were joint proprietors of the lease as shown on the land register and, as trustees of the legal estate, both had to join in the s.8 notice.

Held, dismissing the application, that both joint tenants as trustees of the legal estate had to join in the notice or one might serve a notice with the authority of the other as provided by s.6(3) of the 1967 Act.

WAX v. CHELSEA (VISCOUNT) [1996] 41 E.G. 169, Judge Green Q.C., CC (Central London).

3737. Leasehold valuation tribunals–rent assessment committees

RENT ASSESSMENT COMMITTEE (ENGLAND AND WALES) (LEASEHOLD VALUATION TRIBUNAL) (AMENDMENT) REGULATIONS 1996, SI 1996 2305; made under the Rent Act 1977 s.74. In force: October 1, 1996; £1.10.

The jurisdiction of leasehold valuation tribunals is extended by the Housing Act 1996 to include applications under the new Landlord and Tenant Act 1987 s.8C. Leasehold valuation tribunals also have jurisdiction to determine questions arising under s.13 of the 1987 Act which is amended by the Housing Act 1996. These Regulations amend the Rent Assessment Committee (England and Wales) (Leasehold Valuation Tribunal) Regulations 1993 by substituting, for the reference in Reg.2 (interpretation) of those Regulations to s.13 of the 1987 Act, a reference to the new s.13. They also add Sch.1 para.15A to those Regulations. The new paragraph relates to applications to the tribunal under the new s.8C(4) of the 1987 Act, which may be made where a landlord has offered to dispose of property for a consideration that does not consist, or does not wholly consist, of money, and has received a notice indicating an intention to accept that offer. The tribunal may be asked to determine the equivalent monetary value of the non-monetary consideration so that, as s.8C(4) provides, that consideration may be treated for the purposes of s.11 to s.17 of the 1987 Act as an amount in money. The particulars to be provided to the tribunal in accordance with the new para.15A are of the non-monetary consideration.

3738. Leaseholds–enfranchisement–freehold reversion–landlord's costs–valuation costs–fees claimed not related to disbursements

[Leasehold Reform Act 1967 s.9.]

Following the determination of the price payable for a freehold reversion by the Land Tribunal, AE, a property investment company, claimed in addition to its solicitors' conveyancing costs, "vendor's surveyor's fees of £262 and fees in connection with the service of the Leasehold Reform Act notice £100". An accompanying bill for £100 listed eight heads, including "Receiving Leasehold Reform notice, checking property register, letter to your solicitor asking for information in respect of title". J, the tenant, claimed that as AE's valuer was one of its directors, AE had not incurred valuation costs, and that if there was a valuation it had been made after an application was made by J to the Land Tribunal, and was thus not payable by J. As to the other costs claimed, these were not disbursements incurred by AE, being items not referred to in the Leasehold Reform Act 1967 s.9(4)(a) and were unreasonable. AE submitted that its director was an independent self-employed valuer who had prepared a valuation prior to J's application to the Land Tribunal (not disclosed by discovery) and who was entitled to be reimbursed for the time spent in investigating AE's right to enfranchise.

Held, disallowing AE's valuation costs, that they were entirely artificial. The valuation was carried out in AE's offices by the director who ran the leasehold enfranchisement side of the business. A system had been established whereby once the director had received a notice of leaseholder's claim, he would get his brother, also a director, to write him a letter requesting from him a valuation of the property concerned. In that letter, the brother would give the director information on the lease and ground rent, which the director had in fact supplied to his brother in the first place. It was not a professional valuation, but a calculation of the property's worth completed from the information readily available in AE's offices. The court also disallowed AE's costs of investigating J's right to acquire the freehold, holding that AE's request for fees implied that AE had had to pay fees to somebody else. Many of the items mentioned in AE's bill would simply have incurred no cost whatever and none necessitated any payment of a third party by AE.

JONES v. AVON ESTATES, January 12, 1996, H.H.J. Hall, CC (Stratford-on-Avon). [*Ex rel.* Margetts & Ritchie, Solicitors].

3739. Leaseholds–enfranchisement–landlord selling freehold without offering tenants of flats first option–meaning of "premises"–landlord's duty to comply with purchase notice

[Landlord and Tenant Act 1987 s.1, s.12.]

K and other tenants of flats appealed against the dismissal of their application for a declaration that they were entitled to buy the reversionary interest from T, the landlords. The original landlord sold the freehold without complying with his duty under the Landlord and Tenant Act 1987 to offer the tenants first refusal and T failed to comply with a purchase notice served by the tenants under s.12 of the Act. T submitted that landlords were under no duty to comply with a s.12 notice even if it were valid, and, moreover, that the notice was invalid because it had not been served by the requisite majority of qualifying tenants. T argued that premises within the meaning of the Act included not only the tenants of the building concerned but also an adjoining property purchased at the same time and held under separate registered title.

Held, allowing the appeal, that (1) a freehold landlord served with a valid purchase notice under s.12 was under a duty to comply with the notice, and although the Act did not specifically refer to such duty, to interpret the legislation otherwise would fail to give effect to the intention stated in s.1. If there was no duty to comply, s.12 would otherwise have no purpose, and (2) whether a building was included in one or more registered titles was irrelevant to the question of whether the tenants formed a requisite majority. The word premises did not have the special meaning for which T contended, but meant only real property of some kind. Whether a relevant disposal of premises had taken place was therefore to be determined on a building by building basis.

KAY GREEN v. TWINSECTRA LTD [1996] 1 W.L.R. 1587, Aldous, L.J., CA.

3740. Leaseholds–enfranchisement–residential tenancies–reversion–valuation–assessment of freeholder cost factor using "Delaforce" effect

[Leasehold Reform Act 1967.]

A and his wife held a 99 year leasehold on a semi-detached house in Redditch built in 1971. W were the freehold owners of the property. In 1992 A served notice under the Leasehold Reform Act 1967 to take the freehold interest. At that time the unexpired portion of the lease was 77 years, with a rising ground rent. The local leasehold valuation tribunal determined that the price to be paid for the freehold was £680. W appealed, contending on the basis of the sale of the freehold interest in 500 other properties in the same area that the correct price was £1,150.

Held, allowing the appeal and substituting a price of £796, that although the unexpired portion of the lease was 77 years, the reversion still had some value. The percentage increase in value attributable to the effect described in *Delaforce v. Evans* (1970) 215 E.G. 315, [1971] C.L.Y. 6633 allegedly comparable sales lay for somewhere between the five per cent contended for by W and the 45 per cent contended for by A, and was related mainly to the freeholder costs factor. Some variation of risk rate is called for to reflect the significantly different length of the periods for which the income is fixed; at the second and third stages where the income is fixed for 33 years the highest risk rate of seven per cent should be applied. Since the first stage relates to income fixed for only 11.75 years the risk rate of 5.5 per cent should apply. The reversion, which relates to a substantially increased rental income, justifies a rate of 6.5 per cent. The resultant figure of £796 represents a *Delaforce* factor of 31 per cent.

WINDSOR LIFE ASSURANCE LTD v. AUSTIN [1996] 2 E.G.L.R. 169, M St J Hopper, FRICS., Lands Tr.

3741. Leaseholds–enfranchisement–unreliable guides to valuation for purchase of lease–Lands Tribunal evaluating importance of evidence presented

[Leasehold Reform Act 1967.]

The leasehold valuation tribunal determined the purchase price payable by W, the lessees of three semi-detached houses. W sought to acquire the freeholds under the Leasehold Reform Act 1967. S, the landlord, appealed against the purchase price decision on the basis that it should be reached solely on the basis of unchallenged evidence put before the tribunal by S's valuer. These valuations had been prepared on the basis of the sale prices of 10 similar houses let on the same terms but outside the 1967 Act and without professional advice, and also on the basis of the sale of a block of 14 ground rents secured on houses close to the houses at issue in this appeal.

Held, dismissing the appeal, that the decision of the leasehold valuation tribunal must stand until proved to be wrong. The Lands Tribunal, as an expert body, was entitled to evaluate the evidence placed before it. The valuations put forward by S's valuer were based on two categories of comparables which were unreliable pointers as to price.

SWANN v. WHITE (1996) 71 P. & C.R. 210, PH Clarke, FRICS., Lands Tr.

3742. Leaseholds–right to buy–flats

[Housing Act 1996.]

The Department of the Environment issued a press release entitled *Strengthened rights for leaseholders* (News release 399), published on October 1, 1996. New provisions under the Housing Act 1996 give new rights to leaseholders. These include changes to the right of first refusal making it a criminal offence to fail to offer the property to tenants; restriction of forfeiture of a lease for non payment of service charges; the right of a residents' association to appoint a surveyor with access to both building and landlord's documents; new grounds for the appointment by a court of a manager for a block of flats; and extending collective enfranchisement to flats where there are "flying leaseholds". Environment Secretary John Gummer, announcing the reforms, said that good landlords would welcome the measures and leaseholders would not lose their rights simply through ignorance.

3743. Leases–breach of covenant against subletting and commercial use–whether landlord held right to forfeit

K was the tenant of premises comprising a flat and lock-up garage. Under the lease terms of the lease K covenanted, inter alia, with H to (1) "Not at any time during the term hereby granted to divide the possession of the demised premises by an assignment or underletting or parting with part only" and (2) "Not to use the demised premises nor permit the same to be used for any purpose whatsoever other than as a private residential flat in the occupation of one family only". In late 1988 K sub-let the garage for commercial purposes. In 1992 H first became aware of the fact of the sub-letting. Thereafter H continued to accept rent but indicated to K that the commercial user was unacceptable. A s.146 notice was served for breach of both covenants. It was conceded at trial that breach of the non-continuous covenant (1) was waived but contended that at the date of commencement of proceedings there was a continuous breach of user which was not remedied so that H's right to forfeiture was still operative. K relied upon *Downey v. Turner* [1950] 2 K.B. 112, [1947-1951] C.L.C. 5396.

Held, giving judgment for H, that H could rely upon the breach of the user covenant because that breach did not follow, ex necessitate, from the mere fact of the sub-letting itself. The commercial user was another act on the tenant's part whereby K was at the commencement of the proceedings in continuous breach of covenant. *Downey v. Turner* was explained as an exception to the general rule and only applicable in directly similar circumstances.

HOUGHTON v. KEMP, March 29, 1994, H.H.J. Hague Q.C., CC (Slough). [*Ex rel.* Paul St J Letman, Barrister].

3744. Leases–breach of covenant not to put up signs–whether negative covenant was capable of remedy

[Law of Property Act 1925 s.146.]

S, a landlord, appealed against the dismissal of a claim for possession against H, the tenant, following H's breach of a covenant not to erect signs or carry out alterations to the premises without S's consent. S had issued a notice under the Law of Property Act 1925 s.146 which stated that the breach was incapable of remedy.

Held, dismissing the appeal, that in cases other than breach of a non-assignment covenant, breach of a negative covenant was capable of remedy. It became incapable of remedy only where a s.146 notice requiring a remedy had been served, and the lessee was permitted a reasonable period of time in which to comply and for the payment of appropriate compensation, but such compliance failed to remedy the harm which the lessor had suffered in consequence of the breach, *Expert Clothing Service and Sales Ltd v. Hillgate House Ltd* [1986] Ch. 340, [1985] C.L.Y. 1875 considered, *Billson v. Residential Apartments Ltd* (1990) 60 P. & C.R. 392, [1992] C.L.Y. 2678 not followed. S's notice should have stated the remedial action which H had to take in order to remedy the mischief and was invalid for not doing so.

SAVVA v. HUSSEIN [1996] 47 E.G. 138, Staughton, L.J., CA.

3745. Leases–effect on subtenancy on termination of superior tenancy

[Rent Act 1977 s.137.]

L granted a headlease in respect of a large divided property to K, who sublet to J. The headlease was forfeited for non-payment of rent and J claimed statutory protection for the subtenancy under the Rent Act 1977 s.137(2). The judge held that J continued to have a statutorily protected tenancy. L appealed.

Held, dismissing the appeal, that after the forfeiture of a headlease, s.137(2) of the 1977 Act operated to make a subtenant's relationship with the landlord the same as it had been with the head lessee. Accordingly, if the subtenant had been a statutory tenant of the tenant, he became a statutory tenant of the landlord and if he had been a protected tenant of the tenant he became a protected tenant of the landlord, *Leith Properties Ltd v. Springer* [1982] 3 All E.R. 731, [1982] C.L.Y. 1792 considered.

KEEPERS AND GOVERNORS OF THE POSSESSIONS, REVENUES AND GOODS OF THE FREE GRAMMAR SCHOOL OF JOHN LYON v. JAMES; SUB NOM. KEEPERS AND GOVERNORS OF THE FREE GRAMMAR SCHOOL OF JOHN LYON v. JORDAN [1995] 3 W.L.R. 908, Rose, L.J., CA.

3746. Leases–elaborate arrangement involving merger of underlease with headlease–whether tenant of a underlease allowed to acquire headlease without breach of covenant.

[Landlord and Tenant Act 1927 s.19.]

ANH applied for an order stating that it could acquire its headlease without committing a breach of covenant. ANH sought to avoid certain unfavourable conditions in the underlease by acquiring the headlease, thus extinguishing the headlease. D agreed to sell the lease to ANH with a retention of the purchase price and ANP was then to initiate proceedings to secure an order stating that the merger would not be unlawful. If successful, the retention would be paid over. Following a number of transactions and an apparent oversight, legal title to the headlease became vested in ANP on trust for ANH. ANH now wanted to acquire the legal title in order to terminate the underlease by merger. A clause existed obliging the lessee "not to be a party privy to any agreement or arrangement or commutation in whole or in part of any annual rent to be reserved and made payable on any underletting of the Premises or any part thereof in consideration thereof".

Held, granting the order, that (1) under the Landlord and Tenant Act 1927 s.19(1)(b), D lost the power to object to the assignment of the lease; (2) ANP was privy to the agreement or arrangement. There was no commutation of the annual rent because commutation required the relevant sublease to continue in existence. The retention of money was not a lump sum because it was not paid in consideration of the supposed commutation of rent; (3) there was no covenant by ANP or ANH to bring about the merger and the retention was payable whether or not the merger went ahead and (4) the vendor of the underlease was not a party to any merger and could not prove that it was privy to the agreement between ANP and the original headlessee.

ASSOCIATED NEWSPAPERS PROPERTY LTD v. DRAPERS CO [1995] N.P.C. 127, Ferris, J, Ch D.

3747. Leases–forfeiture–breach of covenant known by landlord–relief against forfeiture on condition tenant paid landlord costs–whether sufficient to show breach to establish waiver

C, the landlord, brought an action against S, the tenant, seeking possession for breach of covenant by subletting the property in contravention of the terms of the lease. The judge held that S had forfeited the lease by reason of the breach, but granted relief from forfeiture on the ground that S pay C's costs. The building society, as second defendant and to whom it seemed payment of costs would fall thus increasing the existing negative equity on the flat, appealed, requesting an order that C's claim to possession be dismissed on the grounds that she had sufficient knowledge of the breach to waive the right to forfeit the lease before she purported to do so.

Held, allowing the appeal, that it was sufficient to show that there had been a breach of covenant to establish waiver, *Metropolitan Properties Co Ltd v. Cordery* [1979] 2 E.G.L.R. 78, [1980] C.L.Y. 1645. The landlord must then do some positive act which recognised continuance of the lease. Where a covenant prohibited subletting the landlord need only know that there had been such a subletting; he was not required to establish the terms of that agreement. In the present case, there was evidence that the landlord had waived the right to forfeit.

CORNILLIE v. SAHA (1996) 72 P. & C.R. 147, Hirst, L.J., CA.

3748. Leases–forfeiture–failure to obtain consent before assignment–equitable assignee of underlease can derive title from lease

[Rules of the Supreme Court Ord.5 r.4; Law of Property Act 1925 s.146.]

B held the head lease of a flat and had granted an underlease for 53 years at a premium. The underlease was assigned to J and a mortgage was transferred to the second plaintiffs, Finance for Mortgages Ltd, F. No payments having been made under the mortgage, F exercised its powers of sale. The buyer effected a subsale to H. There was a covenant in respect of assignment in the underlease which required consent and appeared to have been overlooked by H's solicitor. B served a notice under the Law of Property Act 1925 s.146 on J, who had disappeared, and B then re-entered the property. H sought relief from forfeiture as equitable assignees of the underlease, under s.146(2), or as mortgagees, under s.146(4). The Master granted relief to F, but on appeal relief from forfeiture was granted to H. B appealed and F cross-appealed.

Held, dismissing the appeal and the cross-appeal, that (1) the decision was not merely beyond challenge but completely right and the appeal devoid of all merit. Neither party had suffered any loss and, if H had suffered loss, they were protected by the Solicitors Indemnity Fund. Any advantages to B appellants in resisting relief against forfeiture were out of all proportion to any damage caused by the breach of covenant. The decision in *Lock v. Pearce* [1893] 2 Ch. 271 had been negatived by Rules of the Supreme Court Ord.5 r.4, *Fawsitt, Re* (1885) 30 Ch D. 231 considered. Accordingly, it was not the case that the instant proceedings could only have been brought by action rather than originating summons which was a common and convenient method of obtaining relief from forfeiture and (2) B had contended that there had been no power to grant H relief under s.146(2) since they were not lessees under s.146(5)(b). A lease, however, included an agreement where the lessee had become entitled to the grant of a lease. Accordingly, an equitable assignee of an underlease was one who could derive title from a lease under s.146(5)(b) of the 1925 Act, *Escalus Properties Ltd v. Robinson* [1995] 3 W.L.R. 524, [1995] 1 C.L.Y. 2991 followed.

HIGH STREET INVESTMENTS LTD v. BELLSHORE PROPERTY INVESTMENTS LTD (1997) 73 P. & C.R. 143, Leggatt, L.J., CA.

3749. Leases–forfeiture–rent not paid–landlord asking for payment of specified sum–whether waiver of breach–whether leave of court required for re-entry

[Insolvency Act 1986 s.252.]

Tenants failed to pay two instalments of rent under a lease containing a common form provision for re-entry and determination of lease if the rent was unpaid 14 days beyond the due date, whether formally demanded or not. Sixteen days after the second instalment was due, the landlords' solicitor asked for payment of a specified sum, failing which immediate steps were to be taken to enforce all the arrears. A writ was issued after no payment was made. The tenants obtained an interim order under the Insolvency Act 1986 s.252 preventing legal proceedings without the leave of the court. The landlords entered judgment in default of defence and peaceably re-entered the premises. They obtained a declaration that their entry did not require the leave of the court and the lease was forfeit for non-payment of rent. The tenants appealed on the grounds that the solicitor's letter waived the failure to pay rent due and the re-entry was in breach of the 1986 Act because it was without leave.

Held, dismissing the appeal, that (1) there was no waiver of any right to re-entry because the solicitor's letter demanded rent accrued before the right to forfeiture arose in respect of the second instalment and (2) peaceable re-entry was a non-judicial remedy which did not require the leave of the court and was therefore not prevented by the interim order, *McMullen & Sons Ltd v. Cerrone* [1994] 1 B.C.L.C. 152, [1994] C.L.Y. 2788 applied; *Segal Securities Ltd v. Thoseby* [1963] 1 Q.B. 887, [1963] C.L.Y. 1953 distinguished.

DEBTOR (NO.13A-IO-1995), *Re*; DEBTOR (NO.14A-IO-1995), RE; DEBTORS v. JOYNER [1995] 1 W.L.R. 1127, Rattee, J., Ch D.

3750. Leases–guarantors–whether guarantor liable to reimburse original tenant who has assigned the lease

[Insolvency Rules 1986 r.6.5.]

An original tenant sought reimbursement from the guarantor of the last assignee of a lease after he had paid the outstanding rent due under a covenant of the lease. The tenant served a statutory demand on the guarantor and the judge refused to set it aside.

Held, that (1) the guarantor of the assignee had ultimate responsibility for payment of the rent and must reimburse the original tenant, *Beckton Dickinson v. Zwebner* [1989] 1 Q.B. 208, [1989] C.L.Y. 2095 followed and (2) as the assignee in possession was ultimately responsible the position that he occupied in the chain was irrelevant. His guarantor was in the same position.

DEBTOR (NO.21 OF 1995), *Re* [1995] N.P.C. 170, Evans Lombe, J, QBD.

3751. Leases–lease in name of ex-partner–fire due to defendant's negligence–shortfall in insurance payout–whether landlord could claim against defendant

C occupied a unit in a building owned by S. A was originally the partner of C and the lease was in A's name. C had bought out A's share of the business. There was a fire on the premises which the court held was due to C's negligence. There was a shortfall between the amount recovered under the insurance policy and the rebuilding cost, and the question was whether S could recover against C. C argued that he was an equitable assignee of the lease and had paid the insurance contributions, therefore he could claim the benefits of the covenants and S was precluded from claiming damages in negligence. C contended that, as he had performed the tenant's obligations, he should have the benefit of the covenants. C also argued that both parties had a common assumption to that effect and S was estopped from denying its truth.

Held, giving judgment for S, that (1) S's covenants were construed as meaning that, if C was entitled to step into the lessee's shoes, relief would only be available in relation to C's unit; (2) the ruling in *Mark Rowlands Ltd v. Berni Inns Ltd* [1986] Q.B. 211, [1986] C.L.Y. 1787 that a tenant of part of a building in multiple occupation, with only a limited interest in the property, had an insurable interest in the continued existence of the whole building, did not apply in this case because C was never a tenant; (3) C could not claim estoppel by convention as his payments under the lease were payments of A's debts. C's position had not materially changed so as to show that he was entitled to the same benefits under the lease as A and (4) C could not claim subrogation under the policy. The insurers were only concerned that the premiums were paid, not who paid them.

SADLERS v. CLEMENTS [1995] E.G.C.S. 197, Judge Bursell Q.C., QBD.

3752. Leases–management company of block of flats struck off–headlease disclaimed by Crown–residents sought restoration of company–new leases granted on three flats–whether company should be restored–effect on new leases

The company was established by the developer of a block of flats to act as the residents' management company. The company took a head lease from the developer but was not properly administered, ground rent was not passed on and the company was struck off the register. The freehold reversion was acquired by the respondent who was aware that no ground rent had been paid. The respondent offered new leases but none of the residents accepted. They sought a vesting order in relation to the head lease after the Crown had disclaimed it. New leases had been granted on three of the flats. The vesting order application was stayed pending an application to restore the company to the register.

Held, restoring the company to the register, that there would be no injustice to the respondent. It would be wrong to disturb the three new leases save insofar as was necessary to in order to restore a practical system of management. That was achieved by directing that the restored company's lease took effect subject to the three new leases, those leases continuing with the company as intermediate landlord.

SHIRE COURT RESIDENTS LTD v. REGISTRAR OF COMPANIES [1995] B.C.C. 821, Carnwath, J., Ch D.

3753. Leases–nominated insurer–following takeover insurer succeeding in title not shown–landlord serving s.146 notice–breach of covenant–whether action amounted to implied waiver of forfeiture–whether Landlord and Tenant Act 1987 s.40 permitted variation of lease

[Law of Property Act 1925 s.146; Landlord and Tenant Act 1987 s.40.]

H were tenants of a flat owned by JL. Under the lease, H was required to insure with a nominated insurer. SA took over the named company in 1985, but this was not referred to in the lease. In 1995 H took out a policy with another insurer and JL treated this as a breach of covenant. JL served a notice under the Law of Property Act 1925 s.146 and commenced proceedings. H alleged that by commencing the action, JL had effected an implied waiver of the right to forfeit as it indicated an ongoing relationship under the tenancy. H further claimed that the court was empowered to vary the insurance provision under the Landlord and Tenant Act 1987 s.40 which allowed variation of leases making unsatisfactory provision for specified dwellings.

Held, allowing the application, that cancellation of the insurance with SA and consequent reinsurance with another was a breach of covenant. This remained the situation up to service of the s.146 notice and commencement of the proceedings. The dispute was an artificial one to which waiver offered little protection as JL did not want forfeiture. Such matters would be left for any subsequent litigation ensuing from the present proceedings. The Landlord and Tenant Act 1987 s.40 did not apply to flats, which were not dwellings within the meaning of the Act.

JOHN LYONS CHARITY v. HAYSPORT PROPERTIES LTD [1995] N.P.C. 165, Carnwath, J., Ch D.

3754. Leases–nominated insurers–right of landlord to nominate insurer of leasehold property–recoverability of premiums as service charges

[Landlord and Tenant Act 1985 s.18, s.19, s.30; Landlord and Tenant Act 1987.]

B and 13 others, each a management company and representative tenant of a block of flats appealed against the refusal to grant a declaration that insurance premiums for leasehold flats were excessive and irrecoverable. Alternatively they sought an order in terms of the Landlord and Tenant Act 1985 s.19 and s.30(A) that S were not entitled to recover expenditure and that the sums incurred by S were not costs reasonably incurred in the assessment of service charges in terms of the 1985

Act s.18 and s.19. The respondent, S, acquired the reversions of each block of flats and new arrangements were made for the insurance of the buildings, requiring the management companies to insure with a nominated insurer who charged a higher premium than they could arrange. B argued that there was no justification for the change in insurer, S had no right to nominate an insurance company and it was unreasonable that they should be required to pay more since the management companies were already insuring with insurers of repute. B argued that an implied term in the leases stated that the sum charged by the nominated insurer should not be unreasonable or, alternatively, that the tenant could not be required to pay a substantially higher sum than he could himself arrange with an insurance office of repute.

Held, dismissing the appeal, that (1) in terms of the leases in each case, there was no reason to imply the term submitted by B on the landlord's right to nominate the insurance company or agent through which the insurance would be placed. The management company and tenant were protected by the requirement that the company should be one of repute, *Bandar Property Holdings v. JS Darwen* [1968] 2 All E.R. 305, [1968] C.L.Y. 2167, *Havenridge Ltd v. Boston Dyers Ltd* [1994] 49 E.G. 111, [1994] C.L.Y. 2745 and *Tredegar v. Harwood* [1929] A.C. 72 applied. The fact that the rates proposed by the chosen company were higher than those the management company could have secured was irrelevant, and (2) in terms of the 1985 Act as amended by the Landlord and Tenant Act 1987, the management company could not be regarded as the landlord to the exclusion of the landlord defined in the lease, and as the tenant covenanted directly with the landlord to pay the service charge, the landlord had a right to enforce payment and was the landlord for the purposes of the 1985 Act. On the facts, the quotations for insurance were competitive and not unreasonable.

BERRYCROFT MANAGEMENT CO LTD v. SINCLAIR GARDENS (KENSINGTON) LTD [1996] E.G.C.S. 143, Beldam, L.J., CA.

3755. Leases–offer and acceptance–whether an offer can be unilaterally accepted after a counter-offer has been made

N appealed against a decision which held that letters written to D by N had failed to revoke an offer made earlier by the landlord to vary the date for determining the lease and, that offer being still available, was accepted by N in a subsequent letter. The question was whether the term of the lease had been varied.

Held, allowing the appeal, that (1) the correspondence was between the parties themselves and not their lawyers therefore *Hollington v. Rhodes* [1947-1951] 2 T.L.R. 691, C.L.C. 5265 did not apply; (2) on the facts there was a rejection of a previous offer, accompanied by a counter-offer which could not be considered to be a mere inquiry or request for information. A subsequent letter amounted to a clear rejection of the counter-offer, so there was no agreement to vary the lease and issues of whether any such agreement was void for informality did not arise, and (3) to be capable of binding acceptance an offer must be explicit and exact. If the offer is met by a counter-offer, it lapses and cannot be revived by subsequent correspondence.

DENCORA v. NORFOLK CC [1995] N.P.C. 173, Nourse, L.J., CA.

3756. Leases–rectification–entire agreement clauses–whether lease could be rectified on grounds of unilateral mistake even where there is an "entire agreement" clause

J appealed against a refusal to rectify a commercial lease, in which the agreed rent was stated as £80,000 p.a. exclusive, after an inexperienced solicitor had failed to make the tenants, P, liable for the payment of rates. P's solicitors spotted the mistake but failed to inform J. Two years later, following the receipt of a rate demand, J sought to rectify the lease. P claimed that an entire agreement clause in the agreement for the lease precluded rectification.

Held, allowing the appeal, that (1) the purpose of an entire agreement clause was to set out where the contractual terms were to be found. It did not provide a defence against rectification, *McGrath v. Shah* (1989) 57 P. & C.R. 452, [1990] C.L.Y. 650 applied; (2) where circumstances make it inequitable or unconscionable to force the contract on the plaintiff a unilateral mistake will support rectification, *Bates v. Wyndhams* [1981] 1 W.L.R. 505, [1981] C.L.Y. 1584 applied; (3) it would be inequitable to force on another party something contrary to the agreed basis on which the parties were proceeding in the knowledge that he did not intend it. There must, however, be actual knowledge, mere suspicion is not sufficient, *Nai Genova, The* [1984] 1 Lloyd's Rep. 353, [1984] C.L.Y. 378; *Commissioners for the New Towns v. Cooper* [1995] 2 W.L.R. 677, [1995] 1 C.L.Y. 780 applied; (4) the burden was one of "convincing proof" and, where there was an "entire agreement clause", the court needed to be especially careful and (5) on the facts, it was inequitable for P not to draw J's attention to the mistake and there were no factors which would justify the court exercising its discretion to refuse rectification.

JJ HUBER (INVESTMENTS) LTD v. PRIVATE DIY CO LTD [1995] E.G.C.S. 112, Cooke, J., Ch D.

3757. Leases–retention fund–jointly held by lessor and lessee–interpretation of agreement governing fund

A appealed against a decision ordering the payment of £2,000, standing in a joint account, to be paid to K. A and K were formerly the lessor and lessee of a shop and the £2,000, paid into the account by K, was subject to a written agreement stating that the K could withdraw the £2,000 if he vacated the shop, but if he remained and took a further lease of "say three, five or seven years", A would be entitled to the money. The parties attempted to negotiate a further lease over a number of years but failed, and K quit the premises. A contended that the agreement meant that if K remained in the premises after 12 months, he was entitled to the money.

Held, dismissing the appeal, that (1) A's interpretation was incorrect because mention would not have needed to be made of the length of the new lease and would just have said that the money was A's if K remained in the premises after 12 months and (2) the judge was wrong to conclude that this was a breach of contract case, although she made the correct order. A would have been entitled to the money if that provision of the agreement had come into effect and K had taken a further lease.

ABROL v. KENNY [1996] E.G.C.S. 93, Nourse, L.J., CA.

3758. Leases–tenant defaulting on mortgage, rent and service charges–relief from forfeiture–whether service charge treated as rent

[Law of Property Act 1925 s.146; Supreme Court Act 1981 s.38; County Courts Act 1984 s.138.]

The tenants had all mortgaged their properties and had defaulted in making mortgage repayments as well as payments required under the lease. In three cases there were arrears of service charges and two of these were under a lease that provided that service charges were to be treated as rent and recoverable as such. The landlords commenced proceedings for possession and the mortgagees were joined as defendants seeking relief against forfeiture. The actions were brought in the County Court and the High Court. The mortgagees sought relief under the County Courts Act 1984 s.138 and the Supreme Court Act 1981 s.38. The landlords conceded that the mortgagees were entitled to relief against forfeiture but only as from the court's order on condition that they paid all arrears of rent up to the date of forfeiture and all mesne profits thereafter. The mortgagees sought and obtained retrospective relief on payment of arrears but not mesne profits. The landlords appealed.

Held, dismissing the appeals, that (1) "rent" in the Acts of 1981 and 1984 was a periodical sum paid in return for occupation of land, issuing out of the land where a distress would be levied for non-payment. Where a lease provided that a service charge was to be treated as rent it invested the charge with the character of rent and it was to be treated as such for the purposes of obtaining relief against forfeiture; (2) in proceedings brought for forfeiture of a lease for non-payment of rent by the tenant, the mortgagee was entitled to retrospective relief on payment of all arrears without any liability for mesne profits, *United Dominions Trust Ltd v. Shellpoint Trustees Ltd* [1993] 4 All E.R. 310, [1993] C.L.Y. 2476 applied and (3) such relief was restricted to cases of forfeiture for non-payment of rent and could not assist a mortgagee where there was non-payment of a service charge that had not been invested with the character of rent in the lease. In such circumstances the court had a discretion under the Law of Property Act 1925 s.146(2) to grant relief to the lessee or a person claiming as an underlessee which included the mortgagees, *Nind v. Nineteenth Century Building Society* [1894] 2 Q.B. 226 not followed.

ESCALUS PROPERTIES LTD v. ROBINSON; ESCALUS PROPERTIES LTD v. DENNIS; ESCALUS PROPERTIES LTD v. COOPER-SMITH; SINCLAIR GARDENS INVESTMENTS (KENSINGTON) LTD v. WALSH [1995] 3 W.L.R. 524, Nourse, L.J., CA.

3759. Leases–variation–covenant not ended where there was no intention to surrender and re-grant lease–obligation to pay increased rent reverses to original lessee

In 1957 A granted B an underlease of premises for 21 years and a reversionary underlease from 1978 for a similar term, B covenanting for itself and its successors in title and assigns to pay the "rents hereinbefore reserved". C replaced B as lessee in 1961 then, in 1984, assigned the remainder of the term to D. A's interest had passed to E who, in February 1985, executed with D a deed of variation substantially increasing the rents and altering covenants as to user and alienation. In 1988 E's interest passed to F, and D assigned the remainder of the term to G, who went into liquidation. F sued C on C's personal covenant to pay the rent, contending C was bound by the covenant to pay the increased rent or alternatively pay the original rent. At first instance C successfully contended that the 1985 variations were so fundamental that, notwithstanding the parties' intentions, the deed effected a surrender and re-grant by operation of law, which determined C's liability. F appealed.

Held, allowing the appeal, that (1) when construing a deed of variation the court would give effect to the intention of the parties unless it was compelled to conclude there was a surrender and re-grant by the fact that the variation affected the legal estate, by increasing the extent of either the premises or the legal term; it followed that the variation in obligations had not brought C's personal covenant to an end; (2) obligations accepted by a lessee could not be varied or increased by a later agreement between the lessor and an assignee, so C could not be liable for the higher rent, but (3) the variation of the level of rent could not be construed as granting an assignee, and therefore the lessee, from the original obligation to pay rent.

FRIENDS PROVIDENT LIFE OFFICE v. BRITISH RAILWAYS BOARD [1996] 1 All E.R. 336, Beldam, L.J., CA.

3760. Leases–whether disposal of reversionary leases amounting to evidence of 1987 Act was an incumbrance to tenant's right to buy–whether landlord served proper notice of disposal

[Landlord and Tenant Act 1987 Part 1.]

Landlords of a purpose built block of flats exchanged contracts with F for the sale of a 99 year underlease commencing in 1936, and a 1992 year headlease commencing in 1969, without notifying the tenants as required by the Landlord and Tenant Act 1987 Part 1. F then served notice on the tenants under s.18 of the Act; the majority of tenants served counter notices seeking to exercise their rights of first refusal. F completed the purchase, and sold 150 year leases of parts of the block, its curtilege and airspace to A. Before the last of the leases to A was granted, the tenants served a notice on F under s.12 of the 1987 Act requiring F to dispose of its interest to the management company of the block, M. M sought a declaration that it was entitled to acquire F's interest unincumbered by the leases to A. The county court judge ruled that the A leases were not a sham, but were an artificial device intended to circumvent the mandatory provisions of the Act and that since the leases were "incumbrances" within the meaning of s.12(4) of the 1987 Act, the court could exercise its discretion to make the declaration in favour of M. F appealed.

Held, allowing the appeal in part by limiting the declaration to the F's estate or interest in the underlease, that (1) in the field of real property, the fact a transaction was an artificial device designed to circumvent the effects of a statute did not mean it was a sham that the court could disregard; (2) Part 1 of the 1987 Act which gave qualifying tenants an overriding right to buy was triggered when the landlord parted with the reversion, and s.16 enabled the tenants to pursue their claim against the original and new landlords, and the purchaser A; the grant of the lease was not therefore an "incumbrance" but an event which triggered s.16; (3) F, as the new landlord who intended to dispose of his interest had failed to comply with the notice requirements of s.16(1) of the 1987 Act, and could not avoid his obligation under s.12 by disposing of the reversion; M could therefore compel compliance with the notice provisions and then, if it wished, take appropriate steps against A and (4) the Act was however only concerned with the tenants' rights against their immediate landlord, ie. owner of the underlease not the headlease.

BELVEDERE COURT MANAGEMENT LTD v. FROGMORE DEVELOPMENTS LTD [1996] 3 W.L.R. 1008, Sir Thomas Bingham, M.R., CA.

3761. Leases–whether letter offering rented accommodation amounted to formal offer of tenancy

R, the second appellant, appealed against an order for him to deliver up possession of a flat to B. H and R had been married and were attempting a reconciliation. They negotiated the lease of the flat to be taken as a joint tenancy. H then contacted B and asked for the lease to be a sole tenancy in her name with R merely as an occupier. This was done and the couple moved in. R spent £4,000 on furnishing the flat and then H wrote to B within a month stating that she had bought another flat and requested that the sole tenancy be transferred to R. B served notice to quit on the couple which was the first R knew about H's action. H moved out but R remained. B claimed in trespass against R. R argued that there was a binding agreement for a joint tenancy contained in a letter from B and that the letter did not merely contain an invitation to treat as found by the judge. The letter contained an offer accepted by H on behalf of them both.

Held, dismissing the appeal, that B made it clear from the start that the agreement would be in writing and the written agreement was a precondition to the contract between the parties. Even if there had been an offer, H's refusal to enter the joint tenancy meant that B were no longer obliged to make the contract on the terms stated.

BATTERSEA CHURCHES HOUSING TRUST v. HUNTE, Trans. Ref: FC2 96/5954/H, May 7, 1996, Simon Brown, L.J., CA.

3762. Licences–grant of licence for purposes of waste disposal–rights did not grant exclusive possession

N appealed against a judgment in relation to the interpretation of deeds which were held to have granted a licence of the relevant land. N argued that it had been granted a tenancy with a limited user provision.

Held, dismissing the appeal, that (1) the judge was entitled to find that N did not have exclusive possession and that the agreement was not a tenancy, *Street v. Mountford* [1985] A.C. 809, [1985] C.L.Y. 1893 followed and (2) clause 1 of the agreement provided N with a licence to enter and use the land for the purpose of waste disposal. Those limited rights did not grant exclusive possession, *Addiscombe Garden Estates Ltd v. Crabbe* [1958] 1 Q.B. 513, [1957] C.L.Y. 1937 distinguished. N argued that the other clauses, stating, inter alia, how the agreement could be determined, were consistent with a tenancy. The clauses, however, were ambiguous and showed that the agreement was capable of being construed as either a tenancy or a licence and none of those clauses were strong enough to displace the indication of a licence in cl.1.

HUNTS REFUSE DISPOSALS LTD v. NORFOLK ENVIRONMENTAL WASTE SERVICES LTD [1997] 03 E.G.139, Hutchison, L.J., CA.

3763. Licences–sureties–whether surety who guaranteed obligations contained in licence was liable after subsequent assignment varied licence

B appealed against a decision that B was liable as surety of the last sitting tenant along with the assignee of the lease. A licence of 1988 made MP and B, the then tenant and the assignee parties to the assignment of a lease. B's business was reorganised and it was agreed to transfer the lease into the name of a new company. A further assignment took place in 1990 followed by a licence and deed of variation which removed an absolute prohibition on assignment or sharing of possession and permitted the tenant to allow another company from the same group to occupy part of the premises. The tenant defaulted and M sued B who refuted liability on the grounds that they had not been parties to the 1990 licence nor approved the terms of the variation of the lease, which increased their liability as sureties.

Held, dismissing the appeal, that, (1) the principle on which the sureties relied was set out in *Ward v. National Bank* (1883) 8 A.C. 755, the sureties had guaranteed performance of the 1988 licence. The obligations of the proposed assignee to perform the covenants on the part of the tenant in the lease were guaranteed. A change in the terms of the lease did not alter the obligations which the assignee undertook in the 1988 licence, unless it consented to the variation or consented to consequential variation of its own obligation; (2) an increase in rent agreed between the landlord and a later tenant under the rent review provisions would affect the assignee's liability as the assignee had covenanted to pay the rent so due from time to time. B was also liable for the increased rent, and (3) the assignee who was a party to the 1990 licence was presumed to have sought M's consent to the further assignment but it it did not follow that he sought permission for the variation in the obligations under the 1988 licence and was therefore bound by it. The variation to which the assignee consented affected the new assignee only and since the terms of the principal contract remained unchanged the defendants were not discharged.

METROPOLITAN PROPERTIES CO (REGIS) LTD v. BARTHOLOMEW; METROPOLITAN PROPERTIES CO (REGIS) LTD v. DILLON (1996) 72 P. & C.R. 380, Sir Stephen Brown, CA.

3764. Licences–tenancies–exclusive possession–agreement of indeterminate duration–no tenancy created on basis of licence–no variation of licence by erection of new building

O claimed possession of club buildings under the terms of a 1957 agreement, terminable by either party with one month's notice. In 1993 London Borough of Brent, L, claimed possession, giving the required notice, and the land was subsequently transferred to O, who argued that, (1) the 1957 agreement was the sole basis upon which the club occupied the premises; (2) the club had a mere licence terminable with one month's notice; (3) there was an implied variation of the agreement when a new building had been constructed, in that the new building occupied land not included in the 1957 agreement, and (4) there had been a termination of that licence. B contended that it enjoyed exclusive possession of the premises whatever the status of the 1957 agreement and that it had been granted a tenancy of the new buildings and the site.

Held, giving judgment for O, that (1) the test for exclusive possession did not rule out the possibility of the occupier being a licensee, *Cobb v. Lane* [1952] 1 All E.R. 1199, [1952] C.L.Y. 1974 considered; (2) the lack of a payment provision in the 1957 agreement indicated that it was not of a commercial nature and a question arose as to whether it might be a form of licence, *Street v. Mountford* [1985] 1 E.G.L.R. 128, [1985] C.L.Y. 1893 considered; (3) the grant of a continuous term, determinable by either party, failed for uncertainty, *Prudential*

Assurance v. London Residuary Body [1992] 2 E.G.L.R. 56, [1992] C.L.Y. 2688 considered; (4) the purported grant of a licence, to all club members "for the time being" formed no basis on which a valid tenancy could be granted, *Jarrett v. Ackerley* (1915) 113 L.T. 371 considered, and (5) the implied variation, needed to accommodate the new building, did not create any material change in the relationship between the parties.

ONYX (UK) LTD v. BEARD [1996] E.G.C.S. 55, Michael Hart Q.C., Ch D.

3765. Licences–whether chalets were statutory tenancies protected by the Rent Act 1977

[Rent Act 1977.]

This appeal concerned five lead actions involving property rights to chalets on land purchased by E for development purposes. E's offer of fixed term licences was rejected by the defendants and proceedings for possession were commenced. The defendants occupying units two, 12, 18 and 22 appealed against the order for possession of their units and E appealed against dismissal of the claim for possession of unit six. Four issues were considered; (1) E argued that the occupier of unit six, M, was not a protected statutory tenant under the Rent Act 1977. The chalet was not a fixture but a chalet which failed to pass with the freehold so M's tenancy did not include the chalet itself. Alternatively, if the chalet was a fixture in law, M was estopped from asserting his rights under the 1977 Act; (2) the defendants argued that the trial judge's decision, that the tenancies were not protected tenancies but fixed period tenancies for one year with no notice to quit necessary, was wrong. The true position was that the tenancies were periodic and not lasting for a fixed term of six months as stated in clause four of the agreement. This was compared to the finding that the agreements, although expressed to be licences, were in fact tenancies; (3) the defendants argued that the tenancy of unit 12 did not preclude subletting and the current occupiers W were lawful subtenants. S was granted a licence and then sublet the unit without occupying it herself so she was not a statutory tenant under the 1977 Act. If the subletting was lawful W had the protection of the 1977 Act s.137. The defendants argued that, as there was payment of rent and exclusive possession, there was a tenancy under the rule established in *Street v. Mountford* [1985] 1 A.C. 809, [1985] C.L.Y. 1893, and, as there was no prohibition against subletting in the tenancy, it was lawful, and the defendants argued that an equity by estoppel existed as there was an expectation that the status quo would continue as long as the defendants continued to pay the due fee.

Held, allowing the appeal in relation to unit six and dismissing the appeal of the other defendants, that (1) relying on the test of degree of annexation and purpose of annexation, unit six was not a fixture. It was not annexed to the ground and the defendants believed that they owned the chalets but not the sites. That conclusion meant the estoppel question was not considered; (2) the tenancy was for a fixed term. It was reviewed annually and that was always expected by the parties; (3) the agreement between S and W was personal. Clause two of the agreement between S and the owners only permitted her and her family to occupy the unit, therefore the subletting was unlawful, and (4) there could be no expectation of the status quo continuing indefinitely as the defendants had annual reminders that the tenure needed annual renewal and was by consent. The action of E was not unconscionable as no equity arose.

ELITESTONE LTD v. MORRIS AND DAVIES; ELITESTONE LTD v. DAVIES (1996) 71 P. & C.R. D6, Aldous, L.J., CA.

3766. Local authorities powers and duties–sale of council houses–authority owed no duty of care in respect of overvaluation

[Housing Act 1985 s.125.]

B was a council tenant who had opted to purchase his home under the right to buy scheme, and the local authority, under the Housing Act 1985 s.125, valued the property for the purposes of sale. B contended that the value of the property had been so exaggerated by the council that it was liable in damages for negligence, breach of statutory duty or negligent misrepresentation.

Held, dismissing the claim, that s.125 merely provided for the council to give its opinion as to the price of the property as part of the scheme of compulsory sale under the Act; it imposed no statutory or common law duty of care towards the tenant.

BLAKE v. BARKING AND DAGENHAM LBC [1996] E.G.C.S. 145, Douglas Brown, J., QBD.

3767. Local authority housing–possession orders–tenant's son causing annoyance and offence to neighbours–whether possession order could be made

[Housing Act 1985 Sch.2.]

S, a single parent living in a council maisonette, appealed against a decision to grant the local authority a suspended possession order in respect of her flat after her son, aged 13, was found to have caused annoyance and offence to neighbours amounting to a breach of the tenancy agreement. S argued that because she, as the tenant, was not personally at fault, the possession order should not have been made.

Held, dismissing the appeal, that the Housing Act 1985 Sch.2 Part I specifically referred to the behaviour of the tenant or other persons living in the property as a ground for possession. Moreover, it would go against common sense and the interests of justice for neighbours to be left without a remedy just because a tenant was unable to control her children.

KENSINGTON AND CHELSEA RLBC v. SIMMONDS [1996] 3 F.C.R. 246, Simon Brown, L.J., CA.

3768. Management–codes of practice

APPROVAL OF CODES OF MANAGEMENT PRACTICE (RESIDENTIAL PROPERTY) ORDER 1996, SI 1996 2839; made under the Leasehold Reform, Housing and Urban Development Act 1993 s.87, s.100. In force: March 17, 1997; £0.65.

In this Order the Secretaries of State approve two codes of practice relating to the management of residential property by landlords and others who discharge management functions.

3769. Misrepresentation–licensed premises–previous sale details–whether revealed business features–reasonableness of exclusion clause

I applied for a possession order and rent arrears from W, who counterclaimed contending that an agreement to rent a pub from I had been based on a misrepresentation. W had taken the pub on a yearly rent of £31,000, with a minimum purchasing obligation of 300 barrels for the first year. During negotiations, figures showed annual barrels sold were 370 for the year ending March 1990 and 356 for the year to March 1991. On taking over the tenancy in September 1991, W found the business had declined and sought relief of the full burden of rent, arguing that I should have disclosed full trading figures up to their take over.

Held, allowing the application and dismissing the counterclaim, that the details of the barrels sold did not amount to a feature of the business, but were specific figures up to a specified date, which actually revealed a fall in business over the period. On a balance of probabilities it was likely that even if W had discovered the true figures the agreement would have contained the same terms. The evidence showed that references to increased barrel sales were not misrepresentations on the part of I, but figures which W was willing to persuade themselves they could achieve. However, the agreement contained an exclusion clause which, if the counterclaim had been allowed, I could not have relied on, due to its unreasonableness at the time the agreement was entered.

INNTREPRENEUR ESTATES (CPC) LTD v.WORTH [1996] 1 E.G.L.R. 84, Laddie, J., Ch D.

3770. Mobile homes–whether owner liable to occupier for unreasonably withholding consent to assign

[Mobile Homes Act 1983.]

L and N were parties to an agreement with B whereby L and N stationed a mobile home on B's land. In 1989 L wished to sell the home and B agreed to the sale on the ground that certain alterations were made to the home. However whilst this was being investigated the purchasers lost interest and B discovered that L was in arrears with his pitch fee and was no longer occupying the home as his main residence. B sought to terminate the agreement on these grounds. L claimed that N should have been joined as a defendant and that either one of them occupied the home as their main residence. L then counterclaimed against B on the ground that B had unreasonably withheld consent to the assignment of the home to N and as a result he had suffered loss. L appealed against the decision that B had no liability in damages.

Held, dismissing the appeal, that L was not entitled to claim damages against B. The Mobile Homes Act 1983 imposed a duty on the owner to offer an agreement to the occupier. This agreement resembled a tenancy agreement and consequently the occupier could assign only with the consent of the owner which could not be unreasonably withheld. However, the Act did not give the occupier a right to damages if the consent was unreasonably withheld. The solution of disputes was intended to be via application to the court.

BERKELEY LEISURE GROUP LTD v. LEE AND NEATE [1995] N.P.C. 159, Beldam, L.J., CA.

3771. Notice of termination–periodic tenancy–expiry of fixed term–last day of period failed to expire on last day of period of tenancy–notice complied with requirements of a different section to that given in heading–whether notice valid

[Housing Act 1988 s.21.]

D was an assured shorthold tenant. Following the expiry of the six months' term certain provided for in the tenancy agreement, D remained in the property as a statutory periodic (weekly) tenant. P, the landlord, sought to terminate the tenancy. The notice of termination served on D was headed "Section 21 (4) (a) Notice". The notice satisfied the requirements of the Housing Act 1988 s.21 (1) (b), because it gave D not less than two months' notice that P required possession. However, it did not comply with the provisions of s.21 (4) of the 1988 Act, because the last day of the period set out in the notice did not expire on the last day of a period of the tenancy. D's periodic tenancy ran from Tuesday to Monday, while the last day of the notice was a Thursday.

Held, that a notice complying with either s.21 (4) (a) or a notice complying with s.21 (4) (b) would suffice to terminate D's statutory periodic tenancy after the expiry of the fixed term. The heading of the notice in this case did not render it invalid, given that the notice provided D with "not less than two months notice" pursuant to s.21 (1) (b), and that no form is prescribed for a notice under either section.

UJIMA HOUSING ASSOCIATION v. RICHARDSON, November 29, 1995, Graham, J., CC. [*Ex rel.* Paul Michell, Barrister].

3772. Notice to quit–insufficient particulars given–whether just and equitable to dispense with notice

[Housing Act 1988 s.8.]

K appealed against the dismissal of his application to dismiss a summons for possession of his home on the grounds that the notice did not comply with the

Housing Act 1988 s.8 in that it did not contain sufficient particulars of allegations made against the family. K argued that the judge had wrongly exercised his discretion in deciding that it was just and equitable to dispense with the requirements of the notice.

Held, dismissing the appeal, that (1) where a landlord's notice to quit failed to comply with s.8, a judge had discretion under s.8(1)(b) to dispense with the service of notice if, on the facts of the case, it was just and equitable to do so. The court questioned the position taken on the subject by Sweet & Maxwell's Housing Encyclopedia (vol.1, 1987, p.897), but agreed with that in Megarry on the Rent Act (vol. 3, 11th ed, 1989, p.140); (2) the words "just and equitable" should not have a restrictive meaning but embraced all the circumstances of the case. The judge considered the allegations relating to nuisance against K and his family and the effect of the delay that had occurred before K made the application. He decided that the failure to give appropriate particulars had not created any prejudice. The judge was entitled to reach such a conclusion.

KELSEY HOUSING ASSOCIATION LTD v. KING (1996) 28 H.L.R. 270, Aldous, L.J., CA.

3773. Notices–acquisition of freehold interest–plan omitted–invalidating notice–no declaratory relief available

[Leasehold Reform (Housing and Urban Development) Act 1993 s.13.]

M was a company formed by a number of the residents of a block of six flats held on long leases, with a view to acquiring the freehold interest from B. On March 24, 1995, M served a notice which purported to be a notice pursuant to the Leasehold Reform (Housing and Urban Development) Act 1993 s.13. The notice complied in all respects with s.13, save that, although it referred to a plan, no plan accompanied the notice. On May 24, 1995, B served a counter-notice. This denied that M was entitled to acquire the freehold, stating inter alia, that the purported s.13 notice was invalid. Further, the counter-notice was served under cover of a letter of the same date stating that it was served without prejudice to B's contention that the s.13 was invalid. M subsequently issued an originating application seeking leave to amend the s.13 notice, pursuant to the terms of Sch.3 para.15(2) of the 1993 Act. The application was dismissed on September 24, 1995. The judge held that the court had no jurisdiction under para.15(2) to amend a s.13 notice when a plan had been omitted and the decision was not appealed. M applied for a s.22 declaration claiming that (1) the s.13 notice was not rendered invalid by the omission of a plan; (2) in any event, para.15(1) of the 1993 Act applied as the wording was wide enough to cover this situation and (3) in any event, as a counter-notice had in fact been served, M was entitled to declaratory relief pursuant to s.22, whatever the status of the s.13 notice.

Held, that (1) the omission of the plan rendered the s.13 notice invalid; (2) the wording of para.15(1) was not wide enough to cover the non-inclusion of a plan as the words "inaccuracy in any of the particulars" or "misdirection" were not wide enough to cover an omission and (3) in the circumstances, M was not entitled to declaratory relief pursuant to s.22, as relief under that section was subject to there being a valid notice pursuant to s.13.

MUTUAL PLACE PROPERTY MANAGEMENT v. BLAQUIERE, February 7, 1996, H.H.J. Hallgarten Q.C., CC (Central London). [*Ex rel.* David Holland, Barrister].

3774. Options–lease renewed–licensed premises–whether agreement of new business plans–condition precedent–whether failure to formulate business plan rendered conditions unnecessary

L entered into a five year lease of licensed premises from C. At the same time L entered into a business agreement with C pursuant to which L was obliged to meet specified performance targets and restrict sales to specified products all marketed by C. The lease contained an option exercisable by L to take a further lease for another five years. The option was exercisable if, inter alia, L had agreed with C a further business plan and a further business agreement. When L sought to exercise his option C decided it would rather grant him a 20 year lease. C refused to agree a new business plan or enter into a new business agreement and as a result refused to grant L a new tenancy on the ground that the condition precedent to the exercise of the option had not been fulfilled. L sought a declaration that C was bound to grant him a new lease. L's claim was dismissed.

Held, allowing L's appeal, that it was impossible to imply any terms into the option clause requiring C to negotiate a new business plan and business agreement and impossible to import any requirement for C to use its best endeavours to do so. The object to reach an agreement, was an uncertain object and the option agreement, being a unilateral contract, was not susceptible to the implication of terms which required both parties to agree. In reality there would have been no real negotiation as to the contents of the business plan and business agreement. L would in the ordinary course of events have been presented by C with an agreement that he was required to sign. In the circumstances the words "if required" should be incorporated into the option clause. That being the case, as C did not now require L to enter into a new business plan or a new business agreement, the option was exercisable by L without his having done so.

LITTLE v. COURAGE LTD (1995) 70 P. & C.R. 469, Millett, L.J., CA.

3775. Petrol–service station–breach of covenant to buy petrol from landlord–landlord attempted to forfeit lease–injunction against disturbance to quiet enjoyment and relief from forfeiture sought–whether injunction should stand

EO applied to discharge an interlocutory injunction restraining them from forfeiting a lease. D, the tenant of a petrol filling station, had breached a covenant under the lease which required him to purchase fuel exclusively from EO. EO stopped accepting rent and served a s.146 notice. D alleged discriminatory pricing. Following a further order of third party petrol, EO re-entered. D obtained an ex parte injunction restraining EO from disturbing D's quiet enjoyment. The interlocutory injunction was granted when the court held that D had an arguable case for relief from forfeiture or for an injunction. EO argued that compliance with the covenants should be a minimum requirement for relief and that the allegation of discriminatory pricing had to be answered.

Held, allowing the application, that (1) there was no evidence supporting the discriminatory pricing allegation so there was no reason for the injunction to remain and (2) D proposed to act in breach of the covenant and refused to give an undertaking to purchase fuel solely from EO. This meant that it was impossible to grant relief from forfeiture and an injunction would have the effect of allowing a breach of contract.

DAVIS v. ELF OIL UK PROPERTIES LTD [1995] E.G.C.S. 196, Malcolm Spence Q.C., QBD.

3776. Planning permission–need for landlord to show reasonable prospect of obtaining permission–meaning of "reasonable prospect"

[Landlord and Tenant Act 1954 s.30.]

M, the landlord, appealed against a decision that it had not established an intention to develop a site, occupied by C and others, the tenants, as a tennis club, under the grounds set out in the Landlord and Tenant Act 1954 s.30(1)(f). Following the service of a notice to determine the lease, C served a notice that they would not give up possession and made an application for a new tenancy. M did not have planning permission and the judge found that it did not have a reasonable prospect of obtaining it.

Held, allowing the appeal, that the judge was right to consider whether a landlord had a reasonable prospect of obtaining planning permission. However, the correct test was not whether it was more likely than not that consent would be obtained but whether there was a real chance, a prospect sufficiently strong to support a proposed course of action on which a reasonable landlord would be likely to embark, *Gregson v. Cyril Lord* [1963] 1 W.L.R. 41, [1962] C.L.Y. 1717 considered.

CADOGAN v. McCARTHY & STONE (DEVELOPMENTS) LTD [1996] E.G.C.S. 94, Butler-Sloss, L.J., CA.

3777. Possession–automatic directions–court order that automatic directions apply–whether action struck out for failure to comply with automatic directions

[County Court Rules Ord.17 r.11.]

In a claim for possession on grounds of rent arrears, the court ordered on December 1, 1993, that "On close of pleadings the automatic directions referred to in the County Court Rules Ord.17 r.11 shall apply but with the further directions contained in this order taking precedence where such directions are inconsistent with those in the County Court Rules Ord.17 r.11". The order further required that "The plaintiffs do request a date for trial within nine months from today with a certificate of readiness from both parties".

Held, that although the strike out provision of Ord.17 r.11 (9) does not apply automatically to possession actions, the court had ordered that it apply in this case. Accordingly, P should have requested a trial date by September 1, 1994, and were automatically struck out nine months later, June 1, 1995. He made a declaration to that effect and ordered P to pay D's costs of the action.

HACKNEY LBC v. HAMILL, November 17, 1995, Silverman, CC. [*Ex rel.* Jon Holbrook, Barrister].

3778. Possession–failure to pay service charges–forfeiture for breach of covenant to pay–mortgagee seeking relief from forfeiture after order granted

[Law of Property Act 1925 s.146.]

Following a breach of covenant by the tenant, in failing to pay a service charge, the landlord gained a possession order, pursuant to a Law of Property Act 1925 s.146 warning notice. Although the tenant's mortgagee had been sent a copy of the warning notice, they failed to act until after the landlord gained possession when they applied for relief from forfeiture.

Held, dismissing the application, that the right to relief was restricted under s.146(2),(4) to the period during which possession proceedings were under way, or in which a right of re-entry was being enforced. Once lawfully executed, the right to relief ceased, *Rogers v. Rice* [1892] 2 Ch 170 considered. Only in rare cases could a mortgagee or sub-tenant successfully claim relief from forfeiture where a lease had already been forfeit, or an order for possession granted, *Billson v. Residential Apartments Ltd* [1992] 1 E.G.L.R. 43, [1992] C.L.Y. 2678 considered.

REXHAVEN LTD v. NURSE AND ALLIANCE AND LEICESTER BUILDING SOCIETY (1996) 28 H.L.R. 241, Cloyer, J., Ch D.

3779. Possession–landlord intending to create assured shorthold tenancy–proper notice not given–court's discretion to grant possession

[Housing Act 1988 Sch.2, s.20.]

Held, that it was open to a court to exercise its discretion to grant a possession order where a landlord had erred in not fulfilling the requirements of the Housing Act 1988 s.20 as to the serving of notice to create an assured shorthold tenancy, as had been intended, and had not given formal oral notice. It was not the case that the court could exercise its discretion to grant possession under ground 1 (b) of Part I of Sch.2 to the Act only in exceptional circumstances.

BOYLE v. VERRALL [1996] E.G.C.S. 144, Auld, L.J., CA.

3780. Possession–notice for possession proceedings did not specify rent arrears–validity of notice–requirement specification of rent arrears unnecessary

[Landlord and Tenant Act 1987 s.48; Landlord and Tenant Act 1988 Sch.2; Housing Act 1988 s.8.]

MacG, the tenant, appealed against an order of, inter alia, possession of a flat obtained under the Landlord and Tenant Act 1988 Sch.2 Ground 8. MacG argued that the notice for possession proceedings issued under the Housing Act 1988 s.8 was invalidated as M, the landlord, had failed to specify in the schedule exactly how much rent arrears were owing.

Held, dismissing the appeal, that (1) the 1988 Act s.8 notice could only be served once rent of at least three months was unpaid. Rent was not due until a notice under the Landlord and Tenant Act 1987 s.48 had been served which contained the landlord's address for service of notices; (2) as long as the 1988 Act s.8 notice stated that rent had not been paid for at least three months and enabled the tenant to calculate the amount allegedly overdue, the notice was valid, *Torridge DC v. Jones* (1985) 18 H.L.R. 107, [1986] C.L.Y. 1933 *Dudley MBC v. Bailey* [1990] 22 H.L.R. 424, [1991] C.L.Y. 2253 considered. That had occurred in this case and (3) a notice which complied with the requirements of a 1987 Act s.48 notice was served before the relevant date.

MARATH & MARATH v. MacGILLIVRAY (1996) 28 H.L.R. 484, Sir Iain Glidewell, CA.

3781. Possession–squatting–promissory estoppel only available as an equitable remedy when demanded by justice

[Rules of the Supreme Court Ord.113.]

S sought possession of a house occupied by L. In 1986, an order for possession had been made in proceedings brought under the Rules of the Supreme Court Ord.113, but not enforced. In 1985, L had left another council property after suffering racial harassment and moved into the appeal property without any formal offer of accommodation having been made. In 1994 it was ordered that S should recover possession. L appealed, relying on a letter written by an official in 1986, and claiming that she was a secure tenant. It was S's case that L was a squatter.

Held, dismissing the appeal, that (1) the official's letter was no contract because there was no term agreed as to payment, L having paid no rent since 1985. Any forbearance must be at the request of the other party in order to support a contract as an express or implied consideration. L had left the flat she had occupied until 1985 with no intention of returning and the amended defence raised no matter sufficient to amount to consideration; (2) having left a secure tenancy voluntarily, L had suffered no detriment in accepting an assurance that she would not be evicted from the appeal property, *Jones v. Jones* [1977] 1 W.L.R. 438 considered and (3) promissory estoppel was only available as an equitable remedy where justice so demanded. It could not be said that it was inequitable for S to recover possession, *Central London Property Trust v. High Trees House Ltd* [1947] K.B. 130, [1947-1951] C.L.C. 5601 and *WJ Alan & Co v. EL Nasr Export* [1972] 2 Q.B. 189, [1972] C.L.Y. 3138 considered.

SOUTHWARK LBC v. LOGAN (1996) 8 Admin. L.R. 315, Neill, L.J., CA.

3782. Possession–suspension of warrant of execution–payment of rent arrears–need to clarify housing benefit entitlement

P appealed against an order dismissing her application for the suspension of a warrant of execution of a possession order. H had originally obtained a possession order in November 1992 when P was an estimated £3,500 in arrears on her rent. This was suspended on the basis that P pay off the arrears at an agreed rate. H had later obtained a warrant of execution in November 1994 on the ground that the arrears had risen by about £1,000 since the original order. The level of arrears was disputed, as the position was complicated by the difficulty in establishing P's entitlement to housing benefit as P had been in and out of low paid employment. P's application for the warrant to be suspended had been adjourned in order to clarify her housing benefit entitlement. She appealed against the order arguing that (1) there was doubt as to whether the housing benefit situation had been resolved; (2) H's housing benefit department had not given sufficient and proper credit in respect of benefit; (3) the order was inappropriate for the circumstances and (4) if correct, her figures would have a substantial effect on the court's exercise of its discretion.

Held, that the order dismissing P's application for suspension of the warrant of execution be set aside and that the hearing of the suspension application be adjourned. There should be a further opportunity for the matter to be clarified in respect of P's housing benefit entitlement and the correct version of the rent account. It was also necessary to take account of the up to date position, including the extent to which P had been able to comply with the various court orders made. It was noted that there had been a degree of blame on both sides in terms of progress with the case. H were to indicate within 14 days in clear terms what decisions had been made about her housing benefit claim and were to supply an up to date rent position.

HARINGEY LBC v. POWELL (1996) 28 H.L.R. 798, Evans, L.J., CA.

3783. Possession–tenancy agreement requiring one month's notice of decision to determine tenancy–notice requiring possession of property was effective as notice of determination

[Housing Act 1988 s.21.]

Held, that where a tenancy agreement provided that the tenant had to be given one month's notice of a landlord's decision to determine the tenancy, it was reasonable to interpret the giving of notice requiring possession of the property, under the Housing Act 1988 s.21 (2) (b), as giving the required notice of determination.

FAWAZ v. AYLWARD; SUB NOM. AYLWARD v. FAWAZ [1996] E.G.C.S. 199, Nourse, L.J., CA.

3784. Possession–warrant gained after reinstatement–reinstatement terms differed from earlier suspended order

S sued G for damages for illegal eviction. In April 1993, G obtained a suspended possession order against S. S breached the terms of the suspension and in March 1994 she went abroad. The arrears accumulated, and after service of a notice to quit, G boarded up the flat and treated the tenancy as void. When S returned to the flat in November 1994, G removed the boards, and gave S a set of keys. The council stated that they would not seek to evict S if she paid £200 towards her arrears, which stood at over £5,000, together with current rent, and £10 per week. S's arrears increased, and after G had applied for a warrant (pursuant to the April 1993 possession order) S's application to suspend its execution was dismissed and the order was executed by bailiffs.

Held, giving judgment for S, that by agreeing to reinstate her in November 1994, on terms that differed from those of the suspended order, G had granted S a fresh tenancy, and that accordingly the suspended possession order was of no effect, and the eviction was illegal. It was also directed that the action be set down for assessment of damages.

SACKEY v. GREENWICH LBC, December 20, 1995, Cox, J., CC (Woolwich). [*Ex rel.* Jon Holbrook, Barrister].

3785. Possession proceedings–premises–subtenant at will or licensee–substantial arrears of rent–not protected under Landlord and Tenant Act 1954

[Landlord and Tenant Act 1954.]

C was the lessee of a lock up shop and flat. He entered into an oral agreement for B to occupy the shop pending negotiations for the grant of a sublease or an assignment of the term. After negotiations broke down, C sought possession on the basis that C was a subtenant at will or licensee. At an interlocutory application, the County Court judge ordered possession. B appealed to the Court of Appeal. She contended that the County Court judge should have allowed her to argue that the tenancy was protected under the Landlord and Tenant Act 1954.

Held, dismissing the appeal, that it was unnecessary to consider whether it was right to interfere because there was a further overriding ground for the court not to allow the proceedings to go on any longer. The arrears were now £12,335 and B's plans to pay them off were in large part speculative. The defence would in practice be bound to fail. The 1954 Act would not protect B from the consequences of being unable to repay the very considerable arrears within a reasonable time.

CLARKE v. BANKS, March 4, 1996, Nourse, L.J., CA. [*Ex rel.* Mark Loveday, Barrister].

3786. Property insurance–malicious damage–whether landlords and their solicitors owed tenant duty of care to inform them of withdrawal of insurance cover

F claimed rent arrears of £467,500 from E. E leased premises for which they covenanted to pay for insurance cover taken by the landlord. In 1981 the landlord purportedly procured malicious damage cover which was accepted by E. F bought the freehold of the premises in 1987, without knowledge of the 1981 events, and took out a new policy containing an unoccupied building exclusion. E did not see the policy and from September 1988 the premises were unoccupied. To prevent any problems arising, E requested a copy of the policy and forwarded it to the company arranging top up cover. F's insurance broker told F's insurers that the property was vacant. An endorsement to the policy was sent to F's insurance broker withdrawing the rent cover, on the mistaken assumption that there was no tenant obliged to pay rent, and withdrawing cover for malicious damage. F's solicitors claimed not to have received the endorsement. In December 1988 E discovered that the rent cover had been excluded from the policy. Malicious damage was subsequently suffered and E was informed that the damage was not covered by the policy and that rent was owed despite the damage.

Held, giving judgment for the defendants, that (1) the lease had not been varied in 1981 nor by subsequent conduct so as to add malicious damage to the list of perils in the provisions for additional rent, regardless of the vacant state of the property. Neither were the facts strong enough to show a collateral contract or any estoppel to the same effect; (2) F had breached the duty of care owed to their tenants, *Argy Trading Development Co v. Lapid Developments* [1977] 1 W.L.R. 444, [1977] C.L.Y. 2032 considered; (3) F should have given accurate information to E. Knowledge that malicious damage cover had been withdrawn would have led E to seek alternative cover. However, liability still existed but E had the excess cost, which would have been incurred, deducted from their damages. F's agent had told E that rent cover had been withdrawn so the damages did not include loss of rent and (4) F's solicitors did not owe E a duty of care as there was no assumption of responsibility by them.

FLEETWOOD v. ENGINEERING CONSTRUCTION INDUSTRY TRAINING BOARD [1995] N.P.C. 114, May, J., QBD.

3787. Protected tenancies–lessee failed to serve notice on sub-lessee–sub-lessee relied on failure when purchaser of lease issued possession proceedings–whether just and equitable to treat tenancy as shorthold tenancy

[Housing Act 1980 s.52; Rent Act 1977 Sch.15 case.19.]

By an underlease in 1984, W let a flat in the property to T. The tenancy was expressed to be for "a protected shorthold tenancy" and set out some of the rules apply to shorthold tenancies. In 1994, L purchased the long lease of the property from W, and then issued possession proceedings against T, pursuant to the Rent Act 1977 Sch.15 case 19 on the basis that T occupied his flat as a protected shorthold tenant. For a tenancy granted in 1984 to be a protected shorthold tenancy, under the Housing Act 1980 s.52(1)(b), the landlord had, before the grant of the tenancy, to give the tenant a notice in writing in the prescribed form. T alleged that no such notice had ever been served on him, although a copy notice had been filed with the Rent Officer and had been inspected by L before its purchase of the long lease. T gave evidence that, at the time when his tenancy was granted, he had researched the position in his local library and had therefore been fully aware that W had mistakenly failed to serve the notice, and that such failure would mean that a shorthold tenancy could not be created. He knew that in the absence of a notice he would be a fully protected tenant under the Rent Act 1977, and he would not have entered into the tenancy on any other basis.

Held, making the possession order, that although no notice had been served, s.55(2) gave the court power to treat the tenancy as a shorthold tenancy if satisfied that it was just and equitable to do so. Before purchasing the long lease L had taken reasonable steps to ensure that it only held a shorthold tenancy. In contrast, T had acted disgracefully in deliberately seeking to take advantage of W's mistake. No significant weight should be given to T's assertion that he would not have entered into a shorthold tenancy, since it was unlikely that W would have agreed to grant him a tenancy on any other basis.

ARCWOOD v. DOW, December 1, 1995, Rich, J., CC (Central London). [*Ex rel.* Sarah Lacey, Barrister].

3788. Protected tenancies–tenant moved from one property to another owned by same landlord–whether tenant had transitional protection–whether the Rent Act applied to the second tenancy

[Housing Act 1980 s.55; Housing Act 1988 s.34; Rent Act 1977.]

In 1989, T's landlord failed to establish a valid protected shorthold tenancy for want of the prescribed notice. In November 1989, T moved into another flat owned by the same landlord. Unless T could rely upon the transitional protection of the Housing Act 1988 s.34 this second tenancy would have been an assured shorthold. After E increased T's rent, T sought a declaration that her second tenancy was Rent Act 1977 protected. E relied upon the working of s.34(2) of the 1988 Act, which excluded from transitional protection, a tenancy "which in proceedings for possession under [the mandatory shorthold ground] is treated as a protected shorthold tenancy". Under the Housing Act 1980 s.55(2) a tenancy was to be treated as a protected shorthold tenancy "if in proceedings for possession under [the mandatory shorthold ground] it is just and equitable to make an order for possession".

Held, allowing T's appeal, that T's second tenancy was *Rent Act* protected. A tenancy could only be treated as a protected shorthold tenancy in actual possession proceedings, and it was not permissible to read s.34 as excluding from transitional protection a tenancy "which if proceedings for possession under the mandatory shorthold ground had been brought would have been treated as a protected shorthold tenancy".

THALMANN v. EVANS, March 3, 1996, H.H.J. Rutherford, CC (Bristol). [*Ex rel.* Jon Holbrook, Barrister].

3789. Remedies–assignor of houses let them without knowledge of assignee–profits accounted for–whether assignee entitled to further remedies

T, prior to his death agreed by deed to assign houses to C, which he later let without C's knowledge. On an application for summary judgment, C obtained a declaration that from at least the date of the lease it was the equitable owner of the houses and an order that T's personal representative, R, assign them to C free of incumbrances, to account for the profits from the let of the same and pay such profits to C. C received certain profits, then proceeded to the assessment of damages claiming for loss of use and occupation, comprising loss of market rental, deducting the profits already paid, and damages for diminution in the value of the houses arising out of the wrongful occupation. The Court of Appeal of Hong Kong allowed R's appeal in part, holding that, by receiving the payments on account of profits, C elected to take that remedy and could not also recover damages for wrongful occupation. C and R appealed.

Held, allowing C's cross-appeal and dismissing R's appeal, that C's remedies for loss of profits and damages for loss of use and occupation were in the alternative, but C had not made an election in the circumstances of the judge's order for both an account of profits and damages; C had therefore been entitled to proceed with the assessment of damages and was subsequently entitled to make an election in favour of damages for loss of use and occupation. R's appeal was dismissed as C was entitled to damages for loss of market rental as well as loss resulting from the over use of the houses which had deteriorated as a result.

TANG MAN SIT (DECEASED) v. CAPACIOUS INVESTMENTS LTD; SUB NOM. PERSONAL REPRESENTATIVES OF TANG MAN SIT v. CAPACIOUS INVESTMENTS LTD [1996] 1 A.C. 514, Lord Nicholls of Birkenhead, PC.

3790. Rent–arrears–landlord re-entered premises before judgment–value of goods distrained exceeded rent arrears–landlord with profit motive–exemplary damages awarded

B was the tenant of a shop selling electrical goods. For convenience, he traded through a limited company. B was sentenced to a term of imprisonment, during which no one managed the business. Rent arrears accrued, and WI, the landlord, obtained judgment for £8,906, and an order for possession in the High Court in October 1991. Before judgment, however, WI's agents re-entered the premises and removed all the contents, which belonged to the company, and the fixtures and fittings, which belonged to B. Interlocutory judgment for B and the company against WI was given by the district judge, and an assessment of damages was ordered. Shortly before the assessment of damages, WI returned some of the contents, but by then the goods were obsolete, and only fetched £2,000 at auction.

Held, giving judgment for B and an assessment of damages, that the landlord may have been entitled to re-enter the premises, but not to remove the contents without a warrant of execution. The shop had been stripped, and the value of what had been taken was far in excess of the rent arrears. WI had refused to return the goods in correspondence, and had been evasive about the whereabouts of what was taken. The court was entitled to infer that WI had acted with a view to making a profit. Both B and the company were entitled to exemplary damages. The trial judge awarded B £10,000 general damages (the value of the fixtures and fittings) plus £5,000 exemplary damages. The company was awarded £44,500 (the value of the contents) plus £7,500 exemplary damages. Credit was to be given by B for the unsatisfied High Court judgment against his total award of £19,350 and by the company for auction proceedings against its award of £71,419, both awards including interest.

BHATNAGAR AND ELANRENT v. WHITEHALL INVESTMENTS, November 15, 1995, Quentin Edwards, J., CC (Central London). [*Ex rel.* Martyn Berkin, Barrister].

3791. Rent assessment committees–determination of a fair rent

[Rent Act 1977 s.70.]

This case concerned three appeals against decisions of a rent assessment committee. The first appeal related to one of three identical ground floor flats. It was the only flat subject to a regulated tenancy. The rent was determined at £854 per quarter. The second appeal related to a second floor flat. It was the only flat of four which was subject to a regulated tenancy. The other flats were let on furnished assured tenancies and were centrally heated. By using the other flats as comparables the landlord suggested £85 per week. The committee confirmed the rent at £46 per week. The third appeal related to a self-contained maisonette. The landlord requested a rent of £120 per week and the committee decided it should be £70 per week.

Held, quashing the decision in relation to the first appeal and upholding the decision in relation to the second and third appeals, that (1) to reach a fair rent under the Rent Act 1977 s.70 it was necessary to adjust the market rent for the scarcity element and disregard personal circumstances and other matters, *Spath Holme Ltd v. Chairman of the Greater Manchester Rent Assessment Committee* [1995] 49 E.G. 128, [1995] 1 C.L.Y. 3054 considered; (2) the various methods of assessing a fair rent included the use of registered fair rent comparables and assured tenancy comparables although the methods of the committees could vary according to circumstances; (3) in the first appeal the committee applied an uplift from the flat's previous registered rent with no explanation. The decision was quashed and remitted to a differently constituted committee and (4) in the second and third appeals assured tenancies were rejected as comparables. The committee was entitled to reach its decision but committees should expect the court to look carefully at that type of bare assertion following the *Spath Holme* decision.

CURTIS v. LONDON RENT ASSESSMENT COMMITTEE; SUSANDS v. LONDON RENT ASSESSMENT COMMITTEE (1996) 28 H.L.R. 841, Latham, J., QBD.

3792. Rent assessment committees–rent increase of 41 per cent–whether there was a procedural irregularity–whether the decision was perverse

W applied for judicial review of a decision of the London Rent Assessment Panel to increase his rent from £2,478 per annum to £3,500. This was after W had objected to the Rent Officer's determination of £2,800 per annum. At the hearing before the panel the landlord had submitted that the rent should be £3,050. W's grounds for judicial review described a number of complaints of procedural irregularity and the conclusion that the panel's decision was perverse because the rent had increased by 41 per cent when most comparables had risen by 16 per cent.

Held, allowing the application, that (1) complaints of procedural irregularity raised questions of fact, and the court preferred the statements of the chairman of the panel and (2) perversity did exist due to the large increase in rent which was in excess of what the landlord sought. The decision was an arbitrary decision ignoring the rules of natural justice. The decision was quashed and a rehearing, before a different rent assessment panel, was ordered.

R. v. LONDON RENT ASSESSMENT PANEL, *ex p.* WELLS (1996) 71 P. & C.R. D4, Turner, J., QBD.

3793. Rent officers–functions

RENT OFFICERS (ADDITIONAL FUNCTIONS) (AMENDMENT) ORDER 1996, SI 1996 959; made under the Housing Act 1988 s.121. In force: October 7, 1996; £1.10.

This Order amends the Rent Officers (Additional Functions) Order 1995 (SI 1995 1642) which conferred functions on rent officers, in connection with housing benefit and rent allowance subsidy, and requires them to make determinations and re-determinations in respect of tenancies and licences of dwellings. Article 3 and Art.4 add a requirement for rent officers to make a single room rent determination where a local authority, when applying for a determination, states that the housing benefit claimant is or may be a young individual. Article 6 specifies the notice which the rent officer is to give to the local authority where the rent under a single room rent determination is equal to or more than the rent under the claimant's tenancy or licence. Article 5 makes a correction. Article 7 stops the amendments applying to applications for a determination made before the Order comes into force.

3794. Rent reviews–agricultural holdings–basis for arbitration–permissible factors in assessing rent after reorganisation of tenancies

[Agricultural Holdings Act 1948; Agricultural Holdings Act 1958; Agricultural Holdings Act 1986 s.12, Sch.2.]

A appealed against the decision that a single rent payable in respect of two adjoining plots of land, leased by the trustees, T, to A, was created by an agreement of 1985 operating by surrender by operation of law. Both leases were subject to the Agricultural Holdings Act 1948 and the Agricultural Holdings Act 1958. In 1989 A entered into a management agreement with the Nature Conservancy Council, for a large consideration, which regulated the conduct of agricultural operations on the land. A dispute arose concerning a rent review and T demanded an arbitration under the Agricultural Holdings Act 1986. A denied that there had been any surrender and re-grant and that it had not been intended that the 1985 agreement should amalgamate the two plots.

Held, allowing the appeal, that (1) the arbitrator was required to fix a rent for two separate holdings. The fiction of surrender and re-grant only applied when the intention of the parties could not be implemented without it. The fiction applied to cases concerned with altering the nature of the pre-existing items of property. It did not apply to cases such as this where a rent relating to the original land was converted into rent relating to the original holding with extra land added to it. The property comprised two leases, and no requirement existed that a rent had to change in respect of a lease. The items of property were unaltered by the 1985 agreement and no single lease at an aggregate rent was created, *Jenkins v. Kerman* [1971] Ch. 477 considered; (2) s.12(2) and Sch.2 of the 1986 Act provided a complete statutory code for rent fixing which should be applied without alteration; (3) the arbitrator was entitled to consider the management agreement and the extent to which he did so was a matter for him, and (4) the arbitrator was entitled to investigate the "marriage value" of the land, arising due to the farming use of other nearby land, and give it such weight as he considered appropriate.

TRUSTEES OF JW CHILDERS WILL TRUST v. ANKER (1996) 71 P. & C.R. D5, Neill, L.J., CA.

3795. Rent reviews–arbitration–contract terms–whether arbitrator had made an improper award–whether estoppel affecting subsequent proceedings was created

[Arbitration Act 1979 s.1.]

B, the tenant, applied for leave to appeal against an arbitration award under the Arbitration Act 1979 s.1 relating to the interpretation of cl.5 of their sub-underlease setting out the rent review provisions and defining "the market rent". This was defined by reference to a hypothetical grant of a lease subject to provisions like those of the sub-underlease, including its rent review clause. The arbitrator's award was higher than market rent in order to reflect gains created through the geared rent review clause.

Held, refusing the application for leave, that it was impossible to conclude that the arbitrator had made an improper award, even though it might be possible to make the court take a different construction of the clause based upon commercial common sense, *Ipswich BC v. Fisons Plc* [1990] 1 E.G.L.R. 17, [1990] C.L.Y. 193 applied. However, this did not create an estoppel affecting the rest of the 125 year sub-underlease and R, the landlord, had given an undertaking that estoppel would not be used as an objection in any subsequent proceedings.

BRITISH RAILWAYS BOARD v. RINGBEST LTD [1996] 30 E.G. 94, Sir Richard Scott V.C., Ch D.

3796. Rent reviews–arbitration–whether failure of arbitration to inspect comparables was misconduct–extension of time justified

[Arbitration Act 1950 s.23.]

O applied for an extension of time under the Arbitration Act 1950 s.23 to have an award remitted or set aside after the arbitrator failed to inspect comparables contrary to his own directions during rent review proceedings.

Held, allowing the application for an extension of time, remitting the case back to the arbitrator and setting aside the arbitration award, that the arbitrator's failure to follow his own directions was sufficient to amount to misconduct and it was proper for the arbitrator to reconsider his award in the light of his inspection of the comparables and other evidence so as to determine what the right award should be, *Zermalt Holdings v. Nu-Life Upholstery Repairs Ltd* [1985] 2 E.G.L.R. 14, [1985] C.L.Y. 95 considered.

OAKSTEAD GARAGES LTD v. LEACH PENSION SCHEME (TRUSTEES) LTD [1996] 1 E.G.L.R. 26, Sir Donald Nicholls V.C., Ch D.

3797. Rent reviews–construction–whether "tenant" referred to is hypothetical or actual

A, as landlords, let to P, as tenants, a casino and licensed restaurant for a term of 25 years. Failing agreement on a rent review, an arbitrator was appointed to determine market rent in accordance with assumptions set out in the lease. A point of law was raised before the judge as to whether, on a true construction of the lease, a reference to "the Tenant" was a reference to the tenant under the lease, or a reference to the willing tenant to whom the premises might be let. One of the assumptions stated that "the Tenant" was to be regarded as having been granted all the necessary licences. The judge declared that the reference was to the willing tenant to whom the premises might be let in contrast with the actual tenant under the lease. P appealed against that decision.

Held, allowing the appeal, that this was a simple and narrow point of construction. The lease stipulated at the outset that P were to be called "the Tenant" and that the expression should, where appropriate, include successors in title and assignees. The Court could not see how the term could then be construed as meaning something else, at any rate unless in context it would be absurd to treat it as referring to the actual tenant. The Court was quite unable to see why the rent should be assessed on the assumption that the incoming tenant had been granted the necessary licences. The true construction of the assumption was that the reference to "the Tenant" was a reference only to the actual tenant under the lease.

PARKSIDE CLUBS (NOTTINGHAM) LTD v. ARMGRADE LTD [1995] 48 E.G. 104, Leggatt, L.J., CA.

3798. Rent reviews–construction of clause

A question arose on the construction of an inelegantly drafted rent review clause. The problem had arisen because there had been a sharp rise in the rental value of office properties followed by a dramatic fall. The plaintiff appellant lessee, ANH, argued that the lease provided for an upward only rent review on the first review and on subsequent reviews the rent might be increased or reduced but not so as to fall below the rent payable at the commencement of the term (threshold provision). The defendant respondent lessor, the Secretary of State, argued that the clause provided only for upward rent reviews on each review date, the rent being incapable of being reduced below that previously payable (ratchet provision). The judge found for the Secretary of State and ANH appealed.

Held, dismissing the appeal, that the judge had been correct to conclude that it was a ratchet provision. Had there been a clear mistake on the face of the document, and it was clear what the correction should be, the Court should make the correction. Alternatively, in the absence of rectification, the Court should reach what answer it could on the basis of the uncorrected wording, *East v. Pantiles Plant Hire Ltd* [1982] 2 E.G.L.R. 111, [1982] C.L.Y. 1803 considered. In the instant case, there was no obviously correctable error. A presumption against superfluous language was not necessarily useful, *Tea Trade Properties Ltd v. Cin Properties Ltd* [1990] 1 E.G.L.R. 155, [1990] C.L.Y. 2861 considered. Both threshold and ratchet provisions were not uncommon in commercial leases and whether rent review clauses gave landlords windfall gains must yield to the actual wording of the relevant clause, *British Gas Corp v. Universities Superannuation Scheme Ltd* [1986] 1 W.L.R. 398, [1986] C.L.Y. 1911 considered. There was a provision, in the instant lease, which appeared to counter the possibility that a rent review might lead to a lower rent. Its emphatic terms showed that it was intended to have substantive effect and the judge had been entitled to attach importance to them. That the expression "rent hereby reserved" had been used in this provision (rather than the figure of the annual rent at the commencement of the term) indicated that it was the rent to have been agreed at each review and not the original rent.

SECRETARY OF STATE FOR THE ENVIRONMENT v. ASSOCIATED NEWSPAPER HOLDINGS LTD (1996) 72 P. &. C.R. 395, Peter Gibson, L.J., CA.

3799. Rent reviews–different calculations for ascertaining "annual rack rent" in different paragraphs of the schedule to the lease–whether definition omitting service charges should be read as including them

During the second of four rent review dates specified in a lease lasting 96 years and three months, questions arose in relation to a schedule to the lease and a deed of variation. The tenant, B, sought determination of those questions. The schedule stated that additional rent should be one third of an amount by which the annual rack rent exceeded £185,000, and thereafter, one third of the amount by which the annual rack rent exceeded the previously determined sum. The "annual rack rent" was defined in Para.1 (c) to the Schedule and was to be the amount payable by those in occupation under leases or licences and amounted to the rent, including the service charges, less the cost of "central heating, hot water, porterage, lighting, cleaning or other services and the annual cost of maintenance, repair insurance management and all other outgoings". Where no leases or licences subsisted at the relevant time or the landlord or the tenant thought that the rent was less or more, respectively, than the full market rent, Para.2 provided for arbitration. In such a case the "annual rack rent" was the rent less the cost of "maintenance repair insurance management and all other outgoings other than outgoings borne by those persons in actual occupation".

Held, allowing the application and making declarations accordingly, that the purpose of Para.2 was to provide a default provision if the parties could not agree or if no leases or licences existed at the review date. It would make no sense to calculate the annual rack rent by deducting the service charges in one case but not in the other. Therefore the calculation in Para.2 should also take account of the service charges.

BATH HOUSE ESTATES LTD v. CROWN ESTATES COMMISSIONERS [1996] E.G.C.S. 72, Blackburne, J., Ch D.

3800. Rent reviews–failure to appoint arbitrator within time limit in lease–whether review increase failed as result–time limit sought under s.27 operation–conditions necessary before time extension allowed

[Arbitration Act 1950 s.27.]

F, the landlords, applied under the Arbitration Act 1950 s.27 for a time limit extension allowing them to appoint a rent review arbitrator after the expiry of the time limit stipulated in the lease. Following a failure to agree a rent review increase from £13,450 to £30,000 per annum, F's surveyors failed to appoint an arbitrator in line with the stipulated time limit. N, the tenants, sought to rely on a lease term which provided that, in the event of such a failure, the previous rent should remain in force and the review figure was to be of no effect.

Held, allowing the application, that (1) s.27 granted the court power both to extend a time limit and to reinstate a claim, *Sioux Inc v. China Salvage* [1980] 1 W.L.R. 996, [1980] C.L.Y. 96 followed; (2) the wording of the term did not limit the application of s.27, as it conveyed the same meaning as the term in *Aspen Trader, The* [1981] 1 Lloyd's Rep. 273 and *Comdel Commodities v. Siporex Trade SA (No.2)* [1991] 1 A.C. 148, [1990] C.L.Y. 210 and (3) in allowing a time extension under s.27 it was necessary to consider the following factors, as laid down in *Comdel*: (a) delay, on the facts a 10 week delay was of short duration; (b) review amount, the sum involved suggested hardship for F if deprived of the increased rent; (c) fault, here the fault lay with F's surveyors, and showed a circumstance beyond their control; (d) no evidence showed that F had been misled by any other party and (e) no evidence suggested that N had been prejudiced by the delay. As a result the extension was granted, subject to F paying the costs and no interest being charged for the period preceding the decision.

FORDGATE (BINGLEY) LTD v. NATIONAL WESTMINSTER BANK PLC [1994] 39 E.G. 135, Carnwath, J., Ch D.

3801. Rent reviews–fixtures–principles governing a rent review where tenant has improved premises–rentalisation of fixtures where there is no express agreement governing fixtures

[Arbitration Act 1979 s.1.]

N applied for an extension of time to apply for leave to appeal against the decision of an arbitrator in relation to a disputed rent review. L sought leave to appeal against a decision of another arbitrator which was found in N's favour. The issue of both reviews was whether N's fixtures should be rentalised and included in the review.

Held, that (1) time to apply for leave to appeal should be extended because although there was a delay of two weeks, there was an absence of prejudice to the landlords and an unsatisfactory situation would arise if time were not extended; (2) leave should be given to L although it would normally be refused. However, the issue was the same for a number of leases between the parties and this would avoid inconsistent arbitration awards and allow, if necessary, a single judgment on a further appeal to the Court of Appeal and (3) N's fixtures should not be rentalised. As there were no express terms to the contrary the premises should be valued with improvements considered, *Laura Investment v. Havering* [1992] E.G.L.R. 155, [1992] C.L.Y. 2739 and *Cooperative Wholesale Ltd v. National Westminster Bank Plc* [1995] 1 E.G.L.R. 97, [1995] 1 C.L.Y. 3073 applied. However, it would not be fair to include improvements made by N at his own expense and without obligation. Trade fixtures should not be considered if they could be lawfully removed at the end of the tenancy, even if affixed under obligation, *Young v. Dalgety Plc* [1987] 1 E.G.L.R. 116, [1987] C.L.Y. 2155 and *New Zealand v. HM & S Sand* [1982] 1 Q.B. 1145, [1982] C.L.Y. 1808 applied.

OCEAN ACCIDENT AND GUARANTEE CORP v. NEXT PLC; COMMERCIAL UNION ASSURANCE CO PLC v. NEXT PLC [1996] 33 E.G. 91, Stanley Burnton Q.C., Ch D.

3802. Rent reviews–government departments–clause without ratchet–whether on "arm's length commercial terms"

The State Insurance Office was privatised in 1990 and the New Zealand government sold the shares in the company to NU and retained the assets. Among the assets was a number of office buildings. A clause of the sale and purchase agreements with NU stated that the Crown should use its best endeavours to procure that formal leases were executed in respect of the properties on arms length commercial terms. State Insurance Office's previous leases had but included a provision that rent reviews would be upwards only. The formal lease, however, did not include ratchet provision. NU argued that the lease was not on an arms length commercial terms because most commercial leases executed did include a ratchet.

Held, dismissing the appeal there had been an intention that the terms of the lease, taken as a whole, should be such as would have been negotiated between commercial parties bargaining at arms length. The evidence that only a small minority of commercial leases negotiated in the open market lacked ratchet provision was not inconsistent with the lease having being negotiated on commercial terms. In these circumstances, there was nothing to displace the prima facia assumption that the formalised lease should incorporate the terms actually agreed.

NORWICH UNION LIFE INSURANCE SOCIETY v. ATTORNEY GENERAL [1995] E.G.C.S. 85, Lord Goff of Chieveley, PC.

3803. Rent reviews–interpretation of clause–whether words limited clause

M sought a declaration as to the length of a hypothetical lease term referred to in a rent review clause, contending it should be the residue of the term remaining at the review date.

Held, refusing the declaration, that the matter was to be resolved by construing the document as a whole to ascertain the parties' intentions. Where these were in doubt, a fair and sensible result was to be achieved, mindful of the commercial nature of the clause concerned. Any uncertainty was to be resolved by interpreting the clause by giving it as close a resemblance to reality as possible *Cooperative Wholesale Society Ltd v. National Westminster Bank Plc* [1995] 1 E.G.L.R. 97, [1995] 1 C.L.Y. 3073 considered. On the facts, P's contention as to the limiting effect of the words "not exceeding" was accepted, ruling out M's interpretation as meaning equal to the residue of the lease term, *Prudential Assurance Co Ltd v. Salisburys Handbags Ltd* [1992] 1 E.G.L.R. 153, [1992] C.L.Y. 2735 considered. The declaration provided, therefore, that the term was not to exceed the residue, being one the lessor would reasonably be expected to draft and the lessee to accept, giving the best rent reasonably obtainable on the open market.

MILLSHAW PROPERTY CO LTD v. PRESTON BC [1995] E.G.C.S. 186, R C Kaye Q.C., Ch D.

3804. Rent reviews–interpretation of lease provision–inclusion of gearing formula–whether intention relevant to interpretation process

A dispute arose between NU, as landlord, and BT the successor in title of the original tenant, as to the application of a rent review gearing formula in respect of two parts of leased premises. NU contended that the assessment of comparable open market rent values, as provided for in the review clause, was to be carried out on a basis that did not include the formula included in the lease review clause.

Held, giving judgment for BT, that it was necessary to decide whether the parties had intended to exclude the gearing formula when applying the rent review provision. The wording of the clause was inclusive in nature and in attempting to ascertain the parties' intentions the court would be re-writing the agreement, rather than merely interpreting it.

NORWICH UNION LIFE ASSURANCE SOCIETY v. BRITISH TELECOMMUNICATIONS PLC [1995] E.G.C.S. 148, Knox, J., Ch D.

3805. Rent reviews–interpreted as allowing upwards and downwards reviews–whether valuer appointment provision mandatory in absence of agreement–business efficacy requirements–excess interim rent repayment implied

R was the tenant of warehouse premises demised to R by J for a term of 20 years at a rent to be reviewed in accordance with the provisions of the fourth schedule to the lease. Those provisions provided that the reviewed rent should be the best yearly rent obtainable on the grant of a new lease in the same terms (except as to the reserved rent). The provisions also provided that the reviewed rent should be determined by agreement between R and J and in default by a specialist valuer "such valuer to be agreed between the parties or nominated by the President for the time being of the Royal Institute of Chartered Surveyors upon the application of the landlord". It was also provided that R was to continue paying rent at the highest level paid prior to the review date until the reviewed rent had been determined, with an obligation on R to pay any shortfall between the existing rent and the reviewed rent. The provisions did not make any provision for repayment of any surplus to R in the event that the reviewed rent was less than that payable pending the determination of the reviewed rent. On the rent review date the market rent ascertained in accordance with the review provisions was less than the rent then payable under the lease. R sought to initiate a rent review but J refused to agree a new rent, refused to concur in the appointment of a specialist valuer and refused to seek the nomination of a valuer by the President of the RICS. R sought a declaration that J was bound to apply for the nomination of a valuer by the President and directions as to the repayment of any surplus rent paid between the review date and the date upon which the reviewed rent was finally determined. J contended that in effect the provisions created an upwards only rent review over which J had final control by deciding whether or not to seek the nomination of a valuer.

Held, granting the declaration sought, that had the parties intended the rent review provisions to create an upwards only rent review, the provisions of the lease would have said so. The fact that the review provisions expressly provided for the payment of any shortfall but did not expressly provide for the repayment of any surplus did not assist in determining whether the review required by the lease was an upwards only review. Those provisions were simply administrative and accounting provisions. The rent review provisions placed an enforceable requirement on J to seek the nomination of a specialist valuer by the President of the RICS. If that were wrong, in order to give business efficacy to the rent review provisions so as to provide for the downwards review that the provisions clearly contemplated, there was an implied obligation on the part of J to secure the nomination of a valuer. *Sudbrook Trading Estate Ltd v. Eggleton* [1983] 1 A.C. 444, [1982] C.L.Y. 1776 applied, *Basingstoke and Deane BC v. Host Group* [1988] 1 W.L.R. 348, [1988] C.L.Y. 2069 considered. In the circumstances, the absence of any provision requiring repayment of excess interim rental payments was to be remedied by implying a term that was liable to repay any such excess, should the agreed market rent be less than that presently charged.

ROYAL BANK OF SCOTLAND v. JENNINGS (1995) 70 P. & C.R. 459, Evans-Lombe, J, Ch D.

3806. Rent reviews–leave to appeal from arbitration awards–wrong test applied at first instance–whether strong prima facie case showed arbitrator made error of law–whether assessment of evidence disclosed prima facie error of law

[Arbitration Act 1979.]

GH appealed against a decision granting leave to appeal out of time, in respect of a rent review award of June 1992. Lease rent review clauses provided that improvements by the tenant, other than under the terms of the lease, were to be disregarded for both review and arbitration purposes. In default of agreement, an arbitrator was appointed who made an interim award in June 1992, based on all improvements carried out during the leasehold term. However, the tenant did not see the award details until November 1992 and in February 1993 sought leave to appeal out of time on an error of law.

Held, allowing the appeal, that judges had to ensure that the intention behind the Arbitration Act 1979, to promote quick and final arbitration awards, was not thwarted by the exercise of the discretion conferred by s.1 of the Act. At first instance, the test used to determine the issue of leave required it to be granted if the court was left in real doubt as to the arbitrator being correct in law, *Lucas Industries Plc v. Welsh Development Agency* [1986] 1 E.G.L.R. 147, [1986] C.L.Y. 1907 applied. However, this test had been disapproved, as Parliament's preference for finality in rent review matters required a strong prima facie case to be made out when applying for leave to appeal from rent review arbitration awards, *Ipswich BC v. Fisons Plc* [1990] 1 E.G.L.R. 17, [1990] C.L.Y. 193; *Prudential Assurance Co Ltd v. Trafalgar House Group Estates Ltd* [1991] 1 E.G.L.R. 1277, [1991] C.L.Y. 201 followed. Considering the arbitrator's decision in the light of this more stringent test, it could not be found that a point of law had arisen on the alleged improper conduct of the review. Further, the assessment of evidence by the arbitrator was a matter for him alone and could not be deemed to constitute a prima facie error of law.

EURIPIDES v. GASCOYNE HOLDINGS LTD (1996) 72 P. & C.R. 301, Glidewell, L.J., CA.

3807. Rent reviews–notice–whether notice of rent increase given two clear periods of year before effective–determination of review date expiry time

B leased premises to S from June 24, 1982 for 20 years until June 23, 2002. The landlords gave the tenants notice of a rent increase on October 9, 1991, eight and a half months prior to the date it was to commence. The tenants claimed that the notice was invalid as it was not sent a clear period of two quarters of a year immediately preceding the review date as the lease specified. Validity depended on the fact that the review date fell on June 24, 1992. The landlord alleged that the tenth year had not expired until the night of June 23-24 and, as such, the notice was in time. The tenant claimed that expiry was on the next day. At first instance the notice was found to be invalid.

Held, allowing the appeal, that the review date was on the expiry of the tenth year of the term which occurred at midnight between June 23 and 24. The tenth year had not expired until the night of June 23-24 and therefore the notice was in time. The landlord's interpretation construed the lease provisions according to common sense. The issue centred around identification of the quarters and, as such, the landlord was entitled to have served the notice any time before December 24, 1991.

SUPASNAPS LTD v. BAILEY (1995) 20 P. & C.R. 450, Nourse, L.J., CA.

3808. Rent reviews–notice served under break clause–meaning of "the term" to determine operation of rent review

[Landlord and Tenant Act 1954 s.25.]

W, the tenant, appealed against a declaration that, despite the fact that CE, the landlord, had served notice on W to determine the tenancy under a break clause and also under the Landlord and Tenant Act 1954 s.25, the rent review clause was still operative. The question was whether the words "the term" meant 20 years or earlier determination as defined in the lease, or whether they should be construed as referring to the continuation of the tenancy, which appeared to be the case in clauses concerning the payment of insurance and covenants for quiet enjoyment.

Held, allowing the appeal, that in the case of the rent review clause, it was operated within the contractual term of the lease and so could not be relied upon once the term had been determined. The reviews were to take place at equal periods and so rent could not be ascertained if there was not an equal period left to run.

WILLISON v. CHEVERELL ESTATES LTD [1996] 1 E.G.L.R. 116, Balcombe, L.J., CA.

3809. Rent reviews–rent free period–application for extension of time to apply for remission of award to arbitration refused

[Arbitration Act 1950 s.22.]

B granted leases to L and after failing to agree on rent the two parties went before an arbitrator. The arbitrator found in favour of L but refused to grant the 10 per cent discount in rent which they sought. Harman, J. reversed the arbitrator but refused to remit the decision back to arbitration. This decision was upheld in the Court of Appeal. L now applied for an extension of time in which to apply for the remission of the award to the arbitrator under the Arbitration Act 1950 s.22.

Held, dismissing the application, that the delay of seven months in applying for the extension could not be regarded as minor. No injustice had been caused by the decision and the court could not remit the case in the absence of an injustice. Under the Act defective reasoning was not a ground for remitting a case.

BROADGATE SQUARE PLC v. LEHMAN BROTHERS LTD (NO.2) [1995] 33 E.G. 89, Stanley Burnton Q.C., Ch D.

3810. Rent reviews–right to buy–secured tenant's right to buy freehold property irrelevant in determining reasonable rent–definition of "improvements"–statutory interpretation

[Housing Act 1985.]

D, a secure tenant of E, appealed against a decision granting declarations in E's favour on issues arising from a property valuation in connection with D's right to buy and rent review. D contended that: (1) works undertaken by him to make the property habitable were improvements in terms of the Housing Act 1985 Part V and should be disregarded for valuation purposes. Alternatively the works exceeded mere repair or renewal and, viewed as a whole, constituted improvements and (2) improvement works previously agreed between the partners and scheduled to the lease should be disregarded for rent review purposes under his statutory tenancy. E submitted that regard should be paid, at the valuation date, to D's right to buy the reversion.

Held, dismissing the appeal, that (1) the definition of "improvements" in s.187 of the 1985 Act was exhaustive, and unless work was specified in that section, nothing could be an improvement unless it was an addition or alteration to the property; repairs, renewal and decoration work could not therefore qualify as an improvement and (2) whether improvements specified in a lease schedule amounted to improvements was a matter of interpretation of the rent review clause. The judge at first instance had erred in finding that s.101 of the 1985 Act was inapplicable where a rent review clause was provided. Section 102 and s.103 provide the means whereby a landlord can increase the rent, where a rent review clause is provided s.101 requires that improvements, as defined in s.97(2), carried out by the tenant are to be disregarded when the review provisions become operable. The existence of a right to buy serves to make a tenancy more attractive to a tenant, but less so for a landlord, thus creating a relevant factor in determining the market rent. However, the review clause merely required that the rent be set at a reasonable, as opposed to a market, level, *Ponsford v. HMS Aerosols Ltd* [1979] A.C. 63, [1978] C.L.Y. 1813 considered. The right to buy had been conferred on secure tenants as an inducement to buy the freehold of their homes. It was not reasonable that a landlord could use the existence of the right to buy to increase the rent charged, or for the tenant to be required to pay an increased rent whilst still in the public sector purely because he had been offered a discounted purchase price as an inducement. Therefore, the discount should not be taken into account in determining the rent level.

DICKINSON v. ENFIELD LBC [1996] 49 E.G. 108, Millett, L.J., CA.

3811. Rent reviews–subsequent deed giving landlord option to require surrender–whether option terms relevant to review

C granted W a lease of certain premises. The lease contained a rent review provision providing for the rent to be reviewed with reference to the annual rental value of the premises in the open market on the review date on a lease for a term of years certain "on the same terms and conditions... as this present demise" other than as to the amount of the rent and the duration of the term. Thereafter, C and W entered into a deed pursuant to which W surrendered part of the demised premises to C and granted C an option to require the surrender of further parts of the premises. An issue arose on the rent review as to whether "the same terms and conditions" in the hypothetical lease included the obligations imposed on the parties by the deed. C sought a declaration as to the interpretation of the rent review provisions.

Held, that the words "the same terms and conditions" meant the terms and conditions prevailing at the date of the rent review. As by that time the terms and conditions included the terms of the deed of surrender, they were to be taken into account for the purposes of the rent review. There was a presumption in favour of reality which favoured the construction of the provision in the light of the rights and obligations actually enjoyed by the parties at the review date rather than the rights and obligations that they enjoyed when the lease was originally granted, *Lynnthorpe Enterprises Ltd v. Sidney Smith (Chelsea) Ltd* [1990] 1 E.G.L.R. 148, [1990] C.L.Y. 279 considered.

COMMERCIAL UNION LIFE ASSURANCE CO LTD v. WOOLWORTHS PLC [1996] 1 E.G.L.R. 237, Stanley Burnton Q.C., Ch D.

3812. Rent reviews–upward review with reference to a notional premises within a 35 mile radius–construction of clause disputed–whether landlord entitled to refer to best rent in the area

D, the landlord, sought a declaration on the construction of a rent review clause within a lease for a warehouse granted to S, the tenant, during a sale and leaseback transaction. Alternatively, D sought rectification of the clause to give effect to what D claimed the parties had intended when the lease was granted. The clause allowed for an upwards only rent review which could be based on the open market rental value of the actual premises or could refer to a notional premises which was to be a warehouse unit of 50,000 sq ft within a 35 mile radius of Ross-on-Wye. The problem was that the clause did not specify where the notional premises was located within the 35 mile radius. Rents varied greatly within that area and D argued that the highest rent should apply.

Held, allowing the application and giving the declaration sought by D but dismissing the claim for rectification, that (1) the language of the clause favoured D's interpretation that the notional unit could be situated anywhere within the specified radius. The language could not support S's contention that the notional premises should be located within Ross-on-Wye, but with reference to comparables within the radius. S's argument, that a distortion of the language could be permitted owing to the presumption of reality which interpreted a rent review clause with reference to the actual premises, was rejected. Such a presumption did not apply when a notional premises was referred to as an alternative to the use of the actual premises as in this case; (2) although D had believed that the review would be based on the best rent within the area, this intention was not communicated to their solicitors and D could not rely on estoppel as the judge found, as a matter of fact, that S had not explained the rent review clause in such a way and (3) rectification could not be ordered on the basis of unilateral mistake as it was clear that S had not acted unconscionably. The court did not believe that D was approaching the transaction under a mistaken belief which had arisen during a telephone conversation made to arrange for the property to be viewed.

DUKEMINSTER (EBBGATE HOUSE ONE) LTD v. SOMERFIELD PROPERTY CO LTD (FORMERLY GATEWAY PROPERTIES LTD) [1996] E.G.C.S. 56, Michael Hart Q.C., Ch D.

3813. Rent reviews–whether relevant evidence considered–whether calculations revealed inconsistency in determining award

A applied to set aside a rent review award in respect of a site, one half of which operated as a petrol station; the other as a truck stop. The lease provided for a five yearly, upwards only, rent review, based on prevailing open market values. The tenant appealed against the 1990 review, which the arbitrator had set at £102,750, whereas the landlord and tenant sought £179,808 and £42,750 respectively. The tenant contended that the arbitrator had failed both to take account of evidence regarding the separate use of both parts of the premises and to allow for relevant factors stated in the award.

Held, dismissing the application, that (1) although disregarding evidence amounted to misconduct on the part of the arbitrator, *Unit Four Cinemas Ltd v. Tosara Investment Ltd* [1993] 2 E.G.L.R. 11, [1994] C.L.Y. 208 and *Handley v. Nationwide Anglia Building Society* [1992] 2 E.G.L.R. 114, [1993] C.L.Y. 169 considered, read as a whole, the award showed the evidence had been considered before being rejected. Clear reasons had been given for the decision, which was expressed in neither a technical nor a legalistic manner, allowing the parties to understand how the arbitrator had reached his conclusion and (2) however the award was remitted for reconsideration due to inconsistencies in the calculation arising from the mixed use.

ATKINSON v. WSFS LTD [1995] E.G.C.S. 152, Coyler, J., Ch D.

3814. Rent reviews–whether time of essence in serving nature of review–lease giving timetable after service to allow tenant to decide if links to determine tenancy–relationship between review and break clauses

C's predecessor in title granted a lease of office premises to the Secretary of State for a term of 42 years from September 1971. Four rent review clauses were provided for in the lease and one break clause; September 29, 1991 was the last date for service of a notice requiring a rent review, while March 29, 1992 was the latest date for the service of a notice to determine the lease. However, C did not give notice to review the rent until April 14, 1992. The Secretary of State argued that the notice was invalid. The judge below held that it was valid as time was not of the essence for the service of the notice as the prospect of a rent increase would not be the sole factor in influencing the Secretary of State's decision to determine the lease. The Secretary of State appealed, arguing that relevant authorities showed that time was of the essence where the lease laid down a timetable which gave the tenant a period after the service of the rent review notices before he had to decide whether to serve a notice to determine the tenancy.

Held, allowing the appeal, that the Secretary of State's argument was correct, *United Scientific Holdings Limited v. Burnley BC* [1978] A.C. 904, [1977] C.L.Y. 1758 applied. If time was not of the essence, the period allowed for the service of the break notice for which time was of the essence was eliminated or eroded. The fact that the lease provided for four rent reviews and only one break and the fact that the lease provided for rent reviews both upwards and downwards was irrelevant. The interrelation between the rent review clause and the other provisions of the lease displaced the presumption that time was not of the essence.

CENTRAL ESTATES LTD v. SECRETARY OF STATE FOR THE ENVIRONMENT (1996) 72 P. & C.R. 482, Morritt, L.J., CA.

3815. Rent reviews–whether upward only intended–whether rectification allowed for lease to reflect parties' continuing common intention

BI applied for rectification of a nine year underlease. The lease contained a rent review provision, but did not mention whether it applied to upwards only reviews. By the 1993 review date, the value of the premises had fallen, but BI claimed rectification based on the fact that an earlier lease had proceeded on the same basis.

Held, allowing rectification of the lease, that on the balance of probabilities it was found that a common intention of the parties had been for upward only reviews. Such intention had continued until execution of the lease, but surveyors acting for the parties showed the lease was to follow the earlier one. Additionally, a clause in the new lease providing for arrears created during the review process to be paid as from the review date indicated the upwards only nature of the agreement. Rectification was granted, allowing for a nil increase, where market values were shown to be less than the rent charged for the preceding period.

BRIMICAM INVESTMENTS LTD v. BLUE CIRCLE HEATING LTD [1995] E.G.C.S. 18, Chadwick, J., Ch D.

3816. Repair covenants–lessee to pay half the cost of repair of main structure–disagreement as to whether roofing works reasonably necessary–whether injunction available to lessee to prevent works

[Law of Property Act 1925 s.146; Landlord and Tenant Act 1985 s.17, s.18.]

H leased a flat to T for a term of 99 years. The freehold was subsequently vested in H and the second plaintiffs. T, as lessee, covenanted to carry out interior decorations and to pay half the cost The surveyors drew up a list of dilapidations which included some small external works and later the landlords gave notice to T that builders had reported that the roof was in need of attention. The landlords served notice under the Law of Property Act 1925 s.146, requiring T to amend these alleged breaches of covenant. Tenders for the cost of the work showed the cost of the work to be in the region of £10,840 to £11,450. T's surveyors advised that the roof repairs required were only in the region of £1,500 to £2,000. The landlords served a summons on T for re-entry and sent in builders to erect scaffolding preliminary to the roofing works. T sought and obtained an injunction to restrain the landlords from proceeding with the work pending the resolution of main issue and the landlords appealed.

Held, allowing the appeal, that the injunction had been wrongly granted. Applying the principles Lord Diplock in *American Cyanamid Co v. Ethicon Ltd* [1975] A.C. 396, [1975] C.L.Y. 2640, a plaintiff must establish at least a good arguable claim to the rights he seeks to protect, a requirement not met by T. The decision as to how to repair was the landlord's but that decision must be reasonable. The injunction could not be sustained by an argument that it was not based solely on the roofing works but also on a fear of trespass by the landlords into the flat. T had an alternative remedy under the terms of the Landlord and Tenant Act 1985 s.17 and s.18 on the basis of a declaration that the cost of the works was unreasonably high.

HI-LIFT ELEVATOR SERVICES v. TEMPLE (1996) 28 H.L.R. 1, Glidewell, L.J., CA.

3817. Repair covenants–time when breach arises–whether breach as soon as defect arises

BT was the tenant of premises on the sixth and seventh floors of a building owned by SL. The lease required SL to keep the whole of the premises in good repair. A bulge developed in the walls at fifth floor level in the building and, when informed, SL took steps to remedy the defect. In the meantime BT brought proceedings alleging a breach of the repairing covenant and the judge, on a preliminary issue of construction, ruled that there was a breach as soon as a defect arose, not after the expiry of some reasonable period within which SL could perform repairs. SL appealed.

Held, dismissing the appeal, that a covenant to keep the premises in good repair which extended to the whole building obliged the landlord to keep the premises in repair at all times and there was a breach as soon as a defect occurred, *Makin v. Watkinson* (1861-73) All E.R. Rep 281; *O'Brien v. Robinson* [1973] 1 All E.R. 583, [1973] C.L.Y. 1900 considered.

BRITISH TELECOMMUNICATIONS PLC v. SUN LIFE ASSURANCE SOCIETY PLC [1995] 3 W.L.R. 622, Nourse, L.J., CA.

3818. Repair covenants–underleases–privity of contract–third party cannot take benefit of covenant–statutory interpretation

[Law of Property Act 1925 s.56.]

H was the subtenant of a property who, by cl.3 of an underlease, had covenanted with the tenant to repair the property and to allow the superior landlords, A's predecessor in title, or their agents, to enter the property to examine the repairs and to recover the cost of carrying them out where they had been improperly executed. In the absence of privity of estate or contract between the superior landlord and subtenant, A could not recover these costs directly from the subtenant. A brought an action against H, arguing that it could enforce the covenant because of the express mention of "the superior landlords" in the covenant and because the covenants were clearly meant to be for the benefit of the superior landlord, seeking to rely on the Law of Property Act 1925 s.56 (1) which provided that a person could take the benefit of any covenant in relation to property even if he was not named as a party to the conveyance.

Held, dismissing the action, that A could not enforce the covenants. Someone who was not a party to a contract could take advantage of it under s.56 only where it had been made for his benefit, and a third party could not rely on the provision unless the covenant actually purported to be made with him.

AMSPROP TRADING LTD v. HARRIS DISTRIBUTION LTD [1996] N.P.C. 154, Neuberger, J., Ch D.

3819. Residential tenancies–breakdown of marriage of joint tenants–husband in occupation–injunction forbidding his exclusion–wife terminating joint tenancy–whether council entitled to possession

H and W were joint tenants of residential council property under an agreement which stated that either party could terminate the tenancy by giving four weeks' written notice. Following the breakdown of the marriage, W left the house. H remained in occupation. H obtained an injunction to forbid W from attempting to exclude him or actually excluding him from the house. W applied to the council to be rehoused and signed a notice to terminate the joint tenancy. The council, with knowledge of the injunction, brought proceedings in the county court against H for possession of the house. H argued that the council was in contempt of court and the claim for possession was dismissed. The council appealed.

Held, dismissing the appeal, that in giving notice to terminate the tenancy, W was in breach of the injunction and therefore in contempt of court. The council, in bringing proceedings for possession of the house with knowledge of the injunction, was in contempt of court in that the proceedings were an abuse of the process of the court. Therefore, the notice could not be relied upon to terminate the tenancy while the injunction remained in force.

HARROW LBC v. JOHNSTONE (1996) 28 H.L.R. 83, Russell, L.J., CA.

3820. Residential tenancies–hotel apartments–tenant wrongfully excluded from possession–trespass–measure of damages where landlord derived no benefit

H bought the long leasehold of 30 apartments in a hotel in the Bahamas. The apartments continued to be managed on H's behalf as an integral part of the hotel. The hotel owners, I, ejected H in 1974 and did not give up possession until 1990. H claimed damages for trespass. The registrar awarded damages representing H's original investment at 12.5 per cent simple interest over the period of trespass. H appealed and I cross-appealed. The Court of Appeal of the Bahamas held by a majority that the appropriate measure of damages was a sum representing the notional gross revenue of the 30 apartments on the basis of 100 per cent occupancy throughout the period of trespass. I appealed to the Privy Council, arguing that damages should have been assessed on the basis that the hotel had an occupancy rate of only 35 per cent during the relevant period and was running at a loss.

Held, dismissing the appeal, that a person who let out goods on hire, or the landlord of residential property, was entitled to recover damages from a trespasser who had wrongfully used his property whether or not he could show that he would have let the property to anybody else or used it himself. It was irrelevant that the landlord had not suffered any actual loss by being deprived of the use of his property and that the trespasser had not derived any actual benefit. On the facts, a reasonable rental value for the 30 apartments for 365 days a year was the rate normally paid by tour operators, which exceeded the amount awarded by the Court of Appeal, *Swordheath Properties Ltd v. Tabet* [1979] 1 All E.R. 240, [1979] C.L.Y. 1626 and Nicholls L.J. in *Stoke-on-Trent City Council v. W&J Wass Ltd* [1988] 3 All E.R. 394, [1988] C.L.Y. 3269 applied.

INVERUGIE INVESTMENTS LTD v. HACKETT [1995] 1 W.L.R. 713, Lord Keith of Kinkel, PC.

3821. Residential tenancies–managing agents–harassment of tenant–liability to contribution in respect of damages

[Housing Act 1988 s.27, s.28.]

L3 owned premises which he let to T before emigrating to the USA and arranging informally for L1 to manage the premises. When L1 became ill, he handed management to L2, who harassed T into leaving. The judge awarded damages under the Housing Act 1988 s.27 and s.28 against L2 and L3. The judge also awarded damages against L3 for breaches of his covenant to repair and against L2 and L3 for L2's torts. The judge appointed T equitable receiver of all causes of action vested in L3, including claims against L1 for breaches of duty as managing agent, and gave T leave to serve a contribution notice in L3's name against L1 but dismissed the claim for contribution.

Held, varying the judge's order, that a landlord's liability under the 1988 Act could be founded on his own actions or those of an agent, but only the landlord was liable to pay damages. The formula for compensation provided by the Act was not apt for an agent, so there was a conclusive bar to any claim under the Act against L1. However, since the claim for contribution required further investigation the matter would be remitted.

SAMPSON v. WILSON [1995] 3 W.L.R. 455, Sir Thomas Bingham, M.R., CA.

3822. Residential tenancies–notice to quit–service not required under tenancy agreement–validity

[Law of Property Act 1925 s.196; Protection from Eviction Act 1977.]

In 1975 D was granted a weekly tenancy by W for which he signed an "Acceptance of Offer of Accommodation" document. D emigrated to the United States leaving A as a caretaker. On the basis of this, W served a notice to quit on D on December 14, 1992 as required by the Protection from Eviction Act 1977 and effective on January 18, 1993. The notice was served both at the house and at D's address in the United States. The notice to quit was deemed valid as it had been served at the premises and under the requirements of the Law of Property Act 1925 s.196. Possession was given to W and D appealed.

Held, allowing the appeal, that service of a notice to quit was not required by the terms of the tenancy agreement which D had signed, as no express provision had been made for it. Section 196(5) was only applicable where notices to quit were required to be served by an instrument. This did not include a statute and therefore the council could not argue that a notice was required under the 1977 Act.

WANDSWORTH LBC v. ATWELL (1995) 27 H.L.R. 536, Glidewell, L.J.: Waite, L.J., CA.

3823. Residential tenancies–rent reviews–definition of fair rent–whether rent assessment committee decision was perverse

[Rent Act 1977; Housing Act 1988.]

S owned a block of flats which were let on regulated tenancies under the Rent Act 1977. Any flats which fell vacant were relet on assured tenancies under the Housing Act 1988. S considered that such tenancies justified a higher fair rent. G disagreed. S appealed against G's decision and argued that it had erred in law because (1) G had not appreciated that a fair rent was the market rent discounted to remove the effect of scarcity; (2) G had considered that it could only use the rents payable under the assured tenancies for similar flats as comparables and (3) G had decided such rents could not be used as comparables as the security of tenure would have to be reflected in a discount.

Held, allowing the appeal, that G's decision was perverse and should be quashed as (1) a fair rent was the market rent but G had used "fair" in the sense of reasonable; (2) discounted rents could be used by G to determine a fair rent because a market rent adjusted for scarcity was the definition of a fair rent and (3) if G had regarded the fair rent as the market rent less the disregards and discounts for scarcity then the existence of scarcity was not a reason to reject the comparables.

SPATH HOLME LTD v. GREATER MANCHESTER AND LANCASHIRE RENT ASSESSMENT COMMITTEE (1996) 28 H.L.R. 107, Morritt, L.J., CA.

3824. Residential tenancies–tenant in occupation without being asked for rent–adverse possession

P sought possession of a house which had been rented by H on the basis of an oral weekly tenancy since 1967. H last paid rent in 1971 but continued in possession until his death in 1988. The defendant was his successor who relied on an agreement between H and his then landlord which requested H not to pay any rent until further notice.

Held, dismissing P's claim, that a tenant who remained in possession without paying rent was treated as a trespasser with adverse possession and if, after 12 years, no attempt had been made to gain possession, the owner would be statute barred from claiming his title. H had not acknowledged P's title in that period and therefore P's title had been extinguished.

PRICE v. HARTLEY [1995] N.P.C. 80, Nourse, L.J., CA.

3825. Restitution–leases–mistaken payment to tenant–solicitors' liability to landlord

R&N, a firm of solicitors, appealed against an order giving judgment for PIM for a sum of £4,019 plus interest. PIM were the plaintiffs in an action against R&N in respect of money sent to R&N by a solicitor acting for B, as payment of sums due to PIM under a lease. PIM owned an office building and wanted to terminate two of the leases of the third floor, held by F&J and B, and grant one lease to F&J who would then grant an underlease to B. The aim was to reorganise the management of the building. R&N acted for F&J and inadvertently paid to F&J the sum due to PIM.

Held, dismissing the appeal, that (1) the facts justified the application of the laws of attornment and restitution; (2) R&N had satisfied the conditions in Goff and Jones, *The Law of Restitution* (4th ed) and were accountable or had attorned to PIM in respect of the £4,019. R&N had received the money as solicitors for completion of the transaction on behalf of their clients. They were not agents and so the fund was in their hands. B's solicitors had requested that R&N hold the money for PIM's use on completion. R&N had assented by implication to hold the money for the use of PIM. That assent had been communicated via B's solicitor.

PROPERTY & INVESTMENT MANAGEMENT CO (ANGLIA) LTD v. ROGERS & NORTON [1995] N.P.C. 75, Sir Ralph Gibson, CA.

3826. Restrictive covenants–shopping centres–tenant mix policies–landlord refusing tenant's application for change of use–injunction restraining use of tenant's premises pending trial

C applied for an injunction pending trial restraining B from trading in electrical goods on the grounds that this would be a breach of qualified restricted user clauses in the tenant's lease and because the change of use by B involving the sale of electrical goods would be a breach of C's "tenant mix" policy. B contended that C's consent had been unreasonably withheld.

Held, allowing the application, that (1) there was not a serious issue to be tried. The evidence adduced by B was directed at B's position and no evidence was adduced that no reasonable landlord of such premises would pursue a non-specific tenant mix policy; (2) damages would not be an adequate remedy for either party and the balance of convenience was in favour of a grant. Disadvantages to B were all short term, C had not delayed and (3) the status quo favoured C's position. B had taken a calculated commercial risk and the relevant status quo was the one before the dispute arose.

CHELSFIELD MH INVESTMENTS LTD v. BRITISH GAS PLC [1995] N.P.C. 169, Knox, J., Ch D.

3827. Right to buy–public sector tenancy–applicability of discount–validity of notice to complete–whether citing incorrect statutory provision matter of form–waiver of notices–whether estoppel prevented denial of waiver

[Housing Act 1980; Housing Act 1985 s.140, s.141.]

M sought a ruling as to the right to buy a council property at a discounted price under the Housing Act 1980. M accepted T's offer to sell the freehold but a dispute arose as to their entitlement to buy at the discounted sum. In 1989, T served two notices of completion. The first referred to M's rights under the Housing Act 1985 s.140, which M contended was invalid as s.140 was not in force on the date they accepted the offer. M drew this to T's attention and T served a final notice to complete which referred to s.141 of the 1985 Act.

Held, giving judgment for M, that although the onus lay with T to establish the validity of the notices, *Lemon v. Lardeur* [1946] K.B. 613 considered, citing the wrong statute was merely a matter of form, as the correct statute should have been s.16 of the 1980 Act, which had substantially the same effect, *Morris v. Patel* [1987] 1 E.G.L.R. 75, [1987] C.L.Y. 2133 considered. Both notices told M all that was necessary and neither could be shown to have been a nullity. On the facts, however, the notices were of no effect, as T had waived the right to rely on them and being procedural in nature, estoppel applied to prevent the denial of waiver, *Kammins Ballrooms Co Ltd v. Zenith Investments (Torquay) Ltd* [1971] A.C. 850, [1970] C.L.Y. 1525 applied.

MILNE-BERRY v. TOWER HAMLETS LBC (1996) 28 H.L.R. 225, Sir Haydn Tudor Evans, QBD.

3828. Right to buy–standard form contract–local authority powers to prevent amendment of terms by tenant–validity of counter-notice–rent payments not made on account of purchase price

[Housing Act 1985 s.122, s.138, s.153; Landlord and Tenants (Covenants) Act 1995 s.1.]

G appealed against an order specifying the terms of a lease granted to him by E under the Housing Act 1985 s.122 right to buy provisions. G had submitted that parts of the draft lease were unreasonable and inequitable and as a consequence sought inter alia to treat payments of rent as such and on account of the purchase price under s.153B of the 1985 Act. E contended that amendments to the standard terms of the lease would undermine council policy which aimed to provide the same rights and responsibilities for all tenants exercising their right to buy.

Held, allowing the appeal in part and making certain that amendments were made to the terms of the lease, that (1) Sch.5 para.6 of the 1985 Act could not be used to introduce new landlord's repairing covenants; (2) release from forfeiture, although absent from the lease offered by E, would be implied under the Landlord and Tenant (Covenants) Act 1995 s.1 (3). However, it was not unreasonable that this had not been provided in favour of an assignor in the past; (3) the lease provisions should expressly refer to reasonable regulations that E may make, therefore "reasonable" was ordered to be added to cl.4(25) of the lease; (4) express powers permitting E to deal "as they think fit" with adjoining land were to be deleted from cl.6(2) as, in the absence of a legal right on the part of G to restrain E from so doing, such powers were unnecessary, and if he had such a right, it was unreasonable to remove it; (5) no breach of statutory duty had occurred and no damages were due in terms of s.138 of the 1985 Act as no obligation arose until all the lease terms had been agreed or determined; (6) although s.153A(5) of the 1985 Act was silent as to the requirements for a valid counter-notice, the notice was valid if the landlord believed, in good faith, that he had a right to insist upon the terms offered. On the facts, therefore, the counter-notice issued by ELBC was valid and had been served in time, and G could not claim credit for rent paid against the purchase price under s.153B and (7) the judge below had correctly exercised his discretion in ordering G to pay one third of E's costs as G had failed on three grounds, but succeeded on his challenges to the lease terms, *Elgindata (No.2), Re* [1992] 1 W.L.R. 1207, [1993] C.L.Y. 3144 and *Semco Salvage & Marine Pte Ltd v. Lancer Navigation Co Ltd*

(The Nagasaki Spirit) [1996] 1 Lloyd's Rep. 449, [1996] C.L.Y. 5364 considered.

GUINAN v. ENFIELD LBC [1996] N.P.C. 131, Staughton, L.J., CA.

3829. Secure tenancies–agreement to continue occupation after possession order obtained–revival of tenancy

[Housing Act 1985 s.82, s.85.]

B was a secure tenant of a flat owned by BLBC but had fallen behind with her rent. BLBC obtained a possession order under the Housing Act 1985 s.82, but before the order was due to take effect B made an agreement to make regular payments towards the arrears in return for BLBC's agreement not to execute the order. B failed to make the specified payments and BLBC obtained and executed a possession warrant. B successfully argued that the agreement between herself and BLBC revived her secured tenancy and obtained an injunction requiring BLBC to re-admit her to the flat. BLBC appealed against the dismissal of its appeal by the Court of Appeal.

Held, allowing the appeal, that when a secure tenancy had come to an end due to the granting of a possession order under s.82 of the Act, the tenant could, under s.85, apply to the court to make an order postponing the date given for possession at any time up until the order was executed and thereby revive the tenancy. In making the agreement the parties had merely intended that the execution of the possession order be deferred until either B applied for such an order or failed to comply with the conditions of the agreement. There had been no intention to create a new tenancy; B was merely a trespasser whom BLBC had agreed not to evict, subject to conditions.

BURROWS v. BRENT LBC [1996] 1 W.L.R. 1448, Lord Browne-Wilkinson, HL.

3830. Secure tenancies–possession–alterations to particulars in notice

[Housing Act 1985 s.84.]

Held, that in possession proceedings for property held under a secure tenancy, where the grounds for the proceedings could be "altered or added to with leave of the court" under the Housing Act 1985 s.84(3), such changes would be facilitated by altering or adding to the particulars of the grounds specified in the notice. The ability to alter the grounds conferred the power to alter the particulars and any proposed changes would be appraised by the court when deciding whether to grant leave.

CAMDEN LBC v. OPPONG (1996) 28 H.L.R. 701, Leggatt, L.J., CA.

3831. Secure tenancies–possession–foster child not entitled to succeed to tenancy

[Housing Act 1985 s.87, s.113.]

The secure tenant of local authority accommodation died in October 1994. She had fostered O throughout his childhood, except for periods amounting to just over one year, by arrangement with his natural parents and under the supervision of the local authority. She and O treated one another as mother and son. They maintained a close relationship until her death, when he was aged 44. After her death, the local authority applied for possession of the premises. O claimed that he was entitled to succeed to the tenancy as a member of the tenant's family, within the Housing Act 1985 s.113, asserting also that he had both been occupying the premises as his only or principal home at the time of the tenant's death, and had resided with her throughout the 12 months preceding her death, for the purposes of s.87 of the 1985 Act.

Held, granting the local authority a possession order, that O was not a member of the tenant's family within s.113 as O was not the tenant's "child": *Reading BC v. Ilsley* [1981] C.L.Y. 1323 had been wrongly decided, since s.113(1) and (2) defined exhaustively the relationships which could qualify. It was not the intention of Parliament to include a foster child. On the facts, O's occupation of the premises had also been insufficient for the purposes of s.87.

HEREFORD CITY COUNCIL v. O'CALLAGHAN, July 16, 1996, Judge not specified, CC (Worcester). [*Ex rel.* Christopher Baker, Barrister].

3832. Secure tenancies–possession–nuisance–annoyance to neighbours–statutory notice–particulars of conduct relied upon

[Housing Act 1985 s.83; Housing Act 1988 s.8.]

R were secure tenants of S. On August 19, 1996, S issued a summons for possession. In the particulars of claim, S averred that R had been guilty of nuisance and annoyance to neighbours and that a notice pursuant to the Housing Act 1985 s.83 had been served. Paragraph 3 of the notice read "Possession will be sought on Ground One of Sch.2 to the 1985 Act", para.4 of the notice read "Particulars of each Ground are as follows: Numerous complaints have been received over a period of time that annoyance and nuisance is being caused to your neighbours by noise and disruptive behaviour. This annoyance has been investigated by the staff and I believe the complaints to be substantiated." R submitted that four essentials of a valid notice were that it should: (a) be in the prescribed form; (b) specify the ground(s) for possession relied upon by the landlord; (c) provide proper and sufficient particulars of each of those grounds, and (d) specify a proper date before which proceedings would not be commenced. R submitted that the notice failed to give particulars of the conduct relied upon at all, thereby failing to satisfy the purpose of the notice which was, in this context, to put R upon notice of the manner and degree to which S contended they ought to moderate their behaviour. If, upon its true construction, the notice properly specified Ground 2 as a ground upon which the court would be asked to make an order for possession, the "particulars" amounted to little more than a repetition of the ground upon which possession was sought. In either case, the words "noise and disruptive behaviour" were too general and unparticularised for R to know what was alleged against them so that they could either dispute the allegation or moderate their behaviour to the appropriate degree. The want of proper particulars meant that the notice did not comply with the requirement of s.83(2)(c) and that, therefore, it was not a valid notice. The effect of an invalid notice was that the court could not entertain the proceedings; there was no provision analogous to the Housing Act 1988 s.8(1)(b), permitting the court to dispense with the requirement of a valid notice.

Held, dismissing the proceedings, that Ground 2 of Sch. 2 to the 1985 Act was available to S. However, the consequences to R of the proceedings subsequent to the notice could be most serious. R must be told very clearly in such a notice of the nature of the case against them. The present notice did not do that. It was a defective notice which was invalid.

SLOUGH BC v. ROBBINS AND ROBBINS, September 27, 1996, District Judge Fortgang, CC (Slough). [*Ex rel.* Christopher Maynard, Barrister].

3833. Secure tenancies–redundant employee tenant re-employed by same employer–remaining in occupation–tenancy secure prior to resignation from new post

[Housing Act 1985 s.79, Sch.1 para.2.]

G appealed against a decision that his accommodation had not become a secure tenancy. G, a school caretaker, was employed by B and required to live in accommodation provided by the terms of his employment for the better performance of his duties. G was then made redundant and given notice to vacate the premises. G did not leave and B threatened possession proceedings. G then obtained a job at another school which required him to occupy certain premises when they became available. He was still employed by B who postponed the possession proceedings. G later resigned and a possession order was made. G argued that the tenancy had become a secure tenancy by the time the proceedings had begun because of the Housing Act 1985 s.79(2) which provided that a dwellinghouse let as a separate dwelling was a secure tenancy. In addition,

Sch.1 para.2(1) of the 1985 Act provided that when an employee was required to live in accommodation under his contract of employment he did not have a secure tenancy.

Held, allowing the appeal, that (1) tenancies could become secure as the circumstances changed. Paragraph 2(1) referred to the circumstances in the present tense, *Elvidge v. Coventry City Council* [1994] Q.B. 241, [1993] C.L.Y. 2107 considered; (2) a secure tenancy could be prevented if para.2(1) was partly satisfied and if the occupation was still referable to employment needs and the better performance of duties without any change in the nature of the employment, *South Glamorgan City Council v. Griffiths* [1992] 2 E.G.L.R. 232, [1992] C.L.Y. 2329 considered; (3) G's continued occupation after the termination of his employment did not meet the requirements of the referable test as it was for the convenience of B rather than for G and (4) G's tenancy had become secure and had not been correctly determined.

BERKSHIRE CC v. GREENFIELD; SUB NOM. GREENFIELD v. BERKSHIRE CC (1996) 28 H.L.R. 691, Kennedy, L.J., CA.

3834. Secure tenancies–rent arrears–suspended possession order–new tenancy not created on waiver of breach of suspended order

[Housing Act 1985 s.85.]

R, a tenant, appealed against the dismissal of his application to stay the execution of a warrant of possession. R had a secure tenancy with G. The proceedings for possession were due to nonpayment of rent. A possession order was granted and suspended on condition of payment of rent and arrears in instalments. R argued that a new order for possession was required since he had been in breach of the suspended possession order and he had reached a new arrangement with G for payment of rent and a lesser amount of arrears. Thus, the change in circumstances amounted to the grant of a new tenancy or licence to occupy regardless of the parties' intentions.

Held, dismissing the appeal, that (1) in the case of a suspended order, the tenancy should be determined when the conditions were breached. However, G were entitled to waive the breach and the tenancy then continued as if no breach occurred. This applied to situations where there was agreement to waive the breach after the breach had occurred, as well as to agreement in anticipation of breach; (2) acceptance of payments could not create a new tenancy. It would be against public policy to require the landlord to apply to court for a variation every time a payment was merely a day late; (3) G were entitled to vary the terms of the order and it was a question of fact whether that variation constituted a new tenancy or the tenancy continued without being determined. It was necessary to consider the parties' conduct, and (4) in this case, the tenancy was determined on two occasions by breach of the suspended order and on both occasions G waived the breach and the tenancy was treated as not being determined. If an application had been made by R under the Housing Act 1985 s.85 to postpone possession to allow the agreement with G, the court would have had to have granted the application, *Burrows v. Brent LBC* (1995) 27 H.L.R. 748, [1995] 1 C.L.Y. 3075 distinguished.

GREENWICH LBC v. REGAN (1996) 28 H.L.R. 469, Millett, L.J., CA.

3835. Secure tenancies–subletting–tenant had not parted with possession of his flat–whether tenant occupying premises as only or principal home at expiry of notice to quit

H was the secure tenant of a flat owned by C. Possession was sought against him on the basis that he had sublet the whole of the premises to the second defendant, B. At trial, the judge found that H had occupied other premises as his only or principal home in the latter part of 1986 and 1987 and from 1989 to 1990. C was unable to prove that there was a tenancy agreement between H and B or that rent was paid. There was also no evidence that H did not occupy the flat as his only or principal home on the expiry of the notice to quit. The judge ordered possession. H appealed.

Held, allowing the appeal, that even though, for some periods, H had ceased to occupy the flat as his principal home, he was not shown to have parted with possession of it. Since there was no evidence that H was not occupying the flat, the tenant condition was satisfied and the possession order ought not to have been made.

HUSSEY v. CAMDEN LBC (1995) 27 H.L.R. 5, Leggatt, L.J., CA.

3836. Secure tenancies–succession of grandson to grandmother's tenancy–whether temporary absence broke continuity of residence required for succession to tenancy

[Housing Act 1985 s.87.]

B, who had lived with his grandmother, G, at her flat since 1991, appealed against a refusal to allow her secure tenancy to be assigned to him when she went into a nursing home. He contended that his absence from the flat, while looking after a house belonging to friends, had not displaced his intention to return, even though he had intended moving to other accommodation if somewhere suitable could be found, and that he qualified under the Housing Act 1985 s.87 for assignment of the secure tenancy as a member of the tenant's family who had resided with her during the year prior to her removal.

Held, allowing the appeal, that absence from the flat did not break the continuity required under s.87 where a continuing connection with the property remained, along with an intention of sufficient quality to return, *Crawley BC v. Sawyer* (1987) 86 L.G.R. 629, [1988] C.L.Y. 2078 and *Brickfield Ltd v. Hughes* (1987) 20 H.L.R. 108, [1988] C.L.Y. 2083 considered. On the facts, B had retained the flat as his postal address and any prospect of his finding anywhere else to live following his period of house-sitting had not displaced his intention to return.

CAMDEN LBC v. GOLDENBERG (1996) 28 H.L.R. 727, Thorpe, L.J., CA.

3837. Secure tenancies–surrender–repossession–significance of handing in keys on termination of tenancy–no minimum period elapsing immediately prior to grant of new tenancy–no statutory protection for wife jointly acting with husband

[Matrimonial Homes Act 1983.]

C appealed against a decision that he was not a shorthold tenant, following the end of a previous protected tenancy of a flat which he occupied with his wife. The judge decided that the surrender of the keys showed C's intention to terminate the tenancy and that the fact that his wife kept her set of keys to obtain temporary access did not negate this intention. C took out a three year lease of a flat and remained in possession as a protected tenant. C fell into arrears and B brought proceedings for repossession. Subsequently proceedings were suspended, and C agreed that a protected shorthold tenancy could be substituted for the existing tenancy on payment of outstanding arrears. To effect this C handed over his keys and vacated the flat for a 24 hour period in order to establish a break between the ending of the statutory tenancy and the grant of the new protected shorthold tenancy. The following day C moved back in and signed the new tenancy agreement after paying his arrears, and this procedure was then repeated on C's application for a six month extension of the tenancy.

Held, dismissing the appeal, that (1) it was not possible to terminate a statutory tenancy by contract or deed, whereas a protected tenancy could be ended by another tenancy, containing new or inconsistent terms; (2) when C gave back his keys when faced with immediate eviction, which would only be avoided by surrendering the existing tenancy and accepting a new shorthold tenancy, this was a symbolic surrender of possession; (3) statute defined no minimum period which had to elapse before the tenant became subject to statutory protection "immediately before" the grant; this was a question of fact and degree, there being no rule of law excluding a 24 hour period, *Dibbs v.*

Campbell [1988] 2 E.G.L.R. 122, [1989] C.L.Y. 2200 affirmed; (4) a determination as to whether B sought to avoid the operation of the Rent Acts could not be reached as the shorthold tenancy had been created by the parties' compliance with the statutory requirements for doing so and (5) the right of a spouse not to be evicted under the provisions of the Matrimonial Homes Act 1983 had no application in a case where husband and wife acted jointly, so it was not possible for C's wife to exercise any rights under the Act.

BOLNORE PROPERTIES LTD v. COBB [1996] E.G.C.S. 42, Waite, L.J., CA.

3838. Service charges–reimbursement of repair costs–experts' fees–reasonably incurred–structural defects discovered during repairs–consultation procedure not complied with–whether service charge limit applied to each item or all items

[Landlord and Tenant Act 1985 s.19, s.20.]

L was landlord of two blocks of flats with 31 flats on long leases, and ground floor shops. L covenanted to repair and insure. The lessees covenanted to pay service charges to reimburse L's expenditure. L claimed repayment from eight lessees of their share of (a) experts' fees for investigating concrete defects and supervising their repair; (b) the concrete repairs themselves; (c) replacing windows; (d) penthouse canopy repairs; (e) repairing balcony rails and (f) shop beam repairs which were done later to remedy serious structural defects discovered during the earlier repairs. The lessees contended that the experts' fees were not reasonably incurred and so were irrecoverable under the Landlord and Tenant Act 1985 s.19, as the experts failed to identify and quantify the cost of concrete repairs before they started. They relied upon L's failure to comply with the consultation procedure in s.20 to limit the service charges to £50 a flat. L argued that the £50 limit applied to each of the six components individually and that s.20 only applied to works, not to related expert services. L also asked the court to invoke s.20(9) to dispense with the obligation to consult.

Held, that (1) the expert had acted reasonably, and could not identify all areas of disrepair before the execution of the works revealed hidden defects; (2) the limit of £50 per flat applied to each of the six components, because they were distinct and separate works; (3) s.20 applied to the expert services rendered in relation to works; (4) the court could only exercise its dispensing power under s.20(9) if L had acted reasonably, and even if he had, the court still had a discretion whether to dispense; (5) the court was not restricted to whether L acted reasonably in not complying with s.20, but should consider whether, in all the circumstances, he had acted reasonably; (6) L had acted reasonably in relation to all the works except the shop beam. L had kept the lesees informed and listened to their views regarding the earlier works, but he did not allow the statutory period for response. However, his expedition much reduced the cost of the works as it made it possible to utilise scaffolding that was already in place. L had not acted reasonably over the shop beam repairs. By this time the resident's association had collapsed through dissension, and some lessees wanted full consultation. There was less consultation than with the earlier works, and there was no need to do the concrete beam works quickly and (7) in the exercise of its discretion, the court would dispense with the requirements of s.20 in respect of all works except the concrete beam works. There, the court had no power to dispense as L had not acted reasonably.

GARDNER v. JONES, September 20, 1995, Rutherford, J., CC. [*Ex rel.* Philip Walter, Barrister].

3839. Service charges–repairs–business tenancies–shopping centres–cost of roof and window repair recoverable under service charge–work of type reasonable owner would undertake

P owned a shopping centre and carried out repairs to the roofs and windows. B, a tenant, contended that the cost of the work was not recoverable under the service charge provisions of the leases because the roofs (which had been constructed in 1975, and had a life expectancy of 20 years) were recovered under a phased programme and so the replacement of the roof coverings had been premature. It was submitted that the work to the windows was needed because of rust which could have been avoided with proper maintenance.

Held, allowing P to recover the cost except for 45 pence per square metre on the roofs, that the roof repairs were work of a type which a reasonable owner might have undertaken and did not give back to the landlord something which had not previously existed. It was reasonable to commence the repairs even though some parts of the roof had not yet failed. However, no purpose had been served by priming galvanised sections of the roof. Although the works to the windows may have been needed as a result of P's failure to repaint earlier any delay was balanced out by the cost saved.

POSTEL PROPERTIES LTD v. BOOTS THE CHEMIST [1996] 41 E.G. 164, Ian Kennedy, J., QBD.

3840. Shorthold tenancies–student accommodation deposit paid by tenant–dilapidations

Five students were granted a shorthold tenancy for six months and paid a deposit of £750. The tenancy having terminated, S argued that she had spent more than the deposit on cleaning and making good defects. B claimed the £750 deposit and S counterclaimed for £143. At first instance, B was given judgment in default, S not having been notified of the date of the hearing. An application to set aside the judgment was dismissed when S did not appear because of ill-health. When S appealed the judge set aside the judgment, reheard the case and allowed S £158 set off against B's claim. S sought a retrial on the basis that she was taken by surprise and had further evidence to adduce.

Held, dismissing the appeal, that there had been no miscarriage of justice. The proposed evidence would have added little to the oral evidence. The parties must have consented to the case being dealt with in the way it had been without an adjournment for further preparation. It was equally clear that the judge must have preferred B's evidence.

BRITTAIN v. SLOT, Trans. Ref: 93/1776/G, November 27, 1995, Stuart-Smith, L.J., CA.

3841. Statutory tenancies–landlord disposing of interest in property–notice of first refusal served on tenants–notice of acceptance invalidated by tenant's withdrawal of consent–right to withdraw consent extant until binding contract made

[Landlord and Tenant Act 1987 s.6, s.9.]

M and another appealed against a declaration that their landlord was entitled to proceed with the sale of the property to another party. M and four others were statutory tenants of flats, qualifying under the Landlord and Tenant Act 1987 and had signed notices under s.6 accepting the landlord's offer of first refusal in acquiring the freehold. One tenant, A, had later withdrawn so that the qualifying tenants lacked the majority required to accept the offer. M contended that A should not be permitted to withdraw because he had signed an irrevocable agreement.

Held, dismissing the appeal, that, under the statutory framework, it was open to a tenant to withdraw his consent and this freedom to withdraw could not be overridden by a written agreement. M had been aware of A's withdrawal before service of the s.6 notice on the landlord and, until there was a binding contract, she had been obliged under s.9(3) to inform the landlord that there was no longer a majority.

MAINWARING v. TRUSTEES OF HENRY SMITH'S CHARITY (NO.2) (1997) 73 P. & C.R. D20, Pill, L.J., CA.

3842. Statutory tenancies–tenant's right of first refusal–contract to sell property subject to the right–completed conveyance forming "relevant disposal"–liability of landlord to serve s.5 notice–statutory interpretation

[Landlord and Tenant Act 1987 s.5, s.18.]

M was a statutory tenant of premises forming part of T's estate. The Landlord and Tenant Act 1987 s.5 provided that, where the landlord proposed to make a relevant disposal affecting the premises, he should serve notice on qualifying tenants offering them first refusal. T agreed to sell the estate to W, the contract acknowledging that no s.5 notices had been served and providing that W would inquire, pursuant to s.18 of the 1987 Act, whether tenants would assert their rights and, if they would, that T would serve s.5 notices once an estate management scheme had been determined. M asserted that she would wish to avail herself of the right of first refusal, and sought a county court order that T serve s.5 notices to enable her to pursue her rights. The application was refused on the ground that the time for such notice would not come until the outcome of the estate management scheme application. M appealed.

Held, allowing the appeal, that (1) a "relevant disposal" within the meaning of s.5 of the 1987 Act was a completed conveyance and not an exchange of contracts for sale. In this case, no such completed conveyance had taken place, but (2) the word "proposes" denoted something short of a fixed and irrevocable determination, and it could not be suggested that T did not "propose" to do that which he bound himself by contract. There was, therefore, on the facts a "proposal" to make a disposal for the purposes of s.5 and (3) while there was no set time limit for a s.5 notice after a proposal, s.18 envisaged that it should have been served before a prospective purchaser became entitled to serve a s.18 notice, and so T should have served a notice within a few days of contracting with W and possibly even sooner.

MAINWARING v. TRUSTEES OF HENRY SMITH'S CHARITY [1996] 3 W.L.R. 1033, Sir Thomas Bingham, M.R., CA.

3843. Surety–guarantors for company's obligations under a lease–surrender of lease–contribution claimed from co-surety–equitable remedy–whether co-surety acquiesced in negotiations

[Mercantile Law Amendment Act 1856 s.5.]

H appealed against the dismissal of his appeal against summary judgment given in favour of BSE. H, BSE and a third party were the guarantors of the obligations of a company, the tenant, under a lease. BSE paid outstanding rent when the tenant defaulted and then negotiated the surrender of the lease by the tenant for £207,100 plus outstanding insurance premiums and the landlord's legal fees. BSE then claimed a contribution from H who, it claimed, was jointly and severally liable in terms of the guarantee in the lease. Summary judgment for £101,181.45 was granted, this being for one third of the payments made by BSE, excluding the landlord's legal fees. H argued that, owing to the rule of equity and the Mercantile Law Amendment Act 1856 s.5, BSE could not claim a contribution from H. H contended that, under the decision of *Lord Harberton v. Bennett* (1829) Beatty 386, as the guarantor who settled the liability of the principal debtor, BSE was entitled, by means of subrogation, to the remedies against the principal debtor. In this case, BSE was the surety for the performance of covenants and so was entitled to recoup payments out of the land. Additionally, even if the land was worthless to the surety, the creditor still had no right to judge what was best for the surety. H further argued that the judge had been wrong to find that he was willing to be bound by the negotiations for the surrender of the lease.

Held, allowing the appeal in part, that (1) the decision of *Lord Harberton v. Bennett* and s.5 of the 1856 Act could not be applied to a case where the creditor was a lessor and the principal debtor was the tenant. The remedy of distress and re-entry for nonpayment of rent could not be used by the surety as, in the case of re-entry, the lease would be terminated and the creditor's title over the land had to be preserved, *Lord Harberton v. Bennett* considered and (2) on the facts, the judge was wrong to find that H had acquiesced in the terms of the surrender of the lease. BSE rejected the proposals of H and proceeded with the negotiations independently. Consequently, H had an arguable defence to the contribution claimed in connection with amounts paid under the surrender and unconditional leave was granted to defend the claim for that amount, but not the amount paid by BSE before the surrender.

BSE TRADING LTD v. HANDS (1997) 73 P. & C.R. D5, Peter Gibson, L.J., CA.

3844. Surety–tenant's insolvency–obligation to take lease for residue of term–surety serving notice to complete on landlord–whether obligation enforceable after expiry

A, was the tenant of office premises, sublet to X (UK) for a term of 10 years from June 1989. XSA was a party as a guarantor of X (UK)'s obligations. By its surety covenant XSA undertook to take a new lease for the residue of the term within three months in the event that X (UK) went into liquidation and the liquidator disclaimed. On March 1, 1993 X (UK) went into liquidation and the lease was disclaimed. Seven months later no new lease had been granted. A had prepared a document setting out the tenant's covenants but excluding the landlord's covenants, which it wished XSA to complete. XSA served notice requiring completion of the new lease by December 3, 1993 failing which XSA would consider itself discharged from its obligation under the surety covenant to take a new lease for the residue of the term. Nothing happened and in consequence XSA sought a declaration that it was discharged from its obligations to A.

Held, giving judgment for XSA, that XSA was no longer obliged to take a new lease for the residue of the term. At all material times XSA had been willing to execute a new lease in compliance with its obligations. XSA was entitled to reject the draft document which A had prepared. In the absence of express provision in the surety covenant XSA was not obliged to pay A the costs incurred in obtaining licence to demise the premises to XSA. There had been extreme delay in completion and XSA was not responsible for that delay.

XEY SA v. ABBEY LIFE ASSURANCE CO LTD [1994] E.G.C.S. 190, Stanley Burnton Q.C., Ch D.

3845. Tenancies–disabled persons–discrimination

DISABILITY DISCRIMINATION (SUB-LEASES AND SUB-TENANCIES) REGULATIONS 1996, SI 1996 1333; made under the Disability Discrimination Act 1955 s.16, Sch.4 para.4. In force: June 7, 1996; £0.65.

These Regulations modify and supplement the provisions of the Disability Discrimination Act 1995 s.16 and Sch.4 in relation to cases where premises are occupied under a sub lease or sub tenancy. Section 16 and Sch.4 para.1 are modified so that the lessor refers to the occupier's immediate landlord. The effect of this is that any consent to alterations has to be sought from the immediate landlord rather than a superior landlord. Section 16 is also supplemented to cover the position with regard to the obligations of lessors and lessees under superior leases and tenancies. Schedule 4 para.2 (joining lessors in industrial tribunal proceedings) and para.3 (regulation making power) are modified so that references to the lessor include any superior landlord. They define sub lease and sub tenancy for the purposes of s.16.

3846. Tenancies–occupancy–business activities–judge seeking opinion of others in determining business purposes–reaction of an informed or reasonable person was a suitable test to apply

[Landlord and Tenant Act 1954 Part II, s.23.]

M applied for leave to appeal against a decision that W was not occupying the maisonette, of which M was the landlord, for business purposes. M sought to determine the tenancy under the Landlord and Tenant Act 1954 Part II on the ground that W was using the maisonette for the purposes of his profession as an art historian, private client adviser and exhibition organiser. The judge found that there was no office equipment in the flat and that the main purpose of W's occupation was not the conduct of business. W claimed that the judge had taken a merely subjective view and should not have had regard to the opinion of any other person and that the property was subject to a business tenancy regime under the provisions of 1954 Act.

Held, dismissing the application, that (1) it was hard to determine the nature of W's aim in occupying the flat where no view was taken as to why W took the premises and continued living there; (2) in deciding what was a matter of fact and degree the reaction of the informed or reasonable person was a suitable test to apply; (3) the court had to find that business purposes played an important role in the occupation before it could be determined that they amounted to business purposes under s.23 which was a matter for the trial judge to decide, *Cheryl Investments v. Saldanha* [1978] 1 W.L.R. 1329, [1978] C.L.Y. 1771 and *Gurton v. Parrot* [1991] E.G.L.R. 98, [1991] C.L.Y. 2217 considered and (4) the type of business was not one involving advertising or geographical location and concerned the selling of personal services as an expert in a particular field.

WRIGHT v. MORTIMER (1996) 28 H.L.R. 719, Beldam, L.J., CA.

3847. Tenancies–tenant sharing use of kitchen with landlord–restricted contract–warrant for possession–significance of new corporate landlord being incapable of using kitchen

[Rent Act 1977 s.21.]

U, a tenant, appealed against a possession order in favour of the new landlord, MC, who took over when the original landlord defaulted on mortgage payments. The original landlord bought the property, a maisonette, and rented part to U on terms that included the right to share the kitchen with the landlord and his family, who stayed at the property occasionally. U accepted that under the Rent Act 1977 s.21 he was not entitled to security of tenure because he shared a kitchen with his landlord, but argued that when MC succeeded to the landlord's position the tenancy ceased to be a restricted contract because, as a limited company, MC was incapable of using the kitchen.

Held, dismissing the appeal, that it was unnecessary to rule as to whether, through its officers or employees, a mortgage company was capable of using a kitchen, because, even if a limited company was not so capable, the landlord retained the right to use the kitchen. The tenancy did not cease to be restricted under s.21 because a limited company succeeded an individual as landlord, just as it did not cease to be restricted if, through ill health or absence, an individual landlord became incapable of enjoying his rights to use the shared parts.

MORTGAGE CORP LTD v. UBAH, *The Times*, March 21, 1996, Waite, L.J., CA.

3848. Tenants powers and duties

TENANT'S RIGHTS OF FIRST REFUSAL (AMENDMENT) REGULATIONS 1996, SI 1996 2371; made under the Landlord and Tenant Act 1987 s.20, s.53. In force: October 3, 1996; £0.65.

These Regulations amend the Landlord and Tenant Act 1987 Part I which relates to tenants' rights of first refusal. They extend the period for tenants to serve notices in response to a prospective purchaser's notice under s.18 of that Act (which relates to notices served by prospective purchasers to ensure that rights of first refusal do not arise).

3849. Underleases–assignment–landlord's refusal to consent–reasonableness–failure to provide reasons in writing–foreign company as surety

[Landlord and Tenant Act 1988.]

The tenant of an underlease for a hotel defaulted on his mortgage and the bank's receivers assigned the underlease to K. Clause 5.23 of the lease contained a covenant requiring the tenant not to disclaim without the written consent of the landlord (this consent was not to be unreasonably withheld) and to procure acceptable sureties. K applied to the landlord for consent to assign the underlease to Realco and for its parent company to become the surety in place of the bank. The landlord refused consent.

Held, granting K's application, that K was entitled to apply for the lease to be assigned and the landlord's refusal of consent had been unreasonably withheld. The Landlord and Tenant Act 1988 required a landlord to state his reasons for withholding his consent and the burden of proof is placed on the landlord to show that his refusal was reasonable. If a landlord failed to provide a reason in writing, it casts doubt upon the importance of that reason. The fact that the parent company was registered in Luxembourg did not justify withholding consent.

KENED LTD AND DEN NORSKE BANK PLC v. CONNIE INVESTMENTS LTD (1995) 70 P.&C.R. 370, Nourse, L.J., CA.

3850. Underleases–break clauses–assignment of underlease then reassignment to original tenant–construction of break clause–recovery of tenant's rights on reassignment

M, the tenant, appealed against a decision that it had lost its right, under cl.5.09, to terminate an underlease made with W, the landlord, once it assigned the underlease by licence to P&G, despite the fact that the underlease was reassigned by licence to M.

Held, dismissing the appeal, that (1) the right to determine the underlease under cl.5.09 was personal to M and did not pass to P&G on assignment, *Olympia & York Canary Wharf Ltd v. Oil Property Investments Ltd* [1994] 2 E.G.L.R. 48, [1994] C.L.Y. 2751 considered. On assignment the right ceased to exist and could not be brought back into existence when the underlease was reassigned to M; (2) the judge was correct to find that the words "for the avoidance of doubt", which related to the proviso that the tenant's right to determine the lease ended upon assignment, showed that the parties intended cl.5.09 to be restricted to use when M held the underlease as original grantee and (3) such an interpretation made commercial sense, because, if the contrary were true, the landlord could refuse consent to the reassignment.

MAX FACTOR LTD v. WESLEYAN ASSURANCE SOCIETY [1996] E.G.C.S. 82, Staughton, L.J., CA.

3851. Underleases–onerous condition to licence underlease

[Landlord and Tenant Act 1954 s.1.]

D, the landlord, appealed against an order that it was in breach of its duty under the Landlord and Tenant Act 1954 s.1 (1) by requiring an unreasonable condition from DBM, the tenant, on a request for a licence to underlet and was liable for unsettled damages for the failure of the proposed underletting. D had required an undertaking that DBM indemnify it against specified costs of £4,500 for a standard licence to underlet.

Held, dismissing the appeal, that although it might be acceptable for a landlord to require an undertaking as to his reasonable costs before consenting to an underlease, in the instant case the estimated fees were unreasonable and the landlord was in breach of its statutory duty.

DONG BANG MINERVA (UK) LTD v. DAVINA LTD [1996] 31 E.G. 87, Balcombe, L.J., CA.

3852. Voluntary arrangements–whether liability to pay future rent subject to arrangements already entered into

[Insolvency Act 1986; Companies Act 1985 s.425; Insolvency Rules 1986 r.1.17.]

The landlord of a company which entered into a company voluntary arrangement with its creditors claimed that future rent was not subject to that arrangement and was therefore payable in full.

Held, dismissing the application, that a CVA under the Insolvency Act 1986 could bind those entitled to future or contingent debts, within which future rent was included, *Doorbar v. Alltime Securities* [1994] B.C.C. 994, [1995] 1 C.L.Y.

2842 followed. The court's powers under the Companies Act 1985 s.425 covered future debts. Special reasons existed for determining that under the Insolvency Rules 1986 r.1.17(1) the term "creditor" could include landlords with rights to future rent under existing leases and the CVA could not be altered at the landlord's request. The creditor was not required to place a minimum value on the claim and it was not unfair prejudice to deal with future creditors differently on the terms of the CVA.

CANCOL LTD, *Re*; SUB NOM. CAZALY IRVING HOLDINGS LTD v. CANCOL LTD [1996] 1 All E.R. 37, Knox, J., Ch D.

3853. Articles

1995 Act: liability of former tenants for lease variations *(Simmons & Simmons)*: I.H.L. 1996, 39(Apr), 38. (Liability of former tenant and guarantor for rent under tenancy which was varied after assignment and s.18 provisions in force January 1, 1996 introduced to relieve unfairness).

Another view of AGA's *(John Adams)*: E.G. 1996, 9632, 68. (Whether s.24 releases guarantor from subguarantee of authorised guarantee agreement by tenant on assignment of lease).

Assignment of leases - update *(Delyth W. Williams)*: E.G. 1996, 9601, 92-95. (1995 rulings on liability of original tenants and sureties and effect of variation or liquidators' disclaimers and landlords' obligations to consent to assignments).

Avoiding protection under Part II of the Landlord and Tenant Act 1954 *(Mark Pawlowski)*: R.R.L.R. 1996, 16(2), 29-35. (Methods of excluding security of tenure, with precedents for originating application for order authorising agreement excluding Part II and draft clause embodying agreement in tenancy).

Business leases: excluding security of tenure *(Peter Glover)*: S.J. 1996, 140(24), 605. (Application procedure for landlords and business tenants to obtain orders under LTA 1954 s.38 to authorise agreements to exclude security of tenure).

Case 9 and grounds for eviction: E.G. 1996, 9619, 120, 122. (Remedy in damages for former protected tenant against landlord who obtained possession order by omitting to disclose material facts).

Commercial tenants in individual voluntary arrangement *(Mark Wonnacott)*: E.G. 1996, 9602, 104-105. (Effect of individual voluntary arrangement on rent arrears).

Criminal liability for damage *(Neil Turner)*: E.G. 1995, 9547, 143-145. (Extent of landlords' criminal liability for contamination and pollution caused by tenants and steps they should take to mitigate).

Dealing with non-UK resident landlords? *(Ruth Anderson)*: E.G. 1996, 9613, 121. (Rules taking effect on April 6, 1996 dealing with taxation of rental income of landlords not resident in UK).

Defending tenants in rent possession actions: best practice *(Karen Ashton)*: Q.A. 1995/96, 38(Win), 3-5. (Four types of orders that may be made in possession actions and defences available to tenant with particular regard to avoiding suspended possession orders).

Distress and forfeiture as the property manager's options *(Philip Pennicott)*: R.R.L.R. 1996, 16(1), 7-12. (Use of distress as effective means of resolving non-payment of commercial property rent).

Former tenants, future liabilities and the privity of contract principle: the Landlord and Tenant (Covenants) Act 1995 *(Stuart Bridge)*: C.L.J. 1996, 55(2), 313-357. (Provisions in force January 1, 1996 disallow landlords' right to rely on privity of contract principle in new leases).

Health warning–your lease *(Vivien King)*: C.S.R. 1996, 19(25), 2-4. (Implications for tenants of courts' strict interpretation of common clauses in leases).

Intention to develop–three bites at the cherry? *(Mark Pawlowski)*: R.R.L.R. 1996, 16(3), 7-13. (Three opportunities for landlord to challenge tenant's claim for new tenancy on ground of intention to develop property under s.30(1)(f), s.31(2) and s.33 of 1954 Act).

Is a breach of covenant capable of remedy? *(Joy Harcup)*: S.J. 1996, 140(35), 898-899. (Practical approach to breaches of positive and negative covenants and whether Scala House decision on covenants against alienation is out of line).

Keeping tabs on former tenants *(Stephen Elvidge* and *Peter Williams)*: E.G. 1996, 9624, 140-142. (Action to be taken by landlords to preserve right to sue former tenants and their guarantors for rent arrears in event of default by current tenant).

Landlord and Tenant Covenants Act 1995–s.17 notices and overriding leases *(Peter Taylor)*: Corp. Brief. 1996, 10(7), 22-24. (Landlords' obligations to serve notices on former tenants and sureties to preserve rights to claim assignees' rent arrears accrued before December 31, 1995).

Landlord and tenant: responsibility for state and condition of property: H.L.M. 1996, 3(5), 1-6. (Law Commission Report No.238 proposals to modernise implied covenant of fitness for habitation and improve conditions for short term tenants have grave financial implications for local authorities as well as private landlords).

Landlords beware–the government is after you! *(Barry Shaw)*: E.G. 1996, 9612, 122-123. (Proposed changes to protect private sector tenants in relation to rights to buy reversion, excessive service charges, forfeiture and termination of shorthold tenancies).

Law Commission report on lease repairs: Comm. Leases 1996, 10(5), 1-3. (Law Com No.238 *Landlord and Tenant: Responsibility for State and Condition of Property*, which includes draft Bill).

Lease guarantees after Hindcastle *(Peter Burfoot)*: S.J. 1996, 140(12), 302-303. (Implications of case on liability of guarantor of tenant following disclaimer of lease by liquidator, overruling 1901 CA decision *Stacey v Hill*).

Lease renewals after the 1995 Act *(Richard Bunce* and *Peter Williams)*: E.G. 1996, 9615, 96-97. (Interaction between abolition of privity of contract from January 1, 1996 and business tenants' rights to renew under 1954 legislation as amended affect rent and provision for assignment when pre-1996 leases fall due for renewal).

Life post privity? *(David Sands)*: E.G. 1996, 9607, 54-55. (Draft lease clauses proposed by British Association of Insurers to protect landlords now privity of contract is no longer available).

Measure of damages for breach of pre-emption: Comm. Leases 1996, 10(6), 7-9. (Approach to be taken when assessing loss where landlord fails to comply with pre-emption covenant).

Must a surety guarantee an AGA? *(Sue Cullen* and *Ralph Potterton)*: E.G. 1996, 9619, 118-119. (Whether following prospective abolition of privity in force January 1, 1996 sureties will be liable where former tenants have entered authorised guarantee agreement).

New protection for leaseholders *(James Driscoll)*: S.J. 1996, 140(35), 889. (Benefits for residential long leaseholders under Housing Act 1996 from September 24 and October 1, 1996).

New rules for assured shorthold tenancies *(Richard Smith)*: E.G. 1996, 9642, 150-151. (How 1996 Act reverses position of 1998 Act by ensuring new assured tenancies automatically become shortholds unless fall within exception).

Overpaid housing benefit and the private landlord *(Neil Hickman)*: N.L.J. 1996, 146(6767), 1620-1621. (Local authorities powers to recover housing benefit paid to private sector landlords where the tenant was not entitled to benefit and whether this amount can be treated as rent arrears).

Private-sector lettings *(Christopher Jessel)*: E.G. 1996, 9631, 80-81. (Effect of 1996 Act on lessors and lessees in private sector).

Privity of contract: the way ahead *(Peta Dollar)*: P.R. 1996, 6(1), 10-12. (Practical difficulties for property managers arising from provisions to reform original tenant liability in force January 1, 1996).

Privity on parade *(Robert Porter* and *Jon Vivian)*: E.G. 1996, 9641, 154-157. (Survey suggests wide variety of assignment clauses still being used since 1995 Act with development of industry standards taking longer than anticipated).

Property income: new rules and non-residents *(David Marks)*: Tax J. 1996, 338, 5-6. (FA 1995 transitional rules on income tax treatment of Sch. A property income and rules on deduction of tax from rental payments to non-residents effective April 5, 1996).

Putting it right? The Law Commission and the condition of tenanted property *(Stuart Bridge)*: Conv. 1996, Sep/Oct, 342-351. (Whether proposals in Law Com 238 would achieve objective of marked improvement in state of rented property given emphasis on rights over remedies, and absence of security of tenure for private sector tenants).

Recovery of
service charges *(Andrew Myers)*: E.G. 1996, 9644, 174-175. (Effect of 1996 Act's provisions that freeholder can no longer forfeit residential lease simply because tenant is in arrears with service charge).

Residential reform *(Gary Murphy)*: E.G. 1996, 9635, 49-50. (Legislation expected in force October 1, 1996 introduces criminal sanctions for vendors who fail to comply with statutory formalities of offering residential tenants first refusal but relieves vendors who sell by public auction).

Rights of first refusal *(Jane Fox-Edwards)*: E.G. 1996, 9636, 138-139. (Basic guide to changes to the 1987 Act introduced by Housing Act 1996, stressing importance of understanding timing and procedures as laid down when selling freehold residential property).

Tenants' repairing obligations in leases–a recent change *(Robin Mitchell* and *Sian Williams)*: S.J. 1996, 140(30), 768-769. (Benefit to landlord's position from decision that costs claimed by him for repairs by him after breach of repair covenant were debt so 1938 Act did not apply and leave of court not required).

Tenants' voluntary arrangements *(Hamish Anderson)*: I.L. & P. 1996, 12(4), 114-119. (Options available to landlords when insolvent tenants enter voluntary arrangements and conflicting case law).

The expert's role in rent disputes *(Christopher Austin)*: S.J. 1996, 140(14), 362. (Liabilities and duties of independent expert appointed to resolve rent disputes).

The Landlord and Tenant (Covenants) Act 1995–the lender's perspective *(Sian Williams)*: B.J.I.B. & F.L. 1996, 11(5), 230-233. (Impact on investors and bankers of legislation in force January 1, 1996 to repeal original tenants' privity of contract prospectively).

The Law Society's business lease (1996): Comm. Leases 1996, 10(8), 1-3. (New version of forms taking account of Landlord and Tenant (Covenants) Act 1995).

The licensee's period of grace: Bellotti reconsidered *(Tamara Kerbel)*: C.L.J. 1996, 55(2), 229-240. (Rights of licensee ordered to leave at unreasonably short notice by landlord).

The nightmare of s.17 claims *(Geoffrey Silman)*: E.G. 1996, 9640, 128-130. (Practical advice for those in receipt of notice claiming arrears of rent or service charge under lease).

Turnover rent leases: are they the way forward? *(David Smith)*: S.J. 1996, 140(38), 978-979. (Advantages and disadvantages of rent based upon turnover of tenant in retail trade).

Valuation and compensation: E.G. 1996, 9637, 135, 137-138. (How to account for future receipts and liabilities arising from compensation for improvements, loss of security of tenure and renewal of leases when making valuations).

3854. Books

Adams, John F.; Clarke, David N.–Rent Reviews Manual. Unbound/looseleaf: £165.00. ISBN 0-7520-0005-5. FT Law & Tax.

Aldridge, Trevor M.–Letting Business Premises. Practitioner series. Paperback: £44.00. ISBN 0-7520-0237-6. FT Law & Tax.

Bridge, S.–Statutes on Landlord and Tenant. £15.95. ISBN 1-85431-493-9. Blackstone Press.

Butt, Paul–Residential Landlord and Tenant. Legal Practice Course resource books. Paperback: £17.50. ISBN 0-85308-345-2. Jordan.

Dowding, Nicholas; Reynolds, Kirk–The Modern Law and Practice of Dilapidations: 1. Supplement. £27.00. ISBN 0-421-56260-9. Sweet & Maxwell.

Driscoll, James–Butterworths Residential Landlord and Tenant Guide. Paperback: £37.50. ISBN 0-406-00252-5. Butterworth Law.

Freedman, Philip; Shapiro, Eric; Slater, Brian–Service Charges. Paperback: £30.00. ISBN 0-85308-383-5. Jordan.

Kemp, Margaret–Drafting and Negotiating Rent Review Clauses. Drafting. Paperback: £55.00. ISBN 0-7520-0182-5. FT Law & Tax.

Kenny, P.–Landlord and Tenant Covenants: the New Law in Practice. £19.95. ISBN 1-85431-487-4. Blackstone Press.

Lewison, Kim–Drafting Business Leases. Drafting series. Paperback: £55.00. ISBN 0-7520-0306-2. FT Law & Tax.

Luba, Jan–Repairs: Tenants' Rights. Paperback. ISBN 0-905099-49-4. The Legal Action Group.

Riley, A.; Rogers, P.–Commercial Property and Business Leases. Legal Practice Course resource books. Paperback: £17.50. ISBN 0-85308-337-1. Jordan.

Smith, P. F.–Evans and Smith: the Law of Landlord and Tenant. Paperback: £23.95. ISBN 0-406-06563-2. Butterworth Law.

LEGAL AID

3855. Assignment–causes of action–substitution of plaintiff–companies in liquidation–whether assignment was a sham to permit proceedings with benefit of legal aid–whether fact that company was ineligible was ground for refusing substitution

As part of an action involving three joined appeals, R, as director and shareholder of a company, N, had sought to be substituted as plaintiff in causes of action brought on behalf of N which had gone into liquidation, on the basis that none of the money recovered would be paid first to the liquidator. The application had been dismissed on the basis that the assignment of the causes of action was a sham designed to permit the proceedings to go ahead with the benefit of legal aid. R appealed.

Held, allowing the appeal, that the assignment of a right of action to a person who was entitled to legal aid, conducted with the object and effect of obtaining legal aid for parties where it was not available to N, was not contrary to public policy or unlawful. The transfer of the cause of action was a valid exercise of a statutory power and appeared to be a sensible course in that it relieved N of liability for the costs of the action. The fact that N was ineligible for legal aid was an issue for the Legal Aid Board. It was not a ground for refusing to substitute R as plaintiff. Nor was the arrangement necessarily a sham in circumstances where R had a sufficient interest in the prosecution of the action as a director and major shareholder of the company, *Grovewood Holdings Plc v. James Capel & Co Ltd* [1994] 4 All E.R. 417, [1995] 1 C.L.Y. 2824, *Stein v. Blake* [1995] 2 All E.R. 961, [1995] 1 C.L.Y. 422 and *Joyce v. Sengupta* [1993] 1 All E.R. 897, [1993] C.L.Y. 3097 considered; *Eurocross Sales Ltd v. Cornhill Insurance Plc* [1995] 4 All E.R. 950, [1995] 2 C.L.Y. 4011 not followed.

NORGLEN LTD (IN LIQUIDATION) v. REEDS RAINS PRUDENTIAL LTD; MAYHEW-LEWIS v. WESTMINSTER SCAFFOLDING GROUP PLC; LEVY v. ABN AMRO BANK NV [1996] 1 W.L.R. 864, Sir Thomas Bingham, M.R., CA.

3856. Barristers–advice on chances of success on appeal–written advice given in absence of request from client–whether counsel could claim standard fees–work was reasonably done

[Legal Aid in Criminal and Care Proceedings (Costs) Regulations 1989 Reg.16.]

The Lord Chancellor appealed under the Legal Aid in Criminal and Care Proceedings (Costs) Regulations 1989 Reg.16 against a decision allowing the claim of B, a barrister, for £29 legal aid fees for the preparation of written advice regarding appeal for a client who was sentenced to a period of detention upon conviction. The determining officer had refused her claim on the ground that, applying *R. v. Neill* (Unreported, 1986), the work was not reasonably done as B's client had not requested written advice as to his chances of success on appeal in addition to the oral advice B had already given.

Held, dismissing the appeal, that pursuant to para.1 of *A Guide to Proceedings in the Court of Appeal Criminal Division* (HMSO, 1990), there was no requirement to provide written advice if counsel had expressed a final view at the conclusion of the case as to the likely outcome of an appeal. If counsel had not expressed a final view then they were required to give advice on appeal within 14 days of conviction and Annex H to the Code of Conduct for the Bar of England and Wales (5th ed. (1990) revised 1995) should be amended in accordance with the Court of Appeal Guide. Furthermore, if a client had requested advice in writing, counsel was obliged to give it, and the determining officer would take that work into account as work reasonably done. In the circumstances the work was reasonably done in view of the client's youth and the disparity issue raised.

LORD CHANCELLOR v. BRENNAN, *The Times*, February 14, 1996, Hooper, J., QBD.

3857. Certificates–nominated solicitor replaced–certificate should be amended

[Civil Legal Aid (General) Regulations 1989 Reg.51.]

N had been granted legal aid to be represented in divorce proceedings relating to ancillary relief. The practice of the nominated solicitor was subsequently taken over by new solicitors on a Law Society intervention. N was notified of this. Following judgment, a costs dispute arose and the new solicitors were asked to produce evidence of their right to seek legal aid taxation for their costs. The Board had previously advised that such an amendment was unnecessary. The Board subsequently wrote to the new solicitors to say that the certificate had been amended to nominate the new solicitors under the Civil Legal Aid (General) Regulations 1989 Reg.51 (a). N challenged the amendment, contending that the Board had no power to amend the certificate since the mistake had been that of the Board and the new solicitors as to whether a change was required. The Board contended that there was a mistake within the meaning of the regulation since the certificate failed to reflect accurately who the solicitor with the conduct of the case was.

Held, refusing the application, that considering the phraseology of the regulation and the facts of the case, there was a mistake in the certificate and Reg.51 (a) could be used in the instant case to make the amendment sought. The contrary view would have been perverse.

R. v. LEGAL AID BOARD, *ex p.* NICOLSON [1994] C.O.D. 511, Popplewell, J., QBD.

3858. Certificates–proceedings issued after completion of defined steps–whether plaintiff remained legally assisted person–certificate spent without being discharged

[Legal Aid Act 1988 s.17.]

T appealed against a refusal to grant an order limiting his liability for costs as if the Legal Aid Act 1988 s.17 applied. In his action against P for breach of patent rights T's legal aid certificate was limited to obtaining further evidence and counsel's opinion as to merits and quantum. However, on completion of the permitted procedural steps, T issued proceedings without gaining an extension of the certificate. He later sought to discontinue the proceedings following counsel's advice on receipt of P's defence and counterclaim. T argued that he remained a legally assisted person and should be protected against costs under s.17.

Held, dismissing the appeal, that (1) in the absence of a legal aid certificate covering the issuing of proceedings, T did not have the benefit of legal aid. He could only claim assistance up to the accomplishment of the relevant procedural steps and once those steps were completed his certificate was spent. There was no need for it to be discharged, *Littaur v. Steggles Palmer* [1986] 1 W.L.R. 287, [1986] C.L.Y. 1968 applied and (2) T could not claim protection as a legally assisted person under s.17 for actions taken in excess of the permitted steps unless he gained an extension to the certificate from the legal aid committee, *Dugon v. Williamson* [1964] Ch. 59, [1963] C.L.Y. 2799 considered, *Boorman v. Godfrey* [1981] 1 W.L.R. 1100, [1981] C.L.Y. 1609 distinguished.

TURNER v. PLASPLUGS LTD [1996] 2 All E.R. 939, Sir Thomas Bingham, M.R., CA.

3859. Certificates–revocation–test for determining material facts

[Civil Legal Aid (General) Regulations 1989 Reg.78.]

D sought judicial review of the dismissal of his appeal against the revocation of his legal aid certificate. When proceeding to appeal, the Civil Legal Aid (General) Regulations 1989 Reg.78 required the appellant to be told of any matters likely to be of concern to the committee and if there was any likelihood of the committee failing to believe any material advanced by the appellant. Knowledge was required because the appellant would be likely to want to attend a hearing where his honesty was in question.

Held, allowing the application, that an objective test had to be applied to determine whether a fact was material. It did not depend on its effect on the result of the appeal but was material if it could influence a reasonable legal aid officer when considering the resources available for granting legal aid.

R. v. LEGAL AID BOARD, *ex p.* DORAN, *The Times*, July 22, 1996, Collins, J., QBD.

3860. Civil procedure

The Lord Chancellor's Department issued a press release entitled *Striking the balance: the future of legal aid in England and Wales*, published on July 2, 1996. The Lord Chancellor, launching the Government's White Paper on legal aid, said that he wanted to create a cost effective, better system which targets services only on cases deserving of support and which is fairer to the opponents of legally aided people. The main changes set out in the Paper are: replacing the present open ended system with predetermined budgets allocated to meet local demand; extending the scheme to new types of providers and services; introducing contracts between service providers and the Legal Aid Board for specified services of defined quality at an agreed price; introducing a new test for determining whether civil cases should be granted legal aid to concentrate on the most deserving cases; and changing the rules on financial conditions to increase the potential liability of assisted persons to contribute to their own costs, and, in civil cases, their opponents' costs. The White Paper, entitled *Striking the Balance: the Future of Legal Aid in England and Wales* is published by HMSO (Cm 3305), price £11.80.

3861. Civil procedure–assessment of resources

CIVIL LEGAL AID (ASSESSMENT OF RESOURCES) (AMENDMENT) REGULATIONS 1996, SI 1996 434; made under the Legal Aid Act 1988 s.15, s.16, s.34, s.43. In force: June 1, 1996; £1.10.

These Regulations amend the provisions of the Civil Legal Aid (Assessment of Resources) Regulations 1989 concerning the computation of the income and capital of an applicant for legal aid by providing for a power to take into account all or part of the resources of a person to whom the applicant has transferred assets, or who has been maintaining or assisting the applicant; limiting the amount of the mortgage instalments to be deducted in computing the applicant's income to the proportion attributable to the first £100,000 of the mortgage debt; limiting the total amount deductible in respect of any mortgage debts on one or more homes of the applicant to £100,000; and limiting the amount to be disregarded in respect of his only or principal home to the first £100,000 of the value, as assessed after deduction of any amount allowable in respect of a mortgage debt.

3862. Civil procedure–assessment of resources

CIVIL LEGAL AID (ASSESSMENT OF RESOURCES) (AMENDMENT) (NO.2) REGULATIONS 1996, SI 1996 642; made under the Legal Aid Act 1988 s.15, s.16, s.34, s.43. In force: April 8, 1996; £0.65.

These Regulations amend the Civil Legal Aid (Assessment of Resources) Regulations 1989 (SI 1989 338) by increasing the income limit for non-contributory civil legal aid from £2,425 to £2,498. The upper income limit is increased from £7,187 to £7,403; for personal injury cases the upper limit is increased from £7,920 to £8,158 (Reg.2).

3863. Civil procedure–assessment of resources

CIVIL LEGAL AID (ASSESSMENT OF RESOURCES) (AMENDMENT) (NO.3) REGULATIONS 1996, SI 1996 2309; made under the Legal Aid Act 1988 s.34, s.43. In force: October 7, 1996; £1.10.

These Regulations amend the Civil Aid (Assessment of Resources) Regulations 1989 (SI 1989 338) so that the income and capital of a person in receipt of income based jobseeker's allowance are to be taken not to exceed the contribution limit for the time being; so that any back to work bonus treated as payable by way of a jobseeker's allowance, and all earning top-up, is excluded from the computations of income and capital; and so that the assessment officer is to notify the Area Director of any amended assessment under Reg.14, so that he may discharge or amend the legal aid certificate.

3864. Civil procedure–costs–payment on account to solicitors

CIVIL LEGAL AID (GENERAL) (AMENDMENT) REGULATIONS 1996, SI 1996 649; made under the Legal Aid Act 1988 s.34, s.43. In force: April 1, 1996; £0.65.

These Regulations amend the Civil Legal Aid (General) Regulations 1989 (SI 1989 339) to enable a solicitor to receive a payment on account of his costs where taxation of those costs has not been completed within six months of the institution of the taxation proceedings.

3865. Civil procedure

CIVIL LEGAL AID (GENERAL) (AMENDMENT) (NO.2) REGULATIONS 1996, SI 1996 1257; made under the Legal Aid Act 1988 s.34, s.43. In force: June 1, 1996; £0.65.

These Regulations amend the Civil Legal Aid (General) Regulations 1989 (SI 1989 399) to prevent legal aid being granted to persons who are entitled to bring a cause of action only by reason of an assignment made to obtain legal aid and to require persons who have been granted civil legal aid to provide information or to attend for an interview when requested to do so.

3866. Civil procedure–remuneration rates

LEGAL AID IN CIVIL PROCEEDINGS (REMUNERATION) (AMENDMENT) REGULATIONS 1996, SI 1996 645; made under the Legal Aid Act 1988 s.31, s.34, s.43. In force: April 1, 1996; £1.10.

These Regulations increase the rates of remuneration for work done to which the Legal Aid in Civil Proceedings (Remuneration) Regulations 1994 (SI 1994 228) apply and provide higher rates for franchisees.

3867. Contempt of court–remuneration

LEGAL AID IN CONTEMPT PROCEEDINGS (REMUNERATION) (AMENDMENT) REGULATIONS 1996, SI 1996 643; made under the Legal Aid Act 1988 s.25, s.34, s.43. In force: April 1, 1996; £0.65.

These Regulations amend the Legal Aid in Contempt Proceedings (Remuneration) Regulations 1995 (SI 1995 948) to increase the standard fee which is payable in contempt proceedings where representation is granted under the Legal Aid Act 1988 s.29.

3868. Costs–"Newton" hearing into factual basis of guilty plea was not contested hearing for purposes of costs claim

[Legal Aid in Criminal and Care Proceedings (Costs) Regulations 1989 Sch.1.]

GD, solicitors representing a legally aided client, sought judicial review of the Legal Aid Board's costs appeal committee decision that a *Newton* hearing was not a contested trial for the purposes of the Legal Aid in Criminal and Care Proceedings (Costs) Regulations 1989 Sch.1 Part III para.2(2). GD contended that a *Newton* hearing should come under category 2 of para.2(2) of the Regulations, thereby attracting a higher fee than for a guilty plea within category 1.1.

Held, dismissing the application, that a *Newton* hearing's function was to determine issues of fact where a defendant had pleaded guilty, and even though it was conducted in a similar manner to a trial because facts were disputed, it was not a trial of criminal guilt and therefore not a contested hearing for the purposes of the Regulations.

R. v. LEGAL AID BOARD, *ex p.* GRAHAM DOBSON & CO, *The Times*, October 9, 1996, Simon Brown, L.J., QBD.

3869. Costs–application for judicial review–legal aid award benefited institutional creditors–parties to pay costs where outcome rendered academic

Two applicants sought judicial review of a decision of the Legal Aid Board Appeal Committee to reinstate legal aid to R in order for her to continue proceedings against them in relation to the termination of a partnership. R had made an individual voluntary arrangement to avoid bankruptcy so that she could continue the proceedings under her own name and continue receiving legal aid. The applicants objected, arguing that it was *Wednesbury* unreasonable for legal aid to finance a claim brought mainly for the benefit of creditors who included banks and the Inland Revenue, ie. institutions able to finance the action themselves. The outcome of the proceedings was then rendered academic by R's request that the legal aid certificate be discharged. The applicants declined to withdraw the application for judicial review contending that R was still an assisted person as the certificate had not actually been discharged, that it would be prevented from applying for taxation of costs for the interlocutory applications and, although R would cease to be legally assisted, she would still have the protection of the certificate up until that date.

Held, staying the proceedings, that (1) when the financial contribution required by a legal aid certificate was not complied with, it was automatically discharged. In this case, that had happened and R was no longer legally assisted; (2) judicial review should not proceed to hear academic arguments; (3) if R lost the proceedings the applicants would have to join the rest of her creditors in respect of a judgment debt so the outcome of the judicial review would have no effect on the payment of costs and (4) the parties to the application should bear their own costs upon a stay of proceedings.

R. v. LEGAL AID BOARD, *ex p.* CLEMENT GARAGE LTD, *The Times*, June 3, 1996, Popplewell, J., QBD.

3870. Costs–children cases–appeals–wasted costs orders–procedure to be adopted where assisted party unsuccessful

[Legal Aid Act 1988 s.18.]

In care proceedings the judge awarded continuous staying contact to the grandparents, and suspended contact with the father. The local authority objected to the orders, and on appeal, where the grandparents were legally aided, the Court of Appeal held that the orders should not have been made. The local authority applied for costs against either the Legal Aid Board or for wasted costs against the grandparents' legal advisers. The court indicated that an order would be made against the grandparents, but, since they had no assets, an order would instead be made against the LAB, who objected to the decision.

Held, dismissing in part the LAB's objection, that the general rule in the Legal Aid Act 1988 s.18 that the unsuccessful party should pay the costs of the successful party was not always appropriate in children cases where the welfare of the child was paramount but, in relation to appeals, parties must be prepared for a costs order to be made against them. The procedures to be adopted in the making of costs orders or wasted costs orders at the conclusion of appeals were as follows: (1) the successful party should consider whether circumstances justified an order for costs against the assisted party who was not legally aided or whether they justified a wasted costs order against the assisted party's legal representatives, and if so such an application should be made; (2) if the court considered that a case so clearly merited a wasted costs order that it would not be equitable to make an order nisi against the LAB the court should pursue that order, and in such a case there would normally be no reason to continue with the application against the LAB; (3) if the action against the LAB continued, it was for the court to decide whether the s.18 requirements were met and make any appropriate order against the legally aided party, whose lawyers should inform the court of any relevant matters in relation to s.18. If the LAB objected to an order for costs it could argue that a wasted costs order could be sought, and (4) if an application against the LAB was adjourned while a wasted costs application was investigated, but not subsequently made, the application could be restored.

O (A MINOR) (COSTS: LIABILITY OF LEGAL AID BOARD), *Re*; SUB NOM. O (A MINOR) (LEGAL AID COSTS), *Re* [1997] I.R.L.R. 110, Lord Woolf, M.R., CA.

3871. Costs–legally aided party could not recover costs on an indemnity basis

[Civil Legal Aid (General) Regulations 1989.]

R appealed against a costs order that they should pay costs on an indemnity basis to W, a legally aided plaintiff. R submitted that it would be an incorrect use of the court's discretion to order costs to be paid on an indemnity basis rather than on a standard basis.

Held, allowing the appeal, that, whilst on the facts of the case, given that the defendants had put forward an unsustainable defence, an order for costs on an indemnity basis would not be inappropriate, the effect of the statutory provisions, particularly the Civil Legal Aid (General) Regulations 1989 was to preclude the exercise of a judge's discretion to order that defendants pay costs on an indemnity basis to a party who was legally aided.

WILLIS v. REDBRIDGE HA [1996] 1 W.L.R. 1228, Beldam, L.J., CA.

3872. Costs–taxation of costs–legal aid in wardship proceedings–statutory interpretation of "reasonable amount"

[Civil Legal Aid (General) Regulations 1989 Reg.107; Rules of the Supreme Court Ord.62 r.12.]

L's solicitors appealed against the taxation of their costs in a case where they had been instructed to act in wardship proceedings. A bill of costs for taxation was submitted under the Civil Legal Aid (General) Regulations 1989 Reg.107 and the Rules of the Supreme Court Ord.62 r.12 claiming £60 per hour for a partner and £50 for a legal executive. This was reduced to £45 and £30 respectively. The appellant firm argued that the judge had erred by relying too heavily on past claims and national figures, had failed to consider properly a survey by the local Law Society and had erred by stating that a fair amount would be achieved by a care and control uplift.

Held, allowing the appeal, that (1) the words "reasonable amount" in RSC Ord.62 r.12 were used to represent the hypothetical solicitor by looking at the costs incurred by other solicitors in the locality. The taxing officer must use his own knowledge and experience of the level of costs in the area and be aware that his past taxations could be out of date, *KPMG Peat Marwick McLintock v. HLT Group Ltd* [1995] 2 All E.R. 180, [1994] C.L.Y. 3616 considered; (2) in the instant case, too much importance had been attached to the average figure whereas the survey provided evidence of comparables. The reasonable costs were those initially claimed and (3) direct costs should not be set artificially low with the general amount for care and conduct then being marked up in order to arrive at a fair amount, *Loveday v. Renton (No.2)* [1992] 3 All E.R. 184, [1992] C.L.Y. 3452 followed.

L v. L (LEGAL AID TAXATION) [1996] 1 F.L.R. 873, Neill, L.J., CA.

3873. Criminal procedure–care proceedings–assessment of resources

LEGAL AID IN CRIMINAL AND CARE PROCEEDINGS (GENERAL) (AMENDMENT) REGULATIONS 1996, SI 1996 436; made under the Legal Aid Act 1988 s.21, s.23, s.34, s.43. In force: June 1, 1996; £1.10.

These Regulations amend the provisions of the Legal Aid in Criminal and Care Proceedings (General) Regulations 1989 (SI 1989 344) concerning the computation of the income and capital of an applicant for legal aid by providing for a power to take into account all or part of the resources of a person to whom the applicant has transferred assets, or who has been maintaining or assisting the applicant; limiting the amount of the mortgage instalments to be deducted in computing the applicant's income to the proportion attributable to the first £100,000 of the mortgage debt; limiting the total amount deductible in respect of any mortgage debts on one or more homes of the applicant to £100,000 and limiting the amount to be disregarded in respect of his only or principal home to the first £100,000 of the value, as assessed after deduction of any amount allowable in respect of a mortgage debt.

3874. Criminal procedure–care proceedings

LEGAL AID IN CRIMINAL AND CARE PROCEEDINGS (GENERAL) (AMENDMENT) (NO.2) REGULATIONS 1996, SI 1996 646; made under the Legal Aid Act 1988 s.21, s.23, s.34, s.43. In force: April 8, 1996; £0.65.

These Regulations amend the Legal Aid in Criminal and Care Proceedings (General) Regulations 1989 (SI 1989 344) so as to (a) amend Form 6 in Sch.2 to reflect the changes made by Reg.3 (Reg.2); (c) increase the income limit for non-contributory criminal legal aid from £47 a week to £48 per week (Reg.3).

3875. Criminal procedure–care proceedings

LEGAL AID IN CRIMINAL AND CARE PROCEEDINGS (GENERAL) (AMENDMENT) (NO.3) REGULATIONS 1996, SI 1996 1258; made under the

Legal Aid Act 1988 s.21, s.34, s.43. In force: Reg.2, Reg.4, Reg.9, Reg.11: October 7, 1996; Remainder: June 1, 1996; £1.95.

These Regulations amend the Legal Aid in Criminal and Care Proceedings (General) Regulations 1989 (SI 1989 344) to take into account the introduction of the income based jobseeker's allowance, to strengthen provisions requiring applicants for criminal legal aid to provide information about their financial circumstances so that legal aid orders can be withdrawn when information is not provided or when false information is given and to make amendments to forms resulting from the changes.

3876. Criminal procedure–care proceedings

LEGAL AID IN CRIMINAL AND CARE PROCEEDINGS (GENERAL) (AMENDMENT) (NO.4) REGULATIONS 1996, SI 1996 2307; made under the Legal Aid Act 1988 s.34, s.43. In force: October 7, 1996; £1.10.

These Regulations amend the Legal Aid in Criminal and Care Proceedings (General) Regulations 1989 (SI 1989 344) so that any back to work bonus treated as payable by way of a jobseeker's allowance, and any earnings top-up, are excluded from the computations of disposable income and disposable capital. Reg.41A(2), which provides for a defence of due care or diligence for mis-statements or omissions in connection with legal aid applications, is amended to refer to para.(1)(a) instead of para.(1).

3877. Criminal procedure–care proceedings–costs

LEGAL AID IN CRIMINAL AND CARE PROCEEDINGS (COSTS) (AMENDMENT) (NO.2) REGULATIONS 1996, SI 1996 2655; made under the Legal Aid Act 1988 s.25, s.34, s.43. In force: January 1, 1997; £4.70.

These Regulations amend the Legal Aid in Criminal and Care Proceedings (Costs) Regulations 1989 (SI 1989 343) by instituting a new system for the payment of graduated fees for advocacy and preparation work on the occasion of a trial or guilty plea in the Crown Court, with fixed fees for appeals to the Crown Court against conviction or sentence and for committals for sentence. The graduated fees vary with the nature of the offence and a number of indicators designed to reflect the complexity of the case, and apply to both barrister and solicitor advocates. They further amend the Legal Aid in Criminal and Care Proceedings (Costs) Regulations 1989 (SI 1989 343) by introducing staged payments in long Crown Court cases, consisting of one payment for each block of 100 hours' preparation; introduce interim payments for attendance at trial by solicitors and for counsel's refreshers, consisting of one payment for each period of 20 days' attendance at the trial; allow an advance payment of £100 to the advocate (£250 to a Queen's Counsel, £170 to a leading junior) where substantial preparation for the trial had been done five days before the pleas and directions hearing; and introduce hardship payments for legal representatives engaged in a case for six months or more when final payment is not likely to be received within three months and staged, interim and advance payments are not available.

3878. Criminal procedure–care proceedings–remuneration rates

LEGAL AID IN CRIMINAL AND CARE PROCEEDINGS (COSTS) (AMENDMENT) REGULATIONS 1996, SI 1996 644; made under the Legal Aid Act 1988 s.25, s.34, s.43. In force: April 1, 1996; £1.55.

These Regulations increase the rates of remuneration for legal aid work in criminal proceedings done on or after April 1, 1996. The Regulations also alter the date after which certain work may be remunerated at discretionary instead of prescribed rates from June 30, 1996 to June 30, 1997.

3879. Criminal procedure–care proceedings–solicitors and barristers

LEGAL AID IN CRIMINAL AND CARE PROCEEDINGS (GENERAL) (AMENDMENT) (NO.5) REGULATIONS 1996, SI 1996 2656; made under the Legal Aid Act 1988 s.2, s.34, s.43. In force: January 1, 1997; £1.10.

These Regulations amend the Legal Aid in Criminal and Care Proceedings (General) Regulations 1989 (SI 1989 344) by allowing legal aid orders to provide for the services of authorised litigators and authorised advocates, and by providing that references in those Regulations to solicitors and barristers extend to authorised litigators and authorised advocates respectively.

3880. Criminal procedure–Crown Courts–remuneration rates

The Lord Chancellor's Department issued a press release entitled *New criminal legal aid fees system to be introduced for Crown Court advocates* (Press notice 264/96), published on October 25, 1996. To help control costs, the Government has announced a new graduated fees system for the payment of advocates carrying out criminal legal aid work. The move to standard fees paves the way for the introduction of fixed price contracts as proposed in the White Paper, *Striking the Balance*.

3881. Criminal procedure–failure to submit evidence supporting statement of means at trial–whether submission after trial valid

[Legal Aid in Criminal and Care Proceedings (General) Regulations 1989 Reg.11; Legal Aid in Criminal and Care Proceedings (General) Regulations 1989 Reg.23; Legal Aid in Criminal and Care Proceedings (General) Regulations 1989 Reg.44.]

Solicitors acted for E in summary criminal proceedings and applied for legal aid on E's behalf under the Legal Aid in Criminal and Care Proceedings (General) Regulations 1989 Reg.11 and Reg.23. Regulation 23 required that a statement of means supported by documentary evidence be considered by the justices' clerk before a legal aid order could be made. However E did not have the documentary evidence. After the trial E submitted the evidence which was sent on to the court by the solicitors. The clerk rejected the application for legal aid on the basis that it had been made after the trial had been concluded so no valid order for legal aid could be made. The solicitors sought judicial review of that decision.

Held, granting the application, that where an applicant was unable to furnish the relevant documents before his trial, a legal aid order could still be made on the date at which the documents were eventually produced and any earlier advice or representation could be deemed to have been given under the terms of that order. There were three preconditions before such a course could be taken: the advice and representation must have been required as a matter of urgency, there must have been no undue delay in the making of the application and the representation must have been provided by the same solicitor who sought the legal aid order. On the facts the order should have been made as the preconditions in Reg.44(7) were satisfied.

R. v. HIGHBURY CORNER MAGISTRATES' COURT, *ex p.* DJ SONN & CO [1995] 1 W.L.R. 1365, Simon Brown, L.J., QBD.

3882. Criminal procedure–magistrates' courts

The Lord Chancellor's Department issued a press release entitled *Criminal legal aid in the magistrates' courts* (22.96), published on January 30, 1996. In a written answer to a Parliamentary Question by Viscount Montgomery of Alamein, the Lord Chancellor has announced that responsibility for granting criminal legal aid will remain with magistrates' courts. In the light of uncertainty expressed by the Comptroller and Auditor General in December 1993 about the rigour with which regulations governing the grant of criminal legal aid were being applied, Lord Mackay launched an examination of the feasibility of transferring the function to the Legal Aid Board. Statutory and administrative changes made during the last two years have produced significant improvements. The Lord Chancellor therefore concludes that a change in the arrangements is not necessary, particularly in the light of the fundamental reform of the legal aid scheme proposed in the Green Paper *Legal Aid–Targeting Need* (Cm 2854).

3883. Family proceedings–remuneration

LEGAL AID IN FAMILY PROCEEDINGS (REMUNERATION) (AMENDMENT) REGULATIONS 1996, SI 1996 650; made under the Legal Aid Act 1988 s.34, s.43. In force: April 1, 1996; £2.40.

The Regulations increase the rates of remuneration for work done under a legal aid certificate in family proceedings and provide higher rates for franchisees.

3884. Family proceedings–remuneration

LEGAL AID IN FAMILY PROCEEDINGS (REMUNERATION) (AMENDMENT) (NO.2) REGULATIONS 1996, SI 1996 1555; made under the Legal Aid Act 1988 s.34, s.43. In force: July 8, 1996; £0.65.

These Regulations revise some of the rates of remuneration for work done under a legal aid certificate in family proceedings provided by the Legal Aid in Family Proceedings (Remuneration) (Amendment) Regulations 1996 (SI 1996 650).

3885. Fitness to plead–hospital order but no restriction order imposed–appellant not a convicted person–no legal aid available for criminal appeal

[Legal Aid Act 1988 s.21; Criminal Procedure (Insanity) Act 1964 s.5.]

E, aged 21, appealed against the finding of fact as to theft having been found unfit to plead but, despite that disability having committed theft. A hospital order was made under the Criminal Procedure (Insanity) Act 1965 s.5(5) but was not accompanied by a restriction order. A woman had her bag taken whilst on a train and the issue for the jury was whether it had been proved that E did it. E contended that all the ingredients of the offence of theft must be proved and that he should have been allowed to call psychiatric evidence to determine whether or not he was capable of forming a dishonest intent. He also argued that the summing up was defective as the jury was not directed as to whether he was capable of acting dishonestly. E was granted legal aid to appeal by the Registrar of Criminal Appeals.

Held, quashing the legal aid order, that under the Legal Aid Act 1988 s.21 E was not a convicted or accused person. By virtue of the hospital order made under the 1964 Act, E could not be considered a convicted person. Furthermore, as no restriction order was made at the time of the hospital order, the Secretary of State had no power to require E to stand trial if he recovered.

R. v. EGAN (MICHAEL), *The Times*, October 14, 1996, Ognall, J., CA (Crim Div).

3886. Judicial review–refusal–leave to apply–prospective defendants were not persons "directly affected"

[Rules of the Supreme Court Ord.53 r.5.]

M had obtained leave to apply for judicial review of the Board's decision to refuse them legal aid to pursue actions for personal injuries against various tobacco companies. M had given notice of the proceedings to the tobacco companies but had not served them with the notice of motion and supporting documents. The companies by notice of motion sought an order directing M to serve them on the ground that they were persons "directly affected" under the Rules of the Supreme Court Ord.53 r.5(3).

Held, refusing the tobacco companies' application, that having regard to the statutory regime, prospective defendants in proceedings brought as a consequence of legal aid being granted are not obliged to provide any information nor do they have the right to appear or make representations at the stage when the Legal Aid Board considers whether to grant or to refuse legal aid, let alone at the stage when an appeal against refusal of legal aid is considered. It was only if a full legal aid certificate was granted permitting proceedings against the tobacco companies that anything might happen so far as they were concerned. In the circumstances, the companies were not "directly affected" by the application.

Observed, there was much to commend the view that material given to the Board by M for legal aid is confidential.

R. v. LEGAL AID BOARD, *ex p.* MEGARRY (NO.1) [1994] C.O.D. 468, Turner, J., QBD.

3887. Judicial review–seletion of law firm to manage litigation–multi-party action concerning Gulf War Syndrome–public law element of selection procedure

D, a law firm, applied for judicial review of the decision of the multi-party operational committee of the Legal Aid Board to award a contract for the Gulf War Syndrome litigation to two other firms. D argued that the selection process contained a sufficient element of public law as to make the committee's decision amenable to judicial review, since the litigation involved hundreds of legally aided plaintiffs in a matter of great public importance and that it was clearly in the public interest that the most appropriate firms were selected.

Held, allowing the application, that it was important to consider, as a whole, both the significance of the task to be performed and the public interest in having a fair and regular selection procedure. The committee's decision involved issues justiciable in public law, independent of whether a private law remedy was also available.

R. v. LEGAL AID BOARD, *ex p.* DONN & CO [1996] 3 All E.R. 1, Ognall, J., QBD.

3888. Legal advice–assessment of resources

LEGAL ADVICE AND ASSISTANCE (AMENDMENT) REGULATIONS 1996, SI 1996 435; made under the Legal Aid Act 1988 s.9, s.34, s.43. In force: June 1, 1996; £0.65.

These Regulations amend the provisions of the Legal Advice and Assistance Regulations 1989 (SI 1989 340) concerning the computation of the capital of an applicant for legal advice and assistance by limiting the total amount deductible in respect of any mortgage debts on one or more homes of the applicant to £100,000; and limiting the amount to be disregarded in computing the applicant's capital in respect of his only or principal home to the first £100,000 of the value, as assessed after deduction of any amount allowable in respect of a mortgage debt

3889. Legal advice–assessment of resources–remuneration rates

LEGAL ADVICE AND ASSISTANCE (AMENDMENT) (NO.2) REGULATIONS 1996, SI 1996 641; made under the Legal Aid Act 1988 s.9, s.34, s.43. In force: Reg.2(1), Reg.3: April 8, 1996; Remainder: April 1, 1996; £1.10.

These Regulations amend the Legal Advice and Assistance Regulations 1989 (SI 1989 340). Regulation 3 increases, with effect from April 8, 1996, the income limits for legal advice and assistance (other than assistance by way of representation ABWOR) from £72 to £75; for non-contributory ABWOR from £64 to £67, and for contributory ABWOR from £156 to £162. Regulation 4 provides increased rates of remuneration for legal advice and assistance given on or after April 1, 1996.

3890. Legal advice–assessment of resources

LEGAL ADVICE AND ASSISTANCE (AMENDMENT) (NO.3) REGULATIONS 1996, SI 1996 2308; made under the Legal Aid Act 1988 s.34, s.43. In force: October 7, 1996; £1.10.

These Regulations amend the Legal Advice and Assistance Regulations 1989 (SI 1989 340), so that a person in receipt of income based jobseeker's allowance need not provide details of his financial resources when applying for advice and assistance, and that his financial resources are to be taken not to exceed the eligibility limit for the time being; so that any back to work bonus treated as payable by way of a jobseeker's allowance is excluded from the computation of capital or income; and so that earnings top-up is excluded from the computation of income.

3891. Legal advice–duty solicitors–remuneration rates

LEGAL ADVICE AND ASSISTANCE (DUTY SOLICITOR) (REMUNERATION) (AMENDMENT) (NO.2) REGULATIONS 1996, SI 1996 647; made under the Legal Aid Act 1988 s.34, s.43. In force: April 1, 1996; £1.10.

These Regulations amend the Legal Advice and Assistance (Duty Solicitor) (Remuneration) Regulations 1989 (SI 1989 341) to increase the remuneration which is payable under those Regulations.

3892. Legal advice–police stations–remuneration rates

LEGAL ADVICE AND ASSISTANCE AT POLICE STATIONS (REMUNERATION) (AMENDMENT) REGULATIONS 1996, SI 1996 648; made under the Legal Aid Act 1988 s.34, s.43. In force: April 1, 1996; £1.10.

These Regulations amend the Legal Advice and Assistance at Police Stations (Remuneration) Regulations 1989 (SI 1989 342) to increase the rates of remuneration for work done on or after April 1, 1996.

3893. Legal advice–police stations–remuneration rates

LEGAL ADVICE AND ASSISTANCE AT POLICE STATIONS (REMUNERATION) (AMENDMENT) (NO.2) REGULATIONS 1996, SI 1996 1554; made under the Legal Aid Act 1988 s.34, s.43. In force: July 8, 1996; £0.65.

These Regulations amend the Legal Advice and Assistance at Police Stations (Remuneration) Regulations 1989 (SI 1989 342) to revise some of the rates of remuneration for work done on or after July 8, 1996.

3894. Real property–property recovered or preserved–joint ownership–proceedings by former partner for immediate sale compromised by consent order to postpone sale–charge attached

[Law of Property Act 1925 s.30; Legal Aid Act 1988 s.16.]

P was the co-owner of a property with her partner in an unmarried relationship. In 1988 the relationship ended and shortly afterwards B, P's former partner, commenced proceedings seeking an order under the Law of Property Act 1925 s.30 for a sale of the property and division of the proceeds. P obtained legal aid to defend the proceedings, which were eventually compromised by a consent order permitting P to remain in the house and postponing sale until specified events occurred, the sale proceeds to be divided equally. The Legal Aid Board claimed a charge on P's beneficial interest to secure repayment of the costs incurred on her behalf. The Board argued that the proceedings had involved a dispute as to the beneficial interests, or alternatively, that through the consent order P had "recovered or preserved property" within the meaning of the Legal Aid Act 1988 s.16. At first instance the judge held that there had been no dispute as to the beneficial interests but that P had recovered or preserved property and so the Board was entitled to the charge. P appealed.

Held, dismissing the appeal, that (1) there was ample material for the judge, viewing the matter in the round and taking note of the absence of any serious indications of controversy over the proportions of ownership, to conclude that the beneficial interests were not in issue and (2) the principles concerning married couples as stated in *Hanlon v. Law Society* [1980] 2 All E.R. 199, [1980] C.L.Y. 1664 and *Curling v. Law Society* [1985] 1 All E.R. 705, [1985] C.L.Y. 1988 should be followed. From the date of the consent order, P's rights under the trust for sale of the home, under the Law of Property Act 1925 s.30 were preserved to the extent that she continued to enjoy a right of possession.

Moreover, P's rights were recovered to the extent that where her possession had been formerly shared, it was now exclusive, and where postponement of the sale had formerly been consensual, it was now imperative.

PARKES v. LEGAL AID BOARD [1996] 4 All E.R. 271, Waite, L.J., CA.

3895. Recognisances–forfeiture–criminal or civil legal aid not available

[Legal Aid Act 1988 s.14, s.19, s.21, Sch.2.]

C applied for judicial review of two decisions which held that neither criminal nor civil legal aid was available to enable a surety to be represented in connection with proceedings on a proposed forfeiture of a recognisance. C had stood as surety in the sum of £20,000 for T, who was charged with the illegal importation of drugs. Shortly before T's trial was due to start, C became concerned as to T's whereabouts. He made a written statement to the police indicating that he wished to withdraw as a surety. T failed to surrender for his trial but was later arrested and convicted. C was summoned to attend the court to show cause as to why his recognisance should not be forfeited. By then C had become bankrupt. The judge purported to grant him legal aid to enable C to be represented. However the chief clerk refused legal aid on the grounds that the Legal Aid Act 1988 provided legal aid only in relation to criminal proceedings and that proceedings in relation to forfeiture of a recognisance were not criminal proceedings. C then applied for civil legal aid. This was refused on appeal by the Legal Aid Board and C now sought orders of certiorari to quash both refusals and orders of mandamus to oblige each respondent to reconsider their decisions.

Held, dismissing both applications, that criminal legal aid was only available for proceedings covered by s.19 of the 1988 Act and an application to forfeit a recognisance was not within s.19, *R. v. Southampton Justices, ex p. Green* [1976] Q.B. 11, [1975] C.L.Y. 2038 applied. Forfeiture of recognisance proceedings are not listed in s.19(2), as this was limited only to an accused or convicted person, under s.19(1) and s.21. Regarding civil proceedings, s.14(1) states that Part IV of the Act applies only to those matters specified in Sch.2 Part 1, where no mention is made of Crown Court proceedings, therefore civil legal aid was unavailable. The conclusion that both applications had to be dismissed was reached with considerable reluctance as there might well be occasions when it would be of assistance if a surety whose recognisance was liable to be forfeited could be represented.

R. v. MAIDSTONE CROWN COURT, *ex p.* CLARK; SUB NOM. R. v. LEGAL AID BOARD, *ex p.* CLARK [1996] 1 Cr. App. R. 617, Kennedy, L.J., QBD.

3896. Remand–withdrawal of legal aid by justices' clerk–remand prisoner's failure to produce evidence of means

[Legal Aid in Criminal and Care Proceedings (General) Regulations 1989 Reg.24.]

D and another challenged decisions to withdraw legal aid orders granted to them in relation to a charge of robbery. The orders were withdrawn on the failure by D and B to provide statements of means and documentary evidence in relation to their applications. Both had explained that they could not provide the evidence as they were in custody.

Held, allowing the applications and quashing the decisions, that (1) the proper officer of the court was entitled to require the applicants to complete a statement of means although the applicants had stated they were in receipt of benefits, and (2) however, the Legal Aid in Criminal and Care Proceedings (General) Regulations 1989 Reg.24 did not entitle the justices' clerk to require evidence, based upon an assessment of when the applicants could reasonably be expected to provide the evidence. The Regulations made it necessary for the court to make a formal requirement for the production of the necessary evidence after time had passed within which it was reasonably practicable for the applicant to produce it. The requirement could not be made before that passage of time. Although the procedure adopted by the clerk was administratively convenient, it was unlawful.

R. v. SOUTH WESTERN MAGISTRATES, *ex p.* DOYLE [1996] C.O.D. 309, Latham, J., QBD.

3897. Articles

Alone and franchised: L.S.G. 1996, 93(10), 10. (Experiences of sole practitioners who have successfully applied for legal aid franchises).

Arbitration avoidance *(Peter Glover)*: S.J. 1996, 140(12), 312-313. (Whether cases can be retrieved from small claims courts to promote justice and entitle parties to legal aid in light of increase in jurisdiction of small claims court).

Compulsory welfare benefits training - and legal aid *(Neil Bateman)*: L. Ex. 1996, Jan, 16. (Importance of knowledge of welfare law for legal aid franchise holders).

Death to the standard fees plan *(Guy Mansfield)*: Lawyer 1996, 10(30), 13. (Whether proposals in LCD paper Civil Standard Fees for Advocates will lead to vast discrepancies in payments).

Do costs really follow the event? *(Jane Weakley)*: N.L.J. 1996, 146(6744), 710-711. (Whether legally aided litigants are at disadvantage in not being entitled to recover indemnity costs).

Focus on legal aid *(James Dirks)*: C.L.W. 1996, 4(37), 2a-2b. (Block funding and Woolf fixed costs proposals raise practice management issues for solicitors which require strategic review).

Funding legal services: new lawyers, new money? *(Richard Moorhead)*: Litigator 1996, Sep, 270-276. (Reform proposals for legal aid system contained in Government White Paper *Striking the Balance*, Cm 3305, and in Labour Party's policy document *Access to Justice*, February 1995, and their significance for legal profession).

Getting legal aid for JR *(Stephen Cragg)*: J.R. 1996, 1(1), 5-7. (Guidelines on obtaining legal aid in civil cases, practicalities of applying and applicability of legal merits and general reasonableness tests in judicial review cases).

Has there been supplier-induced demand for legal aid? *(Gwyn Bevan)*: C.J.Q. 1996, (Table of standard fees in civil and criminal proceedings) 15(Apr), 98-114. (Economic analysis of growth in legal aid expenditure, examining changes in total expenditure and regional variations, and implications for reform of legal aid system).

If at first *(Martyn Day)*: L.S.G. 1996, 93(08), 20. (Advice to solicitors to persevere when first refused legal aid, with author's experiences in obtaining legal aid for group actions concerning smoking related diseases and electromagnetic fields).

Keep legal aid coming *(Sarah Brennan)*: Legal Times 1996, 38, 16-17. (Implications of decreasing financial eligibility for legal aid for medical negligence claims).

Law for the poor: the relationship between the agencies and solicitors in the development of poverty law *(Tamara Goriely)*: I.J.L.P. 1996, 3(1/2), 215-248. (Development of legal aid in light of needs of legal profession and rise of legal advice centres).

Legal aid - defendant on benefits - requirement to produce documentary evidence: J.P. 1996, 160(1), 19-20. (Question and answer. Whether applicant for legal aid should provide written explanation as to why information relating to benefits cannot be furnished at time of application).

Legal aid administration–time for a real change? *(Graham Potter)*: N.L.J. 1996, 146(6744), 712-713. (Arguments for new single body to administer legal aid).

Legal aid and injunctions *(Helen L. Conway)*: Fam. Law 1996, 26(Sep), 529. (Legal Aid Board amendment of guidance issued to franchise holders on granting of legal aid for injunctions in domestic violence situations).

Legal aid and tribunals–the Government's proposals: Tribunals 1996, 3(1), 1-3. (Present position in relation to legal aid for representation before tribunals and issues raised by Green Paper on legal aid (Cm. 2854).

Legal aid and welfare benefits: revised guidance: W.B. 1996, 2(Apr), 3-5. (Use of green forms for welfare benefits advice and amount of time LAB expects solicitors to spend on each matter when advising on reviews and appeals).

Legal Aid Board adds details to plans *(Steve Orchard)*: Legal Action 1996, Jan, 9. (Board's response to Lord Chancellor's Green Paper and role of regional legal services committees in allocating funds).

Legal aid eligibility from April 8, 1996 and remuneration rates from April 1: N.L.J. 1996, 146(6738), 479-482.

Legal aid franchising and the White Paper *(Sally Moore)*: S.J. 1996, 140(38), 966-967. (Requirements and incentives involved balanced against costs and need for new initiatives in making it simpler and promoting it to public).

Legal aid future: L.S.G. 1996, 93(25), 8. (White paper on legal aid *Striking the Balance* proposes targeting on priority need and all aided litigants to pay minimum contribution).

Legal aid losers in civil proceedings *(J.N. Spencer)*: J.P. 1996, 160(23), 381-382. (Problems of successful unassisted party in recovering costs from legally aided opponent).

Legal aid proposals for criminal work *(Lee Bridges)*: Legal Action 1996, Oct, 8-9. (Implications of legal aid White Paper proposals on contracting, with particular reference to restrictions on defendant's choice of solicitor).

Legal aid remuneration rates from April 1: N.L.J. 1996, 146(6739), 517-518.

Legal Aid White Paper: Fam. Law 1996, 26(Aug), 455-456. (Objectives and proposals outlined in *Striking the Balance*, published July 1996, including targeting, use of contracts and provisions on financial eligibility and contributions from capital and winnings).

Legal aid–controlling the budget or controlling the lawyers? *(Julian Gibbons)*: N.L.J. 1996, 146(6731), 220-221. (Failure by Legal Aid Board to address problems of Government's Green Paper on Legal Aid in its response, particularly proposals for block contracting).

Legal aid–luxury or necessity? *(Marlene Winfield)*: Litigator 1996, Jan, 15-17. (Speech to 1995 Bar Conference on Lord Chancellor's green paper and Woolf Civil Justice Review, legal aid's role in access to justice, spiralling costs of civil legal aid and need for coherent dispute resolution strategy).

Legal aid: Fam. Law 1996, 26(Aug), 514-522. (Remuneration rates from April 1, 1996 for work done under legal aid certificate in family proceedings, with amended table).

Legal aid: Fam. Law 1996, 26(Sep), 589-593. (Lord Chancellor's proposals for standard fee scheme for litigators undertaking family legal aid work and for fees for specialist advocates undertaking civil legal aid work, with tables of proposed levels).

Legal aid: who benefits? *(Anthony Barton)*: P.I. 1996, 3(3), 212-220. (Legal Aid Board's assessment of claims using merits and reasonableness tests and drawbacks of this system for medical and pharmaceutical claims).

Multi-party actions and the Legal Aid Board *(Paul Balen)*: J.P.I.L. 1996, Oct, 231-246. (Problems in obtaining legal aid funding for group applicants).

PFI for legal aid? *(Brian Raincock)*: L.S.G. 1996, 93(27), 25. (Whether insurance industry should be used as way of financing legal aid by providing legal expenses cover).

Plucking the golden goose's feathers *(Gervase MacGregor)*: Accountancy 1996, 117(1234), 98-99. (Solicitors' fraudulent misuse of legal aid scheme).

Striking the balance or hitting the poor? *(Vicki Chapman)*: Legal Action 1996, Aug, 8-9. (Effects of proposed changes to legal aid scheme in government White Paper).

Striking the wrong note *(Russell Wallman)*: L.S.G. 1996, 93(26), 12-13. (Four lawyers give views on legal aid White Paper *Striking the Balance*).

The Green Paper on legal aid and international human rights law *(Michael J. Beloff* and *Murray Hunt)*: E.H.R.L.R. 1996, 1, 5-17. (Whether state is required to provide legal aid under international human rights law and extent to which proposals in Government's Green Paper contravene these obligations).

Trouble in class *(Mark Mildred)*: Litigator 1996, Jul, 235-236. (Power of Legal Aid Board to enter into contracts for multi-plaintiff personal injury actions and use of judicial review to challenge awards of contracts).

When legal aid starts to go by the board *(Christie Davies)*:

Lawyer 1996, 10(14), 12. (Whether legal aid funding cutbacks will lead to reduction in availability of criminal lawyers).

3898. Books

Coates, Reginald Ian; Parry, James N.R.–Parry: a Practical Guide to Criminal Legal Aid. Paperback: £19.95. ISBN 0-406-04605-0. Butterworth Law.

Edwards, Anthony; Clegg, John; Dawson, Stephen–Profitable Legal Aid. Paperback: £29.95. ISBN 0-85459-950-9. Tolley Publishing.

Legal Aid Handbook: 1996. Paperback: £12.70. ISBN 0-421-57550-6. Sweet & Maxwell.

LEGAL PROFESSION

3899. Abuse of process–solicitors acting pro bono–absence of fee did not affect duty to client and court

[Supreme Court Act 1981 s.51.]

A firm of solicitors, who acted free of charge for T in a case which was struck out as an abuse of process, appealed against a costs order made under the Supreme Court Act 1981 s.51(1) and s.51(3) in favour of A, by which they were ordered to pay 60 per cent of A's costs. A sought confirmation of the original order, contending also that it should have been made as a wasted costs order under s.51(6) and s.51(7) of the 1981 Act. A argued that the solicitors' conduct had been improper and unreasonable, even though they had acted on a pro bono basis.

Held, dismissing the appeal, that (1) s.51(1) and s.51(3) did not confer jurisdiction to make a costs order against legal representatives when acting in that capacity, irrespective of whether they acted for a fee or not; (2) the solicitor could not be treated as third party funder nor a quasi party. However, whether acting for a fee or pro bono, a solicitor had a duty to both client and court, a breach of which could justify the issue of a wasted costs order under s.51(6) and s.51(7). Both solicitor and counsel had chosen to offer their services free of charge to T, believing he had a bona fide case, but the action amounted to an abuse of process. Although acting without a fee in a hopeless case could not on its own justify a wasted costs order, taking account of all the facts and circumstances of the case, there had been a lack of propriety in the conduct of the litigation which showed that the solicitor had failed to act reasonably in pursuing the action, *Ridehalgh v. Horsefield* [1994] Ch. 205, [1994] C.L.Y. 3623 considered.

TOLSTOY MILOSLAVSKY v. ALDINGTON [1996] 1 W.L.R. 736, Rose, L.J., CA.

3900. Administration of estates–executor of estate also a partner in firm of solicitors–transfer of funds from testator's estate to solicitors' account–whether amounted to payment of bill

[Solicitors Act 1974 s.70.]

C, a firm of solicitors in which J, the executor of an estate, was a partner, appealed against a refusal to strike out a summons for taxation brought by G, the principal beneficiary under the same estate, on the grounds that the 12 month time limit contained in the Solicitors Act 1974 s.70 under which G could challenge the bill of costs had expired. C had completed administration of the estate and presented a final bill to G for the sum of £5,500 plus VAT, which was then paid in March 1993 by way of transfer from the account held by the estate to C's office account with the knowledge and consent of the trustees. In May 1993 G informed C that he intended to apply for taxation.

Held, allowing the appeal, that the transfer of funds from the estate to C's account amounted to satisfaction of the bill with the consent of the payers, with the effect that the time limit to apply for taxation expired at the end of March 1994. The fact that J was a partner in the firm was of no relevance to the issue of payment.

GOUGH v. CHIVERS & JORDAN; SUB NOM. CHIVERS & JORDAN v. GOUGH, *The Times*, July 15, 1996, Aldous, L.J., CA.

3901. Bar Council–equal treatment–codes of practice

The Bar Council issued a press release entitled *Bar Council launches ground-breaking new equality code*, published on April 20, 1996. The Bar's new equality code, launched on April 20, 1996 at the Woman Lawyer Conference, provides a standard against which allegations of discrimination can be judged. The code, which will be incorporated into the Bar's Code of Conduct, covers discrimination on grounds of race, sex, disability, sexual orientation, religion and political belief. The code is part of a package of measures to tackle discrimination. Other measures include the validation of educational establishments to teach the Bar vocational course and the promotion of the Pupillage Application Clearing House scheme. The new code provides detailed advice on measures to enhance equality of opportunity, including recommendations on the fair selection of pupils and tenants; equality of opportunity in chambers; harassment; disability; and sexual orientation.

3902. Barristers–free movement of services–freedom of establishment–German barrister suspended from practising in Italy

[Treaty of Rome 1957; Council Directive 77/249 to facilitate the effective exercise by lawyers of freedom to provide services.]

On a reference under Art.177 of the Treaty of Rome 1957 the ECJ were asked to give guidance on the interpretation of Council Directive 77/249 following a challenge by G, a German barrister, of a decision of the Milan Bar Council suspending him from professional activities undertaken from chambers he had set up in Italy.

Held: The provision of services by a Community national in another Member State governed by Art.60 of the EC Treaty was intended to be on a temporary basis, its temporary nature to be determined in the light of the duration, regularity or continuity of the activities pursued, although Art.60 did not preclude the setting up of some kind of professional base or infrastructure to facilitate the performance of such services. However, a national of a Member State who took up and pursued a professional activity on a stable and continuous basis in another Member State came within the freedom of establishment provisions contained in Art.52 to Art.58 of the Treaty and was not required to belong to any professional body of the host state in order to pursue his activities. A host state might lay down conditions for the exercise of the right of establishment which had to be complied with in principle, but in the absence of any specific rules a Community national was entitled to set up business on that territory and his right was determinable in the light of the activities he intended to pursue there. The host state had to recognise the equivalence of professional qualifications of Community nationals and any national measures likely to hinder establishment had to be non-discriminatory and in the general interest and could not go beyond what was necessary to attain the objective sought.

GEBHARD v. CONSIGLIO DELL'ORDINE DEGLI AVVOCATI E PROCURATORI DI MILANO (C55/94) [1996] All E.R. (EC) 189, GC Rodriguez Iglesias (President), ECJ.

3903. Barristers–judges–whether barrister's duty to client extended to putting forward client's unsubstantiated allegations of bias on part of trial judge

D appealed against a decision which held that his neighbour, T, had the right to use a concrete slipway leading down to tidal mudflats in the area of their common boundary. There were a number of grounds of appeal and D instructed his barrister, at a late stage in the appeal, to make serious allegations of bias and corruption against the trial judge which were presented to him in the form of what amounted to interrogatories.

Held, dismissing the appeal, that (1) there was no evidence to support the allegations which were presented in an inappropriate manner and (2) counsel made a grave error of judgment in complying with his client's instructions. He should have either refused to act on those instructions or withdrawn from the case. His duty to his client did not extend to putting forward such allegations of corruption.

THATCHER v. DOUGLAS, *The Times*, January 8, 1996, Nourse, L.J., CA.

3904. Barristers–legal education–vocational training

The General Council of the Bar issued a press release entitled *Bar moves to broaden access to legal education*, published on February 2, 1996. The Bar Vocational Course, which is presently available only at the Inns of Court School of Law, is to be available at eight teaching institutions around the country from autumn 1997. BPP Law School, De Montfort University, Birmingham University, The Inns of Court School of Law, Manchester Metropolitan University, Nottingham Trent University, University of Northumbria at Newcastle and the University of the West of England and Cardiff Law School have successfully completed the first stage of the validation which will enable them to run the course.

3905. Legal Services Ombudsman–annual reports

The Lord Chancellor's Department issued a press release entitled *Law Society must improve its complaints handling if it wants to keep self regulation, says Ombudsman*, published on June 12, 1996. *The Annual Report of the Legal Services Ombudsman* issues a warning to the Law Society that if it does not improve on its complaints handling procedure, it will lose its self regulating role for the profession. The Ombudsman said that there must be a culture change in solicitors' approach to complaints, away from the "natural tendency" to adopt a legalistic and defensive stance when faced with complaints, instead of tackling them quickly and efficiently if they are justified. The report also welcomes the changes to the Bar Council's complaints system requiring barristers to pay compensation for poor service. It also details statistics of complaints, investigations and recommendations made to and by the legal profession's professional bodies. Copies of the report are available from HMSO, price £8.25.

3906. Liens–solicitors–client's papers–client needing papers to continue litigation–solicitors requesting fee–court's jurisdiction to restrict exercise of lien

[Rules of the Supreme Court Ord.29 r.6.]

I appealed against an order that he make a payment into court and that RB deliver up papers held by them against this payment. RB had for a long time acted as I's solicitors, but following a dispute concerning fees, I instructed new solicitors and requested that RB hand over papers so that ongoing litigation would not be prejudiced. RB refused to hand over the papers without being paid in full and issued a writ to recover its fees. In reply I issued a summons seeking delivery of the papers, submitting that the court had erred in requiring I to pay substantial sums to RB and into court. RB argued that the case came within the ambit of the Rules of the Supreme Court Ord.29 r.6 and therefore the court could only order delivery of the papers if I paid in the claim in full. RB further contended that, because I had retained them in other matters concluded some time ago, there existed a general and concurrent lien in relation to retainers which had not been discharged by RB but which had expired naturally, and that this case therefore differed from previous case law which dealt exclusively with situations where liens arose only from a single piece of litigation which was still outstanding.

Held, that Ord.29 r.6 did not prevent the court from exercising its jurisdiction to grant relief in equity against retention of papers by solicitors. The court therefore had the power to order delivery, but to do so would in reality diminish the value of RB's lien. In the interests of justice the court would require I to provide some security for RB's claim and the appropriate amount would be £450,000, being the full amount claimed by RB.

ISMAIL v. RICHARDS BUTLER [1996] Q.B. 711, Moore-Bick, J., QBD.

3907. Liens–solicitors–documents–breach of lien by copying documents and sending copies to client

B had been retained by China Everbright Co, C, to represent them as their solicitors in an arbitration. This retainer was ended by C, who instructed B to send relevant documents to G as their new solicitors. G undertook to hold the documents to the order of B in the interest of preserving B's retaining lien in respect of fees owed by C, but subsequently copied them all and sent copies to C, due to concern at the way the arbitration had been handled by B and on the basis that G understood the undertaking to extend only to the return of the original documents on demand. The judge, holding that the undertaking had three limbs: preservation of the original documents; retention of possession of them; and return of them on demand, found that there was no undertaking not to copy the documents. B's action against G was dismissed, and B appealed.

Held, allowing the appeal, that G had acted in breach of B's lien, and a declaration would be issued to that effect. G's power to deal with documents did not rest on the express extent of the undertaking. The solicitor claiming the lien was to be given every security, so long as it was not "inconsistent with the progress of the cause", *Heslop v. Metcalfe* [1937] 3 My. & C. 183 applied, and that wide principle extended to the making and sending of document copies.

BENTLEY v. GAISFORD, *The Times*, November 4, 1996, Roch, L.J., CA.

3908. Liens–solicitors had lien over client money for unpaid bill–transfer and retransfer of monies did not destroy lien

[Insolvency Act 1986 s.11, s.234.]

C, a firm of solicitors, held a sum of money for E, in their client account. C delivered a bill to E for an amount exceeding the amount held in the client account. An administration order was made against E. C transferred the money into their office account. The administrators brought proceedings under Insolvency Act 1986 s.234 to recover the money. The court held that C had held a lien over the money but that the assertion of the lien was a "step to enforce their security over the company's property" and so pursuant to s.11 of the 1986 Act could be effected only with the consent of the administrators or leave from the court. The judge suggested that the money be transferred back to the client account and an application made to the court to apply it in payment of the bill. The administrators argued that any lien over the funds had been extinguished when the money had been transferred out of the client account.

Held, granting C's application, that when the money was paid back into the client account it became E's property and C acquired a fresh lien in respect of unpaid fees.

EURO COMMERCIAL LEASING LTD v. CARTWRIGHT & LEWIS [1995] 2 B.C.L.C. 618, Evans-Lombe, J., Ch D.

3909. Solicitors–acting for purchaser and lender–mortgage advance held by solicitors in trust for lender–building society alleging breach of duty to disclose facts relevant to decision to lend–entitlement to summary judgment

BWBS brought an action against 13 defendant firms of solicitors, S, who had acted for both purchasers of domestic properties and for BWBS as mortgage lenders. When those properties were repossessed BWBS sought recovery from S as the borrowers' indebtedness was not covered by the reduced house prices. In each case BWBS paid an advance to S on completion of a report on title and a request form for an advance, subject to the requirement that S investigate title and prepare the mortgage deed. This advance was then held in trust for the lender. BWBS alleged that S were in breach of their obligations by failing to disclose material facts which might have influenced their decision to lend money, by failing to investigate and report on title, or by basing their request for an advance cheque on a warranty or representation which they knew to be misleading. S argued that the court must investigate whether BWBS would have proceeded if all relevant matters had been disclosed, the approach adopted in *Target Holdings Ltd v. Redferns* [1995] 3 W.L.R. 352, [1995] 1 C.L.Y. 2195. If BWBS would have proceeded with the loan, S argued, then no loss could be said to have arisen as a result of the breach of trust.

Held, that where solicitors had misled BWBS in confirming that details of the loan transaction accorded exactly with the terms of their advance, BWBS was entitled to summary judgment and it was irrelevant to consider whether they would have proceeded had the misrepresentation not been made, *Brickenden v. London Loan and Savings Co* [1934] 3 D.L.R. 465 applied. However, in cases where solicitors had failed to disclose certain matters and payment had been made in breach of BWBS's instructions but no misrepresentation was alleged, those solicitors should be granted unconditional leave to defend as there was a triable causation issue as to whether BWBS would have proceeded irrespective of the non-disclosure.

BRISTOL & WEST BUILDING SOCIETY v. MAY MAY & MERRIMANS [1996] 2 All E.R. 801, Chadwick, J., Ch D.

3910. Solicitors–breach of contract to employ trainee solicitor

S, a solicitor, appealed against a judgment awarding damages of £5,629 for breach of a contract to employ D as an articled clerk. S wrote a letter confirming that he would offer D articles after a probationary period of four to eight weeks, but evaded every attempt by D to get him to sign the articles. S dismissed D after six months. S contended that the judge below had erred, that (1) in holding that D's employment was beyond the probationary stage and (2) in his finding that the termination of D's contract was justified by complaints about his competence or his taking of holiday leave.

Held, dismissing the appeal, that (1) the judge below had been correct to determine that a contract for articles had been made and breached and (2) was entitled to hold that the complaints were not the reason for the dismissal, especially as they were not mentioned in the brief letter of dismissal.

DALEY v. SOLOMON, Trans. Ref: CCRTF/94/0931/C, October 17, 1995, Hirst, L.J., CA.

3911. Solicitors–confidentiality–duty to client–concern about an improper influence on the client–misconduct of case by Official Solicitor–no damages for disappointment and frustration

H appealed against a judgment ordering the Official Solicitor to pay her damages restricted to a single head and a judgment striking out her claim against her former solicitor. H suffered from periods of mental illness and was a patient of Dr P. Dr P controlled H's business affairs and held £73,000 belonging to H for investment in a nursing home that he intended to open. H's solicitor, P, was suspicious of Dr P's influence on H and demanded the return of the money and reported Dr P to the administrator of his hospital which resulted in Dr P's suspension. P commenced proceedings against H for his fees and a guardian ad litem to H was appointed by the Official Solicitor. In respect of the proceedings against the Official Solicitor, H argued that she was entitled to damages for disappointment and frustration caused by Dr P's suspension which arose when P acted beyond his instructions. In the case of the proceedings against P, H argued that the judge was wrong to strike out the proceedings owing to an estoppel rem judicatam.

Held, dismissing the appeals, that (1) P, as a solicitor, had a duty to his client to protect her. In certain circumstances, such as when a solicitor was concerned about an improper influence on his client, it would be appropriate to break a duty of confidence in order to protect the client by reporting the suspicion to the authorities; (2) the misconduct of H's case by the Official Solicitor was not such as to come within the category described in *Heywood v. Wellers* [1976] Q.B. 446, [1975] C.L.Y. 2350. H claimed damages for mental distress which was incidental to the misconduct; it was not a case where the reason for the contract or duty in tort was to provide freedom from stress and (3) the doctrine of issue estoppel applied in the action against P, because each of the claims made by H could have been dealt with in the action against her. H could not argue that there were special circumstances leading to the doctrine not applying as H was represented by the Official Solicitor, *Talbot v. Berkshire CC* [1994] Q.B. 290, [1993] C.L.Y. 1851 followed.

HOWELL-SMITH v. OFFICIAL SOLICITOR TO THE SUPREME COURT, Trans. Ref: QBENF 95/0325/C, April 26, 1996, Pill, L.J., CA.

3912. Solicitors–disciplinary tribunal–appeal to tribunal seeking to challenge criminal conviction by relying on civil burden of proof–whether abuse of process

[Civil Evidence Act 1968 s.11; Solicitors (Disciplinary Proceedings) Rules 1994 r.16; Solicitors (Disciplinary Proceedings) Rules 1994 r.30.]

A solicitor appealed against a Solicitor's Disciplinary Tribunal decision to strike him off the solicitors' roll following conviction for 15 dishonesty offences involving fraud against the Legal Aid Fund. He argued that, under the Civil Evidence Act 1968 s.11 and the Solicitors (Disciplinary Proceedings) Rules 1994 r.16 and r.30, he should be allowed to adduce evidence before the tribunal to show he had been wrongly convicted in the Crown Court.

Held, dismissing the appeal, that it was a matter of public policy that a collateral attack on a criminal conviction by way of civil proceedings would amount to an abuse of process unless fresh evidence, obtained after conviction, was of such probative value that it justified an exception being made, *Hunter v. Chief Constable of the West Midlands Police* [1982] A.C. 529, [1982] C.L.Y. 2382 followed. It was always preferable to seek to have the conviction reviewed, *Smith v. Linskill* [1996] 1 W.L.R. 763, [1996] C.L.Y. 4496 considered. On the facts of the instant case, the tribunal had correctly refused the application as no new admissible evidence or exceptional circumstances of the type required had been shown to exist.

SOLICITOR, *Re*, *The Times*, March 18, 1996, Lord Taylor of Gosforth, C.J., QBD.

3913. Solicitors–duty solicitor scheme–suspension–breach of statutory duty might give rise to a claim for damages–no claim in contract or quasi contract

[Legal Aid Board Duty Solicitor Arrangements 1992.]

A sought judicial review of the failure of the LAB to reinstate her on the duty solicitor scheme following a decision that she had been unlawfully suspended. A had been reinstated by the time the case was heard and A changed the claim to one for damages for breach of statutory duty by the LAB. A also argued that there was a cause of action in contract or quasi contract relating to lost earnings while she was not on the scheme.

Held, giving judgment for LAB, that (1) there was an arguable case for breach of duty but that did not automatically entitle the injured party to damages; (2) the breach of a statutory duty might give rise to a private law remedy if it could be shown in the legislation that Parliament intended to protect a limited class of the public and there was no other remedy stated in the legislation, *X (Minors) v. Bedfordshire CC* [1995] 3 W.L.R. 152, [1995] 2 C.L.Y. 3452 followed; (3) the Legal Aid Board Duty Solicitor Arrangements 1992 was designed to benefit those who required assistance, not those who provided it and (4) since no contract existed, the solicitor had merely lost the opportunity of earning, not actual earnings, *Roy v. Kensington and Chelsea and Westminster Family Practitioner Committee* [1992] A.C. 624, [1992] C.L.Y. 30 distinguished.

R. v. LEGAL AID BOARD, *ex p.* AMOO-GOTTFRIED, Trans. Ref: CO/2579/95, June 20, 1996, Jowitt, J., QBD.

3914. Solicitors–duty to mortgagee when acting for mortgagor

H claimed that D, solicitors for B, had failed to advise them correctly in relation to a £487,000 mortgage which they had supplied to B. B defaulted and the property, on which the mortgage was secured, was sold for £240,000. H argued that D had failed to advise them that B had two other mortgages. They were also not notified of a defect in title relating to B's common law wife's transfer of her interest in the property to B by deed of gift. It was alleged that D knew that the common law wife's finances were not sound and if she had become bankrupt within five years of the transfer, the transfer could have been displaced. D also knew that B did not live in the property but intended to convert it into flats, although it was a condition of the mortgage that B should reside at the property.

Held, giving judgment to D, that (1) it was the duty of the mortgagor's solicitor to inform the mortgagee of all matters concerning the mortgagee's decision to lend the money. In the case of confidential information, if the solicitor could not obtain the mortgagor's consent to inform the mortgagee, he must decline to act for his client. However, there was no duty on the solicitor to investigate his client's finances in relation to any aspect other than the mortgage; (2) there was no foundation to the argument that the deed of gift could be displaced in the event of bankruptcy since the exact continuation of each party could not be determined and (3) the evidence did not determine how much time the mortgagor spent at the property nor that he did not intend to reside there in the future.

BIRMINGHAM MIDSHIRES MORTGAGE SERVICES LTD v. PARRY; SUB NOM. HYPO-MORTGAGE SERVICES LTD v. DAVID PARRY & CO [1996] P.N.L.R. 494, Sir John Vinelott, Ch D.

3915. Solicitors–fees–London firm instructed in case transferred to Sheffield–disparity of hourly rates–Sheffield rates disregarded–choice of solicitor reasonably made

W was injured at his workplace in Sheffield and his union instructed on his behalf, London solicitors who specialised in personal injury claims and usually handled the union's cases. Proceedings were started in London but transferred by consent to Sheffield. W obtained an order for costs on the standard basis, and the deputy district judge allowed W's solicitors' claim for the hourly charging rate applicable to central London; the defendants applied for a review of that allowance, contending for the lower Sheffield charging rates to apply.

Held, refusing the application, that it had been reasonable, having regard to the extent and importance of the litigation for a reasonably minded litigant, and given that the union usually instructed the solicitors and had confidence in them; the fact that there were less expensive solicitors in the Sheffield area was to be disregarded, *KPMG Peat Marwick McLintock v. HLT Group* [1995] 2 All E.R. 180, [1995] 2 C.L.Y. 4024 applied.

WRAITH v. SHEFFIELD FORGEMASTERS LTD [1996] 1 W.L.R. 617, Potter, J., QBD.

3916. Solicitors–mortgage fraud–compensation–Law Society policy on compensation flawed–extent of duty of disclosure

The applicants sought certiorari to quash decisions by the Law Society Compensation Fund sub-committee refusing compensation for losses in a mortgage fraud involving a dishonest solicitor. The applicants' ground was that the Law Society's policy led to the wrong test being applied to determine the culpability of the solicitor. The Law Society claimed that the role of the solicitor when acting for both borrower and lender was to ensure that effective security was obtained and that although the conduct of the solicitor was a cause of the mortgage advances made, it was not a cause of the ultimate loss as that involved fluctuations in property prices. The Law Society's policy was that losses caused principally by inflated valuation or a fall in property prices would not be met by compensation from the fund.

Held, allowing the application for certiorari, that the sub-committee had misdirected itself regarding the role of the solicitor. Over and above the common law duty of disclosure, the solicitor acted as trustee in holding funds received from the lender by way of proposed mortgage advance and should have disclosed the discrepancy in sale price to the lender, or advised the lender he could no longer act for him. He also had a duty not to part with the advance without the consent of the lender, *Mortgage Express Ltd v. Bowerman & Partners* [1996] 2 All E.R. 836, [1996] C.L.Y. 4497 considered. Certiorari was granted and it was ordered that the issues be redetermined by a different sub-committee.

R. v. LAW SOCIETY, *ex p.* MORTGAGE EXPRESS LTD; R. v. LAW SOCIETY, *ex p.* ALLIANCE AND LEICESTER BUILDING SOCIETY [1997] P.N.L.R. 82, Ognall, J., QBD.

3917. Solicitors–no right to particulars of alleged dishonesty at time intervention notice served

[Solicitors Act 1974 Sch.1; Solicitors Accounts Rules 1991.]

G, a sole practitioner, appealed against a refusal to order the withdrawal of a Law Society intervention notice which stated that there was reason to suspect he had acted dishonestly. The notice resolved to vest his clients' funds in the Law Society and refer G to a disciplinary tribunal. G argued that a solicitor served with a notice of intervention under the Solicitors Act 1974 had the right to be given particulars of the suspected dishonesty and reasons for it contemporaneously with the notice, and that otherwise the notice was invalid and had to be withdrawn. He also sought the withdrawal of a second notice which notified him of failure to comply with the Solicitors Accounts Rules 1991.

Held, dismissing the appeal, that there was no requirement that a solicitor be given particulars of suspected dishonesty at the time a notice of intervention was given nor any requirement that principles of natural justice be considered. The essential feature of the statutory procedure was that any action could be taken swiftly, enabling the Law Society to act on any possible misconduct and the solicitors in question to respond quickly by seeking to suspend that course of action, *Yogarajah v. Law Society* [1982] S.J. 430, [1982] C.L.Y. 3082 followed. Under para.6 of Sch.1 to the 1974 Act, G could apply to the High Court and he would then have the opportunity of hearing the case against him. The same reasoning also applied to the second intervention notice.

GILES v. LAW SOCIETY (1996) 8 Admin. L.R. 105, Nourse, L.J., CA.

3918. Solicitors–professional conduct–conflict of interest–solicitor acted for vendor and purchaser–oral hearing unnecessary–meaning of "provided no conflict of interest appears"

[Solicitors Practice Rules 1988 r.6.2.]

The SCB appealed against a decision to allow an application for judicial review of a decision by the SCB's Conduct Appeal Committee to severely rebuke H, a solicitor, when he acted for both vendor and purchaser in a situation where there was a conflict of interest. SCB argued that the judge was wrong to find that the committee had misconstrued the Solicitors Practice Rules 1988 r.6.2 by applying it objectively. The question of whether H should have been given an oral hearing was also raised.

Held, allowing the appeal, that (1) the judge erred in applying a subjective test to r.6.2. Principles 11.01 and 11.03 prevented a solicitor from acting for two or more clients where there was a conflict of interest or a significant risk of conflict. Those principles imposed an objective test and were overriding principles in relation to the professional conduct of solicitors. In the light of the principles the phrase "provided no conflict of interest appears" in r.6.2 had to mean that which was apparent to a reasonable solicitor in the same position as the solicitor in the particular case. The judge's construction was contrary to principles 11.01 and 11.03 and would result in providing a defence for the more incompetent solicitor who was not alert to his professional duty and (2) it was not the practice of the committee to order oral hearings to be held. The decision was one for the committee to make considering the interests of justice.

R. v. SOLICITORS COMPLAINTS BUREAU, *ex p.* HERMER, Trans. Ref: QBCOF 95/0198/D, February 26, 1996, Sir Thomas Bingham, M.R., CA.

3919. Solicitors–professional conduct–conflict of interest–solicitor retained in patent litigation–former partner joined firm retained by other party–burden of proof

The plaintiff retained a firm of solicitors to act in UK patent litigation concerning the Hepatitis C Virus. For 11 months after this retainer X was a partner in the intellectual property department of the firm, but was not involved in the plaintiff's matter. X then joined another firm. Over two years later one of the defendants in the patent litigation, Y, retained X to act as its solicitor in the litigation. The plaintiff brought proceedings against X, his new firm and Y seeking an injunction preventing X from acting as Y's solicitor in the litigation in the UK and abroad.

Held, refusing the injunction, that (1) the basis of the court's intervention was not a perception of possible impropriety: it was the protection of confidential information, *Rakusen v. Ellis, Munday & Clarke* [1912] 1 Ch. 831; *David Lee & Co (Lincoln) Ltd v. Coward Chance* [1991] Ch. 259, [1991] C.L.Y. 3372; *Firm of Solicitors, Re* [1992] 1 Q.B. 959, [1992] C.L.Y. 4082 followed; (2) insofar as solicitors were constrained from acting against the interests of former clients, the law was concerned with the protection of information which firstly, was originally communicated in confidence; secondly, was still confidential and might reasonably be considered remembered or capable, on the memory being triggered, of being recalled; and thirdly, was relevant to the subject matter of the subsequent proposed retainer; (3) having regard to the fiduciary solicitor client relationship, the burden of proof was on X to establish that there was no risk of him misusing confidential information. X must also show that there was no reasonable prospect of any conflict between his duty to his previous client and his duty to his new client and that there was no real risk that he possessed any confidential information, *Firm of Solicitors, Re* [1992] 1 Q.B. 959, [1992] C.L.Y. 4082 followed and (4) in the instant case there was no real possibility that confidential information was ever communicated to X. Further, the overwhelming probability was that if any confidential information was ever communicated to X, with the lapse of time, the progress of the proceedings and having regard to the highly technical issues, there could be no real risk that such information would any longer have been confidential, relevant and recallable.

Observed, the same principles applied to barristers. Stricter regulation, if necessary, could be adopted by the Law Society or by agreement between partners. A solicitor could be restrained from acting against a former client if he possessed relevant confidential information. However, a solicitor who gained illegitimate possession of such information, in the absence of a former relationship could be restrained from using it but not from acting.

SOLICITORS (A FIRM), *Re* [1996] 3 W.L.R. 16, Lightman, J., Ch D.

3920. **Solicitors–retainers–contingency fees–public policy–recoverability of bills paid–enforceability of outstanding bills**

The litigation concerned certain preliminary issues relating to a solicitor's retainer. The retainer was on the basis that a 20 per cent reduction from solicitor/client fees was given for any lost cases. When the retainer was terminated by A, who was a leading importer of potatoes into the UK, they owed T almost £200,000 in fees and £57,000 in disbursements. The main issues were whether the retainer was void and/or unenforceable, whether A had to pay the outstanding costs and disbursements, and whether A were obliged to pay T on some other basis and if so what principles should be used to calculate the payment. T argued that the retainer was not for a contingency fee as it did not contain an uplift for success but rather a concession for the lack of success.

Held, that (1) this was a differential fee dependant on the outcome of litigation and was included in the definition of a contingency fee. A contingency fee was champertous and unenforceable as it was contrary to public policy; (2) in the case of bills already paid the judge decided that where services had been rendered and paid for under an unenforceable contract and, apart from the agreement itself, the payee had not acted unconscionably towards the payer nor been unjustly enriched, the consideration had not completely failed and it would be unrealistic to expect the plaintiff to recover the cost of the services while retaining the benefit of them and (3) A were not liable for unpaid bills.

ARATRA POTATO CO LTD v. TAYLOR JOYNSON GARRETT [1995] 4 All E.R. 695, Garland, J., QBD.

3921. **Solicitors–rights of audience–whether magistrates' court experience could be taken into account to obtain Higher Courts Criminal Proceedings certificate**

[Higher Court Qualification Regulations 1992 Sch.1 para.1.]

A solicitor appealed against a decision refusing him a Higher Courts Criminal Proceedings qualification. He had 36 years' experience in a vast quantity of work in the magistrates' courts in the London area. He undertook work for the CPS including heavy commitals in serious cases. The refusal was on the grounds that, although he had wide experience in the lower courts, he had limited experience in the higher courts and could not show a sufficient totality of advocacy experience to be granted an exemption from the course of tests under the Higher Court Qualification Regulations 1992 Sch.1 para.1 (iii).

Held, varying the order of the Law Society, that the applicant should be relieved of the requirement to undergo the test, but that he should attend the course. In deciding on whether a solicitor's totality of experience of advocacy satisfies para.1 (iii), his experience in the magistrates' court should not be excluded. However, it was experience in the higher courts which must weigh heaviest in the balance. The decision reflected the applicant's enormous experience.

SOLICITOR, *Re* (1995) 145 N.L.J. Rep. 1222, Sir Thomas Bingham, M.R., CA.

3922. **Articles**

An open hand *(Colin Passmore* and *Nicola Pittam)*: L.S.G. 1996, 93(02), 23. (Solicitors' duty of confidentiality and when legal professional privilege should be waived in disclosure of documents).

Balance of payments: Legal Bus. 1996, 67(Sep), 14, 26-29. (Trend away from lockstep remuneration system for law firm partners towards merit based systems with details of systems used in various top UK firms).

Client care: a balanced view *(Matthew Moore)*: S.J. 1996, 140(33), 843. (Public's perception of legal profession is not as poor as stock media image may portray following publication of Law Society Research Studies on complaints and clients' perceptions).

EMAIL: managing the legal risks *(Michael Hart)*: P.L.C. 1996, 7(4), 17-22. (Suggestions for staff email policy to reduce legal risks, including problems of confidential information, vicarious liability of employer and legal professional privilege).

From cramming to skills–the development of solicitors' education and training since Ormrod *(Nicholas Saunders)*: Law Teach. 1996, 30(2), 168-186. (Trends and changing structure of legal education during past 25 years).

Glass slippers and glass ceilings: women in the legal profession *(Eleni Skordaki)*: I.J.L.P. 1996, 3(1/2), 7-43. (Study of women in solicitors' profession, way in which profession works and how this determines what women do within it).

Hot property: L.S.G. 1996, 93(01), 25. (Legal recruitment industry experiences brisk demand from law firms for young solicitors with specialist commercial expertise).

How to profit from conditional fees *(Kerry Underwood)*: S.J. 1996, 140(33), 837, 840. (How they work and whether solicitors' would benefit from entering such arrangements for personal injuries work as system replaces role of legal aid).

In conversation–David Penry Davey QC–Chairman, the General Council of the Bar *(Rupert Kendrick)*: L. Ex. 1996, May, 42-45. (Interview with Chairman of Bar Council concerning recent developments affecting legal profession such as legal aid and mediation in divorce).

Interpreters and the legal process *(Ruth Morris)*: N.L.J. 1996, 146(6759), 1310-1311. (Need for higher standards demands greater understanding by all members of court of both link between competent interpreting and justice and of proper role and responsibilities of interpreters).

Is adequate professional liability insurance available for lawyers rendering cross-border services in Europe? *(Caroline Van Schoubroeck)*: I.J.I.L. 1996, 2, 171-176. (How completion of Single Market makes it necessary to pay more attention to whether lawyers have adequate liability insurance cover).

Is there a future for lawyers in divorce? *(Janet Walker)*: Int. J. Law & Fam. 1996, 10(1), 52-73. (Whether emphasis on mediation in reform proposals will restrict lawyers' involvement in divorce process).

Lawyers of the next millennium *(Peter Goldsmith)*: Bracton L.J. 1996, 28, 51-58. (Expected changes to role of lawyers and structure of practice and need for awareness and training in EEC and international law).

Lawyers? Aren't they boring? *(Clare Willis)*: Lawyer 1996, 10(13), 12. (Need for lawyers to acquire presentation and communications skills to improve relations with clients and public image).

Learning to compete *(Nicholas Saunders)*: L.S.G. 1996, 93(01), 28. (Whether firms can take active role in improving standard of training for all solicitors).

Litigation risk management: surviving the legal jungle: P.L.C. 1996, 7(8), 25-32. (Advice for in-house lawyers on how to minimise risk of litigation and handle disputes when they do arise).

Litigation will never be the same again *(James Burnett-Hitchcock)*: I.H.L. 1996, 43(Sep), 32-37. (Woolf report proposals, prosect of recommendations being put into practice and implications for practitioners and general public).

Managing the leap *(Diana Bentley)*: G.L. & B. 1996, Apr, 44-45. (Career moves for lawyers to business management, skills required and how move should be made).

Not for the faint-hearted *(Malcolm Fowler)*: L. Ex. 1996, Mar, 38-39. (Need for legal profession to devote more time and thought to lobbying, media handling and practice management).

Older but not yet wiser: S.J. 1996, 140(2), 37. (Growth in solicitors' work relating to older persons, including mental incapacity and community care problems, and inadequacies of existing law).

Plot a path to laptop land *(Kevin Mackay)*: Lawyer 1996, 10(35), 18. (Advice for lawyers intending to invest in laptops).

Preventing product liability: the lawyer's role *(Randall L. Goodden)*: P.L.I. 1996, 18(5), 67-68. (Role of lawyers as product liability prevention consultants for manufacturing companies).

Rethink, repackage and reform *(Frances Burton)*: Lawyer 1996, 10(12), 16. (Need for creative reform of legal profession and coordinated training to modernise legal services).

Sex discrimination at the margins *(Clare McGlynn)*: N.L.J. 1996, 146(6735), 379-381. (US report on sex discrimination in legal profession and comparison with UK).

Solicitors' discrete investment business *(Wilde Sapte)*: F.S.B. 1995, 10, 7-8. (Law Society's rules on conduct of investment business).

Solicitors–competitors or partners? *(Michael McCabe)*: Accountancy 1996, 118(1236), 64. (Ways in which accountants can be of assistance to law firms in advising on accounting and control systems and benefits of solicitors and accountants joining forces as partners).

The Cleveland Street Scandal 1889-90: the conduct of the defence *(Martin Dockray)*: J. Leg. Hist. 1996, 17(1), 1-16. (Prosecution of solicitor for conspiracy to pervert the course of justice and subsequent resumption of his practice).

The cultural time-bomb...and the lawyer *(David Chatterton)*: L. Ex. 1996, Jan, 54. (Lawyers should take advantage of opportunities to give pensions advice).

The ethics of witness coaching *(Richard C. Wydick)*: IALS Bull. 1996, 23, 8-14. (Conduct by lawyer that alters story witness will tell under oath, different forms which it may take and how to identify and avoid it).

The Internet: an introduction for legal practitioners *(Robin Widdison)*: Comp. and Law 1996, 6(6), 6-12. (Key features of Internet and how may be used by legal profession).

The mediation of trade in legal services: the General Agreement on Trade in Services interface *(Christopher Arup)*: W. Comp. 1996, 19(4), 81-108. (Regulatory problems posed by globalisation of legal services as envisaged by GATS and reception of foreign lawyers by host countries).

The rise of the solicitor advocate *(Nicholas Fletcher* and *Iain Roxborough)*: I.C. Lit. 1996, Jul/Aug, 31-33. (Background to 1990 Act granting solicitors rights of audience in higher courts, practical evaluation of new system and need for legal profession to adapt to changes).

The woman lawyer–changing the culture *(Antoinette Curran)*: Writ 1996, 71 (Jul/Aug), 1-2. (English Law Society and Bar joint conference, April 20, 1996 concerning practical ways of changing culture of legal profession in fields of equal opportunities and sexual and ethnic discrimination).

Things are looking up *(Kerry Stephenson)*: S.J. 1996, 140(3), 82. (Views of law firms on prospects for commercial property market in 1996).

Time to consider incorporation? *(I.G.C. Stratton)*: S.J. 1996, 140(2), 40-41. (Advantages and disadvantages of incorporation for legal partnerships).

Who's on the Web (and why) *(Nick Holmes)*: Comp. & Law 1996, 6(6), 12-14. (Lawyers, law firms and other legal institutions publishing on World Wide Web).

3923. Books

Armytage, Livingston–Educating Judges. Hardback: £72.50. ISBN 90-411-0256-6. Kluwer Law International.

Baigent, A.–Pervasive Topics. Legal Practice Course resource books. Paperback: £15.00. ISBN 0-85308-370-3. Jordan.

Ball, Howard–Hugo L. Black: Cold Steel Warrior. Hardback: £25.00. ISBN 0-19-507814-4. Oxford University Press Inc, USA.

Bibliographic Guide to Law: 1995. Hardback: £350.00. ISBN 0-7838-1332-5. G.K. Hall.

Birks, Peter–What Are Law Schools For?: Vol 2. Pressing Problems in the Law. Paperback: £25.00. ISBN 0-19-826293-0. Oxford University Press.

Blake, Susan–A Practical Approach to Legal Advice and Drafting. Paperback: £17.00. ISBN 1-85431-541-2. Blackstone Press.

Blakemore, Timothy–Law for Legal Executives Part 1. Year 1. Paperback: £17.95. ISBN 1-85431-583-8. Blackstone Press.

Bourne, C.; Popat, P.–On Your Feet!. Paperback: £11.95. ISBN 1-874241-12-0. Paperback: £11.95. ISBN 1-874241-12-0. Cavendish Publishing Ltd.

Comyn, Sir James–Advocacy and Practical Skills: Textbook. Paperback. ISBN 1-85836-054-4. Old Bailey Press.

Comyn, Sir James–The Young Barrister's Handbook. Paperback: £15.95. ISBN 1-85836-054-4. Old Bailey Press.

Cumper, Peter–Learning Exam Skills. £11.00. ISBN 1-85431-451-3. Blackstone Press.

Cumper, Peter–Learning Exam Techniques. Paperback: £11.00. ISBN 1-85431-451-3. Blackstone Press.

Cupit, Geoffrey–Justice As Fittingness. Hardback: £27.50. ISBN 0-19-823901-7. Clarendon Press.

Cutler, Andrew; Read, Anne–General Paper II: Textbook 1996-1997. Bar Examinations. Paperback: £21.95. ISBN 0-7510-0712-9. HLT Publications.

Cutler, Andrew; Read, Anne.–General Paper II: Casebook 1996-1997. Bar Examinations. Paperback: £21.95. ISBN 0-7510-0678-5. HLT Publications.

Flenley, William; Leech, Thomas–Flenley and Leech: Solicitors' Negligence. Paperback: £40.00. ISBN 0-406-05225-5. Butterworth Law.

Freeman, John H.–Client Management for Solicitors. Paperback: £16.95. ISBN 1-85941-039-1. Cavendish Publishing Ltd.

General Paper I: Suggested Solutions - Single Paper (Trinity 1995). Bar Examinations. Paperback: £3.95. ISBN 0-7510-0639-4. HLT Publications.

General Paper II: Suggested Solutions (1991-1995). Bar Examinations. Paperback: £9.95. ISBN 0-7510-0740-4. HLT Publications.

General Paper II: Suggested Solutions - Single Paper (Trinity 1995). Bar Examinations. Paperback: £3.95. ISBN 0-7510-0640-8. HLT Publications.

Hall, Jean Graham; Martin, Douglas F.–Haldane. Hardback: £25.00. ISBN 1-872328-29-6. Barry Rose Law Publishers Ltd.

Harris, Olivia–Inside and outside the Law. EASA series. Hardback: £40.00. ISBN 0-415-12928-1. Paperback: £13.99. ISBN 0-415-12929-X. Routledge.

Hogan, Brian; Seago, Peter; Bennett, Geoffrey–"A" Level Law. Concise course texts. Paperback: £12.50. ISBN 0-421-54880-0. Sweet & Maxwell.

Inns of Court Bar Manuals: Advocacy 1996/1997. Paperback: £16.95. ISBN 1-85431-568-4. Blackstone Press.

Inns of Court Bar Manuals: Case Preparation 1996/1997. Paperback: £16.95. ISBN 1-85431-569-2. Blackstone Press.

Inns of Court Bar Manuals: Conference Skills 1996/1997. Paperback: £16.95. ISBN 1-85431-566-8. Blackstone Press.

Inns of Court Bar Manuals: Criminal Litigation and Sentencing 1996/1997. Paperback: £16.95. ISBN 1-85431-573-0. Blackstone Press.

Inns of Court Bar Manuals: Drafting 1996/1997. Paperback: £16.95. ISBN 1-85431-571-4. Blackstone Press.

Inns of Court Bar Manuals: Evidence 1996/1997. Paperback: £16.95. ISBN 1-85431-572-2. Blackstone Press.

Inns of Court Bar Manuals: Negotiation 1996/1997. Paperback: £16.95. ISBN 1-85431-567-6. Blackstone Press.

Inns of Court Bar Manuals: Opinion Writing 1996/1997. Paperback: £16.95. ISBN 1-85431-570-6. Blackstone Press.

Inns of Court Bar Manuals: Professional Conduct 1996/1997. Paperback: £16.95. ISBN 1-85431-576-5. Blackstone Press.

Inns of Court Bar Manuals: Remedies 1996/1997. Paperback: £16.95. ISBN 1-85431-575-7. Blackstone Press.

Irons, Peter; Guitton, Stephanie–May It Please the Court. ISBN 1-56584-337-1. I.B. Tauris.

Johnson, R.–Printed Teaching Materials. Hardback: £30.00. ISBN 1-85941-233-5. Cavendish Publishing Ltd.

Jones, Philip A.–Lawyers' Skills 1996/1997. Legal Practice Course Guides. Paperback: £15.55. ISBN 1-85431-542-0. Blackstone Press.

Linowitz, Sol M.; Mayer, Martin–The Betrayed Profession. Paperback: £13.00. ISBN 0-8018-5329-X. The Johns Hopkins University Press.

McLean, Ian; Morrish, Peter; Greenhill, John–Magistrates' Court Index: 1997. Court indexes. Hardback: £42.00. ISBN 0-7520-0375-5. FT Law & Tax.
Nathanson, Stephen; Carver, Anne–What Lawyers Do. Paperback: £7.95. ISBN 0-421-54890-8. Sweet & Maxwell.
Parker, Stephen; Sampford, Charles–Legal Ethics and Legal Practice. Hardback: £35.00. ISBN 0-19-825945-X. Clarendon Press.
Pierce, Jennifer L.–Gender Trials. Paperback: £13.95. Hardback: £40.00. University of California Press.
Pitchfork, E.; Molan, M.–General Paper I: Casebook 1996-1997. Bar Examinations. Paperback: £20.95. ISBN 0-7510-0677-7. HLT Publications.
Pitchfork, Ernie; Molan, Mike T.–General Paper I: Textbook 1996-1997. Bar Examinations. Paperback: £21.95. ISBN 0-7510-0711-0. HLT Publications.
Q & A: Law. Questions and answers series. Paperback: £3.50. ISBN 0-85660-272-8. Trotman.
Rovere, Richard H.–Howe and Hummel. Paperback: £11.50. ISBN 0-8156-0366-5. Syracuse University Press.
Rowley, Graham–Law for Legal Executives Part 1. Year 2. Paperback: £17.95. ISBN 1-85431-590-0. Blackstone Press.
Seron, Carroll–The Business of Practicing Law. Labor and Social Change Series. Hardback: £39.95. ISBN 1-56639-406-6. Paperback: £18.50. ISBN 1-56639-407-4. Temple University Press.
Skordaki, Eleni–Social Change and the Solicitors' Profession. Hardback: £35.00. ISBN 0-19-825753-8. Clarendon Press.
Stevens, Robert–The Independence of the Judiciary. Paperback: £14.95. ISBN 0-19-826263-9. Clarendon Press.
Susskind, Richard E.–The Future of Law. Hardback: £19.99. ISBN 0-19-826007-5. Oxford University Press.
The Bar Directory: 1997. Hardback: £35.00. ISBN 0-7520-0399-2. FT Law & Tax.
Vandevelde, Kenneth J.–Thinking Like a Lawyer. New perspectives on law, culture & society. Hardback: £41.50. ISBN 0-8133-2203-0. Paperback: £12.95. ISBN 0-8133-2204-9. Westview Press.
Volcansek, Mary L.; Franciscis, Maria Elisabetta de; Lafon, Jacqueline Lucienne–Judicial Misconduct. Hardback: £31.95. ISBN 0-8130-1421-2. University Presses of Florida.
Warren, Suzanne–Legal Research in England and Wales. Guides to legal research. Paperback: £20.50. ISBN 1-870369-03-3. Sweet & Maxwell.
Webb, Julian; Maughan, Caroline–Webb & Maughan: Teaching Lawyers' Skills. Paperback: £27.00. ISBN 0-406-05216-6. Butterworth Law.

LEGAL SYSTEMS

3924. Books

Abdullahi Ahmed An-Na'im–Toward an Islamic Reformation. Contemporary Issues in the Middle East. Paperback: £13.50. ISBN 0-8156-2706-8. Syracuse University Press.
Aldrich, George H.–The Jurisprudence of the Iran-United States Claims Tribunal. Hardback: £75.00. ISBN 0-19-825805-4. Clarendon Press.
Arjava, Antti–Women and Law in Late Antiquity and the Early Middle Ages. Hardback: £35.00. ISBN 0-19-815033-4. Clarendon Press.
Bailey, S.H.; Gunn, M.–Smith and Bailey on the Modern English Legal System. Paperback: £27.00. ISBN 0-421-50840-X. Sweet & Maxwell.
Baldwin, Robert; Cane, Peter–Law and Uncertainty. Hardback: £99.00. ISBN 90-411-0942-0. Kluwer Law International.
Beatson, Jack–Has the Common Law a Future? Paperback: £4.95. ISBN 0-521-58675-5. Cambridge University Press.
Benjamin, Joanna–Benjamin: Global Custody-an English Analysis. Paperback: £130.00. ISBN 0-406-04836-3. Butterworth Law.

Bennett, Michael J.–When Dreams Came True. Hardback: £19.95. ISBN 1-57488-041-1. Brassey's US.

Birkinshaw, Patrick–Freedom of Information - the Law, the Practice and the Ideal. Hardback: £23.95. ISBN 0-406-04972-6. Butterworth Law.

Bland, Randall W.–The Black Robe and the Bald Eagle. Hardback: £53.95. ISBN 1-880921-40-5. Paperback: £35.95. ISBN 1-880921-06-5. Austin and Winfield.

Butler, W.E.–Russian Legal Theory. International Library of Essays on Law and Legal Theory. Hardback: £110.00. ISBN 1-85521-249-8. Dartmouth.

Cale, Michelle–Law and Society. Public Record Office readers' guides, No 14. Paperback: £12.99. Public Record Office.

Charman, Mary; Martin, Jacqueline–Longman A-level Revise Guide: Law. Longman A-level revise guides. Paperback: £10.99. ISBN 0-582-28701-4. Addison-Wesley Longman Higher Education.

Clark, Robert–Legal Skills and System: Textbook 1996-1997. Bachelor of Laws (LLB). Paperback: £17.50. ISBN 0-7510-0649-1. HLT Publications.

Collected Courses of the Academy of European Law/ Recueil des Cours de L'Academie de Droit Europeen: Vol V. Book 1: 1994 European Community Law. Collected Courses of the Academy of European Law. Hardback: £88.00. ISBN 90-411-0230-2. Martinus Nijhoff Publishers.

Cownie, Fiona; Bradney, Anthony–The English Legal System in Context. Paperback: £21.95. ISBN 0-406-51181-0. Butterworth Law.

Cracknell, Doug G.–English Legal System: Textbook 1996-1997. Bachelor of laws (LLB). Paperback: £16.95. ISBN 0-7510-0687-4. HLT Publications.

Cracknell, Doug G.–English Legal System: Casebook 1996-1997. Bachelor of Laws (LLB). Paperback: £14.95. ISBN 0-7510-0653-X. HLT Publications.

Dadamo, Christian; Farran, Susan–The French Legal System. Paperback: £18.95. ISBN 0-421-53970-4. Sweet & Maxwell.

Darbyshire, Penny–Eddey on the English Legal System. Concise course texts. Paperback: £12.95. ISBN 0-421-55500-9. Sweet & Maxwell.

Darrow, Clarence S.–The Story of My Life. Paperback: £14.50. ISBN 0-306-80738-6. Da Capo Press.

Davis Jr, Joseph W.S.–Dispute Resolution in Japan. Hardback: £95.00. ISBN 90-411-0974-9. Kluwer Law International.

Dawson, Norma–One Hundred and Fifty Years of Irish Law. Hardback: £31.50. ISBN 0-85389-615-1. SLS Legal Publications.

Edge, Ian D.–Islamic Law and Legal Theory. International Library of Essays on Law and Legal Theory (Legal Cultures). Hardback: £105.00. ISBN 1-85521-140-8. Dartmouth.

El-Zeyn, Samih Atef–Islam and Human Ideology. Hardback: £45.00. ISBN 0-7103-0539-7. Kegan Paul International.

Elliott, Catherine; Quinn, Frances–English Legal System. Paperback: £14.99. ISBN 0-582-23868-4. Addison-Wesley Longman Higher Education.

English Legal System: Suggested Solutions (1991-1995). Bachelor of Laws (LLB). Paperback: £6.95. ISBN 0-7510-0721-8. HLT Publications.

English Legal System: Suggested Solutions - Single Paper (June 1995). Paperback: £3.00. ISBN 0-7510-0620-3. HLT Publications.

Feenstra, Robert–Legal Scholarship and Doctrines of Private Law, 13th-18th Centuries. Collected studies series. Hardback: £55.00. ISBN 0-86078-616-1. Variorum.

Feofanov, Yuri; Barry, Donald D.–Politics and Justice in Russia. Hardback: £50.50. ISBN 1-56324-344-X. Paperback: £17.50. ISBN 1-56324-345-8. M.E. Sharpe.

Firmin-Sellers, Kathryn–The Transformation of Property Rights in the Gold Coast. Political Economy of Institutions and Decisions. Hardback: £35.00. ISBN 0-521-55503-5. Cambridge University Press.

Foster, Nigel–German Legal System and Laws. £26.95. ISBN 1-85431-450-5. Blackstone Press.

Freeman, Michael D.A.–Current Legal Problems 1996: Vol 49. Part 2. Hardback: £35.00. ISBN 0-19-826280-9. Clarendon Press.

Gessner, Volkmar; Hoeland, Armin; Varga, Casba–European Legal Cultures. Tempus Textbook Series on European Law and European Legal Cultures. Hardback: £45.00. ISBN 1-85521-526-8. Dartmouth.

Gierke, Otto–Political Theories of the Middle Age. Key texts. Paperback: £12.99. ISBN 1-85506-478-2. Thoemmes Press.
Gleave, Robert; Kermeli, Eugenia–Islamic Law. Hardback: £50.00. ISBN 1-86064-119-9. I.B. Tauris.
Hall, Kermit L.; Wiecek, William M.; Finkelman, Paul–American Legal History. Paperback: £15.99. ISBN 0-19-509764-5. Oxford University Press Inc, USA.
Harding, Andrew–Law, Government and the Constitution in Malaysia. Law and administration in developing countries. Hardback: £79.00. ISBN 90-411-0918-8. Kluwer Law International.
Hinton, Martin; Johnston, Elliott; Rigney, Daryle–Indigenous Australians. Paperback: £35.00. ISBN 1-85941-235-1. Cavendish Publishing Ltd.
Hudson, John–The History of English Law. Proceedings of the British Academy, 89. Hardback: £19.95. ISBN 0-19-726165-5. Oxford University Press.
Hudson, John–The Formation of the English Common Law. The medieval world, Vol 2. Hardback: £42.00. ISBN 0-582-07027-9. Paperback: £13.99. ISBN 0-582-07026-0. Addison-Wesley Longman Higher Education.
Hunt, Alan–Governance of the Consuming Passions. Language, discourse, society. Hardback: £45.00. ISBN 0-333-63332-6. Macmillan Press.
Hutchinson, Dennis J.; Strauss, David A.; Stone, Geoffrey R.–The Supreme Court Review: 1995. Supreme Court review, 1995. Hardback: £43.25. ISBN 0-226-36312-0. University of Chicago Press.
Jackson, Bernard S.–Making Sense in Law. Legal semiotics monographs, Vol V. Hardback: £45.00. ISBN 0-9513793-6-4. Deborah Charles Publications.
James, Philip S.–James's Introduction to English Law. Paperback: £15.95. ISBN 0-406-02445-6. Butterworth Law.
Jenkins, Pamela J.; Kroll-Smith, Steve–Witnessing for Sociology. Hardback: £51.95. ISBN 0-275-94852-8. Praeger Publishers.
Johnston, David–The Renewal of the Old. Paperback: £4.95. ISBN 0-521-58756-5. Cambridge University Press.
Just, Peter–Dou Donggo Justice. Paperback: £15.95. ISBN 0-8476-8328-1. Hardback: £43.95. ISBN 0-8476-8327-3. Rowman & Littlefield.
Kaufman, Kenneth C.–Dred Scott's Advocate. Missouri Biography Series. Hardback: £23.95. ISBN 0-8262-1092-9. University of Missouri Press.
Kirk, E.–LLB Cases and Materials: the English Legal System. Paperback: £12.95. ISBN 1-85431-585-4. Blackstone Press.
Kirkby, Diane–Sex, Power and
Justice. Paperback: £18.99. ISBN 0-19-553734-3. OUP Australia.
Law Update: 1996. Paperback: £6.95. ISBN 0-7510-0609-2. HLT Publications.
Lea, David–Melanesian Land Tenure in a Contemporary and Philosophical Context. Hardback: £27.50. ISBN 0-7618-0456-0. University Press of America.
Ledford, Kenneth F.–From General Estate to Special Interest. Hardback: £35.00. ISBN 0-521-56031-4. Cambridge University Press.
Manchester, C.; Salter, D.; Moodie, P.; Lynch, B.–Exploring the Law - the Dynamics of Precedent and Statutory Interpretation. Paperback: £16.50. ISBN 0-421-47180-8. Sweet & Maxwell.
McKenzie, S.–Q & A English Legal System. Paperback: £8.95. ISBN 1-85431-533-1. Blackstone Press.
McLeod, Ian–Legal Method. Macmillan law masters. Paperback: £9.99. ISBN 0-333-67696-3. Macmillan Press.
Mei-fun, Priscilla Leung–China Law Reports: 1991: Vol 1. Civil Law. Hardback: £579.00. Butterworth Law.
Mei-fun, Priscilla Leung–China Law Reports: 1991: Vol 2. Criminal Law. Hardback: £579.00. Butterworth Law.
Mei-fun, Priscilla Leung–China Law Reports: 1991: Vol 3. Administrative and Economic Law. Hardback: £579.00. Butterworth Law.
Morewitz, Stephen–Sexual Harassment and Social Change in American Society. Paperback: £39.95. ISBN 1-880921-76-6. Hardback: £58.50. ISBN 1-880921-77-4. Austin and Winfield.
Muhammad Khalid Masud; Messick, Brinkley; Powers, David S.–Islamic Legal Interpretation. Harvard Law School legal studies/Harvard Middle Eastern studies. Hardback: £28.50. ISBN 0-674-46870-8. Harvard University Press.

Nagel, Robert F.–Judicial Power and American Character. Paperback: £10.99. ISBN 0-19-510662-8. Oxford University Press Inc, USA.

Nelken, David–Comparing Legal Cultures. Socio-legal studies. Hardback: £37.50. ISBN 1-85521-718-X. Dartmouth.

Nielsen, Marianne O.; Silverman, Robert A.–Native Americans, Crime, and Justice. Paperback: £13.50. ISBN 0-8133-2989-2. Hardback: £48.50. ISBN 0-8133-2988-4. Westview Press.

Orucu, Esin; Attwooll, Elspeth; Coyle, Sean–Studies in Legal Systems. Hardback: £70.00. ISBN 90-411-0906-4. Kluwer Law International.

Palmier, Leslie–State and Law in Eastern Asia. Hardback: £39.50. ISBN 1-85521-781-3. Dartmouth.

Posner, Richard A.–Law and Legal Theory in England and America. Clarendon law lectures. Hardback: £17.99. ISBN 0-19-826471-2. Clarendon Press.

Posner, Richard A.–Overcoming Law. Paperback: £11.95. ISBN 0-674-64926-5. Harvard University Press.

Posner, Richard A.–The Federal Courts. Hardback: £24.95. ISBN 0-674-29626-5. Harvard University Press.

Purdy, Jeannine M.–Common Law and Colonised Peoples. Law, social change and development. Hardback: £39.50. ISBN 1-85521-916-6. Dartmouth.

Robinson, O.F.–The Sources of Roman Law. Approaching the ancient world. Paperback: £10.99. ISBN 0-415-08995-6. Hardback: £35.00. ISBN 0-415-08994-8. Routledge.

Rogowski, Ralf–Rogowski: German Law. Paperback: £21.95. ISBN 0-406-02291-7. Butterworth Law.

Roskams, Julian–The Lawyer's Remembrancer: 1997. Hardback: £20.50. ISBN 0-406-06510-1. Butterworth Law.

Rowland, C.K.; Carp, Robert A.–Politics and Judgment in Federal District Courts. Hardback: £23.95. ISBN 0-7006-0776-5. University Press of Kansas.

Rowley, Graham; North, Lee–Law and Practice: NVQ3 for Para-legals. Paperback: £29.50. ISBN 0-7487-2508-3. Stanley Thornes.

Schwartz, Bernard–The Unpublished Opinions of the Rehnquist Court. Hardback: £32.50. ISBN 0-19-509332-1. Hardback: £32.50. ISBN 0-19-509332-1. Oxford University Press Inc, USA.

Shahabuddeen, Mohamed–Precedent in the World Court. Hersch Lauterpacht Memorial Lectures, 12. Hardback: £40.00. ISBN 0-521-56310-0. Cambridge University Press.

Sharifah Zaleha Syed Hassan; Cederroth, Sven–Managing Marital Disputes in Malaysia. NIAS monographs, No 75. Paperback: £15.99. ISBN 0-7007-0454-X. Hardback: £40.00. ISBN 0-7007-0432-9. Curzon Press.

Sharpston, Eleanor–European Legal Studies. Paperback: £21.95. ISBN 0-406-00490-0. Butterworth Law.

Slapper, Gary; Kelly, David–Sourcebook on English Legal System. Sourcebook Series. Paperback: £19.95. ISBN 1-85941-106-1. Cavendish Publishing Ltd.

Smith, Chuck–The New Mexico State Constitution. Reference Guides to the State Constitutions of the United States, No 23. Hardback: £63.50. ISBN 0-313-29548-4. Greenwood Press.

Smith, Gordon B.–Reforming the Russian Legal System. Cambridge Soviet Paperbacks, 11. Hardback: £45.00. ISBN 0-521-45052-7. Paperback: £16.95. ISBN 0-521-45669-X. Cambridge University Press.

Solomon, Peter H.–Reforming Justice in Russia, 1864-1994. Hardback: £66.50. ISBN 1-56324-862-X. M.E. Sharpe.

Sugarman, David–Law in History: Vols I and II. Between History and the Law: on the Writing of Histories of Law and Society/Law and Society. International Library of Essays in Law and Legal Theory (Schools). Hardback: £180.00. ISBN 1-85521-403-2. Dartmouth.

Taniguchi, Nancy J.–Necessary Fraud. Legal History of North America, No 3. Hardback: £31.95. ISBN 0-8061-2818-6. University of Oklahoma Press.

Thakur, Shivesh C.–Religion and Social Justice. Library of philosophy and religion. Hardback: £35.00. ISBN 0-333-60990-5. Macmillan Press.

Thompson, Bankole–The Constitutional History and Law of Sierra Leone (1961-1995). Hardback: £35.50. ISBN 0-7618-0473-0. University Press of America.

Thornton, Margaret–Dissonance and Distrust. Paperback: £18.99. ISBN 0-19-553661-4. OUP Australia.
Tushnet, Mark–The Warren Court in Historical and Political Perspective. Constitutionalism and Democracy. Paperback: £11.50. ISBN 0-8139-1665-8. University Press of Virginia.
Watson, Alan–Jesus and the Law. Hardback: £19.95. ISBN 0-8203-1813-2. University of Georgia Press.
White, R.S.–Natural Law in English Renaissance Literature. Hardback: £35.00. ISBN 0-521-48142-2. Cambridge University Press.
Wieacker, Franz; Zimmermann, Reinhard–A History of Private Law in Europe. Hardback: £55.00. ISBN 0-19-825861-5. Clarendon Press.
Wunder, John R.–Law and the Great Plains. Contributions in Legal Studies, No 82. Hardback: £47.95. ISBN 0-313-29680-4. Greenwood Press.
Zamir, Itzhak; Zysblat, Allen–Public Law in Israel. Hardback: £50.00. ISBN 0-19-825853-4. Clarendon Press.
Zander, Michael–Cases and Materials on the English Legal System. £18.95. ISBN 0-406-08176-X. Butterworth Law.
Zimmermann, Reinhard; Visser, Daniel–Southern Cross. Hardback: £50.00. ISBN 0-19-826087-3. Clarendon Press.

LEGISLATION

3925. Deregulation–annual reports

The Cabinet Office issued a press release entitled *Deregulation Task Force report published*, published on September 13, 1996. Deregulation Task Force chairman Francis Maude has launched the second report on how unnecessary regulation can be removed. He said that all regulation is costly, imposing higher prices, less choice, lower wages and fewer jobs. The report makes 90 specific recommendations among which are the proposal for more exchanges between civil servants and business, more use of alternatives to regulation, amendment to Building Regulations to allow greater choice in compliance, pressure on local authorities to improve their performance in dealing with planning applications, a reduction of £100m in the regulation of the financial services industry, simplification of PAYE and NICS for small businesses, and the abolition of at least 50 per cent of business licences. Mr. Maude said that too many unnecessary regulations were being introduced, and that the Task Force would seek to control this more carefully in the forthcoming year.

3926. Law Commission–annual reports

The Lord Chancellor's Department issued a press release entitled *The Law Commission–Annual Report for 1995: a record year for implementation of reports*, published on April 22, 1996. The annual report of the Law Commission for 1995 shows that 10 Law Commission reports were implemented during the year under review. There are currently over 20 projects in progress including reforms to damages, shareholder remedies, previous misconduct, trade secrets, trustee investments, land registration and property rights of home sharers. *Thirtieth Annual Report* (Law Com. No.293, HC 318) is available from HMSO, £10.60).

3927. Local and Personal Acts

The Law Commission issued a press release entitled *A key to all local statute laws*, published on July 2, 1996. The Law Commission and the Scottish Law Commission have published *The Chronological Table of Local Legislation*, which charts all the 26,500 local Acts passed since 1797, identifying which remain in force, how they have been amended and which have been repealed. Simultaneously, the Commissions have published their *Report on the*

Chronological Table of Local Legislation, which outlines the history and function of local legislation and shows how the absence of such a table has led to uncertainty. *The Chronological Table of Local Legislation* is published by HMSO, £180 (£145 until August 1, 1996). *Report on the Chronological Table of Local Legislation*, Law Com No 241, Scot Law Com No 155 (Cm 3301), is published by HMSO, £8.50.

3928. Parliamentary debates–admissibility for statutory interpretation–intention behind a particular statute

[Banking Act 1979; Banking Act 1987.]

In their action against the Bank of England for alleged failures in its role as banking supervisor of the insolvent Bank of Credit and Commerce International, BCCI, T and other depositors of BCCI applied during a preliminary hearing for leave to have admitted in evidence parliamentary debates and speeches during the passing of both the Banking Act 1979 and the Banking Act 1987. They intended to use the documents to rebut the Bank of England's contention that it had no obligation to protect depositors of banks.

Held, allowing the application, that to be able to ascertain the true purpose of the statutes in question would assist in the hearing of the preliminary issues which arose. There was nothing in the authorities to prevent evidence of parliamentary speeches being admitted to aid a court in interpreting not only statutory provisions but also the intention behind a particular statute, *Pepper v. Hart* [1993] A.C. 593, [1993] C.L.Y. 459, *Melluish v. BMI (No.3) Ltd* [1995] S.T.C. 964, [1995] 1 C.L.Y. 381 considered.

THREE RIVERS DC v. GOVERNOR AND COMPANY OF THE BANK OF ENGLAND (NO.2) [1996] 2 All E.R. 363, Clarke, J., QBD (Comm Ct).

3929. Royal Assents

These Acts received Royal Assent in 1996:

Allied Irish Banks Act 1996 (c.vii)
Appropriation Act 1996 (c.45)
Arbitration Act 1996 (c.23)
Armed Forces Act 1996 (c.46)
Asylum and Immigration Act 1996 (c.49)
Audit (Miscellaneous Provisions) Act 1996 (c.10)
Australia and New Zealand Banking Group Act 1996 (c.ii)
Belfast Charitable Society Act 1996 (c.vi)
Broadcasting Act 1996 (c.55)
Channel Tunnel Rail Link Act 1996 (c.61)
Chemical Weapons Act 1996 (c.6)
City of London (Approved Premises for Marriage) Act 1996 (c.iv)
City of Westminster Act 1996 (c.viii)
Civil Aviation (Amendment) Act 1996 (c.39)
Commonwealth Development Corporation Act 1996 (c.28)
Community Care (Direct Payments) Act 1996 (c.30)
Consolidated Fund Act 1996 (c.4)
Consolidated Fund (No.2) Act 1996 (c.60)
Criminal Procedure and Investigations Act 1996 (c.25)
Damages Act 1996 (c.48)
Defamation Act 1996 (c.31)
Dogs (Fouling of Land) Act 1996 (c.20)
Education (Student Loans) Act 1996 (c.9)

Education Act 1996 (c.56)
Employment Rights Act 1996 (c.18)
Energy Conservation Act 1996 (c.38)
Family Law Act 1996 (c.27)
Finance Act 1996 (c.8)
Health Service Commissioners (Amendment) Act 1996 (c.5)
Henry Johnson, Sons & Co Limited Act 1996 (c.v)
Hong Kong (Overseas Public Servants) Act 1996 (c.2)
Hong Kong (War Wives and Widows) Act 1996 (c.41)
Hong Kong Economic and Trade Office Act 1996 (c.63)
Housing Act 1996 (c.52)
Housing Grants, Construction and Regeneration Act 1996 (c.53)
Humber Bridge (Debts) Act 1996 (c.1)
Industrial Tribunals Act 1996 (c.17)
Law Reform (Year and a Day Rule) Act 1996 (c.19)
London Local Authorities Act 1996 (c.ix)
London Regional Transport Act 1996 (c.21)
Marriage Ceremony (Prescribed Words) Act 1996 (c.34)
National Health Service (Residual Liabilities) Act 1996 (c.15)
Noise Act 1996 (c.37)
Non-Domestic Rating (Information) Act 1996 (c.13)
Northern Ireland (Emergency Provisions) Act 1996 (c.22)
Northern Ireland (Entry to Negotiations, etc) Act 1996 (c.11)
Nursery Education and Grant-Maintained Schools Act 1996 (c.50)
Offensive Weapons Act 1996 (c.26)
Party Wall etc. Act 1996 (c.40)
Prevention of Terrorism (Additional Powers) Act 1996 (c.7)
Prisoners' Earnings Act 1996 (c.33)
Public Order (Amendment) Act 1996 (c.59)
Railway Heritage Act 1996 (c.42)
Rating (Caravans and Boats) Act 1996 (c.12)
Reserve Forces Act 1996 (c.14)
School Inspections Act 1996 (c.57)
Security Service Act 1996 (c.35)
Sexual Offences (Conspiracy and Incitement) Act 1996 (c.29)
Social Security (Overpayments) Act 1996 (c.51)
Statutory Instruments (Production and Sale) Act 1996 (c.54)
Theft (Amendment) Act 1996 (c.62)
Trading Schemes Act 1996 (c.32)
Treasure Act 1996 (c.24)
Trusts of Land and Appointment of Trustees Act 1996 (c.47)
University College London Act 1996 (c.iii)
Wild Mammals (Protection) Act 1996 (c.3)

3930. Statutory Instruments (Production and Sale) Act 1996 (c.54)

An Act to make provision (with retrospective effect) for the printing and sale of statutory instruments under the authority of the Queen's printer, for their issue under the authority of HMSO and for the reception in evidence of lists of such instruments which do not bear the imprint of the Queen's printer.

This Act received Royal Assent on July 24, 1996.

3931. Articles

Analysis and comparison of the Exxon Valdez and Sea Empress disasters *(Stephen Laino)*: Trans. L. & P. 1996, 3(7), 133-135. (Whether inappropriate for UK government to respond to Sea Empress disaster in the same way as US government by passing legislation such as the 1990 Act regarding double hulled tankers and liability issues).

Coping with Community legislation: a practitioner's reaction *(James O'Reilly)*: Stat. L.R. 1996, 17(1), 15-26. (Advice on understanding, interpreting and using EC legislation).

Copyright: HMSO and UK crown copyright: B.L.E. 1996, 3, 10. (Government publication of all new Acts of Parliament on Internet and copyright implications).
English as she is spoke *(Arthur Sellwood)*: Tax. 1996, 136(3537), 362-364. (Need for tax simplification, concise drafting and removal of vague and imprecise terms from tax legislation).
Is it in force? Must it be brought into force? *(Alec Samuels)*: Stat. L.R. 1996, 17(1), 62-65. (Problems of piecemeal implementation of legislation).
Keeping national parliaments informed: the problem of European legislation *(Vaughne Miller* and *Richard Ware)*: J.L.S. 1996, 2(3), 184-197. (Difficulties in tracking progress of EU legislation and need for more information links with Member States' national parliaments, focusing on Westminster's EU information technology requirements).
Plain English in the law *(Martin Cutts)*: Stat. L.R. 1996, 17(1), 50-61. (Need for clearer drafting of legislation using plain language, with example of author's redrafting of Timeshare Act 1992).
Problems of reforming labor legislation in the Republic of Kazakhstan *(E.N. Nurgalieva)*: Rev. C.E.E. Law 1995, 21(2), 149-161. (Progress towards free market economy and reduction of centralised regulation).
Secondary legislation: definitions: E.G. 1996, 9603, 118-119. (Guide for students on differences between statutory rules, orders and regulations).
Simplifying the system *(Christopher Wallworth)*: Tax. 1996, 136(3539), 411-414. (Inland Revenue tax simplification report examines drafting time constraints, structure, order and numbering of present tax legislation, need for rewrite in plain English and use of purpose clauses and examples in legislation).
We must get it right *(Maurice Parry-Wingfield)*: Tax. 1996, 137(3571), 605-607. (Inland Revenue consultation on project to rewrite tax legislation raises issues of approach to anti-avoidance and need for precision and certainty which potentially conflicts with requirements of clarity and everyday language).
What went where: FA 1996 *(John Jeffrey-Cook)*: Tax. P. 1996, Jun, 15-18. (Changes to original Bill clause numbering, with destination table showing amendments, Standing Committee E sitting numbers and relevant Hansard references, along with actual place in final Act).

3932. Books

Gifford; Salter–Understanding an Act of Parliament. Essential series - revision. Paperback: £9.95. ISBN 1-85941-206-8. Cavendish Publishing Ltd.
Is It in Force?: 1996. Paperback: £22.00. ISBN 0-406-06423-7. Butterworth Law.
Thornthon, G.C.–Legislative Drafting. Hardback: £70.00. ISBN 0-406-04521-6. Butterworth Law.

LEISURE INDUSTRY

3933. Football–membership criteria to join league–challenge to rules–whether rules open to review

S appealed against the dismissal of its application to restrain F from imposing their membership criteria which would have the effect of denying S admission to the football league. S sought a declaration that they were entitled to promotion as they had fulfilled the membership criteria pertaining to ground capacity and financial accounts, albeit after the deadlines set by F.

Held, dismissing the appeal on the ground of delay, that any challenge to F's rules governing promotion to and membership of the football league should have been commenced before the season ended. S's failure to do so was contrary to notions of justice and fair play. The court considered that certain questions needed to be answered in the affirmative before any challenge to the rules could be upheld: (1) whether any of the rules were invalid; (2) if so, whether a declaration should be made to that effect, and (3) whether an order should be made giving effect to modified rules. It would, in any case, only be in exceptional circumstances that retrospective effect could be given to modified rules in order to allow S to be promoted.

STEVENAGE BOROUGH FOOTBALL CLUB LTD v. FOOTBALL LEAGUE LTD, *The Times*, August 9, 1996, Millett, L.J., CA.

3934. Football–safety–spectators

FOOTBALL SPECTATORS (SEATING) ORDER 1996, SI 1996 1706; made under the Football Spectators Act 1989 s.11. In force: July 31, 1996; £1.10.

This Order directs the Football Licensing Authority to include in any licence to admit spectators to the football grounds, both in England, listed in Sch.1 a condition imposing requirements specified in Sch.2 as respects the seating of spectators at designated football matches at those premises. Designated football matches are those association football matches designated by the Secretary of State, under powers conferred by the Football Spectators Act 1989 s.1 (2), in the Football Spectators (Designation of Football Matches in England and Wales) Order 1993 (SI 1993 1691) and they include all association football matches played at the premises listed in Sch.1 of the Order.

3935. Recreational services–licensing–young persons–safety

ADVENTURE ACTIVITIES LICENSING REGULATIONS 1996, SI 1996 772; made under the Activity Centres (Young Persons' Safety) Act 1995 s.1, s.2, s.3. In force: April 16, 1996; £2.80.

These Regulations provide for the licensing of persons in respect of the provision of facilities for adventure activities.

3936. Recreational services–licensing–young persons–safety

ADVENTURE ACTIVITIES (ENFORCING AUTHORITY AND LICENSING AMENDMENT) REGULATIONS 1996, SI 1996 1647; made under the Health and Safety at Work etc. Act 1974 s.18; and the Activity Centres (Young Persons' Safety) Act 1995 s.1. In force: July 19, 1996; £0.65.

These Regulations apply with modifications the Health and Safety (Enforcing Authority) Regulations 1989 (SI 1989 1903) which allocate enforcement responsibilities between local authorities and the Health and Safety Executive in respect of the enforcement of the Adventure Activities Licensing Regulations 1996 (SI 1996 772) and amend those Regulations by altering cross references in Reg.7 (1) (a).

3937. Recreational services–licensing–young persons–safety

ADVENTURE ACTIVITIES (LICENSING) (DESIGNATION) ORDER 1996, SI 1996 771; made under the Activity Centres (Young Persons' Safety) Act 1995 s.1. In force: April 16, 1996; £0.65.

The Activity Centres (Young Persons' Safety) Act 1995 s.1 (1) provides that the Secretary of State shall designate a person to exercise prescribed functions relating to the licensing of persons providing facilities for adventure activities. A person designated is referred to in the Act as "the licensing authority". This Order designates Tourism Quality Services Ltd.

3938. Safety–recreational craft

RECREATIONAL CRAFT REGULATIONS 1996, SI 1996 1353; made under the European Communities Act 1972 s.2. In force: June 16, 1996; £4.70.

These Regulations implement provisions of Directive 94/25 ([1994] OJ L164) relating to recreational craft and apply to any product which is a recreational craft, partly completed recreational craft or component. The requirements which products must satisfy if they are to be placed on the market are prescribed, requirements for CE markings and other markings and inscriptions are set out, conformity assessment procedures are laid down along with procedures for the appointment of notified bodies, essential safety requirements for the design and construction of recreational craft are detailed, components are identified, a declaration by the builder or his authorised representative established in the community or the person responsible for placing on the market is set out. In addition EC type examinations, conformity to type, production quality assurance, product verification, unit verification, full quality assurance, technical documentation, written declaration of conformity and enforcement are dealt with.

3939. Safety–sports facilities

SAFETY OF SPORTS GROUNDS (ACCOMMODATION OF SPECTATORS) ORDER 1996, SI 1996 499; made under the Safety of Sports Grounds Act 1975 s.1. In force: March 25, 1996; £0.65.

The Safety of Sports Grounds Acts 1975 s.1 (1) provides that the Secretary of State may by order designate as a sports ground requiring a certificate under that Act any sports ground which in her opinion has accommodation for more than the specified number of spectators. This Order substitutes the number 5,000 as the specified number of spectators for sports grounds at which association football matches are played and which are occupied by a club which is a member of the Football League Ltd or the Football Association Premier League Ltd. The specified number for all other classes of sports ground remains 10,000.

3940. Safety–sports facilities

SAFETY OF SPORTS GROUNDS (DESIGNATION) ORDER 1996, SI 1996 2648; made under the Safety of Sports Grounds Act 1975 s.1, s.18. In force: November 13, 1996; £0.65.

This Order designates the Deva Stadium, the Sixfields Stadium, and the Plainmoor Ground as sports grounds requiring a safety certificate under the Safety of Sports Grounds Act 1975. It also varies the Safety of Sports Grounds (Association Football Grounds) (Designation) Order 1985 (SI 1985 1063) by omitting an entry which is no longer a sports ground.

3941. Articles

Activity centres: Government ignores cost benefit analysis in outdoor activities scheme: H. & S.B. 1996, 245, 4. (New licensing and inspection scheme for adventure activities despite fact that benefits unlikely to exceed costs).

Can sport move in mysterious ways? *(Warren Phelops)*: C.W. 1996, 63, 17-20. (Whether body movements by sporting personalities, such as bowling actions or football tackles, can be protected by copyright as dramatic works).

Child sex tourism: the new law *(Alan Davenport)*: T.L.J. 1996, 3, 110-112. (Implications for tour operators of 1996 Act which creates offences of conspiracy and incitement to commit sexual acts abroad).

Culture, change, commodity and crisis: cricket's timeless test *(Steve Greenfield* and *Guy Osborn)*: Int. J. Soc. L. 1996, 24(2), 189-209. (Historical development of structure of English cricket, change in perceptions of amateur and professional status and increasing commercialisation of both game and players).

International sports law as a process for resolving disputes *(James A.R. Nafziger)*: I.C.L.Q. 1996, 45(1), 130-149. (Normative trends in resolving disputes arising out of international sports activity, role of national courts and situations when judicial review is appropriate).

Key issues in Europe's lucrative sports market *(Adrian Barr-Smith* and *Darren Berman)*: M.I.P. 1996, 60, 39-42. (Recent issues in sports law including broadcasting rights, defamation, model sponsorship agreement, effect of trade mark legislation and regulation of advertising).

Replay for sporting negligence *(Edward Grayson)*: S.J. 1996, 140(21), 533, 535. (Principles for assessing negligence in sports related actions).

Solicitors 1: agents 0 *(Mel Goldberg)*: Legal Bus. 1996, 67(Sep), 75. (Importance of players obtaining advice from qualified lawyer before entering into sporting contracts).

Sporting negligence *(Graham Dunning)*: S.J. 1996, 140(2), 38-39. (Standard of duty of care and consent to risks).

Tackling drugs in sport: the role of the UK Sports Council Doping Control Unit *(Michele Verroken)*: S.L.A. & P. 1996, Sep/Oct, 10-11. (Legal issues surrounding drug testing by governing bodies of various sports).

Taking care of coaches *(Darren Bailey)*: S.L.A. & P. 1996, Sep/Oct, 1, 3-4. (Guidelines for sports coaches on good practice to avoid negligence claims).

The referees' fear of a penalty *(Steve Greenfield* and *Guy Osborn)*: P.N. 1996, 12(2), 63-66. (Appropriateness of legal action as means of settling sports disputes following case on referee's duty of care to young rugby player injured in scrum).

The sporting life: I.H.L. 1996, Jul/Aug, 15-19. (Solicitors who have acted in sports related cases give their views on development of sports law, including broadcasting rights, flotation of clubs on Stock Exchange and AIM and drugs offences).

3942. Books

Biederman, Donald E.; Pierson, Edward P.; Silfen, Martin E.; Glasser, Jeanne A.; Berry, Robert C.; Sobel, Lionel S.–Law and Business of the Entertainment Industries. Hardback: £47.95. ISBN 0-275-95064-6. Praeger Publishers.

Pannett, Alan; Boella, Michael–Principles of Hospitality Law. Hardback: £45.00. ISBN 0-304-33574-6. Paperback: £19.99. ISBN 0-304-33575-4. Cassell.

LICENSING

3943. Alcohol–weights and measures–deregulation

DEREGULATION (LONG PULL) ORDER 1996, SI 1996 1339; made under the Deregulation and Contracting Out Act 1994 s.1. In force: May 17, 1996; £0.65.

This Order repeals the Licensing Act 1964 s.165 which makes it an offence to sell or supply to a person a measure of intoxicating liquor which is more than the amount for which he asks.

3944. Clubs–council refusing to extend licensing hours–justices hearing appeal were entitled to hear evidence arising between council's decision and appeal

[Local Government (Miscellaneous Provisions) Act 1982 Sch.1.]

RBC appealed against the justices' decision to allow R's appeal against the refusal of an extension to his nightclub licence. RBC sought to adduce evidence of events which had taken place outside the club since their decision on the extension and which purported to show that the club was being badly run. The justices refused to admit that evidence on the basis that the appeal was merely a rehearing and should be conducted on the same original evidence.

Held, allowing the appeal, that on an appeal under the Local Government (Miscellaneous Provisions) Act 1982 Sch.1 para.17 the court was entitled to consider all relevant evidence and this included any evidence which arose between the original decision and the appeal. The later evidence of the club being badly run was therefore admissible.

RUSHMOOR BC v. RICHARDS (1996) 160 L.G. Rev. 460, Tuckey, J., QBD.

3945. Excise duty–licences–gambling

AMUSEMENT MACHINE LICENCE DUTY (SMALL-PRIZE MACHINES) ORDER 1996, SI 1996 1422; made under the Betting and Gaming Duties Act 1981 s.22. In force: July 1, 1996; £0.65.

This Order increases from £8 to £10 the maximum amount (in money or money's worth) which an amusement machine may pay out for a single game before it ceases to qualify as a small-prize machine.

3946. Excise duty–licences–gambling

AMUSEMENT MACHINE LICENCE DUTY (SPECIAL LICENCES) REGULATIONS 1996, SI 1996 1423; made under the Betting and Gaming Duties Act 1981 s.21, Sch.4 para.5. In force: July 1, 1996; £1.10.

These Regulations determine who may apply for a special amusement machine licence. They also allow the Commissioners to make directions concerning the display of a special amusement machine licence and the marking of any machine to which a special licence applies. The Schedule applies except that: special licences will only be transferable where the holder dies; a person may not surrender a special licence if he would be left holding between one and nine special licences after that surrender; the requirements to be observed by a licence holder imposed para.12 of the Schedule will not apply.

3947. Gambling–charges

GAMING CLUBS (HOURS AND CHARGES) (AMENDMENT) REGULATIONS 1996, SI 1996 1109; made under the Gaming Act 1968 s.14, s.51. In force: May 13, 1996; £0.65.

These Regulations increase the maximum charges which may be made for admission to gaming and bingo club premises in England and Wales from £6.80 to £8.00.

3948. Gambling–deregulation

DEREGULATION (GAMING MACHINES AND BETTING OFFICE FACILITIES) ORDER 1996, SI 1996 1359; made under the Deregulation and Contracting Out Act 1994 s.1. In force: June 20, 1996; £1.95.

This Order reduces restrictions on business in three areas. Article 3 and Art.4 amend the Betting, Gaming and Lotteries Act 1963 to increase the facilities ancillary to betting which may be provided in a licensed betting office. Article 5 increases the number of jackpot gaming machines which may be used in premises licensed or registered under the Gaming Act 1968 from the present limit of two. Article 6 relaxes the restrictions on use of machines for amusement purposes in the Gaming Act 1968 by permitting a cash only machine which gives a maximum prize of £10 in premises to which children have restricted access. Article 7, Art.8, Art.9 and Art.10 make various consequential and transitional provisions.

3949. Gambling–Horserace Totalisator Board

HORSERACE TOTALISATOR BOARD (EXTENSION OF POWERS) ORDER 1996, SI 1996 2906; made under the Horserace and Totalisator and Betting Levy Boards Act 1972 s.1. In force: December 20, 1996; £0.65.

This Order extends the corporate powers of the Horserace Totalisator Board so as to enable it, by way of business, to receive or negotiate fixed odds bets on the outcome of any lottery conducted outside the United Kingdom.

3950. Gambling–Horserace Totalisator Board–fees–extent of discretion as to amount of charges

[Betting, Gaming and Lotteries Act 1963 s.14.]

Held, that under the Betting, Gaming and Lotteries Act 1963 s.14(1) the Horserace Totalisator Board had a sole wide discretion to determine the amount of charges provided that they were made in good faith, were rational and enforceable and that any differentiation in fees had a legitimate basis.

R. v. HORSERACE TOTALISATOR BOARD, *ex p.* WILLIAM HILL, Trans. Ref: CO/559/95, December 15, 1995, Macpherson, J., QBD.

3951. Gambling–prizes–variation of monetary limits

AMUSEMENTS WITH PRIZES (VARIATION OF MONETARY LIMITS) ORDER 1996, SI 1996 3208; made under the Lotteries and Amusements Act 1976 s.18, s.24. In force: January 27, 1997; £0.65.

This Order raises the limit on money prizes for amusements governed by the Lotteries and Amusements Act 1976 s.16.

3952. Gambling–whether licence application for bingo club not yet built could be heard by justices

[Gaming Act 1968 Sch.2.]

GL applied for judicial review of a refusal by the licensing committee to determine an application for a licence for a bingo club which had not yet been built.

Held, allowing the appeal, that it was clear from the Gaming Act 1968 Sch.2 that the committee could hear applications relating to unbuilt premises provided those premises were situated within the petty sessional area of the licensing authority. If, however, the building was not constructed in accordance with the plan considered by the committee, the building would not be licensed.

R. v. GAMING LICENSING COMMITTEE OF NORTH HERTFORDSHIRE, *ex p.* GALA LEISURE LTD [1996] C.O.D. 312, Sedley, J., QBD.

3953. Licences–revocation–casinos–allegation of bias against Gaming Board

[Betting, Gaming and Lotteries Act 1963 s.16, s.19.]

K was the managing director and chief executive of London Clubs International, LCI, the holding company for London Clubs Ltd, LCL, who were owners of several casinos. K applied for judicial review of a decision of the GBGB to revoke his certificates of approval under the Betting, Gaming and Lotteries Act 1963 s.19. K contended that (1) the GBGB could only take into account matters prohibited under the 1963 Act, or under the guidelines laid down by the British Casino Association, BCA, in assessing that he was not a fit person to be a certificate holder; (2) GBGB were *Wednesbury* unreasonable in their attribution of so much responsibility to him, as a director, for contraventions of the 1963 Act; (3) K claimed that GBGB were wrong to consider that certain cheques were "shams" and should have noted that the cheques, though delayed, had been honoured; (4) GBGB were *Wednesbury* unreasonable to consider that good practice required that enquiries should be instigated before reinstatement of a cheque cashing facility, CCF, after receipt of a cheque marked "Return to drawer please represent" even though it was honoured later, and to require that proper enquiries should be made before granting large CCF's, or had their CCF's reinstated, after cheques had been dishonoured without adequate financial investigation, in breach of LCI's own procedures for taking up new bank references and making enquiries of other casinos; (5) GBGB erred by deciding, without evidence, that he was concerned in four transactions breaching Japanese exchange control regulations, but which were not in breach of the Bretton Woods agreement and therefore not unlawful; (6) GBGB were *Wednesbury* unreasonable to disapprove of a deposit facility enabling members to lend to each other; (7) GBGB were unreasonable to object to some £200,000 spent on gifts to three players made over a 10 month period, and (8) GBGB were unconsciously biased against him and that the doctrine of necessity requested that on independent tribunal be set up to minimise possible bias.

Held, dismissing the application, that (1) GBGB was entitled to consider matters outside the 1963 Act, and those outside the guidelines laid down by the BCA; (2) *R. v. City Equitable Fire Assurance* [1925] 1 Ch. 407, *Dovey v. Cory* [1901] 1 A.C. 477 and *Huckerby v. Elliott* [1970] 1 All E.R. 189, [1969] C.L.Y. 850

were distinguished on the grounds that they related to non-executive directors. GBGB made reasonable decisions that K should bear responsibility, (a) for the procedures that allowed bad practice, (b) for defective monitoring and upward communication, and (c) for management laxity; (3) it was not necessary for there to be a "sham" for a breach of s.16 of the 1963 Act to occur, but the judgment in *R. v. Knightsbridge Crown Court, ex p. Marcrest Properties* [1983] 1 W.L.R. 300, [1983] C.L.Y. 1747 indicated that s.16 would be breached if there was a lack of a "common expectation of payment" within the requisite two days and GBGB were entitled to consider that there was such an arrangement; (4) GBGB were entitled to find, as a matter of fact, that K was responsible for serious breaches in the control of CCF's; (5) GBGB were entitled to make an assessment that K either knew or turned a blind eye to what was taking place. Whether or not the transactions were illegal, GBGB were entitled to consider that they were relevant to the question of whether K was a fit and proper person; (6) GBGB had disapproved of the fact that this facility had frequently been used by members in debt to the casino, which was plainly against the policy of the 1963 Act; (7) GBGB were entitled to rely on their analysis of the general level of gifts in the industry to conclude that the gifts were excessive, and (8) it was common ground that there was evidence establishing an appearance of bias, but there was no evidence of a real danger of injustice arising from it.

R. v. GAMING BOARD FOR GREAT BRITAIN, *ex p.* KINGSLEY (NO.3), Trans. Ref: CO/2506/94, January 11, 1996, Jowitt, J., QBD.

3954. Licences–revocation–meaning given to expression "any person"

[Licensing Act 1964 s.20A.]

H applied for judicial review to quash the Crown Court's decision, on appeal from a decision of the Licensing Justices, whereby it ruled that the expression "any person" in the Licensing Act 1964 s.20A is apt to include a limited company and an unincorporated association. A leisure company and a local licensing victuallers association had sought to make an application under the section seeking the revocation of a licence held by H who submitted that the word "person" should be presumed to bear the same meaning throughout the Act, and that elsewhere it bore the narrow meaning of a natural person.

Held, dismissing the application and remitting the matter to the Crown Court for hearing, that the argument in favour of giving a word the same meaning throughout the Act was not as strong where the word was used in a consolidating Act covering a large number of situations as when dealing with a term of art. Here there was no reason for not giving the word "person" the wide meaning which it had acquired over the past century so as to include bodies corporate and incorporate. Nor was there any policy reason for restricting the class of those entitled to apply under the section, *Farrel v. Alexander* [1977] A.C. 59, [1976] C.L.Y. 1557 considered.

R. v. MAIDSTONE CROWN COURT, *ex p.* HARRIS AND DE MELLO [1994] C.O.D. 514, Schiemann, J., QBD.

3955. Licensed premises–sale of alcohol to minors–licensee absent–whether offence committed by helper

[Licensing Act 1964 s.169.]

B, joint proprietor of a grocery and off licence store, appealed against conviction for selling alcohol to a customer under the legal age, contrary to the Licensing Act 1964 s.169(1). B's wife, the licensee, was absent at the time of the sale.

Held, allowing the appeal, that B did not commit an offence because, on the evidence, he sold the alcohol as an agent for the licensee rather than as her servant. A master servant relationship could not be held to exist because B worked in the store rather than for it and his remuneration came from the business rather than from his wife, *Brandish v. Poole* [1968] 1 W.L.R. 544, [1968] C.L.Y. 2111 followed.

BOUCHER v. DPP (1996) 160 J.P. 650, Leggatt, L.J., QBD.

3956. Lotteries–gaming board fees

LOTTERIES (GAMING BOARD FEES) ORDER 1996, SI 1996 468; made under the Lotteries and Amusements Act 1976 s.18, s.24, Sch.1A para.6, Sch.2 para.7. In force: April 1, 1996; £1.10.

Provision is made as to the fees payable to the Gaming Board for Great Britain by societies and local authorities under the Lotteries and Amusements Act 1976. The fee for registration of a scheme by those wishing to promote a lottery is increased to £570 and the fee payable every three years in respect of continued registration is increased to £60.00. Fees payable for each society's lottery promoted on behalf of a society while registered with the Gaming Board and for each lottery promoted under a local authority scheme registered with the Board ranges from £65 to £515 depending upon the total value of tickets or chances sold. No fee is payable in respect of the eighth and any subsequent lottery promoted by a society in a calendar year provided that the turnover does not exceed £20,000 and an exemption fee applies to lotteries with a turnover of £2,000 or less. The fee payable by members of the public inspecting returns made in respect of societies and local authorities remains set at £2.00 but the fee payable on application for certification as a lottery manager is increased to £2,215.

3957. Lotteries–national lottery

NATIONAL LOTTERY ETC. ACT 1993 (AMENDMENT OF SECTION 23) ORDER 1996, SI 1996 3095; made under the National Lottery etc. Act 1993 s.29, s.60. In force: January 1, 1997; £0.65.

This Order amends the National Lottery etc Act 1993 s.23(2)(a) by substituting the English Sports Council for the Sports Council. The English Sports Council is an incorporated body established by Royal Charter. It also makes provision relating to sums held in the National Lottery Distribution Fund.

3958. Lotteries–registration–charity with 100 branches operating lotteries as single national operation–lottery to be registered with Gaming Board

[Lotteries and Amusements Act 1976 s.5, s.23, Sch.1A.]

B, a trustee of the National Hospital Trust sought judicial review of a decision by K purportedly revoking the registration of 100 NHT societies and thereby revoking lotteries which were run under the banner of NHS Lotto, a weekly lottery run as a society lottery under the Lotteries and Amusements Act 1976 s.5(1). K contended that the lotteries amounted to a single national operation, which, by virtue of its annual takings for 1994, required registration with the Gaming Board under Sch.1A to the 1976 Act, as distinguished from the authority. B submitted that the structure of NHS Lotto amounted to 100 separate lotteries, each run by a separate society sharing a central administration, with each lottery falling below the threshold for Gaming Board registration.

Held, dismissing the application, that given the true nature of the NHS Lotto, sharing common publicity, management and financial arrangements, the operation amounted to a single lottery, not 100 separate bodies, *WT Ramsay Ltd v. Inland Revenue Commissioners* [1982] A.C. 300, [1981] C.L.Y. 1385 and *Singette Ltd v. Martin* [1971] A.C. 407, [1971] C.L.Y. 5148 considered. Each branch in reality only amounted to a paper exercise in the running of the weekly draw and did not fulfil the separate branch requirement under s.23 of the 1976 Act, which meant it was not validly registered with the authority.

R. v. KENSINGTON AND CHELSEA RLBC, *ex p.* BLENNERHASSET, Trans. Ref: CO/922/96, July 19, 1996, Hidden, J., QBD.

3959. Lotteries–sale of tickets

LOTTERIES (AMENDMENT) REGULATIONS 1996, SI 1996 1306; made under the Lotteries and Amusements Act 1976 s.12. In force: June 6, 1996; £0.65.

These Regulations amend the Lotteries Regulations Act 1993 so as to remove the prohibition on the sale of tickets or chances by a person in the discharge of any official, professional or commercial function not connected with lotteries, when visiting another person at his home.

3960. Lotteries–unlawful "snowball scheme"–whether scheme amounted to a "game" and therefore participants not entitled to recovery of money

[Lotteries and Amusements Act 1976 s.1; Gaming Act 1845; Gaming Act 1968.]

The liquidator of O applied for summary judgment against R, the owners of the issued share capital of the company, seeking recovery of sums withdrawn by R as dividends and salary. The liquidator contended that O's only trading activity was the conduct of an unlawful lottery and consequently it made no profits which were capable of distribution. The "snowball scheme" operated by the company redistributed money paid by members around the scheme structure with the founder members gaining most. R argued that the scheme was not a lottery and, if it was, it was "gaming" within the terms of the Lotteries and Amusements Act 1976 and the Gaming Act 1968 and so was excluded from s.1 of the 1976 Act relating to lotteries. R further argued that the Gaming Act 1845 stated that money paid as a wager could not be recovered by court proceedings and therefore the money, advanced under a gaming agreement, was treated as a gift in law and the participants were not entitled to the recovery of their contributions.

Held, giving judgment against R, that the scheme amounted to a lottery for the purposes of the legislation, *Company (No.002613 of 1996), Re* [1996] C.L.Y. 1010 applied. The scheme was not regarded as a game in any sense of the word by the participants and so the scheme was not "gaming" within the 1845 or the 1968 Act and the participants were entitled to recover their money.

ONE LIFE LTD (IN LIQUIDATION) v. ROY [1996] 2 B.C.L.C. 608, Carnwath, J., Ch D.

3961. Markets–cancellation of registration for trading–allegations of bribery–appellants refused sight of witness statements–breach of natural justice

P and three others, all market traders in a street market in Holborn, appealed against the decision by C to cancel their registration for trading in the market. It was thought that the traders had been bribing market inspectors rather than buying tickets from C and handing them to the inspectors. At a hearing before C's Public Health and Environmental Services (Licensing and Control) Subcommittee, the appellants were refused the opportunity to see evidence in the form of 10 witness statements of other market traders on the grounds that the witnesses might be intimidated. The refusal formed a ground of the appeal.

Held, allowing the appeal, that fairness and justice demanded that those accused were entitled to know the evidence against them, *Kanda v. Government of the Federation of Malaya* [1962] A.C. 322, [1962] C.L.Y. 254 followed. The refusal amounted to an irregularity in the procedure. Such an irregularity would not lead to a breach of natural justice unless it could be shown that the irregularity caused the appellants to be deprived of something of substance, *Malloch v. Aberdeen Corp* [1971] 1 W.L.R. 1578, [1971] C.L.Y. 3866 followed. In this case, the evidence would have enabled the appellants to see that the 10 statements were not made by 10 different people and that they added little to a statement already made by a police officer. This would have been of assistance to the appellants. The decisions were quashed.

CAMDEN LBC v. PADDOCK, Trans. Ref: QBCOF 94/1321/D, October 31, 1995, Staughton, L.J., CA.

3962. Public entertainments–statutory interpretation–whether Leicester Square was "premises" within the London Government Act 1963

[London Government Act 1963 Sch.12.]

M, a busker, applied for judicial review of a stipendiary magistrate's decision to grant WCC a warrant to enter and search premises and forfeit equipment under the provisions of the London Government Act 1963, as amended, which required public entertainers to obtain a licence to perform in "premises". M busked in

Leicester Square and argued that Leicester Square was not "premises" within the terms of the Act.

Held, allowing the application, that Sch.12 of the Act described "premises" as including "any place" and M busked in approximately the same place every day. However, the Act could not be stretched to apply to buskers. M did not have a right to his spot in Leicester Square and Sch.12 did not apply to public places but to places to which the public was invited. WCC had applied the Act artificially. Powers to control buskers would require new legislation specifically addressed to that problem.

R. v. BOW STREET MAGISTRATES' COURT, *ex p.* MCDONALD, *The Times*, March 27, 1996, Schiemann, L.J., CA.

3963. Special hours licences–deregulation

DEREGULATION (SPECIAL HOURS CERTIFICATES) ORDER 1996, SI 1996 977; made under the Deregulation and Contracting Out Act 1994 s.1. In force: Art.1, Art.2: March 26, 1996; Remainder: May 1, 1996; £1.10.

This Order amends the Licensing Act 1964 to provide that in premises where a special hours certificate is in force an hour is not lost on the day the clocks go forward. It also enables licensing justices and magistrates' courts to grant provisional special hours certificates.

3964. Special hours licences–deregulation

LICENSING (SPECIAL HOURS CERTIFICATES) (AMENDMENT) RULES 1996, SI 1996 978; made under the Licensing Act 1964 s.91. In force: May 1, 1996; £1.10.

These Rules amend the Licensing (Special Hours Certificates) Rules 1982 (SI 1982 1384) to make provision for the grant of provisional Special Hours Certificates.

3965. Special hours licences–fees

LICENSING (FEES) (AMENDMENT) ORDER 1996, SI 1996 1063; made under the Licensing Act 1964 s.29, s.198. In force: May 1, 1996; £0.65.

This Order amends the Licensing (Fees) Order 1978 by prescribing the fees chargeable for the grant of a provisional special hours certificate (£10.00) and for declaring the provisional grant of such a certificate (£4.00). The Licensing Act 1964 s.77A and s.78ZA which relate to provisional special hours certificates, were inserted by the Deregulation (Special Hours Certificates) Order 1996 (SI 1996 977).

3966. Street trading–Hong Kong–Urban Council had power to prohibit itinerant hawkers

[Public Health and Municipal Services Ordinance 1960 (Hong Kong); Hawker (Urban Council) (Amendment) (No.3) By-Law 1994 (Hong Kong).]

N, the manufacturers and sellers of ice cream, appealed against the decision of the Court of Appeal of Hong Kong that U had validly removed its itinerant hawkers licences. The regulations relating to hawkers were contained in the Public Health and Municipal Services Ordinance 1960 (Hong Kong) as amended and, following a policy to reduce the number of itinerant hawkers who were causing congestion problems in the streets, the category of itinerant hawkers was removed from the licensing scheme by the Hawker (Urban Council) (Amendment) (No.3) By-Law 1994 (Hong Kong). N argued that U did not have the power to prohibit absolutely an activity under the legislation provided to regulate it.

Held, dismissing the appeal, that (1) an activity could not be totally prohibited by a power to regulate it although the effective regulation of the activity might require its partial prohibition. U's power in respect of the regulation of hawkers was very wide and covered those operating in a fixed place and itinerant hawkers. U had the power to amend the regulations in relation to one or both of the categories and were entitled to delete one of the categories, and

(2) U was not under a duty to licences itinerant hawkers, it was rather the case that the activity was unlawful unless licensed by U, *Slattery v. Naylor* (1888) 13 App. Cas. 446, *Municipal Corporation of the City of Toronto v. Virgo* [1895] A.C. 88, *Attorney General for Ontario v. Attorney General for the Dominion* [1896] A.C. 348 and *Cooperative Brick Co Proprietary Ltd v. Mayor of the City of Hawthorn* (1909) 9 C.L.R. 301 considered.

NG ENTERPRISES LTD v. URBAN COUNCIL [1996] 3 W.L.R. 751, Lord Slynn of Hadley, PC.

3967. Taxis–licences–determination of significant unmet demand in area–Crown Court's power–issue of licences on appeal

[Transport Act 1985 s.16; Supreme Court Act 1981 s.48; Public Health Acts Amendment Act 1907 s.7.]

K, whose application for 10 taxi licences had been refused by W, appealed against a decision that Liverpool Crown Court, which dealt with his appeal, was wrong to issue him with the licences following its finding that there was a significant unmet demand in the area concerned. K contended that the Transport Act 1985 s.16 required a Crown Court to grant a licence unless it concluded that there was no significant unmet demand. S, who also applied for a taxi licence, was told that the council would take no action on his application until K's case had been determined in the High Court. The Crown Court ruled that this amounted to withholding a licence in respect of which there was a right of appeal under the Public Health Acts Amendment Act 1907 s.7(1)(b) and granted him a licence. W successfully appealed against the Crown Court's decision and S appealed.

Held, dismissing the appeals, that (1) it was part of the function of a licensing authority, whether a local authority or the Crown Court under the Supreme Court Act 1981 s.48(2), to employ a system for determining applications or appeals that was fair to all applicants. Where a local authority stated that no significant unmet demand existed, but there was such a demand, a determination could only be made by considering the extent to which it could be met by all the current applicants, including the appellant in a particular appeal. As a result, further enquiries were needed before a decision could be reached regarding K's application and it was correctly remitted to W for reconsideration, and (2) there was a right of appeal under s.7(1)(b) of the 1907 Act where a local authority failed to make a determination and therefore withheld a licence, though there would inevitably be difficulties in determining a date of withholding for the purposes of fixing the start of the time limit for appeals, and the Crown Court should therefore take into account the circumstances of each case. S's application should be remitted to W in the light of the Crown Court's decision as to the existence of unmet demand.

KELLY v. WIRRAL MBC; SMITH (DEREK) v. WIRRAL MBC, *The Times*, May 13, 1996, Auld, L.J., CA.

3968. Taxis–licensing conditions imposed on taxis–whether point of hire commenced when drivers stopped plying for hire

[London Cab Order 1934 Part 31.]

Within the Metropolitan Police District licensing conditions impose geographical restrictions on the areas in which taxis can ply for hire. Taxis with green badges were entitled to ply for hire anywhere in the District and those with yellow badges were entitled to ply for hire only within a particular sector which excluded the central London area. It was alleged that the yellow badge drivers had permitted their taxis to be hired within the central area, contrary to their licences, as set out in the London Cab Order 1934 Part 31(1)(ii). It was alleged that C had aided and abetted the drivers to commit these offences. C operated a system whereby jobs in the central area were given to drivers licensed outside the area, although all drivers were in their licensed area when they accepted the calls; the "For Hire" light was simply switched off. The magistrates referred to the High Court the point whether for the purposes of Part 31, the drivers permitted their cabs to be hired at the time and place at which the customer was physically picked up. DPP argued that the hiring took place at the pick-up point. C submitted that the hiring took place once the driver ceased plying and had turned off the "For Hire" sign.

Held, dismissing the appeal, that (1) hiring was a matter of agreement between the customer and the driver. Whether or not hiring took place in an area where drivers were not licensed depended on what remained to be agreed between driver and customer in that area. Once terms had been agreed, the driver ceased to ply for hire, considering himself hired and contractually bound to pick up the customer, and (2) where nothing remained to be agreed then it was clear that hiring had taken place in the area where drivers were licensed. The allegations must therefore fail.

DPP v. COMPUTER CAB COMPANY LTD [1996] R.T.R. 130, Rose, L.J., QBD.

3969. Taxis–revocation of Hackney carriage licence–failure to reveal guilty plea to offences of dishonesty–conviction valid to revocation

[Local Government (Miscellaneous) Provisions Act 1976 s.61.]

B sought judicial review of a decision of C to revoke his hackney carriage licence under the Local Government (Miscellaneous) Provisions Act 1976 s.61. B had failed to reveal that he had pleaded guilty to four offences of dishonesty involving an MOT certificate. He only revealed the convictions once he had been sentenced which was after the licence had been granted. B argued that the council was not entitled to consider the convictions when exercising its power under s.61 (1) (b), as there had been no conviction until the sentence was passed.

Held, dismissing the application, that C was entitled to consider the convictions when exercising its power under s.61 (1) (b).

R. v. CREWE AND NANTWICH LBC, *ex p.* BARKER, Trans. Ref: CO/2045/95, March 8, 1996, Macpherson, J., QBD.

3970. Tour operators–air transport

CIVIL AVIATION (AIR TRAVEL ORGANISERS' LICENSING) (AMENDMENT) REGULATIONS 1996, SI 1996 1390; made under the Civil Aviation Act 1982 s.71. In force: June 21, 1996; £0.65.

These Regulations make minor changes to the Civil Aviation (Air Travel Organisers' Licensing) Regulations 1995 (SI 1995 1054).

3971. Articles

2001–an end to the licensing odyssey? *(David Young)*: I.H.L. 1996, 41 (Jun), 38-40. (Eccentricity of liquor licensing laws demonstrated by different procedures for obtaining licences in different geographical areas and need for change).

British beer and Brussels *(Paul Spink* and *Claire Milne)*: J.L.S.S. 1996, 41 (10), 395-396. (CEC plans to investigate whether UK guest beer arrangements are an illegal trade barrier).

Costs in licensing matters and the Licensing Act 1964 (Amendment) Bill: J.P. 1996, 160 (35), 691. (Ten minute rule Bill to restrict licensing justices' discretion to award costs by providing exemption for residents' associations).

Further progress on deregulations and a reminder of older bureaucratic powers *(Eversheds)*: I.H.L. 1996, Feb, 61. (Proposals aimed at reducing restrictions on gaming machines and amending Licensing Act to permit employment of 16-17 year olds in bars and procedures for suspension of justices' licences).

Game over? The Video Recordings Act and computer games *(David C. Wilkinson)*: C.W. 1996, 59, 14-15. (Exemption from film classification system no longer guaranteed for video or computer games if breach certain public morality criteria).

Judicial review: C.L. 1996, 1 (4), 4. (Virgin Television's proposed challenge to award of Channel 5 licence to Channel 5 Broadcasting on ground that ITC's decision was irrational and failed to comply with s.16 (2).

Licensing for conveyancers update *(Alan Pendlebury)*: S.J. 1996, 140 (20), 505-507. (Trends among licensing justices to publish policies and to limit frequency of transfer and rulings on special hours certificates, irregular licensing conditions, surrenders and tenants' rights to renewal).

Liquor licensing update *(Lawrence E. Stevens)*: S.J. 1996, 140(18), 455-456. (Children's certificate application procedure and qualification requirements, conditions imposed by magistrates, permitted Sunday hours and further possible relaxation).

Proposed changes to Friday and Saturday night drinking: J.P. 1996, 160(30), 536. (Home Office paper on extension of permitted hours licences and procedure likely to be introduced for obtain a licence).

Putting the brakes on depot development *(Philip Taylor)*: E.G. 1996, 9620, Supp Dis 20-21. (Consideration for warehouse operators when applying for goods vehicles operators' licences).

Regulation and the public interest: commercial gambling and the National Lottery *(David Miers)*: M.L.R. 1996, 59(4), 489-516. (Whether public interest in expanding gambling opportunities in name of good causes threatens to compromise regulatory structure of lottery).

Special orders of exemption: an explanatory note *(Alan Thompson)*: J.P. 1996, 160(32), 601-602. (Occasions which magistrates should regard as "special" for purposes of making special orders to extend permitted licensing hours for parties).

Streamlining of liquor licensing transfers and protection orders: J.P. 1996, 160(38), 777-778. (Home Office proposals for new system of interim licences, grant of licence transfers without need to attend court and naming of more than one person on licence).

Streetwise *(Christine Clayson)*: J.P. 1996, 160(31), 573-575. (Whether pavement displays by shop and holder of pedlar's certificate were street trading and whether buskers could be required to be licensed or were soliciting without permission).

Synchronisation licences in existing and new media *(Jeffrey E. Jacobson* and *Bruce E. Colfin)*: C.W. 1996, 63, 28-31. (Licences permitting use of musical works in conjunction with moving images and impact of new media such as home video).

UK: digital audio broadcasting (DAB): I.L.P. 1996, 20(4), 117-118. (Government proposals in White Paper Cm.2946 for licensing and ownership requirements for digital television and radio).

Unlicensed lending *(Anthony Sharp)*: Q.A. 1996, 40(Summer), 16. (Problems caused by existence of unlicensed lenders and role of trading standards departments in combatting their activities).

3972. Books

Cassidy, Constance–The Licensing Acts 1833-1995. Hardback: £137.50. ISBN 1-899-73811-8. Round Hall Sweet & Maxwell.

Davis, Marcia–The Licensing Referencer: 1997. Paperback: £14.95. ISBN 0-421-58180-8. Sweet & Maxwell.

Stevens, Lawrence; Green, Les; Mehigan, Simon–Paterson's Licensing Acts: 1997. Paterson's Licensing Acts, 1997. Hardback: £140.00. ISBN 0-406-99743-8. Butterworth Law.

LOCAL GOVERNMENT

3973. Air pollution–pollutants in excess of international guidelines on days of temperature inversion–road traffic regulations could not be used to restrict traffic for the good of the public health

[Road Traffic Regulation Act 1984 s.14.]

W, by his mother, applied for leave to appeal against the dismissal of his motion that G should exercise its power under the Road Traffic Regulation Act 1984 s.14. The power enabled local authorities to restrict traffic when there was a danger to the public and W, as a representative of children in the area, argued that the power should be exercised when there was a danger to the public from pollutants in the air which were in excess of international guidelines on days when there was temperature inversion. W argued that there was no restriction on what constituted a danger to the public.

Held, dismissing the appeal, that s.14 of the 1984 Act did not extend a local authority's power to dangers to public health. The section applied only to the risk of damage caused directly by vehicles or pedestrians by way of accidents.

R. v. GREENWICH LBC, *ex p.* W (A MINOR); SUB NOM. R. v. GREENWICH LBC, *ex p.* WILLIAMS [1997] Env. L.R. D2, Leggatt, L.J., CA.

3974. Boundaries

BRIDGEND AND THE VALE OF GLAMORGAN (AREAS) ORDER 1996, SI 1996 2915; made under the Local Government Act 1972 s.58, s.67. In force: in accordance with Art.1; £2.40.

The Order makes changes in the boundary between the county borough of the Vale of Glamorgan and the county borough of Bridgend following a review by the Local Government Boundary Commission for Wales.

3975. Boundaries

DENBIGHSHIRE AND WREXHAM (AREAS) ORDER 1996, SI 1996 2914; made under the Local Government Act 1972 s.58, s.67. In force: in accordance with Art.1; £2.40.

The Order makes changes in the boundary between the county of Denbighshire and the county borough of Wrexham following a review by the Local Government Boundary Commission for Wales.

3976. Boundaries

RUNNYMEDE AND SPELTHORNE (BOROUGH BOUNDARIES) ORDER 1996, SI 1996 1684; made under the Local Government Act 1992 s.17, s.26. In force: Art.2 (2): July 26, 1996; Art.1 (3): February 1, 1997; Remainder: April 1, 1997; £1.10.

This Order gives effect to recommendations of the Local Government Commission for England for the making of small changes to the boundary between the boroughs of Runnymede and Spelthorne in the county of Surrey. The recommendations have been modified to correct the name of an electoral area affected by the change.

3977. Care–local authority providing care for brain damaged child–whether local authority could recover cost of care

[Health and Social Services and Social Security Adjudications Act 1983 s.17.]

H, administratrix of the estate of her son, appealed against the decision that ACC were entitled to recover the cost of care provided by them for her brain damaged son. A negligence action had been settled previously by Bristol and District HA and this action was effectively between ACC and BDHA to recover ACC's costs under the Health and Social Services and Social Security Adjudications Act 1983 s.17 which gave a local authority the power to recover charges for care in such circumstances as were reasonable.

Held, dismissing the appeal, that ACC were entitled to recover their costs provided they could show they were acting reasonably and the person concerned had sufficient means. Section 17(3) of the 1983 Act provided no obligation to pay if it could be shown that a person's means were insufficient for them to be reasonably expected to pay.

AVON CC v. HOOPER [1997] 1 All E.R. 532, Hobhouse, L.J., CA.

3978. Charter Trustees

CHARTER TRUSTEES REGULATIONS 1996, SI 1996 263; made under the Local Government Act 1992 s.19, s.26. In force: March 4, 1996; £2.40.

These Regulations establish charter trustees for the city of Bath and the towns of Beverley, Cleethorpes, Great Grimsby and Scunthorpe on April 1, 1996. General provision is made in relation to privileges and rights of the trustees, precepts, the appointment of local government electors as trustees, meetings between the trustees, the chairman and vice-chairman, discharge of functions, accommodation and property of charter trustees, accounts and audit, payment of subscriptions and circumstances in which charter trustees cease to act.

3979. Charter Trustees–reorganisation–transfer of assets

CHARTER TRUSTEES (AMENDMENT) REGULATIONS 1996, SI 1996 610; made under the Local Government Act 1992 s.19, s.26. £1.10.

These Regulations amend the Charter Trustees Regulations 1996 (SI 1995 263) (the 1996 Regulations). Regulation 2(2) and Reg.2(5) amends incorrect cross references in the 1996 Regulations, and Reg.2(3) substitutes Reg.7(7) to clarify the position regarding the application the Local Government Act 1972 s.80(1)(e) to charter trustees established under Local Government Finance Act 1982 to local government electors holding office as charter trustees. Regulation 2(4) inserts Reg.11A into the 1996 Regulations. The new provision operates to transfer historic and ceremonial property held by abolished authorities to charter trustees established under the 1996 Regulations; charter trustees may dispose of certain of that property to the relevant council (defined in Reg.2(1) of the 1996 Regulations).

3980. Churches–funds

WELSH CHURCH ACT FUNDS (DESIGNATION AND SPECIFICATION) ORDER 1996, SI 1996 344; made under the Local Government (Wales) Act 1994 s.50, s.63. In force: April 1, 1996; £1.10.

The Local Government (Wales) Act 1994 reorganises local government in Wales with effect from April 1, 1996. From that date new principal councils established under the 1994 Act take over the administration of Welsh local government from the old principal councils. Section 50 of the 1994 Act makes general provision for the transfer of Welsh Church Act funds, held by old county councils, which are required to be administered in accordance with schemes made under the Welsh Church Act 1914 s.19. For the purpose of the operation of s.50, this order designates the new councils who are to hold those funds, and specifies the manner in which the funds are to be allocated amongst councils so designated. The Order also provides that any rights and liabilities in respect of Welsh Church Act funds are to transfer to the new councils who hold those funds.

3981. City of London–elections–decision by Court of Aldermen as to whether fit and proper person–reasons for decision–whether procedures fair

[Representation of the People Act 1983 s.191.]

M appealed against the refusal of his application for judicial review to quash a decision of the Court of Aldermen of the City of London not to confirm his election as an alderman. The election procedure took the form of an election by voters, recognised as a local government election under the Representation of the People Act 1983 s.191(1), which was subject to confirmation by the Court of Aldermen. M was elected by a majority, having received 78 per cent of the vote, but, after interviewing him and holding a secret ballot, the Court of Aldermen refused to confirm his election.

Held, allowing the appeal, that although the Court of Aldermen had considered M's suitability, they had failed to give reasons for their decision and it was impossible, on the limited information available, to say that their decision was unfair. However, natural justice required that reasons should be given in order that M might know whether to stand for public office again and upon

what basis he had been rejected, *R. v. Secretary of State for the Home Department, ex p. Doody* [1994] 1 A.C. 531, [1995] 1 C.L.Y. 213 followed.
R. v. CITY OF LONDON CORP, *ex p.* MATSON 94 L.G.R. 443, Neill, L.J., CA.

3982. City of Westminster Act 1996 (c.viii)

An Act to make further provision for the control of unlicensed sex establishments in the City of Westminster.
This Act received Royal Assent on July 24, 1996.

3983. Committal orders–community charge default–conditions for imprisonment–powers of High Court to remit sentence when dismissing appeal

P sought judicial review of a decision of the magistrates' court to commit him to prison for 90 days owing to his wilful neglect to pay his community charge pursuant to liability orders totalling £614.86. P argued that the magistrates had been wrong to order an immediate committal to prison and to order that the maximum term be fixed.

Held, dismissing the appeal, that (1) community charge defaulters could be imprisoned if five conditions were satisfied: (a) the correct procedures in terms of liability orders and warrants had been followed; (b) there had been an inquiry into the means of the defaulter; (c) there had been a finding of wilful refusal or culpable neglect; (d) other measures had been considered and (e) the imprisonment was used as a means of securing the payment rather than as a punishment, *R. v. Cannock Justices, ex p. Ireland* (Unreported, 1995) followed; (2) in this case, the magistrates did not err in their application of the law. The first three conditions had been satisfied and the magistrates also considered the alternatives. In addition, imprisonment was not being used primarily as a form of punishment. P had told the magistrates that he would be starting a job soon and so income support deductions were not appropriate and there was also reason to believe that P had the means to pay the debt. P had frequently lied to those chasing the debt and it was important that the threat of imprisonment was not seen as an empty threat, and (3) although the application was dismissed, the period of imprisonment was reduced to the 42 days already served by P, *R. v. Thanet DC, ex p. Haddow* [1992] R.A. 245, [1993] C.L.Y. 2630, *R. v. Nantwich Justices, ex p. Burton* [1993] C.O.D. 460, [1994] C.L.Y. 2934 followed.

Observed, that it was necessary to review and define the powers of the High Court to remit the period of committal in respect of fines or rates while dismissing the appeal.

R. v. KINGSTON UPON THAMES MAGISTRATES' COURT, *ex p.* PETERSEN, Trans. Ref: CO/2907/93, April 18, 1996, Brooke, J., QBD.

3984. Compensation–new fire station built–diminution in value of houses–assessment

Held, that the fire authority was ordered to pay compensation for the diminution in value of three houses in southwest London where a new fire station was built, such compensation being assessed at 6.25 per cent and based on values at the date of the complaints.

WAKELEY v. LONDON FIRE AND CIVIL DEFENCE AUTHORITY [1996] 2 E.G.L.R. 148, M St J Hopper, FRICS., Lands Tr.

3985. Competitive tendering–catering–exemptions–Reigate and Banstead BC

LOCAL GOVERNMENT ACT 1988 (DEFINED ACTIVITIES) (EXEMPTION) (REIGATE AND BANSTEAD BOROUGH COUNCIL) ORDER 1996, SI 1996 2715;

made under the Local Government Act 1988 s.2, s.15. In force: November 21, 1996; £0.65.

Under the Local Government Act 1988 Part I (competition), work falling within certain defined activities may be carried out by local authorities only if specified conditions are fulfilled. This Order exempts from the requirements of Part I the carrying out by Reigate and Banstead BC of school and welfare catering undertaken during the period beginning with November 21, 1996 and ending with November 31, 1997 and consisting of catering for meals provided, as part of a statutory welfare service, to persons in their own homes; and other catering at the premises named in Art.3 during the period beginning with April 1, 1997 and ending with December 31, 1997

3986. Competitive tendering–cleaning–exemptions

LOCAL GOVERNMENT ACT 1988 (DEFINED ACTIVITIES) (EXEMPTION) (CLEVELAND POLICE AUTHORITY) ORDER 1996, SI 1996 2965; made under the Local Government Act 1988 s.2, s.15. In force: December 24, 1996; £0.65.

Under the Local Government Act 1988 Part I (competition), work falling within certain defined activities may be carried out by police authorities only if particular conditions are fulfilled. This Order exempts from the requirements of Part I the cleaning of police buildings by the Cleveland Police Authority so long as it is undertaken within their area before June 30, 1997.

3987. Competitive tendering–cleaning–exemptions–Merton LBC

LOCAL GOVERNMENT ACT 1988 (DEFINED ACTIVITIES) (EXEMPTION) (MERTON LONDON BOROUGH COUNCIL) ORDER 1996, SI 1996 2746; made under the Local Government Act 1988 s.2, s.15. In force: November 27, 1996; £0.65.

Under the Local Government Act 1988 Part I (competition), work falling within certain defined activities may be carried out by local authorities only if particular conditions are fulfilled. This Order exempts from the requirements of Part I cleaning by Merton LBC, so long as it consists of the cleaning (other than by the emptying of gullies) of any street in their area, and it is carried out before July 16, 1997.

3988. Competitive tendering–construction and property services–exemptions–Greenwich

LOCAL GOVERNMENT ACT 1988 (DEFINED ACTIVITIES) (EXEMPTION) (LONDON BOROUGH OF GREENWICH) ORDER 1996, SI 1996 1244; made under the Local Government Act 1988 s.2, s.15. In force: June 4, 1996; £0.65.

Under the Local Government Act 1988 Part I which deals with competition, work falling within certain defined activities may be carried out by local authorities only if certain conditions are fulfilled. This Order exempts from the requirements of Part I the provision of construction and property services by the council of the Borough of Greenwich so long as it is carried out before February 1, 1997.

3989. Competitive tendering–defined activities–exemptions

LOCAL GOVERNMENT ACT 1988 (DEFINED ACTIVITIES) (EXEMPTIONS) (ENGLAND AND WALES) ORDER 1996, SI 1996 770; made under the Local Government Act 1988 s.2, s.15. In force: April 1, 1996; £1.10.

This Order provides that certain defined activities which may only be carried out by local and other authorities if certain conditions are fulfilled under the Local Government Act 1988 need not be treated as such if certain conditions are fulfilled. Article 2 extends the exemption from the requirements of the Act in relation to supervision of parking, management of vehicles and security work where the work costs no more than £100,000 each year. Article 3 makes special provision in relation to police services and provides that legal service and construction and property services, financial services, information technology services and personnel services should not be treated as defined activities if they are undertaken under works contracts and certain conditions are fulfilled. The period of exemption relating to works contracts entered into by county councils in areas undergoing reorganisation is extended by Art.4.

3990. Competitive tendering–defined activities–exemptions

LOCAL GOVERNMENT ACT 1988 (DEFINED ACTIVITIES) (EXEMPTIONS) (WALES) (AMENDMENT) ORDER 1996, SI 1996 3179; made under the Local Government Act 1988 s.2, s.15. In force: January 14, 1997; £1.10.

The Local Government Act 1988 (Defined Activities) (Exemptions) (Wales) Order 1994 (SI 1994 339 as amended by SI 1995 2996) provides an exemption from the competition requirements of the Local Government Act 1988 Part I for the new Welsh County and County Borough Councils during the period of local government reorganisation. Generally, the exemption provided for by the 1994 Order is to continue until September 30, 1997, although for certain councils in respect of certain defined activities the exemption period is only until March 31, 1997. This Order amends the 1994 Order by extending the exemption period for Powys County Council and for the County Council of the City and County of Cardiff until September 30, 1997. It also changes the exemption period for Merthyr Tydfil and Torfaen County Borough Council. The Local Government Act 1988 (Exemptions) (Wales) (Amendment) Order 1995 (SI 1995 2996) is revoked.

3991. Competitive tendering–defined activities–exemptions–Braintree DC and South Bedfordshire DC

LOCAL GOVERNMENT ACT 1988 (DEFINED ACTIVITIES) (EXEMPTION) (BRAINTREE AND SOUTH BEDFORDSHIRE DISTRICT COUNCILS) ORDER 1996, SI 1996 2542; made under the Local Government Act 1988 s.2, s.15. In force: November 4, 1996; £0.65.

Under the Local Government Act 1988 Part I (competition), work falling within certain defined activities may be carried out by local authorities only if particular conditions are fulfilled. This Order exempts from the requirements of Part I the maintenance of ground by Braintree DC so long as it is carried out within any cemetery in their area before January 1, 1998 and exempts from the requirements of that Part, the cleaning of buildings by South Bedfordshire DC so long as it is carried out before October 1997 in relation to buildings within their area other than The District Offices, High Street North, Dunstable and public conveniences.

3992. Competitive tendering–defined activities–exemptions–Gosport BC

LOCAL GOVERNMENT ACT 1988 (DEFINED ACTIVITIES) (EXEMPTION) (GOSPORT BOROUGH COUNCIL) ORDER 1996, SI 1996 1657; made under the Local Government Act 1988 s.2, s.15. In force: July 24, 1996; £0.65.

Under Part I of the Local Government Act 1988, which relates to competition, work falling within certain defined activities may be carried out by local authorities only if particular conditions are fulfilled. This Order exempts from the requirements of Part I, cleaning (other than the cleaning of buildings) and the repair and maintenance of vehicles by the Gosport BC, so long as those activities are carried out in the authority's area before April 1, 1997, and the maintenance of ground, so long as it is carried out by that authority in their area during the period beginning on January 1, 1997 and ending with March 31, 1997.

3993. Competitive tendering–defined activities–exemptions–Hertfordshire DC

LOCAL GOVERNMENT ACT 1988 (DEFINED ACTIVITIES) (EXEMPTION) (NORTH HERTFORDSHIRE DISTRICT COUNCIL AND HERTSMERE BOROUGH COUNCIL) ORDER 1996, SI 1996 2961; made under the Local Government Act 1988 s.2, s.15. In force: April 1, 1997; £0.65.

Under the Local Government Act 1988 Part I (competition), work falling within certain defined activities may be carried out by local authorities only if specified conditions are fulfilled. This Order exempts from the requirements of Part I the management of, and catering at, the sports and leisure facilities named in that article by North Hertfordshire DC during the period beginning with April 1, 1997 and ending with December 31, 1997. It also exempts from those requirements the management of the sports and leisure facilities named in that article by Hertsmere BC during the period beginning with January 1, 1998 and ending with December 31, 1999.

3994. Competitive tendering–defined activities–exemptions–Lambeth LBC

LOCAL GOVERNMENT ACT 1988 (DEFINED ACTIVITIES) (EXEMPTION) (LAMBETH LONDON BOROUGH COUNCIL) ORDER 1996, SI 1996 1750; made under the Local Government Act 1988 s.2, s.15. In force: August 5, 1996; £1.10.

Under the Local Government Act 1988 Part I, which relates to competition, work falling within certain defined activities may be carried out by local authorities only if specified conditions are fulfilled. This Order exempts a number of activities from the requirements of Part I so long as they are carried out by the Lambeth LBC before April 1, 1997. The activities are: the collection of refuse; other catering; the cleaning of buildings in one or more specified wards or consisting of the cleaning of drains or refuse chutes in council housing; and other cleaning consisting of street cleaning or the emptying of gullies.

3995. Competitive tendering–defined activities–exemptions–Lewisham LBC

LOCAL GOVERNMENT ACT 1988 (DEFINED ACTIVITIES) (EXEMPTION) (LEWISHAM LONDON BOROUGH COUNCIL) ORDER 1996, SI 1996 2520; made under the Local Government Act 1988 s.2, s.15. In force: October 31, 1996; £0.65.

Under the Local Government Act 1988 Part I (competition), work falling within certain defined activities may be carried out by local authorities only if particular conditions are fulfilled. This Order exempts from the requirements of Part I catering by Lewisham LBC so long as it is carried out in their area during the period beginning January 1, 1997 and ending with March 31, 1998.

3996. Competitive tendering–defined activities–specified periods–Wales

LOCAL GOVERNMENT ACT 1988 (DEFINED ACTIVITIES) (SPECIFIED PERIODS) (WALES) REGULATIONS 1996, SI 1996 265; made under the Local Government Act 1988 s.8, s.15. In force: April 1, 1996; £1.10.

These Regulations specify new minimum and maximum working periods for which defined authorities may invite offers to carry out functional work of certain descriptions which must be open to competition under the Local Government Act 1988 Part 1. The Regulations make different provision in respect of work all or the majority of which is undertaken at or connected with educational establishments, and work which is not undertaken at those establishments or does not substantially involve such work.

3997. Competitive tendering–direct labour and service organisations

LOCAL GOVERNMENT CHANGES FOR ENGLAND (DIRECT LABOUR AND SERVICE ORGANISATIONS) (AMENDMENT) REGULATIONS 1996, SI 1996 1882; made under the Local Government Act 1992 s.19, s.26. In force: August 12, 1996; £0.65.

These Regulations amend the Local Government Changes for England (Direct Labour and Service Organisations) Regulations 1994 (SI 1994 3161) which make provision for the application of the competition provisions of the Local Government, Planning and Land Act 1980 Part III and the Local Government Act 1988 Part I in relation to authorities affected by orders made under the Local Government Act 1992 s.17. The relevant orders are those implementing recommendations made to the Secretary of State by the Local Government Commission for England pursuant to directions given under s.13 of the 1992 Act. The definition of relevant order in the 1994 Regulations is amended by substituting

August 12, 1996 for May 17, 1995 as the date before which directions should have been given for authorities to fall within the description of relevant authorities. Transitional provisions in respect of orders made before August 12, 1996 which implement recommendations made pursuant to directions given on or after May 17, 1995 are made.

3998. Competitive tendering–gardening–exemptions–Worthing BC

LOCAL GOVERNMENT ACT 1988 (DEFINED ACTIVITIES) (EXEMPTION) (WORTHING BOROUGH COUNCIL) ORDER 1996, SI 1996 1391; made under the Local Government Act 1988 s.2, s.15. In force: June 27, 1996; £0.65.

Under the Local Government Act 1988 Part I (competition), work falling within certain defined activities may be carried out by local authorities only if specified conditions are fulfilled. This Order exempts from the requirements of Part I the tending by the Worthing BC of trees having a stem circumference which, if measured at one metre above ground level, exceeds 350 millimetres so long as the work is carried out at the Hillbarn Golf Course or in any of the wards specified in the Order Art.2(b)(i) before April 1, 1997 or so long as it is carried out in any of the wards specified in Art.2(b)(ii) during the period beginning with September 1, 1996 and ending with March 31, 1997.

3999. Competitive tendering–ground maintenance–exemptions–Brent

LOCAL GOVERNMENT ACT 1988 (DEFINED ACTIVITIES) (EXEMPTION) (LONDON BOROUGH OF BRENT) ORDER 1996, SI 1996 2417; made under the Local Government Act 1988 s.2, s.15. In force: October 16, 1996; £2.40.

Under the Local Government Act 1988 Part I (competition), work falling within certain defined activities may be carried out by local authorities only if particular conditions are fulfilled. This Order exempts from the requirements of Part I the maintenance of ground by the London Borough of Brent so long as it is undertaken within their area at the sites specified in Sch.I before July 1, 1997. It also exempts from the requirements of Part I, cleaning (other than cleaning of buildings) by the Borough as long as it is undertaken within their area in the streets listed in Sch.II before April 1, 1997.

4000. Competitive tendering–housing management–exemptions–City of London

LOCAL GOVERNMENT ACT 1988 (DEFINED ACTIVITIES) (EXEMPTION) (THE COMMON COUNCIL OF THE CITY OF LONDON) ORDER 1996, SI 1996 2469; made under the Local Government Act 1988 s.2, s.15. In force: April 1, 1997; £0.65.

Under the Local Government Act 1988 Part I (competition), work falling within certain defined activities may be carried out by local authorities only if particular conditions are fulfilled. This Order exempts from the requirements of Part I of the 1988 Act housing management by the Common Council of the City of London so long as it is carried out in relation to housing within the Barbican Estate before April 1, 2002.

4001. Competitive tendering–housing management–Rossendale

LOCAL GOVERNMENT ACT 1988 (COMPETITION) (HOUSING MANAGEMENT) (ROSSENDALE) REGULATIONS 1996, SI 1996 154; made under the Local Government Act 1988 s.6, s.15. In force: February 28, 1996; £0.65.

These Regulations provide that the date for compliance with certain conditions relating to housing management under the Local Government Act 1988 (Competition) (Housing Management) (England) Regulations 1994 (SI 1994 2297) shall be postponed from April 1, 1996 to December 1, 1996.

4002. Competitive tendering–legal services–exemptions

LOCAL GOVERNMENT ACT 1988 (DEFINED ACTIVITIES) (EXEMPTION) (BROMLEY LONDON BOROUGH COUNCIL) ORDER 1996, SI 1996 1449; made under the Local Government Act 1988 s.2, s.15. In force: July 3, 1996; £1.10.

Under Part I of the Local Government Act 1988 (competition), work falling within certain defined activities may be carried out by local authorities only if particular conditions are fulfilled. This Order exempts from the requirements of Part I the provision of legal services by the Bromley LBC so long as it consists of work of the type described in Art.2(2) of the Order (that is, broadly, legal services work in connection with specified social services functions of the authority) and is carried out before April 1, 1997.

4003. Competitive tendering–local authority ground maintenance work–indemnity requirement not applicable to DSO–anti-competitive behaviour

[Transfer of Undertakings (Protection of Employment) Regulations 1981; Local Government Act 1988 s.6, s.7.]

SL sought judicial review of a direction of the Secretary of State that ground maintenance work could be carried out by their Direct Service Organisation, DSO, only on three conditions. The conditions, relating to the retendering of the work, arose due to the Secretary of State's view that SL had acted in an anti-competitive manner by requiring tenderers to provide an indemnity against any possible effects of the Transfer of Undertakings (Protection of Employment) Regulations 1981 and a guarantee of the indemnity. SL awarded the contract to their DSO, the lowest bidder. SL argued that the Secretary of State's decision was *Wednesbury* unreasonable or illegal as the Secretary of State could find no evidence to substantiate his allegation and, in any case, the tender was awarded to the lowest bid.

Held, dismissing the application, that (1) the tendering condition was contrary to the fifth condition of the Local Government Act 1988 s.7 and therefore the DSO could not carry out defined acts, in accordance with s.6(1) of the 1988 Act. It was up to the Secretary of State to decide whether the condition had been complied with and the court would not become involved in what amounted to a disagreement between the Secretary of State and the local authority, *R. v. Secretary of State for the Environment, ex p. Knowsley MBC* [1991] C.L.Y. 2384. There was sufficient material upon which the Secretary of State could have reached his conclusion, and (2) the obligation placed upon tenderers, which the DSO did not have to consider, put the other tenderers at a disadvantage as they had to include the cost of the indemnity in their bids, regardless of whether or not TUPE would apply to their proposal. In such circumstances the Secretary of State had cause for concern over the competitiveness of the tender. The question of the application of TUPE should have been addressed at the time the contract was awarded so that it was easier to determine whether TUPE would apply, rather than at the stage when tenders were invited, *R. v. Secretary of State for the Environment, ex p. Oswestry BC* [1996] C.L.Y. 4063 considered.

R. v. SECRETARY OF STATE FOR THE ENVIRONMENT, *ex p.* SOUTH LAKELAND DC, Trans. Ref: CO/2218/95, April 2, 1996, Tucker, J., QBD.

4004. Competitive tendering–parking–exemptions–Kingston-upon-Thames RBC

LOCAL GOVERNMENT ACT 1988 (DEFINED ACTIVITIES) (EXEMPTION) (ROYAL BOROUGH OF KINGSTON-UPON-THAMES) ORDER 1996, SI 1996 138; made under the Local Government Act 1988 s.2, s.15. In force: February 23, 1996; £0.65.

This Order exempts from the requirements of Local Government Act 1988 Part I the supervision of parking by Kingston-upon-Thames R.B.C. so long as it is carried out in their area before September 1, 1996.

4005. Competitive tendering–personnel management–exemptions

LOCAL GOVERNMENT ACT 1988 (PERSONNEL SERVICES) (EXEMPTION) (ENGLAND AND WALES) ORDER 1996, SI 1996 857; made under the Local Government Act 1988 s.2, s.15. In force: April 16, 1996; £1.10.

Under the Local Government Act 1988 Part I (competition), work falling within certain defined activities may be carried out by defined authorities only if particular conditions are fulfilled. Article 2 exempts from the requirements of Part I personnel services carried out for the purposes of the provision (by a local authority in England Wales acting jointly with any other person) of training in social work by way of a course approved or promoted by or other training promoted by, the Central Council for Education and Training in Social Work, in accordance with the Health and Social Services and Social Security Adjudications Act 1983 s.10. Article 3 exempts from the requirements of Part I personnel services carried out by a local authority in England and Wales in conjunction with a training and enterprise council ("TEC") and the TEC is acting pursuant to an arrangement with the Secretary of State under the Employment and Training Act 1973 s.2.

4006. Competitive tendering–refuse collection–exemptions

LOCAL GOVERNMENT ACT 1988 (DEFINED ACTIVITIES) (EXEMPTION) (HARBOROUGH DISTRICT COUNCIL) ORDER 1996, SI 1996 2902; made under the Local Government Act 1988 s.2, s.15. In force: December 18, 1996; £0.65.

This Order exempts from the requirements of the Local Government Act 1988 Part I the collection of refuse by the Harborough DC so long as it is undertaken within their area before October 1, 1997.

4007. Competitive tendering–school catering–exemptions–Stockport BC

LOCAL GOVERNMENT ACT 1988 (DEFINED ACTIVITIES) (EXEMPTION) (STOCKPORT BOROUGH COUNCIL) ORDER 1996, SI 1996 1064; made under the Local Government Act 1988 s.2, s.15. In force: May 8, 1996; £1.10.

Under the Local Government Act 1988 Part I which deals with competition, work falling within certain defined activities may be carried out by local authorities only if certain conditions are fulfilled. This Order exempts from the requirements of Part I catering for purposes of schools by the Stockport BC so long as it is carried out in certain schools before September 1, 1997.

4008. Competitive tendering–sports and leisure facilities–exemptions

LOCAL GOVERNMENT ACT 1988 (DEFINED ACTIVITIES) (EXEMPTIONS) (BEDFORD BOROUGH COUNCIL AND SUFFOLK COASTAL DISTRICT COUNCIL) ORDER 1996, SI 1996 2068; made under the Local Government Act 1988 s.2, s.15. In force: September 3, 1996; £0.65.

Under the Local Government Act 1988 Part I, work falling within certain defined activities may be carried out by local authorities only if particular conditions are fulfilled. This Order exempts from the requirements of Part I the management of sports and leisure facilities by the Bedford BC so long as it is undertaken at the site named in the Order before April 1, 1998 and by Suffolk Coastal District Council so long as it is undertaken at the site named in the Order before January 1, 1999.

4009. Competitive tendering–sports and leisure facilities–exemptions–Bexley

LOCAL GOVERNMENT ACT 1988 (DEFINED ACTIVITIES) (EXEMPTION) (LONDON BOROUGH OF BEXLEY) ORDER 1996, SI 1996 1579; made under the Local Government Act 1988 s.2, s.15. In force: July 17, 1996; £0.65.

Under Part I of the Local Government Act 1988, which relates to competition, work falling within certain defined activities may be carried out by local authorities only if particular conditions are fulfilled. This Order exempts from the requirements of Part I the management of sports and leisure facilities by the London Borough of

Bexley so long as it is undertaken at the site named in the Order before October 19, 1996.

4010. Competitive tendering–sports and leisure facilities–exemptions–Hillingdon LBC

LOCAL GOVERNMENT ACT 1988 (DEFINED ACTIVITIES) (EXEMPTION) (LONDON BOROUGH OF HILLINGDON COUNCIL) ORDER 1996, SI 1996 208; made under the Local Government Act 1988 s.2, s.15. In force: April 1, 1996; £0.65.

This Order exempts from the requirements of Local Government Act 1988 Part 1 (competition) the management of sports and leisure facilities by the Hillingdon LBC so long as it is undertaken at the Hayes Stadium Sports Centre, Hayes before October 31, 1996.

4011. Competitive tendering–sports and leisure facilities–exemptions–Horsham DC and Wealdon DC

LOCAL GOVERNMENT ACT 1988 (DEFINED ACTIVITIES) (EXEMPTION) (HORSHAM DISTRICT COUNCIL AND WEALDEN DISTRICT COUNCIL) ORDER 1996, SI 1996 1658; made under the Local Government Act 1988 s.2, s.15. In force: July 24, 1996; £0.65.

Under Part I of the Local Government Act 1988 which relates to competition, work falling within certain defined activities may be carried out by local authorities only if particular conditions are fulfilled. This Order exempts from the requirements of Part I the management of sports and leisure facilities by the Horsham DC so long as it is carried out in their area during the period beginning January 1, 1997 and ending with March 31, 1998 and such management by the Wealden DC so long as it is undertaken at the Goldsmiths Leisure Centre, Crowborough, before April 1, 1997.

4012. Competitive tendering–sports and leisure facilities–exemptions–Kettering BC

LOCAL GOVERNMENT ACT 1988 (DEFINED ACTIVITIES) (EXEMPTION) (KETTERING BOROUGH COUNCIL) ORDER 1996, SI 1996 1813; made under the Local Government Act 1988 s.2, s.15. In force: August 8, 1996; £0.65.

Under the Local Government Act 1988 Part I, which relates to competition, work falling within certain defined activities may be carried out by local authorities only if particular conditions are fulfilled. This Order exempts from the requirements of Part I the management of sports and leisure facilities by the Kettering BC so long as it is undertaken at named sites before April 1, 1999.

4013. Competitive tendering–sports and leisure facilities–specified periods–Redbridge LBC

LOCAL GOVERNMENT ACT 1988 (DEFINED ACTIVITIES) (SPECIFIED PERIOD) (REDBRIDGE LONDON BOROUGH COUNCIL) REGULATIONS 1996, SI 1996 823; made under the Local Government Act 1988 s.8, s.15. In force: April 16, 1996; £0.65.

Under the Local Government Act 1988 Part I (competition), the management of sports and leisure facilities may be carried out by local authorities only if certain conditions are fulfilled. The Local Government Act 1988 (Defined Activities) (Competition) (England) Regulations 1990 Reg.3 provides that one of those conditions shall not be treated as fulfilled in respect of this type of work if the period included in the specification of the work, required to be made available in accordance with the Local Government Act 1988 s.7 (3) (b), is less than four years or exceeds six years. In these Regulations a period of two years is substituted for the four years which would otherwise be the period applicable (in respect of the management of sports and leisure facilities carried out by the Redbridge LBC at the sites listed in Reg.2 (3)) during the period beginning with the commencement of the Regulations and ending on March 31, 1998.

4014. Competitive tendering–vehicle maintenance–exemptions–Waltham Forest LBC

LOCAL GOVERNMENT ACT 1988 (DEFINED ACTIVITIES) (EXEMPTION) (WALTHAM FOREST LONDON BOROUGH COUNCIL) ORDER 1996, SI 1996 1578; made under the Local Government Act 1988 s.2, s.15. In force: July 17, 1996; £0.65.

Under Part I of the Local Government Act 1988, which relates to competition, work falling within certain defined activities may be carried out by local authorities only if specified conditions are fulfilled. This Order exempts from the requirements of Part I the repair and maintenance of vehicles by the Waltham Forest LBC so long as the work is carried out during the period beginning with July 1, 1996 and ending with March 31, 1997.

4015. Contracting out–community care

CONTRACTING OUT (MANAGEMENT FUNCTIONS IN RELATION TO CERTAIN COMMUNITY HOMES) ORDER 1996, SI 1996 586; made under the Deregulation and Contracting Out Act 1994 s.70, s.77. In force: March 6, 1996; £1.10.

This Order makes provision to enable a local authority in England and Wales to authorise another person, or that person's employees, to exercise the function of managing community homes for children which are provided by that Local authority, other than homes or parts of homes providing secure accommodation.

4016. Contracting out–competitive tendering–local authority housing–allocation

LOCAL AUTHORITIES (CONTRACTING OUT OF ALLOCATION OF HOUSING AND HOMELESSNESS FUNCTIONS) ORDER 1996, SI 1996 3205; made under the Deregulation and Contracting Out Act 1994 s.70, s.77. In force: Art.1, Art.3: January 20, 1997; Art.2: April 1, 1997; £1.10.

This Order makes provision to enable a local housing authority in England and Wales to authorise another person, or that person's employees, to exercise certain of the authority's functions relating to the allocation of housing accommodation and to homelessness. It enables the authority to authorise the exercise by another person of those functions conferred by or under the Housing Act 1996 Part VI (allocation of housing accommodation) other than those listed in Sch.1 to the Order, which include the adoption of an allocation scheme. It also enables the authority to authorise the exercise by another person of those functions conferred by or under Part VII (homelessness) other than those listed in Sch.2, which include the giving of assistance to voluntary organisations concerned with homelessness.

4017. Contracting out–guardian ad litem

CONTRACTING OUT (FUNCTIONS IN RELATION TO THE PROVISION OF GUARDIANS AD LITEM AND REPORTING OFFICERS PANELS) ORDER 1996, SI 1996 858; made under the Deregulation and Contracting Out Act 1994 s.70. In force: March 19, 1996; £0.65.

This Order makes provision to enable a local authority in England and Wales to authorise another person, or that person's employees, to exercise the authority's functions in relation to the provision of a panel of guardians ad litem and reporting officers for their area. Article 2(2) makes a consequential modification to the Guardians Ad Litem and Reporting Officers (Panels) Regulations 1991 (SI 1991 2051).

4018. Contracting out–local authorities–Inland Revenue

LOCAL AUTHORITIES (CONTRACTING OUT OF TAX BILLING, COLLECTION AND ENFORCEMENT FUNCTIONS) ORDER 1996, SI 1996 1880; made under the

Deregulation and Contracting Out Act 1994 s.70, s.77, Sch.16 para.3. In force: July 18, 1996; £4.70.

This Order makes provision for a billing authority in relation to the council tax and non-domestic rates, and a local authority which has the functions of a charging authority in relation to community charges, to authorise another person, or that person's employees, to exercise functions relating to the administration and enforcement of the council tax, community charges and non-domestic rates. The following local authorities are billing authorities, and have the functions of a charging authority: the council of a district or London borough, the Common Council of the City of London, the Council of the Isles of Scilly, a county council which has the functions of a district council by virtue of an order under the Local Government Act 1992 Part II making provision for local government changes in England, and, in relation to Wales, a county council or county borough council.

4019. Contracting out–local authorities–investments

LOCAL AUTHORITIES (CONTRACTING OUT OF INVESTMENT FUNCTIONS) ORDER 1996, SI 1996 1883; made under the Deregulation and Contracting Out Act 1994 s.70. In force: July 18, 1996; £1.55.

This Order makes provision for certain bodies to authorise another person, or that person's employees, to exercise any functions consisting of, or relating to, the investment of sums of money. The sums in question do not include sums forming a trust fund or pension fund, but do include, in the case of a local authority in England which is a billing authority for the purposes of the council tax and non-domestic rates, sums paid into the authority's collection fund which are not immediately required for making payments or transfers from that fund, and sums transferred from their collection fund to their general fund. The bodies which may give an authorisation under this Order are in England, county councils, district councils, London borough councils, the Common Council of the City of London, the Council of the Isles of Scilly and parish councils, and in Wales county councils, county borough councils and community councils.

4020. Coroners–reorganisation

LOCAL GOVERNMENT CHANGES FOR ENGLAND (AMENDMENT) REGULATIONS 1996, SI 1996 611; made under the Local Government Act 1992 s.19, s.26. In force: April 1, 1996; £1.10.

These Regulations amend the Local Government Changes for England Regulations 1994 (SI 1994 867) (the 1994 Regulations). Regulation 5 of the 1994 Regulations is amended by the substitution of more detailed provision to deal with the application and construction of provisions of enactments which relate to areas affected by local government reorganisations in England. Regulation 23 of the 1994 Regulations is revoked. On and after April 1, 1996, compensation for coroners affected by local government reorganisation will be governed by the Local Government Reorganisation (Compensation for Loss of Remuneration) Regulations 1995 (SI 1995 2837) as amended by SI 1996 660. Other minor and drafting amendments are made.

4021. Coroners–reorganisation

LOCAL GOVERNMENT REORGANISATION (AMENDMENT OF CORONERS ACT 1988) REGULATIONS 1996, SI 1996 655; made under the Local Government Act 1992 s.19, s.26. In force: in accordance with Reg.1; £1.10.

These Regulations amend various provisions in the Coroners Act 1988 ("the 1988 Act") by exercise of powers contained in the Local Government Act 1992 ("the 1992 Act"). These amendments ensure that the provisions of the 1988 Act are consistent with various provisions in relation to coroners which it is proposed to include in Orders under s.17 of the 1992 Act in consequence of changes to local government in England under the 1992 Act.

4022. Council tax–liability

LOCAL GOVERNMENT REORGANISATION (WALES) (COUNCIL TAX REDUCTION SCHEME) REGULATIONS 1996, SI 1996 309; made under the Local Government Finance Act 1992 s.13, s.113. In force: March 11, 1996; £2.40.

These Regulations set out a scheme for reducing the liability of certain individuals in Wales to pay council tax for the financial year beginning April 1, 1996, the first full financial year for the new local authorities established under the Local Government (Wales) Act 1994. Regulation 3 provides for the reduction of a person's liability to be determined by reference to the appropriate reduction, if any, for the community area and the relevant valuation band for the chargeable dwelling. Regulation 4 to Reg.6 provide for appeals regarding the application or operation of these Regulations by billing authorities. The Schedule lists the community areas in relation to which a reduction is prescribed, together with the appropriate reduction for each council tax valuation band.

4023. Council tax–reorganisation–transitional reduction

LOCAL GOVERNMENT CHANGES FOR ENGLAND (COUNCIL TAX) (TRANSITIONAL REDUCTION) REGULATIONS 1996, SI 1996 176; made under the Local Government Finance Act 1992 s.13, s.113; and the Local Government Act 1992 s.19, s.26. In force: Reg.4: February 22, 1996; Remainder: February 23, 1996; £2.40.

These Regulations provide for the reduction in certain cases of the amount of council tax that a person is liable to pay to a billing authority which is subject to a reorganisation order or is in the area of a county affected by such an order. They have effect for the financial year beginning April 1, 1996 and, for this year, the Local Government Finance Act 1992 s.13 is modified.

4024. Council tax–local authorities

LOCAL GOVERNMENT CHANGES FOR ENGLAND (COUNCIL TAX) (TRANSITIONAL REDUCTION) (AMENDMENT) REGULATIONS 1996, SI 1996 333; made under the Local Government Finance Act 1992 s.13, s.113. In force: February 23, 1996; £0.65.

The Local Government Changes for England (Council Tax) (Transitional Reduction) Regulations 1996 (SI 1996 176) provide for the reduction in certain cases of the amount that a person is liable to pay by way of council tax to a billing authority which is subject to a reorganisation order, made under the Local Government Act 1992 s.17, or is in the area of a county affected by such an order. They have effect in relation to the financial year beginning on April 1, 1996. These Regulations amend the 1996 Regulations and provide for the calculation of the amount to be deducted in a case where a discount is provided for in the local Government Finance Act 1992 s.11.

4025. Council tax–Wales

LOCAL GOVERNMENT REORGANISATION (WALES) (CALCULATION TAX REDUCTION SCHEME) REGULATIONS 1996, SI 1996 335; made under the Local Government (Wales) Act 1994 s.54. In force: February 21, 1996; £1.10.

The Local Government (Wales) Act 1994 provides for local government changes in Wales. The new Welsh county councils and county borough councils, which were elected on May 4, 1995, are the Welsh billing authorities for the financial year commencing on and after April 1, 1996. Under the Local Government Finance Act 1992 s.33 the billing authorities are required to calculate the basic amount of council tax. This Order amends s.33 to require the new Welsh billing authorities, when making their calculations, to take account of that portion of discretionary non domestic rate relief which will be funded by council tax payers.

4026. Employees–indemnities–no contractual indemnity where employees' act was ultra vires

[Local Government (Miscellaneous Provisions) Act 1976 s.19; Insolvency Act 1986 s.214.]

W undertook to indemnify its employees for claims arising against them for defaults they committed "in or about the pursuit of their duties on behalf of the council while acting within the scope of their authority". This indemnity was included in the contract of B, the assistant chief executive. Using its powers to provide recreational facilities pursuant to the Local Government (Miscellaneous Provisions) Act 1976 s.19, W formed a company to establish a public water park, with B acting as a director. The creation of the company was subsequently agreed, following a number of judicial cases, to be ultra vires and void. The company being in liquidation, the liquidators sought to recover money from B by means of a wrongful trading action under the Insolvency Act 1986 s.214. B denied liability and sought to rely on the indemnity. The district auditor argued that the indemnity did not cover the claims against B, and W was not prepared to indemnify B on this basis. A summons was issued by B against W and the district auditor.

Held, that the contractual indemnity could not be relied upon by B in relation to the insolvency proceedings. In working as a company director it could not be said that B was pursuing his duties on behalf of the council of acting within the scope of his authority when W had no power to appoint him as director or to confer authority upon him. On its proper construction the indemnity did not cover the defaults of employees for acts authorised by W where that authorisation was ultra vires, *Credit Suisse v. Allerdale BC* [1996] 3 W.L.R. 894, [1996] C.L.Y 4060 considered.

BURGOINE v. WALTHAM FOREST LBC, *The Times*, November 7, 1996, Neuberger, J., Ch D.

4027. Equal treatment–sex discrimination–public transport–concessionary fares for elderly–social security–European Union

[Council Directive 79/7 on equal treatment for men and women in matters of social security Art.3.]

A was a male aged 63. The defendant local authority ran a concessionary travel scheme available to retired persons: in the case of men at age 65 and women at age 60. A contended that he was the victim of sexual discrimination. The action was stayed and the question whether the concessionary scheme fell within the Council Directive 79/7 on the progressive implementation of the principle of equal treatment for men and women in matters of social security Art.3(1) was referred to the European Court of Justice.

Held, that on a proper interpretation of Art.3(1) a scheme such as that organised by W did not fall within the scope of the Directive. The purpose of the scheme was to facilitate access to public transport for persons considered to be in need of concessionary travel arrangements, including being financially less well-off. The fact that the recipient was within one of the situations envisaged by the Directive was not sufficient to bring the scheme within the Directive.

ATKINS v. WREKIN DC (C228/94) [1996] All E.R. (EC) 719, GC Rodriguez Iglesias (President), ECJ.

4028. Finance

LOCAL AUTHORITIES (CAPITAL FINANCE) (AMENDMENT NO.2) REGULATIONS 1996, SI 1996 2121; made under the Local Government and Housing Act 1989 s.49, s.59, s.61, s.190. In force: September 4, 1996; £1.10.

These Regulations further amend the Local Authorities (Capital Finance) Regulations 1990 (SI 1990 432). They make further provision for the initial cost of leases of dwellings let or occupied as accommodation for the homeless or temporary accommodation, and leases of land, other than dwellings, for a term, or the residue of a term, of not more than 10 years, make different provision about the price at which the land must be offered to a tenant under a tenancy before a disposal and provide that capital receipts are to be treated as reduced for the purposes of the Local Government and Housing Act 1989 s.59.

4029. Finance

LOCAL AUTHORITIES (CAPITAL FINANCE) (AMENDMENT NO.3) REGULATIONS 1996, SI 1996 2539; made under the Local Government and Housing Act 1989 s.49, s.61, s.190, Sch.3 para.11. In force: October 31, 1996; £1.95.

These Regulations further amend the Local Authorities (Capital Finance) Regulations 1990 (SI 1990 432) for purposes connected with the Private Finance Initiative.

4030. Finance

LOCAL AUTHORITIES (CAPITAL FINANCE) (RATE OF DISCOUNT FOR 1996/97) REGULATIONS 1996, SI 1996 581; made under the Local Government and Housing Act 1989 s.49. In force: April 1, 1996; £0.65.

The Local Government and Housing Act 1989 Part IV makes provision for the capital finance of local authorities. Section 49(2) sets out a formula for determining for the purposes of Part IV the value of the consideration falling to be given by a local authority under a credit arrangement in any financial year after the one in which the arrangement comes into being. The percentage rate of discount prescribed for a financial year is one of the factors referred to in the formula. For the Financial year beginning on April 1, 1996 these Regulations prescribe 9.1 per cent which is the same as the rate of discount prescribed for 1995/96.

4031. Finance

LOCAL GOVERNMENT CHANGES FOR ENGLAND (CAPITAL FINANCE) (AMENDMENT) REGULATIONS 1996, SI 1996 2826; made under the Local Government Act 1992 s.19, s.26. In force: November 5, 1996; £1.10.

These Regulations amend the Local Government Changes for England (Capital Finance) Regulations 1995 (SI 1995 798) which make provision with respect to the application of the Local Government and Housing Act 1989 Part IV (revenue accounts and capital finance of local authorities) for the purposes or in consequence of local government changes in England.

4032. Finance–council tax–calculations

LOCAL AUTHORITIES (ALTERATION OF REQUISITE CALCULATIONS) REGULATIONS 1996, SI 1996 175; made under the Local Government Finance Act 1992 s.32, s.113. In force: February 2, 1996; £1.10.

These Regulations amend the definition in the Local Government Finance Act 1992 s.32 of "police grant" and "relevant special grant" for the financial year beginning in 1996. The amended definitions apply to that section and also to s.33, s.43 and s.44 of the 1992 Act. These sections relate to how a billing authority and a major precepting authority are to calculate their budget and the basic amount of their council tax.

4033. Finance–investments

LOCAL AUTHORITIES (CAPITAL FINANCE AND APPROVED INVESTMENTS) (AMENDMENT) REGULATIONS 1996, SI 1996 568; made under the Local Government and Housing Act 1989 s.48, s.49, s.58, s.59, s.61, s.64, s.66, s.190, s.191, Sch.3 para.10, Sch.3 para.15. In force: March 30, 1996; £3.20.

These Regulations further amend the Local Authorities (Capital Finance) Regulations 1990 (SI 1990 432) (the principal Regulations) and also amend the Local Authorities (Capital Finance and Approved Investments) Regulations 1990 (SI 1990 426), as amended. Provisions are made in respect of the initial cost of leases of land acquired by a local authority; the initial cost of certain credit arrangements is reduced if certain conditions are met; the reserved part of certain capital receipts is reduced if certain conditions are met; and the principal Regulations are amended in respect of the treatment of a capital receipt derived from a disposal of recently acquired land.

4034. Finance–reorganisation

LOCAL GOVERNMENT CHANGES FOR ENGLAND (COLLECTION FUND SURPLUSES AND DEFICITS) (AMENDMENT) REGULATIONS 1996, SI 1996 2177; made under the Local Government Act 1992 s.19, s.26. In force: September 17, 1996; £0.65.

The Local Government Changes for England (Collection Fund Surpluses and Deficits) Regulations 1995 (SI 1995 2889) make consequential and transitional provisions in relation to the surplus or deficit in the collection fund of a billing authority where that authority, or a major precepting authority in relation to that authority, is subject to a reorganisation order under the Local Government Act 1992 s.17. These Regulations substitute a new paragraph in the 1995 Regulations to provide that what is to be excluded from the calculation of the estimate of the surplus or deficit in the collection fund for the first year of reorganisation and subsequent years is a billing authority's share in its own collection fund, as calculated under Reg.4, Reg.5, Reg.6 or Reg.7 of the 1995 Regulations. In addition a new definition of final surplus or deficit is substituted.

4035. Fire services–appointments

FIRE SERVICES (APPOINTMENTS AND PROMOTION) (AMENDMENT) REGULATIONS 1996, SI 1996 2096; made under the Fire Services Act 1947 s.18. In force: September 1, 1996; £0.65.

These Regulations amend the Fire Services (Appointments and Promotion) Regulations 1978 (SI 1978 436) by removing the ineligibility to sit a written promotion examination of a person who has failed that examination on the two previous occasions, and who has failed, on each occasion, to score more than 25 per cent. They also ensure that a person cannot enter Part II of the examination for promotion to leading fire-fighter or sub-officer unless he has passed Part I of the examination.

4036. Fire services–Bedfordshire

BEDFORDSHIRE FIRE SERVICES (COMBINATION SCHEME) ORDER 1996, SI 1996 2918; made under the Fire Services Act 1947 s.6, s.8, s.10; and the Fire Services Act 1959 s.7. In force: November 20, 1996; £1.55.

This Order makes a scheme which combines the areas of the council of the borough of Luton and the Bedfordshire County Council into a combined fire area to be known as the Bedfordshire and Luton Combined Fire Authority.

4037. Fire services–Buckinghamshire

BUCKINGHAMSHIRE FIRE SERVICES (COMBINATION SCHEME) ORDER 1996, SI 1996 2924; made under the Fire Services Act 1947 s.6, s.8, s.10; and the Fire Services Act 1959 s.7. In force: November 20, 1996; £1.55.

This Order makes a scheme which combines the areas of the council of the borough of Milton Keynes and the Buckinghamshire County Council into a combined fire area to be known as the Buckinghamshire and Milton Keynes Fire Authority.

4038. Fire services–Derbyshire

DERBYSHIRE FIRE SERVICES (COMBINATION SCHEME) ORDER 1996, SI 1996 2919; made under the Fire Services Act 1947 s.6, s.8, s.10; and the Fire Services Act 1959 s.7. In force: November 20, 1996; £1.55.

This Order makes a scheme which combines the areas of the council of the city of Derby and the Derbyshire CC into a combined fire area to be known as the Derbyshire Fire Authority.

4039. Fire services–Dorset

DORSET FIRE SERVICES (COMBINATION SCHEME) ORDER 1996, SI 1996 2920; made under the Fire Services Act 1947 s.6, s.8, s.10; and the Fire Services Act 1959 s.7. In force: November 20, 1996; £1.55.

This Order makes a scheme which combines the areas of the councils of the boroughs of Bournemouth and Poole and the Dorset CC into a combined fire area to be known as the Dorset Fire Authority.

4040. Fire services–Durham

DURHAM FIRE SERVICES (COMBINATION SCHEME) ORDER 1996, SI 1996 2921; made under the Fire Services Act 1947 s.6, s.8, s.10; and the Fire Services Act 1959 s.7. In force: November 20, 1996; £1.55.

This Order makes a scheme which combines the areas of the council of the borough of Darlington and the Durham County Council into a combined fire area to be known as the County Durham and Darlington Fire and Rescue Authority.

4041. Fire services–East Sussex

EAST SUSSEX FIRE SERVICES (COMBINATION SCHEME) ORDER 1996, SI 1996 2922; made under the Fire Services Act 1947 s.6, s.8, s.10; and the Fire Services Act 1959 s.7. In force: November 20, 1996; £1.55.

This Order makes a scheme which combines the areas of the council of the district of Brighton and Hove and the East Sussex County Council into a combined fire area to be known as the East Sussex Fire Authority.

4042. Fire services–Hampshire

HAMPSHIRE FIRE SERVICES (COMBINATION SCHEME) ORDER 1996, SI 1996 2923; made under the Fire Services Act 1947 s.6, s.8, s.10; and the Fire Services Act 1959 s.7. In force: November 20, 1996; £1.55.

This Order makes a scheme which combines the areas of the councils of the cities of Portsmouth and Southampton and the Hampshire CC into a combined fire area to be known as the Hampshire Fire Authority.

4043. Fire services–Leicestershire

LEICESTERSHIRE FIRE SERVICES (COMBINATION SCHEME) ORDER 1996, SI 1996 2912; made under the Fire Services Act 1947 s.6, s.8, s.10; and the Fire Services Act 1959 s.7. In force: November 20, 1996; £1.55.

This Order makes a scheme which combines the areas of the councils of the city of Leicester and the district of Rutland and the Leicestershire CC into a combined fire area to be known as the Leicester, Leicestershire and Rutland Combined Fire Authority.

4044. Fire services–Staffordshire

STAFFORDSHIRE FIRE SERVICES (COMBINATION SCHEME) ORDER 1996, SI 1996 2917; made under the Fire Services Act 1947 s.6, s.8, s.10; and the Fire Services Act 1959 s.7. In force: November 20, 1996; £1.55.

This Order makes a scheme which combines the areas of the council of the city of Stoke on Trent and the Staffordshire County Council into a combined fire area to be known as the Stoke-on-Trent and Staffordshire Fire Authority.

4045. Fire services–Wiltshire

WILTSHIRE FIRE SERVICES (COMBINATION SCHEME) ORDER 1996, SI 1996 2916; made under the Fire Services Act 1947 s.6, s.8, s.10; and the Fire Services Act 1959 s.7. In force: November 20, 1996; £1.55.

This Order makes a scheme which combines the areas of the council of the borough of Thamesdown and the Wiltshire County Council into a combined fire area to be known as the Wiltshire and Swindon Fire Authority.

4046. Health authorities–reorganisation

LOCAL GOVERNMENT REORGANISATION (WALES) (SWANSEA BAY PORT HEALTH AUTHORITY) (AMENDMENT) ORDER 1996, SI 1996 409; made under the Local Government (Wales) Act 1994 s.54. In force: March 20, 1996; £1.10.

This Order makes consequential amendments to the Swansea Bay Port Health Authority Order 1991 (SI 1991 1773) arising as a result of Welsh local government reorganisation. The Order specifies which new Welsh principal councils are to be the riparian authorities for the purposes of the 1991 Order and the numbers of members that those councils are to appoint to the Swansea Bay Port Health Authority (Art.2). The Order also makes transitional provision with respect to membership of the Swansea Bay Port Health Authority (Art.3).

4047. Local authorities–allowances–residential accommodation

NATIONAL ASSISTANCE (SUMS FOR PERSONAL REQUIREMENTS) REGULATIONS 1996, SI 1996 391; made under the National Assistance Act 1948 s.22, s.87. In force: April 8, 1996; £0.65.

The weekly sum which local authorities are to assume, in the absence of special circumstances, that residents in accommodation arranged under the National Assistance Act 1948 Part III, the Social Work (Scotland) Act 1968 or the Mental Health (Scotland) Act 1984 s.7 will need for their personal requirements is set at £13.75 from April 8, 1996. The National Assistance (Sums for Personal Requirements) Regulations 1995 (SI 1995 443) are revoked.

4048. Local authorities–armorial bearings

LOCAL AUTHORITIES (ARMORIAL BEARINGS) (WALES) ORDER 1996, SI 1996 733; made under the Local Government Act 1972 s.247. In force: March 14, 1996; £0.65.

This Order authorises the Borough Council of Newport to bear and use the armorial bearings of the former corporation of the borough of Newport.

4049. Local authorities–armorial bearings

LOCAL AUTHORITIES (ARMORIAL BEARINGS) (NO.2) (WALES) ORDER 1996, SI 1996 1930; made under the Local Government Act 1972 s.247. In force: July 24, 1996; £1.10.

This Order transfers the right to bear and use the armorial bearings to local authorities established under the Local Government (Wales) Act 1994.

4050. Local authorities–benefits–reorganisation

LOCAL GOVERNMENT CHANGES FOR ENGLAND (HOUSING BENEFIT AND COUNCIL TAX BENEFIT) AMENDMENT REGULATIONS 1996, SI 1996 547; made under the Local Government Act 1992 s.19, s.26. In force: April 1, 1996; £0.65.

These Regulations amend the Local Government Changes for England (Housing Benefit and Council Tax Benefit) Regulations 1995 (SI 1995 531) in order to make incidental, consequential, transitional and supplementary provision for housing benefit and council tax benefit for the purposes of and in consequence orders made under the Local Government Act 1992 s.17 following local government changes in England relating to the payment of subsidy for benefits granted or allowed before reorganisation.

4051. Local authorities–benefits–reorganisation

LOCAL GOVERNMENT REORGANISATION (WALES) (HOUSING BENEFIT AND COUNCIL TAX BENEFIT) ORDER 1996, SI 1996 549; made under the Local Government (Wales) Act 1994 s.54, s.63. In force: April 1, 1996; £0.65.

The Local Government (Wales) Act 1994 makes provision with respect to local government in Wales. This Order makes incidental, consequential, transitional and supplementary provision for housing benefit and council tax benefit for the purposes of, and in consequence of, that Act by providing power for a successor authority to terminate any benefit period granted by an old authority.

4052. Local authorities–charges–foreign aid–rights of way

LOCAL AUTHORITIES (CHARGES FOR OVERSEAS ASSISTANCE AND PUBLIC PATH ORDERS) REGULATIONS 1996, SI 1996 1978; made under the Local Government and Housing Act 1989 s.150, s.152, s.190. In force: Reg.3(2): April 1, 1997; Remainder: July 28, 1996; £1.10.

These Regulations enable local authorities in England, Wales and Scotland to make charges for providing advice or assistance in accordance with the Local Authorities (Overseas Assistance) Act 1993. The amount of the charges is to be at the discretion of the charging authority having regard to the costs of providing the advice or assistance in question. They also amend the Local Authorities (Recovery of Costs for Public Path Orders) Regulations 1993 (SI 1993 407) so that the ceiling on charges for the making of a public path order is removed.

4053. Local authorities–companies

LOCAL AUTHORITIES (COMPANIES) (AMENDMENT) ORDER 1996, SI 1996 621; made under the Local Government and Housing Act 1989 s.39. In force: March 30, 1996; £1.10.

The Local Authorities (Companies) Order 1995 (SI 1995 849) provides for the regulation of companies which are subject to the influence or control of local authorities within the meaning of the Local Government and Housing Act 1989 Part V ("regulated companies"). Part V of that Order, which is amended by this Order, applies the provisions of Part IV of the 1989 Act (revenue accounts and capital finance of local authorities), subject to modifications, to a regulated company and the local authority by whom the company is influenced or controlled.

4054. Local authorities–discretionary payments

LOCAL GOVERNMENT (DISCRETIONARY PAYMENTS) REGULATIONS 1996, SI 1996 1680; made under the Superannuation Act 1972 s.7, s.12, s.24. In force: July 25, 1996; £6.10.

These Regulations consolidate, with amendments, the provisions of the Local Government (Compensation for Premature Retirement) Regulations 1982 (SI 1982 1009), Part II of the Local Government (Compensation for Redundancy and Premature Retirement) Regulations 1984 (SI 1984 740) and Part II of the Local Government (Compensation for Redundancy) Regulation 1994 (SI 1994

3025), all of which have been amended. They also revoke the extant Parts K and L of the Local Government Superannuation Regulations 1986 (SI 1986 24). Parts V and VI of these Regulations replace them as part of local authority discretionary awards. These Regulations contain all the provisions relating to discretionary payments that may be made to persons engaged in local government employment other than teachers and those engaged in the police and fire services (excluding those under Part III of the Local Government (Compensation for Redundancy) Regulations 1994).

4055. Local authorities–members interests

LOCAL AUTHORITIES (MEMBERS' INTERESTS) (AMENDMENT) REGULATIONS 1996, SI 1996 1215; made under the Local Government and Housing Act 1989 s.19, s.190. In force: July 1, 1996; £1.10.

The Local Authorities (Members' Interests) Regulations 1992 require an elected member of a local authority to give to the local authority of which he is a member written notice of any interest he holds which is described in the Regulations. Regulation 2 to Reg.5 of these Regulations extend with modifications this requirement to members of National Park authorities and to members of police authorities in England and Wales who are elected members of local authorities or who are appointed from a short-list prepared by the Secretary of State. The 1992 Regulations are also modified in consequence of local government reorganisation in Wales.

4056. Local authorities–procedure

LOCAL AUTHORITIES' TRAFFIC ORDERS (PROCEDURE) (ENGLAND AND WALES) REGULATIONS 1996, SI 1996 2489; made under the Road Traffic Regulation Act 1984 s.35C, s.46A, s.124, Sch.9 Part III; and the Local Government Act 1985 Sch.5 para.6, Sch.5 para.7. In force: December 1, 1996; £3.70.

These Regulations prescribe the procedure to be followed by local authorities in England and Wales for making the main types of traffic and parking orders under the Road Traffic Regulation Act 1984. They replace with significant modification the Local Authorities' Traffic Orders (Procedure) (England and Wales) Regulations 1989 (SI 1989 1120) and the Local Authorities' Traffic Orders (Procedure) (England and Wales) (Amendment) Regulations 1993 (SI 1993 1500).

4057. Local authorities–registration

LOCAL GOVERNMENT (CHANGES FOR THE REGISTRATION SERVICE IN BEDFORDSHIRE, BUCKINGHAMSHIRE, DERBYSHIRE, DORSET, DURHAM, EAST SUSSEX, HAMPSHIRE, LEICESTERSHIRE, STAFFORDSHIRE AND WILTSHIRE) ORDER 1996, SI 1996 3118; made under the Local Government Act 1992 s.17, s.26. In force: January 8, 1997; £1.55.

This Order provides for changes to the local registration service in Bedfordshire, Buckinghamshire, Derbyshire, Dorset, Durham, East Sussex, Hampshire, Leicestershire, Staffordshire and Wiltshire, in consequence of structural and boundary changes in those areas made by Orders under the Local Government Act 1992 s.17.

4058. Local authorities powers and duties–duty of care–road safety–no common law duty to compensate injured party on failure to improve highway

[Highways Act 1980 s.79.]

N, in its capacity as highway authority, appealed from a finding that, in failing to propose the expeditious removal of a dangerous obstruction near a road it was in breach of a common law duty of care to road users. N had become aware of a visibility problem caused by a bank of land at a road junction where three accidents had previously occurred in the past 12 years. The matter had been discussed with the land owners, and it had been agreed that N would carry out the necessary work. However, no action had been taken to remove the obstruction by the date on which S was seriously injured as a result of a collision with a car driven by W, who joined N as second defendant to S's claim for damages.

Held, allowing the appeal, that under the Highways Act 1980 s.79 a highway authority had discretionary powers to require the removal of such obstructions. However, a statutory power did not give rise to a common law duty of care and N had not acted unreasonably in failing to proceed under that power. Even if the work ought to have been carried out, it could not be found that a public law duty gave rise to an obligation to compensate those suffering loss due to its non-performance. The creation of a duty of care in the circumstances posed an unacceptable risk to local authority budgetary decision making in an area where road users themselves were subject to compulsory insurance requirements.

STOVIN v. WISE AND NORFOLK CC [1996] A.C. 923, Lord Hoffmann, HL.

4059. Local authorities powers and duties–loan guarantee–loan to local authority established company guaranteed by authority–whether loan ultra vires

[Local Government Act 1972 s.102, s.111.]

WF appealed against a decision that a guarantee and an indemnity, given by the council in respect of a loan granted by CS to NELP, a property company established and partly owned by WF, were enforceable. The loan was made to enable NELP to purchase properties which would be leased to WF, thus permitting the council to discharge its statutory function to house the homeless. However, the collapse of the property market meant that a deficit arose in respect of the proceeds of sale of the properties at the end of the lease period and NELP could not finance the loan repayments. CS argued that the scheme establishing NELP and the provision of the guarantee and indemnity were within the council's powers under the Local Government Act 1972 s.111 as facilitating the discharge of its statutory functions in respect of providing accommodation for homeless people.

Held, allowing the appeal, that WF had no implied power to guarantee the loan or to indemnify NELP against losses. The limited powers provided under s.102 of the Act did not extend to discharging statutory functions via the operations of a partly owned company, and as Parliament had made detailed express legislative provisions for the exercise and discharge of local authority statutory functions, there was no scope to imply additional powers beyond those already provided, *Credit Suisse v. Allerdale BC* [1996] 3 W.L.R. 894, [1996] C.L.Y. 4060 considered.

CREDIT SUISSE v. WALTHAM FOREST LBC [1996] 3 W.L.R. 943, Neill, L.J., CA.

4060. Local authorities powers and duties–loan guarantees–establishment of company to obtain loan for finance of time share and leisure pool complex–local authority's powers to guarantee loan

[Local Government (Miscellaneous Provisions) Act 1976 s.19; Local Government Act 1972 s.111.]

CS appealed against a decision that they were not entitled to payment under a guarantee given by ABC for sums borrowed by a company which ABC had established to carry out the development of a time share and leisure pool complex. The company had gone into liquidation and the guarantee was held to be void. CS argued that the Local Government (Miscellaneous Provisions) Act 1976 s.19 and the Local Government Act 1972 s.111 conferred powers on ABC to assist the financing of the development and to guarantee a loan drawn by the company.

Held, dismissing the appeal, that under s.19 of the 1976 Act a local authority had the power to provide recreational facilities and to provide buildings, supplies and assistance. However, the development of time share accommodation did not constitute a recreational facility and s.19 was not to be construed as permitting assistance to those providing it. Furthermore, s.111 (1) did not confer on ABC an implied power to extend the exercise of its statutory functions beyond a power of a local authority itself to borrow money. The 1972 Act was intended to regulate the discharge of local authorities' statutory functions, including their power to borrow, and the establishment of a company and the giving of a guarantee to circumvent the restriction it laid down was ultra vires.

CREDIT SUISSE v. ALLERDALE BC [1996] 3 W.L.R. 894, Neill, L.J., CA.

4061. Local authorities powers and duties–loan guarantees–validity of guarantees and indemnities to unregistered housing association–express and implicit powers

[Housing Associations Act 1985 s.4; Local Government Act 1972 s.111.]

S used W, an unregistered housing association, in a scheme to provide temporary accommodation to the homeless. W borrowed money from MG to buy houses which S leased for three years. S indemnified W against any losses it might suffer under the scheme and guaranteed the bank against any loss on the sale of the houses after expiration of the leases. W defaulted on its repayments to the bank and went into liquidation. S obtained a declaration that the guarantee and indemnity were void and unenforceable. MG and W appealed.

Held, dismissing the appeal, that the Housing Associations Act 1985 only enabled a local authority to guarantee loans taken out by housing associations registered under s.4 of the Act, which implicitly prevented S providing an indemnity to an unregistered association. Whilst the Local Government Act 1972 s.111 allowed local authorities to incur financial obligations where it would facilitate the discharge of their functions, in this case the provision of accommodation for the homeless, it could not be used to override the express provisions in the 1985 Act as to how local authorities were to carry out that duty, *Credit Suisse v. Waltham Forest LBC* [1996] 4 All E.R. 176, [1996] C.L.Y. 4059 followed. Local authorities could provide guarantees and indemnities only where there were specific statutory provisions permitting them to do so.

SUTTON LBC v. MORGAN GRENFELL & CO LTD, *The Times*, November 7, 1996, Peter Gibson, L.J., CA.

4062. Local authorities powers and duties–parking–parking scheme charges set to make a profit–whether local authority acting within its powers–inadequate consultation with residents

[Road Traffic Regulation Act 1984 s.55; Local Authorities' Traffic Orders (Procedure) (England and Wales) Regulations 1989.]

CLBC sought to introduce a controlled parking zone further to the Road Traffic Regulation Act 1984. Local residents and businesses were to be charged for parking permits even though it was anticipated that CLBC would be able to meet the anticipated cost of the scheme from enforcement and pay and display machines. C sought to quash CLBC order on the basis that it constituted a revenue raising exercise which was outside its powers under the 1984 Act and CLBC had not consulted C and other residents and businesses further to the Local Authorities' Traffic Orders (Procedure) (England and Wales) Regulations 1989.

Held, allowing the application, that (1) a local authority could not have regard to s.55(4) of the 1984 Act relating to the manner in which surpluses from parking control could be spent in making the decision as to determining charges. Instead, when setting charges, on street parking had to be looked at in isolation; (2) although CLBC had not acted unlawfully in the circumstances, it was unlawful for them to introduce controlled parking zones throughout the borough without considering each scheme on its own merits. The consultation could only be fair and effective if it were carried out when the plans were at a formative stage, and (3) on the facts, C had been substantially prejudiced by defects in the consultation process and therefore the order would be quashed.

R. v. CAMDEN LBC, *ex p.* CRAN; SUB NOM. CRAN v. CAMDEN LBC 94 L.G.R. 8, McCullough, J., QBD.

4063. Local authorities powers and duties–tenders for refuse collection–awarded to own unit–whether transfer clause unreasonable

[Transfer of Undertakings (Protection of Employment) Regulations 1981; Council Directive 77/187 Art.3; Council Directive 77/187 Art.4 Local Government Act 1988 s.7; Local Government Act 1988 s.13, s.14.]

O advertised for tenders for its refuse collection contract. The applications included one from O's own Direct Works Unit, DWU. The tender documentation stipulated that in the event the successful tenderer was not O's own DWU, the Transfer of Undertakings (Protection of Employment) Regulations 1981 would apply so that the successful tenderer would have to employ O's existing workforce on their present terms and conditions. O awarded the tender to its own DWU. Complaints regarding the tendering process were made to the respondent claiming that the clause in question was anti-competitive and made it impossible to submit competitive bids. The respondent served O with a notice under the Local Government Act 1988 s.13 stating that it was in breach of s.7(7) in that their action had the effect of restricting, distorting or preventing competition. O maintained that TUPE would apply and that their action was not anti-competitive. The respondent subsequently issued a direction under s.14 of the 1988 Act that O could only have the power to carry out refuse collection if it removed the offending term. O applied for judicial review of the decision to issue the direction on the grounds that it was unlawful because TUPE applied and it was unreasonable in the *Wednesbury* sense to have concluded that it had acted anti-competitively. O also requested an Art.177 reference to the European Court on whether under the proper interpretation of Council Directive 77/187 Art.3(1) and Art.4(1) it was necessary to wait until after a successful tender had taken place before determining whether or not there would be a transfer of an undertaking or whether this could be done at the tender stage.

Held, dismissing the appeal, that (1) the respondent's direction was lawful. However it was accepted in principle that it was possible to conclude at the invitation to tender stage that a transfer would necessarily be involved provided it could be shown on the established facts. Having regard to the characteristics of the transaction known at the invitation stage, it could not be said with certainty that a transfer would necessarily be involved here. The contract document provided scope for significant differences in inter alia the workforce, premises, plant and equipment to make it impossible to say with certainty that there would be a transfer; (2) the respondent's decision that the clause was anti-competitive was not irrational, perverse or unreasonable given the material before it, and (3) given it was accepted in principle that it was possible to conclude at the invitation to tender stage whether a transfer would be involved, and therefore an Art.177 reference was unnecessary. Moreover no point of principle or interpretation of the Directive was involved. The European Court had set out clear principles which a national court should follow.

R. v. SECRETARY OF STATE FOR THE ENVIRONMENT, *ex p.* OSWESTRY BC [1995] C.O.D. 357, Harrison, J.

4064. Local Government Act 1992–Commencement No.5 Order

LOCAL GOVERNMENT ACT 1992 (COMMENCEMENT NO.5) ORDER 1996, SI 1996 1888 (C.40); made under the Local Government Act 1992 s.30. In force: bringing into force various provisions of the Act on August 8, 1996; £0.65.

This Order brings into force the Local Government Act 1992 Sch.1 Part I which repeals parts of the Local Government, Planning and Land Act 1980.

4065. Local Government and Housing Act 1989–Commencement No.18 Order

LOCAL GOVERNMENT AND HOUSING ACT 1989 (COMMENCEMENT NO.18) ORDER 1996, SI 1996 1857 (C.39); made under the Local Government and Housing Act 1989 s.195. In force: bringing into force various provisions of the Act on July 22, 1996; £1.10.

This Order brings into force provisions of the Local Government and Housing Act 1989 which repeal the Education (Grants and Awards) Act 1984 s.2 and references to that section in s.1 of that Act, the Education (Amendment) Act 1986 s.1 which had increased the limit originally imposed by s.2 of the 1984 Act and s.3, the only remaining provision of the 1986 Act.

4066. Local government officers–expenses–allowances

LOCAL AUTHORITIES (MEMBERS' ALLOWANCES) (AMENDMENT) REGULATIONS 1996, SI 1996 469; made under the Local Government Act 1972 s.173, s.175, s.177, s.178, s.270; the Local Government and Housing Act 1989 s.18, s.190; and the Environment Act 1995 s.120. In force: April 1, 1996; £1.10.

The Local Authorities (Members' Allowances) Regulations 1991 (SI 1991 351) are amended by these Regulations. Regulation 2 makes provision for National Park authorities to pay their members travelling allowances, subsistence allowances and allowances for attendance of conferences and meetings, and requires them to make schemes for the payment of allowances. The maxima which may be payable to parish and community councillors and non-elected members of local authorities as attendance allowances are increased by 2.9 per cent and the maximum payable as financial loss allowance is increased by 3.6 per cent.

4067. Local government officers–information

LOCAL GOVERNMENT (PUBLICATION OF STAFFING INFORMATION) (WALES) REGULATIONS 1996, SI 1996 1899; made under the Local Government, Planning and Land Act 1980 s.3. In force: September 1, 1996; £0.65.

These Regulations require local authorities and certain other authorities in Wales to publish the information about their staffing levels which is specified in the Local Government (Publication of Staffing Information) (Wales) Order 1996 in the manner and form and on the occasions specified in the Code. The Code is set out in the Annex to Welsh Office Circular 26/96, which is obtainable from the Welsh Office, Local Government Finance Division.

4068. Local government officers–reorganisation

SOUTH GLOUCESTERSHIRE DISTRICT COUNCIL (STAFF TRANSFER) ORDER 1996, SI 1996 387; made under the Local Government Act 1992 s.17, s.26. In force: April 1, 1996; £1.55.

This Order is supplemental to the Avon (Structural Change) Order 1995 (SI 1995 493) which alters the structure of local government in the county of Avon. This Order specifies the staff employed by the Kingswood BC and the North Avon DC's whose employment is to be transferred to the South Gloucestershire DC.

4069. Local Government (Wales) Act 1994–Commencement No.7 Order

LOCAL GOVERNMENT (WALES) ACT 1994 (COMMENCEMENT NO.7) ORDER 1996, SI 1996 396 (C.7); made under the Local Government (Wales) Act 1994 s.66. In force: April 1, 1996; £1.10.

This is the final Commencement order in respect of the Local Government (Wales) Act 1994. The provisions commenced by this Order come into force on April 1, 1996.

4070. Local Valuation and Community Charge Tribunal–reorganisation

LOCAL GOVERNMENT CHANGES FOR ENGLAND (VALUATION AND COMMUNITY CHARGE TRIBUNALS) REGULATIONS 1996, SI 1996 43; made under the Local Government Finance Act 1988 s.140, s.143, Sch.11; and the Local Government Act 1992 s.19, s.26. In force: February 5, 1996; £1.95.

These Regulations amend valuation tribunal arrangements in areas undergoing structural or boundary changes as a result of reorganisation Orders made by the Secretary of State on the recommendation of the Local Government Commission in the Local Government Act 1992 Part II, by amending the Valuation and Community Charge Tribunals Regulations 1989 (SI 1989 439) which established such tribunals. Schedule 1, entitled establishment of tribunals, sets out the current names of the tribunals, corresponding jurisdiction and the appointing body or bodies.

4071. London Local Authorities Act 1996 (c.ix)

An Act to confer further powers upon local authorities in London.

This Act received Royal Assent on October 17, 1996.

4072. Magistrates' courts–reorganisation

LOCAL GOVERNMENT CHANGES FOR ENGLAND (MAGISTRATES' COURTS) REGULATIONS 1996, SI 1996 674; made under the Local Government Act 1992 s.19, s.26. In force: April 1, 1996; £1.55.

As a result of local government reorganisation in England, these Regulations make amendments to primary legislation. The amendments relate to commission areas, petty sessions areas and magistrates' courts committee areas. Provisions governing certain functions of local authorities relating to magistrates' courts are amended to cover cases in which the authority concerned is a unitary authority other than a county council or where the commission area or petty sessions area concerned falls within the area of more than one authority. Provision is made for commissions of the peace to continue after orders are made creating, abolishing or altering commission areas until new commissions are issued.

4073. National parks–levies

NATIONAL PARK AUTHORITIES (LEVIES) (ENGLAND) REGULATIONS 1996, SI 1996 2794; made under the Local Government Finance Act 1988 s.74, s.140, s.143; and the Environment Act 1995 s.71. In force: November 28, 1996; £1.95.

These Regulations provide for the issue of levies by a National Park authority for a National Park in England. National Park authorities may issue a levy to any principal authority the whole or part of whose area falls within the National Park Authority. These are county councils and district councils. The Regulations include provisions as to the issue of levies, apportionment, the maximum amount of levies, the issuing of substituted levies, the payment of levies and interest on unpaid levies.

4074. National parks–levies

NATIONAL PARK AUTHORITIES (LEVIES) (ENGLAND) (AMENDMENT) REGULATIONS 1996, SI 1996 2976; made under the Government Finance Act 1988 s.74, s.140, s.143. In force: November 28, 1996; £0.65.

The National Park Authorities (Levies) (England) Regulations 1996 (SI 1996 2794) apply to the issue of levies by National Park authorities to meet their expenses in respect of financial years beginning on or after April 1, 1997. Regulation 4 of the 1996 Regulations provides for apportionment of the amount which is to be raised by a National Park authority in respect of any financial year by way of levies. These Regulations amend the definition of the relevant proportion in Reg.4(3) of the 1996 Regulations.

4075. National parks–levies–Wales

NATIONAL PARK AUTHORITIES (LEVIES) (WALES) (AMENDMENT) REGULATIONS 1996, SI 1996 2913; made under the Local Government Finance Act 1988 s.74, s.140, s.143. In force: December 18, 1996; £1.10.

The Regulations amend the National Park Authorities (Levies) (Wales) Regulations 1995 (SI 1995 3019) which provide for the issue of levies to Welsh county and county borough councils as billing authorities by National Park authorities for National Parks in Wales. The Regulations amend the 1995 Regulations insofar as they relate to financial years beginning on and after April 1, 1997.

4076. Occupational pensions

LOCAL GOVERNMENT PENSION SCHEME (AMENDMENT) REGULATIONS 1996, SI 1996 1428; made under the Superannuation Act 1972 s.7, s.12. In force: June 28, 1996; £2.40.

These Regulations make various amendments to the Local Government Pension Scheme Regulations 1995 (SI 1995 1019) which constitute the Local Government Pension Scheme. Provisions contained in the Local Government Superannuation Regulations 1986, in connection with the right of certain members to count service where there has been a return of contributions, is reintroduced and a new provision is introduced so that members are allowed to freeze pension entitlements without having to leave the Scheme on changing jobs within local government employment due to Local Government Reorganisation. Persons are entitled to nominate the recipient or recipients of their death benefits. Where magistrates court committees or probation committees merged, the Regulations allow for bulk transfer provisions to apply and the National Park authorities are added to the list of LGPS employers. Other amendments relate to the treatment of leased care, protected rights for part-timers, employer contributions of National Parks in Wales and the definition of transferred members.

4077. Occupational pensions

LOCAL GOVERNMENT PENSION SCHEME (APPROPRIATE PENSION FUND) REGULATIONS 1996, SI 1996 185; made under the Superannuation Act 1972 s.7. In force: Reg.2: April 1, 1996; Reg.3: April 1, 1997.

These Regulations amend the Local Government Pension Scheme Regulations 1995 (SI 1995 1019), which specifies the appropriate pension fund for the employees of certain employing authorities. The additions made to the Schedule by these Regulations are in respect of employing authorities who, following local government reorganisation in England, will from April 1, 1996 or April 1, 1997, no longer be situated within the local government area of the local authority who is or is to become the administering authority of the fund to which they and their employees contribute. The amended Schedule specifies which is to be the appropriate pension fund for such authorities.

4078. Occupational pensions–civil service–Crown Prosecution Service–transfer

LOCAL GOVERNMENT PENSION SCHEME (CROWN PROSECUTION SERVICE) (TRANSFER OF PENSION RIGHTS) REGULATIONS 1996, SI 1996 2180; made under the Superannuation Act 1972 s.7, s.12. In force: September 17, 1996; £1.10.

These Regulations apply to persons who left local government employment between March 31, 1996 and September 30, 1996 and who thereupon joined the Crown Prosecution Service and became subject to the Principal Civil Service Pension Scheme. They determine the method by which transfer payments to the Principal Civil Service Pension Scheme in respect of such persons are to be calculated, and how such amounts are to be revalued from the date of transfer to the date when payment is effected.

4079. Occupational pensions–Environment Agency

LOCAL GOVERNMENT PENSION SCHEME (ENVIRONMENT AGENCY) REGULATIONS 1996, SI 1996 711; made under the Superannuation Act 1972 s.7. In force: April 1, 1996; £1.55.

These Regulations make provision in relation to the Local Government Pension Scheme constituted under the Local Government Pension Scheme Regulations 1995 (SI 1995 1019) in connection with the abolition of the National Rivers Authority, the establishment of the Environment Agency, and the transfer of staff to the Environment Agency from both the Civil Service and local authority bodies.

4080. Prosecutions–busking on London Underground–solicitation of reward without permission–whether contravention of bylaw established when music had not annoyed the public

D appealed by way of case stated against his conviction of soliciting a reward without permission, while busking at a London Underground station contrary to a general misconduct bylaw of the London Transport Executive. He argued that contravention of the bylaw was established only if the music was annoying to members of the public and that, as he had not actively sought a reward, there had been no solicitation.

Held, dismissing the appeal, that the bylaw was intended to prevent all conduct which might have undesirable consequences and it was not necessary to prove that such conduct had annoyed the public. Furthermore, each case had to be decided on its own facts and, although no express request had been made for money, the magistrate had been entitled to find that, on the basis of having an open container into which passers by dropped money and by shaking a tray of coins, D had been soliciting a reward.

DE CRISTOFARO v. BRITISH TRANSPORT POLICE, *The Times*, May 7, 1996, Newman, J., QBD.

4081. Public procurement–award of public works contracts–failure to state required criteria in invitations to tender–council awarding contract

[Public Works Contracts Regulations 1991 Reg.20; Council Directive 71/305 on the coordination of procedures for the award of public works contracts Art.1.]

C and G, private sector building contractors, appealed against the dismissal of their applications for judicial review of a local authority decision to award the majority of its contracts relating to maintenance and improvement of local authority housing to its own direct labour department, PCS. They argued that, as the local authority had failed to state in the invitations to tender the criteria upon which the awards were to be made, it had breached its obligations under the Public Works Contracts Regulations 1991 and Council Directive 71/305, as amended, and was therefore required to make an award to the contractor submitting the lowest offer.

Held, allowing the appeals in part, that the local authority was prevented from awarding contracts governed by the 1991 Regulations on the basis of criteria which had not been disclosed as this breached Reg.20(3). However, it was not obliged to accept the lowest offer over that of PCS because, under the terms of Council Directive 71/305 Art.1, public works contracts were contracts made for "pecuniary consideration", and a council could not enter into a contract with its own department. The appeal against the contract to which the Directive applied was accordingly dismissed.

R. v. PORTSMOUTH CITY COUNCIL, *ex p.* COLES; R. v. PORTSMOUTH CITY COUNCIL, *ex p.* GEORGE AUSTIN (BUILDERS) LTD, *The Times*, November 13, 1996, Leggatt, L.J., CA.

4082. Rates–advertising hoarding fixed to wall–entry on non-domestic rating list

[Local Government Finance Act 1988 s.64.]

O appealed against a Lands Tribunal decision that a right to display advertisements on a side wall of premises amounted to a hereditament capable of entry on the non-domestic rating list under the Local Government Finance Act 1988 s.64. O contended that the structure fixed to the wall, upon which advertisements were mounted, qualified as "land" occupied by him for the purposes of s.64(2) and s.64(11).

Held, dismissing the appeal, that, from an examination of legislation prior to the 1988 provisions, it had to be concluded that it was the wall to which the structure was affixed that was the "land", not the structure itself, and s.64 was applicable, *Imperial Tobacco Ltd v. Pierson* [1961] A.C. 463, [1960] C.L.Y. 2676 considered.

O'BRIEN v. SECKER (VALUATION OFFICER) [1996] R.A. 409, Roch, L.J., CA.

4083. Redundancy–compensation

LOCAL GOVERNMENT (COMPENSATION FOR REDUNDANCY) (AMENDMENT) REGULATIONS 1996, SI 1996 456; made under the Superannuation Act 1972 s.24. In force: March 20, 1996; £2.40.

The Local Government (Compensation for Redundancy) Regulations 1994 (SI 1994 3025), which make provision for compensation to local government employees when the termination of their employment is due to redundancy or a reorganisation which is in the interests of the employer's functions, are amended by these Regulations. New definitions of continuous and qualifying employment are introduced by Reg.2, Reg.3 provides that periods of qualifying employment may be used for the calculation of compensation and introduces a condition that the employee must not be one whose employment terminates because of the expiry of a fixed term contract. Regulation 4 substitutes a new Part III of the 1994 Regulations which covers payment of compensation during periods of local government reorganisation. Regulation 6 adds a condition that an employee is not eligible for compensation if he receives an offer to renew his contract or an offer of suitable employment to commence within four weeks of the termination and unreasonably refuses such an offer.

4084. Redundancy payments

REDUNDANCY PAYMENTS (LOCAL GOVERNMENT) (MODIFICATION) (AMENDMENT) ORDER 1996, SI 1996 372; made under the Employment Protection (Consolidation) Act 1978 s.149, s.154. In force: April 1, 1996; £1.10.

This Order amends various orders which modified certain redundancy payments provisions of the Employment Protection (Consolidation) Act 1978 in their application to persons employed in relevant local government service so that their employment in that service is to be treated as though it were continuous.

4085. Rent–registration areas

LOCAL GOVERNMENT CHANGES (RENT ACT REGISTRATION AREAS) ORDER 1996, SI 1996 2547; made under the Local Government Act 1992 s.17, s.26. In force: April 1, 1997; £0.65.

This Order redefines registration areas which are the organisational units for the rent officer service and rent assessment committees, as a consequence of the reorganisation of the counties named in Art.2 of this Order under the provisions of the Local Government Act 1992.

4086. Reorganisation

BERKSHIRE (STRUCTURAL CHANGE) ORDER 1996, SI 1996 1879; made under the Local Government Act 1992 s.17, s.18, s.26. In force: Art.2(2), Art.4(2)(3), Art.6, Art.9, Art.10, Art.11, Art.12 Art.13; Art.14; Art.15: July 19, 1996; Remainder: April 1, 1998; £2.80.

This Order gives effect to recommendations by the Local Government Commission for England for the making of structural and electoral changes in the Royal County of Berkshire. It effects the structural change by providing for the abolition of Berkshire county council and the transfer of its functions, in relation to each district in the county, to the council of that district; makes provision for the purposes of subordinate legislation which may be made under the Fire Services Act 1947 in respect of fire services; makes provision in relation to the Berkshire structure plan and to enable the local plans prepared by the district councils under the Town and Country Planning Act 1990 to contain minerals and waste policies; designates the council of the borough of Reading for the purposes of regulations relating to finance and the transfer of property, rights and liabilities, and the council of the district of Newbury for the purposes of regulations relating to certain employment liabilities. It also vests the county council's superannuation fund in the council of the Royal Borough of Windsor and Maidenhead, makes provision in relation to the Berkshire Act 1986, makes provision for electoral arrangements in Newbury, including provision for whole council elections in 1997, 2000 and 2003 and every fourth year after 2003, provides for there to be an additional councillor for the Colnbrook and Poyle ward in the borough of Slough, makes provision for whole council elections in Bracknell Forest and Windsor and Maidenhead in 1997, 2000 and 2003 and every fourth year after 2003, makes provision for elections in Reading, Slough and Wokingham, respectively, in 1997 and subsequent years, provides for the suspension of county council elections in 1997 and extends the term of office of county councillors until April 1, 1998.

4087. Reorganisation

CARDIFF (ST MELLONS COMMUNITY) ORDER 1996, SI 1996 494; made under the Local Government Act 1972 s.58. In force: purposes described in Art.1 (2): March 15, 1996; Remainder: April 1, 1996; £1.10.

This Order constitutes a new community, to be known as Pentprennau in the City of Cardiff (or the County of Cardiff) with effect from April 1, 1996, by virtue of the Local Government (Wales) Act 1994. The new community is formed by the separation from the community of St. Mellons of part of its area. The remaining area continues as a community and is renamed Old St. Mellons. The Pontprennau community does not have a community council. The community council for the Old St. Mellons community continues but with nine councillors and without wards. Supplementary provision is made in relation to councillors for the former Llandedeyrn ward of the St. Mellons community. The map forming part of this note gives a general indication of the areas affected by the Order. Prints of the boundary map referred to in Art.2 of the Order are deposited and may be inspected during normal office hourse at City Hall, Cathays Park, Cardiff; County Hall, Atlantic Wharf, Cardiff and the Welsh Office, Cathays Park, Cardiff. The Local Government Area Changes Regulations 1976 referred to in Art.2 of the Order contain further provisions about the effect and implementation of orders such as this one.

4088. Reorganisation

CHESHIRE (BOROUGHS OF HALTON AND WARRINGTON) (STRUCTURAL CHANGE) ORDER 1996, SI 1996 1863; made under the Local Government Act 1992 s.17, s.18, s.26. In force: Art.2(2), Art.5(1) (3) (4), Art.7, Art.8: July 19, 1996; Remainder: April 1, 1998; £1.55.

This Order gives effect to recommendations by the Local Government Commission for England in respect of the structure of local government in Cheshire. It effects two structural changes by providing for the transfer of functions of Cheshire CC in relation to the boroughs of Halton and Warrington to their respective councils, provides that the councils of Halton and Warrington shall each prepare a unitary development plan for its area instead of separate structure and local plans, makes provision for the purposes of subordinate legislation which may be made under the Fire Services Act 1947 in respect of fire services. It also provides for Halton and Warrington to cease to form part of Cheshire and for new counties of Halton and Warrington to be constituted, makes provision for whole council elections in Halton and Warrington in 1997, provides for councillors so elected for Halton to revert to retirement by thirds and for councillors elected for Warrington in 1997 to retire in 2000 and for those so elected in 2000 to retire in 2003, and makes provision for the suspension of county council elections in 1997 in electoral divisions in Halton and Warrington and extends the term of office of councillors for such divisions until April 1, 1998.

4089. Reorganisation

COMMISSION AREAS (GWENT, MID GLAMORGAN AND SOUTH GLAMORGAN) ORDER 1996, SI 1996 676; made under the Local Government (Wales) Act 1994 s.55. In force: April 1, 1996; £0.65.

This Order is made in connection with the abolition of the existing counties of Gwent, Mid Glamorgan and South Glamorgan by the Local Government (Wales)

Act 1994. It provides for the replacement of the Gwent, Mid Glamorgan and South Glamorgan commission areas by two commission areas to be known as Gwent and South Wales, and comes into force on April 1, 1996.

4090. Reorganisation

DEVON (CITY OF PLYMOUTH AND BOROUGH OF TORBAY) (STRUCTURAL CHANGE) ORDER 1996, SI 1996 1865; made under the Local Government Act 1992 s.17, s.18, s.26. In force: Art.2(2), Art.4(1)(3)(4), Art.7, Art.8: July 19, 1996; Remainder: April 1, 1998; £1.55.

This Order gives effect to recommendations by the Local Government Commission for England in respect of the structure of local government in the City of Plymouth and the borough of Torbay. It effects two structural changes by providing for the transfer of the functions of Devon CC in relation to Plymouth and Torbay to their respective councils, makes provision for the purposes of subordinate legislation which may be made under the Fire Services Act 1947 in respect of fire services, makes provision in relation to the structure plan applying to Devon and makes provision to enable the local plan prepared by the councils of Plymouth and Torbay under the Town and Country Planning Act 1990 to contain minerals and waste policies. It also provides for Plymouth and Torbay to cease to form part of Devon and for new counties of Plymouth and Torbay to be constituted, makes provision for a whole council election in Plymouth and Torbay in 1997, 2000 and 2003 and every fourth year after 2003, makes provision for the suspension of county council elections in 1997 in electoral divisions in Plymouth and Torbay and extends the term of office of councillors for such divisions until April 1, 1998.

4091. Reorganisation

HEREFORD AND WORCESTER (STRUCTURAL, BOUNDARY AND ELECTORAL CHANGES) ORDER 1996, SI 1996 1867; made under the Local Government Act 1992 s.17, s.18, s.26. In force: Art.2(2), Art.3, Art.4, Art.6, Art.7, Art.8, Art.9, Art.10, Art.11, Art.14, Art.15, Art.19, Art.20, Art.21, Art.22, Art.23: July 19, 1996; Remainder: April 1, 1998; £3.20.

This Order gives effect to the recommendations by the Local Government Commission for England in respect of the structure of local government in the county of Hereford and Worcester by providing for the abolition of the existing county, the constitution of a new district of Herefordshire and the constitution of a new county of Worcestershire and provides for the constitution of a new district of Malvern Hills within the new county of Worcestershire.

4092. Reorganisation

KENT (BOROUGH OF GILLINGHAM AND CITY OF ROCHESTER UPON MEDWAY) (STRUCTURAL CHANGE) ORDER 1996, SI 1996 1876; made under the Local Government Act 1992 s.17, s.18, s.26. In force: Art.2(2), Art.3, Art.6(1)(3)(4), Art.9, Art.10, Art.11, Art.12, Art.13, Art.14, Art.15, Art.16: July 19, 1996; Remainder: April 1, 1998; £1.95.

This Order gives effect to recommendations by the Local Government Commision for England in respect of the borough of Gillingham and the City of Rochester upon Medway, in the county of Kent. It provides for the constitution of the district of the Medway Towns, comprising the existing areas of Gillingham and Rochester, and establishes a new district council for that area; effects the structural change by providing for the transfer of the functions of the Kent County Council in relation to Gillingham and Rochester to the council of the Medway Towns; provides for the district of the Medway Towns to cease to form part of Kent and for a new county of the Medway Towns to be constituted; makes provision for the purposes of subordinate legislation to be made under the Fire Services Act 1947 in respect of fire services and makes provision in relation to the Kent structure plan and to enable the local plan prepared by the new council of the Medway Towns under the Town and Country Planning Act 1990 to contain minerals and waste policies. It also provides for the abolition of Gillingham and

Rochester and their councils, makes provision in respect of electoral areas for the Medway Towns, provides for whole council elections to the new council of the Medway Towns in 1997, 2000, 2003 and every four years after that year, makes provision in respect of returning officers and election expenses for the first elections in 1997, makes provision for the suspension of county council elections in 1997 in electoral divisions in Gilligham and Rochester and extends the term of office of councillors for such divisions until April 1, 1998. It also provides that the new council of the Medway Towns established by the Order shall be a shadow authority for the purposes of the Local Government Changes for England Regulations 1994 (SI 1994 867).

4093. Reorganisation

LANCASHIRE (BOROUGHS OF BLACKBURN AND BLACKPOOL) (STRUCTURAL CHANGE) ORDER 1996, SI 1996 1868; made under the Local Government Act 1992 s.17, s.18, s.26. In force: Art.2(2), Art.4(1)(3)(4), Art.7, Art.8: July 19, 1996; Remainder: April 1, 1996; £1.55.

This Order gives effect to recommendations of the Local Government Commission for England in respect of the structure of local government in the county of Lancashire. Article 3 effects two structural changes by providing for the transfer, on April 1, 1998, of the functions of Lancashire County Council in relation to the borough of Blackburn and the borough of Blackpool to their respective councils. Provisions are made in respect of fire services; in relation to the structure plan applying to Lancashire; for whole council elections in Blackburn and Blackpool in 1997 and for the suspension of county council elections in 1997 in electoral divisions in Blackburn and Blackpool.

4094. Reorganisation

LEICESTERSHIRE (CITY OF LEICESTER AND DISTRICT OF RUTLAND) (STRUCTURAL CHANGE) ORDER 1996, SI 1996 507; made under the Local Government Act 1992 s.17, s.18, s.26. In force: Art.2(2), Art.4, Art.6(1), Art.6(3), Art.9, Art.10: March 1, 1996 Remainder: April 1, 1997; £1.55.

Recommendations relating to the structure of local government in Leicester and Rutland made by the Local Government Commission for England are implemented by this Order. Functions of Leicestershire CC relating to Leicester and Rutland are transferred to their respective councils.

4095. Reorganisation

LOCAL GOVERNMENT REORGANISATION (MISCELLANEOUS PROVISION) (RUSH COMMON) ORDER 1996, SI 1996 1690; made under the Local Government Act 1985 s.101. In force: July 26, 1996; £0.65.

This Order makes provision consequential on the abolition of the Greater London Council by the Local Government Act 1985 s.1. It amends the Local Government Reorganisation (Miscellaneous Provision) Order 1988 (SI 1988 1955) Art.6 so as to enable Lambeth BC to exercise functions in relation to an area of land forming part of Rush Common, Brixton which were formerly exercisable by the Greater London Council but not included among the functions transferred by that article.

4096. Reorganisation

NOTTINGHAMSHIRE (CITY OF NOTTINGHAM) (STRUCTURAL CHANGE) ORDER 1996, SI 1996 1877; made under the Local Government Act 1992 s.17, s.18, s.26. In force: Art.2(2), Art.4(1)(3)(4), Art.7, Art.8: July 19, 1996; Remainder: April 1, 1998; £1.55.

This Order gives effect to recommendations by the Local Government Commission for England in respect of the city of Nottingham. They effect the structural change by providing for the transfer on April 1, 1998, of the functions of Nottinghamshire CC in relation to Nottingham to the council of that city, make provision for the purposes of subordinate legislation to be made under the Fire

Services Act 1947 in respect of fire services, make provision in relation to the Nottinghamshire structure plan and to enable the local plan prepared by the council of Nottingham under the Town and Country Planning Act 1990 to contain minerals and waste policies, provide for Nottingham to cease to form part of Nottinghamshire and for a new county of Nottingham to be constituted, make provision for a whole council election in Nottingham in 1997, 2000 and 2003 and for the councillors so elected to retire in 2000 and 2003 and every fourth year after 2003, and make provision for the suspension of county council elections in 1997 in electoral divisions in Nottingham.

4097. Reorganisation

SHROPSHIRE (DISTRICT OF THE WREKIN) (STRUCTURAL CHANGE) ORDER 1996, SI 1996 1866; made under the Local Government Act 1992 s.17, s.18, s.26. In force: Art.2(2), Art.4(1)(3)(4), Art.7, Art.8: July 19, 1996; Remainder: April 1, 1998; £1.55.

This Order gives effect to recommendations by the Local Government Commission for England in respect of the structure of local government in the district of The Wrekin. It effects the structural change by providing for the transfer of the functions of Shropshire CC in relation to The Wrekin to the council of that district, makes provision for the purposes of subordinate legislation which may be made under the Fire Services Act 1947 in respect of fire services, makes provision in relation to the Shropshire structure plan and to enable the local plan prepared by the council of The Wrekin under the Town and Council Planning Act 1990 to contain minerals and waste policies and provides for The Wrekin to cease to form part of Shropshire and for a new county of The Wrekin to be constituted. It also makes provision for a whole council election in The Wrekin in 1997, 2000 and 2003 and every fourth year after 2003, provides for the suspension of county council elections in 1997 in electoral divisions in The Wrekin and extends the term of office of councillors for such divisions until April 1, 1998.

4098. Reorganisation–compensation for loss of remuneration

LOCAL GOVERNMENT REORGANISATION (COMPENSATION FOR LOSS OF REMUNERATION) (AMENDMENT) REGULATIONS 1996, SI 1996 660; made under the Superannuation Act 1972 s.24. In force: April 1, 1996; £0.65.

These Regulations amend the Local Government Reorganisation (Compensation for Loss of Remuneration) Regulations 1995 (SI 1995 2837) (the 1995 Regulations) so as to provide for the payment of compensation to coroners who suffer a loss or reduction of remuneration as a consequence of any provision of an order made under the Local Government Act 1992 s.17, implementing local government changes for England or any provision made by or under the Local Government (Wales) Act 1994, implementing local government changes for Wales. The new Reg.2(2)(a)(i) and Reg.2(2)(a)(ii) of the 1995 Regulations repeat provisions in the existing Reg.2(2).

4099. Reorganisation–council tax reduction scheme

LOCAL GOVERNMENT REORGANISATION (WALES) (COUNCIL TAX REDUCTION SCHEME) ORDER 1996, SI 1996 56; made under the Local Government (Wales) Act 1994 s.54. In force: February 7, 1996; £1.10.

This Order modifies the Local Government Finance Act 1992 s.13 which empowers the Secretary of State to make regulations for council tax reduction. The 1992 Act is amended for the financial year beginning April 1, 1996 so that council tax grant is not counted as income for the purpose of an authority's budget requirement calculation.

4100. **Reorganisation–education**

LOCAL GOVERNMENT CHANGES FOR ENGLAND (EDUCATION) (MISCELLANEOUS PROVISIONS) REGULATIONS 1996, SI 1996 710; made under the Local Government Act 1992 s.19, s.26. In force: April 1, 1996; £1.55.

As a result of boundary and structural changes to local government areas made by orders under the Local Government Act 1992 s.17, these Regulations make incidental and transitional provision of general application in the field of education. Part II relates to determination of applications by standing advisory councils on religious education where the requirement for Christian collective worship does not apply. Part III relates to the extension of periods applicable to decisions made by local education authorities relating to the assessment of educational needs, Part IV relates to grants paid to transferor authorities for educational support and training and to the education of Travellers and displaced persons. Part V modifies the Education Act 1944 s.114(1) by changing the definition of minor authority.

4101. **Reorganisation–elections–boundaries**

CAMBRIDGESHIRE (CITY OF PETERBOROUGH) (STRUCTURAL, BOUNDARY AND ELECTORAL CHANGES) ORDER 1996, SI 1996 1878; made under the Local Government Act 1992 s.17, s.18, s.26. In force: arts.2(2), Art.6(1)(3)(4), Art.8, Art.9, Art.10, Art.11: July 19, 1996; Remainder: April 1, 1998; £1.95.

This Order gives effect to recommendations by the Local Government Commission for England in respect of the structure of local government in the city of Peterborough. It provides for Peterborough to cease to form part of Cambridgeshire and for a new county of Peterborough to be constituted, makes certain changes to the boundary between Peterborough and the district of Huntingdonshire, effects the structural change by providing for the transfer of the functions of Cambridgeshire County Council in relation to Peterborough to the council of the city, makes provision for the purposes of subordinate legislation which may be made under the Fire Services Act 1947 in respect of fire services, makes provision in relation to the Cambridgeshire structure plan and to enable the local plan prepared by the council of Peterborough under the Town and Country Planning Act 1990 to contain minerals and waste policies, make provision for new electoral areas for Peterborough for the purposes of an election held on or after May 1, 1997 and makes provision for a whole council election in Peterborough in 1997 and for reversion to election by thirds in subsequent years, including a transitional period during which elections will be held after three years instead of the usual four.

4102. **Reorganisation–elections–boundaries**

ESSEX (BOROUGHS OF COLCHESTER, SOUTHEND-ON-SEA AND THURROCK AND DISTRICT OF TENDRING) (STRUCTURAL, BOUNDARY AND ELECTORAL CHANGES) ORDER 1996, SI 1996 1875; made under the Local Government Act 1992 s.17, s.18, s.26. In force: Art.2(2): July 19, 1996; Art.4(1)(2)(3): July 19, 1996; Art.7: July 19, 1996; Art.8: July 19, 1996; Art.9: July 19, 1996; Art.11: July 19, 1996; Art.10: April 1, 1997; Remainder: April 1, 1998; £2.80.

This Order gives effect to recommendations by the Local Government Commission for England in respect of the structure of local government in the boroughs of Southend-on-Sea and Thurrock and recommendations in relation to boundaries and electoral arrangements in other districts in the county of Essex. It effects the structural changes by providing for the transfer of the functions of Essex County Council in relation to Southend and Thurrock to their respective councils, makes provision for the purposes of subordinate legislation which may be made under the Fire Services Act 1947 in respect of fire services and makes provision in relation to the structure plan applying to Essex and to enable the local plan prepared by the council of Southend under the Town and Country Planning Act 1990 to contain minerals and waste policies. It provides that the council of Thurrock, as local planning authority, shall prepare a unitary development plan for its area instead of separate structure and local plans, and makes consequential modifications of the 1990 Act. It also provides for Southend and Thurrock to cease to form part of Essex and for new counties of Southend-on-Sea and Thurrock to be constituted, makes provision for a whole council election in Southend in 1997 and for reversion to election by thirds in subsequent years, makes provision for a whole council election in Thurrock in 1997 and for reversion to election by thirds in subsequent years, and provides for the retirement of existing county councillors elected for divisions in Southend and Thurrock.

4103. Reorganisation–finance

LOCAL GOVERNMENT CHANGES FOR ENGLAND (FINANCE) (AMENDMENT) REGULATIONS 1996, SI 1996 563; made under the Local Government Act 1992 s.19, s.26. In force: April 1, 1996; £0.65.

These Regulations and amend the Local Government Changes for England (Finance) Regulations 1994 (SI 1994 2825) Reg.54A to provide for the treatment of grants made by the Secretary of State under the Rent Act 1977 s.63 (rent officer schemes) to an authority which is abolished under the Local Government Act 1992 Part II.

4104. Reorganisation–miscellaneous provisions

LOCAL GOVERNMENT CHANGES FOR ENGLAND (MISCELLANEOUS PROVISION) ORDER 1996, SI 1996 446; made under the Local Government Act 1996 s.17, s.26. In force: Art.4: March 20, 1996; Remainder: April 1, 1996; £1.55.

Miscellaneous amendments are made in consequence of orders made under the Local Government Act 1992 s.17 relating to structural or boundary changes to local authorities.

4105. Reorganisation–miscellaneous provisions

LOCAL GOVERNMENT CHANGES FOR ENGLAND (MISCELLANEOUS PROVISION) REGULATIONS 1996, SI 1996 330; made under the Local Government Act 1992 s.19, s.26. In force: Reg.3(2): April 1, 1996; Remainder: March 11, 1996; £2.40.

For the purposes of, or in consequence of orders made under the Local Government Act 1992 s.17, these Regulations make general incidental, consequential, transitional and supplementary provisions relating to local government changes. The amendments relate to the transfer of armorial bearings, maps and statements of rights of way and interests in companies controlled or influenced by local authorities, claims by employees of abolished authorities and rights and privileges of existing areas affected by reorganisation.

4106. Reorganisation–rent officers

LOCAL GOVERNMENT REORGANISATION (WALES) (RENT OFFICERS) ORDER 1996, SI 1996 533; made under the Local Government (Wales) Act 1994 s.54. In force: April 1, 1996; £1.10.

On April 1, 1996 the new principal councils established under the Local Government (Wales) Act 1996 take over the responsibility for the administration of Welsh local government from the old principal councils which cease to exist. This Order makes provision in respect of rent officers in Wales as a result of that reorganisation. The Order gives effect to agreed arrangements for the transfer of rent officers in Wales. It treats rent officers as having been duly appointed to office on or after April 1, 1996 in those cases where they have not been so appointed (Art.3) and preserves continuity in respect of their terms and conditions of appointment (Art.4).

4107. Reorganisation–sea fisheries districts

LOCAL GOVERNMENT REORGANISATION (WALES) (COMMITTEES FOR SEA FISHERIES DISTRICTS) (AMENDMENT) ORDER 1996, SI 1996 618; made under the Local Government (Wales) Act 1994 s.54. In force: April 1, 1996; £1.10.

This Order makes consequential amendments to the constitutions of the Committees (the Committees) for the South Wales Sea Fisheries District and the North Western and North Wales Sea Fisheries District arising as a result of Welsh local government reorganisation. The Order specifies which new Welsh principal councils are to be constituent councils of the Committees. Consequential adjustments are also made to the membership of the Committees and the liability of Welsh principal councils to contribute to the expenses of the Committees.

4108. Reorganisation–Secretary of State's powers to modify recommendations of Local Government Commission

[Local Government Act 1992 s.17.]

The Secretary of State appealed against a decision allowing B's challenge to his decision which gave effect to the Local Government Commission's recommendations for Berkshire. The report recommended that the present two tier structure consisting of seven councils be replaced by a single tier structure of five unitary authorities. Such change required the abolition of the county council, the combination of two existing authorities and structural changes for existing district or borough councils facilitated by boundary alterations. The Secretary of State sought to modify the changes by ordering that two existing councils remain separate. B contended that, under the Local Government Act 1992 s.17(1), which gave the Secretary of State the power to accept, reject or implement the proposal in a modified form, he did not have the power to reject the recommendation and implement something different.

Held, allowing the appeal, that the structure and purpose of the 1992 Act should be looked at as a whole. The Act allowed for a review of the whole county to be conducted by the Local Government Commission, for recommendations to be made, and for the Secretary of State to give effect to these with or without modification. Section 17(1) was intended to be given a wide interpretation so as not to tie the Secretary of State's hands. Therefore, the Secretary of State, who was prepared to give effect to the proposed structural changes, did not exceed his powers in rejecting a boundary change which he felt was unnecessary to facilitate those changes.

R. v. SECRETARY OF STATE FOR THE ENVIRONMENT, *ex p.* BERKSHIRE CC; R. v. SECRETARY OF STATE FOR THE ENVIRONMENT, *ex p.* BRACKNELL FOREST BC, *The Times*, January 25, 1996, Kennedy, L.J., CA.

4109. Reorganisation–sheriffs

LOCAL GOVERNMENT CHANGES FOR ENGLAND (SHERIFFS) ORDER 1996, SI 1996 2009; made under the Local Government Act 1992 s.17, s.26. In force: April 1, 1997; £0.65.

This Order makes incidental, consequential, transitional or supplementary provision in relation to Orders already made under the Local Government Act 1992 s.17 which effect structural and boundary changes in relation to local government areas in England. It amends the Sheriffs Act 1887 Sch.2A which makes provision in respect of the meaning of county for the purposes of the Act and excludes in the case of the appointment as high sheriff of Rutland of the person appointed as high sheriff of Leicestershire, a provision that a person shall not be appointed as sheriff of a county unless he has sufficient land in the county.

4110. Reorganisation–staff

LOCAL GOVERNMENT CHANGES FOR ENGLAND (STAFF) (AMENDMENT) REGULATIONS 1996, SI 1996 455; made under the Local Government Act 1992 s.19, s.26. In force: March 20, 1996; £0.65.

This Order amends the Local Government Changes for England (Staff) Regulations 1995 (SI 1995 520) which provide that Local Government staff whose employment would have continued but for the winding up and abolition of employing authorities are entitled to treat themselves as having being dismissed on grounds of redundancy. The amendments extend the scope of the Regulations to cover authorities subject to structural or boundary changes and provide that employees receiving offers for renewal of contracts of employment or re-engagement under a new contract with a local government employer are not covered by the Regulations.

4111. Reorganisation–transfer of assets–payments

LOCAL GOVERNMENT CHANGES FOR ENGLAND (PROPERTY TRANSFER AND TRANSITIONAL PAYMENTS) (AMENDMENT) REGULATIONS 1996, SI 1996 312; made under the Local Government Act 1992 s.19, s.26. In force: March 12, 1996; £1.55.

These Regulations amend the Local Government Changes for England (Property Transfer and Transitional Payments) Regulations 1995 (SI 1995 402) which provide for the transfer of property, rights and liabilities of local authorities subject to structural or boundary changes. The amendments relate to the transfer of dwellings and other property accounted for within the Housing Revenue Account (HRA) of authorities and the rights and liabilities relating to such property and dwellings.

4112. Reorganisation–transfer of assets

LOCAL GOVERNMENT CHANGES FOR ENGLAND (PROPERTY TRANSFER AND TRANSITIONAL PAYMENTS) (AMENDMENT) (NO.2) REGULATIONS 1996, SI 1996 2825; made under the Local Government Act 1992 s.19, s.26. In force: December 5, 1996; £1.10.

These Regulations amend the Local Government Changes for England (Property Transfer and Transitional Payments) Regulations 1995 (SI 1995 402) which make provision of general application for the transfer of the property, rights and liabilities of local authorities which are subject to structural or boundary changes under the Local Government Act 1992.

4113. Reorganisation–transfer of staff

AVON (STAFF TRANSFER) ORDER 1996, SI 1996 400; made under the Local Government Act 1992 s.17, s.26. In force: April 1, 1996; £1.10.

This Order is supplemental to the Avon (Structural Change) Order 1995 (SI 1995 493) which alters the structure of local government in the county of Avon. It specifies the staff employed by the Avon CC whose employment is to be transferred to the four Avon district councils.

4114. Reorganisation–transfer of staff

BATH AND NORTH EAST SOMERSET DISTRICT COUNCIL (STAFF TRANSFER) ORDER 1996, SI 1996 377; made under the Local Government Act 1992 s.17, s.26. In force: April 1, 1996; £1.10.

This Order is supplemental to the Avon (Structural Change) Order 1995 (SI 1995 493) which alters the structure of local government in the county of Avon. This Order specifies the staff employed by the Bath City Council or the Waynsdyke District Council whose employment is to be transferred to the Bath and North East Somerset Council.

4115. Reorganisation–transfer of staff

CLEVELAND (STAFF TRANSFER) ORDER 1996, SI 1996 398; made under the Local Government Act 1992 s.17, s.26. In force: April 1, 1996; £0.65.

This Order is supplemental to the Cleveland (Structural Change) Order 1995 (SI 1995 187) which alters the structure of local government in the county of Cleveland. This Order specifies the staff employed by the Cleveland County council whose employment is to be transferred to the four Cleveland borough councils.

4116. Reorganisation–transfer of staff

EAST RIDING OF YORKSHIRE DISTRICT COUNCIL (STAFF TRANSFER) ORDER 1996, SI 1996 378; made under the Local Government Act 1992 s.17, s.26. In force: April 1, 1996; £0.65.

This Order is supplemental to the Humberside (Structural Change) Order 1995 (SI 1995 600) which alters the structure of local government in the county of Humberside. This Order specifies the staff employed by the Beverley BC, the East Yorkshire BC, and the Holderness BC whose employment is to be transferred to the East Riding of Yorkshire DC.

4117. Reorganisation–transfer of staff

HUMBERSIDE (STAFF TRANSFER) ORDER 1996, SI 1996 397; made under the Local Government Act 1992 s.17, s.26. In force: April 1, 1996; £0.65.

This Order is supplemental to the Humberside (Structural Change) Order 1995 (SI 1995 600) which alters the structure of local government in the county of Humberside. This Order specifies the staff employed by the Humberside CC whose employment is to be transferred to the four Humberside district councils.

4118. Reorganisation–transfer of staff

NORTH EAST LINCOLNSHIRE DISTRICT COUNCIL (STAFF TRANSFER) ORDER 1996, SI 1996 386; made under the Local Government Act 1992 s.17, s.26. In force: April 1, 1996; £1.10.

This Order is supplemental to the Humberside (Structural Change) Order 1995 (SI 1995 600) which alters the structure of local government in the county of Humberside. This Order specifies the staff employed by the Cleethorpes or Great Grimsby BC whose employment is to be transferred to the North East Lincolnshire DC.

4119. Reorganisation–transfer of staff

NORTH LINCOLNSHIRE AND EAST RIDING OF YORKSHIRE DISTRICT COUNCILS (STAFF TRANSFER) ORDER 1996, SI 1996 408; made under the Local Government Act 1992 s.17, s.26. In force: April 1, 1996; £1.55.

This Order is supplemental to the Humberside (Structural Change) Order 1995 (SI 1995 600) which alters the structure of local government in the county of Humberside. This Order specifies the staff employed by the Boothferry BC whose employment is to be transferred to the East Riding of Yorkshire DC and the North Lincolnshire DC.

4120. Reorganisation–transfer of staff

NORTH LINCOLNSHIRE DISTRICT COUNCIL (STAFF TRANSFER) ORDER 1996, SI 1996 384; made under the Local Government Act 1992 s.17, s.26. In force: April 1, 1996; £1.10.

This Order is supplemental to the Humberside (Structural Change) Order 1995 (SI 1995 600) which alters the structure of local government in the county of Humberside. This Order specifies the staff employed by the Glanford BC and Scunthorpe BC whose employment is to be transferred to the North Lincolnshire DC.

4121. Reorganisation–transfer of staff

NORTH YORKSHIRE (DISTRICT OF YORK) (STAFF TRANSFER) ORDER 1996, SI 1996 388; made under the Local Government Act 1992 s.17, s.26. In force: April 1, 1996; £1.10.

This Order is supplemental to the North Yorkshire (District of York) (Structural and Boundary Changes) Order 1995 (SI 1995 610) which alters the structure of local government in the county of North Yorkshire and the District of York. This Order specifies the staff employed by the North Yorkshire CC, the Harrogate BC, the Ryedale DC, the Selby DC and the York City Council whose employment is to be transferred to the York DC.

4122. Reorganisation–Wales

LOCAL GOVERNMENT REORGANISATION (WALES) (CONSEQUENTIAL AMENDMENTS) ORDER 1996, SI 1996 525; made under the Local Government (Wales) Act 1994 s.47, s.54, s.57, s.58. In force: April 1, 1996; £1.55.

The Local Government (Wales) Act 1994 creates unitary authorities in Wales which will carry out the functions of the former district and county councils as from April 1, 1996. This Order makes amendments to primary and subordinate legislation (including local legislation) in consequence of this. The amendments update references to the old local government structure in Wales so that they apply to the new structure. The amendments are mainly confined to situations where the general provision contained in s.17 of the 1994 Act (references to the old structure to be construed as references to the new structure) will not apply.

4123. Reorganisation–Wales

LOCAL GOVERNMENT REORGANISATION (WALES) (CONSEQUENTIAL AMENDMENTS NO.2) ORDER 1996, SI 1996 1008; made under the Local Government (Wales) Act 1994 s.54. In force: April 29, 1996; £1.55.

This Order makes amendments to primary and subordinate legislation in consequence of the creation of unitary authorities in Wales which will carry out the functions of the former district and county councils from April 1, 1996. The amendments update references to the old local government structure in Wales so that they apply to the new structure which was created under the Local Government (Wales) Act 1994.

4124. Reorganisation–Wales

LOCAL GOVERNMENT REORGANISATION (WALES) (CONSEQUENTIAL AMENDMENTS NO.3) ORDER 1996, SI 1996 3071; made under the Local Government (Wales) Act 1994 s.54. In force: January 7, 1997; £1.10.

The Local Government (Wales) Act 1994 created unitary authorities in Wales which have, as from April 1, 1996, carried out the functions of the former district and county councils. This Order makes amendments to the Local Government (Miscellaneous Provisions) Act 1976, the Local Government Finance Act 1988, the Local Government and Housing Act 1989 and the Local Government Finance Act 1992 in consequence of this.

4125. Reorganisation–Wales

LOCAL GOVERNMENT REORGANISATION (WALES) (STAFF) ORDER 1996, SI 1996 501; made under the Local Government (Wales) Act 1994 s.42, s.63. In force: April 1, 1996; £1.95.

This Order designates, for the purposes of the Local Government (Wales) Act 1994 s.42, staff of district and county councils and the Milford Port Health Authority which are subject to abolition on April 1, 1996. It specifies a new county council, county borough council or National Park authority in Wales as their new employer. Section 42 provides that the employment contract of staff so designated has effect as if originally made between them and the new employer specified in the last Order.

4126. Reorganisation–Wales

LOCAL GOVERNMENT REORGANISATION (WALES) (STAFF) (NO.2) ORDER 1996, SI 1996 905; made under the Local Government (Wales) Act 1994 s.42, s.63. In force: April 1, 1996; £2.80.

This Order supplements and amends the Local Government Reorganisation (Wales) (Staff) Order 1996 (SI 1996 501) (the principal Order) which makes provision for the designation of employees of district and county councils which are abolished by virtue of the Local Government (Wales) Act 1994 and specifies new employers for employees so designated. Article 4 of the Order disapplies the principal Order in relation to employees described in Parts I and II of the Schedule and effects a minor amendment to the Schedule to the principal Order. Article 5 of the Order designates employees described in Parts II and III of the Schedule and specifies new employers for such employees.

4127. Reorganisation–Wales

LOCAL GOVERNMENT REORGANISATION (WALES) (STAFF) (NO.3) ORDER 1996, SI 1996 1214; made under the Local Government (Wales) Act 1994 s.42, s.63. In force: May 28, 1996; £1.55.

This Order supplements and partly supersedes the Local Government Reorganisation (Wales) (Staff) Order 1996 (SI 1996 501) and the Local Government Reorganisation (Wales) (Staff) (No.2) Order 1996 (SI 1996 905) which designated staff of the district and county councils and of the Milford Port Health Authority which ceased to exist on April 1, 1996 and specified a new county or county borough council or a National Park authority as the new employer of such staff. It designates the staff described in the Schedule for the purposes of the Local Government (Wales) Act 1994 s.42 and specifies a new county or county borough council or a National Park authority as the new employer for such staff.

4128. Reorganisation–Wales–charities

LOCAL GOVERNMENT REORGANISATION (WALES) (CHARITIES) ORDER 1996, SI 1996 183; made under the Local Government (Wales) Act 1994 s.49, s.63. In force: April 1, 1996; £1.10.

This Order supplements the provision in Local Government (Wales) Act 1994 s.49 for the transfer of charitable property and related powers from old authorities to new principal councils. Under this Order, provision is additionally made for the transfer of powers exercisable in relation to a charity where those powers are vested in an old authority rather than an office holder of an old authority; the identity of transferee councils to be determined in accordance with the principles stated in s.49(4) and (5) in the above case and in accordance with s.49(4) in those cases where local authority officers have powers with respect to a charity whose property is not vested in an old authority, or where an old authority or any of its officers are included among the trustees of a charity; references to "the greater part" in s.49(4) and (5) to be construed as references to "the greatest part" in those cases where there are more than two new principal councils whose areas comprise either the specified area under s.49(4) or the area of the old authority in question under s.49(5); refernces in Art.2(2) and s.49(2) to a power with respect to a charity not to include references to a power of an old authority or an office holder of an old authority by virtue of being a trustee of a charity; the transfer of rights and liabilities in connection with charitable property held by an old authority as trustee to the new principal council in which the property is vested.

4129. Reorganisation–Wales–finance

LOCAL GOVERNMENT REORGANISATION (WALES) (CAPITAL FINANCE) ORDER 1996, SI 1996 633; made under the Local Government (Wales) Act 1994 s.54. In force: Art.1: March 1, 1994; Art.2: March 1, 1996; Art.3: March 1, 1996 Remainder: April 1, 1996; £1.55.

This Order which amends the Local Government and Housing Act 1989 (1989 c.42) and the Local Authorities (Capital Finance) Regulations 1990 (SI 1990 432), makes supplementary and transitional provision in respect of capital finance controls as a result of the creation of new county borough councils. The Local Government and Housing Act 1989 s.39 is amended by Art.2 to include Welsh combined fire authorities in the list of authorities subject to the revenue accounts and capital finance controls of Part IV of the 1989 Act. Article 3 ensures that the new authorities will have sufficient time to determine their borrowing limits under s.45 of the 1989 Act, and relieves authorities to be abolished from that duty. Article 4 relates to the register of loan instruments, Art.5 relates to later credit approvals issued to successor authorities, Art.6 empowers the Secretary of State to issue supplementary credit approvals to designated authorities, Art.7 exempts certain payments by the Residuary Body for Wales to a new authority and Art.8 makes amendments to the 1990 Regulations to exclude contracts for the transfer of land to an authority from the Residuary Body for Wales from s.48 of the 1989 Act.

4130. Reorganisation–Wales–finance

LOCAL GOVERNMENT REORGANISATION (WALES) (CAPITAL FINANCE) (AMENDMENT) ORDER 1996, SI 1996 1366; made under the Local Government (Wales) Act 1994 s.54. In force: June 1, 1996; £0.65.

This Order makes amendments to the Local Government Reorganisation (Wales) (Capital Finance) Order 1996 (SI 1996 633) and the Local Government Reorganisation (Wales) (Capital Finance and Miscellaneous Provisions) Order 1996 (SI 1996 910). It deletes superfluous definitions from the interpretation provisions of the Local Government Reorganisation (Wales) (Capital Finance) Order 1996. The Local Government Reorganisation (Wales) (Capital Finance and Miscellaneous Provisions) Order 1996 modified the application of Part IV of the Local Government and Housing Act 1989 in relation to money transferred under some agreements made under the Local Government (Wales) Act 1994 s.56. The agreements are those concerning land, buildings or other structures (except roads), made between certain public bodies affected by area changes made by the 1994 Act (relevant authorities). Paragraph 3 of that Article (which provides that any receipt by a relevant authority under a s.56 agreement shall be treated as a capital receipt) is not however restricted to agreements concerning land, buildings or other structures (except roads). Article 3 of that Order amends that paragraph to restrict its application to such agreements.

4131. Reorganisation–Wales–finance

LOCAL GOVERNMENT REORGANISATION (WALES) (CAPITAL FINANCE AND MISCELLANEOUS PROVISIONS) ORDER 1996, SI 1996 910; made under the Local Government (Wales) Act 1994 s.54; and the Environment Act 1995 s.64. In force: April 1, 1996; £2.80.

This Order, which amends the Local Authorities (Capital Finance) Regulations 1990 (SI 1990 432) and the Local Authorities (Borrowing) Regulations 1990 (SI 1990 767), makes further provision in relation to financial matters resulting from the reorganisation of the local government in Wales. Part II makes provision for successor authorities in relation to capital finance controls under the Local Government and Housing Act 1989 Part IV, Part III of the Order makes provision for the opening balance for the Housing Revenue Account for a new principal council and Part IV makes further transitional provision relating to rating.

4132. Reorganisation–Wales–finance

LOCAL GOVERNMENT REORGANISATION (WALES) (FINANCE) ORDER 1996, SI 1996 88; made under the Local Government (Wales) Act 1994 s.54. In force: February 9, 1996; £2.40.

This Order makes transitional provision in relation to general rates, community charge, non domestic rates, council tax, accounts and grants in consequence of the Local Government (Wales) Act 1994.

4133. Reorganisation–Wales–finance

LOCAL GOVERNMENT REORGANISATION (WALES) (FINANCE) (MISCELLANEOUS AMENDMENTS AND TRANSITIONAL PROVISIONS) ORDER 1996, SI 1996 619; made under the Local Government (Wales) Act 1994 s.54. In force: April 1, 1996; £0.65.

This Order makes supplementary and transitional provision in respect of local government finance following the abolition of county and district councils and the creation of new county and county borough councils in Wales on April 1, 1996. Consequential and transitional provisions for regulations relating to non-domestic rating, as regards references to non-domestic rating lists are made by Art.3, Art.4 and Art.5. Consequential and transitional provision for regulations relating to council tax, as regards references to valuation lists are made by Art.7 and Art.8. Article 6 and Art.9 make transitional provision regarding the actions and duties of valuation officers and listing officers of old and new authorities and Art.10 makes consequential provision as regards recoupment of housing revenue account subsidy. Article 11 empowers the Secretary of State to make commuted payments to new authorities or the Public Works Loan Commissioners and Art.12 revokes, with savings, demand notice regulations relating to local taxation, which are now spent.

4134. Reorganisation–Wales–transfer of assets

LOCAL GOVERNMENT REORGANISATION (WALES) (PROPERTY ETC.) ORDER 1996, SI 1996 532; made under the Local Government (Wales) Act 1994 s.54, s.63. In force: April 1, 1996; £3.20.

Provision is made by these Regulations for the transfer of property, rights and liabilities of the existing district and county councils and a joint board which cease to exist on April 1, 1996 by virtue of the Local Government (Wales) Act 1994. Part I provides for the vesting of property in one Successor Authority, Part II provides for the vesting of property where there is more than one Successor Authority and Part III provides for the vesting of miscellaneous property, rights and liabilities. The Schedules to the Order provide for payments made by the Secretary of State, transfers of loan debt, transfers of a specific nature and coroners.

4135. Reorganisation–Wales–transfer of assets

LOCAL GOVERNMENT REORGANISATION (WALES) (PROPERTY ETC.) (AMENDMENT) ORDER 1996, SI 1996 906; made under the Local Government (Wales) Act 1994 s.54, s.63. In force: April 1, 1996; £0.65.

This Order amends the Local Government Reorganisation (Wales) (Property etc) Order 1996 (SI 1996 532) which makes provision for the transfer of property, rights and liabilities of local authorities and other bodies which are subject to abolition by virtue of the Local Government (Wales) Act 1994. Article 2 of this Order effects minor amendments to Sch.2 and Sch.3.

4136. Residuary bodies–Wales–levies

RESIDUARY BODY FOR WALES (LEVIES) REGULATIONS 1996, SI 1996 2900; made under the Local Government Finance Act 1988 s.74, s.140, s.143. In force: December 18, 1996; £1.55.

The Regulations confer a power on the Residuary Body for Wales to issue levies to certain new principal councils created by the Local Government (Wales) Act 1994 for the purpose of meeting the Body's expenditure in respect of financial years beginning on or after April 1, 1997. They include provisions as to when levies are to be issued, the issue of substituted levies, the payment of levies and interest on unpaid levies. The Residuary Body for Wales (Levies) Regulations 1995 (SI 1995 2306) are disapplied in respect of any financial year beginning on or after April 1, 1997.

4137. Residuary bodies–Wales–transfer of assets

RESIDUARY BODY FOR WALES (PENLAN ROAD OFFICES CARMARTHEN) ORDER 1996, SI 1996 2819; made under the Local Government Act 1994 s.54, s.63. In force: December 11, 1996; £1.10.

The Order makes provision for the transfer of land, known as Penlan Road Offices, Brewery Road, Carmarthen, and associated rights and liabilities from the Residuary Body for Wales to Carmarthenshire CC.

4138. Road traffic

LOCAL AUTHORITIES (GOODS AND SERVICES) (PUBLIC BODIES) (TRUNK ROADS) (NO.2) ORDER 1996, SI 1996 1814; made under the Local Authorities (Goods and Services) Act 1970 s.1. In force: August 7, 1996; £1.10.

This Order designates the Secretary of State for Transport and the Secretary of State for Wales under the Local Authorities (Goods and Services) Act 1970. The effect of the designation is to allow local highway authorities to provide goods and services, in connection with trunk roads and trunk road connected land, to either Secretary of State.

4139. Social services–grants–reorganisation

LOCAL GOVERNMENT CHANGES FOR ENGLAND (FINANCE - SOCIAL SERVICES GRANTS) REGULATIONS 1996, SI 1996 691; made under the Local Government Act 1992 s.19. In force: April 1, 1996; £0.65.

The Local Government Act 1992 Part II makes provision for Local Government changes in England. The Local Government Commission for England makes recommendations to the Secretary of State for the Environment about such changes and where recommendations for change are made the Secretary of State may make an order giving effect to those recommendations. These Regulations provide for the transfer of functions and liabilities concerning certain social services grants or other payments, upon the dissolution of a local authority by such an Order. The grants or other payments concerned are those payable under the Health Services and Public Health Act 1968, the Local Government Grants (Social Need) Act 1969, The Local Authority Social Services Act 1970, the Children Act 1989 and the Child Care Act 1980.

4140. Statutory duty–breach–grant of planning permission–whether grant established duty

[Environmental Protection Act 1990; Town and Country Planning Act 1971; Town and Country Planning Act 1980.]

L claimed compensation for breach of statutory duty and for negligence from T in relation to the exercise of planning and environmental functions. B carried on business as a toy factory, adjacent to L's premises from which they traded as a restaurant. L alleged that their trade and health were damaged due to emission of chemicals from B's premises, and claimed damages for loss of profit for the business, and for personal injuries in respect of their children. Subsequently they alleged that T was liable in damages for exercising or failing to exercise its functions under the Town and Country Planning Act 1971 and the Town and Country Planning Act 1980, and under the Environmental Protection Act 1990. T issued an application to strike out P's claim as disclosing no reasonable cause of action.

Held, that a grant of planning permission to B did not establish a duty of care in relation to his use of that permission, and that it would not be just or reasonable to impose such a duty on a local authority. Similarly, the court held that it was not just or reasonable to impose a duty of care on the council as environmental authority, because a variety of remedies were available to L. L's claims against T were struck out as disclosing no cause of action, *M v. Newham LBC: X (Minors) v. Bedfordshire CC* [1994] C.L.Y. 4296.

LAM v. BRENNAN AND TORBAY BC, January 24, 1996, Collins, J., Court not stated. [*Ex rel.* Veitch Penny, Solicitors].

4141. Street trading–licensing–local authorities powers and duties–no proof that legislation brought into force–conviction unlawful

[London Local Authorities Act 1990 s.22, s.38.]

C appealed by way of case stated against five convictions of unlicensed street trading contrary to the London Local Authorities Act 1990 s.38(1)(a). C contended that, as the procedural steps necessary to bring Part III of the 1990 Act into force in WCC's area had not been advertised as required by s.22 of the Act, no street trading offence could be committed.

Held, allowing the appeal and remitting the matter for reconsideration, that unless the court had been satisfied that Part III had been properly brought into force by WCC, C could not be convicted of an offence under the statute. The stipendiary magistrate had erred in inferring that the 1990 Act had been brought into force in the absence of its advertised adoption in the prescribed manner. The fact that WCC was listed as a "participating council" in Sch.1 to the Act, and that its trading standards officers had purportedly been discharging their functions under it, did not entitle the stipendiary magistrate to infer the 1990 Act had been validly adopted by WCC in the absence of effective and advertised adoption.

COOPER v. WESTMINSTER CITY COUNCIL, Trans. Ref: CO 1328/96, July 19, 1996, Smith, J., QBD.

4142. Street trading–London–whether exposing goods for sale on pavement outside shop amounted to street trading–statutory interpretation

[London Local Authorities Act 1990 s.21, s.38; Local Government (Miscellaneous Provisions) Act 1982.]

W appealed by way of case stated against the dismissal by a stipendiary magistrate of charges against R for unlicensed street trading outside his shop contrary to the London Local Authorities Act 1990 s.38(1).

Held, allowing the appeal, that whereas exposing goods for sale outside a shop which were to be paid for inside the shop was specifically excluded from the definition of "street trading" under the Local Government (Miscellaneous Provisions) Act 1982, applicable to areas outside London, omission in the 1990 Act showed that Parliament intended it to be included in London. Section 21 of the 1990 Act contained a dichotomy between "selling" or "exposing" or "offering for sale". As a result, exposing goods for gain or reward amounted to street trading and this was clearly an activity in which R had been engaged.

WANDSWORTH LBC v. ROSENTHAL (1996) 160 J.P. Rep. 734, Sir Iain Glidewell, QBD.

4143. Street trading–pedlars–requirment to sell whilst travelling

E appealed by way of case stated against three convictions of unlicensed street trading. E contended that he moved his barrow around as he sold hot dogs from it. Therefore, he argued, he was acting as a pedlar and was covered by a valid pedlar's certificate.

Held, dismissing the appeal, that the judge was correct to find that E travelled around in order to sell his wares. He did not trade as he travelled, which was required of a pedlar, but moved to a position and waited for customers to come to him, *Watson v. Malloy* [1988] 1 W.L.R. 1026, [1989] C.L.Y. 2343 followed.

R. v. WESTMINSTER CITY COUNCIL, *ex p.* ELMASOGLU [1996] C.O.D. 357, Forbes, J., QBD.

4144. Street trading–pedlars–valid certificate–trading from pitch in street–prohibition on street trading applied

[Pedlars Act 1871 s.3; Local Government (Miscellaneous Provisions) Act 1982 Sch.4.]

S appealed by way of case stated against W's acquittal of two offences of trading in a prohibited street contrary to the Local Government (Miscellaneous Provisions)

Act 1982 Sch.4 para.10(1). The magistrates had found that when W sold wrapping paper from a shopping bag in a prohibited street he was not street trading as he was in possession of a valid pedlar's certificate. Trading as a pedlar amounted to an exception under Sch.4 para.2(2) of the 1982 Act.

Held, allowing the appeal, that W stood in one place for a significant period of time and exhorted those passing to buy his goods. Acting in such a way did not amount to acting as a pedlar within the Pedlars Act 1871 s.3 and did not, therefore, come within the proviso in Sch.4 para.2(1) of the 1982 Act. W was consequently subject to the prohibition on street trading contained in Sch.4 para.10(1) of the Act, *Watson v. Malloy* [1988] 1 W.L.R. 1026, [1989] C.L.Y. 2343, *Normand v. Alexander* [1994] S.L.T. 274, [1993] C.L.Y. 5530 considered.

STEVENAGE BC v. WRIGHT (1997) 161 J.P. Rep. 13, Leggatt, L.J., QBD.

4145. Street trading–use of wheeled trolley–prohibited area–pedlar's certificate–whether use of trolley meant acting as street trader rather than pedlar

[Local Government (Miscellaneous Provisions) Act 1982 s.3, Sch.4; Pedlars Act 1871 s.3.]

S appealed by way of case stated against a decision of the justices whereby they acquitted V of engaging in street trading in a prohibited street contrary to the Local Government (Miscellaneous Provisions) Act 1982 s.3 and para.10(1)(a) Sch.4. V had contended that, notwithstanding the fact that he sold his goods from a wheeled trolley, he was not a street trader but rather a pedlar and this had a defence under para.1(2)(a) Sch.4 of the Act.

Held, dismissing the appeal, that the term "pedlar" in the Pedlars Act 1871 s.3 was not completely defined. The question here was whether, as a matter of law, a person was taken out of the definition if he used an appendage, such as a trolley, for carrying his goods. In the court's judgment, while it was plain not only that a pedlar must be a pedestrian but also that the goods he sold must be small goods, there was nothing in s.3, nor in the ordinary meaning of the term "pedlar", to exclude a person who could assist the transport of his goods. Ultimately it would be a matter of fact for the justices to decide in each case whether the apparatus was of such a scale to take the defendant out of the definition of pedlar. In the present case, there was no basis for holding that the justices had not been perfectly entitled to acquit V, *Watson v. Malloy* [1988] 1 W.L.R. 1026, [1989] C.L.Y. 2343 considered.

SHEPWAY DC v. VINCENT [1994] C.O.D. 451, Mann, L.J., QBD.

4146. Supply of services–local authorities

LOCAL AUTHORITIES (GOODS AND SERVICES) (PUBLIC BODIES) (THE JULIE ROSE STADIUM) ORDER 1996, SI 1996 2534; made under the Local Goods and Services Act 1970 s.1. In force: November 1, 1996; £0.65.

This Order designates the Julie Rose Stadium under the Local Authorities (Goods and Services) Act 1970 thereby allowing local authorities to provide goods and services to that body.

4147. Supply of services–local authorities–sport facilities

LOCAL AUTHORITIES (GOODS AND SERVICES) (PUBLIC BODIES) (SPORTS COUNCILS) ORDER 1996, SI 1996 3092; made under the Local Authorities (Goods and Services) Act 1970 s.1. In force: January 1, 1997; £0.65.

This Order designates the English Sports Council, the United Kingdom Sports Council and the Scottish Sports Council as public bodies under the Local Authorities (Goods and Services) Act 1970. This enables local authorities to supply certain goods and services to the Councils.

4148. Supply of services–trunk roads

LOCAL AUTHORITIES (GOODS AND SERVICES) (PUBLIC BODIES) (TRUNK ROADS) ORDER 1996, SI 1996 342; made under the Local Authorities (Goods and Services) Act 1970 s.1. In force: March 14, 1996; £1.10.

This Order designates the Secretary of State for Transport, the Secretary of State for Wales and a DBFO contractor under the Local Authorities (Goods and Services) Act 1970. The effect of the designation is to allow local highway authorities to provide certain services in connection with trunk roads and trunk road connected land to DBFO contractors; the Secretary of State for Transport and the Secretary of State for Wales.

4149. Swap agreements–local authority interest rate swap agreements ultra vires and void–equitable jurisdiction to award compound interest or simple interest only

I appealed against the Court of Appeal's award of compound interest on repayments which I was obliged to make to W in respect of an invalid swap agreement into which the parties had entered. Swap agreements involving local authorities were declared ultra vires and void in *Hazell v. Hammersmith and Fulham LBC* [1992] 2 A.C. 1, [1991] C.L.Y. 2420. I contended that simple interest only, not compound interest, was payable on the repayments.

Held, allowing the appeal, that the court had jurisdiction to award compound rather than simple interest only if the defendant was a fiduciary, *Burdick v. Garrick* (1870) L.R. 5 Ch. App. 233, *Wallersteiner v. Moir (No.2)* [1975] Q.B. 373, [1975] C.L.Y. 2602 applied. I did not owe a fiduciary duty to the bank to account for profits from the invalid swap agreement when the authority did not know, at the time when payment was received, that the agreement was ultra vires and void. To find I personally liable as a trustee would necessarily entail creating an equitable proprietary interest in the moneys received, which would have undesirable implications for third party rights in other cases. Commercial transactions would be impeded by uncertainty as to ownership of assets. Claims for moneys had and received were not based on implied contract, *Sinclair v. Brougham* [1914] A.C. 398 overruled. Despite the bank's strong moral claims, the courts should not develop principles that conferred new powers to award compound interest in circumstances where Parliament, having considered the issue, had made clear that there was no jurisdiction to award compound interest. Simple interest only could be awarded on repayment in respect of ultra vires swap agreements.

WESTDEUTSCHE LANDESBANK GIROZENTRALE v. ISLINGTON LBC [1996] A.C. 669, Lord Browne-Wilkinson, HL.

4150. Teachers–compensation for redundancy

LOCAL GOVERNMENT REORGANISATION (COMPENSATION FOR REDUNDANCY OR LOSS OF REMUNERATION) (EDUCATION) REGULATIONS 1996, SI 1996 1240; made under the Superannuation Act 1972 s.24. In force: June 1, 1996; £2.80.

Provision is made by these Regulations for the payment of compensation to certain teachers, administrative and support staff employed by the local education authority who have been adversely affected by local government reorganisation. Provision is made for a lump sum payment to those who have been made redundant in the interests of efficiency or by certain conditions having been satisfied by their employer. Provision is also made for payment of compensation to those suffering a loss or reduction of remuneration.

4151. Tenders–award of public service contracts–housing management contracts–whether restriction of tenders was unlawful

[Housing Act 1985 s.27; Council Directive 92/50 on coordination of procedures for the award of public service contracts Art.30, Art.32, Art.36; Public Service Contracts Regulations 1993.]

H applied for judicial review of the Secretary of State's refusal to approve its proposals, under the Housing Act 1985 s.27, that housing management contracts should be awarded to UK housing associations capable of later accepting transfer of ownership of the properties managed. The Secretary of State's ground for refusal was, inter alia, that H's actions were contrary to Council Directive 92/50 and the Public Service Contracts Regulations 1993 in excluding those organisations capable of providing housing management services but not able, under UK law, to fulfil H's intentions in relation to voluntary transfers. H argued that the Secretary of State had failed to appreciate the ambit of Art.30 and Art.32 of the Directive. It was further argued that Art.36(1)(2) allowed the contract to be awarded to the "most economically advantageous tender", which, according to H, was one from a tenderer who could fulfil H's long term intentions.

Held, refusing the application, that the Secretary of State had been entitled to refuse approval. H had not correctly construed the Directive, Art.30 and Art 32 of which were concerned with the performance of the public service contract, in this case the provision of housing management. Article 36 did not allow fresh selection criteria to be introduced. Consideration of the suitability of tenderers and the award of the contracts were two different operations, *Gebroeders Beentjes BV v. Netherlands* [1990] 1 C.M.L.R. 287, [1991] C.L.Y. 3987 considered. The Secretary of State was right to conclude that the practical effect of H's proposal would be to introduce a restriction which was unlawful in terms of the provisions of Directive 92/50.

R. v. SECRETARY OF STATE FOR THE ENVIRONMENT, *ex p.* HARROW LBC [1996] E.G.C.S. 2, Judge, J., QBD.

4152. Travellers–exercise of statutory powers–whether local authorities made proper inquiries and followed proper procedure when issuing removal directions–whether removal order effective to prevent further trespass after date of issue

[Criminal Justice and Public Order Act 1994 s.77, s.78, s.79.]

In pursuance of their duties under the Criminal Justice and Public Order Act 1994 s.77, s.78 and s.79 the local authorities gave removal directions to travellers who had camped unlawfully and then obtained from the justices removal orders against those who had not left. The complaint was that the removal directions were not validly given because the authorities failed to give proper consideration to their duties in relation to children's welfare, housing and health. The court was required to determine whether the local authorities had taken into account the correct criteria at the correct stage, whether defects could be cured by due consideration at a later stage and whether a removal direction affected persons who arrived on the land after it was given.

Held, that (1) at the initial stage of deciding whether or not to give a removal direction, and if so to whom, the local authority was required to consider the relationship of its proposed action to statutory and humanitarian considerations and to make its decision accordingly. The dispute was whether the inquiries made by the authorities were too little, too late or both; (2) by the date of the direction, Lincolnshire had made no meaningful inquiries into the needs of the persons to whom the intended direction would apply; (3) between that date and the application for the order it did discharge its obligations; (4) Wealden did make inquiries, but unlike Lincolnshire, only after acquiring a removal order, and (5) the effect of a removal direction under s.77 of the 1994 Act did not apply to a locality but could only apply to persons who were on the land at the time when the direction was made.

R. v. LINCOLNSHIRE CC, *ex p.* ATKINSON; SUB NOM. R. v. WEALDEN DC, *ex p.* WALES; R. v. WEALDEN DC, *ex p.* STRATFORD (1996) 8 Admin. L.R. 529, Sedley, J., QBD.

4153. Waste land–information

LOCAL GOVERNMENT (PUBLICATION OF INFORMATION ABOUT UNUSED AND UNDERUSED LAND) (ENGLAND) (REVOCATION) REGULATIONS 1996, SI 1996 585; made under the Local Government, Planning and Land Act 1980 s.3. In force: April 3, 1996; £0.65.

These Regulations revoke the Local Government (Publication of Information about Unused and Underused Land) (England) Regulations 1992 (SI 1992 73), which required local authorities to publish the information specified in the Code of Recommended Practice for the Publication of Information about Unused and Underused Land owned by the Secretary of State for the Environment under the Local Government Planning and Land Act 1980 s.2.

4154. Welsh language–names

LOCAL GOVERNMENT (WALES) (ALTERNATIVE COMMUNITY NAMES) (PRESCRIBED STEPS) REGULATIONS 1996, SI 1996 179; made under the Local Government Act 1972 s.27, s.270. In force: April 1, 1996; £0.65.

These Regulations prescribe the steps to be taken by the principal council of a community to give it a name in the other language where it has been given a name in English or Welsh only, provided that there is a generally accepted alternative form of that name in that language. The council within whose area such a community lies is required to take these steps before October 1, 1997.

4155. Articles

A new paradigm *(Clive Grace)*: L.G.C. 1996, May 24, Supp Law, 6-7. (Changed relationship between central and local government, evolving nature of local authorities' corporate status in face of structural changes including CCT and need for revised legal and constitutional role).

Allerdale and Waltham Forest: their impact on PFI and local authorities *(Jason Fox)*: C.L. 1996, 1 (9), 45-46. (Regulations that have been made relaxing rules on local authority interests in companies and their transactions with private sector in order to encourage them to consider Private Finance Initiative and effect of ultra vires cases).

Compulsory competitive tendering for white collar services *(John Bennett* and *Stephen Cirell)*: P.P.L.R. 1996, 3, 67-76. (Extension of CCT to local authority white collar activities, legal framework of regime, effect on local government finance procedures and outcome of first round).

Compulsory competitive tendering: regulation and the tender process *(Stephen Cirell* and *John Bennett)*: P.L.C. 1996, 7(6), 17-23. (Background to CCT regime, legislative framework and procedure).

Council watchdog *(Bill Church)*: L.S.G. 1996, 93(23), 25. (Role and statutory reporting responsibilities of local government monitoring officers).

Do not dismiss dismissals *(Alan Fowler)*: L.G.C. 1996, Apr(12), 14-15. (Redundancy consultation requirements in local government context).

End of the legal hegemony *(Nicky Willmore)*: L.G.C. Law & Admin. 1996, 4(Oct), 8-9. (Views of six local government legal experts on changing role of council lawyer).

Inspired direction *(Richard Clayton)*: L.G.C. Law & Admin 1996, 3(Sep), 6-7. (How changing nature of central and local government relationship has generated dramatic growth of judicial review cases, fuelled also by individuals gaining new rights and by fragmentation of local government functions).

Judicial use–a year in judgment *(Charles Cross)*: L.G.C. 1996, Jan 19, 16-17. (Review of 1995 cases on local authorities' statutory duties).

Little love lost at House of Lords: L.G.C.1996, Jul 5,16-17. (HL Select Committee on relations between central and local government heard evidence from Local Government Commissioners, academics and officers' associations calling on central government to allow councils more freedom).

Local government law: an (ex) practitioner's perspective *(Clive Grace)*: L.A.L. 1996, 1, 6-8. (Judicial and Government decisions curbing local authority powers during 1980's and possible end to that era).

New local authority capital finance rules *(David Ryland)*: E.G. 1996, 9616, 108-109. (Amended rules in force March 30, 1996 to relieve restrictions on local authority capital finance and facilitate Private Finance Initiative).

Obligations and liabilities *(Charles Cross)*: L.G.C. 1996, July 12, Supp Law, 10-11. (Councils' liability for breach of statutory duty, criteria for determining existence of duty, public policy grounds for exemption in some circumstances and public and personal liabilities for misconduct in public office).

Public authorities and the duty of care *(Douglas Brodie)*: Jur. Rev. 1996, 2, 127-143. (Difficulties in recovering damages for negligence or breach of statutory duty by local authorities).

Public authorities' powers *(John Sissons* and *Andrew Lidbetter)*: C.L. 1996, 1 (9), 43-44. (Principles on local authorities powers arising out of cases on whether they could set up companies and give guarantees and whether ultra vires acts are void or voidable).

Structural "solutions" for local government: an exercise in chasing shadows? *(David Wilson)*: Parl. Aff. 1996, 49(3), 441-454. (Whether any underlying rationale for continual emphasis on structural change of local government and whether tackling resultant fragmentation and lack of accountability is more important).

The laws of good practice *(David Carter)*: L.G.C. 1996, Apr 19, Supp CCT 20-21. (Advice for local authority legal departments in preparing for competitive tendering. Includes known law firms who have won contracts).

The local authority can't afford it–is lack of resources a legal defence to failure to carry out a statutory duty? *(Alec Samuels)*: J.P. 1996, 160(37), 758-760.

The reasonable limits of local authority powers *(Robert Carnwath)*: P.L. 1996, Sum, 244-265. (Role of courts in restraining powers of local government and development of Wednesbury principles regarding reasonableness in administrative decision making).

Transactions with public bodies: P.L.C. 1996, 7 (6), 6. (Financial Law Panel paper on establishing independent tribunal to assess validity of proposed financial transactions involving local authorities).

4156. Books

Aisbett, Alan; Harrison, Alan; Grace, Clive–Local Government Precedents and Practice. Unbound/looseleaf: £175.00. ISBN 0-7520-0100-0. FT Law & Tax.

Monkkonen, Eric H.–The Local State. Stanford Series in the New Political History. Hardback: £30.00. ISBN 0-8047-2412-1. Stanford University Press (CUP).

MEDIA

4157. Broadcasting–applications for Channel 5 licence–funding proposals–whether Independent Television Commission was entitled to inquire into financial status of applicant after date of application–financial sustainability of applicant

[Broadcasting Act 1990 s.15, s.28.]

VT and two other television companies applied for judicial review of ITC's decision to award the licence for Channel 5 to Channel 5 Broadcasting, C5B. The business plan contained in C5B's application for the licence showed a funding commitment from their shareholders of £206 million, but before the licence was granted ITC requested further clarification of a bank debt facility and

C5B then committed their shareholders to a further £100 million finance which satisfied ITC's requirements that £307 million should be available. The applicants argued that C5B had failed to provide sufficient information as to funding by the application date and that therefore the application should have been rejected. It was further argued that ITC's statutory power was limited by the terms of the invitation to apply and by the need to act in the interests of fairness between the applicants.

Held, dismissing the applications, that ITC, obliged under the Broadcasting Act 1990 s.28 to secure provision of Channel 5, was entitled to accept C5B's funding proposals and be satisfied that they would be implemented by the date the licence would be granted. Furthermore, under the Broadcasting Act 1990 s.15(4) ITC could require further financial information after the applications were received and in answering their request C5B had not introduced any new material inconsistent with the construction of s.15(4). The questions of credit worthiness and commitment were inherent in considering the issue of financial sustainability, and as they were liable to change, the time of inquiry could not be limited to the date of application for the licence. There was no procedural unfairness in requesting further information from one applicant if required but not from the others.

R. v. INDEPENDENT TELEVISION COMMISSION, *ex p.* VIRGIN TELEVISION LTD [1996] E.M.L.R. 318, Henry, L.J., QBD.

4158. Broadcasting–Channel 3 transmission–distribution costs

BROADCASTING (CHANNEL 3 TRANSMISSION AND SHARED DISTRIBUTION COSTS) ORDER 1996, SI 1996 3067; made under the Broadcasting Act 1990 s.66. In force: December 27, 1996; £0.65.

This Order extends by six years the period during which all Channel 3 services must be broadcast by a single person, which is also that during which all Channel 3 licensees must share the distribution costs of those services in such manner as may be approved by the Secretary of State.

4159. Broadcasting–Channel 4–excess revenues

CHANNEL 4 (APPLICATION OF EXCESS REVENUES) ORDER 1996, SI 1996 3093; made under the Broadcasting Act 1990 s.27. In force: December 11, 1996; £0.65.

This Order reduces from 50 per cent to nil the percentage of the excess revenue of the Channel Four Television Corporation which must be carried to the credit of a reserve fund of the Corporation under the Broadcasting Act 1990 s.27(3).

4160. Broadcasting–digital technology

INDEPENDENT ANALOGUE BROADCASTERS (RESERVATION OF DIGITAL CAPACITY) ORDER 1996, SI 1996 2760; made under the Broadcasting Act 1990 s.200; and the Broadcasting Act 1996 s.28. In force: November 20, 1996; £1.55.

This Order disapplies, or modifies the application of, certain provisions of the Broadcasting Act 1996 in relation to the multiplex licences to be granted in respect of the frequencies on which capacity is reserved for the broadcasting of Channel 3, Channel 4, Channel 5 and S4C in digital form.

4161. Broadcasting–licences–Gaelic language

MULTIPLEX LICENCE (BROADCASTING OF PROGRAMMES IN GAELIC) ORDER 1996, SI 1996 2758; made under the Broadcasting Act 1996 s.32. In force: November 20, 1996; £0.65.

The Broadcasting Act 1996 Part I provides for licensing digital television programme services and, in particular, for licensing the provision of "multiplex services", by means of which such programme services are broadcast. This Order requires the Independent Television Commission to include in the multiplex licence under which the Channel 5 and S4C Digital are to be broadcast a condition requiring the holder to broadcast at least 30 minutes of Gaelic programming every day in Scotland during peak evening viewing time. It also requires the licence holder to broadcast at least 30 hours of Gaelic programmes per year supplied by the BBC and, currently, Scottish Television and Grampian Television.

4162. Broadcasting–licensing

BROADCASTING (PERCENTAGE OF TELEVISION MULTIPLEX REVENUE) ORDER 1996, SI 1996 2759; made under the Broadcasting Act 1996 s.13. In force: November 20, 1996; £0.65.

This Order provides that no percentage of multiplex revenue will be payable by the holder of a multiplex licence granted by the Independent Television Commission pursuant to any notice published by them during the period for which this Order remains in force.

4163. Broadcasting–prescribed countries

BROADCASTING (PRESCRIBED COUNTRIES) ORDER 1996, SI 1996 904; made under the Broadcasting Act 1990 s.43. In force: April 15, 1996; £0.65.

The Broadcasting Act 1990 describes one type of television programme service under that Act as a non-domestic satellite service. Part of the definition of this service is that it consists in the transmission of television programmes by satellite for general reception in the United Kingdom or in any prescribed country (or both) where the programmes are transmitted from a place which is either in the United Kingdom or is neither in the United Kingdom nor in any prescribed country. This Order revokes the Broadcasting (Prescribed Countries) Order 1994 (SI 1994 454) (which prescribed most European countries) and instead specifies as prescribed countries every country of the world except the United Kingdom.

4164. Broadcasting–satellite television services–broadcasting controls–jurisdiction–failure to fulfil obligations under Council Directive 89/552–European Union

[Council Directive 89/552 on the coordination of certain provisions concerning the pursuit of television broadcasting activities Art.2; Broadcasting Act 1990 s.43.]

The CEC applied to the ECJ for a declaration that the UK had failed to implement correctly Council Directive 89/552 by applying different regimes to domestic and non-domestic satellite services under the Broadcasting Act 1990 s.43 and by exercising control over broadcasters falling under the jurisdiction of another Member State. The CEC alleged that, in determining which broadcasters fell within UK jurisdiction, s.43 applied incorrect criteria since it provided that the jurisdiction of a Member State was determined by the territory from which broadcasts were transmitted, instead of the Member State in which the broadcaster was established. The UK argued that the first part of Art.2(1) of the Directive referred to terrestrial broadcasting and the second to satellite broadcasting. The UK also contended that a broadcaster could be established in more than one Member State and thus would be subject to the jurisdiction of two countries.

Held, that (1) the word "jurisdiction" was to be given the same meaning throughout Art.2(1) so that if no Member State had jurisdiction under the first part of Art.2(1), a Member State broadcasting via a satellite up-link situated in another Member State could assert the same jurisdiction over television broadcasters using that link; (2) Member States could avoid the problem of double control where broadcasters were established in more than one country by either concluding international agreements or interpreting establishment as meaning the place in which broadcasting activities were centred and programming policy decisions made; (3) s.43 applied irrelevant criteria in that it referred to reception of broadcasts and also failed to ensure that broadcasters from non-member countries using a frequency allocated in the UK complied with the law applicable to domestic broadcasts. In distinguishing between domestic and non-domestic services, s.43 made the latter subject to a less stringent regime contrary to Art.2(1) and (4) the UK also failed to fulfil its obligation under Art.2 by exercising control over the licensing of non-domestic satellite services falling under the jurisdiction of other Member States.

COMMISSION OF THE EUROPEAN COMMUNITIES v. UNITED KINGDOM (C222/94) [1997] E.M.L.R. 1, GC Rodriguez Iglesias (President), ECJ.

4165. Broadcasting–statement on involvement by IRA in political violence–whether supported, solicited or invited support for IRA–subtitles substituted for voice–judicial review

M applied for judicial review of the respondent's decision to substitute subtitles for her voice in discussion programmes broadcast in September 1992. The Secretary of State had issued a directive to the BBC requiring it to refrain from broadcasting any words spoken by a person representing a proscribed organisation (including the IRA) or where the words "support or solicit or invite the support for such an organisation". In the course of the programme M stated, inter alia, that the involvement of the IRA in political violence was understandable. The BBC concluded that her words supported or solicited or invited support for the IRA and therefore subtitles were substituted. M argued that her words distinguished between justifying violence and understanding how it could arise.

Held, refusing the application, that (1) the words used by M were capable of falling within the definition of "support or solicit or invite support" regardless of M's intention in speaking them. It was strongly arguable that in many of its activities the BBC would not be susceptible to judicial review; (2) M's words did not support, solicit or invite support for the IRA but, even if the BBC was technically guilty of an error of law, the decision was not irrational nor procedurally improper. The error was well within the field of permissible judgment and, although of considerable importance to M, was of no general or public importance.

R. v. BBC, *ex p.* MCALISKEY [1994] C.O.D. 498, Staughton, L.J., QBD.

4166. Broadcasting Act 1996 (c.55)

An Act to make new provision about the broadcasting in digital form of television and sound programme services and the broadcasting in that form on television or radio frequencies of other services; to amend the Broadcasting Act 1990; to make provision about rights to televise sporting or other events of national interest; to amend in other respects the law relating to the provision of television and sound programme services; to provide for the establishment and functions of a Broadcasting Standards Commission and for the dissolution of the Broadcasting Complaints Commission and the Broadcasting Standards Council; and to make provision for the transfer to other persons of property, rights and liabilities of the British Broadcasting Corporation relating to their transmission network.

This Act received Royal Assent on July 24, 1996.

4167. Broadcasting Act 1996–Commencement No.1 and Transitional Provisions Order

BROADCASTING ACT 1996 (COMMENCEMENT NO.1 AND TRANSITIONAL PROVISIONS) ORDER 1996, SI 1996 2120 (C.49); made under the Broadcasting Act 1996 s.149. In force: bringing into force various provisions of the Act on October 8, 1996, October 1, 1996 and November 1, 1996; £1.10.

This Order brings into force immediately those provisions of the substituted Part IV of Schedule 2 to the Broadcasting Act 1990 which empower the Independent Television Commission and the Radio Authority to determine whether certain prospective alliances between broadcasting licence holders or service providers and newspaper proprietors could be expected to operate against the public interest, and those provisions of the Broadcasting Act 1996 which require the Independent Television Commission to draw up a code relating to the televising of listed events. Further provisions of the Broadcasting Act 1996 are brought into force on October 1, 1996 and November 1, 1996.

4168. Broadcasting Complaints Commission–privacy–jurisdiction to hear complaint before programme broadcast–statutory interpretation

[Broadcasting Act 1990 s.143.]

The application for judicial review was made by two brothers who lived on a private island and had refused landing permission to the BBC. After a journalist landed on the island, intent on interviewing them, a complaint was made to the Broadcasting Complaints Commission which held the view that it had no power to consider a complaint before the programme to which it related had been broadcast.

Held, refusing the application, that the Broadcasting Act 1990 s.143 clearly restricted the jurisdiction of the Broadcasting Complaints Commission so that it could only adjudicate upon complaints of unfair treatment or invasion of privacy if the material concerned was included in a programme which had already been broadcast.

R. v. BROADCASTING COMPLAINTS COMMISSION, *ex p.* BARCLAY [1997] E.M.L.R. 62, Sedley, J., QBD.

4169. Films–cinematic co-production agreements–additional countries

EUROPEAN CONVENTION ON CINEMATOGRAPHIC CO-PRODUCTION (AMENDMENT) ORDER 1996, SI 1996 2600; made under the Films Act 1985 Sch.1 para.4. In force: November 5, 1996; £0.65.

The European Convention on Cinematographic Co-production Order 1994 (SI 1994 1065) provides that films made in accordance with the European Convention on Cinematographic Co-production are to be treated as British films for the purposes of the Films Act 1985 Sch.1. For the Convention to apply where there are only two co-producers one must be established in the United Kingdom and the other in one of the countries set out in the Schedule to the 1994 Order. For the Convention to apply where there are three or more co-producers one must be established in the United Kingdom and at least two others in different countries set out in the Schedule to the 1994 Order. This Order amends the Schedule to the 1994 Order by adding Luxembourg to the countries set out therein.

4170. Films–cinematic co-production agreements–additional countries

EUROPEAN CONVENTION ON CINEMATOGRAPHIC CO-PRODUCTION (AMENDMENT) (NO.2) ORDER 1996, SI 1996 3169; made under the Films Act 1985 Sch.1 para.4. In force: February 2, 1997; £0.65.

The European Convention on Cinematographic Co-production Order 1994 (SI 1994 1065) provides that films made in accordance with the European Convention on Cinematographic Co-production are to be treated as British films for the purposes of the Films Act 1985 Sch.1. This Order amends the Schedule to the 1994 Order by adding Spain and Hungary to the countries set out therein.

4171. Press Complaints Commission–privacy–breach of code of practice–judicial review of PCC decision inappropriate

S, a convicted murderer being treated in a special hospital, applied for leave to move for judicial review of a decision by the Press Complaints Commission (PCC) not to censure a photograph of him in the hospital taken using a long lens camera, and published alongside a newspaper article on the appropriate form of treatment for those convicted of serious offences. Whilst accepting that the article could be justified, S complained that publishing the photograph without consent amounted to breaches of cl.4 of the PCC's Code of Practice (1993) on privacy, which states that such photographs are generally unacceptable unless in the public interest, and also of cl.6 and cl.8, relating to hospital premises and harassment respectively.

Held, dismissing the application, that (1) it was arguable that the PCC was a body which could be subject to judicial review, but that would not be determined on an application for leave, and (2) the article itself was justified because there was a public interest in seeing how criminals were treated, and the publication of the photograph alongside the article was not a serious breach of the code, nor would it affect S any more than if a previously taken photograph had been used. Any jurisdiction which the court had over the PCC should be reserved for clear breaches of the code, and not merely matters of technical interpretation.

R. v. PRESS COMPLAINTS COMMISSION, *ex p.* STEWART-BRADY; SUB NOM. STEWART-BRADY, ex p., *The Times*, November 22, 1996, Lord Woolf, M.R., CA.

4172. Programmes–contracting out

CONTRACTING OUT (FUNCTIONS RELATING TO WIRELESS TELEGRAPHY) ORDER 1996, SI 1996 2290; made under the Deregulation and Contracting Out Act 1994 s.69. In force: September 4, 1996; £0.65.

This Order makes provision to enable the Secretary of State to authorise another person, or that person's employees, to exercise the Secretary of State's functions under the Wireless Telegraphy Act 1949 s.1 (c.54) insofar as they relate to programme making. Programme making is defined in Art.(1) of the Order to include the making of a programme for broadcast, the making of a film, presentation, advertisement or audio or video tape, and the staging or performance of an entertainment, sporting or other public event. Radio may be used in programme making in a variety of ways, for example: to allow directors to communicate with performers and technicians; to transmit programme material at outside broadcast locations to mobile control rooms, for recording or onward routing to a studio centre; to link mobile cameras (for example those used in news gathering) to fixed reception points for onward routing; and for radio microphones, which are extensively used in broadcasting and in film production and entertainment generally.

4173. Registration–television dealers–deregulation

DEREGULATION (WIRELESS TELEGRAPHY) ORDER 1996, SI 1996 1864; made under the Deregulation and Contracting Out Act 1994 s.1. In force: August 16, 1996; £1.10.

This Order amends the Wireless Telegraphy Act 1949 with the effect that television dealers will no longer be required to have a licence for demonstrating, testing or repairing receivers. It also repeals the Wireless Telegraphy Act 1967 s.1 with a consequential amendment of s.2 with the effect that television dealers will no longer be required to register with the BBC.

4174. Satellites–broadcasting

FOREIGN SATELLITE SERVICE PROSCRIPTION ORDER 1996, SI 1996 2557; made under the Broadcasting Act 1990 s.177. In force: October 31, 1996; £0.65.

The Broadcasting Act 1990 s.177 empowers the Secretary of State to make orders proscribing unacceptable foreign satellite services for the purposes of s.178. This Order proscribes the foreign satellite service known as Rendez-Vous.

4175. Television–industrial property rights

ADVANCED TELEVISION SERVICES (INDUSTRIAL PROPERTY RIGHTS) REGULATIONS 1996, SI 1996 2185; made under the European Communities Act 1972 s.2. In force: August 23, 1996; £1.10.

These Regulations make provision in respect of licensing industrial property rights to conditional access products and systems for digital television services.

They implement in the United Kingdom Art.4 (d) of Directive 95/47 of the European Parliament and of the Council on the use of standards for the transmission of television signals (the Advanced Television Services Directive), as it applies to the holders of such rights.

4176. Television–licences–fees

WIRELESS TELEGRAPHY (TELEVISION LICENCE FEES) (AMENDMENT) REGULATIONS 1996, SI 1996 379; made under the Wireless Act 1949 s.2; the Wireless Telegraphy (Channel Islands) Order 1952; and the Wireless Telegraphy (Isle of Man) Order 1952. In force: April 1, 1996; £1.10.

These Regulations increase the television licence fees from £28.50 to £30.00 for monochrome and from £86.50 to £89.50 for colour. In addition the issue fee for Standard Instalment Licences is increased to £44.76 with instalments increased to £22.37, the issue fee for the Premium Instalment License is increased to £23.64 with instalments increased to £23.62 and amendments made in relation to the Budget Instalment Licence.

4177. Television–licences–fees

WIRELESS TELEGRAPHY (TELEVISION LICENCE FEES) (AMENDMENT) (NO.2) REGULATIONS 1996, SI 1996 1772; made under the Wireless Telegraphy Act 1949 s.2. In force: August 1, 1996; £0.65.

These Regulations make provision for an additional type of colour television licence for which fees are payable by instalments. The easy entry licence will only be available to those who are in receipt of an income related state benefit. Provision is made for the payment of an issue fee and of weekly instalments thereafter, the total amount payable being £89.50.

4178. Television–transmission of signals

ADVANCED TELEVISION SERVICES REGULATIONS 1996, SI 1996 3151; made under the European Communities Act 1972 s.2. In force: January 7, 1997; £3.20.

These Regulations implement in part the provisions of Council Directive 95/47 on the use of standards for the transmission of television signals ([1995] OJ L281/51). Part I of the Regulations comprises introductory provisions, Part II implements the provisions of the Directive other than those concerning conditional access and Part III of the Regulations implements Art.4 of the Directive, which concerns conditional access, and Part IV concerns enforcement.

4179. Television–transmission of signals

ADVANCED TELEVISION SERVICES (AMENDMENT) REGULATIONS 1996, SI 1996 3197; made under the European Communities Act 1972 s.2. In force: January 7, 1997; £1.95.

These Regulations amend the Advanced Television Services Regulations 1996 (SI 1996 3151) by substituting a new Sch.1 and a new Sch.2. The new Sch.1 has the same effect as that in the principal Regulations but the provisions of para.3 by which existing Telecommunications Act Licences cease to authorise the running of telecommunication systems by means of which conditional access services other than those purely self provided are provided are clarified. The new Sch.2 repeats the forfeiture procedures in respect of Reg.6, Reg.9 and Reg.14 of the principal Regulations and enables their operation in Scotland as well as in England and Wales and Northern Ireland.

4180. Articles

A human right to broadcast "television speech"? *(Charles Black)*: Comms. L. 1996, 1 (1), 8-16. (Whether there should be a human right to broadcast, as opposed to current licensing restrictions, in light of development of internet cable broadcasting which technically allows unlimited number of broadcasters).

Devil's advocates: Legal Bus. 1996, 61 (Jan/Feb), 54-57. (Solicitors who have represented high profile serial killers discuss problems in coping with media obsession with violent crime).

Exclusive licensing of television programmes: the Cable and Satellite Directive *(Elizabeth McKnight)*: Ent. L.R. 1995, 6(7), 287-291. (Purpose of Directive 93/83 and issues arising from proposed implementing rules, in particular application of national copyright law to satellite broadcasting and collective licensing of cable retransmission rights).

Fashionable plaintiffs *(Steve Greenfield* and *Guy Osborn)*: N.L.J. 1996, 146(6746), 819-820. (Importance of independent legal advice for recording deals).

Fundamental rights, fair trials and the new audio-visual sector *(Clive Walker)*: M.L.R. 1996, 59(4), 517-539. (Dangers which new broadcasting technologies pose to right to fair trial and possible national and international regulatory responses).

Hard core skies *(Susan Edwards)*: N.L.J. 1996, 146(6756), 1213-1214, 1216. (Extent to which existing legislation can protect public from pornography received in UK via satellite).

Legal protection for encrypted services: the EU Green Paper and current UK legislation *(Tim Johnson)*: I.M.L. 1996, 14(10), 77-79. (Ensuring that suppliers of pay to view television channels can enforce payment through civil and criminal remedies against manufacture, supply, possession and use of decoding equipment without authorisation of encryptor).

Lights, camera, action–a review of the proposed changes to UK broadcasting law *(Simon Jones)*: Comms. L. 1996, 1(4), 158-161. (Changes affecting digital television, sporting and other events and ownership rules).

Media ownership: the UK government's proposals *(Jeremy Scholes* and *Lorna Woods)*: Ent. L.R. 1996, 7(1), 7-15. (Policy document Cm.2872 on regulation of cross media ownership proposing that media should be treated as single market for purposes of regulation).

Money advice and the media: M. Advice 1996, 40, 6-8. (Methods of using media to obtain maximum publicity for money advice agencies and raise profile of important issues).

No comment *(Diana Cotton)*: Counsel 1996, Mar/Apr, 33. (Advice on how barristers should answer questions from journalists concerning current matters).

Pre-trial publicity and its treatment in the English courts *(David Corker* and *Michael Levi)*: Crim. L.R. 1996, Sep, 622-632. (Historical development of criminal courts' approach to publicity and its impact on jurors, and difficulties in handling media prejudice).

Reflections of a humble media man *(Robin Day)*: Med. Leg. J. 1996, 64(2), 49-54. (Talk to Medico Legal Society on dangers of allowing televising of trials).

Regulating for media concentration: the emerging policy of the European Union *(Alison J. Harcourt)*: U.L.R. 1996, 7(5), 202-210. (Use of competition law to control concentrations, background to proposals for specific media concentration legislation and Directorate Generals concerned with such policy).

Sting in the tale *(David Morgan)*: Policing T. 1996, 2(2), 28-29. (Pre-trial briefings for press, associated miscarriage of justice risks, inability of police to respond to criticisms if briefings not given as illustrated by Rosemary West murder trial and ACPO guidance on briefings).

Table of EC media related measures *(Freshfields)*: Ent. L.R. 1996, 7(1), E19-20. (Current status of EC measures relating to media law).

Table of EC media related measures *(Freshfields)*: Ent. L.R. 1996, 7(2), E39-40. (Status of EC legislation relating to audio visual, satellite and copyright).

The Broadcasting Bill: copyright implications *(Serena Tierney)*: C.W. 1996, 58, 28-34. (Copyright considerations of proposals for regulation of independent digital broadcasting services and cross media ownership).

The good life: Legal Bus. 1996, 66 (Jul/Aug), 53-55. (Profile of Cheltenham based private client firm Wiggin & Co and growth of its media based commercial practice).
Using the media: Legal Bus. 1996, 63 (Apr), 40-42. (Using media for case research, illustrated by use of press in search for missing family fortune).
Wilkes and the Sunday Sport–a legal link between libertarians? *(John Cooke)*: Comms. L. 1996, 1 (4), 164-171. (History of use of summary procedure for dealing with constructive contempt of court by media).

4181. Books

Albertstat, Philip–Media Production Agreements. Blueprint. Hardback: £50.00. ISBN 0-415-13668-7. Routledge.
Barendt, Eric–Yearbook of Media and Entertainment Law: Vol II. 1996. Hardback: £125.00. ISBN 0-19-826277-9. Oxford University Press.
Campbell, Christian–International Media Liability. Hardback: £75.00. ISBN 0-471-96578-2. Chancery Wiley Law Publications.
Carey, Peter–Media Law. Paperback. ISBN 0-421-57140-3. Sweet & Maxwell.
Creech, Kenneth C.–Electronic Media Law and Regulation. Paperback: £27.50. ISBN 0-240-80216-0. Focal Press (an imprint of Butterworth-Heinemann).
Halloran, Mark–The Musician's Business and Legal Guide. Paperback: £29.75. ISBN 0-13-237322-X. Prentice Hall US.
Henry, Michael–Henry: Entertainment Law. Paperback: £29.50. ISBN 0-406-04969-6. Butterworth Law.
Jarvis, Peter–The Essential Television Handbook. Paperback: £14.99. ISBN 0-240-51445-9. Focal Press: an imprint of Butterworth-Heinemann.
McGonagle, Marie–Law and the Media. Paperback: £25.00. ISBN 1-85800-059-9. Round Hall Sweet & Maxwell.
Mosawi, Anthony–EC Media Law. Paperback: £90.00. ISBN 0-406-00253-3. Butterworth Law.
Murphy, Yvonne–Journalists and the Law. Paperback. ISBN 1-89973-836-3. Round Hall Sweet & Maxwell.

MEDICINE

4182. Artificial insemination–written consent of donor required to store and use sperm–no discretion to allow treatment without written consent

[Human Fertilisation and Embryology Act 1990 Sch.3, s.24.]

B sought judicial review of the H's decision to refuse to release sperm, taken from B's unconscious husband just before his death to enable B to become pregnant by artificial insemination, on the ground that the donor had not consented. The Human Fertilisation and Embryology Act 1990 Sch.3 required that, for B to have treatment in the UK, written consent had to be obtained from the donor or the couple must be treated together so that consent could be inferred from their conduct. B contended that, as she and her husband were trying to start a family when he died, there was a joint enterprise from which his consent could be inferred. In the alternative, B argued that H should have exercised its discretion under s.24 of the Act to enable the sperm to be exported to a country where written consent to treatment was not required. B also relied upon the freedom of an individual to obtain medical treatment in another Member State under EC law as authorising export of any resources required to have treatment in another Member State.

Held, dismissing the application, that (1) B and her husband had not actually started treatment together before he died as, being unconscious, he was not involved in the decision to take the sperm, which was in fact a unilateral decision by his wife. As such, consent could not be inferred from conduct and H had no discretion to derogate from the requirement of written consent; (2) H had acted within its discretion in refusing to allow the sperm to be exported as it had followed written guidelines stating that sperm could not be exported for a purpose that would be unlawful in the UK and, in any case, the donor's express consent to export would be required and (3) EC provisions could not override national law where public policy matters were in issue and it was clear that the intention of the 1990 Act was that written consent be obtained for storage and use of sperm.

R. v. HUMAN FERTILISATION AND EMBRYOLOGY AUTHORITY, *ex p.* BLOOD [1996] 3 W.L.R. 1176, Sir Stephen Brown, QBD.

4183. Dental auxiliaries

DENTAL AUXILIARIES (AMENDMENT) REGULATIONS 1996, SI 1996 2998; made under the Dentists Act 1984 s.45. In force: December 1, 1996; £0.65.

These Regulations amend the Dental Auxiliaries Regulations 1986 (SI 1986 887) to increase, from December 1, 1996, the fees prescribed by the General Dental Council for first enrolment of a name in a roll from £7 to £10, for retention of a name in a roll from £10 to £20, and for the restoration of a name to a roll from £2 to £5.

4184. Dentists–qualifications

DENTAL QUALIFICATIONS (RECOGNITION) REGULATIONS 1996, SI 1996 1496; made under the European Communities Act 1972 s.2. In force: July 1, 1996; £1.95.

These Regulations implement European obligations relating to primary dental qualifications contained in Council Directive 89/594 ([1989] OJ L345/19) and in Council Directive 90/658 ([1990] OJ L353/73) which concern German qualifications following reunification of Germany and implement obligations under the European Economic Area Agreement and take into account the accession of Austria, Finland and Sweden to the European Union. The list of primary dental qualifications entitled to automatic recognition in the United Kingdom is extended. These are qualifications which were awarded in an EEA State following training which satisfied the minimum training requirements set out in Council Directive 78/687 ([1978] OJ L233/10) concerning the co-ordination of provisions in respect of activities of dental practitioners, but which are not listed in Part II of Sch.2 to the Act. The list of Scheduled European diplomas listed in Part II of Sch.2 to the Act is also amended so as to include qualifications awarded in Austria, Finland, Sweden, Iceland, Liechtenstein and Norway and the formal titles of qualification in Italy and Spain.

4185. Doctors–professional conduct–failure to examine patient precluded "wait and see" approach to treatment

[National Health Service (General, Medical and Pharmaceutical Services) Regulations 1974.]

T, a doctor, sought judicial review of the Secretary of State's decision that he had acted in breach of his terms of service in respect of his treatment of a patient, R, and that £500 should be deducted from his remuneration. A medical services committee found that T had failed to refer R to hospital when he attended the patient's home and that the follow up management should not have been left to R's mother. T argued that, in dismissing his appeal, the Secretary of State had acted unlawfully by failing to consider T's argument that, in line with responsible medical practice, T was entitled to adopt a "wait and see" approach to R's treatment.

Held, dismissing the application, that (1) the exercise of a doctor's professional judgment was regulated by the National Health Service (General, Medical and Pharmaceutical Services) Regulations 1974 which state that a doctor is expected to exercise the degree of care and skill that general practitioners as a class would reasonably be expected to exercise and (2) the Secretary of State was entitled to find, on the facts, that because T did not perform an adequate examination of R, he had not put himself in a position to consider properly R's future treatment and therefore was not legitimately entitled to adopt a "wait and see" approach.

R. v. SECRETARY OF STATE FOR HEALTH, *ex p.* TRIVEDI, Trans. Ref: CO/2100/94, April 25, 1996, Potts, J., QBD.

4186. Doctors–professional conduct–registration

[Medical (Professional Performance) Act 1995]

The Department of Health issued a press release entitled *Medical (Professional Performance) Act: General Medical Council given further powers to act to protect patients* (96/44), published on February 16, 1996. New powers have come into effect which allow the GMC to restrict a doctor's practice pending a full hearing of his or her case. The GMC Preliminary Proceedings committee will have powers to suspend or impose conditions on a doctor's registration for up to six months, extendable for three months periods if the case has not been cleared within six months. The GMC's health committee will be able to suspend indefinitely doctors who have been suspended for two years, so that they are not required to appear before the committee every year whilst trying to recover their health. As a first step towards the introduction of professional performance procedures in 1997, the GMC will be empowered to advise doctors on standards or professional performance.

4187. Doctors–professional misconduct–doctors–medical negligence–doctor's removal from register–whether correct test applied

[Medical Act 1969.]

M, having admitted providing seriously negligent medical treatment, appealed against a finding of serious professional misconduct by the GMC and the removal of his name from the register of medical practitioners. M contended that the reasons given for the findings of the professional conduct committee showed the wrong test had been used in reaching the decision, and that without a subjective determination of morally blameworthy conduct on his part the finding that the standard of treatment had fallen deplorably short could not amount to serious professional misconduct.

Held, dismissing the appeal, that although older precedents supported M's argument, the Medical Act 1969 had replaced the old standard of "infamous conduct in a professional respect" with the new offence of professional misconduct, and had increased the range of sanctions available to the GMC, which implied that the new offence was intended to include serious negligence. The public looked to the medical profession's governing bodies for protection against both incompetent and deliberate acts by practitioners. Misconduct was to be assessed using an objective standard which required that the conduct in question be measured by the standard of a practitioner of reasonable skill exercising reasonable care. On the facts, therefore, the decision to erase M's name from the register was correct and would not be interfered with, *Doughty v. General Dental Council* [1988] A.C. 164 approved.

McCANDLESS v. GENERAL MEDICAL COUNCIL [1996] 1 W.L.R. 167, Lord Hoffmann, PC.

4188. Doctors–suspension for professional misconduct–bias of GMC–relevance of late evidence

M appealed against a decision by the Health Committee of GMC that his fitness to practise as a doctor was seriously impaired and his registration should be suspended for a further 12 months. M argued that a member of the committee had been biased in asking questions relating to M's competence in the English language. M also argued that late evidence produced showing M seeking to prescribe when he was not authorised to do so, was not relevant.

Held, dismissing the appeal, that (1) on the evidence, the committee was entitled to conclude that M had a cognitive impairment and should be suspended for 12 months; (2) the questions of the committee showed no bias.

In fact they showed concern that competency tests had been culturally fair and (3) the committee were entitled to take the late evidence into account.

MALLIWAL v. GENERAL MEDICAL COUNCIL, Trans. Ref: No.20 of 1995, December 18, 1995, Lord Goff of Chieveley, PC.

4189. Doctors–suspension for professional misconduct–no grounds to interfere in decision of the Professional Conduct Committee

[Medical Act 1983 s.38.]

G, a doctor, applied to terminate an order, made under the Medical Act 1983 s.38, for suspension owing to a direction that he be erased from the register following a finding of serious professional conduct by GMC's Professional Conduct Committee. G appeared in person and swore an affidavit which complained of his treatment by the committee.

Held, dismissing the application, that, despite making allowances for the fact that G appeared in person, G's affidavit contained no facts or explanation of the offences of which he was charged. G's complaint of the hardship which would be caused to him by suspension could not justify interference with a decision made by a committee, in possession of the facts, who had held that G should be suspended in order to protect members of the public.

GUPTA v. GENERAL MEDICAL COMMITTEE, Trans. Ref: CO 1046/96, April 3, 1996, Leggatt, L.J., QBD.

4190. Drugs–gel-filled Temazepam capsules placed on list of drugs prohibited from prescription–ban justified by reasons of health and safety

[National Health Service Act 1977 s.2, s.29; National Health Service (General Medical Services) (Amendment No.2) Regulations 1995 Sch.10; Council Directive 89/105 Art.7.]

RPS, a pharmaceutical company, sought judicial review of a decision by the Secretary of State to place gel-filled Temazepam capsules on the list of drugs which were not allowed to be prescribed to NHS patients. The reason was to prevent drug abuse as the gel could be removed by inserting a needle into the capsule and abusers then injected the drug. RPS were the only manufacturers of capsules in the UK. They argued that the National Health Service Act 1977 and the National Health Service (General Medical Services) (Amendment No.2) Regulations 1995 gave the Secretary of State the power to prevent prescription of the capsules for reasons of cost, but not for health and safety considerations. RPS also argued that the decision breached Council Directive 89/105 and that the process leading up to the decision was procedurally unfair as a government laboratory report was not disclosed to RPS until after the decision was made.

Held, dismissing the application, that (1) under the 1977 Act the Secretary of State had a duty to improve health, prevent illness and provide adequate services. The scope of the 1977 Act permitted the Secretary of State to consider health and safety when discharging his duties. Section 2(b) allowed him to "do any other thing" to fulfill his duties. Nothing in the statute restricted the Secretary of State to considerations of cost, and regulations made under s.29 could be used to exclude prescriptions to reduce the dangers of drug abuse; (2) the 1992 Regulations also contained nothing to suggest that inclusion of a drug on the list in Sch.10, prohibiting prescription, should be limited to considerations of cost. Although an explanatory note to the 1992 Regulations dealt exclusively with cost, the language of the Regulation was not ambiguous and clearly permitted considerations of health and safety. Recourse to the explanatory note would be necessary only when the meaning was unclear or resulted in an absurdity and the note could then be used to discover parliamentary intention, *Pepper v. Hart* [1993] A.C. 593, [1993] C.L.Y. 459 followed; (3) Council Directive 89/105 Art.7 required reasons, showing justifiable criteria, to be given for the prohibition of a product. This requirement was no more onerous than the requirement of administrative authorites to give reasons in public law. The decision letter was short but contained adequate reasons, especially when considering the correspondence between the Secretary of State and RPS leading up to the decision; (4) the Secretary of State considered the expert evidence and his conclusion that the capsules had to be banned to reduce the risk to drug abusers was not disproportionate. The harsh consequence of the decision on RPS could not provide a reason for setting aside the decision as the overriding consideration was the Secretary of State's duties under the 1977 Act and (5) although the government laboratory report was not disclosed to RPS until after the decision was made, no new issues were revealed by it.

R. v. SECRETARY OF STATE FOR HEALTH, *ex p.* RP SCHERER LTD (1996) 32 B.M.L.R. 12, Judge, J., QBD.

4191. General Medical Council–committees

GENERAL MEDICAL COUNCIL (CONSTITUTION OF FITNESS TO PRACTISE COMMITTEES) RULES ORDER OF COUNCIL 1996, SI 1996 2125; made under the Medical Act 1983 Sch.1 para.20, Sch.1 para.21, Sch.1 para.21A, Sch.1 para.21B, Sch.1 para.22. In force: r.2, r.8(1)(4), r.9, r.10, r.11, r.16(1): September 1, 1996 Remainder: January 1, 1997; £1.95.

The Rules approved by this Order revoke and replace earlier Rules governing the constitution of the General Medical Council's Fitness to Practise Committees. They regulate the constitutions of the Preliminary Proceedings Committee, the Professional Conduct Committee, the Health Committee, the Assessment Referral Committee and the Committee on Professional Performance, the last two of which Committees were provided for in the Medical (Professional Performance) Act 1995 which amends the Medical Act 1983.

4192. General Medical Council–committees–procedure

GENERAL MEDICAL COUNCIL HEALTH COMMITTEE (PROCEDURE) (AMENDMENT) RULES ORDER OF COUNCIL 1996, SI 1996 1219; made under the Medical Act 1983 Sch.4 para.1. In force: June 30, 1996; £1.10.

This Order amends the General Medical Council Health Committee (Procedure) Rules 1987 (SI 1987 2174) and give effect to provisions brought into force by the Medical (Professional Performance) Act 1995 (Commencement No.1) Order 1996 (SI 1996 271) relating to the powers of the General Medical Council, through its appropriate committees regarding interim orders for suspension or conditional registration and orders for the indefinite suspension of doctors.

4193. General Medical Council–committees–professional conduct–procedure

GENERAL MEDICAL COUNCIL PRELIMINARY PROCEEDINGS COMMITTEE AND PROFESSIONAL CONDUCT COMMITTEE (PROCEDURE) (AMENDMENT) RULES ORDER OF COUNCIL 1996, SI 1996 1218; made under the Medical Act 1983 Sch.4 para.1, Sch.4 para.5. In force: May 30, 1996; £1.10.

The rules approved by this Order amend the General Medical Council Preliminary Proceedings Committee and Professional Conduct Committee (Procedure) Rules 1988 (appended to SI 1988 2255). They give effect to the provisions brought into force by the Medical (Professional Performance) Act 1995 (Commencement No.1) Order 1996 (SI 1996 271) relating to the powers of the General Medical Council, through its appropriate Committees, to permit interim orders for suspension or conditional registration to be made for an initial period of six months rather than the original two months, and to make further interim orders for periods of up to three months at a time. The amended rules also update the definition of persons in a public capacity who may refer cases to the General Medical Council, reflecting changes to the structure of the National Health Service.

4194. General Medical Council–constitution

GENERAL MEDICAL COUNCIL (CONSTITUTION) AMENDMENT ORDER 1996, SI 1996 1630; made under the Medical Act 1983 s.1, Sch.1 para.3, Sch.1 para.5. In force: Art.3: October 31, 1996; Remainder: November 1, 1996; £1.10.

This Order amends the General Medical Council (Constitution) Order 1979 (SI 1979 112). Article 2(2) of this Order provides for the number of appointed members of the General Medical Council to be reduced from 35 to 25, and for the maximum number of nominated members to be increased from 13 to 25, with effect from November 1, 1996. By Art.2(3) and Art.2(4), the arrangements for appointing the appointed members are also altered: from November 1, 1996, the two groups of appointing bodies set out in the Schedule to the Constitution Order, as substituted by this Order, will respectively appoint 15 and 10 members. Article 3 provides that all the appointed members holding office on October 31, 1996 cease to hold office at the end of that day.

4195. Licensing–medicinal products–statutory duty of licensing authority to grant marketing authorisation to similar products–implementation by different Member States of EC Directive–statutory interpretation

[Council Directive 65/65 on proprietary medicinal products Art.4.8; Medicines Act 1968.]

M applied for judicial review of the grant of marketing authorisation to G for a pharmaceutical product called Tramake, a form of tramadol hydrochloride, pursuant to the abridged procedure under Council Directive 65/65 Art.4.8. M, who held marketing authorisation, issued under the full application procedure, for a product called Zydol, a tramadol based analgesic, contended that, although Tramake and Tramal were "essentially similar" under Art.4.8.(a)(iii), the 1980 German authorisation on which G's abridged application was based had not been made in accordance with the relevant EC provisions in force between 1990-94, the point in time when M's application was made. M contended that the licensing authority had failed in its duty by not investigating the validity of the German authorisation. M also sought reference to the European Court of Justice under Art.177 for an interpretation of Art.4.8(a)(iii).

Held, dismissing the application, that Council Directive 65/65 had been correctly implemented in Germany prior to granting the authorisation in 1980. M's arguments that the licensing authority should have reconsidered the abridged application in the light of scientific and technical knowledge between 1990-94 overlooked the fact that the authority had referred to data M supplied in connection with its own application, when considering G's abridged application. Use of M's data in confirming the "essential similarity" requirement under Art.4.8(a)(iii) fulfilled the authority's duty under the Medicines Act 1968 as decided in *R. v. Licensing Authority, ex p. Smith Kline & French Laboratories Ltd* [1990] 1 A.C 64, [1989] C.L.Y. 2383. The procedures adopted by the authority in deciding G's abridged application satisfied the substantive duty requirement to ensure that products were "safe, efficacious and of appropriate quality" under Art.4.8(a)(iii), being necessary for the protection of public health and safety. M's investment was protected by the use of the six year authorisation period established under Directive 65/65 and the 10 year equivalent period in the UK, as this was designed to allow partial recovery of research investment costs and the prevention of generic copying of products without the backing of expensive data. However, the authority could refer to data supplied in support of an earlier application in later applications of essentially similar nature. Any difference in treatment accorded by the authority to the two applicants under Art.4.8.(a)(iii) arose from their different situations and was not due to discrimination against M. It was not open for one Member State to question the validity of another Member State's implementation of EC law, as to do so would conflict with the principle of trust between Member States in the performance of legal obligations, *R. v. Ministry of Agriculture,*

Fisheries and Food, ex p. Hedley Lomas (Ireland) Ltd (C5/94) [1996] All. E.R. (EC) 493, [1996] C.L.Y 292 considered.

R. v. LICENSING AUTHORITY ESTABLISHED UNDER THE MEDICINES ACT 1968, *ex p.* MONSANTO PLC, Trans. Ref: CO-1593-96, June 28, 1996, Keene, J., QBD.

4196. Medical profession–qualifications

EUROPEAN PRIMARY MEDICAL QUALIFICATIONS REGULATIONS 1996, SI 1996 1591; made under the European Communities Act 1972 s.2. In force: July 10, 1996; £2.80.

These Regulations, which amend the Medical Act 1983, make provision for primary medical qualifications and registration by virtue of those qualifications and implement Council Directive 93/16 Art.42. The amendments relate to registration by virtue of primary United Kingdom or primary European legislation, primary qualifications obtained in ther EEA states and to EEA nationals whose primary qualifications are from non-EEA States.

4197. Medical profession–supplementary professions–registration rules

PROFESSIONS SUPPLEMENTARY TO MEDICINE (REGISTRATION RULES) (AMENDMENT) ORDER OF COUNCIL 1996, SI 1996 2945; made under the Professions Supplementary to Medicine Act 1960 s.2. In force: September 11, 1996; £1.10.

The Rules confirmed by this Order further amend the Schedule to the Registration Rules 1962 (SI 1962 1765) set out in the Schedule to the Professions Supplementary to Medicine (Registration Rules) Order of Council 1962. In the 1962 Rules, column 3 of the Schedule specifies a date in respect of the annual period of registration of, and payment of fees by, members of each of the professions to which the Professions Supplementary to Medicine Act 1960 relates. The Rules confirmed by this Order substitute, for each profession, a date approximately one month later than that previously specified.

4198. Medical treatment–fees

MEDICAL DEVICES (CONSULTATION REQUIREMENTS) (FEES) AMENDMENT REGULATIONS 1996, SI 1996 622; made under the Finance Act 1973 s.56. In force: April 1, 1996; £0.65.

These Regulations amend the Medical Devices (Consultation Requirements) (Fees) Regulations 1995 (SI 1995 449). The principal Regulations prescribe the fees which are payable where a notified body consults the competent body in accordance with Council Directive 93/42 of June 14, 1993 concerning medical devices. Regulation 2 amends Reg.3 of the principal Regulations by reducing the amounts of all the fees specified in that Regulation. Therefore an assessment of the cost to business of complying with these Regulations has not been made.

4199. Medical (Professional Performance) Act 1995–Commencement No.1 Order

MEDICAL (PROFESSIONAL PERFORMANCE) ACT 1995 (COMMENCEMENT NO.1) ORDER 1996, SI 1996 271 (C.5); made under the Medical (Professional Performance) Act 1995 s.6. In force: bringing into force various provisions of the Act on May 1, 1996; £1.10.

Certain provisions of the Medical (Professional Performance) Act 1995 are brought into force by this Order. They are s.3, preliminary proceedings and interim orders, s.4, supplementary and consequential amendments to the Medical Act 1983, so far as it related to the provisions of the Schedule to the Act brought into force by this order, s.5, expenses, s.6, commencement, s.7(1), short title, s.7(2), extent, so far as it relates to the provisions of the Act brought into force by this Order, para.1 of the Schedule, so far as it relates to the other provisions of the Schedule brought into force by this Order, and para.4, para.5, para.6, para.10(c), para.22(b), para.28(a), para.29(a) and para.30(a) of the Schedule.

4200. Medical (Professional Performance) Act 1995–Commencement No.2 Order

MEDICAL (PROFESSIONAL PERFORMANCE) ACT 1995 (COMMENCEMENT NO.2) ORDER 1996, SI 1996 1631 (C.34); made under the Medical (Professional Performance) Act 1995 s.6. In force: bringing into force various provisions of the Act on September 1, 1996 and January 1, 1997; £0.65.

This Order brings into force certain provisions of the Medical (Professional Performance) Act 1995, which amends the Medical Act 1983. Certain provisions are brought into force on September 1, 1996, first so as to provide that rules made by the GMC shall not come into force until they have been approved by the Privy Council, and secondly for the limited purpose of enabling the GMC to determine, in accordance with rules, who will be the members of its statutory committees from January 1, 1997. The provisions brought into force on January 1, 1997 provide for the establishment, in accordance with rules, of two new Committees of the GMC, namely the Assessment Referral Committee and the Committee on Professional Performance.

4201. Medicines–advertising

MEDICINES (ADVERTISING) AMENDMENT REGULATIONS 1996, SI 1996 1552; made under the Medicines Act 1968 s.95, s.129. In force: July 12, 1996; £0.65.

These Regulations concern the advertising of medicinal products for human use and amend the Medicines (Advertising) Regulations 1994 (SI 1994 1932). They exempt any medicinal product for the treatment of symptoms of sprains or strains or the pain or stiffness of rheumatic and non-serious arthritic conditions from the general prohibition against advertisements of medicinal products referring to specified diseases and add joint, rheumatic and collagen diseases to the diseases subject to the prohibition on advertisements.

4202. Medicines–animal feeding stuffs

MEDICINES (ANIMAL FEEDING STUFFS) (ENFORCEMENT) (AMENDMENT) REGULATIONS 1996, SI 1996 1261; made under the Medicines Act 1968 s.117. In force: June 1, 1996; £2.40.

These Regulations amend the Medicines (Animal Feeding Stuffs) (Enforcement) Regulations 1985 (SI 1985 273) in order to implement the Eleventh Commission Directive 93/70 establishing Community analysis methods for official control of feeding stuffs ([1993] OJ L234/17) which establishes a Community method of analysis to be used in the course of official checks on animal feeding stuffs to identify their halofuginone content and the Twelfth Commission Directive 93/117 establishing Community analysis methods for official control of feeding stuffs ([1993] OJ L329/54) to be used in the course of official checks on animal feeding stuffs to identify their robenidine and methyl benzoquate content. Other amendments increase the amount of concentrated hydrochloric acid which is used as a reagent in the method of analysis for the determination of nifursol from 24 millilitres to 25 millilitres, omit methods of analysis specified for acinitrazole, nitrofurazone and nitrovin from Sch.3 of the 1985 Regulations and prescribe methods of analysis for halofuginone, robenidine and methyl benzoquate.

4203. Medicines–animal feeding stuffs

MEDICINES (MEDICATED ANIMAL FEEDING STUFFS) (AMENDMENT) REGULATIONS 1996, SI 1996 769; made under the Medicines Act 1968 s.40, s.129. In force: April 3, 1996; £1.10.

These Regulations, which come into force on April 3, 1996, amend the Medicines (Medicated Animal Feeding Stuffs) (No.2) Regulations 1992 (SI 1992 1520). The fees payable in respect of the entry or retention in, or restoration to, the Register of Manufacturers of Animal Feeding Stuffs are increased by approximately five per cent.

4204. Medicines–animal tests certificates–exemptions

MEDICINES (EXEMPTIONS FROM ANIMAL TEST CERTIFICATES) (REVOCATION) ORDER 1996, SI 1996 2197; made under the Medicines Act 1968 s.35, s.129. In force: September 13, 1996; £1.10.

This Order, together with the Medicines (Exemptions from Licences) (Revocation) Order 1996, effects the revocation of the Medicines (Exemptions from Licences and Animal Test Certificates) Order 1986 (SI 1986 1180) and the Medicines (Exemption from Licences and Animal Test Certificates) (Amendment) Order 1991 (SI 1991 633).

4205. Medicines–data sheets

MEDICINES (DATA SHEET) AMENDMENT REGULATIONS 1996, SI 1996 2420; made under the Medicines Act 1968 s.96, s.129. In force: October 10, 1996; £1.10.

The Medicines (Data Sheet) Regulations 1972 (SI 1972 2076) Reg.2 prescribe the form of data sheets falling within the Medicines Act 1968 s.96. These Regulations remove certain requirements relating to the compilation of data sheets for medicinal products for human use by inserting a new Reg.2A into the 1972 Regulations.

4206. Medicines–exemptions from licences–revocation

MEDICINES (EXEMPTIONS FROM LICENCES) (REVOCATION) ORDER 1996, SI 1996 2195; made under the Medicines Act 1968 s.15, s.129. In force: September 13, 1996; £1.10.

This Order, together with the Medicines (Exemptions from Animal Test Certificates) (Revocation) Order 1996, effect the revocation of the Medicines (Exemptions from Licences and Animal Test Certificates) Amendment Order 1991 (SI 1991 633).

4207. Medicines–fees

MEDICINES (PRODUCTS FOR HUMAN USE-FEES) AMENDMENT REGULATIONS 1996, SI 1996 683; made under the Medicines Act 1971 s.1. In force: April 1, 1996; £1.55.

These Regulations amend the Medicines (Products for Human Use– Fees) Regulations 1995 (SI 1995 1116) (the principal Regulations). The principal Regulations make provision for the fees payable under the Medicines Act 1971 in respect of marketing authorisations, licences and certificates relating to medicinal products for human use. These Regulations (Reg.3 and the Schedule) vary some of the fees payable for applications for marketing authorisations, clinical trial certificates and export certificates; for variations and renewals of clinical trial certificates; and periodic fees in connection with the holding of such authorisations and licences. They also vary the fees payable in respect of inspections of sites carried out in connection with applications for, or during the currency of, such authorisations and licences. The overall effect of these changes is a reduction of two per cent in fee levels. Some application fees and inspection fees are reduced by five or 20 per cent; the capital fee for complex applications is increased by 7.5 per cent. Periodic fees relating to new and complex drugs are reduced by five and 20 per cent respectively; those for prescription only medicines are increased by five per cent. These Regulations also make a number of miscellaneous amendments.

4208. Medicines–homeopathic medicinal products–fees

MEDICINES (HOMEOPATHIC MEDICINAL PRODUCTS FOR HUMAN USE) AMENDMENT REGULATIONS 1996, SI 1996 482; made under the European Communities Act 1972 s.2. In force: April 1, 1996; £1.10.

These Regulations amend the Medicines (Homeopathic Medicinal Products for Human Use) Regulations 1994 (SI 1994 105) which relate to the simplified registration procedure for the marketing of homeopathic medicinal products for human use. New provisions for fees payable in respect of applications for certificates of registration under Part III of the Regulations are made by Reg.3. Schedule 2, which prescribes fees for certificates of registration, is substituted by a new Sch.2 which prescribes fees ranging from £100 to £650 determined by the number of homeopathic stocks used in the preparation of homeopathic medicinal products and by criteria relating to whether the licensing authority has previously assessed stocks and formulations identical to those proposed.

4209. Medicines–prescription only

MEDICINES (PRODUCTS OTHER THAN VETERINARY DRUGS) (PRESCRIPTION ONLY) AMENDMENT ORDER 1996, SI 1996 1514; made under the Medicines Act 1968 s.58, s.129. In force: July 5, 1996; £1.10.

This Order amends the Medicines (Products Other Than Veterinary Drugs) (Prescription Only) Order 1983 (SI 1983 1212) which specifies descriptions and classes of prescription only medicines. Under the Order products are included in a class of such medicines by reason of the substances contained in them, subject to their being excluded in specified circumstances. The amendments made by this Order are the inclusion of radioactive medicinal products and products containing bacillus salmonella typhi vaccine, fenticonazole nitrate and tramadol hydrochloride; exclusions for certain products containing azelastine hydrochloride and nitzatidine and an exclusion for Perinal Spray; clarification of the exclusion for products containing codeine and its salts.

4210. Medicines–prescription only–classes

MEDICINES (PRODUCTS OTHER THAN VETERINARY DRUGS) (PRESCRIPTION ONLY) AMENDMENT (NO.2) ORDER 1996, SI 1996 3193; made under the Medicines Act 1968 s.58, s.129. In force: January 13, 1997; £1.10.

This Order further amends the Medicines (Products Other Than Veterinary Drugs) (Prescription Only) Order 1983 (SI 1983 1212) which specifies descriptions and classes of prescription only medicines. Under the principal Order products are included in a class of such medicines by reason of the substances contained in them, subject to their being excluded in specified circumstances.

4211. Medicines–prohibition–revocation

MEDICINES (PHENACETIN PROHIBITION) (REVOCATION) ORDER 1996, SI 1996 3269; made under the Medicines Act 1968 s.62, s.129. In force: January 21, 1997; £1.10.

This Order revokes the Medicines (Phenacetin Prohibition) Order 1979 (SI 1979 1181) which prohibited the sale, supply or importation of any medicinal product consisting of or containing phenacetin, subject to specified conditions.

4212. Opticians–fees–registration and enrolment

GENERAL OPTICAL COUNCIL (REGISTRATION AND ENROLMENT (AMENDMENT) RULES) ORDER OF COUNCIL 1996, SI 1996 3021; made under the Opticians Act 1989 s.10. In force: April 1, 1997; £1.10.

The rules approved by this Order increase with effect from April 1, 1997 the fees payable to the General Optical Council by ophthalmic and dispensing opticians and bodies corporate carrying on business as opticians for registration, enrolment or retention in, restoration to and transfer within the register of opticians. The fees were last fixed in April 1994 and the order of increase is approximately 4 per cent. The General Optical Council (Registration and Enrolment (Amendment) Rules) Order of Council 1994 (SI 1994 729) is revoked.

4213. Pharmaceutical industry–fees–registration and application

MEDICINES (PHARMACIES) (APPLICATIONS FOR REGISTRATION AND FEES) AMENDMENT REGULATIONS 1996, SI 1996 3054; made under the Medicines Act 1968 s.75, s.76, s.129. In force: January 1, 1997; £0.65.

These Regulations further amend the Medicines (Pharmacies) (Applications for Registration and Fees) Regulations 1973 (SI 1973 1822) by increasing the fees for registration of premises at which a retail pharmacy business is, or is to be, carried on from £124 to £128 and, where the premises are in Northern Ireland, from £66 to £69. They also increase subsequent annual fees (retention fees) from £80 to £82 and, where the premises are in Northern Ireland, from £61 to £64. The penalty for failure to pay retention fees is increased from £256 to £264 and where the premises are in Northern Ireland from £189 to £197. The Medicines (Pharmacies) (Applications for Registration and Fees) Amendment Regulations 1995 (SI 1995 3029) are revoked.

4214. Pharmacies–training–Italian requirements–Council Directive 85/432–European Union

[Council Directive 85/432 concerning the coordination of provisions laid down by law, regulation or administrative action in respect of certain activities in the field of training in pharmacy Art.5.]

The CEC sought a declaration that Italy had failed to implement properly Council Directive 85/432.

Held, that by postponing from October 1, 1987 to November 1, 1990 the time limit laid down in Council Directive 85/432 Art.5 and by retaining until the latter date curricula for training in pharmacy which were incompatible with the Directive, Italy had failed in its obligations under Art.1, Art.2 and Art.5 of the Directive.

COMMISSION OF THE EUROPEAN COMMUNITIES v. ITALY (C307/94), February 29, 1996, Judge not specified, ECJ.

4215. Pharmacists–qualifications

PHARMACEUTICAL QUALIFICATIONS (RECOGNITION) REGULATIONS 1996, SI 1996 1405; made under the European Communities Act 1972 s.2. In force: June 28, 1996; £1.10.

These Regulations amend the Pharmacy Act 1954 which regulates the practice of pharmacy in Great Britain. Regulation 2(2) amends s.4A to apply subsection (1) to persons who are not nationals of a Member State so far as is necessary to enable a right under Art.11 of Council Regulation 1612/68 (workers' families), or any other enforceable Community right, to be exercised. Paragraphs (3) and (6) of Reg.2 amend s.4A of the 1954 Act by providing for further qualifications to be regarded as appropriate European diplomas for the purposes of that section. They implement Art.6(2) and Art.6a of Council Directive 85/433, inserted by Art.7(2) and Art.7(3) of Council Directive 90/658. That Directive makes amendments consequent on the unification of Germany to Directives on the recognition of professional qualifications. It also provides for the recognition of other pharmaceutical qualifications awarded in Member States. Regulation 2(7) makes a minor amendment to the definition of competent authorities in s.4A(6). Regulation 3 repeals part of the entry relating to Germany in Sch.1A to the 1954 Act in implementation of Council Directive 90/658 Art.7(1).

4216. Practice Directions–persistent vegetative state–procedure for applying for order to terminate artificial feeding and hydration–basis for diagnosis–wording of originating summons–Official Solicitor's role–validity of advance directions

Directions have been issued for an order permitting the withdrawal of artificial feeding and hydration where the condition is diagnosed in accordance with Royal College of Physicians guidelines, with reference to the time a patient has been in a vegetative state. Applications are to be by way of originating summons to be brought by the next of kin, other close relative, district health authority or NHS Trust in the terms stated in the direction. The Official Solicitor is to be invited to act as the patient's guardian ad litem or joined as defendant or respondent. Independent reports by two neurologists or doctors experienced in consciousness disturbance are required, at least one of which is to be commissioned by the Official Solicitor. The Official Solicitor's representatives will normally interview the next of kin and others close to the patient, in addition to seeing the patient and those taking care of him. Previously expressed advance directions of the patient, in writing or otherwise, will be an important factor, and the High Court may determine the effect of advance directives as to future medical treatment. The Official Solicitor's staff are prepared to discuss cases prior to the issue of proceedings and can be contacted during office hours by telephoning 0171 911 7127.

PRACTICE NOTE (OFFICIAL SOLICITOR TO THE SUPREME COURT: VEGETATIVE STATE) [1996] 4 All E.R. 766, Official Solicitor, Sup Ct.

4217. Veterinary medicines–fees

MEDICINES (PRODUCTS FOR ANIMAL USE - FEES) (AMENDMENT) REGULATIONS 1996, SI 1996 2196; made under the Medicines Act 1971 s.1. In force: September 13, 1996; £1.10.

These Regulations amend the Medicines (Products for Animal Use-Fees) Regulations 1995 so as to alter the fees payable in connection with the grant, variation and renewal of animal test certificates, consequential on the Animal Test Certificates Regulations 1996. Two new fees, of £600 and £250, are set for different types of application for the grant of a certificate. Formerly there was a single fee of £40.00. A new fee of £200 is set for applications for the variation of certificates. Formerly there was a range of fees from £110 to £1,150. A new renewal fee of £90 is set. These Regulations do not apply to applications made before their coming into force.

4218. Veterinary medicines–product licences–fees

MEDICINES (VETERINARY DRUGS) (PHARMACY AND MERCHANTS' LIST) (AMENDMENT) ORDER 1996, SI 1996 3034; made under the Medicines Act 1968 s.57, s.129. In force: January 1, 1997; £3.20.

This Order further amends the Medicines (Veterinary Drugs) (Pharmacy and Merchants' List) Order 1992 (SI 1992 33) so as to alter the fees payable on registration, retention of registration and restoration of registration of agricultural merchants and saddlers under that Order, and to take account of product licences or marketing authorisations granted, withdrawn or expired since the Order was last amended.

4219. Veterinary medicines–prohibition on importation–European Union

[Council Directive 81/851 Art.4; Treaty of Rome 1957 Art.30, Art.36.]

A question arose in proceedings in a Belgian court as to whether the provisions of Council Directive 81/851 and the Treaty of Rome 1957 Art.30 and Art.36 permitted a Member State to prohibit the import of a medicinal product, the marketing of which has not been the subject of a prior authorisation by the competent national authority.

Held, that Council Directive 81/851 Art.4 must be interpreted as prohibiting the importation into a Member State of a medicinal product by that Directive with a view to placing it on the market of that state or of administering it there in the absence of prior authorisation issued by the competent authority of the Member State.

BRUYERE v. BELGIUM (C279/94), March 21, 1996, Judge not specified, ECJ.

4220. Articles

Beyond the fringe: integrating complementary therapies within the NHS: Med. L. Mon. 1996, 3(3), 9-11. (Changing attitude of medical profession to complementary therapies and distinction between delegation and referral in relationship between doctors and complementary therapists).

Consent to medical and surgical treatment: the Law Commission's recommendations *(Peter Alldridge)*: Med. L. Rev. 1996, 4(2), 129-143. (Consultation Paper No.139 on liability of person who performs medical or surgical treatment where absence of consent would result in criminal offence).

Decisions and responsibilities at the end of life: euthanasia and clinically assisted death *(Hazel Biggs)*: Med. L. Int. 1996, 2(3), 229-245. (Ethical dilemma faced by doctors attempting to provide appropriate terminal care while respecting patient autonomy).

Harmonisation of the performance of the medico-legal autopsy as agreed to by the European Council in Legal Medicine: M.L.J.I. 1996, 1 (3), 113-116.

Legal medicine in Europe–the past and the future *(Anthony Bussutil)*: M.L.J.I. 1996, 1 (3), 110-112. (Role of European Council of Legal Medicine in harmonising training and procedure in legal aspects of forensic and clinical medicine).

Public health and private lives *(Margaret Brazier* and *John Harris)*: Med. L. Rev. 1996, 4(2), 171-192. (Legal and moral dilemmas affecting rights of patients in relation to HIV and other communicable diseases).

Radioactive substances in pharmaceutical industry: H.S. 1996, 7(3), 10-11. (Guidelines on use of radioactive substances in research and development of new medicines issued by Association of British Pharmaceutical Industry (ABPI).

Resource allocation in medicine and professional liability–the final nail? *(Michael Davies)*: P.N. 1996, 12(1), 15-20. (Whether legal action can be effective in enforcing obligations to treat patients in current financial climate).

The European Agency for the Evaluation of Medicines and European regulation of pharmaceuticals *(John S. Gardner)*: E.L.J. 1996, 2(1), 48-82. (Development of EU regulatory framework for human and veterinary medicines, role and procedure of Agency, regulation of biotechnology, advertising of medicinal products and effect of free movement rules).

The withdrawal and withholding of medical treatment *(Pamela R. Ferguson* and *Alastair Bissett-Johnson)*: Fam. Law 1996, 26(Sep), 563-565. (Recent cases illustrating court's approach to request for leave to discontinue treatment).

4221. Books

Danzon, Patricia M.–Pharmaceutical Price Regulation. Hardback: £23.95. ISBN 0-8447-3982-0. AEI Press.

Fletcher, Nina; Holt, Janet; Brazier, Margaret; Harris, John–Ethics, Law and Nursing. Paperback: £14.99. ISBN 0-7190-4050-7. Manchester University Press.

Khan, Malcolm; Robson, Michelle–Medical Negligence. Medico-Legal Series. Paperback: £25.00. ISBN 1-85941-022-7. Cavendish Publishing Ltd.

Lee, Robert; Morgan, Derek–Death Rites. Paperback: £12.99. ISBN 0-415-14026-9. Routledge.

Pace, Nicholas A.; McLean, Sheila–Ethics and the Law in Intensive Care. Hardback: £35.00. ISBN 0-19-262520-9. Oxford University Press.

Stark, Margaret M.; Payne-James, J. Jason–Symptoms and Signs of Substance Misuse. Paperback: £9.95. ISBN 1-900151-10-3. Greenwich Medical Media.

Steinbock, Bonnie–Life Before Birth. Paperback: £14.95. ISBN 0-19-510872-8. Oxford University Press Inc, USA.

Stone, Julie; Matthews, Joan–Complementary Medicine and the Law. Hardback: £30.00. ISBN 0-19-825970-0. Paperback: £12.99. ISBN 0-19-825971-9. Oxford University Press.

Wacker Guido, Ginny–Legal Issues in Nursing. Paperback: £24.95. ISBN 0-8385-5647-7. Appleton & Lange.

MENTAL HEALTH

4222. Community care

[Mental Health (Patients in the Community) Act 1995.]

The Department of Health issued a press release entitled *New mental health Act comes into force* (Press release 96/108), published on April 1, 1996. Legislation to ensure more effective care and supervision for patients with mental illness took effect from April 1, 1996. A new power of supervised discharge is introduced for patients detained under the Mental Health Act 1983 and in need of special supervision; the provisions for returning patients to hospital if they go absent without leave are tightened up; and the maximum period of leave of absence from hospital which may be allowed to detained patients for rehabilitation before discharge is extended to one year.

4223. Community care–supervision of after care

MENTAL HEALTH (AFTER-CARE UNDER SUPERVISION) REGULATIONS 1996, SI 1996 294; made under the National Health Service Act 1977 s.16; and the Mental Health Act 1983 s.32. In force: April 1, 1996; £3.70.

These Regulations enable specified functions of Health Authorities and local social services authorities under the Mental Health Act 1983 to be performed by other persons or bodies on their behalf. The functions relate to after care under supervision introduced by the Mental Health (Patients in the Community) Act 1995. The Regulations also prescribe forms for use in connection with after care supervision.

4224. Community care–transfer of patients

MENTAL HEALTH (PATIENTS IN THE COMMUNITY) (TRANSFERS FROM SCOTLAND) REGULATIONS 1996, SI 1996 295; made under the Mental Health Act 1983 s.25J. In force: April 1, 1996; £1.10.

These Regulations prescribe modifications to the Mental Health Act 1983 to enable patients who are subject of community care orders made under the Mental Health (Scotland) Act 1984, and who wish to move to England or Wales, to become subject to after care under supervision. Community care orders and after-care under supervision were introduced by the Mental Health (Patients in the Community) Act 1995 which amends the Mental Health Act 1983 and the Mental Health (Scotland) Act 1984.

4225. Foreign nationals–mental health–whether incapacitated foreign national should be removed to country of domicile–jurisdiction–effect of appointment of foreign guardian

S, a wealthy Norwegian citizen with a wife and son in Norway, set up home in England with A. He then suffered a disabling stroke and was admitted to hospital. S's son sought to remove him back to Norway but A, who had been granted power of attorney, resisted and secured an injunction restraining the son from removing S. A guardian was appointed by the Norwegian courts. A applied for a declaration that it would be unlawful for the guardian to remove S from England. The Norwegian guardian became a party to the proceedings.

Held, dismissing A's application, that the English courts' jurisdiction to decide on the legality of any proposed action in relation to an incapable adult was based on the presence of that person within the jurisdiction regardless of nationality. The appointment of a guardian in the country of that person's nationality or domicile did not remove that jurisdiction. The courts should, in the absence of any agreement between the nations involved, consider the comity of nations and the presumption was in favour of returning a person to the country of domicile. The burden of proof fell on those who asserted the contrary. On the facts of the case it was in S's best interests to be returned to Norway.

S (HOSPITAL PATIENT: FOREIGN CURATOR), *Re*; SUB NOM. S (HOSPITAL PATIENT: COURT'S JURISDICTION) (NO.2), *Re* [1996] Fam. 23, Hale, J., Fam Div.

4226. Guardianship–medical treatment–consent

MENTAL HEALTH (HOSPITAL, GUARDIANSHIP AND CONSENT TO TREATMENT) (AMENDMENT) REGULATIONS 1996, SI 1996 540; made under the Mental Health Act 1983 s.32. In force: April 1, 1996; £3.70.

These Regulations amend the Mental Health (Hospital, Guardianship and Consent to Treatment) Regulations 1983 (SI 1983 893) by prescribing Form 14 in place of Form 15 for records made under Reg.4(4) and by substituting new forms for those numbered 2, 3, 4, 7, 9, 10, 11, 12, 14, 15, 21, 22, 24, 28, 29, and 30.

4227. Mental Health Review Tribunals

MENTAL HEALTH REVIEW TRIBUNAL (AMENDMENT) RULES 1996, SI 1996 314; made under the Mental Health Act 1983 s.78. In force: April 1, 1996; £1.55.

These Rules amend the Mental Health Review Tribunal Rules 1983 (SI 1983 942) to provide for applications to Mental Health Review Tribunals in respect of patients subject to after care under supervision under the Mental Health Act 1983 as amended by the Mental Health (Patients in the Community) Act 1995. Rule 2, r.7 and r.8 of the principal Rules are amended to include reference to National Health Service trusts which were introduced by the National Health Service and Community Care Act 1990.

4228. Mental Health Review Tribunals

MENTAL HEALTH REVIEW TRIBUNALS (REGIONS) ORDER 1996, SI 1996 510; made under the Mental Health Act 1983 s.65. In force: April 1, 1996; £1.10.

This Order determines the regions of England for which Mental Health Review Tribunals are to exercise jurisdiction under the Mental Health Act 1983 from April 1, 1996. It also provides that an earlier determination of Tribunals' regions is to cease to have effect and makes transitional provision in relation to Tribunals in existence immediately before the Order comes into force.

4229. Mental patients–detention of conditionally discharged patient–whether Part II and Part III of Mental Health Act 1983 mutually exclusive of each other–statutory interpretation

[Mental Health Act 1983 s.3, s.118.]

S applied for judicial review of a decision by the trust to detain him compulsorily in hospital under the Mental Health Act 1983 s.3. When detained, S was already subject to a detention order and a restriction order, made pursuant to Part III of the Act. As such he had been conditionally discharged but not recalled when he was detained under s.3. S contended that Part II and Part III of the Act were mutually exclusive, thereby preventing his detention under powers contained in Part II when he was already subject to orders made under Part III.

Held, dismissing the application, that although there was no authority governing the issue, it was established practice to detain conditionally discharged patients in this way, as confirmed by guidance notes issued by both the Secretary of State for the Home Department and the Secretary of State for Health and also the code of practice issued pursuant to s.118, and there was nothing in the Act itself which served to exclude Part II powers applying to a restricted patient. The provisions relied on by S related only to patients liable to detention under a hospital order, and did not apply to admissions or detentions carried out under s.3. If such a patient were discharged by the tribunal, the discharge would be subject to a detention liability under s.3, which would not affect the Secretary of State's recall powers over a restricted patient. This interpretation allowed patients to have the benefit of treatment conferred by s.3(2)(c).

R. v. NORTH WEST LONDON MENTAL HEALTH NHS TRUST, *ex p.* STEWART, *The Times*, August 15, 1996, Harrison, J., QBD.

4230. Mental patients–discharge–mandatory duty to discharge patient–Mental Health Review Tribunal entitled to defer discharge

[Mental Health Act 1983 s.72.]

The mother of a mental patient, P, sought judicial review of the decision of a Mental Health Review Tribunal to defer the discharge of her daughter when exercising its mandatory duty under the Mental Health Act 1983 s.72(1)(b)(iii). P argued that, as the 1983 Act was meant to protect the vulnerable, if there had been power to defer the discharge in the case of the mandatory duty, it would have been clearly stated by Parliament.

Held, dismissing the application, that (1) a tribunal was entitled to defer the discharge of a mental patient when exercising its mandatory duty under s.72(1)(b)(iii). The section was unambiguous and it would have been clearly stated if the power to defer was restricted to the discretionary duty and (2) it was doubtful whether deferment would be lawful if it would expose a patient to further treatment to which he might be opposed.

R. v. MENTAL HEALTH REVIEW TRIBUNAL, *ex p.* PIERCE [1996] C.O.D. 467, Harrison, J., QBD.

4231. Mental patients–restriction orders–patient recalled to same hospital in which already detained–Secretary of State's jurisdiction to issue warrant–statutory interpretation

[Mental Health Act 1983 s.3, s.41, s.42.]

D, a mental patient recalled to hospital under a warrant issued under the Mental Health Act 1983 s.42(3), appealed against the refusal of his application for a writ of habeas corpus. Found not guilty of murder by reason of insanity in 1985, D had been conditionally discharged from hospital following a mental health review tribunal's decision in 1993, but had been re-admitted under s.3 of the 1983 Act when his condition deteriorated. While D was still in hospital, the Secretary of State issued a recall warrant for his detention in the same hospital, and D argued that the Secretary of State lacked jurisdiction to issue the warrant as D could not be recalled to a hospital in which he was already detained.

Held, dismissing the appeal, that where a patient was subject to a restriction order under s.41 of the Act, the Secretary of State had wide powers relating to re-admission and was entitled to issue a recall warrant extending the period of detention in the same hospital and also resuming the regime of control authorised by s.41. Any other interpretation would be absurd.

R. v. SECRETARY OF STATE FOR THE HOME DEPARTMENT, *ex p.* D; SUB NOM. DLODLO v. MENTAL HEALTH REVIEW TRIBUNAL FOR THE SOUTH THAMES REGION; DLODLO, RE, *The Times*, May 10, 1996, Sir Thomas Bingham, M.R., CA.

4232. Articles

A psychiatrist's comments on the White Paper on a new Mental Health Act *(Marcus Webb)*: M.L.J.I. 1996, 1(3), 83-85. (Proposals for Mental Health Review Board and criteria and procedures for committal).

Assessing mental patients in less secure environments *(Fenella Morris* and *Mark Mullins)*: N.L.J. 1996, 146(6747), 855-856. (Use of trial leave of absence to less secure hospital and effect on renewal of detention).

Can the law serve as the solution to social ills? The case of the Mental Health (Patients in the Community) Act 1995 *(Herschel Prins)*: Med. Sci. Law 1996, 36(3), 217-220. (Public and patient protection developments in mental health culminating in Act in force April 1, 1996 providing for supervised discharge requiring patient's consent and whether legislation can provide adequate levels of protection).

Caring for patients in the community *(Alan Parkin)*: M.L.R. 1996, 59(3), 414-426. (Background to 1995 Act which introduces legal state of supervised discharge for mental patients returning to community).

Challenging myths: counteracting prejudice and discrimination against psychiatric patients: the need for legal and social change *(Michael Potter)*: Writ 1996, 68(Apr), 6-7, 22. (Compulsory admissions to hospitals under 1961 Act and 1986 Order, right to medical confidentiality and protection against employment discrimination).

Characteristics of young offenders detained under section 53(2) at a young offenders' institution *(B.K. Puri)*: Med. Sci. Law 1996, 36(1), 69-76. (Findings of case study highlighting lack of information as to social and medical characteristics of offender group).

Clients' care *(Denzil Lush)*: L.S.G. 1996, 93(03), 24. (Guidance from Law Society and British Medical Association on assessment of mental capacity of clients).

Displacement of the nearest relative under the Mental Health Act 1983 *(Ajit Shah)*: Med. Sci. Law 1996, 36(4), 325-327. (Case study on dispensing with consent of nearest relative for detention of mental patient and criticism of procedures).

Mental incapacity *(Suzanne Woollard)*: S.J. 1996, 140(14), 360-361. (Inadequacy of law in relation to mental incapacity, property and affairs and medical treatment and Law Commission's draft bill addressing problems which will not be enacted).

Mentally disordered patients *(David Wells)*: Health Law 1996, Jul/Aug, 1-4. (Orders available to courts for dealing with mentally disabled people convicted of criminal offences).

Munchausen Syndrome *(David Smallwood)*: Fam. Law 1996, 26(Aug), 478-483. (Characteristics of syndrome and proxy variant with case history illustrating practical issues involved in representing, in both criminal and care proceedings, father alleged to have administered noxious substances to son).

Pilot mental health assessment and diversion scheme for an English Metropolitan Petty Sessional Division *(N.M. Greenhalgh)*: Med. Sci. Law 1996, 36(1), 52-58. (Findings of three month assessment scheme carried out by Leeds Magistrates' Courts showing 77 per cent of defendants suffering from psychiatric disorders).

Place of safety and section 136 at Gatwick airport *(Francesca L. Lowe-Ponsford* and *Ayaz Begg)*: Med. Sci. Law 1996, 36(4), 306-312. (Study of process by which people are picked up by police for behavioural reasons under s.136 and are removed to place of safety).

Psychopathology and civil commitment criteria *(John Dawson)*: Med. L. Rev. 1996, 4(1), 62-83. (Approaches to definition of mental state of person for purposes of commitment to mental hospital).

Still vulnerable after all these years *(Clare Palmer)*: Crim. L.R. 1996, Sep, 633-644. (Effectiveness of PACE codes of practice safeguards for protecting mentally ill or mentally disabled suspects detained in police custody).

The right to vote? *(Camilla Parker)*: N.L.J. 1996, 146(6759), 1328, 1330. (Extent to which voting rights unlawfully withdrawn from detained patients).

4233. Books

Dimond, Bridgit; Barker, Frances H.–Mental Health Law for Nurses. Paperback: £14.99. ISBN 0-632-03989-2. Blackwell Science (UK).

Eldergill, Anselm–The Law Relating to Mental Health Review Tribunals. Hardback: £48.00. ISBN 0-421-48330-X. Sweet & Maxwell.

Jones, Richard–Mental Health Act Manual. £35.00. ISBN 0-421-56430-X. Sweet & Maxwell.

Lorion, Raymond P.; Iscoe, Ira; DeLeon, Patrick H.; VandenBos, Gary R.–Psychology and Public Policy. Paperback: £23.95. ISBN 1-55798-347-X. American Psychological Association.

Prichard, Jane–Mental Health Law for Nurses. Central health studies series. Paperback: £9.95. ISBN 1-85642-012-4. Quay Books.
Smith, R.C.–A Case about Amy. Health, Society, and Policy. Hardback: £43.95. ISBN 1-56639-411-2. Paperback: £15.95. ISBN 1-56639-412-0. Temple University Press.

NATIONAL HEALTH SERVICE

4234. Committees

JOINT CONSULTATIVE COMMITTEES ORDER 1996, SI 1996 2820; made under the National Health Service Act 1977 s.22, s.126. In force: november 29, 1996; January 1, 1997; April 1, 1997; £1.55.

This Order makes provision for matters relating to Joint Consultative Committees set up under the National Health Service Act 1977 to advise Health Authorities and their associated local authorities on the performance of their duty to co-operate with one another in order to secure and advance the health and welfare of the people of England and Wales, and on the planning and operation of services of common concern to those bodies. It revokes and replaces the Joint Consultative Committee Order 1985 (SI 1985 305) in the light of the changes to National Health Service bodies introduced by the Health Authorities Act 1995.

4235. Community Health Councils–membership–proceedings

COMMUNITY HEALTH COUNCILS REGULATIONS 1996, SI 1996 640; made under the National Health Service Act 1977 s.17, s.126, s.128, Sch.7 para.2, Sch.7 para.3. In force: April 1, 1996; £2.40.

These Regulations supersede the Community Health Councils Regulations 1985. They make provision in connection with the establishment by the Secretary of State of Community Health Councils, and provide for their membership (Reg.2 to Reg.9), proceedings (Reg.10 to Reg.12, and Schedule), staff (Reg.13), premises (Reg.14), expenses (Reg.15) and functions (Reg.16 to Reg.21). These Regulations also make transitional provisions in relation to the membership of Community Health Councils (Reg.22), and revoke the Regulations which they replace, as well as the amending instruments (Reg.23).

4236. Consultants–appointments

NATIONAL HEALTH SERVICE (APPOINTMENT OF CONSULTANTS) REGULATIONS 1996, SI 1996 701; made under the National Health Service Act 1977 s.126, Sch.5 para.10, Sch.5 para.12. In force: April 1, 1996; £1.95.

These Regulations provide for the procedure to be followed by the Health Authorities and Special Health Authorities when appointing medical and dental practitioners to consultant posts in their employment. As respects those appointments to which the Regulations apply (Reg.3 and Reg.5), provision is made for the advertisement of vacant posts (Reg.6), for the constitution and procedure of Advisory Appointments Committees to select candidates and candidates' subsequent appointments by Authorities to consultant posts (Reg.9). These Regulations revoke the National Health Service (Appointment of Consultants) Regulations 1982, and two amending instruments, which are superseded by these Regulations (Reg.10), and make transitional provision in relation to appointments processes begun, but not completed, before April 1, 1996 (Reg.11).

4237. Consultants–appointments–Wales

NATIONAL HEALTH SERVICE (APPOINTMENT OF CONSULTANTS) (WALES) CONTINUATION AND TRANSITIONAL PROVISIONS ORDER 1996, SI 1996 433;

made under the National Health Service Act 1977 s.126; and the Health Authorities Act 1995 Sch.2 para.19, Sch.2 para.20. In force: March 28, 1996; £1.10.

These Regulations continue in force the National Health Service (Appointment of Consultants) (Wales) Regulations 1983 (SI 1983 1275) so that they apply to the new Welsh Health Authorities which were established under the Health Authorities Act 1995 and take over responsibility on April 1, 1996 for the discharge of health functions previously discharged by District Health Authorities and Family Health Service Authorities. The 1983 Regulations make provisions concerning procedures to be followed with respect to the appointment of consultants by Welsh District Health Authorities. Transitional provision is made with respect to appointments to the Chief Administrative Medical Officer and Director of Public Health Medicine, enabling action taken with respect to such an appointment to be treated for the purposes of the 1983 Regulations as action taken by new Welsh Health Authorities.

4238. Consultants–appointments–Wales

NATIONAL HEALTH SERVICE (APPOINTMENT OF CONSULTANTS) (WALES) REGULATIONS 1996, SI 1996 1313; made under the National Health Service Act 1977 s.126, Sch.5 para.10, Sch.5 para.12. In force: June 11, 1996; £1,95.

These Regulations provide for the procedure to be followed by Health Authorities and Special Health Authorities in Wales when appointing medical and dental practitioners to consultant posts. As respects those appointments to which the Regulations apply, provision is made for the advertisement of vacant posts, for the constitution and procedure of Advisory Appointments Committees to select candidates for appointment, and for the candidates' subsequent appointment by Authorities to consultant posts. They replace and revoke the National Health Service (Appointment of Consultants) (Wales) Regulations 1983 (SI 1983 1275) and make transitional provision in relation to those cases where Advisory Appointments Committees have been constituted under the 1983 Regulations but where the appointment process has not been completed by June 11, 1996.

4239. Dental services–dentists–terms of service

NATIONAL HEALTH SERVICE (GENERAL DENTAL SERVICES) AMENDMENT REGULATIONS 1996, SI 1996 704; made under the National Health Service Act 1977 s.15, s.35, s.36, s.37, s.126. In force: April 1, 1996; £1.95.

These Regulations further amend the National Health Service (General Dental Services) Regulations 1992 (SI 1992 661) (the 1992 Regulations). Part I includes in the 1992 Regulations what was formerly Regulation 19 of the National Health Service (Service Committees and Tribunal) Regulations 1992 (SI 1992 664) (the Services Committees and Tribunal Regulations). Part II amends dentists' terms of service contained in Sch.1 to the 1992 Regulations, to require dentists to establish and operate a complaints procedure within their practice. Part III makes various amendments consequential upon amendments to the Service Committees and Tribunal Regulations, and makes minor amendments to the terms of service in Sch.I regarding computerised estimate forms, information to be displayed in practice premises, and the correct name of the Northern Ireland equivalent of a Health Authority.

4240. Dental services

NATIONAL HEALTH SERVICE (GENERAL DENTAL SERVICES) AMENDMENT (NO.2) REGULATIONS 1996, SI 1996 2051; made under the National Health Service Act 1977 s.35, s.36, s.126. In force: September 1, 1996; £1.10.

These Regulations further amend the National Health Service (General Dental Services) Regulations 1992 (SI 1992 661). They reduce from two years to 15 months the period of all continuing care arrangements starting or extended on or after September 1, 1996 and provide for the period of capitation arrangements, starting or extended on or after September 1, 1996, to be 15 months. They also make provision, equivalent to that relating to continuing care arrangements, that the dentist shall provide a new treatment plan if during the currency of a current capitation arrangement the care and treatment given to a patient includes a specified item of treatment.

4241. Dental services–health authorities

NATIONAL HEALTH SERVICE (FUNCTIONS OF HEALTH AUTHORITIES IN ENGLAND) (GENERAL DENTAL SERVICES INCENTIVE SCHEMES) REGULATIONS 1996, SI 1996 2069; made under the National Health Service Act 1977 s.15, Sch.5 para.16; and the National Health Service Act 1997 s.126. In force: September 1, 1996; £0.65.

These Regulations give Health Authorities the additional functions of proposing to the Secretary of State schemes for making payments to general dental practitioners in the Authority's area to increase the provision of general dental services there and where the Secretary of State has approved such a scheme the Health authority is given the function of implementing it.

4242. Dentistry–charges

NATIONAL HEALTH SERVICE (DENTAL CHARGES) AMENDMENT REGULATIONS 1996, SI 1996 389; made under the National Health Service Act 1977 s.79A, Sch.12 para.3. In force: April 1, 1996; £0.65.

These Regulations further amend the National Health Service (Dental Charges) Regulations 1989 (SI 1989 394) to increase from £300 to £325 the maximum charge payable by the patient for dental treatment and appliances, where the contract or arrangement leading to the provision of such treatment or appliances is made on or after April 1, 1996.

4243. Disabled persons–wheelchairs–charges

NATIONAL HEALTH SERVICE (WHEELCHAIR CHARGES) REGULATIONS 1996, SI 1996 1503; made under the National Health Service Act 1977 s.81, s.126, s.128. In force: July 1, 1996; £0.65.

These Regulations provide for charges to be made and recovered by an NHS trust for the supply, at the request of a user, of a wheelchair of a more expensive type than, in the opinion of the NHS trust, is clinically necessary for the user.

4244. Dispute resolution–service contracts

NATIONAL HEALTH SERVICE CONTRACTS (DISPUTE RESOLUTION) REGULATIONS 1996, SI 1996 623; made under the National Health Service Act 1977 s.126, s.128; and the National Health Service and Community Care Act 1990 s.4. In force: April 1, 1996; £1.10.

These Regulations provide for the procedure to be followed where the Secretary of State has appointed a person to consider and determine a dispute between Health Service bodies regarding an NHS contract or the proposed terms of such a contract, and supersede earlier Regulations governing the determination of such disputes. They make provision for the person appointed to give both parties to the dispute and the Secretary of State an opportunity to make written representations. The person appointed may make oral representations and may consult experts. There are time limits for the various stages of the dispute resolution procedure. Provision is made for the adjudicator to record his determination in writing, give reasons for his determination and send it and the reasons for it to the parties and the Secretary of State.

4245. Doctors–disciplinary procedures

NATIONAL HEALTH SERVICE (GENERAL MEDICAL SERVICES) AMENDMENT REGULATIONS 1996, SI 1996 702; made under the National Health Service Act 1977 s.15, s.29, s.126. In force: April 1, 1996; £1.95.

These Regulations further amend the National Health Service (General Medical Services) Regulations 1992 (SI 1992 635) which regulate the terms on which general medical services are provided under the National Health Service Act 1977. Amendments are made to doctors' terms of service, disciplinary procedures and the system for dealing with complaints.

4246. Doctors–fund holding practices

NATIONAL HEALTH SERVICE (FUND-HOLDING PRACTICES) REGULATIONS 1996, SI 1996 706; made under the National Health Service Act 1977 s.126, Sch.5 para.16; and the National Health Service and Community Care Act 1990 s.14, s.15, s.16, s.17. In force: April 1, 1996; £4.15.

These Regulations consolidate, with amendments, the National Health Service (Fund-holding Practices) Regulations 1993 (SI 1993 567), the National Health Service (Fund-holding Practices) Amendment Regulations 1994 (SI 1994 640), National Health Service (Fund-holding Practices) Amendment Regulations 1995 (SI 1995 693), and the National Health Service (Fund-holding Practices) (Functions of Family Health Services Authorities) Regulations 1995 (SI 1995 3280). The Regulations contain provision relating to the recognition and operation of fund-holding practices. A fund-holding practice means a practice of one or more medical practitioners who are providing general medical services in accordance with arrangements under National Health Service Act 1977 s.29 and which has been recognised as a fund-holding practice in accordance with the National Health Service and Community Care Act 1990 s.14. A fund-holding practice is entitled to be paid an allotted sum in accordance with s.15(1) of the 1990 Act and may use that sum for purposes specified in these Regulations.

4247. Expenses–repayments

NATIONAL HEALTH SERVICE (TRAVELLING EXPENSES AND REMISSION OF CHARGES) AMENDMENT REGULATIONS 1996, SI 1996 410; made under the National Health Service Act 1977 s.83A, s.126, s.128. In force: March 18, 1996; £2.40.

The National Health Service (Travelling Expenses and Remission of Charges) Regulations 1988 (SI 1988 551), which provide for the remission of repayment of certain charges and for the payment of travelling expenses incurred in attending hospitals, are amended by these Regulations.

4248. Expenses–repayments

NATIONAL HEALTH SERVICE (TRAVELLING EXPENSES AND REMISSION OF CHARGES) AMENDMENT (NO.2) REGULATIONS 1996, SI 1996 1346; made under the National Health Service Act 1977 s.83A, s.126, s.128. In force: June 11, 1996; £0.65.

These Regulations further amend the National Health Service (Travelling Expenses and Remission of Charges) Regulations 1988 (SI 1988 551) which provide for the remission and repayment of certain charges which would otherwise be payable under the National Health Service Act 1977 and for the payment of travelling expenses incurred in attending a hospital. The financial disregards applied in calculating student income are amended.

4249. Expenses–repayments

NATIONAL HEALTH SERVICE (TRAVELLING EXPENSES AND REMISSION OF CHARGES) AMENDMENT (NO.3) ORDER 1996, SI 1996 2362; made under the

National Health Service Act 1977 s.83A, s.126, s.128. In force: October 7, 1996; £1.10.

These Regulations further amend the National Health Service (Travelling Expenses and Remission of Charges) Regulations 1988 (SI 1988 551), which provide for the remission and repayment of certain charges which would otherwise be payable under the National Health Service Act 1977 and for the payment of travelling expenses incurred in attending a hospital. Regulation 2 amends the definition of family and adds a definition of income based jobseeker's allowance. Regulation 3 amends Reg.4 of the principal Regulations, which contains a list of descriptions of persons entitled to full remission and payment, by removing the capital restriction which applied to persons in receipt of disability working allowance and certain members of their family. The list is also amended to include persons who are in receipt of an income based jobseeker's allowance of less that 10 pence (and therefore do not actually receive such an allowance), and certain members of their family. Regulation 4 amends Reg.7 of the principal Regulations by removing the requirements for certain persons in receipt of disability working allowance to make a claim on a form provided for that purpose and for the Secretary of State to calculate the capital resources of such persons. Regulation 5 amends Sch.1A to the principal Regulations, so as to specify the period for which a notice of entitlement is effective for a person whose entitlement to an income based jobseeker's allowance is less than 10 pence. The amendments also omit the period previously specified for persons in receipt of disability allowance whose capital did not exceed £8,000.

4250. Health authorities

HEALTH AUTHORITIES ACT 1995 (TRANSITIONAL PROVISIONS) ORDER 1996, SI 1996 709; made under the National Health Service Act 1977 s.126; and the Health Authorities Act 1995 Sch.2 para.4, Sch.2 para.7, Sch.2 para.13, Sch.2 para.14, Sch.2 para.16, Sch.2 para.18, Sch.2 para.19, Sch.2 para.20. In force: April 1, 1996; £3.20.

This Order makes transitional provision in connection with the abolition, by the Health Authorities Act 1995 on April 1, 1996, of Regional Health Authorities, District Health Authorities and Family Health Services Authorities, and the establishment under that Act of Health Authorities to exercise functions, principally on behalf of the Secretary of State, in relation to the National Health Service. In particular, the Order identifies the bodies which are to be the successors, for specified purposes, of bodies abolished on April 1, 1996 (Art.1 (2) and Sch.1 to Sch.4). Provision is made for the transfer to new employers of staff employed by the abolished bodies on March 1, 1996 (Art.2 and Art.3), for the transfer of property held on charitable trusts (Art.4), for the accounts and the winding up of affairs of abolished bodies (Art.5), and for their responsibilities in relation to charities connected with the health service (Art.6 and Art.7). The Order also provides for the investigation on and after April 1, 1996 of complaints made against, or made to, an abolished body before that date (Art.9 and Art.10), for the continuation of Community Health Councils in existence on March 31, 1996 (Art.11), for the appointment of members by voluntary organisations to Joint Consultative Committees between April 1, 1996 and September 30, 1996 (Art.12), and for securing continuity in the exercise from April 1, 1996 of functions previously exercised by abolished bodies (Art.13 and Art.14).

4251. Health authorities

HEALTH AUTHORITIES ACT 1995 (TRANSITIONAL PROVISIONS) AMENDMENT ORDER 1996, SI 1996 2310; made under the National Health Service Act 1977 s.126; and the Health Authorities Act 1995 Sch.2 para.19, Sch.2 para.20. In force: September 30, 1996; £0.65.

This Order further amends the Health Authorities Act 1995 (Transitional Provisions) Order 1996 (SI 1996 709), which makes transitional provision in connection with the abolition, by the Health Authorities Act 1995 on April 1, 1996, of Regional Health Authorities, District Health Authorities and Family

Health Services Authorities, and the establishment under that Act of Health Authorities to exercise functions, principally on behalf of the Secretary of State, in relation to the National Health Service. This Order extends until December 31, 1996 the period during which certain persons who were members of Joint Consultative Committees on March 31, 1996 are to be given the opportunity to serve on such Committees, under the transitional arrangements made by the 1996 Order.

4252. Health authorities

HEALTH AUTHORITIES ACT 1995 (AMENDMENT OF TRANSITIONAL PROVISIONS AND MODIFICATION OF REFERENCES) ORDER 1996, SI 1996 971; made under the National Health Service Act 1977 s.126; and the Health Authorities Act 1995 s.2, Sch.2 para.4, Sch.2 para.7, Sch.2 para.18, Sch.2 para.19, Sch.2 para.20. In force: April 1, 1996; £1.95.

This Order, which amends the Health Authorities Act 1995 (Transitional Provisions) Order 1996 (SI 1996 709), is made in connection with the abolition of Regional Health Authorities, District Health Authorities and Family Health Services Authorities on April 1, 1996 and the establishment of Health Authorities to exercise functions in relation to the National Health Service. Article 2 makes further provision for the transfer of staff employed by the District Health and Family Health Services Authorities, for the transfer of trust property held by District Health Authorities and for continuity in the exercise of functions. Further amendments to the principal Order relate to Local Representative Committees, pharmaceutical services, general dental services, the National Health Service Tribunal and fund holding practices. Article 3 makes provision in relation to references to the bodies abolished on April 1, 1996 and the areas for which they were established to act.

4253. Health authorities

HEALTH AUTHORITIES (MEMBERSHIP AND PROCEDURE) REGULATIONS 1996, SI 1996 707; made under the National Health Service Act 1977 s.126, s.128, Sch.5 para.1, Sch.5 para.2, Sch.5 para.3, Sch.5 para.4, Sch.5 para.12, Sch.5 para.12A. In force: April 1, 1996; £3.20.

These Regulations make provision concerning the membership and procedure of Health Authorities established under the National Health Service Act 1977 as amended by the Health Authorities Act 1995. They include in Part II provisions relating to the number of members and conditions of membership (Reg.2, Reg.3 and Sch.1), the tenure of office of members and termination of tenure of office and eligibility for reappointment (Reg.4 to Reg.9) and disqualification for appointment and cessation of disqualification. (Reg.10, Reg.11 and Sch.2). In Part III provisions are included relating to vice-chairmen (Reg.12 and Reg.13), the appointment of committees and sub-committees (Reg.14) and meetings and proceedings on account of pecuniary interest (Reg.15, Reg.16 and Sch.3). The Regulations relating to the membership and procedure of Regional Health Authorities, District Health Authorities and Family Health Services Authorities, which are abolished by the Health Authorities Act 1995, and revoked (Reg.17 and Sch.4). Amendments are also made to Regulations which make provision for the membership and procedure of certain special Health Authorities by reference to these Regulations of the revoked Regulations (Reg.17 and Sch.5).

4254. Health authorities–abolition–transitional provisions–Wales

HEALTH AUTHORITIES ACT 1995 (TRANSITIONAL PROVISIONS) (WALES) AMENDMENT ORDER 1996, SI 1996 3019; made under the National Health Service Act 1977 s.126; and the Health Authorities Act 1995 Sch.2 para.19, Sch.2 para.20. In force: December 31, 1996; £1.10.

This Order further amends the Health Authorities Act 1995 (Transitional Provisions) Order 1996 (SI 1996 709) which makes transitional provision in connection with the abolition of Regional Health Authorities, District Health

Authorities and Family Health Services Authorities, and the establishment of Health Authorities to exercise functions in relation to the National Health Service. This Order further extends until March 31, 1997 the period during which certain persons who were members of Joint Consultative Committees in Wales on March 31, 1996 are to be given the opportunity to serve on such Committees, under the transitional arrangements made by the 1996 Order.

4255. Health authorities–establishment

HEALTH AUTHORITIES (ENGLAND) ESTABLISHMENT ORDER 1996, SI 1996 624; made under the National Health Service Act 1977 s.8, s.126. In force: April 1, 1996; £2.40.

This Order establishes, for the purposes of the National Health Service Act 1977, Health Authorities to act for the areas of England which are specified in the Schedule to the Order.

4256. Health authorities–establishment–Wales

HEALTH AUTHORITIES (WALES) ESTABLISHMENT ORDER 1996, SI 1996 146; made under the National Health Service Act 1977 s.8, s.126; and the Welsh Language Act 1993 s.25. In force: April 1, 1996; £0.65.

This Order establishes five health authorities in Wales, namely, Bro Taf Health Authority, Dyfed Powys Health Authority, Gwent Health Authority, Morgannwg Health Authority and North Wales Health Authority and specifies the areas for which the Authorities are to act. The combined area for which the Authorities are to act comprises the whole of Wales.

4257. Health authorities–functions

NATIONAL HEALTH SERVICE (FUNCTIONS OF HEALTH AUTHORITIES AND ADMINISTRATION ARRANGEMENTS) REGULATIONS 1996, SI 1996 708; made under the Health Services and Public Health Act 1968 s.63; and the National Health Service Act 1977 s.13, s.16, s.17, s.18, s.51, s.126. In force: April 1, 1996; £1.95.

These Regulations make provision for the Secretary of State's functions relating to the health service to be exercised by Health Authorities (Reg.3 and Sch.1) and for certain restrictions on the Health Authorities' exercise of those functions (Reg.4). The Regulations also provide for the arrangements which may be made by Health Authorities and Special Health Authorities for their functions to be exercised jointly with other bodies, or on their behalf by their committees, sub-committees or officers, or by the committees, sub-committees or officers of other bodies (Reg.5). These Regulations also revoke three earlier instruments which were concerned with the exercise of functions by Regional Health Authorities, District Health Authorities and Family Health Services Authorities (bodies which have been abolished as a result of amendments made to the National Health Service Act 1977 by the Health Authorities Act 1995) and provisions in two other instruments concerned with the exercise of functions by particular Special Health Authorities (Reg.6 and Sch.2).

4258. Health authorities–functions–complaints

NATIONAL HEALTH SERVICE (FUNCTIONS OF HEALTH AUTHORITIES) (COMPLAINTS) REGULATIONS 1996, SI 1996 669; made under the National Health Service Act 1977 s.15, s.126. In force: April 1, 1996; £0.65.

These Regulations confer on Health Authorities the function of establishing and operating procedures for dealing with complaints about family health service practitioners (definition in Art.1 of the Regulations) in accordance with directions made by the Secretary of State under the National Health Service Act 1977.

4259. Health authorities–functions–London initiative zones

NATIONAL HEALTH SERVICE (FUNCTIONS OF HEALTH AUTHORITIES IN LONDON) REGULATIONS 1996, SI 1996 654; made under the National Health Service Act 1977 s.15, s.17, s.126. In force: April 1, 1996; £1.10.

These Regulations replace the National Health Service (Functions of Family Health Services Authorities in London) Regulations 1994 (SI 1994 284) and reflect the abolition of Family Health Services Authorities and the creation of Health Authorities by the Health Authorities Act 1995. The Regulations provide for the Health Authorities in a certain area of London (called the London Initiative Zone) to make practice premises available to doctors providing general medical services as part of the National Health Service. Their powers to acquire property for this purpose do not extend beyond March 31, 1999. The area of the London Initiative Zone is defined in the Schedule to the Regulations.

4260. Health authorities–functions–transitional arrangements

NATIONAL HEALTH SERVICE (TRANSITIONAL FUNCTIONS OF HEALTH AUTHORITIES) (ADMINISTRATION ARRANGEMENTS) REGULATIONS 1996, SI 1996 2285; made under the National Health Service Act 1977 s.16, s.126. In force: September 26, 1996; £0.65.

These Regulations make further provision for the arrangements which may be made by Health Authorities for their functions to be exercised jointly with other Health Authorities or on their behalf by their committees, sub-committees or officers, or by other Health Authorities or by the committees, sub-committees or officers of other Authorities. The Regulations enable such arrangements to be made in the case of certain transitional functions conferred on Health Authorities by Orders made under the Health Authorities Act 1995 Sch.2 in connection with the abolition by that Act of District Health Authorities and Family Health Services Authorities.

4261. Health authorities–investigation of complaints–mental hospitals

HEALTH SERVICE COMMISSIONERS FOR ENGLAND (AUTHORITIES FOR THE ASHWORTH, BROADMOOR AND RAMPTON HOSPITALS) ORDER 1996, SI 1996 717; made under the Health Service Commissioners Act 1993 s.2. In force: April 15, 1996; £0.65.

This Order designates the Ashworth, Broadmoor and Rampton Hospital Authorities as relevant bodies within the meaning of the Health Service Commissioners Act 1993 s.2 so that the Health Service Commissioner for England may investigate complaints which relate to these Special Health Authorities or their officers. The Order also revokes the Health Service Commissioner for England (Special Hospitals Service Authority) Order 1990 consequentially upon the abolition of the Special Hospitals Service Authority.

4262. Health authorities–teaching hospitals–abolition

AUTHORITIES FOR LONDON POST-GRADUATE TEACHING HOSPITALS (ABOLITION) ORDER 1996, SI 1996 511; made under the National Health Service Act 1977 s.11, s.126. In force: April 1, 1996; £1.10.

This Order abolishes, on April 1, 1996, the Board of Governors of the National Hospital for Neurology and Neurosurgery and the Board of Governors of the Eastman Dental Hospital which are special health authorities continued in being by the Authorities for London Post-Graduate Teaching Hospitals Order 1990. The Order makes provision for the transfer of property, rights and liabilities from those special health authorities to the Secretary of State (Art.3). It also makes further provision consequential on the abolition of those special health authorities.

4263. Health authorities–teaching hospitals–revocation

AUTHORITIES FOR LONDON POST-GRADUATE TEACHING HOSPITALS (REVOCATION) REGULATIONS 1996, SI 1996 512; made under the National

Health Service Act 1977 s.16, s.17, s.18, s.80, s.126, s.128, Sch.5 para.12, Sch.5 para.12A. In force: April 1, 1996; £0.65.

These Regulations revoke the Authorities for London Post-Graduate Teaching Hospitals Regulations 1990 (SI 1990 1526) which provided for the membership and procedure of the special health authorities for London post-graduate teaching hospitals.

4264. Health authorities–transfer of assets

SOLIHULL HEALTH AUTHORITY (TRANSFER OF TRUST PROPERTY) ORDER 1996, SI 1996 2360; made under the National Health Service Act 1977 s.92. In force: October 8, 1996; £0.65.

This Order transfers to the Solihull Health Authority on October 8, 1996 trust property held by the Birmingham Health Authority.

4265. Health authorities–transfer of assets–Wales

HEALTH AUTHORITIES (WALES) (TRANSFER OF TRUST PROPERTY) ORDER 1996, SI 1996 495; made under the National Health Service Act 1977 s.126; and the Health Authorities Act 1995 Sch.2 para.4. In force: April 1, 1996; £1.10.

On April 1, 1996, as a result of the Health Authorities Act 1995, Welsh District Health Authorities will cease to exist. Health Authorities established under that Act will come into existence at the same time. This Order, subject to a limited exception, transfers trust property held by those old authorities to the new Welsh authorities.

4266. Health Service Commissioners (Amendment) Act 1996 (c.5)

An Act to make provisions about the Health Service Commissioners.

This Act received Royal Assent on March 21, 1996.

4267. Health Service Commissioners (Amendment) Act 1996 Commencement Order

HEALTH SERVICE COMMISSIONERS (AMENDMENT) ACT 1996 (COMMENCEMENT) ORDER 1996, SI 1996 970 (C.15); made under the Health Service Commissioners Act 1996 s.14. In force: April 1, 1996; £0.65.

This Order brings the Health Service Commissioners (Amendment) Act 1966 into force on April 1, 1996. It also brings certain actions, begun before April 1, 1996 and continuing after that date, within the scope of the Health Service Commissioners Act 1993 as amended by the Act.

4268. Hospitals–abolition

SPECIAL HOSPITALS SERVICE AUTHORITY (ABOLITION) ORDER 1996, SI 1996 490; made under the National Health Service Act 1977 s.11, s.126. In force: April 1, 1996; £1.10.

This Order revokes the Special Hospitals Service Authority (Establishment and Constitution) Order 1989 (SI 1989 948) and abolishes the Special Hospitals Service Authority established under that Order. It makes supplemental provision relating to the winding up of the affairs of the old Authority and the transfer of rights and liabilities.

4269. Hospitals–establishment

AUTHORITIES FOR THE ASHWORTH, BROADMOOR AND RAMPTON HOSPITALS (ESTABLISHMENT AND CONSTITUTION) ORDER 1996, SI 1996 488; made under the National Health Service Act 1977 s.11, s.126, Sch.5 para.9. In force: April 1, 1996; £1.10.

Provision is made for the establishment, constitution and remuneration of members of the Special Health Authorities of Ashworth Hospital Authority, Broadmoor Hospital Authority and Rampton Hospital Authority. The purpose of establishment of the Authorities is to manage the respective hospitals and for the purposes of providing mental health and other services as directed by the Secretary of State.

4270. Hospitals–functions and membership

ASHWORTH, BROADMOOR AND RAMPTON HOSPITAL AUTHORITIES (FUNCTIONS AND MEMBERSHIP) REGULATIONS 1996, SI 1996 489; made under the National Health Service Act 1977 s.13, s.16, s.18, s.126, Sch.5 para.10, Sch.5 para.12, Sch.5 para.16. In force: April 1, 1996; £3.20.

Provision is made for the functions, membership and proceedings of Special Health Authorities established to manage the Ashworth, Broadmoor and Rampton special hospitals. The Regulations cover the functions of hospital authorities, appointment of members and officers, tenure of membership, termination and suspension of membership of members, disqualification, cessation of disqualification, appointment and powers of vice chairman, the exercise of functions, meetings and proceedings, disability on grounds of pecuniary interest and public meetings. The Schedules to the Regulations set out provisions of the National Health Service Act 1977 conferring functions exercisable by the hospital authorities and rules as to meetings and proceedings of the hospital authorities.

4271. Liability–personal injuries

NATIONAL HEALTH SERVICE (EXISTING LIABILITIES SCHEME) REGULATIONS 1996, SI 1996 686; made under the National Health Service Act 1977 s.126; and the National Health Service and Community Care Act 1990 s.21. In force: April 1, 1996; £1.10.

These Regulations establish a Scheme (to be known as the Existing Liabilities Scheme) whereby bodies providing services under the National Health Service Act 1977 may make provision for meeting liabilities to third parties in connection with personal injury arising out of negligence in the carrying out of functions under that Act (Reg.2, Reg.3, and Reg.4). The Scheme is to be administered by the Secretary of State (Reg.5). Provision is also made for payments by the Secretary of State under the Scheme (Reg.6) and for the provision of information by bodies to the Secretary of State for the purposes of the Scheme (Reg.7).

4272. Liability–transfer

[National Health Service (Residual Liabilities) Act 1996.]

The Department of Health issued a press release entitled *Royal Assent for NHS (Residual Liabilities) Bill* (Press release 96/177), published on May 23, 1996. Royal Assent has been given to the Bill which sets out arrangements for outstanding liabilities if an NHS Trust, Health Authority or Special Health Authority ceases to exist. The Act places a duty on the Secretary of State for Health to ensure that all liabilities are transferred to other specified bodies or to the Secretary of State. Health Secretary Stephen Dorrell said that the Act would be of particular importance to the Private Finance Initiative and would be of benefit to both taxpayers and patients.

4273. Litigation

NATIONAL HEALTH SERVICE LITIGATION AUTHORITY (AMENDMENT) REGULATIONS 1996, SI 1996 968; made under the National Health Service Act 1977 s.126, Sch.5 para.12. In force: April 19, 1996; £0.65.

These Regulations amend the National Health Service Litigation Authority Regulations 1995 (SI 1995 2801) which provide for the membership and procedure of the National Health Service Litigation Authority, a special health authority established under the National Health Service Act 1977, to correct the provision in those Regulations governing the number of members who must be present before business may be transacted at meetings of the authority.

4274. Medical negligence–compensation

NATIONAL HEALTH SERVICE (CLINICAL NEGLIGENCE SCHEME) REGULATIONS 1996, SI 1996 251; made under the National Health Service Act 1977 s.126; and the National Health Service and Community Care Act 1990 s.21. In force: March 1, 1996; £1.95.

The Clinical Negligence Scheme for Trusts, which will be administered by the Secretary of State, is established by these Regulations so that NHS trusts and certain other bodies providing services under the National Health Service Act 1977 may make provision for meeting liabilities to third parties in connection with personal injury arising from negligence whilst carrying out their functions. Provision is made for bodies to be admitted, withdrawn and expelled from the scheme and for bodies to provide information to the Secretary of State for the purposes of the Scheme.

4275. Medicines–charges

NATIONAL HEALTH SERVICE (CHARGES FOR DRUGS AND APPLIANCES) AMENDMENT REGULATIONS. 1996, SI 1996 583; made under the National Health Service Act 1977 s.77, s.126. In force: April 1, 1996; £1.10.

These Regulations further amend the National Health Service (Charges for Drugs and Appliances) Regulations 1989 (SI 1989 419) (the principal Regulations) which provide for the making and recovery of charges for drugs and appliances supplied by doctors and chemists providing pharmaceutical services, and by the Health Authorities and NHS trusts to out-patients. Amendments made to the principal Regulations by Reg.2 alter the specified description of a nurse or health visitor mentioned in the definition of "nurse prescriber" in Reg.2(1) of the principal Regulations to include a nurse employed by a medical practitioner whose name is included in a medical list. Amendments made to the principal Regulations by Reg.3 and the Schedule increase the charge for items on prescription or supplied to out-patients from £5.25 to £5.50. The charge for elastic stockings is increased from £5.25 to £5.50 each (from £10.50 to £11.00 per pair) and that for tights from £10.50 to £11.00. The charges for partial human hair wigs and modacrylic wigs are increased from £115.00 to £120.00 and from £44.00 to £46.00 respectively. The charge for full human hair wigs is increased from £167.00 to £175.00. The charge for fabric supports is increased from £27.00 to £28.30 and the charge for surgical brassieres is increased from £19.00 to £19.25. The sums prescribed for the grant of pre-payment certificates are increased from £27.20 to £28.50 for a four monthly certificate and from £74.80 to £78.40 for a 12 monthly certificate. These Regulations also make transitional arrangements in Reg.4 in respect of pre-payment certificates and appliances ordered before the coming into force of these Regulations.

4276. National Health Service (Amendment) Act 1995–Commencement No.3 Order

NATIONAL HEALTH SERVICE (AMENDMENT) ACT 1995 (COMMENCEMENT NO.3) ORDER 1996, SI 1996 552 (C.11); made under the National Health Service (Amendment) Act 1995 s.14. In force: bringing into force various provisions of the Act on April 1, 1996; £0.65.

This Order brings into force on April 1, 1996 all the remaining provisions of the National Health Service (Amendment) Act 1995, so far as they are not already in force. That Act amends the National Health Service Act 1977 (1977 c.49) and the National Health Service (Scotland) Act 1978 (1978 c.29). The provisions brought into force relate to powers of the National Health Service Tribunal in relation to opticians, ophthalmic medical practitioners and pharmacists; to direct the interim suspension of practitioners providing family health services under the National Health Service Act 1977 and under the National Health Service (Scotland) Act 1978; and to declare when disqualifying them from inclusion in any list of such practitioners kept, in England and Wales, by a Family Health Services Authority or, in Scotland, by a Health Board that they are not fit to be engaged in any capacity in the provision of those services.

4277. National Health Service (Residual Liabilities) Act 1996 (c.15)

An Act to make provision with respect to the transfer of liabilities of certain National Health Service bodies in the event of their ceasing to exist.

This Act received Royal Assent on May 22, 1996.

4278. NHS trusts

NATIONAL HEALTH SERVICE TRUSTS (MEMBERSHIP AND PROCEDURE) AMENDMENT REGULATIONS 1996, SI 1996 1755; made under the National Health Service Act 1977 s.126; and the National Health Service and Community Care Act 1990 s.5. In force: July 29, 1996; £1.10.

These Regulations amend the National Health Service Trusts (Membership and Procedure) Regulations 1990 (SI 1990 2024) which make provision in connection with the membership and procedure of NHS trusts established under the National Health Service and Community Care Act 1990 Part I. The 1990 Regulations are amended to require that all non-executive directors of NHS trusts in England and Wales are to be appointed by the Secretary of State. In consequence of this change, references to the appointing authority are amended in parts of the 1990 Regulations which are concerned with the tenure of office of directors and the removal of disqualification for appointment as a chairman or director.

4279. NHS trusts–ambulance service–establishment

ESSEX AMBULANCE SERVICE NATIONAL HEALTH SERVICE TRUST (ESTABLISHMENT) AMENDMENT ORDER 1996, SI 1996 2602; made under the National Health Service Act 1977 s.126; and the National Health Service and Community Care Act 1990 s.5. In force: October 28, 1996; £0.65.

This Order amends the constitution of an NHS trust established by Order under the National Health Service and Community Care Act 1990 Part I, by reducing the number of non-executive directors from five to four and the number of executive directors from five to four.

4280. NHS trusts–ambulance service–establishment

LONDON AMBULANCE SERVICE NATIONAL HEALTH SERVICE TRUST (ESTABLISHMENT) ORDER 1996, SI 1996 90; made under the National Health Service and Community Care Act 1990 s.5, Sch.2. In force: January 28, 1996; £1.10.

The London Ambulance Service National Health Service Trust is established as an NHS trust under the National Health Service and Community Care Act 1990 s.5. Article 5 of this Order specifies the operational date as April 1, 1996 and the accounting date of March 31 for the new trust, Art.7 makes provision for the trust to receive assistance from health authorities prior to its operational date, Art.8 specifies the value of assets above which the Secretary of State must consider the disposal of the asset to be £1,000,000 and Art.6 and Art.3 provide for the functions of the trust before and after its operational date.

4281. NHS trusts–ambulance service–establishment–Wales

SOUTH AND EAST WALES AMBULANCE NATIONAL HEALTH SERVICE TRUST (ESTABLISHMENT) (AMENDMENT) ORDER 1996, SI 1996 2288; made under the National Health Service Act 1977 s.126; and the National Health Service and Community Care Act 1990 s.5. In force: September 5, 1996; £0.65.

This Order amends the South and East Wales Ambulance National Health Service (Establishment) Order 1992 (SI 1992 2740) by providing that the number of executive and non-executive directors of the NHS trust established by that Order shall, in each case, be four.

4282. **NHS trusts–ambulance service–transfer of assets**

OXFORDSHIRE AMBULANCE NATIONAL HEALTH SERVICE TRUST (TRANSFER OF TRUST PROPERTY) ORDER 1996, SI 1996 1777; made under the National Health Service Act 1977 s.92. In force: July 31, 1996; £1.10.

This Order transfers to the Oxfordshire Ambulance National Health Service Trust on July 31, 1996 trust property held by Oxfordshire Health Authority.

4283. **NHS trusts–ambulance service–transfer of assets**

SUSSEX AMBULANCE SERVICE NATIONAL HEALTH SERVICE TRUST (TRANSFER OF TRUST PROPERTY) ORDER 1996, SI 1996 91; made under the National Health Service Act 1977 s.92. In force: February 16, 1996; £0.65.

Trust property formerly held by the East Sussex Health Authority is transferred to the Sussex Ambulance Service National Health Service Trust on February 16, 1996.

4284. **NHS trusts–ambulance service–transfer of assets**

WEST WALES AMBULANCE NATIONAL HEALTH SERVICE TRUST (TRANSFER OF TRUST PROPERTY) ORDER 1996, SI 1996 522; made under the National Health Service Act 1977 s.92. In force: April 1, 1996; £0.65.

This Order transfers to the West Wales Ambulance National Health Service Trust on April 1, 1996 trust property formerly held by Dyfed Health Authority.

4285. **NHS trusts–ambulance service–transfer of assets**

WEST WALES AMBULANCE NATIONAL HEALTH SERVICE TRUST (TRANSFER OF TRUST PROPERTY) (NO.2) ORDER 1996, SI 1996 523; made under the National Health Service Act 1977 s.92. In force: April 1, 1996; £0.65.

This Order transfers to the West Wales Ambulance National Health Service Trust on April 1, 1996 trust property formerly held by West Glamorgan Health Authority.

4286. **NHS trusts–change of name**

CORNWALL AND ISLES OF SCILLY LEARNING DISABILITIES NATIONAL HEALTH SERVICE TRUST (CHANGE OF NAME) ORDER 1996, SI 1996 1768; made under the National Health Service Act 1977 s.126; and the National Health Service and Community Care Act 1990 s.5. In force: July 18, 1996; £1.10.

This Order changes the name of the Cornwall and Isles of Scilly Learning Disabilities National Health Service Trust to the Trecare National Health Service Trust.

4287. **NHS trusts–change of name**

GRIMSBY HEALTH NATIONAL HEALTH SERVICE TRUST (CHANGE OF NAME) ORDER 1996, SI 1996 2034; made under the National Health Service Act 1977 s.126; and the National Health Service and Community Care Act 1990 s.5. In force: August 12, 1996; £0.65.

This Order changes the name of the Grimsby Health National Health Service Trust to the North East Lincolnshire National Health Service Trust.

4288. **NHS trusts–change of name**

LINCOLN HOSPITALS NATIONAL HEALTH SERVICE TRUST (CHANGE OF NAME) ORDER 1996, SI 1996 872; made under the National Health Service Act 1977 s.126; and the National Health Service and Community Care Act 1990 s.5. In force: April 1, 1996; £0.65.

This Order changes the name of an NHS trust established by Order under the National Health Service and Community Care Act 1990 Part I from the Lincoln Hospitals National Health Service Trust to the Lincoln and Louth National Health Service Trust, and makes consequential amendments to that Order and transitional provisions.

4289. NHS trusts–change of name

ROYAL LIVERPOOL CHILDREN'S HOSPITAL AND COMMUNITY SERVICES NATIONAL HEALTH SERVICE TRUST (CHANGE OF NAME) ORDER 1996, SI 1996 539; made under the National Health Service Act 1977 s.126; and the National Health Service and Community Care Act 1990 s.5. In force: March 15, 1996; £0.65.

This Order changes the name of an NHS trust established by Order under the National Health Service and Community Care Act 1990 Part I from the Royal Liverpool Children's Hospital and Community Services National Health Service Trust to the Royal Liverpool Children's National Health Service Trust, and makes consequential amendments to that Order and transitional provisions.

4290. NHS trusts–change of name

ROYAL SURREY COUNTY AND ST. LUKE'S HOSPITALS NATIONAL HEALTH SERVICE TRUST (CHANGE OF NAME) ORDER 1996, SI 1996 2860; made under the National Health Service Act 1977 s.126; and the National Health Service and Community Care Act 1990 s.5. In force: April 1, 1997; £0.65.

This Order changes the name of an NHS trust established by Order under the National Health Service and Community Care Act 1990 Part I from the Royal Surrey County and St Luke's Hospitals National Health Service Trust to the Royal Surrey County Hospital National Health Service Trust, and makes consequential amendments to that Order and transitional provisions.

4291. NHS trusts–change of name

WEST LAMBETH COMMUNITY CARE NATIONAL HEALTH SERVICE TRUST (CHANGE OF NAME) ORDER 1996, SI 1996 1769; made under the National Health Service Act 1977 s.126; and the National Health Service and Community Care Act 1990 s.5. In force: July 18, 1996; £1.10.

This Order changes the name of West Lambeth Community Care National Health Service Trust to the Lambeth Healthcare National Health Service Trust.

4292. NHS trusts–debts

NATIONAL HEALTH SERVICE TRUSTS (ORIGINATING CAPITAL DEBT) ORDER 1996, SI 1996 350; made under the National Health Service and Community Care Act 1990 s.9. In force: March 1, 1996; £1.10.

This Order determines the amount of the originating capital debt provided for in the National Health Service and Community Care Act 1990 s.9 of NHS trusts established under that Act with an operational date of April 1, 1995. It provides also for the splitting of the originating capital debts into loan and public dividend capital.

4293. NHS trusts–dissolution

BIRMINGHAM HEARTLANDS HOSPITAL NATIONAL HEALTH SERVICE TRUST (DISSOLUTION) ORDER 1996, SI 1996 882; made under the National Health Service Act 1977 s.126; and the National Health Service and Community Care Act 1990 s.5, Sch.2 para.29. In force: April 1, 1996; £0.65.

This Order provides for the dissolution on April 1, 1996 of the Birmingham Heartlands Hospital National Health Service Trust.

4294. NHS trusts–dissolution

BRIDGEND AND DISTRICT NATIONAL HEALTH SERVICE TRUST (DISSOLUTION) ORDER 1996, SI 1996 255; made under the National Health Service Act 1977 s.126; and the National Health Service and Community Care Act 1990 s.5, Sch.2 para.29. In force: April 1, 1996; £0.65.

This Order provides for the dissolution on April 1, 1996 of the Bridgend and District National Health Service Trust established on November 16, 1992.

4295. **NHS trusts–dissolution**

GLAN HAFREN NATIONAL HEALTH SERVICE TRUST (DISSOLUTION) ORDER 1996, SI 1996 256; made under the National Health Service Act 1977 s.126; and the National Health Service and Community Care Act 1990 s.5, Sch.2 para.29. In force: April 1, 1996; £0.65.

This Order provides for the dissolution on April 1, 1996 of the Glan Hafren National Health Service Trust established on November 16, 1992.

4296. **NHS trusts–dissolution**

HARTLEPOOL AND PETERLEE HOSPITALS NATIONAL HEALTH SERVICE TRUST (DISSOLUTION) ORDER 1996, SI 1996 879; made under the National Health Service Act 1977 s.126; and the National Health Service and Community Care Act 1990 s.5, Sch.2 para.29. In force: April 1, 1996; £0.65.

This Order provides for the dissolution on April 1, 1996 of the Hartlepool and Peterlee Hospitals National Health Service Trust.

4297. **NHS trusts–dissolution**

HARTLEPOOL COMMUNITY CARE NATIONAL HEALTH SERVICE TRUST (DISSOLUTION) ORDER 1996, SI 1996 887; made under the National Health Service Act 1977 s.126; and the National Health Service and Community Care Act 1990 s.5, Sch.2 para.29. In force: April 1, 1996; £0.65.

This Order provides for the dissolution on April 1, 1996 of the Hartlepool Community Care National Health Service Trust.

4298. **NHS trusts–dissolution**

ISLE OF WIGHT COMMUNITY HEALTHCARE NATIONAL HEALTH SERVICE TRUST DISSOLUTION ORDER 1996, SI 1996 2766; made under the National Health Service Act 1977 s.126; and the National Health Service and Community Care Act 1990 s.5, Sch.2 para.29. In force: April 1, 1997; £0.65.

This Order provides for the dissolution on April 1, 1997 of the Isle of Wight Community Healthcare National Health Service Trust established on November 4, 1992.

4299. **NHS trusts–dissolution**

LOUTH AND DISTRICT HEALTHCARE NATIONAL HEALTH SERVICE TRUST (DISSOLUTION) ORDER 1996, SI 1996 877; made under the National Health Service Act 1977 s.126; and the National Health Service and Community Care Act 1990 s.5, Sch.2 para.29. In force: April 1, 1996; £0.65.

This Order provides for the dissolution on April 1, 1996 of the Louth and District Healthcare National Health Service Trust.

4300. **NHS trusts–dissolution**

NORTH EAST WORCESTERSHIRE COMMUNITY HEALTH NATIONAL HEALTH SERVICE TRUST (DISSOLUTION) ORDER 1996, SI 1996 885; made under the National Health Service Act 1977 s.126; and the National Health Service and Community Care Act 1990 s.5, Sch.2 para.29. In force: April 1, 1996; £0.65.

This Order provides for the dissolution on April 1, 1996 of the North East Worcestershire Community Health Care National Health Service Trust.

4301. **NHS trusts–dissolution**

ROYAL NATIONAL THROAT, NOSE AND EAR HOSPITAL NATIONAL HEALTH SERVICE TRUST DISSOLUTION ORDER 1996, SI 1996 886; made under the

National Health Service Act 1977 s.126; and the National Health Service and Community Care Act 1990 s.5, Sch.2 para.29. In force: April 1, 1996; £0.65.

This Order provides for the dissolution on April 1, 1996 of the Royal National Throat, Nose and Ear Hospital National Health Service Trust.

4302. NHS trusts–dissolution

SOUTH DURHAM HEALTH CARE NATIONAL HEALTH SERVICE TRUST (DISSOLUTION) ORDER 1996, SI 1996 880; made under the National Health Service Act 1977 s.126; and the National Health Service and Community Care Act 1990 s.5, Sch.2 para.29. In force: April 1, 1996; £0.65.

This Order provides for the dissolution on April 1, 1996 of the South Durham Health Care National Health Service Trust.

4303. NHS trusts–dissolution

SOUTH WORCESTERSHIRE COMMUNITY NATIONAL HEALTH SERVICE TRUST DISSOLUTION ORDER 1996, SI 1996 884; made under the National Health Service Act 1977 s.126; and the National Health Service and Community Care Act 1990 s.5, Sch.2 para.29. In force: April 1, 1996; £0.65.

This Order provides for the dissolution on April 1, 1996 of the South Worcestershire Community National Health Service Trust.

4304. NHS trusts–dissolution

ST. MARY'S HOSPITAL NATIONAL HEALTH SERVICE TRUST DISSOLUTION ORDER 1996, SI 1996 2767; made under the National Health Service Act 1977 s.126; and the National Health Service and Community Care Act 1990 s.5, Sch.2 para.29. In force: April 1, 1997; £0.65.

This Order provides for the dissolution on April 1, 1997 of the St. Mary's Hospital National Health Service Trust established on November 4, 1992.

4305. NHS trusts–dissolution

UNIVERSITY COLLEGE LONDON NATIONAL HEALTH SERVICE TRUST (DISSOLUTION) ORDER 1996, SI 1996 881; made under the National Health Service Act 1977 s.126; and the National Health Service and Community Care Act 1990 s.5, Sch.2 para.29. In force: April 1, 1996; £0.65.

This Order provides for the dissolution on April 1, 1996 of the University College London Hospitals National Health Service Trust.

4306. NHS trusts–establishment

BEXLEY COMMUNITY HEALTH NATIONAL HEALTH SERVICE TRUST (ESTABLISHMENT) AMENDMENT ORDER 1996, SI 1996 1000; made under the National Health Service Act 1977 s.126; and the National Health Service and Community Care Act 1990 s.5. In force: April 6, 1996; £0.65.

This Order amends the Order which established the Bexley Community Health National Health Service Trust (now called the Oxleas National Health Service Trust) to alter the purpose for which the trust was established, and to amend its functions. (The trust has, in exercise of its existing functions, assumed responsibility for the management of community health services from Bexley Hospital, which were previously managed by the former Bexley Health Authority, and for the ownership of the associated premises). This Order confers on the trust the purpose specified in the National Health Service and Community Care Act 1990 s.5(1)(b), to provide and manage hospitals or other establishments or facilities. It also alters the trust's functions to enable it to provide community health services from premises not previously provided or managed by a health authority, and so that the trust is no longer required to own the premises from which it is to provide such services.

4307. NHS trusts–establishment

BIRMINGHAM HEARTLANDS AND SOLIHULL (TEACHING) NATIONAL HEALTH SERVICE TRUST (ESTABLISHMENT) ORDER 1996, SI 1996 883; made under the National Health Service and Community Care Act 1990 s.5, Sch.2 para.1, Sch.2 para.3, Sch.2 para.4, Sch.2 para.5, Sch.2 para.6. In force: April 1, 1996; £0.65.

This Order establishes the Birmingham Heartlands and Solihull (Teaching) National Health Service Trust, an NHS trust provided for in the National Health Service and Community Care Act 1990 s.5. It also provides for the functions of the trust. It specifies the operational date and the accounting date of the trust, and the value of assets in excess of which the Secretary of State is to consider the disposal of the asset.

4308. NHS trusts–establishment

BISHOP AUCKLAND HOSPITALS NATIONAL HEALTH SERVICE TRUST (ESTABLISHMENT) AMENDMENT ORDER 1996, SI 1996 989; made under the National Health Service Act 1977 s.126; and the National Health Service and Community Care Act 1990 s.5. In force: April 6, 1996; £0.65.

This Order amends the Order which established the Bishop Auckland Hospitals National Health Service Trust to alter the purpose for which the trust has been established and to amend its functions. (The trust has, in exercise of its existing functions, assumed responsibility for the ownership and management of the Bishop Auckland General Hospital and associated hospitals, previously managed by the South Durham Health Authority). This Order confers on the trust the purpose specified in the National Health Service and Community Care Act 1990 s.5(1)(b) to provide and manage hospitals or other establishments or facilities and amend the trust's functions so that it is no longer required to own the premises at which it is to provide hospital accommodation and services.

4309. NHS trusts–establishment

BRIDGEND AND DISTRICT NATIONAL HEALTH SERVICE TRUST (ESTABLISHMENT) ORDER 1996, SI 1996 257; made under the National Health Service and Community Care Act 1990 s.5, Sch.2 para.1, Sch.2 para.3, Sch.2 para.4, Sch.2 para.5, Sch.2 para.6. In force: April 1, 1996; £0.65.

This Order establishes the Bridgend and District National Health Service Trust, an NHS trust provided for in the National Health Service and Community Care Act 1990 s.5. It also provides for the functions of the trust. It specifies the operational date and the accounting date of the trust. It specifies the value of assets in excess of which the Secretary of State is to consider the disposal of the asset.

4310. NHS trusts–establishment

CENTRAL NOTTINGHAMSHIRE HEALTHCARE NATIONAL HEALTH SERVICE TRUST (ESTABLISHMENT) AMENDMENT ORDER 1996, SI 1996 2588; made under the National Health Service Act 1977 s.126; and the National Health Service and Community Care Act 1990 s.5. In force: November 12, 1996; £0.65.

This Order amends the Central Nottinghamshire Healthcare National Health Service Trust (Establishment) Order 1992 (SI 1992 2477) to change the address at which hospital accommodation and services and community health services are to be provided.

4311. NHS trusts–establishment

DARTFORD AND GRAVESHAM NATIONAL HEALTH SERVICE TRUST (ESTABLISHMENT) AMENDMENT ORDER 1996, SI 1996 994; made under the National Health Service Act 1977 s.126; and the National Health Service and Community Care Act 1990 s.5. In force: April 6, 1996; £0.65.

This Order amends the Order which established the Dartford and Gravesham National Health Service Trust, to alter the purpose for which the trust was established, and to amend its functions. (The trust has, in exercise of its existing functions, assumed responsibility for the ownership and management of the Joyce Green Hospital, Dartford and associated hospitals, previously managed by the former Dartford and Gravesham Health Authority). This Order confers on the trust the purpose specified in the National Health Service and Community Care Act 1990 s.5(1)(b), to provide and manage hospitals or other establishments or facilities and amend the trust's functions so that they are no longer confined to the ownership and management of establishments or facilities previously managed or provided by health authorities, but are now to include the provision and management of accommodation and services at other premises.

4312. NHS trusts–establishment

EAST YORKSHIRE COMMUNITY HEALTHCARE NATIONAL HEALTH SERVICE TRUST (ESTABLISHMENT) AMENDMENT ORDER 1996, SI 1996 1002; made under the National Health Service Act 1977 s.126; and the National Health Service and Community Care Act 1990 s.5. In force: April 6, 1996; £0.65.

This Order amends the Order which established the East Yorkshire Community Healthcare National Health Service Trust to alter the purposes for which the trust has been established and to amend its functions. The Order confers on the trust the purpose specified in the National Health Service and Community Care Act 1990 s.5(1)(b) and, in pursuance of that purpose, extends the functions of the trust to include the function of providing and managing hospital accommodation and services from Castle Hill Hospital, Cottingham, previously managed by the East Riding Health Authority and from associated premises.

4313. NHS trusts–establishment

ESSEX RIVERS HEALTHCARE NATIONAL HEALTH SERVICE TRUST (ESTABLISHMENT) AMENDMENT ORDER 1996, SI 1996 993; made under the National Health Service Act 1977 s.126; and the National Health Service and Community Care Act 1990 s.5. In force: April 6, 1996; £0.65.

This Order amends the Order which established the Essex Rivers Healthcare National Health Service Trust to alter the purpose for which the trust has been established and to amend its functions. (The trust has, in exercise of its existing functions, assumed responsibility for the management of hospital and community health services provided from Colchester General Hospital, previously managed by the North Essex Health Authority, and for the ownership of the associated premises.) This Order confers on the trust the purpose specified in the National Health Service and Community Care Act 1990 s.5(1)(b) to provide and manage hospitals or other establishments or facilities and amend the trust's functions so that it is no longer required to own the premises at which it is to provide hospital and community health services.

4314. NHS trusts–establishment

GLAN HAFREN NATIONAL HEALTH SERVICE TRUST (ESTABLISHMENT) ORDER 1996, SI 1996 258; made under the National Health Service and Community Care Act 1990 s.5, Sch.2 para.1, Sch.2 para.3, Sch.2 para.4, Sch.2 para.5, Sch.2 para.6. In force: April 1, 1996; £0.65.

This Order establishes the Glan Hafren National Health Service Trust, an NHS trust provided for in s.5 of the National Health Service and Community Care Act 1990. It also provides for the functions of the trust. It specifies the operational date and the accounting date of the trust. It specifies the value of assets in excess of which the Secretary of State is to consider the disposal of the asset.

4315. NHS trusts–establishment

GLOUCESTERSHIRE ROYAL NATIONAL HEALTH SERVICE TRUST (ESTABLISHMENT) AMENDMENT ORDER 1996, SI 1996 986; made under the

National Health Service Act 1977 s.126; and the National Health Service and Community Care Act 1990 s.5. In force: April 6, 1996; £0.65.

This Order amends the Order which established the Gloucestershire Royal National Health Service Trust to alter the purpose for which the trust has been established and to amend its functions. (The trust has, in exercise of its existing functions, assumed responsibility for the ownership and management of the Gloucestershire Royal Hospital and associated hospitals, previously managed by the Gloucestershire Health Authority.) This Order confers on the trust the purpose specified in the National Health Service and Community Care Act 1990 s.5(1) (b) to provide and manage hospitals or other establishments of facilities and amend the trust's functions so that it is no longer required to own the premises at which it is to provide hospital accommodation and services.

4316. NHS trusts–establishment

HARTLEPOOL AND EAST DURHAM NATIONAL HEALTH SERVICE TRUST (ESTABLISHMENT) ORDER 1996, SI 1996 873; made under the National Health Service and Community Care Act 1990 s.5, Sch.2 para.1, Sch.2 para.3, Sch.2 para.4, Sch.2 para.5, Sch.2 para.6. In force: April 1, 1996; £0.65.

This Order establishes the Hartlepool and East Durham National Health Service Trust, an NHS trust provided for in the National Health Service and Community Care Act 1990 s.5. It also provides for the the functions of the trust. It specifies the operational date and the accounting date of the trust, and the value of assets in excess of which the Secretary of State is to consider the disposal of the asset.

4317. NHS trusts–establishment

HEREFORD HOSPITALS NATIONAL HEALTH SERVICE TRUST (ESTABLISHMENT) AMENDMENT ORDER 1996, SI 1996 990; made under the National Health Service Act 1977 s.126; and the National Health Service and Community Care Act 1990 s.5. In force: April 6, 1996; £0.65.

This Order amends the Order which established the Hereford Hospitals National Health Service Trust to alter the purpose for which the trust has been established and to amend its functions. (The trust has, in exercise of its existing functions, assumed responsibility for the ownership and management of the Hereford County Hospital and associated hospitals, previously managed by the former Herefordshire Health Authority.) This Order confers on the trust the purpose specified in the National Health Service and Community Care Act 1990 s.5(1) (b) to provide and manage hospitals or other establishments or facilities and amends the trust's functions so that it is no longer required to own the premises at which it is to provide hospital accommodation and services.

4318. NHS trusts–establishment

HULL AND HOLDERNESS COMMUNITY HEALTH NATIONAL HEALTH SERVICE TRUST (ESTABLISHMENT) AMENDMENT ORDER 1996, SI 1996 988; made under the National Health Service Act 1977 s.126; and the National Health Service and Community Care Act 1990 s.5. In force: April 6, 1996; £0.65.

This Order amends the Order which established the Hull and Holderness Community Health National Health Service Trust to alter the purpose for which the trust has been established and to amend its functions. (The trust has, in exercise of its existing functions, assumed responsibility for the management of community health service provided from Victoria House, Hull, previously managed by the East Riding Health Authority, and for the ownership of the associated premises). This Order confers on the trust the purpose specified in the National Health Service and Community Care Act 1990 s.5(1) (b) to provide and manage hospitals or other establishments or facilities and amends the trust's functions so that it is no longer required to own the premises from which it is to provide community health services.

4319. NHS trusts–establishment

ISLE OF WIGHT HEALTHCARE NATIONAL HEALTH SERVICE TRUST (ESTABLISHMENT) ORDER 1996, SI 1996 2768; made under the National Health Service and Community Care Act 1990 s.5, Sch.2 para.1, Sch.2 para.3, Sch.2 para.4, Sch.2 para.5, Sch.2 para.6. In force: November 11, 1996; £1.10.

This Order establishes the Isle of Wight Healthcare National Health Service Trust, an NHS trust provided for in the National Health Service and Community Care Act 1990 s.5. It also provides for the functions of the trust, both before and after the operational date and the accounting date of the trust and makes provision for assistance to the trust by a Health Authority before its operational date. It specifies the value of assets in excess of which the Secretary of State is to consider the disposal of the assets.

4320. NHS trusts–establishment

MID ESSEX COMMUNITY AND MENTAL HEALTH NATIONAL HEALTH SERVICE TRUST (ESTABLISHMENT) AMENDMENT ORDER 1996, SI 1996 3012; made under the National Health Service Act 1977 s.126; and the National Health Service and Community Care Act 1990 s.5. In force: December 12, 1996; £0.65.

This Order amends the constitution of an NHS trust established by Order under the National Health Service and Community Care Act 1990 Part I by increasing the number of non-executive directors from four to five and the number of executive directors from four to five.

4321. NHS trusts–establishment

NORFOLK AND NORWICH HEALTH CARE NATIONAL HEALTH SERVICE TRUST (ESTABLISHMENT) AMENDMENT ORDER 1996, SI 1996 1001; made under the National Health Service Act 1977 s.126; and the National Health Service and Community Care Act 1990 s.5. In force: April 6, 1996; £0.65.

This Order amends the Order which established the Norfolk and Norwich Health Care National Health Service Trust to alter the purpose for which the trust has been established and to amend its functions. (The trust assumed responsibility for the management of the Norfolk and Norwich Hospital, and associated hospitals, previously managed by the former Norwich Health Authority). This Order confers on the trust the purpose specified in the National Health Service and Community Care Act 1990 s.5(1)(b), to provide and manage hospitals or other establishments or facilities. The functions of the trust are also amended so that it is no longer required to own premises at which it provides hospital accommodation and services, and so that it may provide such accommodation and services from premises not previously managed by a health authority, and may cease to provide such information and services from certain of its existing premises.

4322. NHS trusts–establishment

NORTH DURHAM ACUTE HOSPITALS NATIONAL HEALTH SERVICE TRUST (ESTABLISHMENT) AMENDMENT ORDER 1996, SI 1996 984; made under the National Health Service Act 1977 s.126; and the National Health Service and Community Care Act 1990 s.5. In force: April 6, 1996; £0.65.

This Order amends the Order which established the North Durham Acute Hospitals National Health Service Trust to alter the purpose for which the trust has been established and to amend its functions. (The trust has, in exercise of its existing functions, assumed responsibility for the ownership and management of the Dryburn Hospital, Durham and associated hospitals, previously managed by the former North Durham Health Authority). This Order confers on the trust the purpose specified in the National Health Service and Community Care Act 1990 s.5(1)(b) to provide and manage hospitals or other establishment or facilities and amend the trust's functions so that it is no longer required to own the premises at which it is to provide hospital accommodation and services.

4323. NHS trusts–establishment

NORTH GLAMORGAN NATIONAL HEALTH SERVICE TRUST (ESTABLISHMENT) ORDER 1996, SI 1996 259; made under the National Health Service and Community Care Act 1990 s.5, Sch.2 para.1, Sch.2 para.3, Sch.2 para.4, Sch.2 para.5, Sch.2 para.6. In force: February 19, 1996; £1.10.

This Order establishes North Glamorgan National Health Service Trust, an NHS trust provided for in the National Health Service and Community Care Act 1990 s.5. It also provides for the functions of the trust both before and after its operational date.

4324. NHS trusts–establishment

ROCHDALE HEALTHCARE NATIONAL HEALTH SERVICE TRUST (ESTABLISHMENT) AMENDMENT ORDER 1996, SI 1996 991; made under the National Health Service Act 1977 s.126; and the National Health Service and Community Care Act 1990 s.5. In force: April 6, 1996; £0.65.

This Order amends the Order which established the Rochdale Healthcare National Health Service Trust to alter the purpose for which the trust has been established and to amend its functions. (The trust has, in exercise of its existing functions, assumed responsibility for the management of hospital and community health services provided from the Birch Hill Hospital, Rochdale, previously managed by the former Rochdale Health Authority, and for the ownership of the associated premises). This Order confers on the trust the purpose specified in the National Health Service and Community Care Act 1990 s.5(1) (b) to provide and manage hospitals or other establishments or facilities and amend the trust's functions so that it is no longer required to own the premises at which it is to provide hospital and community health services.

4325. NHS trusts–establishment

ROYAL FREE HAMPSTEAD NATIONAL HEALTH SERVICE TRUST (AMENDMENT) ORDER 1996, SI 1996 871; made under the National Health Service Act 1977 s.126; and the National Health Service and Community Care Act 1990 s.5. In force: April 1, 1996; £0.65.

This Order amends the Royal Free Hampstead National Health Service Trust (Establishment) Order 1990 (SI 1990 2435) to include in Art.3(2) (a) the Royal National Throat, Nose and Ear Hospital, and its associated hospitals and premises and their teaching and research facilities, as establishments which are owned and managed by the Royal Free Hampstead National Health Service Trust.

4326. NHS trusts–establishment

SOUTH BUCKINGHAMSHIRE NATIONAL HEALTH SERVICE TRUST (ESTABLISHMENT) AMENDMENT ORDER 1996, SI 1996 998; made under the National Health Service Act 1977 s.126; and the National Health Service and Community Care Act 1990 s.5. In force: April 7, 1996; £0.65.

This Order amends the Order which established the South Buckinghamshire National Health Service Trust to alter the purpose for which the trust has been established and to amend its functions. (The trust has, in exercise of its existing functions, assumed responsibility for the management of hospital and community health services provided from the Oakengrove Hospital, High Wycombe, and other premises, previously managed by the former Wycombe Health Authority, and for the ownership of the associated premises). This Order confers on the trust the purpose specified in the National Health Service and Community Care Act 1990 s.5(1) (b) to provide and manage hospitals or other establishments or facilities and amend the trust's functions so that it is no longer required to own the premises at which it is to provide hospital and community health services.

4327. NHS trusts–establishment

SOUTH DEVON HEALTH CARE NATIONAL HEALTH SERVICE TRUST (ESTABLISHMENT) AMENDMENT ORDER 1996, SI 1996 999; made under the National Health Service Act 1977 s.126; and the National Health Service and Community Care Act 1990 s.5. In force: April 7, 1996; £0.65.

This Order amends the Order which established the South Devon Health Care National Health Service Trust to alter the purpose for which the trust has been established and to amend its functions. (The trust has, in exercise of its existing functions, assumed responsibility for the management of hospital accommodation and services provided from Torbay District General Hospital, and community health services formerly provided from St Michael's House, Newton Abbot Hospital, but now provided from Torbay District General Hospital, previously managed by the former Torbay Health Authority and for the ownership of the associated premises.) This Order confers on the trust the purpose specified in the National Health Service and Community Care Act 1990 s.5(1) (b), to provide and manage hospitals or other establishments or facilities and amends the trust's functions so that it is no longer required to own the premises at which it is to provide hospital services, and to alter the premises from which it is to provide community health services.

4328. NHS trusts–establishment

SOUTH DURHAM NATIONAL HEALTH SERVICE TRUST (ESTABLISHMENT) ORDER 1996, SI 1996 875; made under the National Health Service and Community Care Act 1990 s.5, Sch.2 para.1, Sch.2 para.3, Sch.2 para.4, Sch.2 para.5, Sch.2 para.6. In force: April 1, 1996; £1.10.

This Order establishes the South Durham National Health Service Trust, an NHS trust provided for in the National Health Service and Community Care Act 1990 s.5. It also provides for the functions of the trust. It specifies the operational date and the accounting date of the trust, and the value of assets in excess of which the Secretary of State is to consider the disposal of the asset.

4329. NHS trusts–establishment

SOUTH MANCHESTER UNIVERSITY HOSPITALS NATIONAL HEALTH SERVICE TRUST (ESTABLISHMENT) AMENDMENT ORDER 1996, SI 1996 983; made under the National Health Service Act 1977 s.126; and the National Health Service and Community Care Act 1990 s.5. In force: April 6, 1996; £0.65.

This Order amends the Order which established the South Manchester University Hospitals National Health Service Trust to alter the purpose for which the trust had been established and to amend its functions. (The trust has, in exercise of its existing functions, assumed responsibility for ownership and management of the Wythenshawe Hospital, Wythenshawe, Withington Hospital, West Didsbury and associated hospitals, previously managed by the former South Manchester Health Authority). This Order confers on the trust the purpose specified in the National Health Service and Community Care Act 1990 s.5(1) (b) to provide and manage hospitals and other establishments or facilities and amends the trust's functions so that it is no longer required to own the premises at which it is to provide hospital accommodation and services.

4330. NHS trusts–establishment

ST. JAMES'S AND SEACROFT UNIVERSITY HOSPITALS NATIONAL HEALTH SERVICE TRUST (ESTABLISHMENT) AMENDMENT ORDER 1996, SI 1996 996; made under the National Health Service Act 1977 s.126; and the National Health Service and Community Care Act 1990 s.5. In force: April 7, 1996; £0.65.

This Order amends the Order which established the St. James's and Seacroft University Hospitals National Health Service Trust to alter the purpose for which the trust has been established and to amend its functions. The Order confers on the trust the purpose specified in the National Health Service and Community Care Act 1990 s.5(1) (b) and, in pursuance of that purpose, extends the functions of the trust to include the function of providing and managing hospital accommodation and services from St. James's Hospital, Leeds previously managed by the Leeds Eastern Health Authority and from associated premises.

4331. **NHS trusts–establishment**

SWINDON AND MARLBOROUGH NATIONAL HEALTH SERVICE TRUST (ESTABLISHMENT) AMENDMENT ORDER 1996, SI 1996 987; made under the National Health Service Act 1977 s.126; and the National Health Service and Community Care Act 1990 s.5. In force: April 6, 1996; £0.65.

This Order amends the Order which established the Swindon and Marlborough National Health Service Trust to alter the purpose for which the trust has been established and to amend its functions. (The trust has, in exercise of its existing functions, assumed responsibility for the management of hospital and community health services provided from the Princess Margaret Hospital, Swindon, previously managed by the Swindon Health Authority, and for the ownership of the associated premises). This Order confers on the trust the purpose specified in the National Health Service and Community Care Act 1990 s.5(1)(b) to provide and manage hospitals or other establishments or facilities and amend the trust's functions so that it is no longer required to own the premises at which it is to provide hospital and community health services.

4332. **NHS trusts–establishment**

THAMESIDE COMMUNITY HEALTH CARE NATIONAL HEALTH SERVICE TRUST (ESTABLISHMENT) AMENDMENT ORDER 1996, SI 1996 997; made under the National Health Service Act 1977 s.126; and the National Health Service and Community Care Act 1990 s.5. In force: April 7, 1996; £0.65.

This Order amends the Order which established the Thameside Community Health Care National Health Service Trust (now called the Thameside Community Healthcare National Health Service Trust) to alter the purpose for which the trust has been established and to amend its functions. (The trust has, in exercise of its existing functions, assumed responsibility for the management of hospital accommodation and services provided at Thurrock Hospital, Grays, Essex and community health services formerly provided from South Ockenden Hospital, Essex, but now provided from Thurrock Hospital, Grays, Essex and for the ownership of the associated premises, previously managed by the former Basildon and Thurrock Health Authority). This Order confers on the trust the purpose specified in the National Health Service and Community Care Act 1990 s.5(1)(b) to provide and manage hospitals or other establishments or facilities and amend the trust's functions so that it is no longer required to own the premises at which it is to provide hospital and community health services.

4333. **NHS trusts–establishment**

UNIVERSITY COLLEGE LONDON HOSPITALS NATIONAL HEALTH SERVICE TRUST (ESTABLISHMENT) ORDER 1996, SI 1996 401; made under the National Health Service and Community Care Act 1990 s.5, Sch.2 para.1, Sch.2 para.3, Sch.2 para.4, Sch.2 para.5, Sch.2 para.6. In force: March 4, 1996; £1.10.

This Order establishes the University College London Hospitals National Health Service Trust, an NHS trust provided for in the National Health Service and Community Care Act 1990 s.5. It also provides for the functions of the trust both before and after its operational date. It specifies the operational date and the accounting date of the trust and makes provision for assistance to the trust by health authorities before its operational date. It specifies the value of assets in excess of which the Secretary of State is to consider the disposal of the asset.

4334. **NHS trusts–establishment**

WALTON CENTRE FOR NEUROLOGY AND NEUROSURGERY NATIONAL HEALTH SERVICE TRUST (ESTABLISHMENT) AMENDMENT ORDER 1996, SI 1996 982; made under the National Health Service Act 1977 s.126; and the

National Health Service and Community Care Act 1990 s.5. In force: April 6, 1996; £0.65.

This Order amends the Order which established the Walton Centre for Neurology and Neurosurgery National Health Service Trust, to alter the purpose for which the trust was established, and to amend its functions. (The Trust has, in exercise of its functions, assumed responsibility for the ownership and management of the Walton Hospital, Liverpool and associated hospitals, previously managed by the former South Sefton Health Authority). This Order confers on the trust the purpose specified in the National Health Service and Community Care Act 1990 s.5(1)(b), to provide and manage hospitals or other establishments or facilities. It also alters the trust's functions so that they are no longer confined to ownership and management of establishments or facilities previously managed or provided by health authorities, but include the provision and management of accommodation and services at other premises.

4335. NHS trusts–establishment

WELLHOUSE NATIONAL HEALTH SERVICE TRUST (ESTABLISHMENT) AMENDMENT ORDER 1996, SI 1996 992; made under the National Health Service Act 1977 s.126; and the National Health Service and Community Care Act 1990 s.5. In force: April 6, 1996; £0.65.

This Order amends the Order which established the Wellhouse National Health Service Trust to alter the purpose for which the trust has been established and to amend its functions. (The trust has, in exercise of its existing functions, assumed responsibility for the ownership and management of the Edgware General Hospital and associated hospitals, previously managed by the Barnet Health Authority). This Order confers on the trust the purpose specified in the National Health Service and Community Care Act 1990 s.5(1)(b) to provide and manage hospitals or other establishments or facilities and amend the trust's functions so that it is no longer required to own the premises at which it is to provide hospital accommodation and services.

4336. NHS trusts–establishment

WEST MIDDLESEX UNIVERSITY HOSPITAL NATIONAL HEALTH SERVICE TRUST (ESTABLISHMENT) AMENDMENT ORDER 1996, SI 1996 985; made under the National Health Service Act 1977 s.126; and the National Health Service and Community Care Act 1990 s.5. In force: April 6, 1996; £0.65.

This Order amends the Order which established the West Middlesex University Hospital National Health Service Trust to alter the purpose for which the trust has been established and to amend its functions. (The trust has, in exercise of its existing functions, assumed responsibility for the ownership and management of the West Middlesex University Hospital and associated hospitals, previously managed by the former Hounslow and Spelthorne Health Authority). This Order confers on the trust the purpose specified in the National Health Service and Community Care Act 1990 s.5(1)(b) to provide and manage hospitals or other establishment or facilities and amend the trust's functions so that it is no longer required to own the premises at which it is to provide hospital accommodation and services.

4337. NHS trusts–establishment

WORCESTERSHIRE COMMUNITY HEALTHCARE NATIONAL HEALTH SERVICE TRUST (ESTABLISHMENT) ORDER 1996, SI 1996 874; made under the National Health Service and Community Care Act 1990 s.5, Sch.2 para.1, Sch.2 para.3, Sch.2 para.4, Sch.2 para.5, Sch.2 para.6. In force: April 1, 1996; £0.65.

This Order establishes the Worcestershire Community Healthcare National Health Service Trust, an NHS trust provided for in the National Health Service and Community Care Act 1990 s.5. It also provides for the functions of the trust. It specifies the operational date and the accounting date of the trust, and the value of assets in excess of which the Secretary of State is to consider the disposal of the asset.

4338. NHS trusts–establishment and dissolution

NATIONAL HEALTH SERVICE TRUSTS (CONSULTATION ON ESTABLISHMENT AND DISSOLUTION) REGULATIONS 1996, SI 1996 653; made under the National Health Service Act 1977 s.126, s.128; and the National Health Service and Community Care Act 1990 s.5, Sch.2 para.29, Sch.2 para.30. In force: April 1, 1996; £1.10.

These Regulations prescribe the consultation which must be completed before the Secretary of State may make or amend an Order under the National Health Service and Community Care Act 1990 s.5(1) establishing an NHS trust. They also prescribe the consultation required before the Secretary of State may make an order dissolving an NHS trust or an order transferring to another person or body the property, rights, liabilities and staff of a dissolved trust. Where the dissolution of one trust is to be associated with the establishment of a new trust, the consultation prescribed in connection with the dissolution may be combined with that required in relation to the establishment of the new trust. These Regulations also revoke the National Health Service Trusts (Consultation on Dissolution) Regulations 1991 (SI 1991 1347) and the National Health Service Trusts (Consultation on Dissolution) Amendment Regulations 1992 (SI 1992 2905).

4339. NHS trusts–mental health–dissolution

SOUTH WEST DURHAM MENTAL HEALTH NATIONAL HEALTH SERVICE TRUST (DISSOLUTION) ORDER 1996, SI 1996 876; made under the National Health Service Act 1977 s.126; and the National Health Service and Community Care Act 1990 s.5, Sch.2 para.29. In force: April 1, 1996; £0.65.

This Order provides for the dissolution on April 1, 1996 of the South West Durham Mental Health National Health Service Trust.

4340. NHS trusts–transfer of assets

BRIDGEND AND DISTRICT NATIONAL HEALTH SERVICE TRUST (TRANSFER OF PROPERTY) ORDER 1996, SI 1996 2260; made under the National Health Service Act 1977 s.92. In force: October 1, 1996; £0.65.

This Order transfers to Bridgend and District National Health Service Trust on October 1, 1996, trust property formerly held by Bro Taf Health Authority.

4341. NHS trusts–transfer of assets

CARDIFF COMMUNITY HEALTHCARE NATIONAL HEALTH SERVICE TRUST (TRANSFER OF TRUST PROPERTY) ORDER 1996, SI 1996 526; made under the National Health Service Act 1977 s.92. In force: April 1, 1996; £0.65.

This Order transfers to Cardiff Community Healthcare National Health Service Trust on April 1, 1996 trust property formerly held by South Glamorgan Health Authority.

4342. NHS trusts–transfer of assets

CHICHESTER PRIORITY CARE SERVICES NATIONAL HEALTH SERVICE TRUST (TRANSFER OF TRUST PROPERTY) ORDER 1996, SI 1996 571; made under the National Health Service Act 1977 s.92. In force: March 28, 1996; £0.65.

This Order transfers to the Chichester Priority Care Services National Health Service Trust on March 28, 1996 trust property formerly held by West Sussex Health Authority.

4343. NHS trusts–transfer of assets

COMMUNITY HEALTH CARE: NORTH DURHAM NATIONAL HEALTH SERVICE TRUST (TRANSFER OF TRUST PROPERTY) ORDER 1996, SI 1996 352; made under the National Health Service Act 1977 s.92. In force: March 21, 1996; £0.65.

This Order transfers to the Community Health Care: North Durham National Health Service Trust on March 21, 1996 trust property formerly held by the North Durham Health Authority.

4344. NHS trusts–transfer of assets

COMMUNITY HEALTH SERVICES, SOUTHERN DERBYSHIRE NATIONAL HEALTH SERVICE TRUST (TRANSFER OF TRUST PROPERTY) ORDER 1996, SI 1996 2359; made under the National Health Service Act 1977 s.92. In force: October 8, 1996; £0.65.

This Order transfers to the Community Health Services, Southern Derbyshire National Health Service Trust on October 8, 1996 trust property held by the Southern Derbyshire Health Authority.

4345. NHS trusts–transfer of assets

COVENTRY HEALTHCARE NATIONAL HEALTH SERVICE TRUST (TRANSFER OF TRUST PROPERTY) ORDER 1996, SI 1996 380; made under the National Health Service Act 1977 s.92. In force: March 22, 1996; £0.65.

This Order transfers to the Coventry Healthcare National Health Service Trust on March 22, 1996 trust property formerly held by the Coventry Health Authority.

4346. NHS trusts–transfer of assets

DORSET HEALTH AUTHORITY (TRANSFERS OF TRUST PROPERTY) ORDER 1996, SI 1996 2731; made under the National Health Service Act 1977 s.92. In force: November 25, 1996; £0.65.

This Order transfers on October 25, 1996 to the National Health Service trusts specified in the Schedule to the Order, trust property held by the Dorset Health Authority.

4347. NHS trusts–transfer of assets

EAST GLAMORGAN NATIONAL HEALTH SERVICE TRUST (TRANSFER OF TRUST PROPERTY) ORDER 1996, SI 1996 423; made under the National Health Service Act 1977 s.92. In force: April 1, 1996; £0.65.

This Order transfers to the East Glamorgan National Health Service Trust on April 1, 1996 trust property formerly held by the Mid Glamorgan Health Authority.

4348. NHS trusts–transfer of assets

EAST YORKSHIRE COMMUNITY HEALTHCARE NATIONAL HEALTH SERVICE TRUST (TRANSFER OF TRUST PROPERTY) ORDER 1996, SI 1996 2866; made under the National Health Service Act 1977 s.92. In force: December 16, 1996; £0.65.

This Order transfers to the East Yorkshire Community Healthcare National Health Service Trust on December 16, 1996 trust property held by the East Riding Health Authority.

4349. NHS trusts–transfer of assets

EASTBOURNE AND COUNTY HEALTHCARE NATIONAL HEALTH SERVICE TRUST (TRANSFER OF TRUST PROPERTY) ORDER 1996, SI 1996 2732; made under the National Health Service Act 1977 s.92. In force: November 25, 1996; £0.65.

This Order transfers to the Eastbourne and County Healthcare National Health Service Trust on November 25, 1996 trust property formerly held by the Eastbourne Hospitals National Health Service Trust.

4350. NHS trusts–transfer of assets

GATESHEAD HEALTHCARE NATIONAL HEALTH SERVICE TRUST (TRANSFER OF TRUST PROPERTY) ORDER 1996, SI 1996 149; made under the National Health Service Act 1977 s.92. In force: February 29, 1996; £0.65.

This Order transfers to the Gateshead Healthcare National Health Service Trust on February 29, 1996 trust property formerly held by the South Tyne Health Authority.

4351. NHS trusts–transfer of assets

GATESHEAD HOSPITALS NATIONAL HEALTH SERVICE TRUST (TRANSFER OF TRUST PROPERTY) ORDER 1996, SI 1996 148; made under the National Health Service Act 1977 s.92. In force: February 29, 1996; £0.65.

This Order transfers to the Gateshead Hospitals National Health Service Trust on February 29, 1996 trust property formerly held by the South of Tyne Health Authority.

4352. NHS trusts–transfer of assets

GRANTHAM AND DISTRICT HOSPITAL NATIONAL HEALTH SERVICE TRUST (TRANSFER OF TRUST PROPERTY) ORDER 1996, SI 1996 1433; made under the National Health Service Act 1977 s.92. In force: July 1, 1996; £0.65.

This Order transfers to the Grantham and District Hospital National Health Service Trust on July 1, 1996 trust property held by the Lincolnshire Health Authority.

4353. NHS trusts–transfer of assets

GWENT COMMUNITY HEALTH NATIONAL HEALTH SERVICE TRUST (TRANSFER OF TRUST PROPERTY) ORDER 1996, SI 1996 524; made under the National Health Service Act 1977 s.92. In force: April 1, 1996; £0.65.

This Order transfers to the Gwent Community Health National Health Service Trust on April 1, 1996 trust property formerly held by Gwent Health Authority.

4354. NHS trusts–transfer of assets

HEATHLANDS MENTAL HEALTH NATIONAL HEALTH SERVICE TRUST (TRANSFER OF TRUST PROPERTY) ORDER 1996, SI 1996 1704; made under the National Health Service Act 1977 s.92. In force: July 31, 1996; £0.65.

This Order transfers to the Heathlands Mental Health National Health Service Trust on July 31, 1996 trust property held by the West Surrey Health Authority.

4355. NHS trusts–transfer of assets

HORTON GENERAL HOSPITAL NATIONAL HEALTH SERVICE TRUST (TRANSFER OF TRUST PROPERTY) ORDER 1996, SI 1996 1771; made under the National Health Service Act 1977 s.92. In force: July 31, 1996; £1.10.

This Order transfers to the Horton General Hospital National Health Service Trust on July 31, 1996 trust property held by the Oxfordshire Health Authority.

4356. NHS trusts–transfer of assets

HULL AND HOLDERNESS COMMUNITY HEALTH NATIONAL HEALTH SERVICE TRUST (TRANSFER OF TRUST PROPERTY) ORDER 1996, SI 1996 92;

made under the National Health Service Act 1977 s.92. In force: February 16, 1996; £0.65.

Trust property formerly held by the Royal Hull Hospitals National Health Service Trust is transferred to the Hull and Holderness Community Health National Health Service Trust on February 16, 1996.

4357. NHS trusts–transfer of assets

HULL AND HOLDERNESS COMMUNITY HEALTH NATIONAL HEALTH SERVICE TRUST (TRANSFER OF TRUST PROPERTY) (NO.2) ORDER 1996, SI 1996 2647; made under the National Health Service Act 1977 s.92. In force: November 14, 1996; £0.65.

This Order transfers to the Hull and Holderness Community Health National Health Service Trust on November 14, 1996 trust property held by the East Riding Health Authority.

4358. NHS trusts–transfer of assets

KENT AND CANTERBURY HOSPITALS NATIONAL HEALTH SERVICE TRUST (TRANSFER OF TRUST PROPERTY) ORDER 1996, SI 1996 1701; made under the National Health Service Act 1977 s.92. In force: July 31, 1996; £0.65.

This Order transfers to the Kent and Canterbury Hospitals National Health Service Trust on July 31, 1996 trust property held by the East Kent Health Authority.

4359. NHS trusts–transfer of assets

KING'S MILL CENTRE FOR HEALTH CARE SERVICES NATIONAL HEALTH SERVICE TRUST (TRANSFER OF TRUST PROPERTY) ORDER 1996, SI 1996 35; made under the National Health Service Act 1977 s.92. In force: February 8, 1996; £0.65.

Transfers trust property formerly held by the North Nottinghamshire Health Authority to the King's Mill Centre for Health Care Services National Health Service Trust on February 8, 1996.

4360. NHS trusts–transfer of assets

LEEDS COMMUNITY AND MENTAL HEALTH SERVICES TEACHING NATIONAL HEALTH SERVICE TRUST (TRANSFER OF TRUST PROPERTY) ORDER 1996, SI 1996 2861; made under the National Health Service Act 1977 s.92. In force: December 12, 1996; £0.65.

This Order transfers to the Leeds Community and Mental Health Services Teaching National Health Service Trust on December 12, 1996 trust property formerly held by the Wakefield and Pontefract Community Health National Health Service Trust.

4361. NHS trusts–transfer of assets

LEWISHAM HOSPITAL NATIONAL HEALTH SERVICE TRUST (TRANSFER OF TRUST PROPERTY) ORDER 1996, SI 1996 1713; made under the National Health Service Act 1977 s.92. In force: July 31, 1996; £0.65.

This Order transfers to the Lewisham Hospital National Health Service Trust on July 31, 1996 trust property held by the Lambeth, Southwark and Lewisham Health Authority.

4362. NHS trusts–transfer of assets

LLANDOUGH HOSPITAL AND COMMUNITY NATIONAL HEALTH SERVICE TRUST (TRANSFER OF TRUST PROPERTY) ORDER 1996, SI 1996 424; made under the National Health Service Act 1977 s.92. In force: April 1, 1996; £0.65.

This Order transfers to the Llandough Hospital and Community National Health Service Trust on April 1, 1996 trust property formerly held by South Glamorgan Health Authority.

4363. NHS trusts–transfer of assets

MANCHESTER CHILDREN'S HOSPITALS NATIONAL HEALTH SERVICE TRUST (TRANSFER OF TRUST PROPERTY) ORDER 1996, SI 1996 2033; made under the National Health Service Act 1977 s.92. In force: August 29, 1996; £0.65.

This Order transfers to the Manchester Children's Hospitals National Health Service Trust on August 29, 1996 trust property held by the Salford and Trafford Health Authority.

4364. NHS trusts–transfer of assets

MERTON AND SUTTON COMMUNITY NATIONAL HEALTH SERVICE TRUST (TRANSFER OF TRUST PROPERTY) ORDER 1996, SI 1996 1710; made under the National Health Service Act 1977 s.92. In force: July 31, 1996; £0.65.

This Order transfers to the Merton and Sutton Community National Health Service Trust on July 31, 1996 trust property held by the Merton, Sutton and Wandsworth Health Authority.

4365. NHS trusts–transfer of assets

MID ESSEX HOSPITAL SERVICES NATIONAL HEALTH SERVICE TRUST (TRANSFER OF TRUST PROPERTY) ORDER 1996, SI 1996 1709; made under the National Health Service Act 1977 s.92. In force: July 31, 1996; £0.65.

This Order transfers to the Mid Essex Hospital Services National Health Service Trust on July 31, 1996 trust property held by the South Essex Health Authority.

4366. NHS trusts–transfer of assets

MID-SUSSEX NATIONAL HEALTH SERVICE TRUST (TRANSFER OF TRUST PROPERTY) ORDER 1996, SI 1996 1711; made under the National Health Service Act 1977 s.92. In force: July 31, 1996; £1.10.

This Order transfers to the Mid-Sussex National Health Service Trust on July 31, 1996 trust property held by the West Sussex Health Authority.

4367. NHS trusts–transfer of assets

NATIONAL BLOOD AUTHORITY (TRANSFER OF TRUST PROPERTY) ORDER 1996, SI 1996 33; made under the National Health Service Act 1977 s.92. In force: February 9, 1996; £0.65.

Transfers trust property formerly held by the Anglia and Oxford Regional Health Authority to the National Blood Authority on February 9, 1996.

4368. NHS trusts–transfer of assets

NATIONAL BLOOD AUTHORITY (TRANSFER OF TRUST PROPERTY) (NO.2) ORDER 1996, SI 1996 34; made under the National Health Service Act 1977 s.92. In force: February 9, 1996; £0.65.

Transfers trust property formerly held by the Anglia and Oxford Regional Health Authority to the National Blood Authority on February 9, 1996.

4369. NHS trusts–transfer of assets

NORTH DOWNS COMMUNITY NATIONAL HEALTH SERVICE TRUST (TRANSFER OF TRUST PROPERTY) ORDER 1996, SI 1996 1707; made under the National Health Service Act 1977 s.92. In force: July 31, 1996; £0.65.

This Order transfers to the North Downs Community Health National Health Service Trust on July 31, 1996 trust property held by the West Surrey Health Authority.

4370. NHS trusts–transfer of assets

NORTH DURHAM ACUTE HOSPITALS (TRANSFER OF TRUST PROPERTY) ORDER 1996, SI 1996 351; made under the National Health Service Act 1977 s.92. In force: March 21, 1996; £0.65.

This Order transfers to the North Durham Acute Hospitals National Health Service Trust on March 21, 1996 trust property formerly held by the North Durham Health Authority.

4371. NHS trusts–transfer of assets

NORTH GLAMORGAN NATIONAL HEALTH SERVICE TRUST (TRANSFER OF PROPERTY) ORDER 1996, SI 1996 2261; made under the National Health Service Act 1977 s.92. In force: October 1, 1996; £0.65.

This Order transfers to North Glamorgan National Health Service Trust on October 1, 1996 trust property formerly held by Bro Taf Health Authority.

4372. NHS trusts–transfer of assets

NORTH HAMPSHIRE HOSPITALS NATIONAL HEALTH SERVICE TRUST (TRANSFER OF TRUST PROPERTY) ORDER 1996, SI 1996 1739; made under the National Health Service Act 1977 s.92. In force: August 1, 1996; £1.10.

This Order transfers to the North Hampshire Hospitals National Health Service Trust on August 1, 1996 trust property held by the North and Mid Hampshire Health Authority.

4373. NHS trusts–transfer of assets

NORTH HAMPSHIRE, LODDON COMMUNITY NATIONAL HEALTH SERVICE TRUST (TRANSFER OF TRUST PROPERTY) ORDER 1996, SI 1996 2384; made under the National Health Service Act 1977 s.92. In force: October 4, 1996; £0.65.

This Order transfers to the North Hampshire, Loddon Community National Health Service Trust on October 4, 1996 trust property held by the North and Mid Hampshire Health Authority.

4374. NHS trusts–transfer of assets

NORTH STAFFORDSHIRE COMBINED HEALTHCARE NATIONAL HEALTH SERVICE TRUST (TRANSFER OF TRUST PROPERTY) ORDER 1996, SI 1996 124; made under the National Health Service Act 1977 s.92. In force: February 23, 1996; £0.65.

This Order transfers to the North Staffordshire Combined Healthcare National Health Service Trust on February 23, 1996 trust property formerly held by the North Staffordshire Health Authority.

4375. NHS trusts–transfer of assets

NORTH TEES HEALTH NATIONAL HEALTH SERVICE TRUST (TRANSFER OF TRUST PROPERTY) ORDER 1996, SI 1996 1858; made under the National Health Service Act 1977 s.92. In force: August 15, 1996; £0.65.

This Order transfers to the North Tees Health National Health Service Trust on August 15, 1996 trust property formerly held by the Southmead Health Services National Health Service Trust.

4376. NHS trusts–transfer of assets

NORTHUMBERLAND HEALTH AUTHORITY (TRANSFER OF TRUST PROPERTY) ORDER 1996, SI 1996 2862; made under the National Health Service Act 1977 s.92. In force: December 12, 1996; £1.10.

This Order transfers on December 12, 1996 to the National Health Service trusts specified in the Schedule to the Order trust property held by the Northumberland Health Authority.

4377. NHS trusts–transfer of assets

NORTHWICK PARK AND ST MARK'S NATIONAL HEALTH SERVICE TRUST (TRANSFER OF TRUST PROPERTY) ORDER 1996, SI 1996 2672; made under the National Health Service Act 1977 s.92. In force: November 15, 1996; £0.65.

This Order transfers to the Northwick Park and St Mark's National Health Service Trust on November 15, 1996 trust property formerly held by the Special Trustees for St Bartholomew's and St Mark's Hospitals.

4378. NHS trusts–transfer of assets

NOTTINGHAM COMMUNITY HEALTH NATIONAL HEALTH SERVICE TRUST (TRANSFER OF TRUST PROPERTY) ORDER 1996, SI 1996 1714; made under the National Health Service Act 1977 s.92. In force: July 31, 1996; £0.65.

This Order transfers to the Nottingham Community Health National Health Service Trust on July 31, 1996 trust property formerly held by the special trustees for Nottingham University Hospitals.

4379. NHS trusts–transfer of assets

NOTTINGHAM HEALTHCARE NATIONAL HEALTH SERVICE TRUST (TRANSFER OF TRUST PROPERTY) ORDER 1996, SI 1996 1432; made under the National Health Service Act 1977 s.92. In force: July 1, 1996; £0.65.

This Order transfers to the Nottingham Healthcare National Health Service Trust on July 1, 1996 trust property formerly held by the Nottingham City Hospital National Health Service Trust.

4380. NHS trusts–transfer of assets

NOTTINGHAM HEALTHCARE NATIONAL HEALTH SERVICE TRUST (TRANSFER OF TRUST PROPERTY) (NO.2) ORDER 1996, SI 1996 1842; made under the National Health Service Act 1977 s.92. In force: August 13, 1996; £0.65.

This Order transfers to the Nottingham Healthcare National Health Service Trust on August 13, 1996 trust property formerly held by the special trustees for Nottingham University Hospitals.

4381. NHS trusts–transfer of assets

OPTIMUM HEALTH SERVICES NATIONAL HEALTH SERVICE TRUST (TRANSFER OF TRUST PROPERTY) ORDER 1996, SI 1996 2462; made under the National Health Service Act 1977 s.92. In force: October 21, 1996; £1.10.

This Order transfers to the Optimum Health Services National Health Service Trust on October 21, 1996 trust property formerly held by the Lambeth, Southwark and Lewisham Health Authority.

4382. NHS trusts–transfer of assets

OXFORD RADCLIFFE HOSPITAL NATIONAL HEALTH SERVICE TRUST (TRANSFER OF TRUST PROPERTY) ORDER 1996, SI 1996 1773; made under the National Health Service Act 1977 s.92. In force: July 31, 1996; £1.10.

This Order transfers to the Oxford Radcliffe Hospital National Health Service Trust on July 31, 1996 trust property held by the Oxfordshire Health Authority.

4383. NHS trusts–transfer of assets

OXFORDSHIRE COMMUNITY HEALTH NATIONAL HEALTH SERVICE TRUST (TRANSFER OF TRUST PROPERTY) ORDER 1996, SI 1996 1775; made under the National Health Service Act 1977 s.92. In force: July 31, 1996; £1.10.

This Order transfers to the Oxfordshire Community Health National Health Service Trust on July 31, 1996 trust property held by the Oxfordshire Health Authority.

4384. NHS trusts–transfer of assets

OXFORDSHIRE LEARNING DISABILITY NATIONAL HEALTH SERVICE TRUST (TRANSFER OF TRUST PROPERTY) ORDER 1996, SI 1996 1776; made under the National Health Service Act 1977 s.92. In force: July 31, 1996; £1.10.

This Order transfers to the Oxfordshire Learning Disability National Health Service Trust on July 31, 1996 trust property held by the Oxfordshire Health Authority.

4385. NHS trusts–transfer of assets

OXFORDSHIRE MENTAL HEALTHCARE NATIONAL HEALTH SERVICE TRUST (TRANSFER OF TRUST PROPERTY) ORDER 1996, SI 1996 1774; made under the National Health Service Act 1977 s.92. In force: July 31, 1996; £1.10.

This Order transfers to the Oxfordshire Mental Healthcare National Health Service Trust on July 31, 1996 trust property held by the Oxfordshire Health Authority.

4386. NHS trusts–transfer of assets

PATHFINDER NATIONAL HEALTH SERVICE TRUST (TRANSFER OF TRUST PROPERTY) ORDER 1996, SI 1996 1740; made under the National Health Service Act 1977 s.92. In force: August 1, 1996; £1.10.

This Order transfers to the Pathfinder National Health Service Trust on August 1, 1996 trust property held by the Merton, Sutton and Wandsworth Health Authority.

4387. NHS trusts–transfer of assets

PLYMOUTH COMMUNITY SERVICES NATIONAL HEALTH SERVICE TRUST (TRANSFER OF TRUST PROPERTY) ORDER 1996, SI 1996 2463; made under the National Health Service Act 1977 s.92. In force: October 21, 1996; £1.10.

This Order transfers to the Plymouth Community Services National Health Service Trust on October 21, 1996 trust property formerly held by the Cornwall Healthcare National Health Service Trust.

4388. NHS trusts–transfer of assets

RADCLIFFE INFIRMARY NATIONAL HEALTH SERVICE TRUST (TRANSFER OF TRUST PROPERTY) ORDER 1996, SI 1996 1770; made under the National Health Service Act 1977 s.92. In force: July 31, 1996; £1.10.

This Order transfers to the Radcliffe Infirmary National Health Service Trust on July 31, 1996 trust property held by the Oxfordshire Health Authority.

4389. NHS trusts–transfer of assets

REGIONAL HEALTH AUTHORITIES (TRANSFER OF TRUST PROPERTY) AMENDMENT ORDER 1996, SI 1996 969; made under the Health Authorities Act 1995 Sch.2 para.3. In force: April 1, 1996; £0.65.

This Order amends the Regional Health Authorities (Transfer of Trust Property) Order 1996 (SI 1996 666) (the principal Order) which transfers to certain Health Authorities, Special Health Authorities and National Health Service trusts, the property held on trust by Regional Health Authorities immediately before their abolition on April 1, 1996. This Order substitutes in Sch.7 to the principal Order (which is concerned with the transfer of trust property held by the West Midlands Regional Health Authority) a reference to the Birmingham Heartlands and Solihull (Teaching) National Health Service Trust (which is to be established on April 1, 1996) for the references to the Solihull Health Authority and to the Birmingham Heartlands National Health Services Trust (which is to be dissolved on that date).

4390. **NHS trusts–transfer of assets**

REGIONAL HEALTH AUTHORITIES (TRANSFER OF TRUST PROPERTY) ORDER 1996, SI 1996 666; made under the National Health Service Act 1977 s.126; and the Health Authorities Act 1995 Sch.2 para.3. In force: April 1, 1996; £3.20.

This Order transfers on April 1, 1996 to certain Health Authorities, Special Health Authorities and National Health Service trusts the property held on trust by Regional Health Authorities immediately before their abolition on that date by the Health Authorities Act 1995.

4391. **NHS trusts–transfer of assets**

RHONDDA HEALTH CARE NATIONAL HEALTH SERVICE TRUST (TRANSFER OF TRUST PROPERTY) ORDER 1996, SI 1996 531; made under the National Health Service Act 1977 s.92. In force: April 1, 1996; £0.65.

This Order transfers to the Rhondda Health Care National Health Service Trust on April 1, 1996 trust property formerly held by Mid Glamorgan Health Authority.

4392. **NHS trusts–transfer of assets**

ROYAL SURREY COUNTY AND ST LUKE'S HOSPITALS NATIONAL HEALTH SERVICE TRUST (TRANSFER OF TRUST PROPERTY) ORDER 1996, SI 1996 1708; made under the National Health Service Act 1977 s.92. In force: July 31, 1996; £0.65.

This Order transfers to the Royal Surrey County and St Luke's Hospitals National Health Service Trust on July 31, 1996 trust property held by the West Surrey Health Authority.

4393. **NHS trusts–transfer of assets**

ROYAL WEST SUSSEX NATIONAL HEALTH SERVICE TRUST (TRANSFER OF TRUST PROPERTY) ORDER 1996, SI 1996 570; made under the National Health Service Act 1977 s.92. In force: March 28, 1996; £0.65.

This Order transfers to the Royal West Sussex National Health Service Trust on March 28, 1996 trust property formerly held by the West Sussex Health Authority.

4394. **NHS trusts–transfer of assets**

SALFORD COMMUNITY HEALTH CARE NATIONAL HEALTH SERVICE TRUST (TRANSFER OF TRUST PROPERTY) ORDER 1996, SI 1996 503; made under the National Health Service Act 1977 s.92. In force: March 28, 1996; £0.65.

This Order tranfers to the Salford Community Health Care National Health Service Trust on March 28, 1996 trust property formerly held by the Salford and Trafford Health Authority.

4395. **NHS trusts–transfer of assets**

SALFORD ROYAL HOSPITALS NATIONAL HEALTH SERVICE TRUST (TRANSFER OF TRUST PROPERTY) ORDER 1996, SI 1996 2032; made under the National Health Service Act 1977 s.92. In force: August 29, 1996; £0.65.

This Order transfers to the Salford Royal Hospitals National Health Service Trust on August 29, 1996 trust property held by the Salford and Trafford Health Authority.

4396. NHS trusts–transfer of assets

SOUTH TYNESIDE HEALTH CARE NATIONAL HEALTH SERVICE TRUST (TRANSFER OF TRUST PROPERTY) ORDER 1996, SI 1996 383; made under the National Health Service Act 1977 s.92. In force: March 22, 1996; £0.65.

This Order transfers to the South Tyneside Health Care National Health Service Trust on March 22, 1996 trust property formerly held by the South of Tyne Health Authority.

4397. NHS trusts–transfer of assets

SPECIAL TRUSTEES FOR THE MIDDLESEX HOSPITAL (TRANSFER OF TRUST PROPERTY) ORDER 1996, SI 1996 2263; made under the National Health Service Act 1977 s.92. In force: October 1, 1996; £0.65.

This Order transfers to the special trustees for the Middlesex Hospital on October 1, 1996 trust property formerly held by the special trustees for St Peter's Hospital.

4398. NHS trusts–transfer of assets

ST. HELIER NATIONAL HEALTH SERVICE TRUST (TRANSFER OF TRUST PROPERTY) ORDER 1996, SI 1996 1702; made under the National Health Service Act 1977 s.92. In force: July 31, 1996; £0.65.

This Order transfers to the St Helier National Health Service Trust on July 31, 1996 trust property held by the Merton, Sutton and Wandsworth Health Authority.

4399. NHS trusts–transfer of assets

ST. JAMES'S AND SEACROFT UNIVERSITY HOSPITALS NATIONAL HEALTH SERVICE TRUST (TRANSFER OF TRUST PROPERTY) ORDER 1996, SI 1996 2734; made under the National Health Service Act 1977 s.92. In force: November 25, 1996; £0.65.

This Order transfers to the St. James's and Seacroft University Hospitals National Health Service Trust on November 25, 1996 trust property held by the Leeds Health Authority.

4400. NHS trusts–transfer of assets

SWINDON AND MARLBOROUGH NATIONAL HEALTH SERVICE TRUST (TRANSFER OF TRUST PROPERTY) ORDER 1996, SI 1996 2553; made under the National Health Service Act 1977 s.92. In force: November 6, 1996; £0.65.

This Order transfers to the Swindon and Marlborough National Health Service Trust on November 6, 1996 trust property held by the Wiltshire Health Authority.

4401. NHS trusts–transfer of assets

TEDDINGTON MEMORIAL HOSPITAL NATIONAL HEALTH SERVICE TRUST (TRANSFER OF TRUST PROPERTY) ORDER 1996, SI 1996 2385; made under the National Health Service 1977 s.92. In force: October 4, 1996; £0.65.

This Order transfers to the Teddington Memorial Hospital National Health Service Trust on October 4, 1996 trust property held by the Ealing, Hammersmith and Hounslow Health Authority.

4402. NHS trusts–transfer of assets

UNITED LEEDS TEACHING HOSPITALS NATIONAL HEALTH SERVICE TRUST (TRANSFER OF TRUST PROPERTY) ORDER 1996, SI 1996 2733; made under the National Health Service Act 1977 s.92. In force: November 25, 1996; £0.65.

This Order transfers to the United Leeds Teaching Hospitals National Health Service Trust on November 25, 1996 trust property previously held by the former Leeds Health Authority.

4403. NHS trusts–transfer of assets

UNIVERSITY HOSPITAL OF WALES HEALTHCARE NATIONAL HEALTH SERVICE TRUST (TRANSFER OF TRUST PROPERTY) ORDER 1996, SI 1996 530; made under the National Health Service Act 1977 s.92. In force: April 1, 1996; £0.65.

This Order transfers to the University Hospital of Wales Healthcare National Health Service Trust on April 1, 1996 trust property formerly held by South Glamorgan Health Authority.

4404. NHS trusts–transfer of assets

VELINDRE HOSPITAL NATIONAL HEALTH SERVICE TRUST (TRANSFER OF TRUST PROPERTY) ORDER 1996, SI 1996 527; made under the National Health Service Act 1977 s.92. In force: April 1, 1996; £0.65.

This Order transfers to the Velindre Hospital National Health Service Trust on April 1, 1996 trust property formerly held by South Glamorgan Health Authority.

4405. NHS trusts–transfer of assets

WANDSWORTH COMMUNITY HEALTH NATIONAL HEALTH SERVICE TRUST (TRANSFER OF TRUST PROPERTY) ORDER 1996, SI 1996 1703; made under the National Health Service Act 1977 s.92. In force: July 31, 1996; £0.65.

This Order transfers to the Wandsworth Community Health National Health Service Trust on July 31, 1996 trust property held by the Merton, Sutton and Wandsworth Health Authority.

4406. NHS trusts–transfer of assets

WILTSHIRE HEALTH CARE NATIONAL HEALTH SERVICE TRUST (TRANSFER OF TRUST PROPERTY) ORDER 1996, SI 1996 737; made under the National Health Service Act 1977 s.92. In force: April 1, 1996; £0.65.

This Order transfers to the Wiltshire Health Care National Health Service Trust on April 1, 1996 trust property formerly held by the Wiltshire and Bath Health Authority.

4407. NHS trusts–transfer of assets

WORTHING AND SOUTHLANDS HOSPITALS NATIONAL HEALTH SERVICE TRUST (TRANSFER OF TRUST PROPERTY) ORDER 1996, SI 1996 127; made under the National Health Service Act 1977 s.92. In force: February 23, 1996; £0.65.

This Order transfers to the Worthing and Southlands Hospitals National Health Service Trust on February 23, 1996 trust property formerly held by the West Sussex Health Authority.

4408. Occupational pensions–provision of information

NATIONAL HEALTH SERVICE PENSION SCHEME (PROVISION OF INFORMATION AND ADMINISTRATIVE EXPENSES ETC.) REGULATIONS 1996, SI 1996 2424; made under the Pensions Act 1995 s.172, s.174. In force: October 14, 1996; £1.10.

These Regulations make provision for the Secretary of State to provide information in certain circumstances in respect of individuals who have chosen to participate in a personal pension scheme instead of the NHS Pension Scheme and to impose reasonable fees on prescribed persons in connection with administrative expenses incurred in providing such information. They also make provision for the Secretary of State to impose reasonable fees in respect of administration expenses incurred in connection with the admission or re-admission of such individuals to the NHS Pension Scheme or with the administration by him of a compensation payment in respect of such an individual in the circumstances described in s.172(2) of the Act.

4409. Opticians–charges–payments

NATIONAL HEALTH SERVICE (OPTICAL CHARGES AND PAYMENTS) AMENDMENT REGULATIONS 1996, SI 1996 582; made under the National Health Service Act 1977 s.126, Sch.12 para.2A. In force: April 1, 1996; £1.10.

These Regulations further amend the National Health Service (Optical Charges and Payments) Regulations 1989 (SI 1989 396) (the principal Regulations), which provide for payments to be made by means of a voucher system in respect of costs incurred by certain categories of persons in connection with the supply, replacement and repair of optical appliances. Regulation 2 amends Reg.20 of the principal Regulations (redemption value of voucher for replacement or repair) to increase the value of an optical voucher issued towards the cost of replacing a single contact lens, and to increase the maximum contribution by way of voucher to the cost of repairing a frame. Regulation 3(1) amends Sch.1 to the principal Regulations to increase the value of vouchers issued towards the cost of the supply and replacement of glasses and contact lenses. Regulation 3(2) increases the additional values for vouchers for prisms, tints, photochromic lenses and special categories of appliances. Regulation 3(3) and the Schedule substitute a new Sch.3 in the principle Regulations to increase the value of vouchers issued towards the cost of the repair and replacement of optical appliances. The rate of increase is, on average, approximately one per cent.

4410. Opticians–charges–payments

NATIONAL HEALTH SERVICE (OPTICAL CHARGES AND PAYMENTS) AMENDMENT (NO.2) REGULATIONS 1996, SI 1996 2328; made under the National Health Service Act 1977 s.126, Sch.12 para.2A. In force: October 7, 1996; £0.65.

These Regulations further amend the National Health Service (Optical Charges and Payments) Regulations 1989 (SI 1989 396), which provide for payments to be made by means of a voucher system in respect of costs incurred by certain categories of persons in connection with the supply, replacement and repair of optical appliances. Regulation 2 of these Regulations amends Reg.1 of the principal Regulations in order to include a definition of an income based jobseeker's allowance. Regulation 3(2)(a) of these Regulations removes the capital restriction relating to disability working allowance so that everyone in receipt of this, and certain of their relatives, will be eligible for payments towards the cost of optical appliances. Regulation 3(2)(b) and (3) of these Regulations extends the categories of eligibility for payments towards the costs of optical appliances to include people in receipt of an income based jobseeker's allowance, and also certain relatives of such people.

4411. Opticians–charges–payments

NATIONAL HEALTH SERVICE (OPTICAL CHARGES AND PAYMENTS) AMENDMENT (NO.3) REGULATIONS 1996, SI 1996 2574; made under the National Health Service Act 1977 s.126, Sch.12 para.2A. In force: November 1, 1996; £0.65.

These Regulations further amend the National Health Service (Optical Charges Payments) Regulations 1989 (SI 1989 396). They amend the definition of NHS sight test fee which is set at two levels depending on whether the sight test was carried out at the patient's home or not, and the appropriate figure is used to calculate the value of assistance towards the cost of a private sight test; and the value of vouchers towards the cost of private sight test or towards the supply of glasses or contact lenses. The figure used where the sight test was carried out at the patient's home is increased to £37.83 and the figure used in all other cases is increased to £13.71.

4412. Opticians–disciplinary procedures

NATIONAL HEALTH SERVICE (GENERAL OPHTHALMIC SERVICES) AMENDMENT REGULATIONS 1996, SI 1996 705; made under the National Health Service Act 1977 s.15, s.38, s.39, s.49E, s.126. In force: April 1, 1996; £1.55.

These Regulations further amend the National Health Service (General Ophthalmic Services) Regulations 1986 (SI 1986 975) to make provision relating to opthalmic medical practitioners and opthalmic opticians ("contractors") who have been suspended from the provision of general opthalmic services by the NHS Tribunal or whom the Tribunal has declared not fit to be engaged in any capacity in the provision of those services. The Regulations also provide for payments to suspended contractors and amend Schedule 1 of the 1986 Regulations (contractors' terms of service).

4413. Opticians–transitional provisions

NATIONAL HEALTH SERVICE (GENERAL OPHTHALMIC SERVICES) AMENDMENT (NO.2) REGULATIONS 1996, SI 1996 2320; made under the National Health Service Act 1977 s.38, s.126. In force: October 7, 1996; £0.65.

These Regulations further amend the National Health Service (General Ophthalmic Services) Regulations 1986 (SI 1986 975). They amend Reg.2(1) of the 1986 Regulations in order to include a definition of an income based jobseeker's allowance, remove the capital restriction relating to Disability Working Allowance so that everyone in receipt of this, and certain of their relatives, will be eligible for ophthalmic services and extend the categories of eligibility for general ophthalmic services to include people in receipt of an income based jobseeker's allowance, and also certain relatives of such people.

4414. Pharmacy

NATIONAL HEALTH SERVICE (PHARMACEUTICAL SERVICES) AMENDMENT REGULATIONS 1996, SI 1996 698; made under the National Health Service Act 1977 s.41, s.42, s.43, s.49E, s.126. In force: April 1, 1996; £1.95.

These Regulations further amend the National Health Service (Pharmaceutical Services) Regulations 1992 (SI 1992 662) which govern the arrangements to be made by Health Authorities for the provision in their area of pharmaceutical services under the National Health Service Act 1977.

4415. Pharmacy–supply of pharmaceutical services–consideration of extent and adequacy of existing services

[National Health Service (Pharmaceutical Services) Regulations 1992 Reg.4.]

M and other GPs applied for judicial review of the FHSA's decision to grant preliminary consent for the establishment of a pharmacy within the locality of their practice. M argued that the FHSA had misconstrued the National Health Service (Pharmaceutical Services) Regulations 1992 Reg.4(4) and the test to be applied when considering the provision of pharmaceutical services. M also argued that the FHSA failed to consider the effect of the grant on the provision of existing pharmaceutical services and that the FHSA failed to consider all relevant matters.

Held, allowing the application, that (1) when considering a pharmacist's application for permission to establish a pharmacy in a particular locality, a FHSA was obliged under Reg.4(4) of the 1992 Regulations to consider not only the existing provision of pharmaceutical services in that locality, but also the adequacy of provision by listed pharmacists outside the locality but within the area covered by the FHSA. Services provided by GP's had to be taken into account in the decision making process; (2) the FHSA had to consider whether certain information was relevant before they took account of it in their decision and (3) in general, as doctors were not included on pharmaceutical lists, evidence relating to the prejudice they would suffer from the success of the application would be irrelevant.

R. v. HUMBERSIDE FAMILY HEALTH SERVICES AUTHORITY, *ex p.* MOORE; R. v. HUMBERSIDE FAMILY HEALTH SERVICES AUTHORITY, *ex p.* CRUMP (1996) 30 B.M.L.R. 68, Potts, J., QBD.

4416. Pharmacy–supply of pharmaceutical services–desirability of additional services–applicability of statutory test–consideration of desirability

[National Health Service (Pharmaceutical Services) Regulations 1992 Part II.]

PJN sought leave to apply for judicial review of a decision by the Lincoln Family Services Authority and the Appeal Unit of the Northern and Yorkshire RHA to allow an application by a pharmaceutical firm to provide pharmaceutical services 50 yards from PJN's pharmacy. The FHSA did not find that the pharmacy was a "necessity" under the National Health Service (Pharmaceutical Services) Regulations 1992 Part II para.4(4), but that it was "desirable" as the population served by PJN was large and increasing. Patient choice was also a consideration. PJN argued that the statutory test was not applied to the consideration of desirability.

Held, dismissing the application, that the FHSA properly considered the statutory test when dealing with the question of desirability and correctly exercised their discretion.

PJ NORTON LTD, *Re*, Trans. Ref: 96/6171/D, January 18, 1996, Butler-Sloss, L.J., CA.

4417. Pharmacy–supply of pharmaceutical services–no obligation to consult local doctors where applicant already on local pharmaceutical list

[National Health Service (Pharmaceutical Services) Regulations 1992 Reg.4, Reg.12.]

W and other doctors from a medical practice in a rural area, who had for a number of years been allowed to provide pharmaceutical services from their practice, applied for judicial review of the FHSA's decision to allow G, a pharmacist already on the pharmaceutical list for the area, to establish an additional pharmacy, to be located in the same village as their surgery. The doctors, concerned about loss of income and the effect that would have on their practice, contended that, in the interests of fairness, the FHSA should have consulted them over the matter of whether it was "necessary or desirable" to grant G's application under the National Health Service (Pharmaceutical Services) Regulations 1992 Reg.4(4) and that, by not notifying them of the hearing or allowing them to put forward their views, the FHSA had acted unfairly.

Held, dismissing the applications, that it was only under Reg.12 of the 1992 Regulations, where an application was made by someone not already on the area's pharmaceutical list, that local doctors had an express right of representation. No such right arose under Reg.4(4).

R. v. NORTH YORKSHIRE FAMILY HEALTH SERVICES AUTHORITY, *ex p.* WILSON (1996) 8 Admin. L.R. 613, Carnwath, J., QBD.

4418. Pharmacy–supply of pharmaceutical services–relocation–interpretation of "minor relocation"–effect on competitors

[National Health Service (Pharmaceutical Services) Regulations 1992 Reg.4.]

S and G, the owners of pharmacies, appealed against the dismissal of their applications for judicial review of YRHA's decision to allow three pharmacists to relocate their premises. The proposed relocation would have result in the pharmacies being situated close to S and Gs' premises. The appeal centred on the interpretation of the National Health Service (Pharmaceutical Services) Regulations 1992 Reg.4(3) which allowed relocation where the change of premises was a minor relocation. S and G argued that YRHA should have considered the potential effect of the relocation on competitors.

Held, dismissing the appeal, that (1) whether a relocation was minor was a question of fact and degree to be determined by the Family Health Services Authority, taking into account the distance of the move and any obstacles preventing the patient's easy access from the original location to the new one; and (2) there was no obligation on YRHA to consider the potential commercial effect of the relocation on competitors. The DHSS's 1987 guidelines, enjoining authorities to take into account any detriment to competitors, were misconceived, *R. v. Cumbria Family Practitioner Committee, ex p. Boots the Chemists* [1989] C.O.D. 322, [1988] C.L.Y. 2244 applied.

R. v. YORKSHIRE RHA, *ex p.* SURI; R. v. YORKSHIRE RHA, *ex p.* GOMPELS (1996) 30 B.M.L.R. 78, Russell, L.J., CA.

4419. Pharmacy–supply of pharmaceutical services–shopping centre could be neighbourhood in determining adequacy of provision–statutory interpretation

[National Health Service (Pharmaceutical Services) Regulations 1992 Reg.4.]

B, who wished to establish a pharmacy in its store at a new shopping centre, applied for judicial review of F's decision not to give consent for B to be included in Avon FHSA's pharmaceutical list. B contended that F had misdirected itself, and thus erred in law, in deciding that a shopping and leisure complex could not be a "neighbourhood" for the purposes of the National Health Service (Pharmaceutical Services) Regulations 1992 Reg.4(4).

Held, allowing the application, that F was required to consider the shopping centre as a neighbourhood in its own right, even though no people lived there. An assessment of the adequacy of provision for the purposes of Reg.4(4) required consideration of the various needs of all those people who were likely to visit the centre and of whether the needs of shoppers could be met by existing pharmacies. F's decision would be quashed and the case remitted for further consideration.

R. v. FAMILY HEALTH SERVICES APPEAL AUTHORITY, *ex p.* BOOTS THE CHEMIST LTD, *The Times*, June 28, 1996, Tucker, J., QBD.

4420. Pharmacy–supply of pharmaceutical services–test for allowing supply–adequacy of current provision–meaning of "necessity" and "desirability" in decision making process

[National Health Service (Pharmaceutical Services) Regulations 1992 Reg.4.]

Held, that when considering a pharmacist's application for permission to supply pharmaceutical services in a particular locality, a Family Health Services Authority was required, under the National Health Service (Pharmaceutical Services) Regulations 1992 Reg.4(4), to address, first and foremost, the adequacy of the current provision. It was only if the provision of services in the neighbourhood was inadequate that the concepts of necessity or desirability, in terms of filling the gap in the service provision, had to be considered. If the current provision of pharmaceutical services was wholly inadequate, then it would be necessary to secure services. If the service provision was borderline, then the desirability of granting the application would fall to be considered. The words "necessary" and "desirable" did not have to be interpreted disjunctively.

R. v. YORKSHIRE RHA, *ex p.* BAKER, *The Times*, May 6, 1996, Sir Louis Blom-Cooper Q.C., QBD.

4421. Tribunals–service committees

NATIONAL HEALTH SERVICE (SERVICE COMMITTEES AND TRIBUNAL) AMENDMENT REGULATIONS 1996, SI 1996 703; made under the National

Health Service Act 1977 s.16, s.29, s.36, s.39, s.42, s.45, s.126, s.127, Sch.5 para.12, Sch.5 para.16. In force: April 1, 1996; £4.70.

These Regulations amend the National Health Service (Service Committees and Tribunal) Regulations 1992 (SI 1992 664) by substituting new Reg.3 to Reg.13 for Reg.3 to Reg.14, replacing Sch.2 and Sch.4, revoking Sch.3 and Sch.6 and making consequential amendments. These provisions replace the system whereby complaints made against practitioners providing services under the National Health Service Act 1977 Part II were dealt with by service committees. Service committees are abolished and are replaced by discipline committees to which Health Authorities will refer matters for investigation which raise allegations that a practitioner has failed to comply with his terms of service or concern overpayments made to such a practitioner. Unlike service committees, discipline committees will not deal with complaints made by or on behalf of patients.

4422. Articles

Complaints procedures in the NHS: all change *(Christa Christensen)*: Med. L. Int. 1996, 2(3), 247-269. (NHS complaints procedures up to April 1, 1996 and ways they have changed since this date, identifying potential difficulties).

Disputes in the NHS internal market: regulation and relationships *(J.V. McHale)*: Med. L. Int. 1996, 2(3), 215-227. (Research on how disputes regarding NHS contracts, which are excluded from judicial enforcement, have been resolved in practice).

Employment of complementary therapists in NHS: Med. L. Mon. 1996, 3(1), 6-8. (Guidelines for employing practitioners of complementary medicines).

Health complaints *(Olive Braman)*: Adviser 1996, 57, 42-43, 46. (Procedure for approaching health service ombudsman).

Healthcare risk management training: Health Law 1996, Jul/Aug, 7. (Application of risk management strategies in NHS).

NHS complaints: Med. L. Mon. 1996, 3(4), 5-6. (Complaints procedure in force April 1, 1996).

The Health and Safety at Work Act and the health service *(David Wenham)*: Health Law 1996, May, 3-6. (Responsibilities imposed on employers).

The Health Service Commissioner: an extended role in the new NHS *(Vivienne Harpwood)*: E.J.H.L. 1996, 3(3), 207-229. (Extension of powers to investigate patients' complaints under 1996 Act detailing complaints procedures, extension of jurisdiction to make recommendations or order remedies and remaining limitations on powers).

The new magistracy: Health Law 1996, Jun, 9. (Whether NHS trust directors and senior managers adequately protected under s.265 which gives them immunity from civil liability for misperformance of duties).

When is a "trust" not a trust? the National Health Service Trust *(Roy T. Bartlett)*: Conv. 1996, May/Jun, 186-192. (Whether NHS trust is enforceable under courts' equitable jurisdiction or whether it is in fact new species of corporate body).

4423. Books

Harpwood, Vivienne–NHS Complaints: Litigation and Professional Discipline. Medico-legal. Paperback: £19.95. ISBN 1-85941-012-X. Cavendish Publishing Ltd.

NEGLIGENCE

4424. Accidents–accident at work–back injury–other injuries to back–conflicting medical evidence–measure of damages

The PO appealed against an award of £73,000 in damages to B in respect of an injury sustained at his work in January 1989 when aged 32, and to which the PO admitted liability. The complicating feature of the case was that B had suffered three injuries to his back. The first was in 1982 when he was lifting a heavy weight, the second in January 1989, and a third in November 1989 when he was repairing his car. B was left with a moderate disability which meant that he had had to be moved on to lighter duties at work which involved a loss of earnings. The principal concern at the hearing was a conflict between the medical evidence of two orthopaedic consultants. H, on behalf of B, submitted that the second accident in January 1989 had caused permanent damage. T, on behalf of the PO, submitted that no permanent damage had been caused by the second accident at work but that this resulted in an episode of back pain really no different from earlier episodes, and that his current symptoms were due to a subsequent accident, combined with a pre-existing low back pain problem. There were seven grounds of appeal. Six of these were largely argumentative and referred to the judge's preference for the evidence of H over T. The remaining ground of appeal was that the judge failed to make allowance for B's pre-existing back condition in assessing the quantum of damages to be awarded to B.

Held, dismissing the appeal, that (1) in respect of six of the grounds of appeal, the judge below found that on the balance of probabilities he preferred the evidence of H over T. He was quite entitled to come to that conclusion on the material before him; (2) on the question of H's medical evidence that, the Court decided that whilst B had a vulnerable back prior to the second accident, it had not proved a serious problem and there was little evidence from T to put in the balance regarding what impact this should have on the quantum of damages. Further, T was not questioned about H's evidence that, but for the second and third accidents, B would have remained fit for full duties and (3) with regard to the measure of damages, there was no basis on which the propensity to injury could be used to discount the award. Per Pill L.J. dissenting, that the medical evidence preferred by the court below allowed for the conclusion that B's back was vulnerable to future traumas and the vicissitudes principles, *Jobling v. Associated Dairies Ltd* [1982] A.C. 794, [1981] C.L.Y. 1835 should have been applied, the appropriate discount being 25 per cent.

BOOTH v. POST OFFICE, Trans. Ref: CCRTF 95/0083/C, November 8,1995, Henry, L.J., CA.

4425. Accidents–accident at work–plaintiff held to be author of his own misfortune–fellow employee found to be negligent–failure of trial judge to make finding on causation

Q appealed against the dismissal of his negligence claim against J, having suffered minor injuries in the course of his employment with them. When moving a cupboard, a metal flange fell off the top of it and struck him. The trial judge dismissed Q's claim, holding him to be the author of his own misfortune. However, during argument on costs, the judge stated the metal flange had been negligently placed on the top of the cupboard by a fellow employee.

Held, allowing the appeal and remitting the matter back for a new trial, that the judgment was inadequate as it failed to address a crucial part of the case. The trial judge should have made a finding about whether the negligence of the fellow employee had caused the accident.

QUANT v. JI CASE (EUROPE) LTD [1995] P.I.Q.R. P225, Butler-Sloss, L.J., CA.

4426. Accidents–causation–measure of damages–chronic fatigue syndrome–aggravation of existing condition

S appealed against a decision that he was liable for damages for the exacerbation of P's condition of "Chronic Fatigue Syndrome" (CFS) following a car accident in which P's car was written off, but no physical injuries were suffered. S contended that (1) the judge below had used the wrong test of causation and (2) he had reached the wrong decision on the facts.

Held, dismissing the appeal, that (1) although the judge below might have erred by referring to an increase in the risk that P's symptoms would be aggravated, he had correctly concluded that S's negligence was a material cause of the aggravation itself. He had been entitled to consider whether the accident was a more than minimal cause of the exacerbation and whether there existed any other sole cause and (2) on the medical evidence, the judge below had been entitled to find that CFS could be aggravated by the trauma associated with an accident and, on the totality of the available evidence, that it had been so aggravated in the instant case, *McGhee v. National Coal Board* [1972] 3 All E.R. 1008, [1972] C.L.Y. 2356 and *Page v. Smith* [1996] 1 A.C. 155, [1995] 2 C.L.Y. 3682 considered.

PAGE v. SMITH (NO.2) [1996] 1 W.L.R. 855, Sir Thomas Bingham, M.R., CA.

4427. Accidents–foreseeability–accident to dentist cleaning dental equipment–inference of risk drawn from accepted facts

R was employed as a dentist by W. On arriving at the surgery R found that the floor had been replaced, cleaning had not been undertaken, furniture was in disarray and equipment dirty. No dental surgery assistant being available, R set to work to clean the equipment knowing that patients would soon arrive. R, who lacked vision in one eye, claimed that she slipped or stumbled on a wet patch and fell against a piece of furniture suffering injury which led to the removal of the sightless eye. The judge found that liability had not been made out because there had been no reasonably foreseeable risk that the injury could occur. R appealed.

Held, dismissing the appeal, that it had been open to the judge to refuse to infer that the wet patch had caused the accident. Having reached that conclusion, it had not been necessary for the judge to consider whether W would have been negligent had the wet patch been causative of the accident. On the basis of the evidence, the judge was entitled to conclude that the accident could not have been reasonably foreseeable notwithstanding R's monocular vision. The judge had asked herself the right question and dealt with the risk of personal injury rather than the circumstances of the accident and mechanism of the injury, *Hughes v. Lord Advocate* [1963] A.C. 837, [1963] C.L.Y. 970 considered. Even were this not so, the issue did not concern reliability or credibility, but inference from accepted facts with which the Court of Appeal could not interfere.

RENNER v. WIRRAL HA, Trans. Ref: CCRTF 94/1363/C, October 5, 1995, Henry, L.J., CA.

4428. Accidents–road traffic accident–collision with cyclist–car drivers–liability in negligence

D appealed against an order entering judgment for G. The action arose from a road traffic accident which occurred at night. D, then 17, was riding a bicycle with which G, driving a car in the same direction, collided. D suffered a severe head injury and was grievously handicapped as a result. The only issue before the judge was liability. D had submitted that G was negligent in failing to observe or heed the fact that D was turning, or about to turn, right. G had maintained that he was not negligent or in any way responsible for the collision or injuries. The judge found that G was not to blame and that D was wholly to blame. It was submitted that the judge's approach could be criticised, that he should have found G guilty of negligence, and therefore should have apportioned liability between the parties.

Held, dismissing the appeal, that in respect of the judge's approach to issues of fact, he examined all the evidence with considerable care. There was no justification for the suggestion that the judge, when considering causation and blameworthiness, failed to analyse G's conduct in the same manner as he had considered D's actions. The concession that D must bear part of the blame by his counsel did not detract from his analysis or distract the judge. There was no force in the criticism that G should have made the same observations as a witness, the fact he did not notice D's "off balance cycling" did not indicate a poor lookout. The judge's finding was essentially a finding of fact which he was entitled to make on the evidence before him. Even if G had been negligent, this would not have caused the accident or the resultant damage, the immediate and direct cause of the accident was D's swerve to the right. G could not have reasonably anticipated the possibility of danger, in the given circumstances, *London Passenger Transport Board v. Upson* [1949] A.C. 155, [1947-1951] C.L.C. 6618. The judge correctly identified the principles involved here and his conclusions were unassailable. Finally, the judge could not be criticised for exonerating G from any negligence based on his findings of fact in respect of G's response to the danger as it built up and occurred.

DAVIDSON v. GARNER, Trans. Ref: FC3 95/5669/D, November 1, 1995, Otton, L.J., CA.

4429. Accidents–road traffic accident–contributory negligence

B's car was involved in a collision with M's Mercedes. B sued M, and M counterclaimed. It was agreed that B was travelling at about 30 m.p.h. along a main road in wet weather. Visibility was very bad, and the road was lined with parked cars. It was further agreed that M was emerging very slowly from a smaller road on B's right. Because of the parked cars, it was necessary for M to edge forward into the main road to ensure that no cars were coming. Upon seeing B approaching, M stopped. B attempted to brake and steer round M, but his car went into a skid and a collision occurred. M alleged that B had braked too hard, causing the collision. It was accepted by B that M was stationary when the accident occurred. It was suggested that, even if M were found to be negligent, there might be scope for finding that B had been contributorily negligent, as he should have exercised greater care when driving along a main road lined with cars.

Held, dismissing the counterclaim, that this was not a case in which a finding of contributory negligence could properly be made. The court must either prefer the evidence of M and accept that B, startled by the sudden appearance of M, panicked, braked and skidded, or it must accept B's evidence, and find that, as soon as he saw M, B did all he reasonably could in the circumstances. Preferring the evidence of B, the court held that M had been negligent in emerging too far from the smaller road, and in stopping too late and accordingly judgment was given for B.

BLUNDEN v. MARSH, February 13, 1996, Assistant Recorder Towler, CC (Aldershot). [*Ex rel.* Isabella Zornoza, Barrister].

4430. Accidents–road traffic accidents–contributory negligence

A car driven by D and a motor cycle ridden by M were involved in a collision. D claimed damages in respect of the car and M counterclaimed for personal injuries. The judge apportioned liability as 75 per cent against M and 25 per cent against D. M appealed.

Held, allowing the appeal in part, that the apportionment should be reversed. The judge had failed to take account of the fact that D had been turning right into a major road and had been under a continuing obligation to give way. Although M was travelling in excess of the speed limit and had failed to take evasive action, the motorcycle had been visible from 95 yards away and D ought to have seen it.

DOLBY v. MILNER, Trans. Ref: 9204126, January 16, 1996, Russell, L.J., CA.

4431. Accidents–road traffic accidents–contributory negligence

P sought damages as a result of a road traffic accident when a vehicle owned by P, but driven by F, was in collision with a car driven by R. P's claim was dismissed and judgment entered for R. P appealed.

Held, allowing the appeal in part, that when turning right into a major road, R should have seen that F was driving towards him at excessive speed. On the basis of the evidence, R had been negligent even though F's driving had been irresponsible, the negligence of both drivers having caused the accident. It was sufficient to determine the appeal that R's negligence was significant. The parties having agreed that should an apportionment be made, the blame should be 75 per cent against F and 25 per cent against R.

PAUL FARRAH SOUND LTD (IN LIQUIDATION) v. ROOKLEDGE, Trans. Ref: No reference given, May 23, 1995, Otton, L.J., CA.

4432. Accidents–road traffic accidents–contributory negligence–duty of driver emerging from minor road onto major road–judge's findings of fact

G appealed against judgment on liability in relation to a claim arising out of a collision between a motorcycle driven by S and a motor car driven by G. The judge found that G was 70 per cent to blame and S was 30 per cent to blame. G argued that the judge had erred in a number of his findings of fact and that the judge's apportionment of blame was erroneous because S was more to blame than G.

Held, dismissing the appeal, that (1) G was emerging from a minor road onto a major road and therefore owed a high degree of duty. The judge was entitled to find that if G had kept a proper lookout to his right he would have noticed S and (2) none of the criticisms of the judge's findings of fact raised by G vitiated the judge's decision.

SMITH v. GOSS, Trans. Ref: 94/1198/C, November 21, 1995, Swinton Thomas, L.J., CA.

4433. Buildings–defective remedial work to existing building–whether complex structure exception applied–whether Defective Premises Act 1972 applied to remedial work to existing building

[Defective Premises Act 1972 s.1.]

J's predecessors in title retained M to advise them upon, to design and to supervise the implementation of a scheme to rectify cracking due to ground movement affecting their property. M carried out this work and it was completed in October 1987. J purchased the property in June 1988. In November 1988 further cracking was detected at the property which was found to be due to heave. J started proceedings claiming damages for negligence. Preliminary issues were tried raising the questions whether M owed J a duty of care at common law in negligence or under the Defective Premises Act 1972.

Held, that (1) the complex structure exception existed as an exception, to the general exclusionary rule preventing the recovery of economic loss due to defects in buildings, *Murphy v. Brentwood DC* [1991] 1 A.C. 398, [1991] C.L.Y. 2661 applied; (2) whether one item of a building was to be treated as separate from the remainder, so that damage caused to the remainder was to be regarded as damages to separate property, ie. as a complex structure, was a question of fact and degree to be determined by reference to the circumstances including who constructed the relevant part structure, whether it retained its separate identity, whether it positively inflicted damage on the building or simply failed to perform and when it was constructed and (3) rectification of an existing dwelling was not the "provision of a dwelling" within the meaning of the Defective Premises Act 1972 s.1 (1) and therefore J had no cause of action under that Act.

JACOBS v. MORETON 72 B.L.R. 92, Recorder Jackson, Q.C., QBD (ORB).

4434. Contributory negligence–valuation–whether defence available in law–burden of proof–applicability where loss due to negligent valuation proved

P appealed against a decision rejecting their defence of contributory negligence. U asked P to value a commercial property. The valuation figure of £2.5 million was used as the basis for a long term finance arrangement with the owners SDL, allowing them to pay off a previous charge, in return for a charge in U's favour. On default by SDL, the property was sold for £950,000 and U contended the loan would not have been made, but for the negligent valuation given. P sought to show that U contributed to the loss by failing to carry out sufficient inquiry into SDL's capacity to service the debt.

Held, dismissing the appeal, that the applicability of contributory negligence had been decided in P's favour as a matter of law at first instance. Where it was admissible, the question needing to be answered was whether a prudent banker would have made this loan at the time U made it, and later, when the loan was drawn down. However, the burden lay with P throughout and their evidence failed to satisfy it on the balance of probabilities. A highest non-negligent figure could not be relied upon by P, and even if such was admitted, the figure given by them had been excessive.

UNITED BANK OF KUWAIT PLC v. PRUDENTIAL PROPERTY SERVICES LTD [1995] E.G.C.S. 190, Peter Gibson, L.J., CA.

4435. Damages–plumbing work performed negligently

H purchased a substantial two storey flat in need of extensive renovation. She engaged consultants to prepare plans and schedules of work and employed D to carry out the required plumbing works and others to carry out the general building and electrical works. On taking up occupation in January 1993 H found numerous defects in the plumbing work. In particular there were extensive leaks from defective connections in concealed piping resulting in dampness at low level in the walls and floors of the bathroom and adjacent master bedroom. H could not afford to carry out all the necessary remedials because of debts incurred in paying for the works. After one year she had repaired some pipe connections and this reduced the dampness in the walls, mould growth and unpleasant smells, but the dampness in the floors persisted so that the master bedroom could not be used for hanging clothes or sleeping. H was obliged to share another smaller bedroom with her young daughter. Proceedings against the general building and electrical contractors were defended, and continue, but, in default of a defence, judgment was entered against D with damages to be assessed.

Held, that (1) judgment was given for sums overpaid to D plus interest and the present estimated costs of remedials to the plumbing works in the total sum of £6,968, and (2) the court could assess general damages for distress and inconvenience caused by and exclusively referrable to the defects in the plumbing works and awarded the sum of £2,000 under this head.

HARPER v. DOMANSKI (T/A WORKHORSE) & OTHERS, October 14, 1996, H.H.J. Butter Q.C., CC (Central London). [*Ex rel.* Paul St J Letman, Barrister].

4436. Economic loss–liability of builder liable to successor–proximity of relationship–Australia

In 1979 B, a professional builder, built a house on land then owned by M's predecessor in title. Subsequently, the house was sold and M became the second subsequent purchaser. Before purchase she inspected the house but found no defects. About six months after the purchase cracks began to appear in the walls of the house. At trial it was established that the reason for the cracking was that the house had been built on footings which were inadequate to withstand seasonal changes in the clay soil. M sued B for damages in negligence. The trial judge awarded damages in an amount which he held would necessarily be expended in remedying the inadequate footings and the consequential damage to the fabric of the house. B appealed. The issue in the appeal was whether B owed M, as the subsequent purchaser, a relevant duty of care in negligence.

Held, dismissing B's appeal, that (1) there was sufficient proximity between M and B to found a duty of care in relation to the loss she had suffered and (2) there were no significant policy considerations which mitigated against the existence of a proximate relationship and the consequent duty of care with respect to the particular kind of economic loss suffered.

BRYAN v. MALONEY 74 B.L.R. 35, Mason, C.J., HC (Aus).

4437. Economic loss–liability of contractors to successor in title–Canada

W appealed against a decision to strike out a negligence claim on the ground that no cause of action was disclosed. T, W's predecessor in title, engaged B to construct a 15-storey apartment building. T engaged S as architects. B engaged K as masonry sub-contractors. The work was completed by December 1974. W bought the property in October 1978. In May 1989 a storey-high section of the cladding fell to the ground from the ninth floor of the building. Remedial works comprising the removal and replacement of the stone cladding cost $1.5million. W sued B, S and K in negligence alleging inadequate design and workmanship.

Held, allowing the appeal, that the type of economic loss claimed by W was recoverable as damages for the negligence insofar as it was the reasonable cost of putting the building into a non-dangerous state. *D & F Estates Ltd v. Church Commissioners for England* [1989] A.C. 177, [1988] C.L.Y. 3410 distinguished.

WINNIPEG CONDOMINIUM CORP NO.36 v. BIRD CONSTRUCTION CO LTD AND SMITH CARTER PARTNERS 74 B.L.R. 1, La Forest, J., Sup Ct (Can).

4438. Economic loss–local authorities–New Zealand–negligent inspection of defective house foundations–time limits–claim arose when defects became apparent

ICC appealed against a decision of the New Zealand Court of Appeal upholding an award of damages to H for economic loss arising from the depreciation in value of his property after the negligent inspection of defective foundations by a council building inspector. ICC argued that they owed no duty of care to H and that any cause of action accrued at the time the defects came into existence, with the effect that H's claim was time-barred.

Held, dismissing the appeal, that although English common law was governed by *Murphy v. Brentwood DC* [1991] 1 A.C. 398, [1991] C.L.Y. 2661, which had not established a duty of care in respect of local authorities, New Zealand courts had developed case law differently so that to bring New Zealand law into line with *Murphy* would require a significant departure from previous decisions. New Zealand courts were much better placed to decide matters pertaining to their own country. H's cause of action accrued only when the defective foundations became apparent after a second builder had been consulted, as any claim for economic loss occurred when the market value became known to have diminished, *Pirelli General Cable Works Ltd v. Oscar Faber and Partners* [1983] 2 A.C. 1, [1983] C.L.Y. 2216 disapproved. The limitation period ran from the time that a reasonably prudent home owner would have discovered the structural problems, as no economic loss could occur before that time.

INVERCARGILL CITY COUNCIL v. HAMLIN [1996] A.C. 624, Lord Lloyd of Berwick, PC.

4439. Economic loss–unnecessary alterations to guest house–duty of care owed by environmental health officers

[Food Act 1984; Food Safety Act 1990.]

N appealed against an award of £39,522 in damages to W, the proprietor of a guest house, for economic loss caused by the negligence of an environmental health officer employed by N who had wrongly stipulated, upon threat of closure, that costly building work and alterations were required in order to comply with the Food Act 1984 and the Food Safety Act 1990. N argued that environmental health officers did not owe the public a duty of care as their function was similar to that of the police and since they exercised their powers under statutory authority a duty of care did not arise.

Held, dismissing the appeal, that the position of an environmental health officer was not analogous with that of a police officer and the fact that he exercised his functions under statutory powers did not preclude the existence of a duty of care. The officer concerned had assumed responsibility and induced reliance by W, thereby creating a relationship from which a duty of care at common law arose, *Hedley Byrne & Co Ltd v. Heller & Partners Ltd* [1964] A.C. 564, [1963] C.L.Y. 2416 followed.

WELTON v. NORTH CORNWALL DC; SUB NOM. NORTH CORNWALL DC v. WELTON [1997] P.N.L.R. 108, Rose, L.J., CA.

4440. Fire services–duty of care–failure to ensure adequate water supply–duty of care neither just nor reasonable–imposition contrary to public policy

[Fire Services Act 1947.]

The Fire Authority sought to strike out a claim by the Church alleging negligence and a breach of statutory duty in failing to secure an adequate water supply which, the Church contended, had led to the spread of a fire which totally destroyed its premises.

Held, allowing the application and striking out the claim, that (1) the Fire Services Act 1947 conferred no private law right of action and (2) while at common law the damage was foreseeable and a relationship of sufficient proximity existed between the parties, it was neither fair nor reasonable to impose a common law duty of care on the fire authority, *Caparo v. Dickman* [1992] A.C. 605, [1990] C.L.Y. 3266 applied. The case authorities showed that negligence claims against both the police and coastguard were barred on public policy grounds, except in cases where the danger was created by the emergency service itself. Permitting such claims risked imposing burdens detrimental to the efficiency of the fire service and also ran the risk of creating financial claims amounting to an unreasonable burden on the taxpayer.

CHURCH OF JESUS CHRIST OF LATTER DAY SAINTS (GREAT BRITAIN) v. WEST YORKSHIRE FIRE AND CIVIL DEFENCE AUTHORITY, *The Times*, May 9, 1996, William Crawford Q.C., QBD.

4441. Fire services–duty of care–public policy considerations

[Fire Services Act 1947.]

A preliminary question as to the existence of a common law duty of care arose in a negligence action brought by J against L. The fire brigade attended J's premises following an explosion caused by the second and third defendants on adjoining land. The initial fire had been extinguished by the second defendants' staff, and the brigade inspected the area but failed to examine a unit close to the site of the explosions. J contended that the statutory duty, under the Fire Services Act 1947, to make arrangements to respond to calls, carried with it an implied duty on the brigade to respond to emergency calls and also to act with care whilst doing so, or, alternatively, that by responding, the brigade placed itself within sufficient legal proximity to an owner of burning premises in relation to the foreseeable danger from fire. The fire authority compared itself to the police and submitted that the duty owed was to the general public and not to private individuals.

Held, that there was no sufficient proximity or relationship between a fire brigade and an owner of burning premises to give rise to a personal duty to respond to a call for help. As for public policy considerations, a court had to decide whether it was fair, just and reasonable to impose a common law duty, *Clerk & Lindsell on Torts* (17th ed, 1995, p.229) and *Hill v. Chief Constable of West Yorkshire* [1989] 1 A.C. 53 considered. In the instant case, bearing in mind also that compensation claims would have to be met by the general public, the arguments in favour of the imposition of a duty of care were more than counterbalanced by those against, *M (A Minor) v. Newham LBC* [1995] 2 A.C. 633, [1995] 2 C.L.Y 169 considered. On the question of whether responding to the call brought the fire brigade into the range of legal proximity, it was necessary to show that a personal responsibility, going beyond the performance of a public duty, had been assumed towards an individual owner, *Alexandrou v. Oxford* [1993] 4 All E.R. 328, [1994] C.L.Y. 3384 followed.

JOHN MUNROE (ACRYLICS) LTD v. LONDON FIRE AND CIVIL DEFENCE AUTHORITY [1996] 3 W.L.R. 988, Rougier, J., QBD.

4442. Fire services–liability to owner of property on fire–fire brigade not immune on grounds of public policy–considerations applicable to liability of police distinguished

C, the lessee of a property destroyed by fire, brought an action against H claiming damages for negligence arising from a fire officer's decision to turn off the sprinkler system serving the roof space, on the basis of his belief that it did not serve that part of the building. H argued that on grounds of public policy the fire brigade should be immune from liability in the same way as the police service.

Held, giving judgment for C, that the public policy considerations which applied to the fire brigade were different from those relating to police investigations, as the fire brigade had exclusive control of the service provided and made operational decisions in emergency situations which were unlikely to lead to firefighters acting defensively. It was therefore reasonable that the fire brigade owed a duty of care to lessees of property which was on fire, *Alexandrou v. Oxford* [1993] 4 All E.R. 328, [1994] C.L.Y. 3384 distinguished.

CAPITAL & COUNTIES PLC v. HAMPSHIRE CC; DIGITAL EQUIPMENT CO LTD v. HAMPSHIRE CC [1996] 1 W.L.R. 1553, Richard Havery Q.C., QBD (OR).

4443. Footpaths–cattle–footpath across farmland–walker injured

O sustained a shoulder injury, bruising, grazing and shock due to being charged and headbutted by a Limousin-cross cow with suckling calf whilst walking on a right of way through a field. O contended that S was negligent in that a competent farm manager should have known that the breed was prone to temperamental difficulties and therefore should not have been placed in a relatively small field through which a well used public footpath ran. Witnesses for O submitted that the known propensity for aggression in such animals meant that they should not be placed in such a field within two months of calving.

Held, giving judgment for S, that given the total divergence of views between the experts called by O and S as to the risk posed by the Limousin breed, on balance O had failed to discharge the burden of proof as to probable risk posed to passers-by, or that S had unreasonably failed to take the necessary precautions. The evidence of B, S's farm manager, and a witness who was a former veterinary surgeon now working as a dairy farmer, showed that B had correctly considered the possible dangers in the light of the information available to him when finding there was no identifiable risk of injury to the public. In the absence of any known dangerous character in a particular animal, that animal could be used in any ordinary way without a responsibility arising for injury to others, *Manton v. Brocklebank* [1923] 2 K.B. 212 followed. Furthermore, following *Draper v. Hodder* [1972] 2 Q.B. 556, [1972] C.L.Y. 2335, there was no foreseeable risk that the cows would cause damage.

OSTLE v. STAPLETON (T/A LAZONBY ESTATE FARMS), Trans. Ref: 1994 O No.4, July 31, 1996, Sachs, J., QBD.

4444. Footpaths–duty of care–horses kept in field which footpath crossed–no breach of duty

M was walking his dog along a public footpath which crossed a field owned by D, and in which several of D's horses were kept. M suffered personal injuries as a result of being surrounded by the horses and pushed to the ground. M argued that D was negligent and in breach of his duty of care to those who might use the footpath by allowing horses to be kept in this field.

Held, dismissing the claim, that D had acted with the standard of care required by a reasonable horse keeper, having no reason to suspect that these horses, who had a previous untarnished history of behaviour, would act in this way. Horses cannot be said to be a dangerous species in themselves, and D was not in breach of his duty of care.

MILLER v. DUGGAN, June 14, 1996, District Judge Perry, CC (Warrington). [*Ex rel.* Hill Dickinson Davis Campbell, Solicitors].

4445. Franchising–financial projections for franchise operation–details prepared under direction of managing director on whose expertise company relied–director personally liable to franchisee for losses

W sought to obtain and operate a health food shop franchise and approached N, a company operated by D, its managing director. As a result of predictions as to income W entered into a franchise agreement with N. The predictions were overly optimistic and W ran into financial difficulties. W brought an action against N and D in negligence. N was wound up and W pursued the action against D personally.

Held, giving judgment for W, that N had been negligent in giving advice to W, having held itself out as being skilled in and capable of giving such advice. N knew that W would rely upon the advice. N was in breach of its duty of care to W. D was also personally liable even though there was little direct contact between him and W. D was taken to have assumed a personal responsibility to W for the preparation of the predictions, knowing that W was relying on D's experience and skill. N's business was based on that skill and expertise and D owed W a duty of care as a result.

WILLIAMS v. NATURAL LIFE HEALTH FOODS LTD [1996] 1 B.C.L.C. 288, Langley, J., QBD.

4446. Health authorities–standard of care–warning patients by letter of HIV risk did not breach duty of care

T appealed against a decision that they were in breach of their duty of care to patients who had received obstetric treatment from a health worker who was subsequently diagnosed as HIV positive. T had informed all patients by means of a letter stating that there was a very remote risk of infection. The judge had found that they had not exercised due care as the best method of communicating the warning would have been for the patients to be informed face to face by a suitably qualified person to avoid the foreseeable risk of shock and distress which some individuals might suffer.

Held, allowing the appeal, that the standard of care applied by the judge was too stringent. The relevant standard was to take reasonable care in all the circumstances to a standard shown by the ordinary skilled medical practitioner, *Whitehouse v. Jordan* [1981] 1 W.L.R. 246, [1981] C.L.Y. 1844 considered. By sending letters to patients' general practitioners asking if there were any reasons why the standard letter should not be sent to a particular patient, T had discharged their duty to take reasonable steps to warn of the risk and had directed their attention to the possibility that some patients might suffer psychiatric injury. As no comparable situation had arisen before, there was no body of experience from which a standard practice could be drawn, but by weighing up all the factual evidence, T were not negligent in informing patients in the manner they did.

AB v. TAMESIDE AND GLOSSOP HA (1996) 15 Tr. L.R. 78, Brooke, L.J., CA.

4447. Industrial accident–accidents–contributory negligence–foot and ankle caught in revolving rollers of road gritter

B appealed against a decision relating to his claim for damages for personal injuries sustained in an industrial accident during his employment by MoD. The accident occurred when B fell from the hopper of a road gritter and caught his foot and ankle in the revolving gritter rollers. Although primary negligence was found by the judge, he also held that the award of damages should be discounted by one third due to the contributory negligence of B. B appealed against the finding of contributory negligence.

Held, dismissing the appeal, that the trial judge had to decide between B's contention that it was common practice for people to perch on top of the hopper, and the evidence of the driver and the chargehand that it was not so and that they had not given their permission for B to do so. The judge was entitled to place reliance on the evidence of the driver and chargehand.

BURNS v. MINISTRY OF DEFENCE, Trans. Ref: QBENF 94/0282/C, November 17, 1995, Russell, L.J., CA.

4448. Local authorities–approval of works by local authority–duty of care in relation to exercise of statutory powers

[Building Act 1984; Building Regulations 1985.]

T were the tenants of a shopping centre. Maidstone BC was the local authority responsible for the area in which the shopping centre was situated for the enforcement of the Building Act 1984 and the regulations made thereunder following a fire, started by vandals, which spread rapidly throughout the store. T issued proceedings claiming damages for negligence by Maidstone BC in approving plans and inspecting the works in respect of physical damage to stock, fixtures and fittings and consequential business losses. There was no claim in respect of physical injury or risk of harm to the health and safety or welfare of persons or in respect of the building's shell. A preliminary issue was ordered to be tried raising the question whether on the assumed facts Maidstone BC owed T a common law duty of care in or about the exercise of their statutory powers and duties to avoid causing damage to property.

Held, giving the judgment for Maidstone BC, that (1) the statutory regime of the Building Act 1984 and the Building Regulations 1985 was concerned with questions of health, safety and the welfare of persons and not with the protection of property or chattels, *Murphy v. Brentwood DC* [1991] 1 A.C. 398, [1991] C.L.Y. 2661 considered and (2) although, on the assumed facts, damage to T was reasonably foreseeable, it was not fair, just and reasonable that a duty of care at common law be imposed on the assumed facts, *Marc Rich & Co AG v. Bishop Rock Marine Co Ltd* [1995] 3 W.L.R. 227, [1995] 2 C.L.Y. 3730 applied.

TESCO STORES LTD v. WARDS CONSTRUCTION (INVESTMENT) LTD; CLARK CARE GROUP LTD v. MAIDSTONE BC 76 B.L.R. 94, Recorder Mauleverer Q.C., QBD.

4449. Local authorities–defective answer to local land search–whether loss and damage suffered

S, commercial developers, acquired a property, marketed at £245,000, in exchange for another property which S was attempting to sell for £185,000. Prior to entering into the transaction S made a local land search which failed to reveal that the local development plan allowed for the construction of an access road over part of the land belonging to the property. The local authority admitted that they were liable in negligence for that failure but denied that S had suffered loss and damage as a result.

Held, giving judgment for S, that S had satisfied the court on the balance of probability that they would not have proceeded with the transaction had they been made aware of the contents of the local development plan. As a result of the planning proposals the property was worth £17,000 less than S paid for it. In addition S was entitled to the costs and expenses incurred in connection with the acquisition and subsequent disposal of the property.

SMITH v. MID DEVON DC [1994] E.G.C.S. 212, Blackburne, J., Ch D.

4450. Medical negligence–anaesthesia–awareness of preoperative procedures–reliability of patient's memory–res ipsa loquitur

J appealed against a decision dismissing her claim for damages against G. J claimed that she had been injured when a preoperative anaesthetic was negligently administered before a hysterectomy. She claimed that the anaesthetist had missed her vein and thus, although a subsequent injection paralysed her, she was conscious and aware of the operation. This affected her nervous system. J argued that the judge should not have concluded, on the evidence, that her memory was likely to be unreliable after the operation. She also argued that her recollection of events could only sensibly be explained as a pre-operation memory. If the recollection was found to be pre-operational then the doctrine of res ipsa loquitur would mean that negligence had occurred.

Held, dismissing the appeal, that (1) there was sufficient evidence to prove that a person's memory could be unreliable after receiving various forms of drugs; (2) although J's recollection suggested, on a balance of probabilities, a pre-operative memory, the judge did not have to make that assessment. Having weighed up all the evidence, he was entitled to reach the conclusion he did and (3) the prima facie case presented by J had been answered by G and so an inference of negligence could not be drawn. The judge concluded that J had a degree of pre-operative awareness which was unusual in the ordinary patient.

JACOBS v. GREAT YARMOUTH AND WAVENEY HA [1995] 6 Med. L.R. 192, Griffiths, L.J., CA.

4451. Medical negligence–anaesthesia–piercing of dura by guide needle during spinal anaesthetic–whether post operative care was defective

M claimed that N were negligent due to the actions of an anaesthetist who had administered spinal anaesthetic before M had a caesarian section and had pierced the dura with the guide needle, thus causing severe spinal headaches. M also claimed that her post operative care had been negligently defective as a blood patch, which would have cleared the spinal headaches, was not administered.

Held, dismissing the claim, that (1) the anaesthetist had not been negligent but had taken all reasonable care and (2) post operatively it had been reasonable to continue with conservative treatment and not to administer a blood patch.

MUZIO v. NORTH WEST HERTS HA [1995] 6 Med. L.R. 184, Douglas Day, Q.C., QBD.

4452. Medical negligence–anaesthethesia–defendant exercised reasonable care

D appealed against the dismissal of her claim for damages against S. D successfully underwent a routine operation under general anaesthetic but three or four days later complained of pains in her left hand and fingers. A further examination revealed that D had suffered a lesion of the brachial plexus. D claimed that the lesion had occurred as a result of a failure by the anaesthetist to take account of an earlier injury D had suffered which would make her susceptible to this kind of lesion. D alternatively claimed that her arm had been placed in an incorrect position during the operation and that had resulted in the discomfort she now suffered.

Held, dismissing the appeal, that the anaesthetist had established that he had followed the correct procedure during the operation. The judge in the lower court had accepted that the defendant had shown that he had exercised all reasonable care and the court could find no reason to interfere with that decision.

DELANEY v. SOUTHMEAD HA [1995] 6 Med. L.R. 355, Stuart-Smith, L.J., CA.

4453. Medical negligence–birth–cerebral palsy–midwives–causation

M was born suffering from cerebral palsy as a result of acute oxygen starvation immediately prior to birth caused by placental abruption. M brought an action in negligence against W, alleging that the midwives responsible for her mother's care failed to appreciate that there had been a secondary arrest of labour which required referral to a doctor. M argued that had a doctor been called, syntocinon, a drug used to stimulate uterine activity, would have been prescribed, causing M to be born before the abruption of placenta that was causative of her condition.

Held, giving judgment in favour of M, that the midwives caring for M's mother were negligent in failing to carry out a further vaginal examination within two hours of the last examination. Had they done so, a secondary arrest of labour would have been revealed and a doctor called who would have administered syntocinon. M would have been born at the very latest within 10 minutes of the placental abruption. On the balance of probabilities M would then have been born without the disability from which she now suffered.

MURPHY v. WIRRAL HA [1996] 7 Med. L.R. 99, Kay, J., QBD.

4454. Medical negligence–birth–cerebral palsy–suffocation with umbilical cord–doctor failed to attend and midwife failed to summon help

W claimed damages for alleged obstetric mismanagement which resulted in cerebral palsy. The issues were whether an obstetrics doctor was negligent in failing to attend and relying on a midwife who was overconfident and not qualified to make the clinical judgment required. When W was born the umbilical cord tightened around his neck for 13 minutes and he had to be resuscitated. He was left with cerebral palsy. It was submitted that the labour had been managed negligently and that if signs of distress to the fetus had been attended to by the doctor a Caesarean section would have been carried out and the resultant brain damage would not have occurred. It was alleged that the midwife present was overconfident in her abilities and had not called the doctor to attend when procedure dictated that she should.

Held, in favour of W, that it was negligent for the doctor not to attend and no responsible body of medical opinion would support a decision not to attend. Further the doctor was negligent in relying on the midwife. If the doctor had attended at the appropriate time he would have proceeded to a Caesarean section and not allowed the labour to continue, *British Railways Board v. Herrington* [1972] A.C. 877, [1972] C.L.Y. 2344 applied. The cerebral palsy was a direct cause of the way the labour was managed and the harm caused to W was foreseeable, *Joyce v. Merton, Sutton and Wandsworth HA* [1996] 7 Med. L.R. 1, [1996] C.L.Y. 4459 considered.

WISZNIEWSKI v. CENTRAL MANCHESTER HA [1996] 7 Med. L.R. 248, Thomas, J., QBD.

4455. Medical negligence–cancer–diagnosis–failure by surgeon to pay attention to patient and general practitioner–failure by surgeon to make fine needle biopsy or ultrasound available

J claimed against H for negligence in delaying the diagnosis for J's breast cancer. J argued that the consultant surgeon had been negligent when she was referred to him, by her general practitioner, because he failed to make fine needle biopsy or ultrasound available and failed to detect a five millimetre lump. This resulted in J losing an 80 per cent chance of cure.

Held, allowing the claim, that (1) the surgeon was negligent in not paying sufficient attention to what J had told him about the lump and to what the general practitioner had said in his referral letter; (2) failure to make fine needle biopsy or ultrasound available was not negligent but the non-availability of those treatments meant that it was more important to ensure that a mistake was not made and (3) if treatment had taken place following discovery, when J was first examined by the surgeon, this would have led to an 80 per cent chance of a successful result and a full life expectation.

JUDGE v. HUNTINGDON HA [1995] 5 Med. L.R. 223, R Tetheridge Q.C., QBD.

4456. Medical negligence–causation–10 month old baby with hydrocephalus–ventricular peritoneal shunt fitted–symptoms indicating shunt blockage–failure to refer to neurological unit

R, a 10 month old baby, was diagnosed as suffering from G6PD deficiency and hydrocephalus. He was fitted with a ventricular peritoneal shunt, following which he became very ill. S, a paediatrician, diagnosed shunt blockage and spoke to a neurosurgical registrar, Mr. Simpson, about R's case. Mr. Simpson informed S that shunt blockage was unlikely. R's care was continued by A, a consultant paediatrician, who despite close observation of R's signs and symptoms, failed to refer him to the neurological unit at London Hospital for a CT scan. R suffered brain damage due to shunt infection and blockage and brought an action against the medical practitioners involved in his case.

Held, giving judgment for R against A, that neither S nor Mr. Simpson was negligent in their actions. Mr. Simpson was wrong to advise S not to refer R for neurosurgical investigation, but his decision could not be described as one which no neurosurgical registrar of ordinary skill would have taken. However, A failed to give adequate consideration to the signs and symptoms displayed by R indicating neurological problems and was negligent in failing to refer him to a neurological unit for a CT scan. Had he been referred promptly, he would have received treatment which would have prevented the brain damage that occurred.

ROBINSON v. JACKLIN [1996] 7 Med. L.R. 83, G Hamilton Q.C., QBD.

4457. Medical negligence–causation–acoustic neuroma of the ear–failure to refer to specialist or make detailed enquiry of history

R, the widow and administratrix of the deceased patient's estate, brought a claim against K, the patient's general practitioner, in negligence. An acoustic neuroma, which had caused the patient deafness, was initially incorrectly diagnosed. When it was diagnosed an operation was performed to remove it which resulted in the death of the patient. R argued that K failed to implement his own advice to see an ear, nose and throat specialist, who would have given the correct diagnosis, and also that K failed to establish an adequate history in relation to the deafness with which the patient presented. It was a matter of causation as to whether if performed earlier the operation would heave been successful.

Held, dismissing the claim, that (1) the patient had raised isolated points on his three relevant visits to K and his medical assessment was that the patient was suffering from middle ear disease. There would have been no urgency relating to a referral in those circumstances; (2) when the patient was admitted to hospital it was clear that he was not suffering from middle ear disease and the symptoms were worse. Questions about the patient's history of deafness were appropriate at that stage. When the patient saw K there was no reason for him to make such searching enquiries and (3) R had not proved in evidence that the result of the operation would have been different had it been performed earlier, *Hotson v. East Berkshire HA* [1987] A.C. 750, [1987] C.L.Y. 2604 and *Bonnington Castings Ltd v. Wardlaw* [1956] A.C. 613, [1956] C.L.Y. 3489 applied.

RICHARDSON v. KITCHING [1995] 6 Med. L.R. 257, Mance, J., QBD.

4458. Medical negligence–causation–infection resulting in abscess and syringomyelia–not caused by administration of epidural anaesthetic

EM alleged that as a result of B's negligence in the 1970s she suffered from syringomyelia which left her severely disabled. EM claimed that a procedure involving the administration of epidural anaesthetic was carried out negligently and that when she later went to the casualty department an epidural abscess was not detected until a later hospital visit by which time the infection became established and led to the syringomyelia. EM argued that had the condition been detected earlier than 1989 then it would have been more susceptible to effective treatment. The trial was restricted to the issue of liability. It was common ground that one bacterium caused EM's acute illness and B argued that the infection was blood borne and probably picked up after EM left hospital. The infection was characterised by a rapid increase in symptoms after it had taken root which was incompatible with an unrelieved epidural infection.

Held, dismissing EM's claim, that the absence of symptoms when EM was seen in casualty pointed strongly against the introduction of the infection dating back to the period of the epidural anaesthetic. EM was not showing signs of infection when she went to casualty and medical causation was not established.

EL-MORSSY v. BRISTOL & DISTRICT HA [1996] 7 Med. L.R. 232, Turner, J., QBD.

4459. Medical negligence–causation–investigative surgery causing upper brain stem infarction–sutures causing partially blocked artery–procedure in accordance with accepted medical practice

J appealed against an adverse judgment in an action for damages for personal injuries following a mild heart attack. J, aged 57, underwent a cardiac catheterisation to investigate arterial disease but during the procedure upper brainstem infarction was caused by the surgeon picking up the lining of the back wall of the brachial artery during stitching which caused a partial occlusion. This left J in a condition known as "locked in syndrome" with the effect that J could not see or hear but could speak. He could understand speech and was aware of his condition. It was alleged that the doctors had been negligent in failing to reopen the artery when symptoms of J's condition became apparent. There was a general criticism that the trial judge had considered too many irrelevant medical questions, had made incorrect findings of fact, had given misdirections as to the law regarding the rules on accepted clinical practice and that he was wrong to find that instructions given to J on leaving the hospital were adequate. J also argued that the dicta in *Bolitho v. City and Hackney HA* [1993] 4 Med. L.R. 381, [1994] C.L.Y. 3368, that the burden of proof, that the plaintiff's condition was caused by a doctor's negligence lay with the plaintiff, was misapplied.

Held, dismissing the appeal, that (1) all questions needed to be determined in order to discover whether total occlusion of the artery had occurred immediately after the operation or two weeks later; (2) the judge's factual conclusions were unassailable. For example, he was entitled to give more weight to the nurse and doctor's description of their usual practice than to J and his daughter's actual recollections after seven and a half years; (3) the issue was not one of omission, but of whether the doctor's decision not to re-explore the artery because there was a palpable pulse was in line with accepted clinical practice. The doctor was correct to wait and see rather than reopen the artery, as was the usual practice according to eminent expert witnesses; (4) instructions given to J were inadequate but had he immediately returned to hospital it was likely that no action would have been taken, and (5) *Bolitho* was correctly applied by the judge.

JOYCE v. MERTON SUTTON & WANDSWORTH HA [1996] P.I.Q.R. P121, Roch, L.J., CA.

4460. Medical negligence–causation–manic depressive patient–general practitioner's awareness of medical history and failure to arrange assessment or follow up–patient injuring himself

M had a history of manic depression of which S was made aware. M consulted him on two occasions about the deterioration in his mental state. On the last such occasion M stated that he felt like a volcano about to explode. S failed to explore this observation any further with M, who then walked out of the consultation. S did not see M again, and some weeks later M jumped from a balcony, seriously injuring himself. M brought an action against S, alleging negligence causative of his injuries.

Held, allowing M's action, that S had underestimated the gravity of M's condition, and bearing in mind his medical history should have questioned him further at the consultation, and arranged a follow up and assessment as a matter of urgency. Had M received the appropriate treatment and support he was unlikely to have injured himself as he did.

MAHMOOD v. SIGGINS [1996] 7 Med. L.R. 76, H.H.J. Butter Q.C., QBD.

4461. Medical negligence–causation–no proof that kinking of ureter due to negligence

Y, a consultant gynaecologist, appealed against a judgment awarding £96,024 agreed damages to Y for damage to her left ureter sustained during a hysterectomy. The judge below found that the damage resulted from an unintended kinking of the ureter caused by the proximity of a suture of the blood vessels which was the result of negligence. Y contended that the decision was incorrectly based on statistical evidence and the doctrine of "res ipsa loquitur".

Held, allowing the appeal, that there was ample evidence from expert witnesses that kinking of the ureter could occur without negligence and H had failed to discharge the burden of proving negligent causation.

HOOPER v. YOUNG, Trans. Ref: QBENF 94/1654/C, July 26, 1996, Stuart-Smith, L.J., CA.

4462. Medical negligence–causation–paraplegia–unique operating technique

W brought a claim of negligence against WSHA after undergoing an operation at one of their hospitals. In April 1990 W underwent an operation to decompress her spine. W had been warned of the risk of paraplegia but still continued. After the operation W was found to be paraplegic. W sued WSHA for negligence alleging that (1) the neurosurgeon had undertook a unique method of performing the operation involving several complex procedures and (2) he had failed to take into consideration the proper and recommended practices as laid down by the profession.

Held, dismissing the claim, that W had failed to establish that the neurosurgeon had been negligent in performing the operation. No material or body of professional opinion existed which confirmed that the operation had been performed negligently and the court found that neither the surgeon's decision making nor his operative technique were negligent.

Observed, even if W had succeeded in proving a prima facie case of negligence, she was unable to show the necessary element of causation in relation to her injuries.

WATERS v. WEST SUSSEX HA [1995] 6 Med. L.R. 362, Buxton, J., QBD.

4463. Medical negligence–causation–plaintiff contracting chickenpox during pregnancy–child born handicapped–limitations–British Columbia

[Limitation Act 1979 (British Columbia).]

A contracted chickenpox in the twelfth week of pregnancy. She consulted her doctor, S, who failed to inform her of serious risks to the unborn child associated with the virus. A gave birth to a child, M, suffering from congenital varicella syndrome, and brought an action against S. A's claim made on behalf of M for wrongful life was discontinued. Under the Limitation Act 1979 (British Columbia), a claim for damages in respect of injury to a person was barred after two years. The trial judge held that although S was negligent in failing to warn A, the issue of whether A would, if warned, have had an abortion was to be determined objectively, and it was held that A would have continued with her pregnancy. Thus the claim failed on causation, but in any event was statute-barred. A appealed.

Held, allowing the appeal and ordering a new trial, that (1) the trial judge was wrong to find on the evidence that A would not have had an abortion had she been aware of the risks and (2) the claim was for special damages and losses and expenses relating to the cost of M's care and was therefore not a claim for injury to the person. Accordingly, the limitation period was six years and the claim was not statute barred.

ARNDT v. SMITH [1996] 7 Med. L.R. 108, Lambert, J.A., CA (British Columbia).

4464. Medical negligence–causation–plaintiff suffering from raised intracranial pressure due to blocked shunt–failure to diagnose

In 1959 R was diagnosed as suffering from hydrocephalus and fitted with an intracranial shunt. In 1984 she began to suffer headaches and consulted her doctor, F, on a number of occasions. F believed R's symptoms to be stress related and prescribed tranquillisers. R's condition worsened and she suffered double vision, vomiting, slurred speech and other symptoms, all of which F failed to record. In 1987, R had a blackout and F referred her to a consultant neurologist, S, whom he failed to inform of R's medical history. S concluded R suffered from nerves and anxiety and only on R's second visit to him referred her for a CT scan, which revealed the presence of the blocked intracranial shunt that was causing R's symptoms. R brought an action against F and S for the delay in diagnosis and treatment of her condition.

Held, giving judgment for R against F, that F was negligent in failing to suspect that R was suffering from intracranial pressure when he should have had in mind the presence of the shunt. His failure to mention the shunt to S when R was referred was also a breach in his duty of care. Although S was negligent in failing to take a full medical history from R when he first saw her, this had no appreciable effect on R's condition.

RHODES v. SPOKES AND FARBRIDGE [1996] 7 Med. L.R. 135, Smith, J., QBD.

4465. Medical negligence–hypoxia–whether judge should have described the obvious manifestation of hypoxia more precisely–judge should have given reasons for rejecting one of the consultants' evidence in part

H appealed against a judgment against it in negligence in respect of a patient, R, who suffered a respiratory arrest which resulted in significant ischaemic brain damage. R, a Jordanian, suffered a ruptured trachea during a car accident. His condition deteriorated so his relatives arranged to have him treated in the UK at Harefield Hospital. The judge found that the nurse in charge of the high dependency unit where he was awaiting an operation, and the senior house officer, SHO, on duty at the time, had failed to observe that R was suffering from signs of hypoxia during the two hours before he suffered from the respiratory arrest. The judge also found that the nurse and the SHO then failed to administer an arterial blood gas analysis, ABGA, which would have shown whether or not he was hypoxic. H argued that the judge failed to state what the manifestations of hypoxia were that the nurse and the SHO had failed to notice. It further argued that, in the case of the failure to administer an ABGA, the judge had failed to give reasons for rejecting the evidence of D the consultant in charge of R, but accepting the evidence of two other experts.

Held, allowing the appeal, that (1) there was no finding as to what the symptoms of hypoxia were that the nurse and the SHO should have noticed. The hypoxia and the degree of hypoxia in this case would not necessarily have been evident to a competent nurse and doctor. R's symptoms were distress and high respiration which were symptoms manifested by R on a number occasions previously and which had been successfully treated by medication and re-assurance and (2) the judge had stated that he held D in high regard as a witness and a doctor and had accepted his evidence on all the other matters apart from the hypoxia matter. There were no reasons given for such a rejection and that was an error.

RAJI ABU SHKARA v. HILLINGDON HA, Trans. Ref: QBENF 95/1307/C, May 23, 1996, Waite, L.J., CA.

4466. Medical negligence–limitations–plaintiff undergoing unsuccessful operation–date of knowledge

[Limitation Act 1980 s.11, s.14.]

W appealed against a preliminary ruling that F's personal injury claim was not statute barred. In 1982 F underwent an unsuccessful heart bypass operation. F had further surgery the following morning which was also unsuccessful and, in order to save his life, F's leg was amputated to prevent gangrene. F's statement of claim alleged negligence due to W's omission to perform the second operation earlier. However, F did not issue a writ until December 1992 after consulting a vascular surgeon. The preliminary issue was whether the claim was statute barred by the Limitation Act 1980 s.11, the issue turning on the "date of knowledge" which, under s.14 of the 1980 Act, was the date at which the person was aware that the injury was (a) significant and (b) attributable to an act or omission which constituted negligence. The lower court found for F on the ground that he was not aware that the injury was due to negligence until receiving expert medical opinion in 1991. W submitted that the injury in question was the amputation which was significant with F being aware of this immediately and able to decide quickly whether it arose as a result of negligence.

Held, allowing the appeal, that although there was no actual knowledge on F's part that there had been negligence, it was reasonable to expect that F, once aware of his injury, should take steps to acquire the relevant knowledge. Therefore, as soon as F had recovered from the shock of the operation and its consequences, it would have been reasonable to seek professional advice as to whether he had a suitable claim. The court estimated a period of 12-18 months after the operation. The construction of the 1980 Act allowed plaintiffs time to decide whether or not they had a claim. If they decided they did not then they could not later change their minds and seek advice which showed they had a claim. Such a construction was essential to prevent defendants from being exposed to delayed claims which they could not contest. The court granted leave to appeal to the House of Lords.

FORBES v. WANDSWORTH HA [1996] 3 W.L.R. 1108, Stuart-Smith, L.J., CA.

4467. Medical negligence–prescription of oral contraceptives–warning of contra indications not heeded–subsequent death of patient

[Fatal Accidents Act 1976; Law Reform (Miscellaneous) Provisions Act 1934.]

C had received treatment for raised blood pressure which later resolved itself. Her general practitioner proceeded to prescribe oral contraceptives to C, as a result of which she suffered middle cerebral thrombosis and died. Actions were brought under the Fatal Accidents Act 1976 and the Law Reform (Miscellaneous) Provisions Act 1934, on behalf of C's child and her estate, against the health authority and the general practitioners who had been involved in C's treatment.

Held, dismissing the actions, that the general practitioners had given C full and careful warnings of the contra-indications to the oral contraceptives. The evidence of C's father, that C had attended the surgery on a number of occasions prior to her death, complaining of various symptoms, was not accepted.

COKER v. RICHMOND, TWICKENHAM AND ROEHAMPTON AHA [1996] 7 Med. L.R. 58, R Jackson Q.C., QBD.

4468. Medical negligence–standard of care–senior houseman–diagnosis–failure to make enquiries regarding case history

D claimed that a senior houseman at one of B's hospitals was negligent in failing to make sufficient enquiries about D's case history when he was seen in the A&E department. This resulted in an incorrect diagnosis. D was suffering from epiglottitis, but it was diagnosed as a viral upper respiratory tract infection and so he was sent home. D subsequently suffered hypoxic brain damage which meant he remained in a persistant vegetative state.

Held, allowing the claim to succeed, that (1) the standard of care to be applied was that of a reasonably competent senior houseman acting as a casualty officer regardless of length of experience, *Wilsher v. Essex AHA* [1987] 1 Q.B. 730, [1988] C.L.Y. 2415 applied; (2) the doctor was negligent in that he failed to notice the spitting and pooling due to an inability to swallow saliva and (3) by failing to obtain a proper case history, the doctor was deprived of information which would have led a reasonably competent casualty officer to send D for further examination.

DJEMAL v. BEXLEY HA [1995] 6 Med. L.R., Tudor Evans, L.J., QBD.

4469. Medical negligence–sterilisation–two alternative possibilities of what occurred for failure–whether plaintiff had to prove res ipsa loquitur–whether Bolam test applied

R appealed against a judgment against him whereby F, aged 26 at the date of the incident and 32 at the date of the trial, was awarded £5,000 in damages as a result of medical negligence. F was a mother of three and, on discovering she was pregnant, decided to have an abortion and sterilisation. Both operations were conducted together. Five months later F discovered she was pregnant and had to undergo an abortion and sterilisation again. When the second operation was carried out the Fallope ring used in the first operation was not found to be in the correct place. There was only one non-negligent explanation for this which was put forward by experts called by R but rejected by F's expert and the judge. The only other explanation was that R had not fitted the ring to the fallopian tube but had fitted it somewhere else. R argued that F had to establish that this was a case of res ipsa loquitur and that she had failed to do so because there was a non-negligent explanation. R further argued that the court should have adopted the *Bolam* approach as there was a conflict of medical evidence.

Held, dismissing the appeal, that (1) this was not a case of res ipsa loquitur as there were two alternatives for what had happened and it was necessary for the judge to choose the most likely. The judge was entitled to decide that R had been negligent on the facts, having heard the evidence of F's expert witness and preferring it to the evidence of R's expert and (2) the judge would have made an error of law if he had made a choice between different bodies of distinguished professional opinion as that would not have established negligence. In this case, though, the judge determined which of the two explanations, on balance, was most probable. That was a question of fact, *Maynard v. West Midlands RHA* [1984] 1 W.L.R. 634, [1984] C.L.Y. 2324 and *Bolam v. Friern Hospital Management Committee* [1957] 1 W.L.R. 582, [1957] C.L.Y. 2431 distinguished.

FALLOWS v. RANDLE, Trans. Ref: CCRTF 95/0417/C, May 7, 1996, Stuart-Smith, L.J., CA.

4470. Medical negligence–sterilisation–vasectomy–failure to advise–no duty of care to future sexual partner

B appealed against the refusal to strike out G's claim for financial loss which alleged that B was in breach of its duty of care towards her in respect of advice given to her sexual partner concerning his vasectomy. G began her relationship with the man three years after he had undergone the vasectomy and been advised by B that he no longer needed to use contraception. G consulted her own GP who advised her that there was a minute possibility of becoming pregnant, after which she stopped using contraceptives. However, the vasectomy underwent a spontaneous reversal and G became pregnant. G argued that B had breached their duty of care to her by failing to warn her partner of the possibility of reversal and claimed damages for financial loss.

Held, allowing the appeal, that to sustain a case in negligence for financial loss there had to be a proximity of relationship between the adviser and the person acting on the advice. B was not in a relationship of sufficient proximity to give rise to a duty of care, as when the advice was given G was not the man's partner but merely a member of an immeasurably large class of women who might in future have sexual relations with him. G's claim would be struck out.

GOODWILL v. BRITISH PREGNANCY ADVISORY SERVICE [1996] 1 W.L.R. 1397, Peter Gibson, L.J., CA.

4471. Medical negligence–sterilisation–vasectomy–natural reversal–failure to advise

N brought a negligence claim against G following a vasectomy performed by G. N underwent the operation in September 1985 believing it to have been successful. However Mrs N later became pregnant after the vasectomy naturally reversed itself. N alleged that G was negligent in failing to warn of the risk that the vasectomy could reverse itself. G accepted that he had not given a warning, as he usually did, but he claimed that he had adopted the practice of a responsible body of medical opinion which did not give warnings in such cases. Therefore he had not fallen below the standard of care expected of a reasonably competent doctor who performs vasectomies.

Held, allowing the claim, that G had been negligent in failing to give a warning. G knew of the risk and made a practice of warning his patients therefore, by failing to warn N he had fallen below the acceptable standard. It was possible in 1985 that certain doctors still did not give warnings but such doctors would not be considered to be acting reasonably. The court awarded £500 in damages on the basis that in any event N would still have proceeded with the operation.

NEWELL v. GOLDENBERG [1995] 6 Med. L.R. 371, Mantell, J., QBD.

4472. Medical negligence–sterilisation–vasectomy–subsequent pregnancy–no statutory liability of Department of Health for failure to warn of risks–statutory duty

[Ministry of Health Act 1919 s.2.]

D had a vasectomy in 1983. By 1984 the Department of Health knew or ought to have known of the risk of pregnancy following a vasectomy operation. D's wife became pregnant in 1990, and later gave birth to a healthy baby boy. D brought an action against the Department of Heath alleging that it was in breach of its statutory duty under the Ministry of Health Act 1919 s.2 in failing to warn him that the operation might not guarantee permanent and irreversible sterility.

Held, dismissing the claim, that s.2 of the 1919 Act did not give rise to a private law action against the Department of Health in respect of any alleged breach of its provisions. The terms of the section, in so far as they imposed a duty, conferred a discretion upon the Minister of Health to decide what steps he should or should not take in discharge of his ministerial function, and Parliament did not intend to create a private law action by s.2. Although a common law action in negligence could, in very limited circumstances, be based upon the exercise by a public authority of its statutory function, this was not such a case.

DANNS v. DEPARTMENT OF HEALTH [1996] P.I.Q.R. P69, Wright, J., QBD.

4473. Medical negligence–total pelvic clearance–carried out based on misleading pathology report–patient consenting to exploratory operation–no negligence in view of facts aware of at time

A was diagnosed as suffering from cancer of the right ovary. She consulted K, who was misled into believing the diagnosis was correct by pathology reports. He performed an exploratory operation upon A, during which he discovered a lump which he believed to be malignant, causing him to carry out a total pelvic clearance. Subsequently it became evident that the lump was not cancerous. A brought an action against K, claiming that he was negligent in carrying out the total pelvic clearance, and that she had not consented to it.

Held, dismissing A's claim, that K had explained to A that the standard treatment for ovarian cancer was total pelvic clearance, and A was aware that if during the exploratory operation, it appeared that the cancer had spread, this treatment would be employed. As such, it could not be said she did not consent. K was not negligent in performing the total pelvic clearance in view of the facts he was aware of at the time.

ABBAS v. KENNEY [1996] 7 Med. L.R. 47, Gage, J., QBD.

4474. Occupiers' liability–elderly lady falling on council path–whether reasonable steps taken to remove danger

[Occupiers' Liability Act 1957 s.2.]

W claimed damages under the Occupiers' Liability Act 1957 for negligence. W, aged 73, suffered a broken hip when she tripped on a paving stone whilst visiting G premises to pay her rent. In keeping with the character of the building the pathway was york paving which was by its nature uneven. W claimed that there was a differential of less than one inch between two of the paving stones and that this was dangerous. G had no system of inspecting the path and relied upon staff or visitors to bring any defects to their attention. Minor repairs were carried out following the accident.

Held, that s.2 of the 1957 Act applied. The occupier has a duty to take care, to see that a visitor will be reasonably safe in using the premises for the purposes for which he is invited or permitted to be there. In determining whether the occupier took reasonable steps to protect his visitors from danger, the court must consider all the circumstances. The relevant circumstances will include how obvious the danger is, warnings, lighting, the age of the visitor and the purpose of the visit. A significant number of elderly people regularly used the path. The unevenness and variations at the point where W tripped were such that G had failed to take such care as in all the circumstances was reasonable to ensure the safety of the visitors using the premises. It was of particular importance that the path was used by many elderly people and that elderly people are likely to be unsteadied and upset by variations in the path with potentially serious consequences. It was found that the pathway could easily and cheaply be rectified by pointing and relaying.

WRIGHT v. GREENWICH LBC, July 16, 1996, H.H.J. Edwards, CC (Brentford). [*Ex rel.* Rachel Tetzlaff-Sarfas, Solicitor].

4475. Occupiers' liability–loss of sight in one eye caused by golfing accident–liability of golfer–liability of golf club

[Occupiers' Liability Act 1957 s.2.]

J appealed against a decision that the second defendants, B, a golf club, had not been negligent or in breach of their duty under the Occupiers' Liability Act 1957. J was ordered to pay £24,000 damages to H for personal injuries owing to J's negligence when playing a golf shot. H lost the sight of one eye when the golf ball hit him. J conceded that the finding against him was correct, but that B was more responsible for the accident. J argued that the judge was wrong to find that if a screen between the ninth tee and the sixth green had been extended the accident would still have happened and that B's notice giving priority to those on the sixth green was a sufficient enough warning and they had not been negligent in failing to enforce the rule.

Held, dismissing the appeal, that (1) the judge was entitled to accept the expert evidence of an amateur golfer and past chairman of the Rules of Golf Committee of the Royal and Ancient Golf Club of St. Andrews, that the extension to the screen would have made no difference; (2) the judge was also entitled to conclude that B had not breached their duty of care under s.2(2) of the 1957 Act as only two accidents had occurred in 800,000 rounds of golf played there and (3) B could not have prevented the accident with a different sign and the one in existence was reasonable in the circumstances.

HORTON v. JACKSON, Trans. Ref: CCRTF 95/0930/C, February 28, 1996, Douglas Brown, J., CA.

4476. Occupiers' liability–workman injured by fall from roof–no evidence that accident caused by defective roof

[Occupiers' Liability Act 1984 s.2.]

G appealed against a judgment against him in relation to a claim brought by P who was badly injured when he fell from the pitched roof of property owned by G whilst carrying out repair work for G. P claimed that he fell from a crawling ladder when some of the timber supporting the roof moved. G argued, inter alia, that the judge had made errors of fact and law. The evidence failed to support the judge's conclusion that G was in breach of the common duty of care under the Occupiers' Liability Act 1984 s.2(2), by virtue of the fact that the roof was unsupported causing the ladder to tilt and P to fall. However that conclusion was contradicted by P's evidence that he stood up immediately prior to the fall.

Held, allowing the appeal, that, on the evidence available to the judge, P's claim should not have succeeded. The judge failed to make a finding on how much the roof had tilted and to assess that measurement with the amount of movement reasonable for such a roof without its being defective. Thus, causation of the accident was not established.

PATON v. GILMAN, Trans. Ref: QBENF 94/1187/C, March 5, 1996, Neill, L.J., CA.

4477. Personal injuries–duty of care–bus drivers

G, aged 78 at the date of the accident, was a passenger on one of UCO's bus motor vehicles which was travelling from Market Harborough to Clipston. The road on which the bus was travelling had several bends and while the bus was negotiating one of these bends, G was thrown from her seat and sustained injury. G had been sitting with her husband and had not been properly seated on her seat. G argued, inter alia, that UCO had been negligent in failing to (1) warn G by means of a sign or otherwise that it was dangerous for her to sit where she was; (2) advise G by means of a sign or otherwise that she should brace her feet or hold onto a handrail; (3) advise G upon entering the bus at the start of the journey by means of a sign or otherwise that she should choose a different seat to the one which she did and (4) advise G by means of a sign or otherwise that it was unsafe to sit with her husband.

Held, dismissing the claim, that for UCO to owe a duty of care to passengers to ensure that they did not sit inappropriately would place an impossible burden on bus drivers to ensure that all of their passengers were properly seated before and during a journey and were properly safeguarding themselves. In relation to whether signs should have been put up, the court was not certain against what hazard the sign would have been of any help.

GARDNER v. UNITED COUNTIES OMNIBUS CO LTD, January 18, 1996, District Judge Lacey, CC (Northampton). [*Ex rel.* Matthew E Mawdsley].

4478. Personal injuries–mesothelioma contracted due to childhood exposure to asbestos–liability of factory owner–reasonable foreseeability of risk of harm established from state of contemporary knowledge

JWR appealed against a decision awarding £50,000 and £65,000 respectively to M's estate and to another plaintiff, H, who developed mesothelioma as a result of exposure to asbestos dust from JWR's premises during their childhood when they played in the factory loading bay.

Held, dismissing the appeal, that both plaintiffs had played in areas of high contamination and JWR's dust alleviation measures had been totally inadequate. Given the state of knowledge about the risks of asbestos that existed as early as 1925, which should have operated on JWR's corporate mind at the time of the plaintiffs' childhood, it was reasonably foreseeable that the plaintiffs would be exposed to the risk of pulmonary injury, although not necessarily mesothelioma, *Page v. Smith* [1995] 2 W.L.R. 644, [1995] 2 C.L.Y. 3682 considered. No distinction arose between the duty owed to the plaintiffs and that owed to JWR's own employees. This was not a test case upon which the outcome of other possible future claims could be prejudged.

MARGERESON v. JW ROBERTS LTD; HANCOCK v. JW ROBERTS LTD; HANCOCK v. T&N PLC [1996] P.I.Q.R. P358, Russell, L.J., CA.

4479. Personal injuries–plaintiff slipped on some spilled drink on hospital stairs–evidence supported finding of liability

S appealed against a decision giving judgment to B, a doctor, in a trial of liability only. B was awarded 40 per cent damages to be assessed. B had contended that he had slipped on a spilled drink on the stairs of a hospital. S argued that, on the evidence, the judge should have given judgment for S. The judge had decided that a nurse who inspected the stairs shortly after the accident was mistaken and must have examined them later in the day.

Held, dismissing the appeal, that (1) the judge was entitled to reject the nurse's evidence and accept B's and reach the conclusion he did; (2) he was also entitled to reach a finding of negligence on the basis that the spillage should have been dealt with immediately, as was the policy of the hospital and (3) a finding that B was 60 per cent contributorily negligent was the best that S could hope for.

BALACHANDRA v. SOUTHAMPTON AND SOUTH WEST HAMPSHIRE HA, Trans. Ref: CCRTF 94/1592/C, January 23, 1996, Kennedy, L.J., CA.

4480. Personal injuries–tripping over clump of weeds in pavement–highway inspections adequate

[Highways Act 1980 s.58.]

L alleged that she tripped over a large clump of weeds or grass growing in a crack on the footway and sued B as the highway authority for the pavement concerned.

Held, that the clump of grass, with a spread of five inches and a height of four inches at the edge of the footway close to the wall of a property, was not a danger. The judge relied on *Mills v. Barnsley* [1992] P.I.Q.R. 291, [1993] C.L.Y. 2967 for the general principles, but distinguished the present case from "run of the mill" trip cases insofar as it was a potential hazard which was immediately obvious. The position of the clump of grass was also a matter of great significance. The judge also held that R's annual weed control programme satisfied the requirements of the Highways Act 1980 s.58, by taking all practical measures to bring weeds under control and a s.58 defence was therefore established. The judge also referred to the regular highway inspections.

LLOYD v. REDBRIDGE LBC, January 29, 1996, H.H.J. Platt, CC (Ilford). [*Ex rel.* Barlow Lyde & Gilbert, Solicitors].

4481. Personal injuries–young man knocked down by bus–findings of fact did not accord with evidence

L appealed against judgment in favour of R following an accident whereby R, aged 21, was struck by a bus driven by one of L's employees. L argued that the judge below had been wrong to find that the driver was at fault and, alternatively, that if the driver was at fault, the judge was wrong not to find that R was contributorily negligent. The judge should have found that R had walked into the side of the bus and he should have accepted the independent evidence of two defence witnesses to that effect.

Held, allowing the appeal, that it was rare for the Court of Appeal to differ from a trial judge on a question of fact, particularly in a personal injury case where liability depended on the evaluation of evidence given by witnesses. However, the judge's findings of fact, that R had been struck whilst standing six to eight feet to the rear of a parked car and about one foot further out into the road from it, could not be supported. It would have meant that the car would also have been struck by the bus, and it clearly was not. It was difficult to understand why the judge had attached so much weight to a witness who had given evidence which was plainly wrong, and little weight to the evidence of other witnesses.

RUNGHASWAMI v. LONDON BUSES LTD, Trans. Ref: QBENF 93/1093/C, May 1, 1995, Swinton Thomas, L.J., CA.

4482. Professional negligence–accountants–finance of property development–assurances by accountants–measure of damages–collapse in property prices

F financed a property development by G, a client of accountants CA. In June 1990 they became concerned as to whether G had sufficient net worth to service the debt and were informed by CA that he did. However, in August CA admitted this was not the case and they had been negligent in their dealings with F. Damages were held to be £2.7 million, being the difference between the price F obtained on the sale of the property in September and the price they would have obtained if the property had been sold in June, before the collapse in property prices. The sale would undoubtedly have happened if F had been made aware of the true state of G's finances. CA appealed. The question was whether F should have been compensated for the loss of a chance and, if so, to what amount.

Held, allowing the appeal, that (1) it was necessary to decide whether, knowing the truth, F would have marketed the property sooner and that there was a real, not speculative, chance of a sale at the valuation price in June, *Allied Maples Group Ltd v. Simmons & Simmons* [1995] 1 W.L.R. 1602, [1996] C.L.Y. 4489 considered and (2) it was then necessary to produce a valuation of the chance. In this case, there was a real and substantial chance of a sale. The judge found, on the evidence, that there was a 67 per cent chance of selling the whole property for £3 million. The damages were reduced to £2 million.

FIRST INTERSTATE BANK OF CALIFORNIA v. COHEN ARNOLD & CO [1996] 1 P.N.L.R. 17, Nourse, L.J., CA.

4483. Professional negligence–architects–failure to disclose prior knowledge–whether breach of professional duty–liability–duty to comply with building regulations

P sought damages in both contract and tort for M's breach of duty as an architect. P had retained M to undertake alteration and modernisation work on her home and contended that M was liable for failing to comply with building regulations in respect of her design work. She also claimed that M should have warned her of previous difficulties experienced with a building firm, whose work on P's house proved to be unsatisfactory. This meant P had to engage a second building firm, who subsequently became insolvent. M denied liability, counterclaiming for the balance of unpaid fees.

Held, allowing the claim, that the measure of damages was the sum needed to put her in the position she would have been in if the wrong had not occurred *Livingstone v. Rawyards Coal* (1880) 5 App. Cases 25 and *Robinson v. Harman* (1848) 1 Exch. 850 considered. Establishing the measure required a comparison between the end result, following the breach by M, with the result that would have been achieved had it not occurred. On the facts, M had been negligent in failing to disclose her own knowledge as to the builder's previous shortcomings. As a result, P had entered a transaction she otherwise would not have entered and therefore M's breach was the cause of P's losses arising from engaging both sets of builders and the extra costs incurred in making good the defective work, *Bank Bruxelles Lambert SA v. Eagle Star Insurance Co Ltd* [1995] 1 E.G.L.R. 129, [1994] C.L.Y. 3379 applied.

PARTRIDGE v. MORRIS [1995] E.G.C.S. 158, Hicks, J., QBD (OR).

4484. Professional negligence–auditors–investors' monies held on trust–directors improperly using monies–auditors under no duty to investors

The plaintiffs were investors who had invested monies with a company called GAA. The monies were received and held by GAA on trust for the investors and paid into a separate designated client account at GAA's bank. Thereafter the monies were improperly used by the directors of GAA to meet their own and the company's liabilities. GAA in due course collapsed. The plaintiffs sued the directors of GAA and its auditors. They contended that the auditors owed them a duty of care in auditing GAA's accounts and that if they had exercised reasonable skill and care the directors' defalcations would not have gone unnoticed. The auditors' application to strike out the claim as disclosing no reasonable cause of action was dismissed by the master. The auditors appealed.

Held, allowing the appeal and striking out the claim, that the investors did not fall within the class of persons to whom the auditors owed a duty of care. It could not be said that such a duty arose out of the fact that the auditors knew the plaintiffs' money was held by GAA on trust for the them. There was no apparent assumption on the part of the auditors of any responsibility to the plaintiffs nor any reliance by the plaintiffs on their auditing of GAA's accounts, *Caparo Industries Plc v. Dickman* [1990] 2 A.C. 605, [1990] C.L.Y. 3266 applied; *White v. Jones* [1993] 3 W.L.R. 730, [1993] C.L.Y. 2990 considered.

ANTHONY v. WRIGHT [1995] 1 B.C.L.C. 236, Lightman, J., Ch D.

4485. Professional negligence–banks–bank manager–advice on property investment–whether bank owed clients duty of care–damages recoverable

V and S borrowed money from L for the purpose of buying a house for renovation as a business venture in 1988. The investment failed and the losses were aggravated by falling house prices. The questions for determination were whether the bank owed a duty of care to advise as to the prudence of purchasing the house as a business investment; whether the bank was in breach of that duty, if it arose; whether V and S relied on that advice and whether the loss caused by that reliance was foreseeable.

Held, awarding V and S damages, that (1) V and S had specifically sought the manager's advice on the prudence of the transaction and were advised to proceed with it. If bankers gave such advice they were subject to the same duty of care as other professionals. No careful advisor would have advised V and S to proceed with the project. If the manager had advised V and S correctly, they would never have entered into the transaction; (2) the fall in the equitable value of the property would be included in the loss on a "no transaction" basis, *Banque Bruxelles Lambert SA v. Eagle Star Assurance Co Ltd* [1995] 2 All E.R. 769, [1995] 1 C.L.Y. 1834 considered and (3) damages for loss of earnings were not allowed insofar as the claim was based on the damaging effect of stress and strain, but in principle there was a claim for work lost as a result of furthering the project. No damages were possible for emotional stress *Hayes v. Dodd* [1990] 2 All E.R. 815, [1990] C.L.Y. 1524 applied.

VERITY AND SPINDLER v. LLOYDS BANK PLC [1996] Fam. Law 213, Robert Taylor, J., QBD.

4486. Professional negligence–barristers–breach of statutory duty not included in negligence claim–plaintiff within class statutorily protected–application to strike out failed

[Offshore Installations (Operational Safety, Health and Welfare) Regulations 1976 Reg.34; Mineral Workings (Offshore Installations) Act 1971.]

M alleged that he had suffered psychiatric harm as a result of W's negligence as operators of the Piper Alpha oil rig. He had been a painter on board a ship from which he witnessed the Piper Alpha oil rig disaster. The issue arose as to whether W, M's counsel, had been professionally negligent in not including an alternative claim for breach of statutory duty in addition to the claim in negligence; W applied to strike out the professional negligence claim, contending that it disclosed no ensurable cause of action.

Held, dismissing the application, that the appropriate duty was found in the Offshore Installations (Operational Safety, Health and Welfare) Regulations 1976, made pursuant to the Mineral Workings (Offshore Installations) Act 1971. M fell within the category of persons envisaged by Reg.34 of the 1976 Regulations and the 1971 Act, and the 1976 Act Regulations specifically envisaged someone in this situation. Therefore the summons to strike out the whole of the claim failed.

McFARLANE v. WILKINSON [1996] 1 Lloyd's Rep. 406, Rix, J., QBD.

4487. Professional negligence–defective building work–settlement by solicitors–whether reliance on instructions of one partner adequate authority–whether settlement was reasonable–costs

G were partners of a building firm until October 1984. In May 1984 they built an extension on the rear of a bungalow belonging to M. The foundations were defective and in October 1988 M sued the partners for negligence and breach of contract. CJ were the solicitors instructed to act for G. After receipt of an expert's report which was pessimistic on the issue of liability CJ accepted the instructions of one of the partners, to admit liability and the case was settled in the amount claimed by M. Subsequently, G sued CJ for breach of contract and negligence for settling M's action without their authority and on a basis which was, it was alleged, negligently excessive. CJ admitted liability and the action was tried as to quantum. The judge held that the settlement with M was a reasonable settlement and awarded nominal damages of £3. He ordered G to pay CJs costs. G appealed.

Held, dismissing the appeal, that there was no ground on which the judge's conclusion, that the settlement with M was a reasonable settlement, could be challenged. Liability and quantum overlapped and the judge had been entitled in the exercise of his discretion, to order G to pay the costs of the action, *Blank v. Footman, Pretty & Co* (1888) 39 Ch. D. 678 distinguished.

GREEN v. CUNNINGHAM JOHN & CO (1996) 46 Con. L.R. 62, Rose, L.J., CA.

4488. Professional negligence–estate agents–negligent misrepresentation as to size of land–duty of care–effect of disclaimer

[Unfair Contract Terms Act 1977 s.11.]

M, the purchaser of a property, appealed from a decision that he was not entitled to damages for negligent mis-statement against LF, a firm of estate agents, who had misrepresented the size of a plot of land adjoining the property. It was decided that a duty of care was established but that M had failed to show that he had suffered financial loss

Held: appeal dismissed. LF did not owe a duty of care to M because they had included a disclaimer in their sales particulars which negatived the element of proximity and the assumption of responsibility for the statement required to establish negligence, *Hedley Byrne & Co Ltd v. Heller & Partners Ltd* [1964] A.C. 465, [1963] C.L.Y. 2416 followed. Furthermore, it was not unfair within s.11 of the Unfair Contract Terms Act 1977 to allow LF to rely on the disclaimer.

McCULLAGH v. LANE FOX AND PARTNERS LTD [1996] P.N.L.R. 205, Hobhouse, L.J., CA.

4489. Professional negligence–solicitors–acquisition of shares–failure to advise on protection clause against first tenant liability–privity of contract–business tenancies–causation

AM acquired shares in the Gillow Group and subsequently incurred first tenant liabilities from leases originally held by a Gillow company, Kingsbury. SS devised a scheme whereby AM could acquire shares in Kingsbury and transfer out the unwanted properties but claims arose against AM of assignees' defaults. AM sought to recover substantial damages from SS as they argued that SS had failed to advise them of the potential claims against them and that they had been properly advised they would not have continued with the acquisition. SS argued that the AM adviser with whom they were negotiating was a chartered accountant who should have been aware of the possible dangers. The judge below found for AM on the basis of causation and SS appealed.

Held, dismissing the appeal, that a causal link had been established between the negligence of SS's advice and the losses suffered by AM. AM had shown that there was a substantial chance that if they had received proper advice they would have been successful in negotiating a protection clause with Gillow.

ALLIED MAPLES GROUP LTD v. SIMMONS & SIMMONS [1995] 1 W.L.R. 1602, Stuart Smith, L.J., CA.

4490. Professional negligence–solicitors–appointment of receiver–whether act complained of changed presentation of case

O brought an action against his solicitors, M, contending negligence in their handling of a case leading to the appointment of a receiver whom they recommended for his partnership.

Held, dismissing the action that where an action was brought against an adviser contending negligence or omission, the matter could only succeed where the act complained of completely changed the presentation of the case. Following *Hunter v. Chief Constable of the West Midlands Police* [1982] A.C. 529, [1982] C.L.Y. 2382 and *Somasundaram v. M Julius Melchior & Co* [1988] 1 W.L.R. 1394, [1988] C.L.Y. 2768, such actions were restricted where the main thrust would serve to undermine the considered decision of another court on the same matter. On the facts, the issue was whether the decision to appoint the receiver was correct, not whether later events justified his removal.

OLIVER v. McKENNA & CO, *The Times*, December 20, 1995, Laddie, J., Ch D.

4491. Professional negligence–solicitors–bridging loan provider–failure of loan made beyond terms of agreed lending criteria–whether solicitor liable to banks backing own client–foreseeability of loss–proximity of relationship–conflicting duties owed to two separate parties

CFL provided bridging loans to individual purchasers of land for residential purposes. B were CFL's solicitors. Finance was obtained from Barclays Bank with the backing of other banks. One loan to TPL, which subsequently collapsed, included departures from the lending criteria in that it was not made to an individual for residential purposes and an unsatisfactory security compromise was made by B beyond the terms of the criteria. However, B stated that the criteria had been complied with, as confirmed in the request form. As a result of the failure to make proper security arrangements, the money was lost and CFL went into receivership. Barclays and the other banks alleged that B owed a duty of care for negligent misrepresentation or a breach of duty leading to economic loss.

Held, dismissing the claim, that (1) the damage was foreseeable and of a kind likely to occur if the criteria were not kept to. Adding a link to the chain did not lessen this foreseeability with B sufficiently proximate to Barclays for the duty to extend to all the banks as a clearly identifiable class and (2) however, the plaintiffs were not entitled to rely upon the request form as a representation that all the requirements of the scheme had been complied with as the form shared the transaction to be outside the established lending criteria. The request form itself negated two of these criteria and could not be held as an assertion that all the criteria had been complied with. Conflicting duties required by CFL and the banks created a difficult situation for B and it was doubtful how far these distinct duties could be owed by B to the two individual parties.

ROTHSCHILD & SONS LTD v. BERENSON (1995) 70 P. & C.R. D45, Knox, J., Ch D.

4492. Professional negligence–solicitors–causation–failure to advise client company of need for members' approval for property transactions involving directors–liability for losses flowing from negligent advice

[Companies Act 1985 s.320.]

H acted as solicitors to B, but failed to advise B about the requirement under the Companies Act 1985 s.320 for company members in a general meeting to approve a transaction where a director had a personal interest. The director in question owned shares in T in which B was to acquire half the shares. H denied that the loss was suffered as a result of deficient legal advice and that it was in fact suffered because of the directors' flawed commercial judgement. Further, H denied liability for the costs incurred in professional fees without taxation to ensure that they were reasonable.

Held, giving judgment for B and referring the matter to the taxing master, that the purpose of s.320 of the 1985 Act was to safeguard a company against the losses resulting from transactions in which the directors had an interest. H deprived the companies of this safeguard by failing to advise the companies of the need to comply with s.320. The directors' negligence could not be relied upon by H to reduce their liability to the companies because the transaction was well within s.320. H would therefore be liable for the entire amount because there had been no failure by the plaintiffs to mitigate their loss. Expenditure by B on professional fees was reasonable mitigation of their loss.

BRITISH RACING DRIVERS CLUB LTD v. HEXTALL ERSKINE & CO [1996] 3 All E.R. 667, Carnwath, J., Ch D.

4493. Professional negligence–solicitors–claims of failure to call favourable expert evidence or to advise that case was hopeless

N, a beneficiary of her grandfather's estate, commenced proceedings against the trustees of the estate alleging breach of trust resulting from negligent mis-investment of trust monies. The action was dismissed in part because the expert evidence adduced by N's solicitors did not establish any breach of trust. An appeal against this finding was also dismissed, after which N began an action against her solicitors and barristers on the basis that they should have found a better or different expert, or in the alternative, that as the action proved to be hopeless they should have warned her at the outset of the likelihood of failure and the consequent costs she would face. B applied successfully to strike out the claims on the basis that they were frivolous and vexatious. N sought leave to appeal.

Held, dismissing the appeal, that (1) as regards N's contention that her advisers were negligent in not adducing better expert evidence concerning the alleged negligence of the trustees' stewardship of the estate, the judge had been correct to strike out this claim on the basis of the test stated in *Walpole v. Partridge & Wilson* [1994] Q.B. 106, [1994] C.L.Y. 3517 since N had completely failed to provide any evidence of what such better or further expert evidence might have established and (2) it was clear from the Court of Appeal's judgment that N's original case was not bound to fail as she suggested and the judge had also been correct to strike out this part of the claim.

NESTLE v. BEST [1996] P.N.L.R. 444, Hutchison, L.J., CA.

4494. Professional negligence–solicitors–consent orders–alleged failure to provide up to date information to court–alleged failure to advise plaintiff properly–whether writ action was abuse of process of court

In ancillary relief proceedings a consent order was made whereby the wife received £150,000 by way of lump sum in order to purchase a home and would transfer her shares in a company to the husband for £15. Subsequently W issued proceedings against her solicitors, alleging that they had negligently failed to provide an up to date valuation of the former matrimonial home which had in fact been sold in the same year for £750,000 and they had failed to inform the court that the shares were not in W's name and that H and W were jointly indebted to W's parents in the sum of $50,000. She complained that she had relied on their negligent advice when agreeing to the terms of the consent order. The solicitors, M, sought to strike out her claim on the grounds that it amounted to a collateral attack on an order of a court of competent jurisdiction and was therefore abuse of the process of the court.

Held, dismissing the application, that a consent order in ancillary relief proceedings was not the same as an order following a contested hearing. The present action was not a collateral attack on a court of competent jurisdiction since when approving the consent order, the judge would not have examined the proposed order in any purposeful way and W's case would not have been put properly before the court. The basis of W's case was that M had failed to ensure that all relevant information was before the court and that they had given her negligent advice. Failure to seek alternative remedies might be held to constitute a failure by W to mitigate her loss but did not mean that she was not entitled to continue with her action.

B v. MILLER & CO [1996] 2 F.L.R. 23, McKinnon, J., QBD.

4495. Professional negligence–solicitors–conveyance of defective lease–property rendered unsaleable–measure of damages

D, a firm of solicitors, appealed against the amount of damages awarded against them for negligence when they failed to discover that a valid leasehold title had not been conferred upon their clients on the purchase of two flats. One of the flats was bought for £38,950 and the other for £38,000. Damages of £76,202 and £74,890 inclusive of interest and costs were awarded respectively.

Held, dismissing the appeal, that (1) the judge had correctly assessed the value of the lease at the time of the transaction and was correct to measure the damage by the amount of the purchase price without a discount for any value in the defective lease; (2) the respondents had not been overcompensated. They owned properties with no equity and of no value as security for the repayment of their mortgages; (3) compensation for mere disappointment due to a breach of contract was distinct from active discomfort and distress due to breaches which were reasonably foreseeable and (4) the distress caused to a young couple by purchasing a flat which was unsaleable and would lead to them having to start a family in cramped conditions was not too remote.

WAPSHOTT v. DAVIS DONOVAN & CO; KIDD v. DALE & NEWBERRY (1996) 72 P. & C.R. 244, Beldam, L.J., CA.

4496. Professional negligence–solicitors–conviction of aggravated burglary–allegation of negligence was contrary to public policy as a collateral challenge to the conviction

S was sentenced to seven years' imprisonment for aggravated burglary. On his release he brought an action for damages against the firm of solicitors who had acted for him, alleging that, but for their negligence, fresh evidence would have been available at the trial. The judge applied the rule of public policy that the use of a civil action to mount a collateral attack on a decision of a criminal court was an abuse of process, and held that the action should not be allowed to proceed. On appeal, S argued that his purpose in bringing the action was not to attack his conviction but to recover damages for professional negligence.

Held, dismissing the appeal, that the soundness or otherwise of S's criminal conviction was central to his claim that, but for the solicitors' negligence, he would not have been convicted. The existence of an ulterior motive such as the avoidance of a sentence of imprisonment was an additional ground for holding proceedings to be an abuse of process but was not a necessary ingredient of an abuse. On the facts, there were no grounds for disapplying the prima facie rule of public policy invoked by the judge, *Hunter v. Chief Constable of the West Midlands Police* [1982] A.C. 529, [1982] C.L.Y. 2382 and *Walpole v. Partridge & Wilson (A Firm)* [1994] Q.B. 106, [1994] C.L.Y. 3517 applied.

SMITH v. LINSKILLS [1996] 1 W.L.R. 763, Sir Thomas Bingham, M.R., CA.

4497. Professional negligence–solicitors–duty of care–solicitor acting for purchaser and lender–failure to disclose matters affecting valuation

M, a mortgage company, brought negligence proceedings against B, a firm of solicitors, who were instructed by the purchaser to act in arranging a mortgage based on a valuation report valuing a flat at £199,000. M proposed to lend £180,000 based on the valuation. Subsequently the partner found that the sale to H was a sub sale and also discovered from the vendor's vendor that the flat was worth less than £150,000. B's report to M failed to disclose these other transactions. H defaulted and the flat was sold for £96,000. B denied acting in breach of duty to make disclosure to M. The judge held that if M had known the full circumstances they would have asked for a second valuation. No aspersion was cast on the integrity of the partner and it was not alleged that H was dishonest. B appealed against the finding of liability to M.

Held, dismissing the appeal, that (1) the fact that the partner was acting for both purchaser and lender did not affect the duty he owed to either; (2) the terms of the instructions were considered. B was not instructed merely to report on title. The instructions referred also to the normal duties which a solicitor owed to a mortgagee. Although it was a matter of fact and degree there were some facts that would need to be passed on; (3) a solicitor was under a duty to inform the lender of facts which a reasonably competent solicitor might realise would have a material bearing on the value of the lender's security and (4) the case was limited to the facts and did not extend the duties to which solicitors were generally subject.

MORTGAGE EXPRESS LTD v. BOWERMAN & PARTNERS [1996] 2 All E.R. 836, Sir Thomas Bingham, M.R., CA.

4498. Professional negligence–solicitors–expert witnesses–conveyancing–failure to discover defective title–whether expert witnesses should be heard

[Rules of the Supreme Court Ord.38 r.4, Ord.38 r.36.]

In an action for professional negligence against his former solicitors, GS. B appealed against a decision in a pre-trial review refusing leave to call an expert witness. When B bought a domestic property he understood there was a right of way over neighbouring land giving access to the highway. It was alleged that the vendors had no title to a right of way because the grantor had none. B claimed that GS had been negligent in failing to discover defective title and submitted that a conveyancing expert could assist in establishing best practice in conveyancing matters. GS denied that they should have inspected the land or were on notice as to whether the grantor had title.

Held, dismissing the appeal, that the judge had been correct to view the proposed evidence as irrelevant and inadmissible in usurping the function of the trial judge. There was no merit in a point that there was no jurisdiction under Rules of the Supreme Court Ord.38 r.4 or r.36 to rule evidence inadmissible when the question was whether the proposed evidence should be disclosed, *Sullivan v. West Yorkshire Passenger Transport Executive* [1985] 2 All E.R. 134, [1985] C.L.Y. 1506 relied on. The instant appeal concerned a pre-trial review arranged specifically to consider the admissibility of the proposed evidence and it would be wrong if no such procedure existed. There had been no application for disclosure under RSC Ord.38 r.36. It was not a question of interlocutory directions so that the argument was misplaced. In any event, the parties had clearly consented to a ruling which resolved an issue between them. What solicitors should do in such a conveyancing transaction did not concern best practice. These were issues of law for the judge to resolve. To hear what the expert might have done did not advance matters. All the issues which had been raised by B were either of law or of fact, *Midland Bank Trust Co Ltd v. Hett, Stubbs & Kemp* [1979] 1 Ch. 384, [1978] C.L.Y. 2822 followed. It was for B to establish the want of title, transferring the burden to GS to show that it could not have been discovered by the investigation of title. There was no question of notice. In the absence of instructions, it could not be argued that GS were under a duty to carry out a site inspection as part of the process of investigating whether the vendors had deduced title as contractually obliged. Were it necessary to assist with an understanding of the deduction and investigation of title the proper recourse were to the standard conveyancing textbooks rather than the evidence of conveyancing solicitors.

BOWN v. GOULD & SWAYNE [1996] P.N.L.R. 130, Simon Brown, L.J., CA.

4499. Professional negligence–solicitors–failure to inform clients of restrictive covenant–cost of release of covenant–measure of damages

B, in an action in negligence against CF, a firm of solicitors, appealed against a decision to strike out the paragraphs of their particulars of claim relating to damages. CF had acted for B in the purchase of a dwelling house. B alleged that, before the purchase, they had made it known to CF that they intended to build another property in the garden of the house, and that CF had failed to bring to their attention the fact that the property was subject to a restrictive covenant which would prevent such building. B claimed that the amount necessary to secure the release of the restrictive covenant amounted to £3,505 paid to the local authority plus £470 in legal fees. CF successfully argued that the measure of damages was the difference between the amount paid for the house and its market value at that time. B argued that the case amounted to a "no transaction" case or, if not, the facts pleaded in the particulars of claim justified the measure of damages.

Held, dismissing the appeal, that the facts pleaded in the particulars of claim could not sustain the measure of damages claimed. The correct measure of damages in tort was to put the injured party in the position he would have been in if the other party had not acted negligently. If B could not show that they had paid more for the property than it was worth at the time then the damages claimed would have the effect of putting them in a better position. The facts showed that B would have gone ahead with the purchase in any event, *Watts v. Morrow* [1991] 1 W.L.R. 1421, [1992] C.L.Y. 1548 applied.

BROWN v. CUFF ROBERTS, Trans. Ref: CCRTI 95/1285/G, February 12, 1996, Roch, L.J., CA.

4500. Professional negligence–solicitors–grant of restaurant lease–failure to ascertain opening hours permitted and extent of permitted use–whether negligent

P, a firm of solicitors, acted for LR in the grant to LR of a lease of restaurant premises. The landlord lived next door to the restaurant. Planning permission existed for restaurant use subject to a limitation on the opening hours. LR wished to expand the function room side of the business but the lease as granted restricted those activities. Relations with the landlord deteriorated, LR was not able to use the premises as he had originally envisaged and after two years he was obliged to sell. LR sued P for negligence in failing to advise him of the restrictions on the use of the premises and contended that if he had been properly advised he would not have taken the lease at all.

Held, entering judgment for LR, that P acted negligently in failing to take adequate instructions at the outset as to LR's plans for the restaurant and in consequence failed to ensure that the user covenants in the draft lease permitted LR to realise his objectives. P were also negligent in failing to ascertain that the opening hours were restricted by the planning permission applicable to the premises. The court was satisfied that if P had acted competently LR would not have entered into the lease at all.

LE ROUX v. PICTONS [1994] E.G.C.S. 168, Nicholls, J., QBD.

4501. Professional negligence–solicitors–hotel purchase–no duty to advise on commercial aspects of access arrangements

R purchased an hotel, with T acting as his solicitors. At the rear of the hotel was a car park. The car park could be reached only by crossing neighbouring land. T advised R that there was no right of way for access to the car park, but only a licence agreement, which could be terminated without any right to renew. R brought an action in negligence against T for failing to inform him that there would be no secure right of way over the neighbouring land. On a trial of preliminary issues it was decided that T were not in breach of a duty of care on the basis of the advice given and that any damages were to be assessed on the cost of acquiring a right of way to the car park. R appealed.

Held, dismissing the appeal, that T had clearly discharged their obligation to R by explaining that the right of way was dependent upon the former owner's licence. No duty arose on T to advise as to any commercial implications due to the access arrangements, or the risks posed to future development, operations or sale of the hotel.

REEVES v. THRINGS & LONG [1996] P.N.L.R. 265, Sir Thomas Bingham, M.R., CA.

4502. Professional negligence–solicitors–illegal premium paid for underlease–no actual loss–whether entitled to damages

[Rent Act 1977 s.127.]

K, who in 1983 paid a premium of £49,500 for the transfer of an underlease of a flat, brought a claim of professional negligence against her solicitor. The solicitor was found to have been negligent in failing to advise K that the premium was unlawful, since the underlease in question did not come within the Rent Act 1977 s.127 and could not be assigned for a premium. As a result of a legislative amendment, however, K was able, after 1988, to validly assign the underlease. K argued that she should be awarded the difference between the premium she paid and the value of the underlease as at the date of the solicitor's breach of duty. However, the judge declined to apply the diminution in value rule and found that the damages should be assessed at the date of the trial. He concluded that K had suffered no loss and K appealed.

Held, dismissing the appeal, that although the principles set out in *County Personnel (Employment Agency) Ltd v. Alan R Pulver & Co* [1987] 1 W.L.R. 916, [1987] C.L.Y. 3551 favoured the application of the diminution in value rule in cases of solicitors' negligence and the general rule that damages should be assessed at the time of the breach, the judge was right not to apply those rules in the instant case. K now had an assignable underlease and the court should not award compensatory damages where no actual loss had occurred.

KENNEDY v. KB VAN EMDEN & CO; JORDAN v. GERSHON YOUNG FINER & GREEN; BURDGE v. JACOBS [1996] P.N.L.R. 409, Nourse, L.J., CA.

4503. Professional negligence–solicitors–lender's reliance on negligently given incorrect information–lender must prove loss

M, a solicitor who had acted for both the lender and borrower in the purchase of a property, appealed against a judgment in favour of the lender, B, in the sum of £59,000, less the sum received upon sale of the property, after the purchaser defaulted on repayments. M had negligently given information to B which failed to state the purchaser's arrangement to take out a second charge over the property, but argued that had B been aware of the second charge it would still have proceeded with the transaction and suffered the same loss, with the effect that no damages were recoverable at common law. B submitted that it could recover the whole net loss without having to prove that it would have proceeded had it known the true facts, and that it would therefore be unnecessary to establish whether M had been guilty of breach of trust or fiduciary duty in equity.

Held, allowing the appeal, that it was necessary to show that B had relied on the negligently given information in relation to the second charge, ie. a causal link had to be established but B did not need to prove that it would not have proceeded with the transaction had it been in receipt of the true facts, *Downs v. Chappell* [1996] 3 All E.R. 344, [1996] C.L.Y. 5689 followed. However, B had to establish the loss which it had suffered arising from the second charge. The equitable claim that M had breached its fiduciary duty could not be maintained as M had never acted in bad faith or breached the conflict rule, nor could a claim for breach of trust be accepted as M's authority to apply the mortgage money was not vitiated by his misrepresentations. The judgment for damages for breach of contract to be assessed remained the same and the money judgments were set aside.

BRISTOL & WEST BUILDING SOCIETY v. MOTHEW (T/A STAPLEY & CO) [1996] 4 All E.R. 698, Millett, L.J., CA.

4504. Professional negligence–solicitors–misrepresentation–use of standard of forms–effect of disclaimer

[Unfair Contract Terms Act 1977 s.11.]

F claimed damages for negligent mis-statement from L, a firm of solicitors, who had replied to inquiries in relation to a mortgage agreement between a client of L as the borrower and F as the lender using a standard Oyez form. It was accepted by L that some of the replies were not correct, and F claimed to have suffered a substantial loss. L claimed either that no duty of care was owed to F, or, if there was such a duty, that the disclaimer on the form, which had been widely used for conveyancing purposes for a number of years, excused them from any duty that would have been owed in the circumstances, and that under the Unfair Contract Terms Act 1977 s.11 it was fair and reasonable for the solicitors to rely on the disclaimer. The judge struck out F's claim against L as disclosing no reasonable cause of action, and F appealed.

Held, allowing the appeal, that L were not entitled to have the negligence action struck out and a trial of the action was ordered. Whether a duty of care was owed was uncertain in law, and could not be decided separately from the issue of the efficacy of the disclaimer. The true question under the Unfair Contract Terms Act 1977 s.11 (3) was not the fairness and reasonableness of the disclaimer itself, but whether it was fair and reasonable to allow L to rely on it in all the circumstances. This was for L to establish, and all the pertinent facts should be considered at trial.

FIRST NATIONAL COMMERCIAL BANK PLC v. LOXLEYS (A FIRM) [1996] E.G.C.S. 174, Nourse, L.J., CA.

4505. Professional negligence–solicitors–offer to buy house withdrawn after conveyancing documents delayed–necessary to prove real or substantial chance of sale–measure of damages

S instructed B, a firm of solicitors, to act in the sale of his house. On September 13, 1989 S accepted an offer, subject to contract, and the purchaser requested the title deeds and draft contract to be delivered to his solicitors the following day. They failed to arrive and a second deadline was also missed, which meant contracts could not be exchanged by September 22 as the purchaser wished, so the offer was withdrawn and the purchaser bought a different property. At first instance it was decided that B had been negligent in not sending the documents on time and B appealed against an award of £96,312 damages, including interest.

Held, allowing the appeal in part. It was wrong to require S to show, on a balance of probabilities, that if the documents had arrived then the purchaser would have gone ahead with the transaction. The proper approach, founded on *Allied Maples Group Ltd v. Simmons & Simmons* [1995] N.P.C. 83, [1995] 1 C.L.Y. 119, was for S to prove a real or substantial chance of sale had existed if the documents had arrived as requested, with loss being evaluated if the plaintiff succeeded. In assessing quantum, account needed to be taken of the fact that the deeds would not necessarily have arrived even if B had posted them on time. Additionally, even if they had arrived on time, the purchaser could still have decided to withdraw his offer. Accordingly, damages were reduced by 50 per cent.

STOVOLD v. BARLOWS [1996] 1 P.N.L.R. 91, Stuart-Smith, L.J., CA.

4506. Professional negligence–solicitors–property wrongly described in Land Register–solicitor failing to correct–subsequent freeholder refusing to cooperate in rectification–contributory liability of freeholder–measure of damages

[Civil Liability (Contribution) Act 1978.]

The plaintiffs purchased a maisonette which had formed part of refurbished premises and were advised in the purchase by the freeholder's former solicitor Mr Rose, D2. It emerged that the property was not as described in the Land Register and therefore did not correspond with what the plaintiffs thought they were buying. The discrepancy had been known to Mr Rose but he had forgotten about it. The freehold was then purchased by D1 without knowledge of the plaintiffs' overriding interest in rectification of the Land Register. D1 refused to cooperate in the rectification of the Land Register and therefore the plaintiffs suffered loss in losing potential purchasers of the property. The issue arose as to the quantum of the plaintiffs' claim with respect to the negligence of the solicitor.

Held, allowing the plaintiffs' claim in part, that in assessing the quantum of economic loss arising from professional negligence claims, the principle to be applied depended on all the circumstance, including the cause of the error and its import on the plaintiff. A choice can arise, in an action against a solicitor, between a value diminution due to the error, and the cost of putting it right. Difficulties can also arise where the loss is due to a title defect, as, although it may never be challenged, it can prevent any future sale. Any diminution in value test could also involve considerations of both speculative and unreal valuations. Quantum also depends on a distinction between a "no transaction" and a "successful transaction" approach. The measure of damage being to put the plaintiff in the same position as if the wrong had not been committed, but the issue arises whether the plaintiff would have refused to proceed with the transaction, or only gone ahead at a reduced price. On the facts, this was a no transaction case, as the plaintiffs would have withdrawn. Where it is reasonable not to sell, as here, additional costs incurred can be added to the extrication cost without any breach of a duty to mitigate. However, loss of profit on the sale could not be allowed, as this was a no transaction case where the purchase had been funded mainly by borrowed money, and the plaintiffs were not able to sell the property with a defective title in 1986. Damages were allowed to reflect the difference between acquisition and improvement costs and the assessed present day value of the property. Assessing D1's liability under the Civil Liability (Contribution) Act 1978, culpability as well as causation had to be considered. As the facts showed their intransigence and disregard for legal advice had created a long and expensive litigation, they were liable for 80 per cent of the total damages.

CONNOR & LABRUM v. REGOCZI-RITZMAN AND HM ROSE & CO; SUB NOM. CONNOR v. RITZMAN (1995) 70 P. & C.R. D41, Robert Walker, J., Ch D.

4507. Professional negligence–solicitors–valuation–third parties–valuer and solicitor equally liable for mortgagee's losses

B claimed damages in respect of negligent valuation and negligence on the part of C, the purchaser's solicitor. D, the purchaser, applied for a loan of £168,000 from B for the purchase of the leasehold of a flat. B engaged a valuer to value the flat and the money was advanced to D on the basis of their valuation of £198,000. The sale of the flat was intended to include the lease of car parking space and C accepted liability for failing to secure a charge over that land, thus reducing the resale value of the property and the value of B's security. None of the mortgage payments were met by D and the property was repossessed by B and sold for £62,500.

Held, giving judgment for B, that (1) the valuation was negligent. In assessing the value of a property a valuer had to use his own judgement supplemented by his knowledge and experience of current market conditions. Evidence derived from similar transactions formed only a part of this assessment and there was no evidence that market conditions were considered in making the valuations; (2) under the terms of an insurance policy B recovered the sum of £39,524 which was to be disregarded in the assessment of damages, *Banque Bruxelles Lambert SA v. Eagle Star Insurance Co Ltd* [1994] 2 E.G.L.R. 108, [1994] C.L.Y. 3379 applied; (3) as a matter of principle and justice it was wrong that the negligent valuers should be able to reduce the extent of their liability to B in respect of losses caused by their breach of duty; (4) the insurance monies paid to B could not be deducted from their loss and (5) C and the valuer were equally liable for B's loss in all the circumstances, although the solicitors had accepted sole responsibility for the diminution of value of the parking space on the resale of the flat.

BRISTOL & WEST BUILDING SOCIETY v. CHRISTIE [1996] E.G.C.S. 53, Judge Esyr Lewis Q.C., QBD (OR).

4508. Professional negligence–solicitors–wasted costs orders–partner's failure to instruct junior clerk correctly–inaccurate affidavit concerning legal aid grant

H, former solicitors for the plaintiffs P, submitted representations against a wasted costs order where re-trial of a county court action was ordered on appeal. Because of P's fault legal aid was not granted until the day before the hearing. The partner involved reviewed the case some days earlier, and instructed a junior litigation clerk to swear an affidavit to the effect that legal aid had not been granted, attend court on the hearing date and apply to have H removed from the record. However, he did not advise the clerk when legal aid was granted that she must first of all inform the court of the grant. The clerk failed to tell the court of the grant but proceeded on the basis of the affidavit, which was no longer accurate.

Held, allowing the appeal, that in view of the clerk's position and qualifications it was unreasonable and negligent to fail to instruct her exactly what to do in court. She could not be expected to know without being told, *Ridehalgh v. Horsefield* [1994] 3 W.L.R. 462, [1994] C.L.Y. 3623 considered.

SHAH (CHANDRAKANT KESHAVLAL) v. SINGH (GURDIP) [1996] 1 P.N.L.R. 83, Glidewell, L.J., QBD.

4509. Professional negligence–solicitors–witness statements–whether pre-trial advice on evidence covered by immunity

B was charged with conspiracy in 1986. In the preparation of his defence he consulted a firm of solicitors, O, who in turn instructed counsel, D. At a pre-trial hearing the judge made the usual order that the defence should notify the prosecution within 21 days of which witnesses they required to attend at trial. The defence gave notice that they required five witnesses to attend. A number of witnesses were abroad, but the defence did not require the attendance of any of these witnesses. At trial statements given by witnesses who were abroad were read out, without that procedure having been expressly consented to by the defence as required by court rules. B was convicted and sentenced to six years' imprisonment. In 1991 he successfully appealed against his conviction on the grounds that the statements from the overseas witnesses should not have been read out in the absence of agreement from O and D. He then commenced an action for negligence against O and D, alleging inter alia that they had been negligent in failing to advise him that the reading of the statements of the overseas witnesses could have been objected to by the rules. B's claim was struck out at first instance on the basis that the negligence alleged was covered by the immunity from suit that both solicitors and barristers enjoy as described in *Saif Ali v. Sidney Mitchell & Co* [1980] A.C. 198, [1978] C.L.Y. 2323. B sought leave to appeal.

Held, dismissing the application for leave to appeal, that the rule in English law protecting barristers and solicitors from actions for negligence in the conduct of a case at trial extends advice given on evidence prior to the trial, *Saif Ali v. Sidney Mitchell & Co* [1980] A.C. 198, [1978] C.L.Y. 2323 followed. In such a case the advice was so closely connected with the conduct of the case that it was covered by the immunity. The negligence alleged by B in the instant case fell clearly within the scope of that immunity.

BATEMAN v. OWEN WHITE [1996] 1 P.N.L.R. 1, Evans, L.J., CA.

4510. Professional negligence–surveyors–causation–overvaluation of land–common sense approach to whether negligence caused lenders' loss–"but for" test problematic

In 1989 B, a surveyor employed by J, provided a valuation of an office building to BBL, a bank, and E, an insurance company. B valued the building at £82 million and subsequently BBL advanced money to a company to buy the building. The company defaulted on the loan and BBL commenced proceedings against J in tort, claiming that B's valuation was negligent as a reasonably competent surveyor would have valued the building at no more than £63 million and that BBL had acted in reliance on B's valuation to their detriment. Prior to obtaining B's valuation BBL had received another valuation from a different firm of surveyors, which stated that the property was worth £83.5 million. BBL stated that they would not have provided the loan unless they were secured against loss in the amount of the advance, so the question of what part, if any, B's valuation had in E's decision to provide the cover became a crucial issue. At first instance the judge dismissed BBL's claim, holding that E did not rely substantially upon B's valuation, although at one passage the judge found that E would not have provided the cover had they not received B's valuation. BBL appealed, arguing that the judge erred by concentrating too heavily on the issue of reliance rather than applying the "but for" test of causation.

Held, dismissing the appeal, that the "but for" test did not provide much assistance in determining whether the necessary causal link between the negligent act and the action which resulted in the loss had been established. The correct approach was to apply a common sense notion of causation, as stated in *Alexander v. Cambridge Credit Corp Ltd* (1987) 9 N.S.W.L.R. 310, and determine what was the effective cause of the loss. In the instant case there were sufficient findings of fact to support the judge's finding that B's valuation was not the effective cause of E's decision to provide the insurance cover.

BANQUE BRUXELLES LAMBERT SA v. EAGLE STAR INSURANCE CO LTD (1996) [1996] P.N.L.R. 380, Saville, L.J., CA.

4511. Professional negligence–surveyors–mortgage valuation survey–failure to detect inadequately supported chimney

G were instructed to carry out a mortgage valuation survey for a fee of £30 which S subsequently relied upon in buying the house surveyed. The house had recently been refurbished before the surveyor's inspection. In the course of the refurbishment the chimney breast in the kitchen had been removed and the chimney above supported on two pieces of angle iron and an old door which was subsequently plastered over. Had the surveyor looked in the kitchen cupboard he would have noticed the angle iron. Instead he looked at the chimney breast in the room above. He did not see any signs of distress and therefore concluded that the chimney breast was properly supported and reported that the structure and condition of the house was satisfactory. At first instance the Official Referee found that G had been negligent because the surveyor failed to look further and discover that the chimney was inadequately supported. G appealed contending that the Official Referee had placed too high a duty upon them.

Held, dismissing the appeal, that on the facts of the case G had been negligent. Having recognised the need to ascertain whether the chimney was properly supported it was not sufficient for the surveyor to only look for signs of distress in the room above the kitchen. The absence of signs of distress was not necessarily a safe guide where the refurbishment works were recent. G was not justified in assuming, from the fact that the works had been carried out with the benefit of a local authority improvement grant, that the works had been carried out properly. A negligence finding did not mean that the surveyor was incompetent. Perfectly competent surveyors still took risks, but if a surveyor took a risk which a reasonable surveyor would not have taken the firm or its insurers should be liable for compensation.

SNEESBY v. GOLDINGS 45 Con. L.R. 11, Sir Thomas Bingham, M.R., CA.

4512. Professional negligence–surveyors–mortgage valuation survey–whether negligent–quantum–inconvenience and distress

E paid for a mortgage valuation report undertaken by M upon which he relied in purchasing a house. The surveyor carried out a "head and shoulders" inspection of the roof space but failed to notice a gap of 40mm at the end of one of the two purlins forming an integral part of the roof structure. M reported that there was no evidence of any serious defect in the examined areas. The defect came to light five years later when a sale of the property fell through on account of the presence of the defect. Thereafter, the property was repossessed by the building society and sold at auction. E sued M for negligence. The trial judge, after carrying out his own "head and shoulders" inspection, decided that M should have noticed the gap and reported its existence. In consequence, he found M to have been negligent and awarded E damages including, inter alia, £6,000 for inconvenience and distress.

Held, dismissing the appeal on liability but reducing the damages awarded, that (1) the Court of Appeal could not interfere with the judge's finding of fact that M should have noticed the gap. Although he did not expressly find that the defect was serious the judge was entitled to conclude that E would not have bought the property if it had been drawn to his attention and (2) the damages awarded for inconvenience and distress were excessive and would be reduced to £4,000.

EZEKIEL v. McDADE [1995] 47 E.G. 150, Nourse, L.J., CA.

4513. Professional negligence–surveyors–negligent survey–whether claim statute barred

[Limitation Act 1980 s.2, s.14.]

M appealed against a decision that they had provided a negligent survey. C wished to buy their neighbour's house and instructed M to survey it. M's report revealed no problems and C purchased the house in 1985. C subsequently discovered subsidence damage and sued M for negligence. M submitted that the action was statute barred under the Limitation Act 1980 s.2. C relied on s.14A of the Act to argue that the limitation period ran from May 17, 1991 being the date that C discovered the subsidence damage. M claimed that the limitation period ran from August 1986, on the ground that it was the point when C was informed that a neighbouring house required underpinning to cure subsidence. The loss adjusters in those circumstances had understood that the previous owners of C's house had been aware of the possible underpinning and subsidence.

Held, dismissing the appeal, that C's claim was in time as the limitation period ran from May 17, 1991. The issue of what was reasonable for C to do was a question of fact and when C was contacted in 1986, they could not reasonably be expected to pay for another survey as they were in possession of one which was only 20 months old and which they should have been able to rely on.

CAMPBELL v. MEACOCKS [1995] N.P.C. 141, Nourse, L.J., CA.

4514. Professional negligence–surveyors–residential property–measure of damages–values inflated between dates of report and sale

In 1988, relying on a valuation report by H, S bought a residential property. H were negligent in failing to identify and report on defects such that the property was actually worth £5,000 less than H's valuation. As a result of a property boom, the market value rose by £5,000 by the date of the sale and H claimed there was no loss. In determining a preliminary issue, the Official Referee decided that S had suffered a £5,000 loss. H appealed.

Held, dismissing the appeal, that the measure of damage was the difference between the reported and true market values of the property, *Phillips v. Ward* [1956] 1 W.L.R. 471, *Watts v. Morrow* [1991] 1 W.L.R. 1421, [1992] C.L.Y. 1548 and *Dodd Properties (Kent) Ltd v. Canterbury City Council* [1982] 1 W.L.R. 1297 followed. Increases in market value between the date of the report and the completion of the sale did not affect this principle.

Observed, that the difficulties which had arisen in the instant case flowed from treating as a preliminary issue what would have been better dealt with at the substantive hearing.

SHAW v. HALIFAX (SOUTH WEST) LTD (T/A HARTNELL TAYLOR COOK RESIDENTIAL) [1996] P.N.L.R. 451, Pill, L.J., CA.

4515. Professional negligence–surveyors–residual valuation–failure to inspect site or do proper research–reliance on property market prediction

N lent £3.5 million to L to purchase land on the basis of a valuation from E. L defaulted and the land was sold for £345,000. N successfully sued E for negligence and breach of contract. E appealed with regard to liability.

Held, dismissing the appeal, that E had been negligent in compiling a residual valuation. E's surveyors were in breach of contract as they had failed to inspect the site, failed to research the site history or demand for office accommodation in the area and had relied on a prediction as to the future of the property market.

NYKREDIT MORTGAGE BANK PLC v. EDWARD ERDMAN GROUP LTD [1996] 1 E.G. 119, Staughton, L.J., CA.

4516. Professional negligence–surveyors–valuation–buoyant market–sale following possession during recession–expert evidence showed complied with RICS guidelines–figure within acceptable margin

C valued a flat for M in 1987 for £269,000 in reliance upon which M agreed to loan the mortgagor £202,500. On default, M gained possession and the property was sold, following refurbishment, for £167,000 in 1991. A valuation undertaken for M stated that C's figure was an overvaluation and that the property concerned was not a sound investment. C contended that the valuation provided fell within an acceptable margin, with expert evidence showing C to have acted in accordance with RICS guidelines, and giving another valuation of £250,000, established by reference to similar properties valued in 1987.

Held, giving judgment for C, that whereas the sale had taken place at the depth of the recession, C's valuation occurred during a time of market buoyancy. Expert evidence showed that the figure fell within an acceptable margin and there was no negligence on the part of C.

MORTGAGE FUNDING CORP PLC v. CONWAY [1995] E.G.C.S. 47, Judge Crawford, QBD.

4517. Professional negligence–surveyors–valuation–contributory negligence–failure to exercise reasonable care and skill in valuation of property

[Law Reform (Contributory Negligence) Act 1945 s.1.]

C claimed damages from H in respect of their negligent valuation of property which formed the security for a loan. C was a bank specialising in short-term high risk finance at a high rate of interest. On the basis of H's report C loaned £750,000. H's report valued the property at £1,525000 with a forced sale value of £1,342000, but the property was now valued at only £87,500. H admitted that the valuation failed to meet the criteria of reasonable skill and care and the court were restricted to causation, contributory negligence and assessment of damages.

Held, giving judgment for C, that (1) C's reliance on H's valuation had "a real and substantial part in inducing" C to make the loan, *JEB Fasteners Ltd v. Marks Bloom & Co* [1983] 1 All E.R. 589, [1983] C.L.Y. 2534 considered; (2) on the balance of probabilities, C would not have advanced money to M had they been in possession of a competent valuation, having regard to C's operating conditions on the value to loan ratios for securities; (3) the case was subject to the Law Reform (Contributory Negligence) Act 1945, *Banque Bruxelles Lambert SA v. Eagle Star Insurance Co Ltd* [1994] 2 E.G.L.R. 108, [1995] 1 C.L.Y. 1834 and *United Bank of Kuwait v. Prudential Property Services Ltd* [1995] 2 E.G.L.R. 100, [1995] 2 C.L.Y. 3708 considered; (4) C was entitled to advice from an expert valuer exercising proper care and skill even where the loan took place at the high risk end of the property market, *HIT Finance Ltd v. Lewis and Tucker Ltd* [1993] E.G.L.R. 231, [1994] C.L.Y. 3378 and *Britannic Securities & Investments Ltd v. Hirani Watson* [1995] E.G.C.S. 46, [1996] C.L.Y. 4527 considered; (5) H must have known that speed was of the essence in the transaction; if the valuation had been substantially correct C would have had a generous margin of protection for the loan; (6) H had not made out a case for C's damages to be reduced on contributory negligence grounds, *HIT Finance Ltd v. Lewis and Tucker Ltd* [1993] 2 E.G.L.R. 231, [1994] C.L.Y. 3378 considered and (7) C was entitled to recover the value of the loan, less the current value of the property, thereby placing C in the position in which they would have been prior to H's breach of contract.

CAVENDISH FUNDING LTD v. HENRY SPENCER & SONS LTD [1996] P.N.L.R. 554, Evans-Lombe, J., Ch D.

4518. Professional negligence–surveyors–valuation–death-watch beetle–failure to mention infestation–measure of damages

O engaged C to carry out a survey and valuation of a house which they proposed to buy. The report failed to mention that the house was infested with death-watch beetle and in consequence extensive and immediate remedial works were required to all the oak timbers in the house. The house was valued in the report at £215,000. O paid a purchase price of £225,000.

Held, giving judgment for O, that (1) C had been negligent in failing to specify in its report the infestation by death-watch beetle that the surveyor had noticed and which he ought to have appreciated and stated might have been active and (2) the negligence caused O to purchase the house at a price of £225,000 when its true worth was no more than £165,000. O were entitled to the difference of £60,000. Betterment should be deducted for the cost of remedial work where that was the starting point of the calculations, *Watts v. Morrow* [1991] 1 W.L.R. 1421, [1992] C.L.Y. 1548 applied.

OSWALD v. COUNTRYWIDE SURVEYORS LTD 47 Con. L.R. 50, Judge Havery Q.C., QBD.

4519. Professional negligence–surveyors–valuation–information given on which lender based loan–whether loss from market fall recoverable as well as loss from negligent information

In three joined appeals three valuers were required by three lenders to provide open market valuations of properties on which the lenders were considering advancing money on mortgage. In each case the borrowers defaulted, the property was negligently over valued and the market price fell. In the first case, A advanced £11 million on a property valued at £15 million. The true value at the time of the valuation was found to be £5 million. The property was eventually sold for £2,500,000; A was awarded £10 million less 25 per cent for contributory negligence. In the second case B advanced £1,750,000 on a property valued at £2,500,000. The true value at the time of valuation was found to be £1,800,000 and the property was sold for £950,000. B was awarded £1,300,000 including interest. In the third case C advanced £2,450,000 on a property valued at £3,500,000. The correct value was £2 million and the property sold for £345,000. C was awarded £3,000,050 including unpaid interest. The Court of Appeal decided that in a case in which the lender would not, but for the negligent valuation, have lent, he is entitled to recover the difference between the sum which he lent, together with a reasonable rate of interest, and the net sum which he actually recovered, including loss attributable to a fall in the market. Such "no-transaction" cases were to be distinguished from "successful transaction" cases, where the lender, if provided with the correct valuation, would still have lent a lesser sum on the same security. In those cases the lender can only recover the difference between what he actually lost and what he would have lost had he lent a lesser amount; any fall in the market is to be ignored. The valuers appealed.

Held, dismissing the appeal in the first case and allowing the appeals in the second and third cases, that the nature of a valuer's duty of care to a lender, which is the same in tort as in contract, is to provide an estimate of the price which the property might reasonably be expected to fetch if sold on the open market at the date of the valuation. The extent of a valuer's liability if negligent in the provision of the information is for all the foreseeable consequences of the information being wrong. In this sense it was important to appreciate the distinction between the scope of a duty to provide information and the scope of a duty to advise, *Banque Keyser Ullmann SA v. Skandia (UK) Insurance Co Ltd* [1991] 2 A.C. 249, [1990] C.L.Y. 2696 applied. It was also necessary to distinguish a duty to provide accurate information from a warranty that the information is accurate, *Swingcastle Ltd v. Alastair Gibson* [1991] 2 A.C. 223, [1991] C.L.Y. 1322 considered. The distinction between the "no-transaction" and "successful transaction" cases in this context was unhelpful, not based on any principle and should be abandoned. The valuer was not liable for any loss suffered by the lender as a result of a fall in the market, since such a loss was not a foreseeable consequence of the valuer's negligence in providing inaccurate information. Accordingly, the consequence of the negligent valuation in the first case was that A had £10 million less security than it thought and the whole loss was within the scope of the valuer's duty. In the second and third cases the valuers were only liable for the consequences of the valuation being wrong, namely the difference in the amount of security that B and C thought they had and the security they actually had. The correct figures were £700,000 and £1,500,000 respectively.

SOUTH AUSTRALIA ASSET MANAGEMENT CORP v. YORK MONTAGUE LTD; UNITED BANK OF KUWAIT PLC v. PRUDENTIAL PROPERTY SERVICES LTD; NYKREDIT MORTGAGE BANK LTD v. EDWARD ERDMAN GROUP LTD; BANQUE BRUXELLES LAMBERT SA v. EAGLE STAR INSURANCE CO LTD [1996] 3 W.L.R. 87, Lord Hoffmann, HL.

4520. Professional negligence–surveyors–valuation–loan made on strength of valuation–"no transaction" case–whether damages representing fall in value recoverable

B instructed W to value a residential property in connection with a prospective loan to be secured by a mortgage on the property. The loan was made but the mortgagor defaulted. It was common ground at trial that the case was a "no transaction" case, ie. on a proper valuation there would have been no loan transaction. B alleged that the valuation was negligent and claimed damages. Part of the loss represented the fall in the value of the house reflecting a fall in the property market.

Held, allowing the claim, that (1) W had been negligent; (2) B had acted prudently and reasonably and therefore were not contributory negligent and (3) a loss reflecting the fall in the market was recoverable as damages, *Banque Bruxelles Lambert SA v. Eagle Star Insurance Co Ltd* [1995] 2 W.L.R. 607, [1994] C.L.Y. 3379 followed.

GOVERNOR AND COMPANY OF THE BANK OF SCOTLAND v. W G EDWARDS (A FIRM) 44 Con. L.R. 77, Richard Havery Q.C., QBD (OR).

4521. Professional negligence–surveyors–valuation–mortgage lender–13 per cent within acceptable range of valuation

The BC was a firm of valuers and BNP was a mortgage lender. In 1990, a partner in BC provided BNP with a report and valuation on a property. In consequence of the report, BNP lent a sum of money to the purchasers of the property secured by a first charge over that property. The mortgagors defaulted on their repayments under the mortgage. BNP sold the property for considerably less than BC's valuation. BNP sued BC for negligent valuation.

Held, dismissing the claim, that having regard to the type of property, an acceptable range within which a competent valuer should approach the true value of the property is 15 per cent on either side. On the basis of the evidence, the true value of the property was £155,000. As BC's valuation was just under 13 per cent in excess of the true value, it was within the range of valuations which a reasonably competent surveyor could have arrived at with reasonable skill and care.

BNP MORTGAGES LTD v. BARTON COOK & SAMS [1996] 1 E.G.L.R. 239, Judge Hicks Q.C., QBD (OR).

4522. Professional negligence–surveyors–valuation–mortgagee alleging negligence by valuer–failure to mitigate loss–reliance on guarantor–contributory negligence by mortgagee

[Law Reform (Contributory Negligence) Act 1945.]

In mid 1988, introducing brokers applied to F on behalf of H for a loan to finance a proposed redevelopment of office and retail property which H owned in London. F instructed A to value the property. In its valuation report of August 1988, A valued the property at £410,000. In January 1989, in reliance on that valuation, F advanced £340,000 to H. The loan was secured by a charge over the property, and guaranteed by H's prime mover and by its company secretary. Although H fell into substantial arrears almost immediately, F did not increase its interest rate until October 1989, and did not issue a formal demand on H and on the guarantors until December 1989. The property was eventually sold in February 1991 by private sale for £210,000, although it was resold for £280,000 and again for £315,000 on the same day. F accepted £15,000 in full and final settlement under the guarantees, and issued proceedings against A to recover its shortfall. F claimed that it had made the advance in reliance on A's negligently high valuation, that if the valuation had been carried out carefully it would have refused the loan, and that, accordingly, it was entitled to recover the whole shortfall. A denied negligence, and in the alternative alleged that the bank was contributorily negligence and had failed to mitigate its loss.

Held, giving judgment for A, that all the sale and valuation evidence, both before and after, supported A's valuation and they were not negligent in making it. There was no reason in principle why the provisions of the Law Reform (Contributory Negligence) Act 1945 should not apply to a lender who fails to investigate the borrower or take proper care to protect the loan. In any lending transaction the primary concern of the lender must be with the borrower, the security is of secondary importance and guarantors come third. F bank had blithely ignored all the warning signals it had received and had taken no steps to obtain the information which its own guidelines suggested it ought to receive. If A's valuation had been negligent, a reduction of 75 per cent would have been made for contributory negligence. F was very largely the author of its own misfortune. F had failed to mitigate its loss, in respect of which failure a reduction of £75,000 would have been made, comprising £10,000 for failing to sell the property earlier, £40,000 for selling the property at least £40,000 below its market value, £25,000 for not instituting bankruptcy proceedings against the guarantors instead of accepting only £15,000 in full and final settlement under the guarantee, *Kendall Wilson Securities v. Barraclough* [1986] 1 N.Z.L.R. 576 approved.

FIRST NATIONAL COMMERCIAL BANK v. ANDREW S TAYLOR (COMMERCIAL) LTD, December 1, 1995, Anthony Thompson Q.C., QBD. [*Ex rel.* Bruce Gardiner, Barrister].

4523. Professional negligence–surveyors–valuation–open market value–exercise of care and skill of a reasonably competent surveyor and valuer–margin of error

R, a surveyor and valuer, valued a three bedroomed maisonette for mortgage purposes on B's instructions. R did not usually value properties in the locality and obtained comparables from four local agents. He valued the property at £205,000. B alleged that R was negligent and that a reasonably competent valuer would have valued the property at £140,000 and would not have valued the property greater than £155,000 or lower than £130,000.

Held, giving judgment for B, that (1) without detailed knowledge of the area, R should have been aware of the need to inform himself of any cause of variation in values between adjacent areas. One or more of the principal agents in the area should have been approached. R failed to do either and thus failed to give himself the opportunity to assess whether the information he had received was reliable; (2) the value of the property at the date of valuation was assessed at £165,000. A comparable property did not have to be identical, it had to have a number of similar characteristics to make the information relevant to the valuation and (3) considering the property's characteristics, there could be a margin of error of 11 per cent. This meant that the highest non-negligent valuation of the property was £183,150.

BIRMINGHAM MIDSHIRES BUILDING SOCIETY v. RICHARD PAMPLIN & CO [1996] E.G.C.S. 3, Newman, J., QBD.

4524. Professional negligence–surveyors–valuation–open market value–valuation based on comparable asking prices and local knowledge

M contended that S had acted negligently in carrying out a mortgage valuation for them. S stated that the property provided reasonable security, giving an open market value of £75,000 in 1990, in reliance upon which M granted a mortgage of £48,750. On default, M gained possession and the property was sold for £35,500 in 1993.

Held, giving judgment for S, that in preparing the valuation figure, S had taken account of the property itself, as well as its surrounding location and in coming to the final figure S had also consulted a local estate agent about comparative asking prices in the area. The valuation process admitted a degree of leeway and S had taken account of variables in the particular area concerned.

On the facts, S showed that he knew his business and had made use of local knowledge. He had acted reasonably in determining the valuation figure and on balance his evidence was preferred.

MAES ECP NO.1 PLC v. STIMSON [1995] E.G.C.S. 90, Paynter Reece, J., QBD.

4525. Professional negligence–surveyors–valuation–standard of care–whether negligent in discharging duty to lender where subsequent sale realised less than valuation figure

UCB contended that the valuation figure given by RN, on the purchase of the property in 1989 was not a true reflection of its value at that time, claiming RN were in breach of a duty of care owed to UCB as a result.

Held, giving judgment for RN, that the duty of a valuer was to give an informed open market valuation at the date of valuation, to a professional standard, which allowed a lender to decide if the property provided sufficient security for the loan. Negligence could not be shown merely by the existence of a contrary opinion and the valuation process did not call for a consensus of expert opinion as a margin of difference was acceptable between equally competent valuers. On the basis of the evidence given, the valuation was such as to fall within a 12 to 15 percent approximate figure, and as such did not lie beyond the band of reasonable figures achievable by a competent valuation at the time it was made.

UCB HOME LOANS CORPORATION LTD v. ROGER NORTH & ASSOCIATES [1995] E.G.C.S. 149, Orde, J., QBD.

4526. Professional negligence–surveyors–valuation requested by broker–whether duty owed to lender–whether negligent valuation

A&Co provided a mortgage valuation at the request of a mortgage broker for a fee of £50 in 1989. At the height of the property market, A&Co valued the property at £215,000. In reliance of the valuation AAL, a licensed moneylender, advanced £37,000 secured on the property. The property was subsequently sold for £110,000. AAL sued A&Co for negligence alleging that if the property had been properly valued it would have lent less, or nothing at all.

Held, dismissing AAL's claim, that (1) the valuation was commissioned by the broker. A&Co knew it was for the purposes of obtaining a loan secured against the property and therefore, there was sufficient proximity of relationship to found a duty of care owed to the lender who might actually advance moneys on the strength of it and (2) A&Co was under a duty to use such care and skill as was reasonable in the circumstances taking into account that the valuer had been asked to do a quick valuation for a modest fee. To challenge a valuer's professional skill and judgment was a serious matter and more evidence would be required. The figure of £215,000 might raise eyebrows a little, but in the absence of any evidence as to the value which should, in the exercise of reasonable care and skill, have been placed on the property, it was impossible to conclude that A&Co had been negligent.

ASSURED ADVANCES LTD v. ASHBEE & CO [1994] E.G.C.S. 169, Gareth Edwards Q.C., QBD.

4527. Professional negligence–surveyors–valuer grossly overvaluing land–breach of standard required–second loan–sale by first mortgagee took priority–damages allowed for total sum advanced plus lost interest

B sought damages from H, contending they acted negligently in making a gross overvaluation of land offered to B as loan security. On default by the borrower, the first mortgagee took priority and B lost £520,000.

Held, giving judgment for B, that H admitted an overvaluation of between £600,000 to £700,000, in breach of their duty to give a reliable and informed opinion as to the open market value, *Banque Bruxelles Lambert SA v. Eagle Star Insurance Co Ltd* [1995] 12 E.G. 144, [1994] C.L.Y. 3379 applied. On the facts, careful and competent valuer would have given a figure no higher than

£250,000 for the land. Therefore B were entitled to damages equal to the total sum advanced with interest, less any instalments received from the borrower. Although the loan took place at the riskier end of the loan market, B were still entitled to a valuation using the exercise of skill and care of competent valuers, *HIT Finance Ltd v. Lewis & Tucker Ltd* [1993] 2 E.G.L.R. 231, [1994] C.L.Y. 3378 considered, and BS's failure to inquire into the borrower's ability to repay did not allow HW a defence of contributory negligence, *United Bank of Kuwait v. Prudential Property Services Ltd* [1994] 2 E.G.L.R. 100, [1995] 1 C.L.Y. 284 followed.

BRITANNIC SECURITIES & INVESTMENTS LTD v. HIRANI WATSON [1995] E.G.C.S. 46, Evans-Lombe, J., Ch D.

4528. Professional negligence–surveyors–whether valuer admitting breach of duty could rely on plaintiff's contributory negligence–no breach of plaintiff bank's internal guidelines–imputed nature of bank's knowledge insufficient

BFG retained B&M to supply a valuation for a 7.6 acre site, for which BFG had been asked to supply a loan facility. The loan allowed the discharge of an earlier loan and the purchase of the land, with a view to its resale for a hotel development. B&M's report stated that, as a reasonably high chance existed that the necessary permission would be granted on appeal, the value was between £450,000 and £500,000. BFG subsequently found the value to be no more than £15,000, with an eventual sale price of only £6,000. B&M admitted negligence but contended contributory negligence on BFG's part. B&M argued that the loan had breached internal bank guidelines and therefore BFG had acted on its own assessment and not the valuation supplied. B&M also argued that BFG should have imputed knowledge of the use the borrower intended to make of the money advanced.

Held, giving judgement for BFG, that the valuation was contained in a letter giving the value of the land for agricultural use, the value with the prospect of permission and the value if permission was granted. However, although B&M put the prospect of such permission as reasonably high, in reality there was only a remote chance of it being granted. On the facts, reliance on the valuation was reasonable. The terms of the loan had not breached BFG's guidelines, as such rules were to be interpreted in a flexible manner, and the sums involved were small compared with the funds available. Contributory negligence could not be based on imputed knowledge, *Banque Bruxelles Lambert SA v. Eagle Star Insurance Co Ltd* [1994] 2 E.G.L.R. 198, [1994] C.L.Y. 3379 followed.

BFG BANK AG v. BROWN & MUMFORD LTD [1995] E.G.C.S. 21, Judge John Baker, QBD.

4529. Professional negligence–valuation–mortgage indemnity guarantee policy–whether damages could be reduced

[Rules of the Supreme Court Ord.18 r.19.]

EM applied, under the Rules of the Supreme Court Ord.18 r.19(1)(a), to strike out part of HEA's amended defence in an action brought in respect of the negligent valuation of a property which provided security for a loan advanced by EM. The relevant part of the defence was that in which HEA sought credit, in the assessment of damages if judgment went against them, for any sums received by EM under a mortgage indemnity guarantee policy taken out before the money was advanced.

Held, allowing the application, that although *Cleaver v. Parry* [1970] A.C. 1 stated that it was neither just nor reasonable that moneys paid under a contract of insurance should benefit a tortfeasor, it was necessary to look at the nature of the contract itself. The policy proceeds could be said to result as much from HEA's breach as EM's prudent decision to effect the cover. However, it was not the consequences of the breach that mattered, but whether the insurer or guarantor qualified for subrogation against the negligent valuer. Having the nature of a guarantee, as the policy had not been effected for HEA's benefit, the valuer should not receive a benefit from it.

EUROPE MORTGAGE CO v. HALIFAX ESTATE AGENCIES [1996] E.G.C.S. 84, May, J., QBD.

4530. Professional negligence–valuation–valuation confirmed by defendants–whether innocent misrepresentation negligent–determination of true value on relevant date–damages allowed where valuation relied on

Four plaintiff banks financed the purchase of a building valued at £24 million by JDW. The value was endorsed by S and JM, one of its directors in January 1989 and the banks claimed to have relied on this advice in deciding to lend the money. The banks alleged that the property was only worth £18.8 million, a value which eventually dropped to £10 million. They claimed that the valuation was negligent and sued JDW, S and JM.

Held, allowing the case, that this was a negligent valuation. S owed a duty to take reasonable care in advising the banks that they could rely on JDW's valuation of £24 million. JM's endorsement was an innocent misrepresentation which was materially misleading. Whether the advice was negligent depended on the true value at the relevant date, which was £18.8 million. Consequently, his advice was negligent. In respect of damages, each bank could recover substantial damages, subject to contributory negligence, as they had relied on the report endorsing JDW's valuation and it had played a real and substantial part in their decision to participate. Further devaluation was dependent on a new valuation which did not involve S.

CHARTERHOUSE BANK LTD v. ROSE [1995] N.P.C. 108, Rimer, J., Ch D.

4531. Professional negligence–whether duty in tort could be wider than contractual duty

DGC, the second defendant in an action for professional negligence, appealed against a finding that they were liable in negligence to H in relation to the purchase of a property in addition to being liable in respect of H's claim for breach of contractual duty. DGC argued that where a contract between the parties existed, all duties and responsibilities in both contract and tort were limited by either express or implied terms in the contract.

Held, allowing the appeal that, there was no reason why a duty of care in tort could not be imposed by the general law which was wider in scope than the duty which arose from the contractual relationship, which was limited by the factual basis of the contract. Provided that the required assumption of responsibility and concomitant reliance were shown, a duty of care in tort was established. However, on the present facts such a duty was not made out as H had not acted to his detriment on advice given, *Hedley Byrne & Co Ltd v. Heller & Partners Ltd* [1964] A.C. 465, [1963] C.L.Y. 2416 considered.

HOLT v. PAYNE SKILLINGTON [1996] P.N.L.R. 179, Hirst, L.J., CA.

4532. Psychiatric injuries–duty of care–witness to Piper Alpha disaster not within category of rescuer–no duty owed in absence of reasonable fear

[Offshore Installations (Operational Safety, Health and Welfare) Regulations 1976; Mineral Workings (Offshore Installations) Act 1971.]

H alleged that he had suffered psychiatric harm as a result of E's negligence as owners and operators of the Piper Alpha oil rig. He had been a painter on board a ship from which he witnessed the Piper Alpha oil rig disaster. The alleged harm was post traumatic stress syndrome. The issue arose whether E owed H a duty of care.

Held, dismissing the action, that H was never nearer than 100 metres to the Piper Alpha and therefore there was no reasonable fear on his part. H did not come within the category of a rescuer and was not a person to whom a common law duty of care was owed. Nor was there an absolute duty owed to the plaintiff under Offshore Installations (Operational Safety, Health and Welfare)

Regulations 1976 made pursuant to the Mineral Workings (Offshore Installations) Act 1971.

HEGARTY v. EE CALEDONIA LTD [1996] 1 Lloyd's Rep. 413, Popplewell, J., QBD.

4533. Psychiatric injuries–police officers–disasters–Chief Constable had duty of care to avoid causing–proximity

Five police officers appealed against the dismissal of their claims for damages for psychiatric injury following their involvement in the Hillsborough football ground disaster. The officers claimed that there had been a breach of the duty of care owed to them by the Chief Constable to avoid exposing them to unnecessary risk of physical or psychiatric injury either in their capacity as officers acting under his direction or as rescuers. The Chief Constable admitted negligence in respect of the actions that had caused the disaster but argued that no duty of care existed towards the plaintiffs.

Held, allowing four of the appeals and dismissing one, that (1) people could be affected by negligence, even if they had not suffered its physical consequences and this particularly applied to rescuers as members of a special category. It was a question of fact, taking into account all the circumstances, whether a person was a rescuer; (2) the liability of an employer for negligently causing psychiatric injury to an employee through fear for his safety or through witnessing injuries caused to another was no different from the employer's liability for causing him physical injuries; (3) the standard of care and degree of proximity required depended on the type of job and the amount of resilience the employee might be expected to show; (4) people who witnessed an incident but were not rescuers or employees owed a duty of care by the tortfeasor had to meet more stringent tests in order to qualify for damages and (5) a duty of care was owed to four of the officers either as employees or rescuers, taking into account their roles after the disaster, but not to the fifth officer as her participation was not sufficiently proximate.

FROST v. CHIEF CONSTABLE OF SOUTH YORKSHIRE; DUNCAN v. BRITISH COAL CORP [1997] 1 All E.R. 540, Rose, L.J., CA.

4534. Sports–rugby–player injured when scrummage collapsed during match–referee owed a duty of care to prevent such an incident

S, who was injured during a colts rugby match when the scrummage collapsed, claimed damages from W, a player of the opposing team, and from N, who was refereeing the match.

Held, that W was not liable to S but, on the specific facts of the case and considering the modified laws of rugby for colts games and the customs of the 1991/1992 rugby season, the referee owed a duty of care to players to make sure that scrummages did not collapse. The imposition of such a duty was reasonable given the known high risk of neck and spinal injury from such incidents. The judgment had no effect on colts matches played by different rules nor on international or senior rugby.

SMOLDON v. WHITWORTH, *The Times*, April 23, 1996, Curtis, J., QBD.

4535. Subcontractors–liability–cracks in foundations–contractors not liable for damage to building–skill and judgment not expected in the selection of materials

F appealed against an official referee's decision in a damages claim against F for damage to a building said to arise from the breach of an implied warranty as to the fitness and merchantable quality of the materials used in the foundation construction. The building had been constructed over the top of a number of cellars and after completion cracks appeared in the ground floor slab as a result of the unsuitable nature of the fill used around the foundations. At trial the issue was whether the type of fill material used was dependent on the skill and discretion of F.

Held, allowing the appeals, that (1) where a person contracted to do work and supply material they gave an implied warranty that that material was fit for the purpose for which it was used, unless such warranty was excluded by the circumstance of the contract, *GH Myers & Co v. Brent Cross Service Co* [1934] 1 K.B. 46 considered; (2) where efficient operation of a building depended upon a designer, the designer had an obligation to ensure the suitability of components used in it. That liability could in turn be passed on to a specialist on whom the designer relied for the supply of those materials; (3) there were specifications as to the type of hardcore material made by R's architect and engineer which contained the grading and sulphate content of fill material and any freedom of choice regarding material selection was present only where the architect felt no further specification was necessary; (4) the architect was right to regard himself as more expert than the contractors who did not have any special material selection experience and (5) the contractors were obliged to provide the hardcore as specified. The fill provided was within R's specification and was of merchantable quality. Contract terms showed that R comprehensively specified their hardcore requirements and were therefore not relying on the contractors' skill or judgement.

ROTHERHAM MBC v. FRANK HASLAM MILAN & CO LTD 78 B.L.R. 1, Leggatt, L.J., CA.

4536. Articles

A lost chance recovered *(Charles Foster)*: S.J. 1996, 140(21), 534-535. (Consequences of CA decision on whether damages were recoverable in tort for loss of chance).

A second chance *(Margaret Noble)*: N.L.J. 1996, 146(6733), 310-311. (Assessment of damages for negligence for plaintiff's loss of chance).

A single standard of care *(Lauren Sutherland)*: Reparation 1995, 6, 11-12. (Whether length of doctor's experience is relevant to standard of care in medical negligence cases).

Acts of omission in medical professional negligence *(Margaret Hemsworth)*: S.J. 1996, 140(34), 870-872. (Significance of case for assessment of plaintiff's having acquired constructive knowledge under s.14 of 1980 Act and need to take speedy medical advice where patient has undergone "unsuccessful" medical treatment).

All quiet on the legal front: E.G. 1996, 9601, 88-89. (Property and valuation rulings in 1995 including measure of damages, duty of care and variation of leases).

Are solicitors liable for damages resulting from a fall in the market? *(David Halpern* and *Teresa Rosen Peacocke)*: P.N. 1996, 12(3), 77-79. (Implications of decision on liability for negligent overvaluation of property securing loan for solicitors who cause loss to lender through negligence).

Asbestos: recent case law: H. & S.M. 1996, 19(11), IF i-ii. (Liability of employers and manufacturers for activities involving exposure to asbestos and prosecutions for breach of regulations relating to use of asbestos).

Careful handling of asbestos evidence *(Rachel Pairman)*: Legal Times 1996, 32, 8, 14. (Investigations undertaken by solicitors to assemble evidence of historic asbestos pollution and state of company's knowledge).

Case study: never go on holiday... professional negligence: Litigator 1996, Jul, 190-204. (Case study of mortgage fraud involving negligence of solicitor with legal analysis from lender's, solicitor's and estate agent's positions).

Deeds of variation and duties of care *(Philip Laidlow)*: C.T.P. 1996, 15(7), 82-84. (Developing duty of care for solicitors to advise beneficiaries of relevant tax planning opportunities for post death variations and liability limitations for solicitors acting as executors or when advising lay personal representatives).

Fire case opens door to massive liabilities *(Edward Dimbylow)*: L.G.C. 1996, Apr (4), 5. (Liability of fire services for negligence following two High Court decisions where deficient fire fighting methods held to be negligent).

Lessons for professional advisers after Binder Hamlyn *(Mark R. Chapman)*: Litigator 1996, May, 175-176. (Implications of decision that auditors of target company owed duty of care to bidders when making statements as to accuracy of accounts).
Liability for overvaluation *(David Halpern* and *Teresa Rosen Peacocke)*: N.L.J. 1996, 146(6755), 1157-1159. (Whether damages recoverable for negligent overvaluation of property could include amount for loss owing to fall in property market and extent to which HL decision affects solicitors).
Liability of professional advisers: Caparo and beyond *(David Kershaw)*: P.L.C. 1996, 7(3), 42-43. (Principles of liability for negligent misstatement and type of circumstances in which duty of care has been found to exist with particular reference to auditors).
Medical malpractice in England and Wales–a postcard from the edge *(Michael A. Jones)*: E.J.H.L. 1996, 3(2), 109-126. (Risk management practices in NHS trusts to obviate claims for medical negligence and their associated costs).
Medical notes *(David Grundy)*: P.I. 1996, 3(1), 31-33. (Reasons for increase in medical negligence claims and preventive measures including continuing medical education).
Mental distress: should lawyers pay more for their mistakes? *(Laurence Marsh)*: S.J. 1996, 140(33), 848-849. (How cases raise two key issues: distinction between physical and non-physical damage and whether measure of damages is too low).
Negligence: duty of care *(Stephen Fietta)*: I.C.C.L.R. 1996, 7(7), C136-138. (Whether defendants owed duty of care for illness caused by asbestos emissions from factory when plaintiffs were children).
Negligent professionals and mortgage indemnity insurance *(Hugh Tomlinson* and *Thomas Grant)*: S.J. 1996, 140(10), 260-261. (Whether solicitors and valuers who were liable to mortgagees for professional negligence were entitled to benefit from MIG mortgage indemnity guarantee policy in terms of quantum of damages).
Negligent valuation–the proper measure of damages *(H.W. Wilkinson)*: N.L.J. 1996, 146(6759), 1316-1317. (Principles and policy issues behind HL decision in South Australia v York Montague reversing Banque Bruxelles case).
Of new orders and new dawns: freewheeling returns to negligence? *(Guy Osborn* and *Teresa Sutton)*: P.N. 1996, 12(1), 2-6. (Whether changing composition of judiciary has led to more proactive approach to law in negligence cases).
Police liability in negligence *(Margaret Noble)*: N.L.J. 1996, 146(6761), 1395-1396. (Circumstances in which police may have duty of care for third parties' actions and whether public policy immunity applies).
Procedure: throwing down the gauntlet *(John Peysner)*: P. & M.I.L.L. 1996, 12(4), 31-32. (Proposed fast track procedure for medical negligence claims put forward by Lord Woolf's Medical Negligence Working Group).
Property finance negligence damages after BBL *(Hugh Tomlinson* and *Thomas Grant)*: S.J. 1996, 140(26), 654-655. (HL decision limiting damages for negligent valuations to amount of over valuation, and its implications for negligence cases against solicitors).
Public authorities and the duty of care *(Douglas Brodie)*: Jur. Rev. 1996, 2, 127-143. (Difficulties in recovering damages for negligence or breach of statutory duty by local authorities).
Reasons to be careful *(Mark Chapman)*: Lawyer 1996, 10(10), 6. (Implications for professional advisers of decision concerning auditors' liability for oral statements as to accuracy of accounts).
Suing for the loss of a chance *(Nicholas Isaac)*: C.L. 1996, 1(9), 7. (Recovery of damages for loss of chance, particularly where third parties involved, with reference to case involving assessment of percentage chance law firm client would have had of negotiating better contract terms if advised properly).
Surveyors' and valuers' guide *(Laura Storey)*: E.G. 1996, 9626, 124-125. (Importance of insurance against claims for damages in negligence and precautions to avoid claims).
The Bar immunity: private interest or public policy? An examination of barristers' immunity *(Jacquetta Castle* and *Francis Tregear)*: Int. I.L.R. 1996, 4(8), 234-

244. (Origins and justification for barrister's immunity from liability for negligence and its application in practice).

The doctor and the mountaineer's knee *(Ian Grainger)*: C.L. 1996, 1 (9), 56-57. (Extent to which negligent valuer is liable for increased loss resulting from fall in property prices).

The ingredients of negligence: Health Law 1996, Sep, 7-8. (Elements necessary to negligence claims and applicability in medical context).

The patients' obstacle course *(Charles Lewis)*: Legal Times 1996, 38, 16. (Difficulties facing patients in medical negligence claims including biased opinions of defence expert witnesses).

Valuers can breath a sign of relief *(Phillip Brown)*: I.H.L. 1996, 43(Sep), 38-40. (Significance of decision on valuers' liability for economic loss in terms of scope of duty of care, assessment of damages, breach of warranty and causation).

"Waste" and civil liability *(John Bates)*: Env. Law 1996, 10(1), 26-27. (Whether residents had claim in negligence for loss and damage resulting from dust, emanating from development, entering their homes).

4537. Books

Campbell, Dennis–International Personal Injury Compensation. Hardback: £115.00. ISBN 0-421-57060-1. Sweet & Maxwell.

Dugdale, A.M.; Stanton, K.M.; Parkinson, J.E.–Professional Negligence. Hardback: £13.95. ISBN 0-406-03257-2. Butterworth Law.

Dugdale, A.M.; Stanton, K.M.; Parkinson, J.E.–Dugdale and Stanton: Professional Negligence. Hardback: £110.00. ISBN 0-406-03257-2. Butterworth Law.

Garfield, John; Earl, Christopher J.–Medical Negligence. Hardback: £95.00. ISBN 0-443-04958-0. Churchill Livingstone.

Harris, David; Maddison, David; Tetlow, Christopher; Wood, Graham–Bingham's Negligence Cases. Hardback: £125.00. ISBN 0-421-46500-X. Sweet & Maxwell.

Jackson, Rupert; Powell, John–Jackson and Powell on Professional Negligence: Fourth Cumulative Supplement to the Third Edition. Paperback: £24.00. ISBN 0-421-52190-2. Sweet & Maxwell.

Johnson, David–Head Injuries Litigation. Hardback: £60.00. ISBN 0-421-48350-4. Sweet & Maxwell.

Leigh, Sarah–Managing Medical Negligence Actions. Personal injury library. Paperback: £50.00. ISBN 0-85121-984-5. FT Law & Tax.

Minns, Tracy–Quantum in Medical Negligence. Paperback. ISBN 0-7520-0048-9. FT Law & Tax.

Percy, R.A.–Charlesworth and Percy: on Negligence. The common law library, no 6. Hardback: £180.00. ISBN 0-421-56990-5. Sweet & Maxwell.

Phillips, Andrew Fulton–Medical Negligence Law: Seeking a Balance. Medico-legal series. Hardback: £37.50. ISBN 1-85521-643-4. Dartmouth.

PARTNERSHIPS

4538. Actuaries

PARTNERSHIPS (UNRESTRICTED SIZE) NO.11 REGULATIONS 1996, SI 1996 262; made under the Companies Act 1985 s.716, s.744. In force: March 15, 1996; £0.65.

The Companies Act 1985 s.716 prohibits the formation of partnerships of more than 20 persons. These Regulations exempt from that prohibition partnerships formed for the purpose of carrying on practice as actuaries and consisting of persons at least three quarters of whom are Fellows of the Institute of Actuaries or Fellows of the Faculty of Actuaries. They replace, and revoke, earlier Regulations (SI 1970 835) which provided for an exemption in relation to partnerships consisting of persons all of whom were Fellows of either the Institute of Actuaries or Faculty of Actuaries.

4539. Agreements–fundamental breach of partnership–mistaken voluntary VAT declaration not a material breach of a partnership agreement

A partnership was formed and the partnership agreement included a clause that each partner would be just and faithful to the other partners and should at all times act in the best interests of the partnership. By a further clause any material breach by one partner entitled the other to purchase the interest of the partner in breach. The partners fell out and both brought claims that the other had been in breach of the agreement and claimed the right to buy the other's interest. The judge rejected all claims save one, that the appellant had been in breach of the clause by making a voluntary disclosure to Customs and Excise of an apparent under declaration of VAT relating to invoices from a company controlled by the respondents without first telling the respondents. The judge held that such conduct was a material breach of the agreement. The appellants appealed.

Held, allowing the appeal, that it was unnecessary to determine whether or not a breach showed an indication to repudiate the agreement, "material" was to be defined as something serious or important. The voluntary disclosure letter was not a material breach of the agreement because, although there had, in fact, been no under declaration, it was in the partnership's best interests that any potential under declaration be declared voluntarily to avoid possible criminal prosecution of penalties. As no actual loss resulted it was not possible to say that the sending of the letter was so unreasonable as to amount to a material breach.

DB RARE BOOKS LTD v. ANTIQBOOKS [1995] 2 B.C.L.C. 306, Stuart Smith, L.J., CA.

4540. Dissolution–appointment of receiver and manager–no presumption in favour of appointment on dissolution where assets not in danger

A appealed against an order appointing a receiver and manager in respect of a kebab restaurant run by a partnership. The receiver had express power to sell. The partnership had been dissolved and there was a dispute as to the share of the business to which T was entitled. The judge had decided that in cases where the partnership had been dissolved, a receiver should be appointed "almost as a matter of course".

Held, allowing the appeal, that the power to appoint a receiver was discretionary and contained no presumption in favour of the appointment when the partnership had been dissolved. The order was not appropriate to the circumstances of this case where the assets of the business were not in danger. The settlement of the accounts of the business did not require such an extreme order. An inquiry into the partnership assets should have been ordered and an independent arbitrator or valuer should have been appointed to settle the accounts, *Hugh Stephenson & Sons Ltd v. Aktiengesellschaft fur Carton-Nagen-Industrie* [1918] A.C. 239 considered.

TOKER v. AKGUL, Trans. Ref: CHANI 94/0943/B, November 2, 1995, Evans, L.J., CA.

4541. Articles

CYB, SA and new partners *(Mark N. Lee)*: Accountancy 1996, 117(1232), 146-147. (Tax considerations for partnerships where new partners join in 1996/97 and 1997/98 in light of introduction of current year basis and self assessment).

Foreign aspects of partnerships under self assessment *(Nigel Eastaway* and *Paula Higgleton)*: P.T.P.R. 1996, 5(1), 29-42. (Loss of distinct entity status for partnerships and application of Sch.D for use by both resident and non-resident partners for self assessment purposes).

Germany offers lawyers new partnership vehicle *(Karl H. Pilny)*: I.F.L. Rev. 1996, 15(2), 14-16. (Structure and liability of partnership structure intended for freelance professions and available since July 1, 1995).

Incorporation of partnerships *(Mark Nichols)*: E.G. 1996, 9638, 129-131. (Commercial advantages of company structure for professional partnerships and implications in terms of income tax, CGT and stamp duty).

Investment enterprise partnerships: venture capital funds formed in Japan *(Hideki Ebata)*: B.J.I.B. & F.L. 1996, 11(7), 345-346. (Characteristics of investment enterprise partnerships and main provisions of IEP agreements).

Jersey: limited liability for partners *(Beverley Lacey)*: I.C. Lit. 1996, Feb, 22-24. (Proposals to extend law to permit personal asset protection for partners actively involved in management of partnerships).

Jersey: partnership–limited partnerships *(Edward Quinn)*: I.C.C.L.R. 1996, 7(7), C128-129. (Provisions of draft legislation permitting professional partnerships to establish themselves in Jersey with limited liability status).

Limited liability partnerships: P.L.C. 1996, 7(5), 9-10. (Provisions of draft Jersey law which seeks to limit liability of professional partnerships to firms' business assets excluding partners' personal assets).

Limited partnerships *(Philip Mitchell)*: C.M. 1996, 8(12), 112-113. (Benefits of using limited partnership as investment vehicle as alternative to unit trusts).

Partners in law *(Roderick C. I'Anson Banks)*: C.L. 1996, 1(5), 25-26. (Indications of partnership status within professional firms, including sharing of profits, sharing losses, capital contribution, participation in management and agreement).

Partners' deeds: L.S.G. 1996, 93(37), 19. (Different roles of partners and considerations in joining partnerships).

Pulling the safety net *(Ronnie Fox* and *Clare Murray)*: L.S.G. 1996, 93(17), 18. (Whether consultative proposals to restrict protection for partnerships holding professional indemnity policies would leave solicitors exposed to financial ruin should their insurers go into liquidation).

The CYB: which year end? *(Mark Lee)*: Accountancy 1996, 117(1229), 71-72. (Whether sole traders and partnerships should stay with existing accounting date on introduction of current year basis of assessment or change to March 31, or April 30).

The extension of the doctrine of "de facto" contracts to management relationships in German limited partnerships *(Stefan Simon)*: I.C.C.L.R. 1996, 7(2), 64-65.

The problem of older and underperforming partners: C.L. 1996, 1(10), 40-42. (How to recognise and deal with varying levels of performance of partners in law firms).

The uses of junior partnership: C.L. 1996, 1(5), 24-25. (Advantages and disadvantages of salaried or fixed share partnerships in law firms).

Who needs a partnership agreement? *(Michael Simmons)*: P.P.M. 1995, 13(10), 175-177. (Provisions which need to be included in partnership agreement for them to be effective).

4542. Books

Smith; Williamson–Professional Partnership Handbook. Paperback: £35.00. ISBN 1-86012-327-9. Tolley Publishing.

Steiner, Michael; Davis, Glen; Cohen, Malcolm–Insolvent Partnerships. Hardback: £60.00. ISBN 0-85308-351-7. Jordan.

PATENTS

4543. Amendments–personal stereos–apparatus was obvious and did not require invention–amendments to the claims not allowed–excessive pleadings and interlocutory hearings–increased costs–purpose of Patents County Court frustrated

P, the holder of a patent for a personal stereo, appealed against orders by the Patents County Court dismissing his action, revoking his patent and refusing amendment of the patent.

Held, dismissing the appeal, that (1) new amendments to the claim were not permissible as they had not been before the judge in the court below and had not been properly advertised. To allow such amendments would be unfair to those who would wish to object to the amendments. The alternative amendments which had been rejected by the judge had the effect of producing a new combination which changed the patent claim. Fairness required the amendments to be advertised and to do that would prejudice the defendants, therefore the amendments would not be permitted at this late stage and (2) the claims were invalid as they were obvious and did not involve inventiveness. When considering obviousness, the claim must not be considered in hindsight, *British Westinghouse v. Braulik* 27 R.P.C. 209 and *Windsurfing International Inc v. Tabur Marine (GB) Ltd* (1985) R.P.C. 59 followed. In this case the claim was obvious with reference to what was known or used in this country at the time of the claim. When the patent was granted there was apparatus which did a similar job, but in mono and there were stereo radios and recorders which could be carried around. It was an obvious step at the time to upgrade the mono recorders to stereo and to carry the apparatus attached to a belt.

Observed, although the patent description was short and the language and concept both easy to understand, the action had been prolonged and costs increased far more than was reasonable because of the approach the parties had adopted to the litigation. By excessively long pleadings, pursuing all points, whether material or not, and failing to use preparatory procedures to limit the points at issue, the parties had been able to frustrate the purpose of the Patents County Court, which was established to deal with more straightforward patent cases with less cost and delay than the Patents Court, *Chaplin Patents Holding Co Inc v. Group Lotus Plc* [1994] C.L.Y. 3452 considered.

PAVEL v. SONY CORP, *The Times*, March 22, 1996, Aldous, L.J., CA.

4544. Damages–interim relief–complex dispute with issues still outstanding but minimum damages entitlement could be ascertained

[Rules of the Supreme Court Ord.29 r.11; Patents Act 1977 s.46.]

C applied under the Rules of the Supreme Court Ord.29 r.11 (1) (b) for an interim payment of £7 million on the grounds that C had obtained judgment for damages to be assessed. C was the proprietor of a patent, relating to the Hepatitis C virus, which had its most important commercial application in the manufacture of kits for screening blood. The other plaintiffs were licensees. M had been found liable for infringement in two actions. There were two relevant periods of time under the claim, called the M1 period and the M2 period. The plaintiffs main claims were for a reasonable royalty on M's screening kits. Other heads of claim involving difficult questions of fact and law were ignored for the purposes of the application. At the hearing, M applied to strike out the summons as an abuse of process, arguing that it should be dismissed as an inappropriate diversion of resources from the task of preparing for the substantive hearing. The main arguments centred on the appropriate royalty and the appropriate number of screening kits to which the royalty ought to be applied.

Held, granting the interim payment, that (1) although interim payments were not suitable where factual issues were complicated or where difficult points of law arose, an interim payment in relation to an irreducible minimum part of a claim capable of being established without venturing into disputed areas of fact and law could be ordered, *Schott Kem v. Bentley* [1991] 1 Q.B. 61, [1991] C.L.Y. 2892 referred to; (2) two days of court time was not extravagant for a £7 million application. This, together with the fact that M had made an open offer and that the inquiry had been pending for 20 months, was to be taken into account in deciding to hear the application, *Newport (Essex) Engineering Co Ltd v. Press & Shear Machinery* 24 B.L.R. 74, [1984] C.L.Y. 2654 referred to; (3) the court could not hope to resolve questions on whether C's licensing agreements in relation to screening kits for the hepatitis B virus and HIV were appropriate comparables for royalty rates other than to say that they provided useful comparables; (4) as the best available comparable the court should have regard to licences of right under the Patents Act 1977 s.46 for important pharmaceutical patents relating to inventions requiring lengthy and expensive research. A royalty rate of 30 per cent was within the range on which the parties agreed and would be applied to this application, *Chiron Corp v. Organon Teknika Ltd (No.3)* [1994] F.S.R. 202, [1995] 2 C.L.Y. 3777 referred to; (5) as to the volume on which the nominal royalty should be ordered for the M2 period, C's figures for M's sales were not directly challenged and were to be regarded as more reliable. Nevertheless, the court was satisfied only that damages would be established in respect of the basic sales figures and it was not right to take a higher figure. In respect of the M1 period a further 30 per cent should be added, making a total volume of 130 per cent of the basic sales, and (6) taking the nominal royalty and sales figures gave a figure of approximately £6.3 million. The court was entitled to take comfort from its chosen figure being substantially lower than that previously offered to the court and the total sum being less than the total provision in the audited accounts. The court ordered that £6 million was a reasonable proportion of the minimum likely award.

CHIRON CORP v. MUREX DIAGNOSTICS LTD (NO.13) [1996] F.S.R. 578, Robert Walker, J., Ch D.

4545. Disclosure–experiments–no need to disclose all unsuccessful experiments in patent litigation

[Rules of the Supreme Court Ord.104 r.12.]

The patent in suit in E's infringement action related to lawn mowers which hovered over the ground on a cushion of air created by an impeller fan mounted above the cutting blade on the drive shaft. The specification of E's patent modified the standard hover mower so that air flowing towards the fan was also used to suck up cut grass. B's mower had two fans mounted on the same shaft, with the cushion of air created mainly by the lower fan while the upper fan sucked air through a collecting nozzle lifting up cut grass. The upper and lower fans were separated in the mower but some of the air sucked through the collecting nozzle by the upper fan passed through gaps to the lower fan. E argued that infringement resulted from the flow of air into the lower fan. B denied that the flow was significant. Both parties conducted experiments relating to the flow of air and collection of grass.

Held, finding the patent valid but not infringed, that (1) the claim should be construed to cover apparatus which contained all the mechanical features specified and in which it was the stream of air to the hover fan which had the effect of lifting cut grass; (2) when a party served a notice of experiments and the opponent did not ask for a repeat, the account of how the experiment had been conducted and the results obtained were generally taken to be proved. The opponent could still challenge the relevance of the experiment and its appropriateness; (3) if the opponent asked for the experiment to be repeated, primary importance and weight should be given to the outcome of the repeats. However, this did not make the results set out in the notice inadmissible. Factors such as the absence of representatives of the other side at the first experiment went to weight rather than admissibility, *American Cyanamid Co v. Ethicon Ltd* [1978] R.P.C. 667, [1978] C.L.Y. 2233 considered; (4) where a party intended to rely on experiments it was mandatory to serve a notice as required by the Rules of the Supreme Court Ord.104 r.12. Experiments would not be admissible in the absence of such a notice unless, in special circumstances, the court exercised its discretion to allow them in; (5) the admission or disclosure by a party that he had conducted experiments which he had chosen not to rely on should not normally lead the court to draw any adverse inferences as to what those experiments might have proved. It was not in the interests of the administration of justice to force parties to disclose all the unfruitful avenues they had pursued on the off chance that some of them might arguably be supportive of their opponent's case, *Pall Corp v. Commercial Hydraulics (Bedford) Ltd* [1990] F.S.R. 329, [1990] C.L.Y. 3459 referred to; (6) in this case the extent and effect of air flow between the chambers of B's mower was important. Air flow between the chambers could be substantial only if it could at least be shown to make a discernible contribution to picking up the grass. E had failed to show the air flow was used to any substantial extent, and (7) the attack based on obviousness failed. There was no evidence to indicate that anyone had been likely to make the jump from the cited prior art to the patent in suit.

ELECTROLUX NORTHERN LTD v. BLACK & DECKER [1996] F.S.R. 395, Laddie, J., Pat Ct.

4546. European patent–Council Regulation 1768/92–medicinal product patents–legal basis for Regulation–whether competency of Member States excluded–European Union

[Council Regulation 1768/92 concerning the creation of a supplementary protection certificate for medicinal products; Treaty of Rome 1957.]

On June 18, 1992 Council Regulation 1768/92 was enacted, taking as its legal basis the Treaty of Rome 1957 Art.100a. Spain, supported by Greece, applied for the annulment of the Regulation. France and the CEC intervened in support of the validity of the Regulation. Spain, relying in particular upon Art.36 and Art.222 of the Treaty, argued that the EU did not have the competence to legislate to create a new patent right and that in any event Art.100a was not the correct legal basis for the Regulation. In its preamble, the Regulation was said to address the problem of the long period between the filing of a patent application and the authorisation to place the product on the market, which made the period of protection under the patent insufficient to cover the investment put into the research. The CEC argued that this lack of protection penalised pharmaceutical research.

Held, dismissing the application for annulment, that (1) the purpose of Art.222 of the Treaty was to allow general freedom to Member States in the organisation of their property regimes, but it did not prohibit EU intervention in the property rights of individuals, *Commission of the European Communities v. United Kingdom (C30/90)* [1992] E.C.R. I-829, [1992] C.L.Y. 4760 followed; (2) the purpose of Art.36 of the Treaty was not to reserve certain matters to the exclusive competence of Member States, *Simmenthal v. Italian Minister for Finance (35/76)* [1976] E.C.R. 1871, [1971] C.L.Y. 1311 followed; (3) neither Art.222 nor Art.36 of the Treaty reserved a power to regulate substantive patent law to the national legislature to the exclusion of any EC action in the matter. The EU was competent in the field of intellectual property to harmonise national laws and to create new rights superimposed upon national rights, *Opinion 1/94* [1994] E.C.R. I-5267 applied and (4) the Regulation was enacted in order to achieve completion of the internal market, following the objectives set out in Art.8a, and was thus validly adopted on the basis of Art.100a. The Regulation aimed to prevent the heterogeneous development of national laws leading to disparities which would be likely to create either distorted competition conditions or obstacles to the free movement of medicinal products within the EU.

SPAIN v. EUROPEAN COUNCIL (C350/92) [1996] F.S.R. 73, Rodriguez Iglesias (President), ECJ.

4547. European patent–translations–corrections–statutory interpretation

[Patents Act 1977 s.80, s.117; Patents Rules 1990 s.80.]

R applied under the Patents Act 1977 s.117(1) for correction of an English translation of a European patent having French as the language of the proceedings. The translation mistakenly referred to a quantity of 35 to 50 per cent instead of 35 to 80 per cent as in the original claim. The official letter from the Patent Office, signed by an Administrative Officer, stated that the allowance of the corrections would be deferred until the nine month opposition period had expired. At the end of the opposition period, the Administrative Officer wrote saying that since the English translation conferred narrower protection than the French version due to the mistake the rules of the Patents Act 1977 s.80(3) and the Patents Rules 1990 s.80 applied, as opposed to s.117(1). R filed a corrected translation under s.80(3) without prejudice to the s.117(1) correction.

Held, refusing the application, that (1) the correction under s.117(1) had not been already decided by the letter from the Administrative Officer because such a grade of official did not have authority to act for the Comptroller in deciding a request under s.117; (2) s.80(3) was applicable prior to the translation having been published; (3) publication occurred when the translation was made available for public inspection in the Patent Office 14 days after filing and not only when the translation was made available for inspection at the British Library, Science Reference and Information Service. The translation was therefore published before the application for correction under s.117 was filed and the provisions of s.80(3) were applicable on the date of the s.117 application and (4) there was no distinction between correcting a translation and filing a corrected translation and therefore no distinction between the activities covered by s.80(3) and s.117. Accordingly, to allow a correction under s.117 when s.80(3) applied would be in contravention of the established canon of construction generalia specialibus non derogant. It would be inappropriate for the Comptroller to exercise his discretion to allow correction under s.117 which would effectively circumvent the express safeguards of s.80(3) and s.80(4) provided for third parties when the translation offered narrower protection.

RHONE-POULENC SANTE'S EUROPEAN PATENT, *Re* [1996] R.P.C. 125, L Lewis, PO.

4548. Fees

PATENTS (FEES) RULES 1996, SI 1996 2972; made under the Patents Act 1977 s.123, Sch.4 para.14; and the Department of Trade and Industry (Fees) Order 1988. In force: January 1, 1997; £1.95.

These Rules revoke and replace the Patents (Fees) Rules 1995 (SI 1995 2164). The fees remain unchanged except that the fee payable for a substantive examination (Form 10/77) is reduced from £130 to £70.

4549. Genetic engineering–techniques–breadth of claim too broad

[Patents Act 1977 s.1, s.3, s.5, s.72.]

In 1978 B applied for a UK patent of their method of using genetic engineering techniques to produce the antigens of the hepatitis B virus which could then be used to diagnose the disease and to produce vaccines against infection. This application was the basis of a claim to priority in their application for a European patent in 1979. B claimed that M had infringed their patent by proposing to market a hepatitis B vaccine which also relied on genetic engineering methods. M counterclaimed that the patent should be revoked because: (1) the claimed invention had been obvious at the time when the UK patent was applied for and when the European patent was applied for, contrary to the Patents Act 1977 s.1 (1) (b) and s.3; (2) the material disclosed by B did not support the invention claimed in the patent as required by s.5(2) (a) of the Act and therefore B was not entitled to priority with respect to the European patent; (3) the patent claimed was not an invention within the meaning of s.1 (1), and (4) the description claimed in the patent was not sufficient under s.72(1) (c). Judgment in favour of B was overturned by the Court of Appeal and B appealed.

Held, dismissing the appeal, that in order to decide whether a development was inventive, it was necessary to examine the state of the art at the time that the patent was applied for. The court was prepared to assume that B's method of producing the antigens was not obvious to those skilled in genetic engineering techniques in 1978. However, B's disclosure did not support what was claimed in the patent in that it purported to cover methods of producing antigens that did not rely on any of the principles or teaching of B's invention. B had been the first to make hepatitis antigens using their method but this did not justify giving B a monopoly over all methods of doing so as this would discourage competition and research which might lead to further valuable developments. B was therefore not entitled to the priority with regard to the European patent as they had already conceded that its development was obvious when that application was filed in 1979.

BIOGEN INC v. MEDEVA PLC, *The Times*, November 1, 1996, Lord Hoffmann, HL.

4550. Harassment–threats to proceed with action for infringement–patentee not liable for actions of UK licensee–proof that threats addressed to plaintiff's customers caused plaintiff more than minimal damage–right to injunction

[Patents Act 1977 s.70.]

Dimplex (UK) Ltd, P, proceeded for relief against unjustifiable threats. The action originally included allegations of infringement but, as a result of the making of a *See v. Scott-Paine* order, the patentee Miralfin, M, decided to abandon its UK patent. P started to market a new design of oil-filled radiator. This resulted in M's associated company De'Longhi, D, sending letters to P and its customers stating that D would take any legal action necessary against any manufacturer, distributor or retailer of P's new product. It was agreed that the letters were threatening in nature. The issues were whether: (1) P had any case against M; (2) P was a person aggrieved under the Patents Act 1977 s.70 in respect of the customers and was entitled to any form of relief and (3) P was entitled to relief in respect of the threats made against itself.

Held, finding against D, that (1) M was not a joint tortfeasor with D. M had not sent any letters and there was no evidence it was aware of the letters sent by D; (2) a person aggrieved had to establish that the threats complained of had or were likely to cause P more than minimal damage. This was the case here. A large number of extremely well known, large retailers had been contacted with the intention of scaring off customers. Evidence of the reaction of a French distributor, who had sought an indemnity from P against the costs of any infringement proceedings, was admissible as evidence of the reaction of a normal customer faced with a threatening letter. There was a likelihood that such letters would inflict greater than minimal damage on P, who was entitled to relief, *Brain v. Ingledew Brown Bennison & Garrett* [1996] F.S.R. 341, [1996] C.L.Y. 4558 and *Reymes-Cole v. Elite Hosiery Co Ltd* [1965] R.P.C. 102, [1965] C.L.Y. 2948 referred to, and (3) s.70 did not take away from the court its discretion in respect of any equitable relief but did illustrate a general policy that, prima facie, where the tort of threats was made out, P was entitled to relief unless there were good reasons for deciding otherwise. D had denied that the letters were threatening until trial. Although there was no need to make a declaration it was right and proper that an injunction should be granted.

DIMPLEX (UK) LTD v. DE'LONGHI LTD [1996] F.S.R. 622, Laddie, J., Ch D.

4551. Human rights–hearings–appeal procedure–no violation of Art.6 as claim not referred to civil courts

[European Convention on Human Rights 1950 Art.6.]

B filed a patent application with the Netherlands patent office. The application was examined by the Examination Division and then the Appeals Division of the Patent Office. The latter declared the application unsuccessful because it related to non-patentable material. B claimed that there had been a violation of the European Convention on Human Rights Art.6(1) in that there had not been a fair hearing before an independent tribunal. B also claimed violation of Art.1 of Protocol 1 of theTreaty in that it had been deprived of its possessions without an examination by an independent and impartial tribunal.

Held, that there had been no violation of Art.6(1) in that even if the proceedings were considered not to comply with Art.6(1), B had recourse to the civil courts, an independent tribunal with sufficient jurisdiction which itself provided the safeguards required by Art.6. B had chosen not to submit its claim to the civil courts and the Court was thus unable to find in the abstract that the remedies available did not meet the requirements of Art.6(1).

BRITISH AMERICAN TOBACCO CO LTD v. NETHERLANDS (1996) 21 E.H.R.R. 409, R Ryssdal (President), ECHR.

4552. Infringement–application to amend patent–court's jurisdiction after challenge to validity of patent withdrawn

[Patents Act 1949 s.30; Patents Act 1977 s.75.]

N sued E for infringement of their patent for a deboning machine, but E challenged the patent's validity by way of defence and counterclaim. N subsequently applied for leave to amend the patent and the application was to be heard at the infringement trial. E subsequently decided against challenging the validity of the patent, although they continued to deny infringement. The question for the court was whether, in the light of the withdrawal of E's validity claim, the court retained jurisdiction to entertain the application for amendment.

Held, that in *Lever Brothers and Unilever's Patent, Re* (1955) 72 R.P.C. 198, [1955] C.L.Y. 1996 it was held that the effect of the Patents Act 1949 s.30(1) was that the court relinquished jurisdiction to allow an amendment as soon as proceedings for revocation of a patent ceased. However, the Patents Act 1977 s.75(1) gave the court jurisdiction to allow an amendment in any proceedings where "the validity of a patent is put in issue". Once the validity of the patent was challenged, the court had jurisdiction to amend the patent and remained seised of the issue, even if the challenge was subsequently withdrawn.

NORLING v. EEZAWAY (UK) LTD, *The Times*, November 27, 1996, Jacob, J., Pat Ct.

4553. Infringement–application to transfer from High Court to Patents County Court–principles applicable to transfer

SI sued MS for infringement of a patent relating to the digital monitoring of physical phenomena. SI was a substantial US company whereas MS was a relatively new company and less substantial. Before service of its defence MS applied to transfer the case to the Patents County Court, the main argument being that the interlocutory stages would be cheaper there, as counsel would not be required.

Held, refusing the application, that (1) the general principles which applied in deciding whether to transfer an action involved a consideration of the financial position of the parties, the financial substance and importance of the action with particular reference to persons not party to it, the complexity of the matters raised and whether the transfer was likely to result in a more speedy trial; (2) MS's arguments as to costs during the interlocutory stages were rejected. MS would be able to make financial savings anyway as it had instructed a solicitor who had limited rights of audience in the High Court as opposed to instructing a patent agent with no such rights and (3) the only factor of significance was the financial substance of the claim. The patent, if valid, would be immensely valuable. As all the other considerations were neutral, the application was refused, *Mannesmann Kienzle GmbH v. Microsystem Design Ltd* [1992] R.P.C. 569 considered.

Observed, to prevent SI gaining any advantage from the commercial uncertainty, due to the longer time periods involved in a High Court action, it might be necessary to order that their claims to the patent's independent validity be set out after service of the defence.

SLOPE INDICATOR v. MONITORING SYSTEMS LTD [1995] F.S.R. 867, Jacob, J., Pat Ct.

4554. Infringement–defences–genetic engineering

[Patents Act 1977.]

The patent in suit, filed in the United States in 1987, used recombinant DNA technology to develop a diagnostic test for the Hepatitis C Virus, HCV. In 1992 C claimed infringement of the patent against six co-defendants. The defendants denied infringement, counterclaimed for revocation and raised a defence under the Patents Act 1977 s.44. The judge below decided that the patent was valid and had been infringed but that the defence had been made out. Having taken avoidance measures, C served further writs and obtained summary judgment. Two of the defendants appealed and C cross-appealed. The appellant defendants argued that (1) C's claims were discoveries under s.1 (2); (2) there could not be a patentable invention because there was no industrial application under s.1 (1) (c); (3) there was insufficient disclosure under s.72(1) (c) and s.14(5) (c); and (4) a licensing agreement was void under s.44(1) (c), giving a defence under s.44(3), as the judge held in the case of a second agreement.

Held, allowing the appeals and cross-appeals in part, (1) all of C's claims covered inventions and not discoveries as such. C had found a polypeptide which was the physical expression of the part of the genetic sequence of the HCV virus containing an antigenic determinant. Other claims used that physical expression in conjunction with further physical attributes to constitute immuno-assays; (2) the judge below fell into error by giving s.1 (1) (c) and s.4 too literal a construction and in considering what could be made and used by industry rather than what could be made and used in any kind of industry. Accordingly part of C's claim was invalid, because an industry did not exist to make or use what was useless for any known purpose; (3) a failure to comply with s.14(5) (c) was not a ground for revocation. The allegations under s.72(1) (c) had not been established on the facts and the patent did comply with s.14(3). The "one way rule" followed by the judge was wrong in law *Biogen Inc v. Medeva* [1995] F.S.R. 4, [1995] 2 C.L.Y. 3776 applied; *Genentech Inc's Patent* [1989] R.P.C. 147, [1990] C.L.Y. 3472, *May & Baker v. Boots Pure Drug Co* (1950) 67 R.P.C. 23 and *Elliott Bros (London)'s Application* [1967] R.P.C. 1, [1966] C.L.Y. 9114 considered, and (4) neither agreement offended s.44 so as to give rise to a defence under s.44(3). The licensee had not been a party to any form of tie and had not consented to a tie.

Observed that, more documents had been provided than had been used. In future, greater attention should be paid to the exclusion of documents which could not sensibly be required.

CHIRON CORP v. MUREX DIAGNOSTICS LTD (NO.12); CHIRON CORP v. ORGANON TEKNIKA LTD (NO.12) [1996] F.S.R. 153, Morritt, L.J., CA.

4555. Infringement–interlocutory injunctions–only loss which would sound in damages need be considered–parties–joinder

P1 was a French manufacturer of disposable nappies and the proprietor of a patent relating to those nappies. P2 was the UK distributor of the nappies under an alleged exclusive licence. P2 had subsequently transferred its assets to X, which sought to be joined as a third plaintiff. Various associated companies of P1 which were not parties to the action sold the nappies in other European countries. P1 applied for an interlocutory injunction to restrain KC from manufacturing its nappies in the UK without a licence in respect of the patent, alleging that P1 and its other associated companies would suffer irreparable harm if the injunction was not granted.

Held, refusing to grant interlocutory relief, but granting leave to add X as a third plaintiff, that (1) an application for leave to join a further plaintiff should be granted unless the arguments in support of such application were plainly unsustainable; (2) where an exclusive licence was granted to a wholly owned subsidiary, the exclusion even of the proprietor may not be inconsistent with the proprietor retaining some measure of control of sub-licences, perhaps through an agency relationship. P1 should not be shut out from pursuing its contentions with respect to P2's alleged exclusive licence on the pleadings and at trial, *Bank of Tokyo Ltd v. Karoon* [1987] A.C. 45, [1986] C.L.Y. 2637 referred to; (3) P's claim for an injunction included a claim for protection against irrecoverable loss suffered by its associated companies. This approach was wrong in principle. Injunctions were generally granted in order to protect a plaintiff from loss which would sound in damages, not from loss which would not sound in damages. Those damages should not be too remote. The Court had to look at what economic damage the plaintiff had suffered, while being properly sceptical of a company and its shareholder, individual or corporate, seeking to recover duplicated damages in respect of the same wrong, *Polaroid Corp v. Eastman Kodak Co* [1977] R.P.C. 379, [1977] C.L.Y. 2171 applied and *Gerber Garment Technology Inc v. Lectra Systems Ltd* [1995] R.P.C. 383, [1995] 2 C.L.Y. 3780 considered; (4) with respect to the balance of convenience and adequacy of damages as a remedy, in an action which was basically about money, it was actual or reasonably apprehended wrongs that sound in monetary damages, and no other, which were material, and (5) where a patentee held a patent valid in territory B, which manufactured and sold in territory A, sold but did not manufacture in B, and did neither in territory C, loss sustained by infringing manufacture in B had to be ascertained on a case by case basis. For goods to be exported to C, the patentee's damages would be restricted to a royalty basis. For infringing acts in A or B, the patentee could claim loss of profits on sales, unless the sales were made by an exclusive licensee which might join as a co-plaintiff.

PEAUDOUCE SA v. KIMBERLY CLARK LTD [1996] F.S.R. 680, Robert Walker, J., Pat Ct.

4556. Infringement–order for delivery up–purpose of order–protection of patentee

K made a successful claim against R for the infringement of their valid patent over certain material. An order was made for an injunction and for delivery up of certain material. There was then a dispute as to whether the order should be stayed pending an application for leave to appeal. K objected to the stay. K sought leave to join GPB, who now owned the infringing machines and who were an associated company of R, as a defendant. GPB stated it would not object to the order for delivery up if the order was made in different terms. It was agreed that the machines should be rendered non-infringing pending the appeal, but R wanted to keep them to avoid having them destroyed, thereby losing GPB equipment worth £1million. The question was whether the order for delivery up was to prevent R from profiting from their wrongful acts by being able to use the machines when the patent expired or whether it was merely to ensure compliance with the injunction.

Held, granting the order suggested by R, that (1) delivery up was a discretionary remedy granted to suit the facts of each individual case. Its purpose was to protect the plaintiff rather than to punish the defendant, *Merganthaler Linotype Co v. Intertype Ltd* (1926) 43 R.P.C. 381 approved. The injunction had the effect of preventing R from infringing the patent, past infringements were compensated for by damages and the order for delivery up put R in the same position as a member of the public, as the specification of the machines was fully described in the patent; the order for delivery up was not an additional remedy but merely for the protection of the patentee and (2) the argument that for R to keep the machines mothballed gave an unfair competitive advantage when the patent ran out was rejected. The patent was in the public domain, the information concerning the machines was not confidential, *Seager v. Copydex Ltd* [1967] 1 W.L.R. 923, [1967] C.L.Y. 1294 and *Roger Bullivant Ltd v. Ellis* [1987] F.S.R. 172, [1987] C.L.Y. 1486 distinguished.

KASTNER v. RIZLA LTD, Trans. Ref: FC7 95/7027/C, December 15, 1995, Aldous, L.J., CA.

4557. Infringement–rubber or plastic backed floor mats–added matter and novelty considerations–prior use invalidated claim–patent infringed but invalid

This was an action for infringement of a UK patent relating to rubber or plastic backed washable floor mats, used in the doorways of public buildings. The mats required regular washing and spin drying in commercial spin driers that developed large forces sometimes causing the rubber backing to burst. The patent in suit concerned the use of perforations in the backing of mats which opened when subjected to mechanical forces thereby easing the bursting problem. The parties were in dispute over several aspects of construction of claim 1 of the patent in suit. W also attacked the validity of the patent on the grounds of insufficiency and alleged that the matter disclosed in the specification of the patent extended beyond that disclosed in the application as filed by way of addition and deletion and adduced evidence as to prior use. Finally, W claimed that the patent was obvious, relying on the prior use.

Held, finding the patent infringed but invalid, that (1) the skilled man was entitled to have recourse to the priority document or specification to resolve matters in the published patent specification; (2) in construing the patent, "closed" and "open" were used to mean not permitting or permitting the water flow. The skilled man would not understand the patent as requiring an opening or closing mechanism, or see the perforations as mechanical valves; (3) although claims could be imagined which had no meaning to the skilled man, the concept of "normal use" was unambiguous and clear. The claim did not call for perfection. Excessive leakage of mats occurred in normal use, but did not empty the claim of a reasonable degree of certainty for third parties, *General Tire & Rubber Co v. Firestone Tyre & Rubber Co Ltd* [1972] R.P.C. 457, [1975] C.L.Y. 2503 applied; (4) the patent's validity was not susceptible to attack on the ground of claim ambiguity. The Patent Office could reject claims on that ground, but if a patent were granted for an ambiguous claim, this was not a ground for revocation; (5) on a purposive construction, the fact that W's mats let a little water through was not enough to take them outside the scope of infringement, *Henrikson v. Tallon Ltd* [1965] R.P.C. 434, [1965] C.L.Y. 2949 followed; (6) W's attacks failed on insufficiency, as the skilled man could have performed the invention even with an error in the first claim. It was also clear that the same needle could be used for mats of different thickness; (7) W's attacks on added matter grounds also failed, as these had sought to construe real substance differences from mere language or emphasis changes, *Bonzel v. Intervention Ltd (No3)* [1991] R.P.C. 553, [1992] C.L.Y. 3292 referred to; (8) use of the mats by MD's customers before the priority date invalidated the claim, as use from which knowledge could be gained was not uninformative, *Lux Traffic Controls Ltd v. Pike Signals Ltd* [1993] R.P.C. 107 followed; (9) KT's activities, as rubber backed mat originators, were a prior use which anticipated the patent, and (10) MD's evidence of commercial success did not establish an invention and did not answer questions of anticipation or obviousness

MILLIKEN DENMARK AS v. WALK OFF MATS LTD [1996] F.S.R. 292, Jacob, J., Pat Ct.

4558. Infringement–threat of proceedings–entitlement of judge to make declarations of his own motion

[Patents Act 1977 s.70; Rules of the Supreme Court Ord.14A.]

IBB appealed against four declarations that actionable threats of proceedings for infringement of a patent, within the Patents Act 1977 s.70, had been made and that B was an aggrieved person within the meaning of the 1977 Act. The declarations were made when IBB's application for B's statement of claim to be struck out was dismissed. B cross appealed against the first declaration which gave IBB the opportunity to justify the threats by showing that an infringement would occur. The other three declarations stated that letters sent by IBB amounted to threats within s.70, that B was a person aggrieved and that the threats were actionable. IBB argued that the issues were issues of fact to be determined at trial, whereas the judge only had jurisdiction, under the Rules of the Supreme Court Ord.14A, to determine issues of law.

Held, allowing the appeal in relation to the second, third and fourth declarations and dismissing the cross-appeal in relation to the first declaration, that (1) as long as the patent was granted before the action reached trial, under s.70(2)(b) of the 1977 Act, the defendant was entitled to justify the threat of action while the patent was pending, and (2) the judge was entitled to deal with the construction of what was said in letters which purported to threaten proceedings, but the declaration dealt with an issue of fact which could not be properly determined until placed in context with the other evidence at the trial. Similarly, the judge was entitled to determine in law the scope of the word "aggrieved", but to conclude that B was a person aggrieved was a question of fact.

BRAIN v. INGLEDEW BROWN BENNISON & GARRETT [1996] F.S.R. 341, Aldous, L.J., CA.

4559. Infringement–threat of proceedings–statutory definition of infringing acts–alleged infringer seeking damages for costs incurred–action not an abuse of process

[Patents Act 1977 s.70.]

CT appealed against the striking out of a claim for abuse of process in respect of proceedings brought against RMC seeking compensation in damages for costs incurred as a result of a patent infringement action commenced by RMC. CT having been threatened with infringement proceedings, the action was discontinued after RMC's solicitor discovered, on the day of the hearing, that RMC might not have exclusive licence in the product concerned and was unable to give sufficient cross-undertakings in damages.

Held, allowing the appeal, that (1) although the Patents Act 1977 s.70(4) allowed a patentee to warn off a potential infringer, it did not allow proceedings to be brought for threats consisting of the making or importing of a product or the use of a process. The restriction in s.70(4) defined the acts alleged to infringe a patentee's rights, not the persons who might be threatened, and provided an exception to the monopoly relief provisions of s.70, and (2) on the facts, as no proceedings were brought by RMC, it was not an abuse of process for CT to commence an action alleging unlawful threats in an attempt to recover in damages the costs incurred after receiving the threat of proceedings from RMC.

CAVITY TRAYS LTD v. RMC PANEL PRODUCTS LTD [1996] R.P.C. 361, Aldous, L.J., CA.

4560. Infringement–toner cartridges intentional imitations–right to repair–spare parts exception–right of action–Hong Kong

[Registration of Patents Ordinance (Hong Kong) s.6.]

C made printer and photocopier cartridges for its laser printers and photocopiers. The cartridges were intended by C to be thrown away after the toner contained in them had been used. C had a number of patents relating to the cartridges and a number of plans and drawings in which copyright subsisted. G, a Hong Kong company, manufactured and sold cartridges which were intentionally a detailed imitation of C's cartridges so that the cartridges were interchangeable with those of C. C sued for patent infringement and for infringement of copyright. G denied infringement and claimed that C was not entitled to enforce its rights in so far as such enforcement interfered with an inherent right to repair. It was accepted that G was entitled to supply spare parts for broken cartridges. However, C argued that the supply of complete cartridges by G did not fall within the spare parts exception set out in *British Leyland Motor Corp Ltd v. Armstrong Patents Co Ltd* [1986] 1 A.C. 577, [1986] C.L.Y. 432 as the main reason for replacing a cartridge was that the toner was depleted, not because the cartridge was defective.

Held, that (1) the Registration of Patents Ordinance (Hong Kong) s.6 impliedly give a proprietor a right of action in the Hong Kong courts for infringements committed in Hong Kong. The Hong Kong court could grant such relief as would be available to the proprietor as if he were conducting proceedings in the UK in respect of an infringement occurring there, including relief for a partially valid patent; (2) there was no power vested in the Hong Kong court to amend or revoke a patent or to grant a declaration for non-infringement under the Patents Act 1977 s.71. Common law proceedings for a declaration could be brought if the appropriate circumstances existed; (3) the *British Leyland* decision specifically related to repair of machinery which the owner has acquired directly or indirectly from the person required not to derogate from grant. The word "repair" meant to restore to good condition by renewal or replacement of decayed or damaged parts. It would be an extension of the *British Leyland* principle to debar an action for copyright infringement in circumstances other than where there was a repair, *Gardner and Sons Ltd v. Paul Sykes Organisation Ltd* [1981] F.S.R. 284, [1981] C.L.Y. 370 referred to; (4) it is not repair simply to replace cartridges where the toner is depleted when neither the laser printer nor the photocopier nor the cartridge could be described as decayed or damaged. *Flogates Ltd v. Refco Ltd* [1996] F.S.R. 935 considered; (5) the *British Leyland* doctrine should not, in the circumstances, be extended to give protection to G. On the facts, it was within the reasonable contemplation of the purchaser of one of C's photocopiers or laser printers that he would have to purchase replacement cartridges from C, and (6) the *British Leyland* doctrine did not apply to patents. To hold otherwise would mean that a patent holder in Hong Kong would not enjoy the same rights in Hong Kong as he would in the UK. The right of repair that has always existed in patent law was sufficient protection for the owner of a patented article, *British Leyland* considered.

CANON KABUSHIKI KAISHA v. GREEN CARTRIDGE CO (HONG KONG) LTD [1995] F.S.R. 877, Rogers, J., HC (Hong Kong).

4561. Jurisdiction–Patents Court–limitation of claim for non-infringement declaration under the Patent Act 1977 s.74(2) did not affect patent validity or power of European Patent Office by virtue of s.77(1) of the Act–statutory interpretation.

[Patents Act 1977 s.71, s.74, s.77; Rules of the Supreme Court Ord. 104 r.4; European Patent Convention 1973.]

In the course of litigation in the Netherlands, H asserted that O's sales of HIV testing kits were infringing H's UK patent. O issued proceedings in the UK, pursuant to the court's inherent jurisdiction, seeking a declaration that it had not infringed any valid claim of the patent. The statement of claim put the validity of the patent in issue and particulars of objection were served. H applied to strike out those aspects of the statement of claim relating to validity as the Patents Act 1977 s.74(1) set out a list of proceedings, which did not include proceedings for a declaration of non-infringement under the inherent jurisdiction, in which the validity of a patent may be put in issue and s.74(2) of the 1977 Act provided that validity may not be put in issue in any other proceedings. Accordingly, all references to the validity of the patent should be struck out. O argued that the patent's validity was central to all the other proceedings listed in s.74(1) and it would be absurd to omit a claim under the inherent jurisdiction. O also submitted that H's construction would have the effect of excluding oppositions in the European Patent Office. Alternatively, O applied to amend the statement of claim to seek revocation of the patent.

Held, allowing both the strike out and amendment applications, that (1) validity and infringement were part of the same questions in English law; it was not possible to infringe an invalid claim, even if you fell within its language. However, s.74(2) could not be construed as allowing questions of validity to arise in a claim for declaration of non-infringement pursuant to the inherent jurisdiction; (2) s.74(2) therefore had the effect, probably accidentally, of limiting the non-statutory claim for a declaration to a dispute about the scope of the claim. Those parts of the statement of claim referring to validity were struck out; (3) s.74(2) did not have the effect of excluding oppositions in the European Patent Office, as s.77(1) treated European Patents (UK) as if they were granted by the British Patent Office, and subject to the provisions of the European Patent Convention, thereby specifically preserving the jurisdiction of the European Patent Office to revoke a patent, and (4) in general, under the Rules of the Supreme Court Ord.104 r.4(1), proceedings for revocation of a patent had to be initiated by petition rather than by writ action. There was no such requirement where an application to revoke was made in pending proceedings. As the language of the rule did not limit the nature of pending proceedings in any way, the court had jurisdiction to allow amendment to include a claim for revocation of the patent.

ORGANON TEKNIKA LTD v. HOFFMANN LA ROCHE AG [1996] F.S.R. 383, Jacob, J., Pat Ct.

4562. Medicines–byproduct of existing patented drug–no novelty

[Patents Act 1977 s.60.]

M, a pharmaceutical company, appealed against the dismissal of their claim to patent the acid metabolite which was created in the livers of people taking the drug terfenadine, as invalid. In 1972 M had successfully patented the anti-histamine drug terfenadine. The patent expired in 1992 and other companies, including N, began producing terfenadine. M claimed their monopoly in terfenadine continued on the basis of a later patent obtained to protect the acid metabolite, which M had discovered was a byproduct of terfenadine. M brought the action against N and others under s.60(2) of the Patents Act 1977 for infringement of the acid metabolite patent.

Held, dismissing the appeal, that a chemical composition could be judged to be part of the state of the art only if it was part of a process which had been disclosed as a specification of an invention. The composition of acid metabolite was therefore not new because it was already part of the 1972 patent for terfenadine, even though it was not appreciated at the time the patent was granted. If the specifications of the patent were followed then the production of acid metabolite was inevitable and therefore it was not novel, which was the main precondition for the grant of a patent.

MERRELL DOW PHARMACEUTICALS INC v. HN NORTON & CO LTD; MERRELL DOW PHARMACEUTICALS INC v. PENN PHARMACEUTICALS LTD [1996] R.P.C. 76, Lord Hoffmann, HL.

4563. Medicines–Canada–statutory licences–essential features of invention–obvious chemical equivalents–claims–catnic test–purposive interpretation

[Patent Act 1985 s.41 (Canada); Patented Medicines (Notice of Compliance) Regulations 1993 (Canada).]

N applied to the Minister of National Health and Welfare for a notice of compliance, which if granted would be equivalent to a statutory licence, in respect of the marketing of the drug, Prozac. E objected to the issue of the certificate, claiming that N's product was an infringement of E's patent.

Held, granting judicial review and prohibiting the Minister from issuing the certificate, that (1) since E's patent included claims for any process which was "an obvious chemical equivalent", the court had to decide whether N's process for producing the drug was an obvious chemical equivalent to the processes described in E's patent; (2) the words of the claim were plain and unambiguous; (3) in deciding whether the pith and marrow of the claimed invention had been taken, the first approach would be to determine the essential features of the claimed invention. If these essential features had been taken and if only unessential features had been substituted or omitted, there was infringement, *McPhar Engineering Co of Canada Ltd v. Sharpe Instruments Ltd* (1960) 35 C.P.R. 105 applied; (4) no recourse need be had to the doctrine of equivalents in order to construe the patent, as the court should take a purposive approach. Further, the Patent Act 1985 s.41(1) (Canada) at the time provided express protection for obvious equivalent processes and the Patented Medicines (Notice of Compliance) Regulations 1993 (Canada) included express reference to the inclusion of obvious chemical equivalents, *Beecham Canada Ltd v. Proctor & Gamble Co* (1982) 61 C.P.R. (2d) 1 and *Catnic Components Ltd v. Hill and Smith Ltd* [1982] R.P.C. 183, [1983] C.L.Y. 2776 applied; (5) to determine whether a variant between steps in the respective processes was an obvious chemical equivalent depended on the purpose of the step and the function it fulfilled in the process, and (6) N's ether formation process was an obvious chemical equivalent to that claimed in E's patent. The purpose of both reactions was to form the same type of bond, and E's process was sufficiently known at the time to be obvious.

ELI LILLY & CO v. NOVOPHARM LTD [1996] R.P.C. 1, Richard, J., Fed Ct (Can).

4564. Ownership–employees inventions–electric cable–business development manager made invention in course of normal duties–job description

[Patents Act 1977 s.39.]

N sought an order naming him as sole inventor of, and granting him all rights in the UK and European patents relating to an invention concerned with securing an electric cable sheathing to a connector backshell adaptor. The patents were in the name of S, a company in the business of designing and developing cable harnesses and backshell adaptors. N's employer, Hellermann, H, was a much larger company than S involved in the provision of cable markers and heat shrink products for the cable industry. S and H worked very closely with each other and after the invention H acquired S. R, an employee of S at the time of the invention, regularly visited N at H's premises. At one of these visits, R asked N if he could think of an alternative way of holding the cable screen to the adaptor. N devised a spring to perform this function. It was accepted that N was an inventor of the spring, with the only issue in respect of inventorship being whether he was the sole inventor.

Held, dismissing the application, that (1) N did not come up with the idea of using a spring unprompted, and would have been unlikely to have done so without R having spoken to him in the first place. N and R were therefore joint inventors; (2) N was given a wide-ranging brief, including finding new products for H. It would have been a normal part of the normal business contact between N and R for them to explore possible developments and modifications of products of common interest. Backshell connectors lay within the broad field of H's business. Accordingly, N made the invention in the course of his normal duties as an employee and the circumstances were such that an invention might reasonably be expected to result from the carrying out of his duties. Under the Patents Act 1977 s.39(1)(a) the invention must therefore belong to N's employers H, *Harris' Patent, Re* [1985] R.P.C. 19 considered and (3) as Business Development Manager, N enjoyed a position of high status and responsibility, so that the nature of his duties and the particular responsibilities arising from them were such that he had a special obligation to further the interests of H's undertaking, within the meaning of s.39(1)(b) of the 1977 Act.

STAENG LTD'S PATENTS, *Re* [1996] R.P.C. 183, P Ferdinando, PO.

4565. Ownership–employees inventions–ophthalmoscope–hospital registrar did not make invention in course of normal duties–job description

[Patents Act 1977 s.39.]

M, a Registrar in the Department of Ophthalmology at the Western Infirmary in Glasgow, made an invention relating to an ophthalmoscope. M conceived of the idea for the invention during private study for examinations at home. M's job description stated that he was expected to avail himself of the facilities provided for basic and clinical research. M applied to the Comptroller to determine who was entitled to the rights in the invention. The hearing officer found for GG and M appealed.

Held, allowing M's appeal, that (1) M's duties were to treat patients. M made the invention in his own time, when he was not treating a patient. He was considering the problem of eye examination generally. M therefore made the invention when he was not acting in the course of his normal duties as a registrar. GG was wrong to seek to rely on a proposition advanced in *Harris' Patent, Re* [1985] R.P.C. 19 which would have resulted in the conclusion that it was the duty of a doctor to devise, if he could, new ways of diagnosing and treating patients, because his duty was to treat patients; (2) the second limb of the Patents Act 1977 s.39(1)(a) did not apply because the particular circumstances surrounding the making of the invention were nothing to do with M carrying out his duties. M's invention may have been a useful accessory to his contracted work but it was not really a part of it, *Byrne v. Statist* [1914] 1 K.B. 622 considered, and (3) doctors frequently devised new treatments and most doctors were employed. Doctors would be placed in the difficult position of having to ask their employers for permission to publish their discoveries if the inventions became the employers' property.

GREATER GLASGOW HEALTH BOARD'S APPLICATION, *Re* [1996] R.P.C. 207, Jacob, J., Pat Ct.

4566. Parallel imports–free movement of goods–accession of Spain and Portugal to EU–transitional provisions

[Treaty of Rome 1957 Art.177.]

P was the owner of patents relating to various pharmaceuticals. D purchased in Spain and Portugal pharmaceuticals that had been made by the patentees or under their licence and imported them into the UK for subsequent sale. P sought interlocutory relief to restrain the infringement. The parties then applied for a reference of two questions to the European Court of Justice pursuant to Art.177 of the Treaty of Rome 1957. The first question was whether the case of *Merck v. Stephar* [1981] E.C.R. 2063, which held that if a patentee markets a product in a Member State where the law does not provide patent protection he must accept the consequences of his choice as regards the free movement of the product within the Common Market, should be reconsidered or modified to have regard to changed circumstances. The second question concerned the construction of the transitional provisions of the Acts of Accession to the European Union of Spain and of Portugal. Under the Acts both countries had to make patent protection for pharmaceuticals available and provide transitional arrangements in relation to the free circulation rule. The transitional provisions of both countries provided that a patentee could rely on a patent granted in a Member State to prevent the import into that Member State of products made in Spain or Portugal until the end of the third year after the country in question had made that product patentable. Patent protection for pharmaceuticals first became available in Spain on October 7, 1992 and in Portugal on January 1, 1992.

Held, referring both questions to the European Court, that (1) no specific findings of fact would be made. The matters raised by the case of *Merck v. Stephar* were matters of general application to the pharmaceutical industry and of Spanish and Portuguese law and practice. *R. v. Pharmaceutical Society of Great Britain* [1987] 3 C.M.L.R. 951, [1988] C.L.Y. 1530 referred to; (2) D's arguments in relation to the construction of the transitional provisions, ie. that the phrase used was a reference to three calendar years taken from the date that pharmaceuticals were made patentable, were very strong but a reference would still be made and (3) further argument was required as to whether it was proper to take a revised view of *Merck v. Stephar* into account when considering interim relief. Either the rule in *Merck v. Stephar* represented the law as it stood and should be followed unless and until a higher court declared otherwise or a possible change in law by the European Court was just as much a matter of uncertainty as any other uncertain matter at the interlocutory stage and should be treated in just the same way for the purposes of the rules in *American Cyanamid Co v. Ethicon Ltd* [1975] A.C. 396, [1975] C.L.Y. 2640.

MERCK & CO LTD v. PRIMECROWN LTD [1995] F.S.R. 909, Jacob, J., Pat Ct.

4567. Plant varieties–supplementary protection certificates

PATENTS (SUPPLEMENTARY PROTECTION CERTIFICATE FOR PLANT PROTECTION PRODUCTS) REGULATIONS 1996, SI 1996 3120; made under the European Communities Act 1972 s.2. In force: Reg.1, Reg.2, Reg.4(2): January 2, 1997; Remainder: February 8, 1997; £1.10.

These Regulations extend the power of the Secretary of State to make rules under the Patents Act 1977 s.123 in respect of patents and applications for patents so as to enable him to make rules relating to the procedure to be applied to, and the fees in respect of, supplementary protection certificates for plant protection products and applications thereof, and extend and apply in the appropriate cases existing provisions of the Patents Act 1977 and the Patents Act 1949 and rules made thereunder, relating to patents and applications for patents, to certificates and applications for certificates.

4568. Revocation–amendment by deletion–metal connections–whether patent was infringed–whether invalid for obviousness–Gillette defence

JE brought an action for revocation of MM's patent for electric motor brush arms and sought a declaration that its brush arm design did not infringe the patent in suit. Soon after the petition for revocation was served in September 1986, MM was advised that claim 1 was invalid as it stood. However, no application to amend was made until September 1988. The amendments proposed were designed to avoid the prior art whilst catching JE's design. JE admitted it had not suffered any detriment due to the delay, but argued that the amended claims were invalid for obviousness because there were only so many ways of joining two pieces of metal, with crimping, the method used in the patent in suit, being one of them. JE also contended that its device was an obvious development over the prior art and accordingly it had a good *Gillette* defence.

Held, allowing the amendment and finding the patent valid but not infringed, that (1) a patentee who sought to delete claims would not be deprived of the fruits of his invention unless very compelling reasons existed. MM and its patent agents had not deliberately tried to get a monopoly to which MM was not entitled. In the context of a worldwide dispute, the delay was not blameworthy. Accordingly, the amendment would be allowed, *Chiron Corp v. Organon Teknika Ltd (No.7)* [1994] F.S.R. 458, [1995] 2 C.L.Y. 3750 and *C Van der Lely NV v. Bamfords Ltd* [1964] R.P.C. 54 applied; (2) however, because the patent was not framed with reasonable skill and knowledge MM would be penalised in costs; (3) JE's brush arm did not involve crimped projections within the meaning of the patent since riveting was the primary means of connection; (4) the skilled man would have concluded that strict compliance with the stipulation of more than one projection was intended to be an essential requirement of the patent and that the flap on JE's design, which had a relief hole in it, was an immaterial variant on two flaps. Accordingly, on this point JE's design did fall within the claim, *Improver Corp v. Remington Consumer Products Ltd* [1990] F.S.R. 181, [1991] C.L.Y. 2698 applied; (5) the inventive step arose in the combined use of two metal strips, one resilient and the other not, which were overlapped, crimped and bent into an L shape. It had not been shown that the solution of crimping would occur naturally to the skilled man. The patent as amended was therefore valid, *Windsurfing International Inc v. Tabur Marine (Great Britain) Ltd* [1985] R.P.C. 50 and *Molnlycke AB v. Proctor & Gamble Ltd (No.5)* [1994] R.P.C. 49, [1995] C.L.Y. 3778 applied and (6) riveting and the provision of bent over projections to prevent rotation about the rivet was obvious. If the claim was wide enough to cover a protrusion which was bent over to provide some support without any real grip, it would be obvious and a *Gillette* defence would succeed, *Gillette Safety Razor Co v. Anglo-American Trading Co Ltd* [1913] 30 R.P.C. 465 applied.

JOHNSON ELECTRIC INDUSTRIAL MANUFACTORY LTD v. MABUCHI MOTOR KABUSHIKI KAISHA; SUB NOM. MABUCHI MOTOR KK'S PATENT, *Re* [1996] F.S.R. 93, Judge not specified, Pat Ct.

4569. Revocation–petition–amendment seeking to rely on further prior art–appropriate use of See v Scott-Paine orders

Three weeks before trial D applied to amend its particulars of objection to the validity of P's patent so as to rely on a further piece of prior art. P did not object but argued that the amendment should be allowed on *See v. Scott-Paine* terms, meaning that P would be given a limited time in which to elect whether or not to abandon the patent. If it did, it would have to pay D's costs in the petition up to the date of the original particulars of objection and D would have to pay the costs from that date to the date of amendment. As the particulars of objection were served with the petition D would have to bear virtually all the costs of the petition. D argued that either the question of costs should be stood to the trial or that it be ordered to pay only the costs of and occasioned by the amendment.

Held, allowing the amendment, that (1) in exercising the court's discretion as to the appropriate order for costs, account must be taken of all the relevant facts including whether there had been unnecessary wastage of cost and whether a defendant had been reasonably diligent in relation to the prior art inquiries made, *Williamson v. Moldline Ltd* [1986] R.P.C. 556, [1987] C.L.Y. 2794 considered; (2) the factors to be considered included: the timetable of the proceedings; how late the amendment was; the extent to which that lateness had been explained and to what extent the patentee was likely to have been taken by surprise by the reliance on the new prior art, and (3) although the application was late and D had been aware of the prior art for some time, D had not been unreasonably dilatory and P was not surprised or disadvantaged by the application to amend. Accordingly, an order in *See v. Scott-Paine* form would not be made. D should bear the costs occasioned by the amendment.

Observed: *See v. Scott-Paine* orders could work a major injustice as they could seriously affect the freedom of the party attacking the validity of a patent to run the best possible case.

GEC ALSTHOM LTD'S PATENT, *Re* [1996] F.S.R. 415, Laddie, J., Pat Ct.

4570. Software–design of chemical compounds–computer controlled process was not patentable invention

[Patents Act 1977 s.1.]

F appealed against the rejection of its patent application relating to computer software designed to aid chemists in the creation of new "hybrid" chemical compounds. The application was rejected on the basis of the Patents Act 1977 s.1(2) which excluded "a scheme, rule or method for performing a mental act....or a program for a computer". F argued that the invention dealt with the arrangement of the representation of physical entities which was a technical problem and, therefore, according to *VICOM Systems Inc's Application, Re* [1987] E.P.O.R. 74, could be assumed to contribute to the known art.

Held, dismissing the appeal, that the software, by presenting information on the computer screen, was manipulating visual images. When analysing what the computer was doing when controlled by the software, rather than the manipulation of the computer by the software, it was clear that the patent came within the scope of s.1(2) of the 1977 Act.

PATENT APPLICATION NO.9204959.2 BY FUJITSU LTD, *Re* [1996] R.P.C. 511, Laddie, J., Pat Ct.

4571. Supplementary protection certificates–medicines–date of first authorisation–unnecessary to differentiate authorisations for human and veterinary use

[Council Regulation 1768/92 concerning the creation of a supplementary protection certificate for medicinal products Art.4, Art.13.]

F, the proprietor of a basic patent protecting the product cabergoline, applied for a supplementary protection certificate, SPC. First authorisation to place the product on the market in the Community for human use was a Netherlands authorisation dated October 21, 1992, but there was an earlier Italian authorisation dated January 7, 1987 for veterinary use. The examiner took the view that the duration of the SPC was determined by the date of the first authorisation in respect of the product, regardless of whether that authorisation was in respect of human or veterinary use. F sought to rely on the date of the Netherlands authorisation, submitting that the intention of Council Regulation 1768/92 required differentiation between authorisations for human and veterinary use.

Held, granting an SPC based on the Italian authorisation date, that (1) on a plain interpretation of the words of Art.13(1) of the Regulation the Italian date was the correct one to use. However, for the reasons set out in *Yamanouchi*

Pharmaceutical Co's Application, Re (Unreported, 1993) (PO) it was also necessary to have regard to the intention of the Regulation before finally deciding on its interpretation; (2) The provision in Art.4 for automatic extension of an SPC if new authorisation was granted by the Member State concerned was considered, and (3) if F's submissions were followed, different durations of protection in different Member States would result, which would clearly be contrary to the intention of the Regulation. In addition, if the Netherlands date were relied on, the holder of the patent and SPC could enjoy protection for veterinary use for a period in excess of the maximum of 15 years specified in the recitals to the Regulations. The plain meaning of Art.13(1) was the correct one.

FARMITALIA CARLO ERBA SRL'S SPC APPLICATION, *Re* [1996] R.P.C. 111, L Lewis, PO.

4572. Supplementary protection certificates–medicines–patent for combined preparation of anti-microbial agent and antibody–basic patent did not protect antibody for which SPC was claimed

[Council Regulation 1768/92 concerning the creation of a supplementary protection certificate for medicinal products Art.3.]

C applied for a supplementary protection certificate, SPC, in respect of a patent which claimed a product comprising an anti-microbial agent and an antibody as a combined preparation. The authorisation to put the antibody on the market stated that the antibody should be given in hospital, along with the appropriate antibiotics and supportive therapy. Council Regulation 1768/92 Art.3(a) required an SPC to be granted if the product was protected by a basic patent. The examiner reported that the antibody was not protected by the basic patent.

Held, rejecting the application, that (1) the patent claimed a combined preparation and did not protect the antibody per se, and (2) neither did the patent protect an application of the antibody.

CENTOCOR INC'S SPC APPLICATION, *Re* [1996] R.P.C. 118, L Lewis, PO.

4573. Supplementary protection certificates–medicines–patent holder obtained more than one product licence–new improved formulations for same compound covered by same patent–relevant date was that of first product licence

[Council Regulation 1768/92 concerning the creation of a supplementary protection certificate for medicinal products.]

AD, a patent holder, appealed against the refusal of a five year supplementary protection certificate for their medicine Budesonide in the form of a dry powder. AD first obtained a product licence for the medicine in aerosol form eight years after obtaining their patent and, after carrying out further research, developed a powdered form to be taken by inhaler for which a further product licence was obtained, 17 years after the original patent. The Comptroller of Patents' examiner ruled that for supplementary protection purposes the relevant date was that of their first product licence.

Held, dismissing the appeal, that (1) the purpose of the supplementary protection scheme under Council Regulation 1768/92 was to compensate holders of pharmaceutical patents for lost time when they could not exploit their patented medicines because health and safety investigations required to obtain the product licences were continuing. The scheme was not intended to provide general additional protection for the products of research; (2) for any particular chemical compound, the relevant date for supplementary protection was the date when its first product licence was granted rather than any subsequent dates when further licences for new formulations may have been granted. The supplementary protection scheme was not intended to protect formulation research unless the new formulation was patentable in its own right, and (3) no ECJ reference would be made because the examiner's decision was acte claire.

DRACO AB'S SPC APPLICATION, *Re* [1996] R.P.C. 417, Jacob, J., Ch D.

4574. Articles

A dangerous world for patent owners *(James Nurton)*: M.I.P. 1996, 60, 19-26. (Results of world survey of patent owners showing lack of protection or appropriate enforcement in many countries and high costs of patent protection and litigation).

Compulsory disclosure of abortive in-house experiments in UK patent actions *(Mark Finn)*: P.W. 1996, 82, 17-19. (Proposals of Patents Court that all experiments conducted must be disclosed).

Drafting claims around morality *(Derek Harms)*: E.I.P.R. 1996, 18(7), 424-425. (Validity of ethical objections to biotechnology patenting, whether "capable of industrial application" criterion could be exchanged for American "usefulness" concept and harm caused by grant of wide ranging bio patents).

EU industrial property policy: priority for patents? *(Edward Armitage)*: E.I.P.R. 1996, 18(10), 555-558. (Whether EC concern with utility models a distraction from real priority of developing Community wide patent protection at reasonable cost which would be competitive with federal US patent).

First decision on licences of right *(Andrew Inglis* and *Clive Gringras)*: C.W. 1996, 62, 17-21. (Decision of Comptroller General of Patents on terms of licence of right including sub licensing, principles on which to judge terms and royalty rates).

Grounds for revocation of European patents: C.I.P.A.J. 1996, 25(3), 198-202. (Paper prepared by UK Patent Office for submission to European Patent Office on why Art.84, requiring that claims should be supported by description, should provide grounds for opposition and revocation).

High Court patent litigation–discovery reform *(Taylor Joynson Garrett)*: I.H.L. 1996, 41 (Jun), 64-65. (Changes made by amendments to Ord.104 r.11 so as to reduce need for discovery on patent issues of infringement, validity and commercial success).

Novelty of use claims *(Robin Jacob)*: IIC 1996, 27(2), 170-179. (Novelty as applied to patentability expressed in form of series of examples and "available to the public" concept).

Novelty under the EPC and the Patents Act 1977: a unified view of Merrell Dow and Mobil *(Richard Doble)*: E.I.P.R. 1996, 18(9), 511-516. (Circumstances in which prior disclosure of product or process makes "matter" form part of "the state of the art" such that an "invention" relating to "matter" is deprived of novelty).

Of patents and professors: intellectual property, research workers and universities *(Patricia L. Loughlan)*: E.I.P.R. 1996, 18(6), 345-351. (Problems arising from conflict between intellectual property law and values of universities and research workers and whether publicly funded universities should be required to take part in monopoly based patent system).

Patenting plants around the world *(Tim Roberts)*: E.I.P.R. 1996, 18(10), 531-536. (Focus on US and European position regarding law on patentability of plants, distinguishing between plants and plant varieties, value of UPOV protection regarding plant variety rights and effect of TRIPs).

Patents and parallel trade in prescription medicines within the EU *(Ian Senior)*: P.W. 1996, 86, 26-32. (Significance of imminent ECJ judgments regarding volume and value of parallel trade).

Patents county court–ADR pilot schemes project: C.I.P.A.J. 1996, 25(5), 347-348. (Two ADR pilot schemes being introduced at Patents County Court to produce low cost fast solutions to IP disputes).

Patents online at the British Library *(Sue Ashpitel)*: Law Lib. 1996, 27(2), 84-85. (Scope and cost of patent research service).

Pharma companies challenge parallel imports: M.I.P. 1996, 60, 5-6. (Challenge by pharmaceutical companies in CFI against European Commission's decision on December 13, 1995 to reject applications from 10 Member States to maintain safeguards against parallel imports of unpatented medicines from Spain).

Prior use as prior art and evidence thereof *(Monika Auz Castro)*: IIC 1996, 27(2), 190-202. (Prior use as state of art in European patent opposition proceedings).

Proposal for a European Parliament and Council Directive (EC) on the legal protection of biotechnological inventions: IIC 1996, 27(4), 495-502. (Text of proposal).

Recent developments in technology exploitation *(Susan E. Singleton)*: L. Ex. 1996, Feb, 38-39. (Licensing of patents and know how and relevant EU competition legislation).

Report on search comparison: UK, Europe and USA *(Derek Haselden)*: C.I.P.A.J. 1996, 25(4), 250-261. (Results of exercise to assess quality of UK Patent Office searches in comparison with corresponding searches carried out by European Patent Office and United States Patent and Trade Mark Office).

Revocation of a patent due to the claims lacking support in the description *(Arthur V. Huygens)*: C.I.P.A.J. 1996, 25(9), 655-657. (European Patent Institute's March 1996 paper on whether failure to meet Art.84 requirements can be used as ground for revocation).

Software patents in the United Kingdom *(Jeremy Newton)*: Comms. L. 1996, 1(5), 202-205. (Comparison of application of s.1 of 1977 Act and EPO's guidelines to software related inventions and Pat Ct's attempt to reconcile inconsistencies between UK and EU approaches).

Software patents–who needs 'em? *(Clifford Miller)*: Comms. L. 1996, 1(4), 141-142. (Risks and problems for software developers posed by extension of patent protection).

The demise of old-style patent litigation *(Jeremy Phillips)*: M.I.P. 1996, 60, 2. (Reasons for unfashionability of litigating large patent infringement cases).

The future of patent litigation in England and Wales–the impact of the Woolf proposals *(David Barron)*: P.W. 1996, 85, 15-23.

The future of the European patent system *(Paul Braendli)*: IIC 1995, 26(6), 813-828. (Developments at European Patent Office 1973-1995 and future prospects for international cooperation).

The model myth: the relevance of the proposal EC utility model system to the United Kingdom *(Margaret Llewelyn)*: P.W. 1996, 79, 32-38. (CEC's Green Paper on protection of utility models and possible effect on UK patent system).

The new draft Biotechnology Directive *(Nigel Jones)*: E.I.P.R. 1996, 18(6), 363-365. (Amendments intended to overcome Parliament's objections to former proposal include specific exclusion of patents for human body parts and germ line gene therapy and revised ethical criteria for genetically engineered animals).

The new technology transfer block exemption–a whiter shade of grey? *(Justine Antill* and *Michael Burdon)*: P.W. 1996, 80, 14-21. (Theory behind Regulation, general format of block exemption, summary of exempted and non exempted clauses, market share limits, territorial provisions and application of s.44 of 1977 Act).

Towards a European utility model *(Jeremy Newton)*: E.I.P.R. 1996, 18(8), 446-449. (EC Green Paper on protection of utility models in the single market (COM(95) 370), national systems of protection, problems with current structure, advantages of utility model systems and need to harmonise national laws).

Translations–costs and compromise: C.I.P.A.J. 1996, 25(3), 177-190. (Report by CIPA committee on procedure for requiring translation of specification of European patents into official language of each designated state at grant stage and suggested alternative procedures).

Trends in intellectual property damages in the US and UK *(Richard Boulton* and *Mark Bezant)*: I.C. Lit. 1995/96, Dec/Jan, 22-25. (Analysis of damages for patent infringement).

UK Patent Office: new section 16 publication procedures *(Bridie Collier)*: C.I.P.A.J. 1996, 25(8), 564-565. (Introduction of five week cycle for publication of patent applications).

4575. Books

A User's Guide to Patents. Paperback: £35.00. ISBN 0-406-01307-1. Butterworth Law.

Dulken, S. van–British Patents of Invention, 1617-1977. Key resource series. Paperback: £30.00. ISBN 0-7123-0817-2. British Library (Science Reference and Information Service).

PENOLOGY

4576. Administrative decision making–prisoner serving discretionary life sentence released on licence–recall by Secretary of State–whether confirmation by Parole Board was lawful–test to be applied when considering recall

[Criminal Justice Act 1991 s.34, s.39.]

W, a prisoner serving a discretionary life sentence for buggery and indecent assault, who had been released on licence but was subsequently recalled by the Secretary of State for the Home Department after revocation of the licence under the Criminal Justice Act 1991 s.39(2), appealed against the refusal of his application for judicial review of the Parole Board's decision confirming his recall. W argued that the board's confirmation denied him a fair hearing, presented a risk of bias and compromised its position as an independent review body. He further argued that it was not appropriate to apply the same test when considering a review under s.39, namely the risk of serious injury to the public if a prisoner was not recalled, as that prescribed by the Criminal Justice Act 1991 s.34 when considering a person's initial release.

Held, dismissing the appeal, that under s.39(2) the Secretary of State for the Home Department was not required to consult the Parole Board, whose confirmation procedure could not be criticised for unfairness as it was a provisional step subsequent to the Secretary of State's decision. The Board was not limited to considering the Secretary of State's reasons for W's recall. Although there was no statutory test laid down in s.39, the public safety test in s.34 was equally applicable.

R. v. PAROLE BOARD, *ex p.* WATSON [1996] 1 W.L.R. 906, Sir Thomas Bingham, M.R., CA.

4577. Juvenile offenders–prisons

YOUNG OFFENDER INSTITUTION (AMENDMENT) RULES 1996, SI 1996 1662; made under the Prison Act 1952 s.47. In force: July 22, 1996; £1.10.

These Rules amend the Young Offender Institution Rules 1988 (SI 1988 1422). They clarify the definition of inmate for the purposes of the 1988 Rules and para.2 corrects a wrong reference in r.6; make revised provision for the regime activities in a young offender institution; extend the regime day and expands the scope of what are to be regarded as regime activities; make new provision for physical education and revised provision for time in the open air for female inmates aged 21 and over; enable the establishment of regimes providing for stricter order and discipline and which emphasise strict standards of dress, appearance and conduct, subject to certain safeguards; enable the Secretary of State to direct when an inmate should be searched; create two new disciplinary offences relating to alcohol; make revised provision for the appointment of the chairman and vice chairman of a board of visitors for a young offender institution and for the making of reports by such a board to the Secretary of State; introduce new provision for training for members of a board to the Secretary of State; introduce new provision for training for members of a board of visitors and for their suspension from membership on grounds of suspected serious misconduct; and introduce new provision for the termination of office of a chairman or vice chairman of a board of visitors.

4578. Parole–decision letter of Parole Board–inadequate reasons given

[Criminal Justice Act 1991 s.34; Parole Board Rules 1992 r.15.]

L applied for judicial review of the Parole Board's decision not to order his immediate release on licence under the Criminal Justice Act 1991 s.34(4). He was serving a life sentence for rape, buggery and indecent assault. His sentence was originally set at 10 years to expire in 1986 when his first Parole Board review took place. Meanwhile L had begun a relationship with a female probation officer, B. She resigned from the Probation Service and their relationship continued, but in June 1988 B informed L that she had met another man whom she wished to marry. Following L's transfer to open conditions he unsuccessfully attempted to contact B through friends. She then wrote to the prison governor indicating that she felt endangered by L's attempts to contact her. As a result, L was returned to closed conditions, where he remained until a further Parole Board hearing in June 1993. The decision letter which followed indicated that the panel considered that L remained a risk until his progress could be tested in less severe conditions and recommended that he be transferred to a category D prison. L sought an order of certiorari to quash that decision on the grounds, inter alia, that the reasons set out in the letter were so defective as to invalidate the decision.

Held, allowing the application, that the decision did not comply with the requirement under the Parole Board Rules 1992 r.15(2) that adequate reasons be given. The Panel had referred to L's background history of difficulties in relationships with women but there was no reference to this in the papers before them, nor was B mentioned specifically. If the Panel had felt any concern about whether L had come to terms with the ending of that relationship, they should have said so. L had already gone six years past the expiry date of his tariff period and had received universally favourable reports. In the circumstances, the reasons of the Panel were grossly deficient.

R. v. PAROLE BOARD, *ex p.* LODOMEZ [1994] C.O.D. 525, Leggatt, L.J., QBD.

4579. Parole–offender serving longer than normal fixed term sentence under the Criminal Justice Act 1991–right to oral hearing before Parole Board

[Criminal Justice Act 1991 s.2, s.34.]

M applied for judicial review of a Parole Board decision to deny him an oral hearing when deciding his suitability for parole. M was serving five years' imprisonment for indecent assault, imposed as a sentence over and above the normal limit under the Criminal Justice Act 1991 s.2(2)(b). He contended that, as at the time of the Board's decision he had already served the two and a half year punitive element of his sentence, he was now into the preventive phase and the board should have only considered whether continued detention was necessary for the protection of the public.

Held, dismissing the application, that apart from the provisions relating to discretionary life sentences under s.34(1)(b) of the 1991 Act, there was no legal requirement to set determinate lengths to the deterrent or retributive elements of a sentence. In M's case the sentence consisted of two parts: a sentence under s.2(2)(a) deemed to be commensurate with the seriousness of his offence and a longer than normal term under s.2(2)(b) to protect the public, as determined by the opinion of the court. This was not the same as the test provided for parole applications by discretionary lifers where, under s.34(4)(b), it was for the Parole Board to decide whether detention was still needed for public protection. Bare parole review provisions could be added to in the interests of fairness as required by those prisoners, *R. v. Parole Board, ex p. Wilson* [1992] Q.B. 740, [1992] C.L.Y. 3643 and *R. v. Secretary of State for the Home Department, ex p. Doody* [1994] 1 A.C. 531, [1993] C.L.Y. 1213 considered. However, an offender sentenced under s.2(2)(b) had no right to release, even if the public protection element of their sentence could be identified. To grant an oral hearing to M would be illogical and risked creating injustice for other determinate sentence prisoners not sentenced under s.2(2)(b).

R. v. PAROLE BOARD, *ex p.* MANSELL [1996] C.O.D. 327, Otton, L.J., QBD.

4580. Prisoners–wages–deductions

[Prisoners' Earnings Act 1996.]

HM Prison Service issued a press release entitled *Prisoners' Earnings Act receives Royal Assent* (Press release 24n/96), published on July 18, 1996. The Prisoners' Earnings Act provides a framework for deductions which may be made from the wages of prisoners who are participating in enhanced wages schemes or who are working for outside employers. The Act allows governors to make deductions from wages provided they are used for specified purposes. These are payments to voluntary organisations concerned with victim support or crime prevention; contributions towards the prisoner's own upkeep; contributions to the upkeep of the prisoner's dependents; or payments into an investment account for the prisoner's benefit on release.

4581. Prisoners rights–legal advice–prisoner's cardphone telephone calls monitored–not amounting to ultra vires interference with rights

[Prison Act 1952 s.47.]

K, a prisoner, sought leave to move for judicial review by way of a declaration that stipulations contained in a circular relating to the monitoring and use of cardphones in prisons impeded the free flow of communication between the solicitor and his prisoner client and were outside the powers of the Prison Act 1952 s.47. K complained, inter alia, that cardphone telephone calls between him and his solicitor in the course of preparing his defence were recorded, monitored to an unknown extent and that the confidentiality of those conversations was not guaranteed. K also complained that he had been unable to call a mobile phone used solely by his solicitor.

Held, refusing leave to move for judicial review, that the prison service was only entitled to interfere with the free access of a prisoner to his legal advisers and with the confidentiality of such discussions to the extent necessary to maintain security. Notices by the cardphones warned that conversations would be recorded. Since there was no evidence to show that the cardphone system was used as an excuse to reduce prisoners' access to legal advisers through the official telephone system, visits and letters, the monitoring could not be described as ultra vires interference with prisoner's rights. Nor was the prison's policy of prohibiting calls to mobile telephone numbers, which by their nature were difficult to monitor, either ultra vires or *Wednesbury* unreasonable.

R. v. SECRETARY OF STATE FOR THE HOME DEPARTMENT, *ex p.* KANIOGLULARI [1994] C.O.D. 526, Latham, J., DC.

4582. Prisoners rights–prevention of physical contact–prisoner and his family and lawyers separated by glass screen lawful–no breach of civil rights or confidentiality

[Prison Act 1952 s.47; Prison Rules 1964 r.37.]

O, and another in a joined case, applied for judicial review of the imposition by the Secretary of State at two prisons of a "closed conditions" regime on visits to Category A prisoners who presented an exceptional escape risk. The conditions related to visits by the prisoner's family and lawyers and prevented physical contact by a glass screen. O contended that the imposition of a physical barrier between the lawyer and the prisoner amounted to breach of a prisoner's civil rights to which they were entitled unless withdrawn either expressly or by implication. There was also a breach of privilege in relation to an interview between a prisoner and his lawyer by the requirement to give reasons in advance for an interview which was not "closed". O also contended that a prisoner retained the right to open family visits as part of his residual liberty as a citizen which was not taken from him by imprisonment nor the Prison Act 1952 s.47(1).

Held, dismissing the applications, that (1) there was a statutory power to regulate the conduct of prison visits implied in the 1952 Act s.47(1); (2) the facilities provided for visits between the prisoner and his lawyer had to be reasonable within the Prison Rules 1964 r.37(1). All the circumstances had to be considered, including the category of the prisoner and the type of contraband being smuggled into the prison, balanced against the prisoner's right to confidential communication with his lawyer. In this case the facilities were reasonable when considering that they applied only to Category A prisoners and in the light of recent escapes and evidence of the quantity of contraband currently entering the prison and (3) the effects of the loss of physical contact on the prisoner's family were regrettable. However they did not outweigh the security considerations and the need to protect the public.

R. v. SECRETARY OF STATE FOR THE HOME DEPARTMENT, *ex p.* O'DHUIBHIR; R. v. SECRETARY OF STATE FOR THE HOME DEPARTMENT, *ex p.* O'BRIEN (1996) 8 Admin. L.R. 121, Rose, L.J., QBD.

4583. Prisoners rights–urine tests–detection of drug abuse in prisons–Home Secretary's powers ultra vires–whether its random nature breached the European Convention on Human Rights 1950

[European Convention on Human Rights 1950 Art.6, Art.8; Prison Act 1952 s.16A, s.47; Prison Rules 1964 r.46A.]

T sought leave to move for judicial review of the Secretary of State's decision to introduce random urine sampling of prisoners and a notice of the Governor of Risley Prison to introduce mandatory drug testing. T sought to have the notice quashed and also sought mandamus to require the Secretary of State to withdraw the mandatory scheme. T argued that the notice was ultra vires. T further argued that the random element of the notice was ultra vires and was in breach of the European Convention of Human Rights 1950.

Held, dismissing the application, that (1) the Prison Act 1952 s.47 gave the Secretary of State an extremely wide power to make rules on the management of prisons. Section 47 of the 1952 Act could be used to bring into operation s.16A of the 1952 Act, which dealt with drug testing, via the introduction of the Prison Rules 1994 r.46A; (2) the random element of the testing was not irrational nor was it ultra vires, because it was acting as a deterrent. Section 16A conferred a general power which was not restricted in such a way, and (3) the testing did not infringe Art.8 of the European Convention as testing was in the interests of all prisoners generally. Neither was Art.6 infringed as random testing did not amount to self incrimination.

R. v. SECRETARY OF STATE FOR THE HOME DEPARTMENT, *ex p.* TREMAYNE, Trans. Ref: CO/3550/95, May 2, 1996, Buxton, J., QBD.

4584. Prisoners' Earnings Act 1996 (c.33)

An Act to authorise deductions from or levies on prisoners' earnings; and to provide for the application of such deductions or levies.

This Act received Royal Assent on July 18, 1996.

4585. Prisons–administration

PRISON (AMENDMENT) RULES 1996, SI 1996 1663; made under the Prison Act 1952 s.47. In force: July 22, 1996; £1.10.

These Rules amend the Prison Rules 1964 (SI 1964 388), as amended. They make revised provision for physical education and time in the open air for prisoners; enable the Secretary of State to direct when a prisoner should be searched; create two new disciplinary offences relating to alcohol; make revised provision for the appointment of the chairman and vice chairman of a board of visitors for a prison and for the making of reports by such a board to the Secretary of State; introduce new provision for training for members of a board of visitors and for their suspension from membership on grounds of suspected serious misconduct; and introduce new provision for the termination of office of a chairman or vice chairman of a board of visitors.

4586. Prisons–closure–HM Prison Oxford

CLOSURE OF PRISONS (H.M. PRISON OXFORD) ORDER 1996, SI 1996 2126; made under the Prisons Act 1952 s.37. In force: September 7, 1996; £0.65.

This Order provides for the closure of HM Prison Oxford on September 7, 1996.

4587. Young offender institutions–closure

CLOSURE OF PRISONS (HM YOUNG OFFENDER INSTITUTION FINNAMORE WOOD) ORDER 1996, SI 1996 1551; made under the Prisons Act 1952 s.37. In force: September 1, 1996; £0.65.

This Order provides for the closure of HM Young Offender Institution Finnamore Wood on September 1, 1996.

4588. Articles

Capital punishment: a dead duck? *(Helen L. Conway)*: Criminologist 1996, 20(3), 130-136. (Whether death penalty can be justified in murder cases in terms of deterrence, or on grounds of either incapacitation of dangerous individuals or retribution).

Continuity and change in the criminal law *(Lord Taylor of Gosforth)*: J.P. 1996, 160(11), 190-192. (Full transcript of Lord Chief Justice's address to King's College London on March 6, 1996 on recent changes to criminal law and sentencing and statement issued in response by Home Office).

Drugs and imprisonment: challenging misconceptions and some general observations *(Phil Hassan)*: Prison Serv. J. 1996, 107, 2-6. (Misconceptions concerning drug users and how prison staff can best be trained to assist inmates overcome problems of drug abuse).

Drugs and violence in a young offender establishment *(Sarah Skett)*: Prison Serv. J. 1996, 106, 9-13. (Findings of research projects on levels of drug use and its effects, patterns of violence and attendant punishment).

Howard's stance on crime unwelcome: S.J. 1996, 140(14), 343-344. (Criminal lawyers and prison reform groups criticise Home Secretary Michael Howard's White Paper *Protecting the Public* recommending minimum sentences for certain crimes).

Longer than commensurate sentences *(D. A. Thomas)*: Arch. News 1996, 5, 5-8. (Four main criticisms raised by operation of s.2(2)(b) of 1991 Act which allows imposition of longer than normal sentences in order to protect public).

Maximum security, zero tolerance *(Gary Slapper)*: N.L.J. 1996, 146(6749), 914. (Whether law is best means of dealing with social problems in light of rising crime, rising fear of crime and increase in prison population).

Mixed-offence groupwork: a practitioner's viewpoint *(Dave Morrison)*: J.P. 1996, 160(10), 167-168. (Advantages of rehabilitation programmes for offenders which consist of group of offenders with mixed offences).

Playing tag *(Alan Berg)*: Magistrate 1996, 52(5), 108-109. (Benefits of electronic tagging orders despite criticisms of pilot schemes).

Prisoners released on licence *(Martin Gosling)*: Pol. J. 1996, 69(2), 147-148. (CJA 1991 reforms to arrangements for release of sentenced prisoners, introduction of concept of early release and national standard for probation service when dealing with offenders released on licence).

Rehabilitation in prisons: a study of Grendon Underwood *(Elaine Genders* and *Elaine Player)*: C.L.P. 1993, 46(2), 235-256. (Empirical research into prison's therapeutic regime).

Rule 47(21)–the survival of the prison catch all *(Peter M. Quinn)*: Prison Serv. J. 1996, 105, 5-8. (Arguments for abolition of widely drafted provision concerning prison disciplinary offences).

Services for mentally disturbed offenders: Howard Journal 1996, 35(2), 183-184. (NACRO policy reports on how prison service and resettlement service should deal with mentally disturbed prisoners).

Stick or carrot? *(Dick Whitfield)*: Magistrate 1996, 52(2), 36-37. (Role of probation service in developing effective community based penalties for offenders).

The future of the probation service: the case for the compulsive understander *(Cedric Fullwood)*: Probat. J. 1996, 43(3), 118-126. (Alternative policy directions for probation service and whether concept of probation as corrective system should be abandoned and replaced by more community based approach).

The law concerning supervision orders imposed in criminal proceedings *(Charles Bell)*: J.P. 1996, 160(33), 638-640. (Legislative framework on supervision orders, relevant statutory procedures and variation and revocation of orders).

The state of our prisons research: an international perspective *(Roy King)*: Prison Serv. J. 1996, 104, Supp R & D 8-9. (Comparative study of strategic operational demands placed on prison service, increasing levels of incarceration and increase in prisons research).

Users' rights and the probation service: some opportunities and obstacles *(Bob Broad* and *David Denney)*: Howard Journal 1996, 35(1), 61-77. (Proposals for, and possible consequences of, extension of legal and social rights for users of probation service).

Why new "guideline" judgments are needed after the Criminal Justice Act 1991 *(Gavin Dingwall)*: Arch. News 1996, 2, 5-7. (Need for new sentencing judgments which reflect fundamental changes in 1991 Act).

4589. Books

Creighton, Simon; King, Vicky–Prisoners and the Law. Paperback: £45.00. ISBN 0-406-02514-2. Butterworth Law.

Hood, Roger–The Death Penalty. Hardback: £40.00. ISBN 0-19-826282-5. Paperback: £12.99. ISBN 0-19-826281-7. Clarendon Press.

Oxley, Deborah–Convict Maids. Studies in Australian History, 23. Hardback: £40.00. ISBN 0-521-44131-5. Cambridge University Press.

Shoemaker, Donald Joseph–International Handbook on Juvenile Justice. Hardback: £79.95. ISBN 0-313-28895-X. Greenwood Press.

PENSIONS

4590. Civil servants–Hong Kong

HONG KONG (OVERSEAS PUBLIC SERVANTS) (PENSION SUPPLEMENTS) ORDER 1996, SI 1996 1294; made under the Hong Kong (Overseas Public Servants) Act 1996 s.4. In force: July 1, 1996; £3.20.

This Order makes provision for certain supplementary payments to overseas public servants and their dependents if their income from Hong Kong service, from dependant's pensions, or the value of pensionable officers' gratuities is significantly reduced due to the fall in exchange rates between the HKD and GBP.

4591. Contracting out–occupational pensions–Civil Service

CONTRACTING OUT (ADMINISTRATION OF CIVIL SERVICE PENSION SCHEMES) ORDER 1996, SI 1996 1746; made under the Deregulation and Contracting Out Act 1994 s.69, s.79. In force: July 5, 1996; £1.10.

This Order enables the Minister for the Civil Service and other Ministers and office-holders who have functions in relation to the administration of Civil Service Pension Schemes under the Superannuation Act 1972 to authorise private contractors to carry out those functions on their behalf to such extent as is specified in the authorisation.

4592. Contracting out–pensions

SOCIAL SECURITY (CONTRACTING-OUT AND QUALIFYING EARNINGS FACTOR) REGULATIONS 1996, SI 1996 2477; made under the Pension Schemes Act 1993 s.48A, s.182. In force: April 6, 1997; £0.65.

These Regulations modify the application of the Social Security Contributions and Benefits Act 1992 s.44(5) (Category A retirement pension) in relation to an earner who has earnings in a tax year beginning on or after April 6, 1997, part of which are in respect of contracted-out employment and part of which are not, or an earner in respect of whom minimum contributions are paid for part of a tax year. The calculation of the qualifying earnings factor in relation to such a tax year, so that entitlement to additional pension is not affected, is modified.

4593. Divorce–financial provision

DIVORCE ETC. (PENSIONS) REGULATIONS 1996, SI 1996 1676; made under the Matrimonial Causes Act 1973 s.25D. In force: August 1, 1996; £1.55.

These Regulations make provision in relation to orders for ancillary relief in proceedings for divorce, judicial separation or nullity of marriage, so far as they relate to the pension right of a party to the marriage. They provide for: the valuation of pension rights by the court, notices of change of circumstance to be provided by the pension scheme to the party without pension rights, or by that party to the scheme, information concerning the value of pension rights to be provided by the pension scheme to its member, and the recovery by the pension scheme of the costs of complying with these Regulations.

4594. Divorce–overlapping of pensions benefits–awarded by different Member States–whether benefits of the "same kind" and exempt from national rules of overlapping–European Union

[Council Regulation 1408/71 on the application of social security schemes to employed persons and their families moving within the Community; Treaty of Rome 1957 Art.177.]

S worked in Germany for 11 years. After marrying a Belgian, S worked in Belgium for seven years and her husband worked there for 33 years. They separated in 1981 and divorced in 1991. In 1981 at the age of 60, S received a Belgian pension as a single person based on her employment in Belgium. At the age of 65, S received a German pension based on her employment in Germany. In 1991, the Belgian pensions office recalculated her pension entitlement, applying national rules against the overlapping of pensions, and granted her a pension as a divorcee. S challenged that decision, arguing that pursuant to Council Regulation 1408/71 Art.12(2), the overlapping rules could only be applied where they would result in the grant of a higher pension than that calculated under Art.46 of the Regulation. S sought calculation of her pension under Art.46 for comparative purposes, on the grounds that the Belgian divorcee's pension and the German pension to which she was entitled constituted benefits of the "same kind" and were thus exempt from national rules on overlapping unless they exceeded the amount calculated under Art.46. The Arbeitsrechtsbank Antwerp asked the ECJ for a preliminary ruling under the Treaty of Rome 1957 Art.177.

Held, that the retirement pension of one Member State granted on the basis of periods of insurance personally completed by the person concerned, with the aim of ensuring that the worker had adequate income from the date of her retirement, was not a benefit of the same kind as the retirement pension for a divorcee of another Member State, which was calculated on the basis of periods of insurance completed by that person's former spouse with the aim of compensating the recipient for the loss of access to the former spouse's income. Thus, Art.12(2) and Art.46a of Council Regulation 1408/71 did not apply to such benefits to exclude the national rules against overlapping.

SCHMIDT v. RIJKSDIENST VOOR PENSIOENEN (C98/94) [1995] All E.R. (EC) 833, P Jann (President), ECJ.

4595. Earnings cap–indexation

RETIREMENT BENEFITS SCHEMES (INDEXATION OF EARNINGS CAP) ORDER 1996, SI 1996 2951; made under the Income and Corporation Taxes Act 1988 s.590C. £0.65.

The earnings cap for the year of assessment 1997-98 specified by this Order is £84,000.

4596. Expatriates

OVERSEAS SERVICE (PENSIONS SUPPLEMENT) (AMENDMENT) REGULATIONS 1996, SI 1996 1476; made under the Pensions (Increase) Act 1971 s.11, s.11A, s.12, s.13. In force: July 1, 1996; £1.10.

These Regulations amend the Overseas Service (Pensions Supplement) Regulations 1995 (SI 1995 238) which provide for payment of inflation-proofing supplements on pensions paid to officers who have served overseas. The amendments relate to the allocation of pensions to spouses or dependents following the death of the claimant and the method of calculation of the total overseas increase and the position when a person receives several pensions.

4597. Extra statutory concessions–lump sum payments

The Inland Revenue issued a press release entitled *Small lump sum retirement benefits schemes: extra statutory concession*, published on October 11, 1996. A new extra statutory concession allows members of certain small lump sum retirement benefit schemes who are also contributing to personal pensions or retirement annuities to maintain their pensions provided they give up their entitlement to the lump sum benefits.

4598. Final salary schemes–contracted out schemes–national insurance contributions

SOCIAL SECURITY (REDUCED RATES OF CLASS 1 CONTRIBUTIONS) (SALARY RELATED CONTRACTED-OUT SCHEMES) ORDER 1996, SI 1996 1054; made under the Pension Schemes Act 1993 s.42. In force: April 6, 1997; £0.65.

This Order is made as a consequence of a review by the Secretary of State under the Pension Schemes Act 1993 s.42 following a report by the Government Actuary in relation to the contracted out percentages under s.41 of the 1993 Act. It specifies with effect from April 6, 1997 the contracted out percentages to be deducted from primary and secondary Class 1 contributions in respect of members of salary related contracted out schemes. A consequential provision altering the percentage specified in para.2(3)(a) of Sch.4 to the 1993 Act (priority in bankruptcy: calculation of employer's contribution to an occupational pension scheme) is made by Art.3 of this Order. In accordance with s.42 of the 1993 Act, a copy of a report by the Government Actuary on the percentages which, in his opinion, are required to reflect the cost of providing benefits of an actuarial value equivalent to that of the benefits which, under s.48A (effect of reduced contributions and rebates on social security benefits), are forgone by or in respect of members of salary related contracted out schemes, together with a copy of a report by the Secretary of State, was laid before Parliament with a draft of this Order. These reports are contained in a Command Paper published by Her Majesty's Stationery Office (Cm.3221).

4599. Guaranteed minimum pension

GUARANTEED MINIMUM PENSIONS INCREASE ORDER 1996, SI 1996 485; made under the Pension Schemes Act 1993 s.109. In force: April 6, 1996; £0.65.

This Order specifies three per cent as the percentage by which that part of any guaranteed minimum pension attributable to earnings factors for the tax year 1988-89 and subsequent years and payable by occupational pension schemes is to be increased. Under the Pension Schemes Act 1993 s.109(3) the percentage to be specified is the actual percentage increase in the general level of prices in the period under review or 3 per cent, whichever is less.

4600. Human rights–state pension payable to invalided public servant–no enhancement for illness–state obligation–right to enhanced pension amounted to a civil right

[European Convention on Human Rights 1950 Art.6.]

L claimed entitlement to an enhanced ordinary pension on the grounds that he had been invalided out of the Italian Carabinieri by two illnesses. L was granted an enhancement for two years on account of one of his illnesses, but not for the other. L alleged a violation of the European Convention on Human Rights 1950 Art.6(1).

Held, allowing the claim, that there had been a violation of Art.6(1). Notwithstanding the public law features of the employment and pension relationship between L and the state, the obligation to pay a pension to a public servant in accordance with the regulation in force was akin to the obligation on a private individual. The right to receive an enhanced ordinary pension was to be regarded as a civil right.

LOMBARDO v. ITALY (1996) 21 E.H.R.R. 188, R Ryssdal (President), ECHR.

4601. Indexation

PENSIONS INCREASE (REVIEW) ORDER 1996, SI 1996 800; made under the Social Security Pensions Act 1975 s.59. In force: April 8, 1996; £1.10.

This Order prescribes the increase in the rate of public service pensions, deferred lump sums, and reductions in respect of guaranteed minimum pension.

4602. Maladministration–pensions–trustees' exercise of discretion to award lump sum payment to cohabitee of deceased–whether Pensions Ombudsman entitled to finding of maladministration–personal liability of trustee to pay compensation for pecuniary loss and distress

W, a former trustee of a pension scheme, appealed against a finding of the Pensions Ombudsman that the trustees' decision to award a lump sum payment to S, the cohabitee of a deceased member of the scheme, H, constituted maladministration. H had nominated his son and daughter as recipients of the lump sum payable in the event of his death, but the trustees had exercised their discretion to make a payment of £80,000 to S and establish a trust fund in respect of a further £60,000, with S to receive the income and the capital from the fund to be shared equally between H's two children in the event of S's death. The Ombudsman found that the trustees had exercised their discretion unlawfully since, on the evidence, S was dependent upon H out of choice rather than necessity. The trustees were ordered to pay compensation of £500 each to the son and daughter for pecuniary loss and distress.

Held, dismissing the appeal, that the Pensions Ombudsman was entitled to conclude that S was not financially dependent on H and that consequently the trustees' decision did constitute maladministration. However, as W was no longer a trustee, it was wrong to make him personally liable for inconvenience and distress, particularly as the trust deed provided that personal liability should only arise in cases of dishonesty or wilful breach. Such a payment should only be made from the trust fund.

WILD v. PENSIONS OMBUDSMAN; SUB NOM. WILD v. SMITH [1996] C.O.D. 412, Carnwath, J., QBD.

4603. Money purchase schemes–contracted out schemes–national insurance–contributions

SOCIAL SECURITY (REDUCED RATES OF CLASS 1 CONTRIBUTIONS AND REBATES) (MONEY PURCHASE CONTRACTED-OUT SCHEMES) ORDER

1996, SI 1996 1055; made under the Pension Schemes Act 1993 s.42B. In force: April 6, 1997; £1.10.

This Order specified the appropriate flat rate percentage and the appropriate age related percentages in respect of members of money purchase contracted out schemes. In accordance with s.42B of the 1993 Act, a copy of a report by the Government Actuary on the percentages which, in his opinion, are required so as to reflect the cost of providing benefits of an actuarial value equivalent to that the benefits which, under s.48A (effect of reduced contributions and rebates on social security benefits), are forgone by or in respect of members of contracted out money purchase schemes, together with a copy of a report by the Secretary of State, was laid before Parliament with a draft of this Order. These reports are contained in a Command Paper published by Her Majesty's Stationery Office (Cm.3221)

4604. Occupational pensions–application to transfer interest to new scheme–whether application was valid when new scheme was not in existence–trustees' duties to beneficiary

[Pension Schemes Act 1993 s.95, s.99, s.151.]

HL, trustees of a pension scheme, appealed under the Pension Schemes Act 1993 s.151 (4), against the Pensions Ombudsman's decision that HL had failed to transfer F's interest in the scheme to another pension scheme on F's request, as required by s.99(2). HL argued that F's purported request for the transfer was not a valid application under s.95.

Held, allowing the appeal, that (1) the Pensions Ombudsman had made an error by treating a letter from F to HL as a valid application for transfer. The option could only be exercised if there was another occupational pension scheme in existence into which the funds could be transferred. F's letter referred to a new scheme which had not yet been set up and (2) F's contention that his claim could be saved because HL had failed in his duty as a trustee to inform the beneficiary of his rights, and that his letter was not a valid application, was dismissed. This would go beyond the trustees' duty to give information to the beneficiary by showing him documents. It was up to the beneficiary to follow the correct statutory procedure in the exercise of his statutory rights.

HAMAR v. PENSIONS OMBUDSMAN; SUB NOM. HAMAR v. FRENCH [1996] O.P.L.R. 55, Collins, J., QBD.

4605. Occupational pensions–armed forces–committees

WAR PENSIONS COMMITTEES (AMENDMENT) REGULATIONS 1996, SI 1996 1790; made under the Social Security Act 1989 s.25, s.29; and the Social Security Contributions and Benefits Act 1992 s.175. In force: Reg.2(5)(7)(10): August 5, 1996; Remainder: April 1, 1997; £1.10.

These Regulations make further provision for the constitution of War Pensions Committees as a result of the further changes to the structure of local government in England and Wales. They also adjust the areas of the Committees which cover the West Midlands, and change the name of the West Midlands, Warwickshire and Northamptonshire Committee.

4606. Occupational pensions–armed forces–disabled persons–death

NAVAL, MILITARY AND AIR FORCES ETC. (DISABLEMENT AND DEATH) SERVICE PENSIONS AMENDMENT ORDER 1996, SI 1996 732; made under the Naval and Marine Pay and Pensions Act 1865 s.3; the Pensions and Yeomanry Pay Act 1884 s.2; the Air Force (Constitution) Act 1917 s.2; and the Social Security (Miscellaneous Provisions) Act 1977 s.12, s.24. In force: April 1, 1996; £3.20.

This Order further amends the Naval, Military and Air Forces etc. (Disablement and Death) Service Pensions Order 1983 (SI 1983 883) (the principal Order) which makes provision for pensions and other awards in respect of disablement or death due to service in the naval, military and Air Forces during the First World War and after September 2, 1939. Article 2 of this Order raises the maximum amount of annual earnings which may be received by a disabled person while he is deemed to be unemployable for the purposes of unemployability allowances under Art.18 of the principle Order. Article 3 increases the amount of a widow's pension payable under Art.29 of the principal Order. Article 4 makes an amendment to Art.42 of the principal Order which is consequential on the Pensions Act 1995 s.168 which provides for the restoration of a war widow's pension on the termination of a subsequent marriage or judicial separation of the parties to such a marriage. Article 5 substitutes tables in Sch.1 and Sch.2 to the principal Order, thereby varying the rates of retired pay, pensions, gratuities and allowances in respect of disablement or death due to service in the armed forces.

4607. Occupational pensions–armed forces–disabled persons–death

NAVAL, MILITARY AND AIR FORCES ETC. (DISABLEMENT AND DEATH) SERVICE PENSIONS AMENDMENT (NO.2) ORDER 1996, SI 1996 1638; made under the Naval and Marine Pay and Pensions Act 1865 s.3; the Pensions and Yeomanry Pay Act 1884 s.2; the Air Force (Constitution) Act 1917 s.2; and the Social Security (Miscellaneous Provisions) Act 1977 s.12, s.24. In force: July 29, 1996; £1.55.

This Order amends the Naval, Military and Air Forces Etc. (Disablement and Death) Service Pensions Order 1983 (SI 1983 883), so as to bring within its scope pensions payable as a result of death or disablement of members of the armed forces of the Crown in right of the United Kingdom due to service before the First World War or between September 30, 1921 and September 2, 1939. It is made in consequence of a transfer of responsibilities for these pensions from the Ministry of Defence to the Department of Social Security.

4608. Occupational pensions–armed forces–disabled persons–death

NAVAL, MILITARY AND AIR FORCES ETC. (DISABLEMENT AND DEATH) SERVICE PENSIONS AMENDMENT (NO.3) ORDER 1996, SI 1996 2882; made under the Naval and Maritime Pay and Pensions Act 1865 s.3; the Pensions and Yeomanry Pay Act 1884 s.2; the Air Force (Constitution) Act 1917 s.2; and the Social Security (Miscellaneous Provisions) Act 1977 s.12, s.24. In force: December 20, 1996; £1.95.

This Order amends the Naval, Military and Air Forces Etc (Disablement and Death) Service Pensions Order 1983 (SI 1983 883) so as to make clear which pensions, allowances and supplements are required to be claimed expressly, to provide for claims to be made through certain authorised agents and to provide for claims to be treated as being made on earlier dates in specified circumstances. It also makes minor corrections to the titles to certain articles in consequence of changes in their scope by earlier amending Orders.

4609. Occupational pensions–armed forces–widower's pension–equal treatment under EC law–time limits–meaning of equivalent claim

[Treaty of Rome 1957 Art.119.]

H claimed that, in refusing to pay him a widower's pension in respect of his wife's death, the MoD had acted in breach of the Treaty of Rome 1957 Art.119. H's wife served in the armed forces from 1953 to her retirement in 1973. She died in 1979. H pursued his claim for a widower's pension with various individuals in correspondence but did not commence legal proceedings until 1994. His claim was rejected by the industrial tribunal as being time-barred.

Held, dismissing the appeal, that (1) the effect of the judgment in *Barber v. Guardian Royal Exchange Assurance Group Ltd* [1990] I.R.L.R. 240, [1990] C.L.Y. 1915 was that the direct effect of Art.119 might be relied upon for the purpose of claiming equal treatment in occupational pensions, but only in relation to benefits payable in respect of periods of employment subsequent to May 17, 1990, unless the applicant had launched legal proceedings before that date or raised an equivalent claim under the applicable national law. An "equivalent claim" meant a claim equivalent to legal proceedings, not the mere assertion of a claim through correspondence; (2) even if H had raised an equivalent claim prior to May 17, 1990 the effect of the judgment in *Defrenne v. Sabena* [1976] E.C.R. 455, [1976] C.L.Y. 1164 was that, except for those who had already brought legal proceedings or made an equivalent claim, the direct effect of Art.119 could not be relied upon to support claims concerning pay periods prior to April 8, 1976, and (3) in any event, the direct effect of Art.119 could not be relied upon to claim entitlement to an occupational pension in connection with periods of employment served prior to January 1, 1973, the date when the UK acceded to the EC Treaty.

HOWARD v. MINISTRY OF DEFENCE [1995] I.C.R. 1074, Mummery, J., EAT.

4610. Occupational pensions–audited accounts

OCCUPATIONAL PENSION SCHEMES (REQUIREMENT TO OBTAIN AUDITED ACCOUNTS AND A STATEMENT FROM THE AUDITOR) REGULATIONS 1996, SI 1996 1975; made under the Pensions Act 1995 s.41, s.116, s.124, s.174. In force: April 6, 1997; £1.10.

These Regulations make provision in respect of documents which the trustees or managers of an occupational pension scheme must obtain. They require trustees or managers to obtain accounts and the auditor's statement within a prescribed time. Trustees or managers who fail to obtain accounts or the auditor's statement without reasonable excuse are guilty of an offence and liable to a fine. They also make provision in respect of the form and content of accounts and in respect of the auditor's statement.

4611. Occupational pensions–compensation–limit

OCCUPATIONAL PENSION SCHEMES (PENSIONS COMPENSATION BOARD LIMIT ON BORROWING) REGULATIONS 1996, SI 1996 1976; made under the Pensions Act 1995 s.78, s.124. In force: August 1, 1996; £0.65.

The Pensions Compensation Board is established under the Pensions Act 1995 s.78(5) which enables the Board to borrow sums to exercise their functions. These Regulations provide that the aggregate amount outstanding in respect of the principal of any money borrowed must not exceed £15 million.

4612. Occupational pensions–contracting out

OCCUPATIONAL PENSION SCHEMES (CONTRACTING-OUT) REGULATIONS 1996, SI 1996 1172; made under the Pension Schemes Act 1993 s.7, s.8, s.9, s.11, s.12, s.12A, s.12B, s.12C, s.12D, s.16, s.17, s.21, s.25, s.34, s.35, s.36, s.37, s.42A, s.45B, s.50, s.51, s.53, s.55, s.56, s.57, s.61, s.113, s.155, s.156, s.178, s.179, s.181, s.182, s.183, Sch.2 Part 1; and the Pensions Act 1995 s.174, s.180. In force: April 6, 1996; £6.75.

These Regulations, which supplement changes introduced by the Pensions Act 1995 to the Pensions Act 1992 Part III, replace the Occupational Pension Schemes (Contracting-out) Regulations 1984. The procedure for employers to make elections to contract out employments, for notice and consultation requirements and the issue of contracting-out certificates by the Secretary of State is dealt with by Part II of the Regulations, Part III is concerned with new requirements for salary-related contracted-out schemes, Part IV relates to money purchase contracted out schemes, additional and special requirements relating to all schemes and overseas schemes are dealt with by Part V, Part IV is concerned with the restoration of rights in the State scheme, requirements applying to guaranteed minimum pensions accrued up until April 6, 1997 are dealt with in Part VII and Part VIII covers transitional arrangements and savings.

4613. Occupational pensions–contracting out

OCCUPATIONAL PENSION SCHEMES (CONTRACTING-OUT) AMENDMENT REGULATIONS 1996, SI 1996 1577; made under the Pension Schemes Act 1993 s.7, s.12, s.181; and the Pensions Act 1995 s.174, s.180. In force: July 12, 1996; £1.10.

These Regulations, which amend the Occupational Pension Schemes (Contracting-out) Regulations 1996 (SI 1996 1172), enable certain salary-related contracted-out schemes not meeting the requirements of the Pension Schemes Act 1993 s.9(2B) to remain contracted out from the day that those requirements come into force.

4614. Occupational pensions–contracting out

OCCUPATIONAL PENSION SCHEMES (MIXED BENEFIT CONTRACTED-OUT SCHEMES) REGULATIONS 1996, SI 1996 1977; made under the Pensions Act 1995 s.149, s.174. In force: June 4, 1997; £1.55.

These Regulations enable certain schemes which provide both salary-related and money purchase benefits to be contracted-out under the Pension Schemes Act 1993 Part III after April 6, 1997. In particular they provide for a scheme to which the Pensions Act 1995 s.149 applies, being a scheme which provides both such pensions as would satisfy the Pension Schemes Act 1993 s.9(2) and such pensions as would satisfy s.9(3) of that Act to be treated as if those pensions were provided by separate parts of the scheme. They provide for a relevant scheme to be treated, for the purposes of the Pension Schemes Act 1993 Part III, as if the separate parts of the scheme were separate schemes and modifies some provisions in Part III of that Act and also provides for the separate parts of a relevant scheme to be treated as though they were separate schemes for the purposes of any regulations made under that Part. The Occupational Pension Schemes (Contracting-out) Regulations 1996 (SI 1996 1172), the Contracting-out (Transfer and Transfer Payment) Regulations 1996 (SI 1996 1462) and the Protected Rights (Transfer Payment) Regulations 1996 (SI 1996 1461) are modified.

4615. Occupational pensions–disclosure of information

OCCUPATIONAL PENSION SCHEMES (DISCLOSURE OF INFORMATION) REGULATIONS 1996, SI 1996 1655; made under the Pension Schemes Act 1993 s.113, s.168, s.181, s.182; and the Pensions Act 1995 s.10, s.41, s.124, s.174. In force: April 6, 1997; £3.70.

The Regulations set out conditions for their application to an occupational pension scheme; provide for trustees to make available for inspection by specified persons documents containing information about the constitution and about individual entitlement, the audited accounts and actuarial valuations; provide for a limited disclosure requirement to be imposed on trustees of schemes which are not tax-approved or public service pension schemes; provide for the service of documents by post; and provide for the imposition of penalties by the Occupational Pensions Regulatory Authority. The Regulations also deal with the referral of an independent trade union to an industrial tribunal for the purposes of collective bargaining.

4616. Occupational pensions–dispute resolution

OCCUPATIONAL PENSION SCHEMES (INTERNAL DISPUTE RESOLUTION PROCEDURES) REGULATIONS 1996, SI 1996 1270; made under the Pensions Act 1995 s.10, s.50, s.124, s.174. In force: April 6, 1997; £1.55.

These Regulations set out procedures for internal dispute resolution in relation to occupational pension schemes. Provisions as to the persons to whom the arrangements made for the resolution of disagreements shall apply and as to who may bring complaints are made by Reg.2; Reg.3 enables representatives to act on behalf of complainants; Reg.4 to Reg.7 relate to the manner in which applications are to be made and decisions given; Reg.8 and Reg.9 make provision for the arrangements made for the resolution of disagreements not to apply in certain cases; and Reg.10 provides the maximum penalty which may be imposed by the Occupational Pensions Regulatory Authority in cases where arrangements required by the Pensions Act 1995 s.50 have not been made or are not being implemented by a scheme.

4617. Occupational pensions–early retirement–extra statutory concessions

The Inland Revenue issued a press release entitled *Pensions to employees disabled at work: extra statutory concession A62*, published on July 17, 1996. A revised version of extra statutory concession (ESC) A62 on pensions paid to employees who retire because of work related illness or injury, exempts only that part of the pension which exceeds that payable had retirement been on ordinary ill health grounds.

4618. Occupational pensions–European Parliament

EUROPEAN PARLIAMENTARY (UNITED KINGDOM REPRESENTATIVES) PENSIONS (AMENDMENT) ORDER 1996, SI 1996 1493; made under the European Parliament (Pay and Pensions) Act 1979 s.4. In force: July 4, 1996; £1.55.

This Order amends the European Parliamentary (United Kingdom Representatives) Pensions (Consolidation and Amendment) Order 1994 (SI 1994 1662), improving the accrual rate for service as a Representative before July 20, 1983 from sixtieths to fiftieths for Representatives in service on April 1, 1995 and changing the provisions relating to gratuities payable in respect of Representatives who die in service on or after that date.

4619. Occupational pensions–exclusion from schemes–part time employment–sex discrimination–membership qualifications based on number of hours worked–determination of applicable time limits and relevant EC law

[Council Directive 75/117 on the application of the principle of equal pay for men and women; Treaty of Rome Art.119; Equal Pay Act 1970 s.2.]

Over 40,000 applications were made to industrial tribunals by part-time workers complaining of unlawful exclusion from occupational pension schemes with qualifications dependent on the number of hours worked per week. The exclusion was alleged to amount to indirect sex discrimination. The test cases covered male and female applicants, those still in employment and those who had ceased, those employed in public and private sectors, and contributory and non-contributory schemes.

Held, that (1) where the employment has ended, claims will only be in time if brought within six months of the end of the contract of employment or before the end of the contract containing the breached equality clause. This applies to all contracts including term and academic year contracts; (2) the relevant domestic law is the Equal Pay Act 1970. The relevant European law is the Treaty of Rome Art.119 and Council Directive 75/117. The applicants cannot rely on the Equal Pay Directive either in parallel with or instead of Art.119; (3) the domestic time limit of six months for bringing an action under s.2(4) of the 1970 Act, does not provide terms making the Community rule less favourable than the domestic rule; (4) claims do not lie in respect of periods of employment before April 8, 1976; (5) part-time male employees had a right to bring claims, subject to the rights of employers to re-argue individual cases at a later stage, and (6) the Secretary of State for the Environment was a proper respondent to these proceedings by virtue of his responsibility as rule maker for the local government pension scheme.

PRESTON v. WOLVERHAMPTON HEALTH CARE NHS TRUST [1995] O.P.L.R. 205, JK Macmillan, IT.

4620. Occupational pensions–Fireman's Pension Scheme–notice of date and time of appeal following adjournment

[Firemen's Pension Scheme Order Sch.9 para.4.]

HCC applied for judicial review of a decision by S, acting as a medical referee nominated by the Secretary of State. The application concerned an appeal to S by W, who retired from the Hampshire Fire and Rescue Service after 29 years of service. The appeal was under the Fireman's Pension Scheme and related to his retirement due to cervical spondylolysis allegedly caused by his occupation. HCC contended that S had failed, pursuant to his duty under the Firemen's Pension Scheme Order 1992 Sch.9 para.4(2), to notify them of the date and time of the adjourned appeal.

Held, allowing the application, that on the balance of probabilities, HCC's account of what had happened when the hearing was adjourned should be believed and that a genuine mistake about the arrangements of the new hearing had occurred. S's decision would be quashed.

R. v. SHEARER AND SECRETARY OF STATE FOR HOME AFFAIRS, *ex p.* HAMPSHIRE CC, Trans. Ref: CO/3419/94, November 13, 1995, Brooke, J., QBD.

4621. Occupational pensions–investments

OCCUPATIONAL PENSION SCHEMES (INVESTMENT) REGULATIONS 1996, SI 1996 3127; made under the Pensions Act 1995 s.35, s.40, s.56, s.118, s.123, s.124, s.174. In force: April 6, 1997; £3.20.

These Regulations impose restrictions on the amount of the resources of an occupational pension scheme which may be invested in employer-related investments. They also exempt certain schemes from the requirement imposed on trustees of trust schemes by the Pensions Act 1995 s.35 to obtain a statement of the principles governing decisions about investments for the purposes of the scheme. They revoke and replace the Occupational Pension Schemes (Investment of Scheme's Resources) Regulations 1992 (SI 1992 246).

4622. Occupational pensions–judiciary

JUDICIAL PENSIONS (MISCELLANEOUS) (AMENDMENT) REGULATIONS 1996, SI 1996 2893; made under the Judicial Pensions and Retirement Act 1993 s.1. In force: December 16, 1996; £1.10.

These Regulations substitute a new Judicial Pensions (Miscellaneous) Regulations 1995 (SI 1995 632) Part II, which relates to elections for new pension arrangements. They make new provision when an election for the Judicial Pensions and Retirement Act 1993 Part I to apply to an office-holder is to take effect. They extend the time limit within which personal representatives have to make an election on behalf of a deceased office-holder. They also permit an election to be made by a personal representative, notwithstanding that a children's pension or, in certain circumstances, a surviving spouse's pension under an existing judicial pension scheme, has come into payment.

4623. Occupational pensions–judiciary–additional voluntary contributions

JUDICIAL PENSIONS (ADDITIONAL VOLUNTARY CONTRIBUTIONS) (AMENDMENT) REGULATIONS 1996, SI 1996 52; made under the Judicial Pensions and Retirement Act 1993 s.10, s.29. In force: February 2, 1996; £1.55.

These Regulations provide for the further application of Inland Revenue limits to the amount of additional benefits which may be purchased, additional children's pension under the Judicial Added Benefits Scheme in return for the purchase of added units of benefit, a revised basis for calculating contributions costs for the purchase of surviving spouses pension under the Judicial Added Surviving Spouse's Pension Scheme and for the deduction from voluntary contributions of administrative expenses incurred by the authorised provider by making amendments to the Judicial Pensions (Additional Voluntary Contributions) Regulations 1995 (SI 1995 639).

4624. Occupational pensions–Members of Parliament

PARLIAMENTARY PENSIONS (AMENDMENT) REGULATIONS 1996, SI 1996 2406; made under the Parliamentary and other Pensions Act 1987 s.2. In force: October 10, 1996; £1.10.

These Regulations amend the Parliamentary Pensions (Consolidation and Amendment) Regulations 1993 (SI 1993 3253) and the Parliamentary Pensions (Amendment) Regulations 1995 (SI 1995 2867). The amendments relate to the determination of a member's ordinary salary, an increase in accrual rate and a change in provisions relating to gratuities payable in respect of Ministers and the office holders who die in service.

4625. Occupational pensions–modification of schemes

OCCUPATIONAL PENSION SCHEMES (MODIFICATION OF SCHEMES) REGULATIONS 1996, SI 1996 2517; made under the Pensions Act 1995 s.10, s.67, s.68, s.124, s.125, s.174. In force: April 6, 1997; £1.10.

These Regulations extend the meaning of member for the purposes of the Pensions Act s.67; make provision in respect of the certification requirements which an actuary must provide before any person can exercise a power to modify the scheme; make provision in respect of obtaining the consent of a member before any person can exercise a power to modify the scheme; make provision in respect of the circumstances in which consent of a member may be treated as given in respect of a power to modify the scheme; provide that the restriction on the power to modify does not apply to the exercise of the power in a prescribed manner; exempt certain schemes from the provisions which allow trustees of trust schemes to modify the scheme by resolution; and provide for civil penalties to be imposed by the Occupational Pensions Regulatory Authority where the requirements of specified Regulations have not been complied with.

4626. Occupational pensions–payments–employers

OCCUPATIONAL PENSION SCHEMES (PAYMENTS TO EMPLOYERS) REGULATIONS 1996, SI 1996 2156; made under the Pensions Act 1995 s.37, s.69, s.76, s.77, s.124, s.125, s.174. In force: April 6, 1997; £1.95.

These Regulations concern the requirements which must be satisfied before the employer may receive a payment or distribution of assets from an occupational pension scheme. The requirements are applicable only to exempt approved trust schemes.

4627. Occupational pensions–payments–transfer

PROTECTED RIGHTS (TRANSFER PAYMENT) REGULATIONS 1996, SI 1996 1461; made under the Pension Schemes Act 1993 s.28, s.181, s.182, Sch.6, para.17. In force: April 6, 1997; £1.95.

These Regulations make provision for the circumstances in which, and the conditions subject to which, effect may be given to the protected rights of a member of a scheme which is or was a money purchase contracted out scheme or an appropriate personal pension scheme by the making of a transfer payment to another pension scheme and modify Part III of the 1993 Act where a transfer payment has been made to a salary related contracted out scheme, in order to accommodate the guaranteed minimum pensions to which a member of such a scheme becomes entitled in consequence of that payment.

4628. Occupational pensions–pension schemes–indexation

OCCUPATIONAL PENSION SCHEMES (INDEXATION) REGULATIONS 1996, SI 1996 1679; made under the Pensions Act 1995 s.51, s.124, s.174. In force: April 6, 1997; £1.10.

These Regulations provide for the indexation of occupational pensions derived from the acceptance of transfer payments from pension schemes and the indexation of occupational pensions derived from the acceptance of payments from insurance policies or annuity contracts.

4629. Occupational pensions–pension schemes–pensions management

OCCUPATIONAL PENSION SCHEMES (SCHEME ADMINISTRATION) REGULATIONS 1996, SI 1996 1715; made under the Pensions Act 1995 s.27, s.32, s.47, s.49, s.87, s.88, s.124, s.174. In force: April 6, 1996; £2.80.

These Regulations are the first to be made in respect of the administration of occupational pension schemes under the Pensions Act 1995. They make provisions relating to the appointment of professional advisers; the qualification and experience of the auditor or actuary; the manner and terms of appointment of removal of advisers; the duty to disclose information; the ineligibility to act as actuary or auditor; the meaning of trustee or trust scheme; the functions of trustees; receipts; payments and records; and money purchase schemes.

4630. Occupational pensions–pension schemes–transfer value

OCCUPATIONAL PENSION SCHEMES (TRANSFER VALUES) REGULATIONS 1996, SI 1996 1847; made under the Pension Schemes Act 1993 s.93, s.93A, s.94, s.95, s.97, s.98, s.99, s.113, s.153, s.168, s.181, s.182, s.183; and the Pensions Act 1995 s.10, s.124. In force: April 6, 1997; £3.70.

These Regulations revoke and replace the Occupational Pension Schemes (Transfer Values) Regulations 1985 (SI 1985 1931) in order to supplement the changes introduced by the Pensions Act 1995 to the Pension Schemes Act 1993 Part IV Chapter IV. The provisions relate to restrictions on the right to a cash equivalent, guaranteed statements of entitlement and calculation of transfer values, receiving schemes, annuities and arrangements, time limits for payment of cash equivalents, the modification of the 1993 Act and penalties under the 1995 Act.

4631. Occupational pensions–pension schemes–trustees–directors

OCCUPATIONAL PENSION SCHEMES (MEMBER-NOMINATED TRUSTEES AND DIRECTORS) REGULATIONS 1996, SI 1996 1216; made under the Pensions Act 1995 s.17, s.18, s.20, s.21, s.49, s.68, s.118, s.124, s.125, s.174; and the Pensions Act 1996 s.19. In force: Reg.1, Reg.2, Reg.11, Reg.22, Reg.24, Sch.2 para.8: October 6, 1996; Remainder: April 6, 1997; £4.70.

These Regulations, which amend the Pensions Act 1995, are concerned with the selection and appointment of member nominated trustees and directors under the Pensions Act 1995 s.16 to s.21. Arrangements and rules, proposals by employers for alternative arrangements, powers to modify schemes by resolution and cessation of application of requirements in relation to member nominated trustees are dealt with in Part II and for member nominated directors are dealt with in Part III. Part IV provides general and supplementary provisions relating to modifications for special cases, rules and arrangements, records and notices.

4632. Occupational pensions–pension schemes–valuation

OCCUPATIONAL PENSION SCHEMES (MINIMUM FUNDING REQUIREMENT AND ACTUARIAL VALUATIONS) REGULATIONS 1996, SI 1996 1536; made under the Pensions Act 1995 s.41, s.49, s.56, s.57, s.58, s.59, s.60, s.61, s.68, s.75, s.118, s.119, s.124, s.125, s.174. In force: April 6, 1997; £6.10.

These Regulations concern the minimum funding requirement for occupational pension schemes under the Pensions Act 1995 s.56 to s.61 and ongoing actuarial valuations under s.41. They relate to determination, valuation and verification of assets and liabilities, rights under insurance contracts, excluded assets, time limits for minimum funding valuations and duty to obtain such valuations in certain circumstances, Schedules of contributions and certification, inadequate contributions, and authority's powers to extend periods for making payments.

4633. Occupational pensions–pension schemes–winding up

OCCUPATIONAL PENSION SCHEMES (DISCHARGE OF PROTECTED RIGHTS ON WINDING UP) REGULATIONS 1996, SI 1996 775; made under the Pension Schemes Act 1993 s.32A, s.181, s.182. In force: April 6, 1996; £1.55.

These Regulations provide for the conditions on which effect may be given to protected rights of a member of a scheme on winding up by means of an appropriate policy of insurance. Requirements which insurance companies must satisfy, conditions which the policies of insurance must satisfy before they can be surrendered or commuted and requirements which the polices of insurance must satisfy are prescribed.

4634. Occupational pensions–Pensions Ombudsman

PERSONAL AND OCCUPATIONAL PENSION SCHEMES (PENSIONS OMBUDSMAN) REGULATIONS 1996, SI 1996 2475; made under the Pension Schemes Act 1993 s.146, s.151A, s.181, s.182. In force: April 6, 1997; £1.10.

These Regulations revoke and replace the Personal and Occupational Pension Schemes (Pensions Ombudsman) Regulations 1991 (SI 1991 588 as amended by SI 1994 1062 and SI 1996 1271). The jurisdiction of the Ombudsman is extended to cover complaints between actual or potential beneficiaries and the administrators of occupational and personal pensions schemes. In addition certain cases, in certain circumstances, are excluded from his jurisdiction. A time limit for complaints to be referred to the Ombudsman is prescribed together with the rate of interest to be applied under the Pension Schemes Act 1993 s.151A.

4635. Occupational pensions–pensions ombudsman–procedure

PERSONAL AND OCCUPATIONAL PENSION SCHEMES (PENSIONS OMBUDSMAN) (PROCEDURE) AMENDMENT RULES 1996, SI 1996 2638; made under the Pension Schemes Act 1993 s.149. In force: April 6, 1997; £1.10.

These Rules amend the Personal and Occupational Pension Schemes (Pensions Ombudsman) (Procedure) Rules 1995 (SI 1995 1053) which make provision as to the procedure to be followed where a complaint or dispute relating to an occupational or personal pension scheme is referred to the Pensions Ombudsman under the Pension Schemes Act 1993 Part X. They insert a new rule 15A, which makes provision for the Pensions Ombudsman to pay travel subsistence expenses and compensation for lost earnings in certain cases to those who attend oral hearings in connection with an investigation by the Pensions Ombudsman of a complaint or dispute.

4636. Occupational pensions–personal pensions

PERSONAL AND OCCUPATIONAL PENSION SCHEMES (MISCELLANEOUS AMENDMENTS) REGULATIONS 1996, SI 1996 776; made under the Pension Schemes Act 1993 s.28, s.28A, s.29, s.44, s.48, s.113, s.115, s.155, s.181; and the Pensions Scheme Act 1993 s.182. In force: April 6, 1996; £1.55.

These Regulations amend the Occupational Pension Schemes (Contracting-out) Regulations 1984 (SI 1984 380), the Personal and Occupational Pension Schemes (Protected Rights) Regulations 1987 (SI 1987 1117), the Personal Pension Schemes (Disclosure of Information) Regulations 1987 (SI 1987 1110), the Personal and Occupational Pension Schemes (Abatement of Benefit) Regulations 1987 (SI 1987 1113), and the Personal Pension Schemes (Appropriate Schemes) Regulations 1988 (SI 1988 137).

4637. Occupational pensions–personal pensions–benefits

PERSONAL AND OCCUPATIONAL PENSION SCHEMES (PRESERVATION OF BENEFIT AND PERPETUITIES) (AMENDMENTS) REGULATIONS 1996, SI 1996

2131; made under the Pension Schemes Act 1993 s.71, s.73, s.74, s.77, s.82, s.113, s.153, s.163, s.165, s.168, s.181, s.182. In force: April 6, 1997; £1.55.

These Regulations amend the Occupational Pension Scheme (Preservation of Benefit) Regulations 1991 (SI 1991 167) providing for removal of provision for the OPB to exercise its discretion in certain cases, the transfer of rights to an overseas arrangement to be an alternative to short service benefit, a test to determine whether uniform accrual is to be applied in relation to money purchase benefits, requirements for members to be furnished with information in relation to any transfer of accrued rights without consent or in relation to rights on termination of pensionable service, and a civil penalty for failure to comply with the requirements to provide such information. They also amend the Personal and Occupational Pension Schemes (Perpetuities) Regulations 1990 (SI 1990 1143) in relation to the extension of the time limit under that regulation, by substituting a reference to the Secretary of State for a reference to the OPB.

4638. Occupational pensions–police officers

POLICE PENSIONS (AMENDMENT) REGULATIONS 1996, SI 1996 867; made under the Police Pensions Act 1976 s.1. In force: March 31, 1996; £1.10.

These Regulations amend the Police Pensions Regulations 1987 (SI 1987 257). Regulation 4 of the these Regulations abolishes the requirement on a police authority to pay a transfer value when a police officer transfers from the police force maintained by that police authority to a police force maintained by some other police authority or to the Royal Ulster Constabulary. In its place the Regulation inserted by Reg.5 of these Regulations requires the former police authority to provide the new police authority a certificate of pension entitlements of the police officer who transfers. The other amendments are consequential on these changes.

4639. Occupational pensions–retirement benefits schemes

OCCUPATIONAL PENSION SCHEMES (TRANSITIONAL PROVISIONS) (AMENDMENT) REGULATIONS 1996, SI 1996 3115; made under the Income and Corporation Taxes Act 1988 Sch.23 para.1. In force: January 1, 1997; £1.10.

These Regulations amend the Occupational Pension Schemes (Transitional Provisions) Regulations 1988 (SI 1988 1436) by disapplying certain provisions of the Income and Corporation Taxes Act 1988 Sch.23 in circumstances where, as a result of bad investment advice, an employee who was a member of a retirement benefits scheme before March 17, 1987 ceased to be a member of the scheme and instead became a member of a personal pension scheme or entered into an annuity contract, and subsequently as part of compensation for loss suffered is reinstated as a member of the retirement benefits scheme.

4640. Occupational pensions–retirement benefits scheme

OCCUPATIONAL PENSION SCHEMES (TRANSITIONAL PROVISIONS) (AMENDMENT NO.2) REGULATIONS 1996, SI 1996 3234; made under the Income and Corporation Taxes Act 1988 Sch.23 para.1. In force: January 13, 1997; £0.65.

These Regulations correct an error made in the Occupational Pension Schemes (Transitional Provision) (Amendment) Regulations 1996 (SI 1996 3115) Reg.4. That Regulation, by inserting the Occupation Pension Schemes (Transitional Provisions) Regulations 1988 (SI 1988 1436) Reg.42A failed sufficiently to specify a date.

4641. Occupational pensions–revaluation

OCCUPATIONAL PENSIONS (REVALUATION) ORDER 1996, SI 1996 2926; made under the Pension Schemes Act 1993 Sch.3 para.2. In force: January 1, 1997; £0.65.

This Order is made, as required by the Pensions Schemes Act 1993 Sch.3 para.2(1), in the revaluation year beginning on January 1, 1996. The revaluation percentages specified are relevant to the revaluation of benefits under occupational pension schemes, as required by s.84 of, and Sch.3 to, that Act.

4642. Occupational pensions–surplus mergers–employer purported to exercise power to amend scheme but exceeded power–holiday contributions–distribution of surplus on termination–Canada

In 1959 C, a company, started a defined contribution pension scheme subject to a trust providing that on termination the fund should be distributed among the members, which in 1966 became a defined benefit scheme. C's broad power to amend was subject to the proviso that funds could not be diverted for members' exclusive benefit. In 1978 C purported to amend to give itself a discretion to distribute any surplus on termination. In 1970 S, a company, started a defined benefit plan which provided that on termination any surplus could at S's discretion be returned to S or used for the benefit of members. S's broad power to amend was subject to a similar restriction to C's. In 1983, C and S merged to become APC and the merged pension plan provided for any surplus after maximum benefits had been paid to the members to be refunded to APC. APC was obliged to contribute an annual sum sufficient to provide the retirement benefits accruing in the current year, with the actuary taking into account the fund's assets. From 1985 to 1988, APC met this obligation from the surplus in the fund. In 1988 the fund was terminated. APC and the members, through their representative, Schmidt, applied to the court for a declaration of entitlement to the surplus. Lower courts found that the portion of the surplus derived from C's fund had to be paid to members and that C's funds should not have been used by APC for the contributions holiday, but that APC was entitled to the portion of the surplus derived from S's fund. APC appealed and Schmidt cross-appealed.

Held, allowing APC's appeal in part and dismissing the cross-appeal, that (1) the purported amendment to C's plan in 1978 was invalid as it was beyond the scope of the control which C had reserved to itself in 1959. One of the purposes of the trust was to use any money for the benefit of employees. There was no resulting trust in favour of APC and on termination the members of C's fund were entitled to the surplus by reason of the continuing trust in their favour; (2) however, the contributions holiday was permissible because the actuary was permitted to consider the surplus when calculating the funding obligation, *CUPE-CLC, Local 100 v. Ontario Hydro* (1989) 58 D.L.R. (4th) 552 distinguished, and (3) S's fund was not impressed with a trust, expressly or by implication. The 1972 brochure contained only a declaration of intent and, as there was no evidence to suggest that Schmidt had been induced to join S in reliance on the brochure, no estoppel could arise. The limitation on S's power to amend applied only to the defined benefits to which members were contractually entitled. However, the 1983 amendment dealt only with funds in which the members had no interest until the company in its discretion gave them one and was therefore within S's power. By reason of the contract, therefore, APC was entitled to take that part of the surplus which could be traced to S's plan.

SCHMIDT v. AIR PRODUCTS CANADA LTD [1995] O.P.L.R. 283, La Forest, J., Sup Ct (Can).

4643. Occupational pensions–teachers–superannuation

TEACHERS' SUPERANNUATION (AMENDMENT) REGULATIONS 1996, SI 1996 2269; made under the Superannuation Act 1972 s.9, s.12, Sch.3. In force: October 1, 1996; £3.20.

These Regulations further amend the Teachers' Superannuation (Consolidation) Regulations 1988 (SI 1988 1652). The miscellaneous amendments in the main relate to the payment and refund of additional contributions and interest payable.

4644. Occupational pensions–teachers–superannuation–provision of information

TEACHERS' SUPERANNUATION (PROVISION OF INFORMATION AND ADMINISTRATIVE EXPENSES ETC.) REGULATIONS 1996, SI 1996 2282; made under the Pensions Act 1995 s.172, s.174. In force: October 1, 1996; £1.10.

These Regulations are made under the Pensions Act 1995 s.172 and relate to certain individuals who have been active members of the Teachers' Superannuation Scheme. Section 172(1) of the 1995 Act provides that the Secretary of State may supply certain information relating to individuals in prescribed circumstances to any prescribed person and impose on that person reasonable fees in respect of administrative expenses incurred in providing that information. Regulation 3 prescribes circumstances and persons for the purposes of s.172(1) of the 1995 Act. Section 172(2) of the 1995 Act provides that the Secretary of State may in certain circumstances impose on any prescribed person reasonable fees in respect of administrative expenses incurred in the admission or re-admission of individuals to schemes, or incurred in connection with the administration of certain compensation payments. Regulation 4 prescribes, in relation to the Teachers' Superannuation Scheme, the persons on whom fees may be imposed for the purposes of s.172(2) of the 1995 Act.

4645. Occupational pensions–war pensions–fresh evidence–backdating of pension to date of first claim

F applied for judicial review of a decision of the Secretary of State that his father's war pension entitlement would not be backdated to the date of his original claim in 1941 or to any period before 1985. F's father had successfully appealed against the refusal of a war pension when new evidence of a consultant psychiatrist was produced. However, the pension was only backdated for six years as the Secretary of State concluded that the previous decision had been correct on the evidence then available. F argued that any evidence which arose after 1941 was related to 1941 and must be taken into account as at that date.

Held, dismissing the application, that, on the facts of the case, the Secretary of State was entitled to exercise his discretion not to backdate the pension for more than six years. The decision was not illogical as the earlier rejections were correct when they were made.

R. v. SECRETARY OF STATE FOR SOCIAL SECURITY, *ex p.* FOE [1996] C.O.D. 505, Macpherson of Cluny, J., QBD.

4646. Occupational pensions–winding up–deficiency in assets

OCCUPATIONAL PENSION SCHEMES (DEFICIENCY ON WINDING UP ETC.) REGULATIONS 1996, SI 1996 3128; made under the Pensions Act 1995 s.68, s.75, s.89, s.118, s.119, s.124, s.125, s.174. In force: in accordance with Reg.1; £2.80.

These Regulations concern the treatment under the Pensions Act 1995 s.75 of a deficit in the assets of occupational pension schemes as a debt owed by the employer to the trustees or managers of the scheme. Section 75 replaces the Pension Schemes Act 1993 s.144 and these Regulations replace the Occupational Pension Schemes (Deficiency on Winding Up etc) Regulations 1994 (SI 1994 895).

4647. Occupational pensions–winding up–trustees–discharge of liabilities

OCCUPATIONAL PENSION SCHEMES (WINDING UP) REGULATIONS 1996, SI 1996 3126; made under the Pension Schemes Act 1993 s.97, s.113, s.168, s.181, s.182; and the Pensions Act 1995 s.38, s.49, s.68, s.73, s.74, s.118, s.119, s.124, s.125, s.174. In force: April 6, 1997; £2.80.

These Regulations concern the application of the statutory priority order set out in the Pensions Act 1995 s.73; the ways in which the trustees can be treated as having discharged their liabilities in respect of scheme members under s.74 of the Act and the cases in which the statutory power to defer winding up under s.38 of the Act is not to apply.

4648. Pension schemes–contracting out–payments–transfer

CONTRACTING-OUT (TRANSFER AND TRANSFER PAYMENT) REGULATIONS 1996, SI 1996 1462; made under the Pension Schemes Act 1993 s.12C, s.20, s.181, s.182. In force: April 6, 1997; £3.20.

These Regulations replace the Contracting-out (Transfer) Regulations 1985 which are now subject to transitional provisions revoked. The Regulations supplement changes introduced by the Pensions Act 1995 to Part III of the Pension Schemes Act 1993 and consolidate and amend those provisions of the 1985 Regulations which remain relevant.

4649. Pension schemes–disclosure of information

PENSION SCHEMES (APPROPRIATE SCHEMES AND DISCLOSURE OF INFORMATION) (MISCELLANEOUS AMENDMENTS) REGULATIONS 1996, SI 1996 1435; made under the Pension Schemes Act 1993 s.43, s.45B, s.113, s.181, s.182. In force: April 6, 1997; £1.10.

The Regulations amend the Personal Pension Schemes (Appropriate Schemes) Regulations 1988 and the Personal Pension Schemes (Disclosure of Information) Regulations 1987. They amend the Appropriate Schemes Regulations to provide circumstances in which, except where provided, minimum contributions shall not be payable and amend the Disclosure Regulations so as to require trustees to disclose information relating to the date of birth used in determining the appropriate age-related percentage to scheme members. A transitional provision is provided in the case of the payment of minimum contributions in respect of the period up to and including the tax year 1966/97.

4650. Pension schemes–independent trustees–whether administrators had power to remove trustees

[Social Security Pensions Act 1975 s.57C; Insolvency Act 1986 s.14; Occupational Pension Schemes (Independent Trustee) Regulations 1990 Reg.4.]

P was appointed as a company trustee of the staff pension fund of S Ltd, established by a definitive trust deed on April 1, 1985. On January 22, 1991 an administration order was made and administrators were appointed to S Ltd. On May 24, 1991, pursuant to a deed entered into by the administrators and S Ltd, D was appointed as an independent trustee in accordance with the Social Security Pensions Act 1975 s.57C(2). By December 24, 1992 the scheme was paid-up and there were no more employees. On July 4, 1994, the administrators purported to remove D and replace him with another trustee. P issued a summons seeking an order that D had not been validly removed as a trustee.

Held, granting the relief sought by P, that (1) the powers conferred on administrators by the Insolvency Act 1986 s.14 include the power to do acts which relate to the affairs of the company's pension scheme. The company's pension scheme is an intimate part of the company's "affairs" within the meaning of s.14(1) of the 1986 Act, *Edgar, Re* [1971-76] A.C.L.C. 27, 492 and *Simpson Curtis Pension Trustees (in receivership) v. Readson Ltd* [1994] O.P.L.R. 231 applied, and (2) since the scheme was paid up by December 24, 1992, the Occupational Pension Schemes (Independent Trustee) Regulations 1990 Reg.4 operated so as to remove the power of the administrators under s.57C(2) of the

1975 Act to remove and appoint independent trustees. The phrase "if and so long as" contemplated a period beginning when s.57C applied and ending when it disapplied. Such a construction was consistent with commonsense, as there was no need for an independent trustee when the employer no longer had any trust connection with the fund.

DENNY v. YELDON [1995] 3 All E.R. 624, Jacob, J., Ch D.

4651. Pension schemes–Pensions Ombudsman

PERSONAL AND OCCUPATIONAL PENSION SCHEMES (PENSION OMBUDSMAN) AMENDMENT REGULATIONS 1996, SI 1996 1271; made under the Pension Schemes Act 1993 s.146, s.181, s.182. In force: July 1, 1996; £0.65.

These Regulations, which amend the Personal and Occupational Pension Scheme (Pensions Ombudsman) Regulations 1991 (SI 1991 588) by inserting a new Reg.2A, extend the jurisdiction of the Pensions Ombudsman to include complaints against scheme administrators.

4652. Pension schemes–retired trustee–Pensions Ombudsman's investigation of complaint of maladministration–duty to consult previous trustee–failure to give right to reply a breach of natural justice

[Pension Schemes Act 1993 s.149.]

D, a retired trustee of a company pension scheme, appealed against a finding of the Ombudsman, that he and two other trustees were liable to pay £300,000 into the pension fund. The Ombudsman had investigated a complaint of maladministration and found that the transfer values paid into a new scheme, set up when the company was sold, were insufficient to cover the accrued liabilities, and the trustees were subsequently unable to pay members' pensions in full. D argued that the decision was invalid as he had not been notified of any allegations of maladministration against him and knew nothing of the investigation until the Ombudsman's determination that he was guilty of recklessness and wilful neglect was issued.

Held, allowing the appeal, that, under the Pension Schemes Act 1993 s.149, the Ombudsman was required to consult not only current trustees but also previous trustees who were under investigation. The Ombudsman had circumvented a fundamental part of the statutory procedure by denying D a right to reply to the complaints made against him, and the failure to comply with s.149 vitiated the Ombudsman's decision, *London and Clydeside Estates Ltd v. Aberdeen DC* [1980] 1 W.L.R. 182, [1980] C.L.Y. 315 considered. Additionally, the fact that D was not given a chance to answer the accusations until the provisional determination was sent to him was a serious breach of the rules of natural justice. The Ombudsman's decision was set aside.

DUFFIELD v. PENSIONS OMBUDSMAN [1996] C.O.D. 406, Carnwath, J., QBD.

4653. Pensions Act 1995–Commencement No.3 Order

PENSIONS ACT 1995 (COMMENCEMENT NO.3) ORDER 1996, SI 1996 778 (C.13); made under the Pensions Act 1995 s.180. In force: bringing into force various provisions of the Act; £1.55.

This Order provides for the coming into force of further provisions of the Pensions Act 1995 on the following dates: March 13, 1996 for the purpose only of authorising the making of Orders under the Pension Schemes Act 1993 specifying the reduction in the rates of State scheme contributions and rebates payable in respect of members of contracted-out occupational pension schemes and appropriate personal pension schemes; March 13, 1996 for the purpose only of authorising the making of certain Regulations, in particular, under provisions relating to interim arrangements in relation to appropriate personal pension schemes and the discharge of protected rights by money purchase occupational schemes (the provisions in question are brought fully into force on April 6, 1996); April 1, 1996 for provisions relating to the establishment of the Occupational Pensions Regulatory Authority; April 6, 1996 for provisions relating to the disclosure of information by the Secretary of State, the aggregation of earnings in relation to Class 1 contributions and certain other general provisions of the 1995 Act; April 6, 1996 for the purpose only of authorising the making of certain Regulations under the 1995 Act concerning the regulation of occupational pension schemes, contracting-out and transfer values; June 1, 1996 for the purpose only of authorising the making of Regulations about contracting-out by "hybrid schemes"; April 6, 1997, insofar as not already in force, for s.136 of the 1995 Act (new contracting-out requirements) and that day is designated as the principal appointed day for the purposes of Part III of the Act.

4654. Pensions Act 1995–Commencement No.4 order

PENSIONS ACT 1995 (COMMENCEMENT NO.4) ORDER 1996, SI 1996 1412 (C.26); made under the Pensions Act 1995 s.180. In force: bringing into force various provisions of the Act on June 1, 1996 and August 1, 1996; £1.10.

This Order provides for the coming into force of further provisions of the Pensions Act 1995 on the following dates: on August 1, 1996, for provisions relating to the establishment of the Pensions Compensation Board; on June 1, 1996 for the purpose only of authorising the making of certain regulations, in particular, under provisions relating to time limits for paying civil penalties, the requirement for an independent trustee, the Pensions Compensation Board, the proceedings of the Occupational Pensions Regulatory Authority and the review of its decisions and the jurisdiction of the Pensions Ombudsman and his powers as regards costs, expenses and interest.

4655. Pensions Act 1995–Commencement No.5 Order

PENSIONS ACT 1995 (COMMENCEMENT NO.5) ORDER 1996, SI 1996 1675 (C.36); made under the Pensions Act 1995 s.175, s.180. In force: bringing into force various provisions of the Act on June 27, 1996 and August 1, 1996; £1.10.

This Order brings into force the Pensions Act 1995 s.166 on August 1, 1996, with the following exceptions: the inserted Matrimonial Causes Act 1973 s.25D(2) to (4), empowering the Lord Chancellor to make regulations, comes into force on the day after the making of the Order; periodical payments made by a pension fund to a spouse without pension rights may not be ordered so as to commence before April 6, 1997; the inserted Matrimonial Causes Act 1973 s.25B and s.25C do not apply to proceedings commenced by petition before July 1, 1996.

4656. Pensions Act 1995–Commencement No.6 Order

PENSIONS ACT 1995 (COMMENCEMENT NO.6) ORDER 1996, SI 1996 1853 (C.38); made under the Pensions Act 1995 s.180. In force: bringing into force various provisions of the Act on July 16, 1996; £1.10.

This Order provides for the coming into force of the Pensions Act 1995 s.116 which relates to penalties for breach of regulations.

4657. Pensions Act 1995–Commencement No.7 Order

PENSIONS ACT 1995 (COMMENCEMENT NO.6: SI 1996/1853: C.38) (AMENDMENT) ORDER 1996, SI 1996 2150 (C.51); made under the Pensions Act 1995 s.180. In force: bringing into force various provisions of the Act on August 16, 1996; £0.65.

This Order amends the Pensions Act 1995 (Commencement No.6) Order 1996 made July 15, 1996 and registered as SI 1996 1853 (C.38) by re-numbering it the Commencement No.7 Order.

4658. Pensions Act 1995–Commencement No.8 Order

PENSIONS ACT 1995 (COMMENCEMENT NO.8) ORDER 1996, SI 1996 2637 (C.73); made under the Pensions Act 1995 s.180. In force: bringing into force various provisions of the Act on October 16, 1996; £1.55.

This Order brings into force on October 16, 1996 further regulation and rule making powers contained in the Pensions Act 1995. The powers concerned are those contained in s.3(2) (prohibitions orders), s.74 (discharge of liabilities by insurance, etc), s.118 (powers to modify Part I of the Act), s.125 (powers supplementary to the interpretation section), s.158 (amendments to s.149 of the Pensions Scheme Act 1993), s.165 (levy), Sch.2 para.12 (functions and procedures of the Pensions Compensation Board), Sch.3 para.23 (disclosure of information by the Registrar of Occupational and Personal Pension Schemes) and Sch.3 para.44 (definition of the Regulatory Authority, and Sch.5 para.80(f) (consultation about regulations).

4659. Pensions Ombudsman–local authority reducing redundant employee's pension entitlement–order that payment be reinstated and compensation paid–whether had jurisdiction to order payment when such payment was ultra vires–whether order constituted maladministration–compensation not excessive

[Pension Schemes Act 1993; Personal and Occupational Pension Schemes (Pensions Ombudsman) Regulations 1991.]

W appealed against a decision of the Pensions Ombudsman directing that the local authority reinstate the amount of pension paid to H, whose pension entitlement they had reduced after becoming aware that a compensation annuity, paid to him in respect of his redundancy and in addition to his annual retirement pension, was unlawful. W argued that the Ombudsman had no jurisdiction, under the Pension Schemes Act 1993, to investigate H's complaint or to pay him £1000 in compensation for distress or inconvenience because the payment did not relate to funds subject to the Personal and Occupational Pension Schemes (Pensions Ombudsman) Regulations 1991, but to payments out of the rates under the compensation scheme. It was also argued that he wrongly concluded that the ultra vires payment constituted maladministration and that he was not justified in directing the resumption of payments when such payment was unlawful.

Held, allowing the appeal in part, that for the purposes of the 1991 Regulations it was not necessary to make a distinction between the types of payment made or to classify whether the matter was a complaint or a dispute before it fell to be considered by the Ombudsman. However, the Ombudsman erred in assuming that W were guilty of maladministration simply because they had acted on a wrong legal view, *Rowling v. Takaro Properties Ltd* [1988] A.C. 473, [1988] C.L.Y. 2441 followed. Although the level of compensation awarded by the Ombudsman for distress and inconvenience was high, it was not so excessive as to be perverse.

WESTMINSTER CITY COUNCIL v. HAYWOOD [1996] 3 W.L.R. 563, Robert Walker, J., Ch D.

4660. Pensions Ombudsman–pension schemes–maladministration–measure of damages–no award for distress and inconvenience–requirements for such an award

NHS appealed against two determinations of the Ombudsman. In the first case the Ombudsman upheld a complaint of maladministration when NHS gave an estimate of the value of W's pension based on 40 years' service, although he was entitled to only 36 years' service. The Ombudsman ordered the pension to be paid as if 40 years had been served and damages for distress and inconvenience were awarded. NHS argued that, according to, *Westminster City Council v. Haywood* [1996] C.L.Y. 4659, the measure of damages in such a case should be on the basis that the information had not been given, not on the basis that the information had been correct. That argument was accepted and a consent order was drawn up. NHS also argued that the Ombudsman had no power to make an award for distress and inconvenience, and that if there was such a power, there was no justification for exercising it in this case. In the second case, N changed jobs owing to the offer of a higher pensionable salary and informed his new employers, a regional health authority, at the interview, that he was taking the job for that reason and would be transferring his entitlement to the new scheme. However, he was prevented from doing so because he was over the age of 60, but alleged that his new employers had said that he could. A complaint of maladministration was upheld against the regional health authority and also against NHS because N had received a booklet prepared by NHS which dealt with transfer, but made no mention of what the position was for the over 60's. N was awarded the transfer value which he had missed out on and damages of £450 for distress and inconvenience.

Held, allowing the appeals, that (1) in both cases, there was no evidence upon which the Ombudsman could justify the award for distress and inconvenience. Evidence was needed to show more than the mere distress of a dispute. The Ombudsman was obliged to specify the loss for which the compensation was being awarded, and (2) in the second case, N had suffered no loss and, additionally, if he had not received the incorrect advice and not changed jobs, he would have been worse off, *Westminster City Council v. Haywood* [1996] C.L.Y. 000 followed.

NHS PENSIONS AGENCY v. PENSIONS OMBUDSMAN [1996] C.O.D. 321, Carnwath, J., QBD.

4661. Pensions Ombudsman–pension schemes–maladministration–ombudsman failed to comply with statutory fairness procedures and with principles of natural justice

[Pension Schemes Act 1993 s.149.]

S, L and H, former trustees of the Seifert Group pension scheme, and FTS, independent trustee appointed by the Seifert Group's administrative receivers, appealed against the Ombudsman's order in favour of a scheme member, K, on a complaint of maladministration. The trustees objected that the Ombudsman failed to give them an opportunity to reply to the allegations as stipulated by the Pension Schemes Act 1993 s.149. He sent copies of the complainant's early letters and received the trustees' replies, but failed to send copies of a further letter from K containing new and very serious allegations before he proceeded to make his provisional determination. He proposed to order the trustees to pay K his full benefit entitlement and reduce benefits to S and L accordingly. The trustees protested that the order was not an appropriate response to the allegations they had seen and that a clause exonerating the trustees from liability except for wilful default or neglect was disregarded. However, they were not informed of K's further allegations and the provisional order was made final.

Held, allowing the appeal, that the Ombudsman's order was affected by maladministration, ie. failure to observe justice in the decision making process, as well as by errors of law. He was wrong to disregard the clause in the scheme deed which exonerated the trustees and to order that K receive more than his fair share. Moreover, he failed to allow the trustees the opportunity to answer the allegations, upheld a complaint that was not made and granted relief which was not claimed. Costs were awarded against the Ombudsman.

SEIFERT v. PENSIONS OMBUDSMAN; LYNCH v. PENSIONS OMBUDSMAN [1997] 1 All E.R. 214, Lightman, J., QBD.

4662. Personal injuries–reduced life expectancy–loss of pension rights where plaintiff had choices on receipt of pension

V appealed against an award for damages in the sum of £199,961 awarded to W for personal injuries. The appeal was in relation to the part of the award relating to loss of pension rights and concerned the question of what impact the exercise of the plaintiff's choices, made under a pension policy giving him a number of choices, should have on the award of damages. V chose to take his pension at the age of 60 rather than 65, and for it to be paid on a surviving spouse basis because of his illness, and as a result he received a pension of £18,885 a year rather than £39,306. The judge awarded damages for the loss as a result of his choices for the years from age 65 to his death. He was also awarded damages for the years of lost pension, owing to his death being anticipated to occur 10 years prematurely, calculated on the basis of the pension he actually received. V argued that the sum awarded for the lost years was incorrectly calculated as it failed to take into account the amount received by W's wife after W's death. V further argued that the amount awarded for lost years amounted to double recovery as he had received damages for the reduction caused by his choices.

Held, dismissing the appeal, that (1) W's pension rights and the choices he made in exercising them should not be accounted for by a reduction in the damages awarded as W had paid for these rights, including the right to exercise a choice himself; (2) W's loss of earnings owing to his early retirement should be assessed without deducting pension contributions that he would have made if he had carried on working. There was no genuine loss as the amount would have been paid for his own benefit; (3) no damages should have been recoverable for the reduction in his pension during his lifetime as he elected himself to receive a pension for his widow in return for the reduction; (4) the loss of future contributions was accounted for in the award for loss of earnings, and (5) the widow's pension should not be deducted as it was bought and paid for by W by the reduction in his own pension. W was not compensated for that loss and so to have damages deducted for the widow's pension would mean that he would have suffered a double reduction for a single disbursement.

WEST v. VERSIL LTD, *The Times*, August 31, 1996, Phillips, L.J., CA.

4663. Personal pensions–contributions

SOCIAL SECURITY (MINIMUM CONTRIBUTIONS TO APPROPRIATE PERSONAL PENSION SCHEMES) ORDER 1996, SI 1996 1056; made under the Pension Schemes Act 1993 s.45A. In force: April 6, 1997; £1.10.

This Order is made as a consequence of a review by the Secretary of State, under the Pension Schemes Act 1993 s.45A, following a report by the Government Actuary, in relation to minimum contributions under s.43 of the 1993 Act. It specifies, with effect from April 6, 1997, the appropriate age related percentages of earnings payable as minimum contributions in respect of members of appropriate personal pension schemes. In accordance with s.45A of the 1993 Act, a copy of a report by the Government Actuary on the percentages which, in his opinion, are required so as to reflect the cost of s.48A (effect of reduced contributions and rebates on social security benefits), are foregone by or in respect of members of appropriate personal pension schemes, together with a copy of the report by the Secretary of State, was laid before Parliament with a draft of this Order.

4664. Personal pensions–contributions–deferred annuities

PERSONAL PENSION SCHEMES (DEFERRED ANNUITY PURCHASE) (ACCEPTANCE OF CONTRIBUTIONS) REGULATIONS 1996, SI 1996 805; made under the Income and Corporation Taxes Act 1988 s.638. In force: April 6, 1996; £1.10.

By virtue of the Income and Corporation Taxes Act 1988 s.638(7(A)) ("subsection 7A"), the Board of Inland Revenue may not approve a personal pension scheme for the purposes of Chapter IV of Part XIV of the 1988 Act which fails to prohibit (except in such cases as may be prescribed in Regulations made by the Board) the acceptance of further contributions and the making of transfer payments in respect of a member of the scheme after the date ("the pension date") on which the member elects to defer the purchase of an annuity under the scheme and to make income withdrawals from the scheme during the deferral period. These Regulations prescribe as a case for the purposes of subsection 7(A) the acceptance after the pension date of minimum contributions paid by the Department of Social Security in respect of the member.

4665. Personal pensions–deferred annuities–income

PERSONAL PENSION SCHEMES (TABLES OF RATES OF ANNUITIES) REGULATIONS 1996, SI 1996 1311; made under the Income and Corporation Taxes Act 1988 s.630. In force: June 5, 1996; £0.65.

These Regulations make provision for the basis on which the Government Actuary is to prepare tables of rates of annuities for the purposes of the Income and Corporation Taxes Act 1988 Part XIV Chapter IV relating to personal pension schemes. They provide that tables shall be prepared with respect to protected rights of a member under a personal pension scheme in accordance with certain provisions of the Personal and Occupational Pension Scheme (Protected Rights) Regulations 1987 (SI 1987 1117, as amended by SI 1996 776), and that separate tables shall be prepared with respect to rights of a member of a personal pension scheme other than protected rights in accordance with the basis provided by Reg.4 of these Regulations.

4666. Personal pensions–occupational pensions–protected rights

PERSONAL AND OCCUPATIONAL PENSION SCHEMES (PROTECTED RIGHTS) REGULATIONS 1996, SI 1996 1537; made under the Pension Schemes Act 1993 s.9, s.10, s.27, s.28, s.28A, s.29, s.32, s.155, s.181, s.182, s.183. In force: April 6, 1997; £3.20.

These Regulations consolidate the Personal and Occupational Pension Schemes (Protected Rights) Regulations 1987 (SI 1987 1117) with its amendments (SI 1988 474, SI 1990 1142, SI 1992 1531, SI 1994 1062, SI 1995 35, SI 1996 776). They relate to the calculation and verification of protected rights; the rights which schemes may designate as protected; conditions applying to pensions and annuities giving effect to protected rights; circumstances in which and periods for which a pension or annuity is to be paid to certain persons; conditions and requirements applying to interim arrangements; circumstances in which lump sum benefits may be provided or in which protected rights may be surrendered or forfeited; conditions relating to insurance companies and annuities; the death of scheme members and prevention of discrimination by a scheme.

4667. Personal pensions–review of pension transactions authorised by Securities and Investment Board–application by pension companies to stay actions against them

[Supreme Court Act 1981 s.49; Rules of the Supreme Court Ord.18 r.19.]

Various pension companies applied to stay six separate actions brought against them in respect of wrong advice given by them in relation to personal pension schemes. The applications followed a review of pension transactions authorised by the Securities and Investments Board.

Held, dismissing the applications, that the review was an administrative process which did not amount to an arbitration or an alternative dispute resolution. As there was no legal obligation to submit to the review, the claims were not an abuse of process within the Rules of the Supreme Court Ord.18 r.19. Nor were the circumstances such that an action could be stayed under the Supreme Court Act 1981 s.49(3).

COCKING v. PRUDENTIAL ASSURANCE CO LTD [1996] O.P.L.R. 35, Raymond Jack Q.C., QBD.

4668. Superannuation–criminal injuries compensation

SUPERANNUATION (ADMISSION TO SCHEDULE 1 OF THE SUPERANNUATION ACT 1972) ORDER 1996, SI 1996 608; made under the Superannuation Act 1972 s.1. In force: March 27, 1996; £0.65.

This Order adds the office of Chairman of the Criminal Injuries Compensation Board to the offices listed in the Superannuation Act 1972 Sch.1 so that s.1 of the Act (under which the Principal Civil Service Pension Scheme and the Civil Service Compensation Scheme have been made) may apply to it. Provision for the appointment of the Chairman of the Criminal Injuries Compensation Board was made jointly by the Home Secretary and the Secretary of State for Scotland under the terms of the Criminal Injuries Compensation Scheme brought into existence by the exercise of the Royal Prerogative and announced in Parliament on June 24, 1964. Under the power conferred by the Superannuation Act 1972 s.1 (8) (a) the Order takes effect from March 1, 1989.

4669. Superannuation–National Forest Company

SUPERANNUATION (ADMISSION TO SCHEDULE 1 OF THE SUPERANNUATION ACT 1972) (NO.2) ORDER 1996, SI 1996 1029; made under the Superannuation Act 1972 s.1. In force: April 23, 1996; £0.65.

This Order adds employment by the National Forest Company to the employments listed in the Superannuation Act 1972 Sch.1 so that s.1 of that Act (under which the Principal Civil Service Pension Scheme, the Civil Service Additional Voluntary Contribution Scheme and the Civil Service Compensation Scheme have been made) may apply to it. Provision for the employment of staff of the National Forest Company was made pursuant to the Articles of Association of the National Forest Company, a company limited by guarantee and incorporated on November 18, 1994. Under the power conferred by the Superannuation Act 1972 s.1 (8) (a) the Order takes effect from April 1, 1995.

4670. Superannuation–teachers–contracting out

CONTRACTING OUT (ADMINISTRATION OF THE TEACHERS' SUPERANNUATION SCHEME) ORDER 1996, SI 1996 178; made under the Deregulation and Contracting Out Act 1994 s.69. In force: January 31, 1996; £0.65.

This Order enables the Secretary of State to authorise another person, or that person's employees, to carry out on her behalf her functions regarding the teachers' superannuation scheme and the payment generally of pensions, allowances or gratuities to or in respect of teachers, to such extent as is specified in the authorisation.

4671. Articles

A tale of caution *(Peter Docking)*: Pen. World 1996, 25(11) Supp DC, 9-11. (Investment duties of money purchase pension scheme trustees and importance of communication with members).

Actuaries attempt to please everyone with disclosure rules: Occ. Pen. 1996, 109, 6-8. (Actuaries' revised recommendations arising from Greenbury report that costs of directors' final salary schemes should be shown in company accounts by either accrued benefit or transfer value method allow more flexibility).

Advising on pensions *(Michael J. Wilson)*: S.J. 1996, 140(19), 490. (Guidance on pensions advice for solicitors offering discrete investment business).

After the Act *(John Hayward)*: Tax J. 1996, 358, 19-20. (Provisions in 1996 FA affecting pension schemes which were not in Budget, including changes to personal pension schemes and retirement annuity contracts, s.172 post death repayments income withdrawal facility and IHT liabilities).

Annuity deferral: P.T. 1996, 19(4), 6-7. (Inland Revenue temporary solution for members of schemes wanting to transfer money to personal pensions following delay in announcements on deferral options and PIA rules on pension fund withdrawals).

Another brick in the wall? *(Amyas Mascarenhas* and *Jeff Highfield)*: Pen. World 1996, 25(5), 57-59. (Impact that FRS 8 Related Party Disclosures will have on trustees and reports and accounts they distribute to scheme members).

Article 119 and retrospective pension rights *(Victor Craig)*: Emp. L. 1996, 11 (Feb), 7-10. (Time limits for actions to enforce Art.119 rights and relationship between EC law and implementing legislation).

Breaking free *(Allan Martin)*: Pen. World 1996, 25(8), 39-40. (Introduction of earmarking of pension benefits under 1995 Act involving cash equivalent transfer values and debate on pensions splitting during passage of 1996 Family Law Bill).

Changes to the Disclosure Regulations: P.S.T. 1996, 3(7), 2-5. (Revised Regulations in force April 6, 1997 empower OPRA to fine defaulting trustees).

Contracting out for occupational pension schemes: the new regime *(Catherine McKenna)*: B.P.L. 1996, 71, 1-3. (SI 1996 1172 in force April 5, 1997 will prospectively dissociate SERPS from contracted out schemes, require all schemes to re-elect to remain contracted out and introduce statutory standard test for final salary schemes).

Contracting-out after April 1997 *(Tony Bannard)*: T.N.I.B. 1996, 5(8), 63-64. (New rules on pension schemes' ability to contract out of SERPS and NI rebates).

Disclosing board members' pensions: the alternatives: Occ. Pen. 1996, 105, 5-7. (Five methods of valuing directors' pensions in accounts proposed by Faculty of Actuaries in discussion paper *Disclosure of Directors Pensions: Possible Methods of Calculation of Entitlements*).

Drafting solutions to specific problem areas in pension scheme deeds *(David Pollard)*: J.P.M. 1996, 1(4), 297-312. (Common pitfalls when drafting provisions regarding classification of employers' powers, conflicts of interest, trustee indemnities, amendment powers, consolidation and ill health).

Fiduciary, moi? *(Robin Ellison)*: Pen. World 1996, 25(2), 61. (Consequences of provisions in Act which extend fiduciary obligations of trustees to other professionals).

Funding directors' pension schemes *(John Hayward)*: Tax J. 1996, 347, 8-10. (Inland Revenue small self administered pension scheme and executive pension plan funding proposals, based on NAO 1991 report, embodying five and six year transitional periods, respectively, with insurance and index linking provisions).

GMPs under UK pension funds: the impact of Article 119 *(John Southern)*: Tru. L.I. 1996, 10(3), 70-77. (Problems which arise with regard to guaranteed minimum standard for contracted out schemes in relation to requirement to equalise occupational scheme benefits following Barber decision).

Insured schemes–your money or your life? *(Penny Webster* and *Raj Mody)*: B.P.L. 1996, 70, 1-3. (Advantages, costs and problems with deferred annuity and deposit administration contracts).

Internal dispute procedures: a means to an amicable end? Occ. Pen. 1996, 111, 8-11. (Requirements for establishing grievance procedures for occupational pension schemes).

Member-nominated trustees *(Chris Johnson* and *Samantha Buxton)*: C.S.R. 1996, 20(4), 25-27. (Provisions of SI 1996 1216 introducing requirement for member representation on trustee boards of pension schemes which came fully into force on April 6, 1997).

My pension: destitution! divorce! death! *(Roger Smith)*: Counsel 1996, Sep/Oct, 26-28. (Importance of monitoring personal pensions and effects of death or divorce).

Paying rapt attention to pensions *(Ian Purves)*: T.P.T. 1996, 17(18), 137-140. (Interaction of tax reliefs between retirement annuity policies and personal pension policies and effect of self assessment).

Pension schemes–keeping the peace *(Helen Powell)*: C.S.R. 1996, 20(9), 65-66. (Provisions of SI 1996 1270 setting out two stage procedure for dealing with disputes between pension scheme members and trustees).

Pensions accounting *(Mike Jones* and *Martin Lowes)*: J.P.M. 1996, 1(3), 213-224. (FRS 7 on acquisitions deals for first time with pension surplus and deficits, proposed reforms to SSAP 24 on pension costs in employers' statements and SORP 1 on schemes' accounts and Greenbury recommendations on directors' disclosure).

Personal pension scheme protective trusts: marketing manna or legal morass? *(Martin Scott)*: Int. I.L.R. 1996, 4(7), 217-220. (Advantages for personal pension contributors of PSO policy that schemes will be allowed to include forfeiture clause or protective trust for purchasers to shelter assets from risk of bankruptcy).

Post-divorce splitting accepted: P.S.T. 1996, 3(7), 7-8. (Regulations on pension splitting expected in force August 1, 1996 will provide for earmarking or attachment orders).

Setting the stage *(Steven Mendel)*: Pen. World 1996, 25(9), 5-6. (How pension scheme trustees may carry out their investment strategy whilst complying with provisions of 1995 Act).

Sex discrimination: part-time workers pension claim in the industrial tribunal and new legislation: Bus. L.R. 1996, 17(2), 42-43. (Time limits for part time workers' claims regarding exclusion from pension schemes and resulting changes to UK legislation in SI 1995 3183).

Target practice *(Lee Jagger)*: Pen. World 1996, 25(11) Supp DC, 3-5. (Options available to trustees and employers who decide to provide money purchase occupational pension scheme and importance of communication with members).

Taxing the fat *(Clive Briggs)*: Pen. World 1996, 25(1), 46-47. (Inland Revenue rules on pension funds surplus, with particular reference to money purchase and hybrid schemes).

The class of '97 *(Mark Grant)*: Pen. World 1996, 25(8), 37-38. (Changes made by 1995 Act affecting pension trustees from April 1997 with particular reference to trustee liability).

The lawyer's lawyer *(Tim Cooper)*: Pen. World 1996, 25(1), 21-23. (Qualities needed to be successful pensions lawyer and lawyers' recommendations for best all round lawyer).

The National Bus pension scheme: P.S.T. 1996, 3(10), 2-3. (Whether amendment of scheme's winding up rules and payment of surplus to Government following privatisation was breach of trust).

The pension lawyer *(Anna Kelly)*: Pen. World 1995, 24(12), 63. (Role of lawyers in pension scheme administration).

The Pensions Act: safeguarding employee pensions *(Andrew White)*: P.L.C. 1996, 7(5), 41-47. (Main provisions of 1995 Act and practical steps to be taken by companies to prepare for its coming into force on April 6, 1997).

The pensions aspects of sales and acquisitions *(Maria Stimpson)*: I.H.L. 1996, Feb, 25-30. (Employees' pension rights on share
sales and business sales, warranties, documentation, negotiating interim participation period and calculation and payment of transfer value).

The tax free market *(Robin Ellison)*: Pen. World 1996, 25(1), 49. (Whether there will ever be competition between Member States to offer simplest and most efficient tax relief system for pension funds).

The value of choice *(Sarah Milner)*: Pen. World 1996, 25(11) Supp DC, 12-14. (Implications of move to money purchase occupational pension schemes for choice of investments and whether trustees are providing members with right information).

There's a fraudster about! *(Ann Hearn)*: Pen. World 1996, 25(1), 29-30. (Danger areas for pension schemes and steps which can be taken by trustees and managers to avoid fraud).

Valuing early leavers' benefits *(Paul Greenwood)*: Occ. Pen. 1996, 107, 12-14. (What transfer values are, how current legislative regime works and problems which occur).

When can a liquidator get his hands on surplus on the winding-up of an occupational pensions scheme? *(Ian Greenstreet)*: I.L. & P. 1996, 12(2), 35-38. (Powers of liquidator to acquire surplus of pension schemes on winding up of company under six different provisions which may be made).

When can a trustee in bankruptcy get his hands on your pension? *(Ian Greenstreet)*: Tru. L.I. 1996, 10(1), 6-14. (Effectiveness of forfeiture clauses, whether member's rights vest in trustee under s.306, whether lump sum benefit vests in trustee and impact of 1995 Act).

You will comply *(Roy Harding)*: Tax. P. 1996, Oct, 7-8. (Stricter reporting and record keeping requirements for approved pension schemes, automatic disclosure to PSO, time limits and default penalties in force January 1, 1996).

4672. Books

Arthur, Hugh–Pensions Trusteeship Issues. Pensions reports. Hardback: £125.00. ISBN 0-7520-0178-7. FT Law & Tax.

Cooper, Neil; Hand, Sean–Pension Schemes and Liquidation. Hardback: £60.00. ISBN 0-85308-233-2. Jordan.

Ellison, Robin–European Pensions Law. Hardback: £60.00. ISBN 0-406-02449-9. Butterworth Law.

Ellison, Robin–The Pensions Practice: 1996. Hardback: £60.00. ISBN 0-85308-350-9. Jordan.

Ellison, Robin; Rae, Maggie–Ellison and Rae: Family Breakdown and Pensions. Paperback: £25.00. ISBN 0-406-03766-3. Butterworth Law.

Ghosh, Julian–Taxation of Pensions Schemes. Pensions reports. Hardback: £125.00. ISBN 0-7520-0236-8. FT Law & Tax.

Lewis, Roger; Kelloway, Ros–Jacques and Lewis: Sex Discrimination and Occupational Pension Schemes. Current EC legal developments. Paperback: £90.00. ISBN 0-406-00344-0. Butterworth Law.

Pensions Law. Paperback: £42.00. ISBN 0-406-04933-5. Butterworth Law.

Reardon, Anthony–Allied Dunbar Pensions Handbook. Hardback: £24.99. ISBN 0-273-62506-3. Pitman Publishing.

Salter, David–Pensions and Insurance on Family Breakdown. Paperback: £32.50. ISBN 0-85308-331-2. Family Law.

Shulman, Gary; Kelley, David I.–Learning from the Pension Experts. Family law. Hardback: £90.00. ISBN 0-471-12406-0. John Wiley and Sons.

White, Andrew; Punter, Jonathan–Pensions Issues in Mergers and Acquisitions. Pensions reports. Hardback: £95.00. ISBN 0-7520-0293-7. FT Law & Tax.

PLANNING

4673. Advertisements–notice to discontinue–deemed consent for display–whether notices valid due to irregularity of service

[Town and Country Planning Act 1990 s.288; Town and Country Planning (Control of Advertisements) Regulations 1992.]

The applicants sought under the Town and Country Planning Act 1990 s.288 to quash a decision of the Secretary of State dismissing their appeal against a discontinuance notice concerning an advertising hoarding which had been in use since 1927 and had deemed consent under the Town and Country Planning (Control of Advertisements) Regulations 1992. The applicants had appealed on the merits but the inspector found for the local planning authority. Nine identical notices were issued. It was submitted that the service had not been good but, if it had, service of copies of the notice on different dates rendered the notice a nullity and the Secretary of State's decision was undated and therefore prejudicial to the applicants.

Held, dismissing the application, the appeal had been unsuccessful and had been dismissed. The question was whether, given the technical irregularities, there was discretion to grant relief. In the instant case, the applicants had not been prejudiced. Any uncertainty in the original notices could have been resolved by taking the last date on which they might have taken effect. Although it was inefficient that SSE's decision had been undated, it bore a post mark and the applicants had received it in time to challenge its validity within the time limits. Accordingly, the applicants had suffered no prejudice, *Bambury v. Hounslow LBC* [1966] 2 Q.B. 204, *Swishbrook Ltd v. Secretary of State for the Environment* [1990] P.L.R. 824, [1990] C.L.Y. 4359 and *Miller v. Weymouth and Melcombe Regis Corp* (1974) 27 P. & C.R. 468 considered.

NAHLIS, DICKEY & MORRIS v. SECRETARY OF STATE FOR THE ENVIRONMENT (1996) 71 P. &. C.R. 553, G Moriarty Q.C., QBD.

4674. Advertisements–planning appeals–meaning of "substantial injury to amenity"–removal or alteration an appropriate remedy

[Town and Country Planning (Control of Advertisement) Regulations 1992 Reg.8.]

C applied to challenge the decision of the Secretary of State dismissing their appeal against a discontinuance notice served under the Town and Country Planning (Control of Advertisement) Regulations 1992 Reg.8. The notice related to an advertisement hoarding. C argued that the planning inspector failed to deal with whether the notice was necessary to remedy substantial injury to the amenity of the locality, which was the main issue of the appeal. The meaning of "substantial" was not defined and it was not determined whether remedy could be achieved by removal of the whole sign or an alteration to it. C also argued that the decision letter did not contain sufficient reasons for the decision.

Held, dismissing the application, that (1) there was no misdirection in relation to the meaning of "substantial injury to amenity". The decision was clear and the Secretary of State did not have to consider the meaning independently; (2) the Secretary of State was not obliged to consider any lesser form of remedy than removal; (3) the Secretary of State was not required to deal expressly with every point raised in the appeal, *Bolton MDC v. Secretary of State for the Environment* [1995] E.G.C.S. 94, [1995] 2 C.L.Y. 4760 applied, and (4) the decision letter dealt with all the main issues with clear reasons. There was no error of law.

CHEQUEPOINT UK LTD v. SECRETARY OF STATE FOR THE ENVIRONMENT (1996) 72 P. & C.R. 415, Gerald Moriarty Q.C., QBD.

4675. Agricultural property–planning permission–dwelling for agricultural worker–regard to suitability and availability of existing accommodation

K sought, under the Town and Country Planning Act 1990 s.288, to quash a decision of the Secretary of State's inspector dismissing an appeal against the refusal of planning permission for the erection of a dwelling to accommodate an agricultural worker. K wished to employ a stockman so that he could withdraw from active farming. It was essential that the stockman should live close enough to be available to tend the stock around the clock when necessary. It was submitted that it was unreasonable for the inspector to have concluded that a stockman could have been accommodated in the existing farmhouse either by the applicant moving out, or by sharing, or that a stockman could have lived elsewhere.

Held, allowing the application, it could not be accepted that the putative local development plan and PPG 7 could have been reasonably interpreted and applied with the results identified by the inspector. In order to test the need for the appealed development, it was necessary to ask whether there was existing accommodation which was both suitable and available. The decision letter did not disclose the basis upon which this exercise had been carried out. The mere existence of the farmhouse was not itself sufficient and there was no material to suggest that a stockman could have been accommodated there. There were many matters requiring detailed consideration including the issue of planning permission for the shared accommodation. On the basis of the material identified in the decision letter the conclusion was manifestly unreasonable.

KEEN v. SECRETARY OF STATE FOR THE ENVIRONMENT (1996) 71 P. & C.R. 543, Sir Graham Eyre Q.C., QBD.

4676. Agricultural property–planning permission–dwelling for worker–whether use essential for needs of agriculture–nature and location of site–whether racehorse grazing capable of being agricultural use

[Town and Country Planning Act 1990 s.336.]

R applied to quash a decision by a planning inspector to refuse outline planning permission for a dwelling as essential to the needs of agriculture. The four and a half hectare site was situated on agricultural land beyond the boundary of an established settlement, on ground used for grazing racehorses. In her decision, the inspector found that, given the small area and the type of animals involved, the use was not an agricultural enterprise. She also stated that, as there was no need for a worker to be readily available for the horses, the application did not show exceptional circumstances capable of outweighing the harm such a development would cause to the rural character.

Held, refusing the application, that as the application sought to quash a decision based on a subjective determination of matters of fact and degree, it could be allowed only if perversity was found. On the facts, the proposal did not constitute an infill development essential for agricultural needs under the Town and Country Planning Act 1990 s.336, *Sykes v. Secretary of State for the Environment* (1981) 257 E.G. 821, [1981] C.L.Y. 2735 considered. In addition, even if the inspector had been wrong on this point, she had then gone on to find that there was no need for a house on the site for agricultural purposes in any event.

RETTER v. SECRETARY OF STATE FOR THE ENVIRONMENT [1995] E.G.C.S. 33, Nigel Macleod Q.C., QBD.

4677. Agricultural property–planning permission–new farmhouse refused–whether sufficient agricultural need–failure to consider policy in local plan–whether unreasonable refusal to hear representations–whether perverse to refuse site inspection

[Town and Country Planning (Inquiries Procedure) Rules 1992 Reg.11.]

B appealed against the refusal of planning permission to build a farmhouse for a tenant farmer. The main issue of the inquiry was whether there was sufficient agricultural need for the new farmhouse. B argued that the inspector (1) failed to consider policy H/S 14 of the local plan; (2) that, contrary to the Town and Country Planning (Inquiries Procedure) Rules 1992 Reg.11 (2), to hear the representations by the tenant farmer, and (3) by refusing to inspect a farm dwelling on an adjacent farm, had acted perversely. If this application was unsuccessful, B would apply, under Ord.53, for an order for costs against B, to be quashed.

Held, refusing the applications, that (1) the subject matter of policy H/S 14 was considered in the decision letter. Even if the inspector had failed to take account of the policy, he would have been unlikely to have reached a different decision; (2) the inspector had to balance a range of considerations to maintain fairness, natural justice and promptness in decision making. The court would intervene if the inspector had acted unreasonably within the ordinary meaning of the word. The inspector had not acted unreasonably or in breach of Reg.11 (2) by not allowing the tenant farmer to speak. Even if there was a breach, B had suffered no substantial prejudice; (3) it was not perverse of the inspector to refuse to make a site visit central to the case, and (4) in relation to costs, there was no reliance upon policy as justification for maintaining the appeal.

BARNETT v. SECRETARY OF STATE FOR THE ENVIRONMENT [1996] E.G.C.S. 6, R Purchas Q.C., QBD.

4678. Bias–refusal of reviewed matters–appeal to planning inquiry–witness speaking to inspector–whether breach of natural justice occurred–whether real danger of bias

[Town and Country Planning Act 1990 s.288.]

M applied under the Town and Country Planning Act 1990 s.288 for an order quashing a planning inspector's refusal of a reserved matters application, including the site, design and appearance of a proposed development already subject to outline planning permission. During the public inquiry, the inspector was seen talking to a person who later gave evidence as an objector to the development. M submitted, inter alia, that this amounted to a breach of natural justice.

Held, dismissing the application, that (1) on the facts, the incident fell below that needed to show evidence of a real danger of bias on the part of the inspector, *R. v. Gough* [1993] 2 W.L.R. 883, [1993] C.L.Y. 849 considered, and (2) no concern had been expressed at the time by M, and the witness had not been cross-examined about the matter.

MARSH v. SECRETARY OF STATE FOR THE ENVIRONMENT (1995) 70 P. & C.R. 637, Hidden, J., QBD.

4679. Bias–urban development corporations–pecuniary and personal interests of body exercising planning powers–duty not to participate–interpretation of participation

[Local Government Planning and Land Act 1980 Part XVI.]

KVC, a community action group, applied for judicial review of decisions of the Leeds Development Corporation, LDC, granting planning permission for the development of a supermarket on a rugby ground owned by Headingley Football Club. The chairman of LDC owned land to which the rugby club was considering moving and other members of LDC had connections with the rugby club. KVC argued that there was apparent bias and the decisions were contaminated by such undeclared interests and therefore were vitiated.

Held, dismissing the application, that LDC was a statutory body created under the Local Government Planning and Land Act 1980 Part XVI and members were under a duty not to participate in decisions in which they had an interest, either personal or pecuniary, *R. v. Gough* [1993] A.C. 646, [1993] C.L.Y. 849 followed. This rule was not restricted to judicial or quasi-judicial bodies but was generally applicable in public law. Members of a body exercising planning powers could not participate in a decision if they had a personal or pecuniary interest unless the interest was too remote. Non-participation meant more than merely declaring the interest and abstaining from the discussion and the vote; withdrawal from the meeting was necessary. On the facts, the plan to move the rugby club to land owned by the chairman was no longer an option at the time the decision was made. The decision did not arise out of previous tainted decisions but was a new proposal considered afresh by LDC. Membership of the rugby club did not constitute an attachment capable of leading to bias, *R. v. Rand* (1866) L.R. 1 Q.B. 230 considered.

R. v. SECRETARY OF STATE FOR THE ENVIRONMENT, *ex p.* KIRKSTALL VALLEY CAMPAIGN LTD; SUB NOM. R. v. SECRETARY OF STATE FOR THE ENVIRONMENT, *ex p.* WILLIAM MORRISON SUPERMARKET PLC [1996] 3 All E.R. 304, Sedley, J., QBD.

4680. Blight notices–counter notice–whether land was blighted land

Held, that a counter notice served in response to a blight notice in east London was upheld where the local authority was not the only possible developer and the land was not allocated in the local development plan for the purposes of the local authority's functions.

ELCOCK v. NEWHAM LBC (1996) 71 P. & C.R. 575, AP Musto, FRICS., Lands Tr.

4681. Blight notices–subsequent sale of property–sale constituting deemed withdrawal of notice

Held, that where a claimant had served a blight notice and subsequently sold the property which was the subject of his claim for compensation, the sale amounted to a deemed withdrawal of the notice.

CARREL v. LONDON UNDERGROUND LTD [1995] R.V.R. 234, M St J Hopper, FRICS., Lands Tr.

4682. Blight notices–whether garden ground could be taken for road improvement purposes–effect on the amenity or convenience of a house–whether council obliged to take whole hereditament–impact of scheme to be considered in its entirety

[Town and Country Planning Act 1990 s.150, s.151, s.166.]

S owned a semi detached residential property. K were proposing to acquire nine square metres of the front garden and 21 square metres of the garden temporarily as additional working space during a highway widening scheme, involving the felling of mature trees. A proposed purchaser of the property pulled out of the transaction on hearing of the highway widening scheme. S served a blight notice under the Town and Country Planning Act 1990 s.150, requiring the council to purchase the whole property. K served a counter notice, under s.151 of the 1990 Act, to the effect that it proposed to acquire only a part of the hereditament unless otherwise compelled to do so. S contended, further to s.166(2) of the 1990 Act, that part of the garden could not be acquired without "seriously affecting the amenity or convenience of the house".

Held, upholding the blight notice and dismissing the counter-notice, that the impact of the highway scheme fell to be considered in its entirety and this could not be done by taking facets of the proposals or the works necessary to complete the scheme in isolation. Although the amenity of the house would not be seriously affected by the execution of the works, the loss of privacy arising from the felling of mature trees would affect the quality of residence in the house. This would not be remedied by the planting of semi mature trees. On the evidence, the execution of the works in the highway improvement scheme would have a serious effect on the convenience of the house.

SMITH AND SMITH v. KENT CC (1995) 70 P. & C.R. 669, T Hoyes, FRICS., Lands Tr.

4683. Bridleways–diversions–new application made by developers–whether it was a device to circumvent Circular 2/93

[Town and Country Planning Act 1990 s.78, s.247, s.257.]

C appealed against the dismissal of her application to quash an order for the diversion of a bridleway in Avon. The developers had planning permission to build 37 houses, but discovered that a bridleway crossed the plots of three houses. A diversion order obtained by the developer in 1989 was quashed. The developers then applied, under the Town and Country Planning Act 1990 s.257, for another diversion order which was refused. The Secretary of State also refused to exercise his powers under s.247 of the 1990 Act. In 1993 the developers applied for planning permission in relation to the three houses with the additional features of the removal of a hedge, the repositioning of a boundary fence, a cattle grid and a kissing gate. Upon refusal, the developer appealed, under s.78 of the 1990 Act, and requested the Secretary of State to exercise his discretion to publish a notice of the draft order in advance of the grant of permission, which he did. Following an inquiry the inspector recommended that the permission should be granted and the bridleway diverted. The Secretary of State accepted the recommendations, but with conditions that the grid and gate should not be included. C argued that, in dismissing her application, the judge had erred by not finding that the 1993 application was merely a device to circumvent Circular 2/93 which stated that s.247 orders should be made only in exceptional circumstances unless there was an application for planning permission before the Secretary of State. C further argued that the developers had already obtained planning permission for the three houses and should have applied for permission only for the grid and the gate. The judge failed to consider the real reason behind the application and therefore failed to give adequate reasons for allowing it.

Held, dismissing the appeal, that the Secretary of State had a duty to deal with the application and the request under s.253. The Secretary of State did not know at that stage that, in the end, the grid and gate would be excluded. The judge was entitled, on the facts, to conclude that the application was not a device and gave adequate reasons for his decision.

CALDER v. SECRETARY OF STATE FOR THE ENVIRONMENT [1996] E.G.C.S. 78, Hutchison, L.J., CA.

4684. Bridleways–governed by an Inclosure Act award–whether width could be altered–whether s.29 of the 1981 Act and s.41 of the 1980 Act were compatible

[Wildlife and Countryside Act 1981 s.29; Highways Act 1980 s.41.]

W sought judicial review of a decision of an inspector appointed by the Secretary of State. The decision related to the width of a bridleway governed by an Inclosure Act award. W contended that the bridleway should not be altered in contravention of the award. The inspector contended that the right of way could be altered to a limited extent. W argued, inter alia, that the obligations imposed on the authority by the Wildlife and Countryside Act 1981 s.29 and the Highways Act 1980 s.41 were incompatible.

Held, dismissing the application, that both statutory provisions could be read together and reconciled, as a matter of law. There was no conflict between conservation and highway maintenance where the statutes were interpreted correctly.

WARD v. SECRETARY OF STATE FOR THE ENVIRONMENT [1996] J.P.L. 200, Turner, J., QBD.

4685. Change of use–amalgamation of planning units–validity of certificate of lawful use–use classes–auction house as retail shop

[Town and Country Planning Use Classes Order 1987 Class A1.]

EF, a supermarket, sought judicial review of the grant of a certificate of lawful proposed use to CI, their landlord and the property-holding arm of the auctioneers, Christies. EF had a 10 year underlease. CI occupied the adjoining premises and planned to use EF's premises for storage, sales and a viewing room with access either from the street or directly from the adjoining saleroom. The certificate stated that planning permission for change of use was not required as it was within the Town and Country Planning Use Classes Order 1987 Class A1. EF argued that the order did not apply as two existing planning units were being amalgamated.

Held, refusing the application, that (1) the present use as a supermarket and the proposed use as auction rooms both fell within Class 1. The certificate applied to one planning unit but the proposed combined use was considered and held not to constitute a change of use. The proposed combined use did not vitiate the certificate; (2) KC's decision that the amalgamation did not constitute a change of use or the start of a new planning history was one of fact and degree and was justifiable, and (3) the question of whether the auction house was a shop within the meaning of Class A was one of fact. A sale of goods did take place, *Cawley v. Secretary of State for the Environment* [1990] 2 P.L.R. 90, [1991] C.L.Y. 3437 considered.

R. v. KENSINGTON AND CHELSEA RLBC, *ex p.* EUROPA FOODS LTD [1996] E.G.C.S. 5, Macpherson, J., QBD.

4686. Change of use–consideration of existing planning permission–application of provisions of Use Classes Order on multiple use sites

[Town and Country Planning (Use Classes) Order 1987.]

K applied to have set aside the Secretary of State's dismissal of its appeal against the refusal to grant planning permission for the erection of a 22 bed hostel and a four bedroom house for use as a drug rehabilitation centre. The hostel was intended to take over the activities of existing medication, dispensing and social support facilities on the site. The inspector held that those facilities constituted a day centre and their substantial intensification was a material change of use and therefore not lawful. This led the inspector to treat the application as establishing a new use. K argued that the inspector had erred by concluding that the day centre use was not lawful. He had failed to consider planning permission for the existing development on the site and had failed correctly to apply the provisions of the Town and Country Planning (Use Classes) Order 1987 Class D1. K argued that the site should not have been split into a site carrying a number of uses.

Held, dismissing the application, that (1) the inspector was entitled to consider the fact that the existing use, which amounted to an intensification of the use of a day centre, was unlawful, and (2) K had close links with a church occupying the site, but they were separate legal entities and the land and buildings were partly owned by the church and partly owned by K. In the case of a site with more than one ownership the inspector had correctly applied the 1987 Order to the independent uses of the site.

KALEIDOSCOPE HOUSING ASSOCIATION LTD v. SECRETARY OF STATE FOR THE ENVIRONMENT, Trans. Ref: CO/2236/94, October 31, 1995, Gerald Moriarty Q.C., QBD.

4687. Change of use–enforcement notices–mixed use as scrap yard and agricultural use without planning permission–whether immune from enforcement action due to 10 years user–need for regulation of use

[Town and Country Planning Act 1990 s.171B; Waste Management Licensing Regulations 1994.]

An enforcement notice was issued in respect of an allegedly unauthorised change of use without planning permission of land and buildings to a mixed use of scrap yard, agricultural and private domestic use. L appealed, claiming immunity from the notice, by virtue of the Town and Country Planning Act 1990 s.171B (3), on the basis that no enforcement action may be taken 10 years after the beginning of the breach. The issue arose as to whether the land had been consistently used as a "scrap yard".

Held, dismissing the appeal, whether a material change of use has taken place is a matter of fact and degree for the Secretary of State and Inspectors. It is important that the business of scrap metal dealers be controlled due to the associated loss of amenity and in the light of the exemptions conferred by the Waste Management Licensing Regulations 1994. On these facts, it appeared that the court was being asked to go beyond the legislation and to usurp the Inspector's findings of fact.

LILLEY v. SECRETARY OF STATE FOR THE ENVIRONMENT AND NORTH YORKSHIRE CC [1996] 1 P.L.R. 28, Sir Graham Eyre Q.C., QBD.

4688. Change of use–planning permission–flying of model aircraft–whether need for trial period

W appealed against C's decision to grant planning permission for a change in the use of land from agricultural land to use for model aircraft flying and associated parking, subject to conditions that the permission would only continue for a limited period, flying could not take place within certain times and the flying of model aircraft over a given weight could not take place at certain times. The main issue was whether or not the conditions were reasonable and necessary. W argued that, because the proposed use had continued for some time without authorisation, there was no need for a trial period.

Held, allowing the appeal, that the conditions should be altered to allow for a two year period for the permission and specifications as to time of use and the weight and decibel output of aircraft at given times.

CHILTERN DC v. WATFORD WAYFARERS MODEL AIRCRAFT CLUB (1995) 10 P.A.D. 802, Judge not specified.

4689. Change of use–whether solicitor's office fell within Class A2–whether solicitor operated appointments system or if clients came in off the street

[Town and Country Planning (Use Classes) Order 1987.]

K, a solicitor, appealed against the upholding of the dismissal of his appeal against the local planning authority's refusal to grant planning permission for change of use from a shop to a solicitor's office within Class A2 of the Town and Country Planning (Use Classes) Order 1987.

Held, allowing the appeal, that Class A2 required services to be provided "principally for visiting members of the public" and, although some solicitor's offices would definitely not fall within this category because their services were provided almost entirely by way of telephones and correspondence, it was quite feasible that a solicitor wishing to offer advice along the lines of a Citizens' Advice Bureau or a Law Centre, albeit on a profit basis, would fall within Class A2. The existence of an appointments system did not preclude a solicitor's office from qualifying under A2. The difficulties of administering those solicitors who chose to run an A2 office were for the local authority to deal with and should not be a bar to a grant of planning permission.

KALRA v. SECRETARY OF STATE FOR THE ENVIRONMENT AND WALTHAM FOREST BC (1996) 72 P. & C.R. 423, Henry, L.J., CA.

4690. Compensation–acquisition of land as if by compulsory purchase–consideration of betterment to retained land

[Highways Act 1980 s.261.]

Held, in determining the amount of compensation payable on the acquisition of a claimant's freehold interest in land, where consideration was to be the same as that payable on compulsory purchase, the Highways Act 1980 s.261 (1) (a) required the tribunal to set off any betterment to the land retained by the claimant, due to the development.

LEICESTER CITY COUNCIL v. LEICESTERSHIRE CC (1995) 70 P. & C.R. 435, T Hoyes, FRICS., Lands Tr.

4691. Compensation–costs–consent to fell tree subject to the tree preservation order refused–compensation for remedial work due to root damage–extent of tribunal power to award damages

Consent to fell a mature ash tree, protected by a tree preservation order, was refused in October 1990. B sought expert advice and contended that the roots of the tree were damaging the foundations of his property. He sought compensation for the cost of remedial foundation works carried out as a consequence of the refusal of the permission. HBC argued that no compensation was payable since remedial measures to the property would have been required in any event, even if permission to fell the tree had been granted.

Held, awarding compensation to B, that £13,000 would be awarded for the remedial works to the property and some related minor works, and also the costs of the appeal on the basis that they flowed from the refusal of the consent. It was reasonable and foreseeable that the claimant would pursue an appeal in an attempt to mitigate his loss. The tribunal did not have the same power as an adjudicator or court to award interest under its rules, *British Coal Corp v. Gwent CC* [1995] E.G.C.S. 104, [1996] C.L.Y. 2141 followed. The question of interest was subject to separate statutory provisions beyond the tribunal's jurisdictions.

BUCKLE v. HOLDERNESS BC (1996) P. & C.R. 428, T Hoyes, FRICS., Lands Tr.

4692. Compulsory purchase–administrative law–highway development–effect of prior knowledge on valuation

[Highways Act 1980 s.246.]

O sought judicial review of the Secretary of State's refusal to purchase his house under the Highways Act 1980 s.246(2A) when acquiring land affected by proposed highway development. O argued that if he had bought the property at a discounted price he would not be entitled to require the Secretary of State to spend public money at a profit to him. However, as he bought the property at its full value, he should be entitled to have the house purchased by the Secretary of State.

Held, dismissing the application that, (1) the Secretary of State was entitled to conclude that O had either knowledge or access to knowledge, so as to have sufficient information of the proposed road scheme, and (2) in the exercise of his discretion to purchase property, the Secretary of State was entitled to take into account, as a matter of law, the principle of foreseeability. This could be applied irrespective of purchase price and the fact that O would not be entitled to public money if he had purchased the property at a discount did not mean that the converse was true.

R. v. SECRETARY OF STATE FOR TRANSPORT, *ex p.* OWEN (NO.2) (1996) 72 P. &.C.R. 368, Popplewell, J., QBD.

4693. Compulsory purchase–compensation–tenant refused alternative premises–compensation based on notional costs of removal to those premises

Held, that compensation for the compulsory purchase of motor repair premises in south east London was assessed at approximately £13,000 by reference to the notional costs of removal of the business to other premises offered by LLBC as the compensating landlord LLBC, occupation of which the business tenant had wrongly refused.

LANDREBE v. LAMBETH LBC [1996] 36 R.V.R. 112, M St J Hopper, FRICS., LandsTr.

4694. Compulsory purchase–hairdressing salon–compensation

Held, that the compulsory purchase of a hairdressing salon at Waterloo Station in London attracted compensation of £46,200 based on 3.25 year's purchase on annual net profits together with a sum to reflect the forced sale of fixtures and fittings.

KLEIN v. LONDON UNDERGROUND LTD [1996] 36 R.V.R. 94, AP Musto, FRICS., LandsTr.

4695. Compulsory purchase–local authority acquiring derelict land–whether work had to be carried out on all parts of land subject to compulsory purchase order

[National Parks and Access to the Countryside Act 1949 s.89.]

Held, that where a local authority acquired derelict land pursuant to the National Parks and Access to the Countryside Act 1949 s.89 under a compulsory purchase order, it did not have to show that it intended to work on all of the component parts of the land which were subject to the compulsory purchase in order to justify the acquisition.

THOMAS v. SECRETARY OF STATE FOR WALES (1996) 160 J.P. Rep. 1104, Macpherson of Cluny, J., QBD.

4696. Compulsory purchase–unoccupied dwelling–compensation assessment

Held, that compensation for the compulsory purchase of an unoccupied dwelling in Liverpool at which some works had been carried out from time to time but which was little more than a shell at the date of notice of entry was assessed at £3,000.

KINSELLA v. ST HELENS MBC [1996] 36 R.V.R. 144, JC Hill, TD, FRICS., LandsTr.

4697. Compulsory purchase–valuation–established light industrial use continued due to compulsory purchase order

Held, that premises subject to compulsory purchase which had the benefit of established light industrial use until two years before the valuation date fell to be valued as premises with that use since it had not been abandoned. Occupation had ceased due to the uncertainty of the compulsory purchase order.

ULLAH v. LEICESTER CITY COUNCIL (1996) 71 P. & C.R. 216, AP Musto, FRICS., LandsTr.

4698. Compulsory purchase–valuation for compensation–Newcastle upon Tyne

Held, that six parcels of land in Newcastle upon Tyne zoned for residential development, subject to compulsory purchase and totalling over 27.5 acres were valued for compensation purposes at £1,175,570

WILLIAM LEECH (INVESTMENTS) LTD v. SECRETARY OF STATE FOR TRANSPORT [1995] R.V.R. 242, M St J Hopper, FRICS., Lands Tr.

4699. Compulsory purchase–valuation of compensation–Great Yarmouth

Held, that compensation for the compulsory purchase of two contiguous buildings used primarily for retail purposes in a secondary shopping area of Great Yarmouth totalling about 600 square feet was assessed at £20,000 after deducting from the value of the premises the costs of repair and redevelopment.

BELLAMY v. GREAT YARMOUTH BC [1996] 36 R.V.R. 41, PH Clarke, FRICS., Lands Tr.

4700. Conservation areas–planning decision–effect of large modern commercial and residential development on area of historic interest–irrationality–court slow to interfere with decision–judicial review

O applied for judicial review of a decision by S designating the area encompassing the Brooklands racing track and airfield as a site of historic interest. This was despite the presence of a large scale commercial and residential development on the site extending to over two million square feet. O alleged that S had failed to have regard to the area which should be properly designated as being of historic interest. Further, it was alleged that the decision was irrational on the basis that there were few features interest beyond the Brooklands museum and that there had already been extensive commercial development of the site.

Held, dismissing the appeal, that if there was to be a conservation area, it would be appropriate that the area should be broadly contained by the racing track. The line that had been drawn was not irrational. The whole of the area was of historic interest despite the fact that it was largely covered by a modern development. The presence of large scale commercial and residential development did not remove the site's historic interest. The court would be slow to interfere with a decision made after proper consultation in circumstances where there had been no allegation of procedural impropriety and where the authority had considerable local knowledge, especially where one of the grounds of the application was irrationality, *R. v. Hillingdon LBC, ex p. Puhlhofer* [1986] 1 A.C. 484, [1986] C.L.Y. 1619 considered.

R. v. SURREY CC, *ex p.* OAKIMBER LTD (1995) 70 P. & C.R. 649, Tucker, J., QBD.

4701. Costs–appeals–adequacy of reasoning–whether council guilty of unreasonable conduct

The Secretary of State granted planning permission on appeal for certain land to be used as a residential nursing home for the elderly. The development did not proceed but a further application was made for planning permission to build residential flats on the land. The land was not within the areas designated for residential development in the local development plan. The application was refused whereupon the applicant successfully appealed to the Secretary of State. The inspector who conducted the appeal inquiry directed that the council should pay the applicant's costs. The council appealed and sought judicial review of the costs order.

Held, allowing the appeal and quashing the costs order, that where a decision was challenged on the ground of inadequate reasons, the question for the court to answer was whether the interest of the appellant had been substantially prejudiced by the deficiency of the reasons given. It was not appropriate to subject a planning inspector's reasoning in his decision letter to detailed examination in search of the slightest infelicity of expression. However, in this case, the decision letter did not sufficiently disclose the reasoning that led to the inspector's decision nor demonstrate that he had properly considered the points made by the council as justifying their refusal of planning permission. Such reasoning as there was seemed to suggest that, simply because permission had been granted for a residential home for the elderly, there were no proper planning considerations to prevent development of the site for residential flats. The council's objections merited closer consideration and analysis before being rejected. The council's refusal of permission and consequent behaviour could not be described as unreasonable and, therefore, the council should not have been ordered to pay the applicant's costs.

WEST OXFORDSHIRE DC v. SECRETARY OF STATE FOR THE ENVIRONMENT [1994] E.G.C.S. 210, Judge, J., QBD.

4702. Costs–planning appeals–unreasonable conduct by local authority–evidential threshold

W had refused planning permission to a company, C, to extract coal from an opencast site within its area. The planning inspector dismissed C's appeal but ordered the local authority to pay the costs C had incurred in adducing evidence on noise, dust and vibration, and in concluding a planning obligation, on the basis that W's objection to the noise that might be caused by C's operations was unsubstantiated. W applied for judicial review of the decision, contending, inter alia, that the planning inspector was obliged to give reasons for his departure from a decision made by a different planning inspector not to make a costs order against W in similar circumstances.

Held, dismissing the application, that (1) in order for WMBC to avoid a costs order there must be sufficient evidence of real substance to support their objection to the proposed development so as to prevent a finding that they had behaved unreasonably, although it was not necessary that the evidence be enough to decide the appeal. On the facts, the planning inspector had exercised his discretion correctly and was entitled to find that the local authority had behaved unreasonably in relation to the noise issue, although this test might not be applicable in every case, and (2) the planning inspector was not obliged to give reasons for his departure from other costs decisions brought to his attention unless a matter of principle or public interest was involved, *North Wiltshire DC v. Secretary of State for the Environment and Clover* [1992] 3 P.L.R. 113, [1993] C.L.Y. 3930 distinguished, although he might be expected to consider similar costs decisions put before him.

R. v. SECRETARY OF STATE FOR THE ENVIRONMENT, *ex p.* WAKEFIELD MBC, *The Times*, October 29, 1996, Jowitt, J., QBD.

4703. Development plans

TOWN AND COUNTRY PLANNING (GENERAL PERMITTED DEVELOPMENT) (AMENDMENT) ORDER 1996, SI 1996 528; made under the Town and Country Planning Act 1990 s.59, s.60, s.61, s.333. In force: April 1, 1996; £1.10.

The Local Government (Wales) Act 1994 creates unitary authorities in Wales which will carry out the functions of the existing district and county councils as from April 1, 1996. As a consequence of this the distinction between county planning authorities and district planning authorities will no longer be relevant in Wales. This Order makes amendments to the Town and Country Planning (General Permitted Development) Order 1995 (SI 1995 418) in consequence of the local government changes in Wales, and the fact that there will no longer be county and district planning authorities in Wales. Additionally, corrections are made to the descriptions of the areas of land in Wales which are specified in Sch.1 Part 3 to the 1995 Order, in that the references to the communities of Llansanffraid Glan Conwy, Porthmadog, Ffestiniog and Mawddwy have not been repeated.

4704. Development plans–local authorities–reorganisation

The Department of the Environment, DoE, issued a press release entitled *New circular on local government change and the planning system* (News release 150), published on March 28, 1996. The DoE Circular advises local planning authorities on how local government changes taking effect on April 1, 1996 affect the planning process. In addition, a guidance note published by the Association of County Councils, the Association of District Councils and the Association of Metropolitan Authorities provides practical advice on the preparation of development plans following the changes. In areas of more than one authority, plans will be maintained by voluntary joint working. DoE Circular 4/96, *Local Government Change and the Planning System*, ISBN 0 11 753275 4, £4.00 is published by HMSO; tel: 0171 873 9090. The guidance note, *Development Plans: Responding to Local Government Change*, is available from Michael Ashley, Association of District Councils, 26 Chapter Street, London, SW1P 4ND; tel: 0171 233 6868; fax: 0171 233 6551.

4705. Development plans–refusal of planning permission–weight given to newly approved policies

[Town and Country Planning Act 1990 s.54A.]

The Secretary of State appealed against the decision to quash his refusal of an application for outline planning permission for the construction of a bypass together with 400 houses.

Held, allowing the appeal, that although the Town and Country Planning Act 1990 s.54A did not reveal what weight to accord to the development plan as opposed to other material considerations, Planning Policy Guidance Note PPG1 clearly stated that newly approved policies would carry more weight. The Secretary of State arrived at his decision by a proper process of reasoning which depended on the weight he gave to the housing policies, *Save Britain's Heritage v. Number 1 Poultry Ltd* [1991] 1 W.L.R. 153, [1991] C.L.Y. 3494 followed.

LOUP v. SECRETARY OF STATE FOR THE ENVIRONMENT AND SALISBURY DC (1996) 71 P. & C.R. 175, Glidewell, L.J., CA.

4706. Development plans–whether adoption outweighed previous acceptance in principle–policy adopted in intervening period since last planning application

[Town and Country Planning Act 1990 s.54A.]

A 1988 planning application was refused, although the development was accepted in principle. However, an area plan was adopted in 1990, and PPG7 issued in 1992. Both required that current settlement limits be observed and the countryside safeguarded. The Town and Country Planning Act 1990 s.54A also required that any determination had to be in accordance with the development plan, unless material considerations indicated to the contrary. The applicant appealed, following the refusal of two renewed applications, which took account of the reasons given in 1988, on the grounds that the proposed development fell beyond the adopted settlement boundary.

Held, dismissing the appeal, that since 1988 legislative and policy changes required that the countryside be protected for its own sake, and that local area plans were of fundamental importance in deciding planning applications. As a result, the acceptance in principle had been given in different circumstances, and the local plan had served to create a presumption against development in the area concerned.

KIRKMAN v. SECRETARY OF STATE FOR WALES [1995] E.G.C.S. 127, Nigel McLeod Q.C., QBD.

4707. Enforcement notices–appeals to planning inspector and High Court–whether inspector an independent and impartial tribunal

[European Convention on Human Rights 1950 Art.6.]

B was made the subject of an enforcement notice requiring him to demolish two buildings on his property which had been erected in breach of planning control. He appealed unsuccessfully to a planning inspector and then to the High Court on points of law and now applied to the ECHR, contending that the proceedings by which he challenged the enforcement notice were in violation of Art.6.1 of the European Convention on Human Rights 1950 which provided that in the determination of civil rights an individual was entitled to a fair and public hearing by an independent and impartial tribunal.

Held, that the inspector exercised a quasi-judicial function in considering planning appeals. Although B had received a fair hearing the inspector's review did not of itself satisfy the requirement that matters be heard by "an independent and impartial tribunal", as the Secretary of State, whose policies were often in issue, could at any time during proceedings revoke the inspector's power to determine an appeal. However, the subsequent review by the High Court did comply with Art.6. The court did not rehear the original complaint and could not substitute its own findings of fact for those of the inspector but considered whether the inspector's decision had been lawfully reached in accordance with the principles of openness, fairness and impartiality. The scope of its jurisdiction was enough to satisfy the requirements of Art.6.1.

BRYAN v. UNITED KINGDOM (1996) 21 E.H.R.R. 342, R Ryssdal (President), ECHR.

4708. Enforcement notices–breach of notice–amount of fine–financial circumstances of offender

[Town and Country Planning Act 1990 s.179; Criminal Justice Act 1991 s.18, s.18.]

B pleaded guilty to being in breach of an enforcement notice contrary to the Town and Country Planning Act 1990 s.179. B appealed against his fine of £25,000 and an order to pay costs of £1,000.

Held, allowing the appeal, that the judge had erred in assessing the fine. Section 179(9) requires the court to have regard to the financial benefit which had accrued or was likely to accrue as a result of the offence. However the Criminal Justice Act 1991 s.18(2) and s.18(3) requires a court to have regard to the financial circumstances of the offender. The judge in the instant case had failed to do so and the fine and the order were reduced.

R. v. BROWNING (DEREK) [1996] 1 P.L.R. 61, Pill, L.J., CA (Crim Div).

4709. Enforcement notices–breach of notice–extension of time for compliance–no extension of planning permission–criminal liability for breach of notice

[Town and Country Planning Act 1990 s.179; Town and Country Planning General Development Order 1990 Art.3.]

An enforcement notice was served on a landowner requiring the cessation of use of the land for shooting purposes for more than 28 days per calendar year as permitted by the Town and Country Planning General Development Order 1988 Art.3 Sch.2 Pt.4 Class B. Despite an unsuccessful appeal against the order, the planning inspector extended the period of compliance from seven days to four months. After two shooting events held on the land, the landowner was charged with breach of the enforcement notice in terms of the Town and Country Planning Act 1990 s.179(2). The case was dismissed on the ground that certain shooting days had occurred before the enforcement notice took effect and therefore did not count towards the computation of 28 days permitted under the Order. The Attorney General referred the question of whether or not such computation was correct in law.

Held, allowing the application, that it was clear that the calendar year ran from January 1 to December 31 and planning permission use was only lawful if exercised on 28 days. The extension of the period for compliance did not extend that permission. Shooting taking place before the expiry date was unlawful because it was in breach of planning permission, but was not a criminal offence. After the date of compliance, the landowner was in breach of the enforcement notice and was guilty of a criminal offence under the 1990 Act s.179(2).

ATTORNEY GENERAL'S REFERENCE (NO.1 OF 1996), *Re* [1996] E.G.C.S. 164, Lord Bingham of Cornhill, L.C.J., CA (Crim Div).

4710. Enforcement notices–breach of planning conditions–height of fence–proposal to plant hedge to shield fence

BBC issued an enforcement notice alleging a breach of planning control concerning the erection of a fence 1.8m high adjoining the highway. The permission granted by BBC allowed a fence of only 1m.

Held, allowing the appeal, that the notice should be corrected by deleting the permissible height of the fence and that the appellant should plant vegetation to shield the fence. It was preferable that there be a fence 1.8m high shielded by a hedge than a 1m fence without a hedge to screen it.

BRENTWOOD BC v. SHARP (1995) 10 P.A.D. 812, Judge not specified.

4711. Enforcement notices–breach of planning conditions–shop opening for longer hours on Sundays

[Town and Country Planning Act 1990 s.174.]

S issued two enforcement notices. The first related to a breach of planning control in that condition 3 stated that the property was to be used as a newsagent shop and was not to remain open after 1 pm on Sundays. The second alleged a breach of planning control in opening the shop between 5 pm and 11 pm on Sundays. It was suggested that there was some noise between 1 pm and 5 pm on Sundays but that noise after 5 pm on Sundays was unacceptable. Appeals were issued against both notices under the Town and Country Planning Act 1990 s.174(2) on the basis that condition 3 should be discharged. M contended that the town had trebled in size since the making of the condition and there had been legislative alterations to Sunday trading.

Held, allowing the appeal in part, that while the nature of the town and the law relating to Sunday trading had altered, opening the shop after 5 pm caused disturbance to neighbours and exceeds generally acceptable levels. The appeal was allowed replacing condition 3 with a condition that the shop should not open for business after 5 pm on Sundays.

SOUTH NORFOLK DC v. MISSELBROOK AND WESTON LTD (1995) 10 P.A.D. 711, Judge not specified.

4712. Enforcement notices–defences–personal circumstances to be taken into account–standard of proof–remedy open to local planning authority

[Town and Country Planning Act 1990 s.179.]

B was convicted of non-compliance with an enforcement notice. He was charged with a further offence of failing to put right the matters listed in the enforcement notice. The magistrates accepted his defence of physical inability to comply with the notice. KCC sought judicial review arguing that B's personal circumstances were not relevant to the Town and Country Planning Act 1990 s.179(3).

Held, dismissing the application, that the plain meaning of the words permitted personal circumstances to be taken into account. Genuine incapacity was a defence in such cases, although the court should be rigorous as to the necessary proof required, to avoid being hoodwinked by false protestations. If unconvinced as to B's financial ability to put matters right KCC had the remedy of going onto the land and doing the work.

KENT CC v. BROCKMAN [1996] 1 P.L.R. 1, Buckley, J., QBD.

4713. Enforcement notices–extensions–whether notice valid under limitation period–whether extension of time permitted

[Planning and Compensation Act 1991 s.171B; Planning and Compensation Act 1991 (Commencement No.5 and Transitional Provisions) Order 1991.]

The Secretary of State for the Environment appealed against the finding that two enforcement notices issued by Hounslow LBC were out of time and should be quashed. The enforcement notices concerned alleged breaches of planning control that occurred between 1963 and July 1982, which was the relevant date for the purposes of the 10 year limitation period contained in the Planning and Compensation Act 1991 s.171B(3). The Planning and Compensation Act 1991 (Commencement No.5 and Transitional Provisions) Order 1991 Art.5(2) introduced transitional provisions referring to s.171B(4)(b) of the 1991 Act which allowed the issue of a further enforcement notice within four years of an earlier notice if the first notice proved invalid or was withdrawn. Both enforcement notices in question were further notices issued on August 19, 1993 after the withdrawal of earlier notices issued three days before the transitional provisions ceased to have effect in July 1992. The Secretary of State submitted that the first notices were valid under the transitional provisions and that the further notices were issued within the four year extension period under s.171B(4)(b). WB contended that the cut off date for notices was July 24, 1982, 10 years before the date on which the first notices were issued and as the first notices were invalid, s.171B(4) could not be used to issue further notices out of time.

Held, dismissing the appeal, that the 10 year time limit under s.171B was mandatory, subject only to s.171B(4). Therefore, the action "taken or purported to be taken" under s.171B must be within the 10 year limit in s.171B(3) or within the four year extension period allowed under s.171B(4), after a valid first notice had been given. Section 171B(4) operated only if the original notices were not time barred under s.171B(3). In this case the first notices were issued outside the 10 year period and therefore any further notices issued were not valid and could not be saved by the transitional provisions in Art.5.

WILLIAM BOYER (TRANSPORT) LTD v. SECRETARY OF STATE FOR THE ENVIRONMENT [1996] 1 P.L.R. 103, Evans, L.J., CA.

4714. Enforcement notices–fines–sufficient means to pay fine of £2,000

[Town and Country Planning Act 1990 s.179.]

A appealed against fines of £2,000 on a guilty plea to each of two charges of failing to comply with enforcement notices, contrary to the Town and Country Planning Act 1990 s.179(2), and costs of £2,252. The charges related to the use of a field for storage of scrap and building materials.

Held, dismissing the appeal, that A had displayed a wanton disregard for the law, the land still not having been cleaned up, and the sentences were appropriate. It was apparent from his affidavit of means that A had sufficient assets; the land subject to the notice could be sold to pay the fines, and he would be given one month to pay.

R. v. AYLING (JOHN) [1996] 2 Cr. App. R. (S.) 266, Butterfield, J., CA (Crim Div).

4715. Enforcement notices–indictment for failure to comply–whether notice ultra vires–whether vires could be raised as defence to indictment

[Town and Country Planning Act 1990 s.179.]

W was charged on indictment with contravention of the Town and Country Planning Act 1990 s.179(1) by failing to take timeous steps required by an enforcement notice. W argued that the decision to issue an enforcement notice was ultra vires. The trial judge held that W could only raise an argument with reference to the vires of the enforcement notice if it appeared to be invalid on its face. W pleaded guilty but appealed against conviction on the question whether it was proper to challenge the decision to issue an enforcement notice by way of defence to an indictment.

Held, dismissing the appeal, that the enforcement was not a nullity on its face and therefore remained valid until quashed. Only the High Court had the power to quash an enforcement notice: no criminal court had that power. The trial judge was correct in that W could only raise an argument with reference to the vires of the decision to issue the enforcement notice if it appeared to be invalid on its face, *Smith v. East Elloe Rural DC* [1956] A.C. 736, [1956] C.L.Y. 1290 considered.

R. v. WICKS (PETER EDWARD) 93 L.G.R. 377, Keene, J., CA (Crim Div).

4716. Enforcement notices–leave to appeal against inspector's decisions dismissed–applicant's liability for costs against two respondents

R sought leave to appeal against a decision of the Planning Inspectorate that a concrete crushing machine could only be sited within a prescribed area of land. A consent was obtained in 1984 which permitted the siting of the crusher on the land for use only in connection with the backfilling of quarry land. A further consent in 1985 permitted the siting of a spoil heap in connection with the crusher and the re-exportation of the crushed material from the site. R argued that the 1985 consent allowed him to locate the crusher outside the site.

Held, dismissing the application for leave, that (1) the 1985 consent was ancillary to the 1984 consent and so the restriction in the 1984 consent limiting the crusher's use to the prescribed area remained. The Inspector's finding was not fundamentally flawed, and (2) costs would be awarded in favour of the Secretary of State because the application amounted to an opposed ex parte hearing and his participation was appropriate and necessary, *R. v. Secretary of State for Wales, ex p. Rozhon* 91 L.G.R. 667, [1994] C.L.Y. 3558 considered.

RANDALL v. SECRETARY OF STATE FOR THE ENVIRONMENT AND BUCKINGHAMSHIRE CC (1995) 70 P. & C.R. 422, Sedley, J., QBD.

4717. Enforcement notices–mistake as to dimensions of building–power to alter notice–agricultural need for building

[Town and Country Planning Act 1990 s.176.]

M issued an enforcement notice in respect of a prefabricated barn-type building located in a field. The field was originally used for the cultivation of Christmas trees and strawberries. There were suggestions that the building would be used in relation to extensive woodland cultivation in the future. M alleged that the erection of a building measuring 76 metres by 5 metres by 5 metres was without planning permission and demanded its demolition. The measurements of the building in the notice were incorrect. The agreed measurement was 18 metres by 9 metres by 3.7 metres. S contended that the notice was void due to the error on its face and should therefore be quashed, and furthermore, that the planning unit was reasonably necessary for the purposes of agriculture.

Held, allowing the appeal, that (1) the issue was not whether the building as erected differed materially from that which was permitted but whether the notice could be altered without injustice. The power to alter a notice under the Town and Country Planning Act 1990 s.176 was to be exercised deliberately and not restrictively, provided that it could be done without injustice. There was only one building in this field and therefore the amendment could take place without causing injustice, and (2) with reference to the reasonable agricultural use of the unit, the appropriate test was set out in *Clarke v. Secretary of State for the Environment* [1993] J.P.L. 32, [1993] C.L.Y. 3813, being whether the building was reasonably necessary for the purposes of agricultural activities which would reasonably be conducted on this unit. This was a matter of fact and degree and could also relate to future use of the land. On these facts, the proposed future use of the land with reference to woodlands constituted a reasonable agricultural use.

MAIDSTONE BC v. SCHROEDER (1995) 10 P.A.D. 691, Judge not specified.

4718. Enforcement notices–no appeal against validity–evidence concerning validity inadmissible at hearing of formation of non-compliance

[Town and Country Planning Act 1990 s.174, s.179, s.285.]

An enforcement notice had been served by V on T alleging a breach of planning control. The notice stated that there had been a change of use from agriculture or garden use to business use without planning permission. T was given three months to comply. Breach of an enforcement notice was a criminal offence, under the Town and Country Planning Act 1990 s.179, but magistrates dismissed two informations served by V. V appealed by way of case stated. The issue concerned evidence showing the storage of vehicles on the land more than 10 years before the notice was served and whether the magistrates were precluded from admitting the evidence under s.285(1) of the 1990 Act.

Held, allowing the appeal, that (1) to succeed, T had to show that the magistrates had made a decision on whether the use was either lawful or had ceased; (2) although the magistrates had found that vehicles had been stored on the land for over 10 years, they had not made a finding that the use had reverted to a lawful use, and (3) T's remedy had been an appeal under s.174 of the 1990 Act. As they had failed to take that course, s.285(1) precluded T from making these points to the magistrates. The acquittal was set aside and the case remitted to the magistrates' court.

VALE OF WHITE HORSE DC v. TREBLE-PARKER [1996] E.G.C.S. 40, Otton, L.J., QBD.

4719. Enforcement notices–non-compliance–availability of defence under Town and Country Planning Act 1990 s.179(3)

[Town and Country Planning Act 1990 s.179.]

Held, that where an owner of land was charged with failing to comply with an enforcement notice under the Town and Country Planning Act 1990 s.179(2) and he had the power to comply on his own, the defence under s.179(3), as amended, was not available to him as it implied that compliance with the notice would require the assistance of others.

R. v. BEARD (JOHN), Trans. Ref: 96/0168/Z2, May 10, 1996, Hobhouse, L.J., CA (Crim Div).

4720. Enforcement notices–Secretary of State's powers to vary notice on appeal–unlawful mixed use–two notices forbidding individual constituents of mixed use–whether misleading

[Town and Country Planning Act 1990 s.176.]

M appealed against the dismissal of their appeals against two enforcement notices relating to breaches of planning control. The notices differed over steps to be taken and the activities requiring cessation. Notice A demanded that buildings on specified land should cease to be used for residential purposes and Notice B that the buildings and land cease to be used for kennelling, breeding and the training of dogs. The intention of the local authority was that the unlawful mixed use of the land should stop. M appealed to the Secretary of State on the grounds that the service of two notices identical in all respects but differing as to requirements gave rise to such confusion and imprecision as to render them invalid. The inspector dismissed the appeals on the grounds that the notices complied with statutory provisions and that although they could have been contained in one notice, this was not essential.

Held, allowing the appeal, that the breach of planning control alleged in Notice B related to the mixed use. Clear potential conflict as a result of the confusion caused by two notices was sufficient to vitiate the decision in respect of Notice B and the matter should be remitted to the Secretary of State for reconsideration; (2) the Secretary of State had power to vary notices on appeal under the Town and Country Planning Act 1990 s.176(1). Notice A should be varied so as to combine the requirements of both notices and require that the breach of planning control common to both Notices should cease, and (3) the matter was capable of resolution by quashing Notice B and varying the requirements of Notice A.

MILLEN v. SECRETARY OF STATE FOR THE ENVIRONMENT [1996] J.P.L. 735, Sir Graham Eyre, Q.C., QBD.

4721. Enforcement notices–service–whether appellant prejudiced by late service

[Town and Country Planning Act 1990 s.289.]

P issued enforcement notices against D in respect of land and buildings he owned. D appealed to the Inspector arguing that the enforcement notices were not served in accordance with the statutory provision and that there was substantial prejudice as a result. His appeal was dismissed. D appealed under the Town and Country Planning Act 1990 s.289. It was further argued that in coming to his conclusion, the inspector clearly treated what was in fact a range of buildings as a single building and that accordingly he failed to take into account or give consideration to the possibility that part of the development may have been substantially completed prior to December 1989 and thus immune from enforcement action due to the four year rule.

Held, dismissing the appeal, that while D was prejudiced, it was not the result of the late service of the notices, but due to his failure to take legal advice. The inspector was entitled, on the evidence, to treat the development as one building rather than a range of buildings. There was also evidence that the building had not been completed by the relevant time and so was not protected by the four year rule. There was no substance in the challenges made to the notices.

DYER v. SECRETARY OF STATE FOR THE ENVIRONMENT AND PURBECK DC [1996] J.P.L. 740, Sir Graham Eyre, QBD.

4722. Enforcement notices–temporary planning permission granted–DoE Circular 1/85, para.83 a material consideration

D appealed against the decision of a planning inspector allowing an appeal against an enforcement notice requiring the cessation of the use of land for the importation and processing of waste materials, and the carrying out of restoration works. Planning permission was granted for a two year period although the inspector stated that permanent permission should not be granted due to the proximity of the site to housing and the inadequacy of the access road. D argued that the inspector failed to have regard to a material consideration which was guidance in DoE Circular 1/85, para.83 which stated that permission should not be limited due to the effect on the neighbourhood and if permission could not be granted with conditions it should be refused.

Held, dismissing the appeal, that the planning inspector concluded that to enable the cessation of the use to be controlled by D, it was better to quash the notice and grant temporary planning permission rather than extend the period for compliance with the notice. This was in the interests of both parties and therefore reasonable. The circumstances were different from the standard circumstances envisaged by para.83 and therefore it could not be concluded that the inspector had disregarded para.83.

DONCASTER MBC v. SECRETARY OF STATE FOR THE ENVIRONMENT, Trans. Ref: CO/2622/95, November 22, 1995, George Bartlett Q.C., QBD.

4723. Enforcement notices–whether decision to quash in part revealed perversity–mixed use of land–whether planning inspector directed himself correctly in law and applied correct test for determining main use of land

W appealed against a decision by a planning inspector regarding two enforcement notices issued by W and relating to a change of use from agriculture to recreational purposes and certain buildings and operational developments. Notice A was quashed on the ground that the matters it pertained to had either not taken place or did not breach planning regulations, while notice B was allowed in respect of ordering the removal of certain specified buildings and structures. W contended that the decision reached by the inspector as to the recreational use being ancillary to a main agricultural use was perverse.

Held, dismissing the appeal, that (1) the determination of ancillary use was a matter of subjective judgment for the inspector involving questions of fact. The court was primarily concerned with issues of law and could not decide such factual findings were perverse or absurd, *Clarke v. Secretary of State for the Environment* [1992] 3 P.L.R. 146, [1993] C.L.Y. 3813 considered; (2) the inspector had been correct in law when deciding that the planning unit's main purpose was agricultural and the evidence showed that he was entitled to find that this remained the primary purpose throughout, *ELS Wholesale (Wolverhampton) Ltd v. Secretary of State for the Environment* (1987) 56 P. & C.R. 69, [1987] C.L.Y. 2898 considered, and (3) although there might be grounds for finding the inspector's views surprising, that did not amount to perversity. The court had to be wary of usurping the function of a tribunal of fact, which had based its decision on the evidence, seen the land and heard the parties involved.

WYRE FOREST DC v. SECRETARY OF STATE FOR THE ENVIRONMENT AND SPOONER [1995] E.G.C.S. 115, R M K Gray Q.C., QBD.

4724. Enterprise zones–North East

TYNE RIVERSIDE ENTERPRISE ZONES (NORTH TYNESIDE) (DESIGNATION) (NO.1) ORDER 1996, SI 1996 106; made under the Local Government, Planning and Land Act 1980 Sch.32. In force: February 19, 1996; £1.55.

The area which has been the subject of the Tyne Riverside Enterprise Zone No.1 (Hadrian Business Park South) Scheme adopted by the North Tyneside MBC is designated as an enterprise zone for a period of 10 years.

4725. Enterprise zones–North East

TYNE RIVERSIDE ENTERPRISE ZONES (NORTH TYNESIDE) (DESIGNATION) (NO.2) ORDER 1996, SI 1996 1981; made under the Local Government, Planning and Land Act 1980 Sch.32 para.5. In force: August 26, 1996; £1.10.

This Order designates six areas in the metropolitan borough of North Tyneside as enterprise zones for a period of 10 years. The designated areas are the subject of the six enterprise zone schemes adopted by the North Tyneside MBC relating to Silverlink North, Silverlink Business Park, Middle Engine Lane, New York Industrial Park, Balliol Business Park West and Balliol Business Park East respectively.

4726. Enterprise zones–North East

TYNE RIVERSIDE ENTERPRISE ZONES (NORTH TYNESIDE AND SOUTH TYNESIDE) (DESIGNATION) ORDER 1996, SI 1996 2435; made under the Local Government, Planning and Land Act 1980 Sch.32 para.5. In force: October 21, 1996; £1.10.

This Order designates as enterprise zones, four areas located within the Metropolitan Borough of South Tyneside and the Metropolitan Borough of North Tyneside. The designated areas are the subject of the four enterprise zone schemes adopted by the Tyne and Wear Development Corporation. Three of the schemes relate to the Viking Industrial Park, and the remaining one to the Baltic Enterprise Park. The designations are effective for a period of 10 years.

4727. Footpaths–definitive map modification orders–adequacy of reasons for addition of public footpath to map

M applied to quash the decision of an inspector to confirm the Kent CC Definitive Map Modification Order 1991 which added a public footpath across Hawkshill Down. M argued that the inspector had failed to give adequate reasons for his decision and M was substantially prejudiced. Specifically, the inspector had failed to consider the evidence of a brigade major of the Jewish Lads and Girls Brigade who objected to the footpath for safety reasons.

Held, dismissing the applications, that the inspector set out the conflicting cases and was entitled to prefer one body of evidence to the other. The reasons given by the inspector for reaching that conclusion were adequate, intelligible and dealt with the principal issues, *Parkinson v. Secretary of State for the Environment* (Unreported, 1992) considered.

MARTINE v. SECRETARY OF STATE FOR THE ENVIRONMENT, Trans. Ref: CO/996/95, November 27, 1995, Hidden, J., QBD.

4728. Green belt–emerging development plan designation–Sunday market sited within designated area–whether slight harm created special circumstances

[Town and Country Planning Act 1990 s.288.]

WM applied to quash a planning inspector's decision that the operation of a Sunday market on land proposed for green belt amounted to an inappropriate retail use. WM contended that the use created little permanent impact on the site, while allowing weekly shopping and recreation for those attending. The inspector, although conceding that the use created little impact, decided that the use was inappropriate given the proposed green belt designation in the emerging local plan.

Held, refusing the application, that where a development was of an inappropriate nature in the green belt, by definition it was harmful to interests of acknowledged importance, *Vision Engineering Ltd v. Secretary of State for the Environment* [1991] J.P.L. 951, [1992] C.L.Y. 4249 considered. In such cases it was open to the applicant to go on and show how the advantages of the development could outweigh any harm caused. Where the harm was slight, the overall situation could amount to a very special circumstance, justifying the development, and rebutting the presumption against inappropriate development in green belt areas. Such a finding of very special circumstance was a matter of judgment for the inspector. On the facts, the inspector had found that the site fulfilled a green belt function in separating two neighbouring towns, the importance of which outweighed the slight harm caused by the use.

WENDY FAIR MARKETS LTD v. SECRETARY OF STATE FOR THE ENVIRONMENT AND ELMBRIDGE BC; HUGGETT v. SECRETARY OF STATE FOR THE ENVIRONMENT; BELLO v. SECRETARY OF STATE FOR THE ENVIRONMENT [1995] E.G.C.S. 17, Sir Graham Eyre Q.C., QBD.

4729. Green belt–local plans–challenge to allocation of development in local plan–whether a second inquiry should have been held when 1982 Regulations were breached

[Town and Country Planning (Structure and Local Plan) Regulations 1982 Reg.29.]

HE challenged HDC proposals in the local plan to retain land, Gilden Way, within the proposed green belt, against the local plan inspector's recommendations that it be allocated as a housing site, whilst permitting the development of another piece of land, New Hall Farm, in the same area. HE requested either the substitution of the Gilden Way land or that a second inquiry, to compare the merits of each area, be held. HDC rejected the application for a second inquiry as unnecessary and adopted the plan. HE applied to quash HDC's proposals.

Held, allowing the application, that (1) HDC had breached the Town and Country Planning (Structure and Local Plan) Regulations 1982 Reg.29(1) by failing to give adequate reasons for rejecting the inspector's recommendation that the land be removed from the proposed green belt. The proposals for New Hall Farm were different from the proposals considered at the first inquiry; (2) the objections of HE involved new evidence also not presented at this inquiry. The inspector failed to address the site specific objections raised in the objection of HE. According to guidelines, a second inquiry should have been held. In failing to do so HDC was in breach of the 1982 Regulations, and (3) regard must be had to material considerations. HE were substantially prejudiced by this breach and the plan was quashed in relation to the development of the New Hall Farm land.

HARLOWBURY ESTATES LTD v. HARLOW DC [1996] E.G.C.S. 28, R Purchas Q.C., QBD.

4730. Green belt–local plans–council decided irrationally to include land in green belt

[Town and Country Planning (Development Plan) Regulations 1991.]

S applied to quash B's decision to adopt a local plan which included S's land in the designated green belt on the grounds that B had failed to comply with the Town and Country Planning (Development Plan) Regulations 1991 Reg.16, Reg.17 and Reg.18. S complained that B rejected S's objections to the plan without proper consideration and failed to give proper, adequate and intelligible reasons for their decision. The issues were whether B gave adequate consideration to the inspector's report in relation to S's objection and gave sufficient reasons for the decision and whether B had acted fairly by not holding a further inquiry.

Held, allowing the application, that the inadequate decision making process had substantially prejudiced S. B's statement that the matter had been adequately debated at the inquiry showed that they had not appreciated the full significance of the inspector's recommendation. B had not dealt with the problems identified by the inspector and no reasonable authority could have reached a decision in this way. B had irrationally decided merely to reiterate the initial grounds for the decision, and therefore the decision was quashed.

STIRK v. BRIDGNORTH DC [1995] N.P.C. 134, Gerald Moriarty Q.C., QBD.

4731. Green belt–local plans–inclusion of land not ultra vires–local planning authority

T appealed against a refusal of his appeal against the A's inclusion of his land within the green belt area of a local plan. T had already successfully challenged an earlier decision to include his land within the green belt area on the ground that A had not given adequate reasons. A reconsidered the matter and again included T's land within the green belt area. T argued that A's decision was ultra vires and failed to give adequate reasons.

Held, dismissing the appeal, that (1) the Master of the Rolls had previously rejected T's argument, that A's decision was ultra vires, in the previous challenge. The point could not be considered again by the court, and (2) the plan was not procedurally improper for inadequate reasons.

TYLER v. AVON CC (NO.2) (1996) 71 P. & C.R. 405, Staughton, L.J., CA.

4732. Green belt–local plans–whether proposed supermarket site needing bypass–whether nature conservation needs taken into account

[Town and Country Planning Act 1990 s.287; Council Directive 79/409 on the conservation of wild birds; Council Directive 92/43 on the conservation of natural habitats and of wild fauna and flora.]

R objected, inter alia, to the allocation in the deposit draft local plan of a site as green belt, which they sought for retail purposes. P accepted the planning inspector's recommendation not to uphold R's objections. R applied under the Town and Country Planning Act 1990 s.287 to quash the plan, alleging that the other site where P had proposed a supermarket development was entirely dependent on the construction of a bypass. P had failed to have regard to the areas of outstanding nature conservation interest along its route, or to Council Directive 92/43 and Council Directive 79/409 and the true uncertainty of the road proposals.

Held, dismissing the application, that the road should be in the local plan as a proposal. P would still have to go through an environmental assessment and make a planning application. If the application failed, they would have to think again. On the evidence, the nature conservation interests had been taken into account.

RETAIL DEVELOPMENTS LTD v. PURBECK DC [1995] Env. L.R. 336, Malcolm Spence Q.C., QBD.

4733. Green belt–planning permission–enforcement notices

[Town and Country Planning Act 1990 s.288, s.289; Town and Country Planning General Development Order 1988.]

Under the Town and Country Planning Act 1990 s.288 and s.289, B sought to quash a decision of a planning inspector quashing an enforcement notice and granting planning permission for the retention of an outbuilding in an area of green belt. Under the Town and Country Planning General Development Order 1988, express planning permission would not have been required had the building been sited five metres away from the existing dwelling. As a result of an oversight, however, it was only two metres away. B had refused planning permission on the basis that there were no very special circumstances and the building was detrimental to the character and visual amenities of the area. The inspector found that the breach was technical.

Held, allowing the application, the balancing exercise which the inspector was required to perform concerned the harm caused by the inappropriate development and the factors which outweighed the harm. Under PPG2, the inspector was required to consider such factors as were in the balance against harm. In concluding that the harm from the instant development was slight, the inspector had failed to understand and apply the relevant policy. It was not a question of whether the decision was unreasonable. A supposition that the building would be re-erected, in accordance with the 1988 order, was not a finding that the householders had a fall back position to implement planning permission. This was not an issue of inadequate reasons because an essential step in the decision making process had been omitted, *Vision Engineering Ltd v. Secretary of State for the Environment* [1991] J.P.L. 951, [1992] C.L.Y. 4249, *Pehrsson v. Secretary of State for the Environment* (1991) 61 P. & C.R. 226, [1992] C.L.Y. 4252 and *Stewart v. Secretary of State for the Environment* [1991] J.P.L. 121, [1992] C.L.Y. 4252 considered.

BRENTWOOD DC v. SECRETARY OF STATE FOR THE ENVIRONMENT AND GRAY (1996) 72 P. & C.R. 61, Christopher Lockhart-Mummery Q.C., QBD.

4734. Green belt–planning permission–presumption in development plan and PPG 2 against development

[Town and Country Planning Act 1990 s.288; Town and Country Planning Appeals (Determination by Inspectors) (Inquiries Procedure) Rules 1992.]

T sought to challenge, under the Town and Country Planning Act 1990 s.288, a decision whereby LDS had been granted outline planning permission to erect residential accommodation, being an institutional development within extensive grounds located in the green belt. It was argued that the decision had not been made within the powers under the 1990 Act, that the Town and Country Planning Appeals (Determination by Inspectors) (Inquiries Procedure) Rules 1992 had not been complied with and that T had been prejudiced as a result. It was submitted that the inspector had misconstrued and misapplied the relevant planning policies, had failed to take account of the draft replacement PPG2 and had given inadequate reasons. LDS contended that, under the approved development plan, it was open to an inspector to find that a proposal was either "appropriate" or necessary. There was a question, however, as to the meaning of what was appropriate. LDS contended that the proposed development was an essential requirement for the purposes of the institution.

Held, allowing the application and quashing the decision, there had been a misconstruction and misapplication of the planning policies. What was appropriate involved a test both of character and necessity. So far as the appeal proposal was concerned, the presumption against it, under the development plan, as an institutional development within extensive grounds, was greater than under the general green belt policy in PPG2. The inspector had been entitled to base his decision on the extant PPG2 rather than its draft replacement. He had misdirected himself, however, in concluding that the policies all recognised the appeal proposal as appropriate within the green belt. His starting point had been whether there was a connection between the appeal proposal and the existing institution. He ought to have applied a test of strict necessity. As a result, the matter had not been determined according to the development plan as required under the 1990 Act. It was not sufficient to have applied the tests in PPG2. Although a court should be slow to quash a planning inspector's decision, the instant decision was flawed by a misdirection which was fundamental to the decision itself. There were no exceptional circumstances, moreover, for upholding the decision, *Save Britain's Heritage v. Number 1 Poultry Ltd* [1991] 1 W.L.R. 153, [1991] C.L.Y. 3494, *South Somerset DC v. Secretary of State for the Environment* [1993] 1 P.L.R. 80, [1993] C.L.Y. 3927 and *Bolton MBC v. Secretary of State for the Environment* (1990) 61 P. & C.R. 343, [1991] C.L.Y. 94 considered.

TANDRIDGE DC v. SECRETARY OF STATE FOR THE ENVIRONMENT AND THE CHURCH OF JESUS CHRIST OF LATTER DAY SAINTS (1996) 72 P. & C.R. 83, Gerald Moriarty Q.C., QBD.

4735. Green belt–planning permission–storage of reclaimed materials–special circumstances

W refused planning permission for a compound for the storage of reclaimed materials pending their reuse or sale for a period of five years. The issue arose whether this development was appropriate on green belt land, or if not, whether there were special circumstances which would justify the granting of consent.

Held, allowing the appeal and granting planning permission subject to conditions, that the minor nature and short term effect of the proposals would not in themselves constitute special circumstances. The opportunity to facilitate recycling and reuse of waste was something which might amount to special circumstances. The conditions specified that the use should be permitted for five years only, that materials should not be stored to a height of more than 102m, that there should be no effluent discharged, and that a plan of the scheme be submitted to the local planning authority.

WARWICKSHIRE CC v. LANDFILL DEVELOPMENT CO LTD (1995) 10 P.A.D. 790, Judge not specified.

4736. Green belt–planning permission–use of existing car park for garage parking

C appealed against W's refusal to grant planning permission to use part of an existing car park for parking vehicles in association with a garage located nearby. The site lay wholly within the Metropolitan Green Belt. The main issue was whether the proposal would harm the character or appearance of the site and its surroundings or undermine any of the purposes of the green belt. There had been an earlier grant of planning permission over this land.

Held, allowing the appeal subject to conditions, that the proposal would not harm the character or appearance of the site. The conditions imposed were that the use of land would be wholly ancillary to the garage: that no servicing or repairs to vehicles should take place on the site; that no vehicles should be advertised for sale on the site; that the site should not be enclosed by fences, gates or walls and that security equipment should only be erected on the site with the approval of the local planning authority. W had failed to take into the account the effect of the earlier planning permission in precluding the site from being a green field site.

WINDSOR AND MAIDENHEAD RBC v. CLOVER LEAF CARS (1995) 10 P.A.D. 796, Judge not specified.

4737. Green belt–planning permission–whether fall back extant planning permission was likely to go ahead–whether this constituted a material consideration

An inspector, appointed by the SSE, allowed an appeal against NF's refusal of planning permission for 48 timber lodges within green belt land. Part of the site enjoyed extant planning permission for hotel development. The second respondent argued that the hotel development would be completed if the timber lodge development were not completed. The inspector concluded that the hotel development formed a fall back position if the lodge development was not completed and therefore constituted a material consideration. NF contested whether this did constitute a material consideration.

Held, dismissing the application, that for the fall back position to be a material consideration there was no distinction between a test of "real likelihood" and one of "real possibility". The contrast was between a real likelihood or a real possibility on the one hand and no such possibility on the other. It was not appropriate to apply a higher standard than the "real possibility" test. Furthermore, there was no general rule that no consideration could be treated as material unless the harm which was of concern was shown to be more likely to occur than not.

NEW FOREST DC v. SECRETARY OF STATE FOR THE ENVIRONMENT (1996) 71 P. & C.R. 189, Nigel MacLeod Q.C., QBD.

4738. Gypsies–caravan sites–green belt land–statutory definition of gypsy–decision of planning inspector

[European Convention on Human Rights 1950 Art.8; Caravan Sites Act 1968 s.16.]

W sought to quash the decision of the Secretary of State dismissing his appeal against the refusal of planning permission in green belt by Epping Forest DC for a caravan site for one gypsy family. An inspector had recommended that the appeal be allowed. W argued that the Secretary of State and the inspector failed to apply the correct test in deciding whether W was a statutory gypsy under the Caravan Sites Act 1968 s.16; and that he failed to give adequate reasons when considering whether the site complied with the criteria adopted for selection of gypsy sites. He also contended that the Secretary of State should have had regard to the European Convention on Human Rights 1950 Art.8 on the right to respect for private and family life and the home.

Held, dismissing the application, that (1) the inspector's decision was one of fact on the information he had before him. He carefully considered the information and was entitled to reach the conclusion that, although W was of Romany origin and it was possible for gypsies to travel seasonally, W's nomadic lifestyle was not merely in abeyance, but had been abandoned; (2) the criteria had been considered and it was not necessary for the inspector to go through the criteria as a checklist, and (3) this argument should have been before the inspector and leave to amend the notice of motion to include this ground was refused.

WOOLHEAD v. SECRETARY OF STATE FOR THE ENVIRONMENT AND EPPING FOREST DC (1996) 71 P. & C.R. 419, Jeremy Sullivan Q.C., QBD.

4739. Gypsies–caravan sites–refusal of permission–balance between character of neighbourhood and need for authorised caravan sites

G applied for planning permission for a caravan site for use by gypsies. His application was refused by the local planning authority and his appeals to the Secretary of State and the High Court were dismissed. G appealed contending that the inspector, in reaching his decision, had failed to pay sufficient regard to the need for a gypsy caravan site.

Held, dismissing the appeal, that it was clear from the inspector's decision letter that he had in mind the contents of the local structure plan and Circulars 28/77 and 57/78. Having satisfied himself that the application did not satisfy the structure plan requirements for gypsy caravan sites in policy 3/6 he was entitled to apply the restriction in policy 10/2 of the plan ie. permission was not normally to be given for development outside the limits of existing built up areas and that any such development should not adversely affect the countryside. The inspector was entitled to find that the proposed development was one for which permission should not be granted.

GASKIN v. SECRETARY OF STATE FOR THE ENVIRONMENT [1994] E.G.C.S. 171, Glidewell, L.J., CA.

4740. Gypsies–caravan sites–refusal of planning permission–whether the policy was discriminatory

[Town and Country Planning Act 1990 s.284, s.287, s.288; Caravan Sites and Control of Development Act 1960 s.24; European Convention on Human Rights 1950 Art.8.]

Under the Town and Country Planning Act 1990 s.288, H sought to quash a planning inspector's decision dismissing an appeal from N's refusal of planning permission for a mobile home to house a gypsy family. H was a gypsy within the meaning of the Caravan Sites and Control of Development Act 1960 s.24(8). The application had been for a material change of use of the site concerned within the New Forest Heritage Area. The inspector, having regard to *Department of the Environment Circular 1/94*, concluded that H had no compelling personal circumstances which justified a departure from policies which were strongly preventative of new development. It was submitted, that (1) there was a blanket policy against the provision of gypsy sites; (2) the policy was partial, unequal and discriminatory against a national minority and destructive of a traditional way of life and therefore ultra vires; (3) it was contrary to common law following *Kruse v. Johnson* [1898] 2 Q.B. 91; (4) the local policy was contrary to Circular 1/94; (5) it should be assumed that NFDC would not have adopted a discriminatory policy such that it should be interpreted as not applying to gypsy caravans, and (6) under the European Convention on Human Rights 1950 Art.8 the policy should not be interpreted as applying to gypsy caravans.

Held, dismissing the application, that (1) the inspector had been concerned about the impact of breaches of the policy on the character and appearance of the area and of the precedent implications of granting permission in a sensitive area. There was nothing to vitiate the decision, and (2) no point relating to the 1950 Convention had been made to the inspector and the court would be unwilling to entertain a point of law which could have been raised earlier, *West Cheshire Caravan Co Ltd v. Ellesmere Port BC* [1976] 1 E.G.L.R. 143, [1976] C.L.Y. 2689 followed. H had sought to challenge the validity of the policy under s.287 of the 1990 Act and its consistency with s.284. The purpose of the preclusive provisions in s.284, however, was precisely to prevent such an ad hoc attack. The policy applied to all caravans irrespective of whether they were occupied by gypsies, but whether this was discriminatory was not a matter upon which the court could make a finding, the point not having been raised before. The 1950 Convention could be deployed only to resolve an ambiguity in English legislation, *R. v. Secretary of State for the Home Department, ex p. Brind* [1991] 1 A.C. 696, [1991] C.L.Y. 71 followed. Whether there would be a remedy for H under Art.8(2) if N took enforcement action, the Court would express no view. It was unclear whether part of the text of the policy, providing that permission would not normally be given for residential caravans, was supplementary, and therefore having a wider meaning, or explanatory, applying only to sites where a permanent dwelling would be permitted.

HUGHES v. SECRETARY OF STATE FOR THE ENVIRONMENT AND NEW FOREST DC (1996) 71 P. & C.R. 168, Lockhart-Mummery Q.C., QBD.

4741. Gypsies–caravan sites–whether local plan area covered by national Circular

[Criminal Justice and Public Order Act 1994.]

W applied to quash a refusal of planning permission for a gypsy caravan. In his decision letter the inspector had relied on the repeal by the Criminal Justice and

Public Order Act 1994 of the local authority statutory duty to provide site accommodation and Department of the Environment Circular 1/94 Gypsy Sites and Planning. This set out the planning requirements needed to provide accommodation for a nomadic gypsy lifestyle, but stated that such sites were inappropriate "in areas of open land where development is severely restricted including Green Belts and other protected areas". However, the land concerned was sited within a landscape area in the local plan, and W contended the ejusdem generis rule operated to restrict Circular 1/94 designations only to nationally recognised areas.

Held, dismissing the application, that the decision letter had given effect to considerations regarding W's family circumstances, but found these did not outweigh the harm the site could cause. Circular 1/94 clearly stated such sites were not appropriate on open areas of land and the use of the ejusdem generis rule could not be justified where it would restrict development in cases of national, as opposed to local, designation.

Observed, the Secretary of State may consider amending Circular 1/94, to avoid misleading planning authorities in the future.

WEBB v. SECRETARY OF STATE FOR THE ENVIRONMENT [1995] E.G.C.S. 147, Rich, J., QBD.

4742. Gypsies–mobile homes–material considerations–no policy for gypsies in statutory development plans

J appealed against a decision dismissing his appeal against refusal of planning permission for the retention of a gypsy mobile home, drive, concrete hardstanding, gateposts, septic tank and filter bed system and an implement shed. J argued that the Secretary of State failed to take account of a material consideration, namely the absence of any policy on gypsy sites within the statutory development plan. J also argued that the Secretary of State failed to weigh J's family's special needs against harm to the character of the countryside and the interests of highway safety.

Held, dismissing the appeal, that (1) the fact that the policies contained no provision for gypsy accommodation was a material consideration which was inherent in the planning inspector's reasoning, and (2) the planning inspector's consideration of J's overriding need based upon his status as a gypsy incorporated matters relating to J's family circumstances.

JONES v. SECRETARY OF STATE FOR ENVIRONMENT, Trans. Ref: CO/602/95, November 7, 1995, Gerald Moriarty Q.C., QBD.

4743. Gypsies–mobile homes–whether council could obtain injunction to remove gypsy family from their own freehold land in order to restrain breach of planning control

[Caravan Sites Act 1968 s.6; Town and Country Planning Act 1990 s.187.]

H appealed against a refusal to grant them an injunction, under the Town and Country Planning Act 1990 s.187(b), restraining B, a gypsy, from retaining caravans on land which he had purchased after planning permission had been refused on the grounds that there was environmental damage. On completion of an official site H required B to leave and B was successfully prosecuted for breach of an enforcement notice. The inspector reported that he had taken into account whether the special needs of B outweighed the planning disadvantages under the Caravan Sites Act 1968 s.6. The judge was not referred to consultative circular 1/94 and was not told that the Appendix in 57/78 had been cancelled and was further told that a further planning application was contemplated. The judge was also told that B had an arguable case so far as planning permission was concerned. The judge, taking into account that the families had been on the site since 1987, that there were no acceptable sites available and that they could not go to a council site, refused to grant an injunction to restrain breach.

Held, allowing the appeal and granting an injunction to be complied with within three months of determination of the planning permission by H, that (1) the judge was not entitled to approach an application for an injunction in the way he did; (2) H's duty to provide sites was since repealed but H had refrained from seeking an injunction until the alternative site was available; (3) the possibility of a future grant of planning permission was not enough to refuse the injunction, and (4) B's demand for planning permission was inconsistent with a desire to remain at the site and break the law.

HAMBLETON DC v. BIRD AND FLOYD [1995] 3 P.L.R. 8, Balcombe, L.J., CA.

4744. Injunctions–delay–judicial review refused due to delayed application–county court discretion in proceedings for injunctive relief sufficient to deal with matters raised

C was prosecuted three times for ignoring enforcement notices requiring him to stop using his land for a mobile home. In 1994 B's planning committee decided to seek an injunction but proceedings were not commenced until 1995. At the hearing the judge refused C's application for an adjournment to enable him to seek judicial review of the decision to seek an injunction and C applied for judicial review.

Held, dismissing the application, that the delay in bringing the application was enough to merit dismissal. In any event, the county court using its discretion to determine whether or not to grant an injunction could have dealt with the matters raised by C in his application for judicial review. It was unnecessarily expensive and slow to seek to delay the county court's decision by seeking judicial review.

R. v. BASILDON DC, *ex p.* CLARKE [1995] J.P.L. 866, Carnwath, J., QBD.

4745. Land use–whether buildings on agricultural land within scope of general development order–differing conclusions from same facts

[Town and Country Planning General Development Order 1977 Sch.1 Class VI.]

K appealed against a decision by the Secretary of State, quashing an enforcement notice issued by K, in respect of buildings erected on agricultural land in apparent breach of planning control. K contended that, as the Secretary of State and the planning inspector had differed with regard to certain facts, the authority should be allowed to make extra representations.

Held, dismissing the appeal, that (1) under the Town and Country Planning General Development Order 1977 Sch.1 Class VI, general planning permission existed for buildings on land of one acre and above designated for agricultural purposes, *Jones v. Stockport MB* [1984] 269 E.G. 408, [1985] C.L.Y. 3462 considered; (2) although the Secretary of State and the inspector had reached differing conclusions, their respective decisions had been determined on the basis of the same facts, with no disagreement as to what took place on the land at all material times, and (3) the Secretary of State's findings had been arrived at using the correct test as to the nature and use of land, mindful of the fact that the low income did not conclusively prove that the use amounted merely to a hobby or eccentric purpose.

KERRIER DC AND STEVENS v. SECRETARY OF STATE FOR THE ENVIRONMENT [1995] E.G.C.S. 40, Nigel McLeod Q.C., QBD.

4746. Listed buildings–consent for alterations refused–whether external appearance materially affected

[Town and Country Planning Act 1990 s.55.]

BD owned three Grade II listed buildings. They applied for listed building consent to carry out substantial internal work, including a lift shaft, works to the roof and replacement windows. An appeal against the refusal of consent was dismissed. BD argued that the works were internal or, alternatively, that they did not "materially affect the external appearance of the building" within the Town and Country Planning Act 1990 s.55. They sought a declaration to the effect that the works did not constitute development.

Held, giving judgment for BD, that (1) it was not sufficient merely for the exterior surface to be affected, the external appearance had to be changed; (2) the change had to be visible from a number of normal vantage points and was not limited to aerial views or those from a single building; (3) the material nature of the alteration depended on the type of building. A change to a factory might not be material but if the building was an 18th century house the same change would have a different effect, and (4) none of the changes constituted development.

Observed: the court expressed concern at the reports produced by expert witnesses which flew in the face of the requirements of their duties. The witnesses were not required to act as advocates and reach conclusions on the interpretation of statutory provisions.

BURROUGHS DAY v. BRISTOL CITY COUNCIL [1996] 1 E.G.L.R. 167, Richard Southwell, QBD.

4747. Listed buildings–demolition–consent required–addition to listed building built without planning permission–developer acquitted

[Town and Country Planning Act 1990 s.88, s.187B.]

H appealed against an injunction to demolish part of a dwelling built without planning permission. The alleged breach was the erection of guest accommodation against the walls of listed lime kilns. An enforcement notice was issued under the Town and Country Planning Act 1990 s.88(10). Subsequently the kilns were added to the county list of buildings of special historical interest. The dwelling was now attached to a listed building and listed building consent was required before it could be demolished. On appeal before the inspector, it was concluded that the building should be demolished, but that a stay of execution should be granted to secure the listed building consent. Before the due date for compliance, an application was made to demolish only part of the guest accommodation. Three months later, the description was amended to take account of the new building and one day later the listed building consent order for partial demolition was granted. H failed to comply and was prosecuted but acquitted. An injunction was then sought to demolish the part of the building identified in the listed building consent. H contended that the enforcement notice was void, the application for an injunction was an abuse of process because H had been acquitted and that mandatory injunctions did not fall within s.187B of the Act.

Held, dismissing the appeal, that (1) there were no defects in the enforcement notice which was not ambiguous and which made it clear what H had to do to comply with it; (2) the decision of the court in H's criminal trial did not bind the High Court in civil proceedings, and (3) s.187B of the Act was intended to have a wider application than the common law.

SOUTH HAMS DC v. HALSEY [1996] J.P.L. 761, Glidewell, L.J., CA.

4748. Listed buildings–enforcement notices–removal of carillon clock and bronze chandeliers from Grade II Listed building–test to be applied as to fixtures–clock not "plant and machinery"

[Town and Country Planning Act 1990 s.336.]

K appealed against enforcement notices issued against the removal, from a Grade II listed building, of a carillon clock and three bronze chandeliers without an application for listed building consent. K argued that the inspector had taken into account an irrelevance when applying the second limb of the test for fixtures in *Berkley v. Poulett* [1977] 1 E.G.L.R. 86, [1976] C.L.Y. 2303. When considering the object and purpose of annexation the inspector had taken into account the fact that the clock was part of the building's folklore in that its bells rang out across the countryside.

Held, dismissing the appeal, that (1) the test for determining whether a chattel was a fixture, ie. degree of annexation and purpose applied to listed building legislation as to other areas of planning law, *Berkley v. Poulett* applied; (2) the free standing nature of the clock did not conclusively prove that it was not a fixture, *Leigh v. Taylor* [1902] A.C. 157 applied; (3) there was no evidence that irrelevant considerations had been taken into account. Even if this had been established, it would not have vitiated the inspector's overall decision, and

(4) the clock was not "plant and machinery" under the Town and Country Planning Act 1990 s.336.

KENNEDY v. SECRETARY OF STATE FOR WALES; SUB NOM. R. v. SECRETARY OF STATE FOR WALES, *ex p.* KENNEDY [1996] J.P.L. 645, Ognall, J., QBD.

4749. Listed buildings–jurisdiction–whether enforcement notice barred when grounds of appeal made out–judicial review

[Planning (Listed Buildings and Conservation Areas) Act 1990 s.39, s.64; European Convention on Human Rights 1950.]

C applied for judicial review to quash two enforcement notices in respect of work done to his hotel, a listed building. He argued that, under the terms of the Planning (Listed Buildings and Conservation Areas) Act 1990, it would not be open to him to appeal against an enforcement notice on the grounds that the building was not listed, or listed only in part.

Held, refusing the application, that, where the grounds relied on were capable of forming the basis of an appeal to the Secretary of State under the Planning (Listed Buildings and Conservation Areas) Act 1990 s.39, s.64 of that Act operated as an absolute bar so that judicial review was not available. The European Convention on Human Rights 1950 could not be used as it was only an aid to interpretation where the meaning of the legislation was ambiguous and, in this case, the legislation was clear.

R. v. DACORUM BC, *ex p.* CANNON [1996] 2 P.L.R. 45, Saville, L.J., QBD.

4750. Local authorities powers and duties–acquisition of land for planning purposes–interference with third party rights–statutory interpretation

[Town and Country Planning Act 1990 s.237.]

M applied for judicial review of the decision of C, owners of Shelley House, to demolish it and construct a new building which would interfere with M's right to light. C originally acquired land to construct the first Shelley House and conveyed part to M, covenanting not to build anything which would obstruct M's light. Subsequently C obtained planning permission to re-develop the site and maintained that, under the Town and Country Planning Act 1990 s.237(1), the intended re-development was justified by the planning permission, regardless of M's right to light. M challenged the decision on the ground that s.237(1) no longer applied once the purpose for which the local authority purchased the land in the first place had been achieved, ie. the section applied when Shelley House was first built but not when re-development was planned. M contended, alternatively, that s.237(1) did not authorise interference with third party rights granted by the local authority itself.

Held, dismissing the application, that (1) the words "acquired... for planning purposes" in s.237(1) could not mean that the immunity was limited to the first development of the site. The immunity had to extend to all work by the local authority or successors in title which related in some way to the planning purposes for which the local authority acquired the land, and (2) the local authority was entitled to interfere with third party rights under s.237 even where those rights did not exist when the land was acquired but were granted by the local authority itself. Provided planning permission was granted and compensation was payable, there was no scope for adding any qualification to the statutory provisions.

R. v. CITY OF LONDON CORP, *ex p.* MYSTERY OF THE BARBERS OF LONDON; SUB NOM. R. v. MAYOR AND COMMONALITY AND THE CITIZENS OF LONDON, *ex p.* MYSTERY OF THE BARBERS OF LONDON [1996] J.P.L. B125, Dyson, J., QBD.

4751. Local plans–housing policy–consultation on housing and development of Stansted airport–absence of new issues justified refusal to grant further inquiry

The applicants sought to quash parts of a local plan because major housing allocations were alleged to have been included without the opportunity for objections to be heard. When the consultation draft was published, it was proposed that new housing development linked to the expansion of Stansted airport would be concentrated at two sites, but this was replaced in the deposit version with a proposal for 2,500 units at a single site. A public local inquiry was held at which the applicants were refused permission to present their case as objectors to the dispersed site strategy, but were reminded of their option to make written representation. The inspector's recommendation of dispersed sites was accepted by the local authority, but challenged on the basis that a further inquiry should be held. The grounds of appeal, were (1) that the decision not to hold a further inquiry was *Wednesbury* unreasonable and procedurally unfair; (2) the local authority misdirected itself in applying the wrong test to determine whether a further inquiry should be held; (3) there was a failure to exercise discretion, and (4) the issues raised by a transport policy favouring the single site strategy were not taken into consideration. The applicants claimed that a number of issues combined to make the decision unreasonable, including that the nature of the proposed development in the area was dramatic, the obligation to consult parish councils at pre-deposit stage was not honoured and new issues were raised to those considered at the inquiry. They further submitted that the local authority wrongly considered "exceptional circumstances", as defined in government planning policy guidance notes, as the primary consideration for granting a further inquiry and relied solely on legal advice instead of exercising their discretion.

Held, refusing the application, that (1) there were numerous consultation opportunities and the request for a further inquiry had to be judged in the light of the local plan procedures as a whole; (2) because no new issues were raised it was not unreasonable to refuse a further inquiry, *Bushell v. Secretary of State for the Environment* [1981] A.C. 75, [1980] C.L.Y. 1337 considered. There was no misdirection on the part of the local authority in concluding that in the absence of any new issues raised there were no circumstances so exceptional as to justify a further inquiry, *British Railways Board v. Slough BC* [1993] J.P.L. 678, [1994] C.L.Y. 4349 considered. There was no basis for assuming that, because legal advice was sought, it was applied without consideration by the local authority, and (4) the transport policy was in draft form at the time of the inquiry, but was taken into account in its final form by the inspector.

WARREN v. UTTLESFORD DC [1996] J.P.L. B127, Judge Bartlett Q.C., QBD.

4752. Local plans–modification–adequacy of reasons–requirement for second inquiry

[Town and Country Planning (Structure and Local Plans) Regulations 1982 Reg.31.]

L and others applied to quash certain parts of the Review of the Adopted Colchester Borough Local Plan which related to the allocation of an employment zone. L wanted land owned by them to be included within the employment zone. They argued that C had failed to consider that the land allocated might be inappropriate if a suitable road junction could not be provided within the time constraints affecting the draft plan. Also C had failed to consider problems such as planning permission and funding for the road junction and the possibility of the need for compulsory purchase orders. L also argued that C's decision was perverse as it was unreasonable for C to conclude that the development would be ready in time to make a significant contribution during the period of the plan. The second applicants, local residents, LR, objected to the modification of the plan to allow the land within the employment zone to be used for park and ride purposes. LR argued that C had failed to give adequate reasons for the modification under the Town and Country Planning (Structure and Local Plans)

Regulations 1982 Reg.31(1)(a). LR also argued that its allocation was unreasonable and that failure to hold an inquiry into the modification was unreasonable.

Held, dismissing the applications, that (1) consideration was given to the time constraints affecting the provision of the road junction either explicitly or implicitly by C; (2) C was entitled to weigh the possible delay in implementing the plan against the consequences of the failure to develop the land. There was nothing within the material relied upon by C to indicate that their assessment of the time constraints was unreasonable; (3) the reasons given for the modification of the plan were inadequate as they were contrary to the inspector's recommendations. However, LR were not substantially prejudiced as they had seen the report and were aware of the C's reasons, and (4) failure to hold a second inquiry was not *Wednesbury* unreasonable as no new arguments against the allocation had been raised.

LINDMAR TRUST CO LTD v. COLCHESTER BC [1995] E.G.C.S. 169, George Bartlett Q.C., QBD.

4753. Local plans–modification–rural areas–planning inspector's finding on whether property part of village or surrounding countryside

[Town and Country Planning Act 1990 s.287.]

D sought, under the Town and Country Planning Act 1990 s.287, to challenge a decision of the local planning authority refusing to amend the provisions of a local plan having rejected the recommendations of a local plan inspector. The dispute concerned whether D's property should be designated part of the village envelope or the surrounding rural area. D had wished to turn barns, for which there was an existing employment use consent, into residential accommodation. The inspector had concluded that the site had become part of the village area. M heard a deputation from the village who objected to more housing, but did not allow D to respond. It was submitted that M's reasons were inadequate.

Held, allowing the application, that the decision would be quashed, (1) the explanation of policy given by an official in an affidavit was correct but was materially different from the advice he had given to M. As a result, a misdirection or misunderstanding had been adopted; (2) whatever reasons had caused consent to be given for the conversion of D's barns to employment use, no reasons had been given for how those reasons could be undermined by including the site in the village envelope (as D contended) rather than the rural area, as decided by M. M had not dealt with the inspector's view of the situation on the ground. Whether M had reasons for reaching different conclusions was nothing to the point. They had to deal with the inspector's recommendations and reasons so that an informed reader would understand why they had been rejected, yet it remained unclear whether M had accepted the findings of fact or not, and (3) the residents had properly exercised their right to make representations under M standing orders. As a result of those standing orders, however, D had been denied an opportunity to comment. This was all the more significant because M's position, prepared in advance by an official, could not have taken into account the representations of the residents, *Wiseman v. Borneman* [1971] A.C. 297, [1969] C.L.Y. 1748 considered, *Save Britain's Heritage v. Number 1 Poultry Ltd* [1991] 1 W.L.R. 153, [1991] C.L.Y. 3494 and *Bolton MBC v. Secretary of State for the Environment* [1995] J.P.L. 1043, [1995] 2 C.L.Y. 4760 followed.

DAVIES v. MILTON KEYNES BC, Trans. Ref: CO/641/95, November 23, 1995, Gerald Moriarty Q.C., QBD.

4754. Markets–planning permission–draft local plan a material consideration

[Town and Country Planning Act 1990 s.54.]

WM applied for judicial review of decisions of CBC granting planning permission for a temporary change of use for a Sunday market and refusing to revoke that permission. WM argued that CBC had failed to take into account material considerations when making their decisions. They had not considered the draft local plan, particularly in relation to shopping, markets and employment.

Held, dismissing the application, that (1) the local plan was not formally adopted and so was not the primary consideration under the *Town and Country Planning Act 1990* s.54(A). However, the plan was near adoption and so was a material consideration, *Bolton MBC v. Secretary of State for the Environment* (1991) 61 P.& C.R. 343, [1991] C.L.Y. 94 considered; (2) the policies in the local plan were not considered by CBC when permission was granted. The decision was therefore defective. However, the decision should not be quashed. The court, in the exercise of its discretion had regard to money spent on the market, the two year delay between the grant of permission and relief sought and the use made of it by traders who relied on its lawfulness. In addition, CBC would have been likely to have reached the same decision if they considered the local plan, and (3) the planning officer who made the decision not to revoke the permission acted under delegated power and considered the policies underlying the local plan. He was entitled to conclude, that if the market was restricted to Sundays, there would not be a conflict with the policies which protected the town centre.

R. v. CORBY BC, *ex p.* WENDY FAIR MARKETS, Trans. Ref: CO/1188/95, December 19, 1995, Carnwath, J., QBD.

4755. Mining–old mining permission–conditions of the permission not met–operations unauthorised–enforcement notices–Secretary of State correctly interpreted policy guidance on mineral development in green belt areas

[Planning and Compensation Act 1991 s.22, Sch.2; Town and Country Planning Act 1971 Sch.24.]

D appealed against against decisions of the Secretary of State to first, dismiss its appeal against S's refusal to register its old mining permission, obtained in 1947, and secondly, to dismiss its appeal against an enforcement notice issued by S. A developer could not rely on permission which was not registered. The application to register the old mining permission was made under the Planning and Compensation Act 1991 s.22 and Sch.2 which stated that the application should be refused unless the permission authorised the development. The old mining permission had a similar status to outline planning permission and was granted to D's predecessors in title on the condition that details of the proposed operations were submitted to and approved by S. This was not done, the operations were carried out but no enforcement action was taken until recently. In relation to the enforcement notice, D argued that the permission ought to be granted and the Secretary of State had incorrectly interpreted policy promulgated in PPG2 by finding that there was a general presumption against allowing mineral works to take place within the green belt area.

Held, dismissing the appeal, that (1) the Town and Country Planning Act 1971 Sch.24 para.19 stated that permission could be authorised only if it related to operations which were started before April 1, 1979. Although, in this case, operations had begun before that date, they could not be said to be authorised as they were commenced without meeting the conditions of the permission; (2) operations occurring in contravention of the permission could not amount to operations commencing the development which the permission authorised. The operations were in breach of planning control and unauthorised and consequently unlawful, *Oakimber Ltd v. Elmbridge BC* (1991) 62 P. & C.R. 594, [1992] C.L.Y. 4338 and *Whitley & Sons v. Secretary of State for Wales and Clwyd CC* (1992) 64 P. & C.R. 296, [1992] C.L.Y. 4352 considered, and (3) PPG 2 only contained a presumption against inappropriate mineral development in the green belt area. The Secretary of State recognised that and was entitled to decide that the lateral expansion of the operations was inappropriate to the area.

DANIEL PLATT LTD v. SECRETARY OF STATE FOR THE ENVIRONMENT AND STAFFORDSHIRE CC [1996] E.G.C.S. 113, Schiemann, L.J., CA.

4756. National parks–establishment of authorities

NATIONAL PARK AUTHORITIES (ENGLAND) ORDER 1996, SI 1996 1243; made under the Local Government Act 1992 s.241, s.266, Sch.17 Part 1; the Town and Country Planning Act 1990 s.4A; and the Environment Act 1995 s.63, s.75, Sch.7 para.1, Sch.7 para.2. In force: June 4, 1996; £3.70.

This Order establishes National Park Authorities for each of the National Parks in England, makes provision for the number of members to be appointed to each authority and deals with the appointment of members, resignation of office, vacancies and notification of appointments. Provision is made for an acting proper officer, for reports and returns to be made by an Authority, for funds and accounts, for the continuity in the exercise of functions and for the transfer of staff, property, rights and liabilities. Provision is also made, from April 1, 1997, for each authority becomes the sole local planning authority for the area of its Park except for certain functions which must be exercised concurrently with appropriate district councils.

4757. National parks

NATIONAL PARK AUTHORITIES (ENGLAND) (AMENDMENT) ORDER 1996, SI 1996 2546; made under the Environment Act 1995 s.63, s.75. In force: November 6, 1996; £0.65.

These Regulations correct an error in the National Park Authorities (England) Order 1996 (SI 1996 1243) Sch.7 para.10. The substituted sub-para.(2) provides for the application of provisions of the Local Authorities (Standing Orders) Regulations 1993 (SI 1993 202) on April 1, 1997, rather than the non-application of those provisions.

4758. National parks–Wales

NATIONAL PARK AUTHORITIES (WALES) (AMENDMENT) ORDER 1996, SI 1996 534; made under the Environment Act 1995 s.63, s.75. In force: April 1, 1996; £1.55.

This Order amends the National Park Authorities (Wales) Order 1995 (SI 1995 2803). Article 18 of and Sch.5 to the principal Order apply to the National Park authorities in Wales certain enactments and instruments, some with modifications. This Order applies to those authorities the further enactments and instruments some with modifications, which are specified in the Schedule to this Order.

4759. National parks–Wales

NATIONAL PARK AUTHORITIES (WALES) (AMENDMENT NO.2) ORDER 1996, SI 1996 1224; made under the Environment Act 1995 s.63, s.75. In force: May 31, 1996; £0.65.

The Environment Act 1995 Part III provides for the establishment of National Park authorities which will be the local planning authority for their respective National Parks. The National Park Authorities (Wales) Order 1995 (SI 1995 2803) established National Park authorities for National Parks in Wales on November 23, 1995 and these became the local planning authorities for their respective National Parks on April 1, 1996. This Order amends the 1995 Order to provide for a modification in the application of the Local Government (Wales) Act 1994 Sch.5 Part III, which contains provisions whereby work may be continued in relation to the preparation and adoption of local plans and of structure plan alterations, notwithstanding the provision for the introduction of unitary development plans, in relation to the National Park authorities in Wales. The 1995 Order is also amended so that it applies the Local Government Reorganisation (Compensation for Loss of Remuneration) Regulations 1995 (SI 1995 2837) to the National Park Authorities in Wales.

4760. Nuclear power–land use–revocation

TOWN AND COUNTRY PLANNING (ATOMIC ENERGY ESTABLISHMENTS SPECIAL DEVELOPMENT) (REVOCATION) ORDER 1996, SI 1996 3194; made under the Town and Country Planning Act 1990 s.59, s.60, s.333. In force: January 10, 1997; £0.65.

This Order revokes the Town and Country Planning (Atomic Energy Establishments Special Development) Orders 1954 (SI 1954 982), 1957 (SI 1957 806) and 1961 (SI 1961 1295). These Orders permitted the development of land to which the Orders applied, for the purposes of the United Kingdom Atomic Energy Authority.

4761. Planning agreements–Grampian condition–validity

[Town and Country Planning Act 1990 s.106; Town and Country Planning (Use Classes) Order 1987.]

E appealed against a decision of a planning inspector and applied for an order to quash a decision of the inspector whereby he dismissed an appeal against the failure of Blaenau Gwent BC to decide a planning application within the statutory time limit. The case related to the expansion of a used car garage which was the subject of an enforcement notice. E appealed on three grounds; (1) the inspector had made an error in law to find that a *Grampian* condition (which precluded development until a condition precedent is satisfied) was inappropriate; (2) the inspector's decision was perverse. His finding that a waiting lane of a highway proposal was too short could not have reasonably been concluded on the evidence. This was argued on the basis of an affidavit of a chartered engineer who had computed the traffic flow and concluded that the waiting lane was of sufficient length, and (3) the inspector was wrong to fail to reopen the inquiry.

Held, dismissing the appeal and the application, that (1) the inspector was correct to address this matter as one of policy and commonsense rather than of law and to find that, in this case, as development could not occur until certain highway works had been carried out, E would immediately be in breach of this condition as they were already continuing an unlawful use. This would amount to a breach of planning control. If E then did not carry out the works, a new enforcement notice procedure would need to be commenced allowing the unlawful use to continue for a further period; (2) the affidavit was produced after the inquiry. On the evidence given by the engineer at the inquiry and the plan itself the inspector was entitled to take the view he did, and (3) in terms of natural justice E had had plenty of opportunity to reach agreement and state its case.

EMPRESS CAR CO (ABERTILLERY) LTD v. SECRETARY OF STATE FOR WALES [1995] E.G.C.S. 22, Sir Graham Eyre Q.C., QBD.

4762. Planning appeals

The Department of the Environment, DoE, issued a press release entitled *Planning appeal procedures: DoE Circular 15/96*, published on September 20, 1996. A circular offering best practice guidance on local inquiries and other appeal procedures has been published by the Department of the Environment. The main provisions of the circular include the wider use of hearings and pre-inquiry discussions, the importance of agreeing and adhering to timetables, and the need for stricter control over cross examination.

4763. Planning appeals–informal hearing–change of use from guest house to hotel–legitimate complaint

DF applied to quash the decision of an inspector dismissing their appeal against refusal of planning permission relating to their hotel. The permission was for change of use of a neighbouring residential dwelling to form an extension to the existing guest house. DF argued that the informal hearing which took place was unsuitable for the complex issues raised. They also argued that the inspector failed to give sufficient weight to their contentions and gave unreasonable weight to the objectors' contentions. DF contended that the planning inspector was wrong to distinguish between hotels and guest houses.

Held, dismissing the appeal, that (1) although the planning inspectorate failed to advise DF over the telephone of the inappropriateness of an informal hearing for deciding complex issues, a brochure entitled "Planning Appeals Code of Practice for Hearings" was sent to them and referred to that particular point. In any event, there was no evidence that the issues raised were complex; (2) the inspector's findings were not wrong in law and presented a fair picture. The ground for legitimate complaint did not fit within the principles set out in *Ashbridge Investments v. Minister of Housing and Local Government* [1965] 1 W.L.R. 1320, [1965] C.L.Y. 522, and (3) the inspector's conclusion that the extension would result in the creation of a "substantial hotel" as opposed to a guest house for which DF had existing permission was well founded on the facts.

DE FARIA v. SECRETARY OF STATE FOR THE ENVIRONMENT, Trans. Ref: CO/760/94, November 30, 1995, Malcolm Spence Q.C., QBD.

4764. Planning appeals–informal hearing–inspector obliged to give reasons and observe rules of natural justice–no evidence to support a conclusion–whether a real possibility that this influenced the decision

[Town and Country Planning Appeals (Determination by Inspectors) (Inquiries Procedure) Rules 1992.]

RH had appealed against the decision of the District Council to refuse planning permission for the erection of 16 homes. The appeal was heard by an inspector under the informal hearing process as set out in Department of the Environment circular 10/88. The inspector refused the appeal on the grounds of a potentially harmful effect to three trees which were the subject of a tree preservation order. RH appealed to the High Court on the basis that it had not been given the opportunity to present evidence or argument on the effect of the layout on the protected trees and an assumption as to the impervious surface of the road next to the trees.

Held, allowing the application and quashing the decision, that while an informal hearing should be "inspector led" and inquisitorial, it must obey the rules of natural justice, with each party being able to contribute freely to the discussion and the decision letter should include a statement of reasons. In reaching a decision the inspector was entitled to use his own expertise, combined with a site visit and the evidence he had heard. His decision on the layout was amply justified. It was not incumbent on the inspector to spell out those parts of the evidence which were and were not accepted. However reading the decision letter as a whole, even on its most benevolent construction, there was a possibility that it was influenced by a conclusion that the road surface would be impervious. On the basis that there was a difference of opinion as to whether this conclusion would alter the ultimate decision, the parties were entitled to know what the finding was and how it affected the decision, *Bolton MBC v. Secretary of State for the Environment* [1991] J.P.L. 241, [1991] C.L.Y. 94 applied.

RYDON HOMES LTD v. SECRETARY OF STATE FOR THE ENVIRONMENT AND SEVENOAKS DC (1995) 70 P. & C.R. 657, RMK Gray Q.C., QBD.

4765. Planning appeals–property improvement notices–notice withdrawn after partial compliance–whether planning authority liable for all costs

[Town and Country Planning Act 1990 s.215.]

B appealed, by way of case stated, against a decision of the magistrates to award him the sum of £100 for costs relating to his successful appeal against a notice under the Town and Country Planning Act 1990 s.215. The notice related to actions to be done by B to improve the condition of his land which was adversely affecting the amenity of the area. B appealed against the notice but, before the hearing, had partially complied with it. This led to U withdrawing the notice. B went ahead with the hearing in order to recover costs incurred by him in relation to the appeal. B argued that, although the justices did not discuss the grounds of the appeal, they must have impliedly decided on one ground or another in allowing the appeal. This meant that U should not have served the notice and they were, therefore, liable for all costs incurred after service.

Held, dismissing the appeal, that the magistrates had been correct in law in determining the costs in the way that they did. They allowed costs incurred in seeking legal advice once the notice had been withdrawn, as the withdrawal was as a direct result of B's actions.

R. v. UTTLESFORD DC, *ex p.* BARNES, Trans. Ref: CO 3816/94, July 20, 1995, Brooke, J., QBD.

4766. Planning applications–shopping centres–application for certificate of lawfulness for one shop–meaning of "planning unit"

[Town and Country Planning Act 1990 s.192.]

C, the owners of the MetroCentre, a large shopping and entertainment complex, applied to the local planning authority for a certificate of lawfulness pursuant to the Town and Country Planning Act 1990 s.192 in respect of a shopping unit within the centre, which they wished to use as a restaurant. The application was refused. C's appeal to the Secretary of State was dismissed. They applied to quash the Secretary of State's decision on the basis of an error of law, in that the appropriate "unit" for the purpose of s.192 should have been taken to be the whole of the MetroCentre, which was in one occupation.

Held, dismissing the application, that the question of whether the shop was the appropriate planning unit was essentially a matter of fact and degree for the Secretary of State to determine, in accordance with the working rule of Bridge, J. in *Burdle v. Secretary of State for the Environment* [1972] 1 W.L.R. 1207, [1972] C.L.Y. 3335. It was only if the Secretary of State was unable to discern what the planning unit was that he had to go on to consider the specific questions set out in that case.

CHURCH COMMISSIONERS FOR ENGLAND v. SECRETARY OF STATE FOR THE ENVIRONMENT AND GATESHEAD MBC (1996) 71 P. & C.R. 73, R M K Gray Q.C., QBD.

4767. Planning applications–whether letter amounted to an application–whether council had approved planning application–council not obliged to give written response–whether estoppel a rose due to detrimental reliance

[Town and Country Planning Act 1990 s.55, s.57, s.58; Town and Country Planning Act 1990 Part III Town and Country Planning General Development Order 1988.]

T appealed against TDC's refusal to grant planning permission to erect a multi antenna mast for a mobile telephone service. The proposal amounted to a development under the Town and Country Planning Act 1990 s.55, s.57 and Part 111, but under s.58 of the Act planning permission could be granted by a development order. T sent TDC notice of their proposal with drawings, which they claimed satisfied the conditions of the Town and Country Planning General Development Order 1988 thereby allowing permission to be granted for certain developments without the need for an application. The Order also provided an embargo on development for 28 days unless it had been determined that prior approval was not required or had been given. TDC stated that consent was required and would not be forthcoming. T sent details of an amended site with a letter, which was not referred to as an application, stating that everything appeared to be agreed and was awaiting approval. TDC acknowledged receipt and purported to accept the validity of the notification, but remained ambiguous as to whether the letter was an application and prevented work commencing for 28 days provided no further notification was sent. TDC then informed T that the site was not approved. TDC contended that T's letter did not amount to a valid application and that acknowledgement of the letter did not allow T to claim estoppel as there was no evidence that T had relied upon it to his detriment.

Held, dismissing the appeal, that (1) planning permission had not been granted by the Secretary of State by virtue of the Order. This was not an application for planning permission but an application under the Order A2(4) (ii) the original application had been rejected and could not be amended, and (2) the acknowledgement did acknowledge receipt of the notification as a valid application but there was no evidence of reliance on it to T's detriment. Oral notice was sufficient for the refusal of approval to the siting and appearance of the antenna and T had conceded that oral notification had been given, *Lever Finance v. Secretary of State for the Environment* [1971] 1 Q.B. 222; *Western Fish Products v. Penwith DC* [1981] 2 All E.R. 204, [1981] C.L.Y. 2732, *Camden LBC v. Secretary of State for the Environment* (1994) 67 P. & C.R. 59, [1994] C.L.Y. 4460 considered.

TANDRIDGE DC v. TELECOM SECURICOR CELLULAR RADIO [1996] J.P.L. B128, Sir Graham Eyre Q.C., QBD.

4768. Planning authorities–application included a county matter–which authority should deal with the application–construction of Sch.1 para.3 of 1990 Act–statutory interpretation

[Town and Country Planning Act 1990 Sch.1 para.1, Sch.1 para.2, Sch.1 para.3.]

A planning application was made to WDC which included but was not restricted to a county matter as defined by the Town and Country Planning Act 1990 Sch.1 para.1 and para.2. The question was who should deal with such an application and the answer depended upon a proper construction of the phrase "such application...which related to a county matter" in Sch.1 para.3 of the 1990 Act. WDC applied for an order declaring that BCC had no power to deal with the planning application.

Held, refusing the application, that, where the predominant purpose of the planning application was, as it was in this case, a county matter as defined by Sch.1 para.1 and para.2, the county planning authority should determine the whole application.

R. v. BERKSHIRE CC, *ex p.* WOKINGHAM DC [1996] Env. L.R. 71, Latham, J., QBD.

4769. Planning blight–compulsory purchaser–ownership of subsoil formed part of hereditament–within curtilage of dwelling home–whole of hereditament to be purchased

[Town and Country Planning Act 1990 s.150, s.151, s.171; Local Government Finance Act 1988 s.64.]

N contended that, as the land freeholder, he owned the subsoil under the A35 onto which his property abutted. The Department of Transport owned the surface to a depth necessary for highway purposes. N did not occupy the subsoil. The Department of Transport purported to acquire the subsoil under a draft CPO. The Department issued a counter-notice under s.151 of the 1990 Act, submitting that N review a blight notice under the Town and Country Planning act 1990 s.150, requiring the Department of Transport to purchase the property, contending that the sale price had been adversely affected due to blight. They were not acquiring the claimants' hereditament, within the definition of "hereditament" in s.171 (1) of the 1990 Act and Local Government Finance Act 1988 s.64(1).

Held, that the objection in the counter notice was not well founded. Whether the highway subsoil was part of the hereditament in this case was a question of fact and degree requiring a common sense assessment. Following the principle that occupation of part constitutes occupation of the whole, N must be deemed to be in occupation of the highway subsoil; the cottage and the subsoil were within the same curtilage; they were contiguous and prima facie one hereditament; and further the highway subsoil was not capable of being let separately. Therefore the cottage and the subsoil of the highway formed part of a single hereditament and the Department was required to purchase the whole of Ns' interest.

NORMAN v. DEPARTMENT OF TRANSPORT (1996) 72 P. & C.R. 210, PH Clarke, FRICS., LandsTr.

4770. Planning control–advertising–rural areas

The Department of the Environment issued a press release entitled *No relaxation of advertising control in rural areas* (News release 494), published on November 19, 1996. Planning Minister Robert Jones has announced that restrictions on outdoor advertisements in Areas of Special Control of Advertisements, ASCAs, are to be retained. The removal of the ASCA regime was proposed in a consultation paper earlier this year but local authority associations, planning practitioners and amenity societies favoured the regime's retention. Mr Jones said that removal of the scheme would not have resulted in a loss of control over advertising since the special controls largely duplicate controls available to local planning authorities, which would still have to give consent for new poster hoardings. The ASCA regime will be continued for the time being and consideration will be given to modifications to ensure the same level of protection with less bureaucracy.

4771. Planning inquiries–costs

TOWN AND COUNTRY PLANNING (COSTS OF INQUIRIES ETC.) (EXAMINATION IN PUBLIC) REGULATIONS 1996, SI 1996 2382; made under the Town and Country Planning Act 1990 s.35B, s.303A. In force: October 10, 1996; £1.10.

These Regulations, apply in relation to any person who is appointed to conduct, or is appointed as one of the persons who are to conduct, an examination in public under the Town and Country Planning Act 1990 s.35B (1) and whose remuneration, and travelling or subsistence allowances, in respect of the appointment are to be paid by the local planning authority. Examinations in public are a form of administrative hearing which are usually held before the adoption of proposals for the alteration or replacement of a structure plan. These Regulations specify a standard daily amount which may be charged for each day the person appointed to hold it is engaged on the examination in public or work connected with it. The amount is £273 a day.

4772. Planning inquiries–costs–standard daily amount

TOWN AND COUNTRY PLANNING (COSTS OF INQUIRIES ETC.) (STANDARD DAILY AMOUNT) REGULATIONS 1996, SI 1996 24; made under the Town and Country Planning Act 1990 s.303A. In force: February 6, 1996; £0.65.

The standard amount which may be charged each day for a person conducting or undertaking work in connection with any "qualifying inquiry" and which may be recovered by the Secretary of State as costs borne by him is set at £340 by these Regulations. A "qualifying inquiry" is a unitary development plan or simplified planning zone inquiry or other hearing or examination heard in public in respect of structure plans.

4773. Planning inspectors–whether single decision in respect of three appeals breached Regulation–shared factors–adjacent premises

[Town and Country Planning (Appeals) (Written Representations Procedure) Regulations 1987 Reg.9.]

An appeal was made against a decision by a planning inspector, refusing D's applications to vary the opening hours of three adjacent retail units. D contended that by giving his decision in one letter, without separate decisions in respect of each unit, the inspector was in breach of the Town and Country Planning (Appeals) (Written Representations Procedure) Regulations 1987 Reg.9.

Held, dismissing the appeal, that there was no requirement for a separate decision in respect of each application. As each application referred to hours of opening restrictions, originally imposed to prevent disturbance to other occupiers, the inspector had obviously applied the same factors in all three appeals. Considering the matter in one operation did not breach Reg.9, as the Secretary of State had permission to base a decision taking account of only those written representations and other documents supplied, *Geha v. Secretary of State for the Environment* [1993] E.G.C.S. 202, [1994] C.L.Y. 4415 followed.

DIXON v. SECRETARY OF STATE FOR THE ENVIRONMENT [1995] E.G.C.S. 185, George Bartlett Q.C., QBD.

4774. Planning permission–access to parking area–access site near roundabout on main road–erection of safety barriers across site

M appealed against S's refusal to grant planning permission for hardstanding and a garage. The proposal was subject to an objection direction issued by the Secretary of State for Transport, given on the basis that the proposal included an access to be constructed 25m from roundabout on the A34. The Secretary of State had recently erected safety barriers across the site of the proposed access as a result of a 10 year safety audit of that section of the road which was close to a pedestrian subway. The matter was returned to the Secretary of State for the Environment for decision.

Held, dismissing the appeal, that it could not be suggested that the safety barriers had been erected to prevent the development.

STAFFORD BC v. MOLTON (1995) 10 P.A.D. 734, Judge not specified.

4775. Planning permission–adverse effect of development mitigated by public gain–required contents of developer's submissions

[Town and Country Planning Act 1990 s.106.]

Outline planning permission was refused for an application for six acres of housing and 119 acres of community woodland and parkland in Teesville. A non-statutory plan, including development of woodland and parkland, had been produced in June 1993 for consultation. On appeal, the inspector expressed views as to the visual impact of the proposed development and on the restrictive planning policies which would apply to the development. The developer contended that public gain would result.

Held, dismissing the application, that it was necessary, where a developer proposed to mitigate the effects of his development by reference to some form of public gain, that the public gain was identified with precision and that it was demonstrated to be capable of implementation or achievement by reference to the terms of the Town and Country Planning Act 1990 s.106.

COLLINS v. SECRETARY OF STATE FOR THE ENVIRONMENT AND LANGBAURGH ON TEES BC [1996] J.P.L. 303, Sir Graham Eyre Q.C., QBD.

4776. Planning permission–amendment to condition–requirement of emerging local plan–whether correct test used by inspector–validity of grounds for appeal not raised at planning inquiry

P appealed against a refusal to amend a restriction imposed in a caravan site planning permission, requiring removal of caravans each year. P contended that in refusing the amendment, the inspector had applied a different test to that laid down in Department of the Environment Circular 1/85. The Circular required an answer to the question "if planning permission would be granted today, would such a condition need to be attached" whereas the inspector had based his decision on whether the amendment would cause harm to the character of the surrounding land. P also argued, in a point not raised at the planning inquiry, that the objection could have been resolved by imposing conditions on caravan size and fences and sheds allowed on the site.

Held, dismissing the appeal, that (1) the test applied by the inspector complied with the requirements of the emerging local plan. Static caravans were not usually allowed in landscaped areas, a need directly related to the area's character, and (2) the inspector could only consider matters raised by the parties, not search for conditions omitted by them, *Top Deck Holdings v. Secretary of State for the Environment* [1991] J.P.L. 961, [1992] C.L.Y. 4234 considered. Failure to raise a matter at the inquiry did not allow an appellant to base an appeal on something not mentioned to the inspector.

PRATTS DEVELOPMENTS v. SECRETARY OF STATE FOR THE ENVIRONMENT [1995] E.G.C.S. 26, Malcolm Spence Q.C., QBD.

4777. Planning permission–application to expand existing site–importance of risk to established business if refused

R appealed against a refusal of outline planning permission in respect of warehouse, storage and parking facilities. R had a long history on the site, employed 58 people there and contended that the refusal had failed to deal with the risk to the present business if a modest expansion was not permitted.

Held, dismissing the appeal, that in reaching a decision, the Secretary of State had to have regard to all material considerations, but no statutory duty required him to deal specifically with each one. Reasons given for a decision had to contain sufficient detail to show the conclusion reached on the principal and important issues. The matter had been correctly decided at first instance, with the issues being correctly approached and as a result it was inappropriate for the inspector to be cross-examined, *Bolton MBC v. Secretary of State for the Environment* [1995] E.G.C.S. 94, [1996] C.L.Y. 4834 considered.

Observed: In the absence of a formal inquiry record, the parties should reduce the relevant facts to writing. While oral evidence was not to be disregarded, this approach ensured that the inspector had a written form of the main points, thereby the increasing quality of decision making and avoiding misunderstandings

RICHARD READ (TRANSPORT) LTD v. SECRETARY OF STATE FOR THE ENVIRONMENT [1995] 3 P.L.R. 66, Butler-Sloss, L.J., CA.

4778. Planning permission–area of outstanding natural beauty–construction of dam to form fishing lakes–impact on area–effect on traffic

R appealed against S's refusal of planning permission to form fishing lakes by damming a river and for car parking, access and toilet facilities. The main issue raised by S was the effect of the proposal on the character and appearance of the area, having regard to its location within an area of outstanding natural beauty. S argued that there would be an impact on highway safety on local roads caused by the increased traffic. There were considerations about archaeological potential in the area and the potential consequences to local residents if the dam broke.

Held, allowing the appeal, that provision would be made for archaeological investigation and the structural integrity of the dam. Permission would be conditional on woodland planting, landscaping to screen the access track and car park and to soften the impact of the pools. To cope with the problems of highway safety, passing places were to be installed on the road.

STROUD DC v. RACTLIFFE (1995) 10 P.A.D. 754, Judge not specified.

4779. Planning permission–bail and probation hostel–consideration of residents' fears justified

W applied to quash the decision refusing planning permission to extend a bail and probation hostel. The grounds of appeal were that the planning inspector should not have taken into account the apprehensions of local residents as their fear was not relevant to land use and was unjustified. W also questioned whether the need for more bed spaces in the area was given full consideration by the inspector and whether he erred in his application of Home Office guidance in assessing the nature of the locality. W submitted that the guidance was treated as planning policy and strictly adhered to, instead of considering more general points about the locality.

Held, dismissing the application, that (1) the inspector was entitled to take into account the particular character of the residential estate and the likely impact an extension to the hostel would have on residents' fears, *Stringer v. Minister for Housing and Local Government* [1970] 1 W.L.R. 1281, [1970] C.L.Y. 2778 followed; (2) the inspector considered the identified need for further hostel provision in the area, but it was his discretion as to what weight it should carry, *Tesco Stores Ltd v. Secretary of State for the Environment* [1995] 1 W.L.R. 759, [1995] 2 C.L.Y. 4784 applied, and (3) the guidance on locality was taken into account, but the inspector also considered the residential nature of the hostel site, and was justified in reaching his decision that the extension would be incongruous.

WEST MIDLANDS PROBATION COMMITTEE v. SECRETARY OF STATE FOR THE ENVIRONMENT AND WALSALL MBC [1996] N.P.C. 135, Robin Purchas Q.C., QBD.

4780. Planning permission–business park adjacent to airport–whether inconsistent with local plan

H was a developer who applied for planning permission to develop two sites adjacent to East Midlands Airport. On appeal the inspector decided permission should be granted for site A but not site B. The local structure plan expressly provided that the long term future development of the airport was not to be prejudiced by grants of planning permission for other developments. E applied unsuccessfully to the High Court to quash the permission granted for site A and thereafter appealed to the Court of Appeal.

Held, dismissing the appeal, that it was clear from reading the decision letter as a whole that the inspector had in mind that permission should not be granted if the development would interfere with the long term future development of the airport. It was also clear from his decision letter that he considered the development proposed for site B would interfere but that the development proposed for site A would involve only minimal interference or none at all on land that could, in the meantime, be usefully used as a business park. That being the case, the decision could not be quashed.

EAST MIDLANDS INTERNATIONAL AIRPORT LTD v. SECRETARY OF STATE FOR THE ENVIRONMENT [1994] E.G.C.S. 181, Glidewell, L.J., CA.

4781. Planning permission–caravan accommodation for pig farmer–whether inspector acted in excess of powers–whether inspector wrong to fail to suggest conditions

B applied to quash the dismissal of an appeal against the refusal of planning permission to retain a caravan for use as living accommodation. The caravan was required so that B could live near his enterprise which involved the raising of sows for profit. B argued that the inspector failed to consider proper considerations, took into account improper considerations and acted in excess of his powers.

Held, dismissing the appeal, that (1) the inspector was entitled to reach the decision that he did on the material before him, and (2) the inspector was not under a duty to suggest that a condition be attached to the planning permission giving B, for example, three years' temporary permission to prove that his enterprise could be sustained.

BRIGHTWELL v. SECRETARY OF STATE FOR THE ENVIRONMENT, Trans. Ref: CO/1757/95, October 19, 1995, Rich Q.C., QBD.

4782. Planning permission–caravan site licence–could apply in respect of land not within planning permission–nature of "existing site"–whether original application correctly decided

[Caravan Sites and Control of Development Act 1960 s.13.]

B appealed against the High Court's refusal to grant judicial review of a decision by E that they had no power to grant a site licence in respect of a site without planning permission for its proposed use. B's predecessor in title had originally applied for a caravan site licence under the Caravan Sites and Control of Development Act 1960, in respect of all 19.75 acres of the site. However, E had only granted a licence for 10.8 acres, excluding a 4.75 acre recreation area. B sought a caravan site licence for two acres of this area but E refused, contending that they could not issue a licence in respect of land without planning permission for such use.

Held, dismissing the appeal, that (1) it was a question of fact and degree whether land comprised part of an existing site, under s.13 of the Act, *R. v. Axbridge RDC, ex p. Wormald* [1964] 1 W.L.R. 442, [1964] C.L.Y. 3559 considered, and only land forming part of a site could be subject to deemed planning permission, *Williams-Denton v. Watford RDC* (1963) 15 P. & C.R. 11, [1963] C.L.Y. 3377 considered, and (2) a planning authority determining an application made under the Act could validly decide that a licence should apply to a smaller area than that contended for, and such determination could be open to challenge by the applicant. However, the terms used in the original permission showed that the authority had applied the correct test when granting permission for the 10.8 acre site.

R. v. EPPING FOREST DC, *ex p.* BERKELEY LEISURE GROUP LTD [1995] E.G.C.S. 27, Glidewell, L.J., CA.

4783. Planning permission–condition that occupants be of retirement age–removal of condition justified by evidence before planning inspector

[Town and Country Planning (Use Classes) Order 1987.]

B challenged the decision of the Secretary of State to allow the second respondents, E, to use buildings without complying with a restriction, imposed by B, which only allowed the accommodation to be occupied by those of retirement age. The use was subject to a condition that it should be discontinued in two years' time. B argued that the variation would create an unencumbered residential use within Class C3 of the Town and Country Planning (Use Classes) Order 1987.

Held, dismissing the application, that (1) to argue a theoretical Class C3 use was not the same as presenting evidence to support a Class C3 use. Planning permission was granted on the evidence available, and (2) there was no evidence of an unencumbered use within Class C3 or evidence of a theoretical Class C3 use. If there had been a theoretical Class C3 use then it might have been correct to impose a condition preventing a Class C3 use, but that had not been argued.

BROMLEY LBC v. SECRETARY OF STATE FOR THE ENVIRONMENT [1996] E.G.C.S. 41, Christopher Lockhart-Mummery Q.C., QBD.

4784. Planning permission–condition that occupied by agricultural employee–application to remove condition–whether council acted unreasonably in refusing application–costs

A bungalow was built with the benefit of planning permission subject to a condition that the property was to be occupied by a person locally employed in agriculture. Twenty years later the property was within the settlement limits of the neighbouring village. Application was made to remove the condition. Notwithstanding the fact that planning permission would have been granted without the condition, had the application been made in 1992, the council refused to remove the condition. The applicant appealed successfully and the council were ordered to pay the applicant's costs of the appeal. The council appealed against the decision and sought judicial review of the order for costs.

Held, dismissing the appeal and the application for judicial review, that on the evidence before him the inspector was entitled to reach the decision that there was no continuing need to restrict the use of the property in line with the condition. The council had grossly underestimated the weight to be given to the fact that the condition would not be imposed had an application for planning permission been made in 1992. In doing so they had ignored the reality of the case. The inspector was entitled to conclude that the council had behaved unreasonably and put the applicant to unnecessary expense.

HAMBLETON DC v. SECRETARY OF STATE FOR THE ENVIRONMENT (1995) 70 P. & C.R. 549, May, J., QBD.

4785. Planning permission–decision letter revealing matters upon which objector had no opportunity to make comments–test to be applied to establish breach of natural justice

[Town and Country Planning Act 1990 s.288.]

RH applied under the Town and Country Planning Act 1990 s.288 to quash two outline planning permissions granted by the Secretary of State. RH had been the principal objectors to the schemes at the planning inquiry. The Secretary of State had granted permission contrary to the inquiry inspector's recommendation. RH contended that the decision reached was in breach of natural justice, as the decision letter revealed the existence of correspondence upon which they had not had the opportunity to comment.

Held, dismissing the application, that for a breach of the rules of natural justice to occur, the test was whether an objective viewing of the matter by a reasonable person, knowing all the facts before the court, showed that the procedure adopted would cause injury and unfairness to the applicant. Although RH's objection had been allowed to be raised at the inquiry at the discretion of the inspector, it did not arise as of right. On the facts, it could not be found that a reasonable person, knowing all the circumstances, would consider that RH had been placed at the risk of injustice or unfairness. They had not suffered substantial prejudice by not having the opportunity to comment on the matters raised.

ROBERT HITCHIN LTD v. SECRETARY OF STATE FOR THE ENVIRONMENT (1996) 72 P. & C.R. 579, Harrison, J., QBD.

4786. Planning permission–development controlled adequately by HMIP–adequate reasons given why the Secretary of State rejected the inspector's recommendation

[Environmental Protection Act 1990.]

The local planning authority, G, had refused NWG planning permission for a clinical waste incinerator in a semi-rural location. The inspector had decided that the impact on air quality and agriculture had been insufficiently defined although an appropriate plant could be built on this site. The Secretary of State rejected this recommendation on the basis that there were sufficient controls under the Environmental Protection Act 1990. As a prescribed process, separate authorisation for the incineration would be required from Her Majesty's Inspectorate of Pollution, HMIP. G appealed on the basis that the Secretary of State had failed to explain adequately the reason for the difference in his decision from that of the inspector, and that he had reached an irrational conclusion and/or breached the precautionary principle.

Held, dismissing the appeal, that the Secretary of State's reasoning was adequate, proper and intelligible. Just as the environmental impact of emissions was an adequate consideration, so was the presence of controls under the 1990 Act. The Secretary of State was justified in concluding that the areas of concern which led the inspector to recommend refusal could properly be decided by HMIP and that its powers were adequate to meet these concerns.

GATESHEAD MBC v. SECRETARY OF STATE FOR THE ENVIRONMENT AND NORTHUMBRIAN WATER GROUP PLC (1996) 71 P. &. C.R. 350, Glidewell, L.J., CA.

4787. Planning permission–development of countryside site–emerging plan revealed housing land deficit–whether PPG 3 allowed consideration of emerging plan–whether local plan correctly construed in regard to housing land policy

G applied to quash a planning inspector's decision granting permission for a residential development in a green belt area. G contended that the proposed development was contrary to both the existing and emerging structure plans, as well as the local area plan, which all stated opposition to developments in "countryside beyond the green belt". The emerging structure plan, whose approval was imminent at the time of the inquiry, increased the area housing requirement. As a result G submitted that the inspector had been wrong to rely on the emerging plan as opposed to the current structural plan. G also claimed that the inspector had misconstrued the local plan policy of deciding applications for sites of at least one acre by reference to their individual merits, using it to allow the proposed development, contrary to the requirements of the structural plan.

Held, refusing the application, that as the emerging plan gave rise to a large deficit of housing land and was nearly in place, the inspector could depart from the requirements of PPG 3 where a strict application would give a misleading housing land supply picture. In correctly using the local plan to assess the site on its individual merits, the inspector had considered all the relevant factors when finding the scheme to be acceptable.

GUILDFORD BC v. SECRETARY OF STATE FOR THE ENVIRONMENT [1995] E.G.C.S. 100, R.M.K. Gray, QBD.

4788. Planning permission–dual carriageway–impact on area–need for road

S's Highway Committee applied for planning permission to construct a dual carriageway and associated side roads, overbridges and landscaping. The question arose as to the impact on green belt land, conservation areas, listed buildings, heritage landscape, agricultural land, woodland, people living and taking recreation in the area, and wildlife.

Held, dismissing the application, that need for the road required investigation and alternative routes must be examined. The proposed road would harm several interests of acknowledged importance. The need for the road scheme and the benefits it would bring were outweighed by the harm that it would cause.

SEFTON MBC'S HIGHWAYS COMMITTEE'S APPLICATION, *Re* (1995) 10 P.A.D. 776, Judge not specified.

4789. Planning permission–equestrian events–traffic–consistency with previous decision affecting neighbouring land

The local planning authority served an enforcement notice in respect of the use of a farm as an equestrian centre. Access to the farm was along a narrow country road and one other minor road. Previously, planning appeals by a neighbouring farm for use as an equestrian centre and by the present farm for commercial vehicle operations had been refused on the ground that the proposed uses would create unacceptable traffic conditions along the same roads. On an appeal against the enforcement notice, the inspector decided that permission should be granted subject to conditions limiting the number of horses and the number of equestrian events to be held. B and other residents appealed contending that the inspector had improperly ignored or failed to consider the earlier decisions.

Held, allowing the appeal, that it was common sense that the earlier decisions, based as they were on the effect of traffic using the same access roads on the character of the area and residential amenity, were material to the present application. It was open to the inspector to reach a different decision on the present application but as that decision conflicted with the earlier appeal decisions it was incumbent on him to explain why he had come to a different conclusion on the same matters. The inspector had not done so. Previous appellate decisions were not to be legalistically distinguished but should be treated with common sense in order to preserve consistency of approach in the appellate process.

BABER v. SECRETARY OF STATE FOR THE ENVIRONMENT [1994] E.G.C.S. 200, Jeremy Sullivan Q.C., QBD.

4790. Planning permission–floating heliport–construction of "development"–whether planning permission required

[Town and Country Planning Act 1990.]

TH Plc wished to operate a floating heliport at various sites on the tidal waters of the River Thames. It sought the determination of the court on the question of whether or not such an activity was a development for which planning permission was required. Inter alia, TH Plc argued that, as it sought to use the waters of the river, the proposed activity was not a development of land for which planning permission was required.

Held, declaring that planning permission was required, that the purpose of the Town and Country Planning Act 1990 was to control development. In construing the Act the court was bound to take a broad view given that the Act was aimed at controlling the adverse effects and mischief caused through development. The environmental consequences of the proposals were substantial and of the nature that the Act was designed to control. The proposals involved points on land at which passengers would embark and disembark. The word "land" in the Act was not to be construed so as to exclude water which rested on the bed of a river, *Attorney-General v. Brotherton* [1992] 1 All E.R. 230, [1992] C.L.Y. 1801 considered.

THAMES HELIPORT PLC v. TOWER HAMLETS LBC [1994] E.G.C.S. 208, Sir Haydn Tudor Evans, QBD.

4791. Planning permission–Lake District National Park–boathouse on lake–whether it would detract from appearance

L appealed against the refusal of LD to grant planning permission for the construction of a boathouse on land adjoining Lake Windermere. Policy C4 of the Cumbria and Lake District Joint Structure Plan sought to protect lakeshores from inappropriate development and to allow only development which was essential for access to the lake and acceptable in terms of its scale, detailed design and location. The main issue was whether the proposed building would detract from the character and appearance of the locality, contrary to the aims of national and local planning policies.

Held, granting planning permission subject to conditions, that development must take place within five years of the permission being granted. No development could take place without local planning authority approval for a scheme of landscaping to be carried out within the first planting season after the occupation of the buildings. This planning permission was to replace other permissions granted with reference to the land and was not to be in addition to it.

LAKE DISTRICT SPECIAL PLANNING BOARD v. LOWICK (1995) 10 P.A.D. 763, Judge not specified.

4792. Planning permission–landfill sites–risks to aircraft in proposed scheme–whether risk had to be quantified by comparison with previous proposal

The applicant was refused planning permission for use of his quarry, situated next to an RAF landing ground and Cardiff Airport, as a waste disposal site. The inspector appointed to investigate issues of percolating liquid disposal and aviation safety found that increased risks to aircraft safety through bird strikes incidents were associated with landfill sites and that the applicant's schemes to overcome the problem were fundamentally flawed. The applicant challenged the decision on the basis that the inspector had not applied the correct test of comparing the number of birds likely to be attracted if the existing permission were carried out with that of the proposed permission.

Held, refusing the application, that only the issue of aviation safety was to be considered as this was the reason for denial of permission and not the waste problem. The inspector had concluded that the comparison required by the applicant could not be made as it was subject to a great deal of uncertainty relating to numbers of birds, species and their positions at certain times. According to *Small Pressure Castings Ltd v. Secretary of State for the Environment* (1972) 223 E.G. 1099, an inspector was required to compare present and previous use to the extent which the evidence permitted a proper comparison to be made. The inspector was not required to make such a comparison in the present circumstances.

BLUE CIRCLE INDUSTRIES PLC v. SECRETARY OF STATE FOR WALES [1996] E.G.C.S. 26, Owen, J., QBD.

4793. Planning permission–landfill sites–whether material considerations taken into account

HJB applied to quash the decision rejecting a planning appeal for permission to allow the tipping of controlled wastes upon the site of a disused colliery with the condition that the site, thereafter, be properly cleared, covered, wooded and grassed ready for incorporation into the National Forest. HJB argued that the planning inspector failed to take account of material considerations and to give adequate reasons for his decision.

Held, allowing the appeal, that although the planning inspector gave adequate reasons for his decision, he failed to take account of a material consideration. It was acknowledged by the inspector that the proposed development was better for the site in the long run. This he balanced against the obviousness of the scheme and the delay to the redevelopment. From this, he was entitled to conclude that the policy for the Priority Area, within which the site fell, would be breached. However, he only considered the advantage of the proposal in relation to a possible breach of the policy, and failed to consider it in relation to the balancing of the need for a landfill site against a breach of the policy. The decision was quashed and remitted for re-determination.

HJ BANKS & CO LTD v. SECRETARY OF STATE FOR THE ENVIRONMENT [1996] N.P.C. 146, Rich Q.C., QBD.

4794. Planning permission–local plans–whether adequate reasons given

W refused outline planning permission for residential development on land in Berkshire. LE contended that the decision of the Secretary of State to uphold the decision of the inspector, despite the fact that the proposed development appeared to be in accordance with the local plan, was a breach of natural justice and *Wednesbury* unreasonable and the Secretary of State had failed to give adequate reasons for his decision.

Held, allowing the application, that while a planning application can be refused on grounds that the grant might interfere with the preparation of the development plan, the decision maker must explain why the granting of planning permission would prejudice the plan preparation. The Secretary of State failed to explain how the present decision accorded with PPG1 and PPG3.

LEIGH ESTATES (UK) LTD v. SECRETARY OF STATE FOR THE ENVIRONMENT AND WOKINGHAM BC [1996] J.P.L. 217, Roy Vandermeer Q.C., QBD.

4795. Planning permission–location of waste transfer site near food products factory–decision making processes–whether reasons given for preference of certain parts of evidence and rejection of others

E applied, in February 1992, for permission to erect and operate a facility for the collection, bulking up and transfer of liquid and containerised industrial waste to appropriate final disposal facilities. H refused permission on the ground that the proposed developments could prejudice the operation of a nearby food processing factory in the event of malodorous emissions. E appealed. Evidence was presented that the risk of a small spill at the site leading to a tainting incident at B lay within the range of one in 3,000 to one in 300,000. Evidence was presented that the construction of an enclosed drum handling area would substantially reduce the risk of spillage. B gave evidence that any tainting of their cocoa products could have disastrous economic consequences. The inspector dismissed the appeal. He held that a tainting incident at B would sooner or later be likely to occur if the proposed development went ahead and that the risk of such an incident should not be ignored even if it was at the lower end of the range agreed between the experts. He concluded that even if a covered enclosure was added there would be no circumstances in which the risk was not present at all. He further concluded that the worst case scenario presented by B was so serious in an area of high social deprivation that it presented a risk that was too great to take. E appealed against the inspector's decision, arguing that the inspector failed to consider, or to consider adequately, the proposal to construct an enclosed drum handling area, that he was wrong to direct himself that any risk of an incident, however trivial, was not acceptable and that his reasons were inadequate or unintelligible or that his conclusion was perverse.

Held, allowing the appeal, that E were entitled as a matter of law to receive clear, intelligible reasons, and these they did not receive. From the inspector's report, the court was unable to understand how he could have reached the conclusion that the risk posed by unloading and loading drums within the proposed covered area was one which warranted serious consideration, let alone one which entitled him to reach the conclusion in the terms he adopted. The court also failed to understand the thought process by which the inspector focused on the worst case scenario without attempting to assess its likely incidence, nor those by which he reached the unambiguous conclusion that malodorous emissions were likely to have a materially adverse effect on the B factory. There was a substantial breach of the requirements of the Town and Country Planning Appeals (Determination by Inspectors) (Inquiries Procedure) Rules 1992 r.18(1). The inspector also failed to give adequate consideration to the effect of the covered enclosure proposals on the overall risks posed by the proposed developments and that these were material considerations that he ought to have taken into account. These failures substantially prejudiced E.

ENVIROCOR WASTE HOLDINGS LTD v. SECRETARY OF STATE FOR THE ENVIRONMENT, *ex p.* HUMBERSIDE CC AND BRITISH COCOA MILLS (HULL) LTD [1996] Env. L.R. 49, Brooke, J., QBD.

4796. Planning permission–meaning of "sewer"–statutory interpretation

[Town and Country Planning General Development Order 1988 Sch.2 Part 10.]

DBC appealed against a decision of a planning inspector who determined that a drain in Doncaster was a sewer within the meaning of the Town and Country Planning General Development Order 1988 Sch.2 Part 10 and therefore did not need express planning permission.

Held, dismissing the appeal, that (1) the word "sewer" should have its ordinary meaning within the context of planning policy as a whole; (2) the inspector was correct in his wide definition of the word. It was in line with the ordinary meaning as described in the 1978 version of the Oxford English Dictionary which was in use at the time of the drafting of the GDO; (3) authorities showed that the word had a wider meaning than the word "drain" and the ditch in this case could be termed a "sewer", *Mayor, Alderman and Citizens of Newcastle upon Tyne v. Houseman* (1898) 43 S.J. 140, *British Railways Board v. Tonbridge and Malling DC* (1981) 79 L.G.R. 589, [1982] C.L.Y. 2631 considered, and (4) the purpose of the GDO was to allow landowners to maintain their land without having to obtain planning permission.

DONCASTER BC v. SECRETARY OF STATE FOR THE ENVIRONMENT AND LEE [1996] 2 P.L.R. 39, Malcolm Spence Q.C., QBD.

4797. Planning permission–multiple applications relating to separate parts of one property–whether properly considered separately

[Town and Country Planning Act 1990 s.177.]

The council served five enforcement notices in respect of the use and occupation of a group of redundant agricultural buildings. Appeals were lodged in consequence of which there were deemed applications for planning permission under the Town and Country Planning Act 1990 s.177. The inspector considered the cumulative effect of the uses to which the buildings had been put and rejected the applications. B appealed.

Held, allowing the appeal, that giving the decision letter its most benevolent construction it was clear that each of the applications had been interlinked by the inspector and in consequence he failed to consider each separately on an individual basis. That amounted to an error of law sufficient to justify remission for reconsideration.

BRUSCHWEILLER v. SECRETARY OF STATE FOR THE ENVIRONMENT AND CHELMSFORD BC (1995) 70 P. & C.R. 150, RMK Gray Q.C., QBD.

4798. Planning permission–outline permission–application for reserved matters–construction–whether local centre within permission

[Town and Country Planning Act 1990 s.288.]

Applications were made under the Town and Country Planning Act 1990 s.288 to quash two decisions of the Secretary of State allowing appeals against refusal of B's reserved detailed planning applications. The applications concerned outline planning permission for a "local centre", comprising shopping, community and school provision on a new housing development. The centre was to include a supermarket and other shops, occupying a defined area and not exceeding defined maximum net sales areas, as set out in the development brief. In allowing the earlier appeals, the Secretary of State decided that the schemes fell within the scope of reserved matters and no condition contained within the outline planning permission required such matters to comply with the development brief. B appealed, contending as matters of law that the Secretary of State had (1) erred in failing to construe properly "local centre" within the conditions laid down in the outline planning permission; (2) been unreasonable in the *Wednesbury* sense in deciding that the schemes were within the scope of the outline planning permission, and (3) failed to give adequate reasons for his decision.

Held, allowing the applications, that (1) the interpretation of outline planning permission was a matter of law, *Wyre Forest DC v. Secretary of State for the Environment* [1990] 2 A.C. 357, [1990] C.L.Y. 4372 considered. It was for the court to decide whether an application for detailed approval was within the scope of outline planning permission. In doing so, regard must only be paid to the permission itself, and the application could only be used as an aid to construction if deemed to be incorporated into the permission, *Miller-Mead v. Minister of Housing and Local Government* [1963] 2 Q.B. 196, [1963] C.L.Y. 3406 considered. Whether a detailed approval application was within the scope of outline planning permission was a matter of fact and degree for the decision maker to decide, *R. v. Hammersmith and Fulham LBC, ex p. Greater London Council* (1985) 51 P. & C.R. 120, [1986] C.L.Y. 3336 followed, and (2) on the facts, the term "local centre", as found in the development brief, carried no precise meaning, but interpreted in light of the surrounding words, it was effectively limited to the ambit of the new development, not as a retail centre for a wider area. As a result, the size of the approved schemes meant they were in excess of the local requirement. No reasons had been given by the Secretary of State to indicate what features of the proposal led him to conclude that the applications fell within the scope of the permission, such an omission giving doubts as to whether he based the decision only on relevant considerations.

BRAINTREE DC v. SECRETARY OF STATE FOR THE ENVIRONMENT; CARTER COMMERCIAL DEVELOPMENTS LTD v. SECRETARY OF STATE FOR THE ENVIRONMENT AND BRAINTREE DC; ASHFIELD LAND LTD v. SECRETARY OF STATE FOR THE ENVIRONMENT AND BRAINTREE DC (1996) 71 P. & C.R. 323, George Bartlett Q.C., QBD.

4799. Planning permission–permission granted after earlier identical application refused–planning authority was not under a duty to give reasons for change of mind

C applied for judicial review of A's decision to grant planning permission to P following an application identical to one which had earlier been refused. C contended that reasons should have been given for the change of mind inherent in the decision-making process and argued that the planning sub-committee should not have reconsidered a decision on which an appeal was pending.

Held, dismissing the application, that the need for reasons to be given was not a principle which could be universally applied, *R. v. Higher Education Funding Council, ex p. Institute of Dental Surgery* [1994] 1 W.L.R. 242, [1995] 1 C.L.Y. 162 considered, and no general duty existed to give reasons. The present application centred on the change of mind of the planning sub-committee, not the reasons for the grant of permission. Reasons for such a change could not be easily given, as the issue amounted to an individual and not a collective change of mind, *R. v. Poole BC, ex p. Beebee* [1991] 2 P.L.R. 27, [1992] C.L.Y. 4389 considered. In that sense, the decision itself was clear and contained no element of unfairness. Whilst an increasing number of authorities pointed to the need for consistency in decision-making, in the planning sphere, such an approach might lead to a planning authority unnecessarily resisting appeals, a state of affairs which would be contrary to the interests of the taxpayer, *R. v. Inland Revenue Commissioners, ex p. MFK Underwriting Agents Ltd* [1990] 1 W.L.R. 1545, [1990] C.L.Y. 2651 considered.

R. v. AYLESBURY VALE DC, *ex p.* CHAPLIN [1996] E.G.C.S. 126, Keene, J., QBD.

4800. Planning permission–redevelopment–use as probation hostel–effect on local amenities

E appealed against H's refusal to grant outline planning permission for the redevelopment of a tyre and exhaust fitting centre and the erection of a two storey linked extension to a property for use as a probation hostel. The main issues were whether the proposed development would be likely to affect adversely the amenities of nearby residents by reason of an incidence of increased crime in the area and whether the size, location and immediate surroundings would provide a suitable environment for the proposed hostel.

Held, allowing the appeal, that permission would be granted subject to conditions that use be restricted to a probation hostel to ensure a level of prior assessment and continuous supervision of residents appropriate to the location. The number of beds and levels of staffing were essentially matters for the Probation Service.

HARLOW DC v. ESSEX PROBATION SERVICE (1995) 10 P.A.D. 737, G R Holland.

4801. Planning permission–refusal–green belt area–inspector's decision letter

K applied to quash the decision of the Secretary of State dismissing K's appeal against a refusal of planning permission, on the ground that the inspector had failed to balance the proposed harm to the green belt and the circumstances of K's case.

Held, dismissing the application, that no justifiable reason could be seen for criticising the inspector's decision letter. He had demonstrated that he had considered the issues raised by K and made an informed decision on that basis.

KNOWLSON v. SECRETARY OF STATE FOR THE ENVIRONMENT AND NEW FOREST DC (1996) 71 P. & C.R. D13, Sullivan Q.C., QBD.

4802. Planning permission–refusal–importance of previous refusal of application for wider use

K appealed against the decision of an inspector, appointed by the Secretary of State, refusing planning permission for the retention of a building for use for storage and exhaust fitting and the retention of a building and its continued use as a "quick fit" and MOT workshop. An application for planning permission for wider use of the buildings had been refused the previous year and K argued that the inspector had misdirected himself in the manner in which he had dealt with the earlier refusal by another inspector.

Held, allowing the appeal, that (1) the material issue was the impact that the planning permission would have had on the parking and highway conditions. It was contended that the second inspector had dealt with that issue by considering the broader issue of the impact on the amenity. However, highway safety was such an important issue that it needed to be considered independently; (2) the second inspector had correctly attached great importance to the first inspector's decision, but then had failed to understand its true significance. The lesser level of planning permission sought by K was accepted by the first inspector as not causing demonstrable harm to the amenity, and (3) the second inspector had misdirected himself by failing to decide upon the issues that he had defined. The decisions were quashed and remitted for reconsideration.

KANLI v. SECRETARY OF STATE FOR THE ENVIRONMENT, Trans. Ref: CO/866/95; CO/867/95, November 17, 1995, Gerald Moriarty Q.C., QBD.

4803. Planning permission–retail parks–outline permission–relevant considerations on applications to extend time for approval of reserved matters

[Town and Country Planning Act 1990 s.73.]

Held, that on an application to extend the time in which an application for approval of reserved matters could be made where outline planning permission for a retail park had been granted, it was not open to a planning authority to consider whether variation of a condition would be contrary to new planning policies implemented since outline permission was granted. Under the Town and Country Planning Act 1990 s.73 the authority had to consider the acceptability of existing and proposed conditions and was precluded from considering whether the development was acceptable in principle.

ALLIED LONDON PROPERTY INVESTMENT LTD v. SECRETARY OF STATE FOR THE ENVIRONMENT (1996) 72 P. & C.R. 327, Christopher Lockhart-Mummery Q.C., QBD.

4804. Planning permission–retail parks–outline permission for five units–approval of reserved matters allowing subdivision into 70 units–application of Furniss v Dawson

[Town and Country Planning Act 1990 s.55.]

The applicants sought to quash a detailed planning permission granted to PRT to build a retail park on the ground that it would take trade away from local shops and would cause traffic problems. Outline permission for five units in the park had already been given. PRT made two applications for detailed planning permission, one for 70 units and one for five units. The 70 unit application was withdrawn and replaced with a plan showing five units but demonstrating that the units might be subdivided. The applicants claimed that planning permission could not be granted where the reserved matters would allow the creation of the 70 units which were previously opposed.

Held, dismissing the application, that (1) planning permission should be granted as the council had no option but to approve matters if they were within the outline permission for the retail park, *Heron Ltd v. Manchester City Council* [1978] 1 W.L.R. 937, [1978] C.L.Y. 2893 and *R. v. Castlepoint* [1985] J.P.L. 473, [1985] C.L.Y. 3456 considered. Once the five units were built then the later interior subdivision of the units would not constitute development, and (2) the tax principle that where there were a series of preordained transactions it was the end result, not the intervening steps, that was important, had no application to planning law, *Furniss v. Dawson* [1984] 1 A.C. 474, [1984] C.L.Y. 270 considered.

R. v. BOLSOVER DC, *ex p.* ASHFIELD DC AND NOTTINGHAMSHIRE DC (1995) 70 P. & C.R. 507, Owen, J., QBD.

4805. Planning permission–retail parks–warehouses–relevant planning policy

B appealed against P's refusal to grant outline planning permission for the development of a retail warehouse park of up to 10,000 square metres, with access and car parking. It was contended that the most relevant planning policy was the well advanced City of Plymouth Local Plan First Alteration. The appeal site was shown as a "general development site" on the proposals map.

Held, allowing the appeal, that outline planning permission should be granted subject to conditions as to approval of design, siting and external appearance, the time of the commencement of the development, drainage, parking, use classes and landscaping. P had acted unreasonably in causing delay to the application and a full award as to costs would be made to B.

PLYMOUTH CITY COUNCIL v. BRITISH GAS PLC (1995) 10 P.A.D. 726, Judge not specified.

4806. Planning permission–retail store–misconstruction of development plans–development within existing shopping centres

K applied to quash a decision of a planning inspector dismissing their appeal against the refusal of planning permission for a supermarket. K argued that the inspector erred in law by misconstruing the development plan policies dealing with the promotion and maintenance of the existing hierarchy of shopping centres, by permitting development proposals located therein. These policies did not refer to development outside those centres.

Held, allowing the appeal, that the planning inspector misconstrued the policies. They did not justify the rejection of development outside the existing centres.

KWIK SAVE GROUP PLC v. SECRETARY OF STATE FOR THE ENVIRONMENT, Trans. Ref: CO/1577/95, November 28, 1995, Malcolm Spence Q.C., QBD.

4807. Planning permission–retail store–national and local policy guidance–no impact on existing shopping centre–existence of demonstrable harm

[Town and Country Planning Act 1990 s.54A.]

JS sought to challenge the report of a planning inspector and the decision of the Secretary of State refusing two applications for planning permission for retail development in Aylesbury. JS argued that the report and decision letter failed to show that demonstrable harm would arise as there was a finding that the proposed development would not cause an adverse impact on Aylesbury town centre. It also argued that the local and national planning policies were not correctly construed or applied and the reasoning was defective or non-existent.

Held, dismissing the applications, that (1) the planning inspector was entitled to give weight to an up to date development plan which was adverse to the proposal when deciding whether there would be demonstrable harm; (2) the planning inspector and the Secretary of State correctly balanced the policy aims as enshrined in the development plan policy guidance and other significant factors to reach their decisions, *Loup v. Secretary of State for the Environment* (1996) 71 P. & C.R. 175, [1996] C.L.Y. 4705 considered, and (3) the reasons given for the decision were adequate enough for JS to understand why the application was refused and what problems would have to be overcome on a further application.

J SAINSBURY PLC v. SECRETARY OF STATE FOR THE ENVIRONMENT [1996] J.P.L. B132, Popplewell, J., QBD.

4808. Planning permission–retail store–permission refused–demonstrable harm a material consideration–regard to sustainability policies

AS and BG sought to quash a decision of the Secretary of State's inspector dismissing an appeal against the refusal of planning permission for the construction of a retail store. It was submitted that the inspector: (a) failed to have regard to a material consideration that there was no demonstrable harm; (b) failed to have regard to a material consideration, or was perverse, in concluding that the proposal was contrary to sustainability policies; (c) misunderstood the evidence on noise, and (d) failed to have regard to a material consideration in his conclusions as to overshadowing and impact on visual amenity.

Held, dismissing the application, that (1) the inspector had found demonstrable harm in respect of sustainability and the effects on local amenity, set out his conclusions on the principal controversial issues and had not been bound to refer to every material consideration, *Loup v. Secretary of State for the Environment and Salisbury DC* [1996] J.P.L. 22 considered; (2) the inspector had regard to sustainability policies, there being express references to PPG 13 and other policy guidance, and there was neither perversity nor lack of reasons. There was evidence for him to conclude that this was not an "edge of centre" site within the context of the relevant policies; (3) on noise, the inspector had the advice in PPG 24 in mind and was entitled to rely on the evidence of the local authority as to unacceptable disturbance likely to be caused by delivery vehicles, and (4) the assessment of the view from adjoining residential property was entirely a matter for the inspector. The inspector had to decide whether the demonstrable harm was temporary, until screening trees had grown, or was permanent, because of the size of the proposed structure.

ALDI STORES LTD AND BRITISH GAS PLC v. SECRETARY OF STATE FOR THE ENVIRONMENT [1996] E.G.C.S. 11, R Purchas Q.C., QBD.

4809. Planning permission–retail store–whether contrary to development plan–effect on existing shops and plans for new centre

B appealed against T's refusal to grant planning permission for the erection of a retail supermarket and car park. The main issues were whether the proposal would constitute a decentralised form of shopping provision which would be contrary to prevailing development plan policies and whether it would be harmful to the vitality and viability of the town centre, to the continued function of the existing local shopping centres and whether it would be harmful to the prospects of achieving the provision of a new local centre.

Held, dismissing the appeal, that the proposed development was relatively inaccessible to those who did not have a private car, which brought the proposal into conflict with guidance PPG 13 and structure plan policy SHP1. This scheme would have offered no opportunity to make multi-purpose trips to different types of shops and other service uses. The effect on the town centre could have been considered on a cumulative basis, taking into account recent and proposed developments. The impact of the proposal was the greater likelihood of an existing store closing. Those who did not live within convenient walking distance of the proposed supermarket would most probably have been deprived of convenient access to adequate local food shops.

TORBAY BC v. BICKFIELD ASSOCIATES AND MRC DEVELOPMENTS LTD (1995) 10 P.A.D. 717, SRB Amos.

4810. Planning permission–rural areas–conflicting planning policies–erection of organic food production building

[Town and Country Planning Act 1990 s.54A.]

M made an application for outline planning permission for an organic food production unit building on land to the rear of a barn. The new building was to be used as a granary producing organic fruit bread from sprouted grain. The main issue concerned two conflicting planning policies: PPG7 *The Countryside and the Rural Economy* set out the guiding principle that development should benefit the rural economy and maintain or enhance the environment, whereas PPG 4 *Industrial and Commercial Development and Small Firms* provided that development control should not place unjustifiable obstacles in the way of development which was necessary to provide homes, investment and jobs. M contended that refusal of permission for the development would lead to the loss of local jobs. W argued that the proposed development would be detrimental to an area of outstanding natural beauty.

Held, refusing permission, that further to the Town and Country Planning Act 1990 s.54A, the Secretary of State was required to determine the application in accordance with the development plan unless material considerations indicate otherwise. The development would lead to material harm to the objectives of national planning guidance which sought to protect the countryside for its own sake. While there were other material considerations to be taken into account they were not sufficient to outweigh the harm which would be done to the relevant objectives of the development plan.

WEALDEN DC v. MANNA FOOD CO LTD (1995) 10 P.A.D. 702, Judge not specified.

4811. Planning permission–shopping centres–noise reduction–conditions removed–Sunday trading–affect on amenity

H applied to quash a decision by the Secretary of State's inspector to allow an appeal by the second respondent, TS, to remove a condition attached to planning permission for the erection of a shopping centre. The condition prevented trading taking place on a Sunday or a Bank Holiday. The inspector allowed the appeal on condition that acoustic fencing be erected and retained for the purpose of sound attenuation. H argued, inter alia, that the inspector confused the noise attenuation role of the fence between protection from the noise on public roads, for which there was no evidence, and noise from the car park. Secondly, the inspector misunderstood the noise assessment methodology used by H and was in error in dismissing the DMRB method.

Held, dismissing the application, that (1) very clear evidence of such a fundamental mistake was required before such a submission would be upheld. The inspector's decision letter showed that there was no confusion as to the role of the fence. It was required to protect the area from an increase in noise from traffic on public roads, and (2) the inspector took into account the methodology used by H but dismissed it as unreliable. He was entitled on the evidence to reach that decision.

HILLINGDON LBC v. SECRETARY OF STATE FOR THE ENVIRONMENT AND TESCO STORES LTD, Trans. Ref: CO/523/95, July 13, 1995, Nigel Macleod Q.C., QBD.

4812. Planning permission–site for motor services area chosen over applicant's site–whether planning authority entitled to change of view–whether material considerations were taken into account

C challenged the decision of E to grant planning permission for a motor services area. There had been two different applications for permission for two different sites, both previously rejected. Both applications were re-submitted and C argued that their site should have been chosen rather than the other site. C argued that there was a volte face by E and the wrong material was relied upon by E in reaching their final decision. The decision was contrary to the opinion of the principal planning officer.

Held, dismissing the application, that E were not bound by previous decisions or the recommendations of planning officers. The decision was valid provided it was reached by consideration of all the relevant planning criteria and material put before E. In this case, there was a remarkable change of view in relation to the suitability of the site but there was a marked difference of opinion between various officers, experts and councillors. There was no evidence to suggest that all the material considerations were not taken into account.

R. v. EAST DEVON DC, *ex p.* CHURCH COMMISSIONERS FOR ENGLAND, Trans. Ref: CO/547/95, December 5, 1995, Macpherson of Cluny, J., QBD.

4813. Planning permission–time limits–whether unadopted area plan amounted to material consideration

An appeal was made against a refusal to renew unimplemented planning permission beyond a five year time limit in respect of planned residential development in a rear garden site. N sought extension, contending no material change had occurred which meant that renewal of original permission should not have been refused

Held, dismissing the application, that although the area plan had not been formally adopted, it required new developments to have regard to the environment. The proposed development represented a material change in planning policy, in that it would entail the loss of garden or green space. In refusing the application, the planning inspector had correctly balanced the material change of use, considered the weight the expired permission played in the planning history of the site and given proper reasons for the decision.

NAWAR v. SECRETARY OF STATE FOR THE ENVIRONMENT [1995] E.G.C.S. 151, Kennedy, L.J., CA.

4814. Planning permission–Town and Country Planning Act s.52 agreement to demolish existing building–new building not substantially different from original permission–specific performance available to compel agreed demolition

[Town and Country Planning Act 1990 s.52.]

WDC sought an order for specific performance for the demolition of a property, subject to an agreement under the Town and Country Planning Act 1990 s.52. W had obtained planning permission for a building on land owned by them as replacement for an existing property, demolition to take place within one month of the rateable occupation of the new property. W sold the land with the benefit of the permission but retained the land on which the existing property stood. Construction of the new building embodied amendments to the originally permitted scheme and the new owners sought retrospective permission in respect of added walls and a storage tank. In failing to carry out the agreed demolition, W contended that the new building was different from that forming the basis of the original permission and sought a declaration as to the interpretation of the s.52 agreement. In reliance upon *Lever Finance Ltd v. Westminster City Council* [1971] 1 Q.B. 222, [1970] C.L.Y. 2781, WDC contended that a permission covered both the original specification and subsequent immaterial variations.

Held, allowing the order for specific performance, that there was no substantial difference between the building actually constructed and that originally envisaged in the s.52 agreement. As W was in breach of the agreement, WDC was entitled to the order enforcing its performance.

WYCOMBE DC v. WILLIAMS [1995] 3 P.L.R. 19, Alliott, J., QBD.

4815. Planning permission–variation of conditions–notification of application–failure to notify not maladministration

[Town and Country Planning Act 1971 s.209.]

O, the principal shareholder and managing director of W, applied for judicial review of a decision of the Commissioner to dismiss O's compliant of maladministration in relation to Canterbury City Council, CCC. Planning permission was granted by the Secretary of State for the Environment for development of a business park near O's premises. The permission contained a condition that work should not begin on the development until an order under the Town and Country Planning Act 1971 s.209 had been made to stop up vehicular rights on a road next to the site. The developers began work on the site before the order was obtained and then successfully applied for a variation of the condition which had only prevented occupation of the units of the site before the order was made. O argued that the variation had been made without his knowledge and had denied him the opportunity to object to the proposed order to stop up the road. He also argued that CCC had varied the condition without due consideration of the consequences to W. The variation was a manifest absurdity as the Secretary of State would have no choice but to stop up the road as it would be too late to vary the development once the units had been built.

Held, dismissing the application, that (1) it was reasonable for the Commissioner to conclude that the variation made little difference to the permission as the condition only referred to the making of the order and not when the road would actually be stopped up. The variation was technical rather than substantive; (2) the Commissioner was also entitled to find that the variation had not deprived O of an opportunity to object. O had not objected to the original condition which was not much different in substance to the varied condition, and (3) the Commissioner considered O's arguments and the information given to him by CCC. It was for him to decide what weight to give to the information. His conclusion that there was not evidence of maladministration was not *Wednesbury* unreasonable.

R. v. COMMISSIONER FOR LOCAL ADMINISTRATION IN ENGLAND, *ex p.* ODDS [1996] J.P.L. B129, McCullough, J., QBD.

4816. Planning permission–views of inspector when inquiry into local plan–whether inspector failed to consider a material consideration

H applied to challenge the decision of the Secretary of State to allow an appeal for planning permission to build a number of houses. H argued that the Secretary of State failed to have regard to a material consideration and that the inspector had misapplied *Jeantwill Ltd v. Secretary of State for the Environment* [1992] E.G.C.S. 128, [1994] C.L.Y. 4406 which held that an inspector's rejected view, when a plan had been adopted, was not a material consideration against the adopted plan. The inspector should have applied *Ravebuild Ltd v. Secretary of State for the Environment* [1995] 2 C.L.Y. 4751 which held that the recent recommendations of a local plan inspector were material considerations.

Held, dismissing the application, that (1) this case was distinguishable from *Ravebuild* on its facts, and (2) it was for the decision maker to apply what weight he considered fit to a material consideration and the court could only interfere where the decision was *Wednesbury* unreasonable.

HART DC v. SECRETARY OF STATE FOR THE ENVIRONMENT [1996] E.G.C.S. 12, R Purchas Q.C., QBD.

4817. Planning permission–whether judicial review available–failure to use right under Town and Country Planning Act 1990 s.192–certificate of lawfulness–availability of test for damages

[Children Act 1989; Town and Country Planning Act 1990 s.192.]

W applied for planning permission to construct a temporary building on church property for the purposes of a children's day nursery. This was granted subject to the condition that the permission would expire after five years and the building was then to be restored to its previous condition. On this basis, W proceeded and applied for registration of the nursery under the Children Act 1989. W was then informed by a social services inspector that fresh permission was needed to cover the nursery and this was confirmed by the planning officer. W was informed of his right to apply for a certificate of lawfulness of proposed use under the Town and Country Planning Act 1990 s.192. H later informed W that the temporary permission did in fact permit the use of the premises as a nursery and W applied for judicial review of the previous statements and damages relating to H's unreasonable behaviour, causing financial loss as a result of the delay in opening of the nursery.

Held, refusing the application, that the planning officer's expression of viewpoint was not open to judicial review. W could have tested the view under s.192 of the 1990 Act but failed to do so. No recognised principle of civil law, on which damages could be based, existed. W had a potential claim in negligent mistake. However, no duty of care extended to expressions of opinion and the court was unable to decide whether the loss resulted from H's negligence as the nursery's opening was likely to have been delayed by the Children Act 1989 registration requirements and the applicant had refused the opportunity to assess his position under s.192 of the 1990 Act. A second option of misfeasance in public office was possible but the court was not in a position to consider whether the planning officer was guilty of the required malice or unlawful decision making.

R. v. HOUNSLOW LBC, *ex p.* WILLIAMSON [1996] E.G.C.S. 27, Tuckey, J., QBD.

4818. Planning permission–whether permission valid where not conforming to development plan–validity of overriding material consideration–whether inspector's misdirection material to decision reached

[Town and Country Planning Act 1990 s.54A.]

N appealed against planning permission granted by the Secretary of State. In his decision, the inspector had allowed the appeal on the basis of the proposed development's effect on the area's character and appearance, allowing this to override the requirements of the area development plan. N contended that the effect of the Town and Country Planning Act 1990 s.54A required a decision maker to follow the requirements of the local development plan unless material considerations indicated otherwise.

Held, dismissing the appeal, that although the inspector had incorrectly stated s.54A in his decision, the consideration given to the existence of a material consideration, namely the need to ensure continued village viability, showed that he had correctly applied the test. Whilst the decision reached, therefore, was not in accord with the plan, it had correctly given effect to relevant material considerations.

NORTH YORKSHIRE CC v. SECRETARY OF STATE FOR THE ENVIRONMENT AND GRIFFIN [1995] 3 P.L.R. 54, Butler-Sloss, L.J., CA.

4819. Planning permission–whether precedent sufficient to base decision on–similar proposals for area possible–whether use of precedent perverse

W appealed against a decision by the inspector refusing planning permission for the conversion of a shop adjoining its existing market square office, on the grounds that similar proposals were likely to be made and that granting this request would weaken the local authority's position. W alleged that there was no evidence to support the use of precedent as a basis for dismissing the appeal and that it was perverse to do so.

Held, dismissing the appeal, that the inspector's findings were not irrational. The decision in *Poundstretcher, Harris Queensway v. Secretary of State for the Environment and Liverpool City Council* [1988] 3 P.L.R. 69, [1989] C.L.Y. 3560 that "fear of or generalised concern about a precedent effect is an insufficient basis upon which to refuse planning permission without evidence to support it", which W had relied upon was not to be construed too narrowly. Relevant matters included circumstances which were material to the case, taking into account the reasonable application of planning decisions. There was evidence on which a conclusion on precedent could be reached and it was therefore not irrational.

WOOLWICH BUILDING SOCIETY v. SECRETARY OF STATE FOR THE ENVIRONMENT AND SOUTH BEDFORDSHIRE DC [1995] N.P.C. 109, Nigel MacLeod Q.C., QBD.

4820. Planning policy–interpretation of planning policy to rural area

[Town and Country Planning Act 1990 s.54, s.70; Town and Country Planning (Development Plan) Regulations 1991 Reg.33.]

C sought under the Town and Country Planning Act 1990 s.288 to quash a decision of the Secretary of State's inspector dismissing an appeal against the refusal of planning permission for the erection of a dwelling on land within the curtilage of a farmhouse. The District Council had approved proposed modifications to the local plan such that the appeal site should not be in a special restraint area which was shown on the map as without notation. The inspector concluded, in the light of planning policy, that it was a rural area not included in the green belt. C had contended that the policy referred to rural areas beyond the green belt with the appeal site in white land lying between a built up area and the inner boundary of the green belt. It was submitted on behalf of C that: (1) the proposed modifications of the local plan formed part of the statutory local plan, for the purposes of the 1990 Act s.70(2) and s.54A, and that the inspector had failed to treat them on this basis; (2) the inspector failed to have regard to the modifications as a material consideration; (3) the appeal site was in the designated built up area of Harlow and should be treated as such; (4) it was not open to the inspector to apply structure plan policy relating to rural areas beyond the green belt to the appeal site, and (5) that policy could not apply to the appeal site in the light of its explanatory memorandum.

Held, dismissing the application, that the policy applied to the appeal site; (1) the text of the proposed modifications did not form part of the local plan for statutory purposes but part of the process of plan making; (2) the inspector had been aware of this and had been entitled to give it little or no weight, (3) there was no designated area of the built up area of Harlow so the merits of the proposed development was a matter for the inspector's planning judgment; (4) it was not unreasonable for the inspector to conclude that the appeal site was in a rural area and part of the countryside, and (5) the explanatory memorandum to the policy did refer exclusively to rural areas beyond the outer boundary of the green belt but was separate from the structure plan and not part of the development plan, *Severn Trent Water Authority v. Secretary of State for the Environment* [1989] J.P.L. 21, [1989] C.L.Y. 3570 followed. The interpretation of development plan policy often called for the exercise of planning judgment and was not necessarily a matter of law. Policies provided guidelines and principles within which discretion could be exercised. When a policy was unclear an inspector could look at an explanatory memorandum as a material consideration but not as an aid to construction. Under the Town and Country Planning (Development Plan) Regulations 1991 Reg.33, material not forming part of the structure plan could not prevail over statutory policy. On the wording of the policy alone, the inspector was entitled to find that it applied to the appeal site, *Northavon DC v. Secretary of State for the Environment* [1993] J.P.L. 761, [1994] C.L.Y. 4387 applied. On a proper analysis, the instant case was not a matter of the memorandum contradicting a policy but a policy with a clear meaning having an incomplete justification. Accordingly, the partial justification of the policy could not restrict its natural scope.

COOPER v. SECRETARY OF STATE FOR THE ENVIRONMENT (1996) 71 P. & C.R. 529, Lockhart-Mummery Q.C., QBD.

4821. Planning policy–landslides

The Department of the Environment issued a press release entitled *New guidance on avoiding landslide damage* (News release 149), published on March 28, 1996. A guidance note has been published on avoiding the danger of landslides. Unwise development in the wrong place is often a trigger to landslides, a problem which can be avoided if developers are aware of the potential danger. The guidance provides practical advice to planners on the identification and assessment of landslide hazards in their area. Planning Policy Guidance Note 14: *Development on Unstable Land–Annex 1: Landslides and Planning,* ISBN 0 11 753259 2 is available from HMSO outlets at £6.00. A complementary report published by the DoE provides a non-technical introduction to the subject. *Landslide Investigation and Management in Great Britain: a Guide for Planners and Developers,* ISBN 0 11 753180 4, is available at HMSO outlets at £28.00 and can be ordered by telephoning 0171 873 9090.

4822. Planning policy–local plans–whether correct to base decision on planning presumption due to be withdrawn–misinterpreting local plan provision–quashing decision based on policy misapplication

The developer appealed and Scross-appealed against a decision of the Secretary of State granting planning permission for residential housing on land adjoining a green belt area. The decision was in line with part of PPG3, since withdrawn, which established a presumption releasing land for housing use where a five year housing land supply was not identified. The developer's appeal sought the reinstatement of permission, and S cross-appealed, contending that the inspector had based his decision to allow an initial appeal on a misapplication of the local area plan.

Held, allowing both the appeal and cross-appeal, that although it could be assumed that the Secretary of State should follow his own policies, the inspector's decision omitted any reference to the presumption contained in PPG3. Whilst using the presumption, in light of its proposed withdrawal, may have been an unsound basis for the decision, it was wrong to quash the Secretary of State's decision on an inference that the inspector's failure to mention the presumption showed it had not been relied upon. The local area plan provided a restraint on development in the area concerned which the inspector had failed to observe in his decision. Both the inspector, in his initial misapplication, and the Secretary of State in relying on the inspector's decision were in error, and the decision based on that error was quashed.

STRATFORD UPON AVON DC v. SECRETARY OF STATE FOR THE ENVIRONMENT [1995] E.G.C.S. 15, Sir Thomas Bingham M.R., CA.

4823. Planning policy–minerals–development plans

The Department of the Environment issued a press release entitled *Mineral planning guidance on silica sand published* (News release 390), published on September 23, 1996. Mineral Planning Guidance Note 15 (MPG 15), *Provision of Silica Sand in England,* published on September 23, 1996, provides guidance to help mineral planning authorities to develop policies for provision of silica sand in development plans and help industry to bring forward development proposals which satisfy environmental concerns. The guidance is intended to ensure that there is an adequate supply of silica sand, used in industries such as glass, foundry castings and ceramics, while ensuring that developments are consistent with sustainable development principles. The MPG is published by HMSO; tel: 0171 873 9090, price £7.50, ISBN 0 11 753320 3.

4824. Planning policy–mining–development plans–land reclamation

The Department of the Environment issued a press release entitled *Revised minerals planning guidance published* (News release 249), published on June 11, 1996. The revised *Minerals Planning Guidance Note 1: General Considerations and the Development Plan System* has been published, replacing that first published in 1988. It sets out principles and key planning policy objectives for minerals mining and provides advice for planning authorities on issues including the preparation of minerals development plans and the determination of minerals planning applications. Copies of the guidance note are available from HMSO, price £9. The press release *Revised guidance on reclaiming mineral workings published* (Press release 519), published on November 29,1996, draws attention to the revision of MPG7. This guidance on returning land to a condition for further use following the mining of minerals has been revised in the light of important changes to legislation and Government policy affecting the extraction of minerals. MPG 7, which was first published in 1989, has been published by HMSO, ISBN 0 11 753347 5, price £12.00.

4825. Planning policy–modification order–definitive map and statement–whether map prepared–whether way enjoyed as a public right of way

[Wildlife and Countryside Act 1981 s.27, s.53, s.54.]

O sought to quash a confirmation on an order by the Secretary of State on the grounds that the order was not within the powers granted to the Secretary of State by the Wildlife and Countryside Act 1981 s.53 and s.54 and that the requirements of Sch.15 of the 1981 Act had not been complied with. The issue arose as to whether IWCC had prepared the definitive map and statement, and further, whether the way was being enjoyed as a public right of way.

Held, that s.27(4) of the 1981 Act did not require a particular form of document. The principal requirement was that the material served the purpose of the 1981 Act by providing sufficient information. Further to s.53(3) of the 1981 Act, a way could be established by a long user as of right even though at the time of the user, the way was not included in the definitive map. Proof of an intention not to dedicate a right of way was not by itself enough and that intention must be manifested by overt actions, *R. v. Secretary of State for the Environment, ex p. Cowell* [1993] J.P.L. 851, [1994] C.L.Y. 4372.

O'KEEFE v. SECRETARY OF STATE FOR THE ENVIRONMENT AND ISLE OF WIGHT CC [1996] J.P.L. 42, Pill, J., QBD.

4826. Planning policy–proposed extension contrary to policy–term defined in glossary–glossary not incorporated into emerging local plan–planning inspector refusing to rely on material contained in unincorporated glossary to local plan

R applied to quash a planning inspector's decision granting planning permission for a dwelling house extension. R had initially refused permission for the extension, on the grounds that the total size of the extended property would be above that for a "small family dwelling", contrary to both the area plan and emerging local plan. However, as the definition of such a dwelling only appeared in the unincorporated glossary to the local plan, the inspector had refused to consider it in his determination of the appeal, relying instead on PPG12 as the basis for his decision about the glossary's status. R sought to have his decision quashed contending he had erred in law in failing to give effect to the glossary definition.

Held, dismissing the application, that where a glossary was not incorporated into the local plan, it formed part of the plan's explanatory material. As such it did not operate either to expand or restrict local plan policies and the inspector could decide how much weight to accord to this type of material in his decision. The inspector's understanding of PPG12 had been correct and his determination of the appeal was correct in law.

REIGATE AND BANSTEAD BC v. SECRETARY OF STATE FOR THE ENVIRONMENT AND WATTS [1995] 3 P.L.R. 1, Sir Graham Eyre, Q.C., QBD.

4827. Planning policy–redevelopment–change from industrial to retail use–whether local and national policy prevented change–detrimental effect of proposed development on nearby town centre

[Town and Country Planning Act 1990.]

P appealed against a refusal of outline planning permission, relating to the redevelopment of an industrial estate as Use Classes B1, B2 and B8 and a non-food retail warehouse. The refusal had cited the loss of existing employment land to be contrary to both national and local planning policy, and that the retail warehouse would have a detrimental impact on nearby town centre trading.

Held, dismissing the appeal, that (1) although the proposed development covered only part of the site, the change from industrial to retail use amounted to a large percentage of the appeal site. Such a change would adversely affect the available amount of industrial land available, contrary to the local development plan and PPG6 of 1992, para.47; (2) the retail warehouse would have an unacceptable impact on nearby town and district centres, and (3) as the inspector had correctly dealt with the questions of fact, in line with the established policy, there was nothing in the decision with which the court could intervene.

PINHILL LTD AND WEALDOVAL LTD v. SECRETARY OF STATE FOR THE ENVIRONMENT AND GILLINGHAM BC [1995] E.G.C.S. 28, Sir Graham Eyre, Q.C., QBD.

4828. Planning policy–towns–shops–transport policy

The Department of the Environment issued a press release entitled *John Gummer announces new guidance to revitalise town centres* (Press release 267), published on June 20, 1996. New guidance has been issued to Planning Authorities by the Environment Secretary John Gummer in an attempt to revitalise town centres. The main features of the guidance on planning for town centres emphasises planned approaches to developing town centres both through policies and the identification of locations and sites for development, suggests a sequential approach to selecting sites for development for retail, employment, leisure and other key town centre uses, and urges support for local centres. On town centres it urges the promotion of mixed use development and retention of key town centre uses, emphasises the importance of a coherent town centre parking strategy, promotes town centre management to develop clear standards of service and improve quality for town centre users, and promotes good urban design including attractive and secure car parks. On the assessment of retail proposals it suggests three key tests for assessing retail development: impact on vitality and viability of town centres, accessibility by various methods of transport, and impact on overall travel and car use. It sets out how to assess out of town development and how certain types of retail development should be assessed.

4829. Planning procedures–compromise by parties at inquiry–party resiling from agreement as to costs–costs amount immeasurable as fault wrongly attributed to council

B refused an application for planning permission for the redevelopment of an existing industrial estate. R appealed whereupon a public inquiry lasting some 17 days took place. In the course of the inquiry settlement negotiations took place and agreement was reached as to the permission that should be granted. In the course of the negotiations R had agreed that they would bear their own costs of the inquiry. The inquiry was adjourned pending B's formal approval of the proposals. In the meantime R resiled from their willingness to bear their own costs and at the resumed hearing of the inquiry disputed the basis of the agreement which the parties had been prepared to reach. The Inspector refused to adjourn the inquiry pending High Court litigation as to whether or not a binding compromise had been reached between the parties. After considering the position the council withdrew their arguments on R's appeal and left the Inspector to deal with the questions of costs without prejudice to their contention that the parties were each bound by their agreement to bear their own costs. In the light of B's concessions the Inspector concluded that the appeal should be allowed subject to conditions and also concluded that the council had acted unreasonably in contesting the appeal. He directed the council to pay R's costs. The council applied for judicial review of the decision as to costs.

Held, granting judicial review, that the inspector was wrong to conclude that the failure to arrive at a negotiated resolution of the appeal was wholly attributable to B. He ignored the fact that R had originally agreed to bear their own costs and then resiled from that agreement. By failing to take that factor into account he acted unreasonably and reached a decision that was perverse.

R. v. SECRETARY OF STATE FOR THE ENVIRONMENT AND RICH INVESTMENTS LTD, *ex p.* BEXLEY LBC (1995) 70 P. & C.R. 522, Tucker, J., QBD.

4830. Planning procedures–development

TOWN AND COUNTRY PLANNING (GENERAL DEVELOPMENT PROCEDURE) (AMENDMENT) ORDER 1996, SI 1996 1817; made under the Town and Country Planning Act 1990 s.59, s.61, s.74, s.333. In force: August 5, 1996; £1.10.

This Order amends the Town and Country Planning (General Development Procedure) Order 1995 (SI 1995 419). It introduces a requirement to consult, in England, the Sports Council for England and in Wales, the Sports Council for Wales, before the grant of planning permission for development which may have a detrimental effect on the provision of playing fields.

4831. Planning procedures–draft local plan amendment–rejection of inspector's recommendation based on objector's proposal–inadequate reasons created risk of substantial prejudice

[Town and Country Planning Act 1990 s.287; Town and Country Planning (Structure and Local Plans) Regulations 1982 Reg.29; Town and Country Planning (Structure and Local Plans) Regulations 1982 Reg.31.]

L applied to quash an inset to the local plan deposit draft under the Town and Country Planning Act 1990 s.287 on the grounds that her interest had been substantially prejudiced by a failure to comply with the Town and Country Planning (Structure and Local Plans) Regulations 1982 Reg.29 and Reg.31 when considering objections to the draft plan which had been approved by the planning inspector. L's objection sought a modification of a village environmental limit to permit a small development on derelict farmland. However, H decided not to accept the inspector's recommendation to incorporate L's changes, opting for a more restricted change to the village limit instead, and in giving reasons for this decision stated that the recommended change amounted to an alien development in the part of the village concerned.

Held, allowing the application and quashing that part of the inset referred to in the objection, that whereas the explanation given by H was adequate for the decision not to include the site, the reasons were insufficient as they failed to explain why the proposal's disadvantages outweighed the advantages identified by the inspector. The giving of reasons enabled an objector to know why a decision had been made and also acted as a discipline on the part of the decision maker, ensuring that appropriate matters were addressed in the decision making process. Under Reg.29 of the 1982 Regulations, H was required to consider the inspector's report in deciding whether action was required in respect of the plan in the light of each recommendation. The planning authority was not required merely to make a decision on a recommendation, but also to consider the report and to base its decision in the light of any considerations that arose. A failure to give reasons on a crucial issue contained in the report created the likelihood of substantial prejudice to an objector, when the objection had been accepted by the inspector at the inquiry, even though the inspector's consideration of such matters was a recommendation only and H were the final arbiters.

LOPEZ DE CARRIZOSA v. HUNTINGDONSHIRE DC, Trans. Ref: CO/133/96, October 3, 1996, Judge Rich Q.C., QBD.

4832. Planning procedures–permission sought for residential development on pig farm site–history of smell nuisance–whether detriment amounted to very special circumstance–failure of decision to deal with substantive issues

[Town and Country Planning Act 1990 s.288.]

N applied under the Town and Country Planning Act 1990 s.288 to quash a decision of a planning inspector who rejected N's application for planning permission to redevelop a pig and cattle farm which was a source of noise and smell nuisance to local residents and which had been the subject of seven abatement notices by Leeds City Council, LCC. The inspector found that the smell nuisance did not amount to special circumstances sufficient to allow planning permission for residential development on a green belt site but drew attention to the previous expansion of the site and the action by LCC to minimise the nuisance.

Held, allowing the application, that a proper consideration of the issue of removing the smell nuisance (leaving out the irrelevant matters the inspector chose to include) might be thought a very special circumstance. The reasons given for refusing the appeal were unintelligible and did not support the inspector's conclusion. That the farm had been expanded near housing in the past could not diminish the desirability of removing the smell; the two considerations had no logical connection. Accordingly, the conclusion was invalid and the decision not made in terms of the 1990 Act, *Save Britain's Heritage v. Number 1 Poultry Ltd* [1991] 1 W.L.R. 153, [1991] C.L.Y. 3494 followed and *Batchelor v. Kent CC* (1990) 59 P. & C.R. 357, [1990] C.L.Y. 582 considered.

NORTH v. SECRETARY OF STATE FOR THE ENVIRONMENT AND LEEDS CITY COUNCIL [1995] E.G.C.S. 34, Malcolm Spence Q.C., QBD.

4833. Planning procedures–structure plans–development plans–local authorities–reorganisation

[Local Government Act 1992; Local Government Planning Act 1990.]

The Department of the Environment issued a press release entitled *Local Government Act 1992 and the Town and Country Planning Act 1990: local government change and the planning system* (Circular 4/96), published on March 28, 1996. The circular sets out changes in planning procedures necessitated by local government review, particularly in areas of structural change and boundary change.

4834. Planning procedures–whether refusal of inquiry amounted to failure to take account of material considerations–extent of reasons to be given for decision

[Town and Country Planning Act 1990 s.288.]

The Secretary of State appealed against the Court of Appeal's decision (Times, August 4, 1994) in favour of a consortium of district councils who opposed the grant of planning permission for a shopping centre and sports complex which Manchester Ship Canal Co (MSC) intended to build at Trafford Park. The Secretary of State granted planning permission following two public inquiries. After the first inquiry he issued an interim decision letter in favour of the project but subject to concerns about motorway traffic problems. Following a change in motorway building plans a second inquiry was held on the specific issue of motorway congestion, and the Secretary of State accepted the inspector's recommendation and granted planning permission. BMDC and other district councils complained that in the decision the need for urban regeneration (particularly the development's effect on other shopping centres), and the alternative option of reserving the Trafford Park site for high technology industrial development, were not taken properly into account.

Held, allowing the appeal, that the Secretary of State's planning decisions had to include reasons in sufficient detail to show what conclusion had been reached on the principal controversial issues. They did not have to refer to every material consideration, however insignificant, or deal with every argument, however peripheral, *Hope v. Secretary of State for the Environment* (1975) 31 P. & C.R. 120 followed. In the instant case, the Secretary of State had dealt with the issue of urban regeneration and the reasons he gave, although not very full and badly expressed, were adequate. The question of whether to reopen a full public inquiry because the balance of advantage had shifted since the interim decision was for the Secretary of State's judgment. The suggestion about industrial use was not disregarded altogether but did not require to be dealt with in greater detail, *R. v. Secretary of State for Trade and Industry, ex p. Lonrho Plc* [1989] 1 W.L.R. 525, [1989] C.L.Y. 41 followed.

BOLTON MDC v. SECRETARY OF STATE FOR THE ENVIRONMENT; BOLTON MDC v. MANCHESTER SHIP CANAL CO; BOLTON MDC v. TRAFFORD PARK DEVELOPMENT CORP (1996) 71 P. & C.R. 309, Lord Lloyd of Berwick, HL.

4835. Quarries–planning permission–determination of extent of permission–extrinsic evidence relevant to determination

SM, successors in title to the owners of two quarries, applied to quash a decision of the Secretary of State which determined the extent of planning permission granted in relation to the quarries. The permission included the words "and shown on the accompanying plans" which had been crossed out, and at the top of the document was written "Plan No. M16". The inspector determined the use at the material time to be less than put forward by the authority who granted the permission, LRDC. SM argued that the permission was unambiguous and the inspector misdirected himself by looking at extrinsic evidence to interpret the extent of the permission.

Held, allowing the application, that (1) extrinsic evidence should not have been considered unless the permission was ambiguous or the extrinsic evidence was expressly incorporated. The inclusion of a map reference number was not sufficient to incorporate it into the permission; it was necessary to include words such as "in accordance with plans and application", *R. v. Secretary of State for the Environment, ex p. Slough BC* (1995) 70 P. & C.R. 560, [1995] 2 C.L.Y. 4867 applied, and (2) in this case the permission was unambiguous and therefore neither the plan nor the application should have been referred to by the inspector.

SPRINGFIELD MINERALS LTD v. SECRETARY OF STATE FOR WALES (1996) 72 P. & C.R. 70, Popplewell, J., QBD.

4836. Quarries–work commenced after 20 years lapse–whether county council acted as mineral authority when making prohibition order–jurisdiction–whether failure to give sufficient reasons substantially prejudiced plaintiff–possible use of erroneous criteria in decision making process

[Town and Country Planning Act 1990 Sch.9; Local Government Act 1972 Sch.17.]

V's quarry, which prior to his use had remained unused for 20 years, was the subject of a prohibition order, confirmed by the Secretary of State. The order prohibiting resumption of mineral workings was made by Dartmoor NPA but sealed by D. V contended that (1) under the Town and Country Planning Act 1990 Sch.9(3)(2)(b), the making of a prohibition order was a function D could only exercise in its capacity as a mineral authority, not as planning authority. Jurisdiction to do so was conferred on D as the mineral authority by the Local Government Act 1972 Sch.17 and (2) the Secretary of State had failed to appreciate facts at the date of the inquiry. The mineral authority was to be satisfied under Sch.9(3)(2)(b) that work had permanently ceased and the inspector was not prepared to consider the fact that the quarry was actually in use at this time.

Held, allowing the application, that (1) D did have jurisdiction as National Park Authority to make the order in a non-metropolitan National Park Area, but (2) the decision was to be quashed. "Permanently ceasing work" was to be interpreted as ceasing to "any substantial extent". The Secretary of State had given no indication of why the workings of the quarry were not substantial. To this extent, he failed to give sufficient reasons. For the decision to be quashed, the plaintiff had to be substantially prejudiced by the failure, *Save Britain's Heritage v. Number 1 Poultry* [1991] 1 W.L.R. 153, [1991] C.L.Y. 3494 considered. Although the decision was not irrational, there was a possibility that it could have been based on erroneous criteria and the matter should be reconsidered in light of the judgment.

VAN LEEUWEN v. SECRETARY OF STATE FOR THE ENVIRONMENT AND DEVON CC [1995] N.P.C. 157, Rich, J., QBD.

4837. Restrictive covenants–discharge–building schemes–obsolete covenants

[Law of Property Act 1925 s.84.]

KP sought discharge or modification of a restrictive covenant imposed under a building scheme in 1853 so that houses could be built on the site following planning permission. The issues were whether under the Law of Property Act 1925 s.84(1) the restrictive covenant was obsolete or whether some reasonable user would be impeded without securing practical benefits of substantial value. The issue of injury to those with the benefit of restriction was also considered. The objectors argued that the housing development would affect the value of their properties and make the area less desirable though some development of the site had taken place in breach of the covenant including eight bungalows and a tennis pavilion.

Held, allowing the application, that the covenant was obsolete as its original purpose was no longer possible. The development plan had been considered. It was recognised that an obsolete covenant might be valuable so that its discharge would cause injury and here that was the case. The principal covenant was discharged and other covenants modified so that the permitted development could proceed. Some objectors were awarded compensation but not those living in houses built in breach of the covenant. KP was ordered to bear the costs of objectors represented at the hearing.

KENNET PROPERTIES' APPLICATION, *Re* (1996) 72 P. & C.R. 353, Judge Rich, Q.C., Lands Tr.

4838. Right of abode–refusal of planning permission to gypsy for caravan on land she owned–no breach of Art.8 on Human Rights

[European Convention on Human Rights 1950 Art.8, Art.14; Town and Country Planning Act 1990.]

The ECHR was asked to determine whether, in refusing an application for planning permission, the UK had breached the European Convention on Human Rights 1950 Art.8, which guaranteed a right to respect for one's home, taken in conjunction with Art.14, which prohibited discrimination. B, a gypsy, sought planning permission for three caravans for herself and her family on land which she owned. This was refused but she declined an invitation to apply for a place on an official caravan site. B was subsequently fined for failure to comply with enforcement notices. The UK government argued that there was no issue under Art.8 as B's home was not legally established.

Held, that the ECHR had jurisdiction to deal with the issue under Art.8 as it concerned B's right to respect for her home on land which she had specifically bought for that purpose, and on which she had lived continuously since 1988, *Gillow v. United Kingdom* [1986] C.L.Y. 1654 followed. The refusal of planning permission to B and her prosecution under the Town and Country Planning Act 1990 constituted interference by a public authority, but such interference was justified as the interests of the community had to be balanced against B's rights under Art.8. The UK authorities had a wide margin of discretion in implementing planning policies and the decision-making process was fair and gave full consideration to B's representations. The procedural safeguards in place were sufficient to give due respect to her interests and took into account her special needs as a gypsy. B had been offered an alternative site and continued to reside on her land without being forcibly evicted. Therefore there had been no violation of Art.8 as the measures used to achieve the aim pursued were not disproportionate. Article 14 had not been breached as B had not suffered discriminatory treatment under the procedure involved.

BUCKLEY v. UNITED KINGDOM [1996] J.P.L. 1018, R Bernhardt (President), ECHR.

4839. Rights of way–modification order designating lane on private land as byway–whether inspector exceeded his powers–whether local authority had conducted inquiry properly

[Wildlife and Countryside Act 1981.]

I applied for judicial review of a Definitive Map Modification Order made by D under the Wildlife and Countryside Act 1981 designating a lane on I's land as a byway open to all traffic. I claimed that it was a private road over which the only rights of passage appertained to his land and two other houses in the lane. I claimed that the inspector's reasoning was flawed and that D's decision making process was defective.

Held, allowing the application, that (1) the decision of D did not simply merge with that of the inspector which meant that once the inquiry was over, an objector could still challenge proceedings at council level, *R. v. Cornwall CC, ex p. Huntington* [1994] 1 All E.R. 694, [1994] C.L.Y. 65 applied; (2) an inspector's confirmation of the order could be challenged if the council could be shown to have acted without lawful power to act or the inspector could be shown to have exceeded his powers and to have erred in law, *Anisminic v. Foreign Compensation Commission* [1969] 2 A.C. 147, [1969] C.L.Y. 1866 applied; (3) the principal challenge to D had been that its sub-committee abdicated in favour of a working party composed only of a handful of its members. This was not accepted as the procedure had been a practical approach not involving abdication; (4) I's argument that he had not had sufficient time to digest the material going before the committee was also rejected. The modification order was within the powers of D and not in justiciable breach of the procedures, but (5) the inspector had erred in law in excluding admissible evidence and in his process of reasoning from the evidence. He had refused to admit a county court judgment holding that the lane was a private road subject only to private rights of way and also had not appreciated that a road shown as untitheable was not necessarily a public road. However, the court might not have decided to quash the order if the error had occurred at council level and had been properly reviewed at the inquiry, the court had no power to divide up the order and quashed it in its entirety.

ISAAC v. SECRETARY OF STATE FOR THE ENVIRONMENT AND DEVON CC [1995] N.P.C. 176, Sedley, J., QBD.

4840. Roads–public highway–emergency only access erected–whether obstruction unlawful

[Highways Act 1980 s.137.]

Oakland Drive, a public highway, passed across Elmsdale Estate. Oakland Drive stopped 10 feet short of a hedge which formed the boundary with the neighbouring estate, Deer Park Estate, and another public highway, Biddulph Way. H Strategic Planning and Consultation Committee decided to create an emergency access link between Oakland Drive and Biddulph Way with a locked gate. Before erection of the gate, staggered wooden barriers were erected to prevent cyclists and motorcyclists from passing through without dismounting. An information was laid by a local resident, the respondent, P, under the Highways Act 1980 s.137, alleging that H had wilfully obstructed free passage between the two roads. H were convicted and appealed.

Held, allowing the appeal, that there was only a right of way for all purposes along Oakland Drive to the point where it stopped short of the hedge. The track passing through the hedge was not part of a designated public highway for all purposes. There was no evident intention that the track was to be such a public highway. Public rights could not be based on long user. Accordingly, the gate was not an obstruction.

HEREFORD AND WORCESTER CC v. PICK (1996) 71 P. & C.R. 231, Stuart-Smith, L.J., QBD.

4841. Rural areas–development–local authorities–reorganisation

DEVELOPMENT BOARD FOR RURAL WALES (AREA) ORDER 1996, SI 1996 535; made under the Development of Rural Wales Act 1976 s.1. In force: March 31, 1996; £1.10.

This Order includes in the area for which the Development Board for Rural Wales is responsible under the Development of Rural Wales Act 1976 the areas of three communities of Llanrhaedr-ym-Mochnant, Llansilin and Llangedwyn. This extension is to take account of changes made to the boundary of the area of the County of Powys under the Local Government (Wales) Act 1994. The Development of Rural Wales Act 1976 s.1(2) is amended by the Local Government (Wales) Act 1994 Sch.16 para.53(1) which comes into force on April 1, 1996 by substituting for the existing words "the county of Powys and the districts of Ceredigion and Merionnydd" the words "the area for which it was so responsible before April 1, 1996".

4842. Structure plans–recommendations of the Examination in Public Panel–adequate reasons for rejection of recommendations

H applied for an order to quash Policy H1 of the Structure Plan adopted on November 4, 1995. The policy sought to restrict the building of dwellings to 40,000 between 1991 and 2006. H argued that the number of dwellings should be 48,000. H argued that R had not adequately considered the recommendations of the Examination in Public Panel, EIP, that 48,000 houses should be included, and did not give adequate reasons for rejection.

Held, dismissing the application, that the proposed plan, along with the EIP Panel's recommendations and the response of R to them, was placed on deposit draft. There was also an explanatory memorandum of the policies, read with the memorandum, R's reasons were relevant and adequate. It was clear that R considered the issues raised by the recommendations.

HOUSE BUILDERS FEDERATION v. BERKSHIRE CC [1996] E.G.C.S. 79, Gerald Moriarty Q.C., QBD.

4843. Tree preservation orders–application to fell trees refused–compensation–validity of certificate

[Town and Country Planning Act 1971 Art.5.]

H sought compensation when S refused an application to fell trees subject to a tree preservation order. H contended that the Town and Country Planning Act 1971 Art.5 certificate was invalid as it had not been signed by the officer who considered the application. H further argued that the question of whether the refusal was in the interests of good forestry had not been investigated.

Held, giving judgment for S, that where a planning authority refused an application to fell trees subject to a tree preservation order, it was entitled to sign the relevant document by the facsimile of an administrative officer and it was further entitled to certify that the purpose of the refusal was in the interests of good forestry.

HENRIQUES v. SWALE BC [1996] 36 R.V.R. 162, T Hoyes, FRICS., Lands Tr.

4844. Tree preservation orders–variation–emergency order confirmed as woodland order

[Town and Country Planning Act 1990 s.199.]

E appealed against a tree preservation order. The emergency order referred to trees specified by reference to an area but the confirmation order was made in terms of woodlands. E objected that W had no power to vary the tree preservation order in this way.

Held, allowing the appeal, that (1) the power of the council to confirm an emergency order under the Town and Country Planning Act 1990 s.199(1) included such modifications as it considered expedient and this power should not be construed narrowly, *R. v. Secretary of State for the Environment, ex p. Lancashire CC* [1994] 4 All E.R. 165, [1994] C.L.Y. 2986 considered; (2) however, a good deal of the area covered was not woodland and to designate it as such would have involved a change of use, and (3) the council had no power to convert such land into woodland by the making of a woodland tree preservation order.

EVANS v. WAVERLEY BC [1995] 3 P.L.R. 80, Hutchison, L.J., CA.

4845. Urban development corporations–alteration of boundaries

LONDON DOCKLANDS DEVELOPMENT CORPORATION (ALTERATION OF BOUNDARIES) (LIMEHOUSE AND WAPPING) ORDER 1996, SI 1996 3148; made under the Local Government, Planning and Land Act 1980 s.134. In force: January 31, 1997; £1.95.

This Order removes from the London Docklands urban development area an area of approximately 183.6 hectares comprising part of the London borough of Tower Hamlets.

4846. Urban development corporations–alteration of boundaries

LONDON DOCKLANDS DEVELOPMENT CORPORATION (ALTERATION OF BOUNDARIES) (SURREY DOCKS) ORDER 1996, SI 1996 2986; made under the Local Government Planning and Land Act 1980 s.134. In force: December 20, 1996; £1.55.

This Order removes from the London Docklands urban development area an area of approximately 266.3 hectares comprising part of the London borough of Southwark which becomes the local planning authority for the excluded area.

4847. Urban development corporations–dissolution

CENTRAL MANCHESTER DEVELOPMENT CORPORATION (DISSOLUTION) ORDER 1996, SI 1996 966; made under the Local Government, Planning and Land Act 1980 s.166. In force: April 1, 1996; £0.65.

By virtue of the Local Government, Planning and Land Act 1980 s.166(3), on the coming into force of this Order the Central Manchester Development Corporation will cease to act except for the purpose of preparing its final accounts and report and winding up its affairs. The corporation will be dissolved on July 1, 1996.

4848. Urban development corporations–revocation

CENTRAL MANCHESTER DEVELOPMENT CORPORATION (AREA AND CONSTITUTION) ORDER 1996, SI 1996 851; made under the Local Government, Planning and Land Act 1980 s.134, s.135, Sch.26 para.1. In force: April 1, 1996; £0.65.

This Order revokes the Central Manchester Development Corporation (Area and Constitution) Order 1988 (SI 1988 1144) which designated the Central Manchester urban development area and established the Central Manchester Development Corporation. Article 2 and Art.3 of that Order are revoked from April 1, 1996 and the remainder from July 1, 1996.

4849. Urban development corporations–transfer of assets

CENTRAL MANCHESTER DEVELOPMENT CORPORATION (TRANSFER OF PROPERTY, RIGHTS AND LIABILITIES) ORDER 1996, SI 1996 233; made under the Local Government, Planning and Land Act 1980 s.165A. In force: March 26, 1996; £0.65.

This Order transfers to the Secretary of State any residual property, rights and liabilities of the Central Manchester Development Corporation. It is proposed that the Central Manchester Development Corporation will be dissolved on July 1, 1996.

4850. Urban development corporations–transfer of functions

CENTRAL MANCHESTER DEVELOPMENT CORPORATION (PLANNING FUNCTIONS) ORDER 1996, SI 1996 232; made under the Local Government, Planning and Land Act 1980 s.148, s.149; and the Town and Country Planning Act 1990 s.59, s.333. In force: March 25, 1996; £1.10.

This Order revokes the Central Manchester Development Corporation (Planning Functions) Order 1988 (SI 1988 1552) and the Town and Country Planning (Central Manchester Urban Development Area) Special Development Order 1989 (SI 1989 2203) and makes transitional provisions in connection with the transfer of planning functions from the Central Manchester Development Corporation to the councils of the City of Manchester and the Metropolitan Borough of Trafford.

4851. Waste disposal–enforcement notice served on tipping site operated without planning permission or relevant licence–conditional permission granted on appeal–extent of interaction between Control of Pollution Act 1974 and Town and Country Planning Act 1990

[Control of Pollution Act 1974 s.5; Town and Country Planning Act 1990.]

R ran a waste tipping business without planning permission or a waste disposal licence under the Control of Pollution Act 1974 s.5. C served an enforcement notice under the Town and Country Planning Act 1990. The Secretary of State granted conditional planning permission on appeal. C applied to quash this decision, alleging that the Secretary of State should have upheld the notice, considering the pollution control powers available under the 1974 Act and that the planning conditions relating to past pollution problems on the site were invalid.

Held, dismissing the application, that (1) the Secretary of State only had to determine the planning issues under the 1990 Act. No submission on the effect of the 1974 Act had been made to him, *Secretary of State for the Environment and Rochester upon Medway City Council v. Hobday* (1990) 61 P. & C.R. 225, [1991] C.L.Y. 3514 considered. The interaction with the 1974 Act could only be relevant if that was a reason for upholding the notice, and (2) the conditions clearly and reasonably related to the development.

CHESHIRE CC v. SECRETARY OF STATE FOR THE ENVIRONMENT [1995] Env. L.R. 316, R M K Gray Q.C., QBD.

4852. Waste dumping–whether permission for industrial process included permission to import and deposit waste

[Town and Country Planning Act 1990 s.58; Town and Country Planning General Development Order 1988 Sch.2.]

K appealed against the dismissal of enforcement proceedings in respect of waste dumping on M's land. It was alleged that M had no planning permission for this use of their land, but M claimed that waste dumping was authorised by an order under the Town and Country Planning Act 1990 s.58(1). K contended that the inspector's conclusion that the importation, processing and deposit of waste amounted to development by virtue of the Town and Country Planning General Development Order 1988 Sch.2 Part 8 Class D was wrong in law. The waste deposited on the site did not result from an "industrial process" as defined in the Order and Class D did not apply because the waste was imported and not generated on the land.

Held, dismissing the appeal, that (1) the decision turned on the construction of "industrial process" in the Order. The term "articles" in the definition had to be given a broad interpretation and was capable of including land, and (2) it was not accepted that Class D of the Order did not give permission for the deposit of waste which resulted from an industrial process on other land. Such an interpretation was not justified on a reading nor was it justified by any reason of policy.

KENT CC v. SECRETARY OF STATE FOR THE ENVIRONMENT AND MARCHANT AND SONS LTD [1995] J.P.L. 931, Nigel MacLeod Q.C., QBD.

4853. Wind farms–need for balance between harm and benefit in PPG 22–whether harm outweighed benefit of exploiting renewable energy sources–whether noise potential detriment to residents of rural area

W sought to challenge a planning inspector's decision refusing planning permission in respect of two wind farm sites. The inspector had found that the proposals would adversely affect the appearance and physical amenities of the surrounding landscape, creating noise and disturbance to residents. He also stated that the policy contained in Department of the Environment PPG22, requiring the development of renewable energy sources, could be met in other ways and did not outweigh the serious harm presented by the proposed developments in the two locations. W contended that he had taken into account an irrelevant consideration regarding the reduction of carbon dioxide emissions other than by wind energy, and misapplied both the policy on renewable energy sources and government guidance on noise levels.

Held, dismissing the application, that the wording of PPG22 required a balance to assess the relative weight created by the need for renewable energy sources and the harm potential of a proposed development. In carrying out the balancing exercise, the inspector had found the harm outweighed the benefit of exploiting wind energy in the two locations. As to noise, this would reduce the peaceful aspect of a rural area, to the detriment of local residents.

WEST COAST WIND FARMS LTD v. SECRETARY OF STATE FOR THE ENVIRONMENT [1996] Env. L.R. 29, Nigel Macleod, QBD.

4854. Articles

Applying the "sequential test" following the Trowbridge decision *(Martin H. Goodall)*: J.P.L. 1996, Nov, 913-915. (Whether Secretary of State's approach to determining availability of alternative sites closer to town centre before granting planning permission was too rigid).

Archaeology and planning: recent trends and potential conflicts *(John Pugh-Smith* and *John Samuels)*: J.P.L. 1996, Sep, 707-724. (How PPG 15 has widened range of specified material considerations to add to changes brought in with PPG 16, trends in decision making, and emergent problems as archaeology plays growing role in development control process).

Blight: loss of part of property due to proposed public works "seriously affecting the amenity or convenience" *(H.C. Abraham)*: J.P.L. 1996, Jan, 8-12. (Whether owners can compel local authorities to compulsorily purchase whole property where significant blighting occurs).

Changing priorities in urban regeneration? *(Stephen Tromans)*: Env. Law 1996, 10(2), 7-9. (Impact of environmental policy on urban regeneration and application of principle of sustainable development).

Clarifying affordable housing *(Martin Edwards* and *John Martin)*: E.G. 1996, 9611, 132. (Draft Circular on Planning and Affordable Housing provides fuller definitions to planners seeking to implement PPG 3).

Contaminated land investigations–how will they work under PPG 23? *(Tom Graham)*: J.P.L. 1996, Jul, 547-553. (Role of site investigations in determination of planning applications for development of contaminated land).

Control of development adjacent to trunk roads: J.P.L. 1996, Sep, B109-B111. (Text of new guidelines on access to trunk roads where development planned and payments involved).

Crisis of identity *(David Sands)*: E.G. 1996, 9637, 62-63. (Recent inquiry into extension of Merry Hill centre where it was suggested that it should be treated as normal town centre is seen to question definition of town centre under revised PPG 6).

Crisis on the home front *(Ian Shiner* and *David Sheinman)*: E.G. 1996, 9631, 68-69. (Proposals requiring developers to include some affordable housing in their development plans).

Derelict land prevention and the planning system: J.P.L. 1996, Feb, B17-B18. (DoE commissioned report recommends revisions for PPG 1 and 12, better utilisation of rehabilitation conditions and financial guarantees and extended charging powers for local authorities).

Discretionary purchase of land under Highways Act 1980 s.246(2A) *(Kathleen Shorrock* and *Pamela Hargreaves)*: E.L.M. 1996, 8(5), 179-185. (Department of Transport guidelines and how they relate to Owen case regarding assessment of serious effect of proposed roadworks on property and exercise of discretion).

Draft circular on planning and affordable housing: J.P.L. 1996, Apr, B41-47. (Text of Secretary of State's draft circular issued February 26, 1996 supplementing PPG 3).

Enforcement time limits relating to residential conversions: J.P.L. 1996, Mar, 271-272. (Question and answer. Whether unauthorised change to use to mix of self contained flats and multiple occupation is subject to four year or 10 year time limit for enforcement).

Estate agents' boards *(Alec Samuels)*: J.P.L. 1996, Apr, 286-287. (Restrictions on use of "for sale" boards).

Go forth and multiplex? *(John Robertson)*: E.G. 1996, 9622, 108-110. (Concern over threat to town centres from out of town multi screen cinemas).

Identifying the planning unit *(H.W. Wilkinson)*: N.L.J. 1996, 146(6735), 375-376. (Whether landowners' plans to start new projects on part of their properties amounted to material change of use which required planning permission depended on whether parts affected were planning units in own right).

Implications of development plans: P.P.L. 1996, 1(4), 8-11. (Importance of development plans when planning applications and appeals are considered).

Is a garden centre a shop? *(Christopher Lockhart-Mummery)*: J.P.L. 1996, Sep, 725-728. (Whether despite Cawley decision, garden centre is a shop in light of Circular 13/87 para.6, explanatory note to the 1987 order, and Fisher case).

Is the system working? *(Saleem Shamash)*: E.G. 1996, 9635, 77-79. (Use of planning policy guidance to implement government policy up to draft revised PPG 1 and whether objectives including reduction of private motoring would be better achieved by fiscal policy).

Local plans and UDPs: is there a better way? *(Martin Wood)*: J.P.L. 1996, Oct 807-815. (Criticism of local plans and urban development plans procedures as lacking fairness and flexibility).

New planning obligations consultation paper *(Simon Ricketts)*: P.R. 1996, 6(2), 63-64. (DoE draft guidance on criteria for determining when planning obligations are acceptable).

Options to purchase *(Tom Graham)*: E.G. 1996, 9637, 132-134. (How to protect developers with options to purchase from avoiding problems arising from planning obligations and suggested draft "co-operation" clauses).

Overburdened or underinformed? *(Martin Edwards)*: E.G. 1996, 9629, 106-107. (Material considerations in planning decision letters and when they should be treated as "principal important controversial issues" and problems of length of time involved in planning process).

Painless extraction: P.E.L.B. 1996, 5(10), 79-80. (Introduction of new review regime for categorisation of mineral extraction sites).

Planning and development update: Planning obligation deeds *(Denton Hall)*: Corp. Brief. 1996, 10(4), 22-24. (Recent cases illustrating what can be made subject to planning obligation).

Planning and Environment Bar Association: J.P.L. 1996, Jan, 18-19. (Guidelines on better presentation of proofs of evidence, summaries and appendices in public inquiries).

Planning appeal procedures: J.P.L. 1996, May, 357-358. (Draft circular to consolidate and update existing guidance aimed to achieve reduction of delay and expense).

Planning application procedure: statutory consultees–the Sports Council: J.P.L. 1996, Mar, 198-199. (Proposal to require planning authorities to consult with Sports Council on any development affecting playing fields or other sports facilities).

Planning obligations: draft revision of circular 16/91: J.P.L. 1996, Feb, B9-B16. (Guidelines on use of planning obligations in determining planning applications and developing local planning policy).

Planning Policy Guidance Note 1: General policy and principles *(Tim Jewell)*: E.L.M. 1996, 8(5), 171-172. (How July consultation paper, based on series of principles, gives more explicit statements of government objectives and how it places new emphasis on role of strategic central direction in forming development plans).

PPG 13: a guide to better practice? *(Jeremy Hinds)*: P.R. 1996, 6(1), 18-20. (DoE guidance to planning authorities on implementing PPG 13 clarifies policy of restricting out of town development and reducing need to travel but anomalies remain).

PPG 23 and the duplication of controls *(Tom Graham)*: J.P.L. 1996, Oct 816-820. (Application of planning guidance on planning and pollution control to real life situations and relationship between overlapping regulatory regimes).

PPG6–at long last!: P.P.L. 1996, 1 (5), 9-10. (Main features of PPG 6 on town centre planning).

Protecting our heritage: J.P.L. 1996, Jul, 537-538. (Government consultation paper on listed building control).

Protecting the "familiar and cherished local scene" *(Carolyn Shelbourn)*: J.P.L. 1996, Jun, 463-470. (Recent changes in policy and practice which can restrict local authorities and conservationists in preserving local buildings and monuments with particular reference to PPG 15).

Rule (5): equivalent reinstatement: E.G. 1996, 9625, 164-166. (Circumstances in which compulsory purchase compensation may be assessed on basis of equivalent reinstatement

rather than open market value applying s.5 r.5 of the 1961 Act).

Ryde's Scale (1996): E.G. 1996, 9622, 111-115. (Valuation Office's revised scale of charges for work done in preparing compulsory purchase compensation claims).

Stoking up the gravy train *(Paul Strohm)*: E.G. 1996, 9611, 104-106. (Increase in objections by out of town supermarkets against competitors' proposed developments due to increased pressure from planning guidance restrictions).

Stop notices and the cost benefit assessment *(Shona E. Emmett)*: J.P.L. 1996, Jan, 3-7. (Circumstances where cost benefit assessments are necessary or advisable).

Sustainable and low impact developments in the countryside *(Simon Fairlie)*: J.P.L. 1996, Nov, 903-912. (Extent to which planning system recognises need for sustainable development, with particular reference to permaculture and low impact development).

Team players take all *(Martyn Chase)*: E.G. 1996, 9632, 58-59. (Implications for local authorities and other public sector bodies of PPG 6 on town centre strategies).

The best laid plans of mice and men: suing the local planning authority *(Mark Watson-Gandy)*: J.P. 1996, 160(36), 729. (Grounds on which complaint may be brought against planning authority).

The practical uses of planning obligations *(John Martin)*: E.G. 1996, 9607, 132-134. (Extent to which planning obligations can be utilised by developers to achieve their intended projects and enforced by local planning authorities).

4855. Books

Bryan, Helen–Planning Applications and Appeals. Paperback: £14.99. ISBN 0-7506-2792-1. Architectural Press: an imprint of Butterworth-Heinemann.
Duxbury, R.M.C.–Telling and Duxbury: Planning Law and Procedure. Paperback: £20.95. ISBN 0-406-99374-2. Butterworth Law.
Gilg, Andrew–Countryside Planning. Paperback: £14.99. ISBN 0-415-05490-7. Hardback: £45.00. ISBN 0-415-05489-3. Routledge.
Grant, Malcolm–Permitted Development. Green's practice library. Paperback: £42.00. ISBN 0-421-55380-4. Sweet & Maxwell.
Hart, Garry; Williams, Anne; Carnworth, R.; Robinson, P.; Dobry, Judge–Blundell and Dobry: Planning Applications, Appeals and Proceedings. Hardback: £50.00. ISBN 0-421-53540-7. Sweet & Maxwell.
Heap, Desmond–An Outline of Planning Law. Paperback: £42.00. ISBN 0-421-57520-4. Sweet & Maxwell.
Maddock, Malcolm; Norris, Martin–Planning and Environmental Law. Legal Practice Course resource books. Paperback: £17.50. ISBN 0-85308-342-8. Jordan.
Pugh-Smith, John; Samuels, John–Archaeology in Law. Hardback: £48.00. ISBN 0-421-50340-8. Sweet & Maxwell.

POLICE

4856. Arrest–powers of arrest under Public Order Act 1986–whether officer not administering warning can exercise powers of arrest

[Public Order Act 1986 s.5.]

The DPP appealed by way of case stated against a decision to dismiss charges relating to the resisting of two police constables in the execution of their duty and assaulting a police constable. The issue was whether the power of arrest under the Public Order Act 1968 s.5(4) could be exercised only by the officer who personally gave the warning necessary under the section. If this was correct, it was necessary to decide whether an officer making an arrest under s.5 who did not administer the warning, was acting otherwise than in the execution of his duty.

Held, dismissing the appeal, that the magistrates had correctly construed s.5, and an officer who had not administered the warning was acting otherwise than in the execution of his duty by effecting an arrest under the section. The power of arrest was exercisable only by an officer who had personally given the warning.

DPP v. HANCOCK; DPP v. TUTTLE [1995] Crim. L.R. 139, Kennedy, L.J., QBD.

4857. Conditions of employment

POLICE (AMENDMENT) REGULATIONS 1996, SI 1996 699; made under the Police Act 1964 s.33. In force: in accordance with Reg.1 (3); £1.95.

These Regulations amend the Police Regulations 1995 (SI 1995 215). The amendments include the insertion in the principal Regulations of a new Regulation conferring a right on a female member of a police force to take special leave to receive ante-natal care; the making of fresh provision in respect of maternity leave; and alterations to the rates of pay for all ranks and amendments to the categories which determine pay for members of police forces of the rank of superintendent.

4858. Conditions of employment

POLICE (PROMOTION) REGULATIONS 1996, SI 1996 1685; made under the Police Act 1964 s.33. In force: August 1, 1996; £1.95.

These Regulations consolidate with amendments the Regulations revoked by Reg.8 and Sch.3. Regulation 2(2) has been amended to reflect amendments made by the Police and Magistrates' Courts Act 1994. Regulation 6 and Reg.7(5) (a) have been amended because the Police Regulations 1995 no longer provide for the authorised establishment of a police force. Regulation 2(3) has been amended to add references to maternity leave in reckoning service. Under Reg.3(4) probationary service in various constabularies counts as probationary service for the purposes of Reg.3(1). This provision has been changed by adding to the constabularies listed. The drafting of Sch.1 has been changed to refer to persons acting on behalf of the examinations board (and references to the examination agency accordingly omitted). Paragraph 5(5) of that Schedule imposes a new restriction on the circumstances in which a member of a police force can re-sit Part I of the qualifying examination. Schedule 2 to the Regulations is amended to end the recognition of Scottish examinations for promotion to the rank of sergeant or inspector unless the examination had been passed before the coming into force of these Regulations. Schedule 2 has also been amended so that, where a member of the Royal Parks Constabulary, the States of Jersey Police, the Ministry of Defence Police or Dover Harbour Board Police has passed an examination which is the same as the examination for the time being constituting a qualifying examination under these Regulations (or the Regulations revoked by these Regulations), that examination is treated as a pass for the purposes of Reg.3 if that member subsequently becomes a member of a police force (within the meaning of the Police Act 1964). Regulation 3(5) has been added to allow a person who has passed the Scottish examination after the coming into force of these Regulations and has served no less than a year in the rank in question in a Scottish force to qualify for promotion to that rank in an English force.

4859. Disciplinary procedures–senior officers charged by Chief Constable–Chief Constable also exercising judicial function–need for separation of police functions

H and the Police Complaints Authority applied for judicial review of the decision by G, a senior police officer of a neighbouring force, who acted on behalf of the Chief Constable in dismissing disciplinary charges against A, a chief inspector, as an abuse of process, where A had been in charge of a siege in which police officers had shot a man dead. M, another senior officer involved in the siege, was given notice to retire on grounds of ill health.

Held, allowing the applications, that the Chief Constable had not given adequate reasons for his decision to retire M and was required to balance the case for retirement with the public interest issue that the police force carry out disciplinary proceedings to their conclusion. In A's case, a stay of proceedings on the grounds of abuse of process should only have been imposed in exceptional circumstances where a fair trial had become impossible, *Attorney General's Reference (No.1 of 1990)* [1992] 1 Q.B. 630, [1992] C.L.Y. 615 considered. The Chief Constable had a responsibility to fulfil his duty to prosecute the disciplinary charge brought against A. Most importantly, the administrative and prosecutorial roles of the Chief Constable were incompatible and there was clearly a need to separate the power to charge police officers and the judicial functions also exercised by the Chief Constable, as well as the administrative function of overseeing the force as a whole.

R. v. CHIEF CONSTABLE OF DEVON AND CORNWALL, *ex p.* HAY; R. v. CHIEF CONSTABLE OF DEVON AND CORNWALL, *ex p.* POLICE COMPLAINTS AUTHORITY, *The Times*, February 19, 1996, Sedley, J., QBD.

4860. European Police Office–legal capacities

EUROPEAN POLICE OFFICE (LEGAL CAPACITIES) ORDER 1996, SI 1996 3157; made under the International Organisations Act 1968 s.1. In force: in accordance with Art.1; £0.65.

This Order confers the legal capacities of a body corporate on the European Police Office (Europol). This legal capacity is conferred in accordance with Art.26 of the Convention based on Art.K.3 of the Treaty on European Union, on the Establishment of a European Police Office (Europol Convention) (Cm 3050). The Order will enable Her Majesty's Government to give effect to Art.26 of that

Convention, and will come into force on the date on which the Convention enters into force in respect of the United Kingdom.

4861. Pensions–forfeiture after criminal conviction–police officer did not have to be a serving officer when the offences were committed–meaning of "in connection with" in Reg.K5(4) of the Police Pensions Regulations 1987–statutory interpretation

[Police Pensions Regulations 1987 Reg.K5.]

W appealed by way of case stated and applied for judicial review of the Home Secretary's decision resulting in the forfeiture of 75 per cent of his police pension. W received the pension following his retirement from the police force on the grounds of ill health caused by his employment. The forfeiture followed W's conviction on 11 charges including blackmail, contamination of goods with intent to cause economic loss, making a threat to kill and attempting to obtain property by deception. He was subsequently sentenced to a total of 17 years' imprisonment. W was on sick leave from July 1, 1988 and retired from the police force on October 3, 1988. The offences were committed between August 3, 1988 and October 20, 1989. The appeal by way of case stated related to the Police Pensions Regulations 1987 Reg.K5(4). W argued that the words, "offence committed in connection with his service as a member of a police force" should be construed to mean offences committed by a serving police officer during the course of his duties or, alternatively, by a serving police officer whether during the course of his duties or not. W argued that the Home Secretary had erred in law by finding that there merely had to be a real connection between the commission of the offences and the police officer's service and the officer did not need to be a serving officer at the time of the offence. As the regulation was penal, W argued that, according to *Tuck & Sons v. Priester* (1887) 19 Q.B. 629, a reasonable construction should be given if it avoided the penalty. The application for judicial review related to the Home Secretary's decision that the offences could lead to a serious loss of confidence in the police service. W argued that the decision was *Wednesbury* unreasonable as most of the offences were committed while W was no longer a serving member of the police force.

Held, dismissing the appeal and the application, that (1) the approach of the court in *Tuck & Sons v. Priester* was not a principle of law. It should apply only in cases of real doubt over interpretation, *DPP v. Ottewell* [1970] A.C. 642, [1968] C.L.Y. 837 followed; (2) the words "in connection with" should have an ordinary English meaning and should not be limited to cases where the officer was a serving officer and the offence was committed during the course of his duties. There had to be a connection between the commission of the offence and the officer's service as a police officer. In this case W could not have obtained the knowledge he required to commit the offence if he had not been a police officer; (3) if the regulation required the commission of an offence by a police officer, whether in the course of his duties or not, the scope would be too wide and would apply to offences which had nothing to do with the officer's employment, and (4) the fact that the offences occurred after W had retired was not a relevant consideration for the Home Secretary.

WHITCHELO v. SECRETARY OF STATE FOR THE HOME DEPARTMENT; R. v. SECRETARY OF STATE FOR THE HOME DEPARTMENT, *ex p.* WHITCHELO, Trans. Ref: CO 3254/95, April 2, 1996, Dyson, J., QBD.

4862. Pensions–retirement from the police owing to psychiatric illness–injury sustained during course of duties as a police officer

[Police Pensions Regulations 1987.]

M, a medically retired police officer, sought judicial review of a decision of F and T, medical referees, that M's psychiatric illness was not caused by the circumstances of his employment as a police officer. F and T believed that the employment had a contributory role, but failed to issue a certificate to the effect that M was entitled to an injury award under the Police Pensions Regulations 1987.

Held, allowing the application and quashing the decision of the referees, that (1) there had to be a relationship between the injury and the work performed by M in order to show that the injury was received in the execution of his duty, *Garvin v. Police Authority for City of London* [1944] 1 Q.B. 358 and *Police Authority for Huddersfield v. Watson* [1947] 1 K.B. 842 considered. In this case, there was no doubt that the illness was brought on by the conditions of M's work, and (2) in cases of physical injury, an injury could be caused in the execution of a police officer's duties even if he was predisposed to such an injury. The same theory related to claims in tort under the "eggshell skull" principle. The same had to be said of psychiatric illness, *Page v. Smith* [1995] 2 All E.R. 736, [1995] 2 C.L.Y. 3682 considered. In this case, whether or not M was predisposed to psychiatric illness, it was clear that as a result of his duties, he suffered an illness which he had never before experienced.

R. v. FAGIN, *ex p.* MOUNTSTEPHEN [1996] C.O.D. 416, Brooke, J., QBD.

4863. Police and Magistrates' Courts Act 1994–Commencement No.9 Order

POLICE AND MAGISTRATES' COURTS ACT 1994 (COMMENCEMENT NO.9 AND AMENDMENT) ORDER 1995, SI 1995 3003 (C.67); made under the Police and Magistrates" Courts Act 1994 s.94. In force: bringing into force various provisions of the Act on December 13, 1996; £1.10.

This Order brings into force the provisions of s.47(1), s.47(2),(4) and (5) of the Police and Magistrates' Courts Act 1994 which deal with constitution of police forces in Scotland and related appeals and the partial repeal of Sch.4 para.11 of the Police and Criminal Evidence Act 1984.

4864. Police officers–alleged falsification of evidence incriminating appellant–whether police protected from civil action by absolute immunity conferred by public policy

S, whose convictions for the murder of a police officer and of riot had been quashed on the basis that they were unsafe, appealed against an order striking out his claims for conspiracy to prevent the administration of justice and misfeasance in public office against two police officers, who had allegedly created false notes of an interview which incriminated S. A claim for malicious prosecution had also been brought, but S sought re-instatement of the first two actions as, to be able to prosecute, they did not require proof of absence of reasonable and probable cause. The case raised the issue of whether the actions of the police officers were protected by a rule of absolute immunity as a matter of public policy. S argued that the fabrication of evidence was not part of the investigatory process and so could not attract immunity.

Held, dismissing the appeal, that the protection afforded by the immunity rule applied not only to the presentation of evidence but also to its preparation, and its purpose was not to protect those who falsified evidence but those who might be falsely accused of doing so. If the persons who allegedly carried out the wrongdoing were also responsible for bringing the prosecution, a claim for malicious prosecution could be brought, as in the instant case. However, a civil remedy was not available if the actions of the miscreant were not the determinative factor in the decision to prosecute.

SILCOTT v. COMMISSIONER OF POLICE OF THE METROPOLIS (1996) 8 Admin. L.R. 633, Simon Brown, L.J., CA.

4865. Police officers–insufficient resources to attend protests against livestock exports–Chief Constable only allowing exporters' lorries through two days a week–contravening EC rules on restriction of exports–whether Chief Constable's decision unreasonable

[Treaty of Rome 1957 Art.34, Art.36.]

The Chief Constable decided to limit police assistance for livestock exporters from Shoreham, which resulted in turning back lorries on all but two days a week, on the basis that he had insufficient manpower to police animal rights protests. ITF applied for judicial review of his decision.

Held, allowing the application, that (1) under domestic law, the Chief Constable's decision could not be described as unreasonable, having regard to his manpower and financial constraints and the restrictive Home Office policy on special assistance payments and (2) the decision contravened the Treaty of Rome 1957 Art.34 because it had the effect of a quantitative restriction on exports which was not justified on public policy grounds within the meaning of Art.36 of the Treaty. The Chief Constable, in accepting the Home Office policy, had not done enough to establish that the cost was disproportionate, *R. v. Coventry City Council, ex p. Phoenix Aviation* [1995] 3 All E.R. 37, [1995] 1 C.L.Y. 148 followed.

R. v. CHIEF CONSTABLE OF SUSSEX, *ex p.* INTERNATIONAL TRADER'S FERRY LTD [1995] 3 W.L.R. 802, Balcombe, L.J., QBD.

4866. Police powers–contract between police authority and company organising vehicle recovery scheme–no delegation of statutory powers

[Local Government Act 1972 s.111; Police Act 1964 s.4.]

CM, a vehicle recovery operator, applied for judicial review of the lawfulness of a contract between the police authority and Automobile Association Developments Ltd, AAD, under which AAD organised a vehicle recovery scheme in the police authority's area. CM questioned whether the police authority had the power to enter into the contract.

Held, refusing the application, that under the Police Act 1964 s.4, as amended, the police authority had a duty to secure the adequate provision of an efficient police force, the direction and control of which was the responsibility of the Chief Constable, and the Local Government Act 1972 s.111(1) empowered the authority, in discharging its function of maintaining an efficient force, to engage contractors for the recovery of vehicles, *Hazell v. Hammersmith and Fulham LBC* [1992] 2 A.C. 1, [1991] C.L.Y. 2420 considered. The arrangement did not prevent the Chief Constable from maintaining control. Provided that the function of deciding whether or not to exercise their powers in relation to the recovery of vehicles remained with the police, there was no delegation of statutory duty, *Rivers v. Cutting* [1982] 1 W.L.R. 1146, [1980] C.L.Y. 2374 followed. Although there was no express provision to levy charges for the scheme, it was a necessary implication that the police authority was entitled to do so.

R. v. GREATER MANCHESTER POLICE AUTHORITY, *ex p.* CENTURY MOTORS (FARNWORTH) LTD, *The Times*, May 31, 1996, Popplewell, J., QBD.

4867. Police service–disciplinary procedures

[Police and Magistrates' Courts Act 1994.]

The Home Office issued a press release entitled *New police procedures to be introduced* (News release 217/96), published on July 11, 1996. which announces new personnel and disciplinary procedures for the police, to be introduced in 1997. Following discussions with police associations and police authorities, Mr Howard has decided that there will be a new standard of proof at disciplinary hearings; that disciplinary proceedings should be allowed to take place before criminal proceedings in exceptional circumstances; that chief officers should investigate cases involving Superintendents; and that civilian managers should be enabled to initiate action into police officers' conduct. The package also includes a new code of conduct, new procedures for dealing with unsatisfactory performance; and a new appeals tribunal for disciplinary and performance cases. The changes are made under the provisions of the Police and Magistrates' Courts Act 1994.

4868. Race discrimination–vicarious liability of Police Commissioner for actions of police officers–police officers subject to Race Relations Act 1976–statutory interpretation

[Race Relations Act 1976 s.20, s.53, s.75.]

The Commissioner appealed against a refusal to strike out certain passages in a statement of claim in an action for damages against him for false imprisonment, assault and battery, malicious prosecution and racial discrimination brought by F, a Somali refugee, who had been arrested after having summoned police assistance following an attack on her by white teenagers. Instead of assisting F, the police arrested her and charged her with affray. She was acquitted after no evidence was adduced. F amended her claim to include unlawful racial discrimination against the Commissioner, claiming that the officers were acting as his agents and he was therefore vicariously liable for their actions. The time in which an action could have been brought against the individual officers had expired. The Commissioner submitted that the Race Relations Act 1976 s.20 did not apply to a police officer performing his duties, and further that police officers are office holders and not employees, and that under s.53 there would only be vicarious liability if a constable acted with the Commissioner's authority as his agent, which was not so in the present case.

Held, allowing the appeal, that (1) the police were subject to the Race Relations Act 1976 s.20(2)(g) in assisting and protecting members of the public in the same way as any other public service and it was therefore unlawful for them to discriminate racially in the course of providing these services, *Savjani v. Inland Revenue Commissioners* [1981] Q.B. 458, [1981] C.L.Y. 1420 considered. The performance of a public duty did not preclude the provision of a service, *R. v. Entry Clearance Officer, Bombay, ex p. Amin* [1983] 2 A.C. 818, [1983] C.L.Y. 1935 approving Templeman L.J. in *Savjani* supra, considered; (2) although public policy was an issue, the prospect of racial discrimination claims was less serious than the risk that members of the public, faced with racial discrimination by public service providers, could be denied an effective remedy. However, the restriction on proceedings contained in s.53(1) of the 1976 Act was clearly drafted and in the absence of express provisions to the contrary, did not permit claims for ordinary vicarious liability against the Commissioner. Claims could be made against individual officers, but their chief officer could not be held vicariously liable for their acts, *Hawkins v. Bepey* [1980] 1 W.L.R. 419, [1980] C.L.Y. 558 distinguished and (3) leave to appeal to the House of Lords would be granted.

FARAH v. COMMISSIONER OF POLICE OF THE METROPOLIS [1997] 1 All E.R. 289, Hutchison, L.J., CA.

4869. Security Service Act 1996 (c.35)

An Act to give the Security Service the function of acting in support of the prevention and detection of serious crime.

This Act received Royal Assent on July 18, 1996.

4870. Security Service Act 1996–Commencement Order

SECURITY SERVICE ACT 1996 (COMMENCEMENT) ORDER 1996, SI 1996 2454 (C.64); made under the Security Service Act 1996 s.4. In force: bringing into force various provisions of the Act on October 14, 1996; £0.65.

This Order brings into force on October 14, 1966 all the provisions of the Security Service Act 1996.

4871. Articles

Arrest for breach of the peace and the European Convention on Human Rights *(Donald Nicolson* and *Kiron Reid)*: Crim. L.R. 1996, Nov, 764-775. (Extent to which common law powers of police to arrest for breach of the peace may be challenged under Art.5 and possibly under Art.10 and Art.11).

Attrition in rape and sexual assault cases *(Jeanne Gregory* and *Sue Lees)*: Brit. J. Criminol. 1996, 36(1), 1-17. (Findings of research project investigating changing police policies and practices at two London police stations in relation to classification of rape and sexual assault cases and dropping cases without prosecuting).

Beating the JR trap *(Alan Beckley)*: Policing T. 1996, 2(2), 14-18. (Judicial review procedure and review of cases involving police including those concerning natural justice, public interest immunity, police operations and procedures and powers of arrest).

Child protection by bail condition *(Andrew Grand)*: Fam. Law 1996, 26(May), 308-309. (Implications for child protection procedures of powers given to police custody officers under 1994 Act to impose bail conditions when releasing people charged with criminal offences).

Community attitudes regarding police responsibility for crime control *(Richard C. Lumb)*: Pol. J. 1996, 69(4), 319-329. (Public perceptions of comparative responsibility of police and public for crime control in context of community problem solving policing concept).

Covert policing: a comparative view *(Sybil Sharpe)*: Anglo-Am. L.R. 1996, 25(2), 163-187. (Judicial attitudes towards evidence obtained improperly through covert police operations in England and US).

Crime affects our health *(Keith Hellawell)*: Med. Leg. J. 1996, 64(1), 6-22. (Talk by Chief Constable of West Yorkshire on issues facing provincial police forces and impact of drug abuse on rise in crime, with subsequent audience discussion).

Ethics: a moral dilemma *(Brian F. Kingshott)*: Pol. J. 1996, 69(2), 163-166. (Whether police personnel and training professionals should be making greater effort to promote ethical behaviour in their organizations).

Getting burnt *(Christopher Porteous)*: Policing T. 1996, 2(3), 26-28. (Review of 20 years' case law on whether and when police are open to charges of negligence, focusing on fires started negligently, motor vehicle situations, and cases where public policy issues have arisen).

In favour of compliance *(Stephen P. Savage* and *Sarah Charman)*: Policing T. 1996, 2(1), 10-17. (Role of Association of Chief Police Officers within police service and as lobbying influence on government policy and factors contributory to ACPO's evolution).

Law enforcement in Spain *(Colin Waters)*: Pol. J. 1996, 69(1), 77-78. (Public attitudes to police and low rate of serious crime).

Mentally disordered suspects and the right to silence *(Ed Cape)*: N.L.J. 1996, 146(6728), 80, 82-83, 101. (Implications of right to silence provisions in 1994 Act for mentally disordered suspects and ways in which defence lawyers can mitigate worst effects in police interviews).

Part of the Union *(Jurgen Storbeck)*: Policing T. 1996, 2(1), 28-31. (Establishment of Europol for coordinated investigation of cross border crime and plans to develop better equipped and more effective organisation with more extensive powers).

Police accountability in 1996 *(Ian Oliver)*: Crim. L.R. 1996, Sep, 611-621. (Constitutional position of police in England and Wales and whether 1994 Act has altered balance of political control).

Police contact with mentally disordered persons in the Northumbria force area *(Richard Berry)*: Pol. J. 1996, 69(3), 221-226. (Survey of Surgeons' records and incident logs in criminal and other situations).

Police liability in negligence *(Margaret Noble)*: N.L.J. 1996, 146(6761), 1395-1396. (Circumstances in which police may have duty of care for third parties' actions and whether public policy immunity applies).

Police news: Howard Journal 1996, 35(3), 271-272. (Recent developments concerning police including use of CS gas, Metropolitan police response to calls, public satisfaction with police and establishment of National Forensic Science Service).

Policing cyberspace *(David Blakey)*: Policing T. 1996, 2(1), 18-21. (Need for police to join information superhighway both to tackle computer crime and to share knowledge).

Policing low level disorder: police use of section 5 of the Public Order Act 1986 *(David Brown* and *Tom Ellis)*: Res. B. 1996, 38, 51-56. (Results of 1994 research study into policing of offensive behaviour).

Policing youth crime: children's views *(Karen Pfeffer* and *Bankole A. Cole)*: Pol. J. 1996, 69(1), 5-11. (Survey of young childrens' views on youth crime, role of police and control or prevention of such crime).

Prosecutors' code *(Sharon Grace* and *Deborah Crisp)*: Policing T. 1996, 2(2), 37-41. (Police response to revised Code for Crown Prosecutors which was published in June 1994 and impact code has on decision making).

Psychological profiling: red, green or amber? *(Paul Wilson* and *Keith Soothill)*: Pol. J. 1996, 69(1), 12-20. (Background to psychological profiling in police investigations, scientific basis and dangers of approach).

Services to victims: findings from the 1994 British Crime Survey *(Catriona Mirlees Black* and *Tracey Budd)*: Res. B. 1996, 38, 27-35. (Results of survey on police treatment of victims and effectiveness of victim support schemes).

The impact of equal opportunities policies on the day-to-day experiences of women police constables *(Carol Martin)*: Brit. J. Criminol. 1996, 36(4), 510-528. (Focus on recent research and study of women police officers in one police division).

The impact of local policing plans: a study in West Yorkshire *(Patricia K. Barton)*: Pol. J. 1996, 69(4), 289-298. (Background to introduction of local policing plans by 1994 Act and extent to which public aware of them).

The jurisdiction and powers of police constables to arrest and detain *(Wilson Finnie)*: S.L.P.Q. 1996, 1(2), 131-136. (Powers of police in UK to arrest and detain outwith their own jurisdiction).

Use and misuse of data *(Diane Rowland)*: N.L.J. 1996, 146(6734), 332,349. (Definition of "use" of data within s.5 where police officer used data on police computer for reasons not connected with police work).

4872. Books

Brewer, John D.; Guelke, Adrian; Hume, Ian; Moxon-Browne, Edward; Wilford, Rick–The Police, Public Order and the State. Hardback: £40.00. ISBN 0-333-65487-0. Paperback: £14.99. ISBN 0-333-65488-9. Macmillan Press.

Clayton, Richard; Tomlinson, Hugh–Police Actions. Paperback: £19.99. ISBN 0-471-96865-X. Chancery Wiley Law Publications.

English, Jack; Card, Richard–Butterworths Police Law. Paperback: £20.95. ISBN 0-406-02436-7. Butterworth Law.

Levenson, Howard; Fairweather, Fiona; Cape, Ed–Police Powers: a Practitioners' Guide. Paperback: £32.00. ISBN 0-905099-62-1. Legal Action Group.

Rose, David–In the Name of the Law. Paperback: £7.99. ISBN 0-09-930116-4. Vintage.

Sloan, Kenneth–Sloan: Police Law Primer. Paperback: £17.95. ISBN 0-406-99611-3. Butterworth Law.

RATES

4873. Bankruptcy–magistrate committing bankrupt to prison for breach of payment terms–no remedy against bankrupt permitted by Insolvency Act 1986 s.285(3)–no power to commit

[Insolvency Act 1986 s.285.]

L was in default with his rates on 12 properties with a total debt of £8,404. A warrant of commitment was issued on September 8, 1992 but was suspended on terms. L breached the payment terms and on February 5, 1993 the magistrates committed him to prison for 28 days. The magistrates were told that the failure to pay on terms had commenced before the end of 1992 but that on January 27, 1993 L had been declared bankrupt. L appealed.

Held, allowing the appeal, that the magistrates had no power to commit L by reason of the Insolvency Act 1986 s.285(3), whereby no creditor of a bankrupt has a remedy against the property or the person of the bankrupt in respect of that debt.

LEWIS v. OGWR BC [1996] R.A. 124, Hidden, J., QBD.

4874. Community charge–committal for non-payment–further means inquiry required–further consideration of offer to pay instalments

[Community Charges (Administration and Enforcement) Regulations 1989 Reg.46; Council Tax (Administration and Enforcement) Regulations 1992 Reg.52.]

G sought judicial review to quash a decision committing him to prison for 28 days for non-payment of community charge totalling £691 over a period of three years. G had been found guilty of culpable neglect and the magistrates had fixed the term of imprisonment, but postponed the issue of the warrant on condition that G pay £10 per fortnight toward the arrears. Four months later G had paid only £10, his income support had been decreased and his outgoings had increased owing to repayments on a loan. The magistrates therefore activated the term of imprisonment. G argued that the magistrates had failed to consider the option of deducting the arrears directly from his income support rather than deciding on a term of imprisonment. G also submitted that the magistrates had erred by deciding that his offer of £5 per fortnight amounted to gross contempt rather than a means of payment.

Held, allowing the appeal, that (1) once a term of imprisonment had been fixed under either the Community Charges (Administration and Enforcement) Regulations 1989 Reg.46 or the Council Tax (Administration and Enforcement) Regulations 1992 Reg.52 then no action could be taken under the Income Support Regulations, and (2) once the magistrates had ordered a further means inquiry, they were not entitled to reach the conclusion that G's attitude amounted to gross contempt without further inquiries into the reduction in his income support and the need for the loan. The magistrates should have considered whether the offer of £5 per fortnight was an alternative to activating the term of imprisonment, as the power of imprisonment should not have been used as a method of punishment, but as a means of obtaining payment.

R. v. WELLINGBOROUGH MAGISTRATES' COURT, *ex p.* GAUNT, Trans. Ref: CO 876/95, January 31, 1996, McCullough, J., QBD.

4875. Community charge–committal for non-payment–magistrates did not adequately inquire into the applicant's means–inquiry into the applicant's wilful refusal or culpable neglect was not adequate

[Community Charges (Administration and Enforcement) Regulations 1989 Reg.41.]

G sought judicial review of a decision by the justices to commit her to prison for a total of 89 days for non-payment of community charge. G argued that the magistrates had failed to inquire adequately into her means as required by the Community Charges (Administration and Enforcement) Regulations 1989 Reg.41(2). G further argued that the magistrates erred in their inquiry into whether her failure to pay was owing to wilful refusal of culpable neglect because they failed to consider the two separate periods of non-payment relating to the two liability orders.

Held, allowing the appeal and quashing the decisions, that (1) the means inquiry was central to the enforcement procedure under the Regulations and it was not adequately completed by the magistrates. G was 22 years old with learning difficulties and without legal representation. In such a case the magistrates should have made further inquiries into her means especially considering that there were a number of obvious items of expenditure missing. A means inquiry form would have aided the inquiry, and (2) the question of whether failure to pay was owing to wilful refusal or culpable neglect should have been addressed separately for each liability order. The magistrates did not satisfy their obligation to make such inquiries.

R. v. DERWENTSIDE MAGISTRATES' COURT, *ex p.* GALLIMORE, Trans. Ref: CO/2522/95, June 12, 1996, Harrison, J., QBD.

4876. Community charge–committal for non-payment–method of challenging committal–whether committal of female ratepayer looking after children was proper course

[Magistrates' Courts Act 1980 s.113.]

The applicants failed to pay suspended orders for community charge and were committed to prison. They all had small children and had appeared unrepresented at the hearing where the suspended order was imposed. Two were unrepresented at the second hearing as well. In two of the three cases the justices had conducted a means inquiry. In the third the justices had ruled that they could not re-open the inquiry conducted at the hearing which resulted in a suspended order.

Held, allowing B's application and quashing the committal order, but dismissing the other two applications, that (1) the proper method of appeal was not by judicial review but by way of case stated. This did not prevent an application for bail which could be made under the Magistrates' Courts Act 1980 s.113, and (2) the ruling of the justices in B's case was incorrect and they had thereby wrongly fettered their discretion and the decision would be quashed. In the other two cases the decisions of the justices could not be described as outside the bounds of what might reasonably be expected.

R. v. WOLVERHAMPTON JUSTICES, *ex p.* BASTABLE [1995] R.A. 372, Buxton, J., QBD.

4877. Community charge–committal for non-payment–standard of proof for culpable neglect

[Community Charge (Administration and Enforcement) Regulations 1989 Art.41.]

B appealed against sentence of 21 days' imprisonment for failure to pay community charge. B argued that her actions did not amount to culpable neglect when applying the correct standard of proof under the Community Charge (Administration and Enforcement) Regulations 1989 Art.41.

Held, allowing the appeal, that when considering whether someone was guilty of culpable neglect and the threat of imprisonment existed, the standard of proof was higher than the ordinary civil standard of balance of probabilities. In this case, the evidence did not sufficiently establish culpable neglect. The magistrates should have considered whether B was guilty of culpable neglect when she was previously before them and they had imposed a suspended sentence *R. v. South Tyneside Justices, ex p. Martin* [1995] 1 C.L.Y. 992 considered.

R. v. KINGSTON-UPON-HULL JUSTICES, *ex p.* BROOM, Trans. Ref: CO-1042-94, November 15, 1995, Carnwath, J., QBD.

4878. Community charge–council tax–jobseeker's allowance

COMMUNITY CHARGE AND COUNCIL TAX (ADMINISTRATION AND ENFORCEMENT) (AMENDMENT) (JOBSEEKER'S ALLOWANCE) REGULATIONS 1996, SI 1996 2405; made under the Local Government Finance Act 1988 s.143, Sch.4 para.1, Sch.4 para.12; and the Local Government Finance Act 1992 s.113, Sch.4 para.1, Sch.4 para.12. In force: October 8, 1996; £0.65.

Under the Community Charges (Administration and Enforcement) Regulations 1989 (SI 1989 438) and the Council Tax (Administration and Enforcement) Regulations 1992 (SI 1992 613) where a liability order has been made for the payment of community charge or council tax, certain steps for the enforcement of the liability may not be taken while deductions are being made for that purpose from any amount payable to the debtor by way of income support. These Regulations amend both sets of Regulations so that this restriction also applies in respect of amounts payable by way of jobseeker's allowance under the Jobseekers Act 1995 Part I.

4879. Community charge–designation of house for homeless–tribunal discretion to revoke designation

[Local Government Finance Act 1988 s.5.]

S appealed against the dismissal of his appeal to a valuation and community charge tribunal against the designation of his house, which had 40 rooms occupied by the homeless, under the Local Government Finance Act 1988 s.5(3) for the purpose of collective community charge.

Held, allowing the appeal, that the tribunal seemed to decide that it had no discretion to revoke the designation on the ground of hardship and unfairness to S. That amounted to a fetter on its discretion. The designation was quashed and remitted to the tribunal.

SUMAL v. ISLINGTON LBC [1996] R.V.R. 11, Dyson, J., QBD.

4880. Council tax–"granny flats"–whether self contained units–appropriate deciding criteria

[Council Tax (Chargeable Dwellings) Order 1992 Art.2, Art.3.]

Inland Revenue listing officers sought orders to quash the separate decisions of four valuation tribunals to the effect that an annexe of a house was to be treated as part of the principal dwelling for council tax purposes and was not liable to separate assessment. They argued that there had been errors of law in the decision making process as to what constituted a dwelling to be assessed as liable to tax under the Council Tax (Chargeable Dwellings) Order 1992 Art.2 and Art.3. They contended, firstly, that a valuation tribunal was wrong to look exclusively at terms of planning consent and planning restrictions placed on the form of use to determine whether an annexe or granny flat constituted a "self contained unit" as defined by the 1992 Order Art.2.; secondly, that it was wrong to treat the degree of communal living of the family as a relevant consideration; and, thirdly, that whether the annexe was capable of being sold separately was not a relevant consideration.

Held, allowing the appeals, that (1) although planning consent could be taken into account, it should not be relied on as the only way of determining use; (2) looking at the degree of communal living did not properly test the definition of a self contained unit in the 1992 Order Art.2, and (3) saleability helped to confirm that the property was self contained, but the fact that it could not be sold separately confirmed that the property was not self contained. Also there was no suggestion that it was legally impossible to sell the property. The decisions of the valuation tribunals would be remitted for reconsideration of the issue of whether the annexes in question were self contained units.

RODD v. RITCHINGS; BATTY v. BURFOTT; BATTY v. MERRIMAN; GILBERT v. CHILDS [1995] R.A. 299, Ognall, J., QBD.

4881. Council tax–alteration of valuation band–Council Tax (Alteration of Lists and Appeals) Amendment 1994 Regulations not retrospective

[Council Tax (Alteration of Lists and Appeals) Regulations 1993; Council Tax (Alteration of Lists and Appeals) Amendment Regulations 1994.]

S, a listing officer, appealed against a determination of the London (Northwest) Valuation Tribunal in relation to D and five joined cases. The issue was the same in all the cases. The tribunal had determined that, when D's council tax valuation band was altered, the alteration took effect from April 1, 1994, when the Council Tax (Alteration of Lists and Appeals) Amendment Regulations 1994 took effect. S argued that the alteration should be backdated with reference to the Council Tax (Alteration of Lists and Appeals) Regulations 1993 as the 1994 Regulations were not in force when notice of the alterations was given.

Held, allowing the appeals, that there was a presumption against giving retrospective effect to legislation, *Secretary of State for Social Security v. Tunnicliffe* [1991] 2 All E.R. 712, [1991] C.L.Y. 3351 followed. There was nothing in the 1994 legislation to rebut such a presumption and in fact the legislation appeared to say otherwise.

SIMMONDS v. DOWTY; KEITH CLIFFORD SIMMONDS v. HEXTER; KEITH CLIFFORD SIMMONDS v. RICHARDSON; KEITH CLIFFORD SIMMONDS v. HOULT; KEITH CLIFFORD SIMMONDS v. MACE; KEITH CLIFFORD SIMMONDS v. SPRIGGS, Trans. Ref: CO/1696/95, February 26, 1996, Jowitt, J., QBD.

4882. Council tax–arrears–income support deductions

COUNCIL TAX (DEDUCTIONS FROM INCOME SUPPORT) REGULATIONS 1993 AMENDMENT ORDER 1996, SI 1996 712; made under the Local Government etc. (Scotland) Act 1994 s.181. In force: April 1, 1996; £0.65.

The Council Tax (Deductions from Income Support) Regulations 1993 Reg.3 makes provision whereby, in Scotland, arrears of council tax and water charges may be recovered by deductions from income support. From April 1, 1996 local authorities in Scotland will cease to be water authorities, their functions in that respect being taken over by new authorities established by the Local Government etc (Scotland) Act 1994. However, by virtue of an Order made under s.79 of that Act, local authorities will continue for the time being to collect water charges on behalf of the new authorities. This Order amends the 1993 Regulations so as to enable arrears of water charges to continue to be recoverable by means of deductions from income support.

4883. Council tax–demand notices–Wales

COUNCIL TAX (DEMAND NOTICES) (WALES) (AMENDMENT) REGULATIONS 1996, SI 1996 310; made under the Local Government Finance Act 1992 s.113, s.116, Sch.2 para.1, Sch.2 para.2, Sch.2 para.14. In force: March 11, 1996; £1.10.

The Local Government (Wales) Act 1994 (c.19) makes provision for local government reorganisation in Wales. These Regulations amend the Council Tax (Demand Notices) (Wales) Regulations 1993 to allow for changes resulting from local government reorganisation. Regulation 2 makes amendments to show the fact that from April 1, 1996 the only major precepting authorities in Wales will be police authorities. Regulation 3 takes account of the fact that before April 1, 1996 new billing authorities will not have a valuation list, and that the requirements to supply, with demand notices, certain information relating to the previous year, will be inappropriate in the new billing authorities' first year. Regulation 3 also makes provision for demand notices relating to the financial year 1996/97 to include information as to the effect (where applicable) of the council tax reduction scheme for that year.

4884. Council tax–discounts

COUNCIL TAX (ADDITIONAL PROVISIONS FOR DISCOUNT DISREGARDS) AMENDMENT ORDER 1996, SI 1996 637; made under the Local Government Finance Act 1992 Sch.1 para.9. In force: April 1, 1996; £0.65.

Under the Local Government Finance Act 1992 Part 1 the amount payable for council tax is reduced where a person resident in a dwelling falls to be disregarded for discount. Schedule 1 to the 1992 Act provides for classes of persons to qualify for the purpose of discount. The Council Tax (Additional Provisions for Discount Disregards) Regulations 1992 make additional provisions in relation to certain of those classes. These Regulations amend the provision to permit the disregard of care workers where they provide care for a person entitled to one of the benefits specified in the 1992 Regulations; under the existing Regulations the person must be in receipt of such a benefit.

4885. Council tax–discounts

COUNCIL TAX (DISCOUNT DISREGARDS) AMENDMENT ORDER 1996, SI 1996 636; made under the Local Government Finance Act 1992 s.113, Sch.1 para.2, Sch.1 para.4. In force: April 1, 1996; £0.65.

Under the Local Government Finance Act 1992 Part I the amount payable for council tax is reduced where a person resident in a dwelling falls to be disregarded for the purposes of discount. Schedule 1 to the 1992 Act provides for classes of persons to qualify for the purpose of discount. The Council Tax (Discount Disregards) Order 1992 makes further provision in relation to certain of those classes. The amendments in Art.2(2) and Art.2(3) of this Order ensure that severely mentally impaired people eligible for certain benefits do not cease to be disregarded when they reach retirement age. The amendment in Art.2(4) provides that a severely mentally impaired person is disregarded if in receipt of incapacity benefit. The amendment in Art.2(5) enables students to qualify even during a period when they are not attending the course.

4886. Council tax–discounts

COUNCIL TAX (DISCOUNT DISREGARDS) (AMENDMENT) (NO.2) ORDER 1996, SI 1996 3143; made under the Local Government Finance Act 1992 s.113, Sch.1 para.2, Sch.1 para.4. In force: January 8, 1997; £0.65.

The amount of council tax payable under the Local Government Finance Act 1992 Part I is reduced where a person resident in a dwelling falls to be disregarded for the purposes of discount. Schedule 1 to the Act provides for classes of persons to qualify for the purposes of discount, and the Council Tax (Discount Disregards) Order 1992 (SI 1992 548) makes further provision in relation to certain of those classes. This Order amends the 1992 Order so that a person who is the partner of a jobseeker whose jobseeker's allowance is increased on grounds of that person's incapacity for work may qualify for the purposes of the discount.

4887. Council tax–floating home–definition of "dwelling"–and "hereditament"

[Local Government Finance Act 1992 s.1, s.3; General Rate Act 1967 s.115.]

N appealed against the determination of W that council tax was payable on his dwelling. N claimed the property in question was a floating home and was not a boat since it had no means of propulsion. No such premises were mentioned in legislation and, accordingly, it was not subject to council tax. N also argued that the home was a chattel and not real property. W held that the disputed premises fell within the definition of "dwelling" as defined by the Local Government Finance Act 1992 s.1 in respect of which rates must be paid under the Local Government Finance Act 1992 s.3(2) and that the dwelling which N occupied was liable to tax as it fell within the definition of a "hereditament" as defined by the General Rate Act 1967 s.115.

Held, dismissing the appeal, that (1) whether the home was a chattel or real property was not a determining factor under s.115 of the 1967 Act, and (2) this was an issue of fact and W had reached the correct decision according to the points of law raised.

NICHOLLS v. WIMBLEDON VALUATION OFFICE AGENCY [1995] R.V.R 171, Buxton, J., QBD.

4888. Council tax–limits

COUNCIL TAX LIMITATION (ENGLAND) (MAXIMUM AMOUNTS) ORDER 1996, SI 1996 1371; made under the Local Government Finance Act 1992 s.57. In force: May 23, 1996; £0.65.

This order states the amount which the amount calculated by each of the councils named in the Schedule as its budget requirement for the financial year beginning in 1996 is not to exceed.

4889. Council tax–non-domestic rates–demand notices

COUNCIL TAX AND NON-DOMESTIC RATING (DEMAND NOTICES) (ENGLAND) AMENDMENT REGULATIONS 1996, SI 1996 504; made under the Local Government Finance Act 1988 s.143, Sch.9 para.1, Sch.9 para.2; and the Local Government Finance Act 1992 s.113, Sch.2 para.1, Sch.2 para.2, Sch.2 para.14. In force: March 27, 1996; £0.65.

These Regulations amend the Council Tax and Non Domestic Rating (Demand Notices) (England) Regulations 1993 (SI 1993 191) in order to take account of the establishment of new police authorities under the Police Act 1964 s.3. Transitional modifications relate to the council tax demand notices served by billing authorities and to non domestic rating demand notices for the financial year 1996/7.

4890. Council tax–valuation–conversion of two separate dwellings into single unit

[Council Tax (Alteration of Lists and Appeals) Regulations 1993 Reg.4; Council Tax (Situation and Valuation of Dwellings) Regulations 1992.]

S, who had converted two flats into a single dwelling and applied for the council tax valuation list to be altered so as to have the property valued as a single unit, sought judicial review of a valuation tribunal's decision that the property was rightly placed in a higher band.

Held, dismissing the application, that the single dwelling was to be treated as a new dwelling for council tax valuation purposes. Valuation was made by reference to certain irrebuttable assumptions under the Council Tax (Situation and Valuation of Dwellings) Regulations 1992 to achieve uniformity, and reference to the precise facts of individual cases was not permitted. S's claim that a reduction in valuation was justified because of the demolition of some internal walls during conversion could not be supported, because the Council Tax (Alteration of Lists and Appeals) Regulations 1993 Reg.4 was only relevant where demolition work had reduced the value of a dwelling which was already on the valuation list.

R. v. EAST SUSSEX VALUATION TRIBUNAL, *ex p.* SILVERSTONE [1996] 36 R.V.R. 203, Carnwath, J., QBD.

4891. Council tax–valuation–whether the whole composite hereditament had to be valued before the value of the dwelling portion could be ascertained–statutory interpretation

[Council Tax (Situation and Valuation of Dwellings) Regulations 1992 Reg.7.]

A and five others appealed against decisions of C in respect of valuations of part of a composite hereditament for the purposes of council tax. A hereditament was composite if only part of it amounted to domestic property. In this case the properties were farmhouses and the composite hereditament was the farm as a whole. The question of construction was whether the composite hereditament had to be valued before the value of the dwelling part of it could be ascertained. A argued that it had to be valued under the requirements of the Council Tax (Situation and Valuation of Dwellings) Regulations 1992 Reg.7 and, because it was not, the valuation was fatally flawed. The Regulations required the dwelling to be taken as the "portion of the relevant amount" reasonably attributed to it. A argued that the whole hereditament had to be valued in order for the portion to be ascertained by deducting the value of all the property apart from the dwelling, ie. the residual approach.

Held, dismissing the appeals, that (1) it was not necessary to value the whole before the value of a portion could be ascertained. The word "portion" did not require such an approach although to ascertain the "proportion" of the whole, the whole would need to be valued first. A monetary figure had to be determined rather than a proportion or a percentage, and (2) the residual approach would be cumbersome and time consuming in valuations for other composite hereditaments which would otherwise be straightforward, eg. a farm worker's cottage on a large farm amounting to a small percentage of the valuation of the whole.

ATKINSON v. CUMBRIA VALUATION TRIBUNAL; RICHARDSON v. CUMBRIA VALUATION TRIBUNAL; RANDALLS v. CUMBRIA VALUATION TRIBUNAL; DOBSON v. CUMBRIA VALUATION TRIBUNAL; PARK v. CUMBRIA VALUATION TRIBUNAL; WILSON v. CUMBRIA VALUATION TRIBUNAL [1996] R.A. 422, Jowitt, J., QBD.

4892. Distress–irregular levy of goods–compensation under Reg.15(3) of the 1989 Regulations–method of valuation by magistrates

[Non-Domestic Rating (Collection and Enforcement) (Local List) Regulations 1989 Reg.15.]

H and L sought judicial review of an order made in relation to the irregular levy of goods belonging to them. Distraint was mistakenly levied on various hand tools owned by H and a DAF skip unit owned by L. H and L objected to the amount of compensation awarded under the Non-Domestic Rating (Collection and Enforcement) (Local List) Regulations 1989 Reg.15(3) by the magistrates. The applicants criticised the adequacy of the evidence relied upon by the magistrates to assess compensation and the level of compensation.

Held, allowing the application, that the method used by the magistrates to reach their valuation particularly of the skip was unexplained and appeared to be a guess. The magistrates had acted unreasonably as there was no evidence to justify the valuations. A rehearing of the claims for compensation was ordered.

R. v. EPPING MAGISTRATES' COURT, *ex p.* HOWARD, Trans. Ref: CO/379/94, April 18, 1996, Turner, J., QBD.

4893. Electricity supply industry–water industry

ELECTRICITY SUPPLY INDUSTRY AND WATER UNDERTAKERS (RATEABLE VALUES) AMENDMENT ORDER 1996, SI 1996 912; made under the Local Government Finance Act 1988 s.140, s.143, Sch.6 para.3. In force: March 31, 1996; £1.10.

Under the Local Government Finance Act 1988 Sch.6 para.3(2), the Secretary of State may by order provide that, in the case of non-domestic hereditaments to be shown in the central rating lists for England and Wales (central list hereditaments), the basis of valuation contained in Sch.6 para.2 to para.2B shall not apply, and that instead their rateable value shall be such as is specified or determined in accordance with rules set out in the Order. The Electricity Supply Industry (Rateable Values) Order 1994 (SI 1994 3282) (as amended by SI 1995 962) prescribes rateable values for electricity generation, transmission and supply hereditaments. This Order amends it to reflect changes taking place in the electricity industry and the coming into existence on March 31, 1996 of AGR & PWR Co Ltd. The Water Undertakers (Rateable Values) Order 1994 (SI 1994 3285) prescribes rateable values for water supply hereditaments. This Order alters the value of the hereditaments occupied by Bournemouth and West Hampshire Water Plc on April 1, 1996.

4894. Liability–validity of liability orders for non-payment of non-domestic rates–whether applicant was a rateable occupier

[Non-Domestic Rating (Collection and Enforcement) (Local Lists) Regulations 1989 Reg.13; Local Government Finance Act 1988 s.43.]

S sought leave, out of time, to apply for judicial review of liability orders made by WJ relating to non-payment of non-domestic rates in respect of a business run by his wife from whom he had since separated. He had received summonses for his committal to prison for the non-payment and attended a hearing before WJ who told him that they could not review the liability orders. The application was out of time as S was unaware that the orders had been made until he was told at the hearing. S argued that the application should be allowed due to the prejudice caused to him by facing imprisonment if he did not pay a debt for which he was not liable. His case was that his name was on the lease of the premises, but he did not occupy them. The liability orders were not effectively served on him as required by the Non-Domestic Rating (Collection and Enforcement) (Local Lists) Regulations 1989 Reg.13(2) and the notices prior to the liability orders were not served upon him.

Held, allowing the application, that S was not a rateable occupier of the premises under the Local Government Finance Act 1988 s.43 and the liability orders should be set aside.

R. v. WARRINGTON JUSTICES, *ex p.* SHONE (1996) 72 P. & C.R. D7, Brooke, J., QBD.

4895. Moveable dwellings–chalets–domestic property

Held, that chalets used as holiday homes delivered to freehold plots ready assembled or almost ready assembled were properly removed from the non-domestic rating list since they were not caravans but domestic property.

ATKINSON (VALUATION OFFICER) v. FOSTER [1996] R.A. 246, AP Musto, FRICS., Lands Tr.

4896. Non-domestic rates

NON DOMESTIC RATING (DEMAND NOTICES) (WALES) (AMENDMENT) REGULATIONS 1996, SI 1996 311; made under the Local Government Finance Act 1988 s.140, s.143, s.146, Sch.9 para.1, Sch.9 para.2, Sch.9 para.6A; and the Welsh Language Act 1993 s.26. In force: March 11, 1996; £1.10.

The Local Government (Wales) Act 1995 makes provision for local government reorganisation in Wales. These Regulations amend the Non Domestic Rating (Demand Notices) (Wales) Regulations 1993 (SI 1993 252) to take account of the changes resulting from local government reorganisation. In particular, as from April 1, 1996 the only major precepting authorities in Wales will be police authorities, and that the requirements to supply, with demand notices, certain information relating to the previous year, will be inappropriate in the new authorities' first year.

4897. Non-domestic rates–chargeable amounts

NON DOMESTIC RATING (CHARGEABLE AMOUNTS) (AMENDMENT) REGULATIONS 1996, SI 1996 911; made under the Local Government Finance Act 1988 s.58, s.143. In force: April 1, 1996; £1.55.

These Regulations amend the Non Domestic Rating (Chargeable Amounts) Regulations 1994 (SI 1994 3279) which made provision for the five year period beginning on April 1, 1995 in relation to non domestic rates under the Local Government Finance Act 1988 Part III as to the chargeable amount for which a ratepayer is liable in certain circumstances. These Regulations amend the 1994 Regulations by introducing new rules for the determination of the chargeable amount where a hereditament has split or merged after the start of the five year period. An interested person has the option of applying to the appropriate valuation officer for him to certify the value which the new hereditament would have had on March 31, 1995; that value is important in determining the chargeable amount.

Regulation 2(8) and Reg.2(14) introduce a new Regulation and Schedule to provide for this. The Regulations also amend the 1994 Regulations to ensure that where the chargeable amount for a hereditament was not previously determined under those Regulations it will not subsequently fall to be determined under those Regulations.

4898. Non-domestic rates–chargeable amounts

NON-DOMESTIC RATING (CHARGEABLE AMOUNTS FOR SMALL HEREDITAMENTS) REGULATIONS 1996, SI 1996 3214; made under the Local Government Finance Act 1988 s.58, s.143. In force: December 20, 1996; £1.10.

These Regulations make amendments to the Non-Domestic Rating (Chargeable Amounts) Regulations 1994 (SI 1994 3279) which made provision for the five year period beginning on April 1, 1995 in relation to non-domestic rates under the Local Government Finance Act 1988 Part III as to the chargeable amount for which a ratepayer is liable in certain circumstances. The effect of the amendments is to bring about for 1997/8 a freeze or a further reduction in the chargeable amount payable in respect of hereditaments to which those Regulations apply for which the rateable value is below a certain level. They make consequential changes to the 1994 Regulations to deal with small hereditaments the value of which alters during the remainder of the relevant period and add a new Part VII to the 1994 Regulations which specifies an additional category of hereditaments for which those Regulations will have effect for finding the chargeable amount.

4899. Non-domestic rates–contributions

NON-DOMESTIC RATING CONTRIBUTIONS (ENGLAND) (AMENDMENT) REGULATIONS 1996, SI 1996 561; made under the Local Government Finance Act 1988 s.140, s.143, Sch.8 para.6. In force: March 27, 1996; £0.65.

The Non-Domestic Rating Contributions (England) Regulations 1992 contain rules for the calculation of the non-domestic rating contributions required to be made by the English billing authorities to the Secretary of State under the Local Government Finance Act 1988 Sch.8 Part.II. Regulation 6 of the 1992 Regulations provides that where prescribed conditions are fulfilled the provisional amount of an authority's contributions may be recalculated. Regulation 2 of these Regulations amends Reg.6 by inserting a condition that notification of a recalculation, which is accepted by the Secretary of State, can be given only once in each three month period.

4900. Non-domestic rates–contributions

NON-DOMESTIC RATING CONTRIBUTIONS (ENGLAND) (AMENDMENT) (NO.2) REGULATIONS 1996, SI 1996 3245; made under the Local Government Finance Act 1988 s.140, s.143, Sch.8 para.4, Sch.8 para.6. In force: December 31, 1996; £1.10.

These Regulations amend the rules for calculation of contributions contained in the Non-Domestic Rating Contributions (England) Regulations 1992 (SI 1992 3082) with effect from 1997/98. They alter certain figures used in the calculation of contributions and provisional amounts.

4901. Non-domestic rates–contributions–Wales

NON-DOMESTIC RATING CONTRIBUTIONS (WALES) (AMENDMENT) REGULATIONS 1996, SI 1996 3018; made under the Local Government Finance Act 1988 s.140, s.143, Sch.8 para.4, Sch.8 para.6. In force: December 31, 1996; £1.10.

Under the Local Government Finance Act 1988 Sch.8 Part II, billing authorities are required to pay non-domestic rating contributions to the Secretary of State. Provisional amounts are paid during the year, final calculations and payments being made after the year ends. They are calculated in accordance with the Non-Domestic Rating Contributions (Wales) Regulations 1992 (SI 1992 3238). These

Regulations which apply to Wales make various technical amendments to the 1992 Regulations for financial years beginning with 1997/98.

4902. Non-domestic rates–disabled persons–workshop adjacent to house–exemption requirements

Held, that a workshop used by a disabled person for the purposes of his business and attached to his dwelling was not exempt from non-domestic rates since it was not an hereditament provided by him for the provision of facilities for the training or suitable occupation of disabled persons.

O'KELLY v. DAVEY (VALUATION OFFICER) [1996] R.A. 238, Judge Rich, Q.C., Lands Tr.

4903. Non-domestic rates–floating hotel moored to area of land–proposal failing to give valid description of hereditament

Held, that a two storey hotel floating on pontoons which was moored to an area of land used for guest car parking, was a chattel for rating purposes and not a hereditament.

FLOATELS (UK) LTD v. PERRIN (VALUATION OFFICER) [1995] R.A. 326, JC Hill, TD, FRICS., Lands Tr.

4904. Non-domestic rates–non-payment–three months' imprisonment–no remission available

G applied for judicial review of his sentence of three months' imprisonment for a finding of culpable neglect in respect of the payment of business rates. The sentence was postponed provided G paid £50 per week. The sentence was passed following evidence by way of a means enquiry which G contended was procedurally flawed.

Held, allowing the appeal, that the magistrates had not been aware that there was no remission in cases of this kind and G would have had to serve the full three months. A sentence of 21 days was one which the magistrates would probably have wanted to impose.

R. v. THAMES MAGISTRATES' COURT, *ex p.* GRANT, Trans. Ref: CO/711/95, November 9, 1995, Macpherson of Cluny, J., QBD.

4905. Non-domestic rates–possession of premises let as storage units–liability for rates where some units unlet

[General Rate Act 1967 s.16.]

H appealed against the dismissal of his appeal by way of case stated from the magistrates' decision to issue a distress warrant in respect of unpaid business rates. The premises concerned were operated by H as self-contained storage units let on conventional terms and separated into seven individual sections for rating purposes. H contended that no liability arose over four of the sections which, for various reasons, remained unlet for the whole or part of the period in question. The local authority successfully contended that H was liable as he had a continuing intention to use those areas within the main business and that amounted to rateable occupation within the General Rate Act 1967 s.16.

Held, allowing the appeal, that possession of premises did not equate with occupation for rating purposes. Before liability for business rates could be established, there had to be actual occupation or possession which was exclusive for the purposes of the occupier, and the possession, which had to be more than transient, must provide some value or benefit to the possessor, *Ryde on Rating and the Council Tax* (Issue 0, Vol.1, section B at para.61) and *Arbuckle Smith & Co Ltd v. Greenock Corp* [1960] A.C. 813, [1960] C.L.Y. 2677 considered.

HAMPSON (T/A ABBEY SELF STORAGE) v. NEWCASTLE UPON TYNE CITY COUNCIL [1996] R.A. 325, Roch, L.J., CA.

4906. Non-domestic rates–proposal applied to wrong premises–construction of the proposal

A valuation officer misunderstood a ratepayer's proposal concerning a cold storage depot and had applied the proposal to another property in the valuation list. The ratepayer appealed.

Held, allowing the appeal, that the proposal was to be construed according to the ordinary principles of construction. An informed reader with local knowledge would have identified the premises as those intended by the ratepayer.

EXEL LOGISTICS LTD v. OLIVER (VALUATION OFFICER) [1995] R.A. 336, AP Musto, FRICS., Lands Tr.

4907. Non-domestic rates–rateable value of shop in listed building–factors considered for deductions

K appealed against the assessment of the rateable value of shop premises in a listed building situated in a conservation area during and following building works.

Held, dismissing the appeal, that on the evidence deductions should not be made for repairs, security and a divided sales area. The onerous repair obligations of a listed building would be met by a tenant who would reduce the rent to meet the obligations. Additionally, the age and status of the building could attract tenants. The loss of a security gate did not affect security which was improved by the new houses.

KIRKHAM v. CANT (VALUATION OFFICER) [1995] R.A. 372, PH Clarke, FRICS., Lands Tr.

4908. Non-domestic rates–reduction–council entitled to have details of solicitor's personal assets

[Local Government Finance Act 1988 s.49.]

Held, that where a solicitor, establishing a business as a sole practitioner, sought a reduction in her non-domestic rates, the local authority was entitled to require her to provide details of her personal assets in order to determine whether she was suffering hardship in terms of the Local Government Finance Act 1988 s.49(2).

R. v. BIRMINGHAM CITY COUNCIL, *ex p.* MUSHTAQ, *The Independent*, January 1, 1996 (C.S.), Dyson, J., QBD.

4909. Non-domestic rates–show houses owned by development company–whether rateable as non-domestic hereditaments–four requirements of rateable occupation

I, a property development company, owned a number of show houses on larger sites. W appealed against a tribunal's decision to delete the houses from the rating list.

Held, allowing the appeal, that the houses were rateable as non-domestic hereditaments as they fulfilled the four requirements of rateable occupation. These were (1) actual occupation; (2) exclusive occupation; (3) that the occupation was of some benefit to the occupier and (4) the occupation for commercial activities was not transient, having a degree of permanence necessary to I's sales operation.

WALKER (VALUATION OFFICER) v. IDEAL HOMES CENTRAL LTD [1995] R.A. 347, AP Musto, FRICS., Lands Tr.

4910. Non-domestic rates–use of house for conduct of business–effect on hereditament

Held, that where a ratepayer whose house was used by him in the conduct of his profession so that one room was used mainly for his business and another partly so, and where he had no other place of practice, the degree of business user was one which turned the premises into a composite hereditament and was validly entered in a rating list as non-domestic property.

FOTHERINGHAM v. WOOD (VALUATION OFFICER) [1995] R.A. 315, PH Clarke, FRICS., Lands Tr.

4911. Non-domestic rates–valuation–cash and carry warehouse–rateable value

Held, that a wholesale cash and carry warehouse in Leeds was assessed at a total of £329,000 rateable value, made up mostly as to two main warehouse areas which were assessed at £19 and £7 per square metre with an added two and a half per cent for the sprinkler system.

MAKRO SELF SERVICE WHOLESALERS LTD v. BRENNAN (VALUATION OFFICER) [1996] R.A. 341, M St J Hopper, FRICS., Lands Tr.

4912. Non-domestic rates–whether units used partially by disabled persons qualified for exemption

[Local Government Finance Act 1988.]

D owned holiday accommodation units which had been designed and adapted for use by physically handicapped people. The units were let out to disabled guests but also to able bodied people. The valuation tribunal held that the units were exempt from non-domestic rates by virtue of the Local Government Finance Act 1988 and deleted them from the valuation list. The valuation officer appealed against the decision on the ground that the units were not "used wholly" to provide facilities for disabled people as they were also let to able bodied people both when accompanying disabled holidaymakers and in their own right.

Held, allowing the appeal, that the property should be returned to the non-domestic rating list as the units could not be said to be "used wholly" for physically disabled people. Where the units were let to disabled people, it was D's policy that they had to have an able bodied person with them. Therefore, the property could not justifiably be said to be used exclusively by disabled people and an exemption could not be granted. The units were restored to the valuation list with a rateable value of £1,875.

CHILCOTT (VALUATION OFFICER) v. DAY [1995] R.A. 285, Judge Marder, Q.C. (President), Lands Tr.

4913. Non-Domestic Rating (Information) Act 1996 (c.13)

An Act to make provision for and in connection with the disclosure by persons who are valuation officers or assessors to other such persons of information connected with non-domestic rating.

This Act received Royal Assent on May 22, 1996.

4914. Railways–premises–space within railway arch forming separate hereditament for rate valuation purposes

Held, that premises situated within and enclosed by a railway arch formed an hereditament separate from the arch structure and were entered on the rating list with a rateable value of £3,020. The tenant undertook to maintain and repair the space within the arch, with repairs to the archway structure itself being unrelated to the hereditament by virtue of the essential purpose of the structure to the lessor's operational function.

HEADINGS (VALUATION OFFICER) v. BRITISH RAILWAYS PROPERTY BOARD [1996] R.A. 144, JC Hill, TD, FRICS., Lands Tr.

4915. Rating (Caravans and Boats) Act 1996 (c.12)

An Act to make provision about liability for non-domestic rates in England and Wales in relation to certain caravans and boats.

This Act received Royal Assent on April 29, 1996.

4916. Receivers–agents for company–liability for non domestic rates of unoccupied property

[Local Government Finance Act 1988 s.65; Law of Property Act 1925 s.109; Companies Act 1985 s.458.]

In 1989 two Dutch companies, financed by a syndicate of banks including Long Term Credit Bank of Japan Ltd, LTCB, bought the freehold of two office blocks in the City of London. The loans were secured by debentures under which the LTCB, as trustee of the banks, could appoint receivers to exercise powers on behalf of and in the name of the company which was the absolute owner. Clause 14.04 of the debenture deed empowered the receivers to take possession of, collect and get in the charged property, and cl.14.07 provided that every receiver so appointed shall be deemed at all times and for all purposes to be the agent of the company. Receivers were appointed under the terms of the debenture by LTCB in 1993. For rating purposes, the properties became unoccupied on November 21, 1993. The properties were sold by the receivers in February 1995. The City of London Council claimed that the receivers were liable for unpaid rates during the period of the receivership, amounting to approximately £3.5 million. LTCB issued a summons for directions, seeking a determination of the following issues: (1) whether the receivers were persons "entitled to possession of" the properties for the purposes of the Local Government Finance Act 1988 s.65(1); (2) whether the receivers were under an obligation to pay the rates by virtue of cl.14.06 of the debenture and the Law of Property Act 1925 s.109(8); (3) whether the rates were payable as an expense of the receivership, and (4) whether the court should direct the receivers to pay the rates because otherwise they would or might incur liability for fraudulent trading?

Held, answering the questions in the negative, that (1) the general principle of rating law, as stated in *Ratford v. Northavon DC* [1987] Q.B. 357, [1986] C.L.Y. 2813, was that the possession of an agent was to be attributed to his principal and by parity of reasoning, entitlement to possession, the touchstone of liability for unoccupied rates under s.65(1) of the 1988 Act was also attributed to the principal. Following the *Ratford* case the receiver is not, by reason only of his appointment, liable for unoccupied property rates where he was appointed as the agent of the company. The fact that he had "power to act on his own behalf" had no effect until he exercised such power, *Banister v. Islington LBC* (1972) 71 L.G.R. 239, [1973] C.L.Y. 2764 distinguished; (2) there was no policy reason which required the receivers to exercise their discretion under the Law of Property Act 1925 s.109(8) in favour of the council. The obligation to pay rates arose out of the acquisition by the company of property prior to receivership and in that respect was similar to the obligation to pay rates. The law did not regard the conduct of an administrative receiver who per se did not pay rent which accrued after his appointment as unfair or unjust *Atlantic Computer Systems Plc, Re* [1992] Ch. 505, [1991] C.L.Y. 2127 followed. *Sargent v. Customs and Excise Commissioners* [1995] 1 W.L.R. 821, [1995] 2 C.L.Y. 5106 distinguished; (3) rates accruing after the appointment of the receiver for property previously acquired by the company were not payable by the receiver as an expense of the receivership, and (4) there was no intent to defraud by the receivers contrary to the Companies Act 1985 s.458. The receivers' decision to postpone the sale of the properties did not deprive the council of its right to have recourse against the assets of the companies and there was no suggestion that the receivers, in postponing the sale, did not act in the proper performance of their duties or dishonestly took a risk which they were not entitled to take.

BROWN v. CITY OF LONDON CORP [1996] 1 W.L.R. 1070, Arden, J., Ch D.

4917. Receivers–liability for non-domestic rates of unoccupied property

[Finance Act 1988 s.65; Law of Property Act 1925 s.109; Companies Act 1985 s.458.]

Receivers applied for a determination as to whether they were liable to pay £3.5 million in respect of unpaid non-domestic unoccupied property rates. The receivers were appointed by trustees acting under powers given in debentures issued in order to finance the purchase of the freehold of two office blocks. The trustees undertook the responsibility for all costs associated with the running and disposal of the properties. The trustees sold the properties but they had been unoccupied for rating purposes since the appointment of receivers. The receivers argued that they were not persons "entitled to the possession of" the properties under the Local Government and Finance Act 1988 s.65(1). They also argued that the terms of the debentures did not require them to pay the rates and neither did the Law of Property Act 1925 s.109(8).

Held, that (1) the receivers were agents for the company and therefore not liable for unoccupied property rates by reason of their appointment alone, *Ratford v. Northavon DC* [1986] 1 Q.B. 357, [1986] C.L.Y. 2813 applied; (2) the receivers were not under an obligation to pay rates under the terms of the debentures as no funds had been paid to the receivers by third parties on the faith that the receivers would account for them to the authority. The obligation to pay rates was due to the acquisition by the company of the property prior to receivership. No policy required receivers to exercise their discretion under s.109(8); (3) the receivers were not bound to pay the rates as an expense of the receivership and (4) the receivers had no authority to pay unsecured debts and there was no intent to defraud and therefore no liability under the Companies Act 1985 s.458 for fraudulent trading.

SOBAM BV, *Re*; SUB NOM. SATELSCOOP BV, *Re* [1996] 1 B.C.L.C. 446, Arden, J., Ch D.

4918. Valuation–domestic property–council tax bands–tribunal's findings of fact unappealable

[Local Government Finance Act 1988 Sch.11.]

R appealed, under the Local Government Finance Act 1988 Sch.11 para.11 (1) (a), against a decision of the Hampshire South Valuation Tribunal on a question of whether his residence was within band G or F for council tax purposes. It was R's case that the tribunal had been misled as to the measurements of the appeal property and the value of the properties with which comparisons were made were not true comparators.

Held, dismissing the appeal, that there were no grounds for interfering with the tribunal's findings of fact. All the arguments had been heard, there had been no misdirection and the decision was neither irrational nor perverse. The tribunal had not been misled and had taken account of the better amenities enjoyed by the owners of some of the properties the respondents had relied on as comparators.

RIGBY v. FRANKS (VALUATION OFFICER), Trans. Ref: CO/1507/95, December 8, 1995, Popplewell, J., QBD.

4919. Valuation–electricity industry

CENTRAL RATING LISTS (AMENDMENT) REGULATIONS 1996, SI 1996 620; made under the Local Government Finance Act 1988 s.53, s.140, s.143. In force: March 31, 1996; £0.65.

These Regulations amend the Central Rating Lists Regulations 1994 (SI 1994 3121) which, among other things, designate persons and prescribe in relation to such persons descriptions of hereditaments, with a view to securing the central rating en bloc of those hereditaments. These Regulations, in consequence of changes taking place in the electricity industry on March 31, 1996, designate for England, AGR & PWR Co Ltd which will own certain electricity hereditaments from that date. These Regulations make changes to those 1994 Regulations to reflect the mergers of certain water undertakers.

4920. Valuation–local authority car parks–choice of applicable comparables

Held, that 13 public car parks owned or operated by W were assessed at rateable values between £45 and £110 per space, based on comparables including occupancy levels, parking charges and the presence of nearby offices, shops and railways, along with the incidence of vandalism, the facilities provided at each site and the availability of local on street parking,

WALTHAM FOREST LBC v. ANDREWS (VALUATION OFFICER) [1996] R.A. 155, AP Musto, FRICS., LandsTr.

4921. Valuation–office premises–discount for deficiency in the number of lifts

Held, that office premises in Aldershot amounting to a total of 8,013 square metres, of which 7,770 square metres was main space, were assessed at £63 per square metre for main space after making an overall allowance of 12 per cent to allow for a discount for size and a small allowance for a deficiency in the number of lifts although the latter had already formed part of the quality assessment.

BRITISH TELECOMMUNICATIONS PLC v. BROADWAY (VALUATION OFFICER) (NO.2) [1996] R.A. 297, T Hoyes, FRICS., LandsTr.

4922. Valuation–premises–shop premises used as office–valued on open market basis for shop use

Held, that shop premises in East Ham, London, which were used as an office, fell to be assessed on the basis of the value of the premises in the open letting market, which included possible use as a shop, and accordingly, were assessed at a rateable value of £4,600 based on shop use rather than £2,900 which was the applicable value for office use.

IRVING BROWN & DAUGHTER v. SMITH (VALUATION OFFICER) [1996] 2 E.G.L.R. 183, PH Clarke, FRICS., LandsTr.

4923. Valuation–premises part used for bed and breakfast business–balance of probabilities showed domestic ratings provisions complied with for part of period

[Local Government Finance Act 1988 s.66.]

Held, that an hereditament in Llandudno used in part for bed and breakfast business was assessed to non-domestic rates for 1990/91 and to domestic rates for 1991/92 because the ratepayer had shown on a balance of probability that he had arranged his affairs so as to avoid more than six persons staying at any one time, as provided under the Local Government Finance Act 1988 s.66(2).

HODKINSON v. HUMPHREYS-JONES (VALUATION OFFICER) [1996] R.A. 69, Judge Marder, Q.C. (President), LandsTr.

4924. Valuation–public lavatories in shopping centre–basis of valuation

Held, that public lavatories in a shopping centre were properly entered in the rating list but should have been assessed at £1 since there was no hypothetical tenant other than the owner.

HODGKINSON (VALUATION OFFICER) v. STRATHCLYDE REGIONAL COUNCIL SUPERANNUATION FUND [1996] R.A. 129, Judge Rich, Q.C., LandsTr.

4925. Valuation–quantity allowance

Held, that the ratepayer failed to provide sufficient evidence to show that there should be discount or end allowance for quantity in respect of a building of 6,528 square metres situated in a business park, and being considerably larger than any other hereditament on the site.

BRITISH TELECOMMUNICATIONS PLC v. BROADWAY (VALUATION OFFICER) [1996] R.A. 272, JC Hill, TD, FRICS., LandsTr.

4926. Valuation–quarry–rate for processed material–differential for other materials

Held, in the assessment of the rateable value of a quarry, taking into account the comparables, the rate for processed materials had to be increased. In addition, the other materials should have a differential royalty of 50 per cent in line with past practice, as there was no evidence to disturb such a valuation.

HODGKINSON (VALUATION OFFICER) v. ARC LTD [1996] R.A. 1, Judge Marder, Q.C. (President), LandsTr.

4927. Valuation–solicitor's office in residential area–reduced value

Held, that the agreed value of solicitors offices in Islington, north London, was reduced by 2.5 per cent to reflect the personal nature of the permission for office use in a residential area.

OLDSCHOOL v. COLL (VALUATION OFFICER) [1996] R.A. 265, Judge Rich, Q.C., LandsTr.

4928. Articles

Improving the system–the Bayliss report *(Dennis Mabey)*: E.G. 1996, 9610, 154-156. (Terms of reference and recommendations of Bayliss Committee regarding business rating system).

Phasing: fudge or farce *(David Vestergaard)*: S.J. 1996, 140(34), 873. (Practical impact of SI 1994 3279, brought in with 1995 rating re-valuation).

Rates in company receivership: new answers for old questions? *(Gabriel Moss)*: Insolv. Int. 1996, 9(3), 17-19. (Receiver's liability for business rates including position while in occupation as agent of company and liability for unoccupied property rates).

Relief measures still hamper rating: E.G. 1996, 9620, Supp OT 82-84. (Criticism of transitional relief on business rates which has distorted UK's rating system and created two tier market in London).

REAL PROPERTY

4929. Adverse possession–factors to be taken into account

B brought an action to recover possession of a parcel of land adjacent to C's rented home which was registered in B's name. C claimed title by adverse possession as he had enjoyed at least 12 years' adverse possession of the land prior to the commencement of the action in 1994, having kept geese on the land for a period of two years, for which purpose he had erected a chestnut paling fence and subsequently he had dug a vegetable patch, stored and sawed wood on the land and was currently storing vehicles and plant. The court noted that the holder of the paper title is deemed to be in possession in the absence of contrary evidence. It was for the person seeking to establish adverse possession to produce contrary evidence which must be cogent and compelling evidence of a single degree of occupation and physical control of the land unimpeded by others, with the relevant animus possidendi and for a period of 12 years.

Held, that C had made use of the land as alleged, but that such use was not sufficient for C to maintain that the land had been in adverse possession for the requisite period. Although he had used the land at times after 1976, such use was neither consistent nor continuous until 1993, when C substantially cleared the land of trees and put it to its current use. Whilst in some cases the act of deliberate enclosure of land was unequivocal, here it was not, since the fencing was a short term practicality to contain the geese, such fencing being abandoned once the geese were removed. Furthermore, since C had made an enquiry of the local authority with a view to purchasing the land, he had recognised the superior rights of the paper owner, and could not establish that his use of the land was accompanied by the requisite animus. Accordingly, B were entitled to an order for possession.

BASILDON DC v. CHARGE, May 2, 1996, Recorder Ludlow, CC (Brentwood). [*Ex rel.* Kelvin Rutledge, Barrister].

4930. Agreements–developer with adjoining land–ramp built for access to road on plaintiff's land–construction of option agreement

N appealed against the dismissal of his claim against ME and an order to pay ME's costs. ME were developers of land adjoined N's land. The dispute concerned an option agreement between N and ME in relation to a road on the development. In return for a parcel of N's land ME were required, inter alia, to create a new entrance for N to give them access to their property via a new road. During construction, it became apparent that a larger ramp was needed than that described in the option. ME constructed it on N's land. N contended that it should have been constructed on ME's land.

Held, allowing the appeal, that (1) in finding in favour of ME, the Recorder had misconstrued a clause in the agreement which stated that N should make no "objection or hindrance to the Application". However, that clause related only to the period during which ME was seeking planning permission for the development, and before exercise of the option. The clause did not require N to submit to what amounted to trespass on his land and (2) the test of the officious bystander, to create an implied term into the agreement, was not satisfied. N would not, as a reasonable man, have agreed to the term when the agreement was created. The matter was remitted for assessment of damages.

NUNN v. MULBERRY ESTATES LTD, Trans. Ref: CCRTF 94/0225/C, November 16, 1995, Simon Brown, L.J., CA.

4931. Agreements–sale and development of freehold property–interpretation of clause concerning capitalisation of rent–solicitors and surveyors under no duty to advise commercial client of VAT implications of transaction

DMG and the second defendants, F, surveyors and solicitors respectively, were instructed by Virgin Management and Virgin Development Ltd in respect of the development and sale of a freehold property owned by V. A dispute arose in relation to the payment due under a sale and development agreement. DMG and F appealed against the judge's finding on the construction of the agreement. The judge found it to be unambiguous and that F were negligent in their drafting by failing to include the capitalisation of the base rent and that DMG had been negligent in failing to explain the agreement fully. V appealed against the judge's refusal to allow them to amend their pleadings in order to claim that, even if the agreement did account for the capitalisation, DMG and F should have made sure that it could not be interpreted ambiguously. They also applied for leave to appeal against the striking out of a writ which sought to argue the same matters included in the amendment. V also appealed against the rejection of their claim that DMG and F had failed to advise them on their liability for VAT under the agreement.

Held, allowing DMG and F's appeal and dismissing V's appeals and application, that (1) different calculations for payment applied depending on what phase of work had been completed. The judge had erred by deciding that a clause stating the calculation method only applied to the first phase of the works. The clause, in fact, applied to the calculation of the rent if the second phase was or was not completed and the capitalisation of the rent if Phase 2 proceeded or not. The clause was then to be interpreted in accordance with the circumstances prevailing at the time; (2) the judge had correctly exercised his discretion in refusing to allow the amendment to V's pleadings in the light of the delay which would have occurred as a consequence; (3) the judge was correct to find that issue estoppel prevented V from proceeding with their second writ, *Yat Tung Investment Co Ltd v. Dao Heng Bank Ltd* [1975] A.C. 581, [1975] C.L.Y. 211 followed. Additionally, there were no special circumstances which would allow the principle to be disregarded and the writ amounted to an abuse of process and (4) as V was an experienced commercial client, DGM and F were not under a duty to advise them in relation to their VAT liability.

VIRGIN MANAGEMENT LTD v. DE MORGAN GROUP PLC [1996] E.G.C.S. 16, Leggatt, L.J., CA.

4932. Boundaries–disputes–property development–conveyancing plans

There was a dispute as to the proper boundary between two properties in a new residential estate. Prior to the development there had been a hedge marking the boundary between two parcels of land. T contended that the boundary was the line drawn on the conveyance whereas F maintained that it was the line of the hedge which had now disappeared. T instituted proceedings and F counterclaimed for rectification of the conveyance. The judge found for T concluding that there was no conflict between the plan and the express words of the conveyance. He also found against F on the rectification issue having formed an unfavourable impression of F's evidence. Costs were awarded on the indemnity basis. F had been given leave to appeal out of time on the construction of the conveyance.

Held, dismissing the appeal, that the judge was clearly right. Although the parcels clause was insufficiently explicit to identify the boundary, answers to preliminary enquiries, the conveyance plan and the fencing covenants showed that T's claim was correct, *Wigginton & Milner Ltd v. Winster Engineering Ltd* [1978] 1 W.L.R. 1462, [1978] C.L.Y. 2500 and *Spall v. Owen* (1981) 44 P. & C.R. 36, [1982] C.L.Y. 2661 followed. At the material time there had been nothing on the ground to show where the boundary lay. The relevant test was what a reasonable person would have thought was being conveyed, *Toplis v. Green* [1992] E.G.C.S. 20, [1992] C.L.Y. 550 followed. It was doubtful whether the order for costs could be enforced given F's impecuniosity and prima facie there were criticisms which could be made of the judge's unfavourable view of F. The plaintiffs should have 88 per cent of their costs below.

TARGETT v. FERGUSON (1996) 72 P. & C.R. 106, Balcombe, L.J., CA.

4933. Boundaries–inferences from conveyancing documents decisive–hedge and ditch presumption applied in absence of evidence to rebut it

H was the owner of a freehold consisting of an arable field adjoining D's land. A 1926 ordnance survey sheet attached to a 1963 conveyance showed a ditch and the land one foot beyond as land which had been conveyed. D sought planning permission for a number of houses on the site, but the application was rejected. H had always maintained that the ditch represented the boundary between the two pieces of land. D attempted to negotiate a purchase of the disputed land, but this failed and proceedings commenced. The judge held that the boundary ran down the centre of the ditch. H contended that in the absence of evidence to the contrary the hedge and ditch presumption applied, thus making the boundary the lip of the ditch on D's side.

Held, allowing the appeal, that (1) the case turned on the presence of evidence in conveyancing documents, from which changes in boundary position between the parties' land could be inferred; (2) the judge had examined the 1963 conveyance and the 1926 ordnance survey sheet to which it was attached, but had erred when he sought to draw conclusions from the plan; (3) no effective conveyance of the land on the site of the ditch could have been made if the land was owned by H; (4) it was plain from the Land Registry's explanatory memoranda that the title plan did not define the exact location of boundaries but indicated only general boundaries of the registered land and (5) except for the interpretation of the defendant's conveyancing documents the judge would have applied the hedge and ditch presumption, providing that the hedge was on H's side of the ditch and that the boundary fell on the lip of the ditch on D's side.

HALL v. DORLING [1996] E.G.C.S. 58, Beldam, L.J., CA.

4934. Canals–riparian rights–development of land–successors in title

[Grand Junction Canal Act 1793.]

S owned land adjacent to a canal which it wished to develop. The Grand Junction Canal Act 1793 provided for the rights of landowners adjacent to the canal. S wished to exercise its rights under the Act without having to obtain permission from B and the preliminary issue was whether present owners of land adjacent to the canal could exercise rights conferred on the original owners.

Held, that S was entitled to exercise its rights to develop the land without having to obtain permission from B, as the rights granted by the Act did not extend to successors.

SWAN HILL DEVELOPMENTS LTD v. BRITISH WATERWAYS BOARD [1995] N.P.C. 79, Walker, J., Ch D.

4935. Commons–rectification of register–user as of right–recreational use by children

[Commons Registration Act 1965 s.14.]

The Ministry of Defence sought an order under Commons Registration Act 1965 s.14 to delete an entry from the register. The entry concerned Boscombe Down which was owned by the Ministry but could be used by the public when not being used for military purposes. In 1992 it was registered as a village green on the ground that it was used for recreational purposes mainly by the children of service personnel.

Held, that to be registered as a village green user as of right for 20 years must be shown and recreational use by children was not sufficient to prove the right existed. Allowing children to play on the land was merely toleration of incidental use.

MINISTRY OF DEFENCE v. WILTSHIRE CC [1995] 4 All E.R. 931, Harman, J, Ch D.

4936. Commons–registration–failure to register town green did not extinguish customary rights

[Commons Registration Act 1965 s.1.]

Held, that a town green which had not been registered as common land under the Commons Registration Act 1965 s.1 (2) (a) could still be proved on evidence to be a green and the failure to register did not extinguish customary rights over it.

R. v. SUFFOLK CC, *ex p.* STEED; SUB NOM. STEED v. SUFFOLK CC [1996] E.G.C.S. 122, Pill, L.J., CA.

4937. Compulsory purchase–compensation–cancellation of notice to treat after entering into possession

[Land Compensation Act 1961 s.31; Land Compensation Act 1973 s.52.]

A, the owners of land subject to a compulsory purchase order, applied for judicial review of the decision by N, the acquiring authority, to withdraw a notice to treat in respect of the land and to request the return of an advance payment of compensation.

Held, dismissing the application, that N was entitled to withdraw its notice to treat as the withdrawal was served within six weeks of the notice of delivery pursuant to the Land Compensation Act 1961 s.31. As N had entered into possession following the notice to treat, any loss occasioned by the cancellation of the notice to treat was compensatable and the parties were entitled to specific performance as under any contract for the sale of land. A would not be entitled to retain the advance payment as it was made in respect of an acquisition which did not in fact occur. Both the Land Compensation Act 1973 s.52(5) and s.31 (1) of the 1961 Act were intended to provide for ordinary compensation for the acquisition of land and compensation for non-acquisition was not envisaged.

R. v. NORTHUMBRIAN WATER LTD, *ex p.* ABLE UK LTD (1996) 72 P. & C.R. 95, Carnwath, J., QBD.

4938. Compulsory purchase–compensation time limit inoperative–continuing negotiations amounting to estoppel by convention or waiver of statutory time limit

[Compulsory Purchase (Vesting Declarations) Act 1981 s.10.]

Held, that where a local authority compulsorily acquired an interest in land pursuant to a general vesting declaration made under the Compulsory Purchase (Vesting Declarations) Act 1981 s.10(3) and thereby established a six year limitation period for compensation claims, the authority was unable to rely upon the expiry of the limitation period where an estoppel by convention arose as a result of the continuing negotiations between it and the former property owner. Although the authority could have relied on the expiry of the time limit after October 1992 to extinguish a compensation claim, the evidence of negotiations conducted after that date amounted to a waiver of the time bar, *Kammins Ballrooms Co Ltd v. Zenith Investments Ltd* [1971] A.C. 850, [1970] C.L.Y. 1525 applied.

COOPERATIVE WHOLESALE SOCIETY v. CHESTER LE STREET DC [1996] 36 R.V.R. 185, Judge Marder, Q.C. (President), LandsTr.

4939. Compulsory purchase–issue estoppel–appeal against nil certificate of appropriate alternative development–Secretary of State's decision not binding in subsequent compensation proceedings

[Land Compensation Act 1961 s.18.]

The Secretary of State, appealed against a lands tribunal preliminary ruling that in principle a decision of the Secretary of State for the Environment on an appeal under the Land Compensation Act 1961 s.18 could be the basis for issue estoppel in subsequent proceedings to determine whether compensation was payable. The Secretary of State acquired P's land to build a road. P applied to the local authority for a certificate of appropriate alternative development and asserted that, but for the road building, planning permission would have been granted for residential development. However, the local authority issued a nil certificate and P appealed, successfully, to the Secretary of State for the Environment under s.18.

Held, allowing the appeal, that (1) the Secretary of State's decision on a s.18 appeal was incapable of forming the basis of an issue estoppel and could not be binding in the course of assessment of compensation. A decision to grant or refuse planning permission could not form the basis of estoppel per rem judicatam, and (2) the issue determined by the lands tribunal was different from the issue determined on the s.18 appeal.

PORTER v. SECRETARY OF STATE FOR TRANSPORT [1996] 3 All E.R. 693, Stuart-Smith, L.J., CA.

4940. Compulsory purchase–payments–owner occupier supplement dealt with in same way as compensation for purposes of entitlement to interest

[Housing Act 1969 Sch.5.]

S appealed against a decision denying a claim for interest to be paid on the owner-occupier supplement paid to S as the owner of land compulsorily purchased in 1985. S submitted that the supplement amounted to compensation or should be treated as compensation under the deeming provision in the Housing Act 1969 Sch.5, and as such he was liable to receive interest on it. B contended, however, that the statutory scheme distinguished between compensation and payments under Sch.5, and that if Parliament had intended owner-occupier supplement payments to bear interest this would have been expressly provided for in Sch.5.

Held, allowing the appeal, that it was accepted that the 1969 Act maintained a distinction between payments, including owner-occupier supplements, and compensation but that distinction was not determinative of the matter, for Sch.5 para.3(2) required a payment under Sch.5 para.1 to be dealt with "as if it were compensation". Such a requirement was not limited to the introduction of the procedures of the Lands Tribunal and, as a result, interest was payable on owner-occupier supplements.

SHAIKH v. BOLTON MDC (1996) 72 P. & C.R. D43, Pill, L.J., CA.

4941. Compulsory purchase–purchase of land for highway–calculation of compensation for surrendered lease

The Secretary of State appealed against a lands tribunal decision in relation to compensation payable for the surrender, by T and S of their interest in land. The Secretary of State owned the freehold, T owned a lease and S owned a sublease. In order to widen the M5, the Secretary of State entered into an agreement with T and S whereby they surrendered their interests in return for compensation, calculated as if the land had been compulsorily purchased. The deed of surrender stated that T should be paid "the amount of compensation... appropriate at the date of entry on the premises". The tribunal held that the interest was one with an immediate right to vacant possession and that compensation should be paid on the assumption that S's interest did not exist.

Held, allowing the appeal, that (1) "entry on the premises" preceded the surrender in each case so at the time of entry both interests subsisted and (2) for the calculation of a period of time, as a general rule, the law was not concerned with parts of the day. In this case, the court was concerned with a sequence of events on the same day and that should be considered when construing the deed of surrender, *Eaglehill Ltd v. J Needham Builders Ltd* [1973] A.C. 992, [1972] C.L.Y. 210 considered.

TOZER KEMSLEY & MILBOURNE ESTATES PLC v. SECRETARY OF STATE FOR TRANSPORT; SUB NOM. SECRETARY OF STATE FOR TRANSPORT v. TOZER KEMSLEY & MILBOURNE ESTATES PLC [1996] E.G.C.S. 7, Stuart-Smith, L.J., CA.

4942. Compulsory purchase–St Vincent and the Grenadines–valuation–interpretation of Land Acquisition Act 1990 s.19 and s.22–interpretation of Constitution of Saint Vincent and the Grenadines s.6 and Sch.2

[Constitution of Saint Vincent and the Grenadines 1990 s.6, Sch.2; Land Acquisition Act 1990 (Saint Vincent and the Grenadines) s.19, s.22.]

On February 25, 1985 OH agreed to sell an estate to W for ECD 4.32 million. On March 19, 1985 the Government of St.Vincent gazetted its intention to acquire the land for public purposes. In June 1985 W submitted a claim for compensation for a total of ECD 22.5 million. In March 1986 the Government made an unconditional offer of ECD 4.7 million and, agreement not being reached, a board of assessment was appointed to assess compensation. By a majority, it awarded W ECD 4.7 million. The Court of Appeal allowed W's appeal, holding that the rules concerning the assessment of compensation set out in the Land Acquisition Act s.19(a) were an infringement of the right to adequate compensation conferred by the Constitution of Saint Vincent and the Grenadines s.6(1), but only awarded an additional ECD 516,000 for disturbance. W appealed and the Government cross-appealed against the additional award.

Held, dismissing the appeal and allowing the cross-appeal, that (1) the two categories of law which were excluded by para.11 of the transitional provisions in Sch.2 of the Constitution were (a) any law in force immediately before October 27, 1969, and (b) any subsequent amendment that falls outside para.11 (a) (b) and (c) of Sch.2. The Land Acquisition Act fell within the first category and consequently was not affected by s.6 of the Constitution; (2) s.19 of the Act required that compensation should be assessed on the basis of a notional sale at the prescribed date, assuming an "open market" and a "willing seller". Although to arrive at the price likely to be obtained on such a sale a valuer normally undertook a study of sales of comparable land, the comparison used in the instant case was invalid because, inter alia, there was a rapidly diminishing market for large estates in the island; (3) the Court of Appeal erred in making the award for disturbance since no claim had been made for these sums nor had any argument been addressed to the Court on them and (4) since the board of assessment had not considered, in awarding costs to W under s.22 of the Act, whether special reasons existed for that award, the matter should be referred back to the board of assessment.

WINDWARD PROPERTIES LTD v. SAINT VINCENT AND THE GRENADINES [1996] 1 W.L.R. 279, Lord Goff of Chieveley, PC.

4943. Constructive trusts–express common intention to share joint beneficial interest in property–property on trust for sale

It was declared that (a) C held a property on trust for sale and that the net proceeds of the sale on trust were to be 75 per cent to C and 25 per cent to K; (b) K to be appointed an additional trustee; (c) the sale of the property was ordered; (d) C was ordered to pay the second and third plaintiffs, WS and RS, £6,223 plus interest, and (e) costs be awarded against C. C appealed against the award to WS and RS. K cross-appealed claiming a 50 per cent share. The judge had found that C and K were to have set up home in a farm. So that C could obtain a mortgage, K had signed a disclaimer on the understanding that she and C would marry and occupy the property together. The property included a cottage which, when renovated, was to be sold to WS and RS who were K's parents. K gave evidence that she had paid £12,500 into C's bank account and had spent £5,343 on the home. K had also been heavily involved in restoration work on the property. The relationship having broken down, K commenced the instant proceedings claiming a joint beneficial interest in the property having acted on a common intention to her detriment. The property had a current market value of between £140,000 and 150,000. WS and RS claimed that they had spent £6,223 on fixtures and fittings for the cottage which was to be offset against the eventual purchase price and that the sale had been frustrated when C demanded too high a price.

Held, allowing the appeal and the cross-appeal, that (1) there was evidence that K had acted to her detriment and the judge had accepted K's evidence that the express common intention between the parties was that there should have been a joint interest. There was a constructive trust although the case could have been equally well argued on the basis of proprietary estoppel. C should not be allowed to resile from his promise of equal shares, whether or not the common intention had been formed after the acquisition, and K should have a 50 per cent share of the net proceeds, *Grant v. Edwards* [1986] Ch. 638, [1986] C.L.Y. 3034, *Lloyds Bank Plc v Rosset* [1991] 1 A.C. 107, [1990] C.L.Y. 706 and *Gissing v. Gissing* [1971] A.C. 806, [1970] C.L.Y. 1243 followed. Given the express common intention, it was not appropriate to adopt a broad brush approach, assessing K's share on the basis of her labour and actual contribution, *Eves v. Eves* [1975] 1 W.L.R. 1338, [1975] C.L.Y. 3110 distinguished, and (2) the judge rejected the frustration argument, but found for WS and RS on a restitutionary basis they had not pleaded, that C had been unjustly enriched. The expenditure had been incurred voluntarily for their own purposes and they had repudiated the agreement to buy the cottage when the relationship between C and K appeared to have broken down. The cottage could have been purchased and then resold if WS and RS had not wanted to live in it themselves.

CLOUGH v. KILLEY (1996) 72 P. & C.R. D22, Peter Gibson, L.J., CA.

4944. Contract for sale of land–Barbados–compulsory purchase notice issued prior to completion–notice not conferring right of immediate possession–vacant possession unaffected by notice–purchaser's rescission amounting to breach

[Land Acquisition Act (Barbados) s.3, s.5.]

Prior to the completion of a contract for the sale of land between E and N, a notice was issued under the Land Acquisition Act s.3 (Barbados), warning that the land concerned might be needed for Crown purposes. N purported to rescind the contract, contending that E could no longer grant vacant possession on sale and that the decision in *Cook v. Taylor* [1942] Ch. 349 created a dichotomy between supervening events expressly or impliedly accepted by a purchaser and events which prevented a vendor carrying out previously accepted obligations. E appealed against the judgment of the Court of Appeal of Barbados in favour of N.

Held, allowing the appeal, that E could give effective vacant possession on completion, as a s.3 notice did not confer a right of immediate possession on the Crown authorities. The risk posed by compulsory purchase was a normal risk of ownership, and the s.3 notice had not altered the contract, but merely increased the chance of a remote risk becoming an eventuality. Therefore, N had been in breach by their purported rescission. However, as the land had now been vested in the Crown by a notice issued under s.5 of the Act, the correct remedy lay in damages and not specific performance.

E JOHNSON & CO (BARBADOS) LTD v. NSR LTD [1996] 3 W.L.R. 583, Lord Jauncey of Tullichettle, PC.

4945. Contract for sale of land–purchaser's lien–right of recovery of deposit from successor in title

[Land Registration Act 1925.]

C had contracted to buy a lease on a flat which was under construction and had paid 20 per cent of the purchase price by way of deposit. The contract was conditional on the vendor obtaining satisfactory planning permission, which was later granted. Money had been borrowed from the bank to pay for the construction work and when the vendor became insolvent the bank insisted that the development was sold. C claimed a purchaser's lien which entitled him to recover his deposit from F, now the owner of the development, in priority to the bank and their successors in title. The claim failed and C appealed. F argued that for there to be a purchaser's lien it was necessary for the equitable interest in the property contracted to be purchased to have passed to C, but this had not happened because (1) the contract was conditional and was not specifically enforceable until planning permission was obtained and (2) even if the contract was unconditional, a contract for the grant of a new lease had no subsisting equitable interest which could be vested in C as it was property that had not existed before.

Held, allowing C's appeal, but dismissing S's, that the purchaser had an equitable interest or estate in land, albeit future and conditional, *London and South Western Railway Co v. Gomm* (1882) 20 Ch. D. 562 applied. The circumstances in which a purchaser's lien could arise were not restricted to those in which the contract was specifically enforceable. There was no express agreement that the lien should be modified and no implied term in the contract. The registrar was duty bound to note on the title to the underlease when registering the rights of those purchasers whose contracts were signed before the application for registration but he was not entitled to include a similar note in respect of those contracts signed after that date, the consequence being that C's rights had priority over the defendant's, but S's rights did not. The fact that the defendant had notice of prior contracts was insufficient to impose an obligation on them and it was not fraud on their part to rely on the provisions of the Land Registration Act 1925 as conferring on them an unincumbered title.

CHATTEY v. FARNDALE HOLDINGS INC [1997] 06 E.G. 152, Morritt, L.J., CA.

4946. Contract for sale of land–specific performance–whether oral variation effective

K agreed to purchase a freehold property from M subject to a condition that he would carry out certain building works to convert the same into flats one of which was to be let to M on a 999 year lease at a peppercorn rent. The contract was completed but K failed to comply with the condition. M sought specific performance of the condition. The trial judge dismissed the claim after hearing evidence from K to the effect that he and M had agreed orally that M would take a smaller flat than that originally earmarked for him. That point had not been put to M and M appealed.

Held, allowing M's appeal, that the contemporaneous correspondence showed that there was no firm and binding oral variation of the contract because the matter was still being negotiated between the parties. In any event, as the variation was oral with no evidence of any part performance whereas the original contract was in writing, any oral variation could have no effect. The identity of the subject matter of the 999 year lease was sufficiently clearly identified and, in the absence of express provision to the contrary, the lease would contain the usual covenants. Accordingly, there was no obstacle to granting an order for specific performance of the conditions contained in the written agreement. Whilst the court should be conscious of the difficulties experienced by litigants in person it was essential to maintain an even handed approach between the two sides.

MORRALL v. KRAUSE [1994] E.G.C.S. 177, Sir Thomas Bingham, M.R., CA.

4947. Equitable interests in land–conveyance stated property split one tenth/nine tenths–owner of one tenth paid interest on mortgage and endowment premiums–extent of entitlement on sale to sale proceeds and endowment

[Law of Property Act 1925 s.30.]

H and P cohabited in a house which H had purchased from the council. In 1985 they purchased a new house for £74,000. A clause in the conveyance stated that H and P were tenants in common and H owned nine tenths and P one tenth of the property. P paid the interest on a £27,000 mortgage together with the endowment premium. Following their separation, H commenced proceedings under the Law of Property Act 1925 s.30. P appealed against the judge's decision that the proceeds of sale should be split as stated in the conveyance and that the surrender value of the endowment policy should be split in half. P argued that he should be entitled to benefit from the fact that he had made the interest payments and that the judge was wrong to find that such a claim had not been adequately pleaded. P further argued that the judge had wrongly divided the endowment proceeds in light of the fact that P had made all the payments.

Held, dismissing the appeal, that (1) a prayer, in a defence and counterclaim, which asked for all necessary accounts to be taken between the parties, could not be relied upon to plead a substantive claim which had not been mentioned elsewhere in the pleadings; (2) P could not claim an equitable right to have H account for the interest payments he made without an express or implied agreement to reimburse him and (3) the judge's decision in relation to the endowment proceeds was generous to P. He could have split it one tenth/nine tenths as its purpose was to cover the mortgage and benefit the parties in such a division.

HEMBURY v. PEACHEY (1996) 72 P. & C.R. D47, Staughton, L.J., CA.

4948. Equitable interests in land–enforcement of charging order–deposit of title deeds as security–absence of agreement in writing–whether mere deposit sufficient to create equitable mortgage

[Law of Property (Miscellaneous Provisions) Act 1989 s.2.]

SGA, the third defendants in proceedings to enforce a charging order to secure a judgment debt in relation to S's property, appealed against a declaration, that they did not hold an equitable mortgage over S's undivided share in the proceeds of sale. SGA contended that the Law of Property (Miscellaneous Provisions) Act 1989 s.2 had not affected the rule, applicable since *Russel v. Russel* (1783) 1 Bro C.C. 269, that the deposit of the title deeds by way of security could be taken as creating an equitable mortgage without any writing and was not dependent on any actual contract between the parties.

Held, dismissing the appeal, that under s.2 of the 1989 Act a disposition of an interest in land had to be by way of a written document, signed by both parties, containing all the terms of the agreement. The section was intended to provide certainty and the parties' intention to enforce a common agreement could not be inferred from the mere deposit of title deeds.

UNITED BANK OF KUWAIT PLC v. SAHIB [1996] 3 W.L.R. 372, Peter Gibson, L.J., CA.

4949. Equitable interests in land–non-assignable and non-transmissible licence to occupy property

S appealed against a decision dismissing her claim for possession of a house and granting D, her son in law, a right to continue in occupation, rent free, for the rest of his life. After their marriage, D and his wife paid a favourable rent until 1976, when D became unemployed and his wife was diagnosed with cancer, and thereafter paid no rent. D contributed in part to major improvements to the property. S and her husband subsequently made wills leaving the property solely to D's wife, their daughter. S's husband died leaving the property to S and D's wife also died. S paid for substantial renovations to the property and asked D for rent, which he refused. A proper notice to quit was served in 1990. D's 27 year old daughter lived in the property to which D returned only two nights per week, having alternative accommodation elsewhere with his partner. S, aged 71, was in receipt of income support and had fallen into arrears with the mortgage on her own house, which was too large and in need of repair. She wished to sell it and required the property for her own occupation. The judge below found that D had acquired an equitable interest, by reason of his expenditure on the property together with, at the least, acquiescence on the part of S. When S acquired the house from her husband, she was neither a purchaser for value nor a purchaser without notice of D's equitable interest and was therefore bound by his equity. S claimed that the judge below had erred in holding that D was, therefore, entitled to the "minimum equity, shaping it to the facts of the case", namely, a non-assignable, and non-transmissible licence to occupy for his lifetime, based on proprietary estoppel by reason of his expenditure. S contended that she had always intended D to have an interest only so long as he was with his wife and that would have concluded a reasonable time after her death. D's equity was provided for by the wills leaving the property to D's wife, although her predecease had prevented it accruing and that equity had now expired. D countered by claiming that proprietary estoppel lasted so long as his equitable interest endured.

Held, allowing the appeal, that an order for possession was granted. S's will did not satisfy D's legitimate expectation that the family should be allowed to remain in the house, but the circumstances and needs of D and S must be balanced. D was in employment and had alternative accommodation and his daughter was also employed, whereas S had a pressing need for the property, *Inwards v. Baker* [1965] 2 Q.B. 29, [1965] C.L.Y. 1487, *Crabb v. Arun DC* [1976] Ch. 179, [1975] C.L.Y. 1191 and *Pascoe v. Turner* [1979] 1 W.L.R. 431, [1979] C.L.Y. 1083 considered. The principle of an equitable remedy should not produce injustice. D had lived rent free for 20 years and the equity of his limited expenditure on the property had now expired, *Australia v. Verwayen* (1990) 95 A.L.R. 321 followed.

SLEDMORE v. DALBY (1996) 72 P. & C.R. 196, Roch, L.J., CA.

4950. Equitable interests in land–oral agreement–property under lease owned by another–lease charged as security for a loan–bank claiming possession–whether occupier who had paid whole of purchase price had equitable interest

[Land Charges Act 1972; Land Registration Act 1925 s.70.]

L appealed against the dismissal of its claim for possession in relation to a legal charge over a leasehold property. The lease was owned by RC, who had received the proceeds of sale as payment for the property under an oral agreement with his sister-in-law, MC, who was in possession. The judge below had held that the lease was held in trust for MC, but the bank argued that no equitable interest had been established, either by way of bare trust, constructive trust or proprietary estoppel, and that MC's interest under the estate contract was unregistered and therefore void under the Land Charges Act 1972.

Held, allowing the appeal, that although no agreement had been made in writing, the contract became enforceable when MC paid the purchase price which removed any beneficial interest RC had. A bare trust could not be established simply as an equitable consequence of that contract. Furthermore, once a specifically enforceable contract had been made it was not possible to establish a constructive trust in addition to the rights of MC under the contractual relationship. Nor was it possible to apply principles of proprietary estoppel, by arguing that MC carried out improvements to the property believing that she owned it, as a trust already arose from the contract, *Lloyds Bank v. Rosset* [1991] A.C. 107, [1990] C.L.Y. 706 considered. However, if the title to the property had been registered MC would have had an overriding interest binding on the bank under the Land Registration Act 1925 s.70(1)(g) as no enquiries had been made and MC was in possession.

LLOYDS BANK PLC v. CARRICK [1996] 4 All E.R. 630, Morritt, L.J., CA.

4951. Equitable interests in land–pre-contract inquiries–vendor's lien capable of being an overriding interest

[Land Registration Act 1925 s.20, s.70.]

UCB appealed against an order that F, the unpaid vendor, had priority over UCB, the mortgagee in possession and proceeds of sale of property sold by F to B who charged the property as security to UCB. The property was a cafe with flat above. In her replies to enquiries and requisitions on title, F stated B would gain vacant possession on completion. However, F and B agreed, with UCB's knowledge, that F would remain in a flat above and continue to run the business as manageress. F agreed, contrary to usual conveyancing practice, to accept half the purchase price on completion, with the remainder being paid into an overseas bank account in her name by B. However, that transfer did not take place, B defaulted with the repayments and UCB sought an order for possession. F claimed that she was entitled to an unpaid vendor's lien conferring an overriding interest.

Held, allowing the appeal and granting UCB an order for possession, that in determining the question of priority it was accepted, following *Lysaght v. Edwards* [1876] 2 Ch. 499, *London & Cheshire Insurance Co v. Laplagrene Property Co* [1971] 1 Ch. 499, [1971] C.L.Y. 1917 and *Nationwide Anglia Building Society v. Ahmed and Balakrishnan* [1996] C.L.Y. 4953, that an unpaid vendor's lien was capable of constituting an overriding interest. However, one had not arisen here. F's replies to the enquiries and requisitions did not disclose the existence of an overriding interest in the sense of the Land Registration Act 1925 s.70, and she could not execute a transfer and then turn round and attempt to claim an entitlement based on an undisclosed lien. Referring to the 1925 Act s.20, it was stated that F's interest in the property was a minor interest which failed for lack of registration, allowing UCB to take priority over her.

UCB BANK PLC v. BEASLEY AND FRANCE; SUB NOM. UCB BANK PLC v. FRANCE [1995] N.P.C. 144, Morritt, L.J., CA.

4952. Equitable interests in land–prior agreement to share property beneficially–whether defeated constructive trust

Held, that the ownership of property by a wholly owned company did not affect the principle laid down in *Lloyds Bank Plc v. Rosset* [1991] 1 A.C. 107, [1990] C.L.Y. 706 that reliance by a partner upon a prior agreement to share the property beneficially gave rise to a constructive trust.

TRUSTEE IN BANKRUPTCY OF SCHUPPAN v. SCHUPPAN, *The Independent*, November 18, 1996 (C.S.), Judge Maddocks, Ch D.

4953. Equitable interests in land–purchase price of property not fully paid–vendor's contractual licence to occupy–whether vendor's lien was overriding interest against mortgagee

[Land Registration Act 1925 s.70.]

N were given possession of industrial premises against B who appealed. It was submitted that B had a vendor's lien which was an overriding interest under the Land Registration Act 1925 s.70. It was further submitted that when B agreed to sell the premises to A, in acquiring a second charge on the property and a first charge over the machinery, B had not impaired his overriding interest which existed at the date of the agreement. N contended that there was no vendor's lien but, in any case, the terms of the agreement were such that any overriding interest merged in the legal mortgage. N further contended that B was estopped, by reason of the terms of the agreement, from contending that his interest had priority over their own charge.

Held, dismissing the appeal, that (1) B obtained all that he bargained for with A (the charges and the use of the premises as an office) so that a vendor's lien probably never came into existence and, in any event, was given up in consideration of the rights under the agreement, *Capital Finance Co Ltd v. Stokes* [1969] 1 Ch. 261, [1969] C.L.Y. 403 followed; (2) the right to use the premises was only a contractual licence which did not give B an overriding interest. Had the right to occupy amounted to an overriding interest there was no scintilla temporis between the agreement, completion of purchase and creation of the charge to enable occupation to take place; (3) s.70 of the 1925 Act was concerned with proprietary rights which were not mere personal rights, *Ashburn Anstalt v. Arnold* [1989] Ch. 1, [1989] C.L.Y. 2061 followed; (4) B's contractual right to occupy the premises did not give him an estate or interest in the land, *Errington v. Errington* [1952] 1 K.B. 290, [1952] C.L.Y. 624 considered, and (5) the right to occupy did not accrue before N's charge, *Abbey National Building Society v. Cann* [1991] 1 A.C. 56, [1990] C.L.Y. 707 applied. Thus, the right to occupy was not an overriding interest even had it been a proprietary right. B's submissions were, in effect, that his loan to A should be paid in full before that of N. That would be contrary to the terms of the agreement. The conclusion would be that he was estopped from contending that he had a right to retain possession, *Habib Bank v. Habib Bank AG* [1981] 1 W.L.R. 1265, [1982] C.L.Y. 8262 followed. The agreement between B and A was a clear representation that N's charges would have priority to those of B. It would be unconscionable to allow B to resile from the position he encouraged N to assume to be correct.

NATIONWIDE ANGLIA BUILDING SOCIETY v. AHMED AND BALAKRISHNAN (1995) 70 P. & C.R. 381, Aldous, L.J., CA.

4954. Equitable interests in land–trusts for sale–whether overreached when land was mortgaged but no capital money was advanced

[Law of Property Act 1925 s.2; Land Registration Act 1925 s.70.]

The first and second defendants were registered proprietors of land on which they executed a second legal charge in favour of S as security for all their present and future liabilities. S, claiming that substantial debts under the legal charge remained unsatisfied, brought possession proceedings in which the third to seventh defendants argued that they had equitable interests in the property as their main residence and that they had overriding interests under the Land Registration Act 1925 s.70(1)(g). They also contended that, because no capital money had been paid over by S at the time the mortgage was made, their interests were not overreached by the legal charge in terms of the Law of Property Act 1925 s.2(1)(ii). S argued that there was no requirement that capital money and disposition should arise at the same time. The judge refused to strike out parts of the defence to the claim for possession, and S appealed.

Held, allowing the appeal, that, on the true construction of the Law of Property Act 1925 s.2(1)(ii), compliance with the statutory requirements concerning the payment of capital money was only required if capital money arose. It followed that it was not necessary for capital money to have arisen under the conveyance. Notwithstanding their occupation of the property, the beneficial interests of the third to seventh defendants were overreached.

STATE BANK OF INDIA v. SOOD, *The Times*, November 7, 1996, Peter Gibson, L.J., CA.

4955. Estate agents–prohibition–interpretation of "convicted of an offence"

[Estate Agents Act 1979 s.3, s.7.]

A appealed against an order made under the Estate Agents Act 1979 s.7 prohibiting him from working as an estate agent because he had been convicted of an offence in 1971 in Detroit and again in 1991 in Warrington.

Held, dismissing the appeal, that "convicted of an offence" in s.3(1)(a)(i) of the 1979 Act applied to offences committed before its commencement and to offences committed outside the UK. Both convictions were relevant to deciding A's fitness for work and should be taken into account.

ANTONELLI v. SECRETARY OF STATE FOR TRADE AND INDUSTRY [1996] E.G.L.R. 229, Buxton, J., QBD.

4956. Estoppel–registration of charge–purchaser mortgaged land before becoming legal owner

[Land Registration Act 1925 s.25, s.26.]

F appealed against refusal of a declaration that a legal charge executed by T on property of which, at the time of the execution, he was not the registered proprietor nor the person entitled to be registered as proprietor, should be registered. After T was registered as proprietor F applied for the charge to be registered. F was held not to be entitled to have the charge registered, but could apply for leave to amend their pleadings to claim specific performance of T's obligation to create a new legal charge which F could then register. F argued that this would be detrimental to them in terms of the priority of charges and the original charge should be a legal mortgage by estoppel. When T became the registered proprietor the estoppel had been fed and F was entitled to register the charge.

Held, allowing the appeal, that this was not a case of estoppel by representation which would require an express assertion of the grantor's title. This was a case of estoppel by deed. When T became the registered proprietor of the property the estoppel was fed, therefore F had a valid charge, *Universal Permanent Building Society v. Cooke* [1952] Ch. 95, [1947-1951] C.L.C. 6348 followed. There was nothing in the provisions of the Land Registration Act 1925 s.25 and s.26 which precluded registration of a legal charge granted by the person who was afterwards registered as proprietor but executed before he became entitled to be so registered.

FIRST NATIONAL BANK PLC v. THOMPSON [1996] Ch. 231, Millett, L.J., CA.

4957. Fieri facias–sheriff breaking into property–whether unlawful or continuation of walking possession

M sought an injunction to restrain B, the High Sheriff of Greater London, from selling goods which had been removed from her home and from entering her home without a court order. M owed money to a judgment creditor, and when she failed to pay, the creditor issued a writ of fieri facias. On January 24, 1995 B's officers obtained peaceable entry to M's house and formally seized various goods. On December 13, 1995 the court confirmed that this amounted to walking possession of the goods. On December 19, 1995, B's officers returned to M's house to find it locked. A locksmith was called to gain entry and goods were removed. M sought to restrain B on the ground that his actions were unlawful and therefore the goods should not be sold. The issue before the court was whether, after gaining walking possession, B was entitled to break into the house to continue the walking possession and seize further goods. B submitted that the "castle" principle in *Semayne's Case* (1604) 5 Co. Rep. 919 applied solely to original entry, and that once B had walking possession he could return at a later date to continue the possession, and if prevented from so doing could break in to seize goods which were lawfully his.

Held, dismissing the motion, that B was entitled to break in to seize goods under walking possession. In the situation where a sheriff was debarred from gaining entry, he had not acted unlawfully by breaking in as he was merely continuing the execution of the walking possession.

Observed: the court was of the view that this principle had been established at a time when it was unusual for householders to lock their homes and consequently gaining access was not unlawful as it did not require breaking in, and urged that the practice should be reviewed as soon as practicable by the Law Commission.

McLEOD v. BUTTERWICK [1996] 1 W.L.R. 995, Judge Roger Cooke, Ch D.

4958. Land registers–British Virgin Islands–mistake on entry for dominant land showing right of way–no mistake on servient land–whether purchaser entitled to rely on entry in register–whether rectification available

[Registered Land Ordinance (British Virgin Islands) s.140.]

R appealed against a decision of the Court of Appeal of the British Virgin Islands which set aside an order for judgment in its favour in relation to a right of way over neighbouring land. S, the previous owners, had been granted a lease for five years of a strip of road passing over T's land. When S registered their land under the Registered Land Ordinance, the lease was mistakenly entered by the adjudication officer as a right of way. When T's title was registered the lease was also entered as a right of way, but for a duration of five years. R argued that, as a subsequent purchaser for value without notice, it was entitled to rely on the register. R further contended that T should have sought rectification, that the register could no longer be rectified owing to R's purchase and that the appropriate remedy was to claim compensation from the Ordinance.

Held, dismissing the appeal, that T could not have applied for rectification under the Registered Land Ordinance s.140(1) as a fraud or a mistake was required and T's entry was substantially correct. Without an application for rectification there could be no claim for compensation. It would be wrong for R to be able to enforce a right which was imposed on T's land without his knowledge, which he was powerless to prevent and for which he could obtain no compensation. Before R purchased the land, it should have checked the entry in relation to T's land. R therefore was deemed to have knowledge of the error.

RACOON LTD v. TURNBULL [1996] 3 W.L.R. 353, Lord Jauncey of Tullichettle, PC.

4959. Land registration–mortgages–freeholds–defendant's charges took priority over those of plaintiff owing to failure to note obligation on charges register

[Land Registration Act 1925 s.30.]

L sought a declaration under the Land Registration Act 1925 s.30(1) that their mortgage had priority over N's mortgage because a registered charge putting N under an obligation to pay an additional £1,608,000 was not noted. L sold a freehold to a development company owned by H and to whom N agreed to advance £1,608,000 which formed a charge over the property. H could not pay L's purchase price of £863,000. However, £750,000 was paid and the remainder was secured by a legal charge over the property of £127,812. L's charge and N's charge were registered on the same day.

Held, giving judgment for N, that (1) N's advances received priority under s.30(1) of the 1925 Act; (2) N was informed by the Land Registry of the s.30(1) notice on July 30, 1991 and further advances were made prior to this date, but not afterwards and (3) therefore, N remained unaffected by L's further advances regardless of any obligation to note them on the register.

LLOYD v. NATIONWIDE ANGLIA BUILDING SOCIETY [1996] E.G.C.S. 80, Sir John Vinelott, Ch D.

4960. Lands tribunal

LANDS TRIBUNAL RULES 1996, SI 1996 1022; made under the Lands Tribunal Act 1949 s.3; and the Law of Property Act 1925 s.84. In force: May 1, 1996; £4.15.

These Rules make provision for the procedure to be followed in respect of cases before the Lands Tribunal. They replace the Lands Tribunal Rules 1975 (SI 1975 299). The Rules consolidate the procedure in relation to appeals. They no longer provide for prescribed forms to be used except in relation to applications under the Rights of Light Act 1959 s.2. The main changes to the general procedure of the Tribunal are; a simplification of the procedure for the determination of proceedings without a hearing; a new simplified procedure is introduced for appropriate cases; the Arbitration Act 1950 s.19A is applied to proceedings allowing the Tribunal to award interest on compensation; the Tribunal's powers of sanction in the event of failure to pursue proceedings diligently or to comply with the Rules are strengthened; and provision is made for solicitors to be placed formally on the record when acting for a party to proceedings with responsibility to the Tribunal for fees.

4961. Lands tribunal–fees

LANDS TRIBUNAL (FEES) RULES 1996, SI 1996 1021; made under the Lands Tribunal Act 1949 s.3, s.8. In force: May 1, 1996; £1.55.

These Rules provide for a new scale of fees to be taken in proceedings before the Lands Tribunal, following the revocation of the Lands Tribunal Rules 1975 (SI 1975 299) by the Lands Tribunal Rules 1996, which contain the rules of procedure of the Tribunal. The 1975 Rules incorporated both rules of procedure and fees. The Lands Tribunal (Amendment) Rules 1977, 1984, 1986 and 1990 (SI 1977 1820, SI 1984 793, SI 1986 1322, and SI 1990 1382) are revoked. The fee for lodging an appeal or a reference is increased to £50, the fee for lodging an absent owner application is increased to £100 and the fee for lodging a restrictive covenant application is increased to £200. A summary of old and new fees payable is contained in the explanatory note appended to the Rules.

4962. Lands tribunal–valuation–compensation for profits lost due to compulsory purchase–forced move of business established for 120 years–choice of smaller alternative premises considered

H sought compensation following the compulsory purchase of a glazing business situated in the same premises in Burnley for 120 years. Alternative premises offered all presented access or storage problems and H chose to move to an industrial unit in Nelson, but found that he had incurred a loss after the first year due to the lack of facilities.

Held, that compensation was assessed at £102,392 to include the freehold interest, removal costs and loss of profits. The choice of smaller property in Nelson was hard to explain, given the fact that H had been offered the chance to stay in the property as a tenant and that it must have been obvious that the move to smaller premises in another location would reduce trading opportunities. However, the transfer of such a long established business was not a simple matter of loading and transport so that the claim for loss due to forced sale was allowed in full at £3,221 and permanent loss of profit was set at £20,000 allowing for H's unfortunate choice of alternative premises.

HESELDON (T/A JAMES SHOESMITH) v. LANCASHIRE CC [1996] 36 R.V.R. 220, JC Hill, TD, FRICS., Lands Tr.

4963. Lands tribunal–valuation–determination of compensation payable in respect of former warehouse converted for use as office accommodation and licensed premises

O sought compensation of £500,000 from C under a 1993 agreement in respect of their freehold interest in a public house and office development housed in a converted former warehouse and based on valuations carried out using three valuation methods: (1) rent at 15 per cent of an adjusted turnover figure of

£350,000 capitalised at 11 per cent giving a value of £477,225; (2) a notional rent of £52,000 plus barrelage of 460 at a wholesale price of £80 each taken at 5.5 yp giving £491,150 and (3) a goodwill aggregation of three year's purchase of net adjusted profit, plus agreed fixtures and fittings, giving a total of £525,000.

Held, that the compensation payable by C was £412,000, including £4,539 and £14,000 for stock and redundancy costs respectively, based on an upper floor valuation of £93,000 on a net annual rental income of £12,150 with 13 per cent yield rate given the likelihood of a lease renewal for the office accommodation. The public house value was assessed at £300,000 including fixtures and fittings given its potential to attract independent purchasers, although its reliance on entertainment and uncertain car parking arrangements were characteristics limiting its value to no more than once its turnover.

O'SULLIVAN AND SEAL AND BUILDINGS LTD v. CARDIFF BAY DEVELOPMENT CORP [1996] 36 R.V.R. 205, M St J Hopper, FRICS., Lands Tr.

4964. Leases–oral agreement–whether agreement was enforceable–whether the doctrine of part performance applied

[Law of Property (Miscellaneous) Provisions Act 1989 s.2; Law of Property Act 1925 s.40.]

S renewed her application for leave to appeal against judgment in a case in which she had sought specific performance. S and B had agreed to form a company to buy the freehold of their flats and take long leases on the property. S claimed to have made an oral agreement with B to take a lease on the flat S occupied for £10,000. B suggested taking on the negotiations on S's behalf. S discovered that she was offered her flat for £24,000 which she could not afford.

Held, dismissing the application, that (1) an oral agreement was not enforceable, in the absence of any writing to support it, under the Law of Property (Miscellaneous) Provisions Act 1989 s.2. There was no merit in a submission that s.2 did not apply because the agreement was an executory agreement before B had any proprietary interest in the property and (2) the Court of Appeal doubted that the doctrine of part performance had been abolished. Although s.2(8) of the 1989 Act provided that the Law of Property Act 1925 s.40 would cease to have effect, nevertheless the doctrine was an equitable doctrine on which reliance might be placed in certain circumstances. In the instant case, however, the fact that S allowed B to negotiate on her behalf could not amount to part performance of the alleged oral agreement.

SINGH v. BEGGS (1996) 71 P. & C.R. 120, Neill, L.J., CA.

4965. Liens–unpaid vendor's lien–objective test for existence of lien

B, the second defendant, appealed against an order for possession granted to BB. B had sold his property to his son for £70,000, of which £19,000 was paid by the son, and it was agreed that B would receive a half share in the profits following redevelopment. The redevelopment was not a precondition to the payment of the outstanding balance of £51,000. B was to remain in the property rent free until redevelopment. The property was sold to E&C who granted BB a legal charge on the property. B's occupation of the property was not investigated and therefore not discovered. B's claim for an unpaid vendor's lien over the property, which would have ranked higher in priority than BB's legal charge, was rejected.

Held, allowing the appeal, that (1) the existence of a lien did not rely on completion of the contract, but existed once a binding contract was formed, *Birmingham, Re* [1959] Ch. 523, [1958] C.L.Y. 1280 and *London and Cheshire Insurance Co Ltd v. Laplagrene Property Co Ltd* [1971] 1 Ch. 499, [1971] C.L.Y. 1917 considered and (2) the judge was wrong to apply a subjective test to the intention of the parties in relation to whether a lien existed. The existence of a lien was demonstrated by an objective test. Nothing in this transaction amounted to an inference that the lien had been excluded. B's consent would have given the charge priority over the lien but that was not obtained, *Winter v. Lord Anson*

(1827) 3 Russ. 488, *Davies v. Thomas* [1900] 2 Ch. 462 and *Kettlewood v. Watson* (1884) 26 Ch. D. 501 considered.

BARCLAYS BANK PLC v. ESTATES AND COMMERCIAL LTD (IN LIQUIDATION), *The Times*, March 13, 1996, Millett, L.J., CA.

4966. Listed buildings–closing orders–residential tenancies–short term tenants–entitlement to proceed for judicial review–prompt action required

[Housing Act 1985 s.264.]

A was a Rent Act protected tenant in a listed building. W considered it to be unfit for human habitation and served a demolition order. On realising that the building was listed, W served repair notices on A's landlord M, as A had originally requested. M appealed. On counsel's advice that there were no prospects of successfully opposing M's appeal, W consented to an order allowing the appeal which contained a declaration that the most satisfactory course of action would be to serve a closing order under the Housing Act 1985 s.264. W made the closing order and M issued a summons for possession against A. A sought leave to apply for judicial review of W's decision to make the order.

Held, dismissing the application for leave, that (1) given counsel's advice and the declaration contained in the consent order, it would have been irrational for W to serve further repair notices; (2) any initial error by W had long been overtaken by events and (3) a person who had only short term rights of occupation and did not have a statutory right of appeal could nevertheless seek judicial review of a closing order, but only where the decision was on its face irrational or otherwise improper and promptly challenged.

R. v. WOKING BC, *ex p.* ADAM (1996) 28 H.L.R. 513, Simon Brown, L.J., CA.

4967. Matrimonial home–charge against family home executed by wife as security for business of husband and son–legal advice–whether bank put on enquiry as to undue influence

W appealed against a decision allowing a claim against her in respect of a charge executed by W, H and their son against a home owned by all three of them. H and the son owned the shares of a company which was experiencing cash flow problems. Their solicitor witnessed the execution of the charge which contained a certificate stating that they had been advised of the effect of the charge and informed of their right to independent legal advice. The court found that the presumption of undue influence between H and W had not been rebutted and the transaction was to W's disadvantage. However, it was decided that B had not been put on inquiry that W's surety had been improperly obtained and that the bank was entitled to rely on the competence of the solicitor.

Held, dismissing the appeal, that the judge had correctly applied the rules laid down in *Barclays Bank Plc v. O'Brien* [1994] 1 A.C. 180, [1994] C.L.Y. 3300 and was correct in applying them to the facts of this case. B knew that W, H and the son were receiving legal advice from a solicitor throughout the transaction and was entitled to assume that the advice was correct. In particular, the existence of the certificate showed that W was aware of the importance of separate legal advice and to query the correctness of the certificate would have gone beyond what B was required to do as it would have questioned the honesty of the solicitor. The nature and extent of advice given by the solicitor was a matter between the solicitor and the client.

BANK OF BARODA v. RAYAREL (1995) 27 H.L.R. 387, Hirst, L.J., CA.

4968. Matrimonial home–husband and wife as joint tenants–forgery of wife's signature on sale deed–husband and purchaser colluding to defraud building society–whether building society's charge valid–husband's solicitors liable for breach of warranty of authority to building society

[Law of Property Act 1925 s.52, s.63, s.115.]

H and W owned a property in their joint names as beneficial joint tenants, subject to a mortgage in favour of a building society, X. In 1991, H ran into financial difficulties and formed a plan to raise money by selling the house to a purchaser, D2 who would obtain a mortgage to buy the property and then split the net amount advanced by B. The fourth defendants, D4, were a firm of solicitors who acted for H in the sale. To this end, H and D2 forged W's signature on the contract for sale and the deed of transfer. Solicitors acted for D2 in the purchase and as agents for B. They assumed that D4 had W's authority to act in the sale and B&W therefore advanced the purchase price, part of which went to repay X's charge. In April 1992, W divorced H and obtained an order for the transfer of the house. W subsequently discovered the forged transfer. She sought a declaration that the purported transfer of the house and B's legal charge were null and void by reason of H's forgery of her signature. She also sought an order that the applications for registration in D2's name and for registration of B's charge be refused. She further sought damages against D4 in negligence. B&W counterclaimed that the deed had severed the beneficial joint tenancy and that therefore their charge subsisted over H's beneficial interest to secure the balance of the advance. They also sought damages from D4, claiming that they relied on D4's implied warranty that they acted for W and that they would not have advanced the monies had they known the true position.

Held, granting the declarations and the order and damages in favour of W and refusing B's claim for a charge but allowing their action against D4, that (1) no interest could be registered at the Land Registry as the deed upon which D2 relied was a nullity under the Law of Property Act 1925 s.52 due to the forged contract for sale and conveyance. The transaction amounted to a sham so did not sever the joint tenancy. The property transfer order in the divorce could be executed under s.63 of the 1925 Act as H's beneficial interest had not passed to D2 by means of the forged conveyance, *Ahmed v. Kendrick* [1988] 2 F.L.R. 22, [1987] C.L.Y. 470 distinguished; (2) D4 were liable to W in negligence. She was not their client but they owed her a duty of care due to her status as co-owner which was sufficiently proximate to the transaction; (3) under s.115(2) of the 1925 Act B was subrogated to the rights of X because part of the money lent to D2 was used to discharge the original mortgage. However, due to the sham nature of the transaction, B had no charge over H's interest in the equity of redemption and (4) D4 had induced B to enter the transaction due to their representation that they had H and W's authority. Therefore, D4 were liable to B for breach of warranty of authority.

PENN v. BRISTOL & WEST BUILDING SOCIETY [1995] 2 F.L.R. 938, Kolbert, J., Ch D.

4969. Matrimonial home–mortgages–wife as surety–undue influence

W appealed against the repossession of the family home. H the sole owner, charged the house to secure a loan. W had signed a consent form undertaking not to assert an interest in the property, having received independent advice to the effect that she might lose her home. W claimed that she signed the form under undue influence.

Held, dismissing the appeal, that she had not signed the form under undue influence. The bank were aware of her interest in the property and had taken reasonable steps to ensure that she was aware of her rights. She would still have signed the form and therefore the bank could not be held responsible for her.

MIDLAND BANK PLC v. KIDWAI [1995] N.P.C. 81, Stuart-Smith, L.J., CA.

4970. Matrimonial home–mortgages–wife mortgaged family home on basis of misrepresentation–solicitors also acting for mortgagee–whether implied or constructive knowledge

[Law of Property Act 1925 s.199.]

W, a wife, appealed against an order granting possession of the family home to HMS. HMS had advanced money to W and her husband, H, on the security of a charge over their home. W claimed that her consent was given due to a misrepresentation by H that the loan was to be for home improvements. The money had in fact been used to pay off his business debts. W claimed that she had not read the mortgage deed but had relied entirely on H. The solicitors, acting for both parties, were aware of the true purpose of the loan and it was claimed that HMS had imputed or constructive knowledge of what the solicitors knew.

Held, dismissing the appeal, that (1) W could not rely on the principles in *Barclays Bank Plc v. O'Brien* [1994] A.C. 180, [1994] C.L.Y. 3300 and *CICB Mortgages v. Pitt* [1994] A.C. 200, [1994] C.L.Y. 3293 for a defence, although she might have had a case against her husband on these grounds; (2) W had not proved that the solicitors knew that the real purpose of the loan was not that which was expressed to HMS, that they had acquired that knowledge during a transaction in which they had acted for HMS and during which they were under a duty to communicate the knowledge to HMS and that such knowledge had been imputed to the lender, and (3) under the Law of Property Act 1925 s.199(ii)(b) knowledge of the relevant matters had not come to the solicitors as solicitors for HMS. The lender was a purchaser within the meaning of the Act and therefore s.199(ii)(b) precluded the solicitors' knowledge being imputed to the lender.

HALIFAX MORTGAGE SERVICES LTD (FORMERLY BNP MORTGAGES LTD) v. STEPSKY [1996] Ch. 207, Morritt, L.J., CA.

4971. Matrimonial home–repossession–wife claiming mortgage unenforceable against her–not advised to seek independent advice–whether circumstances existed from which undue influence could be presumed–existence of invalidating tendency needed–relevancy of loan purpose

S sought repossession of H's family home. W claimed the mortgage was voidable and unenforceable on the grounds that it was obtained by improper means and that she was not advised to take independent legal advice. The judge held that W had to prove actual undue influence by the husband, under certain circumstances. At the hearing W tried to introduce further evidence. S argued that the hearing had been a trial on the merits.

Held, dismissing the application, that S was entitled to its mortgage remedies. The hearing was a trial on the merits, *Langdale v. Danby* [1982] 1 W.L.R. 1123, [1982] C.L.Y. 2576 followed. Evidence must have been known at the time of the hearing for it to be introduced at such a late stage. The trial judge went too far in his finding; it was sufficient for W to show circumstances from which undue influence could be presumed. In seeking to set aside the transaction, W had to show an invalidating tendency and that the third party was aware. It is the purpose for which the loan is sought which is relevant and not actual application of the funds, *CIBC Mortgages v. Pitt* [1994] 1 A.C. 200, [1994] C.L.Y. 3293. Although the husband was solely responsible for the statement of this, it would be unfair to allow W to rely on a stated purpose which proved not to be the actual one.

SCOTLIFE HOME LOANS (NO.2) LTD v. HEDWORTH (1996) 28 H.L.R. 771, Neill, L.J., CA.

4972. Matrimonial home–undue influence–joint ownership–charge over property–wife to repay half purchase price before charge could be set aside

H took out a loan for £260,000, of which £50,000 was to secure his personal debt to the bank and the rest to purchase leasehold property jointly with W. When H defaulted on payments and DB brought an action for possession of the property, W argued that there had been undue influence on the part of H of which DB had constructive notice, and that DB's charge over the property should be set aside. DB contended that the charge could not be set aside unless W paid the bank a sum of money representing the benefit she had received from the loan in terms of acquiring a joint interest in the property.

Held, that the transaction was sufficiently disadvantageous to W for DB to be alerted to the possibility of undue influence, and it had not taken reasonable steps to ensure W had independent advice about the nature of the transaction. However, because of the nature of the loan, it was appropriate to require W to repay £105,000, half the sum used to purchase the property, plus interest, before the charge would be set aside, *Erlanger v. New Sombrero Phosphate Co* (1878) 3 App. Cas. 1218 considered.

DUNBAR BANK PLC v. NADEEM [1997] 1 F.C.R. 197, Robert Englehart Q.C., Ch D.

4973. Matrimonial home–wife offering security on basis of husband's misrepresentation–bank having constructive knowledge of misrepresentation–transaction set aside

A claimed, from W, sums in excess of £200,000 under a finance agreement for which W had provided security. W was divorced from H but, following a partial reconciliation, W entered the agreement in the mistaken belief that she was entering a joint venture with H relating to a wine bar and that the charge executed against her home was limited to £35,000.

Held, dismissing A's action, that W had relied on H's misrepresentations when entering the agreement. A had failed to explain W's liability to her and, given the couple's history, should have advised her to seek independent legal advice. The solicitor who had dealt with the agreement was not independent as he was retained by A. This resulted in A having constructive knowledge of H's misrepresentation and W was entitled to have the transaction set aside. A's contention that they were entitled to recover the debt to the extent of £35,000, as that was the sum which W had intended to secure, was dismissed. W had not received the £35,000 and H was not entitled to require W to accept liability for it. A were in no better position due to their constructive knowledge. The transaction should be set aside in full in order to put W in the position in which she would have been if the misrepresentation had not occurred, *Barclays Bank Plc v. O'Brien* [1994] 1 A.C. 180, [1994] C.L.Y. 3300 considered.

ALLIED IRISH BANK PLC v. BYRNE [1995] 2 F.L.R. 325, Ferris, J., Ch D.

4974. Matrimonial home–wife secured loan and executed further charge over house–husband fraudulently used house as security for further loan–wife and plaintiff did not know of the fraud–subrogation–set aside

W used the matrimonial home, of which she was the sole freehold owner, as security for a loan made to H and as security for his overdraft with Lloyds Bank. She executed a further charge over the house which she believed to be a loan to pay for roof repairs, but was actually used to pay off H's debts with Barclays. Barclays discharged the debt to Lloyds with this charge. H took money from the roof repair account and other bank accounts. Barclays called in all of H's debts. He then fraudulently used the house as security for a further loan from CPF to pay off Barclays. W and CPF did not know of the fraud. The issue which arose was whether W's claim was subrogated to that of Barclays. The county court judge ordered that W had no contractual liability to CPF and that she was bound by the Barclays charge only to the extent that she had a full understanding of the transaction. W appealed and CPF cross-appealed.

Held, allowing the appeal in part, that the judge had been wrong to set aside the Barclays charge in part only, on the basis that a new equitable mortgage in a limited sum be created, *TSB Bank Plc v. Camfield* [1995] 1 W.L.R. 430, [1995] 1 C.L.Y. 2447 applied. The charge must be totally set aside. When CPF discharged the debt to Barclays it became entitled only to the same security as Barclays, that is to the extent of the charge in favour of Lloyds from the outset. CPF was therefore entitled to be subrogated to the Lloyds charge and the order that W pay 35 per cent of CPF's costs was upheld.

CASTLE PHILLIPS FINANCE v. PIDDINGTON (1995) 70 P. & C.R. 592, Peter Gibson, L.J., CA.

4975. Misrepresentation–availability of main drainage–whether negligence or breach of contract involved–derogation from grant–damages for innocent misrepresentation

[Misrepresentation Act 1967 s.2.]

D sought damages contending misrepresentation and breach of contract against the CEC, in respect of land purchased for house building purposes. The draft contract of sale and attached plan showed main drainage was available for the site when in reality it was not and D argued that he had entered into the contract in reliance on this misrepresentation, suffering loss as a result.

Held, allowing D's claim, that, although there was no evidence of negligence on CEC's part and they were not in breach of contract for purporting to grant a right they did not have, D was entitled to damages under the Misrepresentation Act 1967 s.2(1). Under s.2(1) D could recover damages in respect of all losses caused by the misrepresentation, whether foreseeable or not, subject to a limit for remoteness, *Royscot Trust v. Rogerson* [1991] 2 Q.B. 297, [1991] C.L.Y. 1311 applied. On the facts, due to the misrepresentation D had lost use of the capital involved in construction for six months. Of the two houses involved, it could not be shown that a higher price would have been achieved if the first had been sold six months earlier, but a loss could be attributed to the delay in respect of the second.

DODD v. CROWN ESTATE COMMISSIONERS [1995] E.G.C.S. 35, R. Owen, Q.C., QBD.

4976. Mortgagees–equitable relief–mortgagee's relief entitlement not subject to landlord's intention to grant new lease.

[County Courts Act 1984 s.138.]

B applied for relief from forfeiture against S, their mortgagor's landlord, following an order for possession and forfeiture of a flat on a 125 year lease. Peaceable entry to the flat was obtained by S and B was duly informed that S intended to grant the tenant a new long lease. B gave an undertaking to S to pay arrears and entitlement to relief was claimed on the usual terms. Subsequently, B claimed relief under the County Courts Act 1984 s.138(9), the original leasehold title was cancelled by HM Land Registry and a new lease was granted to the tenant.

Held, giving judgment for B and ordering S to pay the mortgagee's premium of £48,000 on the new lease, that there was no absolute bar in law to relief. S acted unreasonably after receiving the undertaking from B and B was entitled to relief from forfeiture and a reversionary lease on the new lease.

BANK OF IRELAND HOME MORTGAGES v. SOUTH LODGE DEVELOPMENTS [1996] 1 E.G.L.R. 91, Lightman, J., Ch D.

4977. Mortgagees–possession order obtained–agreement not to execute warrant of arrears paid–warrant executed when arrears not paid–whether warrant could be set aside while order still in force

O was in arrears with her mortgage instalments. C obtained an order for possession, but agreed not to execute the warrant for possession if O continued to pay an agreed sum towards the arrears. O then missed a payment and the warrant was executed. O applied to suspend the warrant.

Held, dismissing the application, that once warrant for possession has been executed, the court may no longer exercise its powers to stay or suspend the operation of the warrant, where the order for possession itself is not set aside, unless the execution of the warrant amounts to an abuse of process or oppression, *Hammersmith and Fulham LBC v. Hill* (1994) 27 H.L.R. 368, [1994] C.L.Y. 2778 applied.

CHELTENHAM AND GLOUCESTER BUILDING SOCIETY v. OBI (1996) 28 H.L.R. 22, Kennedy, L.J., CA.

4978. Mortgagees–power of sale–sale completed before mortgagor's application against repossession heard–whether court can interfere

[Administration of Justice Act 1970 s.36.]

N appealed against an order suspending sale of a repossessed property. A borrowed from N to purchase the lease of a flat from Westminster City Council. A defaulted on the mortgage and N brought possession proceedings. A obtained an order under Administration of Justice Act 1970 s.36 to suspend the repossession on terms but fell into arrears. N informed A that they intended to execute the suspended order and took possession. A sought to set aside the possession order on the ground that the lease was void and that he was entitled to the return of his premium plus interest and with this he would be able to repay his mortgage. N contracted to sell the property in the face of A's application and the sale was completed before A's application had been heard. At A's application the court made an order allowing A back into occupation and prohibiting the registration of the title of the purchaser.

Held, allowing the appeal, that the judge had been wrong to prohibit the registration of the sale. Once the mortgagee's power of sale arose the court had no power to deal with the property except under statute and no such grounds arose in this case. A's claim that the grant of the lease was void was also rejected as it was not clear whether the grant was ultra vires.

NATIONAL AND PROVINCIAL BUILDING SOCIETY v. AHMED [1995] 38 E.G. 138, Millett, L.J., CA.

4979. Mortgagees' powers and duties–possession sought–monthly arrears repayment offer–costs

AN sought possession claiming arrears of £4,800 on a loan of £39,000 entered into in April 1993. AN failed to produce the mortgage conditions and there was doubt as to the monthly repayments due, because the monthly sum claimed was greater than had been stated in the mortgage quotation. In correspondence, AN's solicitors had failed to give a satisfactory explanation.

Held, that the claim for possession be adjourned upon terms that the borrowers pay the monthly sum stated in the monthly quotation. In correspondence, A's offer to pay off the arrears over a period of eight years, £50 per month, had been refused on the grounds that AN usually required arrears to be cleared over a period of two years. Since AN's approach was inconsistent with that outlined by the Court of Appeal in *Cheltenham & Gloucester Building Society v. Norgan* [1996] 1 W.L.R. 343, [1996] C.L.Y. 2913, it was further ordered that the lenders should pay the costs of the hearing, which should not be added to the security, *Cheltenham & Gloucester Building Society v. Norgan* applied.

ABBEY NATIONAL v. ACHARYA, January 24, 1996, District Judge Brown, CC (Croydon). [*Ex rel.* Jon Holbrook, Barrister].

4980. Mortgages–forced sale of residential property–whether building society could take over conduct of sale where sale price less than amount owed

[Law of Property Act 1925 s.91.]

H applied to take over the conduct of a sale negotiated by B under the Law of Property Act 1925 s.91. B had mortgaged their home to H and fell into default. H's possession order was suspended on the basis that B should continue to live in the house for the purpose of selling it. B had found a purchaser for some £250,000 against a debt of £324,000. H did not suggest that a better price could be obtained and offered no explanation for the application other than to say that it would be inappropriate to break its established policy to refuse sales by mortgagors where there was a deficiency. B feared that this might cause delay and possible failure and that, if it were known to be a forced sale, this might also drive down the price.

Held, ordering a sale subject to safeguards for the mortgagee in case it did not proceed as planned, that (1) it was not disputed that s.91 conferred on the court a discretion at the instance of the mortgagor to order a sale against the wishes of the mortgagee if justice required it, *Palk v. Mortgage Services* [1993] Ch. 330, [1992] C.L.Y. 3154 followed, and (2) on the evidence there was no discernible advantage to the mortgagee in declining this sale while there was an obvious advantage to the mortgagors in selling at this price, which would also eliminate the accrual of further arrears.

BARRETT v. HALIFAX BUILDING SOCIETY (1996) 28 H.L.R. 634, Evans Lombe, J, Ch D.

4981. Mortgages–indemnities–recognised bodies

MORTGAGE INDEMNITIES (RECOGNISED BODIES) ORDER 1996, SI 1996 161; made under the Housing Act 1985 s.444. In force: February 20, 1996; £0.65.

This Order specifies four additional bodies as recognised bodies for the purposes of Housing Act 1985 s.442 and s.443 (agreements to indemnify mortgagees and contributions to mortgage costs). The bodies are: Bradford and Bingley Loans Ltd; Bradford and Bingley Management Ltd; Bradford and Bingley Secured Loans Ltd and Bradford and Bingley Secured Loans Management Ltd.

4982. Mortgages–money judgment for amount of outstanding mortgage–suspension of judgment appropriate except in exceptional circumstances

[Administration of Justice Act 1970 s.36; Administration of Justice Act 1973 s.8.]

CG applied for a possession order against J when he fell behind with his mortgage repayments. A suspended order was granted on terms that J should pay the arrears by instalments. CG appealed against the dismissal of an appeal against the refusal of the judge to grant a suspended order on the same terms but for payment of the total amount of the mortgage which was over £40,000. The judge ordered that the application should be adjourned with liberty to restore. CG argued that the practice of adjourning the claim, which was a routine procedure for district judges, was contrary to the binding authority of *Cheltenham and Gloucester Building Society v. Grattidge* (1993) 25 H.L.R. 454, [1993] C.L.Y. 2884, which held that a judge had the discretion to make a suspended order for payment of the full amount, but the discretion must be exercised consistently with the Administration of Justice Act 1970 s.36 and the Administration of Justice Act 1973 s.8 and so a money order should be suspended for the same length of time as the possession order.

Held, allowing the appeal, that CG was entitled to a money judgment which should have been suspended in accordance with the suspension of the possession order, *Cheltenham and Gloucester Building Society v. Grattidge* followed. The common procedure of granting an adjournment was contrary to the ratio of *Grattidge* which permitted such practice only in special circumstances.

CHELTENHAM & GLOUCESTER BUILDING SOCIETY v. JOHNSON (1996) 28 H.L.R. 885, Hirst, L.J., CA.

4983. Mortgages–possession order suspended–meaning of "reasonable period" under Administration of Justice Act 1970 s.36–evidence required from mortgagor of ability to repay debt from sale proceeds

[Administration of Justice Act 1970 s.36.]

L, an estate agent, was appointed by N in May 1992 to act as its agent and in June 1992 borrowed £280,000 from N. The loan was secured by charges on L's farm and premises in Dorset. Mortgages were executed in respect of both properties. L soon fell into arrears on the loan and in March 1994 N obtained an order for possession. L appealed against this order. L's appeal was upheld in May 1995, on the basis of affidavit evidence which showed that L expected to complete sales of sufficient portions of his farm and other properties to repay the entire debt to N by June 1996, and the possession order was suspended until June 1996. N appealed.

Held, allowing the appeal and removing the suspension, that (1) there was no rule of law to the effect that the power under the Administration of Justice Act 1970 s.36 to adjourn or suspend a possession order would only be exercised, in the case of the sale of mortgaged property, if the sale would be taking place within a short period of time. The question was whether the sale would take place within a "reasonable period", and that depended on the individual facts of each case. If there was clear evidence that the completion of the sale of a property would take place in six months or even a year there was no reason why a court could not conclude that the "mortgagor was likely to be able within a reasonable period to pay any sums due under the mortgage" and (2) where the mortgaged property was to be sold and there were no known outside assets, a mortgagor must put clear evidence before a court to establish that he was "likely" to be able to repay the sums due within a reasonable period, *Royal Trust Co of Canada v. Markham* [1975] 3 All E.R. 433, [1975] C.L.Y. 2222 applied. A mortgagor's affidavit in which it is simply stated that property was being or had been put on the market was not sufficient. The evidence in the instant case in relation to the critical part of the relevant property took the form of a mere intention to place that property on the market.

NATIONAL & PROVINCIAL BUILDING SOCIETY v. LLOYD [1996] 1 All E.R. 630, Neill, L.J., CA.

4984. Mortgages–possession proceedings–sale of property–whether mortgagee owed duty to spouse to obtain best available price

M made an interlocutory appeal against an order granting leave to appeal to C and setting aside a judgment entered in default of notice of intention to defend. M, as first mortgagees, took possession proceedings after C and her husband fell into arrears on jointly owned properties. Mr C, consequent to his bankruptcy, did not challenge the judgment obtained against himself and C for a shortfall of £103,000. In the course of the possession proceedings it was common ground that Mr C authorised M to deal with W as potential buyer of the properties for £150,000. Mr C was anxious to arrange the sale with W on the basis that, although there would be a shortfall on the charge to the plaintiffs, W would be in a position to negotiate with the second mortgagees so as to relieve Mr C and C of their responsibilities under the second mortgage. C sought to set aside the judgment on the grounds that M had been in breach of their separate duty to her, to use their best endeavours to obtain the best price available for the property in the open market and that if she were permitted to defend the proceedings, there would be "an arguable defence carrying some degree of conviction" on the authority of *Saudi Eagle, The* [1986] 2 Lloyd's Rep. 221, [1987] C.L.Y. 3044.

Held, allowing the appeal, that the central issue was whether C gave actual or ostensible authority to her husband. Her affidavit made it plain that she regarded her husband as authorised to conclude the transaction on his own as well as her behalf and that she had made her husband her agent. The case was not concerned with a mortgagee achieving the best available market price, but with a mortgagee achieving a price acceptable to the mortgagors, in this case a man and wife. The court differed from the judge's view that there was an arguable defence on the grounds that M owed a duty of care to C and that she was unaffected by the conduct of her husband. Further, the judge was too generous in saying that the issue could only be resolved by oral evidence, the affidavit evidence was all one way and settled the issue against C. The court was entitled to interfere because the wrong test had been applied and there was no duty on M to obtain more than £150,000. It was also significant that C advanced no alternative case as to whether she would have acted differently had she been acquainted with all the circumstances.

MERCANTILE CREDIT CO LTD v. CLARKE (1996) 71 P. &. C.R. D18, Russell, L.J., CA.

4985. Mortgages–property owned by company owned by guarantor–whether possession could be sought against guarantors

S was the mortgagee of property belonging to G. G was wholly owned by M who, along with her mother, was a guarantor of the mortgage. S had obtained possession against G on the grounds of arrears and now sought possession against the two guarantors. The guarantors claimed that the property had been charged without their consent and therefore the charge could not be enforced against them.

Held, allowing the application, that S was entitled to possession against the guarantors. They had transferred the property to G with informed consent with the intention that G would own the house and the guarantors would have the benefit of shares. There were no special rules of law applicable to family property.

STOCKHOLM FINANCE LTD v. GARDEN HOLDINGS INC [1995] N.P.C. 162, Walker, J., Ch D.

4986. Mortgages–repossession–judgment given in husband's absence–adduction of new evidence

[County Court Rules 1981 Ord.37 r.2.]

A appealed against a repossession order made in favour of N after they had fallen into arrears with their mortgage. The order was challenged by Mr A on the ground that there were no arrears; and Mrs A claimed that she had a beneficial interest by virtue of her contribution to the purchase price and that Mr A's undue influence had caused her to enter the mortgage. The possession order was confirmed in the lower court and Mr A appealed on the ground that the judgment had been given in his absence as he had not attended the hearing. Mrs A appealed on the basis that she had further evidence of her beneficial interest.

Held, dismissing the appeal, that (1) Mr A could not have the judgment set aside because he had failed to attend court *Shocked v. Goldschmidt* [1994] C.L.Y. 1023 followed; (2) the court had a wide discretion under the County Court Rules 1981 Ord.37 r.1 to order a rehearing but the lower judge's decision was unassailable on the grounds of diligence, evidence and hardship *Stone v. Stone* [1971] 1 W.L.R. 810 applied and (3) the court would not set aside the orders because although Mrs A raised new points and the court did have the power to hear them, the trial court was the proper place to do so.

NATIONAL COUNTIES BUILDING SOCIETY v. ANTONELLI [1995] N.P.C. 177, Otton, L.J., CA.

4987. Mortgages–repossession–party to be joined–establishing non est factum

[County Court Rules 1981 Ord.15.1.]

HB, the mortgagee, appealed against a decision which allowed D to be joined as a party in HB's action for possession of properties owned by B, the mortgagor. D was B's predecessor in title and occupied one of the properties. D had transferred the property to B for £1 but claimed the defence of non est factum. He argued that, due to his illiteracy, it was not his deed. He had not believed he was selling his house, but merely signing an agreement to repair it to obtain grants from state agencies. D was then told that it would cost £51,000 to buy back the house.

Held, allowing the appeal, that (1) in accordance with the County Court Rules 1981 Ord.15.1 D had to show a triable issue to be joined to the case; (2) to establish non est factum D had to satisfy three requirements; first, that he was illiterate, this he had established; secondly, that the document he had signed was fundamentally different from the one he believed he was signing. D did not read the document. He could not rely on the defence if he signed it after his solicitor had put it before him without comment; thirdly, D must have exercised proper care. An illiterate plaintiff must be careless if he does not ask for documents to be read to him and their nature explained, *Barclays Bank v. Schwartz* [1995] 1 C.L.Y. 2492 applied, a defence of non est factum can only be raised if D asked for the document to be read to him and was then misled. D's present claim fitted very badly with his claim that the resale fell through because he did not have enough money.

HAMBROS BANK LTD v. BRITISH HISTORIC BUILDINGS TRUST [1995] N.P.C. 179, Stuart Smith, L.J., CA.

4988. Mortgages–sale by mortgagee–whether assets should have been sold separately–extent of mortgagor's duty–whether valuers owed duty to mortgagor

H was a milk farmer whose assets were a farm and buildings and a milk quota. H got into financial difficulties and the bank appointed a receiver to sell the farm. The farm and the quota were sold for £425,000 and H claimed that the land and the quota should have been sold separately which would have required his co-operation. H also claimed that the valuers who advised the bank owed him a duty.

Held, dismissing the claim, that (1) no cause of action existed. The bank did not have the power to sell the land and the quota separately. The bank owed no duty to H in deciding whether to sell the quota separately or together with the land. The only duty owed by the bank was to obtain a reasonable price for the farm when selling the quota with it, *Downsview Nominees Ltd v. First City Corp Ltd* [1993] B.C.C. 46, [1993] C.L.Y. 2881 applied and (2) an agent employed by a mortgagee to give advice owed no duty to the mortgagor.

HUISH v. ELLIS [1995] B.C.C. 462, Jack, J., QBD.

4989. Party Wall etc. Act 1996 (c.40)

An Act to make provision in respect of party walls, and excavation and construction in proximity to certain buildings or structures.

This Act received Royal Assent on July 18, 1996.

4990. Party walls–London–nuisance–liability for damage prior to obtaining statutory consent–measure of damages–special damages for overseas property costs and mortgage interest repayments

[London Building Acts (Amendment) Act 1939 s.47, s.50.]

S carried out extensive building work on his property which caused damage to the party and front walls of the adjoining property, owned by L. L successfully gained an interlocutory injunction restraining S from carrying out further work until he complied with the requirements of the London Building Acts (Amendment) Act 1939 in providing support for the front elevation of L's property and making good all damage. L failed to sell the property due to the damage and incurred extra costs concerning a proposed move to Guadeloupe, as a result of which L claimed special damages for extra mortgage interest, building costs in Guadeloupe and general damages for nuisance. S appealed against the general damages awards contending that there was no basis for them, and in any event, L's losses were not caused by him or were too remote or excessive in amount.

Held, dismissing the appeal, that the work was carried out without first giving notice or obtaining consent as required under ss.47 and 50 of the 1939 Act and was actionable in private nuisance, *Thompson Schwab v. Costaki* [1956] 1 W.L.R. 335, [1956] C.L.Y. 6178 considered. Nothing in the 1939 Act served to reduce or exclude common law liability for acts committed in breach of the statutory requirements for notice or consent, and subsequently obtaining permission did not relieve S from liability for acts committed prior to consent being granted in the absence of agreement to this effect between S and L, *Adams v. Marylebone BC* [1907] 2 K.B. 822 followed. The judge at first instance had correctly decided that the sale could have been concluded if work lawfully carried out under the 1939 Act was in progress, and it was reasonably foreseeable on S's part that unlawful work carried out by him could prevent L making a sale and result in extra costs to L on the overseas property and additional mortgage interest payments.

LOUIS v. SADIQ [1996] E.G.C.S. 180, Evans, L.J., CA.

4991. Possession–mortgage arrears–suspended execution of warrant for possession–borrower intending to sell property within three to five year period to discharge debt–reasonableness of repayment period–order for immediate possession

[Administration of Justice Act 1970 s.36.]

B appealed against a decision upholding the suspended execution of a warrant for the possession of a property occupied by the second defendant, E, whose husband had moved out leaving substantial arrears. E had failed to comply with an initial order that she pay £5000 immediately and £200 per month thereafter, in addition to interest, but the possession order was suspended on terms that she paid £5000 and discharged the mortgage debt by selling the property within three to five years, after her children had finished their education. B submitted that the suspension order was contrary to the Administration of Justice Act 1970 s.36 which provided that the period for repayment should be reasonable.

Held, allowing the appeal, that as E could not discharge the arrears by periodic payment it was important to consider whether the period before sale was reasonable as, if it was not determined, B could be left with the order until the expiry of the mortgage and with arrears still unpaid. However, a reasonable period was not strictly definable and depended on the facts of the case, having regard to the delay in selling the property which had already occurred and the adequacy of the security if the debt was close to the value of the property. In the circumstances there was insufficient evidence for the judge to exercise his discretion and find that the property could be sold at a high enough price to discharge E's debt within a three to five year period and the appropriate order was an order for immediate possession, *National and Provincial Building Society v. Lloyd* [1996] 1 All E.R. 630, [1996] C.L.Y. 4978 followed.

BRISTOL & WEST BUILDING SOCIETY v. ELLIS (1996) 73 P. & C.R. 158, Auld, L.J., CA.

4992. Possession–registered charges–bank entitled to possession even where serious misconduct was alleged

MB obtained a possession order for a hotel owned by M after M fell behind with loan repayments. M took out a loan with MB for the purposes of refurbishment and a charge was duly registered in favour of the bank. M was subsequently investigated by the police for corruption on the basis of inaccurate information which M alleged had been supplied to the police by the bank. M applied for leave to appeal against the possession order, contending that misconduct on MB's part precluded enforcement of the legal charge.

Held, dismissing the application, that (1) MB's claim was for possession, not payment. Unless statute or contract provided to the contrary, a mortgagee could seek possession at any time after execution of the legal charge, *National Westminster Bank Plc v. Skelton* [1993] 1 W.L.R. 72, [1993] C.L.Y. 2885 applied; (2) a cross claim by the mortgagor could not defeat the mortgagee's right of possession, even if it were for liquidated damages greater than the mortgage arrears, *Ashley Guarantee v. Zacaria* [1993] 1 W.L.R. 62, [1993] C.L.Y. 2886 applied and (3) the court was bound by precedent and the bank was therefore entitled to judgment no matter what the nature of M's allegations might be. There was no hope of success on appeal and granting leave served no purpose.

MIDLAND BANK PLC v. McGRATH [1996] E.G.C.S. 61, Butler-Sloss, L.J., CA.

4993. Property rights–equitable interests in land–whether payment of deposit constitutes second limb of "Lloyd's Bank v Rosset"–undue influence–whether chargee had constructive notice

In 1959, W and her husband, H, purchased a property, the deposit being lent to them by H's mother. H purchased the freehold of their next home in his sole name and to secure loans he granted a charge to HBS and a second charge to RZH. Prior to the second charge, the solicitors acting on behalf of RZH wrote to H's solicitors requesting them to arrange for W to sign a letter postponing any interest she might have in the property. The solicitors forwarded the letter to H and requested that W should take independent legal advice on it, if she so chose. W signed the letter but had not read it, simply relying on assurances given by H. H fell into arrears with both lenders and a suspended order for possession was made in favour of HBS, with a postponed order for possession in favour of RZH. W applied to be joined in both actions and to suspend the warrant for possession. The district judge determined that W had an overriding interest in the property. RZH and HBS appealed successfully and the judge restored the warrant for possession. W appealed.

Held, allowing the appeal, that (1) the payment of a deposit could be an example of the application of the second limb of *Lloyd's Bank Plc v. Rosset* [1991] A.C. 107, [1990] C.L.Y. 706 applied. Accordingly, there was a triable issue on whether W had a beneficial interest in the property, *McHardy v. Warren* [1994] 2 F.L.R. 338, [1994] C.L.Y. 2189 considered; (2) there was just enough evidence to raise a triable issue of undue influence and (3) it was not possible to say categorically that there was no triable issue on the question of constructive notice.

HALIFAX BUILDING SOCIETY v. BROWN; SUB NOM. RAPHAEL ZORN HEMSLEY LTD v. BROWN (1995) 27 H.L.R. 511, Balcombe, L.J., CA.

4994. Property rights–listed building–Crown property–statutory repair obligations–local authority powers and duties

[Planning (Listed Buildings and Conservation Areas) Act 1990; Insolvency Act 1986 s.320; London Building Acts (Amendment) Act 1939; Prevention of Damage by Pests Act 1949.]

H appealed against the refusal to grant a vesting order in respect of a listed building of special architectural interest. Following the bankruptcy of the previous owner, the property had been disclaimed by the trustee in bankruptcy and vested in the Crown but was now derelict. H was responsible under the Planning (Listed Buildings and Conservation Areas) Act 1990 for the prevention of deterioration or damage to the building. Under s.54 and s.55 of the Act, H was authorised to carry out necessary repair work and recover the cost from the owners. However, under s.83 such powers were only to be exercised in respect of Crown land to the extent of the interest held by the Crown. Further, s.47 prevented the compulsory acquisition of such land, without the consent of the commissioners. As the only other interest in the property was an unexercised bank charge, s.83 precluded H from exercising any powers conferred on it by the Act.

Held, allowing the appeal, that for H to succeed, it had to show an interest in the property and that no other claim existed in priority, as required under the Insolvency Act 1986 s.320(2)(a) and (3)(a). Evidence showed that H's interest arose from local land charges registry entries, detailing work carried out under the London Building Acts (Amendment) Act 1939 and the Prevention of Damage by Pests Act 1949, amounting to a total value of £14,781.36. The other interests in the property were a bank charge for £133,000 and the freehold held by the Crown. However, in light of the passive attitude of both the bank and the commissioners, and a property valuation of only £10,000, the property was to be vested in H, free from either of the other two interests.

HACKNEY LBC v. CROWN ESTATE COMMISSIONERS (1996) 72 P. & C.R. 233, Knox, J., Ch D.

4995. Property rights–occupancy rent free with promised option to purchase–rights enforceable against subsequent purchaser–proprietary estoppel

[Land Registration Act 1925 s.70.]

K occupied a house rent free, from 1980, with a further promise that it could later be purchased from the then owner, J, at the price he had paid. J in fact sold the property to H in 1991 and H demanded possession. The promises made by J arose from his attempt to start a commodity business with K's assistance. Since J could not pay any profits to K, and K was threatened with eviction, having no income, the occupation of the house was offered instead. The judge found that K's option to purchase could only remain open for a reasonable time, which he determined as one year after the cessation of the business venture in 1981. K appealed.

Held, allowing the appeal and remitting the case for rehearing, that the real issues appeared not to have been properly explored. In the present unsatisfactory state it would not be appropriate for the Court of Appeal to resolve the outstanding issues. The judge had erred, because J's promise was that K could occupy the house during J's lifetime. K's acquiescence to the charging of the property to another in 1981 did not deny a right to exercise the option to purchase. The correct approach was to establish what the original promise meant, before going on to determine what rights could be enforced against a subsequent purchaser of the land. The central issue was the applicability of the Land Registration Act 1925 s.70(1)(g). This gave rise to questions as to whether enquiry had been made of K prior to H's purchase of the property so that K's alleged rights were disclosed, and if that were resolved in K's favour, whether equity created by proprietary estoppel against J was a right under s.70(1)(g). It was open to argument whether an oral option, not appearing in a lease and only enforceable by proprietary estoppel, was such a right, *Webb v. Pollmount Ltd* [1965] Ch. 584, [1966] C.L.Y. 6733, *Ashburn Anstalt v. WJ Arnold & Co* [1989] Ch. 1, [1988] C.L.Y. 2061 and *Lloyds Bank Plc v. Rosset* [1991] 1 A.C. 107, [1990] C.L.Y. 706 considered.

HABERMANN v. KOEHLER (1996) 72 P. & C.R. D10, Evans, L.J., CA.

4996. Property rights–right to buy council house–transfer of tenancy to joint names–whether discount to be shared jointly

[Housing Act 1985 s.118.]

H appealed against a decision of the court in relation to his beneficial entitlement in a property jointly purchased by him and E. The tenancy of the property had passed to E on her divorce, having been previously in the sole name of her husband. H moved in to the property and E decided to purchase it under the right to buy scheme. E could not raise the mortgage so the tenancy was transferred into H and E's joint names and a joint mortgage was obtained. The discount under the right to buy scheme was calculated in proportion to E's tenure at 41 per cent. When the relationship ended and H applied to force the sale of the property, it was decided that each party had contributed half of the sum borrowed but that E's discount represented a financial contribution. This meant that the beneficial interest was divided in such a way that E had 69.322 per cent and H had 30.678 per cent. H argued that, under the Housing Act 1985, the discount belonged to both of them once the tenancy had been transferred into joint names. H also argued that the discount was not part of the price of the property.

Held, dismissing the appeal, that (1) the Housing Act 1985 s.118 conferred the right to buy on both parties when the tenancy was transferred into joint names. However, this did not have the effect of attributing the discount to them in equal shares. The Act was concerned with the position between the occupying tenants and the local authority, not with the position between the parties. The discount was calculated with reference to E's occupation of the property. H had resided there for less than a year and was not entitled to a discount and (2) the court had been correct to take the discount into account when considering the financial contributions of the parties. The judge had made an inference about the parties' intentions in line with *Marsh v. von Sternberg* [1986] 1 F.L.R. 526, [1986] C.L.Y. 1857, but would have been entitled to reach the same conclusion by regarding it as part of the purchase price using the authority of *Springette v. Defoe* [1992] 2 F.L.R. 388, [1992] C.L.Y. 2031.

EVANS v. HAYWARD [1995] 2 F.L.R. 511, Staughton, L.J., CA.

4997. Property rights–stint holders claiming ownership of moorland–failure to disclose existence of 1867 case establishing ownership–costs penalty

B appealed against a decision that P and others, stint holders on Burnhope Moor, Durham, were also owners of the soil and therefore had the right to shoot grouse over it. B argued that ownership of the soil belonged to them, as *Ecclesiastical Commissioners v. Peart* Times, February 13, 1867 had established that the soil belonged to the Bishop of Durham to whom they were successors in title.

Held, allowing the appeal, that the ownership of the soil vested in B as successors in title to the Bishop. The decision in *Ecclesiastical Commissioners* established that the land belonged to the Bishop and such a long standing decision would be overruled only if it was clearly wrong. Costs were awarded against the respondents, as their failure to disclose the existence of the 1867 case, which they had known about as far back as 1974, had been the direct cause of the instant litigation.

BRACKENBANK LODGE LTD v. PEART; SUB NOM. BRACKEN BANK LODGE LTD, *Re* [1996] E.G.C.S. 134, Lord Browne-Wilkinson, HL.

4998. Redemption–unauthorised tenant–shorthold tenancy agreement–extinguished by warrant for possession obtained by mortgagee–whether tenant an assignee of equity of redemption–whether warrant should be suspended to allow tenant to pursue warrant for redemption

X was a former unauthorised tenant of the mortgagor under a shorthold tenancy agreement. The mortgagee obtained an order and warrant for possession of the property, thereby extinguishing the shorthold tenancy. On receiving a bailiff's notice of the warrant for possession, X applied, ex parte on notice, to set aside, vary or suspend the warrant on the grounds that, by the tenancy agreement, she was an assignee of, and interested in, the equity of redemption. Therefore, it was argued, X was entitled to pursue an action for redemption of the mortgage, but had not had the opportunity to do so, since she was unaware of the proceedings prior to the bailiff's notice. There was evidence that X had a genuine interest in seeking to redeem the mortgage.

Held, that there was an arguable case that X could pursue an action for redemption, and, in the circumstances, she could therefore have the warrant of possession suspended to enable her to issue and pursue a warrant for redemption, with liberty to the mortgagee to apply to restore.

NATIONAL WESTMINSTER HOME LOANS v. LEE RICHES, October 12, 1995, Pellys, CC. [*Ex rel.* Barry O'N McAlinden, Pupil barrister].

4999. Repossession–fixtures–whether mortgagee entitled to sell household articles–degree of permanence and annexation

B appealed against a decision, that a series of 108 items, including, inter alia, fitted carpets, light fittings, gas fires, bathroom fittings, curtains, kitchen units and white goods, oven, dishwasher, extractor, hob, fridge and freezer, were fixtures and subject to TSB's mortgage charges under a repossession order.

Held, allowing the appeal in part, that the evidence as to the nature of the items concerned was limited to photographs, as the schedule and inventory supplied had not been proved with TSB's affidavit evidence. The bathroom fittings and kitchen units were fixtures, given that they were necessary for the use of the rooms concerned, based on the degree of annexation and permanence involved. Apart from some light fittings recessed into the ceiling, the remainder did not have the degree of annexation or permanence to be electrical installations, *British Economical Lamp Co Ltd v. Empire Mile End Ltd,* Times, April 18, 1913 considered. The carpets and curtains were not capable of becoming fixtures, due to their temporary attachment and lack of permanent improvement to the building. Gas fires, although having both functional and decorative effects, were not capable of being fixtures, having a low degree of annexation. Whilst the kitchen white goods formed part of the kitchen, along with the units, they had only a slight degree of annexation which was not sufficient for them to become fixtures, given their intended purpose, relatively short working life and the fact that, if they had been acquired by hire purchase, ownership would not have passed immediately to the householder, *Holland v. Hodgson* [1872] L.R. 7 C.P. 328 and *Berkley v. Poulett* [1977] 241 E.G. 911.

BOTHAM v. TSB BANK PLC; SUB NOM. TSB BANK PLC v. BOTHAM (1997) 73 P. & C.R. D1, Roch, L.J., CA.

5000. Repossession–fraud–suspense accounts–whether fraudulent mortgagor could keep the proceeds of sale on a mortgaged property

[Law of Property Act 1925 s.105; Criminal Justice Act 1988 Part IV.]

HBS appealed against a decision that it could not recover surplus monies generated after the sale of a house on the default of a fraudulent mortgagor. T obtained a mortgage from HBS by making false representations as to his identity and creditworthiness. On his subsequent default the property was sold and the surplus was placed in a suspense account. T was convicted and the CPS sought a confiscation order and a charging order on the suspense account. HBS argued that to allow T to keep the money would be an unjust enrichment brought about by the commission of a wrong against it. HBS also argued that it might recover the money through waiver of tort or on the basis of being a beneficiary to a constructive trust.

Held, dismissing the appeal, that (1) the relationship of lender and borrower was that of debtor and creditor and it was never contemplated by the parties that T would incur liability other than debt. On the sale, he became entitled to the proceeds. The effect of condition 23 of the Law Society's Mortgage conditions operating on the Law of Property Act 1925 s.105 was not to make T liable to account to HBS for the money as money "due under the mortgage" and secured by the mortgage; (2) it was inconsistent with the mortgage to argue that T could sue in tort for deceit to recover any shortfall which the security did not cover. T did not need to rely on illegality to support his claim and his rights were not denied, *Tinsley v. Milligan* [1994] A.C. 340, [1993] C.L.Y. 1839 followed and (3) having affirmed the mortgage HBS remained only a secured creditor. The Criminal Justice Act 1988 Part IV prevented the criminal from keeping the benefits of his crime and the courts also had power to confiscate that benefit. A remedy for unjust enrichment was not provided by a constructive trust.

HALIFAX BUILDING SOCIETY v. THOMAS [1996] Ch. 217, Peter Gibson, L.J., CA.

5001. Repossession–mortgages–whether bank could claim interest as equitable chargee

[Law of Property Act 1925 s.30.]

B applied for a repossession order on N's house over which it claimed to have a valid charge. N and his wife were co-owners of the house which over a period of seven years had been involved in a series of financial dealings with B. B claimed to have a valid charge over either the house or N's beneficial interest in it. B argued it had rights either through subrogation as B's loan paid off an earlier charge or as an equitable chargee because N had agreed to procure a charge to secure a German bank's right to be indemnified by him.

Held, allowing the application, that B was entitled to possession and an order for sale under the Law of Property Act 1925 s.30. B's right to possession was based on its position as an equitable chargee. N had a beneficial interest in the house and the doctrine of partial performance would not be used to prejudice a third party such as B.

BANKERS TRUST CO v. NAMDAR (1996) 60 Conv. 371, Evans Lombe, J., Ch D.

5002. Repossession–sale of property–county court's power to suspend execution of possession warrant and give conduct of sale to lender

[Administration of Justice Act 1970 s.36.]

CG appealed against a county court's decision postponing the execution of a warrant for possession of mortgaged property until completion of the sale of the property, but giving them conduct of the sale. CG questioned whether the court had a residual jurisdiction to suspend execution of the warrant separate from the power conferred by the Administration of Justice Act 1970 s.36(2) and, if such jurisdiction existed, whether it could be used to suspend a warrant for an indeterminate period. CG also queried whether suspension pending sale was appropriate where conduct of the sale was entrusted to the lender.

Held, allowing the appeal, that whereas a limited residual jurisdiction to postpone the giving of possession did exist, *Birmingham Citizens Permanent Building Society v. Caunt* [1962] Ch. 883, [1962] C.L.Y. 1938 and *Royal Trust Co of Canada v. Markham* [1975] 1 W.L.R. 1416, [1975] C.L.Y. 2222 considered, this must depend on whether certain conditions were satisfied, namely that: (1) possession would not be required pending completion; (2) the borrowers would co-operate in the sale and their presence would not depress the sale price and (3) the borrowers would give up possession to the purchasers on completion. However, experience showed that the criteria were seldom met and the exercise of the inherent jurisdiction would rarely be appropriate. Given the inherent illogicality of granting conduct of the sale to the lender while permitting the borrower to remain until completion, it was difficult to envisage the circumstances where the jurisdiction could apply. On the facts of the instant case, it was very doubtful whether B would cooperate with CG, and the order staying possession was not appropriate.

CHELTENHAM AND GLOUCESTER PLC v. BOOKER, *The Times*, November 20, 1996, Millett, L.J., CA.

5003. Repossession–suspension–possession order could not be stayed to enable borrower to apply to High Court for order for sale of property

[Law of Property Act 1925 s.91; Administration of Justice Act 1973 s.8; Administration of Justice Act 1970 s.36.]

K defaulted on his mortgage and a possession order was obtained against him. Warrant for execution was set aside on four occasions, but K breached the terms of each occasion. A fifth warrant fell due for execution on June 12, 1995. The mortgage debt amounted to £83,000 and K had obtained a written valuation on the property of £65,000, which K did not accept, asserting it had a value of about £90,000. K applied on June 9, 1995 for an order suspending the warrant on the grounds of having found a purchaser and that an application would be made to the High Court for an order pursuant to the Law of Property Act 1925 s.91(2). The application was unsuccessful but K's appeal was allowed and execution of the warrant stayed pending an application by K to the High Court under s.91(2) of the 1925 Act. C appealed on the ground that the Court did not have jurisdiction to make the order, or alternatively that even if it had jurisdiction it should not have been exercised.

Held, allowing the appeal, that (1) under common law the court strictly observes the right of a mortgagee to enter into possession of a mortgaged property on default, *Birmingham Citizens Permanent Building Society v. Caunt* [1962] 1 Ch. 883, [1962] C.L.Y. 1938 applied and (2) by virtue of the Administration of Justice Act 1970 s.36 as amended by the Administration of Justice Act 1973 s.8 the court could, inter alia, suspend execution of the possession order if the mortgagor could within a reasonable period pay the sum due under the mortgage. Thus, there is an opportunity for a mortgagor to make an application for sale in terms of s.91 of the 1925 Act. However, s.36 did not extend the circumstances for suspension where there were insufficient funds to discharge the mortgage debt, *Palk v. Mortgage Services Funding Plc* [1993] Ch. 330, [1992] C.L.Y. 3154 distinguished and doubted.

CHELTENHAM AND GLOUCESTER PLC v. KRAUSZ; SUB NOM. CHELTENHAM & GLOUCESTER BUILDING SOCIETY v. KRAUSZ [1997] 1 All E.R. 21, Phillips, L.J., CA.

5004. Repossession–whether house sold at undervalue–sale of personal effects to meet cost of clearance–whether correct to use two estate agents to handle sale

M appealed against the sale of his home by B. Following proceedings brought by B, the property was sold for £39,000 and M's personal effects sold to meet the cost of the clearance. M contended that the house had been undervalued and should have been sold for £57,000. M also argued that the use of two estate agents had led to excessive costs and sought compensation for the loss of his possessions.

Held, dismissing the appeal, that the sale figure was justified, as the bank had valued the property twice prior to sale, once for £45,000 and the second time for £40,000. As M had adduced no evidence in support of his figure, the bank was justified in accepting £39,000. The use of two estate agents increased the chance of a sale and the commission percentage charged as a result was justified in the circumstances. On the facts, M had been requested to remove his personal effects from the property after being given sufficient notice of the bank's intention to clear it out prior to marketing it.

MINAH v. BANK OF IRELAND [1995] E.G.C.S. 144, H Wolton Q.C., QBD.

5005. Residential tenancies–Italy–government policy of postponing or suspending eviction against tenants–policy not interfering with owner's property rights–no discrimination between residential and non-residential owners

[European Convention on Human Rights 1950 Protocol 1 Art.1 European Convention on Human Rights 1950 Art.14.]

S bought two residential flats in Milan that were occupied by tenants. He obtained eviction orders for the tenants. However, in accordance with the Government policy of postponing or suspending enforcement of eviction orders against residential tenants, the orders were suspended on several occasions. S claimed unjust interference with his property rights and unfair discrimination between owners of residential and non-residential property and alleged breaches of the European Convention on Human Rights 1950 Protocol 1 Art.1 and Art.14 of the Convention read in conjunction with Protocol 1 Art.1.

Held, that there had been no violation of Art.1 of Protocol 1 or Art.14 read in conjunction with that article. Suspending the enforcement of eviction orders did amount to the State having a controlling use of the properties and the court would only interfere where the judgment was manifestly without reasonable foundation. The facts showed that the suspensions had the reasonable aim of preventing a large number of people from becoming homeless at the same time. As regards proportionality, it was found that a fair balance had been struck between the general interest of the community and the rights of the individuals. Discrimination only occurred where people in similar situations were treated differently. Owners of residential and non-residential property were not sufficiently similar and thus there had been no breach of Art.14.

SPADEA v. ITALY (1996) 21 E.H.R.R. 482, R Ryssdal (President), ECHR.

5006. Restrictive covenants–modification–parkland to be used as public park and sports ground–whether use of part as commercial nursery and training area should be allowed

Gunnersbury Park in London was conveyed to H and E in 1925 subject to a covenant that it would not be used other than as a public park or sports ground, and that the buildings would not be used other than for purposes ancillary thereto. The covenant had been modified to permit use of a small mansion in the park for training local authorities' park and teaching staff, and to permit an art gallery and studio workshops. H and E sought a further modification to allow (1) a nursery to be used as a commercial nursery for wholesale trade only, and (2) part of the ground floor of the mansion and an acre of ground to be used as a horticultural training area. No objections were raised by the beneficiaries of the covenant.

Held, allowing the application, that it would be against the public interest to impede the proposed uses. The commercial use would be in an area that was unlikely to be put to other use, being surrounded by high walls and occupied largely by greenhouses; further the letting would result in rent which could be used for the maintenance of the park. The horticultural training would affect an area not presently in public use and held out a prospect of practical work of conservation in the park by the students, as well as potential income, given that local authorities now subcontracted such training.

HOUNSLOW AND EALING LBC'S APPLICATION, *Re* (1996) 71 P. & C.R. 100, Judge Rich, Q.C., Lands Tr.

5007. Restrictive covenants–modification–residential estates–whether second house should be allowed on plot in low density estate–value of covenants to residents

[Law of Property Act 1925 s.84.]

S and D owned a plot of land on a substantial low density residential estate laid out in accordance with a building scheme of mutually binding covenants. They wished to modify the covenant to enable the building of a second house on the plot; planning permission had been obtained and foundations laid. Objectors who had the benefits of the restrictive covenants argued that maintenance of the covenants was essential, as they maintained high standards in the estate which planning policies were not protecting and that if this application was granted it would afford a precedent for others on the site. S and D argued that the modification posed no threat to the scheme overall, as it would bring the present site into line with the development of that part of the estate, where other breaches of covenants had been unchallenged, or the subject of releases; and further that the objectors could be compensated by a money payment.

Held, dismissing the application, that the restriction of building was of substantial value or advantage to the objectors and other residents within the meaning of the Law of Property Act 1925 s.84(1)(aa). The development of other houses rendered the preservation of this part of the estate more, not less, important. Whilst each application should be treated on its own merits, it was relevant that the granting of an application would have the effect of opening a breach in a carefully maintained and successful scheme of development, and alter the context for future applications.

SNAITH AND DOLDING'S APPLICATION, *Re* (1996) 71 P. & C.R. 104, Judge Marder, Q.C. (President), Lands Tr.

5008. Restrictive covenants–NHS trusts–extent of enforceability given trust's statutory nature and intended purpose of building

[Compulsory Purchase Act 1965 s.10.]

By an indenture dated December 24, 1912 land was given to the trustees of the Chelsea Hospital for Women by C's predecessor in title. The indenture was subject to two covenants: (1) that the land be used only for the purposes of the Chelsea Hospital for Women and (2) that the plans for the erection of any building be submitted to the surveyor to the Cadogan Estate. The land eventually became the property of the NHS trust. C sought a declaration that the covenants were enforceable against the trust.

Held, that the NHS trust was a body created by statute and the first covenant was contrary to that statutory intention. Therefore, the first covenant would not be enforceable. There was a right to compensation under the Compulsory Purchase Act 1965 s.10. The second covenant could be enforced against the trust to prevent the erection of a building without plans first being submitted. However, the covenant might not be sufficient to restrain the trust from constructing a building for a statutory purpose.

CADOGAN v. ROYAL BROMPTON HOSPITAL NHS TRUST [1996] 37 E.G. 142, Judge Rich Q.C., Ch D.

5009. Restrictive covenants–owner restricted to dwelling house or surgery–discharge sought to allow demolition for access to development–whether building scheme existed

[Law of Property Act 1925 s.84.]

B owned a property which comprised a plot of land and a house built in the 1930s as part of an estate known as the Hill House Estate. The property backed on to a triangular shaped plot of land which was entirely enclosed by houses forming part of the Hill House Estate. B's property was subject to a covenant restricting its use to a private dwelling house or a doctor's or dentist's surgery. The covenant contained a proviso permitting the vendor to deal with his retained land in any way he saw fit. Planning permission had been granted for the construction of eight houses on the triangular plot of land. B intended to provide access to the triangular plot of land by demolishing the house constructed on his property and constructing an access road in its place. That would have constituted a breach of the restrictive covenant. B sought the discharge or modification of the covenant pursuant to the Law of Property Act 1925 s.84(1)(aa). Other property owners in the locality objected on a number of grounds based on the assertion that the change of use would result in a detrimental alteration to the amenity of their own properties and the area in which they lived. The objectors contended that the Hill House Estate was the subject of a building scheme which should be enforced by maintaining the restrictive covenant.

Held, dismissing the application, the Hill House Estate was the subject of a building scheme. The proviso to the covenant was not inconsistent with the existence of a building scheme. The existence of the building scheme gave rise to a greater presumption that the restrictive covenants would be upheld. In the present case the applicant had failed to establish grounds for the discharge or modification of the covenant. The covenant, in impeding the applicant's proposed use for the property, secured practical benefits of substantial advantage to the objectors and it could not be said that preventing the proposed user of the property was contrary to the public interest, *Elliston v. Reacher* [1908] 2 Ch. 374, 665, *Gilbert v. Spoor* [1983] Ch. 27, [1982] C.L.Y. 2664, *Allen v. Veranne Builders Ltd* (Unreported, 1988) considered.

BROMOR PROPERTIES LTD'S APPLICATION, *Re* (1995) 70 P. & C.R. 569, PH Clarke, FRICS., Lands Tr.

5010. Restrictive covenants–prohibition of sale of vehicle fuel–access to unburdened land–intention to erect filling station

E sold land to a local authority subject to a restrictive covenant that the authority and its successors in title should not permit the sale of vehicle fuel on the land. S purchased part of the land from a successor in title and wished to use it for access to land which was not the subject of a restrictive covenant on which S intended to erect and run a petrol filling station. E sought a declaration that such conduct would be a breach of the restrictive covenant.

Held, refusing the declaration, that using the land for access to facilitate a business did not constitute carrying on that business on the land; and the restrictive covenant did not extend to preventing S's customers coming on to the land with a view to using land not burdened by the covenant.

ELLIOTT v. SAFEWAY STORES PLC [1995] 1 W.L.R. 1397, Paul Baker Q.C., Ch D.

5011. Restrictive covenants–right to buy–future disposal subject to local residence or employment qualification–beneficial nature of restrictions

[Law of Property Act 1925 s.84; Housing Act 1985 s.157, Part V.]

M purchased a three bedroomed flat and ground floor shop from the local authority pursuant to the Housing Act 1985 Part V, Right to Buy provisions. Prior to the purchase the applicants had occupied the shop for their newsagents and general store business and had lived in the flat above. In common with all other conveyances entered into by the local authority pursuant to the Right to Buy provisions the conveyance of the property to M contained a provision preventing disposal without the consent of the local authority, which could not be withheld in the case of a disposal to a person who had throughout the preceding three years had his place of work or his only or principal home within the rural areas of the Isle of Anglesey designated as such by the Secretary of State. The restriction was imposed pursuant to the Housing Act 1985 s.157 and approved by the Secretary of State. The purpose of the restriction was to ensure that an affordable supply of accommodation remained available to local people. The applicants had sought to sell their property but had been unable to find a buyer because, they alleged, the restriction rendered the property an unsuitable security from a mortgage lender's point of view. They applied to the Lands Tribunal for the release of the restriction on the ground set out in the Law of Property Act 1925 s.84(1)(aa).

Held, dismissing the application, assuming, but without deciding, that the restriction on the disposal of the property imposed pursuant to s.157 of the Act was a restrictive covenant amenable to the jurisdiction of the Lands Tribunal, no ground for the discharge of the restriction had been made out. There was evidence that the local authority had sold and was still selling properties subject to the restriction to purchasers who were assisted by mortgage lenders. The evidence produced by M did not demonstrate that it was the restriction on disposal that caused concern to potential mortgage lenders. M had never sought the consent of the local authority to any disposal of the property. On the evidence the restriction did secure to the local authority and the public within the area a practical benefit of substantial advantage or value for which money could not provide adequate compensation. It could not be said that the restriction was against the public interest as it was adopted by an elected authority pursuant to a lawful policy approved by Parliament.

MILIUS'S APPLICATION, *Re* (1995) 70 P. & C.R. 427, Judge Marder, Q.C. (President), Lands Tr.

5012. Restrictive covenants–sale of land–whether restrictive covenant applied to annexed land

[Law of Property Act 1925 s.78.]

R sought to enforce a restrictive covenant against B after parcels of land on an estate were sold off and B obtained planning permission and sought to build two houses on a plot of land contrary to a restrictive covenant of 1938 between predecessors in title and the then vendors.

Held, giving judgment for R, that (1) in determining whether a covenant applied to annexed land the court had to look at the whole of the schedule to discover the parties' intentions; (2) there were clear indications that the covenant was intended to apply to the entire estate; (3) despite the fact that the covenant was not specifically annexed to every plot on the estate it would have been so assigned if it was drafted under the Law of Property Act 1925 s.78(1) which deemed covenants concerning land "to be made with the covenantee and his successors in title...and shall have effect as if such successors and other persons were expressed"; (4) the effect of the covenants would have had a discernible relationship to the value of the premises in 1938; (5) annexation was achieved under s.78 unless it purported to effect a different purpose; (6) the vendors were acting as trustees when they sold the land, thus implying that the adjoining land also received the benefit of the covenants; (7) all R needed to show was that the covenants concerned the land, and this they had done and (8) it was a question of fact whether the covenant was obsolete due to changes. In the present case the onus was on the defence to show that such a change had not occurred and the onus had not been discharged.

ROBINS v. BERKELEY HOMES (KENT) LTD [1996] E.G.C.S. 75, Judge Colyer Q.C., Ch D.

5013. Restrictive covenants–whether covenant restricting use of house overrides statutory duty of NHS trust to provide for patients–whether injunction can restrain trust

[National Health Service and Community Care Act 1990 s.5.]

H, a trust established under the National Health Service and Community Care Act 1990 s.5, acquired a property to house five adult patients. B owned adjoining premises benefiting from a covenant that restricted the user of the property by requiring the purchaser to covenant "that no building be erected... shall be used otherwise than as a private dwellinghouse only or as a professional residence of a Medical Practitioner Dentist Solicitor or Architect". B applied for an injunction to restrain H from using the property in any way other than as a private dwelling house.

Held, refusing the injunction, that private rights affecting land were not to be enforced by injunction or damages where the legislature had provided for an exclusive remedy by way of statutory compensation.

BROWN v. HEATHLANDS MENTAL HEALTH NHS TRUST [1996] 1 All E.R. 133, Chadwick, J., Ch D.

5014. Right to buy–whether notices of completion valid–whether notices waived by election or barred by statute

[Housing Act 1985.]

B claimed that their right to buy offer, which had been accepted by the council was to include repairs prior to purchase. The council issued a notice of completion. B alleged this was invalid on the grounds that it referred to the Housing Act 1985 which came into force after the acceptance stage. They claimed breach of contract and statutory duty to repair and notified the council of their intention to start proceedings. The council issued a final notice to complete but no further correspondence was received by B who learned through their own endeavours that the right to buy was to be kept on foot and they confirmed by letter that it was still operative. B claimed that the council had accepted that the notices were invalid or had elected to waive the notices or was estopped from denying them.

Held, allowing the application, that B had the right to buy at the agreed price. The test of whether the notices were misleading was objective. B were not misled and therefore neither notice was a nullity. The council had waived the notices. Waiver and estoppel could apply to cases of procedure, *Kammins Ballrooms Case* [1971] A.C. 850, [1970] C.L.Y. 1525 followed. The council had allowed the state of affairs to continue without correction and consequently had waived by election.

BERRY AND MADDEN v. TOWER HAMLETS LBC [1995] N.P.C. 90, Sir Haydn Tudor Evans, QBD.

5015. Rights of way–administrative decision making–refusal to dedicate footpath as public right of way–public inquiry should have been held in interests of fairness

[Highways Act 1980 s.31; Wildlife and Countryside Act 1981 Sch.14, Sch.15.]

E applied for judicial review of a decision by the Secretary of State refusing to direct the modification of a definitive map to show a public footpath. The Secretary of State had dismissed an appeal against the council's decision not to dedicate the path as a right of way and declined to exercise his powers under the Wildlife and Countryside Act 1981 Sch.14. He concluded that statements made to support a right of way by usage, showing use for walking and access purposes over the requisite time period, were outweighed by the former owner's statement denying an intention to dedicate a public right of way in terms of the Highways Act 1980 s.31.

Held, allowing the application, that although the decision could not be faulted on substantive grounds, such a conflict of documentary evidence should, in the interests of fairness, have been tested by a public inquiry. On examination of the statutory provisions, an imbalance could be seen between Sch.14 and

Sch.15 of the 1981 Act, which seemed to favour private rights at the investigation stage. The Secretary of State could, therefore, be deemed to have acted unfairly by following the statutory procedure without giving due consideration to the individual facts of the case and in not convening a public inquiry.

R. v. SECRETARY OF STATE FOR WALES, *ex p.* EMERY [1996] 4 All E.R. 1, Sir Louis Blom-Cooper Q.C., QBD.

5016. Rights of way–conveyance did not include access via "layby"–whether buyer entitled to a quasi easement

E was the owner of a large house, coach house and surrounding land. In 1987 E sold the large house and some land to M. The driveway which gave M access to the main road ran almost parallel to the main road and ended in a "layby". M asserted he had the right to use the layby to go to and from the main road, because otherwise the corner was dangerous for vehicles. The conveyance from E to M stipulated "a right of way over such part of the land coloured green on the plan as is vested in the vendor". The green land was a thin strip which excluded most of the layby.

Held, allowing the appeal, that (1) under the rule in *Wheeldon v. Burrows* (1879) 12 Ch. D. 31 M was entitled to a quasi easement over the layby when he purchased part of E's property. The criteria of quasi easement were satisfied; (2) the fact that the driveway and layby, at the time of purchase, were both covered in a single unbroken tarmac coating was proof that the right of way was continuous and apparent. They had been used together by E to gain access for years and it was obvious that they had so been used; (3) although the judge's local knowledge of rural Herefordshire was relevant to the issue of whether the right of way was necessary for reasonable and convenient enjoyment of the house, more relevant was the fact that access to the road was safer with a right of way over the layby than without it; (4) the wording of the grant to M, which specifically granted M a right over the driveway and made no reference to the layby, was not inconsistent with the implied grant of a right over the layby, *Borman v. Griffith* [1930] 1 Ch. 493 and *Gregg v. Richards* [1926] Ch. 521 followed and (5) the language of the conveyance did not otherwise exclude the implied grant, although no specific reference was made to the tenement "as it is now used and enjoyed", *Sovmots Investments Ltd v. Secretary of State for the Environment* [1979] A.C. 144 considered.

MILLMAN v. ELLIS (1996) 71 P. & C.R. 158, Sir Thomas Bingham, M.R., CA.

5017. Rights of way–footpaths–definitive map modification order for deletion of footpath–part incorrectly shown–uncertainty of route–whether inspector had power to confirm order

[Wildlife and Countryside Act 1981 s.53.]

K, the surveying authority for the county of Kent, made and published a definitive map modification order under the Wildlife and Countryside Act 1981 s.53(2) which proposed the deletion of the entire length of a footpath running from points A to B to C. The path between B and C had been incorrectly delineated as a footpath but there was no dispute that a footpath existed between points A and B. The Ramblers Association objected. A public inquiry was held by an inspector appointed by the Secretary of State for the Environment. The inspector proposed that the order be confirmed with two alterations. After a further inquiry, the inspector refused to confirm the original deletion order on the basis that the uncertainty of the line was a matter for K and that it could not be resolved under s.53(2) of the 1981 Act because s.53(3)(c)(iii) only applied where "there was no public right of way shown on the map and statement". The applicant sought judicial review of the inspector's refusal to confirm the order to delete the entire footpath.

Held, refusing the application, that (1) the 1981 Act was not concerned with the extinction or deletion of public rights where the existence of those rights was not in issue, although the precise line was in issue between the parties. Where the issue was whether or not a right of way known to exist should be stopped up the matter could not be resolved under s.53. Therefore, the inspector was right to conclude that he had no power to confirm the order and (2) the fact that the precise point of law on which he based his decision had not been canvassed by K did not mean that the rules of natural justice had not been observed, *R. v. Secretary of State for the Environment, ex p. Burrows* [1991] 2 Q.B. 354, [1991] C.L.Y. 3554 considered.

R. v. SECRETARY OF STATE FOR THE ENVIRONMENT, *ex p.* KENT CC [1995] C.O.D. 198, Turner, J., QBD.

5018. Rights of way–footpaths–power to create new public footpath–whether award was ultra vires

Under a Local Inclosure Act 1802, Commissioners were given the power to make awards for the establishment and maintenance of public and private roads and paths. In 1805 the Commissioners made an award regarding an alleged public foothpath in Suffolk, but it was not shown on the definitive maps, nor was there evidence of user of the footpath. The surveying authority refused N's application to modify the definitive map and N's appeal to the Secretary of State was dismissed. The Secretary of State resisted N's application for judicial review of his decision on the basis that the Commissioners had not had the power to create a new public footpath, and their award was therefore ultra vires.

Held, dismissing the application, that the only express power of the Commissioners came from the Inclosure Act 1801 which required new highways to be over 30 feet wide; that could not to be taken to give an express power to create a public right of way on foot unless it was part of a general right of passage. Only new private, not public, footpaths were addressed by the 1801 Act. Not only was there therefore no express power to create a new public footpath, but such a power could not be implied.

R. v. SECRETARY OF STATE FOR THE ENVIRONMENT, *ex p.* ANDREWS (1996) 71 P. & C.R. 1, Schiemann, J., QBD.

5019. Rights of way–footpaths–rights of way–evidence of use during 20 year prescriptive period–effect of notices stating privacy of ground not evidence of intention to deny right of way

[Wildlife and Countryside Act 1981 Sch.15; Highways Act 1980 s.31.]

The Secretary of State appealed against a decision quashing, on *Wednesbury* grounds, the decision of a planning inspector after a public local inquiry into the existence of a public right of way. The inspector had been appointed following objections by B, the landowners, after an order confirming the right of way in terms of the Wildlife and Countryside Act 1981 Sch.15 para.12. B contended that steps taken by their predecessors in title, in erecting notices and effectively turning local children off the path, demonstrated that no right of way had been established between 1955 and 1975.

Held, allowing the appeal, that a public right of way could arise on evidence of 20 years' uninterrupted use, in the absence of evidence showing that there was not an intention to permit use as a highway under the Highways Act 1980 s.31. However, evidence put forward by B as to the existence of a notice stating the right of way was private and that, at the commencement of the 20 year period, gardeners on the estate had chased away local children using the path, was rebutted by witnesses who showed they were unaware of the sign during the material time. Evidence from those who, as children, were chased away showed that they were actually being kept away from the private grounds of the house, not prevented from using the path itself. The apparent acceptance of the footpath's private status at a public meeting in 1975 was not sufficient to show that use of the right of way had been disrupted during the period 1955 to 1975. Fencing placed along the north edge of the path prior to 1976 had been for the purposes of keeping livestock on neighbouring farmland, and not to prevent use of the path during the material time.

SECRETARY OF STATE FOR THE ENVIRONMENT v. BERESFORD TRUSTEES [1996] N.P.C. 128, Hobhouse, L.J., CA.

5020. Rights of way–presumption that land up to the centre of a road or river passes with the transfer of land–rebuttal of the presumption

Mr and Mrs W, the third and fourth defendants, appealed against a declaration that none of the six defendants to the action had any interest or right which entitled them to prevent CO from using a lane adjoining their respective properties as none of the defendants owned half of the lane. CO intended to build a house on land adjoining the lane and the only access was via the lane. CO commenced proceedings to prevent the defendants from obstructing the lane. The judge held that the defendants did not own the subsoil of half of the lane and also that CO had not established that they had a right of way along it.

Held, allowing the appeal, that (1) when land adjoining a road or a river was transferred, half of the road or river was presumed to pass with the grant of the land. Such a presumption could be rebutted by an intention in the language of the deed or in the nature of the grant or in the surrounding circumstances, *Micklethwait v. Newlay Bridge Co* (1886) 33 Ch. D. 133 and *Commissioners for Land Tax for the City of London v. Central London Railway Company* [1913] A.C. 364 followed; (2) the judge was wrong to find that the presumption had been rebutted in this case as there was nothing in the history of the conveyances to that effect and (3) it was not necessary for the land to be described as being bounded by the road for the presumption to apply.

COLLETT v. CULPIN, Trans. Ref: CCRTF 95/0415/C, May 22, 1996, Morritt, L.J., CA.

5021. Roads–compromise agreement giving access to development site–compensation payable pursuant to agreement

S wished to develop certain land for light industrial and residential use. An access road was required which had to pass over land belonging to C. An agreement was entered into by which C agreed to give S a right of access in return for 30 per cent of the difference between the value of the land, taking into account its development potential, and the value in current use. The agreement provided for the payment to be determined in accordance with the approach of the Lands Tribunal in *Stokes v. Cambridge* (1961) 180 E.G. 839, [1962] C.L.Y. 402. S subsequently obtained outline planning permission for a residential development, then sold the land with the benefit of the permission. By notice of motion S raised questions as to how the sum payable to C was to be calculated.

Held, that as a matter of construction the surveyor was required to adopt, insofar as it was practicable to do so, the approach adopted in *Stokes v. Cambridge* starting with an opening valuation on a serviced plot basis.

CHALLOCK PARISH COUNCIL v. SHIRLEY [1995] 2 E.G.L.R. 137, Jonathan Parker, J., Ch D.

5022. Sale of business–leasehold business and residential property–failure to deliver vacant possession of premises–rescission of contract–no affirmation of contract

In 1989 D had acquired a leasehold property used as a news agency with a residential flat above. Part of the the flat was sublet to A in breach of covenant and had given rise to an assured tenancy. In 1991 G sought to obtain the property and the goodwill, fixtures and fittings of the business. She insisted on vacant possession, wishing to occupy the flat as a principal residence and also because of the risk of forfeiture of the lease. A purchase price of £15,000 was agreed. D's solicitors represented that the flat was vacant, but A remained in occupation after the formalities had been completed. G instituted proceedings and the judge found that a letter from her solicitors was a rescission of the contract or an acceptance of D's repudiation which discharged the obligations under the contract. G was awarded damages and D appealed. The question was whether G had lost the right of rescission between the date of completion and the institution of proceedings.

Held, dismissing the appeal, that G had been entitled to rescind the contract because of D's failure to give vacant possession. The letter from G's solicitors, however, did not show that she was unwilling to continue with the contract. It showed that she sought reimbursement of a financial loss and had not accepted that the contract had been terminated by D's breach. The right to rescission should be exercised reasonably promptly and could be lost by delay should the other party act to his detriment having reasonable grounds for believing that the contract had been affirmed. In the instant case, there was no evidence either that D had suffered detriment or that there was belief. A delay of some three months was not sufficient to reasonably induce such belief. G had embarked upon running the business but had done so before the assignment of the lease because of the representation by D's solicitors and because she had not wished to lose the goodwill were the business to cease to trade. Accordingly, G's conduct did not amount to affirmation. As there was no evidence that D's actions had been influenced the case did not give rise to any estoppel. The business now having ceased to trade, the goodwill was lost but G had been under no obligation to carry on with it having rescinded the contract and instituted proceedings.

GUNATUNGA v. DEALWIS (1996) 72 P. & C.R. 147, Sir Christopher Slade, CA.

5023. Sale of land–completion–standard forms of contract–purchaser not in breach where notice allowed only one day for completion–vendor not entitled to forfeit deposit or claim deposit balance

[Law of Property Act 1925 s.49.]

C contracted to sell registered land to T, the contract incorporating condition 6.8 of the Standard Conditions of Sale (2nd ed). Under condition 6.8, on or after the completion date the vendor became entitled to serve notice to complete. The purchaser would become liable to pay whatever balance was outstanding to make up a 10 per cent deposit. The contract purported to exclude the application of the Law of Property Act 1925 s.49(2), which gave the court a discretion to order the return of a deposit. C had not acquired title to the property by the original date for completion. Subsequently C acquired title and received the land certificate. On May 4, C sent T a notice to complete by May 9, giving T effectively one working day in which to complete, which T did not. C wrote that the contract was at an end and that the five per cent deposit paid was forfeit, and sued for the outstanding five per cent. T required the return of its deposit and, when C sold the property elsewhere, counterclaimed for damages. At first instance C's claim for summary judgment was refused and judgment given for T on the counterclaim. C appealed.

Held, dismissing the appeal, that (1) condition 6.8 provided an exhaustive scheme notice to complete and thereby excluded the general law. C's notice, requiring completion within less than 10 days, was therefore ineffective. Under the general law C could not serve a notice to complete with time of the essence when the original date for completion had been missed because of C's inability to complete. It was C, therefore, who wrongfully repudiated the contract and (2) the discretion under s.49(2) of the 1925 Act was to enable the court to order return of a deposit to a defaulting purchaser. To exclude s.49(2) did not affect the purchaser's rights if the vendor defaulted. Therefore, T was entitled to the return of the deposit paid.

COUNTRY AND METROPOLITAN HOMES SURREY LTD v. TOPCLAIM LTD [1996] Ch. 307, Timothy Lloyd Q.C., Ch D.

5024. Sale of land–exercise of sale option–proviso limiting inclusion of further land holdings in sale option–whether proviso operative where development abandoned–implied term giving effect to intention of parties regarding interest payments

Under an agreement M was to obtain planning permission for a retail development by a target date of December 31, 1994, on land held by B as trustee. The agreement also contained a sale option, whereby B, on serving notice at any time up to one month after the target date, created an obligation for M to purchase both the development land and any further agreed land. Valuation, as provided for by the agreement, was to be either the open market value, or the amount given by applying a valuation formula, whichever was higher. B served notice on M when planning permission could not be obtained by the set date, with the valuation formula being used to calculate the price and B contended that two further interests were included. However, M sought to rely on a proviso in the agreement, that excluded such further land if it was no longer required for the development, arguing also that net holding costs, being the notional interest on the further land costs should be excluded as well.

Held, allowing the appeal in favour of BB, that further land had to be defined by construing the agreement as a whole. As a result, the proviso did not apply where the entire development was not going ahead, therefore both the further land interests fell within the terms of the agreement. A term was implied, under the requirement of business efficacy, in respect of the net holding costs, as it was clearly the intention of the parties that these were to be paid irrespective of the form taken by the sale notice.

BARCLAYS BANK PLC v. MEPC DEVELOPMENTS LTD [1995] E.G.C.S. 49, Aldous, L.J., CA.

5025. Sale of land–form of contract–whether letter and plan were a single document–whether typing of name sufficient

[Law of Property (Miscellaneous Provisions) Act 1989 s.2.]

F orally agreed to purchase land from J. F prepared a letter bearing J's name as addressee, and setting out the agreement to purchase the land "shown on the enclosed plan". J signed the accompanying plan only, F signed both the plan and the letter. J died and F sought specific performance of the contract against J's personal representatives. The personal representatives sought to strike out the claim because there was no contract satisfying the requirements of writing under the Law of Property (Miscellaneous Provisions) Act 1989 s.2, which required written terms, in one document, signed by or on behalf of each party. The district judge dismissed the application on the basis that it was arguable that the letter and plan were one document, the judge overruled this and F appealed, further contending that if there were two documents, the purchaser had signed the letter by causing his name to be typed on it as addressee.

Held, dismissing the appeal, that (1) for the purposes of s.2 of the 1989 Act, a letter and a plan enclosed with it were separate documents; the letter contained the terms and so was the document which needed to be signed; (2) the same section required each party to write his name on the document in his own handwriting, so that the typing of J's name was not sufficient.

FIRSTPOST HOMES LTD v. JOHNSON [1995] 1 W.L.R. 1567, Peter Gibson, L.J., CA.

5026. Sale of land–notice to complete with time to be of essence–failure to complete–whether specific performance of sale could be granted–reasonableness of notice

[Conveyancing and Law of Property Ordinance s.7 (Trinidad and Tobago); Law of Property Act 1925 s.49.]

S agreed to sell land to B with completion due on July 31, 1977. B did not complete and on March 20, 1979 S gave him notice to complete within six days, with time to be of the essence. B failed to complete and S sold the land on. B appealed against the dismissal of his claim for specific performance on the ground that no reasonable tribunal would have reached such a decision and that even though time was of the essence, the court could still grant specific performance following the judgment in *Legione v. Hateley* (1983) 57 A.L.J.R. 292. Finally the court should exercise its discretion under the Law of Property Act 1925 s.49(2) to award the return of D's deposit.

Held, dismissing the appeal, that (1) the demand for completion had not come out of the blue and it was open to the court to conclude that reasonable notice had been given, *Stickney v. Keeble* [1915] A.C. 386 considered. B could not rely on the work which had been done to the land because of the lack of evidence of what might have added value, and discretion could not be exercised on the basis of speculation; (2) without evidence as to added value there was no material to found a conclusion that it would be unconscionable for S to treat the agreement as at an end or that it would be equitable to order specific performance. Accordingly, a submission based on *Legione v. Hateley* (1983) 57 A.L.J.R. 292 was hopeless and it was unnecessary to consider whether there should be a departure from the decisions in *Steedman v. Drinkle* [1916] 1 A.C. 275 and *Brickles v. Snell* [1916] 2 A.C. 599 and (3) the gain by retaining the deposit was more than offset by the amount of interest S had lost. Without more, there was insufficient reason to exercise discretion in favour of the defaulting buyer. Following *Workers Trust & Merchant Bank Ltd v. Dojap Investments* [1993] A.C. 573, [1993] C.L.Y. 526, equity did not regard a lost deposit as a penalty against which it granted relief and s.49(2) of the 1925 Act did not overrule this principle.

BIDAISEE v. SAMPATH [1995] N.P.C. 59, Lord Goff of Chieveley, PC.

5027. Sale of land–threat of compulsory purchase–subsequent disposal–pre-emption rights of consortium of former owners–Crichel Down rules–meaning of "special consideration"

W applied for judicial review of T's decision to withdraw W's contract to purchase land and to submit the land to tender. In 1986 T purchased land from W and another party under the threat of compulsory purchase. In 1991 T decided they no longer required the land and decided to resell it. Under the Crichel Down Rules para.9 the former owner should be given the first opportunity to repurchase the land. However, by para.14(7) if the site was formerly under multiple ownership and a fragmented sale would produce a loss on the sale, then special consideration should be given to former owners who formed a consortium. W formed a consortium and offered £1.1 million. T rejected the Crichel Down Rules and treated W as a single owner with no special consideration.

Held, allowing the application, that para.14(7) was a guide as to the meaning of "special consideration" which required treating a consortium as being in the same position as a single former owner. A valid consortium existed in this case and T ought to have given a right of pre emption to W.

R. v. TRENT RHA, *ex p.* WESTERMAN LTD (1996) 72 P. & C.R. 448, Turner, J., QBD.

5028. Sale of land–transfer to purchasers as equitable joint tenants–purchasers not executing transfer–whether transfer effective to create trust of land–whether transfer reflected true intentions of purchasers

[Law of Property Act 1925 s.53.]

P and D were brothers of Bangladeshi origin who in 1968 jointly purchased a house in North London. The purchase was completed by a registered transfer, which conveyed the property to P and D "as joint tenants both in law and in equity" but was executed by the vendor only. The application for the mortgage was made by both P and D, and they each executed the mortgage. D paid the premium on a policy provided as additional security, and paid the shortfall in the purchase price. Soon afterwards, both P and D moved in, but a few months later P moved away and never lived in it again for any period of time. Various people stayed there over the years as lodgers. D made all the mortgage repayments. In 1973 D paid off the loan, although P subsequently paid D a quarter of that amount to help. In 1979 D and his family moved out into a new house which was subsequently sold, and in 1986 D returned with his family. Over the years D spent £19,000 in improvements on the property. P and D were in dispute as to the ownership of the property from 1979 onwards. In 1985 P gave notice severing the joint tenancy; in 1986 he issued an originating summons seeking (1) a declaration that they held the property as joint tenants in trust for themselves in equal shares and (2) an order for sale. D counterclaimed for a declaration that the parties held the property in trust for themselves in shares proportional to their respective contributions, and rectification of the transfer accordingly. The judge found that the purpose of the purchase was to provide a home in this country for both P and D; he concluded that there was no basis for rectification, ordered the sale and the equal division of the proceeds of sale, subject to some equitable accounting. D appealed, contending that since neither P nor D executed the transfer, P could not enforce the trust thereby created, and that the document did not accord with the parties' true intentions.

Held, dismissing the appeal, that (1) although the Law of Property Act 1925 s.53(1)(b) required that a declaration of trust in relation to land must be in writing, P was not relying on D's declaration of trust, but on an absolute transfer by the vendor to P and D jointly. The fact that the purchasers did not sign the transfer did not prevent it being an effective disposition, provided it accurately reflected the parties' intentions and (2) rectification of the transfer would be ordered where it does not accurately reflect the true intentions of the parties. The judge was entitled to find that the parties' true intention had been to effect a joint purchase, and to infer that the solicitors had done no more than give effect to the parties' instructions, *Gorman (A Bankrupt), ex p. Trustee of the Bankrupt, Re* [1990] 1 W.L.R. 616, [1990] C.L.Y. 277 applied, *Robinson v. Robinson* (1976) 241 E.G. 153, [1977] C.L.Y. 2489, *Pink v. Lawrence* (1978) P. & C.R. 98, [1978] C.L.Y. 1785 and *Goodman v. Gallant* [1986] Fam. 106, [1986] C.L.Y. 8037 considered.

ROY v. ROY [1996] 1 F.L.R. 541, Fox, L.J., CA.

5029. Settlements–undertaking by beneficial owner allowing father and stepmother occupation for life–whether agreement created life interest under Settled Land Act 1925

[Settled Land Act 1925 s.1.]

J, the tenant for life of a large estate, surrendered his life interest and vested part of the estate upon trust for one of his sons, P, absolutely. J remarried in 1977 and, with his new wife, M, moved into a farmhouse situated on P's share of the estate as their marital home. In response to M's concerns that she would not be adequately provided for in the event of J's death, P signed an undertaking under seal in 1988, permitting J and, after his death, M to have exclusive occupation of the farmhouse for the duration of their lives or for such period as they required. Following J's death, M sought an order under the Settled Land Act 1925 vesting the farmhouse in her as life tenant.

Held, refusing the application, that (1) on its proper construction and read in context, the undertaking did not create a life interest but rather an irrevocable licence. The language used in the undertaking was one of personal obligation rather than of conferring any interest in J or M. There was no rule of law that a right of occupancy for life or for so long as the person resided in the property would always constitute a tenancy under the Settled Land Act 1925 and (2) if the undertakings had created a strict settlement under the Act, then s.1 (7) of the Act would not have applied so as to exclude the effect of that settlement. The life interest held by J and M on trust for sale could only have been exercised under the Settled Land Act 1925 if the trustees' powers under the original settlement were postponed, *Bacon v. Bacon* [1947] 2 All E.R. 327, [1947-1951] C.L.C. 3031 followed.

DENT v. DENT [1996] 1 W.L.R. 683, David Young Q.C., Ch D.

5030. Sheltered housing–compensation for depreciation caused by noise from bypass–whether restrictions on disposal and use affected value and therefore depreciation

CA was a registered housing association which owned a block of flats providing sheltered accommodation. Planning permission over the property restricted its use to sheltered accommodation with a single flat for a warden. CA claimed compensation for reduction in the value of the property as a result of traffic noise from a bypass opened in January 1989. The compensating authority contended that there was insufficient noise to cause a reduction in the value of the property and that the freehold value of this particular building would not be reduced in any event due to the planning permission restricting its use.

Held, giving judgment for the authority, that the claim failed in any event due to lack of evidence. The property was affected by noise from the bypass but had also benefited from being located in a cul-de-sac. CA's case had failed to take account of the fact that the property was subject to 15 secure tenancies, that there was a restriction on the use of the building, and that CA were limited as to their powers of disposal. Further, the limited evidence on rents did not show any depreciation as a result of the bypass. Evidence relating to private houses in the area was irrelevant because this property contained sheltered accommodation.

CLWYD ALYN HOUSING ASSOCIATION v. WELSH OFFICE (1996) 71 P. & C.R. 195, PH Clarke, FRICS., Lands Tr.

5031. Statutory tenancies–registered land–occupation before mortgage registered–statutory tenancy binding on lender

[Land Registration Act 1925 s.70; Rent Act 1977 s.2.]

The registered proprietors mortgaged the property to provide security on a loan obtained from BB, who failed to register the charge. The proprietors, in writing, then granted P a six month tenancy of the property with an option to renew, but did not obtain the consent of BB as required by the terms of the mortgage. P had no knowledge of the mortgage and entered into occupation of the property. When P's contractual tenancy expired, it was followed by a statutory tenancy by virtue of the Rent Act 1977 s.2(1)(a). Some time after the expiry of the contractual tenancy, BB finally registered the charge and later obtained an order for possession of the property. P appealed.

Held, allowing the appeal, that if the contractual lease had still been in operation when BB registered the charge, P would have had an overriding interest under the Land Registration Act 1925 s.70(1)(k) as the owner of a lease granted for a term of 21 years or less, but the statutory tenancy was not a lease falling within s.70(1)(k). Further, P could not claim an overriding interest under s.70(1)(g), even if a statutory tenant was protected under that subsection, because P was not in occupation when the registered proprietors executed the mortgage, *Abbey National Building Society v. Cann* [1991] A.C. 56, [1990] C.L.Y. 707 and *National Provincial Bank Ltd v. Hastings Car Mart Ltd* [1964] Ch. 665, [1965] C.L.Y. 1850 considered. However, whilst a statutory tenancy could not bind a person with a title paramount, whether BB had a title paramount would be judged by comparing its title to that of the contractual tenancy from which the statutory tenancy had stemmed. As the contractual tenancy would have allowed P to take priority, the statutory tenancy would also be binding on the mortgagee so as to be consistent with the protection afforded to statutory tenants under the 1977 Act, although this would not be the case where the charge was registered before the contractual tenancy was granted.

POURDANAY v. BARCLAYS BANK PLC [1996] N.P.C. 161, Sir Richard Scott, V.C., Ch D.

5032. Surety–spouses–undue influence–independent legal advice–no knowledge of undue influence imputed to lender

[County Court Rules 1981 Ord.7 r.10.]

B appealed against a decision to set aside a possession order on the basis that its legal charge on a joint account had been obtained by the undue influence and misrepresentations of T's husband, of which B had constructive knowledge. T contended that the solicitor who had explained the nature of the charge to her had been acting, not as her agent, but as an agent of B and therefore the solicitor's deficient advice should be imputed to B. T also contended that the original possession order was deficient, because she had never received a summons, though her husband had attended the hearing.

Held, allowing the appeal that, (1) solicitors giving independent advice were acting exclusively for the signatory despite having been introduced and retained by the lender, who would therefore be entitled to rely on a certificate manifesting that the signatory had been given independent advice, *Banco Exterior Internacional v. Mann* [1995] 1 All E.R. 936, [1995] 1 C.L.Y. 2443, *Bank of Baroda v. Rayarel* [1995] 2 F.L.R. 376, [1995] 1 C.L.Y. 2452, *Midland Bank Plc v. Serter* [1995] 1 F.L.R. 1034, [1995] 1 C.L.Y. 2450, *Halifax Mortgage Services Ltd v. Stepsky* [1996] 2 W.L.R. 230, [1996] C.L.Y. 4970 considered, *Bank of Credit and Commerce International SA v. Aboody* [1990] 1 Q.B. 923, [1989] C.L.Y. 1829 followed and (2) service was valid under the County Court Rules 1981 Ord.7 r.10. It was fatal to T's claim that she had failed to challenge the judgment within a reasonable time and, by making an application to set aside the judgment, had taken a step in the proceedings with knowledge of the irregularity.

BARCLAYS BANK PLC v. THOMSON; SUB NOM. BARCLAYS BANK PLC v. THOMPSON [1996] 5 Bank. L.R. 402, Simon Brown, L.J., CA.

5033. Tenancies in common–oral agreement of share value–offer before proceedings withdrawn–costs–award equalled original offer

P appealed against an award of £17,500, in respect of his share in a tenancy in common and an order to pay two thirds of D's costs. In September 1986 P and D purchased premises in their joint names, with an express declaration that they held as tenants in common, in equal shares. By early 1989, their friendship had broken down and P required repayment of his interest in the premises. The judge found that in early 1988 P and D made an oral agreement that D would pay P £17,500 in full resolution of the matter, upon sale of the premises. In mid 1989 D took a banker's draft made out to £17,500 to P, who refused to accept this sum, on legal advice. In October 1989, P issued proceedings claiming half the beneficial interest in the premises. At this stage D denied that P was entitled to any share in the equity. In August 1993 the property was sold and net proceeds of £51,856.51 were realised. P continued to claim half this sum, and D continued to claim that P was not entitled to any of the net equity. On the second day of the trial, D obtained leave to amend his pleading that, in the alternative, P was entitled to £17,500 but not to half the equity.

Held, allowing the appeal, that P should have all his costs of the action and of the appeal. The lateness of D's concession in amendment did not entitle him to anything other than an adverse costs order. Furthermore, the fact that D had, before issue of proceedings, offered an identical sum to that which was finally awarded by the judge, could not bear upon costs. D should have repeated that offer once costs began to accrue following the issue of proceedings. In fact, he withdrew the offer, only repeating it on the second day of a three day trial.

MILLS v. MIFSUD, December 7, 1995, Otton, L.J., CA. [*Ex rel.* Edmund G Farrell, Barrister].

5034. Treasure Act 1996 (c.24)

An Act to abolish treasure trove and make fresh provision in relation to treasure. This Act received Royal Assent on July 4, 1996.

5035. Treasure trove

[Treasure Act 1996.]

The Department of National Heritage issued a press release entitled *Lord Inglewood welcomes Royal Assent for Treasure Act* (DNH 200/96), published on July 5, 1996. The Treasure Act, which provides a better definition of treasure and the procedures for dealing with finds, has received Royal Assent. It will come into force after a code of practice has been devised by both Houses of Parliament. The Act provides for the first time that failure to report finds within 14 days of discovery will be a criminal offence.

5036. Undue influence–deed of gift and will transferring home and leaving estate to son and daughter in law–nature of transfer and relationship–criteria for setting aside–whether influence actual or presumed

The plaintiff applied for a deed of gift in favour of his son and his son's wife, the defendants, to be set aside on the ground of undue influence. The plaintiff had served a life sentence for the murder of his wife and had had no contact with his son until five years after his release from prison. The defendants' business collapsed and about a year later they established contact with the plaintiff. The plaintiff was in poor health and living alone and the defendants moved into the plaintiff's house, which he had bought and improved, and looked after him. Via his solicitor, the plaintiff made a new will and transferred his house to the defendants by deed of gift. Eight months later relations between the parties had begun to deteriorate and the defendants stopped looking after the plaintiff.

Held, granting the application, that (1) whether actual undue influence existed was a question of fact. The plaintiff must show that the defendants' conduct, whether by word, deed or omission, had forced him to enter the deed of gift. Actual undue influence was established on the facts of this case and (2) alternatively, presumed undue influence also existed. The plaintiff had been made dependent on the defendants by his deed of gift and a non-exclusive licence protecting his right of residence after the gift. A presumption of undue influence existed due to the relationship of the parties and the defendants had failed to rebut that presumption by showing that the plaintiff had entered the deed on independent advice. The gift was set aside on the alternative grounds. The defendants claimed the return of money they had spent on the house in order to restore the status quo. This was refused as the expenditure of the plaintiff was taken into account, including his legal costs for the transfer of the property and the fact that the plaintiff continued to pay his attendance allowance over to the defendants.

LANGTON v. LANGTON [1995] 2 F.L.R. 890, AWH Charles Q.C., Ch D.

5037. Valuation–leasehold enfranchisement–onus for proving tenant's improvements on leaseholder

[Landlord and Tenant Act 1954; Leasehold Reform Act 1967.]

The leasehold valuation tribunal determined the purchase price payable by the leaseholder of a substantial semi-detached late 19th century house under the Leasehold Reform Act 1967 at £258,000. A ballroom and garage had been added which increased the value by £38,000; however, the freeholder contended that these should not have been considered as tenant's improvements. The property was structurally sound but in a poor state of repair. The leaseholder contended that the price was too high.

Held, allowing the freeholder's cross-appeal, that the price to be paid should be £310,000. That amount was arrived at after considering comparables; the vacant freehold less the tenant's improvements would be £347,500. Deduction also fell to be made for Landlord and Tenant Act 1954 rights, the proper size of which was a matter for agreement or a matter of evidence. The onus of disproving that the ballroom and garage were not tenant's improvements fell on the leaseholder but this had not been discharged, and the value of the tenant's interest was accepted at £25,000.

VIGNAUD v. KEEPERS AND GOVERNORS OF JOHN LYON'S FREE GRAMMAR SCHOOL (1996) 71 P. & C.R. 456, H.H.J. Rich Q.C., LandsTr.

5038. VAT–extra statutory concessions–real property–development

HM Customs & Excise issued a press release entitled *Property conversion–Customs correct VAT anomaly* (News Release 9/96), published on February 13, 1996. An anomaly in VAT regulations has been rectified with the issue of an extra statutory concession, taking effect on February 12, 1996, so that sellers of commercial property for conversion to residential use can elect to sell on a standard rated supply basis and recover VAT on their costs. Also convertors will be able to recover VAT charged on the purchase of the property providing they make a zero rated supply on the first sale of the conversion.

5039. VAT–small self administered schemes–extra statutory concessions

[Value Added Tax (Buildings and Land) Order 1994 (SI 1994 3013).]

HM Customs & Excise issued a press release entitled *Customs give new concession on property transactions* (11/96), published on February 28, 1996. An extra statutory concession has been published to mitigate the effect of the VAT (Buildings and Land) Order 1994 on property transactions which are not taken as a tax avoidance measure. The Order, introduced to counter tax avoidance, had the unintended effect of preventing recovery of tax incurred on the acquisition of trading premises by small self administered pension schemes for use of the associated trading business. Under the extra statutory concession, a small self administered pension scheme may be treated as a fully taxable person, allowing for full recovery of the tax. The concession is effective retrospectively from November 30, 1994.

5040. Articles

Commercial property–the best ten: Legal Times 1996, 38, 12-13. (Most significant commercial property developments in 1995).

Crossing the border for better returns: E.G. 1996, 9610, 144-145. (Comparison of costs of buying and selling commercial property in Member States, with table showing rates of agents' fees and taxes).

Curtilage–a pernicious lack of certainty? *(Neil Stanley)*: Conv. 1996, Sep/Oct, 352-365. (Need for robust definition of curtilage which will be applicable in every statutory context and proposal to resolve problem by use of statutory duty contained in s.70(2) of 1990 Act).

Guide to the World's leading real estate lawyers: I.F.L. Rev. 1996, 15(3), Supp REL1-59. (Directory of leading real estate lawyers including professional biographies).

I've been misrepresented!–more decision on disclaimers *(John E. Adams)*: Conv. 1996, Mar/Apr, 84-85. (Circumstances in which payments made in relation to land transactions may be recoverable and effect of exclusion clauses and disclaimers on liability of payee for misunderstood statements).

Introduction to Hong Kong property law *(Charles Picken)*: A.C.L.R. 1996, 1 (4), 185-188. (History of property law in Hong Kong and implications for future after June 1997 changeover).

Local government reorganisation: E.G. 1996, 9609, 125-126. (Effects of local government reorganisation on property professions and developments to date).

Mistaken payments and proprietary claims *(Gerard McCormack)*: Conv. 1996, Mar/Apr, 86-97. (Proprietary aspects of mistaken payments made in relation to land and retention of equitable interests enforceable against insolvent payee, notion of destroyed proprietary base, passing of property and presumptive proprietary claims).

Owner-occupiers: recent developments *(Derek McConnell)*: Legal Action 1996, Apr, 16-20. (Proposed legislation and recent cases on mortgage possession proceedings, sale of mortgaged properties, ownership of property, undue influence, negligence and breach of contract affecting owner occupiers).

"The bouncing ball"–developers saving stamp duty for their purchasers *(Patrick C. Soares)*: P.L.B. 1996, 16(10), 79. (Arrangement for reducing property developers' liability to stamp duty by granting long lease at low rent to builder subsidiary).

The Internet and the property professional *(Michael Haddock)*: P.R. 1996, 6(3), 77-79. (Effect of Internet on real property business including use for communication, marketing and collection and dissemination of information).

5041. Books

Bell, Cedric D.–Land Law: Textbook 1996-1997. Bachelor of Laws (LLB). Paperback: £16.95. ISBN 0-7510-0688-2. HLT Publications.

Bridges, Paul–Land Law: Casebook 1996-1997. Bachelor of Laws (LLB). Paperback: £17.95. ISBN 0-7510-0655-6. HLT Publications.

Chesworth, Niki–"The Daily Express" Guide to Buying a Property Abroad. "Daily Express" guides. Paperback: £7.99. ISBN 0-7494-2017-0. Kogan Page.

Dalton, Patrick J.–Land Law. Paperback: £23.95. ISBN 0-273-61423-1. Pitman Publishing.

Densham, H.A.C.; Evans, Della–Scammell and Densham's Law of Agricultural Holdings. Hardback: £139.00. ISBN 0-406-00904-X. Butterworth Law.

Dixon, Martin–Land Law. Lecture notes. Paperback: £14.95. ISBN 1-85941-170-3. Cavendish Publishing Ltd.

Gaunt, Johnathan; Morgan, Paul–Gale on the Law of Easements. Property and conveyancing library. Hardback: £125.00. ISBN 0-421-44470-3. Sweet & Maxwell.

Harris, Jim–Property and Justice. Hardback: £50.00. ISBN 0-19-825957-3. Clarendon Press.

Heller, Lawrance; Levine, Marshall; Cuthbert, Neil–Commercial Property Development Precedents. £230.00. ISBN 0-7520-0427-1. FT Law & Tax.

Kodilinye, Gilbert; Owusu, Sampson–Commonwealth Caribbean Real Property Law: Text, Cases and Materials. Paperback: £20.00. ISBN 1-85941-116-9. Cavendish Publishing Ltd.

Land Law - LLB: Suggested Solutions (1991-1995). Bachelor of Laws (LLB). Paperback: £6.95. ISBN 0-7510-0723-4. HLT Publications.

Land Law: Suggested Solutions - Single Paper (June 1995). Paperback: £3.00. ISBN 0-7510-0622-X. HLT Publications.

Mackenzie, Judith-Anne–A Practical Approach to Land Law. Paperback: £16.95. ISBN 1-85431-550-1. Blackstone Press.

Megarry, Robert; Wade, William; Harpum, Charles; Bridge, S.; Grant, M.–The Law of Real Property. Hardback: £45.00. ISBN 0-421-47460-2. Paperback: £28.00. ISBN 0-421-47470-X. Sweet & Maxwell.

Murphy, J. David–Plunder and Preservation. Hardback: £30.00. ISBN 0-19-586874-9. Oxford University Press.

Reynolds, Kirk; Clark, Wayne–Renewal of Business Tenancies. Hardback: £100.00. ISBN 0-421-52960-1. Sweet & Maxwell.

Sexton, R.–LLB Learning Text: Land Law. Paperback: £17.95. ISBN 1-85431-525-0. Blackstone Press.

Skogen, Larry C.–Indian Depredation Claims, 1796-1920. Legal History of North America, No 2. Hardback: £27.95. ISBN 0-8061-2789-9. University of Oklahoma Press.

Smith, Roger–Property Law. Longman law. Hardback: £50.00. ISBN 0-582-09011-3. Paperback: £28.50. ISBN 0-582-09140-3. Addison-Wesley Longman Higher Education.

Sydenham, Angela–Trusts of Land - the New Law. Paperback: £30.00. ISBN 0-85308-395-9. Jordan.

T. Hussain–Land Rights in Bangladesh. Hardback: £14.95. ISBN 984-05-1280-3. The University Press.

Thomas, Meryl–Statutes on Property Law 1996-7. Paperback: £12.00. ISBN 1-85431-563-3. Blackstone Press.

Tromans, Stephen–Commercial Leases. Hardback: £45.00. ISBN 0-421-52350-6. Sweet & Maxwell.
Waite, Andrew–Waite & Jewell: Environmental Law in Property Transactions. Paperback: £45.00. ISBN 0-406-02293-3. Butterworth Law.
Watt, G.–LLB Cases and Materials: Land Law. Paperback: £18.95. ISBN1-85431-532-3. Blackstone Press.
Webber, Gary–Possession of Business Premises. Practitioner series. Paperback: £50.00. ISBN 0-7520-0294-5. FT Law & Tax.

ROAD TRAFFIC

5042. Airports–whether "airside" part of airport terminal was public place for purposes of Road Traffic Act 1988

[Road Traffic Act 1988 s.3.]

Held, that the driver of an electric buggy who knocked down a child whilst driving on the "airside" part of an airport terminal, could be convicted of an offence under the Road Traffic Act 1988 s.3 as that part of the airport was a public place for the purposes of the Act.

DPP v. NEVILLE (FRANCIS JOHN) [1996] C.O.D. 229, Schiemann, L.J., QBD.

5043. Bridges–construction

COUNTY COUNCIL OF NORFOLK (RECONSTRUCTION OF ACLE WEY BRIDGE) SCHEME 1995 CONFIRMATION INSTRUMENT 1996, SI 1996 158; made under the Highways Act 1980 s.106. In force: date on which notice that it has been confirmed is first published in accordance with the Highways Act 1980 Sch.2 para.1; £1.55.

This Instrument confirms the County Council of Norfolk (Reconstruction of Acle Wey Bridge) Scheme 1995, details of which are given in the Schedule and accompanying plans.

5044. Bridges–construction

COUNTY COUNCIL OF NORFOLK (RECONSTRUCTION OF ACLE WEY BRIDGE - TEMPORARY BRIDGE) SCHEME 1995 CONFIRMATION INSTRUMENT 1996, SI 1996 159; made under the Highways Act 1980 s.106. In force: date on which notice that it has been confirmed is first published in accordance with Highways Act 1980 Sch.2 para.1; £1.55.

This Instrument confirms the County Council of Norfolk (Reconstruction of Acle Wey Bridge - Temporary Bridge) Scheme 1995, details of which are given in the Schedule and accompanying plan.

5045. Bridges–construction

COUNTY COUNCIL OF NORFOLK (RECONSTRUCTION OF STOW BRIDGE) SCHEME 1995 CONFIRMATION INSTRUMENT 1996, SI 1996 1960; made under the Highways Act 1980 s.106. In force: in accordance with Art.1; £1.10.

This Instrument confirms the scheme set out in the Schedule for the reconstruction of the Stow Bridge in Norfolk.

5046. Bridges–construction

COUNTY COUNCIL OF NORTHUMBERLAND (DUPLICATE NORTH SEATON BRIDGE) SCHEME 1995 CONFIRMATION INSTRUMENT 1996, SI 1996 1178; made under the Highways Act 1980 s.106. In force: on the date on which notice that it has been confirmed is first published, in accordance with Highways Act 1980 Sch.2 para.1; £2.80.

This Order confirms, with modifications, the County Council of Northumberland (Duplicate North Seaton Bridge) Scheme 1995. The confirmed scheme is set out in the Schedule to the Order and the plans and specifications of the bridge crossing the River Wansbeck at North Seaton are attached.

5047. Bridges–Hunslet Viaduct

LEEDS CITY COUNCIL (HUNSLET VIADUCT) SCHEME 1992 CONFIRMATION INSTRUMENT 1996, SI 1996 73; made under the Highways act 1980 s.106. In force: in accordance with Highways Act 1980 Sch.2 para.1; £2.80.

The Leeds City Council (Hunslet Viaduct) Scheme 1992 is confirmed, with modifications, by this Instrument. The modified scheme is set out in the attached Schedule and a site plan is enclosed.

5048. Bridges–Pomona Bridge

CITY OF SALFORD (POMONA BRIDGE) SCHEME 1995 CONFIRMATION INSTRUMENT 1996, SI 1996 1809; made under the Highways Act 1980 s.106. In force: in accordance with Art.1; £2.40.

This instrument confirms the City of Salford (Pomona Bridge) Scheme 1995.

5049. Bridges–tolls–Dartford-Thurrock Crossing

DARTFORD THURROCK CROSSING TOLLS ORDER 1996, SI 1996 2046; made under the Dartford Thurrock Crossing Act 1988 s.17. In force: September 1, 1996; £1.10.

This Order fixes the amounts of the tolls to be paid to use the Dartford-Thurrock Crossing.

5050. Bridges–tolls–Dartford-Thurrock Crossing

DARTFORD THURROCK CROSSING (AMENDMENT) REGULATIONS 1996, SI 1996 2047; made under the Dartford Thurrock Crossing Act 1988 s.25, s.26, s.44, s.46. In force: September 1, 1996; £1.10.

These Regulations increase the charges payable to the crossing operator in addition to tolls for the passage of abnormal loads through the tunnels or across the bridge and for removing or assisting broken down vehicles.

5051. Bridges–tolls–Severn Bridge

SEVERN BRIDGES REGULATIONS 1996, SI 1996 1316; made under the Severn Bridges Act 1992 s.14, s.21, s.24, s.25, s.37(5); the Road Regulation Traffic Act 1984 s.17; and the Road Traffic Regulation Act 1984 s.99. In force: June 5, 1996; £1.95.

These Regulations revoke and replace the Severn Bridge Regulations 1993 (SI 1993 1595) and the Severn Bridge (Amendment) Regulations 1995 (SI 1995 1677). They apply to the new Severn Bridge and relate to the payment of tolls, the regulation of traffic on the bridge, the use of the cycleway and the footway and the prevention of injury on the bridge and damage to the bridge.

5052. Bridges–tolls–Severn Bridge

SEVERN BRIDGES TOLLS ORDER 1996, SI 1996 3212; made under the Severn Bridges Act 1992 s.9. In force: January 1, 1997; £0.65.

This Order fixes the tolls payable for use of the Severn Bridge and the Second Severn Crossing during 1997.

5053. Confessions–defendant twice admitted to being disqualified–admissions amounted to prima facie evidence of commission of the offence

The DPP appealed against the acquittal of H of driving whilst disqualified from holding or obtaining a driving licence. A submission of no case to answer was accepted on the grounds that the driver of the car was not identified as a person driving whilst disqualified in the manner required by *R. v. Derwentside Magistrates' Court, ex p. Heaviside* (1995) 11 Road L.R. 557.

Held, allowing the appeal, that H was acquitted on a point which had no substance in law. H twice admitted that he was disqualified from driving. That amounted to prima facie evidence that he had been driving whilst disqualified, *R. v. DPP, ex p. Mansfield* [1997] R.T.R. 96, [1996] C.L.Y. 5068 considered. The case was remitted to the justices for a rehearing.

DPP v. HANSON, Trans. Ref: CO 219/95, April 2, 1996, Leggatt, L.J., QBD.

5054. Drink driving offences–blood tests–breath analysis device unavailable–legality of constable's request for blood sample given stated aversion to needles and diabetes–need for medical advice

[Road Traffic Act 1988 s.7.]

A constable sought a blood sample from a motorist. The constable did not have a breathalyser available. The motorist refused to give a blood sample on the ground that he was diabetic and had an aversion to needles. The issue arose whether the request was lawful and whether there was a reasonable excuse for the failure to provide a specimen. The DPP appealed against the magistrates' ruling of no case.

Held, dismissing the appeal, the motorist had presented a reason based on his medical condition, even though it was unconvincing, so the constable should have waited until a medical practitioner had expressed an opinion pursuant to the Road Traffic Act 1988 s.7(4). It was not for the constable to replace that opinion with his own. Therefore the request was unlawful. The issue whether the excuse was reasonable was irrelevant because the motorist had been denied his rights.

DPP v. WYTHE [1996] R.T.R. 137, Butterfield, J., QBD.

5055. Drink driving offences–blood tests–breath specimen–availability of Lion Intoximeter–reasonable belief in unreliability

[Road Traffic Act 1988 s.5, s.7, s.8, s.15, s.16.]

R was arrested for driving a motor vehicle having consumed alcohol in excess of the prescribed limit contrary to the Road Traffic Act 1988 s.5(1)(a). One breath specimen taken on the Lion Intoximeter registered 58 microgrammes of alcohol in 100 millilitres of breath, but there was no printout. In a manuscript note appended to Police Booklet (Form) 152, the officer in charge stated, "Three subsequent attempts to provide a second reading proved fruitless... [R] was then invited to give further specimens of breath, but declined saying, "I'll go for blood". A blood sample was taken, analysis of which showed 120 milligrammes of alcohol in 100 millilitres of blood. No physician's certificate was served on the defence, nor did the physician give oral evidence. R argued that the established subjective test as to an Intoximeter's non-availability required a "reasonable belief" in the device's unreliability on the part of the officer using it. In the instant case, the officer formed no belief at all, reasonable or otherwise, as evidenced by the appellant's sworn affidavit, the magistrates' clerk's notes and the officer's own manuscript note. Even after three attempts to provide a second Intoximeter reading, R was still invited to give further specimens of breath. Had the officer in fact believed that the device was not available, he would have had no reason to ask for further specimens. The officer's manuscript note should take precedence over the printed or typed portions of Form 152, and therefore the officer was not authorised to obtain a blood or urine sample. R argued that he could not himself legally choose to give a blood sample rather than a second breath specimen. Section 7(4) and s.8(2) of the 1988 Act allowed the accused this choice only when the lower breath reading was below 50 microgrammes per 100 millilitres of breath. Inadequate evidence of the blood sample tests should exclude these results in any event. The statutory provisions concerning the doctor's certificate, s.15(4) and s.16(2), should not be regarded as merely enabling. Affidavits showed that nobody even identified the doctor by way testimony in the magistrates' court.

Held, dismissing the appeal, that the case stated asserted that the officer did in fact have a reasonable belief that the Intoximeter was unavailable; the court would not go behind a case stated. Form 152, appended to the case stated, indicated that the officer came to believe that the device was unavailable and his appended note should be construed in terms of the body of the document. *DPP v. Dixon* [1993] R.T.R. 22, [1993] C.L.Y. 3506 could be distinguished on the particular facts of that case, where the Intoximeter produced an impossibly high reading and the magistrates, in their case stated, assumed more than the officer had in fact indicated as to his reasonable belief. The provision relating to a medical certificate was enabling only, and the case stated declared that the physician was in fact identified adequately. The court categorically refused to go behind the magistrates' statement of the case.

RATHBONE v. DPP, January 20, 1995, Kennedy, L.J., QBD. [*Ex rel.* Professor Dr John Warwick Montgomery, Barrister].

5056. Drink driving offences–blood tests–defendant discharged from hospital before giving sample–whether obligation discharged at same time

[Road Traffic Act 1988 s.5, s.7, s.9.]

W appealed against her conviction for driving with excess alcohol contrary to s.5(1) (a) of the Road Traffic Act 1988. After a car accident W was taken to hospital where she refused to give a breath specimen and was required to give a blood sample instead pursuant to s.7(1) (b) and s.9(1) of the Act. Before she could do so she was discharged from hospital. She was subsequently arrested, provided a blood sample at the police station and was charged. W claimed her obligation to provide a sample had been discharged at the same time as her discharge from hospital and therefore the sample was unlawfully taken.

Held, dismissing the appeal, that once the s.9(1) procedure had been initiated then W's change of location was irrelevant. The requirement for a blood sample was only discharged if an officer set in action the s.7(1) (a) procedure. W was still obliged to provide the specimen as required under s.9(1).

WEBBER v. DPP, *The Times*, December 20, 1995, Holland, J., QBD.

5057. Drink driving offences–blood tests–failure to explain correct procedure for blood test following failed breath test–failure to comply with established formula

A breath specimen was provided for analysis which showed 50 microgrammes of alcohol in 100 millilitres of breath. The constables informed the defendants of their right to elect to give a specimen of blood or urine. The constables failed to explain that such sample would be taken by a medical practitioner and the effect of failure to comply. On appeal, two defendants were acquitted on the basis that the breath test had not been conducted properly.

Held, allowing the DPP's appeal and dismissing five other appeals, that the specimen of breath was untainted by the later failure to comply with the formula given in *DPP v. Warren* [1993] A.C. 319, [1992] C.L.Y. 3788 and there was no evidence that any of the defendants would have exercised their election any differently had the formula been used properly.

DPP v. CHARLES (NOTE); DPP v. KUKADIA; RUXTON v. DPP; REAVELEY v. DPP; HEALY v. DPP; McKEAN v. DPP; EDGE v. DPP [1996] R.T.R. 247, Kennedy, L.J., QBD.

5058. Drink driving offences–blood tests–failure to explain rights and consequences of election to give blood

A breath specimen was provided for analysis which showed 50 microgrammes of alcohol in 100 millilitres of breath. The constable informed the defendant of the right to elect to give a specimen of blood or urine. The constable failed to explain that in the event of any refusal to give such a sample on medical grounds, a medical practitioner would decide on such reason. On appeal the issue arose whether the defendant had been denied the full effect of the right.

Held, allowing the appeal, that the conviction would be quashed for failing to give the driver timeous detailed explanations of his rights and the consequences of exercising his options.

TURNER v. DPP (NOTE) [1996] R.T.R. 274, Balcombe, L.J., QBD.

5059. Drink driving offences–blood tests–whether lawful to use average result of sub-samples

[Road Traffic Act 1988 s.5.]

Held, that, under the Road Traffic Act 1988 s.5(1), where a blood sample was taken for the purpose of analysing the alcohol content, and the sample was divided into a number of sub-samples, it was lawful for the average result to be used. There was no principle in law that the lowest result should be used.

DPP v. WELSH (1997) 161 J.P. 57, Kay, J., QBD.

5060. Drink driving offences–breath tests–capacity–detention under mental health legislation

[Road Traffic Act 1988 s.7; Mental Health Act 1983 s.136.]

F appealed against conviction for failing to supply a breath specimen contrary to the Road Traffic Act 1988 s.7 and for resisting a constable in the exercise of his duty. F was detained at the police station under the Mental Health Act 1983 s.136. No appropriate person was present at any time and he was not examined by the police surgeon. F refused a request for a breath specimen but the police officer formed the opinion that he understood the request and its significance.

Held, dismissing the appeal, that police officers were not precluded from administering a breath test to a drink driving suspect who was detained under s.136 of the 1983 Act. Although they had formed an opinion about his mental state which justified detention under s.136, nevertheless they were entitled to reach the conclusion that he understood the request for a breath test. Having satisfied themselves that he understood what was happening, they had the right to test him.

FRANCIS v. DPP, *The Times*, May 2, 1996, Newman, J., QBD.

5061. Drink driving offences–breath tests–failure to give specimen–motorist did not require full three minutes for test

Held, that there was no authority to support the argument that a motorist being breath tested for suspected drink driving must be informed that the Intoximeter would operate for a three minute period and must be allowed the full three minutes to give a specimen. The police officer conducting the test was entitled to conclude before three minutes had expired that the suspect was failing to provide a specimen and to stop the test, *DPP v. Coyle* [1996] R.T.R. 287, [1995] 2 C.L.Y 4424 considered.

COSGROVE v. DPP, *The Times*, March 29, 1996, Sir Iain Glidewell, QBD.

5062. Drink driving offences–disqualification–domestic dispute did not qualify for discretionary non-disqualification

The DPP appealed against a magistrate's decision not to impose the mandatory period of disqualification from driving following C's conviction of driving with excess alcohol. C's wife suffered from postnatal depression and, following a violent attack by her, C left the house, having consumed excess alcohol, and got into his car. His wife followed him and ordered him to leave under the threat of breaking the car window. C drove for 12 miles. He pulled over and fell asleep.

Two hours later a resident woke him and called the police. He was found to have 52mg of alcohol per 100ml of breath.

Held, allowing the appeal, that (1) for the magistrates to exercise their discretion, they must consider the seriousness of the emergency which caused C to drive, whether there were alternative methods of coping with the crisis, the manner in which C drove and whether, generally, he acted responsibly during the crisis. The overall circumstances must be considered objectively, *Taylor v. Rajan* [1974] Q.B. 424, [1974] C.L.Y. 3268 followed; (2) in this case, C did have to deal with an emergency, but there were alternative ways of dealing with it. C admitted that with hindsight he could have attempted to walk to a hotel. If it was necessary for C to drive the car, there was no need for him to drive for 12 miles; (3) the magistrates had erred in finding that C's alcohol reading was low. It was extremely high, at four o'clock in the morning when he had not been drinking for a few hours and (4) in all the circumstances the magistrates had reached a decision to which, properly directing themselves, they could not have reasonably come.

DPP v. CRADDOCK, Trans. Ref: CO 3836/95, April 2, 1996, Sir Iain Glidewell, QBD.

5063. Drink driving offences–disqualification–emergency–keyholder alerted by burglar alarm after consuming alcohol at home–300 yards driven from home to premises

C pleaded guilty to driving having consumed excess alcohol. He contended that as steward and keyholder of a club he was alerted that there were intruders at the club. He had been at home after midnight consuming alcohol. Without giving thought to other methods of transport he drove 300 yards to the club, of which 150 yards contained no other traffic. The magistrates accepted that there were special reasons for not imposing disqualification. The DPP appealed.

Held, dismissing the appeal, that the situation at the club could not have been stable and therefore greater harm could have been caused. C could not know how long it would be before the police arrived. Therefore the justices were entitled to take the view that the matter was an emergency.

DPP v. COX [1996] R.T.R. 123, McCowan, L.J., QBD.

5064. Drink driving offences–disqualification–special reason for non-disqualification–objective test

[Road Traffic Act 1988 s.5; Road Traffic Offenders Act 1988 s.34.]

The DPP appealed against a decision allowing B's plea of special reasons against disqualification after pleading guilty to a charge of driving with excess alcohol contrary to the Road Traffic Act 1988 s.5(1)(a). B had reacted to news that his daughter and a friend had been indecently assaulted and were being held against their will, driving immediately to the address he had been given. This was found to constitute a special reason under the Road Traffic Offenders Act 1988 s.34(1), and he was not disqualified.

Held, allowing the appeal and remitting the case, that (1) a special reason must be special to the facts of the case, which must be viewed objectively, and it is the defendant's burden to prove those facts on the balance of probabilities; (2) if proven, the special reason provides the court with a discretion as to whether or not to disqualify, or alternatively, to disqualify for a period less than the obligatory 12 months and the discretion should be exercised only in compelling circumstances, *Taylor v. Rajan* [1974] 1 All E.R. 1087, [1974] C.L.Y. 3268 followed. Regard must be given to: (a) how much the defendant had had to drink; (b) what threat would he pose driving in that condition, considering also the condition of the vehicle and the roads, and the distance he would drive; (c) how acute was the emergency, and (d) any alternatives open to the defendant to deal with the emergency. The court should ask itself what a sober, reasonable and responsible friend, himself unable to drive, would have advised in the circumstances. B was over twice the permitted limit and there were reasonable alternatives open to him, in those circumstances the court's discretion should not have been exercised.

DPP v. BRISTOW (1997) 161 J.P. 35, Simon Brown, L.J., QBD.

5065. Drink driving offences–driver's option to give a blood or urine specimen–no duty to warn that breath alcohol level above statutory limit–failure to warn did not invalidate test procedure

The DPP appealed by way of case stated against a magistrates' decision to acquit O of a charge of driving with excess alcohol. It was held that there was no case to answer on the grounds that O, when offered the option of having a blood or urine test, was not told that the level of alcohol in his breath was above the statutory limit. The DPP argued that *DPP v. Hill Brookes* [1997] 1 C.L. 165 should be followed because such an omission would not render the further specimen inadmissible. O argued that *DPP v. Hill Brookes* was not binding, it was wrongly decided and inconsistent with Lord Bridge's guidance in *DPP v. Warren* [1993] A.C. 319, [1992] C.L.Y. 3788.

Held, allowing the appeal, that (1) there was not a conflict of authority. In other, earlier cases, statutory requirements had been omitted when the driver was given his option. These cases could not be relied upon as authority for saying that Lord Bridge's guidance had to be followed literally, *DPP v. Charles* (Unreported, 1994) and *Brennen and Noscoe v. DPP* (Unreported, 1994) distinguished and (2) the decision in *DPP v. Hill Brookes* was correctly decided and binding. Although *R. v. Cheshire Justices, ex p. Cunningham* [1995] R.T.R. 287 stated that Lord Bridge's requirements should be adhered to and subsequent cases had attempted to blur those requirements, this only referred to those parts of the guidance which related to the statutory requirements. There was no statutory requirement to tell a driver that his specimen was above the statutory limit.

DPP v. ORMSBY, Trans. Ref: CO 3390/95, March 12, 1996, Leggatt, L.J., QBD.

5066. Drink driving offences–intoximeter reading wrongly deemed unreliable by police officer–urine sample request unlawful–breath test evidence not sufficiently probative of excess alcohol in urine as charged

[Road Traffic Act 1988 s.5.]

E appealed by way of case stated against conviction of driving with excess alcohol in his urine, contrary to the Road Traffic Act 1988 s.5(1)(a). Disparate Lion Intoximeter test results from two breath specimens led the police officer to believe the machine was unreliable and a urine sample was requested. However, on appeal to the Crown Court, the intoximeter was found to have functioned correctly, and, the request for a urine sample being deemed unlawful as a result, E was convicted on the basis of the breath test evidence.

Held, allowing the appeal, that probative and relevant evidence was necessary for a charge of driving with a proportion of alcohol in urine in excess of the prescribed limit. On deciding that the urine sample had been unlawfully obtained, the evidence from the breath tests was not sufficiently probative of the s.5 offence.

EVANS v. DPP, *The Times*, May 30, 1996, Newman, J., QBD.

5067. Drink driving offences–judicial decision making–magistrate using judicial knowledge of police stations' intoximeter availability–evidence of police sergeant should have been accepted

J was arrested after a positive breath test. At the police station the intoximeter failed to operate. The sergeant required another form of specimen. J agreed to give a specimen of blood but then declined when the doctor arrived. J submitted no case to answer, but the magistrate took notice of judicial knowledge from other cases that there was only one intoximeter at the police station. J appealed.

Held, dismissing the appeal, that it was wrong for a magistrate to use personal knowledge of evidence from one case in the trial of another. The evidence of the sergeant was sufficient in this instance and there was no need for judicial knowledge to fill a gap in the evidence. The magistrate was therefore correct to convict the defendant for failure to provide a specimen.

JARVIS v. DPP [1996] R.T.R. 192, McCowan, L.J., QBD.

5068. Driving–disqualification–justices to determine sufficiency of evidence to prove defendant person disqualified

M had appeared before the justices charged with driving whilst disqualified. M had previously been arrested by a police officer, C, for a motoring offence. However, C had not been in court to see the man described as M in the certificate of conviction and could not say of his own knowledge that the man, M, was previously disqualified because of that earlier offence. The justices dismissed the information against M on the basis that the prosecution did not prove that M was the person disqualified in any of the three ways given in *R. v. Derwentside Magistrates' Court, ex p. Heaviside* (1995) 11 Road L.R. 557. The Crown appealed.

Held, allowing the appeal and remitting the matter to the justices to continue the hearing, that *R. v. Derwentside Magistrates' Court, ex p. Heaviside* did not establish the exclusive methods for proof of identity of the person disqualified. It was a matter for the justices to determine whether there was sufficient evidence to prove that the defendant was the person previously disqualified. In this case there was more than mere coincidence of names and the case should proceed.

R. v. DPP, *ex p.* MANSFIELD (1996) 160 J.P. 472, Staughton, L.J., QBD.

5069. Driving–offences

[Road Traffic Act 1988.]

The Crown Prosecution Service (CPS) issued a press release entitled *Charging the right driving offence: new guidance published* (Press release 002/96), published on March 7, 1996. A new charging standard has been published, providing guidance to police and prosecutors on how to make the right choice when more than one charge is available. The new standards remind police and prosecutors that the charges brought should reflect the seriousness of the offendce, provide the court with adequate sentencing powers and enable the case to be clearly presented. The decision must be taken strictly on available evidence, including reports from police accident investigation officers. The main offences defined in the Standard, the legal requirement to be met in respect of each charge and the maximum penalties for each are detailed in an appendix to the press release. The offences are careless driving (RTA 1988 s.3); dangerous driving (RTA 1988 s.2); causing death by careless driving while under the influence of drink or drugs (RTA 1988 s.3A); and causing death by dangerous driving (RTA 1988 s.1).

5070. Driving licences

MOTOR VEHICLES (DRIVING LICENCES) REGULATIONS 1996, SI 1996 2824; made under the Road Traffic Act 1988 s.88, s.89, s.91, s.92(, s.97, s.98, s.99, s.99A, s.101, s.105, s.108, s.114, s.115, s.115A, s.117, s.118, s.120, s.121, s.164, s.183, s.192. In force: Reg.20 to Reg.32, Sch.5, Sch.6: December 2, 1996 Reg.34(2) (a) (ii) (4) (b), Sch.6: March 1, 1996; Reg.39(6): April 1, 1997; Remainder: January 1, 1997; £8.70.

These Regulations consolidate with amendments the Motor Vehicles (Driving Licences) Regulations 1987 (SI 1987 1378), the Motor Vehicles (Driving Licences) (Large Goods and Passenger-Carrying Vehicles) Regulations 1990 (SI 1990 2612) and Regulations amending those Regulations. The amendments have been made for the purpose of implementing Council Directive 91/439 on Driving Licences ([1991] OJ L237/1) and for general purposes.

5071. Driving licences

MOTOR VEHICLES (DRIVING LICENCES) (AMENDMENT) REGULATIONS 1996, SI 1996 211; made under the Road Traffic Act 1988 s.89, s.91, s.97, s.105, s.108. In force: February 26, 1996; £1.10.

These Regulations amend the Motor Vehicles (Driving Licences) Regulations 1987 Reg.18, Reg.19, Reg.20 and Reg.23A in relation to driving tests.

5072. Driving licences–buses

COMMUNITY BUS (AMENDMENT) REGULATIONS 1996, SI 1996 3087; made under the Public Passenger Vehicles Act 1981 s.60; and the Transport Act 1985 s.23, s.137. In force: January 1, 1997; £1.10.

These Regulations amend the Community Bus Regulations 1986 (SI 1986 1245) by altering the driving licence requirements which must be met by a person driving a bus under a community bus permit. A driver who does not hold a full licence to drive a passenger-carrying vehicle must be 21 or over and hold either a full British driving licence, a full Northern Ireland licence or an equivalent licence issued by a state or territory within the European Economic Area which authorises the driving of motor cars. If, however, a full British licence was not held before January 1, 1997, the licence must have been held for at least two years in aggregate.

5073. Driving licences–buses

MINIBUS AND OTHER SECTION 19 PERMIT BUSES (AMENDMENT) REGULATIONS 1996, SI 1996 3088; made under the Public Passenger Vehicles Act 1981 s.60; and the Transport Act 1985 s.21, s.137. In force: January 1, 1997; £1.10.

These Regulations amend the Minibus and Other Section 19 Permit Buses Regulations 1987 (SI 1987 1320) by altering the conditions which must be met by a person driving a small bus under a section 19 permit. A driver of a small bus under a permit must be 21 or over and hold either a full British driving licence, a full Northern Ireland licence or an equivalent licence issued by a state or territory within the European Economic Area which authorises the driving of motor cars. If, however, a full British licence was not held before January 1, 1997, two additional conditions must be fulfilled, namely that the licence must have been held for at least two years in aggregate and the driver must not receive any payment for driving other than out-of-pocket expenses.

5074. Driving licences

MOTOR VEHICLES (DRIVING LICENCES) (AMENDMENT) REGULATIONS 1996, SI 1996 3198; made under the Road Traffic Act 1988 s.105, s.108. In force: January 1, 1997; £0.65.

These Regulations amend the Motor Vehicles (Driving Licences) Regulations (SI 1996 2824) Reg.70 which enacts transitional arrangements consequent upon the change in the classification of vehicles on January 1, 1997. They extend the classes of vehicles which the holder of a licence authorising, on December 31, 1996, the driving of vehicles in category D otherwise than for the hire or reward may drive. From January 1, 1997 the classes include vehicles in category D which are driven under a permit granted under the Transport Act 1985 s.19.

5075. Driving licences

MOTOR VEHICLES (DRIVING LICENCES) (AMENDMENT) (NO.2) REGULATIONS 1996, SI 1996 536; made under the Road Traffic Act 1988 s.97, s.105, s.108. In force: April 1, 1996; £1.10.

These Regulations relate to Wales. They amend the Motor Vehicles (Driving Licences) Regulations 1987 (SI 1987 1378) to allow provisional licence holders driving in Wales to display 'D' plates (as the Welsh word for learner is dysgwr) as an alternative to 'L' plates, if they so wish.

5076. Driving licences

MOTOR VEHICLES (DRIVING LICENCES) (AMENDMENT) (NO.3) REGULATIONS 1996, SI 1996 1259; made under the Road Traffic Act 1988 s.89, s.91, s.97, s.105, s.108. In force: for purpose of enabling persons to apply for tests: June 1, 1996 Remainder: July 1, 1996; £4.70.

These Regulations amend the Vehicles (Driving Licences) Regulations 1987 (SI 1987 1378) and give effect to the Second Council Directive 91/439 ([1991] OJ L237) regarding driving tests for motor vehicles. The main changes concern the dividing of driving tests for motor bicycles, motor cars, small goods vehicles and mopeds in to two parts, a practical test and a theory test.

5077. Driving licences

MOTOR VEHICLES (DRIVING LICENCES) (AMENDMENT) (NO.4) REGULATIONS 1996, SI 1996 1997; made under the Road Traffic Act 1988 s.97, s.105, s.108. In force: September 9, 1996; £0.65.

These Regulations further amend the Motor Vehicles (Driving Licences) Regulation 1987 (SI 1987 1378) Reg.9(6) by providing that any person with a disability may be a qualified driver for the purpose of supervising a learner driver in a motor car providing that he is able to take control of the braking and steering of the car in an emergency.

5078. Driving licences–European Union

DRIVING LICENCES (COMMUNITY DRIVING LICENCE) REGULATIONS 1996, SI 1996 1974; made under the European Communities Act 1972 s.2. In force: july 23, 1996, January 1, 1997; £4.15.

These Regulations amend the Road Traffic Act 1988, the Road Traffic Offenders Act 1988, the Transport Act 1985 and the Motor Vehicles (International Circulation) Order 1975 (SI 1975 1208) in order to give effect to Council Directive 91/439 ([1991] OJ L237) on driving licences. The Directive applies by virtue of Decision 7/94 of the EEA Joint Committee ([1994] OJ L160) to states within the EEA. The changes relate to the validity of Community driving licences.

5079. Driving licences–heavy goods and passenger vehicles

MOTOR VEHICLES (DRIVING LICENCES) (LARGE GOODS AND PASSENGER CARRYING VEHICLES) (AMENDMENT) REGULATIONS 1996, SI 1996 212; made under the Road Traffic Act 1988 s.89, s.91, s.105, s.108. In force: February 26, 1996; £1.10.

These Regulations amend the Motor Vehicles (Driving Licences) (Large Goods and Passenger-Carrying Vehicles) Regulations 1990 (SI 1990 2612) in relation to driving tests.

5080. Driving licences–reciprocal arrangements–Isle of Man and Channel Islands

DRIVING LICENCES (DESIGNATION OF RELEVANT EXTERNAL LAW) ORDER 1996, SI 1996 3206; made under the Road Traffic Act 1988 s.88, s.89. In force: January 1, 1997; £0.65.

With effect from January 1, 1997, the Driving Licences (Community Driving Licence) Regulations 1996 (SI 1996 1974) amend the Road Traffic Act 1988 s.89 so that a licence under Part III of that Act may not be granted to a person who has passed a driving test under the law applicable in the Isle of Man or the Channel Islands. Licences granted in any of those islands authorising the driving of classes of goods or passenger carrying vehicle continue to be exchangeable for corresponding licences in Great Britain if the relevant law makes satisfactory provision for the grant of those licences. This Order revokes earlier Orders, which applied to both driving tests and licences, and re-enacts the designation of the laws of the Isle of Man and Jersey as making satisfactory provision for granting all classes of goods and passenger carrying vehicle licence.

5081. Heavy goods vehicles–fees–international journeys

GOODS VEHICLES (AUTHORISATION OF INTERNATIONAL JOURNEYS) (FEES) REGULATIONS 1996, SI 1996 131; made under the Finance Act 1973 s.56. In force: January 22, 1996; £1.55.

These Regulations consolidate, with amendments, the Goods Vehicles (Authorisation of Internationall Journeys) (Fees) Regulations 1983 (SI 1983 1831). The Regulations prescribe the fees to be paid for the issue of documents authorising the operation of goods vehicles on journeys between the 7 and (a) other member countries of the European Conference of Ministers of Transport, and (b) certain states with whom bilateral agreements or arrangements have been concluded.

5082. Heavy goods vehicles–licensing

GOODS VEHICLES (LICENSING OF OPERATORS) (TEMPORARY USE IN GREAT BRITAIN) REGULATIONS 1996, SI 1996 2186; made under the Goods Vehicles (Licensing of Operators) Act 1995 s.57. In force: September 26, 1996; £3.70.

These Regulations which consolidate Regulations relating to the licensing of operators of goods vehicles, modify the requirements of the Goods Vehicles (Licensing of Operators) Act 1995 as to operators' licences in relation to certain foreign goods vehicles and Northern Ireland goods vehicles.

5083. Heavy goods vehicles–standards

MOTOR VEHICLES (TYPE APPROVAL FOR GOODS VEHICLES) (AMENDMENT) REGULATIONS 1996, SI 1996 2331; made under the Road Traffic Act 1988 s.54, s.61. In force: October 1, 1996; £2.80.

These Regulations amend the Motor Vehicles (Type Approval for Goods Vehicles) (Great Britain) Regulations 1982 (SI 1982 1271) in compliance with Council Directive 70/156 (as amended by Directives 87/403, 92/53 and 93/81), Council Directive 70/157 (as amended by Directives 73/350, 81/334, 84/424, 92/97 and 96/20). Council Directive 70/220 (as amended by Directive 83/351), Commission Directive 95/54, Council Directive 88/77 (as amended by Directives 91/542 and 96/1) and UN/ECE Regulation 49. The amendments relate to standards of noise, exhaust emissions and electromagnetic compatibility.

5084. Heavy goods vehicles–type approval

MOTOR VEHICLES (TYPE APPROVAL FOR GOODS VEHICLES) (GREAT BRITAIN) (AMENDMENT) (NO.2) REGULATIONS 1996, SI 1996 3014; made under the Road Traffic Act 1988 s.54, s.61, s.63, s.66. In force: July 1, 1997; £1.10.

These Regulations amend the Motor Vehicles (Type Approval for Goods Vehicles) (Great Britain) Regulations 1982 (SI 1982 1271) and together with Motor Vehicles (Approval) Regulations 1996 (SI 1996 3013) establish a statutory scheme for approving the construction of single light goods vehicles before such vehicles are brought into service.

5085. Heavy goods vehicles–time–road safety

COMMUNITY DRIVERS' HOURS (PASSENGER AND GOODS VEHICLES) (TEMPORARY EXCEPTION) REGULATIONS 1996, SI 1996 239; made under the European Communities Act 1972 s.2. In force: February 9, 1996; £0.65.

Article 13(2) of Council Regulation 3820/85 of the December 20, 1985 on the harmonisation of certain social legislation relating to road transport provides that Member States may in urgent cases grant a temporary exception for a period not exceeding 30 days to transport operations carried out in exceptional circumstances. These Regulations provide that until February 18, 1996 any time spent driving in the exceptional circumstances occasioned by severe weather conditions in Great Britain or the effects or consequences of such exceptional circumstances shall not be taken into account for the purposes of the application of Art.6, Art.8 and Art.9 of the Council Regulation.

5086. Heavy goods vehicles–time–road safety

DRIVERS' HOURS (PASSENGER AND GOODS VEHICLES) (EXEMPTION) REGULATIONS 1996, SI 1996 240; made under the Transport Act 1968 s.96. In force: February 9, 1996; £0.65.

These Regulations exempt, until February 18, 1996 from the requirements of the Transport Act 1968 s.96(1) to s.96(6) a driver who during any working day or any working week spends time in driving passenger or goods vehicles and spends time driving or on duty during that day or week to meet the special need occasioned by severe weather conditions in Great Britain or the effects or consequences of such severe weather conditions in respect of that day or week.

5087. Magistrates' courts–complaint that conviction procedurally unfair–whether judicial review or appeal to Crown Court appropriate

[Magistrates' Courts Act 1980 s.108.]

D applied for judicial review to quash his conviction by magistrates for driving without due care and attention, on the ground that failure to disclose a potentially helpful witness statement had rendered the conviction procedurally unfair. D had also commenced an appeal to the Crown Court under the Magistrates' Courts Act 1980 s.108. The magistrates argued that the conviction ought not to be quashed and the case remitted for retrial when an appeal to the Crown Court provided a suitable remedy.

Held, dismissing the application, that it was unnecessary to grant judicial review of a conviction by magistrates when the procedural unfairness complained of could be rectified by a fair hearing before the Crown Court. Otherwise, if a case was remitted to the magistrates after the Crown Court had fairly convicted, the procedurally fair conviction would be subsequently invalidated if the magistrates set aside the original conviction, *R. v. Bradford Justices, ex p. Wilkinson* [1991] 1 W.L.R. 692, [1990] C.L.Y. 1007 not followed.

R. v. PETERBOROUGH MAGISTRATES' COURT, *ex p.* DOWLER; SUB NOM. R. v. PETERBOROUGH JUSTICES, *ex p.* DOWLER [1996] 2 Cr. App. R. 561, Turner, J., QBD.

5088. Motor vehicles–ambulances–no offence where emergency vehicle used for non-emergency purposes–blue emergency light fitted but not illuminated

[Road Vehicles Lighting Regulations 1989 Reg.16.]

H was stopped driving a child to school in a Volvo vehicle which had been adapted for use as an ambulance. There was a blue light on the vehicle but it was not illuminated. The issue arose whether the blue light should be covered up when not in use as an "emergency vehicle" and whether the vehicle was properly an "emergency vehicle". The DPP appealed.

Held, dismissing the appeal, that a vehicle adapted for the purpose of conveying the sick and used for that purpose from time to time was an emergency vehicle within the Road Vehicles Lighting Regulations 1989 Reg.16. H was not committing an offence by using an emergency vehicle for other purposes when a blue light was fitted but not illuminated.

DPP v. HAWKINS [1996] R.T.R. 160, McCowan, L.J., CA.

5089. Motor vehicles–construction–standards

MOTOR VEHICLES (APPROVAL) REGULATIONS 1996, SI 1996 3013; made under the Road Traffic Act 1988 s.54, s.61, s.63, s.66. In force: July 1, 1997; £7.35.

These Regulations establish a statutory system for approving the construction of single vehicles before they enter into service. The Regulations apply to passenger cars, dual-purpose vehicles and light goods vehicles which are amateur-built or personally imported or which enter into service in Great Britain in very low numbers. The Regulations also apply to motor ambulances and motor caravans, but approval is optional for these and for some other vehicles.

5090. Motor vehicles–construction and use

ROAD VEHICLES (CONSTRUCTION AND USE) (AMENDMENT) REGULATIONS 1996, SI 1996 16; made under the Road Traffic Act 1988 s.41. In force: February 1, 1996; £0.65.

These Regulations further amend the Road Vehicles (Construction and Use) Regulations 1986 (SI 1986 1078). Regulation 57A requires original (as opposed to replacement) silencers fitted to motor bicycles (and certain light three wheeled vehicles) first used on or after February 1, 1996 to comply with Council Directive 78/1015 ([1978] OJ L349/21) as amended by Council Directive 87/156 ([1987] OJ L24/42) and Council Directive 89/235 ([1989] OJ L98/1), subject to some modifications set out in the Regulation. An effect of this requirement is that the original silencer fitted to any such vehicle would have to meet the technical requirements of the amended Directive (subject to some modifications) and would bear a mark indicating that the silencer is of a type that has been officially approved under the amended Directive. Regulation 57A is amended so that the original silencer fitted to a vehicle with a design speed not exceeding 50 kilometres per hour will have not to bear such an approval mark. The requirement to meet the technical requirements of the amended Directive (subject to some modifications) will not be affected. The amendments do not affect the requirements of Reg.57A relating to replacement silencers or to original silencers fitted to vehicles with a design speed exceeding 50 kilometres per hour.

5091. Motor vehicles–construction and use

ROAD VEHICLES (CONSTRUCTION AND USE) (AMENDMENT) (NO.2) REGULATIONS 1996, SI 1996 163; made under the European Communities Act 1972 s.2; and the Road Traffic Act 1988 s.41, s.195. In force: Reg.4: June 3, 1996; Remainder: February 10, 1997; £1.10.

These Regulations further amend the Road Vehicles (Construction and Use) Regulations 1986 (SI 1986 1078) in relation to seat belts and anchorages. Regulation 47 para.7 of the 1986 Regulations is amended so that all seat belts to which the paragraph applies have the option of bearing a mark indicating that they have been approved as complying with one of the British Standards or that they comply with the requirements of a corresponding standard. These Regulations also insert a new Reg.48A which prohibits the use of a coach or minibus for the purpose of carrying a group of three or more children in connection with an organised trip unless at least as many forward facing passenger seats as there are children are fitted with seat belts. A disabled child in a wheelchair is disregarded for this purpose. For the purposes of the regulation a "child" is a person aged 3 years or more but under 16. The new Reg.48A does not apply to a vehicle providing a transport service for the general public.

5092. Motor vehicles–construction and use

ROAD VEHICLES (CONSTRUCTION AND USE) (AMENDMENT) (NO.3) REGULATIONS 1996, SI 1996 2064; made under the Road Traffic Act 1988 s.41. In force: Reg.4: September 1, 1997; Remainder: September 1, 1996; £1.10.

These Regulations further amend the Road Vehicles (Construction and Use) Regulations 1986 (SI 1986 1078) Reg.36B which required certain heavy goods vehicles to be fitted with a speed limiter and for the limiter to be so set that the stabilised speed of the vehicle is less than 56 mph. These Regulations amend Reg.36B so that in general the stabilised speed of these vehicles will have to be not more than 90 kilometres per hour and the limiter will have to be set at not more than 85 kilometres per hour. However, it will be permissible for a limiter to be set at a particular speed above 85 kilometres per hour if the processes used in the construction of the vehicle, the limiter and its other equipment are such as to ensure that the stabilised speed of the vehicle is not more than 90 kilometres per hour when the limiter is set at that speed.

5093. Motor vehicles–construction and use

ROAD VEHICLES (CONSTRUCTION AND USE) (AMENDMENT) (NO.4) REGULATIONS 1996, SI 1996 2085; made under the Road Traffic Act 1988 s.41. In force: September 2, 1996; £1.10.

These Regulations further amend the Road Vehicles (Construction and Use) Regulations 1986 (SI 1986 1078), so that they refer to the second edition of In-Service Exhaust Emissions Standards for Road Vehicles (ISBN 0 9526457 1 8) instead of the first edition. The main effect is to revise the requirements of para.10AA for most models. The description of some models in the second edition of the publications differs from the description in the first edition. The Regulations also amend the 1986 Regulations so that the requirements of para.10AA no longer apply to any vehicle that is not a passenger car unless it is of a model listed in the substituted publication. The vehicles that no longer have to comply with para.10AA will instead have to comply with para.10A.

5094. Motor vehicles–construction and use

ROAD VEHICLES (CONSTRUCTION AND USE) (AMENDMENT) (NO.5) REGULATIONS 1996, SI 1996 2329; made under the Road Traffic Act 1988 s.41. In force: October 1, 1996; £3.20.

These Regulations amend the Road Vehicles (Construction and Use) Regulations 1986 (SI 1986 1078) in compliance with Council Directive 70/156 (as amended by Directives 87/403, 92/53 and 93/81), Council Directive 70/157 (as amended by Directives 73/350, 77/212, 81/334, 84/372, 84/424, 92/97 and 96/20), Council Directive 70/220 as amended by Directive 83/351), Council Directive 72/245 as amended by Directives 75/332 and 95/54, Council Directive 78/1015 as amended by Directives 87/56 and 89/235), Council Directive 82/890 and Council Directive 88/77 as amended by Directives 91/542 and 96/1) and UN/ECE Regulation 10 and Regulation 51. The amendments relate to exhaust systems, emission standards, noise limits, silencers and electrical and electronic sub-assembly.

5095. Motor vehicles–construction and use

ROAD VEHICLES (CONSTRUCTION AND USE) (AMENDMENT) (NO.6) REGULATIONS 1996, SI 1996 3017; made under the Road Traffic Act 1988 s.41. In force: July 1, 1997; £1.55.

These Regulations amend the Road Vehicles (Construction and Use) Regulations 1986 (SI 1986 1078) consequentially upon the making of the Motor Vehicles (Approval) Regulations 1996 (SI 1996 3013). They insert a new Sch.2A which relates to vehicles which are the subject of a Minister's approval certificate issued under the Approval Regulations.

5096. Motor vehicles–construction and use

ROAD VEHICLES (CONSTRUCTION AND USE) (AMENDMENT) (NO.7) REGULATIONS 1996, SI 1996 3033; made under the Road Traffic Act 1988 s.41. In force: January 1, 1997; £1.55.

These Regulations further amend the Road Vehicles (Construction and Use) Regulations 1986 (SI 1986 1078). The main amendments relate to braking systems for vehicles, couplings on trailer pneumatic braking systems, marking weights on vehicles and marking dates of manufacture on vehicles.

5097. Motor vehicles–construction and use

ROAD VEHICLES (CONSTRUCTION AND USE) (AMENDMENT) (NO.8) REGULATIONS 1996, SI 1996 3133; made under the Road Traffic Act 1988 s.41. In force: January 3, 1997; £1.10.

These Regulations further amend the Road Vehicles (Construction and Use) Regulations 1986 (SI 1986 1078) by inserting a new Reg.93A which applies with modifications to certain vehicles carrying explosives, the supplementary braking requirements contained in the European Agreement concerning the International Carriage of Dangerous Goods by Road. They also amend Reg.4 of the 1986 Regulations so as to exempt vehicles in the service of a visiting force or a headquarters from the new Reg.93A and make a consequential amendment.

5098. Motor vehicles–documentation

MOTOR VEHICLES (INTERNATIONAL CIRCULATION) (AMENDMENT) ORDER 1996, SI 1996 1929; made under the Motor Vehicles (International Circulation) Act 1952 s.1. In force: August 6, 1996; £1.55.

This Order amends the Motor Vehicles (International Circulation) Order 1975 (SI 1975 1208). The changes relate to documents for drivers and goods vehicles going abroad, visitors' driving permits and vehicle excise exemption.

5099. Motor vehicles–driving–training

MOTOR CARS (DRIVING INSTRUCTION) (AMENDMENT) REGULATIONS 1996, SI 1996 1983; made under the Road Traffic Act 1988 s.123, s.125, s.125A, s.125B, s.127, s.129, s.132, s.133B, s.135, s.141; and the Department of Transport (Fees) Order 1988. In force: September 9, 1996; £1.55.

These Regulations amend the Motor Cars (Driving Instruction) Regulations 1989 (SI 1989 2057) in consequence of amendments made to the Road Traffic Act 1988 Part V by the Road Traffic (Driving Instruction by Disabled Persons) Act 1993 which come into force on September 9, 1996 and enable those with certain physical conditions to give paid driving instruction in certain circumstances.

5100. Motor vehicles–fees

MOTOR VEHICLES (TYPE APPROVAL AND APPROVAL MARKS) (FEES) REGULATIONS 1996, SI 1996 958; made under the Finance Act 1973 s.56; the Road Traffic Act 1988 s.61; the Department of Transport (Fees) Order 1988; and the Finance Act 1990 s.128. In force: April 22, 1996; £7.30.

These Regulations revoke and re-enact the Motor Vehicles (Type Approval and Approval Marks) (Fees) Regulations 1995 (SI 1995 925). They prescribe fees payable for the examination of vehicles and vehicle parts, the examination of complete vehicles, the issue of documents, the type approval of vehicles and parts for the purposes of Community Instruments, ECE Regulations and the national scheme for vehicle type approval, the examination of premises with a view to their being approved for carrying out type approval examinations and for advising manufacturers whether their arrangements for securing conformity of production are likely to be accepted. Changes made to the 1995 Regulations include an increase in fee amounts, the addition of a new provision relating to charges made for work carried out in Japan, China, South Korea or Taiwan by a person resident in Japan, and the introduction of new fees and standards resulting from new or amended ECE Regulations and Community Instruments.

5101. Motor vehicles–lighting

ROAD VEHICLES LIGHTING (AMENDMENT) REGULATIONS 1996, SI 1996 3016; made under the Road Traffic Act 1988 s.41. In force: July 1, 1997; £1.10.

These Regulations insert a new Reg.9B into the Road Vehicles Lighting Regulations 1989 (SI 1989 1796) the effect of which is to modify those Regulations in relation to certain passenger vehicles which are the subject of a Minister's approval certificate given pursuant to the Motor Vehicles (Approval)

Regulations 1996 (SI 1996 3013). These Regulations have been notified to the European Commission pursuant to Council Directive 83/189 laying down a procedure for the provision of information in the field of technical standards and regulations ([1983] OJ L109/9) as amended by Council Directive 88/182 ([1988] OJ L81/75) and European Parliament and Council Directive 94/10 ([1994] OJ L100/30).

5102. Motor vehicles–MOT certificates

MOTOR VEHICLES (TESTS) (AMENDMENT) REGULATIONS 1996, SI 1996 1751; made under the Road Traffic Act 1988 s.45, s.46; and the Department of Transport (Fees) Order 1988. In force: August 1, 1996; £1.10.

These Regulations further amend the Motor Vehicles (Tests) Regulations 1981 (SI 1981 1694) which make provision for certain motor vehicles to be examined by persons authorised by the Secretary of State and for test certificates to be issued for vehicles that are found to meet certain requirements. They increase the fees payable for examinations of vehicles.

5103. Motor vehicles–MOT certificates–deregulation

DEREGULATION (MOTOR VEHICLES TESTS) ORDER 1996, SI 1996 1700; made under the Deregulation and Contracting Out Act 1994 s.1. In force: July 1, 1996; £1.10.

The Road Traffic Act 1988 s.47 makes it an offence for a vehicle to which the section applies to be used on a road unless a MOT test certificate has been issued for it within the previous twelve months. The section does not in general, apply to any vehicle until a specified period after it is first registered, the specified period being three years in some cases and one year in other cases. However, where a vehicle is tested within one month (two months in the case of a public service vehicle) before the expiration of a current certificate, the twelve month period is extended to twelve months from the expiration of that certificate. This Order amends the 1988 Act so that where a vehicle is tested within one month (two months in the case of a public service vehicle) before the date by which it is first required to have a certificate, the twelve month period is extended to twelve months from that date.

5104. Motor vehicles–registration–sale of information

VEHICLE REGISTRATION (SALE OF INFORMATION) REGULATIONS 1996, SI 1996 2800; made under the Vehicle Excise and Registration Act 1994 s.22, s.57. In force: December 30, 1996; £0.65.

These Regulations enable the Secretary of State to sell to any person he thinks fit information derived from the Great Britain register of mechanically propelled vehicles kept by him under the Vehicle Excise and Registration Act 1994. The terms of a sale are at the discretion of the Secretary of State, but the information sold must not identify any person or contain anything enabling any person to be identified.

5105. Motor vehicles–standards

MOTOR VEHICLES (TYPE APPROVAL) (GREAT BRITAIN) (AMENDMENT) REGULATIONS 1996, SI 1996 2330; made under the Road Traffic Act 1988 s.54, s.61. In force: October 1, 1996; £2.40.

These Regulations amend the Motor Vehicles (Type Approval) (Great Britain) Regulations 1984 (SI 1984 981) in compliance with Council Directive 70/156 (as amended by Directives 87/403, 92/53 and 93/81), Council Directive 70/157 (as amended by Directives 73/350, 77/212, 81/334, 84/372, 84/424, 92/97 and 96/20), Council Directive 70/220 (as amended by Directive 83/351), Commission Directive 95/54, Council Directive 88/77 (as amended by Directives 91/542 and 96/1) and UN/ECE Regulation 49. The amendments relate to standards of noise, exhaust emission and electromagnetic compatibility.

5106. Motor vehicles–type approval

MOTOR VEHICLES (TYPE APPROVAL) (GREAT BRITAIN) (AMENDMENT) (NO.2) REGULATIONS 1996, SI 1996 3015; made under the Road Traffic Act 1988 s.54, s.61, s.63, s.66. In force: July 1, 1997; £1.10.

These Regulations amend the Motor Vehicles (Type Approval) Regulations 1984 (SI 1984 981) and, together with the Motor Vehicles (Approval) Regulations 1996 (SI 1996 3013) establish a statutory scheme for approving the construction of single passenger vehicles before such vehicles are brought into service.

5107. Motorways–A1

A1 MOTORWAY (NORTH OF LEEMING TO SCOTCH CORNER SECTION AND CONNECTING ROADS) SCHEME 1996, SI 1996 1830; made under the Highways Act 1980 s.16, s.17, s.19. In force: July 24, 1996; £0.65.

This Order provides that the special roads described in the Schedules shall become trunk roads.

5108. Motorways–A57(M)

CITY OF MANCHESTER (MANCUNIAN WAY A57(M)) (CHESTER ROAD ROUNDABOUT) MOTORWAY SCHEME 1995 CONFIRMATION INSTRUMENT 1996, SI 1996 2201; made under the Highways Act 1980 s.16, s.17. In force: on the date on which notice that it has been confirmed is first published in accordance with the Highways Act 1980 Sch.2 para.1; £1.55.

This Instrument confirms with amendments, the Scheme set out in the Schedules.

5109. Motorways–A64(M)

LEEDS CITY COUNCIL (A64(M) MOTORWAY SLIP ROAD AT MABGATE) SCHEME 1995 CONFIRMATION INSTRUMENT 1996, SI 1996 2724; made under the Highways Act 1980 s.16. In force: in accordance with Art.1; £1.55.

This Statutory Instrument confirms the A64(M) Motorway Slip Road at Mabgate Scheme 1995.

5110. Motorways–A556(M)–connecting roads

A556(M) MOTORWAY (M6 TO M56 LINK) AND CONNECTING ROADS SCHEME 1996, SI 1996 1648; made under the Highways Act 1980 s.16, s.17, s.19. In force: June 28, 1996; £1.10.

This Scheme provides that certain connecting roads set out in Sch.2 shall become trunk roads.

5111. Motorways–A556(M)–connecting roads

A556(M) MOTORWAY (M6 TO M56 LINK) SUPPLEMENTARY CONNECTING ROADS SCHEME 1996, SI 1996 1649; made under the Highways Act 1980 s.16, s.17, s.19. In force: June 28, 1996; £0.65.

This Scheme provides that certain connecting roads set out in the Schedule shall become trunk roads.

5112. Motorways–M1–Leeds

LEEDS CITY COUNCIL (M1 MOTORWAY JUNCTION 46 SLIP ROAD CONNECTING ROAD) SCHEME 1992 CONFIRMATION INSTRUMENT 1996, SI 1996 72; made under the Highways Act 1980 s.16. In force: in accordance with Highways Act 1980 Sch.2 para.1; £1.95.

The Leeds City Council (M1 Motorway Junction 46 Slip Road Connecting Road) Scheme 1992 is confirmed, without modifications, by this Instrument. The confirmed scheme is set out in the attached Schedule and a site plan is enclosed.

5113. Motorways–M1–Leeds–inner ring road

LEEDS CITY COUNCIL (LEEDS INNER RING ROAD STAGES 6 AND 7 (A61) TO M1 MOTORWAY (JUNCTION 46) CONNECTING ROAD) SCHEME 1994 CONFIRMATION INSTRUMENT 1996, SI 1996 71; made under the Highways Act 1980 s.16. In force: in accordance with Highways Act 1980 Sch.2 para.1; £3.20.

The Leeds City Council (Leeds Inner Ring Road Stages 6 and 7 (A61) to M1 Motorway (Junction 46) Connecting Road) Scheme is confirmed, with modifications, by this Instrument. The modified confirmed scheme is set out in the attached Schedule and a site plan is enclosed.

5114. Motorways–M2

M2 MOTORWAY (WEST OF ROCHESTER SECTION) SCHEME 1996, SI 1996 854; made under the Highways Act 1980 s.16, s.17. In force: April 9, 1996; £0.65.

This Scheme provides for a special road, for the exclusive use of traffic of Classes I and II of the classes of traffic set out in the Highways Act 1980 Sch.4, along the route of the A2 Trunk Road, from the western limit of the M2 Motorway, westwards for a distance of 816 metres.

5115. Motorways–M4–flood alleviation scheme

M4 MOTORWAY (MAIDENHEAD WINDSOR AND ETON FLOOD ALLEVIATION SCHEME) (TEMPORARY DIVERSION) SCHEME 1996, SI 1996 2639; made under the Highways Act 1980 s.16, s.17, s.19. In force: October 30, 1996; £0.65.

This Order authorises the provision of a special road for the exclusive use of Class I and Class II of traffic along the route of a temporary highway at Dorney Reach, Buckinghamshire.

5116. Motorways–M11

M11 MOTORWAY (JUNCTION 5, LOUGHTON, ESSEX, NORTH FACING SLIP ROADS) SCHEME 1996, SI 1996 1538; made under the Highways Act 1980 s.16, s.17, s.19. In force: June 25, 1996; £0.65.

This Order provides that the special roads detailed in the Schedule shall become trunk roads.

5117. Motorways–M23

M23 MOTORWAY (BALCOMBE ROAD INTERCHANGE) CONNECTING ROADS SCHEME 1996, SI 1996 2854; made under the Highways Act 1980 s.16, s.17, s.19. In force: December 16, 1996; £0.65.

This Order prescribes the route of connecting roads.

5118. Motorways–M62–M606 link

M62 (EAST) TO M606 LINK AND CONNECTING ROADS SCHEME 1996, SI 1996 2130; made under the Highways Act 1980 s.16, s.17, s.19. In force: September 6, 1996; £0.65.

This Order authorises the provision of roads set out in the Schedules.

5119. Motorways–M66–connecting roads

M66 MOTORWAY (BURY EASTERLY BYPASS NORTHERN SECTION) AND CONNECTING ROADS SCHEME 1973 (VARIATION) SCHEME 1996, SI 1996 2159; made under the Highways Act 1980 s.16, s.17, s.19. In force: September 13, 1996; £0.65.

This Order varies the 1973 scheme.

5120. Motorways–M66–detrunking

M66 MOTORWAY (BURY EASTERLY BYPASS NORTHERN SECTION) (JUNCTION 2 SOUTHBOUND OFF-SLIP) (DETRUNKING) ORDER 1996, SI 1996 2158; made under the Highways Act 1980 s.10, s.12. In force: September 13, 1996; £0.65.

This Order re-classifies the trunk road described in the Schedule as a classified road.

5121. Motorways–passenger vehicles–heavy goods vehicles–driving tests

MOTORWAYS TRAFFIC (ENGLAND AND WALES) (AMENDMENT) REGULATIONS 1996, SI 1996 3053; made under the Road Traffic Regulation Act 1984 s.17. In force: January 1, 1997; £1.10.

By virtue of the Motor Vehicles (Driving Licences) Regulations 1996 (SI 1996 2824), separate driving tests are introduced in respect of motor cars with trailers, trucks and vans of between 3.5 and 7.5 tonnes maximum authorised mass and buses having between 9 and 16 passenger seats whether or not they carry passengers for hire or reward. Provisional licences to drive these categories of vehicle may, however, only be issued to persons holding at least a licence to drive motor cars. These Regulations amend the Motorways Traffic (England and Wales) Regulations 1982 (SI 1982 1163) so as to enable a person who holds a provisional licence for such vehicles to drive them on a motorway.

5122. Motorways–Wainscott Northern Bypass

KENT COUNTY COUNCIL (WAINSCOTT NORTHERN BYPASS) MOTORWAY SCHEME 1992 CONFIRMATION INSTRUMENT 1996, SI 1996 53; made under the Highways Act 1980 s.16, s.17. £1.55.

This Order confirms the Kent County Council (Wainscott Northern Bypass) Motorway Scheme 1992 without modifications. The Schedules to this Instrument set out the Scheme and the routes of the connecting roads and are accompanied by a plan detailing the route of the special road without widths or construction details.

5123. Obstruction of highway–mobile food cabinet in pedestrianised street–relevance of pavement cafes–whether obstruction de minimis

[Highways Act 1980 s.137.]

WCC appealed by way of case stated against the Stipendiary Magistrate's dismissal of an information against A alleging wilful obstruction of the highway contrary to the Highways Act 1980 s.137. The respondent had placed a mobile food cabinet, measuring six feet seven inches long by three feet wide, and an advertisement board in a pedestrianised street. The Stipendiary Magistrate considered, that (1) the obstruction was de minimis and (2) prosecution was oppressive in that it discouraged summer street activity and there was evidence of tables and chairs outside neighbouring catering premises without objection by the appellant.

Held, allowing the appeal and directing the magistrate to enter a conviction, that the evidence of tables and chairs outside neighbouring establishments was not relevant and did not create authority or excuse for this obstruction. It was clear from *Wolverton UDC v. Willis* [1962] 1 W.L.R. 205, [1962] C.L.Y. 1376 and *Hinchon v. Briggs* (1963) 61 L.G.R. 315, [1963] C.L.Y. 1609 that any encroachment which is more than trivial could not in law be de minimis. In this case the counter clearly constituted an obstruction preventing the public from exercising their entitlement to unobstructed user of the whole footway.

WESTMINSTER CC v. ALLADIN LTD [1994] C.O.D. 488, McCowan, L.J., QBD.

5124. Obstruction of highway–shop displaying goods outside–whether obstruction de minimis

[Highways Act 1980 s.137.]

T appealed against a magistrates' decision that C's window display, which extended to no more than 5 per cent of the total width of the road, did not constitute a wilful obstruction within the meaning of the Highways Act 1980 s.137.

Held, allowing the appeal and remitting the case to the justices with a direction to convict, that (1) although the de minimis principle applied to obstruction cases under s.137 of the Act, the obstruction in this case could not be said to satisfy that principle, which was reserved for cases of fractional obstructions, *Seekings v. Clarke* (1961) 59 L.G.R. 268; *Hirst v. Chief Constable of West Yorkshire* (1987) 85 Cr. App. R. 143, [1988] C.L.Y. 809 applied and (2) the use of the highway was not reasonable in all the circumstances of this case.

TORBAY BC v. CROSS (1995) 159 J.P. 682, McCowan, L.J., QBD.

5125. PACE codes of practice–admissibility–unlicensed driving instructor charging for instructions–evidence excluded where based on conversations in breach of PACE codes–invalid registration

[Police and Criminal Evidence Act 1984 s.78; Road Traffic Act 1988 s.123.]

T, the prosecutor, appealed by way of case stated against a justices' decision dismissing charges against H and his employee, L, of giving driving instruction for payment when not licensed as approved driving instructors contrary to the Road Traffic Act 1988 s.123. Evidence of admissions by H to the Traffic Examiner were excluded by the justices under the Police and Criminal Evidence Act 1984 s.78, because they were obtained in breach of the PACE codes of practice on the duty to caution.

Held, allowing the appeal, that there had been a breach of the codes of practice. The examiner had already questioned L and established that H owned the car and the only reason for questioning H further was to obtain an admission that H employed L. There was no need for the prosecutor to prove the invalidity of the registration certificate given that it was an official document prescribed under the terms of 1988 Act. There was evidence on which the justices should have concluded that H was a party to the display of the certificate.

TOMS v. HURST; TOMS v. LANGTON [1996] R.T.R. 226, Curtis, J., QBD.

5126. Parking–City of Westminster

ROAD TRAFFIC (SPECIAL PARKING AREA) (CITY OF WESTMINSTER) (AMENDMENT) ORDER 1996, SI 1996 2284; made under the Road Traffic Act 1991 s.76, s.77. In force: October 1, 1996; £0.65.

This Order amends the Road Traffic (Special Parking Area) (City of Westminster) Order 1994 (SI 1994 1504) so as to add Thorney Street and parts of South Eaton Place, Horseferry Road and Millbank to the roads excluded from the special parking area designated by that Order

5127. Parking–deregulation

DEREGULATION (PARKING EQUIPMENT) ORDER 1996, SI 1996 1553; made under the Deregulation and Contracting Out Act 1994 s.1. In force: September 13, 1996; £1.10.

The Road Traffic Regulation Act 1984 contains various provisions giving local authorities power to make orders regulating the use of on and off street parking places. Such orders may require anyone wishing to park a vehicle to use a parking meter, pay and display ticket machine or other parking device such as a voucher or permit, which is capable of indicating how much has been paid and the period for which the vehicle may be parked. Previously an order could require the use of such apparatus or such a device only if it was of a type or design approved by the

Secretary of State. This Order removes the need for the Secretary of State's approval.

5128. Parking–Kingston upon Thames

ROAD TRAFFIC (SPECIAL PARKING AREA) (ROYAL BOROUGH OF KINGSTON UPON THAMES) ORDER 1996, SI 1996 3038; made under the Road Traffic Act 1991 s.76, s.77. In force: January 1, 1997; £1.95.

This Order consolidates (with amendments) the Road Traffic (Special Parking Area) (Royal Borough of Kingston upon Thames) Order 1994 (SI 1994 1497 as amended by SI 1995 617, SI 1995 1333 and SI 1996 1110) by re-designating the Royal Borough of Kingston upon Thames as a special parking area.

5129. Parking–Kingston upon Thames

ROAD TRAFFIC (SPECIAL PARKING AREA) (ROYAL BOROUGH OF KINGSTON UPON THAMES) (AMENDMENT) ORDER 1996, SI 1996 1110; made under the Road Traffic Act 1991 s.76, s.77. In force: May 20, 1996; £0.65.

This Order amends the Schedule to the Road Traffic (Special Parking Area) (Royal Borough of Kingston upon Thames) Order 1994, which lists the roads excluded from the special parking area designated by that Order.

5130. Parking–Newham

ROAD TRAFFIC (SPECIAL PARKING AREA) (LONDON BOROUGH OF NEWHAM) (AMENDMENT) ORDER 1996, SI 1996 1112; made under the Road Traffic Act 1991 s.76, s.77. In force: May 20, 1996; £1.55.

This Order amends the Schedule to the Road Traffic (Special Parking Area) (London Borough of Newham) Order 1994, which lists the roads excluded from the special parking area designated by that Order.

5131. Parking–offences

ROAD TRAFFIC ACT 1991 (AMENDMENT OF SCHEDULE 3) (ENGLAND AND WALES) ORDER 1996, SI 1996 500; made under the Road Traffic Act 1991 Sch.3 para.1, Sch.3 para.2. In force: April 1, 1996; £1.10.

The Road Traffic Act 1991 Sch.3 is amended with respect to parking contraventions which give rise to civil liability by the imposition of a penalty charge instead of being dealt with as criminal offences. It will no longer be an offence to contravene an order under the Road Traffic Regulation Act 1984 s.35 relating to off-street parking places or a provision of an order relating to an on-street parking place included by virtue of s.53 of that Act. Certain contraventions of temporary traffic orders and loading area orders in special parking areas under the 1984 Act cease to be criminal offences.

5132. Parking–Oxford–North Hinskey

ROAD TRAFFIC (PERMITTED PARKING AREAS AND SPECIAL PARKING AREAS) (CITY OF OXFORD AND PARISH OF NORTH HINKSEY) ORDER 1996, SI 1996 2650; made under the Road Traffic Act 1991 Sch.3 para.1, Sch.3 para.2, Sch.3 para.3. In force: February 3, 1997; £2.40.

This Order designates permitted parking and special parking areas and makes modifications to the Road Traffic Act 1991 Part II and Sch.3 and the Road Traffic Regulation Act 1984.

5133. Parking–penalty notices–appeal–owner not consenting to vehicle being left

[Road Traffic Act 1991 Sch.6, s.66.]

Under the Road Traffic Act 1991 Sch.6 (5) (1), a motorist may appeal to a parking adjudicator against a local authority's rejection of representations following issue of a penalty charge notice under s.66 (1) of the Act. A valid ground of appeal against the issue of a penalty charge notice is "that the vehicle had been permitted to remain at rest in the place in question by a person who was in control of the vehicle without the consent of the owner". O, the owner of a vehicle issued with a penalty charge notice, was being held in custody on remand at the time of issue of the notice, from the day before its issue until two days afterwards. He claimed not to have parked the car at the location where the notice was issued, nor to have any knowledge as to who might have driven it there.

Held, the adjudicator accepted O's explanation that he could not have been the driver of the car at the time, and that the evidence sufficed to show, in the absence of evidence to the contrary, that he did not give consent for the car to be driven by another person at that time.

PARKING APPEALS SERVICE (NO.1950156173), *Re*, 1996, Judge not specified, Parking Appeals Service. [*Ex rel.* Gordon Bell, Barrister].

5134. Parking–Redbridge

ROAD TRAFFIC (SPECIAL PARKING AREA) (LONDON BOROUGH OF REDBRIDGE) (AMENDMENT) ORDER 1996, SI 1996 3059; made under the Road Traffic Act 1991 s.76, s.77. In force: January 8, 1997; £0.65.

This Order amends the Road Traffic (Special Parking Area) (London Borough of Redbridge) Order 1994 (SI 1994 1509) by omitting para.79 from the Schedule to the Order. The Schedule lists the roads in the London Borough of Redbridge which are excluded from the special parking area. The road referred to in para.79 of the Schedule is accordingly no longer so excluded.

5135. Parking–Winchester

ROAD TRAFFIC (PERMITTED PARKING AREA AND SPECIAL PARKING AREA) (COUNTY OF HAMPSHIRE, CITY OF WINCHESTER) ORDER 1996, SI 1996 1171; made under the Road Traffic Act 1991 Sch.3 para.1, Sch.3 para.2, Sch.3 para.3. In force: May 20, 1996; £1.55.

This Order designates the City of Winchester in Hampshire as a permitted parking area and a special parking area in accordance with the Road Traffic Act 1991 Sch.3. It provides that persons appointed as parking adjudicators in London may so act in relation to the designated area and the Road Traffic (Parking Adjudicators) (London) Regulations 1993 are made to apply with modification to parking adjudicators so acting.

5136. Parking–Winchester

ROAD TRAFFIC (PERMITTED PARKING AREA AND SPECIAL PARKING AREA) (COUNTY OF HAMPSHIRE, CITY OF WINCHESTER) (AMENDMENT) ORDER 1996 1996, SI 1996 2017; made under the Road Traffic Act 1991 Sch.3 para.1, Sch.3 para.2, Sch.3 para 3. In force: September 9, 1996; £0.65.

This Order amends the Road Traffic (Permitted Parking Area and Special Parking Area) (County of Hampshire, City of Winchester) Order 1996 (SI 1996 1171) so as to provide that any order and regulations made under the Road Traffic Act 1991 s.78 which relate to the enforcement of parking charges payable in relation to the permitted and special parking areas designated by that Order.

5137. Parking penalties–keeper of the vehicle–rebuttable presumption that the keeper of the vehicle is the person in whose name it is registered

[Road Traffic Act 1991 s.66, s.82, Sch.6; Vehicle Excise and Registration Act 1994 s.21, s.22, s.46A; Vehicle (Registration and Licensing) Regulations 1971 Reg.3; Vehicle (Registration and Licensing) Regulations 1971 Reg.12.]

W appealed against the decision to dismiss its application for judicial review. The Parking Adjudicator allowed F s appeal against penalty charge notices issued by W. Notices had been served on F following non-payment of penalty charge notices that had been incurred whilst F's car was at a garage being repaired. There were no penalty notices affixed to the car, nor was F made aware that any had been issued when she collected the car from the garage. The case concerned the proper construction of the provisions relating to parking penalties contained in the Road Traffic Act 1991 s.66, s.82 and Sch.6, the Vehicle Excise and Registration Act 1994 s.21, s.22 and s.46A, and the Vehicle (Registration and Licensing) Regulations 1971 Reg.3 and Reg.12 were also considered.

Held, allowing the appeal, that the questions the Parking Adjudicator must consider are those set out in Sch.6 para.2(4) to the 1991 Act. There is a presumption in s.82(3) of the 1991 Act, which is rebuttable, that the owner of the vehicle is the person by whom the vehicle is kept and for determination of who is the owner it is presumed that person to be the registered owner, s.82(3). Section 21 and s.22 of the 1994 Act provides for registration on disposition or acquisition of a vehicle. Thus, the presumption can only be rebutted where there is an error in the register, the person has ceased to be the owner or he became the owner after the relevant date. The Parking Adjudicator did not address the matter in those terms, by defining the word "keep" in terms of "bailee" he erred in law. The garage owner could not be held to be the keeper of the car because the concept of ownership in the 1991 Act is associated with what appears on the public record.

R. v. PARKING ADJUDICATOR, *ex p.* WANDSWORTH LBC, *The Times*, November 26, 1996, Stuart-Smith, L.J., CA.

5138. Passenger vehicles–capacity

PUBLIC SERVICES VEHICLES (CARRYING CAPACITY) (AMENDMENT) REGULATIONS 1996, SI 1996 167; made under the Public Passenger Vehicles Act 1981 s.26, s.60. In force: May 1, 1996; £0.65.

These Regulations amend the Public Services Vehicles (Carrying Capacity) Regulations 1984 (SI 1984 1406) Reg.5 so that three seated children count as two passengers only if none of them is occupying a seat provided with a seat belt.

5139. Road safety–road humps

HIGHWAYS (ROAD HUMPS) REGULATIONS 1996, SI 1996 1483; made under the Highways Act 1980 s.90C, s.90D. In force: July 9, 1996; £1.10.

These Regulations revoke and replact the Highways (Road Humps) Regulations 1990 (SI 1990 703). They relate to the construction of road humps in any highway subject to a speed limit of 30 miles per hour or less, the height, positioning, shape and lighting of road humps and the prescription of traffic signs. Humps of any height between 25 millimetres and 100 millimetres are permitted.

5140. Road traffic offences–withholding of identity–meaning of "driver" for purpose of offence

D appealed against conviction of failing to provide information as to the identity of the driver of a car which was seen illegally parked. The car had broken down and was pushed into a "pay and display" car park, steered by a man unknown to D. It had been left there without a valid ticket displayed. An excess charge was not paid and the local authority wrote to D requesting the name and address of the driver. D claimed that she had informed the authority that the car could not be driven and that it therefore had no driver, although she admitted that she knew she was being asked for the name of the person in charge of the car.

Held, dismissing the appeal, that this disclosed no defence. "Driver" in this context meant the person who was responsible for parking the vehicle.

ROCHESTER UPON MEDWAY CITY COUNCIL v. DERBYSHIRE, September 19, 1996, H.H.J. Coombe, Maidstone Crown Court. [*Ex rel.* Alexander Nesbitt, Barrister].

5141. Road Traffic (Driving Instruction by Disabled Persons) Act 1993–Commencement Order

ROAD TRAFFIC (DRIVING INSTRUCTION BY DISABLED PERSONS) ACT 1993 (COMMENCEMENT) ORDER 1996, SI 1996 1980 (C.43); made under the Road Traffic (Driving Instruction by Disabled Persons) Act 1993 s.7. In force: bringing into force various provisions of the Act on September 9, 1996; £0.65.

This Order brings the Road Traffic (Driving Instruction by Disabled Persons) Act 1993 into force on September 9, 1996.

5142. Roads–accidents–pub car park constituted a road

[Road Traffic Act 1988 s.145, s.192.]

P having already obtained judgment in default of defence against an uninsured driver, asked the court to decide as a preliminary issue whether the accident occurred on a road for the purposes of the Road Traffic Act 1988, s.145. This question was relevant to the liability of the authorised insurers. A road is defined in s.192 of the 1988 Act as "any highway and any other road to which the public has access" and in the Oxford English Dictionary as a "line of communication between places". In this case, P was standing in the car park of a public house when the accident occurred. The surface of the car park was tarmac. There were two entrances/exits. A driver could lawfully drive in one and out the other (and thus off the main road into the car park and back onto the main road). Drivers to and from an adjacent garage could and did use the surface of the car park to drive over. Customers intending to use the pub drove into the car park in order to park their cars; others parked their cars and walked into Epping Forest. D conceded that this was a place to which the public had access, so the court was solely concerned with whether or not the car park was a road.

Held, that it was a question of fact whether or not in a particular case the material place was a road. On the facts of this case, the car park was a road within the meaning of the Act, and the insurer was liable, *Oxford v. Austin* [1981] R.T.R. 416, [1981] C.L.Y. 2388 applied.

O'CONNOR v. ROYAL INSURANCE, September 30, 1996, Recorder Jones, CC (Central London). [*Ex rel.* Amery Parkes, Solicitors].

5143. Roads–experimental weight restriction order imposed on landfill site access road–suitability of experimental order for preventing road damage or controlling heavy goods access–order in breach of statutory duty to maintain reasonable access

[Road Traffic Regulation Act 1984 s.9, s.122.]

UKWM applied for the quashing of an experimental weight restriction order, made by W under the Road Traffic Regulation Act 1984 s.9, effectively preventing the use of heavy goods vehicles exceeding seven and a half tonnes on a 350 metre stretch of the sole access road to UKWM's landfill site. UKWM needed to implement a short term clay importation scheme to alleviate rain water penetration problems on the site. However, W had imposed the experimental order, which had a maximum life of 18 months, after complaints about increased heavy goods traffic to the landfill site.

Held, allowing the application and quashing the order, that the purpose of the order was prohibitive and not experimental in nature, and also breached W's duty to maintain reasonable access to the site under s.122(2)(a) of the Act. Given the maximum permitted life of the order, it neither addressed the short term nature of UKWM's operations nor met the council's stated objective of road damage prevention, and WLDC had failed to address the problems which would be created by the use of the order in this particular location.

UK WASTE MANAGEMENT LTD v. WEST LANCASHIRE DC; ST HELENS MBC v. WEST LANCASHIRE DC, *The Times*, April 5, 1996, Carnwath, J., QBD.

5144. Special roads–North West

TAMESIDE (ASHTON NORTHERN BY-PASS STAGE 1 ASHTON-UNDER-LYNE) (SPECIAL ROADS) SCHEME 1994 CONFIRMATION INSTRUMENT 1996, SI 1996 142; made under the Highways Act 1980 s.16. In force: in Accordance with Highways Act 1980 Sch.2 para.2; £1.10.

This Instrument confirms with modifications the Tameside (Ashton Northern By-pass Stage 1 Ashton-Under-Lyne) (Special Roads) Scheme 1994. Details of the Scheme are given in the Schedule and a plan of the Scheme is attached to the Order.

5145. Street trading–no licence–braziers mounted on barrows–whether unlawfully deposited on highway as danger to public–meaning of "deposit"

[Highways Act 1980 s.149.]

S sold chestnuts from hot braziers mounted on barrows on the highway. S did not have a street trading licence. Officers of WCC formed a view that the barrows constituted a danger and in purported exercise of their powers under the Highways Act 1980 s.149(2) they seized and removed the braziers. Section 149(2) provided that where the highway authority officers had "reasonable grounds for considering that (a) any thing unlawfully deposited on the highway constituted a danger to users of the highway... the authority may remove the thing". S brought an action to reclaim his goods and claimed damages in detinue on the basis that the seizure had been wrongful. An application for the return of the braziers was granted. WCC appealed.

Held, allowing the appeal, that (1) "to deposit" was a common term of wide connotation that should be interpreted in a broad sense. The number of contexts in which it could occur were almost limitless. Although in the case of s.149 of the 1980 Act there might be some borderline cases where it would be difficult to say whether some objects had been "deposited" on the highway, the braziers mounted on the highway with their owners standing beside them were clearly "deposited" on it according to the plain English meaning of the word and (2) given that the highway authority officers has reasonable grounds for regarding the braziers as a danger to the public, the unlawfulness for the purpose of s.149 of the 1980 Act had been established.

SCOTT v. WESTMINSTER CITY COUNCIL; KICZYNSKI v. WESTMINSTER CITY COUNCIL 93 L.G.R. 370, Waite, L.J., CA.

5146. Tachographs–passenger and goods vehicles

PASSENGER AND GOODS VEHICLES (RECORDING EQUIPMENT) REGULATIONS 1996, SI 1996 941; made under the European Communities Act 1972 s.2. In force: April 25, 1996; £1.10.

In order to take into account the amendments made to Council Regulation 3821/85 ([1985] OJ L370/8) by Commission Regulation 2479/95 ([1995] OJ L256/8), these Regulations amend the definition of "the Community Recording Equipment Regulation" in the Transport Act 1968 s.97(7), the Road Traffic Act 1988 s.85, the Passenger and Goods Vehicles (Recording Equipment) Regulations 1979 Reg.1(3) and the Passenger and Goods Vehicles (Recording Equipment) (Amendment) Regulations 1984 Reg.3(3). The amendment, made to the Council Regulation to take account of technical changes in recording equipment in road transport, require electronic recording equipment to be capable of detecting interruptions in the power supply and to record driving time automatically, allow the removal, and subsequent refitting by an approved centre, of recording equipment seals to enable speed limiters to be fitted and require the cable connecting electronic recording equipment to the transmitter to be protected by a continuous steel sheath which may include a joint comprising sealed connections.

5147. Taxis–licences

LONDON CAB ORDER 1996, SI 1996 960; made under the Metropolitan Public Carriage Act 1869 s.6. In force: April 22, 1996; £1.10.

This Order is supplemental to the London Cab Order 1934 and supersedes the London Cab Order 1995. Under the 1934 Order, where a person applies for a cab licence under the Metropolitan Public Carriage Act 1869, he is required to submit the cab for examination by a Public Carriage Examiner. This Order applies to applications for a cab licence in respect of a motor cab registered on or after August 1, 1979 and propelled by a diesel engine. It requires a certificate to be handed to the Public Carriage Examiner when the cab is presented to him for examination. The certificate has to indicate that the vehicle had passed the exhaust emission test for diesel engined vehicles specified in the publication entitled *The MOT Inspection Manual Car and Light Commercial Vehicle Testing*. A copy of this publication can be obtained from Her Majesty's Stationery Office. The Order prescribes the form of certificate, the time within which it must be signed and the persons who can sign it. This Order gives a Public Carriage Examiner power to require a further certificate to be produced in certain circumstances.

5148. Taxis–increase in fares

LONDON CAB (NO.2) ORDER 1996, SI 1996 1176; made under the Metropolitan Public Carriage Act 1969 s.9; the London Cab and Stage Carriage Act 1907 s.1; and the London Cab Act 1968 s.1. In force: April 27, 1996; £1.10.

This Order increases the fares payable for hiring a motor cab in the Metropolitan Police District and the City of London in respect of all journeys beginning and ending there. It also increases the extra charge payable for carrying additional passengers.

5149. Taxis–prohibition against stopping–length of road with double white lines along centre–applicability to vehicles stopping to pick up or set down passengers

[Road Traffic Act 1988 s.36; Traffic Signs Regulations and General Directions 1994 Reg.26; Traffic Signs Regulations and General Directions 1981.]

M, a taxi driver, appealed by way of case stated against conviction of an offence contrary to the Road Traffic Act 1988 s.36(1). He had stopped on a road, on which double white lines were painted along the centre, to pick up a taxi fare. M argued that the words "if the vehicle could not be used for such a purpose without stopping on the length of road", which qualified the purposes for which a vehicle could stop in the Traffic Signs Regulations and General Directions 1994 Reg.26(2)(a), did not apply to the picking up or dropping off of a passenger.

Held, allowing the appeal, that, in view of the fact that the previous regulations, the Traffic Signs Regulations and General Directions 1981, made it clear that the qualifying words did not apply in such circumstances and the 1994 Regulations merely amended the structure of those regulations, the words clearly did not apply to a vehicle which stopped to pick up or drop off a passenger.

McKENZIE v. DPP, *The Times*, May 14, 1996, Newman, J., QBD.

5150. Trunk roads–A5

CHESTER-HOLYHEAD TRUNK ROAD (A5) (LLANFAIR PWLLGWYNGYLL TO BRYNGWRAN) ORDER 1996, SI 1996 976; made under the Highways Act 1980 s.10, s.12, s.41. In force: April 1, 1996; £1.10.

This Order provides that the new highways proposed for construction along the routes described in Sch.1 and Sch.2 to this Order shall become trunk roads from April 18, 1996.

5151. Trunk roads–A16

A16 TRUNK ROAD (FOTHERBY BYPASS) ORDER 1996, SI 1996 926; made under the Highways Act 1980 s.10, s.41. In force: April 12, 1996; GBp 1.10.

This Order provides that the road proposed for construction and detailed in Sch.1 shall become a trunk road from April 12, 1996 and that the existing trunk road described in Sch.2 shall cease to be a trunk road from the date on which the Secretary of State notifies the Lincolnshire CC that the new trunk road is open for traffic.

5152. Trunk roads–A21

A21 TRUNK ROAD (LAMBERHURST BYPASS) ORDER 1996, SI 1996 1845; made under the Highways Act 1980 s.10, s.41. In force: August 1, 1996; £1.55.

This Order provides for a new trunk road.

5153. Trunk roads–A21

A21 TRUNK ROAD (TONBRIDGE BYPASS TO PEMBURY BYPASS DUALLING) ORDER 1996, SI 1996 802; made under the Highways Act 1980 s.10, s.41. In force: April 5, 1996; £0.65.

The route of the new trunk road is 3.9 kilometres in length, starting at a point on the trunk road 280 metres southwest of its junction with A1014 Pembury Road, and proceeding generally southwards to join the trunk road (Pembury Bypass) at a point 100 metres south of its junction with Longfield Road.

5154. Trunk roads–A21

A21 TRUNK ROAD (TONBRIDGE BYPASS TO PEMBURY BYPASS DUALLING SLIP ROADS) ORDER 1996, SI 1996 807; made under the Highways Act 1980 s.10, s.41. In force: April 5, 1996; £0.65.

The routes of the slip roads at Southborough in the Royal Borough of Tunbridge Wells in the County of Kent area as follows: Junction with Pembury Road, Tonbridge Road and Longfield Road (a) a route from the southbound carriageway of the main new road to a new roundabout forming part of a junction to be constructed by the Secretary of State (the slip road along this route being given reference number one on the plan); (b) a route from the said roundabout to the southbound carriageway of the trunk road (the slip road along this route being given the reference number two); (c) a route from the northbound carriageway of the trunk road to a new roundabout forming part of the junction to be constructed by the Secretary of State (the slip road along this route being given reference number three on the plan); and (d) a route from the said roundabout to the northbound carriageway of the main new road (the slip road along this route being given reference number four).

5155. Trunk roads–A38–A3064

A38 TRUNK ROAD (A3064 ST BUDEAUX BYPASS SLIP ROADS) (TRUNKING) ORDER 1996, SI 1996 201; made under the Highways Act 1980 s.10. In force: March 1, 1996; £0.65.

This Order provides that the slip roads described in the Schedule to this Order shall become trunk roads from the date when this Order comes into force.

5156. Trunk roads–A47

A47 TRUNK ROAD (HARDWICK ROUNDABOUT FLYOVER AND SLIP ROADS) ORDER 1996, SI 1996 1800; made under the Highways Act 1980 s.10, s.41. In force: August 8, 1996; £1.10.

This Order creates a new trunk road.

5157. Trunk roads–A66

A66 TRUNK ROAD (LONG NEWTON GRADE SEPARATED JUNCTION SLIP ROADS) ORDER 1996, SI 1996 2977; made under the Highways Act 1980 s.10, s.41. In force: December 13, 1996; £0.65.

This Order prescribes the routes of slip roads.

5158. Trunk roads–A303

A303 TRUNK ROAD (SPARKFORD TO ILCHESTER IMPROVEMENT AND SLIP ROADS) ORDER 1996, SI 1996 1191; made under the Highways Act 1980 s.10, s.41. In force: May 17, 1996; £1.10.

This Order states that the main new roads and the slip roads defined in the Schedules to the Order shall become trunk roads on May 17, 1996.

5159. Trunk roads–A449–A456 bypass

A449 AND A456 TRUNK ROADS (KIDDERMINSTER, BLAKEDOWN AND HAGLEY BYPASS AND SLIP ROADS) ORDER 1996, SI 1996 1937; made under the Highways Act 1980 s.10, s.41. In force: July 30, 1996; £1.10.

This Order creates new trunk roads as detailed in the Schedules.

5160. Trunk roads–A556

A556 TRUNK ROAD (CHURCH FARM - TURNPIKE WOOD, OVER TABLEY) ORDER 1996, SI 1996 1650; made under the Highways Act 1980 s.10. In force: June 28, 1996; £0.65.

This Order proposes the construction of a new highway along the route set out in the Schedule. This highway will become a trunk road from the date when this Order comes into force.

5161. Trunk roads–A629

A629 TRUNK ROAD (SKIPTON TO KILDWICK IMPROVEMENT AND SLIP ROADS) ORDER 1996, SI 1996 1100; made under the Highways Act 1980 s.10, s.41. In force: April 26, 1996; £1.10.

This Order provides that the new highways proposed for construction, and detailed in the Schedule to the Order, shall become trunk roads from April 26, 1996.

5162. Trunk roads–A4060

EAST OF ABERCYNON-EAST OF DOWLAIS TRUNK ROAD (A4060) (IMPROVEMENT OF MOUNTAIN HARE TO DOWLAIS TOP) ORDER 1996, SI 1996 60; made under the Highways Act 1980 s.10. In force: January 25, 1996; £0.65.

The proposed new highway following a route which is 2.82 kilometres long starting on the northern side of the roundabout at Mountain Hare and extending northward to the south side of the trunk road roundabout at Dowlais Top at its junction with the A465 Neath to Abergavenny Trunk Road shall be a trunk road.

5163. Trunk roads–bus lanes–A1

A1 TRUNK ROAD (ISLINGTON) (BUS LANES) RED ROUTE EXPERIMENTAL ORDER 1996, SI 1996 589; made under the Road Traffic Regulation Act 1984 s.9, s.10. In force: March 15, 1996; £0.65.

This Order amends the A1 Trunk Road (Islington) Red Route (Bus Lanes) Traffic Order 1993 (SI 1993 897) which prohibits, with certain exemptions, persons from causing vehicles to enter or proceed in specified bus lanes between specified hours.

5164. Trunk roads–bus lanes–A10

A10 TRUNK ROAD (ENFIELD) RED ROUTE (BUS LANES) (NO.2) TRAFFIC ORDER 1996, SI 1996 1463; made under the Road Traffic Regulation Act 1984 s.6. In force: June 14, 1996; £1.10.

This Order provides that between 4.00 pm and 7.00 pm on Mondays to Fridays, vehicles are not permitted to enter or proceed in the specified bus lane. The Enfield (Bus Lanes) (No.1) Traffic Order 1977 (GLC TMO 1977 238) as amended, is hereby revoked in so far as its provisions relate to any part of the trunk road red route.

5165. Trunk roads–bus lanes–A10

A10 TRUNK ROAD (ENFIELD AND HARINGEY) RED ROUTE (BUS LANES) (NO.1) TRAFFIC ORDER 1996, SI 1996 1459; made under the Road Traffic Regulation Act 1984 s.6. In force: June 14, 1996; £1.10.

This Order provides that between the hours of 7.00 am and 10.00 am on Mondays to Fridays no person shall cause any vehicle to enter or proceed in specified bus lanes. It revokes the Enfield and Haringey (Bus Lanes) (No.1) Traffic Order 1984 (GLC TMO 1984 193) so far as it relates to any part of the trunk road red route.

5166. Trunk roads–bus lanes–A23

A23 TRUNK ROAD (CROYDON) RED ROUTE (BUS LANES) TRAFFIC ORDER 1996, SI 1996 3050; made under the Road Traffic Regulation Act 1984 s.6. In force: December 16, 1996; £1.10.

This Order prevents traffic from entering or proceeding along the bus lane during prescribed hours.

5167. Trunk roads–bus lanes–A41

A41 TRUNK ROAD (CAMDEN AND WESTMINSTER) RED ROUTE (BUS LANES) EXPERIMENTAL TRAFFIC ORDER 1996, SI 1996 2165; made under the Road Traffic Regulation Act 1984 s.9, s.10. In force: August 30, 1996; £1.10.

This Order provides that no person shall cause a vehicle to enter or proceed in any bus lane in a length of road specified in the Schedule to this Order during the hours specified in the Schedule.

5168. Trunk roads–bus lanes–A41

A41 TRUNK ROAD (CAMDEN AND WESTMINSTER) RED ROUTE (BUS LANES) (NO.2) EXPERIMENTAL TRAFFIC ORDER 1996, SI 1996 2687; made under the Road Traffic Regulation Act 1984 s.9, s.10. In force: November 4, 1996; £1.10.

This Order prohibits, with certain exemptions, any person from causing any vehicle to enter or proceed in any bus lane specified in the Schedules to the Order, at any time.

5169. Trunk roads–bus lanes–A205

A205 TRUNK ROAD (HOUNSLOW) RED ROUTE (BUS LANES) EXPERIMENTAL TRAFFIC ORDER 1996, SI 1996 2335; made under the Road Traffic Regulation Act 1984 s.9, s.10. In force: September 21, 1996; £1.10.

This Order revokes the A205 Trunk Road (Hounslow) Red Route (Bus Lanes) Experimental Traffic Order (SI 1995 125) and provides that no person shall cause a vehicle to enter or proceed in any bus lane in a length of road specified in the Schedule to this Order during the hours specified in the Schedule.

5170. Trunk roads–bus lanes–A501

A501 TRUNK ROAD (CAMDEN) RED ROUTE (BUS LANE) (NO.1) EXPERIMENTAL TRAFFIC ORDER 1996, SI 1996 1344; made under the Road Traffic Regulation Act 1984 s.9, s.10. In force: May 31, 1996; £1.10.

This Order provides, with certain exemptions, that no person shall cause any vehicle to enter or proceed in any bus lane specified in the Schedule between specified hours on Mondays to Fridays.

5171. Trunk roads–bus lanes–A501

A501 TRUNK ROAD (CAMDEN AND ISLINGTON) RED ROUTE (BUS LANES) EXPERIMENTAL TRAFFIC ORDER 1996, SI 1996 1343; made under the Road Traffic Regulation Act 1984 s.9, s.10. In force: May 31, 1996; £1.10.

This Order provides, with certain exemptions, that no person shall cause any vehicles to enter or proceed in the bus lane specified in the Schedule.

5172. Trunk roads–bypass–A35

A35 TRUNK ROAD (CHIDEOCK MORECOMBELAKE BYPASS) ORDER 1996, SI 1996 1230; made under the Highways Act 1980 s.10, s.41. In force: May 24, 1996; £0.65.

This Order creates a new trunk road, the route of which is described in Sch.1 to the Order, on May 24, 1996.

5173. Trunk roads–Carmarthen Eastern Bypass

MONMOUTH-FISHGUARD TRUNK ROAD (A40) (CARMARTHEN EASTERN BYPASS) ORDER 1996, SI 1996 3043; made under the Highways Act 1980 s.10, s.12, s.106, s.108. In force: December 19, 1996; £1.10.

This Order provides for a new trunk road.

5174. Trunk roads–classification–bypass–A66

A66 TRUNK ROAD (STAINBURN AND GREAT CLIFTON BYPASS) (DE-TRUNKING) ORDER 1996, SI 1996 1430; made under the Highways Act 1980 s.10, s.12. In force: June 21, 1996; £0.65.

This Order reclassifies the length of trunk road described in the Schedule to the Order as a classified road from the date on which the Secretary of State notifies Cumbria CC that the new trunk road is open for traffic.

5175. Trunk roads–construction–bypass–A66

A66 TRUNK ROAD (STAINBURN AND GREAT CLIFTON BYPASS) ORDER 1996, SI 1996 1429; made under the Highways Act 1980 s.10, s.41. In force: June 21, 1996; £0.65.

This Order provides that the road proposed for construction and detailed in the Schedule to the Order shall become a trunk road from June 21, 1996.

5176. Trunk roads–cycle tracks

TRUNK ROAD (A4) (GREAT WEST ROAD, HOUNSLOW) (RESTRICTION OF TRAFFIC) ORDER 1984 (VARIATION) ORDER 1996, SI 1996 357; made under the Road Traffic Regulation Act 1984 s.6, Sch.9 Part IV. In force: January 15, 1996; £0.65.

This Order varies the Trunk Road (A4) (Great West Road, Hounslow) (Restriction of Traffic) Order 1994 by substituting the definition of "the cycle tracks" in Art.2.

5177. Trunk roads–detrunking–A1

A1 TRUNK ROAD (LENGTHS OF A1 CARRIAGEWAY BETWEEN CATTERICK AND BARTON) (DETRUNKING) ORDER 1996, SI 1996 1831; made under the Highways Act 1980 s.10, s.12. In force: July 24, 1996; £0.65.

This Order provides that the lengths of road specified in the Schedule shall cease to be trunk roads.

5178. Trunk roads–detrunking–A2

A2 TRUNK ROAD (WEST OF ROCHESTER) DETRUNKING ORDER 1996, SI 1996 853; made under the Highways Act 1980 s.10, s.12. In force: April 9, 1996; £0.65.

The lengths of road described in the Schedule to this Order shall cease to be trunk roads and shall be classified as classified roads from the date on which this Order comes into force.

5179. Trunk roads–detrunking–A6

A6 TRUNK ROAD (ROTHWELL AND DESBOROUGH BYPASS AND DETRUNKING) ORDER 1996, SI 1996 2661; made under the Highways Act 1980 s.10, s.12, s.41. In force: November 14, 1996; £1.10.

This Order re-classifies the roads described in the Schedules.

5180. Trunk roads–detrunking–A21

A21 TRUNK ROAD (LAMBERHURST BYPASS DETRUNKING) ORDER 1996, SI 1996 1846; made under the Highways Act 1980 s.10, s.12. In force: August 1, 1996; £0.65.

This Order provides for a trunk road described in the Schedule to become a classified road when a new trunk road opens for traffic.

5181. Trunk roads–detrunking–A21

A21 TRUNK ROAD (TONBRIDGE BYPASS TO PEMBURY BYPASS DUALLING) (DETRUNKING) ORDER 1996, SI 1996 808; made under the Highways Act 1980 s.10, s.12. In force: April 5, 1996; £0.65.

The length of the trunk road ceasing to be a trunk road is situated between a point 280 metres southwest of its junction with A2014 Pembury Road and a point 100 metres south of its junction with Longfield Road and is shown by Broad black dashes on the plan numbered HA 10/1/SWM/126, marked the A21 Trunk Road (Tonbridge Bypass to Pembury Bypass Dualling) (Detrunking) Order 1996, signed by authority of the Secretary of State for Transport and deposited at the Department of Transport, Great Mister House, 76 Marsham Street, London SW1P 4DR.

5182. Trunk roads–detrunking–A41

A41 LONDON-BIRMINGHAM TRUNK ROAD (EAST OF AYLESBURY TO WEST OF TRING) DETRUNKING ORDER 1991 (AMENDMENT) ORDER 1996, SI 1996 2667; made under the Highways Act 1980 s.10, s.12. In force: October 31, 1996; £0.65.

This Order amends the definition of the length of trunk road ceasing to be a trunk road.

5183. Trunk roads–detrunking–A47

A47 TRUNK ROAD (HARDWICK ROUNDABOUT TO NORTH RUCTON) (DETRUNKING) ORDER 1996, SI 1996 1801; made under the Highways Act 1980 s.10, s.12. In force: August 8, 1996; £1.10.

This Order prescribes that the length of trunk road described in the Schedule shall cease to be a trunk road on the date on which the new trunk roads are open for traffic.

5184. Trunk roads–detrunking–A57

A57 TRUNK ROAD (ROTHERHAM/SHEFFIELD BOUNDARY TO SWALLOWNEST ROUNDABOUT) (DETRUNKING) ORDER 1996, SI 1996 443; made under the Highways Act 1980 s.10, s.12. In force: March 29, 1996; £1.10.

This Order states that the trunk road described in the Schedule to the Order and shown on a map attached shall cease to be a trunk road and classifies it as a classified road from March 29, 1996.

5185. Trunk roads–detrunking–A61

A61 TRUNK ROAD (B6131 BAR LANE, MAPPLEWELL TO BARNSLEY/ WAKEFIELD METROPOLITAN BOUNDARY) (DETRUNKING) ORDER 1996, SI 1996 1401; made under the Highways Act 1980 s.10, s.12. In force: June 21, 1996; £0.65.

This Order reclassifies the length of trunk road described in the Schedule to the Order as a principal road.

5186. Trunk roads–detrunking–A303

A303 TRUNK ROAD (SPARKFORD TO ILCHESTER IMPROVEMENT AND SLIP ROADS) (DETRUNKING) ORDER 1996, SI 1996 1190; made under the Highways Act 1980 s.10, s.12. In force: May 17, 1996; £1.10.

This Order states that the lengths of trunk road described in the Schedule to the Order shall cease to be trunk road.

5187. Trunk roads–detrunking–A556

A556 TRUNK ROAD (TURNPIKE WOOD, OVER TABLEY - A56 BOWDON ROUNDABOUT) (DETRUNKING) ORDER 1996, SI 1996 1651; made under the Highways Act 1980 s.10, s.12. In force: June 28, 1996; £0.65.

This Order prescribes that the length of road described in the Schedule shall cease to be a trunk road and shall be classified as a principal road on the date on which the new trunk roads are open for traffic.

5188. Trunk roads–detrunking–Wales–A55

CHESTER-BANGOR TRUNK ROAD (A55) (PORT DAFYDD TO WAEN IMPROVEMENT, DETRUNKING) ORDER 1996, SI 1996 2142; made under the Highways Act 1980 s.10. In force: November 9, 1996; £0.65.

This Order removes the status of trunk road from the road described in the Schedule.

5189. Trunk roads–improvements–A13

A13 TRUNK ROAD (MOVERS LANE JUNCTION IMPROVEMENT, TRUNK ROAD AND SLIP ROADS) ORDER 1996, SI 1996 2841; made under the Highways Act 1980 s.10, s.41. In force: November 27, 1996; £1.10.

This Order prescribes the route of a new main road and slip roads.

5190. Trunk roads–improvements–A13–A117

A13 TRUNK ROAD (A117 JUNCTION IMPROVEMENT, TRUNK ROAD AND SLIP ROADS) ORDER 1996, SI 1996 2840; made under the Highways Act 1980 s.10, s.41. In force: November 27, 1996; £0.65.

This Order prescribes the route of a new main road and slip roads.

5191. Trunk roads–improvements–A19–A64

A19 TRUNK ROAD (A19/A64 FULFORD INTERCHANGE IMPROVEMENT) ORDER 1996, SI 1996 1491; made under the Highways Act 1980 s.10, s.41. In force: June 27, 1996; £1.10.

This Order provides that the main new roads and slip roads specified in the Schedules shall become trunk roads.

5192. Trunk roads–improvements–A23

A23 TRUNK ROAD (PURLEY CROSS JUNCTION IMPROVEMENT) TRUNKING ORDER 1996, SI 1996 1046; made under the Highways Act 1980 s.10. In force: April 16, 1996; £0.65.

This Order provides that the highway described in the Schedule to the Order shall become a trunk road on April 16, 1996.

5193. Trunk roads–improvements–A23

A3 TRUNK ROAD (WOOLMER ROAD JUNCTION IMPROVEMENT SLIP ROAD) ORDER 1996, SI 1996 2559; made under the Highways Act 1980 s.10, s.41. In force: November 1, 1996; £1.10.

This Order provides for a new highway to become a trunk road.

5194. Trunk roads–improvements–A494

DOLGELLAU TO SOUTH OF BIRKENHEAD TRUNK ROAD (A494) (DRWS Y NANT IMPROVEMENT) ORDER 1996, SI 1996 1437; made under the Highways Act 1980 s.10. In force: June 27, 1996; £0.65.

This Order prescribes the route of the new trunk road at Drws y Nant, Dolgellau in Gwynedd as about 0.37 kilometres in length, starting at a point on the trunk road 374 metres southwest of Pont Drws y Nant and terminating at a point on the trunk road at the northwest corner of Pont Drws y Nant.

5195. Trunk roads–improvements–A629

A629 TRUNK ROAD (INGS LANE TO CONONLEY LANE) (DETRUNKING) ORDER 1996, SI 1996 1101; made under the Highways Act 1980 s.10. In force: April 26, 1996; £0.65.

This Order stipulates that the length of trunk road described in the Schedule to the Order, the A629 North-West of Doncaster to Kendal, shall cease to be a trunk road from the date on which the Secretary of State notifies the County Council of North Yorkshire that the new trunk road, constructed in pursuance of the A629 Trunk Road (Skipton to Kildwick Improvement and Slip Roads) Order 1996, is open for through traffic.

5196. Trunk roads–King's Lynn Southern Bypass

BIRMINGHAM-GREAT YARMOUTH TRUNK ROAD (KING'S LYNN SOUTHERN BYPASS) ORDER 1971 PARTIAL REVOCATION ORDER 1996, SI 1996 1802; made under the Highways Act 1980 s.10. In force: August 8, 1996; £0.65.

This Order revokes the Birmingham-Great Yarmouth Trunk Road (King's Lynn Southern Bypass) Order 1971 (SI 1971 294) insofar as it authorises the Secretary of State to construct certain new lengths of road and slip roads.

5197. Trunk roads–motor vehicles–height restrictions–A205

A205 TRUNK ROAD (MORTLAKE ROAD, RICHMOND UPON THAMES) (VEHICLE HEIGHT RESTRICTION) ORDER 1996, SI 1996 925; made under the Road Traffic Regulation Act 1984 s.6, Sch.9 Part IV. In force: March 25, 1996; £0.65.

This Order revokes and replaces the London Borough of Richmond upon Thames (Mortlake Road, Kew) (Vehicle Height Restriction) Order 1988 (LBO 1988 13). It stipulates that no person shall cause or permit any vehicle over 4.5 metres from entering the carriageway beneath the railway bridge in Mortlake Road, Kew.

5198. Trunk roads–prescribed routes–A4

A4 TRUNK ROAD (HILLINGDON) (PRESCRIBED ROUTES) ORDER 1996, SI 1996 2157; made under the Road Traffic Regulation Act 1984 s.6, Sch.9 Part IV. In force: August 7, 1996; £0.65.

This Order, which repeals the Trunk Road (M4 Motorway, Heathrow Airport Spur Road) (Prohibition of Traffic) Order 1978 (SI 1978 50), prescribes routes along the Excelsier slip road.

5199. Trunk roads–prescribed routes–A23

A23 TRUNK ROAD (STREATHAM HIGH ROAD AND STREATHAM HILL, LAMBETH) (PRESCRIBED ROUTES) ORDER 1996, SI 1996 2799; made under the Road Traffic Regulation Act 1984 s.6, Sch.9 Part IV. In force: November 8, 1996; £0.65.

This Order prescribes the traffic flow in and around Streatham Hill, Lambeth.

5200. Trunk roads–prescribed routes–A30

A30 TRUNK ROAD (GREAT SOUTH WEST ROAD) (TEMPORARY RESTRICTION OF TRAFFIC) ORDER 1996, SI 1996 215; made under the Road Traffic Regulation Act 1984 s.14. In force: February 2, 1996; £1.10.

Prescribes traffic flow in relation to the Great South West Road in Hounslow for a temporary period whilst road works are completed along or near the specified length of road.

5201. Trunk roads–prescribed routes–A1400

A1400 TRUNK ROAD (SOUTHEND ROAD, REDBRIDGE) (PROHIBITION OF RIGHT TURN AND U-TURNS) ORDER 1996, SI 1996 2387; made under the Road Traffic Regulation Act 1984 s.6, Sch.9 Part IV. In force: September 13, 1996; £0.65.

This Order prescribes the flow of traffic in and around Southend Road, Redbridge.

5202. Trunk roads–prohibition of traffic–A4

A4 TRUNK ROAD (GREAT WEST ROAD, HOUNSLOW) (PROHIBITION OF USE OF GAP IN CENTRAL RESERVE) ORDER 1996, SI 1996 1113; made under the Road Traffic Regulation Act 1984 s.6. In force: April 22, 1996; £0.65.

This Order, which amends the Trunk Roads (Various Roads, Hounslow) (Prescribed Routes) Order 1973 (SI 1973 1856) and revokes the London Borough of Hounslow (Prescribed Routes) (No.5) Traffic Order 1988 (TMO 1988 16) and the Trunk Road (Great West Road, Hounslow) (Prescribed Routes) Order 1977 (SI 1977 1599), prohibits any person from causing or permitting any vehicle to enter or proceed through the gap in the central reserve which lies opposite Lionel Road, London W3.

5203. Trunk roads–prohibition of traffic–A41

A41 TRUNK ROAD (GLOUCESTER PLACE, WESTMINSTER) (TEMPORARY PROHIBITION OF TRAFFIC) ORDER 1996, SI 1996 903; made under the Road Traffic Regulation Act 1984 s.14; and the Road Traffic Act 1989 s.58. In force: March 18, 1996; £0.65.

This Order provides that, owing to the execution of works, no person shall cause or permit vehicles to enter or proceed in the lengths of road specified in the Schedule to the Order during the period starting at 8.00 hours on March 18, 1996 for a period of three months or when the works have been completed, whichever is the earlier.

5204. Trunk roads–prohibition of traffic–A41

A41 TRUNK ROAD (GLOUCESTER PLACE/IVOR PLACE, WESTMINSTER) (TEMPORARY PROHIBITION OF TRAFFIC) ORDER 1996, SI 1996 1077; made under the Road Traffic Regulation Act 1984 s.14. In force: April 8, 1996; £0.65.

This Order provides that, owing to the execution of works, no person shall cause or permit vehicles to enter or exit Gloucester Place from Ivor Place (West) during the period starting at 8.00 hours on April 8, 1996 and ending when the works have been completed or at 8.00 hours on July 8, 1996, whichever is the earlier.

5205. Trunk roads–prohibition of traffic–A41

A41 TRUNK ROAD (PARK ROAD, WESTMINSTER) (TEMPORARY PROHIBITION OF TRAFFIC) ORDER 1996, SI 1996 929; made under the Road Traffic Regulation Act 1984 s.14; and the Road Traffic Act 1991 s.58. In force: March 25, 1996; £0.65.

This Order provides that, owing to works being executed, no person shall cause or permit a vehicle to enter Park Road from Ivor Place during the period starting at 8.00 hours on March 25, 1996 and ending when the works have been completed or at 8.00 hours on June 25, 1996, whichever is the earlier.

5206. Trunk roads–prohibition of traffic–A41

A41 TRUNK ROAD (WATFORD WAY/HENDON WAY, BARNET) TEMPORARY PROHIBITION OF TRAFFIC ORDER 1996, SI 1996 2942; made under the Road Traffic Regulation Act 1984 s.14. In force: November 23, 1996; £0.65.

This Order, with certain exemptions, prohibits persons from causing or permitting vehicles to enter or proceed along the roads specified in the Schedule to this Order during the specified period.

5207. Trunk roads–prohibition of traffic–A406

A406 TRUNK ROAD (HANGER LANE, EALING) (TEMPORARY PROHIBITION OF TRAFFIC) ORDER 1996, SI 1996 1569; made under the Road Traffic Regulation Act 1984 s.14. In force: June 17, 1996; £0.65.

This Order provides that during the period starting at 00.01 hours on June 17, 1996 and ending at 23.59 on July 31, 1996 or when those works have been completed, no person shall permit any vehicle to enter Hanger Lane from any road specified in the schedule or to enter any road specified from Hanger Lane.

5208. Trunk roads–prohibition of traffic–A501

A501 TRUNK ROAD (EUSTON ROAD, CAMDEN) (TEMPORARY PROHIBITION OF TRAFFIC) ORDER 1996, SI 1996 1622; made under the Road Traffic Regulation Act 1984 s.14. In force: June 24, 1996; £0.65.

This Order prohibits traffic in Midland Road, Camden from turning left eastbound into Euston Road whilst works are being carried out from 8.00 hours on June 24, 1996 to 23.59 hours on September 23, 1996, or when those works have been completed.

5209. Trunk roads–prohibition of traffic–A501

A501 TRUNK ROAD (EUSTON ROAD/GOWER STREET, CAMDEN) (TEMPORARY PROHIBITION OF TRAFFIC) ORDER 1996, SI 1996 1222; made under the Road Traffic Regulation Act 1984 s.14. In force: May 9, 1996; £0.65.

This Order states that owing to road works being carried out in the area, no person shall cause or permit any vehicle to exit Euston Road at its north-eastern most junction with Gower Street during the period starting at 17.00 hours on May 9, 1996 and ending when those works have been completed or at 10.00 hours on May 11, 1996, whichever is sooner.

5210. Trunk roads–prohibition of traffic–A501

A501 TRUNK ROAD (GRAYS INN ROAD, CAMDEN) (TEMPORARY PROHIBITION OF TRAFFIC) ORDER 1996, SI 1996 1078; made under the Road Traffic Regulation Act 1984 s.14. In force: April 8, 1996; £0.65.

This Order provides that, owing to the execution of works, no person shall cause or permit vehicles to enter or exit Grays Inn Road from Britannia Road during the period starting at 8.00 hours on April 8, 1996 and ending when the works have been completed or at 8.00 hours on July 8, 1996, whichever is the earlier.

5211. Trunk roads–prohibition of traffic–A501

A501 TRUNK ROAD (MARYLEBONE ROAD, WESTMINSTER) (TEMPORARY PROHIBITION OF TRAFFIC) ORDER 1996, SI 1996 1027; made under the Road Traffic Regulation Act 1984 s.14. In force: April 1, 1996; £0.65.

This Order provides that, owing to the execution of works, no person shall cause or permit vehicles to enter or exit Marylebone Road from Luxborough Street during the period starting at 8.00 hours on April 1, 1996 and ending when the works have been completed or at 8.00 hours on July 1, 1996, whichever is the earlier.

5212. Trunk roads–prohibition of traffic–A501

A501 TRUNK ROAD (MARYLEBONE ROAD, WESTMINSTER) (TEMPORARY PROHIBITION OF TRAFFIC) ORDER 1996, SI 1996 822; made under the Road Traffic Regulation Act 1984 s.14. In force: March 11, 1996; £0.65.

This Order prohibits, with certain exemptions, persons from causing or permitting vehicles from entering or proceeding along the lengths of road specified in the Schedule to the Order for a period of three months, starting at 8.00 hours on March 11, 1996.

5213. Trunk roads–prohibition of traffic–A501

A501 TRUNK ROAD (MARYLEBONE ROAD/GLENTWORTH STREET, WESTMINSTER) (TEMPORARY PROHIBITION OF TRAFFIC) ORDER 1996, SI 1996 1223; made under the Road Traffic Regulation Act 1984 s.14. In force: May 13, 1996; £0.65.

This Order states that owing to roadworks being carried out in the area, no person shall cause or permit any vehicle to enter or exit Marylebone Road from Glentworth Street during the period starting at 8.00 hours on May 13, 1996 and ending when the works have been completed or at 8.00 hours on August 13, 1996, whichever is sooner.

5214. Trunk roads–prohibition of traffic–A501

A501 TRUNK ROAD (MARYLEBONE ROAD/NOTTINGHAM PLACE, WESTMINSTER) (TEMPORARY PROHIBITION OF TRAFFIC) ORDER 1996, SI 1996 1157; made under the Road Traffic Regulation Act 1984 s.14. In force: April 29, 1996; £0.65.

This Order provides that as road works are being carried out in Marylebone Road, no person shall cause or permit any vehicle to enter or exit Marylebone Road from Nottingham Place during the period starting at 8.00 hours on April 29, 1996 and ending when the works are completed or at 8.00 hours on July 29, 1996, whichever is earlier.

5215. Trunk roads–prohibition of traffic–A501

A501 TRUNK ROAD (MARYLEBONE ROAD/PARK CRESCENT MEWS WEST, WESTMINSTER) (TEMPORARY PROHIBITION OF TRAFFIC) ORDER 1996, SI 1996 1340; made under the Road Traffic Regulation Act 1984 s.14. In force: May 28, 1996; £0.65.

This Order provides, with certain exemptions, that no person shall cause any vehicles to enter or proceed in the bus lane specified in the Schedule.

5216. Trunk roads–prohibition of traffic–A501

A501 TRUNK ROAD (SWINTON STREET, CAMDEN) (TEMPORARY PROHIBITION OF TRAFFIC) ORDER 1996, SI 1996 1135; made under the Road Traffic Regulation Act 1984 s.14. In force: April 18, 1996; £0.65.

This Order provides that, owing to the execution of works, no person shall cause or permit vehicles to enter or exit Swinton Street from Swinton Place during the period starting at 8.00 hours on April 18, 1996 and ending when the works have been completed or at 8.00 hours on July 18, 1996, whichever is the earlier.

5217. Trunk roads–red routes–parking prohibition–A205

A205 TRUNK ROAD (HOUNSLOW) RED ROUTE TRAFFIC ORDER 1996, SI 1996 2336; made under the Road Traffic Regulation Act 1984 s.6. In force: September 21, 1996; £1.95.

This Order partly revokes the Hounslow (Waiting and Loading Restrictions) Order 1977 (GLC 1977 642) and the A205 Trunk Road (Hounslow) Red Route Experimental Traffic Order 1995 (SI 1995 126) and places a general prohibition on stopping during restricted hours in the trunk road red route described in the Schedules.

5218. Trunk roads–red routes–parking prohibitions–A1

A1 TRUNK ROAD (BARNET) RED ROUTE (CLEARWAY) TRAFFIC ORDER 1996, SI 1996 819; made under the Road Traffic Regulation Act 1984 s.6. In force: March 19, 1996; £1.55.

This Order introduces a general prohibition on stopping, with certain exemptions, on a section of the A1 Trunk Road.

5219. Trunk roads–red routes–parking prohibitions–A1

A1 TRUNK ROAD (HARINGEY) RED ROUTE TRAFFIC ORDER 1993 EXPERIMENTAL VARIATION ORDER 1996, SI 1996 98; made under the Road Traffic Regulation Act 1984 s.9, s.10. In force: January 29, 1996; £0.65.

This Order varies the A1 Trunk Road (Haringey) Red Route Traffic Order 1993 (SI 1993 896).

5220. Trunk roads–red routes–parking prohibitions–A1

A1 TRUNK ROAD (HARINGEY) (BUS LANES) RED ROUTE EXPERIMENTAL ORDER 1996, SI 1996 591; made under the Road Traffic Regulation Act 1984 s.9, s.10. In force: March 15, 1996; £0.65.

This Order amends the A1 Trunk Road (Haringey) Red Route (Bus Lanes) Traffic Order 1993 (SI 1993 897).

5221. Trunk roads–red routes–parking prohibitions–A1

A1 TRUNK ROAD (ISLINGTON) RED ROUTE TRAFFIC ORDER 1993 EXPERIMENTAL VARIATION NO.3 ORDER 1996, SI 1996 99; made under the Road Traffic Regulation Act 1984 s.9, s.10. In force: February 5, 1996; £1.10.

This Order varies the A1 Trunk Road (Islington) Red Route Traffic Order 1993 (SI 1993 891).

5222. Trunk roads–red routes–parking prohibitions–A1

A1 TRUNK ROAD (ISLINGTON) RED ROUTE TRAFFIC ORDER 1993 VARIATION ORDER 1996, SI 1996 1881; made under the Road Traffic Regulation Act 1984 s.6. In force: July 31, 1996; £0.65.

This Order amends the A1 Trunk Road (Islington) Red Route Traffic Order 1993 (SI 1993 891) and revokes the A1 Trunk Road (Islington) Red Route Traffic Order 1993 Experimental Variation Order 1995 (SI 1995 2743).

5223. Trunk roads–red routes–parking prohibitions–A2

A2 TRUNK ROAD (BEXLEY) RED ROUTE TRAFFIC ORDER 1996, SI 1996 2726; made under the Road Traffic Regulation Act 1984 s.6. In force: November 1, 1996; £1.95.

This Order, which revokes the Bexley (Waiting and Loading Restriction) Order 1991 (in part) and the A2 Trunk Road (Bexley) Red Route Experimental Order 1995 (SI 1995 2444), prohibits persons from causing or permitting vehicles to stop during the restricted hours in the trunk road red route specified in the Schedules to this Order.

5224. Trunk roads–red routes–parking prohibitions–A3

A3 TRUNK ROAD (KINGSTON UPON THAMES) RED ROUTE TRAFFIC ORDER 1996, SI 1996 2332; made under the Road Traffic Regulation Act 1984 s.6. In force: September 16, 1996; £2.80.

This Order partly revokes the Kingston-Upon-Thames (Waiting and Loading Restriction) (No.1) Traffic Order 1994 and the A3 Trunk Road (Kingston Upon Thames) Red Route Experimental Traffic Order 1995 (SI 1995 339) and places a general prohibition on stopping in the trunk road red route during restricted hours.

5225. Trunk roads–red routes–parking prohibitions–A3

A3 TRUNK ROAD (KINGSTON UPON THAMES) RED ROUTE (CLEARWAY) TRAFFIC ORDER 1996, SI 1996 2339; made under the Road Traffic Regulation Act 1984 s.6. In force: September 16, 1996; £1.55.

This Order partly revokes the Kingston-Upon-Thames (Waiting and Loading Restriction) (No.1) Traffic Order 1994 and the A3 Trunk Road (Kingston Upon Thames) Red Route (Clearway) Experimental Traffic Order 1995 (SI 1995 337) and places a general prohibition on stopping at any time in the trunk road red route clearway.

5226. Trunk roads–red routes–parking prohibitions–A3

A3 TRUNK ROAD (MERTON) RED ROUTE TRAFFIC ORDER 1996, SI 1996 2334; made under the Road Traffic Regulation Act 1984 s.6. In force: September 16, 1996; £1.95.

This Order partially revokes the Merton (Waiting and Loading) Order 1977 GLC 1977 107) and the A3 Trunk Road (Merton) Red Route Experimental Traffic Order 1995 (SI 1995 336) and places a general prohibition on stopping in the trunk road red route during restricted hours.

5227. Trunk roads–red routes–parking prohibitions–A3

A3 TRUNK ROAD (MERTON) RED ROUTE (CLEARWAY) TRAFFIC ORDER 1996, SI 1996 2333; made under the Road Traffic Regulation Act 1984 s.6. In force: September 16, 1996; £1.55.

This Order partly revokes the Merton (Waiting and Loading Restriction) Order 1977 (GLC 1977 107) and the A3 Trunk Road (Merton) Red Route (Clearway) Experimental Traffic Order 1995 (SI 1995 338) and places a general prohibition on stopping with certain exemptions, at any time in the trunk road red route clearway described in the Schedules.

5228. Trunk roads–red routes–parking prohibitions–A3

A3 TRUNK ROAD (WANDSWORTH) RED ROUTE (CLEARWAY) TRAFFIC ORDER 1996, SI 1996 2338; made under the Road Traffic Regulation Act 1984 s.6. In force: September 16, 1996; £1.55.

This Order partly revokes the Wandsworth (Waiting and Loading Restriction) Order 1976 and the A3 Trunk Road (Wandsworth) Red Route (Clearway) Experimental Traffic Order (SI 1995 335) and places a general prohibition on stopping at any time in the trunk road red route clearway.

5229. Trunk roads–red routes–parking prohibitions–A4

A4 TRUNK ROAD (HILLINGDON) RED ROUTE (CLEARWAY) TRAFFIC ORDER 1996, SI 1996 1163; made under the Road Traffic Regulation Act 1984 s.6. In force: April 29, 1996; £1.95.

This Order, which amends Hillingdon (Waiting and Loading Restrictions) (Consolidation) Order 1994, places a general prohibition on stopping, with certain exemptions, at any time in the trunk road red route clearway described in the Schedules to the Order.

5230. Trunk roads–red routes–parking prohibitions–A4

A4 TRUNK ROAD (HOUNSLOW) RED ROUTE (CLEARWAY) TRAFFIC ORDER 1996, SI 1996 1170; made under the Road Traffic Regulation Act 1984 s.6. In force: May 1, 1996; £1.95.

This Order, which amends the Hounslow (Waiting and Loading Restriction) Order 1977 (GLC 1977 642), places, with certain exemptions, a general prohibition on stopping at any time in the trunk road red route clearway described in the Schedules to the Order.

5231. Trunk roads–red routes–parking prohibitions–A12

A12 TRUNK ROAD (REDBRIDGE) RED ROUTE TRAFFIC ORDER 1996, SI 1996 1893; made under the Road Traffic Regulation Act 1984 s.6. In force: July 31, 1996; £1.95.

This Order, which revokes the A12 Trunk Road (Redbridge) Red Route Experimental Traffic Order 1995 (SI 1995 1695) and the London Borough of Redbridge Waiting and Loading Restriction and Consolidation Order 1993 (TMO 1993/LBR No.3), places a general prohibition on stopping in the trunk road red route described in the Schedules during restricted hours.

5232. Trunk roads–red routes–parking prohibitions–A12

A12 TRUNK ROAD (REDBRIDGE) (NO.1) RED ROUTE TRAFFIC ORDER 1996, SI 1996 1624; made under the Road Traffic Regulation Act 1984 s.6. In force: July 1, 1996; £2.40.

This Order, which revokes the A12 Trunk Road (Redbridge) (No.1) Red Route Experimental Traffic Order 1995 (SI 1995 1692), places a general prohibition on stopping in the specified trunk road red route during restricted hours.

5233. Trunk roads–red routes–parking prohibitions–A13

A13 TRUNK ROAD (BARKING AND DAGENHAM) RED ROUTE TRAFFIC ORDER 1996, SI 1996 1896; made under the Road Traffic Regulation Act 1984 s.6. In force: July 31, 1996; £1.95.

This Order, which revokes the A13 Trunk Road (Barking and Dagenham) Red Route Experimental Traffic Order 1995 (SI 1995 1700) places a general prohibition on stopping in the trunk road red route described in the Schedules during restricted hours.

5234. Trunk roads–red routes–parking prohibitions–A13

A13 TRUNK ROAD (HAVERING) RED ROUTE TRAFFIC ORDER 1996, SI 1996 1894; made under the Road Traffic Regulation Act 1984 s.6. In force: July 31, 1996; £1.95.

This Order, which revokes the A13 Trunk Road (Havering) (Waiting and Loading Restriction) Order 1995 (SI 1995 1703), places a general prohibition on stopping in the trunk road red route described in the Schedules during restricted hours.

5235. Trunk roads–red routes–parking prohibitions–A13

A13 TRUNK ROAD (TOWER HAMLETS) RED ROUTE TRAFFIC ORDER 1996, SI 1996 1891; made under the Road Traffic Regulation Act 1984 s.6. In force: July 31, 1996; £1.95.

This Order, which revokes the A13 Trunk Road (Tower Hamlets) Red Route Experimental Traffic Order 1995 (SI 1995 2245) and the London Borough of Tower Hamlets Waiting and Loading Order 1976 (No.394), places a general prohibition on stopping in the trunk road red route described in the Schedules during restricted hours.

5236. Trunk roads–red routes–parking prohibitions–A13

A13 TRUNK ROAD (TOWER HAMLETS) RED ROUTE (NO.2) EXPERIMENTAL TRAFFIC ORDER 1996, SI 1996 1841; made under the Road Traffic Regulation Act 1984 s.9, s.10. In force: July 29, 1996; £1.95.

This Order places a general prohibition on stopping in the prescribed trunk road red route during restricted hours.

5237. Trunk roads–red routes–parking prohibitions–A20

A20 TRUNK ROAD (BEXLEY AND BROMLEY) RED ROUTE TRAFFIC ORDER 1996, SI 1996 2728; made under the Road Traffic Regulation Act 1984 s.6. In force: November 1, 1996; £1.95.

This Order, with certain exemptions, prohibits persons from causing or permitting vehicles to stop during the restricted hours in the trunk road red route specified in the Schedules to this Order. It also revokes the A20 Trunk Road (Bexley and Bromley) Red Route Experimental Traffic Order 1995 (SI 1995 2445).

5238. Trunk roads–red routes–parking prohibitions–A20

A20 TRUNK ROAD (GREENWICH) RED ROUTE TRAFFIC ORDER 1996, SI 1996 2727; made under the Road Traffic Regulation Act 1984 s.6. In force: November 1, 1996; £1.95.

This Order, with certain exemptions, prohibits persons from causing or permitting vehicles to stop during the restricted hours in the trunk road red route specified in the Schedules to this Order.

5239. Trunk roads–red routes–parking prohibitions–A23

A23 TRUNK ROAD (CROYDON) RED ROUTE (CLEARWAY) TRAFFIC ORDER 1996, SI 1996 3051; made under the Road Traffic Regulation Act 1984 s.6. In force: December 16, 1996; £1.55.

This Order places a general prohibition of stopping in the trunk road red route at any time.

5240. Trunk roads–red routes–parking prohibitions–A41

A41 TRUNK ROAD (BARNET) RED ROUTE (CLEARWAY) (NO.1) TRAFFIC ORDER 1996, SI 1996 815; made under the Road Traffic Regulation Act 1984 s.6. In force: March 19, 1996; £1.55.

This Order introduces a general prohibition on stopping, with certain exemptions, on a section of the A41 Trunk Road.

5241. Trunk roads–red routes–parking prohibitions–A41

A41 TRUNK ROAD (BARNET) RED ROUTE (CLEARWAY) (NO.2) TRAFFIC ORDER 1996, SI 1996 817; made under the Road Traffic Regulation Act 1984 s.6. In force: March 19, 1996; £1.55.

This Order introduces a general prohibition on stopping, with certain exemptions, on a section of the A41 Trunk Road.

5242. Trunk roads–red routes–parking prohibitions–A41

A41 TRUNK ROAD (BARNET) RED ROUTE (CLEARWAY) (NO.3) TRAFFIC ORDER 1996, SI 1996 818; made under the Road Traffic Regulation Act 1984 s.6. In force: March 19, 1996; £1.55.

This Order introduces a general prohibition on stopping, with certain exemptions, on a section of the A41 Trunk Road.

5243. Trunk roads–red routes–parking prohibitions–A41

A41 TRUNK ROAD (BARNET) RED ROUTE (NO.1) EXPERIMENTAL TRAFFIC ORDER 1996, SI 1996 41; made under the Road Traffic Regulation Act 1984 s.9, s.10; and the Road Traffic Act 1991 s.58. In force: January 19, 1996; £2.40.

This Order introduces a general prohibition on stopping on the A41 trunk road (Barnet) red route, with certain exemptions for parking, loading and unloading, disabled persons' vehicles, and bus stops and stands.

5244. Trunk roads–red routes–parking prohibitions–A41

A41 TRUNK ROAD (BARNET) RED ROUTE (NO.2) EXPERIMENTAL TRAFFIC ORDER 1996, SI 1996 42; made under the Road Traffic Regulation Act 1984 s.9, s.10. In force: January 19, 1996; £1.95.

This Order prohibits, with certain exemption, persons from causing or permitting vehicles to stop during restricted hours in the trunk road red route specified in the Schedule to the Order.

5245. Trunk roads–red routes–parking prohibitions–A41

A41 TRUNK ROAD (CAMDEN) RED ROUTE EXPERIMENTAL TRAFFIC ORDER 1996, SI 1996 216; made under the Road Traffic Regulation Act 1984 s.9, s.10. In force: February 16, 1996; £2.80.

This Order prohibits, with certain exemptions, persons from causing or permitting vehicles to stop during restricted hours in the trunk road red route specified in the Schedule to the Order.

5246. Trunk roads–red routes–parking prohibitions–A41

A41 TRUNK ROAD (WESTMINSTER) RED ROUTE EXPERIMENTAL TRAFFIC ORDER 1996, SI 1996 2166; made under the Road Traffic Regulation Act 1984 s.9, s.10. In force: August 30, 1996; £2.80.

This Order, which suspends the City of Westminster (Waiting and Loading) Restriction Order 1976, with certain exemptions, prohibits persons from causing or permitting vehicles to stop during the restricted hours in the trunk road red route specified in the Schedules to this Order.

5247. Trunk roads–red routes–parking prohibitions–A41

A41 TRUNK ROAD (WESTMINSTER) RED ROUTE (NO.2) EXPERIMENTAL TRAFFIC ORDER 1996, SI 1996 2688; made under the Road Traffic Regulation Act 1984 s.9, s.10. In force: November 4, 1996; £1.95.

This Order, which suspends the City of Westminster (Waiting and Loading Restriction) Order 1976, with certain exemptions, prohibits persons from causing or permitting vehicles to stop during the restricted hours in the trunk road red route specified in the Schedules to this Order.

5248. Trunk roads–red routes–parking prohibitions–A205

A205 TRUNK ROAD (RICHMOND AND WANDSWORTH) RED ROUTE EXPERIMENTAL TRAFFIC ORDER 1995 (AMENDMENT NO.1) ORDER 1996, SI 1996 217; made under the Road Traffic Regulation Act 1984 s.9, s.10. In force: February 13, 1996; £0.65.

This Order amends certain provisions of the A205 Trunk Road (Richmond and Wandsworth) Red Route Experimental Traffic Order 1995 (SI 1995 124).

5249. Trunk roads–red routes–parking prohibitions–A205

A205 TRUNK ROAD (RICHMOND AND WANDSWORTH) RED ROUTE TRAFFIC ORDER 1996, SI 1996 2164; made under the Road Traffic Regulation Act 1984 s.6. In force: September 3, 1996; £1.10.

This Order provides that no person shall cause any vehicle to stop in the trunk road red route during the restricted hours.

5250. Trunk roads–red routes–parking prohibitions–A205

A205 TRUNK ROAD (WANDSWORTH AND RICHMOND) RED ROUTE EXPERIMENTAL TRAFFIC ORDER 1996, SI 1996 3254; made under the Road Traffic Regulation Act 1984 s.9, s.10. In force: January 5, 1997; £2.40.

This Order prohibits, with certain exemptions, any person from causing or permitting a vehicle to stop during the restricted hours in the trunk road red route specified in the Schedules to this Order. It also suspends the Wandsworth (Waiting and Loading Restriction) Order 1976.

5251. Trunk roads–red routes–parking prohibitions–A316

A316 TRUNK ROAD (RICHMOND) (NO.1) RED ROUTE TRAFFIC ORDER 1996, SI 1996 3052; made under the Road Traffic Regulation Act 1984 s.6. In force: December 16, 1996; £1.95.

This Order places a general prohibition of stopping in the trunk road red route during restricted hours.

5252. Trunk roads–red routes–parking prohibitions–A316

A316 TRUNK ROAD (RICHMOND) (NO.2) RED ROUTE EXPERIMENTAL TRAFFIC ORDER 1996, SI 1996 264; made under the Road Traffic Regulation Act 1984 s.9, s.10. In force: March 5, 1996; £2.80.

This Order prohibits, with certain exemptions, persons from causing or permitting vehicles to stop during restricted hours in the trunk road red route clearway specified in the Schedule to the Order.

5253. Trunk roads–red routes–parking prohibitions–A406

A406 TRUNK ROAD (BARNET) RED ROUTE EXPERIMENTAL TRAFFIC ORDER 1996, SI 1996 821; made under the Road Traffic Regulation Act 1984 s.9, s.10. In force: March 22, 1996; £1.95.

This Order introduces a general prohibition on stopping, with certain exemptions, on a section of the A406 Trunk Road.

5254. Trunk roads–red routes–parking prohibitions–A406

A406 TRUNK ROAD (BARNET) RED ROUTE (CLEARWAY) TRAFFIC ORDER 1996, SI 1996 820; made under the Road Traffic Regulation Act 1984 s.6. In force: March 22, 1996; £1.55.

This Order introduces a general prohibition on stopping, with certain exemptions, on a section of the A406 Trunk Road.

5255. Trunk roads–red routes–parking prohibitions–A406

A406 TRUNK ROAD (EALING AND HOUNSLOW) RED ROUTE EXPERIMENTAL TRAFFIC ORDER 1996, SI 1996 1088; made under the Road Traffic Regulation Act 1984 s.9, s.10. In force: April 22, 1996; £2.40.

This Order stipulates that, with certain exemptions, no person shall cause any vehicle to stop in the trunk road red route described in Sch.4 to the Order.

5256. Trunk roads–red routes–parking prohibitions–A406

A406 TRUNK ROAD (ENFIELD) RED ROUTE TRAFFIC ORDER 1996, SI 1996 2543; made under the Road Traffic Regulation Act 1984 s.6. In force: October 18, 1996; £1.95.

This Order partly revokes the A406 Trunk Road (Enfield) Red Route Experimental Traffic Order 1995 (SI 1995 2246), the Enfield (Waiting and Loading Restriction) (Priority Routes and Side Roads) Order 1994 and the Enfield (Restrictions of Waiting on Bus Stops) (Priority Routes and Side Roads) Order 1994. It places a general prohibition on stopping in the trunk road red route during restricted hours.

5257. Trunk roads–red routes–parking prohibitions–A406

A406 TRUNK ROAD (ENFIELD) RED ROUTE (CLEARWAY) TRAFFIC ORDER 1995 VARIATION ORDER 1996, SI 1996 2792; made under the Road Traffic Regulation Act 1984 s.6. In force: November 15, 1996; £0.65.

This Order varies the A406 Trunk Road (Enfield) Red Route (Clearway) Traffic Order 1995 (SI 1995 2532).

5258. Trunk roads–red routes–parking prohibitions–A406

A406 TRUNK ROAD (NEWHAM AND BARKING AND DAGENHAM) RED ROUTE TRAFFIC ORDER 1996, SI 1996 1895; made under the Road Traffic Regulation Act 1984 s.6. In force: July 31, 1996; £1.95.

This Order, which revokes the A406 Trunk Road (Newham and Barking and Dagenham) Red Route Experimental Traffic Order 1995 (SI 1995 1699), places a general prohibition on stopping in the trunk road red route described in the Schedules during restricted hours.

5259. Trunk roads–red routes–parking prohibitions–A501

A501 TRUNK ROAD (CAMDEN AND ISLINGTON) RED ROUTE EXPERIMENTAL TRAFFIC ORDER 1996, SI 1996 1136; made under the Road Traffic Regulation Act 1984 s.9, s.10. In force: May 7, 1996; £1.95.

This Order, which amends the Camden (Waiting and Loading Restriction) (No.2) Order 1993 and the Islington (Waiting and Loading Restriction) Order 1976, with certain exemptions, places a general prohibition on stopping in the trunk road red route described in the Schedules during restricted hours.

5260. Trunk roads–red routes–parking prohibitions–A501

A501 TRUNK ROAD (CAMDEN AND WESTMINSTER) RED ROUTE EXPERIMENTAL TRAFFIC ORDER 1996, SI 1996 2155; made under the Road Traffic Regulation Act 1984 s.9, s.10. In force: August 30, 1996; £2.40.

This Order places a general prohibition of stopping in the trunk road red route during restricted hours.

5261. Trunk roads–red routes–parking prohibitions–A501

A501 TRUNK ROAD (CAMDEN, ISLINGTON AND WESTMINSTER) RED ROUTE EXPERIMENTAL TRAFFIC ORDER 1996, SI 1996 1137; made under the Road Traffic Regulation Act 1984 s.9, s.10. In force: May 7, 1996; £2.40.

This Order which amends the Camden (Waiting and Loading Restriction) (No.2) Order 1993, the Islington (Waiting and Loading Restriction) Order 1976 and the City of Westminster (Waiting and Loading Restriction) Order 1976, with certain exemptions, places a general prohibition on stopping in the trunk road red route described in the Schedules to the Order during restricted hours.

5262. Trunk roads–red routes–parking prohibitions–A1400

A1400 TRUNK ROAD (REDBRIDGE) RED ROUTE TRAFFIC ORDER 1996, SI 1996 1892; made under the Road Traffic Regulation Act 1984 s.6. In force: July 31, 1996; £1.95.

This Order, which revokes the A1400 Trunk Road (Redbridge) Red Route Experimental Traffic Order 1995 (SI 1995 1996) and the London Borough of Redbridge Waiting and Loading Restriction and Consolidation Order 1993 (TMO 1993/LBR No.3), places a general prohibition on stopping in the trunk road red route described in the Schedules during restricted hours.

5263. Trunk roads–red routes–parking prohiitions–A30

A30 TRUNK ROAD (HOUNSLOW AND HILLINGDON) RED ROUTE (CLEARWAY) TRAFFIC ORDER 1996, SI 1996 63; made under the Road Traffic Regulation Act 1984 s.6. In force: January 17, 1996; £1.95.

This Order (which amends Hounslow (Waiting and Loading Restriction) Order 1977) prohibits, with certain exemptions, persons from causing or permitting vehicles to stop at any time in the trunk road red route clearway specified in the Schedule to the Order.

5264. Trunk roads–red routes–prescribed routes–A23

A23 TRUNK ROAD (CROYDON) RED ROUTE (PRESCRIBED ROUTE) TRAFFIC ORDER 1996, SI 1996 3060; made under the Road Traffic Regulation Act 1984 s.6. In force: December 16, 1996; £0.65.

This Order, with certain exemptions, prescribes a certain route on the A23 trunk road, Croydon.

5265. Trunk roads–red routes–prescribed routes–A30

A30 TRUNK ROAD (GREAT SOUTH WEST ROAD, HOUNSLOW) RED ROUTE (PRESCRIBED ROUTES AND PROHIBITIVE TURNS NO.1) TRAFFIC ORDER 1996,

SI 1996 69; made under the Road Traffic Regulation Act 1984 s.6. In force: January 17, 1996; £1.10.

This Order amends GLC 1973 293 which prescribes traffic flow in relation to the Great South West Road in Hounslow.

5266. **Trunk roads–red routes–prescribed routes–A30**

A30 TRUNK ROAD (GREAT SOUTH WEST ROAD, HOUNSLOW) RED ROUTE (PRESCRIBED ROUTES AND PROHIBITIVE TURNS NO.2) TRAFFIC ORDER 1996, SI 1996 70; made under the Road Traffic Regulation Act 1984 s.6. In force: January 17, 1996; £0.65.

This Order prescribes traffic flow in relation to the Great South West Road in Hounslow.

5267. **Trunk roads–red routes–prescribed routes–A406**

A406 TRUNK ROAD (NORTH CIRCULAR ROAD, EALING) RED ROUTE (PRESCRIBED ROUTES AND TURNS NO.1) EXPERIMENTAL TRAFFIC ORDER 1996, SI 1996 1089; made under the Road Traffic Regulation Act 1984 s.9. In force: April 22, 1996; £0.65.

This Order prescribes certain routes and turns in and around the North Circular Road.

5268. **Trunk roads–red routes–prescribed routes–A406**

A406 TRUNK ROAD (NORTH CIRCULAR ROAD, EALING) RED ROUTE (PRESCRIBED TURNS NO.2) EXPERIMENTAL TRAFFIC ORDER 1996, SI 1996 1134; made under the Road Traffic Regulation Act 1984 s.9. In force: April 22, 1996; £0.65.

This Order prescribes traffic routes and turns in and around the North Circular Road, Ealing.

5269. **Trunk roads–red routes–prescribed routes–A406**

A406 TRUNK ROAD (NORTH CIRCULAR ROAD, HOUNSLOW) RED ROUTE (PRESCRIBED ROUTE NO.1) EXPERIMENTAL TRAFFIC ORDER 1996, SI 1996 1090; made under the Road Traffic Regulation Act 1984 s.9. In force: April 22, 1996; £0.65.

This Order provides that no person shall cause any vehicle to proceed in the unnamed service road fronting No.127 to No.139 and the International School for London, Gunnersbury Avenue in the London Borough of Hounslow in a direction other than from south to north.

5270. **Trunk roads–red routes–prescribed routes–A501**

A501 TRUNK ROAD (MARYLEBONE ROAD, WESTMINSTER) RED ROUTE (PRESCRIBED ROUTES AND PROHIBITED TURNS) (NO.1) TRAFFIC ORDER 1996, SI 1996 2689; made under the Road Traffic Regulation Act 1984 s.6. In force: October 29, 1996; £0.65.

This Order, which amends the City of Westminster (Prescribed Routes) (No.10) Traffic Order 1984 (GLC 1984 516), with certain exemptions, prohibits vehicles from turning left or right into Upper Harley Street or making a U-turn through the gap in the central reservation, from Marylebone Road.

5271. Trunk roads–red routes–prescribed routes: A501

A501 TRUNK ROAD (EUSTON ROAD, CAMDEN) RED ROUTE (PRESCRIBED ROUTES) EXPERIMENTAL TRAFFIC ORDER 1996, SI 1996 1625; made under the Road Traffic Regulation Act 1984 s.9, s.10. In force: July 8, 1996; £0.65.

This Order prescribes that no person shall cause any vehicle on entering the A501 Euston Road from Midland Road, Camden, on the eastern side of eastern island, to proceed in any direction other than south into Judd Street.

5272. Trunk roads–red routes–prohibition of traffic–A41

A41 TRUNK ROAD (BARNET) RED ROUTE (PRESCRIBED ROUTE) EXPERIMENTAL TRAFFIC ORDER 1996, SI 1996 64; made under the Road Traffic Regulation Act 1984 s.9, s.10. In force: January 25, 1996; £0.65.

This Order prohibits motor vehicles proceeding west-bound from entering the area of carriageway situated at or adjacent to the junction of the A41 Hendon Way and Ridge Hill in the London Borough of Barnet which lies between the eastern kerb line of A41 Hendon Way and a line between the western boundaries of 60 and 73 Ridge Hill, except with the permission of a police officer or traffic warden.

5273. Trunk roads–revocation–A46

BATH-LINCOLN TRUNK ROAD A46 (UPPER SWAINSWICK TO A420 COLD ASHTON ROUNDABOUT) ORDERS 1987 REVOCATION ORDER 1996. 1996, SI 1996 1097; made under the Highways Act 1980 s.10, s.41. In force: May 3, 1996; £0.65.

This Order revokes the Bath-Lincoln Trunk Road A46 (Upper Swainswick to A420 Cold Ashton Roundabout) Order 1987 (SI 1987 1799) and the Bath-Lincoln Trunk Road A46 (Upper Swainswick to A420 Cold Ashton Roundabout) (Detrunking) Order 1987 (SI 1987 1800).

5274. Trunk roads–road works–revocation–A40

A406 LONDON NORTH CIRCULAR TRUNK ROAD POPES LANE (B4491) TO WESTERN AVENUE (A40) IMPROVEMENT ORDERS 1988 REVOCATION ORDER 1996, SI 1996 3002; made under the Highways Act 1980 s.10, s.41. In force: December 19, 1996; £0.65.

This Order revokes the A406 London North Circular Trunk Road (Popes Lane (B4491) to Western Avenue (A40) Improvement, Trunk Road) Order 1988 (SI 1988 1525) and the London North Circular Trunk Road (Popes Lane (B4491) to Western Avenue (A40) Improvement, Detrunking) Order 1988 (SI 1988 1526).

5275. Trunk roads–slip roads–A41

A41 TRUNK ROAD (LEAVESDEN SLIP ROAD) ORDER 1996, SI 1996 3026; made under the Highways Act 1980 s.10, s.41. In force: January 3, 1997; £0.65.

This Order specifies the route of a new slip road and provides that it shall be a trunk road.

5276. Trunk roads–speed limits–A1

A1 TRUNK ROAD (BARNET) (50 MPH SPEED LIMIT) ORDER 1996, SI 1996 285; made under the Road Traffic Regulation Act 1984 s.84, s.124, Sch.9 para.27. In force: February 19, 1996; £0.65.

The length of the A1 Trunk Road in the London Borough of Barnet known in part as the Great North Way, in part as Watford Way and in part as Barnet Way which extends from its junction with the London North Circular Trunk Road (A406) to a point 200 metres north of the centre line of the pedestrian subway opposite Courtland Avenue, Mill Hill, a distance of approximately 6.2 kilometres.

5277. **Trunk roads–speed limits–A40**

A40 TRUNK ROAD (WESTERN AVENUE, HILLINGDON) (30 MPH SPEED LIMIT) ORDER 1996, SI 1996 2910; made under the Road Traffic Regulation Act 1984 s.84, s.124, Sch.9 para.27. In force: November 22, 1996; £0.65.

This Order implements a 30 mph speed limit on part of the A40 trunk road.

5278. **Trunk roads–temporary prohibition of turns–A501**

A501 TRUNK ROAD (MARYLEBONE ROAD/UPPER HARLEY STREET, WESTMINSTER) (TEMPORARY PROHIBITION OF TURNS) TRAFFIC ORDER 1996, SI 1996 2162; made under the Road Traffic Regulation Act 1984 s.14. In force: August 19, 1996; £0.65.

This Order provides that, during the period starting at 00.01 on August 19, 1996 and ending at 23.59 hours on November 19, 1996 or when those works have been completed, whichever is the sooner, subject to certain provisions (a) no person shall cause or permit any vehicle on reaching Marylebone Road from Upper Harley Street (i) to turn right into Marylebone Road; (ii) to proceed ahead into Harley Street; (b) no person shall cause or permit any vehicle proceeding in Marylebone Road (i) to turn left into Upper Harley Street; (ii) to turn right into Upper Harley Street.

5279. **Trunk roads–traffic flow–A13**

A13 TRUNK ROAD (NEW ROAD, HAVERING) (PROHIBITION OF U-TURNS AND USE OF GAPS IN CENTRAL RESERVE) ORDER 1996, SI 1996 3112; made under the Road Traffic Regulation Act 1984 s.6. In force: December 9, 1996; £0.65.

This Order prohibits certain manoeuvers by motor vehicles using and entering the A13.

5280. **Articles**

A review of recent road traffic developments *(J.N. Spencer)*: J.P. 1996, 160(42), 898-903. (Changes to driving licences and driving test, revocation of licences of new drivers who receive six penalty points, vehicle excise offences and cases on wheel clamping and other road traffic offences).

At the roadside *(Bill Thomas)*: L. Ex. 1996, Oct, 22-23. (Cases on obstruction on highways by dogs, cattle and inanimate objects and road traffic offences related to parking of vehicles).

Diabetes as a defence in road traffic offences *(Alec Samuels)*: J.P. 1996, 160(14), 233-235. (Availability of automatism as defence for diabetics).

Government's air quality strategy puts transport on the spot: ENDS 1996, 257, 15-18. (DoE proposals for air quality targets for eight priority pollutants for year 2005, with implications for local authority traffic management).

Motoring offences England and Wales 1994 *(Linda Dobbs)*: R.T.I. 1996, 1, 2-3. (Statistical analysis).

Obstruction of the highway and unauthorized campers *(Christine Clayson)*: J.P. 1996, 160(18), 301-302. (Meaning of "obstruction" in Reg.3, whether permitted removal of vehicles not only actually obstructing but also potentially obstructing road users and application to travellers).

Road Traffic (New Drivers) Act 1995 *(T.A. Iles)*: J.P. 1996, 160(35), 692-694. (Act providing for newly qualified drivers to retake test if they exceed prescribed number of penalty points up to two years after passing test).

Road traffic–a look at some recent decisions *(Philip Brown)*: L. Ex. 1996, May, 13-15. (Recent cases on drink driving, including defence of duress, aggravated vehicle taking and sentencing guidelines for causing death by driving).

Road works *(Ann Flintham)*: Magistrate 1996, 52(5), 1999. (Training programme designed to raise magistrates' awareness of certain aspects of road traffic law).

Rows over smog: Env. Man. 1996, 3(9), 1-2. (Draft National Air Quality strategy and criticism of failure to tackle problem of road traffic).

Technological advances and the duty to disclose information under s.172 of the Road Traffic Act 1988, as amended *(J.N. Spencer)*: J.P. 1996, 160(33), 632. (Vehicle owner's liability to disclose identity and particulars of driver suspected of driving offence).

Temporary temptations *(Alan Harrison)*: S.J. 1996, 140(20), 502-503. (Proper considerations to be taken into account by local authorities contemplating introduction of temporary and experimental orders to regulate road traffic).

The licence to clamp comes up for renewal *(John Cooper)*: Lawyer 1996, 10(3), 13. (Whether activities of car clampers will be restrained following CA decision setting out circumstances in which clamps can lawfully be used).

5281. Books

Davis, Marcia; Hamed, Odette–The Road Traffic Referencer: 1997. Paperback: £14.95. ISBN 0-421-58220-0. Sweet & Maxwell.

SALE OF GOODS

5282. Conditions and warranties–implied term of fitness abnormal use of goods not made known to seller

See SALE OF GOODS Slater v. Finning Ltd. §7318

5283. Contract of sale–capacity–contracting parties–non-delivery of goods–act of contractive party in good faith

P, were sugar traders who had certain dealings with A Group of companies. A Group communicated on letterheaded paper in the name of AM. P were never aware of the precise nomenclature or structure of the A Group. AM did not, in fact, exist as a separate legal entity. R acted on behalf of A Group and contracted to deliver sugar to P seemingly in the name of AM. P became concerned as to the legal personality of AM and therefore brought an action against R on the basis that he was personally liable for purporting to act on behalf of a company which did not exist. AMFH were sued in the alternative.

Held, dismissing the action against R, that the identity of the defendant company within the A Group was not a matter which was vital to P. P had intended to contract with the appropriate corporate supplier within A Group. The standing of A Group had not previously given rise to any question in P's mind. R knew nothing of P's understanding and had dealt in good faith on the basis of the corporate structure at the time. There was no reason why R should stand as principal to a contract where he had acted in good faith and where it was intended that a corporate entity stand as principal.

CORAL (UK) LTD v. RECHTMAN AND ALTRO MOZART FOOD HANDELS GmbH [1996] 1 Lloyd's Rep. 235, Potter, J., QBD (Comm Ct).

5284. Retention of title–clauses–company in receivership–whether subsale valid

[Factors Act 1889 s.9; Companies Act 1985 s.395.]

C sold a quantity of meat to H on terms that included a retention of title clause which provided C with a right to repossess the meat in the event of non-payment by H. The meat was delivered to H in December 1992, H sold the meat on to K again on terms which included a retention of title clause. The meat was delivered to K in early January 1993. Shortly thereafter C and K agreed that C would re-possess the meat pursuant to its contract with H and sell it to K for the same price it had agreed to sell it to C. C purported to carry that agreement into effect at the end of January 1993, although the meat never left K's premises. By that time part of the meat had been incorporated by K into products it manufactured. On February 2, 1993, H went into receivership. The receivers contended that K was liable to pay C for the meat and sought directions as to whether C or H was entitled to receive the purchase price for the meat.

Held, that C was entitled to receive the purchase price of the unincorporated meat. By reason of the retention of title clause in the agreement between H and K, K could not acquire a good title to the meat until it had paid H. In consequence there was no effective sale of the meat to K which might have had the effect of passing title to the meat from C onto H pursuant to the Factors Act 1889 s.9 and thence onto K as a disposition made as if expressly authorised by C. As the meat remained the property of C at the end of January 1993, C was entitled to repossess the meat and sell it directly to K. So far as the incorporated meat was concerned C was only entitled to recover from H the purchase price payable to it by K. C's interest in that sum was a security interest which was void for want of registration pursuant to the Companies Act 1985 s.395.

HIGHWAY FOODS INTERNATIONAL LTD (IN ADMINISTRATIVE RECEIVERSHIP), *Re*; SUB NOM. MILLS v. C HARRIS (WHOLESALE MEAT) LTD [1995] B.C.C. 271, Edward Nugee Q.C., Ch D.

5285. Supply of goods–resale to third party–breach of warranty–loss of future profits

[Sale of Goods Act 1979 s.35, s.53; Sale of Goods (Amendment) Act 1994.]

AD contracted with AAB, through AD's specialist wholesale department to supply a total of 3,700 one piece telephones at a total price of £18,500, excluding VAT, in the full knowledge that AAB was reselling to a third party, a local newspaper in South Wales, for use in a promotional supply to the newspaper's customers. AAB was not supplied with a sample of the goods. The newspaper promotion went ahead but at least 75 per cent of the telephones proved to be defective. The internal design and construction were markedly different from the advertised telephone which could be purchased "over the counter" at AD's stores. The newspaper received many complaints and placed no further orders with AAB. AD sued for the price of the telephones. AAB sought a set off and counterclaimed for lost profits on (a) the instant contract with the newspaper for £294 and (b) loss of future profits on expected repeat orders with the newspaper, estimated at £12,000 (a further eight months' profit). AAB had only been trading for four months, but expert accountants' evidence had been given of projected earnings and later accounts.

Held, dismissing AD's claim on the basis of a total failure of consideration, that AAB was prevented from rejecting the goods under the Sale of Goods Act 1979 s.35. However s.53 of the 1979 Act allowed the court to extinguish the contract price totally where there had been, as here, a fundamental breach of warranty. Judgment was given for AAB in full on the counterclaim in the sum of £12,294, with costs on both claim and counterclaim to AAB, *Aerial Advertising v. Batchelor Peas* [1938] 2 All E.R. 788 applied.

ARGOS DISTRIBUTORS v. ADVERTISING ADVICE BUREAU, February 15, 1996, District Judge Meredith, CC (Torquay). [*Ex rel.* Peter Telford, Barrister].

5286. Articles

Are you being served satisfactorily? *(Denis Keenan)*: Accountancy 1996, 117(1232), 150. (Provisions of 1994 and 1995 Acts changing consumer law relating to sale of goods).

Better late than never: the reform of the law on the sale of goods forming part of a bulk *(Tom Burns)*: M.L.R. 1996, 59(2), 260-271. (Reasons for delay in reform, reform of passing of property rules in North America and nature of reforms under 1995 Act).

Caveat venditor! *(Brian Clapham)*: Arbitration 1996, 62(1), 50-52. (Effect of legislation on sale of goods, with particular regard to unfair contract terms, resulting in more protection for the consumer).

Connected party transactions *(David O'Keeffe)*: Tax J. 1996, 361, 11-13. (Section 839 connected party definition and effect of connected party transactions on capital allowance availability arising on sale or transfer of machinery plant and buildings).

Consumer law 1995: a review and update *(Sandra Silberstein)*: L. Ex. 1996, Apr, 24-25. (Changes to sale of goods law including replacement of condition of merchantable quality by satisfactory quality and SI 1994 3159 on exclusion clauses).

"New" *(Alec Samuels)*: Trad. L. 1996, 15(1), 45-47. (Sale of goods that are "new" and application of trade descriptions legislation).

Recent developments in the law of sale and unfair contract terms *(Howard Johnson)*: Man. L. 1996, 38(2), 1-32. (Background to legislation on sale of goods and implications of Unfair Contract Terms Directive for national law).

Romalpa clauses and trust funds *(Nicholas Bourne)*: Bus. L.R. 1996, 17(5), 96-98. (Requirements for valid clauses reserving title until goods paid for).

Sales without titles: Cons. L. Today 1996, 19(1), IF ii-iv. (Exceptions to the buyer beware principle in 1964 and 1979 Acts where sale to third party transfers good title).

Vienna Convention: when is it applicable? *(Hans Van Houtte)*: I.B.L. 1996, 24(7), 331-332.

SCIENCE

5287. Genetic engineering–biotechnology

GENETICALLY MODIFIED ORGANISMS (CONTAINED USE) (AMENDMENT) REGULATIONS 1996, SI 1996 967; made under the European Communities Act 1972 s.2; and the Health and Safety at Work etc. Act 1974 s.15, Sch.3 para.1, Sch.3 para.4, Sch.3 para.15. In force: April 27, 1996; £1.10.

These Regulations amend the Genetically Modified Organisms (Contained Use) Regulations 1992 (SI 1992 3217). Regulation 2(1) is amended as Council Directive 90/219 ([1990] OJ L117/1) now applies to the States of the EEA by virtue of the Agreement on the EEA and the definition of organism in that Regulation is amended to exclude humans and human embryos, which are now outside the scope of the 1990 Directive. Regulation 2(2) and Sch.2 are replaced in order to implement the new classification criteria for micro-organisms contained in Commission Directive 94/51 ([1994] OJ L297/29) which adapts to technical progress Council Directive 90/219. The exemptions contained in Reg.6(2)(a) of the principal Regulations are extended to exclude from the prohibitions in Reg.6(1) certain medicinal products marketed in accordance with Council Regulation 2309/93 ([1993] OJ L214/1). Regulation 8(2) of the principal Regulations is amended to provide that a separate notification is not required where a consent for Group II micro-organisms has already been granted and it is intended to use the premises for activities involving Group I micro-organisms, or where simultaneous notification is being given for activities involving Group I and Group II micro-organisms at the same premises. Regulation 16(4)(b), which specified the location where a copy or the register of notifications is held, is amended to specify the current address for the HSE in London.

5288. Genetic engineering–risk management–exemptions

GENETICALLY MODIFIED ORGANISMS (RISK ASSESSMENT) (RECORDS AND EXEMPTIONS) REGULATIONS 1996, SI 1996 1106; made under the Environment Protection Act 1990 s.108, s.126. In force: May 9, 1996; £1.10.

These Regulations, which revoke and replace the Genetically Modified Organisms (Contained Use) Regulations 1993 (SI 1993 15) make provision in relation to the Environmental Protection Act 1990 s.108(1)(a) which restricts the import and acquisition of genetically modified organisms (GMO's). The amendments take account of amendments made to Genetically Modified Organisms (Contained Use) Regulations 1992 (SI 1992 3217) and the Genetically Modified Organisms (Contained Use) (Amendment) Regulations

1996 (SI 1996 967). Regulation 2 prescribes the period for which records of risk assessments, carried out under the Environmental Protection Act 1990 s.108(1)(a) before importing or acquiring GMO's, must be kept. Regulation 3 relates to exemptions from the requirement to carry out risk assessments and exemptions where persons import or acquire GMO's which are contained in medical products subject to market authorisation under Council Regulation 2309/93 ([1993] OJ L241).

SHIPPING

5289. Admiralty Court–jurisdiction–claim for repayment of money paid to sub-agents who had supplied goods for the benefit of shipowners

[Supreme Court Act 1981 s.20, s.21.]

The defendants, D, applied to set aside a claim by the plaintiffs, P, financiers, for want of jurisdiction. The claim was for the recovery of payments in respect of invoices from sub-agents for goods supplied to D's ship, addressed to D, which P had paid. D argued that the claim did not come within the Supreme Court Act 1981 s.20(2)(m) and did not refer to a particular ship so the Admiralty Court did not have jurisdiction to hear the action.

Held, dismissing the application, that to come within s.20(2)(m) the claim had to be "in respect of goods or materials supplied to those ships for their operation or maintenance". It was, therefore, necessary to consider the agreement between P and D. P had arranged for the sub-agents to supply the goods and had an obligation to pay the sub-agents' invoices. The claim clearly came within s.20(2)(m) and did so even if it was proved that money had been paid on account in respect of the invoices as the claim still related to the supply of the goods. In addition, invoices showed that the claims related to specific ships and were therefore within s.21(4) of the Act.

CENTRO LATINO AMERICANO DE COMMERCIO EXTERIOR SA v. OWNERS OF THE SHIP KOMMUNAR (NO.1); SUB NOM. CLACE v. OWNERS OF THE SHIP KOMMUNAR (NO.1) [1997] 1 Lloyd's Rep. 1, Clarke, J., QBD (Adm Ct).

5290. Arbitration–charterparties–whether agreement to arbitrate made–when arbitrator commenced

[Limitation Act 1980 s.34.]

T appealed against a judgment against them relating to the appointment of an arbitrator in connection with claims under a number of charterparties. P time chartered a vessel from DK. Subsequently T were substituted as owners. P time chartered the vessel to S who voyage chartered the vessel to N. N commenced arbitration proceedings against S under the charterparty due to contamination of their product by a product previously carried by the vessel. S proposed a single arbitration between all parties but, when T failed to appoint an arbitrator, N obtained judgment against S for DM 500,000. P indemnified S and issued third party proceedings against T. T argued, inter alia, that firstly, they had agreed by telex that all the disputes should be arbitrated, but that was an ambiguous statement rather than an agreement to arbitration. Secondly, suit was not brought within the time limit under the Hague Rules because P had not appointed their own arbitrator. Thirdly, P's proposed arbitrator was given the owner's name as DK rather than T; therefore they failed to appoint an arbitrator in relation to their dispute with T.

Held, dismissing the appeal, that T's arguments lacked merit but it was necessary to determine whether or not they were technically irresistible; (1) the word "should" was not ambiguous. There was an agreement to arbitrate but no agreement about when T's arbitrator would be appointed. In a commercial contract such as a proposal for arbitration strict offer and acceptance was not required. What was necessary was an adherence by each party to a common arrangement; (2) suit had been brought against T under the Hague Rules because under the Limitation Act 1980 s.34 arbitration had commenced once one party had served notice on the other to appoint an arbitrator or agree to the appointment of an arbitrator. P's letter to T requiring such was deemed to be commencement of arbitration and (3) the mistake as to ownership of the vessel was not material and even if it was it did not invalidate the arbitrator's appointment.

PETREDEC LTD v. TOKOMARU KAIUN CO LTD, Trans. Ref: QBCMF 93/1562/B, February 8, 1995, Leggatt, J., CA.

5291. Arbitration–delay–appointment of arbitrator refused–court's discretion to appoint arbitrator in cases of delay unfettered

[Arbitration Act 1950 s.10.]

F, owner of the vessel Frotanorte, appealed against a decision not to appoint an arbitrator to conduct their dispute with S, their P&I Club, in an action arising out of a collision with another vessel in 1978. The appointment of an arbitrator, under the Arbitration Act 1950 s.10(1), was refused owing to inordinate and inexcusable delay on the part of F, who argued that the principles established in cases of striking out for want of prosecution should be applied to the discretion of the court under s.10 of the Act, which would mean that the discretion would be exercised except where prejudice was demonstrated.

Held, dismissing the appeal, that the discretion in s.10(1) was totally unfettered, *Bjornstad v. Ouse Shipping Ltd* [1924] 2 K.B. 673 followed, and there was no need to show prejudice in cases of striking out. It was important to preserve the court's power to exercise its discretion as it wished. Principles developed in one area in respect of the exercise of discretion should not be extended to another, and it would be unacceptable if an application to appoint an arbitrator could be defeated only where the delay had caused serious prejudice.

FROTA OCEANICA BRASILIERA SA v. STEAMSHIP MUTUAL UNDERWRITING ASSOCIATION (BERMUDA) LTD (THE FROTANORTE) [1996] 2 Lloyd's Rep. 461, Hirst, L.J., CA.

5292. Arbitration–scope of arbitration clause–whether arbitrator had jurisdiction–whether tortious claim fell within clause

G claimed demurrage from C, the receiver of cargo, on the basis of a demurrage clause incorporated into the bill of lading from a charterparty. G also claimed arbitration under the bill of lading in which the relevant clause covered "any dispute or difference arising under this bill of lading". C arrested G's vessel. A settlement agreement was reached under which it was agreed to cease the arbitration proceedings. G later claimed to void the settlement as a result of duress. C asked for a declaration that the arbitration was void and that the arbitrator had no jurisdiction.

Held, that (1) by commencing the declaratory proceedings C had submitted themselves to the jurisdiction of the court to determine the issues raised therein, including the validity of the agreement and whether it was voidable; (2) applying English law, the settlement agreement, if valid, operated as more than a defence in the arbitration, but as a complete bar to the jurisdiction of the arbitrator. Accordingly, the arbitrator could not determine G's case on duress; (3) the language "arising under" was narrower than "arising out of" and it was doubtful whether a tortious claim could give rise to a dispute "under" the bill of lading and (4) in any event, the tortious claims pleaded could not fall within the clause as they themselves depended upon the validity of the settlement agreement.

CHIMIMPORT PLC v. G D'ALESIO SAS (THE PAULA D'ALESIO) [1994] 2 Lloyd's Rep. 366, Rix, J., QBD.

5293. Arrest–dispute over yacht–whether transferor was "interested person"

[Merchant Shipping Act 1894 s.30.]

D agreed to exchange his Portuguese discotheque with P's yacht, which was registered in Jersey. A bill of sale was duly completed and the yacht transferred. P complained that D was unable to transfer the discotheque because it was on land owned by a third party. P also alleged various misrepresentations by D and claimed rescission. The yacht had been moved to Southampton where she had been arrested by one of D's creditors. P issued a writ in England and obtained an order in Jersey, under the Merchant Shipping Act 1894 s.30, which prevented any dealing with the yacht for one year. The order was discharged in Jersey and P appealed.

Held, allowing the appeal, that (1) although a mere creditor is not an "interested person" within s.30, *Mikado, The* [1992] 1 Lloyd's Rep. 163, [1992] C.L.Y. 3515 applied, P was more than a mere personal creditor; (2) P had a more immediate interest in the yacht than in any other asset of D and if the claim for rescission succeeded then property in the yacht would revert to him and (3) s.30 gave a discretion to the court even in cases in which some right in the ship was claimed, but not yet established and, in the absence of any answer to P's allegations, the court would exercise its discretion to make the order as P had a direct interest and close connection with the yacht.

HUGHES v. VAIL BLYTH CLEWLEY (THE SIBEN) [1994] 2 Lloyd's Rep. 420, Sir Godfray Le Quesne Q.C., Jersey Court of Appeal.

5294. Arrest–long term shipping agreement–whether agreement for particular vessel

[Supreme Court Act 1981 s.20, s.21; Rules of the Supreme Court Ord.75.]

P issued a writ in rem against D's ship, LP, and 15 other ships named in a Schedule. The LP was arrested by other claimants and although P issued a caveat against release, it later arrested the vessel. P's claim arose out of a long term agreement to carry containers of coffee using D's services, "within Conference agreements, joint services or independent", in respect of which it claimed that about 1,000 containers had been shut out. D sought a declaration that the Admiralty Court had no jurisdiction and an order setting aside the arrest. The question was whether there was jurisdiction to grant arrest against the LP under the Supreme Court Act 1981 s.20(2)(h) or (p), or against a sister ship under s.21(4).

Held, granting D the declaration and order, that (1) under the Supreme Court Act 1981 s.20(2)(h) the claim could not relate to the carriage of goods in an unidentified ship, but had to arise out of an agreement relating to the use or hire of a particular ship, or to the carriage of goods in a particular ship, and the claim had to arise in connection with that ship, *Eschersheim, The* [1976] 2 Lloyd's Rep. 1, [1976] C.L.Y. 2512 applied; (2) the instant agreement did not have a reasonably direct connection with the use or hire of the LP in particular, or the carriage of goods in her, as the contract contemplated the use or operation of vessels which would be identified in due course and which need not necessarily be vessels owned or operated by D, *River Rima, The* [1988] 1 W.L.R. 758, [1987] C.L.Y. 3360 considered.

Observed, that the position might have been different if particular containers had been booked to the LP; (4) the contract became a contract for a particular vessel within s.21(4) once the vessel was nominated for a particular service; (5) although P had affidavit evidence that certain vessels had been nominated, there was no evidence that they were owned or chartered by D at the time that the alleged causes of action arose, within s.21(4) and the arrest could not be maintained; (6) the same defects applied to the claim under s.20(2)(p); (7) claimants should not arrest a vessel without complying properly with Rules of the Supreme Court Ord.75 r.5(4) and (8) the affidavit to lead the warrant of arrest must state clearly whether the claim is put on a sister ship basis or not.

LLOYD PACIFICO, THE [1995] 1 Lloyd's Rep. 54, Clarke, J., QBD (Adm Ct).

5295. Bills of lading–cargo–bill of lading not prima facie evidence of quantity and weight–tally documents admissible

A cargo of steel billets was loaded in Russia with bills of lading specifying the number of bundles and the weight of the cargo. N acquired the billets from the exporters subject to an f.o.b. contract. A second set of bills were prepared with the quantity and weight expressed as being "unknown". N argued that the weight and quantity of billets were less than disclosed in the first set of bills. The issue arose whether the bill of lading was prima facie evidence of these facts and whether the tally documents were admissible evidence of weight.

Held, dismissing the application, that the bills of lading must be construed to see whether or not they constituted evidence of quantity and weight and whether an assertion that the weight was unknown could be an assertion or representation of the weight shipped. The bills were not assertions of the quantity or weight because they were not prepared to disclose such information; as shown by the expression "quantity unknown". Neither the first nor the second bills constituted prima facie evidence of the quantity or weight shipped. The tally documents did afford admissible evidence of quantity and weight, being prepared on behalf of the port authority on the basis of information given by someone claiming to have such knowledge. On the basis of such evidence, on the balance of probabilities, the amounts documented were the amounts shipped. N could therefore sue in tort on the terms of the bills.

NOBLE RESOURCES LTD v. CAVALIER SHIPPING CORP (THE ATLAS) [1996] 1 Lloyd's Rep. 642, Longmore, J., QBD (Comm Ct).

5296. Bills of lading–cargo claim–bareboat charterparty–identity of carrier–time bar–extension of time requested for "owners"–whether "owners" included bareboat charterer

[Hague Rules Art. III r.6.]

P's cargo was carried in a vessel owned by D, but bareboat chartered to B. D and B were part of the same group and insured by G. The bills of lading were signed by B's master and incorporated the one year time bar under the Hague Rules Art. III r.6. P sued B and D. In the course of settlement negotiations, P asked for, and was granted, a time extension for the claim against "owners". G was aware that P had made a mistake in assuming that the expression included B. It was accepted that the bill of lading contracts were with B and that D could not be liable in contract. B claimed that the extension did not apply to the claim against it and a writ issued outside the Hague Rules period was therefore time barred. The judge held that the claim against B was not time barred, as the expression "owners" meant those concerned as owners, including B. B appealed.

Held, dismissing the appeal, that (1) the expression "owners" did not necessarily have a fixed and absolute meaning and, although it could refer to the registered shipowner, D, in the context of a bill of lading it could also mean the party which had the liabilities of the Conlinebill under the contract of affreightment; (2) the bills made a number of references to "owner" and "shipowner", which, in context, included B and (3) in the context of the communications, the word owner was understood to mean the company which was the owner for the purposes of the bill of lading and a reasonable person would have understood that the request for an extension was required from the person who would be liable under the bill, namely B.

STOLT LOYALTY, THE [1995] 1 Lloyd's Rep. 598, Hoffmann, L.J., CA.

5297. Bills of lading–claim for damage to cargo–amendment of pleading–whether claim time barred

[Hague Rules Art. III r.6.]

CF claimed against PS for damage to cargo within the Hague Rules Art. III r.6 one year time limit and originally pleaded that there was a contract on the terms of a bill of lading, but amended the claim to refer to a charterparty contract. PS showed that it had time chartered its ship to ASG and produced a sub-voyage charterparty on the Gencon form between CF and ASG "as t/c Owners" and PS. CF had been misled by an alternative version of the Gencon charter which indicated that the charter was made by ASG "as agents to owners". CF now accepted that PS was not a party to the Gencon charter and was merely a contracting carrier under the bill. CF applied to re-amend the statement of claim to sue PS under the bill, but PS contended that the Hague Rules one year time limit had now expired and applied for the claim to be struck out.

Held, dismissing PS's application to strike out the claim, that (1) a suit would satisfy the Hague Rules provided that it was brought by a party entitled to sue before a competent court which alleged that the carrier was liable for breach of duty owed in relation to the cargo; (2) CF's claim was always on the basis of breaches of duty as bailee, negligence and breach of contract and these general allegations were sufficient to satisfy the Hague and Hague-Visby Rules, despite errors of detail in the pleaded case, *Kapetan Markos, The* [1986] 1 Lloyd's Rep. 211, [1986] C.L.Y. 2732 applied and (3) accordingly, an application after the expiry of the one year time bar to amend a pleading to refer to a claim against the carrier under a bill of lading, rather than under a charterparty, did not render the suit incompetent under Art. III r.6.

CONTINENTAL FERTILIZER CO LTD v. PIONIER SHIPPING CV (THE PIONIER) [1995] 1 Lloyd's Rep. 223, Phillips, J., QBD (Comm Ct).

5298. Bills of lading–exclusive jurisdiction clause–shipowner not party to contract between shipper and charterer relying on exclusive jurisdiction clause–whether shipowners could rely on Himalaya clause or principles of bailment on terms

[Hague Visby Rules 1968.]

The owners of the vessel M appealed against a decision setting aside an order granting a stay of proceedings issued in reliance upon an exclusive jurisdiction clause contained in a bill of lading between the ship's charterers and the cargo owners, who had issued a writ in respect of damage to the cargo. Although not party to the bill of lading, the shipowners sought to rely on a Himalaya clause in it stating that all "exceptions, limitations, provisions, conditions and liberties herein benefiting the carrier" expressly accrued to the benefit of agents and sub-contractors, or alternatively to rely on their status as bailees under bailment on terms principles. The extension contended for by the shipowners was in accordance with the exceptions to the doctrine of privity of contract recognised in some cases of carriage by sea, which granted the benefit of contractual terms to shipowners and stevedores, but which had been subject to pendulum like changes during the recent past, *Elder Dempster & Co Ltd v. Paterson Zochonis & Co Ltd* [1924] A.C. 522, *Midland Silicones Ltd v. Scruttons Ltd* [1962] A.C. 446, [1962] C.L.Y. 2502 and *New Zealand Shipping Co Ltd v. AM Satterthwaite & Co Ltd (The Eurymedon)* [1975] A.C. 154, [1974] C.L.Y. 3532 considered.

Held, dismissing the appeal, that the Himalaya clause did not allow the shipowners to take advantage of the exclusive jurisdiction clause. Bills of lading usually incorporated the Hague Visby Rules 1968, which segregated carriers' responsibilities and liabilities from their rights and immunities. An exclusive jurisdiction clause could not be equated with such terms as it did not benefit one party over another, but constituted a mutual agreement on the relevant jurisdiction for dispute resolution. It could therefore not be classed as an "exception, limitation, condition or liberty" or a "provision" for the carrier's benefit, as provided for in the Himalaya clause, *The Pioneer Container* [1994] A.C. 324, [1994] C.L.Y. 255 distinguished. Further, the shipowner could not benefit from the exclusive jurisdiction clause on bailment principles, as the present bill of lading's Himalaya clause limited the availability of benefits accruing to the shipowner. Therefore any attempt to claim under the jurisdiction clause for matters arising from the shipowner's obligation as bailee was inconsistent with an express provision contained in the bill of lading.

MAHKUTAI, THE [1996] A.C. 650, Lord Goff of Chieveley, PC.

5299. Bills of lading–responsibility for cost of discharge from hold to ship's sail–receivers' obligations

This appeal concerned the issue of whether a clause in a bill of lading obliged the receiver of goods discharged from the carrying vessel to pay the costs of the discharging from the hold to the ship's rail. If the receivers were responsible for the costs they would be entitled to recover an indemnity from the sellers of the goods. In the court below it was held that the receivers were not liable to pay those costs, *Ceval International Ltd v. Cefetra BV* [1994] 1 Lloyd's Rep. 651, [1995] 2 C.L.Y. 4485.

Held, upholding the awards of the appeal arbitrators, that the receivers were required to pay the whole of the costs of discharge despite the fact that the terms of delivery between themselves and the shipowners were "liner out" (meaning that discharge was free). On the correct construction of the clause the receivers were obliged to pay the costs under the delivery orders tendered by the sellers.

CEVAL INTERNATIONAL LTD v. CEFETRA BV; CEFETRA BV v. SOULES CAF [1996] 1 Lloyd's Rep. 464, Evans, L.J., Peter Gibson, L.J., CA.

5300. Cargo–contamination–cattle poisoned by cattle feed–shipper discharged duty of care by arranging for destruction

H and others appealed against judgment in favour of A in relation to the poisoning of cattle by feed contaminated with lead during transportation by ship. The total loss was £11 million. On discovery that the feed had been poisoned, A arranged for a reputable salvor to destroy it. The salvor in fact sold the cargo. The judge held that A owed H a duty of care, but had not breached it.

Held, dismissing the appeal, that no fresh approach to the questions of this case were advanced in the appeal; it was merely a rerun of the trial. The trial judge had come to the correct conclusion that A had performed their duty by arranging for a reputable contractor to destroy the cargo.

HANFORD FEEDS LTD v. ALFRED C TOEPFER INTERNATIONAL GmbH, Trans. Ref: QBCMF 94/1046/B, March 12, 1996, Simon Brown, L.J., CA.

5301. Cargo–contamination–evidence of previous incidents adduced in evidence–owner's failure to prove due diligence in facts of previous contamination evidence

A cargo of oil was found to contain trace elements of styrene monomer as a result of a previous cargo. The oil was therefore contaminated and sold at a discount to its uncontaminated price. The receivers sought to recover their loss from the shipowners on the basis that the tank into which the oil had been loaded was uncargoworthy. The owners appealed against the decision of the arbitrators contending that the arbitrators had reached their decision based on arguments raised by counsel in closing submissions but which had not formed part of the pleaded case.

Held, dismissing the appeal, that it was plain that in pursuing the question of due diligence with the owners' expert witness, counsel for the recipients raised the issue of the owners' previous experience in contamination cases. There was an opportunity for the owners to meet these arguments, albeit late in the day. This they did not do. The award was based on the overall failure of the owners to discharge the burden of proving due diligence, particularly in the face of evidence of previous contamination cases. There was no evidence that the arbitrators had misunderstood or misapplied the law.

LA FONTANA NOVELA v. EG CORNELIUS & CO LTD (THE PEACEVENTURE L) [1996] 2 Lloyd's Rep. 75, Potter, J., QBD (Comm Ct).

5302. **Cargo–dangerous cargo causing explosion–whether shipowner entitled to indemnity under Hague Visby Rules 1968**

[Hague Visby Rules 1968 Art.IV r.6; Carriage of Goods by Sea Act 1971.]

S's tanker was damaged by an explosion while unloading a cargo of fuel oil shipped by D. S claimed an indemnity from D, for shipping a dangerous cargo, under the Hague Visby Rules 1968 Art.IV r.6 as incorporated into the Carriage of Goods by Sea Act 1971. Fuel oil was not considered dangerous by carriers and there had been no recorded explosions, but oil company shippers were aware it could produce an explosive mixture. Carriers were not warned of the possibility. The fuel had been contaminated by residual condensate carried on a previous voyage, although D did not complain of this until one year after the date of delivery, outside the Hague Visby Rules time bar. The judge held that the condensate and the fuel oil were contributory causes of the explosion, but that S was not entitled to be indemnified under the Hague Visby Rules. S appealed. It was accepted that S's failure was a breach of the duty to make the ship seaworthy under Art.III r.1.

Held, dismissing S's appeal, that (1) Hague Visby Rules 1968 Art.IV r.6 was an indemnity provision, not a mere contractual duty on the shipper to disclose the nature and character of the goods, and was to be construed as not applying to loss caused by S's negligence, *Canada Steamship Lines v. R.* [1952] A.C. 192, [1952] C.L.Y. 610; *Smith v. South Wales Switchgear Co Ltd* [1978] 1 W.L.R. 165, [1978] C.L.Y. 339 followed; (2) neither the language nor context of Art.IV r.6 showed that it should apply even when S was negligent and it was irrelevant that it related to safety matters or covered loss arising directly or indirectly; (3) as S was negligent in failing to exercise due diligence under Art.III r.1 in respect of the condensate then it could not claim the indemnity; (4) a shipper which placed dangerous goods on board without the carrier's consent, contrary to Art.IV r.6, was not prevented from relying on Art.III r.1 and the latter was the overriding article and (5) the one year time bar in Art.III r.6 was directed to the liability of the ship and operated as a discharge of a suit by D, but did not bar a defence raised by D, *Aries Tanker Corporation v. Total Transport Ltd* [1977] 1 W.L.R. 34, [1977] C.L.Y. 2741 distinguished.

MEDITERRANEAN FREIGHT SERVICES LTD v. BP OIL INTERNATIONAL LTD (THE FIONA) [1994] 2 Lloyd's Rep. 506, Hirst, L.J., CA.

5303. **Cargo–dangerous goods–infested cargo dumped at sea–shippers' liability for loss and damage arising–whether liability qualified by Hague Visby Rules Art.IV r.3**

[Hague Visby Rules Art.IV r.3, Art.IV r.6; Bills of Lading Act 1855 s.1.]

Sonacos of Dakar, SD, shippers who were second defendants in an action brought by ES, the owners of the ship G, for damages for expenses and delay caused by the dumping at sea of a cargo of groundnuts infested with khapra beetle, appealed against a decision allowing ES's claim for damages. The judge below had concluded that the goods were a dangerous cargo under the Hague Visby Rules Art.IV r.6 and that SD were therefore liable for all damages arising from the shipment. SD argued that Art.IV r.6 was qualified by Art.IV r.3 which provided that the shipper was not responsible for loss or damage which occurred without his fault or neglect and also contended that the Bills of Lading Act 1855 s.1 divested them of liability to the owner.

Held, dismissing the appeal, that the infested cargo clearly fell within Art.IV r.6 and although it did not present any physical danger to the ship the carriers had little choice but to dump it. Thus Art.IV r.3 could not be relied on to exonerate SD from liability and nor could the Bills of Lading Act 1855 s.1, since it would require very clear wording to divest the shipper of his obligation to the owner with whom he had entered into a contractual relationship.

EFFORT SHIPPING CO LTD v. LINDEN MANAGEMENT SA (THE GIANNIS NK) [1996] 1 Lloyd's Rep. 577, Hirst, L.J., CA.

5304. Carriage by sea–due diligence–seaworthiness of vessel–whether shipowner exercised due diligence

[Hague Rules.]

D's ship suffered a fracture to its shell plating in bad weather and ultimately became a total loss. P claimed for the loss of its cargo on the basis of a breach of the Hague Rules, which were incorporated into the contract of carriage.

Held, awarding judgment for P, that (1) although no classification society surveyor ever required repairs, or made any class recommendation, the cause of the fracture was fatigue caused by serious damage to frames and brackets when the vessel was used in the log trade; (2) the damage existed at the start of the voyage, even though cracks were not at that stage visible, and the vessel was unseaworthy under the Hague Rules and (3) D failed to exercise due diligence under the Hague Rules to make the vessel seaworthy because it did not have a proper system for maintenance and had failed to repair the damage through complacently regarding it as normal.

TOLEDO, THE [1995] 1 Lloyd's Rep. 40, Clarke, J., QBD (Adm Ct).

5305. Carriage by sea–hazardous substances

MERCHANT SHIPPING (DANGEROUS OR NOXIOUS LIQUID SUBSTANCES IN BULK) REGULATIONS 1996, SI 1996 3010; made under the Merchant Shipping (Prevention and Control of Pollution) Order 1987 Art.3; the Merchant Shipping Act 1995 s.85, s.86; and the Merchant Shipping (Prevention of Pollution) (Law of the Sea Convention) Order 1996 Art.2. In force: January 1, 1997; £2.80.

These Regulations replace with some changes the Merchant Shipping (IBC Code) Regulations 1987 (SI 1987 549); the Merchant Shipping (BCH Code) Regulations 1987 (SI 1987 550) and the Merchant Shipping (Control of Pollution by Noxious Liquid Substances in Bulk) Regulations 1987 (SI 1987 551). The consolidation takes into account the 1992 amendments to the IBC Code, BCH Code and Annex II of MARPOL 1973/78 as set out in MEPC Resolutions, MEPC 55(33), which allow port state control inspection of operational requirements. A number of the detailed technical requirements and specifications are now contained in a Merchant Shipping Notice.

5306. Carriers liabilities–loss of cargo–bill of lading specifying number of items in container–interpretation of "package" in Hague Rules

[Hague Rules Art.IV r.5.]

The cargo owners sought judgment on preliminary issues in their action for damages against the carriers, N, whose vessel sank with the loss of the cargo following an engine breakdown. The cargo had been shipped in containers under the UK West Africa Line bills of lading and was subject to the Hague Rules, under Art.IV r.5 of which a carrier was entitled to limit liability to "£100 per package or unit". The carriers claimed their liability was limited because, although the bill of lading stated that the container included a number of items, for the purposes of Art.IV r.5 the container itself was the "package". However, the cargo owners argued that "package" referred to the separate packages within the containers and not the container itself.

Held, giving judgment for the cargo owners, that in construing Art.IV r.5 "package" referred to separate items shipped within a container where the number of packages in the container was noted in the bill of lading. In the instant case the bill of lading clearly stated the number of packages and therefore, in the event of loss, the carriers could not limit their liability to the container when they were aware of the existence of separate items within it.

OWNERS OF CARGO LATELY ABOARD THE RIVER GURARA v. NIGERIAN NATIONAL SHIPPING LINE LTD [1996] 2 Lloyd's Rep. 53, Colman, J., QBD (Adm Ct).

5307. Charterparties–bills of lading–whether owner of sub-chartered vessel entitled to intercept bill of lading to claim unpaid freight from sub-charterer

Held, that where an insolvent time charterer had failed to pay the time charter hire, although moneys due under the time charter had been paid to him by the sub-charterer, an owner of a sub-chartered vessel was not entitled to intercept a bill of lading and claim the freight from the sub-charterer on the basis that it remained unpaid, as "freight payable as per charterparty" included all the details of the payment clause of the sub-charter and payment to the time charterer amounted to payment under the charter.

INDIA STEAMSHIP CO LTD v. LOUIS DREYFUS SUGAR CO LTD (THE INDIAN RELIANCE) [1997] 1 Lloyd's Rep. 52, Rix, J., QBD (Comm Ct).

5308. Charterparties–contract terms–interpretation of laycan narrowing provision–clause inoperative in absence of requisite notice being given

A charter party was effected over a ship: the contract included a term which enabled the owners to narrow the laycan period within given parameters on 25 day's notice, "the laycan clause". The charterers appealed against a majority arbitration decision that the term was an intermediate one giving rise only to relief in damages.

Held, giving judgment for the charterers, that as a matter of contractual construction the laycan clause was a condition precedent to delivery and running time. It was a provision which had to be complied with before any delivery could be valid. The aim of the provision was to enable charterers to arrange their affairs by not allowing delivery with short notice. If the laycan clause had not been a condition precedent, then the onus would have been on the charterers to prove that they had lost valuable employment opportunities. However, on these facts there had not been 25 days' notice and therefore the laycan clause was not operative.

HYUNDAI MERCHANT MARINE CO LTD v. KARANDER MARITIME INC (THE NIZURU) [1996] 2 Lloyd's Rep. 66, Mance, J., QBD (Comm Ct).

5309. Charterparties–diversion clause–alternative port nomination to avoid former Yugoslavia–diversion clause incorporated into bill of lading

By a sale contract, goods were to be shipped from the sellers, CA, to the buyers, AT, and delivered in the former Yugoslavia. The terms and conditions of the charterparty were to be incorporated into the sale contract. CA chartered the Northern Progress and agreed with the owners on a special diversion clause to the effect that, if Yugoslavian ports became subject to insurance premiums because of war risks, CA should nominate an alternative destination. Subsequently the former Yugoslavia was added to the areas designed by the London insurance market for additional premiums because of war risk. Dispute arose when AT contacted CA as to the preferred diversion port. The issue arose whether the special diversion clause in the charterparty was incorporated into the sale contract and the bill of lading.

Held, dismissing the appeal, that the duty on CA was to procure a reasonable and usual contract of carriage. It was argued that the term in the sale contract as to diversion was not usual or reasonable and provided for what would otherwise be breach of CA's basic duties. Therefore, the arbitrator's award that the special diversion clause should not be incorporated into the sale contract should be upheld. It was too late for CA to contend that the special diversion clause had not been included in the bill of lading. CA's contention that AT had waived the right to elect that the ship did not go to Hamburg could not be maintained.

CEVAL ALIMENTOS SA v. AGRIMPEX TRADING CO LTD (THE NORTHERN PROGRESS) (NO.2) [1996] 2 Lloyd's Rep. 319, Rix, J., QBD (Comm Ct).

5310. Charterparties–drydocking requirements–measure of damages–quantifying charterers loss–whether drydocking period considered in arbitration decisions

Under a charter agreement, the defendant charterers N agreed to drydock the ship at certain times for certain periods. The owners, M, entered into a binding drydocking agreement but in January 1994, before the agreed date for drydocking, M breached the agreement. N sought and obtained employment for the vessel to mitigate their loss. The vessel was eventually drydocked in July 1994. The dispute was referred to arbitration. On appeal, M contended that the arbitrators had erred in law in not taking the July 1994 drydocking of the vessel into account when they calculated damages.

Held, dismissing the appeal, that clearly the arbitrators did not take the July 1994 drydocking into account and it could not be shown that they erred in law by disregarding it. On the facts it was clear that the arbitrators had reached a conclusion on the two periods of drydocking in calculating damages. The question the arbitrators were asking was what loss was suffered by the charterers. This was a question of fact.

MEDORA SHIPPING INC v. NAVIX LINE LTD AND NAVIOS CORP (THE TIMAWRA) [1996] 2 Lloyd's Rep. 166, Waller, J., QBD (Comm Ct).

5311. Charterparties–time charterparties–managers of a pool of vessels–name appearing in box for owners in charterparty–whether personally liable as owners

G, the charterers, appealed against a decision that S, who managed a pool of vessels and were authorised to enter into contracts for the use of the vessels on behalf of the owners, were not liable as owners under a time charterparty in respect of the vessel "Frost Express". The managing director of S had signed the charterparty in a space marked "Owners", but the signature was not qualified in relation to S or the disponet owners of the vessel. In addition, box 3 of the charterparty for "owners/place of business" contained S's name and address followed by the words "as agents to Owners or as Disponet Owners". The court found that S acted as agents and were therefore not owners and not liable for the poor condition of the cargo.

Held, allowing the appeal, that (1) S was personally liable under the chartering contract between them and G which was incorporated into the charterparty naming the parties as "Owners" and "Charterers"; (2) as S were not disponet owners of the Frost Express, the relevant part of box 3 was "as agents to Owners". These words did not adequately exclude S from personal liability and (3) it would be absurd to find the managing director to be personally liable owing to his unqualified signature.

SEATRADE GRONINGEN BV v. GEEST INDUSTRIES LTD (THE FROST EXPRESS) [1996] 2 Lloyd's Rep. 375, Evans, L.J., CA.

5312. Charterparties–time charterparties–master under orders of charterer–delivery of cargo without production of bill–whether owner entitled to reasonable time to consider orders–whether time charterer could order delivery of cargo without production of bill

S time chartered its tanker to a Kuwaiti time charterer, C, on the Shelltime 4 form under which the master was to be under the orders of C as regards the employment of the vessel. Clause 13 of the charter provided an express indemnity for obeying orders to deliver without production of a bill. During the charter, Iraq invaded Kuwait, and the tanker was forced to sail from Kuwait with only a part cargo of oil, leaving behind signed, partially completed, negotiable bills of lading made out to C or order. C moved its offices to London after the invasion. On August 8, C gave orders to proceed to the Red Sea, but S was concerned about the authority of the orders and possible conflicts with UN sanctions and stated that it was seeking legal advice. S refused orders of August 13, to allow a surveyor to go on board. A court order was obtained on August 17, under which inspection was allowed, but C agreed not to demand delivery of the cargo without the consent of S or the court. Eventually the vessel was made available to C on August 20, but a dispute arose in September when it was sought to discharge the cargo without production of the bills of lading. The judge found that the vessel was off hire and S appealed. The questions were whether S was entitled to a reasonable time in which to obey an order and whether C could lawfully demand that S deliver the cargo without production of a bill of lading.

Held, allowing the appeal, that (1) the duty of the master was to act reasonably on receipt of orders and such orders would normally require immediate compliance; (2) however, it was necessary to ask how a reasonably prudent master would have acted and there may be circumstances where it was the master's right and duty to pause in order to seek further information, to clarify an ambiguous order, or to verify its authenticity, even where there was no immediate physical threat to the safety of the ship or cargo; (3) the question of the reasonableness of the particular orders would be remitted to the judge; (4) cl.13 did not impose a contractual duty on S to deliver without production of a bill, but merely provided an indemnity if such delivery took place and (5) once the order had been given to sign negotiable bills of lading, rendering S potentially liable to a third party holder, C could no longer order S to deliver otherwise than on presentation of the bills even where C was entitled to possession of the cargo, and S was entitled to refuse any such order.

KUWAIT PETROLEUM CORP v. I&D OIL CARRIERS LTD (THE HOUDA) [1994] 2 Lloyd's Rep. 541, Neill, L.J., CA.

5313. Charterparties–time charterparties–standard form NYPE–cargo not in apparent good order and condition–no implied term obliging the master to clause the mate's receipt

[Hague Rules r.3.]

M, time charterers, appealed against a decision that the standard form NYPE time charterparty did not contain an implied term that the master was under an obligation to the charterers to clause the mate's receipt for the cargo if it was not in apparent good order and condition. The dispute concerned a contaminated cargo of salt causing loss to M owing to the disruption of their trading programme.

Held, dismissing the appeal, that (1) the term should not be implied into the charterparty; (2) the mate's receipt did not have a separate contractual identity, in the same way as a bill of lading, but related to the charterparty and the shipowner's liabilities once the cargo was on board the ship; (3) the receipt demarcated the authority of the master, the charterers or their agents to issue bills of lading which had to be in accordance with the receipt; (4) the Hague Rules r.3(3) imposed an obligation on the master to make an accurate statement as to the apparent order and condition of the goods; (5) when the charterer shipped goods for a third party shipper and, therefore, was unlikely to know the condition of the cargo, then the shipper should be treated as the charterer's agent and the shipper's knowledge should be attributed to the charterer and (6) consequently, there was no reason for an implied term that the master would tell the charterer information which it already knew or was deemed to know through its agent, *Oetkar v. IFA International Fractagentur AG Almak, The* [1985] 1 Lloyd's. Rep. 557, [1985] C.L.Y. 3158 and *Naviera Mogor SA v. Societe Metallurgique de Normandie Nogar Marin, The* [1988] 1 Lloyd's. Rep. 412, [1988] C.L.Y. 3207 distinguished.

TRADE STAR LINE CORP v. MITSUI & CO LTD (THE ARCTIC TRADER); MITSUI & CO LTD v. J LAURITZEN A/S [1996] 2 Lloyd's Rep. 449, Evans, L.J., CA.

5314. Charterparties–voyage charterparty–breach by charterer–whether benefit of higher rate should be taken into account

[Arbitration Act 1950 s.22; Arbitration Act 1979 s.1.]

MR breached a charterparty with BP by shipping dangerous cargo on BP's vessel. BP's vessel was detained, but BP managed to obtain a substitute fixture at a freight rate which was higher than typical hire rates. The arbitrator awarded damages against MR and recorded that it was common ground between the parties that MR was not entitled to the benefit of the higher freight actually earned on the substitute voyage. It was agreed that this was a misunderstanding which merited a remittal to the arbitrator under the Arbitration Act 1950 s.22. MR appealed asking for a lesser sum to be substituted, taking into account the benefit gained, or for the appeal to be remitted under s.22.

Held, remitting the award, that (1) it was not possible to find an error of law which gave the court jurisdiction under the Arbitration Act 1979 s.1, as the arbitrator had expressly stated that the parties were agreed; (2) in any event, there was no obligation to take such benefits into account, *Fanis, The* [1994] 1 Lloyd's Rep. 633, [1995] 2 C.L.Y. 4510 followed, and it could not therefore be said that the arbitrator would necessarily have decided the case in MR's favour and (3) the case would be remitted to the arbitrator in order for the benefit issues to be considered.

MARC RICH & CO AG v. BEOGRADSKA PLOVIDBA (THE AVALA) [1994] 2 Lloyd's Rep. 363, Tuckey, J., QBD.

5315. Charterparties–voyage charterparty–notice of readiness given in good faith but vessel unready–whether laytime commenced but subject to deduction

C chartered a vessel from S under the "Worldfood" voyage charterparty, as used by the UN's World Food Programme. Clause 8 provided that before tendering (NOR), the master should ensure that all holds were clean and in all respects suitable to receive the cargo to the shipper's satisfaction. Clause 9 provided that if the vessel was found to be unready after berthing the actual time lost was not to count as laytime. The vessel arrived at the loadport on August 10/11 when NOR was given. As there were no berths available she waited at the anchorage. On August 28 the master was ordered to remove insect infestation, of which he had been unaware. On September 7 the vessel shifted to a vacant berth. On September 8 an inspection revealed that the infestation was still present and the holds were fumigated. By September 9 the vessel was fit. Loading commenced on September 10. A dispute arose as to when laytime commenced and the question was (1) whether the NOR was a nullity as the vessel was not ready, so that laytime commenced on September 10, or (2) whether laytime commenced, but was subject to a deduction for time lost. The arbitrators found for S on the basis of (2) and C appealed.

Held, dismissing the appeal, that (1) in construing the laytime cl.9, there was a strong presumption that there was to be consistency between the treatment of physical unreadiness and free pratique; (2) cl.8 imposed the same duties as at common law, namely to ensure that the holds were fit to receive cargo before giving NOR and (3) the effect of cl.8 and cl.9 was to require C to pay for waiting time at the anchorage when they had not provided a berth, but that S would bear the risk of delay if the vessel caused delay after arrival at the berth because she was unready, *Linardos, The* [1994] 2 Lloyd's Rep. 28, [1994] C.L.Y. 4068 followed.

UNITED NATIONS FOOD AND AGRICULTURE ORGANISATION v. CASPIAN NAVIGATION INC (THE JAY GANESH) [1994] 2 Lloyd's Rep. 358, Colman, J., QBD (Comm Ct).

5316. Civil procedure–procedural defects in writ–time limits expired–whether writ should be amended

[Maritime Conventions Act 1911 s.8; Rules of the Supreme Court Ord.2.]

A ship, owned by NM and managed by LM, collided with MC's ship on July 22, 1990. On July 2, 1992 a writ in personam was issued in the name of LM, rather than NM. The writ had other procedural defects, namely that the writ was issued in the Commercial Court rather than the Admiralty Court, LM were named as a Greek company, not a Liberian company and MC's address was given in the wrong state. The writ was also served on MC's managers in Monaco, although MC was incorporated in Gibraltar. The time bar under the Maritime Conventions Act 1911 s.8 had expired. NM applied to amend the writ and for an extension of time.

Held, that (1) the general procedural defects were not of sufficient consequence to merit the setting aside of the proceedings under the Rules of the Supreme Court Ord.2 r.1 and could be cured by the transference of the proceedings to the Admiralty Court and a costs order; (2) although the service on MC's managers, rather than MC, was irregular, it was not a nullity within the RSC Ord.2 r.1 and the judge had a discretion to allow the service to stand; (3) the service would be allowed to stand as, inter alia, the parties had agreed jurisdiction, leave to serve in Gibraltar could have been obtained, all communications to D were in practice forwarded to its managers and D had suffered no prejudice; (4) although an amendment to the writ would substitute a new party, there would be no relation back to the time of issue of the writ and the claim would be time barred, *Jay Bola, The* [1992] 2 Lloyd's Rep. 62, [1992] C.L.Y. 3628 applied; (5) under the Maritime Conventions Act 1911 time limit was not a "relevant period of limitation" under Ord.15 r.6 or Ord.20 r.5, although there was a "mistake" within Ord.20 r.5 which would otherwise have allowed an amendment; (6) an extension of time could be granted under the Maritime Conventions Act 1911 s.8, even where there was a misnomer in the writ attributable to the fault of the plaintiff's solicitor, and there was a good reason to extend time as MC had suffered no prejudice and (7) accordingly, the present action would be struck out, but NM would be granted an extension of time in order to enable a new writ to be issued.

LEOND MARITIME INC v. MC AMETHYST SHIPPING LTD (THE ANNA L) [1994] 2 Lloyd's Rep. 379, Phillips, J., QBD (Comm Ct).

5317. Collisions at sea–apportionment of liabilitly–overtaking manoeuvres–good seamanship requirements–need for avoiding action by overtaken vessel

[International Regulations for Preventing Collisions at Sea 1972 r.17.]

The defendant owners of the vessel HS appealed against the Admiralty Court's finding that the vessel K was not at fault in the collision between the two ships. K was overtaken by HS and HS's stem struck the aft transom of K on the starboard side of central line. The weather was fine and visibility was about four miles at the time of the incident. HS was considerably larger than K and was moving at about twice K's speed. The owners objected that K was partly at fault for failing to take avoiding action when about to be overtaken.

Held, allowing the appeal in part, that although the International Regulations for Preventing Collisions at Sea 1972 r.17(a)(iii) was expressed in permissive terms situations might arise in which good seamanship required a vessel being overtaken to take avoiding action before the stage at which r.17(b) came into operation. The overtaken vessel K was at fault for failing to alter course to port between 20 and 30 degrees when HS was a mile away and failed to alter course despite K's sound and light signals. However, the great bulk of the blame lay with the overtaking vessel HS and therefore 15 per cent of the blame only would be apportioned to the overtaken vessel K.

KOSCIERZYNA, THE AND HANJIN SINGAPORE, THE [1996] 2 Lloyd's Rep. 124, Sir Thomas Bingham, M.R., CA.

5318. Collisions at sea–apportionment of liability

D's vessel collided with the port side of P's vessel in the access channel to Buenos Aires in good visibility. The question was whether either or both were to blame.

Held, that (1) P was in a position to starboard of the midchannel; (2) D was at fault in overshooting a bend and allowing herself to approach too close to a bank at excessive speed so that she altered her heading to port and collided with P in P's part of the channel and (3) accordingly, D was wholly responsible for the collision.

SAN NICHOLAS, THE AND FRATERNITY L, THE [1994] 2 Lloyd's Rep. 582, Clarke, J., QBD (Adm Ct).

5319. Collisions at sea–apportionment of liability

[International Regulations for Preventing Collisions at Sea 1972 r.15.]

P and D's vessels collided at night in good visibility, the starboard bow of D striking the port side of P. D claimed to have taken action to avoid a tug and tow which P denied existed. The question was whether either or both were to blame and the appropriate apportionment of liability.

Held, that (1) P was not keeping a good lookout; (2) D did see a radar echo of vessels other than P; (3) D did alter course to port to avoid the tug and tow and went hard aport shortly before the collision; (4) D was not keeping a good lookout and the vessels were shaping to pass too close; (5) the vessels were crossing so as to involve the risk of collision within the International Regulations for Preventing Collisions at Sea 1972 r.15 and it was the duty of D to keep out of the way of P; (6) even if it was necessary for D to avoid the tug and tow, it was imprudent of D to attempt to pass in front of P and D should have altered course to starboard; (7) the failure of D to take early and substantial action under r.16 to keep well clear of P was a significant cause of the collision; (8) P altered course slightly to port when the vessels were two miles apart and failed to stop engines, thus constituting a breach of r.17; (9) failure by both vessels to sound signals was not causative and (10) P was 30 per cent to blame and D 70 per cent.

ANGELIC SPIRIT, THE AND Y MARINER, THE [1994] 2 Lloyd's Rep. 595, Clarke, J., QBD (Adm Ct).

5320. Collisions at sea–apportionment of liability–admissibility of expert evidence

Two ships collided in the Lynn Cut, a narrow channel on the River Ouse. The issue arose whether responsibility lay with the negligence of the defendants or with that of the plaintiffs. There were issues raised as to the admissibility of expert evidence.

Held, that the court considered the evidence of the Nautical Assessors, the place of the collision, the angle of collision and the navigation of the vessels. Evidence would be admitted in this case, not only of "speed and angle of blow report", but also expert evidence containing or commenting on reconstructions. On the facts, the plaintiffs were 25 per cent at fault for the collision and the defendants 75 per cent. The defendants had proceeded down the channel at speed without the pilot on board being able to ascertain the ship's position or heading nor the position of the plaintiff's vessel. However, the plaintiffs failed to move to the starboard side of the channel and proceed with utmost caution.

ANTARES II AND VICTORY, THE [1996] 2 Lloyd's Rep. 482, Geoffrey Brice Q.C., QBD (Adm Ct).

5321. Collisions at sea–apportionment of liability–admission of computer evidence

The Devotion, D, was entering a narrow channel southbound at the entrance to the Panama Canal and was in the process of picking up the pilot to the west of the channel. The Golden Polydinamos, G, had been proceeding in the centre of the channel. D's heading drifted to port and a collision took place, with the starboard bow of G and the starboard shoulder of D coming into contact. Disputes arose as to the place of collision and the angle of the blow. The judge held that the principal cause of the collision was failures by D and that the liabilities would be apportioned 75 per cent to D and 25 per cent to G. D appealed.

Held, dismissing the appeal, that (1) the court would not admit fresh evidence of plots produced by a computer program, as the evidence was available at the time of the trial, *Ladd v. Marshall* [1954] 1 W.L.R. 1489, [1954] C.L.Y. 2507 applied; (2) a party who wishes to use such a program should disclose it an early stage, so that experts on either side can agree on its validity or formulate any criticisms and the judge should be given the opportunity to test any proposed finding against the program; (3) the judge was right to reject that possibility as the validity of the program had not been agreed and it would not have been material to his decision; (4) the judge was correct to find that G was approximately in the centre, or just to the west of, the centre line of the channel when she altered course and (5) the judge was correct to find that both vessels were at fault and the court would not interfere with his apportionment on appeal, *Koningen Juliana, The* [1975] 2 Lloyd's Rep. 111, [1975] C.L.Y. 3181, applied.

DEVOTION, THE AND GOLDEN POLYDINAMOS, THE [1995] 1 Lloyd's Rep. 589, Glidewell, L.J., CA.

5322. Collisions at sea–apportionment of liability–application of international rules for preventing collisions

[International Regulations for Preventing Collisions at Sea 1992.]

Two vessels, CD and AE, collided off Singapore. The collision occurred within a traffic separation scheme. The evidence from the two vessels was contradictory with each contending that the other was at fault at the time of the collision. Both vessels had been unaware of the other. CD had altered course to change to the west-bound lane. AE had altered course, remaining in the west-bound lane.

Held, that (1) CD was at fault in failing to keep a good look-out and in failing to appreciate the presence of AE until a very late stage. On either of the sets of evidence, CD would have been at fault in crossing into the west-bound lane of traffic at an angle of between 100 degrees and 120 degrees rather than at right angles. AE was at fault in failing to detect CD at the latest when she was about to enter the west-bound lane. It was not sufficient to say that if CD had been keeping a good look-out, it would have noticed AE's change of course and (2) the actions of both vessels were at fault. Under the International Regulations for Preventing Collisions at Sea 1992 r.15 and r.16 it was incumbent on AE to take early and substantive action to avoid the collision. AE was more to blame for the collision than CD. AE failed to take urgent action and in fact turned towards the CD. Fault was therefore apportioned as to 60 per cent and 40 per cent respectively between them.

CENTURY DAWN AND ASIAN ENERGY, *Re* [1996] 1 Lloyd's Rep. 125, Hirst, L.J., CA.

5323. Collisions at sea–choice of forum–collision occurring in Netherlands–Chinese defendant shipowners claiming Netherlands forum non conveniens–relevant factors in determining forum

[Supreme Court Act 1981 s.21, s.22; Brussels Convention on Jurisdiction and the Enforcement of Judgments in Civil and Commercial Matters 1968 Art.4.]

The XY caused a collision between vessels in the Netherlands. The XY and its sister ship, the AKJ were arrested in the Netherlands. Actions were brought in England and Rotterdam. The defendants applied for the English action to be stayed in favour of the action in Rotterdam on the ground of forum non conveniens. The plaintiffs argued that the action should not be stayed because the English court was the court first seised of the matter and had a discretion to hear the matter in any event.

Held, granting a stay that the English court had jurisdiction under the Supreme Court Act 1981 s.21 and s.22. This jurisdiction was not displaced by the Brussels Convention on Jurisdiction and the Enforcement of Judgments in Civil and Commercial Matters 1968 Art.4. However, notwithstanding the Convention the court retained the right and duty to decide whether to exercise jurisdiction or to decline on the grounds of forum non conveniens. The defendant was not domiciled within the EU. The Netherlands was the more appropriate forum for deciding issues of quantum on the basis that the plaintiff's vessel was managed there and the collision had occurred there. Furthermore, neither party had any connection with England.

XIN YANG, THE AND AN KANG JIANG, THE [1996] 2 Lloyd's Rep. 217, Clarke, J., QBD (Adm Ct).

5324. Collisions at sea–choice of forum–stay of proceedings–limits of recovery different in England and Singapore–where best to proceed on issues of quantum and liability

[Convention on Limitation of Liability of Owners of Sea-going Ships 1957; Merchant Shipping Act 1894 s.503; Merchant Shipping Act 1979 s.17; Singapore Merchant Shipping Act 1970 s.272.]

A British vessel collided with C's jetty in Singapore waters causing considerable damage. C's claim was estimated at $10.5 million. B admitted liability but applied for a stay of the action in England on the basis that the limit on recovery in Singapore would be lower than that in England. C contended that if the action proceeded in Singapore, they would be unable to recover the difference between their loss and the limit in Singapore. The defendants submitted that there was no relevant juridical advantage because the English court would apply the lex loci delicti.

Held, that (1) Singapore would not be the more appropriate forum if the only issues in the action were as to fault and privity. However, the true issue of fact here was the quantum of C's claim. The collision took place in Singapore waters, C were based in Singapore, the vessel was a British ship, B was an English company. On these facts it would be much more convenient for the trial of the issues of quantum to take place in Singapore; (2) the Singapore Merchant Shipping Act 1970 s.272, in material respects the same as the Merchant Shipping Act 1894 s.503, conferred only procedural rights. Therefore, if the claim were litigated in England, the English court would not apply the Singapore limit; (3) the effect of the Merchant Shipping Act 1979 s.17 was to give the Convention on Limitation of Liability of Owners of Sea-going Ships 1957 direct effect in England. The purpose of the Convention was to introduce a new limitation regime regardless of where the incident occurred and (4) the ends of justice would be best served if C were permitted to proceed in England. C had established a juridical advantage in having the matter heard in England. The most appropriate solution would be to stay the action temporarily. The issue of quantum would be heard in Singapore. The issue as to a permanent stay would be heard thereafter.

CALTEX SINGAPORE PTE LTD v. BP SHIPPING LTD [1996] 1 Lloyd's Rep. 286, Clarke, J., QBD (Adm Ct).

5325. Collisions at sea–pilot negligence–domestic legislation retrospectively depriving compensation claim–proportionality–financial justifications insufficient to justify retrospective legislation

[European Convention on Human Rights 1950 Protocol 1 Art.1, Art.50.]

P's ships were involved in a collision which they submitted was due to the negligence of Belgian pilots. Deprived of their claims for compensation by retrospective legislation, they claimed a violation of the European Convention on Human Rights 1950 Protocol 1 Art.1 and sought just satisfaction under Art.50 of the Convention.

Held, that there had been a violation of Art.1 of Protocol 1. Claims for compensation under rules of tort came into existence as soon as the damage had occurred and constituted an asset amounting to a possession within the meaning of Art.1. The subsequent legislation exempting the State from liability for negligent acts resulted in an interference with the right to the peaceful enjoyment of possessions. As regards the notion of proportionality, national authorities were allowed a certain margin of appreciation in determining what was in the public interest. The notion of public interest was necessarily extensive and laws enacting the expropriation of property necessarily involved political, economic and social issues which allowed a wide margin of appreciation. Any interference with property must strike a balance between the interests of the community and the protection of the individual's fundamental rights and there must be reasonable proportionality between the means employed and the aim sought to achieve this. In this case, the taking of property without the payment of any amount reasonably related to its value would amount to a disproportionate interference and justifiable only in exceptional circumstances.

The Act extinguished claims for very high damages that P could have pursued against the pilots. The financial justifications cited by the Government were not sufficient to justify the retrospective legislation. The question of pecuniary damages under Art.50 was reserved to take account of any agreement that might be reached between the parties.

PRESSOS COMPANIA NAVIERA SA v. BELGIUM (1996) 21 E.H.R.R. 301, R Ryssdal (President), ECHR.

5326. Conflict of laws–relationship between Arrest Convention 1952 and Brussels Convention–jurisdiction of court

[Brussels Convention on Jurisdiction and the Enforcement of Judgments in Civil and Commercial Matters 1968 Art.57; Arrest Convention 1952 Art.7.]

D, a German shipowner, carried a cargo of steel from the UK to Spain. P made a claim against D for cargo damage. D entered a caveat against arrest with a praecipe undertaking to acknowledge any writ and to give bail. P issued a writ in rem and arrested the vessel in order to obtain jurisdiction under the Arrest Convention 1952. She was released on provision of a bail bond and D acknowledged service. D applied to set aside the writ and for an order that the Admiralty Court had no jurisdiction under the Brussels Convention of Jurisdiction and the Enforcement of Judgments in Civil and Commercial Matters 1968 Art.2 because D was domiciled in Germany and that the Arrest Convention 1952 did not apply.

Held, dismissing D's appeal, that (1) there would have been no jurisdiction against D unless granted by the Jurisdiction and Judgments Convention 1968 Art.57; (2) the Arrest Convention 1952 and the Jurisdiction and Judgments Convention 1968 were to be read together and there was no reason to impose any implicit restriction on the effect of Art.57. Where there was a special provision in the Arrest Convention 1952 it would govern and the jurisdiction available under that Convention would apply even where the shipowner was domiciled in another EC state; (3) the definition of "arrest" within the Convention related to the character of the legal process and not to the motivation of the party which initiated the process. It was irrelevant that the purpose of the arrest was not to obtain security, but to found jurisdiction, *Deichland, The* [1990] 1 Q.B. 361, [1990] C.L.Y. 4048 considered and (4) the reference to "domestic law" in Art.7 of the Arrest Convention 1952 could not be read as a reference to the Jurisdiction and Judgments Convention 1968 as incorporated into English law and the enactment of the Civil Jurisdiction and Judgments Act 1982 had not restricted the power of the Admiralty Court to determine the merits of a maritime claim once it had jurisdiction founded on arrest.

ANNA H, THE [1995] 1 Lloyd's Rep. 11, Hoffmann, L.J., CA.

5327. Contracts–repudiation–ship building contracts–interpretation of the contract in relation to non-payment and repudiation

S, a Polish shipyard, contracted under English law to build ships for the second defendants, A, a Liberian company owned by L. The ships were to be purchased in four instalments and the first instalment was paid on all six vessels. Following a fall in freight rates, A informed S that they wished to renegotiate the contracts as they could not finance the deal. S finished work on the laying of the keel, after which the second instalment was due, and claimed the amount due. When it was not received, they notified A that they were treating the contract as repudiated. The same thing happened in respect of the second ship. Summary judgment was given against A for $11,055,600 in respect of the two ships and A appealed. The second action was for the instalments following keel-laying in the remaining four ships and for damages for all six ships. Leave to defend was granted for the claim for the instalments and the claim for damages was dismissed for being premature. S appealed. The questions were whether the contract provided for circumstances when the instalments were unpaid and when the contract was treated as repudiated, and whether S was entitled to the second instalments.

Held, allowing A's appeal and dismissing S's appeal, that (1) the contract allowed S to treat the contract as repudiated. However, S were then required to sell the ship and distribute the proceeds as detailed in the contract. A was not entitled to repayment of instalments already paid and S was not entitled to the outstanding instalments owing to the repudiation. The contract displaced any common law remedies, *Hyundai Heavy Industries Co Ltd v. Papadopoulos* [1980] 1 W.L.R. 1129, [1980] C.L.Y. 2504 distinguished and (2) for the first two contracts S had a legitimate interest in keeping the contracts open until the second instalments became due so it was not bound to treat the contracts as repudiated under the doctrine in *White & Carter (Councils) Ltd v. McGregor* [1962] A.C. 413.

STOCZNIA GDANSKA SA v. LATVIAN SHIPPING CO; SUB NOM. STOCZNIA GDANSKA SA v. LATREEFERS INC [1996] 2 Lloyd's Rep. 132, Staughton, L.J., CA.

5328. Contracts–sale of ship–agreement subject to "terms to be mutually agreed"–whether binding agreement concluded orally

KSC alleged that MS had agreed to buy a ship and to submit any disputes to arbitration. MS was a state organisation which co-ordinated the purchase of ships for scrapping with brokers submitting particulars to regular meetings of MS's negotiating committee. The committee would make "firm" offers or offers "sub recon" which needed confirmation by the committee. On acceptance of an offer, a memorandum of agreement, MOA, on the Norwegian Saleform would be drawn up and signed by the committee. KSC offered a ship to MS which orally agreed to the offer, "subject to the terms to be agreed upon". KSC sent a confirmatory letter stating "otherwise usual [MS] terms to be mutually agreed". No MOA was ever drawn up as MS withdrew from the sale. KSC contended that there was a binding contract and that the terms were to be the MOA used for a number of previous sales between the parties, with London arbitration, subject to logical amendments. MS argued that each MOA needed separate negotiation and signature and that nothing had been finalised.

Held, that (1) the court's task was to establish the objective intentions of the parties, *Pagnan SpA v. Feed Products Ltd* [1987] 2 Lloyd's Rep. 601, [1988] C.L.Y. 429, applied; (2) although the scrap market may have required quick decisions, no final agreement had been reached by the time MS withdrew, as both parties contemplated that further negotiations would be needed on matters of detail; (3) it was not intended that a "firm" offer was to be binding from the moment of acceptance and the distinction between the "firm" and "sub recon" offers was here an indication merely of the speed with which matters would progress to a formal signing of the MOA and (4) if there had been an agreement, the expression "usual [MS] terms to be mutually agreed" would have included provision for London arbitration.

METAL SCRAP TRADE CORP LTD v. KATE SHIPPING CO LTD (NO.2) (THE GLADYS) [1994] 2 Lloyd's Rep. 402, Potter, J., QBD (Comm Ct).

5329. Contracts–sale of ship–Norwegian Saleform 1983–obligation to notify classification society of defects arising before delivery–whether seller obliged to give notification of defects arising before contract

S sold a vessel to B and disputes arose as to the condition of the vessel on delivery. In March certain equipment had been surveyed. On May 10 the vessel was inspected by B and a Norwegian Saleform 1983 contract was signed on May 14. On May 18 the equipment was again surveyed by B so as to provide a certificate with six months' validity as required by additional cl.19. Under cl.11 S was obliged to deliver the vessel "with present class fully maintained, free of recommendations" made by the classification society. The question was whether under cl.11 S was obliged to notify their classification society "prior to delivery" of matters which affected class "coming to their knowledge", (1) as from the contract date, or (2) as from the date of the last classification survey before contract, or (3) some other date, e.g. that of B's last inspection. The arbitrators found that the relevant date was either (1), or possibly (3) and that S was not in breach as their knowledge of the defect arose before the date of contract. The judge held that the relevant date was (2), but the Court of Appeal held that the words referred to knowledge of which S had become aware after the date of contract. B appealed.

Held, allowing the appeal, that (1) there was no commercial reason for confining the words "coming to their knowledge" to the period subsequent to the contract and the contractual obligation was intended to be co-extensive with the obligation of the classification society and (2) as a matter of construction, the words had no temporal significance and were apt to cover knowledge acquired both before and after the contract.

NIOBE MARITIME CORP v. TRADAX OCEAN TRANSPORTATION SA (THE NIOBE) [1995] 1 Lloyd's Rep. 579, Lord Mackay, L.C., HL.

5330. Discovery–evidential significance of material sought–documents related to site of fire and explosion relevant

Explosions and a fire occurred on M's ship while at anchor. The vessel subsequently sank and its cargo was irredeemably damaged or lost. O sought discovery of documents of a particular class. Inter alia, O sought discovery of documents which did not relate to those parts of the ship where the explosions and fire occurred.

Held, ordering discovery in less broad terms than sought that the issue of relevant documents was related to the pleadings and the issue of whether or not they would advance O's case. In such a case as this, the great number of documents would differ in their comparative evidential significance. The documents must be shown to offer the applicant a real possibility of evidential materiality. Documents which were not shown to relate to the parts of the ship where the explosions or fire occurred were not relevant.

O CO v. M CO [1996] 2 Lloyd's Rep. 347, Colman, J., QBD (Comm Ct).

5331. Dundee Port Authority. See SHIPPING. §7365

5332. Ferries–safety at sea–standards

The Department of Transport issued a press release entitled *UK signs Stockholm Agreement on ferry safety* (Press notice: 208), published on July 1, 1996. Shipping Minister Lord Goschen has signed the Stockholm Agreement, which applies higher survivability standards to roll on roll off ferries operating in northern Europe. All ferries must meet the new standard by October 1, 2002. A timetable has been published showing the date by which each ferry operating from UK ports is required to meet the standard.

5333. Fishing vessels–decommissioning grants

FISHING VESSELS (DECOMMISSIONING) SCHEME 1996, SI 1996 1242; made under the Fisheries Act 1981 s.15. In force: May 9, 1996; £2.40.

This Scheme provides for grants in respect of the decommissioning of fishing vessels registered in the United Kingdom. It sets out requirements to be met in respect of applications for grants and deals with the consideration and approval of applications; the eligibility and claims for payment of grant; the procedure for the decommissioning of a vessel; the surrender of licences and removal from the register; damaged or destroyed vessels; the amount of grant; the method of payment of the grants and powers and assistance granted to authorised officers.

5334. Fishing vessels–safety at sea

FISHING VESSELS (SAFETY PROVISIONS) (AMENDMENT) RULES 1996, SI 1996 2419; made under the Merchant Shipping Act 1995 s.122. In force: October 31, 1996; £0.65.

These Rules further amend the Fishing Vessels (Safety Provisions) Rules 1975 (SI 1975 330). They provide that surveys of radio equipment on fishing vessels carried out in the United Kingdom or elsewhere shall be carried out by surveyors appointed by an appropriate Certifying Authority authorised by the Secretary of State. The reference to British Telecom in relation to the appointment of surveyors for such surveys is removed.

5335. Harbours–Newlyn–constitutions

NEWLYN PIER AND HARBOUR (REVISION OF CONSTITUTION OF COMMISSIONERS) ORDER 1996, SI 1996 197; made under the Harbours Act 1964 s.15. In force: March 1, 1996; £1.95.

The constitution of the Newlyn Pier Harbour Commissioners is altered by the revision of the Newlyn Pier and Harbour Order 1906. The maximum number of Commissioners is increased from nine to ten and of those ten, three must be Boat-owner Commissioners, one a Fish Merchant Commissioner, one a County Council Commissioner, four must be appointed by the Minister for Agriculture, Fisheries and Food and the option of one coopted Commissioner is given. Further changes relate to the voting rights, the election of Commissioners, the quorum for meetings of Commissioners and the availability to the public of records of proceedings. The Schedule to the Order details election procedure for Boat-owners Commissioners and Fish Merchant Commissioners.

5336. Harbours–revision–Aberystwyth

ABERYSTWYTH HARBOUR REVISION ORDER 1996, SI 1996 1183; made under the Harbours Act 1964 s.14. In force: December 19, 1995; £0.65.

This Order amends Aberystwyth Harbour Act 1987 s.5(4)(5) which relates to powers to construct works, so as to provide for only one means of access to the development authorised by that Act. The applicants for the Order are Cyngor Dosbarth Ceredigion and those trading as IMP Developments, who are Meirion Ellis Jones, Ian Alexander and Ifan Prys Edwards all of Glanyrafon Industrial Estate, Llanbadarn Fawr, Aberystwyth, Dyfed.

5337. Harbours–revision–Bridlington

BRIDLINGTON HARBOUR REVISION ORDER 1996, SI 1996 3040; made under the Harbours Act 1964 s.14. In force: December 12, 1996; £1.55.

This Order authorises the reclamation of part of the upper section of Bridlington harbour, the construction of a slipway adjoining that reclaimed part and provides for increases in the amounts which the Harbour Commissioners may borrow both permanently and temporarily.

5338. Harbours–revision–Harwich

HARWICH PARKESTON QUAY HARBOUR REVISION ORDER 1996, SI 1996 2037; made under the Harbours Act 1964 s.14. In force: August 6, 1996; £2.40.

This Order empowers Harwich International Port Ltd to construct a new berth and associated facilities for vessels, including the replacement of an existing linkspan at Parkeston Quay.

5339. Harbours–revision–Ilfracombe

ILFRACOMBE HARBOUR REVISION ORDER 1996, SI 1996 2103; made under the Harbours Act 1964 s.14. In force: August 19, 1996; £1.95.

This Order enables the North Devon DC to provide a launchway for the lifeboat from the new lifeboat station in The Strand, Ilfracombe and extending into the bed and foreshore of Ilfracombe Harbour.

5340. Harbours–revision–Weymouth

WEYMOUTH HARBOUR REVISION ORDER 1996, SI 1996 15; made under the Harbours Act 1964 s.14. In force: January 15, 1996; £0.65.

This Order permits the leasing of part of the Inner Harbour of the harbour of Weymouth by the Weymouth and Portland BC in order to construct and operate a marina.

5341. Harbours–revision–Whitehaven

WHITEHAVEN HARBOUR REVISION ORDER 1996, SI 1996 1627; made under the Harbours Act 1964 s.14. In force: July 8, 1996; £3.20.

This Order authorises the Whitehaven Harbour Commissioners to construct works at the harbour, including a new lock between the Outer and Inner Harbour, the extension and strengthening of the harbour walls, and the provision of piled moorings together with pontoon systems in the Inner Harbour, Custom House Dock, South Harbour and Queens Dock. It excludes certain commercial vessels from the use of the harbour and restricts the Inner Harbour, Custom House Dock and South Harbour to pleasure craft and certain other vessels. It also makes provision for the management of the harbour.

5342. Harbours–revision–Yarmouth

YARMOUTH (ISLE OF WIGHT) HARBOUR REVISION ORDER 1996, SI 1996 2480; made under the Harbours Act 1964 s.14. In force: October 14, 1996; £1.10.

This Order extends the limits within which the Yarmouth (Isle of Wight) Harbour Commissioners have authority.

5343. Hovercraft–transfer of responsibility–consequential amendments

HOVERCRAFT (GENERAL) (AMENDMENT) ORDER 1996, SI 1996 3173; made under the Hovercraft Act 1968 s.1. In force: February 1, 1997; £1.10.

This Order further amends the Hovercraft (General) Order 1972 (SI 1972 674) by removing references to the Civil Aviation Authority, and includes references to the Secretary of State consequential upon the Marine Safety Agency of the Department of Transport taking over responsibility for the certification of the safety of hovercraft. In addition Part II and Part III of the 1972 Order cease to apply to certain hovercraft to which the High-Speed Craft Code applies as they are now regulated by the Merchant Shipping (High Speed Craft) Regulations 1996. Experimental Certificates and Types Certificates will no longer be issued.

5344. Insurance–reinsurance pooling agreement–whether jurisdiction to grant anti suit injunction

[Rules of the Supreme Court Ord.29, Ord.16; Brussels Convention on Jurisdiction and the Enforcement of Judgments in Civil and Commercial Matters 1968 Art.6.]

Disputes arose about an environmental impairment reinsurance pool set up to provide cover for US pollution risks. "Front" insurers would provide direct cover in the US, although all the claims handling and underwriting was administered in London. Some parties began actions in the US, with claims for punitive damages, and the question arose whether these parties could be restrained by injunction from proceeding in the US and whether the court had jurisdiction to make such orders. The orders were sought by a third party domiciled in the EC.

Held, declining to make the orders, that (1) Rules of the Supreme Court Ord.29 r.1, contemplated applications for interlocutory injunctions only, in which a separate inter partes trial was anticipated, rather than final injunctions; (2) the wording of RSC Ord.29 r.1 was wide enough to cover a third party seeking interlocutory relief against a foreign plaintiff, as the latter had submitted to the risk of counterclaims and third party claims, provided that leave was obtained under RSC Ord.16; (3) it followed that the court in its inherent jurisdiction could permit a third party to apply for an anti-suit injunction within the confines of an existing action to which a foreign plaintiff was already party, without the need to issue new proceedings by way of originating summons; (4) the inherent jurisdiction arose if it was just and equitable to prevent improper vexation or oppression and/or to do justice between the parties, and was a general power exercisable even where the foreign forum was the sole rather than alternative forum for proceedings, *Societe National Industrielle Aerospatiale ("SNIA") v. Lee Kui Jak* [1987] A.C. 871, [1987] C.L.Y. 3024 considered; (5) alternatively, if it was necessary for the third party to proceed by originating summons, the prosecution of the US proceedings was no breach or invasion of the third party's right to be sued in accordance with the Brussels Convention on Jurisdiction and the Enforcement of Judgments in Civil and Commercial Matters 1968 Art.6, *Harrods (Buenos Aires) Ltd, Re* [1992] Ch. 72, [1991] C.L.Y. 476, applied; (6) there was no need to exclude from the Brussels Convention on Jurisdiction and the Enforcement of Judgments in Civil and Commercial Matters 1968 Art.6 a claim for an anti-suit injunction and Art.6 could apply to many of the foreign domiciled defendants which were sued as a number of defendants in the courts for the place where a number of other defendants were domiciled. The burden was on the foreign domiciled defendants to show that it was not expedient to hear the actions together so as to avoid the risk of "irreconcilable judgments", *Athanasios Kalfelis v. Bankhaus Schroder, Munchmeyer, Hengst & Co* [1988] E.C.R. 5565, [1991] C.L.Y. 3936 applied and (7) on the facts there was no relevant vexation or oppression.

ERAS EIL ACTIONS, THE [1995] 1 Lloyd's Rep. 64, Potter, J., QBD (Comm Ct).

5345. Law of the sea–tribunals

INTERNATIONAL TRIBUNAL FOR THE LAW OF THE SEA (IMMUNITIES AND PRIVILEGES) ORDER 1996, SI 1996 272; made under the International Organisations Act 1968 s.5. In force: in accordance with Art.1; £0.65.

This Order confers privileges and immunities on the members of the International Tribunal for the Law of the Sea. These privileges and immunities are conferred in accordance with Annex VI of the United Nations Convention on the Law of the Sea (Cmnd 8941). The Order will enable Her Majesty's Government to give effect to that Convention and will come into force on the date on which the Convention enters into force in respect of the United Kingdom.

5346. Liens–mortgagees powers and duties–mortgagees' rights taking precedence over charterers' claim for lien–jurisdiction of Admiralty Court where claim brought in Panamanian Maritime Court

B lent money to the owners of the Rama on mortgage. The ship had insufficient bunkers on board to complete a charter. The ship was arrested by B who brought Panamanian proceedings seeking an order for sale. C, the charterers of the Rama, brought Panamanian proceedings seeking damages from the owners on grounds of deceit and negligent misrepresentation, alleging that the owners knew the ship had a shortage of bunkers and was incapable of completing the voyage. The issue arose whether C had a maritime lien which took priority over B's claim under the mortgage under English law. B applied for a declaration.

Held, granting a declaration, that in the interests of justice the Admiralty Division of the High Court was a better forum than the Panamanian Maritime Court to determine the issues concerned. None of the loss suffered by C was done or caused by the Rama as a physical object. None of C's claims gave rise to a maritime lien under English law whether formulated in deceit, negligence, conversion or breach of contract.

BERLINER BANK AG v. C CZARNIKOW SUGAR LTD (THE RAMA) [1996] 2 Lloyd's Rep. 281, Clarke, J., QBD (Adm Ct).

5347. Merchant Navy–fees

MERCHANT SHIPPING (FEES) REGULATIONS 1996, SI 1996 3243; made under the Merchant Shipping Act 1995 s.302. In force: February 1, 1997; £3.20.

These Regulations revoke and replace the Merchant Shipping (Fees) Regulations 1995 (SI 1995 1893 as amended by SI 1996 2419). They prescribe changes in some of the rates charged, and introduce new fees.

5348. Merchant Navy–fees

MERCHANT SHIPPING (FEES) (AMENDMENT) REGULATIONS 1996, SI 1996 2632; made under the Merchant Shipping Act 1995 s.302. In force: November 1, 1996; £0.65.

These Regulations amend the Merchant Shipping (Fees) Regulations 1995 (SI 1995 1893). The fees charged for services performed pursuant to the Radio Rules are reduced to £23 per hour for fishing vessels and £26 per hour for other ships in respect of time occupied by the survey and to £32 in respect of all administrative and other work for all vessels.

5349. Merchant Navy–fishing vessels–medical stores

MERCHANT SHIPPING AND FISHING VESSELS (MEDICAL STORES) (AMENDMENT) REGULATIONS 1996, SI 1996 2821; made under the Medicines Act 1968 s.103; the European Communities Act 1972 s.2; and the Merchant Shipping Act 1995 s.85, s.86. In force: December 5, 1995; £0.65.

These Regulations amend the Merchant Shipping and Fishing Vessels (Medical Stores) Regulations 1995 (SI 1995 1802). The amendment adopts the wording of Council Directive 92/29 of March 31, 1992 ([1992] OJ L113/19), which the 1995 Regulations implement, in defining the area of operation for vessels carrying category C stores as "very close to shore".

5350. Merchant Navy–Gibraltar

MERCHANT SHIPPING (CATEGORISATION OF REGISTRIES OF OVERSEAS TERRITORIES) (GIBRALTAR) ORDER 1996, SI 1996 280; made under the Merchant Shipping Act 1995 s.18. In force: March 19, 1996; £0.65.

Gibraltar is added to the list of overseas territories contained in the Merchant Shipping (Categorisation of Registries of Overseas Territories) Order 1992 (SI 1992 1736) which are assigned to Category 1 of the category of registries. This category places no restriction on the tonnage or types of ships which may be registered.

5351. Merchant Navy–Gibraltar

MERCHANT SHIPPING (GIBRALTAR COLOURS) ORDER 1996, SI 1996 281; made under the Merchant Shipping Act 1995 s.2. In force: March 19, 1996; £1.10.

Ships registered in Gibraltar are authorised to fly a flag consisting of the red ensign defaced with the arms of Gibraltar. The Red Ensign Flag of Gibraltar is detailed in the Schedule to the Order with the Union Flag occupying the upper left quartile of the flag and the castle shield and motto centred within the right hand half of the flag.

5352. Merchant Navy–high speed craft

MERCHANT SHIPPING (HIGH-SPEED CRAFT) REGULATIONS 1996, SI 1996 3188; made under the Merchant Shipping Act 1995 s.85, s.86. In force: February 1, 1997; £1.95.

These Regulations give effect to the International Code of Safety for High-Speed Craft, made mandatory by the Safety of Life at Sea Convention 1974.

5353. Merchant Navy–radio installations

MERCHANT SHIPPING (SURVEY AND CERTIFICATION) (AMENDMENT) REGULATIONS 1996, SI 1996 2418; made under the Merchant Shipping Act 1995 s.85, s.86. In force: October 31, 1996; £1.10.

These Regulations amend the Merchant Shipping (Survey and Certification) Regulations 1995 (SI 1995 1210). The principal amendment provides that the Secretary of State may authorise any person as an appropriate Certifying Authority in relation to radio installations for cargo ships. The reference to British Telecom in relation to such surveys is removed.

5354. Merchant Navy–safety at sea–distress signals

MERCHANT SHIPPING (DISTRESS SIGNALS AND PREVENTION OF COLLISIONS) REGULATIONS 1996, SI 1996 75; made under the Merchant Shipping act 1995 s.85; and the Merchant Shipping Act 1995 s.86. In force: May 1, 1996; £1.10.

These Regulations, which replace the Merchant Shipping (Distress Signals and Prevention of Collisions) Regulations 1989 (SI 1989 1798), give effect to the International Regulations for Preventing Collisions at Sea 1972. The International Regulations, as amended by the Maritime Organisation Resolution A736(18) are set out in Merchant Shipping Notice No. M.1642/COLREG 1 which can be obtained from the Marine Information Centre, Marine Safety Agency, Spring Place, 105 Commercial Road, Southampton, Hampshire SO15 1EG.

5355. Merchant Navy–safety at sea–equipment

MERCHANT SHIPPING (DELEGATION OF TYPE APPROVAL) REGULATIONS 1996, SI 1996 147; made under the Merchant Shipping Act 1995 s.85, s.86; and the Merchant Shipping (Prevention of Oil Pollution) Order 1983. In force: March 1, 1996; £0.65.

These Regulations enable certain bodies specified in a Merchant Shipping Notice to give type approval of safety equipment and arrangements for ships under regulations having effect as if made under the Merchant Shipping Act 1995 s.85(1)(a)(b) and under regulations made under the Merchant Shipping (Prevention of Oil Pollution) Order 1983 (SI 1983 1106).

5356. Merchant Navy–safety at sea–navigation–warnings

MERCHANT SHIPPING (NAVIGATIONAL WARNINGS) REGULATIONS 1996, SI 1996 1815; made under the Merchant Shipping Act 1995 s.85, s.86. In force: August 8, 1996; £1.10.

These Regulations give effect to certain provisions of the Safety of Life at Sea Convention 1974 Chapter V. They require the master of every United Kingdom ship to send warnings of navigational hazards encountered. They replace the Merchant Shipping (Navigational Warnings) Regulations 1980 (SI 1980 534), as amended. The warnings to be sent of certain hazards to navigation are now to be specified in a Merchant Shipping Notice, firstly Merchant Shipping Notice No. M.1641/NW1.

5357. Merchant Navy–safety at sea–reporting procedures

MERCHANT SHIPPING (MANDATORY SHIP REPORTING) REGULATIONS 1996, SI 1996 1749; made under the Merchant Shipping Act 1995 s.85, s.86. In force: August 1, 1996; £1.10.

These Regulations implement Reg.8-1 of Chapter V of the Safety of Life at Sea (SOLAS) Convention 1974, which was added by Maritime Safety Committee Resolution MSC.31 (63) adopted on May 23, 1994. They require United Kingdom ships to comply with ship reporting systems adopted by the International Maritime Organisation (IMO) pursuant to Reg.8-1 of Chapter V of SOLAS which are specified in Part 1, 2 or 3 of Volume 6 of the Admiralty List of Radio Signals and annotated as Mandatory System under SOLAS Regulation V/8-

1. Other ships are required to comply with any such system which was submitted to IMO by the United Kingdom, when in United Kingdom waters.

5358. Merchant Navy–surveys–inspections

MERCHANT SHIPPING (SHIP INSPECTION AND SURVEY ORGANISATIONS) REGULATIONS 1996, SI 1996 2908; made under the European Communities Act 1972 s.2; and the Merchant Shipping Act 1995 s.85, s.86. In force: December 31, 1996; £1.10.

These Regulations implement, in part, Council Directive 94/57 on common rules and standards for ship inspection and survey organisations. They provide for local representation of organisations authorised by the Marine Safety Agency pursuant to the Council Directive, provide for reciprocity of authorisation of recognised organisations and lay down duties of authorised organisations and recognised organisations. They also provide for withdrawal of recognition from organisations where the United Kingdom is satisfied the organisation no longer fulfills the criteria set out in a Directive required for recognition.

5359. Merchant Shipping Act 1995–Commencement and Appointed Day No.1 Order

MERCHANT SHIPPING ACT 1995 (APPOINTED DAY NO.1) ORDER 1996, SI 1996 1210 (C.20); made under the Merchant Shipping Act 1995 s.171, s.182. In force: bringing into force various provisions of the Act on May 3, 1996; £0.65.

This Order appoints May 30, 1996 as the day on which the Merchant Shipping Act 1995 Chapter III and Part VI Chapter IV come into force, and Sch.4 to the Act ceases to have effect. This date is the day on which the 1992 Protocols to the International Convention on Civil Liability for Oil Pollution Damage 1969, and the International Convention on the Establishment of an International Fund for Compensation for Oil Pollution Damage 1971, come into force.

5360. Ownership–action in rem against vessel not the subject of the claim–beneficial interest in vessel owned by Ukrainian state

[Supreme Court Act 1981 s.20.]

P, appealed against a decision that D were not the beneficial owners in relation to all the shares in the vessel "Zorinsk" at the time that the writ in this claim, for goods damaged during carriage on the ship Nazym Khikmet, was issued. D was sued and the Zorinsk was arrested. As the Zorinsk was not the ship involved in this claim, for an action in rem against the ship under the Supreme Court Act 1981 s.20(4) (b) (ii) and the arrest to be valid, P had to prove that D owned it. P argued that the judge had failed to address the contentions of their expert, that the powers that the Ukraine had over the vessel were the powers of a sovereign state imposed for ideological reasons rather than the property rights of an owner.

Held, dismissing the appeal, that (1) it was necessary to determine whether D was, under its own Ukrainian law, what an English court would regard as the beneficial owner, at the time the writ was issued and (2) once the Ukraine became independent the terms of state ownership were loosened but were not actually severed. The state retained the power to make ultimate decisions in relation to the use of the vessel. D's discretion in its use was wide in scope but did not amount to rights of a beneficial owner as recognised by English law.

OWNERS OF THE CARGO LATELY ON BOARD THE SHIP NAZYM KHIKMET v. OWNERS OF THE SHIP NAZYM KHIKMET [1996] 2 Lloyd's Rep. 362, Sir Thomas Bingham, M.R., CA.

5361. Pleasure craft

PLEASURE CRAFT (ARRIVAL AND REPORT) REGULATIONS 1996, SI 1996 1406; made under the Customs and Excise Management Act 1979 s.35, s.42. In force: June 28, 1996; £1.10.

These Regulations revoke and re-enact with changes the Pleasure Craft (Arrival and Report) Regulations 1990 (SI 1990 1169) as amended by the Customs and Excise (Single Market etc.) Regulations 1992 (SI 1992 3095). Under the 1990 Regulations, the requirement to notify arrival was confined to certain vessels based in the United Kingdom which arrived from a place outside the European Community. Also, the person responsible for a pleasure craft not based in the United Kingdom which arrived from a place outside the European Community was obliged in all cases to remain on board the vessel until an officer had boarded. These Regulations remove the distinction between United Kingdom and non-United Kingdom based vessels, require notification of arrival of all vessels and permit anyone on board to disembark if and when the person giving notification is told that an officer is not to board.

5362. Ports–Cromarty Firth Port Authority. See SHIPPING. §7364

5363. Practice Directions–caveats–release of vessel when court offices closed–praecipe for caveat may be filed by fax

The following Practice Direction was published by the Lord Chancellor's Department on January 15, 1996. When the Admiralty and Commercial Registry Office is closed, a praecipe for caveat against release may be filed by fax. The purpose of this direction is to avoid prejudice to those claimants seeking release of a vessel or cargo when court offices are closed to the public. The 24 hour manned fax number to be used is 0171 936 6056 and the fax should be accompanied by a note in the following form so that security staff can identify it easily: "Caveat against release" "Please find praecipe for caveat against release of the (name ship/identify cargo) for filing in the Admiralty and Commercial Registry"

PRACTICE DIRECTION (ADMIRALTY COURT: CAVEAT BY FAX) [1996] 2 All E.R. 210, P Miller (Admiralty Registrar), QBD (Adm Ct).

5364. Salvage–vessel threatening damage to environment–expenses incurred in salvage operation–whether fair rate should be remunerative or compensatory–whether expenses should continue to be paid for salvage operation once environmental risk removed

[International Convention on Salvage 1989 Art.13, Art.14.]

Held, that where expenses were payable to salvors under the International Convention on Salvage 1989 Art.14 in respect of an operation to salvage a vessel which threatened to cause environmental damage, the "fair rate" payable was to compensate for expenses incurred in the operation for equipment and personnel used, provided they were readily available and the services were rendered promptly in accordance with the criteria in Art.13 of the Convention, rather than on a remuneration basis. The fair rate was not therefore a reward for the salvage but a calculation of expenses by which the salvor would be out of pocket. The expenses only became payable once the environmental threat had arisen, but thereafter the salvors were entitled to payment throughout the whole operation, notwithstanding that the risk to the environment may have ceased at an earlier stage.

SEMCO SALVAGE AND MARINE PTE LTD v. LANCER NAVIGATION CO LTD (THE NAGASAKI SPIRIT) [1996] 1 Lloyd's Rep. 449, Staughton, L.J., CA.

5365. Sea pollution–environmental liability–compensation

MERCHANT SHIPPING (LIABILITY AND COMPENSATION FOR OIL POLLUTION DAMAGE) (TRANSITIONAL PROVISIONS) ORDER 1996, SI 1996

1143; made under the Merchant Shipping Act 1995 s.171, s.182. In force: May 30, 1996; £1.55.

This Order makes transitional provision for the period following entry into force of the 1992 Protocols to the International Convention on Civil Liability for Oil Pollution Damage, 1969, and the International Convention on the Establishment of an International Fund for Compensation for Oil Pollution Damage, 1971. The Order provides that if an incident occurs during the transitional period, compensation may be available under the original conventions and the 1992 Convention.

5366. Sea pollution–environmental protection–law of the sea

MERCHANT SHIPPING (PREVENTION OF POLLUTION) (LAW OF THE SEA CONVENTION) ORDER 1996, SI 1996 282; made under the Merchant Shipping Act 1995 s.129. In force: February 28, 1996; £1.10.

This Order enables Regulations to be made implementing provisions in the United Nations Convention on the Law of the Sea 1982 (Cmnd. 8941) relating to pollution of the sea by ships. It enables regulations to be made relating to the protection and preservation of the marine environment from pollution from ships caused beyond the territorial sea of the United Kingdom. Such regulations could, for example, extend the effect of regulations which apply to ships in the territorial sea of the United Kingdom to ships in other waters within which the United Kingdom may exercise jurisdiction over pollution from ships. Regulations may also be made to specify the extent of the United Kingdom's jurisdiction in this regard.

5367. Sea pollution–oil pollution–pollution control

MERCHANT SHIPPING (PREVENTION OF OIL POLLUTION) REGULATIONS 1996, SI 1996 2154; made under the Merchant Shipping (Prevention of Oil Pollution) Order 1983 Art.3; and the Merchant Shipping (Prevention of Pollution) (Law of the Sea Convention) Order 1996 Art.2. In force: September 17, 1996; £6.10.

These Regulations consolidate the Merchant Shipping (Prevention of Oil Pollution) Regulations 1983 (SI 1983 1106) and subsequent amendments.

5368. Sea pollution–pollution control–territorial waters–boundaries

MERCHANT SHIPPING (PREVENTION OF POLLUTION) (LIMITS) REGULATIONS 1996, SI 1996 2128; made under the Merchant Shipping (Prevention of Pollution) (Law of the Sea Convention) Order Art.2. In force: September 5, 1996; £2.40.

These Regulations define the limits of the zone beyond the territorial sea around the United Kingdom and the Isle of Man in which jurisdiction is exercisable in order to prevent pollution by discharges from ships. The limits follow agreed maritime boundaries with Norway, Denmark, Germany, Netherlands, Belgium, France and the Republic of Ireland.

5369. Shipping contracts–breach of contract–force majeure–whether sellers could rely on force majeure clause in contract between buyer and its associated company

Judgment was given against V for breach of contract when it failed to deliver a cargo of fuel oil to C. V appealed against the assessment of damages in relation to loss suffered by an associated company of C, CAR, who were to use the fuel in their refinery. V argued that there was no liability for loss of yield owing to a force majeure clause in the contract between C and CAR. Although in the judgment on liability, V had been unable to take advantage of a force majeure clause in relation to their liability towards C, C's failure to deliver to CAR was not within its own control. V contended that the judge was wrong to find that the two contracts were made back to back in order to put C and CAR in the same contractual position as V and C.

Held, allowing the appeal, that (1) the judge was wrong to construe the contract in the light of the parties' general intentions. It was necessary for the judge to consider the words and phrases actually used, *Sea Queen, The* [1988] 1 Lloyd's Rep. 500 approved and (2) the clause covered non-performance caused by the default of V.

COASTAL (BERMUDA) PETROLEUM LTD v. VTT VULCAN PETROLEUM SA (NO.2) (THE MARINE STAR) [1996] 2 Lloyd's Rep. 383, Saville, L.J., CA.

5370. Shipping contracts–choice of forum–charter stipulating English law–loss of ship and cargo–stayed to permit Russian claim to proceed

The Vanuatu registered charterers, chartered a ship which was registered in Russia and classed with the Russian Register. Clause 17 provided that there be arbitration in London in accordance with English law. The ship sank and the cargo was lost. The issue arose whether the Admiralty Court in London or the Arbitration Court in St Petersburg was the natural forum for the dispute and further whether there was some special circumstance why the matter should be heard before an English court.

Held, that none of the parties was English or resided in or carried on business in England. The parties had little if any connection with England. While the issues of Russian law could be resolved by expert evidence, it was not satisfactory if issues of Russian law were to be resolved by an English court on an interlocutory basis. It was likely that a significant number of Russian witnesses would be needed. None of the evidence was in England. The plaintiffs contended that the defendants would receive preferential treatment as to costs if the matter proceeded in Russia. However, there was no evidence that the plaintiffs would fail to receive a fair trial in Russia. Therefore, the action before the English court would be stayed provided that the plaintiff's action was secured in Russia and the defendants gave certain undertakings to the court.

POLESSK, THE AND AKADEMIK IOSIF ORBELI, THE [1996] 2 Lloyd's Rep. 40, Clarke, J., QBD (Adm Ct).

5371. Shipping contracts–contract terms–breach of contract terms as to seaworthiness and fitness of holds for cargo–fire caused by welding carried out in breach of terms

VS concluded a contract with AMV for the transportation of goods. The contract included a term as to the seaworthiness of the ship and the condition of the holds. The hold covers required repair during the voyage. The ship caught fire. AMV contended that the fire was caused by welding carried out on deck during the voyage, in breach of the contract.

Held, that on the whole of the evidence, AMV had established that there had been some welding and there was evidence that those who had boarded the ship had seen welding debris. The hold was not fit and safe for the cargo due to the hatch being open and the risk of welding sparks entering the hold. The hold was not unfit or unsafe because of the lack of a CO2 system in the hold.

A MEREDITH JONES & CO LTD v. VANGEMAR SHIPPING CO LTD (THE APOSTOLIS) [1996] 1 Lloyd's Rep. 475, Tuckey, J., QBD (Comm Ct).

5372. Shipping contracts–contracts for sale of rice–breach of contract–contracts for carriage on liner terms–failure to tender conforming bills of lading–whether buyer entitled to reject bills

S, the sellers, appealed against an award of damages for breach of two shipping contracts entered into with G, the buyers, for the sale of rice, after the cargo was lost when the vessel ran aground. Both contracts contained a standard term of the London Rice Brokers' Association as to cost and freight liner terms but G rejected the shipping documents on the ground that they did not conform with the terms of the bills of lading as the relevant inspection of the cargo was not undertaken at the time of loading.

Held, dismissing the appeal, that the scheme for cost and freight liner terms involved the presentation of documents, including bills of lading and invoices, which were also intended to include responsibility for discharge. The provision for discharge on liner terms preceded G's obligation to take up the documents and G's payment under the contract covered the protection of the cargo until it reached its destination. G were justified in rejecting the documents as they failed to cover the procedure for discharge under the contract.

SOON HUA SENG CO LTD v. GLENCORE GRAIN LTD [1996] 1 Lloyd's Rep. 398, Mance, J., QBD (Comm Ct).

5373. Shipping contracts–Cristal Contract–jurisdiction–oil pollution–compensation–whether Cristal's judgment final

C, the administrator of the Cristal Contract (the international agreement entitled the Contract Regarding a Supplement to Tanker Liability for Oil Pollution) and the associated compensation fund appealed against a ruling (Lloyd's List, March 15, 1995) that any determination made by them as to the validity of claims was open to review by an English court, even though a clause of the contract specified that C should be the "sole judge" in accordance with the contract terms. C argued that they had exclusive jurisdiction to determine whether or not the time limit for the plaintiff's claim had expired.

Held, allowing the appeal, that there were many circumstances in which the jurisdiction of the High Court might be restricted, including where the parties to a contract incorporated a term to exclude a right of challenge by the courts. Although it was a general rule of common law that to oust the jurisdiction of the courts completely was contrary to public policy, questions of fact were to be treated differently from questions of law. Given the nature of the international agreement and the functions of C under the contract, it was right that C's decision was final and binding on matters of fact and was not reviewable, provided that C acted fairly and not perversely in making any determination.

WEST OF ENGLAND SHIPOWNERS MUTUAL INSURANCE ASSOCIATION (LUXEMBOURG) v. CRISTAL LTD (THE GLACIER BAY) [1996] 1 Lloyd's Rep. 370, Neill, L.J., CA.

5374. Shipping contracts–fire causing salvage expenses and delay–too late for EC subsidy–whether vessel unseaworthy before voyage–whether defendants showed due diligence–measure of damages–remoteness

[Carriage of Goods by Sea Act 1971; Hague Visby Rules 1968 Art.III r.1; Bills of Lading Act 1855 s.1.]

An engine room fire occurred while D's vessel was at sea, as a result of which P incurred salvage expenses and P's cargo was delayed, thereby arriving too late to receive an EC subsidy. P claimed that the vessel was unseaworthy at the commencement of the voyage, contrary to the Hague-Visby Rules 1968 Art.III r.1, and that this caused the fire and contributed to its spread.

Held, that (1) the fire occurred as a result of mechanical damage to wiring caused by shelving having rubbed against it before the voyage in question; (2) the ship was unseaworthy at the commencement of the voyage because either the wiring, or the shelving, were in such a condition that damage could occur in the ordinary weather which was expected; (3) alternatively, the ship was unseaworthy because inflammable material had been left too close to a hot exhaust prior to the commencement of the voyage; (4) D had not exercised due diligence to avoid damage to the wiring and was therefore liable; (5) although the vessel had a defective smoke alarm and it was impossible to shut off the ventilation, these particular defects in fire-fighting capability did not cause any loss as the fire would have spread too quickly even if they had been working properly; (6) the costs of the salvage service were recoverable as they had been incurred by or on behalf of P; (7) P had title to sue either on the basis of an implied contract, or because property passed to P by reason of endorsement of the bill of lading thereby giving rights of suit under the Bills of Lading Act 1855 s.1 and (8) although D did not have any special knowledge of the particular relief levy, the loss was not too remote because everyone would know that the price and value of goods may be affected by EC subsidies, which vary from time to time, and it was therefore reasonably foreseeable that the net amount payable by buyers for goods could be affected by delay.

OWNERS OF CARGO LATELY LADEN ON BOARD SUBRO VALOUR v. OWNERS OF SUBRO VEGA [1995] 1 Lloyd's Rep. 509, Clarke, J., QBD (Adm Ct).

5375. Shipping contracts–guarantees–plaintiff's requirement not passed to defendant–no agreement for performance guarantee concluded

N bought pig-iron from a supplier and sold it on. KSH confirmed that they would meet N's freight commitments. Through various intermediaries, KSH contacted A, who acted as shipping brokers. A made it plain to KSH that they required a performance guarantee from N. This fact did not pass up the chain of intermediaries to N until a year later. KSH failed to perform and A sought redress against N under the purported performance guarantee. N contended that there had never been a performance guarantee; there were merely inconclusive discussions between N and KSH as to the creation of such a contract.

Held, dismissing A's claim, that the only agreement that could be shown was between A and KSH. Negotiations between KSH and N showed that N would probably have provided a guarantee at some time in the future.

ADRIATIC MARE ENTERPRISES SA v. NEWCO AG (THE ANANGEL EXPRESS) [1996] 2 Lloyd's Rep. 299, Waller, J., QBD (Comm Ct).

5376. Shipping contracts–misdelivery of cargo–no charterparty but reference to the Vegoilvoy form–whether London arbitration limited to general average disputes

[Arbitration Act 1950 s.6, s.27.]

SB, the holder and indorsee of a bill of lading, sued the carrier, NS, for damages for misdelivery of the cargo without production of the bill. The bill incorporated a dated charterparty, including the "Arbitration and General Average clause", but no charterparty was ever drawn up. There was merely a fixture confirmation telex which referred to the Vegoilvoy form (providing for New York arbitration) with alterations including "General average/arbitration in London English law to apply. York-Antwerp Rules 1974, as amended, to apply". SB wrote to NS calling upon NS to agree to the appointment of one of a number of arbitrators. The main question was whether the intention was to limit the London arbitration reference to general average disputes.

Held, granting a declaration in favour of SB, that (1) although it might be possible to provide for arbitration of general average disputes under a different regime from all other disputes arising under the charterparty, there was a presumption against such intention and a presumption in favour of "one stop adjudication", *Ioanna, The* [1978] 1 Lloyd's Rep. 238, [1977] C.L.Y. 1343 distinguished; (2) in the absence of a clear countervailing presumption from the commercial background to the contract, the intention was that there was to be arbitration of all disputes in London; (3) using the Arbitration Act 1950 s.6 gap filling powers, there was reference to a single arbitrator; (4) observed, SB's letter was a clear request to submit the dispute to arbitration and so no extension of time was required and (5) observed, an extension of time would have been granted under s.27 of the 1950 Act as there would have been no hardship to NS.

SWISS BANK CORP v. NOVORISSIYSK SHIPPING CO (THE PETR SHMIDT) [1995] 1 Lloyd's Rep. 202, Potter, J., QBD (Comm Ct).

5377. Shipping contracts–seaworthiness–liability of shipowner to charterer and bill of lading holder–causation–banana cargo lost due to delays caused by engine breakdown

[Hague-Visby Rules Art.III r.1.]

F entered into a contract of affreightment with REL for the carriage of bananas. The ship developed severe engine problems, had to dock at Puerto Cortes as a port of refuge and was therefore unable to make collections from two subsequent ports. The bananas were found to be no longer fit to sell and were donated to a charitable organisation. F argued that REL breached a duty to exercise due diligence to ensure that the vessel was seaworthy under the Hague-Visby Rules Art.III r.1 and further that REL had an obligation to proceed on the voyages with all reasonable dispatch. Caribbean Gold, CG, the holder of the bills of lading, claimed damages against shipowners ReefKrit, RK, for the loss caused by failure to carry the goods to their destination. REL sought contribution from RK.

Held, awarding judgment for F, that (1) the cause of the engine failure was the build-up of particulate in the lubricating oil. Regular independent analysis of this oil was a standard precaution against build-up of foreign matter. Further, there had been regular flushings of the engine filters which indicated a build-up of foreign material. The ship must be considered unseaworthy due to the failure of the owners RK to exercise due diligence; (2) the contract of affreightment was a contract of carriage. From the time REL accepted orders to load at port, the Hague-Visby Rules applied to the voyage. Therefore REL were liable to F for the loss suffered by failing to load at further ports on the route; (3) RK, the owners, were liable to CG, the holder of the bills of lading, for loss caused by the unseaworthiness of the vessel and (4) RK owed a duty to REL, because the contract for carriage was in RK's contemplation at the time the charter was created. The benefit of the saving REL made by not being able to complete the voyage should be taken into account in calculating the overall loss.

FYFFES GROUP LTD v. REEFER EXPRESS LINES PTY LTD [1996] 2 Lloyd's Rep. 171, Moore-Bick, J., QBD (Comm Ct).

5378. Shipping contracts–specific performance–notice of appeal not an encumbrance

Z appealed against a decision that a document giving notice of appeal was not an "encumbrance" from which delivery of a vessel should have been kept contractually free under the memorandum of agreement. Z agreed to purchase a new building vessel. TR, a Liberian corporation had as its only asset that vessel whose price was $21,650,000. There was provision in the agreement between Z and TR for a deposit of $4,000,000, with a contractual requirement that completion would be three banking days after a seven day notice of readiness was served. TR expected completion after the end of the seven day period and when payment was not forthcoming, gave notice of cancellation, expecting to retain the deposit. A hearing on the next day found in Z's favour, ordered specific performance and gave a further three days in which to complete. TR then produced a document, which they invited Z to draw to the attention of third parties, recording their intention to appeal that decision and, if successful, to request an order for rescission. TR claimed that this was to prevent third party interests being subordinated to the rights of Z's mortgagees, but they correctly anticipated that Z's mortgagees would refuse to provide the agreed funds for the purchase in time for completion.

Held, allowing the appeal, that it was unnecessary to determine whether TR's claims were encumbrances. The notice that TR were intending to pursue legal or equitable rights was inconsistent with the order for specific performance which bound both parties and required TR to transfer title and possession unconditionally. TR had in fact chosen neither to appeal, not to seek a stay of execution of the order for specific performance until their claim had been heard.

ZEGLUGA POLSKA SA v. TR SHIPPING LTD [1996] 1 Lloyd's Rep. 337, Evans, L.J., CA.

5379. State security–Jersey

MARITIME SECURITY (JERSEY) ORDER 1996, SI 1996 2881; made under the Aviation and Maritime Security Act 1990 s.51. In force: January 1, 1997; £2.40.

This Order extends those provisions of the Aviation and Maritime Security Act 1990 to the Bailiwick of Jersey. The provisions are subject to modifications.

5380. Statute Law (Repeals) Act 1993–Commencement Order

STATUTE LAW (REPEALS) ACT 1993 (COMMENCEMENT) ORDER 1996, SI 1996 509 (C.9); made under the Statute Law (Repeals) Act 1993 s.4. In force: bringing into force various provisions of the Act on April 1, 1996; £0.65.

This Order brings into force the repeal of the Shipbuilding (Redundancy Payments) Act 1978 (the 1978 Act) and of the Shipbuilding Act 1985 s.1 (the 1985 Act) by the Statute Law (Repeals) Act 1993 s.1 (1) and Sch.1 (Part IX, Group 1) (the 1993 Act). The purpose of the 1978 Act was to provide, for a limited period, schemes to alleviate the hardship caused to redundant employees of British shipbuilders by the contraction of the international shipping market. Section 1 of the 1985 Act extended the period by which schemes under the 1978 Act were to have effect. The legislation is now spent; the schemes have expired and have been replaced by non-statutory schemes. Section 4(3) of the 1993 Act made provision for the repeal of the 1978 Act and of s.1 of the 1985 Act to come into force on a day to be appointed by the Lord Chancellor. This Order made pursuant to s.4(3) of the 1993 Act, provides for April 1, 1996 to be the appointed day.

5381. Wrecks–conservation

PROTECTION OF WRECKS (DESIGNATION NO.1) ORDER 1996, SI 1996 1741; made under the Protection of Wrecks Act 1973 s.1. In force: July 6, 1996; £0.65.

This Order designates as a restricted area for the purposes of the Protection of Wrecks Act 1973, an area situated approximately 5 miles north, northwest off the coast of Rhyl, in the County of Denbighshire, round the site of what is thought to be the wreck of a vessel which is of historical and archaeological importance. No part of the site is above the high water mark of ordinary spring tides.

5382. Articles

A competitive maritime industry for Europe *(Philip Wareham)*: Int. M.L. 1996, 3(5), 164-168. (CEC paper *Shaping Europe's Maritime Future: a Contribution to the Competitiveness of Maritime Industries* issued in conjunction with maritime strategy paper outlining its legislative policy).

ADR in collision and salvage cases *(Richard F. Olsen)*: A.D.R.L.J. 1996, 2(Jun), 83-90. (Relative merits and demerits of alternative dispute resolution procedures in maritime disputes where so far they have been little used).

Alternative dispute resolution *(Graham Harris)*: P & I Int. 1996, 10(1), 16-17. (Potential for ADR in shipping disputes with particular regard to LMAA Conciliation Terms 1991).

An old concept evolves *(Robin Stephens)*: Fairplay 1996, 327(5959), 22. (Liability and jurisdiction in law of bailment and implications for commercial shipping).

Applying the precautionary principle to ocean shipments of radioactive materials *(Jon M. Van Dyke)*: O.D. and I.L. 1996, 27(4), 379-397. (Specific responsibilities that must be met before shipments of unusually hazardous materials may be undertaken and whether these are complied with by states such as Japan).

Arrest of ships in Norway *(Haakon Stang Lund)*: Int. M.L. 1996, 3(1), 11-13. (Legal position of arresting ships in Norway following its adoption of the 1952 Arrest Convention on May 1, 1995).

Arrest: new arrest convention at drafting stage *(Holmes Hardingham Walser Johnston Winter)*: P & I Int. 1996, 10(8), 151-152. (Proposals to widen categories of claim for which ships may be arrested).

Arresting ships in England and Wales *(Corinna Creswell)*: I.J.O.S.L. 1996, 3(Jun), 186-189. (Nature of claims for which security can be obtaining by arresting ship and relevant procedural requirements).

Bills of lading *(John Pople)*: P & I Int. 1996, 10(4), 84-86. (COGSA provisions to recognise transfer of cargo by shipping documents other than bills of lading, title to sue on fraudulently pledged bills and cases on incorporation of charterparty terms and misstatements on face of bills).

Canadian maritime decisions 1994-1995 *(William Tetley)*: L.M.C.L.Q. 1996, 1(Feb), 123-144. (Main developments).

Competition, confusion and common sense *(Conor Maguire* and *Jonathan Dykes)*: I.J.O.S.L. 1996, 3(Jun), 190-195. (Application of EC competition law in shipping sector with particular reference to liner conference agreements and multimodal rate fixing agreements).

Contractual/uncontractual–lawful/unlawful orders under charterparties *(A. Mandaraka-Sheppard)*: I.J.O.S.L. 1996, 4(Sep), 222-228. (Parties' rights when charterer gives uncontractual orders, effect of such orders and whether shipowner has implied indemnity in event of loss caused by compliance).

Damages for the wrongful arrest of a vessel *(Shane Nossal)*: L.M.C.L.Q. 1996, 3(Aug), 368-378. (Need to re-examine accepted interpretation of authority on whether parties who effect wrongful arrest without mala fides or crassa negligentia should enjoy protection from liability for shipowners' economic loss).

Documents only arbitrations in London: P & I Int. 1996, 10(7), 133-135. (LMAA small claims procedure for maritime claims not exceeding $50,000 and advantages as alternative to litigation).

Doubts remain on demurrage liability *(Mike Lax)*: P & I Int. 1996, 10(4), 74-75. (Commencement of laytime, charterparty clauses and charterers' liability to pay demurrage where there has been delay).

Draft Arrest Convention–a swing of the pendulum welcomed by insurers *(Miranda Karali)*: P & I Int. 1996, 10(9), 167-168. (Implications of proposals to broaden scope for effecting arrests).

Equipment Interchange Agreement: Int. M.L. 1996, 3(3), 99-100. (Statement of objections by CEC to proposed agreement by member shipping lines of Transatlantic Conference Agreement to notify each other of container level imbalances).

IMO's International Safety Management Code (the ISM Code) *(Terry Ogg)*: I.J.O.S.L. 1996, 3(Jun), 143-152. (Provisions of Code providing for safe management and operation of ships).

International Safety Management Code: friend or foe? *(Peter D. Murphy)*: I.B.L. 1996, 24(8), 355-356. (Problems surrounding code on best management practice in shipping industry and why so many shipping companies have failed to comply with it).

International Salvage Union *(Michael Lacey)*: P & I Int. 1996, 10(7), 136-137. (ISU Pollution Prevention Survey 1995 statistics show increase in number of salvage operations and corresponding increase in marine pollution incidents).

Investigation, detention and release of foreign vessels under the UN Convention on the Law of the Sea of 1982 and other international agreements *(David H. Anderson)*: I.J.M.C.L. 1996, 11(2), 165-177. (Interaction between expedited procedure provided by Art.292 and substantive provisions on prompt release of vessels detained for fisheries or pollution offences).

Negligence in a commercial context *(Stephen Moriarty)*: C.L. 1996, 1(3), 11-12. (Whether duty of care should be imposed for loss of property when ship sank after having been cleared by ship's surveyor).

Observations on vessel release under the United Nations Convention on the Law of the Sea *(Bernard H. Oxman)*: I.J.M.C.L. 1996, 11(2), 201-215. (Locus standi for bringing applications and use of counsel before tribunal).

Ship arrest under Spanish law *(Carlos Perez)*: I.C.C.L.R. 1996, 7(7), 280-282. (Types of claim for which ships may be arrested, requirements and procedure of arrest and release).

Shipbrokers' commission–a review of charterparty commission clauses *(Andrew Jamieson)*: I.J.O.S.L. 1996, 2, 86-91. (How shipbrokers can influence terms of disadvantageous commission clauses).

Shipbuilding aids: or never say never again *(Philip A. Wareham)*: Int. T.L.R. 1995, 1(6), 223-225. (OECD Agreement proposals for abolition of subsidies by January 1, 1996, implementation in EC and prospect for ratification by mid 1996).

Shipowners' liability to longshoremen: P & I Int. 1996, 10(3), 56-57. (Duty of shipowners to warn stevedores of latent hazards in cargo area only extends to hazards that are neither obvious or foreseeable).

Shipping litigation: highly recommended: Legal Bus. 1996, 68(Oct), 74-76. (Expert lawyers in shipping litigation as recommended by their peers).

The legal status of freight forwarders' bills of lading *(Shane Nossal)*: H.K.L.J. 1995, 25(1), 78-95. (Whether such bills should be considered as genuine bills of lading).

The likely impact of the new IMO Regulations on the ferry industry *(Peter Iles)*: Trans. L. & P. 1996, 3(5), 115-117. (Implications for passenger ferries of requirements concerning ship's ability to stay afloat in event of collision, and operational effects of fitting sponsons or transverse bulkheads).

The new Institute Time Clauses Hulls *(Howard N. Bennett)*: L.M.C.L.Q. 1996, 3(Aug), 305-309. (Changes to Institute of London Underwriters Hulls and Freight clauses as revised 1995 include scope of cover, due diligence, stricter requirements of classification compliance and introduction of time limits for notification of claims).

The new Institute Time Clauses–Hulls 1/11/95 *(Nigel Chapman* and *Paul Jaffe)*: I.J.O.S.L. 1996, 4(Sep), 202-210. (Changes resulting from Joint Hull Committee's review of Institute of London Underwriters' standard clauses regarding classification and due diligence).

The proceedings concerning prompt release of vessels and crews before the International Tribunal for the Law of the Sea *(Tullio Treves)*: I.J.M.C.L. 1996, 11(2), 179-200. (Procedure at tribunal expected to start work October 1996).

The surveyor's role in a crisis *(Dave Spence)*: P & I Int. 1996, 10(8), 150-151. (Checklist for shipping surveyors).

Time charter stowage clauses in a bill of lading contract *(Russell Harling)*:

Denning L.J. 1994, 61-66. (Incorporation of charterparty clause regarding charterer's liability for loading and stowage into bills of lading).

5383. Books

Ambrose, Clare; Maxwell, Karen–London Maritime Arbitration. Lloyd's shipping law library. Hardback: £78.00. ISBN 1-85978-027-X. LLP Limited.

Borgese, Elisabeth Mann; Ginsburg, Norton; Morgan, Joseph R.–Ocean Yearbook: Vol 12. Hardback: £55.95. ISBN 0-226-06615-0. University of Chicago Press.

Boyd, S.C.–Scrutton on Charterparties. Hardback: £130.00. ISBN 0-421-52580-0. Sweet & Maxwell.

Hynds, Paul–Fast Ferries. Lloyd's Business Intelligence Centre. Spiral bound: £325.00. ISBN 1-85978-057-1. LLP Limited.

Jackson, David–Enforcement of Maritime Claims. Hardback: £125.00. ISBN 1-85044-302-5. Lloyd's of London Press.

Lovett, William A.–United States Shipping Policies and the World Market. Hardback: £59.95. ISBN 0-89930-945-3. Quorum Books.

Navias, Martin S.; Hooton, E.R–Tanker Wars. Hardback: £75.00. ISBN 1-86064-032-X. Tauris Academic Studies.

Phillips, Nevil–The Merchant Shipping Act 1995 - an Annotated Guide. Hardback: £65.00. ISBN 1-85978-068-7. LLP Limited.

Roach, J. Ashley; Smith, Robert W.–United States Responses to Excessive Maritime Claims. Publications on ocean development. Hardback: £137.50. ISBN 90-411-0225-6. Martinus Nijhoff Publishers.

Schofield, John–Laytime and Demurrage. Lloyd's shipping law library. Hardback: £90.00. ISBN 1-85044-899-X. LLP Limited.

Snelson, Anthony–The Law of Towage. Hardback. ISBN 1-85044-967-8. Lloyd's of London Press.

Temperley, Robert; Thomas, Michael; Steel, David–Templey's Merchant Shipping Legislation. British Shipping Laws, Vol 11. Hardback: £98.00. ISBN 0-420-46510-3. Stevens & Sons.

Thomas, D. Rhidian–The Modern Law of Marine Insurance. Hardback: £75.00. ISBN 1-85978-033-4. LLP Limited.

SOCIAL SECURITY

5384. Attendance allowance–residential accommodation run by a registered charity–grant paid by local authority–costs of accommodation not paid out of public funds

[National Assistance Act 1948 Part III; Social Security Act 1975 s.35; Social Security (Attendance Allowance) Amendment (No.3) Regulations 1983.]

C appealed against a decision that S, who was severely disabled, was entitled to an attendance allowance under the Social Security Act 1975 s.35, at the higher rate prescribed. S resided in a residential home, formerly run by the Isle of Wight CC but now run by a registered charity. The Social Security (Attendance Allowance) Amendment (No.3) Regulations 1983 Reg.4(1)(a) excluded the payment of attendance allowance to those residing in accommodation provided for them under the National Assistance Act 1948 Part III. C contended that S's accommodation was provided under that statute. C further contended that, under para.4(1)(c) of the 1983 Regulations, S was residing in accommodation whose costs "may be borne wholly or partly out of public or local funds in pursuance of a scheduled enactment" and so was deprived of attendance allowance. C also argued that, as a large grant had been paid by the local authority to the home and the rent had been rebated for a number of years, the Social Security (Attendance Allowance) Regulations 1991 Reg.7, which stated that attendance allowance was not excluded in relation to persons who paid the whole cost themselves, was not applicable.

Held, dismissing the appeal, that (1) accommodation was not provided as s.26 of the 1948 Act required payments to be made by the local authority for the accommodation and, in this case, S paid the charges herself; (2) it was necessary to decide whether para.4(1)(c) of the 1983 Regulations was operative owing to the power to bear the costs of the accommodation out of public funds pursuant to a scheduled enactment, *Jones v. Insurance Officer* (Unreported, 1984) followed. There was no need for the arrangements for the accommodation to be made under the scheduled enactments before the exclusion could come into operation, *Chief Adjudication Officer v. Kenyon* Times, November 14, 1995, [1995] C.L.Y. 4567 not followed and (3) payment of grants and rebates by the local authority had no bearing on Reg.7 of the 1991 Regulations which only required the resident to pay the fixed charge for their accommodation.

STEANE v. CHIEF ADJUDICATION OFFICER [1996] 1 W.L.R. 1195, Lord Slynn of Hadley, HL.

5385. Attendance allowance–threshold conditions–additional laundry due to incontinence did not satisfy conditions for daytime attendance allowance

[Social Security Contributions and Benefits Act 1992 s.64.]

Held, that the task of dealing with additional laundry by a carer as a result of incontinence did not come within the definition of "frequent attention in connection with a bodily function" as required by the Social Security Contributions and Benefits Act 1992 s.64(2)(a) for the provision of daytime attendance allowance. *R. v. National Insurance Commissioners, ex p. Secretary of*

State for Social Services [1981] 1 W.L.R. 1017, [1981] C.L.Y. 2557 and *Woodling, Re* [1984] 1 W.L.R. 348, [1984] C.L.Y. 3273 followed.

COCKBURN v. CHIEF ADJUDICATION OFFICER AND SECRETARY OF STATE FOR SOCIAL SECURITY, *The Times*, July 30, 1996, Butler-Sloss, L.J., CA.

5386. Benefits–computation of earnings

SOCIAL SECURITY BENEFIT (COMPUTATION OF EARNINGS) REGULATIONS 1996, SI 1996 2745; made under the Social Security Contributions and Benefits Act 1992 s.3, s.80, s.89, s.112, s.119, s.175, Sch.7 para.4; and the Social Security Administration Act 1992 s.5, s.71, s.189, s.191. In force: November 25, 1996; £4.15.

These Regulations provide for the way in which the earnings of a person to whom benefit is or may be payable or the earnings of such a person's dependant are to be calculated or estimated for the purposes of those provisions of the Social Security Contributions and Benefits Act 1992, and the Regulations made under that Act, by which the right to or the amount of benefit depends on the amount of those earnings. They make provision for earnings not expressly disregarded to be taken into account on a weekly basis; define earnings and prescribe the manner in which earnings are to be calculated; prescribe the circumstances in which a person is to be treated as possessing earnings which he in fact does not possess; and make transitional provision including for the suspension of benefit until the amount of the earnings is established and for the making of interim payments.

5387. Benefits–equal treatment for men and women–interpretation of Council Directive 79/7 Art.4(1)–European Union

[Council Directive 79/7 on equal treatment for men and women in matters of social security Art.4.]

A challenge was made to provisions of the Netherlands social security system on the ground that it resulted in indirect discrimination against women claimants.

Held, that Council Directive 79/7 Art.4(1) must be interpreted as meaning that a national statutory scheme which provided for a benefit designed to guarantee beneficiaries income at the level of the social minimum, irrespective as to whether claimants had any resources but subject to conditions relating to their previous employment and age, did not involve discrimination on grounds of sex even if more men than women found in that scheme a way of avoiding the means test which had to be satisfied in another scheme, where the national legislature was reasonably entitled to consider that the scheme in question was necessary in order to attain a social policy aim unrelated to any discrimination on the grounds of sex.

LAPERRE v. BESTUURSCOMMISSIE BEROEPSZAKEN IN DE PROVINCIE ZUID-HOLLAND (C8/94), February 8, 1996, Judge not specified, ECJ.

5388. Benefits–immigrants

SOCIAL SECURITY (PERSONS FROM ABROAD) MISCELLANEOUS AMENDMENTS REGULATIONS 1996, SI 1996 30; made under the Social Security Contributions and Benefits Act 1992 s.64, s.68, s.70, s.71, s.123, s.124, s.128, s.129, s.130, s.131, s.135, s.137, s.175; and the Social Security Administration Act 1992 s.5. In force: February 5, 1996; £2.80.

These Regulations amend the Social Security (Attendance Allowance) Regulations 1991 (SI 1991 2740), the Council Tax Benefit (General) Regulations 1992 (SI 1992 1814), the Social Security (Disability Living Allowance) Regulations 1991 (SI 1991 2890), the Disability Working Allowance (General) Regulations 1991 (SI 1991 2887), the Family Credit (General) Regulations 1987 (SI 1987 1973), the Housing Benefit (General) Regulations 1987 (SI 1987 1971), the Social Security (Invalid Care Allowance) Regulations 1976 SI 1976 409), the Income Support (General) Regulations 1987 SI 1987 1967), the Social Security (Payments on Account, Overpayments and Recovery) Regulations 1988 (SI 1988 664) and the Social Security (Severe Disablement Allowance) Regulations 1984 (SI 1984 1303). The purpose of the amendments is to exclude persons whose right to remain in Great Britain is subject to conditions or limitations from entitlement to non-contributory benefits, to make provision for interim payments whilst an appeal is pending, to provide for asylum seekers and sponsored immigrants who are not entitled to income related benefits and to make certain saving provisions.

5389. Benefits–invalidity and sickness benefits–effect of EEC law on national employment policy–European Union

[Council Directive 79/7 on equal treatment for men and women in matters of social security Art.2, Art.4 Treaty of Rome 1957 Art.48.]

M and S, employed as part time cleaners in Germany working 10 hours a week, sought recognition from the German social security authorities that they were subject to compulsory insurance under the statutory sickness and old age insurance scheme and that they were accordingly obliged to pay contributions under the statutory unemployment scheme. The German authorities refused their request on the basis that they were in minor employment, since they worked less than 15 hours per week and earned less than one seventh of the relevant monthly reference amount, and were therefore exempt from compulsory insurance and contributions. On appeal the Social Court referred to the ECJ a question as to whether the Council Directive 79/7 Art.4(1), which provided that there should be no direct or indirect discrimination on the grounds of sex either as to the scope of social security schemes or access thereto or on the obligation to contribute, required a finding that the relevant provisions of German legislation constituted indirect discrimination against women. It was common ground that women were disproportionately affected by the provisions in question.

Held, answering the question in the negative, that (1) the very broad scope of Council Directive 79/7, as set out in Art.2, covered workers in minor employment. The fact that a worker's earnings did not cover all his needs could not prevent him from being a member of the working population for the purposes of Council Directive 79/7, *Ruzuis-Wilbrink v. Bestuur van de Bedrijfsvereniging voor Overheidsdiensten* [1989] E.C.R. 4311, [1991] C.L.Y. 4084a followed, nor did it prevent such a person from being regarded as a worker for the purposes of the Treaty of Rome 1957 Art.48, *Levin v. Staatssecretaris van Justitie* 53/81 [1982] E.C.R. 1035, [1982] C.L.Y. 1235, *Kempf v. Staatssecretaris van Justitie* 139/85 [1986] E.C.R. 1741, [1987] C.L.Y. 1565 and *Rinner-Kuhn v. FWW Spezial-Gebaudereinigung GmbH & Co KG* 171/88 [1989] I.R.L.R. 493, [1990] C.L.Y. 2203a followed. Since the cases on Art.48 of the Treaty concerned the concept of worker in the light of the principle of equal treatment, they were relevant to the interpretation of Council Directive 79/7 Art.2 and (2) the legislation in question was not indirectly discriminatory on the grounds of sex contrary to Council Directive 79/7 Art.4(1). That provision precluded the application of a national term which, although formulated in neutral terms, worked far more to the disadvantage of women than men, unless that measure was justified by objective factors unrelated to discrimination on the grounds of sex, such as the reflection of a legitimate aim of social policy. Social and employment policy was a matter for member states and they had a broad margin of discretion in achieving the aims of that policy, *Commission of the European Communities v. Belgium* [1991] I.R.L.R. 393, [1992] C.L.Y. 4838 followed. The German government argued that the exclusion of persons in minor employment from compulsory insurance fostered the existence of such employment and that to bring such employment within the compulsory insurance scheme would lead to a reduction in such jobs and an increase in unlawful employment. This social and employment policy was objectively unrelated to any discrimination on grounds of sex and in exercising its competence the German legislature was reasonably entitled to consider that the legislation in question was necessary in order to achieve that aim.

MEGNER AND SCHEFFEL v. INNUNGSKRANKENKASSE VORDERPFALZ (C444/93) [1996] I.R.L.R. 236, GC Rodriguez Iglesias (President), ECJ.

5390. Benefits–invalidity and sickness benefits–effect of EEC law on national employment policy–European Union

[Treaty of Rome 1957 Art.48; Council Directive 79/7 on equal treatment for men and women in matters of social security Art.2, Art.4.]

N worked as a cleaner in Germany for less than 10 hours a week from 1977 to 1987. She was then forced to retire on grounds of ill health and in 1988 applied to the German social security authorities for a retirement and invalidity pension. Her application was rejected on the basis that since she worked in minor employment, ie. less than 15 hours per week, and earned less than one seventh of the relevant monthly reference amount, and was therefore exempt from compulsory insurance and contributions under the relevant national legislation, she could not show that she had paid the necessary contributions over the relevant period. On appeal the Social Court took the view that exclusion of minor employment from compulsory old age insurance constituted indirect discrimination contrary to Council Directive 79/7 Art.4(1) and that N should be treated as though she had paid contributions to the old age insurance scheme before the onset of invalidity, but referred to the ECJ the question as to whether the correct interpretation of Art.4(1) did require such a result.

Held, answering the question in the negative, that (1) the very broad scope of Council Directive 79/7 as set out in Art.2 covered workers in minor employment. The fact that a worker's earnings did not cover all his needs could not prevent him from being a member of the working population for the purposes of Council Directive 79/7, *Ruzuis-Wilbrink v. Bestuur van de Bedrijfsvereniging voor Overheidsdiensten* [1989] E.C.R. 4311, [1991] C.L.Y. 4084a followed, nor did it prevent such a person from being regarded as a worker for the purposes of the Treaty of Rome 1957 Art.48, *Levin v. Staatssecretaris van Justitie* 53/81 [1982] E.C.R. 1035, [1982] C.L.Y. 1235 , *Kempf v. Staatssecretaris van Justitie* 139/85 [1986] E.C.R. 1741, [1987] C.L.Y. 1565 and *Rinner-Kuhn v. FWW Spezial-Gebaudereinigung GmbH & Co KG* 171/88 [1989] I.R.L.R. 493, [1990] C.L.Y. 2203a followed. Since the cases on Art.48 of the Treaty concerned the concept of worker in the light of the principle of equal treatment, they were relevant to the interpretation of Council Directive 79/7 Art.2 and (2) the legislation in question was not indirectly discriminatory on the grounds of sex contrary to Council Directive 79/7 Art. 4(1). That provision precluded the application of a national term which, although formulated in neutral terms, worked far more to the disadvantage of women than men, unless that measure was justified by objective factors unrelated to discrimination on the grounds of sex, such as the reflection of a legitimate aim of social policy. Social and employment policy was a matter for member states and they had a broad margin of discretion in achieving the aims of that policy, *Commission of the European Communities v. Belgium* [1991] I.R.L.R. 393, [1992] C.L.Y. 4838 followed. The German government argued that the exclusion of persons in minor employment from compulsory insurance fostered the existence of such employment and that to bring such employment within the compulsory insurance scheme would lead to a reduction in such jobs and an increase in unlawful employment. This social and employment policy was objectively unrelated to any discrimination on grounds of sex and, in exercising its competence, the German legislature was reasonably entitled to consider that the legislation in question was necessary in order to achieve that aim.

NOLTE v. LANDESVERSICHERUNGSANSTALT HANNOVER (C317/93); MEGNER v. INNUNGSKRANKENKASSE VORDERPFALZ [1996] All E.R. (EC) 212, G C Rodriguez Iglesias (President), ECJ.

5391. Benefits–invalidity benefits–pensionable age–difference of treatment between men and women–whether breached Council Directive on equal treatment–European Union

[Social Security Contributions and Benefits Act 1992 s.33, s.34; Council Directive 79/7 on equal treatment for men and women in matters of Social Security Art.4, Art.7.]

Due to ill health, G and others had to stop working before reaching 60, the statutory pensionable age for women in the context of the contributory scheme set up by the Social Security Contributions and Benefits Act 1992 s.33. They received sickness benefit at first and thereafter invalidity pension at the full retirement pension rate. One of them was 58 when she became incapacitated for work and under s.34 of the 1992 Act was not entitled to additional invalidity allowance which was payable only to those who at the time of their incapacity were more than five years below pensionable age. On reaching pensionable age, G and others exercised their rights under the 1992 Act and continued to draw invalidity benefits, deferring receipt of a retirement pension (which unlike an invalidity pension, was taxable) for a further five years. As neither G or the others had fulfilled their contribution conditions for the grant of a full retirement pension, the amount of their invalidity pensions was reduced to the rate of the retirement pension which they would have received had they not elected to defer it. G brought proceedings against the Secretary of State for Social Security claiming discrimination. Their claim was upheld and on appeal the Court of Appeal held that the differences in treatment of men and women regarding eligibility of and calculation of invalidity pensions for men and women between 60 and 65 and the non-availability of invalidity allowances to women whose incapacity began between 55 and 60 amounted to sex discrimination contrary to Council Directive 79/7 Art.4(1). However, the Court of Appeal made an Art.177 reference to the ECJ on the interpretation of Council Directive 79/7 Art.7(1)(a) which allowed Member States to exclude from the scope of the Directive not only the setting of the pensionable age for the purposes of granting old age and retirement pensions but also the possible consequences thereof for other benefits, and its application to the forms of discrimination at issue.

Held, that where a Member State laid down different pensionable ages for men and women for the purposes of granting old age and retirement pensions, the scope of the derogation was limited to the forms of discrimination existing under the other benefit schemes, which were linked to the difference in the pensionable age and were objectively necessary in order to avoid disturbing the financial equilibrium of the social security system or to ensure coherence between the retirement pension scheme and other benefit schemes. Applying those criteria to the forms of discrimination at issue, it was clear that they were objectively linked to the setting of different pensionable ages for men and women since they arose from the fact that this was set at 60 for women and 65 for men. Thus, pursuant to Art.7(1)(a) where a Member State had set different pensionable ages, the derogation allowed it first to limit the rate of invalidity pension to the actual rate of the retirement pension payable when the recipient reached the appropriate pensionable age and second to reserve entitlement to additional invalidity allowance to those who were under 55, in the case of women or 60 in the case of men when they first became incapacitated for work. To find otherwise would not only restrict the very right to set different pensionable ages for men and women, but also undermine the coherence between the retirement pension scheme and the invalidity benefit scheme.

GRAHAM v. SECRETARY OF STATE FOR SOCIAL SECURITY (C92/94) [1995] All E.R. (EC) 736, FA Schockweiler (President), ECJ.

5392. Benefits–maintenance payments

SOCIAL SECURITY BENEFITS (MAINTENANCE PAYMENTS AND CONSEQUENTIAL AMENDMENTS) REGULATIONS 1996, SI 1996 940; made under the Social Security Administration Act 1992 s.74A, s.189, s.191; and the

Social Security Contributions and Benefits Act 1992 s.136, s.137, s.175. In force: April 19, 1996; £1.10.

These Regulations are made by virtue of, and are consequential upon, the Social Security Administration Act 1992 s.74A, which was inserted into that Act by the Child Support Act 1995 s.35, and provides that where the Secretary of State is collecting maintenance payments on behalf of a person who is claiming certain social security benefits, the Secretary of State may disregard those maintenance payments for the purposes of calculating the claimant's benefit entitlement, and may then retain any such maintenance payments collected by him. These Regulations provide definitions of certain terms for the purposes of s.74A, and make consequential amendments to the Income Support (General) Regulations 1987 (SI 1987 1967). These Regulations are made within six months of the coming into force of the Social Security Administration Act 1992 s.74A and are accordingly exempted by s.173(5)(b) of that Act from reference to the Social Security Advisory Committee and have not been so referred.

5393. Benefits–Malta

SOCIAL SECURITY (MALTA) ORDER 1996, SI 1996 1927; made under the Social Security Administration Act 1992 s.179. In force: September 1, 1996; £4.15.

This Order makes provision for the modification of the Social Security Administration Act 1992, the Social Security Contributions and Benefits Act 1992 and the Jobseekers Act 1995 and Regulations made or having effect thereunder so as to give effect to the Convention on social security made between the Government of the United Kingdom and Northern Ireland and the Government of Malta. The provisions relate to sickness and invalidity benefit, unemployment benefit, retirement pension and widow's benefit, orphan's benefit and benefits for industrial accidents and industrial diseases.

5394. Benefits–reciprocity

SOCIAL SECURITY (RECIPROCAL AGREEMENTS) ORDER 1996, SI 1996 1928; made under the Social Security Administration Act 1992 s.179. In force: October 7, 1996; £1.55.

This Order provides for social security legislation to be modified or adapted to take account of changes made by the Jobseekers Act 1995 which replaces unemployment benefit by jobseeker's allowance, in relation to Orders in Council which give effect to agreements made between the Governments of the United Kingdom and other countries providing for reciprocity in certain social security matters.

5395. Benefits–recovery of loans and overpayments–Secretary of State's right to make deductions from benefits–whether right could be exercised where recipient of benefit was bankrupt

[Insolvency Act 1986 s.285; Social Security Administration Act 1992.]

Held, that the Insolvency Act 1986 s.285(3) was not to be interpreted as precluding the Secretary of State from exercising his statutory right under the Social Security Administration Act 1992 to make deductions, in order to recover loans or overpayments, from a person's social security benefits where the person in receipt of benefit was bankrupt, *Bradley-Hole v. Cusen* [1953] 1 Q.B. 300 considered.

R. v. SECRETARY OF STATE FOR SOCIAL SECURITY, *ex p.* TAYLOR; R. v. SECRETARY OF STATE FOR SOCIAL SECURITY, *ex p.* CHAPMAN [1996] C.O.D. 332, Keene, J., QBD.

5396. Benefits–retirement

RETIREMENT BENEFITS SCHEMES (RESTRICTION ON DISCRETION TO APPROVE) (EXCEPTED SCHEMES) REGULATIONS 1996, SI 1996 1582; made under the Income and Corporation Taxes Act 1988 s.591A. In force: July 10, 1996; £0.65.

The Retirement Benefits Schemes (Restriction on Discretion to Approve) (Additional Voluntary Contributions) Regulations 1993 (SI 1993 3016) restrict the discretionary powers of the Commissioners of Inland Revenue (the Board) to approve for tax purposes a retirement benefits scheme under the Income and Corporation Taxes Act 1988 s.591. The Regulations achieve this effect by requiring the scheme, as a condition of tax approval, to contain provisions in its trust deed and rules that comply with the Regulations. By virtue of s.591A of the 1988 Act, the 1993 Regulations also apply to schemes approved before the Regulations came into force, except to the extent that any provisions contained in the 1993 Regulations are disapplied by separate Regulations made under s.591A. These Regulations disapply in relation to existing approved schemes the provisions in the 1993 Regulations that restrict the Board's discretionary powers of approval.

5397. Benefits–up-rating

SOCIAL SECURITY BENEFITS UP-RATING ORDER 1996, SI 1996 599; made under the Social Security Administration Act 1992 s.150, s.189. In force: Art.1, Art.2, Art.22, Art.24: April 1, 1996; Art.9: April 6, 1996 Art.10: April 7, 1996; Art.3, Art.4, Art.5, Art.6, Art.7, Art.8, Art.11, Art.12, Art.13: April 8, 1996; Art.14, Art.15: April 11, 1996 Art.16, Art.17, Art.23: April 9, 1996; Art.18, Art.19, Art.20: April 8, 1996, Art.21: April 8, 1996; £6.10.

This Order specifies certain increases in the sums for rates or amounts of benefit under the Contributions or Benefits Act or the Pension Schemes Act.

5398. Benefits–up-rating

SOCIAL SECURITY BENEFITS UP-RATING REGULATIONS 1996, SI 1996 670; made under the Social Security Contributions Act 1992 s.30E, s.90, s.113, s.122, s.175, Sch.7 para.2; and the Social Security Administration Act 1992 s.155, s.189, s.191. In force: April 8, 1996; £1.10.

These Regulations which amend the Social Security (General Benefit) Regulations 1982 (SI 1982 148), the Social Security Benefit (Dependency) Regulations 1977 (SI 1977 343) and the Social Security (Incapacity Benefit) Regulations 1994 (SI 1994 2946) and revoke the Social Security Benefits Up-rating Regulations 1995 (SI 1995 580), contain provisions in consequence of an Order made under s.50 of the Social Security Administration Act 1992 and have not been referred to the Social Security Advisory Committee or the Industrial Injuries Advisory Council. Regulation 2 provides that where a question has arisen about the effect of the up-rating order on a benefit already in payment, the altered rates will not apply until the question is determined by an adjudicating authority. Regulation 3 relates to the restriction of the application of the increases specified in the up-rating order in cases where the beneficiary lives abroad. Regulation 4 increases the earnings limit which applies to unemployability supplements to £2,366. Reg. 5 raises the earnings limits for child dependency increases payable with invalid care allowance to £130 and to £17 and Reg.6 raises the limit of earnings from a councillor's allowance in relation to incapacity benefit to £45.50.

5399. Child benefit–asylum

CHILD BENEFIT (GENERAL) AMENDMENT (NO.2) REGULATIONS 1996, SI 1996 2530; made under the Social Security Contributions and Benefits Act 1992 s.146A, s.147, s.175. In force: October 7, 1996; £0.65.

These Regulations, made by virtue of provisions introduced by the Asylum and Immigration Act 1996, amend the Child Benefit (General) Regulations 1976 (SI 1976 965 as amended by SI 1996 2327) and prescribe additional conditions when the Social Security Contributions and Benefits Act 1992 s.146A, which disentitles persons who require leave to enter or remain in the United Kingdom from receiving benefit, will not apply.

5400. Child benefit–child support

CHILD BENEFIT, CHILD SUPPORT AND SOCIAL SECURITY (MISCELLANEOUS AMENDMENTS) REGULATIONS 1996, SI 1996 1803; made under the Child Support Act 1991 s.11, s.43, s.51, s.52, s.54, Child Support Act 1991 Sch.1 para.1, Sch.1 para.2, Sch.1 para.4, Sch.1 para.5, Sch.1 para.6, Sch.1 para.9; the Social Security Contributions and Benefits Act 1992 s.123, s.135, s.136, s.137, s.144, s.145, s.147, s.175, Sch.9 para.4; the Social Security Administration Act 1992 s.1, s.5, s.7, s.27, s.73, s.189, s.191; and the Jobseekers Act 1995 s.4, s.12, s.35, s.36. In force: Reg.1, Reg.22, Reg.23, Reg.24, Reg.25, Reg.26, Reg.27, Reg.28, Reg.30, Reg.35: April 1, 1997; Reg.2, Reg.3, Reg.4, Reg.5, Reg.6, Reg.7, Reg.8, Reg.9, Reg.10, Reg.11, Reg.12, Reg.13, Reg.14, Reg.15, Reg.16, Reg.17, Reg.18, Reg,19, Reg.20, Reg.21: April 7, 1997; Reg.37, Reg.38, Reg.39, Reg.40, Reg.41, Reg.42, Reg.43, Reg.44, Reg.45, Reg.46, Reg.47, Reg.48, Reg.49: in accordance with Reg.1 (1); £3.20.

These Regulations amend the Child Benefit and Social Security (Fixing and Adjustment of Rates) Regulations 1976 (SI 1976 1267) so as to specify a composite rate of child benefit to be payable in respect of the only, elder or eldest child of a lone parent rather than two distinct rates. They also make certain other amendments which are consequential on, or relate to, the above. They also replace the premium which is applicable in relation to lone parents in receipt of council tax benefit, housing benefit, income support and jobseeker's allowance, with an additional element to the family premium. They also make amendments to the Child Benefit (General) Regulations 1976 (SI 1976 965). In particular, to provide that unmarried partners shall not be entitled to child benefit in any week where they are exempt from United Kingdom income tax and that no person shall be entitled to child benefit in respect of a child who, in any week, is living with another person as his spouse.

5401. Child benefit–entitlement–child voluntarily placed in local authority accommodation–child benefit–entitlement–statutory interpretation

[Children Act 1989 s.20, s.105; Child Benefit Act 1975; Child Benefit (General) Regulations 1976 Reg.16; Social Security Contributions and Benefits Act 1992 Sch.9.]

M appealed against a decision that she was not entitled to child benefit in respect of two of her sons, for whom the local authority was providing accommodation under the Children Act 1989 s.20. In referring to the Social Security Contributions and Benefits Act 1992 Sch.9 (1) (c) claiming that no benefit was payable in certain prescribed circumstances in respect of children in the care of a local authority, and the Child Benefit (General) Regulations 1976 Reg.16 (5) (f), as amended, provided that one such circumstance was where accommodation was provided under s.20. M argued that there was a distinction between care provided by a local authority following the making of a care order and the provision of accommodation where a child was placed voluntarily in the authority's care under s.20, and that Sch.9 to the 1992 Act referred to the former and therefore Reg.16 (5) (f) was ultra vires the Secretary of State's powers.

Held, dismissing the appeal, that the 1976 Regulations were made under the Child Benefit Act 1975, at which time "care" referred to both care under a court order and voluntary care. The concept of care had changed with the Children Act 1989 s.105 of which defined being in the care of a local authority as having care provided following a court order. The words "in the care of a local authority" in Sch.9 to the 1992 Act were, then, capable of two meanings: either the two kinds of care existing under the 1975 Act or the ordinary meaning of care provided by a local authority, regardless of how the child came to be in local authority accommodation. It would seem that Parliament, in enacting the 1989 Act and the 1992 Act, did not intend to change the law on child benefit, and the ordinary and natural meaning of being in the care of the local authority was to be preferred.

McLAVEY v. SECRETARY OF STATE FOR SOCIAL SECURITY; SUB NOM. McLAVEY v. CHIEF ADJUDICATION OFFICER [1996] 2 F.C.R. 813, Staughton, L.J., CA.

5402. Child benefit–immigration–transitional provisions

CHILD BENEFIT (GENERAL) AMENDMENT REGULATIONS 1996, SI 1996 2327; made under the Social Security Contributions and Benefits Act 1992 s.146A, s.147, s.175. In force: October 7, 1996; £1.10.

The Regulations, made by virtue of provisions introduced by the Asylum and Immigration Act 1996, amend the Child Benefit (General) Regulations 1976 (SI 1976 965) and prescribe conditions when the Social Security Contributions and Benefits Act 1992 s.146A, which dis-entitles persons who require leave to enter or remain in the United Kingdom from receiving child benefit, will not apply.

5403. Child support–adjudication

SOCIAL SECURITY (ADJUDICATION) AND CHILD SUPPORT AMENDMENT REGULATIONS 1996, SI 1996 182; made under the Child Support Act 1991 s.21; and the Social Security Administration Act 1992 s.59, s.189, Sch.3. In force: February 28, 1996; £1.10.

These Regulations amend the Social Security (Adjudication) Regulations 1995 (SI 1995 1801) and the Child Support Appeal Tribunals (Procedure) Regulations 1992 (SI 1992 2641). Regulation 3 of the 1995 Regulations is amended by inserting a new para.3(B) making further provision about an application for an extension of time for making an appeal. A new paragraph is inserted into Reg.23, Reg.29 and Reg.38 of the 1995 Regulations and also into Reg.13 of the 1992 Regulations to provide that the chairman of the various appropriate tribunals shall make a record of the proceedings at the hearing of a case and that copies shall be available to the parties to the hearing on request for 18 months after the hearing.

5404. Child support–adjudication

SOCIAL SECURITY (ADJUDICATION) AND CHILD SUPPORT AMENDMENT (NO.2) REGULATIONS 1996, SI 1996 2450; made under the Child Support Act 1991 s.21, s.51, s.52; and the Social Security Administration Act 1992 s.22, s.33, s.46, s.59, s.189, s.191, Sch.3 para.2, Sch.3 para.3, Sch.3 para.4, Sch.3 para.5. In force: October 21, 1996; £2.80.

These Regulations amend the Social Security (Adjudication) Regulations 1995 (SI 1995 1801) and the Child Support Appeal Tribunals (Procedure) Regulations 1992 (SI 1992 2641) to make certain changes to the procedure of social security appeal tribunals, disability appeal tribunals, medical appeal tribunals and child support appeal tribunals.

5405. Child support–child maintenance bonus

SOCIAL SECURITY (CHILD MAINTENANCE BONUS) REGULATIONS 1996, SI 1996 3195; made under the Social Security Contributions and Benefits Act 1992 s.136, s.137, s.175; the Social Security Administration Act 1992 s.5, s.6, s.71, s.78, s.189, s.191; and the Child Support Act 1995 s.10, s.26. In force: April 7, 1997; £2.80.

The Child Support Act 1995 introduces a child maintenance bonus for persons who are or have been entitled to income support or an income based jobseeker's allowance and who have also been in receipt of child maintenance payments. These Regulations relate to the conditions of entitlement to the bonus, calculation of the amount of bonus, the bonus period and the claiming of a bonus.

5406. Child support–maintenance–claims and payments

CHILD SUPPORT (MAINTENANCE ASSESSMENTS AND SPECIAL CASES) AND SOCIAL SECURITY (CLAIMS AND PAYMENTS) AMENDMENT REGULATIONS 1996, SI 1996 481; made under the Child Support Act 1991 s.51, s.52, s.54, Sch.1 para.5, Sch.1 para.7; and the Social Security Administration Act 1992 s.5, s.189. In force: April 8, 1996; £1.10.

In order to provide for an increase in the minimum amount of child support maintenance payable and the amount payable by an absent parent in receipt of income support or other prescribed benefit, these Regulations amend the Child

Support (Maintenance Assessments and Special Cases) Regulations 1992 (SI 1992 1815) and make consequential amendments to the Social Security (Claims and Payments) Regulations 1987 (SI 1987 1968). The amount is increased to two times five per cent of the income support personal allowance for a single person over 25. An amendment is also made to Sch.2 of the 1992 Regulations in order to increase the disregard in relation to charitable or voluntary payments from £10 to £20 when determining net income

5407. Child support–amendments

CHILD SUPPORT (MISCELLANEOUS AMENDMENTS) REGULATIONS 1996, SI 1996 1945; made under the Child Support Act 1991 s.14, s.21, s.32, s.42, s.46, s.47, s.51, s.52, s.54, Sch.1 para.5, Sch.1 para.6, Sch.1 para.8, Sch.1 para.11. In force: Reg.1, Reg.4, Reg.7, Reg.8, Reg.9, Reg.12, Reg.20, Reg.21, Reg.22, Reg.18(1) (3): August 5, 1996; Remainder: October 7, 1996; £2.80.

These Regulations amend the Child Support Appeals Tribunal (Procedure) Regulations 1992 (SI 1992 2641), the Child Support Fees Regulations 1992 (SI 1992 3094), the Child Support (Information, Evidence and Disclosure) Regulations 1992 (SI 1992 1812), the Child Support (Maintenance Assessment Procedure) Regulations 1992 (SI 1992 1813), the Child Support (Maintenance Assessments and Special Cases) Regulations 1992 (SI 1992 1815) and the Child Support (Collection and Enforcement) Regulations 1992 (SI 1992 1989).

5408. Child support–miscellaneous amendments

CHILD SUPPORT (MISCELLANEOUS AMENDMENTS) (NO.2) REGULATIONS 1996, SI 1996 3196; made under the Child Support Act 1991 s.12, s.17, s.21, s.46, s.47, s.51, s.52, s.54, Sch.1 para.5, Sch.1 para.6, Sch.1 para.8, Sch.1 para.11. In force: January 13, 1997; £2.40.

These Regulations amend the Child Support Appeal (Procedure) Regulations 1992 (SI 1992 2641) to make provision for the notice of appeal to be lodged with the Secretary of State at the Child Support Agency Appeals Unit, the Child Support Fees Regulations 1992 (SI 1992 3094) deferring the reintroduction of fees until April 1999, the Child Support (Maintenance Assessment Procedure) Regulations 1992 (SI 1992 1813), and the Child Support (Maintenance Assessments and Special Cases) Regulations 1992 (SI 1992 1815).

5409. Child support–procedure

CHILD SUPPORT COMMISSIONERS (PROCEDURE) (AMENDMENT) REGULATIONS 1996, SI 1996 243; made under the Child Support Act 1991 s.22, s.24, s.25, Sch.4 para.4A. In force: March 1, 1996; £1.10.

These Regulations amend the Child Support Commissioners (Procedure) Regulations 1992 (SI 1992 2640) to provide for nominated officers to perform certain functions of a Commissioner and to provide for decisions made by a nominated officer to be considered by a Commissioner. They revoke the Child Support Commissioners (Procedure) (Amendment) Regulations1995 (SI 1995 2907) which were defective.

5410. Child Support Act 1995–Commencement No.3 Order

CHILD SUPPORT ACT 1995 (COMMENCEMENT NO.3) ORDER 1996, SI 1996 2630 (C.72); made under the Child Support Act 1995 s.30. In force: bringing into force various provisions of the Act on October 14, 1996 and December 2, 1996; £1.55.

This Order brings into force most of the remaining uncommenced provisions of the Child Support Act 1995 on October 14, 1996 and December 2, 1996.

5411. Claims–payments

SOCIAL SECURITY (CLAIMS AND PAYMENTS) AMENDMENT (NO.2) REGULATIONS 1996, SI 1996 2988; made under the Social Security Administration Act 1992 s.15A, s.189. In force: April 1, 1997; £0.65.

These Regulations amend the Social Security (Claims and Payments) Regulations 1987 (SI 1987 1968) Sch.9A para.7 by reducing from £0.77 to £0.72 the fee which qualifying lenders pay for the purpose of defraying administrative expenses incurred by the Secretary of State in making payments in respect of mortgage interest direct to qualifying lenders.

5412. Claims–payments

SOCIAL SECURITY (CLAIMS AND PAYMENTS ETC.) AMENDMENT REGULATIONS 1996, SI 1996 672; made under the Social Security Administration Act 1992 s.5, s.15A, s.71, s.81, s.189. In force: April 4, 1996; £1.10.

These Regulations amend the Social Security (Claims and Payments) Regulations 1987, the Statutory Sick Pay (General) Regulations 1982, the Social Security (Payments on Account, Overpayments and Recovery) Regulations 1988 and the Social Security (Recoupment) Regulations 1990 to make further provision for the payment of benefit by means of a benefit payment card described as an instrument for benefit payment. In particular, provision is made for the circumstances in which agents and receivers etc. may use the benefit payment card to collect benefit on the beneficiary's behalf (Reg.2(2)(a) and Reg.2(2)(c)) and in which they or the beneficiary may be required to accept payment by this means of all the benefits then due (Reg.2(2)(d)).

5413. Claims–payments–adjudication

SOCIAL SECURITY (CLAIMS AND PAYMENTS AND ADJUDICATION) AMENDMENT REGULATIONS 1996, SI 1996 2306; made under the Social Security Administration Act 1992 s.5, s.61, s.189, s.191. In force: October 7, 1996; £1.10.

These Regulations amend the Social Security (Claims and Payments) Regulations 1987 (SI 1987 1968) in the following respects: they remove the special rules on time limits for claiming incapacity benefit or severe disablement allowance for claimants in hospital; they also amend the time limit for claiming social fund payments; they increase the maximum weekly amount of benefit which may be paid at intervals of up to 12 months; they alter the period of time within which payment of benefit may be suspended in a case where an appeal to a Social Security Commissioner may be made. These Regulations also amend the Social Security (Adjudication) Regulations 1995 (SI 1995 1801) Reg.63 and Reg.63A, which concern reviews of income support and jobseeker's allowance. The Regulations amend the provisions relating to the date that the reviews of income support have effect where reductions in the capital outstanding on a loan or changes in the rate of interest have occurred, and make similar provision for jobseeker's allowance.

5414. Community Care (Direct Payments) Act 1996 (c.30)

An Act to enable local authorities responsible for community care services to make payments to persons in respect of their securing the provision of such services; and for connected purposes.

This Act received Royal Assent on July 4, 1996.

5415. Community Care (Direct Payments) Act 1996 (c.30)

The Department of Health issued a press release entitled *Community Care (Direct Payments) Bill receives Royal Assent* (Press release 96/224), published on July 4, 1996. The Act enables local authorities to grant cash payments to people to make their own arrangements for community care services. Welcoming the new powers, Health Minister John Bowis said that it would allow disabled people to have more choice and control over the care they receive and would be a direct alternative to services arranged by local authorities. The first group to benefit from the Act's provisions will be physically and learning disabled adults under 65. After one year's operation, the Government will consider extending direct payments to other groups.

5416. Contributions

SOCIAL SECURITY (CONTRIBUTIONS) AMENDMENT REGULATIONS 1996, SI 1996 486; made under the Social Security Contributions and Benefits Act 1992 s.117, s.175. In force: April 6, 1996; £0.65.

These Regulations amend the Social Security (Contributions) Regulations 1979 (SI 1979 591) by reducing the special rate of Class 2 contributions payable by share fishermen from £7.30 to £7.20.

5417. Contributions

SOCIAL SECURITY (CONTRIBUTIONS) AMENDMENT (NO.2) REGULATIONS 1996, SI 1996 663; made under the Social Security Contributions and Benefits Act 1992 s.5, s.116, s.175; and the Social Security Contributions and Benefits (Northern Ireland) Act 1992 s.116, s.171. In force: April 6, 1996; £1.10.

These Regulations amend the Social Security (Contributions) Regulations 1979 (SI 1979 591). The weekly lower and upper earnings limits for Class 1 contributions for the tax year beginning on April 6, 1996 are increased and the provision reducing the rate of Class 1 contributions payable in respect of earnings by serving members of the forces and with the Crown as their employer is revoked.

5418. Contributions

SOCIAL SECURITY (CONTRIBUTIONS) AMENDMENT (NO.3) REGULATIONS 1996, SI 1996 700; made under the Social Security Contributions and Benefits Act 1992 s.3, s.122, s.175, Sch.1 para.1. In force: April 6, 1996; £1.10.

These Regulations further amend the Social Security (Contributions) Regulations 1979 (the principal Regulations) (SI 1979 591). Regulation 2 amends Reg.5A(2) of the principal Regulations by inserting a new definition of "designated earnings period" where the earner is, or is not, a person in respect of whom minimum contributions are payable in accordance with the Pension Schemes Act 1993 s.43. Regulation 3 amends Reg.19(1) of the principal Regulations (payment to be disregarded) by excluding various payments and benefits from the computation of a person's earnings for the purposes of earnings-related contributions. Regulation 4 amends Reg.9B(5) of the principal Regulations (disregard of payments to directors) by applying the meaning given to "company" by the Income and Corporation Taxes Act 1988 s.832(1) and s.832(2).

5419. Contributions

SOCIAL SECURITY (CONTRIBUTIONS) AMENDMENT (NO.4) REGULATIONS 1996, SI 1996 1047; made under the Social Security Contributions and Benefits Act 1992 s.1, s.122, s.175, Sch.1 para.6. In force: April 19, 1996; £0.65.

These Regulations further amend the Social Security (Contributions) Regulations 1979 (SI 1979 591) (the principal Regulations). Regulation 2 inserts a new Reg.34A into Sch.1 to the principal Regulations which provides, in relation to the payment of earnings related and Class 1A contributions and the calculation of interest on such contributions which are overdue or repaid, that where any such payment is made by cheque, it shall be treated as made on the day on which the cheque is received by the Collector of Taxes.

5420. Contributions

SOCIAL SECURITY (CONTRIBUTIONS) AMENDMENT (NO.5) REGULATIONS 1996, SI 1996 2407; made under the Social Security Contributions and Benefits

Act 1992 s.1, s.3, s.4, s.17, s.122, s.175, Sch.1 para.1, Sch.1 para.2, Sch.1 para.6, Sch.1 para.8. In force: April 6, 1997; £1.55.

These Regulations further amend the Social Security (Contributions) Regulations 1979 (SI 1979 591).

5421. Contributions

SOCIAL SECURITY (CONTRIBUTIONS) AMENDMENT (NO.6) REGULATIONS 1996, SI 1996 3031; made under the Social Security Contributions and Benefits Act 1992 s.3, s.122, s.175. In force: December 5, 1996; £1.10.

These Regulations make miscellaneous amendments to the Social Security (Contributions) Regulations 1979 (SI 1979 591).

5422. Contributions

SOCIAL SECURITY (CONTRIBUTIONS) (RERATING AND NATIONAL INSURANCE FUND PAYMENTS) ORDER 1996, SI 1996 597; made under the Social Security Administration Act 1992 s.141, s.142, s.143, s.145, s.189; and the Social Security Act 1993 s.2. In force: April 6, 1996; £1.10.

This Order increases the amounts of weekly earnings in the secondary earnings brackets, the rates of classes of contributions, the amount of earnings below which an earner may be excepted from liability and the lower and upper limits of profits or gains specified in the Social Security Contributions and Benefits Act 1992. Provision is also made for the Social Security Act 1993 s.2(2) to have effect for the tax year 1996/7 and for the amount of money provided by Parliament to be paid into the National Insurance Fund not to exceed 6 per cent of benefit expenditure for the year ending March 31, 1997.

5423. Contributions–employers–deductions

EMPLOYER'S CONTRIBUTIONS RE-IMBURSEMENT REGULATIONS 1996, SI 1996 195; made under the Jobseekers Act 1995 s.27, s.34, s.35, s.36. In force: April 6, 1996; £2.40.

These Regulations provide for employers to make deductions from their social security contributions payments in prescribed circumstances where they employ a qualifying employee.

5424. Contributions–self-employed persons–freedom of establishment–European Union

[Treaty of Rome 1957 Art.52; Council Regulation 1390/81 extending to self-employed persons and members of their families the scope of Council Regulation 1408/71; Council Regulation 1408/71 on the application of social security schemes to employed persons and their families.]

K worked as a self-employed lawyer in Frankfurt and Brussels. He had always had his habitual residence in Germany but was also, for part of the time, resident in Belgium. The Belgian social security authorities claimed contributions from him for that period but he refused to pay on the ground that he was already covered by the German social security scheme for self-employed persons and that affiliation to the Belgian scheme would not afford him any additional social security cover. Council Regulation 1390/81 which extended to self-employed persons the scope of Council Regulation 1408/71 was not in force for the applicable period.

Held, that the Treaty of Rome 1957 Art.52 precluded a Member State from requiring contributions to be made to the social security scheme for self-employed persons by persons already working as self-employed persons in another Member State where they had their habitual residence and were affiliated to a social security scheme, that obligation affording them no additional social security cover.

INASTI v. KEMMLER (C53/95), February 15, 1996, Judge not specified, ECJ.

5425. Council tax–housing benefits–supply of information

HOUSING BENEFIT, SUPPLY OF INFORMATION AND COUNCIL TAX BENEFIT (AMENDMENT) REGULATIONS 1996, SI 1996 194; made under the Social Security Contributions and Benefits Act 1992 s.123, s.130, s.131, s.135, s.136, s.137, s.175; and the Social Security Administration Act 1992 s.5, s.6, s.63, s.127, s.128, s.128A, s.138, s.189, s.191. In force: April 1, 1996; £2.80.

These Regulations further amend the Housing Benefit (General) Regulations 1987 (SI 1987 1971), the Housing Benefit (Supply of Information) Regulations 1988 (SI 1988 662) and the Council Tax Benefit (General) Regulations 1992 (SI 1992 1814). They make and further amend provisions relating to maximum benefit in cases where housing benefit or council tax benefit was payable, by providing for a further, extended payment of benefit in prescribed circumstances and make provision for the effect of such payments on any further grant of benefit. They also provide for further claims for housing benefit or council tax benefit to be given priority over other claims in prescribed circumstances and for the Secretary of State to pass information about the matters in these Regulations to local authorities to pass such information to each other.

5426. Council tax benefit–housing benefits

COUNCIL TAX BENEFIT AND HOUSING BENEFIT (MISCELLANEOUS AMENDMENTS) REGULATIONS 1996, SI 1996 2432; made under the Social Security Contributions and Benefits Act 1992 s.123, s.130, s.131, s.135, s.136, s.137, s.175; the Social Security Administration Act 1992 s.5, s.6, s.63, s.134, s.189, s.191; and the Asylum and Immigration Act 1996 s.11. In force: October 15, 1996; £2.80.

These Regulations amend the Council Tax Benefit (General) Regulations 1992 (SI 1992 1814), the Housing Benefit (General) Regulations 1987 (SI 1987 1971) and the Housing Benefit (General) Amendment Regulations 1995 (SI 1995 1644) to provide; that a claim for council tax benefit or housing benefit may be made by a person who has been recorded as a refugee by the Secretary of State in respect of the period from the date of his claim for asylum to the date he is recorded as a refugee; for the date on which such a claim for benefit is to be treated as made; and that any benefit to which the claimant is entitled shall be paid.

5427. Council tax benefit–permitted totals

COUNCIL TAX BENEFIT (PERMITTED TOTALS) ORDER 1996, SI 1996 678; made under the Social Security Administration Act 1992 s.139, s.189. In force: April 1, 1996; £0.65.

This Order sets out the basis for calculating the permitted total of council tax benefit for any year for authorities granting such benefit under the Social Security Administration Act 1992 Part VIII, and limits the amount by which Council tax benefit allowed by an authority may be increased in the case of claimants whose circumstances are exceptional or in the case of war widows where the authority's scheme has been modified.

5428. Deception–benefit fraud–false representations–proof of intention to defraud not required for conviction

[Social Security Administration Act 1992 s.112.]

DSS appealed by way of case stated against the dismissal of an information laid against B by the Metropolitan Stipendiary Magistrate. The information alleged two cases of making a false representation for the purposes of obtaining benefit contrary to the Social Security Administration Act 1992 s.112. B claimed that the representation had occurred due to a misunderstanding. The Magistrate dismissed the case when the prosecution failed to adduce evidence that B had possessed criminal intent. They also failed to adduce authorities to challenge the statutory interpretation that the defendant must have intended to make the false statement.

Held, allowing the appeal, that the finding that it was necessary to prove intention to deceive or to defraud the DSS was erroneous. B knew that the statement he had made was false and this was sufficient. The case was remitted to the Magistrate with a direction that she continue the hearing *Clear v. Smith* [1981] 1 W.L.R. 399, [1981] C.L.Y. 2604 followed.

DEPARTMENT OF SOCIAL SECURITY v. BAVI [1996] C.O.D. 260, Wright, J., QBD.

5429. Deductions

SOCIAL SECURITY (NON-DEPENDANT DEDUCTIONS) REGULATIONS 1996, SI 1996 2518; made under the Social Security Contributions and Benefits Act 1992 s.130, s.131, s.135, s.137, s.175; the Jobseekers Act 1995 s.4; and the Jobseekers Allowance Act 1995 s.35, s.36. In force: Reg.1, Reg.2, Reg.3: April 1, 1997; Reg.4: April 6, 1998 Remainder: April 7, 1997; £1.10.

These Regulations amend the Council Tax Benefit (General) Regulations 1992 (SI 1992 1814), the Housing Benefit (General) Regulations 1987 (SI 1987 1971), the Income Support (General) Regulations 1987 (SI 1987 1967) and the Jobseeker's Allowance Regulations 1996 (SI 1996 207). In particular, they insert new thresholds for non-dependant deductions and amend the maximum amount of such deductions, relating to council tax benefit and housing benefit. Similar provisions are inserted relating to the appropriate applicable amounts for the purposes of income support and jobseeker's allowance.

5430. Disability living allowance–care component–cooking test not necessarily discriminatory against women

[Social Security Contributions and Benefits Act 1992 s.72.]

Held, that the test, in the Social Security Contributions and Benefits Act 1992 s.72, for entitlement to the care component of disability living allowance, which was whether a disabled person could prepare a cooked meal, was not necessarily discriminatory against women, as it was not to be applied only to those who could cook. Those applicants who could not cook must be assumed to be ready to learn.

R. v. SECRETARY OF STATE FOR SOCIAL SECURITY, *ex p.* ARMSTRONG (1996) 32 B.M.L.R. 32, Sir Ralph Gibson, CA.

5431. Disability living allowance–claims and payments

SOCIAL SECURITY (DISABILITY LIVING ALLOWANCE AND CLAIMS AND PAYMENTS) AMENDMENT REGULATIONS 1996, SI 1996 1436; made under the Social Security Administration Act 1992 s.5, s.73, s.189. In force: July 31, 1996; £1.10.

These Regulations amend the Social Security (Disability Living Allowance) Regulations 1991 (SI 1991 2890) by inserting new Reg.12A to Reg.12C so as to provide that it is a condition for the receipt of the mobility component of disability living allowance that a person is not being maintained free of charge whilst undergoing treatment as an in-patient in a hospital or similar institution under the National Health Service or maintained by the Defence Council.

5432. Disability living allowance–exemptions

SOCIAL SECURITY (DISABILITY LIVING ALLOWANCE) AMENDMENT REGULATIONS 1996, SI 1996 1767; made under the Social Security Administration Act 1992 s.73, s.189. In force: July 31, 1996; £1.10.

These Regulations further amend the Social Security (Disability Living Allowance) Regulations 1991 (SI 1991 2890). They provide for a further exemption from the provisions of those Regulations relating to hospitalisation in mobility component cases by providing that certain persons residing in hospices shall continue to receive the mobility component of disability living allowance.

5433. Disability working allowance–family credit

DISABILITY WORKING ALLOWANCE AND FAMILY CREDIT (GENERAL) AMENDMENT REGULATIONS 1996, SI 1996 3137; made under the Social Security Contributions and Benefits Act 1992 s.123, s.128, s.129, s.136, s.137, s.175. In force: January 7, 1997; £1.10.

These Regulations further amend the Disability Working Allowance (General) Regulations 1991 (SI 1991 2887) and the Family Credit (General) Regulations 1987 (SI 1987 1973) with respect to the earnings of employed earners and, in the case of family credit, directors, which are to be taken into account in calculating the normal weekly earnings of a claimant for disability working allowance or family credit. They also amend the manner of calculating deductions from the profits of self-employed earners in respect of social security contributions.

5434. Energy conservation–grants

HOME ENERGY EFFICIENCY GRANTS (AMENDMENT) REGULATIONS 1996, SI 1996 587; made under the Social Security Act 1990 s.15. In force: Reg.4(2): October 7, 1996; Remainder: April 1, 1996; £1.55.

These Regulations amend the Home Energy Efficiency Grants Regulations 1992 (SI 1992 483) which make provision for grants to improve energy efficiency in multiple occupied buildings and for agencies to administer the making of such grants. The eligibility for grants is extended to those receiving attendance allowance, disability living allowance, jobseeker's allowance, war disablement pension or mobility supplement. A reduced amount of grant is now awarded to those only eligible for grants because they are at least 60 years of age.

5435. Family credit

FAMILY CREDIT (GENERAL) AMENDMENT REGULATIONS 1996, SI 1996 1418; made under the Social Security Contributions and Benefits Act 1992 s.123, s.128, s.137, s.175; and the Social Security Administration Act 1992 s.5, s. 27, s.189, s.191. In force: July 2, 1996; £0.65.

These Regulations amend the Family Credit (General) Regulations 1987 (SI 1987 1973) by providing that awards of family credit shall be reviewed and shall terminate where persons between the ages of 16 and 19 leave, or have already left, full-time education during the period those awards are in effect and that person is the only member of that household in respect of whom family credit is payable. They also define what is to constitute full-time education for the purpose of this requirement. The Report of the Social Security Advisory Committee dated May 2, 1996 on the proposals referred to them in respect of these Regulations, together with a statement showing the extent to which these Regulations give effect to the Recommendations of the Committee, and insofar as they do not give effect to them, the reasons why not, are contained in Command Paper Cm.3297, published by Her Majesty's Stationery Office.

5436. Freedom of movement–employment–social security benefits–whether French mother could claim for child in Germany–European Union

[Council Regulation 1408/71 Art.19.]

P was a French national working in France, but resident in Germany with her German husband and two children. P was affiliated to a sickness insurance fund in France. Her husband had a private sickness insurance scheme as his salary disqualified him from membership of the state scheme. In 1989, one of P's children received treatment at a hospital in Germany. P sought reimbursement from a German sickness fund under Council Regulation 1408/71 on the application of social security schemes to employed and self-employed persons and to members of their families moving within the EC. Article 19(1) of the Regulation provided that a person who was resident in one member state but working and insured in another member state and who satisfied the conditions of entitlement to sickness benefit in the latter state was entitled to receive sickness benefit in kind in his state of residence as if he were insured there.

Article 19(2) applied the provisions of Art.19(1) by analogy to the family of such workers so far as they were not entitled to such benefits under the legislation of the state in which they resided. P was refused reimbursement under the German Social Security Code which provided that the children of persons affiliated to a sickness insurance fund were not insured if the spouse of the affiliated person was himself not affiliated to a statutory sickness fund or his income exceeded the statutory limit. P appealed on the grounds that her children were entitled irrespective of their parents' income to receive benefits as if they were insured. P was reimbursed the costs but refused a declaration as sought. P appealed further and the Landessozialgericht referred to the ECJ for a preliminary ruling under Art.177 the question whether certain provisions under the Regulation contained a principle of law that prohibited member states from making affiliation to a social insurance system of the children of a frontier worker in another member state dependent upon the income level of the husband

Held, that Art.19(2) of the Regulation was to be interpreted to mean that when a worker resided with the members of his family in the territory of a member state other than the member state in which he worked, under whose legislation he was insured by virtue of the Regulation, the conditions for entitlement to sickness benefits in kind of members of that person's family were also governed by the legislation of the state in which that person worked in so far as the members of the family were not entitled to those benefits under the legislation of their state of residence.

DELAVANT v. ALLGEMEINE ORTSKRANKENKASSE FUR DAS SAARLAND (C451/93) [1995] All E.R. (EC) 673, Judge not specified, ECJ.

5437. Freedom of movement–family benefits–workers moving within the Community–Member State limiting the retroactive effect of an application for family benefits–European Union

[Council Regulation 574/72; Council Regulation 1408/71 on the application of social security schemes to employed persons and their families moving within the Community Art.73; Council Regulation 2001/83; Council Regulation 3427/89.]

A, a Spanish national, had been employed in Germany since 1978. His wife and his two daughters, born in 1966, lived in Spain. In April 1989, A claimed family benefit in respect of his daughters both for the future and retroactively for the preceding six months. German law limited the retroactive effect of such applications to that period. The Employment Office granted family benefit backdated to October 1988. On October 30, 1989 the Council adopted Council Regulation 3427/89 Art.1 (1) which was applicable from January 15, 1986 and amended Council Regulation 1408/71 Art.73. On the basis of that amendment, A claimed the payment of arrears of family allowance from January 1, 1986 to September 30, 1988. The claim was rejected on account of the domestic limitation on the retroactive effect of applications for family benefits.

Held, that Spanish nationals who worked in a Member State other than Spain, but whose families resided in Spain, were entitled to family benefits in the Member State in which they had been working since January 1, 1986 (the date of accession of Spain to the EEC), but they could rely on that entitlement with retroactive effect only from January 15, 1986 (the date from which regulation 3427/89 applied). However, Regulation 1408/71, as amended, and Council Regulation 574/72 did not prevent a national provision, which limited the retroactive effect of applications for family benefits to a period of six months, from being applied to an application by a Spanish national for payment as from January 15, 1986 of family benefits in respect of the members of his family resident in Spain.

ALONSO PEREZ v. BUNDESANSTALT FUR ARBEIT (C394/93), November 23, 1995, Judge not specified, ECJ (Sixth Chamber).

5438. Freedom of movement–invalidity and old age pensions–migrant workers–European Union

[Council Regulation 1408/71; Council Regulation 574/72 fixing the procedure for implementing Regulation 1408/71 on the application of social security schemes to employed persons.]

I, an Italian national, worked in Italy from 1936 until 1964 and thereafter in Belgium. Following an accident at work in 1977, he claimed an invalidity benefit from the Belgian authorities, INAMI. INAMI contacted the Italian authorities, INPS, with a view to the payment of the invalidity pension under Italian legislation. INPS stated that I was entitled to an Italian invalidity pension. Subsequently, INPS notified INAMI of its decision to grant I an old age pension in lieu of the invalidity pension with effect from the date of his sixtieth birthday. I then waived the invalidity pensions because Italian legislation did not at that time provide for the possibility of converting the invalidity pension into an old age pension. INAMI then discontinued the invalidity benefits payable to I.

Held, that Council Regulation 1408/71 on the application of social security schemes to employed persons, self-employed persons and to members of their families moving within the Community Art.46(1) subpara.2 and Council Regulation 574/72 Art.36(4) did not prevent an institution of a member state, to which an institution of another member state had referred a claim for invalidity pension based on Art.40 of Regulation 1408/71, from awarding a worker an old age pension instead of an invalidity pension which he had waived in order to obtain an old age pension which was more advantageous to him.

IACOBELLI v. INAMI (C275/91), February 3, 1993, Judge not specified, ECJ (Third Chamber).

5439. Freedom of movement–invalidity benefit–pre-existing state of health–determination of applicable legislation–European Union

[Treaty of Rome 1957 Art.51; Council Regulation 1408/71 Art.38; Council Regulation 2001/83.]

An Italian national worked in Belgium, then in the Netherlands and later received Belgian unemployment benefit. Subsequently, he secured work in the Netherlands but soon ceased working on account of psychological problems. He was denied incapacity benefits under Dutch law because, on the date when he commenced his last employment in the Netherlands, his state of health made the onset of incapacity for work within a period of less than six months plainly foreseeable.

Held, that in accordance with the rule on aggregation of insurance, residence or employment periods laid down by the Treaty of Rome 1957 Art.51, which it was designed to implement, Council Regulation 1408/71 Art.38(1) on the application of social security schemes to employed and self-employed persons and to members of their families moving within the EC, as amended by Council Regulation 2001/83, was to be interpreted as meaning that, where the applicable legislation of a Member State made the grant of invalidity benefits subject to the condition that at the time of his joining the scheme established by that legislation the worker's state of health must not have been such as to make it foreseeable that incapacity for work followed by invalidity would occur in the near future, the competent institution must also take into account periods of insurance completed by that worker under the legislation of another Member State, as if those periods had been completed under the legislation which it administered.

MOSCATO v. BESTUUR VAN DE NIEUWE ALGEMENE BEDRIJFSVERENING (C481/93), October 26, 1995, Judge not specified, ECJ.

5440. Freedom of movement–invalidity pension–contract of employment subject to private law–employment subject to insurance through a scheme for civil servants–European Union

[Council Regulation 1408/71.]

A teacher in a private school in the Netherlands under a contract of employment governed by private law was insured under a special scheme for civil servants and persons treated as such. After marrying, she worked in Italy and was subject to insurance there. When she ceased occupational activity for reasons of ill health, she claimed invalidity pensions in both the Netherlands and Italy. The Netherlands' insurance institution refused to recognise the period of employment in the Netherlands when she had been subject to the special scheme for civil servants.

Held, that Point 4(a) of the section on the Netherlands contained in Annex V of Council Regulation 1408/71 on the application of social security schemes to employed persons and their families moving within the EC was to be interpreted as meaning that periods of paid employment included periods in which a person worked as a teacher under a contract of employment with a private establishment, even if that person was insured during that period under a special scheme for civil servants and persons treated as such.

OLIVIERI-COENEN v. BESTUUR VAN DE NIEUWE ALGEMENE BEDRIJFSVERENING (C227/94), October 17, 1995, Judge not specified, ECJ.

5441. Freedom of movement–invalidity pension–replacement of social security conventions concluded between Member States–European Union

[Council Regulation 1408/71 on the application of social security schemes to employed persons and their families moving within the Community Art.6; Council Regulation 2001/83; Treaty of Rome 1957 Art.48, Art.51.]

T, a French national, worked in France and thereafter in Germany in employment subject to social insurance. In 1992, T applied in Germany for an invalidity pension. In order to increase the amount of the pension, the Social Assistance Office argued on behalf of T that the period of employment completed in France had to be taken into account in calculating the level of the pension in accordance with the provisions of the general social security convention concluded by Germany and France. This approach was rejected by the Regional Insurance Office, which considered that the convention had been replaced as a result of Council Regulation 1408/71 Art.6. Pursuant to the provisions of that Regulation, the periods of employment in France were relevant only for the purpose of completion of the qualifying period and not for calculation of the amount of the pension.

Held, that Treaty of Rome 1957 Art.48(2) and Art.51 must be interpreted as meaning that they did not preclude the replacement by Regulation 1408/71 as amended, of a convention binding two Member States where, prior to the entry into force of Regulation 1408/71, an insured person completed insurance periods in only one of the signatory States. T had not exercised his right to freedom of movement until after the entry into force of Regulation 1408/71. This was the case even where the application of the bilateral social security convention would have placed that insured person in a more favourable position.

THEVENON v. LANDESVERSICHERUNGSANSTALT RHEINLAND PFALZ (C475/93), November 9, 1995, Judge not specified, ECJ.

5442. Freedom of movement–retirement pensions–special schemes for civil servants–interpretation and validity of Council Regulation 1408/71–European Union

[Council Regulation 1408/71 on the application of social security schemes to employed persons and their families moving within the Community Art.4; Council Regulation 2001/83; Treaty of Rome 1957 Art.48.]

V, a Greek doctor, challenged the refusal of his employer, a Greek social security institution governed by public law, to take into account, for the purpose of his acquisition of old age pension entitlement, periods between 1964 and 1969 during which he worked in public hospitals in Germany.

Held, that the term "civil servants" in Council Regulation 1408/71 Art.4(4) as amended did not refer only to civil servants covered by the derogation from the principle of freedom of movement for workers provided for in the Treaty of Rome 1957 Art.48(4), as interpreted by the court, but to all civil servants employed by a public authority and persons treated as such. In order to be regarded as "special" within the meaning of Regulation 1408/71 Art.4(4), it was sufficient, without there being any need to take other factors into consideration, that the social security scheme in question was different from the general social security scheme applicable to employed persons in the Member State concerned and that all, or certain categories of, civil servants were directly subject to it, or that it referred to a social security scheme for civil servants already in force in that Member State. Consequently, Art.4(4) excluded from the scope of Regulation 1408/71 schemes such as the one in issue. However, the Treaty of Rome 1957 Art.48 and Art.51 must be interpreted as precluding refusal to take into account, for the acquisition of the right to a pension, periods of employment completed by a person subject to a special scheme for civil servants or persons treated as such in public hospitals in another Member State, where the relevant national legislation allowed such periods to be taken into account if they had been completed in comparable establishments within that State.

VOUGIOUKAS v. IDRIMA KOINONIKON ASPHALISSEON (C443/93) [1996] I.C.R. 913, Judge not specified, ECJ.

5443. Housing benefits

HOUSING BENEFIT (GENERAL) AMENDMENT REGULATIONS 1996, SI 1996 965; made under the Social Security Contributions and Benefits Act 1992 s.123, s.130, s.137, s.175; and the Social Security Administration Act 1992 s.5, s.136, s.189, s.191. In force: October 7, 1996; £1.55.

These Regulations amend the Housing Benefit (General) Regulations 1987 (SI 1987 1971). They create a new maximum rent for those claimants under 25 in respect of whom a rent officer has determined and notified a single room rent and make provision for local authorities to refer applications for a rent allowance by young individuals to rent officers and to inform them that the application is from a young individual. A new rule is created for the period within which payment of housing benefit by way of rent allowance is made and it will now be paid at the end of the period to which it relates.

5444. Housing benefits–amounts payable

HOUSING BENEFIT (PERMITTED TOTALS) (AMENDMENT) ORDER 1996, SI 1996 2326; made under the Social Security Administration Act 1992 s.134, s.189. In force: October 7, 1996; £0.65.

This Order amends the Housing Benefit (Permitted Totals) Order 1996 (SI 1996 677). It increases the total amount which local authorities may in the year commencing April 1, 1996 pay by way of housing benefit in the exercise of their discretion under the Housing Benefit (General) Regulations 1987 Reg.61 (3).

5445. Housing benefits–applicant moved to bungalow purchased by brother in law–dominant purpose of transaction was to provide suitable accommodation–judicial review proceedings–importance of a letter before action

[Housing Benefit (General) Regulations 1987 Reg.7; Housing Benefit (General) Regulations 1987 Reg.86.]

M, aged 73, sought judicial review of MK's Housing Benefit Review Board's refusal to grant her housing benefit. M had been in receipt of housing benefit, but had to move from her former home because she suffered from osteoarthritis. When the local authority was unable to rehouse her, her brother in law, B, bought a bungalow with the aid of a contribution from M. The bungalow was held on trust by B for himself and M. M then paid rent to B which covered the mortgage repayments. The board decided that this case fell within the Housing Benefit (General) Regulations 1987 Reg.7(1)(b) as the liability had been created in order to take advantage of the housing benefit scheme.

Held, allowing the application, that, in order for Reg.7(1)(b) to apply there had to be improper conduct. The board had to consider whether the dominant purpose of the purchase was to take advantage of the housing benefit scheme or to provide suitable accommodation for the applicant, *Solihull MBC Housing Benefits Review Board v. Simpson* (1995) 27 H.L.R. 41, [1995] 1 C.L.Y. 2598 followed. In this instance the board failed to make that assessment. M was in need of suitable accommodation which the local authority were unable to provide. If it had been able to provide the accommodation, housing benefit would have been paid, as it had been at the former property.

Observed, that it was important to send a letter before action before embarking on costly judicial review proceedings. It was always possible that this would enable the respondents to draw to the attention of the applicants a speedier and cheaper route of appeal. In this case Reg.86 of the 1987 Regulations provided an internal review provision and it would be unlikely that having unsuccessfully followed that route a court would refuse an application for judicial review for being out of time.

R. v. HOUSING BENEFITS REVIEW BOARD OF MILTON KEYNES BC, *ex p.* MACKLEN, Trans. Ref: CO 3253/95, April 30, 1996, Brooke, J., QBD.

5446. Housing benefits–availability of alternative accommodation–duty of board to consider availability to applicant

[Housing Benefit (General) Regulations 1987 Reg.11.]

D applied for judicial review of two decisions of a housing benefit review board which restricted her housing benefit to £90 per week on the grounds that her house, with two sitting rooms, was larger than required, and the rent, at £103.85, was unreasonably high. D, aged 24, was a single parent with epilepsy. She could live alone but required the support of her family. She fell into the "vulnerable categories" within the Housing Benefit (General) Regulations 1987 Reg.11 (3). This meant that further relevant factors had to be considered.

Held, allowing the application, that (1) the job of a housing benefit review board was to hear the matter afresh. Although the board appeared to be accepting O's case, it had properly considered the evidence before it; (2) under the 1987 Regulations Reg.11 (3) three requirements had to be satisfied: firstly, that there was cheaper alternative accommodation, secondly, that the accommodation was available to the claimant in particular and not just generally available and thirdly, that it was reasonable for the claimant to move from his or her present accommodation, *R. v. Housing Benefit Review Board for East Devon DC, ex p. Gibson* (1993) 25 H.L.R. 487, [1994] C.L.Y. 2354 followed, and (3) the approach of the board to the question of availability was wrong in law. There was sufficient evidence before the board for them to consider the question of availability of accommodation to D. However, they considered the submissions irrelevant. The decisions were quashed and remitted for reconsideration.

R. v. OADBY AND WIGSTON BC, *ex p.* DICKMAN (1996) 28 H.L.R. 806, Buxton, J., QBD.

5447. Housing benefits–claims by hostel for housing benefit–computation of rent–supervision and counselling provided for occupants–adequacy of reasons for decision

[Housing Benefit (General) Regulations 1987 Reg.83.]

HP, a charity which ran hostels to re-settle young offenders, appealed against the dismissal of its application for judicial review of a decision of the S's Housing Benefit Review Board not to change its determination of the amount of housing benefit to be paid to HP in relation to the occupants of its hostels. HP originally received funding for each occupant via the DSS. In October 1989 the system changed and accommodation charges were payable under the housing benefit scheme. The board found that the full charge made to the occupants could not be entirely attributed to "rent" as part of the expenses went towards the management, supervision and counselling given to the occupants. HP argued that the board's decision letter did not accurately reflect its reasoning. HP also argued that the reasons themselves were not good in law as staff expenses could be deemed to be eligible to come within the housing benefit regulations. HP further argued that the decision letter failed to comply with the Housing Benefit (General) Regulations 1987 Reg.83(4) and Reg.83(5) as the letter was signed by the town clerk, who was a solicitor present at the deliberations, rather than the chairman of the board.

Held, dismissing the appeal, that (1) the reasons given in the decision letter accurately reflected the reasoning of the board as evidenced by contemporaneous written notes; (2) HP failed to satisfy the board that its expenses came within the Regulations. Schedule 1 para.1(f) of the 1987 Regulations specifically excluded counselling and other support services, *R. v. North Cornwall DC, ex p. Bateman* (1995) 27 H.L.R. 622, [1995] 1 C.L.Y. 2593 considered; (3) the reason for the dismissal of the appeal was straightforward and the short letter was therefore adequate and intelligible and (4) although the letter failed to fulfil the requirements of Reg. 83, HP suffered no prejudice, *R. v. Solihull MBC Housing Benefits Review Board, ex p. Simpson* (1995) 27 H.L.R. 41, [1995] 1 C.L.Y. 2598 considered.

R. v. STOKE-ON-TRENT CITY COUNCIL AND SECRETARY OF STATE FOR SOCIAL SECURITY, *ex p.* HIGHGATE PROJECTS; R. v. BIRMINGHAM CITY COUNCIL, *ex p.* CONNOLLY, Trans. Ref: QBOF 95/0445/D, April 24, 1996, Simon Brown, L.J., CA.

5448. Housing benefits–council assessment of capital–duty to examine evidence–duty to give reasons

[Housing Benefit (General) Regulations 1987; Council Tax Benefit (General) Regulations 1992.]

N applied for judicial review of a decision of D's Housing Benefit Review Board. The board had determined that N's capital was too high for him to receive any housing or council tax benefit under the Housing Benefit (General) Regulations 1987 and the Council Tax Benefit (General) Regulations 1992. N owned a cottage which was demolished pursuant to a demolition order. The district valuer valued it at a minimum of £17,500 taking into account possible future development. D's valuation department valued the land at £23,000, adjusted to £20,700 to take account of selling expenses, and that figure was accepted by the board. N argued that the board failed to give reasons for preferring the council's valuation and failed to examine the evidence presented in support of the district valuer's conclusion.

Held, allowing the application, that (1) the board exercised an inquisitorial jurisdiction which meant that it should consider all relevant information whether submitted by the parties or not, *R. v. North Cornwall DC, ex p. Singer* (1994) 26 H.L.R. 360, [1994] C.L.Y. 2351 followed; (2) the board should have considered the different valuations as they were crucial to the outcome of the appeal. The board should have provided reasons, in accordance with its statutory duty, for accepting D's valuation unreservedly; (3) evidence from the board at appeal explaining its reasons should only be accepted in exceptional cases, and not in this case, *R. v. Westminster City Council, ex p. Ermakov* [1996] 2 All E.R. 302, [1995] 1 C.L.Y. 2568 followed, and (4) the decision was quashed and remitted for consideration by a differently constituted board.

R. v. DONCASTER MBC, *ex p.* NORTROP (1996) 28 H.L.R. 862, Brooke, J., QBD.

5449. Housing benefits–council tax–benefit–subsidies

HOUSING BENEFIT AND COUNCIL TAX BENEFIT (SUBSIDY) ORDER 1996, SI 1996 1217; made under the Social Security Administration Act 1992 s.135, s.136, s.140, s.189. In force: June 3, 1996; £8.70.

This Order makes provision for the calculation of housing benefit and council tax benefit subsidy payable under the Social Security Administration Act 1992 to authorities administering housing benefit or council tax benefit. It deals with the amount of subsidy, rebates and allowances, backdated benefit, disproportionate rent increase, treatment of high rents, rent officers' determinations, additions in respect of the homeless and short lease rebates, further additions to subsidies, deductions made in the calculation of subsidies in respect of rebates and allowances, deduction from subsidies and additions to and deductions from subsidies in respect of benefit savings.

5450. Housing benefits–council tax benefit–jobseeker's allowance–information

HOUSING BENEFIT, COUNCIL TAX BENEFIT AND SUPPLY OF INFORMATION (JOBSEEKER'S ALLOWANCE) (CONSEQUENTIAL AMENDMENTS) REGULATIONS 1996, SI 1996 1510; made under the Jobseekers Act 1995 s.35, s.36, s.40. In force: October 7, 1996; £3.20.

These Regulations amend the Housing Benefit (General) Regulations 1987 (SI 1987 1971), the Council Tax Benefit (General) Regulations 1992 (SI 1992 1814), the Council Tax Benefit (Supply of Information) Regulations 1988 (SI 1988 662). The amendments are consequential on the coming into force of the Jobseekers Act 1995, which replaces income support for the unemployed and unemployment benefit with jobseeker's allowance. The Regulations replace references to unemployment benefit with references to a jobseeker's allowance, and add references to a jobseeker's allowance where the existing Regulations refer to income support. They also provide that, in certain circumstances, days on which entitlement to a jobseeker's allowance does not arise in accordance with the Jobseekers Act 1995 Sch.1 para.4 (waiting days) or payment is not made in accordance with s.19 of that Act, are counted as days of payment of a jobseeker's allowance.

5451. Housing benefits–council tax benefit–subsidies

HOUSING BENEFIT AND COUNCIL TAX BENEFIT (SUBSIDY) AMENDMENT REGULATIONS 1996, SI 1996 1314; made under the Social Security Administration Act 1992 s.137, s.140, s.191; and the Social Security Administration 1992 s.189. In force: June 11, 1996; £1.10.

These Regulations amend the Housing Benefit and Council Tax Benefit (Subsidy) Regulations 1994 (SI 1994 781), subject to the saving provisions in Reg.4, to provide for the particulars which are required to be provided by an authority to the Secretary of State on the making of claims for housing benefit subsidy and council tax benefit subsidy.

5452. Housing benefits–determination of claim–duty to give reasons–judicial review inappropriate

C sought leave to apply for judicial review of a decision in relation to C's claim for housing benefit. C argued that L had failed to disclose the reasons for their determination and that by such a failure they had breached their statutory duty.

Held, dismissing the application, that (1) there was a determination made in the course of correspondence and a reason was given for it. Judicial review was inappropriate, because if C believed the reason to be inadequate, he should have written to L for further and better particulars and (2) on application for judicial review, C disclosed only one letter relating to the determination. The nondisclosure of other relevant correspondence caused prejudice to L.

R. v. LIVERPOOL CITY COUNCIL, *ex p.* CONNOLLY, Trans. Ref: CO/1767/95, November 20, 1995, Judge, J., QBD.

5453. Housing benefits–eligible rent–suitable alternative accommodation–authority could not take applicant's impecuniosity into account when assessing benefit entitlement

[Housing Benefit (General) Regulations 1987 Reg.11.]

Held, that there was nothing in the Housing Benefit (General) Regulations 1987 Reg.11 (2) or Reg.11 (6) (a) which obliged a local authority, in determining, for the purposes of assessing housing benefit, whether to reduce a claimant's eligible rent by an appropriate amount if the contractual rent was unreasonably high by comparison with rent payable in suitable alternative accommodation elsewhere, to take into account the fact that applicants were impecunious and that alternative accommodation was therefore not financially available to them because landlords normally required deposits which they were unable to pay.

R. v. WALTHAM FOREST LBC, *ex p.* HOLDER, *The Independent*, February 28, 1996, Brooke, J., QBD.

5454. Housing benefits–judicial review–Secretary of State for Social Security applying to be joined as party to proceedings–not person directly affected

[Rules of the Supreme Court Ord.53 r.5.]

The Secretary of State appealed from the refusal of his appeal against the dismissal of his motion that he be joined as respondent in two applications for judicial review arising out of the alleged failure of the Rent Officer Service and L to determine claims for housing benefit. Since 95 per cent of housing benefit paid represented a subsidy from central government funds, the Secretary of State claimed to be a person "directly affected" within the Rules of the Supreme Court Ord.53 r.5(3) and sought to become a party to the proceedings in order to be in a position to appeal against any judgment in favour of the applicants.

Held, dismissing the appeal, that, whilst the Secretary of State was undoubtedly a person affected in that he would be required to commit extra expenditure by way of subsidy if the applicants were successful, he was only indirectly affected and not directly affected in terms of Ord.53 r.5(3).

R. v. LIVERPOOL CITY COUNCIL, *ex p.* MULDOON; R. v. LIVERPOOL CITY COUNCIL, *ex p.* KELLY [1996] 1 W.L.R. 1103, Lord Keith of Kinkel, HL.

5455. Housing benefits–payments to landlord withheld–local authority not obliged to pay housing benefit into interest bearing account

[Local Government Act 1972 s.111; Housing Benefits (General) Regulations 1987 Reg.95.]

B applied for judicial review of KC's refusal to transfer his housing benefit into an interest bearing account whilst it was being withheld and pending payment out. There was a dispute between B and his landlord, L, rent was refused by the landlord and proceedings were commenced. KC were informed of the dispute and withheld housing benefit under the Housing Benefits (General) Regulations 1987 Reg.95(1). B requested that the money be put in an interest bearing account because L's claim in their dispute included a claim for interest. KC contended that they had no power to place the money in an interest bearing account. B argued that the administration of the local housing benefit scheme was a function of the local authority and the placing of retained payments in an interest bearing account was incidental or conducive to the discharge of such a function pursuant to the Local Government Act 1972 s.111 (1). KC was entitled to determine how it administered the scheme. B also argued that the housing benefit scheme was run for the benefit of the claimants. An interest bearing account was consistent with that object.

Held, dismissing the application, that (1) the scheme's intention was to prevent the poorer members of the community from becoming indebted to their landlords. That could be distinguished from implying that s.111 (1) of the 1972 Act required KC to do whatever was necessary to prevent a claimant from falling into debt with his landlord and being evicted as a consequence. Payment of interest was not conducive to the function of the payment of housing benefit. It could be said to assist the claimant, but not to assist the actual payment of the benefit; (2) the fact that KC could withhold the payment of benefit, if it was in the overriding interests of the claimant under the 1987 Regulations Reg.95(3) meant only that KC should not pay the money, it did not mean that KC should retain the money in an interest bearing account. The overriding interest of the claimant only referred to the withholding of the payment and not to the best way that KC could hold the money; (3) there was an implied prohibition on the payment of interest. Provisions relating to overpayment and withheld payments were precisely defined in the 1987 Regulations. These made no mention of interest, and (4) the judgment would not lead to a serious injustice for claimants, because if they could not pay statutory interest on a claim, the judge would be unlikely to award it.

R. v. KENSINGTON AND CHELSEA RLBC, *ex p.* BRANDT (1996) 28 H.L.R. 538, Dyson, J., QBD.

5456. Housing benefits–permitted totals

HOUSING BENEFIT (PERMITTED TOTALS) ORDER 1996, SI 1996 677; made under the Social Security Administration Act 1992 s.134, s.189. In force: April 1, 1996; £1.10.

This Order sets out the basis for calculating the permitted totals of rebates or allowances for the year 1996/1997 for authorities granting rebates or allowances under the Social Security Administration Act 1992 Part VIII. The Order limits the amount by which the housing benefits payments may be increased on the exercise of the discretions provided by the Housing Benefit (General) Regulations 1987 (SI 1987 1971) Reg.61 (2) and Reg.61 (3), and to war widows through modified schemes.

5457. Incapacity benefit

SOCIAL SECURITY (INCAPACITY FOR WORK) (GENERAL) AMENDMENT REGULATIONS 1996, SI 1996 484; made under the Social Security Contributions and Benefits Act 1992 s.171D, s.175. In force: April 8, 1996; £0.65.

The Social Security (Incapacity for Work) (General) Regulations 1995 (SI 1995 311) Reg.17 prescribes the categories of work which are exempt work for the purposes of Reg.16 which provides that a person is to be treated as capable of work in each day of any week during which he does work and prescribes an earnings limit which must not be exceeded if work is to be exempt work. These Regulations increase that limit from £44 to £45.50.

5458. Incapacity benefit–equal treatment for men and women–European Union

[Council Directive 79/7 on equal treatment for men and women in matters of social security Art.4.]

The Netherlands legislation on incapacity benefits was examined by the ECJ to determine whether it resulted in indirect discrimination against women.

Held, that Council Directive 79/7 Art.4(1) did not preclude the application of national legislation which made receipt of a benefit for incapacity for work subject to the requirement of having received a certain income from or in connection with work in the year preceding the commencement of incapacity, even if it was established that that requirement affected more women than men.

POSTHUMA VAN DAMME v. OZTUERK (C280/94), February 1, 1996, Judge not specified, ECJ.

5459. Incapacity benefit–miscellaneous amendments

SOCIAL SECURITY (INCAPACITY FOR WORK AND MISCELLANEOUS AMENDMENTS) REGULATIONS 1996, SI 1996 3207; made under the Social Security and Contributions Benefits Act 1992 s.171A, s.171C, s.171D, s.171E, s.171G, s.175; the Social Security Administration Act 1992 s.73, s.191; and the

Social Security (Incapacity for Work) Act 1994 s.4, s.7, s.12. In force: January 6, 1997; £1.55.

These Regulations amend the Social Security (Incapacity for Work) (General) Regulations 1995 (SI 1995 311), the Social Security (Incapacity Benefit) (Transitional) Regulations 1995 (SI 1995 310) and the Social Security (Overlapping Benefits) Regulations 1979 (SI 1979 597).

5460. Income–assessment

NATIONAL ASSISTANCE (ASSESSMENT OF RESOURCES) (AMENDMENT) REGULATIONS 1996, SI 1996 602; made under the National Assistance Act 1948 s.22. In force: April 8, 1996; £1.10.

These Regulations amend the National Assistance (Assessment of Resources) Regulations 1992 (SI 1992 2977) which are concerned with the assessment of a person's ability to pay for accommodation arranged by local authorities in order to keep the Regulations aligned with similar provisions of the Income Support (General) Regulations 1987 (SI 1987 1967). The capital limit above which a resident is not entitled to be assessed as unable to pay for accommodation is increased to £16,000 and resident's capital to be used in the calculation of weekly tariff income is increased to between £10,000 and £16,000 and where a resident makes one half of his occupational pension available to his spouse for the spouse's maintenance, the equivalent amount is to be disregarded as income other than earnings.

5461. Income related benefits

INCOME-RELATED BENEFITS SCHEMES (MISCELLANEOUS AMENDMENTS) REGULATIONS 1996, SI 1996 462; made under the Social Security Contributions and Benefits Act 1992 s.123, s.130, s.134, s.135, s.136, s.137, s.175; and the Social Security Administration Act 1992 s.5, s.6. In force: in accordance with Reg.1; £2.40.

The Income Support (General) Regulations 1987 (SI 1987 1967), the Housing Benefit (General) Regulations 1987 (SI 1987 1971), the Council Tax Benefit (General) Regulations 1992 (SI 1992 1814), the Family Credit (General) Regulations 1987 (SI 1987 1973) and the Disability Working Allowances (General) Regulations 1991 (SI 1991 2887) are amended by these Regulations. As far as income support is concerned, provision is made for the preserved rights of persons in residential care homes run by the Abbeyfield Society to cease if arrangements are made for those persons to be provided with personal care. With regard to housing benefit and council tax, provision is made for the payment of disability premium to a couple to continue when one partner is in hospital, for additional family credit and disability working allowance to be payable to persons working 30 hours or more per week and for clarifying regulations relating to backdated claims. Provision for the calculation of normal weekly income when a person is paid fortnightly for the purposes of family credit is made along with amendments relating to charitable or voluntary payments, student loans and grants and payments made to Victoria or George Cross holders are made to all income related benefits. Limits relating to claimants of income support and housing benefits in residential care or nursing homes are amended.

5462. Income related benefits

INCOME-RELATED BENEFITS SCHEMES (MISCELLANEOUS AMENDMENTS) (NO.2) REGULATIONS 1996, SI 1996 1759; made under the Social Security Contributions and Benefits Act 1992 s.123, s.130, s.136, s.137, s.175. In force: in accordance with Reg.1 (1); £1.10.

These Regulations amend the Council Tax Benefit (General) Regulations 1992 (SI 1992 1814), the Disability Working Allowance (General) Regulations 1991 (SI 1991 2887), the Family Credit (General) Regulations 1987 (SI 1987 1973), the Housing Benefit (General) Regulations 1987 (SI 1987 1971), and the Income Support (General) Regulations 1987 (SI 1987 1967). They increase the amount to be allowed in respect of the cost of books and equipment in calculating a student's grant income and increase the amount of deduction to be made in calculating a student's eligible rent in respect of housing benefit only,

5463. Income related benefits–immigrants–Montserrat

INCOME-RELATED BENEFITS (MONTSERRAT) REGULATIONS 1996, SI 1996 2006; made under the Social Security Contributions and Benefits Act 1992 s.123, s.131, s.135, s.137, s.175. In force: August 28, 1996; £1.10.

These Regulations further amend the Housing Benefit (General) Regulations 1987 (SI 1987 1971), the Council Tax Benefit (General) Regulations 1992 (SI 1992 1814) and the Income Support (General) Regulations 1987 (SI 1987 1967). They provide that claimants coming to Great Britain from Montserrat as a result of a volcanic eruption on the island are not to be treated as persons from abroad for the purposes of income support, housing benefit and council tax benefit.

5464. Income related benefits–jobseeker's allowance–personal allowances

INCOME-RELATED BENEFITS AND JOBSEEKER'S ALLOWANCE (PERSONAL ALLOWANCES FOR CHILDREN AND YOUNG PERSONS) (AMENDMENT) REGULATIONS 1996, SI 1996 2545; made under the Social Security Contributions and Benefits Act 1992 s.128, s.129, s.135, s.136, s.137, s.175; and the Jobseekers Act 1995 s.4, s.35, s.36. In force: in accordance with Reg.1; £1.95.

These Regulations amend the Income Support (General) Regulations 1987 (SI 1987 1967), the Jobseeker's Allowance Regulations 1996 (SI 1996 207), the Housing Benefit (General) Regulations 1987 (SI 1987 1971), the Council Tax Benefit (General) Regulations 1992 (SI 1992 1814), the Family Credit (General) Regulations 1987 (SI 1987 1973) and the Disability Working Allowance (General) Regulations 1991 (SI 1991 2887). In particular, they change the date when personal allowances in respect of children and young persons are increased for the purposes of income support, income based jobseeker's allowance, housing benefit and council tax benefit, from the date the child or young person concerned attains the age of 11 or 16 to the first Monday in September after that child or young person attains that age.

5465. Income related benefits–social fund–students

INCOME-RELATED BENEFITS SCHEMES AND SOCIAL FUND (MISCELLANEOUS AMENDMENTS) REGULATIONS 1996, SI 1996 1944; made under the Social Security Contributions and Benefits Act 1992 s.123, s.128, s.129, s.130, s.131, s.135, s.136, s.137, s.175; the Social Security Administration Act 1992 s.63, s.78, s.189, s.191; and the Jobseekers Act 1995 s.36, s.40. In force: Reg.2, Reg.5. Reg.6, Reg.7, Reg.8, Reg.9, Reg.10, Reg.11, Reg.12, Reg.13, Sch: October 7, 1996; Reg.3, Reg.4: October 8, 1996; £3.70.

These Regulations make amendments relating to students to the Council Tax Benefit (General) Regulations 1992 (SI 1992 1814), the Disability Working Allowance (General) Regulations 1991 (SI 1991 2887), the Family Credit (General) Regulations 1987 (SI 1987 1973), the Housing Benefit (General) Regulations 1987 (SI 1987 1971 as amended by SI 1995 1644 and SI 1996 965), the Income Support (General) Regulations 1987 (SI 1987 1967 as amended by SI 1996 206) and the Social Fund (Recovery by Deductions from Benefits) Regulations 1988 (SI 1988 35).

5466. Income support

INCOME SUPPORT (GENERAL) AMENDMENT REGULATIONS 1996, SI 1996 606; made under the Social Security Contributions and Benefits Act 1992 s.136, s.137, s.175. In force: April 8, 1996; £1.10.

These Regulations amend the Income Support (General) Regulations 1987 Sch.9 (SI 1987 1967) to provide that where a claimant for income support is resident in, or is temporarily absent from, a residential care home or nursing home and has preserved rights to higher limits of income support, or is resident in accommodation provided under the Polish Resettlement Act 1947, and at least 50 per cent of any occupational pension of his being paid to, or in respect of, his spouse for the spouse's maintenance, 50 per cent of the pension or pensions concerned shall be disregarded in calculating the claimant's income. This disregard shall not have effect in the case of any occupational pension or part of a pension to which the spouse is legally entitled whether under a court order or not.

5467. Income support–loans–standard rate of interest

INCOME SUPPORT (GENERAL) AMENDMENT (NO.2) REGULATIONS 1996, SI 1996 909; made under the Social Security Contributions and Benefits Act 1992 s.135, s.137, s.175. In force: April 21, 1996; £0.65.

These Regulations amend Sch.3 to the Income Support (General) Regulations 1987 (SI 1987 1967), as substituted and amended, with respect to the standard rate of interest applicable to a loan which qualifies for income support under that Schedule to those Regulations, the new rate being 7.74 per cent (Reg.2) and also revoke, with a saving provision, the Income Support (General) Amendment Regulations 1995 (SI 1995 3320) which made a previous amendment to that standard rate of interest (Reg.3).

5468. Income support

INCOME SUPPORT (GENERAL) AMENDMENT (NO.3) REGULATIONS 1996, SI 1996 2614; made under the Social Security Contributions and Benefits Act 1992 s.135, s.137, s.175. In force: November 8, 1996; £0.65.

These Regulations amend the Income Support (General) Regulations 1987 (SI 1987 1967), so as to provide that a person who is in residential accommodation provided by a local authority and who is still in such accommodation when that accommodation becomes a residential care home for the purpose of those Regulations, will be treated as being in residential accommodation, notwithstanding that the local authority may no longer be under a duty to provide or make arrangements for providing accommodation for that person.

5469. Income support–claims and payments

INCOME SUPPORT AND SOCIAL SECURITY (CLAIMS AND PAYMENTS) (MISCELLANEOUS AMENDMENTS) REGULATIONS 1996, SI 1996 2431; made under the Social Security Contributions and Benefits Act 1992 s.135, s.136, s.137, s.175; the Social Security Administration Act 1992 s.5, s.71, s.189, s.191; and the Asylum and Immigration Act 1996 s.11. In force: October 15, 1996; £1.55.

These Regulations amend the Social Security (Claims and Payments) Regulations 1987 (SI 1987 1968) the Income Support (General) Regulations 1987 (SI 1987 1967) so as to provide with respect to a claimant for income support for his entitlement to that benefit for the period from the date of his claim for asylum or February 5, 1996 if that is later to the date of his being recorded by the Secretary of State as a refugee within the Convention relating to the Status of Refugees signed at Geneva on July 28, 1951 (Cmd 9171).

5470. Income support–disability premium–claimant living with parents in their house–entitlement to severe disability premium–statutory interpretation

[Income Support (General) Regulations 1987 Reg.3, Sch.2.]

CAO appealed against the Court of Appeal's decision that B, a severely disabled person claiming income support and living in her parents' home, was entitled to severe disability premium. The decision turned on the interpretation of non-dependant "who normally resides with a claimant" within the Income Support (General) Regulations 1987 Reg.3(1) and Reg.3(2), because under para.13(2)(a)(ii) of Sch.2 to those Regulations, B would be entitled to the premium only if she had no non-dependants aged 18 or over residing with her.

Since the decision in B's favour, the 1987 Regulations had been amended to clarify the position, but it fell to the House of Lords to determine the meaning of the Regulations at the time when B began to receive income support.

Held, allowing the appeal, that "resides with" should be given its natural meaning of living in the same house, there being no requirement that either the claimant or the other person should have the legal interest in the property. Under Reg.3(2)(c) a person who "jointly occupies" the claimant's dwelling was not to be classed as a non-dependant for the purposes of para.13(2)(a)(ii) of Sch.2. However, B's parents could not be held to jointly occupy their house with her as joint occupation denoted a legal relationship, *Fulwood v. Chesterfield BC* (1993) 92 L.G.R. 160, [1994] C.L.Y. 2350 considered. Consequently, B could not show that she had no non-dependants residing with her, and she was not entitled to the premium.

BATE v. CHIEF ADJUDICATION OFFICER [1996] 1 W.L.R. 814, Lord Slynn of Hadley, HL.

5471. Income support–disability premium–determination of capacity to work by doctors–removal of adjudication officer's discretion ultra vires

[Social Security Administration Act 1992 s.20; Social Security Contributions and Benefits Act 1992 s.171; Social Security (Incapacity for Work) (General) Regulations 1995 Reg.27.]

M, a psoriasis sufferer, sought judicial review of a decision under the Social Security Contributions and Benefits Act 1992 s.171C and the Social Security (Incapacity for Work) (General) Regulations 1995 Reg.27 ending his eligibility for a disability premium as part of his income support payment. M contended that the requirement for incapacity to be based on a doctor's opinion under Reg.27 was ultra vires, or alternatively that the decision was irrational, given the requirements of his preferred, topical method of treatment which rendered him incapable of full time work.

Held, allowing the application and granting a declaration that Reg.27 was ultra vires, that (1) the requirement for a decision under Reg.27 to be based on a doctor's opinion was contrary to the provisions of the Social Security Administration Act 1992 s.20, which stipulated that, in the absence of a specific requirement, such matters must be dealt with by the adjudication officer. Although Reg.27 did not expressly remove the duty of an adjudication officer to decide an issue, the effect of making the doctor's opinion on capacity to work conclusive removed an officer's discretion and negated any appeal rights, thereby making the opinion decisive in all circumstances. Whereas the enabling words of s.171D of the 1992 Act were capable of a wide interpretation, the Regulations made under them could not be inconsistent with, or purport to override, the provisions of s.20 of the Social Security Administration Act 1992 and (2) however, M's challenge on the ground of irrationality failed as the tests established by s.171C and s.171D were not limited to full time employment, and M had failed to show that a substantial risk attached to a systemic form of treatment, which would have rendered him substantially more capable of undertaking full time work, as opposed to the time consuming and restrictive topical method preferred by M.

R. v. SECRETARY OF STATE FOR SOCIAL SECURITY, *ex p.* MOULE, Trans. Ref: CO-934-96, September 12, 1996, Collins, J., QBD.

5472. Income support–disability premium–single parent of disabled child–whether attendance allowance had to be received in respect of parent's own needs

[Income Support (General) Regulations 1987 Sch.2 para.13.]

Held, that the words "in receipt of attendance allowance" in the Income Support (General) Regulations 1987 Sch.2 para.13 were to be construed as meaning that the allowance should be payable in respect of the recipient's own needs. Therefore a lone parent who received attendance allowance in respect of her child who was severely disabled was not entitled under those Regulations to have a severe disability premium included in her income support.

RIDER v. CHIEF ADJUDICATION OFFICER; PALMER v. CHIEF ADJUDICATION OFFICER; DOYLE v. CHIEF ADJUDICATION OFFICER (1996) 31 B.M.L.R. 122, Nourse, L.J., CA.

5473. Income support–elderly residents in residential accommodation formerly run by local authority–liability for provision of accommodation

[National Assistance Act 1948 s.21, National Assistance Act 1948 s.26.]

The CAO appealed against two decisions that higher rate income support was payable to elderly residents in residential accommodation formerly run by the respective local authorities and which had been transferred to the management of voluntary organisations. The CAO argued that the local authorities had made arrangements with the voluntary organisations to provide residential accommodation for persons in need of care and attention within the meaning of the National Assistance Act 1948 s.21 and s.26, and accordingly, the local authorities, not the DSS, should fund the costs of their care.

Held, dismissing the appeal, that higher rate income support was payable because the arrangements between the local authorities and voluntary organisations did not qualify as provision of residential accommodation within the meaning of Part III of the 1948 Act. The arrangements did not specifically require the local authorities to pay the voluntary organisations for providing the elderly residents with residential accommodation.

CHIEF ADJUDICATION OFFICER v. QUINN; CHIEF ADJUDICATION OFFICER v. GIBBON [1996] 1 W.L.R. 1184, Lord Slynn of Hadley, HL.

5474. Income support–housing costs–whether wife's mortgage interest relief was limited to amount paid to husband as housing benefit when tenant–whether separation was major change of circumstances for purposes of income support regulations

[Income Support (General) Regulations 1987 Sch.3.]

K appealed against a decision relating to the restrictions placed on the amount of housing costs added to her weekly applicable amount of income support. While K and her husband were secure tenants, K's husband was in receipt of housing benefit of £50 per week which was the amount of rent payable. K and her husband purchased their home with the help of a mortgage and the interest payments were £88 per week. K's husband left England for India and on his return some months later lived apart from K, the marriage having broken down. Before his return K applied for, and was granted, income support in her own right. After her husband's return to England, K made a claim for additional housing costs to cover her interest payments, but was refused. The adjudication officer claimed that the amount of income support was restricted, under the Income Support (General) Regulations 1987 Sch.3 para.10, to the amount payable before acquisition of the property. An appeal was allowed on the grounds that there had been a major change in the circumstances of the family within the definition of para.10(2)(b). This decision was successfully appealed and it was decided that the removal of the restriction could be allowed only when the change in circumstances occurred after the restriction had been applied. K argued that on the wording of para.10(1)(b), at the time of the purchase, the purchaser must be a claimant. K did not claim income support until a later date. K also argued that the commissioner was wrong to find that the change in circumstances had to occur after the restriction was applied.

Held, dismissing the appeal, that (1) para.10 did not imply a sequential order. It merely stated the three conditions which must exist before the restriction could be applied. The only temporal link was achieved by para.10(2)(a) which prevented the restriction from biting unless the claimant or a member of the family who acquired the interest was in receipt of income support when he became liable to complete the purchase and (2) para.10(2)(b) could only be used after the restriction had been applied. K's separation from her husband was a major change in circumstances but it happened before K had made her claim.

KAUR v. CHIEF ADJUDICATION OFFICER [1995] 2 F.L.R. 559, Morritt, L.J., CA.

5475. Income support–interest rates

INCOME SUPPORT (GENERAL) (STANDARD INTEREST RATE AMENDMENT) REGULATIONS 1996, SI 1996 1363; made under the Social Security Contributions and Benefits Act 1992 s.135, s.137, s.175. In force: June 23, 1996; £0.65.

These Regulations amend the Income Support (General) Regulations 1987 (SI 1987 1967), as substituted and amended, with respect to the standard rate of interest applicable to a loan which qualifies for income support under that Schedule to those Regulations. The new rate is 7.48 per cent. They also revoke, with a saving provision, regulations which made a previous amendment to that rate of interest.

5476. Income support–interest rates

INCOME SUPPORT (GENERAL) (STANDARD INTEREST RATE AMENDMENT) (NO.2) REGULATIONS 1996, SI 1996 1889; made under the Social Security Contributions and Benefits Act 1992 s.135, s.137, s.175. In force: August 25, 1996; £0.65.

These Regulations amend the Income Support (General) Regulations 1987 Sch.3 (SI 1987 1967), with respect to the standard rate of interest applicable to a loan which qualifies for income support under Sch.3. The new rate is 7.16 per cent.

5477. Income support–interest rates

INCOME SUPPORT (GENERAL) (STANDARD INTEREST RATE AMENDMENT) (NO.3) REGULATIONS 1996, SI 1996 2903; made under the Social Security Contributions and Benefits Act 1992 s.135, s.137, s.175. In force: December 15, 1996; £1.10.

These Regulations amend the Income Support (General) Regulations 1987 Sch.2 (SI 1987 1967) with respect to the standard rate of interest applicable to a loan which qualifies for income support under that Schedule. The new rate is 6.89 per cent.

5478. Income support–jobseeker's allowance–consequential amendments

INCOME SUPPORT (GENERAL) (JOBSEEKER'S ALLOWANCE CONSEQUENTIAL AMENDMENTS) REGULATIONS 1996, SI 1996 206; made under the Social Security Contributions and Benefits Act 1992 s.124, s.137, s.175; and the Jobseekers Allowance Act 1995 s.40. In force: October 7, 1996; £3.70.

These Regulations further amend the Income Support (General) Regulations 1987 (SI 1987 1967). The amendments are consequential on the coming into force of the Jobseekers Act 1995, which replaces income support for the unemployed and unemployment benefit with jobseeker's allowance. These Regulations insert a new Reg.4ZA and Sch.1B prescribing the categories of person eligible to claim income support into the 1987 Regulations. All the regulations relating to availability for and actively seeking employment are revoked, as are the special entitlement and registration rules for claimants aged 16 or 17, although special applicable amounts for this age group continue. There is special provision for claimants who may be entitled alternately to income support or jobseeker's allowance, so that entitlement to an income based jobseeker's allowance may count towards satisfaction of any condition where a claimant is entitled to income support for a certain period of time.

5479. Income support–jobseeker's allowance–pilot scheme

INCOME SUPPORT (PILOT SCHEME) REGULATIONS 1996, SI 1996 1252; made under the Social Security Contributions and Benefits Act 1992 s.137, s.175; and the Jobseekers Act 1995 s.29, s.35. In force: July 8, 1996; £1.55.

These Regulations establish a pilot scheme under the Jobseekers Act 1995 which relates to persons claiming income support who fit certain age criteria and who have been receiving benefit continuously. Relevant persons must participate in Project Work if they are or have been receiving benefit in certain circumstances and persons will be treated as not available for employment if they refuse or fail to participate in Project Work or lose their place on Project Work due to misconduct.

5480. Income support–mentally handicapped resident in nursing home–daily care not including treatment for mental illness–whether entitled to income support

[Social Security (Hospital In-Patients) Regulations 1975 Reg.2.]

B, a severely mentally disabled resident in a nursing home, appealed against a social security commissioner's decision rejecting her claim for income support. She argued that, as she did not receive treatment for a mental illness and only received nursing care in her daily life, she was not a person receiving in-patient treatment in a hospital or similar institution for the purposes of the Social Security (Hospital In-Patients) Regulations 1975 Reg.2 as amended, and was therefore entitled to receive income support.

Held, dismissing the appeal, that although B and the other nursing home residents received only nursing care, the attention they received was to be regarded as "medical or other treatment" under the 1975 Regulations, and their degree of mental handicap was such as to fall within the definition of "mental disorder", which was wide enough to encompass malfunction of the mind other than impairment caused by illness.

BOTCHETT v. CHIEF ADJUDICATION OFFICER (1996) 32 B.M.L.R. 153, Evans, L.J., CA.

5481. Income support–overpayments–mortgage interest rate reduced–overpayment not recoverable where claimant unaware of reduction–whether overpayment could be recovered

[Social Security Administration Act 1992 s.71.]

F appealed against a social security commissioner's decision that the Department of Social Security was entitled, under s.71 (1) of the Social Security Administration Act 1992, to recover from her an overpayment of income support. Each time she collected her benefit she was required to sign a declaration stating that she had correctly reported any facts which could affect the amount of income support to which she was entitled. After her initial claim, the interest rate on her mortgage was reduced but it was accepted that F had not known of this reduction. The Secretary of State maintained, however, that the overpayment could be recovered even though the misrepresentation was innocent.

Held, allowing the appeal, that the declaration which F signed should be construed as a representation that there were no facts known to her at the time of signing which could affect the amount of payment but which she had not reported, *Jones v. Chief Adjudication Officer* [1994] 1 W.L.R. 62, [1994] C.L.Y. 4178. On this construction, the overpayment was not recoverable.

FRANKLIN v. CHIEF ADJUDICATION OFFICER, *The Times*, December 29, 1995, Staughton, L.J., CA.

5482. Income support–overpayments–mortgage interest rate reduced–recovery of overpayment direct from mortgage lender

[Social Security (Claims and Payments) Regulations 1987 Sch.9A; Social Security Administration Act 1992 s.71.]

The Secretary of State appealed against a decision refusing recovery of money overpaid to G's mortgage lender, being the mortgage interest portion of G's income support entitlement. The overpayment of £1,261.71 occurred as a result of interest rate reductions during 1994, which were not notified at the time of the reduction, but at the end of the year in reliance upon the Social Security (Claims and Payments) Regulations 1987 Sch.9A para.10. The Secretary of State contended that liability to make repayments arose by virtue of Sch.9A para.11 of the 1987 Regulations, whereas G submitted that the power of recovery conferred by para.11 should only apply in respect of payments that ought not to have been made under the award in force at the time the payment was made and not, as here, where the duty to notify the rate reduction only arose after the payment occurred.

Held, allowing the appeal, that the possibility of a failure to notify a change in the lender's interest rate gave rise to the need for a repayment provision, irrespective of whether the overpayment occurred due to clerical error, oversight on the part of the lender, or the non-notification of an interest rate reduction. In such cases recovery under Sch.9A provided a more satisfactory method of recovery than that available under the Social Security Administration Act 1992 s.71, given the need to effect repayment direct from the lender. Schedule 9A para.10 contained no requirement for notification until the next annual report by the lender, and the claimant was under a duty to inform but might fail to do so, owing either to ignorance or omission, whether deliberately or inadvertently. Given this state of affairs, the power conferred by para.11 enabled the Secretary of State to recover the overpayments from the lender at the time they occurred under the terms of the award in force at that point.

R. v. ADJUDICATION OFFICER, *ex p.* GOLDING; SUB NOM. R. v. SECRETARY OF STATE FOR SOCIAL SECURITY, *ex p.* GOLDING, Trans. Ref: 96/0326/D, July 1, 1996, Henry, L.J., CA.

5483. Income support–person from abroad–Dutch national burden to the taxpayer–standard letter requested to leave–whether "required to leave" UK and therefore not entitled to income support–statutory interpretation

[Income Support (General) Regulations 1987 Sch.7.]

W, a Dutch national, sought judicial review of a decision of an adjudication officer that her income support should be stopped because she was a person from abroad with no entitlement to payment. W came to the UK with her partner, a UK national, and their son. The relationship broke down and W and her son lived with her partner's sister. She received a letter from the Immigration and Nationality Department at Croydon which pointed out that she was allowed into the UK as a citizen of a member state in order to seek or take employment or to reside in a non-economic capacity. However, once she had become a burden on the state she was no longer lawfully resident under EU law. The letter asked her to leave the country, but stated that if she did not leave of her own accord, she would not be deported. The question was whether or not the letter meant she came within the definition of "persons from abroad" under the Income Support (General) Regulations 1987 Sch.7(h) which stated that such a person was "a national of a member state and is required by the Secretary of State to leave the United Kingdom".

Held, allowing the application, that the letter clearly did not require W to leave the UK; therefore she did not come within Sch.7(h) of the 1987 Regulations, Commissioners' decision in *Remilien* distinguished, *R. v. Secretary of State for the Home Department, ex p. Vitale* [1995] 3 C.M.L.R. 605, [1995] 1 C.L.Y. 52 and *R. v. Westminster City Council, ex p. Castelli (No.2)* (1996) 28 H.L.R. 616, [1996] C.L.Y. 3058 considered.

R. v. OXFORD SOCIAL SECURITY APPEAL TRIBUNAL, *ex p.* WOLKE [1996] C.O.D. 418, Popplewell, J., QBD.

5484. Income support–person from abroad–French national burden on public funds–single parent–requirement to leave UK

[Income Support (General) Regulations 1987 Reg.21.]

The Secretary of State appealed against a social security commissioner's decision to allow R's appeal against a decision that she was not entitled to income support. R, a French national and therefore a European Economic Area national, had come to the UK with her partner, but they separated and she, a single parent, had responsibility for the care of two children. R received a letter from the Home Office stating that she had become a burden on public funds and should make arrangements to leave the country, although the letter also stated that no steps would be taken to enforce departure.

Held, allowing the appeal, that, in terms of the Income Support (General) Regulations 1987 Reg.21(3)(h), as amended, the letter amounted to a requirement by the Secretary of State that R should leave the UK, even if there were no immediate plans to enforce that requirement. Therefore, under the 1987 Regulations R was a "person from abroad" whose applicable amount, for income support purposes, was nil under Sch.7 of the 1987 Regulations.

SECRETARY OF STATE FOR SOCIAL SECURITY v. REMILIEN; R. v. SECRETARY OF STATE FOR SOCIAL SECURITY, *ex p.* WOLKE; SUB NOM. R. v. CHIEF ADJUDICATION OFFICER, *ex p.* REMELIEN; CHIEF ADJUDICATION OFFICER v. WOLKE [1996] All E.R. (EC) 850, Kennedy, L.J., CA.

5485. Industrial injuries–compensation

WORKMEN'S COMPENSATION (SUPPLEMENTATION) (AMENDMENT) SCHEME 1996, SI 1996 598; made under the Social Security Contributions and Benefits Act 1992 Sch.8 para.2; and the Social Security Administration Act 1992 Sch.9 para.1. In force: April 10, 1996; £1.10.

This Scheme amends the Workmen's Compensation (Supplementation) Scheme 1982 (SI 1982 1489) by making adjustments to the lower rates of incapacity allowance consequential upon the increase in the maximum rate of that allowance. The scheme also makes transitional provisions.

5486. Industrial injuries–dependants–permitted earnings limits

SOCIAL SECURITY (INDUSTRIAL INJURIES) (DEPENDENCY) (PERMITTED EARNINGS LIMITS) ORDER 1996, SI 1996 671; made under the Social Security Contributions and Benefits Act 1992 s.175, Sch.7 para.4. In force: April 8, 1996; £0.65.

Where a disablement pension with an unemployability supplement is increased in respect of a child and the beneficiary is one of two persons who are spouses residing together or an unmarried couple, the Social Security Contributions and Benefits Act 1992 Sch.7 para.4(4) provides that the increase shall not be payable in respect of the first child if the other person's earnings are £125 a week or more and in respect of a further child for each complete £16 where the earnings exceed £125. This Order substitutes the amount of £130 for the amount of £125 and £17 for the amount of £16. Article 3 contains revocations consequent upon the coming into force of this Order.

5487. Industrial injuries–industrial diseases

SOCIAL SECURITY (INDUSTRIAL INJURIES AND DISEASES) (MISCELLANEOUS AMENDMENTS) REGULATIONS 1996, SI 1996 425; made under the Social Security Contributions and Benefits Act 1992 s.108, s.109, s.113, s.122, s.175, Sch.7 para.13; and the Social Security Administration Act 1992 s.5, s.27, s.189. In force: March 24, 1996; £1.55.

The circumstances in which a person, who is entitled to reduced earnings allowance under the Social Security Contributions and Benefits Act 1992 Sch.7, is to be treated as having given up regular employment for the purposes of that allowance are prescribed by these Regulations, which amend the Social Security (Adjudication) Regulations 1995 (SI 1995 1801), the Social Security (Claims and

Payments) Regulations 1987 (SI 1987 1968), the Social Security (General Benefit) Regulations 1982 (SI 1982 1408), the Social Security (Industrial Injuries) (Prescribed Diseases) Regulations 1984 (SI 1985 967) and the Social Security (Industrial Injuries) (Regular Employment) Regulations 1990 (SI 1990 256). A new definition of regular employment is given and the period in respect of which reduced earnings allowance is payable following a late claim or application for a review is altered. Other amendments include the alteration of the list of prescribed diseases in the 1985 Regulations.

5488. Invalid care allowance

SOCIAL SECURITY (INVALID CARE ALLOWANCE) AMENDMENT REGULATIONS 1996, SI 1996 2744; made under the Social Security Contributions and Benefits Act 1992 s.70, s.175. In force: November 25, 1996; £1.10.

These Regulations substitute throughout the Social Security (Invalid Care Allowance) Regulations 1976 (SI 1976 409) equivalent references to the Social Security Contributions and Benefits Act 1992 for references to the Social Security Act 1975. The 1976 Regulations Reg.8(1) provide that a person is not to be treated as gainfully employed on any day in a week unless his earnings in the immediately preceding week have exceeded a specified amount. Paragraph 2(c) of that Regulation provides that there is to be disregarded for the purposes of para.1, a person's earnings on the week immediately preceding the week in respect of which that person (if his earnings in that week were disregarded) would first become entitled to an invalid care allowance and amends the 1976 Regulations Reg.8(2) by omitting sub-para.(c).

5489. Jobseeker's Act 1995–Commencement No.2 Order

JOBSEEKERS ACT 1995 (COMMENCEMENT NO.2) ORDER 1996, SI 1996 1126 (C.18); made under the Jobseekers Act 1995 s.41. In force: bringing into force various provisions of the Act on April 22, 1996; £0.65.

This Order provides for the coming into force on April 22, 1996 of certain provisions in the Jobseekers Act 1995 Sch.2 which introduce into the Social Security Administration Act 1993 (c.4) and the Local Government Finance Act 1992 (c.14) references to the Jobseekers Act 1995.

5490. Jobseeker's Act 1995–Commencement No.3 Order

JOBSEEKERS ACT 1995 (COMMENCEMENT NO.3) ORDER 1996, SI 1996 1509 (C.29); made under the Jobseekers Act 1995 s.41. In force: bringing into force various provisions of the Act on June 11, 1996; £1.10.

This Order provides for the coming into force on June 11, 1996 of certain provisions in Sch.2 which make consequential amendments to other legislation, including the Social Security Administration Act 1992.

5491. Jobseeker's Act 1995–Commencement No.4 Order

JOBSEEKERS ACT 1995 (COMMENCEMENT NO.4) ORDER 1996, SI 1996 2208 (C.54); made under the Jobseekers Act 1995 s.41. In force: bringing into force various provisions of the Act on September 2, 1996 and October 7, 1996; £1.10.

This Order provides for the coming into force of the Jobseekers Act 1995 Sch.2 para.2, Sch.2 para.12 and Sch.2 para.14 on September 2, 1996 and for the whole of the remainder of the Act, in so far as not already in force, to come into force on October 7, 1996.

5492. Jobseeker's allowance

JOBSEEKER'S ALLOWANCE REGULATIONS 1996, SI 1996 207; made under the Social Security Contributions and Benefits Act 1992 s.171D, s.171G, s.175; the

Social Security Administration Act 1992 s.5, s.22, s.23, s.59, s.189, s.191, Sch.3; and the Jobseekers Act 1995 s.2, s.3, s.4, s.5, s.6, s.7, s.8, s.9, s.10, s.11, s.12, s.13, s.15, s.17, s.19, s.20, s.21, s.22, s.23, s.35, s.36, s.40, Sch.1. In force: October 7, 1996; £13.30.

These Regulations contain provisions relating to the introduction of the new benefit known as jobseekers' allowance. Detailed provisions are made on the requirement to be available for employment. In particular, they provide that a person must normally be available to take up employment of at least 40 hours a week or that the times he is available must offer reasonable prospects of securing employment; or may place other restrictions on his availability provided that he can show that he has reasonable prospects of securing employment notwithstanding those restrictions. The Regulations also deal with the active seeking of employment by the claimant; attendance, information and evidence; the jobseeker's agreement; other conditions of entitlement; young persons; sanctions; membership of a family; the amount of jobseeker's allowance; treatment of income and capital; hardship; urgent cases; part-weeks; and special categories of persons.

5493. Jobseeker's allowance

JOBSEEKER'S ALLOWANCE (AMENDMENT) REGULATIONS 1996, SI 1996 1516; made under the Jobseekers Act 1995 s.4, s.9, s.12, s.13, s.19, s.20, s.35, s.36, Sch.1 para.1, Sch.1 para.3, Sch.1 para.8, Sch.1 para.10, Sch.1 para.12, Sch.1 para.16, Sch.1 para.17. In force: October 7, 1996; £2.80.

These Regulations amend the Jobseeker's Allowance Regulations 1996 (SI 1996 207). They make provisions relating to the jobseeker's agreement, young persons, voluntary redundancy, persons receiving training allowance, remunerative work, persons from abroad, the calculation of tariff income from capital, hardship payments, the provision of information, part-weeks, share fishermen and young persons.

5494. Jobseeker's allowance–adjudication

SOCIAL SECURITY (ADJUDICATION) AMENDMENT REGULATIONS 1996, SI 1996 1518; made under the Social Security Administration Act 1992 s.27, s.59, s.61, s.189, s.191, Sch.3; and the Jobseekers Act 1995 s.31, s.35, s.36, Sch.1 para.4. In force: October 7, 1996; £1.95.

These Regulations make amendments to the Social Security (Adjudication) Regulations 1995 (SI 1995 1801) in consequence of the replacement of unemployment benefit and income support for the unemployed by jobseeker's allowance under the Jobseekers Act 1995. The principal amendments relate to notification of decisions, questions not immediately determinable and reviews of decisions. These are amended so as to make provision in relation to jobseeker's allowance which is comparable to that made in relation to income support. A new Regulation is inserted which provides that where a person is in receipt of jobseeker's allowance and he or his partner wishes to claim income support instead, or vice versa, the adjudication officer may stop the payment of the claimant's current benefit if he is satisfied that the claimant or his partner will become entitled to other benefit. The Regulation also provides that when a person claims jobseeker's allowance under this procedure he will not have to serve the normal three waiting days before he becomes entitled to the allowance.

5495. Jobseeker's allowance–adjudication

SOCIAL SECURITY (ADJUDICATION) AMENDMENT (NO.2) REGULATIONS 1996, SI 1996 2659; made under the Social Security Administration Act 1992 s.61, s.189, s.191. In force: November 8, 1996; £1.10.

These Regulations amend the Social Security (Adjudication) Regulations 1995 (SI 1995 1801), which concern review of jobseeker's allowance. The amendments make provision in respect of those treated as having been awarded a jobseeker's allowance in accordance with the Jobseeker's Allowance (Transitional Provisions) Regulations 1996 (SI 1996 2567) Reg.7 whereby jobseeker's allowance replaces income support and unemployment benefit. They provide for the date on which a determination on a review is to have effect in relation to a person's claim to jobseeker's allowance where reductions in capital outstanding on a loan have occurred generally to be the first and subsequent anniversaries of the date on which housing costs were first met in relation to that person's claim to income support.

5496. Jobseeker's allowance–bonus schemes

SOCIAL SECURITY (BACK TO WORK BONUS) (AMENDMENT) REGULATIONS 1996, SI 1996 1511; made under the Jobseekers Act 1995 s.26, s.35, s.36. In force: October 7, 1996; £0.65.

The Regulations contain amendments to the Social Security (Back to Work Bonus) Regulations 1996 (SI 1996 193). In particular, Reg.20 introduces two new regulations. Regulation 25A provides that, in certain circumstances, a back to work bonus may be claimed, and awarded, in advance of the requirements for a bonus, including the work condition, being satisfied. Regulation 25B provided that where a person satisfied the requirements for a back to work bonus, but died before claiming it, the bonus may be claimed by someone else.

5497. Jobseeker's allowance–bonus schemes

SOCIAL SECURITY (BACK TO WORK BONUS) (NO.2) REGULATIONS 1996, SI 1996 2570; made under the Jobseeker's Act 1995 s.26, s.35, s.36. In force: November 4, 1996; £3.70.

These Regulations revoke the Social Security (Back to Work Bonus) Regulations 1996 (SI 1996 193), the Social Security (Back to Work Bonus) (Amendment) Regulations 1996 (SI 1996 1511), the Child Support (Jobseeker's Allowance) (Miscellaneous Amendments) Regulations 1996 (SI 1996 2538) Reg.4 and consolidates the provisions of those Regulations.

5498. Jobseeker's allowance–child support–consequential amendments

SOCIAL SECURITY AND CHILD SUPPORT (JOBSEEKER'S ALLOWANCE) (CONSEQUENTIAL AMENDMENTS) REGULATIONS 1996, SI 1996 1345; made under the Jobseekers Act 1995 s.35, s.36, s.40. In force: October 7, 1996; £3.20.

These Regulations amend various social security Regulations by replacing references to unemployment benefit with references to jobseeker's allowance and by adding references to jobseeker's allowance where existing Regulations refer to income support. The amendments are made in consequence of the coming into force of the Jobseekers Act 1995 which replaces income support with the jobseeker's allowance.

5499. Jobseeker's allowance–child support–miscellaneous amendments

SOCIAL SECURITY AND CHILD SUPPORT (JOBSEEKER'S ALLOWANCE) (MISCELLANEOUS AMENDMENTS) REGULATIONS 1996, SI 1996 2538; made under the Social Security Administration Act 1992 s.61, s.71; and the Jobseekers Act 1995 s.3, s.4, s.5, s.8, s.12, s.20, s.21, s.26, s.35, s.36, s.40, Sch.1 para.3. In force: October 28, 1996; £2.40.

These Regulations amend the Jobseeker's Allowance Regulations (SI 1996 207), the Jobseeker's Allowance (Transitional Provisions) Regulations 1995 (SI 1995 3276), the Social Security (Back to Work Bonus) Regulations 1996 (SI 1996 193), the Social Security (General Benefit) Regulations 1982 (SI 1982 1408), the Jobseeker's Allowance and Income Support (General) (Amendment) Regulations 1996 (SI 1996 1517) and the Child Support (Maintenance Assessment Procedure) Regulations 1992 (SI 1992 1813).

5500. Jobseeker's allowance–child support–transitional provisions

SOCIAL SECURITY AND CHILD SUPPORT (JOBSEEKER'S ALLOWANCE) (TRANSITIONAL PROVISIONS) (AMENDMENT) REGULATIONS 1996, SI 1996 2378; made under the Child Support Act 1991 s.51; and the Jobseekers Act 1995 s.35, s.36, s.40. In force: October 6, 1996; £1.10.

These Regulations amend the Jobseeker's Allowance (Transitional Provisions) (Amendment) Regulations 1996 (SI 1996 1515) and make provision for awards of unemployment benefit during the period October 7 to October 20, 1996 to be treated as an award of unemployment benefit and thereafter as an award of a jobseeker's allowance. They also amend the Child Support (Miscellaneous Amendments) Regulations 1996 (SI 1996 1945) to insert references to amendments made by the Social Security and Child Support (Jobseeker's Allowance) (Consequential Amendments) Regulations 1996 (SI 1996 1345).

5501. Jobseeker's allowance–claims–payments

SOCIAL SECURITY (CLAIMS AND PAYMENTS) (JOBSEEKER'S ALLOWANCE CONSEQUENTIAL AMENDMENTS) REGULATIONS 1996, SI 1996 1460; made under the Social Security Administration Act 1992 s.1, s.5, s.7, s.15A, s.189, s.191; and the Jobseekers Act 1995 s.26, s.35, s.36. In force: October 7, 1996; £2.80.

These Regulations make amendments to the Social Security (Claims and Payments) Regulations 1987 (SI 1987 1968) which are consequential on the coming into force of the Jobseekers Act 1995 which, inter alia, replaces unemployment benefit and income support for those available for and actively seeking employment with a new benefit called jobseeker's allowance.

5502. Jobseeker's allowance–deductions

SOCIAL SECURITY (JOBSEEKER'S ALLOWANCE CONSEQUENTIAL AMENDMENTS) (DEDUCTIONS) REGULATIONS 1996, SI 1996 2344; made under the Abolition of Domestic Rates Etc. (Scotland) Act 1987 Sch.2 para.7A; the Local Government Finance Act 1988 s.146, Sch.4 para.6; the Criminal Justice Act 1991 s.24; the Social Security Administration Act 1992 s.5, s.189, s.191; and the Local Government Finance Act 1992 s.14, s.97, s.116, Sch.4 para.1, Sch.4 para.6, Sch.8 para.6. In force: October 7, 1996; £2.40.

These Regulations amend the Community Charges (Deductions from Income Support) (Scotland) Regulations 1989 (SI 1989 507), the Community Charges (Deductions from Income Support) (No.2) Regulations 1990 (SI 1990 545), the Fines (Deductions from Income Support) Regulations 1992 (SI 1992 2182) and the Council Tax (Deductions from Income Support) Regulations 1993 (SI 1993 494), which provide that deductions may be made from a person's income support and paid towards arrears of community charges or council tax, or towards fines or compensation orders imposed by a court. The Regulations are amended so that deductions can also be made from the jobseeker's allowance. These Regulations also amend the Social Security (Claims and Payments) Regulations 1987 (SI 1987 1968) to provide that deductions in respect of arrears of child support maintenance can be made from a person's contribution-based jobseeker's allowance.

5503. Jobseeker's allowance–income support

JOBSEEKER'S ALLOWANCE AND INCOME SUPPORT (GENERAL) (AMENDMENT) REGULATIONS 1996, SI 1996 1517; made under the Social Security Contributions and Benefits Act 1992 s.124; the Social Security Administration Act 1992 s.5; and the Jobseekers Act 1995 s.4, s.6, s.7, s.8, s.9, s.19, s.21, s.35, s.36, Sch.1 para.4, Sch.1 para.9, Sch.1 para.12, Sch.1 para.16. In force: October 7, 1996; £2.80.

These Regulations contain amendments to the Jobseeker's Allowance Regulations 1996 (SI 1996 207) and the Income Support (General) Regulations 1987 (SI 1987 1967). The amendments relate to part-time students and volunteers; circumstances in which persons are treated as available; laid off and short time workers; circumstances in which persons are to be treated as actively seeking employment; the provision of information and evidence; the time at which entitlement ceases; the remaining in effect of the jobseeker's agreement; the interpretation of Part IV of the 1995 Act; attendance, information, evidence and sanctions for young persons; the jobseeking period; linking periods; persons approaching retirement; short periods of sickness; persons being treated as being or not being a member of a household; payments by way of pensions; permitted periods; the minimum amount of allowance; earnings of employed earners; the calculation of income other than earnings and grant income; the meaning of person in hardship and circumstances in which an allowance is payable to such a person, the applicable amount in hardship cases, housing costs, applicable amount in special cases, sums to be disregarded in the calculation of earnings and occupational pensions.

5504. Jobseeker's allowance–national insurance contributions–consequential provisions

SOCIAL SECURITY (CREDITS AND CONTRIBUTIONS) (JOBSEEKER'S ALLOWANCE CONSEQUENTIAL AND MISCELLANEOUS AMENDMENTS) REGULATIONS 1996, SI 1996 2367; made under the Social Security Contributions and Benefits Act 1992 s.22, s.122, s.175; and the Jobseekers Act 1995 s.35, s.40. In force: October 7, 1996; £1.95.

These Regulations amend the Social Security (Credits) Regulations 1975 (SI 1975 55) and the Social Security (Contributions) Regulations 1979 (SI 1979 591). Regulation 2 amends the 1975 Regulations in consequence of the coming into force of the Jobseekers Act 1995 and also makes some miscellaneous amendments to those Regulations. In particular, it separates into three Regulations the matters formerly covered by Reg.9 of those Regulations. The new Reg.8A provides for credits to be awarded for weeks in respect of which a jobseeker's allowance is paid or the conditions for receiving that allowance are satisfied. The new Reg.8B replaces the existing provision for entitlement to credits during periods of incapacity for work. The substituted Reg.9 replaces the existing provision for restricting the crediting of earnings in respect of periods of unemployment or incapacity for the purposes of entitlement for short-term incapacity benefit. Regulation 3 amends the 1979 Regulations in consequence of the coming into force of the Jobseekers Act 1995. Regulation 4 provides for savings and transitional arrangement.

5505. Jobseeker's allowance–payments

SOCIAL SECURITY (JOBSEEKER'S ALLOWANCE AND PAYMENTS ON ACCOUNT) (MISCELLANEOUS AMENDMENTS) REGULATIONS 1996, SI 1996 2519; made under the Social Security Administration Act 1992 s.71, s.74, s.189, s.191; and the Jobseeker's Act 1995 s.35, s.36, s.40. In force: October 7, 1996; £1.55.

These Regulations amend the Jobseeker's Allowance (Transitional Provisions) Regulations 1995 (SI 1995 3276) and the Social Security (Payments on Account, Overpayments and Recovery) Regulations 1988 (SI 1988 664).

5506. Jobseeker's allowance–pilot scheme

JOBSEEKER'S ALLOWANCE (PILOT SCHEME) REGULATIONS 1996, SI 1996 1307; made under the Jobseekers Act 1995 s.19, s.20, s.29, s.35, s.36, s.40. In force: October 7, 1996; £1.55.

These Regulations apply the scheme established by the Income Support (Pilot Scheme) Regulations 1996 (SI 1996 1252) to persons claiming a jobseeker's allowance. Regulation 3 sets out the criteria of a relevant person for the purposes of the Scheme and Reg.4 places a sanction of a two week or four week loss or reduction in jobseeker's allowance for those failing to participate in the employment programme known as Project Work or lose their place on the programme due to misconduct.

5507. Jobseeker's allowance–pilot scheme

JOBSEEKER'S ALLOWANCE (PILOT SCHEME) (AMENDMENT) REGULATIONS 1996, SI 1996 1856; made under the Jobseekers Act 1995 s.19, s.20, s.29, s.35, s.36, s.40. In force: October 7, 1996; £0.65.

These Regulations amend the Jobseeker's Allowance (Pilot Scheme) Regulations 1996 (SI 1996 1307) by adding an office to those listed in the Schedule. This has the effect that persons who are required to attend that office may fall within the application of the 1996 Regulations and may thus, subject to certain exceptions, receive a sanction in accordance with the Jobseekers Act s.19 and the Jobseeker's Allowance Regulations 1996 (SI 1996 207) if they fail to participate in the employment programme known as Project Work.

5508. Jobseeker's allowance–recovery from employer

EMPLOYMENT PROTECTION (RECOUPMENT OF JOBSEEKER'S ALLOWANCE AND INCOME SUPPORT) REGULATIONS 1996, SI 1996 2349; made under the Social Security Administration Act 1992 s.58; and the Industrial Tribunals Act 1996 s.16, s.41. In force: October 7, 1996; £2.40.

These Regulations replace the Employment Protection (Recoupment of Unemployment Benefit and Supplementary Benefit) Regulations 1977 (SI 1977 674 as amended by SI 1980 1608, SI 1984 458 and SI 1988 419), make provision for the recovery by the Secretary of State from an employer of sums on account of jobseeker's allowance and income support out of a prescribed part of an amount awarded by an industrial tribunal in certain proceedings brought by an employee against an employer. The new Regulations are in part consequential upon the introduction of jobseeker's allowance on October 7, 1996, but also update the provisions dealing with the determination of any question as to the amount of benefit which is recoverable and for the review of that determination.

5509. Jobseeker's allowance–transitional provisions

JOBSEEKER'S ALLOWANCE (TRANSITIONAL PROVISIONS) REGULATIONS 1996, SI 1996 2567; made under the Jobseeker's Act 1995 s.35, s.36, s.40. In force: November 4, 1996; £3.20.

These Regulations revoke the Jobseeker's Allowance (Transitional Provisions) Regulations 1995 (SI 1995 3276), the Jobseeker's Allowance (Transitional Provisions) (Amendment) Regulations 1996 (SI 1996 1515), the Social Security and Child Support (Jobseeker's Allowance) (Transitional Provisions) Amendment Regulations 1996 (SI 1996 2378) Reg.2, the Social Security (Jobseeker's Allowance and Payments on Account) (Miscellaneous Amendments) Regulations 1996 (SI 1996 2519) Reg.2, the Social Security and Child Support (Jobseeker's Allowance) (Miscellaneous Amendments) Regulations 1996 (SI 1996 2538) Reg.3 and consolidates the provisions of those Regulations. These Regulations provide for continuity between unemployment benefit and income support for those who are required to be available for and actively seeking employment, and jobseeker's allowance.

5510. Jobseeker's allowance–transitional provisions

JOBSEEKER'S ALLOWANCE (TRANSITIONAL PROVISIONS) (AMENDMENT) REGULATIONS 1996, SI 1996 1515; made under the Jobseekers Act 1995 s.35, s.36, s.40. In force: October 7, 1996; £1.95.

These regulations amend the Jobseeker's Allowance (Transitional Provisions) Regulations 1995 (SI 1995 3276). They insert new provisions, in particular relating to the provision of information.

5511. Maternity pay–statutory sick pay

SOCIAL SECURITY CONTRIBUTIONS, STATUTORY MATERNITY PAY AND STATUTORY SICK PAY (MISCELLANEOUS AMENDMENTS) REGULATIONS

1996, SI 1996 777; made under the Social Security Contributions and Benefits Act 1992 s.153, s.156, s.162, s.163, s.170, s.171, Sch.1 para.6; and the Social Security Administration Act 1992 s.130. In force: April 6, 1996; £1.55.

These Regulations further amend the Statutory Sick Pay (General) Regulations 1982 (SI 1982 894), the Statutory Sick Pay (Mariners, Airmen and Persons Abroad) Regulations 1982 (SI 1982 1349), the Statutory Maternity Pay (Persons Abroad and Mariners) Regulations 1987 (SI 1987 418) and the Social Security (Contributions) Regulations 1979 (SI 1979 591). These Regulations make provisions enabling statutory sick pay and statutory maternity pay to be paid to employees (including mariners, airmen and continental shelf employees) who go outside Great Britain on holidays or business; and reduces the extent of the records an employer is required to maintain (Reg.2, Reg.3, Reg.4, and Reg.5). As respects statutory sick pay alone, these Regulations also make provision reducing the time limit within which an employee may notify his employer of sickness absence where there is good cause for delay; and introducing flexibility into the manner in which, and the time limit within which, an employer is required to provide information to his employees (Reg.2 and Reg.5). These Regulations also make a transitional provision in respect of women whose expected weeks of confinement fall before August 18, 1996 (Reg.6).

5512. National Insurance–contributions–employers

The Contributions Agency issued a press release entitled *New court powers to freeze personal assets of company bosses who fail to pay National Insurance contributions* (Press release 96/162), published on August 1, 1996. The Secretary of State for Social Security has announced new statutory powers to freeze the personal assets of employers who fail to pay their own and their employees' NI contributions.

5513. Pensions–contributions

SOCIAL SECURITY (ADDITIONAL PENSION) (CONTRIBUTIONS PAID IN ERROR) REGULATIONS 1996, SI 1996 1245; made under the Social Security Contributions and Benefits Act 1992 s.61A, s.122, s.175, Sch.1 para.8. In force: June 4, 1996; £1.10.

These Regulations, which amend the Social Security (Contributions) Regulations 1979 (SI 1979 591), apply to cases where primary Class 1 contributions have been paid in error because the individual concerned was not an employed earner. Regulation 2 sets out the prescribed conditions for the application of the Social Security Contributions and Benefits Act 1992 s.61A to an individual and Reg.3 sets out the purposes for which primary Class 1 contributions paid in error are to be treated as properly paid.

5514. Pensions–guaranteed minimum pension–valuation of earnings

SOCIAL SECURITY REVALUATION OF EARNINGS FACTORS ORDER 1996, SI 1996 1133; made under the Social Security Administration Act 1992 s.148. In force: May 17, 1996; £1.10.

This Order is made consequent upon a review under the Social Security Administration Act 1992 s.48. It directs that the earnings factors relevant to the calculation of the additional pension in the rate of any long-term benefit or of any guaranteed minimum pensions or to any other calculation required under the Pension Scheme Act 1993 Part III for the tax years specified in that Schedule. The percentage for the tax year 1995/6 is 2.8 per cent and those for earlier tax years have been increased so that the earnings factors for those years are revalued at 1995/6 earnings levels. The Order also provides for the rounding of fractional amounts for earnings factors relevant to the calculation of the additional pension in the rate of any long-term benefit. Rounding for the purposes of the calculation of any guaranteed minimum pensions is not required by virtue of the Social Security Contributions and Benefits Act 1992 s.23(2).

5515. Sickness benefit–pre-existing state of health–aggregation of insurance periods–European Union

[Council Regulation 1408/71 Art.35, Art.18; Council Regulation 2001/83.]

Between 1985 and 1989 a Dutch national worked alternately in the Netherlands and Spain. She did not work for a period of several days between her final post in Spain and that in the Netherlands, but she made no application for unemployment benefit in respect of that period. Having suffered from back pain since December 1986, she became unable to work after November 1989. A medical report showed that she was unfit for work at the time she commenced her final post in the Netherlands. The Dutch agency responsible for implementing the sickness insurance scheme informed her that it would not grant her sickness benefit as from November 1989, because at the time when her sickness insurance cover became effective (upon recommencement of employment in the Netherlands) she was already unfit for work.

Held, that Council Regulation 1408/71 Art.35(3) on the application of social security schemes to employed person, to self-employed persons and to members of their families moving within the Community, as amended by Council Regulation No.2001/83, did not apply to the legislation of a Member State which precluded, in whole or in part, the grant of sickness benefits if the worker concerned was already unfit for work at the time when he became insured under the scheme which it established. Regulation 1408/71 Art.18(1) was to be interpreted as meaning that, where such a condition was applied by the legislation of a Member State relating to the grant of cash sickness benefits, the competent institution must also take into account periods of insurance completed by the person concerned under the legislation which it administered. The fact that, having transferred his residence from one Member State to another, the person concerned was for a short period neither employed nor registered as seeking employment in the latter State, did not interrupt the continuity of the insurance periods completed by that person or preclude application of the aggregation rule laid down by Regulation 1408/71 Art.18(1).

KLAUS v. BESTUUR VAN DE NIEUWE ALGEMENE BEDRIJFSVERENING (C482/93), October 26, 1995, Judge not specified, ECJ.

5516. Social fund–application for review two years after decision–judicial review of refusal–extent of discretionary power

[Social Security Administration Act 1992 s.66.]

H applied for judicial review of a decision of a social fund manager not to review a previous decision to award a loan of £548.46 rather than a grant for the same amount. H applied for a review almost two years after the original decision. The social fund manager purported to rely on the Social Security Administration Act 1992 s. 66(1)(a) and s.66 (1)(b) for his reasons not to review the decision. Judicial review was sought on the grounds that the social fund manager confused s.66(1)(a) and s.66(1)(b) in his rejection letter. He had considered s.66(1)(a) which required an appeal to be requested within 28 days of refusal of the grant. The letter then stated that he had considered if there were "special reasons for the delay". This was purporting to be by way of consideration of s.66 (1)(b). "Special reasons", though, related to application of s.66(1)(a).

Held, granting the application, that the social fund manager failed to distinguish between s.66(1)(a) and s.66(1)(b) and thus recognise his wide discretionary power to review the decision. The previous decisions were set aside and the matter was sent back to be considered further.

R. v. SOCIAL FUND OFFICER, *ex p.* HEWSON, Trans. Ref: CO 1132/92, June 22,1995, Kennedy, L.J., QBD.

5517. Social fund–funeral payments–requirement that funeral must take place in UK constituted indirect discrimination against migrant workers–European Union

[Council Regulation 1612/68 on freedom of movement for workers within the Community; Social Fund (Maternity and Funeral Expenses) (General) Regulations 1987 Reg.7.]

On a reference from the Social Security Commissioner, the ECJ was asked to determine whether the Social Fund (Maternity and Funeral Expenses) (General) Regulations 1987 Reg.7(1)(c), which provided that funeral payments to cover expenses for burial or cremation were payable only where the funeral took place in the United Kingdom, was compatible with EU provisions prohibiting discrimination on the ground of nationality laid down in Council Regulation 1612/68 Art.7. O submitted that the condition of payment indirectly discriminated against migrant workers, but the UK contended that there was no discrimination as the condition applied to both national and migrant workers.

Held, that Art.7 of Council Regulation 1612/68 prohibited not only direct discrimination but also indirect discrimination, unless it could be objectively justified and was proportionate to the objective pursued. Although Reg.7 of the 1987 Regulations was not aimed at migrant workers, a substantial proportion of those affected by the condition of payment would be migrant workers responsible for arranging funerals in their state of origin. The UK could not objectively justify the condition by reference to the cost and difficulty of paying an allowance for a funeral outside the UK, because the expenses incurred would be no different from those incurred within the UK, especially as the payment did not cover the costs of transporting the coffin to the place of burial or cremation. It was always open to the UK to restrict the amount payable to a reasonable sum commensurate with the cost of a funeral within the UK.

O'FLYNN v. ADJUDICATION OFFICER (C237/94) [1996] All E.R. (EC) 541, DAO Edward (President), ECJ.

5518. Social Security (Overpayments) Act 1996 (c.51)

An Act to amend the Social Security Administration Act 1992 s.71 and the Social Security Administration (Northern Ireland) Act 1992 s.69.

This Act received Royal Assent on July 24, 1996.

5519. Training–allowances

PROJECT WORK (MISCELLANEOUS PROVISIONS) ORDER 1996, SI 1996 1623; made under the Employment Act 1988 s.26. In force: July 17, 1996; £1.10.

This Order provides that, for the purposes of the Social Security Contribution and Benefits Act 1992 Part I, the Jobseekers Act 1995 and of the subordinate legislation specified in the Schedule to the Order, a person using facilities provided under the Project Work programme shall be treated as participating in arrangements for training under the Employment and Training Act 1973 s.2. Any payment made to such a person in connection with his use of those facilities shall be treated as a payment of training allowance made in respect of such training.

5520. Unemployment–back to work bonus

SOCIAL SECURITY (BACK TO WORK BONUS) REGULATIONS 1996, SI 1996 193; made under the Jobseekers Act 1995 s.26, s.35, s.36. In force: October 7, 1996; £3.20.

These Regulations contain provisions relating to the back to work bonus for persons who are or have been entitled to income support or a jobseeker's allowance, including period of entitlement to a qualifying benefit; connecting period; periods of entitlement which do not qualify; waiting period; requirements for a bonus; amount payable; Secretary of State's estimates; couples who separate; single persons who become couples; single claimants who are couples; couples both of whom are entitled to a qualifying benefit;

persons attaining pensionable age; trainees; death; trade disputes; share fishermen; treatment of bonus as capital; claims and payments of bonuses.

5521. Articles

Asylum seekers and benefits *(Jonathan Parr)*: Adviser 1996, 55, 18-20. (Changes to entitlement to social security benefits for asylum applicants following implementation of 1995 Regulations).

Beating the Compensation Recovery Unit *(Nigel Spencer Ley)*: L. Ex. 1996, Apr, 38-39. (How to challenge DSS claim for repayment of benefits paid to injured plaintiff following award of damages).

Compulsory welfare benefits training–and legal aid *(Neil Bateman)*: L. Ex. 1996, Jan, 16. (Importance of knowledge of welfare law for legal aid franchise holders).

Deductions from awards in personal injuries cases *(Jack Hickey)*: G.I.L.S.I. 1996, 90(7), 289-292. (Circumstances in which social security benefits are repayable by claimants or deceased victims' families awarded damages under 1993 legislation introduced to reduce cost of employers' liability and vehicle insurance).

Important benefit changes proposed *(Neville Harris)*: J.S.S.L. 1996, 3(2), 49-51. (Changes to lone parents' benefits, housing benefit, mobility component of disability living allowance and family credit).

Incapacity for work: decisions and appeals *(Simon Osborne)*: Welf. R. Bull. 1996, 133, 9-10. (Challenges to interpretation of "all work" test introduced for assessment for incapacity in April 1995).

Income support and changing circumstances: notifying the DSS: W.B. 1996, 2(Apr), 2-3. (Events which claimants have duty to report).

Income support and mortgage interest: the new rules *(Nick Wikeley)*: J.S.S.L. 1995, 2(4), 168-178. (Whether increasing cost of mortgage interest is reflective of economy rather than of generosity of income support scheme itself which has been amended in attempt to reduce claims).

Income support post jobseeker's allowance: Welf. R. Bull. 1996, 132, 5-6. (Claimants who will still be eligible for income support but not required to be available for work after JSA comes into force October 7, 1996).

Lone parent benefits "restructuring": W.B. 1996, 1, 6-7. (New Regulations will provide mechanism for ministers to revise levels of benefits for different types of family and restructure benefits payable to single parents).

National and local guidance: Welf. R. Bull. 1996, 129, 13. (Comparison of guidance issued by Secretary of State and by area social fund officers in relation to community care grants, budgeting loans and crisis loans).

Natural justice and non-disclosure of medical evidence *(Nick Wikeley)*: J.S.S.L. 1996, 3(3), 98-99. (Proper approach to non-disclosure of medical evidence in Social Security Appeal Tribunal hearings).

Out of the mouths of babes and sucklings *(Margaret Greenfields)*: ROW Bulletin 1996, Sum, 21-22. (Background to Social Security Select Committee's review of "good cause" procedure allowing women to refuse to authorise CSA to pursue child's father for maintenance, and Government response).

Recent developments in social security law *(Sally Robertson* and *David Thomas)*: Legal Action 1996, Aug, 11-15. (Cases on administration, means tested benefits, non-means tested benefits, disability benefits and EU law).

Right decisions, speedy appeals: J.L.S.S. 1996, 41 (9), 343-344. (Department of Social Security consultation paper entitled Decision Making and Appeals in Social Security and whether administrative considerations will reduce ability of appeals system to give quality decisions).

Statute of Limitations and benefits *(Marcus Revell)*: M. Advice 1996, 40, 12-13. (Limitation considerations in actions for recovery of overpayments of social security benefits and enforcement of County Court judgments).

Suspension of benefit and judicial review *(Scott Martin)*: SCOLAG 1996, 237, 140-142. (Challenges against exercise of power to suspend social security benefits pending appeal).

Suspension of benefit: possible challenges: Welf. R. Bull. 1996, 129, 11-12. (Legal framework governing power to suspend benefit payments and means of challenging validity of suspension).

The reach of disability benefits: an examination of the disability living allowance *(Michael Daly* and *Michael Noble)*: J. Soc. Wel. & Fam. L. 1996, 18(1), 37-51. (Study shows unpredictability in extent to which benefit is reaching its eligible population).

Too much care *(Geoff Tait)*: Adviser 1996, 56, 31-35. (Difficulties faced by young people looked after by social services departments in claiming social security benefits).

5522. Books

Bedee, Henk–The International Guide to Social Security. Hardback: £117.00. ISBN 90-6544-874-8. Kluwer Law International.

Bonner, David; Hooker, Ian; White, Robin–Non Means Tested Benefits: the Legislation: Supplement 1996. Paperback: £17.95. ISBN 0-421-56800-3. Sweet & Maxwell.

Mesher, John; Wood, Penny–CPAG'S Income Related Benefits: the Legislation: 1996. Paperback: £34.00. ISBN 0-421-56770-8. Sweet & Maxwell.

Mesher, John; Wood, Penny–Income Related Benefits: the Legislation: Supplement 1996. Paperback: £17.95. ISBN 0-421-56780-5. Sweet & Maxwell.

Sohrab, Julia A.–Sexing the Benefit. Hardback: £42.50. ISBN 1-85521-705-8. Dartmouth.

Stagg, Paul–Overpayments and Recovery of Social Security Benefits. Paperback: £17.00. ISBN 0-905099-73-7. The Legal Action Group.

SOCIAL WELFARE

5523. Community care–carer assessment

ISLES OF SCILLY (CARERS) ORDER 1996, SI 1996 693; made under the Carers (Recognition and Services) Act 1995 s.3. In force: April 1, 1996; £0.65.

This Order provides that the Carers (Recognition and Services) Act 1995 (the Act) s.1 applies to the Isles of Scilly as if the Council of the Isles of Scilly were a local authority for the purposes of that section. The Act provides that, where a local authority is to decide whether the needs of a person calls for the provision of community care services and a carer so requests, the local authority must assess that carer's ability to provide and to continue to provide care to that person and shall take the results of that assessment into account when making its decision. For these purposes a carer is a person who provides or intends to provide a substantial amount of care to the person on a regular basis but not pursuant to a contract nor as a volunteer for a voluntary organisation.

5524. Community care–duty of local authority to make assessment dependent on physical availability of services

[National Health Service and Community Care Act 1990 s.47; National Assistance Act 1948 s.29.]

P, a severely disabled person, applied for judicial review of a decision of BCC that it did not owe him a duty to assess his needs under the National Health Service and Community Care Act 1990 s.47(1), because, from December 1991 he was resident in the British Home and Hospital for incurables in Streatham. P's residence at that private home was funded partly by the Berkshire Health Authority and partly by the DSS. BCC contended that s.47(1) presupposed the physical availability of services to the applicant for the duty to assess to be invoked.

Held, allowing the application and declaring that BCC should make the appropriate assessment, that (1) on a proper construction of s.47(1) of the 1990

Act there is no condition that the duty to assessment is dependent upon the physical availability of services. The duty to assess arises where the local authority has the legal power to make provision or provide community care to an individual, and (2) the duty to make arrangements under the National Assistance Act 1948 s.29(1) was confined to persons ordinarily resident within the local authority area, but the power to do so arose whenever the Secretary of State had given his approval, without regard to residence.

R. v. BERKSHIRE CC, *ex p.* P, *The Times*, August 15, 1996, Laws, J., QBD.

5525. Community care–elderly–local authorities duty to provide accommodation–whether duty to make direct provision–arrangements with voluntary organisations

[National Assistance Act 1948 s.21, s.26.]

Local authorities are obliged by the National Assistance Act 1948 s.21 (a) to make arrangements for providing accommodation for persons who, by reason of age, are in need of care and attention not otherwise available to them. The Secretary of State, further to its power under the 1948 Act, directed local authorities to make such arrangements in relation to persons ordinarily resident within their areas. Further to s.26(1) such arrangements "may include arrangements made with a voluntary organisation or with any other person who is not a local authority". W owned and managed four homes for the elderly. In December 1994 W decided to turn three of the homes over into private ownership and to close the fourth. B, aged 75, was resident in the fourth home and sought judicial review of the local authority's decision to close that home on the basis that it had a legal duty to provide accommodation. B appealed against the Court of Appeal's decision in favour of W.

Held, dismissing the appeal, that on the true construction of the National Assistance Act 1948 s.26(1), the arrangements made under s.21 of the 1948 Act might consist wholly of arrangements made with voluntary organisations or other persons and there was no obligation on local authorities to make any direct provision for residential care under their control.

R. v. WANDSWORTH LBC, *ex p.* BECKWITH (NO.1) [1996] 1 W.L.R. 60, Lord Hoffmann, HL.

5526. Community care–elderly–local authorities powers and duties–closure of residential home–whether necessary criteria for consultation had been met–whether mix of private and public care should be considered

B applied for judicial review of a decision of W to close a residential home for the elderly. W had informed interested parties and invited responses after the decision was made. B argued that (1) W had not applied the correct test in making its decision. It dealt with the closure in the context of an excess of homes rather than considering the mix of private and public care provision, and (2) it failed either to consult those interested in the decisions or to consider the representations made.

Held, allowing the application, that (1) W was not required to consider the public and private provision of residential care as the policy guidance on the mix of care was not binding at the time, and (2) W was precluded from taking the consultation into account when making its decision as it had failed to initiate the consultation at the formative stage. Interested parties had not had the opportunity to criticise the proposal contrary to the criteria for fair consultation. A declaration was granted that W's decision to close the home was unlawful, *R. v. Devon CC, ex p. Baker* [1995] 1 All E.R. 73, [1995] 1 C.L.Y. 88 applied.

R. v. WANDSWORTH LBC, *ex p.* BECKWITH (NO.2) (1995) 159 L.G. Rev. 929, Potts, J., QBD.

5527. Community care–elderly–local authorities powers and duties–interaction with private sector

[Registered Homes Act 1984 s.1; Public Service Contracts Regulations 1993; Council Directive 92/50 on coordination of procedures for the award of public service contracts.]

CPC applied for judicial review of decisions of CCC, contending that: (1) placements for respite, day and residential care provision for elderly and mentally disabled patients within CCC's own homes were in breach of both national government guidance and Council Directive 92/50; (2) CCC had unfairly used capital funds to upgrade its homes in order to comply with the necessary registration standards for Significantly Mentally Frail, SMF, residents and had required different staffing levels at their own homes from those in the private sector, and (3) waiting lists denied intending residents free access to their private sector choice of location since the National Health Service and Community Care Act 1990.

Held, dismissing the application with costs, that (1) there was no evidence of any unlawful policy. Both the Directive and the Public Service Contracts Regulations 1993 were relevant only to contracts and could not apply where a contractual relationship was excluded because the local authority provider was part of the same legal entity as the purchaser; (2) the Registered Homes Act 1984 s.1 (5) (j) clearly exempted local authorities from the need for registration of their own homes and there was nothing to prevent the private sector provider from accommodating SMF residents in separate wings. The difference in staffing levels was not a policy decision, but one of internal procedure, and (3) the waiting lists were caused by a shortage of funding and there was no evidence of discrimination against the private sector provider. In any event, the duty to assess and provide accommodation was owed to the resident and not to the care provider.

R. v. CUMBRIA CC, *ex p.* CUMBRIA PROFESSIONAL CARE LTD, Trans. Ref: CO/3677/95, September 30, 1996, Turner, J., QBD.

5528. Community care–local authorities powers and duties–allocation of resources to enable person to live independently–policy and financial considerations–adverse effect of change of carer on user

[National Health Service and Community Care Act 1990 s.47.]

B, a 50 year old male with learning difficulties in receipt of care provided by ECC via a private contractor under the National Health Service and Community Care Act 1990 s.47, sought judicial review of a decision of ECC to change his care provider. To enable B to assume a degree of independent living he required care assistance for 18 hours per week. Following a policy change by ECC, it was decided to change his care provider. B wished to remain with his existing provider, under an exception provided in the new policy, based on his desire to continue receiving care from a male of similar age. It was proposed that B receive care from a younger female. B disliked change and his male carer was concerned that the change could have a detrimental effect on B's health. B submitted that ECC's criteria for exceptions to its policy amounted to an unlawful fetter on its discretion conferred by s.47 (2) (a) of the 1990 Act and, furthermore, that while the availability of resources could be taken into account when deciding how to meet B's needs, ECC's policy had been adopted for money saving purposes, which purposes had been placed in advance of B's needs.

Held, dismissing the application, that although an important aspect of care in the community required recipients to be involved in decisions about future care, and that B's needs were of paramount importance, conflict between needs and resources was a matter to be resolved by ECC. The weight to be given to these considerations was for the local authority to decide, provided that the user's needs were not relegated to the need to save money. Resources were a factor, however, in determining how to meet a need, *R. v. Gloucestershire CC, ex p. Barry* [1996] C.L.Y. 5529 considered. Changes having an adverse effect on a user would not be unlawful, if the user's needs continued to be properly provided for and the correct balancing exercise had been carried out. On the facts, ECC had correctly carried out the balancing exercise when finding that any detriment to B was not sufficiently significant to qualify as an exception to the policy changes. Failure to notifiy B of the changes did not constitute a failure justifying the grant of relief.

R. v. ESSEX CC, *ex p.* BUCKE, Trans. Ref: CO-526-96, July 30, 1996, Collins, J., QBD.

5529. Community care–local authorities powers and duties–disabled person–duty to assess need did not include issue of resource availability

[Chronically Sick and Disabled Persons Act 1970 s.2; National Health Service and Community Care Act 1990 s.47.]

B appealed against a decision allowing his application for judicial review of decisions taken by GCC, following the withdrawal of services under the Chronically Sick and Disabled Persons Act 1970 s.2, but refusing to grant declaratory relief as to the authority's entitlement to take account of available resources in assessing his need. B, a 79 year old severely disabled man, had originally been assessed as requiring cleaning and laundry services, but was informed by GCC that the cleaning provision was to be withdrawn and the laundry provision reduced on financial grounds.

Held, allowing B's appeal for a declaration, that GCC had a duty under s.2 of the 1970 Act to conduct an assessment of a disabled person's needs, pursuant to the National Health Service and Community Care Act 1990 s.47, with a view to making arrangements for the provision of care services. Having identified a need, the authority then had a duty to make provision to meet it. The way in which the need was met remained a discretionary matter for the local authority, and cost could become a relevant consideration at this point. However, the availability of resources was not an issue that should be taken into account in carrying out the duty under s.2(1) of the 1970 Act.

R. v. GLOUCESTERSHIRE CC, *ex p.* BARRY; R. v. LANCASHIRE CC, *ex p.* ROYAL ASSOCIATION FOR DISABILITY AND REHABILITATION [1996] 4 All E.R. 421, Swinton Thomas, L.J., CA.

5530. Community care–local authorities powers and duties–disabled persons–whether provision and assessment failed to comply with government policy and practice guidelines

[Education Act 1944 s.41; National Health Service and Community Care Act 1990 s.47; Chronically Sick and Disabled Persons Act 1970 s.2.]

R, who was severely disabled, applied for judicial review of a decision of I in relation to its provision of community care and educational facilities. R contended that I had failed in its duty to comply with the policy guidance issued by the Department of Health under the Chronically Sick and Disabled Persons Act 1970 s.2, and had acted unlawfully by failing to give adequate reasons for deviating from government policy.

Held, allowing the application, that under the National Health Service and Community Care Act 1990 s.47 a local authority was subject to a duty to assess R's individual needs and decide what care was appropriate. This assessment had to be based on need, not the availability of resources, and the authority was required to follow the Department of Health guidance entitled *Caring for People: Community Care in the Next Decade and Beyond: Policy Guidance* (HMSO, 1990) and also the guidance contained in Care Management and Assessment (HMSO, 1994). If the local authority did depart from the guidelines, it had to provide cogent reasons for doing so. I's assessment was unlawful as it had not tailored its consideration to R's individual requirements and his care plan failed to comply with the guidance issued, *R. v. Gloucestershire CC, ex p. Mahfood* (1996) 8 Admin. L.R. 181, [1995] 1 C.L.Y. 3001 followed. Furthermore, it had failed to meet the target duty under the Education Act 1944 s.41 to secure adequate educational provision for the severely disabled.

R. v. ISLINGTON LBC, *ex p.* RIXON (1996) 32 B.M.L.R. 136, Sedley, J., QBD.

5531. Community care–registration of proposed nursing home–whether financial viability of applicant was relevant criterion in determining registration application

[Registered Homes Act 1984 s.9.]

H sought judicial review of a decision of the Registered Homes Tribunal that financial viability was not a relevant consideration, under the Registered Homes Act 1984 s.9(c), when determining whether to allow registration of a proposed nursing home. The tribunal had concluded that any evidence as to the viability of financial provision by applicants should be limited to showing that the provision proposed for particular "services or facilities" was unreasonable.

Held, allowing the application, that the provisions in s.9(a) and s.9(c) of the 1984 Act overlapped in such a way that the financial means available to fund proposed services should be considered. H's concerns as to the financial viability of the proposed residential home were legitimate in the circumstances and H should be allowed to put its case.

R. v. REGISTERED HOMES TRIBUNAL, *ex p.* HERTFORDSHIRE CC (1996) 32 B.M.L.R. 101, Tuckey, J., QBD.

5532. Contracting out–welfare food

CONTRACTING OUT (FUNCTIONS IN RELATION TO THE WELFARE FOOD SCHEME) ORDER 1996, SI 1996 1670; made under the Deregulation and Contracting Out Act 1994 s.69. In force: June 28, 1996; £0.65.

This Order makes provisions to enable the Secretary of State to authorise another person, or that person's employees, to exercise the functions of reimbursing suppliers of welfare food and requiring and receiving information and evidence which may be reasonably needed in connection with the administration of the welfare food scheme.

5533. Disability Discrimination Act 1995–Commencement No.2 Order

DISABILITY DISCRIMINATION ACT 1995 (COMMENCEMENT NO.2) ORDER 1996, SI 1996 1336 (C.25); made under the Disability Discrimination Act 1995 s.70. In force: bringing into force various provisions of the Act on May 17, 1996; £0.65.

This Order brings into force certain provisions of the Disability Discrimination Act 1995 relating to the definition of disability, past disabilities, guidance, definition of lease, sublease and subtenancy, advice and assistance, statutory authority and national security, restriction of publicity in industrial tribunals and the Employment Appeal Tribunal, regulations and orders, interpretation, financial provisions, House of Commons disqualification and provisions supplementing the definition of disability and past disabilities.

5534. Disability Discrimination Act 1995–Commencement No.3 Order

DISABILITY DISCRIMINATION ACT 1995 (COMMENCEMENT NO.3 AND SAVING AND TRANSITIONAL PROVISIONS) ORDER 1996, SI 1996 1474 (C.27); made under the Disability Discrimination Act 1995 s.67, s.70. In force: bringing into force various provision of the Act on June 5, 1996, July 31, 1996 and December 2, 1996; £1.55.

This Order provides for the coming into force on June 6, 1996 of provisions in the Disability Discrimination Act 1995 authorising the making of Regulations. It also provides for the coming into force on June 6, 1996 of s.53 and s.54, which relate to Codes of Practice issued by the Secretary of State, and of s.56, which relates to help for persons suffering discrimination. It provides for the coming into force on July 31, 1996 of s.29(3), s.30(1) to s.30(6) and s.31, which relate to the education and further education of disabled persons. It further provides for the coming into force on December 2, 1996 of provisions relating to employment, including discrimination against applicants and employees; meaning of discrimination for this purpose; duty of employer to make adjustments; exemption for small businesses; enforcement, remedies and procedure; validity of certain agreements; charities and support for particular groups of persons; advertisements suggesting that employers will discriminate against disabled persons; discrimination against contract workers; discrimination by trade organisations; meaning of discrimination in relation to trade organisations; alterations to premises occupied under leases; occupational pension schemes; and insurance services. It provides for the coming into force on December 2, 1996 of provisions relating to goods, facilities and services, including discrimination in relation to goods, facilities and services; meaning of discrimination for this purpose; discrimination in relation to premises; exemption for small dwellings; meaning of discrimination for these purposes; enforcement, remedies and procedure; and validity and revision of certain agreements. It provides for the coming into force on December 2, 1996 of supplemental and miscellaneous provisions including victimisation; aiding unlawful acts; liability of employers and principals; appointment by Secretary of State of advisers; amendment of Disabled Persons (Employment) Act 1944; application to Crown; application to Parliament; Government appointments outside Part II; interpretation; short title, Commencement, extent; consequential amendments and repeals.

5535. Disability Discrimination Act 1995–Commencement No.4 Order

DISABILITY DISCRIMINATION ACT 1995 (COMMENCEMENT NO.4) ORDER 1996, SI 1996 3003 (C.92); made under the Disability Discrimination Act 1995 s.70. In force: bringing into force various provisions of the Act on December 2, 1996; £1.10.

This Order brings the Disability Discrimination Act 1995 s.16(3) into force to the extent that it is not already in force.

5536. Disabled persons–discrimination

DISABILITY DISCRIMINATION (MEANING OF DISABILITY) REGULATIONS 1996, SI 1996 1455; made under the Disability Discrimination Act 1995 Sch.1 para.1, Sch.1 para.2, Sch.1 para.3, Sch.1 para.4, Sch.1 para.5. In force: July 30, 1996; £0.65.

The Disability Discrimination Act 1995 s.1 provides that, subject to Sch.1, a person has a disability if he has a medical or mental impairment which has a substantial and long-term adverse effect on his ability to carry out normal day-to-day activities. These Regulations have the effect of excluding from the scope of the definition: addictions (other than those medically caused); certain personality disorders; hayfever and similar conditions; tattoos; and piercings. These might otherwise amount to severe disfigurements falling within Sch.1 para.3. The effect of Reg.6 is that a child under six is treated as if he were six or over for the purposes of determining the effect of his disability.

5537. Disabled persons–discrimination–codes of practice

DISABILITY DISCRIMINATION CODE OF PRACTICE (GOODS, SERVICES, FACILITIES AND PREMISES) ORDER 1996, SI 1996 2987; made under the Disability Discrimination Act 1995 s.52. In force: November 26, 1996; £0.65.

This Order appoints December 2, 1996 as the date on which the Disability Discrimination Act 1995 Code of Practice on the Rights of Access to Goods, Facilities, Services and Premises, issued by the Secretary of State for Social Security on July 25, 1996, shall come into force.

5538. Disabled persons–discrimination–codes of practice

DISABILITY DISCRIMINATION (GUIDANCE AND CODE OF PRACTICE) (APPOINTED DAY) ORDER 1996, SI 1996 1996 (C.52); made under the Disability Discrimination Act 1995 s.3, s.54. In force: guidance: July 31, 1996; Code of Practice: July 25, 1996; £0.65.

This Order appoints July 31, 1996 as the day on which Guidance on the matters to be taken into account in determining questions relating to the definition of disability issued by the Secretary of State comes into force. The Code of Practice for the elimination of discrimination in the field of employment against disabled persons or persons who have had a disability comes into force on December 2, 1996.

5539. Disabled persons–National Disability Council

NATIONAL DISABILITY COUNCIL (NO.2) REGULATIONS 1996, SI 1996 1410; made under the Disability Discrimination Act 1995 s.50, s.67, s.68, Sch.5 para.7. In force: June 25, 1996; £0.65.

These Regulations make provision for the Secretary of State to commission research at the request of the National Disability Council established by the Disability Discrimination Act 1995 s.50. They also prescribe the circumstances in which the Council may appoint advisers, and the conditions subject to which such appointments are to be made.

5540. Disabled persons–National Disability Council–removal from office

NATIONAL DISABILITY COUNCIL REGULATIONS 1996, SI 1996 11; made under the Disability Discrimination Act 1995 s.67, s.68, Sch.5. In force: January 29, 1996; £0.65.

The circumstances in which a member of the National Disability Council established under the Disability Discrimination Act 1995 s.50 may be removed from office are prescribed by these Regulations. Provision is also made for the Council's expenses to be met by the Secretary of State with approval from the Treasury.

5541. Food

WELFARE FOOD REGULATIONS 1996, SI 1996 1434; made under the Social Security Act 1988 s.13; and the Social Security Contributions and Benefits Act 1992 s.175. In force: June 27, 1996; £3.70.

These Regulations, which take account of Council Directive 80/181 ([1996] OJ L39/40) on metrication, consolidate, with amendments, the Welfare Food Regulations 1988 (SI 1988 536). Welfare food entitlement to milk, dried milk and vitamins to expectant mothers and children in certain circumstances are prescribed, the issue, use and control of milk tokens, the making of payments to those who do not receive tokens are regulated, the supply of free milk in exchange for tokens is regulated and additional entitlement to free milk or dried milk for children who are provided with day care are provided for. Suppliers of welfare food are required to furnish information connected with reimbursement and applies enactments relating to offences.

5542. Social fund–cold weather payments

SOCIAL FUND COLD WEATHER PAYMENTS (GENERAL) AMENDMENT REGULATIONS 1996, SI 1996 2544; made under the Social Security Contributions and Benefits Act 1992 s.138, s.175. In force: November 4, 1996; £2.40.

These Regulations amend the Social Fund Cold Weather Payments (General) Regulations 1988 (SI 1988 1724 as amended) by providing that income based jobseeker's allowance is to be a qualifying benefit for the purpose of obtaining a cold weather payment; providing a definition of the Meteorological Office and providing that only weather stations accredited by the Meteorological Office may provide forecasts for the purposes of these Regulations; specifying the period during which forecasts are supplied by the Meteorological Office; clarifying the identification of the area of the claimant's home and allowing forecasted periods of cold weather to be provided from the specified or nearest alternative weather station where the primary weather station is not available.

5543. Social fund–maternity and funeral expenses

SOCIAL FUND MATERNITY AND FUNERAL EXPENSES (GENERAL) AMENDMENT REGULATIONS 1996, SI 1996 1443; made under the Social Security Contributions and Benefits Act 1992 s.138, s.175. In force: October 7, 1996; £1.55.

These Regulations amend the Social Fund Maternity and Funeral Expenses (General) Regulations 1987 (SI 1987 481) to provide that income based jobseeker's allowance is to be a qualifying benefit for the purpose of obtaining a maternity payment or a funeral payment. They also provide that claimants who are receiving long term care in residential care or nursing homes are treated as members of the household, exclude children and young persons from consideration when determining whether the responsible person is entitled to a funeral payment, provide that funeral payments are not made in respect of items covered by any pre-paid funeral plan, clarify allowable costs in respect of a burial in respect of fees and donations paid to Ministers or for the use of churches and include a reference to confirmations of estates obtained in Scotland.

5544. Articles

A duty to discharge *(Kate Harrison)*: L.S.G. 1996, 93(12), 20-21. (Civil liberties implications of legislation in force April 1, 1996 to enable mental patients to be discharged from hospital into aftercare under supervision).

Community care update *(Stephen Cragg)*: Legal Action 1996, Sep, 16-18. (Developments since October 1994 including judicial review cases on availability of resources, role of government guidance, assessment process and charging for services).

Contesting the contradictions: needs, resources and community care decisions *(Michael Preston-Shoot)*: J. Soc. Wel. & Fam. L. 1996, 18(3), 307-325. (Relationship between needs and resources in community care, extent to which resources can affect decision making and whether better to use judicial review to challenge how need is defined and assessed).

New rights for carers *(Francine Bates* and *Luke Clements)*: Legal Action 1996, Feb, 19-21. (Provisions and significance of 1995 Act which aims to give proper recognition to role of carers by placing duty on social services departments to assess carer when making decisions as to service provision).

Registration and raising standards *(John Mitchell)*: S.J. 1996, 140(38), 968-970. (Registration by local authorities of private nurseries and residential homes and use of conditions in raising standards).

Social Services Inspectorate standards for leaving care: Childright 1996, 123, 14-15. (Support of young people leaving care system and adequacy of social provision).

The cost of caring *(George Curran)*: L.G.C. 1996, Jan 5, 16. (Councils' right to consider available resources when assessing community care provision for disabled persons).

The rights created by the new Carers Act in force on April 1, 1996 *(Luke Clements)*: L.S.G. 1996, 93(12), 21. (Legislation gives persons who look after disabled ill or elderly family or friends rights to ask social services authorities to assess carers' ability to provide and continue providing care).

W(h)ither social work? Social work, social policy and law at an interface: confronting the challenges and realising the potential in work with people needing care or services *(Michael Preston-Shoot)*: Liverpool L.R. 1996, 18(1), 19-39. (Effect of increasing government regulation of social work).

Welfare benefits for the elderly in residential homes *(Hugh Howard)*: S.J. 1996, 140(34), 862-863. (Implications of two recent HL cases for local authorities, residential homes and the privatisation of old peoples' homes).

Welfare law, families and poverty *(Catherine Shelley)*: Law & Just. 1996, 128/129, 29-34. (Whether state, through welfare, housing and employment laws, supports family institution and whether rising divorce rate reflects deeper social pressures and not simply impact of welfare state).

What is community care? *(Larraine Maitland* and *Di Gilbert)*: P.I. 1996, 3(2), 130-139. (Background to 1990 Act including local authorities' financing of community care and Griffiths report on implementing government policy).

5545. Books

Buck, Trevor–The Social Fund. Paperback: £39.00. ISBN 0-421-50930-9. Sweet & Maxwell.

Burrows, Noreen–European Social Law. Paperback: £22.50. ISBN 0-471-96537-5. Chancery Wiley Law Publications.

Clements, Luke–Community Care and the Law. Paperback: £25.00. ISBN 0-905099-74-5. The Legal Action Group.

Cooper, Jeremy; Vernon, Stuart–Disability and the Law. Paperback: £19.95. ISBN 1-85302-318-3. Jessica Kingsley Publishers.

Cretney, Stephen–Enduring Powers of Attorney. Paperback: £32.50. ISBN 0-85308-314-2. Jordan.

Dimond, Bridgit–Legal Aspects of Care in the Community. Hardback: £45.00. ISBN 0-333-53819-6. Macmillan Press.

Dimond, Bridgit–Legal Aspects of Community Care. Paperback: £19.99. ISBN 0-333-53820-X. Macmillan Press.

Koppelman, Andrew–Anti-discrimination Law and Social Equality. Hardback: £22.00. ISBN 0-300-06482-9. Yale University Press.

Mandelstam, Michael–Equipment for Older or Disabled People and the Law. Paperback: £29.95. ISBN 1-85302-352-3. Jessica Kingsley Publishers.

Richards, Margaret–Community Care. Paperback: £29.50. ISBN 0-85308-293-6. Jordan.

Rowland, Mark–Medical and Disability Appeal Tribunals: 1996 Supplement. Paperback: £9.95. ISBN 0-421-55920-9. Sweet & Maxwell.

Smith II, George P.–Legal and Healthcare Ethics for the Elderly. Paperback: £16.95. ISBN 1-56032-453-8. Hardback: £39.95. ISBN 1-56032-452-X. Taylor & Francis.

Teles, Steven Michael–Whose Welfare? Studies in Government and Public Policy. Hardback: £23.95. ISBN 0-7006-0801-X. University Press of Kansas.

Tomasson, Richard F.; Crosby, Faye J.; Herzberger, Sharon D.–Affirmative Action Pro and Con. American University Press Public Policy Series. Hardback: £31.50. ISBN 1-879383-51-9. Paperback: £15.50. ISBN 1-879383-52-7. University Press of America.

West, Jane–Implementing the Americans with Disabilities Act. Paperback: £35.00. ISBN 1-55786-867-0. Blackwell Publishers.

SUCCESSION

5546. Advancement–property purchased with father's money and mortgage in son's name–property conveyed to son only–father dying intestate–whether father had interest in property which passed to his estate–whether presumption of advancement rebutted

W was a widower and had two children, a son D and a daughter P. D and W were living in the family home when D's mother died in 1985. In 1986, W and D decided to sell the family home as it was too big and too expensive, and to buy another property. W was unemployed, and so a mortgage offer was made to D, and the house was conveyed to D alone. The solicitor acting for W and D drew up a deed which would have been a declaration of trust providing that the house was to be held as to 80 per cent by W and as to 20 per cent by D. For reasons which remained completely unknown, that trust deed was not executed, having never left the solicitor's office. W died intestate in 1990, and P sought a declaration that she was entitled to a share of the property under W's intestacy. The judge found that the solicitor must have been instructed not to proceed with the declaration of trust, the arrangement reflecting the reality of the situation, with the mortgage being D's sole responsibility. He accordingly held that P had not rebutted the presumption of advancement, ie. the presumption that W had intended to make a gift of the house to D. P appealed.

Held, allowing the appeal, that (1) in its application to houses acquired for joint occupation, the equitable presumption of advancement was now a judicial instrument of last resort. In a case between father and son, just as between husband and wife, the presumption could be readily rebutted by comparatively slight evidence, *Pettitt v. Pettitt* [1970] A.C. 777, [1969] C.L.Y. 1639, *Gissing v. Gissing* [1971] A.C. 886, [1970] C.L.Y. 1243 and *Falconer v. Falconer* [1970] 1 W.L.R. 1333, [1970] C.L.Y. 1234 applied and (2) since W was not working at the time of the purchase, only D could have been accepted as a mortgagor of the property. It was an irresistible inference that the real reason for conveying the house into D's sole name was that only he could be the mortgagor. That fact alone was probably sufficient to rebut the presumption of advancement. In addition, W never told D that he had instructed the solicitor not to proceed with the declaration of trust, and W had no real reason for wishing to divest himself of any interest in the property. The evidence to rebut the presumption was therefore markedly more than slight, and there would be a declaration that D held the property as to 30 per cent for himself and as to 70 per cent for W's estate, bringing into account the £2,000 already paid by D to P.

McGRATH v. WALLIS; SUB NOM. McGRATH v. WALLACE [1995] 2 F.L.R. 114, Nourse, L.J., CA.

5547. Family provision–claim by widow that no reasonable provision made for her–basis for calculating reasonable financial provision

[Inheritance (Provision for Family and Dependants) Act 1975.]

Beneficiaries under a will appealed against a decision in relation to an application by K's widow under the Inheritance (Provision for Family and Dependants) Act 1975. The judge found that K's will had failed to make "reasonable financial provision" for his widow and took the starting point for consideration, suggested in *Moody v. Stevenson* [1992] Ch. 486, [1992] C.L.Y. 4584/5, as being the amount that his widow would have been entitled to on divorce. That resulted in an order that all of K's estate, except £7,000 for each appellant, should go to his widow.

Held, allowing the appeal, that a spouse's entitlement on divorce was only one consideration in determining the settlement. The major element was what was reasonable in all the circumstances, *Besterman, Re* [1984] 1 Ch. 458, [1984] C.L.Y. 3671 followed. The approach suggested by *Moody v. Stevenson* was confusing when applied to small estates as, on divorce, two parties had to be considered. In the instant case, the judge had not been justified in effectively rewriting the will and providing more than reasonable provision for K's widow. The widow was aged 90, and it was reasonable for her to be awarded the entire estate absolutely, apart from the matrimonial home in which she should have a life interest.

KRUBERT (DECEASED), *Re*; SUB NOM. KRUBERT v. RUTHERFORD DAVIES [1996] 3 W.L.R. 959, Nourse, L.J., CA.

5548. Family provision–delay in bringing claim on behalf of child against estate–leave granted to apply out of time–prejudicial effect of claim on other beneficiaries

[Inheritance (Provision for Family and Dependants) Act 1975 s.4; Limitation Act 1980 s.28.]

C died in August 1990 leaving a substantial estate. A was aged eight and the daughter of C and M. M and C never married nor lived together. In December 1988, C married a woman with two young children from a previous relationship, and in June 1989 his new wife gave birth to a baby boy. C's will provided for his sister to receive his estate, subject to the will trustees' power to make an appointment, no later than two years following his death, in favour of his wife, his issue and her issue. Probate of the will was granted in January 1992, almost 18 months after C's death.

The trustees exercised their power of appointment on behalf of C's widow, his son and his stepchildren. In February 1993 M consulted solicitors, who intimated to the executors a possible claim by M on A's behalf. In March, the executors' solicitors declined to enter into any negotiations, as any claim would be out of time. Legal aid was applied for on A's behalf, but it was not until January 1994 (following delay both in obtaining legal aid and by the lawyers) that A's claim was issued, with M acting as A's next friend. The district judge refused leave to apply outside the six month time limit imposed by the Inheritance (Provision for Family and Dependants) Act 1975. A appealed.

Held, allowing the appeal, that (1) the burden was on the claimant to establish grounds for applying out of time, and the burden was not trivial, *Salmon, Re* [1981] 1 Ch. 167, [1980] C.L.Y. 2818 applied; (2) there was a delay in total of three years and six months between C's death and A's application, including a delay of eighteen months between the expiry of the six month time limit and the application. M's explanation for this delay was unsatisfactory; (3) however, it was A's claim, not M's. A was blameless and had no redress against any other person. Whilst the six month time limit applied to all categories of applicants under the 1975 Act (unlike the position in relation to children's claims under s.28 of the Limitation Act 1980), it would be an injustice to A to refuse leave on the grounds of M's acts or omissions, *Escritt v. Escritt* [1982] 3 F.L.R. 280 distinguished and (4) this was a very large estate, and the prejudice to the other beneficiaries in allowing the application would not be nearly as great as in cases involving more modest estates. In addition, A's prospects of substantial success were clearer than in any of the reported cases. In all the circumstances, the appeal would be allowed, and leave to apply out of time granted.

C (DECEASED) (LEAVE TO APPLY FOR PROVISION), *Re* [1995] 2 F.L.R. 24, Wilson, J., Fam Div.

5549. Family provision–delay in bringing claim on behalf of illegitimate child–effect of refusal on child due to another's default–grounds on which permission granted

[Inheritance (Provision for Families and Dependants) Act 1975.]

F was a peer of the realm who had a child by M, to whom he was not married. F gave M two lump sums and sought to give her regular maintenance. Fearing litigation, M rejected all such regular payments. F later represented to M that he would place money in a deposit account and take out a life insurance contract on behalf of the child. F married another woman in 1988. F then died in August 1989 in a car accident. Probate was granted in January 1992. Deeds of appointment in favour of F's second family were executed in August 1992. In February 1993, M took advice from solicitors as to her child's interest in F's estate. M's application on behalf of her child under the Inheritance (Provision for Families and Dependants) Act 1975 was issued in January 1994.

Held, allowing the application, that the court had to exercise its own discretion as to whether or not permission to apply should be granted. The delay of two and half years from F's death was very unsatisfactory. However, it was essential to remember that the true claimant was the child and not M. The child should not be in a better position than an adult under the 1975 Act. It would be wrong to discern a general principle in favour of granting permission to a minor. Nevertheless, if, in the instant case, permission were to have been refused, the child would suffer as a result of another's default. It was also necessary to consider whether refusal of the permission would have left the claimant without a claim against another person. On the basis of the child's situation living on social security benefits with M, there was a likelihood of an order being made under the 1975 Act on these facts.

W (A MINOR) (CLAIM FROM DECEASED'S ESTATE), *Re* [1995] 2 F.C.R. 689, Wilson, J., Fam Div.

5550. Family provision–mutual wills–remarriage of survivor–new will–whether law would give effect to mutual intention of parties

[Inheritance (Provision for Family and Dependants) Act 1975.]

In 1988 D and J made similar wills in favour of their son, G, leaving their estate to him after the death of the survivor. J died in 1991 and in 1992 D remarried. In November 1992 D made a new will leaving everything to his second wife, E, and in 1993 he died. G sought a declaration that E held D's estate on trust to give effect to the mutual wills of D and J. G also brought a claim under the Inheritance (Provision for Family and Dependants) Act 1975 as a child of the deceased.

Held, that where there was a clear mutual agreement, the law would give effect to the intention of the parties by means of a floating trust which would not be destroyed by the second testator's remarriage. On the facts of the case it could not be established that the wills, although simultaneous and in the same form, were mutually binding in law. However, in view of the fact that J clearly intended that D would give effect to what she believed were their mutual intentions, there arose a moral obligation to make some provision for G. The case was an exceptional one in this respect. The parties were urged to try to come to some financial arrangement as regards the part of the estate attributable to J's assets in order to make some provision for G.

GOODCHILD v. GOODCHILD; SUB NOM. GOODCHILD (DECEASED), *Re* [1996] 1 W.L.R. 694, Carnwath, J., Ch D.

5551. Financial provision–claim by ex-wife–intestate ex-husband–bona vacantia–no special circumstances showing that lack of provision was unreasonable

[Inheritance (Provision for Family and Dependants) Act 1975.]

TS appealed against a decision awarding the net estate of C's deceased ex-husband, O, to C under the Inheritance (Provision for Family and Dependants) Act 1975. The couple were divorced in 1971. A clean break order was made by consent in 1981. There were no children of the marriage, neither party remarried and O died intestate with his estate devolving upon the Crown as bona vacantia. The estate amounted to £7,677 and C claimed that O had not made reasonable financial provision for her. Due to the fact that the estate was small, it was agreed that if C was successful she should be awarded the entire estate. TS argued that the judge was not entitled in law to find that the estate had not made reasonable financial provision for C when he had not found that O owed any legal or moral obligation to C. C relied on her continued friendship with O after their divorce, her financial circumstances, her worsening ill health and the fact that there were no other beneficiaries apart from the Crown.

Held, allowing the appeal, that (1) the court did not have the power to interfere with an estate merely because it would have been reasonable for the deceased to have made provision for the claimant. It was necessary to show that the lack of provision was unreasonable. The judge was wrong to allude to O's indifference to the disposition of his estate just because he died intestate; that could have been a deliberate choice, *Coventry (Deceased), Re* [1980] Ch.461, [1979] C.L.Y. 2807 considered; (2) the fact that the Crown was the only beneficiary was not relevant to C's claim which had to be considered on its merits. The estate could not be treated as a windfall to be distributed to a person because they were in need; (3) there were no special circumstances to demonstrate that the lack of provision was unreasonable, and (4) a moral claim could not exist merely because of financial difficulties of the claimant and her ill health, *Coventry (Deceased), Re* followed.

CAMERON v. TREASURY SOLICITOR; SUB NOM. O'ROURKE (DECEASED), *Re* [1997] 1 F.C.R. 188, Butler-Sloss, L.J., CA.

5552. Forfeiture–plaintiff convicted of manslaughter of parents on grounds of diminished responsibility–whether precluded from entitlement to father's estate

J, through his next friend, sought the determination of the question whether his conviction for the manslaughter of his parents on the grounds of diminished responsibility precluded him from inheriting his father's estate on intestacy. The forfeiture rule, a well established rule of public policy, disqualified a person from acquiring a benefit from the unlawful killing of another. J argued that the court did not have to apply the forfeiture rule to every case of manslaughter, but, according to *Gray v. Barr* [1971] 2 Q.B. 554, [1971] C.I.Y. 6012, only those cases where the claimant was guilty of deliberate, intentional and unlawful violence or threat of violence.

Held, that the application failed on the grounds of public policy. The court was bound by *Royse v. Royse* [1985] Fam. 22, [1984] C.L.Y. 3666 whose facts could not be distinguished from this case. However, the same conclusion would have been reached even if *Gray v. Barr* could be applied. The test in that case was fulfilled as J was criminally responsible for his actions and had used deliberate, intentional and unlawful violence.

Observed: It was necessary for a higher authority to be established before public policy could be changed.

JONES v. ROBERTS [1995] 2 F.L.R. 422, Kolbert, J., Ch D.

5553. Gifts–donatio mortis causa–son in possession of car and keys while father in hospital–son told to keep keys–whether changed possession as bailee to possession as donee

D's father was admitted to hospital and died four days later. While D's father was in hospital D was in possession of his father's car and a set of keys. Three days before his death D's father told D that he could keep the car keys because he (D's father) would not be driving the car any more. After the father's death, D's mother, P, claimed the proceeds of the sale of the car as an asset of the estate. D gave evidence that, if his father had recovered, he would have had the car back. The county court judge held that there had been an outright gift of the car to D. P appealed.

Held, dismissing the appeal, that since it was D's understanding that if his father had recovered he would have had the car again, there had been no outright gift of the car to D. However, there had been a parting with dominion sufficient to create a donatio mortis causa. It was irrelevant that D already had possession of the car and a set of keys, since the words of gift could operate to change the nature of the donee's possession as bailee to possession as donee under an immediate gift or donatio mortis causa, *Craven's Estate, Re* [1937] 3 All E.R. 33, *Sen v. Headley* [1991] 2 All E.R. 636, [1991] C.L.Y. 3707 applied.

WOODARD v. WOODARD [1995] 3 All E.R. 980, Dillon, L.J., CA.

5554. Gifts–share transfer to son–presumption of advancement–transfer for illegal purpose of avoiding creditors–purpose not carried out–whether presumption could be rebutted by reliance on illegality

P owned 459 out of 500 shares in a family company. Fearing personal litigation brought by the landlords of property occupied by the company as licensee and a claim against his shareholding in the company, P transferred the shares to D, his son, for an expressed consideration of £78,030. In the event, the litigation was settled and P sought a retransfer of the shares. D refused to retransfer. P issued proceedings claiming that D had been holding the shares as bare trustee for P and that he had agreed to retransfer them on completion of the litigation. The judge ordered delivery up of the shares because P could adduce evidence to rebut the presumption of advancement.

Held, dismissing the appeal, that although P had transferred property for an illegal purpose to D in circumstances where the presumption of advancement applied, he was nevertheless entitled to withdraw from the transaction before any part of the illegal purpose had been carried into effect. Having done so, P was entitled to give evidence of the illegality to rebut the presumption and recover the property. This constituted an exception to the rule that no court would lend its aid to one who founded his action on an illegal act. P was able to rebut the presumption of advancement by clear evidence of his intentions and given that he had not defrauded his creditors in any way, the judge had not erred in ordering the delivery up of the share certificates. Per Millett L.J: it had been sufficient for the transferor to withdraw voluntarily from the transaction when it had ceased to be necessary without any need to repent his illegal purpose, *Tinsley v. Milligan* [1993] 3 All E.R. 65, [1993] C.L.Y. 1839 considered; *Perpetual Executors and Trustees Association of Australia Ltd v. Wright* (1917) 23 C.L.R. 185 approved.

TRIBE v. TRIBE [1995] 3 W.L.R. 913, Nourse, L.J., CA.

5555. Wills–claim by cohabitant–reasonable to make no provision

[Inheritance (Provision for Family and Dependants) Act 1975 s.1, s.3.]

R appealed against the dismissal of her application for an order under the Inheritance (Provision for Family and Dependants) Act 1975. R cohabited with the deceased, D, from July 1985. The will, made in April 1986, made no provision for her and left his estate to his two children and his two grandchildren, the respondents. The judge found that R came within s.1 (1) (e) of the 1975 Act, but that it was reasonable for D to have made no provision for her in his will.

Held, dismissing the appeal, that (1) under s.3(4) of the 1975 Act it was necessary for the judge to ascertain the extent of D's responsibility for R's maintenance, the basis upon which D had assumed such a responsibility and the length of time for which he had maintained R; (2) on the evidence, the judge was entitled to find that D's responsibility towards R was by means of accommodation only and did not include her daily living expenses and that their relationship was not like a marriage, and (3) it was reasonable for D to have failed to make provision for R in his will as he had made adequate financial provision of £36,000, in a joint account.

RHODES v. DEAN, Trans. Ref: FC3 96/5333/B, March 28, 1996, Ward, L.J., CA.

5556. Wills–payment for work done by solicitor as executor before will declared invalid–whether sole executor of valid will entitled to recovery of money

G sought recovery of sums paid to RB, a firm of solicitors, for work done by a partner as executor of G's deceased mother's will, which was declared invalid after probate was granted. The two witnesses had not witnessed the will at the same time and the judge pronounced in favour of an earlier will which made G the sole executor. G argued that the sums already paid to RB should be returned as the later will, including its charging clause, had been declared invalid.

Held, giving judgment for G, that three principles of law applied to the case: (1) money paid by personal representatives to those not entitled to it was recoverable by those entitled to the money provided the recipients were not bona fide purchasers; (2) payments under a charging clause of a will amounted to bounty to be treated in the same way as other legacies of the will and (3) the person granted probate was entitled to the powers of a personal representative until the grant was revoked or determined. In the instant case, RB were in the same position as other legatees under an invalid will. They were not third parties so could not rely on common law principles for protection. Neither did the circumstances allow them to rely on the defence of change of position set out in *Lipkin Gorman v. Karpnale Ltd* [1991] 2 A.C. 548, [1991] C.L.Y. 502. A solicitor acting as a personal representative and utilising the services of his firm took the risk that he would be placed in the same position as other legatees should the will prove to be invalid. G knew of problems with the will early on but was not estopped from pursuing the claim as he was acting in a personal capacity at that time and his actions then did not bind him in relation to his activities as a personal representative.

GRAY v. RICHARDS BUTLER, *The Times*, July 23, 1996, Carnwath, J., Ch D.

5557. Wills–proviso restricting class of beneficiaries–intention of testator–failure to delete proviso a clerical error–validity of gifts for charitable purpose–transfer exempt for inheritance tax purposes due to exclusively charitable purpose

[Administration of Justice Act 1982 s.20.]

A solicitor drafted a will on S's behalf establishing a trust fund to be used for the assistance of the poor and needy of a class of persons set out in a schedule to the will. Before the schedule had been drawn up, the solicitor drafted a proviso which stated that if any of the persons named in the schedule died during the testator's lifetime or within 21 years of the testator's death, that person's issue would stand in his place and be eligible to benefit under the trust. The will provided for a gift over to charitable institutions or for charitable purposes in the event that no poor and needy member of the class comprised by the schedule was alive at the expiry of 21 years from the testator's death. The testator subsequently provided the solicitor with a schedule comprising six named family members and the issue of five of them. After the testator's death five of the persons named in the schedule sought rectification of the will pursuant to the Administration of Justice Act 1982 s.20(1) on the ground that, contrary to the testator's intention, the proviso restricted the class of persons in the schedule who were eligible to benefit from the trust by excluding the issue of the named individuals while their named ancestors were still alive. One of the executors issued a construction summons to determine whether the will contained valid charitable gifts for the relief of poverty among members of the class constituted by the schedule, and all three executors appealed against a determination of the Inland Revenue Commissioners that the dispositions were not for exclusively charitable purposes.

Held, allowing the application and the appeal and answering the construction summons in the affirmative, that (1) S's intention was that all the persons described in the schedule, named individuals and issue, would be eligible to benefit throughout the period of the trust. On the proper construction of the proviso, the will failed to give effect to that intention. The solicitor's failure through inadvertence to delete the proviso from the draft will once he had received the schedule could be regarded as a clerical error for the purposes of the 1982 Act s.20(1) and the proviso would accordingly be deleted *Wordingham v. Royal Exchange Trust Co Ltd* [1992] 3 All E.R. 204, [1992] C.L.Y. 4592 considered; (2) the gifts for the assistance of poor and needy family members during the 21 year period from S's death, and for the distribution to the poor and needy of that class on expiration of that period, were valid charitable gifts, *Dingle v. Turner* [1972] 1 All E.R. 878, [1972] C.L.Y. 337 and *Scarisbrick's Will Trusts, Re* [1951] 1 All E.R. 822, [1947-51] C.L.C. 1124 considered and (3) S could not be taken to have intended that the existence of a single needy member of the class defined in the schedule at the expiry of 21 years from his death would defeat the gift over in favour of charitable institutions and charitable purposes. It followed that the gift over could take effect and that the dispositions of the residuary estate were for exclusively charitable purposes.

SEGELMAN (DECEASED), *Re* [1996] Ch. 171, Chadwick, J., Ch D.

5558. Wills–testator giving instructions that will be signed on completion of lifetime transfers–whether undated will lacked testamentary intent

[Wills Act 1837.]

C, T's nephew, appealed against the upholding of T's will which T had intended to take effect conditionally on subsequent events. T signed her will in September 1989 but asked her solicitor, who was drawing up deeds of gift of land to her niece and nephew, to insert the date of her signature after the transfers had been completed. However, the will made no reference to being conditional upon such a contingency occurring and the question arose as to whether the will was valid. The judge in the lower court found, on the basis of evidence of communications and correspondence between T and her solicitor, that T had made a valid conditional will which would take effect on completion of the two lifetime gifts.

Held, allowing the appeal, that the will was not valid as T did not possess the animus testandi required to execute a will, *Berger (Deceased), Re* [1990] Ch. 118, [1989] C.L.Y. 3815 considered. T was acting under the misapprehension that the dating of the will, not the signature, constituted execution. As a result, she lacked the necessary intention to make a valid will in the sense of a will intended to be immediately dispositive. Furthermore, it would be contrary to the Wills Act 1837 to allow extrinsic evidence of T's intentions to be used to add a condition which T had not stated in writing nor signed.

CORBETT v. NEWEY [1996] 3 W.L.R. 729, Waite, L.J., CA.

5559. Wills–witnesses–acknowledgement of signature

[Wills Act 1837 s.9.]

C sought to revoke the grant of probate in respect of the will of his father, SC, who had made a will by filling out a printed will form. He then asked his neighbours, Mr and Mrs B, to attest his will. SC had previously signed the will which was then signed by Mrs B in SC's presence and then by Mr B in the presence of SC and with Mrs B a few feet away. During all of this Mrs B urged SC to take the will to a bank to be checked as she was not convinced it was valid because SC had not signed it in her presence. C argued that the will had not been correctly attested as required by the Wills Act 1837 s.9.

Held, dismissing the action, that the will had been correctly attested for the purposes of s.9, under which a will could be signed by a testator in the absence of witnesses and later acknowledged by him in the presence of two witnesses. The court could see no reason why such a principle should not also apply to a witness. Both witnesses were present at the attestation and, by protesting about the validity of the will, Mrs B was acknowledging her signature.

COUSER v. COUSER [1996] 1 W.L.R. 1301, Judge Colyer Q.C., Ch D.

5560. Articles

Avoiding disinheritance *(John Stevens)*: N.L.J. 1996, 146(6750), 961-963. (Importance of ensuring that clients understand full implications of making mutual wills).

Better drafting: Clarity 1996, 36, 18-19. (Extract from will using complex legal language and suggested revision using simpler terminology).

Dealing with the Benham dilemma *(Margaret Stirling)*: P.C.B. 1996, 3, 150-154. (Restrictive approach taken by Capital Taxes office in applying Benham case on grossing up non exempt shares of residue where estate divided between exempt and non-exempt beneficiaries and simpler method of doing calculations).

Debt after death *(Rachael Braverman)*: Q.A. 1996, 40(Summer), 4-6. (Role of adviser in estate administration including sorting out benefits and housing, gathering assets in and settling outstanding debts).

Discretionary trusts: helping the Cinderella beneficiaries *(Christopher J. Whitehouse)*: Legal Times 1996, 42, Supp 8. (Ways in which beneficiaries can be protected from discrimination by trustees including use of letter of wishes).

Estate planning for non-business clients *(Philip Laidlow)*: C.T.P. 1996, 15(4), 44-48. (Tax planning techniques including appropriate drafting of wills, use of annual exemptions, gifts and trusts, and insurance based methods).

Flexible wills after Frankland *(Chris J. Whitehouse)*: Tax J. 1996, 368, 7-9. (Implications for will drafting of Frankland decision on operation of IHTA s.65(4) time limit for constituting discretionary trust and interaction with two year duration requirement of s.144).

International succession law *(Colin D. Robertson)*: T. and T. 1996, 2(1), 20-25. (Scope and formulation of 1988 Convention aimed at harmonisation of succession law though not yet ratified by any country).

Intestacy reforms–the way things were, 1952 *(Stephen M. Cretney)*: Denning L.J. 1994, 35-51. (Process by which 1952 Act came to be drafted, discussed and passed into law and significance for law reform process).

Just say "I do": Pen. World 1996, 25(6), 21-22, 25-26, 28. (Provision for non-married partners and dependants in private, public and recently privatised sector pension schemes).

Mutual wills *(Philip Laidlow)*: C.T.P. 1996, 15(6), 69-72. (Operation and form of mutual wills, revocation prior to first death and implied trust on first death, effect of automatic revocation of survivor's will by remarriage and suitability of arrangements for clients).

Probate and succession - practitioners' update *(Lindsay Messenger)*: L. Ex. 1996, Jan, 17. (Practice direction on production to court of documents incorporated in will and 1995 Act implementing Law Commission's recommendations on intestacy and family provision).

Senior citizens tax *(John T. Newth)*: Tax. 1996, 137(3552), 95-97. (Case studies on IHT, benefits and succession planning for elderly clients with future nursing fee liabilities, testamentary dispositions and trust considerations).

The irreducible core content of trusteeship *(David Hayton)*: J. Int. P. 1996, 5(1), 3-17. (Extent to which settlors and trustees can restrict beneficiaries' rights to information).

The new estate planning *(Philip Laidlow)*: C.T.P. 1996, 15(8), 93-95. (Tax and succession planning strategy for elderly client's home to minimise estate's exposure and maximise state contribution to costs of long term care).

The Royal Marriages Act 1772: a footnote *(Stephen M. Cretney)*: Stat. L.R. 1996, 16(3), 195-199. (Changes made to 1959 Bill to avoid problem arising from clause that legitimated children of void marriages and consequently affected line of succession to throne).

Trustee charging: Tr. & Est. 1996, 11 (1), 1-3. (Advice for solicitors on methods to ensure payment for work undertaken as executor).

Will drafting after the Succession Act–divorce, survivorship and second death legacies *(R.J. Mitchell)*: Conv. 1996, Mar/Apr, 112-117. (Impact of 1995 Act on s.18A of 1837 Act in relation to drafting of survivorship clauses and second death pecuniary legacies in spouses' wills).

Wills and undue influence: Tr. & Est. 1996, 11 (2), 9-11. (Validity of testamentary provisions where beneficiary involved in will drafting or execution or has exercised undue influence).

5561. Books

Applegate, A.–Wills, Probate and Administration. Legal Practice Course resource books. Paperback: £17.50. ISBN 0-85308-369-X. Jordan.

Carmichael, K.S.–Spicer and Pegler's Executorship Law and Accounts. Hardback: £65.00. ISBN 0-406-03598-9. Butterworth Law.

Finch, Janet; Masson, Judith; Mason, Jennifer; Hayes, Lynn; Wallis, Lorraine–Wills, Inheritance and the Family. Oxford Socio-Legal Studies. Hardback: £25.00. ISBN 0-19-825834-8. Clarendon Press.

Halliwell, Mark–Distribution on Intestacy. Practitioner series. Paperback: £37.00. ISBN 0-7520-0208-2. FT Law & Tax.

Iwobi, A.U.–Essential Succession. Essential series - revision. Paperback: £4.95. ISBN 1-85941-144-4. Cavendish Publishing Ltd.

Jones, Ian–Sourcebook on Succession, Wills and Probate. Sourcebook series. Paperback: £18.95. ISBN 1-85941-104-5. Cavendish Publishing Ltd.

King-Jones, Amanda; Butcher, Christopher–Probate Practice Manual. Unbound/looseleaf: £135.00. ISBN 0-7520-0250-3. FT Law & Tax.

Miles, George.–Wills, Probate and Administration 1996/1997. Legal Practice Course Guides. Paperback: £15.55. ISBN 1-85431-546-3. Blackstone Press.

Miller, Gareth–The Machinery of Succession. Hardback: £45.00. ISBN 1-85521-442-3. Dartmouth.

Rendell, Catherine–Law of Succession. Macmillan law masters. Paperback: £9.99. ISBN 0-333-61735-5. Macmillan Press.

Riddett, Robin–Private Client Work. Legal Practice Course resource books. Paperback: £17.50. ISBN 0-85308-343-6. Jordan.
Spedding, Linda S.–Succession: Casebook 1996-1997. Bachelor of Laws (LLB). Paperback: £18.95. ISBN 0-7510-0666-1. HLT Publications.
Spedding, Linda S.–Succession: Textbook 1996-1997. Bachelor of Laws (LLB). Paperback: £18.95. ISBN 0-7510-0700-5. HLT Publications.
Succession - LLB: Suggested Solutions (1991-1995). Bachelor of Laws (LLB). Paperback: £6.95. ISBN 0-7510-0734-X. HLT Publications.
Succession: Suggested Solutions - Single Paper (June 1995). Paperback: £3.00. ISBN 0-7510-0633-5. HLT Publications.
Taylor, Eric–Parker's Modern Wills Precedents. Hardback: £49.50. ISBN 0-406-08140-9. Butterworth Law.

TAXATION

5562. Air passenger duty–interest rates

AIR PASSENGER DUTY (PRESCRIBED RATES OF INTEREST) (AMENDMENT) ORDER 1996, SI 1996 164; made under the Finance Act 1994 s.42, Sch.6 para.11. In force: February 6, 1996; £0.65.

This Order provides for an increase in the rate of interest from 5.5 per cent per annum to 6.25 per cent per annum for the purposes of Finance Act 1994 Sch.6 para.7 (interest carried on an amount of air passenger duty assessed as duty due by an assessment made under s.12). The new rate of interest will apply to amounts assessed as duty due on or after February 6, 1996 and to amounts assessed as duty prior to that date remaining unpaid on or after that date; but in the latter case the new rate will apply to the amount involved only as from that date.

5563. Capital allowances–buildings–planteria–purpose built structure for raising plants and displaying for sale

[Finance Act 1971 s.41.]

S appealed against a decision refusing to allow a capital expenditure claim for the provision of plant under the Finance Act 1971 s.41 in respect of a planteria.

Held, dismissing the appeal, that the structure, a form of greenhouse, served to nurture and protect growing plants, but it also allowed customers to walk among the benches on which the plants were growing. The fact it had a purpose built structure did not make it "plant" for capital allowance purposes because it formed part of the premises in which the business was carried on and business premises could not be plant, *Wimpey International Ltd v. Warland* [1989] S.T.C. 273, [1990] C.L.Y. 753 followed.

GRAY (INSPECTOR OF TAXES) v. SEYMOURS GARDEN CENTRE (HORTICULTURE) [1995] S.T.C. 706, Nourse, L.J., CA.

5564. Capital allowances–car wash–whether premises or plant

[Finance Act 1971 s.41, s.44.]

The Crown appealed against a special commissioners' decision allowing a claim for capital allowance relief under ss.41 and 44 of the Finance Act 1971 in respect of car wash premises operated by ACW.

Held, allowing the appeal that the distinction between "plant" and "premises", for the purposes of the Act, required an analysis to determine whether the area concerned was part of the premises where the business was undertaken, or part of the plant with which the business was carried on. As the site and buildings in which each car wash operated formed a purpose built unit, they fell under the "premises test" as formulated in *Gray v. Seymours Garden Centre* [1995] S.T.C. 706, [1995] 1 C.L.Y. 880, and could not be regarded as plant. As such, any expenditure on the structure or site of a car wash did not qualify for capital expenditure relief, *Gray* and *Jarrold v. John Good & Sons* [1963] 1 W.L.R. 214, [1963] C.L.Y. 1705 affirmed.

ATTWOOD (INSPECTOR OF TAXES) v. ANDUFF CAR WASH LTD [1996] S.T.C. 110, Carnwath, J., Ch D.

5565. Capital allowances–purpose built premises for data processing centre–whether industrial building for purpose of capital allowances

[Capital Allowances Act 1990 s.18.]

G claimed capital allowances for a purpose built data processing centre. At the centre, with the help of special machines, cheques from post offices were received, sorted and encoded and the data was electronically stored. The Inland Revenue submitted that the premises were not an "industrial building" within the meaning of the Capital Allowances Act 1990 s.18(1)(e).

Held, that, for the purposes of capital allowances, the data processing centre was an industrial building. The criteria of s.18(1)(e) of the Act were satisfied in that the centre was used for the processing of goods or materials, ie. the documents. Because the phrase "any process" used in the statute was so broad, processes which were not necessarily industrial and did not necessarily alter the character of goods and materials subjected to them were included in the definition of industrial buildings. Provided there was substantially uniform treatment or system of treatment it did not matter that the goods were not for sale, *Kilmarnock Equitable Cooperative Building Society Ltd v. Inland Revenue Commissioners* (1966) 42 T.C. 675, [1966] C.L.Y. 5884 and *Vibroplant Ltd v. Holland* [1981] 1 All E.R. 526, [1982] C.L.Y. 472 considered. However, the data processing centre was expressly excluded from capital allowances within the meaning of s.18(4) of the Act because it was used as an "office". Viewed as a whole, and by reference to its predominant use or purpose, the centre was used for document processing, and the staff, aided by machines, performed tasks of a kind once carried out manually by clerks, *Inland Revenue Commissioners v. Lambhill Ironworks Ltd* (1950) 31 T.C. 393, [1947-1951] C.L.C. 4715 followed.

GIROBANK PLC v. CLARKE (INSPECTOR OF TAXES) [1996] S.T.C. 540, Lindsay, J., Ch D.

5566. Capital allowances–underground electricity substation–excavation and construction costs–structure did not function as plant

[Capital Allowances Act 1990 s.24.]

The Crown appealed from a special commissioner's ruling that L was entitled to capital allowances for the full amount expended on providing an underground substation. The Crown agreed to capital allowances for the earthing system and equipment installed in the substation, but denied allowances for the expense of excavating and constructing the substation on the grounds that the structure functioned as the premises from which business was carried on, not as apparatus for carrying on the business. L objected that the structure and equipment were designed to function as as single unit.

Held, allowing the appeal, that, for the purposes of capital allowances under the Capital Allowances Act 1990 s.24, although designed together as a substation, the structure and the equipment it housed could be distinguished. The structure qualified for capital allowances only if it could reasonably be called plant with which the business was carried on rather than the premises in which business was carried on, *Gray v. Seymours Garden Centre (Horticulture)* [1995] S.T.C. 706, [1995] 1 C.L.Y. 880 followed. It was not sufficient to show that features of parts of the structure functioned like plant. To qualify, the structure as a whole had to carry out a specific plant-like function, *Wimpy International Ltd v. Warland* [1989] S.T.C. 273 followed. The structure of the substation functioned as premises and therefore did not qualify for capital allowances.

BRADLEY (INSPECTOR OF TAXES) v. LONDON ELECTRICITY PLC [1996] S.T.C. 1054, Blackburne, J., Ch D.

5567. Capital Allowances Act 1990 s.33A–Appointed Day Order

CAPITAL ALLOWANCES ACT 1990, SECTION 33A (APPOINTED DAY) ORDER 1996, SI 1996 1323 (C.23); made under the Capital Allowances Act 1990 s.33F. £0.65.

The Capital Allowances Act 1990 s.33A allows claims to be made by shipowners for deferment of balancing charges on ship disposals taking place on or after April 21, 1994. The 1990 Act s.33F(3) provides that no claim may be made under s.33A at any time before such date as the Treasury may by order appoint. This Order appoints May 31, 1996 as the date in question.

5568. Capital duty–mergers between companies–exemption–Council Directive 69/335–European Union

[Council Directive 69/335 concerning indirect taxes on the raising of capital Art.7.]

Under French legislation registration duty was payable on contributions of moveable assets at the rate of one per cent. Certain exceptions applied, including that the applicable rate was 1.2 per cent for certain acts recording merger transactions. It was argued that this was prohibited by Council Directive 69/335.

Held, that Council Directive 69/335 Art.7(1) precluded the application of national laws maintaining at 1.2 per cent the rate of registration duty on contributions of moveable property made in the context of a merger. The registration duty constituted a capital duty within the meaning of the Directive and therefore pursuant to Art.7(1) could not exceed the rate of 0.5 per cent from January 1, 1986.

SOCIETE BAUTIAA v. DIRECTEUR DES SERVICES FISCAUX DES LANDES (C197/94), February 13, 1996, Judge not specified, ECJ.

5569. Capital transfer tax–agricultural tenancies–valuation of deceased partner's share–whether attributes of surviving partner to be taken into account

[Finance Act 1975 s.38.]

Held, that in valuing, for the purposes of capital transfer tax under s.38 of the Finance Act 1975, a deceased partner's share in the tenancy of a family farm on the basis of a sale on the open market, there was nothing in the legislation to require that the surviving partner should be treated as a hypothetical person. Whether the attributes and characteristics of the actual surviving partner could be taken into account in the market was a question of fact to be established by the evidence before the tribunal.

WALTON v. INLAND REVENUE COMMISSIONERS; SUB NOM. WALTON'S EXECUTORS v. INLAND REVENUE COMMISSIONERS [1996] S.T.C. 68, Peter Gibson, L.J., CA.

5570. Case stated–appeals–Special Commissioners–whether appropriate to remit for further findings of fact

[Taxes Management Act 1970 s.56.]

LE owned an underground substation. It claimed capital allowances on the entire structure. Uncontroversial evidence was given that the entire structure would not be needed if the substation was operated above ground, but this was not recorded as a fact in the case stated by the special commissioner. B applied for an order under the Taxes Management Act 1970 s.56(7) remitting the case to the special commissioner for amendment. LE opposed the application on the ground that the transcript would be before the court.

Held, allowing the application, that in an appeal by way of case stated a finding of fact, based on additional evidence, should be included in the decision. However, findings of fact were for the commissioners and they could not be instructed as to the facts found nor to the manner in which their findings should be expressed, *Consolidated Goldfields Plc v. Inland Revenue Commissioners* [1990] S.T.C. 357, [1990] C.L.Y. 3767 applied.

BRADLEY (INSPECTOR OF TAXES) v. LONDON ELECTRICITY PLC [1996] S.T.C. 231, Jacob, J., Ch D.

5571. Common Customs Tariff–cable television transmission equipment–appropriate tariff classification

[Finance Act 1994 s.16; Council Regulation 2658/87 on the tariff and statistical nomenclature and on the Common Customs Tariff Annex A.]

CEC decided that equipment imported by T should be classified as "electrical apparatus" under Tariff Classification 85.17 82 90 090, contained in Council Regulation 2658/87 Annex A. T appealed, contending that it should be classified as "transmission apparatus" under Tariff Classification 85.25 10 90. At the hearing, CEC sought to argue in the alternative that the equipment should be classified under Tariff Classification 85.25 20 90.

Held, allowing the appeal, that (1) the equipment should be classified as transmission apparatus for television; (2) the tribunal had no jurisdiction under the Finance Act 1994 s.16(1) to rule on the alternative argument but would not have accepted that Tariff Clarification 85.25 90 090 applied.

TRATEC UK LTD v. CUSTOMS AND EXCISE COMMISSIONERS [1995] V. & D.R. 72, Stephen Oliver Q.C. (Chairman), London Tribunal.

5572. Common Customs Tariff–tariff headings–beverages–preparation of wines of fresh grapes–Sangria–European Union

[Council Regulation 2658/87; Commission Regulation 3174/88.]

The plaintiffs imported in large quantities into France from Spain a drink described as sangria. A dispute arose as to the applicable tariff classification. At the relevant time, customs duties remained in force for a transitional period between Spain and the rest of the European Community.

Held, that Heading 2205 of the Combined Nomenclature for the Common Customs Tariff, in Council Regulation 2658/87 and in Commission Regulation 3174/88 was to be interpreted as covering a beverage described as "sangria" consisting of more than 50 per cent wine of fresh grapes together with water, sugar and fruit extracts.

MINISTRE DES FINANCES v. SOCIETE PARDO ET FILS (C59/94), October 17, 1995, Judge not specified, ECJ (Second Chamber).

5573. Competitions–betting duty–liability of newspaper competitions for pool betting duty

[Betting and Gaming Duties Act 1981 s.6, s.7.]

CEC appealed against a VAT and Duties Tribunal decision that four competitions appearing in newspapers owned by NIN were not subject to pool betting duty under the Betting and Gaming Duties Act 1981 s.6. One of the competitions, Fantasy Fund Manager, required the payment of fees for registration and for changes to a share portfolio, whereas the others allowed competitors to take part by using a BT premium rate telephone line.

Held, allowing the appeal in respect of Fantasy Fund Manager but dismissing it in respect of the other three games, that the tribunal had erred in failing to apply the statutory definition of betting under the 1981 Act, concentrating instead on the commonly accepted notion of a bet. Under the deeming provisions of s.7(3), pool betting duty became payable in the absence of a stake and extended to transactions not having the characteristics of a bet in the commonly accepted sense. It was immaterial whether the entry fee had the characteristics of a stake, as it was deemed to be a bet under s.7(3) for the purposes of pool betting. As regards the other competitions, in the absence of a transaction covered by s.7(3), the deeming provision was inoperative, which meant that a conventional stake-based bet had to exist. As payment of a telephone bill could not be deemed to be a stake, no liability to pool betting duty arose.

CUSTOMS AND EXCISE COMMISSIONERS v. NEWS INTERNATIONAL NEWSPAPERS LTD, *The Times*, October 9, 1996, Kay, J., QBD.

5574. Construction industry–subcontractors

[Finance Act 1995; Finance Act 1996.]

The Inland Revenue issued a press release entitled *Taxation of subcontractors in the construction industry* (Press Release 140/96), published on August 29, 1996. A review by the Inland Revenue sets August 1, 1998 as the date for implementation of changes to the construction industry tax scheme set out in the Finance Acts of 1995 and 1996 suggests that the delay of a year would be in the best interests of all concerned. The delay will allow consultation with industry and other interested parties in the development of the new system and for those affected to plan adequately for the changes.

5575. Customs and excise–release of goods for free circulation–failure to comply with the time limit for assignment of the goods to a customs approved treatment or use–imposition of a levy–European Union

[Council Regulation 4151/88 Art.15, Art.19.]

S objected to the levying of a surcharge (equal to five per cent of the value of the goods imported) by the Portuguese customs authorities for its failure to comply within the time limit for customs clearance of a consignment of computer hardware.

Held, that Council Regulation 4151/88, laying down the provision applicable to goods brought into the customs territory of the Community, did not preclude the customs authority from accepting, after the expiry of the periods provided for in Art.15(1), a declaration for the release for free circulation of goods brought into the Community. Council Regulation 4151/88 Art.19 did not preclude the customs authority from requiring the payment of a sum, other than the customs duties and any expenses arising from temporary storage of the goods, for accepting a declaration for their release for free circulation after expiry of the periods provided for in Art.15(1), if the amount of that sum was determined in accordance with the principle of proportionality and under conditions which were analogous to those applicable in national law to infringements of the same nature and gravity.

SIESSE v. DIRECTOR DA ALFANDEGA DE ALCANTARA (C36/94), October 26, 1995, Judge not specified, ECJ (Fifth Chamber).

5576. Customs duty–clearances–post clearance recovery where certain goods not complying with rules of origin and processing requirements–European Union

[Council Regulation 2051/74; Council Regulation 1697/79; Commission Regulation 3184/74; Council Regulation 802/68.]

F, a company involved in the importation of seafood from the Faroe Islands, sought to challenge UK customs demands pursuant to Council Regulation 1697/79 on the post-clearance recovery of import duties or export duties. A European Commission mission of inquiry had found that the Faroese Customs had issued EUR 1 certificates of origin although the seafood was caught by crews with a higher percentage of third party nationals than the Community's rules of origin permitted, and processed without separation from seafood from non-Member States. The Faroese Customs, however, maintained that the certificates were valid. F contended that the UK Customs had no power to set aside those certificates as proof of origin and that the UK authorities should apply Art.5(2) of Regulation 1697/79 which provided that the competent authorities could waive pos - clearance recovery if non-collection of duties occurred because of their error which could not reasonably have been detected by the person liable and the exporter had complied with the rules regarding his customs declaration. The national court stayed the proceedings referring to the European Court of Justice of the European Communities for a preliminary ruling on the interpretation of relevant Community regulations.

Held, giving the preliminary ruling, that (1) Council Regulation 2051/74 on the customs procedure applicable to certain products originating in and coming from the Faroe Islands, Council Regulation 1697/79 and Commission Regulation 3184/74 concerning the definition of the concept of "originating products" and methods of administrative cooperation for the application of the customs procedure applicable to certain products originating and coming from the Faroe Islands were to be interpreted as meaning that the customs authorities of a Member State were entitled to proceed with post-clearance recovery of customs duties on goods imported from the Faroe Islands on the basis of the mission's conclusion, notwithstanding that customs duties had not been levied because the EUR 1 certificates were issued in good faith, or the Faroese Customs' dispute of the conclusions, and even if the issues disputed had not been referred to the Committee on Origin established pursuant to Council Regulation 802/68 on the coordination of the concept of the origin of goods and (2) under Council Regulation 1697/79 Art.5(2) the EUR 1 certification did not in itself constitute an "error on the part of the competent authorities". However, such an error could occur where the exporter declared the origin of the goods in reliance on the competent authorities' actual knowledge of the facts necessary to apply the customs rules and the authorities then raised no objection to the statements made in the declaration. It was for the national court to determine the extent to which the error was capable of being detected by the persons liable.

R. v. CUSTOMS AND EXCISE COMMISSIONERS, *ex p.* FAROE SEAFOOD CO LTD [1996] All E.R. (EC) 606, DAO Edward (President), ECJ.

5577. Customs duty–common commercial policy–repayment or remission of import duties–European Union

[Council Regulation 1430/79 on the repayment and remission of import or export duties Art.1.]

S, a Portuguese company, bought, from an undertaking established in Germany, certain goods on which customs duties were not charged upon their importation into Portugal, since Germany was stated to be the place of origin of the goods on the EUR 1 certificates of origin. Those certificates were later cancelled by the German customs authorities and the Portuguese customs authorities began proceedings to effect post clearance recovery of the duty. S sought the annulment of this decision and various technical issues arose for consideration by the ECJ.

Held, that the words "duties... which have not yet been paid" appearing in Council Regulation 1430/79 Art.1(2)(d) did not refer only to duties whose payment had been deferred. Where, in an application actually seeking remission of import duties, the person concerned relied on facts capable of constituting a special situation within the meaning of Art.13(1), without expressly mentioning that provision, that omission did not prevent the national customs authority from considering the application with reference to that provision.

SEIM v. SUBDIRECTOR-GERAL DAS ALFANDEGAS (C446/93), January 18, 1996, Judge not specified, ECJ.

5578. Customs duty–whether hydrocarbon oil was for qualifying use–issue of restitution proceedings by plaintiff for repayment of duty–availability of private law remedy

[Hydrocarbon Oil Duties Act 1979 s.6, s.9.]

BS used hydrocarbon oil in its steel manufacturing process, on which it was required to pay duty. BS asserted its entitlement to relief from duty within the Hydrocarbon Oil Duties Act 1979 s.6 further to s.9(1) of that Act on the basis that a delivery could be made to "an approved person" where the oil was used for a "qualifying use". CEC had contended that BS did not have a qualifying use and therefore was not allowed to become "an approved person". BS commenced proceedings for restitution for repayment of the duty paid on the basis that it qualified for relief and that CEC's demands for payment had been unlawful. The preliminary question arose whether BS was entitled to proceed other than by way of application for judicial review.

Held, dismissing the application, that the 1979 Act created a comprehensive code for the grant of relief from duty in this area. Since the Act provided that relief was only available to taxpayers falling within s.6, the decision whether or not an individual taxpayer fell within the section was entirely a matter of public law. A private right to recover the duty would only arise once such a public law decision had been made. A private right would only arise in BS's hands if it could show by judicial review that it ought to be accorded approved status under the terms of the Act, had been granted that status and was using the oil for a qualifying purpose. CEC's demands for duty challenged on grounds of illegality. The restitutionary claim must fail, *Cocks v. Thanet DC* [1982] 3 All E.R. 1135, [1982] C.L.Y. 1465 considered; *Roy v. Kensington and Chelsea Family Practitioner Committee* [1992] 1 All E.R. 705, [1992] C.L.Y. 30 and *Woolwich Building Society v. Inland Revenue Commissioners (No.2)* [1992] 3 All E.R. 737, [1992] C.L.Y. 2508 distinguished.

BRITISH STEEL PLC v. CUSTOMS AND EXCISE COMMISSIONERS [1996] 1 All E.R. 1002, Laws, J., QBD.

5579. Damages–Lloyd's Names eligible for full interest on damages award against negligent underwriters–impractical for effect of taxation to be taken into account

[Supreme Court Act 1981 s.35A.]

D was one of a number of Lloyd's Names who were awarded damages against GW and sought a determination as to the award of interest on the damages under the Supreme Court Act 1981 s.35A. In a previous hearing Potter, J. had ruled that the Names would be liable to tax on any damages awarded, so that in the assessment of damages no account should be taken of the effect of taxation, following *Parsons v. BNM Laboratories Ltd* [1964] 1 Q.B. 95, [1963] C.L.Y. 933. GW contended that interest should be paid only on the net losses after giving credit for the tax savings involved.

Held, awarding interest on 75 per cent of the damages recovered, that (1) s.35A gave a broad discretion to award interest on damages which allowed the court to place the plaintiff in the same position as if the wrong had not occurred. Although issues arising from taxation increased the complexity and cost of the inquiry, the court should not close its eyes to the implications of taxation when awarding interest under s.35A. Each claim for interest should be determined on its own merits, refraining from detailed investigation of the tax position but declining to award interest where the plaintiff was unlikely to have suffered loss of use of the money and (2) many Names would have had significant tax benefits on their losses and it was unfair to treat them as if they had lost out entirely from the time of sustaining the loss until judgment. Conversely, there were other Names who would not be able to enjoy such tax benefits and it was impractical to attempt to identify the extent to which tax benefits had affected losses in each and every case, *British Transport Commission v. Gourley* [1956] A.C. 185, [1955] C.L.Y. 724 considered, *Parsons v. BNM Laboratories Ltd* [1964] 1 Q.B. 95, [1963] C.L.Y. 933 distinguished.

DEENY v. GOODA WALKER LTD (NO.4) [1996] L.R.L.R. 168, Phillips, J., QBD (Comm Ct).

5580. Documents–application for production–statutory power extending to inter parties hearing–statutory interpretation

[Taxes Management Act 1970 s.20.]

T's solicitor was informed of the inspector's intention to apply for consent to issue a notice to T to produce documents under the Taxes Management Act 1970 s.20. The solicitor asked for an inter partes hearing.

Held, refusing the request, that the scheme of the section implied that the application should be made ex parte and could not sensibly be made inter partes, *R. v. IRC, ex p. TC Coombs & Co* [1991] 2 A.C. 283, [1991] C.L.Y. 2104 considered.

TAXPAYER v. INSPECTOR OF TAXES [1996] S.T.C. (SCD) 261, DA Shirley, Sp Comm.

5581. Documents–disclosure for inspection–taxpayer's duty to produce documents at reasonable time and place

[General Commissioners (Jurisdiction and Procedure) Regulations 1994 Reg.10.]

J appealed against penalties imposed by the commissioners for failing to comply with precepts requiring production of documents and accounts served under the General Commissioners (Jurisdiction and Procedure) Regulations 1994 Reg.10(1)(b). The precepts required production of documents by February 25, 1995, and J informed the commissioners that the records would be available for inspection at precisely 23.59 hours on that date.

Held, dismissing the appeal, that such documents had to be made available at a reasonable time. J's response was both inconvenient and unreasonable, in view of the positive duty to make records available, by either taking them to the commissioners or inviting inspection at a designated place, *Campbell v. Rochdale General Commissioners* [1975] S.T.C. 311, [1975] C.L.Y. 1617 considered.

JOHNSON v. BLACKPOOL GENERAL COMMISSIONERS AND INLAND REVENUE COMMISSIONERS [1996] S.T.C. 277, Robert Walker, J., Ch D.

5582. Double taxation–reliefs–foreign investment

DOUBLE TAXATION RELIEF (MANUFACTURED OVERSEAS DIVIDENDS) (AMENDMENT) REGULATIONS 1996, SI 1996 2654; made under the Income and Corporation Taxes Act 1988 s.791. In force: November 6, 1996; £0.65.

These Regulations amend the Double Taxation Relief (Taxes on Income) (General) (Manufactured Overseas Dividends) Regulations 1993 (SI 1993 1957) so as to exclude from the definition of manufactured overseas dividend in those Regulations a manufactured overseas dividend in respect of an overseas security that represents a loan relationship within the meaning of the Finance Act 1996 s.81.

5583. Equal treatment–taxation of income of temporary residents–repayment of excess tax–European Union

[Treaty of Rome 1957 Art.48; Council Regulation 1612/68 on freedom of movement for workers within the Community Art.7.]

Pursuant to Luxembourg tax legislation, excess amounts of income tax deducted were repayable as of right to permanent residents, whilst temporary residents could obtain repayment only by means of a non-contentious procedure. The European Commission considered that this legislation discriminated against taxpayers who exercised their right to free movement.

Held, that by maintaining in force provisions under which excess amounts of tax deducted from the salaries of a national of a Member State who resided in Luxembourg or occupied a salaried position there for only part of the tax year were to remain the property of the Treasury and were not repayable, Luxembourg had failed to fulfil its obligations under the Treaty of Rome 1957

Art.48(2) and under Council Regulation 1612/68 Art.7(2) on freedom of movement for workers within the Community.

COMMISSION OF THE EUROPEAN COMMUNITIES v. LUXEMBOURG (C151/94) [1995] S.T.C. 1047, Kakouris (President), ECJ.

5584. Excise duty–hydrocarbon oil–payment of rebates

HYDROCARBON OIL (PAYMENT OF REBATES) REGULATIONS 1996, SI 1996 2313; made under the Hydrocarbon Oil Duties Act 1979 s.24. In force: October 1, 1996; £4.15.

These Regulations replace the Hydrocarbon Oil Regulations 1973 (SI 1973 1311) Reg.31, Reg.32 and Reg.33 which provide for a regulatory scheme for the advance payment of rebate allowed on gas oil, and other heavy oil under the Hydrocarbon Oil Duties Act 1979 s.11 with a revised similar scheme for advance payments. They also apply that revised scheme additionally to the advance payment of part of the s.11 rebate allowed in respect of kerosene, where the rebated kerosene is to be used as a fuel for certain engines.

5585. Excise duty–hydrocarbon oil–relief

HYDROCARBON OIL DUTIES (MARINE VOYAGES RELIEFS) REGULATIONS 1996, SI 1996 2537; made under the Customs and Excise Management Act 1979 s.127A; the Hydrocarbon Oil Duties Act 1979 s.20AA, s.21, Sch.3 Part I; and the Finance (No.2) Act 1992 s.1. In force: November 1, 1996; £1.95.

These Regulations, implement the provisions of Council Directive 92/81 ([1992] OJ L316/12) Art.8(1)(c). They afford relief from excise duty on all oil used as fuel for the machinery of ships (excluding private pleasure craft) engaged on marine voyages. They amend the Hydrocarbons Oil Regulations 1973 (SI 1973 1311), the Hydrocarbon Oil (Amendment) Regulations 1981 (SI 1981 1134), and the Excise Duties (Deferred Payment) Regulations 1992 (SI 1992 3152).

5586. Excise duty–large quantities of beer and wine–presumption imported for commercial purpose–whether court could not interfere with assessment of Customs and Excise

[Customs and Excise Management Act 1979 s.170A; Excise Duties (Personal Reliefs) Order 1992 Art.5.]

C was stopped by Customs and Excise officers and found to be carrying 3,359 litres of beer and 180 litres of wine. He was charged with carrying wine and beer subject to unpaid excise duty contrary to the Customs and Excise Management Act 1979 s.170A. CEC argued that if a person was found carrying goods in excess of the amounts set out in the schedule to the Excise Duties (Personal Reliefs) Order 1992 then the effect of Art.5 of the Order was to create a presumption that the goods had been brought in for a commercial purpose unless the person satisfied the CEC otherwise. It was argued that the assessment as to whether the goods had been imported for commercial purposes was one for CEC alone. The justices rejected that argument and accepted C's defence that he had intended the beer and wine for his own private use. CEC appealed by way of case stated.

Held, allowing the appeal, that on the wording of the 1992 Order it was for CEC alone to decide whether or not a person had discharged the presumption that the goods were intended for a commercial purpose and if they were not satisfied the court was not entitled to go behind the decision.

CUSTOMS AND EXCISE COMMISSIONERS v. CARRIER [1995] 4 All E.R. 38, Glidewell, L.J., QBD.

5587. Excise duty–oil–identification

HYDROCARBON OIL (DESIGNATED MARKERS) REGULATIONS 1996, SI 1996 1251; made under the Hydrocarbon Oil Duties Act 1979 s.24A. In force: June 1, 1996; £0.65.

These Regulations supplement the provisions of the Hydrocarbon Oil Duties Act 1979 s.24A which relate to penalties for misuse of marked oil. Those markers which are used within the United Kingdom and elsewhere for identifying hydrocarbon oil are not to be used as fuel for road vehicles.

5588. Excise duty–wine–discriminatory internal taxation–Benelux system–European Union

[Treaty of Rome 1957 Art.95, Art.233.]

Importers of alcoholic beverages objected to the application of wine duties and special wine duties to certain products which they imported into the Netherlands from other Member States and alleged that, insofar as Dutch legislation taxed wines differently according to whether they had been made from grapes or other fruit, that legislation was incompatible with Treaty of Rome 1957 Art.95.

Held, that Art.95 guaranteed the complete neutrality of internal taxation as regards competition between domestic products and imported products. Although Art.233 enabled Belgium, Luxembourg and the Netherlands to apply, in derogation from Community rules, the rules in force within their union insofar as it was further advanced than the Common Market, that did not entitle a Member State to avoid its obligations under Art.95 where this was not indispensable for the good functioning of the Benelux system. Thus the Benelux countries were not entitled to favour fruit wines produced in their region to the detriment of beverages which had been found to be similar coming from another Member State. In order to assess the compatibility of a fiscal charge with Art.95(2), the national court must take account of the impact of the charge on the competitive relationships between the products concerned. It was important in particular to ascertain whether the charge could have the effect, on the market in question, of reducing potential consumption of the imported products to the advantage of competing domestic products. The national court must have regard here to the difference between the selling prices of the products in question and the impact of that difference on the consumer's choice, as well as to changes in the consumption of those products. In the present case there were no grounds to justify derogation from the principle that interpretative judgments have retroactive effect.

FG RODERS BV v. INSPECTEUR DER INVOERRECHTEN EN ACCIJNZEN (C367/93), August 11, 1995, Judge not specified, ECJ.

5589. Extra statutory concessions

The Inland Revenue issued a press release entitled *Extra-statutory concessions: Booklet IR1*, published on November 29, 1996. A booklet updating existing extra statutory concessions and incorporating new ones is available free of charge from any Tax Enquiry Centre, Tax Office or the Public Enquiry Room, West Wing, Somerset House, Strand, London WC2R 1 LB.

5590. Extra statutory concessions–profits–national insurance–contributions–computation

The Inland Revenue issued a press release entitled *A deduction for an employer's National Insurance Class 1A contributions when computing profits for tax purposes*, published on May 30, 1996. A new extra statutory concession reflects existing practice in relation to deductions for an employer's secondary share of Class 1A NICs paid in respect of employees in the computation of profits for tax purposes.

5591. Finance Act 1994–Commencement Order

FINANCE ACT 1994, SECTIONS 244 AND 245, (COMMENCEMENT) ORDER 1996, SI 1996 2316 (C.59); made under the Finance Act 1994 s.245. In force: bringing into force various provisions of the Act on November 4, 1996; £0.65.

This Order brings the Finance Act 1994 s.244 and s.245, which relate to the production of documents on the transfer of land in Northern Ireland, into force on November 4, 1996.

5592. Finance Act 1996 (c.8)

An Act to grant certain duties, to alter other duties, and to amend the law relating to the National Debt and the public revenue, and to make further provision in connection with finance.

This Act received Royal Assent on April 29, 1996.

5593. Finance Act 1996 s.5(6)–Appointed Day Order

FINANCE ACT 1996, SECTION 5(6), (APPOINTED DAY) ORDER 1996, SI 1996 2314 (C.58); made under the Finance Act 1996 s.5. In force: bringing into force various provisions of the Act on October 1, 1996; £0.65.

This Order appoints October 1, 1996 as the day on which the Finance Act 1996 s.5 has effect in relation to the use of kerosene as fuel for certain classes of engines, and to the taking in of kerosene as fuel for those engines. It amends the Hydrocarbon Oil Duties Act 1979 inserting two sections, which restricts the use of kerosene, as fuel for certain engines on which there has been allowed a rebate of excise duty and provides penalties in the event of a misuse of rebated kerosene.

5594. Finance Act 1996 s.6–Appointed Day Order

FINANCE ACT 1996, SECTION 6, (APPOINTED DAY) ORDER 1996, SI 1996 2751 (C.80); made under the Finance Act 1996 s.6. In force: bringing into force various provisions of the Act on November 15, 1996; £0.65.

This Order appoints November 15, 1996 as the day on which the Finance Act 1996 s.6 and Sch.1 have effect in relation to the production of a mixture of leaded or unleaded petrol and the supply of a mixture of heavy oils.

5595. Finance Act 1996 s.8–Appointed Day Order

FINANCE ACT 1996, SECTION 8 (APPOINTED DAY) ORDER 1996, SI 1996 2536 (C.70); made under the Finance Act 1996 s.8. In force: bringing into force s.8 of the Act on November 1, 1996; £0.65.

This Order appoints November 1, 1996 as the day on which the Finance Act 1996 s.8 comes into force. Section 8 repeals the Hydrocarbon Oil Duties Act 1979 s.18 and s.19 (in part), which provide for relief from excise duty on heavy hydrocarbon oil used as fuel for ships in home waters and oil used on certain fishing boats.

5596. Finance Act 1996 s.26–Appointed Day Order

FINANCE ACT 1996, SECTION 26, (APPOINTED DAY) ORDER 1996, SI 1996 1249 (C.21); made under the Finance Act 1996 s.26. In force: bringing into force various provisions of the 1996 Act on June 1, 1996; £0.65.

This Order brings into force on June 1, 1996 those provisions of the Finance Act 1996 s.26 and Sch.3 which are not already in force on that date.

5597. Finance Act 1996 s.159–Appointed Day Order

FINANCE ACT 1996 SECTION 159 (APPOINTED DAY) ORDER 1996, SI 1996 2646 (C.75); made under the Finance Act 1996 s.159. £0.65.

This Order appoints November 6, 1996 as the day on which Income and Corportion Taxes Act 1988 s.729, s.737A(2)(6) and s.786(4) (provisions applying to sale and repurchase agreements) shall cease to have effect except in relation to cases where the initial agreement to sell or transfer the securities of other property was made before that date.

5598. Free movement of goods–charge equivalent to a customs duty–provisions applicable to Ceuta and Melilla–European Union

[Treaty of Rome 1957; Act of Accession of Spain and Portugal.]

The ECJ was asked to determine whether a tax levied in Ceuta, a Spanish territory, constituted a charge having effect equivalent to a customs duty or, alternatively, discriminatory internal taxation, contrary to the Treaty of Rome 1957 and the Act of Accession of Spain and Portugal. The tax was nominally applied both to imported goods and to goods produced in the territory but, as a matter of fact, was structured in such a manner that the burden of the tax fell mainly on imported goods.

Held, that a tax would be contrary to EC law where, although having the appearance of internal taxation, it was, either by reason of the wording of the provisions imposing it or by reason of the manner in which the administrative authority applied it, such as to be levied upon imported products to the exclusion of local products in the same category.

CAMARA DE COMERCIO INDUSTRIA Y NAVEGACION CEUTA v. MUNICIPALITY OF CEUTA (C45/94), December 7, 1995, Judge not specified, ECJ.

5599. Free zones

FREE ZONE (SOUTHAMPTON) DESIGNATION (VARIATION OF AREA) ORDER 1996, SI 1996 2615; made under the Customs and Excise Management Act 1979 s.100A. In force: October 21, 1996; £0.65.

This Order varies the area designated a free zone by the Free Zone (Southampton) Designation Order 1991 (SI 1991 1740) and subsequently amended by the Free Zone (Southampton) Designation (Variation) Order 1994 (SI 1994 1410) by increasing it from 2.2254 hectares to 3.2436 hectares and relocating it some four kilometres to the west, to land known as the Western Dock Extension, adjacent to the Prince Charles Container Terminal on the north bank of Southampton Water.

5600. Income and Corporation Taxes Act 1988 s.737A–Appointed Day Order

INCOME AND CORPORATION TAXES ACT 1988, SECTION 737A, (APPOINTED DAY) ORDER 1996, SI 1996 2645 (C.74); made under the Income and Corporation Taxes Act 1988 s.737B. In force: November 6, 1996; £0.65.

The Income and Corporation Taxes Act 1988 s.737A provides for deemed manufactured payments on the sale and repurchase of securities where the agreement for the sale is entered into on or after the appointed day. This Order appoints November 6, 1996 as the appointed day in relation to agreements to sell overseas securities entered into on or after that day.

5601. Income tax–capital gains tax–tax returns–notification

The Inland Revenue issued a press release entitled *Obligation to notify chargeability to income tax and capital gains tax for tax years 1995-96 onwards*, published on February 1, 1996. A new Statement of Practice has been published by the Inland Revenue on the application of new rules on notifying chargeability to income tax or capital gains tax to certain employees. The new rules, which started on April 6, 1995, state that employees who do not receive a tax return have six months from the end of the tax year on April 5 to notify Inland Revenue. The time limit expires on October 5 in any tax year.

5602. Insurance contracts–insurance premium tax

INSURANCE PREMIUM TAX (TAXABLE INSURANCE CONTRACTS) ORDER 1996, SI 1996 2955; made under the Finance Act 1994 s.71. In force: January 1, 1997; £0.65.

This Order amends the Finance Act 1994 Sch.7 para.15(2)(b) by deleting the words "in the United Kingdom". The existing provision states that a contract of insurance shall not be taxable for the purposes of insurance premium tax where it relates only to the provision of a "relevant financial facility" (being a loan or guarantee, etc) to an overseas customer in order that he (the overseas customer) may comply with an obligation to receive goods or services from a person carrying on business in the United Kingdom. The amendment extends the existing provision by stating that an insurance contract will not be taxable for the purposes of insurance premium tax where a "relevant financial facility" is provided to an overseas customer in order that he may comply with an obligation to receive goods or services from a person carrying on business anywhere in the world.

5603. Insurance policies–premiums–professions–casual workers

The Inland Revenue issued a press release entitled *Tax treatment of premiums and benefits under locum and fixed practice expenses insurance policies*, published on April 30, 1996. Following consultation, the Inland Revenue has announced changes to the taxation of premiums on insurance policies to cover the cost of engaging a locum tenens. Hitherto those taking out such policies have had the premiums and benefits excluded from the calculation of taxable professional profits. The Inland Revenue has not received legal advice that this is incorrect and that premiums of this nature are deductible in calculating profits under Case II of Schedule D. In the same way, benefits payable under the policies should be regarded as Case II receipts on the basis that they diminish the allowable expenses of the profession. In the case of a policy which includes insurance against other, non-business, risks, only the proportion of the premium relating to practice expenses will be deductible. These new measures must be taken into account when calculating profits for periods of account beginning on or after October 1, 1996.

5604. Insurance premium tax

INSURANCE PREMIUM TAX (AMENDMENT) REGULATIONS 1996, SI 1996 2099; made under the Finance Act 1994 Sch.7 para.7. In force: September 2, 1996; £0.65.

These Regulations amend the Insurance Premium Tax Regulations 1994 (SI 1994 1774). Regulation 3 inserts a new Reg.A42 by which Job Band is defined for the purposes of Part VIII of the Regulations by reference to the rank given to an officer's job in the pay and grading system of Customs and Excise. Regulation 4 amends Reg.42(1) and Reg.43(a)(b). As a consequence, the minimum rank of officer by whom the powers described in Reg.42(1) and Reg.43(a)(b) may be exercised is an officer of a rank not below that of Job Band 7.

5605. Insurance premium tax–interest–prescribed rates

INSURANCE PREMIUM TAX (PRESCRIBED RATES OF INTEREST) (AMENDMENT) ORDER 1996, SI 1996 166; made under the Finance Act 1994 s.74, Sch.7 para.21. In force: February 6, 1996; £0.65.

This Order increases the prescribed rate of interest for the purposes of the Finance Act 1994 Sch.7 para.21 (interest on insurance premium tax recovered or recoverable by assessment) from 5.5 per cent to 6.25 per cent with effect from February 6, 1996

5606. Interest rates–employee benefits–loans

TAXES (INTEREST RATE) (AMENDMENT) REGULATIONS 1996, SI 1996 54; made under the Finance Act 1989 s.178. In force: February 6, 1996; £0.65.

The general official rate of interest for the purposes of taxation of beneficial loans made to employees under Income and Corporation Taxes Act 1988 s.160 is decreased from 7.75 per cent to 7.25 per cent from February 6, 1996.

5607. Interest rates–employee benefits–loans

TAXES (INTEREST RATE) (AMENDMENT NO.2) REGULATIONS 1996, SI 1996 1321; made under the Finance Act 1989 s.178. In force: June 6, 1996; £0.65.

These Regulations amend the Taxes (Interest Rate) Regulations 1989 Reg.5 (SI 1989 1297 as substituted by SI 1994 1307). That Regulation provides for the official rate of interest for the purposes of the Income and Corporation Taxes Act 1988 s.160 (taxation of beneficial loans made to employees) by first specifying an official rate of interest generally and then specifying, by way of exception, different official rates of interest for certain beneficial loans in the currencies of countries specified in the Table to the Regulation. The amendment made by these regulations specifies, with effect from June 6, 1996, a new general rate of interest of seven per cent per annum, in substitution for the rate of 7.25 per cent per annum specified by SI 1996 54.

5608. Interest rates–employee benefits–loans

TAXES (INTEREST RATE) (AMENDMENT NO.3) REGULATIONS 1996, SI 1996 2644; made under the Finance Act 1989 s.178. In force: November 6, 1996; £0.65.

These Regulations amend the Taxes (Interest Rate) Regulations 1989 (SI 1989 1297) Reg.5 which provides for the official rate of interest for the purposes of the Income and Corporation Taxes Act 1988 s.160 (taxation of beneficial loans made to employees) by first specifying an official rate of interest generally and then specifying, by way of exception, different official rates of interest for certain beneficial loans in the currencies of countries specified in the table to the Regulation. The amendment made by these Regulations specifies, with effect from November 6, 1996, a new general official rate of interest of 6.75 per cent per annum, in substitution for the rate of 7 per cent per annum specified by SI 1996 1321.

5609. Interest rates

TAXES (INTEREST RATE) (AMENDMENT NO.4) REGULATIONS 1996, SI 1996 3187; made under the Finance Act 1989 s.178. In force: January 31, 1997; £1.10.

These Regulations amend the Taxes (Interest Rate) Regulations 1989 (SI 1989 1297) by substituting three new Regulations for Reg.3. The new Regulations specify different interest rates applicable under the Finance Act 1989 s.178 in relation to unpaid income tax, capital gains tax, corporation tax, petroleum revenue tax and development land tax, repayments of petroleum revenue tax, overpaid development land tax and stamp duty reserve tax and repayment supplement. The new Regulations also make provision for changes in the applicable interest rate and for the formula to be used in calculating the new rate.

5610. Investigations–informers–confidentiality of letter making allegations against taxpayer

Held, that a letter written by an informant containing allegations about a taxpayer could be withheld from its subject so that the confidential source of information could be protected. The letter had not been the only information instigating the investigation and all the matters referred to in the letter had been independently investigated.

R. v. REVENUE ADJUDICATOR'S OFFICE, *ex p.* DRUMMOND [1996] S.T.C. 1312, Turner, J., QBD.

5611. Investigations notices–third party disclosure–notices requiring disclosure of conjectural categories of documents invalid–documents must be specifically identified

[Taxes Management Act 1970 s.20.]

Held, allowing the application by NB for certiorari to quash 13 notices against it, that the Inland Revenue had exceeded their statutory powers under the Taxes Management Act 1970 s.20(3) by serving notices on NB to provide information on customers who were the subject of investigations. The notices called not only for specifically identified documents but also for documents which the Inland Revenue conjectured might be in existence. Under the notices, NB was required to exercise judgment to determine whether or not documents, which the Inland Revenue specified only as a category, were in the bank's possession. Section 20 of the Act should be interpreted according to the general rule that a mere witness, who was not a party to the dispute, could not be obliged to comply with the full requirements of discovery. The Inland Revenue had no authority to compel third parties to search through their documents and investigate whether or not conjectural documents existed.

R. v. O'KANE, *ex p.* NORTHERN BANK LTD [1996] S.T.C. 1249, Ferris, J., QBD.

5612. Landfill tax

HM Customs & Excise issued a press release entitled *Less waste– more jobs* (News release 51/96), published on September 30, 1996. The landfill tax takes effect from October 1, 1996. It is intended to encourage waste producers to reduce their use of landfill sites and the money raised from the tax will be used to reduce employers' NI contributions by £500 million from next April. The measure thereby helps to protect the environment while reducing the cost of employment. The tax will be collected from landfill site operators by HMCE at a rate of £7.00 per tonne for active waste such as plastic packaging, with a lower rate of £2.00 per tonne set for inactive waste such as builders' rubble.

5613. Landfill tax

LANDFILL TAX REGULATIONS 1996, SI 1996 1527; made under the Finance Act 1996 s.47, s.48, s.49, s.51, s.52, s.53, s.58, s.61, s.62, s.68, Sch.5 para.2, Sch.5 para.13, Sch.5 para.14, Sch.5 para.20, Sch.5 para.23, Sch.5 para.42, Sch.5 para.43. In force: August 1, 1996; £6.10.

These Regulations make provision for the administration and assurance of landfill tax. They relate to the registration of those intending to make taxable disposals; accounting for tax by making returns; the keeping of landfill tax accounts; payments in respect of credits of tax; credits relating to recycling; incineration and permanent removal of waste; landfill invoices; temporary disposals; methods of determining the weight of materials; the set off of landfill credits and debits and distress.

5614. Landfill tax

LANDFILL TAX (AMENDMENT) REGULATIONS 1996, SI 1996 2100; made under the Finance Act 1996 Sch.5 para.13. In force: September 2, 1996; £0.65.

These Regulations amend the Landfill Tax Regulations 1996 (SI 1996 1527) Part XII. Regulation 3 inserts a new Reg.A48 by which Job Band is defined for the purposes of Part XII of the Regulations by reference to the rank given to an officer's job in the pay and grading system of Customs and Excise. Regulation 4 amends Reg.48(1) and Reg.49(a)(b). As a consequence, the minimum rank of officer by whom the powers described in Reg.48(1) and Reg.49(a)(b) may be exercised is an officer of a rank not below that of Job Band 7.

5615. Landfill tax

LANDFILL TAX (QUALIFYING MATERIAL) ORDER 1996, SI 1996 1528; made under the Finance Act 1996 s.42, s.63. In force: October 1, 1996; £1.10.

This Order has been made with regard to listing qualifying material which is described as inactive or inert in relation to landfill tax. It lists the generic description of the qualifying materials with any conditions which must be satisfied. It also contains the relevant conditions for waste disposals in Great Britain and Northern Ireland.

5616. Landfill tax–contaminated land

LANDFILL TAX (CONTAMINATED LAND) ORDER 1996, SI 1996 1529; made under the Finance Act 1996 s.46. In force: August 1, 1996; £1.95.

This Order amends the Finance Act 1996 to provide for an additional exemption from the new landfill tax. The exemption relates to disposals of waste material resulting from certain land reclamations.

5617. Mistake–codes of practice

The Inland Revenue issued a press release entitled *Code of Practice 1: Mistakes by the Inland Revenue,* published on April 3, 1996. A revised version of the Inland Revenue's Code of Practice 1 has been published, which explains how complaints about Inland Revenue errors can be resolved and outlines the circumstances in which costs arising from errors and delays will be reimbursed or consolatory payments made.

5618. Motor vehicles–discriminatory tax on imports–European Union

[Treaty of Rome 1957 Art.95.]

French law provided for a differential tax which was levied on the sale of motor cars. J purchased a Mercedes which was subject to the highest level of the tax. She claimed that, since this level of tax only applied to imported vehicles, there was an element of discriminatory taxation involved.

Held, that the system of taxation at issue did not appear to involve discrimination. Treaty of Rome 1957 Art.95 did not preclude the application of national taxation which increased according to horsepower as long as the level of taxation did not have the effect of favouring the sale of vehicles of domestic manufacture over the sale of vehicles imported from other Member States.

JACQUIER v. DIRECTEUR GENERAL DES IMPOTS (C113/94), November 30, 1995, Judge not specified, ECJ.

5619. Municipal taxes–free movement of goods–charge having effect equivalent to a customs duty–temporal effects of a preliminary ruling–European Union

[Treaty of Rome 1957 Art.9.]

S sought annulment or amendment of a decision entering her name in the fiscal register for municipal taxes calculated on the value of goods imported into the Dodecanese Islands (which are part of Greece) and imposing fines on her for failure to fulfil her obligations.

Held, that an ad valorem charge levied by a Member State on goods imported from or exported to another Member State by reason of their entering or leaving region of the first Member State's territory constituted a charge having an effect equivalent to a customs duty on imports, contrary to the Treaty of Rome 1957 Art.9. This remained the case where the ad valorem charge was also levied by the Member State on goods moving between its territories. The present judgment could not be relied on in support of claims for refunds of sums levied by way of the contested duty before July 16, 1992, the date of the court's judgment in *Administration des Douanes et Droits Indirect v. Legros (C163/90)* [1992] E.C.R. I-4625, [1992] C.L.Y. 4749, except by claimants who had, before that date, initiated legal proceedings or raised an equivalent claim.

SIMITZI v. KOS (C485/93), September 14, 1995, Judge not specified, ECJ.

5620. Penalties–employers–contractors–delay

The Inland Revenue issued a press release entitled *Employers' and contractors' end-of-year returns*, published on June 14, 1996. Following a review of the new penalty system for returns submitted late by employers and contractors, the Inland Revenue has decided to limit the level of automatic penalties to the total amount of tax and NIC which should be shown on the return or £100, whichever is greater.

5621. Pension schemes–tax exempt scheme capable of obtaining tax advantage within ICTA 1988 s.709

[Income and Corporation Taxes Act 1988 s.709.]

Held, that a tax exempt pension scheme was still capable of obtaining a tax advantage under the Income and Corporation Taxes Act 1988 s.709(1), *Sheppard (Trustees of Woodland Trust) v. Inland Revenue Commissioners (No.2)* [1993] S.T.C. 240, [1993] C.L.Y. 2259 not followed.

INLAND REVENUE COMMISSIONERS v. UNIVERSITIES SUPERANNUATION SCHEME LTD [1997] S.T.C. 1, Sir John Vinelott, Ch D.

5622. Petroleum revenue tax–oil from another field flowing through taxpayer's pipeline–tariff receipts allowance

[Oil Taxation Act 1983 s.9.]

C, a participator in the Ninian oilfield, appealed against assessments for petroleum revenue tax in respect of an agreement allowing passage of oil from the Magnus oilfield through the Ninian pipeline. Under a 1978 agreement, Magnus participators passed 150,000 barrels of oil per day down the line, in return for purchasing a 15 per cent share in it. In 1987 the Magnus flow increased, with the participators paying the Ninian participators an extra tariff charge for each barrel in excess of the 1978 agreed figure. Under the Oil Taxation Act 1983 s.9(1), such tariff receipts were included in assessable profits, with an allowance calculated on a formula basis. The assessments raised against C sought to take account of all the oil from the Magnus field passing through the pipelines in assessing liability for tax.

Held, allowing the appeal, that the purpose of the 1983 Act s.9 and Sch.3, para.1 (2) served to give participators allowing the use of field facilities to participators in other fields an allowance equivalent to 250,000 tonnes before tariff receipts became liable to tax. Under s.9(4) Sch.3 the allowance was determined as the cash equivalent of a participator's share of the tariff receipts over a chargeable period, therefore it was inconsistent to include the 250,000 tonnes in the assessment formula.

CHEVRON UK LTD v. INLAND REVENUE COMMISSIONERS [1995] S.T.C. 712, Sir John Vinelott, Ch D.

5623. Petroleum revenue tax–supplement–non-availability in respect of two separate developments within a single oil field

[Finance Act 1981 s.111; Oil Taxation Act 1975 s.2.]

Y and partners developed an oil field. A further reservoir was discovered later within the same field. Y's claim for expenditure supplement in relation to the second development under the Oil Taxation Act 1975 was rejected by the Revenue in reliance on the Finance Act 1981 s.111 (1). Y appealed.

Held, dismissing the appeal, that on the clear wording of the statute the claim in relation to the second stage must fail inevitably given the stipulations relating to the amount of oil or gas and the net profit owned.

Y CO LTD v. INLAND REVENUE COMMISSIONERS [1996] S.T.C. (SCD) 241, DA Shirley, Sp Comm.

5624. Property tax–appeals–judicial review not applicable where statutory appeal procedure provided–no abuse of power or other exceptional circumstance alleged

[Inland Revenue Ordinance s.5 (Hong Kong).]

The second plaintiff, T, owning a leasehold interest in part of a Hong Kong building, obtained an exemption under the Inland Revenue Ordinance s.5(2)(a) from the property tax chargeable under s.5(1) of the Ordinance for the year 1982-3, on the basis that it could set such property tax off against profits. H acquired a lease in another part of the building. H and T then granted an underlease to a bank. T's entire share capital was acquired by a company in the same group as H. H and T sought to challenge assessments to property tax for 1985-6 to 1988-9 inclusive by way of judicial review on the grounds that they were ultra vires, notwithstanding that there existed a procedure, laid down in s.64 to s.68 of the Ordinance, for an objection to the Commissioner and appeal to the board of review. The judge dismissed the application, and the Court of Appeal upheld his decision; H and T appealed to the Judicial Committee.

Held, dismissing the appeal, that where there was an available statutory procedure for objection and appeal in which the vires of a decision could be questioned, an application for judicial review would only be entertained in exceptional circumstances, typically when an abuse of power was alleged; the assessments involved no unfairness and therefore no abuse of power, and judicial review was therefore inappropriate.

HARLEY DEVELOPMENT INC v. INLAND REVENUE COMMISSIONERS [1996] 1 W.L.R. 727, Lord Jauncey of Tullichettle, PC.

5625. Publications

The Inland Revenue issued a press release entitled *Statements of practice: booklet IR131*, published on November 12, 1996. A new edition of the Practitioners Series booklet IR131 has been published by the Inland Revenue updating existing Statements of Practice and including new ones published up to August 31, 1996. It is available free of charge to personal callers from any Tax Enquiry Centre, Tax Office or the Public Enquiry Room, West Wing, Somerset House, Strand, London WC2R 1LB.

5626. Publications

[Finance Act 1996.]

The Inland Revenue issued a press release entitled *Tax relief for vocational training: explanatory leaflet*, published on June 21, 1996. A revised version of the leaflet IR119 has been published, covering the extension of tax relief for vocational training fees to some courses which do not lead to NVQs or SVQs. The new leaflet reflects changes introduced in the Finance Act 1996, which widened vocational training relief to those aged 30 or over who are paying for full time vocational training courses lasting between four weeks and a year, including courses not linked to NVQ or SVQ. The press release *Approved share schemes for emplyees: revised Inland Revenue publications* (Press release 125/96), published on July 16, 1996, draws attention to the revised versions of leaflets and booklets IR95 to IR98. These publications explain the tax reliefs available for shares and share options acquired through approved employee share schemes. The Inland Revenue has also published a new leaflet IR101 and booklet IR102 (replacing IR99 and IR100 which have been withdrawn) explaining the new Company Share Option Plan introduced in the Finance Act 1996. A further press release *Personal residence rules: Inland Reveue publish revised explanatory booklet*, published on October 30, 1996, indicates that a revised edition of booklet IR20 *Residents and Non-residents–Liability to Tax in the United Kingdom* has been published. This sets out the rules for determining the residence status of individuals for tax purposes. Copies may be obtained from any Tax Enquiry Centre or Tax Office, or from the Public Enquiry Room, West Wing, Somerset House, London WC2R 1LB.

5627. Share dealing–stamp duties–stamp duty reserve tax

HM Treasury issued a press release entitled *Stamp duty reform*, published on October 24, 1996. The Chancellor of the Exchequer has announced changes to the existing stamp duty and stamp duty reserve tax exemptions for market makers and broker dealers in all shares. Stamp duty and SDRT relief will be available to firms registered as intermediaries on any UK recognised exchange or EEA regulated market. Relief will be available for all purchases made on the relevant exchange and will cover all stocks on which stamp duty and SDRT is paid, replacing the current market maker and broker dealer exemptions. The changes are to facilitate the London Stock Exchange's moves towards a new trading system as well as providing a level playing field for different market players and exchanges.

5628. Share transfers–appeals–guiding principles when remitting a case back to the commissioners

[Income and Corporation Taxes Act 1988 s.741; Taxes Management Act 1970 s.56.]

C appealed by way of case stated against a determination by the special commissioners that he had failed to show, under the Income and Corporation Taxes Act 1988 s.741, that a share transfer was bona fide, and not designed to avoid tax liability.

Held, dismissing the appeal, that on an appeal by case stated the court could remit an application by either party under the Taxes Management Act 1970 s.56. However, in doing so, regard must be paid to the principles in *Consolidated Goldfields Plc v. Inland Revenue Commissioners* [1990] S.T.C. 357, [1990] C.L.Y. 3767. Implicit in these principles was that the commissioners should forward copies of proved or admitted documents and oral evidence notes along with the case stated, and if they failed to do so the court could request them to expand the case stated. The court had to decide if a conclusion followed as a logical or practical necessity from the findings of fact, or if the findings disclosed inconsistencies with the conclusion. The commissioners acted as a tribunal of fact, and it was for them to decide the relative weight attached to the facts and to decide which facts were relevant to the appeal. A court could only interfere if their conclusion was irrational on the facts. A case should not be remitted merely to inquire into the relevance of proved facts to the conclusion reached or to determine the weight given to the facts the commissioners considered relevant.

CARVILL v. INLAND REVENUE COMMISSIONERS [1996] S.T.C. 126, Sir John Vinelott, Ch D.

5629. Special commissioners–jurisdiction–expert evidence of Scottish law–legal submissions admissible–whether judicial review not appropriate in absence of special circumstances

[Special Commissioners (Jurisdiction and Procedure) Regulations 1994 Reg.2; Taxes Management Act 1970 s.56A.]

The Inspector of Taxes applied for leave to apply for judicial review of a preliminary decision of the special commissioner not to allow expert evidence of Scottish law to be adduced by the Inspector during an appeal which raised points of Scottish law. The special commissioners had decided that the Inspector could not submit evidence of Scottish law as they were able to hear legal submissions as to the law of Scotland. The Inspector argued that the special commissioner was purporting to exercise his jurisdiction throughout the UK whereas it was divided into three separate jurisdictions. In this case, his jurisdiction extended to England and Wales, and points of Scots law should be treated as questions of fact. The Special Commissioners (Jurisdiction and Procedure) Regulations 1994 Reg.2

showed that there was differentiation between the different jurisdictions in relation to proceedings.

Held, dismissing the application, that (1) as a right of appeal on a point of law was conferred under the Taxes Management Act 1970 s.56A, judicial review should not supplant the normal statutory appeal procedure, *Preston, Re* [1985] 1 A.C. 835 followed. Judicial review would only be invoked in exceptional circumstances. There were no exceptional circumstances in this case and (2) this was not a jurisdictional matter but an evidential matter. The special commissioner had jurisdiction to hear the appeal and receive submissions on Scots law in support of a subsidiary point.

R. v. SPECIAL COMMISSIONERS, *ex p.* INSPECTOR OF TAXES, Trans. Ref: CO 1548/95, June 29, 1995, Hidden, J., QBD.

5630. Stamp duties–documents

STAMP DUTY (PRODUCTION OF DOCUMENTS) (NORTHERN IRELAND) REGULATIONS 1996, SI 1996 2348; made under the Finance Act 1994 s.244, s.245. In force: November 4, 1996; £1.10.

The Finance Act 1994 s.244(1) provides, subject to s.245 of that Act, that on the occasion of any transfer on sale of any freehold interest in land in Northern Ireland, or the grant, or any transfer on sale, of any lease of such land, the instrument by means of which the transfer was affected or the lease was granted shall be produced to the Commissioners of Inland Revenue. Section 244(2) provides that any person required to produce an instrument under s.244(1) shall produce with it a document giving such particulars as may be described by Regulations. Section 245(1) provides that s.244 shall not apply to any instrument falling within any prescribed class; but that Regulations may, in respect of exempt instruments or such descriptions of exempt instruments as may be prescribed, require such a document as is mentioned in s.244(2) to be furnished in accordance with the Regulations to the Commissioner of Valuation for Northern Ireland. These Regulations make provision with respect to the enactments contained in s.244 and s.245.

5631. Stamp duties–leases–tax avoidance scheme

[Stamp Act 1891 s.1.]

L, a landlord, appealed against an assessment of stamp duty in respect of two leases. With a view to minimising stamp duty, L had provided in the leases that the premium to be paid by the tenant should be calculated in accordance with a formula involving the closing price of treasury stock at a date 25 days after the execution of the leases. Since the amount of consideration, for the purposes of the Stamp Act 1891 s.1, could not be ascertained as at the date of execution of the leases, L contended that s.1 did not apply and that the lease was therefore chargeable only with the fixed duty of £2.

Held, dismissing the appeal, that as a general principle, consideration should be ascertained by reference to the circumstances as at the date of the instrument, even where there had been an agreement to ascertain the relevant premium by reference to some external factor, *Underground Electric Railways v. Inland Revenue Commissioners* [1906] A.C. 306 considered. Duty could be chargeable as at the date of the execution of the leases by applying the formula involving the closing price of treasury stock as at that date.

LM TENANCIES 1 PLC v. INLAND REVENUE COMMISSIONERS [1996] S.T.C. 880, Carnwath, J., Ch D.

5632. Stamp duties–pension funds

STAMP DUTY AND STAMP DUTY RESERVE TAX (PENSION FUNDS POOLING SCHEMES) REGULATIONS 1996, SI 1996 1584; made under the Finance Act 1946 s.57; and the Finance (No.2) Act (Northern Ireland) 1946 s.28. In force: July 11, 1996; £0.65.

These Regulations provide for certain unauthorised unit trust schemes (pension funds pooling schemes) to be excepted from the definition of unit trust scheme given by the Finance Act 1946 s.57(1) and the Finance (No.2) Act (Northern Ireland) 1946 s.28(1). A pension funds pooling scheme is a scheme participation in which is restricted to certain pension schemes or funds and which has the characteristics set out in the Income Tax (Pension Funds Pooling Schemes) Regulations 1996 (SI 1996 1585). The effect of these Regulations is that units under the scheme will not be treated as stock for the purposes of stamp duty on transfers or (by virtue of the Finance Act 1986 s.99(9) (c.41)) as chargeable securities for the purposes of stamp duty reserve tax. Corresponding Regulations have also been made for the purposes of income tax (SI 1996 1585) and capital gains tax (SI 1996 1583).

5633. Stamp duties–sale of land–deed transferring equitable estate–vendors holding property as nominees of purchaser–whether executory agreement completed

[Stamp Act 1891 s.54, s.59.]

P appealed against a decision to levy stamp duty on a deed transferring the equitable interest in a farming business from a partnership to P. Under the deed, the legal estate was to remain with the partnership, holding as nominees of P, until the sale of the legal estate to a third party. IRC contended that the agreement was either an agreement for sale of an equitable interest, chargeable under the Stamp Act 1891 s.59(1), or a conveyance on sale of an equitable interest under s.54 of the Act. P asserted that the deed was an agreement for the sale of the legal freehold, and did not fall within the class of agreements covered by either s.54 or s.59.

Held, dismissing the appeal, that all the obligations under the executory agreement had been carried out by the parties, with the partnership holding as bare trustees for P. There was no longer any contractual obligation which remained to be performed. As such it did not matter which of the two sections were applied, as both served to charge stamp duty on agreements for the sale of an equitable interest, *West London Syndicate Ltd v. Inland Revenue Commissioners* [1898] 2 Q.B. 507 approved and *Chesterfield Brewery Co v. Inland Revenue Commissioners* [1899] 2 Q.B. 7 distinguished. Strictly the agreement operated as a transfer of the equitable estate in the freehold property and not as an agreement for the sale of the equitable estate.

PETER BONE LTD v. INLAND REVENUE COMMISSIONERS [1995] S.T.C. 921, Vinelott, J., Ch D.

5634. Statutory demands–recruiting–Inland Revenue entitled to payment where appeal still unsolved against special commissioners–home offer as security unacceptable where Inland Revenue not in possession of security for debt

[Insolvency Act 1986 s.271; Insolvency Rules 1986 r 6.5.]

K was served with a statutory demand following a decision of the special commissioners that he owed money in connection with Schedule D assessments and National Insurance contributions. An appeal against the decision of the special commissioners remained outstanding. On this basis, K appealed seeking the setting aside of the statutory declaration. K contended that the statutory demand was fictitious, that no tax was owed and that he would give his family home as security until the matter was resolved.

Held, dismissing the appeal, that K's appeal was in the nature of a true appeal. However, the result of such appeal would not cause the outcome of the appeal to be any different. The Inland Revenue were entitled to payment even though there was an appeal outstanding against the decision of the special commissioners. K's offer to provide security did not satisfy the Insolvency Rules 1986 r.6.5(4)(c) because the Inland Revenue did not hold security in respect of this debt and the offer was no more than a general offer. The time had not arrived when the Insolvency Act 1986 s.271 (3) could be used in respect of a general offer.

KING v. INLAND REVENUE COMMISSIONERS; SUB NOM. DEBTOR (NO.960 OF 1992), *Re* [1996] B.P.I.R. 414, Mummery, J., Ch D.

5635. Vehicle excise duty

VEHICLE EXCISE DUTY (IMMOBILISATION, REMOVAL AND DISPOSAL OF VEHICLES) REGULATIONS 1996, SI 1996 107; made under the Vehicle Excise and Registration Act 1994 s.57, Sch.2A. In force: February 20, 1996; £2.80.

These Regulations make provision for the immobilisation of unlicensed mechanically propelled vehicles found stationary on public roads in designated clamping areas. Authorised persons are enabled under Reg.5, to fix an immobilisation device to such a vehicle, Reg.6 sets out conditions which must be fulfilled in order for a vehicle to be released, Reg.7 prescribes certain exemptions; and Reg.8 and Reg.9 create offences in connection with such an immobilisation. Reg.10 to Reg.15 deal with the removal and disposal of immobilised vehicles, the recovery of prescribed charges, the taking of possession of a vehicle and related offences and the claim by a vehicle's owner following its disposal. The issue of vouchers and offences relating thereto are covered in Reg.16 and Reg.17; and provision is made by Reg.18 for disputes over charges paid for the release of a vehicle. Prescribed charges are set out in Sch.1; designated clamping areas are named in Sch.2; and Sch.3 details steps to be taken to ascertain ownership of a removed vehicle.

5636. Vehicle excise duty–licences–fees

VEHICLE EXCISE DUTY (FEE FOR TEMPORARY LICENCES) REGULATIONS 1996, SI 1996 2008; made under the Vehicle Excise and Registration Act 1994 s.9. In force: September 2, 1996; £0.65.

These Regulations substitute the sum of £2.35 for the sum of £2 which is payable, under the Vehicle Excise and Registration Act 1994 s.9(3) where an application for a temporary vehicle licence is made to an agent of the Secretary of State.

5637. Vocational training–relief

VOCATIONAL TRAINING (PUBLIC FINANCIAL ASSISTANCE AND DISENTITLEMENT TO TAX RELIEF) (AMENDMENT) REGULATIONS 1996, SI 1996 3049; made under the Finance Act 1991 s.32. In force: January 1, 1997; £0.65.

These Regulations make minor amendments to the Vocational Training (Public Financial Assistance and Disentitlement to Tax Relief) Regulations 1992 (SI 1992 734).

5638. Vocational training–relief

VOCATIONAL TRAINING (TAX RELIEF) (AMENDMENT) REGULATIONS 1996, SI 1996 1185; made under the Finance Act 1991 s.32, s.33. In force: May 6, 1996; £1.10.

These Regulations amend the Vocational Training (Tax Relief) Regulations 1992 (SI 1992 746) (the principal Regulations) following legislative changes made by the Finance Act 1996. They also make amendments of a drafting nature to the principal Regulations. Regulation 1 provides for citation and commencement and Reg.2 for interpretation. Regulation 3 and Reg.4 make amendments to the principal Regulations following legislative changes made by the Finance Act 1996. Those changes provide that vocational training relief shall be available in respect of certain courses of training where the individual has attained the age of 30. Regulation 3 accordingly amends Reg.3 of the principal Regulations to extend the cases and conditions under which relief at source may be given; and Reg.4 inserts a new Reg.4A in the principal Regulations prescribing a new form of notice of entitlement to relief at source. Regulation 5 makes amendments of a drafting nature to Reg.13 of the principal Regulations.

5639. Articles

A bonus for the Revenue? *(Neil Denniss)*: Tax. 1996, 136(3548), 665-666. (CGT liability arising from building society merger bonus payments, availability of indexation relief and annual exemption, and potential test case challenging Inland Revenue decision to tax bonuses as asset derived capital sums).

A tax on philanthropy *(Trevor Johnson)*: Tax. 1996, 138(3576), 29-31. (Tax treatment of housing associations with reference to corporate and charitable status and whether they qualify as investment companies for relief for management expenses).

A thorn in their sides - groups and tax avoidance schemes *(Debbie Sharpe)*: Vat Plan. 1996, 52, 2-3. (New draft Sch.9A on VAT group anti avoidance provisions designed to halt entry and exit schemes by giving Customs power to make directions as to VAT liability on group supplies).

Aligning the PILONs: T.P.T. 1996, 17(21), 161-163. (Inland Revenue guidance on income tax treatment of payments in lieu of notice as emoluments, compensation for breach of contract or redundancy payments).

Arrangements, connected parties and control *(David Wainman)*: Tax J. 1996, 340, 12-14. (Meaning of shareholder control in context of availability of group relief provisions and repayment of tax credits on dividends).

Bad advice *(Francesca Lagerberg)*: Tax. 1996, 136(3545), 592. (Income tax and CGT exemptions for mis-sold pension compensation but Law Society questions proposed definition of bad advice).

Between the taxpayer and the executive: law's inadequacy; democracy's failure? *(David Goldberg)*: B.T.R. 1996, 1, 9-27. (Argues that scope of Revenue administrative powers makes substantive legal control difficult, urging instead greater democratic control and shift in burden of proof to redress present imbalance between individual taxpayers and Revenue).

BSE and farm stocktaking valuations: Tax J. 1996, 356, 6. (Inland Revenue guidance on valuation of livestock in year end stocktaking in light of uncertainties due to BSE centred market slump and slaughter policy).

Business taxation: the transitional year *(John Line)*: Tax J. 1996, 340, 18-19. (Anti avoidance measures in transition to current year assessment, accounting changes to obtain tax benefits and additional tax penalties where profits of transitional period increased in way not exempted).

Changing your residence *(Paul Whitehead)*: T.P.T. 1996, 17(12), 89-92. (Tax planning opportunities of non-resident status, applicable rules for establishing status, available reliefs and double taxation provisions).

Compatibility of limitation on benefits provisions with EC law *(Jacques Malherbe* and *Olivier Delattre)*: Euro. Tax. 1996, 36(1), 12-20. (Van Brunschot lecture on relationship of EC law to tax treaties between Member States and third party states, limited direct tax harmonisation under Treaty and whether US treaty policy conflicts with anti discrimination principle).

DIY tax–self assessment *(Mike Evans)*: C.S.R. 1996, 19(26), 206-207. (Implications of self assessment for employers particularly with regard to expenses payments and benefits in kind).

English as she is spoke *(Arthur Sellwood)*: Tax. 1996, 136(3537), 362-364. (Need for tax simplification, concise drafting and removal of vague and imprecise terms from tax legislation).

Environmental bodies *(Pamela Castle)*: Mck. Env. L.B. 1996, Oct, 3-4. (Rebate scheme for landfill tax to encourage landfill operators to set up non-profit making organisations to fund range of approved environmental projects, under supervision of regulatory body ENTRUST).

Finance Act notes: loans to participators: section 173 *(Guy Brannan)*: B.T.R. 1996, 4, 378-379. (FA 1996 reforms to tax treatment of close company loans extend due date for tax refunds when loans are repaid and amend treatment when participators are non resident).

Foreign owned UK subsidiaries *(Lindsay R. Pentelow)*: Tax J. 1996, 378, 12-14. (Tax efficient methods to reduce profits of UK resident company and repatriate to foreign holding group, qualifying payments deductible on arm's length basis and non-dividend based repatriation methods).
Get wise for a demerger *(Arnold Homer* and *Rita Burrows)*: Tax. 1996, 136(3547), 650-651. (Legislative and ESC provisions applicable to demergers include shareholder reliefs and conditions required for beneficial ACTand CGT treatment).
Gift Aid: don't let it slip away *(Daron H. Gunson)*: T.P.T. 1996, 17(9), 65-67. (Basic rules for obtaining tax relief under Gift Aid for individuals and companies, use of loan or deposit covenants and overseas aspects).
Group transfers at an undervalue *(John Lindsay* and *Ian Saunders)*: Tax J. 1996, 350, 17-18. (Capital distribution status of intra group asset transfers, with reference to shares in assets transferred and historical development of legislative provisions).
How the self employed are taxed *(Sharron West)*: M. Advice 1996, 41, 9. (Change to the "current year" basis of assessment for self employed and transitional rules for old businesses).
If it works don't fix it *(Basil Sabine)*: Tax. 1996, 137(3570), 581-583. (General Commissioners' origins and historical development and increased role for independent review powers with advent of self assessment set against Tax Law Review Committee's appeal system reform proposals).
In the performance of the duties: fact, law or both? *(Abimbola A. Olowofoyeku)*: B.T.R. 1996, 1, 28-45. (Decided cases on applicability of Sch.E deductible expenses rule, including meaning of "in the performance of the duties" and "necessarily incurred" and whether determination requires rigid fact and law dichotomy).
Income tax tips for foreign domicilaries *(John P. Fernandez)*: Tax J. 1996, 340, 8-11. (Tax planning opportunities with consideration of remittance basis, foreign emoluments, qualifying loans, overseas loans used as income and settlor interested offshore trusts).
Inspector's intransigence: Tax. 1996, 136(3546), 634-635. (Question and answer. Whether bad debt relief was available to person holding 99 per cent in two associated companies where one company was owed irrecoverable debt due to liquidation of other).
It's official: Tax. 1996, 137(3563), 388-389. (Extracts from IRTB 23 including 1997 self assessment return dates, charitable trading stock donations, controlled foreign companies, ostrich farming tax treatment and landfill tax payments).
More news for tour operators *(Peter Hewitt)*: Tax J. 1996, 338, 11-13. (Alternative proposals announced by Customs following first phase of consultation to amend TOMS system to facilitate computation under Single Market VAT rules).
New statement of practice: Tax. 1996, 136(3542), 493-494. (Text of SP1/96 on shorter time limits for specified classes of employees, directors and pensioners to notify chargeability to income tax and CGTunder self assessment from 1995-96 tax year).
Pre-transaction rulings: a consultative document *(Simon James)*: B.T.R. 1996, 1, 6-8. (Benefits and operation of proposed pre transaction rulings).
Pre-transaction rulings: Europe's single approach? *(David Chester* and *Joanna Bentley)*: Tax J. 1996, 351, 19-20. (Status of pre transaction rulings provided by other Member States' tax authorities, application procedure, appeal rights and whether PTRs could form part of future EU taxation harmonisation programme).
Problems in store *(Daron H. Gunson)*: Tax J. 1996, 361, 14-16. (Availability of industrial buildings allowance for storage premises including warehouses, definition of qualifying process as applied to storage operations under CAA s.18(1) and structures falling within definition of plant and machinery).
Profit related pay and a change of government *(Nicki Demby)*: Tax J. 1996, 368, 15-16. (Current tax treatment of approved profit related schemes and possible changes under incoming

Labour Government with reference to salary substitution schemes and impact of national minimum wage).

Proprietary estoppel: no need for a PET? Tr. & Est. 1996, 11 (2), 14-15. (Use of proprietary estoppel to prove pre-existing beneficial interest of children in property so as to avoid CGT and IHT charges on transfers).

Restructuring the businesses of multinational groups operating in Europe *(Fred C. De Hosson)*: Intertax 1996, 24(3), 80-92. (Taxation implications for European group restructuring).

Self assessment and discovery: Tax. P. 1996, Feb, 29. (Inland Revenue SP 8/91 on circumstances in which discovery assessments may be made following introduction of self assessment and guidance on discovery requirements under ELS electronic lodgement system).

Self assessment correspondence: Tax. P. 1996, Mar, 34-35. (Correspondence between CIoT and Inland Revenue about apportionment, non-resident trading and trust beneficiary matters, employment, agency and intellectual property royalties under self-assessment system).

Sponsorship and tax: lucky for some! *(Daron Gunson)*: Tax. P. 1996, Feb, 19-20. (Corporation tax and VAT planning implications of corporate sponsorship for charities, performing arts and sport).

Tax bulletin: a summary of the Revenue's latest interpretations of tax law: T.P.T. 1996, 17(10), 80b-80c. (CGT exemption for agricultural tenant compensation payments, tax treatment of foreign income dividends, pay and file interest repayments, foreign loan interest tax credit reliefs and loan finance cost deductions).

Tax efficient structures *(David R. Ryder* and *Lowell D. Yoder)*: I.T.R. 1996, 7(6), Supp US, 48-52. (State and federal corporate tax structure applicable to foreign companies and their US operations and subsidiaries, with tax planning opportunities including asset based acquisitions and stock disposals and foreign sales companies).

Tax law: rules or principles? *(John F. Avery Jones)*: Tax J. 1996, 364, 11-13. (Shortened version of lecture given to Insitute for Fiscal Studies on simplification of taxation and whether EU practice of interpreting tax law in accordance with general principles could be used in UK).

Tax matters: self assessment *(Alan R. Barr)*: J.L.S.S. 1996, 41 (9), 361-364. (Inland Revenue statements on disclosure and discovery, provision of information to agents and key dates for self assessment process).

Tax treaty network: annual update: I.R.T.B. 1996, 22(Apr), 307-310. (Table of double taxation agreements in force and agreements concluded or under negotiation but not yet in force as at March 31, 1996).

Taxation of payments made on job termination *(Alan R. Barr)*: J.L.S.S. 1996, 41 (8), 312-313. (Inland Revenue Statement of Practice SP 3/96 concerning severance payments purportedly in settlement of all employment claims).

Tenants beware *(Christopher Wallworth)*: Tax. 1996, 137(3562), 357-358. (Problems with practical operation of Inland Revenue non-resident landlord scheme, effective from April 6, 1996, for taxation of rental income of persons whose place of abode is outside UK).

Termination payments *(David Wainman)*: Tax J. 1996, 351, 8-10. (Income tax treatment of payments due under employment contracts in light of wrongful dismissal cases on breach of conditions and status of agreements not to pursue action for wrongful or unfair dismissal).

The valuation for tax purposes of controlling holdings of unquoted shares *(Bruce Sutherland)*: B.T.R. 1996, 4, 397-417. (Development of practice on CGT and IHT valuation of majority holdings in family companies and whether Inland Revenue takes sufficient account of commercial law and company's constitution when applying hypothetical open market test).

Work to rules *(Francesca Lagerberg)*: Tax. 1996, 136(3536), 340-342. (Tax Aid report, adjudicator's findings and ICAEW opinion show increased instances of bad advice and malpractice, prompting calls for review of regulatory procedures for tax professionals).

5640. Books

Bradford, David F.–Distributional Analysis of Tax Policy. Paperback: £15.95. ISBN 0-8447-3891-3. Hardback: £31.95. ISBN 0-8447-3890-5. American Enterprise Institute.

Brennan, Frank; Howley, Seamus; Moore, Alan–Brennan, Howley, Moore: Tax Acts Commentary 1996-97. Hardback: £85.00. ISBN 1-85475-637-0. Butterworth Law (Ireland).

British Tax Review Index: 1975-1990. Hardback: £50.00. ISBN 0-421-45970-0. Sweet & Maxwell.

Butterworths Orange Tax Handbook: 1996-97. Paperback: £28.00. ISBN 0-406-06499-7. Butterworth Law.

Butterworths Tax Diary: 1996-97. £25.00. ISBN 1-85475-738-5. Butterworth Law (Ireland).

Butterworths Tax Guide 1996-97. Paperback: £60.00. ISBN 1-85475-708-3. Butterworth Law (Ireland).

Butterworths Yellow Tax Handbook: 1996-97. Paperback: £28.00. ISBN 0-406-06498-9. Butterworth Law.

Campbell, Dennis–Butterworths European Tax and Investment Service. Unbound/looseleaf: £165.00. ISBN 0-406-05199-2. Butterworth Law.

Collison, D.–Self Assessment. Paperback: £43.00. ISBN 1-85355-691-2. Accountancy Books.

Cordara, Roderick; Smouha, Joe; Buckett, Alan–De Voil Indirect Tax Intelligence. Unbound/looseleaf: £150.00. ISBN 0-406-04311-6. Butterworth Law.

Davey, Nigel; Parry-Wingfield, Maurice–Ray: Partnership Taxation. Unbound/looseleaf: £65.00. ISBN 0-406-08183-2. Butterworth Law.

Dolton, Alan; Saunders, Glyn–Tax Cases: 1996. Paperback: £35.95. ISBN 1-86012-246-9. Tolley Publishing.

Doran, Nigel–Doran: Taxation of Corporate Joint Ventures. Hardback: £80.00. ISBN 0-406-07916-1. Butterworth Law.

Eastaway, Nigel; Gilligan, Brian–Tax and Financial Planning for Professional Partnerships. Paperback: £45.00. ISBN 0-406-02303-4. Butterworth Law.

Fisher, Glenn W.–The Worst Tax? Studies in Government and Public Policy. Hardback. ISBN 0-7006-0753-6. University Press of Kansas.

Gee, Paul–Spicer and Pegler's Book-keeping and Accounts. Paperback: £25.95. ISBN 0-406-99088-3. Butterworth Law.

Ghosh, Julian; Johnson, Ian–Ghosh: Tax Treatment of Financial Instruments. Unbound/looseleaf: £95.00. ISBN 0-406-05205-0. Butterworth Law.

Gravestock, Peter; Dolton, Alan–Self Assessment for the Self Employed. Paperback: £18.95. ISBN 1-86012-285-X. Tolley Publishing.

Hall, Robert E.; Rabushka, Alvin; Armey, Dick; Eisner, Robert; Stein, Herbert–Fairness and Efficiency in the Flat Tax. Hardback: £15.95. ISBN 0-8447-7062-0. Paperback: £7.95. ISBN 0-8447-7045-0. American Enterprise Institute.

HMSO Finance Act: 1996. Paperback. ISBN 1-86012-251-5. Tolley Publishing.

Homer, Arnold; Burrows, Rita–Partnership Taxation. Paperback: £36.95. ISBN 1-86012-154-3. Tolley Publishing.

Homer, Arnold; Burrows, Rita; Smailes, David–Tax Guide: 1996-97. Hardback: £24.95. ISBN 1-86012-284-1. Tolley Publishing.

Homer, Arnold; Burrows, Rita; Gravestock, Peter–Taxwise 1996-97: II. Value Added Tax, Inheritance Tax, Taxation of Trusts, Tax Planning. Paperback: £26.95. ISBN 1-86012-302-3. Tolley Publishing.

Jeffrey-Cook, John–Moores Rowland's Orange Tax Guide: 1996-97. Paperback: £31.95. ISBN 0-406-06416-4. Butterworth Law.

Jeffrey-Cook, John–Moores Rowland's Yellow Tax Guide: 1996-7. Paperback: £31.95. ISBN 0-406-06441-5. Butterworth Law.

Lawyers' Tax Companion. Ringbinder. ISBN 0-86325-443-8. CCH Editions.

McCrossan, H.–Revenue Law: Textbook. Bachelor of Laws (LLB). £18.95. ISBN 0-7510-0785-4. HLT Publications.

Moore, Alan–Tax Acts 1996-97. Paperback: £75.00. ISBN 1-85475-718-0. Butterworth Law (Ireland).

Parrington, Sheila–Whillan's Tax Tables: 1996-7. Paperback: £4.95. ISBN 0-406-06448-2. Butterworth Law.

Personal Financial Planning Manual: 1996-7. Paperback: £29.95. ISBN 0-406-99089-1. Butterworth Law.

Pollack, Sheldon D.–The Failure of US Tax Policy. Hardback: £23.95. ISBN 0-271-01582-9. Penn State Press.

Revenue Law - LLB: Suggested Solutions (1991-1995). Bachelor of Laws (LLB). Paperback: £6.95. ISBN 0-7510-0735-8. HLT Publications.

Revenue Law: Suggested Solutions (1991-1995). Bar examinations. Paperback: £9.95. ISBN 0-7510-0747-1. HLT Publications.

Revenue Law: Suggested Solutions - Single Paper. Paperback: £3.00. ISBN 0-7510-0634-3. HLT Publications.

Revenue Law: Suggested Solutions - Single Paper (Trinity 1995). Bar Examinations. Paperback: £3.95. ISBN 0-7510-0647-5. HLT Publications.

Rowes, Peter–Taxation. Paperback: £12.95. ISBN 1-85805-186-X. DP Publications.

Rowland, Moores–Butterworths Budget Tax Tables: 1996. Paperback: £5.95. ISBN 0-406-01449-3. Butterworth Law.

Saunders, Ian–Remedies in Taxation. Hardback: £25.00. ISBN 0-471-96080-2. John Wiley and Sons.

Schnepper, Jeff–How to Pay Zero Taxes: 1996. Paperback: £12.95. ISBN 0-07-057224-0. McGraw-Hill Book Company.

Scott, Jacqueline; Mackley-Smith, Gary B.–Capital Allowances: 1996-97. Paperback: £33.95. ISBN 1-86012-288-4. Tolley Publishing.

Shipwright, Adrian J.; Price, Jeffrey W.–UK Taxation and Intellectual Property. Hardback: £70.00. ISBN 0-421-47560-9. Sweet & Maxwell.

Slemrod, Joel; Bakija, Jon–Taxing Ourselves. Hardback: £21.50. ISBN 0-262-19375-2. The MIT Press.

Smailes, David; Saunders, Glyn; Mackley-Smith, Gary B–Tolley's Schedule D (formerly Taxation of Trades and Professions). Paperback: £49.95. ISBN 1-86012-322-8. Tolley Publishing.

Soares, Patrick–Offshore Investment in UK Property. Special reports. Hardback: £125.00. ISBN 0-7520-0242-2. FT Law & Tax.

Sonneveldt, Frans; Bom, Hans M.; Zuiderwijk, Johan C.L.–Global Estate Planning. Unbound/looseleaf: £112.50. ISBN 90-411-0754-1. Kluwer Law International.

Steward, Clive–The Equitable Life Tax Guide. Paperback: £19.99. ISBN 0-631-20162-9. Blackwell Publishers.

Sullivan, Amanda–Butterworths Schedule E Compliance Manual. Unbound/looseleaf: £150.00. ISBN 0-406-99730-6. Butterworth Law.

Taxation of Foreign Exchange Gains and Losses. Paperback: £49.95. ISBN 1-86012-304-X. Tolley Publishing.

Taylor, Rodney–Double Taxation Relief. Tax series. Paperback: £39.95. ISBN 1-86012-311-2. Tolley Publishing.

Teixeira, Gloria–Business Taxation in the European Union: Update 2. Paperback: £40.00. ISBN 0-471-96458-1. Chancery Wiley Law Publications.

Tiley, John–Butterworths UK Tax Guide: 1996-97. Paperback: £23.95. ISBN 0-406-04857-6. Butterworth Law.

Tingley, K.R.; Mackley-Smith, Gary B.–Roll-over, Hold-over and Retirement Reliefs. Paperback: £42.95. ISBN 1-86012-295-7. Tolley Publishing.

Venables, J.; Impey, Ken–Venables and Impey: Internal Audit. Paperback: £30.00. ISBN 0-406-06673-6. Butterworth Law.

Vincent, Robert–Charity Accounting and Taxation. Paperback: £45.00. ISBN 0-406-02921-0. Butterworth Law.

Vogel, Klaus–Klaus Vogel on Double Taxation Conventions. Hardback: £242.00. ISBN 90-411-0892-0. Kluwer Law International.

White, Jeremy–Butterworths Customs Duties Handbook. Paperback: £55.00. ISBN 0-406-06672-8. Butterworth Law.

Whitehouse, Chris–McCutcheon on Inheritance Tax: 7. Supplement. British tax library. Hardback: £45.00. ISBN 0-421-57930-7. Sweet & Maxwell.

Whitehouse, Chris–Revenue Law - Principles and Practice.
Paperback: £29.95. ISBN 0-406-05686-2. Butterworth Law.

TELECOMMUNICATIONS

5641. Directives–non-implementation of Council Directive 91/263–telecommunications–terminal equipment–Ireland–European Union

[Treaty of Rome 1957 Art.189; Council Directive 91/263 on the approximation of the laws of the Member States concerning telecommunications terminal equipment, including the mutual recognition of their conformity.]

CEC sought a declaration that Ireland had failed to implement Council Directive 91/263.

Held, that Ireland had failed to implement the Directive and was therefore in breach of its obligations under Art.17 thereof and of the Treaty of Rome 1957 Art.189(3).

COMMISSION OF THE EUROPEAN COMMUNITIES v. IRELAND (C239/94), February 29, 1996, Judge not specified, ECJ.

5642. Directives–non-implementation of Council Directive 91/263–telecommunications terminal equipment–Greece–European Union

[Council Directive 91/263 on the approximation of the laws of Member States concerning telecommunications terminal equipment, including the mutual recognition of their conformity; Treaty of Rome 1957.]

CEC brought proceedings against Greece for failure to implement, alternatively for failure to notify to CEC the measures taken to implement, Council Directive 91/263.

Held, that by failing to implement Directive 91/263, Greece had failed to fulfil its obligations under the Treaty of Rome 1957.

COMMISSION OF THE EUROPEAN COMMUNITIES v. GREECE (C260/94), August 11, 1995, Judge not specified, ECJ.

5643. Licences–public telecommunications systems

PUBLIC TELECOMMUNICATION SYSTEM DESIGNATION (ATLANTIC TELECOMMUNICATIONS LIMITED) ORDER 1996, SI 1996 1567; made under the Telecommunications Act 1984 s.9. In force: July 17, 1996; £0.65.

The Secretary of State granted to Atlantic Telecommunications Ltd a licence on June 29, 1995 under Telecommunications Act 1984 s.7 to run the telecommunications systems specified in that Licence in the Strathclyde Region. A copy of the licence was laid before Parliament on June 18, 1996. This Order designates those telecommunication systems as public telecommunication systems. Consequently, by virtue of s.9(3) of that Act, Atlantic Telecommunications Ltd will be a public telecommunications operator when the Order comes into force.

5644. Licences–public telecommunications systems

PUBLIC TELECOMMUNICATION SYSTEM DESIGNATION (NATIONAL TRANSCOMMUNICATIONS LIMITED) ORDER 1996, SI 1996 1677; made under the Telecommunications Act 1984 s.9. In force: June 27, 1996; £0.65.

The Secretary of State granted to National Transcommunications Ltd a licence on February 14, 1996 under the Telecommunications Act 1984 s.7 to run specified telecommunication systems in the United Kingdom. A copy of the licence was laid before Parliament on June 28, 1996. This Order designates those telecommunication systems as public telecommunication systems and consequently National Transcommunications Ltd will be a public telecommunications operator when the Order comes into force.

5645. Licences–public telecommunications systems

PUBLIC TELECOMMUNICATION SYSTEM DESIGNATION (SWEB TELECOMS LTD) ORDER 1996, SI 1996 1384; made under the Telecommunications Act 1984 s.9. In force: June 27, 1996; £0.65.

The Secretary of State granted to SWEB Telecoms Ltd a licence on September 15, 1995 under the Telecommunications Act 1984 s.7 to run the telecommunication systems in the United Kingdom. A copy of the licence was laid before Parliament on May 29, 1996. This Order designates those telecommunication systems as public telecommunication systems and SWEB Telecoms Ltd will be a public telecommunications operator when the Order comes into force.

5646. Licences–public telecommunications systems

PUBLIC TELECOMMUNICATION SYSTEM DESIGNATION (TORCH COMMUNICATIONS LIMITED) ORDER 1996, SI 1996 1203; made under the Telecommunications Act 1984 s.9. In force: May 31, 1996; £0.65.

The Secretary of State granted a licence to Torch Communications Limited under the Telecommunications Act 1984 s.7 to run the telecommunications systems specified in that licence in the United Kingdom. This Order designates those telecommunication systems as public telecommunication systems and consequently, by virtue of s.9(3) of that Act, Torch Communications Limited will be a public telecommunications operator when the Order comes into force in May 31, 1996.

5647. Licences–wireless telegraphy–fees

WIRELESS TELEGRAPHY (LICENCE CHARGES) (AMENDMENT) REGULATIONS 1996, SI 1996 1464; made under the Wireless Telegraphy Act 1949 s.2; and the Department of Trade and Industry (Fees) Order 1988 Art.8. In force: July 1, 1996; £1.10.

These Regulations amend the Wireless Telegraphy (Licence Charges) Regulations 1995 (SI 1995 1331) by varying the fees payable in relation to wireless telegraphy licences granted under the Wireless Telegraphy Act 1949 s.1 in the category headed Public Mobile Communications.

5648. Supply of services–procurement of entities for provision of telecommunications services–incorrect transposition of Council Directive 90/531 into UK law–exclusion of most operators from scope of Regulations–whether operator entitled to compensation for loss suffered–European Union

[Council Directive 90/531 on the procurement procedures of entities operating in the water, energy, transport and telecommunications sectors Art.8; Utilities Supply and Works Contracts Regulations 1992 Sch.2.]

On a reference to the ECJ arising from proceedings brought by BT to annul the Utilities Supply and Works Contracts Regulations 1992 Sch.2 on the basis that the Regulations incorrectly transposed Council Directive 90/531 so as to exclude almost all of the contracting entities in the telecommunications sector from complying with its provisions, the High Court sought determination as to which telecommunications services were so excluded under Art.8(1) of the Directive. Pursuant to the wrongly transposed UK legislation, only BT and the City of Hull were subject to the requirements laid down therein to notify the government about their contracts to supply services and to publish their procurement plans and contracts in the Official Journal of the European Communities. The High Court also asked whether BT could claim compensation for loss suffered as a result of the incorrect implementation of the Directive which, they contended, resulted from their being placed at a commercial disadvantage if they complied with the Regulations.

Held, that under Art.8(1) the contracting entities alone determined the services to be excluded from the Directive and not the government of a Member State, as those entities were responsible for notifying the Commission.

Furthermore, the provision in Art.8(1) that other entities were free to offer similar services subject to the same conditions and in the same geographical area was a matter of fact and law, so that any competing contracting entity had to be able to provide the services in question, and the characteristics of those competing services had to be examined on an individual basis. In the circumstances, compensation was not payable to BT in respect of the incorrect transposition, as the Directive was capable of the construction which had been given and the error did not constitute a serious breach, *Brasserie du Pecheur SA v. Germany* (C46/93) [1996] 2 W.L.R. 506, [1996] C.L.Y. 2803 considered.

R. v. HM TREASURY, *ex p.* BRITISH TELECOMMUNICATIONS PLC (C392/93) [1996] Q.B. 615, G C Rodriguez Iglesias (President), ECJ.

5649. Telephones–exemptions

WIRELESS TELEGRAPHY (CORDLESS TELEPHONE APPARATUS) (EXEMPTION) REGULATIONS 1996, SI 1996 316; made under the Wireless Telegraphy Act 1949 s.1, s.3; and the Telecommunications Act 1984 s.84. In force: March 11, 1996; £1.55.

Certain analogue and digital cordless telephones detailed in Sch.2 of the Regulations are exempt from provisions requiring the holding of a licence in order to establish, install and use such apparatus provided that certain requirements are complied with. The exemption does not apply in relation to apparatus which is used to provide or is capable of providing a local loop by-pass by way of business. Apparatus must be made available for inspection by persons authorised by the Secretary of State and must comply with certain Performance Specifications which are available from the Radiocommunications Agency Library or be approved by certain European Telecommunications Standards which are available from the British Standards Institution.

5650. Articles

1997 price review–new caps and lids, ceilings and floors *(Colin Scott)*: U.L.R. 1996, 7(2), 52-53. (OFTEL's consultation document shows eagerness to set new licence conditions prior to possible MMC investigation).

Australia: telecommunications - regulation *(Peter Leonard)*: C.T.L.R. 1995, 1(6), T130-132. (Policy principles behind likely changes to Australia's telecommunications policy to facilitate full and open competition).

Broad-band switched mass-market services - OFTEL proposals *(Bird & Bird)*: I.H.L. 1995, Oct, 72. (Proposals of and comment on Director General of Telecommunications' consultative document on broad-band switched mass market services entitled *Beyond the Telephone, the Television and the PC)*.

BT and pricing–the saga continues *(Heather Rowe)*: IT L.T. 1996, 4(4), 5-6. (Changes to BT pricing under which BT can raise basic line rentals and introduce pricing packages for different sectors and abolition of acess deficit contributions paid by Mercury to offset BT's obligation to provide universal network).

BT and universal service *(Peter Strickland)*: C.T.L.R. 1996, 2(3), 89-95. (Internal BT research into costs of complying with universal service obligations and analysis of Oftel proposals published in December 1995 in light of this evaluation).

Commission releases communication on universal service *(Bird & Bird)*: I.H.L. 1996, 41(Jun), 74-75. (CEC paper on universal service concept for telecommunications which refers to obligation to provide access to telephone network of specified quality to all users at affordable price).

Deregulation of BT's pricing and the new fair trading requirements *(Colin Scott)*: U.L.R. 1996, 7(5), 176-177. (OFTEL's proposals to relax capping of BT's prices whilst introducing new licence condition giving itself powers to regulate anti-competitive behaviour).

Deutsche Telekom and Belgacom investigated for price increases *(Bird & Bird)*: I.H.L. 1996, 43(Sep), 92. (CEC investigations into changes in pricing of European telecoms services prior to liberalisation in 1998).

Dial "O" for outsourcing *(Rory Graham)*: I.H.L. 1996, 41(Jun), 41-42. (Contractual structure and legal issues relating to transfer of in-house telecoms function to third party supplier and ongoing provision of services to consumer).

DTI proposes full liberalisation of international telecommunications from July 1, 1996 *(Bird & Bird)*: I.H.L. 1996, 40(May), 72-73. (Proposed changes to current framework regulating provision of international services by allowing provision by companies other than BTand Mercury).

European Union regulation of the telecommunications industry *(Leo Flynn)*: I.R.L.C.T. 1996, 10(1), 9-26. (Evolution and progress of EC telecommunications law and policy including liberalisation of market access, harmonised standards, introduction of greater competition and use of Art.90 as basis for Directives).

Is fair trading in telecommunications fair regulation? Condition 18A and the Green Paper on competition law reform *(Nicholas Higham)*: C.T.L.R. 1996, 2(3), 119-122. (Oftel's proposal to introduce fair trading condition into BT's licence and exercise of Director General's discretion in light of proposed reform of competition law).

MMC investigates classified directory advertising services *(Bird & Bird)*: I.H.L. 1996, 40(May), 73-74. (MMC findings and recommendations on possible monopoly by BT Yellow Pages).

New licence condition for BTconcerning anti-competitive conduct: U.L.R. 1996, 7(1), 7-8. (BT's response to OFTEL proposals for increased powers to deal with anti competitive conduct partly through new licence conditions on BT).

OFTEL proposes new rule for promoting competition *(Bird & Bird)*: I.H.L. 1996, 39(Apr), 64-65. (Consultation Document proposals to help independent service providers compete in market for enhanced telecommunications services and review BT's dual role as network and service provider).

OFTEL reacts to BT's concerns over its proposal to legislate against anti-competitive behaviour *(Bird and Bird)*: I.H.L. 1996, Feb, 67-68. (Proposed licence condition provisions on anti-competitive behaviour and whether Director General of Telecommunications has power to introduce such conditions).

OFTEL's price control review *(Vivianne Jabbour)*: IT L.T. 1996, 4(8), 10-11. (Proposals for pricing of telecommunications services from 1997 and fair trading provision to go into BT's licence).

Public v private law: BT in the courts *(Graham Cunningham)*: C.T.L.R. 1996, 2(5), 174-179. (Telecoms cases on right to injunction pending preliminary ruling by ECJ, compensation for incorrect implementation of EC Directive and whether challenge to decisions of regulator should be pursued in public or private law).

Regulatory reform in Britain and France: organizational structure and the extension of competition *(Mark Thatcher)*: J.E.P.P. 1994, 1(3), 441-464. (Differences between France and UK in policy making for regulatory reform of telecommunications sector despite both seeking to create more competitive environment).

Satellite services: the European regulatory framework *(Stephan Le Goueff)*: C.T.L.R. 1996, 2(5), 185-191. (Effect of Directive 94/46 in allowing competition in satellite communications market).

Telecommunications and audio-visual convergence: regulatory issues *(Nicholas Garnham)*: C.L.S.R. 1996, 12(5), 284-287. (Impact of amalgamation of telecommunications and broadcasting sectors on regulation of networks and content and problems caused by attempts to reconcile principles of universal service and public service).

Telecommunications antenna: J.P.L. 1996, Jun, 471-477. (DoE consultation paper on proposals to relax planning controls over installation of TV, phone and business communications antennas on buildings and clarify rules on operators' masts–includes text).

Telecommunications regulation and the Internet *(Amanda Dawson Bannister)*: I.M.L. 1996, 14(6), 44-47. (Telecoms licensing position in UK as it applies to use of Internet and implications for future of international telephony).

Telecommunications–regulation *(Simon Jones)*: C.T.L.R. 1996, 2(1), T15-17. (Electronic dealing systems, consequential amendment of Stock Exchange rules and formation and enforcement of electronic contracts).

Telecommunications: advertising *(Robyn Durie)*: C.T.L.R. 1996, 2(4), T105-106. (MMC findings on classified directory advertising services).

Telecommunications: preparing for 1998 and beyond *(Karel Van Miert)*: Eur. Access 1996, 5, 8-12. (Progress made in liberalising EU telecommunications market, competition policy to combat abuse of dominant position, potential for European Telecoms Agency and EU approach to global market).

Telecommunications: regulation *(Michael H. Ryan)*: C.T.L.R. 1996, 2(2), T48-49. (OFTEL consultative document setting out policy on BT interconnection charges, price control and changes to price capping regime).

The European Union's draft Interconnection Directive *(Mark Sherwood-Edwards and Paul Gladen)*: C.T.L.R. 1996, 2(5), 192-194. (Difficulties of subjecting interconnection to legal control, disparate provisions for small and large operators and costing methods).

The evolution of telecommunications regulation in the transition to a competitive marketplace *(International Chamber of Commerce)*: C.L.S.R. 1996, 12(5), 301-305. (Text of ICC policy statement on competition issues raised by liberalisation of telecommunications services).

The publishing industry faces technological change *(Arnold Vahrenwald)*: Ent. L.R. 1996, 7(2), 50-61. (Development of new digital technologies raises serious legal issues for publishing industry and requires amendment of existing copyright, telecommunications and competition laws at international level).

Tracing and recording telephone calls *(Christopher Atkinson* and *Michael Nicholls)*: Fam. Law 1996, 26(Feb), 104-108. (Possibility of tracing missing children through use of new technology, with reference to legal framework and court orders necessary to obtain information).

Under my wheels: issues of access and social exclusion on the information superhighway *(Andrew Charlesworth* and *Holly Cullen)*: I.R.L.C.T. 1996, 10(1), 27-40. (Whether increased use of information and communication technologies will lead to further concentration of information access, safeguards for universality of information access and concept of social exclusion).

United Kingdom *(Rachel Brandenburger)*: I.F.L. Rev. 1996, 15(7), Tel 63-66. (Development of liberalisation of telecommunications services in light of CEC's legislative provisions for full competition throughout European Union).

United States *(Jeffrey P. Cunard)*: I.F.L. Rev. 1996, 15(7), Tel 67-74. (Changes to US telecommunications market by 1996 legislation removing barriers between local and long distance services and promoting free competition in local market).

5651. Books

Gillies, David; Marshall, Roger J.W.–Telecommunications Law. Hardback: £160.00. ISBN 0-406-02096-5. Butterworth Law.

Hazlett, Thomas W.–Public Policy Towards Cable Television: Vol 1. The Economics of Rate Control. AEI studies in telecommunications deregulation. Hardback: £23.50. ISBN 0-262-08253-5. The MIT Press.

Heldman, Peter K.–Competitive Telecommunications. Hardback: £30.95. ISBN 0-07-028113-0. McGraw-Hill Publishing Company.

Kovacic, William E.–The Postal Service As Competitor. Hardback: £31.95. ISBN 0-8447-3960-X. American Enterprise Institute.

Waterman, David; Weiss, Andrew A.–Vertical Integration in Cable Television. AEI studies in telecommunications deregulation. Hardback: £25.50. ISBN 0-262-23190-5. The MIT Press.

White, Stewart; Bate, Stephen; Johnson, Timothy–Satellite Communications in Europe: Law and Regulation. Hardback: £125.00. ISBN 0-7520-0219-8. FT Law & Tax.

TORTS

5652. Accidents–causation–driver of car fatally injured running across road after vehicle breakdown–plaintiff's injuries were caused by deceased's use of vehicle–insurance company liable under third party liability policy

[Road Traffic Act 1988 s.145.]

CI, an insurance company, appealed against a decision that they were liable to pay damages to D, the driver of a vehicle who sustained serious head injuries after colliding with B, who was fatally injured as she ran across a road following the breakdown of her vehicle. CI argued that they were not liable under B's motor policy, which was in accordance with the terms of the Road Traffic Act 1988 s.145 requiring third party insurance by drivers, as D's injuries were not caused by B's use of her car, but by her actions as a pedestrian.

Held, dismissing the appeal, that the judge below was entitled to infer from the facts of the case that B had run across the road to obtain petrol to restart her car and that consequently her reason for being in the road arose from the use of her vehicle.

DUNTHORNE v. BENTLEY [1996] P.I.Q.R. P323, Rose, L.J., CA.

5653. Accidents–fatality at work–dependency–whether possible for person to live in more than one household at a time under the Fatal Accidents Act 1976 s.1 (3)

[Fatal Accidents Act 1976 s.1.]

P, a trackman for London Transport, was tragically killed in the course of his employment. His mother commenced an action against the defendant for the benefit of his dependants. B claimed to be a dependant, saying P had lived with her for at least two years prior to his death for the purposes of the Fatal Accidents Act 1976 s.1 (3). This claim was hotly disputed by P's mother, who claimed he had lived at her home throughout.

Held, in favour of B, that the continuity of the two year qualifying period in s.1 (3) (b) (ii) of the Act was not broken by brief periods of absence.

POUNDER v. LONDON UNDERGROUND LTD [1995] P.I.Q.R. P217, Judge not specified, QBD.

5654. Animals–owner of horses not liable for damage caused by animals which had been maliciously released on highway

[Animals Act 1971 s.2.]

G appealed against the decision to award damages of £4,869 to J, the driver of a car which was damaged when in collision with horses owned by G which had been maliciously released from their field. G denied liability, but was held to be absolutely liable under the Animals Act 1971 s.2(2).

Held, allowing the appeal, that to prove liability under the 1971 Act s.2(2) (b), a causal link had to be established between the animal's characteristics under s.2 and the damage caused. This had not been established in the instant case, because it was the presence of the horses on the road rather than their individual characteristics which caused the damage.

JAUNDRILL v. GILLETT, *The Times,* January 30, 1996, Russell, L.J., CA.

5655. Contribution–defective reservoir under construction contract–whether engineer overseeing contract liable–whether same damage caused

[Civil Liability (Contribution) Act 1978 s.1.]

N was a construction engineer employed by Anglian Water, AW, to oversee and approve a contract for the construction of a reservoir. AW awarded the contract to BC who retained H as consulting engineers on the project. The reservoir was defective, and by agreement to settle AW's claim BC constructed a second reservoir. The question arose whether N was liable to AW in the same manner as

H was to BC. N appealed against the decision that he was liable and that H could consequently claim a contribution from him towards BC's losses.

Held, allowing the appeal, that under the Civil Liability (Contribution) Act 1978 s.1 (1), to claim a contribution from N the two parties had to be liable for the same damage caused to a third party. The damage suffered by AW was physical but that suffered by BC was financial and therefore the damage sustained was different for each party. The judge in the lower court had erred in his decision as s.1 (1) should be taken at face value and entitlement to a contribution only existed where liability arose from the same damage.

BIRSE CONSTRUCTION LTD v. HAISTE LTD [1996] 1 W.L.R. 675, Sir John May, CA.

5656. Conversion–private purchase of a vehicle subject to a hire purchase agreement–vehicle bailed to partners jointly–meaning of "the debtor"–statutory interpretation

[Hire Purchase Act 1964 s.27, s.29.]

C appealed against judgment in which damages were awarded for the conversion of a Mercedes Benz motorcar. K had bought the vehicle in good faith from his cousin, L, unaware that it was the subject of a finance agreement between C and L and his former partner. C argued that, as the sale was by L alone and did not include his former partner, the requirements of the Hire Purchase Act 1964 s.27 were not satisfied. For K to be protected as a private purchaser he had to buy the car from "the debtor" who was defined in s.29 (4) of the 1964 Act as "the person to whom the vehicle is bailed or hired under that agreement". As L's partner was not involved in the sale no disposition had been made.

Held, dismissing the appeal, that for the purposes of s.27 (1) of the 1964 Act "the debtor" meant the persons to whom the car had been bailed and could include either of the bailees.

KEEBLE v. COMBINED LEASE FINANCE PLC [1996] C.C.L.R. 63, Leggatt, L.J., CA.

5657. Dangerous escape–toxic fumes from spraying work–release into adjoining property

[Control of Substances Hazardous to Health Regulations 1988 Reg.5.]

In November 1991 C, a building contractor, carried out chemical spraying work on timbers in the cellar next door to A's terraced house. During the course of the spraying, toxic fumes were released and escaped into A's living room. A developed mild asthma type symptoms and was forced to leave for a period of five and a half weeks. Liability was denied by the contractors on the basis that no escape had taken place and that all reasonable care had been used.

Held, that there was an escape of dangerous fumes from the adjoining property, which constituted a breach of the Control of Substances Hazardous to Health Regulations 1988 Reg.5 because although A was not an "employee" she was a person who was affected by the work undertaken. An award of general damages was made in the sum of £1,500; £500 was made separately for the inconvenience to A for leaving her home and £390 was awarded in respect of the special damages and interest.

ANDERSON v. CRUMP, August 28, 1996, Recorder Andre Jones, CC (Birmingham). [*Ex rel.* Jeffery Zindani, Solicitor].

5658. Defamation–adequacy of jury direction on malice

O and W, the head of the School of Business at O, appealed against a judgment in favour of H, a senior lecturer in law at O, awarding him damages of £60,000 for defamation. The defamation took place in three memoranda, written by W and circulated to other senior members of staff, which questioned the level of H's performance of his job. The jury found that W had acted out of malice. O and W argued that the trial judge's directions on malice were inadequate.

Held, allowing the appeal and ordering a retrial, that (1) malice could be proved if it was shown that the defamer knew that what he was publishing was false, if he was reckless as to the accuracy of what he was publishing or, in a case of qualified privilege, if he published what he did out of spite rather than in the performance of a duty; (2) H needed to show that the memoranda were written without any honest belief in their truth or to cause harm to H deliberately, and (3) the judge failed to explain to the jury that they should be slow to infer an improper motive in relation to qualified privilege, *Horrocks v. Lowe* [1975] A.C. 135, [1974] C.L.Y. 2144 followed. The judge failed to make it clear that an allegation of actual knowledge was no longer being pursued and failed to specify which evidence was relevant to a finding of malice. A retrial was ordered.

HALPIN v. OXFORD BROOKES UNIVERSITY, Trans. Ref: QBENF 94/0863/C, November 30, 1995, Neill, L.J., CA.

5659. Defamation–defamatory attendance note coming to light through discovery in negligence action–whether subject to implied undertaking–effect of note being read in open court–application for order that undertaking should not cease to apply

[County Court Rules 1981 Ord.14 r.8; Rules of the Supreme Court (Amendment No.2) Rules 1992 Ord.24 r.14A.]

T had commenced an action for slander and three actions for libel. The action for slander concerned remarks made by a solicitor in a telephone conversation with another solicitor. The three libel actions concerned the publication of the attendance note of that conversation between the various firms of solicitors involved and to the costs draughtsmen. The attendance note came to light through discovery procedures during a negligence action. C applied to have the actions struck out on the ground that the attendance note was subject to T's implied undertaking on discovery. In the alternative C relied on an order of the district judge continuing the undertaking. T relied on the fact that the attendance note had been read in open court in the course of the negligence action as having released him from his implied undertaking by the operation of the County Court Rules 1981 Ord.14 r.8 (equivalent to Rules of the Supreme Court (Amendment No.2) Rules 1992 Ord.24 r.14A). T applied for release of the implied undertaking and contended that he could nevertheless rely on a copy of the note or the transcript of the proceedings in the negligence action. Three of the actions were struck out by the district judge and T appealed. The application in the fourth action was referred to the judge hearing the appeals.

Held, dismissing the appeals and allowing the application, that (1) before Ord.24 r.14A took effect, the defendants to the defamation action would have been protected by the implied undertaking which prevented T from making any use of the attendance note other than that for which the discovery was ordered; (2) the document belonged to C who was accordingly able to make an application under r.14A for an order that the undertaking should not cease to apply; (3) r.14A represented a change in the onus of showing why a party should not be released from the implied undertaking where documents have been referred to or read in court; (4) T, at all times, remained subject to the implied undertaking to the court not to use the attendance note for the purpose of bringing libel proceedings; (5) there was no good reason to permit T to use the attendance note for a purpose so far removed from the reasons which led to its disclosure in the negligence action; (6) in any event T was bound by the order of the district judge and (7) it was not open to T to rely on a copy of the attendance note or on the transcript from the negligence action, *Sybron Corp v. Barclays Bank Plc* [1985] 1 Ch. 299, [1984] C.L.Y. 2625 and *Crest Homes Plc v. Marks* [1987] 1 A.C. 829, [1987] C.L.Y. 2885 applied.

TEJENDRASINGH v. CHRISTIE [1995] E.M.L.R. 152, Drake, J., QBD.

5660. Defamation–newspaper stating plaintiff was mastermind of £4 million fraud and illegitimate son of a fugitive criminal–frivolous or vexatious claim

N applied for R's statement of claim, in a defamation action against them, to be struck out as frivolous or vexatious or disclosing no reasonable cause of action. They also asked for two of the allegations of defamation to be tried as preliminary issues. The claim related to an article published by *The Sun* newspaper alleging R to have been the mastermind behind a £4 million mortgage fraud. It also stated that he was the illegitimate son of the fugitive Ronnie Knight.

Held, allowing the application and finding for N on the preliminary issues, that (1) R had been convicted of the mortgage fraud. It had been conclusively proved that he was a conspirator in a substantial fraud. It was frivolous and vexatious of R to complain of being portrayed as the mastermind behind the scam. It was also frivolous and vexatious of him to complain of being accused of defrauding the DSS. The article referred to members of his gang defrauding the DSS and, even if R was implicated, the allegations could not injure his reputation having already been convicted of a substantial fraud and (2) on the preliminary issues, the judge found that it was not defamatory to be referred to as the "son of a criminal", "illegitimate" or a "police informer".

ROBSON v. NEWS GROUP NEWSPAPERS LTD, Trans. Ref: 95/SC/0876, October 9, 1995, Previte, J., QBD.

5661. Defamation–publication of sworn affirmation in pending court case–rule of repetition–availability of defence of justification

S, a plaintiff in an action for defamation, appealed against the refusal to strike out P's defence of justification after he published in the "Mail on Sunday" extracts from a sworn affirmation made in respect of a pending court case against S and alleged that he had debts of £3 million. S contended that the defence of justification was not available as the published words were hearsay and only repeated what was stated in the affirmation, nor was the defence of privilege applicable as the sworn statement had not been made in open court.

Held, allowing the appeal, that the defence of privilege applied only to documents and statements in proceedings which took place in open court, and to fair and accurate newspaper reports of those proceedings which enabled allegations of both sides to be reported, rather than simply those of the defendant. Any extension of the defence could be effected only by statute. The rule of repetition was intended to prevent a jury from deciding that the secondary allegation was true rather than the original, and although, in some circumstances, it might be possible to maintain a defence of justification when a defence of privilege was not available, that rule should be enforced as otherwise the law of privilege would be ineffective, *Cadam v. Beaverbrook Newspapers Ltd* [1959] 1 Q.B. 413, [1959] C.L.Y. 1866 and *Waters v. Sunday Pictorial Newspapers Ltd* [1961] 1 W.L.R. 961, [1961] C.L.Y. 4995 considered.

STERN v. PIPER [1996] 3 W.L.R. 715, Hirst, L.J., CA.

5662. Defamation–qualified privilege attached to newspaper report of Commonwealth judicial inquiry

[Defamation Act 1952 s.7, Sch.1.]

T appealed against a declaration that allegedly defamatory words he complained of in a newspaper article were published on an occasion of qualified privilege. The article published in the Independent newspaper reported that T had been recommended for prosecution by a Ghanaian special inquiry into the kidnap and murder of three High Court judges in 1982 and that he had escaped prosecution. The report of the special inquiry and the Ghanaian Attorney General's comments were widely reported in the Ghanaian media. T argued that the article was not a report within the meaning of the Defamation Act 1952 but a commentary on past events, no part of the article was capable of being protected by the defence of qualified privilege, as the report was submitted to the Attorney General and it was not a public report. T further argued that publication of an old, now retracted allegation was not of public concern or benefit. Part of the article had been defended by common law privilege which T maintained was irrelevant when Parliament had laid down the scope of the protection to be conferred by statute.

Held, dismissing the appeal, that (1) what was published was a fair and accurate report of proceedings in public before a tribunal and the conditions of the 1952 Act s.7(3) were fulfilled; (2) a report concerning past events could still be subject to qualified privilege in terms of the 1952 Act Sch.1 para.5; (3) the omission of further reports on developments following the inquiry did not prevent the report being fair and accurate and for the public benefit, and (4) that part of the report not covered by statutory privilege was protected by qualified privilege at common law, *Perera v. Peiris* [1949] A.C. 1 considered.

TSIKATA v. NEWSPAPER PUBLISHING PLC [1997] 1 All E.R. 655, Neill, L.J., CA.

5663. Defamation–quia timet injunctions–publication of threatened libel–statements alleging criminal offences or civil wrongs–whether wording of statement of claim sufficiently precise–standard to be applied

BCR appealed against a refusal to strike out an action by BDM for a quia timet injunction to restrain the publication of allegedly defamatory statements to the effect that BDM was guilty of criminal offences or civil wrongs concerning their annual reports or accounts. BCR argued that the action should be struck out as the statement of claim failed to specify the exact words of the threatened libel so that they would not know with sufficient certainty the case against them.

Held, allowing the appeal, that although the alleged defamation need not be set out verbatim, the statement of claim had to contain enough particulars to enable the defendant to identify issues and decide appropriate questions and to enable the court to draft a sufficiently precise injunction. The standard would normally require the exact wording to be specified unless the threatened allegation was clearly defamatory. BDM's statement of claim was too vague and imprecise to be clearly defamatory and failed to meet the test. Leave to amend would be granted upon continuance of the action.

BRITISH DATA MANAGEMENT PLC v. BOXER COMMERCIAL REMOVALS PLC [1996] 3 All E.R. 707, Hirst, L.J., CA.

5664. Defamation–reaction of hypothetical reader–defamatory meaning as pleaded not found in law

SK and her brother TK appealed against the determination of a preliminary issue in a defamation case where the judge held that words in an article in a magazine called Business Age, read together with the rest of the article on illicit arms dealings, could not, in law, bear the meaning that SK and TK were corrupt and willing to take advantage of SK's relationship with a former Cabinet Minister, Sir Cecil Parkinson, in order to influence him to their own ends, and that TK only obtained a certain employment owing to SK's relationship with CP. In an amended statement of claim SK and TK argued that the words were capable of meaning that, if they were not actually corrupt, SK and TK were corruptible.

Held, dismissing the appeal, that (1) when approaching the question of whether an article was defamatory, it was necessary to consider the reaction of a hypothetical reader who was somewhere between naive and unduly suspicious and who would not decide on a defamatory interpretation if there were other non-defamatory meanings available; (2) the article made no suggestion that SK and TK were corrupt nor that TK did not get his job on his own merits and such meanings were far fetched and (3) the article did not suggest that SK and TK had failed to act in good faith or were corruptible.

KEAYS v. RUBYTHON, Trans. Ref: QBENF 94/1103/C, April 1, 1996, Neill, L.J., CA.

5665. Defamation–words relating to financial viability of company–capable of being defamatory–amendment to plea of justification within judge's discretion

[Rules of the Supreme Court Ord.82 r.3A.]

A, a limited company selling package holidays, and its directors, sued a rival firm, O, for defamation. O's representatives had told hoteliers and travel agents that A were "going bust" and would be "bankrupt within a few days". A's action was settled and the directors continued as sole plaintiffs. O sought a declaration under the Rules of the Supreme Court Ord.82 r.3A that the words were not capable of any defamatory meaning and sought to amend their defence to plead that the true meaning of the words was that there were reasonable grounds to suspect A's financial viability, which was justified. The directors opposed the amendment and sought to strike out the plea of justification. The judge refused to grant the declaration or to strike out the plea of justification and allowed the amendment. The directors and O appealed.

Held, dismissing both appeals, that (1) the declaration sought was correctly refused because the words used were capable of meaning that the directors knowingly permitted A to trade whilst insolvent and that was capable of being defamatory and (2) on the facts, O's allegations were arguably capable of supporting the plea of justification and the judge's decisions to allow the amendment and not to strike out the plea were within the exercise of his discretion.

ASPRO TRAVEL LTD v. OWNERS ABROAD GROUP PLC [1996] 1 W.L.R. 132, Schiemann, L.J., CA.

5666. Defamation Act 1996 (c.31)

An Act to amend the law of defamation and to amend the law of limitation with respect to actions for defamation or malicious falsehood.

This Act received Royal Assent on July 4, 1996.

5667. Duty of care–driving–no difference in standard of care required in car park and on open road

N's driver alleged that W reversed into his stationary vehicle, whilst he was attempting to exit a parking bay, in the Homebase Car Park, Watford. The arbitration (small claims) hearing held that the standard of care for driving was lower in a car park than on the open road. He held that N's driver should have been aware of W. He went on to find both parties equally liable for the accident. N applied to have the award set aside on the ground that the standard of care for a driver was the same in a car park as on the open road. It was submitted that to hold otherwise would create nonsensical results and amounted to an error of law.

Held, that the deputy district judge had misdirected himself. The perception whether there was a different standard of care in a car park from that on the open road was a matter of law. The judge was wrong to hold that the standard of care was lower in a car park than on the open road, he had erred in law and the award would be set aside. The case was remitted for a new arbitration hearing.

NATIONAL WESTMINSTER BANK PLC v. WOODARD, November 4, 1996, H.H.J. Goldstone, CC (Watford). [*Ex rel.* Gary Blaker, Barrister].

5668. Duty of care–importation of animals–whether MAFF owed duty of care to purchasers of diseased imported animals

[Animal Health Act 1981 s.10.]

Held, that MAFF did not owe a duty of care to purchasers of imported animals found to be suffering from disease, as, although the Animal Health Act 1981 s.10 purportedly gave the Ministry control over imports, animals were often kept in isolation between importation and release from quarantine on premises arranged by the original importer, where they were not subject to health checks by Ministry veterinary officials. The plaintiffs also lacked the required proximity to bring a claim in tort as they could not be identified as subsequent purchasers.

They could, however, pursue a contractual claim of liability against the importer.

GAISFORD v. MINISTRY OF AGRICULTURE, FISHERIES AND FOOD, *The Times*, July 19, 1996, David Barker Q.C., QBD.

5669. False imprisonment–breach of statutory duty–detention in police station–three day remand for inquiry into other offences–plaintiff subsequently acquitted–action for damages

[Magistrates' Courts Act 1980 s.128.]

The Chief Constable appealed against a decision that H, who had been remanded in custody at a police station for three days pursuant to the Magistrates' Courts Act 1980 s.128(7), could bring an action for breach of statutory duty and false imprisonment. H was subsequently acquitted of an offence of going equipped for theft and contended that there had been no need to detain him for the purposes of inquiring into further offences under s.128(8) of the Act.

Held, allowing the appeal, that where the detention was dependent on the refusal of bail, s.128 did not apply and breach of that section was not intended to give a civil right to damages. A remedy lay in either an action for malicious process or an application to the High Court for bail.

HYLAND v. CHIEF CONSTABLE OF LANCASHIRE CONSTABULARY, *The Times*, February 7, 1996, Sir Ralph Gibson, CA.

5670. Footpaths–breach of local authority duty under Highways Act 1980 s.41

[Highways Act 1980 s.41, s.58.]

On October 21, 1993 H, who at the time was a 26 year old housewife and seven and half months pregnant, was out shopping with her mother and toddler, and was descending a steep hill in the local town centre when, at the lower end of the hill where the construction of the footpath changed from flags to tarmac, the latter had broken up. The tarmac itself had different textures; one area had what was referred to as ridges on the surface, and the other was simply uneven. There was no defined trip as such or undulation, and although H was wearing low heeled shoes, she slipped. Higher up the street there were situated non-slip paving stones and evidence from a nearby shopkeeper indicated that there had been a history of falls at the same location. Although the local authority stated that the lower part of the footway was in an ongoing programme of works, following the report of H's accident, it was re-surfaced within 13 days. B's highway supervisor gave evidence the street was a 1:3 gradient, and the authority had previously considered it necessary to have non-slip paving stones. Evidence from a local shopkeeper further confirmed that originally the lower portion of the street was also subject to non-slip paving stones but these were uplifted to replace broken paviors at the top end of the footpath. B recognised that due to the steepness of the street, its location in the town centre and the heavy volume of pedestrian traffic, precautions were necessary. B's highway supervisor claimed the pavement was "not dangerous, merely untidy". However, the decision to re-surface the defective area was taken by senior officers which again, the supervisor agreed in evidence, was carried out to "make safe" the pavement.

Held, that in all the circumstances the pavement was risky and in a dangerous condition and this was caused by failure of B to fulfil its duty under the Highways Act 1980 s.41. Even though some element of contributory negligence was introduced at trial, this was not pursued and neither was a defence under s.58 pleaded or argued, *Mills v. Barnsley BC* [1992] P.I.Q.R. 291, [1993] C.L.Y. 2967, *Littler v. Liverpool Corp* [1968] 2 All E.R. 343, [1968] C.L.Y. 1747; *Meggs v. Liverpool Corp* [1968] 1 W.L.R. 689, [1967] C.L.Y. 1808, *Griffiths v. Liverpool Corp* [1967] 1 Q.B. 374, [1966] C.L.Y. 5600 referred to. Damages were agreed prior to trial at £2,566 with special damages of £189 costs were awarded on Scale 2.

HARTLEY v. BURNLEY BC, July 31, 1996, H.H.J. Newton, CC (Burnley). [*Ex rel.* Paul G Kaye, Solicitor].

5671. Human tissue–brain removed at autopsy–administratrix had no right of possession in deceased's brain

[Coroners Rules 1984 r.9.]

D appealed as administratrix against an order confirming a decision striking out a claim for damages against the second defendant, Newcastle Health Authority, NHA, for disposing of a deceased's brain, which had been removed during the course of an autopsy and fixed in paraffin, and which was required as evidence for a claim in medical negligence against NTHA.

Held, dismissing the appeal, that there was no legal right to possession of the brain, as the administratrix, who was charged in law with the duty of disposing of a body, had not been appointed until after the burial. The brain itself had been legally removed, and the act of setting it in paraffin did not transform it into an item subject to rights in possession, as it could not be said to have undergone a process or application of human skill such as embalming, *Doodeward v. Spence* (1908) 6 C.L.R. 406 considered. There was an obligation of preservation under the Coroners Rules 1984 r.9, but the obligation did not continue after the cause of death had been established and a reasonable period of time to allow for a challenge had elapsed. In the absence of a right of possession in the next of kin, or the establishing of a duty of care on the part of NHA, no rights in the torts of conversion, wrongful interference or negligence could exist and D had no right to bailment of the brain. In the circumstances, it would be incorrect to impose a duty on NHA to retain human tissue purely on the ground that it could be needed as evidence in possible civil proceedings in the future.

DOBSON v. NORTH TYNESIDE HA [1996] 4 All E.R. 474, Peter Gibson, L.J., CA.

5672. Libel–interpretation of statement of claim–determining defamatory nature of words used

K appealed against the dismissal of his application for a ruling that words forming part of B's statement of claim in an action for libel were not capable of meaning that B, a professional cricketer, had cheated by tampering with cricket ball seams.

Held, dismissing the appeal, that examining the passage as a whole it was necessary to determine what B was said to have done, not what K thought was the true nature of his conduct. Whether or not a reader could construe the passage as meaning that anyone tampering with a ball in the manner alleged in the statement had cheated was a question of fact, and B's action would succeed if it could be proved that he had not engaged in the act alleged. Determining the defamatory nature of the words themselves was a question for a jury, but they were capable of a defamatory meaning.

BOTHAM v. KHAN, *The Times*, July 15, 1996, Russell, L.J., CA.

5673. Libel–jury awards

MGN, a newspaper publisher, appealed against a total libel award of £350,000, comprising £75,000 compensatory damages and £275,000 exemplary damages, awarded to J, a musician, in a libel action in respect of an article published in the *Sunday Mirror*.

Held, allowing the appeal in part and reducing the total award to £75,000, that guidance should be given to juries on appropriate awards to be made in defamation cases as it was offensive to public opinion that sums awarded for damage to reputation often well exceeded those awarded in serious personal injury cases. Although juries should not be reminded of previous jury libel awards, reference to such awards was permissible in the absence of any established frame of reference, *Rantzen v. Mirror Group Newspapers (1986) Ltd* [1994] Q.B. 670, [1993] C.L.Y. 2579 and *Broome v. Cassell & Co Ltd* [1972] A.C. 1027, [1993] C.L.Y. 2745 considered. However, a change of practice should be introduced whereby counsel could draw a jury's attention to the maximum conventional award for personal injuries and what would be reasonable in the circumstances, with the proviso that there could be no precise equiparation between an injury such as quadriplegia and injury to reputation. There was no reason why counsel could not make submissions or the judge indicate to the jury the level of award considered appropriate. With regard to assessment of exemplary damages, the jury had to be satisfied that the publisher had no genuine belief in the truth of the article published and that he was motivated by material gain, not merely the publication of a newspaper for profit. An award should never exceed the minimum necessary to satisfy the requirements of punishment and deterrence.

JOHN v. MGN LTD [1996] 3 W.L.R. 593, Sir Thomas Bingham, M.R., CA.

5674. Libel–jury awards–damage to reputation as businessman

N, as former editor of the Sunday Times, appealed against a jury verdict awarding K £45,000 in damages for libel and loss of reputation, following allegations in a business news article that K was a major debtor of a leading bank and had been forced to file for bankruptcy. N submitted that the figure was excessive, given that K had refused an earlier offer by the newspaper and that the summing up of the judge below had failed to give the jury proper guidance as to a reasonable amount of damages.

Held, dismissing the appeal, that (1) the award was not excessive where it was designed to compensate K for damage to his reputation as a businessman, *Jones v. Littler* (1841) 7 M.W. 423 considered. The award reflected the irresponsible nature of the libel, where the facts had not been correctly checked prior to publication in a major national newspaper; (2) the summing up was not so defective, in that no error or omission had been drawn to the attention of the judge, and read as a whole it had directed the jury in the need to compensate for damage to reputation and injury to feelings. In reaching the figure, the jury could take K's position into account when deciding how best to vindicate his reputation in terms of the size of the award and (3) viewed on grounds of reasonableness and proportionality, the award amounted to proper compensation and was not one with which the court could justifiably interfere, *Sutcliffe v. Pressdram* [1991] 1 Q.B. 153, [1990] C.L.Y. 1552, *Rantzen v. Mirror Group Newspapers (1986) Ltd* [1994] Q.B. 670, [1993] C.L.Y. 2579 and *John v. MGN Ltd* [1996] 2 All E.R. 35, [1996] C.L.Y. 5673 considered.

KIAM v. NEILL (NO.2) [1996] E.M.L.R. 493, Beldam, L.J., CA.

5675. Libel–justification–defendant's duty to give discovery was not limited to matters raised in particulars of justification

G appealed against an order for discovery made in a libel action. The grounds were that the discovery sought went beyond what was relevant to the pleaded issues and that discovery was limited to matters particularised in the plea of justification. G broadcast a television programme which suggested that certain police officers, including E, were involved in corruption and pleaded justification. The issue was whether a defendant to an action for defamation who pleaded justification could limit his obligation to give discovery to documents relating to matters raised in his particulars of justification.

Held, dismissing the appeal, that the issue was whether there were reasonable grounds to suspect E of misconduct in the manner alleged and documents relating to that were relevant. E was entitled to adduce matters which might show that on the whole of the material there were no reasonable grounds to suspect him of the misconduct alleged. Any other conclusion would result in injustice, *Hart v. Newspaper Publishing Plc* (Unreported, 1989) approved. Discovery was not limited to matters raised in the particulars of justification but must be of all documents put in issue by the plea itself, *Yorkshire Provident Life Assurance Co v. Gilbert & Rivington* [1895] 2 Q.B. 148 explained.

EVANS v. GRANADA TELEVISION LTD [1996] E.M.L.R. 429, Stuart-Smith, L.J., CA.

5676. Libel–justification–sufficiency of evidence–criteria for defence–use of power to strike out

[Rules of the Supreme Court Ord.18 r.19.]

M issued proceedings against S for libel in relation to leaflets S had distributed about M alleging, inter alia, that it destroyed the environment and exploited its workforce. S entered a defence of justification and fair comment. On the application of M, the trial judge struck out substantial parts of the defence on the basis that it was not supported by clear and sufficient evidence. S appealed

Held, allowing the appeal, that (1) a plea of justification was not required to be supported by clear and sufficient evidence. Such a requirement, if applied literally, would impose an unfair and unrealistic burden on a defendant, *Associated Leisure Ltd v. Associated Newspapers Ltd* [1970] 2 All E.R. 754, [1970] C.L.Y. 1574 and *Mangena v. Edward Lloyd Ltd* (1908) 98 L.T. 640 considered. Nevertheless, before a plea of justification was included in a defence the following criteria should normally be satisfied: (a) the defendant should believe the words complained of to be true; (b) the defendant should intend to support the defence of justification at the trial and (c) the defendant should have reasonable evidence to prove the allegations will be available at the trial and (2) the power to strike out pleadings, whether under the Rules of the Supreme Court Ord.18 r.19 or the inherent jurisdiction of the court was a draconian remedy. It should only be employed in obvious cases where a passage in the defence was incurably bad because there was not and could not be any evidence to support it, whether through interlocutory procedures or during the trial.

McDONALD'S CORP v. STEEL [1995] 3 All E.R. 615, Neill, L.J., CA.

5677. Libel–limitations–causes of action–facts relevant to cause of action were only those which should be pleaded in statement of claim–statutory interpretation

[Limitation Act 1980 s.32A.]

C, the plaintiff in a libel action arising from the newspaper publication of defamatory allegations attributed to the father of her children that she was involved in a drugs gang, appealed against the decision that her claim was statute-barred. She also appealed against the striking out of her claim for malicious falsehood. C had failed to comply with an order to return her children to the UK and the article, published in 1988, had not made clear that the remarks by the father were made out of court. She issued a writ for libel and malicious falsehood within a year of receiving, in August 1993, a letter from the presiding judge which stated that nothing was said in court about drug smuggling. She now argued that the limitation period had not expired since the receipt of the letter was the earliest date on which she knew the facts relevant to her cause of action pursuant to the Limitation Act 1980 s.32A, as before that time she believed that the reporting of court proceedings was protected by privilege.

Held, dismissing the appeal in part, that the words "facts relevant to a cause of action" in s.32A were to be construed narrowly and applied only to facts which should be pleaded in a statement of claim, not to facts which could rebut an anticipated defence, *Johnson v. Chief Constable of Surrey* [1992] C.L.Y. 2817 followed. The fact that drug smuggling had not been mentioned in court had no bearing on the issue of the writ. Parliament would have used more general wording in s.32A if a broader interpretation had been envisaged. However, C's claim for malicious falsehood should not be struck out, as proof of publication and falsity had been admitted and there was an arguable case on damages.

C v. MIRROR GROUP NEWSPAPERS; SUB NOM. CLARE v. MIRROR GROUP NEWSPAPERS (1986) LTD [1996] 4 All E.R. 511, Neill, L.J., CA.

5678. Libel–plaintiff suing under a pseudonym–whether such an action was permitted–order for further and better particulars–classes of people recognising plaintiff from article

[Rules of the Supreme Court Ord.1 r.2, Ord.6 r.1.]

A appealed against an order reversing an order for M to provide further and better particulars of his case in a libel action. The plaintiff, a former member of the SAS, used the name M as a pseudonym under which he wrote a best selling book, "Bravo Two Zero". It was alleged, in the Daily Mail, owned by A, that he mistreated his third wife and daughter. The order was granted on the ground that there was no cause of action unless he could identify readers who knew his true identity.

Held, allowing the appeal, that (1) the Rules of the Supreme Court Ord.6 r.1 (2) required a writ to contain "the plaintiff's Christian or other first names and surname". A breach of the rule could be avoided as long as the defendant had not been deceived, misled or prejudiced owing to a lack of protection in respect of costs should the plaintiff be unsuccessful. In such cases the court could treat the case as an irregularity and permit the action to continue on terms under RSC Ord.1 r.2, or it could exercise its inherent jurisdiction. The possible prejudice in relation to costs was avoided by an order whereby M had to lodge his true name with the court in a sealed envelope. The breach was permitted owing to the exceptional circumstances of this case, ie. a distinguished member of the SAS who had served behind enemy lines should be able to maintain anonymity; (2) M had two reputations to defend in this action: one related to those persons who knew his true identity; the other to the general readership of the newspaper who knew him as M, the successful author and (3) M should not be required to reveal the names and addresses of all the people who knew his true identity. The request for further and better particulars should be re-worded to request details of the class of people who read the Daily Mail and (a) who knew that M was a pseudonym of the plaintiff; (b) who knew that the plaintiff had written "Bravo Two Zero" and (c) who knew that the words of the article referred to the plaintiff.

McNAB v. ASSOCIATED NEWSPAPERS LTD, Trans. Ref: QBENI 95/0925/E, May 17, 1996, Otton, L.J., CA.

5679. Libel–public interest–public figures

Held, that a defendant in a libel action could not rely on the fact that the person indicted was a public figure to argue that publication was in the public interest as, unlike the US, there was no defence of public figure immunity in English law.

BENNETT v. GUARDIAN NEWSPAPERS LTD, *The Times*, December 28, 1995, Sir Michael Davies, QBD.

5680. Libel–qualified privilege–circumstances when defence can be pleaded

A applied to strike out part of G's defence to a libel action which relied on the plea of qualified privilege. The claim arose out of an article in respect of alleged harassment of a Jewish police officer by his colleagues.

Held, allowing the application, that (1) for a newspaper to demonstrate a defence of qualified privilege, it must prove that first, the subject matter of the article was of legitimate public interest and secondly, that there was a moral, legal or social obligation on the newspaper to publish it, and a similar interest in the public receiving such information, *Blackshaw v. Lord* [1984] Q.B. 1, [1983] C.L.Y. 2204 followed and (2) in this case the story was unsubstantiated by any comment from the police force or any indication that the story had led to the implementation of any type of complaints procedure, *Bennett v. Guardian Newspapers Ltd* [1996] 1 C.L. 555 distinguished.

AIKEN v. GUARDIAN NEWSPAPERS LTD, Trans. Ref: JS/96/20, April 2, 1996, Sir Maurice Drake, QBD.

5681. Libel–reputation–derogatory reference to actor's physical appearance–whether words were capable of being defamatory was matter for jury

[Rules of the Supreme Court Ord.14A.]

The defendant appealed against a decision refusing an application under the Rules of the Supreme Court Ord.14A for a ruling that using the term "hideously ugly" was not capable of being defamatory, as alleged in B's statement of claim. Two film reviews, written by the defendant and published in a Sunday newspaper, made deprecatory remarks about the physical appearance of B, an actor and director, who contended that these were intended to mean he was ugly in a way that exposed him to ridicule and that he was liable to be shunned as a result. The defendant argued that injury to feelings or annoyance caused by a statement was not relevant to the issue of defamation, which was defined solely by whether the words used were capable of causing injury to a person's reputation.

Held, dismissing the appeal, that words could be defamatory even if they did not impute disgraceful behaviour or deficiencies in the conduct of business or professional activities. In B's case, the test required was whether the words were defamatory when read in context by an ordinary reader. In libel, the words were not to be construed by reference to the publisher's intention, although this could colour their meaning, but by the reader's reaction to them. As a result, a jury might conclude that the context in which the remarks appeared might give an impression that B, a person in the public eye, was repulsive, and it was wrong to decide such a preliminary issue by withdrawing the matter completely from a jury's consideration. Millett, L.J., dissenting, held that words used in jest should not be actionable. Even though the words used were meant to ridicule B, they did not make him look ridiculous or lower his reputation in the eyes of the public and in this sense they were not defamatory.

BERKOFF v. BURCHILL [1996] 4 All E.R. 1008, Neill, L.J., CA.

5682. Libel–ruling on meaning was more severe than pleaded meaning

S appealed against a ruling that a certain part of a leaflet by her and another contained a defamatory meaning against M. The case was a long running libel action and consent was given to the ruling by S and M at an intermediate stage in order for the trial to proceed efficiently. S argued that the meaning pleaded by M was not as severe as the actual meaning found by the judge. S further argued that the judge's ruling reversed earlier concessions and admissions made by M to avoid the need for expert witnesses. The reversal would mean that such witnesses would need to be called and therefore lengthen the trial.

Held, dismissing the appeal, that (1) the trial judge was fully entitled to give the meaning he did and find that it fell within the defamatory meaning as pleaded and (2) the question of admissions and evidence was a question with which the trial judge should deal as the trial proceeded.

McDONALD'S CORP v. STEEL (NO.2), Trans. Ref: QBENF 96/0192/C, April 2, 1996, Hirst, L.J., CA.

5683. Libel–zero damages for republication of defamatory article–admissibility of commercial dispute between defendant and maintainer

B appealed against dismissal of her claim in damages in respect of M's libellous republication to D of a defamatory French newspaper article. The report named B and referred to the involvement of employees of Chequepoint, C, in Paris with drugs and money laundering. M, who had a fierce professional rivalry with C, sent the newspaper article to C's landlord in Puerto Banus, D, who had allegedly displayed it in his window neighbouring C's office during the summer of 1991. B contended that the trial judge had erred in admitting evidence of an irrelevant dispute between C and M and by intervening unduly both during the trial and in his summing up.

Held, dismissing the appeal, that (1) the dispute between C and M had been expressly pleaded in the statement of claim and had been referred to both by counsel for B, and by B herself when giving her evidence. In addition, C was maintaining B in bringing the action and, had the jury been deprived of such evidence, they could not have made a proper judgement of the issues and (2) despite the robust comments of the trial judge, the trial was not unfair because the jury were clearly instructed to, and did, arrive at their own decision on the facts. Fresh documentary evidence of the alleged display was not admitted because it had been available at trial.

BROXTON v. McCLELLAND, *The Times*, November 27, 1996, Staughton, L.J., CA.

5684. Malicious falsehood–publication of false and malicious article in newspaper–claim against journalists and publisher could not succeed without proof of pecuniary loss suffered

A, a Member of Parliament, brought an action for malicious falsehood against C, a journalist, and Mirror Group Newspapers, MGN, contending that an article allegedly instigated by C and published by MGN was based on a false claim that 50 MP's had signed an early day motion challenging A to hand over £250,000 damages won in an earlier libel action against the employer.

Held, dismissing the claim, that A had not been able to prove that C had been sufficiently involved in the article's publication. Whilst there were elements of misrepresentation and unreported details which showed that MGN had published the article falsely and maliciously, it could not be proved to have caused A any pecuniary loss, and the prompt apology and correction undertaken by the publisher showed that any potential claim had already been settled on terms agreed between the parties.

ALLASON v. CAMPBELL, *The Times*, May 8, 1996, Sir Maurice Drake, QBD.

5685. Malicious prosecution–defendant alleging indecent exposure–prosecution offering no evidence–whether defendant responsible for prosecution

On W's complaint of M's indecent exposure, the police laid an information before the justices, who issued a warrant for M's arrest. M was interviewed and bailed to the magistrates' court where the Crown Prosecution Service offered no evidence. M obtained a judgment against W for malicious prosecution but the Court of Appeal allowed W's appeal on the ground that although the prosecution was based on W's false allegation, W had not taken part in the decision to prosecute. M appealed.

Held, allowing the appeal, that where, as here, the facts of the alleged offence were solely within the complainant's knowledge so that the police could not exercise an independent discretion, that complainant could properly be said to have been responsible for the prosecution having been brought. As M had proved that W was in substance responsible for the prosecution, maliciously and without probable cause, W was liable in damages for malicious prosecution, *Commonwealth Life Assurance Society Ltd v. Brain* (1935) 53 C.L.R. 343, *Watters v. Pacific Delivery Service Ltd* (1963) 42 D.L.R. 2d 661, *Commercial Union Assurance Co of NZ Ltd v. Lamont* [1989] 3 N.Z.L.R. 187 applied.

MARTIN v. WATSON [1996] 1 A.C. 74, Lord Keith of Kinkel, HL.

5686. Malicious prosecution–fraud alleged against bus service operator claiming subsidies–accusations made by local authority employee–employee procured prosecution

M appealed against a decision to strike out his statement of claim as being vexatious and an abuse of process. The claim was for malicious prosecution and required the plaintiff to have been prosecuted by the defendant. The question in this case was whether M was prosecuted by W, an employee of K and the second defendant, despite the fact that the information was laid by the police. M ran bus services for K and was entitled to a guaranteed payment if he did not meet a certain revenue. He was accused of understating his revenue to claim a total of £333.10 in subsidies. This was alleged by W in his witness statement and the police relied on his figures when bringing the charges. At a late stage in the trial W revealed that he had used two different methods of calculation, one which was wrong, and that it was possible that mistakes had been made and that K could actually owe M money. The judge in this application stated that there was an independent filtering system of the

CPS and the police and the committal proceedings so W had not compelled the prosecution.

Held, allowing the appeal, that if a person gave false information to the police which he believed to be true then that person could not be liable to a charge of malicious prosecution. The police would use their independent judgment whether or not to pursue the case. However, W did not reveal important information, helpful to M, at the earlier stages of the prosecution and, in effect, procured the prosecution. He presented the police with detailed information compiled by him over a long period of time which showed a prima facie case of fraud. In such a case there was an argument for saying that the police were prevented from exercising independent discretion regarding the prosecution, *Martin v. Watson* [1996] A.C. 74, [1996] C.L.Y. 5685 followed.

MOON v. KENT CC, Trans. Ref: FC3 96/5172/E, February 15, 1996, McCowan, L.J., CA.

5687. Malicious prosecution–wrongful arrest–police complaints–summing up–evidence did not entitle judge to make finding of no case–pattern of summing up in malicious prosecution trial

F appealed against the dismissal of his claim for assault, wrongful arrest, false imprisonment and malicious prosecution against the Commissioner. The complaints arose from F's arrest outside a public house. He had sustained injuries to his face and head that evening and alleged that they had been caused by police officers during his arrest. The trial was by jury and the grounds of appeal were that the judge erred by ruling at the end of F's evidence that there was no case to answer on malicious prosecution despite evidence of malice and lack of reasonable and probable cause to prosecute and that the trial judge's summing up was unfair, prejudicial and biased.

Held, allowing the appeal, that (1) F's account did show that there was no reasonable or probable cause to prosecute and malice was demonstrated by the absence of such a cause. The evidence showed that there was a case to answer in respect of malicious prosecution and (2) the summing up in malicious prosecution trials should follow the same pattern as in criminal trials. The judge must remind the jury of the evidence and the issues but the trial judge was not impartial in his summing up and made comments more suited to the defence speech. Accuracy was lost due to his failure to set out the evidence properly.

FOSTER v. COMMISSIONER OF POLICE OF THE METROPOLIS, Trans. Ref: CCRTF 94/0882/C, October 17, 1995, Henry, L.J., CA.

5688. Ministry of Defence–byelaws–test of certainty of byelaw–reasonable belief as to validity–capable of providing lawful justification for arrest and detention of plaintiffs

[HMS Forest Moor and Menwith Hill Station Bylaws 1986.]

P brought actions for wrongful arrest and false imprisonment against H and other Ministry of Defence police constables, the Chief Constable and the Attorney General, contending, inter alia, that a series of arrests made by the officers, under the HMS Forest Moor and Menwith Hill Station Byelaws 1986, were unlawful, as the byelaws had been found void for uncertainty in *Bugg v. DPP* [1993] Q.B. 473, [1993] C.L.Y. 2618. The judge below, deciding he was bound by *Bugg,* held that the byelaws were invalid for uncertainty, but that H and the other constables were nonetheless entitled to the common law defence of lawful justification for their actions. The police constables and the Attorney General appealed.

Held, allowing the appeal, that (1) the fact that byelaws were later declared void for uncertainty did not render tortious the actions of police officers who, at the relevant time, reasonably believed that byelaw offences were being committed, and (2) as to the test for uncertainty, the decision in *Bugg,* based on the failure to describe a boundary for the protected area in the byelaws, could not be accepted. Whether applying the test in *Kruse v. Johnson* [1898] 2 Q.B. 91 or that in *Fawcett Properties Ltd v. Buckingham CC* [1961] A.C. 636, [1960] C.L.Y. 3110, of which the latter was to be preferred, the words "lands belonging to the Secretary of State" described the protected area with sufficient certainty to provide adequate information to those who had to obey the byelaws.

PERCY v. HALL [1996] 4 All E.R. 523, Simon Brown, L.J., CA.

5689. Misrepresentation–deceit–purchase of a book shop on false accounts–correct test for establishing causation–correct assessment of damages

D appealed against a judgment for C and S, the second defendants, a firm of accountants. The judge found for D on the question of liability in relation to C for the tort of deceit and S in negligence, but found that D had failed to prove that they had suffered any loss as a result. The action was in relation to the purchase of a book shop by D. The judge held that D failed to prove that they purchased the shop having relied upon false figures given by C and verified by S.

Held, allowing the appeal, that (1) the judge below erred in comparing the figures given by C and S with the true figures and then deciding what D would have done with knowledge of the true figures. In the case of deceit, it was necessary for D to prove that there was a material fraudulent representation which induced them to act as they did, which there clearly was. The judge below used the wrong test when he decided whether D had relied upon the figures; (2) in the case of S, it was also clear that D purchased the shop upon reliance on their verification; (3) the damages should be assessed on a no transaction basis, because if D had been aware of the true figures there would have been no transaction. The judge was influenced in his findings on causation when he considered damages. D had, in fact, purchased a business which was not viable; (4) causation and the assessment of damages should be treated as questions of fact. The plaintiff should be entitled to recover all the losses he had suffered up until the time that he discovered the misrepresentation, *Naughton v. O'Callaghan* [1990] 3 All E.R. 191, [1991] C.L.Y. 1319 considered. After D had discovered the misrepresentation they rejected an offer on the shop of £76,000. Any loss after that was not caused by the torts but was attributable to their failure to sell. D had paid £120,000 for the shop so their loss was £44,000. Changes in the market could be considered as they were not too remote and (5) to prevent D from being over compensated it was necessary to decide whether the torts actually caused the loss despite the fact that it had been proved that the torts had induced D to enter into the transaction. If the figures had been true D would have been able to comfortably finance the purchase. That showed that the compensation would not have provided D with a windfall.

DOWNS v. CHAPPELL; DOWNS v. STEPHENSON SMART (A FIRM) [1996] 3 All E.R. 344, Hobhouse, L.J., CA.

5690. Nuisance–causes of action–local authority convicted of criminal offence for failing to abate nuisance–whether liable in civil action

[Public Health Act 1936 Part III.]

H appealed against a decision to award damages to I, the son of a council tenant, for injury to health caused by living in housing which was damp and subject to mould growth. I claimed that H's conviction, under the Public Health Act 1936 Part III, of failure to comply with an abatement notice, in which proceedings, I's father was awarded compensation, rendered them liable in a civil action for any loss or damage suffered. H contended that Part III, which was a self-contained and comprehensive code on statutory nuisance, should not be construed so as to give rise to tortious liability.

Held, allowing the appeal, that Part III did not give rise to a civil cause of action for failure to comply with an abatement notice. The statute had to be construed as at the date of enactment and the case was exceptional in that normally tenants and their families suffering the effects of statutory nuisance would have a common law remedy, *McCall v. Abelesz* [1976] Q.B. 585, [1976] C.L.Y. 1531 and *Lonrho Ltd v. Shell Petroleum Co Ltd (No.2)* [1982] A.C. 173, [1980] C.L.Y. 2135 considered.

HACKNEY LBC v. ISSA; SUB NOM. ISSA v. HACKNEY LBC [1996] E.G.C.S. 184, Nourse, L.J., CA.

5691. Nuisance–damage to barge during firework display–whether actionable in private nuisance–rule in "Rylands v Fletcher" could extend to facts

C claimed in negligence, nuisance and under the rule in *Rylands v. Fletcher* (1868) L.R. 3 H.L. 330 for damage caused to their floating barge and a passenger vessel moored alongside it following a firework display held by K on the River Thames. The fire authority had been called to a small fire on the barge caused by falling debris during the display and a second fire later damaged both the passenger vessel and the barge.

Held, giving judgment for C, that (1) K had been negligent in putting on the firework display without first checking whether any flammable material was on board the vessels in the vicinity, and expert evidence had shown that the second fire occurred because of the fire authority's negligent failure to ensure that the first fire was properly extinguished; (2) the barge was permanently moored and C owned a licence which gave them exclusive use and occupation. This meant that, as the barge was attached to the land, an action in private nuisance against K was sustainable as the display interfered with C's use and enjoyment of the land and (3) there was a case for extending the rule in *Rylands v. Fletcher* to accumulations in a vessel on a river and to intentional releases, as well as accidental escape, provided the release was not deliberately intended to be aimed at the plaintiff's property. However, a finding of liability under *Rylands v. Fletcher* was not made against K in this case.

CROWN RIVER CRUISES LTD v. KIMBOLTON FIREWORKS LTD [1996] 2 Lloyd's Rep. 533, Potter, J., QBD (Adm Ct).

5692. Nuisance–highway authority proposing temporary closure of road–whether public law element precluded private law remedy–damages not available for losses due to implementation of order

[Road Traffic Regulation Act 1984 s.14.]

B appealed against an injunction prohibiting them from closing a road for one week to implement a traffic calming scheme, following the making of an order under the Road Traffic Regulation Act 1984 s.14. GH had begun proceedings by ordinary writ and had been permitted to proceed on the basis of a private law right to bring an action in nuisance, along with two other businesses affected by the road closure.

Held, allowing the appeal and striking out GH's action in nuisance as an abuse of process, that where a s.14 order had been validly made, no private law challenge on the basis of unfairness or unreasonableness could lie. For the order to be valid, B did not have to refute all criticisms made of their conduct in making or implementing the closure order. The order itself precluded the acts covered from being actionable in nuisance during the period of its validity. Where validity was in issue, the only permissible method of challenge lay by way of judicial review. Saville L.J., dissenting, held that GH were seeking to rely on private law rights to claim damages for losses incurred by the closure, to which GH contended B's defence had no merit. The damages claim did not depend on GH proving that B was not statutorily authorised to obstruct the road, but that the obstruction caused them special damage, *Roy v. Kensington and Chelsea and Westminster Family Practitioner Committee* [1992] 1 A.C. 624, [1992] C.L.Y. 30 considered.

GREAT HOUSE AT SONNING LTD v. BERKSHIRE CC [1996] R.T.R. 407, Hutchison, L.J., CA.

5693. Nuisance–injunctions–jurisdiction–prohibition on entering area around plaintiff's home

[Supreme Court Act 1981 s.37; County Courts Act 1984 s.38.]

B, threatened and harassed by A, began proceedings for nuisance and obtained an interlocutory injunction under the Supreme Court Act 1981 s.37 and the County Courts Act 1984 s.38 restraining him from, inter alia, entering or remaining within 250 yards of B's home. A did not challenge the order, but breached it repeatedly, which led to the imposition of a suspended custodial sentence. Thereafter he twice cycled past A's home, prompting fresh committal proceedings. The judge rejected the contention that the county court had no jurisdiction to impose the term excluding A from the vicinity of B's home and imposed immediate custodial sentences for the latest breaches, and activated the suspended sentence. A appealed.

Held, varying the judge's order, that an exclusion order could lawfully be made if necessary to protect a plaintiff's legitimate interest and as A had not sought to challenge the injunction he was bound by it. However, because A had not repeated his earlier breaches of other parts of the original injunction, the order activating the suspended sentence would be set aside.

BURRIS v. AZADANI [1995] 1 W.L.R. 1372, Sir Thomas Bingham, M.R., CA.

5694. Nuisance–interference with TV reception by tall building not actionable in private nuisance–whether planning consent gave immunity in nuisance–action in negligence required proof of physical damage

H and a number of other plaintiffs living in East London brought two actions claiming damages for nuisance and negligence. Firstly, they claimed damages in nuisance from CW in respect of interference with reception of television broadcasts due to the presence of Canary Wharf Tower. Secondly, they claimed damages in nuisance and negligence against London Docklands Development Corporation in respect of the depositing of dust on their properties due to the construction of the Limehouse Link Road. Both the plaintiffs and defendants appealed against certain findings of Richard Havery, Q.C. on preliminary issues, Independent, December 20, 1994.

Held, that occupation of a property as a home enabled an occupier to sue in private nuisance. It was not necessary to have a right of exclusive possession of the property. In the first action, the plaintiffs' appeal was dismissed and the defendant's cross appeal allowed. The presence of a building in the line of sight to a television transmitter was not actionable as an interference with the use and enjoyment of land, and interference with television reception was not capable of constituting either a private or public nuisance. In the second action, the defendants' appeal was dismissed and the plaintiffs' cross appeal allowed. The deposit of excess dust on the plaintiffs' homes was capable of founding an action in negligence. Whether it did was dependent upon proof of physical damage, such proof being dependent on circumstances and evidence. Both parties were given leave to appeal to the House of Lords.

HUNTER v. CANARY WHARF LTD; SUB NOM. HUNTER v. LONDON DOCKLANDS DEVELOPMENT CORP [1996] 2 W.L.R. 348, Pill, L.J., CA.

5695. Nuisance–wall bulging onto plaintiff's property–cost of rebuilding by plaintiff not recoverable from owner

B appealed against the award to C of £6,056 which was the cost of demolishing and rebuilding B's wall, which had bulged on to C's property. B did not agree that the wall was dangerous but agreed that C could rebuild at their own expense. C did so and sought to recover the cost from B.

Held, allowing the appeal, that the right of abatement and self help was to be limited to cases where lives or property were in danger. C might have regarded its actions as reasonable but B had only given C permission to repair or rebuild at their own expense. The judge's order was varied by substituting £1,400, being the cost of demolition.

COOPERATIVE WHOLESALE SOCIETY LTD v. BRITISH RAILWAYS BOARD [1995] N.P.C. 200, Beldam, L.J., CA.

5696. Occupiers liability–damages–hair catching fire on candle in restaurant

[Occupiers Liability Act 1957 s.2.]

O was visiting M's restaurant with her husband and two friends. They were shown to a table which was on a platform, raised approximately three feet above the rest of the floor. O chose to sit with her back to the balustrade of the platform.

Directly behind and below the balustrade and O's seat was another table which was occupied by two diners. Either as she sat, or while she was sitting, O's hair, which was of waist length, fell onto the table below and in the flame of a candle on that table. The candle was uncovered, having been placed only in the top of a glass bottle. O's hair caught fire which her husband was able to pat out in a matter of seconds. O and her fellow guests continued with their meal, although they were moved by M's manager to another table. As a result of her hair catching alight she had to make a number of visits to a hairdresser so as to put her back into a presentable condition. At the date of the trial, her hair was three to four inches shorter than it had been at the time of her visit to the restaurant. She suffered no damage to her scalp or to any other part of her body.

Held, that M had breached its duty of care pursuant to the Occupiers Liability Act 1957 s.2(2) in that the candle on the table below O had been moved to the side of the table and was thus more likely to come into contact with her hair. With respect to damages, *Leckie v. TJ Hairdressers* [1996] C.L.Y. 2210 was applied which stated that distress and embarrassment caused by the accident were as significant as the physical signs of injury itself. Here O had said she was upset to have lost some of her hair. O had limited her claim to £500 in total on her particulars of claim. Had she not done so she would have been awarded very much more by way of general damages.

O'NEILL v. MONGOLIAN BARBEQUE LTD, November 1, 1996, District Judge Madge, CC (West London). [*Ex rel.* Daniel Cohen, Barrister].

5697. Occupiers liability–injury to child trespasser in disused factory–"reasonable grounds to believe" involves actual not constructive knowledge–duty of care not established–statutory interpretation

[Occupiers Liability Act 1984 s.1.]

S, aged nine years, was injured in a fall from a factory roof on to which he had trespassed. He appealed against the dismissal of his claim for damages. The question was whether P owed a duty of care. It was submitted that, for the purposes of the Occupiers Liability Act 1984 s.1(3)(b), there had been reasonable grounds for believing that children would trespass into the disused factory and that there had been a breach of duty.

Held, dismissing the appeal, that there had been no duty of care and consequently no breach of duty. Notwithstanding that the fences were not intruder proof, they were substantial fences and there was no evidence of previous trespass. Accordingly, the judge had been entitled to take the view that the occupiers had no reason to believe that children would attempt to scale the roof. It would have been a different matter had there been evidence of frequent attempts at trespass. "Reasonable grounds to believe", in s.1(3)(b), meant that it was necessary to show that the respondents had actual knowledge of a relevant fact or knew facts which provided grounds for a relevant belief established by evidence. Constructive knowledge did not arise in the context of s.1(3)(b). Had it been intended that the words of the section meant "ought to have known" those words would have been used, *Harris v. Birkenhead Corp* [1976] 1 All E.R. 341, [1972] C.L.Y. 2344, *Herrington v. British Railways Board* [1972] A.C. 877, [1976] C.L.Y. 1349 and *Compania Maritima San Basilio v. Oceanus Mutual Underwriting Association (Bermuda)* [1977] Q.B. 49, [1976] C.L.Y. 257 considered.

SWAIN v. NATUI RAM PURI [1996] P.I.Q.R. P442, Pill, L.J., CA.

5698. Parking–wheel clamping–tortious liability–distress damage feasant

[Theft Act 1968.]

A, a motorist who had parked his car on private property despite having seen a warning notice that unauthorised vehicles would be wheel clamped and a release fee of £40 charged, appealed against the dismissal of his claim for compensatory and exemplary damages for malicious falsehood and tortious interference after his vehicle was clamped by an employee of an agent company of the car park leaseholders. The agent company did not charge the leaseholders for their services but sought remuneration solely through charges paid by clamped drivers. The employee relied on the defence of consent and the medieval remedy of distress damage feasant, whereby the owner of land was entitled to seize trespassing property to prevent further damage until its owner paid compensation.

Held, dismissing the appeal that, by reading the sign, A had impliedly consented to the clamping of his vehicle as he had voluntarily accepted the risk that it would be immobilised until he paid the fee. Provided that the fee was reasonable, his car would be released without delay and the means were given by which he could communicate an offer to pay A could not complain when the resulting action was taken as his assent rendered an otherwise tortious act lawful. The self-help remedy of distress damage feasant could not be applied in the circumstances as the effect of wheel clamping continued the very damage which the leaseholders sought to prevent, namely the parking of unauthorised vehicles on their property, and furthermore no actual damage was suffered by either the car park leaseholders or the agents, as distrainors, for which they could be compensated. Nor was the employee criminally liable for theft or blackmail under the Theft Act 1968 as he lacked the intention to permanently deprive A of his vehicle, *Black v. Carmichael* [1992] S.C.C.R. 709 distinguished as decided under Scots law, and he had reasonable grounds for demanding payment and keeping the car clamped until such payment was made.

ARTHUR v. ANKER [1996] 2 W.L.R. 602, Sir Thomas Bingham, M.R., CA.

5699. Personal injuries

PERSONAL INJURIES (CIVILIANS) AMENDMENT SCHEME 1996, SI 1996 502; made under the Personal Injuries (Emergency Provisions) Act 1939 s.1, s.2. In force: April 8, 1996; £1.55.

This Scheme further amends the Personal Injuries (Civilians) Scheme 1983 (SI 1983 686) (the principal Scheme) which makes provision for the payment of pensions and allowances to or in respect of civilians who were killed or injured during World War II by increasing the amounts of allowances, pensions and awards payable under that Scheme and also increasing the amounts of income to be disregarded for the purposes of certain parts of the Scheme.

5700. Personal injuries–soldier injured in battle–no duty in tort between soldiers in battle–Ministry of Defence not vicariously liable for negligent act of serving soldier

[Crown Proceedings Act 1947 s.10.]

MoD appealed against the refusal to strike out M's personal injury claim as having no reasonable cause of action. M was a soldier serving in the Gulf War, who suffered damage to his hearing when a fellow soldier fired a shell from a howitzer. M claimed that the MoD were vicariously liable for the negligence of the soldier who fired the shell.

Held, allowing the appeal, that (1) where the Secretary of State had not acted to reintroduce the immunity contained in the Crown Proceedings Act 1947 s.10 the court had to consider whether a duty of care existed at common law and (2) although the instant case did contain the elements of proximity and foreseeability of damage, it was necessary to ask whether it was fair, just or reasonable to impose a duty of care in tort by one soldier for another engaging an enemy in battle conditions. The court's opinion was that no basis existed to extend the scope of the duty of care to such situations and therefore no duty of care existed between soldiers on active service. Nor was the MoD obliged to maintain a safe system of work in battle situations, *Shaw Savill and Albion Co Ltd v. Commonwealth of Australia* (1940) 66 C.L.R. 344 and *Burmah Oil Co Ltd v. Lord Advocate* [1965] A.C. 75, [1964] C.L.Y. 543 followed, *Hughes v. National Union of Mineworkers* [1991] 4 All E.R. 278, [1992] C.L.Y. 3354 considered.

MULCAHY v. MINISTRY OF DEFENCE [1996] Q.B. 732, Neill, L.J., CA.

5701. Tortious liability–misfeasance in public office–requirements and ingredients needed to establish tortious liability

T were depositors with BCCI, licensed by the Bank of England who lost the entire amount of their deposit when BCCI failed and went into liquidation. T brought an action against the Bank for misfeasance in public office in the performance of its duties to supervise banking operations in the UK. The action was brought on the basis either that the Bank had wrongly granted a licence to BCCI or had wrongly failed to revoke BCCI's licence. Two issues arose for preliminary ruling (1) whether the Bank could be liable to T for the tort of misfeasance in a public office and (2) whether T's losses were capable of being caused in law by the Bank's omissions.

Held, that (1) the tort of misfeasance in public office required the deliberate and dishonest wrongful abuse of the powers given to a public officer. The purpose of the tort was to provide compensation for those who suffered loss as a result of an abuse of power. The tort was not to be equated with torts based on an intention to injure. The tort could be established in two different ways: (a) where a public officer performed or omitted to perform an act with the object of injuring the plaintiff and (b) where he performed an act which both knew to be beyond his power and one that would injure the plaintiff; (2) to establish the requirement that the officer had no power to act, it was sufficient that the officer knew the act was unlawful or suspected that it lay beyond his power, *Burngion SA v. Ministry of Agriculture Fisheries and Food* [1985] 3 All E.R. 585 considered; (3) an action could be brought under the tort where it could be established that it was intended to injure either the plaintiff, or a class of persons to which the plaintiff belonged, or that the defendant knew he had no power to do the act and that the plaintiff would suffer loss as a result. The plaintiff must also show that the defendant was a public officer or entity and that there was a link between the wrongful act and the plaintiff's loss; (4) the plaintiffs could bring an action where they could demonstrate the causation between the defendant's act and the plaintiff's loss, in the manner set out at (3) above and (5) the plaintiffs had no relevant Community law rights or domestic statutory provisions upon which they could rely.

THREE RIVERS DC v. GOVERNOR AND COMPANY OF THE BANK OF ENGLAND (NO.3) [1996] 3 All E.R. 558, Clarke, J., QBD (Comm Ct).

5702. Articles

A statutory right to privacy *(David Eady)*: E.H.R.L.R. 1996, 3, 243-253. (Conflict between right to free speech under Art.10 and right to private life under Art.8 and proposal for introduction of statutory tort of unlawfully publishing personal information).

Cambridge Water revisited *(Christopher Hilson)*: W.L. 1996, 7(3), 126-132. (Issues of foreseeability in application of Rylands v Fletcher rule, proprietary rights over water that might be affected, limitation and insurance implications of date of damage and distinction between isolated and continuing escapes).

Claiming or resisting a claim for compound interest *(Nicholas Phillips* and *Timothy Lawson-Cruttenden)*: Litigator 1996, Sep, 285-291. (When compound interest can be claimed as debt or as damages for breach of contract or in tort, defences available to claim and remaining influence of Usury Acts).

Damages for defamation: the jury's role *(Michael Olaseinde)*: L. Ex. 1996, Jan, 56-57. (Role of jury in defamation cases, aim of damages and CA's power to set aside excessive awards).

Defamation Bill *(Andrew Stephenson)*: Comms. L. 1996, 1(3), 98-100. (Need for reforms to include public figure defence of privilege and for reversal of burden of proof for plaintiff to prove falsity).

Doing business on the Internet: the legal issues *(Rory Graham)*: C.L.S.R. 1996, 12(4), 202-213. (Liability for defamation on Internet, effective disclaimers, vicarious liability and regulation of marketing, buying, selling and publishing on Internet).

Expectation losses, negligent omissions and the tortious duty of care *(John Murphy)*: C.L.J. 1996, 55(1), 43-55. (Recovery of economic loss in tort where plaintiff has suffered loss by defendant's failure to act).

Fire brigade liability: L.A.L. 1996, 7, 3-4. (Whether there was sufficient special relationship between property owner and fire brigade giving rise to duty of care).

Gendered harms and the law of tort: remedying (sexual) harassment *(Joanne Conaghan)*: O.J.L.S. 1996, 16(3), 407-431. (Ability of tort law to respond to and redress gender specific harms such as harassment).

Injunction or damages? *(Andrew Westwood)*: S.J. 1996, 140(39), 1002-1003. (Remedies in trespass to land cases where defendant makes permanent encroachment on plaintiff's land and apparent conflict between decisions in Gooden and Harrow cases).

Liability: after Hillsborough *(Simon Allen)*: P. & M.I.L.L. 1996, 12(6), 47-48. (Police claims for nervous shock as result of Hillsborough disaster and status of professional rescuers as claimants).

Noisy neighbours *(Alastair Hudson)*: N.L.J. 1996, 146(6749), 910-911. (Whether tort of nuisance contrary to EPA 1990 could be committed where tortfeasor and complainant lived in same building).

Online service provider liability *(Jonathan Bond)*: I.C. Lit. 1996, Apr, 35-36. (Liability for actions of third parties in respect of copyright infringement, defamation and indecency).

Passing off and the misappropriation of valuable intangibles *(Michael Spence)*: L.Q.R. 1996, 112(Jul), 472-498. (Expansion of tort of passing off and whether tort should be developed into more generalised tort of misappropriation).

Private citizens and media libels *(Ian Loveland)*: N.L.J. 1996, 146(6733), 278. (Whether English libel law in relation to allegations of criminal activities will develop along lines of US law in light of Guardian article mistakenly alleging that innocent Irishman injured in bus bombing was IRA terrorist).

Statutory nuisances: E.G. 1996, 9627, 119, 121, 123. (Local authority powers to deal with nuisances within its area).

Summary of changes to defamation law *(Jane Hyndman)*: I.M.L. 1996, 14(8), 58-59. (Main provisions of 1996 Act including new statutory defence of innocent dissemination, provisions allowing defendant to offer to make amends, introduction of summary procedure and extension of statutory privilege).

Television, tower blocks and nuisance *(Barbara Harvey* and *Andy Robinson)*: Env. Law 1996, 10(1), 24-26. (Whether interference with television reception can amount to nuisance and links required to entitle plaintiff to bring action).

The Defamation Act 1996: potential impact and relationship with the present law of libel *(Alex Wade)*: Comms. L. 1996, 1(5), 186-189. (Criticism of 1996 Act including balance between plaintiff and defendant in libel law, measure of damages, summary procedure, defence of innocent dissemination and procedural issues).

The patients' obstacle course *(Charles Lewis)*: Legal Times 1996, 38, 16. (Difficulties facing patients in medical negligence claims including biased opinions of defence expert witnesses).

The radical change in assessment in libel awards by juries: Elton John v MGN Limited *(Dan Tench* and *Jennifer McDermott)*: Comms. L. 1996, 1(1), 17-18. (Background to Elton John libel suit, implications of ruling on how juries should be addressed regarding measure of damages and how new defamation regime will operate in light of ruling and provisions of 1996 Bill).

The rule in Rylands v. Fletcher *(Michael Olaseinde)*: L. Ex. 1996, Mar, 22-23. (Relevance of rule in Rylands v. Fletcher, erosion of distinguishing features between rule and tort of nuisance and whether rule is independent tort or extension of nuisance).

When do solicitors owe third party duties of care? *(Colin Passmore)*: N.L.J. 1996, 146(6736), 409-410. (Circumstances in which solicitors owe duty of care to people other than their clients).

5703. Books

Baker, C.D.–Baker: Tort. Concise course texts. Paperback: £12.95. ISBN 0-421-55480-0. Sweet & Maxwell.

Banakas, Efstathios K.–Civil Liability for Pure Economic Loss. Hardback: £68.00. ISBN 90-411-0908-0. Kluwer Law International.
Cane, Peter–Tort Law and Economic Interests. Hardback: £50.00. ISBN 0-19-876430-8. Paperback: £22.50. ISBN 0-19-876429-4. Clarendon Press.
Clerk and Lindsell on Torts: Supplement 1 to the 17th Edition. Paperback: £25.00. ISBN 0-421-57560-3. Sweet & Maxwell.
Dornstein, Ken–Accidentally, on Purpose. Hardback: £15.50. ISBN 0-333-67457-X. Macmillan Press.
Elliott, Catherine; Quinn, Frances–Tort Law. Paperback: £10.99. ISBN 0-582-29876-8. Addison-Wesley Longman Higher Education.
General Paper I: Suggested Solutions (1991-1995). Bar Examinations. Paperback: £9.95. ISBN 0-7510-0739-0. HLT Publications.
Hepple, R.A.; Matthews, Martin; Howarth, David–Hepple and Matthews: Tort - Cases and Materials. Paperback: £27.95. ISBN 0-406-06326-5. Butterworth Law.
Heuston, R.E.V.; Buckley, R.A.–Salmon and Heuston on the Law of Torts. Paperback: £28.00. ISBN 0-421-53350-1. Sweet & Maxwell.
Hodgson, J.–Blackstone's LLB: Cases and Materials - Torts. Paperback: £18.95. ISBN 1-85431-530-7. Blackstone Press.
Hodgson, J.–Blackstone's LLB: Learning Text - Torts. Paperback: £17.95. ISBN 1-85431-523-4. Blackstone Press.
Hodgson, J.–LLB Cases and Materials: Law of Tort. Paperback: £18.95. ISBN 1-85431-530-7. Blackstone Press.
Hodgson, J.–LLB Learning Text: Torts. Paperback: £17.95. ISBN 1-85431-523-4. Blackstone Press.
Jones, Michael A.–Textbook on Torts. Paperback: £17.00. ISBN 1-85431-551-X. Blackstone Press.
Kidner, Richard.–Casebook on Torts. Paperback: £16.55. ISBN 1-85431-536-6. Blackstone Press.
Law of Tort - LLB: Suggested Solutions (1991-1995). Bachelor of Laws (LLB). Paperback: £6.95. ISBN 0-7510-0724-2. HLT Publications.
McLachlan, Campbell; Nygh, Peter–Transnational Tort Litigation. Hardback: £50.00. ISBN 0-19-825919-0. Clarendon Press.
Pitchfork, Ernie D.–Tort: Casebook 1996-1997. Bachelor of Laws (LLB). Paperback: £17.95. ISBN 0-7510-0656-4. HLT Publications.
Pitchfork, Ernie D.–Tort: Textbook 1996-1997. Bachelor of Laws (LLB). Paperback: £16.95. ISBN 0-7510-0689-0. HLT Publications.
Scott-Bayfield, Julie–Defamation. Longman practitioner series. Paperback: £45.00. ISBN 0-85121-719-2. FT Law & Tax.
Tiernan, Ralph–Tort Law Nutshell. Paperback: £4.95. ISBN 0-421-54830-4. Sweet & Maxwell.
Tort: Suggested Solutions - Single Paper (June 1995). Paperback: £3.00. ISBN 0-7510-0623-8. HLT Publications.

TRADE MARKS

5704. Community trade mark

COMMUNITY TRADE MARK REGULATIONS 1996, SI 1996 1908; made under the Trade Marks Act 1994 s.52. In force: August 14, 1996; £1.10.

These Regulations make provision for the operation of the Community Trade Mark Regulation (Council Regulation 40/94 of December 20, 1993 ([1994] OJ L11/1)). In particular they provide for the procedures for determining a posteriori the invalidity, or liability to revocation, of the registration of a trade mark from which a Community trade mark claims seniority; the conversion of a Community trade mark, or an application for a Community trade mark, into an application for registration under the Trade Marks Act 1994; the designation of courts in the United Kingdom having jurisdiction over proceedings arising out of the Community Trade Mark Regulations; the application in relation to a Community trade mark of the provisions of the Trade Marks Act 1994 which deal with groundless threat of infringement proceedings, importation of infringing goods, material or articles and offences; privilege for communications with persons on the list of professional representatives maintained in pursuance of Art.89 of the Community Trade Mark Regulation; and the application of the Trade Marks Rules 1994 (SI 1994 2583).

5705. Comparative advertising–mobile telephones–claim for malicious falsehood and trade mark infringement–meaning of advertiser's claim

[Trade Marks Act 1994 s.10.]

V, a telecommunications company, brought an action against O for malicious falsehood and infringement of its registered trade mark "Vodafone" following an advertising campaign by O which stated that users of Orange would save on average £20 per month. V argued that the advertisement would be taken to mean that users of Vodafone or Cellnet would have to pay £20 more per month for the same services or that £20 per month would be saved if they transferred to Orange.

Held, dismissing V's claim, that under the Trade Marks Act 1994 s.10(6) comparative advertising was permitted provided that it was not detrimental to, and did not take unfair advantage of, a registered trade mark. Although the slogan used in O's advertising campaign involved a direct comparison with Vodafone, the ordinary reasonable man would not know whether his proposed usage would save him £20 per month, as it would be assumed that fewer calls would be made under a more expensive tariff. The public would expect usage of either service to be elastic, and therefore it could not be established that most members of the public would conclude that a saving of £20 per month could be made by transferring to Orange.

VODAFONE GROUP PLC v. ORANGE PERSONAL COMMUNICATIONS SERVICES LTD [1997] F.S.R. 34, Jacob, J., Ch D.

5706. Counterfeiting–deception–selling copies–genuine belief that not infringing trade mark

[Trade Marks Act 1994 s.92.]

On November 30, 1994 S was charged by trading standards officers with selling goods bearing registered trade marks without the consent of the proprietor, contrary to the Trade Marks Act 1994 s.92(1)(b). Before a lay bench, S pleaded the defence provided by s.92(5) of the Act, that she believed on reasonable grounds that the use of the sign in the manner in which it was used was not an infringement of the registered trade mark.

Held, finding S not guilty, that she conducted the venture as a social activity and not for a profit. S pleaded that no deception was intended and nobody had been deceived as she advertised the fact that the goods were copies. S successfully pleaded the defence contained in s.92(5) which covered situations of use by "someone acting in ignorance, or in a genuine belief that what he was doing did not require the consent of the proprietor, rather than taking part in deliberate counterfeiting", *Kent CC v. Price (Ralph Robert)* (1994) 158 L.G. Rev. 78, [1993] C.L.Y. 484 and *Hodgkinson & Corby v. Wards Mobility Services* [1994] W.L.R. 1564, [1994] C.L.Y. 4292 considered.

R. v. SARGENT, November 9, 1995, Judge not specified, Enfield Magistrates' Court. [*Ex rel.* Jean-Marie Labelle, Barrister].

5707. Fees

TRADE MARKS (FEES) RULES 1996, SI 1996 1942; made under the Department of Trade and Industry (Fees) Order 1988; and the Trade Marks Act 1994 s.54, s.79. In force: October 2, 1996; £1.10.

These Rules revoke and replace the Trade Marks (Fees) Rules 1994 (SI 1994 2584) and the Trade Marks (International Registration) (Fees) Rules 1996 (SI 1996 715). They also provide for a reduction of the fees in respect of the class fee for applications for registration which cover goods and services falling in more than one class and applications for additional classes following examination of a mark, for each additional class.

5708. Infringement–common descriptive word registered as a trade mark–use on different product did not amount to infringement of mark

[Trade Marks Act 1994 s.10.]

BS brought an action for trade mark infringement against JR. In 1992 BS registered as a trade mark their dessert topping "Treat". In 1995 JR launched a new sweet spread using the word "Treat" in the product name. BS submitted that the use of "Treat" was likely to cause confusion and damage to their goodwill. JR argued that they did not use "Treat" as a trade mark and therefore did not infringe BS's mark under the Trade Marks Act 1994 s.10.

Held, dismissing the action, that there had been no infringement of BS's trade mark. If BS wished to use a common term as a trade mark, that trade mark could not be infringed by another party using the same term in a descriptive way on a different product. The court found no evidence to suggest that confusion had arisen between the two products and upheld JR's counterclaim to strike out BS's trade mark registration.

BRITISH SUGAR PLC v. JAMES ROBERTSON & SONS LTD [1996] R.P.C. 281, Jacob, J., Ch D.

5709. Infringement–QUATTRO–QUADRA–whether protection under national law of a Member State of mark denoting a numeral breached EC law–whether risk of confusion test matter for national or EC law–European Union

[Treaty of Rome 1957 Art.30, Art.36.]

A owned German registrations for the mark Quattro in respect of four wheel drive cars. DR introduced onto the German market a four wheel drive car called the Espace Quadra and applied to remove the Quattro mark from the Register. The Bundesgerichtshof referred to the European Court of Justice the question of whether it was an abuse of the Treaty of Rome 1957 Art.30 and Art.36 to prohibit a company, which was a subsidiary of a car manufacturer established in Member State B and which was trading in Member State A, from using the mark Quadra, which the manufacturer had used without restriction elsewhere, on the ground that another manufacturer in Member State A claimed a trade mark right and/or get-up right in the word Quattro. The Bundesgerichtshof pointed out that Quattro was a numeral in another language and that the number four was significant in the automobile trade.

Held, answering the question in the negative, that (1) the conditions for the protection of a mark such as Quattro were, subject to the limits imposed by the second sentence of Art.36, a matter for national law, *Keurkoop BV v. Nancy Keen Gifts BV* [1982] E.C.R. 2853, [1982] C.L.Y. 1254, *Volvo AB v. Erik Veng (UK) Ltd* [1988] E.C.R. 6211; *Thetford v. Fiamma SA* [1988] E.C.R. 3585, [1987] C.L.Y. 2791 applied; (2) the national legislation for protection of a mark such as Quattro was very strict, and a manufacturer from another Member State was not precluded under German law from claiming the protection granted, nor did the protection vary according to whether or not the goods bearing the mark were of national or foreign origin. Accordingly, the national provisions did not represent either arbitrary discrimination or a disguised restriction on intra Community trade; (3) the adoption of criteria for a finding of confusion were a matter for national law, subject to Art.36, *Centrafarm BV v. Winthrop* [1974] E.C.R. 1183, [1976] C.L.Y. 1194; *SA CNL-SUCAL NV v. HAG GF AG (HAG II)* [1990] I E.C.R. 3711, [1993] C.L.Y. 4236 applied and (4) there was nothing to suggest that the German court's interpretation of the concept of confusion differed depending on whether the proprietor of the mark was German or from another Member State. There was, therefore, no abuse of Art.30 or Art.36.

DEUTSCHE RENAULT AG v. AUDI AG [1995] F.S.R. 738, Due, C.J., ECJ.

5710. Infringement–whether statutory defence covered corporate title–computer software–scope of registration

[Trade Marks Act 1938 s.8; Rules of the Supreme Court Ord.14.]

MC, a well known provider of telecommunications services, was registered proprietor of the trade mark MERCURY, in respect of, inter alia, computers, electronic instruments for processing data and computer programs in class 9. MI marketed computer programs for analysing, testing and debugging computer software under various marks incorporating the word MERCURY. MC commenced a trade mark infringement action and applied for summary judgment under the Rules of the Supreme Court Ord.14. MI contended that there were triable issues as to whether their use of the word MERCURY was protected by the Trade Marks Act 1938 s.8(a) and as to the validity of MC's trade mark. MC submitted that the test of bona fide use under s.8(a) was objective, in that the court should compare MI's actions against those of reasonable traders in their place. MI contended that the test was subjective, ie. the court should look at MI's actions and decide whether they were honest.

Held, dismissing the application for summary judgment, that (1) the test for bona fides under s.8(a) was subjective. Where a trader innocently used his own name he did not need to look over his shoulder to make sure that a registered trade mark was not in the way, unless he had already been warned of its existence. Passing off was a different matter, *Parker-Knoll Ltd v. Knoll International Ltd* [1962] R.P.C. 243, [1962] C.L.Y. 3042; *Baume and Co Ltd v. AH Moore Ltd* [1958] R.P.C. 226, [1958] C.L.Y. 3416 followed; (2) if a company was generally known by a name and used that as its trade mark, it had a defence under s.8(a), even if that name was not its registered corporate title. MI might well establish a defence by proving that Mercury was the usual name by which the company or the products were known in the marketplace. This was a question of fact, which could not be decided on an application for summary judgment, *Parker-Knoll Ltd v. Knoll International Ltd* [1962] R.P.C. 243, [1962] C.L.Y. 3042; *Baume and Co Ltd v. AH Moore Ltd* [1958] R.P.C. 226, [1958] C.L.Y. 3416 considered; (3) there was a strong argument that a registration simply for computer software would normally be too wide. MI also had a significant prospect of succeeding, in forcing MC to restrict the scope of registration for lack of use and (4) MI had an arguable defence to allegations of infringement and a significant prospect of forcing MC to restrict the scope of the trade mark registration.

MERCURY COMMUNICATIONS LTD v. MERCURY INTERACTIVE (UK) LTD [1995] F.S.R. 850, Laddie, J., Ch D.

5711. Isle of Man

TRADE MARKS ACT 1994 (ISLE OF MAN) ORDER 1996, SI 1996 729; made under the Trade Marks Act 1994 s.108. In force: April 1, 1996; £1.10.

Amends Consumer Protection (Trade Descriptions) Act 1970; Copyright Act 1991; Design Right Act 1991; Consumer Protection Act 1991 (all Acts of Tynwald–Isle of Man). This Order specifies the exceptions and modifications to which the Trade Marks Act 1994 extends, by virtue of s.108(2), to the Isle of Man.

5712. Newspapers–banner device marks–no evidence of confusion–alternative usage of word "European" on two publications

[Trade Marks Act 1938; Trade Marks Act 1994 s.10.]

P was the proprietor of a device mark registered under the Trade Marks Act 1938 depicting a newspaper banner consisting of the words "The European". P used the mark on a weekly newspaper which had been published since May 1990 and which had a circulation of approximately 165,000. In October 1995, D started publishing a weekly newspaper upon which appeared a sign, in the form of a device, the prominent part of which consisted of the words "European Voice". The paper had a specialist readership of 200-300 amongst European Union officials. P sought an undertaking from D that it would not use the word European in the title. When such an undertaking was not forthcoming, P sued for trade mark infringement under the

Trade Marks Act 1994. P argued that there was a similarity between its mark and D's sign such as to constitute infringement under s.10(2) of the 1994 Act. P relied on the fact that the essential part of its mark was the word European which was also the first part of D's sign. It also relied on evidence of confusion, based on surveys and queries received about the "European Voice" at its offices.

Held, dismissing the action, that (1) P's device mark and D's sign were not similar. The prominent part of D's sign was the word "Voice" with the word "European" being simply a descriptive adjective not bestowing similarity; (2) P's contention in relation to the essential feature of its mark failed. The word "European" was not a distinctive made up word. It was an ordinary word in common use. In the absence of evidence of confusion, D's title was not similar to P's trade mark and its use could not constitute infringement within s.10(2) of the 1994 Act, *De Cordova v. Vick Chemical Company* (1951) 68 R.P.C. 103 and *Wagamama Ltd v. City Centre Restaurants Plc* [1995] F.S.R. 713, [1996] C.L.Y. 5716 considered and (3) considering the evidence of confusion, P had not established its case. The evidence of calls to P's office did not demonstrate confusion. Evidence from newspaper editors was no more useful or valid than the court's own view. Further, the results of survey evidence were of little, if any, help on the question of the likely reaction of customers in the market place. Although some of the respondents to the survey had come to court to give evidence, their evidence did not establish anything. *Guccio Gucci SpA v. Paolo Gucci* [1991] F.S.R. 89, [1992] C.L.Y. 4437 considered and *Imperial Group Plc v. Philip Morris Ltd* [1984] R.P.C. 293 followed.

EUROPEAN LTD v. ECONOMIST NEWSPAPERS LTD [1996] F.S.R. 431, Rattee, J., Ch D.

5713. Packaging–trade mark proprietor consenting to goods bearing trade mark being placed on market in a Member State–parallel importer placing goods in new external packaging to which trade mark affixed–European Union

[Treaty of Rome 1957 Art. 30, Art. 36; Council Directive 89/104 to approximate the laws of Member States relating to trade marks Art. 7.]

BM and other pharmaceutical trade mark owners opposed the importation and sale of pharmaceutical products, bearing their trade marks, which had been placed on the market in another Member State with their consent, but where the parallel importer had subsequently repackaged the goods without the owner's consent. The Danish and German courts requested preliminary rulings from the ECJ in order to determine whether, and within what limits, it was compatible with EU law for the trade mark owner to exercise its national trade mark rights.

Held, that (1) the position of repackaged goods under the Treaty of Rome 1957 Art.30 and Art.36 and under Council Directive 89/104 Art.7 were the same; (2) where goods bearing a trade mark were placed on the open market in a Member State, with the consent of the trade mark owner and bought by another person who placed them in external packaging bearing the trade mark, before marketing them in another Member State, the trade mark owner could not invoke it to prevent such marketing, unless the repackaging was capable of affecting the goods' original condition or impaired the reputation of the mark, *Hoffman La Roche v. Centrafarm (C102/77)* [1978] E.C.R. 1139, [1978] C.L.Y. 1406 and *Pfizer v. Eurim-Pharm (1/81)* [1981] E.C.R. 2913 applied; (3) the repackager must inform the trade mark owner of his intention and provide a specimen repackaged product. Responsibility for the repackaging must be shown on the product, but the manufacturer or the fact that the trade mark owner has not authorised the repackaging need not be mentioned; (4) national courts were to determine how to apply the principles, subject to the following: if the parallel importer did not cut or open the original packaging and the condition of the goods was unlikely to be affected then an objection by the owner should not be allowed. However, if additions were made to the original goods or blister packaging was opened, creating a contamination risk or if the goods were repackaged in a shoddy manner, the owners' objections may be upheld; (5) where same strength products were sold in different Member States, a parallel importer could add an additional word, ensuring the name corresponds to the product; *Centrafarm v. American Home Products Corp (C3/78)* [1978] E.C.R. 1823, [1978] C.L.Y. 1258 distinguished; *IHT Internationale Heiztechnik v. Ideal Standard (C9/93)* [1994] E.C.R. I-2789, [1994] C.L.Y. 4870 applied, and (6) Directive 89/104 did not affect the question of where the burden of proof lies, which was a procedural matter for national courts which EU law should not make unduly difficult, *Deutsche Milchkontor v. Germany (C205/82)* [1983] E.C.R. 2633, [1984] C.L.Y. 1299 applied and *Enderby v. Frenchay HA (C127/92)* [1993] E.C.R. I-5535, [1994] C.L.Y. 4813 followed.

BRISTOL-MYERS SQUIBB v. PARANOVA (C427/93); EURIM-PHARM v. BEIERSDORF; MPA PHARMA v. RHONE-POULENC [1996] F.S.R. 225, FG Jacobs, AGO.

5714. Passing off–court would not countenance a pre-emptive strike of registering a company with names where others had the goodwill in those names–injunction requiring registered name of company to be changed granted though registered company had not traded

[Companies Act 1985.]

The plaintiffs, P1 and P2, made an interlocutory application for a mandatory order that the defendants D1, D2 and D3, should procure a change in D1's name to one not including the words "Glaxo", "Wellcome" or any other confusingly similar words. P1 and P2 were leading pharmaceutical companies, both with a world-wide reputation and goodwill in their respective names. On January 23, 1995 a press release announced a take-over bid by P1 for P2, which stated that if the bid was successful P1 would be renamed Glaxo Wellcome Plc. On January 24, 1995, D3 a company registration agent, filed an application to register D1 under the name of Glaxowellcome Ltd. When Ps' solicitors discovered the Glaxowellcome registration they tried to persuade D2 and D3 to sell D1 to the Ps at D3's standard price for a shelf company of £1,000. However, in a without prejudice letter, the Ds demanded the sum of £100,000. D3 contended that he had acted totally honestly and did not intend D1 to trade under its registered name or to exploit the choice of name. He claimed that the registration was planned prior to the merger notice and that the name had been chosen without the existence of either of the Ps in mind.

Held, granting the injunction, that (1) the Ds' picture of events would be rejected. The Ds were engaged in a dishonest scheme to appropriate the Ps' goodwill in the names Glaxo and Wellcome, and to extort a substantial sum for not damaging it; (2) the Ds' letter was not truly without prejudice, because it was plainly not a bona fide effort to settle the dispute but a threat to damage the Ps unless the totally unwarranted sum demanded was paid; (3) the court would not countenance a pre-emptive strike of registering a company with names where others had the goodwill in those names. The registration was an abuse of the system of registering companies' names. However, the party prejudiced was not obliged to use the sometimes protracted procedure under the Companies Act 1985 which enabled the Registrar of Companies to require names to be changed. In an action for passing off, an injunction requiring the registered name of the company to be changed would be granted even if the registered company had not traded and (4) in the past, injunctions had been granted in a negative form, restraining the company from continuing to be registered in its existing name. In cases such as this, it was better to grant an express mandatory injunction requiring the company and subscribers to take all such steps as lay within their power to change or facilitate the change of name.

GLAXO PLC v. GLAXOWELLCOME LTD [1996] F.S.R. 388, Lightman, J., Ch D.

5715. Passing off–evidence of confusion and deception

G were restrained from passing off their cosmetics and toiletries as those of N by using the trade mark "Neutralia" and any colourable imitation or infringement of N's "Neutrogena" trade mark. G appealed, arguing that: (a) the judge had adopted too low a test as to the likelihood of deception or confusion in respect of whether N's mark had been infringed, or to establish liability for passing off and (b) there was insufficient evidence to establish sufficient confusion or deception by the use of G's mark. Both product ranges were for hypo-allergenic preparations.

Held, dismissing the appeal, that (1) the judge was right to conclude that the confusion was substantial and the effect on N's goodwill was real. The correct legal principles to be followed were as stated in *Reckitt & Colman Products Ltd v. Borden* [1990] R.P.C. 341, [1990] C.L.Y. 3465. The question was whether a substantial number of members of the public would be deceived into buying G's products assuming they were N's; (2) it was inappropriate to construe a reserved judgment by reference to a judge's observations during or after a trial. In any event, it could not be said that the judge's observations meant that he construed the words "a substantial number" and "real" as meaning "more than de minimis" or "above a trivial level" and there was no reason to suppose that he reduced the required standard. In general terms, it was better to avoid the latter pair of expressions because of the risk of misinterpretation, and (3) there was evidence which demonstrated, on the balance of probabilities, that substantial numbers of the public would have been confused. The judge had approached the issue as a "jury question", *GE Trade Mark, Re* [1973] R.P.C. 297, [1972] C.L.Y. 3435 followed. The evidence consisted of: (a) 320 complaints about a television advertisement considered offensive, of which 26 demonstrated confusion; (b) five witnesses who had communicated with N; (c) a representative witness from some 300 who had contacted G; (d) the staff of N's solicitors; (e) interviews with 131 consumers of whom 11 gave evidence for N. The evidence showed confusion arising from the first five letters of both marks being the same.

NEUTROGENA CORP v. GOLDEN LTD (T/A GARNIER) [1996] R.P.C. 489, Morritt, L.J., CA.

5716. Passing off–likelihood of confusion between WAGAMAMA and RAJAMAMA oriental theme restaurants–Trade Marks Act 1994 and Council Directive 89/104 did not create enlarged basis of infringement

[Trade Marks Act 1994 s.10; Council Directive 89/104 on trade marks Art.5.]

W had operated a successful Japanese style noodle bar in London since 1992 under the name WAGAMAMA and was the proprietor of a number of trade and service marks consisting of that word. W owned a significant reputation in the mark. In April 1995 CC opened a restaurant in London serving Indian style food called RAJAMAMA. W commenced proceedings for trade mark infringement and passing off. CC then changed the name of the restaurant to RAJAMAMA'S. W's argument, based on the Trade Marks Act 1994 which implemented Council Directive 89/104, was that s.10 of the 1994 Act introduced to the UK an enlarged basis for infringement. W asserted that under s.10 infringement included confusion in the classical sense and also a mere association between marks even if there was no possibility of a misunderstanding as to the origin of particular goods or services.

Held, finding that trade mark infringement on the classical basis and passing off had been established, *Ravenhead Brick Co v. Ruabon Brick Co* (1937) 54 R.P.C. 341; *Origins Natural Resources Inc v. Origin Clothing Ltd* [1995] F.S.R. 280, [1995] 2 C.L.Y. 4940 followed, that (1) there was no reason to conclude that the words of s.10(2) to the effect that likelihood of confusion "includes the likelihood of association with the trade mark" must have been included in order to enlarge the scope of infringement. Viewed solely from a linguistic standpoint, the words of s.10(2) pointed away from W's argument, *Hill v. William Hill (Park Lane) Ltd* [1949] A.C. 530, [1947-1951] C.L.C. 4259 considered and (2) the scope of infringement had not been enlarged so as to cover mere association between marks where there was no possibility of a misunderstanding as to the origin of the goods or services. There was little commercial justification for the broader interpretation and both the Act and Council Directive 89/104 Art.5 were consistent with the narrower interpretation.

WAGAMAMA LTD v. CITY CENTRE RESTAURANTS PLC [1995] F.S.R. 713, Laddie, J., Ch D.

5717. Passing off–school assuming similar name to Harrods–need to prove that connection would lead to public confusion–no obvious risk of damage to business

Harrods, H, appealed against the dismissal of their passing off action against the Harrodian School, which was founded upon the site of the Harrodian Club, which had been a sports club for employees of H since 1929. H argued that their name had been taken deliberately to benefit from the goodwill generated by their business and that their reputation would be damaged as a result.

Held, dismissing the appeal, that in order to establish the tort of passing off it was necessary to show that there was a clear risk of damage to a plaintiff's business due to a confusion with another product. The likelihood of damage without such confusion was not sufficient as the focus of the tort was not the protection of a famous name but the value of the goodwill generated. In the circumstances the two fields of activity were sufficiently disparate to avoid confusion in the minds of the public, *Taittinger SA v. Allbev Ltd* [1993] F.S.R. 64, [1994] C.L.Y. 4491 considered.

HARRODS LTD v. HARRODIAN SCHOOL [1996] R.P.C. 697, Millett, L.J., CA.

5718. Register of trade marks–removal–clothing labels–company name–mark invalidated for non-use

[Trade Marks Act 1938 s.30, s.35.]

A applied for removal from the register of P's registration of the trade mark Orient Express in respect of clothing on the ground that there had been no bona fide use of the mark in the UK for a continuous period of 5 years. P relied on evidence from its President that clothing was supplied to him from P's suppliers bearing a label showing the Orient Express mark, and exhibited nine invoices. However, none of the invoices referred to the mark, but all referred to the mark Hunting World. The hearing officer on behalf of the Registrar ordered removal of the mark from the register. The hearing officer found that use of the words "Orient Express Trading Company Ltd" on swing labels was not use of the trade mark Orient Express. Whilst he said the position might have been different had there been evidence from the trade that the full company name was used and recognised as a trade mark, there was no such evidence before him. On an application for directions as to the hearing of P's appeal, A sought an order for cross-examination of one of P's witnesses. The application was refused and the appeal was heard with the same material as was before the hearing officer.

Held, dismissing the appeal, that (1) A had made out a prima facie case of non-use to the effect that extensive enquiries disclosed that P had no business premises, distributor or agency in the UK and had made no use of the mark for at least 5 years. The burden was therefore then on P to adduce evidence of bona fide use during the 5 year period; (2) the mark had not been used on its own in relation to the goods. The hearing officer was entitled to conclude that the words "Orient Express" were used as part of the corporate name to identify P, and were not used as a trade mark. That was a question of fact to be decided in every case. The fact that the words Orient Express were slightly larger and more prominent than the rest of the words in the corporate name did not constitute use in a trade mark sense, *Pompadour Laboratories Ltd v. Stanley Frazer* [1966] R.P.C. 7 and *Duracell International Inc v. Ever Ready Ltd* [1989] F.S.R. 71, [1989] C.L.Y. 3686 considered and (3) the hearing officer was right in his approach under the Trade Marks Act 1938 s.30. He concluded that the Registrar would not have allowed an amendment from Orient Express to Orient Express Trading Company Limited under s.35(1) of the Act because the additional words would substantially affect the identity of the mark. This was a relevant consideration when construing and applying s.30(1).

ORIENT EXPRESS TRADE MARK, *Re* [1996] R.P.C. 1, Mummery, J., Ch D.

5719. Registration

TRADE MARKS (INTERNATIONAL REGISTRATION) ORDER 1996, SI 1996 714; made under the Trade Mark Act 1994 s.54. In force: April 1, 1996; £3.20.

The Order gives effect in the UK to the Protocol relating to the Madrid Agreement concerning the International Registration of Marks adopted at Madrid on June 27, 1989 (the Madrid Protocol) which the UK ratified on April 6, 1995. The arrangements made under the Madrid Protocol become effective on April 1, 1996 and the Order comes into force on that date. The Madrid Protocol provides that the proprietor of, or the applicant for, a national registration of a trade mark may apply through the national trade marks office for a registration of that trade mark in the International Register of the International Bureau of the World Intellectual Property Organisation (WIPO). Protection for an international registration may be requested in any other contracting state to the Madrid Protocol by the holder of the international registration. Where protection is requested in respect of an international registration originating in another contracting state, the state in respect of which protection is requested is entitled to refuse protection where the international registration cannot be granted on the grounds which would apply under the International Convention for the Protection of Industrial Property (Cmnd. 4431). Provided that no refusal has been notified to the International Bureau, contracting states are required to accord the same protection to the international registration of the trade mark as if the trade mark had been registered with the trade mark office of that contracting state.

5720. Registration–fees

TRADE MARKS (INTERNATIONAL REGISTRATION) (FEES) RULES 1996, SI 1996 715; made under the Department of Trade and Industry (Fees) Order 1988; and the Trade Marks Act 1994 s.53, s.54, s.79. In force: April 1, 1996; £1.10.

Fees payable for matters arising under the Trade Marks (International Registration) Order 1996 (SI 1996 714), which implements the Madrid Protocol, are prescribed by these Rules. Provision is made for handling fees for submission of applications for international registration originating in the UK, for handling fees for the transmission by the Patent Office of monies payable to the International Bureau for the renewal of international registrations, fees for transformation applications, fees for the recording of concurrent registrations, fees relating to the supplementary register maintained by the registrar for recording transactions relating to international trade marks, fees for the revocation or invalidation of protected international trade marks and for forms required by the registrar for the payment of prescribed fees.

5721. Registration–oppositions–disclaimers–generic phrase included in mark–proprietorship–confusing similarity–cooking utensils

[Trade Marks Act 1938 s.11, s.12, s.17.]

P applied to register as a trade mark the mark Paton Calvert Cordon Bleu in respect of household and kitchen utensils. Remaud Cointreau et Cie, R, used the mark Cordon Bleu in respect of cookery schools in London, Paris and elsewhere, had the registered mark Constance Spry Cordon Bleu in respect of household and kitchen utensils and had applied to register the mark Le Cordon Bleu in respect of cookery courses. R opposed P's application under the Trade Marks Act 1938 s.11, s.12(1), s.12(3) and s.17(1).

Held, allowing the application to proceed to registration, that (1) P had not applied to register Cordon Bleu as a "name", but rather the mark Paton Calvert Cordon Bleu, and had specifically disclaimed any rights in the words Cordon Bleu. The clash between the parties' marks therefore was not a dispute over ownership under s.17(1) of the Act, but over confusingly similar marks. The phrase Cordon Bleu was in the public domain and therefore the objection under s.17(1) failed; (2) an opposition could be brought on the basis of similarity arising from a disclaimed element in a mark, *GRANADA Trade Mark, Re* [1979] R.P.C. 303, [1979] C.L.Y. 2681 considered; (3) with respect to the opposition under s.11, there was no evidence of use of R's marks in the UK, save in respect of the cookery school. Whilst there were indications that R's cookery school had a good reputation and was associated with many publications on high quality French cuisine, it was not sufficient to displace the ordinary dictionary definition of the words Cordon Bleu as denoting high standards, particularly in the culinary arts. There was no evidence of actual confusion. There was no likelihood that confusion would arise between P's use for kitchen utensils and R's use for cookery schools and publications. There was also no inherent risk of confusion since P's use of the words Cordon Bleu was no more than an indication that P thought its goods were of good quality. The opposition under s.11 therefore failed, *Smith Hayden & Co Ltd's Application, Re* (1946) 63 R.P.C. 97 applied; (4) P's mark and R's registered mark were both visually and phonetically easily distinguishable and so the opposition under s.12(1) failed, *Pianotist Co's Application, Re* (1906) 23 R.P.C. 774 applied and (5) P's mark and R's application for Le Cordon Bleu were also both visually and phonetically distinguishable, with the only common elements being a dictionary phrase which was descriptive, generic and laudatory. Indications given by evidence of user were relevant when considering s.12(3) and it was therefore also relevant that there had been no actual confusion. The opposition under s.12(3) therefore also failed.

PATON CALVERT CORDON BLEU TRADE MARK, *Re* [1996] R.P.C. 94, MJ Tuck, TMR.

5722. Registration–oppositions–fresh evidence–admissibility–whether mark was deceptive–beverages

[Trade Marks Act 1938 s.18.]

H applied for registration of the mark Swiss Miss in respect of chocolate drink mixes. The application was opposed by Chocosuisse, C, an association of Swiss chocolate manufacturers, who claimed that the mark would be deceptive unless a condition were imposed that the goods must come from Switzerland. The opposition was dismissed. C appealed and sought leave to file further evidence that in the United States H's Swiss Miss products were sold in packaging with Swiss motifs, that Swiss chocolate firms sold cocoa in the United Kingdom and a small informal survey of consumer opinion showed people believed the mark had a Swiss connection.

Held, admitting some of the further evidence, that the authorities did not disclose a uniform approach to the exercise of the Court's discretion under the Trade Marks Act 1938 s.18(8) in considering whether to admit further evidence on appeal. *Ladd v. Marshall* [1954] 1 W.L.R. 1489, [1954] C.L.Y. 2507 concerned private litigation, whereas an opposition might determine whether or not a new statutory monopoly was created, affecting all traders in the country. Further, if the evidence was excluded and the opponent failed, he would be able to return again in separate rectification proceedings. To admit the evidence at the appeal stage could therefore avoid a multiplicity of proceedings. Moreover, the hearing before the High Court was a rehearing. It was therefore appropriate to look at all the circumstances, including the factors set out in *Ladd v. Marshall* and the public interest in not allowing registration of invalid marks. Most of the factors pointed towards allowing the further evidence, although there was one factor which went the other way, namely that C was aware of the evidence at the time of the original hearing. Nevertheless, the overall balance was in favour of allowing the further evidence except the consumer opinion survey. Evidence of a survey carried out amongst the staff of C's solicitors was so insubstantial as to be almost valueless and was not admitted.

Observed, the practice of inviting the Registrar to write stating whether any of the new evidence raised any point of public interest which was not considered at the hearing, which was suggested in *Oxon Italia SPA's Trade Mark Application, Re* [1981] F.S.R. 408, [1981] C.L.Y. 2772, was of little value, since the Registrar had not heard what the parties' arguments were and in any event had a right to appear on the hearing, and should no longer be followed.

HUNT-WESSON INC'S TRADE MARK APPLICATION, *Re* [1996] R.P.C. 233, Laddie, J., Ch D.

5723. **Service marks – registration – oppositions – telecommunications consultancy–confusing similarity to registered mark–foreign judgments–estoppel**

[Trade Marks Act 1938 s.10, s.11, s.12.]

ITG applied for registration of the service mark International Telesis Group in Part B in respect of consultancy services relating to voice and data telecommunications. PTI had registrations of its own mark Pacific Telesis International in three classes in respect of telecommunications apparatus and services. PTI opposed ITG's application. A dispute between the parties in respect of service marks in the USA had been resolved in PTI's favour and the evidence and findings in those proceedings were considered by the Registrar.

Held, refusing the application under the Trade Marks Act 1938 s.12(1), that (1) ITG was not estopped from claiming use of the mark Telesis in the UK prior to October 1985, despite the fact that ITG's President had declared in the US proceedings that the first use of the mark International Telesis Group in the USA was in October 1985, since the US Court made no finding on use outside the USA; (2) the inclusion of common words such as "International" and "Group" in a mark was no bar to registration, even though there were many marks on the register including those words. The word "Telesis" was not descriptive of telecommunications systems. ITG's mark was therefore capable of distinguishing ITG's services, and so the opposition under s.10 of the 1938 Act failed; (3) since both marks contained the word "Telesis", any possibility of distinguishing the two marks must arise if at all from the remaining words. The word "Group" strongly implied a connection between the two marks. The marks were therefore confusingly similar, *Smith Hayden & Co Ltd's Application, Re* (1946) 63 R.P.C. 97, *Berlei (UK) v. Bali Brassiere Co* [1969] R.P.C. 472, [1969] C.L.Y. 3565 and *Pianotist Co's Application, Re* (1906) 23 R.P.C. 774 considered; (4) PTI's evidence did not support a claim to any significant reputation in PTI's mark in the UK at the material time, but neither had there been any significant use of ITG's mark. Since the marks were confusingly similar, the absence of evidence of actual confusion meant that one or both of the marks had not been used sufficiently so as to make an instance of confusion likely and the opposition under s.11 therefore failed; (5) consultancy services relating to telecommunications fell within the term telecommunications services and therefore the services covered by the two marks were identical, or services of the same description. Similarly, ITG's consultancy services were sufficiently similar to be associated with PTI's goods, since there was evidence that suppliers of telecommunications equipment also supplied consultancy services. Since the two marks were confusingly similar, the opposition under s.12(1) succeeded *Jellinek's Application, Re* (1946) 63 R.P.C. 59 considered, and (6) there was considerable doubt whether there had been any real honest concurrent use and therefore PTI could not claim the benefits of s.12(2).

INTERNATIONAL TELESIS GROUP SERVICE MARK, *Re* [1996] R.P.C. 45, Alison Brimelow, TMR.

5724. **Articles**

A new European system for protection of names and marks *(Iain C. Baillie)*: S.J. 1996, 140(13), 334-336. (Importance of registration under the Community trade mark registration system in force April 1, 1996 to protect trade marks in three or more EU Member States).

Adducing further evidence on appeal from the Trade Marks Registry *(Katharine Stephens)*: C.I.P.A.J. 1996, 25(1), 48-49. (Consideration of factors other than those set out in Ladd v Marshall).

British Sugar Plc v James Robertson and Sons and other recent decisions on the Trade Marks Act 1994 *(Kevin Mooney)*: C.L. 1996, 1(7), 64-65. (Infringement provisions and honest practices defence reviewed in three cases and practical and commercial consequences of decisions).

Comparative advertising limitations in the UK *(Nicholas Macfarlane)*: M.I.P. 1996, 60, 27-29. (Interpretation of s.10(6) of 1994 Act on whether use of trade mark in comparative advertisement was honest and whether interlocutory relief appropriate).

Fair credit? Comparative advertising post Barclays Bank Plc v RBS Advanta *(John M. Benjamin)*: Ent. L.R. 1996, 7(4), 135-136. (Test for "honest practices" when considering whether trade mark has been infringed by its use in competitor's comparative advertising campaign).

Honest practices in comparative advertising *(Ronald Farrants)*: B.L.E. 1996, 96(6), 7-8. (Whether comparative advertising required fair comparison with rivals and criteria for grant of injunction in such cases).

How important are Internet domain names to trade mark owners? *(Ken Moon)*: C.T.L.R. 1996, 2(3), 79-81. (Need to put into perspective unauthorised use of trade marks as Internet addresses and how problem can be treated within existing legal framework).

Likelihood of association: what does it mean? *(Charles Gielen)*: T.W. 1996, 84, 20-23. (EU criteria for judging whether trade marks confuse or conflict).

Making sense of trademarks: an international survey of non-visual marks *(Daniel Zendel* and *Dennis S. Prahl)*: T.W. 1996, 89, 21-26. (Protection of colour, scent and sound marks in various jurisdictions).

Multinational trademark protection in the European Union *(Alexander Nette)*: T.W. 1996, 86, 22-26. (Competing protection systems of Community trade mark and Protocol to Madrid Agreement and advantages and disadvantages of each).

Names on the Internet: their position in English law *(Nick Gardner)*: C.L. 1996, 1(10), 55. (Problems of individuals using Internet domain names which are registered trade marks).

Pharmaceuticals: the requirement of a single mark for the European Union *(Richard Gilbey)*: T.W. 1996, 90, 19-24. (Whether CEC requirement for single mark for medicines to be authorised is justifiable, whether is contrary to objectives of Regulation 2309/93 and difficulties in obtaining single global marks).

Same old tricks or something new? A view of trade mark licensing and quality control *(Neil J. Wilkof)*: E.I.P.R. 1996, 18(5), 261-270. (Role of trade mark licensing based on quality control in relation to grey market importation, effect of insolvency on licence and continuing role of quality control in protecting licence based business).

The case for amending the EU franchise block exemption *(Mark Abell)*: T.W. 1996, 84, 29-32. (Inconsistencies in Regulation and desirable changes for protecting integrity of brand names and trade marks).

The Community trade mark *(E. Susan Singleton)*: C.S.R. 1996, 20(5), 33-34. (Advantages of CTM, what can be registered, generic marks, functions of Community Trade Mark Office, duration and infringement).

The Community Trade Mark *(Susie Middlemiss* and *Jeremy Phillips)*: P.L.C. 1996, 7(4), 39-44. (Internationalisation of trade mark protection with particular reference to EC harmonisation of national laws and introduction of Community Trade Mark).

The convergence of rights: co-existence of copyright and other intellectual property rights with registered trade marks following the Trade Marks Act 1994 *(Susan Hall)*: C.W. 1996, 58, 35-38.

The judgments to date *(Michael Silverleaf)*: C.L. 1996, 1(4), 34-35. (Important judgments which consider effect of provisions of 1994 Act).

The riddle of well-known marks and other goodwill carriers *(Basile Catomeris)*: T.W. 1995/96, 83, 20-23. (WIPO Committee of Experts convened to consider definition of well known trade marks with particular regard to Art.6 and methods for improving protection for such marks).

The Trade Marks Act: the story so far: C.L. 1996, 1(4), 33-34. (Treatment of applications for new style trade marks since 1994 Act came into force).

Trade mark agreements and EC law *(Elizabeth McKnight)*: E.I.P.R. 1996, 18(5), 271-278. (Application of exhaustion of rights rules to trademarks and of competition rules to agreements for licensing, assignment or delimitation of trade marks).

Trade marks: nothing ventured, nothing gained *(Christopher Benson)*: I.H.L. 1996, 44(Oct), 35-37. (Increase in trade mark applications following extension of scope of registration under 1994 Act to include shapes, colours, sounds and smells as well as marketing slogans).

Trade marks: the repackaging problem: Euro. L.M. 1996, 4(9), 10-11. (Whether trade mark owner distributing goods bearing its mark in EC can prevent repackaging and resale of goods to another EC Member State).

Trade marks: the right to repackage: Euro. L.M.1996, 4(9), 11-12. (Circumstances in which it is lawful to repackage goods distributed in EC Member States without any change of mark).

Trademark infringement in the United Kingdom *(Mark Antingham)*: T.W. 1996, 91, 26-34. (Case law interpreting effect 1994 of Act).

Trademark protection throughout the EU *(Taylor Joynson Garrett)*: I.H.L. 1996, 40(May), 65-66. (Advantages and disadvantages of protecting trade marks under Community Trade Mark system).

Trademark use on the Internet *(Mary M. Squyres)*: T.W. 1996, 85, 30-33. (Analysis by country of protection afforded to trademarks on Internet and World Wide Web and need to register trade marks in more than one country).

Trademarks in cyberspace *(Mark F. Radcliffe* and *Maureen S. Dorney)*: T.W. 1996, 87, 18-21. (Registration and use of domain names on Internet, registration through InterNIC, extent to which can be protected as trademark and dispute policy of InterNIC).

UK trade mark law: recent developments *(Peter J. Groves)*: Bus. L.R. 1996, 17(8/9), 167-169. (Significant cases since enactment of Trade Marks Act 1994 on confusion test, comparative advertising and similarity together with use of own name under 1938 Act).

Vested rights unbuttoned: section 11(3) Trade Marks Act 1994 *(Debrett Lyons)*: E.I.P.R. 1995, 17(12), 608-610. (Difficulties in interpretation of vested rights defence to trade marks infringement).

Wet Wet Wet–the sweet little mystery remains *(Clare Elliott)*: J.L.S.S. 1996, 41 (2), 63-65. (Whether use of pop group's name in book title was breach of trade mark).

"Wet? Wet?"–a little mystery unresolved? *(Charlotte Waelde)*: S.L.T. 1996, 1, 1-7. (Whether book using name of pop group was use "in a trade mark sense", whether sign identical to registered mark and whether infringing word used as description of character of goods).

Whither the pharmaceutical trade mark? *(Alan W. White)*: E.I.P.R. 1996, 18(8), 441-445. (Whether European Medicines Evaluation Agency (EMEA) proposal to require that branded medicines have trade mark protection throughout Europe before being licensed is justifiable or realistic).

5725. Books

Aufenanger, M.–Markengesetz/the German Trade Mark Act. Paperback: £31.50. ISBN 3-527-28804-X. VCH.

Inglis, Andrew; Heath, Guy–Using Trademarks in Business. Paperback: £19.99. ISBN 0-471-96670-3. Chancery Wiley Law Publications.

Michaels, Amanda–A Practical Guide to Trade Marks. Paperback: £26.00. ISBN 0-421-45200-5. Sweet & Maxwell.

TRADE UNIONS

5726. Ballots–industrial disputes–railways–determination of employees place of work–meaning of "occupied by employer"–statutory interpretation

[Trade Union and Labour Relations (Consolidation) Act 1992 s.228.]

IWC and another British Rail subsidiary, NWRR, had been granted leases by Railtrack Plc in respect of two separate buildings which they used as offices. As regards the operation of the train services, the companies had entered into formal access agreements which gave them a licence to use parts of Manchester Piccadilly station for the purposes of those services. An industrial dispute arose between the

RMT union and NWRR and IWC, which concerned those members of the union who were conductors and senior conductors employed by both companies. RMT balloted its members in a single ballot which produced a majority in favour of strike action. When notified of the result, IWC applied for an injunction to restrain the proposed action on the basis that it contravened the provisions of the Trade Union and Labour Relations (Consolidation) Act 1992 s.228. IWC contended that the conductors employed by the two companies did not have the "same place of work" within the meaning of s.228(4) of the 1992 Act because the companies occupied different buildings under exclusive leases and those buildings were the places of work of the employees in question. Accordingly, IWC argued that RMT should have conducted separate ballots for each place of work as required by s.228(1) of the Act. RMT submitted that the relevant place of work was the station itself, and that since both companies had been granted licences to use the station they "occupied" the station for the purposes of s.228(4). IWC obtained an injunction at first instance, and RMT appealed.

Held, allowing the appeal, that in construing s.228(4) of the 1992 Act it is essential to consider carefully the context of the legislation, which deals with industrial relations and the conduct of trade unions. Once it is accepted that the licence granted to IWC is a licence for its staff to use the station for the purpose of business, then, having regard to the business of the train operating company, it is clear that IWC "occupied" the station for the purposes of s.228(4). Similarly, the place at or from which the conductors work, within the meaning of s.228(4), is the operating part of the station itself and not merely the offices held by the two companies under leases.

INTERCITY WEST COAST LTD v. NATIONAL UNION OF RAIL, MARITIME AND TRANSPORT WORKERS [1996] I.R.L.R. 583, Neill, L.J., CA.

5727. Certification officer–fees

CERTIFICATION OFFICER (AMENDMENT OF FEES) REGULATIONS 1996, SI 1996 651; made under the Trade Union and Labour Relations (Consolidation) Act 1992 s.108, s.293. In force: April 1, 1996; £1.10.

These Regulations, which come into force on April 1, 1996, make alterations to the fees payable to the Certification Officer in respect of Trade Unions and Employers' Associations. These fees are altered as follows (a) the fee payable on application for approval of a proposed instrument of amalgamation or transfer of engagements is increased from £1543 to £1885; (b) the fee payable on an application for approval of a change of name is decreased from £89 to £84; (c) the fee for an inspection of documents kept by the Certification Officer in respect of amalgamation or transfers of engagements is increased from £43 to £44; (d) the fee for the entry of the name of an amalgamated organisation in the lists maintained by the Certification Officer where the name of each of the amalgamating organisations is already entered is increased from £51 to £52; (e) the fee on application by an organisation of workers to have its name entered in the list of trade unions maintained by the Certification Officer is increased from £132 to £134; (f) the fee on application by an organisation of employers to have its name entered on the list of employers' associations maintained by the Certification Officer is increased from £132 to £134; (g) the fee payable on an application by a trade union for a certificate of independence is increased from £2583 to £3761.

5728. Disciplinary procedures–amalgamation of trade unions–conduct prior to inception of new union–whether ultra vires

M and others were members of NALGO prior to the amalgamation of COHSE, NUPE and NALGO which resulted in the formation of the new trade union Unison. Complaints were made against the plaintiffs in relation to their conduct prior to the amalgamation whilst they were shop stewards for NALGO and a disciplinary hearing had been arranged. That hearing did not take place but the complainants stated that they wished proceedings to continue under the new rules of Unison. J, the General Secretary of Unison, instructed P to carry out an investigation into the complaints and J made an oral report of the investigation to the NEC. The NEC then agreed to convene a disciplinary subcommittee to hear charges against the plaintiffs. The plaintiffs were charged with disobeying any rules or regulations of the union, Rule I 2.1, acting in a manner prejudicial to the union, Rule I 2.2, and committing deliberate racist and sexist acts, Rule I 2.3. The hearings were adjourned after one day to enable the plaintiffs to apply for an interlocutory injunction to halt the proceedings. An injunction was granted on the basis that Unison was acting ultra vires in conducting the disciplinary proceedings since its rules made no provision for the hearing of charges in relation to pre inception conduct.

Held, granting the injunction in relation to charges under Rule I 2.3 but otherwise dismissing the applications, that (1) a court could imply into a union's rules a power to discipline or expel a member, although the court's power to imply such a term should be exercised with care and only when there were compelling circumstances to justify it. The decisions in *Dawkins v. Antrobus* [1881] 17 Ch. D. 615, *Abbott v. Sullivan* [1952] 1 K.B. 189, [1952] C.L.Y. 2748 and *Spring v. National Amalgamated Stevedores' and Dockers' Society* [1956] 1 W.L.R. 585, [1955] C.L.Y. 2146 could not be regarded as authority for the wide proposition that a power to discipline or expel could never be implied into a union's rules. The existence of an implied power to discipline for pre inception conduct must depend on the presumed intention of the parties. It would have been the expectation of the members that the union should be able to take disciplinary action against a member who had before amalgamation done something which contravened both the rules of his former union and the rules of Unison. To refuse to imply such a power would be contrary both to the expectations of the members and to common sense; (2) the scope of such an implied power should, however, be limited to the power to discipline members for conduct prior to the amalgamation when that member was at the time a member of one of the amalgamating unions and his conduct was contrary both to the rules of the amalgamating union and to the rules of Unison. Since Rule I 2.3 had no counterpart in the old NALGO rules no action could be taken against the plaintiffs under that Rule, and an injunction would be granted accordingly, and (3) although there had been a breach of the procedural rules for initiating investigations in that it was not open for J to initiate the investigation, in the circumstances no relief would be granted since no complaint was made about the manner in which P conducted the investigation and completed his report.

McVITAE v. UNISON [1996] I.R.L.R. 33, Harrison, J., Ch D.

5729. Industrial action–trade union policy–member expelled for breach of union policy–pressure to comply with policy did not amount to industrial action

[Trade Union and Labour Relations (Consolidation) Act 1992 s.65.]

Following the rejection by FBU of the use of retained contracts for full time fire fighters, the union's disciplinary committee recommended that K, a full time fire fighter, be expelled when he enrolled as a retained fire fighter. K appealed, contending that the FBU's policy of opposing the use of such contracts amounted to industrial action under the Trade Union and Labour Relations (Consolidation) Act 1992 s.65(2)(a).

Held, dismissing the appeal, that the question of what constituted industrial action was a mixture of fact and law, set in the context of the 1992 Act. On the facts K had been expelled 18 months after the policy was adopted. However, the policy itself did not require full-time fire fighters to breach their existing contracts of employment, merely to refrain from entering into additional retained contracts. Nothing showed that either the employers or the FBU contemplated that pressure on members to comply with the policy needed a ballot. Compliance with the policy by other members did not amount to an indication that the line had been crossed into industrial action within the meaning of s.65.

KNOWLES v. FIRE BRIGADES UNION [1996] 4 All E.R. 653, Neill, L.J., CA.

5730. Trade union membership–suspension–not an "exclusion" contrary to s.174(1) of the 1992 Act–suspension did not amount to constructive expulsion in absence of repudiatory breach acceptance

[Trade Union and Labour Relations (Consolidation) Act 1992 s.174.]

G was a member and official of the Midland Area Association of the trade union NACODS. NACODS passed a resolution to suspend the Midland Area Association from membership. The suspension was maintained beyond the maximum six month period provided for in the union's rule book. G continued to pay his contributions to the Midland Area Association, which held them as an agent for NACODS. An industrial tribunal found that G had been excluded or expelled from the trade union contrary to the Trade Union and Labour Relations (Consolidation) Act 1992 s.174(1).

Held, allowing the appeal by NACODS, that (1) the word "exclusion" in s.174(1) of the 1992 Act was limited to a refusal to admit a person to membership of a trade union and did not cover a mere suspension of the privileges of trade union membership, *Associated Newspapers v. Wilson* [1995] I.R.L.R. 258, [1995] C.L.Y. 1990 considered, and (2) there was no direct evidence of expulsion from NACODS and, even if constructive expulsion was capable of falling within s.174(1), there was no evidence that G had accepted the alleged repudiatory breach of contract on the part of NACODS by terminating his union membership.

NATIONAL ASSOCIATION OF COLLIERY OVERMEN, DEPUTIES AND SHOTFIRERS (NACODS) v. GLUCHOWSKI [1996] I.R.L.R. 252, Maurice Kay, J., EAT.

5731. Trade union membership–time off work for trade union duties–need for employer to know of request before can "fail to permit"

[Trade Union and Labour Relations (Consolidation) Act 1992 s.168, s.172.]

D, who worked as a plastic moulder for R and was a TGWU shop steward, was rostered to work a night shift from 6 p.m. to 6 am. D requested time off to attend a trade union conference and the industrial tribunal later found that there was no evidence that D had either been granted or refused permission. D left the shift at midnight and was only paid for the six hours he had worked. He made a complaint to an industrial tribunal claiming that R had failed to permit him to take reasonable time off for trade union duties under the Trade Union and Labour Relations (Consolidation) Act 1992 s.168(4) and that he was entitled to compensation in respect of wages deducted under s.172 of the 1992 Act. The tribunal upheld D's claim.

Held, allowing the appeal and remitting the matter to the same tribunal, that as a matter of construction s.168(4) of the 1992 Act plainly required that the employer should know of the request for time off before he could "fail to permit" time off within the meaning of the section. One could only "fail to permit" or "refuse to allow" something if one knew what was being asked. An employee had to establish that his request had come to the knowledge of the appropriated designated representative of the employer before he could say that the employer had failed to permit him to take time off. The matter should be remitted because the tribunal did not make any clear findings of fact on this issue.

RYFORD LTD v. DRINKWATER [1996] I.R.L.R. 16, C Smith Q.C., EAT.

5732. Trade union rules–election of officers and executive–decision of executive operated in breach of rules–rules disregarded where inconsistent with statutory requirements–statutory interpretation

[Trade Union and Labour Relations (Consolidations) Act 1992 s.49, s.51.]

At a meeting of its executive council in July 1995 USDAW decided that a candidate for election to the office of general secretary must be nominated by at least 25 of the union's branches in order to comply with the Trade Union and Labour Relations (Consolidations) Act 1992 s.51. At a second decision taken in November 1995 the national executive determined that, in order to take advantage of government funding for union elections which was to cease on March 31, 1996, ballots for the election of the president and to membership of the executive council should take place between December 1995 and the end of March 1996, but that the declaration of the results should be postponed until after the conclusion of USDAW's annual delegate meeting in April 1996. The effect of the second decision was that the newly elected officers would be unable to take office until the conclusion of the annual delegate conference in April 1997. A number of union members commenced proceedings seeking declarations that the decisions of the executive council were contrary to the union's rules and injunctions to restrain the implementation of those decisions. The applications were resisted by USDAW on the basis, inter alia, that individual members of the union did not have standing to complain of infringements of the rules.

Held, granting the relief sought, that (1) *Heatons Transport (St Helens) Ltd v. Transport and General Workers Union* [1972] I.C.R. 308, [1972] C.L.Y. 3452 applied, the source of the executive council's powers is the contract between all of the members as embodied in the rules of the union. Accordingly, the basis on which a member of the union agrees to be bound by a decision of the executive council is that those decisions will be made in accordance with the rules. If a decision is made in breach of the rules the right to complain about the breach is a contractual right individual to each member of the union, *Edwards v. Halliwell* [1950] 2 All E.R. 1064, [1947-1951] C.L.C. 10390 considered. The rule in *Foss v. Harbottle* (1843) 2 Hare 461 does not apply; (2) although several of the rules concerning the election of the general secretary were inconsistent with the requirements of Chapter IV Part 1 of the 1992 Act, that elections must be by a national vote of all members and effect cannot be given to those rules so long as that Act remains in force. The provision that all branches shall have the right to make nominations was not inconsistent with the statutory requirements and there was no need to disregard it; (3) the phrase "all branches shall have the right to make nominations" means that each branch could make a nomination and that nomination would then be voted upon in an election. The rules therefore provide that a candidate who secures the nomination of a single branch is eligible for election and the decision of the executive council that only candidates who had secured the nominations of 25 or more branches was in breach of the rules, and (4) the effect of the 1992 Act is that an election of union officers is complete when the scrutineer's report specifying the number of valid votes cast is delivered to the union, which in the instant case would be "as soon as is reasonably practicable" after voting ended on March 29, 1996. Declaration of the results does not impact on the completion of the election. The decision of the executive council to postpone the declaration of the result until April 29 was made for the purpose of achieving a particular objective regardless of practicality, and contravened the union's rules.

WISE v. UNION OF SHOP, DISTRIBUTIVE AND ALLIED WORKERS [1996] I.C.R. 691, Chadwick, J., Ch D.

5733. Articles

Collective labour law: current trends *(Martin Edwards)*: L. Ex. 1996, Jan, 10-11. (Developments concerning trade unions including offering of personal contracts to union members, establishment of European works councils and employer's duty to consult trade union on proposed redundancies).

Consulting your workforce: redundancies and business transfers *(Fraser Younson)*: P.L.C. 1996, 7(2), 41-45. (Provisions of new regulations extending obligation to inform or consult beyond those companies who recognise trade unions).

Some legal consequences of union derecognition *(Kenneth Miller)*: Jur. Rev. 1996, 1, 13-24. (Extent to which collective bargaining arrangements and individual employees' contractual or statutory rights may present obstacles to employers' plans to derecognise trade unions).

The productive route to EWC agreements *(John Monks)*: E.W.C.B. 1996, 4, 20. (Development of voluntary arrangements in UK, criticisms of those which are inconsistent with Directive and role of TUC as coordinating body).

Trade union and labour law *(David Antill)*: N.L.J. 1996, 146(6755), 1165-1166, 1170. (Threat posed to activities of trade unions by recent legal developments).

Trade union discrimination: IDS Brief 1996, 572, 7-12. (Extent of employees' and job applicants' right not to be victimised or dismissed on account of trade union membership or activities).

Trade union law: IDS Brief 1996, 556, 12-14. (Cases in 1995 on trade union discrimination, redundancy consultation and information, time off for union duties and industrial action ballots).

5734. Books

Barker, George R.–An Economic Analysis of Trade Unions and the Common Law. Hardback: £35.00. ISBN 1-85972-203-2. Avebury.

Undy, Roger–Managing the Unions. Hardback: £35.00. ISBN 0-19-828919-7. Oxford University Press.

TRANSPORT

5735. Bridges–canals

CITY OF STOKE-ON-TRENT (LICHFIELD STREET CANAL BRIDGE) SCHEME, 1995 CONFIRMATION INSTRUMENT 1996, SI 1996 74; made under the Highways Act 1980 s.106, s.108. In force: in accordance with Art.1; £1.10.

The City of Stoke-on-Trent (Lichfield Street Canal Bridge) Scheme 1995 is confirmed, with modifications, by this instrument. The Schedule details the scheme and a plan of the canal bridge attached.

5736. Canals–reclassification

BRITISH WATERWAYS BOARD (SHEFFIELD AND TINSLEY CANAL) (RECLASSIFICATION) ORDER 1996, SI 1996 2552; made under the Transport Act 1968 s.104. In force: November 6, 1996; £0.65.

This Order adds the Sheffield and Tinsley Canal to the list of cruising waterways in the Transport Act 1968 Sch.12 Part II.

5737. Carriage by rail–hazardous substances–labelling

CARRIAGE OF DANGEROUS GOODS (CLASSIFICATION, PACKAGING AND LABELLING) AND USE OF TRANSPORTABLE PRESSURE RECEPTACLES REGULATIONS 1996, SI 1996 2092; made under the Health and Safety at Work etc. Act 1974 s.15, s.43, s.82, Sch.3 para.1, Sch.3 para.3, Sch.3 para.4, Sch.3 para.6, Sch.3 para.16. In force: Reg.21 (9): January 1, 1999; Remainder: September 1, 1996; £7.40.

These Regulations impose requirements and prohibitions in relation to the classification, packaging and labelling of dangerous goods for carriage by road or on a railway. They repeal and re-enact with modifications the Carriage of Dangerous Goods by Road and Rail (Classification, Packaging and Labelling) Regulations 1994 (SI 1994 669). They implement Council Directive 94/55 ([1994] OJ L319/7) with regard to the transport of dangerous goods by road insofar as the Directive concerns classification, packaging and labelling of dangerous goods other than explosives and radioactive material and Council Directive 96/49 with regard to the transport of dangerous goods by rail insofar as the Directive concerns classification, packaging and labelling of dangerous goods other than explosives and radioactive material.

5738. Carriage by rail–hazardous substances–safety

CARRIAGE OF DANGEROUS GOODS BY RAIL REGULATIONS 1996, SI 1996 2089; made under the Health and Safety at Work etc. Act 1974 s.15, s.43, s.82, Sch.3 para.1, Sch.3 para.3, Sch.3 para.4, Sch.3 para.6, Sch.3 para.12, Sch.3 para.14, Sch.3 para.16. In force: September 1, 1996; £6.50.

These Regulations implement Council Directive 96/49 with regard to the transport of dangerous goods by rail, insofar as it relates to the transport of dangerous goods other than radioactive material. They impose requirements and prohibitions in relation to the carriage of dangerous goods by rail in a container, package, tank container, tank wagon or wagon. They revoke the Explosives Act 1875 s.35 to the extent specified, the Conveyance by Rail of Military Explosives Regulations 1977 (SI 1977 889) and the Carriage of Dangerous Goods by Rail Regulations 1994 (SI 1994 670).

5739. Carriage by rail–radioactive substances–labelling–safety

PACKAGING, LABELLING AND CARRIAGE OF RADIOACTIVE MATERIAL BY RAIL REGULATIONS 1996, SI 1996 2090; made under the Health and Safety at Work etc. Act 1974 s.15, s.82, Sch.3 para.1, Sch.3 para.3, Sch.3 para.4, Sch.3 para.5, Sch.3 para.8, Sch.3 para.12, Sch.3 para.13, Sch.3 para.14, Sch.3 para.15, Sch.3 para.16. In force: September 1, 1996; £6.30.

These Regulations implement Council Directive 96/49 with regard to the transport of dangerous goods by rail insofar as it relates to radioactive material and make provision for the carriage by rail of radioactive material.

5740. Carriage by road–explosives–safety

CARRIAGE OF EXPLOSIVES BY ROAD REGULATIONS 1996, SI 1996 2093; made under the Health and Safety at Work etc. Act 1974 s.15, s.82, Sch.3 para.1, Sch.3 para.3, Sch.3 para.4, Sch.3 para.6, Sch.3 para.7, Sch.3 para.12, Sch.3 para.15, Sch.3 para.16, Sch.3 para.20. In force: September 1, 1996; £6.00.

These Regulations impose requirements and prohibitions with regard to the carriage of explosives by road. They implement Council Directive 94/55 ([1994] OJ L319/7) with regard to the transport of dangerous goods by road, insofar as the Directive concerns explosives.

5741. Carriage by road–freight charges claim–cross claim for short delivery–whether cargo can be set off against freight charges

[Convention on the Contract for the International Carriage of Goods by Road (CMR) 1956.]

UC were carriers who were engaged by the retailers, HF, to transport and deliver Christmas hampers. UC brought proceedings against HF to claim their carrying charges. HF did not deny UC's claim but cross-claimed for short delivery and other breaches of contract by UC. The cross claims were greater than UC's claims and HF sought set off. The district judge held that the rule that there could be no set off in respect of cargo against freight charges in the context of carriage of goods by sea by charterparty applied here and therefore awarded judgment for UC without deduction. HF appealed that such a rule did not apply to this contract.

Held, allowing the appeal in part, that the rule that there could be no set off in respect of cargo against freight charges in the context of carriage of goods by sea by charterparty had consistently been applied to international carriage of goods by road under contracts subject to the Convention on the Contract for the International Carriage of Goods by Road 1956 and therefore should be considered as applying generally to the domestic carriage of goods by land. There was no reason why that rule should not apply to a series of journeys. The existence of ancillary obligations was not important so long as the contract could be characterised as one for carriage. UC were therefore entitled to judgment without deduction, *Aries Tanker Corp v. Total Transport Ltd* [1977] 1 All E.R. 398, [1977] C.L.Y. 2741 applied.

UNITED CARRIERS LTD v. HERITAGE FOOD GROUP (UK) LTD [1996] 1 W.L.R. 371, May, J., QBD.

5742. Carriage by road–hazardous substances–driver training

CARRIAGE OF DANGEROUS GOODS BY ROAD (DRIVER TRAINING) REGULATIONS 1996, SI 1996 2094; made under the Health and Safety at Work etc. Act 1974 s.15, s.43, s.82, Sch.3 para.3, Sch.3 para.4, Sch.3 para.6, Sch.3 para.14, Sch.3 para.16. In force: September 1, 1996; £3.20.

These Regulations impose duties on the operator and driver of a vehicle carrying dangerous goods with respect to the provision of instruction and training to the driver of the vehicle concerned. They re-enact, with modifications, the Road Traffic (Training of Drivers of Vehicles Carrying Dangerous Goods) Regulations 1992 (SI 1992 744) as amended. They also implement Council Directive 94/55 ([1994] OJ L319/7) on the transport of dangerous goods by road, insofar as the Directive concerns the instruction and training of drivers.

5743. Carriage by road–hazardous substances–safety

CARRIAGE OF DANGEROUS GOODS BY ROAD REGULATIONS 1996, SI 1996 2095; made under the Health and Safety at Work etc. Act 1974 s.15, s.43, s.82, Sch.3 para.1, Sch.3 para.3, Sch.3 para.4, Sch.3 para.6, Sch.3 para.9, Sch.3 para.12, Sch.3 para.14, Sch.3 para.15, Sch.3 para.16, Sch.3 para.20. In force: September 1, 1996; £8.50.

These Regulations implement Council Directive 94/55 on the approximation of the laws of the Member States with regard to the transport of dangerous goods by road, insofar as it relates to the transport of dangerous goods but not the classification, packaging and labelling of dangerous goods. They also implement European Parliament and Council Directive 94/63 on the control of volatile organic compound (VOC) emissions resulting from the storage of petrol and its distribution from terminals to service stations insofar as it relates to provisions for bottom loading and vapour recovery systems of mobile containers carrying petrol and the retention of vapours within such containers until reloading takes place at a terminal ([1994] OJ L365/24). They impose prohibitions on and requirements for the carriage of dangerous goods by road in any container, tank or vehicle. They revoke the Road Traffic (Carriage of Dangerous Substances in Packages etc.) Regulations 1992 (SI 1992 742) and the Road Traffic (Carriage of Dangerous Substances in Road Tankers and Tank Containers) Regulations 1992 (SI 1992 743).

5744. Carriage by road–radioactive substances–safety

RADIOACTIVE MATERIAL (ROAD TRANSPORT) (GREAT BRITAIN) REGULATIONS 1996, SI 1996 1350; made under the Radioactive Material (Road Transport) Act 1991 s.2. In force: June 20, 1996; £7.35.

These Regulations, which replace the Radioactive Substances (Carriage by Road) (Great Britain) Regulations 1974 (SI 1974 1735) and the Radioactive Substances (Carriage by Road) (Great Britain) (Amendment) Regulations 1995 (SI 1995 1729), make new provision for the transport of radioactive material by road in Great Britain. They implement the International Atomic Energy Agency Safety Series No.6 Regulations 1985 Edition as amended and additional requirements contained in the European Agreement concerning the International Carriage of Dangerous Goods By Road (ADR). They specify circumstances in which radioactive material can be transported by road, lay down standards for the design and testing of packages used, set maximum levels of radioactive contamination permitted on the surface of packaging, extend the use of quality assurance programmes, introduce consignment documentation and the requirement for vehicles to carry fire extinguishers, specify labelling requirements, lay down duties of a driver during transport and remove exemptions contained in the previous Regulations where in certain circumstances the driver or passenger are experienced in the handling of radioactive materials.

5745. Carriage by road–theft of lorry and semiconductor load–driver's conduct not amounting to wilful misconduct–recovery limited to CMR maximum

[Convention on the Contract for the International Carriage of Goods by Road (CMR) 1956 Art.29.]

A valuable cargo of semiconductors belonging to N was to be delivered by UPS to Milan. The driver of the vehicle carrying the semiconductors parked in a street while waiting for the time when the vehicle could be unloaded. He avoided an area where he knew it was unsafe to park and chose a well lit street, then went to eat at a restaurant from which he could not see the vehicle, contrary to company instructions. On his return, the vehicle had vanished. N claimed they were entitled to recover the full value of the cargo on the grounds of the wilful misconduct of the driver under the Convention on the Contract for the International Carriage by Goods by Road (CMR) 1956 Art.29.

Held, dismissing the application, that for wilful misconduct to be proved, there must be an intention to do something which the actor knew to be wrong or reckless in that the actor knew that loss might result from his act but did not care whether loss resulted or not. Recklessness involved somebody taking a risk he knew he ought not to take. On the facts, N had not established wilful misconduct. There was no conscious taking of risk at all by the driver. Since the Convention limit had already been paid, the action would be dismissed.

NATIONAL SEMICONDUCTORS (UK) LTD v. UPS LTD AND INTER CITY TRUCKS [1996] 2 Lloyd's Rep. 212, Longmore, J., QBD (Comm Ct).

5746. Carriage of goods–food

INTERNATIONAL CARRIAGE OF PERISHABLE FOODSTUFFS (AMENDMENT) REGULATIONS 1996, SI 1996 2765; made under the International Carriage of Perishable Foodstuffs Act 1976 s.3, s.4, s.19. In force: December 2, 1996; £0.65.

These Regulations change the daily fee charged under the International Carriage of Perishable Foodstuffs Regulations 1985 (SI 1985 1701 as amended by SI 1992 2682). The fee for testing units of transport equipment remains at £150. The fee for the use of facilities of a designated station for testing a unit of transport equipment is increased to £405. The fee for certifying a unit of transport equipment which has been tested remains unchanged at £50.

5747. Channel Tunnel–frontier controls

CHANNEL TUNNEL (INTERNATIONAL ARRANGEMENTS) (AMENDMENT) ORDER 1996, SI 1996 2283; made under the Channel Tunnel Act 1987 s.11. In force: October 2, 1996; £0.65.

This Order amends the Channel Tunnel (International Arrangements) Order 1993 (SI 1993 1813) so as to extend the provisions of primary and subordinate legislation relating to transport and road traffic frontier controls to the control zone in France within the tunnel system in the Channel Tunnel terminal at Frethun in France, in accordance with Art.8, Art.9 and Art.11 of the Protocol between the Government of the United Kingdom of Great Britain and Northern Ireland and the Government of the French Republic Concerning Frontier Controls and Policing, Cooperation in Criminal Justice, Public Safety and Mutual Assistance Relating to the Channel Fixed Link signed at Sangatte on November 25, 1991 (Cm 1802) which entered into force on August 2, 1993. A new paragraph is inserted in Art.7 (Enactments modified) so that any reference in those provisions of primary and subordinate legislation to road or public road is a reference to any part of the control zone.

5748. Channel Tunnel–railways

[Channel Tunnel Rail Link Act 1996.]

The Department of Transport issued a press release entitled *Channel Tunnel Rail Link Bill receives Royal Assent* (Press notice 400), published on December 18, 1996. Legislation authorising construction, operation and maintenance of the Channel Tunnel Rail Link and widening of the M23 between Junctions one and four has received Royal Assent. The 67 mile high speed railway is expected to stimulate regeneration of the areas surrounding the stations at Ebbsfleet and Stratford and the St Pancras terminus. The Private Finance Initiative project is being taken forward by London & Continental Railways.

5749. Channel Tunnel Rail Link Act 1996 (c.61)

The Act provides for the construction, maintenance and operation of a railway between St Pancras in London and the Channel Tunnel portal in Folkestone, Kent. It also provides for the improvement of the A2 at Cobham in Kent, and of the M2 between junctions 1 and 4, and makes provision with respect to compensation for blighted land.

This Act received Royal Assent on December 18, 1996.

5750. Compulsory purchase–bus stations

[South Yorkshire Passenger Transport Executive (Barnsley Interchange) Compulsory Purchase Order No.2 1992; Transport Act 1968 s.10.]

The Secretary of State confirmed the South Yorkshire Passenger Transport Executive, SY, (Barnsley Interchange) Compulsory Purchase Order No.2 1992 and YT moved for judicial review. The Passenger Executive had sought the order to incorporate a bus station owned by YT into a new transport interchange. It was contended that SY had no power to make the order nor the Secretary of State to confirm it and that his decision was inadequate in law.

Held, dismissing the application, that (1) under the Transport Act 1968 s.10(3), there was power to acquire land, even if that had the effect of acquiring an undertaking, not subject to s.10(1)(XVII), which provided for acquisition by agreement. SY wanted to create a more effective interchange rather than operate YT's bus station as their own, *Meravale Builders v. Secretary of State for the Environment* (1978) 36 P. & C.R. 87 considered. The Secretary of State had been entitled to conclude that nothing in the order would have the effect of inhibiting competition between bus companies in the area. Although an interchange did already exist, SY's actions were intended to offer facilities provided by no one else because the proposed interchange, fulfilling policy objectives, could only be achieved by SY taking the action it had. There was no discrimination against YT as holders of a public service vehicles operators licence. YT's land was chosen as the only suitable site; (2) there was nothing in a point that the Secretary of State had failed to have regard to YT's role in providing bus services. The provision of an interchange was clearly part of SY's business. The Secretary of State had performed the balancing exercise as between the public interest and YT's private interest. Once it was determined that an order was supported by relevant considerations, it was permissible to take other administrative factors into account in deciding whether to confirm an order, *Proctor and Gamble v. Secretary of State for the Environment* (1991) 63 P. & C.R. 317 considered. The onus had been on SY to demonstrate that it had sufficient resources to carry out the project, rather than on YT to prove otherwise although the Secretary of State's reasons could have been better expressed at that stage and (3) it was clear that the basis for the making of the order had been that the creation of an interchange of benefit to the public could only be achieved by compulsory purchase.

YORKSHIRE TRACTION CO LTD v. SECRETARY OF STATE FOR TRANSPORT [1996] E.G.C.S. 13, Popplewell, J., QBD.

5751. Concession schemes

TRAVEL CONCESSION SCHEMES (AMENDMENT) REGULATIONS 1996, SI 1996 2711; made under the Transport Act 1985 s.100. In force: December 1, 1996; £0.65.

These Regulations amend the Travel Concession Schemes Regulations 1986 (SI 1986 77) so as to remove an ambiguity in the wording of Reg.27 and to simplify the particulars required to be given under certain types of statutory notice relating to travel concession schemes and served or given under the Transport Act 1985 s.96 to s.99.

5752. Department of Transport–fees

DEPARTMENT OF TRANSPORT (FEES) (AMENDMENT) ORDER 1996, SI 1996 1961; made under the Finance (No.2) Act 1987 s.102. In force: July 23, 1996; £1.10.

This Order amends the Department of Transport (Fees) Order 1988 (SI 1988 643) in three respects. It makes further provision for the costs and expenses incurred by the Secretary of State in carrying out his functions relating to the approval of the design, construction, equipment and marking of vehicles and parts to be taken into account in the exercise of his power to prescribe changes for the provision of services and facilities in respect of such approval. It makes provision for the costs and expenses incurred by the Secretary of State in carrying out his functions relating to the plating and testing of goods vehicles to be taken into account in the exercise of his power to prescribe charges for altering the plated weights of vehicles without an examination. It makes provision for the costs and expenses incurred by the Secretary of State in carrying out his functions relating to driving tests to be taken into account in the exercise of his power to prescribe charges for the supply of forms providing evidence of the result of a driving test or a part of such a test.

5753. Driving–heavy goods vehicle–driver's hours–anticipatory derogation from regulations not permitted

[Treaty of Rome 1957 Art.177; Council Regulation 3820/85 Art.6, Art.7, Art.12.]

A reference to the European Court of Justice under the Treaty of Rome 1957 Art.177 for a preliminary ruling relating to the driving time of a heavy goods vehicle driver. B was convicted of driving for over 10 hours between two daily rest periods, contrary to Council Regulation 3820/85 on the harmonisation of certain social legislation relating to road transport Art.6(1), and for driving for more than four and a half hours without a break, contrary to Art.7(1) of the Regulation. B and his employer had agreed in advance that the provisions of Art.6 and Art.7 could not be complied with. The reference to the ECJ asked whether the driver could benefit from the flexibility of Art.12 of the Regulation if it was known before the journey that Art.6 and Art.7 would not be complied with. Article 12 permitted derogation from Art.6 and Art.7 if road safety was not jeopardised, the derogation was required for the safety of persons or the vehicle or the load and it was recorded by the driver. In this case the goods were of high value and road safety had not been jeopardised.

Held, that derogation was not permitted under Art.12 of the Regulations if it was determined beforehand that the conditions could not be complied with. Article 12 operated when an unforeseen event occurred during a journey which justified derogation as long as road safety was not jeopardised.

R. v. BIRD (ALAN) [1996] R.T.R. 49, D.A.O. Edward (President), ECJ.

5754. Driving–heavy goods vehicles–exceeding permitted driving time–method for calculating rest periods

[Transport Act 1968 s.96; Council Regulation 3820/85 on the harmonisation of certain social legislation relating to road transport Art.7.]

S appealed by way of case stated against three convictions of exceeding the permitted hours of lorry driving contrary to the Transport Act 1968 s.96(11)(a). The issue was which was the correct method to calculate the periods of rest that a driver was obliged to take. Council Regulation 3820/85 Art.7(1) required a 45 minute break to be taken after four and a half hours' driving. The 45 minutes could be replaced by breaks of at least 15 minutes distributed throughout the driving period. S's method allowed him to choose which break periods to count. If he had taken more than required, he could ignore some of them in the calculation. He must start a new calculation after four and a half hours and there must be at least a 15 minute break if there had been a continuous period of four and a half hours' driving. DOT's method added up the breaks and when they reached 45 minutes a new calculation began.

Held, dismissing the appeal, that the calculation should begin afresh when a driver had taken a 45 minute break as a single break or as several breaks of at least 15 minutes during or at the end of a period of four and a half hours, *Charlton, Re (C116/92)* [1994] 2 C.M.L.R. 600, [1994] C.L.Y. 4973 followed.

STEVENTON v. DEPARTMENT OF TRANSPORT, Trans. Ref: CO 1950/95, November 27,1995, Staughton, L.J., QBD.

5755. Inland waterways–by laws

NORFOLK AND SUFFOLK BROADS (EXTENSION OF BYELAWS) ORDER 1996, SI 1996 545; made under the Norfolk and Suffolk Broads Act 1988 s.23. In force: March 31, 1996; £0.65.

This Order continues in force, until March 31, 1998, certain by laws relating to the navigation area of the Norfolk and Suffolk Broads. The by laws deal with regulation of navigation and registration and licensing of craft.

5756. International carriage by railway–carriage of goods–hazardous substances

The Department of Transport issued a press release entitled *New edition of Carriage of Dangerous Goods by Rail published* (Press notice 406), published on December 23, 1996. A new edition of *Regulations concerning the International Carriage of Dangerous Goods by Rail* a fully revised section on the carriage of gases, and tables listing all substances covered by the Regulations together with their danger labels, marking and UN identification numbers. The new edition is available from the Stationery Office, ISBN 0 11 551840 1, price £70.

5757. London Regional Transport Act 1996 (c.21)

An Act to extend, and facilitate the exercise of, the powers of London Regional Transport to enter into and carry out agreements; and for connected purposes.

This Act received Royal Assent on June 17, 1996.

5758. Passenger transport authorities–finance

PASSENGER TRANSPORT EXECUTIVES (CAPITAL FINANCE) (AMENDMENT) ORDER 1996, SI 1996 3058; made under the Local Government and Housing Act 1989 s.39. In force: December 31, 1996; £0.65.

This Order amends the definitions of "relevant sum" and "special sum" in the Passenger Transport Executives (Capital Finance) Order 1990 (SI 1990 720) Art.1.

5759. Privatisation–railways–levels of passenger services–minimum service levels set–whether unlawfully reducing service levels–judicial review

SOR appealed against the dismissal of its application for judicial review of the decisions of the Director of Passenger Rail Franchising relating to minimum service levels for railway services. SOR claimed that the Director was using his statutory duty to set minimum passenger service requirements as a way of reducing service level requirements for franchising companies prior to privatisation.

Held, allowing the appeal in relation to four rail lines, but dismissed for another two lines. The initial specification of minimum service levels for railway passenger services was to be based on existing British Rail services, which meant the Director could only make minor changes to services and not major reductions. Where the Director's minimum service requirements departed dramatically from the existing services, he had failed to comply with instructions contained in the Secretary of State's guidelines on Objectives, Instructions and Guidance for the Franchising Director, issued in March 1994, and had therefore breached his statutory duty.

R. v. DIRECTOR OF PASSENGER RAIL FRANCHISING, *ex p.* SAVE OUR RAILWAYS, *The Times*, December 18, 1995, Sir Thomas Bingham, M.R., CA.

5760. Railway Heritage Act 1996 (c.42)

An Act to make further provision for, and in connection with, the preservation of railway records and artefacts.

This Act received Royal Assent on July 18, 1996.

5761. Railway Heritage Act 1996 (c.42)

The Department of Transport issued a press release entitled *Railway Heritage Bill achieves Royal Assent* (Press Notice 231), published on July 18, 1996. The Act to protect artifacts and archives pertaining to railways has received its Royal Assent. The Railway Heritage Act 1996 will extend the powers of the Railway Heritage Committee to protect items of historical significance in private sector ownership and will simplify procedures so that it may work more effectively. The Act has been welcomed by railway historians.

5762. Railways

ELSECAR STEAM RAILWAY ORDER 1996, SI 1996 937; made under the Transport and Works Act 1992 s.1, s.5, Sch.1 para.1, Sch.1 para.2, Sch.1 para.15, Sch.1 para.16, Sch.1 para.17. In force: April 4, 1996; £2.40.

This Order authorises the construction, maintenance and operation of a railway in the Metropolitan Borough of Barnsley consisting of part of the former railway authorised by the South Yorkshire, Doncaster and Goole Railway Act 1847. The Order contains provisions relating to level crossings at Distillery Side, Tingle Bridge Lane and Smithy Bridge Lane. It also includes powers to execute street works and stop up streets temporarily. Copies of the deposited plans and sections may be inspected at all reasonable hours at the offices of Barnsley MBC at the Town Hall, Barnsley, South Yorkshire S70 2TA.

5763. Railways

RAILWAYS ACT 1993 (CONSEQUENTIAL MODIFICATIONS) (NO.5) ORDER 1996, SI 1996 420; made under the Railways Act 1993 s.153. In force: March 20, 1996; £1.10.

In consequence of provisions of the Railways Act 1993 this Order modifies certain statutory provisions. The Transport Act 1968 s.116 to s.122, the Transport Act 1968 s.123 and s.124 and Art.2 of the Railway Bridges (Load-bearing Standards) (England and Wales) Order 1972 (SI 1972 1705) are amended in relation to networks transferred by transfer schemes made pursuant to the Railways Act 1993.

5764. Railways–closure

RAILWAYS (CLOSURE PROVISIONS) (EXEMPTIONS) ORDER 1996, SI 1996 1356; made under the Railways Act 1993 s.49, s.143, s.151. In force: May 24, 1996; £1.10.

This Order provides for the grant of the exemptions from the closure provisions of the Railways Act 1993 in relations to the construction of the proposed Croydon Tramlink light rail system. It provides that provisions relating to the closure of non-franchised passenger services, operational passenger networks and facilities do not apply to specified railway passenger services, networks and stations.

5765. Railways–construction

CHURNET VALLEY LIGHT RAILWAY ORDER 1996, SI 1996 1267; made under the Light Railways Act 1896 s.7, s.10, s.11, s.12, s.18. In force: May 4, 1996; £2.40.

This Order authorises the Churnet Valley Railway (1992) Plc to construct and maintain a railway as described in Sch.1 to the Order. Provision is made for the transfer of railway and rights from the British Railways Board to the Company.

5766. Railways–construction

SOUTH TYNEDALE RAILWAY (LIGHT RAILWAY) ORDER 1996, SI 1996 1829; made under the Light Railways Act 1896 s.3, s.7, s.10, s.11, s.12; and the Transport Act 1968 s.121. In force: July 10, 1996; £1.95.

This Order provides for the construction and maintenance of a railway to be laid on the same levels as, and within formation of the existing railway.

5767. Railways–light railways

BODMIN AND WENFORD LIGHT RAILWAY ORDER 1996, SI 1996 2867; made under the Light Railways Act 1896 s.3, s.7, s.10, s.11, s.12. In force: November 2, 1996; £2.80.

This Order relates to the construction and maintenance of a light railway by Bodmin and Wenford Rail Freight Ltd.

5768. Railways–light railways

DUFFIELD AND WIRKSWORTH LIGHT RAILWAY ORDER 1996, SI 1996 2660; made under the Light Railways Act 1896 s.7, s.10, s.11, s.12, s.18; and the Transport Act 1968 s.121. In force: October 16, 1996; £2.40.

This Order empowers Wyvern Rail Ltd to maintain and work the Duffield and Wirksworth Light Railway.

5769. Railways–light railways

GREATER MANCHESTER (LIGHT RAPID TRANSIT SYSTEM) (ECCLES EXTENSION) ORDER 1996, SI 1996 2714; made under the Transport and Works Act 1992 s.1, s.5, Sch.1 para.1, Sch.1 para.2, Sch.1 para.3, Sch.1 para.4, Sch.1 para.6, Sch.1 para.7, Sch.1 para.8, Sch.1 para.9, Sch.1 para.10, Sch.1 para.11, Sch.1 para.12, Sch.1 para.13, Sch.1 para.15, Sch.1 para.16, Sch.1 para.17. In force: November 11, 1996; £6.75.

This Order authorises Greater Manchester Passenger Transport Executive to construct works and compulsorily to acquire land and rights in land for the purposes of extending the Metrolink light rapid transit system to run from Eccles Town Centre to Salford Quays to connect to a part of the Metrolink light rapid transit system in Salford Quays which is already authorised, but not yet constructed.

5770. Railways–loans–extinguishment

RAILWAYS ACT 1993 (EXTINGUISHMENT OF RELEVANT LOANS) (RAILTRACK PLC) ORDER 1996, SI 1996 664; made under the Railways Act 1993 s.106. In force: March 29, 1996; £1.10.

This Order extinguishes, on March 29, 1996, all of Railtrack Plc's liabilities in respect of the principal of the loans set out in the Schedule to the Order. The sum of the liabilities so extinguished totals £1,229,418,952.48. The loans in question were made to the British Railways Board under the Transport Act 1962 s.20, and were paid out of the National Loans Fund. The Board's liability to repay these loans was transferred to, and vested in, Railtrack Plc on April 1, 1994 by a transfer scheme, dated March 30, 1994, made under the Railways Act 1993 s.85.

5771. Road signs–level crossings

PRIVATE CROSSINGS (SIGNS AND BARRIERS) REGULATIONS 1996, SI 1996 1786; made under the Transport and Works Act 1992 s.52. In force: August 1, 1996; £3.20.

The Transport and Works Act 1992 s.52(1) authorises the operator of a railway or tramway that is crossed by a private road or path to place prescribed signs or barriers near the crossing. These Regulations prescribe signs and barriers for the purposes of s.52(1).

5772. Transport Act 1982–Commencement No.7 Order

TRANSPORT ACT 1982 (COMMENCEMENT NO.7 AND TRANSITIONAL PROVISIONS) ORDER 1996, SI 1996 1943 (C.42); made under the Transport Act 1982 s.76. In force: bringing into force various provisions of the Act on August 1, 1996; £1.10.

This Order brings into force the Transport Act 1982 s.18 which inserts a new Road Traffic Act 1988 s.63A which makes provision for the alteration of plated weights for goods vehicles without examination.

5773. Transport and Works Act 1992–Commencement No.6 Order

TRANSPORT AND WORKS ACT 1992 (COMMENCEMENT NO.6) ORDER 1996, SI 1996 1609 (C.33); made under the Transport and Works Act 1992 s.70. In force: bringing into force various provisions of the Act on July 8, 1996; £1.10.

This Order brings into force on July 8, 1996 the provisions of the Transport and Works Act 1992 specified in the Schedule to the Order. These include provisions as to the placement of signs and barriers at private crossings of railways and tramways, and which authorise the making by the Secretary of State of regulations prescribing signs and barriers which he authorises for use at such crossings. They also authorise the Secretary of State to give to a railway or tramway operator directions for the placing of crossing signs or barriers. The Order also brings into force, subject to a saving, provision for the Transport Act 1968 s.124, which gives power for obligations to be imposed by the Secretary of State in respect of level crossings with roads other than public carriage roads, to cease to have effect in its application in England and Wales. In addition, it brings into force provisions which exclude tramcars from certain legislation that relates to hackney carriages (Metropolitan Public Carriage Act 1869), to private hire-cars (London Cab Act 1968 s.4) and to private hire vehicles (Local Government (Miscellaneous Provisions) Act 1976 Part II), and also from legislation that bestows on local authorities powers in relation to tramway carriages similar to those they possess in relation to hackney carriages (Tramways Act 1870 s.48).

5774. Waste–road transport–social legislation–derogation for refuse vehicles–statutory interpretation–European Union

[Council Regulation 3820/85 on the harmonisation of certain social legislation relating to road transport.]

G was charged with infringing the French rules on drivers' working time. He argued that his activity, the transport of waste, was exempt from the applicable rules contained in Council Regulation 3820/85.

Held, that the words, "vehicles used in connection with... refuse collection and disposal" in Art.4(6) of Council Regulation 3820/85 must be interpreted as covering vehicles used for the collection of waste of all kinds which was not subject to more specific rules and for the transportation of such waste over short distances, within the context of a general service in the public interest provided directly by the public authorities or by private undertakings under their control.

CRIMINAL PROCEEDINGS AGAINST GOUPIL (C39/95), March 21, 1996, Judge not specified, ECJ (First Chamber).

5775. Waste–road transport–social legislation–derogation for refuse vehicles–statutory interpretation–European Union

[Council Regulation 3820/85 on the harmonisation of certain social legislation relating to road transport.]

M was charged with infringing the German rules on drivers' working time. He argued that his activity, the transport of waste, was exempt from the applicable rules contained in Council Regulation 3820/85.

Held, that the words "vehicle used in connection with... refuse collection and disposal" in Council Regulation 3820/85 Art.4(6) must be interpreted as covering vehicles used for the collection of waste of all kinds which was not subject to more specific rules and for the transportation of such waste over short distances, within the contract of a general service in the public interest provided directly by the public authorities or by private undertakings under their control. In areas not covered by the Regulation, Member States remained competent to adopt rules on driving periods.

MROZEK v. JAGER (C335/94), March 21, 1996, Judge not specified, ECJ (First Chamber).

5776. Waste–tachographs–EEC law–exemption for vehicles used in connection with refuse collection and disposal–no exemption for lorry delivering skips

[Council Regulation 3820/85 on the harmonisation of certain social legislation relating to road transport Art.4; Council Regulation 3821/85 on recording equipment in road transport.]

Held, that a lorry solely engaged in the collection and delivery of building waste skips was not involved in refuse collection or disposal under Council Regulation 3820/85 Art.4(6) and was therefore not an exempt vehicle in terms of Council Regulation 3821/85 Art.13 to Art.15. To come within the exemption a vehicle had to perform a general service in the public interest, *Licensing Authority South Eastern Traffic Area v. British Gas Plc (C116/91)* [1992] C.L.Y. 4864 considered. Skip delivery amounted to a commercial service, which, in the absence of evidence to the contrary, was not a service that a local authority or other public body would provide as part of a normally funded collection service.

SWAIN v. McCAUL, *The Times*, July 11, 1996, Auld, L.J., QBD.

5777. Articles

Buses: the "commercialisation" of the industry *(Veronica Palmer)*: Trans. L. & P. 1996, 3(10), 154-156. (Effect of 1985 Act and need for future Government policy in public transport to take account of social and economic considerations with reference to CPT's proposals for Quality Partnerships between bus operators and local authorities).

Dangerous goods by road: H.S. 1996, 7(6), 4-6. (Results of consultation on draft Regulations to bring regime into line with 1995 European Agreement and suggested amendments).

Discretionary purchase of land under Highways Act 1980 s.246(2A) *(Kathleen Shorrock* and *Pamela Hargreaves)*: E.L.M. 1996, 8(5), 179-185. (Department of Transport guidelines and how they relate to Owen case regarding assessment of serious effect of proposed roadworks on property and exercise of discretion).

European Community law: transport *(Rosa Greaves)*: I.C.L.Q. 1996, 45(1), 219-225. (Major developments since July 1994 including policies on Trans European Networks, safety measures, negotiations with non-Community countries and developments in specific sectors).

Getting away with murder again *(Andrew Pawley)*: Trans. L. & P. 1996, 3(9), 151-152. (EU policy on transport seeks to link usage to pricing and whether EU will continue to fund road building).

Green Paper ducks challenge of sustainable transport policy: ENDS 1996, 255, 20-22. (DTp consultation *Transport: the Way Forward* fails to respond directly to Royal Commission on Environmental Pollution 1994, sets no limits on growth in traffic but promises public transport investment and stronger powers for councils).

Illegal bus and lorry operators *(Steven Norris)*: Magistrate 1996, Feb, 8-9. (Need for greater cooperation betwen operator licensing system and courts and for greater powers to enforce system).

Public transport systems: the allocation of risks in construction contracts *(Andrew Pitney* and *Cameron Smith)*: Const. L.J. 1996, 12(4), 240-258. (Documentation of major public infrastructure project including contractual structure of project and sample of risk allocation).

Public v. commercial interests in transport *(P. Fawcett)*: J.P. 1996, 160(15), 253-255. (Effect of deregulation and privatisation of bus and rail passenger networks on provision of services, fares and ticketing).

Regulation and liberalisation in the aviation industry: ground handling *(Klaus Gunther)*: I.B.L. 1996, 24(2), 53-58. (CEC proceedings against airports for abuse of dominant position regarding ground handling services and provisions of draft Directive).

Stuck in a jam? The great transport debate: E.I.B. 1996, 56, 10-12. (Industry criticism of Government Green Paper on *Transport: the Way Forward*, May 1996, on its failure to present coherent, integrated national transport policy).

The Channel tunnel rail link, the Ombudsman and the Select Committee *(Rhoda James* and *Diane Longley)*: P.L. 1996, Spring, 38-45. (Findings and investigations by Select Committee and Ombudsman into hardship and planning blight due to Department of Transport's handling of CTRL planning procedures and failure to pay compensation).

The consequences of bus deregulation–the Transport Select Committee's report *(Nick Maltby)*: J.P. 1996, 160(28), 474-475. (Recommendations of HC Transport Committee on alleviating difficulties experienced by deregulated bus service industry).

Transport of dangerous substances *(Helen Harrison)*: Mck. Env. L.B. 1996, Oct, 5-8. (Seven new regulations implementing EC Directives 94/55 and 96/49 and consolidating and replacing legislation, with list of HSC guidance documents).

5778. Books

Ortiz-Blanco, Luis; Houtte, Ben Van–EC Competition Law in the Transport Sector. Hardback: £65.00. ISBN 0-19-826089-X. Clarendon Press.

Teske, Paul; Best, Samuel; Mintrom, Michael–Deregulating Freight Transportation. Studies in Regulation and Federalism. Hardback: £31.95. ISBN 0-8447-3896-4. Paperback: £10.50. ISBN 0-8447-3897-2. American Enterprise Institute.

TRUSTS

5779. Bankruptcy–personal pensions–common law rule–settlor of property on bankruptcy abrogated by scheme membership prior to statutory provision repeal

[Superannuation Schemes Regulations 1983 (New Zealand).]

A and T were members of a personal pension retirement scheme managed by S. They became bankrupt and under the scheme's trust deed, therefore forfeited their entitlement to pension benefits although the trustees retained residual discretion to make financial provision for them. The Superannuation Schemes Regulations 1983 rendered such a protective trust valid, but were repealed in 1990. The Official Assignee, acting for A and T, sought declarations concerning the validity of the trust.

Held, refusing the declarations, that (1) the common law rule voiding any gift of property by a settlor to a trustee which was liable to be divested on the settlor's bankruptcy had not been superseded by statute; (2) however, the rule was abrogated by the 1983 Regulations; (3) this protective trust was therefore valid, and (4) the 1990 repeal had no effect in this case as A and T had both become members of the scheme before that date.

AITCHISON AND TUIVAITI v. NZI LIFE SUPERANNUATION NOMINEES LTD [1996] B.P.I.R. 215, Blanchard, J., HC (NZ).

5780. Cohabitation–shares in property–constructive trust arose due to undisputed common intention

D, the former cohabitee of a property with W, appealed against a decision that she had a 19.4 per cent share of the beneficial interest in the property by way of resulting trust. The parties had bought the property for £61,254, D providing £25,000, 40 per cent, of the purchase price, with the property conveyed solely into W's name. D had contributed £13,000 to conversion works, out of a total of £129,536, and argued that the shares in the property should not have been decided on the basis of a resulting trust as that required only that costs of acquisition be taken into account, not the costs of conversion, and operated on the basis of presumed, rather than actual, intention.

Held: Appeal allowed. The facts gave rise to the creation of a constructive trust since there was undisputed evidence of a common intention that D should have a beneficial interest in the property and she had acted to her detriment. W's counsel had been wrong to proceed on the basis that there was no common intention and in the circumstances D's fair share was one third.

DRAKE v. WHIPP (1996) 28 H.L.R. 531, Peter Gibson, L.J., CA.

5781. Companies–family company informally liquidated–whether shares bona vacantia–agreements creating implied or constructive trusts not required to be in writing

[Law of Property Act 1925 s.53; Companies Act 1948 s.353, s.354.]

In a dispute between the shareholders of a small family company, JEN, questions arose as to whether there had been an agreement for the informal liquidation of the company and, if there had been such an agreement, what was the effect on the disposal of JEN's equitable interest in the shares of another company, UEC. This amended ground of appeal had not been argued at first instance. JEN was to all intents and purposes defunct in 1969 and had been struck off and dissolved under the Companies Act 1948 s.353(5) in 1970. When proceedings came to trial in 1994, the outstanding issues were the ownership of 120 shares in UEC and the costs of previous litigation. The plaintiffs maintained that they held some of the UEC shares as constructive trustees for the shareholders of JEN in proportions equivalent to their existing JEN share holdings. The judge found that the 120 shares, which were registered in the names of the defendants in 1970, were not part of a distribution of UEC shares agreed in 1965. The judge went on to find that any remaining assets were owned beneficially by JEN and were thus bona vacantia, under s.354 of the 1948 Act, declining to make a declaration that the shares were owned by the defendants. He found for the defendants as to costs. The plaintiffs appealed.

Held, allowing the appeal and adjourning the consequential matters, that there had been ample evidence for the judge to find that, in 1965, JEN had only intended to carry out a distribution of some of the shares in UEC. As a result of the pleadings, the judge had no alternative but to find that, from 1965, JEN was the beneficial owner of the disputed shares. The new issue was whether there had then been an agreement in 1969 for the informal liquidation of JEN which disposed of JEN's equitable interest in those shares. Commonsense suggested that, on the evidence, what had been agreed in 1969 was that JEN's debts and liabilities should be discharged with the remaining assets distributed to shareholders pro rata. Accordingly, the disputed shares must be part of that agreement. The agreement not having been made in writing, what was left was whether it was ineffectual under the Law of Property Act 1925 s.53. In effect each shareholder would have made an individual agreement to assign interest such that each of those agreements constituted an implied or constructive trust *Oughtred v. Inland Revenue Commissioners* [1960] A.C. 206, [1959] C.L.Y. 3162 followed and *Vandervell v. Inland Revenue Commissioners* [1967] 2 A.C.

291, [1967] C.L.Y. 1675 and *Re Vandervell's Trusts (No.2)* [1974] Ch. 269, [1974] C.L.Y. 3501 distinguished. There was no apparent reason why the requirement that the agreement be reduced to writing under s.53(1)(c) should not be dispensed with by virtue of s.53(2). The plaintiffs were entitled to relief and JEN's interest in the shares had not been bona vacantia at the date of dissolution.

NEVILLE v. WILSON [1996] 3 W.L.R. 460, Nourse, L.J., CA.

5782. Income tax–capital gains tax

The Inland Revenue issued a press release entitled *New Inland Revenue leaflet on trusts*, published on September 30, 1996. The new leaflet, *Trusts: An Introduction* (IR152) outlines the common types of trust and their treatment for income tax and capital gains tax purposes. The leaflet is targeted at trustees who are not professionally qualified and beneficiaries of private family trusts. Copies are available, free of charge, from Tax Enquiry Centres, Trust Tax Offices or from the Public Enquiry Room, West Wing, Somerset House, London WC2R 1LB.

5783. Pension schemes–actions–trustees declining to continue–order made allowing willing beneficiaries to continue action

Trustees of a pension scheme took advice from N, a firm of solicitors. They then, at the employer's request, paid them £1.7 million as surplus and lent £1 million, leaving the fund with assets of about £1.6 million; in return the beneficiaries obtained a minor enhancement. The employers later went into administrative receivership, and the trustees sought to sue N. At close of pleadings they were advised that the costs of both sides might exceed the total assets of the scheme, and they would be exposed to personal risk as to costs. On an application for directions an order was made allowing willing beneficiaries to continue the action as plaintiffs, the trustees being joined as defendants. Two beneficiaries applied to be joined as plaintiffs.

Held, dismissing the application, that the trustees' conduct in declining to continue the action did not amount to a breach of their duty to protect the trust estate, and the beneficiaries had no legal or equitable property in the subject matter of the action; there being nothing in the rules of court permitting the handing over of an action which trustees had started but wished to abandon, the court had no jurisdiction to grant the application.

BRADSTOCK TRUSTEE SERVICES LTD v. NABARRO NATHANSON [1995] 1 W.L.R. 1405, Paul Baker Q.C., Ch D.

5784. Rectification–payment to charity–mistake in trust deed providing for payments over three years, not four–no rectification in absence of proof covenant did not give effect to intention

[Income and Corporation Taxes Act 1988 s.338, s.660.]

By a resolution, the parent of a company RGSL resolved that it would pay a gross sum of £70,000 p.a. over four years to RECT, a charitable trust. A solicitor drew up the trust deed but, due to a mistake, provided for payments over only three years. The deed was amended such that the payments would be made over four years. The Revenue discovered that the payments would not fall within the Income and Corporation Taxes Act 1988 s.660(3) because the period over which the payments were to be made was not a period of more than three years. Similarly, the payments were not covenanted donations to charity within s.338 of the 1988 Act. The trust repaid the tax to the Revenue by virtue of an interest free loan extended by RGSL. RGSL sought an order from the court to the effect that payments were to be made over four years. Vinelott, J. held that the action was misconceived on the basis that there was no issue between the parties and RGSL had not satisfied the standard that the covenant did not give effect to its intention.

Held, that (1) the court was able to entertain the application for rectification where there was an issue capable of being contested between the parties. On the facts, there was the issue between RGSL and the trust as to whether or not RGSL was able to deduct tax in making the payments, and (2) the court could not rectify a document simply on the basis that it failed to achieve the fiscal objective of the grantor. The specific intention of the grantor as to how the objective was to be achieved had to be shown if the deed was to be rectified. The evidence did not demonstrate RGSL's intention with reference to the date of making payments. Therefore, RGSL had failed to satisfy the standard that the covenant did not give effect to its intention. *Whiteside v. Whiteside* [1950] Ch. 65, [1947-1951] C.L.C. 9380, *Sherdley v. Sherdley* [1986] S.T.C. 266, [1987] C.L.Y. 2504 and *Thomas Bate v. Wyndhams* [1981] 1 W.L.R. 505, [1981] C.L.Y. 1584 considered.

RACAL GROUP SERVICES LTD v. ASHMORE [1995] S.T.C. 1151, Peter Gibson, L.J., CA.

5785. Secret trusts–need for binding intention to be communicated–New Zealand

SD left her property to her eldest child E who in turn left her property by will to her son P. B contested the will and argued that the bequest by SD to E was subject to a secret trust in favour of SD's whole family, making E a constructive trustee for the rest of the family.

Held, dismissing the application, that there was no secret trust in favour of the family. There had to be a communication to the devisee of the deceased's intentions and an acceptance by that person of the request to hold the property on trust. A binding obligation had to be intended. The communication of the intention was an essential factor.

BROWN v. POURAU (1996) 60 Conv. 302, Hammond, J., HC (NZ).

5786. Trust funds–investments

TRUSTEE INVESTMENTS (DIVISION OF TRUST FUND) ORDER 1996, SI 1996 845; made under the Trustee Investments Act 1961 s.13. In force: May 11, 1996; £0.65.

This Order, which extends to England and Wales and Scotland, contains a direction by HM Treasury that the prescribed proportion under the Trustee Investments Act 1961 s.13(1) shall be a proportion of three to one, with the result that any division of a trust fund under s.2(1) of that Act is to be made so that the value of the wider-range part of the fund, instead of being equal to the value of the narrower-range part of the fund as required by s.2, is three times that value.

5787. Trustees–age

[Family Law Reform Act 1969; Trustee Act 1925 s.31.]

The Inland Revenue issued a press release entitled *Age of majority: withdrawal of statement of practice*, published on September 30, 1996. The Inland Revenue has withdrawn its Statement of Practice E8 about the age of majority in the light of a High Court ruling. The statement of practice sets out Inland Revenue's view that where a trust is set up prior to January 1, 1970, an interest created by an appointment of trusts assets on or after that date should apply the age of majority determined under the 1969 Act.

5788. Trustees' liability–exclusion clauses–trustees deliberate but honest breach excluded by clause in settlement–beneficiary under discretionary trust does not have an interest in possession

[Limitation Act 1980 s.21.]

Allegations against trustees for breach involving reckless or wilful disregard of the terms of the trust, but not dishonesty, were accepted for the purposes of a preliminary issue only. Clause 15 of the trust deed stated "no trustee was liable for any loss or damage caused by his own actual fraud". The trustees argued that they were exonerated by the clause and also that they could rely upon the Limitation Act 1980 in relation to breaches prior to the six years from the date of the writ.

Held, that (1) the trustees were exonerated by cl.15 since the breaches were not caused by actual fraud. The clause was to be construed strictly in favour of the beneficiary against the trustee. It would be impossible to include some non fraudulent breaches and exclude others. The beneficiary argued that there was authority in equity to treat "fraud" as "acts against conscience" which would include deliberate breach, however the word "actual" was inserted to counter this point and (2) the trustees were entitled to rely upon the 1980 Act for "fraud or fraudulent breach" caught by s.21 (1) (a). The Act only excluded a trustee's fraud. However, from the age of 18 to 25 the beneficiary was an object of a discretionary trust and until the age of 25 she only had a future interest, therefore time did not begin to run.

ARMITAGE v. NURSE [1995] N.P.C 110, Jacob, J., Ch D.

5789. Trusts of Land and Appointment of Trustees Act 1996 (c.47)

An Act to make new provision about trusts of land including provision phasing out the Settled Land Act 1925, abolishing the doctrine of conversion and otherwise amending the law about trusts for sale of land; and to amend the law about the appointment and retirement of trustees of any trust.

This Act received Royal Assent on July 24, 1996.

5790. Trusts of Land and Appointment of Trustees Act 1996–Commencement Order

TRUSTS OF LAND AND APPOINTMENT OF TRUSTEES ACT 1996 (COMMENCEMENT) ORDER 1996, SI 1996 2974 (C.91); made under the Trusts of Land and Appointment of Trustees Act 1996 s.27. In force: January 1, 1997; £0.65.

This Order provides that the Trusts of Land and Appointment of Trustees Act 1996 shall come into force on January 1, 1997.

5791. Trusts of Land and Appointment of Trustees Act 1996 (c.47)

The Lord Chancellor's Department issued a press release entitled *Trust law reform: commencement of Trusts of Land and Appointment of Trustees Act* (342/96), published on December 3, 1996. The Trusts of Land and Apportionment of Trustees Act 1996, which comes into force on January 1, 1997, simplifies the law on joint and successive ownership of land and puts trusts of land onto a similar basis as trusts of personal property such as money or shares. Additionally, it introduces for both types of trust a new power which will allow beneficiaries, in certain circumstances, acting unanimously, to have input into the appointment of the trustees who administer the trust on their behalf.

5792. Articles

A new role for resulting trusts? *(William Swadling)*: L.S. 1996, 16(1), 110-131. (Relationship between law of restitution and resulting trusts, particularly regarding mistaken gifts and failure of consideration).

A solution to the section 31 trap? *(David Ewart)*: P.T.P.R. 1996, 4(3), 199-201. (CGT tax planning options for excluding operation of s.31 on disposal where is interest in possession and maintaining holdover relief availability for beneficiaries under discretionary trusts).

Accessory liability *(Peter Birks)*: L.M.C.L.Q. 1996, 1 (Feb), 1-6. (Liability of accessory for breach of trust and requirement of dishonesty).

Accumulated income as addition to a discretionary trust for exit charge purposes: P.C.B. 1996, 2, 75-76. (Question and answer. Determination of rate of tax on exit charge before first 10 year anniversary of discretionary trust under s.68(4) IHTA 1984).

Capital taxation business reliefs and trust property: Tr. & Est. 1996, 11 (1), 3-6. (Extent to which business property held in trust qualifies for IHT and CGT reliefs).

Constructive trustees in commercial fraud *(Sukhninder Parnesar)*: Bus. L.R. 1996, 16(12), 251-254. (Third party liability for assisting in breach of trust, whether dishonesty required, state of mind of third party and implications for application of equitable principles in financial context).

Constructive trusts and the unmarried couple *(Diane Wragg)*: Fam. Law 1996, 26(May), 298-300. (Implications of CA decision for cohabitees seeking to establish beneficial interest in family home).

Constructive trusts: are they unfair to creditors? *(Karen Houston)*: R.A.L.Q. 1996, 2(3), 159-185. (Use of constructive trusts as means of remedying unjust enrichment and consequences for unsecured creditors).

Country house mysteries *(William Goodhart)*: Legal Times 1996, 42, Supp 5. (Replacement of settlements and trusts for sale with trusts of land and widening of trustees powers).

Discretionary trusts–special trusts for special assets: Tr. & Est. 1996, 10(8), 57-59. (Types of property suitable to be held in discretionary trusts in order to avoid CGT and IHT with particular reference to woodlands and works of art).

Fear not: your charging clause is safe *(John Mowbray)*: Tru. L.I. 1996, 10(2), 49-50. (Case law shows trustee can be given express power to distribute fund among class including himself and can benefit from his trust if specifically authorised).

Getting the best return *(Simon Phelps)*: T.P.T. 1996, 17(13), 101-103. (Tax planning opportunities for persons resuming UK residence, implications for gains or income arising from foreign assets or offshore trusts and income tax anti-avoidance measures).

In praise of the flexible life interest trust: lifetime arrangements *(Ralph P. Ray)*: P.T.P.R. 1996, 5(1), 25-27. (CGT and IHT planning advantages of gifts to life interest trusts).

Independent schools, purpose trusts, and human rights *(Joseph Jaconelli)*: Conv. 1996, Jan/Feb, 24-33. (Consequences in trust law of termination of charitable status of public schools with particular reference to non charitable purpose trusts and cy pres).

International recognition of the trust concept *(C. Adair Dyer)*: T. & T. 1996, 2(3), 5-11. (Characterisation of trusts, purpose behind 1984 Convention and definition of trusts in it, and effect of Brussels Convention).

Investing trust funds–a bankers view *(Philip M. Hooper)*: T. & T. 1996, 2(4), 17-21. (High standard of care required of trustees investing trusts' assets and relevant considerations for prudent investment policy including consultation with advisers).

Living up to expectations *(Ann Kenny)*: N.L.J. 1996, 146(6734), 348-349. (Limitations of professional trustees' obligations to beneficiaries and need for reform).

Mitigating IHT for foreign domiciliaries *(John Fernandez)*: Tax J. 1996, 352, 12-14. (Asset siting and trust status qualifying for IHT excluded property treatment, liability for UK based assets, offshore company ownership provisons, offshore settlements, deemed domiciliary rules and concurrent will benefits).

Protectors–fish or fowl? *(Anthony Duckworth)*: P.C.B. 1996, 3, 169-180. (Functions, powers and obligations of trust protectors).

Reforms give trustees greater flexibility *(Angela Sydenham)*: E.G. 1996, 9641, 158-160. (Provisions of 1996 Act covering trusts of property which includes land, including consents and consultation, occupation by beneficiary, court powers, protection of purchaser, and appointment and retirement of trustees).

Residence of trusts *(Donald Pearce-Crump)*: Tax. P. 1996, Aug, 13, 15-17. (Tests which determine trustees' residence status for income tax and CGT purposes, with examples showing operation of rules for trusts comprising resident and non-resident trustees).

Resulting and constructive trusts, advancement and illegal purposes *(Angela Sydenham)*: Farm T.B. 1996, 11 (2), 14-15. (Examples of resulting trusts, presumption of advancement and methods of rebuttal).

Risk assessment in multi-jurisdictional asset protection structures *(David R. McNair)*: T. & T. 1996, 2(3), 15-17. (Potential pit falls in structuring offshore trusts).

Section 13 unlucky for some *(Michael Paynter* and *Tony Granby)*: T.P.T. 1996, 17(5), 33-36. (Anti avoidance proposals affecting attribution of non-resident close company gains to UK resident shareholders and participators, offshore trusts and settlors).

Special trust structures: a helping hand to the professional trustee? *(Timothy Ridley)*: J. Int. P. 1996, 5(1), 44-51. (Legal and business risks affecting professional trustees where assets of offshore trust are part of client's business over which trustee has very limited control and use of "special companies" as solution).

The final flourish *(Malcolm Gunn)*: Tax. 1996, 137(3563), 383-385. (Problems of interpreting FA 1986 provisions regarding deduction at source of income tax on discretionary or accumulation trust deposit interest).

The irreducible core content of trusteeship *(David Hayton)*: J. Int. P. 1996, 5(1), 3-17. (Extent to which settlors and trustees can restrict beneficiaries' rights to information).

The rule against perpetuities *(John Goldsworth)*: T. & T. 1996, 2(1), 13-19. (Development of use of perpetuities rule in modern trusts and assessment of future use).

The STEP International Committee: Colloquium on protectors: P.C.B. 1996, 1, 24-32. (Star Trusts case on determining whether power of trustee or protector is fiduciary, what fiduciary power means and implications for trust concept).

The Trusts of Land and Appointment of Trustees Bill *(Richard Wallington)*: N.L.J. 1996, 146(6750), 959-960. (Main provisions of Bill and its likely implication on drafting of wills).

Trust funds and the personal injury lawyer *(Damian P. Horan)*: S.J. 1996, 140(18), 450-451. (Use of trust deed to protect plaintiff in receipt of means tested benefits in view of income support, family credit and housing benefit capital thresholds, including precedent for trust for personal injury compensation).

Trust law for the twenty first century *(William Goodhart)*: Tru. L.I. 1996, 10(2), 38-44. (Historical overview of trust law and need for reform of trustees' powers and duties).

Trust property and CGT retirement relief: Tr. & Est. 1996, 10(8), 59-61. (Availability of retirement relief on assets held in trust where person carrying on business was beneficiary of trust).

Trustee shareholders: capacity and enforcement *(John Conder* and *Matthew Bennett)*: P.L.C. 1996, 7(9), 21-24. (Problems for purchaser of private company arising from substantial shareholding being held by trusts, and steps which purchasers should take).

Trusts and tax planning for UK residents: the use of employee benefits trusts and FURBS *(Charles Parkinson)*: T. & T. 1996, 2(8), 11-14. (Strategies for using trusts to shelter capital gains for UK residents and domiciled individuals and extent to which trusts set
up by employers can be substitute for classical offshore trusts).

Trusts of land and appointment of trustees *(Donald A. Lockhart)*: L.S.G. 1996, 93(29), 30. (Provisions of 1996 Act effective from January 1, 1997).

When you're in Bradley-Hole, stop digging *(Dermot Turing)*: I.L. & P. 1995, 11 (6), 174-175. (Trust which purports to isolate assets for payment of voluntary arrangement creditors after insolvency should not be upheld).

5793. Books

Aldridge, Trevor M.–Powers of Attorney. Practitioner series. Paperback: £40.00. ISBN 0-7520-0234-1. FT Law & Tax.

Burn, Edward–Maudsley & Burn: Trusts and Trustees - Cases and Materials. Paperback: £32.95. ISBN 0-406-01445-0. Butterworth Law.

Campbell, Dennis–Offshore Trusts. Comparative Law Yearbook of International Business. Hardback: £88.00. ISBN 90-411-0921-8. Kluwer Law International.

Clarke, Giles–Butterworths Offshore Trusts and Materials. Unbound/looseleaf: £320.00. ISBN 0-406-05396-0. Butterworth Law.
Cumper, P.–Blackstone's LLB: Learning Text - Law of Trusts. Paperback: £17.95. ISBN 1-85431-520-X. Blackstone Press.
Glasson, John–International Trust Laws: Update 7. Hardback: £40.00. ISBN 0-471-96468-9. Chancery Wiley Law Publications.
Goodman, Dawn; Hall, Brendan–Probate Disputes and Remedies. Practitioner series. Hardback: £50.00. ISBN 0-7520-0235-X. FT Law & Tax.
Hackney, Jeffrey–Understanding Equity and Trusts. Understanding Law, 6. Paperback: £7.99. ISBN 0-00-686294-2. Sweet & Maxwell.
Hayton, David–Cases and Commentary on the Law of Trusts and Equitable Remedies. Paperback: £28.95. ISBN 0-421-54860-6. Sweet & Maxwell.
Hooper, J.–LLB Cases and Materials: Law of Trusts. Paperback: £18.95. ISBN 1-85431-529-3. Blackstone Press.
Hooper, J.–LLB Learning Text: Law of Trusts. Paperback: £17.95. ISBN 1-85431-522-6. Blackstone Press.
Law of Trusts - LLB: Suggested Solutions (1991-1995). Bachelor of Laws (LLB). Paperback: £6.95. ISBN 0-7510-0725-0. HLT Publications.
Oakley, A.J.–Trends in Contemporary Trust Law. Hardback: £50.00. ISBN 0-19-826286-8. Clarendon Press.
Pearce, Robert A.; Stevens, John–The Law of Trusts and Equitable Obligations. Paperback: £24.95. ISBN 0-406-05246-8. Butterworth Law.
Riddall, John G.–Law of Trusts. Law in context series. Paperback: £23.95. ISBN 0-406-00905-8. Butterworth Law.
Todd, Paul–Cases & Materials on Equity and Trusts. Paperback: £23.95. ISBN 1-85431-555-2. Blackstone Press.
Todd, Paul–Textbook on Trusts. Paperback: £17.95. ISBN 1-85431-552-8. Blackstone Press.

UTILITIES

5794. Compensation–installation of sewer–failure to show depreciation in value of land

Held, that where a new larger sewer was laid along the line of an existing sewer under a parcel of development land a claim for compensation was dismissed since the value of the land was not shown to have been diminished.

A&TF BENNETT v. NORTH WEST WATER [1996] 36 R.V.R. 30, Judge Marder, Q.C. (President), Lands Tr.

5795. Directives–implementation–European Union

UTILITIES CONTRACTS REGULATIONS 1996, SI 1996 2911; made under the European Communities Act 1972 s.2. In force: December 12, 1996; £6.75.

These Regulations implement Council Directive 93/38 ([1993] OJ L199/84) concerning the co-ordination of procedures for the award of supply, works and services contracts by certain entities operating in the water, energy, transport and telecommunications sectors. This Directive replaces Council Directive 90/531 ([1990] OJ L297/1) and the Regulations revoke the Utilities Supply and Works Contracts Regulations 1992 (SI 1992 3279) as amended which implemented the 1990 Directive. The principal change is to extend the provisions to services contracts. The Regulations also implement Council Directive 92/13 ([1992] OJ L76/14) concerning the co-ordination of laws, regulations and administrative provisions relating to the application of Community rules to the procurement of entities operating in the water, energy, transport and telecommunications sector which was amended to apply to the 1993 Directive. The Regulations also implement certain European Treaties with a number of other European states under which the Community provisions relating to public procurement have been extended: Bulgaria, the Czech Republic, Hungary, Iceland, Liechtenstein, Norway, Poland, Romania and Slovakia.

5796. Electricity–landlord and tenant–pricing

The Office of Electricity Regulation issued a press release entitled *Electricity resale prices: advice for landlords and tenants in England and Wales* (R11/96), published on April 3, 1996. The Director General of Electricity Supply has published maximum prices which landlords can charge for the resale of electricity for domestic purposes. The new prices apply to six regional electricity companies which changed their tariffs on April 1, 1996.

5797. Electricity–licence holders–disclosure of information

ELECTRICITY ACT 1989 (DISCLOSURE OF INFORMATION) (LICENCE HOLDERS) ORDER 1996, SI 1996 2716; made under the Electricity Act 1989 s.57. In force: December 1, 1996; £0.65.

This Order relates to disclosure of information made between the holders of licences granted under the Electricity Act 1989 s.6. It adds disclosure made between such licence holders under a licence obligation to the list of exceptions from the restriction on disclosure of information in the Electricity Act 1989 s.57(1).

5798. Electricity supply industry–fees

FOSSIL FUEL LEVY (AMENDMENT) REGULATIONS 1996, SI 1996 1309; made under the Electricity Act 1989 s.33, s.60. In force: June 6, 1996; £1.10.

These Regulations amend the Fossil Fuel Levy Regulations 1990 (SI 1990 226). They substitute a new Sch.2 which makes the following change of substance: it specifies a method for calculating the rate of levy (as defined in Reg.2 of the Principal Regulations) where a revised rate is to apply from the beginning of a month other than April in any year (see the new formula in para 3(b) and the revised formula in para.5). They also provide that money received by the Director General of Electricity Supply pursuant to the Principal Regulations may be invested by him through any one or more of the Bank of England and (in place of the Committee of London and Scottish Bankers) any institution of the classes specified in Reg.3.

5799. Electricity supply industry–restrictive trade practices–exemptions

ELECTRICITY (RESTRICTIVE TRADE PRACTICES ACT 1976) (EXEMPTIONS) ORDER 1996, SI 1996 1327; made under the Electricity Act 1989 s.100. In force: June 10, 1996; £3.70.

This Order specifies an agreement and a description of agreements to which the Restrictive Trade Practices Act 1976 is deemed not to apply and never to have applied. By virtue of the Electricity Act 1989 s.100(1) electricity is treated as goods for the purposes of the 1976 Act. This Order provides that the agreement specified in Art.2(2) of the Order and agreements meeting with the description set out in Art.2(4) thereof, nevertheless fall outside the provisions of the 1976 Act.

5800. Gas–connection and disconnection–notice

GAS METERS (INFORMATION OF CONNECTION AND DISCONNECTION) REGULATIONS 1996, SI 1996 450; made under the Gas Act 1986 s.47, s.48, Sch.2B para.12. In force: March 1, 1996; £1.10.

The Gas Act 1986 Sch.2B para.12 provides that a person proposing to connect a meter with a service pipe through which gas is conveyed to any premises by a public gas transporter, or to disconnect a meter from such a pipe, must give 48 hours' notice of the connection or disconnection to the gas supplier supplying gas to the premises, or to the transporter in question. These Regulations prescribe the form of the notice and the information which it is to contain and includes details of the meter itself and of the person requesting the connection or disconnection.

5801. **Gas–equipment–safety**

GAS SAFETY (INSTALLATION AND USE) (AMENDMENT) REGULATIONS 1996, SI 1996 550; made under the Health and Safety at Work etc. Act 1974 s.15, Sch.3 para.1, Sch.3 para.4. In force: April 1, 1996; £1.95.

These Regulations, which amend the Gas Safety (Installation and Use) Regulations 1994 (SI 1994 1886), relate to definitions, specified premises, self propelled vehicles and specified vessels, propulsion systems for vehicles, bunsen burners, work in respect of gas storage vessels, the replacement of specified hoses and regulators, the storing or keeping of natural gas on domestic premises, gas fittings, the installation of regulators, the reporting of unsafe gas appliances and the duties of landlords to carry out maintenance of gas appliances and make safety checks.

5802. **Gas–equipment–safety**

GAS SAFETY (INSTALLATION AND USE) (AMENDMENT) (NO.2) REGULATIONS 1996, SI 1996 2541; made under the Health and Safety at Work etc. Act 1974 s.15, s.82, Sch.3 para.1, Sch.3 para.16. In force: October 31, 1996; £1.10.

These Regulations amend the Gas Safety (Installation and Use) Regulations 1994 (SI 1994 1886) Reg.35A, the provisions of which include a requirement for a landlord to ensure that a yearly safety check is carried out on specified gas appliances, and flues which serve such appliances, and for a record to be made of that check. They require that record to be preserved for a period of two years; specify the information to be included in that record; and require a landlord to provide existing tenants and new tenants with a copy of the record at specified times.

5803. **Gas–safety**

GAS SAFETY (MANAGEMENT) REGULATIONS 1996, SI 1996 551; made under the Health and Safety at Work etc. Act 1974 s.15, s.82, Sch.3 para.1, Sch.3 para.15, Sch.3 para.16, Sch.3 para.21. In force: April 1, 1996; £3.20.

Provision is made for the preparation and acceptance of safety cases for the conveyance of gas in a network and requirements in respect of gas escapes and the composition and pressure of gas are imposed.

5804. **Gas–safety**

GAS SAFETY (RIGHTS OF ENTRY) REGULATIONS 1996, SI 1996 2535; made under the Gas Act 1986 s.18, s.18A, s.47. In force: November 1, 1996; £1.55.

These Regulations confer rights of entry upon public gas transporters and relevant authorities to enter premises for the purposes of preventing gas escapes, the examination and disconnection of gas fittings and other related purposes. They supersede the Gas Safety (Rights of Entry) Regulations 1983 (SI 1983 1575).

5805. **Gas–safety–rights of entry–repeal of superseded legislation**

GAS ACT 1995 (REPEAL OF SUPERSEDED PROVISIONS OF THE GAS ACT 1986) ORDER 1996, SI 1996 3203; made under the Gas Act 1995 s.9. In force: January 8, 1997; £0.65.

This Order repeals the Gas Act 1986 Sch.2B para.22 which provision has been superseded by the Gas Safety (Rights of Entry) Regulations 1996 (SI 1996 2535) which came into force on November 1, 1996. Regulation 4 of the said Regulations enables a public gas transporter through its authorised officers to enter, in respect of escapes of gas which it conveys, any premises and in respect of escapes or suspected escapes of gas which is conveyed by another person, premises which are or are reasonably believed to be within its authorised area,

5806. Gas Act 1995–Appointed Day and Commencement Order

GAS ACT 1995 (APPOINTED DAY AND COMMENCEMENT) ORDER 1996, SI 1996 218 (C.4); made under the Gas Act 1995 s.18. In force: March 1, 1996; £0.65.

This Order appoints March 2, 1996 as the appointed day for the purpose of the Gas Act 1995 s.18(2), and brings s.12 of the Act into force on the same day. The Order brings into force on March 1, 1996 all the provisions of the Act that were not brought into force on its passing

5807. Gas Act 1995–transitional provisions

GAS ACT 1995 (TRANSITIONAL PROVISIONS AND SAVINGS) (NO.1) ORDER 1996, SI 1996 219; made under the Gas Act 1995 s.17. In force: March 1, 1996; £1.10.

This Order provides for the continued operation of the Gas Quality Regulations 1983 (SI 1983 363) and Gas (Testing) Regulations 1949 under (SI 1949 789) the new regulatory regime established by the Gas Act 1995, except in relation to standards relating to uniformity of calorific value. The Order also provides for appointments of competent and impartial persons under the Gas Act 1986 s.16(3) to continue under the new regime.

5808. Gas supply industry

GAS ACT 1995 (CONSEQUENTIAL MODIFICATIONS OF LOCAL ACTS AND ORDERS) ORDER 1996, SI 1996 362; made under the Gas Act 1995 s.16. In force: March 1, 1996; £2.40.

This Order makes modifications to local Acts and Orders in consequence of the enactment of the Gas Act 1995. Article 2 modifies the local Acts in the manner set out in Sch.1. Article 3 amends the local Acts in Sch.2 so as to substitute references to a public gas transporter within the meaning of the Gas Act 1986 Part I for references to a public gas supplier. Article 4 amends references in the local Acts in Sch.3 to any person authorised to carry on, in a particular area, an undertaking for the supply of gas so as to substitute references to a public gas transporter within the meaning of the Gas Act 1986 Part I whose authorised area includes that area. Article 5 amends the local orders in Sch.4 so as to substitute references to a public gas transporter within the meaning of the Gas Act 1986 Part I for references to a public gas supplier.

5809. Gas supply industry

GAS ACT 1995 (CONSEQUENTIAL MODIFICATIONS OF SUBORDINATE LEGISLATION) ORDER 1996, SI 1996 252; made under the Gas Act 1995 s.16. In force: March 1, 1996; £1.95.

This Order makes modifications to subordinate legislation in consequence of the enactment of the Gas Act 1995. Article 2 amends the subordinate legislation in the manner set out in the Schedule, generally so as to substitute references to a public gas transporter within the meaning of the Gas Act 1986 Part I for references (directly or indirectly) to a public gas supplier or British Gas Plc.

5810. Gas supply industry–competition–licences

GAS (EXTENT OF DOMESTIC SUPPLY LICENCES) (AMENDMENT) ORDER 1996, SI 1996 3275; made under the Gas Act 1995 s.6. In force: January 31, 1997; £0.65.

This Order amends the Gas (Extent of Domestic Supply Licences) Order 1996 (SI 1996 752) under which competition in the supply of gas through pipes to premises at rates not expected to exceed 2,500 therms a year is to be introduced in stages. This Order provides for the introduction of competition in Dorset and the former county of Avon on February 10, 1997 and in Devon, Cornwall, Somerset, Kent, East Sussex and West Sussex on March 7, 1997.

5811. Gas supply industry–consequential modifications

GAS ACT (CONSEQUENTIAL MODIFICATIONS OF SUBORDINATE LEGISLATION) (NO.2) ORDER 1996, SI 1996 470; made under the Gas Act 1995 s.16. In force: March 1, 1996; £0.65.

This Order makes modifications to the Gas Safety Regulations 1972 (SI 1972 1178) in consequence of the enactment of the Gas Act 1995. The Act provides for various functions, carried out at one time by Area Gas Boards and latterly by British Gas Plc as a public gas supplier, to be carried out by public gas transporters. Article 2 of the Order amends various references in the 1972 Regulations to Area Boards and the supply of gas so as to refer to public gas transporters and the conveyance of gas. The 1995 Act also provides, by amendments to the Gas Act 1986 s.10, for the owner or occupier of premises to be able to lay a service pipe connecting his premises to a gas main. In consequence, Art.2 of the Order amends Reg.3(1) of the 1972 Regulations so as to exclude owners, occupiers and their contractors from the restriction imposed by that provision as to the persons who may install service pipes and related apparatus.

5812. Gas supply industry–licences

GAS (APPLICATION FOR LICENCES AND EXTENSIONS AND RESTRICTIONS OF LICENCES) REGULATIONS 1996, SI 1996 476; made under the Gas Act 1986 s.7, s.7B, s.47, s.48. In force: March 1, 1996; £3.20.

The Gas Act 1986, as amended by the Gas Act 1995, introduces a new licensing regime for the conveyance, supply and shipping of gas. These Regulations prescribe the information and other documents that are required to be submitted with applications for the new categories of licences, or for extensions or restrictions of such licences, and the form and manner of such applications. The Regulations also prescribe the manner in which such applications are to be published. The Regulations prescribe a minimum time of 14 days which the Director General of Gas Supply may allow for the making of representations and objections in the case of applications for certain limited extensions to public gas transporter licences (Reg.8).

5813. Gas supply industry–licences

GAS (EXTENT OF DOMESTIC SUPPLY LICENCES) ORDER 1996, SI 1996 752; made under the Gas Act 1995 s.6. In force: April 2, 1996; £1.10.

This Order provides for the phased introduction of competition in the supply of piped gas to premises at rates not expected to exceed 2,500 therms a year (predominately domestic premises). By virtue of Art.3 of the Order, domestic supply licences granted under the Gas Act 1986 s.7A(1)(a) (as amended by the Gas Act 1995) may authorise the supply of gas in Devon, Cornwall and Somerset from April 29, 1996, and elsewhere in the south-west and south-east of England from December 31, 1997 or such earlier date during 1997 as may be determined by the Director General of Gas Supply ("the Director"). By virtue of Art.4, the Director is enabled to provide for domestic supply licences to authorise the supply of gas anywhere in Great Britain from a date during 1998. Article 5 provides for consultation before the Director exercises the power to determine a date under either Art.3 or Art.4. The Order does not affect the rights of British Gas plc or others authorised to supply gas prior to the commencement of the Gas Act 1995. These rights are preserved by provisions in s.6(3) to s.6(5) of that Act.

5814. Gas supply industry–licences–exemptions

GAS ACT 1986 (EXEMPTIONS) (NO.1) ORDER 1996, SI 1996 449; made under the Gas Act 1986 s.6A; and the Gas Act 1995 Sch.5 para.17. In force: March 1, 1996; £1.55.

The Gas Act 1986 s.6A provides for the granting by Order of exemptions from the prohibition contained in s.5 of the 1986 Act from carrying on the conveyance, supply or shipping of gas without a licence. This Order contains a number of such exemptions, in respect of the conveyance of gas previously supplied to certain suppliers; the conveyance of gas produced by certain suppliers as a by-product of other activities; the shipping of gas by a consumer on the failure of existing shipping arrangements; the shipping of gas by a supplier in accordance with an undertaking given in accordance with his licence; supply of gas by a public gas transporter as a result of the arrangements exempted under Art.7; shipping in emergency cases; conveyance of gas, subject to conditions, by a person from one set of premises to another where this represents the continuation of certain arrangements in force before the day on which the new regime introduced by the 1995 Act came into force; supply to premises, subject to conditions, of gas consisting wholly or mainly of propane or butane which is conveyed to the premises from transportable storage containers.

5815. Gas supply industry–licences–exemptions

GAS ACT 1986 (EXEMPTIONS) (NO.2) ORDER 1996, SI 1996 471; made under the Gas Act 1986 s.6A. In force: March 1, 1996; £1.55.

The Gas Act 1986 s.6A, substituted by the Gas Act 1995 s.4, provides for the granting by order of exemptions from the prohibition contained in s.5 of the 1986 Act from carrying on the conveyance and supply of gas without a licence. This Order contains a number of such exemptions in respect of particular premises and addresses. Schedule 1 and Sch.2 (see Art.3 and Art.4) relate to exemptions in respect of the conveyance of gas from the premises and addresses there mentioned to a pipeline system operated by a public gas transporter. The exemptions to which Sch.1 relates are subject to the condition set out in Art.6, whereby the Secretary of State may direct the person so conveying gas to provide information about the calorific value and quantity of the gas to the public gas transporter. Schedule 3 (see Art.5) relates to exemptions in respect of the supply of gas by the persons there specified to certain named premises.

5816. Gas supply industry–licences–exemptions

GAS ACT 1986 (EXEMPTIONS) (NO.3) ORDER 1996, SI 1996 1354; made under the Gas Act 1986 s.6A. In force: June 13, 1996; £1.10.

The Gas Act 1986 s.6A, substituted by the Gas Act 1995 s.4, provides for the granting by Order of exemptions from the prohibition contained in the 1986 Act s.5 from carrying on the conveyance, supply or shipping of gas without a licence. The Order contains an exemption in respect of the conveyance of gas from the premises mentioned in the Schedule to a pipeline system operated by a local gas transporter. The exemption, which continues in force until November 30, 1996, is subject to the condition set out in Art.4, whereby the Secretary of State may direct a person so conveying gas to provide information about the calorific value and quantity of the gas to the public gas transporter.

5817. Gas supply industry–licences–exemptions

GAS ACT 1986 (EXEMPTIONS) (NO.4) ORDER 1996, SI 1996 2795; made under the Gas Act 1986 s.6A. In force: December 1, 1996; £1.10.

The Gas Act 1986 s.6A provides for the granting by Order of exemptions from the prohibition contained in s.5 of the 1986 Act from carrying on the conveyance, supply or shipping of gas without a licence. This Order contains an exemption in respect of the conveyance of gas from the premises mentioned in the Schedule to a pipe-line system operated by a public gas transporter.

5818. Gas supply industry–road works–compensation payments to small businesses

GAS (STREET WORKS) (COMPENSATION OF SMALL BUSINESSES) REGULATIONS 1996, SI 1996 491; made under the Gas Act 1986 s.47, Sch.4 para.1. In force: March 22, 1996; £1.55.

These Regulations require a public gas transporter which executes street works which are not completed within 28 days to pay compensation for loss of turnover sustained by a small business (defined in Reg.3), during a specified period of at least 28 days, in consequence of the works, except where the compensation would be less that £500 or would not exceed 2.5 per cent of the annual turnover of the business. The amount of the compensation is the difference between the profit (or loss) which would have accrued to the business but for the works and the reduced profit (or increased loss) which is a consequence of the works (Reg.5(1), Reg.5(2) and Reg.5(3)). A person must reserve the right to claim compensation within 3 months of the completion of the street works and submit supporting evidence within 6 months of their completion (Reg.5(4)).

5819. Gas supply industry–transitional provisions

GAS ACT 1995 (TRANSITIONAL PROVISIONS AND SAVINGS) (NO.2) ORDER 1996, SI 1996 399; made under the Gas Act 1995 s.17. In force: March 1, 1996; £1.55.

This Order makes a number of transitional provisions and savings in relation to the coming into force of the new regulatory regime for the conveyance, supply and shipping of gas introduced by the Gas Act 1995 as from March 1, 1996. These are in addition to the provisions made by Sch.5 to the 1995 Act and by the Gas Act 1995 (Transitional Provisions and Savings) (No 1) Order 1996 (SI 1996 219). The Order makes provision for a number of rights and obligations acquired and incurred, and other things done, by or in relation to public gas suppliers under the Gas Act 1986 to have effect as if they had been done by or in relation to the appropriate successor entities (public gas transporters or gas suppliers) under the new regime. The Order also provides for outstanding applications for authorisations to supply gas under s.8 of the 1986 Act to have effect after March 1, 1996 as the appropriate applications for licences under the new regime.

5820. Land drainage–National Rivers Authority–basis of charge for local authority subscriptions–repayment permitted where certificated accounts did not fulfil requirement of Rate Product Rules 1981–statutory interpretation

[Land Drainage Act 1976 s.45, s.46; Rate Product Rules 1981 r.3; Rape Product Rules 1981 r.10.]

Under the Land Drainage Act 1976 s.45(1) the NRA was entitled to collect subscriptions in respect of drainage operations conducted in a drainage district, which could include areas controlled by two or more local authorities. C and Wiltshire County Council, W, both had territory within the same district and s.46 of the 1976 Act provided that in such cases the relevant costs fell to be apportioned between the respective authorities. However, in calculating its subscriptions for the years 1985 to 1988, W employed an exclusive and not an inclusive method, as required under the Rate Product Rules 1981 r.3, resulting in a substantial overpayment. C sought repayment of £163,000 having made advance overpayments. It was submitted that C would not be entitled to £3,692 if W had been entitled to substitute the lower figure rather than the actual product of a penny rate. In third party proceedings to decide that matter it was held that W were bound by the actual product of a penny rate based on the erroneous exclusive method. W appealed.

Held, allowing the appeal, that the procedure under s.46 of the 1976 Act amounted to a two stage process, with calculations under s.46(1) being by way of an estimate, carried out at the start of the year, with calculations under s.46(9) forming the final figure and based on facts ascertained at the year end. However, although the final figure produced was to be the actual product of a penny rate spread across the drainage territory, there was no stipulation that the figure was binding in nature and not susceptible to alteration, if subsequently found to have been based on an erroneous calculation. W's certificates did not fulfil the requirement under the Schedule to the 1981 Rules, in that the calculations were to be based on an inclusive product basis as an audit of the actual penny rate, not the inclusive penny rate as W had supplied; neither had the calculations themselves been included in the accounts submitted to the district auditor, as required by r.10.

CAMDEN LBC v. NATIONAL RIVERS AUTHORITY; SUB NOM. NATIONAL RIVERS AUTHORITY v. WILTSHIRE CC, Trans. Ref: QBENI 95/1555/E, October 10, 1996, Staughton, L.J., CA.

5821. **Offshore installations–construction law**

OFFSHORE INSTALLATIONS AND WELLS (DESIGN AND CONSTRUCTION, ETC.) REGULATIONS 1996, SI 1996 913; made under the Health and Safety at Work etc. Act 1974 s.15, s.82, Sch.3 para.1, Sch.3 para.6, Sch.3 para.9, Sch.3 para.10, Sch.3 para.11, Sch.3 para.14, Sch.3 para.15, Sch.3 para.16, Sch.3 para.18. In force: June 30, 1996; £4.15.

These Regulations contain requirements for ensuring that offshore oil and gas installations, and oil and gas wells are designed, constructed and kept in a sound structural state, and other requirements affecting them, for purposes of health and safety. They revoke the Offshore Installations (Construction and Survey) Regulations 1974 (SI 1974 289), the Offshore Installations (Operational Safety, Health and Welfare) Regulations 1976 (in part) (SI 1976 1019), the Offshore Installations (Well Control) Regulations 1980 (SI 1980 1759) and the Offshore Installations (Well Control) (Amendment) Regulations 1991 (SI 1991 308). The Regulations give effect to provisions of Council Directive 92/91 ([1992] OJ L348/9) concerning the minimum requirements for improving the safety and health protection of workers in the mineral-extracting industries through drilling.

5822. **Offshore installations–safety at sea**

INSTALLATIONS (SAFETY ZONES) ORDER 1996, SI 1996 97; made under the Petroleum Act 1987 s.22. In force: February 7, 1996; £1.10.

Safety zones with a radius of 500 metres around certain installations stationed in waters to which the Petroleum Act 1987 s.21 (7) applies are established by this Order. Hovercraft, submersible apparatus and installations in transit are prohibited from entering a specified safety zone unless consent is given by the Health and Safety Executive.

5823. **Offshore installations–safety zones**

OFFSHORE INSTALLATIONS (SAFETY ZONES) (NO.2) ORDER 1996, SI 1996 850; made under the Petroleum Act 1987 s.22. In force: April 8, 1996; £0.65.

This Order establishes, under the Petroleum Act 1987 s.22, safety zones having a radius of 500 metres from the specified point, around the installations specified in the Schedule to this order and stationed in waters to which s.21 (7) of that Act applies (these include territorial waters and waters in areas designated under the Continental Shelf Act 1964 s.1 (7)). Vessels (which for this purpose include hovercraft, submersible apparatus and installations in transit) are prohibited from entering or remaining in a safety zone except with the consent of the Health and Safety Executive or in accordance with Regulations made under s.23(1) of the Act (currently the Offshore Installations (Safety Zones) Regulations 1987 (SI 1987 1331)).

5824. **Offshore installations–safety zones**

OFFSHORE INSTALLATIONS (SAFETY ZONES) (NO.3) ORDER 1996, SI 1996 1194; made under the Petroleum Act 1987 s.22. In force: May 20, 1996; £0.65.

This Order establishes, under the Petroleum Act 1987 s.22, safety zones having a radius of 500 metres from the specified point around the installations specified in the Schedule to this Order and stationed in waters to which s.21 (7) of that Act applies (these include territorial waters and waters in areas designated under the Continental Shelf Act 1964 s.1 (7) (c.29)). Vessels (which for this purpose include hovercraft, submersible apparatus and installations in transit) are prohibited from entering or remaining in a safety zone except with the consent of the Health and

Safety Executive or in accordance with Regulations made under 23(1) of the Act (currently the Offshore Installations (Safety Zones) Regulations 1987 (SI 1987 1331)).

5825. Offshore installations–safety zones

OFFSHORE INSTALLATIONS (SAFETY ZONES) (NO.4) ORDER 1996, SI 1996 1492; made under the Petroleum Act 1987 s.22. In force: June 28, 1996; £0.65.

This Order establishes a safety zone having a radius of 500 metres from the specified point, around the installation specified in the Schedule to this Order and stationed in waters to which the Petroleum Act 1987 s.21 (7) applies, are prohibited from entering or remaining in a safety zone except with the consent of the Health and Safety Executive or in accordance with regulations made under s.23(1) of the Act (currently Offshore Installations (Safety Zones) Regulations 1987 (SI 1987 1331)).

5826. Offshore installations–safety zones

OFFSHORE INSTALLATIONS (SAFETY ZONES) (NO.5) ORDER 1996, SI 1996 1862; made under the Petroleum Act 1987 s.22. In force: August 7, 1996; £0.65.

This Order establishes safety zones having a radius of 500 metres from the specified point, around specified installations stationed in waters to which the Petroleum Act 1987 s.21 (9) applies, including territorial waters and waters in areas designated under the Continental Shelf Act 1964 s.1 (7). Vessels are prohibited from entering or remaining in a safety zone except with the consent of the Health and Safety Executive or in accordance with the Offshore Installations (Safety Zones) Regulations 1987 (SI 1987 1331).

5827. Offshore installations–safety zones

OFFSHORE INSTALLATIONS (SAFETY ZONES) (NO.6) ORDER 1996, SI 1996 2304; made under the Petroleum Act 1987 s.22. In force: September 26, 1996; £0.65.

This Order establishes, under the Petroleum Act 1987 s.22, safety zones having a radius of 500 metres from the specified point, around the installations specified in the Schedule to this Order and stationed in waters to which s.21 (7) of that Act applies (these include territorial waters and waters in areas designated under the Continental Shelf Act 1964 s.1 (7) (c.29)). This Order also amends the Offshore Installations (Safety Zones) (No.5) Order 1966 by deleting the entry relating to one installation, which will accordingly cease to be protected by a safety zone. Vessels (which for this purpose include hovercraft, submersible apparatus and installations in transit) are prohibited from entering or remaining in a safety zone except with the consent of the Health and Safety Executive or in accordance with Regulations made under s.23(1) of the Act (currently the Offshore Installations (Safety Zones) Regulations 1987 (SI 1987 1331)).

5828. Offshore installations–safety zones

OFFSHORE INSTALLATIONS (SAFETY ZONES) (NO.7) ORDER 1996, SI 1996 2859; made under the Petroleum Act 1987 s.22. In force: December 5, 1996; £0.65.

This Order establishes safety zones having a radius of 500 metres around specified installations. Vessels are prohibited from entering or remaining in a safety zone without consent or in accordance with the Offshore Installations (Safety Zones) Regulations 1987 (SI 1987 1331).

5829. **Offshore installations–safety zones**

OFFSHORE INSTALLATIONS (SAFETY ZONES) (NO.8) ORDER 1996, SI 1996 3139; made under the Petroleum Act 1987 s.22. In force: December 31, 1996; £0.65.

This Order establishes a safety zone having a radius of 500 metres around the Kingfisher Production Manifold. Vessels are prohibited from entering or remaining in a safety zone except with the consent of the Health and Safety Executive or in accordance with regulations made under the Petroleum Act 1987 s.23(1).

5830. **Petrol–licences–exploration and production**

PETROLEUM (PRODUCTION) (SEAWARD AREAS) (AMENDMENT) REGULATIONS 1996, SI 1996 2946; made under the Petroleum (Production) Act 1934 s.6. In force: December 16, 1996; £1.95.

These Regulations amend the Petroleum (Production) (Seaward Areas) Regulations 1988 (SI 1988 1213) which relate to applications for offshore petroleum exploration and production licences and the clauses to be incorporated in such licences. The amendments enable the Secretary of State to offer for licence tranches of blocks as well as or in addition to individual blocks and reduce the fee payable upon application for a production licence. The particulars required to support an application for a licence are amended, as are the model clauses for incorporation into petroleum production licences.

5831. **Water authorities**

EAST SURREY AND SUTTON DISTRICT WATER (AMENDMENT OF LOCAL ENACTMENTS ETC.) ORDER 1996, SI 1996 907; made under the Water Industry Act 1991 Sch.2 para.7. In force: April 1, 1996; £0.65.

This Order amends references to Sutton, or to the undertaking of Sutton, in any local statutory provision to have effect as a reference to East Surrey or, as the case may be, to the undertaking of East Surrey. The Order repeals the East Surrey Water Act s.9.

5832. **Water authorities**

NORTHUMBRIAN AND NORTH EAST WATER (AMENDMENT OF LOCAL ENACTMENTS ETC.) ORDER 1996, SI 1996 824; made under the Water Industry Act 1991 Sch.2 para.7. In force: April 1, 1996; £0.65.

This Order provides that any reference to North East, or to the undertaking of North East, in any local statutory provision and in any charges scheme made by North East under the Water Act 1989 s.76 or the Water Industry Act 1991 s.143 shall have effect, subject to para.(2), as a reference to Northumbrian or, as the case may be, to the undertaking of Northumbrian. The Order revokes the Derwent Water Order 1958 (SI 1958 496) s.18 to s.32, the Coquet Water Board Order 1959 (SI 1959 940) s.14 and the Derwent Water Order 1964 (SI 1964 1999).

5833. **Water companies**

CAMBRIDGE WATER COMPANY (CONSTITUTION AND REGULATION) ORDER 1996, SI 1996 713; made under the Statutory Water Companies Act 1991 s.12, s.14. In force: April 1, 1996; £1.10.

The Statutory Water Companies Act 1991 s.12(1) provides for the replacement of provisions relating to the constitution and regulation of a statutory water company contained in local legislation by provisions contained in a memorandum and articles which have been approved by special resolution of the members of the company. The replacement provisions have effect only if they are approved by the Secretary of State and come into force on such date as he determines. This Order approves a proposal by Cambridge Water Company that a memorandum and articles of association should have effect in substitution for provisions contained in the Company's local Acts and Orders (Art.2). It also provides that the date on which the memorandum and articles of association replace those provisions is April 1,

1996 (Art.3) and for the repeal of the superseded provisions and for consequential repeals (Art.4). The Order is associated with the Company's proposal to convert to the status of a registered water company under the Companies Act 1985.

5834. Water companies

The Office of Water Services issued a press release entitled *Water companies take steps to improve their trading practices* (News Release PN 37/96), published on September 24, 1996. A report has been published entitled *Transfer Pricing in the Water Industry* which shows a number of areas where the regulator wishes to see change. The report is concerned with the potential for material cross subsidy between water companies and their parent groups, variation in the degree of competitive tendering by the companies, lack of documentation of post tender negotiations, pricing for specialist services, the potential for conflicts of interests where regulated business directors or senior managers hold directorships in related companies, and some charges paid by the regulated business to the group not being directly linked to the services provided. As a result of these concerns, revised guidelines will be sent to the companies, placing greater emphasis on market testing, requiring companies to report on indirect transactions with associates, and offering further guidance to auditors on compliance with guidelines.

5835. Water industry–customer services–standards

WATER SUPPLY AND SEWERAGE SERVICE (CUSTOMER SERVICES STANDARDS) (AMENDMENT) REGULATIONS 1996, SI 1996 3065; made under the Water Industry Act 1991 s.38. In force: January 1, 1997; £1.10.

These Regulations amend the Water Supply and Sewerage Services (Customer Service Standards) Regulations 1989 (SI 1989 1159) in relation to water undertakers. They require the undertaker to maintain a minimum pressure of seven metres static head in communication pipes. If the pressure falls below that minimum for an hour or more on two occasions in any period of 28 days, the customer is entitled to a payment or credit of £25.

5836. Water supply–byelaws

The Department of the Environment issued a press release entitled *Water byelaws to be extended to 1998* (News release 416), published on October 14, 1996. The current water byelaws are to be extended for two years following a recommendation from the Water Regulations Advisory Committee. This will allow the Committee time to develop proposals for the updating of regulations, taking into account developing technologies. Announcing the decision, Environment Minister Robert Jones said that the current byelaws had been effective for almost 10 years, but were rapidly becoming in need of updating and replacement. He said that he looked forward to the Committee's eventual recommendations. The Committee is seeking the views of interested parties on how the byelaws may be updated. Those having views should write to Mr. P. Kemp, Water Supply & Regulation Division, Department of the Environment, Romney House, 43 Marsham Street, London SW1P 3PY; tel: 0171 276 8343; fax: 0171 276 8534.

5837. Articles

A bid too far? *(Ken Bailey)*: U.L.R. 1996, 7(4), 134-136. (Merger and takeover activity in privatised utilities companies, regulatory issues and Government policy).

A hostile bid: Southern acquires SWEB: C.L. 1996, 1 (4), 49-51. (Successful hostile take over bid by US electricity company for SWEB and tactics involved in funding and structuring of offer).

Consumer representation in utilities *(Martin Fitch)*: Q.A. 1996, 40(Summer), 10-12. (Statutory status and functions of four utility consumer representation bodies, their relationship with industry regulators and need for different models to improve effectiveness).

Deregulation of public utilities: the scope of the exemption in Article 90(2) of the EC Treaty *(Fiona Smith)*: U.L.R. 1996, 7(3), 111-116. (State liability for anti competitive behaviour of deregulated utilities).

Determination of applications for ordinary and emergency drought orders: W.L. 1996, 7(1), 33-37. (Developments arising from applications for drought orders including inspectors' observations and procedural issues).

Emerging competition in gas *(Rachel Ouseley)*: C.P.R. 1996, 6(2), 53-59. (New licensing framework and conditions for gas industry introduced by 1995 Act to be tested in first pilot areas in South West England from April 29, 1996 and consumer issues involved).

Energy: EC electricity market: B.L.E. 1996, 96(10), 8-9. (Progress of draft Directive on liberalisation of electricity market).

Environmental concerns arising from natural resource exploitation in the South Atlantic: regional and Patagonian implications *(Luis Castelli* and *Juan Rodrigo Walsh)*: R.E.C.I.E.L. 1996, 5(1), 30-37. (Problems of balancing protection of environment with oil and gas exploration and fishing in South Atlantic).

For a European doctrine of public utility: towards a single market for utilities? *(Stephane Rodrigues)*: U.L.R. 1996, 7(5), 183-185. (Concept of public services provided by utilities within EU and how principles can help in achieving EU's goals).

Liberalisation of regulated markets and its consequences for trade: the internal market for electricity as a case study *(A.M. Klom)*: J.E.R.L. 1996, 14(1), 1-13.

Licensing of the gas supply industry under the Gas Act 1995 *(Stephen R. Dow)*: U.L.R. 1996, 7(1), 31-34.

Oversupply and imbalance in the UK gas market *(Julian Kennedy)*: O.G.L.T.R. 1995, 13(12), 463-465. (Reasons for oversupply of gas, likely impact of new fields brought on stream in 1995 and evidence of delayed developments).

Power for the people *(Sean Watson)*: Lawyer 1996, 10(1), 6. (Legal problems created by flotation of holding company of National Grid Company).

Power games *(Dominic Maclaine)*: E.G. 1996, 9631, 38-39. (Privatisation of electricity industry).

PowerGen Plc/Southern Electric Plc–April 1996 (Cm 3231) and National Power Plc/Midlands Electricity Plc–April 1996 (Cm 3230): B.M.C.R. 1996, 5(3), 6-10. (Major vertical integration issues raised by bids by major power generators for regional electricity companies leading to Secretary of State's decision to block these as being against public interest).

Recent developments in the UK electricity industry *(Lovell White Durrant)*: I.H.L. 1996, Jul/Aug, 38-39. (Proposed acquisition of regional electricity companies by generators and cross utility acquisitions leading to emergence of multi utilities).

Regulated access to European electricity networks *(Eugene Daniel Cross)*: U.L.R. 1996, 7(1), 22-31. (Comparison of legal frameworks for six of most developed systems of regulated access to electricity networks among EU Member States).

"Take or pay" gas contracts: is disaster looming? *(John S. Huggins)*: O.G.L.T.R. 1996, 14(3), 99-104. (Implications of problem of oversupply of gas and contracts under which it has to be paid for whether taken or not and possible solutions).

The competitive electricity market from 1998 *(Charlotte Villiers)*: U.L.R. 1996, 7(2), 55-58. (OFFER consultation document, January 1995, on consumer protection, regulation and competition).

The development of vendor registration systems for European utilities *(Colin Maund)*: P.P.L.R. 1996, 2, CS49-50. (Development of database of suppliers and contractors in utilities and oil and gas industry as tool in EC public procurement process).

The implications of the Advocate General's opinion in the "leased lines" case for the drafting of the new regulations on utilities *(Sue Arrowsmith)*: P.P.L.R. 1996, 5, CS157-158. (Rules on services in 93/38 not yet implemented in UK partly because awaiting outcome of ECJ decision in "BT" case).

The law and practice of water management offshore *(Keith Hayes)*: O.G.L.T.R. 1996, 14(3), 105-111. (Treaties and domestic law affecting discharges at oil into sea from offshore installations).

The position of privatized utilities under WTO and EC procurement rules *(Marco C.E.J. Bronckers)*: L.I.E.I. 1996, 1, 145-160. (Reasons for including privatised utilities in EC public procurement policy and whether they should be included in WTO Agreement on Government Procurement).

The UK gas contract dilemma: who dares wins? *(Jonathan S.M. Fitzpatrick* and *Stephen R. Dow)*: U.L.R. 1996, 7(2), 82-87. (Whether British Gas should be able to renegotiate long term contracts with North Sea gas producers given changed market conditions).

Towards a unified European electricity market: the Commission's latest proposals *(Leigh Hancher)*: O.G.L.T.R. 1996, 14(3), 112-117. (Background to attempts to liberalise European electricity market and provisions of latest proposed Directive with particular regard to competition in production and supply, unbundling and regulation).

Unfair terms in water supply contracts: implied terms–the Unfair Terms in Consumer Contracts Regulations 1994 *(Tim Kaye)*: W.L. 1996, 7(2), 81-85. (Obligations of water companies to customers under legislation to implement Directive 93/13 effective January 1, 1995 may include rebates for hosepipe bans, repairs to leaks and no compulsory metering).

United they stand, divided they fall *(Paul Garrett)*: E.G. 1996, 9622, 48-50. (Consequences of utility mergers, creating multi utilities, for remaining water companies).

5838. Books

Ball, Simon; Burton, Tim–Water Law. Environmental law. Hardback: £45.00. ISBN 0-471-96577-4. Chancery Wiley Law Publications.

David, Martyn–Oil and Gas Agreements. £165.00. ISBN 0-421-55090-2. Sweet & Maxwell.

Dzurik, Andrew A.–Water Resources Planning. Hardback: £35.95. ISBN 0-8476-8081-9. Rowman & Littlefield.

VALUE ADDED TAX

5839. Accountants–regulation of economic activities did not constitute a business

[Value Added Tax Act 1994 s.4; Sixth Council Directive 77/388 on a common system for VAT Art.4.]

ICAEW appealed against a VAT tribunal's decision that they had failed to establish that, for the purposes of the Value Added Tax Act 1994 s.4(1), the practice regulation activities carried on by three of their committees constituted the carrying on of a business. ICAEW submitted that the regulation activities they performed amounted to a business and therefore the input tax levied on supplies was partially recoverable.

Held, dismissing the appeal, that in terms of the Sixth Council Directive 77/388 Arts.4.1 and 4.2, ICAEW's functions relating to the licensing of investment business, companies' auditing and insolvency practitioners did not amount to an economic activity but were, rather, regulation of economic activities and therefore did not qualify as a business under the 1994 Act.

INSTITUTE OF CHARTERED ACCOUNTANTS OF ENGLAND AND WALES v. CUSTOMS AND EXCISE COMMISSIONERS [1996] S.T.C. 799, Tuckey, J., QBD.

5840. Accounts–annual accounting requirements

VALUE ADDED TAX (ANNUAL ACCOUNTING) REGULATIONS 1996, SI 1996 542; made under the Value Added Tax Act 1994 s.25, Sch.11 para.2. In force: April 1, 1996; £1.55.

These Regulations revoke and replace the Value Added Tax Regulations 1995 Part VII, which relate to the requirements of the annual accounting scheme. The major changes to the accounting scheme relate to the reduction of the number of interim payments required to be made by certain businesses and the permitting of businesses to join the scheme before the start of their first current accounting year.

5841. Acquisitions–transfer of food trading stock–retail scheme B–whether goods received for resale in calculating zero rated takings

[Value Added Tax Act 1983 s.3; Value Added Tax (Special Provisions) Order 1981 Art.12.]

CEC appealed against a tribunal decision contending that the effect of the Value Added Tax Act 1983 s.3(3) and the Value Added Tax (Special Provisions) Order 1981 Art.12 was that a transfer of food trading stock, following an acquisition, was not a supply of goods for resale and could not be deemed a receipt of goods under retail scheme B for the purposes of calculating zero rated takings.

Held, dismissing the appeal, that the two statutory provisions served separate purposes and should not be read together. Under s.3(3) of the 1983 Act "supply" had a particular meaning in the identification of a taxable event. The Regulations, however, were concerned with calculating the value of supplies and the simplification of the determination process for retailers, *GUS Merchandise Corp Ltd v. Customs and Excise Commissioners* [1981] S.T.C. 569, [1982] C.L.Y. 3336 considered.

CUSTOMS AND EXCISE COMMISSIONERS v. CO-OPERATIVE WHOLESALE SOCIETY LTD [1995] S.T.C 983, Carnwath, J., QBD.

5842. Appeals–security for tax–whether decision would have been the same

[Value Added Tax Act 1983 s.40, Sch.7.]

Under powers contained in the Value Added Tax Act 1983 Sch.7 CEC served notice on JD, a company sharing two directors with a group now in receivership and owing VAT in excess of £1 million, requiring security as a condition of its making supplies. Following successful appeals by JD to the VAT tribunal and the High Court, CEC appealed, contending that the judge at first instance had erred in finding that once the tribunal concluded the commissioner's decision was erroneous, due to a failure to take account of relevant matters, it was bound to allow JD's appeal.

Held, dismissing the appeal, that a statutory appeal, under s.40, required an examination into whether the commissioners, in the interests of revenue protection, should have required security. In doing so, issues of reasonableness and the taking account of irrelevant considerations might have to be considered by the tribunal. However, the tribunal did not have discretion to examine issues pertaining to the protection of the revenue, which rested only with the commissioners, *Customs and Excise Commissioners v. J H Corbitt (Numismatists) Ltd* [1980] S.T.C. 231, [1980] C.L.Y. 2780 considered. An appeal could fail, even where a decision was shown to be erroneous, due to a failure to take account of relevant matters, where had they been considered the decision would still have gone the same way.

JOHN DEE LTD v. CUSTOMS AND EXCISE COMMISSIONERS [1995] S.T.C 941, Neill, L.J., CA.

5843. Assessment–date assessment made–power to withdraw or replace existing assessment

[Value Added Tax Act 1983 Sch.7 para.4; Finance Act 1985 s.25.]

CEC raised an assessment on C which was subsequently withdrawn and replaced. The tribunal considered, as a preliminary point, the validity of the second assessment.

Held, that (1) an assessment under the Value Added Tax Act 1983 Sch.7 para.4(1) was made when CEC carried out their assessment functions and not when it was notified to the taxpayer, *Customs and Excise Commissioners v. Le Rififi Ltd* [1995] S.T.C. 103, [1995] 2 C.L.Y. 5027 considered; (2) in view of the complication of the facts, the decision not to make an earlier assessment under Sch.7 para.4(5)(b) of the 1983 Act could not be described as perverse, *Cumbrae Properties (1963) Ltd v. Customs and Excise Commissioners* [1981] S.T.C. 799, [1981] C.L.Y. 2851 applied, and (3) there was nothing in the Finance Act 1985 s.25(1) which served to restrict the powers of CEC to withdraw or replace an assessment.

CLASSICMOOR LTD v. CUSTOMS AND EXCISE COMMISSIONERS [1995] V. & D.R. 1, Stephen Oliver Q.C. (Chairman), London Tribunal.

5844. Assessment–limitation period for assessment of wrongly credited input tax–period ran from when deduction was claimed

[Value Added Tax Act 1983 Sch.7.]

CEC appealed against a ruling that an assessment to recover wrongly credited input VAT from C was out of time under the Value Added Tax Act 1983 Sch.7 para.4(5).

Held, allowing the appeal, that the limitation period to assess wrongly credited input VAT ran not from the accounting period in which the chargeable transaction occurred but from the end of the prescribed accounting period, ie. the subsequent period in which the trader submitted a return claiming credit for the input VAT.

CUSTOMS AND EXCISE COMMISSIONERS v. CROYDON HOTEL AND LEISURE CO LTD [1996] S.T.C. 1105, Thorpe, L.J., CA.

5845. Assessment–time limits–period ran from when commissioners had sufficient evidence to make assessment

[Finance Act 1985 s.22; Value Added Tax Act 1983 Sch.7 para.4.]

CEC appealed and PO cross-appealed on issues arising from two assessments raised following the discovery of long term discrepancies in the calculation of general overheads for output tax purposes. On discovering the errors in 1992, CEC raised two assessments (a) from September 1986 to March 1987 and (b) from June 1987 to March 1992. PO sought to challenge the validity of the assessments on the grounds that (1) the first assessment was not made within the six year time limit under the Finance Act 1985 s.22(1); (2) the second assessment was a global assessment, and (3) both assessments were made a year after CEC had the necessary information to make them, contrary to the Value Added Tax Act 1983 Sch.7 para.4(5).

Held, allowing the appeal by CEC and dismissing the cross-appeal by PO, that (1) determining the one year period under Sch.7 para 4(5) was an issue of mixed law and fact which did not allow for constructive knowledge. The period ran from when CEC received sufficient factual evidence to make an assessment. The matter was to be remitted back to the tribunal, *Spillane v. Customs and Excise Commissioners* [1990] S.T.C. 212, [1990] C.L.Y. 4578 considered; (2) assessment notification was not a fixed or prescribed process and consisted of both the notice of assessment (Form VAT 655) and the schedules detailing the calculations used. The issue of whether the notice and schedule counted as a single assessment, or formed a series of assessments, was a mixture of law and fact, which was to be referred back to the tribunal, *Customs and Excise Commissioners v. Le Rififi Ltd* [1995] S.T.C. 103, [1995] 2

C.L.Y. 5027 followed, and (3) on the facts, the assessments had been completed within the period laid down by s.22 of the 1985 Act and therefore were not out of time.

CUSTOMS AND EXCISE COMMISSIONERS v. POST OFFICE [1995] S.T.C. 749, Potts, J., QBD.

5846. Assessment–validity of global assessment–schedules sent separately–whether taxpayer sufficiently informed of assessment

[Value Added Tax Act 1983 Sch.7 para.4.]

H appealed against an order relating to the validity of a VAT assessment. The notice of assessment was in the form of a global assessment and H argued that the judge below had been wrong to find that the global assessment was permissible. H also argued that schedules sent to H separately were not part of the notice of assessment and consequently he had not been sufficiently informed of the assessment.

Held, dismissing the appeal, that (1) the Value Added Tax Act 1983 Sch.7 para.4 contained nothing to suggest that an assessment period should be confined to a single prescribed accounting period, *SJ Grange Ltd v. Customs and Excise Commissioners* [1979] S.T.C. 183, [1979] C.L.Y. 2740 followed. The judge below did not accept Woolf J's interpretation, in *International Language Centres Ltd v. Customs and Excise Commissioners* [1983] S.T.C. 394, [1982] C.L.Y. 3360 or part of Lord Denning's judgment in the *Grange* case, that global assessments should be confined to cases where it was impossible to identify a specific period for which the tax was due and (2) the relevant statute and regulations gave no specific provision for the form of notification. H could have simply and quickly calculated the total sum due from him, *Bell v. Customs and Excise Commissioners* [1979] V.A.T.T.R. 115 disapproved.

HOUSE (T/A P&J AUTOS) v. CUSTOMS AND EXCISE COMMISSIONERS [1996] S.T.C. 154, Sir John Balcombe, CA.

5847. Consideration–debts

VALUE ADDED TAX (AMENDMENT) (NO.5) REGULATIONS 1996, SI 1996 2960; made under the Value Added Tax Act 1994 s.36. In force: December 17, 1996; £0.65.

These Regulations, which come into force on December 17, 1996, amend the Value Added Tax Regulations 1995 (SI 1995 2518) Reg.172 so that consideration shall not be taken as written off as a bad debt until at least six months have elapsed from the time when the debt becomes due and payable.

5848. Customs and Excise–officials seeking order for production of documents held by banks–application should be made inter partes unless notice of order might hamper investigations

[Value Added Tax Act 1994 Sch.11 para.11.]

A applied to quash orders made by the justices requiring certain banks to allow Customs and Excise officials investigating suspected VAT offences access to information pertaining to A and others.

Held, allowing the application, that the Customs and Excise Commissioners, CEC, should not have applied for the orders ex parte. The Value Added Tax Act 1994 Sch.11 para.11 did not require applications to be made ex parte but allowed for cases where applications on notice were not suitable. In each case CEC should consider the best way to proceed and whenever possible make inter partes applications, so that individuals affected by the orders could make representations before the orders were made. The orders should only be made ex parte if an investigation might be hampered by giving notice of the order. In the instant case the application should have been inter partes and, in any event, the orders were so badly worded they could not stand.

R. v. CITY OF LONDON MAGISTRATES' COURT, *ex p.* ASIF [1996] S.T.C. 611, Kennedy, L.J., QBD.

5849. Customs and Excise officers

VALUE ADDED TAX (AMENDMENT) (NO.4) REGULATIONS 1996, SI 1996 2098; made under the Value Added Tax Act 1994 Sch.11 para.5. In force: September 2, 1996; £0.65.

These Regulations amend the Value Added Tax Regulations 1995 (SI 1995 2518) Part XXV. Regulation 3 inserts a new Reg.A212 by which job band is defined for the purposes of Part XXV of the Regulations by reference to the rank given to an officer's job in the pay and grading system of Customs and Excise. Regulation 4 amends Reg.212(1) and Reg.213(a)(b). As a consequence, the minimum rank of officer by whom the powers described in Reg.212(1) and Reg.213(a)(b) may be exercised is an officer of a rank not below that of job band 7.

5850. Educational institutions–domestic legislation inconsistent with Sixth Council Directive

[Sixth Council Directive 77/388 on a common system for VAT; Finance Act 1989; Value Added Tax Act 1983 Sch.6.]

R appealed against CEC's decision to impose a VAT charge on building works. In 1990-91 R had employed contractors to construct playing fields and ancillary buildings near the college. The contractors' charges were subject to VAT but R as an educational institution was tax exempt. Therefore, R had no output tax from which the cost of the works could be deducted. R, to resolve this, incorporated a subsidiary, C, to which it granted a 12 year lease of the playing fields and buildings and as consideration R was granted a non-exclusive licence for their use. The ECJ decided, in 1989, that the zero rating of buildings constructed other than as dwelling houses was in conflict with the Sixth Council Directive 77/388 and as a result the Finance Act 1989 had limited the zero rating to the construction of buildings designed as dwellings. However, the grant of any kind of interest, other than a fee simple, or a licence to occupy was exempt. Under the Value Added Tax Act 1983 Sch.6A para.2 this exemption was subject to a right of waiver whereby the grantor of a lease or licence could exercise an option to be taxed or not. Both R and C exercised their right to waiver of the exemption in relation to the respective grants. CEC argued that R was liable to pay tax once they began using the playing fields because under para.5 and para.6 of Sch.6A of the 1983 Act, R was deemed to have supplied itself with an interest in the land for the purposes of business.

Held, allowing the appeal, that para.5 and para.6 of Sch.6A of the 1983 Act were inconsistent with the Sixth Council Directive as they produced an arbitrary charge where no charge could justifiably be required to counter market distortions. Therefore, CEC could not rely on Sch.6A to create a self-supply charge which was triggered by R's occupation of the land. The Sixth Council Directive was directly applicable and CEC could not attempt to rely on inconsistent domestic legislation to levy a charge against taxpayers.

ROBERT GORDON'S COLLEGE v. CUSTOM AND EXCISE COMMISSIONERS [1996] 1 W.L.R. 201, Lord Keith of Kinkel, HL.

5851. Exemptions–cultural property

VALUE ADDED TAX (CULTURAL SERVICES) ORDER 1996, SI 1996 1256; made under the Value Added Tax 1994 s.31, s.96. In force: June 1, 1996; £1.10.

In order to implement the Sixth Council Directive 77/388 ([1996] OJ L145/1) Art.13A(1)(n), this Order introduces a new Group 13 into the Value Added Tax Act 1994 Sch.9 which exempts admission charges for certain cultural activities from VAT. Item 1 relates to admission charges to cultural activities made by public bodies providing that exemptions will not disadvantage commercial enterprises in a competitive manner and item 2 exempts admission charges to cultural activities made by certain other bodies which cannot and do not distribute any profit they make, and use any profit made from admission charges to continue or improve the facilities to which admission is given. The exemption to performances put on by public and eligible bodies is limited and Group 12 of Sch.9 is amended by the extension of the exemption for fund-raising to eligible bodies.

5852. Exemptions–culture

[Value Added Tax (Cultural Services) Order 1996.]

HM Customs & Excise issued a press release entitled *Exemption from VAT of cultural services* (News release 33/96), published on June 3, 1996. A new VAT exemption took effect from June 1, 1996, applying to admission charges for cultural places and events run by public authorities and certain other non-profit making cultural bodies administered by unpaid volunteers. Where such an exemption would be disadvantageous, such as in the case of local authorities, which would have to forfeit the right to recover VAT paid on capital projects, bodies will not be compelled to exempt. In certain circumstances it may be possible for bodies qualifying for exemption to reclaim VAT back to January 1, 1990. The new arrangements will be explained in VAT Notice 701/47 Culture, which is available from local VAT Business Advice Centres.

5853. Extra statutory concessions–VAT refund on DIY conversion–jurisdiction of VAT tribunal to determine applicability of extra statutory concession

[Value Added Tax Act 1983 s.21; Value Added Tax Act 1994 s.35, s.84.]

In 1992 A commenced work converting a barn to live in as his own dwelling. In August 1993 the property was registered for council tax and A moved in. He continued to do further work, including some minor work to the drains and he had invoices for £17 and £545 dated in 1994 for supplies for that work. In November 1994 a local authority completion certificate was issued. On December 12, 1994 A claimed a refund of £6,893 for VAT on form VAT431. He asserted that the extra statutory concession, ESC, announced on July 21, 1994 applying to DIY conversions completed after April 21, 1994 applied. The claim was rejected and A appealed to the VAT Tribunal, which found that A was eligible for a VAT refund. The CEC appealed, alleging three errors of law: (1) in the tribunal's assertion of jurisdiction to decide whether A came within the terms of an ESC; (2) in the tribunal's holding that the CEC were wrong not to apply the ESC to A; and (3) that no reasonable tribunal could have found that the property in question was not complete. The CEC asserted that A had no claim as a matter of law to have the CEC decision reversed before the tribunal because A's claim had been based on an ESC. With regard to the jurisdiction issue there is no provision conferring jurisdiction on the tribunal in relation to an ESC. The Value Added Tax Act 1994 s.84 provides that "where an appeal is against a decision of the CEC which depended upon a prior decision taken by them in relation to the appellant, the fact that the prior decision is not within s.83 shall not prevent the tribunal from allowing the appeal on the ground that it would have allowed an appeal against the prior decision". For the tribunal to have had jurisdiction there would need to have been a prior decision of the CEC that was such that the disputed decision would have had a different conclusion if the prior decision had been different.

Held, allowing the appeal, that (1) there was one decision only and no prior decision to which s.84 could apply. An appeal could only be allowed if, on the facts, the decision to reject the refund application was unfair, or there was a disappointment of a legitimate expectation combined with detriment. There was no jurisdiction under the 1994 Act s.84, and no right to exercise jurisdiction with regard to the CEC's decision to reject A's application. The creation of the concession did not create a legal right. The operation of the ESC was a matter only for the CEC for which the tribunal had no jurisdiction, *Purdue v. Customs and Excise Commissioners* [1994] V.A.T.T.R. 387 and *G MacKenzie & Co Ltd v. Customs and Excise Commissioners* (Unreported, 1994) applied; (2) the tribunal had erred in law in concluding that A came within the scope of the ESC; (3) the completion date of the conversion was August 1993 when A first occupied the building as a dwelling. A did not come within the ESC, and the submission that A came within s.35 of the 1994 Act was rejected on the basis that A's application form clearly stated that the claim was under the ESC. The Value Added Tax Act 1983 s.21, as amended, provides for a refund of VAT chargeable on the supply of goods to a person constructing a building provided certain conditions are met. The amendment of the 1983 Act did not imply that conversion work could be zero rated. "Constructing a building" was held to mean erecting a building as a whole, *Customs and Excise Commissioners v. Viva Gas Appliances Ltd* [1983] 1 W.L.R. 1445, [1984] C.L.Y 3612 followed, whilst "constructing a dwelling" could include conversion of an existing building into a dwelling, *Customs and Excise Commissioners v. London Diocesan Fund* [1993] S.T.C. 369, [1993] C.L.Y. 4107 considered. A's submission that whether work carried out on an existing building constituted construction of a building was a question of fact and degree was not accepted as there was no proof of extensive work having been carried out, *Customs and Excise Commissioners v. Marchday Holdings* [1995] S.T.C. 898, [1995] 2 C.L.Y. 5122 distinguished. The supply of goods and services in the present case was standard rated because the supply was made in the course of conversion work, and not construction work.

CUSTOMS AND EXCISE COMMISSIONERS v. ARNOLD [1996] S.T.C. 1271, Hidden, J., QBD.

5854. Fraud–evasion did not require intention to default permanently on tax returns

[Value Added Tax Act 1983 s.39.]

D appealed against conviction of being knowingly concerned in the fraudulent evasion of VAT having been found guilty on four specimen counts. D, as a managing director of a VAT registered company, had failed to make tax returns. Assessments were made and he paid the first and part paid the second but no subsequent payments were made. Customs and Excise inspectors raided the company's premises and found records showing the company was working at a loss. D admitted his failure to submit the VAT returns but denied any intention to defraud. At the trial he claimed his intention had never been dishonest and he had always intended to pay the VAT owing but had chosen to pay his employees while the firm was trading at a loss. In directing the jury, the judge said that the word "evasion" in the Value Added Tax Act 1983 s.39(1) meant simply a deliberate non-payment. The issue at appeal, as certified by the trial judge, was whether the word "evasion" within s.39(1) meant (a) a deliberate non-payment when a payment was due, or (b) a deliberate non-payment when a payment was due with intent to make permanent default in whole or in part of that existing liability.

Held, dismissing the appeal, that the Crown did not have to prove a permanent intention to deprive. No such words appeared in the section and there was no reason why they should be implied. The word "evasion" did not imply any sense of permanence. *R. v. Fairclough* (Unreported, 1982) followed, *R. v. Allen* [1985] A.C. 1029, [1985] C.L.Y. 890, a case of making off without payment, distinguished. The appeal also failed on a second ground which criticised the judge's directions on the fact that D had not gone into the witness box. Taken in context of the entirety of the passages concerned, the directions were fair and not to be criticised.

R. v. DEALY (JOHN CLARK) [1995] 1 W.L.R. 658, McCowan, L.J., CA (Crim Div).

5855. Fuel–increase of consideration

VALUE ADDED TAX (INCREASE OF CONSIDERATION FOR FUEL) ORDER 1996, SI 1996 2948; made under the Value Added Tax Act 1994 s.57. In force: April 5, 1997; £0.65.

This Order, which will apply to taxable persons from their prescribed accounting periods beginning on or after April 6, 1997, amends the Value Added Tax Act 1994 s.57(3) Table A which sets out the fixed scales used as the basis for charging VAT on road fuel provided by businesses for private motoring. The Order increases the scales by an average of 15 per cent in relation to diesel and by an average of 13 per cent in relation to other fuels.

5856. Gold–transactions involving refashioning of customers' gold–whether tribunal entitled to classify transactions in broad categories–whether conclusions findings of fact

S ran a jewellery manufacturing business. In some cases, customers' gold was refashioned. CEC contended that these were transactions of barter with the full value of the object produced being the value of the supply. S contended that the gold remained the customers', and the VAT was due only on the work and labour. On appeal, the tribunal held that where 75 per cent of the gold was supplied by the customers, VAT was due only on the additional materials and labour, but that where gold of a different caratage was returned, VAT was due on the full amount. Both parties appealed.

Held, dismissing the appeal and the cross appeal, that (1) the tribunal was entitled to reach the conclusions that it did and (2) its analysis of the nature of the contracts between S and the customers was a proper inference from the facts, *Liverpool City Council v. Irwin* [1977] A.C. 239, [1976] C.L.Y. 1532 applied.

CUSTOMS AND EXCISE COMMISSIONERS v. SAI JEWELLERS [1996] S.T.C. 269, Macpherson of Cluny, J., QBD.

5857. Hotels–tour operators–whether hoteliers within tour operators' margin scheme–meaning of "travel agents" and "tour operators" under Sixth Council Directive Art.26

[Sixth Council Directive 77/388 on a common system for VAT Art.26; Value Added Tax Act 1983 s.37A.]

M and B ran a hotel in partnership. Nearly all their guests were brought to the hotel by long distance coaches hired by M and B. CEC contended that M and B were tour operators within the terms of the Value Added Tax Act 1983 s.37A. The tribunal allowed M and B's appeal on the basis of English law. Two further points, one of European and one of English law, were stayed. On appeal, CEC contended that the matter should be referred to the ECJ for guidance on the interpretation of the Sixth Council Directive 77/388 Art.26.

Held, referring the matter to the European Court, that it was essential to ascertain the meaning in Community law of the terms "travel agents" and "tour operators", as opposed to the differing approaches taken to this point of interpretation by courts in the Member States. It was also desirable for the case to be reheard by the Tribunal, with the point of European law referred if necessary to the ECJ for consolidation with the present matter.

MADGETT AND BALDWIN (T/A HOWDEN COURT HOTEL) v. CUSTOMS AND EXCISE COMMISSIONERS [1996] S.T.C. 167, Brooke, J., QBD.

5858. Imports–inward processing arrangements–default interest for the period between temporary and definitive importation–European Union

[Sixth Council Directive 77/388 on a common system for VAT Art.10, Art.16.]

P imported a consignment of wheat in 1982 from Canada in order to process it into wheat semolina and re-export it. Subsequently, P released for consumption the byproducts of the processing which were then definitively imported. In respect of the definitive import, the Italian authorities required payment of a levy and value added tax and it also required payment of default interest for the period between temporary importation and definitive importation.

Held, that the EU rules applicable at the time did not preclude the charging of default interest in relation to the agricultural levy. However, pursuant to the Sixth Council Directive 77/388 Art.10(1)(b), Art.10(3) and Art.16(1)(A)(e), a Member State was precluded from requiring default interest to be charged on the VAT payable in the event of declaration for home use in the EU of goods which were previously subject to inward processing arrangements for the period between temporary importation and definitive importation.

PEZZULLO MOLINI PASTIFICI MANGIMIFICI SpA v. MINISTERO DELLE FINANZE (C166/94) [1996] S.T.C. 1236, Puissochet (President), ECJ.

5859. Input tax–apportionment–sale of buildings used for business and private purposes–whether business constituted separate supply–whether could apportion property to business and private use for computing input tax liability–European Union

[Sixth Council Directive 77/388 on a common system for VAT Art.5, Art.13C, Art.17.]

On the sale of a building which included a hotel and a private dwelling, A opted, under the Sixth VAT Directive 77/388 Art.13C for taxation but treated only that part of the premises used for business purposes as subject to VAT, whereas the authorities sought to tax the entire dwelling as an indivisible item. As a result, three questions were referred to the ECJ for a preliminary ruling: (1) whether the portion of an immovable property which was used for business purposes constituted a separate supply, under Art.5(1); (2) whether a taxable person selling property part of which had not been assigned to the business was entitled to deduct the VAT due or paid on the whole of the property under Art.17(2), and (3) whether the adjustment to VAT was limited only to the business portion of the property.

Held, answering the points raised, that (1) while national law could determine the extent of property rights transferred on a sale, the objective of the Sixth VAT Directive was to create a common system for VAT. The Directive, not national law, had to be applied to determine whether a transaction was liable to tax; (2) under Art.2(1) of the Directive a private transaction by a taxable person was not liable to tax and the Directive did not prevent such a person from apportioning parts of his property to business and private use. However, such a division was to be based on the proportions prevailing in the year of acquisition and not by reference to geographical divisions. In addition, during the ownership period, the person must demonstrate an intention to keep a portion among his private assets. The option contained in Art.13C of the Directive did not allow a non-taxable supply to be translated into a taxable one. As a result, a taxable person selling property reserved for his private use did not act as a taxable person under Art.2(1) of the Directive, and (3) if a taxable person chose to exclude a portion from his business assets, that part did not fall within the tax system, and only the business part was to be taken into account when computing input tax liability under Art.17(2), or for adjustment purposes under Art.20(2).

FINANZAMT UELZEN v. ARMBRECHT (C291/92) [1995] All E.R. (EC) 882, G C Rodriguez Iglesias (President), ECJ.

5860. Input tax–apportionment–whether applicable in case of repairs to roof–buildings used business and private purposes.

[Sixth Council Directive 77/388 on a common system for VAT Art.6.]

M carried on business as dairy farmers. They claimed credit for the whole of the input tax paid in respect of repairs to the roof of a farmhouse used both for the farming business and as a home. CEC decided that the allowable input tax credit should be limited to that proportion which business use bore to the total use. M appealed.

Held, dismissing the appeal, that (1) the *Lennartz* decision applied only to goods and not to immovable property, *Lennartz v. Finanzamt Munchen III* [1991] E.C.R. 3795, [1995] 2 C.L.Y. 5057 distinguished, and (2) the Sixth Council Directive 77/388 Art.6(2)(b) did not apply on its wording to supplies made to a registered trader by a third party.

F&M MOUNTJOY & SONS v. CUSTOMS AND EXCISE COMMISSIONERS; WD HURD v. CUSTOMS AND EXCISE COMMISSIONERS [1995] V. & D.R. 128, Malcolm JF Palmer (Chairman), London Tribunal.

5861. Input tax–cars–order excluding deduction

[Value Added Tax (Input Tax) Order 1992 Art.7.]

Held, that pending a further EU Directive establishing which goods were excluded from input tax credit entitlement, the UK could continue to exclude input tax credit for cars purchased for business purposes. However, the Value Added Tax (Input Tax) Order 1992 Art.7, as amended, permitted input tax to be reclaimed in respect of cars obtained by a leasing business.

ROYSCOT LEASING LTD v. CUSTOMS AND EXCISE COMMISSIONERS; ALLIED DOMECQ PLC v. CUSTOMS AND EXCISE COMMISSIONERS; TC HARRISON GROUP LTD v. CUSTOMS AND EXCISE COMMISSIONERS [1996] S.T.C. 898, Turner, J., QBD.

5862. Input tax–cars–order excluding deduction–order valid and compatible with European law–apportionment inapplicable given clear and unambiguous exclusion

[Sixth Council Directive 77/388 on a common system for VAT Art.17.2; Value Added Tax (Input Tax) Order 1992 Art.7; Value Added Tax Act 1983 s.14.]

AL, the parent company of a group of companies carrying on retailing, brewing, food and wine and spirits businesses, appealed against a refusal to permit input tax deductions on car purchases. The cars were supplied to its employees, some on the basis of necessity and others as perquisites. AL contended that the block on input tax deductions, under the Value Added Tax (Input Tax) Order 1992 Art.7, was incompatible with the right of deduction in the Sixth Council Directive 77/388 Art.17.2. Alternatively, even if the order was valid, apportionment should be permitted, as the cars purchased were used partly for business and partly for private purposes.

Held, dismissing the appeal, that (1) the exclusion created by the blocking order was compatible with the Sixth Council Directive 77/388 and validly made under the enabling provisions of the Value Added Tax Act 1983 s.14(10) and (2) the terms of the exclusion were clear and unambiguous and left no room for apportionment.

ALLIED LYONS PLC (NOW ALLIED DOMECQ PLC) v. CUSTOMS AND EXCISE COMMISSIONERS [1995] V. & D.R. 42, Stephen Oliver Q.C. (Chairman), London Tribunal.

5863. Input tax–cars–order excluding input tax deduction–compatibility with European law

[Second Council Directive 95/7 amending Directive 77/388 and introducing new simplification measures with regard to VAT Art.11; Sixth Council Directive 77/388 on a common system for VAT Art.17; Value Added Tax (Input Tax) Order 1992 Art.7.]

TCH engaged in motor dealerships, short term car hire and long term car leasing. It was prevented from deducting input tax on the cars it purchased for demonstration, hire or leasing purposes by the Value Added Tax (Input Tax) Order 1992 Art.7 and its predecessors. TCH appealed, contending that the blocking order was invalid under the Sixth Council Directive 77/388 Art.17.

Held, dismissing the appeal, that the orders preventing deduction of input tax were valid within the permission given by the Second Council Directive 95/7 Art.11 and the Sixth Council Directive 77/388 Art.17.

TC HARRISON GROUP LTD v. CUSTOMS AND EXCISE COMMISSIONERS [1995] V. & D.R. 30, Stephen Oliver Q.C. (Chairman), London Tribunal.

5864. Input tax–health club subscription for company director–subscriptions not made for purposes of business as was in nature of luxury, amusement or entertainment

[Value Added Tax Act 1983 s.40.]

P provided seminars on VAT through his personal company P Ltd. To promote his health P joined a tennis club. The CEC decided that P Ltd was not entitled to credit for input tax in respect of fees paid to the club. P Ltd appealed.

Held, dismissing the appeal, that (1) the basic purpose of the expenditure was not referable to P Ltd's business, *Ian Flockton Developments Ltd v. Customs and Excise Commissioners* [1987] S.T.C. 394, [1987] C.L.Y. 3815 applied, and (2) the expenditure was in the nature of a luxury, amusement or entertainment within the Value Added Tax Act 1983 s.40(32A).

JOHN PRICE BUSINESS COURSES LTD v. CUSTOMS AND EXCISE COMMISSIONERS [1995] V. & D.R. 106, Theodore Wallace (Chairman), London Tribunal.

5865. Input tax–mixed use calculations–whether only direct attribution formula lawful–best judgment assessments by Customs

[Sixth Council Directive 77/388 on a common system for VAT Art.17; Value Added Tax Act 1983 Sch.7; Value Added Tax (General) Regulations 1985 Reg.30.]

D appealed against a best judgment assessment made by Customs under the Value Added Tax Act 1983 Sch.7 para.4(1), following the rejection of D's own calculations in support of a mixed use input tax claim. Customs contended that D should have calculated not the input VAT relating to exempt supplies but the input VAT relating to taxable supplies. D contended that the basis for the assessment was wrong, as under the Sixth Council Directive 77/388 Art.17(5) the UK had opted for the use of supplies to form the basis for deductions and that the method used by Customs was contrary to the Value Added Tax (General) Regulations 1985 Reg.30.

Held, dismissing the appeal, that (1) the power contained within Art.17(5) did not require Customs to base its calculations on only one formula; (2) the Value Added Tax (General) Regulations 1985 Reg.30, made pursuant to Art.17(5), did not require the deductible part of mixed input tax to be calculated only by reference to the direct attribution method; (3) in making best judgment assessments, Customs were not obliged to replicate or mirror D's duty to make returns, nor to establish certain facts before making an assessment, *Van Boeckel v. Customs and Excise Commissioners* [1981] S.T.C. 290, [1981] C.L.Y. 2839 approved and (4) on the facts, D had not given any evidence regarding the attribution of mixed use supplies to their actual use, therefore Customs had done their honest and reasonable best on the basis of the information given.

DWYER PROPERTY LTD v. CUSTOMS AND EXCISE COMMISSIONERS [1995] S.T.C 1035, Laws, J., QBD.

5866. Input tax–mobile homes–expenditure on concrete bases and pipework non-deductible–expenditure not related to the sale of the home or the grant of the licence to occupy

CEC appealed against a decision of a VAT tribunal which allowed that input tax in respect of expenditure incurred by H in the construction of concrete bases for mobile homes was deductible. H owned mobile home parks and, when occupiers wished to move the mobile home was generally sold to H or a third party. The mobile home was usually scrapped and rebuilt. CEC argued that the sale of a mobile home was made up of the taxable supply of the mobile home itself and the exempt supply of the grant of the licence to occupy. CEC contended that the tribunal had erred in law. H argued that the mobile homes were buildings and the provision of the concrete base and pipe work was part of the supply of the home itself.

Held, allowing the appeal, that (1) although an occupier would only purchase a mobile home once he was satisfied that the concrete base reached the standards recommended by such documents as the Homeseeker Owners' Handbook and the requirements of the site licence, the base was owned by the site owner and was not part of the sale of the home. The home was movable and a chattel and the input tax was not deductible as the expenditure related to the licence and (2) it was for the tribunal to decide whether the goods and services had a direct and immediate link with the taxable transaction; whether or not the ultimate purpose was exempt was irrelevant, *Stonecliff Caravan Park v. Customs and Excise Commissioners* [1993] V.A.T.T.R. 464 and *BLP Group Plc v. Customs and Excise Commissioners (C4/94)* [1995] S.T.C. 424, [1995] 2 C.L.Y. 5046 followed.

CUSTOMS AND EXCISE COMMISSIONERS v. HARPCOMBE LTD [1996] S.T.C. 726, Brooke, J., QBD.

5867. Input tax–office block construction–whether a conversion or a new building–whether identity of original building survived

[Value Added Tax Act 1983 Sch.5.]

CEC appealed against a VAT tribunal finding that an office block construction, using the reinforced concrete frame, foundations, internal party walls and other features of an old industrial building on the same site fulfilled the "new building" test. Contending that the work amounted instead to a conversion, alteration or enlargement of an existing building, as stated in the Value Added Tax Act 1983 Note 1A of Group 8 Sch.5, the CEC sought to disallow a claim for the deduction of input tax from the construction costs.

Held, dismissing the appeal, that the evidence showed that the office block had utilised a substantial part of the incomplete skeleton of the former structure creating a new building larger in size and of a different construction. Where such factors existed, it was a question of fact and degree whether the end result amounted to a new building or not. However, the office block construction amounted to more than the "conversion, alteration or enlargement" of an existing structure, as stated in Note 1A. A decision maker approaching the issue had to look at the situation before any work had been done and again when it was completed; the "new building" test not being fulfilled where the identity of the original building still survived at the end, *Wimpey Group Services Ltd v. Customs and Excise Commissioners* [1988] S.T.C. 625, [1988] C.L.Y. 3778 and *Customs and Excise Commissioners v. London Diocesan Fund* [1993] S.T.C. 369, [1993] C.L.Y. 4107 applied.

CUSTOMS AND EXCISE COMMISSIONERS v. MARCHDAY HOLDINGS LTD [1995] S.T.C. 898, Laws, J., QBD.

5868. Input tax–payment of estate agents' fees as an incentive scheme by housebuilders–deductible supply of services for VAT

[Value Added Tax Act 1983 s.14.]

CEC appealed against a decision of a VAT tribunal that a sales incentive scheme operated by RG, housebuilders, whereby RG paid the purchasers' estate agent's fees, was a supply of services to RG and therefore gave them the right to deduct input tax. CEC argued that the tribunal had made an error of law as the services were not supplied to RG within the Value Added Tax Act 1983 s.14(3), but were supplied to the purchaser only and RG indemnified the costs of the services.

Held, dismissing the appeal, that, under the scheme, RG had to choose and instruct the estate agent, RG had to agree the asking price and approve any alteration to the instructions and RG was liable for the fees of the estate agent unless the purchaser pulled out of the transaction. This amounted to a tripartite contract with RG, the client of the estate agent, as the principal. The issue was one of fact and the tribunal was correct to find that services were supplied to RG and the purchaser and that, at the time of supply, supplies had been made to RG by the estate agents within s.14(3) of the 1983 Act.

CUSTOMS AND EXCISE COMMISSIONERS v. REDROW GROUP PLC [1996] S.T.C. 365, Potts, J., QBD.

5869. Input tax–recovery of legal and brokering fees–acquisition of leasing businesses combined with existing leasing operation–taxable supplies

[Value Added Tax (General) Regulations 1985 Reg.30.]

CEC appealed against a decision allowing U to recover input tax amounting to £103,327, paid on brokering and legal fees relating to the acquisition of three leasing companies. Following losses in its own leasing business between 1987-1989, U purchased the companies, transferring the acquired business into its own leasing operation. CEC contended that recovery should be limited to £74,486 in respect of input tax, as the supplies were attributable to non-physical assets and not U's total taxable outputs within the meaning of the Value Added Tax (General) Regulations 1985 Reg.30(1)(b).

Held, dismissing the appeal, that it was a finding of fact that the acquisitions were intended to enable U to make substantial additions to its existing leasing business and to the making of taxable supplies. Although not of a physical nature, the assets included rights passing between the companies and their lessees and amounted to assets for use by U in the making of taxable supplies, *BLP Group Plc v. Customs and Excise Commissioners (C4/94)* [1995] S.T.C. 424, [1995] 2 C.L.Y. 5046 distinguished.

CUSTOMS AND EXCISE COMMISSIONERS v. UBAF BANK LTD [1996] S.T.C. 372, Neill, L.J., CA.

5870. Input tax–recovery sought after taxpayer used less advantageous method of apportionment for business and non-business activities–no error made permitting retrospective claim

The Board of Trustees of VAM appealed against a VAT tribunal decision refusing recovery of input tax paid in previous accounting periods. In agreement with the local VAT office, the appellant had adopted the Notice 700 Appendix J formula for apportionment for its business and non-business activities. Subsequently a more favourable method was devised by the museum's accountants and VAM sought to recover the excess input tax paid under the formula.

Held, dismissing the appeal, that the formula was not mandatory and its use was conditional on producing a fair and reasonable result. Just because the formula was less advantageous for the taxpayer in question did not mean that it should not have been used. No error in fact or law had occurred which would permit a retrospective claim.

VICTORIA AND ALBERT MUSEUM v. CUSTOMS AND EXCISE COMMISSIONERS [1996] S.T.C. 1016, Turner, J., QBD.

5871. Interest–prescribed rate

VALUE ADDED TAX ACT 1994 (INTEREST ON TAX) (PRESCRIBED RATE) ORDER 1996, SI 1996 165; made under the Value Added Tax Act 1994 s.74. In force: February 6, 1996; £0.65.

This Order lowers from 7 per cent per annum to 6.25 per cent per annum the prescribed rate of interest for the purposes of the Value Added Tax Act 1994 s.74 (interest on VAT recovered or recoverable by assessment).

5872. Land use–turnover tax–exemptions–requirements for land to be defined as "building land"–European Union

[Sixth Council Directive 77/388 on a common system for VAT Art.4, Art.13.]

A dispute arose as to whether turnover tax was payable on the supply of vacant land for development by a Dutch municipality. The land was designated for building use and had been equipped with roads, sewers and other services. The Sixth Council Directive 77/388 Art.13B(h) provided that "the supply of land which has not been built on other than building land" was exempt from turnover tax, and "building land" was defined in Art.4(3)(b) as "any improved or unimproved land defined as such by the member states". The regional court of appeal referred to the ECJ the question whether land not built on had to have been subjected to specific improvements in order to be categorised as building land under the Sixth Directive.

Held, that the expression "building land" in Art.4(3)(b) and Art.13B(h) referred to land, irrespective of whether or not it had been improved, which had been defined by the member states as land intended for building. It was for individual member states, and not the court, to define the terms of the exemption, provided that they complied with the objective of exempting from tax only the supply of land which had not been built on and was not intended to support a building.

GEMEENTE EMMEN v. BELASTINGDIENST GROTE ONDERNEMINGEN (C468/93) [1996] All E.R. (EC) 372, Edward (President), ECJ.

5873. Liquidation–concept of economic activity–status of taxable person–profitability study for a project–abandonment of project–recovery of VAT–European Union

[Sixth Council Directive 77/388 on a common system for VAT Art.4.]

I was a company set up with the purpose of developing and exploiting processes to treat sea water and turn it into drinking water for distribution. It acquired certain capital goods and commissioned a study on the profitability of a project to construct a desalination plant. It paid VAT in respect of those activities, in particular on the study, which was subsequently repaid by the Belgian tax authorities. However, the study identified numerous profitability problems with the result that the project was abandoned and I was put into liquidation. Consequently, it never commenced the activity envisaged. The tax authorities sought the recovery of the VAT together with penalties and interest.

Held, that where the tax authorities had accepted that a company which declared an intention to commence an economic activity giving rise to taxable transactions had the status of a taxable person for the purposes of VAT within the meaning of Sixth Council Directive 77/388 Art.4, the commissioning of a profitability study could be regarded as an economic activity even if the purpose was to investigate to what degree the activity envisaged was profitable. Except in cases of fraud or abuse, the status of taxable person for the purpose of VAT could not be withdrawn from that company retroactively where, in view of the results of that study, it was decided not to move to the operational phase but to put the company into liquidation with the result that the economic activity envisaged did not give rise to taxable transactions.

INTERCOMMUNALE VOOR ZEEWATERONTZILTING (IN LIQUIDATION) v. BELGIUM (C110/94); SUB NOM. INZO v. BELGIUM (C110/94) [1996] S.T.C. 569, DAO Edward (President), ECJ.

5874. Listed buildings–alterations–roof replaced with higher roof–whether input VAT recovery excluded–whether work was repair or maintenance

[Value Added Tax Act 1983 Sch.5.]

W replaced the roof on a listed building which needed repair, but the new roof structure differed slightly in height and construction from the one it replaced. W's claim that the work was zero rated was refused, as CEC contended that the work amounted to repair or maintenance under the Value Added Tax Act 1983 Sch.5 Group 8A. CEC appealed against a tribunal ruling in favour of W.

Held, allowing the appeal, that although the work had slightly altered the height of the roof, the remainder of the work undertaken was substantially of a repair and maintenance nature. Any alterations to the physical features were minimal and due largely to modern building techniques and materials. As a result the work was not zero rated under Sch.5 of the Act, *ACT Construction Ltd v. Customs and Excise Commissioners* [1982] S.T.C. 25, [1982] C.L.Y. 3345 considered.

CUSTOMS AND EXCISE COMMISSIONERS v. WINDFLOWER HOUSING ASSOCIATION [1995] S.T.C. 860, Ognall, J., QBD.

5875. Listed buildings–alterations–supply of joinery made off site–site visits to measure up and sort out problems–whether mixed supply of goods and services so as to be zero rated

[Value Added Tax Act 1983 Sch.5.]

CEC appealed against a tribunal decision allowing J's appeal against an assessment to VAT and default interest in respect of wooden joinery items designed in connection with alterations to listed buildings which J claimed qualified as zero rated. CEC contended that, as the articles manufactured were not fitted on site, they did not qualify as a mixed supply of services and goods in the course of an approved alteration and did not fall to be treated as zero rated under the Value Added Tax Act 1983 Sch.5 Group 8. The tribunal found that measuring and making the joinery and any subsequent site visits were a mixed supply of goods and services.

Held, allowing the appeal, that the work amounted to a single supply of goods under contract, with the services supplied by J amounting to no more than the normal obligations incumbent upon a seller of goods. As a result, the goods were not covered by the zero rate exemption under Sch.5 of the 1983 Act. The distinction between a single supply or a supply of goods was a question of law, answerable by the application of common sense to the facts of the situation. The tribunal had misdirected itself as to the legal principles. Having found that the services were an intrinsic part of the supply, it should have concluded that no separate supply of services had occurred apart from the supply of goods.

CUSTOMS AND EXCISE COMMISSIONERS v. JEFFS (T/A J&J JOINERY) [1995] S.T.C. 759, Ognall, J., QBD.

5876. Listed buildings–alterations–zero rating–whether installation of new sewerage system for listed building was an approved alteration

[Value Added Tax Act 1983 Sch. 5.]

W owned a listed building. A new sewerage system was installed which served the building and cottages in its grounds. CEC decided that the works were standard rated. W appealed, contending that the works fell within Value Added Tax Act 1983 Sch.5, Group 8A, item 2 and were zero-rated.

Held, allowing the appeal in part, that (1) the works were part of the listed building or its curtilage; (2) they did not constitute repair or maintenance; (3) they required listed building consent, affected the character of the building and were executed in accordance with the consent and (4) the works relating to the cottages were standard rated requiring an apportionment between the standard and zero rated supplies.

WALSINGHAM COLLEGE (YORKSHIRE PROPERTIES) v. CUSTOMS AND EXCISE COMMISSIONERS [1995] V. & D.R. 141, AW Simpson, Manchester Tribunal.

5877. Mail order–tax assessment of goods sold to agents not registered for VAT–discounts for agents–whether whole or part of business carried on by taxpayer consisted of supplying "goods to be sold by retail"–direction did not contravene EC law

[Value Added Tax Act 1983 Sch.4 para.3; Sixth Council Directive 77/388 on a common system for VAT.]

CEC appealed against a Court of Appeal ruling, [1994] S.T.C. 668, in favour of FAD, a mail order company engaged in selling goods to agents not registered for VAT, who in turn sold on some of the goods to catalogue customers and kept some for their own purposes. The Court of Appeal found that CEC had no power to issue a direction that under the Value Added Tax Act 1983 Sch.4 para.3 FAD's business consisted of supplying goods to non-taxable persons to be sold by retail and that for VAT purposes the relevant value would be the full market value of the goods. The appeal turned on whether the whole or part of FAD's business consisted of supplying goods to non-taxable persons to be sold by retail, and to which supply of goods the direction applied, and further, whether the direction contravened the Sixth Council Directive 77/388 which authorised the UK to derogate from its provisions and simplify tax charging procedures.

Held, allowing the appeal, that the goods sold by agents to customers were already earmarked for onward sale and therefore part of the business concerned an identifiable supply of goods "to be sold by retail". It was not necessary for the purpose of charging VAT to identify which particular supply or which exact percentage of goods was sold on, as Sch.4 para.3 specified that only part of the business need be retail selling. CEC were entitled to base the market value for assessment on the catalogue price at which 70 per cent of goods were sold, as to ascertain the market value of the remaining goods would not be reasonably practical and their assessment direction was not a departure from the derogation authorised under EC law, *Direct Cosmetics Ltd v. Customs and Excise Commissioners* [1988] S.T.C. 540, [1988] C.L.Y. 1569 considered.

FINE ART DEVELOPMENTS v. CUSTOMS AND EXCISE COMMISSIONERS [1996] 1 W.L.R. 1054, Lord Keith of Kinkel, HL.

5878. Medical treatment–care–exemptions

HM Customs & Excise issued a press release entitled *VAT health exemptions: direct supervision* (News Release 23/96), published on April 11, 1996. New guidelines have been published on VAT exemptions for certain healthcare services provided that these services are performed for the medical needs of the client. Providers and recipients of homecare services will benefit from the exemption. Exemption can only be granted if the services are carried out in the presence of a qualified supervisor. The changes come into effect immediately.

5879. Milk–farmer undertaking to discontinue milk production–compensation payment not subject to VAT–European Union

[Council Regulation 1336/86 fixing compensation for the definitive discontinuation of milk production; Sixth Council Directive 77/388 on a common system for VAT.]

A reference was made to the ECJ for a preliminary ruling on whether an undertaking to discontinue milk production under Council Regulation 1336/86 constituted a supply of services for the purposes of the Sixth Council Directive 77/388 Art.6(1). M, a dairy cattle owner, had applied for a grant under the Regulation after undertaking to discontinue milk production. His application was subsequently accepted and he was awarded compensation of DM 385,980. His undertaking was treated as a taxable supply and the compensation was made subject to a VAT payment. M brought proceedings claiming that the compensation payment was not subject to VAT under the Sixth VAT Directive.

Held, that for the purposes of the Sixth VAT Directive Art.6(1) an undertaking to discontinue milk production did not constitute a supply of services, as no benefit was conferred on the Community or the competent national authorities as consideration for the payment. Therefore any compensation received by a farmer under the compensation Regulation was not subject to VAT.

MOHR v. FINANZAMT BAD SEGEBERG (C215/94) [1996] All E.R. (EC) 450, DAO Edward (President), ECJ.

5880. Nurseries–whether exempt as being of social or cultural nature–whether non-profit making–European Union

[Sixth Council Directive 77/388 on a common system for VAT Art.13A.]

BG operated a nursery and sought to claim an exemption from VAT under Dutch law equivalent to the Sixth VAT Directive 77/388 Art.13A(1)(g) on the grounds that the nursery was of a social or cultural nature. BG contended that, as the surplus of income over expenditure was less than a salary level, she was non-profit making and qualified for the exemption. As a result, the question was referred to the ECJ, whether a trader, setting out to achieve an income in excess of expenditure, but less than a reasonable level of remuneration, was still aiming to make a profit, under Art.13A(2)(a).

Held, answering the question, that the operation of Art.13A(1)(g) was limited to social or cultural objectives operated by either recognised charities or public law bodies. Therefore the exemption could not apply to BG with the result that the rest of the reference was of no further relevance.

BULTHUIS-GRIFFIOEN v. INSPECTOR DER OMZETBELASTING [1995] S.T.C. 954, F A Schockweiler (President), ECJ.

5881. Motor vehicles

VALUE ADDED TAX (AMENDMENT) REGULATIONS 1996, SI 1996 210; made under the Value Added Tax Act 1994 s.30, Sch.11 para.2. In force: March 1, 1996; £0.65.

In order that they comply with Art.15.2 of Council Directive 77/388 and its amendments (Council Directive 91/680 and Council Directive 95/7), the Value Added Tax Regulations 1995 (SI 1995 2518), as far as they relate to the supply of used motor vehicles being exported by someone other than the supplier and the requirements for businesses to supply certain information to their EC Sales Lists, are amended. As a result of the amendments it is no longer a requirement for businesses to declare supplies of goods for processing in their EC Sales Lists or to provide information relating to such supplies. Zero-rating of used motor vehicles to be exported outside the European Community by someone other than the supplier is now permitted.

5882. Payments

VALUE ADDED TAX (AMENDMENT) (NO.2) REGULATIONS 1996, SI 1996 1198; made under the Value Added Tax Act 1994 s.25, s.28. In force: June 1, 1996; £0.65.

These Regulations, which amend the Value Added Tax Regulations (SI 1995 2518), provide that where the Commissioners have directed the manner in which a person shall make payments on account under the Value Added Tax Act 1994 s.28 then the person shall also pay any balancing payments due in respect of VAT returns in the same manner; provide that payments on account and payments of balances due in respect of VAT returns by persons in the Payments on Account Scheme will not have been made unless they have been made in time to have cleared to the Commissioners' account; and provide that references to a payment being made by any day include references to the payment being made on that day.

5883. Supply of services

VALUE ADDED TAX (AMENDMENT) (NO.3) REGULATIONS 1996, SI 1996 1250; made under the Value Added Tax Act 1994 s.18B, s.18C, s.18D, s.26, s.46, s.58, Sch.11 para.2, Sch.11 para.6; and the Value Added Tax Act 1994 18F. In force: June 1, 1996; £3.20.

These Regulations amend the Value Added Tax Regulations 1995 (SI 1995 2518) to assist in the implementation of Council Directive 77/388 ([1977] OJ L145/1) (the Sixth VAT Directive) as amended by Council Directive 95/7 ([1995] OJ L102/18). They set out the administrative procedures for the fiscal warehousing regime and contain consequential changes to the treatment of services performed on, or in relation to, goods subject to a fiscal or other warehousing regime.

5884. Payments

VALUE ADDED TAX (PAYMENTS ON ACCOUNT) (AMENDMENT) ORDER 1996, SI 1996 1196; made under the Value Added Tax Act 1994 s.28. In force: June 1, 1996; £1.10.

This Order amends the Value Added Tax (Payments on Account) Order 1993 (SI 1993 2001). Article 3(a) and Art.11 substitute references to the Value Added Tax Act

1994 for references to the Value Added Tax Act 1983 and Art.6 withdraws the seven day extension to the time for making payments on account hitherto afforded to persons paying by credit transfer by revoking Art.10. Article 3(b), Art.4 and Art.5 make consequential amendments to Art.6 by removing further references to Art.10 in the principal Order as the definition of "credit transfer" is no longer required. Article 7 and Art.8 reduce the amount of payment on account by 50 per cent to one twenty-fourth of the liability in the reference period. Article 9 makes consequential amendments and Art.10 adds a new Art.12 which gives persons in the scheme an option to pay the actual VAT liability for the preceding month rather than the predetermined amount.

5885. Penalties–tax evasion–whether assessment for prescribed accounting periods–notification–liability of individual directors for penalty

[Finance Act 1985 s.13; Finance Act 1986 s.14, s.21.]

B was a director of a company found liable for fraudulently concealing VAT liability. The company was found liable under the Finance Act 1985 s.13, for a sum equal to the amount evaded and B was found liable under the Finance Act 1986 s.14 for the full amount of VAT evaded from the date s.14 became effective until October 31, 1990. On appeal, the tribunal stated that s.21 of the 1985 Act, which permitted penalty assessments, required such penalties to be assessed and notified by reference to a set accounting period and not as a global figure and also that B's relative culpability, in relation to his fellow directors, should be taken into account. CEC appealed.

Held, allowing the appeal, that (1) notification and assessment of liability were separate functions under s.21(1). Penalty assessment had to relate to a prescribed period, several of which could be aggregated under s.13(1). Notification of the assessment required only communication of the amount to the person liable and (2) where company directors had collaborated in dishonest conduct of the company each was prima facie liable for the whole penalty. Relative culpability was a material consideration in determining the appropriate proportion of the penalty to be recovered from a particular director. It was necessary to ask whether B was less to blame than the others with whom he had acted. As the evidence showed he was not, he was liable for the full amount.

CUSTOMS AND EXCISE COMMISSIONERS v. BASSIMEH [1995] S.T.C. 910, Sedley, J., QBD.

5886. Pharmaceutical industry

VALUE ADDED TAX (PHARMACEUTICAL CHEMISTS) ORDER 1996, SI 1996 2949; made under the Value Added Tax Act 1994 s.31, s.96. In force: January 1, 1997; £0.65.

This Order amends the Value Added Tax Act 1994 Sch.9 Group 7. It inserts a new Note (2A) so that supplies of services made by a person who is not registered in either of the registers of pharmaceutical chemists kept under the Pharmacy Act 1954 or the Pharmacy (Northern Ireland) Order 1976 (SI 1976 1213 (NI 22)) are included within the exemption contained in item 3 of the Group where those services are wholly performed by a person who is so registered.

5887. Registration–dishonest failure to register for VAT–liable under same statutory provision as for dishonest declaration–statutory interpretation

[Finance Act 1985 s.13.]

S appealed against a decision which overturned a VAT tribunal's decision which had allowed S's original appeal against the imposition of a penalty for VAT evasion by dishonestly omitting to register for VAT contrary to the Finance Act 1985 s.13(1).

Held, dismissing the appeal, that it was obviously Parliament's intention that the phrase "does any act or omits to take any action" in s.13(1) of the Act should apply to a dishonest failure to register and was not limited only to evasion due to dishonest declarations.

CUSTOMS AND EXCISE COMMISSIONERS v. STEVENSON; SUB NOM. STEVENSON AND TELFORD BUILDING & DESIGN LTD v. CUSTOMS AND EXCISE COMMISIONERS [1996] S.T.C. 1096, Brooke, L.J., CA.

5888. Registration–increase of limits

VALUE ADDED TAX (INCREASE OF REGISTRATION LIMITS) ORDER 1996, SI 1996 2950; made under the Value Added Tax Act 1994 Sch.1 para.15, Sch.3 para.9. In force: Art.1, Art.2: November 27, 1996; Art.3: January 1, 1997; £0.65.

This Order increases the VAT registration limits for taxable supplies and acquisitions from other Member States from £47,000 to £48,000, with effect from November 27, 1996, in the case of taxable supplies and January 1, 1997, in the case of acquisitions. The Order also increases the limit for cancellation of registration in the case of taxable supplies from £45,000 to £46,000 with effect from November 27, 1996, and in the case of acquisitions from £47,000 to £48,000 with effect from January 1, 1997.

5889. Repayments–refund to taxable persons not established in the territory of the country–European Union

[Council Directive 79/1072 on arrangements for the refusal of value added tax to taxable persons not established in the territory of the country Art.7.]

The Commission sought a declaration that Spain, by disregarding the six month time limit for the refund of VAT to taxable persons not established in the territory of the country, in accordance with Directive 79/1072 Art.7(4) had failed to comply with its obligations under Community law.

Held, allowing the declaration, that Spain had failed to comply with its obligations under the Eighth VAT Directive.

COMMISSION OF THE EUROPEAN COMMUNITIES v. SPAIN (C16/95), December 14, 1995, Judge not specified, ECJ.

5890. Residential accommodation–reliefs–real property–development–charities

HM Customs & Excise issued a press release entitled *Creation of dwellings and other accommodation by conversion* (News Release 15/96), published on March 13, 1996. Residential accommodation conversions have been virtually VAT free since July 21, 1994 because they are zero rated on the grant of a major interest by a VAT registered company, because of the supply of zero rated goods and services in the course of conversion to a registered housing association, or by refund of VAT to a non-business converter under the DIY VAT refund scheme. There are small number of charitable organisations who fall outside the above measures, either because they are prevented by legal constraints from selling the converted property, or do not qualify for the DIY scheme. However, the Commissioners of Customs and Excise may exercise discretionary powers under the Customs and Excise Management Act 1979, and consider refunds of VAT to such bodies. Any charity which believes it could benefit under the grant of such relief should contact Mr D. Kelly, VAT Construction Branch, Customs and Excise, New Kings Beam House, 22 Upper Ground, London SE1 9PJ.

5891. Sale of goods–interest free credit–VAT liability based on net payment received–Sixth VAT Directive–Retail Scheme A

[Sixth Council Directive 77/388 on a common system for VAT Art.27; Value Added Tax Act 1994 Sch.9.]

P, a retailer, sold goods on "interest free credit" by entering tripartite arrangements with customers and finance companies. The customers paid the finance company, by instalments, an amount which totalled the advertised price of the goods and the finance company made an immediate payment to P, being the price of goods less the discount representing interest. CEC successfully argued in the Queen's Bench Division that P should pay VAT on the full price rather than the net price. P appealed.

Held, allowing the appeal, that a retailer selling goods on "interest free credit" was liable for VAT on the net payment received from the finance company, rather than the full price charged to the customer. The retailer made a supply of credit to the customer. According to the principles of the Sixth Council Directive 77/388 Art.27 supplies of credit were exempt from VAT, and the Value Added Tax Act 1994 Sch.9 Group 5 and Retail Scheme A para.14 had to be interpreted in the light of that principle. There could be no justification for disapplying the exemption because a separate charge for credit was not notified to the customer. Where the national legislation was poorly drafted and confusing, an interpretation which was viable and conformed with general VAT law and the Sixth Directive would be preferred, *Craven (Inspector of Taxes) v. White* [1989] A.C. 398, [1988] C.L.Y. 257 considered, *Chaussures Bally SA v. Ministry of Finance (Belgium)* [1993] E.C.R. I-2871, [1993] C.L.Y. 4408 distinguished.

PRIMBACK LTD v. CUSTOMS AND EXCISE COMMISSIONERS [1996] S.T.C. 757, Hutchison, L.J., CA.

5892. Share option schemes–merger–alterations to schemes–approval refused by commissioners–alteration not amounting to new right–group scheme unavailable where grantor had no control over company

[Income and Corporation Taxes Act 1988 Sch.9, s.135.]

R appealed against a refusal by the IRC to approve proposed alterations to two share option schemes, needed to facilitate R's merger with Elsevier NV. Under the Income and Corporation Taxes Act 1988 Sch. 9 the effect of approval meant that a charge to Schedule E income tax under s.135 would not apply to gains realised on the exercise of the options. The proposed changes sought to remove a merger from a list of triggering events that would permit the exercise of options under the schemes. Approval was withheld, as the IRC contended that the alterations created new rights different from those enjoyed previously and sought to extend them to companies over which the original grantor exercised no control.

Held, allowing the appeal in respect of one scheme but upholding the decision with regard to the other, that the removal of one of the predetermined trigger events did not amount to the obtaining of a new and different right, *Inland Revenue Commissioners v. Eurocopy Plc* [1991] S.T.C. 707, [1992] C.L.Y. 599 distinguished. However, Parliament could not have intended such schemes extending to a company over which the grantor no longer exercised control.

INLAND REVENUE COMMISSIONERS v. REED INTERNATIONAL PLC; SUB NOM. REED INTERNATIONAL PLC v. INLAND REVENUE COMMISSIONERS [1995] S.T.C. 889, Nourse, L.J., CA.

5893. Share sales–charities–made beyond scope of economic activities to which VAT applied–European Union

[Sixth Council Directive 77/388 on a common system for VAT Art.4, Art.13B, Art.17.]

The ECJ was called upon to determine a reference from a VAT tribunal as to whether charity trustees who sold and purchased securities, including shares, engaged in economic activities within the meaning of the Sixth Council Directive 77/388 Art.4(2). W was a trustee of a medical research trust required by its constitution to refrain from engaging in trade. In order to raise funds to invest more widely, the trust undertook a large share sale by the "book building" method which involved considerable professional fees. The trust applied unsuccessfully for a refund of input VAT on the fees. W asserted that under Art.17 and Art.13B of the Sixth Council Directive 77/388 the trust was entitled to reclaim a proportion of the input VAT on fees corresponding to the proportion of shares sold to investors outside the EC. W claimed the sale must be treated as an economic activity because the trust's investment activities were like those of an investment trust or pension fund, which were treated in the UK as coming within the scope of VAT.

Held, that a sale of shares by a charitable trustee in the course of management of the charity's assets was not an economic activity within the meaning of Art.4(2) so it fell outside the scope of VAT. The acquisition and sale of shares by an investor who was not a professional securities dealer could come within the scope of "economic activity" in some circumstances, particularly if undertaken as part of commercial share dealing or to assume a role in the management of the companies concerned, but W was prohibited from engaging in such activities, *Polysar Investments Netherlands BV v. Inspecteur der Invoerrechten en Accijnzen, Arnhem* (C60/90) [1991] E.C.R. I-311 considered.

WELLCOME TRUST LTD v. CUSTOMS AND EXCISE COMMISSIONERS (C155/94) [1996] All E.R. (EC) 589, DAO Edward (President), ECJ.

5894. Small businesses–interim payments

HM Customs & Excise issued a press release entitled *Changes to VAT accounting* (News Release 14/96), published on March 7, 1996. The number of interim payments smaller businesses will have to make on the previous year's VAT liability has been changed from April 1, 1996. This will apply to companies with an annual turnover of £100,000 or less, and will mean that no interim payments are required where the previous year's VAT liability is less than £2,000, and three quarterly payments of 20 per cent of the previous year's VAT liability where annual liability exceeds £2,000. Businesses will also be able to choose the method of credit transfer when making interim payments.

5895. Supply of services

VALUE ADDED TAX (PLACE OF SUPPLY OF SERVICES) (AMENDMENT) ORDER 1996, SI 1996 2992; made under the Value Added Tax Act 1994 s.7. In force: January 1, 1997; £0.65.

This Order amends the Value Added Tax (Place of Supply of Services) Order 1992 (SI 1992 3121) to give full effect to Council Directive 77/388 ([1977] OJ L145/1) Art.28b.F. The 1992 Order seeks to deal with a supply of services where a valuation of, or work on, goods is physically performed in a Member State and the goods then leave that Member State, and the recipient of the services provides, for the purposes of the supply, a VAT registration number issued by a different Member State. In these circumstances the supply should be treated as made in the latter Member State. The main effect of the amendment is to treat the supply as made in the United Kingdom where such services are performed in and the goods leave another Member State, and the recipient provides a United Kingdom VAT registration number for the purpose of the supply.

5896. Supply of services–fiscal warehousing

VALUE ADDED TAX (FISCAL WAREHOUSING) (TREATMENT OF TRANSACTIONS) ORDER 1996, SI 1996 1255; made under the Value Added Tax Act 1994 s.5. In force: June 1, 1996; £0.65.

This Order treats for the purposes of VAT certain supplies as being of goods where they would otherwise technically be supplies of services. This enables them to take advantage of the relief from VAT afforded to trade in certain commodities under a fiscal warehousing regime.

5897. Supply of services–invoiced before trader registered as taxable person–payment received after registration–charge to VAT did not arise prior to registration

[Value Added Tax Act 1983 s.2; Value Added Tax (General) (Amendment) Regulations 1989 Reg.23.]

BJR appealed against a decision that they were liable to pay VAT on services supplied prior to being registered for VAT in October 1986. Having issued an invoice free of VAT, which was subsequently written off as a bad debt, BJR later registered for VAT and eventually received payment of the invoice in 1991. CEC contended that a charge arose under the Value Added Tax Act 1983 s.2(1) and the Value Added Tax (General) (Amendment) Regulations 1989 Reg.23(1), as the nature of the supply was chargeable under Reg.23(1), and the supply occurred at the point when the bill was paid, by which time BJR was a taxable person pursuant to s.2(1). CEC further submitted that any injustice created by the decision was offset by the fact that a trader in BJR's position should foresee they might cross the threshold for registration and order their invoicing and costing procedures to be adapted accordingly.

Held, allowing the appeal, that (1) the solutions put forward by CEC did not obviate the injustice. Although a late payer could be penalised, the penalty did not fall to be determined by reference to the VAT prevailing at the time of payment, or allow the benefit to accrue to CEC rather than the taxable person charging for the supply and (2) no liability for VAT could arise if any of the four elements contained in s.2(1) were missing and only if all were present did the time of supply, as determined by Reg.23(1), become a relevant consideration. Apart from the exception provided for by s.41, a chargeable transaction was to be determined at the time the supply was actually made, as both common sense and justice demanded. Levying tax in respect of a supply not taxable at the time it was made was close to retrospective taxation. Sir Ralph Gibson, dissenting, held that the resulting injustice was not of a magnitude to justify a departure from the plain meaning of the Act.

BJ RICE & ASSOCIATES v. CUSTOMS AND EXCISE COMMISSIONERS [1996] S.T.C. 581, Staughton, L.J., CA.

5898. Supply of services–public transport service–whether provided by licensed operator or drivers owning buses operative on self-employed basis

C obtained an operator's licence to run a bus service. The buses, which were owned by the drivers, ran to timetables published by the county council. The drivers paid for their own fuel and kept the fares paid by the passengers and the subsidy claimed by C on their behalf. C was paid a fee by each driver for the use of terminus facilities. He also claimed and retained a fuel rebate from the Department of Transport. The tribunal held that the bus service was provided by C, since he retained substantial control over the operation. C appealed.

Held, dismissing the appeal, that the conclusion was one to which the tribunal which heard the evidence and conducted the necessary balancing exercises could reasonably have come.

CLARK v. CUSTOMS AND EXCISE COMMISSIONERS [1996] S.T.C. 263, McCullough, J., QBD.

5899. Supply of services–telecommunications–whether overpayments for continuous supply were chargeable to output tax on receipt

[Sixth Council Directive 77/388 on a common system for VAT Art.10; Value Added Tax Act 1983 s.4, s.5.]

CEC appealed against a ruling upholding a VAT tribunal's decision allowing BT's appeal against an output tax assessment in respect of inadvertent overpayments received from customers. BT issued bills and accounted for output tax on a quarterly basis. However, inadvertent overpayments were not repaid to customers, unless specifically requested, the amount being deducted from the next quarterly bill. CEC submitted that the overpayments should be treated as payments on account for future supplies, for which VAT was payable at the date of receipt.

Held, dismissing the appeal, that under the Sixth Council Directive 77/388 Art.10(2) and the Value Added Tax Act 1983 s.4 output tax became chargeable at the time goods were delivered or services performed, with tax chargeable on receipt of payment where goods or services were received on account under s.5(1) of the Act. Where an inadvertent overpayment occurred, in the course of a continuous supply of services, the payment was intended for past supplies and did not amount to either a payment on account in respect of future services or an appropriation towards a future liability. At common law BT were liable to repay such sums on receipt, as they were not made for consideration. The practice of crediting them against the next bill, unless repayment was requested, arose due to the needs of administrative convenience.

CUSTOMS AND EXCISE COMMISSIONERS v. BRITISH TELECOMMUNICATIONS PLC [1996] 1 W.L.R. 1309, Millett, L.J., CA.

5900. Supply of services–unincorporated association–supply not taxable where there was no consideration–nature of relationship between association and its members

[Value Added Tax Act 1994 s.5, Sch.1.]

E, an association of independent private car hire drivers, appealed against the CEC's refusal to cancel their registration for the purposes of VAT. Following revision of its constitution E sought to have its registration cancelled. The Value Added Tax Act 1994 Sch.1 provides that any person making taxable supplies exceeding a given threshold turnover figure must register. The issue was whether E made taxable supplies to its members, and whether it was, therefore, liable to pay VAT. E, a non-profit making organisation, sought to provide a communications network for its members, and to employ an office manager and telephonist as necessary to carry out that objective. E argued that it was an administrative intermediary, obtaining goods on behalf of its members as agents, rather than in its own name for onwards supply. It was submitted that, to be taxed, the subject must come within the letter of the law, and to come merely within the spirit did not suffice, and the resolution of issues relating to VAT legislation was a question of fact. In addition to examining the constitution of the association, therefore, it was necessary to analyse the nature of the supply, and the identity of the employer of the staff. It was claimed that the employer was each of the members of the association existing at the time as provided for in the specimen contract of employment used. If the association itself were the employer, however, there would be a taxable supply of staff to its members.

Held, allowing the appeal, that (1) it was for the court to examine the true legal nature of the association to determine its liability to VAT, *Customs and Excise Commissioners v. Reed Personnel Services Ltd* [1995] S.T.C. 588, [1995] 2 C.L.Y. 5089; (2) where a group of taxi drivers established an unincorporated association to undertake particular functions on behalf of, and using money provided by, its members on a non-profit making basis, the services provided by the association fell within the Value Added Tax Act 1994 s.5(2)(b), as being services supplied other than for consideration and (3) the association did not exist as a separate legal entity, and the employees were employed jointly by the members of the association. The nature of the relationship between E and its members had to be properly considered, *Durham Aged Mineworkers Homes Association v. Customs and Excise Commissioners* [1994] S.T.C. 553, [1994] C.L.Y. 4610 and *Nell Gwynn House Maintenance Fund Trustees v. Customs and Excise Commissioners* [1996] S.T.C. 310, [1997] 1 C.L. 650 followed. The association was not required by the 1994 Act to be registered for the purposes of VAT. Leave to appeal by the CEC was refused.

EASTBOURNE TOWN RADIO CARS ASSOCIATION v. CUSTOMS AND EXCISE COMMISSIONERS [1996] S.T.C. 1469, Turner, J., QBD.

5901. Supply of services–whether law of Member State compatible with Community law–European Union

[Sixth Council Directive 77/388 on a common system for VAT Art.10, Art.22.]

A reference was made to the ECJ on issues arising from the use of the derogation in the Sixth Council Directive 77/388; whether a Member State was entitled, under the derogation, to make VAT chargeable on receipt of a price for all supplies; whether the Member State was required to establish specific time periods within which an invoice was to be issued and to lay down detailed rules for extra documentation regarding the invoicing and payment for supplies covered by it.

Held, answering the questions referred, that (1) the powers contained within Art.10(2) required a broad construction, as they were capable of covering all types of services, under the derogation a Member State was allowed to determine that receipt of the price was an event on which VAT for all supplies of services became chargeable; (2) Art.10(2) did not require specific time periods to be established for the service of documentation and (3) apart from a general obligation to keep accounts, under the Sixth VAT Directive Art.22(2), Art.10(2) did not require any extra documentation to be provided where an invoice was not issued or a price had not been received.

UFFICIO IVA DI TRAPANI v. ITALITTICA SpA (C144/94) [1995] S.T.C 1059, Edward (President), ECJ.

5902. Supply of services–whether restaurant transactions on ferries constituted supply of goods or services–place where supply deemed to have taken place–European Union

[Sixth Council Directive 77/388 on a common system for VAT Art.6, Art.9.]

A reference was made to the ECJ for a preliminary ruling to determine whether restaurant transactions on ferries sailing between Denmark and Germany were to be categorised as supplies of goods or services for VAT purposes under Sixth Council Directive 77/388 Art.6(1), and furthermore to determine where the supply took place, since supply of services was carried out at the place where the business was established by the supplier.

Held, that the supply of food and drink on board ferries comprised a number of services ranging from the preparation of food to the provision of waitress service, so that the service was the predominant factor, bringing the transaction within Art.6(1). This was to be differentiated from the provision of take away food which did not involve the same level of service in a similar setting. The place of supply for VAT purposes under Art.9(1) was the place where the operator of the ship was permanently established, *Berkholz v. Finanzamt Hamburg Mitte-Altstadt* (C168/84) [1985] E.C.R. 2251, [1986] C.L.Y. 1495

FAABORG-GELTING LINIEN A/S v. FINANZAMT FLENSBURG (C231/94) [1996] All E.R. (EC) 656, CN Kakouris (President), ECJ.

5903. Tax planning–fuel

VALUE ADDED TAX (ANTI AVOIDANCE (HEATING)) ORDER 1996, SI 1996 1661; made under the Value Added Tax Act 1994 s.30. In force: June 27, 1996; £0.65.

This Order, which applies to supplies, acquisitions and importations taking place on or after June 27, 1996, varies the Value Added Tax Act 1994 Sch.8 Group 2 so as to remove from the zero rate a supply of heated water, and correspondingly makes acquisitions and importations of heated water chargeable to VAT at the standard rate.

5904. Time limits–repayments

HM Customs & Excise issued a press release entitled *Indirect taxes: 3 year limit on repayment claims* (News Release 42/96), published on July 18, 1996. The Paymaster General has announced a three year limit on refunds of VAT and other indirect taxes following concern over the large amount of revenue at risk in taxation boundary disputes, resulting in large sums, having been collected and paid in good faith, having to be repaid to businesses, often many years after the tax has been collected.

5905. Tribunals–appeal against assessment–findings on a question of law

G, the owners of a fish and chip shop, appealed against the dismissal of their appeal against the decision of a VAT tribunal. G admitted knowingly underdeclaring their takings from about 1985 and they were assessed as owing £61,902. G asked to have their case reconsidered and they admitted declarations totalling £8,754. A revised assessment was then prepared which totalled £56,444 and they were penalised for the underdeclaration by a 95 per cent penalty totalling £53,621. G appealed, arguing that the assessments were invalid or alternatively too high. Following a detailed and lengthy appeal the assessment was reduced to £29,964 and the penalty to £22,473. G appealed, stating that the findings of fact could not be supported by the evidence before the tribunal. The court held that G had raised issues of fact and that there was no point of law on which to challenge the tribunal's decision.

Held, dismissing the appeal, that (1) in order to challenge the tribunal's findings on a question of law, G must ascertain the finding to be challenged, show its importance in relation to the decision, ascertain the evidence relating to the finding and show that the finding could not have been made on that evidence. A general contention that the finding was contrary to the weight of the evidence was not adequate; (2) the tribunal's decision could not be criticised on the evidence that was before it and (3) the issues should have been agreed before the trial in order to make discovery easier and to control the vast amount of detail and evidence adduced.

GEORGIOU (T/A MARIOS CHIPPERY) v. CUSTOMS AND EXCISE COMMISSIONERS; SUB NOM. MARIOS CHIPPERY, *Re* [1996] S.T.C. 463, Evans, L.J., CA.

5906. Tribunals–refusal to refer input tax question to European Court of Justice–appeal on point of law–matter not acte clair

[Tribunals and Inquiries Act 1992 s.11.]

C appealed under the Tribunals and Inquiries Act 1992 s.11 against a refusal by a VAT tribunal to refer a question to the ECJ about the input tax liability arising from the operation of a money off voucher scheme.

Held, allowing the appeal, that an appeal under s.11 of the Act was only allowed on a point of law and it was necessary to assess whether the tribunal decision had been wrong, not merely perverse. At issue was whether a direct link ran between the supply and the consideration received in the form of redemption credits. Although the tribunal might have been correct, the matter was not acte clair, as an arguable point existed which was not so obvious as to leave no room for reasonable doubt, *R. v. International Stock Exchange of the UK and Republic of Ireland Ltd, ex p. Else (1982) Ltd* [1993] Q.B. 534, [1993] C.L.Y. 3774 and *BLP Group Plc v. Customs and Excise Commissioners* [1994] S.T.C. 41, [1994] C.L.Y. 4552 considered. As a result, the matter was to be remitted back to the tribunal for reconsideration.

CONOCO LTD v. CUSTOMS AND EXCISE COMMISSIONERS [1995] S.T.C 1022, Harrison, J., QBD.

5907. Tribunals–take away food business–assessment to the best of Customs and Excise judgment

[Rules of the Supreme Court Ord.55 r.7.]

K appealed against a decision of a VAT tribunal dismissing an appeal against an assessment of £23,758 including interest for the period April 1988 to October 1993. K carried on a business selling take away food. He argued that the tribunal's decision was wrong in law because it failed to address whether CEC had made the assessment to the best of their judgment. K's criticisms were concentrated on how CEC had dealt with the sale of pizzas by the business. K also argued that if the assessment was valid, it was excessive.

Held, allowing the appeal, that following *Van Boeckel v. Customs and Excise Commissioners* [1981] S.T.C. 290, [1981] C.L.Y. 2839, it was apparent that the VAT tribunal did not deal with whether CEC had in accordance with their powers made an assessment to the best of their judgment. It was not for the court to usurp the tribunal's function by exercising its powers under the Rules of the Supreme Court Ord.55 r.7, therefore the case would be remitted for rehearing.

KOCA v. CUSTOMS AND EXCISE COMMISSIONERS [1996] S.T.C. 58, Latham, J., QBD.

5908. Vouchers–money off and cash back coupons issued by manufacturers to consumers–consideration–taxable amount for VAT purposes–European Union

[Sixth Council Directive 77/388 on a common system for VAT Art.11.]

EG, a cosmetics manufacturer, distributed "money off" and "cash-back" vouchers. "Money-off" vouchers were distributed to the public, consumers bought products at a discount and the retailers presented vouchers to EG for reimbursement. "Cash-back" vouchers were distributed along with the products and consumers presented vouchers direct to EG for reimbursement. CEC asserted that the "taxable amount" for VAT was the full nominal price of the product without any deduction for the discount which EG offered by means of the vouchers, but EG claimed that deduction for the discount should be allowed. The VAT and Duties Tribunal requested a preliminary ruling from the European Court of Justice on the meaning of "taxable amount" under the Sixth Council Directive 77/388 Art.11.

Held, that the "taxable amount" should be the full nominal price less the discount represented by the face value of the voucher. The Sixth Directive was based on the principle that VAT should be a neutral tax and the burden of tax should fall only on the ultimate consumer, not on taxable persons. In no circumstances could the taxable amount exceed the price charged to the consumer. Consideration was valued according to subjective not objective criteria, and VAT therefore had to be calculated on the basis of the discounted price.

ELIDA GIBBS LTD v. CUSTOMS AND EXCISE COMMISSIONERS (C317/94) [1996] S.T.C. 1387, GF Mancini (President), ECJ (Sixth Chamber).

5909. Vouchers–offered for sale at discount–goods purchased by third party–VAT payable on voucher sale price–European Union

[Sixth Council Directive 77/388 on a common system for VAT Art.11.]

On a reference for a preliminary ruling on the interpretation of the Sixth Council Directive 77/388 Art.11, A, a retailer, contended that the taxable amount in respect of its receipts from sales of goods bought by means of vouchers offered for sale at discounted prices, for redemption by third parties, should be the difference between the full face value of the voucher and the discount granted to the initial buyer of the vouchers. CEC submitted that the face value represented the consideration for the supply of goods and should be the taxable amount, irrespective of the discount.

Held, that the taxable amount was represented by the consideration actually received, and was to be expressed as a subjective value in each case. On the facts, A regarded the voucher as being capable of satisfying the sale price equal to its face value, but the question as to its money equivalent remained and this fell to be determined by reference to the price paid for the voucher, at either its full face or discounted value. When accepted in payment, the money equivalent was the sum actually received on the sale of the voucher, less any discount, and it was irrelevant that the buyer of the goods did not know the voucher's real money equivalent value, which could be ascertained by reference to the serial number of each voucher, thus enabling A to determine the amount of any discount deductible from the face value. In these circumstances, the consideration forming the taxable amount under Art.11 (A) (1) (a) was ascertainable by reference to the sum received by A on the sale of the voucher.

ARGOS DISTRIBUTORS LTD v. CUSTOMS AND EXCISE COMMISSIONERS (C288/94) [1996] S.T.C. 1359, GF Mancini (President), ECJ.

5910. Zero rating–playground completed 10 years after school construction–temporal link needed between school construction and playground provision

[Value Added Tax Act 1983 Sch.5.]

CEC appealed against a VAT tribunal decision that a school playground, completed 10 years after the school's construction, amounted to a completion of the original construction and was therefore a zero rated supply under the Value Added Tax Act 1983 Sch.5 group 8, item 2. It was submitted by the school that the time lapse amounted only to a long delay in the construction of the whole building.

Held, allowing the appeal, that in order to be included within the zero rating provision, services which were unrelated to the actual construction of the building had to be shown to either facilitate the construction or be a part of the whole building. This was a question of degree, it being necessary to consider the nature of the additional work and the contribution it made toward the building's function and purpose. A temporal link was also required between the building's construction and the provision of other services, with a delay falling to be considered when determining the existence of a sufficient degree of temporal connection. In the instant case the facts showed that the time period was excessive, notwithstanding the explanations put forward as the basis for the temporal link.

CUSTOMS AND EXCISE COMMISSIONERS v. ST MARY'S ROMAN CATHOLIC SCHOOL [1996] S.T.C. 1091, Jowitt, J., QBD.

5911. Articles

A thorn in their sides - groups and tax avoidance schemes *(Debbie Sharpe)*: Vat Plan. 1996, 52, 2-3. (New draft Sch.9A on VAT group anti avoidance provisions designed to halt entry and exit schemes by giving Customs power to make directions as to VAT liability on group supplies).

Beyond acceptable limits *(John Kennedy)*: T.P.V. 1996, 10(10), 73-74, 77. (Introduction of three year time limit on retrospective VAT refunds, range of claims and businesses affected and whether cap contravenes EC law).

Chains of transactions *(Richard Pincher)*: Tax J. 1996, 356, 14-15. (VAT treatment of transfers of going concerns, supplies arising on purchase, effect of intervening supply between purchase and supply and role of purchaser's intention in determining availability of VAT recovery for acquisition fees).

Company cars: have you got the cheapest option? *(Alison Chapman)*: C.S.R. 1996, 20(3), 17-18. (Finance options available to companies for company car fleet and effect of VAT changes and direct tax rules).

Deeming provisions and mixed TOGCs *(Richard Pincher)*: Tax J. 1996, 367, 19-20. (VAT treatment of fees arising on sale of mixed purpose TOGC, with applicable tests under deeming provisions and exemption method advocated by Customs in Business Brief 7/96).

Do you generate extra costs by saving VAT? *(Ron Nattrass* and *Reginald S. Nock)*: Tax J. 1996, 379, 17-18. (Effect of non-VAT based considerations on VAT planning operations with cost and compliance implications inherent across range of activities).

Finance Act notes: the new anti-avoidance provisions for VAT group registrations: section 31 *(Hugh Mainprice)*: B.T.R. 1996, 4, 337-338. (Powers for Customs to curb schemes based on moving companies in and out of group VAT registration and exemption where change of group registration is for genuine commercial purpose).

Finance Bill published *(Michael Conlon)*: VAT Int. 1996, 14(1), 1281-1284. (VAT provisions include new anti avoidance grouping rules, Second VAT Simplification Directive changes, DIY builders relief, extension of Gold Scheme, increased small gift threshold and changes to payments on account).

For the avoidance of simplicity *(Martin Scammell)*: T.P.V. 1996, 10(3), 17-20. (Implications for commercial groups of Budget 1994 anti-VAT avoidance measures to curtail leaseback schemes and concession whereby connected persons can exercise option to tax).

Future progress on the harmonization on taxation within the European Union *(Confederation Fiscale Europeenne)*: Euro. Tax. 1996, 36(2), 61-66. (Recommends implementation of Arbitration Convention, abolition of discriminating direct tax measures and reduction of VAT compliance burdens).

Getting your VAT back: C.S.R. 1996, 20(7), 56. (Effect of proposals to impose three year limit to claim retrospective VAT refunds and expected consultation paper on unjust enrichment following decision that VAT only payable on amount actually received by retailer).

Input tax and the three year limit *(Richard L. Barlow)*: Tax J. 1996, 375, 13-14. (Whether three year limit for reclaiming input VAT was lawful when taxpayer voluntarily disclosed or was assessed for underpayment of output VAT).

Kitchen sink drama: Tax. 1996, 136(3537), 376-377. (Question and answer. Whether input VAT could be recovered in respect of bathroom and kitchen fittings for flat above business premises occupied by directors paying rent).

Partial exemption *(Nick Lawrence)*: Tax. 1996, 138(3575), 12-15. (Input tax partial exemption attribution and apportionment methods, with worked examples of attribution of mixed zero-rated and exempt supplies).

Partial exemption in property and VAT planning *(Cathy Hargreaves)*: VAT Plan. 1996, 53, 4-6. (Operation of exempt income provision, direct attribution calculations, apportionment methods and tax planning options).

Piggy in the middle *(Terry Dockley)*: Tax. 1996, 137(3550), 38, 40-41. (Determination for VAT purposes of place of supply of services between Member States under Sixth Directive, Customs Notice 741 and UK legislation raises potential points of divergence).

Plumbing the depths *(Alan Buckett)*: Tax J. 1996, 377, 15-16. (Input tax attribution of Rolex watches purchased by plumbers to measure gas flow accurately with business value balanced against private status enhancement).

Rebuilding the palace *(Francesca Lagerberg)*: Tax. 1996, 137(3557), 246-247. (VAT treatment of costs of rebuilding Alexandra Palace and whether council's purpose in repairing it stemmed from its statutory duty or from business considerations).

Relieving the burden: simplification of VAT *(John Davison)*: Tax. P. 1996, Jul, 6, 8-9. (Administrative and organisational features of Customs and Excise taxation operations, with need for improved training and record keeping, objective VAT rate distinctions and greater publicity for points of statutory interpretation).

Retail schemes: major changes ahead *(John Ireland)*: VAT Plan. 1996, 54, 5-6. (Customs and Excise consultation paper, published November 1995, proposes reduction and simplification for retail schemes, with price calculation changes, increased use of bespoke schemes for large traders and standard method abolition).

Righting wrongs over rights *(Jack Goldberg)*: Tax J. 1996, 339, 8-9. (Whether shares in rights issue amounting to new capital injection should be treated as a transaction with consideration for VAT purposes).

Simplifying the VAT system *(A. St John Price)*: VAT Int. 1996, 14(2), 1290-1295. (Why VAT is so complex, including poor drafting, lack of information on appeals and vested interests).

Supplies of insurance to become liable to VAT? *(Clive R. Othen)*: VAT Int. 1996, 14(4), 1305-1308. (CEC study on whether supplies of financial services, including insurance, should be liable to VAT using cash flow method and impact on insurance industry).

The impact of the VAT anti avoidance provisions on property transactions *(John Kennedy)*: VAT Plan. 1996, 53, 2-4. (Anti avoidance measure empowers Customs to require compulsory VAT grouping or degrouping and retrospectively impose VAT but subsidiary property companies and leaseback schemes may well remain unaffected).

The Luxembourg hourglass *(Terry Dockley)*: Tax. 1996, 137(3556), 216-218, 220. (Member States' liability to repay overpaid VAT where domestic law contravened EC Treaty or Sixth Directive, applicability of time limits to claims and whether temporal restrictions applied to scope and effect of ECJ decisions).

The mark of the beast *(Malcolm Gunn)*: Tax. 1996, 137(3572), 633-635. (Powers to require security as condition of VAT registration, Customs policy, appeal rights and practical steps for new and phoenix businesses to minimise risk).

The nature of TOGCs *(Richard Pincher)*: Tax J. 1996, 364, 19-20. (Customs' approach to VAT on transfer of going concern).

The recovery of input tax by charitable organisations and the effect of receiving donations *(Philip Jeffrey)*: VAT Int. 1996, 14(6), 1322-1326. (Differences between UK and EC legislation on meaning of "business" and "economic activity" and considerations in determining business and non-business activities for purposes of deductability of input tax).

The tribunal extends its boundaries *(Barry Stocks)*: Tax. 1996, 136(3547), 648-649. (Jurisdiction of VAT tribunals to review Customs on Wednesbury principles where prior decision has been made not to exercise discretion including decisions not to apply extra statutory concessions).

Three year limit on VAT repayment claims *(Deborah Sharp)*: Tax J. 1996, 367, 11-12. (Disadvantages created by Press Release 42/96 proposed time limit for VAT overpayment claims and potential for inequitable results where claims delayed
until outcome of current appeals and whether compatible with Sixth Directive).

Tying down Houdini *(Peter Jenkins)*: Tax. 1996, 136(3537), 358-361. (Potential options for reform to Sixth Directive to combat VAT avoidance and double taxation in connection with information technology and telecommunications services).

Unjust enrichment *(A. St John Price)*: Tax. 1996, 137(3557), 248. (Customs and Excise's refusal to refund VAT overpayment on basis that claimant would be unjustly enriched and application of rule where error occurs in supplies to unregistered persons).

VAT and property *(Peter S. Gravestock)*: Tax. P. 1996, Apr, 7-8. (Zero rating for conversions to residential use and gradual abolition of developers' self supply rules and option to tax).

VAT avoidance *(John Davison)*: VAT Int. 1996, 14(3), 1298-1303. (Definitions and causes of avoidance, development of case law and Ramsay principle, anti avoidance legislation and Customs and Excise approach to avoidance measures).

VAT groupies *(Ron Nattrass)*: Tax J. 1996, 366, 7-8. (VATA Sch.9 anti avoidance provisions and joint Customs/CIoT Practice Statement on VAT group schemes in light of need to maximise VAT revenue).

VAT groups: Customs make their case: T.P.V. 1996, 10(6), 41-42, 46-47. (Customs and CIoT joint Statement of Practice on FA 1996 VAT group anti avoidance measures, application for entry and exit schemes, conditions where directions applicable, VAT charge computation methods and transitional overlap provisions).

VAT–international services *(Barry Stocks)*: P.P.M. 1996, 14(5), 66-68. (Circumstances in which VAT is chargeable in relation to professional advisers' provision of services to international clients).

VAT: original tenants and guarantors *(Tim Steele* and *Mark Baldwin)*: E.G. 1996, 9624, 138-139. (VAT planning in respect of continuing liability of occupiers of business property and their guarantors following disposal of leases in light of 1995 Act).

VAT: retail schemes consultation document: Tax. P. 1996, Apr, 26. (CIoT response to Customs and Excise consultation document welcomes aim of reducing traders' compliance burdens but criticises proposal to reduce number of schemes and calls for availability of bespoke schemes to be better publicised).

What is business entertainment? *(Peter Hewitt)*: Tax J. 1996, 377, 9-11. (Input tax recovery on business entertainment supplies, apportionment for mixed supplies and status of working meals for employees).

5912. Books

Allen, Chris–VAT Handbook: 1996-97. Paperback. ISBN 0-86325-400-4. CCH Editions.

Ball, Andrew; Narain, Lakshmi–Deloitte Ross: VAT - a Business by Business Guide: 1996-7. Paperback: £36.95. ISBN 0-406-99087-5. Butterworth Law.

Butterworths VAT Handbook. Paperback: £20.00. ISBN 0-406-01444-2. Butterworth Law.

Crooks, Robert–VAT on Construction, Land and Property. Ringbinder: £45.00. Tolley Publishing.

Dolton, Alan; Wareham, Robert–VAT Cases: 1996. Paperback: £64.50. ISBN 1-86012-248-5. Tolley Publishing.

Soares, Patrick C.–VAT Planning for Property Transactions. Hardback: £75.00. ISBN 0-7520-0045-4. FT Law & Tax.

NORTHERN IRELAND

ADMINISTRATION OF JUSTICE

5913. Juries

JURIES REGULATIONS (NORTHERN IRELAND) 1996, SR 1996 269; made under the Juries (Northern Ireland) Order 1996 Art.2(2), Art.4(3)(8), Art.30(1). In force: August 1, 1996; £3.70.

These Regulations prescribe the arrangement of the divisional jurors list, the procedure for balloting for jurors from the jury panel, the notice to jurors and the form of return which must be sent out and completed by all those selected for jury service in any year and the form of summons.

5914. Juries–oaths–forms

FORMS OF JURORS OATH ORDER (NORTHERN IRELAND) 1996, SR 1996 268; made under the Juries (Northern Ireland) Order 1996 Art.27(1). In force: August 1, 1996; £0.65.

This Order prescribes the form of oath to be taken by jurors in the Crown Court.

5915. Juries (Northern Ireland) Order 1996 (SI 1996 1141 (NI 6))

This Order, which comes into force on days to be appointed, sets out qualifications for jury service and deals with the preparation of jurors lists, the empanelling, summoning and balloting of jurors and challenges. It also confers additional powers on courts and creates offences.

5916. Juries (Northern Ireland) Order 1996–Commencement Order

JURIES (1996 ORDER) (COMMENCEMENT) ORDER 1996 (NORTHERN IRELAND) 1996, SR 1996 267 (C.12); made under the Juries (Northern Ireland) Order 1996 Art.1. In force: bringing the Order into force on July 31, 1996; £0.65.

This Order appoints July 31, 1996, for the coming into operation of the Juries (Northern Ireland) Order 1996 (SI 1996 1141 (NI 6)).

5917. Juvenile Courts–county courts–assessors

JUVENILE COURTS AND ASSESSORS FOR COUNTY COURTS (AMENDMENT) REGULATIONS (NORTHERN IRELAND) 1996, SR 1996 302; made under the Children and Young Persons Act (Northern Ireland) 1968 s.63, Sch.2. In force: November 4, 1996; £0.65.

These Regulations amend the Juvenile Courts and Assessors for County Courts Regulations (Northern Ireland) 1979 (SR 1979 104) to provide for the jurisdiction of juvenile courts. The Regulations make different provision where a juvenile court is exercising jurisdiction conferred by or under the Children (Northern Ireland) Order 1995 (SI 1995 755 (NI 2)).

ADMINISTRATIVE LAW

5918. Commissioner for Complaints (Northern Ireland) Order 1996 (SI 1996 1297 (NI 7))

This Order, which came into force on July 16, 1996, repeals and re-enacts with amendments the Commissioner for Complaints Act (Northern Ireland) 1969. The principal amendments make provision for removing the Commissioner from office when he is incapable for medical reasons, of carrying out his duties and for appointing a temporary Commissioner and extends the list of bodies subject to investigation.

5919. Deregulation and Contracting Out (Northern Ireland) Order 1996 (SI 1996 1632 (NI 11))

This Order, which comes into force in accordance with Art.1, contains miscellaneous provisions relating to deregulation and the contracting out of functions of Northern Ireland departments and certain office-holders. It also confers power to improve enforcement procedures and requires model provisions to be made about appeals against enforcement action, with a view to their being incorporated in legislation.

5920. Ombudsman (Northern Ireland) Order 1996 (SI 1996 1298 (NI 8))

This Order, which came into force on July 16, 1996, repeals and re-enacts with amendments the Parliamentary Commissioner Act (Northern Ireland) 1969. The principal amendments make provision for renaming the Northern Ireland Parliamentary Commissioner for Administration as the Assembly Ombudsman for Northern Ireland, the removal from office of the Ombudsman where he is incapable, for medical reasons, of carrying out his duties and for the appointment of a person to act as Ombudsman for a temporary period, the extension of the Ombudsman's jurisdiction to include actions taken in the exercise of administrative functions by the administrative staff of certain tribunals, the investigation of complaints where the person aggrieved has exercised his rights before a tribunal, but complains that the injustice sustained remains unremedied and the examination by the Ombudsman of any matter complained of and his power to effect a settlement of that matter or to state what action should be taken to effect such a settlement or remove the cause of complaint.

5921. Ombudsmen–salaries

SALARIES (ASSEMBLY OMBUDSMAN AND COMMISSIONER FOR COMPLAINTS) ORDER (NORTHERN IRELAND) 1996, SR 1996 522; made under the Ombudsman (Northern Ireland) Order 1996 Art.5(1)(2); and the Commissioner for Complaints (Northern Ireland) Order 1996 Art.4(1)(2). In force: November 19, 1996; £0.65.

This Order prescribes the salaries of the Assembly Ombudsman and the Commissioner for Complaints.

AGRICULTURE

5922. Access to the countryside

COUNTRYSIDE ACCESS REGULATIONS (NORTHERN IRELAND) 1996, SR 1996 213; made under the European Communities Act 1972 s.2(2); and the

Agriculture (Conservation Grants) (Northern Ireland) Order 1995 Art.3(1)(2). In force: July 1, 1996; £1.95.

These Regulations provide for the payment of aid to farmers who agree to provide public access through their land and lanes pursuant to Council Regulation 2078/92 ([1992] OJ L215/85) Art.2(1)(g).

5923. Access to the countryside

COUNTRYSIDE ACCESS (AMENDMENT) REGULATIONS (NORTHERN IRELAND) 1996, SR 1996 609; made under the European Communities Act 1972 s.2(2); and the Agriculture (Conservation Grants) (Northern Ireland) Order 1995 Art.3(1)(2). In force: January 1, 1997; £1.95.

These Regulations amend the Countryside Access Regulations (Northern Ireland) 1996 (SR 1996 213) which implement in part a zonal programme approved by the European Commission under Council Regulation 2078/92 ([1992] OJ L215/85) on agricultural production methods compatible with the requirements of the protection of the environment and the maintenance of the countryside. The Regulations make provision to implement, as respects Northern Ireland, Commission Regulation 746/96 ([1996] OJ L102/19) laying down detailed rules for the application of the Agri-environment Regulation. They restrict eligibility where an applicant is excluded from giving an undertaking under an agri-environment scheme as a result of a penalty applied under Commission Regulation Art.20(3) or pursuant to the Commission Regulation Art.20(2); specify that entitlement to payment under the principal Regulations is subject to the provisions of the Commission Regulation Art.10 and Art.20(3); make provision to enable the Department to recover grant and impose penalties in accordance with Commission Regulation Art.11, Art.12 and Art.20, and set a rate of interest where recovery of money is to include interest in accordance with Commission Regulation Art.20(1).

5924. Agricultural policy–farming–conservation grants

FARM AND CONSERVATION GRANT (AMENDMENT) (NO.2) SCHEME (NORTHERN IRELAND) 1995, SR 1995 463; made under the Agriculture and Fisheries (Financial Assistance) (Northern Ireland) Order 1987 Art.16. In force: January 30, 1996; £0.65.

This Scheme amends the 1989 Scheme by extending the closing date for receipt of claims by the Department of Agriculture from January 31, 1996, to January 31, 1997.

5925. Agricultural produce–marketing grants

AGRICULTURAL PROCESSING AND MARKETING GRANT REGULATIONS (NORTHERN IRELAND) 1996, SR 1996 196; made under the European Communities Act 1972 s.2(2). In force: June 24, 1996; £1.55.

These Regulations supplement Council Regulation 866/90 ([1990] OJ L91) as amended by Council Regulation 3669/93 ([1990] OJ L338) on measures for improving the processing and marketing conditions of agricultural products by empowering the making of grants towards expenditure in respect of investments or projects approved for the payment of aid from the Guidance Section of the European Agricultural Guidance and Guarantee Fund.

5926. Animal conservation–game birds

GAME BIRDS PRESERVATION ORDER (NORTHERN IRELAND) 1996, SR 1996 231; made under the Game Preservation Act (Northern Ireland) 1928 s.7C(1), s.7F; and the Northern Ireland Act 1974 Sch.1 para.2(1). In force: August 11, 1996; £0.65.

This Order prohibits the killing or taking of partridge, red-legged partridges and hen pheasants during the normal open season for game birds. It also restricts dealings in those birds and prohibits dealings in grouse.

5927. Animal products–diseases and disorders–bovine material

SPECIFIED BOVINE MATERIAL ORDER (NORTHERN IRELAND) 1996, SR 1996 133; made under the Diseases of Animals (Northern Ireland) Order 1981 Art.2(3), Art.5(1), Art.19(b)(e)(f)(i)(k), Art.29(1)(2), Art.32, Art.44, Art.46(7A), Art.60(1). In force: March 29, 1996; £3.20.

This Order extends the list of animals and birds in the Diseases of Animals (Northern Ireland) Order 1981 (SI 1981 1115 (NI 22)) Sch.1 and prohibits the sale, supply and use of certain feeding stuffs for animals and poultry. It provides for licensing collection centres for storing and handling specified bovine material, rendering plants and manufacturing premises for processing such material. It also regulates the consignment and transport of such material and prohibits its import unless stained and its export to Great Britain, the Isle of Man, the Channel Islands or other Member States, except under licence.

5928. Animal products–diseases and disorders–bovine material

SPECIFIED BOVINE MATERIAL (AMENDMENT) ORDER (NORTHERN IRELAND) 1996, SR 1996 185; made under the Diseases of Animals (Northern Ireland) Order 1981 Art.2(3), Art.5(1), Art.19(b)(e)(f)(i)(k), Art.29(1)(2), Art.32, Art.44, Art.46(7A), Art.60(1). In force: May 7, 1996; £1.10.

This Order amends the Specified Bovine Material Order (Northern Ireland) 1996 (SR 1996 133) to exclude processed blood from the definition of mammalian meat and bone meal, to include in the definition of specified bovine material specified parts of the carcasses of scheme animals, that is, animals slaughtered pursuant to the purchase, slaughter and disposal scheme introduced under Council Regulation 716/96 ([1996] OJ L99/14) adopting exceptional support for the beef market in the United Kingdom, to prohibit the sale, supply or feeding to livestock, fish or equine animals of feeding stuffs in which mammalian meat or bone meal has been incorporated and to amend provisions about rendering plants.

5929. Animal products–diseases and disorders–bovine material

SPECIFIED BOVINE MATERIAL (NO.2) ORDER (NORTHERN IRELAND) 1996, SR 1996 360; made under the Diseases of Animals (Northern Ireland) Order 1981 Art.2(3), Art.5(1), Art.19(b)(e)(f)(i)(k), Art.29(1)(2), Art.32, Art.44, Art.46(7A), Art.60(1). In force: August 1, 1996; £3.70.

This Order revokes and re-enacts the Specified Bovine Material Order (Northern Ireland) 1996 (SR 1996 133) and the Specified Bovine Material Amendment Order (Northern Ireland) 1996 (SR 1996 185). It controls specified bovine material and as such implements various EC Directives. The only changes of substance are: the introduction of certain restrictions on the use, storage, packaging and consignment of mammalian meat and bone meal, including a requirement to keep records relating to production, transport and use of such meal; and requiring that any solid resulting from the slaughter of bovine animals which is found in a drainage trap of the slaughterhall of a slaughterhouse is to be dealt with in the same way as specified bovine material.

5930. Animal products–diseases and disorders–bovine material

SPECIFIED BOVINE MATERIAL (NO.2) (AMENDMENT) ORDER (NORTHERN IRELAND) 1996, SR 1996 538; made under the Diseases of Animals (Northern Ireland) Order 1981 Art.2(3), Art.5(1), Art.19(b)(e)(f)(i)(k), Art.29(1)(2), Art.32, Art.44, Art.46(7A), Art.60(1). In force: November 21, 1996; £1.10.

This Order amends the Specified Bovine Material (No.2) Order (Northern Ireland) 1996 (SR 1996 360) by making provision for the sale of mammalian meat and bone meal products at premises where feeding stuffs for livestock are produced.

5931. Animal products–diseases and disorders–bovine material

SPECIFIED BOVINE MATERIAL (NO.2) (AMENDMENT NO.2) ORDER (NORTHERN IRELAND) 1996, SR 1996 596; made under the Diseases of Animals (Northern Ireland) Order 1981 Art.2(3), Art.5(1), Art.19(b)(e)(f)(i)(k), Art.29(1)(2), Art.32, Art.44, Art.46(7A), Art.60(1). In force: January 8, 1997; £1.10.

This Order amends the definition of "scheme animal" in the Specified Bovine Material (No.2) Order (Northern Ireland) 1996 (SR 1996 360) so that the various requirements of that Order regarding the separation of specified bovine material and other animal parts which are already disapplied in relation to the carcasses of animals slaughtered pursuant to the purchase scheme introduced under Commission Regulation 716/96 ([1996] OJ L99/14), are now similarly disapplied in relation to the carcasses of animals slaughtered in accordance with the Diseases of Animals (Northern Ireland) Order 1981 (SI 1985 1115 (NI 22)) as animals exposed to the infection of bovine spongiform encephalopathy.

5932. Animal products–diseases and disorders–bovine material

SPECIFIED BOVINE MATERIAL (TREATMENT AND DISPOSAL) REGULATIONS (NORTHERN IRELAND) 1996, SR 1996 134; made under the Food (Northern Ireland) Order 1989 Art.15(1)(2)(g)(h)(i), Art.72(4). In force: March 29, 1996.

These Regulations prohibit the sale of specified bovine material, including heads (except tongues), for human consumption, restrict the treatment of such material and rendering whole bovine carcasses, restrict the use of bovine vertebral columns and the removal of the brain, eyes and spinal cord of bovine animals and deal with the approval of incinerators for specified bovine material and with the disposal of such material.

5933. Animal products–diseases and disorders–bovine material

SPECIFIED BOVINE MATERIAL (TREATMENT AND DISPOSAL) (AMENDMENT) REGULATIONS (NORTHERN IRELAND) 1996, SR 1996 186; made under the Food (Northern Ireland) Order 1989 Art.15(1)(2)(g)(h)(i), Art.72(4). In force: May 7, 1996; £1.55.

These Regulations amend the Specified Bovine Material (Treatment and Disposal) Regulations (Northern Ireland) 1996 (SR 1996 134) so as to extend the definition of specified bovine material to scheme animals, that is, animals slaughtered pursuant to the purchase slaughter and disposal scheme introduced under Commission Regulation 716/96 ([1996] OJ L99/14) adopting exceptional support for the beef market in the United Kingdom. They also apply the 1996 Regulations with modifications to specified bovine material from scheme animals, prohibit a person recovering meat by mechanical means from bovine carcasses unless his name and certain particulars are registered and require owners of slaughterhouses to stain carcasses (excluding hides) once such material is removed from the carcasses of scheme animals.

5934. Animal products–diseases and disorders–bovine material

SPECIFIED BOVINE MATERIAL (TREATMENT AND DISPOSAL) (NO.2) REGULATIONS (NORTHERN IRELAND) 1996, SR 1996 361; made under the Food (Northern Ireland) Order 1989 Art.15(1)(2)(g)(h)(i), Art.72(4). In force: August 1, 1996; £2.80.

These Regulations revoke and remake with amendments the Specified Bovine Material (Treatment and Disposal) Regulations (Northern Ireland) 1996 (SR 1996 134) and the Specified Bovine Material (Treatment and Disposal) (Amendment) Regulations (Northern Ireland) 1996 (SR 1996 186). The only change of substance is that solid matter trapped in drainage systems where bovine animals are slaughtered or their carcasses processed shall be deemed to be specified bovine material.

5935. Animal products–diseases and disorders–bovine material

SPECIFIED BOVINE MATERIAL (TREATMENT AND DISPOSAL) (NO.3) REGULATIONS (NORTHERN IRELAND) 1996, SR 1996 390; made under the Food Safety (Northern Ireland) Order 1991 Art.15(1)(3), Art.16(1), Art.18(1), Art.25, Art.26(3), Art.47(2). In force: August 26, 1996; £2.80.

These Regulations re-enact the Specified Bovine Material (Treatment and Disposal) (No.2) Regulations (Northern Ireland) 1996 (SR 1996 361), which cease to have effect following the repeal of the remainder of the Food (Northern Ireland) Order 1989 (SI 1989 846 (NI 6)). They implement various Directives first set out in the Specified Bovine Material (Treatment and Disposal) Regulations (Northern Ireland) 1995 (SR 1995 457) and the Mechanically Recovered Meat Regulations (Northern Ireland) 1995 (SR 1995 470).

5936. Animal products–diseases and disorders–bovine material

SPECIFIED BOVINE MATERIAL (TREATMENT AND DISPOSAL) (NO.3) (AMENDMENT) REGULATIONS (NORTHERN IRELAND) 1996, SR 1996 594; made under the Food Safety (Northern Ireland) Order 1991 Art.15(1)(3), Art.16(1), Art.18(1), Art.25, Art.26(3), Art.47(2). In force: January 8, 1997; £1.10.

These Regulations amend the definition of "scheme animal" in the Specified Bovine Material (Treatment and Disposal) (No.3) Regulations (Northern Ireland) 1996 (SR1996 390) with the effect that various requirements of those Regulations requiring the separation of specified bovine material and other animal parts, which are already disapplied in relation to the carcasses of animals slaughtered pursuant to the purchase, slaughter and disposal scheme introduced under Commission Regulations 716/96 ([1996] OJ L99/14), are now similarly disapplied in relation to the carcasses of animals slaughtered in accordance with the provisions of the Diseases of Animals (Northern Ireland) Order 1991 (SI 1991 762 (NI 7)) Sch.2 as animals exposed to the infection of bovine spongiform encephalopathy.

5937. Animal products–diseases and disorders–bovine offal

SPECIFIED BOVINE OFFAL (TREATMENT AND DISPOSAL) REGULATIONS (NORTHERN IRELAND) 1995, SR 1995 457; made under the Food (Northern Ireland) Order 1989 Art.15(1)(2)(g)(h)(i). In force: December 21, 1996.

These Regulations implement Commission Decision 94/774 ([1994] OJ L310/70) Art 3.3(a) in relation to the sale, use and treatment of specified bovine offal.

5938. Animal products–diseases and disorders–BSE

BOVINE SPONGIFORM ENCEPHALOPATHY (AMENDMENT) ORDER (NORTHERN IRELAND) 1996, SR 1996 362; made under the Diseases of Animals (Northern Ireland) Order 1981 Art.2(3), Art.5(1), Art.10(6), Art.18(7), Art.19(e)(f)(k), Art.44, Art.60(1). In force: August 5, 1996; £1.10.

This Order amends the Bovine Spongiform Encephalopathy Order (Northern Ireland) 1995 (SR 1995 274) by extending the power of the Department of Agriculture to require cleansing and disinfection so that it also relates to vehicles and equipment on or in which there is or has been an affected or suspected animal or the carcase of such an animal and premises, vehicles and equipment on or in which there is or has been mammalian meat and bone meal or material containing it. It also imposes certain new requirements relating to the cleansing and disinfection of premises, vehicles or equipment in or in connection with which mammalian meat and bone meal is produced, stored or transported.

5939. Animal products–diseases and disorders–BSE

BOVINE SPONGIFORM ENCEPHALOPATHY (AMENDMENT) (NO.2) ORDER (NORTHERN IRELAND) 1996, SR 1996 593; made under the Diseases of

Animals (Northern Ireland) Order 1981 Art.2(3), Art.5(1), Art.10(6), Art.18(7), Art.19(e) (f) (k), Art.44, Art.60(1). In force: January 8, 1997; £1.70.

This Order further amends the Bovine Spongiform Encephalopathy Order (Northern Ireland) 1995 (SR 1995 274) so as to allow the Department of Agriculture to impose requirements on the owner or person in charge of animals which have been exposed to the infection of bovine spongiform encephalopathy or the carcasses of such animals. These requirements in particular relate to the detention of the animals or carcasses and to the cleansing and disinfection of the premises on which they are kept and of certain items used in connection with them.

5940. Animal products–diseases and disorders–food safety–beef exports

BOVINE PRODUCTS (DESPATCH TO OTHER MEMBER STATES) REGULATIONS (NORTHERN IRELAND) 1996, SR 1996 563; made under the European Communities Act 1972 s.2(2). In force: January 1, 1997; £1.95.

These Regulations implement in part Council Decision 96/239 ([1996] OJ L78/47) on emergency measures to protect against Bovine Spongiform Encephalopathy, as amended by Commission Decision 96/362 ([1996] OJ L139/17). They control the despatch to other Member States of meat and other products from bovine animals slaughtered outside the United Kingdom; make provision for the Department of Agriculture to charge fees, contain provisions on enforcement, obstruction, offences and penalties; and amend the Products of Animal Origin (Import and Export) Regulations (Northern Ireland) 1993 (SR 1993 304) and the Animals and Animal Products (Import and Export) Regulations (Northern Ireland) 1995 (SR 1995 52) so that those Regulations apply without prejudice to these Regulations.

5941. Animal products–diseases and disorders–food safety–beef exports

BOVINE PRODUCTS (DESPATCH TO OTHER MEMBER STATES) (AMENDMENT) REGULATIONS (NORTHERN IRELAND) 1996, SR 1996 597; made under the European Communities Act 1972 s.2(2). In force: January 2, 1997; £1.10.

These Regulations amend the Bovine Products (Despatch to Other Member States) Regulations (Northern Ireland) 1996 (SR 1996 563) which implement in part Commission Decision 96/239 ([1996] OJ L78/47) on emergency measures to protect against bovine spongiform encephalopathy, as amended by Commission Decision 96/362 ([1996] OJ L139/17) in relation to the despatch to other Member States of meat and other products from bovine animals slaughtered outside the United Kingdom. These Regulations additionally make provision for the control of the production of gelatin from bovine animals.

5942. Animal products–export controls

MECHANICALLY RECOVERED MEAT (EXPORT PROHIBITION) ORDER (NORTHERN IRELAND) 1995, SR 1995 469; made under the Diseases of Animals (Northern Ireland) Order 1981 Art.32. In force: December 18, 1995; £1.10.

This Order prohibits the export to Great Britain, the Isle of Man, the Channel Islands or another Member State of mechanically recovered meat.

5943. Animals–slaughter–compensation

SELECTIVE CULL (ENFORCEMENT OF COMMUNITY COMPENSATION CONDITIONS) REGULATIONS (NORTHERN IRELAND) 1996, SR 1996 595; made under the European Communities Act 1972 s.2(2). In force: January 8, 1997; £1.10.

These Regulations make provision for the enforcement of certain of the requirements of Commission Regulation 1484/96 ([1996] OJ L188/25), adopting exceptional support measures for the beef market in the United Kingdom by the application of Commission Decision 96/385 ([1996] OJ L151/39). That Regulation provides for the co-financing by the European Community of the compensation payable to owners of bovine animals slaughtered under the selective cull set out in the BSE eradication plan drawn up by the United Kingdom and approved by Commission Decision 96/385. Various requirements are specified as to the slaughter, treatment and disposal of animals in respect of which compensation is payable.

5944. Arable land–set aside–grazing

ARABLE AREA PAYMENTS (GRAZING OF BOVINE ANIMALS ON SET-ASIDE LAND) (TEMPORARY PROVISIONS) REGULATIONS (NORTHERN IRELAND) 1996, SR 1996 258; made under the European Communities Act 1972 s.2(2). In force: June 26, 1996; £1.10.

These Regulations implement Commission Regulation 1091/96 ([1996] OJ L144/9), which authorises the United Kingdom, until August 31, 1996, to permit the grazing of bovine animals of more than 30 months under Council Regulation 1765/92 ([1992] OJ L181/12) Art.7 establishing a support system for producers of certain arable crops. They expire on August 31, 1996.

5945. Beef–premiums–protection of payments

BEEF SPECIAL PREMIUM (PROTECTION OF PAYMENTS) REGULATIONS (NORTHERN IRELAND) 1996, SR 1996 611; made under the European Communities Act 1972 s.2(2). In force: January 1, 1997; £2.80.

These Regulations consolidate, with amendments, the Beef Special Premium (Protection of Payments) Regulations (Northern Ireland) 1992 (SR 1992 569, as amended by SR 1993 176, SR 1993 480 and SR 1994 476). The main amendment effected by these Regulations is that there is now payable a higher rate premium for un-castrated male bovines (known as "bull premium"). This reflects Council Regulation 2222/96 ([1996] OJ L296/50) and Commission Regulation 2311/96 ([1996] OJ L313/9).

5946. Beef–premiums–protection of payments

DESEASONALISATION PREMIUM (PROTECTION OF PAYMENTS) REGULATIONS (NORTHERN IRELAND) 1996, SR 1996 605; made under the European Communities Act 1972 s.2(2). In force: January 1, 1997; £1.10.

These Regulations supplement the relevant provisions of certain Council and Commission Regulations relating to payments of deseasonalisation premiums to beef and veal producers in respect of 1997.

5947. Cattle–premiums

SUCKLER COW PREMIUM (AMENDMENT) REGULATIONS (NORTHERN IRELAND) 1996, SR 1996 229; made under the European Communities Act 1972 s.2(2). In force: July 1, 1996; £0.65.

These Regulations amend the Suckler Cow Premium Regulations (Northern Ireland) 1993 (SR 1993 280) by substituting December 6, 1996, as the closing date for Suckler Cow premium applications.

5948. Environmentally sensitive areas

ENVIRONMENTALLY SENSITIVE AREAS DESIGNATED ORDERS (AMENDMENT) REGULATIONS (NORTHERN IRELAND) 1996, SR 1996 606; made under the European Communities Act 1972 s.2(2). In force: January 1, 1997; £1.95.

These Regulations amend the Environmentally Sensitive Areas Designation Orders designating areas in Northern Ireland as environmentally sensitive areas, which implement in part a zonal programme approved by the European Commission in compliance with Council Regulation 2078/92 ([1992] OJ L215/85) on agricultural production methods compatible with the requirements of protection of the environment and the maintenance of the countryside. The

Designation Orders amended by the Regulation are set out in the Schedule. The Regulations implement Commission Regulation 746/96 ([1996] OJ L102/19) laying down detailed rules for the application of Council Regulation 2078/92. They provide that entitlement to payment under the Orders set out in the Schedule is subject to the provisions of Commission Regulation 746/96 Art.10 and Art.20(3); enable the Department of Agriculture to recover grant and impose penalties in accordance with Commission Regulation 746/96 Art.11, Art.12 and Art.20; and set a rate of interest where recovery of money is to include interest in accordance with Commission Regulation 746/96 Art.20(1).

5949. Farming–organic farming–aid

ORGANIC FARMING AID (AMENDMENT) REGULATIONS (NORTHERN IRELAND) 1996, SR 1996 610; made under the European Communities Act 1972 s.2(2). In force: January 1, 1997; £1.95.

These Regulations amend the Organic Farming Aid Regulations (Northern Ireland) 1995 (SR 1995 116) which implement in part Council Regulation 2078/92 ([1992] OJ L215/85) on agricultural production methods compatible with the requirements of the protection of the environment and the maintenance of the countryside. The Regulations implement Commission Regulation 746/96 ([1996] OJ L102/19). They provide that entitlement to payment under the 1995 Regulations is subject to the provisions of Commission Regulation 746/96 Art.10 and Art.20(3); make provision to enable the Department of Agriculture to recover grant and impose penalties in accordance with Commission Regulation 746/96 Art.11, Art.12 and Art.20, and set a rate of interest where recovery of money is to include interest in accordance with Commission Regulation 746/96 Art.20(1).

5950. Fertilisers

FERTILISERS (MAMMALIAN MEAT AND BONE MEAL) REGULATIONS (NORTHERN IRELAND) 1996, SR 1996 165; made under the Agriculture Act 1970 s.66(1), s.74A(1), s.84, s.86(1)(2)(3)(9). In force: April 20, 1996; £1.10.

These Regulations control the composition or content of fertilisers used, or intended for sale for use, on agricultural land.

5951. Fertilisers

FERTILISERS (MAMMALIAN MEAT AND BONE MEAL) (AMENDMENT) REGULATIONS (NORTHERN IRELAND) 1996, SR 1996 458; made under the Agriculture Act 1970 s.66(1), s.74A(1), s.84, s.86(1)(2)(3)(9). In force: November 8, 1996; £1.10.

These Regulations amend the Fertilisers (Mammalian Meat and Bone) Regulations (Northern Ireland) 1996 (SR 1996 165) by replacing the definition of mammalian meat and bone meal and adding definitions of protein and rendering.

5952. Fertilisers–sampling–analysis

FERTILISERS (SAMPLING AND ANALYSIS) REGULATIONS (NORTHERN IRELAND) 1996, SR 1996 513; made under the Agriculture Act 1970 s.66(1), s.74A, s.75(1), s.76(1), s.77, s.78(2)(4)(6), s.79(1)(2)(9), s.84, s.86(1)(2)(3), s.86(6)(7)(9). In force: December 16, 1996; £14.00.

These Regulations revoke and replace, with amendments, the Fertilisers (Sampling and Analysis) Regulations (Northern Ireland) 1991 (SR 1991 540).

5953. Fish–diseases and disorders

DISEASES OF FISH (CONTROL) REGULATIONS (NORTHERN IRELAND) 1996, SR 1996 16; made under the European Communities Act 1972 s.2(2). In force: February 23, 1996.

These Regulations implement Council Directive 93/53 ([1993] OJ L175/23) in relation to the control of certain fish diseases.

5954. Fisheries–licence duties

FISHERIES (LICENCE DUTIES) BYELAWS (NORTHERN IRELAND) 1995, SR 1995 495; made under the Fisheries Act (Northern Ireland) 1966 s.26(1), s.114(1)(b), s.115(1)(b). In force: January 1, 1996; £1.55.

These byelaws increase duties on fishing licences.

5955. Fisheries–licence duties

FISHERIES (LICENCE DUTIES) BYELAWS (NORTHERN IRELAND) 1996, SR 1996 540; made under the Fisheries Act (Northern Ireland) 1966 s.26(1), s.114(1)(b), s.115(1)(b). In force: January 1, 1997; £1.55.

These Byelaws further amend the Fisheries Consolidated and Amendment Byelaws (Northern Ireland) 1989 (SR 1989 483) to increase the licence duties payable from January 1, 1997 for fishing with rod and line and hand line for salmon and freshwater fish and for commercial fishing engines used for the taking of salmon and freshwater fish other than eels together with the fee payable for a licence which authorises the holder to buy and sell salmon, trout and eels.

5956. Fishing–licence duties

EEL FISHING (LICENCE DUTIES) REGULATIONS (NORTHERN IRELAND) 1996, SR 1996 539; made under the Fisheries Act (Northern Ireland) 1966 s.15(1), s.19(1). In force: January 1, 1997; £1.10.

These Regulations increase the licence duties payable from January 1, 1997 to the Fisheries Conservancy Board for Northern Ireland in respect of licences for the use of fishing engines for the taking of eels.

5957. Habitats–conservation

HABITAT IMPROVEMENT (AMENDMENT) REGULATIONS (NORTHERN IRELAND) 1996, SR 1996 608; made under the European Communities Act 1972 s.2(2). In force: January 1, 1997; £1.95.

These Regulations amend the Habitat Improvement Regulations (Northern Ireland) 1995 (SR 1995 134) which implement in part a zonal programme approved by the European Commission under Council Regulation 2078/92 ([1992] OJ L215/85) on agricultural production methods compatible with the requirements of the protection of the environment and the maintenance of the countryside. These Regulations implement, as respects Northern Ireland, Commission Regulation 746/96 ([1996] OJ L102/19) laying down detailed rules for the application of the Agri-environment Regulation. They specify that the entitlement to payment under the 1995 Regulations is subject to the provisions of Commission Regulation 746/96 Art.10 and Art.20(3); make provision to enable the Department of Agriculture to recover grant and impose penalties in accordance with Commission Regulation 746/96 Art.11, Art.12 and Art.20; and set a rate of interest where recovery of money is to include interest in accordance with Commission Regulation 746/96 Art.20(1).

5958. Hill farming–compensatory allowances

HILL LIVESTOCK (COMPENSATORY ALLOWANCES) REGULATIONS (NORTHERN IRELAND) 1996, SR 1996 230; made under the European Communities Act 1972 s.2(2). In force: July 1, 1996; £3.20.

These Regulations replace, with amendments and revoke, the Hill Livestock (Compensatory Allowances) Regulations (Northern Ireland) 1994 (SR 1994 417). They implement Council Directive 75/268 ([1975] OJ L128/1) on mountain and hill farming in less-favoured areas, as amended by Council Directive 80/666 ([1980] OJ L180/34) and Council Directive 82/786 ([1982] OJ L3270/19) and comply with Council Regulation 2328/91 ([1991] OJ L218/1) Art.17, Art.18, Art.19 on improving the efficiency of agricultural structures, as amended by Council Regulation 870/93 ([1993] OJ L91/10), Council

Regulation 1992/93 ([1993] OJ L182/12) and Council Regulation 3669/93 ([1993] OJ L338/26). They also provide for the administration and enforcement of provisions of payment of compensatory allowances contained in Commission Regulation 3887/92 ([1992] OJ L391/36) laying down detailed rules for applying the integrated administration and control system for certain community aid schemes.

5959. Hill farming–compensatory allowances

HILL LIVESTOCK (COMPENSATORY ALLOWANCES) (AMENDMENT) REGULATIONS (NORTHERN IRELAND) 1996, SR 1996 498; made under the European Communities Act 1972 s.2(2). In force: November 15, 1996; £1.10.

These Regulations amend the Hill Livestock (Compensatory Allowances) Regulations (Northern Ireland) 1996 (SR 1996 230) by providing for a longer period for applying for compensatory allowances.

5960. Hill farming–compensatory allowances

HILL LIVESTOCK (COMPENSATORY ALLOWANCES) (AMENDMENT) REGULATIONS (NORTHERN IRELAND) 1996, SR 1996 7; made under the European Communities Act 1972 s.2(2). In force: January 31, 1996.

These Regulations amend the Hill Livestock (Compensatory Allowances) Regulations (Northern Ireland) 1994 (SR 1994 417).

5961. Hill farming–compensatory allowances

HILL LIVESTOCK (COMPENSATORY ALLOWANCES) (AMENDMENT) (NO.3) REGULATIONS (NORTHERN IRELAND) 1995, SR 1995 404; made under the European Communities Act 1972 2(2). In force: November 15, 1995; £1.10.

These Regulations amend the Hill Livestock (Compensatory Allowances) Regulations (Northern Ireland) 1994 (SR 1994 417).

5962. Hill farming–livestock extensification

MOORLAND (LIVESTOCK EXTENSIFICATION) (AMENDMENT NO.2) REGULATIONS (NORTHERN IRELAND) 1996, SR 1996 607; made under the European Communities Act 1972 s.2(2). In force: January 1, 1997; £1.95.

These Regulations further amend the Moorland (Livestock Extensification) Regulations (Northern Ireland) 1995 (SR 1995 239 amended by SR 1996 505 which implement in part a zonal programme approved by the European Commission under Council Regulation 2078/92 ([1992] OJ L215/85) on agricultural production methods compatible with the requirements of the protection of the environment and the maintenance of the countryside. These Regulations implement as respects Northern Ireland, Commission Regulation 746/96 ([1996] OJ L102/19) laying down detailed rules for the application of the Agri-environment Regulation. They provide that entitlement to payment under the 1995 Regulations is subject to the provisions of Commission Regulation 746/96 Art.10 and Art.20(3); enable the Department o Agriculture to recover grant and impose penalties in accordance with Commission Regulation 746/96 Art.11, Art.12 and Art.20; and set a rate of interest where recovery of money is to include interest in accordance with Commission Regulation 746/96 Art.20(1).

5963. Pesticides–crops–maximum residue levels–EEC limits–amendments

PESTICIDES (MAXIMUM RESIDUE LEVELS IN CROPS, FOOD AND FEEDING STUFFS) (EEC LIMITS) (AMENDMENT) REGULATIONS (NORTHERN IRELAND) 1995, SR 1995 460; made under the Food and Environment Protection Act 1985 s.16(2) (k) (l) (15), s.24(3). In force: February 14, 1996; £1.10.

These Regulations amend the Pesticides (Maximum Residue Levels in Crops, Food and Feeding Stuffs) (EEC Limits) Regulations 1995 (SR 1995 33).

5964. Pesticides–crops–maximum residue levels–EEC limits–amendments

PESTICIDES (MAXIMUM RESIDUE LEVELS IN CROPS, FOOD AND FEEDING STUFFS) (EEC LIMITS) (AMENDMENT) REGULATIONS (NORTHERN IRELAND) 1996, SR 1996 527; made under the European Communities Act 1972 s.2(2). In force: December 30, 1996; £3.70.

These Regulations amend the Pesticides (Maximum Residue Levels in Crops, Food and Feeding Stuffs) (EEC Limits) Regulations (Northern Ireland) 1995 (SR 1995 33). They specify maximum levels of pesticide residues which may be left in crops, food and feeding stuffs in implementation of Council Directive 95/38 ([1995] OJ L197/14), Council Directive 95/39 ([1995] OJ L197/29) and Council Directive 95/61 ([1995] OJ L292/27).

5965. Pesticides–crops–maximum residue levels–national limits–amendments

PESTICIDES (MAXIMUM RESIDUE LEVELS IN CROPS, FOOD AND FEEDING STUFFS) (NATIONAL LIMITS) (AMENDMENT) REGULATIONS (NORTHERN IRELAND) 1996, SR 1996 526; made under the Food and Environment Protection Act 1985 s.16(2)(k)(l), s.24(3). In force: December 30, 1996; £1.10.

These Regulations amend the Pesticides (Maximum Residue Levels in Crops, Food and Feeding Stuffs) (National Limits) Regulations (Northern Ireland) 1995 (SR 1995 32) Sch.2 by removing certain maximum levels of pesticide levels. The limits are now included in the Pesticides (Maximum Residue Levels in Crops, Food and Feeding Stuffs) (EEC Limits) Regulations (Northern Ireland) 1995 (SR 1995 33).

5966. Pigs–slaughter

PIG PRODUCTION DEVELOPMENT (LEVY) ORDER (NORTHERN IRELAND) 1996, SR 1996 502; made under the Pig Production Development Act (Northern Ireland) 1964 s.5(1)(2)(3). In force: December 2, 1996; £1.10.

This Order provides for the payment of a levy to the Department of Agriculture on pigs slaughtered in, or exported from, Northern Ireland.

5967. Plant conservation

PLANT HEALTH (AMENDMENT) ORDER (NORTHERN IRELAND) 1996, SR 1996 204; made under the Plant Health Act (Northern Ireland) 1967 s.2, s.3(1), s.3A, s.3B(1), s.4(1). In force: June 24, 1996; £1.55.

This Order amends the Plant Health Order (Northern Ireland) 1967 to provide for the granting of licences by the Department of Agriculture in accordance with Commission Directive 95/44 ([1995] OJ L184/34) establishing the conditions under which certain harmful organisms, plants, plant products and other objects listed in Council Directive 77/93 ([1977] OJ L26/20) Annex 1 to Annex V may be introduced into or moved within the European Union or certain protected zones for trial or scientific purposes and for work on varietal selections.

5968. Plant conservation

PLANT HEALTH (AMENDMENT NO.2) ORDER (NORTHERN IRELAND) 1996, SR 1996 249; made under the Plant Health Act (Northern Ireland) 1967 s.2, s.3(1), s.3A, s.3B(1), s.4(1). In force: July 29, 1996; £1.95.

This Order amends the Plant Health Order (Northern Ireland) 1993 (SR 1993 256) to implement Commission Directive 96/14 ([1996] OJ L68/24) amending certain Annexes to Council Directive 77/93 ([1977] OJ L26/20) on protective measures against the introduction into the Community of organisms harmful to plants or plant products and against their spread within the Community and Commission Directive 96/15 ([1996] OJ L70/35) amending Directive 92/76 ([1992] OJ L305/12) recognising protected zones exposed to particular plant health risks in the Community.

5969. Plant conservation

PLANT HEALTH (WOOD AND BARK) (AMENDMENT) ORDER (NORTHERN IRELAND) 1996, SR 1996 18; made under the Plant Health Act (Northern Ireland) 1967 s.2, s.3(1), s.3A, s.3B(1), s.4(1). In force: March 6, 1996; £5.70.

This Order implements, in relation to plant health and plant products, Commission Directive 93/51 ([1993] OJ L205/24), Commission Directive 93/106 ([1993] OJ L298/34), Commission Directive 93/110 ([1993] OJ L303/19), Commission Directive 95/40 ([1995] OJ L82/14), Commission Directive 95/41 ([1995] OJ L182/17) and Council Decision 95/1 ([1995] OJ L1/1).

5970. Plant varieties

FODDER PLANT SEEDS (AMENDMENT) REGULATIONS (NORTHERN IRELAND) 1996, SR 1996 311; made under the Seeds Act (Northern Ireland) 1965 s.1 (1), s.2. In force: August 23, 1996; £0.65.

These Regulations amend the Fodder Plant Seeds Regulations (Northern Ireland) 1994 (SR 1994 252) by increasing the maximum seed lot weight for seeds of common vetch, field bean, field pea, narrow-leaved lupin (blue lupin), white lupin and yellow lupin to 25 tonnes.

5971. Plant varieties

OIL AND FIBRE PLANT SEEDS (AMENDMENT) REGULATIONS (NORTHERN IRELAND) 1996, SR 1996 312; made under the Seeds Act (Northern Ireland) 1965 s.1 (1), s.2. In force: August 23, 1996; £0.65.

These Regulations amend the Oil and Fibre Plant Seeds Regulations (Northern Ireland) 1994 (SR 1994 255) by increasing the maximum seed lot weight for seeds of sunflower and soya bean to 25 tonnes.

5972. Plant varieties–vegetables

VEGETABLE SEEDS (AMENDMENT) REGULATIONS (NORTHERN IRELAND) 1996, SR 1996 313; made under the Seeds Act (Northern Ireland) 1965 s.1 (1), s.2. In force: August 23, 1996; £0.65.

These Regulations amend the Vegetable Seeds Regulations (Northern Ireland) 1994 (SR 1994 250) by increasing the maximum seed lot weight for seeds of broad beans, French beans and peas to 25 tonnes.

5973. Potatoes–Netherlands

POTATOES ORIGINATING IN THE NETHERLANDS (NOTIFICATION) REGULATIONS (NORTHERN IRELAND) 1996, SR 1996 524; made under the European Communities Act 1972 s.2(2). In force: December 16, 1996; £1.10.

These Regulations impose certain notification requirements in respect of potatoes grown in the Netherlands during 1996 in accordance with Commission Decision 95/506 ([1995] OJ L291/48) authorising Member States to take additional measures against the dissemination of Pseudomonas solanacearum (Smith) Smith as regards the Netherlands

5974. Potatoes–packaging–exports

SEED POTATOES (AMENDMENT) REGULATIONS (NORTHERN IRELAND) 1996, SR 1996 242; made under the Seeds Act (Northern Ireland) 1965 s.1, s.2, s.12(1). In force: July 22, 1996; £0.65.

These Regulations amend the Seed Potatoes Regulations (Northern Ireland) 1981 (SR 1981 243) by removing the requirement to mark the name of the variety on packages and containers of basic seed potatoes produced in Northern Ireland which are exported or intended to be exported from Northern Ireland.

5975. Rural areas

RURAL REGENERATION AND CROSS-BORDER DEVELOPMENT REGULATIONS (NORTHERN IRELAND) 1996, SR 1996 450; made under the European Communities Act 1972 s.2(2). In force: October 24, 1996; £1.55.

These Regulations implement Council Regulation 4253/88 ([1988] OJ L374/1) and Council Regulation 4256/88 ([1988] OJ L374/25) insofar as Sub-programme 2(B) relating to rural regeneration and Measure 3 of Sub-programme 3 relating to cross-border development of the Single Programming Document are concerned. They allow the Department of Agriculture to formulate conditions for making payments and grants.

5976. Seeds–fees

SEEDS (FEES) REGULATIONS (NORTHERN IRELAND) 1996, SR 1996 409; made under the Seeds Act (Northern Ireland) 1965 s.1 (1) (2A), s.2(2) (4). In force: October 7, 1996; £2.40.

These Regulations prescribe fees for certain initial applications, crop inspection fees, seed lot fees, seed testing fees and fees in relation to licensed seed testing establishments. Fees are also prescribed in relation to the making of written representations by, and hearings involving, seed merchants, processors or packers.

5977. Sheep–premiums

SHEEP ANNUAL PREMIUM (AMENDMENT) REGULATIONS (NORTHERN IRELAND) 1996, SR 1996 497; made under the European Communities Act 1972 s.2(2). In force: November 15, 1996; £1.10.

These Regulations amend the Sheep Annual Premium Regulations (Northern Ireland) 1992 (SR 1992 476) by providing for a longer period for applying for premiums.

ANIMALS

5978. Animal products–infectious disease control–imports–birds

DISEASES OF ANIMALS (IMPORTATION OF BIRD PRODUCTS) ORDER (NORTHERN IRELAND) 1996, SR 1996 81; made under the Diseases of Animals (Northern Ireland) Order 1981 Art.24(1), Art.60(1). In force: March 29, 1996; £1.10.

This Order prohibits the importation into Northern Ireland of bird products, other than those subject to specified statutory provisions, except under a licence.

5979. Animal welfare

WELFARE OF ANIMALS (SCHEDULED OPERATIONS) (AMENDMENT) ORDER (NORTHERN IRELAND) 1996, SR 1996 514; made under the Welfare of Animals Act (Northern Ireland) 1972 s.14(3). In force: December 11, 1996; £0.65.

This Order amends the Welfare of Animals Act (Northern Ireland) 1972 Sch.1 so that the disbudding of calves by electro-chemical cautery before the fourth week of life may not be performed without anaesthetic.

5980. Animal welfare–game laws

SPRING TRAPS APPROVAL ORDER (NORTHERN IRELAND) 1996, SR 1996 515; made under the Welfare of Animals Act (Northern Ireland) 1972 s.21 (1) (2) (4). In force: November 20, 1996; £1.55.

This Order specifies approved traps, and others which are equivalent in all respects to those listed, for the purposes of the Welfare of Animals Act (Northern Ireland) 1972 s.21.

5981. Animal welfare–slaughter

WELFARE OF ANIMALS (SLAUGHTER OR KILLING) REGULATIONS (NORTHERN IRELAND) 1996, SR 1996 558; made under the European Communities Act 1972 s.2(2). In force: November 30, 1996; £6.45.

These Regulations apply to the movement, lairaging, restraint, stunning, slaughter and killing of animals bred or kept for the production of meat, skin, fur or other products, to methods of killing animals for the purposes of disease control and to the killing of surplus chicks and embryos in hatchery waste, subject to exceptions for acts done lawfully under the Animals (Scientific Procedures) Act 1986, sporting events and wild game. They amend the Slaughter of Animals Act (Northern Ireland) 1932, the Protection of Animals Act (Northern Ireland) 1952, the Diseases of Animals (Northern Ireland) Order 1981 (SI 1981 1115 (NI 22)) and the Agriculture (Miscellaneous Provisions) (Northern Ireland) Order 1984 (SI 1984 702 (NI 22)) and repeal the Slaughter of Animals (Amendment) Act (Northern Ireland) 1956.

5982. Cattle–community purchase scheme–BSE

BOVINE ANIMALS (ENFORCEMENT OF COMMUNITY PURCHASE SCHEME) REGULATIONS (NORTHERN IRELAND) 1996, SR 1996 182; made under the European Communities Act 1972 s.2(2). In force: May 1, 1996; £1.10.

These Regulations make provision for the enforcement of Commission Regulation 716/96 ([1996] OJ L99/14) adopting exceptional support measures for the beef market in the United Kingdom. The United Kingdom is authorised to introduce a scheme for the purchase of any bovine animal aged over 30 months which does not exhibit any clinical sign of bovine spongiform encephalopathy and which was, during a period of at least three months prior to its sale, present on a holding located on United Kingdom territory. Various requirements are specified as to the slaughter, treatment and disposal of animals subject to that scheme. Offences in respect of the provisions of the Commission Regulation are created by Reg.3.

5983. Cattle–embryology

BOVINE EMBRYO COLLECTION, PRODUCTION AND TRANSPLANTATION REGULATIONS (NORTHERN IRELAND) 1996, SR 1996 389; made under the Welfare of Animals Act (Northern Ireland) 1972 s.2(1); and the Artificial Reproduction of Animals (Northern Ireland) Order 1975 Art.5(1)(2). In force: October 2, 1996; £4.15.

These Regulations implement Council Directive 89/556 ([1989] OJ L302/1) in relation to animal health conditions governing intra-Community trade on and importation from third countries of embryos of domestic bovine animals, Council Directive 93/52 ([1993] OJ L175/21), amending the 1989 Directive, and Commission Decision 94/113 ([1994] OJ L53/23), which further amended it.

5984. Diseases and disorders–horses

EQUINE VIRAL ARTERITIS ORDER (NORTHERN IRELAND) 1996, SR 1996 274; made under the Diseases of Animals (Northern Ireland) Order 1981 Art.5(1), Art.10(6), Art.19(e)(f)(g)(k), Art.44, Art.46(7A), Art.60(1). In force: July 24, 1996; £1.55.

This Order introduces controls on equine viral arteritis in horses.

5985. Diseases and disorders–infectious disease control

BRUCELLOSIS CONTROL (AMENDMENT) ORDER (NORTHERN IRELAND) 1996, SR 1996 239; made under the Diseases of Animals (Northern Ireland) Order 1981 Art.16(1), Art.44, Art.60(1), Sch.2 Part I para.5(1), Sch.2 Part II para.5(1). In force: June 17, 1996; £1.10.

This Order amends the Brucellosis Control Order (Northern Ireland) 1972 (SR & O (NI) 1972 94) so that, in relation to an animal over 30 months old, its market value is the higher of the price which could have been obtained for it in the market or the price which would have applied if it had been slaughtered in accordance with Commission Regulation 716/96 ([1996] OJ L99/14).

5986. Diseases and disorders–BSE

DISEASES OF ANIMALS (MODIFICATION) ORDER (NORTHERN IRELAND) 1996, SR 1996 238; made under the Diseases of Animals (Northern Ireland) Order 1981 Art.16(2). In force: June 17, 1996; £1.10.

This Order amends the Diseases of Animals (Northern Ireland) Order 1981 (SI 1981 1115 (NI 22)) Sch.2 Part II (compensation payable for cattle slaughtered in connection with bovine spongiform encephalopathy) as respects the formula used to calculate the indicative market price, and the definition of market value for animals over 30 months old.

5987. Diseases and disorders–horses

DISEASES OF ANIMALS (MODIFICATION NO.2) ORDER (NORTHERN IRELAND) 1996, SR 1996 273; made under the Diseases of Animals (Northern Ireland) Order 1981 Art.2(3). In force: July 24, 1996; £0.65.

This Order amends the Diseases of Animals (Northern Ireland) Order 1981 (SI 1981 1115 (NI 22)) Sch.1 Part III by adding equine viral arteritis to the list of diseases in that Part, making it a disease regulated by that Order.

5988. Diseases and disorders–infectious disease control

DISEASES OF ANIMALS (MODIFICATION NO.3) ORDER (NORTHERN IRELAND) 1996, SR 1996 399; made under the Diseases of Animals (Northern Ireland) Order 1981 Art.16(2). In force: October 10, 1996; £0.65.

This Order amends the Diseases of Animals (Northern Ireland) Order 1981 (SI 1981 1115 (NI 22)) Sch.2 (power to slaughter animals and to pay compensation) by deleting references to Johne's disease. The amendments remove from the Department of Agriculture its powers of slaughter and payment of compensation in relation to Johne's disease.

5989. Diseases and disorders–infectious disease control

DISEASES OF ANIMALS (MODIFICATION NO.4) ORDER (NORTHERN IRELAND) 1995, SR 1995 466; made under the Diseases of Animals (Northern Ireland) Order 1981 Art.2(3). In force: January 15, 1996; £0.65.

This Order modifies the list of diseases of poultry in the Diseases of Animals (Northern Ireland) Order 1981 (SI 1981 1115 (NI 22)) Sch.1 Part IV.

5990. Diseases and disorders–infectious disease control

DISEASES OF ANIMALS (MODIFICATION NO.4) ORDER (NORTHERN IRELAND) 1996, SR 1996 592; made under the Diseases of Animals (Northern Ireland) Order 1981 Sch.2. In force: January 8, 1997; £1.10.

This Order further modifies the Diseases of Animals (Northern Ireland) Order 1981 (SI 1981 1115 (NI 22)) Sch.2 Part II so that it now prescribes the amount of compensation payable for cattle slaughtered or caused to be slaughtered as a result of being suspected of being affected with Bovine Spongiform Encephalopathy and cattle which are in contact with cattle affected by the disease or which appear to be otherwise exposed to the infection of that disease. The compensation payable for the slaughter of exposed animals will be specially enhanced where the animals slaughtered represent more than 10 per cent of the herd.

5991. Diseases and disorders–infectious disease control

DISEASES OF ANIMALS (MODIFICATION NO.5) ORDER (NORTHERN IRELAND) 1996, SR 1996 591; made under the Diseases of Animals (Northern Ireland) Order 1981 Art.2(3). In force: January 21, 1997; £0.65.

This Order modifies the list of diseases of poultry in the Diseases of Animals (Northern Ireland) Order 1981 (SI 1981 1115 (NI 22)) Sch.1 Part IV by substituting for Turkey rhinotracheitis, the disease Avian rhinotracheitis.

5992. Diseases and disorders–infectious disease control

SPECIFIED DISEASES (NOTIFICATION AND MOVEMENT RESTRICTIONS) (AMENDMENT) ORDER (NORTHERN IRELAND) 1996, SR 1996 398; made under the Diseases of Animals (Northern Ireland) Order 1981 Art.2(3), Art.5(1), Art.10(6), Art.12(1), Art.14, Art.19(e)(f)(k), Art.60(1). In force: October 10, 1996; £0.65.

This Order amends the Specified Diseases (Notification and Movement Restrictions) Order (Northern Ireland) 1991 (SR 1991 455) Sch.1 by adding to the list of diseases Jaagsiekte complex and Johne's disease.

5993. Diseases and disorders–infectious disease control

TUBERCULOSIS CONTROL (AMENDMENT) ORDER (NORTHERN IRELAND) 1996, SR 1996 240; made under the Diseases of Animals (Northern Ireland) Order 1981 Art.16(1), Art.44, Art.60(1), Sch.2 Part I para.4, Sch.2 Part II para.4. In force: June 17, 1996; £1.10.

This Order amends the Tuberculosis Control Order (Northern Ireland) 1964 (SR & O (NI) 1964 31) so that, in relation to an animal over 30 months old, its market value is the higher of the price which could have been obtained for it in the market or the price which would have applied if it had been slaughtered in accordance with Commission Regulation 716/96 ([1996] OJ L99/14).

5994. Diseases and disorders–infectious disease control–approval of disinfectants

DISEASES OF ANIMALS (APPROVAL OF DISINFECTANTS) (AMENDMENT) ORDER (NORTHERN IRELAND) 1995, SR 1995 467; made under the Disease of Animals (Northern Ireland) Order 1981 Art.5, Art.19, Art.60(1). In force: January 15, 1996; £1.10.

This Order amends the Diseases of Animals (Approval of Disinfectants) Order (Northern Ireland) 1972 (SR & O (NI) 1972 16 as amended by SR 1975 69) so as to enable the Department of Agriculture to approve disinfectants for use against Avian influenza infection, Newcastle disease and Paramyxovirus 1 in pigeons.

5995. Diseases and disorders–infectious disease control–poultry

DISEASES OF POULTRY SCHEME ORDER (NORTHERN IRELAND) 1995, SR 1995 464; made under the Diseases of Animals (Northern Ireland) Order 1981 Art.8(1)(2). In force: January 15, 1996; £1.95.

This Order introduces a scheme which, in conjunction with the Diseases of Poultry Order (Northern Ireland) 1995 (SR 1995 465), implements the requirements of Council Directive 92/40 ([1992] OJ L167/1) for the control of Avian influenza and Council Directive 92/66 ([1992] OJ L260/1) for the control of Newcastle Disease and for the prevention of those diseases.

5996. Diseases and disorders–infectious disease control–poultry–imports

DISEASES OF ANIMALS (IMPORTATION OF POULTRY) (AMENDMENT) ORDER (NORTHERN IRELAND) 1996, SR 1996 82; made under the Diseases of

Animals (Northern Ireland) Order 1981 Art.24, Art.30, Art.60. In force: March 29, 1996; £0.65.

This Order revokes part of the Diseases of Animals (Importation of Poultry) Order (Northern Ireland) 1965 (SR & O (NI) 1965 175).

5997. Diseases and disorders–infectious disease control–revocation

JOHNE'S DISEASE (REVOCATION) ORDER (NORTHERN IRELAND) 1996, SR 1996 400; made under the Diseases of Animals (Northern Ireland) Order 1981 Art.5(1), Art.10(6), Art.12, Art.14, Art.19(e)(i), Art.60(1). In force: October 10, 1996; £0.65.

This Order revokes the Johne's Disease Order (Northern Ireland) 1976 (SR 1976 25) and the Johne's Disease (Amendment) Order (Northern Ireland) 1989 (SR 1989 88) so that the Department of Agriculture no longer has certain powers to deal with cases of Johne's disease.

5998. Exports

EXPORT OF ANIMALS (PROTECTION) ORDER (NORTHERN IRELAND) 1996, SR 1996 460; made under the Diseases of Animals (Northern Ireland) Order 1981 Art.5(1)(a)(b), Art.19(h), Art.23(b), Art.23A, Art.44, Art.60(1). In force: November 1, 1996; £2.80.

This Order prohibits the export of farm animals to any place outside Great Britain, the Channel Islands, the Isle of Man or another Member State unless they are rested at approved premises for at least 10 hours before they are exported. It also requires the provision of adequate food, water, shelter and bedding and limits the number of each species which may be put at one time into any one pen or enclosure on approved premises.

5999. Feeding stuffs

FEEDING STUFFS REGULATIONS (NORTHERN IRELAND) 1995, SR 1995 451; made under the Agriculture Act 1970 s.66(1), s.68(1)(1A)(3), s.69(1)(6)(7), s.70(1), s.73(3), s.74(1), s.74A, s.84, s.86; and the European Communities Act 1972 s.2(2). In force: January 15, 1996; £11.90.

These Regulations revoke and replace the Feeding Stuffs Regulations (Northern Ireland) 1992 (SR 1992 270 as amended by SR 1993 349, SR 1994 123 and SR 1994 502) and implement, as respects Northern Ireland, specified Council and Commission Directives in relation to animal feeding stuffs.

6000. Feeding stuffs

FEEDING STUFFS (AMENDMENT) REGULATIONS (NORTHERN IRELAND) 1996, SR 1996 259; made under the European Communities Act 1972 s.2(2); and the Agriculture Act 1970 s.66(1), s.68(1), s.73(3), s.74(1), s.74A, s.84, s.86. In force: July 31, 1996; £1.95.

These Regulations amend the Feeding Stuffs Regulations (Northern Ireland) 1995 (SR 1995 451) and implement Commission Directive 95/33 ([1995] OJ L167/17) amending Council Directive 82/471 ([1982] OJ L213/8) concerning certain products used in animal nutrition, Commission Decision 95/274 ([1995] OJ L167/24) amending Commission Decision 91/516 ([1991] OJ L281/23) establishing a list of ingredients whose use is prohibited in compound feeding stuffs, Commission Directive 96/6 ([1996] OJ L49/29) amending Council Directive 74/63 ([1974] OJ L38/31) on undesirable substances and products in animal nutrition, and Commission Directive 96/7 ([1996] OJ L51/45) amending Council Directive 70/524 ([1970] OJ L270/1) concerning additives in feeding stuffs.

6001. Food safety–sheep–goats

HEADS OF SHEEP AND GOATS ORDER (NORTHERN IRELAND) 1996, SR 1996 427; made under the Diseases of Animals (Northern Ireland) Order 1981 Art.5(1), Art.19(b)(e), Art.29(1)(2), Art.44, Art.60(1). In force: September 16, 1996; £1.10.

This Order requires heads removed from the carcases of sheep or goats to be consigned to specified premises and disposed of as if they were specified bovine material and applies various provisions of the Specified Bovine Material (No.2) Order (Northern Ireland) 1996 (SR 1996 360) to them.

6002. Food safety–sheep–goats

HEADS OF SHEEP AND GOATS (TREATMENT AND DISPOSAL) REGULATIONS (NORTHERN IRELAND) 1996, SR 1996 428; made under the Food Safety (Northern Ireland) Order 1991 Art.15(1)(3), Art.16(1), Art.18(1), Art.25, Art.26(3), Art.47(2). In force: September 16, 1996; £1.55.

These Regulations prohibit the sale for human consumption of any part of the head of a sheep or goat and of food containing any part of such heads. They also prohibit the sale of any part of such heads for use in the preparation of food for human consumption. The prohibitions do not apply in relation to tongues in specified circumstances or to the heads of sheep or goats which were born, reared and slaughtered in Australia or New Zealand.

6003. Marking

MARKING OF ANIMALS ORDER (NORTHERN IRELAND) 1996, SR 1996 9; made under the Diseases of Animals (Northern Ireland) Order 1981 Art.5, Art.60. In force: January 19, 1996; £0.65.

This Order empowers authorised officers to apply marks to certain animals.

6004. Pigeons–vaccination–revocation

RACING PIGEONS (VACCINATION) (REVOCATION) REGULATIONS (NORTHERN IRELAND) 1995, SR 1995 468; made under the European Communities Act 1972 s.2(2). In force: January 15, 1996; £0.65.

These Regulations revoke the Racing Pigeons (Vaccination) Regulations (Northern Ireland) 1995 (SR 1995 168). The Diseases of Poultry Scheme Order (Northern Ireland) 1995 (SR 1995 464) re-enacts the requirement of those Regulations for the organiser of a show or race to ensure that racing pigeons entered in it have been vaccinated against Paramyxovirus 1 infection.

6005. Slaughter houses–licensing

SLAUGHTER-HOUSES (LICENSING) (AMENDMENT) REGULATIONS (NORTHERN IRELAND) 1996, SR 1996 183; made under the Slaughter-Houses Act (Northern Ireland) 1953 s.1(1), s.5, s.11(1). In force: May 3, 1996; £2.40.

These Regulations amend the Slaughter-houses (Licensing) Regulations (Northern Ireland) 1955 (SR & O (NI) 1955 169) to enable slaughter-houses to be used for the slaughter of animals which are not destined for human consumption, but which are slaughtered pursuant to a slaughter scheme introduced by or under Council Regulation 805/68 ([1968] OJ L148/24) as amended. They also amend and update the records which the holder of a licence under the Slaughter-Houses Act (Northern Ireland) 1953 s.1 must retain and furnish to the Department of Agriculture.

ARBITRATION

6006. Unfair arbitration agreements–specified amount

UNFAIR ARBITRATION AGREEMENTS (SPECIFIED AMOUNT) ORDER (NORTHERN IRELAND) 1996, SR 1996 598; made under the Arbitration Act 1996 s.91 (3) (c). In force: January 31, 1997; £0.65.

This Order specifies the amount of £3,000 for the purposes of the Arbitration Act 1996 s.91 which provides that a term which constitutes an arbitration agreement is unfair for the purposes of the Unfair Contract Terms in Consumer Contracts Regulations 1994 (SI 1994 3159), which implement Council Directive 93/13 ([1993] OJ L95/29) on unfair terms in consumer contracts, so far as the term relates to a claim for a pecuniary remedy which does not exceed the amount specified by order for the purposes of that section.

BANKING

6007. Allied Irish Banks Act 1996 (c.vii). See BANKING. §392

CHARITIES

6008. Belfast Charitable Society Act 1996 (c.vi). See CHARITIES. §452

CHILDREN

6009. Adoption

ADOPTION ALLOWANCE REGULATIONS (NORTHERN IRELAND) 1996, SR 1996 438; made under the Adoption (Northern Ireland) Order 1987 Art.10(1), Art.59A. In force: November 4, 1996; £1.95.

These Regulations enable adoption agencies to pay allowances to persons who have adopted, or intend to adopt, a child in pursuance of arrangements made by those agencies.

6010. Care–placement of children

ARRANGEMENTS FOR PLACEMENT OF CHILDREN (GENERAL) REGULATIONS (NORTHERN IRELAND) 1996, SR 1996 453; made under the Children (Northern Ireland) Order 1995 Art.27(2) (a) (f) (ii) (5), Art.28, Art.73(1) (2) (d), Art.75(2) (3), Art.89(1) (2) (g), Art.105(1) (2) (g). In force: November 4, 1996; £3.20.

These Regulations provide for the placement of children by authorities, voluntary organisations and persons carrying on registered children's homes.

6011. Care–registration of activities–exemptions

DAY CARE (EXEMPT SUPERVISED ACTIVITIES) REGULATIONS (NORTHERN IRELAND) 1996, SR 1996 444; made under the Children (Northern Ireland) Order 1995 Art.121 (6). In force: November 4, 1996; £0.65.

These Regulations specify supervised activities which are exempt from registration under the Children (Northern Ireland) Order 1995 (SI 1995 755 (NI 2)) Art.118(1) (b).

6012. Care–representations

REPRESENTATIONS PROCEDURE (CHILDREN) REGULATIONS (NORTHERN IRELAND) 1996, SR 1996 451; made under the Children (Northern Ireland) Order 1995 Art.37(2), Art.45(5)(6), Art.75(4)(5), Art.105(1)(2)(l), Sch.5 para.6(2). In force: November 4, 1996; £2.40.

These Regulations establish a procedure for considering representations made to authorities about the discharge of their functions under the Children (Northern Ireland) Order 1995 (SI 1995 755 (NI 2)) Part IV in relation to children looked after them, where Art.37(1) of the Order (advice and assistance for certain children aged 18 to 21) applies or under Sch.5 para.4 to the Order in relation to exemption from the usual fostering limit.

6013. Care–review of cases

REVIEW OF CHILDREN'S CASES REGULATIONS (NORTHERN IRELAND) 1996, SR 1996 461; made under the Children (Northern Ireland) Order 1995 Art.45(1)(2), Art.75(4)(a)(5), Art.105(1)(2)(l). In force: November 4, 1996; £2.40.

These Regulations provide for the review of the cases of children who are looked after by authorities or provided with accommodation by voluntary organisations or in registered children's homes.

6014. Care orders–reciprocity–Isle of Man–Guernsey

CHILDREN (PRESCRIBED ORDERS-ISLE OF MAN AND GUERNSEY) REGULATIONS (NORTHERN IRELAND) 1996, SR 1996 528; made under the Children (Northern Ireland) Order 1995 Art.180. In force: December 16, 1996; £1.10.

These Regulations provide for reciprocity in certain circumstances in relation to care orders made in the Isle of Man and Guernsey and for certain recovery orders made in the Isle of Man to have effect as if they were recovery orders made under the Children (Northern Ireland) Order 1995 (SI 1995 755 (NI 2)) Art.50.

6015. Child minders–day care

CHILD MINDING AND DAY CARE (APPLICATIONS FOR DAY REGISTRATION) REGULATIONS (NORTHERN IRELAND) 1996, SR 1996 468; made under the Children (Northern Ireland) Order 1995 Art.123(2). In force: November 4, 1996; £1.55.

These Regulations require child minders and providers of day care to provide specified information when applying for registration under the 1995 Order.

6016. Child minders–fostering–disqualification

DISQUALIFICATION FOR CARING FOR CHILDREN REGULATIONS (NORTHERN IRELAND) 1996, SR 1996 478; made under the Children (Northern Ireland) Order 1995 Art.109(1)(2), Art.122(1)(2). In force: November 4, 1996; £1.95.

These Regulations specify circumstances in which persons are disqualified from fostering children privately and from being registered as child minders on domestic premises or for providing day care for children under 12 on non-domestic premises.

6017. Child protection

CONTACT WITH CHILDREN REGULATIONS (NORTHERN IRELAND) 1996, SR 1996 443; made under the Children (Northern Ireland) Order 1995 Art.53(8). In force: November 4, 1996; £1.10.

These Regulations provide for the steps to be taken by an authority which has refused contact between a child in care and his parents and others specified in the Children (Northern Ireland) Order 1995 (SI 1995 755 (NI 2)) Art.53(1), which include notifying those persons and anyone else whose wishes and feelings the authority considers to be relevant.

6018. **Children (Northern Ireland) Order 1995–Commencement No.2 Order**

CHILDREN (1995 ORDER) (COMMENCEMENT NO.2) ORDER (NORTHERN IRELAND) 1996, SR 1996 15 (C.2); made under the Children (Northern Ireland) Order 1995 (NI 2) Art.1. In force: bringing into force various provisions of the Order on February 19, 1996; £1.10.

This Order brings the Children (Northern Ireland) Order 1995 (SI 1995 755 (NI 2)) Art.60(7)(9), Art.185(1) and part of Sch.9 into force on February 19, 1996.

6019. **Children (Northern Ireland) Order 1995–Commencement No.3 Order**

CHILDREN (1995 ORDER) (COMMENCEMENT NO.3) ORDER (NORTHERN IRELAND) 1996, SR 1996 297 (C.17); made under the Children (Northern Ireland) Order 1995 Art.1 (2)(3). In force: bringing into force various provisions of the Order on July 18, 1996 and November 4, 1996; £1.95.

This Order brings provisions of the Children (Northern Ireland) Order 1995 authorising the making of orders, regulations or rules of court into operation on July 18, 1996; it also brings into operation on November 4, 1996 the remaining provisions of the 1995 Order (except those specified in Sch.2) and the Children (Northern Ireland Consequential Amendments) Order 1995 (SI 1995 756).

6020. **Children's Evidence (Northern Ireland) Order 1995–Commencement Order**

CHILDREN'S EVIDENCE (1995 ORDER) (COMMENCEMENT) ORDER (NORTHERN IRELAND) 1996, SR 1996 122 (C.5); made under the Children's Evidence (Northern Ireland) Order 1995 Art.1. In force: April 8, 1996; £0.65.

This Order appoints April 8, 1996, for the coming into operation of the Children's Evidence (Northern Ireland) Order 1995 (SI 1995 757 (NI 3)).

6021. **Children's welfare–residential accommodation**

CHILDREN'S HOMES REGULATIONS (NORTHERN IRELAND) 1996, SR 1996 479; made under the Children (Northern Ireland) Order 1995 Art.73, Art.74(2)(h), Art.77(3), Art.80(2)(3)(4)(5), Art.82(1), Art.89, Art.91(2)(h), Art.93(3), Art.96(2)(3)(4)(5), Art.98(1), Art.105. In force: November 4, 1996; £5.30.

These Regulations provide for the conduct of children's homes.

6022. **Emergency protection–transfer**

EMERGENCY PROTECTION ORDER (TRANSFER OF RESPONSIBILITIES) REGULATIONS (NORTHERN IRELAND) 1996, SR 1996 435; made under the Children (Northern Ireland) Order 1995 Art.71(3)(4). In force: November 4, 1996; £1.10.

These Regulations provide for an authority to be treated as though it, and not the original applicant for an emergency protection order, had applied for and been granted the order.

6023. **Employment**

EMPLOYMENT OF CHILDREN REGULATIONS (NORTHERN IRELAND) 1996, SR 1996 477; made under the Children (Northern Ireland) Order 1995 Art.136(1)(a)(b)(c)(ii)(iii)(iv)(v). In force: November 4, 1996; £1.55.

These Regulations make provision with respect to the employment of children who are not over school leaving age. The employment of children under 13 is prohibited.

6024. **Employment–performing arts**

CHILDREN (PUBLIC PERFORMANCES) REGULATIONS (NORTHERN IRELAND) 1996, SR 1996 481; made under the Children (Northern Ireland)

Order 1995 Art.137(3), Art.138(5)(7), Art.140(1). In force: November 4, 1996; £5.70.

These Regulations make provision with respect to children who take part in performances to which the Children (Northern Ireland) Order 1995 (SI 1995 755 (NI 2)) Art.137(1)(a) applies.

6025. Evidence

CHILDREN'S EVIDENCE (NORTHERN IRELAND) ORDER 1995 (NOTICE OF TRANSFER) REGULATIONS 1996, SR 1996; made under the Children's Evidence (Northern Ireland) Order 1995 Art.4(5), Sch.1 para.3. In force: May 31, 1996; £1.95.

These Regulations set out the form of notices to transfer under the Children's Evidence (Northern Ireland) Order 1995 (SI 1995 757 (NI 3)) Art.4 and forms to be sent to defendants informing them of the effect of a notice of transfer. Copies of notices to transfer and the form must be sent to specified persons.

6026. Family proceedings

CHILDREN (ALLOCATION OF PROCEEDINGS) ORDER (NORTHERN IRELAND) 1996, SR 1996 300; made under the Children (Northern Ireland) Order 1995 Art.164(5), Art.166(4)(a), Sch.7. In force: November 4, 1996; £2.40.

This Order provides for the allocation and transfer of proceedings under the Children (Northern Ireland) Order 1995 (SI 1995 755 (NI 2)) and the Child Support (Northern Ireland) Order 1995 (SI 1995 2702 (NI 13)) as between the High Court, county courts and courts of summary jurisdiction (including family proceedings courts).

6027. Fostering

CHILDREN (PRIVATE ARRANGEMENTS FOR FOSTERING) REGULATIONS (NORTHERN IRELAND) 1996, SR 1996 452; made under the Children (Northern Ireland) Order 1995 Art.108(1)(2), Art.112(1)(2). In force: November 4, 1996; £1.95.

These Regulations provide for the arrangements for fostering children privately and supplement the Children (Northern Ireland) Order 1995 (SI 1995 755 (NI 2)) Part X.

6028. Fostering

FOSTER PLACEMENT (CHILDREN) REGULATIONS (NORTHERN IRELAND) 1996, SR 1996 467; made under the Children (Northern Ireland) Order 1995 Art.27(2)(a), Art.28(1), Art.75(2), Art.77(3). In force: November 4, 1996; £3.20.

These Regulations, which replace and revoke the Children and Young Persons (Boarding-Out) Regulations (Northern Ireland) 1976 (SR 1976 19), apply to placements of children by authorities and voluntary organisations, other than placements to which the Placement of Children with Parents etc. Regulations (Northern Ireland) 1996 (SR 1996 463) apply and placements for adoption or with persons having parental responsibility for a child.

6029. Fostering–refuges

REFUGES (CHILDREN'S HOMES AND FOSTER PLACEMENTS) REGULATIONS (NORTHERN IRELAND) 1996, SR 1996 480; made under the Children (Northern Ireland) Order 1995 Art.70(4). In force: November 4, 1996; £1.10.

These Regulations make provision in respect of voluntary homes and registered children's homes which are used as refuges and foster parents providing refuge under the Children (Northern Ireland) Order 1995 (SI 1995 755 (NI 2)) Art.70. They set out requirements to be complied with while certificates relating to refuges are in force and provide for the withdrawal of those certificates.

6030. Guardian ad litem

GUARDIANS AD LITEM (PANEL) REGULATIONS (NORTHERN IRELAND) 1996, SR 1996 128; made under the Children (Northern Ireland) Order 1995 Art.60(7)(9); and the Adoption (Northern Ireland) Order 1987 Art.66A(1)(2). In force: May 1, 1996; £1.95.

These Regulations provide for the establishment of a panel of guardians ad litem, a complaints board and a panel committee.

6031. Parental responsibility–agreements

CHILDREN (PARENTAL RESPONSIBILITY AGREEMENT) REGULATIONS (NORTHERN IRELAND) 1996, SR 1996 455; made under the Children (Northern Ireland) Order 1995 Art.7(2)(3), Art.183(1). In force: November 4, 1996; £1.95.

These Regulations prescribe the form to be used for parental responsibility agreements under the Children (Northern Ireland) Order 1995 (SI 1995 755 (NI 2)) Art.7(1)(b) and the manner of recording those agreements.

6032. Parents–care

PLACEMENT OF CHILDREN WITH PARENTS ETC. REGULATIONS (NORTHERN IRELAND) 1996, SR 1996 463; made under the Children (Northern Ireland) Order 1995 Art.27(5), Art.28(3). In force: November 4, 1996; £2.80.

These Regulations provide for the placement of children in the care of authorities with a parent, a person who is not a parent but has parental responsibility or a person in whose favour there was a residence order before the care order was made.

6033. Secure accommodation

CHILDREN (SECURE ACCOMMODATION) REGULATIONS (NORTHERN IRELAND) 1996, SR 1996 487; made under the Children (Northern Ireland) Order 1995 Art.44(3)(8), Art.45(1)(2), Art.73(1)(2)(d), Art.89(1)(2)(f)(3), Art.105(1)(2)(f)(3). In force: November 4, 1996; £1.05.

These Regulations supplement the Children (Northern Ireland) Order 1995 (SI 1995 755 (NI 2)) Art.44, which governs the restriction of liberty of children who are being looked after by authorities. They provide for approval by the Department of Health and Social Services to the placement of children under 13 in secure accommodation, the children to whom Art.44 does not apply, the making of applications to court and related matters.

6034. Visitors

DEFINITION OF INDEPENDENT VISITORS (CHILDREN) REGULATIONS (NORTHERN IRELAND) 1996, SR 1996 434; made under the Children (Northern Ireland) Order 1995 Art.31 (7). In force: November 4, 1996; £1.10.

These Regulations prescribe the circumstances in which persons appointed as independent visitors are to be regarded as independent of the authority appointing them.

CIVIL EVIDENCE

6035. Admissibility–children

CHILDREN (ADMISSIBILITY OF HEARSAY EVIDENCE) ORDER (NORTHERN IRELAND) 1996, SR 1996 301; made under the Children (Northern Ireland) Order 1995 Art.169(5). In force: November 4, 1996; £0.65.

This Order specifies the type of court proceedings in which evidence may be given in connection with the upbringing, maintenance or welfare of a child notwithstanding that the evidence would otherwise be inadmissible as hearsay.

CIVIL PROCEDURE

6036. County courts–fees

COUNTY COURT FEES ORDER (NORTHERN IRELAND) 1996, SR 1996 103; made under the Judicature (Northern Ireland) Act 1978 s.116(1)(4). In force: April 1, 1996; £3.20.

This Order revokes and replaces the County Court Fees Order (Northern Ireland) 1994 (SR 1994 280 as amended by SR 1995 221), so as to introduce a new fee for a certificate of readiness, remove several fees and increase fees payable to process servers.

6037. County courts–rules

COUNTY COURT (AMENDMENT) RULES (NORTHERN IRELAND) 1996, SR 1996 19; made under the County Courts (Northern Ireland) Order 1990 Art.47. In force: February 26, 1996; £5.80.

These Rules increase county court costs by 11.25 per cent.

6038. County courts–rules

COUNTY COURT (AMENDMENT NO.2) RULES (NORTHERN IRELAND) 1996, SR 1996 294; made under the County Courts (Northern Ireland) Order 1980 Art.46; and the Criminal Evidence (Northern Ireland) Order 1989 Art.81(5), Art.81A(11). In force: September 2, 1996; £2.80.

These Rules amend the County Court Rules (Northern Ireland) 1981 (SR 1981 225) to provide for applications for leave under the Police and Criminal Evidence (Northern Ireland) Order 1989 (SI 1989 1341 (NI 12)) Art.81 (2) for evidence to be given via live television link by certain child witnesses, and under Art.81A for a video recording of testimony from certain child witnesses to be admitted in evidence, in any appeal to the county court arising from proceedings in a juvenile court for certain offences.

6039. County courts–rules

COUNTY COURT (AMENDMENT NO.3) RULES (NORTHERN IRELAND) 1996, SR 1996 295; made under the County Courts (Northern Ireland) Order 1980 Art.47. In force: September 2, 1996; £1.95.

These Rules amend the County Court Rules (Northern Ireland) 1981 (SR 1981 225) to provide for applications under the County Courts (Northern Ireland) Order 1980 (SI 1980 397 (NI 3)) Art.42A (powers of court exercisable before commencement of action) and Art.42B (power of court to order disclosure of documents, inspection of property etc. in proceedings for personal injuries or death).

6040. County courts–rules

COUNTY COURTS (AMENDMENT NO.4) RULES (NORTHERN IRELAND) 1995, SR 1995 471; made under the County Courts (Northern Ireland) Order 1980 Art.46. In force: January 1, 1996; £1.10.

These Rules amend the County Courts (Northern Ireland) Order 1981 (SR 1981 225) as respects proceedings for debts or liquidated amounts of less than £1,000.

6041. County Courts (Amendment) (Northern Ireland) Order 1996 (SI 1996 277 (NI 3))

This Order, which comes into force on days to be appointed, confers on county courts the power to make certain orders for the discovery or preservation of property or documents which are, or may become, relevant to proceedings in those courts.

6042. County Courts (Amendment) (Northern Ireland) Order 1996–Commencement Order

COUNTY COURTS (AMENDMENT) (1996 ORDER) (COMMENCEMENT) ORDER (NORTHERN IRELAND) 1996, SR 1996 293 (C.16); made under the County Courts (Amendment) (Northern Ireland) Order Art.1 (2). In force: bringing the Order into force on September 9, 1996; £0.65.

This Order brings the County Courts (Amendment) (Northern Ireland) Order 1996 (SI 1996 277 (NI 3)) into operation on September 1, 1996.

6043. Family proceedings–fees

FAMILY PROCEEDINGS FEES ORDER (NORTHERN IRELAND) 1996, SR 1996 495; made under the Judicature (Northern Ireland) Act 1978 s.116 (1) (4). In force: November 4, 1996; £1.95.

This Order prescribes the fees payable in respect of specified family proceedings in the High Court and county courts.

6044. Family proceedings–rules

FAMILY PROCEEDINGS RULES (NORTHERN IRELAND) 1996, SR 1996 322; made under the Family Law (Northern Ireland) Order 1993 Art.12. In force: November 4, 1996; £15.65.

These Rules, which apply to proceedings in the High Court and county courts, provide for applications under the Matrimonial Causes (Northern Ireland) Order 1978 (SI 1978 1045 (NI 5)) and the Matrimonial and Family Proceedings (Northern Ireland) Order 1989 (SI 1989 677 (NI 6)) Art.31 (declaration as to marital status), Art.41 (transfer of tenancy upon divorce) and Part IV (financial relief after overseas divorce) and under the Children (Northern Ireland) Order 1995.

6045. Judgments and orders–enforcement–fees

JUDGMENT ENFORCEMENT FEES ORDER (NORTHERN IRELAND) 1996, SR 1996 101; made under the Judicature (Northern Ireland) Act 1978 s.116 (1) (4). In force: April 1, 1996; £1.95.

This Order revokes and replaces the Judgment Enforcement Fees Order (Northern Ireland) 1992 (SR 1992 19 as amended by SR 1994 278 and SR 1995 217), to increase the majority of fees to be taken in respect of judgments under the Judgments Enforcement (Northern Ireland) Order 1981 (SI 1981 226 (NI 6)).

6046. Magistrates' courts–child abduction

MAGISTRATES' COURTS (CHILD ABDUCTION AND CUSTODY) (AMENDMENT) RULES (NORTHERN IRELAND) 1996, SR 1996 55; made under the Magistrates' Courts (Northern Ireland) Order 1981 Art.13; and the Child Abduction and Custody Act 1985 s.24. In force: March 18, 1996; £0.65.

These Rules insert references to the Isle of Man in the Magistrates' Courts (Child Abduction and Custody) Rules (Northern Ireland) 1986 (SR 1986 219).

6047. Magistrates' courts–children

MAGISTRATES' COURTS (CHILDREN (NORTHERN IRELAND) ORDER 1995) RULES (NORTHERN IRELAND) 1996, SR 1996 323; made under the Magistrates' Courts (Northern Ireland) Order 1981 Art.13; and the Children (Northern Ireland) Order 1995 Art.71, Art.165. In force: November 4, 1996; £9.40.

These Rules provide for applications to magistrates' courts (including family proceedings courts) under the Children (Northern Ireland) Order 1995 (SI 1995 755 (NI 2)).

6048. Magistrates' courts–children–young persons

MAGISTRATES' COURTS (CHILDREN AND YOUNG PERSONS) (AMENDMENT) RULES (NORTHERN IRELAND) 1996, SR 1996 325; made under the Magistrates' Courts (Northern Ireland) Order 1981 Art.13. In force: November 4, 1996; £1.55.

These Rules amend the Magistrates' Courts' (Children and Young Persons) Rules (Northern Ireland) 1969 (SR & O (NI) 1969 221) in consequence of amendments made to the Children and Young Persons Act (Northern Ireland) 1968 by the Children (Northern Ireland) Order 1995 (SI 1995 755 (NI 2)).

6049. Magistrates' courts–family proceedings

MAGISTRATES' COURTS (DOMESTIC PROCEEDINGS) RULES (NORTHERN IRELAND) 1996, SR 1996 324; made under the Magistrates' Courts (Northern Ireland) Order 1981 Art.13; and the Domestic Proceedings (Northern Ireland) Order 1980 Art.8(8), Art.18(8)(9), Art.21(4), Art.25(1), Art.26(2). In force: November 4, 1996; £4.70.

These Rules prescribe the procedure to be followed in applications under the Domestic Proceedings (Northern Ireland) Order 1980, taking into account the Children (Northern Ireland) Order 1995 (SI 1995 755 (NI 2)).

6050. Magistrates' courts–family proceedings

MAGISTRATES' COURTS (FAMILY LAW ACT 1986) (AMENDMENT) RULES (NORTHERN IRELAND) 1996, SR 1996 56; made under the Magistrates' Courts (Northern Ireland) Order 1981 Art.13; and the Family Law Act 1986 s.27. In force: March 18, 1996; £1.10.

These Rules insert references to the Isle of Man in the Magistrates' Courts (Family Law Act 1986) Rules (Northern Ireland) 1988 (SR 1988 113).

6051. Magistrates' courts–fees

MAGISTRATES' COURTS FEES ORDER (NORTHERN IRELAND) 1996, SR 1996 102; made under the Judicature (Northern Ireland) Act 1978 s.116(1)(4). In force: April 1, 1996; £2.40.

This Order revokes and replaces the Magistrates' Courts Fees Order (Northern Ireland) 1994 (SR 1994 279 as amended by SR 1995 222), so as to increase a number of the fees payable in respect of proceedings in magistrates' courts; introduce a new fee, of £40, to be paid on a bingo club grant being declared final; and increase the fees payable for service of a summons or process.

6052. Magistrates' courts–fees

MAGISTRATES' COURTS FEES (AMENDMENT) ORDER (NORTHERN IRELAND) 1996, SR 1996 494; made under the Judicature (Northern Ireland) Act 1978 s.116(1) (4). In force: November 4, 1996; £1.10.

This Order amends the Magistrates' Courts Fees Order (Northern Ireland) 1996 (SR 1996 102) to prescribe the fees payable in respect of certain applications and proceedings under the Children (Northern Ireland) Order 1995 (SI 1995 755 (NI 2)).

6053. Supreme Court–fees

SUPREME COURT FEES ORDER (NORTHERN IRELAND) 1996, SR 1996 100; made under the Judicature (Northern Ireland) Act 1978 s.116(1) (4). In force: April 1, 1996; £3.20.

This Order revokes and replaces the Supreme Court Fees Order (Northern Ireland) 1994 (SR 1994 283 as amended by SR 1995 220), to increase the majority of fees payable in the Supreme Court and to introduce new fees in respect of certain proceedings.

6054. Supreme Court–probate–fees

SUPREME COURT (NON-CONTENTIOUS PROBATE) FEES ORDER (NORTHERN IRELAND) 1996, SR 1996 104; made under the Judicature (Northern Ireland) Act 1978 s.116(1) (4). In force: April 1, 1996; £2.40.

This Order revokes and replaces the Supreme Court (Non-Contentious Probate) Fees Order (Northern Ireland) 1991 (SR 1991 293 as amended by SR 1992 218, SR 1994 282 and SR 1995 219), so as to increase the majority of the fees to be taken in non-contentious probate proceedings and to restructure the fees in respect of personal applications for grants, searches and copy documents.

6055. Supreme Court–rules

RULES OF THE SUPREME COURT (NORTHERN IRELAND) (AMENDMENT) 1996, SR 1996 212; made under the Judicature (Northern Ireland) Act 1978 s.55. In force: June 17, 1996; £1.10.

These Rules amend the Rules of the Supreme Court (Northern Ireland) 1980 (SI 1980 346) Ord.1 to substitute a new r.12 and a new r.17 providing for the allocation of proceedings (including proceedings under the Children (Northern Ireland) Order 1995 (SI 1995 755 (NI 2)) to the Family Division in the High Court and for the allocation of business to the Office of Care and Protection.

6056. Supreme Court–rules

RULES OF THE SUPREME COURT (NORTHERN IRELAND) (AMENDMENT NO.2) 1995, SR 1995 462; made under the Judicature (Northern Ireland) Act 1978 s.55. In force: January 9, 1996; £1.10.

These Rules amend Rules of the Supreme Court in relation to court records, medical examinations and the disclosure of expert evidence in commercial actions.

6057. Supreme Court–rules

RULES OF THE SUPREME COURT (NORTHERN IRELAND) (AMENDMENT NO.2) 1996, SR 1996 282; made under the Judicature (Northern Ireland) Act 1978 s.55. In force: August 25, 1996; £2.80.

These Rules amend Rules of the Supreme Court (Northern Ireland) 1980 (SR 1980 346) Ord.116 to insert r.16 to take account of the Prevention of Terrorism (Temporary Provisions) Act 1989 (Enforcement of External Orders) Order 1995 (SI 1995 760) and to substitute Part II providing for the procedure to be followed in applications to the High Court under the Proceeds of Crime (Northern Ireland) Order 1996 (SI 1996 1299 (NI 9)) and proceedings under the Criminal Justice (International Co-operation) Act 1990 s.9.

6058. Supreme Court–rules

RULES OF THE SUPREME COURT (NORTHERN IRELAND) (AMENDMENT NO.3) 1996, SR 1996 283; made under the Judicature (Northern Ireland) Act 1978 s.55. In force: September 1, 1996; £2.40.

These Rules amend Rules of the Supreme Court (Northern Ireland) 1980 (SR 1980 346) to increase the costs allowed to a litigant in person and the fixed costs recoverable under Ord.62, Appendix 3, to provide for short form taxation in respect of individual items or disbursement in dispute and to substitute Ord.100 for applications under the Trade Marks Act 1994, the Olympic Symbol etc. (Protection) Act 1995 and the Olympic Association Right (Infringement Proceedings) Regulations 1995 (SI 1995 3325).

6059. Supreme Court–rules

RULES OF THE SUPREME COURT (NORTHERN IRELAND) (AMENDMENT NO.4) 1996, SR 1996 321; made under the Judicature (Northern Ireland) Act 1978 s.55. In force: November 4, 1996; £1.95.

These Rules amend Rules of the Supreme Court (Northern Ireland) 1980 (SR 1980 346) by adding a rule to Ord.16 (disability) providing for the appointment in certain circumstances of a guardian of a child's fortune or estate, amending Ord.98 (matrimonial and family proceedings) to prescribe the procedure for an application for a declaration of parentage and revoking Ord.74 (alteration of maintenance agreements) and Ord.90 r.6 to Ord.90 r.8 (applications under the Guardianship of Infants Act 1886).

COMPANY LAW

6060. Accounts–financial statements–form and content

COMPANIES (SUMMARY FINANCIAL STATEMENT) REGULATIONS (NORTHERN IRELAND) 1996, SR 1996 179; made under the Companies (Northern Ireland) Order 1986 Art.253(3)(4), Art.259(1)(2)(3). In force: June 10, 1996; £4.15.

These Regulations revoke and replace the Companies (Summary Financial Statement) Regulations (Northern Ireland) Order 1993 (SR 1993 267). They relate to the conditions for sending out summary financial statement, the form and content of summary financial statement.

6061. Shares–disclosure

DISCLOSURE OF INTERESTS IN SHARES (AMENDMENT) REGULATIONS (NORTHERN IRELAND) 1996, SR 1996 246; made under the Companies (Northern Ireland) Order 1986 Art.218A. In force: July 15, 1996; £1.10.

These Regulations amend the 1986 Order to provide for disregarding, for the purposes of the disclosure of interests in shares pursuant to Art.206 to Art.210 of the Order, certain interests in shares arising from arrangements effected under a computer-based system for the transfer of title to securities otherwise than by a written instrument where the system operator is approved by the Treasury under the Uncertificated Securities Regulations 1995 (SI 1995 3272).

CONSTITUTIONAL LAW

6062. Time. See CONSTITUTIONAL LAW. §1123

CONSTRUCTION LAW

6063. Building regulations

BUILDING (AMENDMENT) REGULATIONS (NORTHERN IRELAND) 1995, SR 1995 473; made under the Building Regulations (Northern Ireland) Order 1979 Art.3(1)(2), Art.5(1)(2)(3), Sch.1 para.1, Sch.1 para.2, Sch.1 para.3, Sch.1 para.4, Sch.1 para.5, Sch.1 para.6, Sch.1 para.9, Sch.1 para.9, Sch.1 para.10, Sch.1 para.11, Sch.1 para.12, Sch.1 para.13, Sch.1 para.17, Sch.1 para.18, Sch.1 para.19, Sch.1 para.20, Sch.1 para.21, Sch.1 para.22. In force: January 15, 1996; £2.40.

These Regulations amend the Building Regulations (Northern Ireland) 1994 (SR 1994 243).

6064. Construction industry–Construction Industry Training Board–levy on employers

INDUSTRIAL TRAINING LEVY (CONSTRUCTION INDUSTRY) ORDER (NORTHERN IRELAND) 1996, SR 1996 276; made under the Industrial Training (Northern Ireland) Order 1984 Art.23(2)(3), Art.24(3)(4). In force: August 31, 1996; £1.95.

This Order imposes a further levy on employers in the construction industry in order to meet the expenses of the Construction Industry Training Board.

CONSUMER LAW

6065. Chemicals–packaging

CHEMICALS (HAZARD INFORMATION AND PACKAGING FOR SUPPLY) (AMENDMENT) REGULATIONS (NORTHERN IRELAND) 1996, SR 1996 376; made under the Health and Safety at Work (Northern Ireland) Order 1978 Art.17(1) to (6), Art.55(2), Sch.3 para.1(1)(4)(5), Sch.3 para.2, Sch.3 para.14, Sch.3 para.15. In force: September 9, 1996; £2.80.

These Regulations amend the Chemicals (Hazard Information and Packaging for Supply) Regulations (Northern Ireland) 1995 (SR 1995 60) to implement part of Council Directive 94/60 ([1994] OJ L365/1), the 14th Amendment to Council Directive 76/769 ([1976] OJ L262/201) implementing Commission Directive 94/69 ([1994] OJ L381/1), and the 21st Adaptation to Technical Progress of Commission Directive 67/548 ([1967] OJ L196/1).

6066. Price marking

PRICE MARKING (AMENDMENT) ORDER (NORTHERN IRELAND) 1996, SR 1996 17; made under the Prices Act 1974 s.4. In force: February 21, 1996; £0.65.

This Order amends the Price Marking Order (Northern Ireland) 1992 (SI 1992 59) which implemented Council Directive 79/581 ([1979] OJ L158/19) as amended by Council Directive 88/315 ([1988] OJ L142/23) and by Council Directive 88/314 ([1988] OJ L142/19) on consumer protection in the indication of the prices of foodstuffs and non-food products, respectively.

6067. Weights and measures

NON-AUTOMATIC WEIGHING MACHINES AND NON-AUTOMATIC WEIGHING INSTRUMENTS (AMENDMENT) REGULATIONS (NORTHERN IRELAND) 1996, SR 1996 320; made under the Weights and Measures (Northern Ireland) Order 1981 Art.13(1). In force: September 2, 1996; £1.55.

These Regulations amend the Weighing Equipment (Non-automatic Weighing Machines) Regulations (Northern Ireland) 1991 (SR 1991 266) to forbid the use for trade of equipment outside its prescribed weighing range in relation to gold and other precious metals, precious stones or pearls and drugs or other pharmaceutical products and to permit the import of non-automatic weighing machines if tested in another Member State or an EEA State on the same basis as required by the Regulations. They also amend the Non-automatic Weighing Instruments (EEC Requirements) (Use for Trade) Regulations (Northern Ireland) 1992 (SR 1992 484) in so far as they relate to instruments in use for trade covered by the Non-automatic Weighing Instruments (EEC Requirements) Regulations 1995 (SI 1995 1907) and to forbid the use for trade of instruments outside their prescribed weighing range in relation to gold and other precious metals, precious stones or pearls and drugs or other pharmaceutical products and to forbid the use for trade on or after January 1, 2000 of instruments having weight scale intervals expressed in decimal parts save by way of supplementary indication of weights.

6068. Weights and measures

WEIGHTS AND MEASURES (GUERNSEY AND ALDERNEY) ORDER (NORTHERN IRELAND) 1996, SR 1996 177; made under the Weights and Measures (Northern Ireland) Order 1981 Art.2(2), Art.9(1)(13). In force: June 1, 1996; £1.10.

This Order declares Guernsey and Alderney to be designated countries for the purposes of these provisions and other provisions of the 1981 Order which refer to designated countries and provides that any weighing or measuring equipment which would otherwise have to be stamped in accordance with the 1981 Order before it could be used for trade in Northern Ireland is, to the exception of certain non-automatic weighing instruments, to be treated as if it were so stamped when it has been stamped under weights and measures legislation in force in Guernsey and Alderney.

CRIMINAL LAW

6069. Explosives

EXPLOSIVES (AMENDMENT) REGULATIONS (NORTHERN IRELAND) 1996, SR 1996 429; made under the Explosives Act (Northern Ireland) 1970 s.3; and the Explosives (Northern Ireland) Order 1972 Art.3. In force: December 2, 1996; £1.10.

These Regulations amend the Explosives Regulations (Northern Ireland) 1972 (SR & O (NI) 1972 118) to provide that the prohibition in Reg.2 (under which, in particular, it is an offence, except in accordance with a licence, to manufacture, sell, purchase or acquire certain mixtures containing ammonium nitrate) applies to any solution containing ammonium nitrate and to any mixture in which the ammonium nitrate content of any particulate component of the mixture exceeds 79 per cent, by weight of that component.

6070. Explosives–fireworks

EXPLOSIVES (FIREWORKS) REGULATIONS (NORTHERN IRELAND) 1996, SR 1996 391; made under the Explosives Act (Northern Ireland) 1970 s.3. In force: September 18, 1996; £1.95.

These Regulations prohibit the possession, sale or use of certain categories of fireworks, except under a licence issued by the Secretary of State, for which a fee is payable. Specified bodies are exempted from the Regulations.

6071. Explosives (Amendment) (Northern Ireland) Order 1996 (SI 1996 1920 (NI 17))

This Order, which came into operation on August 24, 1996, enables Explosives Regulations under the Explosives Act (Northern Ireland) 1970 s.3(1) to make provision for controlling and regulating the manufacture, sale, acquisition, transfer, storing, transportation, handling, use or disposal of fireworks. It also enables Explosives Regulations to exempt fireworks from s.1(1) and s.1(2) of the 1970 Act and increases to 16 the minimum age at which explosives, including fireworks, may be sold to any person.

6072. Terrorism–emergency provisions–codes of practice. See CRIMINAL LAW. §1526

6073. Terrorism–emergency provisions. See CRIMINAL LAW. §1525

CRIMINAL PROCEDURE

6074. Criminal Justice (Northern Ireland) Order 1996 (SI 1996 3160 (NI 24))

This Order, which comes into force on days to be appointed, makes further provision with respect to the powers of courts to deal with offenders, including fresh provision with respect to probation and community service orders and to release on licence sex offenders; makes provision for 28 day remands; makes provision about the jurisdiction of courts in Northern Ireland in relation to certain offences of dishonesty and blackmail; makes provision for an accused to be open to question as to his own character if he impugns the character of a deceased victim of the alleged crime; abolishes the corroboration rules; makes provision relating to the verdict of insanity or unfitness to plead and provides for a trial of the facts in the case of a defendant found to be unfit to plead; creates an offence of witness and juror intimidation; creates new offences with respect to certain knives and other dangerous weapons; and enables rules to provide for the furnishing of information by the prosecution in criminal cases.

6075. Crown Courts–children–offences

CROWN COURT (CHILDREN'S EVIDENCE) (DISMISSAL OF TRANSFERRED CHARGES) RULES (NORTHERN IRELAND) 1996, SR 1996 70; made under the Judicature (Northern Ireland) Act 1978 s.52(1); and the Children's Evidence (Northern Ireland) Order 1995 Sch.1 para.4(8). In force: April 8, 1996; £2.80.

These Rules permit persons charged with certain offences involving children whose cases are transferred to the Crown Court under the Children's Evidence (Northern Ireland) Order 1995 (SI 1995 757 (NI 3)) Art.4 to apply for the charges to be dismissed.

6076. Crown Courts–rules

CROWN COURT (AMENDMENT) RULES (NORTHERN IRELAND) 1996, SR 1996 71; made under the Judicature (Northern Ireland) Act 1978 s.52(1); and the

Police and Criminal Evidence (Northern Ireland) Order 1989 Art.81(5), Art.81A(11). In force: April 8, 1996; £2.80.

These Rules amend the Crown Court Rules (Northern Ireland) 1979 (SR 1979 90) to reflect amendments made to the Police and Criminal Evidence (Northern Ireland) Order 1989 (SI 1989 1341 (NI 12)) by the Children's Evidence (Northern Ireland) Order 1995 (SI 1995 757 (NI 3)) Art.5(1)(2).

6077. Crown Courts–rules

CROWN COURT (AMENDMENT NO.2) RULES (NORTHERN IRELAND) 1996, SR 1996 281; made under the Judicature (Northern Ireland) Act 1978 s.52(1); and the Proceeds of Crime (Northern Ireland) Order 1996 Art.50(7). In force: August 25, 1996; £1.55.

These Rules amend the Crown Court Rules (Northern Ireland) 1979 (SR 1979 90) to take account of the replacement of the Criminal Justice (Confiscation) (Northern Ireland) Order 1990 (SI 1990 2588 (NI 17)) by the Proceeds of Crime (Northern Ireland) Order 1996 (SI 1996 1299 (NI 9)). They substitute a new Part VII in the 1979 Rules to provide for various matters under the 1996 Order.

6078. Magistrates' courts

MAGISTRATES' COURTS (AMENDMENT) RULES (NORTHERN IRELAND) 1996, SR 1996 126; made under the Magistrates' Courts (Northern Ireland) Order 1981 Art.13; and the Police and Criminal Evidence (Northern Ireland) Order 1989 Art.81, Art.81A. In force: April 8, 1996; £3.20.

These Rules amend the Magistrates' Courts (Children and Young Persons) Rules (Northern Ireland) 1969 (SR 1969 221) and the Magistrates' Courts Rules (Northern Ireland) 1984 (SR 1984 225) to reflect certain amendments made to the Police and Criminal Evidence (Northern Ireland) Order 1989 (SI 1989 1341 (NI 12)).

6079. Magistrates' courts–children's evidence–transfer

MAGISTRATES' COURTS (CHILDREN'S EVIDENCE) (NOTICE OF TRANSFER) RULES (NORTHERN IRELAND) 1996, SR 1996 127; made under the Magistrates' Courts (Northern Ireland) Order 1981 Art.13. In force: April 8, 1996; £1.95.

These Rules set out the procedure in connection with notices to transfer under the Children's Evidence (Northern Ireland) Order 1995 (SI 1995 757 (NI 3)) Art.4(1)

6080. Magistrates' courts–drug trafficking

MAGISTRATES' COURTS (DRUG TRAFFICKING ACT 1994) RULES (NORTHERN IRELAND) 1996, SR 1996 54; made under the Magistrates' Courts (Northern Ireland) Order 1981 Art.13; and the Drug Trafficking Act 1994 s.46(1). In force: March 18, 1996; £3.20.

These Rules replace the Magistrates' Courts (Criminal Justice (International Cooperation) Act 1990) (No.2) Rules (Northern Ireland) 1992 (SR 1992 191) to take account of the Drug Trafficking Act 1994.

6081. Northern Ireland (Emergency Provisions) Act 1996 (c.22). See CRIMINAL PROCEDURE. §1523

6082. Probation orders–community service orders–consequential amendments. See CRIMINAL PROCEDURE. §1661

6083. Proceeds of Crime (Northern Ireland) Order 1996 (SI 1996 1299 (NI 9))

This Order, which came into force on August 25, 1996, amends and largely restates the law relating to the confiscation of the proceeds of crime. Part I is introductory and Part II deals with confiscation orders, proceedings in connection with those orders where the defendant has died or absconded, restraint orders, the realisation of property, the insolvency of defendants, protection for insolvency officers and the enforcement of orders made outside Northern Ireland. Part III sets out offences in connection with the proceeds of criminal conduct and Part IV contains miscellaneous and supplementary provisions.

CRIMINAL SENTENCING

6084. Reviews–Court of Appeal–range of offences

CRIMINAL JUSTICE ACT 1988 (REVIEWS OF SENTENCING) ORDER (NORTHERN IRELAND) 1996, SR 1996 40; made under the Criminal Justice Act 1988 s.35(4). In force: April 8, 1996; £1.10.

This Order extends the range of offences in respect of which the Attorney General may refer cases to the Court of Appeal for reviews of sentences imposed in the Crown Court.

DAMAGES

6085. Books

Greer, Desmond S.–Compensation Recovery: Substantive and Procedural Issues. Paperback: £11.50. ISBN 0-85389-618-6. SLS Legal Publications.

EDUCATION

6086. Education (Northern Ireland) Order 1996 (SI 1996 274 (NI 1))

This Order, which comes into force in accordance with Art.1, makes miscellaneous amendments to the law of education and makes new provision for educating children with special needs. Provision is made for an Independent Schools Tribunal to hear appeals concerning independent schools, for the appointment of lay persons to assist in the inspection of educational and other establishments, for new powers for trustees in relation to the proceeds of the disposal of school premises and for the incorporation of Boards of Governors and governing bodies of institutions of further education. Requirements of the curriculum at key stage 4 are amended, the procedure for acquisition of grant-maintained integrated or controlled integrated status is simplified and educational and library boards are given the power to direct the admission of a child to a grant aided school in certain circumstances.

6087. Education (Northern Ireland) Order 1996–Commencement No.1 Order

EDUCATION (1996 ORDER) (COMMENCEMENT NO.1) ORDER (NORTHERN (IRELAND) 1996, SR 1996 329 (C.20); made under the Education (Northern Ireland) Order 1996 Art.1 (3). In force: bringing into force various provisions of the Order on August 1, 1996 and September 1, 1996; £0.65.

This Order brings Art.35(1) to (5) of, and Sch.3 to, the Education (Northern Ireland) Order 1996 (SI 1996 274 (NI 1)) into operation on August 1, 1996 and Art.31, Art.34, Art.40 of, and Sch.4 to, the 1996 Order into operation on September 1, 1996.

6088. Education (Student Loans) (Northern Ireland) Order 1996 (SI 1996 1918 (NI 15))

This Order, which came into force on September 24, 1996, enables the payment of subsidies to private sector financial institutions which provide loans to students in higher education.

6089. Pensions–teachers–additional voluntary contributions

TEACHERS' SUPERANNUATION (ADDITIONAL VOLUNTARY CONTRIBUTIONS) REGULATIONS (NORTHERN IRELAND) 1996, SR 1996 260; made under the Superannuation (Northern Ireland) Order 1972 Art.11 (1) (2) (2A) (3), Art.14 (1) (2) (3), Sch.3 para.1, Sch.3 para.3, Sch.3 para.5, Sch.3 para.6, Sch.3 para.8, Sch.3 para.10, Sch.3 para.11, Sch.3 para.13. In force: July 31, 1996; £4.15.

These Regulations provide for the payment of additional voluntary contributions by teachers who are members of the superannuation scheme constituted by the Teachers' Superannuation Regulations (Northern Ireland) 1977 (SR 1977 260).

6090. Schools–assessment

EDUCATION (ASSESSMENT ARRANGEMENTS FOR KEY STAGES 1 AND 2) ORDER (NORTHERN IRELAND) 1996, SR 1996 363; made under the Education Reform (Northern Ireland) Order 1989 Art.7 (1) (b) (2) (a) (ii) (6). In force: September 1, 1996; £1.55.

This Order prescribes arrangements for the assessment of pupils in English and mathematics in key stages 1 and 2 and, in Irish-speaking schools, arrangements for assessment in Irish and mathematics in key stage 1 and Irish, English and mathematics in key stage 2.

6091. Schools–assessment

EDUCATION (ASSESSMENT ARRANGEMENTS FOR KEY STAGE 3) ORDER (NORTHERN IRELAND) 1996, SR 1996 364; made under the Education Reform (Northern Ireland) Order 1989 Art.7 (1) (b) (2) (a) (ii) (6). In force: in accordance with Art.1 (1) (2); £1.95.

This Order prescribes arrangements for the assessment of pupils in English, mathematics and science in key stage 3.

6092. Schools–assessment

EDUCATION (ASSESSMENT ARRANGEMENTS FOR KEY STAGES 1 AND 2) (EXCEPTIONS) REGULATIONS (NORTHERN IRELAND) 1996, SR 1996 567; made under the Education Reform (Northern Ireland) Order 1989 Art.15(b). In force: January 1, 1997; £0.65.

These Regulations provide that an Irish speaking primary school shall be excepted from the requirements to assess pupils at the end of key stages 1 and 2 in the school year commencing with the date on which the school becomes a grant-aided school. Where such a school becomes a grant-aided school from a date other than the beginning of a school year, it shall be excepted for the remainder of that school year.

6093. Schools–curriculum

CURRICULUM (PROGRAMMES OF STUDY AND ATTAINMENT TARGETS AT KEY STAGES 1 AND 2) ORDER (NORTHERN IRELAND) 1996, SR 1996 346; made under the Education Reform (Northern Ireland) Order 1989 Art.7 (1) (a) (5). In force: in accordance with Art.1 (2) (3); £1.10.

This Order specifies programmes of study and attainment targets for the compulsory contributory subjects of the curriculum at key stages 1 and 2.

6094. Schools–curriculum–art and design

CURRICULUM (PROGRAMMES OF STUDY AND ATTAINMENT TARGET IN ART AND DESIGN AT KEY STAGES 3 AND 4) ORDER (NORTHERN IRELAND) 1996, SR 1996 337; made under the Education Reform (Northern Ireland) Order 1989 Art.7 (1) (a) (5). In force: in accordance with Art.1 (2) (3); £1.10.

This Order specifies programmes of study for key stages 3 and 4 and an attainment target for key stage 3 in relation to art and design.

6095. Schools–curriculum–business studies

CURRICULUM (PROGRAMME OF STUDY IN BUSINESS STUDIES AT KEY STAGE 4) ORDER (NORTHERN IRELAND) 1996, SR 1996 332; made under the Education Reform (Northern Ireland) Order 1989 Art.7 (1) (a) (5). In force: in accordance with Art.1 (2) (3); £1.10.

This Order specifies the programme of study for key stage 4 in relation to business studies.

6096. Schools–curriculum–drama

CURRICULUM (PROGRAMME OF STUDY IN DRAMA AT KEY STAGE 4) ORDER (NORTHERN IRELAND) 1996, SR 1996 336; made under the Education Reform (Northern Ireland) Order 1989 Art.7 (1) (a) (5). In force: in accordance with Art.1 (2) (3); £1.10.

This Order specifies the programme of study for key stage 4 in relation to drama.

6097. Schools–curriculum–economics–politics–environmental studies

CURRICULUM (PROGRAMMES OF STUDY IN ECONOMICS, POLITICAL STUDIES AND SOCIAL AND ENVIRONMENTAL STUDIES AT KEY STAGE 4) ORDER (NORTHERN IRELAND) 1996, SR 1996 333; made under the Education Reform (Northern Ireland) Order 1989 Art.7 (1) (a) (5). In force: in accordance with Art.1 (2) (3); £1.10.

This Order specifies programmes of study for key stage 4 in relation to economics, political studies and social and environmental studies.

6098. Schools–curriculum–English language

CURRICULUM (ENGLISH IN IRISH SPEAKING SCHOOLS) (EXCEPTIONS) REGULATIONS (NORTHERN IRELAND) 1996, SR 1996 350; made under the Education Reform (Northern Ireland) Order 1989 Art.15(b). In force: September 1, 1996; £0.65.

These Regulations exempt primary schools which teach through the medium of Irish, from the requirement to teach English to pupils in the first, second and third years of the first key stage.

6099. Schools–curriculum–English language

CURRICULUM (PROGRAMME OF STUDY AND ATTAINMENT TARGETS IN ENGLISH AT KEY STAGES 3 AND 4) ORDER (NORTHERN IRELAND) 1996, SR

1996 340; made under the Education Reform (Northern Ireland) Order 1989 Art.7 (1) (a) (5). In force: in accordance with Art.1 (2) (3); £1.10.

This Order specifies a programme of study for key stages 3 and 4 and attainment targets for key stage 3 in relation to English.

6100. Schools–curriculum–geography

CURRICULUM (PROGRAMMES OF STUDY AND ATTAINMENT TARGET IN GEOGRAPHY AT KEY STAGES 3 AND 4) ORDER (NORTHERN IRELAND) 1996, SR 1996 348; made under the Education Reform (Northern Ireland) Order 1989 Art.7 (1) (a) (5). In force: in accordance with Art.1 (2) (3); £1.10.

This Order specifies programmes of study for key stages 3 and 4 and an attainment target for key stage 3 in relation to geography.

6101. Schools–curriculum–history

CURRICULUM (PROGRAMMES OF STUDY AND ATTAINMENT TARGET IN HISTORY AT KEY STAGES 3 AND 4) ORDER (NORTHERN IRELAND) 1996, SR 1996 347; made under the Education Reform (Northern Ireland) Order 1989 Art.7 (1) (a) (5). In force: in accordance with Art.1 (2) (3); £1.10.

This Order specifies programmes of study for key stages 3 and 4 and an attainment target for key stage 3 in relation to history.

6102. Schools–curriculum–home economics

CURRICULUM (PROGRAMMES OF STUDY AND ATTAINMENT TARGET IN HOME ECONOMICS AT KEY STAGES 3 AND 4) ORDER (NORTHERN IRELAND) 1996, SR 1996 330; made under the Education Reform (Northern Ireland) Order 1989 Art.7 (1) (a) (5). In force: in accordance with Art.1 (2) (3); £1.10.

This Order specifies programmes of study for key stages 3 and 4 and an attainment target for key stage 3 in relation to home economics.

6103. Schools–curriculum–languages

CURRICULUM (PROGRAMMES OF STUDY AND ATTAINMENT TARGETS IN MODERN LANGUAGES AT KEY STAGES 3 AND 4) ORDER (NORTHERN IRELAND) 1996, SR 1996 342; made under the Education Reform (Northern Ireland) Order 1989 Art.7 (1) (a) (5). In force: in accordance with Art.1 (2) (3); £1.10.

This Order specifies a programme of study for key stages 3 and 4 and attainment targets for key stage 3 in relation to modern languages.

6104. Schools–curriculum–mathematics

CURRICULUM (PROGRAMME OF STUDY AND ATTAINMENT TARGETS IN MATHEMATICS AT KEY STAGES 3 AND 4) ORDER (NORTHERN IRELAND) 1996, SR 1996 341; made under the Education Reform (Northern Ireland) Order 1989 Art.7 (1) (a) (5). In force: in accordance with Art.1 (2) (3); £1.10.

This Order specifies a programme of study for key stages 3 and 4 and attainment targets for key stage 3 in relation to mathematics.

6105. Schools–curriculum–music

CURRICULUM (PROGRAMMES OF STUDY AND ATTAINMENT TARGET IN MUSIC AT KEY STAGES 3 AND 4) ORDER (NORTHERN IRELAND 1996, SR 1996 339; made under the Education Reform (Northern Ireland) Order 1989 Art.7 (1) (a) (5). In force: in accordance with Art.1 (2) (3); £1.10.

This Order specifies programmes of study for key stages 3 and 4 and an attainment target for key stage 3 in relation to music.

6106. Schools–curriculum–physical education

CURRICULUM (PROGRAMMES OF STUDY AND ATTAINMENT TARGETS IN PHYSICAL EDUCATION AT KEY STAGES 3 AND 4) ORDER (NORTHERN IRELAND) 1996, SR 1996 331; made under the Education Reform (Northern Ireland) Order 1989 Art.7(1)(a)(5). In force: in accordance with Art.1(2)(3); £1.10.

This Order specifies programmes of study for key stages 3 and 4 and attainment targets for key stage 3 in relation to physical education.

6107. Schools–curriculum–religious education

CURRICULUM (CORE SYLLABUS FOR RELIGIOUS EDUCATION) ORDER (NORTHERN IRELAND) 1996, SR 1996 351; made under the Education Reform (Northern Ireland) Order 1989 Art.13(1)(6). In force: September 1, 1996; £1.10.

This Order specifies the core syllabus for the teaching of religious education in grant-aided schools.

6108. Schools–curriculum–science

CURRICULUM (PROGRAMMES OF STUDY AND ATTAINMENT TARGETS IN SCIENCE AT KEY STAGES 3 AND 4) ORDER (NORTHERN IRELAND) 1996, SR 1996 335; made under the Education Reform (Northern Ireland) Order 1989 Art.7(1)(a)(5). In force: in accordance with Art.1(2)(3); £1.10.

This Order specifies programmes of study for key stages 3 and 4 and attainment targets for key stage 3 in relation to science.

6109. Schools–curriculum–science and technology

EDUCATION REFORM (AMENDMENT) ORDER (NORTHERN IRELAND) 1996, SR 1996 328; made under the Education Reform (Northern Ireland) Order 1989 Art.5(7), Art.6(6). In force: August 31, 1996; £0.65.

This Order amends the Education Reform (Northern Ireland) Order 1989 (SI 1989 2406 (NI 20)) Sch.1 by adding science and technology to the listed contributory subjects. It also amends Sch.2 so that the contributory subject science (A) at key stages 1 and 2 becomes science and technology.

6110. Schools–curriculum–technology

CURRICULUM (PROGRAMMES OF STUDY AND ATTAINMENT TARGET IN TECHNOLOGY AND DESIGN AT KEY STAGES 3 AND 4) ORDER (NORTHERN IRELAND) 1996, SR 1996 338; made under the Education Reform (Northern Ireland) Order 1989 Art.7(1)(a)(5). In force: in accordance with Art.1(2)(3); £1.10.

This Order specifies programmes of study for key stages 3 and 4 and an attainment target for key stage 3 in relation to technology and design.

6111. Schools–prospectuses

EDUCATION (SCHOOL INFORMATION AND PROSPECTUSES) (AMENDMENT) REGULATIONS (NORTHERN IRELAND) 1996, SR 1996 359; made under the Education Reform (Northern Ireland) Order 1989 Art.31(2)(3), Art.42(3)(6), Art.137(5). In force: September 1, 1996; £1.10.

These Regulations amend the Education (School Information and Prospectuses) Regulations (Northern Ireland) 1993 (SR 1993 370) as respects the information to be given in the annual report of the boards of governors of schools to parents and the information relating to individual schools (other than primary schools) to be published by the board of governors of the school or by the relevant board on their behalf.

6112. Students–grants

STUDENTS AWARDS REGULATIONS (NORTHERN IRELAND) 1996, SR 1996 190; made under the Education and Libraries (Northern Ireland) Order 1986 Art.50(1)(2), Art.134(1). In force: June 10, 1996; £7.05.

These Regulations, which revoke and replace, with amendments, the Students Awards Regulations (Northern Ireland) 1995 (SR 1995 1), govern the making of mandatory awards which it is the duty of education and library boards to make to specified persons in Sch.2 to the Regulations.

6113. Students–grants

STUDENTS AWARDS (NO.2) REGULATIONS (NORTHERN IRELAND) 1996, SR 1996 298; made under the Education (Northern Ireland) Order 1986 Art.50(1), Art.134(1). In force: September 1, 1996; £7.05.

These Regulations replace with amendments, and revoke, the Students Awards Regulations (Northern Ireland) 1996 (SR 1996 190). They govern the making of mandatory awards by education and library boards to persons specified in Sch.2 to the Regulations.

6114. Students–grants

STUDENTS AWARDS (NO.2) (AMENDMENT) REGULATIONS (NORTHERN IRELAND) 1996, SR 1996 546; made under the Education and Libraries (Northern Ireland) Order 1986 Art.50(1)(2), Art.134(1). In force: December 24, 1996; £1.10.

These Regulations amend the Students Awards (No.2) Regulations (Northern Ireland) 1996 (SR 1996 298) and have effect retrospectively from September 1, 1996. Provision has been made for the designation of full-time courses for the initial training of teachers which are not provided wholly by publicly funded institutions in the United Kingdom, or wholly by those certain other institutions. A definition of an EEA migrant worker has been added. Provision has also been made for the payment of awards to spouses of EEA migrant workers. First degrees comparable to a Bachelor of Education degrees are now conferred by some institutions under different names so provision has been made for them to be treated for the purposes of the Regulations as Bachelor of Education degrees.

6115. Students–loans

EDUCATION (STUDENT LOANS) REGULATIONS (NORTHERN IRELAND) 1996, SR 1996 349; made under the Education (Student Loans) (Northern Ireland) Order 1990 Art.3(2), Sch.2 para.1(1)(3)(4), Sch.2 para.2(1), Sch.2 para.3(4). In force: August 1, 1996; £3.20.

These Regulations replace with amendments, and revoke, the Education (Student Loans) Regulations (Northern Ireland) 1995 (SR 1995 279).

6116. Students–loans

EDUCATION (STUDENT LOANS) (AMENDMENT) REGULATIONS (NORTHERN IRELAND) 1996, SR 1996 490; made under the Education (Student Loans) (Northern Ireland) Order 1990 Art.3(2), Sch.2 para.1(1)(3)(4), Sch.2 para.2(1)(1A), Sch.2 para.3(4). In force: November 15, 1996; £0.65.

These Regulations amend the Education (Student Loans) Regulations (Northern Ireland) 1996 (SR 1996 349) to require loan administrators to pay specified fees to institutions of higher education in connection with applications for loans.

ELECTORAL PROCESS

6117. Elections–election of delegates. See ELECTORAL PROCESS. §2507

6118. Elections–returning officers–expenses. See ELECTORAL PROCESS. §2512

6119. Northern Ireland (Entry to Negotiations, etc.) Act (c.11). See ELECTORAL PROCESS. §2514

EMPLOYMENT

6120. Community work–payments

COMMUNITY WORK PROGRAMME (MISCELLANEOUS PROVISIONS) ORDER (NORTHERN IRELAND) 1996, SR 1996 172; made under the Employment and Training (Amendment) (Northern Ireland) Order 1988 Art.4(1)(2). In force: June 3, 1996; £1.55.

This Order provides that, for the purposes of the statutory provisions specified in the Schedule, a person using facilities provided under the Community Work Programme shall be treated as participating in arrangements for training under the Employment and Training Act (Northern Ireland) 1950 s.1. Any payment made to such a person in connection with their use of those facilities shall be treated in the same manner as a payment made in respect of such training. The Order also provides that a payment made to a person in connection with his use of such facilities shall not be treated as earnings for the purposes of the Social Security Contributions and Benefits (Northern Ireland) Act 1992 Part I.

6121. Constructive dismissal–Roman Catholic employed in an establishment frequented by Protestant customers–employers failure to deal with a threat made against employee–discrimination on grounds of religious belief–comparison for the purposes of establishing less favourable treatment

[Fair Employment (Northern Ireland) Act 1976 s.16.]

S, a Roman Catholic, was employed as a barman in a pub with Protestant customers in a loyalist area of Belfast. A message was delivered to the pub saying that S should be advised not to be in the bar in the following week. The employers took no action. S, believing that his life was at risk, resigned and claimed that he had been discriminated against on grounds of religious belief in that he had been constructively dismissed. The Fair Employment Tribunal upheld his claim.

Held, dismissing the employer's appeal, that (1) the tribunal was entitled to find that the employers, in failing to show concern, were in breach of the implied term not to destroy or seriously damage the relationship of trust and confidence with S and that this breach justified S's resignation; (2) the tribunal was entitled to find that the employers had treated S less favourably than they treated or would treat other persons on grounds of religious belief. S would not have been constructively dismissed but for being a Roman Catholic, in that it was being a Catholic which gave rise to his dismissal, dicta of Lord Goff in *R. v. Birmingham City Council, ex p. Equal Opportunities Commission* [1989] I.R.L.R. 173, [1989] C.L.Y. 1371 applied, and (3) the tribunal had not erred in finding that the employers had treated S less favourably than they would have treated a Protestant employee in comparable circumstances. The relevant comparison under the Fair Employment (Northern Ireland) Act 1976 s.16(4A) was between S and a hypothetical Protestant barman working in the same bar who was not dismissed because of his religious belief, rather than a hypothetical Protestant barman working in a Catholic bar in a nationalist area, who would have been treated in the same way.

SMYTH v. CROFT INNS LTD [1996] I.R.L.R. 84, Sir Brian Hutton, L.C.J. (NI), CA (NI).

6122. Employee's rights–continuity of employment–health service

EMPLOYMENT RIGHTS (HEALTH SERVICE EMPLOYERS) ORDER (NORTHERN IRELAND) 1996, SR 1996 547; made under the Employment Rights (Northern Ireland) Order 1996 Art.14(8)(b). In force: December 29, 1996; £0.65.

This Order specifies for the purposes of the Employment Rights (Northern Ireland) Order 1996 (SI 1996 1919 (NI 16)) Art.14(7), the descriptions of employment (being employment in which persons are engaged while undergoing professional training which involves their being employed successively by a number of different health service employers) where the continuity of the employee's period of employment is, by virtue of that Article, maintained on his changing his employer for that purpose.

6123. Employment protection–continuity of employment

EMPLOYMENT PROTECTION (CONTINUITY OF EMPLOYMENT) REGULATIONS (NORTHERN IRELAND) 1996, SR 1996 604; made under the Employment Rights (Northern Ireland) Order Art.15. In force: February 2, 1997; £1.10.

These Regulations revoke and replace the Industrial Regulations (Continuity of Employment) (Northern Ireland) Regulations 1994 (SR 1994 3) which provided for the preservation of continuity of employment for the purposes of employment protection rights now contained in the Employment Rights (Northern Ireland) Order 1996 (SI 1996 1919 (NI 16)) where a dismissed employee was reinstated or re-engaged in certain circumstances. The 1994 Regulations also provided that continuity of employment was not broken in redundancy cases where any such employee repaid a redundancy payment or equivalent payment. The only change of substance in these Regulations is the inclusion of provision for preserving continuity of employment where a dismissed employee is reinstated or re-engaged in consequence of the making of an agreement or contract authorised by the Disability Discrimination Act 1995.

6124. Employment Rights (Northern Ireland) Order 1996–Commencement No.1 Order

EMPLOYMENT RIGHTS (1996 ORDER) (RESIDUARY COMMENCEMENT NO.1) ORDER (NORTHERN IRELAND) 1996, SR 1996 475 (C.23); made under the Employment Rights (Northern Ireland) Order 1996 Sch.2 para.11 (2)(b). In force: bringing into force various provisions of the Order on October 6, 1996; £0.65.

This Order brings the Employment Rights (Northern Ireland) Order 1996 Art.69, Art.86, Art.87, Art.88, Art.133 (employment rights of trustees of occupational pension schemes) into operation on October 6, 1996.

6125. Employment Rights (Northern Ireland) Order 1996 (SI 1996 1919 (NI 16))

The Order came into operation on September 24, 1996 and re-enacts, with minor amendments, the Contracts of Employment and Redundancy Payments Act (Northern Ireland) 1965 and the Industrial Relations (Northern Ireland) Orders 1976 (SI 1976 1043 (NI 16)) to 1993 (SI 1993 2668 (NI 11)) in so far as they relate to employment rights.

6126. Equal opportunities–public authorities

FAIR EMPLOYMENT (SPECIFICATION OF PUBLIC AUTHORITIES) (AMENDMENT) ORDER (NORTHERN IRELAND) 1996, SR 1996 504; made under the Fair Employment Act 1989 s.25(1)(2). In force: January 1, 1997; £1.95.

This Order amends the Fair Employment (Specification of Public Authorities) Order (Northern Ireland) 1989 (SR 1989 475) which specifies persons or bodies as public authorities for certain purposes under the Fair Employment (Northern Ireland) Act 1989 Part II and provides for the persons who are to be treated for such purposes as the employees of some of those authorities.

6127. Equal pay

EQUAL PAY (AMENDMENT) REGULATIONS (NORTHERN IRELAND) 1996, SR 1996 465; made under the European Communities Act 1972 s.2(2). In force: November 3, 1996; £1.10.

These Regulations change the powers of industrial tribunals in certain cases under the Equal Pay Act (Northern Ireland) 1970. They improve provisions implementing Council Directive 75/117 ([1975] OJ L145/19), which provides among other things for equal pay for work of equal value. They alter the procedure for such claims, so that industrial tribunals will no longer have to refer questions of equal value to independent experts and will have no power to do so where satisfied that there are no reasonable grounds for determining that the work in question is of equal value.

6128. Industrial tribunals–discrimination–interest on awards

INDUSTRIAL TRIBUNALS (INTEREST ON AWARDS IN SEX AND DISABILITY DISCRIMINATION CASES) REGULATIONS (NORTHERN IRELAND) 1996, SR 1996 581; made under the European Communities Act 1972 s.2(2); and the Disability Discrimination Act 1995 s.8(6)(7), s.67. In force: January 26, 1997; £1.95.

These Regulations make special provisions in relation to interest on awards and compensation orders made by industrial tribunals. They revoke the Sex Discrimination and Equal Pay (Remedies) Regulations (Northern Ireland) 1993 (SR 1993 478).

6129. Industrial tribunals–procedure

INDUSTRIAL TRIBUNALS (CONSTITUTION AND RULES OF PROCEDURE) REGULATIONS (NORTHERN IRELAND) 1996, SR 1996 173; made under the Industrial Relations (Northern Ireland) Order 1976 Art.58A(1)(5)(6)(7)(8), Art.59(1)(2)(2A)(2B)(2D)(3)(4)(6A)(6B)(7)(8), Art.80(3); the Health and Safety at Work (Northern Ireland) Order 1978 Art.26(1); and the Industrial Training (Northern Ireland) Order 1984 Art.30(1). In force: June 1, 1996; £7.55.

These Regulations revoke and replace Regulations prescribing rules of procedure for industrial tribunals in Northern Ireland.

6130. Industrial tribunals–procedure

INDUSTRIAL TRIBUNALS (CONSTITUTION AND RULES OF PROCEDURE) (AMENDMENT) REGULATIONS (NORTHERN IRELAND) 1996, SR 1996 466; made under the Health and Safety at Work (Northern Ireland) Order 1978 Art.26(1); and the Industrial Tribunals (Northern Ireland) Order 1996 Art.3(1), Art.6(1)(5)(6)(7), Art.9(1)(2)(3)(5), Art.11(1)(2)(4), Art.12(2), Art.13(1)(4), Art.14(2)(5), Art.15(1)(2), Art.21, Art.25(5). In force: Reg.9, Reg.11: December 2, 1996; Remainder: November 3, 1996; £2.80.

These Regulations amend the Industrial Tribunals (Constitution and Rules of Procedure) Regulations (Northern Ireland) 1996 (SR 1996 173) which prescribe procedural rules for proceedings in industrial tribunals.

6131. Industrial Tribunals (Northern Ireland) Order 1996 (SI 1996 1921 (NI 18))

This Order, which came into operation on September 24, 1996, re-enacts, with minor amendments, the enactments relating to the constitution, jurisdiction and procedure of industrial tribunals.

6132. Maternity pay–employers–compensation

STATUTORY MATERNITY PAY (COMPENSATION OF EMPLOYERS) (AMENDMENT) REGULATIONS (NORTHERN IRELAND) 1996, SR 1996 77; made under the Social Security Contributions and Benefits (Northern Ireland) act 1992 s.163(1)(c). In force: April 6, 1996; £0.65.

These Regulations increase the additional amount of statutory maternity pay which small employers may recover.

6133. Sex discrimination

SEX DISCRIMINATION (AMENDMENT) REGULATIONS (NORTHERN IRELAND) 1996, SR 1996 418; made under the European Communities Act 1972 s.2(2). In force: October 20, 1996; £1.10.

These Regulations amend the Sex Discrimination (Northern Ireland) Order 1976 (SI 1976 1042 (NI 15)) to extend the remedies available for sex discrimination pursuant to Council Directive 76/207 ([1976] OJ L39/40). They enable an industrial tribunal to award compensation to a person who has suffered indirect discrimination under the 1976 Order Part III, even where the respondent did not intend to treat the complainant unfavourably on the ground of his or her marital status, where it would not be just and equitable to grant other remedies alone.

6134. Statutory sick pay

STATUTORY SICK PAY (GENERAL) (AMENDMENT) REGULATIONS (NORTHERN IRELAND) 1996, SR 1996 569; made under the Social Security Administration (Northern Ireland) Act 1992 s.122(4), s.165(1). In force: April 6, 1997; £0.65.

These Regulations further amend the Statutory Sick Pay (General) Regulations (Northern Ireland) 1982 (SR 1982 263) by adding a new paragraph which provides that any payment, or payments, of contractual remuneration which equal or exceed the amount of statutory sick pay payable in respect of a day of incapacity, shall not be regarded as a payment of statutory sick pay for the purpose of the record keeping requirements of the 1982 Regulations only.

ENERGY

6135. Domestic Energy Efficiency Schemes (Northern Ireland) Order 1996 (SI 1996 2879 (NI 21))

This Order, which came into force on January 20, 1997, amends the Social Security (Northern Ireland) Order 1990 (SI 1990 1511 (NI 15)) Art.17 to modify and widen the scope of the power to pay grants towards the cost of improving the energy efficiency of dwellings and buildings in multiple occupation.

6136. Energy Conservation Act 1996–Commencement Order

ENERGY CONSERVATION ACT 1996 (COMMENCEMENT) ORDER (NORTHERN IRELAND) 1996, SR 1996 559 (C.26); made under the Energy Conservation Act 1996 s.2(2)(4). In force: bringing the Act into force on December 5, 1996; £0.65.

This Order brings the provisions of the Energy Conservation Act 1996 into force on December 5, 1996.

ENVIRONMENT

6137. Air pollution–standards

AIR QUALITY STANDARDS (AMENDMENT) REGULATIONS (NORTHERN IRELAND) 1996, SR 1996 23; made under the European Communities Act 1972 s.2(2). In force: March 1, 1996; £0.65.

These Regulations amend the Air Quality Standards Regulations (Northern Ireland) 1990 (SR 1990 145) Reg.7.

6138. Environmental impact–construction work–harbours

HARBOUR WORKS (ASSESSMENT OF ENVIRONMENTAL EFFECTS) (AMENDMENT) REGULATIONS (NORTHERN IRELAND) 1996, SR 1996 369; made under the European Communities Act 1972 s.2(2). In force: September 9, 1996; £1.10.

These Regulations make minor amendments to the Harbour Works (Assessment of Environmental Effects) Regulations (Northern Ireland) 1990 (SR 1990 181) which implements, in respect of harbour works, Council Directive 85/337 ([1985] OJ L175/40), on the assessment of the effects of certain public and private projects on the environment. The amendments align the law of Northern Ireland more exactly with the Directive, and make provision for costs of inquiries held under the 1990 Regulations.

6139. Fees

DEPARTMENT OF THE ENVIRONMENT (FEES) ORDER (NORTHERN IRELAND) 1996, SR 1996 87; made under the Fees &c. (Northern Ireland) Order 1988 Art.3. In force: May 1, 1996; £1.95.

This Order specifies functions to be taken into account in the fixing of certain fees by the Department of the Environment.

6140. Plant health

PLANT PROTECTION PRODUCTS (AMENDMENT) REGULATIONS (NORTHERN IRELAND) 1996, SR 1996 456; made under the European Communities Act 1972 s.2(2). In force: November 1, 1996; £0.65.

These Regulations amend the definition of "the Directive" in the Plant Protection Products Regulations (Northern Ireland) 1995 (SR 1995 371)

6141. Water pollution–asbestos

CONTROL OF ASBESTOS IN WATER (AMENDMENT) REGULATIONS (NORTHERN IRELAND) 1996, SR 1996 602; made under the European Communities Act 1972 s.2(2). In force: February 20, 1997; £1.10.

These Regulations amend the Control of Asbestos in Water Regulations (Northern Ireland) 1995 (SR 1995 93) which require the Department of the Environment to reduce and prevent, as far as reasonably practicable, emissions of asbestos into the aquatic environment. The amendment requires the Department to monitor at regular intervals any discharge into the aquatic environment which may contain asbestos.

6142. Water pollution–nitrates

PROTECTION OF WATER AGAINST AGRICULTURAL NITRATE POLLUTION REGULATIONS (NORTHERN IRELAND) 1996, SR 1996 217; made under the European Communities Act 1972 s.2. In force: July 3, 1996; £1.95.

These Regulations implement Council Directive 91/676 ([1991] OJ L375/1) concerning the protection of waters against pollution caused by nitrates from agricultural sources.

6143. Water supply–surface water–abstraction for drinking water–classification of quality

SURFACE WATERS (ABSTRACTION FOR DRINKING WATER) (CLASSIFICATION) REGULATIONS (NORTHERN IRELAND) 1996, SR 1996 603; made under the Water Act (Northern Ireland) 1972 s.4B; and the Water and Sewerage Services Order (Northern Ireland) 1973 Art.56B. In force: February 20, 1997; £4.15.

These Regulations prescribe a system for classifying the quality of waters intended for abstraction for drinking water according to their suitability for abstraction by the Department of the Environment for supply after treatment as drinking water.

ENVIRONMENTAL HEALTH

6144. Litter–waste disposal

LITTER (STATUTORY UNDERTAKERS) (DESIGNATION AND RELEVANT LAND) ORDER (NORTHERN IRELAND) 1996, SR 1996 22; made under the Litter (Northern Ireland) Order 1994 Art.2(1)(3). In force: March 1, 1996; £1.10.

This Order makes provision as to the application of the Litter (Northern Ireland) Order 1994 to statutory undertakers.

6145. Sanitation–interest on expenses

INTEREST ON RECOVERABLE SANITATION EXPENSES ORDER (NORTHERN IRELAND) 1996, SR 1996 211; made under the Public Health and Local Government (Miscellaneous Provisions) Act (Northern Ireland) 1962 s.5(2). In force: July 1, 1996; £1.10.

This Order fixes the rate of interest on certain expenses recoverable from owners of premises under the Public Health (Ireland) Act 1878 as being 0.5 per cent below the base rate quoted by the seven largest banks authorised under the Banking Act 1987 on the reference day falling on July 1, 1996, and on any subsequent days. This Order also revokes the interest on Recoverable Sanitation Expenses Order (Northern Ireland) 1994 (SR 1994 90).

FAMILY LAW

6146. Births–deaths–registration

REGISTRATION (BIRTHS, STILL-BIRTHS AND DEATHS) (AMENDMENT) REGULATIONS (NORTHERN IRELAND) 1996, SR 1996 500; made under the Births and Deaths Registration (Northern Ireland) Order 1973 Art.10(1), Art.14(3), Art.16(1), Art.18(2), Art.19A(2). In force: December 2, 1996; £2.80.

These Regulations amend the Registration (Births, Still-Births and Deaths) Regulations (Northern Ireland) 1973 (SR 1973 373) consequentially on the commencement of the Children (Northern Ireland) Order 1995 (SI 1995 755 (NI 2)) Sch.9 para.83 to Sch.9 para.88. They also amend forms in the 1973 Regulations.

6147. Children–marriage–consent

MARRIAGE OF CHILDREN (CONSENTS) (AMENDMENT) REGULATIONS (NORTHERN IRELAND) 1996, SR 1996 501; made under the Marriages Act (Northern Ireland) 1954 s.5(1); and the Northern Ireland Act 1974 Sch.1 para.2(1)(b). In force: December 2, 1996; £1.55.

These Regulations amend the Marriage of Minors (Consents) Regulations (Northern Ireland) 1954 (SR & O (NI) 1954 134) by substituting "child" for "minor" and substituting the forms used where the consent of the marriage of a child is involved.

6148. Divorce–pensions

DIVORCE ETC. (PENSIONS) REGULATIONS (NORTHERN IRELAND) 1996, SR 1996 296; made under the Matrimonial Causes (Northern Ireland) Order 1978 Art.27D(2)(4). In force: August 10, 1996; £1.95.

These Regulations make provision in relation to orders made for ancillary relief in proceedings for divorce, judicial separation or nullity of marriage as respects the pension rights of a party to a marriage. In particular, they provide for the valuation of pension rights, for notices of change of circumstances to be provided by the pension scheme to the party without pension rights, or by that party to the scheme, for information concerning the value of pension rights to be provided by the pension scheme to its member and for the recovery by the scheme of the costs of complying with these Regulations.

6149. Family Law (Northern Ireland) Order 1993–Commencement No.1 Order

FAMILY LAW (1993 ORDERS) (COMMENCEMENT NO.1) ORDER (NORTHERN IRELAND) 1996, SR 1996 454 (C.22); made under the Northern Ireland Act 1974 Sch.1 para.2(1); and the Family Law (Northern Ireland) Order 1993 Art.1(3). In force: bringing into force various provisions of Family Law (Northern Ireland) Order 1993 and Family Law (Northern Ireland Consequential Amendments) Order 1993 on November 4, 1996; £0.65.

This Order brings the maintenance enforcement provisions in the Family Law (Northern Ireland) Order 1993 (SI 1993 1576 (NI 6)) Art.6 to Art.11, Sch.1 and the Family Law (Northern Ireland Consequential Amendments) Order 1993 (SI 1993 1577) into operation on November 4, 1996.

6150. Matrimonial causes–fees

MATRIMONIAL CAUSES FEES ORDER (NORTHERN IRELAND) 1996, SR 1996 105; made under the Judicature (Northern Ireland) Act 1978 s.116(1)(4). In force: April 1, 1996; £1.95.

This Order revokes and replaces the Matrimonial Causes Fees Order (Northern Ireland) 1991 (SR 1991 292) as amended by the Matrimonial Causes Fees Order (Northern Ireland) 1992 (SR 1992 219), the Matrimonial Causes Fees Order (Northern Ireland) 1994 (SR 1994 281) and the Matrimonial Causes Fees Order (Northern Ireland) 1995 (SR 1995 218). The Order increases the majority of fees to be taken in matrimonial proceedings, whether in the High Court or divorce county courts; restructures the fees in relation to copies of documents; and introduces a new fee in relation to a postal application for a search.

FINANCE

6151. Appropriation (Northern Ireland) Order 1996 (SI 1996 721 (NI 4))

The Order, which came into force on March 13, 1996, authorises the issue, out of the Consolidated Fund, of a further sum for the year ending March 31, 1996 and of sums on account for the year ending March 31, 1997 and appropriates those sums for specified services in Northern Ireland. It also authorises the application of certain further sums as appropriations in aid for the year ending on March 31, 1996 and reduces certain sums already authorised to be applied as appropriations in aid.

6152. Appropriation (No.2) (Northern Ireland) Order 1996 (SI 1996 1917 (NI 14))

The Order, which came into operation on July 23, 1996, authorises the issue out of the Consolidated Fund of a further sum for the year ending March 31, 1997, appropriates that sum and deals with the application of sums as appropriations in aid.

6153. Financial Provisions (Northern Ireland) Order 1995 (SI 1995 2991 (NI 16))

This Order contains various miscellaneous financial provisions. Provision is made for the Department of Finance and Personnel to amend or repeal provisions requiring a statutory body or Northern Ireland Department to obtain the consent of the Department to exercise its functions. The Financial Provisions (Northern Ireland) Order 1993 is amended in relation to the reserves, public dividend capital and borrowing limits of trading funds. Time limits for the preparation and audit of certain accounts under the Exchequer and Financial Provisions Act (Northern Ireland) 1950 are extended. The requirement that a loan made to Enterprise Ulster must be repaid within the same financial year is removed from the Enterprise Ulster (Northern Ireland) Order 1973 (SI 1973 1228 (NI 16)).

FINANCIAL SERVICES

6154. Insolvency–financial markets

FINANCIAL MARKETS AND INSOLVENCY REGULATIONS (NORTHERN IRELAND) 1996, SR 1996 252; made under the Companies (No.2) (Northern Ireland) Order 1990 Art.106(1)(3), Art.107(1). In force: July 15, 1996; £1.40.

These Regulations apply with modifications certain provisions of the Companies (No.2) (Northern Ireland) Order 1990 (SI 1990 1504 (NI 10)) Part V to certain charges (and to property subject to those charges) granted in favour of persons undertaking assured payment obligations in connection with the settlement of transactions through a relevant system in respect of which an operator has been approved under the Uncertificated Securities Regulations 1995 (SI 1995 3272).

FOOD AND DRUGS

6155. Dairy products–food hygiene

DAIRY PRODUCTS (HYGIENE) (AMENDMENT) REGULATIONS (NORTHERN IRELAND) 1996, SR 1996 287; made under the Food Safety (Northern Ireland) Order 1991 Art.15(1)(3), Art.16(1), Art.17(2), Art.18, Art.25, Art.26(3), Art.32, Art.47(2), Sch.1 para.5, Sch.1 para.6(1). In force: August 25, 1996; £1.95.

These Regulations amend the Dairy Products (Hygiene) Regulations (Northern Ireland) 1995 (SR 1995 201). They implement part of Commission Decision 95/165 ([1995] OJ L108/84) establishing uniform criteria for the grant of derogations to certain establishments manufacturing milk-based products and Commission Decision 95/340 ([1995] OJ L200/38) drawing up a provisional list of third countries from which Member States authorise import of milk and milk based products, as amended by Commission Decision 96/106 ([1996] OJ L24/34) and as read with Council Directive 92/46 ([1992] OJ L268/1), correct Reg.10 (heat-treated milk) and Reg.12 (health mark) to reflect Council Directive 92/46 ([1992] OJ L268/1), as amended and clarify provisions relating to risk analysis principles, exemptions and enforcement and supervision.

6156. Drug abuse

MISUSE OF DRUGS (AMENDMENT) REGULATIONS (NORTHERN IRELAND) 1996, SR 1996 353; made under the Misuse of Drugs Act 1971 s.7, s.10, s.31. In force: September 1, 1996; £1.10.

These Regulations amend the Misuse of Drugs Regulations (Northern Ireland) 1986 (SR 1986 52) Sch.4 by adding a new Part I comprising a list of anabolic and androgenic steroids and derivatives, an andrenoceptor stimulant and polypeptide hormones.

6157. Food safety

FOOD PROTECTION (EMERGENCY PROHIBITIONS) (AMENDMENT) ORDER (NORTHERN IRELAND) 1995, SR 1995 472; made under the Food and Environment Protection Act 1985 s.1 (1), s.24(3). In force: January 17, 1996; £1.10.

This Order amends the Food Protection (Emergency Prohibitions) Order (Northern Ireland) 1991 (SR 1991 8) by reducing the size of a designated area in Glenshane, Co. Londonderry from which sheep cannot be taken to provide food for human consumption.

6158. Food safety–additives

MISCELLANEOUS FOOD ADDITIVES REGULATIONS (NORTHERN IRELAND) 1996, SR 1996 50; made under the Food Safety (Northern Ireland) Order 1991 Art.15(1)(a), Art.16(1), Art.17(1), Art.25(1)(3), Art.26(3), Art.47(2), Sch.1 para.1. In force: April 22, 1996; £9.10.

These Regulations implement European Parliament and Council Directive 95/2 ([1995] OJ L61/1), read with Council Directive 89/107 ([1989] OJ L40/27) on food additives authorised for use in foodstuffs intended for human consumption by dealing with the use of additives in or on foods. They also make provision in relation to compound foods.

6159. Food safety–additives–colours

COLOURS IN FOOD REGULATIONS (NORTHERN IRELAND) 1996, SR 1996 49; made under the Food Safety (Northern Ireland) Order 1991 Art.15(1)(a), Art.16(1), Art.25(1)(3), Art.26(3), Art.47(2), Sch.1 para.1. In force: April 22, 1996; £4.15.

These Regulations implement European Parliament and Council Directive 94/36 ([1994] OJ L237/13), read with Council Directive 89/107 ([1989] OJ L40/27) on food additives authorised for use in foodstuffs intended for human consumption and Council Directive 95/45 ([1995] OJ L226/1) on criteria of purity concerning colours for use in foodstuffs by dealing with the use of colours in or on foods. They also make provision in relation to compound foods.

6160. Food safety–additives–sweeteners

SWEETENERS IN FOOD REGULATIONS (NORTHERN IRELAND) 1996, SR 1996 48; made under the Food Safety (Northern Ireland) Order 1991 Art.15(1)(a), Art.25(1)(3), Art.26(3), Art.47(2), Sch.1 para.1. In force: April 22, 1996; £3.70.

These Regulations implement European Parliament and Council Directive 94/35 ([1994] OJ L237/3), on sweeteners for use in foodstuffs, read with Council Directive 89/107 ([1989] OJ L40/27) on food additives authorised for use in foodstuffs intended for human consumption and Council Directive 95/31 ([1995] OJ L178/1) on criteria of purity concerning sweeteners for use in foodstuffs by prohibiting the sale of sweeteners intended for sale to the ultimate consumer of for use in or on foods, other than permitted sweeteners.

6161. Food safety–beef

FRESH MEAT (BEEF CONTROLS) REGULATIONS (NORTHERN IRELAND) 1996, SR 1996 404; made under the Food Safety (Northern Ireland) Order 1991

Art.15(1)(f), Art.25(1)(3), Art.26(3), Art.44(1), Art.47(2). In force: September 1, 1996; £2.40.

These Regulations replace the Beef (Emergency Control) Order (Northern Ireland) 1996 (SR 1996 132), as amended, by prohibiting the sale for human consumption of meat derived from bovine animals slaughtered on or after March 29, 1996, and which, at the time of slaughter, were more than two and a half years of age. Meat from bovine animals which were born, reared and slaughtered in specified countries is exempt from the prohibition, as is meat from bovine animals which belonged to a herd registered under the Beef Assurance Scheme.

6162. Food safety–beef

FRESH MEAT (BEEF CONTROLS) (AMENDMENT) REGULATIONS (NORTHERN IRELAND) 1996, SR 1996 506; made under the Food Safety (Northern Ireland) Order 1991 Art.15(1)(f), Art.25(1)(3), Art.26(3), Art.44(1), Art.47(2). In force: October 24, 1996; £1.10.

These Regulations amend the Fresh Meat (Beef Controls) Regulations (Northern Ireland) 1996 (SR 1996 404) by altering the conditions of eligibility and of continued membership of the Beef Assurance Scheme established under those Regulations.

6163. Food safety–beef–emergency control

BEEF (EMERGENCY CONTROL) ORDER (NORTHERN IRELAND) 1996, SR 1996 132; made under the Food Safety (Northern Ireland) Order 1991 Art.12(1), Art.26(3), Art.47(2). In force: March 29, 1996; £1.10.

This Order prohibits the sale of any meat (as defined in Art.1 (2)) from bovine animals slaughtered after March 28, 1996 and which at the time of slaughter were more than two and a half years of age.

6164. Food safety–beef–emergency control

BEEF (EMERGENCY CONTROL) (AMENDMENT) ORDER (NORTHERN IRELAND) 1996, SR 1996 175; made under the Food Safety (Northern Ireland) Order 1991 Art.12(1), Art.26(3), Art.47(2). In force: April 30, 1996; £1.10.

The Beef (Emergency Control) Order (Northern Ireland) 1996 (SR 1996 132) (the principal Order) prohibited the sale in Northern Ireland of any meat from bovine animals slaughtered after March 28, 1996 and which at the time of slaughter were more than two and a half years of age. This Order amends the principal Order to exclude from the scope of that prohibition meat from bovine animals that were born, reared and slaughtered in countries specified in the Schedule inserted by Art.2(b).

6165. Food safety–beef–emergency controls

BEEF (EMERGENCY CONTROL) (REVOCATION) ORDER (NORTHERN IRELAND) 1996, SR 1996 403; made under the Food Safety (Northern Ireland) Order 1991 Art.12(1), Art.26(3), Art.47(2). In force: September 1, 1996; £0.65.

This Order revokes the Beef (Emergency Control) Order (Northern Ireland) 1996 (SR 1996 132) and the Beef (Emergency Control) (Amendment) Order (Northern Ireland) 1996 (SR 1996 175), which are replaced by measures in the Fresh Meat (Beef Controls) Regulations (Northern Ireland) 1996 (SR 1996 404).

6166. Food safety–bread and flour

BREAD AND FLOUR REGULATIONS (NORTHERN IRELAND) 1996, SR 1996 51; made under the Food Safety (Northern Ireland) Order 1991 Art.15(1)(a), Art.15(1)(e), Art.15(1)(f), Art.16(1), Art.25(1)(a)(3), Art.26(3), Art.47(2). In force: April 22, 1996; £2.80.

These Regulations replace, with amendments, and revoke the Bread and Flour Regulations (Northern Ireland) 1996 (SR 1984 406).

6167. Food safety–bread and flour

BREAD AND FLOUR (AMENDMENT) REGULATIONS (NORTHERN IRELAND) 1996, SR 1996 385; made under the Food Safety (Northern Ireland) Order 1991 Art.15(1)(a)(e)(f), Art.16(1), Art.25(1)(a)(3), Art.26(3), Art.47(2). In force: October 1, 1996; £1.10.

These Regulations amend the Bread and Flour Regulations (Northern Ireland) 1996 (SR 1996 51) by inserting a definition and amending another, by providing more clearly that bread and flour lawfully produced in one Member State and brought into Northern Ireland from another Member State where it was lawfully bought are exempt from those Regulations and by removing a prohibition and restrictions on the use of enzyme preparations as ingredients of flour and bread.

6168. Food safety–dairy products

CHEESE AND CREAM REGULATIONS (NORTHERN IRELAND) 1996, SR 1996 52; made under the Food Safety (Northern Ireland) Order 1991 Art.15(1)(a), Art.15(1)(e), Art.15(1)(f), Art.16, Art.25(1)(3), Art.26(3), Art.47(2). In force: April 22, 1996; £1.95.

These Regulations replace, with amendments, and revoke the Cheese Regulations (Northern Ireland) 1970 (SR & O (NI) 1970 14), the Cream Regulations (Northern Ireland) 1970 (SR & O (NI) 1970 194), the Cheese (Amendment) Regulations (Northern Ireland) 1974 (SR 1974 177), the Cream (Amendment) Regulations (Northern Ireland) 1976 (SR 1976 15), and the Cheese (Amendment) Regulations (Northern Ireland) 1984 (SR 1984 352).

6169. Food safety–fisheries

FOOD SAFETY (FISHERY PRODUCTS AND LIVE BIVALVE MOLLUSCS AND OTHER SHELLFISH) (MISCELLANEOUS AMENDMENTS) REGULATIONS (NORTHERN IRELAND) 1996, SR 1996 264; made under the European Communities Act 1972 s.2(2); and the Food Safety (Northern Ireland) Order 1991 Art.15(1), Art.16(1), Art.25(3), Art.26(3), Art.47(2), Art.48(2). In force: August 12, 1996; £2.80.

These Regulations amend various Regulations. The majority of the amendments implement Commission Decisions concerning the import conditions for fishery products and live bivalve molluscs and other shellfish from specified countries outside the European Economic Area.

6170. Food safety–food hygiene

FOOD SAFETY (GENERAL FOOD HYGIENE) (AMENDMENT) REGULATIONS (NORTHERN IRELAND) 1996, SR 1996 286; made under the Food Safety (Northern Ireland) Order 1991 Art.15(1), Art.16(1), Art.25(1)(3), Art.47(2). In force: August 25, 1996; £1.10.

These Regulations amend the Food Safety (General Food Hygiene) Regulations (Northern Ireland) 1995 (SR 1995 360) so that they apply to a person carrying on the handling in or sale from any catering establishment or shop premises of ice-cream or heat-treated cream.

6171. Food safety–labelling

FOOD LABELLING REGULATIONS (NORTHERN IRELAND) 1996, SR 1996 383; made under the Food Safety (Northern Ireland) Order 1991 Art.15(1)(e)(f), Art.16(1), Art.25(1)(3), Art.26(3), Art.47(2). In force: October 1, 1996; £8.40.

These Regulations replace with amendments, and revoke, the Food Labelling Regulations (Northern Ireland) 1984 (SR 1984 407), as amended and continue to implement Council Directive 79/112 ([1979] OJ L33/8) on the approximation of the laws of the Member States relating to labelling, presentation and advertising of foodstuffs (apart from its provisions relating to net quantity). They also implement Commission Directive 87/250 ([1987] OJ L113/57) on the indication of alcoholic strength by volume in the labelling of alcoholic beverages for sale to the ultimate consumer, implement Council Directive 89/398 ([1989] OJ L186/27) on the approximation of the laws of the Member States relating to foodstuffs intended for particular nutritional uses, implement Council Directive 90/496 ([1990] OJ L276/40) on nutrition labelling for foodstuffs and implement Commission Directive 94/54 ([1994] OJ L300/14) as amended, concerning the compulsory indication on the labelling of certain foodstuffs of particulars other than those provided for in Council Directive 79/112.

6172. Food safety–labelling

FOOD (LOT MARKING) REGULATIONS (NORTHERN IRELAND) 1996, SR 1996 384; made under the Food Safety (Northern Ireland) Order 1991 Art.15(1)(e), Art.16(1), Art.25(1)(a)(3), Art.26(3), Art.47(2). In force: October 1, 1996; £1.10.

These Regulations replace with amendments, and revoke, the Food (Lot Marking) Regulations (Northern Ireland) 1992 (SR 1992 281). Like those Regulations, they implement Council Directive 89/396 ([1989] OJ L186/21) as amended by Council Directive 91/238 ([1991] OJ L107/50) and Council Directive 92/11 ([1992] OJ L65/32). They continue the previous requirements that food which has been produced, prepared or packaged as part of a lot is to be so marked or labelled as to enable the lot to be identified.

6173. Food safety–marketing–standards

SPREADABLE FATS (MARKETING STANDARDS) REGULATIONS (NORTHERN IRELAND) 1996, SR 1996 47; made under the Food Safety (Northern Ireland) Order 1991 Art.15(1), Art.16(2), Art.25(1)(3), Art.26(3), Art.47(2). In force: April 22, 1996; £1.95.

These Regulations provide for the enforcement of Council Regulation 2991/94 ([1994] OJ L316/2) laying down standards for spreadable fats.

6174. Food safety–plastics–contact with foodstuffs

PLASTIC MATERIALS AND ARTICLES IN CONTACT WITH FOOD (AMENDMENT) REGULATIONS (NORTHERN IRELAND) 1996, SR 1996 164; made under the European Communities Act 1972 s.2(2); and the Food Safety (Northern Ireland) Order 1991 Art.15(2), Art.16(1), Art.25(1)(a)(3), Art.26(3), Art.32, Art.47(2). In force: June 3, 1996; £3.20.

These Regulations implement Council Directive 95/3 ([1995] OJ L41/1), amending Directive 90/128 ([1990 OJ L75/19) to be read with corrigendum ([1990] OJ L349) relating to plastic materials and articles intended to come into contact with foodstuffs.

6175. Food safety–plastics–contact with foodstuffs

PLASTIC MATERIALS AND ARTICLES IN CONTACT WITH FOOD (AMENDMENT NO.2) REGULATIONS (NORTHERN IRELAND) 1996, SR 1996 580; made under the European Communities Act 1972 s.2(2); and the Food Safety (Northern Ireland) Order 1991 Art.15(2), Art.16(1), Art.25(1)(a)(3), Art.26(3), Art.32, Art.47(2). In force: January 29, 1997; £2.80.

These Regulations further amend the Plastic Materials and Articles in Contact with Food Regulations (Northern Ireland) 1993 (SR 1993 173) and implement European legislation relating to plastics intended to come into contact with food.

6176. Food safety–premises–improvement notices–enforcement

DEREGULATION (IMPROVEMENT OF ENFORCEMENT PROCEDURES) (FOOD SAFETY) ORDER (NORTHERN IRELAND) 1996, SR 1996 579; made under the

Food Safety (Northern Ireland) Order 1996 Art.9(1)(4), Sch.1 para.3. In force: February 10, 1997; £1.10.

This Order improves enforcement procedures under the Food Safety (Northern Ireland) Order 1991 (SI 1991 762 (NI 7)). Before an authorised officer serves an improvement notice on the proprietor of a food business under the 1991 Order, the officer must give the proprietor a written notice stating that the officer is considering serving an improvement notice, the reasons for this and that the proprietor has the right to make representations; and any representations made and not withdrawn must be considered.

6177. Food safety–revocations

FOOD (MISCELLANEOUS REVOCATIONS AND AMENDMENTS) REGULATIONS (NORTHERN IRELAND) 1996, SR 1996 53; made under the Food Safety (Northern Ireland) Order 1991 Art.15(1), Art.15(2), Art.15(3), Art.16, Art.25(1)(a), Art.25(2)(e), Art.25(3), Art.26(3), Art.32, Art.47(2), Sch.1 para.5; and the European Communities Act 1972 s.2(2). In force: April 22, 1996; £1.95.

These Regulations revoke the Skimmed Milk with Non-Milk Fat Regulations (Northern Ireland) 1961 (SR&O (NI) 1961 190), the Soft Drinks Regulations (Northern Ireland) 1976 (SR&O (NI) 1976 357) and partly revoke the Ice-Cream and Other Frozen Confections Regulations (Northern Ireland) 1968 (SR&O (NI) 1968 13), which relate to labelling and advertising. They make amendments to other Regulations in relation to the use of descriptions of various dairy products and in relation to warnings on certain products regarding their unfitness as food for babies.

6178. Food Safety (Amendment) (Northern Ireland) Order 1996 (SI 1996 1633 (NI 12))

This Order, which came into operation on August 27, 1996, makes miscellaneous amendments to the Food Safety (Northern Ireland) Order 1991 (SI 1991 762 (NI 7)). The principal amendments extend the provisions of that Order to enable the Department of Agriculture to exercise functions under that Order in relation to all foods for which it has responsibility.

GOVERNMENT ADMINISTRATION

6179. Public Record Office–fees–management

PUBLIC USE OF THE RECORDS (MANAGEMENT AND FEES) RULES (NORTHERN IRELAND) 1996, SR 1996 38; made under the Public Records Act (Northern Ireland) 1923 s.9; and the Northern Ireland Act 1974 Sch.1 para.2(1). In force: April 1, 1996; £1.95.

These Rules deal with admission to the Public Record Office and payment of fees for the use of the Northern Ireland records and replace the Public Record Office (Public Use of the Records) Rules (Northern Ireland) 1992 (SR 1992 72) and the Public Use of the Records (Amendment) Rules (Northern Ireland) 1995 (SR 1995 123).

HEALTH AND SAFETY AT WORK

6180. Construction industry

CONSTRUCTION (HEALTH, SAFETY AND WELFARE) REGULATIONS (NORTHERN IRELAND) 1996, SR 1996 510; made under the Health and Safety at Work (Northern Ireland) Order 1978 Art.17(1)(2)(3(5), Art.20(2), Art.55(2), Sch.3 para.1(1)(2), Sch.3 para.6, Sch.3 para.8, Sch.3 para.9, Sch.3 para.10,

Sch.3 para.11, Sch.3 para.13, Sch.3 para.15, Sch.3 para.17(a). In force: January 6, 1997; £5.80.

These Regulations impose requirements with respect to the health, safety and welfare of persons carrying out construction work and of others who may be affected by that work. They implement Council Directive 92/57 ([1992] OJ L245/6) on the implementation of minimum safety and health requirements at temporary or mobile construction sites.

6181. Employees

HEALTH AND SAFETY (CONSULTATION WITH EMPLOYEES) REGULATIONS (NORTHERN IRELAND) 1996, SR 1996 511; made under the European Communities Act 1972 s.2(2). In force: January 1, 1997; £2.80.

These Regulations provide for further implementation of Council Directive 89/391 ([1989] OJ L183/1) on the introduction of measures to encourage improvements in the health and safety of employees at work. They require employers to consult either their employees directly or representatives elected by them where there are employees not represented by safety representatives appointed by trade unions.

6182. Employees–information

HEALTH AND SAFETY INFORMATION FOR EMPLOYEES (AMENDMENTS AND REPEALS) REGULATIONS (NORTHERN IRELAND) 1996, SR 1996 512; made under the Health and Safety at Work (Northern Ireland) Order 1978 Art.17(1)(2)(3)(4), Art.55(2), Sch.3 para.14(1). In force: Reg.2(a): January 1, 1998; Reg.3(2) so far as it relates to Construction (Lifting Operations) Regulations (Northern Ireland) 1963: January 1, 1997; Remainder: December 12, 1996; £1.95.

These Regulations amend the Health and Safety Information for Employees Regulations (Northern Ireland) 1991 (SR 1991 105) so as to specify premises and activities within United Kingdom territorial waters adjacent to Northern Ireland to which those Regulations apply and to add provisions enabling the Department of Economic Development to approve posters or leaflets which are specific to particular classes of employment so that employers in those classes may display or provide them.

6183. Equipment–explosives–components

EQUIPMENT AND PROTECTIVE SYSTEMS INTENDED FOR USE IN POTENTIALLY EXPLOSIVE ATMOSPHERES REGULATIONS (NORTHERN IRELAND) 1996, SR 1996 247; made under the European Communities Act 1972 s.2(2). In force: July 29, 1996; £7.05.

These Regulations implement the European Parliament and Council Directive 94/9 ([1994] OJ L100/1) on the approximation of the laws of the Member States concerning equipment and protective systems intended for use in potentially explosive atmospheres.

6184. Explosives

MARKING OF PLASTIC EXPLOSIVE FOR DETECTION REGULATIONS (NORTHERN IRELAND) 1996, SR 1996 262; made under the Health and Safety at Work (Northern Ireland) Order 1978 Art.17(1)(2), Art.55(2), Sch.3 para.1(1)(b). In force: on a day to be notified in the Belfast Gazette or July 31, 1997, whichever is the earlier; £1.55.

These Regulations implement the Convention on the Marking of Plastic Explosives for the purpose of Detection, done at Montreal on March 1, 1991. They provide for ensuring that plastic explosives are marked in such a way that they are detectable.

6185. Fees

HEALTH AND SAFETY (MISCELLANEOUS FEES AMENDMENT) REGULATIONS (NORTHERN IRELAND) 1996, SR 1996 159; made under the Health and Safety at Work Act 1978 Art.40(2)(4). In force: May 20, 1996; £1.95.

These Regulations amend the Road Traffic (Training of Drivers of Vehicles Carrying Dangerous Goods) Regulations (Northern Ireland) 1992 (SR 1992 262) to increase the fee for the issue of a vocational training certificate, the Notification of New Substances Regulations (Northern Ireland) 1994 (SR 1994 6) to increase certain fees payable by notifiers of new substances and the Genetically Modified Organisms (Contained Use) Regulations (Northern Ireland) 1994 (SR 1994 143) to reduce fees payable by notifiers in relation to the notification of the use of premises and of individual activities involving genetic modification.

6186. Hazardous substances

HEALTH AND SAFETY AT WORK ORDER (APPLICATION TO ENVIRONMENTALLY HAZARDOUS SUBSTANCES) REGULATIONS (NORTHERN IRELAND) 1996, SR 1996 525; made under the European Communities Act 1972 s.2(2). In force: December 16, 1996; £1.10.

These Regulations extend the reference to dangerous substances in the Health and Safety at Work (Northern Ireland) Order 1978 Art.3(1)(c) to include environmentally hazardous substances.

6187. Medical treatment–equipment

HEALTH AND SAFETY (MEDICAL DEVICES) REGULATIONS (NORTHERN IRELAND) 1996, SR 1996 109; made under the Health and Safety at Work (Northern Ireland) Order 1978 Art.17(1)(2)(3)(5), Art.55(2), Sch.3 para.1 (1)(2)(3), Sch.3 para.10, Sch.3 para.12(1), Sch.3 para.13. In force: April 29, 1996; £1.10.

These Regulations amend lists of Directives in the Provision and Use of Work Equipment Regulations (Northern Ireland) 1993 (SR 1993 19) and the Personal Protective Equipment at Work Regulations (Northern Ireland) 1993 (SR 1993 20)

6188. Medical treatment–fees

HEALTH AND SAFETY (MEDICAL FEES) REGULATIONS (NORTHERN IRELAND) 1996, SR 1996 14; made under the Health and Safety at Work (Northern Ireland) Order 1978 Art.49, Art.55. In force: March 4, 1996; £1.55.

These Regulations fix fees for work done under specified Regulations by employment medical advisers.

6189. Offshore and Pipelines, Safety (Northern Ireland) Order 1992–Commencement No.2 Order

OFFSHORE AND PIPELINES, SAFETY (1992 ORDER) (COMMENCEMENT NO.2) ORDER (NORTHERN IRELAND) 1996, SR 1996 251 (C.11); made under the Northern Ireland Act 1974 Sch.1 para.2(1); and the Offshore and Pipelines, Safety (Northern Ireland) Order 1992 Art.1(3). In force: bringing into force various provisions of the Order on July 14, 1996; £0.65.

This Order brings Art.4(3) of the 1992 Order into operation on July 14, 1996.

6190. Petrol–licences–fees

HEALTH AND SAFETY (PETROLEUM-SPIRIT LICENCE FEES) REGULATIONS (NORTHERN IRELAND) 1995, SR 1995 490; made under the Health and Safety at

Work (Northern Ireland) Order 1978 Art.40(2)(3). In force: February 12, 1996; £1.10.

These Regulations, which revoke the Health and Safety (Petroleum-Spirit Licence Fees) Regulations (Northern Ireland) 1994 (SR 1994 260) increase fees in relation to petroleum-spirit licences.

6191. Repeals

HEALTH AND SAFETY (REPEALS AND REVOCATIONS) REGULATIONS (NORTHERN IRELAND) 1996, SR 1996 21; made under the Deregulation and Contracting Out Act 1994 s.37(1)(c). In force: April 1, 1996; £1.10.

These Regulations repeal the Hours of Employment (Conventions) Act 1935 and the Factories Act (Northern Ireland) 1965 Part VIII and revoke certain orders relating to home work.

6192. Safety–information

HEALTH AND SAFETY (SAFETY SIGNS AND SIGNALS) REGULATIONS (NORTHERN IRELAND) 1996, SR 1996 119; made under the Health and Safety at Work (Northern Ireland) Order 1978 Art.17, Art.55, Sch.3 para.1, Sch.3 para.8, Sch.3 para.11, Sch.3 para.13, Sch.3 para.17. In force: May 1, 1996; £4.15.

These Regulations amend the Offshore Installations (Operational Safety, Health and Welfare) Regulations 1976 (SI 1976 1019), the Noise at Work Regulations (Northern Ireland) 1990 (SR 1990 147), and the Dangerous Substances (Notification and Marking of Sites) Regulations (Northern Ireland) 1992 (SR 1992 71) and revoke the Safety Signs Regulations (Northern Ireland) 1981 (SR 1981 352). They impose requirements in relation to the provision and use of safety signs and signals and implement as respects Northern Ireland Council Directive 92/58 ([1992] OJ L245/23) on the minimum requirements for the provision of safety and/or health signs at work. The Regulations do not apply to signs used in relation to the supply of equipment or substances, for the transport of dangerous goods and for the regulation of transport. Safety signs are required to comply with the descriptions in Sch.1 to the Regulations. They must be provided where the required risk assessment indicates that the risk cannot be avoided or adequately controlled in other ways. Fire safety signs must also be provided where they are required to comply with the provisions of any statutory provision. Employees must receive adequate instruction and training in the meaning of safety signs and the measures to be taken in connection with safety signs.

HOUSING

6193. Assured tenancies–investment trusts–tax relief

HOUSING INVESTMENT TRUSTS (ASSURED TENANCIES) REGULATIONS (NORTHERN IRELAND) 1996, SR 1996 537; made under the Income and Corporation Taxes Act 1988 s.508B(7). In force: January 13, 1997; £1.10.

The Income and Corporation Taxes Act 1988 s.508A and s.508B make provision conferring relief from corporation tax on companies that invest in housing. Under the scheme relief from corporation tax will be afforded to a company that is an investment trust and has eligible rental income deriving from lettings by the company of eligible properties let on assured tenancies. These Regulations prescribe the requirements and conditions with which a tenancy of a dwelling-house in Northern Ireland must comply if it is to be an "assured tenancy" within the meaning of the above-noted sections.

6194. Homelessness–immigrants. See HOUSING. §3044

6195. Renovation grants

HOUSING RENOVATION ETC. GRANTS (GRANT LIMIT) ORDER (NORTHERN IRELAND) 1996, SR 1996 148; made under the Housing (Northern Ireland) Order 1992 Art.54(5). In force: May 13, 1996; £0.65.

This Order revokes the Housing Renovation etc. Grants (Grant Limit) Order (Northern Ireland) 1993 (SR 1993 82), and provides new maximum limits on the amount of grant which the Northern Ireland Housing Executive may pay in respect of an application for renovation grant, disabled facilities grant, common parts grant and HMO grant (as defined in the Housing (Northern Ireland) Order 1992 (SI 1992 1725 (NI 15)) Art.39(2)(d)).

6196. Renovation grants

REPAIRS GRANTS (APPROPRIATE PERCENTAGE) ORDER (NORTHERN IRELAND) 1996, SR 1996 387; made under the Housing (Northern Ireland) Order 1992 Art.74(3), Sch.3 para.4(3). In force: September 30, 1996; £1.10.

This Order amends the Housing (Northern Ireland) Order 1992 (SI 1992 1725 (NI 15)) Sch.3 para.4(2) by substituting a sliding scale of percentages (75, 50 and 25 per cent to be determined by reference to the net annual value) for cases not falling within the 1992 Order Sch.3 para.4(2)(a) to para.4(2)(c).

6197. Renovation grants–expenses

REPAIRS GRANTS (ELIGIBLE EXPENSE) ORDER (NORTHERN IRELAND) 1996, SR 1996 147; made under the Housing (Northern Ireland) Order 1992 Art.74(3), Sch.3 para.3(2). In force: May 1, 1996; £0.65.

This Order reduces to £500 the maximum amount of eligible expenses for the purposes of certain applications for repairs grants by owner occupiers.

6198. Renovation grants–reduction

HOUSING RENOVATION ETC. GRANTS (REDUCTION OF GRANT) (AMENDMENT) REGULATIONS (NORTHERN IRELAND) 1996, SR 1996 110; made under the Housing (Northern Ireland) Order 1992 Art.47. In force: April 19, 1996; £3.70.

These Regulations further amend the Housing Renovation etc. Grants (Reduction of Grant) Regulations (Northern Ireland) 1992 (SR 1992 412). The principal changes include amendments to various definitions; an increase to the multipliers used in the assessment of the amount by which a grant is reduced in certain circumstances; a provision that average weekly child care charges must be deducted in determining a person's weekly income; provision for the calculation of weekly earnings of self-employed persons whose earnings fluctuate; and amendments to provisions in respect of income and capital to be disregarded.

INHERITANCE TAX

6199. Accounts. See INHERITANCE TAX. §3427

INSOLVENCY

6200. Companies–directors–disqualification

INSOLVENT COMPANIES (DISQUALIFICATION OF UNFIT DIRECTORS) PROCEEDINGS (AMENDMENT) RULES (NORTHERN IRELAND) 1996, SR 1996 471; made under the Insolvency (Northern Ireland) Order 1989 Art.359; and the Companies (Northern Ireland) Order 1989 Art.24(1). In force: December 1, 1996; £0.65.

These Rules amend the Insolvent Companies (Disqualification of Unfit Directors) Proceedings Rules (Northern Ireland) 1991 (SR 1991 367) as respects the time limit for appealing from orders or decisions of the Master (Bankruptcy) in proceedings for the disqualification of directors under the Companies (Northern Ireland) Order 1989 (SI 1989 2404) Art.10 and Art.11.

6201. Deeds of arrangement

DEEDS OF ARRANGEMENT REGULATIONS (NORTHERN IRELAND) 1996, SR 1996 575; made under the Insolvency (Northern Ireland) Order 1989 Art.212(h), Art.222(1)(a)(2). In force: January 31, 1997; £3.70.

These Regulations re-enact provisions relating to deeds of arrangement formerly contained in the Insolvency Regulations (Northern Ireland) 1991 (SR 1991 388) which were revoked by the Insolvency Regulations (Northern Ireland) 1996 (SR 1996 574). They prescribe the form of statement which sets out the trustee's accounts and proceedings under the deed of arrangement which must be sent to creditors who have assented to the deed and make provision for the submission by the trustee of his receipts and payments as a trustee. They also specify additional particulars to be recorded in the register of deeds.

6202. Fees

INSOLVENCY (FEES) (AMENDMENT) ORDER (NORTHERN IRELAND) 1996, SR 1996 576; made under the Insolvency (Northern Ireland) Order 1989 Art.361(1)(3)(4). In force: January 31, 1997; £1.10.

This Order further amends the Insolvency (Fees) Order (Northern Ireland) 1991 (SR 1991 385). A new provision limits the fees payable for functions carried out by the official receiver as receiver and manager and by the Department of Economic Development where the bankruptcy debts and expenses are paid in full or are secured to the satisfaction of the High Court. The fee payable by the official receiver to an insolvency practitioner appointed by the High Court to prepare and submit a report under the Insolvency (Northern Ireland) Order 1989 (SI 1989 2405 (NI 19)) is increased from £135 to £250.

6203. Partnerships–winding up petitions

INSOLVENT PARTNERSHIPS (AMENDMENT) ORDER (NORTHERN IRELAND) 1996, SR 1996 472; made under the Insolvency (Northern Ireland) Order 1989 Art.364; and the Companies (Northern Ireland) Order 1989 Art.24(1). In force: December 1, 1996; £1.10.

These Rules amend the Insolvent Partnerships Order (Northern Ireland) 1995 (SR 1995 225) to extend the list of persons who may petition for the winding up of an insolvent partnership as an unregistered company to include any person other than a member.

6204. Petitions–deposits

INSOLVENCY (DEPOSITS) (AMENDMENT) ORDER (NORTHERN IRELAND) 1996, SR 1996 577; made under the Insolvency (Northern Ireland) Order 1989 Art.361 (2)(3). In force: January 31, 1997; £0.65.

This Order amends the Insolvency (Deposits) Order (Northern Ireland) 1991 (SR 1991 384) by increasing the deposits payable to the Official Receiver on presentation of a bankruptcy petition to £300, on presentation of a winding up petition to £500 and on presentation of an individual's own bankruptcy petition to £250.

6205. Receivers–liability for costs when defending insolvent company in action

H, receiver to Hub Leisure Ltd, the defendant in an action brought by A, took over the defence and continued the action. Judgment was awarded in favour of A but costs were awarded against the insolvent company only, which had no assets available for unsecured creditors, and not against the receiver. A appealed on the grounds that a liquidator would have been liable for costs if he had taken over the defence, and that a receiver would have been liable if he had taken over an action in which the insolvent company was plaintiff. H resisted on the grounds that A was not entitled to be placed in a better position than the insolvent company's other unsecured creditors.

Held, allowing the appeal, that (1) the receiver who carried on the insolvent company's defence should be liable to costs in the same way a liquidator would have been liable, *Wenborn and Co, Re* [1905] 1 Ch. 413 followed; (2) authority on receivers who continued actions commenced by the debtors could not be distinguished, *Racal Communications Ltd, Re* [1981] A.C. 374 considered, and (3) to allow the receiver to defend on the basis that even if successful the plaintiff would be unable to recover costs would be unjust and inequitable. The effect of a costs order against the receiver would be that A's costs would be paid as an expense of the receivership.

ANDERSON v. HYDE (T/A HYDE PROPERTY SERVICES), February 23, 1996, Carswell, L.J., CA (NI). [*Ex rel.* EJ David McBrien, Barrister].

6206. Regulations

INSOLVENCY REGULATIONS (NORTHERN IRELAND) 1996, SR 1996 574; made under the Insolvency (Northern Ireland) Order 1989 Art.359, Sch.5 para.27, Sch.6 para.28; and the Insolvency Rules (Northern Ireland) 1991 r.12.01. In force: January 31, 1997; £5.80.

These Regulations replace the Insolvency Regulations (Northern Ireland) 1991 (SR 1991 388) and provide for a less onerous regime in respect of administrative matters that were covered by the 1991 Regulations.

LANDLORD AND TENANT

6207. Business Tenancies (Northern Ireland) Order 1996 (SI 1996 725 (NI 5))

This Order, which comes into force on a day to be appointed, repeals and re-enacts with amendments the Business Tenancies Act (Northern Ireland) 1964. It gives effect to recommendations of the Law Reform Advisory Committee for Northern Ireland (Report No.1 on Business Tenancies, LRAC No. 2, 1994).

6208. Rent–registered rents–increase

REGISTERED RENTS (INCREASE) ORDER (NORTHERN IRELAND) 1996, SR 1996 25; made under the Rent (Northern Ireland) Order 1978 Art.33(2). In force: March 4, 1996; £0.65.

This Order increases rents of regulated tenancies registered under the Rent (Northern Ireland) Order 1978 (SI 1978 1050 (NI 20)) Part V by 2.75 per cent.

LEGAL AID

6209. Assessment of resources

LEGAL AID (ASSESSMENT OF RESOURCES) (AMENDMENT) REGULATIONS (NORTHERN IRELAND) 1996, SR 1996 410; made under the Legal Aid, Advice and Assistance (Northern Ireland) Order 1981 Art.14, Art.22, Art.27. In force: October 7, 1996; £1.10.

These Regulations amend the Legal Aid (Assessment of Resources) Regulations (Northern Ireland) 1981 (SR 1981 189) by providing that the income and capital of persons receiving an income based jobseeker's allowance are to be taken not to exceed the prescribed contribution limit and that any back to work bonus treated as payable by way of jobseeker's allowance is excluded from the computation of income and capital.

6210. Children

LEGAL AID, ADVICE AND ASSISTANCE (AMENDMENT) ORDER (NORTHERN IRELAND) 1996, SR 1996 482; made under the Children (Northern Ireland) Order 1981 Art.172(4). In force: November 4, 1996; £0.65.

This Order amends the Legal Aid, Advice and Assistance (Northern Ireland) Order 1981 (SI 1981 228 (NI 18)) to exclude Art.10(5B), (5C) and (5E) (mandatory grant of legal aid in relation to children in certain cases) where the proceedings are before a court of summary jurisdiction and where assistance by way of representation has been granted and to provide that legal aid must be granted irrespective of the means test for appeals against orders under the Children (Northern Ireland) Order 1995 (SI 1995 755 (NI 2)) in certain circumstances.

6211. Criminal procedure–costs

LEGAL AID IN CRIMINAL PROCEEDINGS (COSTS) (AMENDMENT) RULES (NORTHERN IRELAND) 1996, SR 1996 222; made under the Legal Aid, Advice and Assistance (Northern Ireland) Order 1981 Art.36(3). In force: June 29, 1996; £1.95.

These Rules amend the Legal Aid in Criminal Proceedings (Costs) Rules (Northern Ireland) 1992 (SR 1992 314) by increasing the rates of remuneration for certain legal aid work in criminal proceedings done on or after June 30, 1996. They also alter to June 30, 1997, the date after which certain work may be remunerated at discretionary instead of prescribed rates.

6212. Income–conditions

LEGAL AID (FINANCIAL CONDITIONS) REGULATIONS (NORTHERN IRELAND) 1996, SR 1996 97; made under the Legal Aid, Advice and Assistance (Northern Ireland) Order 1981 Art.9(2), Art.12(2), Art.22, Art.27. In force: April 8, 1996; £1.10.

These Regulations amend the Legal Aid, Advice and Assistance (Northern Ireland) Order 1981 (SI 1981 228 (NI 8)) so as to increase the upper income limit to make legal aid available to those with disposable incomes of not more than £7,403 or in connection with proceedings involving a personal injury £8,158 and increase the lower income limit below which legal aid is available without payment of a contribution to £2,498. They revoke the Legal Aid (Financial Conditions) Regulations (Northern Ireland) 1995 (SR 1995 77) with savings.

6213. Legal advice–assistance

LEGAL ADVICE AND ASSISTANCE (AMENDMENT) REGULATIONS (NORTHERN IRELAND) 1996, SR 1996 98; made under the Legal Aid, Advice and Assistance (Northern Ireland) Order 1981 Art.7(2), Art.22, Art.27. In force: April 8, 1996; £1.10.

These Regulations amend the Legal Advice and Assistance Regulations (Northern Ireland) 1981 (SR 1981 366) so as to substitute a new scale of contributions payable for legal advice and assistance under the Legal Aid, Advice and Assistance (Northern Ireland) Order 1981 (SI 1981 228 (NI 8)) Art.7(2) and revoke the Legal Advice and Assistance (Amendment) Regulations (Northern Ireland) 1995 (SR 1995 76).

6214. Legal advice–assistance

LEGAL ADVICE AND ASSISTANCE (AMENDMENT NO.2) REGULATIONS (NORTHERN IRELAND) 1996, SR 1996 411; made under the Legal Aid, Advice and Assistance (Northern Ireland) Order 1981 Art.14, Art.22, Art.27. In force: October 7, 1996; £1.10.

These Regulations amend the Legal Advice and Assistance Regulations (Northern Ireland) 1981 (SR 1981 366) by providing that persons receiving income based jobseeker's allowance, when applying for advice and assistance, must provide information showing they are receiving that benefit, that solicitors need not determine the disposable income of persons receiving income based jobseeker's allowance who apply for advice and assistance and that any back to work bonus treated as payable by way of jobseeker's allowance is excluded from the computation of income and capital.

6215. Legal advice–assistance

LEGAL ADVICE AND ASSISTANCE (AMENDMENT NO.3) REGULATIONS (NORTHERN IRELAND) 1996, SR 1996 483; made under the Legal Aid, Advice and Assistance (Northern Ireland) Order 1981 Art.5(3)(4A), Art.27. In force: November 4, 1996; £1.10.

These Regulations amend the Legal Advice and Assistance Regulations (Northern Ireland) 1981 (SR 1981 366) in relation to proceedings under the Children (Northern Ireland) Order 1995 (SI 1995 755 (NI 2)).

6216. Legal advice–costs

LEGAL ADVICE AND ASSISTANCE (PROSPECTIVE COST) REGULATIONS (NORTHERN IRELAND) 1996, SR 1996 205; made under the Legal Aid, Advice and Assistance (Northern Ireland) Order 1981 Art.6(2), Art.22, Art.27. In force: June 10, 1996; £0.65.

These Regulations revoke and replace the Legal Advice and Assistance (Prospective Cost) Regulations (Northern Ireland) 1992 (SR 1992 104) to increase to £88 the limit on the cost of legal advice and assistance provided under the Legal Aid, Advice and Assistance (Northern Ireland) Order 1981 (SI 1981 228 (NI 8)) Art.3 and Art.4 which solicitors may incur without obtaining the advice of the appropriate authority.

6217. Legal advice–income

LEGAL ADVICE AND ASSISTANCE (FINANCIAL CONDITIONS) REGULATIONS (NORTHERN IRELAND) 1996, SR 1996 96; made under the Legal Aid, Advice and Assistance (Northern Ireland) Order 1981 Art.3, Art.7, Art.22, Art.27. In force: April 8, 1996; £0.65.

These Regulations amend the Legal Aid, Advice and Assistance (Northern Ireland) Order 1981 (SI 1981 228 (NI 8)) so as to vary the upper and lower income limit affecting the availability of legal advice and assistance and revoke the Legal Advice and Assistance (Financial Conditions) Regulations (Northern Ireland) 1995 (SR 1995 75).

LEGAL SYSTEMS

6218. Books

Dickson, Brice–Digest of Northern Ireland Law. £99.00. ISBN 0-85389-586-4. SLS Legal Publications.

LICENSING

6219. Bookmakers–horse racing–charges

HORSE RACING (CHARGES ON BOOKMAKERS) ORDER (NORTHERN IRELAND) 1996, SR 1996 208; made under the Horse Racing (Northern Ireland) Order 1990 Art.9(1). In force: July 1, 1996; £1.10.

This Order, which revokes the Horse Racing (Charges on Bookmakers) Order (Northern Ireland) 1995 (SR 1995 198), increases the charges payable by those intending to apply for the grant or renewal of a bookmaker's licence from £61 to £80 and increases the charge payable by those intending to apply for the grant or renewal of a bookmaking office licence or to have the provisional grant of a bookmaking office licence declared final from £476 to £900.

6220. Gambling–bingo–increase in charges

GAMING (BINGO) (AMENDMENT) REGULATIONS (NORTHERN IRELAND) 1996, SR 1996 573; made under the Betting, Gaming, Lotteries and Amusements (Northern Ireland) Order 1985 Art.76(2). In force: January 27, 1997; £0.65.

These Regulations amend the Gaming (Bingo) Regulations (Northern Ireland) 1987 (SR 1987 8) by increasing the maximum charge which may be made in respect of gaming by way of bingo on bingo club premises from £6.60 to £8. The new reference to VAT does not indicate a change in the position on this tax but has been included for the purpose of clarification. The Gaming (Bingo) (Amendment) Regulations (Northern Ireland) 1995 (SR 1995 344) are revoked as a consequence of these Regulations.

6221. Gambling–prizes–increase in maximum amount

GAMING AND AMUSEMENTS WITH PRIZES (VARIATION OF MONETARY LIMITS) ORDER (NORTHERN IRELAND) 1996, SR 1996 572; made under the Betting, Gaming, Lotteries and Amusements (Northern Ireland) Order 1985 Art.75(2), Art.76(5), Art.77(4), Art.108(16), Art.154(7). In force: January 27, 1997; £1.10.

This Order increases the maximum permitted aggregate amount of winnings in respect of games of bingo played in one week simultaneously on different bingo club premises from £10,000 to £25,000; increases the maximum amount by which weekly winnings on bingo club premises may exceed the stakes hazarded from £2,500 to £5,000; increases, in any one determination of winners in gaming for prizes on bingo club premises, the maximum permitted aggregate amount taken by way of the sale of chances from £27.50 to £30 and the maximum permitted aggregate amount or value of prizes from £27.50 to £30; increases the maximum entitlement to prizes in gaming by means of a gaming machine installed on licensed premises (within the meaning of the Licensing (Northern Ireland) Order 1990) from £8 to £10; increases the maximum permitted aggregate amount taken by way of the sale of chances in any one determination of winners in amusements with prizes at certain commercial entertainments from £25 to £30.

6222. Licensing (Northern Ireland) Order 1996 (SI 1996 3158 (NI 22))

This Order, which comes into force on February 20, 1997, consolidates with amendments the law relating to licences for the sale by retail of intoxicating liquor.

6223. Registration of Clubs (Northern Ireland) Order 1996 (SI 1996 3159 (NI 23))

This Order, which comes into force on days to be appointed, consolidates with amendments the law relating to the registration of clubs.

LOCAL GOVERNMENT

6224. Fire service–employees–promotion examinations

FIRE SERVICES (APPOINTMENTS AND PROMOTION) (AMENDMENT) REGULATIONS (NORTHERN IRELAND) 1996, SR 1996 491; made under the Fire Services (Northern Ireland) Order 1984 Art.9(5). In force: November 25, 1996; £0.65.

These Regulations amend the Fire Services (Appointments and Promotion) Regulations (Northern Ireland) 1979 (SR 1979 167) in relation to promotion examinations.

6225. Local government finance–general grant

LOCAL GOVERNMENT (GENERAL GRANT) ORDER (NORTHERN IRELAND) 1996, SR 1996 189; made under the Local Government etc. (Northern Ireland) Order 1972 Sch.1 Part.1 para.3(1). In force: June 21, 1996; £0.65.

This Order specifies districts to be taken into account in calculating the standard rate product for the year ending March 31, 1997, when computing the resources element of the grant made from central funds to district councils.

MEDICINE

6226. Pharmacists–qualifications

PHARMACEUTICAL QUALIFICATIONS (RECOGNITION) REGULATIONS (NORTHERN IRELAND) 1996, SR 1996 393; made under the European Communities Act 1972 s.2(2). In force: September 28, 1996; £1.10.

These Regulations amend the Pharmacy (Northern Ireland) Order 1976 (SI 1976 1213 (NI 22)). Article 8A is amended to apply para.(1) to persons who are not nationals of a Member State so far as necessary to enable a right under Council Regulation 1612/68 ([1968] OJ L257/2) (workers' families), or any other enforceable Community right, to be exercised. Article 8A is also amended by providing for further qualifications to be regarded as appropriate European diplomas for the purposes of Art.8A, so as to implement Council Directive 85/433 ([1985] OJ L253/37), Art.6(2) and Art.6a, inserted by Council Directive 90/658 ([1990] OJ L353/73) Art.7(2)(3) and as respects the definition of competent authorities. Part of the entry relating to Germany in Sch.2A is repealed.

6227. Pharmacists–society

PHARMACEUTICAL SOCIETY OF NORTHERN IRELAND (GENERAL) (AMENDMENT) REGULATIONS (NORTHERN IRELAND) 1996, SR 1996 187; made under the Pharmacy (Northern Ireland) Order 1976 Art.5. In force: June 1, 1996; £1.10.

These Regulations amend the Pharmaceutical Society of Northern Ireland (General) Regulations (Northern Ireland) 1994 (SR 1994 202) by: increasing fees in respect of registration as a pharmaceutical chemist and as a student;

increasing fees in respect of restoration of a person's name to the register; increasing retention fees payable in respect of members of the Society; increasing penalties for default in payment of retention fees; and increasing fees for the issue of a further certificate of registration where original certificate is lost or destroyed.

NATIONAL HEALTH SERVICE

6228. Consultants–appointment

APPOINTMENT OF CONSULTANTS REGULATIONS (NORTHERN IRELAND) 1996, SR 1996 562; made under the Health and Personal Social Services (Northern Ireland) Order 1972 Art.16(3), Art.89(1), Art.106(b), Art.107(6), Sch.1 para.12(2). In force: January 1, 1997; £2.80.

These Regulations prescribe the procedure relating to the appointment of consultants; provide for the constitution of Advisory Appointments Committees; and provide that specified appointments shall be exempted from the requirements of the Regulations. They also revoke the Appointments of Consultants Regulations (Northern Ireland) 1992 (SR 1992 472).

6229. Dental services

GENERAL DENTAL SERVICES (AMENDMENT) REGULATIONS (NORTHERN IRELAND) 1996, SR 1996 114; made under the Health and Personal Social Services (Northern Ireland) Order 1972 Art.61 (1) (2) (2AA), Art.106, Art.107(6), Sch.II Part I para.8E. In force: April 1, 1996; £1.55.

These Regulations further amend the Health and Personal Social Services General Dental Services Regulations (Northern Ireland) 1993 (the principal Regulations). Regulation 2 amends the dentist's terms of service contained in Sch.2 to the principal Regulations to require dentists to establish and operate a complaints procedure within their practice. Regulation 3 makes minor amendments to the terms of service in Sch.2 regarding computerised estimate forms and information to be displayed in practice premises.

6230. Dental services

GENERAL DENTAL SERVICES (AMENDMENT NO.2) REGULATIONS (NORTHERN IRELAND) 1996, SR 1996 382; made under the Health and Personal Social Services (Northern Ireland) Order 1972 Art.61 (1) (2) (2AA), Art.106, Art.107(6), Sch.11 Part I para.8E. In force: September 1, 1996; £1.10.

These Regulations amend the General Dental Services Regulations (Northern Ireland) 1993 (SR 1993 326) as respects care arrangements and continuing care arrangements.

6231. Dental services–charges

DENTAL CHARGES (AMENDMENT) REGULATIONS (NORTHERN IRELAND) 1996, SR 1996 106; made under the Health and Personal Social Services (Northern Ireland) Order 1972 Art.98, Art.106, Sch.15. In force: April 1, 1996; £1.10.

These Regulations further amend the Dental Charges Regulations (Northern Ireland) 1989 (SR 1989 111 as amended by SR 1995 83), which relate to charges for dental treatment provided and dental appliances supplied as part of health service general dental services. Regulation 2 amends Reg.4(5) of the 1989 Regulations to increase from £300 to £325 the maximum charge which a patient may be required to pay towards the cost of his treatment or appliance under general dental services. Regulation 4 provides that these new charges shall apply only where the arrangements for treatment or supply of a dental appliance are made on or after April 1, 1996.

6232. Doctors–fund holding practices

HEALTH AND PERSONAL SOCIAL SERVICES (FUND-HOLDING PRACTICES) AMENDMENT REGULATIONS (NORTHERN IRELAND) 1996, SR 1996 131; made under the Health and Personal Social Services (Northern Ireland) Order 1972 Art.90(7); and the Health and Personal Social Services (Northern Ireland) Order 1991 Art.17(2)(3), Art.18(4), Art.19, Art.20. In force: April 1, 1996; £2.80.

The Health and Personal Social Services (Fund-Holding Practices Regulations (Northern Ireland) 1993 (SR 1993 142), which regulate the recognition and operation of fund-holding practices, are amended by these Regulations as respects the withdrawal of members from practice, the application of accumulated savings, the amount which may be spent on the provision of goods and services to any on individual in any financial year, the use of allotted sums, payments of management allowances, and the purposes on which a fund-holding practice may spend savings and the size of practices.

6233. Drugs–appliances–charges

CHARGES FOR DRUGS AND APPLIANCES (AMENDMENT) REGULATIONS (NORTHERN IRELAND) 1996, SR 1996 112; made under the Health and Personal Social Services (Northern Ireland) Order 1972 Art.98, Art.106, Sch.15. In force: April 1, 1996; £1.10.

These Regulations further amend the Health and Personal Social Services (Charges for Drugs and Appliances) Regulations (Northern Ireland) 1973 (SR & O (NI) 1973 419), which provide for the making and recovery of charges for drugs and appliances supplied by doctors and chemists providing pharmaceutical services, and by hospitals and HSS Trusts to outpatients. The charge for each item on prescription is increased from £5.25 to £5.50. The sums prescribed for the grant of prepayment certificates of exemption from prescription charges are increased from £27.20 to £28.50 for a four month certificate and from £74.80 to £78.40 for a 12 month certificate. The charge for a partial human hair wig is increased from £115 to £120 and for a stock modacrylic wig from £44 to £46. The charge for a full bespoke human hair wig is increased from £167 to £175. The charge for a surgical brassiere is increased from £19 to £19.25 and for an abdominal or spinal support from £27 to £28.30. Transitional arrangements are made in respect of prepayment certificates and appliances ordered, before the coming into force of these Regulations.

6234. Expenses–travel charges

TRAVELLING EXPENSES AND REMISSION OF CHARGES (AMENDMENT) REGULATIONS (NORTHERN IRELAND) 1996, SR 1996 107; made under the Health and Personal Social Services (Northern Ireland) Order 1972 Art.45, Art.98, Art.106, Art.107(6), Sch.15 para.1 (b). In force: March 18, 1996; £3.20.

These Regulations further amend the Travelling Expenses and Remission of Charges Regulations (Northern Ireland) 1989 (SR 1989 348) which provide for the remission and repayment of certain charges which would otherwise be payable under the Health and Personal Social Services (Northern Ireland) Order 1972 (SI 1972 1265) and for the payment of travelling expenses incurred in attending hospital. They revoke the Health and Personal Social Services Travelling Expenses and Remission of Charges (Amendment No.2) Regulations (Northern Ireland) 1995 (SR 1995 361).

6235. Expenses–travel charges

TRAVELLING EXPENSES AND REMISSION OF CHARGES (AMENDMENT NO.2) REGULATIONS (NORTHERN IRELAND) 1996, SR 1996 209; made under the Health and Personal Social Services (Northern Ireland) Order 1972 Art.45, Art.98, Art.106, Art.107. In force: June 11, 1996; £1.10.

These Regulations amend the Travelling Expenses and Remission of Charges Regulations (Northern Ireland) 1989 (SR 1989 348), which provide for the remission and repayment of certain charges which would otherwise be payable under the Health and Personal Social Services (Northern Ireland) Order 1972 (SI 1972 1265 (NI 14)) and for the payment of travelling expenses incurred in attending a hospital as respects the financial disregards applied in calculating student income.

6236. Expenses–travel charges

TRAVELLING EXPENSES AND REMISSION OF CHARGES (AMENDMENT NO.3) REGULATIONS (NORTHERN IRELAND) 1996, SR 1996 425; made under the Health and Personal Social Services (Northern Ireland) Order 1972 Art.45, Art.98, Art.106, Art.107 (6), Sch.15 para.1 (b), Sch.15 para.1B. In force: October 7, 1996; £1.10.

These Regulations amend the Travelling Expenses and Remission of Charges Regulations (Northern Ireland) 1989 (SR 1989 348), which provide for the remission and repayment of certain charges which would otherwise be payable under the 1972 Order and for the payment of travelling expenses incurred in attending a hospital, as respects two definitions, the description of persons entitled to full remission and payment, claims and periods of validity of notices of entitlement.

6237. Health and Personal Social Services (Amendment) (Northern Ireland) Order 1995–Commencement No.2 Order

HEALTH AND PERSONAL SOCIAL SERVICES (AMENDMENT) (1995) ORDER) (COMMENCEMENT NO.2) ORDER (NORTHERN IRELAND) 1996, SR 1996 123 (C.6); made under the Health and Personal Social Services (Amendment) (Northern Ireland) Order 1995 Art.1; and the Northern Ireland Act 1974 Sch.1 para.2(1). In force: bringing into force various provisions of the Order on March 29, 1996; £0.65.

This Order brings the remaining provisions of the Health and Personal Social Services (Amendment) (Northern Ireland) Order 1995 (SI 1995 2704 (NI 14)) into operation on March 29, 1996 so far as they are not already in operation.

6238. Health and Personal Social Services (Residual Liabilities) (Northern Ireland) Order 1996 (SI 1996 1636 (NI 13))

This Order, which came into force on August 27, 1996, imposes a duty on the Department of Health and Social Services, when certain Health and Social Service bodies cease to exist, to exercise its statutory powers as respects the transfer of property, rights and liabilities of the defunct bodies so as to secure that all of their liabilities are transferred to other Health and Social Services bodies or the Department.

6239. HSS trusts–capital debt

HEALTH AND SOCIAL SERVICES TRUSTS (ORIGINATING CAPITAL DEBT) ORDER (NORTHERN IRELAND) 1996, SR 1996 125; made under the Health and Personal Social Services (Northern Ireland) Order 1991 Art.14(1) (4). In force: March 27, 1996; £1.10.

This Order determines the amount of the original capital debt provided for in the Health and Personal Social Services (Northern Ireland) Order 1991 (SI 1991 194 (NI 1)) Art.14 (1) of HSS trusts established under that Order with an operational date of April 1, 1995. It also provides for the splitting of the original capital debts into interest bearing loan and public dividend capital.

6240. HSS trusts–capital debt

HEALTH AND SOCIAL SERVICES TRUSTS (ORIGINATING CAPITAL DEBT) (AMENDMENT) ORDER (NORTHERN IRELAND) 1996, SR 1996 160; made under the Health and Personal Social Services (Northern Ireland) Order 1991 Art.14(1)(4). In force: April 16, 1996; £0.65.

This Order amends the Health and Social Services Trusts (Originating Capital Debt) Order (Northern Ireland) 1996 (SR 1996 125) which determines the originating capital debt, interest bearing initial loan and public dividend capital of the HSS trusts established under the Health and Personal Social Services (Northern Ireland) Order 1991 (SI 1991 194 (NI 1)) with an operational date of April 1, 1995. The Order varies the originating capital debt, interest bearing initial loan and public dividend capital of Causeway HSS Trust.

6241. HSS trusts–establishment

HEALTH AND SOCIAL SERVICES TRUSTS (ESTABLISHING ORDERS) (AMENDMENT) ORDER (NORTHERN IRELAND) 1996, SR 1996 516; made under the Health and Personal Social Services (Northern Ireland) Order 1972 Art.10(1), Sch.3 para.1, Sch.3 para.3A. In force: November 4, 1996; £1.10.

This Order amends Orders establishing certain Health and Social Services Trusts to take account of the Children (Northern Ireland) Order 1995 (SI 1995 755 (NI 2)) by specifying areas within which the trusts may exercise the functions conferred on a Health and Social Services Board under the 1995 Order and which are delegated to them.

6242. HSS trusts–establishment

HOMEFIRST COMMUNITY HEALTH AND SOCIAL SERVICES TRUST (ESTABLISHMENT) ORDER (NORTHERN IRELAND) 1996, SR 1996 20; made under the Health and Personal Social Services (Northern Ireland) Order 1991 Art.10(1), Sch.3 para.1, Sch.3 para.3, Sch.3 para.3A, Sch.3 para.4, Sch.3 para.5, Sch.3 para.6(2)(d). In force: February 1, 1996; £1.95.

This Order establishes the Homefirst Community Health and Personal Social Services Trust.

6243. HSS trusts–establishment

SPERRIN LAKELAND HEALTH AND SOCIAL SERVICES TRUST (ESTABLISHMENT) ORDER (NORTHERN IRELAND) 1996, SR 1996 116; made under the Health and Personal Social Services (Northern Ireland) Order 1991 Art.10(1), Sch.3 para.1, Sch.3 para.3, Sch.3 para.3A, Sch.3 para.4, Sch.3 para.5, Sch.3 para.6(2)(d). In force: March 25, 1996; £1.10.

This Order establishes the Sperrin Lakeland Health and Social Services Trust and provides for the functions of the trust both before and after its operational date. The Order also specifies the operational date of the trust, makes provision for assistance to the trust by the Western Health and Social Services Board before its operational date and specifies £500,000 as the maximum value of freely disposable assets.

6244. HSS trusts–establishment

SPERRIN LAKELAND HEALTH AND SOCIAL SERVICES TRUST (ESTABLISHMENT) (AMENDMENT) ORDER (NORTHERN IRELAND) 1996, SR 1996 220; made under the Health and Personal Social Services (Northern Ireland) Order 1991 Art.10(1), Sch.3 para.1, Sch.3 para.3, Sch.3 para.3A. In force: June 3, 1996; £0.65.

This Order amends the Sperrin Lakeland Health and Social Services Trust (Establishment) Order (Northern Ireland) 1996 (SR 1996 116) by redefining the headquarters of the Trust.

6245. HSS trusts–establishment–amendments

FOYLE HEALTH AND SOCIAL SERVICES TRUST (ESTABLISHMENT) (AMENDMENT) ORDER (NORTHERN IRELAND) 1996, SR 1996 117; made under the Health and Personal Social Services (Northern Ireland) Order 1991

Art.10(1), Sch.3 para.1, Sch.3 para.3, Sch.3 para.3A. In force: March 25, 1996; £1.10.

This Order amends the Foyle Health and Social Services Trust (Establishment) Order (Northern Ireland) 1995 (SR 1995 423) by redefining the operational area of the trust to take account of redistribution of clinical responsibilities consequent upon the establishment of the Sperrin Lakeland Health and Social Services Trust.

6246. HSS trusts–functions

HEALTH AND SOCIAL SERVICES TRUSTS (EXERCISE OF FUNCTIONS) (AMENDMENT) REGULATIONS (NORTHERN IRELAND) 1996, SR 1996 439; made under the Health and Personal Social Services (Northern Ireland) Order 1994 Art.3(3). In force: November 4, 1996; £0.65.

These Regulations amend the Health and Social Services Trusts (Exercise of Functions) Regulations (Northern Ireland) 1994 (SR 1994 64) to extend the list of relevant functions of health and social services boards to include all functions conferred on such boards under the Children (Northern Ireland) Order 1995 (SI 1995 755 (NI 2)).

6247. Income–capital–assessment

HEALTH AND PERSONAL SOCIAL SERVICES (ASSESSMENT OF RESOURCES) (AMENDMENT) REGULATIONS (NORTHERN IRELAND) 1996, SR 1996 83; made under the Health and Personal Social Services (Northern Ireland) Order 1972 Art.36, Art.99. In force: April 8, 1996; £1.10.

These Regulations amend the Health and Personal Social Services (Assessment of Resources) Regulations (Northern Ireland) 1993 (SR 1993 127) as respects a capital limit, weekly tariff incomes, the disregard of half a resident's occupational pension in certain circumstances and certain interests in property.

6248. Medical treatment–services

GENERAL MEDICAL AND PHARMACEUTICAL SERVICES (AMENDMENT) REGULATIONS (NORTHERN IRELAND) 1996, SR 1996 136; made under the Health and Personal Social Services (Northern Ireland) Order 1972 Art.56, Art.63, Art.106, Art.107(6), Sch.11 para.8E; and the Health and Medicines (Northern Ireland) Order 1988 Art.10. In force: April 1, 1996; £3.20.

These Regulations amend the General Medical and Pharmaceutical Services Regulations (Northern Ireland) 1973 (SR 1973 421) as respects the terms on which general medical and pharmaceutical services are provided. In particular, they reflect the power of the Tribunal established under the Health and Personal Social Services (Northern Ireland) Order 1972 (SI 1972 1265 (NI 14)) to suspend chemists or to declare chemists not fit to be engaged in providing pharmaceutical services.

6249. Ophthalmic services

GENERAL OPHTHALMIC SERVICES (AMENDMENT) REGULATIONS (NORTHERN IRELAND) 1996, SR 1996 135; made under the Health and Personal Social Services (Northern Ireland) Order 1972 Art.62, Art.106, Art.107(6), Sch.16 para.8E; and the Health and Medicines (Northern Ireland) Order 1988 Art.10. In force: April 1, 1996; £2.40.

These Regulations further amend the General Opthalmic Services Regulations (Northern Ireland) 1986 (SI 1986 163) as respects opthalmic medical practitioners and opthalmic opticians suspended from providing general opthalmic services by the Tribunal established under the Health and Personal Social Services (Northern Ireland) Order 1972 (SI 1972 1265 (NI 14)) or declared not fit to be engaged in providing these services. They also amend contractors' terms of service.

6250. Ophthalmic services

GENERAL OPHTHALMIC SERVICES (AMENDMENT NO.2) REGULATIONS (NORTHERN IRELAND) 1996, SR 1996 416; made under the Health and Personal Social Services (Northern Ireland) Order 1972 Art.62, Art.106, Art.107(6). In force: October 7, 1996; £1.10.

These Regulations amend the General Ophthalmic Services Regulations (Northern Ireland) 1986 (SR 1986 163) by inserting a definition, removing the capital restriction relating to disability working allowance so that everyone receiving it, and members of their families, will be eligible for general ophthalmic services and extending the categories of eligibility for general ophthalmic services to include persons receiving income based jobseeker's allowance and members of their families.

6251. Opticians–charges

OPTICAL CHARGES AND PAYMENTS (AMENDMENT) REGULATIONS (NORTHERN IRELAND) 1996, SR 1996 124; made under the Health and Personal Social Services (Northern Ireland) Order 1972 Art.98, Art.106, Sch.15. In force: April 1, 1996; £1.55.

These Regulations increase charges for glasses and contact lenses supplied under the health service and increase the value of certain vouchers for them.

6252. Opticians–charges

OPTICAL CHARGES AND PAYMENTS (AMENDMENT NO.2) REGULATIONS (NORTHERN IRELAND) 1996, SR 1996 424; made under the Health and Personal Social Services Order 1972 Art.98, Art.106, Sch.15. In force: October 7, 1996; £1.10.

These Regulations amend the Optical Charges and Payments Regulations (Northern Ireland) 1989 (SR 1989 114) by inserting a definition, removing the capital restriction relating to disability working allowance so that everyone receiving it, and members of their families, will be eligible for payments towards the costs of optical appliances and extending the categories of eligibility for payments towards the costs of optical appliances to include people receiving income based jobseeker's allowance and members of their families.

6253. Opticians–charges–sight tests–fees

OPTICAL CHARGES AND PAYMENTS (AMENDMENT NO.3) REGULATIONS (NORTHERN IRELAND) 1996, SR 1996 484; made under the Health and Personal Social Services (Northern Ireland) Order 1972 Art.98, Art.106, Sch.15 para.2A. In force: November 1, 1996; £1.10.

These Regulations amend the Optical Charges and Payments Regulations (Northern Ireland) 1989 (SR 1989 114) to increase the fees for health service sight fees to £37.83 where the test is carried out at the patient's home and to £13.71 in all other cases.

6254. Social services–disciplinary procedures

HEALTH AND PERSONAL SOCIAL SERVICES (DISCIPLINARY PROCEDURES) REGULATIONS (NORTHERN IRELAND) 1996, SR 1996 137; made under the Health and Personal Social Services (Northern Ireland) Order 1972 Art.56, Art.61, Art.62, Art.63, Art.106, Sch.1 para.8(5); and the Health and Medicines (Northern Ireland) Order 1988 Art.10. In force: April 1, 1996; £6.45.

These Regulations supersede the Health and Personal Social Services (Services Committee) Regulations (Northern Ireland) 1973 (SR & O (NI) 1973 416) to provide for the investigation and determination by Health and Social Services Boards, of questions whether doctors, dentists, chemists and opticians providing certain services have failed to comply with their terms of service, and for the consideration and determination of appeals from determinations of Boards. Provision is made to replace the system whereby complaints made against practitioners providing such services were dealt with by the Services Committee which has been abolished and replaced by discipline committees to which Boards will refer matters for investigation which raise allegations that a practitioner has failed to comply with his terms of service or concern overpayments made to such a practitioner. The discipline committees will not deal with complaints made by or on behalf of patients. New criteria which must be satisfied for a matter to be referred for investigation, the procedure for investigation, appeals and the imposition of an arrangements to enforce sanctions are provided in these Regulations.

NEGLIGENCE

6255. Personal injuries–discovery–medical records–extent of disclosure

[Administration of Justice Act 1970 s.32.]

I brought an action against D, his former employer, alleging that as a result of his employment he had contracted dermatitis which rendered him virtually unemployable. D applied under the Administration of Justice Act 1970 s.32 for discovery of all I's medical records from his medical practitioners. It was ordered that there be full discovery by list of all I's medical records and in the absence of any objection by I on grounds of privilege all documents were to be disclosed to D. I appealed, arguing that the records were by their nature confidential, and disclosure should be limited to those documents that D's medical advisers considered relevant to the action.

Held, dismissing the appeal, that confidentiality per se was not a ground upon which the Court could refuse or restrict disclosure on an application under s.32. The appropriate order was for I's medical practitioners to serve a list of all the documents they had in their possession upon both I and D and for I then to be given the opportunity to inspect and object to disclosure to D on the grounds of privilege or irrelevancy.

IRVIN v. DONAGHY [1996] P.I.Q.R. P207, Girvan, J., HCJ (NI).

PENSIONS

6256. Occupational pensions

OCCUPATIONAL PENSIONS (REVALUATION) ORDER (NORTHERN IRELAND) 1996, SR 1996 544; made under the Pension Schemes (Northern Ireland) Act 1993 Sch.2 para.2(1). In force: January 1, 1997; £1.10.

This Order specifies appropriate revaluation percentages relevant to the revaluation of benefits under occupational pension schemes, as required by the Pension Schemes (Northern Ireland) Act 1993 s.80 and Sch.2.

6257. Occupational pensions–additional voluntary contributions–judiciary

JUDICIAL PENSIONS (ADDITIONAL VOLUNTARY CONTRIBUTIONS) (AMENDMENT) REGULATIONS (NORTHERN IRELAND) 1996, SR 1996 10; made under the Judicial Pensions Act (Northern Ireland) 1951 s.11A; the County Courts Act (Northern Ireland) 1959 s.127A; and the Resident Magistrates' Pensions Act (Northern Ireland) 1960 s.9A. In force: February 2, 1996; £1.55.

These Regulations amend the Judicial Pensions (Additional Voluntary Contributions) Regulations (Northern Ireland) 1995 (SR 1995 189) by providing for the further application of Inland Revenue limits to the amount of additional benefits which may be purchased, an additional children's pension under the Judicial Added Benefits Scheme and for administrative expenses incurred by authorised providers to be deducted from voluntary contributions received.

6258. Occupational pensions–additional voluntary contributions–judiciary

JUDICIAL PENSIONS (ADDITIONAL VOLUNTARY CONTRIBUTIONS) (NO.2) (AMENDMENT) REGULATIONS (NORTHERN IRELAND) 1996, SR 1996 86; made under the Judicial Pensions Act (Northern Ireland) 1951 s.11A. In force: April 7, 1996; £1.10.

These Regulations amend the Judicial Pensions (Additional Voluntary Contributions) (No.2) Regulations (Northern Ireland) 1995 (SR 1995 255).

6259. Occupational pensions–Civil Service

NORTHERN IRELAND CIVIL SERVICE PENSIONS (PROVISION OF INFORMATION AND ADMINISTRATIVE CHARGES ETC) SCHEME (NORTHERN IRELAND) 1996, SR 1996 582; made under the Pensions (Northern Ireland) Order 1995 Art.164(1)(2)(3)(a). In force: January 27, 1997; £1.10.

This Scheme makes certain provisions in relation to individuals who have been eligible to be members of the Principal Civil Service Pension Scheme (Northern Ireland) but have instead made contributions to a personal pension scheme.

6260. Occupational pensions–contracting-out

OCCUPATIONAL PENSION SCHEMES (CONTRACTING-OUT) REGULATIONS (NORTHERN IRELAND) 1996, SR 1996 493; made under the Pension Schemes (Northern Ireland) Act 1993 s.3, s.5, s.4(3), s.7(5), s.8(3), s.8A(4)(5)(6), s.8B(2)(4), s.8C(1)(3), s.8D, s.12(3)(4), s.13(6), s.17, s.21(2), s.30, s.31(6), s.32(6), s.33, s.38A, s.41B, s.46(1B)(4), s.47(2)(4), s.49(3), s.51(2), s.52(2), s.53(1)(2), s.57(7)(11), s.109(1), s.151, s.152, s.173, s.174, s.177(4), s.178(1), Sch.1 paras.1 to 8; and the Pensions (Northern Ireland) Order 1995 Art.1(5)(a), Art.166(4). In force: April 6, 1997; £8.05.

These Regulations are made in consequence of the revised procedures for contracting-out in the Pensions (Northern Ireland) Order 1995 (SI 1995 3213 (NI 22)). They replace with amendments, and revoke, the Occupational Pension Schemes (Contracting-Out) Regulations (Northern Ireland) 1985 (SR 1985 259).

6261. Occupational pensions–deficit in assets

OCCUPATIONAL PENSION SCHEMES (DEFICIENCY ON WINDING UP ETC) REGULATIONS (NORTHERN IRELAND) 1996, SR 1996 585; made under the Pensions (Northern Ireland) Order 1995 Art.68(2)(e), Art.75(5)(9)(10), Art.87(2), Art.115(1)(a)(b), Art.116, Art.122(2)(3)(4)(a), Art.166(2)(3). In force: in accordance with Reg.1; £3.20.

These Regulations concern the treatment under the Pensions (Northern Ireland) Order 1995 (SI 1995 3213 (NI 22)) of a deficit in the assets of an occupational pension scheme as a debt owed by the employer to the trustees or managers of the scheme. Article 75 of the Order replaces the Pension Schemes (Northern Ireland) Act 1993 s.140 and these Regulations replace the Occupational Pension Schemes (Deficiency on Winding Up etc.) Regulations (Northern Ireland) 1994 (SR 1994 107).

6262. Occupational pensions–disputes

OCCUPATIONAL PENSION SCHEMES (INTERNAL DISPUTE RESOLUTION PROCEDURES) REGULATIONS (NORTHERN IRELAND) 1996, SR 1996 203; made under the Pensions (Northern Ireland) Order 1995 Art.10(2)(b), Art.50(1)(2)(a)(3)(7). In force: April 6, 1996; £1.95.

These Regulations set out procedures for internal dispute resolution in relation to occupational pension schemes. Provisions as to the persons to whom the arrangements made for the resolution of disagreements shall apply and as to who may bring complaints are made by Reg.2, Reg.3 enables representatives to act on behalf of complainants. Regulation 4 to Reg.7 relate to the manner in which applications are to be made and decisions given. Regulation 8 and Reg.9 make provision for the arrangements made for the resolution of disagreements not to apply in certain cases. Regulation 10 provides the maximum penalty which may be imposed by the Occupational Pensions Regulatory Authority in cases where arrangements required by the Pensions (Northern Ireland) Order 1995 (SI 1995 3213 (NI 22)) Art.50 have not been made or are not being implemented by a scheme.

6263. Occupational pensions–equal treatment

OCCUPATIONAL PENSION SCHEMES (EQUAL TREATMENT) REGULATIONS (NORTHERN IRELAND) 1995, SR 1995 482; made under the Pensions (Northern Ireland) Order 1995 Art.63(5), Art.64(2)(3), Art.66(4). In force: January 1, 1996; £2.80.

These Regulations supplement requirements for equal treatment provided for in the Pensions (Northern Ireland) Order 1995 (SR 1995 3213 (NI 22)).

6264. Occupational pensions–funding requirements and actuarial valuations

OCCUPATIONAL PENSION SCHEMES (MINIMUM FUNDING REQUIREMENT AND ACTUARIAL VALUATIONS) REGULATIONS (NORTHERN IRELAND) 1996, SR 1996 570; made under the Pensions (Northern Ireland) Order 1995 Art.41(1)(2)(c)(3)(b)(6), Art.49(2)(3), Art. 56(2)(b)(3), Art.57(1)(2)(b), Art.(4)(b)(5), Art.58(2)(3)(a)(c)(4)(b)(i)(5)(6)(7), Art.59(1)(3), Art.60(2)(b)(3)(4), Art.60(5)(b)(6)(7), Art.61, Art.68(2)(e), Art.75(5), Art.115(1), Art.116, Art.122(3), Art.166(1) to (3). In force: April 6, 1997; £6.45.

These Regulations concern the minimum funding requirement for occupational pension schemes under the Pensions (Northern Ireland) Order 1995 (SI 1995 3213 (NI 22)) Art.56 to Art.61 and ongoing actuarial valuations under Art.41 of the Order.

6265. Occupational pensions–guaranteed minimum pension–indexation

GUARANTEED MINIMUM PENSIONS INCREASE ORDER (NORTHERN IRELAND) 1996, SR 1996 62; made under the Pension Schemes (Northern Ireland) Act 1993 s.105. In force: April 6, 1996; £0.65.

This Order specifies three per cent as the increase for that part of guaranteed minimum pensions attributable to earnings factors for 1988-89 and subsequent tax years and payable by occupational pension schemes.

6266. Occupational pensions–investments

OCCUPATIONAL PENSION SCHEMES (INVESTMENT) REGULATIONS (NORTHERN IRELAND) 1996, SR 1996 584; made under the Pensions (Northern Ireland) Order 1995 Art.35(7), Art.40(1)(2), Art.56(3), Art.115(1)(a), Art.120(2), Art.166(1) to (3). In force: April 6, 1997; £3.20.

These Regulations impose restrictions on the amount of the resources of an occupational pension scheme which may be invested in employer-related investments. They also exempt certain schemes from the requirement imposed on trustees of trust schemes by the Pensions (Northern Ireland) Order 1995 (SI 1995 3213 (NI 22)) to obtain a statement of the principles governing decisions about investments for the purposes of the scheme. The Regulations revoke and replace the Occupational Pension Schemes (Investment of Scheme's Resources) Regulations (Northern Ireland) 1992 (SR 1992 47).

6267. Occupational pensions–personal pensions

PERSONAL AND OCCUPATIONAL PENSION SCHEMES (MISCELLANEOUS AMENDMENTS) REGULATIONS (NORTHERN IRELAND) 1996, SR 1996 95; made under the Pension Schemes (Northern Ireland) Act 1993 s.24(1A)(4)(5), s.24A(3)(5), s.25(4), s.40, s.44(2), s.109, s.151. In force: April 6, 1996; £1.95.

These Regulations amend provisions so as to require trustees of a scheme who are discharging a member's protected rights on winding up of the scheme through insurance policies to notify the Department of Health and Social Services the identity of the member and insurance company; amend the treatment of a scheme member's widow or widower as regards entitlement to a guaranteed minimum pension; and amend the effect to be given to protected rights under a personal pension scheme.

6268. Occupational pensions–personal pensions–benefits and perpetuities

PERSONAL AND OCCUPATIONAL PENSION SCHEMES (PRESERVATION OF BENEFIT AND PERPETUITIES) (AMENDMENT) REGULATIONS (NORTHERN IRELAND) 1996, SR 1996 620; made under the Pension Schemes (Northern Ireland) Act 1993 s.67(6), s.69(2)(4), s.70(8), s.73(5)(c)(6), s.78(1), s.109(1), s.149(2)(c), s.159(6), s.161(5), s.164(1)(4), s.177(2) to (4). In force: April 6, 1997; £1.95.

These Regulations further amend the Occupational Pension Schemes (Preservation of Benefit) Regulations (Northern Ireland) 1991 (SR 1991 37) and the Personal and Occupational Pension Schemes (Perpetuities) Regulations (Northern Ireland) 1990 (SR 1990 204). The Preservation Regulations are amended by the removal of the provision for the Occupational Pensions Board, OPB, which is being dissolved, to exercise discretion in certain cases; by allowing the transfer of rights to an overseas arrangement to be an alternative to short service benefit; by introducing a test to determine whether uniform accrual is to be applied to money purchase benefits; and by inserting requirements for members to be furnished with information in relation to any transfer of accrued rights without consent or in relation to rights on termination of pensionable service. The Perpetuities Regulations are amended in relation to the extension of the time limit under that Regulations, by substituting a reference to the Department of Health and Social Services for the reference to the OPB.

6269. Occupational pensions–personal pensions–Pensions Ombudsman

PERSONAL AND OCCUPATIONAL PENSION SCHEMES (PENSIONS OMBUDSMAN) (AMENDMENT) REGULATIONS (NORTHERN IRELAND) 1996, SR 1996 207; made under the Pension Schemes (Northern Ireland) Act 1993 s.142(4)(b). In force: July 1, 1996; £1.10.

These Regulations amend the Personal and Occupational Pension Schemes (Pensions Ombudsman) Regulations (Northern Ireland) 1991 (SR 1991 93) by inserting a new Reg.2A which extends the jurisdiction of the Pensions Ombudsman to include complaints against scheme administrators.

6270. Occupational pensions–public authorities–indexation

PENSIONS INCREASE (REVIEW) ORDER (NORTHERN IRELAND) 1996, SR 1996 90; made under the Social Security Pensions (Northern Ireland) Order 1975 Art.69(1)(2)(5)(5ZA). In force: April 8, 1996; £1.95.

This Order increases public service pensions.

6271. Occupational pensions–transfer values

OCCUPATIONAL PENSION SCHEMES (TRANSFER VALUES) REGULATIONS (NORTHERN IRELAND) 1996, SR 1996 619; made under the Pension Schemes (Northern Ireland) Act 1993 s.89(1), s.89(IB), s.89A(2)(3), s.90(3), s.91(2)(5)(6), s.93(1) to (3)(4), s.94(1) to (4), s.95(4)(7), s.109(1)(3), s.149(1), s.164(1)(4), s.177(2) to (4), s.178(1)(3). In force: April 6, 1997; £4.70.

These Regulations replace the Occupational Pension Schemes (Transfer Values) Regulations (Northern Ireland) 1985 (SR 1985 358 as amended) which are, subject to transitional provisions, now revoked. The Regulations supplement the changes introduced by the Pensions (Northern Ireland) Order 1995 (SI 1995 3213 (NI 22)) to the Pension Schemes (Northern Ireland) Act 1993. They also consolidate and amend the 1985 Regulations. Provisions carried forward from the 1985 Regulations are amended to take into account new provisions introduced by the Order and changes made by the Order to the Act.

6272. Occupational pensions–trustees–directors

OCCUPATIONAL PENSION SCHEMES (MEMBER-NOMINATED TRUSTEES AND DIRECTORS) REGULATIONS (NORTHERN IRELAND) 1996, SR 1996 431; made under the Pensions (Northern Ireland) Order 1995 Art.17(1)(c)(4)(b), Art.18(1), Art.19(1)(c)(4), Art.20(1)(b)(2)(3)(4)(5), Art.21(3)(4)(5)(6)(7)(b), Art.49(2)(b)(3), Art.68(2)(e), Art.115(1)(a)(b), Art.122(3)(4), Art.166(3). In force: in accordance with Reg.1(2); £5.90.

These Regulations concern the selection and appointment of member-nominated trustees and directors under the Pensions (Northern Ireland) Order 1995 (SI 1995 3213 (NI 22)) Art.16 to Art.21.

6273. Occupational pensions–winding up

OCCUPATIONAL PENSION SCHEMES (WINDING UP) REGULATIONS (NORTHERN IRELAND) 1996, SR 1996 621; made under the Pension Schemes (Northern Ireland) Act 1993 s.93(1)(2), s.109(1)(d), s.164(1)(4), s.177(2) to (4); and the Pensions (Northern Ireland) Order 1995 Art.38(3)(b), Art.49(2)(3)(4), Art.68(2)(e), Art.73(3)(7) to (9), Art.74(2)(3)(a) to (d)(5)(b), Art.115(1)(a)(b), Art.116, Art.112(2)(3), Art.116, Art.122(2)(3), Art.166. In force: April 6, 1997; £3.70.

These Regulations make provision for the application of the statutory priority order set out in the Pensions (Northern Ireland) Order 1995 (SI 1995 3213 (NI 22)) Art.73.

6274. Occupational pensions–winding up–protected rights

OCCUPATIONAL PENSION SCHEMES (DISCHARGE OF PROTECTED RIGHTS ON WINDING UP) REGULATIONS (NORTHERN IRELAND) 1996, SR 1996 94; made under the Pension Schemes (Northern Ireland) Act 1993 s.28A. In force: April 6, 1996; £1.55.

These Regulations provide for the conditions which must be satisfied before effect may be given to protected rights of a member of a scheme on winding up by means of an appropriate policy of insurance.

6275. Pension schemes–contracting out–transfer payments

CONTRACTING-OUT (TRANSFER AND TRANSFER PAYMENT) REGULATIONS (NORTHERN IRELAND) 1996, SR 1996 618; made under the Pension Schemes (Northern Ireland) Act 1993 s.8C(1)(a), s.16(1) to (3), s.17(2) to (4). In force: April 6, 1997; £3.70.

These Regulations replace the Contracting-out (Transfer) Regulations (Northern Ireland) 1985 (SR 1985 243) which are, subject to transitional provisions, now revoked. The Regulations supplement changes introduced by the Pensions (Northern Ireland) Order 1995 (SI 1995 3213 (NI 22)) to the Pension Schemes (Northern Ireland) Act 1993 Part III. They also consolidate and amend those provisions of the 1995 Regulations which remain relevant. In addition to minor and drafting amendments, the Regulations make the following changes of substance: they provide for treating separately rights to guaranteed minimum pensions and rights earned in respect of any period from April 6, 1997 and make provision for the transfer of liability for the latter rights; they set out revised conditions for the making of a transfer payment to an overseas scheme, and they no longer require the Occupational Pensions Board, which is being dissolved, to approve transfers.

6276. Pensions (Northern Ireland) Order 1995–Commencement No.2 Order

PENSIONS (1995 ORDER) (COMMENCEMENT NO.2) ORDER (NORTHERN IRELAND) 1996, SR 1996 91 (C.4); made under the Pensions (Northern Ireland) Order 1995 Art.1(2). In force: bringing into force various provisions of the Order on March 14, 1996, April 6, 1996, June 1, 1996, October 6, 1996 and April 6, 1997; £1.95.

This Order brings into operation provisions of the Pensions (Northern Ireland) Order 1995 (SI 1995 3213 (NI 22)) as follows: March 14, 1996, for the purposes of provisions authorising the making of certain Orders and Regulations; April 6, 1996, for provisions commenced on March 14, 1996 only for the purpose of provisions authorising the making of Regulations, for provisions relating to the disclosure of certain information, the aggregation of certain earnings and certain other general provisions and for the purpose of provisions authorising the making of certain Regulations; June 1, 1996, in relation to Regulations about contracting-out by hybrid schemes; October 6, 1996, for Art.68 and Art.114 for transitional purposes; and April 6, 1997 for Art.133.

6277. Pensions (Northern Ireland) Order 1995–Commencement No.3 Order

PENSIONS (1995 ORDER) (COMMENCEMENT NO.3) ORDER (NORTHERN IRELAND) 1996, SR 1996 284 (C.14); made under the Pensions (Northern Ireland) Order 1995 Art.1(4), Art.166(3). In force: bringing into force various provisions of the Order on August 1, 1996; £1.95.

This Order brings Art.162 (with minor exceptions) of the Pensions (Northern Ireland) Order 1995 (SI 1995 3213 (NI 22)) into operation.

6278. Pensions (Northern Ireland) Order 1995–Commencement No.4 Order

PENSIONS (1995 ORDER) (COMMENCEMENT NO.4) ORDER (NORTHERN IRELAND) 1996, SR 1996 307 (C.18); made under the Pensions (Northern Ireland Order 1995 Art.1(2). In force: bringing into force various provisions of the Order on July 23, 1996 and August 1, 1996; £1.55.

This Order brings specified provisions of the Pensions (Northern Ireland) Order 1995 (SI 1995 3213 (NI 22)) into operation on July 23, 1996 and August 1, 1996.

6279. Pensions (Northern Ireland) Order 1995–Commencement No.5 Order

PENSIONS (1995 ORDER) (COMMENCEMENT NO.5) ORDER (NORTHERN IRELAND) 1996, SR 1996 534 (C.25); made under the Pensions (Northern Ireland) Order 1995 Art.1(2). In force: bringing into force various provisions of the Order on November 19, 1996; £1.55.

This Order brings into operation on November 19, 1996, provisions of the Pensions (Northern Ireland) Order 1995 (SI 1995 3213 (NI 22)) for the purpose of authorising the making of regulations relating to the issue of certain orders by the Occupational Pensions Authority and, on the same day, Art.115 and Art.122(2)(3)(4).

6280. Personal pensions–contributions

SOCIAL SECURITY (MINIMUM CONTRIBUTIONS TO APPROPRIATE PERSONAL PENSION SCHEMES) ORDER (NORTHERN IRELAND) 1996, SR 1996 151; made under the Pension Schemes (Northern Ireland) Act 1993 s.45A. In force: April 6, 1996.

This Order specifies, with effect from April 6, 1997, the appropriate age related percentages of earnings payable as minimum contributions in respect of members of appropriate personal pension schemes.

6281. Personal pensions–disclosure–information

PERSONAL PENSION SCHEMES (APPROPRIATE SCHEMES AND DISCLOSURE OF INFORMATION) (MISCELLANEOUS AMENDMENTS) REGULATIONS (NORTHERN IRELAND) 1996, SR 1996 508; made under the

Pension Schemes (Northern Ireland) Act 1993 s.39(1)(3), s.41B, s.109(1), s.177(2)(3)(4), s.178(1). In force: April 6, 1997; £1.55.

These Regulations amend the Personal Pension Schemes (Disclosure of Information) Regulations (Northern Ireland) 1987 (SR 1987 288) to require trustees to disclose information relating to dates of birth. They also amend the Personal Pension Schemes (Appropriate Schemes) Regulations (Northern Ireland) 1988 (SR 1988 34) to set out circumstances in which, except where provided, minimum contributions are not payable to schemes and by making miscellaneous amendments.

6282. Protected rights–transfer payments

PROTECTED RIGHTS (TRANSFER PAYMENT) REGULATIONS (NORTHERN IRELAND) 1996, SR 1996 509; made under the Pension Schemes (Northern Ireland) Act 1993 s.242(b), s.177(2)(3)(4), Sch.5 para.17(1). In force: April 6, 1997; £2.80.

These Regulations replace the Protected Rights (Transfer Payment) Regulations (Northern Ireland) 1987 (SR 1987 296). They supplement changes introduced by the Pensions (Northern Ireland) Order 1995 (SI 1995 3213 (NI 22)) to the Pension Schemes (Northern Ireland) Act 1993 Part III.

PLANNING

6283. Development

PLANNING (GENERAL DEVELOPMENT) (AMENDMENT) ORDER (NORTHERN IRELAND) 1996, SR 1996 232; made under the Planning (Northern Ireland) Order 1991 Art.13. In force: July 19, 1996; £1.10.

This Order amends the Planning (General Development) Order (Northern Ireland) 1993 (SR 1993 278) to permit, subject to certain qualifications and restrictions, a change of use of a building from Class 1 (shops) or Class 2 (financial, professional and other services) of the Schedule to the Planning (Use Classes) Order (Northern Ireland) 1989 (SR 1989 290) to a mixed use for any purpose within Class 1 or Class 2 and as a single flat and a change of use from a mixed use within Class 1 or Class 2 and a single flat to either Class 1 or Class 2 use.

6284. Development–designated areas–Laganside

LAGANSIDE DEVELOPMENT (ALTERATION OF DESIGNATED AREA) ORDER (NORTHERN IRELAND) 1996, SR 1996 612; made under the Laganside Development (Northern Ireland) Order 1989 Art.3(2)(5). In force: February 1, 1997; £0.65.

The Laganside Development Designation Order (Northern Ireland) 1989 (SR 1989 138) designated an area of about 141.5 hectares lying within the City of Belfast for the purposes of its regeneration by the Laganside Corporation. A further 16 hectares approximately was designated under the Laganside Development (Alteration of Designated Area) Order (Northern Ireland) 1995 (SR 1995 30). This Order alters the designated area by adding five separate areas totalling approximately 45.5 hectares contiguous to the existing area.

6285. Fees

PLANNING (FEES) (AMENDMENT) REGULATIONS (NORTHERN IRELAND) 1996, SR 1996 41; made under the Planning (Northern Ireland) Order 1991 Art.127, Art.129(1). In force: April 1, 1996; £1.95.

These Regulations increase fees under the Planning (Fees) Regulations (Northern Ireland) 1995 (SR 1995 78).

6286. **Use classes**

PLANNING (USE CLASSES) (AMENDMENT) ORDER (NORTHERN IRELAND) 1996, SR 1996 248; made under the Planning (Northern Ireland) Order 1991 Art.11 (2) (e). In force: August 5, 1996; £0.65.

This Order amends the Planning (Use Classes) Order (Northern Ireland) 1989 (SR 1989 290) by omitting Class 7 to Class 10 (Special Industrial) from the Schedule. Industrial processes previously within those Classes will fall within Class 5 (General Industrial).

POLICE

6287. **Pace (Northern Ireland) Order 1989–applications**

POLICE AND CRIMINAL EVIDENCE (APPLICATION TO CUSTOMS AND EXCISE) (AMENDMENT) ORDER (NORTHERN IRELAND) 1996, SR 1996 292; made under the Police and Criminal Evidence (Northern Ireland) Order 1989 Art.85 (1). In force: September 1, 1996; £1.10.

These Regulations amend the Police and Criminal Evidence (Application to Customs and Excise) Order (Northern Ireland) 1989 (SR 1989 465) by applying the equivalent job titles and pay-banding of Customs and Excise officers to equivalent ranks of constables and police officers.

6288. **Police powers–codes of practice**

POLICE AND CRIMINAL EVIDENCE (NORTHERN IRELAND) ORDER 1989 (CODES OF PRACTICE) (NO.2) ORDER 1996, SR 1996 261; made under the Police and Criminal Evidence (Northern Ireland) Order 1989 Art.66 (4). In force: July 29, 1996; £1.10.

This Order appoints July 29, 1996 as the date on which the code of practice under the Police and Criminal Evidence (Northern Ireland) Order 1989 (SI 1989 1341 (NI 12)) Art.60 and the revised codes of practice under Art.65 of that Order come into operation. Those codes of practice are for the tape recording of interviews of persons suspected of the commission of criminal offences which are held by police officers at police stations, the exercise by police officers of statutory powers of stop and search, the searching of premises by police officers and the seizure of property found by police officers, the detention, treatment and questioning of persons by police officers and the identification of persons by police officers.

6289. **Police (Amendment) (Northern Ireland) Order 1995 (SI 1995 2993 (NI 17))**

Provisions of the Police and Criminal Evidence (Northern Ireland) Order 1989 relating to police powers in the investigation of crime are amended by Part II of this Order and provisions of the Police (Northern Ireland) Order 1987 (SI 1987 938 (NI 10)) relating to complaints against the police are amended by Part IV. New provisions for Regulations relating to the conduct, efficiency and discipline of members of the RUC and RUC Reserve are made by Part III. This Order comes into force on days to be appointed under Art.1 (2).

6290. **Police (Amendment) (Northern Ireland) Order 1995–Commencement No.1 Order**

POLICE (AMENDMENT) (1995 ORDER) (COMMENCEMENT NO.1) ORDER (NORTHERN IRELAND) 1996, SR 1996 316 (C.19); made under the Police (Amendment) (Northern Ireland) Order 1995 Art.1 (1) (2) (3). In force: bringing into force various provisions of the Order on July 29, 1996; £0.65.

This Order brings the Police (Amendment) Order (Northern Ireland) 1995 (SI 1995 2993 (NI 17)) Part II into operation on July 29, 1996, subject to transitional provisions in Art.3.

6291. Royal Ulster Constabulary–disciplinary procedures–appeals

ROYAL ULSTER CONSTABULARY (DISCIPLINE AND DISCIPLINARY APPEALS) (AMENDMENT NO.2) REGULATIONS 1996, SR 1996 343; made under the Police Act (Northern Ireland) 1970 s.25, s.26. In force: August 25, 1996; £0.65.

These Regulations amend the Royal Ulster Constabulary (Discipline and Disciplinary Appeals) Regulations 1988 (SR 1988 10) to make failure to comply with a code of practice under the Police and Criminal Evidence (Northern Ireland) Order 1989 (SI 1989 1341 (NI 12)) Art.60, the Northern Ireland (Emergency Provisions) Act 1991 s.61 or the Northern Ireland (Emergency Provisions) Act 1996 s.52 or s.53 a disciplinary offence.

6292. Royal Ulster Constabulary–occupational pensions

ROYAL ULSTER CONSTABULARY PENSIONS (AMENDMENT) REGULATIONS 1996, SR 1996 4; made under the Police Act (Northern Ireland) 1970 s.25, s.34; and the Police Negotiating Board Act 1980 s.2. In force: February 1, 1996; £1.95.

The Royal Ulster Constabulary Pensions Regulations 1988 (SR 1988 374) are amended so that women members are able to make additional payments to ensure that service prior to May 17, 1996 is included in the calculation of widowers' benefits together with service after that date which automatically counts.

6293. Royal Ulster Constabulary–terms and conditions of service

ROYAL ULSTER CONSTABULARY REGULATIONS 1996, SR 1996 473; made under the Police Act (Northern Ireland) 1970 s.25. In force: November 12, 1996; £8.70.

These Regulations consolidate with amendments, and revoke, the Royal Ulster Constabulary Regulations 1984 (SR 1984 62) as amended.

6294. Royal Ulster Constabulary Reserve–disciplinary procedures–appeals

ROYAL ULSTER CONSTABULARY RESERVE (DISCIPLINE AND DISCIPLINARY APPEALS) (AMENDMENT) REGULATIONS 1996, SR 1996 253; made under the Police Act (Northern Ireland) 1970 s.26; and the Police (Northern Ireland) Order 1987 Art.14(6). In force: July 29, 1996; £1.10.

These Regulations make minor amendments to the Royal Ulster Constabulary (Discipline and Disciplinary Appeals) Regulations 1988 (SR 1988 10) Reg.17(12)(b) and Reg.37(9)(b) and substitute revised forms of caution for those in Sch.1A to those Regulations.

6295. Royal Ulster Constabulary Reserve–disciplinary procedures–appeals

ROYAL ULSTER CONSTABULARY RESERVE (PART-TIME) (DISCIPLINE AND DISCIPLINARY APPEALS) (AMENDMENT) REGULATIONS 1996, SR 1996 254; made under the Police Act (Northern Ireland) 1970 s.26; and the Police (Northern Ireland) Order 1987 Art.14(6). In force: July 29, 1996; £1.10.

These Regulations make a minor amendment to the Royal Ulster Constabulary Reserve (Part-time) (Discipline and Disciplinary Appeals) Regulations 1988 (SR 1988 8) Reg.15(12)(b) and substitute revised forms of caution for those in Sch.1A to those Regulations.

6296. Royal Ulster Constabulary Reserve–disciplinary procedures–appeals

ROYAL ULSTER CONSTABULARY RESERVE (PART-TIME) (DISCIPLINE AND DISCIPLINARY APPEALS) (AMENDMENT NO.2) REGULATIONS 1996, SR 1996 344; made under the Police Act (Northern Ireland) 1970 s.26. In force: August 25, 1996; £0.65.

These Regulations amend the Royal Ulster Constabulary Reserve (Part-time) (Discipline and Disciplinary Appeals) Regulations 1988 (SR 1988 8) to make failure to comply with a code of practice under the Police and Criminal Evidence

(Northern Ireland) Order 1989 (SI 1989 1341 (NI 12)) Art.60, the Northern Ireland (Emergency Provisions) Act 1991 s.61 or the Northern Ireland (Emergency Provisions) Act 1996 s.52 or s.53 a disciplinary offence.

6297. Royal Ulster Constabulary Reserve–occupational pensions

ROYAL ULSTER CONSTABULARY RESERVE (FULL-TIME) PENSIONS (AMENDMENT) REGULATIONS 1996, SR 1996 5; made under the Police Act (Northern Ireland) 1970 s.26, s.34. In force: February 1, 1996; £1.10.

These Regulations insert a new Reg.4(5A), Reg.4(5B), Reg.4(5C) and Reg.5(8) into the Royal Ulster Constabulary Reserve (Full-Time) Pensions Regulations 1994 (SR 1994 197) to provide for increases made in certain maxima by the Occupational Pension Schemes (Preservation of Benefit) Regulations (Northern Ireland) 1991 (SR 1991 37) and for any future increases in them.

6298. Royal Ulster Constabulary Reserve–terms and conditions of service–full-time

ROYAL ULSTER CONSTABULARY RESERVE (FULL-TIME) (APPOINTMENT AND CONDITIONS OF SERVICE) REGULATIONS 1996, SR 1996 564; made under the Police Act (Northern Ireland) 1970 s.26. In force: December 30, 1996; £6.45.

These Regulations consolidate the Royal Ulster Constabulary Reserve (Full-Time) (Appointment and Conditions of Service) Regulations 1988 (SR 1988 36 as amended by SR 1988 341, SR 1989 208, SR 1990 75, SR 1990 83, SR 1990 434, SR 1990 436, SR 1991 460, SR 1992 446, SR 1993 208, SR 1993 465, SR 1994 72, SR 1994 187, SR 1994 332, SR 1994 432, SR 1995 339, and SR 1995 401), subject to the savings in Sch.10 Part II. The main amendments relate to maternity and paternity leave.

6299. Royal Ulster Constabulary Reserve–terms and conditions of service–part-time

ROYAL ULSTER CONSTABULARY RESERVE (PART-TIME) (APPOINTMENT AND CONDITIONS OF SERVICE) REGULATIONS 1996, SR 1996 565; made under the Police Act (Northern Ireland) 1970 s.26. In force: December 30, 1996; £3.70.

These Regulations consolidate the Royal Ulster Constabulary Reserve (Part-time) (Appointment and Conditions of Service) Regulations 1988 (SR 1988 35 as amended by SR 1988 342, SR 1989 209, SR 1990 76, SR 1990 437, SR 1991 461, SR 1992 445, SR 1993 209, SR 1994 73, SR 1994 188, and SR 1995 119). They relate to duties, allowances, pay, uniform and equipment as well as the governance of the force.

RATES

6300. Local government finance

RATES (REGIONAL RATE) ORDER (NORTHERN IRELAND) 1996, SR 1996 46; made under the Rates (Northern Ireland) Order 1977 Art.2(2), Art.7(1), Art.27(4). In force: April 1, 1996; £0.65.

This Order fixes the regional rate for the year ending March 31, 1997 and the amount by which it is reduced for dwelling-houses.

6301. Rates (Amendment) (Northern Ireland) Order 1996 (SI 1996 3162 (NI 25))

This Order amends the Rates (Northern Ireland) Order 1977 (SI 1977 (NI 28)) by enabling different rates to be made and levied for different classes of hereditaments;

providing for the date of rate liability, in respect of a newly erected or constructed hereditament, to be the date of occupation; conferring power to provide for transitional rate relief; conferring power to provide for cases in which more than one hereditament are to be treated as a single hereditament and a single hereditament is to be treated as more than one; conferring power to revise the rating of hereditaments used for purposes of water supply and sewerage services; providing for an industrial hereditament not to include any part of a hereditament used as a private dwelling; clarifying the circumstances where a dwelling-house will be considered to be occupied on a commercial basis; providing rate exemption for hereditaments used in association with salmon or eel fishing or as public parks; conferring power to determine a de-capitalisation rate for hereditaments valued using the contractor's basis; and conferring power to revise the rating of hereditaments used for plant and machinery and railways.

REAL PROPERTY

6302. Compulsory purchase–interest

COMPULSORY ACQUISITION (INTEREST) ORDER (NORTHERN IRELAND) 1996, SR 1996 210; made under the Public Health and Local Government (Miscellaneous Provisions) Act (Northern Ireland) 1955 s.12; the Administrative and Financial Provisions Act (Northern Ireland) 1956 s.14(3); and the Local Government Act (Northern Ireland) 1972 Sch.6 para.18. In force: July 1, 1996; £1.10.

This Order fixes the rate of interest on compensation money payable under compulsory purchase enactments mentioned in the Order 0.5 per cent below the base rate quoted by the seven largest banks authorised under the Banking Act 1987 on July 1, 1996 and subsequent reference days. This Order also revokes the Compulsory Acquisition (Interest) Order (Northern Ireland) 1994 (SR 1994 91).

6303. Deeds–registration–fees

REGISTRATION OF DEEDS (FEES) ORDER (NORTHERN IRELAND) 1996, SR 1996 265; made under the Registration of Deeds Act (Northern Ireland) 1970 s.16(1). In force: August 8, 1996; £1.55.

This Order specifies the fees to be taken in respect of documents lodged for registration in the Registry of Deeds and for other work carried out in that Registry.

6304. Land registry–fees

LAND REGISTRY (FEES) ORDER (NORTHERN IRELAND) 1996, SR 1996 157; made under the Land Registration Act (Northern Ireland) 1970 s.84. In force: March 31, 1996; £3.20.

This Order revokes and replaces the Land Registry (Fees) Order (Northern Ireland) 1988 (SR 1988 410) and prescribes the fees to be taken in the Land Registry for the purposes of the Land Registration Act (Northern Ireland) 1970 and the manner in which those fees are to be paid.

6305. Lands tribunal–salaries

LANDS TRIBUNAL (SALARIES) ORDER (NORTHERN IRELAND) 1996, SR 1996 377; made under the Lands Tribunal and Compensation Act (Northern Ireland) 1964 s.2(5); and the Administrative and Financial Provisions Act (Northern Ireland) 1962 s.18. In force: September 23, 1996; £1.10.

This Order provides for changes in the annual salaries payable to members of the Lands Tribunal for Northern Ireland.

ROAD TRAFFIC

6306. Bus lanes

BUS LANE (QUEEN'S SQUARE, BELFAST) ORDER (NORTHERN IRELAND) 1996, SR 1996 59; made under the Road Traffic (Northern Ireland) Order 1981 Art.21 (1). In force: April 4, 1996; £1.10.

This Order provides for a bus lane.

6307. Bus lanes

BUS LANE (SHAFTESBURY SQUARE AND GREAT VICTORIA STREET, BELFAST) ORDER (NORTHERN IRELAND) 1996, SR 1996 531; made under the Road Traffic (Northern Ireland) Order 1981 Art.22(1). In force: January 20, 1997; £1.10.

This Order provides for with-flow bus lanes on part of the citybound carriageway of Shaftesbury Square and part of Great Victoria Street, Belfast.

6308. Bus lanes

BUS LANE (UPPER LISBURN ROAD, BELFAST) ORDER (NORTHERN IRELAND) 1996, SR 1996 530; made under the Road Traffic (Northern Ireland) Order 1981 Art.22(1). In force: January 6, 1997; £1.10.

This Order provides for a with-flow bus lane on part of the citybound section of the Upper Lisburn Road, Belfast.

6309. Bus lanes

BUS LANES (ALBERTBRIDGE ROAD AND WOODSTOCK LINK, BELFAST) ORDER (NORTHERN IRELAND) 1995, SR 1995 498; made under the Road Traffic (Northern Ireland) Order 1981 Art.21 (1) (2). In force: February 12, 1996; £1.10.

This Order specifies bus lanes on Albertbridge Road and Woodstock Link, Belfast.

6310. Driving licences

DRIVING LICENCES (COMMUNITY DRIVING LICENCES) REGULATIONS (NORTHERN IRELAND) 1996, SR 1996 426; made under the European Communities Act 1972 s.2(2). In force: October 18, 1996 and January 1, 1997; £4.15.

These Regulations amend the Road Traffic (Northern Ireland) Order 1981 (SI 1981 154 (NI 1)), certain other Orders, the Transport Act (Northern Ireland) 1967 and the Motor Vehicles (International Circulation) Order (Northern Ireland) 1990 (SR 1990 190) to implement Council Directive 91/439 ([1991] OJ L237/1) on driving licences.

6311. Driving licences–Driver and Vehicle Testing Agency

DRIVER AND VEHICLE TESTING AGENCY TRADING FUND ORDER (NORTHERN IRELAND) ORDER 1996, SR 1996 32; made under the Financial Provisions (Northern Ireland) Order 1993 Art.3(1)(3), Art.4(1)(8), Art.5(1), Art.6(5), Art.11 (a). In force: April 1, 1996; £1.55.

This Order sets up a trading fund to finance the Driver and Vehicle Testing Agency.

6312. Driving licences–driving tests

MOTOR VEHICLES (DRIVING LICENCES) REGULATIONS (NORTHERN IRELAND) 1996, SR 1996 542; made under the Road Traffic (Northern Ireland) Order 1981 Art.4(7)(8), Art.5(3)(4)(5)(7)(8)(10), Art.6(3)(5), Art.8, Art.9(2)(4), Art.11 (4)(5), Art.13(1)(3)(4), Art.14(2)(4), Art.15(1)(2), Art.15A(3)(4),

Art.17(2)(3), Art.19C, Art.19D(1), Art.72(1), Art.73(1)(3), Art.73A(1), Art.74(4), Art.75(3), Art.77, Art.78, Art.194(8), Art.214(1), Art.218(1). In force: Reg.17, Reg.18, Reg.19, Reg.20, Reg.21, Reg.22, Reg.23, Reg.24, Reg.25, Sch.4: December 2, 1996; Reg.27(2)(a)(ii), Reg.27(4)(b), Sch.5: March 1, 1997; Remainder: January 1, 1997; £9.10.

These Regulations consolidate with amendments the Motor Vehicles (Driving Licences) Regulations (Northern Ireland) 1994 (SR 1994 365 as amended) and the Motor Vehicles (Driving Licences) (Large Goods and Passenger-Carrying Vehicles) Regulations (Northern Ireland) 1991 (SR 1991 100 as amended). The amendments have been made for the purpose of implementing that part of Council Directive 91/439 ([1991] OJ L237/1) relating to driving tests and for general purposes.

6313. Driving licences–driving tests

MOTOR VEHICLES (DRIVING LICENCES) (AMENDMENT NO.2) REGULATIONS (NORTHERN IRELAND) 1996, SR 1996 197; made under the Road Traffic (Northern Ireland) Order 1991 Art.5(3)(4)(5)(6)(8), Art.8, Art.13(1), Art.19C(1)(2), Art.19D(1), Art.218(1). In force: June 3, 1996; July 1, 1996; £4.70.

These Regulations replace the Motor Vehicles (Driving Licences) Regulations (Northern Ireland) 1994 Part III. The principal amendments introduce theory and practical driving tests for vehicles in categories A (motor bicycles), B (motor cars and small goods vehicles) and P (mopeds) to implement Council Directive 91/439 ([1991] OJ L237/1). Other tests remain unitary tests.

6314. Driving licences–heavy goods vehicles–passenger vehicles–fees

MOTOR VEHICLES (DRIVING LICENCES) (LARGE GOODS AND PASSENGER-CARRYING VEHICLES) (FEES) (AMENDMENT) REGULATIONS (NORTHERN IRELAND) 1996, SR 1996 305; made under the Road Traffic (Northern Ireland) Order 1981 Art.13(1), Art.218(1). In force: September 2, 1996; £1.10.

These Regulations amend the Motor Vehicles (Driving Licences) (Large Goods and Passenger-Carrying Vehicles) Regulations (Northern Ireland) 1991 (SR 1991 100) by increasing most fees payable for driving licences for large goods and passenger-carrying vehicles.

6315. Driving licences–test fees

MOTOR VEHICLES (DRIVING LICENCES) (AMENDMENT) (TEST FEES) REGULATIONS (NORTHERN IRELAND) 1996, SR 1996 141; made under the Road Traffic (Northern Ireland) Order 1981 Art.5(4), Art.218(1). In force: June 3, 1996; £1.10.

These Regulations further amend the Motor Vehicles (Driving Licences) Regulations (Northern Ireland) 1994 (SR 1994 365) by increasing the fee payable for a driving test on all types of vehicles except invalid carriages (for which no fee is payable).

6316. Driving licences–test fees

MOTOR VEHICLES (DRIVING LICENCES) (FEES) (AMENDMENT) REGULATIONS (NORTHERN IRELAND) 1996, SR 1996 299; made under the Road Traffic (Northern Ireland) Order 1981 Art.13(1), Art.19C(1), Art.218(1). In force: September 2, 1996; £1.10.

These Regulations amend the Motor Vehicles (Driving Licences) Regulations (Northern Ireland) 1994 (SR 1994 365) by increasing fees for driving tests and abolishing the fee for the grant of a licence to a person suffering from a disability.

6317. Heavy goods vehicles–passenger vehicles–tachographs

PASSENGER AND GOODS VEHICLES (RECORDING EQUIPMENT) REGULATIONS (NORTHERN IRELAND) 1996, SR 1996 145; made under the European Communities Act 1972 s.2(2); the Finance Act 1973 s.56(1)(5); and the Road Traffic (Northern Ireland) Order 1981, Art.56(5), Art.58, Art.63, Art.83(1), Art.218(1). In force: June 3, 1996; £2.40.

These Regulations consolidate, with amendments, the Passenger and Goods Vehicles (Recording Equipment) Regulations (Northern Ireland) 1979 (SR 1979 443 as amended). The Regulations impose requirements regarding the installation and use of recording equipment (tachographs) in vehicles, and make provision for the inspection and repair of such equipment.

6318. Heavy goods vehicles–testing–fees

GOODS VEHICLES (TESTING) (AMENDMENT) REGULATIONS (NORTHERN IRELAND) 1996, SR 1996 139; made under the Road Traffic (Northern Ireland) Order 1995 Art.65(1)(2), Art.67(1), Art.110(2). In force: June 3, 1996; £0.65.

These Regulations amend the Goods Vehicles (Testing) Regulations (Northern Ireland) 1995 (SR 1995 450) in relation to the periods referred to in Reg.13(4) for applications for re-tests, and increase the fees payable in respect of a trailer on application for a test or re-test.

6319. Motor vehicles–construction and use

MOTOR VEHICLES (CONSTRUCTION AND USE) (AMENDMENT) REGULATIONS (NORTHERN IRELAND) 1996, SR 1996 275; made under the Road Traffic (Northern Ireland) Order 1995 Art.55(1)(2)(6), Art.110(2). In force: in accordance with Reg.1 (1); £1.95.

These Regulations amend the Motor Vehicles (Construction and Use) Regulations (Northern Ireland) 1989 (SR 1989 299) by removing the 4.2 metre height restriction on the body-work of goods vehicles with a total weight restriction exceeding 35,000 kilograms, omitting Reg.19 (wheels not fitted with pneumatic types), Reg.45 (the power to weight ratio of heavy vehicles) and Reg.60 (noise limits for vehicles first used on or after April 1, 1970) and inserting a new Reg.48A which prohibits the use of a coach or minibus for carrying three or more children in connection with an organised trip unless as many forward facing seats as there are children are fitted with seat belts.

6320. Motor vehicles–construction and use

MOTOR VEHICLES (CONSTRUCTION AND USE) (AMENDMENT NO.2) REGULATIONS (NORTHERN IRELAND) 1996, SR 1996 462; made under the Road Traffic (Northern Ireland) Order 1981 Art.55(1)(2), Art.110(2). In force: November 1, 1996; £1.10.

These Regulations amend the Motor Vehicles (Construction and Use) Regulations (Northern Ireland) 1989 (SR 1989 299) by increasing the maximum overall width of all motor vehicles (except for certain locomotives and for refrigerated vehicles, which are already subject to maximum overall widths) to 2.55 metres. They also apply the same maximum width to certain trailers, agricultural trailed appliances and specified agricultural implements mounted on wheeled agricultural vehicles.

6321. Motor vehicles–control of traffic

CONTROL OF TRAFFIC (ANTRIM) ORDER (NORTHERN IRELAND) 1996, SR 1996 310; made under the Road Traffic (Northern Ireland) Order 1981 Art.23(1)(2). In force: September 2, 1996; £1.95.

This Order prohibits the use of specified roads and a length of road in Antrim by vehicles other than taxis.

6322. Motor vehicles–control of traffic

CONTROL OF TRAFFIC (BELFAST) ORDER (NORTHERN IRELAND) 1996, SR 1996 554; made under the Road Traffic (Northern Ireland) Order 1981 Art.23(1) (2). In force: January 13, 1997; £0.65.

This Order prohibits vehicles travelling in a north-easterly direction along the link road between Newtownbreda Road, Belfast, and Upper Knockbreda Road from making a right-hand turn into the southbound carriageway of Saintfield Road.

6323. Motor vehicles–control of traffic

CONTROL OF TRAFFIC (BELFAST) (NO.2) ORDER (NORTHERN IRELAND) 1996, SR 1996 623; made under the Road Traffic (Northern Ireland) Order 1981 Art.21 (1), Art.22(1). In force: February 9, 1997; £1.10.

This Order prescribes the traffic flow in and around Castle Lane and Callender Street, Belfast.

6324. Motor vehicles–control of traffic

CONTROL OF TRAFFIC (CASTLEDAWSON) ORDER (NORTHERN IRELAND) 1996, SR 1996 552; made under the Road Traffic (Northern Ireland) Order 1981 Art.23(1) (2). In force: January 20, 1997; £0.65.

This Order prohibits vehicles travelling in south-easterly direction along Old Magherafelt Road, Unclassified No.134, Castledawson, upon reaching its north-eastern junction with Castledawson Road, Route A31, from making a right-hand turn into Castledawson Road.

6325. Motor vehicles–control of traffic

CONTROL OF TRAFFIC (NEWRY) ORDER (NORTHERN IRELAND) 1995, SR 1995 408; made under the Road Traffic (Northern Ireland) Order 1981 Art.21 (1) (2). In force: December 6, 1996; £0.65.

This Order prohibits vehicles travelling in a northerly direction along Patrick Street, Newry, from making a right hand turn into Monaghan Street.

6326. Motor vehicles–control of traffic

CONTROL OF TRAFFIC (NEWRY) ORDER (NORTHERN IRELAND) 1996, SR 1996 550; made under the Road Traffic (Northern Ireland) Order 1981 Art.23(1) (2). In force: January 13, 1997; £1.10.

This Order prohibits vehicles travelling in an easterly direction along Craigmore Road, Newry, from making a right-hand turn into Newry By-Pass, Route A1 and in an easterly direction along Camlough Road Link, Route A1, Newry, from making a right-hand turn into Newry By-Pass, Route A1.

6327. Motor vehicles–control of traffic

CONTROL OF TRAFFIC (OMAGH) ORDER (NORTHERN IRELAND) 1996, SR 1996 368; made under the Road Traffic (Northern Ireland) Order 1981 Art.21 (1). In force: September 15, 1996; £0.65.

This Order prohibits right-hand turns in a road in Omagh.

6328. Motor vehicles–emissions–noise

MOTOR VEHICLES (TYPE APPROVAL) (AMENDMENT) REGULATIONS (NORTHERN IRELAND) 1996, SR 1996 156; made under the Road Traffic (Northern Ireland) Order 1981 Art.31A(1), Art.31D(1), Art.31E(1), Art.218(1). In force: May 20, 1996; £1.95.

These Regulations further amend the Motor Vehicles (Type Approval) Regulations (Northern Ireland) 1985 (SR 1985 294) so that, from May 20, 1996, the type approval requirements relating to noise emissions then in force shall apply to a vehicle regardless of the date of manufacture.

6329. Motor vehicles–international circulation–Isle of Man and Jersey–driving licences

MOTOR VEHICLES (INTERNATIONAL CIRCULATION) (AMENDMENT) ORDER (NORTHERN IRELAND) 1996, SR 1996 588; made under the Motor Vehicles (International Circulation) Act 1952 s.2. In force: January 25, 1997; £1.10.

This Order further amends the Motor Vehicles (International Circulation) Order (Northern Ireland) 1990 (SR 1990 190) to allow visitors to Northern Ireland resident in the Isle of Man or Jersey who hold appropriate visitors' driving permits, to drive in Northern Ireland large goods and passenger-carrying vehicles whether or not those vehicles have been brought temporarily into Northern Ireland. The definitions of Convention driving permit and domestic driving permit are amended so that foreign provisional licences do not have the same validity as full driving licences and the provision allowing foreign military personnel to drive large buses and lorries is restored.

6330. Motor vehicles–restrictions

MOTOR VEHICLES (PRESCRIBED RESTRICTIONS) REGULATIONS (NORTHERN IRELAND) 1996, SR 1996 446; made under the Road Traffic (Northern Ireland) Order 1981 Art.19A(3)(9), Art.214(1), Art.218(1). In force: November 4, 1996; £1.10.

These Regulations prescribe restrictions for the purposes of the Road Traffic (Northern Ireland) Order 1981 (SI 1981 154 (NI 1)) Art.19A with respect to newly qualified drivers and drivers disqualified until tested. They require an "R" plate to be displayed on the vehicle and impose a 45 mph speed limit on it.

6331. Motor vehicles–safety–payments–exemptions

MOTOR VEHICLES (PAYMENTS IN RESPECT OF APPLICANTS FOR EXEMPTION FROM WEARING SEAT BELTS) ORDER (NORTHERN IRELAND) 1996, SR 1996 146; made under the Road Traffic (Northern Ireland) Order 1995 Art.25(3), Art.110(1). In force: May 20, 1996; £0.65.

This Order amends the Road Traffic (Northern Ireland) Order 1995 (SI 1995 2994 (NI 18)) Art.25(2)(b) so as to enable the Department of the Environment to make payments in respect of an applicant for exemption from wearing seat belts who is either in receipt of an income based jobseeker's allowance paid under the Jobseekers (Northern Ireland) Order 1995 or is the dependant of such a person.

6332. Motor vehicles–testing

MOTOR VEHICLE TESTING (EXTENSION) ORDER (NORTHERN IRELAND) 1996, SR 1996 12; made under the Road Traffic (Northern Ireland) Order 1995 Art.63. In force: in accordance with Art.2; £1.10.

This Order requires motor vehicles registered or manufactured more than four years ago to be tested.

6333. Motor vehicles–testing–fees

MOTOR VEHICLE TESTING (AMENDMENT) REGULATIONS (NORTHERN IRELAND) 1996, SR 1996 140; made under the Road Traffic (Northern Ireland) Order 1995 Art.61(6), Art.62, Art.75(8), Art.81(8)(9), Art.110(2). In force: June 3, 1996; £1.55.

These Regulations amend the Motor Vehicle Testing Regulations (Northern Ireland) 1995 (SR 1995 448) by altering fees payable in respect of examinations, full inspections under the Road Traffic (Northern Ireland) Order 1995 (SI 1995 2994 (NI 18)) Art.81 and tests under Art.75(5) or a partial inspection under Art.81 of the 1995 Order and by making periods of 21 and 14 days in Reg.10(4) and Reg.15(1) consecutive days.

6334. Motor vehicles–weight restrictions

TRAFFIC WEIGHT RESTRICTION (BRITISH ROAD, ALDERGROVE, CRUMLIN) ORDER (NORTHERN IRELAND) 1996, SR 1996 37; made under the Road Traffic (Northern Ireland) Order 1981 Art.22(1). In force: March 31, 1996; £1.10.

This Order prohibits vehicles exceeding a specified weight from using a road.

6335. Motor vehicles–weight restrictions

TRAFFIC WEIGHT RESTRICTION (KILLYNAMPH ROAD, LISNASKEA) ORDER (NORTHERN IRELAND) 1996, SR 1996 555; made under the Road Traffic (Northern Ireland) Order 1981 Art.23(1)(2). In force: January 13, 1997; £1.10.

This Order prohibits vehicles exceeding 7.5 tonnes maximum gross weight from using Killynamph Road, Unclassified No.9446, Lisnaskea. Vehicles requiring access are excepted from the provisions of the Order.

6336. Motor vehicles–weight restrictions

TRAFFIC WEIGHT RESTRICTION (LONG RIG ROAD, NUTTS CORNER, CRUMLIN) ORDER (NORTHERN IRELAND) 1996, SR 1996 374; made under the Road Traffic (Northern Ireland) Order 1981 Art.22(1). In force: September 18, 1996; £1.10.

This Order prohibits vehicles exceeding 16.5 tonnes maximum gross weight from using a road at Nutts Corner, Crumlin.

6337. Motor vehicles–weight restrictions

TRAFFIC WEIGHT RESTRICTION (MILLBAY ROAD, ISLANDMAGEE) ORDER (NORTHERN IRELAND) 1996, SR 1996 27; made under the Road Traffic (Northern Ireland) Order 1981 Art.22(1). In force: March 19, 1996; £1.10.

This Order prohibits vehicles exceeding a specified weight from using a road.

6338. Motor vehicles–weight restrictions

TRAFFIC WEIGHT RESTRICTION (ROSSCOR VIADUCT BRIDGE) ORDER (NORTHERN IRELAND) 1996, SR 1996 171; made under the Road Traffic (Northern Ireland) Order 1981 Art.23(1). In force: June 5, 1996; £1.10.

This Order prohibits vehicles exceeding 7.5 tonnes maximum gross weight from using Rosscor Viaduct Bridge, Belleek, County Fermanagh.

6339. Parking

OFF-STREET PARKING BYE-LAWS (NORTHERN IRELAND) 1996, SR 1996 237; made under the Road Traffic (Northern Ireland) Order 1981 Art.105(1). In force: July 1, 1996; £10.05.

These Bye-laws revoke and replace with minor amendments, the Off-Street Parking Bye-Laws (Northern Ireland) 1994 (SR 1994 134) as amended.

6340. Parking

ON-STREET PARKING (AMENDMENT) BYE-LAWS (NORTHERN IRELAND) 1996, SR 1996 233; made under the Road Traffic (Northern Ireland) Order 1991 Art.107(1), Art.109(2), Art.110. In force: July 1, 1996; £1.10.

These bye-laws amend the On-Street Parking Bye-Laws (Northern Ireland) 1987 (SR 1987 410) by revising the charges applicable to on-street parking.

6341. Parking

PARKING PLACES ON ROADS (AMENDMENT) ORDER (NORTHERN IRELAND) 1996, SR 1996 241; made under the Road Traffic (Northern Ireland) Order 1981 Art.104 (1) (c). In force: July 26, 1996; £1.95.

This Order amends the Parking Places on Roads Order (Northern Ireland) 1993 (SR 1993 201) by adding and deleting specified parking places.

6342. Parking

PARKING PLACES ON ROADS (AMENDMENT NO.2) ORDER (NORTHERN IRELAND) 1996, SR 1996 309; made under the Road Traffic (Northern Ireland) Order 1981 Art.104 (1) (c). In force: September 2, 1996; £1.55.

This Order amends the Parking Places on Roads Order (Northern Ireland) 1993 (SR 1993 201) by adding and deleting specified parking places.

6343. Passenger vehicles–licences–fees

PUBLIC SERVICE VEHICLES (LICENCE FEES) (AMENDMENT) REGULATIONS (NORTHERN IRELAND) 1996, SR 1996 143; made under the Road Traffic (Northern Ireland) Order 1981 Art.61 (1), Art.66 (1), Art.218 (1). In force: June 3, 1996; £1.10.

These Regulations amend the Public Service Vehicles (Licence Fees) (Amendment) Regulations (Northern Ireland) 1985 (SR 1985 123) by amending the fee payable for certain applications and re-applications for a licence for a taxi or a bus. The Public Service Vehicles (Licence Fees) (Amendment) Regulations (Northern Ireland) 1995 (SR 1995 159) are revoked as a consequence of these Regulations.

6344. Public transport

PUBLIC SERVICE VEHICLES (AMENDMENT) REGULATIONS (NORTHERN IRELAND) 1995, SR 1995 446; made under the Road Traffic (Northern Ireland) Order 1981 Art.61 (1), Art.66 (1), Art.80, Art.218 (1). In force: January 24, 1996; £1.10.

These Regulations amend the Public Service Vehicles Regulations (Northern Ireland) (SR 1985 123).

6345. Public transport–safety

PUBLIC SERVICE VEHICLES (CONDITIONS OF FITNESS, EQUIPMENT AND USE) REGULATIONS (NORTHERN IRELAND) 1995, SR 1995 447; made under the Road Traffic (Northern Ireland) Order 1981 Art.66 (1), Art.218 (1); and the Road Traffic (Northern Ireland) Order 1995 Art.55 (1) (2) (4) (6), Art.110 (2). In force: January 24, 1996; £6.35.

These Regulations revoke and replace the Public Service Vehicles (Construction) Regulations (Northern Ireland) 1960 (SR & O (NI) 1960 91 as amended by SR & O (NI) 1967 224, SR & O (NI) 1969 63, SR 1988 335 and SR 1994 435).

6346. Road safety–road humps

ROAD HUMPS (AMENDMENT) REGULATIONS (NORTHERN IRELAND) 1996, SR 1996 613; made under the Roads (Northern Ireland) Order 1993 Art.65 (4). In force: February 10, 1997; £1.10.

These Regulations amend the Road Humps Regulations (Northern Ireland) 1992 (SI 1992 132) by including cushion type humps in the specification for road humps.

6347. Road safety–traffic signs

TRAFFIC SIGNS (AMENDMENT) REGULATIONS (NORTHERN IRELAND) 1996, SR 1996 69; made under the Road Traffic (Northern Ireland) Order 1981 Art.27. In force: April 22, 1996; £1.10.

These Regulations amend the Traffic Signs Regulations (Northern Ireland) 1979 (SR 1979 386) by inserting a new sign for restricting entry to pedestrian zones and allowing additional permitted variants for a diagram relating to parking places for disabled badge holders.

6348. Road safety–traffic signs

TRAFFIC SIGNS (AMENDMENT NO.2) REGULATIONS (NORTHERN IRELAND) 1996, SR 1996 392; made under the Road Traffic (Northern Ireland) Order 1981 Art.27. In force: October 13, 1996; £4.15.

These Regulations amend the Traffic Signs Regulations (Northern Ireland) 1979 (SR 1979 386) as respects definitions and diagrams for certain signs, by extending the use of the flashing amber warning signal to traffic on dual carriageways, by providing for the use of matrix signs, by permitting the use of blue flashing beacons to warn drivers to take special care, by specifying requirements for a wide range of variable message signs and by prescribing new signs and plates for various purposes.

6349. Road safety–traffic signs

TRAFFIC SIGNS (AMENDMENT NO.3) REGULATIONS (NORTHERN IRELAND) 1996, SR 1996 408; made under the Road Traffic (Northern Ireland) Order 1981 Art.27. In force: October 20, 1996; £1.10.

These Regulations amend the Traffic Signs Regulations (Northern Ireland) 1979 (SR 1979 386) by inserting a sign to indicate a waiting place for police patrol vehicles only.

6350. Road safety–traffic signs

TRAFFIC SIGNS (AMENDMENT NO.4) REGULATIONS (NORTHERN IRELAND) 1996, SR 1996 614; made under the Road Traffic (Northern Ireland) Order 1981 Art.27. In force: February 10, 1997; £1.95.

These Regulations amend the Traffic Signs Regulations (Northern Ireland) 1979 (SR 1979 386) by substituting new diagrams and prescribing a new road marking.

6351. Road Traffic (Northern Ireland) Order 1995 (SI 1995 2994 (NI 18))

This Order sets out the main road safety provisions for Northern Ireland. This includes making provision for offences of causing death or grievous bodily injury by dangerous driving, dangerous driving, careless and inconsiderate driving and causing death or grievous bodily injury by careless driving whilst under the influence of drink or drugs which is contained in Part II of the Order along with protective measures, cycling offences and restrictions in the interests of safety. Part III deals with the construction and use of vehicles and equipment, making offences of using motor vehicles or trailers in a condition which may cause injury, and empowers the Department of the Environment to make regulations relating to the use and construction and testing of vehicles. Miscellaneous amendments are made to the Road Traffic (Northern Ireland) Order 1981 (SI 1981 154 (NI 1)) relating to the extension of its enforcement provisions to include offences under this Order. This Order comes into force in accordance with Art.1 (2) (3).

6352. Road Traffic Offenders (Northern Ireland) Order 1996 (SI 1996 1320 (NI 10))

This Order comes into force in accordance with Art.1 and provides for the prosecution and punishment of road traffic offences. Part II deals with various matters concerning the trial of road traffic offences and Part III with penalties. A court may (and in certain instances must) on convicting a person of some offences order that he be disqualified for driving or that his licence be endorsed. Penalty points may be attributed where a person is convicted of an offence involving obligatory endorsement of his driving licence and are to be taken into account if he is convicted of a further offence. Under Part I, V and VI persons alleged to have committed certain road traffic offences may discharge liability to conviction by payment of a fixed penalty.

6353. Speed limits

EXPERIMENTAL SPEED LIMIT (ROUTE A1) (CONTINUATION) ORDER (NORTHERN IRELAND) 1996, SR 1996 39; made under the Road Traffic (Northern Ireland) Order 1981 Art.51 (5). In force: April 7, 1996; £0.65.

This Order continues the Experimental Speed Limit (Route A1) (Continuation) Order (Northern Ireland) 1995 (SR 1995 66) indefinitely.

6354. Speed limits

ROADS (SPEED LIMIT) ORDER 1996, SR 1996 2; made under the Road Traffic (Northern Ireland) Order 1981 Art.50. In force: February 19, 1996; £1.95.

This Order increases the speed limit on specified restricted roads.

6355. Speed limits

ROADS (SPEED LIMIT) (NO.2) ORDER (NORTHERN IRELAND) 1996, SR 1996 33; made under the Road Traffic (Northern Ireland) Order 1981 Art.50(4)(a). In force: March 21, 1996; £1.55.

This Order varies the speed limits on specified roads.

6356. Speed limits

ROADS (SPEED LIMIT) (NO.3) ORDER (NORTHERN IRELAND) 1995, SR 1995 432; made under the Road Traffic (Northern Ireland) Order 1981 Art.50(4)(c). In force: January 4, 1996; £1.95.

This Order makes certain specified roads and lengths of road restricted roads, thereby imposing a 30 mph speed limit on those roads.

6357. Speed limits

ROADS (SPEED LIMIT) (NO.3) ORDER (NORTHERN IRELAND) 1996, SR 1996 34; made under the Road Traffic (Northern Ireland) Order 1981 Art.50(4)(c). In force: March 25, 1996; £1.10.

This Order makes specified roads restricted roads, thereby imposing a 30 mph speed limit on those roads.

6358. Speed limits

ROADS (SPEED LIMIT) (NO.4) ORDER (NORTHERN IRELAND) 1995, SR 1995 496; made under the Road Traffic (Northern Ireland) Order 1981 Art.50(4)(c). In force: February 8, 1996; £1.10.

This Order makes certain specified roads restricted roads, thus imposing a 30 mph speed limit on those roads.

6359. Speed limits

ROADS (SPEED LIMIT) (NO.4) ORDER (NORTHERN IRELAND) 1996, SR 1996 118; made under the Road Traffic (Northern Ireland) Order 1981 Art.50. In force: May 6, 1996; £1.10.

This Order reduces from 30 mph to 20 mph the speed limit on specified restricted roads.

6360. Speed limits

ROADS (SPEED LIMIT) (NO.5) ORDER (NORTHERN IRELAND) 1996, SR 1996 162; made under the Road Traffic (Northern Ireland) Order 1981 Art.50(4) (c). In force: May 27, 1996; £1.95.

This Order makes specified roads and lengths of road restricted roads subject to a 30 mph speed limit

6361. Speed limits

ROADS (SPEED LIMIT) (NO.6) ORDER (NORTHERN IRELAND) 1996, SR 1996 215; made under the Road Traffic (Northern Ireland) Order 1981 Art.50 (4) (a). In force: July 9, 1996; £1.55.

This Order increases the speed limit on restricted roads.

6362. Speed limits

ROADS (SPEED LIMIT) (NO.7) ORDER (NORTHERN IRELAND) 1996, SR 1996 474; made under the Road Traffic (Northern Ireland) Order 1981 Art.50(4) (c). In force: November 18, 1996; £1.95.

This Order makes specified roads and lengths of road restricted roads, so imposing a 30 mph speed limit on them.

6363. Speed limits

ROADS (SPEED LIMIT) (NO.8) ORDER (NORTHERN IRELAND) 1996, SR 1996 536; made under the Road Traffic (Northern Ireland) Order 1981 Art.50(4) (a). In force: December 31, 1996; £1.95.

This Order increases or reduces speed limits on specified restricted roads.

6364. Speed limits

ROADS (SPEED LIMIT) (NO.9) ORDER (NORTHERN IRELAND) 1996, SR 1996 553; made under the Road Traffic (Northern Ireland) Order 1981 Art.50(4), Art.211A. In force: January 27, 1997; £1.10.

This Order makes the roads and length of roads specified in the Schedule restricted roads, thereby imposing a 30 mph speed limit on those roads.

6365. Speed limits

ROADS (SPEED LIMIT) (NO.10) ORDER (NORTHERN IRELAND) 1996, SR 1996 617; made under the Road Traffic (Northern Ireland) Order 1981 Art.50(4) (c). In force: February 10, 1997; £2.80.

This Order provides for certain roads and lengths of road to be restricted roads, thereby imposing a 30 mph speed limit on those roads.

6366. Speed limits

TEMPORARY SPEED LIMIT (BELFAST) ORDER (NORTHERN IRELAND) 1996, SR 1996 535; made under the Road Traffic (Northern Ireland) Order 1981 Art.51 (1), Art.211A. In force: December 29, 1996; £1.55.

This Order imposes temporary speed limits of 50 mph on part of the M3 and a slip road from it and of 30 mph on the T1 Trunk Road, Belfast, part of the Route A2, Belfast and related slip roads.

6367. Speed limits

TEMPORARY SPEED LIMIT (BELFAST) (NO.2) ORDER (NORTHERN IRELAND) 1996, SR 1996 615; made under the Road Traffic (Northern Ireland) Order 1981 Art.51 (1), Art.211A. In force: February 9, 1997; £1.10.

This Order imposes speed limits on specified roads for a four month period beginning on February 8, 1997.

6368. Speed limits

TEMPORARY SPEED LIMIT (MAGHERAMASON) ORDER (NORTHERN IRELAND) 1996, SR 1996 406; made under the Road Traffic (Northern Ireland) 1981 Art.51 (1). In force: October 21, 1996; £0.65.

This Order imposes a temporary 30 mph speed limit on part of Victoria Road, Route A5 (T3), Magheramason, Londonderry.

6369. Speed limits

TEMPORARY SPEED LIMIT (MAGHERAMASON) (NO.2) ORDER (NORTHERN IRELAND) 1996, SR 1996 568; made under the Road Traffic (Northern Ireland) Order 1981 Art.51 (4). In force: February 21, 1997; £0.65.

This Order continues in force the provisions of the Temporary Speed Limit (Magheramason) Order (Northern Ireland) 1996 (SR 1996 406). It prohibits for a further period of four months commencing on February 21, 1997 the driving of motor vehicles at a speed greater than 30 mph on Victoria Road, Route A5 (T3), Magheramason, Londonderry, from a point approximately 100 metres south-west of its junction with Meenagh Road, Unclassified No.1809, to a point approximately 85 metres north-east of its junction with Clampernow Road, Unclassified No.1157.

6370. Speed limits

TEMPORARY SPEED LIMIT (SYDENHAM BY-PASS, ROUTE A2, BELFAST) (CONTINUATION) (REVOCATION) ORDER (NORTHERN IRELAND) 1996, SR 1996 42; made under the Road Traffic (Northern Ireland) Order 1981 Art.51 (5). In force: April 3, 1996; £0.65.

This Order revokes the Temporary Speed Limit (Sydenham By-pass, Route A2, Belfast) (Continuation) (Revocation) Order (Northern Ireland) 1995 (SI 1995 288), thereby removing the temporary 30 mph speed limit.

6371. Speed limits

TEMPORARY SPEED LIMIT (SYDENHAM BY-PASS, ROUTE A2, BELFAST) ORDER (NORTHERN IRELAND) 1996, SR 1996 178; made under the Road Traffic (Northern Ireland) Order 1991 Art.51 (1). In force: June 10, 1996; £0.65.

This Order prohibits in the interest of safety the driving of motor vehicles at more than 30 mph on part of the Route A2, Belfast.

6372. Speed limits

TEMPORARY SPEED LIMIT (SYDENHAM BYPASS, ROUTE A2, BELFAST) (NO.2) ORDER (NORTHERN IRELAND) 1996, SR 1996 367; made under the Road Traffic (Northern Ireland) Order 1981 Art.51 (4). In force: October 10, 1996; £0.65.

This Order continues for four months a speed limit of 30 mph on part of the Sydenham By-Pass, Route A2, Belfast,

6373. Street Works (Northern Ireland) Order 1995–Commencement No.1 Order

STREET WORKS (1995 ORDER) (COMMENCEMENT NO.1) ORDER (NORTHERN IRELAND) 1996, SR 1996 223 (C.10); made under the Northern Ireland Act 1974 Sch.1 para.2 (1); and the Street Works (Northern Ireland) Order 1995 Art.1 (2). In force: bringing into force various provisions of the Order into force on June 3, 1996; £1.10.

This Order brings specified provisions of the Street Works (Northern Ireland) Order 1995 (SI 1995 3210 (NI 19)) into operation on June 3, 1996.

6374. Taxis

MOTOR HACKNEY CARRIAGES (BELFAST) (AMENDMENT) BY-LAWS (NORTHERN IRELAND) 1996, SR 1996 113; made under the Road Traffic (Northern Ireland) Order 1981 Art.65(1)(2). In force: May 1, 1996; £1.10.

These Byelaws amend the Motor Hackney Carriages (Belfast) By-Laws (Northern Ireland) 1951 made on June 4, 1951 by altering the position of two taxi stands and increasing the number of taxis which may stand.

6375. Taxis

MOTOR HACKNEY CARRIAGES (BELFAST) (AMENDMENT NO.2) BY-LAWS (NORTHERN IRELAND) 1996, SR 1996 523; made under the Road Traffic (Northern Ireland) Order 1981 Art.65(1)(2). In force: December 9, 1996; £1.10.

These byelaws amend the Motor Hackney Carriages (Belfast) By-laws 1951 made on June 4, 1951 by fixing minimum and maximum fares.

6376. Taxis

MOTOR HACKNEY CARRIAGES (BELFAST) (AMENDMENT NO.3) BY-LAWS (NORTHERN IRELAND) 1996, SR 1996 543; made under the Road Traffic (Northern Ireland) Order 1981 Art.65(1)(2). In force: December 30, 1996; £1.55.

These Byelaws revoke and replace the Schedule to the Motor Hackney Carriages (Belfast) Bylaws 1951 made on June 4, 1951. They make provision for new taxi stands at Corporation Square, Great Victoria Street and Donegall Quay, and the alteration of the position of existing stands at Corporation Square and Oxford Street. The number of taxi stands in Corporation Square has been reduced from 18 to seven. The Motor Hackney Carriages (Belfast) (Amendment) By-laws (Northern Ireland) 1991 (SR 1991 298), the Motor Hackney Carriages (Belfast) (Amendment No.2) By-laws (Northern Ireland) 1992 (SR 1992 526) and the Motor Hackney Carriages (Belfast) (Amendment) By-laws (Northern Ireland) 1996 (SR 1996 113) are revoked.

6377. Taxis

TAXIS (NEWTOWNARDS) BYE-LAWS 1996, SR 1996 6; made under the Road Traffic (Northern Ireland) Order 1981 Art.65. In force: February 12, 1996; £1.10.

These byelaws prescribe precise locations to be used as stands or starting places for taxis in Newtownards, the maximum number of taxis which may use the stands or starting places and the hours that they are available for use.

6378. Taxis

TAXIS (STRABANE) (AMENDMENT) BYE-LAWS (NORTHERN IRELAND) 1996, SR 1996 352; made under the Road Traffic (Northern Ireland) Order 1981 Art.65(1)(2). In force: September 9, 1996; £0.65.

These Byelaws amend the Taxis (Strabane) Bye-laws (Northern Ireland) 1988 as respects two taxi stands.

6379. Taxis–driving licences–fees

MOTOR VEHICLES (TAXI DRIVERS' LICENCES) (AMENDMENT) REGULATIONS (NORTHERN IRELAND) 1996, SR 1996 304; made under the Road Traffic (Northern Ireland) Order Art.79A(2)(4), Art.218(1). In force: August 27, 1996; £0.65.

These Regulations amend the Motor Vehicles (Taxi Drivers' Licences) Regulations (Northern Ireland) 1991 (SR 1991 454) by replacing the two tier system of fees for licences by a single fee of £58.50 and revoking the provisions dealing with tests of competence.

6380. Taxis–driving licences–fees

MOTOR VEHICLES (TAXI DRIVERS' LICENCES) (FEES) (AMENDMENT) REGULATIONS (NORTHERN IRELAND) 1996, SR 1996 142; made under the Road Traffic (Northern Ireland) Order 1981 Art.79A(2), Art.218(1). In force: June 3, 1996; £0.65.

These Regulations further amend the Motor Vehicles (Taxi Drivers' Licences) Regulations (Northern Ireland) 1991 (SR 1991 454) by decreasing the fee for a renewal of a licence from £60 to £58.50.

6381. Traffic regulation–one-way traffic

ONE-WAY TRAFFIC (BALLYMENA) (AMENDMENT) ORDER (NORTHERN IRELAND) 1996, SR 1996 45; made under the Road Traffic (Northern Ireland) Order 1981 Art.21 (1). In force: May 13, 1996; £0.65.

This Order amends the provisions of the One-Way Traffic (Ballymena) Order (Northern Ireland) 1982 (SR 1982 33).

6382. Traffic regulation–one-way traffic

ONE-WAY TRAFFIC (BALLYMENA) (AMENDMENT NO.2) ORDER (NORTHERN IRELAND) 1996, SR 1996 63; made under the Road Traffic (Northern Ireland) Order 1981 Art.21 (1). In force: April 15, 1996; £0.65.

This Order amends the One-Way Traffic (Ballymena) Order (Northern Ireland) 1982 (SR 1982 33).

6383. Traffic regulation–one way-traffic

ONE-WAY TRAFFIC (BALLYMENA) (AMENDMENT NO.3) ORDER (NORTHERN IRELAND) 1996, SR 1996 372; made under the Road Traffic (Northern Ireland) Order 1981 Art.21 (1). In force: September 15, 1996; £0.65.

This Order amends the One-Way Traffic (Ballymena) Order (Northern Ireland) 1982 (SR 1982 33) by deleting items relating to Duke Street.

6384. Traffic regulation–one-way traffic

ONE-WAY TRAFFIC (BALLYMENA) (AMENDMENT NO.4) ORDER (NORTHERN IRELAND) 1996, SR 1996 373; made under the Road Traffic (Northern Ireland) Order 1981 Art.21 (1). In force: September 16, 1996; £0.65.

This Order amends the One-Way Traffic (Ballymena) Order (Northern Ireland) 1982 (SR 1982 33) by reversing the flow of traffic in part of Cullybackey Road.

6385. Traffic regulation–one-way traffic

ONE-WAY TRAFFIC (BELFAST) (AMENDMENT) ORDER (NORTHERN IRELAND) 1996, SR 1996 44; made under the Road Traffic (Northern Ireland) Order 1981 Art.21 (1). In force: April 10, 1996; £0.65.

This Order amends the provisions of the One-Way Traffic (Belfast) Order (Northern Ireland) 1986 (SR 1986 6).

6386. Traffic regulation–one-way traffic

ONE-WAY TRAFFIC (BELFAST) (AMENDMENT NO.2) ORDER (NORTHERN IRELAND) 1996, SR 1996 60; made under the Road Traffic (Northern Ireland) Order 1981 Art.23(1), Art.23(2). In force: April 4, 1996; £0.65.

This Order, which amends the One-Way Traffic (Belfast) Order (Northern Ireland) 1986 (SR 1986 6), relates to the traffic flow around the Queen's Square area of Belfast.

6387. Traffic regulation–one-way traffic

ONE-WAY TRAFFIC (KILLYLEAGH) ORDER (NORTHERN IRELAND) 1996, SR 1996 163; made under the Road Traffic (Northern Ireland) Order 1981 Art.23(1), Art.23(2). In force: June 5, 1996; £0.65.

This Order provides for a one-way system in Shore Street, Killyleagh.

6388. Traffic regulation–one-way traffic

ONE-WAY TRAFFIC (OMAGH) (AMENDMENT) ORDER (NORTHERN IRELAND) 1996, SR 1996 161; made under the Road Traffic (Northern Ireland) Order 1981 Art.23(1)(2). In force: May 27, 1996; £0.65.

This Order amends the One-Way Traffic (Omagh) Order (Northern Ireland) 1986 (SR 1986 215) to reverse the flow of traffic in a street in Omagh.

6389. Traffic regulation–urban clearways

URBAN CLEARWAYS (BELFAST) (NO.2) ORDER (AMENDMENT) ORDER (NORTHERN IRELAND) 1996, SR 1996 170; made under the Road Traffic (Northern Ireland) Order 1981 Art.21(1). In force: June 10, 1996; £1.10.

This Order amends the Urban Clearways (Belfast) (No.2) Order (Northern Ireland) 1981 (SR 1981 304).

6390. Traffic regulation–urban clearways

URBAN CLEARWAYS (LONDONDERRY) (AMENDMENT) ORDER (NORTHERN IRELAND) 1996, SR 1996 616; made under the Road Traffic (Northern Ireland) Order 1981 Art.21(1). In force: February 9, 1997; £1.10.

This Order further amends the Urban Clearways (Londonderry) Order (Northern Ireland) 1986 (SR 1986 4) by deleting the items relating to Custom House Street, Waterloo Place and William Street and reducing the extent of the item relating to Shipquay Place, Londonderry.

SCIENCE

6391. Genetic engineering

GENETICALLY MODIFIED ORGANISMS (CONTAINED USE) (AMENDMENT) REGULATIONS 1996, SR 1996 250; made under the European Communities Act 1972 s.2(2). In force: July 29, 1996; £1.95.

These Regulations amend the Genetically Modified Organisms (Contained Use) Regulations (Northern Ireland) 1994 (SR 1994 143) by inserting definitions of Member State (which includes States of the European Economic Area). European Economic Area and the Agreement (on that Area) and amending the definition of organisms, by implementing new criteria for micro-organisms in Commission Directive 94/51 ([1994] OJ L297/29), which adapts to technical progress Council Directive 90/219 ([1990] OJ L117/1), by extending exemptions in Reg.6(2)(a) to exclude from the prohibition in Reg.6(1) certain medicinal products marketed in accordance with Council Regulation 2309/93 ([1993] OJ L214/1) and by amending Reg.8(2) to provide that a separate notification is not required in certain cases where a consent for Group II micro-organisms has already been granted.

6392. Genetic engineering–risk assessment

GENETICALLY MODIFIED ORGANISMS (RISK ASSESSMENT) (RECORDS AND EXEMPTIONS) REGULATIONS (NORTHERN IRELAND) 1996, SR 1996

442; made under the Genetically Modified Organisms (Northern Ireland) Order 1991 Art.5(5)(7). In force: October 31, 1996; £1.10.

These Regulations replace with amendments, and revoke, the Genetically Modified Organisms (Contained Use) (No.2) Regulations (Northern Ireland) 1994 (SR 1994 145).

SOCIAL SECURITY

6393. Adjudication

SOCIAL SECURITY (ADJUDICATION) (AMENDMENT) REGULATIONS (NORTHERN IRELAND) 1996, SR 1996 355; made under the Social Security Administration (Northern Ireland) Act 1992 s.25(1), s.57(1)(2)(5), s.59(1)(2); and the Jobseekers (Northern Ireland) Order 1995 Art.32, Sch.1 para.4. In force: October 7, 1996; £2.80.

These Regulations amend the Social Security (Adjudication) Regulations (Northern Ireland) 1995 (SR 1995 293) to make provision in relation to jobseeker's allowance which is comparable to that in relation to income support. They also insert a new Reg.56B to provide that where a person is in receipt of a jobseeker's allowance and he or his partner wishes to claim income support instead or vice versa, the adjudication officer may end the claimant's current benefit where he is satisfied that the claimant or his partner will be entitled to the other benefit.

6394. Adjudication

SOCIAL SECURITY (ADJUDICATION) (AMENDMENT NO.2) REGULATIONS (NORTHERN IRELAND) 1996, SR 1996 499; made under the Social Security Administration (Northern Ireland) Act 1992 s.59(1)(2), s.165. In force: November 8, 1996; £1.10.

These Regulations amend the Social Security (Adjudication) Regulations (Northern Ireland) 1995 (SR 1995 293) Reg.63A to provide, in respect of a person treated as having been awarded a jobseeker's allowance in accordance with the Jobseeker's Allowance (Transitional Provisions) Regulations (Northern Ireland) 1996 (SR 1996 200) Reg.6, for the date on which a determination on a review is to have effect where a reduction in capital outstanding on a loan has occurred.

6395. Benefits–computation of earnings

SOCIAL SECURITY BENEFIT (COMPUTATION OF EARNINGS) REGULATIONS (NORTHERN IRELAND) 1996, SR 1996 520; made under the Social Security Contributions and Benefits (Northern Ireland) Act 1992 s.3(2)(3), s.80(7), s.89, s.112, s.119, s.171(1)(3)(4), Sch.7 para.4(6); and the Social Security Administration (Northern Ireland) Act 1992 s.5(1)(o)(s), s.69(7), s.165(4)(5). In force: November 25, 1996; £4.70.

These Regulations provide for the way in which the earnings of a person to whom benefit is or may be payable, or the earnings of such a person's dependant, are to be calculated for provisions of the Social Security Contributions and Benefits (Northern Ireland) Act 1992, and regulations under it, by which the right to, or the amount of, benefit depends on the amount of those earnings.

6396. Benefits–foreign nationals

SOCIAL SECURITY (PERSONS FROM ABROAD) (MISCELLANEOUS AMENDMENTS) REGULATIONS (NORTHERN IRELAND) 1996, SR 1996 11; made under the Social Security Contributions and Benefits (Northern Ireland)

Act 1992 s.64, s.68, s.70, s.71, s.122, s.129, s.131, s.133; and the Social Security Administration (Northern Ireland) Act 1992 s.5. In force: February 5, 1996; £2.80.

These Regulations exclude persons from entitlement to certain non-contributory benefits if their right to remain in Northern Ireland is subject to any limitation or condition, make provision regarding interim payments during an appeal and make provision in respect of asylum seekers and sponsored immigrants.

6397. Benefits–maintenance payments

SOCIAL SECURITY BENEFITS (MAINTENANCE PAYMENTS AND CONSEQUENTIAL AMENDMENTS) REGULATIONS (NORTHERN IRELAND) 1996, SR 1996 202; made under the Social Security Administration (Northern Ireland) Act 1992 s.72A(5)(6); and the Social Security Contributions and Benefits (Northern Ireland) Act 1992 s.132(4)(b). In force: July 1, 1996; £1.10.

These Regulations provide that where the Department of Health and Social Services is collecting maintenance payments on behalf of a person claiming certain social security benefits, it may disregard those payments for the purposes of calculating the claimant's benefit entitlement and may then retain any such payments collected by it.

6398. Benefits–revaluation of earnings factors

SOCIAL SECURITY REVALUATION OF EARNINGS FACTORS ORDER (NORTHERN IRELAND) 1996, SR 1996 168; made under the Social Security Administration (Northern Ireland) Act 1992 s.130. In force: May 25, 1996; £0.65.

This Order directs that the earnings factors relevant to the calculation of the additional pension in the rate of any long-term benefit or of any guaranteed minimum pension or to any other calculation required under the Pension Schemes (Northern Ireland) Act 1993 Part III for specified tax years to be increased by specified percentages. It also provides for the rounding of fractional amounts in certain cases.

6399. Benefits–state retirement pensions

SOCIAL SECURITY (GRADUATED RETIREMENT BENEFIT) (AMENDMENT) REGULATIONS (NORTHERN IRELAND) 1995, SR 1995 483; made under the Social Security Contributions and Benefits (Northern Ireland) 1992 s.62(1); and the Social Security Administration (Northern Ireland) Act 1992 s.135(7). In force: January 29, 1996; £1.10.

These Regulations further amend the Social Security (Graduated Retirement Benefit) (No.2) Regulations (Northern Ireland) 1978 (SR 1978 105), which preserve the rights, prospective rights or expectations of persons to graduated retirement benefit by retaining the effect of the National Insurance Act (Northern Ireland) 1966 s.35 and s.36.

6400. Benefits–up-rating

SOCIAL SECURITY BENEFITS UP-RATING ORDER (NORTHERN IRELAND) 1996, SR 1996 73; made under the Social Security Administration (Northern Ireland) Act 1992 s.132. In force: in accordance with Art.1 (1); £6.45.

This Order increases the rates and amounts of certain social security benefits.

6401. Benefits–up rating

SOCIAL SECURITY BENEFITS UP-RATING (NO.2) ORDER (NORTHERN IRELAND) 1996, SR 1996 184; made under the Social Security Administration (Northern Ireland) Act 1992 s.132. In force: May 3, 1996; £0.65.

This Order increases to £60 the maximum amount to be allowed in respect of child care charges relevant to the calculation of housing benefit.

6402. Benefits–up-rating

SOCIAL SECURITY BENEFITS UP-RATING REGULATIONS (NORTHERN IRELAND) 1996, SR 1996 74; made under the Social Security Contributions and Benefits (Northern Ireland) Act 1992 s.30E(1), s.90(b), s.113(1)(a), Sch.7 para.2(3); and the Social Security Administration (Northern Ireland) Act 1992 s.135(3). In force: April 8, 1996; £1.10.

These Regulations restrict the application of the Social Security Administration (Northern Ireland) Act 1992 s.135(3) and the Social Security Benefits Up-rating Order (Northern Ireland) 1996 (SR 1996 73).

6403. Bonus schemes

SOCIAL SECURITY (BACK TO WORK BONUS) (AMENDMENT) REGULATIONS (NORTHERN IRELAND) 1996, SR 1996 319; made under the Jobseekers (Northern Ireland) Order 1995 Art.28, Art.36(2). In force: October 7, 1996; £3.20.

These Regulations amend the Social Security (Back to Work Bonus) Regulations (Northern Ireland) 1996 (SR 1996 201). In particular, under a new Reg.25A,in certain circumstances a back to work bonus may be claimed and awarded in advance of the requirements for a bonus being satisfied and, under a new Reg.25B, where a person satisfied the requirements for a back to work bonus but died before claiming it, the bonus may be claimed by a person appointed by the Department of Health and Social Services.

6404. Bonus schemes

SOCIAL SECURITY (BACK TO WORK BONUS) (NO.2) REGULATIONS (NORTHERN IRELAND) 1996, SR 1996 519; made under the Jobseekers (Northern Ireland) Order 1995 Art.28, Art.36. In force: December 16, 1996; £4.70.

These Regulations supplement the Jobseekers (Northern Ireland) Order 1995 Art.28 which introduced the back to work bonus for persons who are or may not have been entitled to income support or a jobseeker's allowance.

6405. Child benefit

CHILD BENEFIT (GENERAL) (AMENDMENT) REGULATIONS (NORTHERN IRELAND) 1996, SR 1996 422; made under the Social Security Contributions and Benefits (Northern Ireland) Act 1992 s.142A. In force: October 7, 1996; £1.10.

These Regulations amend the Child Benefit (General) Regulations (Northern Ireland) 1979 (SR 1979 5) by prescribing conditions when the Social Security Contributions and Benefits (Northern Ireland) Act 1992 s.142A (which disentitles persons who require leave to enter or remain in the UK from receiving child benefit) will not apply.

6406. Child benefit

CHILD BENEFIT (GENERAL) (AMENDMENT NO.2) REGULATIONS (NORTHERN IRELAND) 1996, SR 1996 469; made under the Social Security Contributions and Benefits (Northern Ireland) Act 1992 s.142A; and the Asylum and Immigration Act 1996 s.10. In force: October 7, 1996; £1.10.

These Regulations amend the Child Benefit (General) Regulations (Northern Ireland) 1979 (SR 1979 5) by prescribing additional conditions when the Social Security Contributions and Benefits (Northern Ireland) Act 1992 s.142A (which disentitles persons who require leave to enter or remain in the United Kingdom from receiving child benefit) will not apply.

6407. Child benefit

CHILD BENEFIT (GENERAL) (AMENDMENT NO.3) REGULATIONS (NORTHERN IRELAND) 1996, SR 1996 470; made under the Social Security

Contributions and Benefits (Northern Ireland) Act 1992 s.139(3)(c), Sch.9 para.1(1)(f)(i). In force: November 4, 1996; £1.10.

These Regulations amend the Child Benefit (General) Regulations (Northern Ireland) 1979 (SR 1979 5) so that a person may be entitled to child benefit notwithstanding the absence of a child who is in residential accommodation provided under the Children (Northern Ireland) Order 1995 and to provide that there will be no title to child benefit in respect of a child who is looked after by an authority in specified circumstances or who is placed for adoption and in respect of whom an authority is making a payment.

6408. Child benefit–child support

CHILD BENEFIT, CHILD SUPPORT AND SOCIAL SECURITY (MISCELLANEOUS AMENDMENTS) REGULATIONS (NORTHERN IRELAND) 1996, SR 1996 288; made under the Child Support (Northern Ireland) Order 1991 Art.40(1)(b), Art.47, Sch.1 para.1(3)(5), Sch.1 para.2(1), Sch.1 para.4(3), Sch.1 para.5(1)(2), Sch.1 para.6(2), Sch.1 para.9; the Social Security Contributions and Benefits (Northern Ireland) Act 1992 s.122(1)(a), s.131(1), s.132(3)(4)(a)(b), s.141(1), Sch.9 para.4; the Social Security Administration (Northern Ireland) Act 1992 s.1(1), s.5(1)(i)(j), s.25(1)(b), s.71(1)(a); and the Jobseekers (Northern Ireland) Order 1995 Art.6(5), Art.14(2)(a)(b). In force: April 7, 1996; £3.20.

These Regulations amend the Child Benefit and Social Security (Fixing and Adjustment of Rates) Regulations (Northern Ireland) 1976 (SR 1976 223) so as to specify a composite rate of child benefit to be payable in respect of the only, elder or eldest child of a lone parent rather than two distinct rates. They also replace the premium which is applicable in relation to lone parents in receipt of income support and jobseeker's allowance with an additional element in the family premium. They also amend the Child Benefit (General) Regulations (Northern Ireland) 1979 (SR 1979 5) to provide that unmarried partners are not entitled to child benefit in any week where they are exempt from UK income tax and that a person is not entitled to child benefit in respect of a child who, in any week, is living with another person as his spouse.

6409. Child support

CHILD SUPPORT (MISCELLANEOUS AMENDMENTS) REGULATIONS (NORTHERN IRELAND) 1996, SR 1996 317; made under the Child Support (Northern Ireland) Order 1991 Art.16(1), Art.23(2), Art.32(1), Art.39(3), Art.43(11), Art.47, Art.48(4), Sch.1 para.5(1)(2), Sch.1 para.6, Sch.1 para.8, Sch.1 para.11. In force: Reg.2, Reg.3(1)(2)(5), Reg.4(1)(2)(4)(5)(6), Reg.5(1)(3): August 5, 1996; Remainder: October 7, 1996; £2.80.

These Regulations amend the Child Support (Information, Evidence and Disclosure) Regulations (Northern Ireland) 1992 (SR 1992 339) to provide for information to be given to the Department of Health and Social Services in certain cases. They amend the Child Support (Maintenance Assessment Procedure) Regulations (Northern Ireland) 1992 (SR 1992 340) as respects maintenance periods, the reference of cases to child support officers, the issue of further reduced benefit directions and the reduction of the income support personal allowance for a single claimant of 25 or over. They amend the Child Support (Maintenance Assessments and Special Cases) Regulations (Northern Ireland) 1992 (SR 1992 341) as respects the net income of absent parents, the maintenance requirement where an application is made in relation to only one of two absent parents and the inclusion of travel expenses in earnings. They also amend the Child Support Appeal Tribunals (Procedure) Regulations (Northern Ireland) 1993 (SR 1993 50) to allow disclosure to the parties to an appeal of an address or information which might lead to a person being located in certain cases.

6410. Child support–adjudication

SOCIAL SECURITY (ADJUDICATION) AND CHILD SUPPORT (AMENDMENT) REGULATIONS (NORTHERN IRELAND) 1996, SR 1996 24; made under the Child

Support (Northern Ireland) Order 1991 Art.23(2); and the Social Security Administration (Northern Ireland) Act 1992 s.57(1), Sch.3 para.2, Sch.3 para.5. In force: February 28, 1996; £1.55.

These Regulations amend the Social Security (Adjudication) Regulations (Northern Ireland) 1995 (SR 1995 293) and the Child Support Appeal Tribunals (Procedure) Regulations (Northern Ireland) 1993 (SR 1993 50).

6411. Child support–adjudication

SOCIAL SECURITY (ADJUDICATION) AND CHILD SUPPORT (AMENDMENT NO.2) REGULATIONS (NORTHERN IRELAND) 1996, SR 1996 457; made under the Social Security Administration (Northern Ireland) Act 1992 s.20(2) (4), s.31 (2), s.44(2), s.57(1), Sch.3 para.2, Sch.3 para.3, Sch.3 para.4, Sch.3 para.5; and the Child Support (Northern Ireland) Order 1995 Art.23(2) (3). In force: October 21, 1996; £3.20.

These Regulations amend the Child Support Regulations (Northern Ireland) 1993 (SR 1993 50) and the Social Security (Adjudication) Regulations (Northern Ireland) 1995 (SR 1995 293) to change the procedure of child support tribunals, social security appeal tribunals, disability appeal tribunals and medical appeal tribunals.

6412. Child support–child maintenance bonus

SOCIAL SECURITY (CHILD MAINTENANCE BONUS) REGULATIONS (NORTHERN IRELAND) 1996, SR 1996 622; made under the Social Security Contributions and Benefits (Northern Ireland) Act 1992 s.132(4) (b), s.171 (1) (3); the Social Security Administration (Northern Ireland) Act 1992 s.5(1) (q), s.69(8), s.74(2), s.165(1) (3) (4); and the Child Support (Northern Ireland) Order 1995 Art.4, Art.19(1). In force: April 7, 1997; £3.20.

The Child Support (Northern Ireland) Order 1995 (SI 1995 2702) (NI 13)) introduces a child maintenance bonus for persons who are or have been entitled to income support or an income based jobseeker's allowance and who have also been in receipt of child maintenance payments. These Regulations make provision relating to the child maintenance bonus.

6413. Child support–consequential amendments

CHILD SUPPORT DEPARTURE DIRECTION AND CONSEQUENTIAL AMENDMENTS REGULATIONS (NORTHERN IRELAND) 1996, SR 1996 541; made under the Child Support (Northern Ireland) Order 1991 Art.2(2), Art.16(3), Art.23, Art.28A(3), Art.28B(2) (b), Art.28C(2) (b) (6) (b), Art.28E(5), Art.28F(3) (4) (8), Art.28G(3) (4) (5), Art.39, Art.47, Art.48(4), Sch.1 para.5, Sch.4A para.2, Sch.4A para.4, Sch.4A para.6, Sch.4A para.7, Sch.4A para.9, Sch.4B. In force: December 2, 1996; £7.05.

These Regulations provide for an application for a departure direction to be made, the effect of which, if given, would be to vary a child support maintenance assessment determined in accordance with the formula provisions of the Child Support (Northern Ireland) Order 1991 (SI 1991 2628 (NI 23)) Sch.1 Part I and the Regulations made under it.

6414. Child support–jobseeker's allowance

SOCIAL SECURITY AND CHILD SUPPORT (JOBSEEKER'S ALLOWANCE) (AMENDMENT) REGULATIONS (NORTHERN IRELAND) 1996, SR 1996 358; made under the Social Security Contributions and Benefits (Northern Ireland) Act 1992 s.123(1) (e), s.167D; the Social Security Administration (Northern Ireland) Act 1992 s.5(1) (h); and the Jobseekers (Northern Ireland) Order 1995 Art.6(1) (4) (5), Art.8(2) (4), Art.9(4), Art.10, Art.11 (10) (12), Art.14(1) (4) (b),

Art.21 (8) (b), Art.22(4), Art.36(2), Art.39, Sch.1 para.3, Sch.1 para.6, Sch.1 para.9, Sch.1 para.10, Sch.1 para.12. In force: October 7, 1996; £3.70.

These Regulations amend the Jobseeker's Allowance Regulations (Northern Ireland) 1996 (SR 1996 198) as respects jobseeking and other matters.

6415. Child support–jobseeker's allowance

SOCIAL SECURITY AND CHILD SUPPORT (JOBSEEKER'S ALLOWANCE) (MISCELLANEOUS AMENDMENTS) REGULATIONS (NORTHERN IRELAND) 1996, SR 1996 503; made under the Child Support (Northern Ireland) Order 1991 Art.43(5) (11); the Social Security Administration (Northern Ireland) Act 1992 s.59, s.69; and the Jobseekers (Northern Ireland) Order 1995 Art.2(2), Art.6(5), Art.9(2), Art.14(1) (4) (b), Art.22(4), Art.28, Art.36(2) (3), Art.39, Sch.1 para.3. In force: October 28, 1996; £3.20.

These Regulations make detailed amendments to the Jobseeker's Allowance Regulations (Northern Ireland) 1996 (SR 1996 198), the Jobseeker's Allowance (Transitional Provisions) Regulations (Northern Ireland) 1996 (SR 1996 200), the Social Security (Back to Work Bonus) Regulations (Northern Ireland) 1996 (SR 1996 201) and the Social Security (General Benefit) Regulations (Northern Ireland) 1984 (SR 1984 92).

6416. Child support–miscellaneous amendments

CHILD SUPPORT (MISCELLANEOUS AMENDMENTS NO.2) REGULATIONS (NORTHERN IRELAND) 1996, SR 1996 590; made under the Child Support (Northern Ireland) Order 1991 Art.4(3), Art.14(2) (3), Art.19(6) (7), Art.23(2) (3), Art.39, Art.43(11), Art.44, Art.47, Art.48, Sch.1 para.5(1) (2) (4), Sch.1 para.6(4), Sch.1 para.8, Sch.1 para.9, Sch.1 para.11. In force: January 13, 1997; £3.20.

These Regulations make miscellaneous amendments to the Child Support (Maintenance Assessment) Procedure Regulations (Northern Ireland) 1992 (SR 1992 340), the Child Support (Maintenance Assessment and Special Cases) Regulations (Northern Ireland) 1992 (SR 1992 341), the Child Support Appeal Tribunals (Procedure) Regulations (Northern Ireland) 1993 (SR 1993 50), and the Child Support Fees Regulations (Northern Ireland) 1993 (SR 1993 73).

6417. Child support–payments

CHILD SUPPORT (MAINTENANCE ASSESSMENTS AND SPECIAL CASES) AND SOCIAL SECURITY (CLAIMS AND PAYMENTS) (AMENDMENT) REGULATIONS (NORTHERN IRELAND) 1996, SR 1996 65; made under the Child Support (Northern Ireland) Order 1991 Art.47, Art.48(4), Sch.1 para.5, Sch.1 para.7; and the Social Security Administration (Northern Ireland) Act 1992 s.5(1) (q). In force: April 8, 1996; £1.10.

These Regulations amend the Child Support (Maintenance Assessments and Special Cases) Regulations (Northern Ireland) 1992 (SR 1992 341) so as to increase the minimum amount of child support maintenance payable. Consequential amendments are made to the Social Security (Claims and Payments) Regulations 1987 (SR 1987 465).

6418. Child support–procedure

CHILD SUPPORT COMMISSIONERS (PROCEDURE) (AMENDMENT) REGULATIONS (NORTHERN IRELAND) 1996, SR 1996 99; made under the Child Support (Northern Ireland) Order 1991 Art.25, Art.26, Sch.4 para.1, Sch.4 para.1A. In force: April 29, 1996; £1.10.

These Regulations amend the Child Support Commissioners (Procedure) Regulations (Northern Ireland) 1993 (SR 1993 42) to provide for nominated officers to perform certain functions of a Commissioner and to provide for decisions made by a nominated officer to be considered by a Commissioner.

6419. Child Support (Northern Ireland) Order 1995–Commencement No.2 Order

CHILD SUPPORT (1995 ORDER) (COMMENCEMENT NO.2) ORDER (NORTHERN IRELAND) 1995, SR 1995 474 (C.10); made under the Northern Ireland Act 1974 Sch.1 para.2(1); and the Child Support (Northern Ireland) Order 1995 Art.1 (3). In force: bringing into force various provisions of the Order on December 18, 1995 and January 22, 1996; £1.10.

This Order brings into force the Child Support (Northern Ireland) Order 1995 (SI 1995 2702 (NI 13)) Art.10, Art.11, Art.21, and part of Sch.3 on December 18, 1995 and Art.5, the remainder of Art.6, Art.7, Art.8 and Art.9 on January 22, 1996.

6420. Child Support (Northern Ireland) Order 1995–Commencement No.3 Order

CHILD SUPPORT (1995 ORDER) (COMMENCEMENT NO.3) ORDER (NORTHERN IRELAND) 1996, SR 1996 492 (C.24); made under the Northern Ireland Act 1974 Sch.1 para.2(1); and the Child Support (Northern Ireland) Order 1995 Art.1 (3). In force: bringing into force various provisions of the Order on October 16, 1996 and December 2, 1996; £1.55.

This Order brings most of the remaining provisions of the Child Support (Northern Ireland) Order 1995 (SI 1995 2702 (NI 13)) into force on October 16, 1996 or December 2, 1996.

6421. Claims–payments

SOCIAL SECURITY (CLAIMS AND PAYMENTS) (AMENDMENT) REGULATIONS (NORTHERN IRELAND) 1996, SR 1996 556; made under the Social Security Administration (Northern Ireland) Act 1992 s.13A(2) (b). In force: April 1, 1997; £1.10.

These Regulations amend the Social Security (Claims and Payments) Regulations (Northern Ireland) 1987 (SR 1987 465) Sch.8B para.6 by reducing from £0.77 to £0.72 the fee which qualifying lenders pay for the purpose of defraying administrative expenses incurred by the Department of Health and Social Services in making payments in respect of mortgage interest direct to those lenders. They revoke the Social Security (Claims and Payments) (Amendment) Regulations (Northern Ireland) 1995 (SR 1995 439).

6422. Claims–payments

SOCIAL SECURITY (CLAIMS AND PAYMENTS ETC.) (AMENDMENT) REGULATIONS 1996, SR 1996 85; made under the Social Security Administration (Northern Ireland) Act 1992 s.5, s.77. In force: April 4, 1996; £1.10.

These Regulations make further provision for the payment of benefit by way of benefit payment cards.

6423. Claims–payments–adjudication

SOCIAL SECURITY (CLAIMS AND PAYMENTS AND ADJUDICATION) (AMENDMENT) REGULATIONS (NORTHERN IRELAND) 1996, SR 1996 432; made under the Social Security Administration (Northern Ireland) Act 1992 s.5(1) (a) (j) (o) (p) (q), s.59 (1) (2). In force: October 7, 1996; £1.95.

These Regulations amend the Social Security (Claims and Payments) Regulations (Northern Ireland) 1987 (SR 1987 465) as respects time limits for claiming incapacity benefit or severe disablement allowance for claimants in hospital, the maximum weekly amount of benefit which may be paid at intervals of up to 12 months, the period within which payment of benefit may be suspended where an appeal to a Social Security Commissioner may be made, the withholding of benefit, the time limit for claiming social fund payments for funeral expenses and deductions in respect of arrears of child support maintenance from a beneficiary's contribution based jobseeker's allowance. They also amend the Social Security (Adjudication) Regulations (Northern Ireland) 1995 (SR 1995 293) as respects the date that reviews of income support have effect where reductions in the capital outstanding on a loan or changes in the rate of interest have occurred and make similar provision for jobseeker's allowance.

6424. Compensation–diseases and disorders–payment of claims

PNEUMOCONIOSIS, ETC., (WORKMENS' COMPENSATION) (PAYMENT OF CLAIMS) (AMENDMENT) REGULATIONS (NORTHERN IRELAND) 1996, SR 1996 485; made under the Pneumoconiosis, etc. (Workmen's Compensation) (Northern Ireland) Order 1979 Art.3(3), Art.4(3), Art.11 (1)(4). In force: November 20, 1996; £1.95.

These Regulations amend the Pneumoconiosis, etc. (Workmen's Compensation) (Payment of Claims) Regulations (Northern Ireland) 1988 (SR 1988 242) to increase certain payments by 2.1 per cent.

6425. Contributions

SOCIAL SECURITY (CONTRIBUTIONS) (AMENDMENT) REGULATIONS (NORTHERN IRELAND) 1996, SR 1996 58; made under the Social Security Contributions and Benefits (Northern Ireland) Act 1992 s.117(1). In force: April 6, 1996; £0.65.

These Regulations further amend the Social Security (Contributions) Regulations (Northern Ireland) 1979 (SR 1979 186) by reducing the rate of Class 2 contributions paid by share fishermen.

6426. Contributions

SOCIAL SECURITY (CONTRIBUTIONS) (AMENDMENT NO.2) REGULATIONS (NORTHERN IRELAND) 1996, SR 1996 79; made under the Social Security Contributions and Benefits (Northern Ireland) Act 1992 s.5. In force: April 6, 1996; £0.65.

These Regulations increase weekly lower and upper earnings limits for Class 1 contributions.

6427. Contributions

SOCIAL SECURITY (CONTRIBUTIONS) (AMENDMENT NO.3) REGULATIONS (NORTHERN IRELAND) 1996, SR 1996 89; made under the Social Security Contributions and Benefits (Northern Ireland) Act 1992 s.3, Sch.1 para.1. In force: April 6, 1996; £1.10.

These Regulations amend the Social Security (Contributions) Regulations (Northern Ireland) 1979 (SR 1979 186) as respects definitions and computation of earnings.

6428. Contributions

SOCIAL SECURITY (CONTRIBUTIONS) (AMENDMENT NO.4) REGULATIONS (NORTHERN IRELAND) 1996, SR 1996 152; made under the Social Security Contributions and Benefits (Northern Ireland) Act 1992 Sch.1 para.6. In force: April 19, 1996; £1.10.

These Regulations further amend the Social Security (Contributions) Regulations (Northern Ireland) 1979 (SR 1979 186) by inserting a new Reg.34A into Sch.1 to the principal Regulations, providing that, in relation to earnings related and Class 1A contributions and the calculation of interest on such contributions which are overdue or repaid, that where any such payment is made by cheque, it shall be treated as made on the day on which the cheque is received by the Collector of Taxes.

6429. Contributions

SOCIAL SECURITY (CONTRIBUTIONS) (AMENDMENT NO.5) REGULATIONS (NORTHERN IRELAND) 1996, SR 1996 433; made under the Social Security

Contributions and Benefits (Northern Ireland) Act 1992 s.3(2)(3), s.4(5), s.17(3)(6), Sch.1 para.1(1), Sch.1 para.2, Sch.1 para.6(1), Sch.1 para.8(1)(m). In force: April 6, 1997; £1.95.

These Regulations amend the Social Security (Contributions) Regulations (Northern Ireland) 1979 (SR 1979 186) as respects definitions, the designation of earnings periods, the order of priority for the return of earnings-related contributions in respect of certain employment, deductions from earnings-related contributions paid in error, periods for applying for the repayment of certain Class 4 contributions paid in error, time limits for recording Class 1A contributions and preparing deductions working sheets and the date for payment of Class 1A contributions.

6430. Contributions

SOCIAL SECURITY (CONTRIBUTIONS) (AMENDMENT NO.6) REGULATIONS (NORTHERN IRELAND) 1996, SR 1996 566; made under the Social Security Contributions and Benefits (Northern Ireland) Act 1992 s.3(2)(3), s.171(1)(3). In force: December 5, 1996; £1.55.

These Regulations make miscellaneous amendments to the Social Security (Contributions) Regulations (Northern Ireland) 1979 (SR 1979 186), and partially revoke the Social Security (Contributions) (Amendment No.3) Regulations (Northern Ireland) 1994 (SR 1994 328) and the Social Security (Contributions) (Amendment No.4) Regulations (Northern Ireland) 1995 (SR 1995 146).

6431. Contributions

SOCIAL SECURITY (CONTRIBUTIONS) (RE-RATING AND NORTHERN IRELAND NATIONAL INSURANCE FUND PAYMENTS) ORDER (NORTHERN IRELAND) 1996, SR 1996 72; made under the Social Security Administration (Northern Ireland) Act 1992 s.129; and the Social Security (Northern Ireland) Order 1993 Art.4(3). In force: April 6, 1996; £1.10.

This Order amends figures in the Social Security Administration (Northern Ireland) Act 1992 relating to secondary earnings brackets and Class 2, Class 3 and Class 4 contributions and deals with estimated benefit expenditure.

6432. Contributions–class 1–contracted out schemes–final salary schemes

SOCIAL SECURITY (REDUCED RATES OF CLASS 1 CONTRIBUTIONS) (SALARY RELATED CONTRACTED-OUT SCHEMES) ORDER (NORTHERN IRELAND) 1996, SR 1996 149; made under the Pension Schemes (Northern Ireland) Act 1993 s.38. In force: April 6, 1996; £1.10.

This Order specifies the percentages to be deducted from Class 1 contributions in respect of members of salary related contracted out pension schemes.

6433. Contributions–class 1–contracted out schemes–money purchase schemes

SOCIAL SECURITY (REDUCED RATES OF CLASS 1 CONTRIBUTIONS AND REBATES) (MONEY PURCHASE CONTRACTED-OUT SCHEMES) ORDER (NORTHERN IRELAND) 1996, SR 1996 150; made under the Pension Schemes (Northern Ireland) Act 1993 s.38B. In force: April 6, 1996; £1.55.

This Order specifies with effect from April 6, 1997 the appropriate flat rate percentage and the appropriate age related percentages in respect of members of money purchase contracted out schemes.

6434. Contributions–credits–consequential amendments

SOCIAL SECURITY (CREDITS AND CONTRIBUTIONS) (JOBSEEKER'S ALLOWANCE CONSEQUENTIAL AND MISCELLANEOUS AMENDMENTS) REGULATIONS (NORTHERN IRELAND) 1996, SR 1996 430; made under the Social Security Contributions and Benefits (Northern Ireland) Act 1992 s.22(5);

and the Jobseekers (Northern Ireland) Order 1995 Art.39. In force: October 7, 1996; £2.80.

These Regulations amend the Social Security (Credits) Regulations (Northern Ireland) 1975 (SR 1975 113) and the Social Security (Contributions) Regulations (Northern Ireland) 1979 (SR 1979 186) in consequence of the Jobseekers (Northern Ireland) Order 1995 and make miscellaneous amendments of the 1975 Regulations by, in particular, separating into three regulations matters formerly covered by Reg.9 of those Regulations.

6435. Contributions–deductions

EMPLOYER'S CONTRIBUTIONS REIMBURSEMENT REGULATIONS (NORTHERN IRELAND) 1996, SR 1996 30; made under the Jobseekers (Northern Ireland) Order 1995 Art.2(2)(b), Art.29, Art.35(3)(7), Art.36(2). In force: April 6, 1996; £2.80.

These Regulations authorise employers to make deductions from social security contributions in prescribed circumstances where they employ qualifying employees.

6436. Credits

SOCIAL SECURITY (CREDITS) (AMENDMENT) REGULATIONS (NORTHERN IRELAND) 1995, SR 1995 479; made under the Social Security Contributions and Benefits (Northern Ireland) Act 1992 s.22(5). In force: January 29, 1996; £1.10.

These Regulations further amend the Social Security (Credits) Regulations (Northern Ireland) 1975 (SR 1975 113) by inserting a new Reg.7C which applies for the purposes of entitlement to a Category A or B retirement pension, widowed mother's allowance or a widow's pension and provides for persons to be credited with earnings equal to the lower earnings limit in respect of weeks for which family credit is paid to them. Provision is made, in cases where family credit is paid to one of a married or unmarried couple, as to which member of the couple is to be credited with earnings.

6437. Disability living allowance

SOCIAL SECURITY (DISABILITY LIVING ALLOWANCE) (AMENDMENT) REGULATIONS (NORTHERN IRELAND) 1996, SR 1996 290; made under the Social Security Administration (Northern Ireland) Act 1992 s.71(1). In force: July 31, 1996; £0.65.

These Regulations amend the Social Security (Disability Living Allowance) Regulations (Northern Ireland) 1992 (SR 1992 32) by providing that certain persons residing in hospices will continue to receive the mobility component of disability living allowance.

6438. Disability living allowance

SOCIAL SECURITY (DISABILITY LIVING ALLOWANCE, ATTENDANCE ALLOWANCE AND CLAIMS AND PAYMENTS) (AMENDMENT) REGULATIONS (NORTHERN IRELAND) 1996, SR 1996 225; made under the Social Security Contributions and Benefits (Northern Ireland) Act 1992 s.67(2), s.72(8); and the Social Security Administration (Northern Ireland) Act 1992 s.5(1)(j), s.71(1). In force: July 31, 1996; £1.55.

These Regulations amend the Social Security (Claims and Payments) Regulations (Northern Ireland) 1987 (SR 1987 465), the Social Security (Attendance Allowance) Regulations (Northern Ireland) 1992 (SR 1992 20) and the Social Security (Disability Living Allowance) Regulations (Northern Ireland) 1992 (SR 1992 32). They impose a restriction on the payment of the mobility component of disability living allowance in respect of a person who is maintained free of charge whilst undergoing treatment as an in patient in a hospital or similar institution under the Health Service or maintained by the

Defence Council. They also provide for exemptions and for benefit to be adjusted in certain cases.

6439. Disability working allowance–family credit

DISABILITY WORKING ALLOWANCE AND FAMILY CREDIT (GENERAL) (AMENDMENT) REGULATIONS (NORTHERN IRELAND) 1996, SR 1996 583; made under the Social Security Contributions and Benefits (Northern Ireland) Act 1992 s.122(1)(b)(c), s.127(5), s.128(8), s.132(3), s.171(1)(3)(4). In force: January 7, 1997; £1.10.

These Regulations further amend the Disability Working Allowance (General) Regulations (Northern Ireland) 1992 (SR 1992 78) and the Family Credit (General) Regulations (Northern Ireland) 1987 (SR 1987 463) with respect to the earnings of employed earners and, in the case of family credit, directors, which are to be taken into account in calculating the normal weekly earnings of a claimant for disability working allowance or family credit. They also amend the manner of calculating deductions from the profits of self-employed earners in respect of social security contributions.

6440. Energy conservation–grants

DOMESTIC ENERGY EFFICIENCY GRANTS (AMENDMENT) REGULATIONS (NORTHERN IRELAND) 1996, SR 1996 417; made under the Social Security (Northern Ireland) Order 1990 Art.17(1)(2)(3)(4)(5)(6)(7)(10). In force: October 7, 1996; £1.10.

These Regulations amend the Domestic Energy Efficiency Grants Regulations (Northern Ireland) 1994 (SR 1994 306) by extending eligibility for grants to cases where individuals receive an attendance or disability living allowance, and income based jobseeker's allowance or both a war disablement pension and either mobility supplement or constant attendance allowance and by replacing references to cases where applicants carry out the grant works themselves with references to cases where the works are not carried out by network installers.

6441. Family credit

FAMILY CREDIT (GENERAL) (AMENDMENT) REGULATIONS (NORTHERN IRELAND) 1996, SR 1996 224; made under the Social Security Contributions and Benefits (Northern Ireland) Act 1992 s.122(1)(b), s.127(3); and the Social Security Administration (Northern Ireland) Act 1992 s.5(1)(l), s.25(1). In force: July 2, 1996; £1.10.

These Regulations amend the Family Credit (General) Regulations (Northern Ireland) 1987 (SR 1987 463) by providing that awards of family credit must be reviewed and terminate where persons between the ages of 16 and 19 leave, or have left, full-time education during the period those awards are in effect and that person is the only member of that household in respect of whom family credit is payable. They also define full-time education for that purpose.

6442. Family credit–wages

SOCIAL SECURITY (EFFECT OF FAMILY CREDIT ON EARNINGS FACTORS) REGULATIONS (NORTHERN IRELAND) 1995, SR 1995 478; made under the Social Security Contributions and Benefits (Northern Ireland) Act 1992 s.45A(2). In force: January 29, 1996; £0.65.

These Regulations specify the person to whom the Social Security Contributions and Benefits (Northern Ireland) Act 1992 s.45A applies, where family credit is payable to one of a married or unmarried couple.

6443. Housing Benefit (Payment toThird Parties) (Northern Ireland) Order1996 (SI 1996 2597 (NI 20))

This Order, which came into force on October 22, 1996, amends the Social Security Administration (Northern Ireland) Act 1992 s.5 to enable the Department of Health and Social Services to prescribe cases in which the Northern Ireland Housing Executive is required to make payments of housing benefit direct to landlords.

6444. Housing benefits

HOUSING BENEFIT (GENERAL) (AMENDMENT) REGULATIONS (NORTHERN IRELAND) 1996, SR 1996 84; made under the Social Security Contributions and Benefits (Northern Ireland) Act1992 s.122, s.129, s.131, s.132. In force: April 1, 1996; £1.55.

These Regulations amend the Housing Benefit (General) Regulations (Northern Ireland) 1987 (SR 1987 461) as respects certain amounts, deductions and sums to be disregarded.

6445. Housing benefits

HOUSING BENEFIT (GENERAL) (AMENDMENT NO.2) REGULATIONS (NORTHERN IRELAND) 1996, SR 1996 111; made under the Social Security Contributions and Benefits (Northern Ireland) Act 1992 s.122(1)(d), s.129(2)(3)(4), s.131(1), s.171(5); and the Social Security Administration (Northern Ireland) Act 1992 s.5(j)(h)(p), s.61(1)(2)(3). In force: April 2, 1996; £4.15.

These Regulations amend the Housing Benefit (General) Regulations (Northern Ireland) 1987 (SR 1987 461). They relate to maximum eligible rent in cases where housing benefit is payable, including conferring a discretion on the Northern Ireland Housing Executive to pay a lesser sum in appropriate cases. They also add a discretion to pay more benefit than would otherwise be payable by reason of these Regulations.

6446. Housing benefits

HOUSING BENEFIT (GENERAL) (AMENDMENT NO.3) REGULATIONS (NORTHERN IRELAND) 1996, SR 1996 181; made under the Social Security Contributions and Benefits (Northern Ireland) Act 1992 s.122(1)(d), s.129(2)(4), s.171(5); and the Social Security Administration (Northern Ireland) Act 1992 s.5(1)(j)(q). In force: October 7, 1996; £1.95.

These Regulations, which amend the Housing Benefit (General) Regulations (Northern Ireland) 1987 (SR 1987 461), create a new maximum rent for single claimants under the age of 25 in respect of whom the Housing Executive has determined a single room rent. They also create a new rule for the period within which payment of housing benefit by way of rent allowance is made, enable the Executive to make first payments of benefit to claimants by way of instruments of payment in favour of landlords and provide for the manner in which single room rents are to be determined.

6447. Housing benefits

HOUSING BENEFIT (GENERAL) (AMENDMENT NO.4) REGULATIONS (NORTHERN IRELAND) 1996, SR 1996 221; made under the Social Security Contributions and Benefits (Northern Ireland) Act 1992 s.122(1)(d), s.129(4). In force: July 8, 1996; £1.10.

These Regulations further amend the Housing Benefit (General Regulations (Northern Ireland) 1987 (SR 1987 461) to require the Northern Ireland Housing Executive to consider all claims for a rent allowance under Reg.10A (determinations).

6448. Housing benefits

HOUSING BENEFIT (GENERAL) (AMENDMENT NO.5) REGULATIONS (NORTHERN IRELAND) 1996, SR 1996 448; made under the Social Security Contributions and Benefits (Northern Ireland) Act 1992 s.122(1)(d), s.129(2)(3)(4), s.131(1), s.132(4)(b), s.133(1)(2)(a)(i), s.171(5); the Social Security Administration (Northern Ireland) Act 1992 s.5(1)(a)(b)(h)(j)(k)(q); and the Asylum and Immigration Act 1996 s.11. In force: October 15, 1996; £2.40.

These Regulations amend the Housing Benefit (General) Regulations (Northern Ireland) 1987 (SR 1987 461) and the Housing Benefit (General) (Amendment No.2) Regulations (Northern Ireland) 1996 (SR 1996 111) to make provision with respect to claims for housing benefit by persons recorded as refugees by the Secretary of State in respect of the period from and including the dates of their claims to the date they are recorded as refugees.

6449. Housing benefits–jobseeker's allowance–information

HOUSING BENEFIT (GENERAL AND SUPPLY OF INFORMATION) (JOBSEEKER'S ALLOWANCE) (CONSEQUENTIAL AMENDMENTS) REGULATIONS (NORTHERN IRELAND) 1996, SR 1996 334; made under the Jobseekers (Northern Ireland) Order 1995 Art.39. In force: October 7, 1996; £2.80.

These Regulations amend the Housing Benefit (General) Regulations (Northern Ireland) 1987 (SR 1987 461) consequentially on the coming into operation of the Jobseekers (Northern Ireland) Order 1995 (SI 1995 2705 (NI 15)), which replaces unemployment benefit and income support for the unemployed with jobseeker's allowance. They also provide that, in certain circumstances, days on which entitlement to a jobseeker's allowance does not arise in accordance with the 1995 Order Sch.1 para.4 (waiting days) or payment is not made in accordance with the 1995 Order Art.21, are counted as days of payment of a jobseeker's allowance.

6450. Housing benefits–payments

HOUSING BENEFIT (GENERAL AND SUPPLY OF INFORMATION) (AMENDMENT) REGULATIONS (NORTHERN IRELAND) 1996, SR 1996 115; made under the Social Security Contributions and Benefits (Northern Ireland) Act 1992 s.122(1)(d), s.129(2)(3)(4), s.131(1), s.132(3)(4)(b), s.133(2)(c)(d)(h), s.171(5); and the Social Security Administration (Northern Ireland) Act 1992 s.5(1)(a)(b)(j), s.61(1)(2A), s.120(1). In force: April 1, 1996; £2.40.

These Regulations further amend the Housing Benefit (General) Regulations (Northern Ireland) 1987 (SR 1987 461) and the Housing Benefit (Supply of Information) Regulations (Northern Ireland) 1988 (SR 1988 118). They make and further amend provisions relating to maximum benefit in cases where housing benefit was payable, by providing for a further, extended payment of benefit in prescribed circumstances and make provision for the effect of such payments on any further grant of benefit.

6451. Incapacity benefit

SOCIAL SECURITY (INCAPACITY FOR WORK) (GENERAL) (AMENDMENT) REGULATIONS (NORTHERN IRELAND) 1996, SR 1996 61; made under the Social Security Contributions and Benefits (Northern Ireland) Act 1992 s.167D. In force: April 8, 1996; £0.65.

These Regulations increase a weekly earnings limit in the Social Security (Incapacity for Work) (General) Regulations (Northern Ireland) 1995 (SR 1995 41) as amended by the Social Security (Incapacity for Work) (Miscellaneous Amendments) Regulations (Northern Ireland) 1995 (SR 1995 149).

6452. Incapacity benefit–amendment regulations

SOCIAL SECURITY (INCAPACITY FOR WORK AND MISCELLANEOUS AMENDMENTS) REGULATIONS (NORTHERN IRELAND) 1996, SR 1996 601;

made under the Social Security Contributions and Benefits (Northern Ireland) Act 1992 s.167A(2), s.167C, s.167D, s.167E, s.171 (2) (3) (4); the Social Security Administration (Northern Ireland) Act 1992 s.59A(4), s.71; and the Social Security (Incapacity for Work) (Northern Ireland) Order 1994 Art.6, Art.9, Art.14(1). In force: January 6, 1997; £1.95.

These Regulations further amend the Social Security (Overlapping Benefits) Regulations (Northern Ireland) 1979 (SR 1979 242), the Social Security (Incapacity Benefit) (Transitional) Regulations (Northern Ireland) 1995 (SR 1995 35) and the Social Security (Incapacity for Work) (General) Regulations (Northern Ireland) 1995 (SR 1995 41). The Overlapping Benefits Regulations are amended to clarify that additional rate under the Transitional Regulations is to be treated the same way as additional pension. The Transitional Regulations are clarified. The General Regulations are amended to make certain clarifications and to correct minor errors and to make provisions consistent with adjudication in respect of the exceptional circumstances for which a person who fails the all work test is to be treated as incapable of work.

6453. Income related benefits

INCOME-RELATED BENEFITS (AMENDMENT) REGULATIONS (NORTHERN IRELAND) 1996, SR 1996 92; made under the Social Security Contributions and Benefits (Northern Ireland) Act 1992 s.122(1), s.132(4)(b). In force: in accordance with Reg.1; £1.10.

These Regulations extend the provision for the disregard of capital arising from the sale of a home to persons who continue to live in the same house following the exercise of compulsory purchase powers.

6454. Income related benefits

INCOME-RELATED BENEFITS (MISCELLANEOUS AMENDMENTS) REGULATIONS (NORTHERN IRELAND) 1996, SR 1996 93; made under the Social Security Contributions and Benefits (Northern Ireland) Act 1992 s.122, s.130, s.131, s.132, s.133; and the Social Security Administration (Northern Ireland) Act 1992 s.5. In force: in accordance with Reg.1; £2.80.

These Regulations amend provisions relating to income support, housing benefit, family credit and disability working allowance.

6455. Income related benefits

INCOME-RELATED BENEFITS (MISCELLANEOUS AMENDMENTS NO.2) REGULATIONS (NORTHERN IRELAND) 1996, SR 1996 291; made under the Social Security Contributions and Benefits (Northern Ireland) Act 1992 s.122(1), s.129(2) (4), s.132(3) (4) (b). In force: in accordance with Reg.1 (1); £1.10.

These Regulations amend the Income Support (General) Regulations (Northern Ireland) 1987 (SR 1987 459), the Housing Benefit (General) Regulations (Northern Ireland) 1987 (SR 1987 461), the Family Credit (General) Regulations (Northern Ireland) 1987 (SR 1987 463) and the Disability Working Allowance (General) Regulations (Northern Ireland) 1992 (SR 1992 78). They increase to £280 the amount to be allowed in respect of the cost of books and equipment in calculating a student's grant income and to £17.45 the amount of the deduction to be made in calculating a student's eligible rent for housing benefit purposes.

6456. Income related benefits–jobseeker's allowance

INCOME-RELATED BENEFITS AND JOBSEEKER'S ALLOWANCE (PERSONAL ALLOWANCES FOR CHILDREN AND YOUNG PERSONS) (AMENDMENT) REGULATIONS (NORTHERN IRELAND) 1996, SR 1996 476; made under the Social Security Contributions and Benefits Act (Northern Ireland) 1992 s.122, s.127(1)(a)(i)(5), s.128(1)(c)(i)(8), s.131(1), s.132(3); and the Jobseekers (Northern Ireland) Order 1995 Art.6(5). In force: in accordance with Reg.1; £1.95.

These Regulations amend the Income Support (General) Regulations (Northern Ireland) 1987 (SR 1987 459), the Housing Benefit (General) Regulations (Northern Ireland) 1987 (SR 1987 461), the Family Credit (General) Regulations (Northern Ireland) 1987 (SR 1987 463), the Disability Working Allowance (General) Regulations (Northern Ireland) 1992 (SR 1992 78) and the Jobseeker's Allowance Regulations (Northern Ireland) 1996 (SR 1996 198). They change the date when personal allowances in respect of children and young persons are increased for the purposes of income support, income based jobseeker's allowance and housing benefit. They also provide that an increase in those allowances will no longer be applicable in respect of young persons aged 18 or over. Similar provisions are made in relation to the assessment of the appropriate maximum amounts of family credit and disability working allowance. Corresponding provisions are also made relating to the period during which childcare charges may be disregarded for the purposes of housing benefit, family credit and disability working allowance.

6457. Income related benefits–Montserrat

INCOME-RELATED BENEFITS (MONTSERRAT) REGULATIONS (NORTHERN IRELAND) 1996, SR 1996 375; made under the Social Security Contributions and Benefits (Northern Ireland) Act 1992 s.122(1)(a)(d), s.131(1), s.133(2)(i). In force: August 28, 1996; £1.10.

These Regulations amend the Housing Benefit (General) Regulations (Northern Ireland) 1987 (SR 1987 461) and the Income Support (General) Regulations (Northern Ireland) 1987 (SR 1987 459) so that claimants coming from Montserrat as a result of a volcanic eruption there are not to be treated as persons from abroad for the purposes of housing benefit and income support.

6458. Income related benefits–social fund

INCOME-RELATED BENEFITS AND SOCIAL FUND (MISCELLANEOUS AMENDMENTS) REGULATIONS (NORTHERN IRELAND) 1996, SR 1996 405; made under the Social Security Contributions and Benefits (Northern Ireland) Act 1992 s.122(1), s.127(3), s.128(6), s.129(2)(3)(4), s.131(1), s.132(3)(4)(b), s.133(2)(a)(d)(i)(1); the Social Security Administration (Northern Ireland) Act 1992 s.61, s.74(2); and the Jobseekers (Northern Ireland) Order 1995 Art.36, Art.39(1). In force: in accordance with Reg.1; £3.20.

These Regulations amend the Disability Working Allowance (General) Regulations (Northern Ireland) 1992 (SR 1992 78) as respects the period over which weekly income is to be determined, the Family Credit (General) Regulations (Northern Ireland) 1987 (SR 1987 463) as respects the calculation of students' grant income and the treatment of overlapping awards of benefits and the Housing Benefit (General) Regulations (Northern Ireland) 1987 (SR 1987 461) as respects definitions and the calculation of students' covenant income. They amend the Income Support (General) Regulations (Northern Ireland) 1987 (SR 1987 459) and the Housing Benefit (General) Regulations (Northern Ireland) 1987 (SR 1987 461) as respects definitions relating to students, the calculation of students' grant income and provisions specifying who is to be treated as a person from abroad. They amend the Income Support (General) Regulations (Northern Ireland) 1987 (SR 1987 459) as respects payment of benefit to persons temporarily absent from Northern Ireland, the entitlement of persons from abroad, the treatment of partners of claimants for income support in certain circumstances, persons detained in custody or on temporary release, days on which arrears of child support maintenance are to be treated as paid, the treatment of prescribed housing costs and sums to be disregarded in calculating income other then earnings. They also amend the Social Fund (Recovery by Deductions from Benefits) Regulations (Northern Ireland) 1988 (SR 1988 21) in consequence of jobseeker's allowance and the Income Support (General) (Jobseeker's Allowance Consequential Amendments) Regulations (Northern

Ireland) 1996 (SR 1996 199) as respects continuity between income support and jobseeker's allowance.

6459. Income support

INCOME SUPPORT (GENERAL) (AMENDMENT) REGULATIONS (NORTHERN IRELAND) 1996, SR 1996 78; made under the Social Security Contributions and Benefits (Northern Ireland) Act 1992 s.122(1)(a), s.132(4)(b). In force: in accordance with Reg.1(1)(2); £1.10.

These Regulations provide for the disregard of half the occupational pension of certain claimants for income support who are in residential or nursing homes if at least half of the pension is being paid for their spouse's maintenance.

6460. Income support

INCOME SUPPORT (GENERAL) (AMENDMENT NO.2) REGULATIONS (NORTHERN IRELAND) 1996, SR 1996 120; made under the Social Security Contributions and Benefits (Northern Ireland) Act 1992 s.122(1)(a), s.131(1). In force: April 21, 1996; £1.10.

These Regulations amend the Income Support (General) Regulations (Northern Ireland) 1987 (SR 1987 459) Sch.3 with respect to the standard rate of interest applicable to a loan which qualifies for income support, the new rate being 7.74 per cent. The Regulations also make consequential revocations together with a saving provision. These Regulations correspond to provision contained in Regulations made by the Secretary of State for Social Security in relation to Great Britain and accordingly, by virtue of the Social Security Administration (Northern Ireland) Act 1992 s.149(3) and Sch.5 para.10, are not subject to the requirement of s.149(2) of that Act for prior reference to the Social Security Advisory Committee.

6461. Income support

INCOME SUPPORT (GENERAL) (AMENDMENT NO.3) REGULATIONS (NORTHERN IRELAND) 1996, SR 1996 489; made under the Social Security Contributions and Benefits (Northern Ireland) Act 1992 s.122(1)(a), s.131(1). In force: November 8, 1996; £0.65.

These Regulations amend the Income Support (General) Regulations (Northern Ireland) 1987 (SR 1987 465) to provide that persons in residential accommodation provided by the Department of Health and Social Services and who are still in it when it becomes a residential care home will be treated as being in residential accommodation although that Department may no longer be under a duty to provide or make arrangements for providing accommodation for them.

6462. Income support–claims and payments

INCOME SUPPORT AND SOCIAL SECURITY (CLAIMS AND PAYMENTS) (MISCELLANEOUS AMENDMENTS) REGULATIONS (NORTHERN IRELAND) 1996, SR 1996 449; made under the Social Security Contributions and Benefits (Northern Ireland) Act 1992 s.131, s.132(4)(b); the Social Security Administration (Northern Ireland) Act 1992 s.5(1)(a)(b), s.69(6)(b); and the Asylum and Immigration Act 1996 s.11. In force: October 15, 1996; £1.95.

These Regulations amend the Income Support (General) Regulations (Northern Ireland) 1987 (SR 1987 459) and the Social Security (Claims and Payments) Regulations (Northern Ireland) 1987 (SR 1987 465) to provide with respect to claimants for income support for their entitlement to that benefit for the period from the date of their claims for asylum, or February 5, 1996, if later, up to the date of their being recorded by the Secretary of State as refugees within the Convention relating to the Status of Refugees (Cmnd.9171).

6463. Income support–interest rates

INCOME SUPPORT (GENERAL) (STANDARD INTEREST RATE AMENDMENT) REGULATIONS 1996, SR 1996 218; made under the Social Security Contributions and Benefits (Northern Ireland) Act 1992 s.122(1)(a), s.131(1). In force: June 23, 1996; £1.10.

These Regulations amend the Income Support (General) Regulations (Northern Ireland) 1987 (SR 1987 459) by prescribing 7.48 per cent as the standard rate of interest applicable to a loan which qualifies for income support.

6464. Income support–interest rates

INCOME SUPPORT (GENERAL) (STANDARD INTEREST RATE AMENDMENT NO.2) REGULATIONS (NORTHERN IRELAND) 1996, SR 1996 318; made under the Social Security Contributions and Benefits (Northern Ireland) Act 1992 s.122(1)(a), s.131(1). In force: August 25, 1996; £1.10.

These Regulations amend the Income Support (General) Regulations (Northern Ireland) 1987 (SR 1987 459) Sch.3 by reducing the standard rate of interest applicable to loans qualifying for income support to 7.16 per cent.

6465. Income support–interest rates

INCOME SUPPORT (GENERAL) (STANDARD INTEREST RATE AMENDMENT NO.3) REGULATIONS (NORTHERN IRELAND) 1996, SR 1996 545; made under the Social Security Contributions and Benefits (Northern Ireland) Act 1992 s.122(1)(a), s.131(1), s.171(1)(3)(4)(5). In force: December 15, 1996; £1.10.

These Regulations amend the Income Support (General) Regulations (Northern Ireland) 1987 (SR 1987 459) Sch.3 with respect to the standard rate of interest applicable to a loan which qualifies for income support. The rate is reduced from 7.16 per cent to 6.89 per cent. They also revoke, with a saving provision, the Income Support (General) (Standard Interest Rate Amendment No.2) Regulations (Northern Ireland) 1996 (SR 1996 318) which made a previous amendment to the standard rate of interest.

6466. Income support–jobseeker's allowance

INCOME SUPPORT (GENERAL) (JOBSEEKER'S ALLOWANCE CONSEQUENTIAL AMENDMENTS) REGULATIONS (NORTHERN IRELAND) 1996, SR 1996 199; made under the Jobseekers (Northern Ireland) Order 1995 Art.39; and the Social Security Contributions and Benefits (Northern Ireland) Act 1992 s.122(1)(a), s.123(1)(e). In force: October 7, 1996; £4.15.

These Regulations amend the Income Support (General) Regulations (Northern Ireland) 1987 (SR 1987 459) consequentially on the coming into operation of the Jobseekers (Northern Ireland) Order 1995 (SI 1995 2705 (NI 15)), which replaces income support for the unemployed and unemployment benefit with jobseeker's allowance.

6467. Industrial injuries–industrial diseases

SOCIAL SECURITY (INDUSTRIAL INJURIES AND DISEASES) (MISCELLANEOUS AMENDMENTS) REGULATIONS (NORTHERN IRELAND) 1996, SR 1996 57; made under the Social Security Contributions and Benefits (Northern Ireland) Act 1992 s.108(2), s.109(2), s.109(3), s.113(1)(b), Sch.7 para.13(8), Sch.7 para.13(9); the Social Security Administration (Northern Ireland) Act 1992 s.5(1)(1); and the Social Security Contributions Administration (Northern Ireland) Act 1992 s.25(1)(b). In force: March 24, 1996; £1.95.

These Regulations prescribe circumstances in which persons entitled to a specified reduced earnings allowance are to be regarded as having given up regular employment, and alter the list of prescribed diseases.

6468. Industrial injuries benefit

WORKMEN'S COMPENSATION (SUPPLEMENTATION) (AMENDMENT) REGULATIONS (NORTHERN IRELAND) 1996, SR 1996 76; made under the Social Security Contributions and Benefits (Northern Ireland) Act 1992 s.171 (4), Sch.8 para.2; and the Social Security Administration (Northern Ireland) Act 1992 Sch.6 para.1. In force: April 10, 1996; £1.55.

These Regulations adjust the lower rates of lesser incapacity allowance.

6469. Industrial injuries benefit–permitted earnings limits

SOCIAL SECURITY (INDUSTRIAL INJURIES) (DEPENDENCY) (PERMITTED EARNINGS LIMITS) ORDER (NORTHERN IRELAND) 1996, SR 1996 75; made under the Social Security Contributions and Benefits (Northern Ireland) Act 1992 Sch.7 para.4(5). In force: April 8, 1996; £0.65.

This Order increases amounts in the Social Security Contributions and Benefits (Northern Ireland) Act 1992 Sch.7 para.4(4).

6470. Invalid care allowance

SOCIAL SECURITY (INVALID CARE ALLOWANCE) (AMENDMENT) REGULATIONS (NORTHERN IRELAND) 1996, SR 1996 521; made under the Social Security Contributions and Benefits (Northern Ireland) Act 1992 s.70, s.171 (1) (3). In force: November 25, 1996; £1.10.

These Regulations amend the Social Security (Invalid Care Allowance) Regulations (Northern Ireland) 1976 (SR 1976 99) Reg.8 by omitting para. (2) (c), under which there is to be disregarded a person's earnings in the week immediately preceding the week in respect of which that person (if his earnings in that week were disregarded) would first become entitled to an invalid care allowance.

6471. Jobseeker's allowance

JOBSEEKER'S ALLOWANCE REGULATIONS (NORTHERN IRELAND) 1996, SR 1996 198; made under the Social Security Administration (Northern Ireland) Act 1992 s.5(1) (h) (j) (k), s.20(4), s.21 (9) (10), Sch.3; the Social Security Contributions and Benefits (Northern Ireland) Act 1992 s.167D; and the Jobseekers (Northern Ireland) Order 1995 Art.2(2), Art.4(1) (c), Art.5(1) (f) (iii) (2) (4), Art.6(1) (b) (2) (4) (5) (12), Art.7(3), Art.8(2) (3) (4) (5) (8), Art.9(2) (3) (4) (5) (6) (8), Art.10, Art.11 (1) (8) (10) (11) (12), Art.12(1) (6) (c) (7), Art.13(2) (5) (7), Art.14, Art.15, Art.17(1) (2) (d) (5), Art.19(1), Art.21 (2) (4) (7) (8) (10) (c), Art.22(3) (4(5) (6) (7) (8), Art.25(1) (3) (4), Art.36(2), Art.39, Sch.1. In force: October 7, 1996; £15.35.

These Regulations introduce a new benefit, to be known as a jobseeker's allowance, for those available for and actively seeking employment. They deal with jobseeking, availability for employment, actively seeking employment, attendance, the jobseeker's agreement, other conditions of entitlement, young persons, sanctions, membership of the family, amounts of allowance, income and capital, liable relatives, child support, full time students, hardship, urgent cases, part-weeks and special categories of claimant.

6472. Jobseeker's allowance

JOBSEEKER'S ALLOWANCE (AMENDMENT) REGULATIONS (NORTHERN IRELAND) 1996, SR 1996 356; made under the Jobseekers (Northern Ireland) Order 1995 Art.6(2) (5), Art.14(1) (4), Art.15(1), Art.21 (7) (8), Art.22(4) (5) (6), Sch.1 para.1, Sch.1 para.5, Sch.1 para.8, Sch.1 para.10, Sch.1 para.16, Sch.1 para.17; and the Jobseekers Northern Ireland) Order 1995 Art.11 (1) (10). In force: October 7, 1996; £2.80.

These Regulations amend the Jobseeker's Allowance Regulations (Northern Ireland) 1996 (SR 1996 198) as respects jobseekers' agreements treated as having been made, the definition of "young person", voluntary redundancy, good cause for the purposes of Art.21(5)(b), persons receiving training allowances, remunerative work, persons from abroad, capital limit, the calculation of tariff income, hardship payments and cases, the provision of information, part weeks, share fishermen, young persons, new housing costs and disregards.

6473. **Jobseeker's allowance–bonus schemes**

SOCIAL SECURITY (BACK TO WORK BONUS) REGULATIONS (NORTHERN IRELAND) 1996, SR 1996 201; made under the Jobseekers (Northern Ireland) Order 1995 Art.28, Art.36(2). In force: October 7, 1996; £4.15.

These Regulations supplement the Jobseekers (Northern Ireland) Order 1995 (SI 1995 2705 (NI 15)) Art.28, which introduced the back to work bonus for persons who are or may have been entitled to income support or a jobseeker's allowance.

6474. **Jobseeker's allowance–child support**

SOCIAL SECURITY AND CHILD SUPPORT (JOBSEEKER'S ALLOWANCE) (TRANSITIONAL PROVISIONS) (AMENDMENT) REGULATIONS (NORTHERN IRELAND) 1996, SR 1996 441; made under the Child Support (Northern Ireland) Order 1991 Art.47; and the Jobseekers (Northern Ireland) Order 1995 Art.36(2), Art.39. In force: October 6, 1996; £1.10.

These Regulations amend the Jobseeker's Allowance (Transitional Provisions) (Amendment) Regulations (Northern Ireland) 1996 (SR 1996 357) as respects the transition from unemployment benefit to jobseeker's allowance during the period October 7 to October 20, 1996, and amend the Child Support (Miscellaneous Amendments) Regulations (Northern Ireland) 1996 (SR 1996 317) to refer to the Social Security and Child Support (Jobseeker's Allowance) (Consequential Amendments) Regulations (Northern Ireland) 1996 (SR 1996 289).

6475. **Jobseeker's allowance–claims–payments**

SOCIAL SECURITY (CLAIMS AND PAYMENTS) (JOBSEEKER'S ALLOWANCE CONSEQUENTIAL AMENDMENTS) REGULATIONS (NORTHERN IRELAND) 1996, SR 1996 354; made under the Social Security Administration (Northern Ireland) Act 1992 s.1(1), s.5(1), s.13A(2), s.165(6); and the Jobseekers (Northern Ireland) Order 1995 Art.28. In force: October 7, 1996; £3.20.

These Regulations amend the Social Security (Claims and Payments) Regulations (Northern Ireland) 1987 (SR 1987 465) consequentially on the coming into operation of the Jobseekers (Northern Ireland) Order 1995 (SI 1995 2705 (NI 15)), which replaces unemployment benefit and income support for the unemployed with jobseeker's allowance.

6476. **Jobseeker's allowance–consequential amendments**

SOCIAL SECURITY AND CHILD SUPPORT (JOBSEEKER'S ALLOWANCE) (CONSEQUENTIAL AMENDMENTS) REGULATIONS (NORTHERN IRELAND) 1996, SR 1996 289; made under the Jobseekers (Northern Ireland) Order 1995 Art.39. In force: October 7, 1996; £4.15.

These Regulations amend various Regulations by replacing references to unemployment benefit with references to jobseeker's allowance and add references to jobseeker's allowance where the existing Regulations refer to income support.

6477. **Jobseeker's allowance–income support**

JOBSEEKER'S ALLOWANCE AND INCOME SUPPORT (AMENDMENT) REGULATIONS (NORTHERN IRELAND) 1996, SR 1996 440; made under the Social Security Contributions and Benefits (Northern Ireland) Act 1992 s.122(1)(a), s.123(1)(e), s.132(4)(b); and the Jobseekers (Northern Ireland)

Order 1995 Art.5(1)(f)(iii), Art.6(5), Art.14(4)(b)(d). In force: October 7, 1996; £1.10.

These Regulations amend the Income Support (General) Regulations (Northern Ireland) 1987 (SR 1987 459) and the Jobseeker's Allowance Regulations (Northern Ireland) 1996 (SR 1996 358) to include references to the Children and Young Persons Act (Northern Ireland) 1968 and remove references to the Children (Northern Ireland) Order 1995 (SI 1995 755 (NI 2)).

6478. Jobseeker's allowance–income support–recoupment–employment protection

EMPLOYMENT PROTECTION (RECOUPMENT OF JOBSEEKER'S ALLOWANCE AND INCOME SUPPORT) REGULATIONS (NORTHERN IRELAND) 1996, SR 1996 459; made under the Social Security Administration (Northern Ireland) Act 1992 s.56(1); and the Industrial Tribunals (Northern Ireland) Order 1996 Art.18, Art.25(5). In force: October 7, 1996; £1.95.

These Regulations replace the Industrial Relations (Recoupment of Unemployment Benefit and Supplementary Benefit) Regulations (Northern Ireland) 1977 (SR 1977 123). They provide for the recovery by the Department of Health and Social Services from employers of sums on account of jobseeker's allowance and income support out of a prescribed part of amounts awarded by industrial tribunals in specified proceedings brought by employees against employers.

6479. Jobseeker's allowance–payments on account

SOCIAL SECURITY (JOBSEEKER'S ALLOWANCE AND PAYMENTS ON ACCOUNT) (MISCELLANEOUS AMENDMENTS) REGULATIONS (NORTHERN IRELAND) 1996, SR 1996 464; made under the Social Security Administration (Northern Ireland) Act 1992 s.69, s.72; and the Jobseekers (Northern Ireland) Order 1995 Art.36(2), Art.39. In force: October 7, 1996; £1.95.

These Regulations amend the Social Security (Payments on account, Overpayment and Recovery) Regulations (Northern Ireland) 1988 (SR 1988 142) to bring income based jobseeker's allowance and, in some cases, contribution-based jobseeker's allowance within the Regulations and deal with them in the same way as income support and to make the maximum amount that can be recovered by way of deductions from contribution based jobseeker's allowance one third of the claimant's age related amount; they also amend the Jobseeker's Allowance (Transitional Provisions) Regulations (Northern Ireland) 1996 (SR 1996 200).

6480. Jobseeker's allowance–transitional provisions

JOBSEEKER'S ALLOWANCE (TRANSITIONAL PROVISIONS) REGULATIONS (NORTHERN IRELAND) 1996, SR 1996 200; made under the Jobseekers (Northern Ireland) Order 1995 Art.36(2), Art.39. In force: October 7, 1996; £3.70.

These Regulations provide for continuity between, on the one hand, unemployment benefit and income support for those who are required to be available for and actively seeking employment and, on the other hand, a jobseeker's allowance. They contain provisions for awards of income support made to those required to be available for and actively seeking employment to be terminated and replaced by awards of a jobseeker's allowance; for continuity between unemployment benefit and a jobseeker's allowance; setting out the conditions a claimant needs to satisfy for an award of a jobseeker's allowance arising under these Regulations to continue; and for transitional protection to be given for a limited period to persons formerly entitled to unemployment benefit or income support.

6481. Jobseeker's allowance–transitional provisions

JOBSEEKER'S ALLOWANCE (TRANSITIONAL PROVISIONS) (AMENDMENT) REGULATIONS (NORTHERN IRELAND) 1996, SR 1996 357; made under the Jobseekers (Northern Ireland) Order 1995 Art.36(2), Art.39. In force: October 7, 1996; £2.80.

These Regulations amend the Jobseeker's Allowance (Transitional Provisions) Regulations (Northern Ireland) 1996 (SR 1996 200); they also insert provisions relating to the provision of information.

6482. Jobseeker's allowance–transitional provisions

JOBSEEKER'S ALLOWANCE (TRANSITIONAL PROVISIONS) (NO.2) REGULATIONS (NORTHERN IRELAND) 1996, SR 1996 518; made under the Jobseekers (Northern Ireland) Order 1995 Art.36, Art.39. In force: December 16, 1996; £4.15.

These Regulations provide for continuity between unemployment benefit and income support for persons who are required to be available for and actively seeking employment, and jobseeker's allowance.

6483. Jobseeker's (Northern Ireland) Order 1995–Commencement No.1 Order

JOBSEEKERS (1995 ORDER) (COMMENCEMENT NO.1) ORDER (NORTHERN IRELAND) 1996, SR1996 26 (C.3); made under the Jobseekers (Northern Ireland) Order 1995 Art.1 (2). In force: bringing into force various provisions of the Order on February 5, 1996, April 1, 1996 and April 6, 1996; £1.10.

This Order brings the Jobseekers (Northern Ireland) Order 1995 (SI 1995 2705 (NI 15)) Art.31 and provisions of the Order authorising the making of Regulations into force on February 5, 1996. It brings Art.30 into force on April 1, 1996 and Art.29, Art.34, Art.35, Art.38(3) of, and part of Sch.2 and a related provision to, the Order into force on April 6, 1996.

6484. Jobseeker's (Northern Ireland) Order 1995–Commencement No.2 Order

JOBSEEKERS (1995 ORDER) (COMMENCEMENT NO.2) ORDER (NORTHERN IRELAND) 1996, SR 1996 180 (C.7); made under the Jobseekers (Northern Ireland) Order Art.1 (2). In force: bringing into force various provisions of the Order on May 3, 1996; £1.10.

This Order brings into operation on May 3, 1996, certain provisions in the Jobseekers (Northern Ireland) Order 1995 (SI 1995 2705 (NI 15)) Sch.2 which amend the Social Security Administration (Northern Ireland) Act 1992 to refer to the 1995 Order.

6485. Jobseeker's (Northern Ireland) Order 1995–Commencement No.3 Order

JOBSEEKERS (1995 ORDER) (COMMENCEMENT NO.3) ORDER (NORTHERN IRELAND) 1996, SR 1996 285 (C.15); made under the Jobseekers (Northern Ireland) Order 1995 Art.1 (2). In force: bringing into force various provisions of the Order on July 17, 1996; £1.55.

This Order brings into operation on July 17, 1996, certain provisions in the Jobseekers (Northern Ireland) Order 1995 (SI 1995 2705 (NI 15)) Sch.2 which make consequential amendments to the Social Security Administration (Northern Ireland) Act 1992.

6486. Jobseeker's (Northern Ireland) Order 1995–Commencement No.4 Order

JOBSEEKERS (1995 ORDER) (COMMENCEMENT NO.4) ORDER (NORTHERN IRELAND) 1996, SR 1996 401 (C.21); made under the Jobseekers (Northern

Ireland) Order 1995 Art.1 (2). In force: bringing into force various provisions of the Order on September 2, 1996 and October 7, 1996; £1.10.

This Order brings the Jobseekers (Northern Ireland) Order 1995 (SI 1995 2705 (NI 15)) Sch.2 para.1 into operation on September 2, 1996 and the remainder of the Order, so far as not already in operation, on October 7, 1996.

6487. Maintenance–allowances–pupils over compulsory school age

MAINTENANCE ALLOWANCES (PUPILS OVER COMPULSORY SCHOOL AGE) REGULATIONS (NORTHERN IRELAND) 1996, SR 1996 578; made under the Education and Libraries (Northern Ireland) Order 1986 Art.50(1)(2), Art.134(1). In force: January 11, 1997; £1.95.

These Regulations, which revoke and replace the Maintenance Allowances (Pupils over Compulsory School Age) Regulations (Northern Ireland) 1994 (SR 1994 298), prescribe the conditions of eligibility for a maintenance allowance. The allowances payable have been increased and are determined by reference to income bands.

6488. Malta

SOCIAL SECURITY (MALTA) ORDER (NORTHERN IRELAND) 1996, SR 1996 345; made under the Social Security Administration (Northern Ireland) Act 1992 s.155(1)(2). In force: September 1, 1996; £5.30.

This Order modifies social security legislation to give effect to the Convention on Social Security between the governments of the United Kingdom and of Malta.

6489. Maternity pay

STATUTORY MATERNITY PAY (GENERAL) (AMENDMENT) REGULATIONS (NORTHERN IRELAND) 1996, SR 1996 206; made under the Social Security Contributions and Benefits (Northern Ireland) Act 1992 s.160(9)(a), s.167(6). In force: June 12, 1996; £1.10.

These Regulations amend the Statutory Maternity Pay (General) Regulations (Northern Ireland) 1987 (SR 1987 30) to include in the calculation of normal weekly earnings any sum payable in respect of a relevant period by virtue of a back dated pay increase received later and to provide that, where a woman is receiving maternity allowance and is entitled to statutory maternity pay due to receiving a backdated pay increase, her employer need only pay statutory maternity pay equal to the amount by which the rate of statutory maternity pay exceeds the rate of maternity allowance received by her.

6490. Maternity pay–statutory sick pay–contributions

SOCIAL SECURITY (CONTRIBUTIONS), STATUTORY MATERNITY PAY AND STATUTORY SICK PAY (MISCELLANEOUS AMENDMENTS) REGULATIONS (NORTHERN IRELAND) 1996, SR 1996 108; made under the Social Security Contributions and Benefits (Northern Ireland) Act 1992 s.149(5)(b), s.152(1), s.158(1), s.159(1), s.166(1), s.167(1); and the Social Security Administration (Northern Ireland) Act 1992 Sch.1 para.6(1), s.122. In force: April 6, 1996; £1.95.

These Regulations make provisions enabling statutory sick pay and statutory maternity pay to be paid to employees (including mariners and airmen) who go outside Northern Ireland for any purpose; and reduce the extent of the records which an employer is required to maintain. For statutory sick pay, they reduce the time within which employees may notify their employers of sickness absence where there is good reason for delay and introduce flexibility into the manner which and the time limit within which, employers must give their employees information.

6491. Pensions–contributions–error

SOCIAL SECURITY (ADDITIONAL PENSION) (CONTRIBUTIONS PAID IN ERROR) REGULATIONS (NORTHERN IRELAND) 1996, SR 1996 188; made under the Social Security Contributions and Benefits (Northern Ireland) Act 1992 s.61A, Sch.1 para.8(1)(m). In force: June 4, 1996; £1.10.

These Regulations, which amend the Social Security (Contributions) Regulations 1979 (SR 1979 186), apply to cases where primary Class 1 contributions have been paid in error because the individual concerned was not an employed earner. They set out conditions to be satisfied before s.61A of the 1992 Act can apply to an individual and provide for the individual's entitlement to additional pension or to the additional pension element in a transitional award of incapacity benefit to be determined as though he had been an employed earner and the contributions had been properly paid.

6492. Reciprocity–agreements

SOCIAL SECURITY (RECIPROCAL AGREEMENTS) ORDER (NORTHERN IRELAND) 1996, SR 1996 327; made under the Social Security Administration (Northern Ireland) Act 1992 s.155(1)(b)(2). In force: October 7, 1996; £1.55.

This Order modifies social security legislation to take account of changes made by the Jobseekers (Northern Ireland) Order 1995 (SI 1995 2705 (NI 15)) (which replaces unemployment benefit by jobseeker's allowance) in relation to Orders in Council and Orders listed in Sch.2 which give effect to reciprocal agreements on social security matters.

6493. Social fund–cold weather payments

SOCIAL FUND (COLD WEATHER PAYMENTS) (GENERAL) (AMENDMENT) REGULATIONS (NORTHERN IRELAND) 1996, SR 1996 488; made under the Social Security Contributions and Benefits (Northern Ireland) Act 1992 s.134(2). In force: November 4, 1996; £1.10.

These Regulations amend the Social Fund (Cold Weather Payments) (General) Regulations (Northern Ireland) 1988 (SR 1988 368) as respects weather forecasts and by providing that an income based jobseeker's allowance is to be a qualifying benefit for the purpose of obtaining cold weather payments.

6494. Social fund–maternity–funerals–expenses

SOCIAL FUND (MATERNITY AND FUNERAL EXPENSES) (GENERAL) (AMENDMENT) REGULATIONS (NORTHERN IRELAND) 1996, SR 1996 423; made under the Social Security Contributions and Benefits (Northern Ireland) Act 1992 s.134(1)(a). In force: October 7, 1996; £1.55.

These Regulations amend the Social Fund (Maternity and Funeral Expenses) (General) Regulations (Northern Ireland) 1987 (SR 1987 150) by providing that income based jobseeker's allowance is to be a qualifying benefit for the purpose of obtaining a maternity payment or a funeral payment, treating claimants or their partners who are receiving long term care in residential care or nursing homes as members of the household, excluding children and young persons from consideration when determining whether responsible persons are entitled to funeral payments, making provision in relation to pre-paid funeral plans, clarifying allowable costs in respect of burials and certain fees and donations and including a reference to confirmation of estates in Scotland.

6495. Social fund–maternity–funerals–expenses

SOCIAL FUND (MATERNITY AND FUNERAL EXPENSES) (GENERAL) (AMENDMENT NO.2) REGULATIONS (NORTHERN IRELAND) 1996, SR 1996 571; made under the Social Security Contributions and Benefits (Northern Ireland) Act 1992 s.134(1)(a), s.171(1)(3)(4). In force: January 1, 1997; £0.65.

These Regulations amend the Social Fund (Maternity and Funeral Expenses) (General) Regulations (Northern Ireland) 1987 (SR 1987 150) by increasing, with effect from January 1, 1997, the amount of funeral expenses allowable in respect of fees or donations paid to ministers of religion or for the use of churches and other places of worship from £57 to £59.

SOCIAL WELFARE

6496. Disability Discrimination Act 1995–Commencement No.1 Order

DISABILITY DISCRIMINATION ACT 1995 (COMMENCEMENT NO.1) ORDER (NORTHERN IRELAND) 1996, SR 1996 1 (C.1); made under the Disability Discrimination Act 1995 s.70. In force: bringing into force various provisions of the Act on January 2, 1996; £0.65.

This Order brings s.50, s.51 and s.52 of, and Sch.5 to, the 1995 Act into force on January 2, 1996.

6497. Disability Discrimination Act 1995–Commencement No.2 Order

DISABILITY DISCRIMINATION ACT 1995 (COMMENCEMENT NO.2) ORDER (NORTHERN IRELAND) 1996, SR 1996 219 (C.9); made under the Disability Discrimination Act 1995 s.70(3). In force: bringing into force various provisions of the Act on May 30, 1996; £1.10.

This Order brings into operation on May 30, 1996, provisions of the Disability Discrimination Act 1995 relating to the specified definitions of disability, past disabilities, guidance, advice and assistance; statutory authority and national security, restriction of publicity in industrial tribunals, Regulations and Orders, interpretation, financial provisions, House of Commons and Northern Ireland Assembly disqualification and definitions of disability and past disabilities.

6498. Disability Discrimination Act 1995–Commencement No.3 Order

DISABILITY DISCRIMINATION ACT 1995 (COMMENCEMENT NO.3 AND SAVING AND TRANSITIONAL PROVISONS) ORDER (NORTHERN IRELAND) 1996, SR 1996 280 (C.13); made under the Disability Discrimination Act 1995 s.67(3), s.70(3). In force: bringing into force various provisions of the Act on July 11, 1996 and December 2, 1996; £1.95.

This Order brings specified provisions of the Disability Discrimination Act 1995 into operation on July 11, 1996 and December 2, 1996.

6499. Disability Discrimination Act 1995–Commencement No.4 Order

DISABILITY DISCRIMINATION ACT 1995 (COMMENCEMENT NO.4) ORDER (NORTHERN IRELAND) 1996, SR 1996 560 (C.27); made under the Disability Discrimination Act 1995 s.70(3). In force: bringing into force various provisions of the Order on December 2, 1996; £1.10.

This Order brings into operation on December 2, 1996 the Disability Discrimination Act 1995 s.16(3) to the extent that it is not already in operation.

6500. Disabled persons–councils

NORTHERN IRELAND DISABILITY COUNCIL REGULATIONS (NORTHERN IRELAND) 1996, SR 1996 13; made under the Disability Discrimination Act 1995 s.67, Sch.5. In force: February 19, 1996; £1.10.

These Regulations prescribe circumstances in which members of the Northern Ireland Disability Council may be removed from office and provide for the expenses of the Council.

6501. Disabled persons–councils

NORTHERN IRELAND DISABILITY COUNCIL (NO.2) REGULATIONS (NORTHERN IRELAND) 1996, SR 1996 272; made under the Disability Discrimination Act 1995 s.50(8), s.67(3), s.68(1), Sch.5 para.7. In force: August 16, 1996; £1.10.

These Regulations authorise the Department of Health and Social Services to commission research at the request of the Northern Ireland Disability Council. They also deal with the appointment of advisers to the Council.

6502. Disabled persons–discrimination

DISABILITY DISCRIMINATION (MEANING OF DISABILITY) REGULATIONS (NORTHERN IRELAND) 1996, SR 1996 421; made under the Disability Discrimination Act 1995 Sch.1 para.1(2), Sch.1 para.2(4), Sch.1 para.3(2)(3), Sch.1 para.4(2)(a), Sch.1 para.5(a). In force: November 4, 1996; £1.10.

These Regulations have the effect of excluding from the scope of the definition of disability addictions (other than those medically caused), certain personality disorders and hayfever and similar conditions. Tattoos and piercings are also excluded. The Regulations also provide that a child under six is to be treated as if he were six or over for the purposes of determining the effect of his disability.

6503. Disabled persons–discrimination

DISABILITY DISCRIMINATION (QUESTIONS AND REPLIES) ORDER (NORTHERN IRELAND) 1996, SR 1996 532; made under the Disability Discrimination Act 1995 s.56(2)(4), s.67(3), Sch.8 para.38, Sch.8 para.46. In force: December 2, 1996; £1.95.

This Order prescribes forms for use in connection with persons who may have been discriminated against by employers for reasons connected with disability. It also specifies the period within which the questions must be served in order to be admissible in proceedings in an industrial tribunal.

6504. Disabled persons–discrimination–codes of practice

DISABILITY DISCRIMINATION CODE OF PRACTICE (GOODS, FACILITIES, SERVICES AND PREMISES) ORDER (NORTHERN IRELAND) 1996, SR 1996 561; made under the Disability Discrimination Act 1995 s.52(8). In force: December 2, 1996; £0.65.

This Order appoints December 2, 1996 as the day for the coming into force of the Disability Discrimination Act 1995 Code of Practice on the Rights of Access to Goods, Facilities, Services and Premises, issued by the Department of Health and Social Services.

6505. Disabled persons–discrimination–codes of practice

DISABILITY DISCRIMINATION (GUIDANCE AND CODE OF PRACTICE) (APPOINTED DAY) ORDER (NORTHERN IRELAND) 1996, SR 1996 549; made under the Disability Discrimination Act 1995 s.3(4), s.54(6). In force: December 2, 1996; £1.10.

This Order appoints December 2, 1996 as the day on which Guidance issued by the Department of Economic Development on matters to be taken into account in determining questions relating to the definition of disability is to come into force. It also provides for the elimination of discrimination in the field of employment against disabled persons or persons who have had a disability.

6506. Disabled persons–discrimination–employment

DISABILITY DISCRIMINATION (EMPLOYMENT) REGULATIONS (NORTHERN IRELAND) 1996, SR 1996 419; made under the Disability Discrimination Act 1995 s.5(6)(7), s.6(8)(a)(c)(d)(e)(f)(g)(10), s.12(3), Sch.4 para.3(a)(b). In force: December 2, 1996; £1.95.

These Regulations set out circumstances where treatment of a disabled employee (or a failure to adjust premises) is justified. These include where pay is linked to performance, where there are uniform rates of contribution to occupational pension schemes regardless of contributions and where building works complied with (and continue to do so) the building regulations on access and facilities for disabled people when the works were carried out. They also deal with the position where the employer's premises are held under a lease or tenancy.

6507. Disabled persons–discrimination–premises

DISABILITY DISCRIMINATION (SERVICES AND PREMISES) REGULATIONS (NORTHERN IRELAND) 1996, SR 1996 557; made under the Disability Discrimination Act 1995 s.19(5)(c), s.20(7)(8), s.24(5), s.67(2)(3), s.68(1). In force: December 2, 1996; £1.95.

These Regulations make provision for unequal treatment of disabled persons to be justified in specified circumstances.

6508. Disabled persons–discrimination–tenancies

DISABILITY DISCRIMINATION (SUB-LEASES AND SUB-TENANCIES) REGULATIONS (NORTHERN IRELAND) 1996, SR 1996 420; made under the Disability Discrimination Act 1995 s.16(3), Sch.4 para.4. In force: November 4, 1996; £1.10.

These Regulations modify and supplement the Disability Discrimination Act 1995 s.16, Sch.4 in relation to cases where premises are occupied under a sub-lease or sub-tenancy. Section 16 and Sch.4 para.1 are modified so that lessor refers to the occupier's immediate landlord. Section 16 is also supplemented to cover the position as respects the obligations of lessors and lessees under superior leases and tenancies. Schedule 4 para.2 and Sch.4 para.3 are modified so that references to the lessor include any superior landlord.

6509. Personal Social Services (Northern Ireland) Order 1996 (SI 1996 1923 (NI 19))

This Order, which comes into operation on days to be appointed, amends the Health and Personal Social Services (Northern Ireland) Order 1972 (SI 1972 1265 (NI 14) to enable the Department of Health and Social Services to make payments to persons in respect of their securing the provision of personal social services.

SUCCESSION

6510. Succession (Northern Ireland) Order 1996 (SI 1996 3163 (NI 26))

This Order, which comes into force on February 20, 1997, provides that the spouse of an intestate will take in accordance with the intestacy rules only if he or she survives the intestate by 28 days; abolishes the "hotchpot" rule, by which certain payments made by a person who dies intestate to his children must be brought into account by the recipient against the share of the estate to which he would otherwise be entitled; and adds to the persons who, under the Inheritance (Provision for Family and Dependants) (Northern Ireland) Order 1979 (SI 1979 924 (NI 8)) may apply for financial provision out of a deceased person's estate, a person who (though not married to the deceased) lived with the deceased as husband or wife.

6511. Books

Grattan, Sheena–Succession Law in Northern Ireland. Hardback: £76.50. ISBN 0-85389-657-7. SLS Legal Publications (NI).

TAXATION

6512. Stamp duties–documents. See TAXATION. §5630

TRADE UNIONS

6513. Certification officer–fees

CERTIFICATION OFFICER (FEES) (AMENDMENT) REGULATIONS (NORTHERN IRELAND) 1996, SR 1996 214; made under the Industrial Relations (Northern Ireland) Order 1992 Art.5(4), Art.6(2), Art.80(1). In force: June 30, 1996; £1.10.

These Regulations amend the Certification Officer (Fees) Regulations (Northern Ireland) 1995 (SR 1995 133) by increasing the fees payable to the certification officer.

TRANSPORT

6514. Carriage of goods–fees

INTERNATIONAL TRANSPORT OF GOODS UNDER COVER OF TIR CARNETS (FEES) (AMENDMENT) REGULATIONS (NORTHERN IRELAND) 1996, SR 1996 144; made under the Finance Act 1973 s.56(1)(5). In force: June 3, 1996; £0.65.

These Regulations further amend the International Transport of Goods under Cover of TIR Carnets (Fees) Regulations (Northern Ireland) 1992 (SR 1992 386) by reducing the fee payable for an inspection of an individual vehicle in respect of the issue of an approval certificate and increasing the fee payable for a duplicate certificate. The International Transport of Goods under Cover of TIR Carnets (Fees) (Amendment) Regulations (Northern Ireland) 1993 (SR 1993 395) are revoked.

UTILITIES

6515. Electricity–non-fossil fuels

ELECTRICITY (NON-FOSSIL FUEL SOURCES) ORDER (NORTHERN IRELAND) 1996, SR 1996 407; made under the Electricity (Northern Ireland) Order 1992 Art.35(1). In force: September 5, 1996; £1.95.

This Order imposes on Northern Ireland Electricity plc an obligation to secure the availability, during specified periods, of specified amounts of generating capacity from certain non-fossil fuel generating stations.

6516. Gas–licences

GAS (APPLICATIONS FOR LICENCES AND EXTENSIONS) REGULATIONS (NORTHERN IRELAND) 1996, SR 1996 447; made under the Gas (Northern Ireland) Order 1996 Art.8(3). In force: September 24, 1996; £3.70.

These Regulations prescribe the manner in which applications for licences to convey, store or supply gas or for the extension of such licences are to be made.

6517. Gas (Northern Ireland) Order 1996 (SI 1996 275 (NI 2))

This Order, which comes into operation on days to be appointed, provides for the regulation of the supply of gas through pipes in Northern Ireland. Provisions relate to licensing of the supply of gas and associated activities, modification of licences, meters, storage and gas processing facilities, consumer protection, investigation of complaints, functions of the Director General of Gas for Northern Ireland and safety of pipe lines.

6518. Gas (Northern Ireland) Order 1996–Commencement Order

GAS (1996 ORDER) (COMMENCEMENT) ORDER (NORTHERN IRELAND) 1996, SR 1996 216 (C.8); made under the Northern Ireland Act 1974 Sch.1 para.2(1); and the Gas (Northern Ireland) Order 1996 Art.1 (2) (3). In force: bringing into force various provisions of the Order on June 10, 1996; £1.10.

This Order brings into operation the provisions of the Gas (Northern Ireland) Order 1996 (SI 1996 275 (NI 2) on June 10, 1996. It also contains transitional provisions allowing the execution work before December 10, 1996, on a major pipeline without the consent of the Director General of Gas for Northern Ireland and in connection with the breaking up of roads pending the commencement of the Street Works (Northern Ireland) Order 1995 (SI 1995 3210 (NI 19).

6519. Offshore installations–design and construction

OFFSHORE INSTALLATIONS AND WELLS (DESIGN AND CONSTRUCTION, ETC.) REGULATIONS (NORTHERN IRELAND) 1996, SR 1996 228; made under the Health and Safety at Work (Northern Ireland) Order 1978 Art.17(1) (2) (3) (4) (5) (6), Art.55(2), Sch.3 para.1 (1) (2), Sch.3 para.5, Sch.3 para.7, Sch.3 para.8, Sch.3 para.9, Sch.3 para.10, Sch.3 para.11, Sch.3 para.12(1) (3), Sch.3 para.13, Sch.3 para.14(1), Sch.3 para.15, Sch.3 para.17, Sch.3 para.19; and the Health and Safety at Work (Northern Ireland) Order 1992 Art.3(2). In force: July 21, 1996; £5.30.

These Regulations contain requirements for ensuring that offshore oil and gas installations, and oil and gas wells are designed, constructed and kept in a sound structural state, and other requirements affecting them, for purposes of health and safety. They implement in relation to offshore installations in United Kingdom territorial waters adjacent to Northern Ireland, certain provisions of Council Directive 92/91 ([1992] OJ L348/9), concerning the minimum requirements for improving the safety and health protection of workers in the mineral-extracting industries through drilling.

SCOTLAND

ACCOUNTANCY

6520. Books

Watson, Robert A.B.; Watson, Louise M.–Business Accounting for Scottish Solicitors. Paperback: £27.00. ISBN 0-406-04655-7. Butterworth Law.

ADMINISTRATION OF JUSTICE

6521. Judges–Land Valuation Appeal Court–appointments

ACT OF SEDERUNT (LANDS VALUATION APPEAL COURT) 1995, SI 1995 3069 (S.223); made under the Valuation of Lands (Scotland) Amendment Act 1879 s.7. In force: December 18, 1995; £0.65.

Judges who may hear appeals under the Valuation of Lands (Scotland) Amendment Act 1879 s.7 are appointed by this Act. The judges named are The Honourable Lord Clyde, The Honourable Lord Cullen, The Honourable Lord Prosser, The Honourable Lord Milligan and The Honourable Lord Gill.

6522. Judges–Lands Valuation Appeal Court–appointments

ACT OF SEDERUNT (LANDS VALUATION APPEAL COURT) 1996, SI 1996 2856 (S.218); made under the Valuation of Lands (Scotland) Amendment Act 1879 s.7. In force: December 4, 1996; £0.65.

This Act of Sederunt appoints the judges who may hear appeals under Valuation of Lands (Scotland) Amendment Act 1879 s.7. It also revokes the Act of Sederunt (Lands Valuation Appeal Court) 1995 (SI 1995 3069).

6523. Juries–provision of information

JURORS (SCOTLAND) ACT 1825 (PROVISION OF INFORMATION) ORDER 1996, SI 1996 626 (S.61); made under the Jurors (Scotland) Act 1825 s.3. In force: March 31, 1996; £0.65.

This Order prescribes the nature and form of information which a sheriff principal may require from a potential juror. In particular, Art.2 provides that the sheriff principal may require from such a person, in written form, that person's name, address and date of birth. In terms of the Jurors (Scotland) Act 1825 s.3(4) it is an offence to fail to comply with any such requirement.

6524. Law Reform (Miscellaneous Provisions) (Scotland) Act 1990–Commencement No.13 Order

LAW REFORM (MISCELLANEOUS PROVISIONS) (SCOTLAND) ACT 1990 (COMMENCEMENT NO.13) ORDER 1996, SI 1996 2894 (C.85; S.222); made under the Law Reform (Miscellaneous Provisions) (Scotland) Act 1990 s.75. In force: bringing into force various provisions of the Act on December 5, 1995; £1.55.

This Order appoints December 5, 1996 for the coming into force of the provisions of the Law Reform (Miscellaneous Provisions) (Scotland) Act 1990 which are specified in the Schedule to the Order insofar as these are not already in force.

6525. Law Reform (Miscellaneous Provisions) (Scotland) Act 1990–Commencement No.13 (Amendment) Order

LAW REFORM (MISCELLANEOUS PROVISIONS) (SCOTLAND) ACT 1990 (COMMENCEMENT NO.13) (AMENDMENT) ORDER 1996, SI 1996 2966 (C.89;

S.226); made under the Law Reform (Miscellaneous Provisions) (Scotland) Act 1990 s.75. In force: bringing into force various provisions of the Act on March 1, 1997; £0.65.

This Order amends the Law Reform (Miscellaneous Provisions) (Scotland) Act 1990 (Commencement No.13) Order 1996 (SI 1996 2894) by substituting the words "March 1, 1997" for the words "December 5, 1996" in Art.3 of and in the headnote to the Schedule. The effect of this is that the provisions of the Law Reform (Miscellaneous Provisions) (Scotland) Act 1990 which are specified in column 1 of the Schedule, and described by reference to the subject matter in column 2 of that Schedule will now come into force on March 1, 1997.

6526. Articles

Court interpreters in Scotland: une reforme s'impose *(Anne-Sylvie Vassenaix)*: S.L.T. 1996, 23, 197-201. (Need to adopt common standard for court interpreters to ensure justice and compliance with human rights).

ADMINISTRATIVE LAW

6527. Judicial review–competency–whether partly implemented decision capable of being subject to judicial review

A prisoner sought judicial review of a decision made in June 1993 which found him guilty of disciplinary offences and imposed various punishments, including cellular confinement, deprivation of use of a mattress, forfeiture of remission, earnings, association and recreation, and exclusion from work, each for a period of 14 days. His petition came before the court in 1995 when all the punishments had been implemented and spent, save for the loss of remission, which, along with the possible payment of lost wages, was the only outstanding live issue with practical consequences for the prisoner. It was argued for the Secretary of State that the decision could not be reviewed because it had been partly implemented.

Held, that (1) judicial review was not available to enable persons to challenge administrative decisions if a successful challenge would not have practical consequences to them; (2) it was inappropriate to deny a remedy where only part of the consequences of an unlawful decision had been implemented and were incapable of being restored or rectified; (3) judicial review was available to any person aggrieved by a decision which affected the rights of that person, so long as a successful challenge would have a practical consequence which would reflect in that person's patrimonial or human rights and (4) the petitioner could point to two such practical consequences, namely the loss of remission and loss of wages and was accordingly entitled to seek judicial review; and case continued for a second hearing.

CONWAY v. SECRETARY OF STATE FOR SCOTLAND 1996 S.L.T. 689, Judge not specified, OH.

6528. Judicial review–natural justice–investigation into sheriff's fitness for office

[Sheriff Courts (Scotland) Act 1971 (c.58) s.12(1) and (2).]

Section 12(1) of the Sheriff Courts (Scotland) Act 1971 provides, *inter alia*, that the Lord President and the Lord Justice-Clerk shall, if requested to do so by the Secretary of State for Scotland, jointly investigate into the fitness for office of a sheriff and, as soon as practicable after completing that investigation, shall report in writing to the Secretary of State either (a) that the sheriff is fit for office; or (b) that he is "unfit for office by reason of inability, neglect of duty or misbehaviour". Section 12(2) provides, *inter alia*, that if the report concludes that the sheriff is unfit for office then the Secretary of State may make an order removing him from office. The Lord President and the Lord Justice-Clerk investigated the conduct of a sheriff in terms of s.12(1) of the 1971 Act. In their report those judges found that there was no basis for saying that the sheriff was unfit by reason of neglect of duty or misbehaviour, but that he was unfit for office by reason of inability on the basis of "an underlying defect in character, which manifests itself in various ways to the severe prejudice of the sheriff's function as a judge". This conclusion was based upon an examination of cases reviewed and other sources. The Secretary of State made an order finding that the sheriff was not fit for office. The former sheriff then brought a petition for judicial review, arguing (a) that "inability" under s.12(1) was confined to mental and physical inability; and (b) that, in any event, he had not been given fair notice of the case against him in that he was not informed that the case against him was one of inability rather than misbehaviour; not having been informed of his character defect, and had not been given fair notice of the fact that the judges had obtained comments from other various sources. The petition was dismissed and the sheriff reclaimed.

Held, that (1) there was no ground for giving the word "inability" the narrow meaning contended for by the petitioner, and the word should be given its ordinary meaning of lack of power, capacity or means; (2) having found that the petitioner had an inability to direct and concentrate his attention on the matter before him and to exercise self-restraint, the judges were entitled to hold that inability in that sense had been demonstrated by the time of the investigation, and (3) the nature and ambit of the investigation had been made clear and ample notice had been given of the particular examples of conduct before the judges for consideration; the accounts of a general nature provided to the judges were only a subsidiary element in their decision, so that there was no obligation to give notice of them to the petitioner; and reclaiming motion refused. *Per* Lord McCluskey: The interpretation placed on "inability" would not open the door to the removal of a judge on the basis of alleged incompetence or mere error in the exercise of the judicial function albeit that incompetence might be a feature, symptom or consequence of "neglect of duty", and either a cause or a consequence of inability, so that the judgment that fell to be made under s.12(1) should not ignore the incompetence of the sheriff if the evidence established it. *Per* Lord Clyde: The "inability" might be one which was restricted to the scope of the judicial function or it might be one which extended beyond it; but whether a particular case of inability brought about an unfitness for office was the question to be addressed by the senior judges. *Per* Lord Coulsfield: What was required to satisfy the test was not that facts should be established which indicated that the judge could not do the job efficiently or well: what had to be shown was that he was not really capable of performing the proper function of a judge at all.

STEWART v. SECRETARY OF STATE FOR SCOTLAND 1996 S.L.T. 1203, Lord McCluskey, IH.

6529. Judicial review–shipping subsides–unreasonableness–decision based on error of fact

[Highlands and Islands Shipping Services Act 1960 (c.31).]

The Highlands and Islands Shipping Services Act 1960 empowers the Secretary of State for Scotland to operate a discretionary scheme to subsidise shippers of freight to the Northern Isles. Applicant companies are required to submit freight projections for each financial year from which the Secretary of State calculates the rate of subsidy. Payments are made on presentation of invoices, and the scheme also allows for capping of the amounts claimed. Two shipping companies submitted erroneous projections for three financial years which were understated due to their being based on wrong information from the Scottish Office. Other companies had submitted projections which had been made on the correct basis, and this resulted in the two companies' subsidies under the scheme being less than if their projections and relevant invoices had been correctly submitted. The two companies brought a petition for judicial review in which they sought reduction of the decisions of the Secretary of State fixing the rates, rebates and caps for the three years in which they had submitted erroneous projections and invoices. It was argued on behalf of the companies that the decisions were unlawful on the grounds that they were irrational, unfair and based on errors of fact. It was not suggested that the Secretary of State had acted in bad faith. If the court decided that the decisions were spent and so could not be reduced, it was argued that the petition should be continued so that remedies of declarator and damages for negligence could be sought.

Held, that (1) although irrationality as a ground of review could involve an error of fact, any such error had to relate to facts material to the decision in circumstances where the opportunity to appreciate the true situation was before a minister or his officials at the time the decision was taken, and it was not sufficient for the error to be discovered with the benefit of hindsight; (2) in the exercise of the court's supervisory jurisdiction a decision had to be reviewed against the background of material before the minister at the relevant time, and not by reference to subsequent events; (3) in the context of judicial review the concept of unfairness (other than a procedural unfairness) was not a substantive ground of review on its own; (4) damages were not awardable in respect of the consequences of a decision of a Minister of the Crown in the absence of misfeasance or an abuse of power amounting to bad faith, although a duty of care might arise in respect of the manner in which a power was exercised; (5) even if there was a claim in negligence, in the circumstances it should be pursued in a separate action for reparation and not by continuing the petition for judicial review and (6) where the decisions were spent the remedy of reduction was not appropriate; and petition dismissed.

SHETLAND LINE (1984) LTD v. SECRETARY OF STATE FOR SCOTLAND 1996 S.L.T. 653, Judge not specified, OH.

6530. Articles

Dunblane public inquiry–preliminary hearing opening statement by Lord Cullen (1 May 1996). : S.L.G. 1996, 64(2), 54-56. (Lord Cullen's statement on matters of representation and procedure for Dunblane public inquiry into use of firearms and school security).

Judicial review in Scotland *(Tom Mullen)*: S.L.P.Q. 1996, 1(5), 366-383. (Summary of research findings into operation of judicial review).

6531. Books

Mullen, Tom; Prosser, Tony–Judicial Review in Scotland. Paperback: £35.00. ISBN 0-471-96614-2. John Wiley and Sons.

AGENCY

6532. Construction–whether provision for contractual payment on failure to perform a penalty clause

The sole-agency agreement between estate agents and a client provided, *inter alia*, that after the termination of the agreement that client had to submit any offer to purchase to the estate agents before it was submitted to the client's solicitor and that, in the event that this was not done, the estate agents would be entitled to their whole remuneration and outlays as if the agreement had not been terminated. The estate agents sought to enforce this provision.

Held, that the stipulated payment was not a genuine pre-estimate of damage but, being a stipulation purely *in terrorem* of the client, amounted to a penalty clause and was unenforceable.

CHRIS HART (BUSINESS SALES) LTD v. MITCHELL 1996 S.C.L.R. 68, Judge not specified, Sh Ct.

6533. Principal and agent–"commercial agent"

[Commercial Agents (Council Directive) Regulations 1993 Reg.2(1), 15(1), (2) and (4), 17(6), (7) and (8).]

Held, that an agent who received commission on the sale by him of bakery products belonging to his principal was entitled to three months' notice of termination of the contract in terms of Reg.15(2)(c) of the 1993 Regulations.

KING v. TUNNOCK 1996 S.C.L.R. 742, Judge not specified, Sh Ct.

6534. Articles

Boyter v Thomson: let the seller beware *(R.F. Hunter)*: S.L.G. 1996, 64(1), 3-6. (HL decision that aggrieved buyer may raise action against either principal or agent where principal was not acting in course of business).

AGRICULTURE

6535. Agricultural holdings–notice to remedy–admissibility of extrinsic evidence to explain notice

Held, in a joint application by the landlord and the tenant of an agricultural holding under the Agricultural Holdings (Scotland) Act 1991 s.60, that the rule as to the inadmissibility of extrinsic evidence for the explanation of writings did not apply to a notice to remedy and that the notice to remedy which had been served by the landlord was not invalid even although it did not specify the condition of which the tenant was purportedly in breach.

CAYZER v. HAMILTON (NO.1) 1996 S.L.T. (Land Ct.) 18, Judge not specified, Land Ct.

6536. Agricultural holdings–notice to remedy–notice to quit–delay in issuing notice to quit

In a joint application the landlord and tenant of an agricultural holding referred various questions to the court arising out of the service by the landlord of a notice to remedy and then a notice to quit. The tenant had been carrying on a business, trading in farm machinery from the holding. The landlord served a notice to remedy and thereafter a notice to quit. Parties agreed to refer the following questions to the court, namely (1) whether the carrying on of the machinery business was a breach by the tenant of any term or condition of his tenancy; (2) whether such condition was inconsistent with the fulfilment of responsibilities to farm in accordance with the rules of good husbandry; (3) whether the period of two months specified in the notice to remedy was in the circumstances reasonable and (4) whether the landlord had acquiesced in any breach and thus barred himself from founding upon the notices.

Held, that (1) the carrying on of the business of the sale and storage of agricultural machinery producing a turnover greatly exceeding that of the farm fell to be regarded as an inversion of possession by the tenant; (2) an implied condition in the lease prohibiting such inversion of possession was not inconsistent with fulfilment of the tenant's responsibilities to farm in accordance with the rules of good husbandry; (3) on the evidence the tenant could have removed the machinery within the two-month-period which was therefore a reasonable one but (4) as the landlord had twice accepted rent after the expiry of the period detailed in the notice to remedy, had allowed 18 months to elapse between service of the notice to remedy and service of the notice to quit, and had acted in certain respects which suggested acceptance of the carrying on of the business provided certain conditions were fulfilled, he had waived his right to terminate the tenancy by serving an incontestable notice to quit.

CAYZER v. HAMILTON (NO.2) 1996 S.L.T. (Land Ct.) 21, Judge not specified, Land Ct.

6537. Agricultural holdings–rent properly payable–arbitration–tenant's improvement

[Agricultural Holdings (Scotland) Act 1991 (c.55) s.5.]

The tenant of an agricultural holding appealed against the award of a statutory arbiter appointed to determine the rent for the holding. The tenant maintained that the arbiter had erred in law in taking into account any increase in the rental value of the holding which was due to the completion by the tenant of a comprehensive drainage scheme in terms of an obligation imposed on him by the lease.

Held, that the landlords had failed to provide the necessary fixed equipment in terms of the Agricultural Holdings (Scotland) Act 1991 s.5(2)(a), that the agreement whereby the tenant undertook to execute on behalf of the landlords work required to fulfil the obligation incumbent upon the landlords should have been constituted in a post lease agreement, that the attempt to transfer the landlord's obligation to the tenant within the lease itself was invalid, and accordingly that the work carried out by the tenant fell to be considered as an improvement which the arbiter was obliged to leave out of account in assessing the rent for the holding; and appeal sustained.

GRANT v. BROADLAND PROPERTIES ESTATES 1995 S.L.C.R. 39, Judge not specified.

6538. Agricultural policy–environmental protection–habitats

HABITATS (SCOTLAND) AMENDMENT REGULATIONS 1996, SI 1996 3035 (S.229); made under the European Communities Act 1972 s.2. In force: January 1, 1997; £1.10.

These Regulations amend the Habitats (Scotland) Regulations 1994 (SI 1994 2710) which implement in part Council Regulation 2078/92 on agricultural production methods compatible with the requirements of the protection of the environment and the maintenance of the countryside. The amendments relate to transfer of holdings, force majeure, transformation of undertakings and reimbursement of aid and penalties.

6539. Agricultural policy–environmental protection–organic aid

ORGANIC AID (SCOTLAND) AMENDMENT REGULATIONS 1996, SI 1996 3083 (S.238); made under the European Communities Act 1972 s.2. In force: January 1, 1997; £1.10.

These Regulations amend the Organic Aid (Scotland) Regulations 1994 (SI 1994 1701) which implement in part Council Regulations 2078/92. The amendments made adapt the 1994 Regulations to conform to Commission Regulation 746/96, laying down detailed rules for the application of the Council Regulation.

6540. Agricultural policy–livestock extensification–environmental protection–heather moorland

HEATHER MOORLAND (LIVESTOCK EXTENSIFICATION) (SCOTLAND) AMENDMENT REGULATIONS 1996, SI 1996 3036 (S.230); made under the European Communities Act 1972 s.2. In force: January 1, 1997; £1.10.

These Regulations amend the Heather Moorland (Livestock Extensification) (Scotland) Regulations which implement in part Council Regulation 2078/92 on agricultural production methods compatible with the requirements of the protection of the environment and the maintenance of the countryside. The amendments relate to transfer of holdings, force majeure, transformation of undertakings and reimbursement of aid and penalties.

6541. Cattle–diseases and disorders–brucellosis and tuberculosis

BRUCELLOSIS AND TUBERCULOSIS COMPENSATION (SCOTLAND) AMENDMENT ORDER 1996, SI 1996 1358 (S.126); made under the Animal Health Act 1981 s.32, s.34. In force: May 23, 1996; £1.10.

This Order amends the Brucellosis and Tuberculosis Compensation (Scotland) Order 1978 which is concerned with the amount of compensation payable for cattle slaughtered by order of the Secretary of State because they are affected with brucellosis or tuberculosis.

6542. Environmentally sensitive areas

ENVIRONMENTALLY SENSITIVE AREAS (SCOTLAND) ORDERS AMENDMENT REGULATIONS 1996, SI 1996 3082 (S.237); made under the European Communities Act 1972 s.2. In force: January 1, 1997; £1.55.

These Regulations amend a series of Orders which designate various areas of land in Scotland as environmentally sensitive areas to conform to Commission Regulation 746/96, laying down detailed rules for the application of Council Regulation 2078/92.

6543. Environmentally sensitive areas–Argyll Islands

ENVIRONMENTALLY SENSITIVE AREAS (ARGYLL ISLANDS) DESIGNATION (AMENDMENT) ORDER 1996, SI 1996 1966 (S.162); made under the Agriculture Act 1986 s.18. In force: August 15, 1996; £1.10.

This Order makes amendments to the Environmentally Sensitive Areas (Argyll Islands) Designation Order 1993 (SI 1993 3136) by changing the maximum rates of payments for expenditure identified to undertake additional farming operations.

6544. Environmentally sensitive areas–Breadalbane

ENVIRONMENTALLY SENSITIVE AREAS (BREADALBANE) DESIGNATION (AMENDMENT) ORDER 1995, SI 1995 3096 (S.227); made under the Agriculture Act 1986 s.18. In force: December 21, 1995; £1.10.

This Order amends the Environmentally Sensitive Areas (Breadalbane) Designation Order 1992 (SI 1992 1920) to increase the ceiling on payments made to persons who undertake additional farming operations as specified in para.10(b) of the Schedule. The limit of £4,000 per annum is increased to an overall five year limit of £25,000 per farm conservation plan.

6545. Environmentally sensitive areas–Breadalbane

ENVIRONMENTALLY SENSITIVE AREAS (BREADALBANE) DESIGNATION (AMENDMENT) ORDER 1996, SI 1996 738 (S.71); made under the Agriculture Act 1986 s.18. In force: April 1, 1996; £0.65.

This Order amends the Environmentally Sensitive Areas (Breadalbane) Designation Order 1992 (SI 1992 1920) by an amendment to paragraph 10(b) of the Schedule to that Order to enable a farmer, if he so wishes, to include in his farm conservation plan a grazing plan and other measures necessary to conserve, enhance or extend water margins in the area affected by the Order.

6546. Environmentally sensitive areas–Cairngorms Straths

ENVIRONMENTALLY SENSITIVE AREAS (CAIRNGORMS STRATHS) DESIGNATION (AMENDMENT) ORDER 1996, SI 1996 1963 (S.159); made under the Agriculture Act 1986 s.18. In force: August 15, 1996; £1.10.

This Order makes amendments to the Environmentally Sensitive Areas (Cairngorms Straths) Designation Order 1993 (SI 1993 2345) by changing the maximum rates of payments for expenditure identified to undertake additional farming operations.

6547. Environmentally sensitive areas–Central Borders

ENVIRONMENTALLY SENSITIVE AREAS (CENTRAL BORDERS) DESIGNATION (AMENDMENT) ORDER 1996, SI 1996 1964 (S.160); made under the Agriculture Act 1986 s.18. In force: August 15, 1996; £1.10.

This Order makes amendments to the Environmentally Sensitive Areas (Central Borders) Designation Order 1993 (SI 1993 2767) by changing the maximum rates of payments for expenditure identified to undertake additional farming operations.

6548. Environmentally sensitive areas–Central Southern Uplands

ENVIRONMENTALLY SENSITIVE AREAS (CENTRAL SOUTHERN UPLANDS) DESIGNATION (AMENDMENT) ORDER 1996, SI 1996 1969 (S.165); made under the Agriculture Act 1986 s.18. In force: August 15, 1996; £1.10.

This Order amends the Environmentally Sensitive Areas (Central Southern Uplands) Designation Order 1993 (SI 1993 996) by changing the maximum rate of payments for expenditure identified to undertake additional farming operations.

6549. Environmentally sensitive areas–Loch Lomond

ENVIRONMENTALLY SENSITIVE AREAS (LOCH LOMOND) DESIGNATION (AMENDMENT) ORDER 1995, SI 1995 3097 (S.228); made under the Agriculture Act 1986 s.18. In force: December 21, 1995; £1.10.

This Order increases the ceiling on payments made to persons undertaking additional farming operations from £4,000 per annum to an overall five year limit of £25,000 per farm conservation plan. A substitution is also made of a definition of "inbye land" for the definition of "enclosed" land along with minor drafting changes.

6550. Environmentally sensitive areas–Machair of the Uists and Benbecula

ENVIRONMENTALLY SENSITIVE AREAS (MACHAIR OF THE UISTS AND BENBECULA, BARRA AND VATERSAY) DESIGNATION (AMENDMENT) ORDER 1996, SI 1996 1962 (S.158); made under the Agriculture Act 1986 s.18. In force: August 15, 1996; £1.10.

This Order makes amendments to the Environmentally Sensitive Areas (Machair of the Uists and Benbecula, Barra and Vatersay) Designation Order 1993 (SI 1993 3149) by changing the maximum rates of payment for expenditure identified to undertake additional farming operations.

6551. Environmentally sensitive areas–Shetland Islands

ENVIRONMENTALLY SENSITIVE AREAS (SHETLAND ISLANDS) DESIGNATION (AMENDMENT) ORDER 1996, SI 1996 1965 (S.161); made under the Agriculture Act 1986 s.18. In force: August 15, 1996; £1.10.

This Order makes amendments to the Environmentally Sensitive Areas (Shetland Islands) Designation Order 1993 (SI 1993 3150) by changing maximum and minimum rates of payments for expenditure.

6552. Environmentally sensitive areas–Stewartry

ENVIRONMENTALLY SENSITIVE AREAS (STEWARTRY) DESIGNATION (AMENDMENT) ORDER 1996, SI 1996 1967 (S.163); made under the Agriculture Act 1986 s.18. In force: August 15, 1996; £1.10.

This Order makes amendments to the Environmentally Sensitive Areas (Stewartry) Designation Order 1993 (SI 1993 2768) by changing the maximum rates of payments for expenditure identified to undertake additional farming operations.

6553. Environmentally sensitive areas–Western Southern Uplands

ENVIRONMENTALLY SENSITIVE AREAS (WESTERN SOUTHERN UPLANDS) DESIGNATION (AMENDMENT) ORDER 1996, SI 1996 1968 (S.164); made under the Agriculture Act 1986 s.18. In force: August 15, 1996; £1.10.

This Order amends the Environmentally Sensitive Areas (Western Southern Uplands) Designation Order 1993 (SI 1993 997) by substituting various references and definitions, amending various maximum rates of payments for expenditure and amends provisions relating to farming operations details for inclusion in conservation plans.

6554. Milk Marketing Board–dissolution

ABERDEEN AND DISTRICT MILK MARKETING BOARD DISSOLUTION ORDER 1996, SI 1996 1094 (S.118); made under the Agriculture Act 1993 s.14. In force: April 29, 1996; £0.65.

Provides that the Aberdeen and District Milk Marketing Board shall be dissolved on April 29, 1996.

6555. Milk Marketing Board–dissolution

NORTH OF SCOTLAND MILK MARKETING BOARD DISSOLUTION ORDER 1996, SI 1996 1093 (S.117); made under the Agriculture Act 1993 s.14. In force: April 29, 1996; £0.65.

Provides that the North of Scotland Milk Marketing Board shall be dissolved on April 29, 1996.

6556. Plant conservation

PLANT HEALTH FEES (SCOTLAND) REGULATIONS 1996, SI 1996 1784 (S.148); made under the European Communities Act 1972 s.2. In force: August 1, 1996; £1.55.

These Regulations supersede the Plant Health Fees (Scotland) Order 1994 (SI 1994 1441), and prescribe fees in respect of inspections carried out for the purpose of conferring authority to issue plant passports under the Plant Health (Great Britain) Order 1993 (SI 1993 1320) under which Order, certain listed plants, plant products and other objects require a plant passport for movement within the European Community including any trade within the United Kingdom. The Regulations also prescribe the fees for the issue of licences under the 1993 Order to permit the importation of those articles which would otherwise by prohibited, including fees for the new licences for the new licences for trial or scientific purposes or for work on varietal selection introduced by the Plant Health (Great Britain) (Amendment) Order 1996 (SI 1996 25). Due to the introduction of this amendment Order, a new fee for the renewal/extension of import licences has been introduced and the £55 charge now applies to licences issued for material moved within the EC. Other fees are unchanged.

6557. Plant health

SOFT FRUIT PLANTS (SCOTLAND) REVOCATION ORDER 1995, SI 1995 3024 (S.217); made under the Plant Health Act 1967 s.39. In force: December 1, 1995; £0.65.

This Order revokes the Soft Fruit Plants (Scotland) Order 1991 which prohibits the a sale of soft fruit propagating material in Scotland unless it conforms to certain standards. The revocation is in consequence of the making of the Marketing of Fruit Plants Regulations 1995 which implement Council Directive 92/34 ([1992] OJ L157) and Dir.93/48 ([1993] OJ L250).

6558. Rural diversification programme

RURAL DIVERSIFICATION PROGRAMME (SCOTLAND) REGULATIONS 1995, SI 1995 3295 (S.244); made under the European Communities Act 1972 s.2. In force: February 1, 1996; £2.80.

These Regulations, which implement provisions of Council Regulation 4256/88 laying down provisions for implementing Council Regulation 2052/88 as regards the European Agricultural Guidance and Guarantee Fund (EAGGF) Guidance Section as amended by Council Regulation 2085/93, enable the receipt of financial assistance from the EAGGF Guidance Section under progammes approved by Commission Decisions and set out in the Single Programming Documents for the four Objective 5b areas in Scotland. Provision is made for financial provision towards the cost of diversification measures which must provide employment opportunities or increase the income of a person eligible who, with certain specifications, is defined as a legal occupier of an agricultural unit within the programme area. Certain restrictions are imposed upon the approval of applications, allowance is made for approval to be given with variations and measures on which financial assistance can be given are detailed along with details of the amount available.

6559. Set aside–access to the countryside–revocation

SET-ASIDE ACCESS (SCOTLAND) AMENDMENT AND REVOCATION REGULATIONS 1996, SI 1996 3037 (S.231); made under the European Communities Act 1972 s.2. In force: January 1, 1997; £1.10.

These Regulations amend the Set-Aside Access (Scotland) Regulations 1994 (SI 1994 3085) which implemented in part Council Regulation 2078/92 ([1992] OJ L215/85) on agricultural production methods compatible with the requirements of the protection of the environment and maintenance of the countryside, provided for the payment of aid to eligible persons who undertook to set aside an area of land, to permit members of the public to have access thereto for the purposes of quiet recreation and to manage it and any adjacent land crossed by an access way in accordance with the requirements set out in the Regulations. The amendments relate to transfer of holdings, force majeure, transformation of undertakings and reimbursement of aid and penalties.

6560. Articles

The Agricultural Holdings (Scotland) Act 1991–is there a course for change? *(Malcolm Strang Steel)*: J.L.S.S. 1996, 41 (7), 249-251 . (Security of tenure in agricultural tenancies in Scotland and its effect on farming compared to the situation in England).

6561. Books

Gill, Hon Lord–The Law of Agricultural Holdings in Scotland. Greens practice library. Hardback. ISBN 0-414-01110-4. W.Green & Son.

AIR TRANSPORT

6562. Carriage by air–domestic flight–helicopter hired by police–claim against carrier at common law–applicability of Warsaw Convention

[Carriage by Air Acts (Application of Provisions) Order 1967 (SI 1967 480) Sch.1.]

The Carriage by Air Act 1961 s.10, provides for the application of the Warsaw Convention of 1929 (as amended) to domestic flights. The Convention provides for strict liability for death sustained by a passenger during any "carriage by air", but also imposes an upper limit on any damages recoverable in respect of the death. A police force chartered a helicopter and pilot for a period of five months in order to use the helicopter for surveillance and detection work. During the course of such work the helicopter crashed, killing a policeman who was on board. His family raised an action for damages at common law and alternatively under the Convention, averring that the accident had been the fault of the helicopter pilot. In terms of the contract between the police force and the helicopter operators, the pilot had been solely responsible for flying the helicopter at the time of the accident, subject to receiving instructions from the deceased to allow for the performance of his duties. The helicopter operators contended that the action was incompetent at common law, arguing that the contract they had entered into with the police force was a contract of carriage and that the deceased had been a passenger in the helicopter at the time of the accident, and therefore that Art.17 of the Convention governed any claim, thus restricting the amount of any damages recoverable. The Lord Ordinary upheld these contentions and dismissed the common law case. The pursuers reclaimed, arguing that Art.17 did not apply, on the grounds that (1) there was no "carriage" within the meaning of the 1967 Order, as there had not been a contract between the operators and the deceased; (2) the deceased had not been a "passenger", having regard to his principal purpose for being on board the helicopter; and (3) the operators had not been a "carrier" since the deceased had been part of the crew, as his purpose was to participate in the operation on which the helicopter had been employed.

Held, that (1) the primary purpose of the contract between the police force and the helicopter operators was the carriage of persons and equipment; (2) on the facts the deceased was a passenger in the helicopter at the time of the accident; (3) the consent of the deceased to his being carried under the terms of the contract arose from the fact of his employment with the police force and his going on board the helicopter in the course of his employment; and reclaiming motion refused. Per Lord Murray dissenting; that the substance of the contract was the chartering of a police helicopter for a police operational role, which was not in substance a contract of carriage.

HERD v. CLYDE HELICOPTERS LTD 1996 S.L.T. 976, Judge not specified, IH.

ANIMALS

6563. Animal welfare–placing poisonous edible matter–defence of destroying vermin–whether vermin included fox

[Protection of Animals (Scotland) Act 1912 (c.14) s.7(b).]

Having pled not guilty to a charge alleging a contravention of s.7(b) of the Protection of Animals (Scotland) Act 1912, at trial an accused entered into a joint minute admitting that he did knowingly put or place edible matter, namely part of a bird carcass which had been rendered poisonous by lacing it with strychnine. The accused had placed part of a chicken carcass containing strychnine, buried to a shallow depth beneath a bush. The bait was eaten by a dog which later died. The accused relied upon the statutory defence that the poison was placed for the purpose of destroying vermin, which he contended included foxes, and that he had taken all reasonable precautions to prevent access thereto by dogs, cats, fowls, or other domestic animals.

Held, that (1) the accused was entitled to regard the fox as vermin; but (2) he had failed to take any precautions to prevent access to the poisonous matter by domestic animals; and accused convicted of the charge. Opinion, that it was doubtful whether such precautions could ever be taken as would satisfy the test in law where the purpose of the exercise was to lay poison in open countryside where a fox could get access to it to eat it.

WALKINGSHAW v. McCLYMONT 1996 S.L.T. (Sh.Ct.) 107, Judge not specified, Sh Ct.

6564. Animal welfare–slaughter houses–deregulation. See ANIMALS. §332

6565. Animal welfare–spring traps

SPRING TRAPS APPROVAL (SCOTLAND) ORDER 1996, SI 1996 2202 (S.178); made under the Agriculture (Scotland) Act 1948 s.50, s.85. In force: August 26, 1996; £1.55.

By virtue of the Agriculture (Scotland) Act 1948 s.50 it is an offence to use in Scotland for the purposes of killing or taking animals, a spring trap other than one approved by an order of the Secretary of State. This Order revokes and replaces the Spring Traps Approval Order 1975 (SI 1975 1722) and subsequent amendments. The Order adds four types of traps to those approved under the previous Orders and attaches conditions to the approval of each type of trap. These have been amended from the conditions in the previous Orders so as to ensure that no trap could operate as a leghold trap as defined in Council Regulations (EEC) 3254/91 Art.1 ([1992] OJ L308/1) prohibiting the use of leghold traps in the Community and the introduction into the community of pelts and manufactured goods of certain wild species originating in countries which catch them by means of leghold traps or trapping methods which do not meet international humane trapping standards.

6566. Deer (Scotland) Act 1996 (c.58)

An Act to consolidate the legislation relating to deer in Scotland.
This Act received Royal Assent on July 24, 1996.

6567. Deer (Amendment) (Scotland) Act 1996 (c.44)

An Act to amend the Deer (Scotland) Act 1959.
This Act received Royal Assent on July 18, 1996.

6568. Dogs–whether dog "attacking or harrying" pursuer–whether behaviour of dog foreseeable

[Animals (Scotland) Act 1987 (c.9) s.1.]

By the Animals (Scotland) Act 1987 s.1 (1), as read with s.1 (3), the owner of a dog shall be liable for any injury or damage caused by the dog caused *inter alia* by "attacking or harrying". A woman then aged 66 raised an action of damages against the owner of a dog arising out of an incident where the defender's dog ran up to her, knocked against her and knocked her down. She sustained a fracture of the lateral tibia plateau of the left knee which continued to cause her pain and restricted mobility over four years later. She had had to give up work as a part-time tourist guide. She alleged that the defender was in breach of the Animals (Scotland) Act 1987 s.1 (1) and of his duty at common law.

Held, that (1) the pursuer had failed to establish that the dog had harried or attacked her, and she had accordingly failed to establish her case under the 1987 Act and (2) the defender did not have such knowledge of the likelihood of his dog behaving in a dangerous manner as to establish negligence; and defender assoilzied. Opinion, that solatium would have been properly valued at £9,000 and four years' loss of earnings at £3,600.

FAIRLIE v. CARRUTHERS 1996 S.L.T. (Sh.Ct.) 56, Judge not specified, Sh Ct.

6569. Wild Mammals (Protection) Act (c.3). See ANIMALS. §347

ARBITRATION

6570. Arbitration clause–whether timeously pleaded

In spring 1993 the owners of a house raised an action against the architects and the builders for breach of contract and negligence in the design and building of the house. The contract with the architects contained a clause providing that any disputes which could not be resolved were to be referred to arbitration. The action was continued for adjustment before being sisted for negotiations. The sist was finally recalled in June 1995 and the record continued for adjustment. The architects added a plea that the action should be sisted to await the result of arbitration and intimated a motion to that effect. Adjustment of the record continued until September 1995 when the motion to sist was heard. The pursuers argued that the right to arbitration had been waived because of (1) the passage of time; (2) the incurring of expense on the basis that the action was proceeding; (3) the agreement of the architects in extending the period of adjustment and (4) correspondence between the parties proceeding on the basis that the dispute was to be litigated if it was not to be settled. The Lord Ordinary refused the motion. The architects appealed.

Held, that (1) waiver connoted the abandonment of a right, which might be express or inferred from the facts and circumstances of the case; (2) the proper test of abandonment was whether the party's actings (including failure to act) were inconsistent with an intention to insist on an arbitration; (3) a plea to sist an action pending arbitration might be competently made at any time before the closing of the record, and no inference of abandonment could be derived from parties' having engaged in the ordinary procedures of litigation before the plea was taken; (4) the circumstances could not be said to constitute a waiver of the right to arbitration; and reclaiming motion granted, *Armia v. Daejan Developments* 1977 S.L.T. (Notes) 9, [1977] C.L.Y. 3475 applied; *Inverclyde (Mearns) Housing Society v. Lawrence Construction Co* 1989 S.L.T. 815, [1989] C.L.Y. 3854 approved.

Observed, that while the question of abandonment had to be determined on an objective assessment of the architects' conduct, their explanation that the plea had only been tendered after the focus of the action had changed to one in which they rather than the builders were principally involved, provided a situation in which the earlier failure to take the plea might be objectively held as not inconsistent with an intention to reserve, rather than to abandon, the right to go to arbitration.

PRESSLIE v. COCHRANE McGREGOR GROUP LTD 1996 S.L.T. 988, Judge not specified, IH.

6571. Decree arbitral–enforcement–decree conform

Held, in an action to enforce a decree arbitral, that the decree arbitral was not final, and action dismissed as irrelevant. Observations, as to the proper style for the cause and plea-in-law in such an action.

GRANT v. GRANT 1996 S.C.L.R. 328, Judge not specified, Sh Ct.

6572. Articles

A new Scottish arbitration procedure *(Ian Christie Strathdee)*: Arbitration 1996, 62(3), 196-198. (Suggested mandatory procedure to be incorporated into Standard Forms Industry for construction industry arbitration).

Arbitration *(Rosalind M.M. McInnes)*: Civ. P.B. 1996, 10(Jul), 2-4. (Why arbitration has survived, when it is appropriate to use it and what can be done to alleviate difficulties in arbitration process).

Cross border aspects of arbitration *(Richard Aird)*: Bus. L.R. 1996, 17(5), 95-96. (Jurisdiction of courts to provide interim protective and security measures to non-Scots parties in arbitrations).

ARMED FORCES

6573. Local government–reorganisation

LORD-LIEUTENANTS (SCOTLAND) ORDER 1996, SI 1996 731 (S.83); made under the Reserve (Forces) Act 1980 s.131. In force: April 1, 1996; £1.55.

This Order divides Scotland up into areas for the purposes of the provisions of the Reserve Forces Act 1980 relating to lieutenancies. Article 3(a) and Sch.1 create and name each of the lieutenancies in Scotland except those lieutenancies which are made up of the four city areas of Aberdeen, Dundee, Edinburgh and Glasgow. Those city areas are in any event lieutenancies by virtue of s.131(2) of the said Act of 1980. Article 3(b) and Sch.2 make provision for certain deputy lieutenants to hold office in a area or city other than that in which they reside.

BANKING

6574. Bank accounts–current account–agents account overdrawn–funds to principal

A company, G, collected sums from third parties owed by them to SFS under a credit card scheme. Such sums were paid into G's bank account with BS but were not earmarked specifically for the scheme. At the material time this account was overdrawn and monies paid into it were swallowed up as payment for the overdraft and therefore ceased to exist. The company went into receivership and SFS raised an action against BS seeking recompense for the sums due to it. In view of issues regarding the fiduciary relationship between the parties, the Lord Ordinary allowed a proof before answer. BS appealed against that decision.

Held, refusing the appeal and proof allowed to establish the facts. While neither BS nor G was in breach of any fiduciary relationship as a result of sums due to SFS being paid into the overdrawn account by G, SFS could seek to recover funds on the basis of unjust enrichment if it could establish that its relationship with G had been of a fiduciary nature, and that BS had known that the sums being paid into the account had been collected on behalf of SFS.

STYLE FINANCIAL SERVICES LTD v. BANK OF SCOTLAND 1996 S.L.T. 421, Lord Ross, L.J.C., IH.

6575. Cautionary obligation–construction–"top slice guarantee"–entitlement to interest

[Law Reform (Miscellaneous Provisions) (Scotland) Act 1985 (c.73) s.8.]

A company granted a guarantee to a bank in relation to sums due to the bank by two other companies. The guarantee related to sums due in excess of the sum of £800,000 and the cautioners' liability was not to exceed £1,000,000 "and interest thereon". Payment having been requested under the guarantee, payment of the sum required (£1,040,589.13) was made on a "without prejudice" basis. The cautioners assigned their right to another company which raised an action against the bank, seeking inter alia: (i) declarator that the guarantee was void; (ii) an accounting by the bank in respect of its realisation of securities in support of the guaranteed debt; (iii) (as an alternative to the previous conclusions) rectification of the guarantee in terms of the Law Reform (Miscellaneous Provisions) (Scotland) Act 1985 s.8 to the effect of providing that any securities realised by the bank were in the first place to be set against the excess over £800,000. The assignees argued that the guarantee was void because of the uncertainty as to whether interest was due on the total indebtedness or only on the excess guaranteed. They also argued that the guarantee was void since the bank had increased the risk to the cautioners by increasing the original debtors' liability under it, the bank having previously agreed that the overdraft facilities of the original debtors were to be £1,800,000 but having thereafter advanced £2,302,669. In support of the alternative conclusion for rectification the assignees argued that the chairman of the cautioners had agreed with the bank's chief executive that any sums realised from the securities over the original debtors' assets would be applied first to reduce the liability under the guarantee. The bank pleaded that the action was irrelevant. At procedure roll the Lord Ordinary held that the pursuers were entitled to a proof before answer on the issue of rectification but dismissed the conclusions for declarator, payment and accounting. The pursuers reclaimed and the defenders took advantage of the reclaiming motion to seek review of the decision to allow a proof before answer. The submissions made to the Lord Ordinary were repeated before the Second Division.

Held, that (1) when the guarantee was read as a whole its meaning was clear and unambiguous and it contained no essential contradiction or ambiguity; (2) the guarantee envisaged additional advances to the principal debtor in excess of £1.8 million, and making such additional advances did not increase the risk or liability of the cautioners because of the stipulation in the guarantee that liability should not exceed £1,000,000 and there was no question of the cautioners' liability having been unilaterally increased by the bank; (3) as there were no averments that the bank held funds belonging to the pursuers from the realisation of securities, there was accordingly nothing on record to justify the conclusion that the bank were under any duty to account to the pursuers regarding their intromissions with the proceeds of the realisation of securities and the Lord Ordinary was well founded in holding that the pursuers had failed to aver any legal basis for an action of count, reckoning and payment; (4) in respect of the conclusion for rectification, the pursuers had insufficient averments of any prior agreement to which the guarantee failed to give effect; further, that rather than contend that some expression in the guarantee should be corrected or altered, the pursuers were in fact maintaining that different contractual terms should be adopted to the application of the proceeds of realisation of debts and securities and they were effectively seeking to rewrite the guarantee, which they were not entitled to do, and the Lord Ordinary erred in allowing a proof before answer in relation to the question of rectification; and, inter alia, conclusion relating to rectification dismissed and proof before answer allowed, restricted to the matter of interest. Opinion, that as a matter of relevancy and specification it was for the pursuers to specify details of any alterations to the document which they maintained would be required in order to give effect to the alleged common intention of the parties and the court must guard against being placed in the position of rewriting the parties' agreement and of taking part in the formulation of that agreement. The Lord Ordinary was incorrect in his opinion that it was a matter for the court to decide whether the document should be rectified and if so in what manner.

HUEWIND LTD v. CLYDESDALE BANK PLC [1996] 5 Bank. L.R. 35, Judge not specified, IH.

6576. Direct debits–direct debit instruction–rights of creditor–failure of bank to transfer funds lodged

M, a finance company, sought payment from C, a bank, of sums paid into accounts with C by G, in respect of debts due by G to M under agreements in terms of which M provided vehicles to G for sale, and G forwarded the sale proceeds to M. M averred that from August 22, 1990 payments were made by G to M by direct debit. In October 1990 C froze G's accounts. When M intimated direct debit requests in respect of sales C refused to pay. M averred that G's managing director, H, agreed with C that H was to lodge the sale proceeds for October to enable telegraphic transfer to take place to M, but, notwithstanding lodgement of the moneys, C did not transfer the funds requested by M and on November 5, 1990, a receiver was appointed. M argued that (1) the direct debit by G to C was a mandate in rem suam in M's favour and that intimation by M to C of the instruction to pay effected assignation to M of the funds available to G; that by analogy with *Sutherland v. Royal Bank of Scotland* 1996 G.W.D. 6-290, although the mandate operated in terms of the contract between C and G, it was not dependent on a credit balance for its assignative effect; M, as mandatory, had the same right as G to enforce obligations within the limits of the direct debit *British Linen Bank v. Carruthers & Fergusson* (1883) 10 R. 923; (2) G had lodged a sum for the specific purpose of payment to M and, since C accepted payment on that basis, C became trustees of the sum for M's purpose as the requirements in *Clark Taylor & Co v. Quality Site Development Ltd* 1981 S.L.T. 308, [1981] C.L.Y. 3722 were satisfied; (3) M suffered loss through C's wrongful interference with G's performance of obligations under the contract with M since C knew that the proposed telegraphic transfer was in pursuance of a contractual obligation owed by G to M; (4) the agreement whereby G lodged funds with C to ensure that telegraphic transfers were made to M involved C accepting specific sums appropriated to M's interests, and M had a ius quaesitum tertio in such circumstances and (5) M were entitled to recompense on the basis of C's unjustified enrichment on the balance of equities and on the basis of C's knowledge.

Held, proof before answer allowed on M's averments based on (4) and (5); (1) a creditor under a direct debit agreement was not put in the debtor's position to operate the account at his own hand. The instruction to pay remained that of the account holder. As with payment by cheque, it was prerequisite of assignative effect that there be funds available at the critical date; (2) the requirements for constitution of trusts as set out in *Clark Taylor* were not met by the lodging of funds in a bank account. Although it was possible for G to have made such an arrangement with C for the lodging and application of specific funds, that was not the ordinary operation of an account current such as M's, and the transactions in question fell within the ordinary operation; (3) the test for wrongful interference on C's part required more than simple failure to perform contractual obligations *British Motor Trade Association v. Gray* 1951 S.L.T. 247, [1951] C.L.Y. 3791; (4) M's averments of ius quaesitum tertio could not be disposed of without inquiry on the tests in Gloag and Henderson *The Law of Scotland* (10th ed.), pp.235-236 and (5) although there were no relevant averments of trust or a fiduciary relationship between C and M, M's averments of C's knowledge of the reasons for lodging the funds to meet specific obligations by G were, with hesitation, sufficient for proof to be heard on M's case of unjustified enrichment where the law was in a state of development.

MERCEDES-BENZ FINANCE LTD v. CLYDESDALE BANK 1996 S.C.L.R. 1005, Lord Penrose, OH.

6577. Guarantee–misrepresentation by debtor against guarantor–constructive knowledge of creditor–relevancy

M and S reclaimed against the Lord Ordinary's decision [1994] C.L.Y. 5881 to dismiss as irrelevant actions brought by them seeking reduction of deeds granted by them to the prejudice of their rights in their respective matrimonial homes, the deeds being granted in favour of a bank, B, which was seeking security for loans to their businessmen husbands and which M and S averred had acted in bad faith since the deeds had been obtained as a result of the husbands' misrepresentations and B had failed to inquire whether M and S had been properly advised. M and S argued that *Barclays Bank v. O'Brien* [1994] 1 A.C. 180, [1994] C.L.Y. 3300, could, contrary to the Lord Ordinary's view, be reconciled with the principles of Scots law: an analogy could be drawn with *Rodger (Builders) Ltd v. Fawdry* 1950 S.L.T. 345, [1950] C.L.Y. 4871, as to failure to make appropriate inquiries giving rise to bad faith, and the cases relied on by the Lord Ordinary concerned different facts, were obiter and out of date, and in any event indicated an overriding principle of fairness.

Held, reclaiming motion refused. There was no doubt that before the *O'Brien* decision the position in Scots law was that a creditor was not liable for representations by the principal debtor made to induce a cautioner to undertake an obligation, unless it was proved that he was privy to the fact that the cautioner was being deceived *Young v. Clydesdale Bank* (1889) 17 R. 231 and *Royal Bank of Scotland v. Greenshields* 1914 S.C. 259. A duty to make inquiry arose only where circumstances were known to the creditor which might reasonably create a suspicion of fraud: Bell, *Principles*, para.251, and not simply because the creditor knew that the transaction was not to the cautioner's financial advantage and that the cautioner would be likely to rely on his or her principal. While the doctrine of constructive notice as explained in *O'Brien* was simply another way of expressing the same principle, the facts which were held to be sufficient to put the creditor on his inquiry were markedly different from the approach of Scots law. The tendency in English law to deal with cases of undue influence by reference to presumptions arising from the fact that the parties were related to each other differed significantly from Scots law, which recognised no presumptions and looked at the effect of the relationship in each case on its own facts, the question being whether the circumstances were such, and the influence exercised by one party so dominant, as to deprive the other of the power of apprehending the considerations applicable to the case. The consequences of accepting *O'Brien* as part of Scots law would be very significant, cf. *Massey v. Midland Bank Plc* [1995] 1 All E.R. 929, [1995] C.L.Y. 2446 for the whole structure of the law in regard to undue influence, and it could not be confined to cases where financial institutions were creditors. If the duties of creditors were thought to be in need of extension, this should be by Parliament after detailed consideration by the Scottish Law Commission.

Observed, that banks and building societies had now adopted a recommendation of the Jack Committee that they issue appropriate warnings to private individuals proposing to give a guarantee or other security for another's liabilities, but that could not be said to be a matter of legal obligation.

MUMFORD v. BANK OF SCOTLAND 1996 S.L.T. 392, Lord Hope, Lord President, IH.

6578. Articles

Black Sheep Music. : I.B.L. 1996, 24(2), 94. (Whether bank was put on notice of forged company mandate used to open account and whether bank had authority to conduct business on behalf of company).

Survivorship destinations and bank accounts *(Michael C. Meston)*: S.L.P.Q. 1996, 1(4), 315-319. (No such thing as survivorship destination in bank accounts under Scots law and strong view that all survivorship destinations should be abolished).

Undue influence: a difference of emphasis *(Paul Fallon)*: B.J.I.B. & F.L. 1996, 11(1), 16-18. (Scottish decision that bank could not be fixed with constructive notice of bad faith of husbands when obtaining consent of wives for charges in contrast to English law).

6579. Books

Crerar, Lorne D.– Banking Law in Scotland. Paperback: £25.00. ISBN 0-406-05458-4. Butterworth Law (Scotland).

BANKRUPTCY

6580. Gratuitous alienations–challenge by trustee after debtor discharged–competency

[Bankruptcy (Scotland) Act 1985 (c.66) s.34, s.54.]

Held, that an action of declarator at the instance of a trustee in bankruptcy that a disposition by the debtor in favour of his former wife was a gratuitous alienation was competent, notwithstanding the fact that the debtor had already been discharged in terms of s.54(1) of the 1985 Act.

OVENSTONE'S TRUSTEE v. OVENSTONE 1995 S.C.L.R. 969, Judge not specified, Sh Ct.

6581. Sequestration–apparent insolvency–expired charge–charge following on decree against arrestee in action of furthcoming

Held, that an expired charge on a decree against the debtor as arrestee in an action of furthcoming provided a good foundation for apparent insolvency; and sequestration granted.

SCOTT OSWALD & CO v. MURRAY 1995 S.C.L.R. 1094, Judge not specified, Sh Ct.

6582. Sequestration–inclusion of property in sequestration order–competency of appeal to sheriff principal

[Bankruptcy (Scotland) Act 1985 (c.66) s.31(6).]

After proof in an application made in terms of s.31(b) of the Bankruptcy (Scotland) Act 1985, the sheriff found that property claimed by the permanent trustee should be excluded. On appeal by the trustee, the applicant submitted the appeal was incompetent as leave had not been granted.

Held, that the appeal of the trustee to the sheriff principal was incompetent, *Ingle's Trustee v. Ingle* 1996 S.L.T. 26, followed.

SMITH v. BERRY'S TRUSTEE 1996 S.L.T. (Sh. Ct.) 31, Judge not specified, Sh Ct.

6583. Sequestration–order that bankrupt attend for private examination–competency of appeal without leave

[Bankruptcy (Scotland) Act 1985 (c.66) s.44; Sheriff Courts (Scotland) Act 1907 (c.51) s.28.]

Section 28 of the Sheriff Courts (Scotland) Act 1907 provides that it shall be competent to appeal to the Court of Session against a judgment of the sheriff if it is a final judgment or if the sheriff grants leave to appeal. A trustee in bankruptcy applied to the sheriff for an order under s.44(2) of the Bankruptcy (Scotland) Act 1985 requiring the bankrupt to attend for private examination before the sheriff. The motion was continued for attendance of the bankrupt. At the continued motion the bankrupt failed to attend. The motion was then granted. The appellant appealed, without leave of the sheriff, to the Court of Session. The trustee contended that, in light of s.28 of the 1907 Act, the appeal was incompetent. The appellant argued that as the order pronounced was incompetent on procedural grounds, leave was not required.

Held, that (1) it was not in all cases of appeal on the ground of incompetency that an appeal was competent without leave but only in those in which the sheriff had no power or right to pronounce the interlocutor sought to be appealed against; (2) the order pronounced by the sheriff was one which he was not only entitled but was bound to make in the exercise of his judicial function; (3) as the appellant's grounds of appeal were not based upon the proposition that the sheriff was acting ultra vires in hearing and determining the application for the order, the appeal was incompetent without leave; and appeal refused, *Lord Advocate v. Johnston* 1983 S.L.T. 290, [1983] C.L.Y. 4958 and *Ingle's Trustee v. Ingle* 1996 S.L.T. 26, applied. Quaere, whether the exercise of the pre-eminent power of the Court of Session to rectify an injustice caused by the sheriff doing something which in the proper exercise of his judicial duty he was not entitled to do could only now be invoked by judicial review.

GUPTA'S TRUSTEE v. GUPTA 1996 S.L.T. 1098, Judge not specified, IH.

6584. Sequestration–realisation of assets–dwelling-house

[Bankruptcy (Scotland) Act 1985 (c.66) s.40.]

Held, in an application by a permanent trustee in bankruptcy for authority to sell the house jointly owned and occupied by the debtor and his wife, where the debtor's total indebtedness amounted to £24,646, his interest in the house, his sole asset, was estimated to be worth £2,863 and the expenses of the trustee amounted to more than £2,500, that the application should be refused as the proposed sale would bring no material benefit to the creditors and would cause trauma and distress to the debtor's wife.

HUNT'S TRUSTEE v. HUNT 1995 S.C.L.R. 973, Judge not specified, Sh Ct.

6585. Sequestration–sheriff courts–bankruptcy rules

ACT OF SEDERUNT (SHERIFF COURT BANKRUPTCY RULES) 1996, SI 1996 2507 (S.196); made under the Sheriff Courts (Scotland) Act 1971 s.32; and the Bankruptcy (Scotland) Act 1985 s.1A, s.14, s.25, Sch.2 para.2, Sch.5 para.2. In force: January 1, 1997; £5.20.

This Act of Sederunt consolidates the Act of Sederunt (Bankruptcy Rules) 1993 (SI 1993 921), making provision for the procedure to be followed, and forms to be used, in proceedings brought in the sheriff court under the Bankruptcy (Scotland) Act 1985. It also makes provision as to the manner of appealing from the sheriff court to the Court of Session under that Act, and repeals the Act of Sederunt (Bankruptcy Rules) 1993.

6586. Sequestration–trustees in bankruptcy–exoneration and discharge

[Bankruptcy (Scotland) Act 1913 (c.20) s.82, s.122, s.158, s.165.]

D, a bankrupt, reclaimed against the Lord Ordinary's decision granting the petition of F, his trustee, for exoneration and discharge, founding on his averments that F could have concluded the sequestration in 1984 if he had (a) recovered a sum due from a local authority in respect of sewers at a development, or (b) sold certain plots of land which were eventually returned to D, or (c) obtained a reasonable price for subjects which D averred were sold for less than their true worth.

Held, reclaiming motion refused, that D had had ample opportunity under the Bankruptcy (Scotland) Act 1913 to question or challenge F's actings, by invoking s.82, s.122, s.158 or s.165. Point (a) could have been raised at adjudication of the authority's claim in the sequestration. Point (b) was of no relevance where D now had the land back. Point (c), if concerning a private sale, would have been a decision under s.111 open to appeal under s.165. Concern about F's fees could have been raised under s.122. No sufficient explanation had been given for failure to raise these matters at an earlier stage and a belated intention to do so was inadequate reason to hold up F's discharge, *Dundas v. Lawrie* (1822) 1 S. 238 distinguished. Nor was it clear what remedy D was seeking; he had no averments adequate for an accounting or for a claim based on negligence; an inference of negligence could not be drawn from the mere fact of delay. Nor had the Lord Ordinary been shown to have erred in refusing to receive the minute of amendment for D.

DUFF'S TRUSTEE, PETITIONER 1993 S.C. 466, Judge not specified.

6587. Sequestration–trustees in bankruptcy–personal liability for expenses–relief from estate–appeal incompetent

An applicant, seeking to have certain funds excluded from a bankrupt debtor's estate, was found entitled to the expenses of an appeal taken by the permanent trustee in the debtor's sequestration. The appeal was refused as incompetent since it was a part of the sequestration proceedings and had been taken without the leave of the sheriff. The applicant submitted that the trustee in bankruptcy was personally liable for litigation expenses, albeit that he might have a right of relief against the bankrupt's estate, and that the right of relief could be denied at the court's discretion if the trustee had engaged in incompetent litigation.

Held, that although a trustee was *primo loco* personally liable for expenses awarded against him, he normally had a right of relief against the trust estate for those expenses, a trustee's right of relief for judicial expenses being denied only when all of the beneficiaries were present in the process and when the trustee had not acted reasonably, prudently or in good faith; and motion refused.

SMITH v. BERRY'S TRUSTEE (NO.2) 1996 S.L.T. (Sh.Ct.) 80, Judge not specified, Sh Ct.

6588. Articles

Apparent insolvency–further developments *(Donna W. McKenzie)*: Bus. L.B. 1996, 22(Jul), 3-4. (Decision that earnings arrestment does not trigger apparent insolvency requires clarification by appeal to Court of Session).

Deferral of debtor's discharge *(Calum S. Jones)*: J.L.S.S. 1996, 41(2), 61-62. (Whether debtor's conduct alone is sufficient ground for deferral).

Poor enough to pay *(Cy Nicol)*: SCOLAG 1996, 232, 33. (Cynical view of sequestration not benefiting extreme poor who are on income related benefits).

Short's Trustee v Chung revisited *(Peter Eager)*: Prop. L.B. 1996, 22(Aug), 2-4. (Whether trustee in bankruptcy could obtain decree of reduction for sale of land at undervalue, whether Keeper of Land Register could refuse to rectify register and whether trustee entitled to indemnity).

Trustee's claim to solatium *(Donna W. McKenzie)*: Bus. L.B. 1996, 22(Jul), 4-5. (Discharge of trustee in bankruptcy does not remove right to claim damages paid to former bankrupt for benefit of creditors).

CAPITAL TAXATION

6589. Inheritance tax–delivery of accounts

INHERITANCE TAX (DELIVERY OF ACCOUNTS) (SCOTLAND) REGULATIONS 1996, SI 1996 1472; made under the Inheritance Tax Act 1984 s.256. In force: July 1, 1996; £0.65.

Substitute a new definition of an excepted estate in respect of deaths on or after April 6, 1996, providing inter alia that the limit for the value of the property situated outside the UK which may form part of the deceased's estate is raised from £15,000 to £30,000.

6590. Articles

An onshore view of forced heirship–domestic conflict and its planning implications: Part 1 *(Simon Mackintosh)*: P.C.B. 1996, 3, 161-166. (Scottish rules on forced heirship and lack of protection of interests of forced heirs).

An onshore view of forced heirship–domestic conflict and its planning implications: Part 2 *(Simon Mackintosh)*: P.C.B. 1996, 3, 197-199. (Posthumous tax planning possibilities under Scots law of forced heirship including variation).

Important developments for curators bonis *(Alan R. Barr)*: J.L.S.S. 1996, 41(11), 444-446. (Taxation changes affecting curators bonis).

CHILDREN

6591. Access–best interests of child–relevant considerations

[Law Reform (Parent and Child) (Scotland) Act 1986 (c.9) s.3.]

S appealed a sheriff principal's refusal of his appeal against a sheriff's decision to refuse S access to B who was born on April 11, 1989 and was the child of S and M, who had cohabited until early 1991. The sheriff principal had decided that he was entitled to review the sheriff's decision, because hearsay evidence of B's statements had been admitted as evidence of the facts contained therein without it being established that B was a competent witness, and had heard further evidence concerning an incident at an access centre on July 31, 1993, while the case was at avizandum, after which B had stated that S had hit him. S argued that the sheriff and sheriff principal had failed to have regard to the intrinsic value of a parent-child relationship, to the efforts which S had made to make access work, and to the principle that the status quo should be maintained unless there were sound reasons to displace it; that criticisms of S that he was only interested in his own rights and had no true interest in B were not justified, given that the sheriff had found that B had a relationship with S and his family and that access visits had gone reasonably well; that the sheriff principal had erred in relying on hearsay evidence of B as a factor adverse to S and in his favourable treatment of the evidence of M and her mother (N); and that there was insufficient material to conclude that it was not in B's interests for S to have access, and that the court should allow limited access at an access centre.

Held, appeal refused. Per Lords Weir and Brand, that as an unmarried father, S did not have parental rights and it was for him to show that he should be allowed access. Factors such as the value of maintaining the parent-child relationship and of preserving the status quo were only of significance insofar as they coincided with B's interest. Both the sheriff and the sheriff principal had formed a favourable view of M and N, and although the sheriff principal had expressed some reservation about their evidence concerning bruising seen on B, there was no ground for suggesting that their whole evidence should have been rejected as unreliable. The sheriff principal had not expressed a view on the veracity of B's statements, and, given that they were made spontaneously after periods of access, he had been entitled to have limited regard to them as colouring other evidence, as it would have been entirely artificial to leave them out of account. The evidence that B had become abusive and made derogatory remarks about M after access, had behaved aggressively and out of character at school and had had bruising on his face on the last occasion access took place, amply justified the view that access by S was not beneficial to B. While there were flaws in the sheriff's analysis, they were not significant, as his approach was clearly based on B's welfare being paramount. The sheriff had erred in holding that the traditional approach to maintaining access between children and their natural parents did not apply and in his treatment of the evidence. These errors were compounded by the sheriff principal who failed to assess matters in the best interests of B. It was necessary to determine whether B's interests would be promoted by severing contact with S.

S v. M (A MINOR: ACCESS ORDER) 1996 S.L.T. 750, Judge not specified, IH.

6592. Adoption–agencies–approval

ADOPTION AGENCIES (SCOTLAND) REGULATIONS 1996, SI 1996 3266 (S.254); made under the Adoption (Scotland) Act 1978 s.3; and the Children (Scotland) Act 1978 s.9, s.27. In force: April 1, 1997; £4.15.

These Regulations regulate adoption agencies and make provision inter alia for how adoption societies shall be approved by the Secretary of State, their appointment of adoption panels, the functions of the adoption panels and the duties of adoption agencies in the adoption process.

6593. Adoption–allowance schemes

ADOPTION ALLOWANCE (SCOTLAND) REGULATIONS 1996, SI 1996 3257 (S.247); made under the Adoption (Scotland) Act 1978 s.9, s.51A. In force: April 1, 1998; £1.55.

These Regulations make provision in respect of adoption allowances schemes prepared by adoption agencies to pay allowances to persons who have adopted or intend to adopt a child in pursuance of arrangements made by such agencies. These new schemes are to replace the existing schemes approved by the Secretary of Sate under the Adoption (Scotland) Act 1978 s.51 (5) which are to be revoked on the coming into force of s.51A which relates to adoption allowances schemes and s.51B which relates to transitional provisions as respects adoption allowances.

6594. Adoption–consent unreasonably withheld–surrogacy

[Adoption (Scotland) Act 1978 (c.28) s.51; Children Act 1975 (c.72) s.53(1); Human Fertilisation and Embryology Act 1990 (c.37) s.30.]

S, the natural mother of X, appealed against a sheriff's decision, granting custody of X to C in terms of s.53(1) (b) of the 1975 Act, and refusing her access to X. C cross-appealed on the ground that the sheriff should have granted an adoption order. S argued that the sheriff erred in dispensing with her agreement in terms of s.16(1) (b) (ii) of the 1978 Act and concluding that she had voluntarily placed X with C. After X's birth she had been too distressed to give free and unconditional agreement. The sheriff had allowed his sympathies for C to colour his judgment, and failed to consider that as X's natural mother, S was obviously committed to him, that she had good parenting qualities and that C had exerted undue pressure on her. The sheriff failed to explain why it would not be in X's best interests to retain some contact with S, and he placed undue weight on the poor relationship between S and C. C submitted that the custody order was not competent in terms of s.53(1) (b) of the 1975 Act since such an order could only be made if the sheriff opined that it was more appropriate than an adoption order and it was clear from the sheriff's note that he considered that an adoption order was more appropriate. He departed from the requirements of s.6 of the 1978 Act in failing to consider the effect that the custody order would have on X. There was no breach of s.51 of the 1978 Act as the payment to S had not been made with a view to adopting X, but arose out of a surrogacy arrangement.

Held, S's appeal refused, C's cross-appeal granted, custody order recalled and order for adoption substituted., that (1) the sheriff did not err in finding that S had withheld her agreement unreasonably. If S had placed X's welfare first, she would have recognised that X had been with C since birth and was happy and that C, who had a secure relationship, could provide a balanced home environment and lifestyle for X. In attempting to recover X, S had displayed a lack of personal responsibility by ignoring professional advice and involving a tabloid newspaper. She had also abused drugs and lied about a previous miscarriage. There was no evidence that C had acted deviously or put undue pressure on S; S understood what she was doing and exercised her judgment freely when she initially agreed to enter into the surrogacy arrangement and give up X; (2) the custody order was incompetent for the reason argued by C. It was not in X's best interest to allow S access; (3) an adoption order was in X's best interests as the custody order did not safeguard and promote his welfare since S would retain all the parental rights and responsibilities mentioned in the Children (Scotland) Act 1995 s.1 and s.2 unless an adoption order was made. Although C could not obtain a parental order under the 1990 Act because of their breach of s.30(7), they were not disabled under the 1978 Act from obtaining an adoption order. At the time the payment was made, C intended to obtain parental rights to X by way of a parental order, not adoption, and although the payment contravened s.30(7)(c), it was not made with a view to C adopting X in terms of s.51 (1) (c) of the 1978 Act. Therefore, the fact that the transaction was tainted by the payment was not enough to prohibit the adoption, *C (A Minor) Adoption Application, Re* [1993] 1 F.L.R. 7, [1993] C.L.Y. 2767 distinguished. If C had been able to apply for a parental order, it was not obvious that authorisation of C's payment to S would have been refused under s.30(7) of the 1990 Act. In any event, the transaction was not so offensive as to be seriously objected to on the grounds of public policy, *Adoption Application AA 212/86 (Payment for Adoption)* [1987] 2 F.L.R. 291, [1987] C.L.Y. 2450; and any pubic policy objection in respect of the payment was outweighed by the need to safeguard and promote X's welfare throughout his childhood.

C AND C v. S; SUB NOM. C, PETITIONER; C v. S 1996 S.C.L.R. 837, Lord Hope, Lord President, IH.

6595. Adoption–procedure–question as to mental capacity of parent–appointment of curator "ad litem"

[Adoption Act 1973 (c.28) s.57; Act of Sederunt (Adoption of Children) 1984 (SI 1984 1013) para.8.]

S, an adoption agency, sought an order freeing M, born October 18, 1994, a child of P, for adoption. S averred that P's consent should be dispensed with on the grounds that (1) P was incapable of giving consent; (2) P's consent was withheld unreasonably and (3) P had persistently failed to discharge her parental duties. P had a history of detention under the Mental Health Act and M had been in S's care since birth through proceedings under the Social Work (Scotland) Act 1968 Pt.III. In those proceedings C was appointed curator ad litem to P. In a report before the court in S's petition, the curator to M and reporting officer, D, stated that he had witnessed P signing her consent to M's freeing for adoption, that P had understood the implications and that he had explained her right to withdraw her consent. C was notified of the hearing and, after consultation with P's psychiatrist, was not satisfied that P had capacity to give her consent in the manner reported. C sought appointment as P's curator in the present proceedings through a colleague, A, who claimed to appear as amicus curiae. The sheriff made the appointment in the face of S's opposition and motion to dispense with P's consent. S appealed the interlocutor as incompetent. S argued that adoption proceedings were sui generis; the hearing was governed by the Act of Sederunt 1984 para.8 and by s.57 of the 1978 Act and so the proceedings should be conducted in private. A should not have been present and the hearing should not have proceeded as a full hearing instead of merely a procedural one. A could not be an amicus curiae as such a person could not have an interest in the proceedings whereas A did have such an interest as she was a colleague in the same firm of solicitors as C. A then appeared as C's agent and argued that natural justice required the court to inquire into P's position and that the only possible capacity in which appearance could be made was of an amicus curiae. The words "in private" in s.57 should not be construed so as to achieve a result contrary to natural justice. The matters were all within the sheriff's discretion.

Held, appeal refused, that (1) there was justification for the sheriff inquiring into P's capacity to consent which was fundamental to the application. There was an apparent incongruity between the grounds for S's application. Adoption procedure was very much at the court's discretion; (2) to insist that A was not entitled to be heard was too rigid an interpretation of "in private". A's appearance was concerned with natural justice. The sheriff had a discretion under s.57 to permit others to be present, and necessarily had a discretion to permit the appearance of any particular individuals at a hearing if he considered it would advance his inquiry; (3) it was the practice of the sheriffdom to set down statutory hearings at 10 minute intervals. If a prolonged hearing was required, the Act of Sederunt para.8(4) provided for a further diet and (4) the sheriff's statutory powers did not displace his common law power to appoint C in order to protect P's interests, *Drummond's Trustees v. Peels Trustees* 1929 S.C. 484; McNeill, *Adoption* (2nd ed.), para.10.09(ii)). The status of amicus curiae was defined by the function performed, offering help to the court, and A was merely a person possessed of the information offering to help the court.

STRATHCLYDE RC, PETITIONERS 1996 S.L.T. (Sh. Ct.) 65, Judge not specified, Sh Ct.

6596. Adoption–public policy–petition by single male in homosexual relationship

[Adoption (Scotland) Act 1978 (c.28) s.16.]

T, aged 34 and unmarried, reclaimed against a Lord Ordinary's decision refusing his petition for adoption because (1) it had not been shown that S's natural mother (M) had withheld her agreement unreasonably and (2) there was a fundamental question of principle since T was a single male who proposed to bring up S jointly with his partner (P), with whom he was cohabiting in a homosexual relationship. S was born on November 11, 1990 with a complex combination of abnormalities including profound deafness and an inability to talk or walk unaided, because of which it was difficult to secure a permanent placement for him. T, who was regarded by the adoption panel and the director of social services as offering the best home for S, had nursed both children and adults with physical and mental disabilities as an enrolled and a registered nurse, and at the time of making his application had lived in a stable relationship with P for 10 years. The High Court in Manchester had granted authority to remove S from the court's jurisdiction with a view to his adoption in Scotland by T. A curator ad litem (F) stated that adoption by T was likely to safeguard and promote S's welfare throughout his childhood. Two reporting officers attempted to obtain M's consent to the adoption, but received no reply to their inquiries; in July 1994 M told social workers that she did not wish any more contact about S. M advised a process server that she had no objection to the adoption and had no intention of attending the hearing.

Held, reclaiming motion allowed and petition granted, that (1) on the information before the Lord Ordinary, there was nothing to cast any doubt on F's conclusions that it was in S's best interest that adoption proceed, *A and B, Petitioners* 1971 S.L.T. 258, [1971] C.L.Y. 5833; (2) the Lord Ordinary should have dispensed with M's agreement. The court could treat M's refusal to have anything to do with the application as an unreasonable withholding of her agreement to it within s.16(2)(b) of the 1978 Act; (3) S's adoption by T did not raise any fundamental question of principle in view of the requirements of s.6 of the 1978 Act. An unmarried single person could apply for an adoption order (s.15(1)(a)) and the statute did not express any fundamental objection to an adoption by a proposed adopter living in a homosexual relationship. Any negative factors associated with his homosexuality had to be balanced against the positive factors in favour of the application in the whole context of S's welfare. Per the Lord President (Hope) that (1) the provisions of the 1978 Act were broadly in line with the European Convention on the Adoption of Children (Strasbourg, April 24, 1967). Parliament should have expressly provided if it intended to prohibit a person living in a homosexual relationship from applying for an adoption order. It was also relevant to consider whether the contrary interpretation would conflict with the European Convention on Human Rights 1950, and the Scottish courts should apply the presumption that Parliament intended to legislate in conformity with the Convention, dicta in *Kaur v. Lord Advocate* 1980 S.L.T. 322, [1980] C.L.Y. 1156, disapproved, though it did not appear that such an approach would have been held in breach of the Convention; (2) adoption orders in favour of homosexual applicants had been granted in a number of unreported cases; and there was no evidence of any adverse effect on a child living with homosexual carers, *B v. B (Minors) (Custody, Care and Control)* [1991] 1 F.L.R. 402, [1991] C.L.Y. 2547; (3) the Lord Ordinary's criticisms of F, an advocate and clinical psychologist, inter alia, for not addressing the issue raised or giving sufficient reasons for his opinion, were not justified. F's report demonstrated that he fulfilled the confidence which was placed in him. Per Lord Weir; that the Lord Ordinary erred in approaching the application like an undefended proof, judging it on the sufficiency of the evidence when his task in considering the petition was restricted to investigating and verifying the relevant facts, *J and J v. C's Tutor* 1948 S.L.T. 479, [1948] C.L.Y. 407.

T, PETITIONER 1996 S.C.L.R. 897, Lord Hope, Lord President, IH.

6597. Aliment–backdating–special cause

A wife appealed against the sheriff principal's interlocutor, inter alia, reversing the sheriff's decision to backdate an award of aliment payable by her former husband in respect of their two children.

Held, that in the absence of findings in fact to the effect that the husband could afford to pay backdated aliment, no case had been made out for backdating the award.

Observed, that it was incompetent in an interlocutor awarding interim aliment to include a provision for backdating, *McColl v. McColl* 1993 S.L.T. 617, [1993] C.L.Y. 5209 referred to.

ADAMSON v. ADAMSON 1996 S.L.T. 427, Lord McCluskey, Ex Div.

6598. Aliment–competency of claim–effect of Child Support Act 1991

[Child Support Act 1991 (c.48), s.8; Child Support Act 1991 (Commencement No. 3 and Transitional Provisions) Order 1992 (SI 1992 2644).]

Held, in an action of custody and aliment raised in September 1992, in which an interim award of aliment had been made in September 1992 and varied in September 1994, that it was competent to make an award of aliment in March 1995 notwithstanding the terms of s.8(3) of the 1991 Act.

POPE v. POPE 1995 S.C.L.R. 963, Judge not specified, Sh Ct.

6599. Aliment–interim aliment–disabled child over 18

[Family Law (Scotland) Act 1985 (c.37) s.1.]

Held, in an action of aliment at the instance of a man aged 20, who was physically and mentally disabled and in receipt of benefits amounting to £98.30 per week, against his father, that he was "reasonably and appropriately undergoing instruction" at an "educational establishment" all within the meaning of the Family Law (Scotland) Act 1985 s.1 (5) (2) by virtue of his attendance at a college and an adult training centre but that he had failed to show that his means were insufficient for his needs; and application for interim aliment refused.

McBRIDE v. McBRIDE 1995 S.C.L.R. 1021, Judge not specified, Sh Ct.

6600. Aliment–variation–change of circumstances–increasing needs of child

Held, in an application for variation of an award of aliment made on divorce, that the changed income of the parties and the additional cost of maintaining the one child still under the age of 18 were both relevant reasons justifying an increase in the award of aliment.

SKINNER v. SKINNER 1996 S.C.L.R. 334, Judge not specified, Sh Ct.

6601. Care plans–children looked after by local authority

ARRANGEMENTS TO LOOK AFTER CHILDREN (SCOTLAND) REGULATIONS 1996, SI 1996 3262 (S.252); made under the Children (Scotland) Act 1995 s.17, s.31, s.103. In force: April 1, 1997; £2.40.

These Regulations make provision with respect to the duties of local authorities for children who are looked after. They provide that a local authority will make a care plan for each child looked after by them and deal with the considerations to which a local authority must have regard in making a care plan. Minimum requirements are specified regarding notifications of placements and incidents, reviews, records, health assessment, and monitoring and provision is made for a looked after child to be cared for by his own parents in certain circumstances.

6602. Child protection–emergency protection orders

EMERGENCY CHILD PROTECTION MEASURES (SCOTLAND) REGULATIONS 1996, SI 1996 3258 (S.248); made under the Children (Scotland) Act 1995 s.62. In force: April 1, 1997; £1.10.

These Regulations make provisions concerning the duties of any person removing a child to, or keeping him in, a place of safety. They specify persons to be notified and information which should be provided where a child has been removed to a place of safety by a constable or where a justice of the peace has granted an authorisation to protect a child. They also provide for a constable keeping a child in a place of safety only so long as he has reasonable cause to believe certain things are satisfied. They also deal with the arrangements for giving notice where an authorisation ceases to have effect; for informing and taking account of the views of the child; and for allowing contact with a child who is subject to such protection measures.

6603. Children in care of local authorities–parental rights–application of local authority–competency

[Law Reform (Parent and Child) (Scotland) Act 1986 (c.9) s.3(1); Social Work (Scotland) Act 1968 (c.49) s.44(1).]

A child was made the subject of a supervision requirement under s.44(1) of the Social Work (Scotland) Act 1968 and was placed with foster parents. Her mother refused to agree to the child travelling abroad or to sign a passport application on the child's behalf to enable her to accompany her foster carers on holiday to Ibiza. The local authority raised an action craving, on the basis of s.3(1) of the Law Reform (Parent and Child) (Scotland) Act 1986, the right to consent to the child travelling abroad and authorising signature of the passport application forms. The sheriff refused decree and the pursuers appealed.

Held, that an application under s.3(1) of the 1986 Act could not competently be brought by a local authority; and appeal refused, *M v. Dumfries and Galloway RC* 1991 S.C.L.R. 481, [1991] C.L.Y. 5210, not followed. Opinion, that (1) the rights to consent to the child travelling abroad and to apply for a passport for the child could properly be regarded as aspects of parental rights; and (2) that it would be in the child's interests to accompany her foster carers on their holiday.

EDINBURGH CITY COUNCIL v. M 1996 S.L.T. (Sh.Ct.) 112, CGB Nicholson Q.C. (Sheriff Principal), Sh Ct.

6604. Children (Scotland) Act 1995–Commencement No.2 and Transitional Provisions Amendment Order

CHILDREN (SCOTLAND) ACT 1995 (COMMENCEMENT NO.2 AND TRANSITIONAL PROVISIONS) (AMENDMENT) ORDER 1996, SI 1996 2708 (C.79; S.210); made under the Children (Scotland) Act 1995 s.105. £0.65.

This Order amends the Children (Scotland) Act 1995 (Commencement No.2 and Transitional Provisions) Order (SI 1996 2203) by omitting from the table of repeals in the Schedule to the Order, the entry relating to the Trusts (Scotland) Act 1921.

6605. Children (Scotland) Act 1995–Commencement No.2 and Transitional Provisions Order

CHILDREN (SCOTLAND) ACT 1995 (COMMENCEMENT NO.2 AND TRANSITIONAL PROVISIONS) ORDER 1996, SI 1996 2203 (C.53; S.179); made under the Children (Scotland) Act 1995 s.105. In force: bringing into force various provisions of the Act on September 1, 1996; £1.95.

This Order brings into force various provisions of the Children (Scotland) Act 1995. Article 3(1) of the Order brings into force on September 1, 1996 s.4 of the Act, but only for the purpose of enabling Regulations to be made under that section to come into force on November 1, 1996. Article 3(2) of the Order brings into force on October 1, 1996 s.91 of the Act (procedural rules in the sheriff court in relation to applications under Part II of the Act). Article 3(3) of, and the Schedule to, the Order bring into force on November 1, 1996, the provisions listed in that Schedule, insofar as they are not then in force. These are mainly concerned with Part I of the Act and related provisions in Part II (s.54 and s.93), together with consequential amendments of the Adoption (Scotland) Act 1978 in Sch.2 to the Act, certain transitional and savings provisions in Sch.3 to the Act and minor and consequential amendments and repeals in Sch.4 and Sch.5 to the Act.

6606. Children (Scotland) Act 1995–Commencement No.3 Order

CHILDREN (SCOTLAND) ACT 1995 (COMMENCEMENT NO.3) ORDER 1996, SI 1996 3201 (C.102; S.241); made under the Children (Scotland) Act 1995 s.105. In force: bringing into force various provisions of the Act on December 12, 1996 and April 1, 1997; £1.10.

This Order brings into force various provisions of the Children (Scotland) Act 1995.

6607. Children's hearings

CHILDREN'S HEARINGS (SCOTLAND) RULES 1996, SI 1996 3261 (S.251); made under the Children (Scotland) Act 1995 s.42. In force: April 1, 1997; £6.75.

These Rules consolidate and amend the Children's Hearings (Scotland) Rules 1986 (SI 1986 2291) taking into account the new provisions introduced by the Local Government etc (Scotland) Act 1994, the Criminal Procedure (Scotland) Act 1995 and the Children (Scotland) Act 1995.

6608. Children's hearings

CHILDREN'S HEARINGS (SCOTLAND) AMENDMENT RULES 1996, SI 1996 1199 (S.121); made under the Social Work (Scotland) Act 1968 s.35, s.36. In force: October 1, 1996; £0.65.

These Rules amend the Children's Hearings (Scotland) Rules 1986 in connection with the provision of documents and information for the purposes of a children's hearing providing for a new obligation on the principal reporter to give each parent of a child whose case is to be considered by the children's hearing a copy of any document, or information, at the same time as the document or information is being given to members of the children's hearing; any reference to a reporter appointed under the 1968 Act s.36 is to be construed on and after April 1, 1996 as a reference to the principal reporter.

6609. Children's hearings

CHILDREN'S HEARINGS (TRANSMISSION OF INFORMATION ETC) (SCOTLAND) REGULATIONS 1996, SI 1996 3260 (S.250); made under the Children (Scotland) Act 1995 s.17, s.40, s.42, s.74. In force: April 1, 1997; £1.10.

These Regulations which re-enact with amendments the Reporter's Duties and Transmission of Information etc (Scotland) Rules 1971 (SI 1971 525) r.11, r.12 and r.13, provide for local authorities to pass on reports or other relevant information to persons responsible for a child under a supervision order. They oblige local authorities in specified circumstances to arrange temporary accommodation when they cannot find an immediate place at an establishment detailed in a supervision order, failing which to refer the matter back to the Principal Reporter to deal with.

6610. Children's hearings

LOCAL GOVERNMENT (TRANSFER OF CHILDREN'S HEARINGS CASES) (SCOTLAND) ORDER 1996, SI 1996 492 (S.43); made under the Local Government etc. (Scotland) Act 1994 s.181. In force: April 1, 1996; £1.10.

This Order makes transitional arrangements for the transfer on April 1, 1996 of cases of children being considered by a children's hearing for the area of a present local authority under the Social Work (Scotland) Act 1968 to the children's hearing for the area of a new council constituted by the Local Government etc. (Scotland) Act 1994.

6611. Children's hearings–appeal to sheriff–appeal of safeguarder–competency

Held, where a children's hearing had failed to grant a continuation to enable an educational psychologist's report to be obtained, that an appeal to the sheriff by the safeguarder who had not consulted the child, aged 11, was competent and should be allowed.

ROSS v. KENNEDY 1995 S.C.L.R. 1160, Judge not specified, Sh Ct.

6612. Children's hearings–grounds for referral–proof of–whether hearing entitled to take account of other information

[Act of Sederunt (Social Work) (Sheriff Court Procedure Rules) 1971 (SI 1971 92) r.10.]

The Act of Sederunt (Social Work) (Sheriff Court Procedure Rules) 1971 r.10, provides: "Where the grounds of referral are alleged to constitute an offence or offences or any attempt thereat the sheriff may find on the facts that any offence established by the facts has been committed". A child aged 15 years was referred to a children's hearing on two grounds, (1) that an offence mentioned in the Criminal Procedure (Scotland) Act 1975 Sch.1, lewd, indecent or libidinous practices, had been committed in respect of her and (2) that she was a member of the same household as a person who had committed such an offence. As the grounds of referral were disputed, the matter was remitted to the sheriff. The evidence disclosed that the child had been subject to full penile penetration, but that this could have taken place at any time between the ages of 12 and 15. Accordingly an offence under either s.3 (intercourse with a child under the age of 13 years) or s.4, intercourse with a child over 13 but under 16 years, of the Sexual Offences (Scotland) Act 1976 had been committed, but it could not be determined which. The sheriff found that this ground of referral had not been established, but remitted the case to the children's hearing in respect that the second ground was no longer disputed. The child appealed by way of case stated to the Court of Session for a determination as to whether the sheriff should have found, in terms of the Act of Sederunt (Social Work) (Sheriff Court Procedure Rules) 1971 r.10, that any offence had been committed against her.

Held, that the sheriff having held the second ground established, the hearing would be entitled to take into account the undisputed fact that the child had been the subject of full penile penetration in considering the appropriate disposal of the case; and appeal refused, *O v. Rae* 1993 S.L.T. 570, [1992] C.L.Y. 5278 followed. Opinion, that there was nothing in the 1968 Act which required a sheriff to hold that the ground of referral had not been established because he could not choose between two offences, either of which would justify a finding under reference to s.32(2)(d), and while it was less clear whether r.10 of the 1971 Act could be read to that effect, it would be unsatisfactory if a sheriff had to find that a ground of referral under s.32(2)(d) had not been established simply because he could not say whether the child was over or under the age of 13 years when the person had sexual intercourse with her, *McGregor v. D* 1977 S.L.T. 182, [1977] C.L.Y. 3239 commented on.

M v. KENNEDY 1996 S.L.T. 434, Judge not specified, IH.

6613. Children's hearings–grounds for referral–proof of additional evidence on appeal

[Social Work (Scotland) Act 1968 (c.49) s.32, s.50.]

A reporter, X, appealed against a sheriff's decision to refuse to find established grounds for referral under the Social Work (Scotland) Act 1968 s.32(2)(d) in respect of J, born in January 1992, and under s.32(2)(c) and s.32(2)(d) in respect of S, born in January 1994, the sheriff having found only the ground under s.32(2)(c) established in respect of J. At the appeal J and S's mother, R, sought leave to lodge further reports relating to J and S prepared after the sheriff's decision. X argued that (1) given medical evidence that a spiral fracture sustained by J to his right femur would probably have been caused by a twisting of the bone and had probably been non-accidental, the sheriff had erred in accepting R's evidence that the injury had been caused by J falling three feet from a chute; (2) evidence from a post mortem examination of R's child, M, who had been born in August 1989 and had died from natural causes in December, showed that M had sustained fractures to four ribs, which were non-accidental, and in the absence of an explanation from R, this was sufficient to show that M had been assaulted and, as S was a member of the same household as M, the ground for referral under s.32(2)(d) had been established in respect of S and (3) as the sheriff had found that a lack of parental care was likely to cause J unnecessary suffering or seriously to impair his health or development, it was illogical not to make the same finding in relation to S.

Held, appeal refused, that (1) it was incompetent in an appeal under s.50 of the 1968 Act to put before the court additional evidence which did not bear upon any alleged irregularity in the conduct of the case and could not assist in determining any point of law raised, *L, Petitioners (No.1)* 1993 S.C.L.R. 693, [1993] C.L.Y. 4787 distinguished; (2) R's evidence had been corroborated by the evidence of other adults who had been in the vicinity when J had sustained the fracture and whose accounts were more consistent with an accidental fall than with an assault to J. Further, the possibility that J's injuries had been caused by a fall was not excluded by the medical evidence, and, given that the sheriff had dealt with all the criticisms made of the reliability of R's witnesses, he had approached R's evidence with the utmost caution, and that he had taken into account the probabilities of the various causes of the injury, the sheriff had been entitled to conclude that it had not been established that J had been assaulted; (3) given that, apart from the injuries to M, no other features of abuse had been found at the time, and no further action had been taken, the sheriff was entitled to conclude that there was insufficient evidence for him to made a finding that M had been assaulted and that accordingly the ground under s.32(2)(d) had not been satisfied. *Observed*, that if the ground under s.32(2)(d) was satisfied in relation to S, it ought to have been satisfied in relation to J and that it was a matter of concern that no similar submission had been made in respect of J and that the grounds of referral had given little indication that the assault founded upon under s.32(2)(d) would be to M and not the one alleged to have occurred to J, the narrative in support of the grounds referring only to the fractures found in the post-mortem being unexplained and (4) S was a normal healthy child, well looked after and cared for by R and there was no evidence that he had suffered any injuries or neglect, which was clearly different from the case of J, who had had several accidents. Notwithstanding the concern about what had happened to M and another child who had been adopted in 1988 when R was still a teenager, the sheriff was entitled to conclude from the recent history that S was not at risk.

STIRLING v. R 1996 S.C.L.R. 191, Judge not specified, IH.

6614. Children's hearings–grounds for referral–review of sheriff's findings–competency–nobile officium

[Criminal Procedure (Scotland) Act 1975 (c.21) Sch.1; Social Work (Scotland) Act 1968 (c.49) s.42, s.50, s.52.]

R applied to the nobile officium for an order directing the sheriff to reconsider whether grounds for referral of his children, S, B and J, to a children's hearing were established. The reporter, K, had referred S, B and J to a children's panel on the grounds that S had been the victim of an offence within Sch. 1 to the Criminal Procedure (Scotland) Act 1975 and that B and J were members of the same household as S. R and his wife, W, did not accept these grounds. S stated that R had had sexual intercourse with her. The sheriff found the facts established. R abandoned his appeal to the Court of Session as it appeared that the material issue before the sheriff was the credibility of S's evidence. The panel made supervision requirements for each child: S was left in care, and B and J were to live with W while R lived elsewhere. S confessed she had fabricated her evidence to protect her boyfriend with whom she had had sexual intercourse. R applied unsuccessfully to the panel for review of the supervision requirements for B and J, there being other reasons why S should remain in care. The panel noted the retraction, but did not see it as their function to question the sheriff's decision. The Secretary of State declined R's request that he exercise his powers under s.52 of the Social Work (Scotland) Act 1968 by terminating the supervision requirements for each child, noting the sheriff's decision, the abandoned appeal and the panel's subsequent decision. R argued that it was the scheme of the 1968 Act that children should only receive compulsory measures of care while they still needed them and at every stage of the case the grounds of referral and whether the conditions mentioned in s.32(1) of the 1968 Act were satisfied remained open to reconsideration. If S's evidence had been false, it was not in the best interests of B and J to be deprived of contact with their father. K opposed the application as incompetent. K averred that such retractions were part of a recognised pattern of behaviour among child victims of sexual abuse.

Held, petition dismissed as incompetent, that the nobile officium might only be exercised in highly special and unforeseen circumstances to prevent injustice and oppression. Under the scheme of the 1968 Act, there were no provisions to return the case to the sheriff to reconsider the grounds of referral. Nor was there any provision for the withdrawal of acceptance of the grounds of referral once the hearing was complete. The Secretary of State had no power to discharge the referral or to order the sheriff to reconsider the question of whether the grounds of referral had been established. This absence in the procedure was not due to an oversight, since such a case was not so exceptional as to be unforeseen. Parliament therefore clearly intended finality on the matter of the grounds of referral. The grounds of referral did not bind the panel to a particular course of action; they were entitled to ask for and consider a wide range of information, some of which might be matters which could have formed an additional ground for referral. A decision that the panel could not continue to hear a case because the original grounds for referral were no longer accepted or established might be quite contrary to the best interests of the child, who might be in need of compulsory measures of care on other grounds. It would be inconsistent with the Act for the hearing to be interrupted in this way. While in exceptional circumstances, such as incomplete or mistaken facts at the time the grounds of referral were accepted or established, it might be appropriate to exercise the nobile officium since neither the Secretary of State nor the panel could review the grounds of referral, this was not the situation here.

R v. KENNEDY 1993 S.C. 417, Judge not specified.

6615. Custody–access–child subject to local authority supervision requirement

[Social Work (Scotland) Act 1968 (c.49) s.44(1) (a).]

In an action of declarator of paternity in which access was sought, the mother of the child sought to have the natural father's access to the child reduced to nil. The child was subject to a supervision requirement under s.44(1) (a) of the Social Work (Scotland) Act 1968, with the condition that the natural father should not have access to the child. The regional council entered the process as party minuter. The sheriff held, distinguishing *D v. Strathclyde RC* 1985 S.L.T. 114, [1985] C.L.Y. 3731, that the natural father's crave was in substance a crave for access at large, a plea for the principle of access to be investigated, and as such could competently be determined by the court. The child's mother and the regional council appealed.

Held, that any order for access in favour of the natural father, even one for access in principle, made during the currency of the supervision requirement would necessarily be in conflict with the discretion in the matter of access exercised by the local authority, which had the responsibility to give effect to the requirement, and accordingly an order for access was incompetent; and appeal allowed and action remitted to the sheriff to proceed as accords, *D v. Strathclyde RC* 1985 S.L.T. 114, [1985] C.L.Y. 3731

A v. G 1996 S.L.T. (Sh.Ct.) 123, Sheriff Kearney, Sh Ct.

6616. Custody–best interests of child–very young child

The mother and father of a young child both sought custody of the child. The parties had separated when the child was four months old. The mother obtained an interim award of custody from the sheriff and the child resided with the mother from that time until the sheriff awarded custody to the father after proof, at which time the child was about 14 months old. In awarding the father custody the sheriff proceeded on his favourable impression of the father's background and his unfavourable impression of the mother's lifestyle. The sheriff principal upheld the award of custody to the father, commenting that the sheriff could only be expected to have regard to the circumstances at the time of the proof, and if these circumstances changed the court could consider the matter of custody afresh. The mother appealed to the Court of Session. The First Division allowed the appeal and awarded custody to the mother on the basis that the sheriff had failed to balance against the long term advantages which he considered that the father's background had to offer, the advantages of maternal care to a very young child especially where the child was already in the care of its mother. The father appealed to the House of Lords, contending, inter alia, that there was neither principle nor practice in Scotland whereby, during its infancy, a child's need for its mother was stronger than for its father.

Held, that (1) the advantage to a very young child of being with its mother was a consideration which had to be taken into account in deciding where its best interests lay in custody proceedings in which the mother was involved: this was neither a presumption nor a principle but rather recognition of a widely held belief based on practical experience and the workings of nature, its importance would vary according to the age of the child and to other circumstances of each individual case and circumstances might be such that it had no importance at all and (2) it would always yield to other competing advantages which more effectively promoted the welfare of the child, but where a very young child had been with its mother since birth and there was no criticism of her ability to care for the child, only the strongest competing advantages were likely to prevail, and the sheriff not having addressed the advantages of preserving the status quo with the availability of maternal care, the First Division had been entitled to interfere with his decision; and appeal dismissed. (Wilkinson and Norrie, *Parent and Child*, p.211-212, approved.)

BRIXEY v. LYNAS 1996 S.L.T. 908, Judge not specified, HL.

6617. Custody–international child abduction–habitual residence

[Child Abduction and Custody Act 1985 (c.60) Sch.1 Art.13.]

F petitioned for an order for the return of his children, R and S, to France after M had taken them to Scotland. In a reclaiming motion it had been held that R and S were habitually resident in France and the case was remitted to the Outer House for consideration of M's remaining arguments which arose under Art.13 of the Hague Convention in the 1985 Act. M was ordained to lead at the proof and submitted that (1) R objected to being returned and it was appropriate to take her views into account given her age (7 3/4 at proof) and maturity, and if S was returned without R, there was a grave risk that S would be in an intolerable situation and (2) in any event there was a grave risk that R and S would be exposed to psychological harm or otherwise placed in an intolerable situation, having already been exposed to the conflict between F and M and suffered psychological damage.

Held, order for return made, that (1) R, who had been witness at the further proof, was accepted as having a genuine objection to returning, but she had not attained the relevant age and degree of maturity. Her reaction was that of a child of her years more comfortable with her immediate security and unable to balance the advantages and disadvantages of returning. In the circumstances no discretion to refuse R's return arose. Opinion, that any such discretion would have been exercised in favour of ordering R's return, since although neither the parties nor their children spoke fluent French, and R's physical connection with France was relatively tenuous, the fact that R and S were habitually resident in France outweighed those concerns having regard to the policy of the

Convention; (2) an argument for M that the French court might refuse jurisdiction was irrelevant, the court being assumed to have jurisdiction as soon as the children were present in France. Opinion, further, that it could only be said that S would be in an intolerable situation if returned without R, if M also chose not to return to France and (3) M's argument that R and S would suffer if M had to return with R and S, was rejected. The risk of harm required to be grave to a severe degree.

CAMERON v. CAMERON 1996 S.C.L.R. 552, Judge not specified, OH.

6618. Custody–international child abduction–habitual residence

[Child Abduction and Custody Act 1985 (c.60) Sch.1 Art.4; Hague Convention on Civil Aspects of International Child Abduction 1985.]

The Child Abduction and Custody Act 1985, by incorporation of the Hague Convention on Civil Aspects of International Child Abduction 1985, provides remedies where a child is wrongfully removed from a country where the child, in terms of Art. 4, was "habitually resident in a Contracting State immediately before any breach of custody or access rights". A father petitioned the Court of Session for an order for the return of his children to France on the ground that their mother had wrongfully retained them in Scotland in breach of his rights of custody in terms of a minute of agreement between the parties. The parties separated in autumn 1994 and in terms of a separation agreement agreed to share custody of their children. The children were taken by F to live with him in France and M had unlimited access in France and residential access in Scotland. If the children became unhappy with F in France, he was immediately to arrange their return to Scotland; further, the arrangements were to be reviewed on the expiry of six months from the date of execution. The children resided in France with F from January to April 1995. In April 1995 they travelled to England with him and, following a period of access with M, were not returned to F but taken by M to Scotland. Before the Lord Ordinary, F argued that it was the parties' intention in the minute of agreement that the children be habitually resident in France; the minute of agreement indicated that the children would remain in France for the long term and it was not tentative or provisional in its character. The Lord Ordinary having refused the prayer of the petition, F reclaimed. M argued that the children were to go to France as an experiment, which view was reflected in the terms of the minute of agreement, and, in any event, they had not resided there for sufficiently long to acquire a habitual residence.

Held, that (1) the Lord Ordinary erred in concluding that the arrangements contained in the minute of agreement were tentative only and not final, and it was plain from looking at the terms of the minute that there was nothing tentative or provisional in what was agreed; (2) there was no minimum period which was necessary in order to establish the acquisition of a new habitual residence; it was sufficient if there was an intention to reside in a place for an appreciable period, and in all the circumstances the children had lived in France for a sufficiently long period to show that they had become habitually resident there; and reclaiming motion allowed. Opinion, that (1) a person could have only one habitual residence at any one time and, if a new habitual residence were to be acquired, the old one would be lost and (2) it was not necessary in all cases that residence had to be voluntarily adopted before there could be habitual residence.

CAMERON v. CAMERON 1996 S.L.T. 306, Lord Ross, L.J.C., IH.

6619. Fostering

FOSTERING OF CHILDREN (SCOTLAND) REGULATIONS 1996, SI 1996 3263 (S.253); made under the Social Work (Scotland) Act 1968 s.5. In force: April 1, 1997; £2.80.

These Regulations apply where a local authority fosters a child who is looked after by them under the Children (Scotland) Act 1995. They supersede the Boarding Out and Fostering of Children (Scotland) Regulations 1985 (SI 1985 1799). They make provision for the establishment of fostering panels and specify the functions of such panels, prescribe the procedures to be followed by local authorities in approving persons as foster carers and the procedures to be followed in making arrangements to foster children. The main change to the Regulations is that provision is made for local authorities collectively to enter into agreements with voluntary organisations to discharge general fostering arrangements on the authorities' behalf.

6620. Judgments and orders–reciprocal enforcement

CHILDREN (RECIPROCAL ENFORCEMENT OF PRESCRIBED ORDERS ETC (ENGLAND AND WALES AND NORTHERN IRELAND) (SCOTLAND) REGULATIONS 1996, SI 1996 3267 (S.255); made under the Children (Scotland) Act 1995 s.33. In force: April 1, 1997; £2.40.

These Regulations provide for the reciprocal enforcement between Scotland and England and Wales and Scotland and Northern Ireland of various Orders in respect of children and young persons.

6621. Parental responsibility–parental rights

PARENTAL RESPONSIBILITIES AND PARENTAL RIGHTS AGREEMENT (SCOTLAND) REGULATIONS 1996, SI 1996 2549 (S.198); made under the Children (Scotland) Act 1995 s.4, s.103. In force: November 1, 1996; £1.55.

These Regulations prescribe the form for the agreement between the father and mother of a child regarding the acquisition of parental responsibilities and parental rights by that child's natural father.

6622. Parental rights–guardianship–purpose of acquiring right to attend children's hearing–competency

[Law Reform (Parent and Child) (Scotland) Act 1986 (c.9); Children's Hearings (Scotland) Rules 1986 (SI 1986 2291) r.14.]

In September 1992 a mother who had at no stage been married to the father of her child was awarded custody of the child in the sheriff court. In August 1993 the father sought and obtained legal aid to vary the interlocutor of September 1992 by awarding him access to the child. In January 1994 the child was made the subject of a supervision requirement. F lodged a minute for variation and a hearing thereon was fixed. Prior to the hearing the father lodged a minute of amendment to seek the parental right of guardianship on a restricted basis. On appeal to the Court of Session, F contended that the amended crave for parental rights of guardianship upon a restricted basis was competent, and that the form of procedure adopted was competent. The purpose of the application was for F, who had no parental rights by operation of law in terms of the Law Reform (Parent and Child) (Scotland) Act 1986, to attend and participate in a children's hearing. In order for F to have a right to attend at all stages of the children's hearing, he would require to be a guardian of the child. F contended that at common law it was recognised that a right of guardianship might be exercised for a limited purpose. F further maintained that his application was in effect an application for variation of the custody order.

Held, that (1) the powers of a guardian were given for the benefit of the child, not the guardian, and the sheriff was accordingly well founded in concluding that the amended crave for parental rights of guardianship upon a restricted basis was incompetent where F was not seeking to represent the child at the children's hearing, but to have the right to attend the hearing in order to obtain an order of access in his own favour; (2) since the interlocutor sought to be varied had been pronounced prior to the coming into force of the Ordinary Cause Rules 1993, procedure fell to be determined according to the rules previously in force and (3) guardianship and custody being entirely different concepts, the seeking of guardianship could not be regarded as varying an order for custody in terms of r.129 of those rules; and appeal refused.

Observed, that the father could apply to the chairman of the children's hearing to be permitted to attend as a person whose presence might be justified by special circumstances, in terms of the Children's Hearings (Scotland) Rules 1986 r.14(d).

L v. H 1996 S.L.T. 612, Judge not specified, IH.

6623. Residential accommodation–designation and approval

REFUGES FOR CHILDREN (SCOTLAND) REGULATIONS 1996, SI 1996 3259 (S.249); made under the Children (Scotland) Act 1995 s.38. In force: April 1, 1997; £1.55.

These Regulations make provisions concerning the designation and approval of establishments or households as refuges and for the review and withdrawal of such designation or approval. They specify requirements to be complied with where designation or approval is in force and persons who should be notified and the information about which they should be notified where a child is provided with refuge. They also prescribe the exceptional circumstances where a child may be provided with a refuge beyond the normal seven day limit to a 14 day limit.

6624. Residential care

RESIDENTIAL ESTABLISHMENTS - CHILD CARE (SCOTLAND) REGULATIONS 1996, SI 1996 3256 (S.246); made under the Social Work (Scotland) Act 1968 s.5, s.60. In force: April 1, 1997; £1.95.

These Regulations make provisions with respect to residential establishments in which a child who is looked after by a local authority under the Children (Scotland) Act 1995 may be placed. They supersede the Social Work (Residential Establishments–Child Care) (Scotland) Regulations 1987 (SI 1987 2233).

6625. Secure accommodation

SECURE ACCOMMODATION (SCOTLAND) REGULATIONS 1996, SI 1996 3255 (S.245); made under the Social Work (Scotland) Act 1968 s.60; the Children (Scotland) Act 1995 s.75; and the Criminal Procedure (Scotland) Act 1995 s.44. In force: April 1, 1997; £1.95.

These Regulations are concerned with the use of secure accommodation for any child who is being looked after by a local authority or for whom the local authority is responsible under Criminal Procedure legislation. They replace the four sets of secure accommodation Regulations which are extant.

6626. Articles

A voice for the child *(Elaine E. Sutherland)*: J.L.S.S. 1996, 41 (10), 391-393. (Implications of provisions of 1995 Act affecting children's welfare and opportunity to recognise child's right to be involved in decision making process).

Adoption: the new law *(Joe Thomson)*: S.L.G. 1996, 64(3), 138. (Amended adoption procedures introduced by the Children (Scotland) Act 1995, making child's welfare paramount consideration).

Children instructing solicitors *(Alison Cleland)*: Fam. L.B. 1996, 19(Jan), 3-4. (Capacity of children under 16 since November 1, 1995).

Custody in separation agreements *(Ian L.S. Balfour)*: Fam. L.B. 1996, 21 (May), 2-3. (Separation agreement between parties should be precise as to arrangements for custody and residence).

D v Grampian Regional Council: parental rights and adoption *(Elaine E. Sutherland)*: S.L.P.Q. 1996, 1 (2), 159-165. (Implications of decision that birth parents whose children have been freed for adoption cannot obtain order granting parental rights).

From access to contact *(Joe Thomson)*: S.L.G. 1996, 64(2), 82-83. (Changed rights and responsibilities of parents in relation to contact with their children under 1995 Act).

Homeless young persons and interim care orders *(Almuth Ernsting)*: SCOLAG 1996, 236, 130-131. (Use of interim order under s.15 to compel local authority to take homeless young person under 17 into care and implications for application of duties under Children (Scotland) Act 1995).

Parental pride: adoption and the gay man *(Kenneth McK. Norrie)*: S.L.T. 1996, 33, 321-325. (Whether consent to adoption had been unreasonably withheld and implications of decision that no bar exists to adoption by male homosexual couple).

Parental responsibilities and parental rights agreements *(Kenneth McK. Norrie)*: SCOLAG 1996, 235, 94-95. (From November 1, 1996 unmarried fathers will be able to acquire parental rights by entering into written agreement with mothers).

Surrogacy and illegal payments *(Neil Gow)*: Fam. L.B. 1996, 24(Nov), 3-4. (Legislation governing surrogacy arrangements, including parental orders and adoption, and cases on illegal payments).

The Children (Scotland) Act 1995–exclusion orders *(Joe Thomson)*: S.L.G. 1996, 64(1), 32-33. (Procedure for removal of alleged abuser from child's home).

The Hague Convention on international child abduction *(Ian L.S. Balfour* and *Elizabeth B. Crawford)*: S.L.P.Q. 1996, 1(5), 411-427. (Implementation of Convention and 1985 Act with reference to recent decisions and including list of contracting states as at September 1996).

Whatever happened to section 37? Emergency child protection and the Children (Scotland) Act 1995 *(Deirdre Watson)*: Fam. L.B. 1996, 24(Nov), 4-6. (Reasons why reform was necessary and introduction of child protection orders under 1995 Act).

CIVIL EVIDENCE

6627. Admissibility–hearsay–child–allegations of sexual abuse

A couple lived together and thereafter married in England in 1984. The wife had moved from Scotland to England for employment reasons in about 1979. Two children, C, aged eight at proof, and D, aged five, were born to the couple. The marriage broke down thereafter and S moved in to live with the wife after the husband had moved out. In 1993 the wife, together with S and the children, moved back to Scotland. She thereafter sought custody of the children and interdict against her husband removing or attempting to remove the children furth of Scotland. At the proof, evidence regarding the relationships between the wife, the husband, the children, and S was led. This included allegations that S, with whom the wife and her children continued to live, had sexually abused his own daughters, H and E, in England. The evidence relied upon to establish these allegations was that of S's wife, M, and a social worker who had interviewed the children at the time. The social worker had at the time of the proof no recollection of her interviews with S's children but referred to a report made up at the time based on her notes from the interview. M had been in the house downstairs when one of the incidents of alleged sexual abuse by S of her two daughters in their upstairs bedroom took place. The two daughters had told her what had happened during this and a previous incident. Neither of the two daughters was called at the proof to give evidence. Nor was evidence led of accounts given by M to her solicitor, a friend, or a psychoanalyst regarding the incidents. Counsel for the husband argued that evidence at proof of statement made by a child extrajudicially was competent evidence of the contents of the statement, under the Civil Evidence (Scotland) Act, 1988 s.2 and that the test of competency was whether at the date of proof the child was likely to give a truthful account; this could be established otherwise than by examination of the child by the judge, such as by evidence of others as to the child's trustworthiness.

Held, that (1) direct oral evidence of a statement made extrajudicially by a child was not admissible within the meaning of s.2(1) of the 1988 Act unless direct evidence of such matter was admissible at proof and the child had been tendered as a witness and undergone a preliminary examination by the judge, and the statements made to the mother and social worker were therefore not admissible as evidence of the matters contained in those statements; (2) notwithstanding the abolition of the rule that corroboration was required for legal sufficiency by s.1 (1) of the 1988 Act, failure to lead other evidence which might have supported a single witness speaking to crucial facts might be material to whether a court was satisfied that that fact had been proved by the evidence led; (3) failure to lead evidence now competent under s.3 of the 1988 Act potentially supportive of a witness's credibility might affect the court's view as to whether a fact had been proved; (4) in the absence of evidence from either of the primary witnesses to the alleged events, and of evidence material to the credibility of the only witness led, the allegations of sexual abuse had not been proved and (5) a permanent order, breach of which could give rise to contempt of court and punishment, was undesirable in custody cases unless the circumstances were compelling, the wife's remedy for protection being registration of the decree of custody; and petition granted for custody only. Opinion, that the standard of proof in a civil action of an allegation of criminal conduct was on a balance of probabilities, *Mullan v. Anderson* 1993 S.L.T. 835, [1993] C.L.Y. 5815 followed.

L v. L 1996 S.L.T. 767, Judge not specified, OH.

6628. Admissibility–surprise witness

[Court of Session Act 1988 (c.36) s.29(1) (b).]

An action relating to a road traffic accident in which a young child was knocked down proceeded to a jury trial. The effect of the jury's verdict was to absolve the defenders of liability. The pursuer sought a new trial on the ground of the undue admission of evidence in terms of s.29(1) (b) of the Court of Session Act 1988. The pursuer contended that certain evidence should not have been allowed by the presiding Lord Ordinary, as this had occasioned an element of surprise. The pursuer's case was that the child had been knocked down while crossing the road to a shop. The evidence in question was from the shopkeeper who stated that the child had visited the shop and was crossing the road in the opposite direction. The pursuer argued that the evidence was not foreshadowed either in the pleadings or in cross-examination of the pursuer's witnesses, nor had a list of witnesses been provided by the defenders.

Held, that (1) if evidence was admitted which was objectionable on the ground of surprise it would be a ground for allowing a new trial; (2) as neither party had offered a list of witnesses as had been recommended, the pursuer had no good ground of complaint on that account; (3) in order to justify the allowance of a new trial the element of surprise had to be of a character which the party allegedly taken by surprise could not reasonably have been expected to anticipate, and having regard to an averment in the defences that the child had crossed from the shop side it would have been a reasonable line of investigation for the pursuer's solicitors to approach the witness led and (4) sufficient notice had been given of the line of defence by a question put in cross-examination; and motion refused.

CHRISTIE'S CURATOR AD LITEM v. KIRKWOOD 1996 S.L.T. 1299, Judge not specified, IH.

6629. Best evidence rule–damaged net not produced–competency of other evidence about damage to net–effect of failure to preserve net

The owners of a fish farm sought damages for an escape of fish from the farm, alleged to have been caused by the fault of manufacturers of nets used in the farm. The negligence founded on was in the method of joining the netting. Fish had escaped after a gap developed in one of the joins. The nets had been removed shortly afterwards and laid out in a field where they had remained in a deteriorating condition. They had not been produced as productions in court. The defenders objected to any evidence about the state of the nets, contending that the best evidence rule precluded evidence being led about the nets (1) when they were available but had not been produced, and (2) when the defenders had not been given the opportunity of inspection shortly after the incident and the nets had not been kept in a presentable state for inspection.

Held, that the best evidence rule existed to prevent prejudice to one party and unfair advantage to the other party to a dispute where better evidence than that before the court existed, and it could not apply to exclude evidence about the nets when they were no longer capable of being examined usefully, but where the nets had not been produced or preserved for inspection, it was appropriate to examine the pursuers' case with greater care, and thereby impose a heavier burden of proof than might otherwise be necessary; and objection repelled.

STIRLING AQUATIC TECHNOLOGY LTD v. FARMOCEAN AB (NO.2) 1996 S.L.T. 456, Judge not specified, OH.

6630. Civil Evidence (Family Mediation) (Scotland) Act 1995–Commencement Order

CIVIL EVIDENCE (FAMILY MEDIATION) (SCOTLAND) ACT 1995 (COMMENCEMENT AND TRANSITIONAL PROVISION) ORDER 1996, SI 1996 125 (C.2; S.9); made under the Civil Evidence (Family Mediation) (Scotland) Act 1995 s.3. In force: bringing into force various provisions of the Act on February 19, 1996; £0.65.

This Order appoints February 19, 1996 for the commencement of the Civil Evidence (Family Mediation) (Scotland) Act 1995 and includes a transitional provision which applies the Act only to evidence given or heard in any civil proceedings after the commencement date.

6631. Letter of request–recovery of documents in hands of third party–competency

[Evidence (Proceedings in Other Jurisdictions) Act 1975 (c.34) s.1; Act of Sederunt (Sheriff Court Ordinary Cause Rules) 1993 (SI 1993 1956).]

Section 1 of the Evidence (Proceedings in Other Jurisdictions) Act 1975 provides for applications to be made to United Kingdom courts for assistance in obtaining evidence for civil proceedings in another court in pursuance of a request. Section 2(4) provides that an order shall not require a person to produce any documents other than particular documents specified in the order. Section 9 defines "request" as including "any commission, order or other process issued by or on behalf of the requesting court". In an action seeking declarator of paternity and custody of children, the pursuer lodged a minute craving the court to issue a letter of request to the High Court in London for the recovery of records from an English hospital in terms of s.1 of the 1975 Act. The letter of request set out alongside the words "Evidence to be obtained or other judicial act to be performed" the words "All medical records, failing principals copies of the same, in the name of the defender as are held at the [hospital]." Alongside the words "Documents or other property to be inspected" it stated "All medical records, failing principals copies of the same, in the name of the defender as are held at the foregoing hospital. To be produced and copied." The sheriff refused the pursuer's motion and granted leave to appeal. The pursuers appealed to the sheriff principal.

Held, that (1) a requesting court had a duty to consider whether the documents requested had been sufficiently specified and could not leave it to the receiving court to determine whether or not to give effect to the request, especially when the requesting court was another court within the United Kingdom; (2) the letter of request was likely to be confusing to the receiving court since there was a clear conflict in asking for documents to be "obtained" and "inspected"; (3) the calls in the letter of request plainly failed to satisfy what would be required before the High Court could give effect to it, in that they were not limited by reference to any dates nor by reference to any treatment for any specified disorder, and the general description of the documents sought to be recovered as "medical records", which was not further specified, was insufficient; and appeal refused. Opinion, that while it appeared that a Scottish commission and diligence was unenforceable outside Scotland, the 1975 Act provided a means by which the purpose of a Scottish commission and diligence procedure could be achieved in respect of documents in other parts of the United Kingdom, and a party who had unsuccessfully tried to secure voluntary compliance with a properly drawn specification of documents forming part of a commission and diligence procedure might then use the same specification as the basis for a letter of request.

Observed, that Form G13 in the Ordinary Cause Rules, although applicable, was inappropriate for the normal operation of commission and diligence.

STEWART v. CALLAGHAN 1996 S.L.T. (Sh.Ct.) 12, Judge not specified, Sh Ct.

6632. Articles

Restriction on proof of contract terms *(Desmond Cheyne)*: Civ. P.B. 1996, 8(Mar), 2-3. (Scottish Law Commission Report No.152 on reform of rule regarding admission of parole evidence as to terms not in written document).

6633. Books

Hunter, Robert–Cases on the Scots Law of Evidence. Paperback: £28.50. ISBN 0-406-02418-9. Butterworth Law (Scotland).

Raitt, Fiona; Field, David–The Law of Evidence in Scotland. Greens' concise Scots law. Paperback. ISBN 0-414-01041-8. W.Green & Son.

Wilkinson–The Scottish Law of Evidence. Paperback: £28.00. ISBN 0-406-01357-8. Butterworth Law (Scotland).

Wilkinson, Sheriff A.B.–Wilkinson: the Scottish Law of Evidence. Paperback: £28.00. ISBN 0-406-01357-8. Butterworth Law (Scotland).

CIVIL PRACTICE

6634. Acts of Sederunt–chancery procedure

ACT OF SEDERUNT (CHANCERY PROCEDURE RULES) 1996, SI 1996 2184 (S.176); made under the Titles to Land Consolidation (Scotland) Act 1868 s.51; and the Sheriff Courts (Scotland) Act 1971 s.32. In force: November 1, 1996; £3.70.

This Act of Sederunt makes new provision in relation to the forms, subscription, publication, taking of evidence and issue of extract in chancery petitions. It revokes the Act of Sederunt (Edictal Citations, Commissary Petitions and Petitions of Service) 1971 (SI 1971 1165) para.3 which made provision for publication of petitions of service. It also repeals the Titles to Land Consolidation (Scotland) Act 1868 (C.101) s.29, s.30 and s.34, and parts of s.33, and part of the Conveyancing (Scotland) Act 1874 (C.94) s.10, which provide for the form, publication and procedure with respect to petitions for service for which new provision is made in this Act of Sederunt.

6635. Appeals–Court of Session, to–competency–failure to find caution

A pursuer was ordained to find caution by the sheriff principal as a condition of being allowed to continue with an appeal against a sheriff's finding the defenders entitled to dismissal of the action against them. The pursuer appealed against that order, without leave, to the Court of Session. The nominated judge refused the appeal as incompetent under r.40.12(6)(b) of the Rules of the Court of Session 1994. After the time limit for finding caution had expired, the sheriff principal dismissed the original appeal. The pursuer appealed that interlocutor to the Court of Session. In the single bills, the pursuer sought a first order and made it clear that he would seek to challenge the interlocutor ordering caution.

Held, that (1) the sheriff principal's interlocutor ordering caution became expressly a final interlocutor when the pursuer's appeal against it was refused by the nominated judge and (2) it then became incapable of being reviewed, notwithstanding the rule in the Sheriff Courts (Scotland) Act 1907 s.29 that an appeal under that Act would be effectual to submit to review the whole of the interlocutors pronounced in the cause, and as it was his failure to find caution which led to his appeal to the sheriff principal being dismissed, there was no purpose to be served by allowing him to proceed further with the present appeal; and motion for first order refused, *Marsh v. Baxendale* 1995 S.L.T. 198, [1995] 2 C.L.Y. 5931 followed.

Observed, that the application for leave to appeal had to be made to the sheriff or sheriff principal, as the case may be, and not to the appeal court *Bulman v. Frost* 1996 S.L.T. 316, referred to.

MOWBRAY v. D C THOMSON & CO LTD 1996 S.L.T. 846, Judge not specified, IH.

6636. Appeals–House of Lords, to–action begun in sheriff court–scope of appeal–construction of findings altered on appeal to Inner House

[Court of Session Act 1988 (c.36) s.32; Occupier's Liability (Scotland) Act 1960 (c.30) s.2.]

An employee slipped on the step of a staircase in his place of work. He raised an action for damages against his employers, claiming that the accident had been caused by the eroded state of the tread of the step and that they had been negligent in not repairing it. The sheriff assoilzied the defenders. On appeal the sheriff principal recalled the sheriff's interlocutor and granted decree in favour of the pursuer. On further appeal an Extra Division recalled the interlocutor of the sheriff principal and affirmed that of the sheriff. The Extra Division made certain alterations to the findings relative to fault. On appeal to the House of Lords it was contended that, on the basis of the findings in fact, the Extra Division had erred in law in concluding that fault was not established. It was submitted that the House was not entitled to look at the judgment as an aid to the construction of a particular finding which had been altered by the Extra Division.

Held, that it was legitimate, and indeed necessary, to consider the opinion of the Extra Division in order to resolve ambiguity in the finding; and appeal dismissed. *Sutherland v. Glasgow Corp* 1951 S.L.T. 185, [1951] C.L.Y. 4325, followed. Observation in *Laing v. Scottish Grain Distillers* 1992 S.L.T. 435, [1992] C.L.Y. 6125, clarified.

MARTINEZ v. GRAMPIAN HEALTH BOARD 1996 S.L.T. 69, Lord Jauncey of Tullichettle, HL.

6637. Appeals–House of Lords, to–regulation of access to child pending appeal–competency

[Court of Session Act 1988 (c.36) s.41.]

The Court of Session Act 1988 s.41 (1) provides, inter alia, that pending an appeal to the House of Lords, "the Inner House... may regulate all matters relating to interim possession, execution and expenses already incurred as it thinks fit". Pending an appeal to the House of Lords on the issue of custody of a child, the pursuer sought variation of an interlocutor of the sheriff on the question of access by motion on the single bills. The defender contended that the wording of s.41 (1) was too narrow to enable the Inner House to deal with a matter relating to access.

Held, that the phrase "all matters relating to interim possession" in s.41 (1) was wide enough to include orders relating to the custody of a child, in a case where that matter was under appeal to the House of Lords, and access to the child by the parent who did not have custody; and the motion was competent.

BRIXEY v. LYNAS (NO.2) 1996 S.L.T. 651, Judge not specified, IH.

6638. Appeals–sheriff court, from–grounds of appeal–adequacy

[Rules of the Court of Session 1994 (SI 1994 1443) r.40.14(2); Rules of the Court of Session 1994 (SI 1994 1443) r.40.14(5).]

The landlord of licensed premises raised an action in the sheriff court against the creditor in a standard security over the tenant's interest under the lease, for payment of unpaid rent and damages for breach of contract. After debate, the sheriff sustained the creditor's plea to the relevancy and dismissed the action. The landlord appealed to the sheriff principal and the appeal was dismissed. He appealed to the Court of Session on the basis that both the sheriff principal and the sheriff had erred.

Held, that the grounds of appeal were wholly inadequate; and appeal refused on the basis that the landlord had failed to lodge proper grounds of appeal.

FERGUSON v. WHITBREAD & CO PLC 1996 S.L.T. 659, Judge not specified, IH.

6639. Appeals–sheriff court, from–grounds of appeal–amendment

[Act of Sederunt (Rules of the Court of Session) 1994 (SI 1994 1443) r.40.14.]

P appealed a sheriff court decision which found P solely at fault for an accident in which P sustained injury after being struck by D's car. Grounds of appeal against liability were lodged in December 1994. P attempted at the start of the hearing to lodge further grounds of appeal against quantum.

Held, that leave to amend the grounds of appeal should be refused as no special cause had been shown under the Rules of the Court of Session 1994 r.40.14(4) and proper notice had not been given so as to get a proper allocation of court time, *Noble Organisation Ltd v. Kilmarnock and Loudoun DC* 1993 S.L.T. 759, [1993] C.L.Y. 5703.

McINNES v. LAWRENCE 1996 S.C.L.R. 169, Judge not specified, IH.

6640. Commission and diligence–recovery of documents–confidentiality–expert report

W sought damages from his employers, M, after developing repetitive strain injury to his elbows. W was a fish processor involved in the heading and trimming of fish, which meant W carrying out rapid pulling and gripping movements causing repeated and traumatic forces to be exerted on W's wrists, forearms and elbows. W's action was based on common law fault. W moved to have a confidential envelope opened up which had been lodged by D in response to an order for recovery. D was an ergonomist who had been instructed by M to investigate the process in 1992. At that time 12 claims by different employees had become the subject of action or been intimated to M. W's action was raised in 1994. M opposed the motion, arguing that the report had been prepared in contemplation of or in preparation for other litigation. W argued that excerpts should be allowed to be taken from the report insofar as those excerpts were narrations of objective scientific fact. D's report was prepared to ascertain facts as opposed to being in contemplation of judicial proceedings, *Marks & Spencer v. British Gas Corp* 1983 S.L.T. 196, [1982] C.L.Y. 4125; *Waddington v. Buchan Poultry Products Ltd* 1961 S.L.T. 428, [1961] C.L.Y. 1088. W could not instruct an ergonomist, the processes having been altered.

Held, motion refused, as the report was compiled post litem motam, *Hunter v. Douglas Reyburn & Co* 1993 S.L.T. 637, [1993] C.L.Y. 5601, could not be distinguished. Such a report remained confidential to the party entitled to protection of the material. Further, some of the actions then in contemplation were still proceeding, and the report might be said to be post litem motam in relation to the present case as W had in 1992 already begun to take time off work as a result of his condition. The fact that videotape evidence of the production operations, as they existed then, was available, and that similar processes still existed in other locations, was of some relevance.

WARD v. MARINE HARVEST 1996 S.C.L.R. 94, Judge not specified, OH.

6641. Commission and diligence–recovery of documents–confidentiality–records of education authority

[School Pupils Records (Scotland) Regulations 1990 (SI 1990 1551).]

B sought to have opened a confidential envelope containing records from M's school lodged by an education authority (S) in response to a commission and diligence granted to B in M's action for damages. M averred that as a result of an accident in June 1991, in which M had fallen from a pipe spanning a railway line onto electric power cables, his personality had changed; that he had become withdrawn, and had few friends; that absence from school for a considerable period meant that he found schooling difficult; and that he had had absences from school which had resulted in him being reported to the children's panel for truancy. B averred that M had shown behavioural and truancy problems since attending his present school in August 1990, for which he had been treated in 1990. S argued that, as the documents contained records of communications with the social work authority relating to the involvement of the reporter, they should remain confidential, as this was essential if S were to function effectively as an education or social work authority; and that S were required by the School Pupils Records (Scotland) Regulations 1990 to keep certain categories of information confidential.

Held, granting the motion, that although M had not opposed B's motion, this was not decisive as the interest S were seeking to protect was quite distinct. The documents clearly might be confidential, as they might contain information which would not have been given to S had it been known to the informant that it might be disclosed to a third party, this confidentiality having been recognised by the 1990 Regulations. However, the cause and effect of M's behavioural problems had a significant bearing on damages, and justice required that B should have the opportunity to prove that M's problems predated the accident, which they could not hope to do effectively without access to the documents, and B's need for access outweighed S's claim for confidentiality. S's concerns would be adequately met by the fact that the call in the specification of documents was restricted to records relating to M's behavioural problems and truancy at his school from August 1990 to date and that the documents were to be produced to a commissioner who would take only excerpts of entries falling within the call, *Parks v. Tayside RC* 1989 S.L.T. 345, [1989] C.L.Y. 4706 followed.

McLEOD v. BRITISH RAILWAYS BOARD 1995 S.C.L.R. 1140, Judge not specified, OH.

6642. Commission and diligence–recovery of documents–recovery sought before record closed

D, manufacturers of a drug, reclaimed against the Lord Ordinary's decision (1992 S.L.T. 344) in an action by P for loss allegedly as a result of using the drug, to grant a motion for recovery of documents before D had lodged defences. After D was granted leave to reclaim the action had been sisted. Subsequently, it was recognised that numerous actions had been raised in England, Scotland and Northern Ireland and that it was more cost effective for a master statement of claim to be prepared with a view to the common issues being resolved in England. The Legal Aid Board in England then withdrew public support for the claimants in February 1994 and the majority of actions fell. The sist in P's action was then recalled. D argued that the Lord Ordinary had misdirected himself. P had called for records relating to pre-marketing research and development and results of clinical trials as well as post-marketing research and monitoring as part of her calls. In terms of *Moore v. Greater Glasgow Health Board* 1979 S.L.T. 42, [1979] C.L.Y. 3296, the test was one of necessity; as P had averred that it was known scientifically and by D by the late 1970s that a risk of dependence existed, this test was not satisfied. P argued that the main thrust of her case was directed to D's own clinical trials and research programme; as it was clear that the documents would be required prior to the record closing, the proper course was to permit recovery without further delay.

Held, allowing the reclaiming motion, that the test was one of necessity, *Moore*. As defences had not yet been lodged it was not a question of whether P needed the documents to reply to D's averments. Further, P had been able to make out her claim in reasonable detail thus recovery was not necessary to enable P to plead her case. The motion should have been refused pending defences being lodged to see what points were truly at issue. If the matter was at large for the court, the possibility that the Scottish Legal Aid Board would also withdraw public funding could not be ignored where granting the order would involve a large public expenditure before a decision had been taken.

McINALLY v. JOHN WYETH & BROTHER 1995 S.C.L.R. 1117, Judge not specified, IH.

6643. Contempt of court–proof

H, the defender in an action of divorce by W, appealed against a finding of contempt by failing to return the parties' child timeously after access. W wrote a letter supporting H's appeal. H argued that where the alleged contempt was said to have occurred outwith the court and the necessary facts were not admitted, the court could not make such a finding without a hearing on the evidence. The court would require to be satisfied that H had wilfully disregarded the court's authority and that the contempt had been proved beyond reasonable doubt. H had given the court an undertaking which had resulted in W's motion that H be found in contempt being withdrawn, and which was incorporated in an interlocutor. H claimed that the interlocutor was unclear and that the sheriff was not entitled to infer from its terms that there had been previous difficulties and that subsequent failures would be regarded seriously.

Held, appeal allowed. The sheriff should have proceeded to proof and was not entitled to rely on ex parte statements in rejecting H's denials of wilful disregard.

Observed, that the court had serious doubts about the wisdom of recording an "undertaking" to obey orders of the court, which parties were bound to do anyway, and that any warning issued to a party should be recorded in unambiguous terms.

JOHNSTON v. JOHNSTON 1995 S.C.L.R. 888, Judge not specified, IH.

6644. Court of Session–family mediation

ACT OF SEDERUNT (CIVIL EVIDENCE) (FAMILY MEDIATION)) 1996, SI 1996 140 (S.12); made under the Civil Evidence (Family Mediation (Scotland) Act 1995 s.1. In force: February 14, 1996; £1.10.

This Act of Sederunt provides the form of certificate of approval granted by the Lord President of the Court of Session to organisations under the Civil Evidence (Family Mediation) (Scotland) Act 1995 s.1 (4) for the purposes of s.1 (2).

6645. Court of Session–rules of court

ACT OF SEDERUNT (RULES OF THE COURT OF SESSION AMENDMENT NO.3) (MISCELLANEOUS) 1996, SI 1996 1756 (S.146); made under the Child Abduction and Custody Act 1985 s.10, s.24; the Court of Session Act 1988 s.5, s.6; the Prevention of Terrorism (Temporary Provisions) Act 1989 Sch.4 para.19; the Merchant Shipping Act 1995 s.177; the Proceeds of Crime (Scotland) Act 1995 s.36; and the Olympics Association Right (Infringement Proceedings) Regulations 1995 Reg.5. In force: August 5, 1996; £3.20.

Makes amendments to the Rules of the Court of Session 1994 (SI 1994 1443) relating, inter alia, to petitions, appeals under statute, appeals from the Child Support Commissioner, the International Oil Pollution Compensation Fund, family actions, referral to family mediation and conciliation service, infringement proceedings relating to intellectual property, recognition, registration and enforcement of foreign judgments, applications under the Child Abduction and Custody Act 1985 and applications under the Financial Services Act 1986.

6646. Court of Session–rules of court

ACT OF SEDERUNT (RULES OF THE COURT OF SESSION AMENDMENT NO.4) (MISCELLANEOUS) 1996, SI 1996 2168 (S.175); made under the Civil Jurisdiction and Judgments Act 1982 s.12, s.48; the Transport Act 1985 Sch.4 para.14; the Court of Session Act 1988 s.5, s.6; the Prevention of Terrorism (Temporary Provisions)

Act 1989 Sch.4 para.11, Sch.4 para.19; and the Proceeds of Crime (Scotland) Act 1995 s.48, Sch.1 para.11. In force: September 23, 1996; £4.70.

This Act of Sederunt amends the Rules of the Court of Session 1994 (SI 1994 1443) relating, inter alia, to first orders in petitions, notices to admit and of non-admission, intimations to parties whose agent has withdrawn, pursuer's offers, optional procedure before executing commission and diligence, Outer House appeals, actions of damages, actions of recovery, recognition, registration and enforcement of foreign jugdments etc. and causes in relation to confiscation of proceeds of crime.

6647. Court of Session–rules of court

ACT OF SEDERUNT (RULES OF THE COURT OF SESSION AMENDMENT NO.5) (FAMILY ACTIONS AND MISCELLANEOUS) 1996, SI 1996 2587 (S.203); made under the Court of Session Act 1998 s.5. In force: November 1, 1996; £3.20.

This Act of Sederunt amends the Rules of the Court of Session 1994 (SI 1994 1443) in relation to, and makes provision for, proceedings under the Children (Scotland) Act 1995. Part I makes new provision for parental responsibilities and parental rights, guardianship, the administration of a child's property and court orders with respect to these matters.

6648. Court of Session–settlement of claims

ACT OF SEDERUNT (RULES OF THE COURT OF SESSION AMENDMENT NO.6) 1996, SI 1996 2769 (S.213); made under the Court of Session Act 1988 s.5. In force: October 14, 1996; £0.65.

This Act of Sederunt revokes the Rules of the Court of Session Chapter 34A which provides for an offer made by a pursuer to a defender to settle a claim by the pursuer against the defender and amends the Rules by omitting the Chapter and such Forms in the appendix to the Rules as are applicable in terms of the chapter. The Chapter is however, to continue to have effect and the forms to be applicable, as respects any such offer made before the Act of Sederunt comes into force.

6649. Decree–absolvitor–non-appearance of pursuer

Proof in an action which had remained on the adjustment roll from August 1993 until June 1994 was allowed on July 27, 1994. The pursuers were ordained on November 22, 1994 to sist a mandatary by January 20, 1995. They failed to do so and were allowed a further 21 days but did not sist a mandatary until March 9, 1995. On April 28, 1995 the pursuers sought discharge of a diet of proof fixed for May 2, 1995. This was refused. Upon the pursuers failing to appear at the proof diet, the defenders moved for absolvitor in the principal action and dismissal of the counterclaim.

Held, that in light of the procedural history of the action, the pursuers should not be given a further opportunity of delaying matters by being ordained to intimate whether they intended to proceed; and motion granted.

MUNRO & MILLER (PAKISTAN) v. WYVERN STRUCTURES LTD 1996 S.L.T. 135, Judge not specified, OH.

6650. Diligence–arrestment–arrestment of aircraft in hands of owner–competency

[Administration of Justice Act 1956 (c.46).]

An aircraft was arrested in the hands of its owners through the use of a style of schedule of arrestment of a ship. The arrestment proceeded upon warrants granted by a sheriff clerk to arrest on the dependence and to found jurisdiction, both as craved in the relative initial writ. Eight days later, the Court of Session, on an appeal from the sheriff, recalled the arrestment on the basis that the initial writ disclosed no colourable case. In a subsequent action the owners of the aircraft sought damages for wrongous diligence in respect of the period between service of the schedule of arrestment and the recall thereof during which the aircraft remained grounded. The owners averred that the form and mode of diligence were irregular but did not offer to prove malice. The arresters sought dismissal of the action, submitting that arrestment of the aircraft in the owner's hands was lawful as it was appropriate to equiparate an aircraft with a ship and that, accordingly, arrestment of an aircraft in the hands of its owner by affixing to it a copy schedule of the kind used for arrestment of ships was regular and correct. In any event, if the arrestment was irregular it constituted a technical informality in the absence of malice. It was further argued that the owners had not suffered any relevant loss since there was no reason for the aircraft to remain grounded if the arrestments were inept. There was no causal connection between any wrongful use of diligence and any losses by the owners.

Held, that (1) the arrestment was an irregular use of diligence as the special common law rule which in certain circumstances allowed for a ship to be arrested in the hands of its owners did not, either as a general proposition or under reference to the provisions of the Administration of Justice Act 1956, extend to aircraft, at least not to aircraft of a kind designed only to land on and take off from terra firma; (2) as the schedule of arrestment bore to arrest the aircraft whether it was in the hands of its owner or a third party it could not be described as a technical informality and rather its use against the aircraft amounted to a fundamental misuse of the warrant, giving rise to liability without the necessity to aver malice; (3) having regard to the arresters' resistance to recall of the arrestment, the arrestees were not obliged to take the risk of treating the purported arrestment as null and void and were entitled to seek judicial recall and (4) that any losses sustained pending such recall were caused by the use of diligence; and defence on merits repelled and proof restricted to quantum. Opinion reserved, on whether or not a seaplane might in some waterborne circumstances be liable to arrestment in the hands of its owner.

EMERALD AIRWAYS LTD v. NORDIC OIL SERVICES LTD 1996 S.L.T. 403, Judge not specified, OH.

6651. Diligence–arrestment–arrestment of ship

[Administration of Justice Act 1956 (c.46) s.47(1).]

Section 47(1) of the Administration of Justice Act 1956 provides that a warrant issued after commencement of that Part of the Act for arrestment on the dependence of an action shall only have effect in relation to detention of a ship where the ship is either the ship with which the action is concerned or all of the shares in the ship are owned by the defender against whom that conclusion is directed. Pursuers executed, to found jurisdiction and on the dependence of an action, an arrestment of a vessel owned by the defenders, and also subsequently of a second vessel. A third party sought recall of the arrestment of the second vessel. The third party argued, first, that the vessel was not competently arrested because they and not the defenders were the owners at the date of arrestment, the ship having been sold to them by the defenders by memorandum of agreement, which memorandum and in particular a bill of sale demonstrated their ownership; secondly, that the purpose of s.47(1) of the 1956 Act in relation to an action was to restrict the right to arrest to one ship, and thirdly, that the prior arrestment afforded ample security for the debt alleged to be due. It was argued for the pursuers that the 1956 Act had not removed the previous common law right to arrest more than one ship on the dependence of an *in personam* action such as the present.

Held, that (1) at the argument that the prior arrestment was sufficient security for the pursuers was only relevant if at the time of the arrestment the vessel remained in the ownership of the defenders and continued to do so, and was thus not open to the third party to advance; (2) any arrestment on the dependence of an action which fell within the definition of a maritime claim in Pt.I of the 1956 Act was restricted to one ship owned by the defenders, there being no substance in any purported distinction between an action *in rem* in England and an action *in personam* in Scotland, *Banco, The* [1971] P.137, [1970] C.L.Y. 2644 followed; (3) there was insufficient material to determine that ownership in the vessel had already passed from the defenders, but there was sufficient to demonstrate that the third party had agreed to purchase the vessel and therefore had title and interest to contest the arrestment and (4) the arrestment was inept as without warrant; and motion for recall granted.

INTERATLANTIC (NAMIBIA) (PTY) v. OKEANSKI RIBOLOV [1995] 2 Lloyd's Rep. 286, Lord Cameron, OH.

6652. Diligence–arrestment–on dependence–breach

[Breach of Arrestment Act 1581 (c.23).]

W sued B, a bank, for breach of arrestment. W had sued H for divorce and arrested £21,000 in the hands of B on the dependence of W's capital claim. The following day H transferred £7,000 from an account with B in Jersey to a branch with B in Paisley. H then withdrew £8,000 from the Paisley branch. W averred B had contravened the 1581 Act. W subsequently obtained decree for £1,500 against H and restricted her claim accordingly. B averred that (1) as at the date of the arrestment H's account was in Jersey and governed by the law of Jersey; B were under a duty to repay the balance at credit of the account only at that branch and their obligation had not been attached by the arrestment; (2) esto the arrestment was effective, H's total indebtedness to B exceeded any sums at credit. On procedure roll B argued W's action was incompetent *et separatim* irrelevant, (1) as the Act of 1581 had been impliedly repealed by desuetude: the Act had been amended but only insofar as deleting alienations made to defraud creditors and those provisions relating to escheat, and was capable of being in desuetude in respect of separate severable matters, *McAra v. Magistrates of Edinburgh* 1913 S.C. 1059 and (2) as W had no relevant averments of loss since W required to aver that the decree had not been satisfied: if W had received payment under the decree she would be suing where W had sustained no loss.

Held, proof allowed, that (1) the argument on desuetude was one of relevancy rather than competency. B's argument failed in respect that (a) B had no averments or plea in law in that respect; (b) contrary to B's argument, the Act had not become obsolete as respects breach of arrestment despite the repeal of the sanctions of corporal punishment and escheat of goods, as other remedies in the Act were enforceable even when there was no escheat in the context of a civil remedy, and (c) the fact that specific parts of the Act had been repealed excluded the theory that the remainder was impliedly repealed by desuetude and (2) W averred that she had suffered loss in consequence and it was an obvious inference that the decree remained unsatisfied.

Observed, that proof before answer was inappropriate where B's plea to relevancy was in an unusual and incorrect form (that W's averments "being irrelevant... should not be admitted to probation") and could not be given effect.

McSKIMMING v. ROYAL BANK OF SCOTLAND 1996 S.C.L.R. 547, Judge not specified, OH.

6653. Diligence–arrestment on dependence–recall–whether nimious and oppressive

A company which had been supplied with materials and against which decree had passed in the sheriff court for payment therefor, raised an action in the Court of Session against the suppliers and effected arrestments on the dependence. The action was for damages allegedly arising from delay in the supply of the materials. It could have been raised as a counterclaim in the sheriff court, where decree had passed against the company undefended. In seeking recall of the arrestments on the ground that they were nimious and oppressive, the suppliers argued that the facts demonstrated that the predominant motive of the company had been to injure or embarrass the suppliers rather than to obtain security for the alleged debt.

Held, that the combination of the features that the summons, and particularly the condescendence on damages, were irrelevant and lacking in specification, that there was no explanation for the absence of a counterclaim in the sheriff court action, and that there had been no demand for payment before the present action had been raised, was sufficient to lead to the inference that the arrestments had been laid predominantly either as an attack on the suppliers' financial credit or as a form of riposte to the sheriff court action, and that they were accordingly nimious and oppressive; and arrestments recalled.

HYDRALOAD RESEARCH & DEVELOPMENTS LTD v. BONE CONNELL & BAXTERS LTD 1996 S.L.T. 219, Judge not specified, OH.

6654. Diligence–inhibition–error in designation of debtor–whether inhibition enforceable

A sought reduction of a disposition by T in favour of C as it was granted and recorded when there was an inhibition outstanding against T at the instance of A. C subsequently disponed the property to M. At the time of T's disposition to C, the interim report on search failed to disclose the inhibition against T since the designation of T's forename in the notice and letters of inhibition was "Steve", whereas in the disposition in his favour and in the disposition in favour of C it was "Stephen John". A argued that (1) reduction was appropriate since M had a remedy against the searchers (S) who had carried out the interim report. M argued that, in the circumstances, reduction would be inequitable. On the evidence, it was established that (1) T was known interchangeably as "Steve" and "Stephen John" or "Stephen J" and was clearly identifiable when associated with the address concerned; (2) the memorandum for search which instructed the interim report designed T as "Stephen John" T and failed to disclose the entries in the personal register; (3) during the period from 1990 to 1991, the developing computer systems would not have disclosed an entry in respect of a diminutive name although a manual search of the register would have linked the diminutive and formal designations with T's address; nor would the official system developed by the Keeper of the Registers have disclosed the diminutive entry on the basis of instructions containing a full designation until 1992 or 1993.

Held, that the facts failed to established a breach of duty by S, or that M had any claim against S; and case put out by order for discussion of further procedure, that (1) previous procedure in the matter had established various tests and, according to them, T would not have been identified in his full name as a debtor affected by the inhibition; (2) the problem also related to registered interests in land, and since the Land Registration (Scotland) Act 1979 s.6(1)(c) required the keeper to maintain a title sheet in respect of a registered interest in land which showed "any subsisting entry in the Register of Inhibitions and Adjudications adverse to the interest". The keeper was not required to seek his information from extrinsic evidence. A person's designation had to be such as to make the identity of the person clear to a third party and that could only be achieved by designation in the context of the public register; (3) the problem was whether T was effectively inhibited as far as third party interests were concerned, and extrinsic evidence could not be employed to establish this since faith in the register was fundamental to the Scots system of land tenure, *Lattimore v. Singleton Dunn & Co.* (1911) 2 S.L.T. 360; (4) although the designation used was sufficiently specific for the purposes of the initial writ in the sheriff court action, A had determined the scope of the inhibition on the dependence thereof, and the inhibition was limited to the identification which A adopted. A had knowledge of the names used by T and chose to use only part of T's designation and was, therefore, not entitled to the benefit of the inhibition, and (5) the search was carried out by S in a reasonable manner using competent and appropriate methods and, on that basis, the keeper would have been in difficulty in 1990 to 1991 if T's interest had required to be registered in the Land Register rather than in the Register of Sasines since the unequivocal link between the registration of particulars and T's designation in the register of inhibitions would have been missing.

ATLAS APPOINTMENTS v. TINSLEY 1996 S.C.L.R. 476, Judge not specified, OH.

6655. Identification of responsible defender–personal injuries action

M, a refuse collector, sustained a back injury while lifting a refuse bag which had allegedly been overfilled by the defenders, H, a married couple. On the basis of the decision in *Caughie v. Robertson & Co* 1897 5 S.L.T. 139 he brought an action for damages against both defenders without specifying which of the defenders was liable, claiming that the accident had been caused through H's fault, ie. by overfilling the bag, and that H had a duty to take reasonable care for the health and safety of persons who would be liable to lift the bag.

Held, dismissing the action, that where damages for personal injuries were sought, the pursuer must identify the person responsible for the negligent act, but where it was possible that more than one person was responsible the process of identification could not be through a process of elimination unless the facts were such that they led to a conclusion as to the responsible person's identity, *Stout v. United Kingdom Atomic Energy Authority* 1979 S.L.T. 54, [1978] C.L.Y. 3598 considered.

MARONEY v. HUGMAN, *The Scotsman*, March 20, 1996, Lord Gill, OH.

6656. Judicial factors–tutor at law–competency of appointment–proper test

[Curators Act 1585 (c.25); Court of Session Act 1868 (c.100) s.101; Court of Session Act 1988 (c.36) s.52(2), Sch.2.]

The Curators Act 1585 provides, *inter alia*, that: "the nearest agnettis and kinsmen of naturall foulis Ideottis and furious Salbe seruit ressauit and preferrit according to the dispositioun of the commoun law to thair tutorie and curatorie". The procedure for the appointment of a tutor at law under that Act was superseded by s.101 of the Court of Session Act 1868 which in turn was repealed by s.52(2) of and Sch.2 to the Court of Session Act 1988. The father of a 23 year old woman who had sustained serious injury resulting in loss of mental capacity from a road traffic accident in 1971 petitioned the Outer House for appointment at her tutor in law in terms of the 1585 Act. The woman was incapable of managing her own affairs or of giving directions for their management. A *curator bonis* had already been appointed. He opposed the petition on the bases that (a) it was incompetent as the 1585 Act had been repealed either expressly or by implication, had fallen into *desuetude* and, in any event, the petition should have been presented to the Inner House, not the Outer House; (b) as the *incapax* was not a "natural fool", "idiot" or "furious", she fell outwith the ambit of the Act and (c) as the father had the *incapax* in his custody, it was incompetent for him to be appointed her tutor at law.

Held, that (1) the 1585 Act had not been expressly or impliedly repealed, and had not fallen into *desuetude*; the replacement of the more detailed procedure of s.101 of the 1868 Act by that provided by the Rules of Court, and the subsequent, unreplaced deletion of those rules was not a reason for denying the existence of the right given under the 1585 Act, and the necessary machinery could be provided by the court; (2) it was competent to bring the petition before the Outer House; (3) the 1585 Act should be construed in modern phraseology, and the test for the appointment of a *tutor dative* or *curator bonis*, that the *incapax* was in such a mental condition as to be incapable of managing his or her affairs or of giving directions for their management, was equally applicable; (4) the *incapax* was not in the custody of the petitioner as she was an adult and, in any event, as the petitioner would be required to find caution and would be subject to the supervision of the Accountant of Court, there would be no conflict of interest arising from the fact that the *incapax* lived in the same house as the petitioner and (5) it was appropriate to deal with the matter in the same way as a petition for the appointment of curator bonis or tutor dative, with a petition containing sufficient averments as to the factual circumstances and the reason why the appointment was sought and the lodging of two recent medical certificates; and the petition granted subject to production of such certificates.

BRITTON v. BRITTON'S CURATOR BONIS 1996 S.L.T. 1272, Judge not specified, OH.

6657. Jury trial–issues–late lodging "on cause shown"

[Act of Sederunt (Rules of the Court of Session) 1994 (SI 1994 1443) r.37.1.]

Rule 37.1 (2) of the Rules of the Court of Session 1994 provides inter alia that where a pursuer fails to lodge a proposed issue, he shall be held to have departed from his right to jury trial unless the court "on cause shown" otherwise orders. A pursuer's solicitors failed to lodge issues for a jury trial timeously and sought their late receipt by the court, explaining that the date for lodging issues had been overlooked because of a change in personnel in their office. The defenders contended that the rule was peremptory in its terms.

Held, that the pursuer had shown just sufficient cause; and late lodging of issues allowed. Opinion, that where a rule provided a specific relief from its peremptory requirements the court should hesitate to apply the wider powers of general relief in r.2.1 (1).

McGEE v. MATTHEW HALL LTD 1996 S.L.T. 399, Judge not specified, OH.

6658. Jury trial–motion for new trial–approach to be taken by appeal court

[Court of Session Act 1988 (c.36) s.29.]

The Court of Session Act 1988 s.29 (1) provides that a party to a jury action may apply for a new trial, inter alia, on the ground of excess or inadequacy of damages. A driver injured in a road traffic accident was awarded solatium of £120,000 by a jury. His most significant injury was a fracture of the right elbow which had repercussions for his work, domestic life and participation at international level in his sport, clay pigeon shooting. A motion by the defenders for a new trial on the ground that the damages were excessive was granted and the verdict of the jury was set aside. At a second trial the jury awarded solatium of £95,000 and the defenders moved to have the verdict set aside on the ground that the damages awarded were excessive.

Held (Lord Abernethy dissenting), that (1) although the award was very high and higher than the pattern of previous judicial awards, that was not of itself sufficient to conclude that the award was excessive and there was possibly some force in the view that judges were increasingly out of touch with awards made by juries in the proper exercise of their function and (2) the jury were entitled to consider the pursuer's injuries as very serious and to make a large award for the consequences upon his whole life and, adopting a broad approach and having regard to all the factors including the fact that this was the second high award, the award could not by described as excessive in the sense of going beyond what a reasonable jury, properly instructed, could have awarded and resulting in a gross injustice to the defenders; and motion refused. Per Lord Abernethy (dissenting): (1) the starting point for assessing the validity of the jury's award was for the court to reach a view as to what a proper figure would be, drawing assistance from previously decided cases, but the fact that a previous award in this case had already been set aside was irrelevant to consideration of the motion and (2) a judge would not be entitled to make an award for solatium in this case which would approach even one half of the figure awarded by the jury and accordingly the award was excessive and the motion for a new trial should be granted.

Observed, (per Lords Kirkwood and Abernethy), that (1) it would be in the interests of justice if juries were now given some guidance in the submissions and directions as to the appropriate level of award; (2) (per Lords Kirkwood and Abernethy) the working rule of 100 per cent permissible error, applied in earlier cases, was of questionable validity particularly where the sums involved were large, and it could not be applied to awards made by juries in addition to any latitude already allowed and (3) (per Lord Abernethy) it might be advisable if the court were given power to assess damages on a successful motion for a new trial and so save a further procedure.

GIRVAN v. INVERNESS FARMERS DAIRY (NO.2) 1996 S.L.T. 631, Judge not specified, IH.

6659. Order for party to undergo psychological examination–competency

An employee allegedly injured in an accident at work raised an action of damages. Her employers averred that her symptoms were caused by psychological problems and sought an order for her examination by a named clinical psychologist.

Opinion, provisionally, that an order for examination by a clinical psychologist was competent.

McLAREN v. REMPLOY 1996 S.L.T. 382, Judge not specified, OH.

6660. Pleadings–construction–fair notice of evidence

L, a health board, reclaimed against the Lord Ordinary's decision awarding their employee, P, damages for loss resulting from a back injury which she allegedly sustained in the course of her employment. At proof, the pleadings were crucial in determining the issues between the parties and the admissibility of certain evidence. P averred that on July 11, 1989, as she and a nursing auxiliary were attempting to lift a severely disabled patient, M, from a wheelchair into an aquajac bath, M went into spasm and threw himself backwards forcing P to support his whole weight, thus causing her injury. L should have known that M was difficult to lift because of his poor medical condition and that in lifting him, P would be required to support an excessive weight. L failed in their duty to provide appropriate equipment, including a hoist to lift M into the bath. L averred that wheeling M into the bathroom and lifting him on to the aquajac from the wheelchair was the simplest solution to permit bathing by M. At proof, L questioned P and the expert witnesses on the use of a pivot lift, P objected on the ground that there was no notice in the pleadings regarding pivot lifting. L argued that their pleadings did not tie their evidence to any particular method of lifting. After allowing the evidence under reservation, the Lord Ordinary sustained P's objection as there was no reference to a pivot lift in the pleadings and the lifting process averred by P clearly described a lifting of the whole weight of M. In addition, there was no case of contributory negligence against P based on using a wrong lift. L moved to amend their pleadings, which was refused. On appeal, L argued that the Lord Ordinary erred in excluding evidence from consideration on the issue of whether P was required to use the type of lift which she did or whether it was foreseeable that P and the auxiliary would engage in a full body lift of the patient from the wheelchair to the bath. The verb "lift" should not have been construed narrowly and their pleadings covered all methods of lifting, including the pivot lift. In addition, the Lord Ordinary erred by failing to have regard to the medical evidence which established a prima facie inference that P's symptoms had cleared up by the date of proof, and in preferring the opinion of P's expert, G, to L's expert.

Held, refusing the reclaiming motion, that the Lord Ordinary correctly excluded the line of evidence regarding a pivot lift as the pleadings, properly construed, did not place in issue the foreseeability of the use by P and the auxiliary of a full body lift of M from the wheelchair to the aquajac and there was no basis in the pleadings for any suggestion that L would have expected P to employ a pivot lift. L's averments had to be read as a whole and in their context of responding to P's pleadings, which were confined to a lift in which the whole weight of the patient was removed from the seat and supported by the nurses without any assistance from M. The pleadings enabled the Lord Ordinary properly to hold that there was no issue between the parties as to the employment of the type of lift that P said she employed. In respect of the medical evidence, there was sufficient and cogent evidence to entitle the Lord Ordinary to conclude that P's condition had not improved, that her symptoms were attributable to the accident and that G's opinions were to be preferred.

PARKER v. LANARKSHIRE HEALTH BOARD 1996 S.C.L.R. 57, Judge not specified, IH.

6661. Pleadings–relevancy and specification–averments of acquittal on certain criminal charges on indictment

An individual raised an action against a chief constable, averring that he had suffered injuries following assaults upon him by police officers. The defender averred that the pursuer had been convicted of certain offences following a trial. The pursuer admitted the indictment and extract convictions incorporated into the pleadings, but averred that he had been acquitted of certain other charges. The defender argued that the averments relating to the pursuer's acquittal were irrelevant and should not be admitted to probation. The pursuer submitted that the averments were relevant as narrative and in response to the defender's averments.

Held, that (1) proof of the fact that in the criminal proceedings the pursuer had been acquitted of certain charges would not yield any relevant inference in the civil proceedings as to whether the facts libelled in those charges had occurred and (2) the disputed averments were of limited relevancy but the full narrative should be clearly before the court as it would touch on issues which the court would require to consider; and proof before answer allowed.

DENNISON v. CHIEF CONSTABLE, STRATHCLYDE POLICE 1996 S.L.T. 74, Judge not specified, OH.

6662. Pleadings–relevancy and specification defences–skeleton defences

In an action of payment in the sheriff court the pursuer sought payment of a sum of money which he maintained was outstanding in respect of a loan made by him to the defender. He averred the dates and amounts of payments made to the defender, the purpose of the loan and the amounts of certain repayments made by the defender to him. The defender met these averments with a general denial. At debate before the sheriff, the defender sought to have proof of the pursuer's averments restricted to writ or oath and the pursuer sought decree de plano on the basis that the defender had not given fair notice of his position and that the defences were irrelevant. The defender maintained that fair notice had been given and he was entitled to put the pursuer to his proof. The sheriff found in the defender's favour and the pursuer appealed to the sheriff principal who allowed the appeal. The defender appealed to the Court of Session, arguing that he was entitled to make use of a bare denial which, in the circumstances, gave the pursuer fair notice of his position. The pursuer relied on *Ellon Castle Estates Co v. Macdonald* 1975 S.L.T. (Notes) 66, [1975] C.L.Y. 4057, and argued that if a denial of averments was not candid it was proper to treat the averments in question as admitted. Accordingly, the general denial of the pursuer's specific averments fell to be regarded as a judicial admission of loan with the result that the sheriff principal had been well founded in pronouncing decree de plano.

Held (Lord Morison dissenting), that while it was a well recognised rule of written pleading that failure to deny an averment of fact within a party's knowledge was to be construed as an admission of that fact, there was no warrant in principle or practice for any corollary to that rule to the effect that where a statement made by one party of a fact within his knowledge was denied, that should be held to constitute an implied admission merely because it was felt that the person making the denial had been less than candid; and appeal allowed. Opinion (per the Lord Justice-Clerk (Ross)), that any practice which had developed since *Ellon Castle Estates Co v. Macdonald* of treating a general denial as amounting to an implied admission, merely because there had been a lack of candour, was not a sound practice. Per Lord Morison (dissenting): While there was no general rule that a bare denial would necessarily be held irrelevant, equally there was no general rule that it would be taken at face value, and to hold the defences relevant in the present case would encourage lack of candour and detract from the advantages of the current system and practice of Scottish pleading.

GRAY v. BOYD 1996 S.L.T. 60, Judge not specified, IH.

6663. Pleadings–separate conclusions directed against different defenders–competency

A company owned the whole recording and performance rights of a group "The Drifters". Certain individuals and companies were managing and promoting a group known as "Sounds of the Drifters" allegedly as "The Drifters"; a singer in "Sounds of the Drifters" had previously sung with "The Drifters" and had contracted with the company not to utilise the name "The Drifters". The company sought, in separate conclusions in the same action, first, an accounting of profits from passing off against the individuals and companies ("the promoters") jointly and severally; secondly, damages for breach of contract against the singer; and thirdly, interdict against the promotion or performance of "Sounds of the Drifters" as "The Drifters". The court having raised the matter *ex proprio motu*, the defenders argued that it was incompetent for a pursuer to sue more than one defender in the same action, with separate conclusions against each defender, based on separate and independent grounds of debt. They also argued that the action was incompetent as leading to double recovery, and irrelevantly pled as an action of passing off. The pursuers argued, that first there were not separate and independent grounds of debt and that the fact that different legal grounds of action appeared together did not render an action incompetent: here there was a single wrong, the performance of "Sounds of the Drifters" in a situation in which a passing off occurred; secondly, a pursuer was entitled to sue defenders one at a time until compensated for the wrong involved: even if there had been separate actions, the same problems would have existed, and the solution lay in a partial sist of proceedings; thirdly, the pursuers had relevantly pled goodwill attaching to services, a misrepresentation by the defenders leading to the public confusing the defenders' services and those of the pursuers, and damage being suffered because of the erroneous belief engendered by the misrepresentation.

Held, that (1) it was incompetent for a pursuer to sue more than one defender in the same action with separate conclusions against each defender based on separate and independent grounds of debt; (2) in their first two conclusions the pursuers sought against different defenders two differed remedies, based on the separate and independent grounds of debt of the delict of passing off and of breach of contract, that injustice would result from permitting the action to continue in two separate procedures following the two separate conclusions and that the action was accordingly incompetent; (3) the absence of a specific plea to competency was not a barrier to dismissal of the action on that ground, and (4) in a passing off action a pursuer might not take both an inquiry as to profits and an inquiry as to damages, as was here attempted by the pursuers, and the action was for this reason also incompetent; and action dismissed as incompetent, *Western Bank Liquidators v. Douglas* (1860) 22 D. 447, followed. Opinion, that the company had stated a relevant case of passing off, *Reckitt & Colman Products v. Borden Inc* [1990] 1 All E.R. 873, [1990] C.L.Y. 3465 followed.

TREADWELL'S DRIFTERS INC v. RCL LTD 1996 S.L.T. 1048, Judge not specified, OH.

6664. Prescription–amendment of pleadings after expiry of prescriptive period–change in basis of case

[Prescription and Limitation (Scotland) Act 1973 (c.52) s.6(1) and s.11 (1).]

A company, M instructed solicitors to raise an action against another limited company, A, for payment of a debt. The solicitors carried out that instruction and arrested funds in the hands of a third party, B, in respect of sums due by B to A. No company existed by name of A but a company was registered in name of AB. On January 23, 1991, more than 60 days after the arrestment was lodged, a petition was presented for the winding up of AB. On March 13, 1991 the solicitors wrote to B, without the authority of M, authorising the loosing of the arrestment. M then raised an action against the solicitors for breach of contract and professional negligence on the basis that the unauthorised loosing of the arrestment caused loss to the pursuers as it prevented them from having a preference in the liquidation of AB and having a share in the liquidator's distribution. The sheriff dismissed the action on the basis that the arrestment was invalid *ab initio* as it was in name of a non-existent company. The liquidator, however, regarded the arrestment as valid and, but for it being loosed, would have allowed the pursuers a share in the distribution. The pursuers appealed to the Court of Session and lodged a minute of amendment in which they sought to add averments of a new ground of fault by which the defenders ought to have verified the registered name of AB prior to arresting. The minute also averred that an action against AB was now time barred and that, accordingly, the defenders' failure to secure a claim against AB resulted in loss to the pursuers. The defenders argued that the ground of fault in the minute was time barred as no relevant claim had been made within the quinquennium. The pursuers argued that the *terminus a quo* for prescription was January 16, 1991, the date of decree in the pursuers' court action against A, and not the date of lodging the arrestment.

Held, that (1) as the right to raise an action of reparation accrued when iniuria concurred with damnum, that occurred at the latest on November 19, 1990 when the action had been raised and the arrestment lodged; (2) although the action would remain one based on breach of contract and negligence if amendment were allowed, the amendment proposed would change the basis of the pursuers' case by adding a new ground of fault resulting in the pursuers seeking damages for a different reason, so that the amendment was time-barred; (3) the liquidator would not have been acting lawfully if he had entertained the pursuers' claim and, in any event, the pursuers would have had to have the agreement of the other creditors to allow them to participate in the distribution, for which there were no averments and (4) the absence of averments of such agreement was fatal to the relevancy of a claim based upon a lost chance to participate in the distribution; and motion to amend and appeal refused. *Yeoman's Executrix v. Ferries* 1967 S.L.T. 332, [1968] C.L.Y. 3719 distinguished.

J G MARTIN PLANT HIRE LTD v. MacDONALD 1996 S.L.T. 1192, Judge not specified, IH.

6665. Prescription–negative–date from which time runs–breach of contract–date when litigation became enforceable

[Prescription and Limitation (Scotland) Act 1973 (c.52) s.6(3), Sch.1 para.1, Sch.2 para.4.]

F appealed against a sheriff's decision to dismiss his action for declarator that he had enforceable rights under a trade union personal insurance plan and decree for payment against U, the insurers of the sick pay part of the plan. F averred that there was a deferred period of 39 weeks under the plan from the time he ceased work, which period expired on June 30 1988. The action was commenced in December 1993. The sheriff sustained U's plea of prescription. F argued that (1) the obligation to pay did not become enforceable in terms of s.6(3) of the 1973 Act until U failed to make payment after being asked to do so, which was by letter of February 13, 1989; while the right of action might have accrued on the expiry of the 39 weeks, it could only be enforced when U had refused to pay and (2) alternatively, the benefit under the plan, in F's case payments of £80 per week, was an obligation on U to make payment by instalments within Sch.2 para.4(1)(a) and did not prescribe so long as F remained incapacitated and entitled to the benefit.

Held, refusing the appeal, that (1) in determining when an obligation became enforceable, it was necessary to have regard to the terms of the contract in question and any principle of law affecting that contract. There was nothing in the present contract to support F's argument. The general principle in *Scott Lithgow v. Secretary of State for Defence* 1989 S.L.T. 236, [1989] C.L.Y. 3970 applied. The obligation became enforceable on the date from which F became entitled to payment. Dicta in certain U.S. and New Zealand cases and statements in some English textbooks founded on by F were not of assistance in interpreting the 1973 Act and (2) Sch.2 para.4(1) applied to an obligation to pay a sum of money payable by instalments; here there was no "sum of money" as, the benefit being payable until recovery, retirement or death, the total payable was not ascertainable.

FLYNN v. UNUM 1996 S.C.L.R. 258, Judge not specified, IH.

6666. Prescription–negative–date from which time runs–obligation to make reparation–knowledge of loss attributable to fault

[Prescription and Limitation (Scotland) Act 1973 (c.52) s.11.]

Housing built for a housing association suffered a failure in the roughcast, of which the association had become aware more than five years before raising an action against their architects and their building contractors. The association argued that their claim had not prescribed because they had not been aware, and could not with reasonable diligence have become aware, more than five years before the action was raised, that the failure had been the result of any act, neglect or default. The architects and contractors contended that it was sufficient for the association's right to have prescribed that the association had been aware for more than five years before raising the action that they had suffered loss.

Held, granting absolvitor, that on the facts the pursuers had been aware more than five years before the raising of the action that they had suffered loss, injury and damage and the loss had been caused by the defenders. Opinion, that it would have been sufficient to prevent prescription of the association's right that they were not aware, and could not reasonably have become aware, more than five years before raising the action that their loss had been caused by act, neglect or default, *Greater Glasgow Health Board v. Baxter Clark & Paul* 1992 S.L.T. 35, [1992] C.L.Y. 6209 and *Dunfermline DC v. Blyth & Blyth Associates* 1985 S.L.T. 345, [1985] C.L.Y. 4601 discussed.

KIRK CARE HOUSING ASSOCIATION LTD v. CRERAR AND PARTNERS 1996 S.L.T. 150, Judge not specified, OH.

6667. Prescription–negative–date from which time runs–obligation to make reparation–sufficiency of averments that pursuers not aware that loss, injury or damage had occurred

[Prescription and Limitation (Scotland) Act 1973 (c.52), s.6(1) and s.11 (3).]

The Prescription and Limitation (Scotland) Act 1973 provides that an action for reparation must be raised within five years from the date when loss, injury or damage occurred, except that where the pursuer was not aware, and could not with reasonable diligence have been aware, that the loss, injury or damage had occurred, the action must be raised within five years from the date when the pursuer first became, or could with reasonable diligence have become, so aware. A husband and wife sought damages from their former solicitors on the ground of their alleged professional negligence. The pursuers' losses were actually sustained on March 20, 1984, when, according to their averments, the title to a hotel they were purchasing was recorded, contrary to their instructions, in name of their son alone. The pursuers, who had resided in England, averred that they did not become aware of this until August 1985 when their son disappeared and a heritable creditor began moves to enforce its security over the hotel. The action was raised just under five years later. The defenders claimed that the case was time-barred. The sheriff allowed a proof before answer. The sheriff principal sustained an appeal by the defenders on the view that the pursuers had not made sufficient averments that they did not know and could not with reasonable diligence have known of their loss at an earlier date. The pursuers appealed to the Court of Session. They contended that taking their averments as a whole, their position was that they were in a continuing state of ignorance that they had sustained loss and damage caused by an act, neglect or default of the defenders, and that their ignorance was not due to any lack of reasonable diligence on their part. The defenders argued that there were no averments to show that the pursuers could reasonably have remained in ignorance of the fact that they had sustained a loss.

Held, that (1) what was required under s.11 (3) was an awareness not only of the fact of loss having occurred but of the fact that it was a loss caused by negligence; (2) where the pursuers averred, as here, that they were not aware that they had sustained a loss at all, the question was whether, in all the circumstances, they had any reason to exercise reasonable diligence in order to discover whether a loss had occurred and (3) the pursuers had averred sufficient facts and circumstances to put the reasonableness of their ignorance in issue; and appeal allowed. Dicta in *Greater Glasgow Health Board v. Baxter Clark & Paul* 1992 S.L.T. 35, [1992] C.L.Y. 6209, approved.

GLASPER v. RODGER 1996 S.L.T. 44, Judge not specified, IH.

6668. Proof or jury trial–special cause

[Court of Session Act 1988 (c.36) s.9.]

A prison officer sought damages arising from a road accident in which he averred he sustained a wrist injury with prospective deterioration which had resulted in the loss of his employment. The defender opposed the allowance of issues on the basis of the extensive averments of loss challenged by the defender in that (1) the pursuer had an extensive medical history independent of the accident, (2) the pursuer had exaggerated his symptoms and had attempted to produce misleading results in tests, and (3) the pursuer had a poor work record and had been recommended for discharge.

Held, that the combination of matters raised constituted special cause to justify withholding the case from jury trial and proof allowed. *Doubted*, whether an analogy drawn by the pursuer between civil and criminal jury trials was appropriate given that juries always judged the facts of serious crimes, whereas s.9 of the Court of Session Act 1988 permitted a proof to be ordered on cause shown.

MEECHAN v. McFARLANE 1996 S.L.T. 208, Judge not specified, OH.

6669. Proof or jury trial–special cause

[Court of Session Act 1988 (c.36) s.9.]

An action arising out of a road accident was raised by an individual who sought damages comprising solatium and loss of earnings. Issues were allowed. The condition of the pursuer subsequently deteriorated and a curator bonis was appointed and sisted in his place as pursuer. At the same time, the pleadings were amended to include the issues of post-traumatic stress syndrome, the ongoing costs of the administration of the curatory estate and special needs of the incapax. The defender argued that introduction of these new issues complicated the pursuer's case and amounted to "special cause" in terms of s.9(b). The pursuer contended that although the condition of the incapax had deteriorated, necessitating the introduction of fresh heads of claim, there had been no material alteration in the character of the cause since issues were first allowed, such as would justify a different course of action.

Held, that as there would be a serious risk of confusion and error on the part of any jury confronted by the numerous and complex issues of fact arising in the case, special cause did exist as to why issues should not be allowed; and proof allowed.

McKECHNIE'S CURATOR BONIS v. GRIBBEN 1996 S.L.T. 136, Judge not specified, OH.

6670. Proof or jury trial–special cause–claim for wage loss and loss of employability

O sought allowance of issues in an action for damages against his employers (M) in respect of an accident at work on October 1, 1992. M attacked as lacking in specification and unsuitable for a jury O's averments that "[O] has been unfit for any work since the date of the said accident. He is permanently unfit for his previous employment or any employment other than of a sedentary nature. His prospects of obtaining alternative employment are poor. He is at a material disadvantage in the labour market... [O] is an upholsterer to trade. He worked in his trade from about 1974 to 1990. He is permanently unfit for upholstery work... He is registered as disabled... he was paid off by [M, for whom he had worked since June 2, 1992], on or about July 30, 1993. He had lost and continues to lose wages." M averred that O would, in any event, have been made redundant on July 30 along with a number of M's other employees. O argued that it was not necessary to aver specific details of wage loss, as wage information would be produced at the trial.

Held, allowing proof before answer, that while standards of specification in averments of loss had become more relaxed in recent years as jury trials had become infrequent, a jury trial was appropriate only if O's pleadings were clearly relevant and specific on all material points. However, O's averments did not provide a specific foundation for either his claim for continuing wage loss or his claim for loss of employability, as there were no averments concerning his pre-accident earnings, the present level of earnings in his pre-accident employment or in any employment for which he was qualified, or on the financial implications of only being fit for sedentary work. Further, it was not clear whether the two heads of claim were alternatives or cumulative, and it was difficult to see how on the present state of the pleadings an adequate and effective direction could be given on how to calculate the two heads of claim and how to discriminate between them, the court being unable to make any assumptions as to the adequacy of the information that might be produced in due course.

O'MALLEY v. MULTIFLEX (UK) 1995 S.C.L.R. 1143, Judge not specified, OH.

6671. Proof or jury trial–special cause–necessary services claim

[Court of Session Act 1988 (c.36) s.9(b).]

Sections 9 and 11 of the Court of Session Act 1988 provide that an action for damages for personal injuries shall be tried by jury unless either the parties agree to a proof or special cause is shown. A woman sustained serious injuries when, as a driver, she was involved in a road accident. She raised an action of damages against the two other drivers involved and sought allowance of issues. Her injuries rendered her severely and permanently disabled and dependent on services provided to her by her parents. At procedure roll the defenders both submitted that the averments in support of the pursuer's services claim were such as to justify withholding the action from trial by jury. The Lord Ordinary held that a jury would be in as good a position as a judge to quantify the pursuer's claim for services, and allowed issues. The second defender reclaimed. Before the Inner House the defender's primary argument was that the pursuer's failure to specify the actual number of hours spent by her parents in looking after her meant that the averments regarding the services claim were without specification and not suitable to go before a jury.

Held, that there was no merit in the criticisms of the pursuer's pleadings, and the Lord Ordinary had not been in error in commenting that a jury was as well placed as a judge to assess a claim of a kind which defied precise quantification; and reclaiming motion refused.

STARK v. FORD (NO.2) 1996 S.L.T. 1329, Judge not specified, IH.

6672. Reclaiming motion–grounds of appeal–motion to amend grounds of appeal at appeal hearing

[Act of Sederunt (Rules of the Court of Session) 1994 (SI 1994 1443) r.38.16(4).]

Suppliers of photocopying machines entered into a contract with a health board. The health board repudiated the contract and the suppliers raised an action seeking declarator of entitlement to terminate the contract in terms of the contractual termination provisions, and for payment of damages as calculated under the terms of the contract. The pursuers had an alternative claim for damages for sums due under the contract prior to the repudiation and for loss, injury and damage sustained subsequent to the date of termination of the contract. After a debate on the parties' preliminary pleas, the Lord Ordinary held that the primary obligations of both parties came to an end when the pursuers accepted the defenders' repudiation of the contract and that the averments relating to a claim for liquidated damages under the contract were irrelevant. A proof before answer was allowed in respect of the remainder of the pursuers' case. The Lord Ordinary commented *obiter* that he considered the contractual measure of damages to be penal. The pursuers reclaimed. The pursuers' appeal was directed solely to the question of whether the contractual measure of damages was penal. At the appeal hearing the pursuers sought leave to amend the grounds of appeal in order that they might argue the relevancy of the excluded averments. The pursuers offered no excuse for not seeking leave earlier, but the question of whether the liquidate damages clause was penal was of considerable importance to them as there had been many disputes on that point.

Held, that as the hearing would require to be discharged and a proof before answer had already been allowed, and as the pursuers still had the opportunity to recover damages at common law, they should not be allowed to amend their grounds of appeal at this stage and it would not be appropriate to hear the reclaiming motion on a matter which was no longer of any practical importance to the case; and reclaiming motion refused. *Observed*, that the case highlighted the importance of the preparation of adequate grounds of appeal and the appearance of the case on the by order roll, and that sufficient opportunity had to be given for the case to be reviewed prior to its appearance on the by order roll to enable counsel to confirm that the grounds of appeal are adequate and to provide a reasonable forecast of the time required.

EUROCOPY RENTALS v. TAYSIDE HEALTH BOARD 1996 S.L.T. 1322, Judge not specified, IH.

6673. Sheriff court decree–judicial review–reduction of decree–competency

[Act of Sederunt (Rules of the Court of Session) 1994 (SI 1994 1443), Chaps. 53, 58 and 60.]

Individuals against whom decree had passed in an undefended action in the sheriff court, sought reduction of the decree and suspension and interdict of diligence on it. They did so by petition for judicial review.

Held, that it was incompetent to seek reduction of a decree of an inferior court by judicial review; and petition dismissed. General notes in Greens Annotated Rules of the Court of Session 1994, at r.53.2 and r.60.6, disapproved.

BELL v. FIDDES 1996 S.L.T. 51, Judge not specified, OH.

6674. Sist–actions of reparation following oil pollution–sist of seventy seven actions pending outcome of four leading actions inappropriate

[Merchant Shipping (Oil Pollution) Act 1971 (c.59); Act of Sederunt (Rules of the Court of Session) 1994 (SI 1994 1443) r.22.3.]

A, along with 76 other parties bringing actions for reparation arising from the wreck of the Braer oil tanker off the Shetland Islands, applied for the actions to be sisted pending the outcome of four leading cases. Payments from the compensation fund had been suspended pending resolution of all the actions, and it was proposed that, by allowing the leading cases to proceed, time, expense and effort could be minimised in the remaining actions.

Held, dismissing the application, that although all the actions had been brought under the Merchant Shipping (Oil Pollution) Act 1971 and arose due to the Braer oil spillage, they contained many different types of claim involving physical injuries, damage to property and financial loss. Even if the Rules of Court r.22.3(6) did not exclude an inherent discretion to order a sist, the actions involved various types of claim, and the proposed four leading actions accounted for only 14 of the 45 heads of claim identified by BC. Further, they did not contain any clear or concise questions of law or fact, the resolution of which would lead to significant savings in time, effort or expense in the other cases. Given that no Lord Ordinary would be bound by a decision reached in the leading actions, and if a sist were granted the remaining parties would be free to adapt their legal strategies in the light of the leading cases' outcomes, if the application were allowed it might delay the settlement of the claims rather than expedite them.

ANDERSON v. BRAER CORP, *The Times*, April 18, 1996, Lord Gill, OH.

6675. Sist–of process–matter to be determined by Lands Tribunal

[Coal Mining Subsidence Act 1991 (c.45) s.40(1).]

The Coal Mining Subsidence Act 1991 makes provision in certain circumstances for payment of compensation to owners of property which has been damaged by subsidence. Section 40(1) of the Act, read with s.52(1), provides that "any question arising under this Act shall, in default of agreement, be referred to and determined by the Lands Tribunal for Scotland". Some owners of properties allegedly damaged by subsidence gave the notice required under the Act to the relevant authority and later raised an action of damages in the Court of Session. The defences admitted that the court had jurisdiction but included pleas in law challenging the competency and relevancy of the action. After procedure roll debate, the Lord Ordinary was satisfied that there was a bar to the court proceeding to determine the issues since the dispute fell to be determined by the Lands Tribunal in terms of the 1991 Act. In view of the terms of the defenders' pleas, he held that it was *pars judicis* to notice and apply a bar to court proceedings and he dismissed the action without sustaining any plea in law. The pursuers reclaimed. The defenders amended their pleadings in the course of the reclaiming motion and the pursuers moved the court to sist the action, which was opposed by the defenders. It was not suggested by the defenders that the effect of s.40(1) of the 1991 Act was to oust the jurisdiction of the court completely.

Held, that (1) having regard to the fact that the jurisdiction of the court was not wholly ousted by s.40(1) of the 1991 Act and to the fact that the principle expounded in *Brodie v. Ker* applied to the present case, it was possible that the court might be called upon at some stage in the process to pronounce an interlocutor even if only to give effect to a decision of the Lands Tribunal and (2) where the pursuers now accepted that the dispute between the parties fell to be referred to the Lands Tribunal, the appropriate disposal was not to dismiss the action but to sist it pending the outcome of the proceedings before the Lands Tribunal; and reclaiming motion granted, *Brodie v. Ker* 1952 S.L.T. 226, [1952] C.L.Y. 3756/4161 followed.

Observed, that where, after making *avizandum*, a Lord Ordinary discovered an authority on some material matter which had not been cited by the parties and upon which he was inclined to proceed, or where an argument occurred to him which had not been discussed by the parties before him, or where a question arose as to the appropriate interlocutor for the Lord Ordinary to pronounce in the light of the conclusions he had reached, the proper practice was for the Lord Ordinary to put the case out by order so that parties might have an opportunity of making further submissions to him on these new matters and, if need be, on the form of interlocutor which should be pronounced. Alternatively, if the only outstanding issue was the form of interlocutor, the Lord Ordinary might give his judgment expressing his conclusions, but continue the matter so that parties could address him on the appropriate interlocutor which in the circumstances he should pronounce.

OSBORNE v. BRITISH COAL PROPERTY 1996 S.L.T. 736, Judge not specified, IH.

6676. Third party notices–after record closed–prejudice to pursuer

An employee raised an action against his employers for damages following an accident at work. The defences admitted the accident but consisted only of denials on the issue of fault. By the closing of the record, there were averments by the defenders of a contract of indemnity. After the record closed the defenders sought to convene the other party to the contract as a third party.

Held, that the pursuer would be prejudiced in his right to an expeditious pursuit of his claim if the third party notice were granted; and motion refused.

HALBERT v. BRITISH AIRPORTS AUTHORITY PLC 1996 S.L.T. 97, Judge not specified, OH.

6677. Articles

Leave to reclaim a summary decree *(Nigel Morrison)*: Civ. P.B. 1996, 9(May), 7-8. (Clarification of rules relating to appeals against summary decrees).

Pursuers' offers *(David Stevenson)*: Civ. P.B. 1996, 11(Sep), 2-4. (Innovative procedure allows pursuers to exercise degree of control over timing and amount of settlement in actions).

Pursuers' offers to settle in the Court of Session *(David Bartos)*: J.L.S.S. 1996, 41(11), 434-435. (Consequences of change in Court of Session rules as to liability for expenses and penalty payments when pursuer makes offer to settle which is unaccepted).

Report on multi-party actions: procedures and funding: S.L.G. 1996, 64(3), 145-147. (Scottish Law Commission Report No.154 proposals for group actions procedure in Court of Session).

Report on multi-party actions: S.L.T. 1996, 25, 219-220. (Scottish Law Commission report No.154 recommending introduction of group proceedings procedure).

The Scottish Commercial Court *(McGrigor Donald)*: I.H.L. 1996, 44(Oct), 73. (Work of Commercial Court with reference to three recent cases).

Trial by jury *(David Taylor)*: Ins. L. & C. 1996, 9, 35-36 . (Problems caused to insurers by juries awarding large damages claims for personal injuries, with particular reference to Scottish system).

Witness from England in the Court of Session *(D.I.K. MacLeod)*: Civ. P.B. 1996, 12(Nov), 9-10. (How to enforce attendance by English witnesses).

COMMERCIAL LAW

6678. Sale of business–whether seller entitled to retention of assignation of lease

Held, where missives provided for an assignation of a lease to be delivered on the entry date in exchange for payment of the purchase price, that the seller was not entitled to withhold delivery of the assignation after the date of entry pending resolution of a dispute regarding valuation of the stock, payment for which was not due until three months after the date of entry.

MOOR v. ATWAL 1995 S.C.L.R. 1119, Judge not specified, Sh Ct.

6679. Sale of shares–disclosure by sellers–construction of contract

P, the registered holders of shares in W, sought declarator that S was obliged to implement the terms of an options agreement and the agreement itself. In March 1994, P and S entered into investment and option agreements whereby P granted to S options to purchase their shares any time between October 1, 1995 and March 31, 1997. To effect their option, S were required to deliver a simple written notice in prescribed form to P. The options contract contained various warranties by P and provided for disclosure, within 45 days of the delivery of S's notice, against any warranty deemed granted in terms of cl.9.3 of the investment agreement. It also gave S the right to withdraw from the written notice if P's disclosures were not accepted. The disclosure letter was defined in the investment agreement as "the disclosure letter addressed to (S) on behalf of the warrantors dated of even date within this Agreement". By letters dated December 14, 1995, S served notice and on January 8, 1996, P sent S the first draft of the disclosure letter and a volume of disclosure documents with a note that additional disclosure documents would be forwarded. On January 26, P advised S, with reference to cl.5(D) of the options agreement and after reviewing the warranties deemed granted by them in terms of cl.9.3, that they declined to made any disclosures. S thereafter notified P in writing that they did not accept some of the disclosures made on January 8, and that their notice was withdrawn. At debate, P sought exclusion of S's averments relating to disclosure, arguing that, reading the options and investment agreements together, disclosure had to be in the form of a single disclosure letter executed by them and delivered to S. The warranties and disclosure were indissolubly linked and disclosure and the delivery of a disclosure letter were indistinguishable. S's right to terminate only arose if they did not accept such disclosures. There would not be sufficient certainty without such a document. Further, S had received all the relevant information before the correspondence relating to disclosure. Even if P's letters constituted disclosure, it was implied that S were obliged to act reasonably in withdrawing their notice. S sought exclusion of P's averments of implied term.

Held, proof before answer allowed under exclusion of P's averment of implied term, that (1) in terms of cl.91 and the definition provisions, P were obliged to provide a disclosure letter executed on the date of the investment agreement, the effect of which was to limit the scope of the warranties. It did not follow that the disclosure letter had to be a single document, a series of documents could meet the requirements of the agreement. Nor did it follow that P were obliged, rather than entitled, to make disclosures on the qualification of the express warranties, and if they did not purport to make them, fairness would be irrelevant as fairness of disclosure was related to the content of the disclosure and not to the decision whether to disclose. The options agreement was different as there was no requirement for a single comprehensive disclosure event as in the investment agreement; on a sound construction of the contract, everything did not have to remain tentative or conditional until a final omnibus disclosure letter was delivered. There was no provision entitling P to offer a disclosure conditionally upon acceptance in the sense that it would fall if not accepted, or otherwise fall outwith the scope of S's rights of withdrawal unless incorporated into a final single disclosure letter and (2) there was nothing in general principle or the contract which implied that S must exercise their right to withdraw reasonably. P were not obliged to make disclosure unless they wished to limit their warranty liabilities; they had no counterpart obligation to act reasonably in deciding to make disclosures and therefore the term argued for by P could not be described as an equitable provision. S could not be assumed to have agreed that they could only withdraw if they could prove that their reasons satisfied some standard of reasonable conduct defined independently of their own judgment. It was not reasonable or necessary to the efficacy of the contract to imply such a term and it was unclear that such a term would have been agreed to as a matter of course. The contract structure was also contrary to such an implication since the agreements expressly provided tests of reasonableness which inferred that P and S were aware of the need to qualify certain provisions and would have applied such a test to S's right to withdraw if one had been intended.

PRENTICE v. SCOTTISH POWER PLC, *The Times*, October 28, 1996, Lord Penrose, OH.

6680. Articles

Swords or shields? Counterclaims and assigned debts *(Anthony F. Deutsch)*: Civ. P.B. 1996, 11 (Sep), 4-7. (Whether debtor who is sued by assignee of creditor can raise counterclaim).

Where now for commercial ADR? *(Bryan Clark)*: S.L.G. 1996, 64(3), 124-127. (Issues of alternative dispute resolution which require to be resolved if it is to develop particularly into commercial disputes).

6681. Books

Cusine, Douglas J.; Forte, A.D.M.–Cusine & Forte: Scottish Cases and Materials in Commercial Law. Paperback: £35.00. ISBN 0-406-04658-1. Butterworth Law.

Macmillan, Moira; Macfarland, Sally–Scottish Business Law. Paperback: £23.99. ISBN 0-273-62035-5. Pitman Publishing.

COMPANY LAW

6682. Edinburgh Merchant Company Order Confirmation Act 1996 (c.xi)

The Act confirms the Provisional Order set out in the Schedule which continues in being the Company of merchants of the City of Edinburgh and consolidates with amendments the Acts relating to the Company.

This Act received Royal Assent on December 18, 1996.

6683. Shareholders–entitlement to receive dividend–director required to surrender shares on resignation–delay in valuation of shares

Held, that where a director was found on resigning to surrender his shareholding, until the shares had been valued and the value paid in exchange for his execution of the document of transfer, he remained a member of the company and entitled to receive payment of any dividend declared.

STRACHAN v. ABERDEEN INDUSTRIAL DOCTORS 1995 S.C.L.R. 1098, Judge not specified, Sh Ct.

6684. Voluntary association–status of Scottish Council of British association incorporated as company limited by guarantee

A former member of the Scottish branch of the British Show Jumping Association raised an action seeking declarator that a decision of the branch's standing committee, preventing him from standing for election to the branch's council, and a further decision removing him from office as a judge, time judge and a member of the council, were invalid as contrary to natural justice and ultra vires. He also sought reduction of these decisions and of the elections of area representatives to the council. The pursuer averred that he had been a prominent member of the defender's organisation, had served on its council, and had been a judge of show jumping events and a time judge in addition to being on the panel of supervisory judges for a number of years. On procedure roll the defender argued a plea to the competency of the action as laid against the defender, who it was maintained was simply a branch of the BSJA, a company limited by guarantee. The pursuer argued that his averments disclosed sufficient contractual arrangements between the defender's members to constitute the defender as a voluntary organisation. The defender also argued that, the pursuer no longer being a member of the defender's association and being therefore ineligible to stand for election as an area representative or serve as a judge, time judge, or member of the council, reduction as sought would achieve nothing for the pursuer and he could demonstrate no sufficient interest; that his averments were insufficient to justify the court exercising what was an equitable jurisdiction to reduce; that the action was incompetent insofar as it was brought against the defender's honourary president who held no executive powers under the defender's constitution; that it was possible to reduce written documents only, not decisions, as here sought; and that the averments anent financial loss were unquantified and irrelevant, there being no conclusion for the payment of damages.

Held, that having regard to the defender's rules and to the articles of association of the BSJA, the defender had no existence separate from the BSJA; and action dismissed as incompetent, *Cassel v. Inglis* [1916] 2 Ch. 211 and *McMillan v. Free Church* (1859) 22 D. 290 distinguished. Opinion, that (1) it was no longer necessary for a pursuer to aver that the question at issue involved his pecuniary rights or status and the pursuer, although no longer a member of association, had averred sufficient to qualify an interest to sue; averring that the defender acted in a manner contrary to natural justice and specifying the basis of those averments was in itself sufficient and it was for the defenders to aver any particular circumstance which stood in the way of an entitlement to reduction; (2) the action would have been competent if directed in the recognised way against a voluntary association by naming the association and its office bearers; (3) that the availability of reduction was not confined to writings but was also available to reduce illegal acts and (4) the averments anent financial loss were relevant to qualify an interest to sue and sufficiently specific, although inadequate to support a claim for damages proper, *Scottish Old People's Welfare Council, Petitioners* 1987 S.L.T. 179, [1987] C.L.Y. 5156 and *Spowart v. Transport & General Workers Union* 1926 S.L.T. 245 applied.

LENNOX v. BRITISH SHOW JUMPING ASSOCIATION (SCOTTISH BRANCH) 1996 S.L.T. 353, Judge not specified, OH.

COMPETITION LAW

6685. Restrictive practices–registrable agreement–arrangement–user of solicitors' property centre

[Restrictive Trade Practices Act 1976 (c. 34) s.11, Sch.1 para. 1.]

A and E, two solicitors' property centres, applied for orders to remove agreements registered as restrictive agreements in terms of s.11 of the 1976 Act from the Register of Agreements maintained by the Director General of Fair Trading (D). The parties agreed (1) that A and E's primary business was the provision of facilities for solicitors to advertise properties in their areas; (2) that solicitors made an annual payment of £60 per partner to use the services of A and E, and paid a registration fee of £145 (or £200 for firms that did not make the annual payment) for each property advertised on behalf of a client. A and E's users were not members of the companies and had no voting rights; (3) that since August 1991, A and E had only accepted properties marketed by solicitors for registration and did not accept properties marketed on a "joint agency" basis by solicitors and estate agents. The issue before the court was whether, in terms of the 1976 Act, there was an "arrangement or agreement" between the users of the centres and if there was could the Sch.1 para.1 exemption applicable to legal service be invoked.

Held, applications granted and agreements removed from the Register of Agreements, that (1) given the purpose of the centres, A and E were the "creatures" of their regular users who were in a real sense accountable for the restrictive rules under which the centres operated, *Royal Institution of Chartered Surveyors v. Director General of Fair Trading* [1986] I.C.R. 550, [1986] C.L.Y. 3401 applied. In terms of the shared expectation or "manifestation of will" it could properly be said that there was an arrangement between the regular users of each centre to the effect that if any users attempted to break the rule against joint agencies, they would be subject to opprobrium by the other users, and (2) the multilateral agreement, however, concerned the supply of legal services and was therefore exempt from the 1976 Act, particularly in view of D's concession that estate agency services provided by solicitors were legal services, and the arrangement containing the restriction was an agreement between solicitors who, although providing estate agency services, did not profess the services of an advertiser.

ABERDEEN SOLICITORS PROPERTY CENTRE LTD v. DIRECTOR GENERAL OF FAIR TRADING 1996 S.L.T. 523, Lord Marnoch, RPC.

CONFLICT OF LAWS

6686. Choice of forum–choice of law–limitations–restitutionary obligation–proper test

B, a bank, sought restitution by repayment of the excess of sums paid by B to C, a district council, under a "forward rate agreement" which was agreed to be void ab initio as C had acted ultra vires, the agreement provided that the law of England was the governing law of the contract. If Scots law applied B's claim had been extinguished by prescription, but if English law applied the claim was extant. B argued that had *Morgan Guaranty Trust Co v. Lothian RC* 1995 S.L.T. 299, [1995] C.L.Y. 5586, 6118 been argued on the basis that the proper law of the obligation was English law; then s.23A(1) of the Prescription and Limitation (Scotland) Act 1973 as amended would required a Scottish court to apply English limitation rules, *Kleinwort Benson v. City of Glasgow DC* [1995] 3 W.L.R. 866, [1995] 2 C.L.Y. 4337; that in the absence of judicial authority, academic authority demonstrated that the obligation of restitution was the sequel to a factual situation or assumed relationship, and the governing law should regulate the obligation since the proper law of the contract regulated a unitary situation whether the contract subsisted or was void ab initio, (Dicey and Morris, *The Conflict of Laws* (11th ed); Anton, *Private International Law* (1st ed); Zweigert and Muller-Gindullis, *International Encyclopaedia of Comparative Law*, Vol.III (1971); and essays by Bird and Brereton in Rose, *Restitution and the Conflict of Laws* (1995); that there were three stages which gave rise to B's claim; (1) the parties acted on the assumption that there was a contract in force governing their relationship; (2) the validity of the contract was determined by the putative proper law of the contract and that rendered the contract void; and (3) in determining the nature and extent of any restitutionary remedy, B and C could elect to invite the court to apply the lex fori by withholding averment or proof of foreign law; or the court could resort to the lex fori on equitable grounds, but consistent treatment of the problem required that the same system of law which rendered the contract void should deal with the consequences in applying the appropriate restitutionary remedies, and that in any event the law of England was the system with which the facts had the closest connection.

Held, proof before answer allowed, that it was incompetent to rely on the direct application of a provision in a void contract to determine the choice of law in the context of restitution, and that view was consistent with the decision in *Morgan Guaranty*, which was concerned exclusively with domestic issues of Scots law and not conflict of laws. In considering the academic authorities and academic debate the choice of law rules relating to the proper law of a restitutionary obligation, there was a fundamental difficulty to be overcome where the original contract was void ab initio, since the restitutionary remedy was only available to B because there was no contract and no obligation at the date of transfer of the assets, and the proper law of the contract had exhausted its purpose and did not validly regulate the relationship between B and C. The application of a different system to that which was determinative of the validity of the contract could give rise, however, to the risk of injustice since the scope for incompatibility between the grounds of nullifying the contract and the restitutionary remedies was greater where they were products of different systems of law. The application of the putative proper law of the contract in the interests of certainty was made difficult by the qualified enactment of the Rome Convention, which implied that within the UK, the determination of the putative proper law of a contract which was held to be void ab initio and the determination of the proper law of any consequential restitutionary claim might identify different systems, and that contradicted the common law theory, as expressed in Dicey and Morris. The analysis of Blaikie in "Unjust Enrichment in the Conflict of Laws", 1984, J.R. 112, provided the broadest and most appropriate test of identification of the proper law of a restitutionary obligation as being the system of law with the closest and most real connection with the enrichment. Only in the light of the whole facts and circumstances of the case, therefore, could the proper law of the obligation be determined. Since both B and C had advanced credible arguments relating to the various facts of the case, there were issues of fact which required to be decided before the proper law of the obligation could be ascertained.

BARING BROTHERS & CO LTD v. CUNNINGHAME DC, *The Times*, September 30, 1996, Lord Penrose, OH.

6687. Foreign judgments–registration–appeal against registration

[Act of Sederunt (Rules of the Court of Session) 1994 (SI 1994 1443) r.62.28.]

In an appeal against the registration in Scotland of a foreign judgment, of decree in absence, the appellant argued that the respondent had failed to serve him notice of the original proceedings and, in any case, had failed to produce an accurate copy of the original document establishing service upon him and thus had failed to comply with the terms of r.62.28(2) of the Rules of Court 1994.

Held, that (1) r.62.28(3) allowed the court either to order the proper documents to be produced or to recall the original interlocutor granting warrant for registration; (2) it was appropriate in this case to continue the appeal for the appellant to lodge affidavits in support of his claim and for the court to be addressed further on the documents produced; and appeal continued accordingly.

ARTIC FISH SALES CO v. ADAM (NO.1) 1996 S.L.T. 968, Judge not specified, OH.

6688. Foreign judgments–registration–appeal against registration

[Civil Jurisdiction and Judgments Act 1982 (c.27) Sch.1 Art.27; Act of Sederunt (Rules of the Court of Session) 1994 (SI 1994 1443) r.62.28.]

An Irish company obtained a decree in absence in an Irish court, against an individual in an action arising from a contractual dispute with a company which had a place of business in Scotland and of which the individual was formerly a director. In the individual's appeal against the registration in Scotland of this decree in absence, the court, in terms of r.62.28(2) of the Rules of Court, allowed a continuation for the purpose of production of the certified copy of the original writ establishing that the appellant had been served with the document initiating the proceedings in which decree in absence had been pronounced against him. At the hearing it was established that the document produced had never in fact been before the court of origin. An accurate photocopy of the original writ was produced at the continued hearing and it was argued, by the appellant, that the present proceedings were vitiated by the respondent's failure to produce the documentation at the stage when application for registration of the judgment was first made. The appellant also made reference to the history of the proceedings. The respondents had initially corresponded with the appellant's employers in April 1993 regarding the dispute and twice subsequently raised proceedings in identical terms against the company which were later dropped. During correspondence, the company confirmed to the respondents that the contractual relationship, regarding the dispute, was between themselves only and not the appellant. Nevertheless the respondents subsequently raised proceedings against the appellant only in August 1993. By this time the appellant had left the employment of the company and was not apprised of the proceedings against him until December 1994 when the original interlocutor granting registration of the decree in Scotland was pronounced. In these circumstances the appellant argued that the document had not been duly served in accordance with Art.27(2) of the Brussels Convention as he had not had sufficient time to arrange for his defence and, in any case, the circumstances of the case offended public policy in terms of Art.27(1) of the Convention and the decree should not be recognised.

Held, that (1) the appellant was not limited to the grounds of challenge in Art.27 and Art.28 of the Convention, and could challenge the decision to grant warrant for registration on the ground that the proper formalities were not observed in presenting the application; (2) having regard to r.62.28(3), the respondents were not prevented from curing any defect by producing the necessary documents, and the fact that a photocopy could be treated as the equivalent of the original document meant that the failure to produce the required documentation in support of the original application was not fatal; (3) any challenge to the judgment of the court in Ireland as having been impetrated by fraud had to be taken in Ireland and there was nothing before the court to suggest that enforcement of the judgment should be refused on grounds of public policy by virtue of Art.27(1) of the Convention and (4) looking at the whole circumstances of the case and, in particular, at the facts that the appellant at no time traded under the company name, the respondents should have been aware that the appellant was a separate entity from the company, and the appellant had no reason to expect to be called to account for this action for which the initiating documents were never received by him, the factors all constituted exceptional circumstances such as to entitle the court to regard the service effected as inadequate for the purposes of causing the time within which the appellant was to be enabled to arrange for his defence, to begin to run in terms of Art.27(2); and appeal sustained.

ARTIC FISH SALES CO v. ADAM (NO.2) 1996 S.L.T. 970, Judge not specified, OH.

6689. Foreign judgments–registration–appeal against registration

[Civil Jurisdiction and Judgments Act 1982 (c.27) Sch.1 Art.27(2).]

Article 27(2) of the Brussels Convention, set out in Sch.1 to the Civil Jurisdiction and Judgments Act 1982, provides that a judgment issued in another contracting state shall not be recognised where it was given in default of appearance, if the defendant was not duly served with the document instituting the proceedings or equivalent in sufficient time to enable him to arrange for his defence. The Belgium judicial code provides in Art.35 that if service cannot be performed personally, it shall take place at a person's domicile, or in default of domicile, at their place of residence. Article 36 defines "domicile" as the place where the person is principally inscribed in the population registers, and "residence" as any other establishment such as the place where the person has an office or carries on business. Article 38 makes provision for service in a case where service cannot be made as provided for in Art.35. A company petitioned for registration and enforcement of a judgment of a Belgian court which had been granted in default of appearance in an action of payment against a Belgian national. After warrant for registration had been granted, the respondent enrolled a motion seeking recall of the warrant for registration on the ground that the action had not been duly served upon him, or alternatively that there had been insufficient time to arrange a defence. His evidence was that he had left Belgium in 1963 and had no property or business there; that in 1980 he had come to Scotland, where he purchased property; that in 1990 he had notified the Belgian embassy of his permanent residence in Scotland; that he was registered in the Belgian national register as domiciled in Scotland; that in the Belgian action he had been designed as resident at the address of a friend in Kraainem, Belgium; that a copy of the summons had been left at that address and with the public prosecutor, on the basis that the respondent had no known domicile or address, but had not been sent to his address; and that he had made an application to the Belgian court for recall of the judgment on the ground that there had been no proper service.

Held, that (1) on the evidence the respondent's principal residence was clearly in Scotland and he had intimated this to the appropriate Belgian authorities, and therefore for the purposes of the Belgian code he was domiciled in Scotland and (2) even if the respondent had a residence in Belgium, service was required to be at his domicile, which was Scotland, and accordingly service had not been properly carried out; and motion granted and warrant for registration recalled.

Observed, that if there had been proper service, a period of about a month between the date of service and the date of judgment did not appear ex facie to be unreasonable.

SELCO LTD v. MERCIER 1996 S.L.T. 1247, Judge not specified, OH.

6690. Articles

New choice of law rules in delict *(Andrew Stewart)*: Civ. P.B. 1996, 12(Nov), 6-7. (Private International Law (Miscellaneous Provisions) Act 1995 Part III that applicable law is that of country in which events occurred with exception of defamation actions).

Recent Scottish cases on habitual residence *(R.D. Leslie)*: S.L.T. 1996, 16, 145-149. (Courts' development of concept of habitual residence by application of increasingly complex rules).

The Halley: holed and now sunk *(Barry J. Rodger)*: S.L.P.Q. 1996, 1 (5), 397-410. (Effect of provisions of Private International Law (Miscellaneous Provisions) Act 1995 Part III in force on May 1, 1996, reforming UK rules in regard to choice of law in delict or tort).

CONSTITUTIONAL LAW

6691. Articles

MacCormick: a double edged sword *(Charles Haggerty)*: SCOLAG 1996, 234, 78-80. (Constitutional issues surrounding Skye Toll Bridge protest campaign).

CONSTRUCTION LAW

6692. Building contract–architect's certificate–failure to pay–alleged breach of contract by contractor

Held, in an action of payment at the instance of building contractors relying on an architect's interim certificate entitling them to payment, that defences alleging breach of contract by the contractors and claiming a right of retention were radically lacking in specification and irrelevant because they failed to aver that the contractors were in breach of contract at the time when payment became due under the certificate.

CAMPBELL & SMITH CONSTRUCTION CO v. BOYLE 1996 S.C.L.R. 335, Judge not specified, Sh Ct.

6693. Building contract–construction–clauses inconsistent with standard conditions–whether part of bills or of appendix

Clause 2.2.1 of the conditions of the Standard Form of Building Contract (Private Edition with Quantities) (1980 ed.), as amended, provides that "Nothing contained in the Contract Bills shall override or modify the application or interpretation of that which is contained in the Articles of Agreement, the Conditions or the Appendix". A building company brought an action against its employer for payment of the balance due under an interim certificate. The employer maintained that he was entitled to deduct the sum in question as liquidate and ascertained damages in terms of the contract. The contract had been formed by means of a tender on the basis of a number of documents referred to as "Conditions of Contract, Specification and Bills of Quantities", and a letter of acceptance. The documents incorporated, inter alia, the 1980 Standard Form of Building Contract. It was argued for the building company that the provisions relating to dates of completion and liquidate and ascertained damages upon which the defender founded comprised part of the bills of quantities, were inconsistent with the corresponding clauses in the standard conditions, and were accordingly of no effect due to the priority accorded to the standard conditions by cl.2.2.1.

Held, that (1) cl.2.2.1 of the 1980 edition was materially different from the corresponding cl.12(1) of the 1963 edition, in that cl.12(1) accorded priority only to the standard conditions over the contract bills, whereas cl.2.2.1 accorded priority to the articles of agreement and the appendix, in addition to the standard conditions, over the contract bills; (2) the conditions, the articles of agreement and the appendix had to be construed together, resolving any conflicts by applying ordinary principle unaided by priority stipulations, before comparing the result with the bills and settling any inconsistency in terms of the priority afforded by cl.2.2.1; (3) the clauses founded upon by the defender in respect of completion dates and liquidate and ascertained damages were part of the appendix, which was an essential part of the contract, despite the fact that the appendix had been included in the volume of documents which contained references and definitions which tended to suggest that it was part of the bills of quantities; (4) when the conditions and the appendix were construed together it was necessary to apply the rule that typewritten elements had priority over inconsistent standard printed conditions, and so the typewritten provisions in question of the appendix took priority and (5) there was no inconsistency between the conditions and the appendix so construed and the bills of quantities, and the provisions founded upon by the defender were enforceable; and action dismissed, *Inverclyde DC v. Hardstock (Scotland)* 1984 S.L.T. 226, [1984] C.L.Y. 3734 distinguished.

BARRY D TRENTHAM LTD v. McNEIL 1996 S.L.T. 202, Judge not specified, OH.

6694. Building regulations

BUILDING STANDARDS (SCOTLAND) AMENDMENT REGULATIONS 1996, SI 1996 2251 (S.183); made under the Building (Scotland) Act 1959 s.3, s.6, s.24, s.29, Sch.4. In force: November 5, 1996; £1.95.

These Regulations amend the Building Standards (Scotland) Regulations (SI 1990 2179) to apply the requirement to provide adequate sanitary facilities to all buildings except school premises, for which provision is made elsewhere, and to clarify the descriptions of some classes of exempted buildings and to expand on the exceptions to certain classes of buildings to ensure that buildings on land which has harmful or dangerous substances within its boundaries remain subject to the Regulations.

6695. Articles

Constructing ambiguities? *(Alan McMillan)*: S.L.T. 1996, 6, 49-50. (Practical difficulties caused by Requirements of Writing (Scotland) Act 1995 in relation to building and construction contracts).

Quantum meruit building construction claim *(Ian Christie Strathdee)*: Cons. Law 1996, 7(3), 101-107. (Whether contractor could found claim under quantum meruit where employer was in material breach of contract; includes flow chart showing Scottish stated case procedure for opinions on points of law arising from arbitration).

Scotland the brave–the written versus the printed word *(Peter A. MacGillivray)*: Cons. Law 1995/96, 6(5), 189-191. (Scottish decision on priority where contract documents incorporate amended standard form conditions).

Scottish construction industry arbitration procedures *(Ian Christie Strathdee)*: A.D.R.L.J. 1996, 1 (Mar), 25-31. (Lack of statutory rules governing arbitration procedures, inflexible nature of adversarial procedures and need to give arbitrators greater powers of investigation).

6696. Books

Hamilton, W.; McLaughlin, R.; MacPherson, A.; Kennedy, Paul–The Scottish Building Regulations. Paperback: £24.95. ISBN 0-632-04115-3. Blackwell Science (UK).

CONSUMER LAW

6697. Hire purchase–car purchased by hire purchase–garage not agent of finance company

[Consumer Credit Act 1974 (c.39) s.56(1)(b).]

The customer in a hire-purchase transaction claimed damages from a finance company in respect of a loss alleged to have resulted from a breach of contract. The pursuer had entered into a hire-purchase agreement in respect of a Vauxhall Cavalier car. He traded that car in when purchasing a Nissan car. He averred that the garage salesman insisted that he make the cheque out to the garage and undertook that the garage would repay the finance company. He went on to aver that the garage had acted as agents for the finance company and had failed to make the payment. A debate was fixed to consider (1) whether the pursuer had relevantly averred that in giving the undertaking to pay the finance company the garage were deemed to have been agents of the defenders by virtue of s.56 of the Consumer Credit Act 1974 and (2) whether the pursuer had relevantly averred that in giving that undertaking the garage were acting as the agents of the defenders at common law.

Held, that (1) negotiations were deemed to be conducted by the dealer in the capacity of agent for the finance company only if they were negotiations falling within s.56(1)(b) of the 1974 Act, and they only fell within that provision if they were conducted by the dealer in relation to goods sold or proposed to be sold by the dealer, which goods in this case were the Nissan car and not the Vauxhall car, *UDT v. Whitfield* [1987] C.C.L.R. 60, [1986] C.L.Y. 375 not followed, and (2) in the absence of special circumstances, the relationship of principal and agent did not arise between a finance company entering into a hire-purchase agreement and the dealer or retailer, and there were no circumstances averred in the present case to take it out of the general rule; and action dismissed.

POWELL v. LLOYDS BOWMAKER 1996 S.L.T. (Sh.Ct.) 117, Judge not specified, Sh Ct.

6698. Trade descriptions–supply of goods with false description–patent breach of contract

[Trade Descriptions Act 1968 (c.29) s.1(1)(6).]

Held, that where goods were ordered in October 1993 and supplied in December 1993, a trade description applied at the time of sale remained attached to the goods to be carried forward to the point of delivery so that any offence of supplying goods to which a false trade description had been applied was committed in December 1993, but that since the alleged false trade description constituted a patent disconformity to contract, the situation was apt for prosecution under the Trade Descriptions Act 1968.

NORMAND v. DM DESIGN BEDROOMS 1996 S.C.C.R. 457, Judge not specified, Sh Ct.

CONTRACTS

6699. Breach of contract–substantial performance–remedy

Held, in a small claim for payment of a restaurant bill, where only a round of liqueurs after the meal was unsatisfactory, that there had been a single contract between the restaurateur and the customers, rather than a series of contracts for each item ordered, but not that there had been substantial performance, so that the restaurateur was entitled to payment for the meal but not for the liqueurs.

CULTER MILL RESTAURANT v. HOGG 1996 S.C.L.R. 182, Judge not specified, Sh Ct.

6700. Construction–sale of business–back letter–whether enforceable by specific implement

The pursuers were formerly the telecommunications rentals division of the defenders. As such they occupied part of premises in Aberdeen and Great Yarmouth which were tenanted by a wholly-owned subsidiary of the defenders. The subsidiary's landlord was an independent company which had a lease of the premises on a tenancy from the head landlord. The premises were also occupied by two other former divisions of the defenders. The defenders sold all three businesses at or about the same time to separate purchasers. The subsidiary's interest in the premises was not one of the assets which were sold as part of the business. The terms of the sale of the business to the pursuers were set out in a formal written agreement. There was in addition an informal back letter containing an undertaking that the subsidiary would co-operate with the pursuers in an application to the landlord and head landlord with a view to negotiation of assignations, assignments or sub-leases on terms and conditions to be agreed among the parties. The purchaser of each of the businesses received a back-letter in identical terms. The landlord and the head landlord became wholly-owned subsidiaries of the pursuers. The only remaining obstacle to the pursuers obtaining a title to occupy the premises was their need to obtain the consent of the defenders' subsidiary for an assignation of their sub-lease to the pursuers. The pursuers brought an action of specific implement, contending that the terms of the back-letter were an undertaking by the defenders to take various measures to assign the subsidiary's interest in the premises to the pursuers. After a procedure roll hearing the Lord Ordinary allowed the pursuers to amend the terms of their conclusion for specific implement and granted decree in terms of the amended conclusion. The defenders reclaimed.

Held, that (1) the agreement distinguished between the business which was being sold and the premises which it occupied; (2) the obligations in the back-letter fell into two parts, and the first part was sufficiently clear to allow the pursuers to seek specific implement of the defenders' obligation to co-operate with the pursuers in application to the landlord and head landlord made through the defenders' subsidiary; (3) the second part defined the purpose of the applications, and as the method of transferring the sub-tenant's interest in the premises, the terms and conditions which were to apply, and the rights and obligations of the other businesses occupying the premises were all to be determined by negotiation, the back-letter could not be enforceable by specific implement and (4) neither could an order for specific implement be made in the terms sought when it was not clear what the precise area of the pursuers' title would be; and reclaiming motion allowed and action dismissed.

EAST ANGLIAN ELECTRONICS LTD v. OIS PLC 1996 S.L.T. 808, Judge not specified, IH.

6701. Construction–termination clause–payments due on termination–whether penalty clause

E, suppliers of photocopying machines raised an action for sums allegedly due under the termination provisions of their contract with T, or alternatively for sums allegedly due under the contract prior to termination and damages for breach of contract. E and T had entered into a supplying and servicing agreement set out on a standard form and concluded on March 26, 1990. Condition 5 provided for an initial hire term of seven years and an "agreed copy volume" at an "agreed price per copy". These were variable within a limit of 15 per cent per annum by the supplier in terms of condition 3(c). In terms of condition 10(a) the contract terminated on the repossession of the copiers by E upon the apparent insolvency or insolvency of T or their failure to comply in any respect with the conditions of the contract.

Condition 10(b) provided a detailed formula for calculating damages on termination. Payments were made under the contract and on January 31, 1991 E advised T that the copy charges were to be increased by just under 15 per cent with effect from March 20, 1991. T protested against this as being contrary to the spirit of the agreement and refused to accept it but made two further payments at the original rate. E raised invoices for three further periods which T did not pay. On November 8, 1991 E' solicitors wrote to T, inquiring if any valid reason existed for the non-payment and indicating that court proceedings would be instituted should no reply giving reasons be received within seven days. T's response on November 19, 1991 stated that they believed they had been induced to sign the agreement by misrepresentation and that they were seeking to resolve the situation through negotiation. In January 1992 E raised an action in the sheriff court, seeking damages in terms of condition 10 and alleging that the contract had been terminated by repudiation. Following removal of the copiers an action was raised in the Court of Session under the provisions of condition 10.

Held, that (1) the questions of whether or when equipment had been installed were questions of fact; the actings of the parties showed that they had regarded the installation as complete on the date of the installation of the last piece of equipment and the contract could be applied on that basis; (2) although certain obligations might continue in force after an accepted repudiation, the primary obligations of performance under the contract came to an end and were replaced by an obligation on the party in breach to pay damages; this had happened by E's acceptance of the repudiation and they could not then claim a right to act under condition 10(a); (3) condition 10(b) could only be relied on where the contract had been brought to an end in terms of condition 10(a), and the contract not having been so terminated, any claim for damages required to be made at common law; and E's averments relative to condition 10 refused probation and quoad ultra proof before answer allowed. Opinion, that the provisions of condition 10 were penal as they purported to provide for termination and payment calculated thereunder for any breach of contract, whether material or otherwise, *Dunlop Pneumatic Tyre Co v. New Garage and Motor Co* [1915] A.C. 79 followed.

EUROCOPY RENTALS v. TAYSIDE HEALTH BOARD 1996 S.L.T. 224, Judge not specified, OH.

6702. Contractual obligations–breach–right of retention–whether right to withhold payment in respect of duly performed obligations–meaning of "contemporaneous"

SE appealed against the dismissal of their appeal in an action arising from the failure to perform a contractual obligation for building work by SM. SE and SM had agreed that no instalments were to be paid until May 15, 1990 and SM assigned all sums payable by SE to BEA as security. It was accepted that work had been carried out negligently prior to that date but when SM became insolvent SE suffered further loss and damage. Although SE had a right to retention, namely a right to withhold payment to the bank in respect of sums due for work done before May 15, they questioned whether they had a right to resist demand for the further sums arising from SM's failure to complete the contract after that date.

Held, dismissing the appeal, that the principle in Scots law that a party to a contract only had a right of retention in respect of a breach before the date when payment fell due was correct, *Redpath Dorman Long Ltd v. Cummins Engine Co Ltd* 1981 S.C. 370, [1982] C.L.Y. 3441 followed. The ascertained claim before May 15, 1990 could only be set off against the latter unascertained claim if the two arose contemporaneously ie. the counter obligations existed at the same time, *Johnston v. Robertson* (1861) 23 D. 646 considered. Therefore the right of retention could be operated against enforceable corresponding obligations which remained unfulfilled but could not be applied to claims arising from obligations which had already been performed.

BANK OF EAST ASIA LTD v. SCOTTISH ENTERPRISE [1996] 5 Bank L.R. 93, Lord Jauncey of Tullichettle, HL.

6703. Formation–sale of computer software–conditions of licence not disclosed to purchaser until package received

A company ordered from a supplier a standard computer software package to upgrade their existing software. The software was delivered in a package which showed that the software was subject to strict end user licence conditions under the name of the author. The conditions could be read through the wrapping. On the package it stated, "Opening the Informix SI software package indicates your acceptance of these terms and conditions". The company attempted to return the package unopened, but the suppliers refused to accept its return and sued for payment of the price. The suppliers argued that there was an unconditional and unqualified order for identified software; that, as they had supplied what was ordered, the defenders were obliged to pay the price; and that the suppliers were not concerned with any conditions imposed by the authors as owners of the intellectual property. The defenders argued that acceptance of the licence conditions was an implied condition suspensive of their agreement with the suppliers.

Held, that (1) the supply of proprietary software for a price was a single contract sui generis, although it contained elements of nominate contracts such as sale and the grant of a licence; (2) that it was an essential feature of the transaction that the supplier undertook to make available to the purchaser both the medium on which the program material was recorded and the right of access to and use of the software, and there could not be consensus in idem until the conditions of use stipulated by the author were produced and accepted by the parties, which could not come earlier than the stage at which the supplier tendered to the defenders an expression of those conditions and (3) in any event, whether the tender by the supplier of software subject to conditions of use was regarded as a breach of a previously unconditional contract, or as being subject to an implied suspensive condition entitling the defenders to reject the software if the conditions of use were unacceptable, or as being made when there was not concluded contract, the defenders were entitled to reject the software; and action dismissed.

BETA COMPUTERS (EUROPE) LTD v. ADOBE SYSTEMS (EUROPE) LTD 1996 S.L.T. 604, Judge not specified, OH.

6704. Hire–destruction of subject of hire in the custody of hirer–burden of proof

Held, in an action of damages at the instance of the owner of a toilet caravan against the hirer in whose custody it had been destroyed by fire, that it was for the defender to aver and prove destruction without fault on her part and that there was no requirement on the pursuer to specify negligent acts causing the loss; and proof before answer allowed.

LEITH v. DOWNIE 1996 S.C.L.R. 336, Judge not specified, Sh Ct.

6705. Offer and acceptance–provision of services–no agreement as to remuneration

P sought declarator that P had entered into a contract with D, to act as middlemen in procuring D business in relation to aircraft engines operated by A, and commission and fees in respect of P's services under that contract. The First Division [1994] C.L.Y. 5492 had previously held, reversing the Lord Ordinary [1993] C.L.Y. 4867 that where there was an arrangement to supply goods at a price "to be agreed" or to perform on terms "to be agreed", then if it was executed on one side, the law would say that there was necessarily implied from that conduct, a contract that in default of an agreement a reasonable price was to be paid. At a further debate, D argued that P still had inadequate averments of contract. P had averred that after a meeting between P and D on May 23, 1990 a contract was entered into but that remuneration was subject to further negotiation. D claimed that the averments upon which P's appeal had been granted had now been radically altered to disclose that P performed services at a time when the alleged contract was likely to come into existence, and had done so merely in pursuit of a contract in the hope of obtaining one. P now sought to aver a course of dealings between 1987 and 1990 not as background but to infer the existence of a contract. P argued that there was no more than a broadening of the spectrum and giving D better notice.

Held, proof before answer allowed, that the court could only compare the pleadings with their state before the Division and there had not been a radical departure. Opinion, that where parties were negotiating on an essential part of a contract such as price and expressly failed to agree it, there was no consensus in idem. That was distinct from a situation where parties either by mistake or deliberately were silent as to price, where the court should then fix a reasonable rate. This was without prejudice to the principles of unjustified enrichment.

AVINTAIR v. AVILL 1995 S.C.L.R. 1012, Judge not specified, OH.

6706. Articles

Delectus personae: you and who else? *(Rosalind M.M. McInnes)*: Bus. L.B. 1996, 21 (May), 2-3. (Delectus personae principle in relation to assignation of commercial contracts in Scotland).

Remoteness and breach of contract *(Hector L. MacQueen)*: Jur. Rev. 1996, 5, 295-303. (Divergence in approach of Scottish courts from English courts when considering test for remoteness in relation to fixing damages for breach of contract).

Remoteness in breach of contract *(William W. McBryde)*: S.L.P.Q. 1996, 1 (5), 341-351. (Conceptual basis of law regarding remoteness of damages for breach of contract and current position in Scots law)

Report on Three Bad Rules in Contract Law (Scot Law Com No 152). *(Enid A. Marshall)*: S.L.G. 1996, 64(1), 37-39. (Recommends abolition of rules on restriction of proof of contract terms, supersession of contract by conveyance and no damages unless property returned).

Scottish Law Commission: contract law : S.L.T. 1996, 2, 19-20 . (Scottish Law Commission report No.152 on "Three Bad Rules in Contract Law" recommends abolition of rules regarding restriction of proof of contract terms, supersession of contract by conveyance and no damages unless property returned).

Shrink wrap licences–breaking the seal–the Beta v Adobe case *(Charlotte Waelde)*: IT L.T. 1996, 4(5), 1-4. (Whether licence conditions for shrink wrapped software could be enforced as part of contract with end user).

Shrink-wrap licensing in the Scottish courts *(Graham P. Smith)*: I.J.L & I.T. 1996, 4(2), 131-150. (Legal enforceability and status of licences and decision that contract not completed until purchaser read and accepted conditions).

The expectation, reliance and restitution interests in contract damages *(Laura J. Macgregor)*: Jur. Rev. 1996, 4, 227-249 . (Analysis of decisions relating to damages for breach of contract against background of Fuller and Perdue's article entitled The Reliance Interest in Contract Damages at 1936, 46 Yale L.J. 52).

The theory of the Scots law of contract *(William J. Stewart)*: Jur. Rev. 1996, 6, 403-413. (Response to article by Laura J. Macgregor at Jur. Rev. 1996, 4, 227-249 on theoretical underpinning of law of contract in relation to damages for breach).

The validity of shrink-wrap licences *(Clive Gringras)*: I.J.L & I.T. 1996, 4(2), 77-111. (Rationale for use their validity under English law in light of precedent from Scotland and US, effect if they are not valid and conflict of laws problems).

COPYRIGHT

6707. Infringement–building plans and designs–damages

[Copyright, Designs and Patents Act 1988 (c.48) s.97(2).]

Section 97(2) of the Copyright, Designs and Patents Act 1988 provides that the court, in an action for infringement of copyright, may, having regard in particular to the flagrancy of the infringement and any benefit accruing to the defender by reason of the infringement, award such additional damages as the justice of the case may require. House builders concluded, inter alia, for an accounting in connection with an action for breach of copyright. They alleged that the defenders had infringed their copyright in relation to the design of different types of houses, in the course of their similar business of housebuilding. They also sought additional damages in terms of s.97(2) of the 1988 Act. At procedure roll, the defenders argued that it was incompetent for an award of additional damages to be made in the absence of a claim for damages under s.96 of that Act. The pursuers argued that the right to additional damages stood alone and was created by Parliament in order to enable a claim for damage or loss which could be identified but not quantified and therefore could not be included within the primary remedy sought.

Held, that s.97(2) should not be interpreted so as to restrict a claim for additional damages to only those cases where a claim for damages was being advanced under s.96(2); and proof before answer allowed on the pursuers' whole case, *Cala Homes (South) v. Alfred McAlpine Homes East Ltd* Independent, October 30, 1995, [1996] C.L.Y. 3632 followed.

Observed, that since damages cannot cover loss twice, the defenders were protected to the extent that whatever they paid under an accounting would have to be taken into consideration when assessing the claim for additional damages. Opinion, that the remedy still had to reflect identifiable damages either unquantifiable or at least not being claimed by other means.

REDROW HOMES v. BETT BROTHERS 1996 S.L.T. 1254, Judge not specified, OH.

CRIMINAL EVIDENCE

6708. Admissibility–bankers' books–proof of copies

[Bankers' Books Evidence Act 1879 (c.11) s.6; Prisoners and Criminal Proceedings (Scotland) Act 1993 (c.9) s.29.]

The Prisoners and Criminal Proceedings (Scotland) Act 1992 Sch.3 s.29 provides for the admissibility in criminal proceedings of copy documents and of evidence contained in business documents. Paragraphs 1 and 2 of Sch.3 deal respectively with the production of copy documents and the proof of the accuracy of such copies. Paragraph 7(1)(b) provides that nothing in Sch.3 shall affect the operation of the Bankers' Books Evidence Act 1879 and para.8 defines "business" as including trade, profession or other occupation. Paragraph 7(3) amends s.6 of the 1879 Act which, as amended, provides that a banker or bank officer shall not, in any legal proceedings to which the bank is not party, be compellable to produce any banker's book the contents of which can be proved under the 1879 Act or the Civil Evidence (Scotland) Act 1988 or Sch.3 to the 1993 Act, or to appear as a witness to prove the matters, transactions, and accounts therein, unless by order of a judge made for special cause. Two accused persons were tried on indictment for embezzlement from a firm of solicitors. The Crown lodged copies of the firm's bank statements to prove that sums of money deposited with the firm by its clients had passed through the accused's hands but had not been credited to the firm's bank accounts. The Crown sought to rely on Sch.3 to the 1993 Act to prove that the bank statements were true copies and that the entries therein were accurate. On objection being taken the sheriff held that Sch.3 did not apply to the proof of bank statements or documents which could be proved under the 1879 Act. The Crown was thereby prevented from leading essential evidence and the sheriff therefore sustained submissions of no case to answer and acquitted the accused. The Lord Advocate presented a petition to the High Court in terms of the Criminal Procedure (Scotland) Act 1975 s.263A(1) to obtain the court's opinion as to whether the provisions of Sch.3 applied to the proof of bank statements or bank documents which could be proved under the 1879 Act.

Held, that bank statements or bank documents could be proved in criminal proceedings either under the 1879 Act or under the 1993 Act; and question answered accordingly.

Observed, that the 1993 Act had produced an alternative and less stringent means than the 1879 Act of proving bank statements or bank documents, *HM Advocate v. Fox* (Unreported, 1995) approved.

LORD ADVOCATE'S REFERENCE (NO.1 OF 1996) 1996 S.L.T. 740, Lord Ross, L.J.C., HCJ.

6709. Admissibility–co-accused's extrajudicial statements

An accused person was tried along with four co-accused for murder. The deceased was set upon in a street and kicked and punched and was fatally stabbed by S. The accused gave evidence but none of his co-accused did. The accused maintained that he did not know of the use of the knife during the attack. At an interview the accused told police that he had walked away from the attack before it was over, because he had had enough, while S was still continuing to punch and kick the deceased. The accused's evidence on this point was contradicted by a Crown witness who identified the accused as one of two youths who kept on hitting the deceased after the others had left. The accused sought to rely on passages in statements by three of his co-accused to the police, which were partly incriminating and partly exculpatory, in order to demonstrate that his evidence was consistent with what his co-accused had said to the police. The co-accused's statements were all made outwith the presence of the other co-accused. The trial judge directed the jury that they should disregard the co-accused's statements for that purpose as they were not evidence in relation to the accused. The accused was convicted of culpable homicide and appealed on the ground of misdirection.

Held, that the co-accused's statements were not admissible against the other accused as they were not present when they were made and, for the same reason they were not admissible for the purpose of assisting the other accused in their defence; and appeal refused, *Morrison v. HM Advocate* 1991 S.L.T. 57, [1991] C.L.Y. 4552 distinguished; dictum of Lord Justice Clerk (Ross) in *McLay v. HM Advocate* 1994 S.L.T. 873, [1994] C.L.Y. 5568.

MURRAY v. HM ADVOCATE 1996 S.L.T. 648, Judge not specified, HCJ.

6710. Admissibility–search–club steward suspecting possession of drugs–search against will–whether illegal–whether excusable

[Misuse of Drugs Act 1971 (c.38) s.5(3).]

An accused person was tried on summary complaint for a contravention of the Misuse of Drugs Act 1971 s.5 (3). The accused was in a club when he was asked by a steward to submit to a search. The accused, who had by then been searched twice with his consent, refused and was put out of the club. After the club had closed two stewards saw the accused with a group of people at the side of the club in an area known to be frequented by drug dealers. The accused had some objects in his hand, but threw them to the ground and they were never recovered by the police. Some short time later, one of the stewards took hold of the accused and having felt something under the accused's shirt, suspected that the accused was carrying drugs. The accused was then detained and during his detention he was searched against his will by the stewards on the ground that it was management policy to do so where it was suspected that the person might have drugs. Seventy eight temazepam tablets were found under the accused's shirt. The sheriff admitted the evidence of the results of the search on the ground that though the search was irregular, it was justified by the accused's prior suspicious behaviour and by it being in the stewards' interests as the accused might have had a weapon. The accused was convicted and appealed.

Held, that the search was illegal as the sheriff's reasons for admitting the evidence were not sound ones and the search was both irregular and inexcusable; and appeal allowed and conviction quashed.

WILSON v. BROWN 1996 S.L.T. 686, Judge not specified, HCJ.

6711. Admissibility–statement by accused

Held, where the interview of a suspect under caution was interrupted by the police to enable them to formulate a charge, and the suspect, who had previously denied the allegations, confessed when the interview resumed and was then questioned in detail about the alleged incident before being charged, it was only when a formal charge was levelled against the citizen that further questioning was automatically precluded as a matter of fairness. The question of whether it was fair for the police to renew the interview should be left to the jury; and objection to the admissibility of the confession statement repelled.

HM ADVOCATE v. PENDERS 1996 S.C.C.R. 404, Judge not specified.

6712. Admissibility–statement by accused–14 year old girl subject to prolonged interview

[Criminal Justice (Scotland) Act 1980 (c.62) s.2.]

C appealed against conviction of murdering D in concert with three coaccused, X. On June 1, 1995 when she was aged 14, C and X allegedly assaulted three men in a park, although the first two victims did not sustain serious injuries. D was stabbed three times in the scrotum with a knife, and beaten and stamped on repeatedly on his head and body with such force that his skull and almost all of the bones in his face were severely fractured. He was left lying unconscious in the park and died soon after being taken to hospital. A policeman who observed C and X in the vicinity of the park about 12.30 am took C home in a police vehicle, although X ran away. All four were detained by the police on June 3 and made detailed statements about the assaults. C was told that she was being questioned as a witness, although she was later advised that she was being detained under the Criminal Justice (Scotland) Act 1980 s.2 because of her potential involvement in the incident. C's father was present, but unwell during the interview. C was detained for about three and a half hours and closely interviewed by two police officers for about two and a half hours. In the course of her interview, C was asked several times if she had kicked D, which she denied until a late stage when she was informed that she might be charged and the police had evidence which suggested that she had kicked D, after which she broke down and admitted that she had kicked D once on the back of his feet. The Crown's case against C was based on her admission of kicking D and her statement that she was present throughout the attack, which was corroborated by evidence of bloodstains on the bottom front of her T-shirt indicating that she was close to D when he was being assaulted. C argued that (1) the trial judge erred in allowing her admission to be admitted in evidence as it was made in circumstances which were as a matter of law unfair to her, in view of her age, the length of time taken at the interview, the fact that her father was unable to protect her interests and the cumulative effect of the pressures which she was subjected to and (2) there was insufficient evidence to entitle the jury to convict her of murder. The Crown argued that the police had been entitled to put to C the matters they did and the jury had been properly directed on the question of fairness.

Held, allowing the appeal and quashing the conviction, that by the time C made the admission, the questioning had become so unfair that her answers were inadmissible. The mere presence of her father, even if unwell, was itself a check on the way the interview was conducted. However, despite her consistent denials, the police repeatedly asked C if she had kicked D, at a time when she had been crying and was clearly at her most vulnerable after a prolonged interview, and the questioning was designed to persuade C to change her answers and to admit what was being put to her. The statements C made at this stage in the interview were therefore obtained under pressure, not voluntarily and therefore were inadmissible, *Brown v. HM Advocate* 1966 S.L.T. 105, [1966] C.L.Y. 13011 and *HM Advocate v. Mair* 1982 S.L.T. 471, [1982] C.L.Y. 3554 applied; (2) even if her admission were admissible, it was insufficient to entitle the jury to convict her of murder, as there was no indication that when she kicked D she had reason to think that she was participating in an attack which was murderous in character as there was nothing in the nature of the earlier assaults to indicate that D was likely to be subjected to an attack of such savagery and wicked recklessness as ensued after he was first kicked. In addition, there was no evidence of blood on C's shoes or lower body and the position of the spots of blood on her T-shirt suggested that they came from D's face when he was still standing; and although the bloodstains would have been enough to corroborate her admission that she had participated in an assault on D, they did not provide the further circumstantial evidence which was needed to convict her of murder, in view of the limited character of her admission.

CODONA v. HM ADVOCATE 1996 S.L.T. 1100, Judge not specified, HCJ.

6713. Admissibility–statement by accused–whether inducement to admit offence

S appealed against conviction of three charges of theft on the grounds that (a) a statement which she gave to a police officer, C, was inadmissible and (b) (conceded by the Crown) there was insufficient evidence to establish charge three that S had taken money from the bank account of her lodger, B. S was charged with stealing money and a letter from B's room and removing £30 from B's bank account. The evidence on charges one and two included a statement which S made to C, after being cautioned, admitting that she had stolen the money and the letter from B. S argued that her statement was obtained under pressure. C had advised her at her residence that she was suspected of theft and that she had to be detained for questioning at the police station. When she told C that she could not leave the house as she was in charge of young children and no one else was present to look after them, C offered to make arrangements for a social worker to look after them, but stated that detention would not be necessary if she made a statement there and then in response to his inquiries, which she did. S argued that C's comment that S would not be detained if she made a statement amounted to an inducement to make the statement and the use which C made of the fact that he was proposing to detain her amounted to unfair pressure.

Held, refusing the appeal except as respects charge three, that S's statement was not unfairly obtained. In proposing that S avoid detention by making a contemporaneous statement, C was attempting to meet S's objection about leaving the young children alone in the house. Her advice was not given as an inducement for her to make a statement, but as an answer to her difficulty; and as she was cautioned, S would have been told that she was not obliged to make a statement.

STEWART v. HINGSTON 1996 S.C.C.R. 234, Judge not specified.

6714. Admissibility–whether evidence irregularly obtained

[Misuse of Drugs Act 1971 (c.38) s.23(2).]

Held, on C's appeal against conviction of unlawfully possessing cannabis resin, where C was a passenger in a car driven by B and the police had received information that B was believed to be in possession of controlled drugs, and where C, after being advised by the police that she would be detained for a search in terms of s.23(2) of the 1971 Act, without waiting to be searched, produced a piece of resinous substance which was apparently adhered to the front passenger seat rather than on her person and said "That belongs to me", that the sheriff did not err in finding that the police were entitled to search C and in admitting the evidence of their search since the power in s.23(2) to search B's vehicle extended to persons travelling with B when his car was stopped, and it was the information relating to the presence of B travelling within the vehicle and in possession of drugs which led the police to stop the vehicle in the first

place, *Campbell v. HM Advocate* 1993 S.L.T. 245 [1992] C.L.Y. 5367 followed; *Lucas v. Lockhart* (1980) S.C.C.R. Supp. 256, distinguished.
COOPER v. BUCHANAN 1996 S.C.C.R. 448, Lord Hope L.J.G., HCJ.

6715. Appeals–fresh evidence

An accused person was tried on indictment for assault and robbery. The accused pled alibi. The Crown's case against the accused relied upon the evidence of four witnesses who identified the accused as the robber. The robbery had been recorded on video tape by means of security cameras. The accused was convicted and appealed on the ground that there existed additional evidence which demonstrated that he was not the person whose face had been captured on the video tape. The High Court allowed the additional evidence to be led. At a continued hearing of the appeal, when the Crown also led an expert witness, who disputed the accused's experts' evidence as to facial comparison, the Crown maintained that a proper foundation had not been laid for the accused's experts' conclusions because their method of working was too imprecise to allow scientific comparison, and the quality of the video films was not sufficiently good.

Held, that (1) the appeal court could reject evidence which it considered that no reasonable jury would have regarded as credible or reliable; (2) in considering questions of credibility and reliability the function of the appeal court was different from that of the trial court, as the appeal court had to act as a court of review; but (3) if the appeal court found that the evidence was capable of being found by a reasonable jury, properly directed, to be both credible and reliable, that would be sufficient for the appeal to succeed, and (4) the additional evidence satisfied the latter test as the Crown's criticisms of the evidence raised questions of fact which should be left to a jury to decide and accordingly the absence of the additional evidence from the trial was a miscarriage of justice; and appeal allowed and retrial authorised.

Observed, that in considering the significance of the additional evidence sought to be led (the Crown having conceded that the evidence in the present case met the required standard), the evidence had to be directed to a matter which was so important, in the context of the whole of the evidence, that its absence from the trial could be said to amount to a miscarriage of justice, and that it could be assumed that evidence which was of no real importance to such an issue, or which related merely to peripheral matters, would not have had any importance attached to it by a jury.
CHURCH v. HM ADVOCATE (NO.2) 1996 S.L.T. 383, Judge not specified, HCJ.

6716. Appeals–fresh evidence–hearsay–time as at which admissibility to be determined

[Criminal Procedure (Scotland) Act 1995 (c.46) s.259.]

C appealed against conviction of murdering M on the ground that A, an incriminee at C's trial who had given evidence that he had taken a knife from C, that M had later assaulted C who did not retaliate and A had got C to run away, and that he did not wish to incriminate himself when asked if he had stabbed M, had since admitted to his solicitor, his wife (C's sister) and C's mother that he had killed M. The appeal was continued on three occasions for an affidavit to be obtained from A. It then appeared that A now sought to retract his confession and had stated that the evidence he had given about having the knife in his possession was not true. C argued that it would still be open to him to lead evidence from the wife, mother and solicitor of A's admissions, and that notwithstanding the decisions in *Perrie v. HM Advocate* [1991] J.C. 27, [1991] C.L.Y. 4548 and *McLay v. HM Advocate* [1994] S.L.T. 873, [1994] C.L.Y. 5568, if the court allowed the appeal and granted authority for a new prosecution the evidence would be admissible at the new trial having regard to s.259 of the 1995 Act.

Held, appeal refused, that (1) when it appeared that A was admitting to murder, that was evidence which could be regarded as additional evidence which was unavailable at trial, *Mitchell v. HM Advocate* 1989 S.C.C.R. 502, [1990] C.L.Y. 4892 followed. However as A sought to contradict evidence given at trial in support of the Crown case, continuation of the appeal was pointless; (2) the evidence of the other witnesses as to A's confession plainly would be hearsay, and (3) the question whether there was a miscarriage of justice on the ground of fresh evidence had to be tested by examining the position if the evidence had been made available at the trial. While s.259 would apply if authority were granted for a new trial, it was not relevant to the trial in which C was convicted and the rules in *Perrie* and *McLay* applied, under which the statements would only have been admissible if they had been put to A and he had denied making them, and could not have been used to establish the truth of their contents.

CONWAY v. HM ADVOCATE 1996 S.C.C.R. 569, Judge not specified.

6717. Appeals–fresh evidence–subsequent admission by co-accused

[Criminal Procedure (Scotland) Act 1975 (c.21) s.228(2).]

M appealed against conviction of attempted murder on the ground that the jury's verdict, which was reached in ignorance of his coaccused's (K) evidence, was a miscarriage of justice. In his initial statement to the police, K denied any responsibility for the assault, although in a second statement he blamed M for it and alleged that he had played only a minor role. Although K did not give evidence at the trial, his defence was to incriminate M. When the jury retired, however, K gave a statement taking sole responsibility for the incident. On the basis of M's argument on appeal that K's statement constituted significant evidence that was not available at trial and which would have had a material bearing on the jury's determination, the court agreed to hear K's evidence in terms of the Criminal Procedure (Scotland) Act 1975 s.252(b) to determine whether there was a miscarriage of justice. On examination, K stated that he was solely responsible for the assault and that M had not been present during the incident. He had lied to the police about M's involvement because he had hoped to be acquitted; however, by the end of the trial he realised that he would be convicted and decided that he did not want an innocent man to be convicted for his crime. On the continued appeal, M argued that K's evidence was capable of being found by a reasonable jury to be credible, *Church v. HM Advocate (No.2)* 1996 S.L.T. 383, [1996] C.L.Y. 6715. His admission was entirely consistent with the forensic evidence. He had nothing to gain by continuing to blame M and the fact that his admission was against his own interest enhanced its credibility. The Crown submitted that K's evidence was wholly incredible because he was a self confessed liar and because it was unreliable when checked against other evidence.

Held, appeal allowed, verdict set aside and authority granted for a new prosecution. A reasonable jury could well have accepted K's admission as credible and concluded that M had been wrongly accused. K's evidence was entirely consistent with M's account to the police and his insistence that he was innocent. K was a brutal and callous man and his initial incrimination of M might be seen as a cynical attempt to escape the consequences of his own crime without regard to what might happen to M.

MITCHELL v. HM ADVOCATE 1996 S.C.C.R. 477, Judge not specified.

6718. Corroboration–chemical analysis

Held, that on M's appeal against conviction on a charge of causing pollution in a stream on the grounds that there had been inadequate corroboration of the evidence of F, an analyst, M claiming that D, F's immediate superior, who had discussed the tests with F, had not been involved in the actual testing but only in the discussion and an arithmetical check of F's calculations, that the appeal would be refused since there had been sufficient corroboration of F's work in that the discussions between D and F had been in some detail regarding the tests to be done, the tests were carried out in accordance with normal laboratory procedures and D had checked the results independently and also against the value of standards before the report of the results was signed by both F and D.

LAW MINING v. CARMICHAEL 1996 S.C.C.R. 627, Judge not specified.

6719. Corroboration–identification

R appealed against conviction for an assault to injury on Y, claiming that, although Y had positively identified R as his attacker, this had not been sufficiently corroborated by S, who had been drinking with Y and spoke to Y, and then R, leaving the bar, and stated that R, on his return to the bar, had said, "You had better make sure your mate is OK." The Crown claimed that R's statement required to be considered together with other evidence particularly that relating to the time at which R and Y left the bar and the time R returned.

Held, allowing the appeal and quashing the conviction, that the point was a narrow one, but it was concluded with hesitation that the sheriff was not entitled to draw the inference which he did. R's statement, although it showed that he was aware that something had happened to Y, could not reasonably be construed as an admission of guilt.

REILLY v. FRASER 1996 S.C.C.R. 26, Judge not specified.

6720. Corroboration–Moorov doctrine–rape

Held, that on A's appeal against conviction of raping a seven-year-old-girl, C, on two occasions in 1989, on one of which C was the only witness to the incident, charge 2, and on another which was allegedly witnessed in its entirety by D, charge 3, where A was also charged but acquitted of raping D when she was aged seven, charge 1, and the Crown relied on the *Moorov* doctrine 1930 S.L.T. 596 in respect of the unwitnessed rapes of C and D, (1) of consent, that the jury erred in acquitting A of charge 1 but convicting him of charge 2 where the trial judge had instructed them that they could not convict A of charge 2 unless they accepted D's evidence in its essentials in relation to charge 1; but (2) that the jury's verdicts on charges 1 and 3 were not so inconsistent and irreconcilable with each other as to require reconstruction of the verdict, *Hamilton v. HM Advocate* 1938 S.L.T. 333, and although their rejection of D's evidence in respect of charge 1 was understandable since she refused to be medically examined and she did not make any allegation against A until July 1995, there was no indication that they did not accept D's evidence about what A did to C, and where a consultant paediatrician opined that C's history and subsequent behavioural patterns in taking an overdose of pills in 1994 were highly suggestive of sexual abuse, the jury must have been satisfied that C's evidence was credible and reliable and it was not necessary to suppose that the jury misunderstood the directions on the need for corroboration of C's evidence as there was sufficient evidence on charge 3 which they were entitled to accept; and verdict set aside on charge 2 only.

AINSWORTH v. HM ADVOCATE 1996 S.C.C.R. 631, Lord Hope L.J.G., HCJ.

6721. Corroboration–Moorov doctrine–sexual offences

An accused person was charged on indictment with six sexual offences involving three complainers. Charge 4 was an assault with intent to rape involving the attempted insertion of the accused's penis in the complainer's private parts. Charge 1 was a charge of using lewd, indecent and libidinous practices and behaviour by attempting to insert his finger in the complainer's private parts. The accused's defence was a denial of the allegations. The sheriff directed the jury that the evidence of the complainers on each of charges 1 and 4, if accepted, could be used to corroborate the other charge. In his directions the sheriff went into the evidence in detail giving over 16 pages of his charge to an analysis of the Crown case but only one-half page to the defence case. In explaining the *Moorov* doctrine the sheriff quoted a passage from the charge in *H.M. Advocate v. AE* 1938 S.L.T. 70 which referred by way of illustration to immoral conduct by a depraved man in the street. The accused was convicted and appealed, contending that (1) the offences in charges 1 and 4 could not corroborate each other and (2) by going into the complainers' evidence in detail, quoting an emotive illustration which was inapposite to the circumstances of the case, giving greater treatment to the Crown case and providing unnecessarily complicated directions on corroboration, the charge had been unfair to the accused.

Held, that (1) despite the differences in the *nomen iuris* of the crimes libelled in charges 1 and 4, there was an underlying similarity in the conduct which it was for the jury, as question of fact and degree, to assess; (2) while the charge was longer and more detailed than necessary, the basic *Moorov* principles and their application to the case had been set out with sufficient clarity, and the matter was one for the sheriff's judgment; and appeal refused.

McMAHON v. HM ADVOCATE 1996 S.L.T. 1139, Judge not specified, HCJ.

6722. Corroboration–Moorov doctrine–theft

Held, on T's appeal against three charges of theft, where in each case an elderly lady had been approached by a young woman offering to sell rose bushes and each of the complainers had been persuaded to go into their gardens while a third party entered their homes and committed the theft, (a) that the Crown was entitled to rely on the *Moorov* doctrine in respect of charges 1 and 2 where T was positively identified by the complainer in charge 2, and although the complainer in charge 1 was not sure about the identification, there was sufficient evidence from which it could be inferred that T was the perpetrator where one of the complainer's neighbours gave evidence that he had seen T in the street and another that had seen her in the street and later in the complainer's garden *Lindsay v. HM Advocate* 1994 S.L.T. 546, [1994] C.L.Y. 5524; and (b) in respect of charge 3, that because of the similarities between the incidents, the Crown were entitled to rely on the proposition that all three crimes had been committed by the same person and that since it was proved that T had committed two of them, it followed from the mixture of identification and circumstantial evidence that the third charge had also been committed by her, *Howden v. HM Advocate* 1994 S.C.C.R. 19, [1994] C.L.Y. 5531.

TOWNSLEY v. LEES 1996 S.C.C.R. 620, Judge not specified.

6723. Corroboration–theft–shoplifting

Held, where S appealed against a conviction for theft of 88 packets of batteries from a shop on the grounds that there was insufficient corroboration of evidence of C, a security officer in the shop, that he had seen S leaning over a counter and filling a black bag with the batteries, that the appeal would be allowed and the conviction quashed since the fact that a theft had taken place was an essential fact which required corroborated evidence *McDonald v. Herron* 1966 S.L.T. 61 [1966] C.L.Y. 13021, and in the present case the only evidence was that from C who spoke to the theft and that of J, who spoke of having seen S behaving in a suspicious manner a short time before and this was not sufficient corroboration without evidence, e.g. that similar packets were missing or that the batteries found had come from the store.

STEWART v. HAMILTON 1996 S.C.C.R. 494, Judge not specified.

6724. Previous convictions–disclosure

[Criminal Procedure (Scotland) Act 1975 (c.21) s.160.]

H appealed against conviction of driving while disqualified, arguing that although he had not challenged the special capacity in which he was charged and therefore no evidence had been led of the reason for him being disqualified, the prosecutor in addressing the jury had referred to his being disqualified as a result of a previous conviction, in breach of the Criminal Procedure (Scotland) Act 1975 s.160(1).

Held, refusing the appeal, that the reference had been unnecessary, but since it was clear that H could only have been disqualified as a result of a conviction there had been no breach of s.160(1), *Russell v. HM Advocate* 1993 S.L.T. 358 [1991] C.L.Y. 4594. In any event the sheriff was entitled to conclude that it would be better to make no further reference to the matter in his charge.

HARKIN v. HM ADVOCATE 1996 S.L.T. 1004, Judge not specified, HCJ.

6725. Previous convictions–perjury–driving while disqualified

[Criminal Procedure (Scotland) Act 1975 (c. 21) s.160(1) and (2).]

M appealed against his conviction of perjury on the ground that the Crown's leading of evidence of M's previous conviction constituted a miscarriage of justice in breach of s.160 of the Criminal Procedure (Scotland) Act 1975. In January 1993, M was tried for driving while disqualified. He gave evidence in the course of the proceedings that he had not driven a motor vehicle on the date libelled, but eventually pled guilty to the charges and was thereafter indicted for perjury in respect of his evidence at trial. Although the indictment for perjury stated that M had falsely deponed in the earlier trial that he had not driven a motor vehicle at the material time, it did not libel that he pled guilty to contravening s.103 of the Road Traffic Act 1988. M argued that it was therefore inappropriate under s.160 of the 1975 Act for the Crown to refer in evidence to his previous conviction as the leading of such evidence was prejudicial.

Held, appeal refused, that the evidence that M had pled guilty to contravening s.103 at his earlier trial was evidence in causa in support of the charge of perjury. The Crown did not require to put their evidence into the charge. It was of critical importance to proof of the charge of perjury to show that M had represented that he had not been in the car or driven it at the material time whereas the truth was that he had done so, and therefore it was competent under s.160(2) for his plea of guilty to be led even though it disclosed that M had a previous conviction.

MILNE v. HM ADVOCATE 1996 S.L.T. 775, Judge not specified, HCJ.

6726. Relevancy–line of cross examination

An accused person was tried on a summary complaint for breach of the peace at a district council housing office. A senior official in the housing office and his superior, M, were called for the Crown. In cross examination M was asked whether he knew a defence witness, who had been present in the housing office and was the accused's girlfriend and secretary of the local tenants' association, and he said that he did. When M was thereafter asked whether he had been charged with making nuisance telephone calls to the accused's girlfriend two years after the incident, the Crown objected. The accused's solicitor explained that the question was put to alert the court to an ongoing feud involving considerable ill feeling and that it related directly to M's credibility and was indirectly connected with the facts of the case because it involved Crown and defence witnesses who were part of the feud. The sheriff disallowed the question as irrelevant. The evidence of Crown witnesses, including M, was accepted by the sheriff as credible and reliable. The accused was convicted and appealed, arguing that the sheriff had erred in disallowing the line of cross examination.

Held, that (1) care had always to be taken when stopping a line of cross examination of a Crown witness but (2) as there was no suggestion that M was being challenged about his recollection of events or was exaggerating, or that the telephone calls had anything to do with the accused being charged, the sheriff was entitled to disallow the line as irrelevant; and appeal refused.

Observed, that had it been suggested to the sheriff that the telephone calls would be relied on to demonstrate ill feeling between M and the accused which might have influenced M's evidence, there might have been some force in the argument that the sheriff had erred.

McALLISTER v. NORMAND 1996 S.L.T. 622, Judge not specified.

6727. Special defence–incrimination of co-accused–whether notice required

[Criminal Procedure (Scotland) Act 1975 (c.21) s.82.]

M and B appealed against conviction of attempted murder of a police constable, D, and murder of P (who was shot by their coaccused, S, arising out of an armed robbery. D gave evidence that M had fired his gun at him or in his direction twice before he was apprehended. A photograph of a mark on D's hand, which was taken at the police station following M's arrest, was described as a powder burn by D and B, a forensic pathologist. There was also evidence that two bullets were found jammed in the barrel of M's gun, and two spent cartridges were found in its revolving chamber. S was the only accused to give evidence and he stated that all of the participants knew that each of them carried a weapon which was loaded with live ammunition, (1) M and B argued that there was a miscarriage of justice in allowing S's evidence as no notice had been given as required under the Criminal Procedure (Scotland) Act 1975 s.82(1), it being evidence which exculpated S and incriminated M and B. It was enough for it to fall within s.82 that S's evidence reduced his responsibility for the offence and materially supported the Crown's case against M and B by undermining their defences, *McCourtney v. HM Advocate* 1977 J.C. 68, [1977] C.L.Y. 3307 and (2) M also argued that the judge erred in law in repelling his plea of no case to answer in respect that D's evidence was uncorroborated. There was no evidence that M's gun had gone off and no one else spoke to seeking a burn on D's hand after the incident. Moreover, the state of M's gun did not corroborate D's evidence since there was a live cartridge between the two spent ones and no explanation as to how this live cartridge could still be in the chamber if the gun had been fired twice during the struggle between D and M.

Held, refusing the appeals, that (1) the Crown were not required to give notice of S's evidence as it did not have the dual character and effect of exculpating S by incriminating M and B, as specified in s.82 of the 1975 Act. To hold otherwise would lead to difficulty and uncertainty as evidence which reduced an accused's responsibility for an offence might be difficult to identify in advance, *McCourtney v. HM Advocate* 1977 J.C. 68, [1977] C.L.Y. 3307 disapproved and (2) there was sufficient evidence in the photograph and the state of the gun to corroborate D's statement that M had twice fired a gun at him or in his direction during the incident. In addition, a ballistics expert opined that the gun had been fired twice and that the revolving chamber could be turned to move a live round from the firing position before the gun was fired if the revolving cylinder was knocked in the course of a struggle. In light of the explanation, there was sufficient for conviction.

McQUADE v. HM ADVOCATE 1996 S.C.C.R. 347, Lord Hope, L.J.G., HCJ.

6728. Sufficiency–bylaws

An accused person was tried on a summary complaint for consuming alcohol in a street which was a designated place in terms of local bylaws. The Crown lodged the bylaws, but not the plan identifying the prohibited areas. The accused was convicted and appealed.

Held, that (1) where byelaws required to be proved by a copy being put in evidence the whole bylaws required to be put in evidence, and that the Crown had failed to comply with this requirement by not having lodged the plan, without which it was not possible fully to understand the description of the area; (2) the Crown's failure could not be made good by the justice's personal knowledge or a police officer's evidence that the street was a designated area and appeal allowed and conviction quashed, *Herkes v. Dickie* 1959 S.L.T. 74, [1959] C.L.Y. 3785 applied.

DONNELLY v. CARMICHAEL 1996 S.L.T. 153, Judge not specified, HCJ.

6729. Sufficiency–attempting to pervert the course of justice

An accused person was charged on a summary complaint with attempting to pervert the course of justice by assisting a man, S, to avoid being taken into lawful custody. Police officers, after having been shown a warrant for the arrest of S, went to his house where they saw him leaving quickly via the back court. The officers gave chase along a street and as they were doing so the accused stopped his motor vehicle and allowed S and another man to get into the vehicle, which was then driven off at speed. Objection was taken to evidence of the police officers' efforts to execute the warrant on the ground that the warrant had not been produced in evidence. The sheriff repelled the objection and convicted the accused, who appealed.

Held, that the course of justice commenced when the police officers were informed of the existence of the warrant and began their pursuit, and was still being pursued when the appellant interrupted it; and the existence or validity of the original warrant was an incidental matter which it was unnecessary for the Crown to establish in order to prove the case against the accused; and appeal refused, *Fletcher v. Tudhope* 1984 S.C.C.R. 267, [1984] C.L.Y. 3896 considered.

McELHINNEY v. NORMAND 1996 S.L.T. 238, Judge not specified, HCJ.

6730. Sufficiency–breach of the peace

Held, on C's appeal against conviction for breach of the peace, that the appeal would be allowed and the conviction quashed since there was no finding to indicate that the two police officers, who had been called by C to her house to investigate a complaint of assault, had been alarmed, upset or annoyed as a result of offensive remarks made to them by C, or that anyone in the vicinity could hear what was being said. For once this was a case in which *Logan v. Jessop* 1987 S.C.C.R. 604, [1988] C.L.Y. 3999, could be followed.

CAVANAGH v. WILSON 1995 S.C.C.R. 693, Judge not specified.

6731. Sufficiency–culpable homicide–concert in criminal law

M and X appealed against conviction of culpable homicide of D. D had been brutally assaulted by a group of youths including M and X during which he was slashed several times and fatally stabbed with a knife by their co-accused, S. M and X denied having any part in the use of the knife, stating they had left the attack before it was over. W, who observed the later stages of the assault from his window, identified X as one of two youths who kept hitting D after the others had gone away, and H, a 16 year old girl who tried to pull one of the assailants off D, identified M and X as participants who were still involved in the attack when D was slashed several times with the knife. Y and L, who observed the incidents from about 100 yards away, stated that all of the assailants were involved until the incident ended with D falling to the ground. The jury found S guilty of murder and M and X guilty of culpable homicide on the basis that they persisted in the attack knowing that S had produced a knife and had used it to inflict injury on D. (1) M and X argued there was insufficient evidence for the jury to hold that they were involved in the use of the knife. H's evidence that M was present until the end of the attack was not supported by other evidence, and her statement that D was slashed and stabbed while standing was inconsistent with the pathologist's opinion that the knife injuries were sustained while D was lying on his back. It was not clear that the knife had been used during the earlier part of the incident when M was still involved, significantly no one other than H saw the knife being used and as there was no evidence to indicate when the blows with the knife had been delivered, there was no basis for inferring that the assailants must have seen the knife, *Walker v. H.M. Advocate* 1985 S.C.C.R. 150, [1985] C.L.Y. 3825/3950; (2) X argued that the judge misdirected the jury in charging them not to consider the statements his co-accused made during their interviews with the police. The statements demonstrated that this evidence was consistent with what his co-accused told the police; he was relying on these for the truth of their contents, but as an incidental benefit, to find support for his account given in evidence; this was a legitimate extension of the rules relating to statements that were partly incriminating and partly exculpatory.

Held, appeals refused, that (1) there was sufficient evidence for the jury to conclude that X and M continued to participate in the assault after D had been stabbed and slashed by S, and although there were differences in the evidence, it was for the jury to decide which parts they would accept, and what inferences to draw. The jury were entitled to hold that the main injuries, including the knife wounds, were inflicted when D was still being assaulted by M and X *Walker*, distinguished. H's evidence was corroborated by the number and distribution of the wounds which, when taken together with the proximity of M and X to D and S, provided a basis for the necessary inference that the knife, which was used to inflict so many different injuries, must have been visible to M and X; (2) the trial judge properly directed the jury not to consider the co-accused's statements. The statements could not be used to incriminate or exculpate S and were not admissible for the purpose of assisting his defence, even for the limited purpose of showing that the co-accused's stories were consistent with his. The rules in *Morrison v. HM Advocate* 1991 S.L.T. 57, [1991] C.L.Y. 4552 did not apply. X was seeking to undermine W's credibility and this was not a purpose which could reasonably be described as an incidental benefit of the kind referred to in *McLay v. HM Advocate* 1994 S.L.T. 873, [1994] C.L.Y. 5568, distinguished.

MATHIESON v. HM ADVOCATE 1996 S.C.C.R. 388, Judge not specified.

6732. Sufficiency–forensic report–witness not responsible for carrying out tests

[Criminal Justice (Scotland) Act 1980 (c.62) s.26.]

O appealed against conviction of being concerned in the supply of diamorphine on the ground that the Crown had failed to prove the nature of the substance in question. The Crown relied on a certificate under the Criminal Justice (Scotland) Act 1980 (c.62) s.26, spoken to by F, one of the signatories, the Crown having given notice under s.26(7) that only F was to be called and O having served no counter notice. O unsuccessfully objected to F's evidence on the ground that as the tests had actually been carried out by the other signatory, C, F's evidence of the analysis was hearsay. F stated in evidence that the results from the tests were given to him and that both he and C examined them. O argued on appeal that while F could say enough to corroborate C, he could not give direct evidence that the results analysed had been obtained by means of the tests carried out by C. Section 26(7) removed the requirement for corroboration but did not remove the need for primary evidence to be given of the facts contained in the report.

Held, refusing the appeal, that the provision that the evidence of the single signatory was to be "sufficient evidence of any fact (or conclusion as to fact) contained in the report" implied that the evidence of one signatory about the work which was done by the other, which would otherwise have been treated as hearsay, was admissible and sufficient so long as it related to a fact or conclusion as to fact in the report. In the absence of a counter notice the Crown were entitled to rely on the single signatory.

O'BRIEN v. HM ADVOCATE 1996 S.C.C.R. 238, Judge not specified.

6733. Sufficiency–identification–circumstantial evidence

Held, where children had described offences committed by a nightwatchman known as "Mike", and their parents had identified in court the accused as a nightwatchman, who was very friendly with the children and their family and was known to them as "Mike", that, having regard to the circumstantial detail to which the parents were able to speak, their evidence was sufficient to enable the jury to draw the inference that the accused was the man described by the children as the offender.

ROBSON v. HM ADVOCATE 1996 S.L.T. 944, Judge not specified, HCJ.

6734. Sufficiency–reset–uttering

An accused was charged with resetting and uttering a number of cheques. The cheques had been stolen one afternoon and were presented between 1.55 pm and 4.35 pm on the same day. The cheques had all been signed by the same person and bore the fingerprints of the accused in places which, according to the fingerprint experts, were consistent with extensive use of the cheques to sign, grip and remove them from the cheque book, but were inconsistent with casual handling. The accused told the police that she had flicked through the cheques when someone had shown her them in a public house, but she did not give evidence.

Held, that the evidence was sufficient for conviction, and accused convicted except in respect of two cheques where the sheriff had a reasonable doubt on the matter.

CROWE v. DEASLEY 1996 S.C.C.R. 1, Judge not specified.

6735. Sufficiency–sexual intercourse with 13 year old girl–defence of reasonable belief

[Sexual Offences (Scotland) Act 1976 (c.67) s.4.]

Held, the Crown not opposing, on M's appeal against conviction of having unlawful sexual intercourse with a 13 year old girl (C) in breach of the Sexual Offences (Scotland) Act 1976 s.4(1), where M argued in terms of s.4(2)(b) of the Act that he had reasonable cause to believe that C was of or above the age of 16 years since she had told him when they met that she was 16, that she had looked to be 16, none of her friends contradicted her when she gave her age, and C's mother stated that M had been very forthcoming and she believed that M had not appreciated C's true age, that the sheriff had erred in concluding that M could not reasonably have believed that she was aged 16, as the basis for his decision was C's appearance in the witness box rather than the evidence of her behaviour and general demeanour at the time of the incident, and in taking this approach he in effect substituted his own views, even if unintentionally, for the views which M could reasonably have formed on the occasion of the incident as there was no evidence that her general appearance in the witness box was the same as it was at the time when M had asked how old she was, and M was entitled to avail himself of the statutory defence in view of the evidence about what he was told and was able to observe for himself at the time; and conviction quashed.

MAIR v. RUSSELL 1996 S.C.C.R. 453, Judge not specified.

6736. Sufficiency–statutory offence–trespass–failure to comply with direction to remove–disputed occupancy of land

[Criminal Justice and Public Order Act 1994 (c. 33) s.61.]

The Crown appealed against a sheriff's decision sustaining a motion of no case to answer against three accused (R) charged with five others with encamping on land and failing to remove from it as soon as reasonably practicable in breach of s.61 after having been directed to do so by representatives of the occupiers and by a senior police officer (C). There was a dispute between F and D as to who was the occupier of the land in terms of s.61 (9); however, representatives of both F and D, as well as C, had directed the accused to leave the land. As a result of the title dispute between F and D, the sheriff concluded that since there was no clear evidence as to who was entitled between F and D to natural possession of the land, the condition in s.61 that C reasonably believed that reasonable steps had been taken by or on behalf of the occupier to ask the accused to leave could not be satisfied and therefore the complaint was incompetent.

Held, appeal allowed, that it was not necessary for the Crown to prove who owned the land as both of the two possible owners had given evidence that they had not consented or given lawful authority to R to enter or remain on the land. It was a question of fact whether C reasonably believed that the occupiers had taken steps to ask R to leave and the issue of which of the two contenders was in fact the occupier was immaterial. There was sufficient evidence to entitle the sheriff to hold that the requirements for a direction under s.61 (1) were therefore satisfied.

NEIZER v. RHODES 1995 S.C.C.R. 799, Judge not specified.

6737. Witnesses–character of prosecution witness–scope of cross examination

[Criminal Procedure (Scotland) Act 1975 (c.21) s.346(1).]

Held, where S appealed against conviction for dangerous driving on the grounds that the sheriff erred in allowing the Crown to cross-examine S as to his character, the prosecutor having intimated to the sheriff that, if S's solicitor continued his line of cross-examination of Crown witnesses, P, it being put to them that not only were they lying but they had conspired to make a false accusation against S, then leave to cross-examine S as to his character would be sought, that the appeal would be refused since, despite claims by S that, had such questions not been put to P, adverse comments might have been made on S's own evidence, the sheriff had a wide discretion to refuse or allow an accused to be cross-examined as to his character *Leggate v. HM Advocate* 1988 S.L.T. 665, [1988] C.L.Y. 3887 and in the present case the sheriff was in the best position to determine whether or not the questions asked of the Crown witnesses were fair and integral to the case.

SINCLAIR v. MacDONALD 1996 S.C.C.R. 466, Judge not specified.

6738. Witnesses–expert witness–alleged misunderstanding of medical publication

An accused person was charged on indictment with, *inter alia,* rape. In evidence in chief at his trial a forensic scientist led for the Crown gave the opinion that prior to intercourse the complainer had been a virgin and the complainer's account of events, coupled with his findings on examination of her, were consistent with sexual intercourse having taken place at the material time. This conclusion was supported by other medical witnesses. In cross-examination it was put to the witness that a tear to the hymen at the five and seven o'clock positions (the tear in this case being at the three o'clock position) favoured digital penetration and that tears at the six o'clock position favoured penile penetration. Reference was made to various medical publications and in particular to a report published in 1975. The witness stated that he was aware of that report but countered that work offering different conclusions had been published since that date. This report was not produced in court. However the witness conceded that the case of a virgin after her first normal sexual intercourse the hymen would usually be ruptured at the five or six o'clock positions. He conceded that the damage in this case could have been caused by a finger if it had been pushed in heavily. The accused was convicted of rape and appealed, seeking to be allowed to lead as additional evidence the more recent report referred to by the witness. The accused argued that the witness had misunderstood this report and that this had resulted in a fundamental flaw in his evidence.

Held, that (1) there was no evidence that the complainer's hymen had ever been penetrated or interfered with by use of a finger, and that there had to be some evidence to support the allegation of digital penetration if this was to affect what was to be required of the medical evidence; (2) the evidence given by the Crown's expert witness was based on his own report based on his 17 years' experience and not on an external report put to him in cross-examination, so that there was no foundation for the allegation that as the external report did not provide a basis for the witness's opinion, his evidence was fundamentally flawed, and there had been no miscarriage of justice; and appeal refused.

DI LUCA v. HM ADVOCATE 1996 S.L.T. 924, Judge not specified, HCJ.

6739. Articles

Corroboration and similar fact evidence *(Peter W. Ferguson)*: S.L.T. 1996, 34, 339-341. (Extent to which recent decisions have weakened protection given by corroboration rule where identification evidence for only one of series of similar incidents).

Corroboration in criminal cases *(Munro D. McCannell)*: S.L.T. 1996, 35, 347-353. (Status of rule in Scotland with particular reference to consistent evidence).

Criminal law: foreign witnesses *(Alastair N. Brown)*: S.L.G. 1996, 64(2), 73-75. (Obtaining evidence from witnesses in other jurisdictions by use of letters of request, procedure for making applications and serving process on witness to attend).

Evidence in criminal trials: the evidential provisions of the Criminal Justice (Scotland) Act 1995 *(David Sheldon)*: J.L.S.S. 1996, 41(1), 25-28. (Agreement of evidence, hearsay, right to silence and cross examination on criminal record or character).

Fresh evidence appeals *(F.A. Mulholland* and *A. Ogg)*: Crim. L.B. 1996, 19(Feb), 2-3. (Circumstances in which additional evidence will be admitted on appeal).

The admissibility of prior statements of witnesses and the accused in criminal trials *(Greg W. Gordon)*: S.L.P.Q. 1996, 1(5), 352-365. (Particular reference to exceptions to hearsay rule).

Trials of the small screen *(John Fotheringham)*: J.L.S.S. 1996, 41(2), 60-61. (Author's experience of use of video links to take children's evidence in Scottish criminal courts).

6740. Books

Field, D.; Raitt, F.–Evidence, Ed.2. Paperback: £24.00. ISBN 0-414-01041-8. W. Green & Son.

CRIMINAL LAW

6741. Breach of the peace–sitting on felled tree being cut up with power saw

An accused person was charged on a summary complaint with breach of the peace. The accused, a protester against a road building project, deliberately sat on a felled tree which was being cut up by a workman using a power operated saw. Both the accused and the workman were facing away from each other as the workman progressed along the length of the tree. The accused was repeatedly asked to move but refused to do so. The sheriff convicted the accused who appealed by stated case.

Held, that the accused's deliberate conduct was such as might reasonably have caused a person to be alarmed by virtue of what might ensue if the accused remained where he was as the work progressed, and the sheriff was accordingly entitled to convict; and appeal refused. Dictum of Lord Justice Clerk Thomson in *Raffaelli v. Heatly* 1949 J.C. 101, [1949] C.L.Y. 4452 applied.

COLHOUN v. FRIEL 1996 S.L.T. 1252, Judge not specified, HCJ.

6742. Breach of the peace–summary complaint–not necessary to state "disorderly conduct" in charge

[Summary Jurisdiction (Scotland) Act 1954 (c. 48) Sch.2. Pt.II; Criminal Procedure (Scotland) Act 1975 (c. 21) s.312.]

The Crown sought advocation of a sheriff's decision to dismiss a complaint against G as incompetent. G was charged with committing a breach of peace by following in a car a bus on which his wife was a passenger and stopping behind it when it stopped at bus stops. At trial, the sheriff refused the Crown's motion to amend the complaint to state that G had "conducted himself in a disorderly manner" and dismissed the case, finding that the complaint was a nullity in that, by failing to specify that G had conducted himself in a disorderly manner, it failed to conform to the appropriate style for a charge of breach of peace in Sched. 2 to the 1954 Act, adopted in s.312 of the 1975 Act, and failed to disclose a crime known to the law of Scotland. G argued that the conduct libelled was not such as would justify the inference of disorderly conduct or conduct likely to cause alarm.

Held, bill passed, that there was no fundamental nullity in the terms of the charge which clearly stated that G had committed a breach of the peace. The

Crown had set out a course of conduct involving G and whether that conduct might reasonably be expected to cause alarm or upset to his wife or to members of the public was a matter for proof rather than style or specification. Sufficient specification was given of the conduct alleged.

Observed, that the style in the 1954 Act simply libelled disorderly conduct without further specification.

LEES v. GREER, *The Scotsman*, February 14, 1996, Lord Hope, L.J.G., HCJ.

6743. Contempt of court–failure to attend for social work interview

Held, that a sheriff was entitled to find U guilty of gross disrespect and in contempt of court where he had failed to attend at the social work department for interview to enable an inquiry report to be prepared: although he had told them he had no money for fares, as a perfectly fit 17 year old he should have been prepared to walk the five miles to the office; he had also failed to inform the department of a change of address as he was bound to. *Held*, further, that the sheriff was entitled to impose a short period of community service where U had no means to pay a fine, there was a serious problem of non cooperation with the department locally and U required to learn some discipline.

URQUHART v. HAMILTON 1996 S.C.C.R. 217, Judge not specified.

6744. Contempt of court–prevarication–record of proceedings

[Criminal Procedure (Scotland) Act 1975 (c.21) s.344.]

R sought suspension of a finding of contempt of court by prevaricating as a witness on the ground that the record of proceedings did not properly minute the statements forming the prevarication as required under the Criminal Procedure (Scotland) Act 1975 s.344(2). The record minuted that R was found guilty of contempt "in respect of his failure to answer questions asked by the procurator fiscal and prevarication". The sheriff provided a report which detailed the passage in R's evidence which led him to conclude that R was prevaricating. R argued that the information in the report should have been contained in the minute as s.344 did not provide for a report to be given by the presiding judge and it was the sheriff's duty to ensure that the minute contained a complete record in order to satisfy the requirements of s.344(2).

Held, refusing the bill, that the minute was sufficient to meet the requirements of s.344(2). As the purpose of s.344(2) was to secure an accurate record for an appeal (Renton and Brown's *Criminal Procedure* (5th ed) para.18-105), it would be unreasonable for the court to close its eye to the contents of a report which it asked the sheriff to produce in order to examine the facts alleged in the bill of suspension. Where the court had the benefit of a report, it was more likely to find the detail of the matter which was found to have constituted the contempt in that report than in a minute taken by the clerk at the trial. The report was consistent with the brief narrative in the minute and it was not necessary that the minute record verbatim the statements forming the prevarication, *Sze v. Wilson* 1992 S.L.T. 569, [1992] C.L.Y. 5462. There was no criticism that the report was inaccurate. The bill had been presented on a technicality which was adequately resolved by reference to the sheriff's report.

RIAVIZ v. HOWDLE 1996 S.C.C.R. 20, Judge not specified.

6745. Contempt of court–solicitors–late arrival at court–inefficiency not wilful disregard

A solicitor omitted to record the altered date of a trial diet in his diary and accordingly failed to appear at the diet at 10 am although, on his mistake being drawn to his attention, he immediately went to the court, arriving there at 11.10 am. The sheriff, taking into account two previous instances when he had had occasion to warn the solicitor about his conduct, concluded that the failure to record the new diet demonstrated a reckless disregard of his duties to the court and found the solicitor in contempt of court. The solicitor sought suspension of the finding and sentence.

Held, that (1) the previous warnings could not convert the solicitor's conduct, which was due simply to inefficiency, into a contempt and (2) though the solicitor could be criticised for inefficiency, his conduct did not amount to the wilful disregard of the authority of the court which was necessary to constitute contempt; and bill passed and finding suspended. *Caldwell v. Normand* 1994 S.L.T. 489, [1993] C.L.Y. 5064 and *Ferguson v. Normand* 1994 S.L.T. 1355, [1994] C.L.Y. 5652 applied. *Observed*, that had the solicitor been guilty of a contempt of court on this occasion, the previous warnings might have had a bearing on sentence.

MURDANAIGUM v. HENDERSON 1996 S.L.T. 1297, Judge not specified, HCJ.

6746. Firearms and explosives–possession–knowledge–extent of knowledge required

[Firearms Act 1968 (c.27).]

Held, on S's appeal against conviction for a firearms offence on the grounds that the sheriff had misdirected the jury that possession of a gun could be established without the Crown proving S's knowledge that the object possessed was a gun and so subject to the Firearms Act 1968 (knowledge that he knew that he had something over which he had some meaningful control being sufficient), that the appeal would be refused since Scots law on the matter was the same as that in England whereby absolute liability was imposed where a person possessed a weapon and proof of knowledge that the object possessed was a firearm was not required, *R. v. Hussain* [1981] 1 W.L.R. 416, [1981] C.L.Y. 1220 and *R. v. Steele* [1993] Crim. L.R. 298 followed.

SMITH v. HM ADVOCATE 1996 S.C.C.R. 49, Judge not specified.

6747. Firearms and explosives–possession with intent to commit robbery–jury acquitting of conspiracy to rob

[Firearms Act 1968 (c. 27) s.18(1) and (3).]

C appealed against conviction under s.18(1) of the Firearms Act 1968 (along with a charge under s.1 (1) and one of possessing an offensive weapon) on the ground that as the jury had acquitted him of a further charge of conspiracy to rob the premises in question, it was not open to them to convict of a charge that at those premises he had a sawn-off shotgun with intent to commit a robbery. The Crown, and the trial judge, had invited the jury to treat these charges as alternative. C argued that while in relation to a s.18(1) charge the Crown did not generally have to specify a particular place, in the present case the whole evidence led had been in relation to specific premises, a bingo hall, and these were the only potential target in the area.

Held, appeal refused, that there was no need for the Crown to establish the prospective victim or the prospective locus. There was evidence of possession of a knife, mask and plastic bags as well as the shotgun and of the flight of C and his co-accused when the police approached, which was sufficient for conviction. *Held*, further, that five years' imprisonment on the s.1 (1) charge, the same as that imposed under s.18(1), was not excessive where C had nine convictions, several for dishonesty and violence, and had been in possession of a loaded sawn-off shotgun in a public place late at night.

CONNER v. HM ADVOCATE 1995 S.C.C.R. 719, Judge not specified.

6748. Misuse of drugs–attempting to possess drugs with intent to supply–drugs not controlled drugs but accused believing that they were

[Misuse of Drugs Act 1971 (c.38) s.5.]

An accused person was charged on a summary complaint with attempting to possess what he erroneously believed were controlled drugs, with intent to supply them to others, contrary to the Misuse of Drugs Act 1971 s.5(3). The accused objected to the charge on the ground that it did not disclose a criminal attempt because the commission of the completed crime was impossible. The sheriff repelled the objection but granted leave to appeal.

Held, (by a bench of five judges) that (1) when considering the relevancy of a charge of attempted crime, it was not necessary to consider whether or not it was impossible for the completed crime to be committed and (2) all that the court required to do was consider whether the accused had the necessary mens rea and had taken matters further by doing some positive act towards execution of his purpose; and appeal refused, *HM Advocate v. Anderson* 1927 S.L.T. 651 overruled, dicta of Lord Sands in *Lamont v. Strathern* 1933 S.L.T. 118 and dicta in *HM Advocate v. Semple* 1937 S.L.T. 48 disapproved. Opinion reserved (per Lord Cameron of Lochbroom), whether, where a crime could be committed only if a person was within a class of persons, such as licensees, it was relevant to libel an attempt to commit such a crime by someone who merely believed himself to be within that class.

DOCHERTY v. BROWN 1996 S.L.T. 325, Judge not specified, HCJ.

6749. Misuse of drugs–being concerned in supply of controlled drug

[Misuse of Drugs Act 1971 (c.38) s.4.]

An accused person was charged on summary complaint with a contravention of the Misuse of Drugs Act 1971 s.4(3)(b). The accused's father supplied a quantity of amphetamine to a Crown witness and two weeks later the accused, who had not been present when the drug was supplied, went to the witness's house and demanded payment for the drug on her father's behalf. The accused later admitted to the police that she had done so. The sheriff sustained a submission of no case to answer and acquitted the accused. The Crown appealed by stated case.

Held, that the process of supply could not be said to have been at an end when the accused demanded payment for the drug, and the sheriff had erred in holding that there was insufficient evidence for conviction; and appeal allowed and case remitted to sheriff to proceed as accords. Dictum of Lord Hunter in *Kerr v. HM Advocate* 1986 S.C.C.R. 81 at p.87, [1986] C.L.Y. 3802/3810/4716 applied.

DOUGLAS v. BOYD 1996 S.L.T. 401, Judge not specified, HCJ.

6750. Murder–mens rea–wicked recklessness

Held, on S's appeal against conviction of murder, that the trial judge did not err in charging the jury that intended murder would ordinarily be considered more wicked than unintended murder, and it would be confusing to compare one with the other, as the direction was merely a response to S's submission, the Crown case resting on the wicked recklessness branch of the definition, that the jury could only convict S of murder if he had acted as wickedly as if he intended to kill. Wickedly reckless conduct was treated as the equivalent of an intention to kill in law rather than in fact, but the degree of wickedness involved in each was not something about which any rule could be laid down and it would not normally be appropriate to direct a jury on that aspect. In any event no miscarriage of justice had occurred where the trial judge's directions otherwise followed the classic definition of murder and indicated that the necessary mens rea could be established through either intentional killing or such a display of wicked recklessness as to imply a disposition depraved enough to disregard the consequences.

SCOTT v. HM ADVOCATE 1995 S.C.C.R. 760, Judge not specified.

6751. Obscene publications–whether liable to corrupt and deprave–magazine sealed in clear wrapper

[Civic Government (Scotland) Act 1982 (c.45) s.51(2), Sch.3 para.2(1); Criminal Procedure (Scotland) Act 1975 (c.21) s.312(f).]

R appealed against conviction of distributing and selling obscene material and operating a sex shop without a licence, after 278 and 123 sex articles were seized from his shop during two police raids, arguing that (1) because no evidence was led of any actual sale taking place on the dates in question he had not "sold" obscene material in terms of s.51 (2) of the 1982 Act, (2) the magazines being sealed in, albeit clear, wrappers, they were not liable to corrupt or deprave, and (3) because no evidence was led on stocks and sales of sex articles compared to non-sex articles, it had not been shown the shop was a "sex shop" within the terms of para.2 of Sch.2 to the 1982 Act.

Held, appeal refused, that (1) the word "sells" in s.51 (2) included "offers for sale", and the sheriff had been entitled to infer that the articles were available for sale from evidence of sale on other occasions. In any event the latitude was covered by s.312(f) of the 1975 Act; (2) the sheriff had been entitled to hold that the obscene magazines and videos visibly displayed with no warnings or age restrictions were liable to corrupt and deprave unsuspecting members of the public who found themselves exposed to the explicit and obscene covers visible through the wrappers, and (3) the Crown did not have to show that the majority of goods sold were sex articles and the sheriff had been entitled to infer that they formed a significant degree of business within para.2(1) of Sch.2 from evidence of the value of the goods and the total sales for the shop as recorded on the till roll.

REES v. LEES 1996 S.C.C.R. 601, Judge not specified.

6752. Theft–housebreaking–smashing security light

Held, on the Crown's appeal against the sheriff's decision to sustain a plea to the relevancy of a complaint against R that he did by means of smashing a security light attempt to break into premises with intent to steal, the sheriff having considered that the action libelled was more likely to draw attention to R and might be no more than an act of vandalism, that the appeal would be allowed since much might depend on the circumstances including the position and nature of the security light, and it was not possible at this stage to say whether or not the act libelled amounted to an attempt to break in.

HEYWOOD v. REID 1995 S.C.C.R. 741, Judge not specified.

6753. Theft–possession of tools with intent to commit

[Civic Government (Scotland) Act 1982 (c.45) s.58(1).]

The Civic Government (Scotland) Act 1982 s.58(1) provides that any person who has two or more convictions for theft which are not spent convictions, and (a) has or has recently had in his possession any tool or object from the possession of which it may reasonably be inferred that he intended to commit theft or had committed theft, and (b) "is unable to demonstrate satisfactorily" that such possession is or was not for the purposes of committing theft, is guilty of an offence. An accused person was charged on summary complaint with a contravention of s.58(1) of the 1982 Act. The accused was observed at about 2 am standing in darkness at the entrance to a common close where he was crouched down with his back to the street, moving his hands about at the position of the door handle. When the police approached him the accused dropped a screwdriver. The police then cautioned the accused at common law and requested him to explain his presence at the door and his possession of the screwdriver. The accused shrugged, looked blankly and said nothing. It was argued that as it had been held in *Mathieson v. Crowe* 1994 S.L.T. 554, [1994] C.L.Y. 5671, that the explanation had to be given when the accused was found in possession of the tool, once the police had cautioned the accused it was unfair for them to rely on his silence. The magistrate rejected the argument and convicted the accused who appealed by stated case.

Held (by a bench of five judges), that (1) there was nothing in s.58(1)(b) which prevented an accused from offering an explanation for the first time at his trial, as long as it was an explanation that could have been provided at the time he was found; (2) as it was not too late for the accused to give an explanation at his trial there was no unfairness in the administration of the caution; but (3) as the accused did not give an explanation at his trial because the defence was conducted on the basis of *Mathieson v. Crowe*, it was unfair to allow the conviction to stand; and appeal allowed and conviction quashed. *Mathieson v. Crowe* 1994 S.L.T. 554, [1994] C.L.Y. 5671 overruled; *Phillips v. MacLeod,* 1996 S.L.T. 259, explained. *Observed,* that the time at which the question whether or not the accused was able to give a satisfactory explanation had to be determined was at his trial but delay in providing the explanation would raise questions of credibility.

DOCHERTY v. NORMAND 1996 S.L.T. 955, Judge not specified, HCJ.

6754. Articles

Art and part guilt: a difference of view. : Crim. L.B. 1996, 23(Oct), 2-4. (Difference of views among HCJ judges on whether jury directions as to concert constituted misdirection by trial judge).

Civic Government (Scotland) Act 1982. : Crim. L.B. 1996, 22(Aug), 4-6. (Whether person accused of having instruments which may have been intended for use in committing theft is able to provide explanation under s.58(2)(b) at any time or must do so before trial).

Criminal liability for sexual harassment *(Sam Middlemiss)*: S.L.G. 1996, 64(2), 58-60. (Forms of criminal liability for sexual harassment in Scotland and whether is need for legislation).

Incidents at sporting events. : Crim. L.B. 1996, 22(Aug), 2-3. (Lord Advocate's advice to police on possible criminal offences committed by players, officials and spectators at sporting events).

Insanity and unfitness to plead *(Clare Connelly)*: Jur. Rev. 1996, 3, 206-211. (Whether new provisions relating to mentally disordered offenders may encourage greater use of unfitness plea and insanity defence).

Insanity in bar of trial *(Alastair N. Brown)*: S.L.G. 1996, 64(1), 23-25. (Procedural aspects of law on insanity and fitness to stand trial as from April 1, 1996).

Stalking and the Scottish courts *(Alistair J. Bonnington)*: N.L.J. 1996, 146(6761), 1394. (Common law crime of breach of the peace covers the modern crime of stalking).

The mens rea of rape *(Peter W. Ferguson)*: S.L.T. 1996, 30, 279-281. (Whether accused has necessary mens rea where has honest albeit unreasonable belief that woman is consenting).

The Proceeds of Crime (Scotland) Act 1995 *(Alastair N. Brown)*: J.L.S.S. 1996, 41(2), 47-49. (New Act, in force April 1, 1995, affords possibility of wider use of confiscation as means of tackling profit motivated criminals).

Unlawful act culpable homicide: a suitable case for reappraisal *(Jenifer Ross)*: S.L.T. 1996, 9, 75-80. (Whether mens rea necessary for conviction of culpable homicide should be more firmly based on concept of recklessness).

Wilful neglect of duty by public officials *(Alastair N. Brown)*: S.L.G. 1996, 64(3), 130-132. (Unusual prosecution of police officer charged at common law with failing timeously to report offences to procurator fiscal where statutory offence was time barred).

Women who kill violent men *(Clare Connelly)*: Jur. Rev. 1996, 3, 215-217. (Development of case law since 1979 in prosecution and sentencing of abused women who kill violent partners).

6755. Books

Brown, Alistair N.–Proceeds of Crime. Green's annotated acts. Paperback. ISBN 0-414-01148-1. W.Green & Son.

Jones, T.H.; Christie, M.G.A.–Criminal Law. Greens' concise Scots law. Paperback. ISBN 0-414-01146-5. W.Green & Son.

Shiels, Robert–Offensive Weapons. Paperback. ISBN 0-414-01171-6. W.Green & Son.

Young, Peter–Crime and Criminal Justice in Scotland. Paperback: £7.00. ISBN 0-11-495808-4. HMSO Books.

CRIMINAL PROCEDURE

6756. 12 months elapsing after first appearance–application for extension–competency

[Criminal Procedure (Scotland) Act 1975 (c.21) s.101 (1), s.101 (5).]

An accused person was committed for trial on a petition and admitted to bail. An indictment was served for a sitting but was adjourned from that sitting to a later one. Subsequently a notice in terms of the Criminal Procedure (Scotland) Act 1975 s.81 was served and, on the Crown's motion, the later diet was deserted *pro loco et tempore*. Therefore the Crown purported to serve an indictment under s.127 of the 1975 Act but, after hearing evidence at a preliminary diet, the sheriff held that the Crown had failed to comply with the provisions of s.127. The Crown thereupon sought an extension for the 12-month period but the sheriff refused to be addressed on the matter. An extension of two months was subsequently granted by a different sheriff at a later diet. The accused appealed against the extension, contending, *inter alia*, that it was incompetent for the Crown to make a fresh application when the sheriff's earlier refusal had not been appealed under s.101 (5) of the 1975 Act or received by way of petition to the *nobile officium*.

Held, that when the sheriff refused to be addressed on the application there was no grant or refusal which could be the subject of an appeal under s.101 (5) or the basis at that stage for invoking the *nobile officium*, and the later application was competent; and appeal refused.

McKNIGHT v. HM ADVOCATE 1996 S.L.T. 834, Judge not specified, HCJ.

6757. 12 months elapsing after first appearance–justification for extension

[Criminal Procedure (Scotland) Act 1975 (c.21) s.101 (1).]

Held, on A's appeal against the sheriff's decision to extend the 12-month time limit under s.101 (1) (ii) of the 1975 Act, where an indictment had been served at A's original address notwithstanding the granting of an application to alter the address on the bail order, which grant had been intimated to the prosecutor, that the appeal would be refused where it was the practice of the procurator fiscal's office to check the domicile of citation with the sheriff clerk's office prior to service and the wrong information had been communicated in this case; the sheriff was entitled to take the view that is was reasonable to rely on the information provided.

ANDERSON v. HM ADVOCATE 1996 S.C.C.R. 487, Judge not specified, HCJ.

6758. 12 months elapsing after first appearance–justification for extension–alleged rape victim not to give evidence twice

[Criminal Procedure (Scotland) Act 1975 (c.21) s.101 (1).]

Held, on A's appeal against a sheriff's decision to grant an extension of the 12-month period from April 13 to May 31, 1996 (after a previous seven-month extension), where A and his co-accused, C, were charged with attempted rape of a young girl, G, and both A and C had been granted postponements of the trial, where the matter was at large for the court, that the extension was justified since if was undesirable for G to give her evidence twice, and it was a material consideration that the Crown had not caused any delay in the proceedings, *Mejka v. HM Advocate* 1993 S.L.T. 1321, [1993] C.L.Y. 4934 distinguished.

ASHCROFT v. HM ADVOCATE 1996 S.C.C.R. 608, Lord Ross, L.J.C., HCJ.

6759. 12 months elapsing after first appearance–whether grant of warrant to arrest interrupted 12-month period

[Criminal Procedure (Scotland) Act 1975 (c.21) s.101 (1).]

Section 101 (1) of the Criminal Procedure (Scotland) Act 1975 provides that failing the commencement, within 12 months of the first appearance of an accused on petition in respect of an offence, of a trial on indictment for that offence, the accused shall be discharged forthwith and thereafter free from all question or process for that offence, provided that (i) nothing in the subsection should bar the trial of an accused for whose arrest a warrant had been granted for failure to appear at a diet in the case. An accused person appeared on a petition charging him with breach of the peace and offences under the Misuse of Drugs Act 1971, and was admitted to bail. An indictment was served for a sitting of the sheriff court commencing within the 12-month period. The accused was absent when the case called and the diet was deserted *pro loco et tempore*. A warrant was granted for the arrest of the accused on the ground of his failure to appear and accordingly the Crown did not seek an extension of the 12-month period. The accused, unknown to anyone, had been in the court building but in another courtroom to which he had been wrongly directed by court officials. The Crown accepted that explanation and undertook not to execute the warrant. The accused was subsequently reindicted for a sitting outwith the 12-month period. At a preliminary diet the sheriff, considering that the proviso to s.101 (1) applied only to cases where the accused had absconded or wilfully absented himself, held that the proceedings were time barred because the Crown were not entitled to rely on the warrant to interrupt the 12-month period. The Crown appealed.

Held, that the circumstances which had led to the granting of the warrant were irrelevant to the application of the proviso to s.101 (1); and appeal allowed and decision recalled. Dictum of Lord Justice General Hope in *HM Advocate v. Lang* 1992 S.C.C.R. 642 at p.645, [1992] C.L.Y. 5424, applied; *HM Advocate v. Campbell* 1988 S.L.T. 72, [1988] C.L.Y. 3921, distinguished.

Observed, that the accused's remedy, as soon as he was aware that proceedings were being continued against him outwith the 12-month period in reliance on the proviso, was to bring the granting of the warrant under the review of the High Court by means of a bill of suspension.

HM ADVOCATE v. TAYLOR 1996 S.L.T. 836, Judge not specified, HCJ.

6760. 110 days elapsing after committal–de facto detention after instructions given for liberation

[Criminal Procedure (Scotland) Act 1975 (c.21) s.101 (2).]

C petitioned the nobile officium to hold that he had been de facto detained in custody for a period in excess of 110 days without a trial being commenced in breach of s.101 (2) (b) of the 1975 Act and for an order that he was free from all question or process in respect of the charges under which he was originally detained. After being fully committed until liberation in due course of law, C was released on bail with a condition of residence in a secure unit in a list D school. In terms of s.101 (2) (b) the 110 days expired on February 7, 1995. On February 3, the Crown Office contacted the school's headmaster requesting that C be transferred as a matter of urgency to open accommodation within the school. In an earlier petition, the court concluded, as a result of information provided by the school, that after February 6 C had complete freedom of movement, that he had not been detained for a period on excess of 110 days and that he was not entitled to found on the provisions of s.101 (2) (b). In the present petition, C maintained that the court's previous decision proceeded on erroneous information as the school log confirmed that he had not been given freedom to leave the facility until February 9. The case was remitted to a judge who heard evidence and found in finding 13 that C had been told that if he left the school on February 7 he would be treated as an abscondee. C argued that as a consequence of this finding, he de facto continued to be detained on February 7 and he was therefore entitled to be free from further process in terms of s.101 (2) *K v. HM Advocate* 1993 S.L.T. 77, [1991] C.L.Y. 4629.

Held, petition refused, that although, in terms of finding 13, C was detained at the school beyond midnight on February 7, that detention was not by virtue of the committal warrant. By sending the communication to the school on February 3, the Crown Office made it clear that C's situation at the school was to be changed and that instruction was in fact given effect when C was transferred to the open unit on February 6. Thereafter, the school authorities and social worker continued to have responsibility for him by virtue of the fact that he had been made the subject of a home supervision order prior to appearing on petition and therefore his continued detention on February 6 and 7 was a result of the attitude of the staff and social worker who were influenced by factors unconnected to the committal warrant.

Observed, that it was undesirable and unacceptable that the Crown had placed false information before the court and invited the court to proceed upon that information, and if the Crown did not have sufficient time to check material, then it should have sought an adjournment to confirm its facts, particularly where the facts were in dispute.

X, PETITIONER; SUB NOM. CAMPBELL, PETITIONER 1996 S.C.C.R. 436, Lord Ross, L.J.C., HCJ.

6761. 110 days elapsing after committal–effect of incompetent sentence

[Criminal Procedure (Scotland) Act 1995 (c.46) s.65(4).]

Section 65(4)(b) of the Criminal Procedure (Scotland) Act 1995 provides, *inter alia*, that an accused who is fully committed shall not be detained by virtue of that committal for a total period of more than 110 days, unless his trial is commenced within that period, which failing he shall be liberated forthwith and thereafter be forever free from all question or process for that offence. An accused person was fully committed on a charge of rape on December 21, 1995 and remanded in custody. On January 24, 1996 the accused was sentenced to six months' imprisonment in respect of a charge on summary complaint of reckless discharge of an air rifle. The accused sought suspension of the sentence on the ground that it was incompetent as being in excess of the sheriff's powers, and on April 17, 1996, the sentence was suspended by the High Court and a sentence of three months' imprisonment was substituted. By that time the accused had served three weeks more than he would have required to serve if he had been sentenced to three months' imprisonment. The accused was indicted for trial on the rape charge on June 17, 1996 when he pled in bar of trial that the proceedings were time barred because he had been detained for a period in excess of 110 days when account was taken of the three weeks served under the incompetent warrant. The trial judge repelled the plea on the basis that the interruption of the 110 day period did not cease until the appeal court suspended the incompetent warrant. The accused appealed.

Held, that so long as the warrant granted on January 24, 1996 remained unaltered by the court, that was the authority under which the accused continued to be detained and as it was not until April 17, 1996 that the warrant was altered, it was only from that date that, the Crown being aware of the court's decision, any further detention of the accused was attributable to the committal warrant for the purposes of s.65(4)(b); and appeal refused. *Observed*, that unless a situation of uncertainty and confusion were to prevail, the detention of an accused had to be regulated according to the status which the court gave from time to time to the warrant which it issued for his detention.

THOMSON v. HM ADVOCATE 1996 S.L.T. 1257, Judge not specified, HCJ.

6762. Acts of Sederunt–proceeds of crime

ACT OF SEDERUNT (PROCEEDS OF CRIME RULES) 1996, SI 1996 2446 (S.191); made under the Sheriff Courts (Scotland) Act 1971 s.32; and the Proceeds of Crime (Scotland) Act 1995 s.31, s.48, Sch.1 para.11. In force: October 7, 1996; £1.95.

The Proceeds of Crime (Scotland) Act 1995 Part III extends the jurisdiction of the sheriff to deal with applications for restraint orders and the appointment of administrators. This Act of Sederunt makes provision for the procedures to be followed in the sheriff court in cases under that Part.

6763. Appeals–bill of suspension–competency–suspension of committal warrant

An accused person was fully committed until liberated in due course of law in terms of a petition charging him, inter alia, with attempting to defeat the ends of justice. The charge alleged that the accused had repeatedly refused to comply with the terms of warrants authorising the taking from him of blood and saliva samples and dental impressions by repeatedly refusing to permit a named doctor and dentist to take samples from him. The accused sought suspension of the committal warrant on the ground that the charge was irrelevant as it did not disclose a crime. Before the High Court a question arose as to the competency of the bill of suspension.

Held, the Crown not opposing, that (1) it was appropriate to entertain the bill in the light of the authorities, *Hume*, ii, 86: *Alison*, ii, 159, considered, but (2) whether or not the accused's conduct amounted to a crime would depend on the circumstances and the inferences which the jury would be entitled to draw from the evidence and accordingly it could not be affirmed at this stage that the conduct could not constitute an attempt to defeat the ends of justice; and bill refused, *Carney v. HM Advocate* 1995 S.L.T. 1208, [1995] C.L.Y. 5782 considered.

MELLORS v. NORMAND 1996 S.L.T. 704, Judge not specified, HCJ.

6764. Appeals–whether conduct of defence case relevant ground of appeal

[Criminal Procedure (Scotland) Act 1975 (c.21) s.228.]

An accused person was charged on indictment with, inter alia, aggravated assault and was represented at his trial in the High Court by a solicitor advocate. He was convicted and appealed on the ground that his solicitor advocate had failed to cross-examine the complainer about his previous convictions as the accused had instructed him to do.

Held, (by a bench of five judges), that (1) the accused had a right to a fair trial including the right to have his defence presented to the court; but (2) the accused's legal representative was not subject to the accused's direction as to how that defence was to be presented although he had to act according to his instructions as to what the defence was, and could not disregard them and conduct the case as he thought best; (3) the way in which the accused's representative conducted the defence within his instructions was a matter for him and as a general rule the accused was bound by that, and (4) decisions as to whether or not to attack the character of a Crown witness were for the accused's legal representative to take, not the accused, and his decision did not deprive the accused of a fair trial and appeal refused, *Turnbull v. HM Advocate* 1948 S.L.T. (Notes) 12, [1948] C.L.Y. 4152 and *McCarroll v. H.M. Advocate* 1949 S.L.T. 74, [1948] C.L.Y. 4153 overruled.

Observed, that it was essential that legal representatives against whom allegations were made were given a fair opportunity to respond in writing to the allegations before the court heard the appeal, although legal representatives were under no obligation to respond at that stage.

ANDERSON v. HM ADVOCATE 1996 S.L.T. 155, Judge not specified, HCJ.

6765. Bail–breach of bail condition–form of charge–transitional statutory provisions

[Interpretation Act 1978 (c.30) s.16; Criminal Procedure (Scotland) Act 1995 (c.46) s.27; Criminal Procedure (Consequential Provisions) (Scotland) Act 1995 (c.40), Sch.3, para.3; Criminal Justice (Scotland) Act 1995 (Commencement No.2 Transitional Provisions and Savings) Order 1996 (SI 1996 517).]

The Crown appealed against a sheriff's decision to uphold a plea to the competency of two charges of breach of bail against R. The charges alleged that R, having been granted bail in November 1995 and March 1996 respectively in terms of the Criminal Procedure (Scotland) Act 1995, committed certain other offences on April 4 and 5, 1996 and thereby failed to comply with a condition of bail, contrary to the Criminal Procedure (Scotland) Act 1995 s.27 (1) (b). The sheriff considered that libelling the offences under s.27 (1) (b) was incompetent as it ignored the existence of s.27 (3), and that the effect of the various enactments by which the Bail etc (Scotland) Act 1980 had been amended and then repealed and re-enacted, was that the Crown could not proceed at all where the bail order had been made before March 31 and the offence was committed after April 1, 1996. The Crown conceded that it was incorrect to narrate that R had been granted bail under the 1995 Act, which was not then in force, but argued that the offences had been correctly libelled under s.27(1)(b) as there was a presumption especially with consolidating legislation that Parliament did not intend to alter the existing law: while with a bail order made since April 1 the new procedure would apply, there had been no change in the position of persons granted bail before March 31. Paragraph 3(2) of Sch.3 to the Consequential Provisions Act made it clear that the effect of the Commencement No.2 Order (amending provisions only to apply in relation to bail granted on or after March 31) continued in force notwithstanding the repeal of the enabling power for that order. Section 3 of the 1980 Act could not be invoked as it had been repealed.

Held, appeal refused, that it was impossible to construe s.27(1)(b) as contended for by the Crown; other provisions in s.27 would have to be disregarded, which was not permissible as a presumption of interpretation could not be used to ignore or alter words used. Section 27 applied only to bail orders made on or after March 31. The commencement order could not have the effect contended for as the 1980 Act was among the Acts repealed by the Consequential Provisions Act 1995; if s.3 were to be saved, an express provision in the latter Act would have been necessary. However it was not the case that no charge could be brought in a case like the present: the conditions attached to pre-March 31 bail orders and the liability to a penalty on their breach, could properly be described as an obligation incurred under the the 1980 Act within the Interpretation Act s.16(1)(c) to which para.(d) and para.(e) and the concluding part of s.16(1) also applied. Thus proceedings could still be taken under the 1980 Act for a breach of an order made before March 31, irrespective of the date of the subsequent offence. *Observed*, that it was to be regretted that the consolidation had been carried out in such a confusing manner that even the Crown had been misled.

HAMILTON v. ROBERTSON 1996 S.C.C.R. 539, Judge not specified.

6766. Child accused–certification as unruly pending trial

[Social Work (Scotland) Act 1968 (c.49) s.44; Criminal Procedure (Scotland) Act 1975 (c.21) s.24.]

M, aged 15, petitioned the nobile officium when he was certified as unruly in terms of the Criminal Procedure (Scotland) Act 1975 s.24 and committed to a remand centre while he awaited trial. M was so certified when he appeared on petition in the sheriff court on October 9, 1995 charged with five charges of assault and robbery. At that time, he was under residential supervision at Kerelaw residential school in terms of the Social Work (Scotland) Act 1968 s.44(1)(b), although prior to the date of the alleged offences he had failed to return from home leave. M's application for bail was again refused on October 13, and on October 17 the sheriff of new certified M as unruly. His application for a review of the orders was refused on November 3. M averred that the sheriff was not entitled to consider the availability of secure accommodation, and that if such had existed he would not have been certified as unruly by the sheriff. The conditions under which he was being held were unsatisfactory.

Held, refusing the application, that in view of the fact that M had previously absconded from Kerelaw and subsequently appeared on petition in respect of serious charges, the sheriff was entitled to certify on both October 9 and 17 that M was of so unruly a character that he could not safely be committed to the local authority. Although it was unfortunate that M was detained under unsatisfactory conditions, there had been no error in the sheriff's approach and it was appropriate to apply the proviso to s.24(1).

M, PETITIONER 1996 S.C.C.R. 92, Judge not specified.

6767. Criminal Justice (Scotland) Act 1995–Commencement No.2 Order

CRIMINAL JUSTICE (SCOTLAND) ACT 1995 (COMMENCEMENT NO.2, TRANSITIONAL PROVISIONS AND SAVINGS) ORDER 1996, SI 1996 517 (C.10; S.51); made under the Criminal Justice (Scotland) Act 1995 s.118. In force: bringing into force various provisions of the Act on March 31, 1996; £1.55.

This Order brings into force: certain provisions of the Criminal Justice (Scotland) Act 1995 which are specified in the Sch.1 to the Order on March 5, 1996 but only for the purpose of enabling subordinate legislation to be made under the provisions specified in that Schedule so as to come into force on or after March 31, 1996 (Art.3(1)); and all the provisions of the Act, except s.66, on March 31, 1996, insofar as they are not then in force (Art.3(2)). Section 66 is the only provision of the Act which is not commenced on March 31, 1996. That section amends the Social Work (Scotland) Act 1968 s.27(1) to make provision for the supervision and care of persons diverted from prosecution or subject to supervision requirement.

6768. Indictment–preamble disclosing crime not libelled–prejudice to accused

[Criminal Procedure (Scotland) Act 1975 (c. 21) s.160(1).]

S appealed against convictions of driving while disqualified, driving without insurance and attempting to defeat the ends of justice by giving false information to the police, on the ground that the preamble to the charges, which disclosed that S had unlawfully removed a car prior to committing the offences, was grossly prejudicial as he had not been charged with theft of the vehicle. The Crown argued that evidence of the unlawful removal of the car was necessary in order to prove the charges libelled against S and the allegation had been included in the preamble to give S fair notice of the evidence which would be led at trial. The police had not seen S driving the car, therefore the Crown were relying on S's admission that he had driven the car, which in its terms did not make sense without the evidence about the car's removal. S was not charged with theft because it would have been a breach of s.160(1) of the Criminal Procedure (Scotland) Act 1975 to do so on the same indictment as that on which he was being charged with driving while disqualified.

Held, appeal allowed and conviction quashed, that it was not necessary for the Crown to prove that S was not the owner of the vehicle or that he had unlawfully removed it in order to prove that he had been driving while disqualified and without insurance, as direct evidence of S driving the car was available from S's passenger (L), and to lead such other evidence was prejudicial to S. This amounted to a miscarriage of justice as L's credibility was crucial to the Crown case and it was difficult to determine whether the jury would have found S guilty of the offences if they had not heard the evidence that he had unlawfully removed the car. Opinion reserved, whether it would have been competent to charge S with theft, or unlawfully removing the car, on the same indictment.

SLACK v. HM ADVOCATE 1995 S.C.C.R. 809, Judge not specified.

6769. Indictment–second indictment while first indictment not deserted–competency of second indictment

[Criminal Procedure (Scotland) Act 1995 (c.46) s.72.]

Held, that on S's appeal against the repelling of his objection to the competency of a second indictment, where (1) the minute of notice on the original indictment cited an erroneous address for the sitting of the High Court and therefore did not constitute a valid citation; (2) a second indictment was served on S while the preliminary diet on the first indictment was pending and (3) at the preliminary diet the Crown accepted that the first indictment was defective and offered to withdraw it and proceed on the second one, that the judge did not err in repelling S's objection to the second indictment as the Crown were not barred from serving a second indictment on S while the first one remained alive since it was not incompetent for two indictments to be extant at the same time *HM Advocate v. Dow* 1992 S.L.T. 577, [1992] C.L.Y. 5435 and in serving the second indictment the Crown had impliedly deserted the first one and were not attempting to proceed against S on two indictments, despite S's argument that written notice of a preliminary diet on the first indictment having been given in terms of s.72(1) of the 1995 Act, the diet then had to proceed and the point raised be disposed of: it remained open to the Crown to intimate that they no longer intended to proceed on that indictment, and it was in the public interest that the Crown remained the master of the instance.

SMITH v. HM ADVOCATE 1996 S.C.C.R. 664, Judge not specified.

6770. Indictment–specification–false trade descriptions–time bar–commencement of proceedings

[Trade Descriptions Act 1968 (c.29) s.19.]

H appealed against a sheriff's decision repelling his pleas to the competency and relevancy of two charges and a plea in bar of trial. H was charged with supplying motor vehicles to which a false trade description of the mileage had been applied in breach of s.1 (1) (a) and s.1 (1) (b) of the 1968 Act. The offences were allegedly committed between June 26, 1992 and November 30, 1993, and August 3, 1992 and January 18, 1994 respectively, and in terms of s.19 (1) the prosecutor, P, certified the discovery on September 7, 1994 that the offences had been committed. A petition for warrant to arrest H was granted on June 26, 1995 and H appeared before the sheriff on petition on July 11. The indictment was served on June 6, 1996. H argued that; (1) the proceedings were incompetent as they were not commenced until service of the indictment, which occurred outside the time limit in s.19(1). Although s.19(1) did not define when the proceedings commenced, the expression should be given the same meaning throughout the UK and be construed narrowly in favour of the accused; (2) as investigations were completed by September 7, 1994 when the matter was first drawn to P's attention, P had delayed unreasonably in serving the indictment, resulting in such severe prejudice that further proceedings were oppressive at common law. The trading standards department had not returned the records which they took from H and no satisfactory explanation had been given for the delay, and (3) charge 2, of supplying goods contrary to s.1 (1) (a), which was concerned with application of a false description was irrelevant, and both charges were lacking in specification as they did not give H fair notice of how the false description was applied.

Held, appeal refused, that (1) the proceedings were not time barred. The prosecution commenced for the purposes of s.19(1) as soon as P brought the matter before the court by means of a petition to arrest and the warrant was granted, *McArthur v. Lord Advocate* 1902 10 S.L.T. 310 applied, which was sufficient to interrupt the running of the time limit. No useful analogy could be drawn from the English authorities; (2) the delay was not unreasonable at common law. P was entitled and obliged to make his own inquiries to satisfy himself that prosecution was appropriate. H was entitled to see the productions which P was relying on, and to seek an adjournment if necessary; and the bare assertion that G had not had access to his records was not enough to show that the prejudice had been so grave that it could not be removed by suitable directions, *McDowall v. HM Advocate* 1996 G.W.D. 12-685 applied; (3) although charge 2 could have been worded better since the offence was a continuing one it was sufficient for P to specify as the date when the offence was committed, any of the dates during which the false descriptions were applied to the vehicles and (4) ample notice was given of the difference between the declared mileage applied to each vehicle and the true mileage. The manner in which the false description was applied to each vehicle was a matter for evidence and did not need to be specified in the charge.

HAMILTON v. HM ADVOCATE 1996 S.C.C.R. 744, Lord Hope L.J.G., HCJ.

6771. Intermediate diets

INTERMEDIATE DIETS (SCOTLAND) ORDER 1996, SI 1996 616 (S.59); made under the Criminal Procedure (Scotland) Act 1995 s.148. In force: April 1, 1996; £1.10.

This Order prescribes certain courts for the purposes of the Criminal Procedure (Scotland) Act 1995 s.148(7) in relation to proceedings commenced after a date which is also prescribed in the Order. The effect of any such prescription is that the prescribed court will be required to hold an intermediate diet under that section in any case where proceedings are commenced after the prescribed date unless the court considers, on a joint application by the parties, that it would be inappropriate to hold an intermediate diet in that case. Article 3 and Art.4 prescribes certain sheriff courts and district courts specified in, respectively, Sch.1 and Sch.2 to the Order, in relation to proceedings commenced after March 31, 1996. Article 5 prescribes the sheriff court for the sheriff court district of Linlithgow in relation to proceedings commenced after September 30, 1996. Article 6 prescribes the district courts for the commission areas of City of Glasgow and South Lanarkshire in relation to proceedings commenced after March 31, 1997.

6772. Nobile officium–prohibition of pre-trial broadcast–broadcast featuring related incident not subject of trial

[Contempt of Court Act 1981 (c.49) s.2(2).]

Held, on the petition of three prison officers (M) to prohibit B from broadcasting a programme before M's trial, M being accused of assaulting inmates transferred after rioting, where the programme showed a prison doctor, D, who would be a crucial Crown witness, stating his opinions, which had the backing of the British Medical Association and the European Committee for the Prevention of Torture, that an assault on another inmate at the same prison but not the subject of prosecution, was consistent with beatings and torture, and D having since been dismissed, that the petition would be granted. The court had power to do so under the nobile officium where there was a more than minimal risk of prejudice to the trial, even if the programme did not constitute a contempt of court under the Contempt of Court Act 1981, *Smith v. Ritchie* (1892) 20 R. 52 applied. There was such a risk here, where the programme could give the impression that the doctor's views were of considerable credit and importance and he had been martyred for them, although they might be challenged at trial, *HM Advocate v. Caledonian Newspapers* 1995 S.L.T. 926, [1995] C.L.Y. 5756 applied. *Observed*, that the defence under s.5 of the 1981 Act was irrelevant when the court was considering the prohibition of the broadcast.

MUIR v. BBC 1996 S.C.C.R. 584, Judge not specified.

6773. Plea–guilty plea–plea allegedly tendered under error

[Criminal Procedure (Scotland) Act 1975 (c.21) s.252.]

C appealed against conviction of murder on the ground that his plea of guilty was tendered under a real error and misconception. C was charged, with M, of murdering L. C lodged a special defence of self-defence. During the trial, M pled guilty to assault and C tendered a plea of guilty of murder. On the day of sentencing, however, C submitted that he was unaware that he had pled guilty to murder and sought to withdraw his plea, and his counsel, A, was granted leave to withdraw. The trial judge refused C's motion as incompetent since the plea had already been recorded in the minute book and C had been convicted. Following a remit by the appeal court under the Criminal Procedure (Scotland) Act 1975 s.252(d) to a single judge to report on all matters including questions of credibility and reliability, the judge concluded that C's plea was not tendered because of any pressure from his legal representatives or under any mistake or misunderstanding, and that C understood the plea which he decided to tender. On further hearing, C maintained that he had not been aware that a plea of guilty had been tendered on his behalf and that it was not in his interest to tender such a plea since he believed that he had a sound defence to the charge. There was room for concern as his instructions to plead guilty to murder were not recorded in writing and neither the plea which was tendered orally on his behalf nor the plea as recorded in the minute book included the word murder. He also questioned the judge's acceptance of A's recollection that C had shouted, "I got life" to a witness after recording his plea of guilty.

Held, refusing the appeal, that the judge's finding that C's plea was not tendered under any mistake or misunderstanding had to be accepted, and it was not for the court to determine whether A's failure to obtain written instructions amounted to misconduct. It was immaterial that the word "murder" was not used or minuted when C's plea was being tendered by A or recorded by the clerk, since C was duly represented at the time by A and A was satisfied that C understood the plea which was being tendered to the court.

CROSSAN v. HM ADVOCATE 1996 S.C.C.R. 279, Judge not specified.

6774. Plea–guilty plea–suggestible accused–whether plea tendered under error

An accused person was charged on summary complaint with lewd, indecent and libidinous practices and behaviour. He had been detained in custody on the day of the offence and admitted to the police that he was guilty. When he appeared in court his solicitor tendered a plea of guilty on his behalf. The diet was adjourned for reports to be prepared and when he appeared for sentence a different solicitor appeared for him and sought leave to withdraw the plea on the ground that the accused had pled guilty under a misconception. He maintained that he had been told by the police that if there had been physical contact of the nature described by him he was guilty and on that basis he had volunteered to his solicitor that he was guilty although the conduct was merely horseplay and not sexually motivated. The sheriff, with the accused's consent, examined the accused's original solicitor whose notes of his interview with the accused showed that the accused had given a version of events to that solicitor which was entirely consistent with what the accused had told the police and with the victim's account. The solicitor was satisfied that the accused, who was of low intelligence and suggestible, nonetheless fully understood his position. The sheriff refused to allow the plea to be withdrawn on the view that the accused had been properly advised and that he had volunteered the information that he was guilty. The accused sought suspension of his conviction.

Held, that the sheriff was right to conclude that since the plea was tendered by the accused with the benefit of his solicitor's advice after interview, it could not be withdrawn because it had not been tendered under any real error or misconception or in circumstances clearly prejudicial to him; and bill refused, *Healy v. HM Advocate* 1990 S.C.C.R. 110, [1990] C.L.Y. 4908 applied.

Observed, that it was an unusual but commendable step for the sheriff to examine the solicitor as he was thereby in a position to satisfy himself that the accused had fully understood his position.

MATHIESON v. MacLEOD 1996 S.L.T. 660, Judge not specified, HCJ.

6775. Plea–guilty plea–whether justice seen to be done

Held, where a suggestible 16 year old charged with theft by housebreaking was approached by his co-accused's solicitor and was persuaded to allow that solicitor to act for him and to change his plea to one of guilty, that justice had not been seen to be done, and bill of suspension passed and conviction and sentence suspended.

McGOUGH v. CROWE 1996 S.C.C.R. 226, Judge not specified.

6776. Police powers–warrant to take bodily samples

[Criminal Procedure (Scotland) Act 1995 (c.46) s.18(6).]

The Criminal Procedure (Scotland) Act 1995 s.18(6) provides, *inter alia*, that a constable may, with the authority of an officer of a rank no lower than inspector, take from a person arrested and in custody or detained, a sample of hair, other than pubic hair, or other material. An accused person was charged on petition with rape and was remanded in custody. Prior to his committal for rape he had been fully committed on a charge of attempted murder and warrants had been granted for samples of blood and saliva and dental impressions to be taken, but he had refused to comply with these warrants. The accused was subsequently charged on petition with, *inter alia*, attempting to defeat the ends of justice by refusing to comply with the warrants and was remanded in custody in respect of that petition but liberated on the rape charge. Thereafter the Crown applied by petition, which referred to s.18 of the 1995 Act, for a warrant to take a sample of the accused's hair, other than pubic hair, for comparison purposes in respect of the rape charge. The sheriff granted the warrant without intimation of the petition being given to the accused, on the basis of information on oath that there was a real danger that the accused would frustrate the purposes of the warrant. The accused, after the warrant had been executed, sought suspension of it and an order for the destruction of the samples which had been obtained under the warrant, on the grounds that he had not been able to make representations to the sheriff who, in any event, had been misled as to the power which she was exercising. It was conceded that while intimation of such warrants was the normal and proper practice, but intimation was not required where it would defeat the purpose for which the warrant was granted.

Held, that (1) the sheriff was entitled to accept and proceed upon the information on oath and while administrative steps might have been taken to prevent the accused's attempts to frustrate the warrant, the sheriff was entitled to decide in the public interest that the attendant risks should not be undertaken by requiring intimation; (2) the sheriff had not been misled as to her powers as the warrant was sought at common law and the reference to s.18 of the 1995 Act indicated that since that statutory power was unavailable, a warrant was necessary in accordance with the common law rules; and bill refused, *Harris, Complainer* 1994 S.L.T. 906, [1994] C.L.Y. 5644 applied.

MELLORS v. NORMAND (NO.2) 1996 S.L.T. 1146, Judge not specified, HCJ.

6777. Rules–High Court of Justiciary–sheriff courts–district courts–consolidation

ACT OF ADJOURNAL (CRIMINAL PROCEDURE RULES) 1996, SI 1996 513 (S.47); made under the Public Records (Scotland) Act 1937 s.305; the Backing of Warrants (Republic of Ireland) Act 1965 s.2A, s.8; the Legal Aid (Scotland) Act 1986 s.38; the Debtors (Scotland) Act 1987 s.90; the Extradition Act 1989 s.10, s.14, Sch.1 para.9; the Computer Misuse Act 1990 s.8; the Criminal Justice (International Co-operation) Act 1990 s.10; the Prisoners and Criminal Proceedings (Scotland) Act 1993 s.19; the Proceeds of Crime (Scotland) Act 1995 s.18; and the Criminal Procedure (Scotland) Act 1995 s.305. In force: April 1, 1996; £15.65.

This Act of Adjournal arises out of the enacting of the Criminal Procedure (Scotland) Act 1995 (c.46) which consolidates enactments relating to criminal procedure including those mentioned below. The Act of Adjournal makes new rules for the High Court of Judiciary, for the sheriff court in exercise of its criminal jurisdiction, and for the district court, consolidating, with amendments the Act of Adjournal (Consolidation) 1988 and certain provisions of the Criminal Procedure (Scotland) Act 1887 (c.35), the Criminal Justice (Scotland) Act 1949 (c.94), the Summary Jurisdiction (Scotland) Act 1954 (c.48) and the Criminal Procedure (Scotland) Act 1975 (c.21). The provisions in the enactments mentioned above which are consolidated in this Act of Adjournal and the respective provisions in the Act of Adjournal which re enact them, are set out in the Table of Destinations attached to this Act of Adjournal.

6778. Rules–notice of witnesses–notice of productions

ACT OF ADJOURNAL (CRIMINAL PROCEDURE RULES AMENDMENT) (MISCELLANEOUS) 1996, SI 1996 2147 (S.171); made under the Proceeds of

Crime (Scotland) Act 1995 s.18; and the Criminal Procedure (Scotland) Act 1995 s.140, s.305. In force: September 9, 1996; £1.10.

This Act of Adjournal amends the Criminal Procedure Rules 1996 (SI 1996 513) in order to provide for a notice by an accused on a co-accused of lists of witnesses or productions to be served on the co-accused's solicitor; to provide in applications for leave of appeal for the judge of the High Court considering the application to remit to the judge at first instance for a report with respect to the grounds of appeal; and to provide for a signature by mechanical or electronic means, or an official stamp of the signature, of the prosecutor of postal citations of accused persons and witnesses served in summary proceedings under the Criminal Procedure (Scotland) Act 1995 s.141.

6779. Search–warrant–validity

[Misuse of Drugs Act 1971 (c.38) s.23(3).]

Two accused persons were charged on separate indictments levelling, *inter alia*, contraventions of the Misuse of Drugs Act 1971 s.5(2). On the day before the alleged offences the police had applied to the sheriff for a search warrant on the basis that there were reasonable grounds for suspecting that controlled drugs were in the possession of a person or persons on the premises of a named public house. The sheriff granted the warrant. The accused in due course sought suspension of the warrant on the ground that as the police intended to search patrons of the public house, whoever they might be, they had no proper basis for seeking the warrant under the Misuse of Drugs Act 1971 s.23(3).

Held, that the crucial point was the connection between controlled drugs and the premises and it was not necessary that a view should be formed as to precisely who was in possession of the drugs; and bill refused.

HAMMOND v. HOWDLE 1996 S.L.T. 1174, Judge not specified, HCJ.

6780. Search–without warrant–suspected possession of stolen property

[Civic Government (Scotland) Act 1982 (c.45) s.60(1).]

C appealed against conviction for possession of drugs on the ground that a search carried out was unlawful. A train en route to Wick was reported to the police as having a quantity of miniature spirits stolen from the buffet. On arriving at Wick, all of the passengers were asked to remain on board the train. M and S were among the investigating officers. C consented to M examining the pockets of his clothing and his holdall, although M did not explain that he could withhold his consent to the search. C's companion, X was also searched and was found to be in possession of some, but not all of the missing spirits and was taken to the police station. M and S offered C a lift to the station to meet up with X, which C accepted. On the way to the car, M advised C that he intended to search the turnups of his jeans, having realised his previous omission to do so, and on commencing the search, a small metal box containing cannabis resin fell out. No statutory authority for the search was stated to C. At trial, the sheriff found that although the initial search, for which there was no statutory basis, was illegal, the search in the car satisfied the conditions for a search without warrant under s.60(1). C argued that the search of his turnups was illegal, *McGovern v. HM Advocate* 1950 S.L.T. 133, [1950] C.L.Y. 4649.

Held, appeal refused, that the police knew a specific crime had been committed and prior to searching C's turnups, they had reasonable cause to suspect that C was in possession of stolen property and were therefore entitled to search him by virtue of s.60(1)(a). C's consent was not required and M and S did not need to intimate to him that his consent could be withheld.

CHASSAR v. MacDONALD 1996 S.C.C.R. 730, Judge not specified.

6781. Summary–adjournment–refusal–whether oppressive

[Criminal Procedure (Scotland) Act 1975 (c.21) s.316(2).]

Section 316(2)(a) of the Criminal Procedure (Scotland) Act 1975 provides, *inter alia*, that it should be deemed a legal citation of a witness to a diet if the citation was delivered to him personally or left for him at his dwellinghouse with some person resident or employed therein. An accused person was charged on a summary complaint with assault and robbery. When the case called for trial the Crown could not proceed because of the absence of two essential witnesses. The police had twice unsuccessfully attempted to serve citations at the witnesses' home addresses as the witnesses were not present. There was no information that anyone else was present at the homes. The police accordingly left calling cards. The Crown sought an adjournment of the trial diet but the sheriff refused the motion and a further motion for leave to desert the diet *pro loco et tempore*, and deserted the *diet simpliciter*. The sheriff criticised the Crown and police for leaving calling-cards instead of the citations on the ground that executions of service of the citations could then have been produced to the court. The Crown sought advocation of the sheriff's decision, contending that he had misdirected himself.

Held, that the sheriff had misdirected himself because had the citations been left at the witnesses' home addresses there would not have been regular citation in accordance with the 1975 Act, and his decision was therefore oppressive and unjust; and bill passed and decision recalled.

NORMAND v. MILNE 1996 S.L.T. 801, Judge not specified, HCJ.

6782. Summary–adjournment after conviction–adjournment under statute or at common law

[Criminal Procedure (Scotland) Act 1975 (c.21) s.380(1).]

Held, on A seeking suspension of sentences passed on him on a complaint, on the ground that sentence had been deferred for a period longer than allowed by s.380(1)(b) of the 1975 Act as amended, that while sentence had been deferred "to be of good behaviour and to ascertain taxi licence situation (what effect the convictions would have on A's licence) and for a social inquiry report and community service assessment", A himself accepted that the primary reason had been the taxi licence question, which did not fall within the terms of s.380(1) despite A's argument that it was to "enable enquiries to be made" and the adjournment had accordingly been at common law; and bill refused.

AIRLIE v. HEYWOOD 1996 S.C.C.R. 562, Judge not specified.

6783. Summary–adjournment after conviction–competency

[Criminal Procedure (Scotland) Act 1995 (c.46) s.201 (1) and (3).]

An accused person was charged on a summary complaint with a contravention of s.1 (1) of the Prevention of Crime Act 1953. On August 19, 1996 he pled guilty and the sheriff adjourned the case until September 16, 1996 to obtain social inquiry and community service reports, and remanded the accused in custody. The accused sought suspension of the order for adjournment and his remand in custody on the ground that the adjournment was in breach of s.201 (3) (a) of the Criminal Procedure (Scotland) Act 1995 as it exceeded three weeks. The procurator fiscal, conceding that the order was incompetent, sought advocation and a remit to the sheriff to adjourn the diet to a date within the three week period.

Held, that as there was nothing improper in the adjournment to obtain reports and all that the sheriff had done wrong was exceed the statutory time limit, it was possible for the Crown to ask the High Court to alter the order before the three week period expired; and proceedings advocated and adjourned diet directed to proceed on September 9, 1996, *HM Advocate v. Clegg* 1991 S.L.T. 192, [1991] C.L.Y. 4848 followed; *Russell v. Wilson* 1994 S.L.T. 660, [1994] C.L.Y. 5592 distinguished.

CONNOLLY v. NORMAND; SUB NOM. NORMAND v. CONNOLLY 1996 S.L.T. 1336, Judge not specified, HCJ.

6784. Summary–citation–delivery at accused's home to person falsely pretending to be resident there

[Criminal Procedure (Scotland) Act 1975 (c.21) s.316(2).]

Held, where a sheriff officer had delivered a complaint and citation to a man at the accused's address who said that he was the accused's flatmate and who accepted the citation on behalf of the accused, that the sheriff officer had acted reasonably and in good faith and that the citation had been lawful.

NORMAND v. HARKINS 1996 S.C.C.R. 355, Judge not specified, Sh Ct.

6785. Summary–citation–delivery to member of family at neighbouring address

[Criminal Procedure (Scotland) Act 1975 (c.21) s.311 (5), s.316(2).]

Held, where B, his mother (M) and his sister (S) were charged with drug offences and after B pled guilty a proof was held on the competence of the service of the notice of penalties, that B had not been lawfully cited nor had the notices of penalty been served on him, where a police officer delivered the citations for M and S at their house (no.131), was told by M that B, who lived at no.135 (his domicile of citation), would not be there and left B's envelope with M to give to B, although it was said in evidence that this was common practice.

NORMAND v. BUCHANAN 1996 S.C.C.R. 363, Judge not specified.

6786. Summary–complaint–designation of accused

R appealed against a sheriff's decision granting the Crown leave to amend a complaint to alter the designation of an accused from "Henry Ralston Limited", which was a non-existent company, to "Henry Ralston". R argued that amendment enabled the Crown to substitute a non-existent entity with an existing person outwith the time limit *Valentine v. Thistle Leisure* 1983 S.C.C.R. 515, [1984] C.L.Y. 3922; *Hoyers (UK) v. Houston* 1991 S.L.T. 934, [1991] C.L.Y. 4676 could be distinguished as it did not involve introducing a different legal entity.

Held, appeal refused. The justice was entitled in terms of s.335(1) to allow the amendments. There was no question of prejudice where there had been correspondence between the fiscal's office and R's solicitor. There was no rule of law that an amendment which involved changing the identity of the person charged could not be allowed, *Hoyers (UK) v. Houston. Valentine v. Thistle Leisure* was expressed too widely and was distinguishable as it involved an amendment substituting an individual for a company originally named in the complaint where both the individual and the company were existing persons. There was sufficient similarity between the name stated in the present complaint and that of R, the address being the same, for it to be clear that R was being charged with the offence.

RALSTON v. CARMICHAEL 1995 S.C.C.R. 729, Judge not specified.

6787. Summary–joint minutes seeking acceleration of diet and fixing new diet–failure of minute to discharge–authority granted to hold that diet to consider application

[Criminal Procedure (Scotland) Act 1975 (c.21) s.314; Road Traffic Act 1988 (c.52).]

The Criminal Procedure (Scotland) Act 1975 s.314(3) provides that where a diet has been fixed in a summary prosecution, it shall be competent for the court, on the joint application in writing by the parties or their solicitors, to discharge the diet so fixed and fix in lieu thereof an earlier diet. Two accused persons were charged on summary complaint with contraventions of the Road Traffic Act 1988. After pleading not guilty their cases were adjourned to a diet on September 7, 1995 at which they were ordained to appear. On May 10, 1995 two joint minutes in terms of s.314(3) of the 1975 Act came before the sheriff who was requested to accelerate the diet of September 7 to May 10 and fix a new diet of trial. The sheriff acceded to the request. The minutes of proceedings contained two separate minutes. The first minute, which was unsigned, discharged the diet of September 7 and assigned May 10 as the new diet. The second minute, which was signed, narrated that the first accused had confirmed his plea of not guilty previously tendered and that the court, on the motion of the defence for the second accused, discharged the diet of trial for September 7. The minute thereafter adjourned the diet for trial to November 14, 1995 and assigned an intermediate diet. A minute relating to the second accused was in similar terms but also recorded the fact that the original trial diet had been discharged because the second accused was to be on holiday on that day. The second accused was present along with his solicitor but the first accused was absent. Objection was taken to the competency of the proceedings on November 14, 1995 on the ground that the signed minutes did not contain authority for holding the diet on May 10 and although the first minute did, it should be disregarded as it was unsigned. The first accused also maintained that he had been prejudiced by the fact that he was absent and the second minute did not record the reason for the discharge of the trial diet in his case. The sheriff repelled the objections but granted leave to appeal.

Held, that (1) authority to hold the diet of May 10 was to be found in the joint minutes under s.314(3) which expressly moved the court to fix May 10 as a diet in lieu of September 7 and (2) any irregularity in the proceedings on May 10 prejudicing the first accused should be remedied by bill of suspension and could not be raised in an appeal under s.334; and appeals refused.

Observed, that the better practice was for a diet for the hearing of a joint application under s.314(3) to be assigned in a minute.

WHITE v. RUXTON 1996 S.L.T. 556, Judge not specified, HCJ.

6788. Summary–minute of proceedings–inaccurate minuting of trial diet

Held, on W and F's appeal against a sheriff's decision refusing their pleas to the competency of fixing a new trial diet, that the sheriff did not err in fixing a new diet where W and F's case had been adjourned to a trial diet announced in court as May 26, 1995 (a date prescribed as a holiday), although the minute of proceedings narrated that the trial diet was fixed for May 15, 1995, on which date the case called and the sheriff fixed a new date in W and F's absence, and that the trial date reflected in the minute was competent until the minute was amended. There was no suggestion of any material prejudice to W or F.

WALKER v. NORMAND 1996 S.C.C.R. 296, Judge not specified.

6789. Summary–oppression–Crown obtaining psychiatric report also disclosing particulars of defence

[Criminal Procedure (Scotland) Act 1975 (c.21) s.376(5).]

M, charged with assault and breach of the peace, appealed against a sheriff's decision to reject his plea in bar of trial. The Crown had instructed a psychiatric report on M's mental condition pursuant to s.376(5). The report, which concluded that M was sane and fit to plead, was made available to the Crown. M argued that the report was prejudicial as it disclosed to the Crown his whole position regarding the charges against him and the nature of his defence, and gave the Crown such an unfair advantage that it would be oppressive to proceed.

Held, appeal refused, that it was undesirable that a psychiatrist instructed under s.376(5) should be restricted in the nature of his inquiry or inhibited in expressing the basis for forming his opinion, *Sloan v. Crowe* 1996 S.C.C.R. 200, [1996] C.L.Y. 6790 and a psychiatrist called upon to provide a report regarding the mental condition of an accused person could hardly do so effectively without including information regarding the accused's background, including interviews with members of his family. Nor would it be satisfactory for the psychiatrist to send part of his report to the Crown in a sealed envelope since the whole report was part of the available evidence of the accused's mental condition which it was the duty of the Crown to bring before the court. In addition, the chances of the sheriff who took the initial plea remembering the terms of the report were remote and any matters contained in it which might be prejudicial to the accused could be expected to be ignored.

MacDONALD v. MUNRO 1996 S.C.C.R. 595, Judge not specified.

6790. Summary–oppression–Crown obtaining psychiatric report also disclosing particulars of defence

[Criminal Procedure (Scotland) Act 1975 (c.21) s.376(5).]

S, charged with assault and breach of peace, appealed against the sheriff's decision to repel his plea in bar of trial. The Crown had sought a psychiatric report on S's mental condition pursuant to the Criminal Procedure (Scotland) Act 1975 s.376(5). The report, which stated that S was sane and fit to plead, was made available to the Crown. S argued that the report, was made available to the Crown. S argued that the report, which provided details of S's position and the nature of his defence, gave the Crown such an unfair (although accidental) advantage that it would be oppressive for the case to proceed to trial.

Held, refusing the appeal, that the prosecutor had a duty under s.376(5) to bring evidence of S's mental condition before the court. It was inaccurate to describe the report as an investigation carried out on behalf of the prosecutor as it was an exercise carried out on his behalf to enable him to perform a statutory duty placed upon him for the protection of S. There was no evidence that the report was not carried out in good faith or that anything was done deliberately to place the Crown in an advantageous position. It was undesirable that a psychiatrist preparing a report pursuant to s.376(5) should be restricted in the nature of his inquiry or inhibited in expressing the basis for his opinion, *Mowbray v. Crowe* 1994 S.L.T. 445, [1993] C.L.Y. 5001, *MacLeod v. Tiffney* 1994 S.L.T. 531, [1994] C.L.Y. 5613 and *Bott v. Anderson* 1995 S.L.T. 1308, [1995] C.L.Y. 5700 distinguished.

SLOAN v. CROWE 1996 S.C.C.R. 200, Judge not specified.

6791. Summary–prosecutor's right of appeal

PROSECUTOR'S RIGHT OF APPEAL IN SUMMARY PROCEEDINGS (SCOTLAND) ORDER 1996, SI 1996 2548 (S.197); made under the Criminal Procedure (Scotland) Act 1995 s.175. In force: November 1, 1996; £0.65.

The Criminal Procedure (Scotland) Act 1995 s.175(4) enables the Secretary of State by order to specify a class of case in summary proceedings in which the prosecutor may appeal to the High Court against the sentence or other disposal passed or made on the grounds that the sentence or disposal is unduly lenient or otherwise inappropriate. This Order specifies the class of case for this purpose as being any case in which, on or after November 1, 1996, the sentence or other disposal is passed or made.

6792. Summary–renunciation of right to prosecute

Two accused persons along with a third person, M, were charged on a summary complaint. After they had pled not guilty and a trial diet had been fixed, they were approached by a police officer who told them that the charges against them had been dropped and they were asked to provide statements as witnesses against their coaccused. The police officer's actions were the result of a letter comprising a computer printout which he had received from the procurator fiscal and which was headed: "A: statements required for: [the two accused]. Case of: [the co-accused, M]." The letter stated, "The above named appeared in court today when a plea of not guilty was tendered. I should be obliged if you will instruct the officer in charge to obtain full statements from the witnesses necessary to establish the charges." Towards the end of the letter was added, "Statements required listed at A: only." At the end of the letter it was stated, "Trial date: [the two accused]." The accused objected in bar of trial that the Crown was precluded from prosecuting them because the letter was capable of being construed as an instruction from the procurator fiscal that the charges were to be dropped. The sheriff repelled the objection and the accused appealed.

Held, that the letter contained no unequivocal and unqualified announcement on the Crown's behalf that no further proceedings were to be taken; and appeals refused, *Thom v. HM Advocate* 1976 J. C. 48, [1976] C.L.Y. 3015, applied.

McGHEE v. MAGUIRE 1996 S.L.T. 1012, Judge not specified, HCJ.

6793. Summary–time bar–effect of previous charges on petition

[Criminal Procedure (Scotland) Act 1975 (c. 21) s.101 (1) and (2).]

G appealed against a sheriff's decision repelling his plea to the competency of a complaint brought against him. On May 28, 1993 G appeared on petition charged with prison breaking. Although no proceedings on indictment were commenced against him within 12 months, on June 30, 1994 he was served with a summary complaint on the same charge. The appeal was remitted to a court of five judges to reconsider the decisions in *MacDougall v. Russell* 1986 S.L.T. 403, [1986] C.L.Y. 3865 and *Whitelaw v. Dickinson* 1993 S.L.T. 599, [1993] C.L.Y. 5038. G argued that although the opening words of s.101 (1) related exclusively to solemn procedure, the remainder of the provision conferred upon the accused a substantive right of immunity from all further prosecution for the offence if trial on indictment was not commenced before the expiry of the 12 month period. In addition, as s.101 (1) and (2) contained the same language, there was no justification in applying s.101 (1) more restrictively to solemn proceedings while s.101 (2) applied to both solemn and summary procedure. The Crown submitted that the words, "and thereafter he shall be forever free from all question or process for that offence" in s.101 (1) and (2) (b) did not necessarily have the same meaning and their meaning depended on their context. The language in s.101 (2) (b) was wider, *C v. Forsyth* 1995 S.L.T. 905, [1995] C.L.Y. 5663.

Held, appeal allowed and complaint dismissed. Per the Lord Justice General (Hope) and Lord McCluskey, Lords Cullen and Cowie concurring: *MacDougall* and *Whitelaw* were wrongly decided and should be overruled, and *C v. Forsyth*, insofar as it proceeded upon the same reasoning, should be disapproved. Although s.101 (1) was included in Pt I of the 1975 Act, the declaration as to the effect of the failure to commence the trial within the 12 month time limit was not necessarily limited to solemn procedure. It was not necessary to add the words "on indictment" to give meaning to the declaration, and such additions which limited the effect of the declaration were inconsistent with the legislative history of the provision. Although the opening words of s.101 (1) and 101 (2) were different, their respective declarations were the same and therefore the protection provided in each section was the same. The declaration in s.101 (1) should be given effect according to the plain and unambiguous meaning of its words, which should not vary according to context. Opinion, that if the Crown obtained a conviction or finding of guilt in summary proceedings within the 12 month period, the declaration would not prevent the court from dealing with the case thereafter. Per Lord Morison: having examined the legislative history of s.101 (1), if the sanction against bringing proceedings outside the 12 month time limit extended to summary proceedings brought on similar or related charges to those previously brought on petition, the time bar extends to any continuation of proceedings and whatever stage. Thus, for example, deferral of sentence or breach of probation could be discharged. Although construing the subsection in this manner is undesirable it does not create absurdity or insistency and the remedy must be with the legislature.

GARDNER v. LEES 1996 S.L.T. 342, Lord Hope L.J.G., HCJ.

6794. Summary–time bar–effect of previous charge on petition

[Misuse of Drugs Act 1971; Criminal Procedure (Scotland) Act 1975 (c.21) s.101.]

Section 101 (1) of the Criminal Procedure (Scotland) Act 1975 provides that an accused shall not be tried on indictment for an offence unless his trial is commenced within 12 months of his first appearance on petition, provided that "(ii)... the sheriff ... may on cause shown extend the said period." An accused person was charged on petition with contravention of the Misuse of Drugs Act 1971 and was committed for further examination and released on bail on January 23, 1995. He was thereafter served with a summary complaint containing these charges. A trial date was fixed but was twice adjourned on the Crown's motion until May 9, 1996. The Crown applied for an extension of the 12 month period but the sheriff refused in on the ground that it was incompetent for an extension to be granted in summary proceedings. The Crown appealed.

Held, that the application was competent because the effect of the time bar and the provisions which were designed to modify its effect were applicable generally to all further proceedings irrespective of the level at which they were taken; and appeal allowed and decision recalled, *Gardner v. Lees* 1996 S.L.T. 342, [1996] C.L.Y. 6793.

NORMAND v. WALKER 1996 S.L.T. 418, Judge not specified, HCJ.

6795. Summary–time bar–effect of previous charge on petition–application for extension of time

[Criminal Procedure (Scotland) Act 1975 (c.21) s.101 (1).]

The Crown brought a bill of advocation in respect of a sheriff's decision refusing to grant an extension of the 12 month time limit following G's appearance on petition on December 5, 1994. On August 3, 1995, the case was reduced to summary and a trial diet was later fixed for January 16, 1996. In the course of the trial, the Crown became aware of the decision in *Gardner v. Lees* 1996 S.L.T. 342, [1996] 3 C.L. 658, and moved for an extension of the 12 month period. The sheriff held that he did not have the power to grant the extension as s.101 (1) related exclusively to solemn proceedings. The Crown argued that it was competent to extend the time period in summary proceedings, *Normand v. Walker* 1996 S.L.T. 418, [1996] C.L.Y. 6794 and that the extension could be granted retrospectively, *McDowall v. Lees* 1996 S.L.T. 871, [1996] C.L.Y. 6796. G submitted that an application for extension had to be made prior to the commencement of the trial, and since the trial had commenced outwith the 12 month period without the grant of an extension, it was a fundamental nullity which could not be cured.

Held, bill passed, that there was no restriction in s.101 (1) on the time at which the Crown could seek an extension of time and therefore G did not have an absolute right to be discharged at the expiry of 12 months, *McDowall v. Lees* applied. Nothing in the wording of s.101 indicated that commencement of the trial barred the Crown from seeking an extension or that an accused's qualified right to be discharged after the expiry of 12 months became absolute as at the date the trial commenced, and the trial could not be a fundamental nullity until G's qualified right had been converted into an absolute right by the court's refusal to extend the time limit.

McDONALD v. GORDON 1996 S.C.C.R. 740, Judge not specified.

6796. Summary–time bar–effect of previous charge on petition–retrospective extension of time

[Criminal Procedure (Scotland) Act 1975 (c.21) s.101 (1).]

Section 101 (1) of the Criminal Procedure (Scotland) Act 1975 provides that an accused shall not be tried on indictment for any offence unless his trial is commenced within 12 months of his first appearance on petition, provided that "(ii)... the sheriff... may on cause shown extend the said period". An accused person was charged on petition with fraud and was committed for further examination and released on bail on June 22, 1994. She was thereafter served with a summary complaint in respect of that charge. A trial diet was fixed for January 18, 1996 when the Crown applied for an extension of the 12 month period in light of the decision in *Gardner v. Lees* 1996 S.L.T. 342, [1996] C.L.Y. 6793. The accused opposed the extension on the ground, inter alia, that it was incompetent to extend the 12 month period retrospectively. The sheriff granted the extension and the accused appealed.

Held, (by a bench of five judges), that having regard to the history of the legislation and the recognition of a power to extend retrospectively the 110 day rule under solemn procedure, there was nothing in the terms of s.101 to indicate that Parliament intended to depart from the principle that a retrospective grant of extension might competently be sought and made; and appeal refused, *HM Advocate v. M* 1987 J.C. 1 approved; *HM Advocate v. Bickerstaff* 1926 S.L.T. 121, *HM Advocate v. McCann* 1977 J.C. 1, [1977] C.L.Y. 3322 and *Farrell v. HM Advocate* 1985 S.L.T. 58, [1985] C.L.Y. 3914 considered.

Observed, that it was inaccurate to describe the right conferred by s.101 of the 1975 Act as "an absolutely unqualified right ". Dictum of Lord McCluskey in *Gardner v. Lees* 1996 S.L.T. 342, [1996] C.L.Y. 6793 disapproved.

McDOWALL v. LEES 1996 S.L.T. 871, Judge not specified, HCJ.

6797. Summary–trial–adjournment–refusal–oppression

N sought suspension of his conviction for driving dangerously and driving while disqualified and without insurance on the ground that the sheriff erred in refusing his motion to adjourn the trial. N had moved for an adjournment in order to trace and cite C, whom he was acquainted with and wished to incriminate as the driver, as his efforts to cite him before trial had been unsuccessful. The sheriff refused N's motion because he was not persuaded that N had a good reason for failing to locate C, and if C, an acquaintance of N, could not be traced within the period to trial, it was unlikely that he could be traced during an adjournment. On appeal N argued that the sheriff failed to take proper account that C was an essential witness and that there was a reasonable explanation, given the short time between the fixing of the date for trial and the trial itself, for his failure to trace and cite C.

Held, refusing the bill, that the sheriff's decision could not properly be interfered with as it was not one which no reasonable sheriff would have taken in view of the information provided, *Sim v. Tudhope* 1987 S.C.C.R. 482, [1987] C.L.Y. 4165.

NASH v. NORMAND 1996 S.C.C.R. 196, Judge not specified.

6798. Summary–trial–adjournment–repeated adjournments

Two accused persons were charged on a summary complaint. They pled not guilty in December 1994 and an intermediate diet was set for March 3, 1995 when the Crown stated that they were prepared for trial. Despite the fact that the Crown's productions included a video tape which had not by then been made available to the defence and had not been edited, a trial date was set for March 21, 1995 when the Crown moved for an adjournment on the ground that the video tape had not been analysed and edited. The accused opposed the motion but the sheriff granted it, fixing an intermediate diet for April 6, 1995 and a trial diet for April 13, 1995. At the intermediate diet the Crown intimated that they were ready for trial but at the trial diet the video tape had not been checked and certain Crown witnesses were also absent. The diet was called at 3.30 pm when the evidence of a formal witness was led and the diet was adjourned until May 11, 1995. On that date the proceedings commenced at 2.15 pm because the Crown required to have a video recorder brought from police headquarters. Further evidence was led and the diet was adjourned, because of the lack of court time, until May 26, 1995 when further evidence was led and at 4 pm the Crown moved for and obtained an adjournment until June 16, 1995. On that date the Crown sought an adjournment due to the absence of certain Crown witnesses, citations for whom had only been sent out on June 15, 1995. The witness whose evidence had been interrupted on May 26 was on leave and only one Crown witness was present. The accused opposed the motion to adjourn. The sheriff initially refused the motion and allowed the evidence of the one available witness to be interposed, but on the Crown renewing its motion, granted an adjournment until July 4, 1995 on the basis that the Crown had acted reasonably on every occasion throughout the case. The accused sought recall of the sheriff's decision. Before the High Court the Crown conceded that the absence of witnesses on June 16, was the result of the Crown's failure to cite them earlier than the night before the trial diet.

Held, that (1) the sheriff had erred in the exercise of his discretion because there had been failures on more than one occasion on the part of the Crown, and (2) the Crown had to accept the consequences of their failures and as the adjournment was prejudicial and oppressive, it should not have been granted; and bills passed and decision recalled, *Skeen v. McLaren* 1976 S.L.T. (Notes) 14, [1976] C.L.Y. 3017 applied.

TIMNEY v. CARDLE 1996 S.L.T. 376, Judge not specified, HCJ.

6799. Summary–trial–conduct of sheriff

An accused person was tried on summary complaint for indecent assault. The accused lived with the complainer's mother in the same house as the complainer, a 15 year old boy. In the course of defence evidence the complainer's mother, after she had stated that the accused had never before made advances on her son when he had had ample time to do so, was asked by the sheriff: "Has a man ever thrown himself at you in the heat of sexual excitement?" When the accused's solicitor suggested that the question might be inappropriate, the sheriff told him that he was being "terribly juvenile about the whole thing". After the sheriff had found the accused guilty, she said to the accused: "You did this, didn't you?" to which the accused replied in the negative, and she then said: "You did this, didn't you? You did it. You did it. You did it. I know that you did it." The accused sought suspension of his convictions.

Held, that the sheriff's conduct was such as to create in the mind of a reasonable man a suspicion that the sheriff was antagonistic to the accused and his witness, and that the accused did not receive a fair trial; and bill passed and conviction quashed, *Hogg v. Normand* 1992 S.L.T. 736, [1992] C.L.Y. 5483 applied.

SNEDDON v. LEES 1996 S.L.T. 294, Judge not specified, HCJ.

6800. Summary–trial–conduct of sheriff–fairness

Held, on D seeking suspension of a conviction of assault and breach of the peace, where the sheriff, after convicting D but before sentencing him, invited the complainer who was a local Member of Parliament into his chambers to meet him, and that the bill would be passed since the meeting, taking place before sentence was imposed or any possible appeal raised, could give rise to suspicion in the ordinary man that the sheriff was not being impartial, and justice had not been seen to be done.

DOHERTY v. McGLENNAN 1996 S.C.C.R. 591, Judge not specified.

6801. Summary–trial–conduct of sheriff–oppression

An accused person was tried on summary complaint for assault and sought to incriminate his brother. The accused's brother had been present in the police station when the accused was charged but he had made no statement. The brother was called as a witness for the defence and was asked why he had made no statement to the police. Before the accused's brother could answer the sheriff interjected, saying that if the witness were to leave his admission until that stage and the incrimination were successful, the Crown would be unable to proceed against the brother and both the accused and his brother would get off scot free. The accused's solicitor replied that since no objection had been taken to the question the brother should be allowed to answer. The sheriff replied that there was little point in having the question answered as the answer was obvious. The examination was however allowed to proceed and the accused's brother explained that he did not make a statement as he wanted to avoid being arrested as it was he who had committed the offence. The sheriff rejected the brother's account. The accused was convicted and sought suspension of the conviction on the ground of oppression.

Held, that the sheriff's remarks went beyond the mark of what was permissible and in their context could properly be thought to reveal, to the dispassionate observer, that the accused was not receiving a fair trial; the bill passed and conviction and sentence suspended.

Observed, that if a sheriff made statements in the course of the evidence indicating that he was disposed not to consider questions of credibility because of the consequences of doing so, or made some other remark indicating that he had diverted himself from his judicial function, then it could be said that he had acted oppressively and that justice was not being seen to be done.

COAKLEY v. CROWE 1996 S.L.T. 867, Judge not specified, HCJ.

6802. Summary–trial–conduct of sheriff–whether justice seen to be done

An accused person was tried on a summary complaint. At the close of the Crown case a submission of no case to answer was made. After an adjournment when other cases were called over, the sheriff announced his decision repelling the submission. The accused's solicitor then sought and was granted an adjournment to take the accused's instructions. The sheriff thereafter dealt with other cases coming before him at the call over. When the accused's case was called again the accused's solicitor intimated that there was no evidence to be led for the defence. The procurator fiscal depute commenced her closing submissions on the evidence at which stage the sheriff asked whether the accused had any previous convictions. The sheriff had wrongly gained the impression that the case was at the post-conviction stage and immediately acknowledged his mistake. He was not provided with a schedule of previous convictions. The accused was convicted and appealed, contending that justice had not been seen to be done.

Held, that the sheriff had made a momentary lapse which he immediately corrected and no bystander could reasonably have concluded that the accused's case was not being dealt with fairly, far less that the sheriff had made up his mind regarding the accused's guilt; and appeal refused *Hogg v. Normand* 1992 S.L.T. 736, [1992] C.L.Y. 5483 distinguished.

PIERCY v. LEES 1996 S.L.T. 906, Judge not specified, HCJ.

6803. Summary–trial–sheriff falling asleep during cross-examination of Crown witness

An accused person was tried on summary complaint for a contravention of s.2 or alternatively s.3 of the Road Traffic Act 1988. During cross-examination of a Crown witness the sheriff fell asleep and on awakening he asked the Crown to re-examine the witness although the cross-examination had not been completed. The questions put to the witness while the sheriff had been asleep were then repeated. The accused was convicted and sought suspension of the conviction.

Held, that although it was not disputed that justice might in fact have been done, justice had not been seen to have been done; and bill passed and conviction suspended.

FREW v. BROWN 1996 S.L.T. 282, Lord Ross, LCJ., HCJ.

6804. Summary–warrant to apprehend–delay in executing warrant–time bar

[Criminal Procedure (Scotland) Act 1975 (c.21) s.331 (3).]

Section 331 (3) of the Criminal Procedure (Scotland) Act 1975 provides that proceedings shall be deemed to be commenced on the date on which a warrant to apprehend or to cite the accused is granted, if the warrant is executed without undue delay. An accused person was charged on a summary complaint with, *inter alia*, contraventions of the Road Traffic Act 1988 allegedly committed on November 3 and 15, 1994. A warrant to apprehend the accused was issued on April 27, 1995 as his whereabouts were then unknown and it was passed to the procurator fiscal's office which transmitted it, marked as priority, to police headquarters. On the basis of the accused's address which was stated in the complaint, the warrant was sent to F division for execution but because of a public holiday weekend intervening, it was not received until May 5. It was then discovered from the police national computer that the accused had an address within E division which received the warrant only on May 12 also because of a national public holiday weekend intervening. When the warrant was received it was learned that the accused was to appear for trial at a High Court sitting in Glasgow. The warrant was executed in accordance with police policy on May 19 when the High Court proceedings had concluded. The magistrate repelled a plea that the warrant had not been executed without undue delay. The accused appealed.

Held, that there was no undue delay in sending the warrant from F to E division; that the police policy of not apprehending persons involved in High Court proceedings was a sound policy; the police had done all that was required of them by keeping watch on the proceedings and acting promptly once they had come to an end; and, accordingly, there were no grounds for interfering with the magistrates' decision; and appeal refused. *Observed*, that in considering whether there had been undue delay, some allowance had to be made for the pressure of circumstances and for the making of decisions under pressure of circumstances.

MELVILLE v. NORMAND 1996 S.L.T. 826, Judge not specified, HCJ.

6805. Summary–warrant to apprehend–duty in executing warrant–time bar

[Criminal Procedure (Scotland) Act 1975 (c.21) s.331.]

The Criminal Procedure (Scotland) Act 1975 s.331 (1) provides that summary proceedings for statutory offences should be commenced within six months of the offence. Subsection 3 provides that proceedings shall be deemed to be commenced on the date on which a warrant to apprehend is granted if such warrant is executed without undue delay. An accused person was charged on summary complaint with, inter alia, a contravention of the Road Traffic Act 1988 s.178 (1) (a) allegedly committed on October 24, 1994. When the complaint called in court on May 2, 1995 the accused objected to the competency of the complaint on the ground that a warrant to apprehend the accused had not been executed without undue delay. The warrant was granted on March 16, 1995 on the ground that the accused's whereabouts were unknown. Subsequently the police reported an address for the accused to the Crown. On April 2 or 3, the police went to that address but were told by the householder that the accused had not lived there for several months and that she did not know where he was. The Crown were informed on April 8 and the warrant to apprehend was received for execution at police headquarters on April 19, but was not executed until April 28. The magistrate, after hearing evidence, disbelieved the accused and the householder whom she considered were lying to prevent the accused being arrested. The magistrate repelled the objection and the accused appealed, arguing that there was undue delay in executing the warrant between March 16 and April 2 or 3.

Held, that (1) it was only where the warrant was executed after the expiry of the time limit that an explanation was called for, and (2) as the visit by the police on April 2 or 3 to clarify the accused's address was within the statutory time limit, it could not be said that there had been undue delay at that stage; and appeal refused, *Smith v. Peter Walker & Son (Edinburgh) Ltd* 1978 J.C. 33, [1980] C.L.Y. 3019 applied.

McKAY v. NORMAND 1996 S.L.T. 624, Judge not specified, HCJ.

6806. Transcripts

TRANSCRIPTS OF CRIMINAL PROCEEDINGS (SCOTLAND) AMENDMENT ORDER 1995, SI 1995 1751 (S.121); made under the Criminal Procedure (Scotland) Act 1975 s.275. In force: August 1, 1995; £0.65.

This Order amends the 1993 Order which makes provision for restrictions on the availability of transcripts of proceedings under Criminal Procedure (Scotland) Act 1975 s.275. Article 2 (1) of this Order amends Art.4 of the 1993 order so that it will restrict the availability of transcripts of proceedings which are conducted in the absence of people from the courtroom by virtue of certain provisions of the 1975 Act; or which may not be published because of an order under Contempt of Court Act 1981 s.4 (2). Article 2 (2) of this Order amends Art.5 of the 1993 Order so that it will enable transcripts to be made available in certain circumstances, for proceedings before the European Court of Justice.

6807. Trial–failure to read the jury declaration at judicial examination

[Criminal Procedure (Scotland) Act 1975 (c.21) s.20B.]

R appealed against conviction for disorderly conduct and breach of peace on the grounds that there had been a miscarriage of justice in that a declaration which he made when the matter first called in court was not read to the jury. In an earlier appeal, R unsuccessfully submitted that the indictment was incompetent because the declaration had not been recorded and certified as required under the Criminal Procedure (Scotland) Act 1975 s.20B. On the further appeal R argued that the declaration had explained that he participated in the incident in order to defend his father's house and that he sustained injuries as a result, and he was prejudiced in not being afforded the opportunity of reading the declaration to the jury. The court remitted the case to the sheriff principal to investigate. The sheriff principal concluded that R's declaration had not related to the charge of which he was convicted but to other charges. In addition, R's counsel, for apparently good reasons, had decided that the declaration should not be read to the jury. At the reconvened hearing, R argued that the sheriff principal's finding should not be accepted as his recollection, which was supported by his solicitor, was that he had referred to his injuries in the declaration and this was at variance with the sheriff principal's conclusion. Since s.20B had not been complied with, R was prejudiced at his trial because the declaration was not available to him and read to the jury, and this constituted a miscarriage of justice.

Held, refusing the appeal, that R's allegations were insufficient to disturb the validity of the sheriff principal's conclusion. The sheriff's notes of the declaration stated that the reference to injuries was in relation to a different charge from that on which R was ultimately convicted. R's present assertion of his recollection did not appear to have been expressed until after his conviction. R's submission that he was prejudiced because s.20B had not been complied with was therefore ill founded. In addition, the argument that he was prejudiced by the non-compliance to the extent that it would be oppressive to allow a trial to proceed was in substance the same argument referred to but not taken in the competency proceedings. Any argument that R was prejudiced by non-compliance was available to him before the trial; and the only remedy for the effects of the admitted non-compliance lay in a plea in bar of trial or in raising the matter during the course of the trial, and R was not entitled to complain after being convicted that he was prejudiced at the trial on the ground which was available but not advance on his behalf before or during the trial.

Observed, that R could not have founded on the facts contained in the alleged statement since it was wholly exculpatory and could not have been founded on by the Crown, *Morrison v. HM Advocate* 1991 S.L.T. 57, [1991] C.L.Y. 4552.

ROBERTSON (NEIL) v. HM ADVOCATE 1996 S.C.C.R. 243, Lord Morison.

6808. Trial–judge's charge–misdirection–comments on evidence led

Held, that on S's appeal against conviction of the murder of D, where H, an essential Crown witness, gave evidence in chief that S was the maker of a statement heard at the time of the murder, but under cross-examination said that she could not be sure of the statement or of its maker, and counsel in his summing up had mentioned only the latter part of H's evidence, S arguing that the judge had been unbalanced in his direction to the jury in reminding them of the evidence in chief but failing to remind them of the charge under cross-examination, that the appeal would be refused since the judge had stated that he did not wish to rehearse all the evidence and would merely draw attention to counsel's comments, and where counsel had made a submission to the effect that there was no evidence on a particular point and the judge's understanding was that there was, it was appropriate for him to remind the jury of the contradictory evidence and invite them to test it against their own recollection.

Observed, that (1) the trial judge was in the best position to understand the real issues of fact and the extent to which clarification was needed and (2) where the judge was summarising a witness's evidence, it was not sufficient for him merely to refer to evidence in chief if the evidence in cross-examination was different.

SHEPHERD v. HM ADVOCATE 1996 S.C.C.R. 679, Judge not specified.

6809. Trial–judge's charge–misdirection–concert in criminal law

H appealed against conviction of assault and robbery in concert with X on the grounds of misdirection. H had lodged a special defence of alibi. None of the witnesses were able to identify the person who committed the robbery, although someone driving H's vehicle allegedly drove the perpetrator from the locus, and shortly after the incident the police found the car's engine warm and H in possession of bags containing £250 in coins. The judge directed the jury that since it was indisputable that the man who entered the shop and the driver of the car were acting in concert, it did not matter what part, if any, H played in the robbery if the jury were satisfied that H was one of the two men involved. On appeal, H argued that the judge failed to direct the jury, that (1) in order to find him guilty they had to be satisfied that the two persons allegedly involved in the robbery were acting in concert and (2) they could alternatively convict H of reset of the money found in his possession. Since there was no evidence as to whether H had gone into the shop or remained in the car, the judge had failed to direct the jury on an essential element of the Crown's case which was that they had to be satisfied that the two persons had been acting in concert. By treating the point that both persons were involved in the robbery as indisputable, the trial judge failed to identify the proper starting point for the issues of fact which the jury had to determine.

Held, verdict set aside and authority granted to bring a new prosecution (Lord Sutherland *dissenting*), that (1) *per* the Lord Justice-General (Hope) and Lord Macfadyen: The issues of fact which the jury had to decide were not confined to the question of whether H was involved in the incident. Since no one was able to identify either of the men involved in the offence, in order to establish as a matter of fact that the two men involved were acting in concert the Crown had to prove beyond a reasonable doubt that both men were engaged on a common criminal purpose, that what occurred in the shop was done in furtherance of that purpose and that it did not go beyond the reasonable expectation of the person who remained in the car. It was for the jury to draw the inferences under proper directions from the trial judge. The effect of the judge's direction was to confine the jury's attention to the question of whether H was one of the two persons who took part in the incident, and remove from them issues of fact relating to the application of the principle of concert; (2) an instruction on reset was unnecessary since the issue was never raised by the Crown or the defence and since the case against H did not depend solely on his possession of the comparatively small sum of money which was considered part of the proceeds of the robbery *Allan v. HM Advocate* 1995 S.C.C.R. 234, [1995] C.L.Y. 5718 followed; *Steele v. HM Advocate* 1992 J.C. 1, [1992] C.L.Y. 5502 distinguished. *Per* Lord Sutherland *dissenting*: In the circumstances, the contention that the driver of the car could in some way have been an innocent bystander was virtually untenable on any common sense point of view and was not part of the defence case. It was not fatal that the judge had failed to remind the jury that although the evidence appeared fairly clear, the matter of whether the Crown had proved that H was one of the two people who took part in the robbery was still a matter for them. The fact that there was a technical misdirection should not, standing the evidence, have led in any way to a miscarriage of justice since in convicting H, the jury must have disbelieved H's defence of alibi.

HOBBINS v. HM ADVOCATE 1996 S.C.C.R. 637, Lord Hope, L.J.G., HCJ.

6810. Trial–judge's charge–misdirection–exculpatory statement containing qualified admission

Held, that on G's appeal against conviction of attempted rape and indecent assault by anal penetration of M, aged 12, on the grounds that (1) the judge had failed to give adequate direction on exculpatory elements of a mixed statement made by G at a police interview, G claiming he believed M had consented, and the judge stating only that evidence of the interview was substantive evidence whether favourable or unfavourable to G; (2) no direction had been given to consider whether this belief was reasonable and (3) corroboration on charge 2 could not be taken from his admission at interview that sexual activity took place, where the issue of anal penetration was never put to him, or from M's distress five days later on having her anus examined, that the appeal would be allowed in respect of charge 2 only since (1) the judge's directions on the mixed statement were clear and placed no restriction on its use; (2) the issue of the honesty of G's belief was clearly before the court and there was no need to raise the question of reasonable grounds in any event to have done so would not have been favourable to G and (3) M's distress was too remote to corroborate her account, and could have been attributable to the examination itself. Opinion reserved, on whether G's admission of sexual activity corroborated him as perpetrator of charge 2. *Held* further, that where G was 19, had a girlfriend and only one previous conviction for theft, that three years' detention for the attempted rape would be substituted for a cumulo sentence of five years.

GEDDES v. HM ADVOCATE 1996 S.C.C.R. 687, Judge not specified.

6811. Trial–judge's charge–misdirection–identification

Held, on W's appeal against conviction of assault to severe injury against C, who was attacked in a lane outside a club at about 2.15 am in February, where K and M (who admitted that they were under the influence of alcohol at the time) were the only witnesses to identify W as one of C's assailants, that the trial judge erred in failing to direct the jury that they should approach the identification evidence with care and to point out the strengths and weaknesses of K and M's evidence, *McAvoy v. HM Advocate* 1991 J.C. 16, [1991] C.L.Y. 4716 and Renton and Brown, *Criminal Procedure* (5th ed.), para.10-54, particularly since M and K identified W from a distance of over 60 yards, when it must have been dark and after consuming a large quantity of alcohol and where M did not know W prior to the evening in question; and since identification was crucial, the trial judge should have suggested that the jury consider when the person identified by M and K was clearly visible to them and for how long he was so visible in order to reduce the risk of mistaken identification, Note by Lord Justice-General Emslie, February 18, 1977 and *McAvoy v. HM Advocate* applied; and verdict set aside and authority to bring a new prosecution under the Criminal Procedure (Scotland) Act 1995 s.119 granted.

WEBB v. HM ADVOCATE 1996 S.C.C.R. 530, Judge not specified.

6812. Trial–judge's charge–misdirection–indecent assault–consent

An accused person was tried on indictment for abduction and indecent assault. The complainer gave evidence that she had been sexually assaulted by the accused who was a taxi driver and had collected her as a fare. In cross-examination she accepted that she had shown no signs of resistance and that an outsider would have seen no signs of resistance. The accused accepted that sexual intimacy had taken place on two occasions but said that there was nothing in the complainer's demeanour to make him think that she was not consenting. The sheriff directed the jury that if they honestly believed that the complainer had consented, or were in doubt on that matter, they had to acquit the accused, but she did not tell them that in assessing the genuineness of the accused's belief, they should consider whether he had reasonable grounds for it. The accused was convicted of indecent assault, but not abduction and appealed on the ground of misdirection.

Held, that while in many cases the trial judge might consider it desirable to remind the jury that when assessing the genuineness of the accused's belief they might wish to consider whether there were reasonable grounds for that belief, it was not the law that in every case such a direction should be given; and appeal refused. Dicta of Lord Justice General Hope in *Jamieson v. HM Advocate (No.1)* 1994 S.L.T. 537 at p.541C-E, [1994] C.L.Y. 5664 applied. *Observed*, that in any event, the sheriff's failure to give the direction could only be favourable to the accused since the direction would have meant that there was a further test which had to be satisfied before they could decide whether the accused's belief was genuine.

MARR v. HM ADVOCATE 1996 S.L.T. 1035, Judge not specified, HCJ.

6813. Trial–judge's charge–misdirection–Moorov doctrine

[Criminal Procedure (Scotland) Act 1975 (c,21) s.255.]

Held, on O's appeal against conviction of armed robbery at a bank at Uddingston and a rail depot in Polmadie 17 days later, that the trial judge had erred in directing the jury on his own initiative that they could apply the rule in *Moorov v. HM Advocate* 1930 S.L.T. 596, where the Crown had not relied on the rule and the only material similarities between the crimes were that they both concerned instances of armed robbery in the Glasgow area in which a sawn-off shotgun had been presented by masked men and menaces had been made, and there was no underlying unity of criminal intent and purpose between the two crimes or anything in the evidence to justify the conclusion that the two robberies were instances of a course of criminal conduct pursued by O. It was not enough merely to show that there had been two or more separate similar offences, *Ogg v. HM Advocate* 1938 S.L.T. 513. Although there was sufficient evidence to justify O's conviction in respect of the armed robbery at the bank without having to resort to the rule in *Moorov*, the misdirection produced a miscarriage of justice since it was impossible to determine whether the jury had relied on the rule in finding O guilty; and verdict set aside and authority to bring a new prosecution in terms of s.255 of the Criminal Procedure (Scotland) Act 1975 granted.

O'NEILL v. HM ADVOCATE 1995 S.C.C.R. 816, Judge not specified.

6814. Trial–judge's charge–misdirection–possession of controlled drug

Held, on S's appeal against possession of temazepam (found in a plastic bag in S's wardrobe) with intent to supply, on the ground that it was a misdirection for the judge to tell the jury that to be in possession one would not require to know the precise character of the bag or its contents, but would need to know that the packet and its contents were in the bag, that the appeal would be refused since a further direction, which was a development of the first in light of the evidence and not contradictory of it, that the Crown had to prove that S knew that the bag and its contents were in his physical control and that he knew the general character of the contents, was sound and in accordance with *McKenzie v. Skeen* 1983 S.L.T. 121, [1983] C.L.Y. 4132 and had made it clear how those principles fell to be applied.

SIM v. HM ADVOCATE 1996 S.C.C.R. 77, Judge not specified.

6815. Trial–judge's charge–misdirection–rape

An accused person was charged on indictment with rape. The complainer's account of the incident was that she did not consent and was crying and battling to keep the accused off her but the accused stated that the complainer consented and that she neither protested nor offered resistance. The accused's wife, who was in an adjacent room throughout, said that she heard no noise of any disturbance. The accused's counsel, in his speech to the jury, did not suggest that the accused might have honestly but mistakenly believed that the complainer was consenting to sexual intercourse, nor was that suggestion put in cross-examination of the complainer. The trial judge, considering that the issue was the straightforward one of whether intercourse took place against the complainer's will or with her consent, did not direct the jury that the accused could not be convicted of rape if he mistakenly believed, however unreasonably, that the complainer was a consenting party. The accused was convicted and appealed on the ground of misdirection.

Held, that (1) a direction about honest belief in rape cases should be given only when that issue had been raised in the evidence; (2) as the accused did not suggest that he had made a mistake about the complainer's attitude, the trial judge was wholly justified in refraining from giving the direction; and appealed refused, *Meek v. H.M. Advocate* 1983 S.L.T. 280, [1983] C.L.Y. 4203 applied.

DORIS v. HM ADVOCATE 1996 S.L.T. 995, Judge not specified, HCJ.

6816. Trial–judge's charge–misdirection–rape–whether miscarriage of justice–duty of trial judge to give opinion on grounds of appeal–retrials

[Criminal Procedure (Scotland) Act 1975 (c.21) s.236A(1).]

Section 236A(1) of the Criminal Procedure (Scotland) Act 1975 provides that as soon as is reasonably practicable after his receipt of the note of appeal, the trial judge shall furnish the Clerk of Justiciary with a report in writing giving his opinion on the case generally and on the grounds contained in the note of appeal. An accused person was tried for, *inter alia*, rape. He maintained that he had had sexual intercourse with the complainer with her consent. The trial judge directed the jury that the Crown had to establish that the accused had no reasonable grounds for believing that the woman consented to his having sexual intercourse with her. The accused was convicted and appealed on the ground of misdirection and also contended that it would not be appropriate to authorise a retrial if the conviction were set aside, because the accused was only 20 years of age and the alleged crime had occurred nearly two years ago. In his report to the appeal court the trial judge stated that he never commented on grounds of appeal unless questions of fact were raised.

Held, that (1) there had been a misdirection (which the Crown conceded), resulting in a miscarriage of justice because the jury might have considered that the accused had no reasonable grounds for believing that the complainer consented without considering whether in fact he genuinely or honestly believed that she consented; but (2) as no fault could be laid at the door of the Crown and the reasons advanced for not authorising a retrial were unconvincing, it was appropriate to grant authority for a new prosecution; and conviction quashed and retrial authorised *Jamieson v. HM Advocate (No.1)* 1994 S.L.T. 537, [1994] C.L.Y. 5664 applied.

Observed, that whether or not it was necessary to give the jury a direction as to the alleged belief of the accused as to the complainer's consent depended upon the circumstances as there were cases where no such direction was called for, *Meek v. HM Advocate*, 1983 S.L.T. 280, [1983] C.L.Y. 4203, considered.

Observed, further, that standing the duty in s.236A(1) of the 1975 Act (s.113 of the Criminal Procedure (Scotland) Act 1995) imposed on trial judges, if it was the trial judge's practice not to comment on grounds of appeal unless questions of fact were raised, that was a practice which he should discontinue.

McPHELIM v. HM ADVOCATE 1996 S.L.T. 992, Judge not specified, HCJ.

6817. Trial–judge's charge–misdirection–withdrawal of defence of self-defence

Held, on W's appeal against conviction of assaulting A to severe injury by punching in the face, breaking his jaw, that the trial judge erred in withdrawing from the jury a special defence of self-defence on the basis that W had admitted in cross-examination having gone too far in attempting to protect A's mother from what he believed to be an imminent assault by A, since a special defence had to be left with the jury if there was some evidence, however slight, on which the jury might properly consider it to have been made out *Crawford v. HM Advocate* 1950 S.L.T. 279, [1950] C.L.Y. 4668, and given that it was difficult to judge precisely how strong the blow needed to be in the circumstances and the level of force with which a blow might strike; it would not be right to hold against W the frank answers he gave having observed the results of the blow when the jury would have been directed not to weigh the matter in too fine a balance. The Crown did not seek authority for a fresh prosecution.

WHYTE v. HM ADVOCATE 1996 S.C.C.R. 575, Lord Hope L.J.G., HCJ.

6818. Trial–judge's charge–murder–provocation

Direction, by the judge in a murder trial where the accused pleaded that she had acted under provocation in that she had killed a man in response to information that he had been sharing her lesbian partner's bed, that the circumstances were capable of constituting provocation.

HM ADVOCATE v. McKEAN 1996 S.C.C.R. 402, Judge not specified.

6819. Trial–judge's charge–murder–whether trial judge bound to direct jury on culpable homicide verdict

An accused person was tried for murder along with two other persons who were the deceased's wife and daughter. The Crown's case was that all three persons had plotted to kill the deceased because for many years he had abused members of his family both physically and verbally, and he had sexually abused another daughter (who was the accused's fiancee) over a seven month period. The accused pled self defence and explained that at no point had he intended to kill the deceased, who had brandished a hammer at him when he had confronted the deceased at his home with abusing his fiancee. The trial judge deliberately did not tell the jury that a verdict of culpable homicide was open to them but suggested that they should first decide whether the accused had intended to kill the deceased and then, but only then, go on to consider the case against the two co-accused. The co-accused were acquitted but the accused was convicted of murder. He appealed contending that the trial judge should have directed the jury on culpable homicide as an alternative verdict because there was evidence to substantiate a finding of provocation.

Held, that had the trial judge mentioned culpable homicide he would have been introducing a point which had not been raised by either side, and since it could have been prejudicial to the accused, the trial judge was not bound to give a direction on culpable homicide; and appeal refused, *Templeton v. HM Advocate* 1961 S.L.T. 328, [1961] C.L.Y. 11193 applied.

WHITESIDE v. HM ADVOCATE 1996 S.L.T. 299, Judge not specified, HCJ.

6820. Trial–judge's charge–sheriff giving additional directions to jury in shorthand writer's absence

[Criminal Procedure (Scotland) Act 1975 (c. 21) s.274(1).]

Section 274(1) of the Criminal Procedure (Scotland) Act 1975 provides that the proceedings at the trial of any person who, if convicted, is entitled to appeal under solemn procedure, shall be recorded by means of shorthand notes or by mechanical means. An accused person was tried on indictment for, inter alia, assault to severe injury. In charging the jury the sheriff gave no directions as to how they should approach the question of whether the aggravation had been proved, but after the jury had retired he reconvened the court and, in the absence of the shorthand writer, gave directions on that matter. The accused was convicted of assault to severe injury and appealed.

Held, (the Crown not opposing the appeal), that it was quite wrong for the sheriff to give directions in the shorthand writer's absence and accordingly there was a clear breach of s.274(1); and appeal allowed and amended verdict of assault substituted, *McColl v. HM Advocate* 1989 S.L.T. 691, [1989] C.L.Y. 4078/9 considered.

McLAUGHLAN v. HM ADVOCATE 1996 S.L.T. 304, Judge not specified, HCJ.

6821. Trial–judge's charge–whether necessary to define self defence

Three accused persons were tried along with others on an indictment for assault to severe injury. They pleaded self defence. The Crown witnesses supported the Crown contention that the accused had been the aggressors and the defence evidence directly contradicted that view. The sheriff did not explain to the jury the legal requirements of self defence, but told them that each accused had satisfied the requirements of the defence and that if they believed the accused or if a reasonable doubt were raised by their evidence, they should acquit the accused. The accused were convicted and appealed on the ground that the sheriff ought to have defined what constituted self defence.

Held, refusing the appeals, that (1) it was a matter of circumstances as to whether a jury required to be directed on the elements which went to make up the defence of self defence and (2) where there were simply two competing accounts of the incident and there were no issues of degree or questions of mixed fact and law, such as whether excessive force had been used, there was no misdirection in not defining the defence.

REID v. HM ADVOCATE 1996 S.L.T. 469, Judge not specified, HCJ.

6822. Trial–productions–recovery of productions after trial–appeal pending by co-accused

[Criminal Procedure (Scotland) Act 1975 (c.21) s.270(2).]

Held, on S's petition to the *nobile officium* seeking an order for the release and return of label productions containing £14,005 which was seized from his dwellinghouse in the course of police investigations regarding the supply of cannabis, where S was acquitted and his co-accused (C), who was convicted under the Misuse of Drugs Act 1971 s.4(3)(b), had appealed against his conviction, that S's petition was incompetent as, although the trial judge or his clerk had taken the view that s.270 did not apply as C had appealed, the trial judge was empowered in terms of the proviso to s.270(2) to grant an order authorising the productions to be released notwithstanding that C had appealed, since the money did not form any part of the case against C and C had confirmed that he had no interest in the money; and petition dismissed as incompetent on the understanding that S would renew his application for an order under s.270(2).

STROCK, PETITIONER 1996 S.C.C.R. 432, Judge not specified.

6823. Trial–seclusion of jury–arrangements for accommodation

[Criminal Procedure (Scotland) Act 1975 (c.21) s.153, s.255.]

S appealed against conviction for assault with intent to rape of the grounds that (1) the trial judge erred in directing the jury that they were entitled to consider the complainer's opinion regarding S's intention, and (2) in asking the foreman at 5.40 pm, after the jury had retired for three hours, about the progress of their deliberations and whether arrangements for overnight accommodation should be made, the trial judge misdirected the jury by failing to explain that they were not being put under any pressure and that the interests of justice required that they be given as much time as they needed to reach their verdict in terms of the Criminal Procedure (Scotland) Act 1975 s.153(3A), *Mackenzie v. HM Advocate* 1986 S.L.T. 389, [1989] C.L.Y. 3837, 3882, *Love v. HM Advocate* 1995 S.C.C.R. 501, [1995] C.L.Y. 5739.

Held, setting aside the verdict and granting the Crown authority to bring a new prosecution in accordance with s.255 of the 1975 Act. The trial judge's failure to explain to the jury that they were not being put under any pressure and that, in the interests of justice, they would be given as much time as they needed to reach their verdict, amounted to a miscarriage of justice which would not have occurred if the trial judge had followed the guidance laid down in *Mackenzie v. HM Advocate*. The fact that the jury returned their verdict one minute after the trial judge inquired about their progress suggested that his inquiry was construed by some of the jury as putting them under pressure and that they succumbed to such pressure. Opinion reserved, on S's first ground of appeal.

SINCLAIR v. HM ADVOCATE 1996 S.C.C.R. 221, Judge not specified.

6824. Trial–seclusion of jury–failure of sheriff to instruct jury that they could return verdict at any time and should feel under no pressure of time–whether misdirection

An accused person along with three co-accused was tried on an indictment libelling 10 charges. The trial lasted 23 days. The jury retired at 2.45 pm and returned to court at 6.08 pm when the sheriff reconvened the court to inquire whether their deliberations were nearly concluded. The sheriff was told that another hour would be necessary for the jury to reach their verdicts and the sheriff allowed them to continue their deliberations. The jury were not told about any arrangements which might have to be made if they took longer than one hour and nothing was said to indicate that they should not feel under pressure to reach their verdict. The jury returned at 6.34 pm when the accused was found guilty. The accused appealed, contending that the jury should have been directed that they could return their verdict at any time and that they were under no pressure of time to reach their verdict.

Held, that the sheriff had not reached the point of raising with the jury whether arrangements should be made for overnight accommodation and as nothing that the sheriff said could have been reasonably construed by the jury as indicating that they were under pressure of time, there was no miscarriage of justice; and appeal refused. [See also Robertson (Neil) v. HM Advocate 1996 S.C.C.R. 243, [1996] C.L.Y. 000].

ROBERTSON (DONALD STEWART) v. HM ADVOCATE 1996 S.L.T. 1119, Lord Hope, L.J.G., HCJ.

6825. Witnesses–precognition on oath

[Criminal Justice (Scotland) Act 1980 (c.62) s.9.]

The Crown sought advocation of a sheriff's decision to order a detective (G) to be precognosced on oath as sought by C, charged with murder. It was averred that G was not a witness at the trial but C believed that one D would give evidence about a conversation between C and D, and that D had advised G of the details. G had refused to answer questions from C's solicitors relevant to this. C's purpose was to obtain information which would enable the defence to cross-examine D if he were called, about other transactions between D and G with a view to attacking D's credibility. The Crown objected to the precognition covering dealings between D and G which were unrelated to the present case.

Held, bill refused subject to undertakings by C, that while it was doubtful whether C's application was appropriate for the purpose described, the decision would be allowed to stand since it was a murder trial and the circumstances were somewhat special. However C undertook that he would not seek to find out the details of any advantages D had received in respect of any earlier transactions, or to whom they related, and that the questioning would be directed to discovering whether D had sought or obtained any advantage in return for providing information in relation to these earlier transactions.

HM ADVOCATE v. CAMPBELL 1996 S.C.C.R. 419, Judge not specified.

6826. Articles

A bouncer's right to search *(Peter W. Ferguson)*: J.L.S.S. 1996, 41 (6), 227. (Nightclub steward's right to search and detain persons suspected of carrying drugs or weapons).

An examination of the sifting system: Part 1 *(Margaret E. Scott.)*: Crim. L.B. 1996, 20 (Apr), 2-3. (Practical guide to new system for criminal appeals).

An examination of the sifting system: Part 2 *(Margaret E. Scott.)*: Crim. L.B. 1996, 21 (Jun), 2-4. (Matters of concern regarding test for allowing criminal appeals to proceed and need for properly drafted grounds of appeal).

Cross borders: cross purposes *(Alistair J. Bonnington)*: N.L.J. 1996, 146(6759), 1312. (Comparison of English and Scottish approaches to prejudicial pretrial publicity).

Detention or arrest revisited *(James Watson)*: S.L.G. 1996, 64(1), 6-9. (Police powers in regard to questioning suspect between arrest and charge in light of decision that arrest does not debar fair questioning).

Diversion of neighbourhood disputes to community mediation *(Robert E. Mackay* and *Susan R. Moody)*: Howard Journal 1996, 35(4), 299-313. (Scottish prosecutors' approaches to neighbourhood disputes, use and effectiveness of courts, and potential for alternative methods of dispute resolution).

Guidelines on bail : S.L.T. 1996, 6, 51-52. (Lord Advocate's revised guidelines on bail for those who reoffend while on bail and reasons for procurator fiscal marking cases "no proceeding").

Incompetent representation *(F.A. Mulholland)*: Crim. L.B. 1996, 20(Apr), 3-4. (Consideration of issues for appellant if he wishes to appeal on grounds of miscarriage of justice arising from solicitor's or counsel's handling of case).

Miscarriages of justice and legal practice : J.L.S.S. 1996, 41(1), 5-8. (Scottish principles on right to fair trial and whether defence's conduct of case resulted in miscarriage of justice).

Out for blood: the Crown's right to seek samples for forensic analysis *(Ian H. Cruickshank)*: J.L.S.S. 1996, 41 (5), 179-181. (Police powers to obtain samples of blood or other material from accused and test to be applied in granting warrant to Crown).

Suspension of arrest warrants *(Peter W. Ferguson)*: J.L.S.S. 1996, 41 (9), 358-360. (Remedies available to accused where warrant for arrest not proceeded with and subsequent reindictment for trial is outside 12 month time limit).

Suspension of committal warrants *(Peter W. Ferguson)*: S.L.T. 1996, 21, 185-187. (Whether decision allowing bill of suspension seeking to suspend committal warrant on grounds of irrelevancy breaches rule that suspension only competent after conclusion of trial).

The case of Anderson v HM Advocate *(R.T. McCormack)*: SCOLAG 1996, 230, 5-7. (Personal view of solicitor advocate involved in case concerning failure of lawyer to present client's defence adequately on background to case and its implications).

6827. Books

Gordon, Sheriff G.–Renton & Brown: Criminal Procedure. Ringbinder. ISBN 0-414-01151-1. W.Green & Son.

Shiels, Robert–Renton and Brown's Criminal Procedure Legislation. Looseleaf: £175.00. ISBN 0-414-01152-X. W.Green & Son.

CRIMINAL SENTENCING

6828. Assault–injury–first offender

Held, that 60 days' detention was not excessive where Y, a 16 year old first offender now employed as an apprentice butcher, was in one of two groups having an altercation, several of Y's group suddenly attacking one of the other group, punching and kicking him repeatedly to substantial bruising and a fractured nose, this being an offence of such gravity that the sheriff was entitled despite Y's circumstances to impose a deterrent sentence.

YOUNG v. HAMILTON 1996 S.C.C.R. 66, Judge not specified.

6829. Assault–injury–player in football match

Held, where F, a professional footballer from a good family background and who did a considerable amount of community work in his own time, whose record, which occurred within a short time frame, included two analogous offences and who was on probation at the time, received three months' imprisonment for assaulting M, an opposing player, in the course of a Premier Division match by lunging at him, seizing hold of his clothing and head butting him causing a minor mouth injury, that sentence was not excessive, although the sheriff had exaggerated in describing F's record as appalling and there had been a recommendation for community service in the pre-sentence report, since F's actions had gone beyond what was regarded as normal physical contact, no leniency was to be expected simply because the offence occurred during a football match and F was a public figure playing in a high profile match of the sort which set standards of conduct throughout the country.

FERGUSON v. NORMAND 1995 S.C.C.R. 770, Judge not specified.

6830. Assault–robbery–juvenile offender with alcohol dependency–deferred sentence unduly lenient

[Criminal Procedure (Scotland) Act 1995 (c.46) s.108.]

An accused person pled guilty to assault and robbery and assault to severe injury, permanent impairment and permanent disfigurement. The complainer in the assault charge was knocked to the ground and kicked and repeatedly struck with knives by the accused and his co-accused, causing wounds to his head, nose, wrist and fingers. He sustained a skull indentation and some metal was imbedded in his skull. After discharge the complainer required to be re-admitted to hospital because of profuse bleeding from his nose. He also had permanent scarring and required to give up his employment. Psychiatric reports stated that the accused, who was 15 and a first offender at the time of the offences, had an early form of alcohol dependency and suffered from clinical depression which required and would benefit from treatment available at a specialised clinic in Glasgow. The trial judge, mistakenly considering that such treatment would not be available in a young offenders institution, deferred sentence for six months for the accused to attend the clinic and to be of good behaviour. The Crown appealed, contending that the order deferring sentence was inappropriate having regard to the circumstances of both offences and the gravity of the assault charge, and that the trial judge had placed undue weight on the accused's background and personal circumstances.

Held, that (1) the fact that it was suggested that the accused would require and benefit from psychiatric treatment was not a ground for refraining from imposing a custodial sentence if the circumstances indicated that such a sentence was appropriate; (2) having regard to the nature of the assault charge, the repeated use of knives, the severity of the injuries and their consequences, an immediate custodial sentence was the only appropriate disposal; and appeal allowed and sentence of three years' detention substituted.

Observed, that when determining sentence the trial judge ought always to proceed on the basis that if psychiatric or medical treatment was required by the accused, he would receive it while in custody. Opinion, that the sentence of five years' detention on the co-accused, who was more than two years older, had a number of previous convictions and had been on deferred sentence and probation at the time of the offences, was very much at the lower end of the appropriate range.

HM ADVOCATE v. McCOLL 1996 S.L.T. 803, Judge not specified, HCJ.

6831. Assault–severe injury–first offender

Held, where M, a first offender aged 19 at the time, received one year's detention for making a quite unprovoked attack with a glass tumbler causing permanent facial disfigurement, that the sentence was excessive notwithstanding the serious nature of the attack, since M claimed that at the time his mother had just died, he did not normally drink but had been drinking on this occasion, his time spent in custody had been a salutary experience, he was a fourth year engineering apprentice earning a good wage, his employers were willing to take him back and he and his sister now cared for their two young brothers; and 240 hours' community service and a compensation order for £750 substituted.

McNAMEE v. HM ADVOCATE 1996 S.C.C.R. 423, Judge not specified.

6832. Assault–severe injury–short concurrent custodial sentences unduly lenient

[Criminal Procedure (Scotland) Act 1975 (c. 21) s.228A.]

The Crown appealed against sentences passed on M as unduly lenient, and as respects breach of bail incompetent. M had been sentenced to three months' imprisonment on each of malicious damage, two charges of breach of the peace, and assaulting his former cohabitee (C) to severe injury by repeated punching and kicking, causing a broken nose and damaged teeth; and to six months for each of a simple assault and two charges of breach of bail. All these sentences, imposed in July 1994, were made concurrent and to run from that date, though M was then serving another sentence from which he was due to be released in December.

Held, that the sentences were unduly lenient but that it would be inappropriate now to impose other sentences. The three month sentence on the assault charge was plainly inadequate where M had a previous three month sentence for assault in 1991 and where he had received six months for the simple assault. The sheriff erred in stating that C was to a large extent the author of her own misfortune having been doing her utmost to entice M away from his current partner. It would have been appropriate to impose concurrent sentences of six months on each assault charge, consecutive to the other three month sentences. The bail sentences were incompetent, and where M had many similar convictions, three months concurrent on each charge, consecutive to the other sentences, would have been appropriate. The sheriff further erred in considering that because M was due to be released in December 1994, it would be appropriate to let him and his family start afresh in 1995, and his order effectively meant that M was receiving no sentence in respect of these offences. However, in determining whether to substitute now the consecutive sentences which would have been appropriate, it was relevant to consider that M had remained in custody having been sentenced on other matters and was due to be released in late August 1995, and that the instant offences all took place in 1993. Although the latest sentences might also have been made consecutive to what should have been imposed, it could be said with some hesitation that it would not be in the interests of justice that M should begin from August to serve a further 12 months for these offences.

HM ADVOCATE v. McVEY 1995 S.C.C.R. 706, Judge not specified.

6833. Assault–severe injury–unduly lenient sentence

[Criminal Procedure (Scotland) Act 1975 (c. 21) s.228A.]

Held, that four years' imprisonment for assaulting C to severe injury and danger of life was unduly lenient in terms of the test in *HM Advocate v. Bell* 1995 S.L.T. 350, [1995] C.L.Y. 5797, where O and F had previous convictions for violent crimes and where the assault was recorded on a security video film which showed that the attack had been a brutal and merciless assault involving kicking and stamping on C's head and body, and while C's injuries were much less severe than would have been expected from the impression given by the film and it was important not to overreact to the film, it was important also to react carefully and responsibly to what was depicted; that it was not necessary for an assault to the danger of life to show that life was in fact at risk, and the sentencing judge took too narrow a view of the nature of the aggravation in concluding that the only danger to C's life was a short lived obstruction to his airway in hospital; and seven years' imprisonment substituted.

HM ADVOCATE v. O'DONNELL 1995 S.C.C.R. 745, Judge not specified.

6834. Assault on police–obstruction

Held, where G received 40 hours' community service for obstructing the police, having been stopped with a defective tyre, and two charges of failure to appear in court, the sentence was excessive since it was inappropriate for the sheriff (1) to discount the imposition of fines on the basis that G, who had a disposable income of £103 per week, would have no difficulty in paying, and (2) to impose community service after discounting imprisonment as being excessive as the former could only be imposed as a direct alternative to custody; and fines of £400 on charge one and £200 on each of the other charges all at £20 per week substituted.

GIUSTI v. WALKINGSHAW 1996 S.C.C.R. 61, Judge not specified.

6835. Automatism–matters not before sentencing court–assault–probation unduly lenient

[Criminal Procedure (Scotland) Act 1975 (c.21) s.228A.]

The Crown appealed against B's sentence of two years' probation (with conditions of 200 hours' unpaid community work and payment of compensation of £7,500) following his conviction for assault on the ground that it was unduly lenient in terms of the Criminal Procedure (Scotland) Act 1975 s.228A. B was taken into custody after punching a man outside a pub. While en route to the police station, B, unprovoked and without warning, lunged at P, one of the arresting officers, and bit and removed a large part of his ear. At trial, B intended to present a defence of non-insane automatism on the ground that his brother in law, L, had put drugs into his beer without his knowledge. L refused to give evidence, however, and B pled guilty to the charges since he was unable to satisfy the requirements for the defence, *Ross v. HM Advocate* 1991 S.L.T. 563, [1991] C.L.Y. 4754. At sentencing, B advised the court, without objection, of the circumstances of his reduced responsibility. The trial judge reported that, in the absence of B's explanation he would have imposed a substantial period of imprisonment. On appeal, the Crown argued that B's submission to the trial judge was inconsistent with his plea of guilty. The defence of non-insane automatism was only available if the evidence showed that it was not self-induced, *Sorley v. HM Advocate* 1992 S.L.T. 396, [1992] C.L.Y. 5531. There was no proper basis for concluding that B's responsibility for his actions was reduced.

Held, refusing the appeal, that although there was merit in the Crown's argument, they should have objected before the trial court to the points being made for B, and as the challenge was not made at the proper time, it was too late for the point to be taken on appeal.

HM ADVOCATE v. BENNETT 1996 S.C.C.R. 331, Judge not specified.

6836. Backdating–competency–order to serve balance of previous sentence

[Criminal Procedure (Scotland) Act 1975 (c. 21), s.431; Prisoners and Criminal Proceedings (Scotland) Act 1993 (c. 9) s.16(2).]

Held, where E received six months' detention on charges of shoplifting and assault to be served after 46 days of an unexpired sentence, that this was excessive since the sheriff, who believed that it was impossible to backdate return sentences (s.16(2)(a)(i) of the 1993 Act) misdirected himself as to the effect of s.431(1) of the 1975 Act, which referred rather to taking into account time spent in custody, and E's period in custody could be taken into account when determining the length of the sentence imposed; and five months substituted.

ENGLISH v. McGLENNAN 1995 S.C.C.R. 767, Judge not specified.

6837. Bail–breach of order–aggravation of other offence

[Criminal Procedure (Scotland) Act 1995 (c.46) s.27(3) and (5).]

Held, that where C, whose record included two bail offences, received consecutive sentences of three months' imprisonment for a breach of the peace and three months for vandalism, one month of each sentence to reflect that the offences were committed while C was on bail, that C's appeal against the consecutive nature of the bail sentences would be refused since, under the new procedure relating to bail offences, s.27(3)(a) of the Criminal Procedure (Scotland) Act 1995, the fact that the offence was committed while on bail was seen as an aggravation of that offence and not as a separate offence as under the old procedure, and as such each offence along with its aggravation would be considered on its own. It followed therefore that if the substantive sentences were made consecutive to each other then the same would apply to the aggravations.

CONNAL v. CROWE 1996 S.C.C.R. 716, Judge not specified.

6838. Community service

COMMUNITY SERVICE BY OFFENDERS (HOURS OF WORK) (SCOTLAND) ORDER 1996, SI 1996 1938 (S.156); made under the Criminal Procedure (Scotland) Act 1995 s.238. In force: July 18, 1996; £0.65.

This Order amends the Criminal Procedure (Scotland) Act 1995 s.238(1) as regards the minimum and maximum number of hours of unpaid work which an offender may be required to perform under a community service order made by the court. The amendments increase the minimum number of hours from 40 to 80 for all cases and increase the maximum number of hours from 240 to 300 for cases where the conviction is on indictment.

6839. Compensation order–competency–payment to charity

[Criminal Justice (Scotland) Act 1980 (c.62) s.58(1).]

The Criminal Justice (Scotland) Act 1980 s.58(1) provides that where a person is convicted of an offence the court may make a compensation order requiring him to pay compensation for any personal injury, loss or damage caused (whether directly or indirectly) by the acts which constituted the offence. An accused person pleaded guilty on indictment to aggravated assault. The sheriff made a compensation order requiring the accused to pay £250 to the complainer and £1,000 to Victim Support, Airdrie. The Lord Advocate appealed against the order requiring payment to the charity on the ground that it was incompetent.

Held, that it was not competent to make a compensation order in favour of the charity as it had no connection either directly or indirectly with the accused and had not itself suffered any personal injury, loss or damage caused by the actions of the accused; and appeal allowed and order quashed.

HM ADVOCATE v. NELSON 1996 S.L.T. 1073, Judge not specified, HCJ.

6840. Consecutive sentences–whether competent–whether appropriate

N, sentenced to six months' imprisonment for assaulting the police, with 28 days concurrent, in default of payment of a fine, for a construction and use offence, and similar terms for driving while disqualified and without insurance charged on a second complaint, these sentences consecutive to those on the first complaint, appealed against the consecutive order, the complaints having been separated for technical reasons and the offences having been committed at the same place one immediately after the other. The sheriff stated that he did not consider that the assault formed part of the same incident as the driving offences. The question of when sentences could properly be made consecutive was referred to a full bench. The Crown accepted that the charges on the second complaint should have been treated as if they had appeared on the first since they had been separated for technical reasons, and that the maximum sentence which could have been pronounced was six months since that was the penalty selected on the assault charge, but invited the court to give some guidance to inferior courts.

Held, sentences ordered to run concurrently, that it was necessary to distinguish the maximum sentencing power of the court from the question whether sentences should run concurrently or consecutively. The rules as to maximum sentencing power of a summary court were: (1) where two or more charges were contained in a single complaint, the court could not competently impose a total period which exceeded the upper limit permitted for that court by common law or statute, *Maguiness v. Macdonald* 1953 S.L.T. 158, [1953] C.L.Y. 4043, *Wishart v. Heatly* 1953 S.L.T. 184, [1953] C.L.Y. 4040. The highest penalty that could be imposed was the maximum for the charge which carried the highest penalty. The foregoing did not apply in the case of fines, *Wann v. Macmillan* 1956 S.L.T. 369, [1956] C.L.Y. 10242. (2) The same rule applied where two or more charges were contained in more than one complaint, but fairness required the two complaints to be treated as if they were one, *Shand v. Normand* 1993 S.C.C.R. 274, [1993] C.L.Y. 5147, which had been decided apparently without reference to *Williamson v. Farrell* 1975 S.L.T. (Notes) 92, [1975] C.L.Y. 3113, was wrongly decided in that respect. The Crown's remedy, if it considered that the summary maximum was inadequate, was to proceed on indictment. (3) Where there was more than one complaint, and fairness did not require that the charges be treated as one, it was competent to impose sentences adding up to more than the maximum on one complaint, *Thomson v. Smith* 1982 S.L.T. 546, [1982] C.L.Y. 3660. The court had a discretion and there was no general rule as to whether sentences should normally be either consecutive or concurrent. The court should look at the reasons why the charges had appeared on separate complaints and various considerations might arise, *Thomson*. The true ratio of *Williamson v. Farrell* was not that sentences in relation to a single course of events had to be made concurrent, but that sentences should not exceed in total the maximum sentence available for a single complaint, *McGuigan v. Wilson* 1988 S.C.C.R. 474, [1989] C.L.Y. 4159, *Sargent v. Henderson* 1993 S.C.C.R. 338, [1993] C.L.Y. 5106 and *Steven v. Lees* 1994 S.C.C.R. 778, [1995] C.L.Y. 6280, disapproved in this respect.

Observed, that nothing said was intended to alter the general rule in relation to consecutive sentences for breach of a condition of bail or failing to attend a diet.

NICHOLSON v. LEES 1996 S.L.T. 706, Judge not specified, HCJ.

6841. Culpable homicide

Held, on S's appeal against eight years' imprisonment for culpable homicide of L, the jury having accepted S's plea of diminished responsibility where L had previously sexually abused S's 10 year old son, X, the offence not being a serious one but having seriously affected X who had attempted suicide, and S having become obsessed with what had happened and with the perceived injustice of L only being placed on probation while believing that L had since been taunting both of them in an obscene manner, that the matter was at large for the court since the trial judge had misdirected himself (a) in not having regarded the circumstances of the diminished responsibility as a mitigating factor in relation to sentence as well as conviction, *Kirkwood v. HM Advocate* 1939 S.L.T. 209, and (b) in attaching weight to evidence of threats by S against L on an earlier occasion when an allegation that he previously evinced malice and ill will was deleted from the charge; and seven years substituted.

STRATHEARN v. HM ADVOCATE 1996 S.C.C.R. 100, Judge not specified.

6842. Culpable homicide–lenient sentence appropriate

Held, on the Crown's appeal against sentences of three years' imprisonment for each of G and F for the culpable homicide of X, where G and F punched, kicked and stamped on X's head after a fight had broken out amongst them, that the appeal would be refused since the judge, who had considered the offence to be at the lower range for culpable homicide, had been lenient but not unduly lenient having taken into account all the mitigating factors, namely that G had never been in trouble before, F had only a minor, non analogous record, all three men had been drinking, X had delivered the first blow, G had lost his temper during the incident and, although the attack had been brutal, there had been no fracture to X's skull, X having died as a result of a serious fracture to his nose.

HM ADVOCATE v. GORDON 1996 S.C.C.R. 274, Judge not specified.

6843. Deferred sentence–whether appropriate

[Criminal Procedure (Scotland) Act 1995 (c.46) s.108.]

Held, on the Crown's appeal, that a deferred sentence was not a disposal which a reasonably judge would have found appropriate *HM Advocate v. Lee* 1996 S.C.C.R. 205, [1996] C.L.Y. 6849 where C, who had a formidable criminal record including convictions analogous to each charge and had been disqualified under three orders at the time, pled guilty to two charges of driving while disqualified and two of driving with excess alcohol, having continued to re-offend despite being given opportunities to take treatment and have community based disposals; that the only appropriate sentence was a custodial one; and having regard to 105 days spent on remand, a total of 18 months' imprisonment and three months consecutive for breach of bail substituted, with disqualification for life.

HM ADVOCATE v. CALLAGHAN 1996 S.C.C.R. 709, Judge not specified.

6844. Fines–inducement of court–offer of admonition on making donation to charity–donation less than proposed fine–competency

[Control of Pollution Act 1974 (c.40) s.32.]

A company was found guilty after trial on a summary complaint libelling a contravention of the Control of Pollution Act 1974 s.32(1). Prior to sentence being imposed the sheriff indicated that he was considering a fine of £2,500 but if the company was willing to donate £1,500 to a local trust fund, he would admonish the company. The company undertook to make the donation whereupon the sheriff admonished the company. The trust fund had no connection with the offence. The Crown sought advocation of the sentence.

Held, that what the sheriff did was wholly incompetent and inappropriate because once the company had been convicted it was for the sheriff to determine the appropriate penalty and he ought to have imposed the fine which he had concluded was appropriate; and admonition suspended and fine of £1,000 substituted.

WILSON v. TRANSORGANICS 1996 S.L.T. 1014, Judge not specified, HCJ.

6845. Fines–interim suspension of payment instalments pending appeal–competency

[Criminal Procedure (Scotland) Act 1975 (c.21) s.443A.]

Section 443A(1)(a) of the Criminal Procedure (Scotland) Act 1975 provides that "any disqualification, forfeiture or disability" attaching to any person by reason of his conviction shall, if the court before which he was convicted thinks fit, be suspended pending the determination of any appeal against conviction or sentence. An accused person pled guilty to a summary complaint libelling two charges of theft. She was fined £3,000 and ordered to pay the fine at the rate of £50 per week. She appealed against sentence and craved the sheriff to suspend payment of the fine ad interim. The sheriff's practice was to consider interim suspension of fines on application being made to him for that purpose when an appeal was intimated. The sheriff refused interim suspension and the accused petitioned the nobile officium to recall his decision and to sist execution of the fine. The Crown opposed the petition as being unnecessary because the practice of sheriff clerks was not to collect fines when appeals were outstanding.

Held, that as there was no statutory authority for the sheriff's practice, there was no injustice which had arisen requiring the court's intervention in exercise of its nobile officium; and petition refused as unnecessary.

Observed, that in the absence of any provision under summary procedure for repayment of fines in the event of an appeal being successful, the practice followed by sheriff clerks was sensible and should continue.

MAGEE, PETITIONER 1996 S.L.T. 400, Judge not specified, HCJ.

6846. Fixed penalties

CRIMINAL JUSTICE (SCOTLAND) ACT1987 FIXED PENALTY ORDER 1996, SI 1996 617 (S.60); made under the Criminal Justice (Scotland) Act 1987 s.56. In force: March 31, 1996; £1.10.

This Order prescribes a scale of fixed penalties for the purposes of section 56 of the Criminal Justice (Scotland) Act 1987 (Art.3 and the Schedule). The effect of the Order will be to enable a procurator fiscal when issuing any conditional offer under that section to specify as the fixed penalty in that offer such amount as he thinks fit being an amount which represents a level on the prescribed scale. Article 4 and Art.5 of the Order make provision as to the payment of any fixed penalty by instalment and as to what should happen when any such instalment is not paid. The Order revokes the Criminal Justice (Scotland) Act 1987 Fixed Penalty Order 1987 (SI 1987 2025) ("the 1987 Order"). The 1987 Order prescribed the amount of the fixed penalty to be £25. The Order comes into effect on March 31, 1996 but Art.1 (3) of the Order provides that it shall not apply in respect of any conditional offer made before that date.

6847. Indecent assault–deferred sentence unduly lenient

[Criminal Procedure (Scotland) Act 1975 (c. 21) s.228A.]

An accused person was found guilty after trial of indecent assault by seizing hold of the complainer, throwing her to the ground, forcing her legs apart and handling her private parts. The offence was committed late at night in a street and the complainer was a stranger to the accused, who was of low intelligence and drunk at the time of the offence. The sheriff, considering that only a short custodial sentence would be appropriate for the offence and that neither the accused nor society would benefit if such a sentence were imposed, deferred sentence for six months for the accused to be of good behaviour. The Lord Advocate appealed against the sentence, arguing that it did not reflect, inter alia, the gravity of the offence.

Held, that the sentence was unduly lenient as the proper starting point for such a crime was a custodial sentence and only if there were significant mitigating factors would a non-custodial sentence be appropriate; and appeal allowed and sentence of nine months' imprisonment substituted.

FALLAN v. HM ADVOCATE 1996 S.L.T. 314, Judge not specified, HCJ.

6848. Misuse of drugs–being concerned in supply

Held, where C received consecutive sentences of eight years in cumulo for several offences in respect of being concerned in the supply of drugs, five years in cumulo for several firearms offences and four years for assault (17 years in total), the sentences on the drug offences were excessive. Although the fact that C was also the subject of a £55,000 confiscation order should not lead to a reduction (since the sum had been agreed between C and the Crown), nor should C's worries that he would lose touch with his children influence the sentence, the judge had not had regard to the fact that C was cooperating with the authorities in relation to cases involving controlled drugs and was to be an important witness at a forthcoming trial; and a total of six years substituted on the drug charges.

CORMACK v. HM ADVOCATE 1996 S.C.C.R. 53, Judge not specified.

6849. Misuse of drugs–being concerned in supply–Class A drug–deferred sentence inappropriate–custodial sentence appropriate

Held, on the Crown's appeal against a judge's decision to defer sentence for two years, where L pled guilty to being concerned in the supplying of a Class A drug in that he had sold Ecstasy tablets at £10 each to young people in the street in the early hours of the morning in the vicinity of a discotheque and was found in possession of 19 more tablets and £590 cash, that (1) the approach in *HM Advocate v. Bell* 1995 S.L.T. 350, [1995] C.L.Y. 5797 applied to a Crown appeal against a decision to defer sentence but (2) the judge erred in rejecting an immediate and substantial custodial sentence as the trafficking in Class A drugs was a very serious offence which required an immediate and substantial custodial sentence to punish the offender, to deter others and to protect the public, *HM Advocate v. McPhee* 1994 S.L.T. 1292, [1994] C.L.Y. 5675, and although L was aged 18 at the time of the offence, with no previous convictions and was currently employed as a joiner, it was inappropriate for the trial judge to consider, and cast doubt on, the deterrent effect of a custodial sentence, which was not a justiciable issue although the aim of deterring others from engaging in similar activity was well established as an important function in reassuring the public that the court appreciated the gravity of the offence, and there was nothing in the circumstances of the case to justify a non-custodial disposal; and four years' detention substituted.

Observed, that it was inappropriate for the appeal to be drafted as an appeal against sentence.

HM ADVOCATE v. LEE 1996 S.L.T. 568, Judge not specified, HCJ.

6850. Misuse of drugs–being concerned in supply–Class A drug–whether sentence excessive

An accused person pled guilty to summary complaint libelling a contravention of s.4(3)(a) of the Misuse of Drugs Act 1971. The accused had been at a discotheque where a friend of his girlfriend had approached him and asked him to buy two Ecstasy tablets for her. The accused at first tried to dissuade the girl from buying drugs but he eventually agreed to do so for her. He bought the drugs and gave them to the girl in exchange for the price which he had paid for them. The girl took the drugs and began to exhibit symptoms of distress which required medical attention. The sheriff attached considerable weight to the effects of the consumption of the tablets and sentenced the accused to six months' detention. The accused appealed and founded on the fact that the girl had taken amphetamine earlier in the evening.

Held, that as the circumstances in which the accused came to be involved in the supply were very unusual, the accused was a first offender in employment and from a good background and supportive family and as the sheriff had not attached sufficient importance to the fact that the earlier consumption of amphetamine must have had some effect, the case was sufficiently special to merit a non-custodial disposal; and sentence quashed and community service order for 240 hours substituted. Dictum of Lord Justice-Clerk Ross in *HM Advocate v. McPhee* 1994 S.L.T. 1292, [1994] C.L.Y. 5675 applied.

McDONALD v. BARBOUR 1996 S.L.T. 1138, Judge not specified, HCJ.

6851. Misuse of drugs–possession–small quantities of cannabis

Held, on M and C's appeals against fines of £250 and £300 respectively, at £10 per fortnight, for simple possession of cannabis, the quantities in each case being minimal, on the grounds that the sheriff misdirected himself in imposing deterrent sentences which were higher than those imposed in other areas for similar offences and had followed a blanket policy without taking into account the circumstances of the offence and the offenders, *Sopwith v. Cruickshank* 1959 J.C. 78, [1960] C.L.Y. 3968, that the appeals would be refused since the sheriff was fully entitled to impose fairly severe penalties to prevent the spread of drugs into his area and account had been taken of the small amount of the drug involved and that neither M nor C, who were both in receipt of benefits, were in a position to pay large fines.

McCLEARY v. WALKINGSHAW; CALDERWOOD v. WALKINGSHAW 1996 S.C.C.R. 13, Judge not specified.

6852. Misuse of drugs–production of cannabis

Held, that 18 months' imprisonment was not excessive for H, in whose house was a room with an elaborate hydroponic system in which she had cultivated cannabis plants over a 15 month period, 13 plants being found in the room and another 113 seedlings in a greenhouse awaiting the stage when they could be transferred indoors, H claiming to smoke 10 cannabis cigarettes a day. Parliament having provided a much higher maximum sentence than for simple possession, the two offences could not be equiparated where production was for H's own use, as contended for H, and the trial judge was entitled to impose the same sentence as on a coaccused, F, whose house had two rooms devoted to production involving a substantial number of plants.

Observed, that whatever view others might take about the purpose and nature of the production of cannabis, the court's duty was to apply the law in accordance with policy disclosed by the sentences provided by Parliament.

HENDERSON v. HM ADVOCATE 1996 S.C.C.R. 71, Judge not specified.

6853. Misuse of drugs–trafficking in drugs in prison–deferred sentence appropriate in exceptional circumstances

[Criminal Procedure (Scotland) Act 1975 (c.21) s.228A.]

The Criminal Procedure (Scotland) Act 1975 s.228A, as amended, provides that where a person has been convicted on indictment, the Lord Advocate may appeal against an order deferring sentence if it appears to him that the deferment is inappropriate or on unduly lenient terms. An accused person pled guilty to an indictment containing five charges of contravention of the Misuse of Drugs Act 1971 s.5(3) within HM Prison, Barlinnie, on January 12, 1994. The accused had been sentenced on January 11, 1994 to imprisonment and on the next day, while in the prison hospital, had been threatened with violence by another inmate unless he conveyed the drugs from the hospital into a hall of the prison. The trial judge deferred sentence for six months for the accused to be of good behaviour. He told the accused that but for exceptional circumstances involving the accused's tenacious fight to free himself from his heroin addiction following his release from the earlier sentence, he would have imposed a sentence of seven years' imprisonment on the basis of the accused's criminal record and the nature of the charges. He also made clear that he was not committing the court to any final disposal at the end of the period of deferment. The Crown appealed, contending that the order was inappropriate having regard to the gravity of the crimes, the accused's criminal record, the value of the drugs and the circumstances of the offences, but no mention was made by way of criticism of the mitigating factors relied on by the trial judge in making the order. Before the appeal court the Crown sought leave to abandon the appeal because the information placed before the trial judge on the accused's behalf, which the trial judge had relied on as evidencing the exceptional circumstances, had only become available to the Crown in the course of the week prior to the appeal hearing.

Held, that (1) on the material placed before the trial judge his decision was entirely justified and (2) whereas from the grounds of appeal it seemed that the appeal court was in effect being invited to lay down a minimum custodial sentence for trafficking in drugs in prison, the court would continue so long as the power rested with it, to assert the right of judges to exercise leniency in sentencing whenever it was appropriate and to take account of exceptional circumstances where a custodial sentence would otherwise be inevitable; and leave to abandon the appeal granted.

Observed, that (1) in view of the Lord Advocate's privilege of direct access to the appeal court without first requiring to obtain leave to appeal, the court was entitled to demand from the Lord Advocate and his advisers a high standard of care and accuracy from the outset in both the selection and presentation of cases for appeal under s.228A of the 1975 Act and (2) had the appeal court been dealing with the appeal as one for which leave was required, in light of the grounds of appeal it was very likely that leave to appeal would not have been granted.

HM ADVOCATE v. McKAY 1996 S.L.T. 697, Judge not specified, HCJ.

6854. Murder–life sentence tariff–minimum recommendation

[Criminal Procedure (Scotland) Act 1975 (c. 21), s.205A.]

Held, where M was sentenced to life imprisonment with a recommendation for a minimum period of 15 years following his conviction for murdering S by twice throwing him out of a fourth floor window, placing him in a bin and abandoning the bin in open ground, that the circumstances were not so grave or brutal to justify the making of a recommendation which would tie the hands of the Parole Board, and therefore the Secretary of State, as to when it would be appropriate to release M on life licence, nor did M's past record indicate that he was a danger to the public, although the trial judge concluded that the offence demonstrated sheer wickedness and a complete lack of normal human feeling; and recommendation set aside.

McGUIRE v. HM ADVOCATE 1995 S.C.C.R. 776, Judge not specified.

6855. Murder–life sentence tariff–minimum recommendation

[Murder (Abolition of Death Penalty) Act 1965 (c.71) s.1; Criminal Procedure (Scotland) Act 1975 (c.21) s.262, s.281.]

D petitioned the nobile officium seeking review of a recommendation made in 1974 in terms of the Murder (Abolition of Death Penalty) Act 1965 s.1 (2) that he serve a minimum period of 25 years before being released on licence, having been convicted of theft of a car, assault, attempted murder (two charges), robbery and murder. Six other persons also convicted received recommendations for minimum periods of 15 to 18 years, apart from B, who was acknowledged at the trial as having fired the fatal shot and who was also recommended for 25 years. In a post-trial note to the Secretary of State, the trial judge described D as "clearly the leader of the experts brought up from London". D averred that there was no basis in the evidence which justified such a statement since he had not taken any greater part in the crimes than his co-accused and on a comparative basis the trial judge's recommendation should have been on par with those of his co-accused, other than B. He had not previously tried to invoke the nobile officium because he was unaware of the content of the post trial note until August 1994, when his solicitors obtained an abridged version. The Crown argued that the petition was incompetent as the nobile officium could only be invoked in extreme cases where the recommendation was based upon a blatant error. D's case did not fall into this category since it sought to review a recommendation which was not binding on S.

Held, allowing the petition and inviting the parties to make submission as to how the disputed questions of fact might be resolved, since the trial judge had died in 1981 and was unable to provide any further report, that (1) the petition was not barred by the Criminal Procedure (Scotland) Act 1975 s.262 and s.281 since a recommendation was not a sentence (as defined in s.279 and s.462) for the purpose of those sections, nor was it an interlocutor; (2) between 1965 and the implementation of s.205A of the 1975 Act a party could have petitioned the nobile officium, on the ground of manifest injustice rather than casus improvisus. Although the trial judge's recommendation was not binding, it plainly affected S's consideration of when D should be released on licence, *R. v. Secretary of State for Home Affairs, ex p. Doody* [1994] A.C. 531, [1993] C.L.Y. 1213. D could invoke the nobile officium if the circumstances were extraordinary and unforeseen and no other procedure or remedy was available, *Wylie v. HM Advocate* 1966 S.L.T. 149, [1966] C.L.Y. 13003 and *Wan Ping Nam v. Minister of Justice of the Federal German Republic* 1972 S.L.T. 200, [1972] C.L.Y. 3667, and if in making his recommendation the trial judge was influenced by a totally erroneous view of the facts for which there was no evidential basis or justification, then D had stated a relevant case for invoking the nobile officium and the court would be entitled to interfere with the purpose of preventing a manifest injustice or oppression.

DRAPER, PETITIONER 1996 S.L.T. 617, Judge not specified, HCJ.

6856. Murder–life sentence tariff–minimum recommendation–discretion of trial judge–whether recommendation necessary

[Criminal Procedure (Scotland) Act 1975 (c.21) s.205A.]

Section 205A(1) of the Criminal Procedure (Scotland) Act 1975 as amended provides that in sentencing any person convicted of murder a judge might make a recommendation as to the minimum period which should elapse before, under s.26 of the Prisons (Scotland) Act 1989, the Secretary of State released that person on licence. An accused person was convicted of murder. He had been involved in a confrontation with the deceased in a discotheque earlier in the evening and had lain in wait for the deceased outside the discotheque after it had closed. The deceased died as a result of two stab wounds from a knife with which the accused had armed himself. The accused had a previous conviction for assault to severe injury, permanent disfigurement and permanent impairment for which he had been sentenced in the High Court to four years' imprisonment. The murder occurred within four years of that conviction. The trial judge sentenced the accused to life imprisonment with a recommendation that he serve a minimum period of 15 years because of the nature of his conduct and his previous conviction for violence. The accused appealed against the making of the recommendation, contending, *inter alia*, that as there was no reference in the libel to the accused's lying in wait for the deceased, the jury did not make a determination on that point, on which there was competing evidence, and the trial judge should not have taken it into account.

Held, that (1) the trial judge was entitled to base his decision on his understanding of the evidence provided that it was within the verdict which the jury returned; (2) the incident itself was not of so grave or brutal and violent a nature as to justify on its own the making of a recommendation but (3) the accused's previous conviction took the case out of the ordinary run of cases and made it appropriate for the trial judge to consider whether, in the exercise of his discretion, to make a recommendation; and appeal refused. *Dictum* of Lord Justice-General Hope in *McGuire v. HM Advocate* 1995 S.C.C.R. 776, [1996] C.L.Y. 6854 applied.

GREENFIELD v. HM ADVOCATE 1996 S.L.T. 1214, Judge not specified, HCJ.

6857. Offensive weapons

Held, that where H, aged 16 with one minor, non-analogous offence, received 90 days' imprisonment for an unprovoked head butt and violent struggle with police when arrested, and six months concurrent for possession of a draper knife, that the sentences were not excessive as H, who owed money for drugs, was carrying the knife for protection and this type of offence was on the increase in the district, despite claims by H that he was now drug-free after three years and the social inquiry report recommended probation.

HAMILTON v. HAMILTON 1996 S.C.C.R. 652, Judge not specified.

6858. Oppression–transfer of case between courts–additional sentencing power

[Criminal Procedure (Scotland) Act 1975 (c.21) s.294; District Courts (Scotland) Act 1975 (c.20) s.3(2).]

Held, where G received three months' imprisonment for attempted theft with one month consecutive for a bail offence, G claiming that, since he pled guilty before a justice, it was unfair and oppressive for a stipendiary magistrate (after a background report had been obtained) then to impose a longer sentence than the justice could have imposed, that it was not oppressive for the magistrate to exercise the powers conferred on him, since it was commonplace that cases be transferred between courts depending on workloads and availability of courts, G's case had originally been called before the magistrate and the sentence which was selected was undoubtedly appropriate in all the circumstances.

GRAHAM v. NORMAND 1996 S.C.C.R. 371, Judge not specified.

6859. Parole Board–prisoner released on licence recalled after committing offence–whether decision to revoke licence was reasonable

[Prisoners and Criminal Proceedings (Scotland) Act 1993 (c.9) s.1 (3).]

M applied for judicial review of the Parole Board's decision to recommend that his licence be revoked a short time after his release from prison. M was sentenced to four years' imprisonment but was released on licence after two years under the Prisoners and Criminal Proceedings (Scotland) Act 1993 s.1 (3). Shortly after his release he was arrested and charged with assault and committed for trial, having pleaded not guilty. As a result the Parole Board recommended that his licence be revoked and he was recalled to prison. The recall was justified by reference to the serious nature of the charge and M's admission that he had been under the influence of drugs at the time of the offence. M argued that the decision to recall him was unreasonable.

Held, dismissing the application, that the Parole Board's decision to recall M had been a reasonable one. The severity of the incident and the proximity of it to M's release on licence had led the Parole Board to conclude that his release would present an unacceptable risk to the public. When disputing a Parole Board decision as being unreasonable the onus lay on the defendant to show that interference by way of judicial review was warranted.

McRAE v. PAROLE BOARD FOR SCOTLAND, *The Times*, March 19, 1996, Lord Weir, OH.

6860. Robbery–use of weapons

Held, on appeals by J and M against seven and six and a half years' imprisonment respectively for (while acting with another) assaulting four employees at certain premises, presenting a knife, locking them in a toilet, compelling one to open a safe and taking £4,193 in cash and also some cheques, that (1) J's sentence was not excessive though he claimed to have taken a lesser part in the offence, where all had pled guilty on the basis of concert, and though his only serious previous conviction (18 months for assault to severe injury) was in 1985, since the court required to protect those at risk from such offences but (2) M's sentence was excessive, not because he was just the driver but because (a) he only had three summary convictions for assault, and (b) the sentence had been made consecutive to three years for reset imposed six months before the present sentence, when the current charge was known to be outstanding, and while it was appropriate in this case for the sentences to be consecutive (cf. Renton and Brown, para.10.73), regard should be had to the total imposed; and five and a half years substituted.

McGILL v. HM ADVOCATE 1996 S.C.C.R. 35, Judge not specified.

6861. Robbery–use of weapons

Held, that a cumulo sentence of 15 years' imprisonment for G, who had convictions for dishonesty but not violence and whose longest previous sentence was three months, for two armed bank robberies on the same day in which a loaded pistol was used and held at the head of a customer (with 10 years concurrent on each of two charges of using a firearm in the course of a robbery), was excessive as outwith the normal range of sentences for such offences; and 12 years substituted, for such offences being towards the top end of the scale.

GRAHAM v. HM ADVOCATE 1996 S.C.C.R. 105, Judge not specified.

6862. Sexual offences–lewd, indecent and libidinous behaviour–lenient sentence

[Sexual Offences (Scotland) Act 1976 (c.67) s.5.]

R was convicted of two charges of lewd, libidinous and indecent practices against his niece, C, and great niece, G, which involved (1) touching C's private parts, inserting a finger, licking and masturbating in front of C approximately once a month when C was between the ages of four and a half and seven, and exposing his penis and placing it in her mouth on two occasions when she was aged 10; (2) separate incidents of (i) kissing G on the lips, (ii) placing his penis on her bottom and (iii) restricting her with toy handcuffs, removing her pants and his own clothing and placing his penis in her private parts and (3) breach of the Sexual Offences (Scotland) Act 1976 s.5 by placing his finger in C's private parts when she was aged between 12 and 13, and was sentenced concurrently to one year's imprisonment for each offences. (R was also charged with rape, but no evidence was led in support of it and the charge was withdrawn in the course of trial). The Crown appealed on the grounds that the sentences were unduly lenient having regard to (1) the grossly indecent nature of the sexual abuse; (2) the gross breach of trust, when R had been babysitting; (3) the ages of C and G when the offences took place; (4) the period of time over which the offences occurred (incorrectly stated in the note of appeal as 13 years) and (5) the absence of any mitigating circumstances other than R's asthma and minor hearing impairment. The trial judge criticised the grounds of appeal as conveying a misleading impression of the evidence and reported in respect of charge one that although he regarded R's conduct towards C as appalling, the conduct had ceased in 1981 when R was aged 25 and the nature and frequency of the proved abuse was not as severe as other cases where the abuse had been more repulsive and regularly maintained over a long period. In respect of charge two, it was not clear whether R had exposed himself in placing his penis on G's bottom and he had not attached any significance to the use of handcuffs, while charge three related to only one occasion. In sentencing R he had taken into account his employment record, his general good character as evidenced by a social inquiry report and most significantly the fact that R had been subject to the ordeal of a rape charge for which the Crown led no evidence.

Held, refusing the appeal, that in respect of charge one, the trial judge's decision was flawed as he gave too little weight to the gravity of the offences and failed to attach sufficient importance to the frequency of the conduct against C when C was aged between four and a half and seven and the sentence was undoubtedly lenient; however, the sentence was not so unduly lenient as to justify interference, *HM Advocate v. Bell* 1995 S.L.T. 350, [1995] C.L.Y. 5797. In addition, he was entitled to consider that R had for a time faced a very serious charge of raping a young child in respect of which the Crown had not led any evidence. The sentence was not outwith the range of sentence which could reasonably be considered appropriate. In respect of charge two, the trial judge was in a much better position to determine and form an impression whether the use of handcuffs was significant and although such conduct did constitute a serious abuse of a child, the sentence was not unduly lenient in view of the nature of the conduct and the number of times it occurred. The sentence for charge three was not unduly lenient where two years was the maximum.

Observed, that it was regrettable that the note of appeal before the Lord Advocate had contained a good deal of inaccurate information, although the court was assured that the Lord Advocate had decided to appeal on the basis of an accurate report from the trial advocate depute.

HM ADVOCATE v. ROSS 1996 S.C.C.R. 107, Judge not specified.

6863. Sexual offences–lewd, indecent and libidinous behaviour–probation order–unduly lenient

[Criminal Procedure (Scotland) Act 1975 (c.21) s.228A; Sexual Offences (Scotland) Act 1976 (c.67) s.4, s.5.]

Held, on the Crown's appeal against a judge's decision to make a probation order for three years with the requirement of 100 hours' unpaid community service during the first 12 months, where B pled guilty to two offences under Sexual Offences (Scotland) Act 1976 s.4 and s.5 of repeatedly using lewd, indecent and libidinous practices and behaviour against two 14 or 15 year old girls (C) during 1976 and 1977 while a schoolteacher, in that he had handled one of the girls' breasts and had induced her to handle his penis and masturbate him and had placed his penis in the other girl's mouth, that in view of the gravity of the two charges, the fact that they were committed by someone in the relationship of teacher and pupil and that B's conduct had had serious consequences on C's lives, the disposal adopted by the trial judge was unduly lenient as the only appropriate disposal was a custodial sentence, and although such offences might normally attract the maximum sentence available, in view of the strong mitigating factors including the considerable delay in bringing the case and the facts that there had been no further offending in over 18 years, that B had given up teaching in 1981 and had devoted a great deal of his time since then to working in his church and assisting the community, and that B had sought psychiatric help and had tried to mend his ways and live a useful life since the date of the offences, 12 months' imprisonment concurrent on each charge would be substituted.

HM ADVOCATE v. BROUGH 1996 S.C.C.R. 377, Judge not specified.

6864. Theft–housebreaking

Held, that three months' detention was not excessive for H for three charges of housebreaking and one attempted housebreaking, the property stolen being valued at £4,000 with no recovery, though H, aged 17 with no analogous record, claimed that at the time he was abusing cannabis and had got into debt in order to finance his habit, and he was now drug free, in full time employment and hoping to go to college in the near future.

HOLLYWOOD v. BROWN 1996 S.C.C.R. 64, Judge not specified.

6865. Theft–housebreaking

Held, where R, aged 32, received concurrent sentences of six months' imprisonment on each of two charges of theft by housebreaking, the total value of goods stolen being £150, that the sentences were not excessive nor should they be backdated, in view of R's record which included some 53 offences of dishonesty and the distress and upset caused, though R claimed that he had been drunk and was uncertain if he committed the offences, and had changed his plea to guilty after the late intimation of fingerprint evidence

ROBERTSON v. ORR 1996 S.C.C.R. 260, Judge not specified.

6866. Theft–housebreaking–forfeiture

Held, that forfeiture of a car bought a year earlier for £4,700 which he used in a housebreaking (with admonition) was excessive where W, a first offender aged 35 and in full time employment, had driven for S and M who actually carried out the housebreaking and was regarded as having acted from naivety, and a £1,000 fine substituted; but that three months' imprisonment for S was not excessive where his record included seven offences of dishonesty, though none since 1989 when he married and though M had a much worse record.

WILSON v. HAMILTON 1996 S.C.C.R. 193, Judge not specified.

6867. Theft–motor vehicle

Held, where D, who had a appalling record with many analogous offences, received two years' imprisonment for theft of a car, one year consecutive for driving while disqualified and an admonition for driving without insurance, together with 142 days as the unexpired balance of a previous sentence, that the sentences were not excessive nor would they be made concurrent though D claimed that the offences occurred in the course of one incident, but that as the sheriff had given no reason for not backdating to take account of 97 days spent on remand, 45 days would be substituted for the 142 days.

DAILLY v. HM ADVOCATE 1996 S.C.C.R. 580, Judge not specified.

6868. Theft–postal packets–first offender

Held, where R, a postman, stole or secreted 1,666 postal packets over a period of six weeks, all the items being recovered, that 60 days' imprisonment was excessive since this was an exceptional case, *Fleming-Scott v. HM*

Advocate 1991 S.C.C.R. 748, [1991] C.L.Y. 4859 as R, a first offender, was a diabetic whose medical condition had been controlled by his family until recently when R had moved into a flat with friends, R had begun to drink heavily and this had affected his condition, he had been unable to carry the heavy bags of mail on his round and had requested and been refused a vehicle by the Post Office and, as a result, he had decided to take the bags home, take out the important looking letters such as giros which he delivered, intending to deliver the other items by car (though he never got round to it); and 200 hours' community service substituted.

ROBERTSON v. MAGUIRE 1996 S.C.C.R. 58, Judge not specified.

6869. Theft–shoplifting

Held, where M, whose record included 38 offences of dishonesty and who had just been released after serving four months for an identical offence, received six months' imprisonment for shoplifting (plus eight days of a previous unexpired sentence), that the sentence was not excessive despite claims by M that the social inquiry report recommended probation and that the case should have been continued to allow for a lay justice who had taken and interest in the case to be further involved.

MAIN v. NORMAND 1996 S.C.C.R. 256, Judge not specified.

6870. Vandalism–compensation order

Held, where E was admonished on charges of breach of the peace and vandalism and ordered to pay compensation of £540 at £7 per week, the cost of the windows of the public house which she broke after being ejected from the bar, that the order was not excessive though E was in receipt of income support, since it was irrelevant whether or not the owners had recovered any money from their insurance and the guidelines which applied to the length of time over which fines were paid should not be regarded as applying to compensation orders.

ELY v. DONNELLY 1996 S.C.C.R. 537, Judge not specified.

6871. Articles

Consecutive sentences: competency and appropriateness *(Peter W. Ferguson)*: J.L.S.S. 1996, 41 (7), 263-264. (Court of five judges gives guidance on consecutive and concurrent sentences).

Crown appeals against lenient sentences *(Daniel Kelly)*: Crim. L.B. 1996, 19 (Feb), 4-5. (Cases show mixed outcome of appeals).

The fiscal fine: how far can it be extended? *(Peter Duff)*: S.L.T. 1996, 19, 167-171. (Introduction of fixed penalties offered by procurators fiscal in Scotland and comparison with wider use of such penalties in Netherlands).

DAMAGES

6872. Measure of damages–loss of use of vehicle–method of calculating loss

In an action of damages relating to a road traffic accident the pursuers claimed for the value of the loss of use of their vehicle while it was being repaired. The pursuers based their claim on a formula by which the operating costs were deducted from the total expenses for a year. The difference, the standing cost, was divided by the average number of vehicles multiplied by the number of days in the year. The resultant figure was said to represent the cost per day of having a substitute vehicle, or the cost of the loss of the vehicle. The defender maintained that the basis of the pursuer's claim was incorrect.

Held, that, there being no special sanctity about any particular method, and the important consideration being that the pursuers were fairly compensated for their loss, the pursuers were entitled to claim for loss of use of their vehicle on a standing cost per day basis; and damages awarded accordingly.

EASTERN SCOTTISH OMNIBUSES v. LESLIE 1996 S.L.T. (Sh.Ct.) 53, Judge not specified, Sh Ct.

6873. Personal injuries or death–measure of damages–arm

S, a machine operator aged 48 at proof, sued his employers, B, after S's dominant right arm became entangled in tape passing through a machine and was torn off from beneath his elbow in April 1993. B admitted liability. The arm was recovered and reconnected. Muscle activity did not recover and two months later the arm was amputated to four inches below the elbow. S also suffered a fracture of the upper arm which healed well. Artificial appliances allowed S a rudimentary grasp which meant he was able to return to employment as a fork lift truck driver. In February 1995 S required to have a painful neuroma removed from the stump of his arm. S required to use a nerve stimulating machine to control the pain and attended a pain clinic. S required help with shaving, clothing and bathing and could not carry out ordinary household tasks. He suffered phantom pain and cramp. He had become depressed and self conscious. He could no longer tend the garden or maintain car engines as he frequently did in the past. His employment appeared to be secure.

Held, that solatium of £42,500 was appropriate, £17,500 to the past, together with agreed past loss of earnings of £5,000; future loss of £16,000 (using an eight year multiplier where S hoped to work until 65); employment disadvantage of £2,500; £5,000 for his wife's services, £1,500 to the past (rejecting a calculation based on rates for paid housekeepers and companions); and £1,500 for loss of S's services, £250 to the past.

STUPPART v. BONAR TEXTILES 1996 S.C.L.R. 763, Judge not specified, OH.

6874. Personal injuries or death–measure of damages–asthma type illness–provisional award

[Administration of Justice Act 1982 (c.53) s.12.]

The Administration of Justice Act 1982 s.12 provides that a provisional award of damages may be made where there is proved or admitted to be a risk that at some definite or indefinite time in the future the injured person will, as a result of the act or omission which gave rise to the cause of action, develop some serious disease or suffer some serious deterioration in his physical or mental condition. A spray painter, aged 36 at proof, sought damages from his employers after he developed incurable industrial asthma in late 1993, some months after his employers started using a new epoxy resin paint which was a known respiratory sensitiser. When using the paint, he experienced uncontrollable coughing, sneezing, an irritated throat and nosebleeds. He also developed a skin rash and had bouts of vomiting and sweating. Although his condition improved greatly at weekends and during holidays, he continued to have symptoms when not working. His sleep was disturbed in that he would wake up with his symptoms at least three times a fortnight. He required to take heavy medication including steroid inhalants, a nasal topical steroid and a bronchial dilator. He became sensitised to other household irritants such as cigarette smoke and aftershave. His family and social life was adversely affected. It was necessary for him to change duties at his place of work and to take extra precautionary measures such as the wearing of masks during the course of his work. The employee continued to work hard although he still experienced discomfort and his work was rendered more strenuous and arduous as a result of his condition. In the event that he required to give up his employment due to his disability, the pursuer, who was not qualified for any other job, would have a reduced employability on the labour market. The pursuer sought, inter alia, an award of provisional damages.

Held, that (1) before an award for provisional damages could be made, it was essential that the court's determination should make it clear to the parties the nature of the deterioration, the occurrence of which would cause the pursuer's final right to damages to emerge; (2) in the present case the court could not identify with sufficient particularity a future event against which a claim for final damages could be preserved, and in any event the risk was not such as to justify provisional damages where the risk of a serious deterioration in the pursuer's condition was agreed to be small and there were numerous potential supervening causes of deterioration; (3) solatium was properly valued at £16,500 with 25 per cent allocated to the past and (4) loss of employability was properly valued at £20,000; and decree pronounced accordingly. Opinion, that an order under s.12 should not be granted without limit of time unless in exceptional circumstances.

BONAR v. TRAFALGAR HOUSE OFFSHORE FABRICATION LTD 1996 S.L.T. 548, Judge not specified, OH.

6875. Personal injuries or death–measure of damages–back

F, aged 44 at proof, sought reparation from L in respect of an injury to her back sustained in a fall on ice and snow during the course of her employment as a nurse at L's hospital in December 1990.

Held, that where F injured her coccyx and damaged her lumbar spine and, although there was no immediate prolapse of a disc, two subsequent accidents culminated in full prolapse and F's full post-accident symptoms were attributable to the accident, solatium would have been awarded at £14,000, with wage loss of £13,800 to the date of proof, inclusive of interest, loss of pension rights of £15,000 and services provided to F at £1,000. In view of F's age and her chances of being fit for work in the future, a multiplier of five would have been applied to the agreed multiplicand of £10,000, giving total damages of £93,800. Opinion, further that for the coccygeal injury only, £1,250 would have been awarded for wage loss, £1,000 for services and £4,000 for solatium.

FINLAYSON v. LANARKSHIRE HEALTH BOARD 1996 S.C.L.R. 774, Judge not specified, OH.

6876. Personal injuries or death–measure of damages–back

A 45 year old nurse injured her back in circumstances which brought to the surface an underlying predisposition to injury. The injury caused pain and disability and was not susceptible to treatment. She was unable to resume working and required occasional assistance from her husband.

Held, that solatium was properly valued at £4,000 and that her husband's services were sufficiently recognised by an award of £500; and decree pronounced accordingly.

HIGGINS v. TAYSIDE HEALTH BOARD 1996 S.L.T. 288, Judge not specified, OH.

6877. Personal injuries or death–measure of damages–back

L, aged 46 at proof, sued among others T, a health board, in respect of an injury which she suffered on August 3, 1990 during the course of her employment as an auxiliary nurse with T. L sustained an injury to her back as a result of lifting a 10 and half stone male patient. The injury L had sustained had progressively worsened. She never returned to work. Spondylitic changes were identified and were operated on in July 1991, but by 1995 L was frequently confined to bed due to the pain, which frequently made her physically sick. Her condition was likely to remain the same.

Held, decree granted. Since L was an active woman whose whole life had been completely altered by the accident, and she suffered pain on a continuing basis, £11,000 was appropriate for pain and suffering, with 50 per cent apportioned to the past. Parties were agreed on wage loss of £7,584.17 (less sick pay of £2, 371.75) for the period between August 3, 1990 and October 18, 1992 when L's employment was terminated, and loss of earnings of £9,768.22 from then to the proof. A multiplier of 8 was appropriate for future wage loss calculation where L would have retired at 60, allowing for the slight possibility of L finding employment, or of her employment having otherwise come to an end, producing a rounded figure of £26,300. Pension loss was agreed at £9,000. In respect of services rendered by L's husband £2,100 was awarded for the period since January 1995 to the date of proof on the basis of British Nursing Association rates for housekeepers and companions and £750 for the period before then. In respect of future services, the appropriate figure was to be calculated having regard to L's husband's life expectancy rather than that of L, producing a figure of £15,000. Total award: £79,094.64 exclusive of interest.

LAING v. TAYSIDE RC 1996 S.C.L.R. 754, Judge not specified, OH.

6878. Personal injuries or death–measure of damages–back

M, a cleansing department driver employed by C, a district council, sued C after sustaining an injury to his back on November 1, 1992 in the course of his employment.

Opinion, where M suffered a prolapsed disc of the lumbar spine which was an exacerbation of a pre-existing condition accelerated by an estimated 18 months, solatium would have been awarded at £4,000, all to the past. Wage loss was agreed at £2,340 from the date of the incident until dismissal, and then at £235 per week until the end of the acceleration period, with interest at half the legal rate until then and at the full legal rate thereafter.

McGINN v. MOTHERWELL DC 1996 S.C.L.R. 359, Judge not specified, OH.

6879. Personal injuries or death–measure of damages–back

A 40 year-old workman sustained injury in an accident at work when the person carrying the other end of a heavy pole let it go. The injury caused was either of transient effect or was the cause of a prolapsed disc which had devastating and permanent consequences to his back, but which the pursuer would have suffered at some point in any event.

Held, that the injury sustained was of a minor nature and solatium was properly valued at £250; and decree pronounced accordingly. Opinion, that had the accident been the cause of the pursuer's symptoms, solatium would properly have been valued at £17,000, discounted to £13,000 because of the inevitability of a disc prolapse; and that the multiplier for loss of earnings would have been reduced from eight years to four years for the same reason.

McKINNON v. BRITISH TELECOMMUNICATIONS PLC 1996 S.L.T. 798, Lord Rodger, OH.

6880. Personal injuries or death–measure of damages–back

S sued her employers, F, a health board, after sustaining an injury to her chest wall involving two fractured ribs and sciatic pain, when she fell backwards over boxes against a window ledge on October 19, 1992. F accepted liability. S ("somewhat older" than the 34 of a pursuer in a similar case) claimed that she continued to suffer pain and, in particular, sciatic pain as a result of the accident. F maintained that S had, in fact, made a good recovery within a few weeks. On S's evidence, as her chest symptoms subsided, S became aware of pain radiating down into her leg which was sciatic pain relating to the accident. The tenderness S suffered in her ribs might be permanent. She could no longer move heavy items and tired more easily. F's evidence was based on a medical expert's report which disputed S's expert medical evidence and which only became available to S's counsel on a Friday, four days before proof commenced.

Held, decree granted, that S had established that her injuries were ongoing and attributable to the accident. No reliance should be placed on F's expert medical report, which was lodged far too late and for which there was no record; in any event its conclusions would not have been preferred. Although S's pain gradually subsided the symptoms were likely to be permanent, and since S's back injury was "moderate", the appropriate award of solatium was £6,000 with interest on two thirds at half the judicial rate (£814). S's claim for disadvantage on the labour market was assessed at £1,250 since S was no longer able to carry out the same tasks as prior to the accident. Since the

evidence relating to S's claim for services was confusing, a token award was made of £200, and £207 was agreed as S's net wage loss. Total award, £8,471.
SMITH v. FIFE HEALTH BOARD 1996 S.C.L.R. 354, Judge not specified, OH.

6881. Personal injuries or death–measure of damages–claims for death of a husband–claims for death of parent–loss of support

A businessman was killed as a result of a road traffic accident in 1990. His widow and children sued for, inter alia, loss of support. The pursuers averred that, had the deceased survived, his business profits were likely to be substantially more than those existing at the time of his death, with the company's progress and estimated turnover. The pursuers also averred that the court should take into account in assessing damages for future loss the anticipated real return on money invested after tax, and made averments concerning yields and index-linked Government securities. The defender argued that the averments were irrelevant. In the first place, the averments about the projected increase in the deceased's income, and thus the sum appropriate for dependency, lacked specification and gave insufficient notice to the defender of the case against her. In the second place, there was no need to depart from the conventional multiplier to ascertain future loss.

Held, that (1) the defender did not have any proper notice of matters in relation to which she could prepare a defence to the general assertions relating to the company's performance and the deceased's actual plans for the future, his ultimate aims and ambitions, by testing the substratum of fact upon which the assertions were made, so that they were irrelevant for want of specification; (2) that as this was a straightforward case, the conventional multiplier was to be used; and averments excluded from probation, *O'Brien's Curator Bonis v. British Steel* 1991 S.L.T. 516, [1991] C.L.Y. 4906 followed; *Thomas v. Burton HA* (Unreported) not followed. Opinion, that multipliers should not be substantially increased on the hypothesis that index-linked securities would be the way in which people would invest their funds, as it would be extremely unlikely than any investment manager would invest any fund of several hundreds of thousands of pounds solely in index-linked securities, which were not a guarantee and had provided a poor investment in real terms since their inception.
CHALMERS v. MARTIN 1996 S.L.T. 1307, Judge not specified, OH.

6882. Personal injuries or death–measure of damages–claims for death of husband–claims for death of parent

The 27 year old widow of a 37 year old coastguard officer sought damages for herself and for her two children, aged about four and a half and almost three, following the death of her husband in a road accident. The claims were for loss of society, loss of services provided by the deceased and loss of support both in relation to the period before the deceased would have retired and thereafter, when he would have been in receipt of an occupational pension. On her husband's death the widow had received a widow's pension and a lump sum death benefit from her husband's employers. In calculating the loss of support related to the period before her husband would have retired, it was agreed that the family dependency should be taken at 70 per cent of earnings. For the period after he would have retired the widow contended that the same 70 per cent dependency should be used and that no account should be taken of her widow's pension. The defenders contended that the existence of the widow's pension demonstrated that she had suffered no loss of support from her husband's pension.

Held, that (1) loss of society was properly valued at £13,500 for the widow, £8,000 for the older child and £9,000 for the younger child; (2) loss of services should be calculated at an average rate of one hour a day at a rate of £4.50 an hour and using a multiplier of 13 years from the date of death; (3) loss of support from the deceased's earnings should be calculated on a multiplier of 13 years from the date of death; (4) the widow's pension fell to be disregarded under s.1 (5) of the Damages (Scotland) Act 1976 in calculating loss of support from her husband's pension, (5) a dependency of 50 per cent should be used in respect of the period after the deceased's retirement with a multiplier of five years to take account of the delay in that loss occurring; (6) the widow should also be awarded 50 per cent of the lump sum that would have been received on retiral, discounted by one third for early payment; and decree pronounced accordingly, subject to abatement of 60 per cent for contributory negligence. *Davidson v. Upper Clyde Shipbuilders* [1990] C.L.Y. 5070, followed.

CAMPBELL v. GILLESPIE 1996 S.L.T. 503, OH.

6883. Personal injuries or death–measure of damages–food poisoning

A diner in her mid-20s suffered from salmonella poisoning after eating a meal in a restaurant. After proof before answer, the sheriff awarded her damages comprising £3,000 solatium, £594 agreed wage loss and £200 in respect of services performed by her husband. The defender appealed challenging, inter alia, the amount of damages awarded.

Held, that (1) taking into account what had been said in *Currie v. Kilmarnock and Loudoun DC* 1996 S.L.T. 481, [1996] C.L.Y. 6891, on the general level of judicial awards for solatium, the dubious authority of the cases founded upon by the defender, the fact that the sheriff's award was not wildly out of line with at least one previous award, and the discretion allowed to the judge of first instance, there was no basis to differ from the conclusion arrived at by the sheriff regarding solatium and (2) the assessment of the award for services was very much within the discretion of the sheriff and it could not be said that the award was one which he was not entitled to make; and appeal refused.

McINULTY v. ALAM 1996 S.L.T. (Sh. Ct.) 71, Judge not specified, Sh Ct.

6884. Personal injuries or death–measure of damages–foot

A 43 year old time-served engineer sustained fracture dislocations in his foot which kept him off work for over six months. The foot remained painful and was a substantial disability which would lead to a need to seek less physically demanding work in his mid-50s.

Held, that solatium was properly valued at £8,000, that potential future loss of earnings and pension was to be reflected by lump sum awards of £15,000 and £1,100 respectively, and that a services award of £1,000 was appropriate; and decree pronounced accordingly.

TAGGART v. SHELL (UK) LTD 1996 S.L.T. 795, Judge not specified, OH.

6885. Personal injuries or death–measure of damages–hand–wrist–elbow–ankle

A 51-year-old shopkeeper and his 45 year old wife suffered injuries in a road accident. The husband's injuries were to his right hand, wrist and elbow. His symptoms remained constant from about six months after the accident. He had restricted movement of his right elbow and some aching discomfort in his arm, made worse by weather and by use. His wife's injuries involved a flake fracture in the ankle. She too experienced constant symptoms with no improvement from about six months after the accident. Her ankle swelled each day and restricted her ability to work.

Held, that solatium was properly valued at £5,000 for the husband and at £6,500 for the wife and that the pursuers were entitled to damages for the reduction in the profits of their business, assessed by comparison with the similar period of the previous year for the first few months and by a lump sum thereafter; and decree pronounced accordingly.

TWEEDY v. NEWBOULT 1996 S.L.T. 2, Judge not specified, OH.

6886. Personal injuries or death–measure of damages–head

Held, that solatium of £2,000 should be awarded to a child aged two who had sustained skull fractures but who, on examination one month after the accident, had no adverse symptoms and was unlikely to have any deficit as a result of the injury.

MOONEY v. CITY OF GLASGOW DC 1996 S.C.L.R. 360, Judge not specified, Sh Ct.

6887. Personal injuries or death–measure of damages–head

A sued his former employer, R, after sustaining a head injury requiring some stitches while carrying out pointing on the external brickwork of R's dwellinghouse on June 3, 1991. There was dispute as to whether post traumatic neurosis suffered by A was attributable to the accident.

Held, as to damages, that the most credible expert evidence showed that for three years after the accident A genuinely suffered symptoms of memory loss, headache, nausea, depression and aggression. The problems stimulated by marital and drink problems had disappeared or been overtaken by those by August 1994. Since there was a material disruption to A's life, solatium would have been £7,500, with interest at half the legal rate until August 1994 and at the full rate thereafter; that since A was earning about £160 per week at the time of the accident, and allowing for inflation over the three year period but deducting 50 per cent as A's employment was irregular, £12,750 would have been awarded for past wage loss, which would have been rounded up to £13,500 to reflect the last few months of the relevant period, with interest as above.

RUINE v. ROGER 1996 S.C.L.R. 353, Lord Johnston, OH.

6888. Personal injuries or death–measure of damages–head

A 33 year old railway worker was injured in a road accident. He sustained a compound fracture of the skull, a compression fracture of the first lumbar vertebra, a cracked left fibula and cuts and bruises. The skull fracture involved no brain damage but did lead to headaches and permanent loss of the senses of taste and smell. The other injuries healed and had no continuing effect.

Held, that solatium was properly valued at £18,000.

THOMSON v. BRITISH RAILWAYS BOARD 1996 S.L.T. 317, Judge not specified, OH.

6889. Personal injuries or death–measure of damages–hernia

A 56 year old nurse suffered an incisional hernia at the site of a previous abdominal operation. The hernia would, even without the accident, have occurred within about nine months. The repair to the hernia was complicated by wound infection.

Held, that solatium was properly valued at £5,500.

GRAY v. LANARKSHIRE HEALTH BOARD 1996 S.L.T. 390, Judge not specified, OH.

6890. Personal injuries or death–measure of damages–interest–whether reason to restrict interest on damages

Damages were sought for medical negligence alleged to have occurred shortly after the birth of a child in 1978.

Held, that, absolvitor was granted. The quantification of damages had been agreed apart from the question of interest. The pursuer sought interest on past solatium at one-half the court rate from time to time from the allegedly negligent event. The defenders contended that any award should be restricted to 2 per cent per annum in line with English decisions. Opinion, that the longstanding Scottish practice would have been followed of awarding interest on past solatium at one-half of the court rate as it had been from time to time from the date of the event in February 1978.

PURRYAG v. GREATER GLASGOW HEALTH BOARD 1996 S.L.T. 794, Judge not specified, OH.

6891. Personal injuries or death–measure of damages–jury awards–whether "excessive"

[Court of Session Act 1988 (c.36) s.29.]

In an action for damages a jury awarded C substantial damages for injury against KLDC. KLDC sought a new trial under the Court of Session Act 1988 s.29 on the grounds that the damages awarded for solatium were excessive.

Held: Motion for new trial refused. Whilst the sums awarded in the present case were excessive when compared with recent awards by judges in similar cases, where the award was made by a jury the court had to be satisfied that it was so extravagant as to cause the defenders gross injustice. A broad approach had to be adopted. The court took the view that the so called working rule, considered in a number of cases culminating in *Girvan v. Inverness Farmers Dairy* 1995 S.L.T. 735, [1994] C.L.Y. 5762, that a jury award should not be interfered with unless it was twice as large as a reasonable jury could be expected to award was no more than a rough guide as to what was excessive.

CURRIE v. KILMARNOCK AND LOUDOUN DC 1996 S.L.T. 481, Lord Hope, Lord President, IH.

6892. Personal injuries or death–measure of damages–knee

C, aged 36 at proof, raised an action against A seeking damages for an injury to his right knee which he suffered during the course of his employment with A on June 22, 1993. C, a rigger on an oil rig, was erecting protective sheeting on scaffolding when he stepped back on to a short section of scaffolding tubing which was lying on the surface where he was working. C fell forward and banged his right knee against horizontal safety rails, causing immediate sharp pain in his right knee. C reported for work for the remainder of his tour of duty which ended on June 28. Thereafter, C returned to work at various points until the end of January 1994 when he was made redundant by A. C had been unable to return to his former work as a rigger during that time since he could not climb, but undertook lighter duties, and had had to be signed off his tour of duty early on two occasions due to the injury. C argued that a chondral lesion over the medial facet of the patella, diagnosed in March 1995, had developed as a result of the injury. A argued that, although C had suffered a soft tissue injury in the accident in June 1993, the lesion was caused by C's fall from a ladder on October 20, 1994.

Held, decree granted. On the medical evidence led on behalf of both C and A, the lesion condition could not be attributed to the fall in June 1993. In any event C was unlikely to suffer arthritic changes in the knee joint in the future and was expected to make a full recovery fairly quickly. Damages would be awarded on the basis that C had experienced considerable sharp, though intermittent, pain in his knee over a period of seven months. Solatium of £2,500 was appropriate, with agreed wage loss of £3,250. Opinion, that in respect of the period from February 1, 1994 to the date of the proof, wage loss would have been assessed on the basis that C would have worked 75 per cent. of the time, in view of employment conditions in the industry.

COULSON v. AMEC OFFSHORE DEVELOPMENTS 1996 S.C.L.R. 35, Judge not specified, OH.

6893. Personal injuries or death–measure of damages–knee

A 37 year old civil servant suffered injuries in a car collision, the main injury being to his left knee. Although he had recovered well, his knee was likely to deteriorate over the period of five to 10 years from the proof. This deterioration could lead to restriction in his activities making it difficult for him to continue in his employment or find alternative employment. He earned about £12,000 net a year.

Held, that the appropriate award to reflect his disadvantage in the labour market was £4,000; and decree pronounced accordingly.

WALLEDGE v. BROWN 1996 S.L.T. 95, Judge not specified, OH.

6894. Personal injuries or death–measure of damages–leg

A 43 year old maintenance electrician sustained serious crush injuries to his pelvis and legs. The injuries left him with permanent incapacity from low back pain. He was also rendered impotent and, to a large extent, incontinent of urine. There was a limited possibility of future employment.

Held, that solatium was properly valued at £32,500; that wage loss to date and, using a multiplier of 7.5 years, for the future, was appropriate; that services rendered by the pursuer's wife were properly assessed at £500 and that the loss of his services in maintaining the house and tending the garden were properly assessed at £750; and decree pronounced accordingly.

McGARRIGLE v. BABCOCK ENERGY 1996 S.L.T. 471, Judge not specified, OH.

6895. Personal injuries or death–measure of damages–loss of earnings–deduction of benefits

[Administration of Justice Act 1982 (c.53) s.10.]

L sought damages from his employers (B) in respect of injuries sustained as a result of an accident at work in November 1992, since when L had been absent from work. Following the accident L received payments from B of £12,663.96 per annum under a long term disability plan, which was funded by an insurance policy arranged by B with an insurance company (S). Although the policy provided for specific benefits for L, as an insured "member", the premiums were paid by B and L had no right to claim against S under the policy. The payments would continue until L returned to work or his normal retirement date. B argued that (1) given that the payments came directly from B, were related to L's previous salary, and were subject to income tax and national insurance, that provision of the plan had been part of L's remuneration package, and that the premiums had been a taxable benefit, the payments had to be regarded as part of L's remuneration or earnings and, therefore, fell to be deducted in terms of s.10(i) of the 1982 Act from any loss of earnings suffered by L; and (2) alternatively, the payments were to be regarded as benevolent payments by B, as the responsible person, and were to be deducted in terms of s.10(iv); and that not to take the payments into account would result in L being compensated twice over by B, which was unjust. L argued that, given that the level of payments depended in part on L's membership of a pension scheme, to which L contributed, and that the payments after the accident depended on provision made before it, whereas s.10(i) was concerned only with payments in respect of post-accident employment, the payments were to be regarded as a benefit and not earnings; the principle that sums received from insurance policies were excluded did not depend on who had paid the premiums, and in arranging and paying for the policy B was only doing what L might have done himself, and, accordingly, the payments were to be excluded in the calculation of damages in terms of s.10(a).

Held, B's averments anent the payments excluded from probation. Section 10 was sufficiently exhaustive to cover L's situation and the matter could not be regulated by the common law. Accordingly, any discussion of principle could only be as an aid to construction of the section. Given that L was entitled to the payments from B in terms of his employment contract, the payments could not be benevolent in terms of s.10(f) or (iv) and, for the reasons given by L, the payments were to be excluded as benefits coming under s.10(a).

LEWICKI v. BROWN & ROOT WIMPEY HIGHLAND FABRICATORS LTD 1995 S.C.L.R. 996, Judge not specified, OH.

6896. Personal injuries or death–measure of damages–loss of earnings–deduction of benefits

[Administration of Justice Act 1982 (c. 53), s.10(a), s.10(i).]

In an action where L sought damages for injury sustained while in B's employ, B reclaimed the decision to exclude B's averments from proof to the effect that sums received by L under B's "long term disability plan" fell to be deducted from L's alleged loss of earnings. B accepted that the payments were not excluded as being of a benevolent nature within s.10(iv), but argued that in terms of s.10(i) the payments fell to be deducted as they were "remuneration of earnings" from L's employment. The payments were made by B under the contract of employment while L was absent due to disability and were dependent on the continuation of L's employment with B. Payment was linked to L's salary, being 75 per cent. of salary under deduction of the single state invalidity benefit. The payments were made under deduction of tax and national insurance and were distinguishable from private insurance arranged by an employee. B should not be penalised for making arrangements with an insurance company. Having regard to the nature of the payments rather than their source, the payments should be treated as sick pay. The underlying principle was of compensation *Parry v. Cleaver* [1970] A.C. 1, [1969] C.L.Y. 906; *Smoker v. London Fire and Civil Defence Authority* [1991] A.C. 502, [1991] C.L.Y. 1327. It was not as if L was being punished for being prudent. L argued that the plan was a benefit as a counterpart of services required to be performed by L in the contract of employment. In any event L had also contributed in that the percentage payable was dependent on whether or not L contributed to the pension scheme. The payment was not sickness pay but a contractual benefit and was thus excluded. Section 10 had not really altered the common law. There was no difference between the situation where L had made the payments and where they had been made for L. It would be unjust to effect a situation whereby a wrongdoer, who might not be the employer, should be entitled to deduct such payments from any claim the injured party might have against that wrongdoer. B was simply passing on to L as a benefit what had been payable to B by the insurers.

Held, reclaiming motion refused subject to exclusion of certain further averments of B's from probation. L's arguments were preferred and *Parry* and *Smoker*, applied. The payments were by nature payments of a contractual pension or benefit rather than remuneration or earnings. Per the Lord Justice-Clerk (Ross) and Lord McCluskey: s.10(a) and s.10(i) were mutually exclusive. Per Lord McCluskey: the concept of remuneration or earnings was not compatible with a payment which was contingent on disability. Per Lord Osborne: the differences in the statutory language were such that the taxation of the payments as income gave rise to no particular inference as to whether they fell within s.10(i).

LEWICKI v. BROWN & ROOT WIMPEY HIGHLAND FABRICATORS LTD 1996 S.C.L.R. 680, Lord Ross, L.J.C., IH.

6897. Personal injuries or death–measure of damages–multiple injuries

S raised an action against W and B in respect of injuries sustained by him on May 13, 1992 while he was working in W's employment as a forklift driver. S suffered a broken cheekbone and broken jaw, lacerations to his neck, a fracture to his left rib and a fracture of the anterior lower border of his second cervical vertebra. He required immediate surgery and further surgery later to reconstruct damaged facial bones. He still had an intermittent swelling in his cheek and was likely to require further surgery. He received psychiatric treatment for post-traumatic stress disorder, which had now cleared.

Held, decree granted against W; B assoilzied. Solatium of £10,000 was appropriate for the period of initial hospitalisation and treatment. The risk of further surgery was assessed at £2,500 and psychiatric damage at £5,000. Interest would run on £15,000. Parties were agreed on £4,000 inclusive of interest for loss of earnings and on £1,500 inclusive of interest for services.

WALTON v. WILKIE-HOOKE 1996 S.C.L.R. 759, Judge not specified, OH.

6898. Personal injuries or death–measure of damages–psychiatric damage

Held, that where a child aged three years and four months suffered a personality change from being peaceful and pleasant to being aggressive as a result of falling 15 feet from the veranda of a house to the ground below, solatium of £4,500 was appropriate.

McCANN v. CITY OF GLASGOW DC 1996 S.C.L.R. 772, Judge not specified, Sh Ct.

6899. Personal injuries or death–measure of damages–respiratory organs

A man, aged 55 at the date of the proof, who had worked as an insulator with asbestos as a young man but who had been unable to work since the age of 47 because of unrelated chronic obstructive airways disease and emphysema, was found to be suffering from some very early fibrotic changes which were noted shortly before the proof. They were held to be indicative of asbestosis. This would result in a few years' reduction in his lifespan. He also had a 2 per cent risk of developing mesothelioma and a 10 per cent risk of developing lung cancer.

Held, that solatium was properly valued at £8,000 and the additional services to be rendered to the pursuer over the remainder of his life resulting from the asbestosis were adequately recognised by an award of £4,000; and decree pronounced accordingly.

McCANCE v. NEWALLS INSULATION LTD 1996 S.L.T. 80, Judge not specified, OH.

6900. Personal injuries or death–measure of damages–scars

A prisoner sued the Secretary of State for Scotland for damages after he had been stabbed by another inmate. Opinion, that solatium would have been assessed at £5,000 having regard to the multiple stab wounds and unsightly scars.

HAMILTON v. SECRETARY OF STATE FOR SCOTLAND 1996 S.C.L.R. 773, Judge not specified, OH.

6901. Personal injuries or death–measure of damages–severe brain damage

A 12 year old boy was seriously injured in a road accident. He had a very severe brain injury involving loss of brain tissue. He was in hospital for more than six months. He had marked physical disabilities including a gross involuntary tremor of all limbs. He also suffered marked intellectual disabilities including limited capacity to concentrate. Damages were sought for solatium, housing costs, special aids and equipment for his needs and extra costs attributable to his disabilities, the cost of caring in the past and for the future and loss of earnings.

Held, that solatium was properly assessed at £70,000, that there was no reason for an award for the cost of housing since that would have to be provided from his earnings in any event, that costs such as the cost of travel by private transport, additional heating, clothing and laundry costs, wear and tear and outlays on a computer and other aids properly amounted to £43,080; that care to date, provided by his parents, was properly assessed at £60,000 and for the future was assessed at £24,000 for care to be supplied by his parents for the next five years and thereafter by use of a multiplicand of £13,100 and a multiplier of 14 years; that loss of earnings was reasonably valued by a lump sum of £15,000 to date and a multiplier of 12 years applied to the agreed multiplicand of £9,734 for the future; and decree pronounced accordingly subject to a 50 per cent reduction in respect of contributory negligence.

O'CONNOR v. MATTHEWS 1996 S.L.T. 408, Judge not specified, OH.

6902. Personal injuries or death–measure of damages–severe brain damage

A 23 year old man (the ward) sustained brain injury when his head was struck in a road accident in 1986. The injury resulted in an altered personality, a decline in his intellectual ability, loss of insight, impaired judgment and some difficulty with short-term memory and speech. There was a slight risk of epilepsy. His condition was permanent and the accident rendered him unemployable. Prior to the accident he had not had steady employment but despite an earlier unstable social and family background, he had become closely involved in voluntary work in the community. After proof the Lord Ordinary awarded, *inter alia*, the sum of £25,000 in respect of loss of employability. The curator bonis reclaimed on the basis that it was more appropriate in the ward's circumstances for an award to be made on the basis of loss of earnings rather than loss of employability. He argued that the evidence showed that his record of voluntary work, the attitude and initiative which he had by then adopted, and the prospect of undertaking training, were such that he would have taken up employment and been successful therein. The respondent argued that the prospects for the future were so speculative that a loss of employability award was the most appropriate one.

Held, that (1) the evidence did not justify the conclusion that the ward's future, but for the accident, was so speculative as to make it appropriate merely to make an award for loss of employability; (2) on the evidence, the probability had been established that the ward would have obtained employment within a relatively short period of the accident and probably would have been in employment at the date of the proof, and hence the award should be one for loss of earnings and (3) in the circumstances it was reasonable to allow £20,000 in respect of past wage loss and £80,000 in respect of future wage loss; and £100,000 substituted as the element in the award in respect of employment.

ROBERTSON'S CURATOR BONIS v. ANDERSON 1996 S.L.T. 828, Judge not specified, Ex Div.

6903. Personal injuries or death–measure of damages–whiplash type injury

P, a former taxi driver, sued K, a bus company, for damages for personal injury sustained on January 27, 1991 when P's taxi was struck from behind by one of K's buses. Liability was not disputed. P averred that he sustained an injury resulting in pain in his neck, radiating into his right shoulder, with a tingling sensation down his right arm. The pain also radiated into the back of his head on movement and was a whiplash type injury. P continued to suffer from pain, dizzy spells and disturbed sleep. Since the accident P had been unable to return to work as a taxi driver and, since his working experience was in exclusively driving related functions, P had been unable to obtain work. Prior to the accident P was very fit, pursuing hobbies such as a swimming, karate and weightlifting, none of which he was now able to do. P, aged 30 at the time of the accident, had suffered injuries to his neck when he was involved in a road traffic accident in 1988 as a result of which he had been prescribed a soft collar and painkillers, and in July 1990 when he slipped on a wet linoleum floor and sustained an injury which was treated similarly. P attended his GP in connection with the latter injury on a number of occasions until early January 1991. K's expert medical evidence was that P's symptoms were caused by the fall in 1990 and that P was fit to return to work by June 1991.

Held, decree granted, that P had recovered from the 1990 injury by the time of the accident in January 1991 and P's current problems were attributable to that later accident. The accident had disrupted P's existence and on the expert evidence it was unlikely that any treatment of P's symptoms would alter the situation. On solatium, £11,000 was reasonable, with interest at half the judicial rate on two thirds of the amount (£1,837). On past wage loss, the evidence disclosed a net profit over the last 12-month period of £12,000 and, since P had been out of work for 4.3 years, the total amounted to £52,332 with interest (reduced by £129 in respect of state benefits of £516) of £12,981. On future wage loss, given that P was unqualified for any form of work other than driving and suffered from dyslexia, he was unlikely to obtain any other employment and the appropriate multiplier was 12, discounted to 10 to take account of the remote possibility of some form of work becoming available. The appropriate multiplicand was £12,600, being the figure of £12,000 increased by 5 per cent as provision for increases in income. Total award, £204,150.

PATERSON v. KELVIN CENTRAL BUSES 1996 S.C.L.R. 358, Judge not specified, OH.

6904. Personal injuries or death–measure of damages–wrist

B, a catering assistant aged 39 at proof, sued her employers, W, after she suffered a colles fracture of her wrist when she fell on May 30, 1993. Liability was admitted. B's wrist was in plaster for six weeks and was painful. B underwent physiotherapy but her wrist remained sore and stiff. B returned to light duties in September 1993 but was unable to cope with wrapping cutlery or making sandwiches due to the pain. Subsequent investigation found that B had suffered a radial shortening requiring a corrective osteotomy. B's wrist was in plaster for a further six weeks;

further physiotherapy relieved some of the pain and restriction of movement. B would have been fit to return to her pre-accident work at the end of 1994, but was retired on health grounds in October 1994. B now had disabling pain in her upper arm which B claimed was first experienced in September 1993. Symptoms were not reported by B until April 1994 although the physiotherapy records did mention secondary problems to the fracture. At proof B led evidence that the upper arm symptoms were as a result of the combined prolonged immobilisation, B's distress and emotional disturbance at her loss of job, B's dependence on others and the treatment. W argued that future earnings loss should be awarded as a lump sum rather than using a multiplier.

Held, that there were no grounds for departing from the multiplier method. On permanent disability a multiplier of 12 would be appropriate; where B wanted to work again and would do what she could to achieve that, but there was a significant risk that treatment would be unsuccessful, a multiplier of seven to a multiplicand of £2,680 was appropriate. Solatium and past wage loss were agreed at £5,500 and £5,200 respectively, including interest. Individual awards of £277.50 (including interest) to each of B's husband and sister and two sons was appropriate in respect of past services of a domestic nature; a composite award of £1,000 was appropriate for the future. Total award, £31,750.

BARKER v. WEST LOTHIAN NATIONAL HEALTH SERVICE TRUST 1996 S.C.L.R. 768, Judge not specified, OH.

6905. Personal injuries or death–necessary services rendered by relative–relative a defender in the action

[Administration of Justice Act 1982 (c.53) s.8.]

A person who has sustained personal injuries may, under the Administration of Justice Act 1982 s.8, recover from the wrongdoer damages representing reasonable remuneration for any necessary services rendered to the injured person by a relative as a consequence of the injury. The injured person has a duty to account to the relative for damages recovered on this ground. A wife sued her husband and a roads authority for damages in respect of injuries suffered when her husband's car skidded on an icy road. The wife's claim included a claim for necessary services rendered to her by her husband and by their children.

Held, that it was incompetent for the wife to recover from her husband remuneration in respect of his own services, but that it was not possible before proof to work out what the rights of parties would be were the roads authority also found liable; and proof before answer allowed, *Hunt v. Severs* [1994] 2 A.C. 350, [1994] C.L.Y. 1530 followed.

KOZIKOWSKA v. KOZIKOWSKI 1996 S.L.T. 386, Judge not specified, OH.

6906. Articles

Excess of damages and civil jury trial: the implications of Currie and Girvan *(Mark Lazarowicz)*: S.L.T. 1996, 28, 251-256. (Differing approaches to test for determining whether new trial is to be allowed on ground of excess or inadequacy of damages awarded by jury).

Juries–quantum of damages.: Rep. B. 1996, 8(Mar), 5-6. (Juries require guidance as to levels of damages awards particularly in view of some recent excessive awards).

Loss of earnings–what about the self employed? *(Gordon Junor)*: Rep. B. 1996, 12(Nov), 6-8. (Recovery of damages for loss of earnings as result of personal injuries by self employed partners).

DEFAMATION

6907. Articles

The Defamation Act 1996: much ado about not very much *(Kenneth McK. Norrie)*: S.L.T. 1996, 32, 311-314. (Effect of changes in law introduced by 1996 Act with particular reference to Scotland).

The Defamation Bill 1996 *(Alistair J. Bonnington)*: J.L.S.S. 1996, 41 (3), 102-104. (Provisions applying throughout UK and those not extending to Scotland).

The Defamation Bill 1996 *(Gillian A. Wade)*: Rep. B. 1996, 9(May), 2-3. (Application to Scotland of proposals to implement Neill Report on distributors' liability, Internet libel and offers of amends and question whether they are required given the flexibility of existing law).

DIVORCE AND CONSISTORIAL CAUSES

6908. Aliment–interim aliment

Observed, in a sheriff court action of divorce, that a claim for interim aliment should not be tagged onto a claim for payment of a periodical allowance but should be the subject of a separate case and should be supported by a distinct and appropriate plea in law.

KERR v. KERR 1995 S.C.L.R. 1130, Judge not specified, Sh Ct.

6909. Decrees–sheriff court practice–undefended decree of divorce–appeal after extract of decree–competency

Held, that in an action of divorce which had proceeded as undefended as a result of the non-appearance of the defenders' solicitor following a failure to advise him of the late making of opposition to a motion to sist for legal aid, that an appeal against the subsequent decree of divorce was incompetent after it had been extracted.

BROWN v. BROWN 1996 S.C.L.R. 527, Judge not specified, Sh Ct.

6910. Financial provision on divorce–matrimonial property–transfer of matrimonial home–pension rights

[Family Law (Scotland) Act 1985 (c.37) s.8(2) (b), s.10(5), s.6(d).]

H appealed against the sheriff's decision in W's divorce action 1994 S.L.T. (Sh.Ct.) 43 to order transfer to her of H's one half share in the matrimonial home and to award W a periodical allowance of £30 a week. H argued that since, apart from the home and contents, the only relevant asset was the capital value of his pension scheme (£100,800 out of matrimonial property of £158,995), the order was manifestly unfair to H, and not reasonable in terms of s.8(2) (b) of the 1985 Act, where he was already dependent on his pension, which should have been regarded purely as income: by s.10(6) (d) the sheriff ought to have had regard to its nature and use. The matrimonial home should have been sold to permit the proceeds to be divided between H and W. In any event, the award of periodical allowance failed to take account of the fact that H would be able to live in the house rent free, or could sell it and receive an income from the proceeds.

Held, appeal refused, that (1) having regard to s.10(5) of the 1985 Act, the sheriff was fully entitled to treat the pension scheme as part of the matrimonial property. The transfer order left W with less than half the value of the whole property, whether or not the widow's pension element was included in the valuation (an issue on which H originally also appealed the sheriff's decision but now conceded that the point was therefore academic), and there was nothing unreasonable in the sheriff's decision and (2) the sheriff had taken H's points into consideration and applied the correct statutory tests. H's net income was £176 as against W's £58.44, and the sheriff had taken account of H's need to rent other accommodation as well as the fact that if W sold the house, she would require to pay rent from the income on the proceeds. The amount fixed was reasonable.

GRIBB v. GRIBB 1995 S.C.L.R. 1007, Judge not specified, IH.

6911. Financial provision on divorce–matrimonial property–transfer of matrimonial home–unequal division

In a divorce action the matrimonial property was valued at £260,000, of which the matrimonial home, the title to which was in joint names, was valued at £154,000 net. The wife wished to continue to live in the former matrimonial home with the two children of the marriage, aged 13 and eight. The husband proposed that the house should be sold and the proceeds divided.

Held, that the husband's share of the home should be transferred to the wife and that she be ordered to grant a standard security over it in favour of the husband for £24,000, payable in the event of the wife disposing of the house or on the younger child's eighteenth birthday, whichever occurred first.

MURLEY v. MURLEY 1995 S.C.L.R. 1138, Judge not specified, OH.

6912. Financial provision on divorce–matrimonial property–unequal division–economic disadvantage

[Family Law (Scotland) Act 1985 (c.37) s.9(1)(b).]

Held, in an action of divorce, that the fact that throughout the marriage the husband had alienated his children from a previous marriage did not constitute "economic disadvantage" on the part of the wife such as would entitle her to more than half the matrimonial property on divorce.

HUNTER v. HUNTER 1996 S.C.L.R. 329, Judge not specified, Sh Ct.

6913. Financial provision on divorce–matrimonial property–valuation

[Family Law (Scotland) Act 1985 (c.37) s.10(1), (2) and (6)(b).]

The Family Law (Scotland) Act 1985 s.10(1) provides that in applying the principle of fair sharing of the matrimonial property, the net value of the property "shall be taken to be shared fairly between the parties to the marriage when it is shared equally or in such other proportions as are justified by special circumstances". By subs.(6)(b) "special circumstances" may include the source of the funds or assets used to acquire any of the matrimonial property where these were not derived from the income or efforts of the parties during the marriage. In an action of divorce the wife sought payment of a capital sum. The parties were married on September 26, 1987 and separated on December 28, 1988. The only matrimonial property to be taken into account was the house in which the parties had been living, which the husband had purchased nine days before the marriage at the discounted price of £11,960, the capital value being £25,500. The husband secured a mortgage of £15,000. By the date of separation the market value of the house was £29,000. After proof the sheriff assessed the net value of the matrimonial property at the relevant date at £14,000 and awarded a capital sum of £5,000, which was the sum sued for. The husband appealed, arguing that in terms of the Family Law (Scotland) Act 1985 s.10(6)(b), he had contributed a special and personal asset to the purchase of the matrimonial home in the form of his entitlement to a discount, which ought to have been taken into account to reduce the value of the house, when the parties separated, by 60 per cent. He also argued that in determining the gross value of the house at the relevant date, account should have been taken of the fact that the full market value would not have accrued to him at that date because of the clawback provision in favour of the local authority. These arguments had not been presented to the sheriff.

Held, that (1) an appeal court was entitled to entertain a new argument where that was necessary in order to do justice between the parties, and as the result of giving effect to the new arguments would reduce the sum awarded by more than half, the arguments would be considered; (2) "special circumstances" in s.10(1) of the 1985 Act did not qualify the way in which the net value of the matrimonial property was to be determined and, further, that an entitlement to a discount on the purchase of a particular thing was not an asset; but (3) the clawback provision in favour of the local authority ought to result in a reduction in the capital sum awarded; and appeal allowed to the extent of reducing the capital sum to £2,333.

LAWSON v. LAWSON 1996 S.L.T. (Sh. Ct.) 83, Judge not specified, Sh Ct.

6914. Financial provision on divorce–pension rights–method of valuation–husband's pension rights relating to widow's pension

[Family Law (Scotland) Act 1985 (c.37) s.9(1)(a), s.6(a), s.10(5).]

In an action of divorce the wife sought transfer to her of the husband's interest in the matrimonial home. The defender had rights to two pensions which, net of tax to include spouse's benefits, were valued at £12,300 and £11,500 respectively. On a continuing service basis net of tax excluding spouse's benefits, they were valued at £10,800 and £9,400 respectively. The wife argued that the widow's benefits should be included in valuing the husband's pensions.

Held, that (1) there was no reason for defining the matrimonial property so as to exclude the wife's interest in the schemes in her capacity as a prospective widow; (2) where the pursuer would have the care of the parties' child after divorce, the house was necessary for the child's welfare, the defender had alternative accommodation and the pursuer would receive no payment from the pension rights or otherwise, special circumstances existed justifying an unequal division of matrimonial property in the pursuer's favour; and pension schemes valued accordingly, *Brooks v. Brooks* 1993 S.L.T. 184, [1993] C.L.Y. 5227, *Bannon v. Bannon* 1993 S.L.T. 99, [1993] C.L.Y. 5226 and *Welsh v. Welsh* 1994 S.L.T. 828, [1994] C.L.Y. 5782, not followed.

MURPHY v. MURPHY 1996 S.L.T. (Sh. Ct.) 91, Judge not specified, Sh Ct.

6915. Financial provision on divorce–pensions

DIVORCE ETC (PENSIONS) (SCOTLAND) REGULATIONS 1996, SI 1996 1901 (S.153); made under the Family Law (Scotland) Act 1985 s.10, s.12A. In force: August 19, 1996; £1.55.

These Regulations relate to the treatment on divorce of any pension rights which either party to the marriage may have. They provide for the calculation and verification of pension benefits, for the provision of information from trustees or managers, for notices in respect of changes in circumstances and for the recovery of administrative expenses incurred by trustees or managers. Divorce actions commenced before August 19, 1996 are not affected by these Regulations.

6916. Financial provision on divorce–periodical allowance–competency–duration and amount

[Family Law (Scotland) Act 1985 (c.37) s.9.]

Section 9(1)(e) of the Family Law (Scotland) Act 1985 provides that "a party who at the time of the divorce seems likely to suffer serious financial hardship as a result of the divorce should be awarded such financial provision as is reasonable to relieve him of hardship over a reasonable period". A 51 year old woman, after 27 years of marriage during which she had been in employment for short periods only, separated from her Norwegian husband and returned to Scotland. Her health was poor. She had poor hearing and chronic high blood pressure and fibrositis. She was also suffering from depression which, on its own, would render her unfit for employment over the next two years. She received no aliment and was wholly reliant on state benefit. Her husband earned about £74,000 net of tax per year and had necessary annual expenditure of, he said, £72,000. On the evidence it was held that there were areas where his expenditure could be reduced by extending the period over which loan repayments could be made. There was also a likelihood of further income by way of bonus payments. His potential excess of income over expenditure was assessed by the Lord Ordinary at £12,000 per year. It was contended for the wife that the whole of that sum should be awarded to her as periodical allowance, without limit of time. It was contended for the husband; (a) that it was incompetent for an award of periodical allowance to be made because no aliment had been paid by the husband following the separation, and therefore hardship suffered was not "as a result of the divorce" in terms of s.9(1)(e), and (b) that any award made should be limited in time.

Held, that (1) the loss of the right to aliment on divorce would itself be a hardship brought about by the divorce rather than by the separation, and that the application for periodical allowance was accordingly competent and (2) this was clearly a case in which an award unlimited in time would be appropriate; and periodical allowance at the rate of £1,000 per month without limit of time awarded.

HAUGHAN v. HAUGHAN 1996 S.L.T. 321, Judge not specified, OH.

6917. Financial provision on divorce–reciprocal enforcement of maintenance orders

ACT OF SEDERUNT (RECIPROCAL ENFORCEMENT OF MAINTENANCE ORDERS) (UNITED STATES OF AMERICA) 1995, SI 1995 3345 (S.247); made under the Sheriff Courts (Scotland) Act 1971 s.32; the Maintenance Orders (Reciprocal Enforcement) Act 1972 s.19; and the Court of Session Act 1988 s.5. In force: January 8, 1996; £1.10.

This Act of Sederunt makes provision for the procedure to be followed in relation to the transmission of maintenance orders made by the Court of Session or sheriff court to, and registration in the sheriff court of maintenance orders made by, courts in the states of the USA specified in the Reciprocal Enforcement of Maintenance Orders (United States of America) Order 1995 Sch.1.

6918. Matrimonial home–occupancy rights–cohabiting couple–interim order–competency

[Matrimonial Homes (Family Protection) (Scotland) Act 1981 (c.59) s.18(1); Act of Sederunt (Ordinary Cause Rules) 1993 (SI 1993 1956) r.33.67(1), r.37.69(1).]

Held, that (1) a non-entitled partner had no existing occupancy rights in a house belonging to the entitled partner but rather a right to apply to the court for a grant of such rights; (2) it was not competent for the court to grant occupancy rights to a non-entitled partner ad interim, and (3) to enable the non-entitled partner to be in a position to seek a grant of occupancy rights as soon as possible, the period of notice should be reduced to six days and the period until the options hearing should be reduced from 10 to six weeks.

SMITH-MILNE v. GAMMACK 1995 S.C.L.R. 1058, Judge not specified, Sh Ct.

6919. Articles

Pensions and divorce: Part 1 *(Sandra Eden)*: Fam. L.B. 1996, 22(Jul), 3-5. (Changes to Scots law on computation of and arrangements for pension rights following divorce).

Pensions and divorce: Part 2 *(Sandra Eden)*: Fam. L.B. 1996, 23(Sep), 3-5. (Valuation of pension rights on divorce).

Recent changes in valuation and division of pensions on divorce. *(Alastair Bissett-Johnson)*: S.L.T. 1996, 31, 295-299. (Reforms to valuation and division of pensions under SI 1996 1901 in force August 19, 1996 suggest confusion as to whether pension is seen as income stream or capital asset).

Rights on divorce of non-working wife with high earning husband. *(Douglas Kinloch)*: Fam. L.B. 1996, 19(Jan), 2-3. (Compensation for economic disadvantages suffered by non working wife).

Survivorship destinations and the family home *(James Hotchkis)*: Fam. L.B.1996, 20(Mar), 2-3. (Implications for separating couples where title to home contains survivorship destination).

EDUCATION

6920. Education (Scotland) Act 1996 (c.43)

An Act to provide for the establishment of a body corporate to be known as the Scottish Qualifications Authority; to provide for the transfer of functions, property, rights, liabilities, obligations and staff to that body and for the conferring of other functions on it; to make provision enabling payment of grant to providers of education for children under school age; and to amend certain legislation relating to school education in Scotland.

This Act received Royal Assent on July 18, 1996.

6921. Education (Scotland) Act 1996–Commencement Order

EDUCATION (SCOTLAND) ACT 1996 (COMMENCEMENT) ORDER 1996, SI 1996 2250 (S.182; C.53); made under the Education (Scotland) Act 1996 s.37. In force: bringing into force various provisions of the Act on September 18, 1996; £0.65.

This Order provides for the commencement of certain provisions in the Education (Scotland) Act 1996 on September 18, 1996. In Part I of the Act, which relates to the Scottish Qualifications Authority (SQA), all provisions are commenced other than those conferring substantive functions on SQA. SQA is to be established by order of the Secretary of State on September 18, 1996, but will not take up its substantive functions immediately. The property, rights, liabilities and obligations of the Scottish Examination Board and the Scottish Vocational Education Council will be transferred to SQA as their successor at a future date to be appointed by the Secretary of State, and the provisions conferring substantive functions will be commenced then. Part II (education for children under school age) and Part III (school boards) of the Act are commenced on September 18, 1996. Part IV is also commenced on that date except for certain minor consequential amendments and repeal of the Education (Scotland) Act 1980 s.129.

6922. Education (Student Loans) Act (c.9). See EDUCATION. §2400

6923. Educational endowments

EDUCATIONAL ENDOWMENTS (BORDERS REGION) TRANSFER SCHEME ORDER 1996, SI 1996 308 (S.22); made under the Local Government etc. (Scotland) Act 1994 s.17. In force: April 1, 1996; £1.10.

A Scheme for the transfer, on April 1, 1996, of interests in educational endowments from Borders Regional Council and Berwickshire, Ettrick and Lauderdale, Roxburgh and Tweeddale District Councils, to the new unitary Scottish Borders Council established under the Local Government etc. (Scotland) Act 1994 is made by this Order. Educational endowments consist of heritable or moveable property which is dedicated to charitable educational purposes. Provision is made for the transfer of interests such as the endowment itself, powers in respect to the endowment or a right to payment of money out of an endowment from the Borders Regional Council to the Scottish Borders Council.

6924. Educational endowments

EDUCATIONAL ENDOWMENTS (CENTRAL REGION) TRANSFER SCHEME ORDER 1996, SI 1996 475 (S.40); made under the Local Government etc. (Scotland) Act 1994 s.17. In force: April 1, 1996; £1.55.

Amends Clackmannanshire Educational Trust Scheme 1957, Stirlingshire Educational Trust Scheme 1957. This Order makes a Scheme for the transfer of interests in educational endowments from Central Regional Council and the district councils within Central Region, namely Clackmannan, Falkirk and Stirling District Councils, to the new unitary Clackmannanshire, Falkirk and Stirling Councils established under the Local Government etc. (Scotland) Act 1994. The transfer takes effect on April 1, 1996, the day when the new unitary Councils take up their functions and the existing Regional and District Councils cease to exist.

6925. Educational endowments

EDUCATIONAL ENDOWMENTS (DUMFRIES AND GALLOWAY REGION) TRANSFER SCHEME ORDER 1996, SI 1996 474 (S.39); made under the Local Government etc. (Scotland) Act 1994 s.17. In force: April 1, 1996; £1.10.

This Order makes a Scheme for the transfer of interests in educational endowments from Dumfries and Galloway Regional Council and the district councils within Dumfries and Galloway Region, namely Annandale and Eskdale, Nithsdale, Stewartry and Wigtown District Councils, to the new unitary Dumfries and Galloway Council established under the Local Government etc. (Scotland) Act 1994. The transfer takes effect on April 1, 1996, the day when the new unitary Councils take up their functions and the existing Regional and District Councils cease to exist.

6926. Educational endowments

EDUCATIONAL ENDOWMENTS (FIFE REGION) TRANSFER SCHEME ORDER 1996, SI 1996 306 (S.20); made under the Local Government etc. (Scotland) Act 1994 s.17. In force: April 1, 1996; £1.10.

A Scheme for the transfer, on April 1, 1996, of interests in educational endowments from Fife Regional Council and Dunfermline, Kirkaldy and North East Fife District Councils, to the new unitary Fife Council established under the Local Government etc. (Scotland) Act 1994 is made by this Order. Educational endowments consist of heritable or moveable property which is dedicated to charitable educational purposes. Provision is made for the transfer of interests such as the endowment itself, powers in respect to the endowment or a right to payment of money out of an endowment from Fife Regional Council to Fife Council.

6927. Educational endowments

EDUCATIONAL ENDOWMENTS (GRAMPIAN REGION) TRANSFER SCHEME ORDER 1996, SI 1996 478 (S.42); made under the Local Government etc. (Scotland) Act 1994 s.17. In force: April 1, 1996; £3.70.

This Order makes a Scheme for the transfer of interests in educational endowments from Grampian Regional Council and the district councils within Grampian Region, namely Aberdeen, Banff and Buchan, Gordon, Kincardine and Deeside and Moray District Councils, to the new unitary Aberdeen City, Aberdeenshire and Moray Councils established under the Local Government etc. (Scotland) Act 1994. The transfer takes effect on April 1, 1996, the day when the new unitary Councils take up their functions and the existing Regional and District Councils cease to exist.

6928. Educational endowments

EDUCATIONAL ENDOWMENTS (HIGHLAND REGION) TRANSFER SCHEME ORDER 1996, SI 1996 307 (S.21); made under the Local Government etc. (Scotland) Act 1994 s.17. In force: April 1, 1996; £1.10.

A Scheme for the transfer, on April 1, 1996, of interests in educational endowments from Highland Regional Council and Caithness, Sutherland, Ross and Cromarty, Skye and Lochalsh, Lochaber, Inverness, Badenoch and Strathspey District Councils, to the new unitary Highland Council established under the Local Government etc. (Scotland) Act 1994 is made by this Order. Educational endowments consist of heritable or moveable property which is dedicated to charitable educational purposes. Provision is made for the transfer of interests such as the endowment itself, powers in respect to the endowment or a right to payment of money out of an endowment from Highland Regional Council to Highland Council.

6929. Educational endowments

EDUCATIONAL ENDOWMENTS (LOTHIAN REGION) TRANSFER SCHEME ORDER 1996, SI 1996 630 (S.65); made under the Local Government etc. (Scotland) Act 1994 s.17. In force: April 1, 1996; £2.40.

This Order makes a Scheme for the transfer of interests in educational endowments from Lothian Regional Council and the district councils within Lothian Region, namely Edinburgh, East Lothian, Midlothian and West Lothian District Councils, to the new unitary City of Edinburgh, East Lothian, Midlothian and West Lothian Councils established under the Local Government etc. (Scotland) Act 1994. The transfer takes effect on April 1, 1996, the day when the new unitary Councils take up their functions and the existing Regional and District Councils cease to exist.

6930. Educational endowments

EDUCATIONAL ENDOWMENTS (STRATHCLYDE REGION) TRANSFER SCHEME ORDER 1996, SI 1996 629 (S.64); made under the Local Government etc. (Scotland) Act 1994 s.17. In force: April 1, 1996; £4.15.

Amends Lanarkshire Educational Trust Scheme 1936; Ayrshire Educational Trust Scheme 1936; County of Argyll Educational Trust Scheme, 1960; Renfrewshire Education Trust Scheme 1961; Bute Educational Trust Scheme 1961; Spier's Trust Scheme 1978; Scheme for the Administration of the Strathclyde Schools Orchestra Trust; The Colonel Maclean Trust Scheme 1980; The Glasgow Educational and Marshall Trust Scheme 1936 to 1991. This Order makes a Scheme for the transfer of interests in educational endowments from Strathclyde Regional Council and the district councils within Strathclyde Region to the new unitary councils established under the Local Government etc. (Scotland) Act 1994. The transfer takes effect on April 1, 1996, the day when the new unitary Councils take up their functions and the existing Regional and District Councils cease to exist.

6931. Educational endowments

EDUCATIONAL ENDOWMENTS (TAYSIDE REGION) TRANSFER SCHEME ORDER 1996, SI 1996 477 (S.41); made under the Local Government etc. (Scotland) Act 1994 s.17. In force: April 1, 1996; £2.80.

Amends Angus Education Trust Scheme 1935, Webster and Davidson Mortification for the Blind Scheme 1963, Perth and Kinross Education Trust Scheme 1964, City of Dundee Educational Trust Scheme 1966, Morgan Trust Scheme 1982 and SI 1980 2037. This Order makes a Scheme for the transfer of interests in educational endowments from Tayside Regional Council and the district councils within Tayside Region, namely Angus, City of Dundee and Perth and Kinross District Councils, to the new unitary Angus, City of Dundee and Perth and Kinross Councils established under the Local Government etc. (Scotland) Act 1994. The transfer takes effect on April 1, 1996, the day when the new unitary Councils take up their functions and the existing Regional and District Councils cease to exist.

6932. Educational endowments

SEX DISCRIMINATION (GEOFFREY SIMPSON BEQUEST MODIFICATION) ORDER 1996, SI 1996 1745 (S.144); made under the Sex Discrimination Act 1975 s.79. In force: August 1, 1996; £0.65.

The educational endowment constituted by the Settlement of Geoffrey Simpson dated October 16, 1981, and registered in the Books of Council and Session on August 17, 1982 is modified by this Order.

6933. Further education

COLLEGES OF EDUCATION (LOCAL GOVERNMENT RE-ORGANISATION CONSEQUENTIAL PROVISIONS) (SCOTLAND) ORDER 1996, SI 1996 1971 (S.167); made under the Local Government etc. (Scotland) Act 1994 s.181. In force: September 1, 1996; £1.10.

This Order makes amendments to the Colleges of Education (Scotland) Regulations 1987 (SI 1987 309) which are consequential on local government reorganisation on April 1, 1996.

6934. Further education

COLLEGES OF FURTHER EDUCATION (CHANGES OF NAME) (SCOTLAND) ORDER 1995, SI 1995 2960 (S.213); made under the Further and Higher Education (Scotland) Act 1992 s.3. In force: January 1, 1996; £0.65.

This Order changes the names of Falkirk College of Technology to Falkirk College of Further and Higher Education and the name of Telford College to Edinburgh's Telford College. The names of each board of management are also changed to reflect the new name of the colleges.

6935. Further education

GLASGOW SCHOOL OF ART (SCOTLAND) ORDER OF COUNCIL 1996, SI 1996 120 (S.8); made under the Further and Higher Education (Scotland) Act 1992 s.45, s.60. In force: February 14, 1996; £2.40.

This Order, which replaces the provisions of the Central Institutions (Scotland) Regulations 1988 (SI 1988 1715) as far as they relate to The Glasgow School of Art, makes new provision for the constitution, functions and powers of the Governors of the Glasgow School of Art, as governing body of the school, and the arrangements to be adopted in discharging its functions.

6936. Further education–staff conditions–decision not to apply to future appointments–whether lawful

[Self Governing Schools Etc (Scotland) Act 1989 (c.39) s.67(1); Education (Scotland) Act 1980 (c.44) s.94(1), s.97A(2).]

T, a trade union, sought judicial review of R's decision to apply new conditions of service to teaching staff appointments made after February 1, 1996, which T claimed was inconsistent with an agreement centrally negotiated under the 1980 Act and effective from January 21, 1988. T sought declarator that R was acting illegally et separatim ultra vires, and reduction of R's decision. The agreement was reached under s.94(1) and s.97A(2) of the Education (Scotland) Act 1980; although these had since been repealed, existing agreements subsisted subject to any agreed variations. The settlement had provided for parity of treatment of staff in comparison to colleagues in the university system as it was recognised that staff in certain areas of specialism might be difficult to recruit. R now proposed to alter teaching hours and annual leave. T argued that such conditions would have universal application and thus the decision was open to judicial review, *Watt v. Strathclyde RC* 1992 S.L.T. 324, [1992] C.L.Y. 5704. R argued that the effect of s.67(1) of the 1989 Act was to render the agreement no longer binding in the case of appointments, including renewals or promotions, after the appeal. Furthermore T had no title to make the application concerned as it should have been at the instance of the individuals affected by R's decision, *D & J Nicol v. Dundee Harbour Trustees* 1915 S.C. (H.L.) 7.

Held, declarator and reduction granted, that (1) T had title to sue as a representative body and it was unrealistic to presume that any new staff would accept an offer of employment and then seek to challenge R's decision. T had power to sue where R made an unlawful decision in breach of statutory requirements, and (2) the agreement had been very much concerned with future recruitment and it was a material term of that settlement that the conditions applied to future as well as existing appointments.

EDUCATIONAL INSTITUTE OF SCOTLAND v. ROBERT GORDON UNIVERSITY, *The Times*, July 1, 1996, Lord Milligan, OH.

6937. Grants

EDUCATION (ASSISTED PLACES) (SCOTLAND) AMENDMENT REGULATIONS 1996, SI 1996 1808 (S.150); made under the Education (Scotland) Act 1980 s.75A, s.75B. In force: August 1, 1996; £1.10.

These Regulations amend the Education (Assisted Places) (Scotland) Regulations 1995 (SI 1995 1713) to lower the age limit for children to participate in the scheme and to increase figures used in the calculation of relevant income

6938. Grants

ST. MARY'S MUSIC SCHOOL (AIDED PLACES) AMENDMENT REGULATIONS 1996, SI 1996 1807 (S.149); made under the Education (Scotland) Act 1980 s.73, s.74. In force: August 1, 1996; £1.10.

These Regulations amend the St. Mary's Music School (Aided Places) Regulations 1995 (SI 1995 1712) to amend the amount deducted from income in calculating relevant income, to increase the amounts of relevant income which qualify for remission of fees and charges and for making clothing and travel grants and to increase the amounts of clothing grants, in the aided places scheme.

6939. Grants

STUDENTS' ALLOWANCES (SCOTLAND) REGULATIONS 1996, SI 1996 1754 (S.145); made under the Education (Scotland) Act 1980 s.73, s.74. In force: August 1, 1996; £1.95.

These Regulations consolidate, with only minor and drafting amendments, the Students' Allowances (Scotland) Regulations 1991 (SI 1991 1522) and subsequent amending instruments. They enable the Secretary of State to pay allowances to persons attending courses of education who fulfil certain criteria as to eligibility and prescribe the conditions and requirements subject to which allowances may be paid. The 1991 Regulations continue to apply as regards allowances awarded before their revocation.

6940. Nursery education–grants

GRANTS FOR PRE-SCHOOL EDUCATION (PRESCRIBED CHILDREN) (SCOTLAND) ORDER 1996, SI 1996 3079 (S.236); made under the Education (Scotland) Act 1996 s.23. In force: August 1, 1997; £0.65.

The Education (Scotland) Act 1996 empowers the Secretary of State to make grants to providers of education for children under school age. This Order prescribes the description of children for this purpose as being those under compulsory school age to whom education is provided at any time, on or after the beginning of the school year preceding the school year in which they would first become eligible to attend a public primary school; and before they attend any school other than a nursery school or a nursery class in a primary school.

6941. Nursery education–grants

GRANTS FOR PRE-SCHOOL EDUCATION (SCOTLAND) REGULATIONS 1996, SI 1996 1783 (S.147); made under the Education (Scotland) Act 1980 s.73, s.74. In force: August 1, 1996; £1.10.

These Regulations enable the Secretary of State to pay grants in respect of the provision of pre-school education in the school year 1996/97 in the North Ayrshire, East Ayrshire, East Renfrewshire and parts of Argyll and Bute and Highland local government areas. Grants can be paid to education authorities, managers of schools or other persons approved by the Secretary of State. The areas concerned are ones in which education authorities have chosen to participate in a trial of funding arrangements relating to pre-school education which do not apply in other areas, and which appear to the Secretary of State suitable for such a trial. Grants can also be paid in respect of pre-school education provided at special schools outwith these areas for children whose parent is ordinarily resident in one of these areas.

6942. Nursery education–grants–social security information

GRANTS FOR PRE-SCHOOL EDUCATION (SOCIAL SECURITY INFORMATION) (SCOTLAND) REGULATIONS 1996, SI 1996 3078 (S.235); made under the Education (Scotland) Act 1996 s.26. In force: December 31, 1996; £0.65.

The Education (Scotland) Act 1996 provides for the making of grants to providers of education for children under school age and authorises the Secretary of State to supply to civil servants and others in the Scottish Office, and to those engaged in the exercise of any function relating to the making of these grants, such "social security information" as the person may require for or in connection with the exercise of that function. These Regulations prescribe information relating to a claim for, or the adjudication of a claim for, child benefit as "social security information" for this purpose.

6943. Schools–duty to maintain–scope of statutory duty–enforceability

[Education (Scotland) Act 1980 (c.44) s.19(2).]

Section 19(1) of the Education (Scotland) Act 1980 empowers the Secretary of State to make regulations prescribing standards for the premises and equipment of educational establishments. Section 19(2) imposes on an education authority a duty to secure that the premises and equipment of educational establishments under their control conform to the standards and requirements applicable to that establishment, and in particular their maintenance in such a condition as to conduce to good health and safety. Section 19(3) empowers the Secretary of State to direct that there be compliance with any prescribed standards and imposes a duty on an education authority to give effect to any such directions. A pupil raised an action of reparation against the local education authority in respect of an accident which occurred at school. Her pleadings contained a ground of fault said to arise from a breach by the defenders of a duty imposed by s.19(2) of the 1980 Act. The defenders challenged the relevancy of this averment on the ground that no regulations had been made by the Secretary of State under s.19. The pursuer submitted that the duty under the second part of s.19(2) could exist independently of such regulations. The sheriff allowed a proof before answer on all matters. The defenders appealed.

Held, that the pursuer could not relevantly found on any duty imposed by s.19(2) in the absence of any regulations having been issued under s.19(1); and appeal allowed to the extent of refusing to remit corresponding averments to probation. Opinion, that averments of failure to "maintain" something which, while not in disrepair, was falling behind current standards, would have been allowed to go to probation. Opinion reserved, on whether s.19(2) could be construed as conferring a civil right of action.

JOHANNESON v. LOTHIAN RC 1996 S.L.T. (Sh.Ct.) 74, Judge not specified, Sh Ct.

6944. Scottish Examination Board

SCOTTISH EXAMINATION BOARD (AMENDMENT) REGULATIONS 1996, SI 1996 579 (S.57); made under the Education (Scotland) Act 1980 s.129. In force: January 1, 1996; £0.65.

These Regulations made a consequential amendment to the Scottish Examination Board Regulations 1981 in light of the abolition, by the Local Government etc (Scotland) Act 1994, of the statutory post of director of education with effect from April 1, 1996.

6945. Scottish Examination Board

SCOTTISH EXAMINATION BOARD (AMENDMENT NO.2) REGULATIONS 1996, SI 1996 1970 (S.166); made under the Education (Scotland) Act 1980 s.129. In force: August 19, 1996; £0.65.

These Regulations amend the Scottish Examination Board Regulations 1981 (SI 1981 1562) to extend the borrowing powers of the board. At present, except in relation to land purchase, the board is only allowed to borrow on a six month overdraft. This amendment authorises other types of borrowing but only if the Secretary of State has first consented to the terms of the borrowing instrument.

6946. Scottish Qualifications Authority

SCOTTISH QUALIFICATIONS AUTHORITY (ESTABLISHMENT) (SCOTLAND) ORDER 1996, SI 1996 2248 (S.180); made under the Education (Scotland) Act 1996 s.1. In force: September 18, 1996; £0.65.

The Education (Scotland) Act 1996 Part I enables the Secretary of State by order to establish a new statutory body called the Scottish Qualifications Authority (SQA). This Order establishes that body on September 18, 1996, when most provisions of Part I of the Act come into force. SQA will not take up its substantive functions immediately. The property, rights, liabilities and obligations of the Scottish Examinations Board and the Scottish Vocational Education Council will be transferred to SQA as their successor at a future date to be appointed by the Secretary of State, and the provisions of the Act giving SQA substantive functions will be commenced then.

6947. Scottish Qualifications Authority–transitional provisions

SCOTTISH QUALIFICATIONS AUTHORITY (TRANSITIONAL PROVISIONS) (SCOTLAND) ORDER 1996, SI 1996 2249 (S.181); made under the Education (Scotland) 1996 s.20. In force: September 18, 1996; £0.65.

The Education (Scotland) Act 1996 Part I enables the Secretary of State by order to establish a new statutory body called the Scottish Qualifications Authority. The SQA was established at September 18, 1996, when most of the provisions of Part I of the Act came into force. The SQA will not take up its substantive functions immediately. The property rights, liabilities and obligations of the Scottish Examination Board and the Scottish Vocational Education Council will be transferred to the SQA as their successor at a future date to be appointed by the Secretary of State (the transfer date), and the provisions of the Act giving the SQA substantive functions will be commenced then. Section 20(1) of the Act provides that prior to the transfer date SQA shall have such of the functions to be conferred on it by Part I of the Act as are necessary or expedient to facilitate the transfer and facilitate or enable the effective carrying on by it of its functions after the transfer. This Order in terms of s.20(2) of the Act sets the date when the transitional period provided for in s.20(1) of the Act shall begin.

6948. Teachers–retirement–redundancy

TEACHERS (COMPENSATION FOR PREMATURE RETIREMENT AND REDUNDANCY) (SCOTLAND) REGULATIONS 1996, SI 1996 2317 (S.185); made under the Superannuation Act 1972 s.24. In force: October 31, 1996; £4.15.

These Regulations consolidate and replace the Teachers' (Compensation for Premature Retirement) (Scotland) Regulations 1980 (SI 1980 1254), the Teachers' (Compensation for Premature Retirement) Amendment Regulations 1982 (SI 1982 918), the Teachers' (Compensation for Redundancy and Premature Retirement) (Scotland) Regulations 1984 (SI 1984 845), the Teachers' (Compensation for Premature Retirement) (Scotland) Amendment Regulations 1986 (SI 1986 412) and amend the Teachers' (Superannuation and Compensation for Premature Retirement) (Scotland) Amendment Regulations 1993 (SI 1993 2513). They provide for compensation for premature retirement of certain teachers and provide for compensation on redundancy to certain teachers in addition to the normal statutory compensation.

6949. Articles

Closing schools *(Jean McFadden)*: J.L.S.S. 1996, 41 (4), 151-153 . (Statutory procedures to be followed before school can be closed or amalgamated).

Teaching quality assessment in Scotland *(Colin T. Reid)*: S.P.T.L. Reporter 1996, 13, 36,38-39. (Framework and procedure of quality assessments carried out on Scottish universities' legal courses).

ELECTORAL PROCESS

6950. European Parliament–constituencies

EUROPEAN PARLIAMENTARY CONSTITUENCIES (SCOTLAND) ORDER 1996, SI 1996 1926 (S.155); made under the European Assembly Elections Act 1978 Sch.2 para.4B. In force: in accordance with Art.1 (2); £1.55.

This Order gives effect without modification to the recommendations contained in the supplementary report of the Boundary Commission for Scotland dated June 6, 1996. It sets out the European Parliamentary Constituencies into which Scotland will be divided, but these constituencies will only have effect from the next European Parliamentary general election.

6951. European Parliament–returning officers

EUROPEAN PARLIAMENTARY ELECTIONS (RETURNING OFFICERS) (SCOTLAND) ORDER 1996, SI 1996 753 (S.84); made under the European Parliamentary Elections Act 1978 s.9, Sch.1 para.4. In force: April 1, 1996; £1.10.

Revokes SI 1984 623. This Order is consequential on the reorganisation of local government in Scotland and directs who shall be the returning officer for an European Parliamentary election in the case of those European Parliamentary constituencies in Scotland which are situated in more than one of the local government areas established by the Local Government etc. (Scotland) Act 1994. The Order comes into force on April 1, 1996 being the date on which the new local government areas have effect in Scotland. The European Parliamentary Elections (Returning Officers) (Scotland) Order 1984 (SI 1984 623), by which returning officers are at present designated for European Parliamentary constituencies which are situated in more than one region or islands area, is revoked.

EMPLOYMENT

6952. Contract of employment–change to contract terms–accrued holiday pay not be paid to those dismissed for gross misconduct–display notice insufficient notice of change

[Wages Act 1986 (c.48) s.1.]

K and P were summarily dismissed by S for gross misconduct. Prior to their dismissals S purported to change the company rules and regulations so that any employee dismissed for gross misconduct would not receive accrued holiday pay. S attempted to notify the change by placing a notice in the factory; employees were not notified individually. Prior to the change K had signed a contract of employment which expressly referred to the company rules and regulations. P had not signed any contract of employment. On their dismissals K and P did not receive their accrued holiday pay, and both made applications to an industrial tribunal claiming that S had made an unlawful deduction from their wages in respect of this amount. In respect of K the tribunal held that, as he had signed a contract of employment, and as S had displayed a notice drawing attention to the change in the terms of employment, K had signified his consent to the deduction in writing, within the meaning of the Wages Act 1986 s.1. The tribunal upheld P's claim on the grounds that he had no signed contract and so had not signified his consent to the deduction. K appealed and S appealed in respect of the finding in favour of P.

Held, allowing K's appeal and dismissing S's appeal, that, in order for a deduction from wages to be lawful, it was not necessary for the employee to have signified his agreement to the deduction in writing. The lawfulness of a deduction could be achieved by means of a relevant provision in the worker's contract, as provided in s.1 (1) (a) of the 1986 Act. Under s.1 (3) (b) of the 1986 Act, it was not necessary for the worker to acknowledge in writing that a relevant term had been incorporated, merely that its existence and effect had been notified to him in writing by the employer. If the worker then did not object and continued to work in accordance with the new provision, his agreement could be inferred with regard to the existence of the provision and its effect. However, the display of a notice within an employer's premises indicating a change in the company's rules and regulations affecting the workers' terms and conditions of employment was not a sufficient means of discharging the statutory obligation to notify relevant provisions in writing. Section 1 (3) (b) of the 1986 Act required that notification be given to each worker individually who was affected by the provision. References to other documents for terms and conditions of employment must be references to the employee in writing, so that he knew where to look. In the case of K, even if the change was verbally drawn to his attention, that was not sufficient. A simple statement accompanying a wages slip, either indicating the change or bringing to the attention of the employee where to find the change, would be sufficient, *Merrell v. Asda Stores Ltd* (Unreported).

KERR v. SWEATER SHOP (SCOTLAND) LTD; SWEATER SHOP (SCOTLAND) LTD v. PARK [1996] I.R.L.R. 424, Lord Johnston, EAT.

6953. Employment Rights Act 1996 (c.18). See EMPLOYMENT. §2544

6954. Industrial tribunals–procedure

INDUSTRIAL TRIBUNALS (CONSTITUTION AND RULES OF PROCEDURE) (SCOTLAND) (AMENDMENT) REGULATIONS 1996, SI 1996 1758; made under the Employment Protection (Consolidation) Act 1978 s.128, s.154, Sch.9 para.1. In force: Reg.9, Reg.13: on date when Disability Discrimination Act 1995 s.8 comes into force; Remainder: July 31, 1996; £1.95.

These Regulations amend the Industrial Tribunals (Constitution and Rules of Procedure) (Scotland) (Amendment) Regulations 1993 (SI 1993 2688) by prescribing the procedural rules for proceedings before industrial tribunals in

Scotland. They provide that a notice of appearance must be presented within 21 days of the respondent receiving a copy of the applicant's originating application instead of 14 days; require tribunals to give extended reasons for their decisions in proceedings brought under the 1995 Act; make provision to enable tribunals to make restricted reporting orders in proceedings brought under the 1995 Act; and amend the procedure applying in equal value cases to the appointment of an expert and the preparation of an expert's report.

6955. Industrial Tribunals Act 1996 (c.17). See EMPLOYMENT. §2563

6956. Redundancy–unfair dismissal–consultation

[Employment Protection (Consolidation) Act 1978 (c.44) s.57(3).]

K, one of a number of E's employees selected for dismissal on grounds of redundancy, discovered at a meeting between E's management and union representatives, of whom K was one, that he was among those to be made redundant. K applied to an industrial tribunal claiming that he had been unfairly dismissed by E. The tribunal decided that he had been unfairly dismissed on the basis that E had not acted reasonably in terms of s.57(3) of the Employment Protection (Consolidation) Act 1978 in that E had failed to show that their method of selection was generally fair or had been applied reasonably. E appealed successfully to the EAT but K appealed.

Held, allowing the appeal, that the decision of the industrial tribunal was restored and the case remitted back for consideration of any remedy. Failure to discuss selection procedures and assessment methods with a trade union demonstrated a lack of proper consultation in selecting employees for redundancy and therefore provided grounds for an unfair dismissal claim. A system of redundancy selection adopted by an employer had to be fair and reasonable and applied fairly and reasonably between employees, per *British Aerospace Plc v. Green* [1995] I.R.L.R. 433, [1995] C.L.Y. 2103 considered, and consultation also had to be fair, ie. at a stage where proposals were still formative, *R. v. British Coal Corp, ex p. Price (No.3)* [1994] I.R.L.R. 72, [1994] C.L.Y. 81 considered. In this case there was no evidence of adequate consultation.

KING v. EATON LTD [1996] I.R.L.R. 199, Lord Ross, L.J.C., Lord Murray, IH.

6957. Sex discrimination–unfair dismissal–part time employee–continuous period of employment

[Treaty of Rome 1957 Art.119; Employment Protection (Consolidation) Act 1978 (c.44) s.64, Sch.13.]

C's contract of employment obliged her to work for five and a half hours on alternate Fridays. Her claim for compensation for unfair dismissal was dismissed as she did not have the requisite two years continuous service needed to claim protection under the provisions of the Employment Protection (Consolidation) Act 1978 s.64(1). The provisions in the 1978 Act Sch.13 relating to the computation of a period of employment meant that the continuity of her employment was taken in each alternate week. C appealed.

Held, allowing the appeal, that the conditions were indirectly discriminatory against women and incompatible with the Treaty of Rome 1957 Art.119 and that periods of part-time employment even of less than eight hours every alternate week counted in the computation of periods of employment for the purposes of the 1978 Act, *R. v. Secretary of State for Employment, ex p. Equal Opportunities Commission* [1994] 1 All E.R. 910, [1994] C.L.Y. 1981 applied.

COLLEY v. CORKINDALE [1995] I.C.R. 965, Mummery, J., EAT.

6958. Sex discrimination–unfair dismissal–pregnancy–dismissal due to illness arising from pregnancy

[Council Directive 76/207 on equal treatment for men and women as regards access to employment; Sex Discrimination Act 1975 (c.44) s.1 (1), s.5(1), s.6(1).]

A female employee worked as a service driver. In August 1990 she advised her employers that she was pregnant. From August 18, 1990 she submitted a series of medical certificates signing her off from work for a number of causes connected to her pregnancy. In November 1990 she was reminded of the respondents' rule that where an employee exceeded 26 weeks' continuous sick leave, that employee would be dismissed, and she was told that she would be dismissed at the expiry of this period if she had not returned to work before then. This rule had previously been applied on at least one occasion in respect of a male employee. She did not return to work and was dismissed at the end of the 26 week period. As she had only been employed for 18 months her employment was not subject to the Employment Protection (Consolidation) Act 1978. She claimed before an industrial tribunal that her dismissal was attributable to sex discrimination. Her application was dismissed. An appeal against that decision to the employment appeal tribunal was refused. In appealing against that refusal it was argued that there had been direct discrimination against the appellant on the ground of her sex. The appellant suggested a question to be referred to the European Court.

Held, that (1) that in terms of the Sex Discrimination Act 1975 the relevant circumstance was the unavailability of the appellant for work because of her illness, and the fact that the reason for her illness was pregnancy was not relevant; (2) there was a distinction between dismissal due to pregnancy and dismissal due to illness caused by pregnancy, and the Equal Treatment Directive 76/207 did not apply in the case of an employee whose illness was attributable to pregnancy unless a provision giving protection applied under national law; (3) as the appellant was not protected by any national legislation the 1976 Directive did not apply; (4) the law was reasonably clear following a previous decision of the European Court, and no reference was necessary; and appeal refused, *Handels-og Kontorfunktionarernes Forbund i Danmark v. Dansk Arbejdsgiverforening* [1992] I.C.R. 332, [1991] C.L.Y. 4077 applied; *Webb v. EMO Air Cargo (UK) (C-32/93)* [1994] C.L.Y. 4825 applied.

BROWN v. RENTOKIL LTD 1996 S.L.T. 839, Lord Allanbridge, IH.

6959. Transfer of undertakings–council employee unhappy about transfer–objection implied from evidence of state of mind and actions

[Transfer of Undertakings (Protection of Employment) Regulations 1981 (SI 1981 1794) Reg.5.]

In November 1994, Argyll & Bute DC transferred its repair and maintenance activities to GH. H, a council employee for several years, was employed in the repair and maintenance division. He was unhappy about the transfer and attempted to resist it, by seeking alternative work within the council and by going on sick leave at the time of the transfer. H failed to respond to a letter from the responsible manager at GH which stated that the manager considered that H was objecting to the transfer. H's claim against GH for unfair dismissal in connection with the transfer was rejected by an industrial tribunal on the basis that H had informed either the council or GH that he objected to his employment being transferred to GH. Under the Transfer of Undertakings (Protection of Employment) Regulations 1981 Reg.5(4A) and Reg.5(4B), the effect of such a finding by the tribunal was that the 1981 Regulations did not operate so as to transfer H's employment to GH, but rather that H's employment was terminated by his own volition and that he was not to be treated for any purpose as having been dismissed by the council. H appealed, contending that Reg.5(4A) of the 1981 Regulations required a clear and unequivocal statement, whether oral or in writing, by the employee that he did not want to be employed by the transferee and that such an objection could not be implied from act or statements which were not unequivocal.

Held, dismissing the appeal, that the word "object" in Reg.5(4)A was to be construed as effectively meaning a refusal to accept the transfer, and it was clear from that regulation that such a state of mind must be conveyed to the transferor or transferee before the date of the transfer. However, it was not necessary to lay down any particular method whereby such a conveyance could be effected. It could be by word or deed or both, and each case must be looked at on its own facts to determine whether there was a sufficient state of mind to amount to a refusal on the part of the employee to consent to the transfer. It should not be difficult in most cases to distinguish between withholding of consent and mere concern or unwillingness, which may still be consistent with accepting the inevitable. The matter should be approached from a common sense perspective, and the fact that in the instant case the tribunal considered evidence of matters which occurred after the transfer did not mean they fell into error, because such evidence could cast light upon the state of mind of the employee and the knowledge of the employer prior to the date of the transfer. On the facts, the tribunal were entitled to conclude that H had objected to the transfer and that this objection had been conveyed to the transferor prior to the transfer date.

HAY v. GEORGE HANSON (BUILDING CONTRACTORS) LTD [1996] I.R.L.R. 427, Lord Johnston, EAT.

6960. Articles

Count reckoning and payment–can it be an employee's remedy? *(Gordon Junor)*: S.L.G. 1996, 64(1), 9-12. (Whether action for payment under employment contract was appropriate means of recovery of sums due rather than action for count reckoning and payment where no duty to account existed).

Equal pay–complaints time-barred after six months *(G. Ian McPherson)*: Emp. L.B. 1996, 12(Apr), 5-6. (Tribunals have no powers to extend time limits for applications).

Restrictive covenants *(Alexandra Davidson)*: Emp. L. Brief. 1996, 3(6), 64-65. (Ensuring appropriateness of restrictive covenants in contract of employment and effect of unlawful termination on enforceability).

ENVIRONMENT

6961. Coast protection–notice of proposed works

COAST PROTECTION (NOTICES) (SCOTLAND) AMENDMENT REGULATIONS 1996, SI 1996 141 (S.13); made under the Coastal Protection Act 1949 s.5, s.8, s.49. In force: April 1, 1996; £0.65.

These Regulations amend the Coast Protection (Notices) (Scotland) Regulations 1988 (SI 1988 957) by adding Scottish Natural Heritage and the Scottish Environment Protection Agency to the list of persons on whom notice of proposed coast protection works must be served. They also revoke the form of notice prescribed for works schemes and make minor drafting changes.

6962. Environment Act 1995–Commencement No.7 Order

ENVIRONMENT ACT 1995 (COMMENCEMENT NO.7) (SCOTLAND) ORDER 1996, SI 1996 2857 (C.84; S.219); made under the Environment Act 1995 s.125. In force: bringing into force various provisions of the Act on January 1, 1997; £1.95.

This Order brings into force on January 1, 1997 s.96(1) (5) (6), Sch.13; Sch.14; s.96(3); part of s.96(4) and part of s.120(3) of the Environmental Protection Act 1995.

6963. Environmental protection–Sustainable Action Fund–grants

FINANCIAL ASSISTANCE FOR ENVIRONMENTAL PURPOSES (NO.2) ORDER 1996, SI 1996 1431 (S.130); made under the Environmental Protection Act 1990 s.153. In force: July 1, 1996; £0.65.

Varies the Environmental Protection Act 1990 s.153(1) so as to enable the Secretary of State, with the consent of the Treasury, to give financial assistance for the purposes of the Sustainable Action Fund whose objectives are to fund research, demonstration projects and other relevant activities in support of sustainable development in Scotland.

6964. Pollution–waste management–managers' qualifications–disapplication of requirements

WASTE MANAGEMENT LICENSING (SCOTLAND) REGULATIONS 1996, SI 1996 916 (S.100); made under the Environmental Protection Act 1990 s.74. In force: May 1, 1996; £1.10.

These Regulations disapply the Waste Management Licensing Regulations 1994 (SI 1994 1056) Reg.4 (qualifications required for a person to be technically competent) to managers of specified waste facilities operated by local authorities, who meet certain criteria as to age and experience. Such managers will be treated as technically competent for the purposes of the Environmental Protection Act 1990 s.74(3)(b).

6965. Pollution–water pollution–agricultural nitrates

PROTECTION OF WATER AGAINST AGRICULTURAL NITRATE POLLUTION (SCOTLAND) REGULATIONS 1996, SI 1996 1564 (S.137); made under the European Communities Act 1972 s.2. In force: July 22, 1996; £1.95.

Transpose for Scotland the requirements of Council Directive 91/676 concerning the protection of waters against pollution caused by nitrates from agricultural sources and gives SEPA a duty to monitor the nitrate concentration of water.

6966. Pollution–water pollution–sentencing

[Control of Pollution Act 1974 (c.40) s.31(1)(a) and (c); Environmental Protection Act 1990 (c. 43) s.145.]

C, a company with a turnover of around £20 million a year, which was in the business of waste disposal and which had several landfill sites, appealed against a fine of £12,000, the maximum being £20,000, imposed for causing or knowingly permitting polluting matter to enter controlled waters in violation of s.31(1)(a) of the Control of Pollution Act 1974. C, which had no previous offences, claimed that they had consent from the river purification board (B) to pump water from a rain filled hole into the river, but had not done so as a nearby quarrying company, Q, had arranged to use the water in their quarrying operations. Q did not require to use all the water and the level began to increase again. If the water was not disposed of there was a risk that it would seep into C's neighbouring landfill site. Although B's consent had lapsed, C decided to pump the water from the hole and into a drain where it would eventually flow into the river. Before doing so C tested the drain and analysed the water which was found to be pollution free. Unknown to C the water seeped out of the drain and into the clay lining of the dam which surrounded the landfill site, and became contaminated, causing pollution in the river. At the first sign of pollution, measures were taken to prevent further contamination.

Held, fine reduced to £5,000, that while C should have sought renewed consent from B to pump the water, C had realised that pollution would occur if the rainwater had been allowed to rise in the hole, had taken precautions against this and had not, as suggested by the sheriff, taken a "calculated risk". Fortunately, no damage to animal life within the water had resulted.

CAIRD ENVIRONMENTAL v. VALENTINE 1995 S.C.C.R. 714, Judge not specified.

6967. Scottish Environment Protection Agency–establishment

ENVIRONMENT ACT 1995 (CONSEQUENTIAL AND TRANSITIONAL PROVISIONS) (SCOTLAND) REGULATIONS 1996, SI 1996 973 (S.104); made under the Environment Act 1995 s.120. In force: April 1, 1996; £1.55.

The Environment Act 1995 Part I establishes the Scottish Environment Protection Agency and transfers to it the functions, property, rights and liabilities of river purification authorities, waste Regulation authorities, disposal authorities, and Her Majesty's Industrial Pollution Inspectorate together with some functions, property, rights and liabilities of the Health and Safety Executive, local authorities and the Secretary of State. Reg.2 and the Schedule to the Regulations make a number of minor and consequential amendments to primary and secondary legislation in consequence of these transfers. Regulation 3 makes transitional provisions for consideration of questions for determination by the Secretary of State under the Control of Pollution Act 1974 s.39.

6968. Scottish Environment Protection Agency–redundancy–early retirement–compensation

COMPENSATION FOR REDUNDANCY OR PREMATURE RETIREMENT (SCOTTISH ENVIRONMENT PROTECTION AGENCY AND RIVER PURIFICATION BOARDS TRANSITIONAL ARRANGEMENTS) (SCOTLAND) REGULATIONS 1996, SI 1996 1360 (S.127); made under the Superannuation Act 1972 s.24. In force: June 12, 1996; £1.55.

These Regulations allow a lump sum payment to be made to certain employees who cease to hold employment with a river purification board or SEPA by reason of redundancy or following dissolution of the river purification board and establishment of SEPA on April 1, 1996; the Regulations have retrospective effect from March 1, 1996.

6969. Scottish Environment Protection Agency–transfer of functions–transfer of assets

SCOTTISH ENVIRONMENT PROTECTION AGENCY (TRANSFER DATE) ORDER 1996, SI 1996 139 (S.11); made under the Environment Act 1995 s.56. In force: April 1, 1996; £0.65.

This Order sets April 1, 1996 as the date of transfer to the Scottish Environment Protection Agency of the functions, property, rights and liabilities of river purification authorities and Her Majesty's Industrial Pollution Inspectorate and of certain functions, property, rights and liabilities of local authorities and the Secretary of State.

6970. Articles

Green light for environment agencies *(Stephen Tromans)*: Legal Times 1996, 39, 4. (Implementation of Part I of 1995 Act on April 1, 1996 and likely impact of new environment agencies in England and Scotland).

Landfill firm loses appeal over analytical tests : ENDS 1996, 253, 49-50. (Verification procedures not necessary for each step of analytical process).

Restructuring pollution control policy in Scotland *(Calum Macleod.)*: Euro. Env. 1996, 6(5), 156-161. (Water pollution enforcement policy and procedures of River Purification Boards and their replacement by Scottish Environmental Protection Agency).

ENVIRONMENTAL HEALTH

6971. Fire precautions–using premises without fire certificate–"occupier"

[Fire Precautions Act 1971 (c.40) s.7(1).]

An accused person was charged on a summary complaint with a contravention of the Fire Precautions Act 1971 in respect that, being the occupier of premises, he used them in such a manner that a fire certificate was required when no certificate was in force. The accused was the owner of a guest house and restaurant and held a restaurant licence for the premises. He was out of the country for two weeks on holiday at the time of the offence and had left two women in charge of the day to day running of the guest house. The sheriff, holding that the accused was in no position to exercise any form of control or supervision when on holiday and was therefore not the occupier of the guest house, acquitted the accused. The Crown appealed.

Held, that somebody who was away temporarily on holiday remained the "occupier" of the premises if he was in fact the owner/occupier before he left and had every intention of remaining as such when he returned; and appeal allowed, *Christison v. Hogg* 1974 S.L.T. (Notes) 33, [1974] C.L.Y. 4349 applied. *Observed,* that if the accused had been away from the business for a lengthy period, of months rather than weeks, then questions might have arisen as to whether there was the necessary degree of permanency.

McCLORY v. MacKINNON 1996 S.L.T. 1180, Judge not specified, HCJ.

6972. Noise–building works–notice requiring all audible work to be carried out at set times–whether notice unreasonable and unnecessary

[Control of Pollution Act 1974 (c. 40) s.60.]

A notice was served by a local authority under s.60 of the Control of Pollution Act 1974 requiring all works which were audible at a site to be carried out only between certain hours. The site developers applied to the sheriff for the recall or variation of the notice. Evidence having been led, the developers submitted that the notice should not be sustained and contended that audibility was inappropriate as a test since it was not objective, some form of measurement of the noise level being required.

Held, that (1) the notice was both reasonable and necessary and would give the residents some respite from the effects of the noise during the weekend and (2) audibility, denoting discernible sound over and above background noise, was not objectionable as being subjective; and application refused.

ADAM (SCOTLAND) LTD v. BEARSDEN AND MILNGAVIE DC 1996 S.L.T. (Sh.Ct.) 21, Judge not specified, Sh Ct.

6973. Sewerage–charges

DOMESTIC SEWERAGE CHARGES (REDUCTION) (SCOTLAND) REGULATIONS 1996, SI 1996 326 (S.26); made under the Local Government etc. (Scotland) Act 1994 s.81. In force: April 1, 1996; £1.10.

With effect from April 1, 1996, responsibility for water and sewerage services in Scotland will transfer from local authorities to three new water authorities, established under the Local Government etc. (Scotland) Act 1994. Charges for services provided by those new water authorities will generally be levied under charges schemes drawn up and approved under s.76 of that Act. These Regulations reduce the amount which would otherwise be payable under a charges scheme in respect of the provision of sewerage services to a dwelling. The reduced amount payable in any case falls to be calculated under Reg.3.

6974. Sewerage–duty to maintain–drainage channel originating on private land adjacent to public pavement and open to public

[Sewerage (Scotland) Act 1968 (c. 47) s.59.]

The Sewerage (Scotland) Act 1968, which provides, inter alia, for the maintenance of sewers by sewerage authorities, defines "sewer" in s.59 as including all drains used for the drainage of buildings except for any drain within the curtilage of premises used solely for or in connection with the drainage of one building or any buildings or yards within the same curtilage. Two persons allegedly injured in separate incidents when they tripped on a broken slab covering a rodding eye at the commencement of a surface water drainage channel, sought damages from the sewerage authority. The area where the channel originated was a tarmacadam area fronting certain shops and adjacent to the pavement, but was not part of the pavement and was not vested in the local authority. The channel drained water from three shops as it passed each in turn, and then reached the main sewer in the street. The pursuers argued that the rodding eye permitted the cleaning of the whole channel, which was a "sewer" within s.59 as it was used for the drainage of more than one building, and the cover was accordingly an accessory of a sewer and within the defenders' responsibility. The defenders argued, inter alia, that as the three shops were part of a single building the entire channel was a "drain" within s.59 and not a "sewer".

Held, that (1) as the various parts of the structure were in separate ownership the channel as a whole could not be regarded as within the curtilage of one building in terms of the statutory exception, but that at the point it originated the channel was a drain within the curtilage of a building (one of the shops in separate ownership) and did not become a sewer until it crossed the notional boundary with the next premises and began to accept water from those premises also; (2) the rodding eye constituted nothing more than the commencement of the drain as it served the first building, and the covering slab was therefore an accessory to that drain and not to the sewer; (3) in any event there was insufficient evidence that the defenders knew or should have known about the condition of the slab as at the dates of the pursuers' accidents; and defenders assoilzied. Opinion, that contributory negligence would have been assessed at 10 per cent in the case of the pursuer who had had no knowledge of the defect and whose accident had occurred in the dark, and at 25 per cent in the case of the pursuer whose accident had happened in daylight and who admitted that he had not been keeping a lookout.

GALLAGHER v. STRATHCLYDE RC 1996 S.L.T. 255, Judge not specified, OH.

6975. Statutory nuisance

STATUTORY NUISANCE (APPEALS) (SCOTLAND) REGULATIONS 1996, SI 1996 1076 (S.116); made under the Control of Pollution Act 1974 s.70, s.104; and the Environmental Protection Act 1990 Sch.3 para.1A. In force: May 2, 1996; £1.55.

Sets out grounds on which appeals may be made to the sheriff against abatement notices served under the 1990 Act may be made, prescribes the procedure to be followed and the cases in which an abatement notice is to be suspended pending the decision of a sheriff on an appeal or until the appeals abandonment.

EXPENSES

6976. Caution for expenses

In M's action against I, the manufacturers of a brand of cigarettes smoked by M's husband, H, who had died of lung cancer, I reclaimed against the Lord Ordinary's refusal to ordain M to lodge caution for expenses. I argued that (1) caution was appropriate where the interests of justice required it: all other rules, including M's right to pursue her claim, were subsidiary to that principle and caution was the only means of protection for I to ensure that M would be capable of meeting any award of expenses made; although mere impecuniosity was not sufficient to warrant an order for caution *per se* but not much more was required, and (2) the Lord Ordinary's decision was plainly wrong since there were exceptional circumstances which required caution such as (a) the nature and scale of the litigation and the costs of defending, (b) M's inability to meet any expenses, (c) that legal aid had already been refused, (d) that M had little prospect of success, (e) that M's claim was of limited value and damages were likely to be low, (f) that M's action was backed by the anti-smoking lobby, (g) that the delay which had occurred between July 1992 and the commission to take H's evidence in March 1993 caused prejudice to I since they were unable to cross-examine H on relevant matters prior to his death, and (h) that there were no other protective remedies available to I.

Held, reclaiming motion refused, that the Lord Ordinary had taken into account the matters advanced by I individually and cumulatively; had balanced these against the general principle of impecuniosity, and applied the appropriate test in *G v. G* [1985] 1 W.L.R. 647, [1985] C.L.Y. 2594 as approved in *Britton v. Central RC* 1986 S.L.T. 207, [1986] C.L.Y. 3641. He did not misdirect himself and it was not appropriate for the court to consider the matter anew.

McTEAR v. IMPERIAL TOBACCO LTD, *The Times*, September 30, 1996, Lord Sutherland, IH.

6977. Caution for expenses–limited company as pursuer–additional caution

[Companies Act 1985 (c.6) s.726.]

M, a limited company, raised an action for implement of missives against D, F and T. Prior to proof, M was ordained to find caution in the sum of £2,000. On December 15, following a hearing at which all the parties agreed that the proof would take eight days, M was ordered to lodge additional caution in the sum of £14,000 each for D and T. On April 12, 1995, after seven days of proof, M had still not closed its case and D and T moved to have M ordained to lodge further caution for expenses. The Lord Ordinary refused this motion and D and T reclaimed. M submitted that the Lord Ordinary had applied the proper test under s.726(2) of the Companies Act 1985 and that as the ordering of caution was discretionary, his decision could only be interfered with if it was completely wrong, *New Mining and Exploring Syndicate v. Chalmers & Hunter*, 1909 2 S.L.T. 236. In addition, it was possible that if additional caution were ordered, M would not be able to find it, and all their expenditure to date would be rendered abortive.

Held, reclaiming motion granted and M ordained to lodge additional caution of £10,000 each in respect of D and T that the Lord Ordinary erred (1) in failing to attach sufficient weight to the fact that D and T were seeking additional caution, not just caution, and (2) in stating that only D and T had seriously underestimated the duration of proof since the sums previously fixed were based on the assessment of all counsel that the proof would last eight days; accordingly the court was entitled to review the Lord Ordinary's exercise of discretion. Additional caution was appropriate since the estimated time for proof was unreliable and it was probable that if the Lord Ordinary had known on December 15, that further time would be needed to complete the proof, he would have fixed caution at a larger figure.

Observed, that there was no general rule that the court should be reluctant to accede to a step by step approach to the ordaining of caution.

MERRICK HOMES LTD v. DUFF [1995] B.C.C 954, Lord Ross, L.J.C., IH.

6978. Court of Session–account of expenses–failure to lodge timeously

[Act of Sederunt (Rules of the Court of Session) 1994 (SI 1994 1443) r.42.1 (2).]

M, the successful respondent in F's appeal, sought to have remitted to the auditor an account of expenses prepared in terms of an interlocutor dated November 16, 1994 although the account had been lodged outwith the four month period specified in r.42.1 (2) (a). M argued that an account had been submitted to F before March 16, 1995 with view to reaching agreement and avoiding the need for taxation; the assistant with M's local agents handling the case had often been absent in early 1995 owing to illness and domestic difficulties; the deadline had passed without being noticed; parties had continued negotiations about various matters throughout the summer; once it became clear that agreement could not be reached the account had been lodged; and there would be no prejudice to F by allowing the account late.

Held, motion refused, that the rule was peremptory and special cause could not be constituted by an assistant solicitor being absent for several months, as it was the responsibility of his superiors to ensure that his work was properly carried out and that time limits were met. In any event, the account could have been lodged within the deadline and a substantial period had elapsed since the expiry of the four-month period, *Smith v. Smith* (Unreported), distinguished.

FANE v. MURRAY 1996 S.C.L.R. 323, Judge not specified, IH.

6979. Court of Session–additional fee

[Act of Sederunt (Rules of the Court of Session) 1994 (SI 1994 1443) r.42.14.]

Z sought an award of an additional fee against G in terms of the Rules of the Court of Session 1994 r.42.14(3) (a), (b), (c) and (e). The action was one of reparation for personal injury after Z contracted a laboratory animal allergy whilst employed by G as an animal technician. The proof was to have been restricted to quantum but the action was settled on the day of the proof. Z argued that the action had been complex in that calculation of wage loss was complicated by Z having requalified after having to give up work, the novelty of the medical questions and the unusual statutory provisions on which it was founded. Z argued that his was the first case of occupational asthma linked to laboratory animals and that medical experts had been hard to find.

Held, refusing the motion, that there was an extensive literature on the subject to which it was not suggested that Z's advisers had difficulty in obtaining access. Z's file had not been produced, *Boal v. Newall's Insulation Co Ltd* 1994 S.C.L.R. 534 and it was not sufficient merely to state that it was very large. Documents lodged were few and did not infer that they were unusual in number or importance. It was not sufficient merely to argue that the cause was important to the client. The court had to be satisfied that in its particular circumstances the cause was of such importance as to justify an additional fee.

ZYSZKIEWICZ v. UNIVERSITY OF GLASGOW 1995 S.C.L.R. 1124, OH.

6980. Court of Session–additional fee–remit to auditor to determine entitlement

[Act of Sederunt (Rules of the Court of Session) 1994 (SI 1994 1443) r.42.14.]

A reparation action by K against B arising from a mining accident was settled at a relatively early stage by joint minute, inter alia, that B would be liable to K in expenses as taxed. K then enrolled, inter alia, to remit his account of expenses to the auditor to enable him to determine; (a) whether an additional fee should be allowed, and (b) the extent of any such fee. The motion was not opposed, but the court required a hearing. K accepted that it was for the court to be satisfied that there could be warrant for allowing an additional fee even where parties were agreed on a remit.

Held, motion granted with hesitation, that while there might be circumstances in which the court did not consider that it was able to make a full and proper assessment of such an application and would remit to the auditor to determine it, it would require something out of the ordinary to persuade the court to do so. If, as K stated, it was B's intention to argue before the auditor that no additional fee should be allowed, they should have opposed the present motion. On the merits, while the action was not out of the ordinary for its type, nor was the settlement figure (£165,000) exceptionally large although K's injuries were serious and would remain disabling, the main factor was that from an early stage there had been a substantial exchange of correspondence between agents under various heads with very little involvement of counsel, including the discussions leading to final settlement. These were matters within the scope of r. 42.14(3)(g) and made it difficult for the court to decide.

KENNEDY v. BRITISH COAL CORP 1995 S.C.L.R. 977, Judge not specified, OH.

6981. Court of Session–fees

ACT OF SEDERUNT (RULES OF THE COURT OF SESSION AMENDMENT NO.1) (FEES OF SOLICITORS) 1996, SI 1996 237 (S.17); made under the Court of Session Act 1988 s.5. In force: April 1, 1996; £1.55.

This Act of Sederunt amends Chapters I and III of the Table of Fees in Chapter 42 of the Rules of the Court of Session 1994 (SI 1994 1443) r.42.16 by increasing the fees payable to solicitors by about 5 per cent. The last increase was in the Act of Sederunt (Rules of the Court of Session 1994 Amendment No.2) (Fees of Solicitors) 1995 (SI 1995 1396).

6982. Court of Session–fees

ACT OF SEDERUNT (RULES OF THE COURT OF SESSION AMENDMENT NO.2) (FEES OF SHORT-HAND WRITERS) 1996, SI 1996 754 (S.85); made under the Court of Session Act 1988 s.5. In force: May 1, 1996; £1.10.

This Act of Sederunt amends Chapter IV of the Table of Fees in r.42.16 of the Rules of the Court of Session 1994 (SI 1994 1443) by increasing the fees payable to shorthand writers in the Court of Session by about 3.3 per cent. The last increase was in the Act of Sederunt (Rules of the Court of Session 1994 Amendment) (Shorthand Writers' Fees) 1995 (SI 1995 1023).

6983. Court of Session–fees

COURT OF SESSION ETC. FEES AMENDMENT ORDER 1996, SI 1996 514 (S.48); made under the Courts of Law Fees (Scotland) Act 1895 s.2. In force: April 1, 1996; £1.95.

This Order increases most of the fees payable in relation to proceedings in the Court of Session and specialised courts and offices.

6984. Court of Session–successful pursuer–modification of award

N reclaimed against the Lord Ordinary's decision in N's action against R for breach of contract, that no award of expenses should be made in relation to the proof or its preparation since N had not been successful in around half of the matters raised at proof, particularly in the quantification of the claim for loss of profits. R argued that the decision was a reasonable one given that the judge could have approached the matter by awarding each side one half of the expenses against the other to reflect the time spent by both sides on unsuccessful aspects of the proof.

Held, allowing the appeal, that N be awarded expenses against R, excluding one half of the expenses occasioned by the proof. The Lord Ordinary's approach to modifying expenses had produced an unreasonable result. The general rule was that the party put to the expense of vindicating his rights was entitled to recover the expense from the person by whom it was created. While it was permissible to take into account time spent on matters on which the party awarded expenses was unsuccessful, that did not necessarily lead to any diminution of expenses, *Howitt v. Alexander & Sons* 1948 S.L.T. 334, [1948] C.L.Y. 4292. In fact N succeeded at the proof in the general assertion of their right, and that the issues on which they were unsuccessful related only to quantification of that right. Any modification should also have taken into account that protection in regard to liability for the expenses of the proof could have been afforded by the lodging of a tender.

NIMMO (WILLIAM) & CO v. RUSSELL CONSTRUCTION CO 1995 S.C.L.R. 1148, Judge not specified, IH.

6985. Curator ad litem–failure to apply timeously for legal aid–payment from public funds

[Legal Aid (Scotland) Act 1986 (c.47) s.14; Civil Legal Aid (Scotland) Regulations 1987 (SI 1987 381) Reg.18.]

C, the curator ad litem to children of P, whose children were ordered to be returned following a rehearing on grounds of referral to a children's hearing, sought an award of expenses against P and the reporter to the children's panel, R. C's motion was opposed by P and R. C had been appointed on February 27 in place of a curator appointed by the sheriff. C in turn had instructed his own solicitor, S, who applied for legal aid to meet C's remuneration. S did not apply to the court for any other direction as to C's remuneration, *Drummond's Trs v. Peel's Trs* 1929 S.L.T. 450. C was to make recommendations as to how best to return P's children to their home after a long absence. On March 6, following C's recommendation, P were granted interim access. S was thought not to have fully understood the legal aid regulations and had a number of abortive attempts to get legal aid cover. S did obtain legal aid cover for C under the Legal Aid (Scotland) Act 1986 s.14 on June 27 and under the Civil Legal Aid (Scotland) Regulations 1987 Reg.18(1)(a) for the period from April 12 to May 10.

Held, refusing the motion, that C's appointment, although requested by P, was not made necessary by any act or omission by P or R, and P no longer had the benefit of legal aid. It was not right that C should not be remunerated, and the necessary steps should be taken to permit recovery from public funds, but not insofar as C's account related to any of S's fees and outlays as it was appropriate that S be found personally liable for that part of the account.

L v. KENNEDY 1996 S.C.L.R. 202, Judge not specified, IH.

6986. High Court of Justiciary–fees

HIGH COURT OF JUSTICIARY FEES AMENDMENT ORDER 1996, SI 1996 516 (S.50); made under the Courts of Law Fees (Scotland) Act 1895 s.2. In force: April 1, 1996; £1.10.

This Order increases from April 1, 1996 certain of the fees payable to the Principal Clerk of Justiciary or any officer acting for him in relation to proceedings in the High Court of Justiciary.

6987. Land Court–award of expenses–additional fee

[Act of Sederunt (Fees of Solicitors in the Sheriff Court) (Amendment and Further Provisions) 1993 (SI 1993 3080) para.5.]

Held, in an application by a crofter to acquire her croft, where expenses had been awarded in her favour against the landlord, that it was for the solicitor moving for a percentage increase in the fees to cover the responsibility undertaken by him in the conduct of the case in terms of the Act of Sederunt (Fees of Solicitors in the Sheriff Court) (Amendment and Further Provisions) 1993 para.5 to satisfy the court that such an increase was justified and it was not for the court to satisfy itself by reference to whatever material might be available to it.

LAWSON v. LORD STRATHCONA 1995 S.L.C.R. 133, Judge not specified.

6988. Land Court–fees

SCOTTISH LAND COURT (FEES) ORDER 1996, SI 1996 680 (S.68); made under the Court of Law Fees (Scotland) Act 1895 s.2. In force: April 1, 1996; £1.10.

This Order regulates the fees payable from April 1, 1996 in respect of proceedings before the Scottish Land Court. In the majority of cases the fees are increased and a fee is prescribed for the first time for searches in the records of the court. The Scottish Land Court (Fees) Order 1995 is revoked.

6989. Lands Tribunal–fees

LANDS TRIBUNAL FOR SCOTLAND (AMENDMENT) (FEES) RULES 1996, SI 1996 519 (S.52); made under the Lands Tribunal Act 1949 s.3. In force: April 1, 1996; £1.55.

These Rules amend the Lands Tribunal for Scotland Rules 1971 from April 1, 1996 by substituting a new table of fees in Sch.2 to those Rules; some of the fees payable to the tribunal are increased.

6990. Lyon Court–fees

LYON COURT AND OFFICE FEES (VARIATION) ORDER 1996, SI 1996 413 (S.29). In force: April 1, 1996; £1.10.

This Order varies the fees for matters listed in the Lyon King of Arms Act 1867 Sch.B. The fees were last varied in 1995 and the fees specified in this Order represent an increase on average of approximately three per cent. They are exclusive of stamp duty when stamp duty is eligible.

6991. Messengers at arms–fees

ACT OF SEDERUNT (FEES OF MESSENGERS-AT-ARMS) 1995, SI 1995 3094 (S.225); made under the Execution of Diligence (Scotland) Act 1926 s.6; and the Court of Session Act 1988 s.5. In force: January 1, 1996; £1.10.

Fees payable to Messengers-at-Arms, as set out in the Act of Sederunt (Fees of Messengers-at-Arms) 1994, are increased by about 3.3 per cent. A table of fees contained in the Schedule to this Act gives details of exact amounts for Service or Intimation of a Document, Inhibitions, Interdicts, Poindings, Poindings of Motor Vehicles, Heavy Plant or Machinery, Sequestrations for Rent, Poinding of the Ground, Sales, Ejections and other Miscellaneous items according to Bands 1, 2 and 3.

6992. Messengers at arms–fees

ACT OF SEDERUNT (FEES OF MESSENGERS-AT-ARMS) 1996, SI 1996 2855 (S.217); made under the Execution of Diligence (Scotland) Act 1926 s.6; and the Court of Session Act 1988 s.5. In force: January 1, 1997; £1.55.

This Act of Sederunt amends the Act of Sederunt (Fees of Messengers-at-Arms) 1994 (SI 1994 391) by increasing the fees payable to Messengers-at-Arms by about three per cent.

6993. Sheriff courts–fees

ACT OF SEDERUNT (FEES OF SOLICITORS IN THE SHERIFF COURT) (AMENDMENT) 1996, SI 1996 236 (S.16); made under the Sheriff Courts (Scotland) Act 1907 s.40. In force: March 1, 1996; £1.95.

This Act of Sederunt amends Chapters I, II, III, IV and VI of the Table of Fees in the Schedule to the Act of Sederunt (Fees of Solicitors in the Sheriff Court) Amendment and Further Provisions) 1993 (SI 1993 3080) by increasing the fees payable to solicitors by about 5 per cent. The last increase was in the Act of Sederunt (Fees of Solicitors in the Sheriff Court) (Amendment) 1995 (SI 1995 1395).

6994. Sheriff courts–fees

SHERIFF COURT FEES AMENDMENT ORDER 1996, SI 1996 628 (S.63); made under the Courts of Law Fees (Scotland) Act 1895 s.2. In force: April 1, 1996; £1.95.

This Order amends the Sheriff Court Fees Order 1985 (SI 1985 827) by specifying new fee levels in substitution for those applicable since January 1, 1994. Many fee levels remain unchanged and the increases represent an average of 4 per cent. A fee is payable for the first time for applications in terms of the Requirements of Writing (Scotland) Act 1995 s.4 and the fee for copying and extracting in respect of commissary proceedings is reduced when a subsequent duplicate confirmation, confirmation and will or will is ordered at the same time as the first copy. The 1985 Order is amended for the purpose of clarification and in particular places beyond doubt that the fee is to be paid on the lodging of a certified copy record, on the lodging of a certified closed record and the endorsing of a minute seeking decree in certain undefended family actions is payable on one occasion only in respect of a cause. The 1985 Order is also amended in making consequential amendments.

6995. Sheriff courts–settlement of action–additional fee

[Act of Sederunt (Fees of Solicitors in the Sheriff Court) (Amendment and Further Provisions) 1993 (SI 1993 3080) Reg.5.]

Held, where an action had been settled on the basis of the payment of a sum of money plus expenses "as agreed by the parties or taxed by the court" in exchange for decree of absolvitor, that it was not open to the court to grant an additional fee under the Act of Sederunt Reg.5 because the terms of the agreement had not yet been exhausted.

GOODWIN v. FARMING AGRICULTURAL FINANCE 1996 S.C.C.R. 545, Judge not specified, Sh Ct.

6996. Sheriff courts–shorthand writers–fees

ACT OF SEDERUNT (FEES OF SHORTHAND WRITERS IN THE SHERIFF COURT) (AMENDMENT) 1996, SI 1996 767 (S.88); made under the Sheriff Courts (Scotland) Act 1907 s.40. In force: May 1, 1996; £1.10.

This Act of Sederunt amends the Table of Fees for shorthand writers in civil proceedings in the Sheriff Court in the Act of Sederunt (Fees of Witnesses and Shorthand Writers in the Sheriff Court) 1992 (SI 1992 1878) by increasing the fees payable by about 3.3 per cent. The last increase was in the Act of Sederunt (Fees of Shorthand Writers in the Sheriff Court) (Amendment) 1995 (SI 1995 1024).

6997. Sheriff officers–fees

ACT OF SEDERUNT (FEES OF SHERIFF OFFICERS) 1995, SI 1995 3095 (S.266); made under the Sheriff Courts (Scotland) Act 1907 s.40. In force: January 1, 1996; £1.55.

Fees payable to Sheriff Officers for service or intimation of documents, interdicts, poindings, poindings of motor vehicles, heavy plant or machinery, sequestrations for rent, poinding of ground, sales, ejections, taking possession of effects, apprehensions, taking possession of children, arresting vessels, aircraft and cargo, and other miscellaneous items are increased by approximately 3.3 per cent from January 1, 1996. The Schedule gives a table of fees payable.

6998. Sheriff officers–fees

ACT OF SEDERUNT (FEES OF SHERIFF OFFICERS) 1996, SI 1996 2858 (S.220); made under the Sheriff Courts (Scotland) Act 1907 s.40; and the Execution of Diligence (Scotland) Act 1926 s.6. In force: January 1, 1997; £1.55.

This Act of Sederunt amends the Act of Sederunt (Fees of Sheriff Officers) 1994 (SI 1994 392) by increasing the fees payable to Sheriff Officers by about three per cent.

6999. Small claims–limit on expenses–tender

In a small claim in which the pursuer sought damages of £750 the defenders stated a defence on the merits and on quantum and tendered £600 "together with the taxed expenses to the date hereof". The pursuer accepted the tender and the sheriff pronounced decree and awarded expenses of £75. The pursuer appealed arguing that he was entitled to expenses on the summary cause scale.

Held, that the tender was not a proper one for a small claim in request of expenses and that, since the defenders had stated a defence with which they did not proceed, the pursuer was entitled to expenses on the summary cause scale.

McKEITCH v. CENTRAL RC 1995 S.C.L.R. 1112, Judge not specified, Sh Ct.

7000. Articles

Bonds of caution or consignation: considering the options for the client *(Angela Grahame)*: Civ. P.B. 1996, 8(Mar), 3-5. (Methods of seeking security for expences).

Counsel's fees–agreement between the Law Society of Scotland and the Faculty of Advocates. : J.L.S.S. 1996, 41 (7), 273 .

Courage mes braves–what the Sheriff should do *(Graham Johnston.)*: Civ. P.B. 1996, 12(Nov), 8-9. (Adjustment of expenses for applications to amend pleadings and problems caused by failure of sheriffs to specialise with particular reference to family proceedings).

Getting money for your value *(Kenneth Campbell)*: S.L.T. 1996, 36, 355-357. (Applications for additional fee uplift by successful party in civil litigation before and interaction with legal aid rules).

Speculative actions insurance *(Graeme Garrett)*: J.L.S.S. 1996, 41 (11), 423-426. (Introduction of new speculative fees insurance scheme to protect personal injury litigants from risk of being found liable for opponents' expenses).

EXTRADITION

7001. Articles

Illegal extradition: the irregular return of fugitive offenders. *(Christopher H.W. Gane and Susan Nash)*: S.L.P.Q. 1996, 1 (4), 277-304. (International, US, English and Commonwealth case law and Scots ruling on whether courts of native country may deal with offender without regard to improper means used to remove him from country of refuge).

FAMILY LAW

7002. Sterilisation–appointment of tutor dative with power to consent to sterilisation–circumstances in which power granted

L, the mother of I, an autistic woman of 32, sought the appointment of a tutor dative with power to consent to the sterilisation of I. I's curator ad litem opposed the power to consent. I had been prescribed the contraceptive pill since the age of 13 to prevent menstruation and pregnancy, both of which were considered too distressing for her to cope with, given her mental state. Sterilisation was thought necessary because of medical worries about long-term use of the pill.

Held, granting the petition, that, in the case of a ward who lacked the capacity to give consent, it was necessary to consider what was in the ward's best interest, *F (Mental Patient: Sterilisation), Re* [1990] 2 A.C. 1, [1989] C.L.Y. 3044 and *A (A Minor) (Wardship: Sterilisation), Re* [1988] A.C. 199 considered. Different circumstances required different measures and precise rules were unwise. In the instant case, although I had probably never had sexual intercourse, she was suggestible and, balancing the disadvantages of major surgery against the fact that a partial hysterectomy was the best way to deal with the dual problem of menstruation and pregnancy, the power of a tutor dative to consent to sterilisation was in I's best interests.

L v. L'S CURATOR AD LITEM, *The Times*, March 19, 1996, Lord MacLean, OH.

7003. Articles

CALMing the waters–two years on *(Richard Ward)*: SCOLAG 1996, 235, 102-103. (Developments since 1995 in mediation including preservation of confidentiality of meetings).

In defence of family mediation *(Ann E. Oswald)*: SCOLAG 1996, 237, 148. (Response to article by Fiona Raitt in Scolag 1996, 234, 68-69, on suitability of mediation for relationship breakdowns).

Limitations of family mediation *(Fiona Raitt)*: SCOLAG 1996, 234, 68-69. (Further discussion on suitability of mediation as form of dispute resolution in response to article by Anne Oswald at J.L.S.S. 1996, 41 (3), 115-117).

Mediation in family disputes *(Anne Oswald)*: J.L.S.S. 1996, 41 (3), 115-117. (Response to criticism by Fiona E. Raitt in J.L.S.S. 1995, 40(5), 182-184, defending use of ADR as means of resolving family disputes on divorce or separation).

7004. Books

Edwards, Lilian; Griffiths, Anne–Family Law. Green's concise Scots law. Paperback. ISBN 0-414-01113-9. W.Green & Son.

Nichols, David; Brown, John L.R.; Kearney, Brian; McInnes, John C.; Norrie, Kenneth McK; Robb, Kenneth; Robson, Peter; Scott, Janys; Stoddart, Charles–Butterworths Scottish Family Law Service. Unbound/looseleaf: £140.00. ISBN 0-406-01354-3. Butterworth Law (Scotland).

Thomson, J.M.–Family Law in Scotland. Paperback: £26.00. ISBN 0-406-07013-X. Butterworth Law.

FINANCE

7005. Audit (Miscellaneous Provisions) Act 1996 (c.10). See FINANCE. §2900

FISH AND FISHERIES

7006. Salmon and freshwater fisheries

DEREGULATION (SALMON FISHERIES (SCOTLAND) ACT 1868) ORDER 1996, SI 1996 1211 (S.122); made under the Deregulation and Contracting Out Act 1994 s.1. In force: April 30, 1996; £1.10.

This Order amends the Salmon Fisheries (Scotland) Act 1868 (c.123) s.18 which makes it a criminal offence in Scotland to buy, sell, expose for sale or possess any salmon roe.

7007. Salmon and freshwater fisheries–baits and lures–River Forth

RIVER FORTH SALMON FISHERY DISTRICT (BAITS AND LURES) REGULATIONS 1996, SI 1996 2641 (S.205); made under the Salmon Act 1986 s.8. In force: January 1, 1997; £0.65.

The Regulations which apply to the River Forth Salmon Fishery District, prohibit the use of natural prawns and shrimps or any part of them as bait and lures when fishing by rod and line for salmon or sea trout.

7008. Salmon and freshwater fisheries–baits and lures–River Stinchar

RIVER STINCHAR SALMON FISHERY DISTRICT (BAITS AND LURES) REGULATIONS 1996, SI 1996 2640 (S.204); made under the Salmon Act 1986 s.8. In force: January 1, 1997; £0.65.

The Regulations, which apply to the River Stinchar Salmon Fishery District, prohibit the use of natural prawns and shrimps or any part of them as baits and lures when fishing by rod and line for salmon and sea trout.

7009. Salmon and fresh water fisheries–baits and lures–River Ythan

RIVER YTHAN SALMON FISHERY DISTRICT (BAITS AND LURES) REGULATIONS 1996, SI 1996 3046 (S.232); made under the Salmon Act 1986 s.8. In force: February 1, 1997; £0.65.

These Regulations, which apply to the River Ythan Salmon Fishery District, prohibit the use of natural prawns and shrimps or any part of them as baits and lures when fishing by rod and line for salmon or sea trout.

7010. Salmon and fresh water fisheries–obstructing water bailiffs–bailiffs unable to show warrant

[Salmon and Freshwater Fisheries Protection (Scotland) Act 1951 (c.26) s.10.]

M was convicted of an offence under s.10 of the Salmon and Freshwater Fisheries Protection (Scotland) Act 1951 of obstructing water bailiffs in the execution of their duty. M had been informed of the identities and intentions of the water bailiffs. He had failed to stop his creel boat and had pulled his net from the bailiffs' boat while they were examining it. M maintained that the bailiffs were acting outwith their powers in that they had not produced the written instrument of appointment. He appealed against conviction.

Held, dismissing the appeal, that provided that the crew of a fishing vessel had been alerted to the identity of the water bailiffs and to their intentions, it was not vital to the proper exercise of the bailiffs' powers to stop and search the vessel under s.10 of the Act that they produced the instruments of their appointment. The circumstances of each case had to be taken into account and the fact that the present incident had taken place in the open sea distinguished it from the decision in *Barnacott v. Passmore* (1887) 19 Q.B. 75.

MACKAY v. WESTWATER, *The Scotsman*, November 16, 1995, Lord Ross, L.J.C., HCJ.

7011. Salmon and freshwater fisheries–River Eachaig close season

ANNUAL CLOSE TIME (RIVER EACHAIG SALMON FISHERY DISTRICT) ORDER 1995, SI 1995 3047 (S.220); made under the Salmon Act 1986 s.6. In force: January 1, 1996; £0.65.

This Order prescribes the date of the annual close time for the River Eachaig Salmon Fishery District as September 1 to April 30, both dates inclusive, and thereby replaces the previous dates which were September 1 to February 15. This Order also prescribes September 1 to October 31, both dates inclusive, as the period within that annual close time during which fishing for salmon by rod and line is permitted.

7012. Salmon and freshwater fisheries–River Tay

RIVER TAY CATCHMENT AREA PROTECTION (RENEWAL) ORDER 1993 VARIATION ORDER 1996, SI 1996 58 (S.3); made under the Freshwater and Salmon Fisheries (Scotland) Act 1976 s.1. In force: February 1, 1996; £1.10.

The River Tay Catchment Area Protection (Renewal) Order 1993 (SI 1993 276), which prohibits fishing in prescribed inland waters without legal right or written permission, is varied so that it continues in force for an unlimited period.

7013. Salmon and freshwater fisheries–Upper Spey

UPPER SPEY AND ASSOCIATED WATERS PROTECTION (RENEWAL) ORDER 1993 VARIATION ORDER 1996, SI 1996 57 (S.2); made under the Freshwater and Salmon Fisheries Act 1976 s.1. In force: February 1, 1996; £1.10.

The Upper Spey and Associated Waters Protection (Renewal) Order 1993 (SI 1993 3216), which prohibits fishing in prescribed inland waters without legal right or written permission, is varied so that it continues in force for an unlimited period.

7014. Sea fishing–fishing methods–Scapa Flow

INSHORE FISHING (PROHIBITION OF FISHING METHODS) (SCOTLAND) AMENDMENT ORDER 1996, SI 1996 1475 (S.131); made under the Inshore Fishing (Scotland) Act 1984 s.1. In force: July 8, 1996; £1.10.

Amends the Inshore Fishing (Prohibition of Fishing and Fishing Methods) (Scotland) Order 1989 (SI 1989 2307) by inserting a new prohibition on certain crab and lobster fishing in Scapa Flow between June 1 and September 15 each year.

7015. Sea fishing–fishing records–monofilament gill nets

INSHORE FISHING (MONOFILAMENT GILL NETS) (SCOTLAND) ORDER 1996, SI 1996 1907 (S.157); made under the Inshore Fishing (Scotland) Act 1984 s.1: Inshore Fishing (Scotland) Act 1984 s.2. In force: August 12, 1996; £1.10.

This Order prohibits fishing for sea fish with a monofilament gill in the specified area and the carriage of monofilament gill net having a mesh size less than 250 millimetres, for any purpose, in any British fishing board, in the specified area. The mesh size of nets is to be determined in accordance with Commission Regulation 2108/84. The Inshore Fishing (Prohibition of Carriage of Monofilament Gill Nets) (Scotland) Order 1986 is revoked.

7016. Shellfish

PROHIBITION OF KEEPING OF LIVE FISH (CRAYFISH) (SCOTLAND) ORDER 1996, SI 1996 1107 (S.119); made under the Import of Live Fish (Scotland) Act 1978 s.1. In force: May 29, 1996; £0.65.

Prohibits the keeping in Scotland of any species of live crayfish except under a licence granted by the Secretary of State, the definition of crayfish does not include the species austropotamobius pallipes, which is native to Scotland.

FOOD AND DRUGS

7017. Dairy products–hygiene

DAIRY PRODUCTS (HYGIENE) (SCOTLAND) AMENDMENT REGULATIONS 1996, SI 1996 2465 (S.194); made under the Food Safety Act 1990 s.6, s.16, s.17, s.18, s.19, s.26, s.48, Sch.1 para.5. In force: October 16, 1996; £1.55.

These Regulations amend the Dairy Products (Hygiene) Scotland) Regulations 1995 (SI 1995 1372). They implement Art.2 of, as read with Annex B to, Commission Decision 95/165 establishing uniform criteria for the grant of derogations to certain establishments manufacturing milk-based products; implement Commission Decision 95/340 drawing up a provisional list of third countries from which Member States authorise imports of milk and milk-based products and revoking Decision 94/70 as amended by Commission Decision 96/106 and as read with Art.22 and Art.23(2)(a) of Council Directive 92/46 laying down the health rules for the production and placing on the market of raw milk, heat-treated milk and milk-based products ([1992] OJ L268/1); make some corrections to the principal Regulations to reflect provisions in Council Directive 92/46 relating to heat-treated drinking milk and the health mark; provide a defence to a charge of selling raw drinking milk that the milk is intended for export; clarify the provisions in the principal Regulations relating to risk analysis principles and exemptions. In addition, they amend the Food Safety (General Food Hygiene) Regulations 1995 (SI 1995 1763) so that those Regulations apply to a person carrying on the handling in or the sale from any catering establishment or shop premises of ice-cream or heat-treated cream in Scotland.

7018. Food–animal products–revocation

FOOD (PREPARATION AND DISTRIBUTION OF MEAT) (SCOTLAND) REVOCATION REGULATIONS 1996, SI 1996 497 (S.46); made under the Food Safety Act 1990 s.16, s.26, s.48, Sch.1 para.5, Sch.1 para.6.. In force: March 31, 1996; £0.65.

These Regulations revoke the Food (Preparation and Distribution of Meat) (Scotland) Regulations 1963 (the 1963 Regulations). The 1963 Regulations originally controlled the construction, equipment and maintenance of slaughterhouses and meat markets. Provisions to ensure the hygienic handling of fresh meat up to the point of retail sale were also included. The measures specifically relating to slaughterhouses were revoked by the Slaughterhouse Hygiene (Scotland) Regulations 1978 (SI 1978 1273), now replaced by the Fresh Meat (Hygiene and Inspection) Regulations 1995 (SI 1995 539), but the provisions which apply to meat markets, meat handlers and distribution of meat still remain in force. These remaining provisions have now been superseded by more recent legislation applicable to Great Britain. The 1963 Regulations therefore no longer serve any useful regulatory purpose.

7019. Articles

Unfit food *(Francis McManus)*: J.L.S.S. 1996, 41 (3), 105-106 . (Problems in interpreting "unfit for human consumption" in connection with food safety offences).

HEALTH AND SAFETY AT WORK

7020. Accidents–foreseeability–employer's statutory duty to keep workplace safe

[Factories Act 1961 (c.34) s.14, s.29.]

M was injured when operating a machine at UET's tyre factory. M's claims for damages and under the Factories Act 1961 s.14 were rejected at first instance on the basis that the accident was not reasonably foreseeable. M's claim under s.29 of the 1961 Act was rejected for the same reason, and against that part of the decision M appealed.

Held, allowing the appeal, that s.29(1) of the 1961 Act places a duty on an employer to make the workplace safe, which means a duty to prevent any injury arising from the state of the workplace. There is nothing whatever in the section to suggest that the obligation is only to prevent risks arising if they are reasonably foreseeable, and the dicta to the contrary in *Keenan v. Rolls Royce Ltd* 1969 S.C. 322, [1970] C.L.Y. 3189 and *Morrow v. Enterprise Sheet Metal Works (Aberdeen) Ltd* 1986 S.C. 96, [1986] C.L.Y. 3618 should be disregarded. The correct approach was contained in *Nimmo v. Alexander Cowan Ltd* 1967 S.C.(HL) 79, [1967] C.L.Y. 4374 and *Larner v. British Steel Plc* [1993] I.R.L.R. 278, [1993] C.L.Y. 2021. Reasonable foreseeability may only be relevant in determining whether the employer has established that it was not reasonably practicable to make the workplace safe, as indicated in *Gillies v. Glynwed Foundries Ltd* 1977 S.L.T. 97, since considerations of reasonable practicability involve weighing the degree and extent of risk against the time, trouble and expense of preventing it.

MAINS v. UNIROYAL ENGLEBERT TYRES LTD [1995] I.R.L.R. 544, Lord Sutherland, IH.

7021. Building operations–negligence–erection of platforms as permanent access to plant in recently constructed building within factory–whether "building operations"

[Factories Act 1961 (c.34); Construction (Working Places) Regulations 1966 (SI 1966 94).]

A plater was injured in an accident at work on January 8, 1986. He was then aged 42. He fell from a ladder which he had placed on a walkway which consisted of metal gratings, the walkway being installed as access to machinery. He sustained a gross fracture dislocation of his ankle which healed with considerable pain requiring further operative treatment and, after about two years, arthrodesis of the ankle joint. He remained unfit for his preaccident work but had taken no steps to seek alternative employment. His case on the merits failed because there was no proof that the metal grating had not been properly placed in position and had moved, causing the fall. His cases of fault included various statutory cases, one of which was based on the Construction (Working Places) Regulations 1966 and a case against the occupiers based on the Factories Act 1961. After proof those defenders contended that the statutory provisions were inapplicable and, even if they were not barred from denying their applicability, the works were "building operations" to which the 1966 Regulations applied, and also that the premises were a factory to which s.29(1) of the 1961 Act applied.

Held, that (1) the employers and the occupiers were not barred from contending that the relevant statutory provisions were inapplicable since, although they had referred to those provisions, they had not inferentially admitted that they were applicable; (2) the 1966 Regulations did not apply to the work since the work was the provision of access to plant and not part of the construction of a building and therefore did not qualify as "building operations" and (3) the 1961 Act did not apply since the area where the accident happened was not being used for factory purposes. Opinion, that solatium was properly valued at £15,000 and that an award for wage loss to date would have been appropriate together with an award for future loss, calculated using a multiplier of three and a half years.

BALLANTYNE v. JOHN YOUNG & CO (KELVINHAUGH) 1996 S.L.T. 358, Judge not specified, OH.

7022. Employer's duty–breach of statutory duty–offshore installation to be "so maintained as to ensure" its safety and safety of persons

[Offshore Installations (Operational Safety, Health and Welfare) Regulations 1976 (SI 1976 1019) Reg.5(1).]

Regulation 5(1) of the Offshore Installations (Operational Safety, Health and Welfare) Regulations 1976 provides that, "All parts of every offshore installation and its equipment shall be so maintained as to ensure the safety of the installation and the safety and health of the persons thereon." A mechanic, employed on a drilling rig in the North Sea, was injured in the course of his employment. While walking from a boiler room to a spare parts department on the offshore installation, his foot slipped on the metal surface of the floor, on which there was a slippery substance similar to dieselene or grease. He raised an action of damages against his employers, one of the bases of the action being a breach of Reg.5(1). The defenders argued that Reg.5(1) was irrelevant where the cause of the accident was a substance on the surface of the installation, but not a defect in the installation itself, which argument was dismissed by the sheriff. The defenders appealed to the Court of Session.

Held, that (1) the obligation of maintenance in Reg.5(1), which imposed an absolute duty, was directed to the structural integrity of the installation, which had to be kept in a proper state of repair and (2) as the pursuer's averments were that the accident was caused by the presence on the floor of a slippery substance which was a transient condition which was not due in any way to a lack of maintenance of the structure of the floor, his averments were insufficient to found a breach of Reg.5(1); and appeal refused, *Breslin v. Britoil* 1992 S.L.T. 414, [1991] C.L.Y. 4880 overruled in part.

BRUCE v. BEN ODECO LTD 1996 S.L.T. 1315, Lord Hope, Lord President, IH.

7023. Employer's duty–criminal procedure–duty to ensure safety–relevancy of complaint

[Health and Safety at Work etc. Act 1974 (c. 37) s.2, s.33; Criminal Procedure (Scotland) Act 1975 (c. 21) s.312; Management of Health and Safety at Work Regulations 1992 (SI 1992 2051) Reg.3.]

S, a store, and its manager, M, were charged on summary complaint with violating s.2(1) and s.33 of the Health and Safety at Work etc Act 1974, whereby an employee instructed to stack boxes stepped onto, and fell through, fragile tiles adjacent to a working platform within a cupboard (charge 1), and S was charged with breaching Reg. 3 of the Management of Health and Safety at Work Regulations 1992, by failing to make a sufficient assessment of risks to the health and safety of S's employees (charge 2). S and M objected to the relevancy of the complaint and, following a hearing, the sheriff dismissed charge 2 and parts (a) and (c) of charge 1. The Crown appealed against the sheriff's decision, arguing that branch (a) of charge 1 contained sufficient notice as it mirrored the words of s.2(1)(b) of the 1974 Act; branch (c) was plainly based on s.2(2)(a) of the Act; and the sheriff had erred in looking at the different branches in isolation instead of as a whole. In terms of s.312(p) of the Criminal Procedure (Scotland) Act 1975, no further specification was required. In respect of charge 2, the Crown only required to prove that S had failed to make an assessment of the risks or that any assessment made was not suitable, and therefore it was inappropriate for the sheriff to conclude that the charge was irrelevant, that it failed to give M fair notice of the charges against him, *Blair v. Keane* 1981 S.L.T. (Notes) 4, [1980] C.L.Y. 3008 or that M was not alive to the allegations, *Walkingshaw v. Robison & Davidson* 1989 S.L.T. 17, [1988] C.L.Y. 3955. M submitted that the sheriff was well founded in dismissing charge 2 and branch (c) of charge 1, while accepting that branch (a) contained sufficient notice. Charge 2 did not state in what respect the assessment of the risks to health and safety was allegedly insufficient, as regards the type of risk, the persons at risk, the nature and extent of any dangers or the measures required to be taken. In addition, branch (c) of charge 1 was obscure, confusing and unintelligible, as it alleged a failure to provide systems of work concerning the storage of boxes but went on to specify an insufficiency in S's training manuals.

Held, appeal allowed of consent in relation to branch (a) of charge 1; quoad ultra appeal refused, S and M's arguments were preferred, (1) the reference to training manuals in the context of systems of work in branch (c) of charge 1 was confusing and unintelligible, since work systems fell under s.2(2)(a) of the 1974 Act, but manuals under s.2(2)(c), and the alleged deficiency in the manuals had nothing to do with systems of work, and (2) on the wording of charge 2, the Crown would be entitled to prove either that no assessment had been made or that an assessment made was not suitable and sufficient, and M was entitled to be told the essential features of the case.

CARMICHAEL v. MARKS & SPENCER 1995 S.C.C.R. 781, Judge not specified.

7024. Employers' duty–failure to ensure health and safety

[Health and Safety at Work etc. Act 1974 (c.37) s.2(1) and (2), s.17 and s.33.]

Section 16 of the Health and Safety at Work etc. Act 1974 provides that for the purposes of providing practical guidance with respect to the requirements of, *inter alia*, s.2 of the Act, the Health and Safety Commission may, with the Secretary of State's consent and after consultation, approve codes of practice issued by outside bodies. Section 17 provides that where in criminal proceedings a party is alleged to have committed an offence by reason of a contravention of any requirement or prohibition of an approved code, any provision of the code which appears to the court to be relevant to the requirement or prohibition shall be taken as proved unless the court is satisfied that the requirement of prohibition was complied with otherwise than by observance of that provision of the code. A limited company was charged on indictment with, and convicted of *inter alia*, a contravention of s.2 and s.33 of the 1974 Act by failing to ensure so far as was reasonably practicable the health, safety and welfare of their employees in that during the transfer of anchor chains by means of a crane they failed to perform duties under subs.(2)(a)-(e) and that as a consequence the crane, while a 15 tonne chain was suspended above their employees, overturned and an employee was struck by the chain and killed. The deceased, who had been engaged by the company for two days prior to the accident, was directed to work under the chain but no instructions were given by the company to the crane driver, an employee of a sub-contractor, to take account of that fact. The company appealed on the ground that the British Code of Practice for the safe use of cranes, published by the British Standards Institution, was inadmissible as hearsay evidence as it was not approved in terms of s.16.

Held, that (1) the unapproved status of the code of practice was immaterial as the Crown was not relying on the code to speak for itself but was relying on the witness's opinion as to whether it was or was not a statement of good practice; (2) the question was whether there was sufficient evidence to convict the company of the charge and the answer to that question did not depend on the court's assessment of the apportionment of blame between the company, the crane driver or his employers; (3) there was ample evidence to show that the company failed to perform the general duty in s.2(1) of the 1974 Act in regard to part at least of each of paras.(a)-(e) of subs.(2) and (4) while the crane overturned without fault on the company's part, a proper risk assessment would have indicated that is was possible that the crane might become overloaded if stretched too far and that no one should have been required to work anywhere near the chain while it was being moved; and appeal refused.

BALMORAL GROUP LTD v. HM ADVOCATE 1996 S.L.T. 1230, Judge not specified, HCJ.

7025. Factories–regulations made under the Factories Act–scope of protection

Held, that in an action of damages against the occupiers of a factory in which action the pursuer founded on regulations made under the Factories Act 1961, that the case based on the regulations was irrelevant because the pursuer had not averred that he had been employed in whatever capacity or by whomsoever while in the factory premises.

BROWN v. CARLIN 1996 S.C.L.R. 739, Judge not specified, Sh Ct.

7026. Master and servant–sufficiency of instruction–moving heavy item

[Factories Act 1961 (c.34) s.72.]

Section 72(1) of the Factories Act 1961 provides: "A person shall not be employed to lift, carry or move any load so heavy as to be likely to cause injury to him." A storekeeper was injured while manhandling reels of paper which weighed about 220 to 245 kg. He was required to roll the reels to their position in the store, which involved turning them through 90, a task for which he had not been trained. As he was turning a reel, he injured his back. His action was raised both at common law and under s.72(1) of the Factories Act 1961.

Held, in considering the statutory case, that the test to be applied was an objective one involving not only consideration of the physical characteristics of the "load" and the means available for moving it but also of the particular employee, his skills and the employer's training and supervision; and decree pronounced in favour of the pursuer.

WATKINSON v. BRITISH TELECOMMUNICATIONS PLC 1996 S.L.T. 72, Judge not specified, OH.

7027. Safe place of work–mobile welding shed moving on wheels fitted into steel channels

[Factories Act 1961 (c.34) s.29.]

D sued his employers, B, for damages after suffering injury on April 11, 1994 whilst working in B's fabrication yard. D was assisting in moving a welding shed formed of metal and mounted on wheels fitted into steel channels set in the ground on each side of a set of rollers. Tubes for the construction of oil rigs were placed on the rollers in order to be welded together. The shed would be moved into a position so that the welding of two tubes together could be carried out from above the joint, from a scaffold platform six feet from ground level. The platform was made up of scaffold poles and planks, and held the welding equipment and cables. Plastic sheeting extended from each end of the shed almost to the ground. The shed was too heavy to be moved manually and was pushed by a forklift truck. The shed was not secured or attached to the truck. The shed was being moved and the driver of the truck was unable to see beyond the side of, or face of, the shed or underneath the platform. The driver was looking to D, on the ground ahead of the truck, for signals. D had pushed aside plastic sheeting to check whether anything would be caught in the tubing, and saw that cables from the platform had fallen where they could be caught and pull the welding equipment. D's arm became trapped between part of the structure and the tubing as he attempted to throw the cables back. As his glove was nipped he shouted to the driver to stop but the shed moved inches more before halting. D's actions had been made on the spur of the moment and to save valuable equipment. D argued that B were at fault at common law and under the Factories Act 1961 s.29(1), in failing to provide a safe place of work. B argued that the danger was a transient and unusual one in that D had put himself at risk of injury and this was not foreseeable by B. D should have stopped the driver before going under the shed. D's expert conceded that a braking system would only have mitigated, not eliminated the risk of injury.

Held, granting the decree, that the mobile shed and the area in which it was travelling formed a place of work in which D was required to check the shed was free from obstruction and prevent damage, which he did. D had made a reasonable decision in the situation. If the shed had been shackled to the truck, the shed would have been halted immediately when D had given the signal. It was dangerous to move a large and heavy piece of metal without being in full control of its movement, thus the statutory duty was breached. Further, it was reasonably foreseeable that workmen would react suddenly to prevent damage in such circumstances, and the risk of injury could have been reduced. The absence of previous prior accident did not excuse B. D had not contributed to the negligence as the assumption of risk D had undertaken was reasonable, *Steel v. Glasgow Iron & Steel Co* 1945 S.L.T. 70. Damages were agreed at £2,500, inclusive of interest.

DOYLE v. BROWN & ROOT HIGHLAND FABRICATORS 1996 S.C.L.R. 192, Judge not specified, OH.

7028. Articles

The Manual Handling Regulations: the story so far *(Ronnie Conway.)*: Rep. B. 1996, 12(Nov), 2-3. (Interpretation and application of Manual Handling Operations Regulations 1992 in personal injury cases).

When stress fractures *(Alan W.D. McLean)*: Rep. B. 1996, 12(Nov), 3-5. (Employer's liability for stress at work with reference to out of court settlement for social worker suffering stress as result of supervisor's actions).

HERITABLE PROPERTY AND CONVEYANCING

7029. Common property–division and sale–division between cohabitees on separation–recompense for mortgage payments

Held, in an action of division and sale at the insistence of one former cohabitee against the other, that the defender should be ordered to sell his one-half share in the property to the pursuer at the agreed price and that he should be ordered to repay to the pursuer one-half of the mortgage payments which had been made by her since the relationship between the parties had broken down.

GRAY v. KERNER 1996 S.C.L.R. 331, Judge not specified, Sh Ct.

7030. Common property–division and sale–effect of prior agreement to divorce

A husband entered into a minute of agreement with his wife by which it was agreed that the husband would transfer two thirds of the reversionary interest in the matrimonial home to his wife and retain one third himself. It was further agreed that the husband would not seek to force a sale of the house for a period of five years from the date of their divorce and that the wife would be entitled to occupy the house so long as it remained unsold. The parties were divorced in October 1989. After five years elapsed the husband raised an action in the sheriff court for the division or sale of the house. The husband sought summary decree. The wife sought to have the action sisted pending the outcome of an action raised by her in the Court of Session against her former solicitors in which she claimed damages for their alleged failure to take into account her husband's interest in a pension fund in their reckoning of the matrimonial property. The sheriff refused to sist the action and granted summary decree. The wife appealed to the Court of Session, arguing that the sale of the house should be deferred and that the sheriff had erred in failing properly to take into account the equitable circumstances in that the husband had a degree of financial security while the wife was in poorly paid employment and had no capital with which to buy her husband's reversionary interest in the property, but was likely to succeed in claim against her former solicitors.

Held, that there was no question of adjusting the financial provisions of the divorce and as the five-year period had expired, the pursuer had an absolute right to insist in the action for division and sale; and appeal refused.

BURROWS v. BURROWS 1996 S.L.T. 1313, Judge not specified, IH.

7031. Disposition–destination–survivorship clause–agreement to sell property as part of settlement on divorce–supervening death of party

A husband and wife purchased a house, both parties contributing to the price and the disposition being granted to them "equally between them and to the survivor of them". The couple subsequently separated and both raised actions of divorce. Thereafter they entered into a minute of agreement in terms of which both actions were to be dismissed and the husband undertook in cl.4 to raise an action of divorce on the grounds of two years' separation to which the wife would consent. The agreement further provided in cl.1, cl.2 and cl.3 for the former matrimonial home to be marketed by estate agents and the proceeds of sale to be divided between the parties, and in cl.5 that "save as provided for in these presents neither party shall have any claim of any nature against the other either now or at any time in the future and the parties hereby relinquish all rights in succession to the estate of the other party in the event of the death of either of them". The house was put on the market but no sale had been effected when the husband died. The wife thereafter refused to agree to the sale of the house. The husband's executors raised an action for declarator that the minute of agreement was a valid and subsisting contract binding on the parties, and for implement by the wife of the agreement to sell the house. At debate the wife sought dismissal arguing that the minute of agreement and in particular cl.4 was so impressed with the character of *delectus personae* that the agreement, had to be performed during the parties' life and that no rights under it could be assigned or transmit to the executors; that the obligations in the agreement was interdependent, and accordingly, as cl.4 had been frustrated by the death of the husband, the executors were not entitled to enforce the obligations in cl.1 to cl.3; and that cl.5 was inept to evacuate the special destination in the disposition, and accordingly, as the husband's share in the house had automatically been transferred to the wife, the executors had no basis for intervening to require her to do something which had never been intended by the parties.

Held, that (1) the minute of agreement comprised two distinct parts, the first to regulate the parties' relationship as married persons and the second to regulate the sale of the matrimonial home, and, given that neither part contained any reference to time for performance or any indication that the obligations under one part were conditional upon performance of the obligations in the other part, it was clear that the intention of the parties had been that the sale of the house should proceed independently of the remaining provisions of the agreement and (2) the effect of cl.5 was that each party had voluntarily waived the bar to evacuation incorporated in the special destination upon a sale to a third party being effected in accordance with the agreement; and decree of declarator granted, and case put out by order for a hearing with regard to the second conclusion for implement. Doubted, that cl.4 involved an element of *delectus personae* as that phrase was properly understood.

REDFERN'S EXECUTORS v. REDFERN 1996 S.L.T. 900, Judge not specified, OH.

7032. Disposition–destination–survivorship clause–divorce–entitlement of former wife on death of former husband

In 1984 a married couple bought a house. The disposition conveyed it to them "equally between them and to the survivor of them and to their respective executors and assignees whomsoever heritably and irredeemably". The couple separated in November 1985 and were divorced in September 1986. In November 1985 the wife conveyed her one-half pro indiviso share in the property to her husband. On the death of the former husband in July 1991 his executors claimed to be entitled to the whole of the subjects, whereas the former wife claimed that the 1985 conveyance had not affected the survivorship provision attaching to the husband's original one-half share.

Held, that the 1985 disposition had conveyed only the former wife's one-half share, with the result that the former husband's original one-half share continued to be subject to the survivorship destination; and executor's action of declarator dismissed as irrelevant.

GARDNER'S EXECUTORS v. RAEBURN 1996 S.L.T. 745, Judge not specified, OH.

7033. Land obligations–variation and discharge–effect of express provision for change of use

[Conveyancing and Feudal Reform (Scotland) Act 1970 (c.35) s.1 (3) (b), s.1 (3) (c), s.1 (4).]

In May 1987 a company purchased an area of land from a development corporation for £100,000 for the purposes of building and operating an ice rink. It was agreed that had the site been sold entirely for retail development, the value would have been around £750,000. Certain land obligations were created by the corporation in a feu disposition to the company dated August 31 and registered in the Land Register on September 4, 1987. These obligations, *inter alia*, restricted the site to use for an ice rink and provided a detailed scheme in cl. Fourth to regulate the situation between superior and feuar in the event of the ice rink becoming financially unviable. The clause resulted from a condition in the original tender made by the company, to the effect that the company would pay the corporation £650,000 if such financial unviability did occur. The ice rink was duly constructed and opened on October 1, 1990. It ceased to operate in April 1993 due to financial difficulties and was closed in October 1993. In January 1994 the receiver of the company sold the subjects for £2,250,000 to another company which proposed to use them as a bingo hall. The corporation having refused to vary the restriction in the 1987 feu disposition, the purchasers applied to the Lands Tribunal. They found in favour of the applicants under heads (b) and (c) of s.1 (3) of the Conveyancing and Feudal Reform (Scotland) Act 1970 and varied the land obligation to allow the subjects to be used as a bingo hall. They also awarded the sum of £206,000 as compensation to the corporation under s.1 (4) (ii) of the 1970 Act, taking the view that the sum of £650,000 related to the circumstances whereby the use of the subjects would be changed to retail and that that sum was an incorrect basis for assessing compensation when the change of use was to a bingo hall. The corporation appealed to the Court of Session and challenged the tribunal's decision in relation to heads (b) and (c), and the matter of compensation, arguing that the tribunal had failed to take into account the availability of cl. Fourth, which was a material consideration when considering the tests under heads (b) and (c), and that compensation should have been awarded under s.1 (4) (i) of the Act in the sum of £864,110, this being the sum of £650,000 as increased by the appropriate indexation.

Held, that (1) in the absence of any mention of cl. Fourth as a factor or any explanation for its absence from the relevant part of their opinion, it could not be said that the Lands Tribunal took proper account of the clause as a factor in balancing the burdens and benefits for the purposes of s.1 (3) (b) of the 1970 Act and that if that factor was taken into account, the tribunal could not have held the obligation to be unduly burdensome; accordingly, the tribunal had erred in law with regard to the head of the application under s.1 (3) (b); (2) the tribunal had taken proper account of cl. Fourth in relation to the head of application under s.1 (3) (c) in considering whether the existence of the obligation impeded some reasonable use of the land and had not fallen into error in that regard, and even if the matter had been open for reconsideration, the conclusion reached by the tribunal would not have been altered; (3) the tribunal had not erred in law in relation to the question of compensation as the proposed change of use was not to retail use and in addition the possibility of recovery under cl. Fourth was only speculative and (4) this was not one of the exceptional cases where variation should be refused because money was not an adequate compensation; and appeal refused.

CUMBERNAULD DEVELOPMENT CORP v. COUNTY PROPERTIES AND DEVELOPMENTS 1996 S.L.T. 1106, Judge not specified, IH.

7034. Land Registers (Scotland) Act 1995–Commencement Order

LAND REGISTERS (SCOTLAND) ACT 1995 (COMMENCEMENT) ORDER 1996, SI 1996 94 (C.1; S.4); made under the Land Registers (Scotland) Act 1995 s.2. In force: April 1, 1996; £0.65.

This Order brings into force the provisions of the Land Registers (Scotland) Act 1995 on April 1, 1996.

7035. Land registration–registrable transactions or events–decree of reduction of disposition

[Bankruptcy (Scotland) Act 1985 (c.66) s.34; Land Registration (Scotland) Act 1979 (c.33) s.2, s.9; Conveyancing (Scotland) Act 1924 (c.27) s.46; Law Reform (Miscellaneous Provisions) (Scotland) Act 1985 (c.73) s.59.]

L, permanent trustee on the sequestrated estates of Alexander Short, sought judicial review of a decision by the Keeper refusing to register a decree of reduction of certain dispositions of two flats in Glasgow. S, as the heritable proprietor, had sold two flats in Glasgow within two years of the date of his sequestration at prices below those on the open market. L challenged the dispositions granted by S on the ground that they were gratuitous alienations, under the Bankruptcy (Scotland) Act 1985 s.34. A decree of reduction was granted. A reclaiming motion was refused *Short's Trustee v. Chung* 1991 S.L.T. 472, [1991] C.L.Y. 4415. L then applied to the Keeper for effect to be given to the decree of reduction showing S as heritable proprietor under the Land

Registration (Scotland) Act 1979 s.2(4)(c). The Keeper refused on the ground that the appropriate procedure was to apply for rectification under s.9(1) of the 1979 Act. The question was whether a decree of reduction was an event falling within the terms of s.2(4)(c) or whether the legislative intent was that a decree of reduction could only receive effect by way of rectification of the register under s.9. The Lord Ordinary pronounced an interlocutor dismissing L's application. L reclaimed and the interlocutor was affirmed. L appealed to the House of Lords.

Held, dismissing the appeal, that indemnification rather than registration was the appropriate remedy. Parliament could not have intended the creation of a situation where a decree of reduction of a deed forming part of the title to unregistered land was capable, by recording in the General Register of Sasines, of vesting the title to the land in the holder of the decree but with no corresponding remedy in the case of registered land. There were two distinct systems for registration of heritable rights in Scotland and the present proceedings would never have taken place had the flats been in Edinburgh rather than Glasgow. The system of land registration involved a guaranteed title with limited scope for rectification and a right of indemnity in suitable cases where rectification was unavailable. With the General Register of Sasines there was no room for rectification and only the recording of further deeds or instruments could affect title. Under the Conveyancing (Scotland) Act 1924 s.46(2) (as amended by the Law Reform (Miscellaneous Provisions) (Scotland) Act 1985 s.59 and Sch.2 para.7), the amended recording in the Register was the appropriate course where a document has been rectified by order, under s.8 of the 1985 Act, in the case of unregistered land. In the case of registered land, in contrast, the appropriate course was rectification under s.9(3)(b) of the 1979 Act, *Gibson v. Hunter Home Designs Ltd* 1976 S.C. 23, [1976] C.L.Y. 3188 considered.

SHORT'S TRUSTEE v. KEEPER OF THE REGISTERS OF SCOTLAND; SUB NOM. LAING v. KEEPER OF THE REGISTERS OF SCOTLAND 1996 S.L.T. 166, Lord Keith of Kinkel, HL.

7036. Land Registration (Scotland) Act 1979–Commencement No.10 Order

LAND REGISTRATION (SCOTLAND) ACT 1979 (COMMENCEMENT NO.10) ORDER 1996, SI 1996 2490 (C.66; S.195); made under the Land Registration (Scotland) Act 1979 s.30. In force: April 1, 1997; £0.65.

This Order brings into force on April 1, 1997 in the areas of the Counties of Ayr, Dumfries, the Stewartry of Kirkcudbright and Wigtown, the Land Registration (Scotland) Act 1979 s.2(1)(2) and s.3(3) which provides for the circumstances in which an interest in land shall be registrable and provides that certain persons are to obtain a real right only by registration.

7037. Possession–rights of possession against holder of ex facie valid title

Held, that the possessors of heritable property could obtain permanent interdict against someone who challenged that possession only if they were able to do so, and that, since the challenger lost an ex facie valid title to the subjects which constituted clear prima facie evidence that he was heritable proprietor of the property and entitled to interfere with the possessors' possession, the possessors were not entitled to interdict against the challenger.

WATSON v. SHIELDS 1996 S.C.L.R. 81, Judge not specified, IH.

7038. Sale–missives–breach–effect of subsequent disposition

Held, where missives of sale contained a warranty, inter alia, that all necessary building warrants had been obtained, and the subsequent disposition expressly saved the continuing obligations to the missives, that the warranty continued to be enforceable.

GLAZIK v. IYER 1996 S.C.L.R. 270, Judge not specified, Sh Ct.

7039. Sale–missives–breach–entitlment to resile

Held, where sellers had failed to exhibit a necessary completion certificate of the date of settlement, that the purchasers were entitled to resile.

HAWKE v. WB MATHERS 1995 S.C.L.R. 1004, Judge not specified, Sh Ct.

7040. Sale–missives–construction–entitlement to rescind

Missives for the sale of heritable property provided, inter alia, that in the event of the purchase price not being paid in full within 21 days of the date of entry, the sellers would be entitled to treat the purchasers as being in material breach of contract and to rescind the missives on giving prior written notice to that effect. No part of the total consideration was in fact made over within the stipulated period. On June 2, 1995, the day upon which the 21 day-period expired, the sellers sent a letter purporting to hold the purchasers in material breach of contract and rescinding the missives with immediate effect. The purchasers did not accept the purported rescission. Further correspondence followed. On July 5, 1995 the sellers wrote two more letters. The first purported to intimate that the sellers held the purchasers in material breach of contract and would resile from the contract. The second stated that the contract constituted by the missives was rescinded. The sellers raised an action for declarator that the missives between the parties were at an end.

Held, that (1) in terms of the clause, failure to pay the purchase price by the due time was a material breach of contract entitling but not obliging the pursuers to take the further steps provided; (2) the written notice had to anticipate a future rescission and in the absence of any defined period between notice and rescission, a reasonable time had to be allowed to elapse, so that the purported immediate rescission contained in the letter of June 2, 1995 was not competent under the provision; (3) on a sound construction of the missives as a whole, notice of the kind given in the first letter of July 5, 1995, followed immediately by intimation of rescission, was not competent; and action dismissed.

Observed, that what constituted a reasonable time would be required to be determined on an objective basis in the circumstances of the case.

CHARISMA PROPERTIES LTD v. GRAYLING (1994) LTD 1996 S.L.T. 791, Judge not specified, OH.

7041. Sale–missives–construction–interest payable by purchaser–whether a "liquidate penalty"

Held, where missives provided for payment of interest on the purchase price in the event of late settlement, and that such interest should be deemed to be a "liquidate penalty" in the event of rescission, that the seller was able to claim other losses in addition to the interest referred to in the missives in the event of late settlement rather than rescission.

FIELD v. DICKINSON 1995 S.C.L.R. 1146, Judge not specified, Sh Ct.

7042. Sale–missives–suspensive conditions–waiver

B reclaimed against the Lord Ordinary's decision, granting declarator to M that their missives for the sale of land to B were at an end. Condition 7.1 of B's offer stated that the missives would remain conditional until B intimated in writing to M that they had received planning permission to use the property as an opencast mine. Under cl.7.4 the missives would fall if intimation pursuant to cl.7.1 was not made within two years of the conclusion of the contract. Two days before the expiry of the (extended) time limit, B wrote to M stating the condition 7 had been "purified", although planning permission had not been granted, which M refused to accept. B argued that they had waived condition 7 of the contract, which they were entitled to do since it was conceived only for their benefit.

Held, reclaiming motion refused, that a party was entitled to waive a condition which was purely in his own interest *Dewar & Finlay Ltd v. Blackwood* 1968 S.L.T. 196, [1968] C.L.Y. 4351, the condition could not be waived if the other party had an interest in its performance. If the question of whether the stipulation was for the sole benefit of the party seeking to waive it was not obvious from the face of the contract, then it could not be struck out unilaterally and it was not for the court to conduct an inquiry outside its terms to ascertain where the benefit lay, *Heron Garage Properties v. Moss* [1974] 1 W.L.R. 148, [1974] C.L.Y. 3943. Therefore, the whole contract had to be examined to determine the intention of the parties from the terms of the contract without the aid of extrinsic evidence, *Hawksley v. Outram* [1892] 3 Ch. 359. Even if a condition was conceived solely for the interests of one party, it could not be waived if it was inextricably connected with other parts of the contract and could not be severed from them, *Zebmoon v. Akinbrook Investment Developments* 1988 S.L.T. 146, [1988] C.L.Y. 4348; each provision had to be read in the context of the whole contract. In terms of cl.7.1 the missives between B and M remained conditional until written intimation was given by B, and therefore condition 7.1 had to be read together with the other conditions in the missives, which revealed that both parties had an interest in the obtaining of the planning permission, thereby excluding B's right to waive the condition since it could not be said to have been inserted into the missives solely in B's own interest. In addition, condition 7 was inextricably linked to the date of entry and if its requirements were waived, the contract would be unworkable. *Per* the Lord President (Hope): *Dewar & Finlay* did not provide much value as guidance regarding the waiver of suspensive conditions generally since it did not discuss the severability of the suspensive condition from the rest of the contract. *Per* Lord Sutherland: In light of the way the law had developed, the decision in *Dewar & Finlay*, which was based on a limited construction of the contract, could no longer be supported.

MANHEATH v. HJ BANKS & CO 1996 S.L.T. 1006, Judge not specified, IH.

7043. Servitude–access–express grant–infringement–whether order to remove buildings should be granted

In 1985 the owner of an hotel property disponed the subjects, excepting therefrom the whole ground floor premises and an access lane, and reserved a servitude right of pedestrian and vehicular access of subjects delineated on a plan. The singular successor of the disponee carried out development work following upon a major fire. Part of the development protruded 4.8 metres into the servitude subjects. The proprietor of the dominant tenement raised an action against the proprietor of the servient tenement seeking interdict against his carrying out further works or placing other obstructions upon the subjects and decree ordaining the defender to remove the works.

Held, that while the pursuer had no practical reason for seeking to exercise access rights over the affected property and although it was neither fair nor just to do so, decree fell to be granted, the defender having effected a unilateral alteration to an urban servitude of passage described in the 1985 disposition; and decree granted, implementation of which in removing the works to be within 12 months, *Hill v. McLaren* (1879) 6 R. 1363 and *Moyes v. McDiarmid* (1900) 2 F. 918, followed. Opinion, that had the court not been bound by the authorities, the appropriate disposal would have been one of absolvitor.

MUNRO v. McCLINTOCK 1996 S.L.T. (Sh.Ct.) 97, Judge not specified, Sh Ct.

7044. Standard security–description of subjects–description by postal address–whether "particular description"

[Titles to Land Consolidation (Scotland) Act 1868 (c.101); Conveyancing (Scotland) Act 1924 (c.27) Sch.D; Conveyancing and Feudal Reform (Scotland) Act 1970 (c.35) Sch.2.]

The Conveyancing and Feudal Reform (Scotland) Act 1970 Sch.2 prescribes the forms of a standard security. Note 1 thereto provides that: "The security subjects shall be described by means of a particular description or by reference to a description thereof as in Schedule D to the Conveyancing (Scotland) Act 1924 or as in Schedule G to the Titles to Land (Consolidation) (Scotland) Act 1868. A couple borrowed money from a bank. In security of the loan the bank requested that a standard security be granted by the couple over certain property owned by them. The security subjects were described as being, "The Heritable subjects known as 57 Longdykes Road, Prestonpans in the County of East Lothian." A question arose as to the validity of the description for the purposes of the 1970 Act. The couple and the bank brought a special case before the Inner House to decide the matter.

Held, that (1) the requirement for a particular description by reference in a standard security was mandatory; (2) it was clear that the amount of detail which was required for a description to be effective in regard to transactions affecting heritable property would very according to circumstances and those descriptions might be classified into a number of generally recognised categories; (3) the test for a particular description was whether sufficient detail was given to define the boundaries, expressly or by necessary implication, in such a way as to remove any need to rely upon the state of possession and the operation of the positive prescription and (4) as the security subjects in the present case comprised a mid terrace villa with adjoining garden ground there was nothing in the postal address which defined the extent of the subjects either expressly or by implication so it could not be held to constitute a particular description of them; and question answered accordingly. Opinion, it would be going too far to assert that a postal address would never constitute a particular description as it might contain within it all that was needed to identify the boundaries.

BENEFICIAL BANK PLC v. McCONNACHIE 1996 S.L.T. 413, Judge not specified, IH.

7045. Standard security–discharge–reduction–relevancy

A bank, B, reclaimed against a temporary judge's decision to allow a proof before answer in S's action for reduction of S's discharge of a standard security which had been granted by F. S averred that the discharge had been signed and issued by mistake and that S had unilaterally and gratuitously conferred a benefit upon F. B argued that S were not entitled to adduce parole evidence to show that the discharge had been granted gratuitously as that would contradict the probative terms of the discharge which showed that it had been granted "in consideration of all sums due or that might become due"; that S could not seek reduction of an onerous deed on the grounds of their own unilateral error; and that there were no averments to show that the error was mutual or induced, how it had come about, or that it had been reasonably entertained. S argued that the phrase "all sums due or that might become due", which was taken from the standard form of standard security, did not reflect any real consideration and that, if there were sums due or which might become due to S, then it did not appear that S had granted the discharge for any consideration; that, accordingly, ex facie the discharge was gratuitous; that, as S had given D a benefit by mistake and sine cause, S's error did not need to be excusable, *Morgan Guaranty Trust Co of New York v. Lothian RC* 1995 S.L.T. 299, [1995] C.L.Y. 5586; and that the error was mutual in that F had been in error when recording the discharge in supposing that they had a right to that benefit.

Held, refusing the reclaiming motion, that S would not necessarily fail to establish that the discharge had been granted as a result of essential error, and, given the curious terms of the discharge, it could not be said that it was plainly mutual and onerous. S were not seeking to use extrinsic evidence to contradict the meaning of the discharge, but to establish the preceding error which resulted in it being sent to F. Further, as many of the relevant authorities involved the application of equitable principles similar to the condictio indebiti, the court would be reluctant to apply or exclude those principles before the facts had been ascertained in what was a complicated and confused situation.

SECURITY PACIFIC FINANCE v. T & I FILSHIE'S TRUSTEES 1995 S.C.L.R. 1171, Judge not specified, IH.

7046. Articles

A ("qualified") conveyancer's responsibilities–Begg revisited? *(Gordon Junor)*: S.L.G. 1996, 64(3), 118-120. (Duties of solicitors as set out in 19th century treatise Begg on Law Agents remain relevant today as statements of professional responsibility).

Alluvio in the Land Register: shifting sands and the thin red line. *(Robert Rennie)*: S.L.T. 1996, 5, 41-44. (Principle of accretion and difficulties of registering land bounded by sea or river where boundaries change from time to time).

Casualties: suitable cases for treatment *(John Sinclair)*: S.L.P.Q. 1996, 1 (2), 125-130. (Commutation of feudal casualties, which are various forms of payments in connection with feus, into feuduties, failure of Act to abolish leasehold casualties and consequent implications for indemnity claims).

Conveyancing quality standards *(John Elliot)*: J.L.S.S. 1996, 41 (11), 436-437. (Results of survey by Law Society of Scotland on views of legal profession as to "kite-marking" conveyancing practice and procedures).

Descriptions in standard securities–where now? *(Douglas J. Cusine.)*: J.L.S.S. 1996, 41 (6), 209-211. (Difficulties still persist as to whether postal address is sufficient particular description, despite IH ruling).

Development sites and a disposition of the superiority *(Roderick Paisley)*: Jur. Rev. 1996, 2, 109-126. (Devices available to deal with adverse title conditions relating to sites).

Development sites and purchasers of the superiority *(Roderick Paisley)*: Jur. Rev. 1996, 5, 331-352. (Different interests and motives of parties who may wish to purchase superiority and consequent need for different and appropriate contracts).

Drainage systems and rural properties *(David M. Preston* and *Mike Jarvie)*: Prop. L.B. 1996, 22(Aug), 4-6. (Practical title problems relating to drainage and drainage rights in rural properties).

Estate agents *(Anthony F. Deutsch)*: Civ. P.B. 1996, 8(Mar), 5-7. (Legality of standard terms in estate agents' contracts).

Estate agents and advertising charges *(Rod McKenzie)*: Civ. P.B. 1996, 12(Nov), 4-6. (Disclosure obligations of estate agents regarding advertising discounts and whether scale charges were part of remuneration).

Metrication and conveyancing descriptions. : Prop. L.B. 1996, 19(Feb), 4-7. (Guidance from Keeper of the Registers as to compliance with EC Directives when submitting documents to Land Register and Sasine Register).

Minerals and the land register *(Alec M. Falconer)*: J.L.S.S. 1996, 41 (7), 266-267. (Issues for consideration when seeking to register mineral rights in the Scottish land register).

Registers of Scotland–requisition policy in the Land Register. : J.L.S.S. 1996, 41 (7), 272. (Rights of Keeper of Land Register to require submission of documentation where original application incomplete but accepted).

Requirements of writing: problems in practice *(Robert Rennie)*: S.L.P.Q. 1996, 1 (3), 187-196. (Review of 1995 Act after eight months suggests no real problems in its operation although different interpretations of certain provisions and different practices in relation to missives require resolution).

Setting missives up–and apart *(Robert Rennie)*: Prop. L.B. 1996, 19(Feb), 2-4. (Practical problems on form of contracts for sale of land in light of 1995 Act).

Special destinations *(John H. Sinclair)*: Prop. L.B. 1996, 22(Aug), 6-7. (Questions that need to be considered before entering special destination in disposition).

The perils of a trusting disposition *(Andrew J.M. Steven* and *Scott Wortley)*: S.L.T. 1996, 37, 365-369. (Efficacy of practice of declaring in conveyance that seller holds property in trust for buyer until registration where seller becomes insolvent or where floating charge is attached).

The scope and meaning of "dwelling-house" in title conditions. *(Douglas J. Cusine)*: S.L.P.Q. 1996, 1 (5), 384-396 .

Void and voidable deeds and the Land Register *(Kenneth G.C. Reid.)*: S.L.P.Q. 1996, 1 (4), 265-276. (Implications for Scots property law of land registration system introduced 1979 in light of decision in Short's Trustee with particular regard to registration–rectification–indemnity triangle).

Winston v Patrick revisited: the two year enforceability clause. *(Gordon Junor)*: Prop. L.B. 1996, 23(Oct), 2-4. (Cases since "Winston v Patrick" show continuing uncertainty as to whether conveyance of land supersedes missives even in relation to collateral matters).

7047. Books

Halliday, J.M.–Conveyancing Law and Practice: Vol 1. Hardback. ISBN 0-414-01085-X. W.Green & Son.

Halliday, J.M.–Conveyancing Law and Practice in Scotland: Vol 2. Hardback. ISBN 0-414-01086-8. W.Green & Son.

Lochnaw, Crispin Agnew–Agricultural Law in Scotland. Hardback: £40.00. ISBN 0-406-11514-1. Butterworth Law (Scotland).

HIGHWAYS AND BRIDGES

7048. Bridges–Forth Road Bridge–Tay Road Bridge

FORTH AND TAY ROAD BRIDGE ORDER CONFIRMATION ACTS (MODIFICATION) ORDER 1996, SI 1996 749 (S.82); made under the Local Government etc. (Scotland) Act 1994 s.59, s.181. In force: April 1, 1996; £1.55.

The Order reconstitutes the membership of the Forth and Tay Road Bridge Joint Boards in consequence of the reorganisation of local government in Scotland effected by the Local Government etc. (Scotland) Act 1994 and makes a number of consequential amendments to the legislation governing each board. The Order provides for the Forth Road Bridge Joint Board to comprise 14 members, of whom seven shall be elected by the City of Edinburgh Council, five by the Fife Council, one by the Midlothian Council and one by the West Lothian Council. The Order similarly provides for the Tay Road Bridge Joint Board to comprise 12 members, of whom six shall be members of the Dundee City Council, five shall be members of the Fife Council and one shall be a member of the Angus Council. For both Boards, the Order makes arrangements for a transitional period during which the new members shall be appointed.

7049. Erskine Bridge–tolls

ERSKINE BRIDGE TOLLS EXTENSION ORDER 1996, SI 1996 1370 (S.128); made under the Erskine Bridge Tolls Act 1968 s.4. In force: in accordance with Art.1; £0.65.

This Order further extends the period during which tolls may be levied by another five years from July 2, 1996 to July 1, 2001.

7050. Motorways

MOTORWAYS TRAFFIC (SCOTLAND) AMENDMENT REGULATIONS 1996, SI 1996 2664 (S.207); made under the Road Traffic Regulation Act 1984 s.17. In force: November 15, 1996; £1.10.

These Regulations, which amend the Motorways Traffic (Scotland) Regulations 1995 (SI 1995 2507) which regulate the use of motorways in Scotland, by exempting from the application of the 1995 Regulations, those special roads, which otherwise would be classed as motorways and covered by the 1995 Regulations.

7051. Motorways–M77–speed limits

AYR ROAD ROUTE (M77) (SPEED LIMIT) REGULATIONS 1996, SI 1996 2863 (S.221); made under the Road Traffic Regulation Act 1984 s.17. In force: in accordance with Reg.1 (1); £1.55.

This Order designates various speed limits along the M77.

7052. Motorways–passenger vehicles–prohibition

MOTORWAYS TRAFFIC (SCOTLAND) AMENDMENT REGULATIONS 1995, SI 1995 3070 (S.224); made under the Road Traffic Regulation Act 1984 s.17. In force: January 1, 1996; £0.65.

The Motorways Traffic (Scotland) Regulations 1995 are amended by these Regulations in order to widen the range of passenger carrying vehicles prohibited from using the right hand lane of a three or more lane motorway. Specifically, passenger vehicles prohibited are those which are constructed or adapted to carry eight or more seated passengers in addition to the driver and have a maximum laden weight exceeding 7.5 tonnes.

7053. Road works

ROAD WORKS (PERMISSION UNDER SECTION 109) (SCOTLAND) REGULATIONS 1996, SI 1996 3199 (S.240); made under the New Roads and Street Works Act 1991 s.109, s.163. In force: January 13, 1997; £0.65.

The New Roads and Streets Works Act 1991 s.109 empowers a road works authority to grant permission to persons to carry out certain road works. These Regulations prescribe that permission may be granted under s.109 to any person carrying out any class of works except works of inspection and maintenance of fire hydrants in roads.

7054. Roads–"way to which public had access"

[Road Traffic Act 1988 (c.52) s.192; Roads (Scotland) Act 1984 (c.54).]

The Road Traffic Act 1988 s.192 (1), as amended, provides that "road" means, inter alia, "any road within the meaning of the Roads (Scotland) Act 1984 and any other way to which the public has access". An accused person was tried on a summary complaint charging him with failing to comply with a road traffic signal. The accused drove his motor car along a road linking docks with the town. The road was within the curtilage of the ground owned and occupied by the port authority but there was nothing to prevent people from driving on to the land and along the road, which carried much traffic between the town and the dock terminals. No passes were required for persons to use the road and there was no physical obstruction of the road, but the port authority had made a byelaw prohibiting access except for business purposes and a notice was erected to that effect. The justice found that the road was a way to which the public had access and convicted the accused who appealed.

Held, that the true question as whether this was a way or road to which the public had access, and this did not depend on the terms of any byelaw or notice but on what in fact happened from day to day; and in light of the justice's finding, it was a road within the meaning of s.192 (1) of the 1988 Act; and appeal refused. *Rodger v. Normand* 1995 S.L.T. 411, [1995] C.L.Y. 6277, applied; *Buchanan v. Motor Insurers Bureau* [1955] 1 W.L.R. 488, [1955] C.L.Y. 2457, distinguished.

RENWICK v. SCOTT 1996 S.L.T. 1164, Judge not specified, HCJ.

7055. Roads–bicycle racing

CYCLE RACING ON HIGHWAYS (SCOTLAND) AMENDMENT REGULATIONS 1996, SI 1996 2665 (S.208); made under the Road Traffic Act 1988 s.31. In force: December 2, 1996; £0.65.

The Cycle Racing on Highways (Scotland) Regulations 1960 (SI 1960 270) authorise the holding of races or trials of speed between bicycles or tricycles, not being motor cycles, on public highways provided that in races, apart from those selected by the Scottish Cyclists Union, the number of competitors must not exceed a maximum of 60. These Regulations increase that maximum to 80 competitors.

7056. Special roads–A1–speed limits

A1 (OLD CRAIGHALL ROUNDABOUT TO EAST OF HADDINGTON) SPECIAL ROAD REGULATIONS 1996, SI 1996 2448 (S.193); made under the Road Traffic Regulation Act 1984 s.17. In force: in accordance with Reg.1 (1); £0.65.

This Order sets the speed limit on the special road at 70 mph.

7057. Trunk roads

ROADS (TRANSITIONAL POWERS) (SCOTLAND) AMENDMENT ORDER 1995, SI 1995 3328 (S.245); made under the Roads (Scotland) Act 1984 s.12A, s.12B, s.143. In force: January 31, 1996; £0.65.

The Roads (Transitional Powers) (Scotland) Order 1995 (SI 1995 1476) provided for a change in status of certain roads as a result of the establishment of new local government areas. Amendments made to that Order mean that the A819 will not become a trunk road, the A828 trunk road will remain a trunk road and the road proposed in Sch.2 Part II to the original Order will, on completion, become part of the A828 trunk road.

7058. Trunk roads–A95–Dulnain Bridge bypass

ROADS (TRANSITIONAL POWERS) (SCOTLAND) AMENDMENT ORDER 1996, SI 1996 496 (S.45); made under the Roads (Scotland) Act 1984 s.12B. In force: March 31, 1996; £0.65.

This Order amends the Roads (Transitional Powers) (Scotland) Order 1995. That Order provided for a change in the status of certain roads, consequential on the establishment of new local government areas on April 1, 1996. The amendment made by this Order will mean that the proposed road to form the A95 Dulnain Bridge bypass will become a trunk road.

7059. Trunk roads–competitive tendering

LOCAL GOVERNMENT ACT 1988 (DEFINED ACTIVITIES) (EXEMPTION OF GROUND MAINTENANCE IN TRUNK ROAD WORK AGREEMENTS) (SCOTLAND) ORDER 1996, SI 1996 2934 (S.223); made under the Local Government Act 1988 s.2, s.15. In force: July 1, 1997; £0.65.

Under the Local Government Act 1988 Part I (competition), work falling within certain defined activities may be carried out by authorities only if particular conditions relating to competitive tendering are fulfilled. This Order exempts from the requirements of Part I ground maintenance so long as it is undertaken following a competitive tender as part of an agreement between an authority and the Secretary of State relating to work on motorways and trunk roads in Scotland.

7060. Trunk roads–contracting out

SECRETARY OF STATE'S TRUNK ROAD FUNCTIONS (CONTRACTING OUT) (SCOTLAND) ORDER 1996, SI 1996 878 (S.99); made under the Deregulation and Contracting Out Act 1994 s.69. In force: March 16, 1996; £1.10.

This Order empowers the Secretary of State to contract out certain of his functions in relation to trunk roads so that these may be exercised by such persons as he may authorise. The functions which may be contracted out are specified in the Schedule to this Order.

7061. Western Isles Council (Berneray Causeway) Order Confirmation Act 1996 (c.xiii)

The Act confirms the Provisional Order set out in the Schedule which authorises the Western Isles Council to construct a causeway for pedestrians and vehicles between the islands of North Uist and Berneray.

This Act received Royal Assent on December 18, 1996.

7062. Wrongful encroachment–construction of access road on land owned by highway authority

[Roads (Scotland) Act 1984 (c. 54) s.21 (2) and (4).]

The Roads (Scotland) Act 1984, s.21 (2) (b) (i) provides that intimation of an application for construction consent shall be made to the owners of any land on or beside which a proposed road is to be built. Section 21 (4) provides, inter alia, that the local roads authority granting the consent is to specify the period within which construction is to be completed. S sued P for alleged wrongful encroachment on land averred to belong to it and on which a road known as Bridge Street had been constructed. In 1988, P started to construct dwellinghouses on neighbouring land which they had purchased, planning permission for the development having previously been granted. They also applied for and were granted construction consent by S under s.21 of the Roads (Scotland) Act 1984 for the building of roads at the development including an access road leading off Bridge Street. S averred that this access road ran across land owned by it. P raised three preliminary pleas to the relevancy and specification of S's pleadings, arguing that S's averments (1) inadequately specified the encroachment; (2) did not disclose that the encroachment was wrongful, and (3) did not disclose circumstances of the exceptional kind required to entitle S to seek damages rather than removal of the road; further, any loss or damage suffered was due to the council's own failure to exercise their rights, and the loss to the council had been incorrectly quantified on the basis of a hypothetical willing seller and the developers' gain, rather than S's own loss.

Held, that (1) S's averments had plainly indicated that the alleged encroachment related to the construction, not use, of the road, and P having themselves built the road they did not require further notice or detail than that given in the pleadings; (2) grant of planning permission by an authority which is also heritable proprietor of land does not infer consent as proprietor (at least without compensation); similarly, the statutory consent under s.21 did not affect the right of the authority as heritable proprietor to refuse consent to the road being built on its land; the condition under s.21 (4) merely requires the period of completion to be inserted, consent allowed an applicant to build a road or do nothing, at his option; (3) waiver was a matter of fact: a party had to be aware of a right and deliberately abandon it; this could not be taken to have occurred in this case as S had averred that it was unaware that the road would be constructed over its land and that P had not intimated their application for construction consent to S as proprietors of affected land in terms of s.21 (2) (b) (i), *Porteous's Trustees v. Porteous* 1991 S.L.T. 129, [1991] C.L.Y. 5346, followed; *Brown v. Baty* 1957 S.L.T. 336, [1957] C.L.Y. 4029, considered; (4) the decision whether to order removal or award damages being essentially one of fact and circumstance and of the exercise of an equitable power of the court, it would be premature to determine the matter purely on the basis of averment without knowing the whole facts; and proof before answer allowed. Opinion, that where both parties (as might prove to be the case here) had acted in good faith and in ignorance of their legal rights it was a question of fact how any compensation should be measured.

STRATHCLYDE RC v. PERSIMMON HOMES (SCOTLAND) LTD 1996 S.L.T. 176, Lord Clyde, OH.

7063. Articles

Responsibility for boundaries and roadside verges and related matters. *(A.H. Anderson)*: Prop. L.B. 1996, 20(Apr), 5-8. (Identification and maintenance of boundaries, and rights and duties of highway authorities and adjourning owners in relation to road verges and boundaries).

The right to roam free *(Nora Kellock)*: S.L.G. 1996, 64(3), 124 . (Legal position of rights of way in Scotland).

HOUSING

7064. Damages–leases–obligations of landlord–obligation to provide house reasonably fit for human habitation

[Housing (Scotland) Act 1987 (c.26) Sch.10, para.1.]

Held, in an action of damages at the instance of tenants against their landlords in which the married couple sought compensation for themselves and for their child, aged three, for loss suffered as a result of the house not being reasonably fit for habitation, that the reasonableness or otherwise of the landlords' conduct was irrelevant in judging whether they had been in breach of their obligation, and damages of £2,175 awarded to the couple, including £600 for inconvenience, and of £2,000 to the child whose asthmatic condition had been exacerbated by the condition of the house.

DOCHERTY v. INVERCLYDE DC 1995 S.C.L.R. 956, Judge not specified, Sh Ct.

7065. Homeless persons–duty of local authority–reasonableness of existing accommodation–duty to consider alternative to own housing stock

A husband and wife claimed that they were homeless on the grounds that it was not reasonable for them to continue occupying their accommodation because of threats and abusive behaviour from neighbours. The neighbours' behaviour was a reaction to the husband's medical condition. The husband and wife had been rehoused before. The housing authority refused the application, taking into account the fact that the authority had no more suitable accommodation to offer. The husband and wife sought reduction of the decision, contending that the housing authority should have taken into account the possibility of rehousing them in accommodation in the area of another housing authority.

Held, that while in an appropriate case it might be necessary for a housing authority to consider accommodation beyond their own stock, there was no suggestion that by doing so they might have discovered accommodation more suitable to the husband and wife and therefore such inquiries were unnecessary, and the petition was dismissed.

McAULAY v. DUMBARTON DC 1996 S.L.T. 318, Judge not specified, OH.

7066. Housing revenue account

HOUSING REVENUE ACCOUNT GENERAL FUND CONTRIBUTION LIMITS (SCOTLAND) ORDER 1996, SI 1996 115 (S.7); made under the Housing (Scotland) Act 1987 s.204. In force: March 1, 1996; £0.65.

This Order provides that contributions from local authorities' general funds to their housing revenue account may not be included in estimates for the year 1996-97.

7067. Housing support grant

HOUSING SUPPORT GRANT (SCOTLAND) ORDER 1996, SI 1996 813 (S.93); made under the Housing (Scotland) Act 1987 s.191, s.192. In force: April 1, 1996; £1.55.

This Order fixes for the year 1996 to 97 the aggregate amount of the housing support grants payable to some local authorities under the Housing (Scotland) Act 1987 s.191; lists the councils among whom the grants will be apportioned; and prescribes the method of apportionment among those councils of the general and hostel portion of the aggregate amount.

7068. Housing support grant

HOUSING SUPPORT GRANT (SCOTLAND) VARIATION ORDER 1996, SI 1996 814 (S.94); made under the Housing (Scotland) Act 1987 s.193. In force: March 14, 1996; £0.65.

This Order varies the Housing Support Grant (Scotland) Order 1995 (SI 1995 470) by reducing the aggregate amounts of housing grant (both general and hostel portions) originally fixed for the year 1995/6. The aggregate amount is reduced by £340,487 to £21,960,220, comprising a reduction of £327,217 to £19,330,435 for the general portion and a reduction of £13,264 to £2,629,785 for the hostel portion.

7069. Rent officers

RENT OFFICERS (ADDITIONAL FUNCTIONS) (SCOTLAND) AMENDMENT ORDER 1996, SI 1996 975 (S.106); made under the Housing (Scotland) Act 1988 s.70. In force: October 7, 1996; £1.10.

Amends the Rent Officers (Additional Functions) (Scotland) Order 1995, which confers functions on rent officers in connection with housing benefit and rent allowance subsidy, and requires them to make determinations and re-determinations in respect of tenancies of dwellings.

7070. Repairs grants–forms

HOUSING (FORMS) (SCOTLAND) AMENDMENT REGULATIONS 1996, SI 1996 632 (S.67); made under the Housing (Scotland) Act 1987 s.237, s.248, s.338. In force: April 1, 1996; £1.10.

These Regulations amend the Housing (Forms) (Scotland) Regulations 1980 (SI 1980 1647) (which prescribe the forms in which applications for improvement and repairs grants must be made) to take account of the change from using rateable values to using council tax valuation bands as a means of imposing valuation limits above which applications for improvement and repairs grants in respect of certain houses will not be approved. (The change was made by the Council Tax (Amendment of Housing) (Scotland) Act 1987) (Scotland) Regulations 1996 and the Housing (Valuation Bands for Improvement and Repairs Grants) (Scotland) Order 1996 (SI 1996 741)). These Regulations make appropriate amendments in the parts of the forms and the notes to them which were framed in terms of rateable values.

7071. Repairs grants–valuation

COUNCIL TAX (AMENDMENT OF HOUSING (SCOTLAND) ACT 1987) (SCOTLAND) REGULATIONS 1996, SI 1996 631 (S.66); made under the Local Government Finance Act 1992 s.111, s.113, s.116. In force: April 1, 1996; £1.10.

These Regulations amend the Housing (Scotland) Act 1987 s.240(2)(c) and s.240(4) which, before amendment, provided that a local authority must not (except in certain exceptional cases) approve an application for an improvement or repairs grant where the rateable value of the house exceeded a limit prescribed by the Secretary of State with consent of the Treasury or, if a house was to be provided by the conversion of two or more houses, the aggregate of the rateable values of those houses exceeded a limit so prescribed. These Regulations make the references to rateable values in these provisions references to council tax valuation bands in respect of applications for improvement or repairs grant made on or after April 1, 1996, so that such a grant must not (except in the exceptional cases) be made (a) if the house is in a higher valuation band than that prescribed; or (b) where two or more houses are to be amalgamated into one house, if the middle values of the council tax valuation bands applicable to each house to be amalgamated, when added together, exceed the highest value of a prescribed valuation band. Transitional provision is made for the previous provisions of s.240 providing for limits in terms of rateable values, and Regulations made under them, to remain in effect in respect of applications for grant to be made before April 1, 1996.

7072. Repairs grants–valuation

HOUSING (VALUATION BANDS FOR IMPROVEMENT AND REPAIRS GRANTS) (SCOTLAND) ORDER 1996, SI 1996 741 (S.74); made under the Housing (Scotland) Act 1987 s.240, s.248. In force: April 1, 1996; £0.65.

The Housing (Scotland) Act 1987 s.240(2) (c) and s.240(4), as amended by the Council Tax (Amendment of Housing (Scotland) Act 1987) (Scotland) Regulations 1996, provides that applications for improvement grant shall not be granted where the values of the premises concerned, expressed in terms of council tax valuation bands, exceed certain limits prescribed by Order. Section 248(5) of the 1987 Act extends these provisions to applications for repairs grant. This Order prescribes the limits for the purpose of these provisions. Under s.240(2) (c) (i), where the application relates to a single house, it cannot be granted if the house is in a valuation band for a range of values higher that the prescribed band. For this purpose, the Order prescribes valuation band E where the single house is being improved or repaired and valuation band F where it is being converted to two or more houses. Under s.240(c) (ii), where the application relates to several houses which are to be converted into one house, it cannot be granted if these houses are in valuations bands, the middle values of which, when added together, exceed the maximum value of the prescribed valuation band. For this purpose the Order prescribes valuation band E.

7073. Repairs notice–competency–tenement building comprising flats and shops

Held, in respect of a tenement building comprising two shops and 11 flats, that it was competent to serve repair notices on the proprietors of the shops as well as on those of the flats and that it was competent to serve different notices in respect of the flats, which included, inter alia, the common stair, and the shops which did not.

WHITELAW v. CITY OF ABERDEEN DC 1995 S.C.L.R. 1167, Judge not specified, Sh Ct.

7074. Right to buy–discount on market value–periods of occupation to be taken into account in calculation of discount

[Housing (Scotland) Act 1987 (c.26) s.62.]

By the Housing (Scotland) Act 1987 s.62(3) it is provided that the discount on its market value at which a house may be purchased by a secure tenant shall be based on the number of years of occupation of a public sector house by the tenant so whoever else may be the appropriate person for that purpose. In s.61 it is provided by ss.(10) (a) that in that section and s.62 references to occupation of a house include occupation (iv) as the child, or the spouse of a child, of a tenant... who has succeeded, directly or indirectly, to the right of that person in a house occupation of which would be reckonable for the purposes of this section; but only in relation to any period when the child, or as the case may be, spouse of the child, is at least 16 years of age. A wife succeeded her husband as tenant of a public sector house. Subsequently their son became a joint tenant along with his mother and on her death became the sole tenant. When he applied to buy the house the landlords' offer to sell allowed discount only in respect of the tenant's occupation since he became a joint tenant along with his mother. The tenant claimed that he was also entitled to discount in respect of his occupation of the house as the child of his mother while she was the sole tenant following his father's death and as the child of his father during his father's tenancy and while he was more than 16 years of age. He contended that he was entitled to such discount as having succeeded directly to the rights in the house of his mother and indirectly to those of his father. In the course of the proceedings it was conceded that, on the authorities, the tenant was entitled to discount in respect of his occupation of the house during his mother's sole tenancy.

Held, that (1) a tenant could not be said to have succeeded indirectly to the rights of a tenant preceding the one whom he had himself followed, in the sense of coming next, in the tenancy and (2) the applicant was not therefore entitled to discount in respect of his occupation of the house during his father's tenancy.

HAMILTON v. CITY OF GLASGOW DC 1996 S.L.T. (Lands Tr.) 14, Judge not applicable, Lands Tr.

7075. Right to buy–discount on market value–periods of occupation to be taken into account in calculation of discount

[Housing (Scotland) Act 1987 (c.26) s.61 (10), s.62(3), s.(4).]

By s.62(3) of the Housing (Scotland) Act 1987 it is provided that the discount on its market value at which a house may be purchased by a secure tenant shall be based on the number of years of occupation of a public sector house by the "appropriate person" as that term is defined in s.62(4) (a). In s.61 it is provided by subs. (10) (a) that in that section and s.62 "references to occupation of a house include occupation... (iii) as the spouse of the tenant". A husband and wife applied to purchase the public sector house of which they were the joint tenants. Since the wife had the longer period of occupation, she was, by s.62(4) (a), the appropriate person on whose period or periods of occupation the discount fell to be based. When calculating the discount the landlords did not take into account a period of occupation by her as the wife of a former husband during his tenancy of public sector houses. They refused to do so on the ground that the only periods of occupation to be taken into account were periods of occupation by the appropriate person in one of the capacities referred to in s.62(4) (a), which did not cover occupation as the spouse of a tenant from whom there had been a subsequent divorce.

Held, that (1) for the purposes of s.62(3) (b) the appropriate person's qualifying occupation might be occupation of any of the kinds listed in s.61 (10) (a); and (2) since one of these was as the spouse of the tenant, the applicants were entitled to discount in respect of the period of the wife's occupation as the spouse of her former husband.

Observed, that one had also to have regard to the provisions of s.61 (10) (a) when deciding which of the persons listed in s.62(4) (a) was the appropriate person to put forward for the purpose of calculating a discount based on the period of occupation.

McLEAN v. CUNNINGHAME DC 1996 S.L.T. (Lands Tr.) 2, Judge not specified, Lands Tr.

7076. Right to buy–dwellinghouse specially designed for the disabled

[Housing (Scotland) Act 1987 (c.26) s.61.]

K, tenants of a district council (H), appealed a decision of the Lands Tribunal for Scotland to refuse K's application to purchase their council house on the grounds that at the date of K's application, March 16, 1994, the house was one of a group provided with facilities specially designed for the needs of paraplegics in terms of s.61 (4) (a) of the 1987 Act. The house had been built in 1984 for occupation by paraplegics, as part of a scheme including housing for the elderly. However, only in 1988 had a call system and warden service been provided for K's house. K argued that for the house to fall within the exclusion in s.61 (4) (a) it had to have a call system and warden service, *Crilly v. Motherwell DC* 1988 S.L.T. (Lands Tr.) 7, [1988] C.L.Y. 4436, that, as the exclusion could not have applied prior to 1988, K had had the right to purchase when they entered into their lease with H in 1984, that it was an implied term of the lease that K would retain that right, that H had no power to remove that right by installing a call system and warden service without obtaining K's consent, and that as installation of the services by H had been ultra vires, the facilities fell to be ignored when considering whether at the time of K's application the exemption applied.

Held, appeal refused, that it was at the date of application that K were seeking to exercise their right to purchase. In order to have that right a number of conditions in s.61 in relation to H, K, the house and any group of houses which included that house, had to be fulfilled as at the date of application, which pointed to that date as the material date. Accordingly, whether the house fell within s.61 (4) (a) was purely a question of fact to be decided by reference to the state of affairs at the date of application, which question had been determined by the tribunal in H's favour. K's interpretation would require an examination of the history of all provision of services to all the houses within the group in case the facilities had been provided at different times, which did not fit in with an ordinary reading of the subsection. There was nothing in the lease which restricted H from adding to or improving the facilities within K's house, there was no basis for implying a term preventing H from altering the premises if that affected K's right to purchase, and in any event, there was no suggestion in s.61 (4) that the result of H's actings should be ignored if they were in breach of such a term. Opinion reserved, on whether *Crilly* was correctly decided.

KENNEDY v. HAMILTON DC 1995 S.C.L.R. 980, Judge not specified, IH.

7077. Right to buy–tenancy terminated prior to acceptance of offer to sell

[Housing (Scotland) Act 1987 (c.26) s.71.]

When the tenant of a public sector house served on her landlords an application to purchase the house, her tenancy was secure, and it was not disputed that she then had a right to purchase, although an action had already been raised in the sheriff court for recovery of possession of the house. The landlords having failed to issue timeously either an offer to sell, or a notice of refusal of the application, the tenant referred the matter to the Lands Tribunal in terms of the Housing (Scotland) Act 1987 s.71 (1) (a). If the tribunal had found that there had been a failure by the landlords, then in terms of s.71 (2) (a) it might itself have taken such steps as were required to effect the sale of the house to the tenant. During the course of the proceedings before the tribunal the landlords obtained an order in the sheriff court for recovery of possession of the house and for the ejection of the tenant. On behalf of the landlords it was submitted that the right to purchase could be exercised only by someone who was at all relevant times a secure tenant; that the right was not exercised until the tenant accepted an offer to sell, and since the tenancy had been brought to an end without an offer having been made or accepted, the applicant no longer had a right to purchase the house. The tenant having appealed to the sheriff principal against the sheriff's decision, a question also arose as to whether the tenancy had been brought to an end at the date appointed by the sheriff or whether it remained in being pending the outcome of the appeal. However, the appeal was unsuccessful, and in any event the tenancy had been terminated before the tribunal could have effected the sale of the house to the tenant.

Held, that (1) it was when a secure tenant accepted an offer to sell that he exercised the right to purchase; (2) in order to exercise the right he accordingly had to remain a secure tenant until that time and (3) the applicant being no longer the tenant, the tribunal could not offer to sell the house to her, nor, if it did, could she validly accept the offer, *Cooper's Executors v. City of Edinburgh DC* 1991 S.L.T. 518, [1991] C.L.Y. 5189 applied. Opinion, that the effect of the appeal to the sheriff principal had been to suspend the operation of the sheriff's order, and that the tenancy had therefore been terminated on the date when the sheriff principal, having refused the appeal, allowed extract of the order.

McKAY v. CITY OF DUNDEE DC 1996 S.L.T. (Lands Tr.) 9, Judge not applicable, Lands Tr.

7078. Articles

No support for "unwelcome and disturbing intrusion" *(Mike Dailly* and *Jamie Finlay)*: SCOLAG 1996, 238, 152-154. (Response to Government consultation on Code of Guidance on Homelessness rejecting view that homeless persons should be placed in temporary accommodation).

Remedies for non-payment of home loss and disturbance payments *(Simon Collins)*: SCOLAG 1996, 238, 158-159. (Whether judicial review is appropriate or best remedy when housing authority refuses to make mandatory home loss payment).

HUMAN RIGHTS

7079. Articles

The European Convention on Human Rights in Scottish courts *(Alastair N. Brown)*: S.L.T. 1996, 29, 267-270. (IH ruling that where domestic legislation is ambiguous, there is presumption that Parliament did not intend legislation to conflict with ECHR).

The European Convention: a Scottish perspective *(Andrew Grotrian.)*: E.H.R.L.R. 1996, 5, 511-523. (Reluctance of Scottish judiciary to use ECHR and implications of changing approach following IH ruling where it was considered to resolve statutory ambiguity).

IMMIGRATION

7080. Leave to re-enter–refusal–whether immigration officer acted in excess or want of jurisdiction

[Immigration Act 1971 (c.77) s.13.]

In terms of the Immigration Rules (HC 251) r.60 a person whose stay in the UK was subject to a time limit and who returns after a temporary absence abroad has no claim to admission as a returning resident. The same time limit and any conditions attached will normally be reimposed if the requirements of the rules are met, unless the person is seeking admission in a different capacity from the one in which he was last given leave to enter or remain. The petitioner held a British passport as a citizen of the British dependent territory, Hong Kong where he lived with his mother until July 1992, when he came to the UK. Before travelling he had obtained an entry certificate until October 31, 1993 as a student for single visit. In November 1992 the petitioner applied for indefinite leave to remain which was refused in April 1993, and the petitioner appealed. In July 1993 he returned to Hong Kong to visit his mother. He came back to the UK in September 1993 to resume his studies. On his return his passport was removed and he was given a notice of temporary admission and asked to attend for interview, on October 3, 1993. Notice of refusal of leave to enter was given on October 5, along with directions for removal to Hong Kong on October 12. The reasons for refusal were that the petitioner was to be treated as a new entrant and that the immigration officer was not satisfied that the petitioner intended to leave the UK on completion of his studies. The decision made no reference to the outstanding appeal. A judicial review was sought on the grounds that the decision to treat the petitioner as a new entrant was ultra vires and illegal, that the decision was not reasonable, and that the circumstances of the interview were oppressive and in breach of natural justice. It was argued that the immigration officer was correct to treat the petitioner as a new entrant, and that as there was an appeal procedure available in terms of the Immigration Act 1971 s.13, the application for judicial review was incompetent. It was also argued that s.14(1) did not assist the petitioner as he had left the country voluntarily, and in seeking to return as a student the petitioner was doing so in a different capacity from that which he had originally been granted leave to enter.

Held, that (1) the immigration officer was not acting in excess or want of jurisdiction in refusing leave to re-enter in the absence of any current entry clearance; (2) while the fact of the petitioner's outstanding appeal against refusal of unlimited leave to remain could not give rise to a legitimate expectation that he could leave and return to the UK at any time, it was a material consideration to be taken into account and (3) the accumulation of grounds of procedural impropriety and irrationality averred in the petition were capable of constituting special circumstance such as to be an exception to the general rule that judicial review was not available when a statutory remedy was otherwise available and was not exhausted; and plea to the competency repelled.

CHOI v. SECRETARY OF STATE FOR THE HOME DEPARTMENT 1996 S.L.T. 590, Judge not specified, OH.

7081. Articles

Homeless asylum seekers in Scotland *(Simon Collins)*: SCOLAG 1996, 238, 160-162. (Whether and in what form asylum seekers may obtain assistance with accommodation from public authorities).

INCOME TAX

7082. Income tax–employee benefits–private use of car–employee paying insurance–whether insurance cost deductible in calculating cash equivalent of benefit

IRC appealed against a decision allowing the deduction of motor insurance costs in respect of private use of a vehicle supplied for business use, under the Income and Corporation Taxes Act 1988 Sched. 6, para. 4. Q was responsible for arranging the insurance for both private and business use though his employers contributed to the insurance cost for each business mile travelled. IRC contended that the ordinary meaning of para. 4 served to confine the reduction of the cash equivalent of the benefit only to where money had been paid in respect of private use, not amounts paid as a condition that the vehicle would be available for such use.

Held, allowing the appeal, that para. 4 allowed a cash equivalent benefit reduction only where the payment was such that the employee had to make a payment as a condition of the car being made available for his private use. On the facts, the payments here were for the insurance of the vehicle not the private use of it, as required under para. 4. Therefore Q was not entitled to claim a reduction of the cash equivalent benefit for his private use.

INLAND REVENUE COMMISSIONERS v. QUIGLEY [1995] S.T.C. 93, Lord Clyde, IH.

7083. Articles

Executory income tax–the first year *(Alan R. Barr)*: J.L.S.S. 1996, 41 (3), 118-120. (Effect of income tax on executory funds on beneficiaries).

INSOLVENCY

7084. Administration orders–consent to proceedings against company–landlords serving notice of irritancy of lease in terms of provision in lease–whether "legal process"

[Insolvency Act 1986 (c.45) s.11.]

Section 11 (3) of the Insolvency Act 1986 provides that during the period for which an administration order is in force, "(d) no other proceedings and no execution or other legal process may be commenced or continued" against the company except with the consent of the administrator or the leave of the court. The landlords of a building, the tenants of which had had administrators appointed under s.8 (3) (a) and (d) of the 1986 Act, obtained leave from the court to bring proceedings against the tenants and subsequently raised an action against the tenants and their administrators seeking declarator that an irritancy had been incurred in terms of the lease on that appointment, notice having been served on the tenants following the initial appointment of the administrators ad interim, and an order for removal. The defenders sought dismissal, arguing, inter alia, that (1) service of the notice was "other legal process" in terms of s.11 (3) (d) and hence required the leave of the court and (2) an appointment ad interim was not an appointment of administrators in terms of the Act and the notice was invalid having been served when the tenants were not in a state of administration.

Held, that (1) "other legal process" did not include the taking of a non-judicial step such as the service of a notice under the contract of lease and (2) the appointment of the administrators ad interim was sufficient to entitle the pursuers to give notice under the irritancy clause; and defenders' relative pleas repelled and proof before answer allowed on whether a fair and reasonable landlord would have enforced the irritancy, *Olympia and York Canary Wharf, Re* [1993] B.C.C. 154, [1993] C.L.Y. 516 followed.

SCOTTISH EXHIBITION CENTRE LTD v. MIRESTOP LTD (IN ADMINISTRATION) (NO.2) 1996 S.L.T. 8, Judge not specified, OH.

7085. Directors–disqualification–procedure–competency

[Company Directors Disqualification Act 1986 (c.46) s.16.]

Two directors, L, of a company, C, appealed a sheriff's decision that applications by the Secretary of State for disqualification orders against L were competent, although the Secretary of State had failed to give L 10 days' notice of the applications as required by the Company Directors Disqualification Act 1986 s.16(1). C had become insolvent on March 18, 1992. The Secretary of State had given L notice of his intention to make the applications on March 7, 1994, and the applications had been made on March 10. Had the Secretary of State waited until March 18 as required by s.16(1), the applications would have required leave of the court under s.7(2). L argued that the requirement for notice under s.16(1) was mandatory; that the reasoning on this point of the dissenting judge, Nourse, L.J., in *Secretary of State for Trade and Industry v. Langridge* [1993] 3 All E.R. 591, [1991] C.L.Y. 403, was to be preferred as the majority in *Langridge* had failed to take into account the fact that the 1986 Act provided criminal penalties for breach of the orders; and that it was clear from *Hansard* that the provision for notice was intended to deal with shadow directors.

Held, refusing the appeal, that there was no ambiguity in s.16(1) which could be explained or resolved by reference to the parliamentary proceedings. The 1986 Act was intended for the protection of the public and was not a purely penal statute, *Jaymar Management Ltd, Re* [1990] B.C.L.C. 617, [1990] C.L.Y. 475. In any event, even if the 1986 Act did require to be construed strictly, s.16(1) was to be regarded as directory and not mandatory for the reasons given by the majority in *Langridge*. Accordingly both applications were competent.

SECRETARY OF STATE FOR TRADE AND INDUSTRY v. LOVAT 1996 S.C.L.R. 195, Judge not specified, IH.

7086. Directors–insolvent companies

INSOLVENT COMPANIES (REPORTS ON CONDUCT OF DIRECTORS) (SCOTLAND) RULES 1996, SI 1996 1910 (S.154); made under the Insolvency Act 1986 s.411; and the Company Directors Disqualification Act 1986 s.21. In force: September 30, 1996; £3.20.

These Rules revoke and replace the Insolvent Companies (Reports on Conduct of Directors) (No.2) (Scotland) Rules 1986 (SI 1986 1916). They make provision for the manner in which liquidators, administrative receivers or administrators of companies are to make reports to the Secretary of State in relation to any persons who have been directors or shadow directors of insolvent companies and whose conduct appears to be unfit to be involved with company management. They also provide for returns to be made to the Secretary of State by office holders in respect of directors and shadow directors of insolvent companies where a report has not already been made.

7087. Winding up–breach of trust by director–whether fraudulent

[Insolvency Act 1986 (c.45) s.212; Prescription and Limitation (Scotland) Act 1973 (c.52) Sch.1 para.1 (d), Sch.3 para. (c).]

R, the liquidator of a property development company (M), sued D, a former director of M, for authorising and making overpayments of £93,379 to S in fraudulent breach of his duty of trust as director. R averred that in terms of the sums certified by the architects, D overpaid S £288,157 on the false pretence that S was entitled to such payment for works carried out and, after various deductions, M's loss of profit as a result of the overpayment was £93,379. R sought to amend his pleadings to state that D, as an officer of M, was accountable for any misapplied funds overpaid to S and separatim was guilty of misfeasance and breach of his fiduciary duty to M. D averred that the building contract had been altered by agreement so that S was paid on stage payment basis for works actually carried out rather than on certification. D contended that R had not averred fraud in terms known to Scots law and therefore the action relating to fraudulent breach of trust was irrelevant. D averred that the action based on non-fraudulent breach of trust had prescribed in terms of the Prescription and Limitation (Scotland) Act 1973 Sch.3(e)(ii). R sought amendment to include an order in terms of the Insolvency Act 1986, which he claimed was not subject to prescription.

Held, amendment allowed in respect of factual matters only and proof before answer allowed on all averments that (1) R's amendment was incompetent insofar as it sought to add a case under s.212 of the 1986 Act. It would be contrary to the structure and spirit of the rules to entertain an application under s.212 in an ordinary action as ordinary rules of pleading were inappropriate in a petition process, *Liquidators of the City of Glasgow Bank v. Mackinnon* (1882) 9 R. 535; *Blin v. Johnstone* 1988 S.L.T. 335, [1988] C.L.Y. 3836; (2) unless the obligation was imprescriptible, the short negative prescription applied as R's claim for damages for breach of trust fell within the ambit of Sch.1, para 1 (d) and in seeking damages for breach of trust in the way R had done, he sought a remedy of reparation. A fraudulent breach of trust was an imprescriptible obligation although it was imported from English law. Many dicta suggested that the diversion of trust funds was of the nature of a fraudulent act and "fraudulent" clearly was capable of supporting a meaning which did not require the false pretence of procuring a practical result. There were sufficient averments on which, if R's case were fully proved, it could be inferred that the payments of sums from the resources of the joint venture belonging in part to M without warrant under contract to S, which was substantially owned by D, involved a dishonest appropriation of funds. If, however, it was established that the building contract was varied and that all of the material transactions were carried out openly and with the concurrence of other directors of the companies involved, R would fail. Opinion, that s.212 did not provide the source of obligation and did not define in any way the scope of remedies available against directors, *Selangor United Rubber Estates v. Cradock (No.2)* [1968] 1 W.L.R. 319, [1968] C.L.Y. 468; (4) as a procedural device s.212 could neither extend nor limit the liability of a director and it was a misconception to attempt to apply the provisions of the 1973 Act to s.212 as if it were a source of remedy. R's approach was predicated on a view that s.212 applied and obviated independent analysis of the grounds of action and (5) where R sought damages for D's wrongful act of diverting funds from M into S's hands M's loss of profit was properly characterised as damages.

ROSS v. DAVY 1996 S.C.L.R. 369, Judge not specified, OH.

7088. Winding up–unfair preference–payment to creditor by third party in exchange for withdrawal of arrestments shortly before liquidation

[Insolvency Act 1986 (c.45) s.243.]

The liquidator of a company sought recovery in terms of the Insolvency Act 1986 s.243 of a payment made to the defender by a third party in exchange for withdrawal of arrestments on the dependence of an action for payment of a commercial account raised by the defender. Recovery was sought on the basis that the payment, which was made a few days before the company went into liquidation, created a preference in favour of the defender. The sheriff granted decree as craved. The defender appealed to the sheriff principal.

Held, refusing the appeal, that (1) the payment which the defender received from the third party clearly had the effect of creating an unfair preference in his favour to the prejudice of the general body of creditors; (2) the arrestment by the defender could not be regarded as a transaction in the ordinary course of business within s.243 and (3) the payment was in effect an assignation of the debt owed by the third party and was not a payment in cash within s.243.

R GAFFNEY & SON LTD (IN LIQUIDATION) v. DAVIDSON 1996 S.L.T. (Sh. Ct.) 36, Judge not specified, Sh. Ct.

7089. Articles

A further cautionary note for conveyancers *(Donna W. McKenzie* and *David O'Donnell)*: J.L.S.S. 1996, 41(7), 255-257. (Problems for conveyancers in establishing whether companies have gone into liquidation, receivership or administration).

Alienations: significant cross border differences *(John Macfarlane* and *Andrew Orr)*: I.H.L. 1996, 40(May), 37-40. (Provisions for dealing with preferences and transactions at an undervalue by insolvent companies in Scottish and English law).

Cross-border liquidations *(Philip St. J. Smart)*: J.L.S.S. 1996, 41(4), 141-143. (Whether Scottish provisions of 1986 Act should not be restricted in operation to Scotland).

Diligence *(George L. Gretton)*: Insolv. L. 1996, Spe Issue, 6-11. (Meaning and types of diligence as procedure for enforcement of unsecured judgment debts, equivalent to Mareva injunctions and interaction with insolvency and foreign insolvency).

Intervening insolvency: how can you know? *(Donna W. McKenzie* and *David O'Donnell)*: S.L.P.Q. 1996, 1(2), 173-185. (How third parties may check to confirm appointment of administrator, receiver or liquidator has been or is about to be made in light of effect of such appointment on dealings between company and third party).

Locus standi to present winding-up petition *(Donna W. McKenzie)*: Bus. L.B. 1996, 22(Jul), 5-6. (Whether petitioner was contributory to the creditor of a company in liquidation).

The assignation of floating charges *(William Lucas)*: S.L.T. 1996, 24, 203-205. (Problems in assigning floating charges under Scots law might be solved by re-registration to ensure effective transfer).

INSURANCE

7090. Indemnity insurance–construction of policy–"value" of premises damaged

S reclaimed against the allowance of proof before answer on K's claim in respect of fire damage to their property for the cost of reinstatement subject to a deduction for betterment. The policy provided for the cost of reinstatement, and as an alternative basis of settlement where reinstatement was not to be carried out, "the value of the buildings at the time of their destruction". K argued that under the alternative basis they were entitled to the cost of reinstatement less betterment, that being the sole measure of loss in terms of the policy. S maintained that the measure of indemnity was market value at the time of destruction, that that was a matter for determination by valuers, that it was unreasonable for K to seek to be indemnified for costs which they were not proposing to incur and that it was not necessary for S to prove that comparable property was in fact available for purchase elsewhere at the relevant time, nor to show that there was a market in which the buildings could be sold.

Held, reclaiming motion refused. The word "value" did not mean "market value", *Carrick Furniture House v. General Accident Fire & Life Assurance Corp* 1978 S.L.T. 65, [1978] C.L.Y. 3441, followed. There was a consistent line of authority that the proper measure of indemnity depended on the facts and circumstances; K's proposition as to the sole measure of value was incorrect. Reinstatement cost was unlikely to be an appropriate measure where a replacement building could readily be found on the open market; the right under the policy to additional costs such as complying with public authorities' requirements would not exclude the possibility of market value applying where this was appropriate, nor did a provision for average in the event of under-insurance. K had averred that no similar property with similar planning permission was available; this was sufficient to entitle them to base a claim on the cost of reinstatement less betterment. It was then for S to put in issue the alternative measure based on market value if they wished to do so. The essential prerequisite to this basis was the existence of a market, not the ability of a valuer to place a valuation on a given hypothesis.

KEYSTONE PROPERTIES v. SUN ALLIANCE AND LONDON INSURANCE 1993 S.C. 494, Judge not specified.

7091. Indemnity insurance–proposal form–breach of warranty as to accuracy and completeness

Following a fire at their premises, a wholesale company sought indemnity from their insurers in respect of the damage. When the insurers' proposal form had been completed by the company two questions had been answered incorrectly. One related to the length of time for which the company had carried on business at the premises and the other to whether they were the sole occupiers. The company had also signed the declaration in the proposal form: "We declare that to the best of our knowledge and belief all statements and particulars contained in this proposal are true and complete and that no material fact had been withheld or suppressed. We agree that this proposal shall be the basis of the contract between us and the insurers." The insurers resisted paying out on the claim. The company raised a commercial action for payment. At debate the insurers argued that as there were the inaccuracies in the proposal form and as the signed declaration amounted to a warranty as to the accuracy of all answers, they were thus entitled to avoid liability under the policy. The company contended that the declaration amounted to no more than a representation that the statements and particulars relating to material facts were true and complete and that no material fact has been withheld or suppressed. The Lord Ordinary dismissed the action, holding that, on a sound construction of the language of the proposal form, the company had warranted the accuracy of their answers to the questions put, to the best of their knowledge and belief, and that, given the breach of that warranty disclosed in the pleadings, the insurers were entitled to avoid the policy. The company reclaimed, arguing that the declaration amounted to no more than an undertaking that no material fact to the best of the knowledge and belief of the proposer had been concealed in respect of matters raised by the questions in the form and that the second clause of the first sentence of the declaration should be read as a qualification of the first clause. They contended that the words used were insufficient to give rise to the construction that the declaration amounted to a warranty as to the truth and accuracy of the answers as the basis of the contract, and that any ambiguity in the declaration fell to be construed against the insurers who had drawn up the form.

Held, that (1) there was no ambiguity in the declaration and the statement to the effect that the proposal was to be the basis of the contract made it clear that the answers contained in the proposal were warranted as being true and complete; (2) the two clauses of the first sentence of the declaration dealt with two distinct matters, namely the warranty and the obligation not to withhold material facts; (3) there was no reason in law why the two contractual provisions could not co-exist or for favouring a construction that one provision qualified the other and (4) while a consequence of this construction might be that the contract would be voidable as a result of an error in the proposal which was not material, that was entirely consistent with freedom of contract; and reclaiming motion refused, *Dawson v. Bonnin* 1922 S.L.T. 444 applied; *Fowkes v. Manchester & London Life Assurance & Loan Association* (1863) 3 B. & S. 917 distinguished; *Hemmings v. Sceptre Life Association* [1905] 1 Ch. 365 doubted.

UNIPAC (SCOTLAND) LTD v. AEGON INSURANCE CO (UK) LTD 1996 S.L.T. 1197, Judge not specified, IH.

7092. Insurable interest–trustee for partnership insuring as an individual

M raised an action against S for payment of £1,077,540.92 under a contract of insurance. M had entered into a contract of partnership with his son to run a nightclub and title to the nightclub's premises was taken in both names as trustees for the firm. The premises were damaged by fire. M had completed the insurance proposal form in his own name only and as an individual trading as the nightclub, failing to mention either the beneficial interest of the firm or the infeftment of his son as trustee, and had warranted that he had not withheld any material information. S argued that M's pleadings were irrelevant in that (1) they revealed an absence of insurable interest, *Arif v. Excess Insurance Group* 1987 S.L.T. 473 [1987] C.L.Y. 4579, (2) they revealed that the proposal form had contained inaccuracies of a kind which amounted to breach of warranty, and (3) in failing to disclose that there had been a previous arson attack on the premises, M had breached a further warranty. M argued that (1) *Arif* was not correctly decided since partnership property was joint property and, though infeft trustees had no separable or individual title, in feudal terms the trustees owned the property and M therefore had an insurable interest, though not the only insurable interest. M was not required to declare the nature of his ownership in the proposal form, but merely that, being a trustee, he was an owner; (2) questions on the form requiring disclosure of other interests were directed at disclosing landlords and creditors; and (3) the statements and particulars in the proposal form were true to the best of M's knowledge and belief: the materiality of any information withheld was a matter requiring proof. No loss had been incurred as a result of the previous arson attack since damage had been minimal and works were being carried out at the time of the attack, and M had been entitled to answer the question regarding previous loss in the negative.

Held, that dismissal was appropriate, that (1) where property was partnership property and title was taken in one or more of the partners' names, the only insurable interest was that of the partnership. None of the joint proprietors individually had an interest which could be identified as insurable; (2) there had been a breach of warranty by M since the answers given in the proposal form regarding interests, occupancy and ownership were untrue, and could not have been true to the best of M's knowledge and belief, and (3) these answers also constituted a withholding of information which had to be regarded as material. Further, irrespective of previous loss, the fact that the previous incident was apparently arson should have been disclosed. Case put out by order for M to consider amendment, having sued as an individual but relying on his status as trustee.

MITCHELL v. SCOTTISH EAGLE INSURANCE CO LTD, *The Scotsman*, February 21, 1996, Lord Prosser, OH.

7093. Articles

A matter of implication *(Rosalind M.M. McInnes)*: Bus. L.B. 1996, 23(Sep), 6-9. (Tests for introducing implied terms into contracts illustrated by attempt to introduce implied terms into fire insurance policy relating to payment for repairs).

Res judicata and excess clauses in insurance contracts *(Alan A. Summers)*: S.L.T. 1996, 22, 189-192. (Whether insurance company and insured should be able to bring separate actions against defender in respect of different heads of loss arising from same incident).

INTELLECTUAL PROPERTY

7094. Edinburgh Assay Office Order Confirmation Act 1996 (c.i)

To confirm a Provisional Order under the Private Legislation Procedure (Scotland) Act 1936 (c.52) relating to Edinburgh Assay Office.

This Act received Royal Assent on February 29, 1996.

7095. Articles

Fixed security rights over intellectual property in Scotland *(Tom Guthrie* and *Alistair Orr)*: E.I.P.R. 1996, 18(11), 597-603 . (Creation of security rights by way of assignation, procedural and conflict of laws considerations and proposals for new type of security over moveable property and creating security by way of trust).

JURISDICTION

7096. Court of Session–prorogation agreement–related proceedings in another state–priority of proceedings

[Civil Jurisdiction and Judgments Act 1982 (c.27) s.49, Sch.1 Art.6, Sch.1 Art.17, Sch.1 Art.21, Sch.1 Art.22.]

A Scottish bank raised an action for payment against a French bank, founding on a guarantee issued by the French bank in respect of the indebtedness to the Scottish bank by one of its customers, a Scottish company. The Scottish company was a subsidiary of a French company which had instructed the French bank to issue the guarantee. In a separate agreement the French company indemnified the French bank against its liability under the Scottish guarantee. The Scottish bank called upon the French bank to make payment under the guarantee on November 4, 1992. The Scottish guarantee provided, inter alia, that it "shall be governed and interpreted in accordance with the Scottish law and shall be subject to the exclusive jurisdiction of the courts of Scotland". Following sundry procedure the action was sisted "pending the outcome of appeals in respect of proceedings before the French courts". Those proceedings consisted of three actions raised by the French company before the Commercial Court of Marseille to which the French and Scottish banks had been called as defenders. The French company obtained, an interim injunction prohibiting the French bank from making payment to the Scottish bank under the guarantee, and declarators that the French bank did not owe the Scottish bank any money under the guarantee and the guarantee provided by the French company to the French bank was null and void. The Scottish bank defended said actions on the grounds of competence or jurisdiction. After further sundry procedure the sist was recalled. The French bank objected and contended the proceedings be sisted because; that (1) the Scottish bank had conceded the jurisdiction of the French courts; (2) Art.21 of the Brussels Convention of 1968 applied in respect that the Commercial Court of Marseille had been first seised of the issues between parties, and sist of the Scottish proceedings was mandatory; (3) alternatively, Art.22 of the Convention was applied and the Scottish proceedings could be sisted in the exercise of the court's discretion and (4) in any event there should be a sist of the Scottish proceedings in exercise of the court's general, or residual, power to avoid duplication of proceedings. The French bank had not pleaded any substantive defence to the Scottish proceedings.

Held, that (1) a concession made in court had to take account of the system of law within which the court was established and which that court had to be expected to apply: the competence of the French courts had, generally, to be a matter for those courts, but as the French Court of Appeal gave limited weight to the concession by the Scottish bank in respect of the competence of the court of first instance to deal with preliminary matters, and as the plea of no jurisdiction remained a substantive issue in the appeal before the Cour de Cassation, which could not be resolved by concession, the French bank had not made out its contention that the present action should be sisted; (2) there was no identity of causes of action and of object between the two litigants and, the requirements of Art.21 had not been met; (3) even if the terms of Art.21 were met, BNP would have been in breach of contract and the prorogation agreement and Art.17 would prevail; (4) although the actions were related Art.22 did not apply as the parallel proceedings in Scotland and France were not both at first instance; (5) even if Art.22 were otherwise applicable Art.17 had priority, and to sist the proceedings would be contrary to the interests of justice on the view that related actions in France focused the same issues without having a proper basis in averment for concluding that the French bank had undertaken the responsibilities towards the court and towards the Scottish bank implied in the allegation of fraud and (6) having regard to the nature and extent of the defence proposed, it would be inappropriate to exercise any residual power to sist at common law.

Observed, that had it been competent for the Lord Ordinary to do so he would have acceded to the suggestion made by counsel that there were important questions on the interpretation and application of the Convention which ought to be referred to the Court of Justice. Doubted, whether the exercise of any residual power of sist at common law would be appropriate, except where an issue of public policy was not raised, standing that the purpose and intent of the Convention was to define more or less comprehensively the rules to be applied in relation to the stay or sist of proceedings.

BANK OF SCOTLAND v. SA BANQUE NATIONALE DE PARIS 1996 S.L.T. 103, Judge not specified, OH.

7097. Sheriff courts–action of reparation–invalidity of prison standing orders–judicial review in sheriff court incompetent

[Prison (Scotland) Rules 1952 (SI 1952 565) r.1.]

The Prison (Scotland) Rules 1952 r.1 (2) provided that any direction under the rules was to be assumed to be given by the Secretary of State for Scotland unless otherwise provided for in the rule. Under r.14 every person was to be searched on admission and at such times subsequently as may be directed. A standing order (Fb5) was issued to governors of prisons whereby the Secretary of State directed circumstances in which prisoners were to be searched. A prisoner raised an action in the sheriff court against the Secretary of State in which he averred that he had been subjected to many illegal searches, and sought declarator, interdict and damages. A motion for interim interdict was refused. The prisoner founded upon standing order Fb5 issued by the Scottish Home and Health Department and contended that that had been issued without parliamentary approval and had no status other that that of guidelines. The sheriff dismissed the action on the basis that it was a case for judicial review which process was incompetent in the sheriff court, so that that court lacked jurisdiction. The pursuer appealed to the sheriff principal who held that the pursuer's averments amounted to an allegation not that the Secretary of State was exceeding or abusing his powers but rather that he was not in fact exercising them, which was properly a matter for inquiry by the sheriff court. The Secretary of State appealed to the Court of Session.

Held, that (1) it was clear that the pursuer had directed the court action against the Secretary of State himself and not against the actings of the prison officers, his claim being that there was no legal justification for the treatment complained of; (2) the pursuer had both acknowledged that the standing orders had been issued and averred that they were of no legal status, so that it could not be said that the Secretary of State had not exercised his powers of issuing them and (3) that raised the question of the validity of the standing orders which could only be challenged by way of judicial review in the Court of Session; and appeal allowed and action dismissed.

McDONALD v. SECRETARY OF STATE FOR SCOTLAND (NO.2) 1996 S.L.T. 575, Judge not specified, IH.

7098. Sist–lis alibi pendens–proceedings in another state

[Civil Jurisdiction and Judgments Act 1982 (c.27) Sch.1 Art.5, Sch.1 Art.21, Sch.1 Art.22.]

I, a limited company, sued M, a company registered in France, for payment in the sum of FF 66,844, 627 or sterling equivalent, averring negligent misrepresentation by M. I averred that I's parent company, L, entered into an agreement with M in 1958 whereby M were the exclusive distributors of L's products in France. Since about 1980, at M's request, L's products were supplied to A, a Swiss subsidiary of M, and L and M caused I and A to enter into individual contracts of sale, with A being invoiced by I for the products which were then distributed by M. When I informed M that the exclusive arrangement was to be terminated on December 31, 1993 M intimated that L were not entitled to do so and I became concerned that if L's products continued to be supplied to M, M would prevent A from paying the purchase price as security for any claim for compensation against I in respect of the termination. I were also concerned that M would fail to pay A sufficient money to enable A to meet I's invoices. On September 8, 1993 M's deputy general manager represented to I that I's invoices to A would be paid in the normal course of business. M could not and would not compensate any claim that M might have against sums due to I or by M or A, and M had no intention of procuring that the sums due would not be paid by the due dates. In reliance on B's representations, I entered into contracts to supply A up to December 31, 1993. The products supplied by I to A between September and December 1993 were not paid for. On December 30, 1993 M raised an action against L and I in the commercial court of Bordeaux in which M sought damages for wrongful termination of the exclusive distribution agreement between L and M. A sequestration order was granted on January 3, 1994 which prevented A from making payment to I of the amount outstanding. Although the rules and procedure of that court provided a mechanism for the counterclaim, L and I adhered to a defence of no jurisdiction, despite being ordered to lodge defences on the merits. On January 27, 1995 a judgment was issued rejecting L and I's plea of no jurisdiction, finding against L and I, and ordaining M to pay to I the sum of FF 66,903,946 which was due to be set of against the substantial damages awarded to M. M argued that the proceedings were separate as the French case was contractual, and that Art.22 of the Brussels Convention required both to be at first instance.

Held, action sisted under Art.21. Under Art.21 of the Convention lis pendens was a concept independent of definitions in national legal systems *Gubisch Maschinenfabrik AG v. Palumbo* [1987] E.C.R. 4861 [1988] C.L.Y. 1466. There was no necessity that the claims made in the two actions were identical since "cause of action" was a broad concept denoting the general factual or legal basis out of which each claim arose *Owners of Cargo Lately Laden on Board Tatry v. Owners of Maciej Rataj* [1994] E.C.R. 5439 [1995] C.L.Y. 704 and Art.21 applied when there was even a partial overlap in the bases of the actions, in order to avoid irreconcilable judgments on similar facts in two contracting states. Since the outcome of I's action might pre-empt the outcome of M's action in France and since M's liability to pay for the goods invoiced to A had been ruled upon, I's current action, in effect, was a counterclaim since the origin of both actions was to be found in the same substantive question. I's arguments were not sufficient to avoid the operation of Art.21 and the French court's determination was to be accepted unless set aside on the pending appeal. Opinion, that (1) I's action and M's action in France were not "related actions" in terms of Art.22 since M's action was not at first instance and it had not been demonstrated to the court that French law permitted consolidation of related actions; and (2) it was open to I to prove that the harmful event averred had occurred in Scotland *Handelskwekerij GJ Bier BV v. Mines de Potasse d'Alsace SA* [1976] E.C.R. 1735, [1976] C.L.Y. 1097, and the delictual liability founded on by I did not overlap necessarily with a term governing the contractual relationship between M and L *Kalfelis v. Schroder, Munchmeyer, Hengst* [1988] E.C.R. 5565 [1988] C.L.Y. 1469, distinguished.

WILLIAM GRANT & SONS v. MARIE-BRIZARD & ROGER INTERNATIONAL SA 1996 S.C.L.R. 987, Lord Gill, OH.

7099. Articles

International jurisdiction: High Court reverses itself following (1994) PILMR issue 2, or "how Drake J didn't duck the issue" *(Peter Kaye.)*: P.I. 1996, 3(1), 19-24. (Whether English courts could stay proceedings in favour of Scottish courts on grounds of forum non-conveniens and whether doctrine inapplicable within contracting states to Brussels Convention).

Whisky galore–por favor: private international law and interdicting whisky exports *(Barry J. Rodger)*: S.L.T. 1996, 12, 105-108 . (Reexamination needed of basis on which courts in UK grant injunctions against export of goods in circumstances giving rise to claim of passing off in foreign jurisdictions and effect of 1995 Act).

7100. Books

Aird, R.E.; Jameson, J.M.St.C.–The Scots Dimension to Cross-Border Litigation. Hardback: £65.00. ISBN 0-414-011309. W. Green & Son.

LANDLORD AND TENANT

7101. Assured tenancies–tenants' rights–recovery of possession by heritable creditor–competency

[Housing (Scotland) Act 1988 (c.43) s.18(1) and Sch.5 ground 2.]

T, tenant under a short assured tenancy, sought interim interdict against eviction by C, the heritable creditors of her landlord, G. G had leased the subjects without C's knowledge. C obtained decree entitling them to repossess the subjects from G. C claimed T ought not to be in occupation without their consent, the standard security being registered before the lease was entered into. As it was on the public record that T's occupation would thus be prohibited T was to be deemed to have been aware of that. T argued that C required to make an application to the court to dispense with the requirement for notice of the possible repossession, Housing (Scotland) Act 1988 s.18, Sch.5 and ground 2, which was not restricted to cases where the creditor knew of the tenancy.

Held, T's argument upheld, that although such a lease was voidable it was not void *ab initio* and required a separate order, *Trade Development Bank v. Warriner & Mason (Scotland)* 1980 S.L.T. 223, [1980] C.L.Y. 3536, (Cusine, Standard Securities, para.508).

TAMROUI v. CLYDESDALE BANK 1996 S.C.L.R. 732, Judge not specified, Sh Ct.

7102. Leases–assignation–invalid lease

[Land Tenure Reform (Scotland) Act 1974 (c.38) s.17; Agricultural Holdings (Scotland) Act 1949 (c.75).]

K, a limited company, heritable proprietors of an estate in Aberdeenshire, sought declarator of their rights under missives which had been concluded with C, the tenant under an agricultural lease of a farm forming part of the estate, and decree ordaining C to vacate the farm in implementation of the missives. K had received title to the estate in September 1979 from a couple, S, who had first granted a lease of the whole estate to E, a limited company, both K and E having been set up in order to mitigate S's tax liability. In October 1979 E assigned the tenant's interest under the lease to S, and Mrs S continued to occupy the estate after her husband's death in 1985 and to pay rent to K and receive rent from the farm occupied by C, conform to the lease. The lease between S and E was declared a fundamental nullity in August 1990, since E had been acting from the outset as S's trustees and agents, and as their nominees S were in effect seeking to enter into a contract with themselves, *Kildrummy (Jersey) Ltd v. IRC* 1992 S.L.T. 787, [1991] C.L.Y. 5730. In May 1990 Mrs S, Mr S's executors and K entered into a minute of agreement which provided that Mrs S would continue to occupy the estate in terms of the lease even if the lease was judicially determined to be invalid. Further, K was obliged immediately to grant a new lease in favour of Mrs S on identical terms and conditions in such an event. C argued that (1) K had no title or interest to pursue the action since they were not C's landlords and (2) the missives fell to be set aside since they were induced by misrepresentation. K argued that there had been no interposed lease at the time of the notice to quit and that the original lease was invalid, Mrs S only having had a licence to occupy the estate and a personal right to receive the rents. The purpose of the assignation was to transfer a lease which was fundamentally null and not to create a new one, and the Land Tenure Reform (Scotland) Act 1974 s.17 was never intended to cover agricultural leases since it did not sit well with the Agricultural Holdings (Scotland) Act 1949 concerning counter-notices. K's right stemmed from the ultimate right of a heritable proprietor to possession of his land, and as such K had title to remove subtenants without the consent of the head tenant, *Wilson v. Wilson* (1859) 21 D. 309 and such a right was not affected by s.17 of the 1974 Act.

Held, absolvitor granted, that the purported assignation by E to S could in law create a new lease since it was a tripartite deed which was clearly designed to effect a relationship of landlord and tenant, *Church of Scotland Endowment Committee v. Provident Association of London* 1914 S.C. 165. The assignation incorporated the terms of the invalid lease and it regulated the legal relationship thereby created. The parties regarded themselves as bound by the terms and conditions, *Morrison-Low v. Paterson* 1985 S.L.T. 255, [1985] C.L.Y. 3660. The operation of s.17(2) of the 1974 Act transferred the right to remove C to Mrs S and superseded *Wilson v. Wilson*. K had therefore been removed from the category of landlord as defined in s.93 of the 1949 Act. The terms of the notice to quit together with K's actings implied an assertion that K was entitled to take such action and C would not have agreed to the missives but for that misrepresentation.

KILDRUMMY (JERSEY) LTD v. CALDER 1996 S.C.L.R. 727, Judge not specified, OH.

7103. Leases–assignation–whether consent unreasonably withheld–whether landlord in material breach

Two partners in a firm of solicitors tenanted office premises from a company. Clause 6 of the lease prohibited the tenants from assigning the lease without the previous consent in writing of the landlords "such consent not to be unreasonably withheld". The firm dissolved and one of the partners sought assignation of the lease into her name as sole tenant. The landlords refused but offered to reconsider the position after two years, when she would have had an opportunity to establish herself in her own business. Nearly four years later the solicitor again sought an assignation in her favour to which the landlords were agreeable in principle. A draft assignation was then finalised but not executed or delivered by the time that an award was made by arbitration which considerably increased the rent payable by the tenants in terms of the lease. Prior to the award, the solicitor had personally discharged the tenants' obligations under the lease, including prompt payment of rent, entirely satisfactorily. The arbitration award was retrospective. The solicitor agreed to pay back the arrears in instalments and vacated the premises for other premises, thereby incurring additional overheads. The landlords then refused an assignation unless a suitable guarantor was found in place of the second tenant. The tenants purported to rescind the lease on the ground that the failure of the landlords to consent to the assignation was unreasonable and that the landlords were, accordingly, in material breach of contract. The landlords sued for payments prestable by the tenants under the lease. The sheriff held that the landlords were entitled to refuse the assignation and granted decree in their favour. The tenants appealed.

Held, that (1) the test to be applied was whether the tenants had discharged the onus of showing that, in failing to consent to the proposed assignation, the landlords had acted in a way in which no reasonable landlord would have acted and (2) the events following the arbitration award were sufficient in the whole circumstances to entitle the landlords to reconsider their previous willingness to depart from what the sheriff had found to be the prudent practice of a commercial landlord in not accepting a single tenant in lieu of two tenants without a guarantor or other independent financial support, and it followed that the tenants had not been entitled to rescind the contact; and appeal refused. Opinion, that the test of materiality of a breach of contract was one which applied to the nature of the breach rather than the actual or anticipated consequences to the party founding on it, although those consequences might be relevant as illustrating the materiality, and, provisionally that any breach of a condition which compelled a landlord to act reasonably in relation to an assignation proposed by a tenant or joint tenant went to the root of the contact.

SCOTMORE DEVELOPMENTS LTD v. ANDERTON 1996 S.L.T. 1304, Judge not specified, IH.

7104. Leases–construction–"common parts"

M, the landlords of a building development, appealed against a sheriff's decision that they were not entitled to recover from the tenant, S, any part of their maintenance expense for the roof and external walls of the building as they were not common parts of the premises in terms of the lease. In 1972, S and M's predecessor in interest entered into a lease whereby S agreed to lease a substantial number of offices within a building and 14 parking spaces in the car park which formed part of the same development. In terms of the introductory clause, S had a right in common with the other tenants to certain subjects and services, referred to as the "common parts"; and in cl. third, S undertook to pay a proportionate share of the expense of the maintenance, cleaning and lighting of the common parts. After a proof before answer, the sheriff held that the roof and external wall did not form part of "the common parts" because these areas were not recognised at common law as common parts and therefore could not be included in cl. third of the lease unless S's obligation to share the expense of maintaining them was stated in clear and unequivocal terms. On appeal, M argued that there was no common law regarding the expression. Therefore its meaning had to be determined by reference to the constitution of the words used by the parties in their contract, and cl. third did not lack clarity.

Held, appeal allowed, that there was no common law as to what was covered by the expression "common parts" in a lease, as opposed to "common property" in the law of the tenement, and the expression had to be construed by the ordinary rules of interpretation. There was no dispute that S was liable for a share of the expense, only as to the scope of the definition. The definition of "common parts" included "all other parts... of the ... development which are common to the premises and other parts of the... development", which included anything shared or which in some way benefited or concerned the occupiers. It was not necessary for the roof and external walls to be expressly mentioned since they fell naturally within the scope of the expression and the definition of common parts was wide enough to include them by implication.

MARFIELD PROPERTIES v. SECRETARY OF STATE FOR THE ENVIRONMENT 1996 S.C.L.R. 749, Judge not specified, IH.

7105. Leases–irritancy–claim by tenant for unjustified enrichment–res judicata

D, developers and tenants of a shopping centre, reclaimed against a Lord Ordinary's decision dismissing their claim against their landlords, P, following P's irritation of their sublease (1996 S.L.T. 186). D accepted the Lord Ordinary's decision except as regards unjust enrichment. In terms of the sublease, D were entitled to retain a portion of the rents they collected from the occupational tenants. D pled that the portion of rents which they were entitled to retain represented a return for their investment in the development. When the sublease was irritated, D lost their entitlement to this return, which was not a counterpart of their right of possession under the sublease. P were unjustly enriched by the capitalised value of that element of D's interest which did not correlate to the rent payable by to P. D argued: (1) regard had to be had to the whole contractual arrangement, the head lease, development agreement and sublease. The commercial reality was that as a result of the irritancy, P received an income which represented D's contribution to the development; (2) since D lost both civil possession and their capital base which allowed them to obtain an anticipated return on their investment, P retained more than what corresponded to possession and were therefore unjustly enriched in a way which exceeded the scope of the irritancy clause; (3) in order to remedy the unjust enrichment, the court could adjust the parties' position after termination where there was no claim available under the contract and the equities favoured adjustment. The scope of the original agreement envisaged a join exploitation of the property and thus P had been unjustly enriched insofar as the sublease contained matters which went beyond the usual terms of landlord and tenant; (4) the authorities on forfeiture on irritancy dealt with the orthodox case of landlord and tenant however relying on *Dorchester Studios (Glasgow) Ltd. v. Stone* 1975 S.L.T. 153, [1975] C.L.Y. 3893 only the strict rule of forfeiture might not be applied where injustice would result and (5) even where forfeiture was involved, the court had an equitable jurisdiction to consider relief, *Stockloser v. Johnston* [1954] 1 Q.B. 476, [1954] C.L.Y. 1463.

Held, reclaiming motion refused. Per Lords Sutherland and Cullen, that (1) D's claim was clearly excluded by the terms of the irritancy clause, which prescribed precisely what was to happen on such an event and barred "all claims" by D, which could not be read as restricted to claims in respect of the use and possession of the premises; (2) the windfall which P received was the result of their contractual entitlement under the irritancy clause and did not constitute enrichment. Any injustice which arose could only by cured by altering the law relating to irritancy clauses or altering the rule that clear contractual terms precluded any equitable consideration such as recompense, and therefore there was no justification in law for D's claim that P had been unjustifiedly enriched and (3) the English law on forfeiture was at best an uncertain guide to Scottish law on irritancy and although *Stockloser* had not been overruled, its dissenting opinion had subsequently been supported. *Cassels v. Lamb* (1885) 12 R. 722 supported the contrary view. *Held*, further, that the Lord Ordinary had correctly rejected P's pleas of res judicata and omitted those which were unsound. opinion, per Lord Rodger (dissenting as regards unjust enrichment), that to succeed, D had to show that P were enriched at D's expense, that there was no legal justification for the enrichment and that it would be equitable to compel P to redress the enrichment.

DOLLAR LAND (CUMBERNAULD) LTD v. CIN PROPERTIES LTD 1996 S.C.L.R. 697, Lord Sutherland, IH.

7106. Leases–irritancy–irritancy on liquidation–irritancy on receivership

A lease provided, in cl.16, for irritancy on any one of a number of events. One such event was where the tenants went into liquidation. On an assignation of the tenants' interest, cl.16 was amended, inter alia, by introducing at the end a declaratory provision on the manner in which the landlords' right might be exercised, which provision made reference to the tenants' receivership. On the new tenants going into receivership, a dispute arose as to whether receivership had become a competent ground upon which the landlords might take proceedings to irritate the lease. The landlords sought declarator to that effect and removing of the tenants. At procedure roll, the tenants argued that the only grounds for irritancy were those in the unamended cl.16. They further argued that while there was no bias for or against the effectiveness of an irritancy clause, one was looking to ascertain the parties' intention. There was, it was submitted, a hostility to such clauses. The landlords argued that receivership had become an additional ground for irritancy. It was contended that one had to discover the intention of the parties, with no presumption that such clauses were unreasonable, and further that there was a distinction between the interpretation of the language of such provisions and the court's attitude towards their enforcement.

Held, dismissing the action, that (1) it was proper to draw the distinction contended for by the landlords and to adopt a fair construction of the language used, with no presumption for or against the effectiveness of the clause and (2) on a proper interpretation, the assignation did not innovate upon the grounds on which the landlords might be entitled to terminate the lease, but simply qualified the way in which the landlords' right to irritate fell to be exercised if an irritancy was incurred as otherwise provided for in the lease.

AUDITGLEN LTD v. SCOTEC INDUSTRIES (IN RECEIVERSHIP) 1996 S.L.T. 493, Judge not specified, OH.

7107. Leases–notice of termination–means of service

S, the tenant of a property owned by C, reclaimed against a Lord Ordinary's decision that S had not validly served a notice of termination of the lease, for which 12 months' notice in writing was required by cl.2 of the lease, because the notice had not been sent to C's registered office as required by cl.7, S having sent notices instead to C's business address and C's agents, A. Another Lord Ordinary held after proof that A did not have authority to receive service on C's behalf. S argued that, while the requirement for 12 months' notice in writing was mandatory, cl.7 was only a procedural provision dealing with methods of service, and was directory rather than mandatory; the words "shall be sent" were not necessarily mandatory, *Howard v. Secretary of State for the Environment* [1975] Q.B. 235, [1974] C.L.Y. 3731; cl.7 was primarily for the benefit of the giver of a notice, as it provided that a notice sent by recorded delivery would be deemed sufficiently served 48 hours after posting and that notice could be served at an individual's last know address, in both of which cases the notice might never be received; and that cl.7 could not be mandatory because if C had been an individual living aboad the clause could not have been complied with.

Held, reclaiming motion refused, cl.2, which was plainly mandatory, had to read as qualified by cl.7. Accordingly "notice in writing" meant a notice served on C at their registered office. Clause 7 was clearly conceived in favour of the recipient of a notice, so that the recipient knew where to look for any notices, and the language of the provisions regarding place of service was plainly intended to be mandatory, *Yates Building Co v. R J Pulleyn & Sons (York)* (1975) 119 S.J. 370, [1975] C.L.Y. 388, distinguished, even though cl.7 contained other deeming provisions. Different considerations applied to the interpretation of statutes as opposed to arms length contracts, *Howard v. Secretary of State for the Environment* [1975] Q.B. 235, [1974] C.L.Y. 3731 distinguished, and the parties, having made specific provision for the places to which notice had to be sent, were entitled to hold each other to them.

CAPITAL LAND HOLDINGS LTD v. SECRETARY OF STATE FOR THE ENVIRONMENT, *The Times*, September 28, 1995, Lord Penrose, OH.

7108. Leases–obligation of tenants–guarantee–effect of conveyance of landlords' interest

W sought declarator that a guarantee granted by D of E's obligations as tenant under a lease was enforceable by W as successors in title to the landlords (S) in whose favour the guarantee was granted. W purchased the premises in February 1993 from S, the statutory successors of A. The premises were burdened by a lease which had been entered into in 1990. E had taken entry to the premises under missives in 1987. D granted the guarantee on July 15, 1987. E went into liquidation in or about March 1994. The guarantee related to payment of rent, other monetary obligations and the performance of all other obligations of E as tenant. D argued that (1) having regard to the language of the guarantee and the fact that W had not pled any relevant case averring that there had been an assignation of the guarantee, the obligation was personal to A as creditor and only enforceable by A; (2) since the guarantee defined A itself as creditor, the obligation undertaken by D to A was one involving delectus personae, (Gloag and Irvine, *Rights in Security*, p.767); *Bowie v. Watson, McNight & Co.* (1840) 2 D. 1061; *Stewart v. Scott* (1803) Hume's Dec. 91. W argued that (1) it was the general rule that rights were assignable and that delectus personae was the exception rather than the rule. There was no reason to infer delectus personae unless there was some clear indication of reliance on trust in the principal creditor and, if the obligant under a guarantee sought special provisions, these should have been stipulated for, otherwise ordinarily there could be no transmission of the benefit of a guarantee in favour of the heir of any individual landlord on death. There could be no basis for confidence or trust in the case of a corporate landlord since the policies of any corporate body were liable to vary depending on who was in control of the organisation at any given time: the confidence in individual judgment necessary for delectus personae could not be predicated of a guarantor in these circumstances; (2) the benefit of the guarantee was assignable by implication in order to give the guarantee business efficacy. The identification of A was merely to identify the lease and obligations thereunder.

Held, action dismissed. (1) The issue depended on the terms of the obligation undertaken in the guarantee in the context of the lease. Where the guarantee was given in gremio of the principal lease it could extend to singular successor of the landlord since, typically, the landlord would be defined for the purposes of the lease including his singular successors (Halliday, *Conveyancing Law and Practice*, Vol.III, p.155). Where the guarantee was undertaken in a separate deed and there were other relevant circumstances, for example that A was a statutory body, the indications favoured a construction pointing to delectus personae and (2) the test applied in *Inverlochy Castle v. Lochaber Power Co* 1987 S.L.T. 466, [1987] C.L.Y. 4507, of whether the contract ran with the land, was applicable. In the absence of express language conferring the benefit of the guarantee on singular successors there was nothing to indicate a right inherent in the owner of the premises for the time being. Where the creditor's right under a guarantee ran with the land, assignation was not required, since the creditor's right did pass to the singular successor by virtue of the disposition in his favour. The guarantee of a tenant's obligation under a lease did not have that character and merely provided protection to the landlord in the event of failure by the particular tenant in his obligations. Such a right terminated upon assignation of a lease in the absence of express language conferring the benefit of the guarantee on singular successors.

WAYDALE v. DHL HOLDINGS (UK) 1996 S.C.L.R. 391, Judge not specified, OH.

7109. Leases–obligations of tenant–obligation to keep premise open for trade–enforcement

Tenants under a lease which included an obligation on them to keep premises open within a shopping centre, proposed to close down their business. The premises which they occupied were located on two floors. Approximately three quarters of the ground floor had been sublet by the tenants and since about January 1995 had been unused. The landlords raised an action seeking a positive order ordaining the tenants to keep the premises open ad interim, and interim interdict against the tenants from vacating or removing therefrom. The tenants argued that as the terms of the lease were too wide, an interim positive order was incompetent, and in any event, on the balance of convenience, both interim orders should be refused as the facts and circumstances weighed against their being forced to trade from the premises. The landlords argued that the terms of the lease were permissive and not the measure of the positive order and that their exposure to the possible adverse consequences rendered the balance of convenience strongly in favour of the status quo.

Held, that (1) the orders were the counterparts one of the other and that interim orders to require that the premises remain open so as to preserve the status quo were competent; (2) the balance of convenience favoured the pursuers as the defenders' proposed action was prima facie a serious and material breach of their contractual obligations and (3) in the whole circumstances interim orders were appropriate to maintain, but not innovate on the status quo and no order would be made compelling the defenders to use or keep open the ground floor premises; and orders granted ad interim interdicting the defenders from vacating or removing from the first floor premises and ad interim ordaining the defenders to keep the first floor premises open.

HIGHLAND & UNIVERSAL PROPERTIES LTD v. SAFEWAY PROPERTIES LTD 1996 S.L.T. 559, Judge not specified, OH.

7110. Leases–obligations of tenant–obligation to keep property open for trade–enforcement

The tenants, a bank, gave notice to the landlords of the bank offices that they intended to cease to operate part of their business carried on in the premises, but that the business carried on by the cash dispensing machines would remain. Clause third of the lease provided that the tenants were bound to use and occupy the premises for use as bank offices and during all normal business hours to keep the premises open for business throughout the duration of the lease. The landlords raised an action seeking a decree ordaining the tenants to use and occupy the premises as bank offices; to keep the premises open for business during specified hours; and to permit the public to have access to the premises for the purpose of transacting banking business during those specified hours. The tenants argued that (1) the obligation in the lease allowed scope for adaptation as to how the basic activities comprised in banking were carried out, and (2) the obligation was insufficiently specific to form the basis of a decree of specific implement.

Held, that (1) it was legitimate in construing cl. third to have regard to the circumstances prevailing when the lease was entered into, and it was clear that the parties would have had in contemplation the operation of a traditional bank branch open to the public during normal business hours and (2) even though the obligation was narrower and more specific than that which was considered in *Grosvenor Developments (Scotland) Plc v. Argyll Stores* 1987 S.L.T. 738, [1987] C.L.Y. 4846, the authority of that case precluded the grant of any decree of specific implement expressed in general terms such as use of the premises as bank offices; and decree of specific implement refused.

Observed, that an obligation, to be binding, did not require to be capable of being expressed in terms of a decree of specific implement. Dictum of Lord President Inglis in *McArthur v. Lawson* (1877) 4 R. 1137, commented on.

RETAIL PARKS INVESTMENTS LTD v. ROYAL BANK OF SCOTLAND (NO. 2) 1996 S.L.T. 52, Judge not specified, OH.

7111. Leases–rent reviews–basis for determination–adjustment of rental evidence

An arbiter, A, appointed to determine the revised rent due in terms of a commercial lease between landlords, C, and tenants, E, stated a case for the opinion of the court on the question of whether or not he was obliged, in considering evidence of comparable rents, to ignore the effect on those rents of any rent free period. Clause 1 of Pt. IV of the schedule to the lease provided that, "The revised open market rent for each Review Period shall be such as may be agreed or determined to be the open market rent at the relevant Review Date for the Property: (1) on the following assumptions at that date:;... (iv) that the Property would be let upon terms that the willing tenant would commence paying rent immediately upon the relevant Review Date and that such rent would not be discounted or reduced to reflect the absence of any rent free period or other concession or consideration which on a new letting of the Property might be granted to an incoming tenant, it being assumed that the willing tenant has been entitled to the benefit of the Property before the relevant Review Date for a period reflecting the value of such rent free period or other concession or consideration and (2) but disregarding:;... (vii) the value of any rent free period or other concession or consideration which might be given to any tenant on the open market for the purposes of applying to the Property evidence of rents passing in the market." C argued that the effect of cl.1 was that when A was examining the rental evidence from comparable properties, he was not to make any adjustment to the headline rent to allow for the effect of any rent free period.

Held, question answered in the negative. A clause which deemed the market rent to be the headline rent obtainable after a rent free period granted to disguise a fall in the rental value was not in accordance with the basic purpose of a rent review clause, as it enabled C to obtain an increase in rent simply by reason of changes in the way rents were structured, and in the absence of unambiguous language a rent review clause would not be construed as having that effect *Co-operative Wholesale Society v. National Westminster Bank* [1995] 01 E.G. 111, [1995] C.L.Y. 3037; *City Offices v. Bryanston Insurance Co* [1993] 11 E.G. 129, [1993] C.L.Y. 2531, applied. Subparagraph (A)(iv) required that the revised rent was not to be discounted to reflect the absence of any rent free period which might be granted on a new letting, which implied that, if A wished to use as comparables market lettings which involved rent free periods, he had to adjust them in order to fix a rent which would be payable from day one *Prudential Nominees v. Greenham Trading Co* joined supra to *Co-operative Wholesale Society*. This was reinforced, rather than contradicted, by subpara.(B)(vii) which was entirely general in its terms and therefore required A to disregard the value of any rent free period irrespective of the purpose to which it was attributable, and accordingly A had to adjust the headline rents of comparable properties to reflect the assumption that there was to be no rent free period granted to E as at the review date.

Observed, that the court agreed with the parties' settlement during the hearing of other questions put: that (1) a provision that C were not to withhold consent unreasonably to a proposed subdivision of the property, if on certain lines, implied that C were entitled to withhold consent in their absolute discretion to a subdivision in any other respect, but that this was not an absolute prohibition against subdivision and (2) a further assumption that there would be disregarded any effect on rental value of the fact that E might have fitted out the property and/or installed and/or paid for, inter alia, staircases, when read in its context, required only the fact that E had paid for staircases to be disregarded and not also the fact that the property had been fitted with internal staircases.

CHURCH COMMISSIONERS FOR ENGLAND v. ETAM 1995 S.C.L.R. 947, Lord Hope (Lord President), IH.

7112. Leases–rent reviews–waiver by landlord

In terms of the missives of let for industrial premises, a rent review was provided for on May 28, 1990 and at five-yearly intervals thereafter. The landlords did not seek a review on or before May 28, 1990. The tenants continued to pay, and the landlords to accept, rent at the original rate until October 1991, when the landlords intimated a rent review with effect from May 28, 1990. The landlords raised an action seeking declarator that they were entitled to insist upon the rent review. Having heard submissions on the agreed evidence, the sheriff granted the declarator craved. The tenants appealed.

Held, that the proper reference to be drawn from the facts was that the landlords had waived their right to a rent review in May 1990; and appeal allowed and defenders assoilzied.

WAYDALE LTD v. MRM ENGINEERING 1996 S.L.T. (Sh.Ct.) 6, Judge not specified.

7113. Leases–tacit relocation–whether implied consent of parties to continuation excluded by actings

The tenants of premises in Dundee sent a notice of termination of tenancy to the landlords. The landlords contended that the tenants ought to have given 40 days' clear notice of their intention to remove. The tenants argued that the implied consent of the parties to the continuation of the lease was excluded by their actings and moreover that the notice of termination, given on April 5, 1993 to take effect from Whitsunday, May 15, was timeous. They submitted that in order to avoid the operation of tacit relocation it was not essential for one of the parties to a lease to take the step of giving notice, and that there might be cases in which the conduct of a party was sufficient by itself to rebut the presumption that renewal of the lease was intended. The tenants founded in particular upon their act of closing down business at the premises and removing well before any date when notice was due. Although this was in breach of the terms of the sublease, the landlords took no steps to require them to resume their occupation and trading.

Held, that (1) the actings relied upon by the tenants so as to exclude tacit relocation were insufficient for that purpose in the absence of any averment that any actings founded upon by the tenants were known to the landlords; (2) in relation to leases 40 clear days were required for notice to be given by a party to a lease so as to avoid tacit relocation, and notice given on the 40th day prior to the termination date was insufficient and accordingly the sublease continued by tacit relocation; and question answered accordingly. *Observed*, that it was very difficult to envisage a case where any actings short of some form of notice, whether communicated verbally or in writing, would ever suffice.

SIGNET GROUP PLC v. C & J CLARK RETAIL PROPERTIES LTD 1996 S.L.T. 1325, Judge not specified, OH.

7114. Leases–validity–pro indiviso proprietors granting lease of subjects to one of their number

By a minute of lease granted in January 1977 the pro indiviso proprietors of certain subjects purported to lease them to one of their number as tenant and on March 5, 1985 they granted a standard security over the subjects in favour of lenders. On October 26, 1988 the lenders served calling up notices on the proprietors and subsequently raised actions seeking declarator that they were entitled to enter into possession of the security subjects and remove the occupants thereof. The pro indiviso proprietors averred that, having granted a lease to one of their number, his occupation of the subjects was protected by the Agricultural Holdings Acts and accordingly the creditors were not entitled to remove him therefrom. After debate the sheriff granted decree and the proprietors appealed to the sheriff principal who refused the appeal, holding that, even if it were possible for pro indiviso proprietors to grant a lease to one of their number, there could not be a valid lease unless the tenant was divested of his rights as coproprietor and that there had been such a merging of the rights and obligations of landlord and tenant as to render the purported lease invalid. The proprietors appealed to the Court of Session and argued that a lease by joint pro indiviso proprietors in favour of one of their number as tenant had the necessary content in law to exist since the obligations of such proprietors arose in solidum and rights could be enforced jointly or severally or, alternatively, the doctrine of pro indiviso ownership admitted the concept of necessity which permitted the enforcement of the proprietor's right in appropriate circumstances even when they were not unanimous.

Held, Lord McCluskey dissenting, that a lease between pro indiviso proprietors and one of their number was a nullity because (1) one of the granters and the grantee would thereby become both creditor and debtor in obligations arising from the same contract, and if the contract was a nullity as regards one of the proprietors, it could not survive so far as the other proprietors were concerned and (2) the grant of such a lease would be inconsistent with the granters' pro indiviso ownership of the land, since acts of management including actions that might require to be taken against the tenant, could only be taken with the consent of all the proprietors; and appeals refused, *Barclay v. Penman* 1984 S.L.T. 376, [1984] C.L.Y. 4238 approved. *Opinion* (per the Lord Justice Clerk (Ross)), (1) that *Pinkerton v. Pinkerton* 1986 S.L.T. 376, [1986] C.L.Y. 4199, on which the defenders relied, was the converse of the present case, and the same considerations did not necessarily apply to pro indiviso landlords as to pro indiviso tenants and (2) it appeared to be contrary to both principle and authority to suggest that joint pro indiviso proprietors had a legal persona distinct from the individuals who were pro indiviso proprietors. Opinion (per Lord McCluskey dissenting): that the authorities did not justify a conclusion that the rule that a legal person could not contract with himself so as to create rights enforceable by the courts, applied to a case in which pro indiviso proprietors voluntarily entered into a formal written contract to lease the subjects to one of their own number: in the case of a dispute the court should permit a majority of the proprietors to act in the common interest.

CLYDESDALE BANK PLC v. DAVIDSON 1996 S.L.T. 437, Judge not specified, IH.

7115. Articles

Assignation: approaches to the reasonable landlord *(Lionel D. Most.)*: S.L.P.Q. 1996, 1 (2), 166-172. (Meaning of expression "consent not to be unreasonably withheld" in Scottish commercial leases).

Commercial leasing: enforcing keep-open clauses *(Andrew McCowan.)*: J.L.S.S. 1996, 41 (6), 228-230. (Whether tenant's obligation to occupy and use leased premises can be enforced in Scotland by specific implement).

Keep open covenants: Part 1 *(Brian Kilcoyne)*: Corp. Brief. 1996, 10(8), 23-26. (Interpretation of positive covenants requiring trader to continue trading from premises and landlords' remedies for breach).

Keep open covenants: Part 2 *(Jonathan Ross)*: Corp. Brief. 1996, 10(9), 22-25. (Implications of cases on enforcement of covenants requiring tenant of retail premises to continue trading, including effect on rent review and lease renewal).

Lease or licence in Scots law? *(Mike Dailly)*: SCOLAG 1996, 236, 126-129. (Extent of recognition of distinction with particular reference to residents in hostels and supported accommodation).

Notices to quit *(Stewart Brymer)*: Prop. L.B. 1996, 22(Aug), 7-8. (Format and service of notices to quit).

Rent review and waiver *(Stewart Brymer)*: Prop. L.B. 1996, 19(Feb), 10-11. (Whether in Scotland acceptance of old level of rent after review date implies waiver by landlord of right to review).

Schedules of condition of repair *(Stewart Brymer)*: Prop. L.B. 1996, 20(Apr), 11-12. (Tenants' liability for meeting landlords' common law obligations for repair must be clearly and unequivocally stated in lease).

Tenant default: what are the landlord's options? *(Stewart Brymer.)*: Prop. L.B. 1996, 23(Oct), 5-7.

Tenant's improvements *(Stewart Brymer)*: Prop. L.B. 1996, 21 (Jun), 4-5. (Ownership of improvements and position regarding improvements at rent review and termination).

LEGAL AID

7116. Advice and assistance

ADVICE AND ASSISTANCE (ASSISTANCE BY WAY OF REPRESENTATION) (SCOTLAND) AMENDMENT REGULATIONS 1996, SI 1996 1011 (S.112); made under the Legal Aid (Scotland) Act 1986 s.9, s.36, s.37. In force: March 31, 1996; £1.10.

Amend the Advice and Assistance (Assistance by Way of Representation) (Scotland) Regulations 1988 (SI 1988 2290) to take into account certain applications and under the Criminal Justice (Scotland) Act 1995.

7117. Advice and assistance

ADVICE AND ASSISTANCE (FINANCIAL CONDITIONS) (SCOTLAND) REGULATIONS 1996, SI 1996 1010 (S.111); made under the Legal Aid (Scotland) Act 1986 s.11, s.36, s.37. In force: April 8, 1996; £1.10.

Increase the disposable income limit for eligibility for advice and assistance under the 1986 Act from £156 a week to £162 a week and the weekly disposable income above which a person is required to make a contribution from £64 to £67; and prescribe the scale of contributions to be paid where the weekly disposable income exceeds £67 but does not exceed £162.

7118. Advice and assistance

ADVICE AND ASSISTANCE (SCOTLAND) AMENDMENT REGULATIONS 1996, SI 1996 811 (S.91); made under the Legal Aid (Scotland) Act 1986 s.33, s.36. In force: April 8, 1996; £1.10.

These Regulations amend the Advice and Assistance (Scotland) Regulations 1987 (SI 1987 382). They provide: that advice and assistance in relation to the recognition or enforcement of a judgment under the Civil Jurisdiction and Judgments Act 1982 s.5 shall be made available free without regard to the income or capital of the applicant where the applicant benefited from complete or partial legal aid or exemption from costs or expenses in the State of origin or, in the case of Denmark or Iceland, fulfilled the economic requirements to qualify for such grant or exemption; that any application for such advice and assistance may be signed on behalf of the applicant by the solicitor to whom the application is made; for the table of fees allowable to solicitors for assistance by way of representation to be amended to take account of amendment made to the conditions applicable to the provision of assistance by way of representation in summary criminal proceedings made by the Advice and Assistance (Assistance by Way of Representation) (Scotland) Amendment Regulations 1996 (SI 1996 1011).

7119. Advice and assistance–consolidation regulations

ADVICE AND ASSISTANCE (SCOTLAND) (CONSOLIDATION AND AMENDMENT) REGULATIONS 1996, SI 1996 2447 (S.192); made under the Legal Aid (Scotland) Act 1986 s.12, s.33, s.36, s.37, s.42. In force: October 7, 1996; £3.20.

These Regulations consolidate with amendments and revoke the Advice and Assistance (Scotland) Regulations 1987 (SI 1987 382) and the Regulations amending those Regulations. The main amendments are in consequence of the Children (Scotland) Act 1995 and the Jobseekers Allowance Act 1995.

7120. Civil legal aid

ACT OF SEDERUNT (CIVIL LEGAL AID RULES) (AMENDMENT NO.2) 1996, SI 1996 3202 (S.242); made under the Legal Aid (Scotland) Act 1986 s.38. In force: January 1, 1997; £0.65.

This Act of Sederunt amends the Act of Sederunt (Civil Legal Aid Rules 1987 (SI 1987 492) by replacing a definition referring to the Civil Legal Aid (Scotland) Regulations 1987 (SI 1987 381) with a definition referring to the Civil Legal Aid (Scotland) Regulations 1996 (SI 1996 2444).

7121. Civil legal aid

CIVIL LEGAL AID (FINANCIAL CONDITIONS) (SCOTLAND) REGULATIONS 1996, SI 1996 1012 (S.113); made under the Legal Aid (Scotland) Act 1986 s.36. In force: April 8, 1996; £0.65.

Increase income limits to make eligible for civil legal aid those with a disposable income not exceeding £8,158 and to make eligible without contribution, those with disposable income not exceeding £2,450; and increases the upper limit from £6,750 to £8,560, above which legal aid may be refunded.

7122. Civil legal aid

CIVIL LEGAL AID (SCOTLAND) REGULATIONS 1996, SI 1996 2444 (S.189); made under the Legal Aid (Scotland) Act 1986 s.17, s.19, s.20, s.36, s.37, s.42. In force: October 7, 1996; £4.70.

These Regulations consolidate with amendments and revoke the Civil Legal Aid (Scotland) Regulations 1987 (SI 1987 381) and the Regulations amending those Regulations. The main amendments are in consequence of the Children (Scotland) Act 1995 and the Jobseekers Allowance Act 1995.

7123. Civil legal aid

CIVIL LEGAL AID (SCOTLAND) AMENDMENT REGULATIONS 1996, SI 1996 812 (S.92); made under the Legal Aid (Scotland) Act 1986 s.36. In force: April 8, 1996; £1.10.

These Regulations amend the Civil Legal Aid (Scotland) Regulations 1987 (SI 1987 381). They: (a) require an applicant or assisted person immediately to inform the Board of any change in his circumstances, or, so far as known, those of any person jointly concerned with, or having the same interest in, the matter (Reg.3); (b) clarify the power of the Board to make legal aid available in relation to applications under the Convention on the Civil Aspects of International Child Abduction and the European Convention on Recognition and Enforcement of Decisions Concerning Custody of Children and on the Restoration of the Custody of Children and modify the provisions of the Legal Aid (Scotland) Act 1986 in relation to the availability of civil legal aid for appeals to the Inner House of the Court of Session or the House of Lords arising from such applications (Reg.4); (c) clarify the power of the Board to make legal aid available in relation to applications under the European Conventions on jurisdiction and the enforcement of judgements in civil and commercial matters (Reg.5).

7124. Civil legal aid–fees

ACT OF SEDERUNT (CIVIL LEGAL AID RULES) (AMENDMENT) 1996, SI 1996 2148 (S.172); made under the Legal Aid (Scotland) Act 1986 s.38. In force: September 9, 1996; £1.10.

This Act of Sederunt amends the Act of Sederunt (Civil Legal Aid Rules) 1987 (SI 1987 492) by making provision for intimation to the Scottish Legal Aid Board of applications for increases in fees which will subsequently be met by the Board. It enables the Board to be represented at any hearing on the application and to cite any party to attend such a hearing. It also provides that in all motions intimated to the Board under the rules, the period of intimation is 14 days.

7125. Contempt of court proceedings

LEGAL AID IN CONTEMPT OF COURT PROCEEDINGS (SCOTLAND) AMENDMENT REGULATIONS 1996, SI 1996 2550 (S.199); made under the Legal Aid (Scotland) Act 1986 s.36. In force: November 1, 1996; £0.65.

These Regulations amend the Legal Aid in Contempt of Court Proceedings (Scotland) Regulations 1992 (SI 1992 1227) by amending the definition of legal representative in consequence of the Children (Scotland) Act 1995, to include a person having parental responsibilities in relation to a child and requiring the prior approval of the Scottish Legal Aid Board for work of an unusual nature or likely to involve unusually large expenditure, but only for work done on or after November 1, 1996.

7126. Criminal legal aid

CRIMINAL LEGAL AID (SCOTLAND) REGULATIONS 1996, SI 1996 2555 (S.200); made under the Legal Aid (Scotland) Act 1986 s.31, s.36. In force: November 1, 1996; £1.95.

These Regulations consolidate with only minor and drafting amendments and revoke the Criminal Legal Aid (Scotland) Regulations 1987 (SI 1987 307 as amended by SI 1988 1126, SI 1992 527, SI 1994 1050, SI 1995 2320 and SI 1996 627). In consequence of the Children (Scotland) Act 1995, the definition of legal representative has been amended to include a person having parental responsibilities in relation to a child. In addition, the prior approval of the Scottish Legal Aid Board will be required for work of an unusual nature or likely to involve unusually large expenditure but only for work done on or after November 1, 1996.

7127. Criminal legal aid

CRIMINAL LEGAL AID (SCOTLAND) AMENDMENT REGULATIONS 1996, SI 1996 627 (S.62); made under the Legal Aid (Scotland) Act 1986 s.36. In force: March 31, 1996; £1.10.

These Regulations amend the Criminal Legal Aid (Scotland) Regulations 1987 (SI 1987 307) to extend the list of proceedings treated as distinct for the purposes of criminal legal aid to take account of amendments made to the Legal Aid (Scotland) Act 1986 s.22(1) (automatic availability of criminal legal aid) by the Criminal Justice (Scotland) Act 1995 s.64 (legal aid in cases involving insanity in bar of trial) and brought into force on March 31, 1996 by the Criminal Justice (Scotland) Act 1995 (Commencement No.2, Transitional Provisions and Savings) Order 1996; and to provide that the board may, in all cases, where it is satisfied that there is good reason for doing so grant authority to an assisted person to nominate another specified solicitor.

7128. Criminal legal aid

CRIMINAL LEGAL AID (SCOTLAND) (PRESCRIBED PROCEEDINGS) AMENDMENT REGULATIONS 1996, SI 1996 1009 (S.110); made under the Legal Aid (Scotland) Act 1986 s.21, s.36. In force: March 31, 1996; £0.65.

Amend the Criminal Legal Aid (Scotland) (Prescribed Proceedings) Regulations 1994 (SI 1994 1001) by adding to the proceedings in relation to which criminal legal aid is not to be available; those to which assistance by way of representation under the Part II of the 1986 Act is made available by the Advice and Assistance (Assistance by Way of Representation) (Scotland) Amendment Regulations 1996 (SI 1996 1011) Reg.3.

7129. Petition to nobile officium–remit to sheriff for hearing–application for direction to sheriff to hear applications for legal aid after conclusion of hearing–competency

[Legal Aid (Scotland) Act 1986 (c.47) s.29(1)(a)(2) and (4); Civil Legal Aid (Scotland) Regulations 1987 (SI 1987 381) Reg.4(2) and Reg.31; Civil Legal Aid (Scotland) (Fees) Regulations 1989 (SI 1989 1490) Reg.5(4).]

Following a petition to the *nobile officium* by the parents of certain children who had been committed to compulsory care, the court ordered a rehearing of the evidence by a sheriff. After the conclusion of the proceedings before the sheriff the petitioners moved for an additional fee in terms of the Civil Legal Aid (Scotland) (Fees) Regulations 1989 Reg.5(4), on the assumption that the whole proceedings in the Court of Session and before the sheriff fell to be regarded as Court of Session proceedings. In the case of the third to sixth petitioners, an application was made for the sheriff to be directed to hear applications for legal aid in terms of the Legal Aid (Scotland) Act 1986 s.29(1)(a), (2) and (4), due to legal aid having been withdrawn from them in the course of the hearing under the Civil Legal Aid (Scotland) Regulations 1987 Reg.31(2)(a). The Scottish Legal Aid Board opposed the motions on the basis of competency on the following grounds: first, the restoration of legal aid would be contrary to the provisions of Reg.31(3)(c) of the 1987 Regulations; secondly, the proceedings which had taken place before the sheriff were Court of Session proceedings and not proceedings to which s.29 of the 1986 Act applied; and thirdly, in any event s.29 gave no power to the sheriff to backdate a grant of legal aid which was made under that section.

Held, that (1) the 1987 Regulations applied only to civil legal aid as defined in s.13(2) of the 1986 Act and not to legal aid in connection with proceedings under the Social Work (Scotland) Act 1968 Part III; (2) the third to sixth petitioners were entitled to the benefit of legal aid under s.29 in connection with the whole of the proceedings before the sheriff, and in the exceptional circumstances where the court had intended that the matter be dealt with at an earlier stage by the sheriff, an order would be made to that effect although the proceedings before the sheriff were now concluded; (3) for the purposes of Reg.5(4) of the 1989 Regulations the proceedings before the sheriff were proceedings in the sheriff court, and that it was for the sheriff to determine what percentage increase should be allowed, subject to the 50 per cent maximum applicable to cases on the ordinary roll; and orders made accordingly.

L, PETITIONERS (NO.3) 1996 S.L.T. 928, Judge not specified, IH.

7130. Articles

Applications for legal aid to pursue actions of interdict (non-matrimonial).: J.L.S.S. 1996, 41 (11), 452-453. (Including approach that Scottish Legal Aid Board will take in assessing merits of applications).

Legal aid: duties of nominated solicitor.: Crim. L.B.1996, 20(Apr), 5-6. (Rights and duties of nominated solicitor where legally aided client seeks another solicitor to act for him).

The cost of legal aid *(Mike Dailly)*: SCOLAG 1996, 236, 119-120 . (Annual report of Scottish Legal Aid Board including proposals to help reduce fraud, use of advice agencies and make system cost effective).

Withdrawal of criminal legal aid.: Crim. L.B.1996, 19(Feb), 3-4. (Circumstances in which legal aid may be restored remain unclear).

LEGAL PROFESSION

7131. Solicitors–confidentiality–fraud by third party–whether client's identity privileged

[Administration of Justice (Scotland) Act 1972 (c.59) s.1.]

CLP, a firm of solicitors, wrote to C intimating that they acted for an unnamed client who had information about a significant overpayment by C to a third party which was aware of the overpayment but had not returned the money. The nature of the payment was such that it would be very difficult to trace. CLP's client would provide the necessary information in return for a proportion of the sum recovered. C sought an order under the Administration of Justice (Scotland) Act 1972 s.1 for disclosure of the name of CLP's client. CLP maintained that the identity of their client was privileged on a solicitor/client basis.

Held, that the fact that CLP's client had attempted to take advantage of a fraud by a third party on C deprived CLP of the right to keep their client's identity confidential as a matter of privilege. CLP was ordered to disclose the name of their client to enable C to bring proceedings against the client to reveal the identity of the third party.

CONOCO (UK) LTD v. COMMERCIAL LAW PRACTICE, *The Times*, February 13, 1996, Lord Macfadyen, OH.

7132. Solicitors–professional misconduct–breach of mandate in favour of other solicitor–effect of nomination for legal aid purposes

[Criminal Legal Aid (Scotland) Regulations 1987 (SI 1987 307) Reg.17.]

S, a solicitor, petitioned for judicial review of the decision of a committee and the Council of the Law Society of Scotland (L) to reprimand S and warn him as to his future conduct. S had been introduced by the duty solicitor to a client, C, who at that time was charged with murder. S was to represent C, but prior to full committal another solicitor, G, had forwarded a mandate to S. Thereafter S visited C in custody and obtained another mandate from C. G had appeared to represent C on the same day but had been denied access to C. C again granted a further mandate to G which was then intimated to S and S responded by sending G the precognitions. Despite that, S visited C on three further occasions. S had also objected to the transfer of the legal aid certificate to G in the knowledge that C wanted other representation. G complained to L that S was guilty of professional misconduct. At a first hearing in the petition, S argued that (1) L had not applied the appropriate test of professional misconduct in that there were differing conclusions about S's conduct but nothing concluding that S had failed to attain the standard of conduct to be expected of a competent and reputable solicitor; (2) L had failed to consider as relevant the legal aid considerations, missed by the Criminal Legal Aid (Scotland) Regulations 1987 Reg.17(2).

Held, petition granted, that the test of professional misconduct had not been properly applied as it was clear that L had concluded that S's behaviour was merely inappropriate. L had been given elaborate reasons for their decision and it was reasonable to examine them, *MacColl v. Council of the Law Society of Scotland* 1987 S.L.T. 524, [1987] C.L.Y. 5168 distinguished. Further, C had not terminated his relationship with S but expressed his desire to nominate another solicitor, Reg.17(3), 1987 Regulations. S did not have the power to appoint G as the authority of the Legal Aid Board was required. S had a duty to render normal services to C once nominated had failed to take S's duties to C and the Legal Aid Board into account. S's actions were no more than was required of him whilst continuing to perform duties as a nominated solicitor. In any event, S's actions were bona fide and could not be regarded as a serious and a reprehensible departure from his duties.

McKINSTRY v. LAW SOCIETY OF SCOTLAND 1996 S.C.L.R. 421, Judge not specified, OH.

7133. Solicitors–professional misconduct–penalty

[Solicitors (Scotland) Act 1980 (c.46) s.53.]

Following a complaint by the Council of the Law Society of Scotland in relation to certain conveyancing transactions, the Scottish Solicitors Discipline Tribunal found a solicitor guilty of professional misconduct, censured and fined her £4,000 and directed in terms of s.53(5) of the Solicitors (Scotland) Act 1980 that she be subject to a restricted practising certificate for five years and until such time as the tribunal thought her fit to hold a full one. The tribunal had found the solicitor guilty of professional misconduct in respect that she had (a) notarised affidavits relative to an individual client when she knew that the person signing them was using a fictitious name; and (b) carried out a conveyancing transaction in the name of the fictitious person when the conveyance was to the same person using his real name. The solicitor had been in general practice for only a short period of time, had not attempted to conceal the transactions and had not been the subject of any other professional complaint.

Held, that (1) a strong case had to be made out before the court could interfere with the decision of a disciplinary tribunal on penalty, as the tribunal was best placed to weigh up the possible consequences of the professional misconduct and to decide what should be done to protect the public and preserve the good name of the profession and (2) the principle underlying all cases on penalty review was that, if the sentence were to be set aside, it had to be shown to have been plainly wrong and unjustified, which was not the case here as the tribunal had been right to regard the solicitor's misconduct as justifying the penalty imposed; and appeal refused, *MacDonald v. Council of the Law Society of Scotland* 1992 S.L.T. 353, [1992] C.L.Y. 6466 and *MacColl v. Council of the Law Society of Scotland* 1987 S.L.T 524, [1987] C.L.Y. 5168 applied.

GRAY v. LAW SOCIETY OF SCOTLAND 1993 S.C. 126, Judge not specified.

7134. Articles

A short history of conveyancing fees *(Brian D. Allingham.)*: J.L.S.S. 1996, 41 (8), 298-300. (Life cycle of provision of conveyancing services based on Boston Matrix management model).

A solicitors' monopoly? : J.L.S.S. 1996, 41 (4), 130-131. (DGFT's referral to Monopolies and Mergers Commission of solicitors' residential estate agency services in Scotland).

Conveyancing fees–the real answer *(Brian D. Allingham)*: J.L.S.S. 1996, 41 (10), 379-380. (Range of solutions identified to improve profitability in conveyancing for law firms).

Conveyancing fees: are we selling ourselves short? *(Brian D. Allingham)*: J.L.S.S. 1996, 41 (9), 341-343. (Downward spiral of conveyancing fees, arguments for increasing fees and methods of calculating scales).

CPD: the final frontier. : J.L.S.S. 1996, 41 (10), 393-395 . (Introduction of continuing professional development requirements for all Scottish solicitors from November 1, 1996).

Incorporation for solicitors' practices *(Bruce A. Ritchie)*: Bus. L.B. 1996, 20(Mar), 3-4. (Provisions for incorporation of legal practices in Scotland).

The 1996 cost of time survey *(John J. McCutcheon)*: J.L.S.S. 1996, 41 (11), 449-450. (Survey of hourly cost rates in legal practices in Scotland in 1996).

The legal profession and ADR *(Bryan Clark* and *Richard Mays)*: Jur. Rev. 1996, 6, 389-402. (Results of survey on role of legal profession in alternative dispute resolution processes).

Training advocates *(John Sturrock)*: J.L.S.S. 1996, 41 (1), 30-31. (Changes in pre-and post admission training for Faculty of Advocates).

LEGISLATION

7135. Royal Assents

These Acts received Royal Assent in 1996:

City of Edinburgh Council Order Confirmation Act 1996 (c.x)
Deer (Scotland) Act 1996 (c.58)
Deer (Amendment) (Scotland) Act 1996 (c.44)
Edinburgh Assay Office Order Confirmation Act 1996 (c.i)
Edinburgh Merchant Company Order Confirmation Act 1996 (c.xi)
Education (Scotland) Act 1996 (c.43)
Licensing (Amendment) (Scotland) Act 1996 (c.36)
Scottish Borders Council (Jim Clark Memorial Rally) Order Confirmation Act 1996 (c.xii)
Western Isles Council (Berneray Causeway) Order Confirmation Act 1996 (c.xiii)

7136. Articles

Schedules in Scotland *(T. St. J.N. Bates)*: Jur. Rev. 1996, 2, 79-96. (Use of schedules in statutes and main cases on interpretation).

LEISURE INDUSTRY

7137. Sports facilities–safety

SPORTS GROUNDS AND SPORTING EVENTS (DESIGNATION) (SCOTLAND) AMENDMENT ORDER 1996, SI 1996 2653 (S.206); made under the Criminal Law (Consolidation) (Scotland) Act 1995 s.18. In force: November 9, 1996; £0.65.

This Order amends the Sports Grounds and Sporting Events (Designation) (Scotland) Order 1985 (SI 1985 1224) Part II which designates certain sports grounds and classes of sporting event for the purposes of the Criminal Law (Consolidation) (Scotland) Act 1995. As a result of the amendments, Telford Street Park, Inverness ceases to be, and Caledonian Stadium, Inverness becomes a designated sports ground.

LICENSING

7138. Appeals–service of writ on chief constable–whether warrant for service required

[Act of Sederunt (Appeals under the Licensing (Scotland) Act 1976) 1977 (SI 1977 1622) para.3; Act of Sederunt (Sheriff Court Summary Application) Rules 1993 (SI 1993 3240) r.17(1).]

The Act of Sederunt (Appeals under the Licensing (Scotland) Act 1976) 1977 para.3, provides that "At the same time as the initial writ is lodged with the sheriff clerk or as soon as may be thereafter, the appellant shall serve a copy of the initial writ" on, inter alia, the chief constable. An appellant obtained a warrant to serve an initial writ only on the clerk to the licensing board, but proceeded to post a copy of the writ to the chief constable who had also appeared at the hearing. Before the sheriff it was argued for the chief constable that the appeal was incompetent because he had not been served with a copy of the writ as required by the Act of Sederunt, a warrant for service being essential. The appellant argued that the warrant for service was contained in the words of the Act of Sederunt, or alternatively that any defect in service had been cured by the appearance of the chief constable in process. The sheriff repelled the chief constable plea to the competency. The chief constable appealed to the Court of Session.

Held, that (1) the provision in para.3 that the initial writ be "served" referred to service in the manner ordinarily adopted in summary procedure; and (2) such service required judicial authority and a copy of the warrant which provided that authority had to be sent to the person on whom the writ was served; (3) the initial writ was not served on the chief constable in the manner required by para.3 of the Act of Sederunt; but (4) the appearance of the chief constable had cured any defect in the service; and appeal refused.

GHANI v. CLYDESDALE DISTRICT LICENSING BOARD 1996 S.L.T. 986, Judge not specified, IH.

7139. Appeals–time limits–extent of right of appeal

An appeal against a decision of a licensing board which is lodged timeously but dismissed as incompetent without a hearing on the merits, exhausts the appellant's right of appeal and it is not open to that appellant to lodge a further appeal out of time.

AHMED v. CHIEF CONSTABLE OF STRATHCLYDE POLICE, *The Scotsman*, January 17, 1996, Judge not specified, IH.

7140. Entertainment licence–application for grant of licence–refusal–over-provision–relevant considerations–nature of facilities to be provided

[Licensing (Scotland) Act 1976 (c.66) s.17.]

The licensing board appealed against a decision allowing an appeal by CN, a company proposing to open a nightclub in respect of which the board had refused an entertainment licence on the ground that it would result in the over-provision of licensed premises in the locality. CN had successfully argued that there was insufficient material to enable the board to reach such a conclusion and that the board's adoption of a 200 metre radius to determine locality was too wide.

Held, allowing the appeal, that the Licensing (Scotland) Act 1976 s.17 gave licensing boards a wide discretion to determine whether the grant of a licence would result in over-provision. The board was entitled to conclude that the large scale development proposed would have an impact on the amenity of the area, as there were 14 other licensed premises within the defined locality. It was not necessary to examine further an existing entertainments licence and the board was justified in adopting a radius of 200 metres in view of its local knowledge and expertise in considering a great number of applications, *Latif v. Motherwell District Licensing Board* 1994 S.L.T. 414, [1994] C.L.Y. 5936 followed.

CALEDONIAN NIGHTCLUBS LTD v. CITY OF GLASGOW DISTRICT LICENSING BOARD 1996 S.L.T. 210, Lord Jauncey of Tullichettle, HL.

7141. Entertainment licence–application for provisional grant of licence–affirmation of application–grant–effect of appeal against grant

[Licensing (Scotland) Act 1976 (c.66) s.26(1), (2), (8), s.30(1), (3), (4) and (5).]

The Licensing (Scotland) Act 1976 s.26 provides, inter alia, that any provisional grant of a licence shall be ineffective unless affirmed by the licensing board on application to them within 12 months of the provisional grant. Section 30(1) provides that where there are objections to the grant of a licence, that licence shall not take effect until any appeal has been abandoned or determined in favour of the applicant. At the March 1995 licensing board meeting a company applied to the licensing board for the provisional grant of an entertainment licence. The board granted the application. An objector appealed against that decision. A year later the appeal was still pending. The clerk to the licensing board, in a letter to the company, gave his opinion that, notwithstanding that the appeal was still ongoing, the company required to have the provisional grant (i) affirmed within 12 months of March 1995, and (ii) renewed at the March 1996 licensing board meeting. The petitioners sought judicial review of that "decision", seeking declarator that until the appeal had been decided, the provisional grant would not come into effect, the 12 month period would not begin to run, and renewal was not required; and that the board erred in law in requiring affirmation of the provisional grant within 12 months, before an application for renewal would be competent. The board agreed, *inter alia*, that s.30(1) did not apply to the provisional grant of a licence, having regard to the terms of s.26(8), and that the duration of the licence prescribed by s.30(3) ran from the grant of the licence by the board and into from its coming into effect.

Held, that (1) s.30(1) of the 1976 Act existed to deal with the date when a new licence came into force and to safeguard the rights of objectors pending an appeal, and applied to the provisional grant of a licence as well as to a full grant; (2) the grant of a licence was not the same as its coming into effect: s.26(1) and (2) concerned the former and not the latter and accordingly a provisional grant could be in effect under s.26(1) and (2) even though the licence was not yet in effect under s.30(1) because the grant was subject to an appeal; (3) as the provisional grant was in effect notwithstanding the appeal, the licence required to be affirmed under s.26(2); (4) the application for affirmation required to be made to the board within 12 months of the grant, but the board did not require to determine the application within that period, *Cunninghame DC v. Payne* 1988 S.L.T. (Sh.Ct.) 21, [1988] C.L.Y. 4511 followed and (5) while the licence, provisionally granted, was not in effect because the appeal was still ongoing, the renewal date was determined by reference to the date on which the provisional grant of the licence was first made, and accordingly the provisional grant required to be renewed at the March 1996 licensing board meeting; and a restricted declarator and reduction granted.

Observed, that while the Lord Ordinary had considerable doubts about the competency of the petition, he was prepared to consider it because there was a real issue that both parties wished to have determined.

FIRST LEISURE TRADING LTD v. CITY OF GLASGOW DISTRICT LICENSING BOARD 1996 S.L.T. 1018, Judge not specified, OH.

7142. Entertainment licence–application for provisional grant of licence–amendment of application–competence

[Licensing (Scotland) Act 1976 (c.66) s.26.]

A appealed against a sheriff's refusal of her appeal against the provisional grant by a licensing board, B, of an entertainment licence under the Licensing (Scotland) Act 1976 s.26(2) in G's favour in respect of premises which had previously been used as a private members' registered club. A argued that (1) the sheriff had erred in hearing the appeal when A was unrepresented and in refusing to adjourn the hearing to enable A properly to instruct legal representation; (2) as G had not applied for confirmation of the licence within 12 months of the provisional grant G's application was ineffective; (3) B had erred in allowing G to change their application from one under s.26(1) to one under s.26(2) and (4) G had created the impression at the hearing that their application concerned simply a continuation of club use, whereas in fact it was to be changed to a discotheque for 650 people.

Held, refusing the appeal, that (1) whether to adjourn the hearing was a matter for the sheriff's discretion and A had not put forward any proper ground of appeal for interfering with that discretion; (2) the dispute as to the expiry of the 12 month period (G maintaining that the period had been suspended while the appeal was outstanding) had arisen since the sheriff had heard the appeal in January 1995 and it would be premature and incompetent for the court to deal with that matter; (3) G had asked for their application to be changed from one under s.26(1) to one under s.26(2) in order to allow further time for discussion with the director of building control and the fire officer about the proposals, and considering that A's solicitor, who had been at the hearing, had not objected or sought an adjournment, and that G had not withdrawn the plans already lodged, which contained more than sufficient information to meet the requirements of s.26(2), B had been entitled to proceed with the application under s.26(2) and (4) although G had put the name of the club, which had previously leased the premises, on the plans and had stated that "virtually the same facilities" would be provided, it was clear that B had been aware that G intended to operate a "proprietary club" as opposed to a members' club, and that other facilities, including a discotheque, were to be provided, and B had been entitled to make the grant on the facts before them.

ACKERMANN v. GLASGOW DISTRICT LICENSING BOARD 1996 S.C.L.R. 168, Judge not specified, IH.

7143. Entertainment licence–provisional grant–appeal to Court of Session–competency

[Sheriff Courts (Scotland) Act 1907 (c.51) s.28; Licensing (Scotland) Act 1976 s.39.]

The Sheriff Courts (Scotland) Act 1907 s.28 provides, inter alia, that subject to the provision of the Act a right of appeal against a sheriff's interlocutor lies to the Court of Session with leave of the sheriff. Section 50 of that Act provides, inter alia, that nothing contained in this Act shall affect any right of appeal provided by any Act of Parliament under which a summary application is brought. The Licensing (Scotland) Act 1976 s.39(8) permits a party to an appeal to the sheriff under the Act to appeal to the Court of Session if dissatisfied on a point of law with a decision of the sheriff. Objectors appeal by summary application to the sheriff against the provisional grant of a new entertainment licence for certain premises. The appellants moved that the sheriff should hear evidence in the appeal under s.39(5) of the 1976 Act. The sheriff refused the motion. Without seeking leave to appeal from the sheriff, the appellants appealed to the Court of Session. The court having doubted the competency of the appeal, the appellants argued that the refusal of the sheriff to hear evidence constituted a decision of the sheriff under s.39(8) of the 1976 Act and so gave them a clear statutory basis or appealing when regard was had to the proviso to s.50 of the 1907 Act.

Held, that s.39(8) of the 1976 Act did not contain any provisions whereby the right of appeal might be exercised independently of the provisions in the 1907 Act, and that the appeal was incompetent in light of the provisions of s.28 of the 1907 Act together with the absence of leave to appeal from the sheriff, as the right of appeal relating to an interlocutory decision of the sheriff could only be exercised by virtue of s.29 of the 1907 Act in an appeal against the final judgment or determination of the sheriff in the summary application, which the interlocutor sought to be appealed against was not; and appeal refused as incompetent, *Cambridge Street Properties Ltd v. City of Glasgow District Licensing Board* 1995 S.L.T. 913, [1995] C.L.Y. 6395 distinguished.

BANTOP v. CITY OF GLASGOW LICENSING BOARD 1996 S.L.T. 552, Judge not specified, IH.

7144. Gambling–amusements with prizes–variation of monetary limits

AMUSEMENTS WITH PRIZES (VARIATION OF MONETARY LIMITS) (SCOTLAND) ORDER 1996, SI 1996 3273 (S.256); made under the Lotteries and Amusements Act 1976 s.18, s.24. In force: January 27, 1997; £0.65.

This Order increases the maximum amount of prize money offered at certain fairs and other commercial entertainments under the Lotteries and Amusements Act 1976 s.16 from £0.30 to £5.00

7145. Gambling–bingo clubs

GAMING CLUBS (HOURS AND CHARGES) (SCOTLAND) AMENDMENT REGULATIONS 1996, SI 1996 1144 (S.120); made under the Gaming Act 1968 s.14, s.51. In force: May 13, 1996; £0.65.

Increase the maximum charges which may be made for admission to gaming on bingo club premises in Scotland in respect of charging periods other than the shorter permitted period on a Sunday to £8.00 and in respect of the shorter permitted period to £6.00.

7146. Late hours catering licence–appeal–licence holder leaving premises–interest to pursue appeal

[Civic Government (Scotland) Act 1982 (c.45) s.42.]

A licensee who had held a late hours catering licence for three years applied for a new licence with extended hours. The licence granted was restricted to the hours of the former licence. The applicant appealed to the sheriff. Thereafter the applicant let the subjects to a tenant. The sheriff sustained a plea for the council that the applicant, having stated that he had disposed of the business to a new proprietor, no longer had an interest in pursuing the matter, holding that as the Civic Government (Scotland) Act 1982 s.42(1) required a licence for the use of premises, the applicant could not seek a licence for premises which he no longer used. The applicant appealed to the Court of Session.

Held, allowing the appeal, that (1) the appeal being taken on the basis that the applicant was the owner of the premises and the holder of a licence under s.42(1), the applicant had a clear interest in pursuing the appeal; (2) a licence holder could conceivably enter into some arrangement with another person whereby the character or detail of his interest in the premises changed, but that would not automatically mean that he lost any interest in the premises, the council then having power under para.11 of Sch.1 to take steps to suspend the licence and (3) there was not enough material to justify the conclusion that while the applicant remained the holder of the licence he had lost any interest in seeking a further extension of late hours and case remitted to sheriff to proceed as accords.

SHAHIN v. ROXBURGH DC 1996 S.L.T. 457, Judge not specified, IH.

7147. Licensing (Amendment) (Scotland) Act 1996 (c.36)

An Act to amend the Licensing (Scotland) Act 1976 to require licensing boards to attach to licences conditions relating to certain events involving music and dancing and to make new provision for the composition of licensing boards for licensing divisions.

This Act received Royal Assent on July 18, 1996.

7148. Licensing (Amendment) (Scotland) Act 1996–Commencement Order

LICENSING (AMENDMENT) (SCOTLAND) ACT 1996 COMMENCEMENT ORDER 1996, SI 1996 2670 (C.78; S.209); made under the Licensing (Amendment) (Scotland) Act 1996 s.3. In force: bringing into force various provisions of the Act on October 21, 1996; £0.65.

This Order brings into force on October 21, 1996 the Licensing (Amendment) (Scotland) Act 1996.

7149. Off licences–appeals–time limits–appeal lodged timeously but copy of writ not served on chief constable–no further right of appeal

A's off sales licence was suspended by the local licensing board for a year following a hearing at which a complaint from the police was considered. A appealed against the suspension within the period of 14 days provided for in the Licensing (Scotland) Act 1976 s.39(2), but his solicitors omitted to serve a copy of the appeal writ on the police as a party to the hearing as required under the relevant regulations. A sought to lodge a further appeal out of time. The original appeal was held by the sheriff to be incompetent. A appealed against the decision.

Held, refusing the appeal, that A had no further statutory right of appeal and no right to lodge a further appeal out of time once his appeal, though lodged within the time limit, had been disposed of as being incompetent.

AHMED v. CHIEF CONSTABLE OF STRATHCLYDE POLICE 1996 S.L.T. 941, Lord Kirkwood, IH.

7150. Off licences–application for grant of licence–refusal–whether onus on applicant to satisfy licensing board that licence should be granted

[Licensing (Scotland) Act 1976 (c.66) s.17.]

An individual applied to the licensing board for the grant of a new off sale licence. The board refused the application in terms of the Licensing (Scotland) Act 1976 s.17(1) on the grounds that the applicant was not a fit and proper person to hold a licence, that it was not satisfied that the applicant's premises were suitable for the sale of alcoholic liquor and that there were sufficient licensed premises within the locality and the grant of the application would result in overprovision. The applicant appealed to the sheriff, who granted the licence. The board appealed to the Court of Session on the grounds that the onus was on the applicant to satisfy the board that he was a fit and proper person to hold a licence and that the premises were suitable for the sale of alcoholic liquor, that in any event there was sufficient material before the board entitling them to make their findings to the contrary and, with regard to overprovision, that on the material before it and taking into account their general knowledge and expertise, the board were entitled to find that the grant of the licence would amount to overprovision.

Held, that (1) there was no onus on an applicant to satisfy the board that he was a fit and proper person to hold a licence or that his premises were suitable, and the board's error in these respects had vitiated its approach; (2) there was not sufficient information before the board to entitle it to find against the applicant on either of these matters and (3) it was not possible to say that because the present facilities were "sufficient", it followed that the addition of one more such facility would result in overprovision, and the licensing board had failed to offer an intelligible explanation which would warrant its conclusion that the grant of the application would result in overprovision; and appeal refused. Opinion, that in determining whether to refuse an application on any of the grounds set out in s.17(1) of the 1976 Act, a board was making a separate decision in respect of each ground, and by s.5(7) was obliged to vote in public on each ground separately.

Observed, that the court disapproved of bland, standard reasons offered in support of a conclusion that the grant of the application would result in overprovision.

DIN v. CITY OF GLASGOW DISTRICT LICENSING BOARD 1996 S.L.T. 363, Judge not specified, IH.

7151. Off licences–application for grant of licence–whether overprovision

[Licensing (Scotland) Act 1976 (c.66) s.18.]

An applicant for the grant of an off sale licence appealed to the sheriff against the refusal of the application. The licensing board held that granting the licence would result in an overprovision of licensed premises within the locality, which the board took as the area within 500 metres of the premises. In its reasons the board stated that it had had regard to the number of licensed premises and in particular the combined number of public house licences and off sale licences, and the distances of the existing off sale licences from the premises, and had considered that information "against its own knowledge and the locality". On appeal the applicant contended that (i) the reasons were inadequate; (ii) the reference to "own knowledge" indicated that the board had acted contrary to natural justice in that they had failed to disclose the knowledge upon which they were acting and (iii) the board had acted unreasonably in adopting a 500 metre radius as the locality. The sheriff upheld the appeal on the first contention, reached no conclusion as to natural justice and rejected the argument on locality, and remitted the application to the board for reconsideration. The board appeal to the Court of Session arguing, inter alia, that the local knowledge on which they relied was general, as opposed to specific, local knowledge and did not require to be disclosed. The applicant cross appealed on the grounds that the sheriff had erred (i) in dismissing the appeal regarding locality, (ii) in failing to hold that G had acted contrary to natural justice, and (iii) in remitting to G for reconsideration.

Held, that (1) the test to be applied in determining the adequacy of reasons was that in *Wordie Property Co v. Secretary of State for Scotland,* and on that test the statement of reasons was adequate; (2) included in a board's knowledge of a locality was a knowledge of the geography of its area, which was an important factor in determining whether an additional licence would lead to overprovision, and which did not require to be disclosed to the applicant; and appeal allowed, *Wordie Property Co v. Secretary of State for Scotland* 1984 S.L.T. 345, [1984] C.L.Y. 4735, and *Pagliocca v. City of Glasgow District Licensing Board* 1995 S.L.T. 180, [1995] C.L.Y. 6048 applied; *Din v. City of Glasgow District Licensing Board,* 1996 S.L.T. 363, [1996] C.L.Y. 7150 and *Save Britain's Heritage v. Secretary of State for the Environment and Number 1 Poultry* [1991] 1 W.L.R. 153, [1991] C.L.Y. 3494 distinguished. Opinion, that (1) the licensing board had properly and reasonably defined the locality by adopting a radius of 500 metres and (2) the court would not have interfered with the sheriff's exercise of discretion in remitting the application to the licensing board for a reconsideration.

MIRZA v. CITY OF GLASGOW LICENSING BOARD; SUB NOM. MIRZA v. GLASGOW DISTRICT LICENSING BOARD 1996 S.L.T. 1029, Lord Ross, L.J.C., IH.

7152. Public house licence–application for regular extension of permitted hours–refusal–judicial review–legitimate expectation

[Law Reform (Miscellaneous Provisions) (Scotland) Act 1990 (c.40) s.47(1).]

Section 47 of the Law Reform (Miscellaneous Provisions) (Scotland) Act 1990 provides that a licensing board "shall not grant an application... for an extension of permitted hours unless it is satisfied by the applicant... (a) that there is a need in the locality.. for a regular extension of the permitted hours; and (b) that such an extension is likely to be of such benefit to the community as a whole as to outweigh any detriment to that locality". Licensees of a public house applied for regular extension of permitted hours in relation to late night and early morning opening. They had originally sought a regular extension of the permitted hours from Monday to Saturday between 5.30 am and 11.30 am. There were written objections to this application including representations from a local residents' association and observations from the chief constable. Immediately prior to the hearing of the application it was amended to restrict the regular extension of permitted hours to between 8.00 am and 11.00 am, a regular extension which the board had permitted in the previous five years. Following this amendment the chief constable withdrew his objections, but the residents' association, maintained theirs. The board was addressed by the objectors and the solicitor for the licensees who made no submission in respect of "need in the locality" or "benefit to the community". The board granted the evening, but refused the early morning regular extension, giving as one of its reasons that is was not satisfied that the early morning extension could have met a need in the locality or would have been of some benefit to the community. The licensees sought judicial review of the board's decision, arguing that the board's ordinary practice in dealing with application for existing extensions was to deal with contentious matters only. The board denied such a practice and argued that the onus was on the applicant to satisfy them as to need and benefit whenever an objection was made to an extension application.

Held, that (1) it could not be said that the licensees must fail even if they established the whole of their averments; (2) it could not be said that on a sound construction of the legislation no alternative to oral presentation could ever satisfy a local authority acting properly as to the factual basis for the exercise of its jurisdiction and (3) it could not be right to require of applicants that in every case they addressed every conceivable issue so as to ensure that there was nothing left uncovered which might form the basis for refusal of the application, not on a matter of substance, but on account of failure properly to address the total range of relevant considerations in that applicant's case; and second hearing allowed for proof of disputed areas of fact.

PERFECT LEISURE LTD v. CITY OF EDINBURGH DISTRICT LICENSING BOARD 1996 S.L.T. 1267, Judge not specified, OH.

7153. Public house licence–consumption during prohibited hours–sale or supply–"sale"

[Licensing (Scotland) Act 1976 (c. 66) s.54(1)(a) and (4).]

An accused person was charged on a summary complaint with selling or supplying alcoholic liquor in a public house outwith permitted hours, contrary to s.54(1)(a) and (4) of the Licensing (Scotland) Act 1976. The accused placed cans of soft drinks, a bottle of vodka and two cans of lager into a carrier bag. The customer placed three £1 banknotes on the counter and counted out seven £1 coins from her purse. The accused pulled the money towards him while he pushed the bag towards the customer. At that stage the accused was told to return the money by the licence holder's husband who placed the bag behind the counter. At the close of the Crown case it was submitted that there was no case to answer because there was insufficient evidence of a sale. The magistrate repelled the submission and convicted the accused, who appealed.

Held, that (1) a "sale" was a contract by which the seller transferred or agreed to transfer the property in goods to the purchaser for a money consideration called the price, and (2) the accused's and the customer's actings were consistent with there having been a completed contract of sale which they were implementing; and appeal refused.

MAJOR v. NORMAND 1996 S.L.T. 297, Judge not specified, HCJ.

7154. Taxicabs–refusal to grant licence–appeal

[Civic Government (Scotland) Act 1982 (c.45) s.10(3), Sch.1 para.4.]

In terms of the Civic Government (Scotland) Act 1982 s.10(3) a licensing authority had taken a policy decision which provided: "without prejudice to the consideration of all taxi licence applications on their merits 1,428 remained the number of taxi licences considered necessary to meet the demand for the services of taxis in the District but that nevertheless there would be no significant unmet demand for the services of taxis in the District until the number of taxi licences issued fell below 1,418". An individual failed to renew his taxi operator's licence. On being reminded of this failure he applied for a new licence. At that date three licences more than the maximum of 1,428 had been issued by the licensing authority or by the courts on appeal. The clerk to the licensing committee informed it that there were three licences in excess of 1,428, but this information was not communicated to the applicant who submitted to the authority that he would suffer substantial financial hardship if the licence were not granted. The application was refused on the ground that the applicant had presented no evidence to show that there was a significant unmet demand for the services of taxis in the area. The authority did not take into account the applicant's submissions regarding hardship on the ground that, having determined that 1,428 licences were sufficient, it had no residual discretion to grant a licence unless satisfied that there was unmet demand. The applicant appealed to the sheriff who allowed the appeal and remitted the application to the authority with the direction to grant it. The authority appealed to the Court of Session, arguing that the sheriff had erred; (1) in holding that it was required to take into account the personal circumstances of the applicant, where it had reached a decision that 1,428 licences satisfied demand; (2) in holding that the fact that the clerk to the committee had informed the committee prior to the hearing that there was an excess of three licences above the 1,428 was a breach of para.4(1) of Sch.1 to the 1982 Act

Held, that (1) while s.10(3) conferred upon a local authority a power to refuse to grant a taxi operator's licence if satisfied that there was no significant unmet demand, nevertheless it conferred upon it discretion as to whether or not to grant a taxi operator's licence in those circumstances; (2) the discretion fell to be exercised at the stage of deciding whether to grant or refuse the licence and not only at the stage of determining whether or not it was satisfied that there was any unmet demand; (3) while s.10(3) of the 1982 Act, as amended, empowered a licensing authority to adopt a policy of limiting the number of taxi licences, the authority ought to have had regard to the personal circumstances of the applicant in considering his application for a new licence, and in failing to do so had acted contrary to the terms of their adopted policy; (4) the authority had erred in failing to give the applicant a chance to comment on the fact that there were three licences above the 1,428 maximum and their expectation that the total would be reduced to that figure and (5) since the authority had acted incorrectly and the circumstances had changed since the application, it was appropriate to remit to the licensing authority with a direction to grant the application; and appeal refused.

DOUGLAS v. CITY OF GLASGOW DC 1996 S.L.T. 713, Judge not specified, IH.

7155. Articles

Taxi!–a licensing saga from the Monklands *(Andrew M. Hajducki)*: S.L.T. 1996, 10, 85-90. (Operation and effect of the Civic Government (Scotland) Act 1982 in relation to objections, deemed grant and judicial review).

LOCAL GOVERNMENT

7156. City of Edinburgh Council Order Confirmation Act 1996 (c.x)

The Act confirms the Provisional Order set out in the Schedule which empowers the City of Edinburgh Council to create and maintain a general reserve fund.

This Act received Royal Assent on December 18, 1996.

7157. Common good–alienation–subjects no longer used for dedicated purposes

[Local Government (Scotland) Act 1973 (c.65) s.51 (2), s.75(2).]

C, a community council, sought review of E's decision of October 24, 1995 to proceed with the demolition of a hall and swimming pool on the grounds that E had acted unlawfully and *ultra vires* in failing to obtain the court's authorisation in terms of s.75(2) of the Local Government (Scotland) Act 1973 before disposing of the property by demolition as the subjects constituted land forming part of the common good and a question had arisen regarding their alienability. The subjects were erected in 1933 as a result of local subscription and the donated services of local tradesmen. C argued that they had become part of the common good under a feu charter disponing the property in favour of the officers of the Burgh of Cockenzie and Port Seton and their successors "as representing the community of the Burgh". In addition, the subjects were inalienable in terms of s.222(2) of the 1973 Act which specified that in administering property, the council was to "have regard to the interests of the inhabitants of the area to which the common good formerly related". Under s.75(2), E's desire to demolish the subjects constituted a desire to dispose of land which was part of the common good and to which there existed a question regarding E's right to alienate. The court had a wide and unfettered discretion to authorise disposal where common good land had the quality of inalienability or where it appeared that it might have that quality, *East Lothian DC v. National Coal Board* 1982 S.L.T. 460, [1982] C.L.Y. 3982. What constituted alienation had to be liberally construed and included any action which effectively deprived the community of something which, by custom or dedication by direct grant, they were entitled to have, and where a building was by custom or dedication by grant devoted to community purpose, it constituted inalienable common good property *Waddell v. Stewartry DC* 1977 S.L.T. (Notes) 35, [1977] C.L.Y. 3484.

Held, petition refused, that (1) C possessed title and interest to raise the present proceedings having regard to their function as defined in s.51 (2) of the Act and to *East Lothian DC v. National Coal Board* and *Kircaldy DC v. Burntisland Community Council* 1993 S.L.T. 753, [1993] C.L.Y. 5504. The restrictive principle in E's argument arose out of a situation obtaining only in former royal burghs, and was confined to accounting for the common good in general and did not prevent objection being raised to a specific unlawful or *ultra vires* act; (2) during the period of the existence of the burgh the subjects did form part of the common good, having regard to the dedication of the property; (3) in terms of s.75(1) E were entitled to dispose of the subjects without court approval and their failure to seek court authority before resolving to demolish the subjects did not constitute an *ultra vires* act; (4) in proceedings such as the present, the true question was whether the subjects were inalienable having been set apart for the general use of enjoyment of the inhabitants *Green's Encyclopedia*, Vol.2, para.1250, and (5) although the subjects were at one time inalienable (when they were used fully for the purposes for which they were established), the inalienable quality no longer attached to the subjects by the time of E's decision as by August 1994 all public functions of the subjects were carried on elsewhere, as to which no complaint was made *Kirkcaldy Magistrates v. Marks & Spencer Ltd* 1937 S.L.T. 574 applied.

COCKENZIE AND PORT SETON COMMUNITY COUNCIL v. EAST LOTHIAN DC 1996 S.C.L.R. 209, Lord Osborne, OH.

7158. **Competitive tendering–accounts**

LOCAL GOVERNMENT (DIRECT LABOUR ORGANISATIONS) (ACCOUNTS) SCOTLAND) REGULATIONS 1996, SI 1996 784 (S.90); made under the Local Government, Planning and Land Act 1980 s.10. In force: April 1, 1996; £0.65.

Local authorities who undertake construction or maintenance work are required by the Local Government, Planning and Land Act 1980 s.10(1) to keep separate accounts in respect of each description of work in s.10(2) of the Act. These Regulations further amend the descriptions of construction or maintenance work in s.10(2) so as to distinguish in Scotland between trunk roads and roads other than trunk roads. The previous amendment to s.10(2) for Scotland was made by the Local Government (Direct Labour Organisations) (Accounts) (Scotland) Regulations 1982 (SI 1982 319) which provides a separate description for general water and sewerage work.

7159. **Competitive tendering–local authorities**

LOCAL GOVERNMENT, PLANNING AND LAND ACT 1980 (COMPETITION) (SCOTLAND) REGULATIONS 1996, SI 1996 2935 (S.224); made under the Local Government, Planning and Land Act 1980 s.7, s.9, s.23. In force: July 1, 1997; £1.95.

These Regulations replace the Local Government, Planning and Land Act 1980 (Competition) (Scotland) Regulations 1995 (SI 1995 677 as amended by SI 1996 2936) by changing the levels above which certain services provided by local authorities require to be exposed to competitive tender. The 1995 Regulations, which required less work to be exposed to competitive tender than had previously been the case, were enacted in recognition of the additional administrative work which local government reorganisation placed upon local authorities.

7160. **Competitive tendering–construction and maintenance work**

LOCAL GOVERNMENT, PLANNING AND LAND ACT 1980 (COMPETITION) (SCOTLAND) AMENDMENT REGULATIONS 1996, SI 1996 2936 (S.225); made under the Local Government, Planning and Land Act 1980 s.9, s.23. In force: Reg.4 (a) (b) (i) (iii): December 13, 1996; Remainder: April 1, 1997; £1.10.

These Regulations amend the Local Government, Planning and Land Act 1980 (Competition) (Scotland) Regulations 1995 (SI 1995 677) so as to introduce further conditions which authorities must comply with before carrying out certain construction and maintenance work at their own hand.

7161. **Competitive tendering–local authorities**

LOCAL GOVERNMENT ACT 1988 (DEFINED ACTIVITIES) (SPECIFIED PERIODS) (SCOTLAND) REGULATIONS 1996, SI 1996 917 (S.101); made under the Local Government Act 1988 s.8, s.15. In force: May 1, 1996; £1.10.

These Regulations specify the minimum and maximum periods for which Scottish local authorities, joint boards and joint committees may invite offers to carry out work in respect of certain of the activities which must be open to competition under the Local Government Act 1988 Part I. The Regulations will apply to the defined activities of collection of refuse, cleaning of buildings (including police buildings), other cleaning, catering for purposes of schools and welfare, other catering, managing sports and leisure facilities, maintenance of ground, repair and maintenance of vehicles, management of vehicles and security work. Regulations relating to specified contract periods for development corporations (which are in the process of being wound up) are revoked.

7162. **Council tax–enforcement**

COUNCIL TAX (ADMINISTRATIVE AND ENFORCEMENT) (SCOTLAND) AMENDMENT REGULATIONS 1996, SI 1996 430 (S.32); made under the Local

Government Finance Act 1992 s.113, s.116, Sch.2 para.1, Sch.2 para.2, Sch.2 para.3, Sch.2 para.8, Sch.2 para.9, Sch.2 para.10, Sch.2 para.12; and the Local Government etc. (Scotland) Act 1994 Sch.10 para.2. In force: March 31, 1996; £1.55.

The Council Tax (Administration and Enforcement) (Scotland) Regulations 1992 (SI 1982 1332) are amended by these Regulations. The amendments, which are mainly consequential on the provisions of the Local Government etc. (Scotland) Act 1994, reflect the move to single-tier local authorities in Scotland from April 1, 1996, and the creation of new Scottish Water Authorities.

7163. Council tax–liability

COUNCIL TAX (REDUCTION OF LIABILITY) (SCOTLAND) REGULATIONS 1996, SI 1996 746 (S.79); made under the Local Government Finance Act 1992 s.80, s.113, s.116, Sch.2 para.1, Sch.2 para.2. In force: April 1, 1996; £1.10.

With effect from April 1, 1996, new single tier authorities will replace regional and district councils in mainland Scotland. In certain cases, the area of the new local authority will consist of the areas, or parts of areas, of more than one district council. These Regulations make provision so as to reduce, in respect of financial years 1996-97 and 1997-98, the amount payable as council tax in respect of dwellings situated in any of the 22 district council areas specified in column 1 of the Schedule to the Regulations. For 1996-97, the amount payable is to be calculated as if the council tax set for a band D dwelling by the relevant new local authority was reduced by the appropriate amount specified in column 2 of the Schedule. In 1997-98, the calculation is to be carried out as if the council tax set was reduced by half the amount specified in the Schedule.

7164. Council tax–valuation–effect of alteration to dwelling

[Council Tax (Valuation of Dwellings) (Scotland) Regulations 1992 (SI 1992 1329) Reg.2; Local Government Finance Act 1992 (c.14) s.86.]

A, an assessor, appealed against a valuation appeal committee's decision upholding R's appeal and placing his property in band A instead of band B. The house had been bought from the local authority in August 1991 on a valuation within band A. Between then and April 1, 1993, R had had double glazing and extra radiators installed, which A considered took the valuation into band B. The committee considered on a construction of the Act and the regulations that these alterations fell to be left out of account. A argued that the effect of the legislation was that he was required to value the dwelling as it stood as at April 1, 1993 but to apply the levels of value which existed as at April 1, 1991. If the committee were correct in reading the Council Tax (Valuation of Dwelling) (Scotland) Regulations 1992 Reg.2(2)(c) as requiring that alterations carried out between those dates, which did not affect the size or layout of a dwelling, be left out of account, there would be an anomaly in that such alterations carried out after April 1, 1993 might lead to a band being altered if the subjects had been sold (s.87). The provisions of Reg.2(2)(c) were explanatory only.

Held, refusing the appeal, that the effect of the Local Government Finance Act 1992 s.86(2) read with Reg.2(1) of the 1992 Regulations was that the value was to be taken as the open market value as at April 1, 1991, and that was the starting point. But for Reg.2(2), A's approach would probably have been correct, but effect had to be given to the terms of the regulations and there was no justification for applying any further assumptions than were contained therein. This did not result in anomalies because A was not required to carry out an individual valuation of each dwelling but to determine which valuation band applied, and the regulations in requiring alterations to the size or layout of a dwelling between the two dates to be taken into account, would cover any significant alteration for that purpose.

ASSESSOR FOR STRATHCLYDE v. REA 1995 S.C.L.R. 1048, Lord Ross, L.J.C., IH.

7165. Fire services–appointments and promotion

FIRE SERVICES (APPOINTMENTS AND PROMOTION) (SCOTLAND) AMENDMENT REGULATIONS 1996, SI 1996 2091 (S.169); made under the Fire Services Act 1947 s.18. In force: September 1, 1996; £1.10.

These Regulations amend the Fire Services (Appointments and Promotion) (Scotland) Regulations 1978 (SI 1978 1727) by removing the ineligibility to sit a written promotion examination of a person who has failed twice previously and who has failed to attain a certain mark.

7166. Fire services–establishment schemes

FIRE SERVICES (NOTIFICATION OF ESTABLISHMENT SCHEMES) (SCOTLAND) REGULATIONS 1995, SI 1995 3176 (S.234); made under the Fire Services Act 1947 s.19. In force: December 31, 1995; £0.65.

The date on which all Scottish fire authorities must notify the Secretary of State of the establishment scheme in force on March 31, each year in their area is prescribed by these Regulations to be April 30,.

7167. Freedom of information

LOCAL GOVERNMENT (ACCESS TO INFORMATION) (SCOTLAND) ORDER 1996, SI 1996 2278 (S.184); made under the Local Government etc. (Scotland) Act 1994 s.181. In force: September 30, 1996; £1.10.

The Local Government etc. (Scotland) Act 1994 provided, in connection with the reorganisation of local government in Scotland at April 1, 1996, for the establishment of new joint boards to be responsible for police, fire and valuation functions in certain areas and for the establishment of a new Strathclyde Passenger Transport Authority. This Order amends the Local Government (Scotland) Act 1973 Part IIIA so that the provisions in that Part relating to access to meetings and documents of local authorities will in future apply equally to meetings and documents of joint boards and the SPTA, and of committees and sub-committees of those bodies.

7168. Local authorities–public expenditure–discretion

LOCAL AUTHORITIES (DISCRETIONARY EXPENDITURE) (SCOTLAND) REGULATIONS 1996, SI 1996 747 (S.80); made under the Local Government (Scotland) Act 1973 s.83. In force: April 1, 1996; £0.65.

The annual limit on the amount of expenditure which a Scottish local authority may incur for purposes not otherwise authorised is, with effect from April 1, 1996, determined under the Local Government (Scotland) Act 1973 s.83(4) by multiplying £3.80 by the relevant population of the authority's area. These Regulations make provision as to how the relevant population is to be calculated for these purposes.

7169. Local authorities–reorganisation

LOCAL GOVERNMENT (TRANSITIONAL FINANCIAL PROVISIONS) (SCOTLAND) ORDER 1996, SI 1996 682 (S.70); made under the Local Government etc. (Scotland) Act 1994 s.15, s.138, s.181. In force: April 1, 1996; £3.20.

This Order makes provision as to certain accounting and financial matters relative to the reorganisation of Scottish local government to replace existing regional and district councils with new single-tier authorities. Article 3 to Art.5 make provision as to the completion of the accounts and certain reports of existing authorities after the date of their abolition. Article 6 deals with the completion of outstanding duties relative to non-domestic rating contributions for 1995-96. Article 8 to Art.19 deal with the allocation of the rights, liabilities and obligations of authorities which are being abolished and Art.7 allows certain of those provisions to be varied by agreement between the relevant new authorities. Article 20 and Art.21 make provision as to financial arrangements where an existing local authority has more than one successor local authority. Article 22 provides that nothing in the Order has effect for determining the new authorities on which the Secretary of State may serve notices or give directions under certain competitive tendering provisions.

7170. Local authorities–reorganisation

LOCAL GOVERNMENT (TRANSITIONAL AMENDMENTS) (SCOTLAND) ORDER 1996, SI 1996 974 (S.105); made under the Local Government etc. (Scotland) Act 1994 s.183. In force: April 1, 1996; £1.55.

As a result of local government reorganisation, substitutes references to new unitary authorities in place of existing Scottish local authorities in certain enactments.

7171. Local authorities–reorganisation–benefits

LOCAL GOVERNMENT CHANGES FOR SCOTLAND (HOUSING BENEFIT AND COUNCIL TAX BENEFIT) ORDER 1996, SI 1996 548 (S.53); made under the Local Government etc. (Scotland) Act 1994 s.181. In force: April 1, 1996; £0.65.

The Local Government etc (Scotland) Act 1994 makes provision with respect to local government in Scotland. This Order makes incidental, consequential, transitional and supplementary provision for housing benefit and council tax benefit for the purposes of, and in consequence of, that Act by providing power for a new authority to terminate any benefit period granted by an old authority.

7172. Local authorities–reorganisation–revocation

LOCAL GOVERNMENT (TRANSITIONAL AND CONSEQUENTIAL PROVISIONS AND REVOCATIONS) (SCOTLAND) ORDER 1996, SI 1996 739 (S.72); made under the Local Government etc (Scotland) Act 1994 s.181. In force: April 1, 1996; £2.80.

This Order makes transitional and consequential provisions pursuant to local government reorganisation in Scotland as at April 1, 1996. The provisions relate to the operation of district courts, warrants issued by Justices of the Peace, duty rotas for Justices of the Peace, planning applications made by local authorities and the re-election of councillors and consequential amendments to various enactments for the purposes of translating references to new authorities or new legislation.

7173. Local authorities–reorganisation–transfer of assets

LOCAL AUTHORITIES (PROPERTY TRANSFER) (SCOTLAND) AMENDMENT ORDER 1996, SI 1996 578 (S.56); made under the Local Government etc. (Scotland) Act 1994 s.181. In force: April 1, 1996; £1.10.

The Order makes additional provision relating to the transfer of heritable property to new Scottish local authorities on April 1, 1996. It enables successor authorities other than the authority in which heritable property vests by virtue of the Local Authorities (Property Transfer) (Scotland) Order 1995 Art.3(2) to be granted (a) user rights; (b) a right to share in the proceeds of disposal of that property; (c) a right to receive a payment from the authority in which the property has vested, where an application for such a grant has been made the Local Government Property Commission (Scotland) before April 1, 1996.

7174. Local government finance–Accounts Commission

ACCOUNTS COMMISSION (SCOTLAND) REGULATIONS 1996, SI 1996 681 (S.69); made under the Local Government etc. (Scotland) Act 1973 s.98, s.106; and the Local Government etc. (Scotland) Act 1975 s.22. In force: April 1, 1996; £1.10.

These Regulations amend the Commissioner for Local Administration in Scotland (Expenses) Regulations 1989 (SI 1989 98) and revoke the Commission for Local Authority Accounts in Scotland Regulations 1988 (SI

1988 133). They make provision as to the payment of expenses incurred after March 31, 1996 by the Accounts Commission for Scotland and apply to all expenses incurred by the Commission, other than expenses met from grants and expenses incurred by that body in carrying out its functions with respect to health service bodies and by virtue of being the designated body under the Local Government (Scotland) Act 1975 Part II (Commissioner for Local Administration in Scotland). The relevant expenses are to be met by local authorities and bodies referred to in the Local Government (Scotland) Act 1973 s.106(1) (a) (b) (the specified bodies) in proportion to the time spent by an auditor, or employee of an auditor, in auditing the accounts of the specified body in question; or a body which is abolished as at April 1, 1996 but for which that specified body is the accounting authority. Provision is made as to the payment of instalments by each specified body.

7175. Local Government etc. (Scotland) Act 1994–Commencement No.7 Order

LOCAL GOVERNMENT ETC. (SCOTLAND) ACT 1994 (COMMENCEMENT NO.7 AND SAVINGS) ORDER 1996, SI 1996 323 (C.6; S.23); made under the Local Government etc. (Scotland) Act 1994 s.184. In force: bringing into force various provisions of the Act on February 19, 1996, March 31, 1996 and April 1, 1996; £3.70.

Certain provisions of the Local Government etc. (Scotland) Act 1994 which amend or repeal provisions of the Local Government Finance Act 1992 are brought into force by this Order. The effect will be to ensure that new Scottish unitary councils will have responsibility for setting and collecting council tax from 1996/7 onwards and sewerage charges will not be set from 1995/6 onwards. The commencement dates for relevant outstanding provisions of the Act relating to the transfer of functions to the new Scottish unitary councils and water and sewerage authorities and the Scottish Children's Reporter Administration are April 1, 1996 and March 31, 1996.

7176. Local Government Finance Act 1992–Commencement No.10 Order

LOCAL GOVERNMENT FINANCE ACT 1992 (COMMENCEMENT NO.10) ORDER 1996, SI 1996 918 (S.102; C.14); made under the Local Government Finance Act 1992 s.119. In force: bringing into force various provisions of the Act on April 1, 1996; £1.10.

This Order brings into force on April 1, 1996 the following provisions of the Local Government Finance Act 1992: (c) the repeal in Sch.13 and 14 of s.111 (1) (a), (b) and (d) of the Local Government (Scotland) Act 1973 (regulation-making powers with respect to rates); and (d) the repeal in Sch.14 of s.9(6) of the Water (Scotland) Act 1980 (recovery of charges for non-domestic supply of water).

7177. Occupational pensions–teachers–National Health Service–information and administrative expenses

LOCAL GOVERNMENT, TEACHERS' AND NATIONAL HEALTH SERVICE (SCOTLAND) PENSION SCHEMES (PROVISION OF INFORMATION AND ADMINISTRATIVE EXPENSES ETC.) REGULATIONS 1996, SI 1996 2809 (S.216); made under the Pensions Act 1995 s.172, s.174. In force: December 1, 1996; £1.10.

The Regulations prescribe the various matters which require to be prescribed under the Pensions Act 1995 s.172 in the cases of local government, teachers' and National Health Service pension schemes in Scotland. They prescribe that the person responsible for providing information and charging fees in the case of local government scheme is an administering authority under the Local Government Superannuation (Scotland) Regulations 1987 (SI 1987 1850); prescribe that the circumstances where the information may be given are where the individual to whom the information relates has made a written request for, or consented in writing to the provision of the information; prescribe the persons to whom the information may be given and who may be required to pay reasonable fees in respect of the administrative expenses incurred in providing the information;

and prescribe the persons who may be required to pay reasonable fees in respect of administrative expenses incurred in connection with an individual's admission or re-admission to a scheme or in connection with any payment made to the scheme to restore his position there.

7178. Redundancy–early retirement–compensation

LOCAL GOVERNMENT (SUPERANNUATION AND COMPENSATION FOR REDUNDANCY OR PREMATURE RETIREMENT) (SCOTLAND) AMENDMENT REGULATIONS 1995, SI 1995 3294 (S.243); made under the Superannuation Act 1972 s.7, s.24. In force: January 18, 1996; £2.80.

As a result of the re-organisation of local government and the establishment of water and sewerage authorities, the Scottish Children's Reporter Administration and the Strathclyde Passenger Transport Authority and the Scottish Environmental Protection Agency, amendments are made to the provisions of the Local Government Superannuation (Scotland) Regulations 1987 (SI 1987 1850) along with amendments to the Local Government (Compensation for Premature Retirement) (Scotland) Regulations 1979 (SI 1979 785) and the Local Government (Compensation for Redundancy or Premature Retirement on Reorganisation) (Scotland) Regulations 1995 (SI 1995 340). Specified new authorities are designated as administering authorities and superannuation funds are transferred to the appropriate designated new administering authority on April 1, 1996 when the new authorities assume responsibility for functions currently under district and regional councils. Superannuation of staff transferring to the employment of the new authorities is provided for, funds are transferred to successor authorities and provision is made for transfer of rights, liabilities and obligations to new authorities. In addition, a right of appeal to industrial tribunals is introduced for persons dissatisfied with payments of mandatory compensation determined by relevant bodies under the Regulations.

7179. Revenue support grant

LOCAL GOVERNMENT FINANCE (SCOTLAND) ORDER 1996, SI 1996 755 (S.86), made under the Local Government Finance Act 1992 Sch.12 para.1, Sch.12 para.9. In force: March 10, 1996; £1.55.

This Order determines the amount of the revenue support grant payable to each local authority in Scotland in respect of the financial year 1996-97; determines the amount of non domestic rate income to be distributed to each local authority in respect of that year; redetermines the amount of the revenue support grant payable to each local authority in respect of the financial years 1995-96, 1994-95 and 1993-94; and makes consequential revocations in the Local Government Finance (Scotland) Order 1994 (SI 1994 528) and the Local Government Finance (Scotland) Order 1995 (SI 1995 391).

7180. Revenue support grant–redetermination

REVENUE SUPPORT GRANT (SCOTLAND) ORDER 1996, SI 1996 756 (S.87); made under the Abolition of Domestic Rates Etc. (Scotland) Act 1987 Sch.4 para.1. In force: March 10, 1996; £1.55.

This Order redetermines for the fourth time the amount of the revenue support grant payable to each local authority in respect of the financial years 1991-92 and 1992-93. As a consequence, the Order revokes those provisions in the Revenue Support Grant (Scotland) Order 1995 which previously redetermined the amount of such grant payable in respect of those financial years.

7181. **Sale of surplus land–land acquired by or under threat of compulsion–whether "Crichel Down rules" applied**

[Local Government (Scotland) Act1973 (c.65) s.71, s.74; Roads (Scotland) Act 1984 (c.54) s.104-107, s.110(1), s.151 (1).]

J petitioned for judicial review of a decision of a regional council (S) to offer for sale on the open market 3.65 hectares of land, which formed part of a former goods yard bought from J in 1985 in connection with a road development project. J sought, *inter alia*, declarator that the "Crichel Down rules" on the disposal of surplus government land applied, and that J was entitled to be given the opportunity to purchase the land. J had purchased the yard in January 1985 in the knowledge that it was affected by S's road proposal. J had subsequently arranged for the sale of the yard by public auction. However, following an approach from S, missives had been concluded, which provided that the purchase of the yard by S was to be treated as if it were in implement of a notice to treat served following upon a confirmed compulsory purchase order, and that, failing agreement, the price was to be determined by the Lands Tribunal for Scotland. Subsequently the road proposal was altered and in June 1995 S decided that the 3.65 hectares were surplus to requirements. The Crichel Down rules, were set out in a circular issued by the Secretary of State for Scotland (F) to S in October 1992. S argued that (1) there was no obligation upon S to follow the rules, as S were only commended to follow the general principles where they thought appropriate, and that the existence of the advice did not give J any right of action; (2) that judicial review was not competent, as S were not exercising a jurisdiction, but merely deciding how to sell their own property and (3) that, as no compulsory purchase order had been obtained, the assumption in para.5 did not apply. J argued (1) that good administrative practice required that S offer back the land to J and that J had a legitimate expectation that it would be so offered; (2) given the terms of the missives, S had to be treated as having the yard by compulsion; and (3) the proviso in para.5 of the Rules did not apply, because, while J might have been willing to sell in 1985, the yard had not been offered for sale, the issuing of a catalogue relative to the auction not amounting to an offer for sale.

Held, petition dismissed, that (1) while F's circular itself imposed no obligation upon S, it had to be considered in the context of s.74(1) of the Local Government (Scotland) Act 1973 under which S were obliged, except with F's consent, not to dispose of land for a consideration less than the best that could reasonably be obtained, and against the background that public bodies could justifiably be criticised if land acquired by or under the threat of compulsion and subsequently found to be surplus to requirements, was not offered back to its original owners; the issue of the circular behoved S at least to consider its contents and to make decisions in relation to surplus land after due consideration of it; (2) S's exercise of powers of compulsory purchase could be subject to judicial review in some circumstances, and at least where S purported to adopt and apply the principles in the circular, their decisions could be viewed as an exercise of a jurisdiction; the matter could not be decided without determining the part played by the circular in S's decision; (3) the missives were clearly consensual. The assumption that the sale was to be treated as a compulsory purchase was only intended to provide a mechanism for determining the price and importing the other legal incidents of serving a notice to treat, and did not translate a consensual bargain into an acquisition by compulsion. In any event, the circular did not apply to transactions contractually to be treated as acquisitions by compulsion. Nor was there any actual threat of compulsion. However, S did have the power under s.104(1) of the Roads (Scotland) Act 1984 to acquire land if the land was required for specified purposes, and although S required authorisation from F to acquire particular land, that did not affect the existence of the power. While the absence of a compulsory purchase order might make it difficult for J to demonstrate that a power to acquire the yard had existed at the time, that was a practical matter to be resolved at inquiry. The circular had to be construed in a colloquial sense rather than a strictly legal one, and advertising the yard for sale by auction constituted offering for sale within the terms of the proviso in para.5. Accordingly, even assuming that the rules applied to S's disposal, as the rules did not require S to offer back the land to J, there was no relevant ground of action.

JDP INVESTMENTS v. STRATHCLYDE RC 1996 S.C.L.R. 243, Judge not specified, OH.

7182. Social services–qualifications of chief social work officers

QUALIFICATIONS OF CHIEF SOCIAL WORK OFFICERS (SCOTLAND) REGULATIONS 1996, SI 1996 515 (S.49); made under the Social Work (Scotland) Act 1968 s.3, s.94. In force: April 1, 1996; £1.10.

These Regulations prescribe the qualifications to be held by the person appointed to the office of chief social work officer by a local authority under the Social Work (Scotland) Act 1968 Part I; the Local Government etc. (Scotland) Act 1994 replaced the obligation on a local authority to appoint a director of social work with a requirement to appoint a chief social work officer.

7183. Superannuation

LOCAL GOVERNMENT SUPERANNUATION (SCOTLAND) AMENDMENT REGULATIONS 1996, SI 1996 414 (S.30); made under the Superannuation Act 1972 s.7, s.12. In force: April 1, 1996; £2.40.

These Regulations amend the Local Government Superannuation (Scotland) Regulations 1987 (SI 1987 1850). The amendments relate to entitlement to and amount of retirement pension, retirement allowance, widows' short-term and long-term pensions, children's short-term and long term pensions, death gratuity, commutation of pension for reason of ill health, interest on late payment, certain persons who become subject to certain other superannuation schemes, transfer of pension rights, the right to opt out of effect of amendments made by certain new regulations, transitional provisions for elections and transitional provisions for transfer of pension rights.

7184. Tourist boards–superannuation–early retirement

LOCAL GOVERNMENT (SUPERANNUATION AND COMPENSATION FOR PREMATURE RETIREMENT) (SCOTLAND) AMENDMENT REGULATIONS 1996, SI 1996 1241 (S.123); made under the Superannuation Act 1972 s.7, s.12, s.24. In force: May 31, 1996; £1.10.

These Regulations amend the Local Government Superannuation (Scotland) Regulations 1987 (SI 1987 1850) and the Local Government (Compensation for Premature Retirement) (Scotland) Regulations 1979 (SI 1979 785) to take into account the establishment of new tourist boards under the Local Government etc. (Scotland) Act 1994, with retrospective effect from April 1, 1996

7185. Articles

Local government reform in Scotland *(Tom Mullen* and *Tony Prosser)*: E.P.L. 1996, 2(1), 40-45. (Changes introduced by 1994 legislation and consultation process include creation of new local authority areas and transfer of responsibility for certain services from local to national level).

Ongoing litigation–the implications of local government reorganisation *(Gordon Junor)*: Civ. P.B. 1996, 10(Jul), 4-6 . (Effect of Scottish local government reorganisation on actions by and against former local authorities).

MEDIA

7186. Articles

SNP v BBC: round 2 *(Colin R. Munro)*: N.L.J. 1996, 146(6762), 1433-1434. (Judicial review of BBC over allocation of broadcasting time to political party conferences).

MEDICINE

7187. Articles

Parens patriae jurisdiction applied *(Ian S. Crerar)*: J.L.S.S. 1996, 41(10), 400-402. (Whether court should allow withdrawal of life sustaining and medical treatment for patient in persistent vegetative state and Lord Advocate's guidance as to how future cases should be dealt with).

MENTAL HEALTH

7188. Community care–hospital orders

ACT OF SEDERUNT (MENTAL HEALTH RULES) 1996, SI 1996 2149 (S.173); made under the Sheriff Courts (Scotland) Act 1971 s.32. In force: September 9, 1996; £1.95.

This Act of Sederunt consolidates the Act of Sederunt (Mental Health (Scotland) Act 1984) 1986 (SI 1986 545) and extends the provisions relating to hospital orders to community care orders, which were introduced by the Mental Health (Patients in the Community) Act 1995 s.4. It also provides rules relating to the variation of community care orders, provides a form of appeal against a community care order, and repeals the Act of Sederunt (Mental Health (Scotland) Act 1984) 1986.

7189. Community care–transfer of patients

MENTAL HEALTH (PATIENTS IN THE COMMUNITY) (TRANSFER FROM ENGLAND AND WALES TO SCOTLAND) REGULATIONS 1996, SI 1996 742 (S.75); made under the Mental Health (Scotland) Act 1984 s.35K, s.58. In force: April 1, 1996; £1.10.

These Regulations prescribe modifications to the Mental Health (Scotland) Act 1984 s.35A to s.35C to enable patients who are subject to after care under supervision under the Mental Health Act 1983 and who wish to move to Scotland to become subject to community care orders there. Community care orders and after care under supervision were introduced into the Mental Health (Scotland) Act 1984 and the Mental Health Act 1983 respectively by the Mental Health (Patients in the Community) Act 1995.

7190. Community care–transfer of patients. See MENTAL HEALTH. §4224

7191. Detention–renewal of authority for–requirement to "furnish" report to managers of hospital

[Mental Health (Scotland) Act 1984 (c.36) s.30.]

Opinion, that a report on the continuing need for a patient's detention in hospital was "furnished" to the hospital managers when it was committed to the internal mailing system operated by those managers.

MILBORROW, APPLICANT 1996 S.C.L.R. 315, Judge not specified, Sh Ct.

7192. Forms

MENTAL HEALTH (PRESCRIBED FORMS) (SCOTLAND) REGULATIONS 1996, SI 1996 743 (S.76); made under the Mental Health (Scotland) Act 1984 s.18, s.30, s.31B, s.35B, s.35C, s.35D, s.35E, s.35G, s.35H, s.37, s.47, s.48B, s.58, s.74, s.86, s.88, s.96, s.97, s.98. In force: April 1, 1996; £5.60.

These Regulations make minor amendments to existing forms and provide new forms to be used under the Mental Health (Scotland) Act 1984 Part V. Existing forms to be used in conjunction with procedures for the compulsory admission to and the detention in hospital of patients, or their reception into guardianship, are amended so that all include the date of birth of the patient. Some modification is made to certificates of consent or second opinion under s.98 of the 1984 Act. New forms are prescribed to be used in connection with procedures for the making of community care orders and for subsequent procedures relating to patients subject to such orders in accordance with s.35A to s.35J inserted into Part V of the 1984 Act by the Mental Health (Patients in the Community Act) Act 1995. Each form in the Schedule shows the reference to the provision of the 1984 Act which requires the form to be prescribed. The Mental Health (Prescribed Forms) (Scotland) Regulations 1984 (SI 1984 1495) are revoked.

7193. Articles

Tutors dative: uses, principles and practicalities *(Adrian D. Ward.)*: Fam. L.B. 1996, 22(Jul), 2-3. (Advantages of flexible guardianship procedure for incapable adults).

NATIONAL HEALTH SERVICE

7194. Dental services

NATIONAL HEALTH SERVICE (GENERAL DENTAL SERVICES) (SCOTLAND) AMENDMENT REGULATIONS 1995, SI 1995 3200 (S.238); made under the National Health Service (Scotland) Act 1978 s.25, s.32E, s.105, s.108. In force: January 1, 1996; £1.55.

Further amendments are made to the National Health Service (General Dental Services) (Scotland) Regulations 1974 in order to make provisions for dentists suspended by the NHS Tribunal from providing general dental services or who have been declared unfit to to engaged in the provision of such services. Health Boards are given the authority to transfer the care and treatment of patients of the suspended dentists to another dentist and transfer them back if the suspended dentist is reinstated. Any dentist suspended by the tribunal is prevented from being employed as an assistant or deputy following changes made to Sch.1 or the 1974 Regulations.

7195. Dental services

NATIONAL HEALTH SERVICE (GENERAL DENTAL SERVICES) (SCOTLAND) REGULATIONS 1996, SI 1996 177 (S.14); made under the National Health Service (Scotland) Act 1978 s.2, s.25, s.28, s.32E, s.34, s.105, s.108. In force: March 11, 1996; £6.75.

These Regulations consolidate, with a number of minor or consequential drafting amendments, the provisions of the National Health Service (General Dental Services) (Scotland) Regulations 1974 (SI 1974 505). The 1974 Regulations and all subsequent amendments, excepting provisions relating to the Scottish Dental Practice Board, are revoked. These Regulations therefore regulate the terms on which general dental services are provided under the National Health Service (Scotland) Act 1978.

7196. Dental services–charges

NATIONAL HEALTH SERVICE (DENTAL CHARGES) (SCOTLAND) AMENDMENT REGULATIONS 1996, SI 1996 472 (S.37); made under the National Health Service (Scotland) Act 1978 s.70, s.71, s.71A, s.105, s.108, Sch.11 para.3. In force: April 1, 1996; £0.65.

These Regulations amend the National Health Service (Dental Charges) (Scotland) Regulations 1989 (SI 1989 363) which provide for the making and recovering of charges for dental appliances supplied or repaired under the National Health Service in Scotland, and for other dental treatment provided as part of NHS general dental services. Regulation 2 amends the principal Regulations to increase from £300 to £325 the maximum contribution which a patient may be required to make towards the aggregate cost of dental treatment and appliances under the National Health Service (Scotland) Act 1978 Part II, where the contract or arrangement leading to the provision of such treatment and the supply of such appliances is made on or after April 1, 1996.

7197. Dental services

NATIONAL HEALTH SERVICE (GENERAL DENTAL SERVICES) (SCOTLAND) AMENDMENT REGULATIONS 1996, SI 1996 841 (S.96); made under the National Health Service (Scotland) Act 1978 s.4, s.25, s.105. In force: April 1, 1996; £1.95.

These Regulations amend the National Health Service (General Dental Services) (Scotland) Regulations 1996 (SI 1996 177) ("the 1996 Regulations"). Part I includes in the 1996 Regulations what was formerly Regulation 20 of the National Health Service (Service Committees and Tribunal) (Scotland) Regulations 1992 (SI 1992 434). Part II amends dentists' terms of service contained in Schedule I to the 1996 Regulations, to require dentists to establish and operate a complaints procedure within their practice. Part III makes minor amendments to the dentists' terms of service including information about NHS charges to be displayed in practice premises.

7198. Dental services

NATIONAL HEALTH SERVICE (GENERAL DENTAL SERVICES) (SCOTLAND) AMENDMENT (NO.2) REGULATIONS 1996, SI 1996 2060 (S.168); made under the National Health Service (Scotland) Act 1978 s.25, s.105, s.108. In force: September 1, 1996; £1.10.

These Regulations amend the National Health Service (General Dental Services) (Scotland) Regulations 1996 (SI 1996 177) by reducing the period of all continuing care arrangements started or extended on or after September 1, 1996 from two years to 15 months and for the period of capitation arrangements, starting or extended on or after that date to be 15 months.

7199. Fund holding practices

NATIONAL HEALTH SERVICE (FUND-HOLDING PRACTICES) (SCOTLAND) AMENDMENT REGULATIONS. 1996, SI 1996 748 (S.81); made under the National Health Service (Scotland) Act 1978 s.2, s.87A, s.87B, s.105, s.108. In force: April 1, 1996; £1.55.

These Regulations further amend the National Health Service (Fund-Holding Practices) (Scotland) Regulations 1993 (SI 1993 488) which regulate the recognition and operation of fund-holding practices.

7200. Health service trusts–originating capital debt

NATIONAL HEALTH SERVICE TRUSTS (ORIGINATING CAPITAL DEBT) (SCOTLAND) ORDER 1996, SI 1996 392 (S.27); made under the National Health Service (Scotland) Act 1978 s.12E. In force: March 14, 1996; £1.10.

This Order determines the amount of the originating capital debt provided for in the National Health Service (Scotland) Act 1978 s.12E of NHS trusts established under that Act with an operational date of April 1, 1995. It provides also for the splitting of the originating capital debts into loan and public dividend capital.

7201. Medical and pharmaceutical services

NATIONAL HEALTH SERVICE (CHARGES FOR DRUGS AND APPLIANCES) (SCOTLAND) AMENDMENT REGULATIONS 1996, SI 1996 740 (S.73); made under the National Health Service (Scotland) Act 1978 s.69, s.75A, s.105, s.108. In force: April 1, 1996; £1.10.

These Regulations further amend the National Health Service (Charges for Drugs and Appliances) (Scotland) Regulations 1989 (SI 1989 326) ("the principal Regulations") which provide for the making and recovery of charges for drugs and appliances supplied by doctors and pharmacists providing pharmaceutical services, and by the Health Boards and NHS trusts to outpatients. Amendments made to the principal Regulations by Reg.2 and the Schedule increase the charge for items on prescription or supplied to outpatients from £5.25 to £5.50. The charge for elastic stockings is increased from £5.25 to £5.50 each (from £10.50 to £11.00 per pair) and that for tights from £10.50 to £11.00. The charges for partial human hair wigs and modacrylic wigs are increased from £115.00 to £120.00 and from £44.00 to £46.00 respectively. The charge for full human hair wigs is increased from £167.00 to £175.00. The charge for fabric supports is increased from £27.00 to £28.30 and the charges for surgical brassieres is increased from £19.00 to £19.25. The sums prescribed for the grant of pre-payment certificates are increased from £27.20 to £28.50 for a four monthly certificate and from £74.80 to £78.40 for a 12 monthly certificate.

7202. Medical and pharmaceutical services

NATIONAL HEALTH SERVICE (GENERAL MEDICAL SERVICES, PHARMACEUTICAL SERVICES AND CHARGES FOR DRUGS AND APPLIANCES) (SCOTLAND) AMENDMENT REGULATIONS 1996, SI 1996 1504 (S.132); made under the National Health Service (Scotland) Act 1978 s.19, s.27, s.28, s.69, s.105. In force: July 1, 1996; £1.55.

These regulations amend the National Health Service (General Medical Services) (Scotland) Regulations 1995 (SI 1995 416) and the National Health Service (Pharmaceutical Services) (Scotland) Regulations 1995 (SI 1995 414) which govern arrangements made for the provision of pharmaceutical services under the 1978 Act; amend the National Health Service (Charges for Drugs and Appliances) (Scotland) Regulations 1989 (SI 1989 326) providing for the making and recovery of charges for drugs and appliances supplied while providing pharmaceutical services and describe the categories of nurse who may prescribe under the National Health Service.

7203. Medical and pharmaceutical services–inclusion in pharmaceutical list–scope of appeal from pharmacy practices committee–reasons for decision

A company applied to a health board to be included in the board's pharmaceutical list for the provision of pharmaceutical services, from supermarket premises operated by the company. Its application was granted by the board's pharmacy practices committee. A number of the objectors to its granting appealed against this decision to the National Appeal Panel. In addition to the company and the objectors, other "interested persons" were heard by the panel. The appeal was upheld and the panel wrote to the company, advising it of the panel's decision and that, having taken into account all the factors, including demand and supply in the area, the granting of the application was not justified at that time. The company applied for judicial review on the grounds that the panel had reached its decision on the basis of matters beyond the limited grounds of appeal, had allowed people who were not objectors to make representations, and had failed to give any reason or sufficient reasons to justify its decision. The Lord Ordinary sustained the panel's pleas in law and dismissed the petition as irrelevant, following *Ian Monachan (Central), Petitioners* 1991 S.L.T. 494, [1991] C.L.Y. 4379. The petitioners reclaimed, submitting that the panel had failed to provide an adequate statement of its reasons, and that neither the petitioners nor the court could be aware of what the reasons were.

Held, that (1) where, as in the present case, there was an obligation to give reasons, the reasons had to deal with the substantial questions in issue in an intelligible way, and not leave the informed reader or the court in any real doubt as to what the reasons for the decision were, and what were the material considerations which were taken into account in reaching it; (2) while the amount of detail which the panel required to give would depend upon the circumstances, where the panel was differing from the committee, the panel had to indicate what material factors it considered in arriving at its decision and what conclusions it reached on these material factors, and it was not sufficient simply to paraphrase the regulations; and petition continued and case remitted to the panel to provide a proper and adequate statement of the reasons for its decision, *Ian Monachan (Central), Petitioners* 1991 S.L.T. 494, [1991] C.L.Y. 4379 distinguished.

SAFEWAY STORES PLC v. NATIONAL APPEAL PANEL 1996 S.L.T. 235, Judge not specified, IH.

7204. Medical services

NATIONAL HEALTH SERVICE (GENERAL MEDICAL SERVICES) (SCOTLAND) AMENDMENT REGULATIONS 1995, SI 1995 3199 (S.237); made under the National Health Service (Scotland) Act 1978 s.2, s.19, s.32E, s.105. In force: January 1, 1996; £1.10.

The Regulations amend the National Health Service (General Medical Services) (Scotland) Regulations 1992 which regulate the terms on which general medical services are provided under the National Health Service (Scotland) Act 1978. Provision is made for cases where general medical practitioners are suspended or disqualified from providing medical services by the NHS Tribunal. Reg.3 provides that in assessment of doctors failing to provide general medical services, the health board shall disregard any prior suspension by direction of the NHS Tribunal. Regulation 4 requires temporary arrangements to be made for the provision of general medical services to a suspended doctor's patients by the Family Health Services Authority, and reg.5 provides for payments to be made to suspended doctors. Doctors' terms of service are amended by reg.6 to stop a doctor engaging a suspended or disqualified doctor as a deputy or assistant. Reg.7 adds "Temazepam Soft Gelatin Gel-Filled Capsules" to this list of drugs which may not be prescribed by GPs.

7205. Medical services

NATIONAL HEALTH SERVICE (GENERAL MEDICAL SERVICES) (SCOTLAND) AMENDMENT REGULATIONS 1996, SI 1996 842 (S.97); made under the National Health Service (Scotland) Act 1978 s.2, s.19, s.105, s.108. In force: April 1, 1996; £1.95.

These Regulations amend the National Health Service (General Medical Services) (Scotland) Regulations (SI 1995 416) which regulate the terms on which general medical services are provided under the National Health Service (Scotland) Act 1978. Regulation 4 amends the terms of service by requiring a doctor to establish and operate a system to deal with complaints and by enabling doctors to transfer all or part of their obligations under the terms of service to another doctor at nights, weekends or public holidays. Regulation 5 requires doctors to include details of any new out of hours arrangements in their practice leaflets and Regulation 6 requires doctors to include the number of complaints received under the new procedures in the annual report which they must submit to their Health Board.

7206. National Health Service (Amendment) Act 1995–Commencement No.2 Order

NATIONAL HEALTH SERVICE (AMENDMENT) ACT 1995 (COMMENCEMENT NO.2 AND SAVING) (SCOTLAND) ORDER 1995, SI 1995 3214 (C.74; S.240); made under the National Health Service (Amendment) Act 1995 s.14. In force: bringing into force various provisions of the Act on January 1, 1996; £1.10.

Provisions of the National Health Service (Amendment) Act 1995 brought into force by this Order on January 1, 1996 relate to the powers of the NHS Tribunal. The provisions include the power to direct interim suspensions of doctors and dentists from providing family health services and to declare such practitioners as not fit to be engaged in the provision of family health services. Provisions relating to the abolition of appeals to the Secretary of State regarding decisions of the NHS Tribunal are brought into force but these amendments will not affect appeals and applications made prior to January 1, 1996.

7207. NHS trusts–establishment

AYRSHIRE AND ARRAN COMMUNITY HEALTH CARE NATIONAL HEALTH SERVICE TRUST (ESTABLISHMENT) AMENDMENT ORDER 1996, SI 1996 1681 (S.143); made under the National Health Service (Scotland) Act 1978 s.12A, Sch.7A para.1, Sch.7A para.3. In force: June 28, 1996; £0.65.

This Order substitutes a new Art.3 in the Ayrshire and Arran Community Health Care National Health Service Trust (Establishment) Order 1992 (SI 1992 3312) to empower the trust to provide a new hospital at Ayr Road, Cumnock.

7208. NHS trusts–establishment

WEST GLASGOW HOSPITALS UNIVERSITY NATIONAL HEALTH SERVICE TRUST (ESTABLISHMENT) (AMENDMENT) ORDER 1996, SI 1996 324 (S.24); made under the National Health Service (Scotland) Act 1978 s.12A, Sch.7A para.1, Sch.7A para.3. In force: February 14, 1996; £1.10.

This Order substitutes a new West Glasgow Hospitals University National Health Service Trust (Establishment) Order 1993 (SI 1993 3025) Art.3 to empower the trust to provide a new hospital to replace Glasgow Homeopathic Hospital.

7209. Opthalmic services

NATIONAL HEALTH SERVICE (GENERAL OPHTHALMIC SERVICES) (SCOTLAND) AMENDMENT REGULATIONS 1996, SI 1996 843 (S.98); made under the National Health Service (Scotland) Act 1978 s.26, s.32E, s.105, s.108. In force: April 1, 1996; £1.95.

To make provision for payments made to ophthalmic medical practitioners and opthalmic opticians who have been suspended by the NHS Tribunal from providing services, the National Health Service (General Ophthalmic Services) (Scotland) Regulations 1986 (SI 1986 965) are amended. The contractor' terms of service are also amended to prevent any suspended contractor from taking employment as an assistant or deputy. Requirements are also made for the display of notices and leaflets relating to the optical voucher scheme and for the establishment and operation of complaints systems and procedures.

7210. Opthalmic services

NATIONAL HEALTH SERVICE (GENERAL OPHTHALMIC SERVICES) (SCOTLAND) AMENDMENT (NO.2) REGULATIONS 1996, SI 1996 2353 (S.186); made under the National Health Service (Scotland) Act 1978 s.26, s.105, s.108. In force: October 7, 1996; £1.10.

These Regulations further amend the National Health Service (General Ophthalmic Services) (Scotland) Regulations 1986 (SI 1986 965). They add a definition of an income based jobseeker's allowance, remove the capital restriction relating to disability working allowance so that everyone in receipt of this, and certain of their relatives, will be eligible for general ophthalmic services, and extend the categories of eligibility for general ophthalmic services to include people in receipt of an income based jobseeker's allowance, and also certain relatives of such people.

7211. Opthalmic services–optical charges and payment

NATIONAL HEALTH SERVICE (OPTICAL CHARGES AND PAYMENTS) (SCOTLAND) AMENDMENT (NO.2) REGULATIONS 1996, SI 1996 2354 (S.187); made under the National Health Service (Scotland) Act 1978 s.105, s.108, Sch.11 para.2A. In force: October 7, 1996; £1.10.

These Regulations further amend the National Health Service (Optical Charges and Payments) (Scotland) Regulations 1989 (SI 1989 392), which provide for payments to be made by means of a voucher system in respect of costs incurred by certain categories of persons in connection with the supply, replacement and repair of optical appliances. They add a definition of an income based jobseeker's allowance; remove the capital restriction relating to disability working allowance so that everyone in receipt of this, and certain of their relatives, will be eligible for payments towards the cost of optical appliances; and extend the categories of eligibility for payments towards the costs of optical appliances to include people in receipt of an income based jobseeker's allowance, and also certain relatives of such people.

7212. Opthalmic services–optical charges and payments

NATIONAL HEALTH SERVICE (OPTICAL CHARGES AND PAYMENTS) (SCOTLAND) AMENDMENT REGULATIONS 1996, SI 1996 473 (S.38); made under the National Health Service (Scotland) Act 1978 s.26, s.70, s.73, s.74, s.105, s.108, Sch.11 para.2, Sch.11 para.2A. In force: April 1, 1996; £1.55.

These Regulations further amend the National Health Service (Optical Charges and Payments) (Scotland) Regulations 1989 (SI 1989 392) ("the principal Regulations"), which provide for payments to be made by means of a voucher system in respect of costs incurred by certain categories of persons in connection with the supply, replacement and repair of optical appliances. Regulation 2 amends Reg.20 of the principal Regulations (redemption value of voucher for replacement or repair) to increase the value of an optical voucher issued towards the cost of replacing a single contact lens, and to increase the maximum contribution by way of voucher to the cost of repairing a frame. Regulation 3(1) amends Sch.1 to the principal Regulations to increase the value of vouchers issued towards the cost of the supply and replacement of glasses and contact lenses. Regulation 3(2) and the Schedule substitute a new Sch.2 in the principal Regulations to increase the value of vouchers issued towards the cost of the repair and replacement of optical appliances. Regulation 3(3) increases the additional values for vouchers for prisms, tints, photochromic lenses and special categories of appliances. The increase in voucher values are approximately one per cent.

7213. Opthalmic services–optical charges and payments

NATIONAL HEALTH SERVICE (OPTICAL CHARGES AND PAYMENTS) (SCOTLAND) AMENDMENT (NO.3) REGULATIONS 1996, SI 1996 2556 (S.201); made under the National Health Service (Scotland) Act 1978 s.70, s.105, s.108, Sch.11 para.2A. In force: November 1, 1996; £0.65.

These Regulations further amend the National Health Service (Optical Charges and Payments) (Scotland) Regulations 1989 (SI 1989 392), which provide for payments to be made, by means of a voucher system, in respect of costs incurred by certain categories of persons in connection with the supply and repair of optical appliances. The definition of NHS sight test fee is amended. This fee is set at two levels depending on whether the sight test was carried out at the patient's home or not, and the appropriate figure is used to calculate the value of assistance towards the cost of a private sight test and the value of vouchers towards the cost of a private sight test or towards the supply of glasses or contact lenses. The figure used where the sight test was carried out at the patient's home is raised to £37.83 and the figure used in all other cases is increased to £13.71.

7214. Pharmaceutical services

NATIONAL HEALTH SERVICE (PHARMACEUTICAL SERVICES) (SCOTLAND) AMENDMENT REGULATIONS 1996, SI 1996 840 (S.95); made under the National Health Service (Scotland) Act 1978 s.27, s.28, s.32E, s.105. In force: April 1, 1996; £1.55.

These Regulations amend the National Health Service (Pharmaceutical Services) (Scotland) Regulations 1995 (SI 1995 414) (the 1995 Regulations) which govern the arrangements to be made by Health Boards for the provision in their area of pharmaceutical services under the National health Service (Scotland) Act 1978. Part II amends the 1995 Regulations to reflect the power of the NHS Tribunal to suspend a pharmacist or to declare a pharmacist not fit to be engaged in any capacity in the provision of pharmaceutical services. The terms of service for pharmacists are amended to prevent the employment of pharmacists in relation to whom such a declaration is in force. The amendments also provide for payments to suspended pharmacists. Part III requires pharmacists to set up and operate (in accordance with the Regulations) a complaints procedure at each of their premises and to co-operate with any investigation of a complaint by a Health Board in accordance with procedures. Part IV makes minor amendments in connection with pharmaceutical discipline committees.

7215. Prescription by Nurses etc. Act 1992–Commencement No.2 Order

MEDICINAL PRODUCTS: PRESCRIPTION BY NURSES ETC. ACT 1992 (COMMENCEMENT NO.2) ORDER 1996, SI 1996 1505 (C.28; S.133); made under the Medicinal Products: Prescription by Nurses etc. Act 1992 s.6. In force: bringing into force various provisions of the Act on July 1, 1996; £0.65.

Brings into force on July 1, 1996.

7216. Service committees and tribunal

NATIONAL HEALTH SERVICE (SERVICE COMMITTEES AND TRIBUNAL) (SCOTLAND) AMENDMENT REGULATIONS 1995, SI 1995 3201 (S.239); made under the National Health Service (Scotland) Act 1978 s.32, s.32C, s.105, s.108, Sch.8. In force: January 1, 1996; £1.55.

These Regulations implement provisions which provide the National Health Service Tribunal with powers to suspend doctors, dentists, pharmacists, opthalmic medical practitioners and opticians from providing their medical, dental, pharmaceutical and opthalmic services. Part II is concerned with officers of the Tribunal, Part III abolished the right to appeal against tribunal decisions, Part IV, which applies only to doctors and dentists, deals with procedures relating to suspensions and Part V makes transitional provisions relating to appeals which are outstanding.

7217. Service committees and tribunal

NATIONAL HEALTH SERVICE (SERVICE COMMITTEES AND TRIBUNAL) (SCOTLAND) AMENDMENT REGULATIONS 1996, SI 1996 938 (S.103); made under the National Health Service (Scotland) Act 1978 s.19, s.26, s.27, s.108; the National Health (Scotland) Act 1978 s.25; and the Nation Health Service (Scotland) Act 1978 s.105. In force: April 1, 1996; £3.70.

These Regulations, which amend the National Health Service (Service Committees and Tribunal) (Scotland) Regulations 1992 (SI 1992 434) by substituting new Reg.2 to Reg.15 and replacing Sch.1 and revoke the National Health Service (Service Committees and Tribunal) (Scotland) Regulation 1994 (SI 1994 3038) Reg.20, replace the system whereby complaints made against practitioners providing services under the National Health Service (Scotland) Act 1978 Part II were dealt with by service committees. Health Boards will refer for investigation matters which raise allegations that a practitioner has failed to comply with his terms of service or concern over payments made by the practitioners to the new discipline committees, which will not deal with complaints made by or on behalf of patients. The Regulations provide criteria which must be satisfied in order for a matter to be referred for investigation, the procedure for investigation, appeals and the imposition of, and arrangements to enforce sanctions.

7218. Travelling expenses–remission of charges

NATIONAL HEALTH SERVICE (TRAVELLING EXPENSES AND REMISSION OF CHARGES) (SCOTLAND) AMENDMENT REGULATIONS 1996, SI 1996 429 (S.31); made under the National Health Service (Scotland) Act 1978 s.75A, s.105, s.108. In force: March 19, 1996; £2.40.

These Regulations further amend the National Health Service (Travelling Expenses and Remission of Charges) (Scotland) Regulations 1988 (SI 1988 546) which provide for the remission and repayment of certain charges which would otherwise be payable under the National Health Service (Scotland) Act 1978 and for the payment of travelling expenses incurred in attending a hospital. The National Health Service (Travelling Expenses and Remission of Charges) (Scotland) Amendment (No.2) Regulations 1995 (SI 1995 2381) are revoked.

7219. Travelling expenses–remission of charges

NATIONAL HEALTH SERVICE (TRAVELLING EXPENSES AND REMISSION OF CHARGES) (SCOTLAND) AMENDMENT (NO.2) REGULATIONS 1996, SI 1996 2391 (S.188); made under the National Health Service (Scotland) Act 1978 s.75A, s.105, s.108. In force: October 7, 1996; £1.10.

These Regulations further amend the National Health Service (Travelling Expenses and Remission of Charges) (Scotland) Regulations 1988 (SI 1988 546), which provide for the remission and repayment of certain charges which would otherwise by payable under the National Health Service (Scotland) Act 1978 and for the payment of travelling expenses incurred in attending a hospital.

NEGLIGENCE

7220. Building and construction–duty of care–house builder and feudal superior–whether economic loss

The owners of a house damaged in a fire sought damages from the builders, who were also the feudal superiors of the owners, on the ground of the builders' alleged negligence in failing to construct a fire stop between the garage and the house. The owners pled that the builders had shown a fire stop in the plans lodged for building control purposes, that such a fire stop complied with the relevant regulations, that the builders had obtained a completion certificate upon the representation that the work had been carried out in accordance with the plans and that the owners had relied upon the fact that a completion certificate had been obtained. The damages sought were (a) the cost of restoring the house, (b) the cost of replacing the destroyed contents, (c) the cost of letting other property to move into while the house was rebuilt and (d) damages for gross anxiety and inconvenience. The builders argued on procedure roll that they owed no duty of care to the owners for economic loss in the absence of any "special relationship", and that the averments of the other alleged losses were irrelevant from lack of specification.

Held, that (1) although it was not clear that the damage to the house was economic loss, even if it was economic loss it was arguable that the averments about the feudal relationship and especially about the obtaining of a completion certificate on a false basis, the completion certificate having been relied upon by the owners, could amount to a "special relationship"; (2) the averments of loss were sufficiently specific to go to proof; and proof before answer allowed.

STEVENSON v. A & J STEPHEN (BUILDERS) LTD 1996 S.L.T. 140, OH, Judge not specified, OH.

7221. Causation–psychological anger and resentment following physical injury

An employee sustained an injury to her back when she slipped on stairs at the place of her employment. The medical evidence was that she should have recovered from the injury within about three months of the accident, but she continued to complain of various symptoms at the date of the proof, about five years after the accident. The Lord Ordinary restricted the amount which he would have awarded the pursuer as solatium to that which reflected his view that she should have recovered within about three months, and that any continuing disability was caused by the pursuer's anger at what she felt was unfair treatment by the defenders after the accident, which had resulted in a psychological disturbance. On appeal the question arose as to whether the accident could properly be regarded as having caused the continuing symptoms.

Held, that the defenders were liable for any psychological injury caused by their negligence, whether or not the pursuer was by nature more susceptible than other persons to such injury, but that it was not the accident which caused her continuing symptoms but what had happened thereafter; and reclaiming motion refused.

GRAHAM v. DAVID A HALL LTD 1996 S.L.T. 596, Judge not specified, IH.

7222. Duty of care–duty of teacher to pupil–remoteness–foreseeability

A P.E. teacher who placed himself so as to assist if necessary a pupil about to perform an exercise was not in breach of his duty to the pupil who chose to perform an exercise he had not previously performed without supervision, when the teacher was suddenly called to the assistance of another pupil.

McDOUGALL v. STRATHCLYDE RC 1996 S.L.T. 1124, Judge not specified, IH.

7223. Duty of care–local authority–grant of completion certificate for new building–whether duty owed to neighbouring proprietors for damage to their property

[Building (Scotland) Act 1959 (c.24) s.24.]

The heritable proprietors of properties within a tenement raised an action for damages against the builders of an adjoining tenement and the local building authority for losses caused by rainwater running off the gutter of the adjoining tenement on to the roof of the pursuers' tenement and into a 100 mm gap between the tenements, causing one of the pursuers' gable walls to become damp and rendering properties on that side of the tenement damp and uninhabitable. The pursuers averred that the builders had been negligent in constructing the building, and that they had acted in breach of building regulations. The pursuers further averred that the building authority knew or ought to have known that the gutter on the new tenement would leak water over the pursuers' property; that the gap between the tenements which should have been at least one metre and should have been sealed at both the front and rear elevations, would cause damage to the pursuers' property; that the new tenement did not conform to the building warrant and approved drawings; that it was the duty of the building authority not to issue a completion certificate to buildings that they knew or ought to have known were dangerous and would cause damage to the pursuers' property; and that they had a duty to take reasonable care to ensure that the new tenement did not cause damage to the pursuers' property. It was agreed that the case against the first defenders should go to a proof before answer. The second defenders challenged the relevancy of the action insofar as directed against them, arguing they owed no duty of care to the pursuers.

Held, that (1) before any duty of care could arise on the part of the local authority it was necessary to discover some statutory duty arising from the statutory functions laid upon it which, looking to the purpose of the statute, could be said to be conceived in favour of the pursuer and which had been breached; (2) the purpose of the building standards regulations was to secure the health and safety of those inhabiting the new building, and there was nothing in the purposes of the Building (Scotland) Act 1959 giving rise to that proximity of relationship between the authority and the pursuers as proprietors of an adjacent building necessary to give rise to a duty of care on the part of the authority, even where defects in the new building were or ought to have been known to the authority and were such that damage to the pursuers' property or health was foreseeable and (3) in any event, as the particular regulation founded on had been revoked in 1981 and not re-enacted, there was no relevant averment that the new tenement had breached any relevant building standards regulation or did not comply with any condition on which the warrant had been granted, and accordingly the authority could not be under any duty to refuse to grant the completion certificate; and action dismissed insofar as directed against the second defenders.

Observed, that, while refusal of the completion certificate alone might have protected those who would otherwise have inhabited the building, it would not have made any difference to the building or prevented rainfall passing on to the pursuers' property, *Murphy v. Brentwood DC* [1991] 1 A.C. 398, [1991] C.L.Y. 2661 considered.

ARMSTRONG v. MOORE 1996 S.L.T. 690, Judge not specified, OH.

7224. Duty of care–ship owner–failure of machinery–duty of inspection and maintenance

A port operator sued the owners of a ship for damages, on the basis of both personal and vicarious liability, after he was struck by a rope which had snapped after the reverse thrust on the engines failed to engage and stop the forward movement of the ship when entering a lock. The grounds of fault included one which alleged that the defenders had a duty, by means of a reasonable system of inspection and maintenance, to see that the engines were operating properly and, in particular, that the reverse thrust mechanism would engage when required. The pursuer contended that the master's failure to stop the ship by means of the reverse thrust raised a prima facie presumption of negligence and that it was for the defenders to explain what had happened and to prove that they had taken all reasonable precautions and that there had been no negligence on their part. He also contended that, as the defenders had not led any evidence and nothing had been adduced by them to explain this failure, they had failed to establish that the cause of the accident had not been attributable to their negligence. The defenders argued that the pursuer, by leading no evidence that a reasonable system of inspection and maintenance would have revealed any fault, had not discharged the onus of proof which he had assumed by basing his claim on that ground. They also pointed out that the engines had been inspected some two months prior to the accident, to which averment the pursuer had responded by stating that it was "believed to be true" which, the defenders argued, was tantamount to an admission. The Temporary Lord Ordinary (Horsburgh, Q.C.) held that the pursuer had not established a prima facie case against the defenders because: (a) the engine failure had not been the cause of the accident but had been merely a sine qua non, the cause of the accident being the parting of the rope under tension, which resulted from the remedial efforts to avoid the bow of the vessel colliding with the lock gates once the engine failure had been appreciated, so that no presumption of negligence arose; and (b) the accident had not been a reasonably foreseeable consequence of the reverse thrust not engaging. The pursuer reclaimed.

Held, that (1) although the accident resulted from the remedial efforts to prevent the ship from colliding with the lock after the engine failure, those actions did not break the chain of causation between the engine failure and the injuries sustained; (2) accordingly, the engine failure was not merely a sine qua non of the accident but was the effective cause of it, everything happening afterwards following directly from the emergency which the engine failure had created; (3) the pursuer's injury had been reasonably foreseeable; (4) the fact of the previous inspection did not mean that the engines were not defective at the time of the accident, and that prima facie this was attributable to negligence and that, even though the pursuer had made averments of fault on that issue, it did not prevent him from saying that the effect of the evidence had been to raise a prima facie inference of negligence which the defenders had to displace, and (5) the defenders having failed to explain the accident, the inferences to be drawn from the evidence were those which were most favourable to the pursuer and the engines' failure to operate when required suggested that there was a defect which ought prima facie to have been prevented by a reasonable system of inspection and maintenance, which had been the pursuer's case on record; and reclaiming motion allowed, *Elliot v. Young's Bus Service* 1945 S.C. 445 followed; *Henderson v. Henry E Jenkins & Sons and Evans* [1970] A.C. 282, [1969] C.L.Y. 2422 (dictum of Lord Pearson at p.301) applied.

Observed that a party whose averment was met by a reply of "believed to be true", together with a denial of other averments, was entitled to take it that the point believed to be true was not disputed and was not one on which evidence was required.

BINNIE v. REDERIJ THEODORO BV 1993 S.C. 1993, Judge not specified.

7225. Master and servant–safe means of access–agency employer

An employee was injured at work while using a wooden walkway which broke as he walked across it. The defective walkway was the only means of access. The pursuer averred that the walkway had been kept in a muddy and waterlogged condition for a year prior to the accident. He raised an action for damages against (1) the occupiers of the site, in overall control of it; (2) the electrical contractors who had subcontracted his services from the third defenders and (3) the agency on whose payroll he was at the time of the accident. The third defenders sought dismissal of the action against them, arguing that as they were not in occupation of the site and did not control the work carried out by the pursuer, in the absence of actual knowledge of the dangerous condition of the site, or reason to suspect it, there was no obligation upon them to inspect the premises of a third party. There was no basis in the pursuer's averments whereby the third defenders ought to have been aware of the dangerous condition of the walkway given that it had been kept in a muddy and wet condition for a year, whereas the pursuer had worked on the first defenders' site for a period of only three months prior to the accident. There were no averments that it was the usual practice in the industry for employers to inspect the premises of third parties before sending their employees there.

Held, that (1) the test was whether in all the circumstances the performance of the employer's duty of reasonable care called for steps to be taken by him to acquaint himself with the physical circumstances in which his employees were to work; (2) the third defenders' duty of care to the pursuer as employers, not to expose him to unnecessary risk, was not negatived by the fact that they had supplied the skilled labour of the pursuer unsupervised by them; (3) the fact that the third defenders did not exercise control of the pursuer's work was only one (albeit important) factor in establishing whether they took reasonable care; (4) the pursuer's averments that the third defenders ought to have acquainted themselves with the pursuer's working conditions and ought thereafter to have taken reasonable steps to secure a safe walkway by providing it themselves or by requesting that the first defenders provide it, were relevant; (5) the pursuer's case was not dependent on the third defenders being aware that the walkway had been muddy for a year since even a single inspection prior to the accident might have been sufficient to alert them to the risk of danger, and (6) the pursuer's case against the third defenders could not be determined without inquiry; case put out by order for a further hearing on certain averments.

Observed, that (1) previous case law concerning stevedores whereby employers were not obliged to safeguard workers against dangers arising from the state of the premises of a third party was not consistent with the principles of modern law and (2) departure from an established industry practice was not a prerequisite for a finding of breach of a duty of reasonable care.

CROMBIE v. McDERMOTT SCOTLAND 1996 S.L.T. 1238, Judge not specified, OH.

7226. Master and servant–safe system of working–duty to enforce

A warehouse operator sought damages from her employers following an accident in which she fell while retrieving a box from a high shelf. The pursuer's duties required her to uplift items of stock stored on shelves. A bonus system was in operation whereby employees were rewarded for the number of items removed from shelves and packed. The pursuer required to obtain a box stored on the topmost of five shelves, which was somewhat over six feet above floor level. There was no stepladder in the immediate vicinity and she clambered on to the third shelf in order to reach the box. As she descended she missed her footing and fell to the ground. There was evidence that although stepladders were available within the workplace, there was no system to ensure that they were available in all areas at all times. Furthermore, whilst the pursuer and other members of staff received training and a booklet on good working practice, both of which instructed employees not to climb on shelves, managerial staff turned a blind eye to breaches of this instruction.

Held, that (1) the accident was caused by the defenders' failure to devise and maintain a safe system of work and (2) there was no reason to find that the pursuer contributed to the accident; and decree pronounced accordingly.

McGREGOR v. AAH PHARMACEUTICALS LTD 1996 S.L.T. 1161, Judge not specified, OH.

7227. Personal injuries–limitations–action raised after expiry of limitation period–equitable power of court to override time limits

[Prescription and Limitation (Scotland) Act 1973 (c.52) s.19A.]

Section 19A of the Prescription and Limitation (Scotland) Act 1973 empowers the court to allow a person to bring an action which would otherwise be time barred under s.17, if it seems to the court to be equitable to do so. An action of damages for personal injuries was raised in September 1991, three days after the expiry of the triennium. At procedure roll, the defenders argued that the action fell to be dismissed as time barred. The pursuer argued that the court should exercise its discretion under s.19A of the 1973 Act and allow the action to proceed. The pursuer argued inter alia that the delay between the expiry of the triennium and the raising of the action was only three days; that the defenders had not suffered any prejudice as a result of the delay since the claim had been intimated to them well before the expiry of the triennium; and that the delay was caused by administrative oversight on the part of the pursuer's agents for which the pursuer himself was not personally responsible.

Held, that (1) the defenders were entitled to rely on the statutory defence afforded by s.17 of the 1973 Act, even if the delay in question was of only one day, and in any event there had been subsequent delay in the prosecution of the action which effectively negated this argument; (2) the fact that the defenders had not suffered any prejudice in terms of opportunity to investigate the pursuer's claim was of no great significance; (3) a pursuer had to be held to act through his agents and to be responsible for their actings and (4) the pursuer had a possible alternative remedy against his agents, and conceivably his counsel, in respect of the delay in bringing the action; and action dismissed.

WILSON v. TELLING (NORTHERN) LTD 1996 S.L.T. 380, Judge not specified, OH.

7228. Personal injuries–limitations–date from which time runs–when pursuer aware that injuries "sufficiently serious" to justify bringing action

[Prescription and Limitation (Scotland) Act 1973 (c.52) s.17, s.19A.]

In an action signeted on June 7, 1989 S sought damages from five former employers (A, B, C, D and E), for whom S had worked between 1939 and 1980, in respect of pleural plaques, pleural thickening and asbestosis developed by S as a result of his exposure to asbestos throughout that period. In a preliminary proof on time bar, S's evidence was that in 1976, S, who smoked about 30 cigarettes per day, had developed breathlessness, that X-rays had revealed several uncalcified pleural plaques, that after a lung biopsy in December 1977 had shown no definite abnormality or malignancy and an asbestos count which was not significant, S had been advised that he did not have true asbestosis and that his symptoms were mostly related to bronchitis and smoking, that a medical board in 1977 had decided that, although some pleural thickening and plaques were present, S was not suffering from asbestosis, that S's solicitor had advised S to withdraw his appeal to the medical appeal tribunal, that in 1983 S had further tests which indicated he had obstructive airways disease, that, although his X-ray showed bilateral pleural thickening, S had been advised that this was not related to his symptoms, that in February 1986 S had applied for disablement benefit on the basis of the pleural thickening, but the application had been refused, and that not until 1987 had S been aware that he had actual asbestosis. B, C and E argued that (1) given that by 1978 S had been aware of physical changes due to asbestos and that there was a risk of asbestosis emerging, in 1983 S had raised the matter of asbestosis with his doctor, and in 1986 S had believed his condition sufficiently serious to justify a further application to the medical board, it was clear that prior to June 7, 1986 S had been aware his condition was sufficiently serious to justify raising an action and (2) that the action should not be allowed to proceed under s.19A, as investigation of the matter had become harder with the lapse of time, S had failed to make reasonable progress with the action, it having been sisted for four years, and C had been prejudiced by the delay in that the power station at which S had worked had been demolished and C had been unable to trace any records of their employers' liability insurers for the period of his employment, 1948-49.

Held, allowing proof before answer, that as the Prescription and Limitation (Scotland) Act 1973 s.17(2)(b)(i) treated the seriousness of the injuries as the justification for raising an action, "sufficiently serious" had to mean more than just fractionally above the de minimis cut off for damages. S had not been aware by 1978 of pleural thickening, and even if he had been, it was not sufficiently serious at that stage to justify raising an action, even taken with the pleural plaques, the change to which could not be described as a disease or impairment. Although pleural thickening had been identified as widespread by 1983, S would have been deterred from raising an action related to his symptoms, and while a change in the social security regulations had encouraged S to reapply for benefit, the earlier advice meant that there was no basis for seeking any material sum of damages. Accordingly S had not been aware prior to 1987 that his condition was sufficiently serious to justify bringing an action of damages. Opinion, (1) that, as pleural plaques, pleural thickening and asbestosis were separate diseases, each had a separate time bar period, and even if the claims in respect of pleural thickening and plaques were time barred, the action could proceed as a claim in respect of asbestosis, from which, in any event, all the damages flowed, and (2) that S would have been allowed to proceed under the 1973 Act s.19A given the complexity of the medical issues, the absence of symptoms clearly attributable to exposure to asbestos, the medical advice given to S, and C's problems in investigating the claim would have arisen even by the 1970s and were limited in that the claim turned on general matters as to the processes carried out at the power station.

SHUTTLETON v. DUNCAN STEWART & CO LTD 1996 S.L.T. 517, Judge not specified, OH.

7229. **Articles**

A live issue: damages for wrongful birth *(Angus Stewart)*: J.L.S.S. 1996, 41 (11), 443-444. (Whether damages due for failed vasectomy and subsequent conception and birth of healthy child).

Medical negligence in Scotland *(John W.G. Blackie)*: E.J.H.L. 1996, 3(2), 127-141. (Background to health care system, interpretation of statistics on claims against Scottish medical profession and hospitals and approach of Scottish courts to cases on negligent diagnosis or treatment).

Professional negligence: the dilatory solicitor and the disappointed legatee *(James Blaikie)*: S.L.P.Q. 1996, 1(3), 245-251. (Effect of decision in White v Jones for Scots law where earlier decisions deny beneficiaries rights to recover damages for solicitors' negligence in preparing wills).

Subsidiarity and subsidence *(Douglas Brodie)*: Rep. B. 1996, 9(May), 3-5. (Implications of PC ruling in New Zealand case concerning council's negligent inspection of building work and consequent economic loss for home buyer).

The lost chance *(Neil Gow)*: Civ. P.B. 1996, 9(May), 3-6 . (Speculative actions for damages for loss of chance in professional negligence and employment actions).

NUISANCE

7230. **"Culpa"–whether equivalent to negligence**

H, consulting engineers, reclaimed against the Lord Ordinary's decision to allow proof before answer in an action by K, the proprietors and tenants of part of a tenement, for damages from G, tenants of the basement, and H arising from settlement within the tenement. H challenged the decision so far as relating to K's averments of nuisance. K averred that G and H had been aware that one of the walls to be removed was load bearing and that its removal caused cracking and settlement of the spine wall. H had advised G that this was likely. Nevertheless the wall was removed and K averred this was done under H's direction and instruction. H argued that K had not averred anything from which fault in terms of H's negligence or a deliberate act could be inferred. As such they lacked specification and the required fair notice. K's claim that H had occupied G's premises at the material time also lacked specification.

Held, reclaiming motion refused. The case of nuisance was appropriate given that H knew the works constituted an interference with the support enjoyed by K. Liability in damages for nuisance was a species of delictual liability and was based on culpa, *RHM Bakeries (Scotland) v. Strathclyde RC* 1985 S.L.T. 214 [1985] C.L.Y. 2493, 4458. Such claim arose where there was an invasion of land which exceeded what was reasonably tolerable. Where that test had been satisfied and culpa established, the requirements for delictual liability were fulfilled. It was sufficient that H instructed and directed hazardous works which they knew constituted an interference with the support enjoyed by K, and K had sufficient averments of fact to support such a case. H's presence on G's premises was not merely transitory in that they were in a substantial sense in control of what was going on when the work was being done at G's request. However, a separate case of fault based on H's knowledge of what was likely to happen was irrelevant if maintained on a ground other than nuisance. Per Lord Murray: Lord Fraser in *RHM* was not adopting Lord Atkin's dictum in *Sedleigh-Denfield v. O'Callaghan* [1940] A.C. 880 as a definition of culpa in Scots law in this field, and if the Lord Ordinary intended to substitute this notion of fault he would disagree.

KENNEDY v. GLENBELLE 1996 S.C.L.R. 411, Judge not specified, IH.

7231. Articles

Remedies in an action for nuisance *(Douglas Kinloch)*: Civ. P.B. 1996, 7(Jan), 2-3. (Interdict may provide more appropriate remedy in actions against nuisance than specific implement).

PARTNERSHIPS

7232. Judicial factor–personal liability

Held, in an action of payment at the instance of creditors against a judicial factor of a partnership in respect of goods supplied to the partnership at the request of the factor, that, in the absence of any suggestion that the factor had acted in bad faith or in breach of his duty, he had not attracted personal liability for the debt; and appeal against dismissal of the action refused.

SCOTTISH BREWERS v. J DOUGLAS PEARSON & CO 1996 S.C.L.R. 197, Judge not specified, Sh Ct.

7233. Articles

Shades of northern difference: the Scots law of partnership as applied to ICTA 1988 section 419 *(Julian Ghosh)*: P.T.P.R. 1996, 4(3), 165-173. (Whether separate legal personality of Scottish partnership precludes tax charge under s.419 where close company loan made to partnership by company in which partnership holds shares).

Stop press: more alarming news for partnerships *(David A. Bennett.)*: Bus. L.B. 1996, 20(Mar), 6-7. (Dissolution of partnership does not allow former partners to escape liability for partnership contracts).

PATENTS

7234. Articles

Rights in security over "Scottish patents" *(David P. Sellar)*: S.L.P.Q. 1996, 1(2), 137-144. (Creating security over patents in Scotland and nature of patent as property).

PEERAGES AND DIGNITIES

7235. Name and arms–succession as chief of clan–succession by alien

Cross petitions were presented to the Lord Lyon seeking confirmation of the plain undifferenced arms of Gunn in the petitioners' name as chief of the name and arms of Gunn. Both petitioners claimed descent from a common ancestor and accepted that the succession to their lines had opened between 1785 and 1807. The second petitioner claimed descent from Lt Col. William Gunn in the Dutch service, whose daughter Margaret, died 1788, married a Dutch national and whose issue thereafter were aliens and bore their Dutch paternal name of Brocades. The first petitioner claimed descent from Esther Gunn, sister of Lt. Col. William Gunn, who married a Gunn and whose issue continued to bear the name Gunn. At a procedure roll hearing before the Lord Lyon it was argued for the first petitioner that (1) when the succession opened to Margaret Gunn or her issue, she or her issue were aliens and therefore barred from succeeding to heritage in Scotland, which included a coat of arms, and the succession had therefore passed to Esther Gunn or her issue and (2) in any event even if the succession had opened to that line, by their failure to adopt the name Gunn within a year and a day of the succession opening, they had forfeited their right to succeed to the plain undifferenced arms of Gunn and the succession had therefore passed to Esther Gunn or her issue. It was argued for the second petitioner that the fact of alienage in an ancestor did not bar the present petitioner from making a claim, because no claim had been made by the first petitioner's line at a time when alienage might have been a bar to the succession.

Held, that (1) the status of alien at the date that the succession opened operated as a bar, like illegitimacy, to prevent the alien or his heirs from succeeding to a coat of arms; (2) the fact that the bar on an alien succeeding to a coat of arms was later removed by statute did not operate so as to bring the heirs of the alien back into the succession and (3) the failure by an heir female and her issue to adopt the family name over a long period of time meant that they were regarded as conventionally dead within the family and accordingly the succession had passed to the next heir; and second petitioner's petition dismissed as irrelevant and first petitioner allowed a proof.

GUNN, PETITIONERS 1996 S.L.T. (Lyon Ct) 3, Judge not specified, Lyon Ct.

7236. Name and arms–territorial designation

[Lyon King of Arms Act 1672 (c.21); Titles to Land Consolidation (Scotland) Act 1868 (c.101) s.3; Conveyancing (Scotland) Act 1874 (c.94) s.3; Conveyancing (Scotland) Act 1924 (c.27) s.2(1).]

Three individuals petitioned the Lord Lyon *inter alia* to recognise them officially in surnames, which included a territorial designation and to grant or matriculate a coat of arms to them in those names as officially recognised. Each petitioner sought to derive his territorial designation from a named dominium directum or superiority title. The Lord Lyon put out the three petitions for a hearing on whether the petitioners titles constituted titles to "lands".

Held, that the petitioners had established that they were infeft in lands in terms of the 19th and 20th century conveyancing legislation and that accordingly they might adject the designation of those lands to their surname when subscribing deeds; and petitioners officially recognised in the names and designations as prayed for.

COWAN OF BLACKBURN, PETITIONER; STEAHLI OF MARCHMONT, PETITIONER; BARTLE JONES OF CRAIGIEBUCKLER, PETITIONER 1996 S.L.T. (Lyon Ct.) 2, Judge not specified, Lyon Ct.

7237. Succession to arms–arms descending with Scots peerage–tailzied successor to arms and peerage with destination over–construction

[Peerage Act 1963 (c.48) s.1 Peerage Act 1963 (c.48) s.3.]

The Earldom of Selkirk was resettled following a resignation by William, 1st Earl of Selkirk (and Duke of Hamilton for life) by diploma dated October 6, 1688 on Lord Charles Hamilton, third but second surviving son of William, 1st Earl, and a series of named heirs, who had died, with a destination over to [in translation]: "all of whom failing to the other heirs male of the said Duke of Hamilton contained in his abovewritten letters patent. Declaring always, as it is provided and declared by the presents, that if it happens that the same Lord Charles, or the heirs male of his body, or any other of his brothers, or their heirs male, succeeds to the title and honour of Duke of Hamilton, then and in that case the aforesaid title and honour of Earl of Selkirk shall always descend and pertain to the immediately younger brother of him who shall succeed to the title of Duke of Hamilton, and to the heirs male of his body, whom failing (as is aforesaid)." On the death of Alfred, who succeeded as 13th Duke of Hamilton and 9th Earl of Selkirk, on March 16, 1940, Lord George Douglas-Hamilton, immediate younger brother of Douglas, succeeded as 14th Duke of Hamilton, and 10th Earl of Selkirk. On the death of the 10th Earl on November 24, 1994 without heirs male of his body, the petitioner, is the eldest son of the 10th Earl's immediate younger brother, the late Lord Malcolm Douglas-Hamilton, petitioned the Lord Lyon for matriculation of the arms and additaments appropriate to him as 11th Earl of Selkirk. this was opposed by Lord James Douglas-Hamilton, the 10th Earl's nephew and immediate younger brother of Angus, 15th and present Duke of Hamilton, and his son Andrew, claiming to be Master of Selkirk. Lord James had executed an instrument of disclaimer of the peerage in terms of s.1 of the Peerage Act 1963 following on from the 10th Earl's death. The petitioner argued that on the death of the 10th Earl the succession opened to him either as the heir male of the body of his father, who would have taken as the next younger brother after the 10th Earl, or as the representer of the immediate younger brother of a duke, who had also succeeded to the earldom. Lord James argued in terms of the 1688 diploma, on the death of the 10th Earl without heirs male of his body, the earldom reverted to the present Duke of Hamilton as heir male of William, 1st Earl of Selkirk, and as he was duke, then descended to Lord James as his immediate younger brother.

Held, that (1) the heir fell to be ascertained at the death of the 10th Earl; (2) on a proper construction of the 1688 diploma, on the death of the 10th Earl, the present Duke of Hamilton succeeded to the earldom, which immediately devolved on his immediate younger brother, Lord James, who succeeded as 11th Earl of Selkirk; (3) the instrument of disclaimer executed by Lord James did not affect his rights to succeed to the ensigns armorial recorded in the Lyon Register for the Earls of Selkirk, but that during his lifetime he was not entitled to use or bear the armorial additaments appropriate to the holder of the Earldom of Selkirk and (4) Andrew Douglas-Hamilton, as heir apparent to the Earldom of Selkirk, as Master of Selkirk was entitled to matriculate the arms of the Earls of Selkirk with the addition of an appropriate label of three points for difference; and petition dismissed.

DOUGLAS-HAMILTON, PETITIONER 1996 S.L.T. (Lyon Ct) 8, Judge not specified, Lyon Ct.

PENSIONS

7238. Pensions Act 1995–Commencement No.6 Order

PENSIONS ACT 1995 (COMMENCEMENT NO.6) ORDER 1996, SI 1996 1843 (C.37; S.151); made under the Pensions Act 1995 s.174, s.180. In force: bringing into force various provisions of the Act on July 15, 1996 and August 19, 1996; £1.10.

This Order brings into force the Pensions Act 1995 s.167 on August 19, 1996, with certain exceptions.

7239. Scottish Transport Group

SCOTTISH TRANSPORT GROUP (PENSION SCHEMES) ORDER 1996, SI 1996 1900 (S.152); made under the Transport Act 1962 s.74. In force: August 14, 1996; £1.10.

This Order provides for the winding up of two Scottish Transport Group Pension Schemes and for the transfer of assets, liabilities, obligations and any surplus funds to Scottish Bus Group.

PLANNING

7240. Ancient monuments

ANCIENT MONUMENTS (CLASS CONSENTS) (SCOTLAND) ORDER 1996, SI 1996 1507 (S.134); made under the Ancient Monument and Archaeological Act 1979 s.3, s.10. In force: July 11, 1996; £1.55.

Revokes and re-enacts the Ancient Monuments (Class Contents) (Scotland) Order 1981 (SI 1981 1468), which grants scheduled monument consent under the Part I of the 1979 Act for the execution of specified works in Scotland.

7241. Compulsory purchase–interest rates

ACQUISITION OF LAND (RATE OF INTEREST AFTER ENTRY) (SCOTLAND) REGULATIONS 1995, SI 1995 2791 (S.206); made under the Land Compensation (Scotland) Act 1963 s.40. In force: December 31, 1995; £1.10.

The rate of interest payable where entry is taken to Scottish land which is being compulsorily purchased is set by these Regulations at 0.5 per cent below the standard rate of interest applying from time to time. The standard rate is the quoted sterling base rate from the seven largest banks authorised under the Banking Act 1987 on whichever of the reference days most recently precedes the date when entry to the land is taken and any following days prior to payment of compensation.

7242. Compulsory purchase–limit of annual value

TOWN AND COUNTRY PLANNING (LIMIT OF ANNUAL VALUE) (SCOTLAND) ORDER 1995, SI 1995 3048 (S.221); made under the Town and Country Planning (Scotland) Act 1972 s.273. In force: January 1, 1996; £0.65.

The Town and Country Planning (Scotland) Act 1972 s.181 relates to the circumstances in which authorities may be obliged to purchase interests of owner-occupiers affected by planning proposals. This Order prescribes £21,500 as the limit of annual value for the purposes of s.181, replacing the previous limit of £12,000 set in 1985.

7243. Housing and Planning Act 1986–Commencement No.19 Order

HOUSING AND PLANNING ACT 1986 (COMMENCEMENT NO.19) (SCOTLAND) ORDER 1996, SI 1996 1276 (C.22; S.125); made under the Housing and Planning Act 1986 s.57. In force: bringing into force various provisions of the Act on June 1, 1996; £1.10.

This Order brings into force on June 1, 1996 the following provisions: s.53(1) and s.53(2).

7244. Listed building–description–scope of protection

[Town and Country Planning (Scotland) Act 1972 (c.52) s.52, s.53.]

E, a district council, appealed under the Town and Country Planning (Scotland) Act 1972 s.233 against the decisions of R, a reporter appointed by the Secretary of State (S), regarding the demolition and redevelopment of a former riding school building mentioned under the description of Redford Barracks in the list of listed buildings. E refused P's application for outline planning permission to erect a foodstore, petrol filling station and ancillary works and for listed building consent to demolish the riding school on the grounds that (a) the proposals would result in the loss of a statutorily listed building, contrary to Government policy, and (b) the statutory development plan, which consisted of the Structure Plan 1985 and the South West Edinburgh Local Plan 1993, "SWELP", effectually prohibited such a development. R concluded that (1) because the former riding school was built after 1915, it was not covered in the list, that listed building consent was not required and that reference to the riding school should be deleted from the description, and (2) material considerations justified departure from the development plan and conditional planning permission should be granted. S and P submitted that, in respect of the first issue, R was only required to consider the "name of the building" in the list, the "description" column being an "optional extra" included for information only. There was a presumption in favour of freedom from restriction on use and any ambiguity in the list should be resolved accordingly. Under the more recent statutory list, only the name of the building was relevant, and the description had no legal significance. In respect of the planning permission, R was entitled to consider that the National Planning Guidelines 1986 and the draft Structure Plan 1994, which encouraged authorities to support the provision of sites for major new retail development in or adjacent to existing centres, amounted to material considerations which justified departure from the development plan. The retail policy had progressed since the date of the development plan. R correctly concluded that there was a deficiency in quantitative terms on the basis that people should be able to meet their shopping needs without going outside the area they lived in and it was not necessary for R to find compelling reasons for his conclusion.

Held, appeal allowed and decisions in relation to the listed building consent and grant of planning permission quashed in respect of the grant of planning permission, that (1) R erred in holding that the former riding school building was not covered by the entry for Redford Barracks in the list and that listed building consent was not required for its demolition. The former riding school was included in the description, which was provided to help identify the subjects, not as an "optional extra". The reference to, "original buildings of 1909 to 15 only" might include buildings designed or planned as well as those built during that period, and any contradiction between the name of the building and the description only became apparent when regard was had to extrinsic information. The newer form of list was distinguishable from and inapplicable to the present appeal. R should now have regard to the further issues mentioned by E, whether the riding school should be removed from the list, and if not, whether a case for permitting demolition had been made out and (2) per the Lord Justice Clerk (Ross) and Lord McCluskey: R was not justified in finding that there were material considerations justifying departure from the provisions of the Structure Plan 1985 and SWELP. Although it was open to R to conclude that the National Planning Guidelines 1986 and the draft Structure Plan 1994 could constitute a material consideration justifying departure from the plan, there was no sound basis in fact for R to conclude that there appeared to be a quantitative case and the fact that certain stores in the area were trading at exceptionally high levels did not justify the conclusion that there was a deficiency in quantitative terms under s.17A in local shopping facilities in the area. It was significant that R had only stated that there "would appear to be" a quantitative case. There was no room for the general presumption in favour of development when strict criteria had to be met for such a development to be permitted.

CITY OF EDINBURGH DC v. SECRETARY OF STATE FOR SCOTLAND 1996 S.C.L.R. 600, Judge not specified, IH.

7245. New towns–dissolution–East Kilbride

NEW TOWN (EAST KILBRIDE) DISSOLUTION ORDER 1996, SI 1996 1066 (S.115); made under the New Towns (Scotland) Act 1968 s.36G. In force: April 4, 1996; £0.65.

This Order appoints April 5, 1996 as the date for the dissolution of the East Kilbride Development Corporation.

7246. New towns–dissolution–Glenrothes

NEW TOWN (GLENROTHES) DISSOLUTION ORDER 1996, SI 1996 1065 (S.114); made under the New Towns (Scotland) Act 1968 s.36G. In force: April 4, 1996; £0.65.

This Order appoints April 5, 1996 as the date for the dissolution of the Glenrothes Development Corporation.

7247. New towns–transfer of property rights–Cumbernauld

NEW TOWN (CUMBERNAULD) (TRANSFER OF PROPERTY, RIGHTS AND LIABILITIES) ORDER 1996, SI 1996 464 (S.33); made under the New Towns (Scotland) Act 1968 s.36D. In force: March 31, 1996; £7.35.

This Order provides for the transfer of certain property, rights and liabilities of the Cumbernauld Development Corporation to Cumbernauld and Kilsyth DC on March 31, 1996 in connection with the winding up of the corporation.

7248. **New towns–transfer of property rights–Cumbernauld**

NEW TOWN (CUMBERNAULD) (TRANSFER OF PROPERTY, RIGHTS AND LIABILITIES) (NO.2) ORDER 1996, SI 1996 3024 (S.228); made under the New Towns (Scotland) Act 1968 s.36D. In force: December 31, 1996; £2.40.

This Order makes provision for the transfer of certain property, rights and liabilities of the Cumbernauld Development Corporation to the North Lanarkshire Council on December 31, 1996, in connection with the winding up of the Corporation.

7249. **New towns–transfer of property rights–East Kilbride**

NEW TOWN (EAST KILBRIDE) (TRANSFER OF PROPERTY, RIGHTS AND LIABILITIES) ORDER 1995, SI 1995 3068 (S.222); made under the New Towns (Scotland) Act 1968 s.36D. In force: December 31, 1995; £6.75.

This Order makes provision for the transfer of certain property, rights and liabilities of the East Kilbride DC in connection with the winding up of the Corporation. The property, rights and liabilities which are the subject of the transfer Order comprise heritable property described in the Schedule and the Corporation's rights and liabilities under the various standard securities, minutes of agreement, policies of assurance and other contracts or agreements specified in the Schedule.

7250. **New towns–transfer of property rights–East Kilbride**

NEW TOWN (EAST KILBRIDE) (TRANSFER OF PROPERTY, RIGHTS AND LIABILITIES) ORDER 1996, SI 1996 465 (S.34); made under the New Towns (Scotland) Act 1968 s.36D. In force: April 1, 1996; £1.10.

This Order makes provision for the transfer of any property, rights and liabilities of the East Kilbride Development Corporation to the South Lanarkshire Council on April 1, 1996. Article 3 to Art.5 specify certain incidental and supplementary provisions.

7251. **New towns–transfer of property rights–Glenrothes**

NEW TOWN (GLENROTHES) (TRANSFER OF PROPERTY, RIGHTS AND LIABILITIES) ORDER 1996, SI 1996 466 (S.35); made under the New Towns (Scotland) Act 1968 s.36D. In force: April 1, 1996; £1.10.

This Order makes provision for the transfer of any property, rights and liabilities of the Glenrothes Development Corporation to Fife Council on April 1, 1996. Article 3, Art.4 and Art.5 specify certain incidental and supplementary provisions.

7252. **Planning control–permitted development**

TOWN AND COUNTRY PLANNING (GENERAL PERMITTED DEVELOPMENT) (SCOTLAND) AMENDMENT ORDER 1996, SI 1996 1266 (S.124); made under the Town and Country Planning (Scotland) Act 1972 s.21, s.273. In force: June 10, 1996; £1.10.

This Order amends the Town and Country Planning (General Permitted Development) (Scotland) Order 1992 by adding a new Part 25 to Sch.1 to grant permitted development rights for the installation, alteration or replacement on a building or other structure of a closed circuit television camera for security purposes.

7253. **Planning control–permitted development**

TOWN AND COUNTRY PLANNING (GENERAL PERMITTED DEVELOPMENT) (SCOTLAND) AMENDMENT (NO.2) ORDER 1996, SI 1996 3023 (S.227); made under the Town and Country Planning (Scotland) Act 1972 s.21, s.273. In force: December 25, 1996; £1.10.

This Order amends the Town and Country Planning (General Permitted Development) (Scotland) Order 1992 (SI 1992 223). It introduces a permitted development right for domestic liquified petroleum gas tanks and extends to the new sewerage authorities established under the Local Government etc (Scotland) Act 1994, and to bodies authorised by those authorities, permitted development rights in relation to certain sewerage works.

7254. Planning inquiries

TOWN AND COUNTRY PLANNING (COSTS OF INQUIRIES ETC.) (STANDARD DAILY AMOUNT) (SCOTLAND) REGULATIONS 1996, SI 1996 493 (S.44); made under the Town and Country Planning (Scotland) Act 1972 s.11, s.273, s.275, Sch.6A para.7. In force: April 1, 1996; £1.10.

These regulations set out a standard daily amount which planning authorities shall pay in respect of each day on which a person appointed to conduct a local plan or simplified planning zone inquiry or hearing is engaged in such work. Regulation 5 sets the standard daily amount at £275. Regulation 6 amends the Town and Country Planning (Structure and Local Plans) (Scotland) Regulations 1983. This minor amendment is necessary to make it clear that remuneration of a person appointed to conduct a local plan inquiry is payable under these new Regulations rather than the 1983 Regulations.

7255. Planning permission–conditions–whether sufficiently certain

[Town and Country Planning (Scotland) Act 1972 (c.52) s.83A, s.85, s.233.]

D, a district council, appealed against S, the Secretary of State's decision to sustain F's appeal against an enforcement notice. D sought reinstatement of the notice. D had granted planning permission for the erection of a clinical waste incinerator and refuse store in the grounds of F's hospital. A condition of the permission was that the incinerator would comply with certain environmental statements. Subsequently F were found not to be complying with the regulations for the emission of smoke and noise, and the enforcement notice was served. A reporter (R) concluded that any breaches of smoke emission were de minimis and that on the issue of noise the provisions were ambiguous as to where the noise level measure should be taken and therefore unworkable. The notice was quashed but R substituted an alternative noise condition providing for the noise level to be measured at the boundary of the site. D argued that (1) the condition was not ambiguous as it made clear that the noise should not exceed 65 dB (A) when all three incinerators were operational in a "worst case" situation. It was clear that the condition applied to the plant and not the site; (2) certainty and enforceability should not have been tested by reference to SDD circular 18/1986; (3) had the noise level been determinable by measuring at the boundaries instead of the plant, D would never have granted permission; further, R had given no explanation of what noise level would be acceptable at the boundary; and (4) R had acted contrary to natural justice in failing to inquire what was an acceptable level of noise and in failing to elicit D's opinion. S did not resist the appeal.

Held, appeal allowed on ground 4; R's decision quashed. The plant consisted of various pieces of machinery and there was no particular point at which noise was generated or from which it could be measured. R's conclusion on this aspect was justified. However as R failed to hear the views of F or D as to acceptable noise levels, the matter should be reconsidered by R and it might be appropriate to obtain an expert opinion. It should also be dealt with by oral rather than written submissions, which would avoid a repetition of the problem.

DUNFERMLINE DC v. SECRETARY OF STATE FOR SCOTLAND 1996 S.L.T. 89, Judge not specified, IH.

7256. Planning permission–deemed refusal–appeal–consistency of application with development plan–prior assessment of local needs

[Town and Country Planning (Scotland) Act 1972 (c.52) s.18A.]

D, a district council, appealed against the decision of the Secretary of State, S, to allow an appeal by C and to grant planning permission for the development of 13 houses in Stirlingshire, following a deemed refusal by D. The appeal was sisted to allow D to assess local and special needs. D failed to carry out the assessment and the appeal proceeded on the basis of written submissions. It was accepted by D that S had correctly set out the issue to be determined and that the relevant provisions of the development plan had been identified. D argued however that S had dealt with each in isolation and wrongly determined that general housing should not be held back pending identification of the demand for local and special needs housing. S had not identified all the criteria and the structure plan had to be read as requiring an assessment of all local and special needs housing before approval could be given for general housing. Failure to assess such needs was an absolute bar to such a development. The proposal did not then accord with the housing proposals and S's decision was therefore ultra vires as not in accordance with the Town and Country Planning (Scotland) Act 1972 s.18A.

Held, appeal refused. The provision requiring identification of the demand for local and special needs housing also required D to carry out the assessment as part of an urgent review of the local plan, but the absence of such a review was not an absolute bar to the granting of planning permission. There would otherwise be an absolute bar to any general needs housing for all the period of D's delay. It was for D to put forward a demonstrable requirement for local or special needs housing which would be prejudiced if the proposed development were approved.

STIRLING DC v. CARVILL (SCOTLAND) 1996 S.C.L.R. 265, Judge not specified, IH.

7257. Planning permission–development plan–whether "material considerations justifying departure from development plan

[Town and Country Planning (Scotland) Act 1972 (c.52) s.50.]

In 1990 a company appealed to the Secretary of State against the refusal of outline planning permission for residential development on land on a greenfield site which lay within the area governed by the Strathclyde Structure Plan as updated. In 1993 the Secretary of State issued an intentions letter intimating that he was minded to sustain the appeal provided an agreement under the Town and Country Planning (Scotland) Act 1972 s.50 was entered into between the company and the district planning authority. No such agreement was entered into. In 1995 the Secretary of State issued a decision letter sustaining the appeal and imposing various purported conditions. The regional and district planning authorities appealed to the Court of Session, arguing that the Secretary of State had failed to have regard to the policy considerations of the development plan in relation to the siting of housing on a greenfield site in the green belt, the specific criteria for which were in policies GB1A and RES2A. They also argued that the Secretary of State had erred in law in seeking to apply conditions to the consent which related to land beyond the control of the company in relation to matters upon which there was no evidence that there was a reasonable prospect that they could ever be fulfilled. In particular, they contended, the conditions were in terms which allowed fulfillment or otherwise to be judged by a party other than the planning authority and certain conditions had been applied defectively. Condition 4 required the approval for arrangements for sewerage to be obtained before development commenced but there was no compulsion to require the sewerage scheme to be carried out. Condition 5 likewise required the submission and details of necessary road schemes but not their completion. Both conditions 4 and 5 provided for the approval of sewerage and road proposals by someone other than the planning authority. Those condition were contrary to the guidance offered in circular No.8/1986 issued by the Scottish Development Department. The appellants also contended that the conditions were irrational in the *Wednesbury* sense.

Held, that (1) the Secretary of State had shown in both his intentions letter and his decision letter that he had assessed the proposed development against the criteria laid down in policies RES2A and GB1A, so that he had had regard to the policy consideration of the development plan and had concluded that there were good grounds for granting outline planning permission despite the fact that what was proposed was contrary to the statutory development plan; (2) there was a crucial difference between a positive condition attached to planning permission that the applicant bring about some circumstance which it was not within his power alone to bring about, and a negative condition that development should not commence until such a result had been achieved, in that the latter was enforceable while the former was not, and conditions 4 and 5 were not invalid or inappropriate, nor were they open to challenge because they related to actions which might take place on land beyond the control of the company or depend upon decision taken by someone other than the planning authority and (3) Circular 8/1986 contained guidance but was not to be taken as laying down any binding rules of law relating to conditions and had always to be read in light of the law laid down by the courts, so that the fact that a condition was negative in character and appeared to have no reasonable prospects of being implemented did not mean that the grant of planning permission subject to it would be irrational in the *Wednesbury* sense; and appeal refused, *Grampian RC v. City of Aberdeen DC* 1984 S.L.T. 197, [1984] C.L.Y. 4734 and *British Railways Board v. Secretary of State for the Environment and Hounslow BC* (1993) 3 P.L.R. 125 followed. Opinion reserved, whether, in the circumstances, it was unnecessary for the Secretary of State to have regard to the criteria laid down in policies RES2A and GB1A.

STRATHCLYDE RC v. SECRETARY OF STATE FOR SCOTLAND 1996 S.L.T. 579, Judge not specified, IH.

7258. Planning permission–refusal–appeal

[Town and Country Planning (Scotland) Act 1972 (c.52) s.233.]

Applications for planning permission and for winning and working of minerals were refused by a planning authority in October 1992. The unsuccessful applicants appealed to the Secretary of State who directed that he would determine the appeal himself, principally because the proposals would constitute a major industrial development which would affect a national scenic area. After a public local inquiry, the reporter recommended that the grant of planning permission was not justified and that the appeal should be dismissed. The Secretary of State followed the recommendation and dismissed the appeal by decision letter dated March 24, 1995. He accepted the findings of fact made by the reporter and agreed with the reporter's reasoning and conclusions for the purposes of his own decision. The reporter had properly taken into account the guidance contained in draft National Planning Policy Guidelines for mineral working, but at the time when the Secretary of State made his decision, the draft had been finalised as National Planning Policy Guideline 4. In an appeal to the Court of Session against the Secretary of State's decision, it was argued that he had fallen into error in failing properly to address the new guidance introduced by the finalised version.

Held, that (1) the differences between the policy guidance contained in the draft guideline and in the finalised version did not appear to be significant and that it was for the Secretary of State, as a matter of planning judgment, to determine whether or not any differences in expression or emphasis were sufficiently material as to affect his overall planning decision; (2) he was entitled to take the view that they were not so material and, in any event, it was for him, as the ultimate planning authority, to make the planning judgment quite apart from the terms of any draft or finalised policy guidance and (3) accordingly there was no error of law in the decision letter; and appeal dismissed.

M-I GREAT BRITAIN LTD v. SECRETARY OF STATE FOR SCOTLAND 1996 S.L.T. 1025, Judge not specified, IH.

7259. Planning permission–refusal–appeal–competing application–Secretary of State not following reporter's recommendations–reasons for decision

[Town and Country Planning (Inquiries Procedure) (Scotland) Rules 1980 (SI 1980 1676) r.12; Town and Country Planning (Inquiries Procedure) (Scotland) Rules 1980 (SI 1980 1676) r.13.]

L appealed against the Secretary of States's (S) decision dated March 23, 1995 refusing their application for outline planning permission for a mixed use development. L's application was one of seven applications and two appeals relating to four sites in Kilmarnock. A conjoined public local inquiry was held in 1994, as a result of which the reporter (R) made recommendations to S. R stated that the most significant factors of the relevant planning considerations were: (1) the proximity of the development to and supportiveness of the town centre, (2) the environmental impact and the potential for environmental improvement, and (3) the potential for economic regeneration. Three of the integrated proposals were placed before S. R noted that of the three proposals, D's application offered the greatest environmental benefit, although the environmental benefits of L's application would not be insignificant. R preferred L's application, however, because he considered that the potential for economic regeneration was the most important factor and implementation of L's proposal would achieve substantial benefits for an existing manufacturing concern in the area and would most closely comply with recommendation R1 of the Strathclyde Structure Plan. S did not accept R's recommendation and granted D's application; and although he accepted R's findings of fact and reasoning, he concluded that the issue of environmental benefits from the redevelopment site was more important than the potential for economic regeneration. L argued that in rejecting R's recommendation and granting outline planning permission to D, S had changed the emphasis without giving a reason for doing so, in breach of the Town and Country Planning (Inquiries Procedure) (Scotland) Rules 1980 r.13. In addition, S had acted unfairly in taking a Draft National Policy Guideline on Retailing (NPPG), issued on February 10, 1995, into account in making his decision without affording the parties an opportunity to make comments on the draft policy guideline and draw attention to its effect upon the applications being considered. The rules of natural justice applied and the way in which S had come to his decision was unfair as the new guidelines were new material upon which, in fairness, the parties should have had an opportunity to comment before S made his decision.

Held, appeal refused, that S had given an adequate reason for his decision where he stated that he attached more weight to environmental benefits and less to the potential for economic regeneration than R had done (R having in turn given no reason for his conclusion as to the most important factor), and S was entitled to determine as a matter of planning judgment what weight should be attached to the material planning factors identified by R. S had not exceeded his powers or acted unreasonably in differing from R. There was no substance to L's submission that S's decision was unfair. The draft NPPG 1995 did not raise any new issues or contain any new material because the issues it raised were the same as those contained in PPG 6, which had been considered by R and made the subject of findings of fact by him. In addition, there was no ground for concluding that there had been a breach of natural justice. There was clearly room for a difference of opinion upon matters of planning judgment and it was within S's power to exercise his own planning judgment and to prefer his own views on the weight to be given to planning considerations to those of R.

LONDON AND MIDLAND DEVELOPMENTS v. SECRETARY OF STATE FOR SCOTLAND 1996 S.C.L.R. 465, Judge not specified, IH.

7260. Planning permission–refusal–appeal–sufficiency of reasons

[Roads (Scotland) Act 1984 (c.54) s.91, s.93; Town and Country Planning (Appeals) (Written Submissions Procedure) (Scotland) Regulations 1990 (SI 1990 507).]

C appealed against the refusal by the Secretary of State's reporter (R) of C's appeal against refusal of planning permission for a housing development. R had considered that safety considerations in the form of a road access with restricted visibility should prevail over what was "an otherwise desirable scheme". A report from the director of highways had stated that even with remedial measures the required sight line of 2.5 metres by 90 metres could not be achieved, but that a sight line of 65 metres was possible, within the minimum sight stopping distance of 85 per cent of the traffic measured there, and that vehicles could also be seen beyond 115 metres. R also had four letters of objection from local residents based on the sight lines, a letter from the director to the district council indicating that the proposed access would be tolerably safe, and the benefit of a site inspection. The council had also refused the application because of traffic concerns. C argued that R had not expressed sufficient grounds for rejecting the director's expert view that the visibility was acceptably safe. Although there was no specific statutory requirement on R, there was a duty to give proper, intelligible and adequate reasons for any decision under the written submissions procedure, this was accepted. R had relied on factual considerations for which there was no basis in the material before her.

Held, appeal refused, that C's contentions were tantamount to saying that the advice of the director of highways had to prevail on a traffic question unless contradicted or qualified by another traffic expert. A question such as raised in the present case was to a degree a matter of judgment and the views of experienced road users could be sufficiently informed. The views of local residents taken with R's own experience and site visit could be put in the balance. In any event R did not require to accept evidence even where uncontradicted. She was entitled to consider that the position, set out by the director, was less than ideal and left no margin for driver uncertainty or error, especially in poor conditions. It was quite clear why she had rejected the appeal and C could have suffered no prejudice from the way the decision was articulated.

CASTLE ROCK HOUSING ASSOCIATION v. SECRETARY OF STATE FOR SCOTLAND 1995 S.C.L.R. 850, Judge not specified, IH.

7261. Planning procedures

TOWN AND COUNTRY PLANNING (GENERAL DEVELOPMENT PROCEDURE) (SCOTLAND) AMENDMENT ORDER 1996, SI 1996 467 (S.36); made under the Town and Country Planning (Scotland) Act 1972 s.28, s.33, s.273. In force: April 1, 1996; £1.10.

The Town and Country Planning (General Development Procedure) (Scotland) Order 1992 (SI 1992 224) is amended by this Order. Article 12 is extended to require planning authorities to send community councils a weekly list giving specified information on all planning applications. Article 15, which deals with consultations before grant of planning permission, is amended to provide for SEPA to take over certain responsibilities in relation to rivers and be consulted where development is likely to result in a material increase in the number of buildings at risk from flooding, to require the new water and sewerage authorities to be consulted when development is likely to make changes or add to their services and to require community councils to be consulted on certain applications.

7262. Structure plans–boundaries

DESIGNATION OF STRUCTURE PLAN AREAS (SCOTLAND) ORDER 1995, SI 1995 3002 (S.216); made under the Town and Country Planning (Scotland) Act 1972 s.4A. In force: April 1, 1996; £1.10.

This Order divides Scotland into 17 areas for the purposes of the functions of preparation and maintenance of structure plans which have fallen on the new unitary authorities as a result of local government reorganisation.

7263. Articles

Compulsory purchase and compensation *(Neil Collar)*: Prop. L.B. 1996, 23(Oct), 7-9 .

Duplicate applications and call-ins *(Bruce Smith)*: S.P.E.L. 1996, 57, 88-90. (Practical and tactical steps which can be taken to win planning consent for development where there is more than one competing application).

Listed buildings–section 18A and quantitative shopping deficiencies: the Redford Barracks case *(Neil Collar)*: Prop. L.B. 1996, 19(Feb), 7-10. (Identification of listed building and failure to have appropriate regard to development plan).

Planning and waste management–NPPG 10. : E.L.M. 1996, 8(5), 176-177 . (How NPPG 10, March 1996, sets out government planning policies in Scotland involving waste, defines content of structure and local plans regarding waste, and in terms of other pollution controls).

Planning inquiries: proposals for new procedure rules *(Jeremy Rowan-Robinson)*: S.P.E.L. 1996, 56, 62-63. (Scottish Office consultation paper on proposals for procedural changes to rules for inquiries where Secretary of State has jurisdiction).

Planning, pollution control and waste management *(Neil Collar)*: S.P.E.L. 1996, 56, 67-72. (How the planning system deals with overlaps with other statutory control systems in regard to potentially polluting development).

Protecting the built heritage (historic Scotland) *(Francis McManus.)*: S.P.E.L. 1996, 57, 82-84. (Green Paper on possible changes to listing procedures, partnership approach to heritage protection and issues relating to heritage legislation).

Retailing *(Iain J. Michie)*: S.P.E.L. 1996, 56, 72-73. (Scottish Office Circular 16/ 1996 and National Planning Policy Guideline No.8 on major retail developments).

Retailing–NPPG 8. : E.L.M. 1996, 8(5), 174-175. (Principal issues in finalised draft NPPG on retailing, April 1996, covering town centre as well as out of town developments).

Review of the use classes order *(Eric Young)*: S.P.E.L. 1996, 56, 63-64. (Scottish Office consultation paper on proposals to reform 1989 Order).

Scottish Office guidance: planning agreements and retailing *(Neil Collar)*: Prop. L.B. 1996, 21(Jun), 5-7. (Guidance notes issued April 29, 1996 on general policy and principles on use of planning agreements and control of retail developments to ensure vitality and viability of town centres).

Section 50 agreements *(Neil Collar)*: J.L.S.S. 1996, 41(8), 302-304. (Legal background to use of planning agreements).

7264. Books

Gill, Hon Lord; Thomson, Malcolm–Scottish Planning Encyclopedia. Paperback. ISBN 0-414-01150-3. W.Green & Son.

Young, Eric; Rowan-Robinson, Jeremy–Permitted Development. Green's practice library. Hardback. ISBN 0-414-01075-2. W.Green & Son.

POLICE

7265. Police and Magistrates' Courts Act 1994–Commencement No.10 Order

POLICE AND MAGISTRATES' COURTS ACT 1994 (COMMENCEMENT NO.10 AND SAVINGS) (SCOTLAND) ORDER 1996, SI 1996 1646 (C.35; S.142); made under the Police and Magistrates' Courts Act 1994 s.94. In force: bringing into force various provisions of the Act on August 1, 1996; £1.55.

This Order brings into force on August 1, 1996 the remaining provisions of Part II of the Police and Magistrates' Courts Act 1994 which concern the arrangements for policing in Scotland. Article 3 makes provision for certain savings in relation to proceedings brought under provisions of the Police (Scotland) Act 1967 which are substituted by provisions of the 1994 Act which are brought into force by this Order.

7266. Police officers–appeals tribunals

POLICE APPEALS TRIBUNALS (SCOTLAND) RULES 1996, SI 1996 1644 (S.140); made under the Police (Scotland) Act 1967 s.30. In force: August 1, 1996; £2.80.

These Rules make provision as to the procedure on appeals by constables to a police appeals tribunal under the Police (Scotland) Act 1967 s.30. Provision is made with respect to the appointment of an officer of the police authority to act as Registrar and for the police authority to act as respondent when an appeal is by a senior officer and the chief constable in other cases.

7267. Police officers–conditions of employment

POLICE (SCOTLAND) AMENDMENT REGULATIONS 1996, SI 1996 3232 (S.244); made under the Police Act 1967 s.26. In force: January 14, 1997; £2.40.

These Regulations make amendments to the Police (Scotland) Regulations 1976 (SI 1976 1073) relating to maternity rights, part time appointees, dog handler's allowance and temporary salaries for constables acting for constables of higher ranks.

7268. Police officers–disciplinary procedures

POLICE ACT 1996 (SCOTLAND) ORDER 1996, SI 1996 2146 (S.170); made under the Police Act 1996 Sch.8 para.11. In force: August 21, 1996; £0.65.

This Order appoints August 22, 1996 as the day when the provisions of the Police Act 1996 s.59 shall cease to have effect subject to the modifications in Sch.8 of the Act.

7269. Police officers–professional conduct

POLICE (CONDUCT) (SCOTLAND) REGULATIONS 1996, SI 1996 1642 (S.138); made under the Police (Scotland) Act 1967 s.26. In force: August 1, 1996; £3.70.

These Regulations replace the Police (Discipline) Regulations 1967 (SI 1967 1021). They make revised provision for the procedures for cases in which a constable below the rank of assistant chief constable who is the subject of an allegation of misconduct may be dealt with by dismissal, requirement to resign, reduction in rank, reduction in rate of pay, fine, reprimand or caution.

7270. Police officers–professional conduct

POLICE (CONDUCT) (SENIOR OFFICERS) (SCOTLAND) REGULATIONS 1996, SI 1996 1645 (S.141); made under the Police (Scotland) Act 1967 s.26. In force: August 1, 1996; £4.15.

These Regulations replace the Police (Discipline) (Senior Officers) (Scotland) Regulations 1990 (SI 1990 1017). They make provision with respect to the procedures for cases in which Chief Constables or Assistant Chief Constables of police forces may be dealt with by dismissal, requirement to resign, reprimand or caution where their conduct constitutes a disciplinary offence, being conduct of any of the kinds described in Sch.1 to the Regulations. In making such provision the Regulations re-enact the 1990 Regulations with minor amendments as a consequence of amendments made to the Police (Scotland) Act 1967 s.26 by the Police and Magistrates' Courts Act 1994 s.52 and the revocation of the Police (Discipline) (Scotland) Regulations 1967 (SI 1967 1021).

7271. Police officers–professional conduct–efficiency

POLICE (EFFICIENCY) (SCOTLAND) REGULATIONS 1996, SI 1996 1643 (S.139); made under the Police (Scotland) Act 1967 s.26. In force: August 1, 1996; £3.20.

These Regulations make provision with respect to the assessment of the efficiency of constables of police forces in Scotland and establish procedures for cases in which a constable who is not performing satisfactorily may be dealt with by way of requirement to resign reduction in rank or warning. Provision is made for interviewing constables where it is considered that their performance is unsatisfactory and identifying areas for improvement and for the holding of an inefficiency hearing.

7272. Police officers–promotion

POLICE (PROMOTION) (SCOTLAND) REGULATIONS 1996, SI 1996 221 (S.15); made under the Police (Scotland) Act 1967 s.26. In force: March 1, 1996.

The Police (Promotion) (Scotland) Regulations 1968 (SI 1968 717) are re-enacted with amendments by these Regulations. The main changes are the termination of the Police (Scotland) Examination Board and the simplification of the functions relating to the arrangement and conduct of the qualifying examination for promotion above the rank of constable. The Regulations still require that for constables to be promoted to the rank of sergeant they must pass the Police (Scotland) Promotion Examination and certain transitional provision are introduced.

7273. Police service

COMMON POLICE SERVICES (SCOTLAND) ORDER 1996, SI 1996 745 (S.78); made under the Police (Scotland) Act 1967 s.36. In force: April 1, 1996; £1.55.

This Order revokes and replaces the Common Police Services (Scotland) Order 1995 (SI 1995 707). The changes effected by this Order are consequential upon the establishment of joint police boards and the reorganisation of police areas by virtue of the Police (Scotland) Act 1967 s.21B (as inserted the Local Government etc. (Scotland) Act 1994 s.34). The Police (Scotland) Act 1967 s.26(3) (as substituted by the Police and Magistrates' Courts Act 1994 s.59) enables the Secretary of State to provide for the recovery from police authorities and joint police boards of expenses incurred by him in providing facilities or services under or by virtue of s.36(1) of the said Act of 1967. Article 2 of the Order provides for the recovery of 50 per cent of the expenses incurred by the Secretary of State in providing under or by virtue of s.36(1) of the said Act of 1967 the facilities and services specified in Art.2(2). Article 3 of the Order also provides for the application of provisions of Art.2 to the expenses incurred by the Secretary of State for the purposes of police forces in Scotland generally on or in connection with the services or institutions specified in Art.3.

7274. Police service–police grant

POLICE GRANT (SCOTLAND) ORDER 1996, SI 1996 780 (S.89); made under the Police (Scotland) Act 1967 s.32. In force: April 1, 1996; £1.55.

This Order replaces the Police Grant (Scotland) Order 1947 (SR&O 1947 1659) and determines the amount of police grant payable under the Police (Scotland) Act 1967 s.32(1) to police authorities and joint police boards in respect of the financial year commencing April 1, 1996. The amount of police grant payable to an authority will be 51 per cent of its net expenditure for the purposes of the Act (calculated under Art.3) except where such expenditure exceeds a prescribed sum in which case the grant will be limited to that sum. The prescribed sum is determined by a formula set out in Art.4 and Sch.1. Article 5 and Art.6 make provision with respect to the timing and manner of payment of police grant and the conditions subject to which it is payable. Article 7 and Sch.2 revoke the said Order of 1947 and Orders amending it.

7275. Police service–police grant

POLICE GRANT (SCOTLAND) (AMENDMENT) ORDER 1995, SI 1995 3025 (S.218); made under the Police (Scotland) Act 1967 s.32. In force: December 20, 1995; £1.10.

Amends the Police Grant (Scotland) Order 1947 by imposing a limit on the amount of expenditure incurred by a police authority or a joint police committee in respect of pay eligible for a grant under the Police (Scotland) Act 1967 (c.77) s.32 where the number of constables in a force and the amount of such pay exceeds specified limits during certain periods in the financial year ending March 31, 1996.

PRISONS

7276. Prison rules

PRISONS AND YOUNG OFFENDERS INSTITUTIONS (SCOTLAND) AMENDMENT RULES 1996, SI 1996 32 (S.1); made under the Prisons (Scotland) Act 1989 s.39. In force: February 5, 1996; £4.15.

These Rules make provision for the amendment of the Prisons and Young Offenders Institutions (Scotland) Rules 1994 (SI 1994 1931), which are amended as follows: r.75 (exercise and time in the open air) is amended to clarify the circumstances when entitlements do not apply and to alter procedures for disapplying its provisions; r.86 (admission and searching of visitors) is amended in consequence of amendments made to the Prisons (Scotland) Act 1989 s.41; a new r.88A is inserted to make provision for compulsory testing of prisoners for controlled drugs; a new r.101A is inserted for the Governor to review certain disciplinary punishments in the case of a prisoner who is removed to hospital for treatment for mental disorder; r.28 to r.39 of the 1996 Rules amend Part 11 (requests and complaints); r.133 (constitution of visiting committees) is amended to make provision for the constitution for prisons of new visiting committees on April 1, 1996 by councils constituted under Local Government etc. (Scotland) Act 1994 s.2; r.120 to r.126 in Part 14 (temporary release) are amended; and a new r.104A and Sch.4A are inserted for the constitution of visiting committees for police cells declared to be legalised police cells under the 1989 Act.

RATES

7277. Council tax–local government reorganisation

RATING, VALUATION AND COUNCIL TAX (MISCELLANEOUS PROVISIONS) (SCOTLAND) ORDER 1996, SI 1996 580 (S.58); made under the Local Government etc. (Scotland) Act 1994 s.181. In force: April 1, 1996; £1.55.

This Order make provisions so as to ensure continuity, in connection with local government reorganisation, in the transition to the new assessors, valuation appeal panels and committees, and valuation rolls and lists and makes minor amendments in subordinate legislation relating to the council tax and valuation appeals.

7278. Non domestic rates

NON DOMESTIC RATE (SCOTLAND) ORDER 1996, SI 1996 95 (S.5); made under the Local Government (Scotland) Act 1975 s.7B, s.37. In force: April 1, 1996; £0.65.

This Order prescribes a rate of 44.9 pence in the pound as the non domestic rate to be levied throughout Scotland in respect of the financial year 1996-97.

7279. Non domestic rates

NON DOMESTIC RATES (LEVYING) (SCOTLAND) REGULATIONS 1996, SI 1996 103 (S.6); made under the Local Government etc. (Scotland) Act 1994 s.153. In force: April 1, 1996; £3.90.

These Regulations, which apply only to the financial year of 1996-7, make provision for the amount payable as non-domestic rates on property in Scotland. Part II deals with lands and heritages on the valuation roll on April 1, 1996; Part III applies to certain property with its rateable value for 1996-7 fixed by order; Part IV applies to lands and heritages which have merged, split, or reorganised after March 31, 1996; and Part V deals with reductions, remissions and exemptions for unoccupied lands, heritages and charities. The Schedules set out base liabilities and notional rateable values for water authorities and the British Railways Board.

7280. Non domestic rates–contributions

NON DOMESTIC RATING CONTRIBUTIONS (SCOTLAND) AMENDMENT REGULATIONS 1995, SI 1995 3177 (S.235); made under the Local Government Finance Act 1992 s.113; and the 116, Sch.12 (part). In force: December 31, 1995; £1.10.

Rules for the calculation of non domestic rating contributions payable by Scottish local authorities to the Secretary of State under Part III of Sch.12 to the Local Government Finance Act 1992 for the financial year 1996/7 and subsequent years are amended. Most amendments are consequential on the reorganisation of Scottish local government which will take place on April 1, 1996 or reinstate provisions inapplicable to the financial year 1995/6 due to that year being a year of revaluation for non-domestic rating purposes.

7281. Non domestic rates–contributions

NON-DOMESTIC RATING CONTRIBUTIONS (SCOTLAND) REGULATIONS 1996, SI 1996 3070 (S.234); made under the Local Government Finance Act 1992 s.113, s.116, Sch.12 para.10, Sch.12 para.11, Sch.12 para.12. In force: December 31, 1996; £2.40.

Under the Local Government Finance Act 1992 Sch.12 Part III Scottish local authorities are required to pay non-domestic rating contributions to the Secretary of State. Payments in respect of a provisional amount of the contributions are made during the financial year, final calculations and payments being made after year ends. These Regulations contain rules for the calculation of those contributions and apply from financial year 1997/98 onwards. The Non-Domestic Rating Contributions (Scotland) Regulations 1992 (SI 1992 3061 as amended by SI 1993 3059, SI 1994 3146 and SI 1995 3177) are revoked.

7282. Non-Domestic Rating (Information) Act 1996 (c.13). See RATES. §4913

7283. Plant and machinery–chill store within warehouse occupying most of warehouse and forming part of one wall

[Lands Valuation (Scotland) Act 1854 (c. 9) s.42.]

Ratepayers appealed against the decision of a valuation appeal committee to include the value of a chill store (hereafter "chill") within a warehouse as a rateable element in the valuation of those subjects. The ratepayers argued that the chill was "plant" which fell to be excluded from the scope of "machinery fixed or attached" for the purposes of s.42 of the Lands Valuation (Scotland) Act 1854, as amended, because it could be removed from its place without necessitating the removal of any part of the building. The chill was constructed for the ratepayers to enable them to store food at a temperature of about 5C for the purpose of their business as distributors of food products. It took the form of a large insulated box set on the floor of the warehouse and attached to it by various types of fixing. The chill could not be removed from the warehouse as a unit; however it could be removed in its component parts.

Held, that (1) whether something had the character of "plant" was a matter of fact in each case and the committee were entitled to hold that the chill was plant because it was something with which the ratepayers carried on business, as distinguished from a place in which business was carried on; (2) the committee were entitled to hold that, notwithstanding the uninsulated floor, the chill was used for the cooling of itself and the food products stored within it, as distinguished from the building or part of it; (3) per Lord Cullen, s.42(2) was intended to bring about the result that certain plant, which otherwise would be treated as rateable because it was heritable, would be excluded from rateability if it satisfied the test as to moveability; (4) it was unnecessary for the ratepayer to demonstrate that an item of plant was capable of being removed in any particular mode, at least where no question of the destruction of the plant or its components arose, and that while ratepayers had to demonstrate that the removability of plant was a practicable and not merely a theoretical exercise, this referred to the physical operations which removal would entail and not the likelihood of re-assembly elsewhere on substantially the same configuration; (5) the breaking out of fixings, or the time taken to dismantle the plant, did not, affect the issue of removability; (6) on the facts found, the only reasonable conclusion was that the door and its framing formed part of the chill, and its removal would not necessitate removal of part of the building even though a hole in the warehouse wall would remain and ratepayers' appeal allowed and the value relating to the chill excluded from valuation, *Inland Revenue Commissioners v. Scottish & Newcastle Breweries* 1982 S.L.T. 407, [1982] C.L.Y. 475 applied, *Michael Nairn & Co Ltd v. Assessor for Kirkcaldy* 1915 S.C. 801 followed.

WATSON & PHILIP PLC v. ASSESSOR FOR GRAMPIAN REGION 1996 S.L.T. 247, Judge not specified, LVAC.

7284. Rateable occupation–division of subjects–whether agreement effective to create separation of subjects

A ratepaying company transferred certain subjects, part of larger subjects, to another company by disposition dated in November 1994. Entry was granted as from August 1, 1993, by which time the subjects had become vacant. The ratepaying company sought to have the subjects treated as a separate entry in the valuation roll as from August 1, 1993. The assessor refused to do this and the ratepaying company appealed to the valuation appeal committee. At the hearing on the appeal the assessor raised a preliminary point on competency, arguing that the basis of the appeal was that the vacant buildings had been transferred to the other company but that no actual transfer would occur until delivery of the disposition in November 1994. The ratepaying company argued that the granting of entry as at August 1993 effected the requisite change requiring separation of entries in the roll at that date. The valuation appeal committee refused the appeal, holding that delivery and recording of the disposition were necessary in order for the subjects to be treated as a separate entity in law. The ratepaying company appealed to the Lands Valuation Appeal Court.

Held, that (1) it was unfortunate and inappropriate that the committee had dealt with the case on the basis of the preliminary point raised as that went to the heart of the merits of the appeal, but that the company had not suffered any prejudice for any further evidence would have been only on matters of detail and the company had acquiesced in the procedure adopted and (2) the primary test for the identification of a unum quid was by reference to actual occupation, and while the delivery and recording of a disposition did not necessarily determine the propriety of making a separate entry in the valuation roll, the deemed possession which the parties to the agreement and the conveyance agreed should regulate their rights retrospectively was not sufficient to constitute a rateable occupation or to justify a splitting of the subjects; and appeal refused.

UNITED MALT AND GRAIN DISTILLERS LTD v. ASSESSOR FOR THE HIGHLAND REGION AND WESTERN ISLES ISLAND AREA 1996 S.L.T. 785, Judge not specified, LVAC.

7285. Rateable values–docks and harbours

DOCKS AND HARBOURS (RATEABLE VALUES) (SCOTLAND) AMENDMENT (NO.2) ORDER 1995, SI 1995 3253 (S.242); made under the Local Government (Scotland) Act 1975 s.6, s.35, s.37. In force: December 12, 1995; £0.65.

The Docks and Harbours (Rateable Values) (Scotland) Order 1990 (SI 1990 817) prescribes the method of calculation of rateable values of certain lands and heritages used for dock and harbour purposes in Scotland. This Order, which takes effect from April 1, 1996, amends Art.5 of the 1990 Order so that such a rateable value for the 1995/96 period will be calculated by referring to the income of the undertaking over the relevant 12 month period ending between December 31, 1992 and March 31, 1993.

7286. Rateable values–water undertakings

WATER UNDERTAKINGS (RATEABLE VALUES) (SCOTLAND) (NO.2) ORDER 1995, SI 1995 3252 (S.241); made under the Local Government (Scotland) Act 1975 s.6, s.35, s.37. In force: April 1, 1996; £1.95.

Provision is made in this Order for the valuation of lands and heritages occupied by or used by water authorities during the financial years 1996/7 to 1999/2000. The aggregate amount of rateable value is prescribed at £33,218,368 by Art.4 and the aggregate amount is also apportioned among the three water authorities and among local authorities by Art.5 and Art.6. and set out in the Schedules to the Order. Certain enactments relating to prescribed classes of lands and heritages are amended by Art.7 to Art.9 and Art.10 revokes the Water Undertakings (Rateable Values) (Scotland) Order 1995.

7287. Retail premises–whether to be valued as shop or retail warehouse

Tenants of retail premises, whose business operated on a self-service basis, with the customer selecting goods and then taking them to a point of sale within the premises, appealed to the valuation appeal committee against the assessor's decision to value the premises on the basis of his shop scheme as opposed to a retail warehouse scheme. The premises were located in a shopping centre and interconnected physically with other units accepted to be shops. There was a substantial glass shop front to the premises and their internal layout involved the creation of room settings. The size of the premises was comparable with other units assessed under the shop scheme of valuation and the only admitted retail warehouse was distinguishable in size, physical appearance and physical separation from the block of units in which the premises were situated. The figures on valuation under each scheme differed widely from one another. The committee refused the appeal and the tenants appealed to the Lands Valuation Appeal Court.

Held, that what mattered was the actual use of the premises, and on their findings in fact the committee had been entitled to conclude that the proper mode of valuation was under the shop scheme; and appeal refused.

Observed, that there was now a huge range of types of retail operation and there would inevitably be cases of premises falling just on one or other side of the dividing line between shop and retail warehouse; that such categorisations should not have the effect of preventing a fair valuation being achieved in particular cases; but that having regard to the approach adopted by the parties and the issue on which the case had been focused, the court was unable to do other than affirm the value contended for by one or other party.

TEXSTYLE WORLD v. ASSESSOR FOR STRATHCLYDE REGION 1996 S.L.T. 782, Judge not specified, LVAC.

7288. Valuation appeal committee–procedure–duty to hear evidence–appellant failing to comply with order for productions

[Lands Valuation (Scotland) Act 1854 (c.9) s.10.]

W appealed against the valuation of a public house. W failed to appear at the appeal hearing. The committee ordered W to produce evidence of annual drawings from the date of entry on the valuation roll and set a date for the continued hearing. At the hearing W did not produce the evidence ordered and argued that the appeal ought to be disposed of on other grounds. The committee held that the request for turnover figures was reasonable and the order for production not having been complied with, the appeal ought to be dismissed. W appealed. The assessor argued, inter alia, that the appeal was incompetent as it did not raise a question of valuation.

Held, allowing the appeal; case remitted to the committee for a hearing, that (1) there was nothing in s.10 of the 1854 Act that required the committee to dismiss the appeal in these circumstances. The committee could not reasonably have held, in the absence of evidence as to drawings, that the assessor's valuation was correct, *Scouller v. Assessor for Glasgow* 1912 S.C. 757, and *Deards v. Assessor for Edinburgh* 1911 S.C. 918, distinguished, and (2) the matter was not purely procedural but incidental to a genuine valuation issue, hence the appeal was competent.

WHITBREAD v. ASSESSOR FOR CENTRAL REGION 1993 S.C. 552, Judge not specified.

7289. Valuation appeal panels

VALUATION APPEAL PANELS AND COMMITTEES (SCOTLAND) REGULATIONS 1996, SI 1996 137 (S.10); made under the Local Government etc. (Scotland) Act 1994 s.29. In force: January 29, 1996; £1.10.

These Regulations constitute 13 valuation appeals tribunals for the valuation areas referred to in Reg.2 for the purpose of hearing appeals under the Valuation Acts and council tax appeals, pursuant to local government reorganisation in Scotland.

REGISTERS AND RECORDS

7290. Adoption

ADOPTED CHILDREN REGISTER AND PARENTAL ORDER REGISTER (FORM OF ENTRY) (SCOTLAND) REGULATIONS 1995, SI 1995 3158 (S.233); made under the Adoption (Scotland) Act 1978 Sch.1 para.1. In force: January 1, 1996; £1.55.

These Regulations specify the revised forms of entry to be made following a direction in an adoption order or a parental order in the Adopted Children Register maintained by the Registrar General for Scotland and the Parental Order Register maintained by the Registrar General for Scotland in consequence of the Parental Orders (Human Fertilisation and Embryology) (Scotland) Regulations 1994.

7291. Marriage–fees

MARRIAGE FEES (SCOTLAND) REGULATIONS 1996, SI 1996 572 (S.54); made under the Marriage (Scotland) Act 1977 s.3, s.19, s.25, s.26. In force: April 1, 1996; £0.65.

These Regulations set out, with effect from April 1, 1996, the fees payable under the Marriage (Scotland) Act 1977 s.3(1) and s.129(2) (fees for the preliminaries to marriage and for the solemnisation of a civil marriage respectively). The fee under s.3(1) is increased from £10 to £11 and the fee under s.19(2) is unchanged at £40. The Marriage Fees (Scotland) Regulations 1993 (SI 1993 3152) are revoked.

7292. Registers of Scotland Executive Agency–finance

REGISTERS OF SCOTLAND EXECUTIVE AGENCY TRADING FUND ORDER 1996, SI 1996 1004 (S.107); made under the Government Trading Funds Act 1973 s.1, s.2, s.2A, s.2C. In force: April 1, 1996; £1.55.

This Order provides for the setting up as from April 1, 1996 of a fund with public money under the Government Trading Funds Act 1973 to finance the operations of the Department of the Registers of Scotland, now known as the Registers of Scotland Executive Agency, described in Sch.1 to the Order. It also provides for the fund to be under the control and management of the Keeper of the Registers of Scotland. The Order designates the National Loans Fund as the authorised lender to the fund and imposes a limit of £40,000,000 on the amount which may be lent to it. It provides for assets (estimated at £13,763,000) and liabilities (estimated at £3,715,000) set out in Sch.2 to the Order to be appropriated to the fund and for 40 per cent of the amount by which the value of the assets exceeds the value of the liabilities to be treated as public dividend capital.

7293. Registration–fees–births, deaths, marriages and divorces

REGISTRATION OF BIRTHS, DEATHS, MARRIAGES AND DIVORCES (FEES) (SCOTLAND) AMENDMENT REGULATIONS 1996, SI 1996 574 (S.55); made under the Registration of Births, Deaths and Marriages (Scotland) Act 1965 s.28A, s.38, s.43, s.47, s.54, s.56. In force: April 1, 1996; £1.10.

The Births, Deaths, Marriages and Divorces (Fees) (Scotland) Regulations 1993 (SI 1993 3153) are amended in order to prescribe new circumstances in which the Registrar General can remit certain fees and to increase certain fees. Fees for inclusive general searches in parochial registers and indexes to the statutory registers in cases where payments are made not less than 14 days in advance are increased to £14.00 per pay, or part. In other cases the fee per afternoon is increased to £10.00, the fee per day is increased to £17.00, the fee per week is increased to £65.00, the fee per four weeks is increased to £220.00 and the fee per quarter is increased to £500.00. The fee for recording change of name or surname is increased to £34.00. As a result of these changes the Registration of Births, Deaths, Marriages and Divorces (Fees) (Scotland) Amendment Regulations (SI 1995 646) Reg.4 is revoked.

7294. Registration–forms–births' stillbirths' deaths and marriages

REGISTRATION OF BIRTHS, STILL-BIRTHS, DEATHS AND MARRIAGES (PRESCRIPTION OF FORMS) (SCOTLAND) AMENDMENT REGULATIONS 1995, SI 1995 3157 (S.232); made under the Registration of Births, Deaths and Marriage (Scotland) Act 1965 s.13; the 19; the 22; the 32; the 40; the 54; and the 56. In force: January 1, 1996; £2.40.

Forms specified in the Registration of Births, Still-births, Deaths and Marriages (Prescription of Forms) (Scotland) Regulations 1965 are substituted with corresponding forms set out in these Regulations which make provision for female occupations to be inserted on such forms where appropriate. Other minor changes are made to the style and layout of the forms.

REPARATION

7295. Articles

Smoking in the courts: there may be trouble ahead *(William J. Stewart)*: Rep. B. 1996, 11 (Sep), 4-7. (Ethical, political and economic considerations in smoking litigation, with particular reference to US, and difficulties in obtaining legal aid in UK).

Suing the fire brigade *(Jane Convery)*: Rep. B. 1996, 10 (Jul), 2-3. (Refusal of English courts to recognise duty of care for fire services on public policy grounds in contrast to situation in Scotland).

RESTITUTION

7296. Articles

Change of position in Scots law *(G.C. Borland)*: S.L.T. 1996, 15, 139-141. (Change of position defence considered as answer to claim for restitution following unjust enrichment).

Commercial remedies: recovering money paid into agent's bank account. : C.L.M. 1996, 4(3), 1-2. (Ability to trace funds where bank account overdrawn and whether agent held money as constructive trustee).

Recompense for interference in Scots law *(Andrew J.M. Steven)*: Jur. Rev. 1996, 1, 51-65. (Whether Scottish principle of restitution should take into account interference by one party where unjust enrichment has occurred).

Scotland *(William J. Stewart)*: R.L.R. 1996, 4, 224-231 . (Developments in law of restitution in past year, including abstracts of cases and articles).

Scottish Law Commission Discussion Paper No.99: judicial abolition of the error of law rule and its aftermath *(Hilary Hiram)*: Jur. Rev. 1996, 5, 353-357. (Whether and on what grounds statutory safeguard is needed against reopening settled transactions on ground of error of law in light of decision on restitution for ultra vires swap agreement).

Swaps and unjustified enrichment *(George L. Gretton)*: J.B.L. 1996, May, 327-328. (Impact of "Hazell v Hammersmith" regarding interest rate swap agreements, restitutionary principles and whether errors in law preclude recovery under swap agreement).

The intention to donate in recompense and Professor Bell's definition. *(William J. Stewart)*: S.L.T. 1996, 29, 270-273. (Critical analysis of definition of recompense in Bell's Principles and comparison with other legal commentaries).

ROAD TRAFFIC

7297. Accident–failure to stop–sentence

Held, that disqualification for 12 months with a fine of £250 plus £150 for careless driving was not excessive where W, a first offender who had been driving for 25 years, failed to stop and exchange particulars after a collision, the sheriff being entitled, though there was no charge arising out of drinking and driving, to take into account W's reply the following day, to caution and charge, that his reason for failing to stop was that he had had a few drinks and was unsure if he was below the limit, *McNamee v. Carmichael* 1985 S.C.C.R. 289, [1986] C.L.Y. 4570 distinguished, and it was within the sheriff's discretion to hold that the nature and circumstances of the offence merited disqualification. On W's claim that he might lose his job if he was unable to drive, his income of £4,000 net per month was sufficient to employ a driver for the length of the ban.

WILLEMS v. VANNET 1996 S.C.C.R. 16, Judge not specified.

7298. Complaints–summary–latitude as to place

[Criminal Procedure (Scotland) Act 1975 (c.21) s.312.]

Section 312(f) of the Criminal Procedure (Scotland) Act 1975 provides, inter alia, that the latitude in use to be taken in stating any place by adding to the word "at", or to the word "in", the words "or near", or the words "or in the near neighbourhood thereof", shall be implied "where the actual place is not of the essence of the charge". An accused person was charged on a summary complaint with a contravention of the Road Vehicles (Construction and Use) Regulations 1986 in respect that he caused and permitted his motor vehicle to stand on a lane near a library so as to cause unnecessary obstruction thereof. There was an area of parking contiguous to the lane. Two vehicles were in the car park and the accused's vehicle was parked in the car park so that neither of the other vehicles could leave. The justices convicted the accused by relying on the latitude implied under s.312(f). The accused appealed.

Held, that what was charged was specifically an obstruction of the lane and as that place was of the essence of the charge, the justices were not entitled to convict; and appeal allowed and conviction quashed.

ALLAN v. McKAY 1996 S.L.T. 223, Lord Sutherland, HCJ.

7299. Complaints–summary–plea to lesser offence not libelled–competency

[Criminal Procedure (Scotland) Act 1975 (c. 21) s.103, s.336; Road Traffic Offenders Act 1988 (c. 53) s.24(1).]

D, charged on summary complaint with dangerous driving in violation of s.2 of the Road Traffic Act 1988, tendered a plea of guilty to careless driving in breach of s.3, which the Crown accepted. As the complaint did not contain an alternative charge of careless driving, the sheriff refused to record the plea on the ground that it was incompetent and, when the Crown intimated that they were not proceeding to trial, found D not guilty on the view that on a construction of s.24(1), D could only be convicted of careless driving after he had gone to trial and been found not guilty of dangerous driving. The Crown raised a bill of advocation, arguing that s.24(1) did not require to be read in this way, which D accepted.

Held, bill passed and case remitted to the sheriff to record D's plea of guilty to s.3 and to proceed as accords. It was competent for D to tender a plea of guilty to s.3 of the Act and, as this was accepted by the prosecutor, the sheriff erred in rejecting it. "Is found not guilty" in s.24(1) did not mean that D had to be tried first. Such an interpretation would be inconsistent with the provisions of s.103 of the 1975 Act in relation to solemn procedure; for summary procedure the words "or any part thereof" in s.336 were understood to include any other offence of which the accused could be convicted under that complaint in terms of s.312, or of s.24 of the 1988 Act. *Held*, further, contrary to D's argument, that by intimating that they were not proceeding to trial when the sheriff refused to record D's plea, the Crown did not depart from their acceptance of D's plea or relinquish their right to proceed further with D's prosecution.

VANNET v. DAVIDSON 1995 S.C.C.R. 792, Judge not specified.

7300. Dangerous driving–causing death–whether imprisonment excessive

Held, that where D, who had held a licence since January 1995 and whose record contained no road traffic offences, received 12 months' imprisonment, disqualification for four years and an order to resit his driving test for causing the death of a passenger, X, a friend and workmate, by driving too fast, going out of control on a bend and colliding head on with a Range Rover, that the custodial sentence was excessive since the charge was restricted to D's driving on the bend and did not refer to a course of dangerous driving, there was no question of D showing off at the time, D himself sustained severe injuries, D felt genuine remorse for what had happened and X's family bore no animosity towards D; and 240 hours' community service substituted.

DAVISON v. HM ADVOCATE 1996 S.C.C.R. 736, Judge not specified.

7301. Dangerous driving–sentence–imprisonment

Held, that three months' imprisonment, disqualification for two years and an order to resit his driving test were not excessive where M, a partner in a garage business, drove at up to 132 mph in a 60 mph zone on the A96 since this was M's second such offence since 1992, it had been less than one year since M's previous disqualification had ended and M had had no regard for his passenger or the general public.

MEARNS v. VANNET 1995 S.C.C.R. 688, Judge not specified.

7302. Disqualification–penalty points–aggregation–offences occurring "on the same occasion"

[Road Traffic Offenders Act 1988 (c.53) s.29(4).]

Held, that where C appealed against the sheriff's decision to aggregate penalty points imposed on C for two road traffic offences, namely, parking on a pelican crossing and failure to provide a breath specimen, C claiming that the offences had arisen out of the same incident *Johnson v. Finbow* [1981] 1 W.L.R. 879, [1983] C.L.Y. 3289, that the appeal would be refused since, though there was an obvious connection, the second offence was wholly separate in that it related to C's refusal to comply with a police request, *Robertson v. McNaughtan* 1993 S.L.T. 1143, [1993] C.L.Y. 5763; *McKeever v. Walkingshaw* 1996 S.C.C.R. 189, [1996] C.L.Y. 7303.

CAMERON v. BROWN 1996 S.C.C.R. 675, Judge not specified.

7303. Disqualification–penalty points–aggregation–offences occurring "on the same occasion"

[Road Traffic Offenders Act 1988 (c.53) s.28.]

Held, that justices correctly imposed aggregate penalty points where the police observed M speeding at 96 mph in a 60 mph limit and, in the course of pursuing him, crossing double white lines, as the offences were of a different nature and were committed at different loci, and under the Road Traffic Offences Act 1988 s.28(4) "on the same occasion" meant during a single incident and not a series of incidents which occurred in an uninterrupted course of driving, *Robertson v. McNaughtan* 1993 S.L.T. 1143, [1993] C.L.Y. 5763 considered.

McKEEVER v. WALKINGSHAW 1996 S.C.C.R. 189, Judge not specified.

7304. Drink or drugs–blood or urine specimen–failure to provide blood specimen–unreliable Camic device

[Road Traffic Act 1988 (c.52) s.7(3)(G).]

An accused person was charged on a summary complaint with failing, without reasonable excuse, to provide a specimen of blood, contrary to the Road Traffic Act 1988 s.7(6). The accused was arrested and taken to a police station, where the Camic device when operated produced a reading of 31 microgrammes and displayed the words "calibration out". The police officers formed the view that the Camic device was unreliable and required the accused to provide a blood specimen, which the accused declined to do. The device had a history of trouble and required to be serviced every two or three months. The police officers made no second attempt to operate the device although they were aware of a standing order which required them to make a further attempt. No other device was available at the police station. The accused was convicted and appealed, arguing that the requirement to provide a blood specimen was illegal because the police were not entitled to consider the device to be unreliable.

Held, that in the light of the history of trouble with the particular device the police officers' opinion that it was not reliable could be regarded as reasonable; and appeal refused.

WIGHAM v. HOWDLE 1996 S.L.T. 1175, Judge not specified, HCJ.

7305. Drink or drugs–breath tests–failure to provide breath specimen–effect of subsequent negative blood test

[Road Traffic Act 1988 (c.52) s.7.]

An accused person was tried on a summary complaint for inter alia a contravention of the Road Traffic Act 1988 s.7(6). On being stopped by the police and asked to take a breath test, the accused had blown down the side of the tube. She was then arrested, taken to the police station, and again blew down the side of the Camic mouthpiece and invalidated the test. The accused stated that she was going to see her doctor about her breathlessness. The police, though doubtful about her explanation, then proceeded to take a blood sample which showed that the proportion of alcohol in her blood sample which showed that the proportion of alcohol in her blood was below the permitted level. The following day when collecting her car the accused voluntarily provided a breath specimen without difficulty. The sheriff rejected a submission of no case to answer and, the accused leading no evidence, convicted her after taking into account the accused's ability on the following day to provide a breath specimen. The accused appealed contending that a blood sample having been taken, the Crown could not rely on the accused's failure to provide a breath specimen.

Held, refusing the appeal, that (1) the Crown were not barred from bringing a prosecution for failing to provide a breath test by having moved on to the blood test procedure; (2) the sheriff was entitled to take into account the accused's conduct on the next day when considering the credibility of her excuse and to conclude that there was no evidence of any valid medical reason for the accused's not blowing into the mouthpiece, *DPP v. Boden* [1988] R.T.R. 188, [1988] C.L.Y. 3092 approved.

LORIMER v. RUSSELL 1996 S.L.T. 501, Judge not specified, HCJ.

7306. Drink or drugs–disqualification–special reasons

[Road Traffic Act 1988 (c.52) s.5; Road Traffic Offenders Act 1988 (c.53) s.34.]

An accused person pleaded guilty to a contravention of the Road Traffic Act 1988 s.5(1) (a) but advanced special reasons in terms of the Road Traffic Offenders Act 1988 s.34(1) for not disqualifying him from driving. The accused was a reformed alcoholic who had not drunk alcohol for four years prior to the offence. On the day of the offence he had attended a golf luncheon where he drank no more than three bottles of non-alcoholic lager which were purchased in rounds with friends. At about 7 pm he began to feel the effects of alcohol and maintained that someone must have bought him ordinary lager which he had drunk unknowingly. A neighbour was babysitting for him and so at 8.15 pm the accused had driven home as he considered himself fit to drive. Only the accused gave evidence as to his consumption of drink. The sheriff, disqualifying the accused, observed that it would be far too easy for anyone to establish special reasons if all he had to do was give evidence not supported by independent evidence. The sheriff also stated that there was insufficient evidence to persuade him that he had heard the whole story, and that he did not fully accept what the accused had said. The accused appealed.

Held, that (1) where corroboration did not exist or was unavailable for some good reason it was still open to the court to hold that special reasons had been established if the accused's evidence were believed; (2) despite some ambiguity it was clear that ultimately the sheriff's conclusion was based on his refusal fully to accept the account given by the accused alone, quite apart from the absence of corroboration; (3) special reasons could be established where an accused's drink had been laced or spiked and where, for some other good reason, the accused was unaware of the amount of alcohol which he had consumed, though the situation would have to be unusual in any particular case and (4) as the clear inference was that the accused, not knowing how much he had consumed, took a risk in driving, special reasons had not been established; and appeal refused.

Observed, that where corroborative material was available, an unexplained failure to lead such evidence might cause the court to pause before deciding to accept an account in support of the establishment of special reasons.

WATSON v. ADAM 1996 S.L.T. 459, Judge not specified, HCJ.

7307. Drink or drugs–driving while unfit through drugs–disqualification

Held, where R was sentenced to 30 days' imprisonment for driving under the influence of drugs (causing two accidents for which he was admonished on charges of careless driving) and disqualified for four years, the disqualification was not excessive since in effect the ban was only for two years as R was currently serving a prison sentence with a release date of January 1998.

RIDDICK v. NORMAND 1996 S.C.C.R. 56, Judge not specified.

7308. Drink or drugs–forfeiture of motor vehicle

Held, that where C, a first offender who would lose his job on the loss of his licence, appealed against an order for forfeiture of his car which was worth £1,500, C also being fined £200 for dangerous driving and £250 and disqualified for one year for drink driving, that the order, though substantial, was not excessive in view of the fact that C had ignored a police warning not to drive, and had sped through six sets of traffic lights causing other road users to take evasive action.

CRAIGIE v. HEYWOOD 1996 S.C.C.R. 654, Judge not specified.

7309. Drivers' records–failure to keep–"refuse collection and disposal"

[Council Regulation 3820/85 Art.4(6); Council Regulation 3821/85.]

The Crown appealed against a sheriff's decision finding S not guilty of failing to use a tachograph. S had been driving a van carrying two 25 litre drums containing waste vegetable oil collected from around Scotland and being taken for recycling. At trial, S produced a letter from a district council showing that his services were known to and approved by the local authority, but not under their control. The sheriff concluded that S was entitled to the benefit of the exception in Art.4(6) of Regulation 3821/85 as his vehicle was being used in connection with refuse collection and disposal and was engaged in the provision of general services performed in the public interest, *Licensing Authority South Eastern Traffic Area v. British Gas (C116/91)* [1992] 3 C.M.L.R. 65, [1992] C.L.Y. 4864, *Nicholls v. Carmichael* 1993 S.C.C.R. 991, [1994] C.L.Y. 6233. The Crown argued under reference to the recent decisions of *Mrozek & Jager (C335/94)* and *Pierre Goupil (C39/95)* that the exception under Art.4(6) only included refuse collection and disposal vehicles used for the transportation over short distances of any waste which was not subject to more specific rules, within the context of a general service in the public interest provided directly by public authorities or by private undertakings under their control.

Held, appeal allowed and case remitted to the sheriff, that in light of the recent decisions, the activities which S carried on did not have the benefit of the exception provided by Art.4(6) since the waste oil was not transported over a short distance, but was conducted on a commercial basis over a wide area, and the service was not provided under public authority control.

REITH v. SKINNER 1996 S.C.C.R. 506, Judge not specified.

7310. Driving while disqualified–forfeiture of motor vehicle

[Criminal Procedure (Scotland) Act 1975 (c.21) s.436(1).]

Held, on D's application to the nobile officium to have quashed a forfeiture order in respect of her car imposed on her husband, H, for driving it while disqualified, D averring that the car had been registered in her name after H was disqualified, she had paid for it in good faith and it was excessive to order its forfeiture, that the petition would be refused since there were no averments that D took any steps to prevent H using the car or to ensure that he could not use it while disqualified, and this was not a special case such as *Lloyds & Scottish Finance Ltd v. HM Advocate* 1974 S.L.T. 3, [1973] C.L.Y. 3600, where the court would be entitled to interfere to prevent an injustice.

DONALD, PETITIONER 1996 S.C.C.R. 68, Judge not specified.

7311. Lighting–emergency lamp–whether "fitted" to vehicle

[Road Vehicles Lighting Regulations 1989 (SI 1989 1796) Reg.16.]

The Road Vehicles Lighting Regulations 1989 provide in Reg.16 that no vehicle other than an emergency vehicle should be fitted with a blue warning lamp or similar device whether in working order or not. B was stopped by the police who noticed a blue lamp on the car's rear parcel shelf. The lamp was not plugged in but was in working order and was similar to the type of lamp used in unmarked police cars. B was convicted of a breach of Reg.16. He appealed on the grounds that as the lamp was not plugged in and could not therefore function, it could not be "fitted" within the terms of the Regulations.

Held, appeal refused, that in interpreting Reg.16 the word "fitted" meant simply "equipped with", and an unauthorised car need only be equipped with a blue warning light or similar device to contravene the prohibition against fitting contained in the Regulations.

BROWN v. McGLENNAN 1995 S.C.C.R. 724, Lord Ross, L.J.C., HCJ.

7312. Road traffic regulations–order restricting access to Royal Mile during specified times–vehicles over certain weight–effect on loading and unloading–requirement for public hearing where objection outstanding

[Road Traffic Regulation Act 1984 (c.27); Local Roads Authorities Traffic Orders (Procedure) (Scotland) Regulations 1987 (SI 1987 2245) Reg.7.]

LRC made an order under the Road Traffic Regulation Act 1984 restricting the hours of access to and waiting in the Royal Mile in Edinburgh of vehicles over a certain weight. The procedures followed were those under the Local Roads Authorities Traffic Orders (Procedure) (Scotland) Regulations 1987. FTA had lodged an objection to the order, contending that its effect would be to prohibit loading and unloading of vehicles between the times stated and that L should have held a public inquiry to consider the objection. This objection remained outstanding and FTA appealed to the Court of Session against the order.

Held, allowing the appeal and quashing the order, that the order would clearly have the effect of preventing loading and unloading between certain specified times even though it contained no specific reference to the matter of loading. It therefore came within Reg.7(1)(a)(i) of the 1987 Regulations and a public hearing was required where an objection was made and not withdrawn.

FREIGHT TRANSPORT ASSOCIATION LTD v. LOTHIAN RC 1996 S.L.T. 666, Lord Kirkwood, IH.

7313. Scottish Borders Council (Jim Clark Memorial Rally) Order Confirmation Act 1996 (c.xii)

The Act confirms the Provisional Order set out in the Schedule which authorises the Jim Clark Memorial Rally to take place on certain public roads.

This Act received Royal Assent on December 18, 1996.

7314. Speeding–proof–nature of road–motorway

[Criminal Procedure (Scotland) Act 1975 (c.21) s.312; Motorways Traffic (Speed Limit) Regulations 1974 (SI 1974 502) Reg.3; Road Traffic Regulation Act 1984 (c.27) s.17; Special Roads (Notice of Opening) (Scotland) Regulations 1964 (SI 1964 1003).]

The Criminal Procedure (Scotland) Act 1975 s.312(q) provides, inter alia, that the statement in a complaint that an act was done contrary to a statute or order shall imply a statement that the statute or order applied to the circumstances existing at the time and place of the offence, and that the order was duly made, confirmed, published and generally made effectual according to the law applicable. Section 454(1) provides, inter alia, that no conviction, where the accused had legal assistance in his defence, shall be set aside in respect of any objections to the competency or admission of evidence at the trial in the inferior court, unless such objections have been timeously stated at the trial. An accused person was charged on summary complaint with speeding contrary to the Motorways Traffic (Speed Limit) Regulations 1974 Reg.3 and the Road Traffic Regulation Act 1984 s.17. The accused was represented by a solicitor. Two police officers gave evidence that the part of the road on which the driving took place was a motorway and referred to it as the M9 although the Crown did not produce a notice published under the Special Roads (Notice of Opening) (Scotland) Regulations 1964. The accused's solicitor did not object to the competency or admissibility of the police officers' evidence and did not challenge it in cross examination. At the close of the Crown case it was submitted that there was no case to answer because it had not been proved that the road was a motorway within the meaning of the Motorway Traffic (Scotland) Regulations 1964 by production of the notice. The justices repelled the submission and no evidence being led for the defence, convicted the accused who appealed. Before the High Court the Crown argued that s.312(q) made it unnecessary to prove publication of the notice and that as no timeous objection had been taken to the police officers' evidence, it was competently before the justices.

Held, that (1) s.312(q) related only to the form of the complaint and did not affect the proof of any order; (2) there was no obligation on the accused's solicitor to challenge at the trial the competency or admissibility of the police officers' evidence but (3) there was sufficient evidence because the police officers' evidence was unchallenged and became evidence in causa upon which the justices were entitled to rely and, in any event, (a) the justices were entitled to hold it to be within judicial knowledge that the prefix M denoted a motorway and (b) the principle omnia rite acta praesumuntur applied and was not rebutted in evidence; and appeal refused.

DONALDSON v. VALENTINE 1996 S.L.T. 643, Judge not specified, HCJ.

7315. Traffic signs–failure to comply with–sufficiency of evidence

[Road Traffic Act 1988 (c.52) s.36.]

Section 36(3) of the Road Traffic Act 1988 provides, inter alia, that a traffic sign placed on or near a road shall be deemed to be of the prescribed size, colour and type, or of another character authorised by the Secretary of State. An accused person was tried on summary complaint with, inter alia, failing to stop at a red light. The Crown led two police officers who stated that the accused failed to comply with red flashing lights situated on the gantry above the lane in which the accused was driving. At the close of the Crown case it was submitted that there was no case for the accused to answer because it had not been proved that the traffic sign was of the size, colour and type libelled in the complaint. The justice repelled the submission and the accused, who gave evidence, was convicted. The accused appealed and when the application for a stated case was made the Crown intimated that it would not oppose the appeal. The justice did not however narrate the Crown and defence evidence in the stated case.

Held, that (1) notwithstanding the Crown's concession, it was the court's responsibility to decide whether or not the submission had been wrongly repelled; (2) there was no necessity to have a narrative of the Crown evidence in this case as it was sufficiently clear that the findings were based on the two police officers' evidence; (3) the complete answer was found in s.36(3) and it was not necessary for the Crown to lead such evidence as that was a matter which required to be addressed in the defence evidence if the accused wished to show that the sign was not of the prescribed type and appeal refused, *Wingate v. McGlennan* 1992 S.L.T. 837, [1991] C.L.Y. 4674 distinguished.

SPIERS v. NORMAND 1996 S.L.T. 78, Judge not specified, HCJ.

7316. Vehicle excise–using vehicle without excise licence

[Vehicle Excise and Registration Act 1994 (c.22) s.29, s.30.]

P appealed against an order to pay back duty of £54.17 for using an unlicensed vehicle in breach of the Vehicle Excise and Registration Act 1994 s.29. The notice of penalties stated that in addition to any penalty which could be imposed under s.29 of the Act, the sum of £54.17 should be imposed against P as keeper of the vehicle in terms of s.30; and following a proof which was held to determine whether P was the keeper of the car, P was admonished and ordered to pay back duty. P argued that it was incompetent for the Crown to endeavour to levy a penalty against her in terms of s.30 as she had not been charged with keeping a vehicle. The Crown submitted that they were entitled to proceed to proof to determine whether P was the keeper of the car since the matter was raised in the notice of penalties. Section 29 constituted the offence and s.30 dealt with the matter of penalties.

Held, quashing the sentence insofar as it related to the payment of back duty, that if the Crown wished to establish as a matter of fact, for the purposes of penalty and for the purpose of obtaining back duty, that P was the keeper as well as the user of the vehicle, then the complaint should have so charged P and they should not have relied on the obscurity of the notice of penalties. It was incompetent to hold a proof to decide whether P was the keeper of the car.

PEACOCK v. HAMILTON 1996 S.L.T. 777, Judge not specified, HCJ.

7317. Articles

Conversion on the road to Auchtermuchty: extrapolating from blood and breath alcohol tests *(J.K. Mason)*: S.L.T. 1996, 4, 33-38 . (Legal issues in calculating blood and breath alcohol readings back to time of incident and of converting from one method of analysis to another).

SALE OF GOODS

7318. Conditions and warranties–implied term of fitness–abnormal feature in circumstances of use of goods by buyer–abnormal feature not made known to seller

[Sale of Goods Act 1979 (c.54) s.14(3).]

Section 14(3) of the Sale of Goods Act 1979, prior to amendment, provided that when goods are sold in the course of a business and the buyer makes known to the seller the purpose for which the goods are being bought, there is an implied term in the contract that the goods "are reasonably fit for that purpose, whether or not that is a purpose for which such goods are commonly supplied, except where the circumstances show that the buyer does not rely, or that it is unreasonable for him to rely, on the skill or judgment or the seller". In 1985 the owners of a fishing vessel arranged for the length of the vessel to be increased and the engine to be uprated. Thereafter the main engine bearings failed. The owners called in a company who were dealers in marine engines. The dealers advised that the camshaft should be replaced. In May 1986 they supplied a new type of camshaft and undertook the work of replacement. The replacement was not a success. In June 1986 the dealers supplied and fitted a second camshaft. Again there were problems, and in November 1986 the dealers supplied and fitted a third camshaft. The problems persisted and in 1987 the owners gave up and sold the engine. They raised an action against the dealers seeking damages for breach of the condition implied by s.14(3) of the 1979 Act. The dealers counterclaimed for payment in respect of goods and services supplied by them to the owners. After proof, the Lord Ordinary held that the cause of the failure of the camshafts was excessive torsional resonance excited by some cause external to the engine and the camshafts themselves. He concluded therefore that the damage observed in the camshafts from time to time was not due to their unfitness to fulfil the purpose, but was the consequence of external factors. He assoilzied the dealers and pronounced decree for payment in the counterclaim. An appeal by the owners to the Inner House was unsuccessful, and they then appealed to the House of Lords, arguing that under s.14(3) a seller who undertook to supply equipment suitable for use in a particular vessel took the risk that performance of the goods might be adversely affected by an unanticipated and unusual feature of the vessel.

Held, that (1) where a buyer purchased goods from a seller who dealt in goods of that description there was no breach of the implied condition of fitness where the failure of the goods to meet the intended purpose arose from an abnormal feature or idiosyncrasy, not made known to the seller, in the buyer or in the circumstances of the use by the buyer, whether or not the buyer himself was aware of that feature and (2) the particular purpose for which the camshafts were required was that of being fitted in the engine of a vessel which suffered from a particular abnormality or idiosyncrasy, namely a tendency to create excessive torsional resonance in camshafts, and the dealers, not having been aware of that tendency, were not in a position to exercise skill and judgment for the purpose of dealing with it, nor were they in a position to make

up their minds whether or not to accept the burden of the implied condition; and appeal dismissed *Griffiths v. Peter Conway* [1939] 1 All E.R. 685 approved.
SLATER v. FINNING LTD [1996] 3 W.L.R. 191, Lord Keith of Kinkel, HL.

7319. Conditions and warranties–implied terms of fitness and merchantable quality–effect of express term

[Sale of Goods Act 1979 (c.54) s.14.]

The Sale of Goods Act 1979, prior to amendment, provided in s.14(2) that where a seller sold goods in the course of a business there was an implied condition that the goods supplied were of merchantable quality. Section 14(3) provided that where the seller sold goods in the course of a business and the buyer, expressly or by implication made known to the seller any particular purpose for which the goods were being bought, there was an implied condition that the goods supplied were reasonably fit for that purpose, except where the circumstances showed that the buyer did not rely on the skill and judgment of the seller. Section 55(2) provided that an express condition or warranty did not negative a condition or warranty implied by the Act unless inconsistent with it. A water authority invited tenders for the supply of pipes which were required in connection with the laying of a trunk water main, specifying that the pipes had to conform to the British standard for unplasticised pipes for cold water services. A tender was accepted from a company which manufactured and supplied the pipes. After the trunk main was brought into service there were a number of failures, which the authority averred were attributable to latent defects in the pipes which made them vulnerable to cracking and which arose as a result of inadequate quality control during the manufacture of the pipes. The authority sought damages from the suppliers, alleging that the pipes were not of merchantable quality and that they were not fit for the purpose of use as unplasticised pipes for cold water services to be used underground. At debate the defenders sought dismissal arguing that by stipulating for compliance with a specified British standard, the pursuers had taken upon themselves the responsibility for selecting the standard for the pipes as suitable for their purpose and so had negatived any implied warranty as to both fitness for purpose and as to quality.

Held, that (1) reference in a contract to a specified standard might still leave other matters not covered in the standard to the warranties implied by the 1979 Act, and, as the pleadings did not disclose what matters the specified British standard covered, this matter could not be decided without proof and (2) s.14(3) placed the burden of showing that there had been no reliance on the supplier, or that the reliance was unreasonable, on the party seeking to establish the exception, and accordingly it was for the defenders to show both that the pipes complied with the specified British standard and that the requirements of the standard were such as to negative the stipulations arising from the implied warranties either as being inconsistent with them or because they would cover all matters which would otherwise be implied by the warranties; and proof before answer allowed, reserving the defenders' pleas to the relevancy and specification.

CENTRAL RC v. UPONOR LTD 1996 S.L.T. 645, Judge not specified, OH.

7320. Trade descriptions–course of trade or business

[Trade Descriptions Act 1968 (c.29) s.1.]

Held, on E's appeal against conviction for offering to supply, in the course of a trade or business, goods to which a false trade description applied regarding the manufacturer, on the grounds that it had not been established that what had taken place had been in the course of a trade or business or that the goods were to be supplied, that the appeal would be refused since a degree of regularity was not always required to establish the existence of a trade and a one off adventure carried out with a view to profit was sufficient, *Davies v. Sumner* [1984] 3 All E.R. 831, [1984] C.L.Y. 3100; E's explanation that he was storing 300 bottles of counterfeit perfume for one G had not been found credible, and in any event the number of bottles involved surely inferred that G was engaged in a trade or business and as such E, who would have been acting in relation to that trade, would still be liable under the Trade Descriptions Act 1968 s.1 (1). *Held*, further, that E's fine of £2,000 with no time to pay was not excessive since sums of money found in E's house could be used, and in fact were used to repay the sum, despite claims by E that this money belonged to third parties who would seek to recover it.

ELDER v. CROWE 1996 S.C.C.R. 38, Judge not specified.

SHERIFF COURT PRACTICE

7321. Acts of Sederunt–copyright designs and patents

ACT OF SEDERUNT (COPYRIGHT, DESIGNS AND PATENTS) (AMENDMENT) 1996, SI 1996 238 (S.18); made under the Sheriff Courts (Scotland) Act 1971 s.32; and the Olympics Association Right (Infringement Proceedings) Regulations 1995 Reg.5. In force: March 1, 1996; £1.10.

This Act of Sederunt amends the Act of Sederunt (Copyright, Designs and Patents) 1990 (SI 1990 380) by making provision for the procedure for an application under the Olympics Association Right (Infringement Proceedings) Regulations 1995 Reg.3 and Reg.5.

7322. Acts of Sederunt–diligence–summary procedure

ACT OF SEDERUNT (PROCEEDINGS IN THE SHERIFF COURT UNDER THE DEBTORS (SCOTLAND) ACT 1987) (AMENDMENT) 1996, SI 1996 2709 (S.211); made under the Local Government (Scotland) Act 1947 s.247; the Taxes Management Act 1970 s.63; the Sheriff Courts (Scotland) Act 1971 s.32; the Car Tax Act 1983 Sch.1 para.3; the Abolition of Domestic Rates Etc. (Scotland) Act 1987 Sch.2 para.7; the Local Government Finance Act 1992 Sch.8 para.2; the Finance Act 1994 Sch.7 para.7; the Value Added Tax 1994 Sch.11 para 5; the Local Government etc. (Scotland) Act 1994 Sch.10 para.2; and the Finance Act 1996 Sch.5 para.13. In force: November 11, 1996; £1.55.

This Act of Sederunt amends the Act of Sederunt (Proceedings in the Sheriff Court under the Debtors (Scotland) Act 1988 (SI 1988 2013) to make general provision for enforcement action for non-payment of monies by summary warrant procedure rather than separate provision dependent on the legislative basis of such recovery, as at present.

7323. Acts of Sederunt–documents–authentication of documents

ACT OF SEDERUNT (REQUIREMENTS OF WRITING) 1996, SI 1996 1534 (S.136); made under the Sheriff Courts (Scotland) Act 1971 s.32. In force: July 1, 1996; £1.55.

Makes provision for the procedure to be followed in respect of applications under the Requirements of Writing (Scotland) Act 1995 to the court for authentication of documents which do not attract the statutory presumptions about subscriptions of a deed.

7324. Acts of Sederunt–family proceedings

ACT OF SEDERUNT (FAMILY PROCEEDINGS IN THE SHERIFF COURT) 1996, SI 1996 2167 (S.174); made under the Sheriff Courts (Scotland) Act 1971 s.32; and the Children (Scotland) Act 1995 s.91. In force: November 1, 1996; £4.15.

This Act of Sederunt amends the Ordinary Cause Rules 1993 and the Judicial Factors Rules of the Sheriff Court in relation to, and makes provision for, proceedings under Part I of the Children (Scotland) Act 1995 (c.36). Part I of the Act makes new provision for parental responsibilities and parental rights, guardianship, the administration of a child's property and court orders with respect to these matters.

7325. Acts of Sederunt–Ordinary Cause Rules

ACT OF SEDERUNT (SHERIFF COURT ORDINARY CAUSE RULES AMENDMENT) (MISCELLANEOUS) 1996, SI 1996 2445 (S.190); made under the Sheriff Courts (Scotland) Extracts Act 1892 s.13; the Sheriff Courts (Scotland) Act 1971 s.32; and the Administration of Justice (Scotland) Act 1972 s.1. In force: November 1, 1996; £4.15.

This Act of Sederunt amends the Ordinary Cause Rules in the Sheriff Court by amending provisions relating to standard procedure in defended cases, interlocutors, applications by minute, procedures for motions, counterclaims, hearing parts of proof separately, appeals and family actions.

7326. Acts of Sederunt–Ordinary Cause Rules

ACT OF SEDERUNT (SHERIFF COURT ORDINARY CAUSE RULES AMENDMENT) (MISCELLANEOUS) (AMENDMENT) 1996, SI 1996 2586 (S.202); made under the Sheriff Courts (Scotland) Act 1971 s.32. In force: October 31, 1996; £0.65.

This Act of Sederunt revokes the Act of Sederunt (Sheriff Court Ordinary Cause Rules Amendment) (Miscellaneous) 1996 (SI 1996 2445) para.2 which provided that nothing in that Act of Sederunt was to affect any cause commenced before November 1, 1996. In consequence, the provisions of the 1996 Act will now apply equally to causes commenced before that date.

7327. Appeals–appeal to sheriff court–abuse of process–public house licence

Held, in an action of damages where it was claimed that an objector had appealed against the grant of a public house licence without justification but for commercial gain, that the principles of abuse of process were applicable to a statutory right of appeal; and proof before answer allowed.

ASHEDEN v. AMBER ENTERTAINMENTS 1996 S.C.L.R. 520, Judge not specified, Sh Ct.

7328. Appeals–appeal to sheriff principal–appeal marked late after decree extracted–competency–effect of error in extract

[Sheriff Courts (Scotland) Act 1907 (c.51) Sch. r.59.]

At a diet of proof in an action, the defenders' agent, after a motion to discharge the proof had been refused, advised the court that he no longer acted and was allowed to withdraw. The sheriff granted decree by default. An extract subsequently issued wrongly designed the defenders as "Scotia International TV/Aeroskip Sports Ltd". The defenders enrolled a motion seeking permission to appeal against the interlocutor, though late, arguing that the extract was not a bar to an appeal because (1) it was not an extract in respect of the true defenders, and (2) the defenders had not failed to appear or be represented at the diet of proof in terms of ordinary cause r.59 and the sheriff had therefore not been entitled to grant decree by default.

Held, that (1) the defenders were not represented at the proof diet, the brief appearance by a solicitor on their behalf being no more than an attempt to have the diet discharged and a courtesy to the court before the withdrawal from acting was intimated; (2) an error in the naming of a party in an extract decree was not fatal to the extract provided that the decree was granted as between the true parties and that the issuing of the extract took place at the appropriate time and in the correct form; and motion refused, *K-X Rentals v. Joyce* 1992 S.L.T. (Sh.Ct) 42, [1992] C.L.Y. 6417 and *Alloa Brewery Co v. Parker* 1991 S.C.L.R. 70, [1991] C.L.Y. 5629 followed.

NORTECH v. AEROSKIP SPORTS 1996 S.L.T. (Sh.Ct) 94, Judge not specified, Sh Ct.

7329. Appeals–appeal to sheriff principal–competency–proceedings for breach of interdict

[Sheriff Courts (Scotland) Act 1907 (c.51) s.3(d), s.27.]

An action for breach of interdict was raised on September 27, 1994. On April 13, 1995, the sheriff repelled a plea by the defenders that the action was time barred and assigned a diet for debate. The interlocutor was not a final judgment within the meaning of the Sheriff Courts (Scotland) Act 1907 s.27 and was not one which could be appealed without leave. Leave to appeal having been refused by the sheriff, the defenders appealed without leave to the sheriff principal who refused the appeal. The sheriff principal was not asked for leave to appeal to the Court of Session, but the defenders took such an appeal. As a result of the decision in *Forbes v. Forbes* 1994 S.L.T. 16, [1993] C.L.Y. 5803, where it was held that proceedings taken by initial writ for breach of interdict were proceedings sui generis and not "civil proceedings" for the purposes of s.3 of the 1907 Act, a question arose as to whether the present proceedings were governed by the provisions of the 1907 Act, in which case an appeal, without leave against a judgment which was not a final interlocutor would be incompetent.

Held, that (1) while *Forbes v. Forbes* was correct in stating that proceedings for contempt of court were always regarded as sui generis, it was not correct to say that proceedings taken by way of initial writ for breach of interdict were not civil proceedings within the meaning of s.3 of the 1907 Act, and the section was wide enough to include such proceedings and (2) the sheriff was wrong to regard the proceedings as sui generis which were not subject to any of the rules provided for by the Act; and appeal allowed to the extent of remitting the case to the sheriff to consider of new the defenders' plea of time-bar, *Forbes v. Forbes* commented on.

MACIVER v. MACIVER 1996 S.L.T. 733, Judge not specified, IH.

7330. Appeals–appeal to sheriff principal–late marking of appeal–dispensing power

[Act of Sederunt (Ordinary Cause Rules) 1993 (SI 1993 1956) r.2.1(1) and r.31.2(2).]

An arrestment on the dependence of an action was recalled by the sheriff. The interlocutor granted leave to appeal and allowed the arrestment to remain in force meantime, but restricted to the sum sued for. An appeal was not marked within the seven days provided for in r.31.2(2) of the Ordinary Cause Rules 1993, there being a delay of some five weeks due to confusion as to which agent was to mark the appeal which delay was not discovered until one of the agents returned from holiday. The pursuers invited the court to exercise its discretionary powers under r.2.1(1) and allow the appeal to be marked, though late. The defenders opposed the motion and contended that the limited arrestment allowed by the sheriff was no longer effective, the days for marking an appeal having by then expired.

Held, that (1) the misunderstanding between agents not being a grave failure in professional duty and the delay being neither excessive nor inexcusable, the discretion to excuse the delay should be exercised in favour of the pursuers; and (2) where an arrestment had been kept in force pending the outcome of an appeal for which leave had been granted and an appeal was not marked, the appropriate remedy was to return to court to have the arrestment revoked; and motion granted.

CRENDON TIMBER ENGINEERING LTD v. MILLER CONSTRUCTION LTD 1996 S.L.T. (Sh.Ct.) 102, Judge not specified, Sh Ct.

7331. Appeals–appeal to sheriff principal–leave to appeal–failure to seek timeously–dispensing power of sheriff

Held, that it was a competent and appropriate use of the dispensing power of the sheriff to allow an application for leave to appeal to the sheriff principal to be made out of time, and case remitted to the sheriff to consider whether leave to appeal should be granted.

THOMPSON v. LYNN 1995 S.C.L.R. 1090, Judge not specified, Sh Ct.

7332. Appeals–appeal to sheriff principal–leave to appeal out of time–decree extracted

[Sheriff Courts (Scotland) Act 1907 (c.51), Sch.r.90.]

G sought leave from the sheriff principal to be allowed to appeal against a final interlocutor in an action against M in which M counterclaimed. After proof, decree in the counterclaim had been granted against G and M had been assoilzied. A subsequent hearing took place on expenses and the matter was again taken to avizandum but two days later a finding against G was issued. Neither G nor M were notified of the decision and the sheriff clerk issued an extract decree, without any prompting, 17 days later. The time limit for appeal had expired and M argued that extract precluded any appeal, *Alloa Brewery Co v. Parker* 1991 S.C.L.R. 70, [1991] C.L.Y. 5629.

Held, motion granted. Neither G nor M had applied for an extract, which had been wrongly issued and was therefore capable of being recalled to allow an appeal *Anderson Brown & Co v. Morris* 1987 S.L.T. (Sh.Ct) 96, [1987] C.L.Y. 5078. The terms of the pre-1993 Rules (r.90) indicated that extract would be issued only on application. The motion succeeded on its merits.

GAUNT v. MARCO'S LEISURE 1995 S.C.L.R. 966, Judge not specified, Sh Ct.

7333. Appeals–appeal to sheriff principal–without leave–competency

Held, in an action of divorce which was proceeding as undefended following upon the defender's failure to appear at a peremptory diet, that the sheriff had no power ex proprio motu to make an award of interim access, that the interlocutor in terms of which he purported to do so was incompetent and that the sheriff principal had power at common law to uphold an appeal without leave against it.

GRAY v. GRAY 1996 S.C.L.R. 531, Judge not specified, Sh Ct.

7334. Appeals–reponing–decree in absence–reason for failure to defend

[Act of Sederunt (Ordinary Cause Rules) 1993 (SI 1993 1956) r.8.1.]

Held, where the sheriff had found neither the proposed defence nor the explanation for failure to enter appearance timeously to the acceptable and had refused a defender's reponing note against a decree in absence for payment, thus the sheriff's refusal had been proper exercise of his discretion and that it was not appropriate at appeal to have regard to material which had not been before the sheriff; and amended reporting note rejected and appeal refused.

RATTY v. HUGHES 1996 S.C.L.R. 160, Judge not specified, Sh Ct.

7335. Counterclaim–effective date of–whether judicial notice necessary

[Sheriff Courts (Scotland) Act 1907 (c.51) Sch. r.51; Prescription and Limitation (Scotland) Act 1973 (c.52) s.4(2), s.6(1), s.11 (3), Sch.2 para1.]

S, a firm of solicitors, sued C for payment of outstanding professional fees. S had carried out work throughout the 1980s. S raised the action in early 1991. By a counterclaim, lodged in process in June 1994, C sought damages and averred that S were in breach of contract for which C pled set off. Although the counterclaim was intimated to S at that time, no further steps were taken until April 1995 when S enrolled and were granted a motion to allow answers to C's counterclaim. In September 1995 S sought dismissal of C's claim arguing it had prescribed. The sheriff subsequently dismissed the counterclaim, finding that (1) the last possible date that S owed C any possible obligation was June 1989, when S sent C a detailed accounting after C had complained to the Law Society, and no judicial notice of the counterclaim had been taken until S's motion in April 1995; (2) in any event the prescriptive period had started before June 1989 even allowing for the leeway allowed by s.11 (3) of the 1973 Act. On appeal, C argued that (1) the sheriff had misunderstood the effect of ordinary cause r.51 in that the rules for lodging a counterclaim were not the same as for amendment procedure: the lodging of the counterclaim and intimation thereof was sufficient to render the counterclaim an effective step in process and thus a relevant claim (s.9(1) (a), 1973 Act); (2) S had charged a continuous account from 1983 to 1988, therefore the relevant date was when that course of action came to an end (Sch.2, para.1 to the 1973 Act). The date of S's final accounting was the relevant date; (3) in terms of s.11 (3) the determination of the date when the loss, injury or damage caused by S's actions occurred was subject to C being aware that C had a claim *Dunlop v. McGowans* 1980 S.L.T. 129, [1980] C.L.Y. 3479; *Greater Glasgow Health Board v. Baxter Clark & Paul* 1992 S.L.T. 35, [1992] C.L.Y. 6209; *Glasper v. Rodger* 1996 S.L.T. 44, [1996] 1 C.L. 716, which also occurred at the time of the final accounting after the Law Society complaint.

Held, refusing the appeal, that (1) for the claim to have been made timeously it was necessary that it be made in appropriate proceedings and that it should be brought to the attention of the other party. On this ground C would have been successful as C had satisfied r.51; (2) however, the sheriff was correct on the second point. C had misunderstood para.1 of Sch.2 in that it related to prescription of rights to payment in respect of services rendered and not to breach of contract and (3) it was impossible to conclude that C was not aware before June 1989 of any loss suffered and negligence committed, where C founded, inter alia, on alleged failures in advice in 1983 and the obtaining of a decree against her in 1986. If acting with reasonable diligence C would have been put on notice long before then. Opinion reserved, whether the ruling on the effect of r.51 would apply also to the comparable r.19.1 of the 1993 Rules, which was expressed in different terms.

BEVERIDGE & KELLAS WS v. ABERCROMBY 1996 S.C.L.R. 177, CGB Nicholson Q.C., Sh Ct.

7336. Decree–recall–summary cause

[Act of Sederunt (Summary Cause Rules, Sheriff Court) 1976 (SI 1976 476) r.18.]

B, the defender in a summary cause action by L, sought recall of a decree granted at a hearing at which B had been present but unrepresented. L argued that r.8(6) applied only where the defender did not appear and was not represented.

Held, minute for recall granted, that r.18(6) provided for two situations, (1) where the defender was not present or represented and (2) where the court was satisfied that the defender did not intend to defend, whether or not (1) applied *City of Edinburgh DC v. MacPhail* (Unreported), followed. There was a previous history of payment arrangements which had broken down and the sheriff had clearly been satisfied that B did not intend to defend.

LINTHOUSE HOUSING ASSOCIATION v. BARCLAY [1995] S.T.C. 93, Judge not specified, Sh Ct.

7337. Diligence–arrestment–on dependence–recall

D sought recall of an additional arrestment on the dependence laid by P, an arrestment on the dependence when the action was raised some two years earlier having been restricted to the sum of £25,000, after which the action was sisted for arbitration. (1) D claimed that the continued use of arrestments was nimious or oppressive, the total sum of £50,000 was disproportionate to the amount being sued for and, though the initial writ craved £50,000, the averments were insufficient to justify the additional sums being arrested, *Gebruder Van Uden v. Burrell* 1914 1 S.L.T. 411. P claimed that a great deal had occurred since the original writ and the claim for arbitration which had now been lodged clearly justified the total sum arrested, the amount claimed being about £40,000 with expenses of around £10,000 and (2) D further argued that the arrestments were invalid as they had been laid while the case was sisted for arbitration. P accepted that although no step could be taken in the process while the action was sisted, there was nothing to stop P laying on arrestments in terms of a warrant already granted.

Held, refusing the motion for recall and restricting the additional arrestment to £25,000, that (1) the sheriff was bound to take account of the arbitration proceedings or any other relevant matter which came to his attention in the course of hearing the case, *Van Uden v. Burrell* supported P's position. In the present case there was a detailed claim in the arbitration process and a great deal of proceedings had taken place, the expenses of which amounted to about £10,000. Given the nature of the claim and the fact that a seven day proof had been fixed, it was appropriate that the pursuers should have security amounting to around £50,000; (2) the additional arrestment was not invalid as a sist of process did not prevent a party laying on arrestments on the dependence of an action, the effect of a sist being to stop further conduct of the proceedings, ie. in the process, until a certain date, event or court order, (Macphail, Sheriff Court Practice, para.13-74). Arrestment on the dependence was not a step in the process.

ROBERT TAYLOR & PARTNERS (EDINBURGH) LTD v. WILLIAM GERARD LTD 1995 S.C.L.R. 1131, Judge not specified, Sh Ct.

7338. Diligence–earnings arrestment–wrong address of employee–employers' duties

[Debtors (Scotland) Act 1987 (c.15) s.57.]

A company, C, attempted to serve an earnings arrestment schedule on employers, S, in respect of one of their employees, D. S employed someone of the same name, but the schedule stated an address for D which did not match the address held by S. S returned the schedule to the sheriff officers with a not: "Not employed by [S]". A further two identical schedules were sent to S. S returned the schedules with the reply that they had no employee who lived at the address stated on the schedule. C's solicitors then telephoned S advising them of D's date of birth. S confirmed that it was that of their employee. S then received a further earnings arrestment schedule in identical terms, but containing an employee wages reference number identical to D's. S then gave effect to the arrestment. D left their employment less than a month later. C made an application for S to be made liable in terms of the Debtors (Scotland) Act 1987 s.57 (1) (a) for the sums that would have been paid if they had complied with the earlier arrestments. C argued that the Act imposed strict liability on an employer and did not provide him with any defence of due diligence. Section 69 allowed employers a period of seven days in which to make any necessary inquiries, and S had not done enough to ascertain whether the person on the schedule was their employee. S replied that it was for the creditor to design the debtor correctly. It would be a serious error to operate an arrestment against the wrong person. S had around three or four earnings arrestments served on them every week and they operated around 50 earnings arrestments. S had failed to ask D whether he was the person referred to in the schedules because it was their view that if he was not the same person, then their inquiry would involve disclosing to him the private affairs of another person. In returning the schedules, S acted promptly and appropriately, while C had continued to serve arrestments in identical terms after periods of delay. The provisions of the Act implied that the debtor had to be accurately identified in the schedule.

Held, refusing the application, that S did not fail to comply with the arrestments. As an employer, they were entitled to expect to find in the earnings arrestment schedule a description of the debtor which was sufficient to enable them to know whose earnings were to be arrested. The seven day period referred to in s.69 did not impose upon an employer a duty to make inquiries, but rather allowed employers a period after service in order to make the necessary administrative arrangements for processing the arrestment order. Even if C were correct to argue that an employer might by under a duty to make inquiries in cases of doubt, there was nothing in the circumstances of the present case which might have imposed such a duty on S.

CLYDESDALE BANK v. SCOTTISH MIDLAND COOPERATIVE SOCIETY 1995 S.C.L.R. 1151, Judge not specified, Sh Ct.

7339. Diligence–poinding–household goods of separated married couple–whether common property

[Family Law (Scotland) Act 1985 (c.37) s.25; Debtors (Scotland) Act 1987 (c.15) s.41.]

W, the wife of H, applied for recall of a poinding carried out by B on furniture formerly in the matrimonial home in respect of debts owed by H. W and H had separated, the matrimonial home had been repossessed and W had obtained the tenancy of another house, at which time W claimed H had told her to take all the furniture. W and H had then been reconciled but subsequently separated "for good". The sheriff officers treated the furniture as common property. W argued that a poinding could be held only in respect of goods in the debtor's own possession; that the tenancy was in W's sole name and the assumption in s.19(2) of the 1987 Act could not apply; that s.25 of the 1985 Act gave rise to a presumption only that each had an equal share in the goods and that ownership was joint rather than common; and that s.41 of the 1987 Act, articles owned in common by debtor and third party, applied only to property which was clearly matrimonial, owned in common by both parties and in possession of both parties. The application was refused. Section 25 related simply to parties to a marriage and did not require that they be living together. Its effect was to give rise to a rebuttable presumption that the parties had equal shares in household goods and that the goods were held in common ownership and not joint: (Gloag and Henderson (9th ed.), para. 40.13). The goods were then poindable in terms of s.41 of the 1987 Act. There was clearly civil possession by H where there was possession by W with presumed common ownership by them in the property. W appealed the sheriff's decision, arguing that s.25(1) of the 1985 Act regulated only the relationship between the spouses and did not affect arrangements with a third party; and that the goods were not in H's possession at the time of the poinding.

Held, appeal refused, that the sheriff was well founded in his interpretation of s.25(1) and that there was civil possession by H although he was not living in the house at the time.

Observed, that the court expected sheriff officers to produce written documentation which was clearly legible, which it was not in the present case.

KINLOCH v. BARCLAY'S BANK 1995 S.C.L.R. 975, Judge not specified, Sh Ct.

7340. Evidence–affidavits–whether discretion to refuse to receive

Held, in an action of delivery, that the sheriff had a discretion to refuse to receive the evidence of a witness resident in New York by way of affidavit.

LOBBAN v. PHILIP 1995 S.C.L.R. 1104, Judge not specified, Sh Ct.

7341. Evidence–copies of production–dispensing power of sheriff

[Act of Sederunt (Ordinary Cause Rules) 1993 (SI 1993 1956) r.2.1; Act of Sederunt (Ordinary Cause Rules) 1993 (SI 1993 1956) r.29.12.]

Held, that a solicitor's ignorance of r. 29.12(1) requiring copies of productions to be lodged for the use of the sheriff at a proof not later than 48 hours before the diet of proof could be an excusable cause for the exercise of the dispensing power under r. 2.1 (1).

HENDERSON v. HENDERSON 1995 S.C.L.R. 856, Judge not specified, Sh Ct.

7342. Initial writ–warrant for citation–refusal to grant–collector of taxes signing initial writ

Held, that warrant to cite the defender should be granted in respect of an initial writ signed by the pursuer who was a collector of taxes seeking recovery in her own name of taxes allegedly due by the defender.

LITTLE v. ASLAM 1995 S.C.L.R. 1158, Judge not specified, Sh Ct.

7343. Interdict–interim interdict granted–whether action fell after a year and a day without any further judicial step

M appealed a sheriff's decision to grant C's minute for perpetual interdict against M on August 18, 1995 in C's action which had been warranted on April 5, 1994. M argued that, as he had not lodged a notice of intention to defend and as C had taken no further steps in the action until July 1995 when the minute had been lodged, the action had fallen a year and a day from the end of the period within which notice of intention to defend should have been lodged, *McCulloch v. McCulloch* 1990 S.L.T. (Sh.Ct.) 63, [1990] C.L.Y. 5130; *McKidd v. Manson* (1882) 2 R. 790; *Home-Drummond v. Norman* (1903) 19 Sh. Ct. Rep. 16; and that the introduction of the new sheriff court rules had not affected that rule. C argued that as interim interdict had been granted on April 5, 1994, the rule did not apply.

Held, appeal allowed, that M's submissions were preferred, *McCulloch, McKidd*, and *Home-Drummond*, followed. The sheriff's interlocutor was incompetent and would be recalled and no further order made.

CRINGEAN v. McNEILL 1996 S.C.L.R. 184, Judge not specified, Sh Ct.

7344. Lawburrows–evidence and procedure

[Civil Imprisonment (Scotland) Act 1882 (c.42) s.6(2).]

The Civil Imprisonment (Scotland) Act 1882 s.6(2) provides, *inter alia*, that on an application for lawburrows being presented the sheriff shall immediately, and without taking the oath of the applicant, order the petition to be served on the person claimed against "and shall at the same time grant warrant to both parties to cite witnesses". A husband and wife brought a summary application for lawburrows against their neighbour. On November 16, 1994 a warrant for service on the defender was granted ordaining him to appear on December 16, 1994 when, despite the defender's opposition, the sheriff granted warrant to cite witnesses and to fix a hearing. After a proof the sheriff found, *inter alia*, that in May 1994 the defender admitted to the pursuers his responsibility for breaking a window in one of their barns and he threatened the husband with further violence, shook his fists at him and said that it was fortunate that it was not his neck that had been broken; that on September 22, 1994 the defender left a gate off its hinges so that it would fall on anyone trying to open it, and a postman was injured when he was delivering mail to the pursuers' house; and that in early October 1994 the defender damaged the pursuers' fence, a barn window and their front door. The sheriff however did not expressly find in fact in the stated case that the pursuers had reasonable cause to apprehend that the defender would harm their persons or property, but in his interlocutor he did find in fact and law that the pursuers had such reasonable apprehension. The defender appealed to the High Court by stated case contending that the proceedings were incompetent because the warrant to cite witnesses had not been granted with the warrant for service in terms of s.6(2) of the 1882 Act, and that the sheriff had not been entitled to hold that the pursuers had reasonable cause to apprehend that the defender would harm their person or property.

Held, that (1) s.6(2) dealt with two separate matters and the granting of a warrant was not essential for the initiating of proceedings since citing witnesses could only arise once proceedings had been initiated; (2) as the defect in the warrant to cite witnesses was a failure to comply with s.6(2) but was cured by the appearance of the defender, the proceedings were competent and (3) on the findings especially relating to May, September and October, the sheriff was entitled to hold that the pursuers had reasonable cause to apprehend further

harm at the defender's hands; and appeal refused, *Morrow v. Neil* 1975 S.L.T. (Sh.Ct.) 65, [1975] C.L.Y. 4133 approved.
LIDDLE v. MORTON 1996 S.L.T. 1143, Judge not specified, HCJ.

7345. Options hearing–failure to appear or be represented

Held, in an action in Inverness Sheriff Court in which the pursuer was represented by Edinburgh solicitors who had timeously lodged a copy of the record, that the sheriff was under no duty of inquiry when the pursuer was neither present nor represented at the options hearing and the action was dismissed.
COLONIAL MUTUAL GROUP (UK HOLDINGS) v. JOHNSTON 1995 S.C.L.R. 1165, Judge not specified, Sh Ct.

7346. Options hearing–failure to appear or be represented–continued hearing held in error–whether parties in default

[Act of Sederunt (Ordinary Cause Rules) 1993 (SI 1993 1956) r.9.2; Act of Sederunt (Ordinary Cause Rules) 1993 (SI 1993 1956) r.9.12(5); Act of Sederunt (Ordinary Cause Rules) 1993 (SI 1993 1956) r.20.6(1).]

Before an options hearing which had been fixed by the sheriff clerk under the Sheriff Courts (Scotland) Act 1907 r.9.2, the defenders in an action enrolled a motion for warrant to serve a third party notice, which was granted. By the time of the options hearing, answers by the third party had been intimated to the pursuer and defenders. The sheriff continued the options hearing under r.9.12(5). After answers for the third party were lodged an amended record was lodged and the sheriff clerk assigned a diet as an options hearing under r.20.6(1). At the continued options hearing, there being no appearance by the solicitors for the pursuer and defenders, who had been advised by the sheriff clerk that the hearing would be discharged, the sheriff concluded that the parties were in default and dismissed the action. An appeal was taken by the pursuer to the sheriff principal, which was not opposed.

Held, that although the rules provided only for one continued options hearing, the continued hearing took place in error and therefore did not fall to be regarded as a continued diet; and appeal allowed and cause continued to a continued options hearing. Opinion, that there would be advantage if the rules made it clear that it would always be open to an appellate court to fix an options hearing or a continued options hearing on allowing an appeal, notwithstanding the provisions of r.9.12.
BLYSZCZAK v. GEC MARCONI AVIONICS LTD 1996 S.L.T. (Sh.Ct.) 54, Judge not specified, Sh Ct.

7347. Options hearing–failure to lodge copy of record timeously

[Act of Sederunt (Ordinary Cause Rules) 1993 (SI 1993 1956) r.9.11.]

Held, in an action in which interim interdict had been pronounced on various occasions but in which no certified copy of the record was lodged in terms of the Ordinary Cause Rules r.9.11(2), that the dispensing power should not be exercised in the pursuer's favour and action was dismissed.
DA BAIRD & SON v. NISBET 1995 S.C.L.R. 1127, Judge not specified, Sh Ct.

7348. Options hearing–failure to lodge copy of record timeously–failure to appear or be represented at options hearing

[Act of Sederunt (Sheriff Court Ordinary Cause Rules) 1993 (SI 1993 1956) r.9.11.]

A pursuer having failed to lodge answers to a defender's counterclaim, adjust the initial writ, lodge the record as required under the Ordinary Cause Rules r.9.11, or appear or be represented at the options hearing, the sheriff dismissed the pursuer's action and granted decree in terms of the counterclaim. The sheriff principal held that the collective catalogue of errors, albeit by the pursuer's solicitor, along with the prejudice suffered by the defender, displaced the court's reluctance to allow a decree to stand where there was prima facie a substantial defence which had never been heard, and refused the pursuer's appeal. The pursuer appealed to the Inner House.

Held, of consent of the parties, that the appeal should be allowed and the pursuer found liable to the defender in the expenses of process to date with payment thereof made a condition precedent of further procedure in the case.

DE MELO v. BAZAZI 1995 S.C.L.R. 1172, Judge not specified, IH.

7349. Options hearing–note of basis for preliminary plea–consequences of failure to lodge

[Act of Sederunt (Ordinary Cause Rules) 1993 (SI 1993 1956) r.9.12; Act of Sederunt (Ordinary Cause Rules) 1993 (SI 1993 1956) r.22.1.]

Held, where defenders in an action had failed to lodge in process a note of the basis for their plea that the action should be sisted for arbitration, as required by r.22.1 (1), that the plea was a preliminary one within the meaning of that rule and that the sheriff had been correct to repel the plea at the options hearing.

DINARDO PARTNERSHIP v. THOMAS TAIT & SONS 1995 S.C.L.R. 941, Judge not specified, Sh Ct.

7350. Pleadings–amendment–reference to a tender

Held, in a reparation action arising out of a road traffic accident, that the record should be allowed to be amended in terms of a minute and answers which contained reference inter alia to a disputed settlement of the action and to a tender which had been lodged by the defender.

RODGERS v. CLYDESDALE 1995 S.C.L.R. 1163, Judge not specified, Sh Ct.

7351. Pleadings–dispensing power of sheriff–deliberate delay in attempting to lodge defence

[Act of Sederunt (Ordinary Cause Rules) 1993 (SI 1993 1956) r.2.1 (1).]

Held, that where an assistant solicitor had deliberately refrained from lodging defences in a sheriff court action, that his action could not be described as a "mistake" or as being "excusable" within the meaning of r.2.1 (1), but that the question under r.2.1 (1) was whether a party should be relieved from the consequences of failure to comply with the rules and accordingly the sheriff should have had regard to the particular facts rather than automatically imputing the solicitor's conduct to his client; and motion for defence to be received late granted.

ELLIS v. AMEC OFFSHORE DEVELOPMENTS 1996 S.C.L.R. 403, Judge not specified, Sh Ct.

7352. Pleadings–dispensing power of sheriff–failure to lodge note of basis for plea when amending to add preliminary plea–ignorance of rule

In an action of payment the defender added by amendment a plea in law that proof should be limited to the writ or oath of the pursuer. No note of the basis of the plea was lodged with the minute of amendment as required by ordinary cause rule 18.8. The defender subsequently sought relief by the exercise of the dispensing power in rule 2.1, on the ground that his agent was ignorant of the terms of rule 18.8. The sheriff granted the motion and the pursuer appealed.

Held, refusing the appeal, that (1) rule 2.1 could be applied in a case of simple ignorance of a rule and (2) the sheriff had not acted in a way in which no reasonable sheriff could have acted.

SUTHERLAND v. DUNCAN 1996 S.L.T. 428, Judge not specified, IH.

7353. Sheriff clerk–failure to act on caveat–whether discharging responsibilities which he had in connection with the execution of judicial process

[Crown Proceedings Act 1947 (c.44) s.2.]

Held, on appeal to the sheriff principal, that a sheriff clerk who had failed to act on a duly lodged caveat in respect of any application for confirmation to an estate was discharging responsibilities which he had in connection with the execution of judicial process, and that in terms of the Crown Proceedings Act 1947 s.2(5) no proceedings lay against the Crown in respect of his failure to act on the caveat.

WOOD v. LORD ADVOCATE 1996 S.C.L.R. 278, Judge not specified, Sh Ct.

7354. Sheriff courts–boundaries

SHERIFF COURT DISTRICTS (ALTERATION OF BOUNDARIES) ORDER 1996, SI 1996 1005 (S.108); made under the Sheriff Courts (Scotland) Act 1971 s.3, s.43. In force: April 1, 1996; £1.95.

The Sheriff Court Districts Reorganisation Order 1975 divided Scotland's six sheriffdoms into 50 sheriff court districts (one of which was subsequently abolished). This Order alters the boundaries of six of these districts with effect from April 1, 1996. Under the Sheriffdoms (Alteration of Boundaries) Order 1996 (SI 1996 1006), an area around Chryston is to be transferred from the sheriffdom of Glasgow and Strathkelvin into the sheriffdom of South Strathclyde, Dumfries and Galloway. This Order makes the consequential transfer of that area from the sheriff court district of Glasgow and Strathkelvin into the sheriff court district of Airdrie. The other changes involve the transfer of three areas from the sheriff court district of Dundee into the sheriff court districts of Arbroath, Forfar and Perth. All changes made by the Order are linked to the reorganisation of local government areas in Scotland which takes effect on April 1, 1996. Since the 1975 Order specified the areas of sheriff court districts for the most part by reference to the areas of district and islands councils (which bodies are to be abolished as at April 1, 1996), that Order is now revoked and Sch.1 to this Order specifies the sheriff court district areas for the most part by reference to new local authority areas and electoral wards.

7355. Sheriff courts–boundaries

SHERIFF COURT DISTRICTS (ALTERATION OF BOUNDARIES) AMENDMENT ORDER 1996, SI 1996 2192 (S.177); made under the Sheriff Courts (Scotland) Act 1971 s.3, s.43. In force: August 26, 1996; £0.65.

The Sheriff Court Districts (Alteration of Boundaries) Order 1996 (SI 1996 1005) made provision as to the boundaries of the sheriff court districts in Scotland. This Order amends that Order so that, with effect from August 26, 1996; electoral ward 23 in the local government area of Angus is transferred from the sheriff court district of Perth to that of Forfar; and Livingston and Lochgilphead are prescribed as additional places at which sheriff courts may be held in the sheriff court districts of Linlithgow and Dunoon respectively.

7356. Sheriff courts–Commissary Court Books

ACT OF SEDERUNT (COMMISSARY COURT BOOKS) (AMENDMENT) 1996, SI 1996 3144 (S.239); made under the Sheriff Courts (Scotland) Act 1971 s.32. In force: January 1, 1997; £0.65.

This Act of Sederunt amends existing provisions for the keeping of records in the Commissary Court Books to allow for the recording of such records by methods other than microfilm. It requires the commissary clerk to seek the prior approval of the Keeper of the Records of Scotland before using new types of equipment to record documents in the Commissary Court Books. It also amends the term "writ" to "document" to reflect more accurately the practice of the commissary clerk.

7357. Sheriffdoms–boundaries

SHERIFFDOMS (ALTERATION OF BOUNDARIES) ORDER 1996, SI 1996 1006 (S.109); made under the Sheriff Courts (Scotland) Act 1971 s.2, s.43. In force: April 1, 1996; £1.10.

By virtue of the Sheriffdoms Reorganisation Order 1974 (SI 1974 2087), Scotland is divided into six sheriffdoms. This Order alters the boundaries of two of these sheriffdoms, so as to transfer an area around Chryston from the sheriffdom of Glasgow and Strathkelvin into the sheriffdom of South Strathclyde, Dumfries and Galloway. The boundaries of the other four sheriffdoms remain unchanged. Since the 1974 Order specified the areas of sheriffdoms by reference to the areas of regional, district and islands councils (which bodies are to be abolished as at April 1, 1996), that Order is now revoked and the Schedule to this Order specifies the areas of the sheriffdoms by reference to new local authority areas and electoral wards.

7358. Sist–whether appropriate during criminal trial relating to the same subject matter

Held, that a motion to sist an action of divorce on the ground of the defender's alleged behaviour pending the conclusion of a criminal trial of the defender relating to the behaviour complained of should be refused.

BENNETT v. BENNETT 1996 S.C.L.R. 736, Judge not specified, Sh Ct.

7359. Articles

Appeal–competency–final interlocutor. : Civ. P.B. 1996, 8(Mar), 10-11. (Whether interlocutor providing for hearing on costs was final judgment for purposes of time limit for appeal).

Ascertaining disputed matters at an options hearing *(A.G. Stevenson.)*: Civ. P.B. 1996, 10(Jul), 6-7. (Criticism of Act of Sederunt SI 1993 1956 r.9.12 on written pleadings in options hearings).

Commentary on changes to ordinary cause rules in family proceedings. *(Alisdair Gordon)*: Civ. P.B. 1996, 12(Nov), 2-4. (Act of Sederunt SI 1996 2176, sheriff court rules for child related cases).

Connected persons joining the limitation buster in the Sheriff Court. *(William J. Stewart)*: Rep. B. 1996, 10(Jul), 9-10. (Procedural difficulties where connected person to deceased, such as relative, wishes to be sisted as additional pursuer a short time before end of limitation period).

Family proceedings: the new Sheriff Court rules *(Andrew M. Cubie.)*: Fam. L.B. 1996, 24(Nov), 2-3. (Act of Sederunt 1996 SI 1996 2176, in force November 1, 1996, including those relating to intimation, recording views of child and child welfare hearings).

Lay-representation in the sheriff court *(Alexis Scott)*: SCOLAG 1996, 234, 70-72. (Small claims actions in Fife sheriff courts).

Minutes for recall of decree in summary cause actions *(James Bauld.)*: SCOLAG 1996, 236, 124-125. (Use of minutes for recall to prevent eviction even after decree granted and eviction scheduled).

Miscellaneous procedure roll *(Graham Johnston)*: Civ. P.B. 1996, 9(May), 6-7. (Unauthorised miscellaneous procedure roll reintroduces unnecessary delay into new civil procedure system).

Sheriff Court practice: three years of the new rules *(Lindsay Foulis)*: J.L.S.S. 1996, 41 (11), 438-441. (Case law pertaining to 1993 Rules).

Solicitor resigning agency shortly before proof or debate *(Graham Johnston)*: Civ. P.B. 1996, 7(Jan), 6-7. (Practice and procedure where solicitor withdraws from action in sheriff court).

SHIPPING

7360. Harbours–Campbeltown

CAMPBELTOWN (FERRY TERMINAL) HARBOUR REVISION ORDER 1996, SI 1996 412 (S.28); made under the Harbours Act 1964 s.14. In force: March 1, 1996; £1.95.

Strathclyde Regional Council is authorised by this Order to carry out certain works connected with the construction of a ferry terminal at Campbeltown Harbour. The Council is permitted to deviate from the plans and sections within certain limits by Art.4 and Art.5 enables the construction of subsidiary works. The Council is empowered to dredge within the defined limits shown on the plans by Art.6 and Art.7 to Art.14 makes provision for safety in relation to any works carried out in tidal waters of lands. Article 15 stipulates that if the authorised works are not completed within 10 years from March 1, 1996, or such extended time as may be allowed, then the powers granted in this Order will cease.

7361. Harbours–Leverburgh

WESTERN ISLES ISLANDS COUNCIL (LEVERBURGH) HARBOUR REVISION ORDER 1995, SI 1995 2971 (S.214); made under the Harbours Act 1964 s.14. In force: November 17, 1995; £2.80.

The Western Isles Islands Council is authorised by this Order to construct new harbour works at Leverburgh in the Obbe Electoral Division, parish of Harris on the Island of Harris in the Western Isles Islands Area. Additional powers of control and administration are vested in the Council in relation to the Harbour.

7362. Harbours–Mallaig

MALLAIG HARBOUR REVISION ORDER 1995, SI 1995 3109 (S.229); made under the Harbours Act 1964 s.14. In force: December 1, 1995; £1.55.

The construction of a new fishery harbour by reclaiming and infilling and constructing a new breakwater and slipway by the Mallaig Harbour Authority is authorised by this Order along with dredging in connection with the proposed works. The application for this Harbour Revision Order, from the Mallaig Harbour Authority, is made in relation to a project under Council Directive 85/337 Annex II on the assessment of the effects of certain public and private projects on the environment.

7363. Harbours–Peterhead

PETERHEAD HARBOURS REVISION ORDER 1996, SI 1996 2755 (S.212); made under the Harbours Act 1964 s.14. In force: November 15, 1996; £1.55.

This Order empowers the trustees of the harbours of Peterhead to construct a dry dock alongside Scott's Pier and to dredge within North Harbour. It also gives the trustees ancillary powers in relation to the works.

7364. Ports–Cromarty Firth Port Authority

CROMARTY FIRTH PORT AUTHORITY HARBOUR REVISION ORDER 1996, SI 1996 1419; made under the Harbours Act 1964 s.14. In force: June 21, 1996; £1.10.

This Order amends the constitution of the Cromarty Firth Port Authority by increasing the total membership of the Authority from six or seven to seven or eight, of whom the number to be appointed otherwise than on the nomination of the Highland Council will be increased from three to four. The power of the Highland Council to nominate three persons for appointment and the power of all the appointed members to co-opt a member are not affected. In addition to making minor and consequential amendments, the Order amends the general powers of the authority in the Cromarty Firth Port Authority Order 1973 s.7(2). The Order also empowers the Authority to appoint a chief executive, to form wholly owned subsidiaries for carrying on activities which the Authority has power to carry on, and to form companies for developing or carrying on business on land within, or formerly within, the port but no longer required for the purposes of the Authority's undertaking.

7365. Ports–Dundee Port Authority

DUNDEE PORT AUTHORITY TRANSFER SCHEME 1995 CONFIRMATION ORDER 1995, SI 1995 3023; made under the Ports Act 1991 Part 1, s.9. In force: November 24, 1995; £1.95.

The Dundee Port Authority Transfer Scheme 1995, made by the Dundee Port Authority under the Ports Act 1991 s.9, as modified by the Secretary of State for Transport, is confirmed by this Order. The Scheme takes effect on November 24, 1994 and on that date all property, rights and liabilities of the Authority, except as stated in para.2(a) of the Scheme, and all functions conferred or imposed on the Authority by any local statutory provision are transferred to the successor company specified in para.3 of the Scheme.

7366. Shipowners–statutory duty of owner–ship in dock being "operated"

[Merchant Shipping Act 1988 (c.12) s.31.]

L, a crew member of a ship, injured himself while carrying out repairs while the ship was docked. He raised an action for damages against W, founding on s.31 (1) of the Merchant Shipping Act 1988 which places a duty on the owner of a ship to take all reasonable steps to secure that the ship is operated in a safe manner and creates a criminal offence if there is a failure to comply. W maintained that the ship was not being operated while in dock, and that where a statute created a criminal offence it could not also create a civil liability, per *Lonrho Ltd v. Shell Petroleum (No.2)* [1982] A.C. 173, [1980] C.L.Y. 2135, and attacked the relevancy of L's action.

Held, that for the purposes of s.31 (1), a ship was being operated when at sea, afloat in port, under repair, or loading and unloading cargo. Although failure to comply with the section was a criminal offence, civil claims for damages could also be allowed as the legislation was aimed at protecting a particular class of persons, ie. all those on board ship, whether at sea or not. L's action was allowed to proceed to a proof.

LITTLEJOHN v. WOOD & DAVIDSON LTD, *The Scotsman*, December 6, 1995, Lord Johnston, OH.

SMALL LANDHOLDER

7367. Cottar–house and garden–acquisition by cottar

Held, that the tenant of a dwellinghouse and garden ground qualified as a cottar and therefore had an incontestable right to a conveyance of the site.

CORBETT v. ASSYNT ESTATES 1995 S.L.C.R. 122, Judge not specified, Land Ct.

7368. Croft–acquisition by crofter

A crofter applied to the Land Court for an order authorising her to acquire the site of the dwellinghouse on her croft. The previous tenant of the croft had purportedly bequeathed it to the applicant's father who then assigned it to her. The landlords refused to grant the appropriate conveyance as they had been led to believe that a member of the deceased's family proposed to challenge the validity of the bequest transferring the croft to the applicant's father.

Held, that the applicant was entitled to a conveyance of the site of the croft dwellinghouse.

Observed, that any such claim by a relative of the deceased crofter would be barred and in any event such a claim would be against the executor of the deceased tenant and not the present applicant.

FOWLER v. SMECH PROPERTIES 1995 S.L.C.R. 83, Judge not specified, Land Ct.

7369. Croft–common grazings–resumption by landlord–unnecessary

Held, where landlords of a common grazing applied to the land court to resume part of the grazings for road widening purposes, that the application should be dismissed as unnecessary because the area in question had been the subject of a compulsory purchase order.

HIGHLAND & ISLANDS OIL & GAS CO v. CROFTERS SHARING IN BOURBLOCK COMMON GRAZINGS 1995 S.L.C.R. 110, Judge not specified, Land Ct.

7370. Croft–conditions of tenure–whether landlord entitled to construct a parking and turning area on croft land

[Crofters (Scotland) Act 1993 (c.44) Sch.2, para.11.]

The landlord of a croft sought an order ordaining the crofter in terms of para. 11 (e) of Sched. 2 to the Crofters (Scotland) Act 1993 to permit him or any person authorised by him to enter upon an area of the croft for the purpose of opening and making a road to permit access from the public road to two decrofted plots of ground which were no longer in the ownership of the landlord. Planning consent had been granted for the erection of a house on a neighbouring plot subject to a condition designed to achieve safe vehicular access, in respect of which the landlord proposed to construct a parking and turning area. Alternatively the landlord sought resumption of the area in terms of s.20 of the Crofters (Scotland) Act 1993. The Divisional Court granted the primary crave for the landlord and its decision was appealed to the full court by the crofter respondent.

Held, that (1) whether or not the landlord was entitled to an order in terms of the primary crave depended on whether the case fell within the terms of para.11 (e), which prima facie conferred an unqualified right on the landlord, and not on questions of reasonableness, and the divisional court having approached the case on the latter basis, the question was at large for the court; (2) the rights conferred by para.11 were more intended to benefit the landlord in his capacity as owner of the estate, not to be exercised for public purposes such as road safety considerations put forward by the planning authority; nor did the creation of an area of ground as a parking and turning area fall within "opening or making roads" in terms of para.11 (e), and the primary crave fell to be refused; (3) the purpose for which resumption was sought was reasonable having regard to the public interest, and as the area in question was to be lost permanently to the croft, resumption was the appropriate course of action; and resumption authorised.

CAMERON v. MacKINNON 1996 S.L.T. (Land Ct.) 4, Judge not specified, Land Ct.

7371. Croft–sublet–duration–whether sublet could continue on tacit relocation

Held, where a sublet in respect of a croft provided that the period of the sublet would be for seven years to the term of Whitsunday 1992 and for such further periods as the sublet might lawfully subsist until terminated in accordance with the due processed of land, that the sublet terminated at Whitsunday 1992 because the doctrine of tacit relocation could not apply to a sublet as the prior written consent of the Crofters Commission was required to any sublet

MARTIN v. MacSWEEN 1995 S.L.C.R. 99, Judge not specified, Land Ct.

7372. Articles

Succession to crofts *(Donald Smith)*: J.L.S.S. 1996, 41 (5), 183-185. (Succession to crofts, difficulties caused by time limits in testate succession and on transfers of deceased crofters' interests and role of Crofters Commission in resolving problems).

SOCIAL SECURITY

7373. Appeal–decision of tribunal–application to set aside–procedural irregularity

[Social Security (Adjudication) Regulations 1986 (SI 1986 2218) Reg.11.]

W, a retired person on income support, sought judicial review of a decision of a social security appeal tribunal to set aside a decision of another tribunal in his favour. W had submitted claims to the Department of Social Security (S) for additional diet payments and laundry costs. An adjudication officer (A) refused W's claim for additional diet payments and apparently failed to consider the claim for additional laundry expenses, and W appealed. S requested a postponement of the hearing because no presenting officers were available for the diet fixed and the interests of natural justice would not be served if the hearing proceeded without one. S's application for a postponement was refused and W's appeal was heard by a tribunal (T) on March 14, 1994 without a representative of S. T overturned A's decision finding that, on the balance of probabilities, W had submitted a doctor's letter regarding his ulcer to S in 1971 and that S knew of W's stomach problems from 1982. Moreover, although W had submitted a laundry addition claim in August 1987, S had never considered this claim. T granted W's claim for a diet addition from 1971, remitting the case to A to determine the amount and to consider the additional laundry claim. A then sought to set aside T's decision under the Social Security (Adjudication) Regulations 1986 Reg.11 on the grounds that it was inappropriate to proceed with the hearing in the absence of a presenting officer. A's application was granted by a further tribunal on August 5, 1994 on the grounds that (1) A's representative was not present and (2) it was in the interest of justice to set aside for procedural irregularity. W sought judicial review of that decision, arguing that A's absence from the hearing did not automatically invalidate the proceedings and did not amount to a procedural mishap.

Held, granting the petition and reducing the decision, that the reasons for setting aside the earlier decision were flawed. The power to set aside under Reg.11 was intended to provide a short, simple and speedy alternative to the appeal process where something had gone wrong with the procedure. It should be confined to cases where there was a readily identifiable error or mishap and should not be used as a substitute for an appeal. The decision suggested that T had failed to consider all relevant issues or adequately express the reasons for its decision, but such matters could only properly be considered on appeal. There were no procedural irregularities where A applied for a postponement, which was refused, and then chose not to attend the hearing.

WARD v. SECRETARY OF STATE FOR SOCIAL SECURITY 1995 S.C.L.R. 1134, Judge not specified, OH.

7374. Child support–application for liability order–competency of application signed by "litigation officer"

[Act of Sederunt (Child Support Rules) 1993 (SI 1993 920) r.2(1).]

Rule 2(1) of the Act of Sederunt (Child Support Rules) 1993 provides that applications by the Secretary of State for a liability order shall be by summary application in form 1 introduced by the rules. In an application by the Secretary of

State for a liability order, the application and minute were signed by departmental officials designed as litigation officers. The sheriff applied r.4 of the pre-1993 Ordinary Cause Rules requiring that an initial writ be signed by the pursuer or his solicitor and dismissed the application. The applicant appealed.

Held, that the intention of the Child Support Rules was to replace the initial writ as the document commencing an application of this kind with an initiating document specific to an application for a liability order, r.4 thus being inapplicable, and that the signatures did not render the application incompetent; and appeal allowed and application remitted to the sheriff, *Carltona v. Commissioners of Works* [1943] 2 All E.R. 560 applied.

SECRETARY OF STATE FOR SOCIAL SECURITY v. LOVE 1996 S.L.T. (Sh.Ct.) 78, Judge not specified, Sh.Ct.

7375. Child support–objection lodged to grant of liability order–procedure

[Act of Sederunt (Child Support Rules) 1993 (SI 1993 920) r.2.]

Rule 2(5) of the Act of Sederunt (Child Support Rules) 1993 provides, where the liable person wishes to object to the grant of an application by the Secretary of State for a liability order, that the sheriff may consider the application and any objection on the date fixed for the hearing or at any continuation, whether or not any of the parties appear. The Secretary of State applied for a liability order. The liable person objected and the cause was put out for a hearing at which the respondent failed to appear. The sheriff, on the applicant's motion and in respect of no appearance by or on behalf of the respondent, made a liability order. The liable person appealed, arguing that the interlocutor was incompetent.

Held, that r.2(5) required the sheriff to consider the application and any objection, the discretion relating merely to whether the sheriff considered the application at the hearing or at any continuation thereof; and appeal allowed and application remitted to the sheriff.

SECRETARY OF STATE FOR SOCIAL SECURITY v. NICOL 1996 S.L.T. (Sh. Ct.) 34, Judge not specified, Sh.Ct.

7376. Social fund–refusal of application for payment–decision of inspector following review of earlier determination–whether inspector entitled to consider matter anew–matters to be taken into account

[Social Security Contributions and Benefits Act 1992 (c.4) s.140; Social Security Administration Act 1992 (c.5) s.66.]

The Social Security Contributions and Benefits Act 1992, and directions issued by the Secretary of State thereunder, make provision for payment out of the social fund to ease "exceptional pressures" on applicants and their families. A single father sought judicial review of the refusal by a social fund inspector of his application for a payment from the fund. The inspector had decided that the original determination by a social fund officer, affirmed by a higher social fund officer, had not been correct and reviewed that determination. The petitioner was, at the time of making his application, aged 37 and a single parent with two children aged six and three. He and the younger child suffered from asthma. The mother of the children had left them in his care. The petitioner was living, and had lived throughout his life, with his parents. The social fund inspector was satisfied that the petitioner's whole family was experiencing exceptional pressure when he made his original application. The petitioner subsequently moved into unfurnished accommodation with his children where he had two single beds, bedding, livingroom carpet and curtains, washing machine and (borrowed) kettle. The petitioner had to sleep on the floor. The family had no cooker and ate at the petitioner's parents' home or had takeaway meals. The social fund inspector considered that the main source of pressure had been removed by the move to the new home, that her office was likely to receive applications from people far more vulnerable and that their budget would not be sufficient to meet all needs. The petitioner argued that the inspector wrongly considered the case de novo, wrongly took account of budget constraints and failed to have regard to all considerations under the Social Security Administration Act 1992 s.66.

Held, that (1) a social fund inspector was entitled to determine such applications de novo; (2) in so doing, regard was properly had to levels of priority and the state of the annual budget, including the likely receipt of applications from claimants far more vulnerable in the year in question, for such grants, and the inspector had properly considered the material before her and had been entitled to reach her decision accordingly and (3) there was no obligation to consider each item of claim made separately or to give specific reasons as to why claims in respect of individual items might have been rejected; and petition dismissed.

MURRAY v. SOCIAL FUND INSPECTION 1996 S.L.T. 38, Judge not specified, OH.

SUCCESSION

7377. Standard securities–repayment by life policy proceeds–death of joint owner–claim of recompense to deceased's estate

A house was owned jointly by two persons. They had granted a standard security in favour of a building society. One of the owners had taken out a life assurance policy which he assigned in favour of the building society. He thereafter died, and the building society applied the proceedings of the policy to discharge the whole sums outstanding in respect of the mortgage by both the deceased and the other joint owner. The deceased's executor then raised an action of relief against the other joint owner on the basis that the deceased was only liable for a one-half share of the debt due to the building society and therefore was entitled to be recompensed to the extent of a sum equivalent to a one-half share of the debt. Following a debate the sheriff held that direct payment by the deceased to the defender was necessary before a right of relief arose, and sustained the defender's plea to the relevancy and dismissed the action. The pursuer appealed to the Court of Session where it was argued that a right of relief was a broad remedy not requiring direct payment by the deceased or his estate.

Held, that (1) actual payment by the deceased or his estate to the building society was not essential before a claim for relief could succeed as such a claim was based on the principle of recompense, and the pursuer had relevantly averred a benefit to the defender as a result of arrangements made by the deceased with the building society, (2) that the claim for relief could only succeed if there had been no intention of donation by the deceased to the defender; and appeal allowed, but case remitted to the sheriff to fix a proof before answer on the question of whether there had been any intention of donation.

CHRISTIE'S EXECUTOR v. ARMSTRONG 1996 S.L.T. 948, Judge not specified, IH.

TRADE MARKS

7378. Trade mark–infringement–words used in "trade mark sense"

[Trade Marks Act 1994 s.10; Trade Mark Harmonisation Directive 89/104.]

B, the owner of a trade mark "Wet Wet Wet" which was the name of a successful pop group, sought interdict against M from infringing the trade mark in terms of the Trade Marks Act 1994 s.10(1) by publishing and marketing a book entitled "A Sweet Little Mystery - Wet Wet Wet - The Inside Story". M argued that (1) Wet Wet Wet was not being used in a trade mark sense, but rather was descriptive of the subject matter of the book, which was the group; that the typeface used was different from that appearing in the registration certificate; and that there was nothing about the book or its get-up to suggest that it was published by B and (2) in any event, as the words were being used as indications of the characteristic of the book, in terms of s.11 (2) (b) there had been no infringement. B argued that, as the offence in terms of s.10 was in "affixing" the mark to the goods, it was only M's use of the words on the dust cover and spine of the book which was an infringement under s.10 and not the use in the text; that s.11 (2) (b) related only to situations where the words were being used in their ordinary sense; and that if M were entitled to use the registered mark simply because the book was about the group then it would be impossible to prevent its use in relation to anything else pertaining to the group, such as a box of pictures.

Held, refusing the petition, that (1) in s.10(1) uses in the course of trade meant use in a trade mark sense. However, the words could be used in both that sense and in a descriptive sense at the same time, and, although the use of "Wet Wet Wet" was appropriate to indicate the subject matter of the book, given that the use of the words was avowedly and obviously a use of the name which the group had registered, the words were being used in a trade mark sense, *Mothercare (UK) v. Penguin Books* [1988] R.P.C. 113, [1987] C.L.Y. 530 distinguished. B had registered the word "wet" repeated three times in combination without punctuation, and, notwithstanding that the registration certificate showed two different typefaces, for which no explanation had been given, the actual typeface was not an integral part of the mark, because words had to be registered in some script or typeface, and otherwise B would have had to register the words in every possible typeface to be protected, *Morny Trade Marks, Re* (1951) 61 R.P.C. 131, [1951] C.L.Y. 10353 followed. Accordingly M were using a mark identical to that registered by B in relation to books, which were goods for which it was registered and (2) however, notwithstanding that the use could be characterised as an infringement of s.10, M's use fell within the terms of s.11 (2) (b), as it was an indication concerning the main characteristic of the book. It would have been a bizarre result if the 1994 Act, which was intended to guarantee the trade mark as an indication of origin, preamble, Trade Mark Harmonisation Directive 89/104, could have been used to prevent M from using the protected name in the title of a book about the group, and s.11 (2) was designed to avoid the risk that trade mark law might be used too restrictively, the proviso in s.11 (2) providing protection for B. Accordingly, M had not infringed B's trade mark.

BRAVADO MERCHANDISING SERVICES v. MAINSTREAM PUBLISHING (EDINBURGH) 1996 S.L.T. 597, Judge not specified, OH.

7379. Articles

Judge puts dampeners on Wet Wet Wet *(McGrigor Donald)*: I.H.L. 1996, 38 (Mar), 68. (Whether use of pop group's name in title of book about them was breach of their trade mark).

Wet Wet Wet—the sweet little mystery remains *(Clare Elliott)*: J.L.S.S. 1996, 41 (2), 63-65. (Whether use of pop group's name in book title was breach of trade mark).

"Wet? Wet?"—a little mystery unresolved? *(Charlotte Waelde)*: S.L.T. 1996, 1, 1-7. (Use by book of pop group name not used "in a trade mark sense").

TRANSPORT

7380. Strathclyde Passenger Transport Authority

STRATHCLYDE PASSENGER TRANSPORT AUTHORITY (CONSTITUTION, MEMBERSHIP AND TRANSITIONAL AND CONSEQUENTIAL PROVISIONS) ORDER 1995, SI 1995 3026 (S.219); made under the Local Government etc.

(Scotland) Act 1994 s.40, s.181, Sch.5. In force: Art.19, Sch.3: December 18, 1995; Remainder: April 1, 1996; £2.80.

The constitution and membership of the Strathclyde Passenger Transport Authority (SPTA) which was established by the Local Government etc. (Scotland) Act 1994, are dealt with by this Order along with the certain transitional and consequential provisions. The Articles cover incorporation, appointment of members, the period of appointment of the members, vacancies, appointment of deputies, notification of appointment or termination of appointment, proceedings of the Authority, allowances and remuneration of officers and staff, appointment of committees, delegation of functions, entitlement of members of the Authority to allowances, application of enactments, provision of accommodation, discharge of functions of officers of the Authority, documents, validity, transitional provisions and consequential provisions relating to concessionary travel. Sch.1 lists the councils entitled to appoint members of the Authority and numbers of members permitted to be appointed by each council. Sch.2 details provisions as to proceedings of the Authority and Sch.3 lists transitional provisions.

TRUSTS

7381. St Andrews Links Trust

LOCAL STATUTORY PROVISIONS (EXEMPTION OF ST. ANDREWS LINKS TRUST) (SCOTLAND) ORDER 1996, SI 1996 1382 (S.129); made under the Local Government etc. (Scotland) Act 1994 s.59. In force: July 1, 1996; £0.65.

This Order exempts the St. Andrews Links Order Confirmation Act 1974 (c.iii) from ceasing to have effect at the end of 1999 in terms of the 1994 Act, the 1974 Act having constituted the St. Andrews Links Trust and vested in that trust the control and management of the Links of St Andrews.

7382. Articles

Intimation: the equivalent delivery of what? *(Kenneth J.M. Young.)*: S.L.T. 1996, 38, 373-376. (How and whether person can successfully make himself trustee of his own property to create effective truster-as-trustee trust with particular regard to what must be delivered).

Scotland *(Andrew S. Biggart)*: T. & T. 1996, 2(2), 47-48. (Scots trust law sources, trust formation and management, powers, responsibilities and remuneration of trustees and treatment of foreign trusts).

UTILITIES

7383. Electricity industry–target investment limit

ELECTRICITY (SCOTTISH NUCLEAR LIMITED) (TARGET INVESTMENT LIMIT) ORDER 1996, SI 1996 3221 (S.243); made under the Electricity Act 1989 s.74. In force: January 14, 1997; £0.65.

This Order fixes the target investment limit for the Government shareholding in Scottish Nuclear Limited which is a privatised Scottish nuclear company. Under that Act the limit must be expressed as a proportion of the voting rights exercisable in all circumstances at general meetings of the company. The Government shareholding must normally be kept within this limit. In this case the limit is fixed as nil.

7384. Electricity supply industry–levy

FOSSIL FUEL LEVY (SCOTLAND) REGULATIONS 1996, SI 1996 293 (S.19); made under the Electricity Act 1989 s.33, s.60, s.64. In force: February 16, 1996; £4.15.

These Regulations make provision for the imposition and payment of a levy on each public electricity supplier in Scotland and on persons authorised by licence to supply electricity within authorised areas under the Electricity Act 1989. Regulation 3 imposes the levy, Reg.4 and Reg.5 prescribe the person responsible for collection and the methods of collection, Reg.6 and Reg.7 deal with the calculation and publication of the rate of levy, and the calculation of quantities of electricity supplies dealt with by Reg.8, Reg.9 and Reg.10. Regulation 11 to Reg.15 cover principal payments in respect of the levy, defaults in the making of payments are dealt with in Reg.16 to Reg.18, provision is made for overpayments in Reg.19 to Reg.22 and the application and distribution of sums collecting in Reg.23 to Reg.27. Provision for information is dealt with in Reg.28 to Reg.32 with supplementary and transitional provisions covered in Reg.33 to Reg.36.

7385. Electricity supply industry–levy

FOSSIL FUEL LEVY (SCOTLAND) AMENDMENT REGULATIONS 1996, SI 1996 1512 (S.135); made under the Electricity Act 1989 s.33, s.60. In force: July 3, 1996; £0.65.

Amend the Fossil Fuel Levy (Scotland) Regulations 1996 (SI 1996 293) so as to permit the Director General of Electricity Supply to utilise a wider range of institutions for the investment of money received under the Regulations.

7386. Energy Conservation Act 1996–Commencement No.1 Order

ENERGY CONSERVATION ACT 1996 (COMMENCEMENT NO.1) (SCOTLAND) ORDER 1996, SI 1996 2796 (C.81; S.214); made under the Energy Conservation Act 1996 s.2. In force: bringing into force various provisions of the Act on December 1, 1996; £0.65.

This Order brings the Energy Conservation Act 1996 into force in Scotland on December 1, 1996.

7387. Home Energy Conservation Act 1995–Commencement No.3 Order

HOME ENERGY CONSERVATION ACT 1995 (COMMENCEMENT NO.3) (SCOTLAND) ORDER 1996, SI 1996 2797 (S.215; C.82); made under the Home Energy Conservation Act 1995 s.9. In force: bringing into force various provisions of the Act on December 1, 1996; £0.65.

This Order brings the Home Energy Conservation Act 1995 into force in Scotland on December 1, 1996.

7388. Stop notice–contravention of–excavation of drain or sewer

[Sewerage (Scotland) Act 1968 (c.47) s.59(1).]

An accused was charged on summary complaint that he, being subject to a stop notice requiring him to stop the unauthorised excavation by him of a public sewer, continued to carry out excavation work contrary to the said stop notice, contrary to the Town and Country Planning (Scotland) Act 1972 s.87(5). He was also charged at common law with malicious mischief. The accused admitted the excavation and blocking of the pipe but argued, *inter alia*, that the pipe under his land was a drain only, not a sewer, notwithstanding that the pipe did not originate from his property, since it served one development only, and that therefore no criminal offence had been committed. After trial the sheriff found the accused guilty of both charges. The accused appealed to the High Court by way of stated case.

Held, that (1) in order to fall within the definition of "drain" in s.59(1) a pipe required to be within the curtilage of the premises to which it related and had also to be used solely for or in connection with the drainage of one building or of any related building or yards within the same curtilage; (2) any "drain" within s.59(1) ceased to be such a drain as soon as it left the curtilage of the premises, at which point it became a "sewer"; (3) if it was a sewer which connected with a public sewer or with sewage treatment works vested in a local authority it was also vested in the local authority from that point onwards in terms of s.16(1)(c) of the 1968 Act and (4) accordingly the sheriff had been well founded in his approach to the whole matter; and appeal refused.

COWIE v. NORMAND 1996 S.L.T. 960, Judge not specified, HCJ.

7389. Water and sewerage–three new authorities

WATER AND SEWERAGE AUTHORITIES (RATE OF RETURN) (SCOTLAND) ORDER 1996, SI 1996 744 (S.77); made under the Local Government etc. (Scotland) Act 1994 s.83. In force: April 1, 1996; £1.10.

Responsibility for the provision of water and sewerage services in Scotland will on April 1, 1996 transfer from local authorities to three new water and sewerage authorities, established under the Local Government etc. (Scotland) Act 1994. This Order makes provision as to the rate of return on the value of their assets which these three authorities require to achieve from financial year 1996/97 onwards.

7390. Water authorities–service charges

WATER SERVICES CHARGES (BILLING AND COLLECTION) (SCOTLAND) ORDER 1996, SI 1996 325 (S.25); made under the Local Government etc. (Scotland) Act 1994 s.79. In force: March 11, 1996; £1.55.

This Order provides that when responsibility for water and sewerage services in Scotland is transferred from local authorities to three new water authorities on April 1, 1996, each local authority will be responsible for demanding and recovering charges payable in respect of services provided by new water authorities to dwellings in the area of the local authority with the exclusion of charges for water supply taken by a meter. Provision is made for the authorities to account for sums collected, for the forms and procedures to be used and followed in the demanding of payment, for chargepayers to have a right of appeal to relevant valuation appeal committees and requirements are made for the local authorities to keep accounts and records of transactions which the water authorities will have the right to inspect.

7391. Water orders–Loch an Sgoltaire

WATER BYELAWS (LOCH AN SGOLTAIRE) EXTENSION ORDER 1995, SI 1995 3155 (S.230); made under the Water (Scotland) Act 1980 s.72. In force: December 10, 1995; £0.60.

This Order extends the period during which the Strathclyde Regional Council, Prevention of Water Pollution (Loch an Sgoltaire) Byelaws 1985 remain in force to December 11, 1996.

7392. Water supply–surface water–abstraction for drinking water–classification of quality

SURFACE WATERS (ABSTRACTION FOR DRINKING WATER) (CLASSIFICATION) (SCOTLAND) REGULATIONS 1996, SI 1996 3047 (S.233); made under the Control of Pollution Act 1974 s.30B, s.41. In force: January 6, 1997; £3.70.

These Regulations prescribe a system for classifying the quality of inland waters according to their suitability for abstraction for supply as drinking water, in implementation of Directive 75/440.

VALUE ADDED TAX

7393. Appeal from VAT tribunal–procedure

[Value Added Tax Tribunal Rules 1986 (SI 1986 590) r.19.]

The commissioners, C, appealed against the allowance of an appeal by Y against C's refusal of his claim for a VAT refund. His appeal was served on March 26, 1992. On May 13, 1992 an extension of time was granted to C for lodging their statement of case and list of documents by June 26, 1992. C failed to comply and did not lodge their statement and list until July 8, 1992. At the hearing the tribunal allowed Y's appeal. The principal question was whether the tribunal had exercised its discretion unreasonably. C appealed on the grounds that they had not wilfully failed to comply with the direction and that Y suffered no prejudice as a result of their failure. It was due to an administrative error that the statement of case had not been lodged on time. The tribunal indicated that it expected a direction to be complied with and required compelling reasons and circumstances to excuse compliance. Y had objected to the extension of time. No reasonable excuse had been given for waiting until the last minute to complete the statement of case, and as C were represented by legal advisers it was reasonable to expect them to carry out their job properly. C argued that the tribunal had closed their minds to the explanations and had simply concentrated on the terms of the rule. It appeared that the tribunal had not been asked specifically to waive the requirement of lodging the statement of case on time.

Held, appeal refused, that the test to be applied was whether the tribunal exercised their discretion reasonably and in a judicial way. The test had to be applied to the facts and circumstances which were before the tribunal at the time when the discretion was exercised *Gault v. Inland Revenue Commissioners* [1990] S.T.C. 612. It appeared that C's representative had not provided the tribunal with a full explanation at the time as to why she had not been instructed until a late date and had then failed to comply with the direction. It was clear that the tribunal were willing to excuse non-compliance had there been compelling reasons and circumstances to justify that, and the fact of non-compliance had not been the sole reason for their decision.

CUSTOMS AND EXCISE COMMISSIONERS v. YOUNG 1993 S.C. 339, Judge not specified.

7394. Return–adjustment–decrease in consideration–void election to waive exemption–whether claimant entitled to obtain repayment by adjusting VAT returns

[Value Added Tax (Accounting and Records) Regulations 1989 (SI 1989 2248) Reg.7; Finance Act 1989 (c.26) s.24.]

A company owned several department stores, parts of which included separate internal shops which had been let to tenants. The rent payable by the tenants for the internal shops was initially exempt from VAT, but in April 1990 the company notified the tenants that, in terms of a recently introduced amendment to the Value Added Tax Act 1983, it had elected to waive the exemption from VAT. Thereafter, for a period of about two and a half years, the tenants paid VAT on their rent and these sums were paid over by the company to the Commissioners of HM Customs and Excise. The company, however, failed to notify the commissioners of its election to waive exemption which, in terms of the amended legislation, meant that the election was invalid. In December 1992 a receiver was appointed to the company. The receiver discovered that the election had not been notified to the commissioners and sought to recover from them the VAT paid by the tenants, arguing that as it had been wrongly charged he was entitled, in terms of the Value Added Tax (Accounting and Records) Regulations 1989 Reg.7, to adjust the amount of the company's output tax on a VAT return, or alternatively that he was entitled to a refund of the VAT under the Finance Act 1989 s.24. The commissioners disallowed the adjustment of the VAT return, and the company appealed to the value added tax tribunal which upheld the appeal. The commissioners appealed to the Court of Session, arguing that no adjustment of the VATreturns was competent and, in relation to the alternative claim, that to refund the VAT would result in the company being unjustly enriched.

Held, that (1) Reg.7 was concerned only with the making of adjustments to the VAT account to reflect an increase or a decrease in consideration which included an amount of tax chargeable on a supply, and was not concerned with the position in this case where the supply was an exempt supply and no VAT was due to be paid on it to the commissioners, and therefore any claim for reimbursement had to be made under s.24 of the 1989 Act; (2) the question of whether the company would be unjustly enriched by the reimbursement of VAT was simply a question of statutory interpretation to be decided without reference to common law concepts, bearing in mind that it was desirable to have a uniformity of approach in Scotland and England; (3) a claimant could be said to be enriched where the amount claimed as overpaid was repaid to the claimant, irrespective of whether he was beneficially entitled to the sum or of the obligations, if any, to which he had subjected himself in the event of its receipt; (4) the question of whether the enrichment could be described as unjust was one of fact and degree which ought to be left to the tribunal, and the tribunal had been entitled to conclude that the company would not be unjustly enriched by reimbursement of the VAT as the money would be used for the benefit of unsecured creditors; and appeal refused.

CUSTOMS AND EXCISE COMMISSIONERS v. McMASTER STORES (SCOTLAND) LTD (IN RECEIVERSHIP) 1996 S.L.T. 935, Judge not specified, IH.

7395. Supply–development of land–deemed self-supply–grant of lease followed by licence-back

[Value Added Tax Act 1983 (c.55), Sch.6A, para.5, Sch.6A, para.6; Sixth VAT Directive 388/77 Title V, Art. 5.]

The Sixth VAT Council Directive and the Finance Act 1989 introduced a charge to VAT on the supply of services and materials for the construction of buildings other than those designed as dwellings or intended to be used solely for residential or certain charitable purposes. Paragraph 5 and para.6 of Sched. 6A to the Value Added Tax Act 1983, introduced a "self supply" charge to deal, inter alia, with the situation of a developer constructing a non-domestic building for his own use to prevent distortion of the market in land. The Sixth Directive provided in Art. 5(7), that Member States might treat as supplies made for consideration: "(a) the application by a taxable person for the purposes of his business of goods produced, constructed, extracted, processed, purchased or imported in the course of such business, where the value added tax on such goods, had they been acquired from another taxable person, would not be wholly deductible". An educational college developed land for the purposes of providing new playing fields, changing accommodation, a house for a groundsman and renovated certain existing buildings there. As a tax planning measure the college incorporated a limited company and entered into an arrangement with that company whereby the college granted a lease of the playing fields and buildings for a term of 12 years to the company in return for a premium of £187,000 and an annual rent of £30,000. The company, in return, gave the college a non-exclusive licence to use the premises in return for an annual licence fee. The effect of which was that the college became taxable at the standard rate upon the premium and rent payable by the company, but was entitled to deduct the whole of the input tax payable upon the construction works, the whole cost of the works being exclusively attributable to the taxable supply, namely the lease to the company. Following sundry procedure the Commissioners successfully appealed against a decision that the self supply provisions of the Value added Tax Act 1983 Sch.6A para.5 and para.6 were not activated. The college argued that in view of the provisions of Art.5 the Directive was of direct effect and binding on the Commissioners.

Held, that the purpose of Art. 5(7)(a) was to permit legislation by member states to prevent distortion in the market which would occur if a taxpayer could gain a tax advantage by acquiring goods in one way rather than another, by supplying them to himself rather than acquiring them from a third party; that, since the use which the college made of the new sports grounds was pursuant to services (ie. the licence) supplied to it by a third party, namely the company, there could be no room for a self supply charge within the terms of the Sixth Directive; and that paras. 5 and 6 of Sched. 6A, as construed by the Court of Session, were not consistent with the Sixth Directive and appeal allowed and decision of the VAT tribunal restored.

CUSTOMS AND EXCISE COMMISSIONERS v. ROBERT GORDON'S COLLEGE 1996 S.L.T. 98, Judge not specified, HL.

7396. Articles

VAT: statement of practice on transfer of a property-letting business as a going concern *(Alan R. Barr)*: J.L.S.S. 1996, 41 (10), 398-399. (Text of Customs and Excise statement of practice with commentary on effect for Scots property law).

WILLS

7397. Attestation–witness signing with wrong surname–whether informality could be cured

[Conveyancing (Scotland) Act 1874 (c.94) s.39.]

W sought reduction of a will signed by his late mother, R on the ground that it had been improperly executed. The document bore to be attested by two witnesses, one of whom signed as "D C R Williamson", although the testing clause stated that it had been signed by "David Carment Reid Wilson". E, the other children and a grandchild of R, averred that the will had been signed by Wilson but that he had inadvertently written "Williamson". E argued that (1) the discrepancy in the surnames was so minor that it should be disregarded; and (2) as the document ex facie had been signed by R and two witnesses, s.39 of the 1874 Act, which was to be given a liberal interpretation, applied, and that, if the document had been witnessed by the person who signed as "D C R Williamson" then reduction should be refused.

Held, decree de plano granted. (1) The discrepancy in the surnames was not so minor that it could be disregarded and, as the signature of a witness with a surname which was not his own was not a "subscription" in terms of the authentication statutes, the will had not been properly executed and (2) while the discrepancy might not be fatal if it was due to an error in the testing clause, s.39 required E to prove that the document had been subscribed "by the witness by whom such deed, instrument or writing bears to be attested", who was D. C. R. Williamson. E were not offering to prove this and a failure to satisfy the express terms of s.39 could not be disregarded on the basis of an argument based on the policy of the section.

WILLIAMSON v. WILLIAMSON 1996 S.L.T. 92, Judge not specified, OH.

7398. Construction–writings sent to solicitor after execution of formal will

A testatrix executed a formal will in 1985 in which various charities were listed as residuary legatees. Shortly before her death in 1991 she wrote to her solicitors enclosing a copy of an earlier will, dated 1983, to which she had made various handwritten additions and alterations which included changing the residuary legatees under the 1985 will into pecuniary legatees to receive specified benefits. She also enclosed various other handwritten papers which included the provision, "any residue to Scottish Cot Death Trust". The covering letter to her solicitors referred to an "extraordinary document" for them to unravel and stated that she had signed it "to be adopted as holograph" in case things did not go well for her. She died a few days later before further action had been taken by the solicitors. The executors, the residuary beneficiaries under the 1985 will, and the Cot Death Trust presented a special case to the Inner House for its judgment on the testamentary effect of these writings. On behalf of the residuary beneficiaries under the 1985 will it was argued that the 1991 bundle amounted only to instructions to the solicitor to alter the will.

Held, that (1) documents which were partly printed and partly handwritten, which were clearly intended to be taken and read together, fell to be treated as a single, properly executed testamentary document if the writer signed the writing and adopted the printed material as holograph; (2) looking to the terms of the covering letter and the close correlation between the handwritten list of bequests and the will with its alterations, it was clear that in the mind of the testatrix she was enclosing a single "document", albeit consisting of a number of parts and (3) while the testatrix was giving her solicitor instructions to change her will, it was also plain from the letter that given the state of her health she wanted the document to constitute an immediate testamentary disposition and the 1991 writings validly bequeathed the residue to the trust and revoked the earlier bequest of residue to the other charities; and questions answered accordingly.

BARKER'S EXECUTORS v. SCOTTISH RIGHTS OF WAY SOCIETY 1996 S.L.T. 1319, Judge not specified, IH.

7399. Books

Meston, Michael C.–Succession Opinions. Green's practice library. Hardback. ISBN 0-414-01121-X. W.Green & Son.

WORDS AND PHRASES

The table below is a cumulative guide to words and phrases judicially considered in 1996:

Law books

published during 1996

1996 Wiley Personal Injury Update. Personal injury. Paperback: £75.00. ISBN 0-471-13510-0. John Wiley and Sons.

A Guide to the Reporting of Injuries, Diseases and Dangerous Occurrences Regulations 1995 (RIDDOR). Guidance booklet, 73. ISBN 0-7176-1012-8. Health and Safety Executive.

A Practical Guide to the Machinery Directive: May 1995 Update. Unbound/looseleaf: £30.00. ISBN 1-86058-005-X. Mechanical Engineering Publications.

A Practical Guide to the Machinery Directive: October 1996 Update. Unbound/looseleaf: £30.00. ISBN 1-86058-008-4. Mechanical Engineering Publications.

A User's Guide to Patents. Paperback: £35.00. ISBN 0-406-01307-1. Butterworth Law.

Abbott, K.–Business Law for GNVQ Advanced Business. GNVQ Business series. Paperback: £8.95. ISBN 1-85805-176-2. DP Publications.

Abdullahi Ahmed An-Na'im–Toward an Islamic Reformation. Contemporary Issues in the Middle East. Paperback: £13.50. ISBN 0-8156-2706-8. Syracuse University Press.

Academie de Droit International de la Haye–Recueil des Cours/Collected Courses: Vol 253. 1995. Recueil Des Cours. Hardback: £96.00. ISBN 90-411-0279-5. Martinus Nijhoff Publishers.

Accessible Design Review Guide. Hardback: £60.95. ISBN 0-07-000189-8. McGraw-Hill Publishing Company.

Adams, Alix–Business Law: a Student Centred Approach. Paperback: £17.99. ISBN 0-273-60707-3. Pitman Publishing.

Adams, John F.; Clarke, David N.–Rent Reviews Manual. Unbound/looseleaf: £165.00. ISBN 0-7520-0005-5. FT Law & Tax.

Adams, John N.–Character Merchandising. Hardback: £105.00. ISBN 0-406-07767-3. Butterworth Law.

Adams, John N.; Pritchard Jones, K.V.–Franchising. Hardback: £95.00. ISBN 0-406-13790-0. Butterworth Law.

Adlam, J.C.–Iran-US Claims Tribunal Reports. Iran-US Claims Tribunal Reports. Paperback: £95.00. ISBN 0-521-46338-6. Cambridge University Press.

Adlem, Nick; Beecher, Graham–Commercial Litigation: 1995/96. Legal Practice Course resource books. Paperback: £17.50. ISBN 0-85308-336-3. Jordan.

Administrative Law - LLB: Suggested Solutions (1991-1995). Bachelor of laws (LLB). Paperback: £6.95. ISBN 0-7510-0732-3. HLT Publications.

Administrative Law: Suggested Solutions - Single Paper (June 1995). Paperback: £3.00. ISBN 0-7510-0631-9. HLT Publications.

Aird, R.E.; Jameson, J.M.St.C.–The Scots Dimension to Cross-Border Litigation. Hardback: £65.00. ISBN 0-414-011309. W. Green & Son.

Aisbett, Alan; Harrison, Alan; Grace, Clive–Local Government Precedents and Practice. Unbound/looseleaf: £175.00. ISBN 0-7520-0100-0. FT Law & Tax.

Albertstat, Philip–Media Production Agreements. Blueprint. Hardback: £50.00. ISBN 0-415-13668-7. Routledge.

Alder, John; Handy, Christopher–Housing Association Law. Hardback: £86.00. ISBN 0-421-54160-1. Sweet & Maxwell.

Aldrich, George H.–The Jurisprudence of the Iran-United States Claims Tribunal. Hardback: £75.00. ISBN 0-19-825805-4. Clarendon Press.

Aldridge, Trevor M.–Letting Business Premises. Practitioner series. Paperback: £44.00. ISBN 0-7520-0237-6. FT Law & Tax.

Aldridge, Trevor M.–Powers of Attorney. Practitioner series. Paperback: £40.00. ISBN 0-7520-0234-1. FT Law & Tax.

Alexiadis, Peter; Kallaugher, John–Alexiadis and Kallaugher: EC Competition Law Yearbook: 1995. Hardback: £65.00. ISBN 0-421-55110-0. Sweet & Maxwell.

Allard, Amanda–Child Abuse Briefing Paper. Paperback: £2.50. The Children's Society.

Allen, Chris–VAT Handbook: 1996-97. Paperback. ISBN 0-86325-400-4. CCH Editions.

Allen, M.–WEB Yearbook. Paperback: £35.00. ISBN 1-85431-515-3. Blackstone Press.

Allen, Michael–Cases and Materials on Constitutional and Administrative Law. Paperback: £20.00. ISBN 1-85431-554-4. Blackstone Press.

Alston, Philip–Human Rights Law. International Library of Essays on Law and Legal Theory. Hardback: £97.50. ISBN 1-85521-236-6. Dartmouth.

Alston, Philip–Promoting Human Rights Through Bills of Rights. Hardback: £50.00. ISBN 0-19-825822-4. Clarendon Press.

Alston, Philip; Steiner, Henry–International Human Rights in Context. Hardback: £60.00. ISBN 0-19-825427-X. Paperback: £30.00. ISBN 0-19-825426-1. Clarendon Press.

Ambrose, Clare; Maxwell, Karen–London Maritime Arbitration. Lloyd's shipping law library. Hardback: £78.00. ISBN 1-85978-027-X. LLP Limited.

Amerasinghe, C.F.–Principles of the Institutional Law of International Organizations. Cambridge Studies in International and Comparative Law, 1. Hardback: £60.00. ISBN 0-521-56254-6. Cambridge University Press.

Amira El Azhary Sonbol–Women, the Family, and Divorce Laws in Islamic History. Contemporary Issues in the Middle East. Hardback: £35.95. ISBN 0-8156-2688-6. Paperback: £15.95. ISBN 0-8156-0383-5. Syracuse University Press.

Amirahmadi, Hooshang–Small Islands, Big Politics. Hardback: £29.50. ISBN 0-333-68019-7. Macmillan Press.

Anaya, S. James–Indigenous Peoples in International Law. Hardback: £32.50. ISBN 0-19-508620-1. Oxford University Press Inc, USA.

Anderson, Mark S.–Technology - the Law of Exploitation and Transfer. Hardback: £48.00. ISBN 0-406-01304-7. Butterworth Law.

Anderson, Michael; Boyle, Alan–Human Rights Approaches to Environmental Protection. Hardback: £35.00. ISBN 0-19-826255-8. Clarendon Press.

Andoh, Benjamin; Marsh, Stephen–Civil Remedies. Hardback: £47.50. ISBN 1-85521-788-0. Dartmouth. Paperback: £21.50. ISBN 1-85521-792-9. Dartmouth.

Andrews, Mark; Barnett, Nigel–Insolvency Litigation Strategies. Paperback: £65.00. ISBN 0-7520-0233-3. FT Law & Tax.

Antle, John M.–Choice and Efficiency in Food Safety Policy. Studies in Agricultural Policy. Hardback: £23.95. ISBN 0-8447-3902-2. American Enterprise Institute.

Applegate, A.–Wills, Probate and Administration. Legal Practice Course resource books. Paperback: £17.50. ISBN 0-85308-369-X. Jordan.

Applying Psychology to the Legal World. £5.99. ISBN 0-340-64759-0. Hodder & Stoughton Educational.

Aquino, T.–Essential Evidence. Essential law series. Paperback: £4.95. ISBN 1-85941-145-2. Cavendish Publishing Ltd.

Arden, Andrew; Hunter, Caroline–Manual of Housing Law. Paperback: £30.00. ISBN 0-421-55390-1. Sweet & Maxwell.

Arjava, Antti–Women and Law in Late Antiquity and the Early Middle Ages. Hardback: £35.00. ISBN 0-19-815033-4. Clarendon Press.

Arlidge, Anthony; Parry, Jacques; Gatt, Ian–Arlidge and Parry on Fraud. Criminal law library. Hardback: £95.00. ISBN 0-421-48500-0. Sweet & Maxwell.

Armytage, Livingston–Educating Judges. Hardback: £72.50. ISBN 90-411-0256-6. Kluwer Law International.

Arthur, Hugh–Pensions Trusteeship Issues. Pensions reports. Hardback: £125.00. ISBN 0-7520-0178-7. FT Law & Tax.

Ashford, Mark; Johnston, Helen; Chard, Alex–Defending Young People. Paperback: £23.00. ISBN 0-905099-76-1. The Legal Action Group.

Ashworth, Allan–Contractural Procedures in the Construction Industry. Paperback: £19.99. ISBN 0-582-28875-4. Addison-Wesley Longman Higher Education.

Aufenanger, M.–Markengesetz/the German Trade Mark Act. Paperback: £31.50. ISBN 3-527-28804-X. VCH.

Austin, John–The Province of Jurisprudence Determined. Classical Jurisprudence. Hardback: £40.00. ISBN 1-85521-649-3. Dartmouth.

Austin, R.C.; Bonner, David; Whitty, Noel–Legal Protection of Civil Liberties. Paperback: £26.95. ISBN 0-406-55511-7. Butterworth Law.

Ayrton, Lyn–Residence and Contact Orders. Practitioner series. Paperback: £29.00. ISBN 0-7520-0113-2. FT Law & Tax.

Bagnall, Gary–Law As Art. Applied legal philosophy. Hardback: £39.50. ISBN 1-85521-758-9. Dartmouth.

Baigent, A.–Pervasive Topics. Legal Practice Course resource books. Paperback: £15.00. ISBN 0-85308-370-3. Jordan.

Bailey, Edward; Groves, Hugo; Smith, Cormac–Corporate Insolvency - Law and Practice. Hardback: £125.00. ISBN 0-406-08142-5. Butterworth Law.

Bailey, F. Lee; Fishman, Kenneth J.–Criminal Trial Techniques. Ring binder: £255.00. ISBN 0-420-55650-8. Stevens & Sons.

Bailey, S.H.; Gunn, M.–Smith and Bailey on the Modern English Legal System. Paperback: £27.00. ISBN 0-421-50840-X. Sweet & Maxwell.

Bainbridge, David I.–An Introduction to Computer Law. Paperback: £21.95. ISBN 0-273-61940-3. Pitman Publishing.

Bainbridge, David–Intellectual Property. Paperback: £27.99. ISBN 0-273-62279-X. Pitman Publishing.

Bainbridge, David; Pearce, Graham; Platten, Nick–Bainbridge, Pearce and Platten: European Data Protection Directive. Paperback: £90.00. ISBN 0-406-01447-7. Butterworth Law.

Bainham, Andrew–The International Survey of Family Law: 1994. Hardback: £112.50. ISBN 90-411-0218-3. Martinus Nijhoff Publishers.

Baker, C.D.–Baker: Tort. Concise course texts. Paperback: £12.95. ISBN 0-421-55480-0. Sweet & Maxwell.

Baldwin, Carl R.–Immigration: Questions and Answers. Paperback: £9.95. ISBN 1-880559-32-3. Allworth Press.

Baldwin, Robert; Cane, Peter–Law and Uncertainty. Hardback: £99.00. ISBN 90-411-0942-0. Kluwer Law International.

Baldwin, Terence–Road Accident Compensation. Paperback: £9.99. ISBN 0-7090-5811-X. Robert Hale.

Ball, Andrew; Narain, Lakshmi–Deloitte Ross: VAT - a Business by Business Guide: 1996-7. Paperback: £36.95. ISBN 0-406-99087-5. Butterworth Law.

Ball, Howard–Hugo L. Black: Cold Steel Warrior. Hardback: £25.00. ISBN 0-19-507814-4. Oxford University Press Inc, USA.

Ball, Simon; Burton, Tim–Water Law. Environmental law. Hardback: £45.00. ISBN 0-471-96577-4. Chancery Wiley Law Publications.

Bamforth, Nicholas–Sexuality, Morals and Justice. Lesbian and gay studies. Hardback: £40.00. ISBN 0-304-33145-7. Paperback: £12.99. ISBN 0-304-33147-3. Cassell.

Banakas, Efstathios K.–Civil Liability for Pure Economic Loss. Hardback: £68.00. ISBN 90-411-0908-0. Kluwer Law International.

Bannister, Jim–How to Manage Risk. A DYP textbook. Hardback. ISBN 1-85978-060-1. DYP Insurance Publications.

Barav, Ami; Wyatt, Derrick–Yearbook of European Law: Vol 14. 1994. Hardback: £110.00. ISBN 0-19-825782-1. Clarendon Press.

Barendt, Eric–Yearbook of Media and Entertainment Law: Vol II. 1996. Hardback: £125.00. ISBN 0-19-826277-9. Oxford University Press.

Barker, George R.–An Economic Analysis of Trade Unions and the Common Law. Hardback: £35.00. ISBN 1-85972-203-2. Avebury.

Barlow, Anne–The Law Relating to Cohabitation. Paperback: £39.95. ISBN 1-86012-047-4. Tolley Publishing.

Barnard, Catherine–EC Employment Law. Hardback: £24.95. ISBN 0-471-96665-7. Chancery Wiley Law Publications.

Barnard, David; O'Cain, Andrea; Stockdale, Michael–Barnard O'Cain and Stockdale: the Criminal Court in Action. Paperback: £21.95. ISBN 0-406-04587-9. Butterworth Law.

Barnett, Daniel–Avoiding Unfair Dismissal Claims. Paperback: £14.99. ISBN 0-471-96564-2. John Wiley and Sons.

Barnsley, D.G.–Barnsley's Conveyancing Law and Practice. Paperback: £29.95. ISBN 0-406-00489-7. Butterworth Law.

Barrett, Richard S.–Fair Employment Strategies in Human Resource Management. Hardback: £47.95. ISBN 0-89930-986-0. Quorum Books.

Barritt, C.M.H.–The Building Acts and Regulations Applied. Paperback: £15.99. ISBN 0-582-25630-5. Addison-Wesley Longman Higher Education.

Barrow, C.A.–Industrial Relations Law. Paperback: £17.95. ISBN 1-85941-115-0. Cavendish Publishing Ltd.

Barson, Kalman A.–Investigating Accounting in Divorce. Family Law. Hardback: £75.00. ISBN 0-471-13513-5. John Wiley and Sons.

Bateman, Mike; King, Brian; Lewis, Paul–The Handbook of Health and Safety At Work. Hardback: £45.00. ISBN 0-7494-1241-0. Kogan Page.

Baum, Andrew; Sams, Gary–Statutory Valuations. Paperback: £16.99. ISBN 0-415-13762-4. International Thomson Business Press.

Bauman, Richard W.–Critical Legal Studies. Hardback: £40.95. ISBN 0-8133-8980-1. Westview Press.

Baums, Theodor; Wymeersch, Eddy–Asset Backed Securitization in Europe. Hardback: £89.00. ISBN 90-411-0916-1. Kluwer Law International.

Baxter, James S.–Child Witnesses. Cassell series: the facts about... Hardback: £35.00. ISBN 0-304-32662-3. Cassell.

Bean, David–Injunctions. Practitioner series. Paperback: £35.00. ISBN 0-7520-0288-0. FT Law & Tax.

Beatson, Jack–Has the Common Law a Future? Paperback: £4.95. ISBN 0-521-58675-5. Cambridge University Press.

Beck, Robert J.; Arend, Anthony Clark; Lugt, Robert D. Vander–International Rules. Hardback: £27.50. ISBN 0-19-508539-6. Paperback: £15.99. ISBN 0-19-508540-X. Oxford University Press Inc, USA.

Bedee, Henk–The International Guide to Social Security. Hardback: £117.00. ISBN 90-6544-874-8. Kluwer Law International.

Bedford, Becky; Tyrell, Alan–Bedford and Tyrrell: Public Procurement in Europe - Enforcement and Remedies. Hardback: £90.00. ISBN 0-406-04783-9. Butterworth Law.

Beeferman, Larry W.–Images of the Citizen and the State. Hardback: £50.50. ISBN 0-7618-0231-2. Paperback: £35.50. ISBN 0-7618-0232-0. University Press of America.

Beier, F.-K; Schricker, G.; Fikentscher, W.–German Industrial Property, Copyright and Antitrust Laws. Unbound/looseleaf: £52.00. ISBN 3-527-28730-2. VCH.

Bell, Cedric D.–Evidence: Casebook 1996-1997. Bar examinations. Paperback: £18.95. ISBN 0-7510-0676-9. HLT Publications.

Bell, Cedric D.–Evidence: Textbook 1996-1997. Bar examinations. Paperback: £19.95. ISBN 0-7510-0713-7. HLT Publications.

Bell, Cedric D.–Land Law: Textbook 1996-1997. Bachelor of Laws (LLB). Paperback: £16.95. ISBN 0-7510-0688-2. HLT Publications.

Bell, Cedric–Land Law. Cracknell's law students' companions. Paperback: £9.95. ISBN 1-85836-039-0. Old Bailey Press.

Benjamin, Joanna–Benjamin: Global Custody-an English Analysis. Paperback: £130.00. ISBN 0-406-04836-3. Butterworth Law.

Bennett, Howard–The Law of Marine Insurance. Hardback: £30.00. ISBN 0-19-826244-2. Paperback: £60.00. ISBN 0-19-825844-5. Clarendon Press.

Bennett, Michael J.–When Dreams Came True. Hardback: £19.95. ISBN 1-57488-041-1. Brassey's US.

Bentham, Jeremy; Burns, J.H.; Hart, H.L.A.–The Collected Works of Jeremy Bentham: an Introduction to the Principles of Morals and Legislation. Paperback: £17.99. ISBN 0-19-820516-3. Clarendon Press.

Bentley, David–English Criminal Justice in the Nineteenth Century. Hardback: £25.00. Hambledon Press.

Bentley, Lionel; Flynn, Leo–Law and the Senses. Law and social theory. Hardback: £45.00. ISBN 0-7453-1069-9. Paperback: £14.99. ISBN 0-7453-1068-0. Pluto Press.

Berg, Albert Jan van den–Planning Efficient Arbitration Proceedings and the Law Applicable in International Arbitration. Icca congress series. Paperback: £104.00. ISBN 90-411-0224-8. Kluwer Law International.

Beswick, Simon; Wine, Humphrey–Buying and Selling Private Companies and Businesses. £45.00. ISBN 0-406-08190-5. Butterworth Law.

Bethlehem, Daniel; Weller, Marc–The Yugoslav Crisis in International Law: Part III. Human Rights and War Crimes. Cambridge International Documents Series. Hardback: £75.00. ISBN 0-521-47509-0. Cambridge University Press.

Bettelheim, Eric; Parry, Helen; Rees, William–Swaps and Derivatives Trading Law and Regulation. Hardback: £95.00. ISBN 0-7520-0159-0. FT Law & Tax.

Bezold, G.–Protection of Biotechnological Matter Under European and German Law. Paperback: £54.00. ISBN 3-527-28781-7. VCH.

Bhandari, Jagdeep S.; Adler, Barry E.; Weiss, Lawrence A.–Corporate Bankruptcy. Hardback: £55.00. ISBN 0-521-45107-8. Paperback: £19.95. ISBN 0-521-45717-3. Cambridge University Press.

Bibliographic Guide to Law: 1995. Hardback: £350.00. ISBN 0-7838-1332-5. G.K. Hall.

Bick, Paul–Construction Contract Law. Paperback: £21.95. ISBN 1-85941-038-3. Cavendish Publishing Ltd.

Biederman, Donald E.; Pierson, Edward P.; Silfen, Martin E.; Glasser, Jeanne A.; Berry, Robert C.; Sobel, Lionel S.–Law and Business of the Entertainment Industries. Hardback: £47.95. ISBN 0-275-95064-6. Praeger Publishers.

Biggs, A.K.–Butterworths Rules of Court - Family Court Practice: 1996. Butterworths rules of court series. Paperback: £37.50. ISBN 0-406-99893-0. Butterworth Law.

Bird, Roger–Child Maintenance. Paperback: £27.50. ISBN 0-85308-320-7. Family Law.

Birds, John–Reminders for Company Secretaries. Paperback: £17.50. ISBN 0-85308-390-8. Jordan.

Birkinshaw, Patrick–Freedom of Information - the Law, the Practice and the Ideal. Hardback: £23.95. ISBN 0-406-04972-6. Butterworth Law.

Birks, Peter–What Are Law Schools For?: Vol 2. Pressing Problems in the Law. Paperback: £25.00. ISBN 0-19-826293-0. Oxford University Press.

Bishop, Gillian; Hodson, David; Raeside, Dominic; Robinson, Sara; Smallacombe, Ruth–Divorce Reform. Paperback: £35.00. ISBN 0-7520-0282-1. FT Law & Tax.

Bix, Brian–Jurisprudence: Theory and Context. Modern legal studies. Paperback: £18.95. ISBN 0-421-52660-2. Sweet & Maxwell.

Blackburn, Robert–The Bill of Rights Debate. Citizenship and the law series. Hardback: £45.00. ISBN 0-7201-2123-X. Mansell.

Blackburn, Robert–The European Convention on Human Rights. Hardback: £50.00. ISBN 0-7201-2229-5. Mansell.

Blake, Susan–A Practical Approach to Legal Advice and Drafting. Paperback: £17.00. ISBN 1-85431-541-2. Blackstone Press.

Blakemore, Timothy–Law for Legal Executives Part 1. Year 1. Paperback: £17.95. ISBN 1-85431-583-8. Blackstone Press.

Blakeney, Michael–Trade Related Aspects of Intellectual Property Rights. Intellectual property in practice. Hardback: £55.00. ISBN 0-421-53630-6. Sweet & Maxwell.

Bland, Randall W.–The Black Robe and the Bald Eagle. Hardback: £53.95. ISBN 1-880921-40-5. Paperback: £35.95. ISBN 1-880921-06-5. Austin and Winfield.

Blanpain, Roger; Engels, Chris–Labour Law in Belgium. Paperback: £45.00. ISBN 90-411-0228-0. Kluwer Law International.

Bloy, Duncan–Criminal Law. Lecture notes. Paperback: £14.95. ISBN 1-85941-168-1. Cavendish Publishing Ltd.

Blum, Francoise; Logue, Anne–State Monopolies Under EC Law. Hardback: £75.00. ISBN 0-471-94353-3. Chancery Wiley Law Publications.

Blumenroder, U.–German Regulations on Industrial Products. Paperback. ISBN 3-527-28780-9. VCH.

Bobb-Semple, Colin–Sourcebook on Criminal Litigation and Sentencing. Sourcebook Series. Paperback: £19.95. ISBN 1-85941-101-0. Cavendish Publishing Ltd.

Bocken, Hubert–Codification of Environmental Law Draft Decree on Environmental Policy. Nijhoff law specials. Paperback: £68.00. ISBN 90-411-0911-0. Hardback: £70.00. ISBN 90-411-0888-2. Kluwer Law International.

Bogle, Andrew; Fuller, John–Successful Debt Collecting. Paperback: £17.50. ISBN 0-85308-323-1. Jordan.

Bojczuk, William; Cracknell, Doug G.–Evidence: Textbook 1996-1997. Bachelor of Laws (LLB). Paperback: £18.95. ISBN 0-7510-0692-0. HLT Publications.

Bologna, Jack; Shaw, Paul–Corporate Crime Investigation. Hardback: £27.50. ISBN 0-7506-9659-1. Butterworth-Heinemann.

Bonner, David; Hooker, Ian; White, Robin–Non Means Tested Benefits: the Legislation: Supplement 1996. Paperback: £17.95. ISBN 0-421-56800-3. Sweet & Maxwell.

Boorstin, Daniel J.–The Mysterious Science of the Law. Paperback: £11.95. ISBN 0-226-06498-0. University of Chicago Press.

Borgese, Elisabeth Mann; Ginsburg, Norton; Morgan, Joseph R.–Ocean Yearbook: Vol 12. Hardback: £55.95. ISBN 0-226-06615-0. University of Chicago Press.

Boumil, Marcia Mobilia; Friedman, Joel–Deadbeat Dads. Paperback: £27.95. ISBN 0-275-95125-1. Praeger Publishers.

Bourantonis, Dimitris; Evriviades, Marios–A United Nations for the Twenty-first Century. Nijhoff law specials. Hardback: £103.00. ISBN 90-411-0312-0. Kluwer Law International.

Bourn, Colin; Whitmore, John–Anti-discrimination Law in Britain. Paperback: £48.00. ISBN 0-421-56420-2. Sweet & Maxwell.

Bourne, C.; Popat, P.–On Your Feet!. Paperback: £11.95. ISBN 1-874241-12-0. Cavendish Publishing Ltd.

Bowers, John–Textbook on Labour Law. Paperback: £17.95. ISBN 1-85431-446-7. Blackstone Press.

Bowers, John; Brown, Damian; Mead, Geoffrey–Industrial Tribunal Practice. Paperback: £40.00. ISBN 0-7520-0351-8. FT Law & Tax.

Bowman, Scott R.–The Modern Corporation and American Political Thought. Hardback: £43.95. ISBN 0-271-01472-5. Paperback: £15.50. ISBN 0-271-01473-3. Penn State Press.

Boyd, S.C.–Scrutton on Charterparties. Hardback: £130.00. ISBN 0-421-52580-0. Sweet & Maxwell.

Boyle, Alan; Marshall, Philip; Jones, Philip; Kosmin, Leslie; Richards, David; Gillyon, Philip–The Practice and Procedure of the Companies Court. Lloyd's commercial law library. Hardback: £110.00. ISBN 1-85044-502-8. LLP Limited.

Boyle, James–Shamans, Software and Spleens. Hardback: £21.95. ISBN 0-674-80522-4. Harvard University Press.

Bracewell, J–The Family Court Practice: 1996. Hardback: £99.00. ISBN 0-85308-367-3. Family Law.

Brack, Duncan–International Trade and the Montreal Protocol. Hardback: £35.00. Earthscan.

Bradford, David F.–Distributional Analysis of Tax Policy. Hardback: £31.95. ISBN 0-8447-3890-5. Paperback: £15.95. ISBN 0-8447-3891-3. American Enterprise Institute.

Bradley–Family Law & Political Culture. Paperback: £18.95. ISBN 0-421-52620-3. Sweet & Maxwell.

Brahm, Laurence; Daoran, Li–The Business Guide to China. Paperback: £11.99. ISBN 981-00-7079-9. Butterworth-Heinemann.

Brayne, Hugh–Legal Practice Course Case Study: Criminal Litigation 1996/1997. Paperback: £10.95. ISBN 1-85431-578-1. Blackstone Press.

Brazier, Gill–Insider Dealing. Paperback: £19.95. ISBN 1-874241-02-3. Cavendish Publishing Ltd.

Bregman, J.I.; Melchor, J.R.–Environmental Compliance Handbook. Hardback: £49.00. ISBN 1-56670-146-5. Lewis (CRC).

Brennan, Frank; Howley, Seamus; Moore, Alan–Brennan, Howley, Moore: Tax Acts Commentary 1996-97. Hardback: £85.00. ISBN 1-85475-637-0. Butterworth Law (Ireland).

Brenner, Daniel L.–Law and Regulation of Common Carriers in the Communications Industry. Hardback: £54.95. ISBN 0-8133-2740-7. Westview Press.

Brewer, John D.; Guelke, Adrian; Hume, Ian; Moxon-Browne, Edward; Wilford, Rick–The Police, Public Order and the State. Hardback: £40.00. ISBN 0-333-65487-0. Paperback: £14.99. ISBN 0-333-65488-9. Macmillan Press.

Bridge, Michael–The Sale of Goods. Hardback: £80.00. ISBN 0-19-825871-2. Oxford University Press.

Bridge, S.–Statutes on Landlord and Tenant. £15.95. ISBN 1-85431-493-9. Blackstone Press.

Bridges, Paul–Land Law: Casebook 1996-1997. Bachelor of Laws (LLB). Paperback: £17.95. ISBN 0-7510-0655-6. HLT Publications.

Brindle, Michael; Cox, Raymond–Law of Banking Payments. Hardback: £95.00. ISBN 0-7520-0037-3. FT Law & Tax.

British Companies Legislation: 1996. British companies legislation. Paperback: £30.00. ISBN 0-86325-438-1. CCH Editions.

British Tax Review Index: 1975-1990. Hardback: £50.00. ISBN 0-421-45970-0. Sweet & Maxwell.

Brooks, Peter; Gewirtz, Paul–Law's Stories. Hardback: £20.00. ISBN 0-300-06675-9. Yale University Press.

Brown, Alistair N.–Proceeds of Crime. Green's annotated acts. Paperback. ISBN 0-414-01148-1. W.Green & Son.

Brown, I–Q & A Law of Contract. £8.95. ISBN 1-85431-494-7. Blackstone Press.

Brownlie, Ian; Crawford, James–The British Year Book of International Law: Vol 66. 1995. Hardback: £95.00. ISBN 0-19-825882-8. Clarendon Press.

Bruce-Radcliffe, Godfrey–Property Development Finance: a Practical Guide. Paperback: £50.00. ISBN 0-7520-0217-1. FT Law & Tax.

Bryan, Helen–Planning Applications and Appeals. Paperback: £14.99. ISBN 0-7506-2792-1. Architectural Press: an imprint of Butterworth-Heinemann.

Buck, Trevor –The Social Fund. Paperback: £39.00. ISBN 0-421-50930-9. Sweet & Maxwell.

Buckley, Richard–Legal Structures. Hardback: £45.00. ISBN 0-471-96631-2. John Wiley and Sons.

Bucknell, Patrick; Ghodse, Hamid–Bucknell and Ghodse on Misuse of Drugs. Criminal law library. £99.00. ISBN 0-421-54990-4. Sweet & Maxwell.

Budden, Michael Craig–Protecting Trade Secrets Under the Uniform Trade Secrets Act. Hardback: £43.95. ISBN 1-56720-016-8. Quorum Books.

Bueno, Antonio; Hedley, Richard; Stallebrass, Paul–Electronic Transfer of Funds. Hardback: £49.00. ISBN 0-421-52060-4. Sweet & Maxwell.

Bulterman, M.K.–Compliance with Judgments of International Courts. Hardback: £61.00. ISBN 90-411-0157-8. Martinus Nijhoff Publishers.

Burgess-Jackson, Keith–Rape: a Philosophical Investigation. Appied Legal Philosophy. Hardback: £42.50. ISBN 1-85521-485-7. Dartmouth.

Burn, Edward–Maudsley & Burn: Trusts and Trustees - Cases and Materials. Paperback: £32.95. ISBN 0-406-01445-0. Butterworth Law.

Burrows, David; Bruce, Simon; Hughes, Judith; Purdie, Robert; Wildblood, Steven–Butterworths Family Law Guide. Paperback: £45.00. ISBN 0-406-08141-7. Butterworth Law.

Burrows, Noreen–European Social Law. Paperback: £22.50. ISBN 0-471-96537-5. Chancery Wiley Law Publications.

Bursell, Rupert D.H.–Liturgy Order and the Law. Hardback: £45.00. ISBN 0-19-826250-7. Paperback: £14.99. ISBN 0-19-826249-3. Clarendon Press.

Burton, Frances–Guide to the Family Law Act 1996. Paperback: £19.95. ISBN 1-85941-312-9. Cavendish Publishing Ltd.

Burton, Imogen; Duffield, Nancy; O'Toole, Dawn–Family Law and Practice. Legal Practice Course resource books. Paperback: £17.50. ISBN 0-85308-340-1. Family Law.

Business Law Guide to Switzerland. Hardback: £75.00. ISBN 0-86325-352-0. CCH Editions.

Busuttil, James J.; Gilbert, Geoff; Wight, Robert; Sunkin, Maurice–Sourcebook on Environmental Law. Sourcebook series. Paperback: £18.95. ISBN 1-85941-109-6. Cavendish Publishing Ltd.

Butler, Henry N.; Macey, Jonathan R.–Using Federalism to Improve Environmental Policy. AEI Studies in Regulation and Federalism. Hardback: £23.95. ISBN 0-8447-3962-6. Paperback: £10.50. ISBN 0-8447-3963-4. American Enterprise Institute.

Butler, W.E.–Russian Legal Theory. International Library of Essays on Law and Legal Theory. Hardback: £110.00. ISBN 1-85521-249-8. Dartmouth.

Butt, Paul–Residential Landlord and Tenant. Legal Practice Course resource books. Paperback: £17.50. ISBN 0-85308-345-2. Jordan.

Butterworths European Information Services–Butterworths Annual European Review: 1995. Hardback: £155.00. ISBN 0-406-06508-X. Butterworth Law.

Butterworths Orange Tax Handbook: 1996-97. Paperback: £28.00. ISBN 0-406-06499-7. Butterworth Law.

Butterworths Tax Diary: 1996-97. £25.00. ISBN 1-85475-738-5. Butterworth Law (Ireland).

Butterworths Tax Guide 1996-97. Paperback: £60.00. ISBN 1-85475-708-3. Butterworth Law (Ireland).

Butterworths VAT Handbook. Paperback: £20.00. ISBN 0-406-01444-2. Butterworth Law.

Butterworths Yellow Tax Handbook: 1996-97. Paperback: £28.00. ISBN 0-406-06498-9. Butterworth Law.

Cairns, Elizabeth–Charities: Law and Practice. Hardback: £56.00. ISBN 0-421-56190-4. Sweet & Maxwell.

Cairns, Elizabeth–Tolley's Raising Funds for Charity. £35.95. ISBN 0-85459-760-3. Tolley Publishing.

Cairns, Walter–Introduction to European Law. Legal Skills Series. Paperback: £8.95. ISBN 1-85941-205-X. Cavendish Publishing Ltd.

Cale, Michelle–Law and Society. Public Record Office readers' guides, No 14. Paperback: £12.99. Public Record Office.

Calfee, John E.; Rubin, Paul H.–Restoring Consumer Sovereignty to Products Liability. Hardback: £15.95. ISBN 0-8447-7065-5. Paperback: £7.95. ISBN 0-8447-7065-5. American Enterprise Institute.

Cameron, James; Werksman, Jacob; Roderick, Peter–Improving Compliance with International Environmental Law. Law and sustainable development, No 2. Paperback: £19.95. ISBN 1-85383-261-8. Earthscan.

Campbell, Brigid; Cross, Ian–Welfare Law and Immigration. Legal Practice Course Resource Books. Paperback: £17.50. ISBN 0-85308-346-0. Jordan.

Campbell, Christian–International Media Liability. Hardback: £75.00. ISBN 0-471-96578-2. Chancery Wiley Law Publications.

Campbell, David; Vincent-Jones, Peter–Contract and Economic Organisation. Hardback: £37.50. ISBN 1-85521-694-9. Dartmouth.

Campbell, Dennis–Butterworths European Tax and Investment Service. Unbound/looseleaf: £165.00. ISBN 0-406-05199-2. Butterworth Law.

Campbell, Dennis–Commercial Alliances in the Information Age. Commercial Law. Hardback: £75.00. ISBN 0-471-96552-9. Chancery Wiley Law Publications.

Campbell, Dennis–International Banking Law and Regulation. Unbound/looseleaf: £195.00. ISBN 0-7520-0192-2. FT Law & Tax.

Campbell, Dennis–International Food and Beverage Law. Hardback: £100.00. ISBN 90-411-0936-6. Kluwer Law International.

Campbell, Dennis–International Information Technology Law. Hardback: £75.00. ISBN 0-471-96871-4. Chancery Wiley Law Publications.

Campbell, Dennis–International Personal Injury Compensation. Hardback: £115.00. ISBN 0-421-57060-1. Sweet & Maxwell.

Campbell, Dennis–Offshore Trusts. Comparative Law Yearbook of International Business. Hardback: £88.00. ISBN 90-411-0921-8. Kluwer Law International.

Campbell, Dennis–Protecting Minority Shareholders. Hardback: £165.00. ISBN 90-411-0922-6. Kluwer Law International.

Campbell, Dennis–Structuring International Contracts. Hardback: £88.00. ISBN 90-411-0935-8. Kluwer Law International.

Campbell, Ian–Compensation for Personal Injury in New Zealand. Paperback. ISBN 1-86940-150-6. Auckland University Press.

Campbell, Tom D.–The Legal Theory of Ethical Positivism. Applied Legal Philosophy Series. Hardback: £39.50. ISBN 1-85521-171-8. Dartmouth.

Canadian Council on International Law/Conseil Canadien de Droit International–Global Forests and International Environmental Law. International environmental law and policy. Hardback: £85.00. ISBN 90-411-0897-1. Kluwer Law International.

Cane, Peter–An Introduction to Administrative Law. Clarendon law series. Hardback: £35.00. ISBN 0-19-876464-2. Paperback: £15.99. ISBN 0-19-876465-0. Clarendon Press.

Cane, Peter–Tort Law and Economic Interests. Hardback: £50.00. ISBN 0-19-876430-8. Paperback: £22.50. ISBN 0-19-876429-4. Clarendon Press.

Card, Richard; Ward, Richard–The Criminal Procedure and Investigations Act 1996. Paperback: £19.50. ISBN 0-85308-379-7. Jordan.

Cardwell, Michael–Milk Quotas. Hardback: £35.00. ISBN 0-19-825940-9. Clarendon Press.

Carey, Peter–Media Law. Paperback. ISBN 0-421-57140-3. Sweet & Maxwell.

Carman, John–Valuing Ancient Things. Hardback: £59.95. ISBN 0-7185-0012-1. Leicester University Press, a Division of Pinter Publishers.

Carmichael, K.S.–Spicer and Pegler's Executorship Law and Accounts. Hardback: £65.00. ISBN 0-406-03598-9. Butterworth Law.

Carr, C.J.–SWOT: Law of Evidence. Paperback: £8.95. ISBN 1-85431-486-6. Blackstone Press.

Carter, Mary E.–Electronic Highway Robbery. Paperback: £18.95. ISBN 0-201-88393-7. Peachpit Press.

Cassidy, Constance–The Licensing Acts 1833-1995. Hardback: £137.50. ISBN 1-899-73811-8. Round Hall Sweet & Maxwell.

Cato, D. Mark–Arbitration Workbook. Unbound/looseleaf: £125.00. ISBN 1-85044-853-1. Lloyd's of London Press.

Chappell, David–Contractual Correspondence for Architects. Hardback: £29.95. ISBN 0-632-04002-5. Blackwell Science (UK).

Charlesworth, Andrew; Cullen, Holly–European Community Law. Paperback: £25.95. ISBN 0-273-61939-X. Pitman Publishing.

Charman, Mary; Martin, Jacqueline–Longman A-level Revise Guide: Law. Longman A-level revise guides. Paperback: £10.99. ISBN 0-582-28701-4. Addison-Wesley Longman Higher Education.

Chatterjee, C. –Public International Law. Cracknell's statutes. Paperback: £7.95. ISBN 1-85836-023-4. Old Bailey Press.

Chatterjee, C.; Davies, D.R.–Public International Law. Cracknell's law students' companions. Paperback: £9.95. ISBN 1-85836-038-2. Old Bailey Press.

Chatterjee, Charles–Legal Aspects of Transnational Marketing and Sales Contracts. Paperback: £19.95. ISBN 1-85941-035-9. Cavendish Publishing Ltd.

Chayes, Abram; Chayes, Antonia Handler–The New Sovereignity. Hardback: £31.50. ISBN 0-674-61782-7. Harvard University Press.

Cheffins, Brian R.–Company Law. Paperback: £19.99. ISBN 0-19-876469-3. Oxford University Press.

Cherry, John–Ear, Nose and Throat. Medico-legal practitioner. Hardback: £34.95. ISBN 1-85941-210-6. Cavendish Publishing Ltd.

Chesworth, Niki–The Daily Express Guide to Buying a Property Abroad. Daily Express guides. Paperback: £7.99. ISBN 0-7494-2017-0. Kogan Page.

Choo, Andrew Li-Teik–Hearsay and Confrontation in Criminal Trials. Oxford Monographs on Criminal Law and Justice. Hardback: £35.00. ISBN 0-19-825891-7. Clarendon Press.

Christou, Richard–International Agency, Distribution and Licensing Agreements. Commercial series. Hardback: £85.00. ISBN 0-7520-0211-2. FT Law & Tax.

Ciambella, Franca–Investment in South East Asia. Hardback: £35.00. ISBN 981-00-6798-4. Butterworth-Heinemann.

Civil and Criminal Procedure: Suggested Solutions - Single Paper (Trinity 1995). Bar Examinations. Paperback: £3.95. ISBN 0-7510-0637-8. HLT Publications.

Clapham, Andrew–Human Rights in the Private Sphere. Oxford Monographs in international law. Paperback: £19.99. ISBN 0-19-876431-6. Clarendon Press.

Clark, F.; Diliberto, K.–Investigating Computer Crime. Hardback: £35.00. ISBN 0-8493-8158-4. CRC Press.

Clark, Robert–Legal Skills and System: Textbook 1996-1997. Bachelor of Laws (LLB). Paperback: £17.50. ISBN 0-7510-0649-1. HLT Publications.

Clark, Robert; Smyth, Shane–Clark and Smyth: Intellectual Property Law. Hardback: £55.00. ISBN 1-85475-138-7. Butterworth Law (Ireland).

Clarke, A.; Dinning, S.–Business Entities. Paperback: £22.95. ISBN 0-421-50490-0. Sweet & Maxwell.

Clarke, Giles–Butterworths Offshore Trusts and Materials. Unbound/looseleaf: £320.00. ISBN 0-406-05396-0. Butterworth Law.

Clarke, Julie–Tolley's Employment and Personnel Procedures. Unbound/looseleaf: £75.00. ISBN 1-86012-355-4. Tolley Publishing.

Clarke, Malcolm A.–The Law of Insurance Contracts: Supplement. Spiral bound: £42.00. ISBN 1-85978-054-7. LLP Limited.

Clayton, Richard; Tomlinson, Hugh–Judicial Review Procedure. Paperback: £19.99. ISBN 0-471-96867-6. Chancery Wiley Law Publications.

Clayton, Richard; Tomlinson, Hugh–Police Actions. Paperback: £19.99. ISBN 0-471-96865-X. Chancery Wiley Law Publications.

Clements, Luke–Community Care and the Law. Paperback: £25.00. ISBN 0-905099-74-5. The Legal Action Group.

Clerk and Lindsell on Torts: Supplement 1 to the 17th Edition. Paperback: £25.00. ISBN 0-421-57560-3. Sweet & Maxwell.

Clore, Jonathan–Civil Litigation. Legal practise course (LPC). Paperback: £12.95. ISBN 1-85941-005-7. Cavendish Publishing Ltd.

Coates, Reginald Ian; Parry, James N.R.–Parry: a Practical Guide to Criminal Legal Aid. Paperback: £19.95. ISBN 0-406-04605-0. Butterworth Law.

Collected Courses of the Academy of European Law/ Recueil des Cours de L'Academie de Droit Europeen: Vol V. Book 1: 1994 European Community Law. Collected Courses of the Academy of European Law. Hardback: £88.00. ISBN 90-411-0230-2. Martinus Nijhoff Publishers.

Collins, Lawrence–Essays in International Litigation and the Conflict of Laws. Paperback: £19.99. ISBN 0-19-826566-2. Clarendon Press.

Collison, D.–Self Assessment. Paperback: £43.00. ISBN 1-85355-691-2. Accountancy Books.

Colliver, Douglas; Proctor, Charles–Norton Rose: Cross Border Security. Hardback: £125.00. ISBN 0-406-05463-0. Butterworth Law.

Comair-Obeid, Nayla–The Law of Business Contracts in the Arab Middle East. Arab and Islamic laws. Hardback: £77.00. ISBN 90-411-0216-7. Kluwer Law International.

Commercial Law: Sale of Goods, Consumer Credit and Agency: Suggested Solutions - Single Paper (June 1995). Paperback: £3.00. ISBN 0-7510-0627-0. HLT Publications.

Commercial Law: Suggested Solutions (1991-1995). Bachelor of Laws (LLB). Paperback: £6.95. ISBN 0-7510-0728-5. HLT Publications.

Company Law. Revision Workbook. Paperback: £9.95. ISBN 0-7510-0597-5. HLT Publications.

Company Law: Suggested Solutions (1991-1995). Bachelor of Laws (LLB). Paperback: £6.95. ISBN 0-7510-0731-5. HLT Publications.

Company Law: Suggested Solutions - Single Paper (June 1995). Paperback: £3.00. ISBN 0-7510-0630-0. HLT Publications.

Comyn, Sir James–Advocacy and Practical Skills: Textbook. Paperback. ISBN 1-85836-054-4. Old Bailey Press.

Comyn, Sir James–The Young Barrister's Handbook. Paperback: £15.95. ISBN 1-85836-054-4. Old Bailey Press.

Conflict of Laws: Suggested Solutions (1991-1995). Bar Examinations. Paperback: £6.95. ISBN 0-7510-0745-5. HLT Publications.
Conflict of Laws: Suggested Solutions - Single Paper (June 1995). Paperback: £3.00. ISBN 0-7510-0636-X. HLT Publications.
Conflict of Laws: Suggested Solutions - Single Paper (Trinity 1995). Bar Examinations. Paperback: £3.95. ISBN 0-7510-0645-9. HLT Publications.
Conforti, Benedetto–The Law and Practice of the United Nations. Hardback: £65.00. ISBN 90-411-0233-7. Kluwer Law International.
Constitutional Law: Suggested Solutions (1991-1995). Bachelor of Laws (LLB). Paperback: £6.95. ISBN 0-7510-0722-6. HLT Publications.
Constitutional Law: Suggested Solutions - Single Paper (June 1995). Paperback: £3.00. ISBN 0-7510-0621-1. HLT Publications.
Contract Administration for the Building Team. Paperback: £12.99. ISBN 0-632-03847-0. Blackwell Science (UK).
Contract Law: Suggested Solutions (1991-1995). Bachelor of laws (LLB). Paperback: £6.95. ISBN 0-7510-0720-X. HLT Publications.
Contract Law: Suggested Solutions - Single Paper (June 1995). Paperback: £3.00. ISBN 0-7510-0619-X. HLT Publications.
Cook, John; Kerse, Chris–EC Merger Control. European competition law monographs. Hardback: £75.00. ISBN 0-421-56160-2. Sweet & Maxwell.
Cooke, Darryl–Venture Capital: Law and Practice. Commercial series. Hardback: £68.00. ISBN 0-7520-0143-4. FT Law & Tax.
Cooper, Jeremy; Vernon, Stuart–Disability and the Law. Paperback: £19.95. ISBN 1-85302-318-3. Jessica Kingsley Publishers.
Cooper, Neil; Hand, Sean–Pension Schemes and Liquidation. Hardback: £60.00. ISBN 0-85308-233-2. Jordan.
Cooper, Neil; Jarvis, Rebecca–Cross-border Insolvency: a Guide to Recognition and Enforcement in International Practice. Commercial law. Paperback: £39.95. ISBN 0-471-96310-0. Chancery Wiley Law Publications.
Cooter, Robert; Ulen, Thomas–Law and Economics. Hardback: £19.99. ISBN 0-673-46332-X. Addison-Wesley Longman Higher Education.
Cordara, Roderick; Smouha, Joe; Buckett, Alan–De Voil Indirect Tax Intelligence. Unbound/looseleaf: £150.00. ISBN 0-406-04311-6. Butterworth Law.
Corley, Robert N.; Reed, O. Lee; Shedd, Peter J.–The Legal and Regulatory Environment of Business. Hardback: £49.95. ISBN 0-07-013337-9. McGraw-Hill Book Company.
Cornish, W.R.–Cases and Materials on Intellectual Property. Paperback: £35.00. ISBN 0-421-53530-X. Sweet & Maxwell.
Cornish, W.R.–Intellectual Property. Paperback: £30.00. ISBN 0-421-53520-2. Sweet & Maxwell.
Cornwell, John–The Power to Harm. Hardback: £18.00. ISBN 0-670-86767-5. Allen Lane The Penguin Press.
Cortner, Richard C.–The Kingfisher and the Constitution. Contributions in political science, No 365. £43.95. ISBN 0-313-29842-4. Greenwood Press.
Cotran, Eugene–The Arab-Israeli Accords. Centre of Islamic & Middle Eastern law series (Cimel). Hardback: £79.00. ISBN 90-411-0902-1. Kluwer Law International.
Cownie, Fiona; Bradney, Anthony–The English Legal System in Context. Paperback: £21.95. ISBN 0-406-51181-0. Butterworth Law.
Cracknell, D.G.–Company Law. Cracknell's statutes. Paperback: £9.95. ISBN 1-85836-063-3. Old Bailey Press.
Cracknell, D.G.–Contract Law. Cracknell's statutes. Paperback: £5.95. ISBN 1-85836-061-7. Old Bailey Press.
Cracknell, Doug G.–English Legal System: Casebook 1996-1997. Bachelor of Laws (LLB). Paperback: £14.95. ISBN 0-7510-0653-X. HLT Publications.
Cracknell, Doug G.–Evidence: Casebook 1996-1997. Bachelor of Laws (LLB). Paperback: £18.95. ISBN 0-7510-0658-0. HLT Publications.

Cracknell, Douglas–Cracknell on Charities. Practitioner series. Hardback: £55.00. ISBN 0-85121-638-2. FT Law & Tax.

Craiger, Andrew–Cause Lawyering in South Africa. Hardback: £51.95. ISBN 1-57292-015-7. Paperback: £35.95. ISBN 1-57292-014-9. Austin and Winfield.

Craighead, David–Financial Analysis of a Reinsurance Office. Spiral bound. ISBN 1-85978-067-9. LLP Limited.

Creech, Kenneth C.–Electronic Media Law and Regulation. Paperback: £27.50. ISBN 0-240-80216-0. Focal Press (an imprint of Butterworth-Heinemann).

Creighton, Brian; Wright, D.–Butterworths Rights and Duties of Directors. Paperback: £35.00. ISBN 0-406-05342-1. Butterworth Law.

Creighton, Simon; King, Vicky–Prisoners and the Law. Paperback: £45.00. ISBN 0-406-02514-2. Butterworth Law.

Crerar, Lorne D.–Crerar: Banking Law in Scotland. Paperback: £25.00. ISBN 0-406-05458-4. Butterworth Law (Scotland).

Cretney, Stephen–Enduring Powers of Attorney. Paperback: £32.50. ISBN 0-85308-314-2. Jordan.

Cretney, Stephen; Masson, Judith–Principles of Family Law. Paperback: £28. ISBN 0-421-50180-4. Sweet & Maxwell.

Criminal Law: Suggested Solutions (1991-1995). Bachelor of Laws (LLB). Paperback: £6.95. ISBN 0-7510-0719-6. HLT Publications.

Criminal Litigation. Legal Practice Course. Paperback: £12.95. ISBN 1-85941-006-5. Cavendish Publishing Ltd.

Criminology: Suggested Solutions - Single Paper (June 1995). Paperback: £3.00. ISBN 0-7510-0635-1. HLT Publications.

Crooks, Robert–VAT on Construction, Land and Property. Ringbinder: £45.00. Tolley Publishing.

Crump, D.W.; Pugsley, David–Dix, Crump and Pugsley: Contracts of Employment. Hardback: £80.00. ISBN 0-406-01146-X. Butterworth Law.

Cumper, P.–Blackstone's LLB: Cases and Materials - Constitutional and Administrative Law. Paperback: £18.95. ISBN 1-85431-527-7. Blackstone Press.

Cumper, P.–Blackstone's LLB: Learning Text - Law of Trusts. Paperback: £17.95. ISBN 1-85431-520-X. Blackstone Press.

Cumper, Peter–Learning Exam Skills. £11.00. ISBN 1-85431-451-3. Blackstone Press.

Cumper, Peter–Learning Exam Techniques. Paperback: £11.00. ISBN 1-85431-451-3. Blackstone Press.

Cunneen, Chris; White, Robert–Juvenile Justice. Paperback: £17.50. ISBN 0-19-553613-4. OUP Australia.

Cupit, Geoffrey–Justice As Fittingness. Hardback: £27.50. ISBN 0-19-823901-7. Clarendon Press.

Curtis, Simpson; McMullen, John–Redundancy Law and Practice. Practitioner series. Paperback: £45.00. ISBN 0-85121-763-X. FT Law & Tax.

Curzon, L.B.–Equity and Trusts. Lecture notes. Paperback: £14.95. ISBN 1-85941-169-X. Cavendish Publishing Ltd.

Cushman, R.F.; Trimble, P.J.–Proving and Pricing Construction Claims. Hardback: £68.00. ISBN 0-471-11424-3. John Wiley and Sons.

Cusine, Douglas J.; Forte, A.D.M.–Cusine & Forte: Scottish Cases and Materials in Commercial Law. Paperback: £35.00. ISBN 0-406-04658-1. Butterworth Law.

Cutler, Andrew J.; Doonan, E.–Equity and Trusts: Casebook 1996-1997. Common Professional Examinations (CPE). Paperback: £17.95. ISBN 0-7510-0674-2. HLT Publications.

Cutler, Andrew; Read, Anne–General Paper II: Textbook 1996-1997. Bar Examinations. Paperback: £21.95. ISBN 0-7510-0712-9. HLT Publications.

Cutler, Andrew; Read, Anne.–General Paper II: Casebook 1996-1997. Bar Examinations. Paperback: £21.95. ISBN 0-7510-0678-5. HLT Publications.

Dadamo, Christian; Farran, Susan–The French Legal System. Paperback: £18.95. ISBN 0-421-53970-4. Sweet & Maxwell.

Dalton, Patrick J.–Land Law. Paperback: £23.95. ISBN 0-273-61423-1. Pitman Publishing.

Danzon, Patricia M.–Pharmaceutical Price Regulation. Hardback: £23.95. ISBN 0-8447-3982-0. AEI Press.

Darbyshire, Penny–Eddey on the English Legal System. Concise course texts. Paperback: £12.95. ISBN 0-421-55500-9. Sweet & Maxwell.

Darrow, Clarence S.–The Story of My Life. Paperback: £14.50. ISBN 0-306-80738-6. Da Capo Press.

Davey, Nigel; Parry-Wingfield, Maurice–Ray: Partnership Taxation. Unbound/looseleaf: £65.00. ISBN 0-406-08183-2. Butterworth Law.

David, Martyn–Oil and Gas Agreements. £165.00. ISBN 0-421-55090-2. Sweet & Maxwell.

Davidson, J.Scott–The Inter-American Human Rights System. Hardback: £45.00. ISBN 1-85521-776-7. Dartmouth.

Davies, Iwan–Sale and Supply of Goods. Practitioner. Paperback: £44.00. ISBN 0-7520-0223-6. FT Law & Tax.

Davies, Margaret–Delimiting the Law. Law and social theory. Hardback: £40.00. ISBN 0-7453-1100-8. Paperback: £12.99. ISBN 0-7453-0769-8. Pluto Press.

Davies, Paul; Lyon-Caen, Antoine; Simitis, Spiros; Sciarra, Silvana–Principles and Perspectives on European Community Labour Law. Hardback: £40.00. ISBN 0-19-826010-5. Clarendon Press.

Davis Jr, Joseph W.S.–Dispute Resolution in Japan. Hardback: £95.00. ISBN 90-411-0974-9. Kluwer Law International.

Davis, Marcia–The Licensing Referencer: 1997. Paperback: £14.95. ISBN 0-421-58180-8. Sweet & Maxwell.

Davis, Marcia; Hamed, Odette–The Road Traffic Referencer: 1997. Paperback: £14.95. ISBN 0-421-58220-0. Sweet & Maxwell.

Dawson, Norma–One Hundred and Fifty Years of Irish Law. Hardback: £31.50. ISBN 0-85389-615-1. SLS Legal Publications.

De Doelder, Hans; Tiedemann Klaus–Criminal Liability of Corporations / La Criminalisation du Comportement Collectif. Hardback: £101.25. ISBN 90-411-0165-9. Kluwer Law International.

De Nooy, Gert –The Role of European Naval Forces After the Cold War. Nijhoff law specials. Paperback: £43.00. ISBN 90-411-0227-2. Kluwer Law International.

Dean, Yvonne–Finishes. Mitchell's building series. Paperback: £17.99. ISBN 0-582-25877-4. Addison-Wesley Longman Higher Education.

Delmas-Marty, Mireille–What Kind of Criminal Policy for Europe? NAFTA law and policy series. Hardback: £99.00. ISBN 90-411-0310-4. Kluwer Law International.

Densham, H.A.C.; Evans, Della–Scammell and Densham's Law of Agricultural Holdings. Hardback: £139.00. ISBN 0-406-00904-X. Butterworth Law.

Denters, Erik M.G.–Law and Policy of IMF Conditionality. Hardback: £65.00. ISBN 90-411-0211-6. Kluwer Law International.

Derham, Rory–Set-off. Hardback: £90.00. ISBN 0-19-825907-7. Oxford University Press.

Dershowitz, Alan M.–Reasonable Doubts. Hardback: £12.99. ISBN 0-684-83021-3. Simon & Schuster (General list, Trade Division).

Devins, Neal–Shaping Constitutional Values. Interpreting American politics. Hardback: £37.00. ISBN 0-8018-5284-6. Paperback: £12.50. ISBN 0-8018-5285-4. The Johns Hopkins University Press.

DeVries, Raymond G.–Making Midwives Legal. Women and Health Series. Paperback: £15.50. ISBN 0-8142-0703-0. Ohio State University Press.

Dewees, Donald; Trebilcock, Michael; Duff, David–Exploring the Domain of Accident Law. Hardback: £50.00. ISBN 0-19-508797-6. Oxford University Press Inc, USA.

Dickson, Brice–Digest of Northern Ireland Law. £99.00. ISBN 0-85389-586-4. SLS Legal Publications.

Dickson, Brice; Connelly, Alpha–Human Rights and the European Convention. Paperback: £18.00. ISBN 0-421-53160-6. Sweet & Maxwell.

Dimond, Bridgit –Legal Aspects of Occupational Therapy. Paperback: £14.99. ISBN 0-632-04074-2. Blackwell Science (UK).

Dimond, Bridgit–Legal Aspects of Care in the Community. Hardback: £45.00. ISBN 0-333-53819-6. Macmillan Press.

Dimond, Bridgit–Legal Aspects of Community Care. Paperback: £19.99. ISBN 0-333-53820-X. Macmillan Press.

Dimond, Bridgit; Barker, Frances H.–Mental Health Law for Nurses. Paperback: £14.99. ISBN 0-632-03989-2. Blackwell Science (UK).

Dimond, Bridgit; Walters, Dorothy–Legal Aspects of Midwifery Workbook. Paperback: £9.95. ISBN 1-898507-43-0. Butterworth-Heinemann.

Dine, Janet–EC Company Law: Update 6. Hardback: £40.00. ISBN 0-471-96467-0. Chancery Wiley Law Publications.

Dine, Janet; Watts, Robert–Discrimination Law. Paperback: £27.50. ISBN 0-582-28909-2. Addison-Wesley Longman Higher Education.

Dixon, John C.; Wareham, Bob–Trading in the European Union. Business law and administration. Paperback: £49.95. ISBN 0-85459-964-9. Tolley Publishing.

Dixon, Martin–Land Law. Lecture notes. Paperback: £14.95. ISBN 1-85941-170-3. Cavendish Publishing Ltd.

Dixon, Martin–Textbook on International Law. Hardback: £16.95. ISBN 1-85431-444-0. Blackstone Press.

Dnes, A.W.–Economics of Law. Paperback: £17.99. ISBN 0-412-62800-7. Chapman and Hall.

Dobinson, Ian; Roebuck, Derek–Introduction to Law in the Hong Kong SAR. Paperback: £30.00. ISBN 0-421-56880-1. Sweet & Maxwell.

Dodds, Malcolm –Family Law: Textbook 1996-1997. Bar examinations. Paperback: £18.95. ISBN 0-7510-0715-3. HLT Publications.

Dodds, Malcolm–Family Law: Casebook 1996-1997. Bachelor of Laws (LLB). Paperback: £18.95. ISBN 0-7510-0662-9. HLT Publications.

Dodds, Malcolm–Family Law: Casebook 1996-1997. Bar examinations. Paperback: £19.95. ISBN 0-7510-0680-7. HLT Publications.

Dodds, Malcolm–Family Law: Textbook 1996-1997. Bachelor of Laws (LLB). Paperback: £18.95. ISBN 0-7510-0696-3. HLT Publications.

Doe, Norman–The Legal Framework of the Church of England. Hardback: £60.00. ISBN 0-19-826220-5. Clarendon Press.

Doek, Jaap–Children on the Move. Hardback: £78.00. ISBN 90-411-0156-X. Martinus Nijhoff Publishers.

Doern, G. Bruce; Wilks, Stephen–Comparative Competition Policy. Hardback: £45.00. ISBN 0-19-828062-9. Oxford University Press.

Dolton, Alan; Saunders, Glyn–Tax Cases: 1996. Paperback: £35.95. ISBN 1-86012-246-9. Tolley Publishing.

Dolton, Alan; Wareham, Robert–VAT Cases: 1996. Paperback: £64.50. ISBN 1-86012-248-5. Tolley Publishing.

Donnellan, Craig–Exploring the Issues: What Are Children's Rights?: Study Guide. Exploring the issues, 13. Paperback: £1.50. ISBN 1-86168-005-8. Independence Educational Publishers.

Doonan, Elmer; Cutler, Andrew J.–Equity and Trusts: Textbook 1996-1997. Bachelor of Laws (LLB). Paperback: £16.95. ISBN 0-7510-0690-4. HLT Publications.

Doran, Nigel–Doran: Taxation of Corporate Joint Ventures. Hardback: £80.00. ISBN 0-406-07916-1. Butterworth Law.

Dornstein, Ken–Accidentally, on Purpose. Hardback: £15.50. ISBN 0-333-67457-X. Macmillan Press.

Dowding, Nicholas; Reynolds, Kirk–The Modern Law and Practice of Dilapidations: 1. Supplement. £27.00. ISBN 0-421-56260-9. Sweet & Maxwell.

Doyle, Brian–Disability Discrimination - the New Law. Paperback: £22.50. ISBN 0-85308-321-5. Jordan.

Doyle, Brian–Disability Discrimination. Paperback: £27.50. ISBN 0-85308-403-3. Jordan.

Drahos, Peter–A Philosophy of Intellectual Property. Applied Legal Philosophy Series. Hardback: £39.50. ISBN 1-85521-240-4. Dartmouth.

Driscoll, James–Butterworths Residential Landlord and Tenant Guide. Paperback: £37.50. ISBN 0-406-00252-5. Butterworth Law.

Driscoll, James–Driscoll: a Guide to the Housing Act 1996. Paperback: £27.00. ISBN 0-406-99894-9. Butterworth Law.

Dromgoole, Sarah–International Trade Law. Paperback: £24.95. ISBN 0-273-61112-7. Pitman Publishing.

Duff, Antony–Criminal Attempts. Oxford monographs on criminal law and justice. Hardback: £50.00. ISBN 0-19-826268-X. Clarendon Press.

Duffy, Peter–Human Rights: Collected Texts. Paperback: £35.00. ISBN 0-421-48130-7. Sweet & Maxwell.

Dugard, John; Wyngaert, Christine van den–International Criminal Law and Procedure. Hardback: £80.00. ISBN 1-85521-835-6. Dartmouth.

Dugdale, A.M.; Stanton, K.M.; Parkinson, J.E.–Professional Negligence. Hardback: £80.00. ISBN 0-406-03257-2. Butterworth Law.

Duggan, Michael; Mann, Jayne; Ingle, Michael–Directors: Termination of Employment. Special reports. Hardback: £125.00. ISBN 0-7520-0311-9. FT Law & Tax.

Dulken, S. van–British Patents of Invention, 1617-1977. Key resource series. Paperback: £30.00. ISBN 0-7123-0817-2. British Library (Science Reference and Information Service).

Dutt, Trevor P.–Gynaecology. Medico-legal practitioner. Hardback: £34.95. ISBN 1-85941-215-7. Cavendish Publishing Ltd.

Duxbury, R.M.C. –Telling and Duxbury: Planning Law and Procedure. Paperback: £20.95. ISBN 0-406-99374-2. Butterworth Law.

Dworkin, Ronald–Freedom's Law. Hardback: £27.50. ISBN 0-19-826470-4. Oxford University Press.

Dzurik, Andrew A.–Water Resources Planning. Hardback: £35.95. ISBN 0-8476-8081-9. Rowman & Littlefield.

Earnshaw, Jill; Cooper, Gary–Stress and Employers' Liability. Law and employment. Paperback: £16.95. ISBN 0-85292-615-4. Institute of Personnel and Development.

Eastaway, Nigel; Gilligan, Brian–Tax and Financial Planning for Professional Partnerships. Paperback: £45.00. ISBN 0-406-02303-4. Butterworth Law.

Edge, Ian D.–Islamic Law and Legal Theory. International Library of Essays on Law and Legal Theory (Legal Cultures). Hardback: £105.00. ISBN 1-85521-140-8. Dartmouth.

Edwards, Anthony; Clegg, John; Dawson, Stephen–Profitable Legal Aid. Paperback: £29.95. ISBN 0-85459-950-9. Tolley Publishing.

Edwards, Lilian; Griffiths, Anne–Family Law. Green's concise Scots law. Paperback. ISBN 0-414-01113-9. W.Green & Son.

Edwards, S.–Sex and Gender in the Legal Process. £15.00. ISBN 1-85431-507-2. Blackstone Press.

Egan, Manus; Rushbrooke, Justin; Lockett, Nick–EC Financial Services Regulation: Update 2. Hardback: £40.00. ISBN 0-471-96466-2. Chancery Wiley Law Publications.

Egan, Paul–Irish Corporate Procedures. Hardback: £35.00. ISBN 0-85308-349-5. Jordan.

Eggleston, Brian–The New Engineering Contract. Hardback: £37.50. ISBN 0-632-04065-3. Blackwell Science (UK).

El-Zeyn, Samih Atef–Islam and Human Ideology. Hardback: £45.00. ISBN 0-7103-0539-7. Kegan Paul International.

Elagab, Omar Y, DPhil–Public International Law. Questions and answers. Paperback: £8.95. ISBN 1-874241-37-6. Cavendish Publishing Ltd.

Eldergill, Anselm–The Law Relating to Mental Health Review Tribunals. Hardback: £48.00. ISBN 0-421-48330-X. Sweet & Maxwell.

Elliott, Catherine; Quinn, Frances–Contract Law. Paperback: £10.99. ISBN 0-582-29878-4. Addison-Wesley Longman Higher Education.

Elliott, Catherine; Quinn, Frances–English Legal System. Paperback: £14.99. ISBN 0-582-23868-4. Addison-Wesley Longman Higher Education.

Elliott, Catherine; Quinn, Frances–Tort Law. Paperback: £10.99. ISBN 0-582-29876-8. Addison-Wesley Longman Higher Education.

Ellison, Julian; Kling, Edward–Joint Ventures in Europe. Hardback: £90.00. ISBN 0-406-05338-3. Butterworth Law.

Ellison, Robin–European Pensions Law. Hardback: £60.00. ISBN 0-406-02449-9. Butterworth Law.

Ellison, Robin–The Pensions Practice: 1996. Hardback: £60.00. ISBN 0-85308-350-9. Jordan.

Ellison, Robin; Rae, Maggie–Ellison and Rae: Family Breakdown and Pensions. Paperback: £25.00. ISBN 0-406-03766-3. Butterworth Law.

Ely, John Hart–On Constitutional Ground. Hardback: £55.00. ISBN 0-691-08644-3. Paperback: £18.95. ISBN 0-691-02553-3. Princeton University Press.

Emiliou, Nicholas–The Principle of Proportionality in European Law. European monographs. Paperback: £72.00. ISBN 90-411-0866-1. Kluwer Law International.

Emsley, Clive; Knafla, Louis A.–Crime History and Histories of Crime. Contributions in the Historiography of Criminology and Penology, No 48. Hardback: £59.95. ISBN 0-313-28722-8. Greenwood Press.

Encyclopedia of European Union Law Constitutional Texts. Ringbinder: £680.00. ISBN 0-421-53440-0. Sweet & Maxwell.

Endeshaw, Assafa–Intellectual Property for Non-industrial Countries. Law, Social Change and Development. Hardback: £45.00. ISBN 1-85521-754-6. Dartmouth.

English Legal System: Suggested Solutions (1991-1995). Bachelor of Laws (LLB). Paperback: £6.95. ISBN 0-7510-0721-8. HLT Publications.

English Legal System: Suggested Solutions - Single Paper (June 1995). Paperback: £3.00. ISBN 0-7510-0620-3. HLT Publications.

English, Jack; Card, Richard–Butterworths Police Law. Paperback: £20.95. ISBN 0-406-02436-7. Butterworth Law.

Enmarch-Williams, Herbert–Environmental Risks and Rewards for Business. Environmental Law. Paperback: £19.99. ISBN 0-471-96437-9. John Wiley and Sons.

Enright, Ian–Professional Indemnity Insurance Law. Insurance practitioners library. Hardback: £135.00. ISBN 0-421-38240-6. Sweet & Maxwell.

Enright, Sean; Grant, Gary–Enright and Grant: Bail. Paperback: £32.50. ISBN 0-406-00250-9. Butterworth Law.

European Community Law and Human Rights: Suggested Solutions (1991-1995). Bar Examinations. Paperback: £9.95. ISBN 0-7510-0741-2. HLT Publications.

European Community Law and Human Rights: Suggested Solutions - Single Paper (Trinity 1995). Bar Examinations. Paperback: £3.95. ISBN 0-7510-0641-6. HLT Publications.

European Community Law: Suggested Solutions (1991-1995). Bachelor of Laws (LLB). Paperback: £6.95. ISBN 0-7510-0729-3. HLT Publications.

European Community Law: Suggested Solutions - Single Paper (June 1995). Paperback: £3.00. ISBN 0-7510-0628-9. HLT Publications.

European Union Law. Paperback: £6.95. ISBN 1-85836-052-8. Old Bailey Press.

Evans, Andrew–The Integration of the European Community and Third States in Europe. Hardback: £40.00. ISBN 0-19-826229-9. Clarendon Press.

Evans, M.–International Law Documents. £13.95. ISBN 1-85431-565-X. Blackstone Press.

Evans, Malcom D.–Aspects of Statehood and Institutionalism in Contemporary Europe. EC/International Law Forum II. Hardback: £45.00. ISBN 1-85521-928-X. Dartmouth.

Evans, Roger–Accident and Emergency. Medico-legal practitioner. Hardback: £34.95. ISBN 1-85941-216-5. Cavendish Publishing Ltd.

Evidence - Bar Finals: Suggested Solutions (1991-1995). Bar examinations. Paperback: £9.95. ISBN 0-7510-0738-2. HLT Publications.

Evidence - LLB: Suggested Solutions (1991-1995). Bachelor of Laws (LLB). Paperback: £6.95. ISBN 0-7510-0727-7. HLT Publications.

Evidence: Suggested Solutions - Single Paper (June 1995). Paperback: £3.00. ISBN 0-7510-0626-2. HLT Publications.

Evidence: Suggested Solutions - Single Paper (Trinity 1995). Bar Examinations. Paperback: £3.95. ISBN 0-7510-0638-6. HLT Publications.

Ewing, Keith; Gearty, Conor–Cases and Materials on Civil Liberties. Hardback: £35.00. ISBN 0-19-825665-5. Paperback: £19.95. ISBN 0-19-876251-8. Clarendon Press.

Fairest, P.B.; Clements, L.M.–Housing Law. Paperback: £19.95. ISBN 1-85941-222-X. Cavendish Publishing Ltd.

Family Law - Bar Finals: Suggested Solutions 1991-1995. Bar examinations. Paperback: £9.95. ISBN 0-7510-0742-0. HLT Publications.

Family Law - LLB: Suggested Solutions (1991-1995). Bachelor of Laws (LLB). Paperback: £6.95. ISBN 0-7510-0730-7. HLT Publications.

Family Law: Suggested Solutions - Single Paper (June 1995). Paperback: £3.00. ISBN 0-7510-0629-7. HLT Publications.

Family Law: Suggested Solutions - Single Paper (Trinity 1995). Bar Examinations. Paperback: £3.95. ISBN 0-7510-0642-4. HLT Publications.

Farmer, Lindsay–Criminal Law, Tradition and Legal Order. Hardback: £35.00. ISBN 0-521-55320-2. Cambridge University Press.

Farran, Sue–The UK Before the European Court of Human Rights: Case Law and Commentary. Paperback: £25.95. ISBN 1-85431-455-6. Blackstone Press.

Farringdon, Jill M.; Morton, Andrew Q.; Farringdon, Michael; Baker, M. David–Analyzing for Authorship. Hardback: £35.00. ISBN 0-7083-1324-8. University of Wales Press.

Farthing, Stuart M.–Evaluating Local Environmental Policy. Avebury studies in green research. Hardback: £30.00. ISBN 1-85972-321-7. Avebury.

Faulhaber, Gregory M.–Politics, Law and the Church. Distinguished Research Series/Catholic Scholars Press. Hardback: £55.95. ISBN 1-57309-103-0. International Scholars Publications.

Faulhaber, Gregory M.–Politics, Law and the Church. Distinguished Research Series/Catholic Scholars Press. Paperback: £39.95. ISBN 1-57309-102-2. International Scholars Publications.

Faundez, Julio–Good Government and Law. Hardback: £40.00. ISBN 0-333-66996-7. Paperback: £14.99. ISBN 0-333-66997-5. Macmillan Press.

Feenstra, Robert–Legal Scholarship and Doctrines of Private Law, 13th-18th Centuries. Collected studies series. Hardback: £55.00. ISBN 0-86078-616-1. Variorum.

Feldman, David –Feldman: Criminal Confiscation Orders. Paperback: £32.50. ISBN 0-406-00217-7. Butterworth Law.

Fentiman, Richard G.–Conflict of Laws. International Library of Essays in Law and Legal Theory. Hardback: £100.00. ISBN 1-85521-191-2. Dartmouth.
Fenwick, Helen–Civil Liberties. Lecture notes series. Paperback: £14.95. ISBN 1-85941-165-7. Cavendish Publishing Ltd.
Fenwick, Helen–Source Book on Civil Liberties. Sourcebook series. Paperback: £21.95. ISBN 1-85941-181-9. Cavendish Publishing Ltd.
Fenwick, Helen–Sourcebook on Public Law. Sourcebook series. Paperback: £17.95. ISBN 1-85941-182-7. Cavendish Publishing Ltd.
Feofanov, Yuri; Barry, Donald D.–Politics and Justice in Russia. Hardback: £50.50. ISBN 1-56324-344-X. Paperback: £17.50. ISBN 1-56324-345-8. M.E. Sharpe.
Field, D.; Raitt, F.–Evidence, Ed.2. Paperback: £24.00. ISBN 0-414-01041-8. W. Green & Son.
Finch, Janet; Masson, Judith; Mason, Jennifer; Hayes, Lynn; Wallis, Lorraine–Wills, Inheritance and the Family. Oxford Socio-Legal Studies. Hardback: £25.00. ISBN 0-19-825834-8. Clarendon Press.
Firmin-Sellers, Kathryn–The Transformation of Property Rights in the Gold Coast. Political Economy of Institutions and Decisions. Hardback: £35.00. ISBN 0-521-55503-5. Cambridge University Press.
Firth, Alison–The Prehistory and Development of Intellectual Property Systems. Perspectives on intellectual property, Vol 1. Paperback: £18.50. ISBN 0-421-58030-5. Sweet & Maxwell.
Fisher, Glenn W.–The Worst Tax? Studies in Government and Public Policy. Hardback. ISBN 0-7006-0753-6. University Press of Kansas.
Fitzgerald, Keith–The Face of the Nation. Hardback: £35.00. ISBN 0-8047-2485-7. Stanford University Press (CUP).
Flenley, William; Leech, Thomas–Flenley and Leech: Solicitors' Negligence. Paperback: £40.00. ISBN 0-406-05225-5. Butterworth Law.
Fletcher, George P.–The Basic Concepts of Legal Thought. Hardback: £25.00. ISBN 0-19-508335-0. Paperback: £10.99. ISBN 0-19-508336-9. Oxford University Press Inc, USA.
Fletcher, Nina; Holt, Janet; Brazier, Margaret; Harris, John–Ethics, Law and Nursing. Paperback: £14.99. ISBN 0-7190-4050-7. Manchester University Press.
Flint, Michael F.–Flint: a User's Guide to Copyright. Paperback: £25.00. ISBN 0-406-04607-7. Butterworth Law.
Flynn, James–EC Law: Implementation and Interpretation. Paperback: £55.00. ISBN 0-406-02898-2. Butterworth Law.
Forbes, Duncan–Action Against Racial Harassment. Paperback: £24.00. ISBN 0-905099-41-9. The Legal Action Group.
Foreman, Tony; Adams, David–Purchase and Sale of a Private Company's Shares. Paperback: £39.95. ISBN 1-86012-291-4. Tolley Publishing.
Forsyth, C.F.–Conflict of Laws: Casebook 1996-1997. Bar Examinations. Paperback: £17.95. ISBN 0-7510-0683-1. HLT Publications.
Forsyth, C.F.–Conflict of Laws: Textbook 1996-1997. Bachelor of Laws (LLB). Paperback: £18.95. ISBN 0-7510-0702-1. HLT Publications.
Fortson, Rudi–The Law on the Misuse of Drugs and Drug Trafficking Offence. Criminal practice. Paperback: £39.50. ISBN 0-421-56550-0. Sweet & Maxwell.
Fosbrook, D.; Laing, A.–A-Z of Contract Clauses. £95.00. ISBN 0-421-50720-9. Sweet & Maxwell.
Foskett, David–The Law and Practice of Compromise (with Precedents). Hardback: £112.00. ISBN 0-421-53670-5. Sweet & Maxwell.
Foster, Charles; Ainley, Nicolas; Wynn, Toby–Privilege: Withholding and Disclosing Information in Civil and Criminal Cases. Practitioner Series. Paperback: £45.00. ISBN 0-7520-0158-2. FT Law & Tax.
Foster, Nigel–German Legal System and Laws. £26.95. ISBN 1-85431-450-5. Blackstone Press.

Franck, Matthew J.–Against the Imperial Judiciary. Hardback: £27.95. ISBN 0-7006-0761-7. University Press of Kansas.

Fransman, Laurie –Fransman's Nationality Law. Hardback. ISBN 1-86012-161-6. Fourmat Publishing.

Franzosi, Mario; Hirsch, Marc Roger; Hoyng, Willem A.; Levin, Marianne; Ohlgart, Dietrich C.; Phillips, Jeremy; Posner, Bernhard; Scordamaglia, Vincenzo–European Design Protection. Hardback: £112.50. ISBN 90-411-0112-8. Kluwer Law International.

Freckleton, Ian; Selby, Hugh–Expert Evidence. Ring binder: £318.00. ISBN 0-420-99740-7. Stevens & Sons.

Freedman, Philip; Shapiro, Eric; Slater, Brian–Service Charges. Paperback: £30.00. ISBN 0-85308-383-5. Jordan.

Freeman, John H.–Client Management for Solicitors. Paperback: £16.95. ISBN 1-85941-039-1. Cavendish Publishing Ltd.

Freeman, Michael D.A.–Current Legal Problems 1996: Vol 49. Part 2. Hardback: £35.00. ISBN 0-19-826280-9. Clarendon Press.

Freeman, Michael–Children's Rights. Issues in Law and Society. Hardback: £35.00. ISBN 1-85521-678-7. Paperback: £15.00. ISBN 1-85521-683-3. Dartmouth.

Freeman, Michael–Divorce: Where Next? Issues in Law and Society. Hardback: £35.00. ISBN 1-85521-677-9. Paperback: £15.00. ISBN 1-85521-682-5. Dartmouth.

French, D–How to Cite Legal Authorities. Paperback: £14.95. ISBN 1-85431-315-0. Blackstone Press.

Fricker, Nigel; Adams, J.D.R.; Pearce, Nasreen; Plumstead, Isobel; Salter, David; Silver, Maggie; Whybrow, Jonathan–Emergency Remedies and Procedures in the Family Courts. Unbound/looseleaf: £90.00. ISBN 0-85308-329-0. Family Law.

Fridman, G.H.L.–Law of Agency. Paperback: £33.95. ISBN 0-406-51820-3. Butterworth Law.

Fry, Michael–A Manual of Environmental Protection Law. Hardback: £40.00. ISBN 0-19-826230-2. Paperback: £22.00. ISBN 0-19-826233-7. Clarendon Press.

Furmston, Michael–Cheshire, Fifoot and Furmston's Law of Contract. Paperback: £24.95. ISBN 0-406-04964-5. Butterworth Law.

Furst, Arthur–The Toxicologist As Expert Witness. Hardback: £39.95. ISBN 1-56032-531-3. Paperback: £15.99. ISBN 1-56032-590-9. Taylor & Francis.

Fysh, M; Wilson-Thomas, R.–Intellectual Property Citator: 1982-1995. Hardback: £135.00. ISBN 0-421-52820-6. Sweet & Maxwell.

Gabriel, M.; Gilles, P.–International Trade and Business Law Annual: Vol II. Paperback: £19.95. ISBN 1-85941-291-2. Cavendish Publishing Ltd.

Gaffney, Paul–Ronald Dworkin on Law As Integrity. Hardback: £49.95. ISBN 0-7734-2268-4. Edwin Mellen Press.

Galligan, Denis–A Reader on Administrative Law. Oxford Readings in Socio-Legal Studies. Hardback: £40.00. ISBN 0-19-876408-1. Paperback: £11.99. ISBN 0-19-876409-X. Oxford University Press.

Galligan, Denis–Due Process and Fair Procedures. Hardback: £55.00. ISBN 0-19-825676-0. Clarendon Press.

Gannon, Sean; O'Floinn, Benedict–Gannon and O'Floinn: Practice and Procedure in the Superior Courts. Hardback: £85.00. ISBN 1-85475-220-0. Butterworth Law (Ireland).

Gardner, Anthony Laurence–A New Era in US-EU Relations. Hardback: £30.00. ISBN 1-85972-530-9. Avebury.

Gardner, Nick–A Guide to United Kingdom and European Union Competition Policy. Hardback: £45.00. ISBN 0-333-63109-9. Macmillan Press.

Garfield, John; Earl, Christopher J.–Medical Negligence. Hardback: £95.00. ISBN 0-443-04958-0. Churchill Livingstone.

Garlick, Helen–The Which? Guide to Divorce. Which? Consumer guides. Paperback: £10.99. ISBN 0-85202-588-2. Which?

Garner, J.F.; Jones, B.L.–Countryside Law. Paperback. ISBN 0-7219-1062-9. Shaw & Sons.

Gaunt, Johnathan; Morgan, Paul–Gale on the Law of Easements. Property and conveyancing library. Hardback: £125.00. ISBN 0-421-44470-3. Sweet & Maxwell.

Gearty, Conor–Terrorism. The international library of criminology, criminal justice and penology. Hardback: £75.00. ISBN 1-85521-548-9. Dartmouth.

Geddes, Andrew–Public Procurement: a Practical Guide. Hardback: £70.00. ISBN 0-421-53890-2. Sweet & Maxwell.

Gee, Paul–Spicer and Pegler's Book-keeping and Accounts. Paperback: £25.95. ISBN 0-406-99088-3. Butterworth Law.

General Paper I: Suggested Solutions (1991-1995). Bar Examinations. Paperback: £9.95. ISBN 0-7510-0739-0. HLT Publications.

General Paper I: Suggested Solutions - Single Paper (Trinity 1995). Bar Examinations. Paperback: £3.95. ISBN 0-7510-0639-4. HLT Publications.

General Paper II: Suggested Solutions (1991-1995). Bar Examinations. Paperback: £9.95. ISBN 0-7510-0740-4. HLT Publications.

General Paper II: Suggested Solutions - Single Paper (Trinity 1995). Bar Examinations. Paperback: £3.95. ISBN 0-7510-0640-8. HLT Publications.

George, Robert P.–Natural Law, Liberalism, and Morality. Hardback: £40.00. ISBN 0-19-825984-0. Clarendon Press.

George, Robert P.–The Autonomy of Law. Hardback: £40.00. ISBN 0-19-825786-4. Clarendon Press.

Gerlis, Stephen; Blackford, Robert–County Court Practice Handbook 1996/1997. Practitioner series. Paperback: £35.00. ISBN 0-7520-0329-1. FT Law & Tax.

Gessner, Volkmar–Foreign Courts: Civil Litigation in Foreign Legal Cultures. Onati International Series in Law and Society. Hardback: £40.00. ISBN 1-85521-808-9. Paperback: £16.50. ISBN 1-85521-812-7. Dartmouth.

Gessner, Volkmar; Hoeland, Armin; Varga, Casba–European Legal Cultures. Tempus Textbook Series on European Law and European Legal Cultures. Hardback: £45.00. ISBN 1-85521-526-8. Paperback: £25.00. ISBN 1-85521-530-6. Dartmouth.

Gething, Heather; O'Shea, James; Fraser, Ron; McKnight, Elizabeth–Demutualisation. Special reports. Hardback: £125.00. ISBN 0-7520-0395-X. FT Law & Tax.

Ghosh, Julian–Taxation of Pensions Schemes. Pensions reports. Hardback: £125.00. ISBN 0-7520-0236-8. FT Law & Tax.

Ghosh, Julian; Johnson, Ian–Ghosh: Tax Treatment of Financial Instruments. Unbound/looseleaf: £95.00. ISBN 0-406-05205-0. Butterworth Law.

Gierke, Otto–Political Theories of the Middle Age. Key texts. Paperback: £12.99. ISBN 1-85506-478-2. Thoemmes Press.

Gifford; Salter–Understanding an Act of Parliament. Essential series - revision. Paperback: £9.95. ISBN 1-85941-206-8. Cavendish Publishing Ltd.

Giles, Marianne–Criminal Law Nutshell. Nutshells. Paperback: £4.95. ISBN 0-421-54840-1. Sweet & Maxwell.

Gilg, Andrew–Countryside Planning. Hardback: £45.00. ISBN 0-415-05489-3. Paperback: £14.99. ISBN 0-415-05490-7. Routledge.

Gill, Dita–Family Law and Practice. Legal practice course companions. Paperback: £12.95. ISBN 1-874241-91-0. Cavendish Publishing Ltd.

Gill, Hon Lord–The Law of Agricultural Holdings in Scotland. Greens practice library. Hardback. ISBN 0-414-01110-4. W.Green & Son.

Gill, Hon Lord; Thomson, Malcolm–Scottish Planning Encyclopedia. Paperback. ISBN 0-414-01150-3. W.Green & Son.

Gillies, David; Marshall, Roger J.W.–Telecommunications Law. Hardback: £160.00. ISBN 0-406-02096-5. Butterworth Law.

Ginsburgs, George; Barry, Donald, D.; Simons, William B.–The Revival of Private Law in Central and Eastern Europe. Law in Eastern Europe, No. 46. Hardback: £142.00. ISBN 0-7923-2843-4. Martinus Nijhoff Publishers.

Glasson, John–International Trust Laws: Update 7. Hardback: £40.00. ISBN 0-471-96468-9. Chancery Wiley Law Publications.

Glazebrook, Peter–Statutes on Criminal Law 1996/97. Paperback: £9.50. ISBN 1-85431-559-5. Blackstone Press.

Gleave, Robert; Kermeli, Eugenia–Islamic Law. Hardback: £50.00. ISBN 1-86064-119-9. I.B.Tauris.

Gold, Joseph–Interpretation: the IMF and International Law. Hardback: £124.00. ISBN 90-411-0887-4. Kluwer Law International.

Gold, Richard; Szemerenyi, Stephen–Schools Legal Guide: 1996/7. Paperback: £24.95. ISBN 0-85308-332-0. Jordan.

Goldenberg, Philip–Guide to Company Law. Paperback: £35.00. ISBN 0-86325-432-2. CCH Editions.

Goldrein, Iain; Wilkinson, Judge Kenneth H.P.; Kershaw, Michael–Commercial Litigation: Pre-emptive Remedies. Litigation library. Hardback: £140.00. ISBN 0-421-53660-8. Sweet & Maxwell.

Goldstein, Robert Justin–Burning the Flag. Hardback: £31.50. ISBN 0-87338-526-8. Kent State University Press.

Gomaa, Mohammed M.–Suspension or Termination of Treaties on Grounds of Breach. Hardback: £65.00. ISBN 90-411-0226-4. Martinus Nijhoff Publishers.

Goodman, Dawn; Hall, Brendan–Probate Disputes and Remedies. Practitioner series. Hardback: £50.00. ISBN 0-7520-0235-X. FT Law & Tax.

Goodrich, Peter–Law in the Courts of Love. Hardback: £45.00. ISBN 0-415-06165-2. Routledge.

Goodwin-Gill, Guy S.–The Refugee in International Law. Hardback: £18.99. ISBN 0-19-826020-2. Paperback: £45.00. ISBN 0-19-826019-9. Oxford University Press.

Gordon, Richard–Judicial Review Deskbook. Hardback: £32.50. ISBN 0-471-96556-1. Chancery Wiley Law Publications.

Gordon, Sheriff G.–Renton & Brown: Criminal Procedure. Ringbinder. ISBN 0-414-01151-1. W.Green & Son.

Gorringe, Timothy–God's Just Vengeance. Cambridge Studies in Ideology and Religion, 9. Hardback: £35.00. ISBN 0-521-55301-6. Paperback: £12.95. ISBN 0-521-55762-3. Cambridge University Press.

Goulding, Simon–Odgers on Civil Court Actions. Hardback: £77.00. ISBN 0-421-51390-X. Sweet & Maxwell.

Goyder, Joanna–EC Distribution Law. European law. Hardback: £65.00. ISBN 0-471-96122-1. Chancery Wiley Law Publications.

Grant, Malcolm–Permitted Development. Green's practice library. Paperback: £42.00. ISBN 0-421-55380-4. Sweet & Maxwell.

Grant, Malcolm; Hawkins, Richard–Concise Lexicon of Environment Terms. Wiley series in environmental law. Paperback: £19.99. ISBN 0-471-96357-7. Chancery Wiley Law Publications.

Grattan, Sheena –Succession Law in Northern Ireland. Hardback: £76.50. ISBN 0-85389-657-7. SLS Legal Publications (NI).

Gravestock, Peter; Dolton, Alan–Self Assessment for the Self Employed. Paperback: £18.95. ISBN 1-86012-285-X. Tolley Publishing.

Gray, Jennifer–Briefcase on Company Law. Briefcase series. Paperback: £9.95. ISBN 1-85941-242-4. Cavendish Publishing Ltd.

Gray, John Chipman–The Nature and Sources of the Law. Classical Jurisprudence. Hardback: £40.00. ISBN 1-85521-651-5. Dartmouth.

Gray, Pamela N.–Artificial Legal Intelligence. Applied Legal Philosophy Series. Hardback: £39.50. ISBN 1-85521-266-8. Dartmouth.

Grayston, Clare; Schmitz, Winifried F.; Abbatescianni, Girolamo–Sale of Private and Public Companies by Auction. AIJA law library. Hardback: £86.00. ISBN 90-411-0925-0. Kluwer Law International.

Greenfield, Jeanette–The Return of Cultural Treasures. Hardback: £55.00. ISBN 0-521-47170-2. Paperback: £19.95. ISBN 0-521-47746-8. Cambridge University Press.

Greensdale, R.–Butterworths Rules of Court - Civil Court Practice: 1996. Butterworths rules of court series. Paperback: £37.50. ISBN 0-406-99891-4. Butterworth Law.

Greer, Desmond S.–Compensation Recovery: Substantive and Procedural Issues. Paperback: £11.50. ISBN 0-85389-618-6. SLS Legal Publications.

Greig, D.W.; Balkin, Rosemary–Grieg: International Law. Paperback: £25.95. ISBN 0-406-59185-7. Butterworth Law.

Gretton, George Lidderdale–The Law of Inhibition and Adjudication. Paperback: £32.00. ISBN 0-406-04497-X. Butterworth Law (Scotland).

Greve, Michael S.–The Demise of Environmentalism in American Law. Hardback: £23.95. ISBN 0-8447-3980-4. Paperback: £7.95. ISBN 0-8447-3981-2. American Enterprise Institute.

Grier, Nicholas–UK Company Law. Paperback: £19.99. ISBN 0-471-95836-0. Chancery Wiley Law Publications.

Griffiths, Margaret–Law for Purchasing and Supply. Paperback: £21.95. ISBN 0-273-62308-7. Pitman Publishing.

Gringras, Clive–Nabarro Nathanson: the Law of the Internet. Paperback: £75.00. ISBN 0-406-00249-5. Butterworth Law.

Grossberg–A Judgement for Solomon. Cambridge Historical Studies in American Law and Society. Hardback: £35.00. ISBN 0-521-55206-0. Paperback: £13.95. ISBN 0-521-55745-3. Cambridge University Press.

Guest, Stephen–Positivism Today. Issues in Law and Society. Hardback: £37.50. ISBN 1-85521-689-2. Dartmouth.

Gulbenkian, Paul–Entry and Residence in Europe. Hardback: £45.00. ISBN 0-471-96664-9. Chancery Wiley Law Publications.

Gulmann, Claus; Hagel-Sorensen, Karsten–European Law. Paperback. ISBN 87-574-1896-9. Djof Publishing.

Gunther, Teubner–Global Law Without a State. Studies in Modern Law and Policy. Hardback: £45.00. ISBN 1-85521-879-8. Dartmouth.

Habermas, Jurgen–Between Facts and Norms. Hardback: £45.00. ISBN 0-7456-1229-6. Polity Press.

Hackney, Jeffrey–Understanding Equity and Trusts. Understanding Law, 6. Paperback: £7.99. ISBN 0-00-686294-2. Sweet & Maxwell.

Hakim, Catherine–Key Issues in Women's Work: Female Heterogeneity and the Polarisation of Women's Employment. Hardback: £35.00. ISBN 0-485-80009-8. Paperback: £14.95. ISBN 0-485-80109-4. The Athlone Press.

Hale, Hon Mrs Justice, QC–From the Test Tube to the Coffin. Hardback: £28.00. ISBN 0-421-58270-7. Paperback: £16.95. ISBN 0-421-58280-4. Sweet & Maxwell.

Hale, Hon Mrs Justice; Pearl, David; Cooke, Elizabeth–The Family, Law and Society. Law in context series. Paperback: £29.95. ISBN 0-406-04588-7. Butterworth Law.

Haley, John Owen–Authority Without Power. Paperback: £10.99. ISBN 0-19-509257-0. Oxford University Press Inc, USA.

Hall, Jean Graham; Martin, Douglas F.–Haldane. Hardback: £25.00. ISBN 1-872328-29-6. Barry Rose Law Publishers Ltd.

Hall, Kermit L.; Wiecek, William M.; Finkelman, Paul–American Legal History. Paperback: £15.99. ISBN 0-19-509764-5. Oxford University Press Inc, USA.

Hall, Robert E.; Rabushka, Alvin; Armey, Dick; Eisner, Robert; Stein, Herbert–Fairness and Efficiency in the Flat Tax. Hardback: £15.95. ISBN 0-

8447-7062-0. Paperback: £7.95. ISBN 0-8447-7045-0. American Enterprise Institute.

Halliday, J.M.; Talman, Iain J.S.–Conveyancing Law and Practice: 1. Hardback. ISBN 0-414-01085-X. W.Green & Son.

Halliday, John M.–Conveyancing Law and Practice in Scotland: Vol 2. Hardback. ISBN 0-414-01086-8. W.Green & Son.

Halliwell, Mark–Distribution on Intestacy. Practitioner series. Paperback: £37.00. ISBN 0-7520-0208-2. FT Law & Tax.

Hallo, Ralph E.–Access to Environmental Information in Europe. International environmental law and policy. Hardback: £77.00. ISBN 90-411-0651-0. Kluwer Law International.

Halloran, Mark–The Musician's Business and Legal Guide. Paperback: £29.75. ISBN 0-13-237322-X. Prentice Hall US.

Halson, Roger–Exploring the Boundaries of Contract. Issues in Law and Society. Hardback: £35.00. ISBN 1-85521-701-5. Paperback: £15.00. ISBN 1-85521-712-0. Dartmouth.

Hamilton, W.; McLaughlin, R.; MacPherson, A.; Kennedy, Paul–The Scottish Building Regulations. Paperback: £24.95. ISBN 0-632-04115-3. Blackwell Science (UK).

Handl, Gunther–Yearbook of International Environmental Law: Vol 6. 1995. Hardback: £85.00. ISBN 0-19-826276-0. Clarendon Press.

Handley, Peter–Business Law. Paperback: £14.99. ISBN 0-631-20183-1. Blackwell Publishers.

Hanlon, J.–European Community Law. Concise course texts. Paperback: £14.50. ISBN 0-421-53870-8. Sweet & Maxwell.

Hansmann, Henry–The Ownership of Enterprise. Hardback: £26.50. ISBN 0-674-64970-2. The Belknap Press of Harvard University Press.

Hapgood, Mark –Paget's Law of Banking. Hardback: £180.00. ISBN 0-406-02598-3. Butterworth Law.

Harding, Andrew–Law, Government and the Constitution in Malaysia. Law and administration in developing countries. Hardback: £79.00. ISBN 90-411-0918-8. Kluwer Law International.

Harding, Christopher; Swart, Bert–Enforcing European Community Rules. Hardback: £39.50. ISBN 1-85521-757-0. Dartmouth.

Hargreaves, S.–Blackstone's LLB: Cases and Materials - European Law. Paperback: £18.95. ISBN 1-85431-528-5. Blackstone Press.

Hargreaves, S.–Blackstone's LLB: Learning Text - Contract. Paperback: £17.95. ISBN 1-85431-521-8. Blackstone Press.

Hargreaves, S.–LLB Cases and Materials: European Law. Paperback: £18.95. ISBN 1-85431-528-5. Blackstone Press.

Hargreaves, S.–LLB Learning Text: European Law. Paperback: £17.95. ISBN 1-85431-521-8. Blackstone Press.

Harper, Mark–Model Letters for Family Lawyers. £47.00. ISBN 0-85308-318-5. Family Law.

Harpwood, Vivienne –NHS Complaints: Litigation and Professional Discipline. Medico-legal. Paperback: £19.95. ISBN 1-85941-012-X. Cavendish Publishing Ltd.

Harris, Bruce; Planterose, Rowan; Tecks, Jonathan–The Arbitration Act: 1996. Paperback: £37.50. ISBN 0-632-04131-5. Blackwell Science (UK).

Harris, David; Maddison, David; Tetlow, Christopher; Wood, Graham–Bingham's Negligence Cases. Hardback: £125.00. ISBN 0-421-46500-X. Sweet & Maxwell.

Harris, Jim–Property and Justice. Hardback: £50.00. ISBN 0-19-825957-3. Clarendon Press.

Harris, Olivia–Inside and outside the Law. EASA series. Hardback: £40.00. ISBN 0-415-12928-1. Paperback: £13.99. ISBN 0-415-12929-X. Routledge.

Harris, Richard A.; Milkis, Sidney M.–The Politics of Regulatory Change. Paperback: £12.99. ISBN 0-19-508191-9. Oxford University Press Inc, USA.

Hart, Garry; Williams, Anne; Carnworth, R.; Robinson, P.; Dobry, Judge–Blundell and Dobry: Planning Applications, Appeals and Proceedings. Hardback: £50.00. ISBN 0-421-53540-7. Sweet & Maxwell.

Hartley, David–Briefcase on Family Law. Briefcase series. Paperback: £9.95. ISBN 1-85941-246-7. Cavendish Publishing Ltd.

Hartley, William M.–Matrimonial Conveyancing. Drafting series. Paperback: £38.00. ISBN 0-7520-0174-4. FT Law & Tax.

Harvey, Brian W.; Parry, Deborah L.–The Law of Consumer Protection and Fair Trading. Paperback: £25.95. ISBN 0-406-08186-7. Butterworth Law.

Harvey, David–Justice, Nature and the Geography of Difference. Hardback: £50.00. ISBN 1-55786-680-5. Paperback: £12.99. ISBN 1-55786-681-3. Blackwell Publishers.

Harwood, Michael–Conveyancing Law and Practice. Paperback: £15.95. ISBN 1-85941-232-7. Cavendish Publishing Ltd.

Hawke, Neil; Parpworth, Neil–Introduction to Administrative Law. Paperback: £12.95. ISBN 1-85941-191-6. Cavendish Publishing Ltd.

Hawkes, Leonard; Snyder, Francis G.–Customs and Commercial Policy in Europe. Hardback: £75.00. ISBN 0-406-16701-X. Butterworth Law.

Hay, David–Words and Phrases Legally Defined: 1996. Supplement. Paperback: £29.50. ISBN 0-406-99731-4. Butterworth Law.

Hayton, David–Cases and Commentary on the Law of Trusts and Equitable Remedies. Paperback: £28.95. ISBN 0-421-54860-6. Sweet & Maxwell.

Hazlett, Thomas W.–Public Policy Towards Cable Television: Vol 1. The Economics of Rate Control. AEI studies in telecommunications deregulation. Hardback: £23.50. ISBN 0-262-08253-5. The MIT Press.

Heap, Desmond–An Outline of Planning Law. Paperback: £42.00. ISBN 0-421-57520-4. Sweet & Maxwell.

Heard, Brian–Handbook of Firearms and Ballistics. Hardback: £45.00. ISBN 0-471-96563-4. Chancery Wiley Law Publications.

Hearle, Liz–World Guide to Intellectual Property Organisations. Key resources series. Paperback. ISBN 0-7123-0819-9. British Library (Science Reference and Information Service).

Heaton, R.–LLB Cases and Materials: Criminal Law. Paperback: £18.95. ISBN 1-85431-531-5. Blackstone Press.

Heaton, R.–LLB Learning Text: Criminal Law. Paperback: £17.95. ISBN 1-85431-524-2. Blackstone Press.

Heldman, Peter K.–Competitive Telecommunications. Hardback: £30.95. ISBN 0-07-028113-0. McGraw-Hill Publishing Company.

Heller, Lawrance; Levine, Marshall; Cuthbert, Neil–Commercial Property Development Precedents. £230.00. ISBN 0-7520-0427-1. FT Law & Tax.

Helmholz, R.H.–The Spirit of Classical Canon Law. The Spirit of the Laws. Hardback: £47.95. ISBN 0-8203-1821-3. University of Georgia Press.

Hendrick, Judith–Legal Aspects of Child Health Care. Paperback: £16.99. ISBN 0-412-58320-8. Chapman and Hall.

Henham, Ralph–Criminal Justice and Sentencing Policy. Hardback: £37.50. ISBN 1-85521-702-3. Dartmouth.

Henkin, Louis–Foreign Affairs and the US Constitution. Hardback: £55.00. ISBN 0-19-826099-7. Paperback: £22.50. ISBN 0-19-826098-9. Oxford University Press.

Henkin, Louis–The Age of Rights. Paperback: £13.00. ISBN 0-231-06445-4. Columbia University Press.

Henry, Michael–Henry: Entertainment Law. Paperback: £29.50. ISBN 0-406-04969-6. Butterworth Law.

Hepple, R.A.; Matthews, Martin; Howarth, David–Hepple and Matthews: Tort - Cases and Materials. Paperback: £27.95. ISBN 0-406-06326-5. Butterworth Law.

Hervey, Tamara K.; O'Keeffe, David–Sex Equality Law in the European Union. Hardback: £50.00. ISBN 0-471-96436-0. Chancery Wiley Law Publications.

Herzfeld, Edgar; Wilson, Adam–Joint Ventures. Hardback: £45.00. ISBN 0-85308-242-1. Jordan.

Heshon, Dennis–Acquisitions and Group Structures: 1995/96. Legal Practice Course resource books. Paperback: £17.50. ISBN 0-85308-334-7. Jordan.

Heuston, R.E.V.; Buckley, R.A.–Salmon and Heuston on the Law of Torts. Paperback: £28.00. ISBN 0-421-53350-1. Sweet & Maxwell.

Heydon, J.D.; Ockelton, Mark–Heydon and Ockelton: Evidence - Cases and Materials. Paperback: £26.95. ISBN 0-406-08180-8. Butterworth Law.

Hiebert, Janet L.–Limiting Rights. Hardback: £28.00. ISBN 0-7735-1431-7. Paperback: £13.95. ISBN 0-7735-1437-6. McGill Queens University Press (UCL Press).

Higgins, Rosalyn; Flory, Maurice–Terrorism and International Law. Hardback: £65.00. ISBN 0-415-11606-6. Routledge.

Hildreth, Steven; Longshaw, Alexis; Riley, Alan; Rogers, Philip; Sewell, Tim; Spencer, Chris–Commercial Law and Practice: 1995/96. Legal Practice Course resource books. Paperback: £17.50. ISBN 0-85308-335-5. Jordan.

Hill, Timothy; Ghaffar, Arshad–EC Air Transport Law. Hardback: £750.00. ISBN 1-85044-969-4. LLP Limited.

Hiller, Tim–Criminology. Lecture notes. Paperback: £15.95. ISBN 1-874241-57-0. Cavendish Publishing Ltd.

Hillier, Tim–Sourcebook on Public International Law. Sourcebook series. Paperback: £20.95. ISBN 1-85941-050-2. Cavendish Publishing Ltd.

Hindley, Brian; Messerlin, Patrick–Antidumping Industrial Policy. Paperback: £7.95. ISBN 0-8447-7046-9. American Enterprise Institute.

Hinton, Martin; Johnston, Elliott; Rigney, Daryle–Indigenous Australians. Paperback: £35.00. ISBN 1-85941-235-1. Cavendish Publishing Ltd.

Hirsch, Andrew von–Censure and Sanctions. Oxford monographs on criminal law and justice. Paperback: £15.99. ISBN 0-19-826216-7. Clarendon Press.

HMSO Finance Act: 1996. Paperback. ISBN 1-86012-251-5. Tolley Publishing.

Hoare, Richard; McCool, Geraldine–Personal Injury Pleadings and Precedents. Unbound/looseleaf: £185.00. ISBN 0-7520-0321-6. FT Law & Tax.

Hoban, Thomas More; Brooks, Richard Oliver–Green Justice. Hardback: £48.50. ISBN 0-8133-2602-8. Paperback: £13.50. ISBN 0-8133-2603-6. Westview Press.

Hobson, Charles F.–The Great Chief Justice. American Political Thought. Hardback: £27.95. ISBN 0-7006-0788-9. University Press of Kansas.

Hockett, Jeffrey D.–New Deal Justice. Studies in American Constitutionalism. Hardback: £55.50. ISBN 0-8476-8210-2. Paperback: £21.50. ISBN 0-8476-8211-0. Rowman & Littlefield.

Hodgkin, Ray–Professional Liability: Law and Insurance. Lloyd's commercial law library. Hardback: £115.00. ISBN 1-85978-034-2. LLP Limited.

Hodgson, J.–Blackstone's LLB: Cases and Materials - Torts. Paperback: £18.95. ISBN 1-85431-530-7. Blackstone Press.

Hodgson, J.–Blackstone's LLB: Learning Text - Torts. Paperback: £17.95. ISBN 1-85431-523-4. Blackstone Press.

Hodgson, J.–LLB Cases and Materials: Law of Tort. Paperback: £18.95. ISBN 1-85431-530-7. Blackstone Press.

Hodgson, J.–LLB Learning Text: Torts. Paperback: £17.95. ISBN 1-85431-523-4. Blackstone Press.

Hoffman, Anthony–Civil Costs Cases: Taxation Handbook: 1995/96. Paperback: £32.00. ISBN 0-421-53650-0. Sweet & Maxwell.

Hogan, Brian; Seago, Peter; Bennett, Geoffrey–A Level Law. Concise course texts. Paperback: £12.50. ISBN 0-421-54880-0. Sweet & Maxwell.

Hogan, Greer–Constitutional and Administrative Law Nutshell. Nutshells. Paperback: £4.95. ISBN 0-421-54850-9. Sweet & Maxwell.

Hogan, Patrick Colm–On Interpretation. Hardback: £35.50. ISBN 0-8203-1724-1. University of Georgia Press.

Holland, James–Learning Legal Rules. Paperback: £13.00. ISBN 1-85431-535-8. Blackstone Press.

Holland, Kenneth M.; Morton, F.L.; Galligan, Brian–Federalism and the Environment. Contributions in Political Science, No 368. Hardback: £47.95. ISBN 0-313-29430-5. Greenwood Press.

Hollinger, Richard–Crime, Deviance and the Computer. The international library of criminology, criminal justice and penology. Hardback: £75.00. ISBN 1-85521-467-9. Dartmouth.

Holmes, Ann–SWOT: Employment Law. Paperback: £8.95. ISBN 1-85431-586-2. Blackstone Press.

Holt, Richard–Conflict of Laws. Question and Answer Series. Paperback: £8.95. ISBN 1-85941-142-8. Cavendish Publishing Ltd.

Holyoak, Jon; Torremans, Paul–Intellectual Property Law. Butterworths student statutes series. Paperback: £8.95. ISBN 0-406-99376-9. Butterworth Law.

Homer, Arnold; Burrows, Rita–Partnership Taxation. Paperback: £36.95. ISBN 1-86012-154-3. Tolley Publishing.

Homer, Arnold; Burrows, Rita; Gravestock, Peter–Taxwise 1996-97: II. Value Added Tax, Inheritance Tax, Taxation of Trusts, Tax Planning. Paperback: £26.95. ISBN 1-86012-302-3. Tolley Publishing.

Homer, Arnold; Burrows, Rita; Smailes, David–Tax Guide: 1996-97. Hardback: £24.95. ISBN 1-86012-284-1. Tolley Publishing.

Hood, Roger–The Death Penalty. Hardback: £40.00. ISBN 0-19-826282-5. Paperback: £12.99. ISBN 0-19-826281-7. Clarendon Press.

Hooper, J.–LLB Cases and Materials: Law of Trusts. Paperback: £18.95. ISBN 1-85431-529-3. Blackstone Press.

Hooper, J.–LLB Learning Text: Law of Trusts. Paperback: £17.95. ISBN 1-85431-522-6. Blackstone Press.

Hopkins, Bruce R.–Business and Legal Strategies for Nonprofit Organizations. Nonprofit law, finance and management. Paperback: £50.00. ISBN 0-471-10606-2. John Wiley and Sons.

Hopt, Klaus J.–Insider Regulation and Timely Disclosure. Forum internationale. Paperback: £22.50. ISBN 90-411-0199-3. Kluwer Law International.

Horton, Michael; Pearson, Philippa; Papps, Laura–Family Homes and Domestic Violence. Paperback: £29.00. ISBN 0-7520-0232-5. FT Law & Tax.

Hospitality and Tourism Law. Tourism and hospitality management. Paperback: £17.99. ISBN 0-412-62080-4. Chapman and Hall.

Howells, Geraint–European Business Law. European Business Law Library. Hardback: £50.00. ISBN 1-85521-587-X. Dartmouth.

Hudson, Barbara–Race, Crime and Justice. The international library of criminology, criminal justice and penology. Hardback: £85.00. ISBN 1-85521-660-4. Dartmouth.

Hudson, John–The Formation of the English Common Law. The medieval world, Vol 2. Hardback: £42.00. ISBN 0-582-07027-9. Paperback: £13.99. ISBN 0-582-07026-0. Addison-Wesley Longman Higher Education.

Hudson, John–The History of English Law. Proceedings of the British Academy, 89. Hardback: £19.95. ISBN 0-19-726165-5. Oxford University Press.

Hugenholtz, P. Bernt–The Future of Copyright in a Digital Environment. Information law series. Paperback: £59.50. ISBN 90-411-0267-1. Kluwer Law International.

Hughes, David–Environmental Law. Paperback: £27.95. ISBN 0-406-08179-4. Butterworth Law.

Humphreys, Nick–Employment Law Referencer: 1997. Paperback: £14.95. ISBN 0-421-58170-0. Sweet & Maxwell.

Hunnings, Neville March–The European Courts. Hardback: £39.00. ISBN 1-86067-010-5. Cartermill Publishing.

Hunt, Alan–Governance of the Consuming Passions. Language, discourse, society. Hardback: £45.00. ISBN 0-333-63332-6. Macmillan Press.

Hunt, Paul–Reclaiming Social Rights. Hardback: £39.50. ISBN 1-85521-845-3. Dartmouth.

Hunter, Robert –Cases on the Scots Law of Evidence. Paperback: £28.50. ISBN 0-406-02418-9. Butterworth Law (Scotland).

Hunter, Susan; Waterman, Richard W.–Enforcing the Law. Bureaucracies, public administration, and public policy. Hardback: £47.40. ISBN 1-56324-682-1. Paperback: £19.40. ISBN 1-56324-683-X. M.E. Sharpe.

Huse, Joseph–Understanding and Negotiating Turnkey Contract. Hardback: £85.00. ISBN 0-421-52340-9. Sweet & Maxwell.

Hutchinson, Dennis J.; Strauss, David A.; Stone, Geoffrey R.–The Supreme Court Review: 1995. Hardback: £43.25. ISBN 0-226-36312-0. University of Chicago Press.

Hynds, Paul–Fast Ferries. Lloyd's Business Intelligence Centre. Spiral bound: £325.00. ISBN 1-85978-057-1. LLP Limited.

Hyung-chan Kim–Asian Americans and Congress. Documentary Reference Collections. Hardback: £98.00. ISBN 0-313-28595-0. Greenwood Press.

Impey, David; Montague, Nicholas–Running a Limited Company. Paperback: £13.50. ISBN 0-85308-381-9. Jordan.

Inglis, Andrew; Heath, Guy–Using Trademarks in Business. Paperback: £19.99. ISBN 0-471-96670-3. Chancery Wiley Law Publications.

Inness, Julie–Privacy, Intimacy, and Isolation. Paperback: £8.99. ISBN 0-19-510460-9. Oxford University Press Inc, USA.

Inns of Court Bar Manuals: Advocacy 1996/1997. Paperback: £16.95. ISBN 1-85431-568-4. Blackstone Press.

Inns of Court Bar Manuals: Case Preparation 1996/1997. Paperback: £16.95. ISBN 1-85431-569-2. Blackstone Press.

Inns of Court Bar Manuals: Conference Skills 1996/1997. Paperback: £16.95. ISBN 1-85431-566-8. Blackstone Press.

Inns of Court Bar Manuals: Criminal Litigation and Sentencing 1996/1997. Paperback: £16.95. ISBN 1-85431-573-0. Blackstone Press.

Inns of Court Bar Manuals: Drafting 1996/1997. Paperback: £16.95. ISBN 1-85431-571-4. Blackstone Press.

Inns of Court Bar Manuals: Evidence 1996/1997. Paperback: £16.95. ISBN 1-85431-572-2. Blackstone Press.

Inns of Court Bar Manuals: Negotiation 1996/1997. Paperback: £16.95. ISBN 1-85431-567-6. Blackstone Press.

Inns of Court Bar Manuals: Opinion Writing 1996/1997. Paperback: £16.95. ISBN 1-85431-570-6. Blackstone Press.

Inns of Court Bar Manuals: Professional Conduct 1996/1997. Paperback: £16.95. ISBN 1-85431-576-5. Blackstone Press.

Inns of Court Bar Manuals: Remedies 1996/1997. Paperback: £16.95. ISBN 1-85431-575-7. Blackstone Press.

Inter-American Commission on Human Rights–Inter-American Yearbook on Human Rights/Anuario Interamericano de Derechos Humanos: Vol 10. 1994. Inter-American yearbook on human rights, 10. Hardback: £350.00. ISBN 90-411-0302-3. Kluwer Law International.

Intern Conventions and Recommendations: 1919-1995. Hardback: £67.50. ISBN 92-2-109192-9. International Labour Office.

Irons, Peter; Guitton, Stephanie–May It Please the Court. ISBN 1-56584-337-1. I.B. Tauris.

Is It 6. Paperback: £22.00. ISBN 0-406-06423-7. Butterworth Law.

Ivamy, E.R. Hardy–Fire and Motor Insurance. Hardback: £98.50. ISBN 0-406-04838-X. Butterworth Law.

Iwobi, A.U.–Essential Succession. Essential series - revision. Paperback: £4.95. ISBN 1-85941-144-4. Cavendish Publishing Ltd.

Jackson, Bernard S.–Making Sense in Jurisprudence. Legal semiotics monographs, Vol V. Hardback: £39.50. ISBN 0-9513793-8-0. Paperback: £16.95. ISBN 0-9513793-9-9. Deborah Charles Publications.

Jackson, Bernard S.–Making Sense in Law. Legal semiotics monographs, Vol V. Hardback: £45.00. ISBN 0-9513793-6-4. Deborah Charles Publications.

Jackson, David–Enforcement of Maritime Claims. Hardback: £125.00. ISBN 1-85044-302-5. Lloyd's of London Press.

Jackson, David–Immigration: Law and Practice. Hardback: £115.00. ISBN 0-421-37790-9. Sweet & Maxwell.

Jackson, Diana; Smith, Alison–Consumer Protection. Legal Practice Course resource books. Paperback: £17.50. ISBN 0-85308-338-X. Jordan.

Jackson, Rupert; Powell, John–Jackson and Powell on Professional Negligence: Fourth Cumulative Supplement to the Third Edition. Paperback: £24.00. ISBN 0-421-52190-2. Sweet & Maxwell.

Jackson, Sherman A.–Islamic Law and the State. Studies in Islamic law and society, 1. Hardback. ISBN 90-04-10458-5. E.J. Brill.

Jacob, Herbert; Blankenburg, Erhard; Kritzer, Herbert M.; Provine, Doris Marie; Sanders, Joseph–Courts, Law and Politics in Comparative Perspective. Hardback: £28.00. ISBN 0-300-06378-4. Paperback: £12.50. ISBN 0-300-06379-2. Yale University Press.

Jacobs, Francis; White, Robin C.A.–The European Convention on Human Rights. Hardback: £45.00. ISBN 0-19-825820-8. Paperback: £18.99. ISBN 0-19-826242-6. Clarendon Press.

Jacobson, David–Rights Across Borders. Hardback: £27.50. ISBN 0-8018-5150-5. The Johns Hopkins University Press.

Jacquemet, Marco–Credibility in Court. Studies in Interactional Sociolinguistics, 14. Hardback: £40.00. ISBN 0-521-55251-6. Cambridge University Press.

James, Philip S.–James's Introduction to English Law. Paperback: £15.95. ISBN 0-406-02445-6. Butterworth Law.

Jarvis, Peter–The Essential Television Handbook. Paperback: £14.99. ISBN 0-240-51445-9. Focal Press: an imprint of Butterworth-Heinemann.

Jefferson, Michael–Restraint of Trade. Paperback: £19.95. ISBN 0-471-96271-6. Chancery Wiley Law Publications.

Jeffrey-Cook, John–Moores Rowland's Orange Tax Guide: 1996-97. Paperback: £31.95. ISBN 0-406-06416-4. Butterworth Law.

Jeffrey-Cook, John–Moores Rowland's Yellow Tax Guide: 1996-7. Paperback: £31.95. ISBN 0-406-06441-5. Butterworth Law.

Jenkins, Pamela J.; Kroll-Smith, Steve–Witnessing for Sociology. Hardback: £51.95. ISBN 0-275-94852-8. Praeger Publishers.

Jennings, Robert; Watts, Arthur–International Law: Vol 1. Peace. International law, Vol 1. Paperback: £75.00. ISBN 0-582-30245-5. Addison-Wesley Longman Higher Education.

Jeremiah, Joanna R.–Merchandising Intellectual Property Rights. Intellectual property law. Hardback: £65.00. ISBN 0-471-96579-0. John Wiley and Sons.

Johansen, Bruce E.–Native American Political Systems and the Evolution of Democracy. Bibliographies and Indexes in American History, No 32. Hardback: £51.95. ISBN 0-313-30010-0. Greenwood Press.

Johnson, David–Head Injuries Litigation. Hardback: £60.00. ISBN 0-421-48350-4. Sweet & Maxwell.

Johnson, R.–Printed Teaching Materials. Hardback: £30.00. ISBN 1-85941-233-5. Cavendish Publishing Ltd.

Johnston, David–The Renewal of the Old. Paperback: £4.95. ISBN 0-521-58756-5. Cambridge University Press.

Joly, Daniele–Haven or Hell? Migrations, minorities and citizenship. Hardback: £40.00. ISBN 0-333-64304-6. Macmillan Press.

Jones, Brian; Thompson, Katharine–Garner's Administrative Law. Paperback: £29.95. ISBN 0-406-99251-7. Butterworth Law.

Jones, C.; Van der Woude, M.; Lewis, X.–EC Competition Law Handbook: 1996. Paperback: £75.00. ISBN 0-421-58450-5. Sweet & Maxwell.

Jones, Gareth; Goodhart, Sir William–Specific Performance. Hardback: £80.00. ISBN 0-406-06561-6. Butterworth Law.

Jones, Hugh–Essential Law for Publishers. Hardback: £35.00. ISBN 1-85713-000-6. Routledge.

Jones, Hugh–Publishing Law. Blueprint. Hardback: £60.00 ISBN 0-415-15110. Paperback: £19.99. ISBN 0-415-15466-9. Routledge.

Jones, Ian–Sourcebook on Succession, Wills and Probate. Sourcebook series. Paperback: £18.95. ISBN 1-85941-104-5. Cavendish Publishing Ltd.

Jones, Mark P.–Electoral Laws and the Survival of Presidential Democracies. Hardback: £26.50. ISBN 0-268-00933-3. University of Notre Dame Press.

Jones, Michael A.–Textbook on Torts. Paperback: £17.00. ISBN 1-85431-551-X. Blackstone Press.

Jones, Philip A.–Lawyers' Skills 1996/1997. Legal Practice Course Guides. Paperback: £15.55. ISBN 1-85431-542-0. Blackstone Press.

Jones, Professor–Environmental Liability Practice Manual. Paperback: £29.95. ISBN 0-471-95554-X. Chancery Wiley Law Publications.

Jones, Richard–Mental Health Act Manual. £35.00. ISBN 0-421-56430-X. Sweet & Maxwell.

Jones, T.H.; Christie, M.G.A.–Criminal Law. Greens' concise Scots law. Paperback. ISBN 0-414-01146-5. W.Green & Son.

Jones–EC Competition Law Handbook. Paperback: £59.00. ISBN 0-421-54020-6. Sweet & Maxwell.

Jordan, Emma Coleman; Hill, Anita F.–Race, Gender, and Power in America. Hardback: £16.99. ISBN 0-19-508774-7. Oxford University Press Inc, USA.

Joseph, Janice–Black Youths, Delinquency, and Juvenile Justice. Hardback: £43.95. ISBN 0-275-94909-5. Praeger Publishers.

Joubert, Chantal–Schengen Investigated. Hardback: £119.00. ISBN 90-411-0266-3. Kluwer Law International.

Juda, Lawrence–International Law and Ocean Management. Ocean management and policy. Hardback: £50.00. ISBN 0-415-11271-0. Routledge.

Julyan, Alan; Jeffries, Simon; McMullen, Jeremy–Employment Precedents and Company Policy Documents. Unbound/looseleaf: £165.00. ISBN 0-7520-0305-4. FT Law & Tax.

Jupp, Kenneth–Private Property & Public Finance. The Georgist paradigm. Paperback: £12.95. ISBN 0-85683-155-7. Shepheard-Walwyn.

Jurisprudence and Legal Theory - LLB: Suggested Solutions (1991-1995). Bachelor of Laws (LLB). Paperback: £6.95. ISBN 0-7510-0726-9. HLT Publications.

Jurisprudence and Legal Theory: Suggested Solutions - Single Paper (June 1995). Paperback: £3.00. ISBN 0-7510-0625-4. HLT Publications.

Jurisprudence and Legal Theory: Textbook 1996-1997. Bachelor of Laws (LLB). Paperback: £16.95. ISBN 0-7510-0691-2. HLT Publications.

Just, Peter–Dou Donggo Justice. Hardback: £43.95. ISBN 0-8476-8327-3. Paperback: £15.95. ISBN 0-8476-8328-1. Rowman & Littlefield.

Kadish, Alon–The Corn Laws. Fine binding: £375.00. ISBN 1-85196-410-X. Pickering & Chatto.

Kalman, Laura–The Strange Career of Legal Liberalism. Hardback: £25.00. ISBN 0-300-06369-5. Yale University Press.

Kaplan, Sandra J.–Family Violence. Hardback: £37.50. ISBN 0-89042-010-6. American Psychiatric Press.

Kapur, Ratna–Feminist Terrains in Legal Domains. Hardback. ISBN 81-85107-83-1. Kali for Women.

Kaufman, Kenneth C.–Dred Scott's Advocate. Missouri Biography Series. Hardback: £23.95. ISBN 0-8262-1092-9. University of Missouri Press.

Kaye, Martin; Salter, David–Family Finance and Tax. Paperback: £36.00. ISBN 0-421-49690-8. Sweet & Maxwell.

Keane, Adrian–Keane: Modern Law of Evidence. Paperback: £20.95. ISBN 0-406-08185-9. Butterworth Law.

Keenan, Denis; Bisacre, Josephine–Smith and Keenan's Company Law for Students. Paperback: £22.99. ISBN 0-273-62034-7. Pitman Publishing.

Kelleher, Denis; Murray, Karen–Kelleher and Murray: Computer Law. Paperback: £50.00. ISBN 1-85475-825-X. Butterworth Law (Ireland).

Kelly, Patrick R.N.–Agency and Distribution Agreements in Europe. Hardback: £90.00. ISBN 0-85308-210-3. Jordan.

Kelly, Patrick; Attree, Rebecca–European Product Liability. Hardback: £98.00. ISBN 0-406-03256-4. Butterworth Law.

Kelly, Patrick; Attree, Rebecca–Kelly and Attress: European Product Liability. Hardback: £100.00. ISBN 0-406-03256-4. Butterworth Law.

Kelsen, Hans–Introduction to the Problems of Legal Theory. Paperback: £16.99. ISBN 0-19-826565-4. Clarendon Press.

Kemp, Margaret–Drafting and Negotiating Rent Review Clauses. Drafting. Paperback: £55.00. ISBN 0-7520-0182-5. FT Law & Tax.

Kempees, Peter–A Systematic Guide to the Case Law of the European Court of Human Rights, 1960-1994. Hardback: £330.00. ISBN 0-7923-3281-4. Kluwer Law International.

Kendall, G. John–Expert Determination. Hardback: £75.00. ISBN 0-7520-0283-X. FT Law & Tax.

Kendall, John; Sutton, David St John; Gill, Judith–Russell on Arbitration. Hardback. ISBN 0-420-48090-0. W.Green & Son.

Kenny, P.–Landlord and Tenant Covenants: the New Law in Practice. £19.95. ISBN 1-85431-487-4. Blackstone Press.

Kenny, Phillip.–Conveyancing 1996/1997. Legal Practice Course Guides. Paperback: £15.55. ISBN 1-85431-545-5. Blackstone Press.

Kent, Penelope–Law of the European Union. M&E handbooks. Paperback: £13.99. ISBN 0-7121-0851-3. Macdonald and Evans.

Kersner, Myra; Wright, Jannet A.–How to Manage Communication Problems in Young Children. Paperback: £12.99. ISBN 1-85346-414-7. David Fulton Publishers.

Keynes, Edward–Liberty, Property, and Privacy. Hardback: £31.95. ISBN 0-271-01509-8. Paperback: £13.50. ISBN 0-271-01510-1. Penn State Press.

Khan, L. Ali–The Extinction of Nation-states. Developments in International Law, 21. Hardback: £74.50. ISBN 90-411-0198-5. Kluwer Law International.

Khan, Malcolm; Robson, Michelle–Medical Negligence. Medico-Legal Series. Paperback: £25.00. ISBN 1-85941-022-7. Cavendish Publishing Ltd.

Kibling, Thomas; Lewis, Tamara–Employment Law. Paperback: £18.00. ISBN 0-905099-71-0. The Legal Action Group.

Kidner, Richard–Blackstone's Statutes on Employment Law. Paperback: £11.95. ISBN 1-85431-561-7. Blackstone Press.

Kidner, Richard.–Casebook on Torts. Paperback: £16.55 . ISBN 1-85431-536-6. Blackstone Press.

Kilpatrick, Alyson–Repairs and Maintenance. Arden's housing library series. Paperback: £16.95. ISBN 1-898001-11-1. Lemos & Crane.

Kime's International Law Directory: 1997. Hardback: £77.00. ISBN 0-7520-0238-4. FT Law & Tax.

King-Jones, Amanda; Butcher, Christopher–Probate Practice Manual. Unbound/looseleaf: £135.00. ISBN 0-7520-0250-3. FT Law & Tax.

Kirk, David N.; Woodcock, Anthony J.J.–Kirk and Woodcock: Serious Fraud-investigation and Trial. Hardback: £110.00. ISBN 0-406-05690-0. Butterworth Law.

Kirk, E.–LLB Cases and Materials: the English Legal System. Paperback: £12.95. ISBN 1-85431-585-4. Blackstone Press.

Kirkby, Diane–Sex, Power and Justice. Paperback: £18.99. ISBN 0-19-553734-3. OUP Australia.

Klabbers, Jan–The Concept of Treaty in International Law. Developments in international law. Hardback: £74.25. ISBN 90-411-0244-2. Kluwer Law International.

Klug, Francesca; Starmer, Keir; Weir, Stuart–The Three Pillars of Liberty. The democratic audit of the United Kingdom. Hardback: £50.00. ISBN 0-415-09641-3. Paperback: £14.99. ISBN 0-415-09642-1. Routledge.

Kodilinye, Gilbert; Owusu, Sampson–Commonwealth Caribbean Real Property Law: Text, Cases and Materials. Paperback: £20.00. ISBN 1-85941-116-9. Cavendish Publishing Ltd.

Konstadinidis, Stratos V.–The Legal Regulation of the European Community's External Relations After the Completion of the Internal Market. EC/International Law Forum I. Hardback: £45.00. ISBN 1-85521-695-7. Dartmouth.

Koppelman, Andrew–Anti-discrimination Law and Social Equality. Hardback: £22.00. ISBN 0-300-06482-9. Yale University Press.

Korah, Valentine–Cases and Materials on EC Competition Law. Paperback: £22.95. ISBN 0-421-54700-6. Sweet & Maxwell.

Korah, Valentine–The Technology Transfer Regulation. Hardback: £50.00. ISBN 0-19-826243-4. Oxford University Press.

Korman, Sharon–The Right of Conquest. Hardback: £40.00. ISBN 0-19-828007-6. Clarendon Press.

Kovacic, William E.–The Postal Service As Competitor. Hardback: £31.95. ISBN 0-8447-3960-X. American Enterprise Institute.

Krause, Elliott A.–Death of the Guilds. Hardback: £27.50. ISBN 0-300-06758-5. Yale University Press.

Kubasek, Nancy K.; Brennnan, Bartley A.; Browne, M. Neil–The Legal Environment of Business. Paperback: £27.95. ISBN 0-13-160517-8. Prentice Hall US.

Kurczewski, Jacek; Maclean, Mavis–Family Law and Family Policy in the New Europe. Onati international series in law and society. Hardback: £40.00. ISBN 1-85521-810-0. Paperback: £17.50. ISBN 1-85521-814-3. Dartmouth.

La Follette, Maryly; Purdie, Robert A.J.–La Follette and Purdie: a Guide to the Family Law Act 1996. Butterworths annotated legislation service. Paperback: £19.00. ISBN 0-406-08160-3. Butterworth Law.

Lai, Jerry P.L.; Martin, Steve; Cranidge, Claire–Company Secretary's Handbook: 1996/97. Paperback: £33.95. ISBN 1-86012-342-2. Tolley Publishing.

Land Law - LLB: Suggested Solutions (1991-1995). Bachelor of Laws (LLB). Paperback: £6.95. ISBN 0-7510-0723-4. HLT Publications.

Land Law: Suggested Solutions - Single Paper (June 1995). Paperback: £3.00. ISBN 0-7510-0622-X. HLT Publications.

Lane, David–Law Relating to Unincorporated Associations. Paperback: £15.95. ISBN 1-85941-028-6. Cavendish Publishing Ltd.

Lane, Jan-Erik–Constitutions and Political Theory. Hardback: £40.00. ISBN 0-7190-4647-5. Paperback: £14.99. ISBN 0-7190-4648-3. Manchester University Press.

Langridge, Nicola–The Family Law Referencer: 1997. Paperback: £14.95. ISBN 0-421-58190-5. Sweet & Maxwell.

Laudati, Laraine–European Competition Forum. European law. Hardback: £50.00. ISBN 0-471-96668-1. Chancery Wiley Law Publications.

Lauterpacht, E.J., QC; Greenwood, C.J.–International Law Reports: Vol 101. Hardback: £85.00. ISBN 0-521-49648-9. Cambridge University Press.

Lauterpacht, E.J.; Greenwood, C.J.–International Law Reports. Hardback: £95.00. ISBN 0-521-56229-5. Cambridge University Press.

Lauterpacht, E.J.; Greenwood, C.J.–International Law Reports: Vol 102. Hardback: £85.00. ISBN 0-521-55199-4. Cambridge University Press.

Lavers, A.–Professional Negligence in the Construction Industry. Hardback: £27.00. ISBN 0-419-17900-3. E & FN Spon (An imprint of Chapman & Hall).

Law of International Trade: Suggested Solutions (1991-1995). Bar examinations. Paperback: £9.95. ISBN 0-7510-0743-9. HLT Publications.

Law of International Trade: Suggested Solutions - Single Paper (Trinity 1995). Bar Examinations. Paperback: £3.95. ISBN 0-7510-0643-2. HLT Publications.

Law of Tort - LLB: Suggested Solutions (1991-1995). Bachelor of Laws (LLB). Paperback: £6.95. ISBN 0-7510-0724-2. HLT Publications.

Law of Trusts - LLB: Suggested Solutions (1991-1995). Bachelor of Laws (LLB). Paperback: £6.95. ISBN 0-7510-0725-0. HLT Publications.

Law of Trusts: Suggested Solutions - Single Paper (June 1995). Paperback: £3.00. ISBN 0-7510-0624-6. HLT Publications.

Law Update: 1996. Paperback: £6.95. ISBN 0-7510-0609-2. HLT Publications.

Lawyers' Tax Companion. Ringbinder. ISBN 0-86325-443-8. CCH Editions.

Lea, David–Melanesian Land Tenure in a Contemporary and Philosophical Context. Hardback: £27.50. ISBN 0-7618-0456-0. University Press of America.

Ledford, Kenneth F.–From General Estate to Special Interest. Hardback: £35.00. ISBN 0-521-56031-4. Cambridge University Press.

Lee, C.C.–Dictionary of Environmental Legal Terms. Hardback: £59.95. ISBN 0-07-038113-5. McGraw-Hill Publishing Company.

Lee, Robert; Morgan, Derek–Death Rites. Paperback: £12.99. ISBN 0-415-14026-9. Routledge.

Lee, Terry–Multi-party Actions. Personal injury library. Paperback: £38.00. ISBN 0-85121-985-3. FT Law & Tax.

Lefeber, Rene–Transboundary Environmental Interference and the Origin of State Liability. Hardback: £86.00. ISBN 90-411-0275-2. Kluwer Law International.

Legal Aid Handbook: 1996. Paperback: £12.70. ISBN 0-421-57550-6. Sweet & Maxwell.

Leibowitz, Arnold H.–Embattled Island. Hardback: £43.95. ISBN 0-275-95390-4. Praeger Publishers.

Leigh, Sarah–Managing Medical Negligence Actions. Personal injury library. Paperback: £50.00. ISBN 0-85121-984-5. FT Law & Tax.

Leighton, Gerald; Lowe, Jim–Jordans Company Secretarial Precedents. Hardback: £50.00. ISBN 0-85308-324-X. Jordan.

Leitner, Peter M.–Reforming the Law of the Sea Treaty. Hardback: £49.50. ISBN 0-7618-0393-9. Paperback: £33.50. ISBN 0-7618-0394-7. University Press of America.

Leng–Guide to the Criminal Procedure and Investigations Act 1996. Paperback: £16.95. ISBN 1-85431-588-9. Blackstone Press.

Leng–Guide to the Family Law Act 1996. Paperback: £17.95. ISBN 1-85431-589-7. Blackstone Press.

Levenson, Howard; Fairweather, Fiona; Cape, Ed–Police Powers: a Practitioners' Guide. Paperback: £32.00. ISBN 0-905099-62-1. Legal Action Group.

Levi, Michael; Nelken, David–Corruption in Public Life. Paperback: £12.99. ISBN 0-631-20014-2. Blackwell Publishers.

Levine, Marshall–Construction and Environmental Law. Hardback: £75.00. ISBN 0-7520-0262-7. FT Law & Tax.

Levy, Allan–Custody and Access. Longman practitioner series. Paperback. ISBN 0-85121-316-2. FT Law & Tax.

Lewis, Roger; Kelloway, Ros–Jacques and Lewis: Sex Discrimination and Occupational Pension Schemes. Current EC legal developments. Paperback: £90.00. ISBN 0-406-00344-0. Butterworth Law.

Lewison, Kim–Drafting Business Leases. Drafting series. Paperback: £55.00. ISBN 0-7520-0306-2. FT Law & Tax.

Ley, Nigel–Drink Driving Law and Practice. Hardback: £75.00. ISBN 0-421-58060-7. Sweet & Maxwell.

Lin Feng–Administrative Law Procedures and Remedies in China. China law series. Paperback: £65.00. ISBN 0-421-56020-7. Sweet & Maxwell.

Lindstein, Tomas; Meteyard, Barry–What Works in Family Mediation. Paperback: £12.95. ISBN 1-898924-85-6. Russell House Publishing Ltd.

Linowitz, Sol M.; Mayer, Martin–The Betrayed Profession. Paperback: £13.00. ISBN 0-8018-5329-X. The Johns Hopkins University Press.

Lister, Charles–European Environmental Law. Environmental law. Paperback: £19.95. ISBN 0-471-96296-1. John Wiley and Sons.

Livens, Leslie–Share and Business Valuation Handbook. Paperback: £44.95. ISBN 1-86012-293-0. Tolley Publishing.

Lloyd, H.; Baatz, N.; Streatfeild-James, D.; Fraser, P.D.; Clay, R.–Building Law Reports: Vol 75. Hardback. ISBN 0-582-29762-1. Addison-Wesley Longman Higher Education.

Lloyd, H.; Baatz, N.; Streatfeild-James, D.; Fraser, P.D.; Clay, R.–Building Law Reports: Vol 76. Hardback. ISBN 0-582-29761-3. Addison-Wesley Longman Higher Education.

Lloyd, H.; Baatz, N.; Streatfeild-James, D.; Fraser, P.D.; Clay, R.–Building Law Reports: Vol 77. Hardback. ISBN 0-582-29763-X. Addison-Wesley Longman Higher Education.

Lloyd, H.; Baatz, N.; Streatfeild-James, D.; Fraser, P.D.; Clay, R.–Building Law Reports: Vol 78. Hardback. ISBN 0-582-29766-4. Addison-Wesley Longman Higher Education.

Lloyd, Stephen; Middleton, Fiona–The Charities Acts Handbook. Paperback: £24.95. ISBN 0-85308-292-8. Jordan.

Lloyd, Stephen; Middleton, Fiona; Randall, Adrian; Gifford, Barry–Charities Administration Service. Unbound/looseleaf. ISBN 0-85308-327-4. Jordan.

Lochnaw, Crispin Agnew–Agricultural Law in Scotland. Hardback: £40.00. ISBN 0-406-11514-1. Butterworth Law (Scotland).

Lockton, Deborah J.–Employment Law. Macmillan master series. Paperback: £9.99. ISBN 0-333-67097-3. Macmillan Press.

Lohman, Hans–Duties and Liability of Directors and Shareholders Under Netherlands Law. Hardback: £62.00. ISBN 90-411-0927-7. Kluwer Law International.

Lonbay, Julian–Remedies for Breach of EC Law. Hardback: £50.00. ISBN 0-471-97109-X. Chancery Wiley Law Publications.

Loose, Peter; Griffiths, Michael–Loose on Liquidators. Hardback: £55.00. ISBN 0-85308-234-0. Jordan.

Lorion, Raymond P.; Iscoe, Ira; DeLeon, Patrick H.; VandenBos, Gary R.–Psychology and Public Policy. Paperback: £23.95. ISBN 1-55798-347-X. American Psychological Association.

Loughlin, Martin–Legality and Locality. Hardback: £50.00. ISBN 0-19-826015-6. Clarendon Press.

Lovett, William A.–United States Shipping Policies and the World Market. Hardback: £59.95. ISBN 0-89930-945-3. Quorum Books.

Lowe, Vaughan; Fitzmaurice, Malgosia–Fifty Years of the International Court of Justice. Cambridge Studies in International and Comparative Law. Hardback: £75.00. ISBN 0-521-55093-9. Cambridge University Press.

Lowenfeld, Andreas F.–International Litigation and the Quest for Reasonableness. Hardback: £40.00. ISBN 0-19-826059-8. Clarendon Press.

Luba, Jan–Repairs: Tenants' Rights. Paperback. ISBN 0-905099-49-4. The Legal Action Group.

Lucas, N.–LLB Learning Text: Contract. Paperback: £17.95. ISBN 1-85431-519-6. Blackstone Press.

Luckman, Michael–Intellectual Property in Commercial Transactions. Commercial series. Hardback: £65.00. ISBN 0-7520-0131-0. FT Law & Tax.

Lush, Denzil–Elderly Clients. Paperback: £39.50. ISBN 0-85308-309-6. Jordan.

Lyon, C.M.; de Cruz, S.P.–Lyon and De Cruz: Parents, Children and the Law. Paperback: £18.95. ISBN 0-406-50800-3. Butterworth Law.

MacCann, Lyndon–MacCann: Companies Acts 1963-1990. Hardback: £75.00. ISBN 1-85475-162-X. Butterworth Law (Ireland).

MacCormack, Geoffrey–The Spirit of Traditional Chinese Law. The Spirit of the Laws. Hardback: £35.50. ISBN 0-8203-1722-5. University of Georgia Press.

Macdonald, Ian A.; Blake, Nicholas J.–Macdonald's Immigration Law and Practice: Supplement. Paperback: £15.00. ISBN 0-406-99732-2. Butterworth Law.

Macfarlane, Julie–Rethinking Disputes - the Mediation Alternative. Hardback: £34.99. ISBN 1-85941-151-7. Cavendish Publishing Ltd.

MacIntyre, Ewan–Business Law: the Soap. Paperback: £19.99. ISBN 0-273-62375-3. Pitman Publishing.

Mackenzie, Judith-Anne–A Practical Approach to Land Law. Paperback: £16.95. ISBN 1-85431-550-1. Blackstone Press.

MacLean, Robert M.–European Community Law and Human Rights: Casebook 1996-1997. Bar Examinations. Paperback: £18.95. ISBN 0-7510-0679-3. HLT Publications.

MacLean, Robert M.–European Union Law. Cracknell's law student companion series. Paperback: £9.95. ISBN 1-85836-056-0. Old Bailey Press.

MacLean, Robert M.–European Union Law: Casebook 1996-1997. Bachelor of Laws (LLB). Paperback: £17.95. ISBN 0-7510-0661-0. HLT Publications.

MacLean, Robert M.–Public International Law: Casebook 1996-1997. Bachelor of Laws (LLB). Paperback: £18.95. ISBN 0-7510-0665-3. HLT Publications.

MacLeod, Iain; Hendry, Ian D.; Hyatt, Stephen–The External Relations of the European Communities. Oxford European Community Law Series. Hardback: £55.00. ISBN 0-19-825929-8. Paperback: £17.99. ISBN 0-19-825930-1. Clarendon Press.

Macleod, J.S.; Levitt, A.R.–MacLeod and Levitt: Taxation of Insurance Business. Unbound/looseleaf: £120.00. ISBN 0-406-04606-9. Butterworth Law.

Macmillan, Moira; Macfarland, Sally–Scottish Business Law. Paperback: £23.99. ISBN 0-273-62035-5. Pitman Publishing.

Maddock, Malcolm; Norris, Martin–Planning and Environmental Law. Legal Practice Course resource books. Paperback: £17.50. ISBN 0-85308-342-8. Jordan.

Madge, Nic–Housing Law Casebook. Paperback: £30.00. ISBN 0-905099-59-1. The Legal Action Group.

Majid, Amir A.–Legal Status of International Institutions. Hardback: £45.00. ISBN 1-85521-761-9. Dartmouth.

Malamud-Goti, Jaime–Game Without End. Hardback: £19.95. ISBN 0-8061-2826-7. University of Oklahoma Press.

Malcolm, Joyce Lee–To Keep and Bear Arms. Paperback: £10.50. ISBN 0-674-89307-7. Harvard University Press.

Manchester, C.; Salter, D.; Moodie, P.; Lynch, B.–Exploring the Law - the Dynamics of Precedent and Statutory Interpretation. Paperback: £16.50. ISBN 0-421-47180-8. Sweet & Maxwell.

Mandelstam, Michael–Equipment for Older or Disabled People and the Law. Paperback: £29.95. ISBN 1-85302-352-3. Jessica Kingsley Publishers.

Mantle, Wendy–Child Support: a Practitioner's Guide. Practitioner series. Paperback: £50.00. ISBN 0-7520-0049-7. FT Law & Tax.

Martin, Denis–Martin and Guild: Free Movement of Persons in the European Union. Hardback: £120.00. ISBN 0-406-06564-0. Butterworth Law.

Martin, Jose Maria Fernandez–The EC Public Procurement Rules. Hardback: £45.00. ISBN 0-19-826017-2. Clarendon Press.

Mastel, Greg–American Trade Laws After the Uraguay Round. Hardback: £47.50. ISBN 1-56324-895-6. Paperback: £19.50. ISBN 1-56324-896-4. M.E. Sharpe.

Maveety, Nancy–Justice Sandra Day O'Connor. Studies in American Constitutionalism. Hardback: £41.95. ISBN 0-8476-8194-7. Paperback: £17.50. ISBN 0-8476-8195-5. Rowman & Littlefield.

Mayor, Bill; Harvey, Andrew–Law of Contract. M&E handbooks. Paperback: £14.99. ISBN 0-7121-1065-8. Macdonald and Evans.

Mayson, Stephen–Company Law. Paperback: £25.95. ISBN 1-85431-549-8. Blackstone Press.

Mayss, Abla J.–Conflict of Laws. Lecture Notes. Paperback: £15.95. ISBN 1-85941-172-X. Cavendish Publishing Ltd.

Mazur, Amy G.–Gender Bias and the State. Pitt Series in Policy and Institutional Studies. Hardback: £39.95. ISBN 0-8229-3902-9. Paperback: £18.50. ISBN 0-8229-5601-2. University of Pittsburgh Press.

McAlhone, Christina; Stockindale, Michael–Evidence Nutshell. Nutshells. Paperback: £4.95. ISBN 0-421-54190-3. Sweet & Maxwell.

McAuley, Finbarr; McCutcheon, Paul J.–The Grammar of Criminal Liability. Hardback: £42.50. ISBN 1-85800-058-0. Round Hall Sweet & Maxwell.

McBride, J. Michael–Purchase and Sale of Assets in Bankruptcy. Hardback: £102.95. ISBN 0-471-13321-3. John Wiley and Sons.

McCahery, Joseph; Bratton, William W.; Picciotto, Sol; Scott, C.–International Regulatory Competition and Coordination. Hardback: £55.00. ISBN 0-19-826035-0. Clarendon Press.

McChesney, Fred; Rubin, Paul–The Role of Economists in Modern Antitrust. Wiley series in managerial economics. Hardback: £45.00. ISBN 0-471-97074-3. John Wiley and Sons.

McColgan, Aileen–The Future of Labour Law. Hardback: £55.00. ISBN 1-85567-405-X. Pinter Publishers.

McCormack, Gerald–Proprietary Claims in Insolvency. Hardback: £65.00. ISBN 0-421-56480-6. Sweet & Maxwell.

McCoubrey, Hilaire–Textbook on Jurisprudence. Paperback: £15.95. ISBN 1-85431-582-X. Blackstone Press.

McCoubrey, Hilaire–The Obligation to Obey in Legal Theory. Hardback: £39.50. ISBN 1-85521-825-9. Dartmouth.

McCoubrey, Hilaire; White, Nigel D.–The Blue Helmets: Legal Regulation of United Nations Military Operations. Hardback: £40.00. ISBN 1-85521-626-4. Dartmouth.

McCracken, Sheelagh–McCracken: the Banker's Remedy of Set-off. Hardback: £95.00. ISBN 0-406-00909-0. Butterworth Law.

McCrossan, H.–Revenue Law: Textbook. Bachelor of Laws (LLB). £18.95. ISBN 0-7510-0785-4. HLT Publications.

McCrudden, Christopher–Public Procurement, Contract Compliance and Social Policy in the European Union. Hardback: £35.00. ISBN 0-19-826267-1. Clarendon Press.

McCullough, Cameron–Foreign Direct Investment in Vietnam. China law series. Paperback: £40.00. ISBN 0-421-56870-4. Sweet & Maxwell.

McCutcheon–McCutcheon on Inheritance Tax. Sixth Cumulative Supplement to the Third Edition. British tax library. Paperback: £36.00. ISBN 0-421-54670-0. Sweet & Maxwell.

McDonald-Ros, M.–The Finance Act 1992. Paperback: £12.95. ISBN 0-7494-0845-6. Kogan Page.

McEldowney, John F.; McEldowney, Sharron–The Environment and the Law. Paperback: £22.99. ISBN 0-582-22712-7. Addison-Wesley Longman Higher Education.

McGonagle, Marie–Law and the Media. Paperback: £25.00. ISBN 1-85800-059-9. Round Hall Sweet & Maxwell.

McHale, J; Murphy, J.; Fox, M.–Health Care Law: Text, Cases and Materials. Paperback: £28.00. ISBN 0-421-51180-X. Sweet & Maxwell.

McKenzie, Master–Butterworths Rules of Court - Criminal Court Practice: 1996. Paperback: £27.50. ISBN 0-406-99892-2. Butterworth Law.

McKenzie, S.–Q & A English Legal System. Paperback: £8.95. ISBN 1-85431-533-1. Blackstone Press.

McLachlan, Campbell; Nygh, Peter–Transnational Tort Litigation. Hardback: £50.00. ISBN 0-19-825919-0. Clarendon Press.

McLean, Ian; Morrish, Peter; Greenhill, John–Magistrates' Court Index: 1997. Court indexes. Hardback: £42.00. ISBN 0-7520-0375-5. FT Law & Tax.

McLean, Sheila A.M.–Contemporary Issues in Law, Medicine and Ethics. Medico-legal series. Hardback: £42.50. ISBN 1-85521-586-1. Dartmouth.

McLeod, Ian–Legal Method. Macmillan law masters. Paperback: £9.99. ISBN 0-333-67696-3. Macmillan Press.

McMullen, Jeremy; Eady, Jennifer–Employment Tribunal Procedure. Paperback: £22.50. ISBN 0-905099-47-8. The Legal Action Group.

McMullen, Jeremy; Eady, Jennifer–Industrial Tribunal Procedure. Paperback: £17.50. ISBN 0-905099-47-8. The Legal Action Group.

Meessen, Karl M.–Extraterritorial Jurisdiction in Theory and Practice. Hardback: £89.00. ISBN 90-411-0899-8. Kluwer Law International.

Megarry, Robert; Wade, William; Harpum, Charles; Bridge, S.; Grant, M.–The Law of Real Property. Hardback: £45.00. ISBN 0-421-47460-2. Paperback: £28.00. ISBN 0-421-47470-X. Sweet & Maxwell.

Mehigan, Simon; Griffiths, David–Restraint of Trade and Business Secrets: Law and Practice. Commercial series. Paperback: £75.00. ISBN 0-7520-0019-5. FT Law & Tax.

Mei-fun, Priscilla Leung–China Law Reports: 1991: Vol 1. Civil Law. Hardback: £579.00. Butterworth Law.

Mei-fun, Priscilla Leung–China Law Reports: 1991: Vol 2. Criminal Law. Hardback: £579.00. Butterworth Law.

Mei-fun, Priscilla Leung–China Law Reports: 1991: Vol 3. Administrative and Economic Law. Hardback: £579.00. Butterworth Law.

Melander, Goran; Alfredsson, Gudmundur–The Raoul Wallenberg Compilation of Human Rights Instruments. The Raoul Wallenberg Institute human rights library. Hardback: £133.00. ISBN 0-7923-3646-1. Martinus Nijhoff Publishers.

Mesher, John; Wood, Penny–CPAG'S Income Related Benefits: the Legislation: 1996. Paperback: £34.00. ISBN 0-421-56770-8. Sweet & Maxwell.

Mesher, John; Wood, Penny–Income Related Benefits: the Legislation: Supplement 1996. Paperback: £17.95. ISBN 0-421-56780-5. Sweet & Maxwell.

Meston, Michael C.–Succession Opinions. Green's practice library. Hardback. ISBN 0-414-01121-X. W.Green & Son.

Michaels, Amanda–A Practical Guide to Trade Marks. Paperback: £26.00. ISBN 0-421-45200-5. Sweet & Maxwell.

Miles, George.–Wills, Probate and Administration 1996/1997. Legal Practice Course Guides. Paperback: £15.55. ISBN 1-85431-546-3. Blackstone Press.

Miller, Gareth–The Machinery of Succession. Hardback: £45.00. ISBN 1-85521-442-3. Dartmouth.

Miller, Grady–The Legal and Economic Basis of International Trade. Hardback: £51.95. ISBN 0-89930-918-6. Quorum Books.

Miller, Jerome G.–Search and Destroy. Hardback: £30.00. ISBN 0-521-46021-2. Cambridge University Press.

Millington, Trevor–Restraint and Confiscation Orders. Practitioner. Paperback: £38.00. ISBN 0-7520-0151-5. FT Law & Tax.

Mills, Shaun–Constitutional and Administrative Law of the EC. Paperback: £15.95. ISBN 1-85941-223-8. Cavendish Publishing Ltd.

Minns, Tracy–Quantum in Medical Negligence. Paperback. ISBN 0-7520-0048-9. FT Law & Tax.

Mitchell, Andrew R.; Talbot, Kennedy; Taylor, Susan M.–Forfeiture, Confiscation and the Proceeds of Crime. Criminal law library. Hardback: £99.00. ISBN 0-421-54490-2. Sweet & Maxwell.

Mitchell, Lawrence E.–Progressive Corporate Law. New perspectives on law, culture, & society. Hardback: £37.00. ISBN 0-8133-2363-0. Paperback: £11.95. ISBN 0-8133-2364-9. Westview Press.

Model Form of Conditions of Contract for Process Plants: Suitable for Lump-sum Contracts - The Red Book. Paperback: £25.00. ISBN 0-85295-326-7. Institution of Chemical Engineers.

Model Form of Conditions of Subcontract for Process Plant. Paperback: £25.00. ISBN 0-85295-375-5. Institution of Chemical Engineers.

Mohammad Hashim Kamali–Principles of Islamic Jurisprudence. Hardback: £45.00. ISBN 0-946621-23-3. Paperback: £18.95. ISBN 0-946621-24-1. The Islamic Texts Society.

Mohr, James C.–Doctors and the Law. Paperback: £13.00. ISBN 0-8018-5398-2. The Johns Hopkins University Press.

Molan, Michael T. –Constitutional Law: Casebook 1996-1997. Bachelor of Laws (LLB). Paperback: £14.95. ISBN 0-7510-0654-8. HLT Publications.

Molan, Michael T.–Administrative Law: Casebook 1996-1997. Bachelor of Laws (LLB). Paperback: £18.95. ISBN 0-7510-0664-5. HLT Publications.

Molan, Michael T.–Administrative Law: Textbook 1996-1997. Bachelor of Laws (LLB). Paperback: £18.95. ISBN 0-7510-0698-X. HLT Publications.

Molan, Michael T.–Constitutional Law: Casebook 1996-1997. Common Professional Examinations (CPE). Paperback: £14.95. ISBN 0-7510-0671-8. HLT Publications.

Molan, Michael T.–Constitutional Law: Textbook 1996-1997. Bachelor of Laws (LLB). Paperback: £16.95. ISBN 0-7510-0686-6. HLT Publications.

Molan, Michael T.–Criminal Law: Casebook 1996-1997. Common Professional Examinations (CPE). Paperback: £17.95. ISBN 0-7510-0669-6. HLT Publications.

Molan, Michael T.–Criminal Law: Suggested Solutions - Single Paper (June 1995). Paperback: £3.00. ISBN 0-7510-0618-1. HLT Publications.

Molan, Michael T.–Criminal Law: Textbook 1996-1997. Common Professional Examinations (CPE). Paperback: £16.95. ISBN 0-7510-0705-6. HLT Publications.

Monet, Jean–The Cassock and the Crown. Hardback: £28.00. ISBN 0-7735-1399-X. Paperback: £12.95. ISBN 0-7735-1449-X. McGill Queens University Press (UCL Press).

Monkkonen, Eric H.–The Local State. Stanford Series in the New Political History. Hardback: £30.00. ISBN 0-8047-2412-1. Stanford University Press (CUP).

Montgomery, Jonathan–Health Care Law. Hardback: £30.00. ISBN 0-19-876260-7. Paperback: £16.99. ISBN 0-19-876259-3. Clarendon Press.

Moore, Alan–Tax Acts 1996-97. Paperback: £75.00. ISBN 1-85475-718-0. Butterworth Law (Ireland).

Moore, Wayne D.–Constitutional Rights and Powers of the People. Hardback: £29.95. ISBN 0-691-01111-7. Princeton University Press.

Moors, Annelies–Muslim Women and Property. Cambridge Middle East Library, 3. Hardback: £40.00. ISBN 0-521-47497-3. Paperback: £14.95. ISBN 0-521-48355-7. Cambridge University Press.

Moran, Leslie–The Homosexual(ity) of Law. Hardback: £50.00. ISBN 0-415-07952-7. Paperback: £16.99. ISBN 0-415-07953-5. Routledge.
Moran, T.–Legal Competence in Environmental Health. Hardback: £35.00. ISBN 0-412-71580-5. Chapman and Hall.
Morewitz, Stephen–Sexual Harassment and Social Change in American Society. Hardback: £58.50. ISBN 1-880921-77-4. Austin and Winfield.
Morewitz, Stephen–Sexual Harassment and Social Change in American Society. Paperback: £39.95. ISBN 1-880921-76-6. Austin and Winfield.
Morison, John; Bell, Christine–Tall Stories? Reading Law and Literature. Applied Legal Philosophy. Hardback: £39.50. ISBN 1-85521-741-4. Dartmouth.
Morris, D. Glynis; Melvin, Claire–Tolley's Manual of Accounting. Ring binder: £95.00. ISBN 1-86012-324-4. Tolley Publishing.
Morris, Debra–Schools: an Education in Charity Law. Hardback: £39.50. ISBN 1-85521-444-X. Dartmouth.
Morris, Gordon–Shaw's Directory of Courts in the United Kingdom: 1996/97. Paperback: £33.50. ISBN 0-7219-1403-9. Shaw & Sons.
Morrish, Peter; McLean, Ian; Selwood, David–Crown Court Index: 1997. Court indexes. Hardback: £49.00. ISBN 0-7520-0376-3. FT Law & Tax.
Morrison, Neil–Private Finance Initiative. Special reports. Hardback: £125.00. ISBN 0-7520-0352-6. FT Law & Tax.
Morrison, Wayne J.–Sourcebook on Criminal Law. Sourcebook Series. Paperback: £19.95. ISBN 1-85941-100-2. Cavendish Publishing Ltd.
Mosawi, Anthony–EC Media Law. Paperback: £90.00. ISBN 0-406-00253-3. Butterworth Law.
Mostert, Frederick–Mostert: Famous and Well-known Marks. Hardback: £100.00. ISBN 0-406-99734-9. Butterworth Law.
Moynihan, Edmund; Hendry, Richard; Nicholas, Mike; Booth, Neil; Self, Roger; Maas, Robert–Remuneration and Benefits - a Managers' Guide to the Law. Unbound/looseleaf: £65.00. ISBN 1-86012-253-1. Tolley Publishing.
Muhammad Khalid Masud; Messick, Brinkley; Powers, David S.–Islamic Legal Interpretation. Harvard Law School legal studies / Harvard Middle Eastern studies. Hardback: £28.50. ISBN 0-674-46870-8. Harvard University Press.
Muhammad Mustafa Azami–On Schacht's Origins of Muhammadan Jurisprudence. Paperback: £14.95. ISBN 0-946621-46-2. The Islamic Texts Society.
Mullen, Tom; Prosser, Tony–Judicial Review in Scotland. Paperback: £35.00. ISBN 0-471-96614-2. John Wiley and Sons.
Muneer Goolam Fareed–Legal Reform in the Muslim World. Hardback: £47.95. ISBN 1-57292-003-3. Paperback: £31.95. ISBN 1-57292-002-5. Austin and Winfield.
Munkman, John–Damages for Personal Injuries and Death. Hardback: £45.00. ISBN 0-406-01481-7. Butterworth Law.
Murdoch, John; Hughes, Will–Construction Contracts. Paperback: £21.99. ISBN 0-419-20760-0. E & FN Spon (an imprint of Chapman & Hall).
Murphy, J. David–Plunder and Preservation. Hardback: £30.00. ISBN 0-19-586874-9. Oxford University Press.
Murphy, P.–Blackstone's Criminal Practice 1996. £99.00. ISBN 1-85431-511-0. Blackstone Press.
Murphy, Tim–Modern Law Review: Vol 58. Hardback: £47.00. ISBN 0-631-20079-7. Blackwell Publishers.
Murphy, Yvonne–Journalists and the Law. Paperback. ISBN 1-89973-836-3. Round Hall Sweet & Maxwell.
Muscat, Andrew–The Liability of the Holding Company for the Debts of Its Insolvent Subsidiaries. Hardback: £52.50. ISBN 1-85521-844-5. Dartmouth.
Musson, Anthony–Public Order and Law Enforcement. Hardback: £39.50. ISBN 0-85115-635-5. The Boydell Press.

Nagel, Robert F.–Judicial Power and American Character. Paperback: £10.99. ISBN 0-19-510662-8. Oxford University Press Inc, USA.

Nathanson, Stephen; Carver, Anne–What Lawyers Do. Paperback: £7.95. ISBN 0-421-54890-8. Sweet & Maxwell.

Navias, Martin S.; Hooton, E.R–Tanker Wars. Hardback: £75.00. ISBN 1-86064-032-X. Tauris Academic Studies.

Neal, A.C.; Wright, F.B.–European Communities' Health and Safety Legislation: Vol 2. Paperback: £45.00. ISBN 0-412-57760-7. Chapman and Hall.

Neal, A.C.; Wright, F.B.–European Communities' Health and Safety Legislation: Vol 3. Paperback: £29.95. ISBN 0-412-57770-4. Chapman and Hall.

Nelken, David–Comparing Legal Cultures. Socio-legal studies. Hardback: £37.50. ISBN 1-85521-718-X. Dartmouth.

Nelken, David–Law As Communication. Issues in Law and Society. Hardback: £35.00. ISBN 1-85521-719-8. Paperback: £15.00. ISBN 1-85521-722-8. Dartmouth.

Newton, Alan–Newton: the Law and Regulation of Derivatives. Hardback: £85.00. ISBN 0-406-04965-3. Butterworth Law.

Nicholls, Paul–CCH Absence Manual. Ring binder. ISBN 0-86325-445-4. CCH Editions.

Nichols, David; Brown, John L.R.; Kearney, Brian; McInnes, John C.; Norrie, Kenneth McK; Robb, Kenneth; Robson, Peter; Scott, Janys; Stoddart, Charles–Butterworths Scottish Family Law Service. Unbound/looseleaf: £140.00. ISBN 0-406-01354-3. Butterworth Law (Scotland).

Nielsen, Marianne O.; Silverman, Robert A.–Native Americans, Crime, and Justice. Hardback: £48.50. ISBN 0-8133-2988-4. Paperback: £13.50. ISBN 0-8133-2989-2. Westview Press.

Noone, Michael–Mediation. Legal skills. Paperback: £10.95. ISBN 1-85941-202-5. Cavendish Publishing Ltd.

Norman, Sandy–Copyright in Further and Higher Education Libraries. Library Association copyright guides. Paperback: £8.95. ISBN 1-85604-196-4. Library Association Publishing.

Norman, Sandy–Copyright in Health Libraries. Library Association copyright guides. Paperback: £8.95. ISBN 1-85604-195-6. Library Association Publishing.

Norman, Sandy–Copyright in Industrial and Commercial Libraries. Library Association copyright guides. Paperback: £8.95. ISBN 1-85604-193-X. Library Association Publishing.

Norman, Sandy–Copyright in Public Libraries. Library Association copyright guides. Paperback: £8.95. ISBN 1-85604-194-8. Library Association Publishing.

Norman, Sandy–Copyright in School Libraries. Library Association copyright guides. Paperback: £8.95. ISBN 1-85604-192-1. Library Association Publishing.

Norman, Sandy–Copyright in Voluntary Sector Libraries. Library Association copyright guides. Paperback: £8.95. ISBN 1-85604-197-2. Library Association Publishing.

O'Dempsey, Declan; Short, Andrew–Disability Discrimination. Practitioner series. Paperback: £38.00. ISBN 0-7520-0281-3. FT Law & Tax.

O'Malley, Stephen; Layton, Alex–European Civil Practice: 1st Supplement to the 1st Edition. Hardback: £55.00. ISBN 0-421-47330-4. Sweet & Maxwell.

Oakley, A.J.–Trends in Contemporary Trust Law. Hardback: £50.00. ISBN 0-19-826286-8. Clarendon Press.

Oditah, Fidelis–Insolvency of Banks. Special reports. Hardback: £137.00. ISBN 0-7520-0290-2. FT Law & Tax.

Oditah, Fidelis–The Future for the Global Securities Market - Legal and Regulatory Aspects. Hardback: £40.00. ISBN 0-19-826219-1. Clarendon Press.

Oldham-Smith, Ken–Electrical Safety and the Law. Paperback: £24.99. ISBN 0-632-04094-7. Blackwell Science (UK).

Oldham, Mika–Statutes on Family Law 1996/1997. Paperback: £12.95. ISBN 1-85431-562-5. Blackstone Press.
Oliver, Dawn; Drewry, Gavin–Reform of the Public Services. Constitutional Reform Series. Hardback: £40.00. ISBN 0-7201-2156-6. Mansell.
Oliver, Peter–Free Movement of Goods in the EC. Hardback: £100.00. ISBN 0-421-51110-9. Sweet & Maxwell.
Oliver, Simon; Austen, Lesley–Special Educational Needs. Paperback: £19.50. ISBN 0-85308-310-X. Jordan.
Olley, Nick–Public Companies and the City. Legal Practice Course resource books. Paperback: £17.50. ISBN 0-85308-344-4. Jordan.
Ortiz-Blanco, Luis–EC Competition Procedure. Hardback: £110.00. ISBN 0-19-825967-0. Clarendon Press.
Ortiz-Blanco, Luis; Houtte, Ben Van–EC Competition Law in the Transport Sector. Hardback: £65.00. ISBN 0-19-826089-X. Clarendon Press.
Orucu, Esin; Attwooll, Elspeth; Coyle, Sean–Studies in Legal Systems. Hardback: £70.00. ISBN 90-411-0906-4. Kluwer Law International.
Osborne, Craig.–Civil Litigation 1996/1997. Legal Practice Course Guides. Paperback: £15.55. ISBN 1-85431-547-1. Blackstone Press.
Osman, Christopher–Butterworths Employment Law Guide. Paperback: £60.00. ISBN 0-406-01652-6. Butterworth Law.
Ough, Richard; McClelland, Alan M.–McClelland and Matheson: Child Abuse. Paperback: £35.00. ISBN 0-406-04980-7. Butterworth Law.
Oxley, Deborah–Convict Maids. Studies in Australian History, 23. Hardback: £40.00. ISBN 0-521-44131-5. Cambridge University Press.
Pace, Nicholas A.; McLean, Sheila–Ethics and the Law in Intensive Care. Hardback: £35.00. ISBN 0-19-262520-9. Oxford University Press.
Pace, Peter J.–Family Law. M&E Handbooks. Paperback: £13.99. ISBN 0-7121-1056-9. Macdonald and Evans.
Painter, Richard–Cases and Materials on Employment Law. Paperback: £25.00. ISBN 1-85431-593-5. Blackstone Press.
Palmer's Corporate Insolvency. Unbound/looseleaf: £195.00. ISBN 0-421-56500-4. Sweet & Maxwell.
Palmer, Camilla–Maternity Rights. Paperback: £15.00. ISBN 0-905099-66-4. The Legal Action Group.
Palmer, Camilla; Moon, Gay–Discrimination At Work. Paperback: £26.00. ISBN 0-905099-70-2. The Legal Action Group.
Palmier, Leslie–State and Law in Eastern Asia. Hardback: £39.50. ISBN 1-85521-781-3. Dartmouth.
Pannett, Alan; Boella, Michael–Principles of Hospitality Law. Hardback: £45.00. ISBN 0-304-33574-6. Paperback: £19.99. ISBN 0-304-33575-4. Cassell.
Park, Semin–The Duty of Disclosure in Insurance Contract Law. Hardback: £42.50. ISBN 1-85521-923-9. Dartmouth.
Parker, Stephen; Sampford, Charles–Legal Ethics and Legal Practice. Hardback: £35.00. ISBN 0-19-825945-X. Clarendon Press.
Parr, Russell L.; Sullivan, Patrick H.–Technology Licensing Strategies. Hardback: £50.00. ISBN 0-471-13081-8. John Wiley and Sons.
Parrington, Sheila–Whillan's Tax Tables: 1996-7. Paperback: £4.95. ISBN 0-406-06448-2. Butterworth Law.
Patel, Chandra K.–Fiscal Reforms in the Least Developed Countries. Hardback: £39.95. ISBN 1-85898-513-7. Edward Elgar.
Pattenden, Rosemary–English Criminal Appeals. Oxford Monographs on Criminal Law and Justice. Hardback: £45.00. ISBN 0-19-825405-9. Clarendon Press.
Patterson, Dennis–Companion to Philosophy of Law and Legal Theory. Blackwell companions to philosophy. Hardback: £65.00. ISBN 1-55786-535-3. Blackwell Publishers.

Patterson, Dennis–Law and Truth. Hardback: £30.00. ISBN 0-19-508323-7. Oxford University Press Inc, USA.

Pawlowski, Mark–Proprietary Estoppel. Hardback: £56.00. ISBN 0-421-56630-2. Sweet & Maxwell.

Payne-James, Jason; Dean, Peter J.; Wall, Ian–Medicolegal Essentials in Healthcare. Paperback: £16.95. ISBN 0-443-05240-9. Churchill Livingstone.

Pearce, Robert A.; Stevens, John–The Law of Trusts and Equitable Obligations. Paperback: £24.95. ISBN 0-406-05246-8. Butterworth Law.

Pease, Ken–Uses and Abuses of Criminal Statistics. The international library of criminology, criminal justice and penology. Hardback: £85.00. ISBN 1-85521-408-3. Dartmouth.

Penn, Graham A.–Banking Supervision. Hardback: £95.00. ISBN 0-406-05212-3. Butterworth Law.

Pensions Law. Paperback: £42.00. ISBN 0-406-04933-5. Butterworth Law.

Percy, R.A.–Charlesworth and Percy: on Negligence. The common law library, no 6. Hardback: £180.00. ISBN 0-421-56990-5. Sweet & Maxwell.

Perritt Jr, Henry H.–Cyber-law. Intellectual property. Hardback: £90.00. ISBN 0-471-12624-1. John Wiley and Sons.

Perry, Michael J.–The Constitution in the Courts. Paperback: £11.99. ISBN 0-19-510464-1. Oxford University Press Inc, USA.

Personal Financial Planning Manual: 1996-7. Paperback: £29.95. ISBN 0-406-99089-1. Butterworth Law.

Peters, Roger–Essential Law for Catering Students. Paperback: £12.99. ISBN 0-340-63078-7. Hodder & Stoughton Educational.

Petersen, Hanne–Home Knitted Law. Socio-legal studies. Hardback: £40.00. ISBN 1-85521-837-2. Dartmouth.

Pett, David; Moss, Leslie–Employee Share Schemes Handbook. Hardback: £195.00. ISBN 0-7520-0218-X. FT Law & Tax.

Phelan, Diarmuid Rossa–Revolt or Revolution. Paperback. ISBN 1-899738-24-X. Round Hall Sweet & Maxwell.

Phillips, Andrew Fulton–Medical Negligence Law: Seeking a Balance. Medico-legal series. Hardback: £37.50. ISBN 1-85521-643-4. Dartmouth.

Phillips, Edward–Briefcase on Law of Evidence. Briefcase series. Paperback: £9.95. ISBN 1-85941-244-0. Cavendish Publishing Ltd.

Phillips, J.–The Inventor's Guide. Information in focus. Paperback: £25.00. ISBN 0-7123-0793-1. British Library (Science Reference and Information Service).

Phillips, Nevil–The Merchant Shipping Act 1995 - an Annotated Guide. Hardback: £65.00. ISBN 1-85978-068-7. LLP Limited.

Pianca, Andrew–Charity Accounts and the New SORP. Paperback: £30.00. ISBN 0-85308-235-9. Jordan.

Pierce, Jennifer L.–Gender Trials. Hardback: £40.00. Paperback: £13.95. University of California Press.

Pitchfork, E.; Molan, M.–General Paper I: Casebook 1996-1997. Bar Examinations. Paperback: £20.95. ISBN 0-7510-0677-7. HLT Publications.

Pitchfork, Ernie D.–Tort: Casebook 1996-1997. Bachelor of Laws (LLB). Paperback: £17.95. ISBN 0-7510-0656-4. HLT Publications.

Pitchfork, Ernie; Molan, Mike T.–General Paper I: Textbook 1996-1997. Bar Examinations. Paperback: £21.95. ISBN 0-7510-0711-0. HLT Publications.

Podgorecki, Adam; Olgiati, Vittorio–Totalitarian and Post-totalitarian Law. Onati Series in Law and Society. Hardback: £40.00. ISBN 1-85521-779-1. Paperback: £17.50. ISBN 1-85521-783-X. Dartmouth.

Pollack, Sheldon D.–The Failure of US Tax Policy. Hardback: £23.95. ISBN 0-271-01582-9. Penn State Press.

Pongo, Kodzp Tita–Expectation As Fulfillment. Hardback: £29.50. ISBN 0-7618-0227-4. University Press of America.

Popple, James–A Pragmatic Legal Expert System. Applied Legal Philosophy. Hardback: £45.00. ISBN 1-85521-739-2. Dartmouth.

Porter, Brenda; Hatherly, David; Simon, John–Principles of External Auditing. Paperback: £16.99. ISBN 0-471-96212-0. John Wiley and Sons.

Posner, Richard A.–Law and Legal Theory in England and America. Clarendon law lectures. Hardback: £17.99. ISBN 0-19-826471-2. Clarendon Press.

Posner, Richard A.–Overcoming Law. Paperback: £11.95. ISBN 0-674-64926-5. Harvard University Press.

Posner, Richard A.–The Federal Courts. Hardback: £24.95. ISBN 0-674-29626-5. Harvard University Press.

Power, Vincent J.G.–Power: Competition Law in Ireland and the EU. Hardback: £85.00. ISBN 1-85475-135-2. Butterworth Law (Ireland).

PowerGen plc–The CDM Regulations. Hardback: £49.50. ISBN 0-632-04087-4. Blackwell Science (UK).

Pozo, Susan–Price Behaviour in Illegal Markets. Hardback: £35.00. ISBN 1-85972-349-7. Avebury.

Practical Conveyancing: Suggested Solutions (1991-1995). Bar Examinations. Paperback: £9.95. ISBN 0-7510-0746-3. HLT Publications.

Practical Conveyancing: Suggested Solutions - Single Paper (Trinity 1995). Bar Examinations. Paperback: £3.95. ISBN 0-7510-0646-7. HLT Publications.

Prais, Vivien–Company Law. Cracknell's law students' companions. Paperback: £9.95. ISBN 1-85836-034-X. Old Bailey Press.

Prichard, Jane–Mental Health Law for Nurses. Central health studies series. Paperback: £9.95. ISBN 1-85642-012-4. Quay Books.

Pring, George W.; Canan, Penelope–SLAPPs. Hardback: £47.95. ISBN 1-56639-368-X. Paperback: £19.95. ISBN 1-56639-369-8. Temple University Press.

Pritchard, Robert–Economic Development, Foreign Investment and the Law. Hardback: £65.00. ISBN 90-411-0891-2. Kluwer Law International.

Public International Law - LLB: Suggested Solutions (1991- 1995). Bachelor of Laws (LLB). Paperback: £6.95. ISBN 0-7510-0733-1. HLT Publications.

Public International Law: Suggested Solutions - Single Paper (June 1995). Paperback: £3.00. ISBN 0-7510-0632-7. HLT Publications.

Pugh-Smith, John; Samuels, John–Archaeology in Law. Hardback: £48.00. ISBN 0-421-50340-8. Sweet & Maxwell.

Purdy, Jeannine M.–Common Law and Colonised Peoples. Law, social change and development. Hardback: £39.50. ISBN 1-85521-916-6. Dartmouth.

Q & A: Law. Questions and answers series. Paperback: £3.50. ISBN 0-85660-272-8. Trotman.

Qureshi, Asif H.–The World Trade Organisation. Melland Studies in International Law. Hardback: £50.00. ISBN 0-7190-3191-5. Manchester University Press.

Rabinowicz, Jack; Widdrington, Tony; Nicholas, Katharine–Education. Practitioner series. Paperback: £38.00. ISBN 0-7520-0201-5. FT Law & Tax.

Radin, Margaret Jane–Reinterpreting Property. Paperback. ISBN 0-226-70228-6. University of Chicago Press.

Raitt, Fiona; Field, David–The Law of Evidence in Scotland. Greens' concise Scots law. Paperback. ISBN 0-414-01041-8. W.Green & Son.

Rajak, Harry; Davis, Richard–Insolvency - a Business by Business Guide. Paperback: £45.00. ISBN 0-406-02231-3. Butterworth Law.

Ramsey, Iain–Advertising, Culture and the Law. Modern legal studies. Hardback: £18.95. ISBN 0-421-52650-5. Sweet & Maxwell.

Ramus, J.W.; Birchall, Simon–Contract Practice for Surveyors. Paperback: £16.99. ISBN 0-7506-2661-5. Laxton's: an imprint of Butterworth-Heinemann.

Rantala, M.L.–O.J. Unmasked. Paperback: £11.50. ISBN 0-8126-9328-0. Open Court Publishing Company.

Read, Anne P.–Contract Law: Textbook 1996-1997. Bachelor of Laws (LLB). Paperback: £16.95. ISBN 0-7510-0685-8. HLT Publications.

Read, P. Anne –Sale of Goods and Credit: Textbook 1996-1997. Bar examinations. Paperback: £18.95. ISBN 0-7510-0717-X. HLT Publications.
Read, P. Anne–Commercial Law: Sale of Goods, Consumer Credit and Agency: Textbook 1996-1997. Bachelor of Laws (LLB). Paperback: £18.95. ISBN 0-7510-0693-9. HLT Publications.
Read, P. Anne–Contract Law: Casebook 1996-1997. Bachelor of Laws (LLB). Paperback: £17.95. ISBN 0-7510-0652-1. HLT Publications.
Read, P. Anne–Contract Law: Casebook 1996-1997. Common Professional Examinations (CPE). Paperback: £17.95. ISBN 0-7510-0670-X. HLT Publications.
Read, P. Anne–Sale of Goods and Credit: Casebook 1996-1997. Bar examinations. Paperback: £18.95. ISBN 0-7510-0682-3. HLT Publications.
Read, P.Anne–Commercial Law: Sale of Goods, Consumer Credit and Agency: Casebook 1996-1997. Bachelor of Laws (LLB). Paperback: £18.95. ISBN 0-7510-0659-9. HLT Publications.
Real, A.–Opinion Writing and Drafting in Equity and Trusts. Paperback: £10.95. ISBN 1-85941-033-2. Cavendish Publishing Ltd.
Reardon, Anthony–Allied Dunbar Pensions Handbook. Hardback: £24.99. ISBN 0-273-62506-3. Pitman Publishing.
Reed, Charles B.–Administrative Law. Revision Workbook. Paperback: £9.95. ISBN 0-7510-0617-3. HLT Publications.
Reich, Peter Lester–Mexico's Hidden Revolution. Hardback: £23.50. ISBN 0-268-01418-3. University of Notre Dame Press.
Rendell, Catherine–Law of Succession. Macmillan law masters. Paperback: £9.99. ISBN 0-333-61735-5. Macmillan Press.
Revenue Law - LLB: Suggested Solutions (1991-1995). Bachelor of Laws (LLB). Paperback: £6.95. ISBN 0-7510-0735-8. HLT Publications.
Revenue Law: Suggested Solutions (1991-1995). Bar examinations. Paperback: £9.95. ISBN 0-7510-0747-1. HLT Publications.
Revenue Law: Suggested Solutions - Single Paper (Trinity 1995). Bar Examinations. Paperback: £3.95. ISBN 0-7510-0647-5. HLT Publications.
Revenue Law: Suggested Solutions - Single Paper. Paperback: £3.00. ISBN 0-7510-0634-3. HLT Publications.
Reynolds, Kirk; Clark, Wayne–Renewal of Business Tenancies. Hardback: £100.00. ISBN 0-421-52960-1. Sweet & Maxwell.
RIBA–Engaging an Architect: Guidance for Clients on Health and Safety: The Construction (Design and Management) Regulations 1994 (CDM Yellow Book). £5.00. ISBN 1-85946-006-2. RIBA Publications.
RIBA–Form of Appointment As Planning Supervisor (PS/95). £4.00. RIBA Publications.
Ribeiro, Robert–Engineering Contracts. Hardback: £35.00. ISBN 0-7506-2498-1. Butterworth-Heinemann.
Richards, Margaret–Community Care. Paperback: £29.50. ISBN 0-85308-293-6. Jordan.
Richards, Margaret; Waddington, Matthew; Cowan, David–The Housing Act 1996: a Practitioner's Guide. Paperback: £22.50. ISBN 0-85308-394-0. Jordan.
Richardson, P.J.; Thomas, D.A.–Archbold: Criminal Pleading, Evidence and Practice: 1997. Hardback: £165.00. ISBN 0-421-56670-1. Sweet & Maxwell.
Richens, N.J.; Fletcher, M.J.G.–Charity Land and Premises. Paperback: £22.50. ISBN 0-85308-326-6. Jordan.
Riddall, John G. –Law of Trusts. Law in context series. Paperback: £23.95. ISBN 0-406-00905-8. Butterworth Law.
Riddett, Robin–Private Client Work. Legal Practice Course resource books. Paperback: £17.50. ISBN 0-85308-343-6. Jordan.
Rider, B.A.K.; Ashe, Michael–Financial Services Law. Paperback: £21.95. ISBN 0-406-04996-3. Butterworth Law.

Rider, Barry–Money Laundering Control. Paperback. ISBN 1-899738-23-1. Round Hall Sweet & Maxwell.

Rider, Barry; Ashe, Michael–Guide to Financial Services Regulation. Paperback: £55.00. ISBN 0-86325-401-2. CCH Editions.

Riley, A.; Rogers, P.–Commercial Property and Business Leases. Legal Practice Course resource books. Paperback: £17.50. ISBN 0-85308-337-1. Jordan.

Roach, J. Ashley; Smith, Robert W.–United States Responses to Excessive Maritime Claims. Publications on ocean development. Hardback: £137.50. ISBN 90-411-0225-6. Martinus Nijhoff Publishers.

Robinson, Daniel N.–Wild Beasts and Idle Humours. Hardback: £19.95. ISBN 0-674-95289-8. Harvard University Press.

Robinson, O.F.–The Criminal Law of Ancient Rome. Hardback: £33.00. ISBN 0-8018-5318-4. The Johns Hopkins University Press.

Robinson, O.F.–The Sources of Roman Law. Approaching the ancient world. Hardback: £35.00. ISBN 0-415-08994-8. Paperback: £10.99. ISBN 0-415-08995-6. Routledge.

Robson, Michelle–Legal Practice Course Case Studies: Civil Litigation 1996/1997. Paperback: £10.95. ISBN 1-85431-579-X. Blackstone Press.

Rodgers, Christopher P.–Nature Conservation and Countryside Law. Hardback: £35.00. ISBN 0-7083-1303-5. University of Wales Press.

Rogers, Major General A.P.V.–The Law of the Battlefield. Melland Schill studies in international law. Hardback: £35.00. ISBN 0-7190-4784-6. Paperback: £16.99. ISBN 0-7190-4785-4. Manchester University Press.

Rogowski, Ralf–German Law. Paperback: £21.95. ISBN 0-406-02291-7. Butterworth Law.

Rogowski, Ralf–Rogowski: German Law. Paperback: £21.95. ISBN 0-406-02291-7. Butterworth Law.

Roney, Alex; Rhodes, John–Appointing Commercial Agents in Europe. Paperback: £19.99. ISBN 0-471-96438-7. Chancery Wiley Law Publications.

Rose, David–In the Name of the Law. Hardback: £17.99. ISBN 0-224-03744-7. Paperback: £7.99. ISBN 0-09-930116-4. Vintage.

Rose, F.D.–Statutes on Contract, Tort and Restitution 1996/7. Paperback: £9.95. ISBN 1-85431-558-7. Blackstone Press.

Rosen, Emanuel; Rosen, William–Ophthalmology. Medico-legal practitioner. Hardback: £34.95. ISBN 1-85941-211-4. Cavendish Publishing Ltd.

Rosenoer, J.–CyberLaw. Hardback: £25.00. ISBN 0-387-94832-5. Springer-Verlag New York Inc.

Roskams, Julian–The Lawyer's Remembrancer: 1997. Hardback: £20.50. ISBN 0-406-06510-1. Butterworth Law.

Rossmanith, H.P.–Structural Failure: Technical, Legal and Insurance Aspects. Hardback: £50.00. ISBN 0-419-20710-4. E & FN Spon (An imprint of Chapman & Hall).

Roth, Peter–Bellamy and Child: Common Market Law of Competition: Supplement 1. Hardback: £55.00. ISBN 0-421-56510-1. Sweet & Maxwell.

Rothwell, Donald R.–The Polar Regions and the Development of International Law. Cambridge Studies in International and Comparative Law. Hardback: £60.00. ISBN 0-521-56182-5. Cambridge University Press.

Rovere, Richard H.–Howe and Hummel. Paperback: £11.50. ISBN 0-8156-0366-5. Syracuse University Press.

Rowes, Peter–Taxation. Paperback: £12.95. ISBN 1-85805-186-X. DP Publications.

Rowland, C.K.; Carp, Robert A.–Politics and Judgment in Federal District Courts. Hardback: £23.95. ISBN 0-7006-0776-5. University Press of Kansas.

Rowland, Mark–Medical and Disability Appeal Tribunals: 1996 Supplement. Paperback: £9.95. ISBN 0-421-55920-9. Sweet & Maxwell.

Rowland, Moores–Butterworths Budget Tax Tables: 1996. Paperback: £5.95. ISBN 0-406-01449-3. Butterworth Law.

Rowley, Graham–Law for Legal Executives Part 1. Year 2. Paperback: £17.95. ISBN 1-85431-590-0. Blackstone Press.

Rowley, Graham; North, Lee–Law and Practice: NVQ3 for Para-legals. Paperback: £29.50. ISBN 0-7487-2508-3. Stanley Thornes.

Rowley; Baker–International Mergers. Anti-trust Procedures. Hardback: £265.00. ISBN 0-421-52220-8. Sweet & Maxwell.

Rowson, John; Slaney, Adrian E.–Dentistry. Medico-legal practitioner. Hardback: £34.95. ISBN 1-85941-212-2. Cavendish Publishing Ltd.

Rubenstein, William B.–Lesbians, Gay Men and the Law. Paperback: £19.95. ISBN 1-56584-322-3. The New Press.

Rudden, Bernard; Wyatt, Derrick–Basic Community Laws. Hardback: £50.00. ISBN 0-19-876428-6. Paperback: £12.95. ISBN 0-19-876427-8. Clarendon Press.

Rumbelow, Peter; Mooneeram, Judith; Heys, Barbara–Employment Law. Legal Practice Course resource books. Paperback: £17.50. ISBN 0-85308-339-8. Jordan.

Rutherford, Andrew–Transforming Criminal Policy. Paperback: £16.00. ISBN 1-872-870-31-7. Waterside Press.

Rutherford, Margaret; Sims, John–Arbitration Act 1996. Paperback: £40.00. ISBN 0-85121-982-9. FT Law & Tax.

Rutherford, Peter; Hodgkinson, Peter–Capital Punishment. Paperback: £32.00. ISBN 1-872-870-32-5. Waterside Press.

Ryan, C.L.; Savla, S.; Scanlan, G.–Ryan, Salva and Scanlan: A Guide to the Criminal Procedure and Investigations Act 1996. Paperback: £17.95. ISBN 0-406-99249-5. Butterworth Law.

Sabalot, Deborah –Butterworths Financial Services Law Guide. Paperback: £65.00. ISBN 0-406-99197-9. Butterworth Law.

Sale of Goods and Credit: Suggested Solutions (1991-1995). Bar examinations. Paperback: £9.95. ISBN 0-7510-0744-7. HLT Publications.

Sale of Goods and Credit: Suggested Solutions - Single Paper (Trinity 1995). Bar Examinations. Paperback: £3.95. ISBN 0-7510-0644-0. HLT Publications.

Salter, David–Matrimonial Consent Orders and Agreements. Longman practitioner series. Paperback: £30.00. ISBN 0-85121-971-3. FT Law & Tax.

Salter, David–Pensions and Insurance on Family Breakdown. Paperback: £32.50. ISBN 0-85308-331-2. Family Law.

Salter, David; Jeavons, Helen; Ayrton, Lyn; Way, Philip–Humphreys' Family Proceedings. Practitioner series. Paperback: £48.00. ISBN 0-7520-0327-5. FT Law & Tax.

Salter, Richard–Salter: the Modern Law of Guarantees. Paperback: £100.00. ISBN 0-406-12781-6. Butterworth Law.

Samuel, Geoffrey–Law of Obligations and Legal Remedies. Paperback: £17.95. ISBN 1-85941-130-4. Cavendish Publishing Ltd.

Sanderson, John–Criminology: Textbook 1996-1997. Bachelor of Laws (LLB). Paperback: £17.95. ISBN 0-7510-0701-3. HLT Publications.

Santa Maria, Alberto–EC Commercial Law. Hardback: £119.00. ISBN 90-411-0885-8. Kluwer Law International.

Sara, Colin–Boundaries and Easements. Hardback: £106.00. ISBN 0-421-53790-6. Sweet & Maxwell.

Sarat, Austin; Felstiner, William–Divorce Lawyers and Their Clients. Hardback: £25.00. ISBN 0-19-506387-2. Oxford University Press Inc, USA.

Sarie-Eldin, Hani–Consortia Agreements in the International Construction Industry. International economic development law. Hardback: £72.00. ISBN 90-411-0912-9. Kluwer Law International.

Sato, Tetsuo–Evolving Constitutions of International Organizations. International Law in Japanese perspective. Hardback: £79.00. ISBN 90-411-0202-7. Kluwer Law International.

Saunders, Ian–Remedies in Taxation. Hardback: £25.00. ISBN 0-471-96080-2. John Wiley and Sons.

Scallan, Andrew; Mates, Rory–Schofield's Election Law. Ringbinder: £175.00. ISBN 0-7219-1490-X. Shaw & Sons.

Scallan, Andrew; Mates, Rory–Schofield's Election Law. Unbound/looseleaf: £150.00. ISBN 0-7219-0345-2. Shaw & Sons.

Scammell, Ernest H.–Scamell: Land Covenants. Hardback: £95.00. ISBN 0-406-08151-4. Butterworth Law.

Schlemminger, Horst; Wissel, Holger–German Environmental Law for Practitioners. Series legislation in translation. Hardback: £145.00. ISBN 90-6544-832-2. Kluwer Law International.

Schlicher, John W.–Licensing Intellectual Property Rights. Intellectual property library. Hardback: £100.00. ISBN 0-471-15312-5. John Wiley and Sons.

Schmitz, Winifried F.–Due Diligence for Corporate Acquisitions. AIJA law library, 3. Hardback: £84.00. ISBN 1-85966-064-9. Kluwer Law International.

Schnepper, Jeff–How to Pay Zero Taxes: 1996. Paperback: £12.95. ISBN 0-07-057224-0. McGraw-Hill Book Company.

Schofield, John–Laytime and Demurrage. Lloyd's shipping law library. Hardback: £90.00. ISBN 1-85044-899-X. LLP Limited.

Schultz, David A.; Smith, Christopher E.–The Jurisprudential Vision of Justice Antonin Scalia. Studies in American Constitutionalism. Hardback: £50.50. ISBN 0-8476-8131-9. Paperback: £19.50. ISBN 0-8476-8132-7. Rowman & Littlefield.

Schwartz, Bernard–Decision: How the Supreme Court Decides Cases. Hardback: £19.50. ISBN 0-19-509859-5. Oxford University Press Inc, USA.

Schwartz, Bernard–The Unpublished Opinions of the Rehnquist Court. Hardback: £32.50. ISBN 0-19-509332-1. Oxford University Press Inc, USA.

Scott-Bayfield, Julie–Defamation. Longman practitioner series. Paperback: £45.00. ISBN 0-85121-719-2. FT Law & Tax.

Scott, Jacqueline; Mackley-Smith, Gary B.–Capital Allowances: 1996-97. Paperback: £33.95. ISBN 1-86012-288-4. Tolley Publishing.

Sealy, L.S.–Cases and Materials in Company Law. £27.95. ISBN 0-406-06327-3. Butterworth Law.

Sebba, Leslie–Third Parties. Hardback: £35.95. ISBN 0-8142-0664-6. Ohio State University Press.

Seidman, Louis Michael; Tushnet, Mark–Remnants of Belief. Hardback: £40.00. ISBN 0-19-509979-6. Paperback: £22.50. ISBN 0-19-509980-X. Oxford University Press Inc, USA.

Sellers, M.N.S.–The New World Order. Baltimore studies in nationalism and internationalism. Hardback: £39.95. ISBN 1-85973-059-0. Paperback: £14.95. ISBN 1-85973-064-7. Berg Publishers.

Sellman, Pamela –Law of International Trade: Textbook 1996-1997. Bar examinations. Paperback: £17.95. ISBN 0-7510-0716-1. HLT Publications.

Sellman, Pamela–Law of International Trade. Cracknell's law students' companions. Paperback: £9.95. ISBN 1-85836-044-7. Old Bailey Press.

Sellman, Pamela–Law of International Trade: Casebook 1996-1997. Bachelor of Laws (LLB). Paperback: £14.95. ISBN 0-7510-0660-2. HLT Publications.

Sellman, Pamela–Law of International Trade: Casebook 1996-1997. Bar examinations. Paperback: £15.95. ISBN 0-7510-0681-5. HLT Publications.

Sellman, Pamela–Law of International Trade: Textbook 1996-1997. Bachelor of Laws (LLB). Paperback: £18.95. ISBN 0-7510-0694-7. HLT Publications.

Sells, Benjamin–The Soul of the Law. Paperback: £9.99. ISBN 1-85230-796-X. Element Books Ltd.

Selman, Andrew; Hunter, Caroline–CCT of Housing Management. Arden's housing library series. Paperback: £16.95. ISBN 1-898001-05-7. Lemos & Crane.

Seplaki, Les –Economic Scarcity and Healthcare Quality. Hardback: £40.00. ISBN 1-85521-841-0. Dartmouth.

Seron, Carroll–The Business of Practicing Law. Labor and Social Change Series. Hardback: £39.95. ISBN 1-56639-406-6. Paperback: £18.50. ISBN 1-56639-407-4. Temple University Press.

Sexton, R.–LLB Learning Text: Land Law. Paperback: £17.95. ISBN 1-85431-525-0. Blackstone Press.

Shahabuddeen, Mohamed–Precedent in the World Court. Hersch Lauterpacht Memorial Lectures, 12. Hardback: £40.00. ISBN 0-521-56310-0. Cambridge University Press.

Sharifah Zaleha Syed Hassan; Cederroth, Sven–Managing Marital Disputes in Malaysia. NIAS monographs, No 75. Hardback: £40.00. ISBN 0-7007-0432-9. Paperback: £15.99. ISBN 0-7007-0454-X. Curzon Press.

Sharp, Isobel; Lennon, Mark–Financial Statements for Smaller Companies: A Guide to Practice and the FRSSE. Paperback: £32.00. ISBN 1-85355-728-5. Accountancy Books.

Sharpston, Eleanor–European Legal Studies. Paperback: £21.95. ISBN 0-406-00490-0. Butterworth Law.

Shaw, Josephine–The Law of the European Union: Vol 1. Institutional and Constitutional Law. Macmillan law masters. Paperback: £9.99. ISBN 0-333-66481-7. Macmillan Press.

Shaw, Josephine–The Law of the European Union: Vols 1 & 2. Macmillan law masters. Paperback: £17.50. ISBN 0-333-66486-8. Macmillan Press.

Sheikh, Saleem–Business Law Transaction Guide. Essential Series - Revision. Hardback: £14.95. ISBN 1-85941-195-9. Cavendish Publishing Ltd.

Sheldon, David–Evidence. Paperback. ISBN 0-414-01142-2. W.Green & Son.

Shenefield, John H.; Stelzer, Irwin M.–The Antitrust Laws. Hardback: £15.95. ISBN 0-8447-3942-1. American Enterprise Institute.

Sheperd, Chris–Commercial Law. Cracknell's statutes. Paperback: £9.95. ISBN 1-85836-019-6. Old Bailey Press.

Shepherd, Chris–Commercial Law. Cracknell's Law Students' Companions. Paperback: £9.95. ISBN 1-85836-033-1. Old Bailey Press.

Shepherd, Chris–Company Law: Casebook 1996-1997. Bachelor of Laws (LLB). Paperback: £18.95. ISBN 0-7510-0663-7. HLT Publications.

Shepherd, Chris–Company Law: Textbook 1996-1997. Bachelor of Laws (LLB). Paperback: £18.95. ISBN 0-7510-0697-1. HLT Publications.

Sherry, Michael–Whiteman on Income Tax: Supplement 8. Paperback: £50.00. ISBN 0-421-57740-1. Sweet & Maxwell.

Shiels, Robert–Offensive Weapons. Paperback. ISBN 0-414-01171-6. W.Green & Son.

Shiels, Robert–Renton and Brown's Criminal Procedure Legislation. Looseleaf: £175.00. ISBN 0-414-01152-X. W.Green & Son.

Shilling, Helen–Shilling and Sharp: Corporate Governance. Paperback: £45.00. ISBN 0-406-04936-X. Butterworth Law.

Shipwright, Adrian J.; Price, Jeffrey W.–UK Taxation and Intellectual Property. Hardback: £70.00. ISBN 0-421-47560-9. Sweet & Maxwell.

Shoemaker, Donald Joseph–International Handbook on Juvenile Justice. Hardback: £79.95. ISBN 0-313-28895-X. Greenwood Press.

Shulman, Gary; Kelley, David I.–Learning from the Pension Experts. Family law. Hardback: £90.00. ISBN 0-471-12406-0. John Wiley and Sons.

Shute, Stephen; Gardner, John; Horder, Jeremy–Action and Value in Criminal Law. Paperback: £15.99. ISBN 0-19-826079-2. Clarendon Press.

Shuy, Roger–Language Crimes. The language library. Paperback: £14.99. ISBN 0-631-20153-X. Blackwell Publishers.

Silvester, Steven; Reeves, Tracy–Sourcebook on Employment Law. Sourcebook series. Paperback: £21.95. ISBN 1-85941-184-3. Cavendish Publishing Ltd.

Simester, Andrew; Smith, A.T.H.–Harms and Culpability. Oxford monographs on criminal law and justice. Hardback: £40.00. ISBN 0-19-826057-1. Clarendon Press.

Simmons, Patterson; Rubin, Elvira–Sourcebook on Business Law. Paperback: £19.95. ISBN 1-85941-036-7. Cavendish Publishing Ltd.

Simple Guide on Management and Control of Wastes. Paperback: £9.95. ISBN 0-85404-990-8. The Royal Society of Chemistry.

Simpson, Struan; Carless, Jacqueline–Business, Pollution and Regulation in the 90s. Key resource series. Paperback: £37.00. ISBN 0-7123-0820-2. British Library (Science Reference and Information Service).

Sinclair, Neil–Warranties and Indemnities on Share and Asset Sales. Commercial series. Hardback: £77.00. ISBN 0-7520-0287-2. FT Law & Tax.

Singer, Simon I.–Recriminalizing Delinquency. Cambridge Criminology Series. Hardback: £40.00. ISBN 0-521-48208-9. Cambridge University Press.

Singhvi, L.M.–A Tale of Three Cities. Paperback: £9.95. ISBN 0-521-57818-3. Cambridge University Press.

Skogen, Larry C.–Indian Depredation Claims, 1796-1920. Legal History of North America, No 2. Hardback: £27.95. ISBN 0-8061-2789-9. University of Oklahoma Press.

Skordaki, Eleni–Social Change and the Solicitors' Profession. Hardback: £35.00. ISBN 0-19-825753-8. Clarendon Press.

Slade, Elizabeth –Tolley's Employment Handbook. Paperback: £34.95. ISBN 1-86012-354-6. Tolley Publishing.

Slapper, Gary; Kelly, David–Sourcebook on English Legal System. Sourcebook Series. Paperback: £19.95. ISBN 1-85941-106-1. Cavendish Publishing Ltd.

Slemrod, Joel; Bakija, Jon–Taxing Ourselves. Hardback: £21.50. ISBN 0-262-19375-2. The MIT Press.

Sloan, Kenneth–Sloan: Police Law Primer. Paperback: £17.95. ISBN 0-406-99611-3. Butterworth Law.

Smailes, David; Saunders, Glyn; Mackley-Smith, Gary B–Tolley's Schedule D (formerly Taxation of Trades and Professions). Paperback: £49.95. ISBN 1-86012-322-8. Tolley Publishing.

Smedinghoff, Thomas J.–The Software Publishers Association Guide to Online Law. Hardback: £36.95. ISBN 0-201-48980-5. Addison-Wesley Longman Higher Education.

Smith II, George P.–Legal and Healthcare Ethics for the Elderly. Hardback: £39.95. ISBN 1-56032-452-X. Paperback: £16.95. ISBN 1-56032-453-8. Taylor & Francis.

Smith, B.J.; Peters, R.J.; Owen, Stephanie–Acoustics and Noise Control. Paperback: £29.99. ISBN 0-582-08804-6. Addison-Wesley Longman Higher Education.

Smith, Chuck–The New Mexico State Constitution. Reference Guides to the State Constitutions of the United States, No 23. Hardback: £63.50. ISBN 0-313-29548-4. Greenwood Press.

Smith, Gordon B.–Reforming the Russian Legal System. Cambridge Soviet Paperbacks, 11.\ Hardback: £45.00. ISBN 0-521-45052-7. Paperbacks, 11. Paperback: £16.95. ISBN 0-521-45669-X. Cambridge University Press.

Smith, Graham J.H.–Internet Law and Regulation. Special reports. Hardback: £85.00. ISBN 0-7520-0286-4. FT Law & Tax.

Smith, Ian; Thomas, Gareth–Industrial Law. Paperback: £28.95. ISBN 0-406-07754-1. Butterworth Law.

Smith, J.C.; Hogan, Brian, LLB–Criminal Law. Paperback: £28.95. ISBN 0-406-08187-5. Butterworth Law.

Smith, J.C.; Hogan, Brian–Criminal Law - Cases and Materials. Paperback: £26.95. ISBN 0-406-08188-3. Butterworth Law.
Smith, John–Smith and Thomas: a Casebook on Contract. Paperback: £28.00. ISBN 0-421-53950-X. Sweet & Maxwell.
Smith, John–Smith and Thomas: a Casebook on Contract: ISE Edition. Paperback: £9.95. ISBN 0-421-53960-7. Sweet & Maxwell.
Smith, P.F.–Evans and Smith: the Law of Landlord and Tenant. Paperback: £23.95. ISBN 0-406-06563-2. Butterworth Law.
Smith, R.C.–A Case about Amy. Health, Society, and Policy. Hardback: £43.95. ISBN 1-56639-411-2. Paperback: £15.95. ISBN 1-56639-412-0. Temple University Press.
Smith, Rodger Hayward; Newton, Clive R.–Jackson's Matrimonial Finance and Taxation. Hardback: £95.00. ISBN 0-406-05426-6. Butterworth Law.
Smith, Roger–Achieving Civil Justice. Paperback: £9.95. ISBN 0-905099-75-3. The Legal Action Group.
Smith, Roger–Property Law. Longman law. Hardback: £50.00. ISBN 0-582-09011-3. Paperback: £28.50. ISBN 0-582-09140-3. Addison-Wesley Longman Higher Education.
Smith; Williamson–Professional Partnership Handbook. Paperback: £35.00. ISBN 1-86012-327-9. Tolley Publishing.
Snelson, Anthony–The Law of Towage. Hardback. ISBN 1-85044-967-8. Lloyd's of London Press.
Snijders, Henk J.–Access to Civil Procedure Abroad. Paperback. ISBN 90-411-0212-4. Kluwer Law International.
Snyder, Francis–Constitutional Dimensions of European Economic Integration. Hardback: £70.00. ISBN 90-411-0914-5. Kluwer Law International.
Soares, Patrick C.–VAT Planning for Property Transactions. Hardback: £75.00. ISBN 0-7520-0045-4. FT Law & Tax.
Soares, Patrick–Offshore Investment in UK Property. Special reports. Hardback: £125.00. ISBN 0-7520-0242-2. FT Law & Tax.
Sohrab, Julia A.–Sexing the Benefit. Hardback: £42.50. ISBN 1-85521-705-8. Dartmouth.
Solomon, Peter H.–Reforming Justice in Russia, 1864-1994. Hardback: £66.50. ISBN 1-56324-862-X. M.E. Sharpe.
Sonneveldt, Frans; Bom, Hans M.; Zuiderwijk, Johan C.L.–Global Estate Planning. Unbound/looseleaf: £112.50. ISBN 90-411-0754-1. Kluwer Law International.
Sorensen, Anker; Omar, Paul J.–Corporate Rescue Procedures in France. Hardback: £95.00. ISBN 90-411-0941-2. Kluwer Law International.
Sparrow, Malcolm K.–License to Steal. Hardback: £40.95. ISBN 0-8133-3067-X. Paperback: £11.50. ISBN 0-8133-3068-8. Westview Press.
Speaight, Anthony–Architect's Legal Handbook. Paperback: £25.00. ISBN 0-7506-2161-3. Butterworth Architecture: an Imprint of Butterworth-Heinemann.
Spedding, Linda S.–Succession: Casebook 1996-1997. Bachelor of Laws (LLB). Paperback: £18.95. ISBN 0-7510-0666-1. HLT Publications.
Spencer–Q & A Evidence. £8.95. ISBN 1-85431-496-3. Blackstone Press.
Stagg, Paul–Overpayments and Recovery of Social Security Benefits. Paperback: £17.00. ISBN 0-905099-73-7. The Legal Action Group.
Stamp, Mark–International Insider Dealing. Hardback: £125.00. ISBN 0-7520-0179-5. FT Law & Tax.
Stapledon, Geoff–Institutional Shareholders and Corporate Governance. Hardback: £45.00. ISBN 0-19-826088-1. Clarendon Press.
Star, Leonie–Counsel of Perfection. Paperback: £13.99. ISBN 0-19-553576-6. OUP Australia and New Zealand.
Stark, Margaret M.; Payne-James, J. Jason–Symptoms and Signs of Substance Misuse. Paperback: £9.95. ISBN 1-900151-10-3. Greenwich Medical Media.

Stavropoulos, Nicos–Objectivity in Law. Hardback: £35.00. ISBN 0-19-825899-2. Clarendon Press.

Steele, Keith–Anti-dumping Under the WTO. Hardback: £85.00. ISBN 90-411-0915-3. Kluwer Law International.

Steinbock, Bonnie–Life Before Birth. Paperback: £14.95. ISBN 0-19-510872-8. Oxford University Press Inc, USA.

Steiner, Josephine–Textbook on EC Law. Paperback: £19.00. ISBN 1-85431-553-6. Blackstone Press.

Steiner, Michael; Davis, Glen; Cohen, Malcolm–Insolvent Partnerships. Hardback: £60.00. ISBN 0-85308-351-7. Jordan.

Stephen, James Fitzjames–A History of the Criminal Law of England. Making of the British legal system. Hardback: £175.00. ISBN 0-415-14952-5. Routledge.

Stern, Carole; Volz, Christian–1996 Wiley Environmental Law Update. Hardback: £75.00. ISBN 0-471-13723-5. John Wiley and Sons.

Stevens, Irving–Constitutional and Administrative Law. M&E handbooks. Paperback: £13.99. ISBN 0-7121-0869-6. Macdonald and Evans.

Stevens, Lawrence; Green, Les; Mehigan, Simon–Paterson's Licensing Acts: 1997. Paterson's Licensing Acts, 1997. Hardback: £140.00. ISBN 0-406-99743-8. Butterworth Law.

Stevens, Robert–The Independence of the Judiciary. Paperback: £14.95. ISBN 0-19-826263-9. Clarendon Press.

Steward, Clive–The Equitable Life Tax Guide. Paperback: £19.99. ISBN 0-631-20162-9. Blackwell Publishers.

Stewart, Stephen; Sandison, Hamish–International Copyright and Neighbouring Rights: Vol 2. Hardback: £120.00. ISBN 0-406-00904-X. Butterworth Law.

Stone, Julie; Matthews, Joan–Complementary Medicine and the Law. Hardback: £30.00. ISBN 0-19-825970-0. Paperback: £12.99. ISBN 0-19-825971-9. Oxford University Press.

Stone, R.–LLB Cases and Materials: Contract. Paperback: £18.95. ISBN 1-85431-526-9. Blackstone Press.

Stott, David–Administrative Law. Lecture notes. Paperback: £16.95. ISBN 1-874241-39-2. Cavendish Publishing Ltd.

Stranks, Jeremy–Food Safety Law and Practice. Practitioner. Paperback: £38.00. ISBN 0-7520-0102-7. FT Law & Tax.

Stranks, Jeremy–Law and Practice of Risk Assessment. Paperback: £16.99. ISBN 0-273-62352-4. Pitman Publishing.

Strier, Franklin–Reconstructing Justice. Paperback. ISBN 0-226-77718-9. University of Chicago Press.

Succession - LLB: Suggested Solutions (1991-1995). Bachelor of Laws (LLB). Paperback: £6.95. ISBN 0-7510-0734-X. HLT Publications.

Succession: Suggested Solutions - Single Paper (June 1995). Paperback: £3.00. ISBN 0-7510-0633-5. HLT Publications.

Sugarman, David–Law in History: Vols I and II. Between History and the Law: on the Writing of Histories of Law and Society / Law and Society. International Library of Essays in Law and Legal Theory (Schools). Hardback: £180.00. ISBN 1-85521-403-2. Dartmouth.

Sullivan, Amanda–Butterworths Schedule E Compliance Manual. Unbound/looseleaf: £150.00. ISBN 0-406-99730-6. Butterworth Law.

Sunstein, Cass R.–Legal Reasoning and Political Conflict. Hardback: £18.99. ISBN 0-19-510082-4. Oxford University Press Inc, USA.

Supperstone, Michael; O'Dempsey, Declan–Immigration. Practitioner series. Paperback: £55.00. ISBN 0-7520-0285-6. FT Law & Tax.

Suratgar, D.; MacDonald, G.–International Project Finance: Law and Practice. Hardback: £85.00. ISBN 0-85121-836-9. FT Law & Tax.

Susskind, Richard E.–The Future of Law. Hardback: £19.99. ISBN 0-19-826007-5. Oxford University Press.

Sutherland, Jon; Canwell, Diane–Consumer Protection. Paperback: £12.99. ISBN 0-340-67407-5. Hodder & Stoughton Educational.

Sutton, Alistair –The Wider European Market. Paperback: £90.00. ISBN 0-406-02131-7. Butterworth Law.

Sweet & Maxwell's Consumer Law Statutes. Hardback: £14.95. ISBN 0-421-41990-3. Sweet & Maxwell.

Sweet, Jonathan J.–Sweet on Construction Industry. Construction Law. Hardback: £150.00. ISBN 0-471-12550-4. John Wiley and Sons.

Swenson, Leland C.–Psychology and Law for the Helping Professions. Hardback: £45.50. ISBN 0-534-34285-X. Brooks/Cole.

Sydenham, Angela–Trusts of Land - the New Law. Paperback: £30.00. ISBN 0-85308-395-9. Jordan.

Szasz, Thomas–Our Right to Drugs. Paperback: £11.95. ISBN 0-8156-0333-9. Syracuse University Press.

T. **Hussain**–Land Rights in Bangladesh. Hardback: £14.95. ISBN 984-05-1280-3. The University Press.

T.M.C. Asser Instituut–Netherlands Yearbook of International Law: Vol 26. 1995. Netherlands yearbook of international law. Hardback: £88.00. ISBN 90-411-0196-9. Martinus Nijhoff Publishers.

Taniguchi, Nancy J.–Necessary Fraud. Legal History of North America, No 3. Hardback: £31.95. ISBN 0-8061-2818-6. University of Oklahoma Press.

Tatham, David; Richards, William; Gielen, Charles–ECTA Guide to EU Trade Mark Legislation. Hardback: £85.00. ISBN 0-421-52880-X. Sweet & Maxwell.

Taverne, Bernard G.–Co-operative Agreements in the Extractive Petroleum Industry. International energy and resources law and policy. Hardback: £68.00. ISBN 90-411-0926-9. Kluwer Law International.

Taxation of Foreign Exchange Gains and Losses. Paperback: £49.95. ISBN 1-86012-304-X. Tolley Publishing.

Taylor, Eric–Parker's Modern Wills Precedents. Hardback: £49.50. ISBN 0-406-08140-9. Butterworth Law.

Taylor, Rodney–Double Taxation Relief. Tax series. Paperback: £39.95. ISBN 1-86012-311-2. Tolley Publishing.

Teixeira, Gloria–Business Taxation in the European Union: Update 2. Paperback: £40.00. ISBN 0-471-96458-1. Chancery Wiley Law Publications.

Teles, Steven Michael–Whose Welfare? Studies in Government and Public Policy. Hardback: £23.95. ISBN 0-7006-0801-X. University Press of Kansas.

Temperley, Robert; Thomas, Michael; Steel, David–The Merchant Shipping Acts. British Shipping Laws, Vol 11. Hardback: £98.00. ISBN 0-420-46510-3. Stevens & Sons.

Tennekoon, Ravi C. –Tennekoon: the Law and Regulation of International Finance. Hardback: £135.00. ISBN 0-406-08158-1. Butterworth Law.

Teske, Paul; Best, Samuel; Mintrom, Michael–Deregulating Freight Transportation. Studies in Regulation and Federalism. Hardback: £31.95. ISBN 0-8447-3896-4. Paperback: £10.50. ISBN 0-8447-3897-2. American Enterprise Institute.

Tettenborn, Andrew–Law of Restitution. Paperback: £17.95. ISBN 1-85941-201-7. Cavendish Publishing Ltd.

Thakur, Shivesh C.–Religion and Social Justice. Library of philosophy and religion. Hardback: £35.00. ISBN 0-333-60990-5. Macmillan Press.

The Bar Directory: 1997. Hardback: £35.00. ISBN 0-7520-0399-2. FT Law & Tax.

The Law Society–The Law Society's Directory of Expert Witnesses: 1997. Hardback: £60.00. ISBN 0-7520-0301-1. FT Law & Tax.

The New Engineering Contract: Flow Charts. Paperback: £10.00. ISBN 0-7277-2080-5. Thomas Telford Ltd.

The New Engineering Contract: Full Set. Paperback: £60.00. ISBN 0-7277-2081-3. Thomas Telford Ltd.

The New Engineering Contract: Guidance Notes. Paperback: £10.00. ISBN 0-7277-2079-1. Thomas Telford Ltd.
The New Engineering Contract: Main Contract. Paperback: £12.00. ISBN 0-7277-2094-5. Thomas Telford Ltd.
The New Engineering Contract: Option A. Paperback: £10.00. ISBN 0-7277-2072-4. Thomas Telford Ltd.
The New Engineering Contract: Option B. Paperback: £10.00. ISBN 0-7277-2073-2. Thomas Telford Ltd.
The New Engineering Contract: Option C. Paperback: £10.00. ISBN 0-7277-2074-0. Thomas Telford Ltd.
The New Engineering Contract: Option D. Paperback: £10.00. ISBN 0-7277-2075-9. Thomas Telford Ltd.
The New Engineering Contract: Option E. Paperback: £10.00. ISBN 0-7277-2076-7. Thomas Telford Ltd.
The New Engineering Contract: Option F. Paperback: £10.00. ISBN 0-7277-2077-5. Thomas Telford Ltd.
The New Engineering Contract: Sub-contract. Paperback: £10.00. ISBN 0-7277-2078-3. Thomas Telford Ltd.
The Supreme Court Practice 1997. £385.00. ISBN 0-421-57620-0. Sweet & Maxwell.
Thomas, Colin–Teach Yourself Company Law. Teach yourself business and finance. £12.99. ISBN 0-340-67362-1. Teach Yourself.
Thomas, D. Rhidian–The Modern Law of Marine Insurance. Hardback: £75.00. ISBN 1-85978-033-4. LLP Limited.
Thomas, David–The Sentencing Referencer: 1997. Paperback: £14.95. ISBN 0-421-58200-6. Sweet & Maxwell.
Thomas, Gareth–Disability Discrimination Act 1995. Sweet and Maxwell legislation handbook. Paperback: £15.50. ISBN 0-421-57880-7. Sweet & Maxwell.
Thomas, Liz; Vincent, Charles; MacNeil, Paul–Medical Accidents and the Law. Hardback: £14.99. ISBN 0-471-96642-8. Chancery Wiley Law Publications.
Thomas, Meryl–Statutes on Property Law 1996-7. Paperback: £12.00. ISBN 1-85431-563-3. Blackstone Press.
Thompson, Bankole–The Constitutional History and Law of Sierra Leone (1961-1995). Hardback: £35.50. ISBN 0-7618-0473-0. University Press of America.
Thompson, Katharine–The Law of Food and Drink. Paperback: £29.95. ISBN 0-7219-1480-2. Shaw & Sons.
Thomson, J.M.–Family Law in Scotland. Paperback: £26.00. ISBN 0-406-07013-X. Butterworth Law.
Thornthon, G.C.–Legislative Drafting. Hardback: £70.00. ISBN 0-406-04521-6. Butterworth Law.
Thornton, Margaret–Dissonance and Distrust. Paperback: £18.99. ISBN 0-19-553661-4. OUP Australia.
Thornton, Margaret–Public and Private. Paperback: £15.99. ISBN 0-19-553662-2. OUP Australia.
Tiernan, Ralph–Tort Law Nutshell. Paperback: £4.95. ISBN 0-421-54830-4. Sweet & Maxwell.
Tiley, John–Butterworths UK Tax Guide: 1996-97. Paperback: £23.95. ISBN 0-406-04857-6. Butterworth Law.
Tillotson, John Patrick–Contract Law in Perspective. Paperback: £9.95. ISBN 1-85941-002-2. Cavendish Publishing Ltd.
Tillotson, John–EC Law: Text, Cases & Materials. Paperback: £15.95. ISBN 1-85941-197-5. Cavendish Publishing Ltd.
Tillotson, John–European Community Law. Paperback: £15.95. ISBN 1-85941-282-3. Cavendish Publishing Ltd.

Tingley, K.R.; Mackley-Smith, Gary B.–Roll-over, Hold-over and Retirement Reliefs. Paperback: £42.95. ISBN 1-86012-295-7. Tolley Publishing.
Todd, Paul–SWOT Equity and Trusts. £8.95. ISBN 1-85431-500-5. Blackstone Press.
Todd, Paul–Cases & Materials on Equity and Trusts. Paperback: £23.95. ISBN 1-85431-555-2. Blackstone Press.
Todd, Paul–Textbook on Trusts. Paperback: £17.95. ISBN 1-85431-552-8. Blackstone Press.
Tokley, Ian; Ravn, Tina–Banking Law in China. China law series. Paperback: £29.00. ISBN 0-421-56860-7. Sweet & Maxwell.
Toman, Jiri–Protection of Cultural Property in the Event of Armed Conflict. Hardback: £40.00. ISBN 1-85521-793-7. Paperback: £28.00. ISBN 1-85521-800-3. Dartmouth.
Tomasson, Richard F.; Crosby, Faye J.; Herzberger, Sharon D.–Affirmative Action Pro and Con. American University Press Public Policy Series. Hardback: £31.50. ISBN 1-879383-51-9. Paperback: £15.50. ISBN 1-879383-52-7. University Press of America.
Tomlinson, Hugh; Seitler, Jonathan; Grant, Thomas–Property Valuation: Law and Liability. Special reports. Hardback: £45.00. ISBN 0-7520-0216-3. FT Law & Tax.
Tonry, Michael–Sentencing Matters. Studies in Crime and Public Policy. Hardback: £25.00. ISBN 0-19-509498-0. Oxford University Press Inc, USA.
Tort: Suggested Solutions - Single Paper (June 1995). Paperback: £3.00. ISBN 0-7510-0623-8. HLT Publications.
Treu, Tizano; Terry, Michael–European Employment and Industrial Relations Glossaries: Denmark. Paperback: £19.95. ISBN 0-421-44890-3. Sweet & Maxwell.
Trickey, G.; Hackett, M.–Presentation and Settlement of Contractors' Claims. Hardback: £39.50. ISBN 0-419-20500-4. E & FN Spon (An imprint of Chapman & Hall).
Tromans, Stephen–Commercial Leases. Hardback: £45.00. ISBN 0-421-52350-6. Sweet & Maxwell.
Tromans, Stephen–The Environment Acts 1990 - 1995. Sweet and Maxwell legislation handbook. Hardback: £35.00. ISBN 0-421-55810-5. Sweet & Maxwell.
Tromans, Stephen; Fitzgerald, James–The Law of Nuclear Installations and Radioactive Substances. Hardback: £80.00. ISBN 0-421-53880-5. Sweet & Maxwell.
Tuitt, Patricia–False Images. Law and social theory. Hardback: £35.00. ISBN 0-7453-0744-2. Paperback: £9.95. ISBN 0-7453-0745-0. Pluto Press.
Turner, Mark; Williams, Alan–Multimedia Contracts Rights and Licensing. Special Report. Hardback: £125.00. ISBN 0-7520-0177-9. FT Law & Tax.
Tushnet, Mark V.–Making Civil Rights Law. Paperback: £11.99. ISBN 0-19-510468-4. Oxford University Press Inc, USA.
Tushnet, Mark–The Warren Court in Historical and Political Perspective. Constitutionalism and Democracy. Paperback: £11.50. ISBN 0-8139-1665-8. University Press of Virginia.
Undy, Roger–Managing the Unions. Hardback: £35.00. ISBN 0-19-828919-7. Oxford University Press.
Unger, Andy–Know-how for Personal Injury Lawyers. Know-how series. Paperback: £47.00. ISBN 0-7520-0325-9. FT Law & Tax.
Unger, Roberto Mangabeira–What Should Legal Analysis Become? Hardback: £34.95. ISBN 1-85984-969-5. Paperback: £11.95. ISBN 1-85984-100-7. Verso.
Uniacke, Suzanne–Permissible Killing. Cambridge Studies in Philosophy and Law. Paperback: £12.95. ISBN 0-521-56458-1. Cambridge University Press.

Upex, Robert; Thomas, Gareth–The Employment Acts 1996. Sweet and Maxwell legislation handbook. Paperback: £26.00. ISBN 0-421-58470-X. Sweet & Maxwell.

Uviller, H. Richard–Virtual Justice. Hardback: £20.00. ISBN 0-300-06483-7. Yale University Press.

Van den Berg, Albert Jan–Yearbook Commercial Arbitration: Vol 21. 1996. Paperback: £142.00. ISBN 90-411-0307-4. Kluwer Law International.

Vandevelde, Kenneth J.–Thinking Like a Lawyer. New perspectives on law, culture & society. Hardback: £41.50. ISBN 0-8133-2203-0. Paperback: £12.95. ISBN 0-8133-2204-9. Westview Press.

Venables, J.; Impey, Ken–Venables and Impey: Internal Audit. Paperback: £30.00. ISBN 0-406-06673-6. Butterworth Law.

Verhellen, Eugeen–Monitoring Children's Rights. Hardback: £158.00. ISBN 90-411-0161-6. Martinus Nijhoff Publishers.

Villiers, Bertus de; Wyk, David van; Dugard, John; Davis, Dennis–Rights and Constitutionalism. Hardback: £60.00. ISBN 0-19-826225-6. Clarendon Press.

Vincent, Robert–Charity Accounting and Taxation. Paperback: £45.00. ISBN 0-406-02921-0. Butterworth Law.

Vincenzi, Christopher–Law of the European Community. Foundation studies in law. Paperback: £21.99. ISBN 0-273-61471-1. Pitman Publishing.

Vogel, Klaus–Klaus Vogel on Double Taxation Conventions. Hardback: £242.00. ISBN 90-411-0892-0. Kluwer Law International.

Volcansek, Mary L.; Franciscis, Maria Elisabetta de; Lafon, Jacqueline Lucienne–Judicial Misconduct. Hardback: £31.95. ISBN 0-8130-1421-2. University Presses of Florida.

Volhard, Rudiger; Arndt, Stengel–German Limited Liability Company. Hardback: £75.00. ISBN 0-471-96581-2. Chancery Wiley Law Publications.

Wacker Guido, Ginny–Legal Issues in Nursing. Paperback: £24.95. ISBN 0-8385-5647-7. Appleton & Lange.

Wai Chee Dimock–Residues of Justice. Hardback: £40.00. ISBN 0-520-20243-0. University of California Press.

Waite, Andrew –Waite & Jewell: Environmental Law in Property Transactions. Paperback: £45.00. ISBN 0-406-02293-3. Butterworth Law.

Waite, Andrew–Butterworths Environmental Law Handbook. £65.00. ISBN 0-406-99154-5. Butterworth Law.

Walker, Gordon; Fisse, Brent–Securities Regulation in Australia and New Zealand. Hardback: £45.00. ISBN 0-19-558290-X. OUP New Zealand.

Walker, Nigel–Dangerous People. Paperback: £20.00. ISBN 1-85431-518-8. Blackstone Press.

Walker, Nigel; Padfield, Nicola–Walker and Padfield: Sentencing: Theory, Law and Practice. Paperback: £28.95. ISBN 0-406-06325-7. Butterworth Law.

Wall, D.–Access to Criminal Justice. £18.95. ISBN 1-85431-502-1. Blackstone Press.

Wallace, R.–International Human Rights. Paperback: £28.00. ISBN 0-421-54210-1. Sweet & Maxwell.

Wallace, Rebecca; Heffernan, Liz–The European Union - Immigration. Current EC legal developments. Paperback: £90.00. ISBN 0-406-04524-0. Butterworth Law.

Wallington, Peter–Butterworths Employment Law Handbook. Paperback: £32.50. ISBN 0-406-05429-0. Butterworth Law.

Wallington, Peter–Statutes on Public Law 1996/97. Paperback: £12.95. ISBN 1-85431-564-1. Blackstone Press.

Ward, Ian–A Critical Introduction to European Law. Law in context. Paperback: £23.95. ISBN 0-406-08192-1. Butterworth Law.

Ward, Ian–The Margins of European Law. Hardback: £40.00. ISBN 0-333-67011-6. Paperback: £14.99. ISBN 0-333-67012-4. Macmillan Press.

Ward, Ian–Ward: a Critical Introduction to European Law. Law in context. Paperback: £23.95. ISBN 0-406-08192-1. Butterworth Law.

Wargo, John–Our Children's Toxic Legacy. Hardback: £22.50. ISBN 0-300-06686-4. Yale University Press.

Warlow, T.A.–Firearms, the Law and Forensic Ballistics. Hardback: £55.00. ISBN 0-7484-0432-5. Taylor & Francis.

Warren, Suzanne–Legal Research in England and Wales. Guides to legal research. Paperback: £20.50. ISBN 1-870369-03-3. Sweet & Maxwell.

Wasik, Martin–The Sentencing Process. The international library of criminology, criminal justice and penology. Hardback: £80.00. ISBN 1-85521-784-8. Dartmouth.

Waterman, David; Weiss, Andrew A.–Vertical Integration in Cable Television. AEI studies in telecommunications deregulation. Hardback: £25.50. ISBN 0-262-23190-5. The MIT Press.

Watson, Alan–Jesus and the Law. Hardback: £19.95. ISBN 0-8203-1813-2. University of Georgia Press.

Watson, Robert A.B.; Watson, Louise M.–Business Accounting for Scottish Solicitors. Paperback: £27.00. ISBN 0-406-04655-7. Butterworth Law.

Watt, G.–LLB Cases and Materials: Land Law. Paperback: £18.95. ISBN 1-85431-532-3. Blackstone Press.

Watterston, Juliana M.; Mackley-Smith, Gary B.; Noakes, Patrick–Capital Gains Tax: 1996 Post-budget Supplement. Paperback: £13.95. ISBN 1-86012-359-7. Tolley Publishing.

Weatherill, Stephen.–Cases and Materials on EC Law. Paperback: £22.55. ISBN 1-85431-556-0. Blackstone Press.

Webb, Julian; Maughan, Caroline–Webb & Maughan: Teaching Lawyers' Skills. Paperback: £27.00. ISBN 0-406-05216-6. Butterworth Law.

Webber, Gary–Possession of Business Premises. Practitioner series. Paperback: £50.00. ISBN 0-7520-0294-5. FT Law & Tax.

Webster, Andrew–Innovation and the Intellectual Property System. Nijhoff law specials. Paperback: £65.00. ISBN 90-411-0907-2. Kluwer Law International.

Weisberg, D. Kelly–Applications of Feminist Legal Theory to Women's Lives: Vol 2. Women in the Political Economy Series. Hardback: £63.95. ISBN 1-56639-423-6. Paperback: £27.95. ISBN 1-56639-424-4. Temple University Press.

West, Jane–Implementing the Americans with Disabilities Act. Paperback: £35.00. ISBN 1-55786-867-0. Blackwell Publishers.

Wetterstein, Peter–Harm to the Environment. Hardback: £45.00. ISBN 0-19-826274-4. Clarendon Press.

Wheatley, S.–SWOT International Law. £8.95. ISBN 1-85431-501-3. Blackstone Press.

White, Andrew; Punter, Jonathan–Pensions Issues in Mergers and Acquisitions. Pensions reports. Hardback: £95.00. ISBN 0-7520-0293-7. FT Law & Tax.

White, G. Edward–Justice Oliver Wendell Holmes. Paperback: £12.99. ISBN 0-19-510128-6. Oxford University Press Inc, USA.

White, Jeremy–Butterworths Customs Duties Handbook. Paperback: £55.00. ISBN 0-406-06672-8. Butterworth Law.

White, John–Regulation of Securities and Futures Dealing. Hardback: £82.00. ISBN 0-421-56170-X. Sweet & Maxwell.

White, Nigel–The Law of International Organisations. Studies in International Law. Hardback: £40.00. ISBN 0-7190-4339-5. Paperback: £14.99. ISBN 0-7190-4340-9. Manchester University Press.

White, Paul, LLB–Personal Injury Litigation. Legal Practice Course resource books. Paperback: £17.50. ISBN 0-85308-341-X. Jordan.

White, R.S.–Natural Law in English Renaissance Literature. Hardback: £35.00. ISBN 0-521-48142-2. Cambridge University Press.

White, Richard; Williams, Richard; Harbour, Anthony; Bingley, William–Safeguards for Young Minds. Paperback: £10.00. ISBN 0-902241-94-X. Gaskell (Royal College of Psychiatrists).

White, Stewart; Bate, Stephen; Johnson, Timothy–Satellite Communications in Europe: Law and Regulation. Hardback: £125.00. ISBN 0-7520-0219-8. FT Law & Tax.

Whitehead, Laurence–The International Dimensions of Democratization. Oxford studies in democratization. Hardback: £35.00. ISBN 0-19-828036-X. Oxford University Press.

Whitehouse, Chris–McCutcheon on Inheritance Tax: 7. Supplement. British tax library. Hardback: £45.00. ISBN 0-421-57930-7. Sweet & Maxwell.

Whitehouse, Chris–Revenue Law - Principles and Practice. Paperback: £29.95. ISBN 0-406-05686-2. Butterworth Law.

Widlake, Brian–Serious Fraud Office. Paperback: £7.99. ISBN 0-7515-1438-1. Warner.

Wieacker, Franz; Zimmermann, Reinhard–A History of Private Law in Europe. Hardback: £55.00. ISBN 0-19-825861-5. Clarendon Press.

Wiethoff, William E.–A Peculiar Humanism. Studies in the Legal History of the South. Hardback: £29.50. ISBN 0-8203-1797-7. University of Georgia Press.

Wilets, James D.–The Human Rights of Sexual Minorities. Lesbian and gay studies. Hardback: £35.00. ISBN 0-304-33540-1. Paperback: £10.99. ISBN 0-304-33541-X. Cassell.

Wilkie–Q & A Equity and Trusts. £8.95. ISBN 1-85431-495-5. Blackstone Press.

Wilkinson, Sheriff A.B. –Wilkinson: the Scottish Law of Evidence. Paperback: £28.00. ISBN 0-406-01357-8. Butterworth Law (Scotland).

Willett, Chris–Public Sector Reform and the Citizen's Charter. Law in its Social Setting Series. Hardback: £35.00. ISBN 1-85898-362-2. Edward Elgar.

Williams, Crispin–Shaw's Directory of Tribunals and Regulatory Bodies: 1996. Paperback: £19.00. ISBN 0-7219-1411-X. Shaw & Sons.

Winter, Gerd–European Environmental Law in Comparison. Tempus textbook series on European law and European legal cultures. Paperback: £25.00. ISBN 1-85521-564-0. Dartmouth.

Winter, Gerd–European Environmental Law. Tempus textbook series on European law and European legal cultures. Hardback: £55.00. ISBN 1-85521-560-8. Dartmouth.

Winter, Jan A.; Curtin, Deirdre M.; Kellerman, Alfred E.; de Witte, Bruno–Reforming the Treaty on European Union. Hardback: £152.00. ISBN 90-411-0133-0. Kluwer Law International.

Wolchover, David; Heaton-Armstrong, Anthony–Confession Evidence. Criminal law library. Hardback: £99.00. ISBN 0-421-54710-3. Sweet & Maxwell.

Wolf, Susan–Briefcase on European Community Law. Briefcase series. Paperback: £9.95. ISBN 1-85941-250-5. Cavendish Publishing Ltd.

Wolfe, Christopher–How to Read the Constitution. Paperback: £18.95. ISBN 0-8476-8235-8. Rowman & Littlefield.

Wolfe, Christopher–How to Read the Constitution: Organisation, Constitutional Interpretation and Judicial Power. Hardback: £49.95. ISBN 0-8476-8234-X. Rowman & Littlefield.

Wolkinson, Richard; Block, Benjamin–Employment Law. Human resource management US. Paperback: £19.99. ISBN 1-55786-832-8. Blackwell Publishers.

Worthington, Sarah–Proprietary Interests in Commercial Transactions. Hardback: £40.00. ISBN 0-19-826275-2. Clarendon Press.

Wright, David–A Guide to the IChemE's Model Forms of Conditions of Contract. Paperback: £30.00. ISBN 0-85295-371-2. Institution of Chemical Engineers.

Wunder, John R.–Law and the Great Plains. Contributions in Legal Studies, No 82. Hardback: £47.95. ISBN 0-313-29680-4. Greenwood Press.
Wunnicke, Brooke; Wunnicke, Diane B.; Turner, Paul S.–Standby and Commercial Letters of Credit: 2 Vol Set. Business practice. Hardback: £155.00. ISBN 0-471-12800-7. John Wiley and Sons.
Wyld, Nicola; Carlton, Nancy–Family Emergency Procedures. Paperback: £22.00. ISBN 0-905099-68-0. The Legal Action Group.
Wynne, Geoffrey–Butterworths Banking Law Guide. Butterworths guide. Paperback: £55.00. ISBN 0-406-04935-1. Butterworth Law.
Yates, Elizabeth–Local Authority Interests in Companies. Hardback: £48.00. ISBN 0-421-56250-1. Sweet & Maxwell.
Yearbook of the European Convention on Human Rights/Annuaire de la Convention Europeenne des Droits de L'Homme: Vol 36. 1993. Yearbook of the European Convention on Human Rights, Volume 36. Hardback: £248.00. ISBN 90-411-0151-9. Kluwer Law International.
York, Stephen–Practical Alternative Dispute Resolution. Practitioner series. Hardback: £55.00. ISBN 0-7520-0296-1. FT Law & Tax.
Young, Eric; Rowan-Robinson, Jeremy–Permitted Development. Green's practice library. Hardback. ISBN 0-414-01075-2. W.Green & Son.
Young, Peter–Crime and Criminal Justice in Scotland. Paperback: £7.00. ISBN 0-11-495808-4. HMSO Books.
Young, Peter–Punishment, Money and Legal Order. Edinburgh law and society series. Hardback: £35.00. ISBN 0-7486-0534-7. Edinburgh University Press.
Zamir, Itzhak; Zysblat, Allen–Public Law in Israel. Hardback: £50.00. ISBN 0-19-825853-4. Clarendon Press.
Zander, Michael–A Bill of Rights? Paperback: £9.00. ISBN 0-421-58430-0. Sweet & Maxwell.
Zander, Michael–Cases and Materials on the English Legal System. £18.95. ISBN 0-406-08176-X. Butterworth Law.
Ziegler, Andreas R.–Trade and Environment Law in the European Community. Hardback: £45.00. ISBN 0-19-826246-9. Clarendon Press.
Zimmermann, Reinhard; Visser, Daniel–Southern Cross. Hardback: £50.00. ISBN 0-19-826087-3. Clarendon Press.
Zweigert, K.–International Encyclopedia of Comparative Law: Instalment 30. International encyclopedia of comparative law. Paperback: £198.00. ISBN 90-411-0174-8. Martinus Nijhoff Publishers.
Zwirn, Jerrold–Accessing US Government Information. Bibliographies and Indexes in Law and Political Science, No. 24. Hardback: £47.95. ISBN 0-313-29765-7. Greenwood Press.

INDEX 1996